Penguin Books

The Penguin Guide to Jazz
on CD, LP and Cassette

RICHARD COOK was born in Kew in 1957 and has lived and worked in London ever since. He heard Jelly Roll Morton's record of 'Doctor Jazz' in his youth, and that was that – although he also listens to rock, classical and other musics to keep up with planetary vibrations. He has been writing about music since the late '70s, initially for the rock press, and until recently was editor of *The Wire*, jazz critic for the *Sunday Times* and music columnist for *Punch*. He also broadcasts every week for the BBC's GLR.

BRIAN MORTON was born in Paisley in 1954 and grew up in the American garrison-town of Dunoon, a kind of New Orleans-on-Clyde, where jazz was invented by his ancestor, Jam Roll Morton, in 1745. He read English (and listened to a lot of records) at Edinburgh University, then researched and taught American literature at the universities of East Anglia and Tromsø, Norway. Between 1981 and 1991 he was features editor, then literary editor, at the *Times Higher Education Supplement*. Now a full-time writer and broadcaster, Morton is co-editor with Pam Collins of *Contemporary Composers* (1991), author of *Sax* (1993) and a novel *Scherzo* (1993), and regularly reviews contemporary literature and music. He lives in London with Pam and their daughter, Fiona.

The Penguin Guide to Jazz
on CD, LP and Cassette

Richard Cook and Brian Morton

Penguin Books

PENGUIN BOOKS

Published by the Penguin Group
Penguin Books Ltd, 27 Wrights Lane, London W8 5TZ, England
Penguin Books USA Inc, 375 Hudson Street, New York, New York 10014, USA
Penguin Books Australia Ltd, Ringwood, Victoria, Australia
Penguin Books Canada Ltd, 10 Alcorn Avenue, Toronto, Ontario Canada M4V 3B2
Penguin Books (NZ) Ltd, 182-190 Wairu Road, Auckland 10, New Zealand

Penguin Books Ltd, Registered Offices: Harmondsworth, Middlesex, England

First published 1992
5 7 9 10 8 6 4

Made and printed in Great Britain by Clays Ltd, St Ives plc

Typeset in 8 on 9½ pt Times by Barbers Ltd, Wrotham, Kent

Contents

Introduction

The origins of jazz are as cloudy and unspecific as those of any other kind of music, but scholars usually agree that the recordings made by the Original Dixieland Jazz Band in 1917 mark the starting point for jazz on record. We shall never know what Buddy Bolden, the first 'King' of New Orleans cornet playing, sounded like, since he never recorded; and many other opportunities were also missed by the American industry. King Oliver and Jelly Roll Morton, both prominent figures before 1917, didn't arrive in the studios until the 1920s; Freddie Keppard, whose band was a sensation in the 1910s, allegedly refused to make records lest anyone steal his sound. In fact, scarcely any significant recording was done in New Orleans, the supposed birthplace of jazz, until the 1940s. So a white band in New York made 'Darktown Strutters' Ball' in January 1917: at that time, they were described on the record labels as 'Original Dixieland Jass Band'.

Seventy-five years later, jazz (or jass) has become as widely documented on record as any music. It has rushed through its history – from traditional jazz to swing to bebop to free jazz and back again – in less than 100 years, and the gramophone has enjoyed the unique position of being able to document it at almost every step along the way. Although jazz itself may still be regarded by many as some kind of specialist music, difficult to comprehend without a wide-ranging knowledge of the form, its impact on twentieth-century music as a whole is incalculable. It has nurtured some of the finest composers and performers of our times, in any musical genre; its influence on other musics, through the principles of jazz improvisation and compositions, is immense; and it paved the way for rock and soul and all their various sub-genres that have emerged in the last 40 years.

Although many will always hold that jazz is primarily a live music, created at its best in the immediacy of a concert setting of some kind, it has long been disseminated, listened to and argued about via the medium of records. Jazz was, indeed, the first music to be dramatically affected *by* records. As the 78-r.p.m. medium gave way to the LP format, the confining bonds of the three-minute disc were abandoned and jazz performance became longer and less proscribed. Jazz records are relatively economical to make as compared with the studio time which rock and classical records seem to demand and, while the major companies have an almost traditional antipathy towards putting significant resources behind a music they tend to see as marginal, countless independent operations have sprung up which have recorded and released the music with an almost obsessive fervour. The advent of the compact disc has brought new life to many a neglected jazz archive, too. Some of the major catalogues of the past – RCA's Bluebird, Warner Bros' Atlantic, the great modern archives of Blue Note and Prestige – have been restored to circulation via CD. As many of the earlier recordings have fallen out of copyright, independent enterprises such as JSP and Classics have embarked on extensive CD reissues of the jazz of the 1920s and '30s. The Original Jazz Classics reissue programme, run by the Fantasy group in the USA, has remastered hundreds of albums from Prestige, Milestone, Contemporary and other labels. While it remains to be seen how long a shelf-life these records will have – jazz records have frequently been reissued and as quickly deleted – the current outlook suggests that the steady flow of reissues will at least be maintained if not accelerated in the foreseeable future, while the thirst for recording new music seems unquenchable.

Our aim in this book has been to try to provide a comprehensive overview of this vast and bewilderingly diverse area of music on record. While a number of selective guides have appeared in the past, this is the first serious attempt to bring the whole spectrum of jazz recording within a single volume. The most difficult problem facing newcomers to this music – and there have been many in recent years, with jazz acquiring a much wider casual listenership than it has had since, perhaps, the trad boom of the 1950s – is where to start, and where to proceed from there. Most will have heard, say, of Miles Davis's *Kind Of Blue* or John Coltrane's *Giant Steps*, two of the most famous jazz LPs ever released. But both those musicians have enormous discographies, and this presents a formidable problem to collectors on a limited budget or to those who wish to acquire just a few examples of Davis or Coltrane on record. At the same time, more experienced fans and collectors have never been provided with the kind of detailed summary and evaluation of what exactly is available by both major and minor figures in the jazz field. That is what we've tried to do here.

The richness and diversity of music covered by the term 'jazz' is extraordinary, and that point has been brought home to us more forcefully than ever in compiling this book. We have attempted to list and discuss all the records currently available in the field – but, since jazz itself is a difficult area to define, this has inevitably brought its own problems: what to include and what to leave out. Although jazz and blues are inextricably bound up in each other, we have omitted such musicians as Bessie Smith and Alberta Hunter, even though their records are listened to and enjoyed by countless 'jazz fans': the blues demands a volume to itself, which should be documented by safer hands than ours. Singers, too, are difficult to make clear judgement calls on: the old argument as to what is a jazz singer has never been resolved, and it could be contended that, if we have included Mel Torme (as we have), then why not Peggy Lee, or even Bing Crosby? Often we have been guided by the nature of the accompaniments, and in some cases we have chosen to include only the jazz-directed output of a particular artist. In the case of Nat Cole, for instance, we've omitted the bulk of his vocal recordings, while his instrumental ones have remained; much the same applies to George Benson. This isn't to imply a snobbish dismissal of the other records as fluff: but we feel confident that Cole's *For Two In Love* cannot claim the jazz status of his *After Midnight*, even if both records are equally enjoyable on their own terms.

The advent of 'free music' has placed a further strain on jazz classification: the work of such musicians as Derek Bailey and Billy Jenkins may, often at their own insistence, have little to do with any jazz tradition. But the connections between jazz and improvised music are indisputable, and there is no feasible reason to discriminate against free music by excluding it from this book. We start, therefore, with the Original Dixieland Jazz Band and continue up to the present day, as exhaustively as possible.

That said, we cannot hope to include in this book every jazz record that is currently available. In a few cases, we have simply been unable to locate a copy of a supposedly 'available' record for review. Where we have been selective, it has been in trying to exclude a number of bargain-priced collections of dubious quality and probably illicit status, the appearance of which in the racks CD has seemed to encourage. Besides these, there are many records which amount to little more than easy- listening, instrumental music with only the vaguest of jazz connotations. While there's an awkward line to draw here, we've attempted to inscribe it. There's a substantial grey area between jazz and contemporary composition: some musicians, such as Fred Rzewski or John Lewis, move freely between these genres, and there are many records – particularly from such companies as Bvhaast and New Albion – which count jazz as an element, though not perhaps the defining one, in their make-up. Again, we've used our discretion here as best we can.

Our intention has been to make this as practical a book as possible. None of the judgements herein are cast in stone: further listening and pondering on the music may yield different opinions in the fullness of time, which may be accounted for in future editions of this *Guide*. In that respect, we share a characteristic that is surely common to all jazz listeners: of living and developing with this music as it continues to evolve and grow. We have tried not to be sentimental about our evaluations: it is all too tempting to overrate some records on the basis that the jazz musician's lot is trying enough without having to endure negative criticism. But the first responsibility of such a guide is to listeners and record-buyers. With full-priced CDs costing more than £10 each, most record collectors and enthusiasts will be able to invest in only a fraction of what is available to them in the current record marketplace. Our primary aim has been to assist in deciding how best to make that choice and to suggest areas of the music which may yield hitherto unrealized pleasures.

EVALUATION

While some may consider it iniquitous to define the merits of a record using a star-system, we feel that it's simply the most useful shorthand as a starting point for discussing the disc in question. The reader is urged to consult the text in addition to the star rating for our overall evaluation of the record. We have chosen to make use of between one and four stars: parentheses round a single star indicate that some small reservation prevents our placing it in the higher category. Parentheses round all the stars indicate that some more fundamental reservation exists which prevents us giving a wholehearted recommendation: usually this will relate to some aspect of the recording or presentation of the disc in question, but again we advise the reader to consult the text.

- **** an outstanding record that demands a place in any comprehensive collection
- *** a very good if middleweight set; one that lacks the stature or consistency of the finest records, but is playable on its own terms
- ** a decent but essentially flawed record; recommended only to those who feel a particular interest in the artist in question
- * a record that does a disservice either to the artist or to the music in general; in both cases, it does a severe disservice to the listener

In a *very* few cases, we have, like our colleagues on *The Penguin Guide To Compact Discs and Cassettes*, chosen to award a special token of merit; in our *Guide*, it takes the form of a fifth star. This is to denote records we feel to be of a desert-island calibre, numbering among the very finest of all jazz recordings. If we were able to recommend only a handful of discs, either to the committed jazz follower or to someone wanting to hear only the very best of the music, it would be these five-star records.

RECORDING QUALITY

Our evaluations also deal with the matter of the sonic qualities of the recording itself, although we have not been quite so zealous in this area as our colleagues on *The Penguin Guide to Compact Discs and Cassettes*, which covers 'classical' music. Our first concern is with the music itself, and most contemporary jazz records are engineered to the customary high standards which are the norm for the industry; they therefore require little further comment – although, whenever there is some particular felicity or problem with the production, we have noted it as such. Far more important, however, is the question of the remastering of older material for CD reissue. We have been disturbed to discover how erratic and unreliable standards of remastering for CD are, particularly among the major companies, where it is basically inexcusable: they have the resources to do the best possible job on their historical material, yet time and again we have encountered examples of shoddy and ill-informed work, particularly with regard to remastering from 78s. Set against this is the magnificent work which has been done by, in particular, the British engineer, John R. T. Davies – for Fountain, Retrieval and JSP – and Robert Parker, some of whose stereo re-creations for BBC records have been outstanding. We have attempted to be as scrupulous as possible in our evaluation of this issue. We might also mention that we have frequently discovered many instances when the CD version of even a relatively modern record offers no noticeable improvement over the LP issue. We leave it to the reader's discretion as to how much hype about CD sound he or she is prepared to believe.

RUNNING TIME: NEVER MIND THE WIDTH ...

Our decision to ignore the question of CD running-time may vex some readers, since it seems to have become a major issue in some quarters. The compact disc can comfortably accommodate some 80 minutes of music, yet most jazz CDs fail to use the full capacity of the disc and, in the case of many reissues, no attempt is made to beef up the running-time of the original LP by adding extra material. That said, a considerable number of issues *do* include extra tracks by way of alternative takes or previously rejected pieces. But such material is often of dubious value, and an ordinary LP is unlikely to become an extraordinary CD by the addition of three or four more-of-the-same tunes. We have usually noted in the text where there is a significant difference in the CD version of a record as compared to its vinyl counterpart. But our criterion has been that the quality of the music determines the desirability of the disc, not its running-time. An outstanding 40-minute record remains outstanding, even if it does run to only half of what could be put on the CD. In many cases we have found that judicious editing of a lengthy CD programme would have improved our overall impression of the record in question. Life is too short, and there are too many records, to worry about whether an extra few minutes would have fulfilled the mysterious means test of 'value for money'.

PRICING

While it is tempting to denote records which are available at less than full price, in practice this is a difficult area to be accurate about. Many reissues are made available in some mid-price range, but the bargain bracket which is a commonplace in the field of classical discs holds very few jazz records, and most of those are frequently of dubious worth. As a general guide, the reader is advised that many reissues from the major record companies are likely to be priced in the 'medium' range of £8–£10; new issues and any issues on the many independent labels are likely to be in the premium-price category. It's clearly a matter of checking with individual retailers.

LAYOUT OF TEXT

Here is a typical record-entry:

***　**Ahmed Abdullah And The Solomonic Quintet** Silkheart 109 CD/LP
Abdullah; David S. Ware (*ts*); Masuhjaa (*g*); Fred Hopkins (*b*); Charles Moffett (*d*). 89.

The star-rating is followed by the title of the record, its label and catalogue number, and the formats in which it's available: compact disc (CD), vinyl album (LP) or cassette (MC). On the next line, we list the musicians who are playing on the disc, together with their instrumental credits, and – where available – the date of the recording (month/year). All personnel are listed collectively – that is, it shouldn't be implied that every musician listed for a record is featured on every track. A full list of instrument abbreviations follows this introduction. Where there are multiple records in an entry, each change in personnel is duly noted – although, rather than listing the same musicians over again, subsequent details may begin with 'As above, except . . .'. Where the recording dates span a number of different sessions, as is the case for many compilations, they are listed as, for example, 5/74–10/80. While we've tried to present the clearest possible picture of who recorded what and when, this is a guide, not a discography, and we've attempted to be sensible over the listing of minutiae.

We have tried to be as accurate as possible over listing catalogue numbers, but neither we nor our publishers can be held responsible for mistakes which may have eluded our checking. By and large, we have attempted to simplify the situation as far as possible by concentrating on the 'core' number which most records are assigned. The RCA Bluebird catalogue, for instance, uses different prefixes to denote different formats – ND for CD, NK for LP, NL for cassette – yet each issue uses the same five-digit number for each format. It has become almost an industry standard to use the suffix -2 to denote a CD issue and -4 to denote a cassette; but we have used those suffixes only where there is but a single format available. In at least one instance – the EMI Blue Note catalogue – all the current catalogue numbers are now ending in an unhyphenated '2', since they are concentrating on releasing CDs only. Many independent companies use very simple systems of cataloguing – which we wish were as available to the major companies!

The situation is further complicated by the inclusion of many America-only or Europe-only releases in the book. The reader is warned that many such releases, from smaller companies in particular, may be much more difficult to obtain. We have usually noted in the text where a major company has American but not UK editions available on certain releases: the Blue Note UK catalogue, for example, has recently been hit by deletions, but the American editions of many of the records are still available, and we have duly listed the US number in those cases and mentioned it in the text. Good retailers – on both sides of the Atlantic! – will still be able to obtain them.

We always advise that, when ordering records, readers state the title and artist and desired format, as well as the catalogue numbers. Most experienced dealers will be able to spot any possible confusion over the number when furnished with these extra details.

FORMATS: VINYL STILL LIVES!

Some readers may be surprised that we still list LPs in this book, at a time when many are predicting the imminent demise of the vinyl album as compact discs take an ever-growing share of the world market. The fact remains, however, that many of the smaller companies are still committed to vinyl to a greater or lesser degree, and the stocks of existing vinyl which are in the hands of many distributors are still substantial. Such important companies as Xanadu, Tax, Splasc(h), Steeplechase and Dragon have confirmed that they will continue to supply vinyl for as long as they have stocks and as long as demand for it continues.

Nevertheless, we have listed LP issues with some trepidation. There is little doubt that fundamentally it is a dying medium. As we go to press, for instance, the important German company, FMP, which has a very large and significant vinyl catalogue, has announced that it will be ceasing to distribute LPs by the end of 1992. Most of the major companies no longer want to have anything to do with vinyl, and the substantial reissue programme handled by the Fantasy group under the title Original Jazz Classics has recently chosen to release no further LPs. Our advice, for vinyl diehards, is simply to stock up now before second-hand LPs are the only alternative.

The cassette format presents a further problem. If the availability of LP and CD for jazz is sometimes erratic, the situation is worse for cassettes: we have again been cautious over listing the cassette issue for many releases and have done so only where we feel reasonably confident that the reader will be able to obtain the cassette in point. Although we've been able to hear only a proportion of those issues listed on cassette, we also note that sound-quality on many such releases frequently leaves much to be desired in the tape format as compared with either LP or CD. Until the Digital Compact Cassette medium takes hold, as it seems likely to do by the end of 1993, we must advise readers to approach this area with caution.

DELETIONS

A work of this kind is, in one sense, out of date as soon as it arrives on the shelves: new records are constantly being issued and old discs are being removed from circulation. As noted above, we are doubtful about even the short-term life of many of the LP issues included here. Even where a record is officially deleted by its issuing company, however, it may still be available by dint of stocks being in the hands of independent distributors. All this will be familiar to experienced collectors, who know how difficult it can be to locate a particular record; but we counsel that a patient reader should try more than one source if confronted with an initial response that a record is deleted and therefore impossible to get. For that purpose we have included a list of distributors at the end of this introduction.

MOSAIC RECORDS

A rather special case has been presented by the work done by Mosaic Records, the company run by Charlie Lourie and Michael Cuscuna in Stamford, Connecticut. Mosaic's remarkable output consists of deluxe boxed-set editions of the complete recordings of major artists in a specific period, such as all the Blue Note recordings of Thelonious Monk or all the 'live' recordings made for Roulette by Count Basie. Remastered to the highest standards, pressed on top-quality vinyl or CD and sumptuously packaged, these editions are designed to please the most demanding of collectors.

Since, however, they are all available only in limited-edition runs and are generally difficult to find in most record stores, we find it somewhat inappropriate to include most of them in the general run of this book. Where there is a special interest – such as the Mosaic edition forming a key part of the work of an artist who is otherwise under-represented by the rest of his or her entry – we have included that edition in the body of the text. Otherwise they have been omitted.

This does not, of course, proclaim any bias against these editions. Our general view is that they are superb feats of reissue scholarship which anyone with a serious interest in the music of the artists in question must investigate. In consequence, we here provide a brief listing of those Mosaic editions which are currently available. As a general rule, each should be considered as at least a four-star record. We would also warn purchasers that each is a limited edition and that as we go to press stocks on several titles are reportedly very low.

The Complete Pacific Jazz And Capitol Recordings Of The Original Gerry Mulligan Quartet And Tentette With Chet Baker Mosaic MD3-102 3CD

The Complete Blue Note And Pacific Jazz Recordings Of Clifford Brown Mosaic MR5-104 5LP

The Complete Pacific Jazz Small Group Recordings Of Art Pepper Mosaic MR3-105 3LP

The Complete Blue Note Small Group Recordings Of Tina Brooks Mosaic MR4-106 4LP

The Complete Blue Note Forties Recordings Of Ike Quebec And John Hardee Mosaic 107 4LP/3CD

The Complete Edmond Hall/James P. Johnson/Sidney De Paris/Vic Dickenson Blue Note Sessions Mosaic 109 6LP/4CD

The Complete Blue Note Recordings Of Sidney Bechet Mosaic M 110 6LP/4CD

The Complete Candid Recordings Of Charles Mingus Mosaic M 111 4LP/3CD

The Complete Black Lion And Vogue Recordings Of Thelonious Monk Mosaic M 112 4LP/3CD

The Complete Pacific Jazz Live Recordings Of The Chet Baker Quartet with Russ Freeman Mosaic M 113 4LP/3CD

The Complete Blue Note Art Hodes Sessions Mosaic M 114 5LP/4CD

The Benny Morton And Jimmy Hamilton Blue Note Swingtets Mosaic M 115 1LP

The Complete Bud Powell Blue Note Recordings Mosaic M 116 5LP

The Complete Verve Recordings Of The Buddy DeFranco Quartet/Quintet With Sonny Clark Mosaic M 117 5LP/4CD

The Complete Blue Note Recordings Of Herbie Nichols Mosaic M 118 5LP/3CD

The Complete Recordings Of The Paul Desmond Quartet With Jim Hall Mosaic M 120 6LP/4CD

The Complete Blue Note 45 Sessions Of Ike Quebec Mosaic M 118 3LP/2CD

The Complete Pacific Jazz Studio Recordings Of The Chet Baker Quartet With Russ Freeman Mosaic M 122 4LP/3CD

The Complete Commodore Jazz Recordings Vol. 1 Mosaic M 123 25LP

The Complete Blue Note Recordings Of Freddie Redd Mosaic M 124 3LP/3CD

The Complete Atlantic And EMI Jazz Recordings Of Shorty Rogers Mosaic M 125 6LP/4CD

The Complete Johnny Hodges Recordings 1951–55 Mosaic M 126 6LP

The Complete Candid Recordings Of Cecil Taylor And Buell Neidlinger Mosaic
M 127 6LP/4CD

The Complete Commodore Jazz Recordings Vol. 2 Mosaic 128 23LP

The Complete Dean Benedetti Recordings Of Charlie Parker Mosaic M 129
10LP/7CD

The Complete Recordings Of T-Bone Walker Mosaic M 130 9LP/6CD

The Complete Recordings Of The Stan Getz Quartet With Jimmy Raney Mosaic
M 131 4LP/3CD

The Complete Blue Note Recordings Of George Lewis Mosaic M 132 5LP/3CD

The Complete Blue Note Recordings Of Grant Green With Sonny Clark
5LP/4CD

The Complete Commodore Jazz Recordings Vol. III Mosaic M 134 20LP

The Complete Roulette Live Recordings Of Count Basie And His Orchestra
Mosaic M 135 12LP/8CD

*Stan Kenton: The Complete Capitol Recordings Of The Bill Holman And Bill
Russo Charts* Mosaic M 136 6LP/4CD

The Complete Blue Note Recordings Of Larry Young Mosaic M 137 9LP/6CD

Mosaic Records are located at 35 Melrose Place, Stamford, CT06902, USA (Tel.:
06902-7533).

ACKNOWLEDGEMENTS

Throughout the writing of this book we have received invaluable assistance from
hardy souls working in the distribution and retailing of jazz records in the UK.
Special thanks must go to John Jack and Hazel Miller of Cadillac, Steve Sanderson at
New Note, Laurie Staff (and his predecessor, Ron Warshaw) at Harmonia Mundi,
Tony Williams at Spotlite, Karen Pitchford at Koch International, Val Rooker and
Jane Chapman at RCA Novus and Bluebird, Ken Ansell at Impetus, Ray Smith and
all at Ray's Jazz Shop, and Peter Taylor at Panther Music; and to a number of overseas residents who helped us in our attempts to show that jazz is indeed a music of
the world, particularly Lars Westin at Dragon. Thanks also to Adele Yaron, whose
assistance in collating our research was indispensable; to Brian Priestley for some further advice; to Roger Wells, our tireless copy editor; and to Ravi Mirchandani and
Liz Bland, our patient editors at Penguin. And for their understanding and good
humour in the face of a colossal mountain of records taking up most of their living
space, our thanks and affection go to Lee Ellen, Pam and Fiona.

Richard Cook
Brian Morton

Distributors

The following UK distributors may be be able to help in obtaining records. We have added the names of the labels they deal with, where appropriate.

New Note Distribution, 2 Orpington Trading Estate, Sevenoaks Way, St Mary Cray, Orpington, Kent BR5 3SR (Tel.: 06898 77884)
> Chesky, Concord, ECM, Enja, Gramavision, Hep, Jazz City, Landmark, Muse, Paddlewheel, Strata East, Theresa, Timeless, Triloka, Tutu

Harmonia Mundi Ltd, 19–21 Nile St, London N1 7LR (Tel.: 071- 253 0863)
> Bebab, Black Saint, Criss Cross, DIW, Flapper, hat ART, Jazzpoint, Jazz View, LRC, Moon, Philology, Red, Soul Note, Sunnyside

Cadillac Distribution, 180 Shaftesbury Ave, London WC2H 8JB (Tel.: 071-836 3646)
> Bvhaast, Capri, Dormouse, Dragon, FMP, Fountain/Retrieval, Fresh Sound, Gemini, ICP, Incus, JSP, Moers, Ogun, Olufsen, Po Torch, Reservoir, Xanadu

Koch International, 23 Warple Way, London W3 0RX (Tel.: 081- 749 7177)
> Black & Blue, Black Lion, Candid, IDA, ITM, Jazz Door, Mainstream, West Wind, Yazoo

Spotlite, 103 London Road, Sawbridgeworth, Herts CM21 9JJ (Tel.: 0279 724572)
> Sackville, Spotlite

Panther Music, Unit 4, Chapman Park Industrial Estate, 387-388 High Road, Willesden, London NW10 2OY (Tel.: 081-459 1212)
> Classics

Conifer Records, Horton Road, West Drayton, Middx UB7 8JL (Tel.: 0895 440450)
> Denon, DMP, Savoy, Telarc

Impetus Distribution, 587 Wandsworth Road, London SW8 3JD (Tel.: 071-720 4460)
> Nine Winds, Splasc(h)

Abbreviations

acc	accordion	g	guitar
acl	alto clarinet	gfs	goofus
af	alto flute	g-syn	guitar synthesizer
ahn	alto horn	hca	harmonica
arr	arranger	hn	horn
as	alto saxophone	hp	harp
b	bass	hpd	harpsichord
ban	bandoneon	ky	keyboards
bar hn	baritone horn	mand	mandolin
bb	brass bass	mar	marimba
bcl	bass clarinet	mel	mellophone
bf	bass flute	ob	oboe
bhn	baritone horn	org	organ
bj	banjo	p	piano
bs	baritone saxophone	perc	percussion
bsn	bassoon	picc	piccolo
bsx	bass saxophone	picc t	piccolo trumpet
b-t	bass trumpet	pkt-t	pocket-trumpet
btb	bass trombone	sno	sopranino saxophone
c	cornet	sou	sousaphone
cbcl	contrabass clarinet	srspn	sarrusophone
cbsrspn	contrabass sarrusophone	ss	soprano saxophone
cbsx	contrabass saxophone	syn	synthesizer
cel	celeste	t	trumpet
cl	clarinet	tb	trombone
clo	cello	tba	tuba
Cmel	C-melody saxophone	thn	tenor horn
comp	composer	ts	tenor saxophone
cond	conductor	uke	ukulele
cor	cor anglais	v	vocal
d	drums	vib	vibraphone
elec	electronics	vla	viola
eng hn	english horn	vn	violin
euph	euphonium	vtb	valve trombone
f	flute	wbd	washboard
flhn	flugelhorn	xy	xylophone
frhn	french horn		

GREG ABATE
ALTO, SOPRANO AND TENOR SAXOPHONES, FLUTE

*** **Bop City – Live At Birdland** Candid CCD 79513 CD
  Abate; James Williams (*p*); Rufus Reid (*b*); Kenny Washington (*d*). 7/91.

Abate is no beginner. He's worked as a section player in big bands for nearly 20 years and has recently begun performing as a small-group leader. This breezy session affirms a basic interest in bebop saxophone which the leader is apparently at home with on any of the models: alto is his main preoccupation, but his tenor features on 'Peaks Beaks' and 'Gemini Mood' are convincing, and the soprano on 'Opportunity' reveals a lesson absorbed from Coltrane. It's a pick-up rhythm section, but they know exactly what they're doing. Very playable.

AHMED ABDULLAH (born 1947)
TRUMPET

*(*) **Abdullah Live At Allen's Alley** Cadence CJR 1000 LP
  Abdullah; Chico Freeman (*ts*); Vincent Chancey (*frhn*); Muneer Abdul Fataah (*clo*); Jerome Hunter (*b*); Rashied Sinan (*d*). 4/78.

(*) **Liquid Magic Silkheart SHLP-104 LP
  Abdullah; Charles Brackeen (*ts*); Malachi Favors (*b*); Alvin Fielder (*d*). 2/87.

Although Abdullah was first influenced by Louis Armstrong, his principal jazz experience is with free playing – in various free collectives in the 1960s and '70s, and with Sun Ra's Arkestra. The earlier recording is typical of the less inspired loft jazz of the period: crashing, ragged ensembles, tunes that start and close arbitrarily, improvisations which offer generous but ill-disciplined opportunities. The indifferent recording doesn't help much.

 The Silkheart record makes a more positive case for his music. Tersely organized, the session's six tunes reflect a Colemanesque feel which suits the folk-like melodies. But the trumpeter is, frankly, the least impressive player here: Brackeen's fierce yet lightly shaded solos make a more powerful impression, and Favors and Fielder generate a splendid swing.

*** **Ahmed Abdullah And The Solomonic Quintet** Silkheart 109 CD/LP
  Abdullah; David S. Ware (*ts*); Masuhjaa (*g*); Fred Hopkins (*b*); Charles Moffett (*d*).

Abdullah's second Silkheart disc has the same problem as the first: the leader is outclassed by his own band. The rhythm section is wonderfully alert and inventive, with Masuhjaa's guitar an especially individual presence, and Ware is a gritty improviser. Abdullah's writing is at its best in the Latin lope of 'El Canto II', and altogether this must be his strongest record.

JOHN ABERCROMBIE (born 1944)
GUITAR, GUITAR SYNTHESIZERS, ELECTRIC MANDOLIN, GUITAR MANDOLIN

***(*) **Timeless** ECM 1047 CD/LP
  Abercrombie; Jan Hammer (*p, ky*); Jack DeJohnette (*d*). 6/74.

*** **Gateway** ECM 1061 (2301061) LP

(*) **Gateway 2 ECM 1105 (2301105) LP
  Abercrombie; David Holland (*b*); Jack DeJohnette (*d*). 3/75 & 7/77.

(*) **Night ECM 1272 LP
  Abercrombie; Mike Brecker (*ts*); Jan Hammer (*ky*); Jack DeJohnette (*d*). 4/84.

ECM had been around for nigh on five years when the first of these top-drawer sets was cut, and all the qualities that distinguish Manfred Eicher's label are firmly in place. *Timeless* is a superb album, brimming with interesting ideas and textures. DeJohnette is probably the finest drummer of his generation – or why not say one of the finest musicians of his generation. Hammer is a vastly underrated keyboard player, with a strong all-round conception (face it, everyone gets a buzz off the *Miami Vice* theme). At this point he still seems to be adjusting to normal altitude, having just descended from Mount Mahavishnu, and there is a tendency to overplay; but DeJohnette and Abercrombie seem to be in complete agreement, and the guitarist's fingering is typically exact and his lyricism more than usually forceful.

Given the variation in personnel, *Gateway* is inevitably a more reflective album, but it is by no means sombre. Abercrombie seems to like the open rhythmic weave and plays acoustically with great confidence and finely controlled timbre and dynamics. Holland is by no means playing at his best, but he is also incapable of mere journeywork and asserts his presence in the harmonic transitions in a way that more than makes up for the absence of keyboards.

Gateway 2, recorded two years later, is less effective, with Abercrombie riffling rather desperately through his electrical shade cards. DeJohnette, as always, is flawless; and he is so again on the surprisingly funky *Night*, a good trio session into which a slightly surprised Brecker seems to have walked out of the darkness. Blinking a little in the sudden glare, he peers at the charts. Edit him out and this fine album would be none the worse.

**   **Sargasso Sea** ECM 1080 LP
       Abercrombie; Ralph Towner (*classical g, 12-string g, p*). 5/76.

Though the abstractions of the title-track are intriguing, this is a slightly disappointing set. In contrast to Towner's duos with Larry Coryell on *The Restful Mind* (Vanguard), which is a magnificent stylistic compromise on both parts, Towner and Abercrombie are perhaps too similar to do more than cancel each other out. Towner's piano, increasingly important to his conception at that point in his career, adds an attractive element, but 'attractive' is the strongest this set merits. Five years later, they met up again and cut *Five Years Later* (ECM 1207); Towner's name came first that time . . .

***   **Characters** ECM 1117 LP
       Abercrombie (*g* solo). 11/77.

Before the advent of Bill Frisell, this was as good as contemporary solo guitar playing got. The mood is generally elegiac, and there are sufficient internal indications to suggest that Abercrombie is working through at least some of his influences. There are strong echoes of Tal Farlow and Jim Hall in the beautiful opening 'Parable', in the writing and conception rather than the articulation, and there are signs elsewhere that Abercrombie has absorbed Django Reinhardt's overlapping rhythm.

*   **Abercrombie Quartet** ECM 1164 LP

*(*)   **M** ECM 1191 LP
       Abercrombie; Richard Beirach (*p*); George Mraz (*b*); Peter Donald (*d*). 11/79 & 11/80.

What a difference a year makes! The first of these is a dismal affair, thinly executed and registered. Uncomfortably bravura and unconvincingly 'thoughtful' by turns, it is probably Abercrombie's poorest recording, the product of a misalliance. Beirach – the guilty party of the first part, as they say in the divorce courts – tries to make a go of it on *M*, adjusting his attack and conveying an impression of having taken a note off each chord. If they had just stuck together, they might have made a go of it.

(*)   **John Abercrombie ECM 1390 CD/LP
       Abercrombie; Marc Johnson (*b*); Peter Erskine (*d*). 4/88.

***   **Animato** ECM 1411 CD/LP
       Abercrombie; Vince Mendoza (*synths*); Jon Christensen (*d*). 10/89.

Not known as a big standards player (but then, that's what they used to say about Keith Jarrett), Abercrombie turns in a beautiful 'Stella By Starlight' here, perfectly weighted this side of sentimentality, and an unforgettable version of the less well-known Dietz/Schwartz 'Haunted Heart'. Johnson and Erskine make a convincing team, though the former shouldn't have been indulged an airing of his 'Samurai Hee-Haw', nor the latter his drum solo.

With *Animato*, the exact opposite applies. Christensen can be listened to all night, the lightest, nimblest drummer Europe has produced, rivalling DeJohnette for sheer swing and intelligence. Mendoza's six (out of eight) compositions are spot-on and he seems to have steered Abercrombie towards a more confident use of electronics. Both albums feature the leader's guitar synthesizer, a machine that too often stands in the way of creative thought. Abercrombie deploys it intelligently, using it to vary the textures, supplying unexpected glissandi and dramatic upward shifts or to add a more forceful chordal pulse. Strongly recommended.

LENNART ÅBERG
SAXOPHONES, FLUTE

***   Green Prints Caprice CAP 1276 LP
Åberg; Jan Kohlin, Gustavo Bergalli, Lars Lindgren, Leif Lindvall (*t, flhn*); Palle Mikkelborg (*t*); Nils Landgren, Lars Olofsson (*tb*); Sven Larsson (*btb, tba*); Håkan Nykvist (*frhn*); Erik Nilsson (*bs*); Jan Erik Kling (*bcl, f*); Dave Wilczewski (*f*); Bobo Stenson, Peter Ljung (*ky*); Jan Schaffer (*g, g-syn*); Örjan Fahlström (*vib, mar*); Palle Danielsson (*b*); Pär Lindvall (*d*); Bengt Berger, Okay Temiz (*perc*). 10/85–1/86.

A two-sided record: the first half is based on 'African' pentatonic scales, Balinese and other world-music influences, the second on what Åberg absorbed from Gil Evans and George Russell. Anyone who knows Palle Mikkelborg's *Aura* score for Miles Davis will find this familiar territory – and Mikkelborg is involved here, too, as both player and conductor. There are many striking moments throughout the seven pieces, such as the brass suddenly bursting in on an improvisation in 'Night Spirits', and, while the writing is perhaps appropriately fragmentary, Åberg has a hand-picked team of players, and his own solos are impassioned. Recommended to all followers of this contemporary movement.

RABIH ABOU-KHALIL
OUD, FLUTE

***   Bitter Harvest MMP 170884 LP
Abou-Khalil; Michael Armann (*p, v*); Jonathan Brock (*perc, v*); Shankar Lal (*tabla*). 2 & 5/84.

****   Between Dusk And Dawn MMP 170886 CD/LP
Abou-Khalil; Charlie Mariano (*as, ss*); Christian Burchard (*mar*); Michael Armann (*p*); Glen Moore (*b*); Glen Velez (*frame d, bodhran, darabukka, perc*); Ramesh Shotham (*tavil, ghatam, mouth hp, dholak, kanjira, perc*). 86.

****   Bukra MMP 170889 CD/LP
Abou-Khalil; Sonny Fortune (*as*); Glen Moore (*b*); Glen Velez (*frame d, perc, v*); Ramesh Shotham (*South Indian d, perc*). 3/88.

***(*)   Al-Jadida Enja 6090 CD
Abou-Khalil; Sonny Fortune (*as*); Glen Moore (*b*); Ramesh Shotham (*South Indian d, perc*); Nabil Khaiat (*frame d, perc*). 10/90.

***   Roots And Sprouts MMP 170890 CD/LP/MC
Abou-Khalil; Selim Kusur (*nay*); Yassin El-Achek (*v*); Glen Moore (*b*); Glen Velez (*frame d*); Mohammad Al-Sous (*darabukka*). 11/90.

Jazz is only one of the world's great improvising traditions. Within Arab music, there has always been a substantial area of freedom for the virtuoso performer and the 11-string oud has occupied a role in classical and more popular forms roughly analogous to that of the piano and guitar in the West. Abou-Khalil is a young Lebanese master forced into exile in 1978 by the increasingly chaotic civil war. A follower of the great Wadih Al-Safi, he has maintained a passionate commitment to the 'new music' (*al-jadida*; 'new' not just in the sense of modern, but also in the sense that Western homophony was once dubbed 'new') while taking account of the singing and playing traditions of Western jazz.

From the point of view of a jazz-literate listener, it is clear that the first and last items above are likely to be the least familiarly accessible and their ratings reflect that rather than their perceived quality. One of the main points of contact on the middle three items is the presence of jazz improvisers Charlie Mariano, Sonny Fortune and Oregon (*q. v.*) bassist, Glen Moore, all of whom have made the same cultural journey as Abou-Khalil, but in reverse, west to east. There is an impressive absence of pastiche or self-conscious eclecticism. A composition like 'Ornette Never Sleeps' (*Al-Jadida*) gives off no obvious irony; like much of Abou-Khalil's work, it is intended as sincere *hommage*. Those well disposed towards Oregon's proto-'world music' will feel most comfortable with the magnificent *Between Dusk And Dawn*, but *Bukra* is in some regards more challenging.

Like early jazz, much of the emphasis is on ensemble improvisation rather than more obviously virtuosic soloing. Apart from the leader's cleanly picked multi-directional lines, it's also worth mentioning Moore's marvellously sonorous bass and Mariano's familiarly 'Eastern' mode. Fortune is more of a revelation; staying mainly with the alto saxophone, which is perhaps a more promising choice in this harmonic context, he sounds absolutely familiar with the idiom, and it's the saxophonist who gives *Bukra* much of its compelling power; his unaccompanied introduction to 'Kibbe' is breathtaking, matched for sheer surprise only by Glen Velez's perfectly controlled overtone singing on 'Remember . . . The Desert'.

(Enthusiasts should keep watch for the deleted *Nafas* [ECM 1359], which features Selim Kusur – see also *Roots And Sprouts* – a leading performer on the bamboo *nay* flute.)

MUHAL RICHARD ABRAMS (born 1930)
PIANO, CLARINET, COMPOSER, EDUCATOR

(*)   **Levels And Degrees Of Light Delmark DD 413 CD
Abrams; Anthony Braxton (*as*); Maurice McIntyre (*ts*); Leroy Jenkins (*vn*); Gordon Emmanuel (*vib*); Charles Clark, Leonard Jones (*b*); Thurman Barker (*d*); David Moore, Penelope Taylor (*v*). 1 & 7/67.

***   **Young At Heart / Wise In Time** Delmark DS 423 LP
Abrams (*p* solo) and with Leo Smith (*t, flhn*); Henry Threadgill (*as*); Lester Lashley (*b*); Thurman Barker (*perc*). 68.

***   **Sightsong** Black Saint BSR 0003 LP
Abrams; Malachi Favors (*b, v, perc*). 10/75.

*(*)   **Duet** Black Saint BSR 0051 LP
Abrams; Amina Claudine Myers (*p*). 5/81.

Hugely, hugely influential, Abrams is one of the most important catalytic forces in contemporary jazz and improvisation and, like any physical catalyst, seems curiously unchanged and unmoved by the forces he has set in motion. His own performing and compositional style remains fixed in his original and very personal synthesis of black music styles. He ranges from stride to freely improvised structures, bebop to a kind of proto-funk, echoes of field hollers to dim annunciations of the European classical avant-garde.

Levels And Degrees Of Light has an oddly prayerful quality, encapsulated on the opening track by Penelope Taylor's wavering *vocalise* (which gives way to Abrams's unvirtuosic but effective clarinet). The lyrical content of the very long 'Bird Song' is much less effective; Jenkins and Jones join the others (Cranshaw sits it out), giving an almost orchestral depth of focus that contrasts with the percussive quality of the other two tracks. Braxton and McIntyre play modestly but with feeling throughout, and Barker is absolutely excellent.

Another valuable reissue, *Young At Heart/Wise In Time* consists of a band performance of considerable intensity (which recalls the high points of the earlier Delmark), and a piano side from Abrams, who is not generally considered a wholly convincing solo performer. 'Wise In Time', though, is a fine articulation of his basic philosophies, with powerfully striding meters and wonderful left-hand geometries that recall Art Tatum, James P. Johnson and Bud Powell.

Sightsong is a series of meditations on tradition, consisting of dedications to the great bassist Wilbur Ware, whose chthonic manner Abrams shares, to Johnny Griffin and to the AACM, the Chicago-based Association for the Advancement of Colored Musicians, of which Abrams is founder and *éminence noire*. Hard to fault either in conception or in execution, it's a perfect example of the radical/traditionalist ethos Abrams has done so much to foster and which the Art Ensemble of Chicago did so much to trivialize.

In sharp contrast to his rapport with Favors, Abrams simply lets Amina Claudine Myers get in his way. Piano duos are rarely successful, and this one seems more laden and leaden than most.

** **1-OQA+19** Black Saint BSR 0017 LP
Abrams; Anthony Braxton (*as, sno, f, cl, v*); Henry Threadgill (*as, ts, f, v*); Leonard
Jones (*b, v*); Steve McCall (*d, perc, v*). 11–12/77.

*** **Spihumonesty** Black Saint BSR 0032 LP
Abrams; George Lewis (*tb, sousaphone, synth*); Roscoe Mitchell (*as, f*); Amina
Claudine Myers (*p, electric p, org*); Leonard Jones (*b*); Jay Clayton (*v*); Youssef
Yancey (*theremin*). 7/79.

Myers's contribution to *Spihumonesty* (a typically punning title that recalls the gnomic and
esoteric titles of bebop, like 'Klactoveesedstene') is a good deal more acute. The drummerless
band moves through the charts like information through a printed circuit, and there is an
intriguing simultaneity to some of the cues that suggests – rightly or wrongly – something like
Braxton's wholly-composed conception. In truth, Abrams isn't a great soloist in the
conventional sense. But that doesn't mean that he attempts to submerge more assertive musical
personalities in a bland collective logic. Here the balance of ensemble and solo is well
maintained and the timbral range impressively extended by Lewis's computer/synth and the
peculiar sound of the theremin (the woo-woo bit in the Beach Boys' 'Good Vibrations').
Abrams did finer things in the '80s, but this is well worth tracking back.
    The earlier set has, on the face of it, a more impressive starting line-up. Though Threadgill is
a much less demanding player than Mitchell, Anthony Braxton is one of the certain masters of
modern jazz and perhaps Abrams's most gifted pupil. The music they make is complex,
scurryingly allusive and seldom directly appealing. Braxton's title composition is compellingly
handled, and so is 'Charlie In The Parker' (compare George Lewis's similarly conceived
homage on Black Saint BSR 0029), but there are question marks over some of the rest. May
take longer to absorb than is strictly worthwhile.

** **Mama And Daddy** Black Saint BSR 0041 LP
Abrams; Baikida Carroll (*t, flhn*); Vincent Chancey (*hrn*); Wallace McMillan (*as, bs, ts,
f, perc*); Andrew Cyrille (*perc*); George Lewis (*tb*); Bob Stewart (*tba*); Leroy Jenkins
(*vn*); Brian Smith (*b*). 12/79.

** **Blues Forever** Black Saint BSR 0061 LP
Abrams; Baikida Carroll (*t, flhn*); Vincent Chancey (*hrn*); Wallace McMillan (*as, bs, ts,
f, perc*); Andrew Cyrille (*perc*); Craig Harris (*tb*); Jimmy Vass (*as, f*); Eugene Ghee
(*ts, cl*); Howard Johnson (*tba*); Jean-Paul Bourelly (*g*); Michael Logan (*b*); Thurman
Barker (*d, mar, perc*). 7/81.

** **Rejoicing With The Light** Black Saint BSR 0071 CD/LP
Abrams; Baikida Carroll (*t, flhn*); Vincent Chancey (*hrn*); Wallace McMillan (*as, bs, ts,
f, perc*); Andrew Cyrille (*perc*); Marty Ehrlich (*as, f, cl*); Patience Higgins (*cl, alto cl,
bs*); Jean-Paul Bourelly (*g*); Abdul Wadud (*clo*); Rick Rosie (*b*); Warren Smith (*vib,
timp, perc*). 1/83.

Three albums recorded at two-year intervals and credited to Abrams's regular – but shifting –
Orchestra. How much more orchestrally they play than some of the larger chamber groups is a
little difficult to judge, and there seems to be little difference in the basic philosophy. These are
slightly uneasy records, by no means his most impressive work. *Blues Forever* has an energy the
other two lack, but it is an energy that remains potential rather than convincingly actual.
Rejoicing With The Light is perhaps the record of choice, better recorded, tauter and more
coherent.

(*) **View From Within Black Saint BSR 0081 CD/LP
Abrams; Stanton Davis (*t, flhn*); John Purcell (*as, ss, f, ts, bcl*); Marty Ehrlich (*picc, f,
as, ts, cl, bcl*); Warren Smith (*vib, mar, perc*); Rick Rosie (*b*); Thurman Barker (*d,
perc*); Ray Mantilla (*perc*). 9/84.

(*) **Colors In Thirty-Third Black Saint BSR 1091 CD/LP
Abrams; John Purcell (*ss, ts, bcl*); Dave Holland (*clo, b*); Fred Hopkins (*b*); Andrew
Cyrille (*d*); John Blake (*v*). 12/86.

View From Within and *Colors In Thirty-Third* sound paradoxically like Abrams's most personal
work of the '80s. The multi-instrumental approach lends the first a fluid, unsettled quality that
is rectified only by Thurman Barker's typically inspirational percussion and by Abrams's own

patient articulation. The slightly later *Colors* has a more meditative and philosophical air, almost as if Abrams is taking careful stock of his 'Inner Lights'; the basic personnel divide into trio, quartet, quintet and, for the title piece and the significantly named 'Introspection', full sextet. Purcell creates counterpoints and high triumphal passages worthy of his distant English namesake. As on the Orchestra albums, Barker is matched for pace and intensity only by Andrew Cyrille, to whom 'Drumman' is dedicated. Plenty of fine things here, though surprisingly little of the much-hinted-at change of artistic direction.

**   **The Hearinga Suite** Black Saint 120 103-2 CD/LP
Abrams; Ron Tooley, Jack Walrath, Cecil Bridgewater, Frank Gordon (*t*); Clifton Anderson, Dick Griffin, Jack Jeffers, Bill Lowe (*tb*); John Purcell (*f, cl, ts*); Marty Ehrlich (*picc, f, cl, as*); Patience Higgins (*bcl, ts*); Courtnay Wynter (*bsn, bcl, ts*); Charles Davis (*bs, ss*); Diedre Murray (*clo*); Fred Hopkins (*b*); Warren Smith (*vib, perc*); Andrew Cyrille (*d*). 1/89.

This is the best possible evidence for the non-progression of Abrams's style, an album that might have been recorded at almost any point over the past fifteen to twenty years and which bears no discernible mark of what has been happening in creative improvisation since 1970.

As E. M. Forster said, though, 'progress' isn't everything in art. Works need to be judged on their own terms. Sadly, perhaps, by that logic *The Hearinga Suite* comes out even less positively. The ingredients are all in place: big, affirmative woodwinds placed against rather more sombre and sceptical statements from the carefully weighted brass. Abrams's synthesizer effects are beautifully executed, but the whole seems to be striving for some totalizing significance; it's interesting to compare Ellington's untroubled conception of the suite as a straightforward sequence of dance themes. Disappointing, but certainly not a technical knockout.

****   **Blu Blu Blu** Black Saint 120 117 CD
Abrams; Joel Brandon (*whistle*); Jack Walrath (*t*); Alfred Patterson (*tb*); Mark Taylor (*frhn*); Joe Daley (*tba*); John Purcell (*as, f, bcl*); Robert De Bellis (*as, cl, bcl*); Eugene Ghee (*ts, cl, bcl*); Dave Fiuczynski (*g*); Lindsay Horner, Brad Jones (*b*); Warren Smith (*vib, tym*); Thurman Barker (*d*). 11/90.

Abrams's best album for some considerable time is a showcase for the extraordinary – and initially unsettling – talents of whistler Joel Brandon (also featured on David Murray's recent big-band album, DIW 851). At first hearing, Brandon's high swooping lines sound remarkably like the MiniMoog features Jan Hammer used to contribute to the Mahavishnu Orchestra, only much more quickly delivered. 'One For The Whistler' is a *tour de force*, but elsewhere on the album Brandon demonstrates his own and his instrument's viability in an improvising context.

Abrams really gets going as a pianist only on the final 'Stretch Time', leaving most of the foreground to a tonally varied and adventurous band. The title-track is a dedication to McKinley Morganfield (better known as the late, great Muddy Waters). Fiuczynski's howling guitar initially sounds out of place, but it settles back into a typically sophisticated and historically aware chart which underlines Abrams's commitment to the wider spectrum of black music. Walrath is forceful among the brasses and Barker moves fluently between abstraction and big-band swing. Set alongside Sun Ra's later work and Butch Morris's 'conduction' experiments, this is among the most important contemporary big-band records. Highly recommended.

GEORGE ADAMS (born 1940)
TENOR SAXOPHONE, FLUTE, BASS CLARINET

**   **Don't Loose Control** Soul Note SN 1004 LP
Adams; Don Pullen (*p*); Cameron Brown (*b*); Dannie Richmond (*d*). 11/79.

***   **Live At The Village Vanguard** Soul Note SN 1094 CD/LP/MC
As above. 8/83.

***   **Live At The Village Vanguard 2** Soul Note SN 1144 CD/LP/MC
As above. 8/83.

***   **Earth Beams** Timeless SJP 147 CD/LP
As above. 81.

***   **Life Line** Timeless SJP 154 LP
As above. 8/80.

***   **City Gates** Timeless SJP 181 LP
As above. 3/83.

***   **Decisions** Timeless SJP 205 CD/LP
As above. 2/84.

**   **Live At Montmartre** Timeless SJP 219
As above, except add John Scofield (*g*). 4/85.

***   **Breakthrough** Blue Note BT 85122 CD/LP
As above. 4/86.

***   **Song Everlasting** Blue Note BLJ 46907 CD/LP
As above. 4/87.

This is certainly one of the most successful long-standing units working in contemporary jazz. Co-led with Don Pullen – the Blue Note sessions list the pianist's name first – the quartet combines a convincing unity of purpose with tremendous individuality of response. Adams is a powerful player with a huge, fruity tone that occasionally overwhelms lesser sidemen. Pullen's forceful right-hand chords are a perfect complement and foil. Richmond, with the weight of many years with Charles Mingus behind him, has no problems with powerful personalities and always plays superbly in these settings, as on the co-led *Hand To Hand* (see below). He is particularly fine on the rumbustious *Village Vanguard* sessions, which see the band stretch out the tight Monk-inspired structures of the studio sets in order to explore some of the freer areas Adams and Pullen enter in their duo work (see below).

Adams has a technique which suggests a hybrid of Albert Ayler and Sonny Rollins. He has Ayler's power, but, more tellingly, much of Rollins's superb instinct for the structural logic of a song or of a chord progression. He is at home with material ranging from Stephen Foster and traditional hymns to the wilder shores of atonality (and Pullen's Taylorish free play describes a similar arc).

Completists will, of course, want the lot. Newcomers might well start with *City Gates*, which includes a version of 'Thank You Very Much, Mr Monk' (the kick-off piece on the slightly later *Village Vanguard* double set), a Mingus tribute, a samba, and a reading of 'Nobody Knows The Trouble I've Seen'. Taken together, that's a fair cross-section of what they do. The subsequent Timeless albums are qualitatively pretty much of a piece, though John Scofield's contribution to *Live at Montmartre* seems a little supernumerary. The Blue Notes are fine, too.

(*)   **Melodic Excursions Timeless SJP 166 CD/LP
Adams; Don Pullen (*p*). 6/82.

This is perhaps more influenced by Pullen's conception than was usually the case in the quartets. It is a curious album, demanding without being particularly involving. There is a hot, gospelly 'God Has Smiled On Me' (the shortest track) and six originals, almost all of which play on the inbuilt dichotomies of the duo format. It's probably unfortunate that the dichotomies insist more strongly than the unities in this case; unusually, and however responsive they seem to be, the two players give every sense of working on parallel tracks rather than in tandem.

**   **Hand To Hand** Soul Note SN 1007 CD/LP

(*)   **Gentlemen's Agreement Soul Note SN 1057 LP
Adams; Jimmy Knepper (*tb*); Hugh Lawson (*p*); Mike Richmond (*b*); Dannie Richmond (*d*). 2/80, 1/83.

Co-led by the drummer, these sets are marked by fine writing and some ambitious structures redolent of Mingus bands, where five could be made to sound like a dozen and every solo suggested an entire section at play. The 'Symphony For Five' on *Gentlemen's Agreement* moves into Dolphy territory, as does 'Prayer For A Jitterbug'. The tonality is broader than on the quartet sessions; Knepper's playing is reminiscent of Vic Dickenson, an almost regressive style that ignores much of the Bebop 'Bone Book and keeps the trombone closer to the saxophone's timbral range and attack. Lawson is an intelligent and lyrical pianist, but he isn't in Pullen's class, and these sets are nowhere like as compelling as the Adams/Pullen quartets.

7

*** **Jazzbühne Berlin '85** Repertoire REPCD 4912 CD
Adams; James Blood Ulmer (g, v); Amin Ali (b); Grant Calvin Weston (d). 6/85.

Ulmer's choke-riffs and dark downward spirals propel Adams to some of his most unbuttoned blowing on 'Black Rock' and 'America', but there's a forced quality to this which one doesn't find on *Revealing* (In + Out 7005 CD, reviewed in the entry on Ulmer). As on many of Repertoire's live sessions from East Berlin, the sound is a bit cavernous. It suits this music better than most.

*(*) **Nightingale** Blue Note CDP 7919842 CD
Adams; Hugh Lawson (p); Sirone (b); Victor Lewis (d). 8/88.

** **America** Blue Note CDP 7938962 CD
Adams; Hugh Lawson (p); Cecil McBee (b); Mark Johnson (d). 5–7/89.

Hard to gauge where Adams's tongue is on these collections of old American songs. Hendrix claimed his 'Star-Spangled Banner' was respectfully straight; Adams's seems too ironic for that. Alongside 'America The Beautiful', played with a little wobble in the voice, and 'Have You Thanked America?', it seems a long way from the anger of the late '60s and early '70s radicalized New Thing, where dialogue with a white populist tradition represented treason. On the other hand, it scarcely seems to represent a comfortable acommodation. The band play well, and the recording is typical blue riband Blue Note, but there are too many question marks over this one.

   Nightingale set out to confront a black spiritual tradition, but eventually included 'Bridge Over Troubled Water' (an astonishingly bland performance), 'Cry Me A River', and 'A Nightingale Sang In Berkeley Square' (which calls into question whose turf he is trying to colonize). Rollins is a masterful vertical and melodic improviser; Adams seems too caught up in textures and gestures.

PEPPER ADAMS (1930–86)
BARITONE SAXOPHONE

*** **My One And Only Love** West Wind 2053 CD
Adams; Stu Williamson (t); Carl Perkins (p); Leroy Vinnegar (b); Mel Lewis (d). 7/57.

*** **10 To 4 At The 5-Spot** Original Jazz Classics OJC 031 LP
Adams; Donald Byrd (t); Bobby Timmons (p); Doug Watkins (b); Elvin Jones (d). 4/58.

The baritone sax was as unpopular with the hard bop musicians as it was with original boppers and, come to that, the swing-era saxophonists. Pepper Adams, more than anyone, came close to making it a congenial instrument in the hothouse environment of hard bop. He had a dry, unsentimental tone – very different to either Serge Chaloff or Gerry Mulligan – and a penchant for full-tilt solos that gave no shred of concession to the horn's 'cumbersome' reputation. The live session, made with a frequent partner at the time, Donald Byrd, is typical of Adams's kind of date, with muscular blow-outs of the order of 'Hastings Street Bounce' sitting next to a clear-headed ballad reading of 'You're My Thrill'. That said, it's sometimes only the novelty value of hearing a baritone in the ensembles that lifts the music out of a professional hard bop routine. *My One And Only Love* is a reissue of an LP first issued on Mode, distinguished by an exceptional rhythm section but marred a little by the glibness which afflicts so many sessions of the period: still, the particularly lyrical Williamson contrasts with Adams's rigour to good effect.

*** **Pepper Adams Plays Charlie Mingus** Fresh Sound FSR-CD 177 CD
Adams; Thad Jones (t); Bennie Powell (tb); Charles McPherson (as); Zoot Sims (ts); Hank Jones (p); Paul Chambers, Bob Cranshaw (b); Dannie Richmond (d). 9/63.

Adams led this date with his usual no-nonsense authority. There are nine Mingus tunes and a mixture of Mingusians and – in the case of Zoot Sims – at least one musician about as far removed from being a Mingus sideman as one could imagine, though Zoot deals with the situation as imperturbably as always. The results, split between a quintet and an octet, are akin to a pocket-size edition of a typical Mingus band: 'Haitian Fight Song' and 'Fables Of Faubus' are as swinging as any Mingus version (Chambers is at the top of his game), but 'Better Git In

Your Soul' (*sic.*) is comparatively watery and Jones is a lot more dapper than a Mingus pianist might have been. A solid jazz record.

(*)   **Ephemera Spotlite PA6 LP
Adams; Roland Hanna (*p*); George Mraz (*b*); Mel Lewis (*d*). 10/73.

**   **Reflectory** Muse MR 5182 LP
As above, except Billy Hart (*d*) replaces Lewis. 6/78.

(*)   **The Master Muse MR 5213 LP
Adams; Tommy Flanagan (*p*); George Mraz (*b*); Leroy Williams (*d*). 3/80.

Adams led few sessions under his own name, and the above three 1970s dates are among the few which are still available (two Enja albums from a similar period have yet to emerge on CD). The Spotlite album was recorded in London and has all concerned in good fettle, although both this and *Reflectory* suffer from a certain fatigue, as if the leader felt that bop figurations, as much as he trusted them, often led him nowhere. *The Master* benefits greatly from the sure, calm hands of Tommy Flanagan, whose thoughtful contributions to 'Chelsea Bridge' and 'My Shining Hour' enhance the leader's own.

***(*)   **Conjuration: Fat Tuesday's Session** Reservoir RSR 113 CD
Adams; Kenny Wheeler (*t, flhn*); Hank Jones (*p*); Clint Houston (*b*); Louis Hayes (*d*). 8/83.

A heartening farewell to Adams's career on record, this live set emphasizes his virtues – the muscularity of sound, oversized tone and plangent phrasing – so decisively that one overlooks any scent of routine in the playing. Kenny Wheeler, an unlikely partner, adds sparkle and some good material, and Hank Jones is sublimely buoyant, as are Houston and Hayes. Three extra tracks have been added to the original LP issue, bringing the running time to 66 minutes.

STEVE ADAMS
SOPRANO, ALTO AND TENOR SAXOPHONES, FLUTE, ALTO FLUTE

***   **Anacrusis** Nine Winds NW 0128 LP
Adams; Vinny Golia (*ts, bs, bcl, cbcl, bf, picc*); Ken Filiano (*b*); Billy Mintz (*d*). 8/88.

This quartet is co-led by Adams and Filiano, and they play free jazz which follows a clear descent from Ornette Coleman: Filiano's '3, 5, 4 Ornette' might be a direct tribute, and most of the material encourages the two horns into energetic train-of-thought solos against simple metres from bass and drums. There's not much obfuscation, just a search for streams of melody: Golia is the garrulous, argumentative player, Adams relatively restrained; between them, they make an interesting pairing, even if some of the tracks don't go anywhere in particular.

JULIAN 'CANNONBALL' ADDERLEY (1928–75)
ALTO SAXOPHONE

***   **Presenting Cannonball** Savoy SV-0108 CD
Adderley; Nat Adderley (*c*); Hank Jones (*p*); Paul Chambers (*b*); Kenny Clarke (*d*). 7/55.

****   **Somethin' Else** Blue Note CDP 7463382 CD/MC
Adderley; Miles Davis (*t*); Hank Jones (*p*); Sam Jones (*b*); Art Blakey (*d*). 3/58.

***   **Portrait Of Cannonball** Original Jazz Classics OJC 361 CD/LP/MC
Adderley; Blue Mitchell (*t*); Bill Evans (*p*); Sam Jones (*b*); Philly Joe Jones (*d*). 7/58.

***(*)   **Things Are Getting Better** Original Jazz Classics OJC 032 CD/LP/MC
Adderley; Wynton Kelly (*p*); Milt Jackson (*vib*); Percy Heath (*b*); Art Blakey (*d*). 10/58.

***   **Cannonball And Coltrane** Emarcy 8345882 CD
Adderley; John Coltrane (*ts*); Wynton Kelly (*p*); Paul Chambers (*b*); Jimmy Cobb (*d*). 2/59.

(*)   **Cannonball Takes Charge Landmark 1306 CD/LP/MC
Adderley; Wynton Kelly (*p*); Paul Chambers, Percy Heath (*b*); Jimmy Cobb, Albert
'Tootie' Heath (*d*). 4–5/59.

***   **Compact Jazz: Cannonball Adderley** EmArcy 842933-2 CD
Adderley; Nat Adderley (*c*); Ernie Royal, Joe Newman, Clark Terry (*t*); J. J. Johnson,
Jimmy Cleveland, Melba Liston, Britt Woodman, Paul Faulise (*tb*); Earle Warren,
John Coltrane, Jerome Richardson, Budd Johnson, Yusef Lateef, Seldon Powell (*ts*);
Cecil Payne (*bs*); Horace Silver, John Williams, Junior Mance, Tommy Flanagan,
Wynton Kelly (*p*); Paul Chambers, Sam Jones, Ray Brown (*b*); Kenny Clarke, Roy
Haynes, Jimmy Cobb, Osie Johnson (*d*). 7/55–1/62.

Long a critically undervalued figure, Cannonball Adderley's status as a great popularizer and
patron spirit of the music has, if anything, increased since his sadly early death. The
blues-soaked tone and hard, swinging delivery of his alto lines is as recognizable and
communicative a sound as anything in the aftermath of bebop and, while many have been quick
to criticize his essentially derivative manner – Cannonball always fell back on clichés, because
he just liked the sound of them – there's a lean, hard-won quality about his best playing which
says a lot about one man's dedication to his craft. Everything was already in place at the time of
his 1955 debut, with brother Nat playing the eternal second fiddle: in sprucely remastered
sound, the music sounds like an excerpt from almost any stage of the leader's career. When he
joined Miles Davis, Adderley's cameo appearances on *Milestones* and *Kind Of Blue* were
somewhat outclassed by the leader's returning-the-favour guest spot on *Somethin' Else*, which
features some of Davis's most pithy improvising. But something else distinguishes the Adderley
sessions of this period: the superb line-up of supporting players. There is marvellous sparring
with Milt Jackson on *Things Are Getting Better*, with Kelly, Heath and Blakey in great form too,
and 'The Sidewalks Of New York' is an inspired revision which only Ellington's incomparable
1940 version can surpass. *Cannonball Takes Charge* is perhaps only ordinary, but *Portrait Of
Cannonball* (which includes three alternative takes on the CD issue) finds Blue Mitchell taking
some welcome limelight – though he sounds no more facile than the oft-maligned Nat – and an
early glimpse of Bill Evans feeling his way through 'Nardis'. The session with Coltrane is really
the Miles Davis band without Miles, and it's a bit of good fun, both horn men flexing their
muscles on the blues and a ballad feature apiece. There isn't really a dud record in this batch.
The *Compact Jazz* compilation picks from six sessions led by Cannonball and one by Nat, some
from otherwise unavailable records (*Sophisticated Swing*, *Cannonball's Sharpshooters*): a useful
primer on the altoman's early days in the studios.

***   **In San Francisco** Original Jazz Classics OJC 035 CD/LP/MC
Adderley; Nat Adderley (*c*); Bobby Timmons (*p*); Sam Jones (*b*); Louis Hayes (*d*).
10/59.

***   **Them Dirty Blues** Landmark 1301 CD/LP/MC
As above, except add Barry Harris (*p*). 2–3/60.

***   **Cannonball And The Poll Winners** Landmark 1304 CD/LP/MC
Adderley; Victor Feldman (*p, vib*); Wes Montgomery (*g*); Ray Brown (*b*); Louis
Hayes (*d*). 5–6/60.

***(*)   **At The Lighthouse** Landmark 1305 CD/LP/MC
Adderley; Nat Adderley (*c*); Victor Feldman (*p*); Sam Jones (*b*); Louis Hayes (*d*).
10/60.

Adderley's regular quintet has often been damned with such faint praise as 'unpretentious' and
'soulful'. This was a hard-hitting, rocking band which invested blues and blowing formulae with
an intensity which helped to keep one part of jazz's communication channels open at the time
of Ornette Coleman, Eric Dolphy and other seekers after new forms. The two live albums, cut
in San Francisco and at the Hermosa Beach Lighthouse, are memorably rowdy and exciting
sessions. *In San Francisco* is a little overstretched, with four tracks nudging the 12-minute mark
and some of the solos running out of steam too soon, but *At The Lighthouse* is crisper and
wittier: Feldman, who contributes the engaging 'Azule Serape' to the band book, is a lot more
interesting than Timmons, and the Adderleys are in rousing form: Cannonball's six choruses on
'Sack O' Woe' distil some of the best of himself. *Them Dirty Blues* introduces two classic
set-pieces in 'Dat Dere' and 'Work Song' – and the originals are still the best – while Barry

Harris sits in for half of the set. Jones and Hayes aren't often remarked on as a rhythm team, but they're as big-hearted and generously propulsive as this music has to be. The *Poll Winners* date is a brief vacation for Cannonball, and he trades licks with Wes Montgomery to piquant effect. The remastering of this series is excellent.

***   **African Waltz** Original Jazz Classics OJC 258 LP/MC
        Adderley; Clark Terry, Ernie Royal, Joe Newman, Nick Travis (*t*); Nat Adderley (*c*);
        Bob Brookmeyer (*vtb*); Melba Liston, Arnette Sparrow, George Matthews, Jimmy
        Cleveland, Paul Faulise (*tb*); George Dorsey (*as, f*); Jerome Richardson, Oliver
        Jackson (*ts, f*); Arthur Clarke (*bs*); Wynton Kelly (*p*); Sam Jones (*b*); Don Butterfield
        (*tba*); Louis Hayes, Charlie Persip (*d*); Ray Barretto, Olatunji (*perc*). 2–5/61.

Disappointingly, this one hasn't yet made it to CD: it's both a departure from and an extension of what the Adderleys were doing in their small groups. Ernie Wilkins arranges a set of fulsome, top-heavy charts which Adderley has to jostle with to create their own space, and the music's worth hearing for its sheer brashness and impact. But the simple clarity of the Adderley small-groups is a casualty of the setting, and the altoman isn't as convincingly at home here as he is in the *Great Jazz Standards* album with Gil Evans, one of his finest hours.

***   **Know What I Mean?** Original Jazz Classics OJC 105 CD/LP/MC
        Adderley; Bill Evans (*p*); Percy Heath (*b*); Connie Kay (*d*). 1–3/61.

***   **Cannonball Adderley Quintet Plus** Original Jazz Classics OJC 306 CD/LP/MC
        Adderley; Nat Adderley (*c*); Victor Feldman (*p, vib*); Wynton Kelly (*p*); Sam Jones
        (*b*); Louis Hayes (*d*). 5/61.

(*)   **In New York Original Jazz Classics OJC 142 CD/LP/MC
        Adderley; Nat Adderley (*c*); Yusef Lateef (*ts, ob*); Joe Zawinul (*p*); Sam Jones (*b*);
        Louis Hayes (*d*). 1/62.

***   **Cannonball In Europe!** Landmark 1307 CD/LP/MC
        As above. 8/62.

(*)   **Jazz Workshop Revisited Landmark 1303 CD/LP/MC
        As above. 9/62.

(*)   **Cannonball's Bossa Nova Landmark 1302 CD/LP/MC
        Adderley; Pedro Paulo (*t*); Paulo Moura (*as*); Sergie Mondez (*p*); Durval Ferreira (*g*);
        Octavio Bielly (*b*); Dom Um Romao (*d*). 12/62.

***   **Nippon Soul** Original Jazz Classics OJC 435 CD/LP/MC
        Adderley; Nat Adderley (*c*); Yusef Lateef (*ts, ob, f*); Joe Zawinul (*p*); Sam Jones (*b*);
        Louis Hayes (*d*). 7/63.

Cannonball continued to turn out records for Riverside at a cracking pace and, while there are no classics here, his own big-hearted playing seldom falters. At this point, though, the regimen of tours and records begins to fossilize some aspects of his own playing. Having stratified bop licks and set the pace for so-called 'soul jazz', Adderley found there wasn't much left to do but play them over again. If he plays with undiminished verve, the power of his improvising declines. The quartet date with Bill Evans was one of the last chances to hear him as sole horn, and he sounds fine; *Plus* brings in Wynton Kelly on a few tracks, enabling Feldman to play some more vibes, but it's otherwise a routine Adderley band date. Bringing in Joe Zawinul and Yusef Lateef energized the band anew, but the records are all vaguely disappointing. Zawinul is still no more than a good bandsman, and Lateef's touches of exotica – such as the oboe solo on 'Brother John' (*Nippon Soul*) or his furry, Roland Kirk-like flute improvisations – are an awkward match for the sunnier disposition of the customary material. Nevertheless *Nippon Soul* and *In Europe* are perhaps the best of this bunch; the *bossa nova* set is a perfunctory nod to prevailing breezes. The men who earn exemption from criticism on most of these records are Sam Jones and Louis Hayes: seldom remembered as a major rhythm section, their unflagging tempos and generosity of spirit centre the music at all times.

**   **Cannonball In Japan** Capitol CDP 7935602 CD
        Adderley; Nat Adderley (*c*); Joe Zawinul (*p*); Victor Gaskin (*b*); Roy McCurdy (*d*).
        8/66.

***   **The Best Of Cannonball Adderley: The Capitol Years** Capitol CDP 7954822 CD
As above, except add Yusef Lateef, Charles Lloyd (*ts*); Sam Jones, Walter Booker (*b*); Louis Hayes (*d*). 8/62–10/69.

**   **Radio Nights** Night VNCD2 CD
As above, except omit Lateef and Booker. 12/67–1/68.

Adderley kept on recording regularly until his death, but his later albums are currently in limbo so far as the catalogues are concerned. Close to 20 Capitol albums have been boiled down to one live set from Tokyo and the best-of, which actually starts with two tracks from Riverside sessions. Given that many of the later records were misfire attempts at fusion of one sort or another, maybe it's not such a bad thing. *Cannonball In Japan* is another live show in a favourite location: the group play well enough, but it won't enrich any who already have other Adderley records. Nor does *Radio Nights*, from the eccentric on-location series which Night are releasing, offer anything out of the ordinary: sound is only middling here. The best-of is short on surprise, and concentrates mostly on Zawinul's additions to the band's book, including their hit 'Mercy Mercy Mercy' and 'Country Preacher', which has a rare glimpse of the leader on soprano. But the most interesting thing is the lengthy '74 Miles Away', which suggests the distant influence of late Coltrane, with Cannonball's solo straying into what are for him very remote regions. That the group finally don't know what to do with the situation says something about the limits of their ambitions.

NAT ADDERLEY (born 1931)
CORNET, TRUMPET

****   **Work Song** Original Jazz Classics OJC 363 CD/LP/MC
Adderley; Bobby Timmons (*p*); Wes Montgomery (*g*); Keter Betts, Sam Jones (*b*); Louis Hayes, Percy Heath (*d*).

***(*)   **In The Bag** Original Jazz Classics OJC 648 CD/LP/MC
Adderley; Julian 'Cannonball' Adderley (*as*); Nat Perrilliat (*ts*); Ellis Marsalis (*p*); Sam Jones (*b*); James Black (*d*).

***   **That's Nat** Savoy SV 0146 CD
Adderley; Jerome Richardson (*ts, f*); Hank Jones (*p*); Wendell Marshall (*b*); Kenny Clarke (*d*). 7/55.

***   **Branching Out** Original Jazz Classics OJC 255 LP/MC
Adderley; Johnny Griffin (*ts*); The Three Sounds: Gene Harris (*p*); Andy Simpkins (*b*); Bill Dowdy (*d*). 9/58.

The Adderley brothers helped keep a light burning for jazz when rock'n'roll was dominating the industry 'demographics'. Neither was ever particularly revolutionary or adventurous in style but saxophonist Cannonball's enormous personality and untimely death, together with his participation in such legendary dates as Miles's *Kind Of Blue* have sanctified his memory with young fans who would have found his live performances rather predictable.

Nat was always the more incisive soloist, with a bright, ringing tone that most obviously drew on the example of Dizzy Gillespie but in which could be heard a whole raft of influences from Clark Terry to Henry 'Red' Allen to the pre-post-modern Miles of the 1950s.

'I Married An Angel', on *That's Nat*, suggests that Bobby Hackett be added to that roster. A gorgeously toned ballad performance which keeps referring to the original tune, it's perhaps the best single track on a beautifully remastered recording. Jones's comping is inch-perfect throughout and Clarke is right on the case, often following Adderley outside the basic count for a phrase or two.

In 1958, the cornetist was playing at his peak and these sessions do genuinely merit the 'classic' tag, though 'original' is probably stretching things a bit. Griffin is, as always, tough and uncompromising, with a devastating technique over the sprint and an underrated touch with ballads and mid-tempo tunes. The Three Sounds virtually wrote the book on this sort of section playing, water-tight but relaxed.

Work Song is the classic, of course. Laced with a funky blues feel, but marked by some unexpectedly lyrical playing (on 'Violets For Your Furs' and 'My Heart Stood Still') from the leader. Montgomery manages to produce something more enterprising than his trademark octave runs and hits a tense, almost threatening groove. Timmons is more predictable, but just right for this sort of set; compare *In San Francisco* (OJC 035) which was made under Cannonball's name. *In The Bag* is welcome for a further glimpse of the brothers playing together, but isn't specially exciting. Watch out for the little-known Perrilliat, who plays a firm-toned and steady tenor, with some interesting quirks. The CD has a couple of rather inconsequential bonus tracks.

*** **On The Move** Theresa TR 117 LP
  Adderley; Sonny Fortune (*as*); Larry Willis (*p*); Walter Booker (*b*); Jimmy Cobb (*d*).

A fair proportion of listeners played this one cold would plump for Cannonball as the altoist, which suggests it may have been an attempt to recreate that cheerfully bouncing sound. In many respects Fortune is a more interesting player, inserting oddly angular ideas and figures into relatively innocuous contexts, stretching out with ideas that Cannonball would have dismissed with the back of his hand. The group as a whole is very strong and while there might be quibbles about the sound quality, there are none whatsoever about the music.

(*) **Don't Look Back Steeplechase SCS 1059 CD/LP
  Adderley; Ken McIntyre (*as, bcl, ob, f*); John Stubblefield (*ts, ss*); Onaje Allan Gumbs (*p, ky*); Fernando Gumbs (*b*); Ira Buddy Williams (*d*); Victor See Yuen (*perc*). 8/76.

Adderley's reputation as a mainstream traditionalist takes a knock with sets like these. Unfortunately, the results aren't by any means commensurate with the daring of the line-up. McIntyre is an important catalyst in the re-voicing of jazz horns, but like a true catalyst he remains largely untouched by what goes on round him and solos as if alone. Stubblefield is fierier and provokes some of the leader's best returns of fire. Whatever Gumbs's qualities, he's patently wrong for this gig and the rest of the group circle round him somewhat uneasily. A bold effort, but not quite there.

*** **A Little New York Midtown Music** Galaxy GXY 5120 LP
  Adderley; Johnny Griffin (*ts*); Victor Feldman (*p, electric p*); Ron Carter (*b*); Roy McCurdy (*d*). 9/78.

The 1978 set finds Adderley in the sort of conducive company he was to find later in the Paris Reunion Band, with Griffin sounding remarkably like Nathan Davis in some passages. Adderley's brass tone is as clean-cut and fleet as ever; Feldman is a quirky asset to any band and the bass and drums combination of Carter and McCurdy, who sound and occasionally play like a firm of mid-town lawyers, manage to relax an initially strict construction of the tempo in time for some fine solos from the horns. Recommended (and great 'blindfold' test material).

(*) **Talkin' About You Landmark LCD 1528 2 CD
  Adderley; Vincent Herring (*as*); Rob Bargad (*p*); Walter Booker (*b*); Jimmy Cobb (*d*). 11/90.

Astonishingly slow to get going (almost as if it were an unedited take of a live set) and marred by intonation problems with both horns, this develops into a storming session with Eddie Vinson's 'Arriving Soon'. Adderley's tone is better on medium tempo themes like Victor Feldman's swinging 'Azule Serape' but he doesn't have a sure enough lip for the moody 'Ill Wind', a theme tailored to Herring's melting delivery. The rhythm section is faultless and the digital recording is of the highest quality.

AFRO-ASIAN MUSIC ENSEMBLE
GROUP

*** **Tomorrow Is Now** Soul Note SN 1117 LP
  Fred Houn (*bs, leader*); Sam Furnace (*as, ts*); Sayyd Abdul Al-Khabyyr, Al Givens (*ss, ts, f*); Richard Clements (*p*); Jon Jang (*p*); Kyoto Fujiwara (*b*); Taru Alexander (*d*); Carleen Robinson (*v*). 85.

(*) **We Refuse To Be Used And Abused Soul Note SN 1167 CD/LP/MC
  Fred Houn (*bs, ss, f*); Sam Furnace (*as, ss, f*); Hafez Modir (*ts, f*); Jon Jang (*p*); Kyoto Fujiwara (*b*); Royal Hartigan (*perc*). 11/87.

This is powerfully advocated activist music from a 'rainbow coalition' of fine young players, led by the young baritone saxophonist Fred Houn. Houn, an Asian-American like pianist Jang, has a big, powerful sound reminiscent of Harry Carney, and this sets the tone for the ensemble, which has a strongly Ellingtonian cast.

The title of the first album sets up all sorts of expectations – from Ornette Coleman's *Tomorrow Is The Question* to Max Roach's *Freedom Now* suite – which are not so much confounded as skirted. There would seem to be little place for prettiness in music as aggressively programmatic as this, but the band plays with surprising delicacy and unfailing taste.

The later album is more bitty and has a much less coherent sound. There is also a degree of stridency completely missing from the earlier set. Together, though, they represent an interesting development beyond the politicized jazz of Charlie Haden's Liberation Music Ensemble. An object lesson for America's new New Frontier in the dismal '80s.

AIR / NEW AIR
GROUP

**   **Live Air** Black Saint BSR 0034 CD/LP
             Henry Threadgill (*as, ts, f, bs f, hubkaphone*); Fred Hopkins (*b*); Steve McCall (*d, perc*). 10/77.

***(*)   **Air Lore** Bluebird ND86578 CD
             As above. 5/79.

***   **Air Mail** Black Saint BSR 0049 CD/LP
             As above. 12/80.

**   **New Air: Live At Montreal International Jazz Festival** Black Saint BSR 0084 CD/LP
             As above, except add Pheeroan AkLaff (*d, perc*). 7/83.

One of the less shambolic units to come out of the AACM, and, on its day, a far more interesting band than the Art Ensemble of Chicago. Though Threadgill, the *de facto* leader, is a far less complex musician than either Roscoe Mitchell or Joseph Jarman, he shows a far clearer and more sophisticated understanding of form, and an awareness (even more noticeable on the earlier, deleted *Air Song*, *Air Raid* and *Air Time*) of the need to conceive music for the band *democratically* but also *dramatically* (Air was formed to provide incidental music for a play about Scott Joplin and *Air Lore* is a fascinating free meditation on compositions by Joplin and Jelly Roll Morton), in such a way that the drums are conceived as another voiced and pitched instrument. Perhaps only with McCall would this have been practicable. Unlike almost any of his contemporaries, he is able to play ametrically, with almost no quantifiable pulse, at the same time as Hopkins is shadowing the saxophonist's marvellous lines. On *Lore*, different sections of original rags and blues are assigned to different players, and in the absence of a piano the drummer was called upon for melodic as well as rhythmic elements.

McCall's successor akLaff is a rather different proposition, motoric, closer to Sunny Murray than to Andrew Cyrille, less concerned with finessing Threadgill's melodic textures than with finding the correct gear ratio that gives the band its undoubted impetus. New Air, almost inevitably, came across rather more immediately and compellingly, but the Montreal sessions do not capture the band at their best. The tributes – to Charles Clarke and Leo Smith on *Live Air*, the late Ronnie Boykins, Cecil Taylor and Jimmy Lyons on *Air Mail* – are heartfelt and very powerful; Hopkins's 'R.B.' is a low, sonorous eulogy to a fellow-bassist. It's one of the finest things in the current Air catalogue, topped only by the wonderful 'Ragtime Dance', 'Buddy Bolden's Blues' and 'Weeping Willow Rag' on *Lore*; time, perhaps, to make available again the wonderful 'No 2' and 'Dance of the Beast' from the missing early albums.

AKILI
GROUP

**   **Akili** M. A. Music NA 730-2 CD
             Bart Van Lier (*tb*); Koen Van Baal (*ky*); Eef Albers (*g*); Dave King (*b*); Victor Lewis (*d*); Eddie Conrad (*perc, v*). 89.

**   **Maasai Mara** M. A. Music A.802-2 CD
        Bart Van Lier (*tb*); John Ruocco (*reeds*); Peter Schon (*ky*); Eef Albers (*g*); Marcel
        Schirmsheimer (*b*); Victor Lewis (*d*); Eddie Conrad (*perc*). 90.

Although he doesn't perform on these dates, the group appears to be the brainchild of
trumpeter/producer Allen Botschinsky, who composed all the music on both records, aside from
a version of 'Speak Low' on *Maasai Mara*. The aim of the music is a portrait of Africa without
recourse to any recognizably 'African' music: what results is European fusion of a faintly
impressionistic bent. It's capably played, without offering anything startling, although Van
Lier's trombone adds an agreeably lugubrious streak to the music. The second LP has
marginally superior material.

TOSHIKO AKIYOSHI (born 1929)
PIANO, COMPOSER

***   **Live At Birdland** Fresh Sound FSRCD 1021 CD
        Akiyoshi; Charlie Mariano (*as*); Gene Cherico (*b*); Eddie Marshall (*d*). 4/60, 10/61.

***   **Toshiko-Mariano Quartet** Candid 9012 CD/LP
        As above. 12/60.

When she moved to the United States in 1956, under Oscar Peterson's patronage, Toshiko
Akiyoshi was already the most highly regarded arranger-composer to emerge in the post-war
commercial music revival in her native Japan.
    Akiyoshi met Charlie Mariano while at Berklee and the couple married in 1959, just over a
year before the Candid session. Her playing, based closely but not slavishly on Bud Powell's, is
forceful and intelligent, and the only sign of 'orientalism' in the small group playing (there are
engaging oddities of scoring in the big band arrangements) is a willingness to mix modes, as on
the Mariano-composed 'Little T', dedicated to her, and on the closing 'Long Yellow Road'.
    Recorded with an established band (the excellent Eddie Marshall had signed up a few
months before), the set has a coherence of tone and enthusiasm which provides Mariano with
the impetus for some of his best recorded playing. Supervised by Nat Hentoff, the balances and
registrations are ahead of their time.
    The Birdland sets, one before and one after the studio recording, are worthwhile in
themselves, but they also offer a useful way of judging how much the band developed in its
short life. A later version of 'Blues For Father' (introduced by stand-in compère Maynard
Ferguson on the April 1960 date as a new composition) is taken rather slower and Mariano's
solo opens on a sequence of held notes that feed directly off Akiyoshi's accompaniment, rather
than varying the melody. Unfortunately, the sound is much poorer on the later session,
roughening his tone and significantly muting the piano and bass.

**   **Finesse** Concord CCD 4069 CD
        Akiyoshi; Monty Budwig (*b*); Jake Hanna (*d*). n. d.

**   **Interlude** Concord CCD 4324 CD/MC
        Akiyoshi; Dennis Irwin (*b*); Eddie Marshall (*d*). 2/87.

It's a pity that Akiyoshi should have cluttered herself with a rhythm section for at least the
second of these sets. She is such an interesting player that she barely needs an external context –
even one as sympathetic as that provided by Irwin and Marshall.
    The earlier set is marginally the more impressive and there is a slightly perfunctory quality to
the 1987 cuts. Working an unpromising theme like 'Solveig's Song', which can turn to mush
without undue trouble, her harmonic rigour is impressive. Nor is she troubled by the demands
of such very different standards as 'Mr Jelly Lord' and 'You Go To My Head'. 'American
Ballad' is one of her best performances, beautifully judged.
    The later trio seems tighter, but much less conscious, as if the whole business had become
second nature. The closing 'You Stepped Out Of A Dream' is the high spot. Some doubts
about the recording levels on both sets (is this endemic to Concord?) but no loss of clarity.

****   **The Toshiko Akiyoshi–Lew Tabackin Big Band** Novus ND 83 106 CD
        Akiyoshi; Lew Tabackin (*ts, f, picc*); Stu Blumberg, Richard Cooper, Steve Huffsteter,
        John Madrid, Lynn Nicholson, Mike Price (*t*); Bobby Shew (*t, flhn*); Charlie Loper,

Bruce Paulson, Bill Reichenbach, Jim Sawyer, Britt Woodman (*tb*); Bill Teele (*btb*); Gary Foster (*as, ss, f, acl*); Dick Spencer (*as, cl, f*); Tom Peterson (*ts, as, ss, cl, f*); Bill Perkins (*bs, ss, cl, f, bcl*); Don Baldwin, Gene Cherico (*b*); Peter Donald (*d*); Kisaku Katada (*kotsuzumi*); Yataka Yazaki (*ohtsuzumi*); Tokuku Kaga (*v*); collective personnel. 4/74, 2 & 3/75, 1, 2 & 6/76.

Akiyoshi's mid-1970s big band, co-led with second husband Lew Tabackin, was remarkable in its almost total concentration on her own compositional output: no standards, no pop tunes or arrangements. Though it's often said, and with some justification, that the orchestra, not the piano, is Akiyoshi's instrument, her unaccompanied intro to the first number, 'Studio J', (taken from the 1976 Insights) suggests that she was still also a formidable keyboard performer. However, it's palpably true that her real genius is for orchestration, with a distinctive use of multi-part harmony in the horn section. The Akiyoshi–Tabackin bands used an enormous range of instruments (particularly in the reeds and flutes); in his useful liner note Leonard Feather points to the highly effective pairing on 'Quadrille, Anyone?' of Bill Perkins's baritone saxophone and Tabackin's piccolo. Akiyoshi is quickly identifiable on tracks such as 'Children In The Temple Ground', with its distinctive vocals, and 'The First Time' (like 'Quadrille, Anyone?' both come from the slightly earlier *Long Yellow Road*, perhaps the most self-consciously 'Eastern' of the albums) for her imaginative and challenging part-writing, which often sounds as if it has moved outside conventional tonality.

Perhaps the most moving of the tracks are 'Kogun', dedicated to the Japanese soldier who didn't know the war had ended, and the skilful linking of 'Since Perry' (a reference to the American naval commodore who 'opened up' Japan to Western influence) and Tabackin's magnificent 'Yet Another Tear'. Both come from the live 1976 album *Road Time*; confusingly, perhaps, 'American Ballad' comes from an earlier set called *Kogun*.

This is a tremendously important compilation, intelligently selected and beautifully remastered; credit for that to Steve Backer, John Snyder and engineer Joe Lopes. Anyone who can dig out the four original albums really should, but for the moment this will do admirably.

***(*) **Wishing Peace** Ken/Bellaphon 660 56 001 CD
Akiyoshi; John Eckert, Brian Lynch, Joe Mosello, Chris Pasin (*t*); Conrad Herwig, Kenny Rupp, Hart Smith (*tb*); Matt Finders (*btb*); Frank Wess (*as, ss, f*); Lew Tabackin (*ts, f, picc*); Jim Snidero (*as, cl, f*); Walt Weiskopf (*ts, cl*); Mark Lopeman (*bs, bcl*); Jay Anderson (*b*); Jeff Hirshfield (*d*)); Daniel Ponce (*perc*). 7/86.

'Liberty Suite', which takes up a substantial proportion of this fine record, was written as part of the centenary celebrations for the Statue of Liberty. It opens with a piano-and-flute duet between Akiyoshi and second husband Tabackin, whose touch on his 'second' horn is now near-perfect. Akiyoshi's preference for high voicings is also reflected in a later segment, entitled 'Wishing Peace', where the flute part is taken by Frank Wess, a bluesier player with a stronger but less sophisticated tone. The preceding 'Lady Liberty' develops the opening duet into a powerful orchestration, marked by fine solos from Brian Lynch (in much better form here than on his disappointing Criss Cross albums) and Jim Snidero (ditto). The East Coast band, recruited when Akiyoshi and Tabackin moved their base to New York, are spot-on throughout, and the two non-suite tracks, Akiyoshi's 'Feast In Milano' and Tabackin's beautiful 'Unrequited Love', are both magnificent performances. For anyone interested in the development of big-band playing in the 1980s, this is an essential purchase.

JOE ALBANY (1924–88)
PIANO, VOCAL

***(*) **The Right Combination** Original Jazz Classics OJC 1749 CD/LP
Albany; Warne Marsh (*ts*); Bob Whitlock (*b*). 57.

Albany was a frustrating enigma. Legendary in his time, as the sleeve to this album proclaims, he was allegedly one of Parker's favourite accompanists but never made a studio recording with him. In fact he didn't make any kind of studio sessions until the 1970s. This reissue was spliced together from an impromptu session at engineer Ralph Garretson's home, which caught Albany and Marsh jamming together on seven standards (the last of which, 'The Nearness Of You', is only a fragment). While the sound is very plain, and the piano in particular is recessed, the music is intermittently remarkable. Albany's style is a peculiar amalgam of Parker and Art

Tatum: the complexity of his lines suggests something of the older pianist, while the horn-like figures in the right hand might suggest a bop soloist. Yet Albany's jumbled, idiosyncratic sense of time is almost all his own, and his solos are cliff-hanger explorations. Marsh is at his most fragmentary, his tone a foggy squeal at some points, yet between them they create some compelling improvisations: 'Body And Soul', done at fast and slow tempos, is as personal as any version, and a dreamy, troubled 'Angel Eyes' shows off Albany's best work. No wonder, with the next 25 years spoiled by narcotic and personal problems, that Albany seemed like a wasted talent.

**   **Joe Albany At Home** Spotlite JA1 LP
Albany (*p* solo). 8–9/71.

**   **Proto-bopper** Spotlite JA3 LP
Albany; Bob Whitlock (*b*); Nick Martinis, Jerry McKenzie (*d*). 2–10/72.

**   **Birdtown Birds** Steeplechase SCS/SCCD 1003 CD/LP
Albany; Hugo Rasmussen (*b*); Hans Nymand (*d*). 4/73.

(*)   **Two's Company Steeplechase SCS 1019 LP
Albany; Niels-Henning Ørsted-Pedersen (*b*). 2/74.

Once rediscovered, first through a home-made tape which forms the basis of *Joe Albany At Home*, and then on subsequent European sojourns and New York appearances, Albany made a dozen or so albums during the 1970s. While much talked-up at the time, none of them are very satisfying now. *At Home* suffers from indifferent recording, and the *Proto-bopper* set has him sounding out of practice; but that difficulty extends to his whole career on record, in that he's always grasping for ideas which are basically beyond his pianistic powers. The best music comes on *Two's Company*, where the duets with bassist Pedersen are elaborately conceived and confidently despatched. But many of his ideas are beset by misfingerings, and the famously off-kilter conception of time can sometimes sound more like clumsiness than anything. It seems churlish to criticize one of the few bop-orientated pianists to take Parker's ideas in a different direction, but Albany's records sound like an unfulfilled ideal.

(*)   **Live In Paris Fresh Sound FSCD-1010 CD
Albany; Alby Cullaz (*b*); Aldo Romano (*d*). 77.

This recent discovery sheds no special new light on Albany, but there are some rather more impressive things here: the long Jerome Kern medley which opens the solo section (six titles; there are five more with the trio) shows the pianist's dense, heavily allusive style at its best, and it's a severe disappointment when he follows this with a terribly maudlin vocal treatment of 'Lush Life' (he also sings 'The Christmas Song'). Cullaz and Romano accompany as best they can, but this was clearly a trio that needed more work. The sound is a bit flat but not too bad, for what seems to be a private club recording.

(*)   **Bird Lives Storyville STCD 4164 CD
Albany; Art Davis (*b*); Roy Haynes (*d*). 1/79.

Davis and Haynes play particularly well, and ensure that there's no loss of focus on what is one of the best sets that Albany laid down. The strong emphasis on blues lines – most of the songs are Parker originals, but most are based on the blues – might have led to a lack of variety, but they're more useful in keeping Albany's mind on the job, perhaps. A decent piano and respectable sound.

HOWARD ALDEN
GUITAR

***   **Swing Street** Concord CCD 4349 CD/MC
Alden; Dan Barrett (*tb*); Chuck Wilson (*as, cl*); Frank Tate (*b*); Jackie Williams (*d*). 9/86.

***   **The A. B. Q. Salutes Buck Clayton** Concord CCD 4395 CD/MC
As above. 6/89.

Alden's polished manner places him in the polite swing-to-modern lineage of Herb Ellis, and he has mastered the style as well as anybody. In this band of young fogeys, the musicians don't so much re-create swing styles as reinvigorate them, adding a modern lick or two to classic material and classy arrangements, and throwing the occasional curve, such as a lucid treatment of Monk's 'Pannonica', into the gameplan. Barrett, a superbly accomplished player, is the star of these sessions, but the group is uniformly commanding and relaxed. The session devoted to material associated with Buck Clayton is marginally superior, if only because of the interesting concept.

(*)   **The Howard Alden Trio Plus Special Guests Concord CCD 4378 CD/MC
      Alden; Warren Vaché (*c*); Ken Peplowski (*ts, cl*); Lynn Seaton (*b*); Mel Lewis (*d*).
      1/89.

Vaché sits in with Alden's trio for five tracks, Peplowski for three, and the music has less cohesion than the ABQ records, although no less freshness. Vaché rewards Ellington's 'Purple Gazelle' with special radiance.

(*)   **Snowy Morning Blues Concord CCD 4424 CD/MC
      Alden; Monty Alexander (*p*); Lynn Seaton (*b*); Dennis Mackrel (*d*). 4/90.

Alexander's customary enthusiasm puts a little more pep into Alden's music, though not enough to coarsen the guitarist's fundamentally lightweight variations on swing material. The programme is well chosen to include some lesser-known Ellington and Monk tunes, but the Concord recording tends to smooth away the most interesting edges.

***   **Misterioso** Concord CCD 4487 CD/MC
      Alden; Frank Tate (*b*); Keith Copeland (*d*). 4/91.

Like such older Concord hands as Scott Hamilton and Warren Vaché, Alden is starting to assume his methods so convincingly that the prettiness and formal grace of his playing are beginning to take on an ironclad quality. This is certainly his most effective record to date: 'We See' and 'Misterioso' don't so much simplify Monk as put the crusty elegance of his tunes in the forefront, and everything else – including such bedfellows as 'Flying Down To Rio' and Jelly Roll Morton's 'The Pearls' – is delivered with the same fine touch.

MONTY ALEXANDER (born 1944)
PIANO

(*)   **Live In Holland Verve 835627 CD/LP

(*)   **Reunion In Europe Concord CJ 231 MC
      Alexander; John Clayton (*b*); Jeff Hamilton (*d*). 3/77, 3/83.

***   **Facets** Concord CCD 4108 CD/MC
      Alexander; Ray Brown (*b*); Jeff Hamilton (*d*). 8/79.

**   **Full Steam Ahead** Concord CCD 4287 CD/MC
      Alexander; Ray Brown (*b*); Frank Gant (*d*). n. d.

**   **In Tokyo** Pablo 2310836 LP
      Alexander; Andrew Simpkins (*b*); Frank Gant (*d*). 1/79.

Long associated with Milt Jackson and Ray Brown, Alexander now has an impressive back-catalogue of (mostly trio) recordings which reveal an exuberant sensibility schooled – sometimes a little too doctrinairely – in the School of Oscar Peterson. Typical of that tendency, he has a tone which is both percussive and lyrical, heavy on the triplets and arpeggiated chords, melodically inspired in the main (i.e. no long chordal ramblings), maximal but controlled.

It's a little difficult to assess the permutations in these bass and drum trios, beyond the observation that Gant seems better suited to the faster tempos, whereas Hamilton plays with a greater feel for the melody on the two European dates. Brown, as always, is so beyond reproach as to be *sui generis*.

CD transfer of *Facets* has significantly brightened the sound.

***   **Trio** Concord CCD 4136 CD/MC

(*) **Triple Treat Concord CCD 4193 CD/MC

(*) **Overseas Special Concord CCD 4253 CD/MC

**   **Triple Treat II** Concord CCD 4338 CD/MC
Alexander; John Frigo (*vn*, on *Triple Treat II* only); Herb Ellis (*g*); Ray Brown (*b*).
8/80, 3/82, 3/82, 6/87.

This is the ideal context for Alexander's playing. Adding a fourth set of strings with John Frigo (three tracks only), was an unnecessary embellishment, though Alexander obviously encourages his bassists to play arco, favouring big-toned pedals against which he can punch out sometimes surprisingly complex augmented chords. Of the group, *Overseas Special* is probably the most successful, but there are wonderful things on *Trio* (the opening 'I'm Afraid The Masquerade Is Over'), and *Triple Treat* ('Body And Soul' and, ahem, the 'Flintstones' theme). The sequel is a shade disappointing, given the weight of campaign medals, but there is a gorgeous quartet reading of 'Smile' and a fine trio 'It Might As Well Be Spring'.

***   **Ivory And Steel** Concord CCD 4124 CD/MC
Alexander; Othello Molineaux (*steel d*); Gerald Wiggins (*b*); Frank Gant (*d*); Robert Thomas Jr (*perc*). 3/80

***   **Jamboree** Concord CCD 4359 CD/MC
Alexander; Othello Molineaux, Len 'Boogsie' Sharpe (*steel d*); Marshall Wood, Bernard Montgomery (*b*); Robert Thomas Jr (*perc*); Marvin 'Smitty' Smith (*d*). 2–3/88.

One of the most interesting aspects of Alexander's career has been his attempt to assimilate the steel drum sound of his native Jamaica to the conventional jazz rhythm section. In the earlier pair, the new sound is still a little tacked-on and Gant in particular seems slightly uneasy, but the balance of instrumentation is good and Alexander finds sufficient space on *Ivory And Steel* to rattle off some of his most joyous solos.

Jamboree is a marvellous record, partly because the playing is so good, but also because of the imaginative selection of covers. Bob Marley's 'No Woman, No Cry' and Joni Mitchell's 'Big Yellow Taxi' have not previously figured too prominently in the average fake book; indeed, with the very considerable exception of avant-garde trumpeter Leo Smith, reggae has made remarkably little impact on contemporary jazz. 'Smitty' Smith was an inspired addition on the later date and lifts the energy level a further notch. Both are highly recommended, but go for *Jamboree*. One–love.

***   **Fridaynight** Limetree MLP 0022 CD/LP

***   **Saturdaynight** Limetree MLP 0024 LP
Alexander; Reggie Johnson (*b*); Ed Thigpen (*d*); Robert Thomas Jr (*hand d*). 10/85.

Two fine quartet sessions, consolidating Alexander's imaginative use of percussion. There is a particularly good version of his staple 'Fungi Mama' (a kind of acid test for an Alexander performance) on *Saturdaynight*, some impressive drumming from Thigpen and an intriguing insight into Reggie Johnson's undersung talent for long melodic lines and taut registration. Recording quality isn't anything to write home about, but the performances carry the day.

***(*) **The River** Concord CCD 4422 CD/MC
Alexander; John Clayton (*b*); Ed Thigpen (*d*). 10/85.

No confusing this with the Bruce Springsteen product of the same name. This is the unsentimental one, played largely in key. Alexander's reading of hymn tunes (all except the title-track and Ellington's 'David Danced') is as bold as anything he has tried since the 'Ivory and Steel' sets. Mostly played with a rolling, gospelly fervour, there is space for a little schmaltz on 'Ave Maria' (aching bowed bass from Clayton) and some surprisingly abstract drum and piano effects on the closing traditional 'How Great Thou Art'. Thigpen is magnificent throughout. A really beautiful record.

***   **Threesome** Soul Note SN 1152 CD/LP
Alexander; Niels-Henning Ørsted-Pedersen (*b*); Grady Tate (*d*, *v*). 11–12/85.

Well used to top-drawer rhythm sections, Alexander makes the most of this one, turning in a sparkling set with sufficient variety to suggest his responsiveness to others. The version of 'All Blues' is interesting, but the material is otherwise a little lacklustre.

BJORN ALKE
BASS, VIOLIN

**(*)   Bjorn Alke Quartet Caprice CAP 1072 LP
Alke; Gunnar Bergsten (*sno, bs, f*); Goran Strandberg (*p*); Fredrik Norén (*d*). 4–5/74.

Although there are touches such as the tinny electric piano which date this music to the early 1970s, Alke's record will provide historical interest as typical of the kind of post-bop explorations which Swedish musicians went on to develop into a major part of European jazz in the 1980s and '90s. There are some oddball touches, such as the 59-second trio reading of 'Kitten On The Keys' which closes the first side, but Strandberg and Bergsten both contribute thoughtful material, and Alke's 'Gun' is a winsome ballad. Bergsten handles both saxes with somewhat heavy-handed aplomb.

GERI ALLEN
PIANO

***(*)   Etudes Soul Note SN 1162 CD/LP/MC

***   Segments DIW-833 CD

****   Live At The Village Vanguard DIW 847E CD
Allen; Charlie Haden (*b*); Paul Motian (*d*). 9/87, 4/89.

Strictly speaking, *Etudes* was credited to the Haden/Motian trio with Geri Allen as featured artist. A single hearing establishes it unequivocally as her album, not because her two senior colleagues merely fulfil backing duties, but because she is so obviously calling the shots. The obvious parallel is Bill Evans, who 'led' by unassertive example, and there are similarities of manner (not least the presence of Paul Motian) with the vintage Evans Trio.

Allen is without equal in her ability to play quietly, sometimes as soft as *ppp*, without becoming indistinct and losing the cool, almost intellectual intensity which is her signature. Only Paul Bley – with whom she shares certain tonal characteristics – manages to invest diminuendo passages with such dramatic freight. Motian almost notoriously inclines to the subliminal, but Haden's ability to play in these registers is seldom acknowledged.

The set isn't without humour. Ornette's 'Lonely Woman' is offset by the much less obvious 'Shuffle Montgomery', a little-played Herbie Nichols tune, and there is an unexpected warmth and gentleness to 'Dolphy's Dance', which belies the sardonic Monkish delivery.

Segments is by no means an anticlimax, though it lacks the immediate impact of the earlier set. It is certainly a more polished and professional performance from a trio rapidly acquiring 'in demand' status from promoters and record producers. There are hints, in the closing original 'Rain', of a slightly soft centre to Allen's playing that bodes ill. On the other hand, 'Segment', a not-quite-canonical Charlie Parker tune from 1949, is given a superb reading, as is 'Marmaduke', two untypical examples of Allen's bebop approach. Haden's 'La Pasionaria', like most of his work, is too vital a tune to suffer fatal damage from a lacklustre performance.

Quite the best of the trio's recordings to date is the live session from 1990. The empathy is closer than ever and each of the three seems to have taken on characteristics of the others' voices: Allen's insistent, slightly anguished bass figures on 'Vanguard Blues', her near-static rhythms elsewhere; Haden's limpid pedals on 'Song For The Whales'; Motian's thorough tunefulness. Expertly recorded and mastered, *Live* is both accessible and inexhaustible, making its appeal at all sorts of unexpected levels, again with a tinge of humour. Even allowing for the head start of Keith Jarrett's 'Standards' trio, this is probably the best piano-led group currently working.

***(*)   The Nurturer Blue Note CDP 7 95139 2 CD
Allen; Marcus Belgrave (*t, flhn*); Kenny Garrett (*as, straight as*); Robert Hurst (*b*); Jeff Watts (*d*); Eli Fountain (*perc*). 5/90.

With *The Nurturer*, Allen develops her interest in structures, the shape and resonance of compositions, as opposed to straightforward soloing on themes. The arrangements are watertight and quite ambitious, distributing emphasis throughout the players. Belgrave's solo on the opening track is masterful and his muted section on the title-piece has the richness of a French horn solo. Garrett's Vinson-influenced blues style works well against Allen's slightly restless, fragmented approach. Watts is in the Smitty Smith mould, but has developed his own signature of bounced rimshots and fast-decaying cymbals. The production is clean and full, with no loss of resolution at higher volumes. Strongly recommended.

HARRY ALLEN
TENOR SAXOPHONE

**(*)   How Long Has This Been Going On? Progressive 7082 CD
Allen; Keith Ingham (*p*); Major Holley (*b*); Oliver Jackson (*d*). 6/88.

Another young fogey looking for mainstream credibility, Allen plays lightly swinging tenor with enough panache to make him stand comfortably with such an experienced rhythm section as this one. But it doesn't go much further than that. A few unusual choices of material suggest a worthy line in archaeology; otherwise, Allen sounds as if he has no particular place to go with this pleasant and forgettable session.

HENRY 'RED' ALLEN (1908–1967)
TRUMPET, VOCAL

****   Henry 'Red' Allen And His New York Orchestra 1929–1930 JSP CD 332 CD
Allen; Otis Johnson (*t*); J. C. Higginbotham (*tb*); Albert Nicholas, William Blue (*cl, as*); Charlie Holmes (*cl, ss, as*); Teddy Hill (*cl, ts*); Luis Russell (*p, cel*); Will Johnson (*bj, g, v*); Pops Foster (*b*); Paul Barbarin (*d*); Victoria Spivey, The Four Wanderers (*v*). 7/29–2/30.

****   Henry 'Red' Allen And His New York Orchestra Vol. 2 JSP CD 333 CD
As above. 29–30.

****   Henry 'Red' Allen & His Orchestra 1929–1933 Classics 540 CD
As above, except add James Archey, Dickie Wells, Benny Morton (*tb*); Russell Procope, Edward Inge (*cl, as*); Hilton Jefferson (*as*); Coleman Hawkins, Greely Walton (*ts*); Don Kirkpatrick, Horace Henderson (*p*); Bernard Addison (*g*); Bob Ysaguire (*bb, b*); Ernest Hill (*bb*); Walter Johnson, Manzie Johnson (*d*). 7/29–11/33.

***   Henry 'Red' Allen–Coleman Hawkins 1933 Hep 1028 CD
As above, except add Russell Smith, Bobby Stark (*t*); Claude Jones (*tb*), John Kirby (*b*), omit Blue, Johnson, Higginbotham, Archey, Russell, Holmes, Walton, Johnson, Foster, Barbarin, Spivey. 3–10/33.

****   Henry 'Red' Allen 1929–1936 BBC 685 CD/LP/MC
Allen; plus groups led by Fats Waller, Luis Russell, Billy Banks, Walter Pichon, Spike Hughes, Horace Henderson, Benny Morton, Mills Blue Rhythm Band. 29–36.

Henry Allen was once described as 'the last great trumpet soloist to come out of New Orleans', but that was before Wynton Marsalis and his followers. He was, though, the last to make a mark on the 1920s, recording his astonishing debut sessions as a leader for Victor in the summer of 1929 and immediately causing a stir. The four tracks are 'It Should Be You', 'Biff'ly Blues', 'Feeling Drowsy' and 'Swing Out', and there is a total of ten takes of them on the first JSP disc, while the Classics CD, which commences a chronological survey of Allen in the 1930s, is content with the master takes in each case. Either way, these four titles are magnificently conceived and executed jazz, with the whole band – actually the nucleus of the Luis Russell Orchestra, where Allen had already set down some superb solos – playing with outstanding power and finesse while Allen's own improvisations outplay any trumpeter of the day aside from Louis Armstrong. While his playing is sometimes a little unfocused, Allen's ideas usually run together with few seams showing, and the controlled strength of his solo on 'Feeling Drowsy' is as impressive as the more daring flights of 'Swing Out'. The beautifully sustained solo on 'Make A Country Bird Fly Wild' sees him through a tricky stop-time passage, and shows how he was both like and unlike Armstrong: there's the same rhythmic chance-taking and nobility of tone, but Allen is often less predictable than Armstrong and can shy away from the signalled high notes which Louis always aimed at. He can even suggest a faintly wistful quality in an otherwise heated passage. The tracks for Victor, though, are abetted by his choice of companions: Higginbotham is wonderfully characterful on trombone, agile but snarlingly expressive, and the vastly underrated Charlie Holmes matches the young Johnny Hodges for a hard-hitting yet fundamentally lyrical alto style. Foster and Barbarin, too, are exceptionally swinging. This was an outstanding band which should have made many more records than it did.

The JSP discs, superbly remastered by John R. T. Davies, are indispensable. Some may prefer the Classics approach, which carries on through the first sessions by the Allen–Coleman Hawkins Orchestra. Both men were then working with Fletcher Henderson, and this could have been an explosive combination, but their records are comparatively tame, with pop-tune material and Allen's admittedly engaging vocals taking up a lot of space. The Hep CD includes all the Allen–Hawkins tracks (the final three are on the next Classics disc), and adds the 1933 session under Horace Henderson's leadership, which includes what might be the most swinging 'Ol' Man River' on record and a splendid feature for Hawkins in 'I've Got To Sing A Torch Song'. More excellent remastering here: the Classics CD is patchy in comparison but most will find it very listenable.

Robert Parker's BBC compilation fills in some useful gaps – the very obscure session with the vaudeville singer Walter Pichon, for instance, and a date under Benny Morton's leadership – and picks some favourites by the Luis Russell band and Allen's own groups. A useful supplement to the Classics series, although concentrating on all the otherwise-unavailable titles would have made it even more collectable. Parker's resonant transfers may not appeal to all, but they're very wide-ranging in their sonic detail.

***   **Henry 'Red' Allen 1933–1935** Classics 551 CD
Allen; Pee Wee Irwin (*t*); J. C. Higginbotham, Dicky Wells, Benny Morton, Keg Johnson, George Washington (*tb*); Buster Bailey, Cecil Scott, Albert Nicholas (*cl*); Edward Inge (*cl, as*); Hilton Jefferson (*as*); Coleman Hawkins, Chu Berry (*ts*); Horace Henderson (*p*); Bernard Addison (*bj, g*); Lawrence Lucie (*g*); Bob Ysaguirre (*bb*); John Kirby (*b, bb*); Elmer James, Pops Foster (*b*); Manzie Johnson, Kaiser Marshall, Walter Johnson, Paul Barbarin, George Stafford (*d*). 11/33–7/35.

***   **Henry 'Red' Allen 1935–1936** Classics 575 CD
Allen; J. C. Higginbotham (*tb*); Albert Nicholas (*cl*); Rudy Powell, Hildred Humphries (*cl, as*); Cecil Scott (*cl, ts*); Pete Clark, Tab Smith (*as*); Happy Caldwell, Joe Garland, Ted McRae (*ts*); Edgar Hayes, Norman Lester, Jimmy Reynolds, Clyde Hart (*p*); Lawrence Lucie (*g*); Elmer James, John Kirby (*b*); O'Neil Spencer, Cozy Cole, Walter Johnson (*d*).11/35–8/36.

***   **Henry 'Red' Allen 1936–1937** Classics 590 CD
Allen; Gene Mikell, Buster Bailey, Glyn Paque (*cl*); Tab Smith (*as*); Ted McRae, Sonny Fredericks, Harold Arnold (*ts*); Clyde Hart, Billy Kyle, Luis Russell (*p*); Danny Barker (*g*); John Kirby, John Williams (*b*); Cozy Cole, Alphonse Steele, Paul Barbarin (*d*). 10/36–4/37.

***(*)   **Henry 'Red' Allen 1937–1941** Classics 628 CD
Allen; Benny Morton, J. C. Higginbotham (*tb*); Glyn Paque, Edmond Hall (*cl*); Tab Smith (*as*); Harold Arnold, Sammy Davis (*ts*); Luis Russell, Billy Kyle, Lil Armstrong, Kenny Kersey (*p*); Danny Barker, Bernard Addison (*g*); John Williams, Pops Foster, Billy Taylor (*b*); Paul Barbarin, Alphonse Steele, Zutty Singleton, Jimmy Hoskins (*d*). 6/37–7/41.

***   **Original 1933–1941 Recordings** Tax S-3-2 CD
As above Classics discs. 33–41.

***   **Henry 'Red' Allen 1939–1941** Everybody's 1000 LP
Allen; J. C. Higginbotham (*tb*); Ed Hall (*cl*); Gene Sedric (*ts*); James P Johnson, Cliff Jackson, Kenny Kersey (*p*); Al Casey, Eugene Fields (*g*); Johnny Williams, Pops

Foster, Billy Taylor (*b*); Sid Catlett, Jimmy Hoskins (*d*); Anna Robinson, Ida Cox (*v*). 3/39–4/41.

Maybe Allen was a man out of time: he arrived just too late to make a significant impact on the first jazz decade, and he had to work through the depression – and the early part of the swing era – recording what were really novelty small-group sessions, most of which are little-known today. Like Armstrong and Waller, he had to record at least as many bad songs as good ones, and though he was an entertaining singer, he couldn't match either Fats or Louis as master of whatever material came his way. Still, the chronological Classics sequence is a valuable and pretty consistent documentation. The groups tend to be rough-and-ready, but whenever he's partnered by the superb Higginbotham, Allen comes up with marvellously exuberant jazz. And sometimes unpromising material releases a classic performance: hear, for instance, the completely wild version of 'Roll Along, Prairie Moon' on Classics 551, where the trombonist blows such a fine solo that Allen insists on handing over his own solo space. The two CDs in the middle of the sequence have too many duff tunes on them, but the 1937–41 set is stronger, since Allen switched labels (to Decca) in 1940 and started recording uncompromised jazz again. Sessions with Ed Hall, Zutty Singleton and Benny Morton are a little too brash, perhaps, but Allen's own playing is stirring throughout.

The Tax CD offers a somewhat mystifying selection of tracks from the period. The sound on all five CDs is mostly very good, with just a few transfers suffering from noticeable blemishes.

The Everybody's LP includes one of Allen's 1941 sessions plus one date under Ida Cox's name and two under James P. Johnson's leadership. With Higginbotham again present throughout there's plenty of fun on the likes of 'Harlem Woogie' and 'Swingin' At The Lido' and Cox shouts the blues with vigour if not much finesse on her four titles. Good transfers.

****   **World On A String** RCA Bluebird ND 82497 CD
        Allen; J. C. Higginbotham (*tb*); Buster Bailey (*cl*); Coleman Hawkins (*ts*); Marty Napoleon (*p*); Everett Barksdale (*g*); Lloyd Trotman (*b*); Cozy Cole (*d*). 3–4/57.

Despite a tendency towards chaos in some of the ride-out choruses, this good-humoured session has the air of an unprompted masterpiece. Allen's singing is marvellous – 'Let me Miss You, Baby' is a wry blues which he phrases so inventively he makes it sound like a new form – but his trumpet playing is even better. The shrillness in his high register is turned to advantage, the squeezed notes and valve effects are flawlessly deployed, and it culminates – in a long solo on 'I Cover The Waterfront' – in one of the great trumpet improvisations of the period. Hawkins, back with Allen for the first time since their 1933 sessions, is in rambunctious form, and Bailey, another old comrade, turns his trickiest playing to advantage. All this and the faithful Higginbotham, too. There are splendid later Allen sessions currently out of the catalogue – Fantasy should certainly think about reissuing the 1962 date for Prestige, *Mr Allen* – but this remains one of the best examples of Red at his most engaging.

MOSE ALLISON (born 1927)
PIANO, VOCAL, TRUMPET

***(*)   **Back Country Suite** Original Jazz Classics OJC 075 LP
        Allison; Taylor LaFargue (*b*); Frank Isola (*d*). 3/57.

***   **Local Color** Original Jazz Classics OJC 457 CD/LP
        Allison; Addison Farmer (*b*); Nick Stabulas (*d*). 11/57.

Mose Allison grew up in Mississippi, played trumpet in high school and listened to a lot of blues and swing; by the time he came to listen to bebop, a little of which creeps into his playing, he was already hooked on the light and steady kind of swing playing which Nat Cole's trio exemplified. Mose has always been a modernist: his hip world-weariness and mastery of the wry put-down ('When you're walking your last mile / Baby, don't forget to smile') have always been paired with a vocal style that is reluctantly knowing, as though he tells truths which he has to force out. Coupled with a rhythmically juddering, blues-directed piano manner, he's made sure that there's been no one else quite like him – aside from such second-generation stylists as Georgie Fame.

Back Country Suite, his debut, remains arguably his best record as an instrumentalist and composer: the deft little miniatures which make up the 'suite' are winsome and rocking by turns, and LaFargue and Isola read the leader's moves beautifully. *Local Color* is nearly as good, with a rare glimpse of Allison's muted trumpet on 'Trouble In Mind', an unusual Ellington revival in 'Don't Ever Say Goodbye'and his first and best treatment of Percy Mayfield's 'Lost Mind'. Both albums were excellently recorded at the time, but the new remastering, while good enough, adds nothing extra to the sound.

LAURINDO ALMEIDA (born 1917)
GUITAR

***(*) **Brazilliance Vol. 1** World Pacific CDP 7963392 CD
Almeida; Bud Shank (*as*); Harry Babasin (*b*); Roy Harte (*d*). 4/53.

***(*) **Brazilliance Vol. 2** World Pacific CDP 7961022 CD
Almeida; Bud Shank (*as, f*); Gary Peacock (*b*); Chuck Flores (*d*). 3/58.

Almeida is a Brazilian guitarist whose work in aligning his native music with jazz materials has been undervalued, partly through his own infrequent appearances in a visible jazz setting. While he recorded frequently with the L. A. Four in the 1970s, most of his records are of more traditionally orientated Brazilian music and fall outside the scope of this book. His early collaborations with Bud Shank for Richard Bock's Pacific Jazz operation were highly successful, though: the records were among the label's best-sellers, and this excellent CD edition collects the 10-inch and 12-inch albums on to two CDs. Although superficially following the same formula, the two discs are quite different from each other. The 1953 sessions are more formal, more dependent on Brazilian themes, and are pitched more coolly in terms of the interplay between Shank and Almeida. The later music includes a number of originals by both principals, some more familiar jazz standards (including a lovely, drowsy 'Round Midnight') and a greater sense of freedom and airiness in Shank's improvisations. The saxophonist never sounded better in his early days than he did on these records, his phrasing lithe and the tone bitingly clear – even though, when he wants, he has the same softness of timbre which Paul Desmond employed. Almeida's harmonies and rhythmic insight into the material are indispensable. This is lovely music. The CD transfers are a bit dry and they sometimes rasp a little, though only those who've heard good-condition original pressings may note much difference.

MAARTEN ALTENA (born 1943)
BASS, CELLO

**   **Quotl** hat Art 6029 CD

(*)   **Rif hat Art 6056 CD

***   **Cities And Streets** hat Art 6082 CD
Altena; Marc Charig (*t, alto horn*); Wolter Wierbos (*tb*); Michael Moore (*as, cl, bcl*); Peter van Bergen (*ts, bcl*); Maartje ten Hoorn (*vn on Rif and Quotl*); Christel Postma (*vn on Cities And Streets*); Guus Janssen (*p, synth on Rif only*); Michiel Scheen (*p on Quotl and Cities And Streets*); Michael Vatcher (*perc*). 8/87, 12/88, 10/89.

Tremendously interesting things have been done in the Netherlands over the past two or three decades by composers deeply influenced by jazz and improvisational traditions. One thinks mainly of Louis Andriessen and Misha Mengelberg. That Altena's writing is much less certain than either of these is evident in *Quotl*'s heavyweight seriousness. Nine densely packed compositions – of which five are credited to the bassist – played by a flexible ensemble that seems to be attempting big-band gestures with insufficient resources. There are rather too many send-for-reinforcements occasions, and too many moments when the already sparse solos come across like desperate vamping while the rest of the band reshuffle their sheet music. Only the most self-effacing curate would fail to baulk at such an egg.

Cities And Streets, by the sharpest of contrasts, is like a walk through the ethnic hotch-potch of the cultural market district. Though again devised as a series of systems for improvisation, it has a steady, ambulatory progress that makes the album resemble a large-scale suite: there are quiet squares, threatening alleys and sudden, barking thoroughfares. The effect resembles Charles Ives and Mingus, filtered back through much of the technical innovation of the last 75 years. The album also features a much-transformed rerun of 'Rif' from the fine 1987 set; put side by side, they provide a useful object lesson in Altena's conception of the borders of composition and improvisation. Unlike the Willem Breuker Kollektief, there is little obvious satirical intent, but there are moments of calculated banality, which must be heard in context. Despite the imbroglio of *Quotl*, Altena's is a music of the highest contemporary significance.

**(*)   Code hat Art CD 6094 CD
Altena; Wolter Wierbos (*tb*); Peter Van Bergen (*ts, bcl, cbcl*); Jacques Palinckx (*g*); Christel Postma (*vn*); Michel Scheen (*p*); Michael Vatcher (*perc*); Jannie Pranger (*v*). 12/90.

With *Code*, Altena's insistent self-examination moves to a new level. The Ensemble line-up has changed again, paring down the sectional feel of the earlier band, adding Palinckx's quite aggressive guitar sound and Pranger's post-Berberian vocabularies, giving the sound a tougher, but also more conservatively Modernist, feel. In keeping with Altena's growing interest in 'coding', three tracks – 'Slange', 'Prikkel' and 'Rij' – are reprised from the excellent *Cities And Streets*. There are also compositions from British 'punk' composer Steve Martland – the opening 'Principia' – and from Gilius van Bergerjik, a companion-piece to the earlier 'Scène Rurale' called 'Scène de Mort'.

Like many current leader/composers, Altena is concerned with the interface between notated and improvised musical language and the title-track (part of a series again) is based on structural cues calling for either imitation of basic materials or else free improvisation. The result there is very much more interesting than the 'squeaky door' effects of earlier tracks. By this point in his career, Altena's music may require more effort and cross-reference than most casual listeners will be prepared to give it. This isn't necessarily a vice, but it is an obstacle – and one has to wonder if the means of communication (successive CDs that overlap, thematically and methodologically) is the right one. For most people, the code will remain not just unbreakable but unappealingly enigmatic.

BARRY ALTSCHUL (born 1943)
DRUMS, PERCUSSION

***   Virtuosi Improvising Artists Inc 123 844 2 CD
Altschul; Paul Bley (*p*); Gary Peacock (*b*). 6/67.

***   For Stu Soul Note SN 1015 LP
Altschul; Ray Anderson (*tb*); Anthony Davis (*p*); Rick Rozie (*b*). 2/79.

**   Somewhere Else Moers Music 01064 LP
Altschul; Ray Anderson (*tb, kalimba, whistles*); Mark Helias (*b*). 6/79.

**(*)   Irina Soul Note SN 1065 LP
Altschul; Enrico Rava (*t*); John Surman (*bs, ss*); Mark Helias (*b*). 2/83.

Altschul is one of the finest percussionists in contemporary jazz, an intelligent, analytical man who has moved from an early free-form and avant-garde idiom to embrace virtually all the major world traditions (except, interestingly, the unaccented musics of East Asia). He has written persuasively about drumming, but if there is anything that mars his recorded output, it is a slightly didactic insistence which can make his playing a little stiff. The early *Virtuosi* sounds – and is – very much like Bley's own trio work of the period. There are two compositions by Annette Peacock, each of which forms the basis for a long, freely associating improvisation. Bley still tends to dominate proceedings, though Altschul's continuous flow of ideas would be impressive were it more distinctly registered; not even CD gives a faithful rendition of some of his softer figures and effects. *For Stu* – dedicated, like 'Martin's Stew' on *Somewhere Else*, to the late Stu Martin – is perhaps still his best record, though the pianoless instrumentation on *Irina* and the twinned, 'European' voices of Rava and Surman seem to suit him better than Ray Anderson's jovial New World blurt. There is a fine version of Mingus's 'Orange Was The

Color Of Her Dress, Then Blue Silk', and the title-track is appropriately cadenced. Punning titles are never a good idea, but 'Drum Role' is in any case somewhat attentuated.

Somewhere Else seems a little like a dialogue of the deaf. Trios of this conformation are always dificult to modulate effectively. What happens here is that three players with strongly rhythmic conceptions of their own manage to cancel each other out. *Irina* is altogether better balanced and the interplay more coherent and appealing. There is no doubt that Altschul has suffered more seriously than most from an endemic lack of understanding of how to record drummers effectively. Much like Stu Martin, who was often faintly disappointing on record, he really needs to be heard live.

FRANCO AMBROSETTI (born 1941)
TRUMPET, FLUGELHORN

***   **Close Encounter** Enja 3017 LP
Ambrosetti; Bennie Wallace (*ss, ts*); George Gruntz (*p*); Mike Richmond (*b*); Bob Moses (*d*). 3/78.

(*)   **Heart Bop Enja 3087 LP
Ambrosetti; Phil Woods (*cl, as*); Hal Galper (*p*); Mike Richmond (*b*); Joe LaBarbera, Billy Hart (*d*). 2/81.

***   **Wings** Enja 4068 LP
Ambrosetti; Michael Brecker (*ts*); John Clark (*frhn*); Kenny Kirkland (*p*); Buster Williams (*b*); Daniel Humair (*d*). 12/83.

Ambrosetti, a Swiss who holds down a regular industrial job in his family's firm, is a fine post-bop trumpeter who is something of an underachiever on record: his series of Enja albums perhaps promise more than they deliver. Enja 3017 and 3087 are both purposeful records which finally miss the last ounce of character which would turn them into great sessions: neat rather than profound compositions account for some lack of intensity, and the date with Woods in particular has a sense of perfunctory blowing. *Wings* is considerably more powerful, though, thanks to the punishing rhythm section and the surprising presence of Brecker and the far-from-outclassed Clark; here Ambrosetti's nods to Miles Davis take on a glowing candour.

***   **Tentets** Enja 4096 LP
Ambrosetti; Lew Soloff, Mike Mossman (*t*); Steve Coleman (*as*); Michael Brecker (*ts*); Howard Johnson (*bs, tba*); Alex Brofsky (*frhn*); Tommy Flanagan (*p*); Dave Holland (*b*); Daniel Humair (*d*). 3/85.

It's a tribute to Ambrosetti's talent that he stands as tall as any of the players on this all-star date: although Brecker has a couple of tempestuous solos, and Coleman spins a beautiful net over 'Ode To A Princess', the leader's flugelhorn playing is a model of lyrical consistency. Although the charts are perhaps not especially inspiring, the musicians perform them with ringing enthusiasm.

***   **Movies** Enja 5035 CD/LP
Ambrosetti; Geri Allen (*p*); John Scofield (*g*); Michael Formanek (*b*); Daniel Humair (*d*); Jerry Gonzalez (*perc*). 11/86.

***   **Movies, Too** Enja 5079 CD/LP.
As above, except add Greg Osby (*ss, as*), omit Gonzalez. 3/88.

Film music – everything from 'Yellow Submarine' and 'The Magnificent Seven' on the first album to 'What's New Pussycat' and 'Steppenwolf' on the second – treated with amused and just slightly irreverent hospitality by Ambrosetti and some American friends. It's hardly as dramatic a disintegration as a John Zorn session, but the players have fun, and Ambrosetti again impresses as an inventive soloist.

AMM
IMPROVISING ENSEMBLE

***(*)   **AMMMusic 1966** Matchless/ReR no number CD
Cornelius Cardew (*p, transistor radio*); Lou Gare (*ts, vn*); Eddie Prévost (*d*); Keith Rowe (*g, transistor radio*); Lawrence Sheaff (*cl, acc, cl, transistor radio*). 6/66.

****   **The Crypt – 12th June 1968** Matchless MRCD05 2CD
Cornelius Cardew (*p, clo*); Lou Gare (*ts, vn*); Christopher Hobbs, Eddie Prévost (*perc*); Keith Rowe (*g, elec*). 6/68.

***   **It Had Been An Ordinary Enough Day In Pueblo, Colorado** ECM Japo 60031 CD
Eddie Prévost (*d*); Keith Rowe (*g, elec*). 79.

***(*)   **Generative Themes** Matchless MR06 LP
Eddie Prévost (*d*); Keith Rowe (*g, elec*); John Tilbury (*p*). 82.

***   **Combine And Laminates** Pogus Productions P 201 LP
Keith Rowe (*g, elec*); Eddie Prévost (*d*); John Tilbury (*p*). 84.

***(*)   **The Inexhaustible Document** Matchless MR 13 LP
Eddie Prévost (*d*); Keith Rowe (*g, elec*); Rohan de Saram (*clo*); John Tilbury (*p*). 87.

****   **The Nameless Uncarved Block** Matchless MR 20 CD
Lou Gare (*ts*); Eddie Prévost (*d*); Keith Rowe (*g, elec*); John Tilbury (*p*). 4/90.

Commercial recording is in almost every practical and ethical respect inimical to this extraordinary music, which has helped shape the instincts of two generations of British improvisers and their supporters. Organized on a collective basis, AMM self-transformed within two years from a free-jazz outfit into a process-dominated improvising group influenced by a very British combination of materialist and spiritualist philosophies (and, somewhat implicitly, by left-wing politics). Performances attained such a level of intensity and rapport, with the 'audience' as well as among the players, that recordings can offer only a very partial and compromised impression of the group's music.

One of the practical problems to be confronted was that before the advent of the CD era, extended improvisations could only be accommodated to LP by heavy editing. *AMMMusic 1966* usefully restores material excluded from the original [Elektra EUK 265] release. Eddie Prévost points out in his superb liner note (which also reproduces the 13 aphorisms that accompanied the original LP) that *Jazz Journal* attributed the record to the 'Cornelius Cardew Quartet', patent nonsense anyway given the non-hierarchical nature of the music, but still more so given Cardew's formal preoccupations and ideological unease.

The music itself, though unremittingly abstract, still calls upon musical and semantic (i.e. radio-sampled) reference points, which give the music an element or irony it entirely lacks later. This may well be down to Cardew's presence; it's also noticeable on the very important Crypt performances recorded in June 1968. Though the 2-LP boxed set [Matchless MR5] is now very collectable, these have recently been digitally restored and reissued with additional material on a double CD set. As a more orthodox composer from the serialist tradition, Cardew found the selflessness and abnegation of AMM performances (which occasionally took place in pitch dark) difficult to comprehend. Cellist Rohan de Saram, a member of the pivotal, new-music Arditti String Quartet, seems to have had no such difficulties in AMM (he appears only on *The Inexhaustible Document*, in an instrumental role similar to Cardew's) but it's perhaps fair to suggest that de Saram comes from a very different philosophical tradition, in which suspension of the self, of ego and intention, is more readily accepted.

Identifying the participants on record (not, after all, so very different from one of the early live performances) is a little like watching for meteor showers on a moonless night. Sources are identifiable, but their incidence is not, and there is constant activity elsewhere on the aural plane; digital sound exposes more and more layers of activity. Over time, though, it becomes clear that the central dialogue is between the stupendously gifted Prévost and Keith Rowe. Their duetting on the wonderfully titled *Pueblo, Colorado*, a rare instance of studio recording under the auspices of a large(*ish*) label, is quite exceptional.

The arrival of pianist John Tilbury reintroduced some of the contradictions experienced at past changes of personnel but Tilbury is so monstrously polymorphous in technique as to overcome any danger of separatism, and his role on *Generative Themes*, *Combine and Laminates*, and on the marvellous recent *Nameless Uncarved Block* is reassuringly seamless.

By 1990, the music has become absolute, physical rather than abstract, calling on nothing outside itself, but not falling into the Cagean formlessness (with its silences and 'found' devices) of earlier years. Uncarved or not, the music is the product of identifiable forces, just as the 'Sedimentary', 'Igneous' and 'Metamorphic' strata of the album's three tracks (two massive, one brief) are the product of enormous proto-historical pressures. Prévost's percussion constantly and logically alters the physical dynamics of performance; to identify him as leader is now more than justified, an empirical response to the music as played.

Critics, who have always found it difficult to describe that music, and who often resort to comment on titles, were quick to dub *Nameless Uncarved Block* as AMM's 'rock album'. The approach has actually and with the important qualifications mentioned above changed remarkably little over 25 years; it certainly hasn't been susceptible to stylistic fashion. AMMmusic is *sui generis* and needs to be encountered not so much with an open mind as a mind from which certain critical blind alleys have been carefully closed off. The 1990 album and the newly restored 1966 debut and Crypt performances are among the essential documents of contemporary free music, and should be heard.

GENE AMMONS (1925–74)
TENOR SAXOPHONE

(*)   **All Star Sessions Original Jazz Classics OJC 014 LP
Ammons; Art Farmer, Bill Massey (*t*); Al Outcalt (*tb*); Lou Donaldson (*as*); Sonny
Stitt (*ts, bs*); Duke Jordan, Junior Mance, Charles Bateman, Freddie Redd (*p*);
Tommy Potter, Gene Wright, Addison Farmer (*b*); Jo Jones, Wes Landers, Teddy
Stewart, Kenny Clarke (*d*). 3/50–6/55.

***   **The Happy Blues** Original Jazz Classics OJC 013 LP
Ammons; Art Farmer, Jackie Mclean (*as*); Duke Jordan (*p*); Addison Farmer (*b*); Art
Taylor (*d*); Candido Camero (*perc*). 4/56.

(*)   **Jammin' With Gene Original Jazz Classics OJC 211 LP
Ammons; Donald Byrd (*t*); Jackie McLean (*as*); Mal Waldron (*b*); Doug Watkins (*b*);
Art Taylor (*d*). 7/56.

***   **Funky** Original Jazz Classics OJC 244 LP
As above, except Art Farmer (*t*) replaces Byrd, add Kenny Burrell (*g*). 1/57.

**   **Jammin' In Hi Fi** Original Jazz Classics OJC 129 LP
Ammons; Idrees Sulieman (*t*); Jackie Mclean (*as*); Mal Waldron (*p*); Kenny Burrell
(*g*); Paul Chambers (*b*); Art Taylor (*d*). 4/57.

***   **The Big Sound** Original Jazz Classics OJC 651 CD/LP/MC
Ammons; John Coltrane (*as*); Paul Quinichette (*ts*); Pepper Adams (*bs*); Jerome
Richardson (*f*); Mal Waldron (*p*); George Joyner (*b*); Arthur Taylor (*d*). 1/58.

(*)   **Blue Gene Original Jazz Classics OJC 192 CD/LP
Ammons; Idrees Sulieman (*t*); Pepper Adams (*bs*), Mal Waldron (*p*); Doug Watkins
(*b*); Art Taylor (*d*); Ray Barretto (*perc*). 5/58.

The son of Albert Ammons made a lot of records, yet many of the best of them are out of print. OJC's series of reissues has so far dealt mainly with his jamming sessions of the mid-and late-1950s; they are entertaining but often flabby blowing sessions which number as many clichés as worthwhile ideas in the playing. The leader's own style had been forged as a first-generation bopper, first with Billy Eckstine, then under his own name, but his early records find him walking a line between bop and R&B honking: he liked to enjoy his music, and perhaps the darker passions of a Parker were beyond him. The earliest tracks on *All Star Sessions* are typical of the kind of stuff he recorded prior to the LP era, roistering through two-tenor battles with Sonny Stitt, a close kindred spirit. A later date with Farmer and Donaldson is more restrained until the collective whoop of 'Madhouse'.

The next six records all follow similar patterns: long, expansive tracks – at most four to a record – and variations on the blues and some standards for the material. Ammons himself takes the leading solos, but he so often resorts to quotes and familiar phrases that one is left wishing for a less open-ended environment; of the other players involved, McLean and Waldron are the most reliably inventive. *Jammin' In Hi Fi* is the weakest of the six, the whole session sounding like a warm-up, while *Jammin' With Gene* has a very long and overcooked 'Not Really The Blues' balancing two superior slow pieces. *Funky* and *Blue Gene* are decent if unremarkable, but *The Big Sound* has a couple of interesting points in featuring one of John Coltrane's only appearances on alto (undistinguished though it is) and some unexpectedly piquant flute solos by Richardson to vary the palette a little. These all count as playable but unexceptional discs; so far, much of the best of Ammons's work for Prestige, such as the excellent *The Soulful Moods Of Gene Ammons*, has yet to appear on CD.

***   **Boss Tenor** Original Jazz Classics OJC 297 CD/LP/MC
      Ammons; Tommy Flanagan (*p*); Doug Watkins (*b*); Art Taylor (*d*); Ray Barretto
      (*perc*). 6/60.

(*)   **Live! In Chicago Original Jazz Classics OJC 395 CD/LP/MC
      Ammons; Eddie Buster (*org*); Gerald Donovan (*d*). 8/61.

***   **Boss Tenors** Verve 837440 CD
      Ammons; Sonny Stitt (*as, ts*); John Houston (*p*); Charles Williams (*b*); George Brown
      (*d*). 8/61.

(*)   **Bad! Bossa Nova Original Jazz Classics OJC 351 CD/LP/MC
      Ammons; Hank Jones (*p*); Bucky Pizzarelli, Kenny Burrell (*g*); Norman Edge (*b*);
      Oliver Jackson (*d*); Al Hayes (*perc*). 9/62.

(*)   **Greatest Hits, Vol. 1: The Sixties Original Jazz Classics OJC 6005 CD/LP/MC
      Ammons; Joe Newman (*t*); Frank Wess (*ts*); Jack McDuff, Johnny Hammond Smith
      (*org*); Richard Wyands, Hank Jones, Tommy Flanagan (*p*); Kenny Burrell, Bucky
      Pizzarelli (*g*); Doug Watkins, Norman Edge, Wendell Marshall (*b*); Art Taylor, Oliver
      Jackson, Walter Perkins (*d*); Ray Barretto, Al Hayes (*perc*). 61–69.

Following Ammons's records can be disheartening, because he's so inconsistent: great performances can follow weary efforts on the same album, and he doesn't seem to respond to a variation in format. It depends entirely on his mood. *Bad! Bossa Nova* is a dull-witted company idea, of setting this full-throated blues player against the fashionable bossa nova rhythms of the day, and yet Ammons sounds loudly on top of the situation. The live album, though, is merely serviceable, and even *Boss Tenor*, which might be the single best introductory album for anyone wishing to get to know Ammons and his playing, is occasionally heavy-handed, although there is fine sax oratory on the likes of 'Close Your Eyes'. The meeting with Stitt is at least lively and full of hearty good fun, with the swaggering 'Blues Up And Down' a great show of strength by both men. The *Hits* collection could have been the ideal way to sample Ammons, but it also suffers from indecisive programming: the title-track off *Angel Eyes* is one interesting inclusion, but that whole album merits reissue. Since Ammons spent much of the 1960s in jail on narcotics charges, it's necessarily a skimpy survey of a decade's work, too.

*(*)   **In Sweden** Enja 3093 LP
      Ammons; Horace Parlan (*p*); Red Mitchell (*b*); Ed Jones (*d*). 7/73.

Boomingly recorded and mixed, this is a sad reminder of Ammons's indifferent final years. He sounds short of breath and unsure of any direction in his solos, and the surprisingly gutsy attack of Parlan and the rhythm section only magnifies his own frailties.

ARILD ANDERSEN (born 1945)
DOUBLE BASS, ELECTRIC BASS, OTHER INSTRUMENTS

**   **Green Shading Into Blue** ECM 1127 LP
      Andersen; Juhani Aaltonen (*ts, ss, f*); Lars Jansson (*p, syn, syn strings*); Pal Thowsen
      (*d, perc*). 4/78.

***   **A Molde Concert** ECM 1236 LP
      Andersen; Bill Frisell (*g*); John Taylor (*p*); Alphonse Mouzon (*d*). 8/81.

One of Europe's finest musicians, and certainly one of a handful of international-class bass players, Andersen is sadly under-recorded. These two albums, though, and the 1985 *Bande A Part* (ECM 1319) by his band Masqualero, are sufficient to establish his credentials.

Like so many Scandinavians, Andersen is powerfully influenced by Miles Davis, writing and adapting oblique melodies which are separated from kitsch only by the most exact intonation and absence of undue elaboration. That being so, Alphonse Mouzon might not seem the happiest choice of drummer (Jon Christensen's delicate touch is one of the trademarks of Masqualero), but he fits in extraordinarily well behind guitarist Frisell, in counterpoint to pianist Taylor (in one of his best recorded live performances) and the leader. One long track, 'The Sword Under His Wings', is one of the finest European group performances of the 1980s, and there are equally good things elsewhere on the album.

The 1978 band clearly lacks the pedigree of the *Molde* supergroup but is still capable of enterprising and occasionally startling music. The synthesized 'string ensemble' – a fixture much used by Terje Rypdal, before he began to hold out for real orchestras – is a shade too lush, and there is little of the bite that Frisell and Taylor bring to the live album, but *Green Shading Into Blue* (and no will miss the Miles allusions) is still a fine and distinctive set, marked by a lovely samba dedicated to the late singer Radka Toneff, who co-wrote 'Lifelines' on *A Molde Concert*.

***(*)   **Sagn** ECM 1435 CD
      Andersen; Bendik Hofseth (*ts, ss*); Frode Alnaes (*g*); Bugge Wesseltoft (*ky*); Nana Vasconcelos (*perc, v*); Kirsten Braten Berg (*v*). 8/90.

Immediately reminiscent of Jan Garbarek's recent explorations in the boundaries of jazz and Nordic folk-music, *Sagn* – 'Saga' – stands up to the comparison remarkably well. Andersen structures his commissioned piece with great care, incorporating Kirsten Braten Berg's reconstructed Telemark folk songs alongside elements of mainstream and modern jazz and rock (the latter largely communicated by Alnaes, not always with perfect taste). Berg hasn't the purity and simplicity of tone of Agnes Buen Garnas, Garbarek's collaborator, but she has considerable presence in the overall shape of the piece, which is deeply moving and satisfying.

CAT ANDERSON (1916–81)
TRUMPET, FLUGELHORN

***   **Cat Anderson** Swing SW 8412 LP
      Anderson; Buster Cooper, Quentin Jackson (*tb*); Russell Procope (*cl, as*); Paul Gonsalves (*ts*); George Arvanitas, Claude Bolling, Joe Turner (*p*); Roland Lobligeois, Jimmy Woode (*b*); Sam Woodyard (*d*). 10/58, 3/64.

***   **Plays W. C. Handy** Black & Blue 59163 2 CD
      Anderson; Booty Wood (*tb*); Norris Turney (*as*); Harold Ashby (*ts*); Gerard Badini (*ts, cl*); Philippe Baudouin, Raymond Fol, André Persiany (*p*); Aaron Bell, Michel Gaudry (*b*); Sam Woodyard (*d*). 6/77, 5/78.

There has long been a tendency to dismiss Anderson as just another high-wire act, an exhibitionist who traded on his extraordinary five-octave reach to the detriment of more thoughtful play in the vital middle trumpet register. Anderson's coloratura solos were features of Ellington shows, and carefully pitched numbers like 'El Gato' were contrived to afford him as much sky as he wanted; at such moments, Anderson was like a cat who had traded souls with a bird.

Underneath, though, he was a tense perfectionist who studied music with an intensity that belied his occasionally histrionic playing. In his solo ventures before and after Ellington's death, he demonstrates an intelligence and sense of structure that utterly confounds the usual complaint that his solo-development was immature or banal. On the 1958 'Concerto for Cootie' – originally written for his arch-rival on the Ellington trumpet benches, Cootie Williams – he demonstrates considerable taste and tact, and the 'Black and Tan Fantasy' from the same 1958 sessions is one of the finest small-group performances on record. Never well served by furiously compensating sound engineers, Anderson's recorded performances can, as on the Swing compilation, sound rather brittle.

Recorded in France with a mixture of locals and Ellingtonians, the Black & Blue CD is much better. The resolute traditionalism of the material allows Anderson to explore harmonic and timbral devices which in the late 1970s were identified with the avant-garde (Anderson had a brief and, by all accounts, productive flirtation with experimental techniques) but which relate back directly to the growls, slurs and squeezed notes of the classic cornetists. The opening cadences of 'Yellow Dog Blues' betray absolutely no stint in his ability to do high-note intros. His wah-wah solo on 'Careless Love' is a rarer, middle-register effort, but none the less impressive for being relatively contained. (The CD reissue brings in two non-Handy numbers from an earlier session.)

There has never been any doubt about Anderson's technique, but there is a nudging sense that, even by the early 1960s, he had become slightly typecast as a high-note man and that his attempts to shake off a tired script and take account of some of the more interesting recent developments in trumpet-playing – Miles and Clifford Brown most obviously – were a little too late. As with Armstrong, people came along to hear him clearing top C and would have been queueing at the refund desk if he hadn't.

ERNESTINE ANDERSON (born 1928)
VOCAL

(*)   **Hello Like Before Concord CCD 4031 CD/MC
Anderson; Hank Jones (*p*); Ray Brown (*b*); Jimmie Smith (*d*). 76.

***   **Never Make Your Move Too Soon** Concord CCD 4147 CD/MC
Anderson; Monty Alexander (*p*); Ray Brown (*b*); Frank Gant (*d*). 8/80.

***   **Big City** Concord CCD 4214 CD/MC
Anderson; Hank Jones (*p*); Monty Budwig (*b*); Jeff Hamilton (*d*). 2/83.

(*)   **When The Sun Goes Down Concord CCD 4263 CD/MC
Anderson; Red Holloway (*ts*); Gene Harris (*p*); Ray Brown (*b*); Gerrick King (*d*).
8/84.

***   **Be Mine Tonight** Concord CCD 4319 CD/MC
Anderson; Benny Carter (*as*); Marshall Otwell (*p*); Ron Eschete (*g*); Ray Brown (*b*);
Jimmie Smith (*d*). 12/86.

***   **Boogie Down** Concord CCD 4407 CD/MC
Anderson; Clayton-Hamilton Jazz Orchestra. 9/89.

Ernestine Anderson isn't the kind of singer one expects to find on Concord: she's more of a rhythm-and-blues shouter (she sang with Johnny Otis's band in the late 1940s), and the suave situations she's been placed in at this suavest of jazz recording operations might on the face of it seem to be inappropriate. Yet the least satisfying session here is the most 'bluesy', *When The Sun Goes Down*, which wastes the subtleties in Anderson's voice on lesser material, with Holloway and Harris also sounding stuck in routine. None of these records counts as a classic, but each has its own particular interest. The two with Hank Jones benefit from the pianist's ingenious accompaniments, although *Hello Like Before* suffers from a couple of weak song-choices. *Never Make Your Move Too Soon* also has too many familiar tunes on it, but Alexander's knowing vivacity is a tonic. Benny Carter's stately appearance on *Be Mine Tonight* adds some extra interest, and here the songs are perfectly chosen, including 'Christopher Columbus', 'London By Night' and 'Sack Full Of Dreams'. Anderson's voice isn't the strong, smoky instrument it was on her Mercury albums from 30 years ago, but she often takes hold of a song with a kind of infectious intensity which is exciting; her ballads, by contrast, are either compelling or heavy-going. The latest session, with a full big band behind her, is suitably rollicking music, and she can show Diane Schuur, for one, how to make such a situation work best for a singer.

RAY ANDERSON (born 1952)
TROMBONE, ALTO TROMBONE, OTHER BRASS AND PERCUSSION

(*)   **Harrisburg Half-Life Moers 01074 LP
Anderson; Allan Jaffe (*g*); Mark Dresser (*b*); Gerry Hemingway (*d*). 6/80.

***   **Old Bottles – New Wine** Enja 4098/807532 LP/MC
Anderson; Kenny Barron (*p*); Cecil McBee (*b*); Dannie Richmond (*d*). 6/85.

***   **Right Down Your Alley** Soul Note 1087 CD/LP
Anderson; Mark Helias (*b*); Gerry Hemingway (*d*). 2/84.

(*)   **It Just So Happens Enja 5037/807546 CD/MC
Anderson; Stanton Davis (*t*); Bob Stewart (*tba*); Perry Robinson (*cl*); Mark Dresser (*b*); Ronnie Burrage (*d*). 86.

***   **Blues Bred In The Bone** Enja 5081/807661 CD/LP
Anderson; John Scofield (*g*); Anthony Davis (*p*); Mark Dresser (*b*); Johnny Vidacovich (*d*). 3/88.

(*)   **What Because Gramavision GV 79453 CD/LP/MC
Anderson; John Hicks (*p*); Allan Jaffe (*g*); Mark Dresser (*b*); Pheeroan AkLaff (*d*). 11/89.

Just over a decade ago, Ray Anderson headed the usually under-contested trombone category in the *down beat* critics' poll and won a 'Talent Deserving Wider Recognition' citation into the bargain. Since then, he has rapidly established himself as the most exciting slide brass player of his generation, effortlessly switching between free improvisation and funk, humorous and intense by turns, always challenging and always identifiably himself.

Though his biggest commercial success has been the Latinized funk of his band Slickaphonics, he has an impressive back-catalogue both as sideman and leader, working with the (un)likes of Barry Altschul, Anthony Braxton, Barbara Dennerlein and others. *Harrisburg Half-Life* is still an impressive set. Its already well-assimilated rock influence became a feature of Anderson's subsequent work. His preferred sidemen – Dresser, Hemingway, Helias, Burrage – all play in what could be described as an advanced rock idiom and Cecil McBee on the outstanding *Old Bottles – New Wine* demonstrates the untroubled eclecticism that made the Charles Lloyd quartets of the late '60s and early '70s so important to the jazz–rock crossover.

Anderson plays very cleanly, almost like a valve player, but has a massive repertoire of smears, multiphonics, huge portamento effects, which fit equally comfortably into his funk and abstract idioms. *It Just So Happens* is perhaps his least well-defined recording to date, but it is adventurous and provocative in its remarkably traditionalist deployment of instrumental voices. By contrast, *Right Down Your Alley* is taut and to the point, and a slap in the face to those who regard solo trombone as a hubristic embarrassment in flight from its 'proper' section role in one of the back rows of the band. Here, as in the similarly constituted Bass Drum Bone, he plays with great discipline and control.

The 1989 Gramavision album is curiously unfocused. At this point in Anderson's career, we might reasonably expect rather stronger original material. Impressive as it is, another run through his extensive phrase-book is neither here nor there. Hicks, Dresser and akLaff play impeccably but with the slightly desperate air of men ordered to make bricks without straw.

Anderson's blues understanding, sharpened by a fruitful stint with saxophonist Bennie Wallace's revivalist project, is strongly featured on the very fine *Blues Bred In The Bone*. Anderson's partnership with Scofield on the haunting, self-written '53rd And Greenwood' is hard to fault, as is the fully-blown 'A Flower Is A Lovesome Thing'. Jazz was bred in the cornet, the clarinet, and the 'bone; Anderson is putting flesh on the tradition.

ANGLASPEL
GROUP

**   **Jazz I Sverige '82** Caprice CAP 1270 LP
Ann-Sofi Soderqvist (*t, flhn*); Mikael Godee (*ss*); Stefan Isaksson (*ts*); Stefan Forssen (*p*); Anders Jormin (*b*); Erik Dahlback (*d*). 3/82.

**   **Lappland** Dragon DRLP 112 LP
       As above. 84.

While the stance of the band suggests a particularly native kind of Scandinavian jazz, Anglaspel play a fairly polite, modal, mainstream sort of music. There is some attractive improvising from the horns and Forssen especially, but the records are at best no more than mildly diverting.

PETER APFELBAUM & THE HIEROGLYPHICS ENSEMBLE
GROUP

***(*)   **Signs Of Life** Antilles 422 848 634 CD/MC
       Apfelbaum (*ts, ss, p, ky, perc*); Bill Ortiz (*t*); Jeff Cressman, James Harvey (*tb, perc*);
       Phil Hanson (*as, ts, bsn*); Tony Jones (*ts*); Peck Allmond (*bs, t, cl, perc*); Norbert
       Stachel (*reeds, f, bf*); Will Bernard, Stan Franks (*g*); Jai Uttal (*g, harmonium, v, perc*);
       David Belove (*b*); Bo Freeman (*b, v*); Josh Jones V (*d, perc*); Deszon X. Claiborne
       (*d*); Buddha Robert Huffman (*perc*); Scheherazade Stone (*v*). 11/90.

Global village music from a West Coast collective which, despite having been around for most of the decade, seems not to have recorded and which came to prominence only on the strength of a guest role on Don Cherry's poly-ethnic *Multi Kulti*. With such an extraordinary instrumental range to call upon (Hanson, Allmond and Stachel replace a dozen session call-ups between them), the group's characteristic sound is difficult to pin down with certainty, but it seems to be compounded of 1960s West-meets-East rock, 1970s soul, Afro-jazz, and a welter of 'world music' reference points that are either highly effective, as on the North African 'The Last Door', or kitsch, as on a funked-up 'Michael, Row The Boat Ashore'; the nearest parallel might be Fred Houn's Afro-Asian Ensemble, though without the political agenda.

Apfelbaum is credited with all the material but takes a relatively modest role as a soloist (he sounds vaguely like Pharoah Sanders on tenor; his piano solo on 'Chant No. 11' prompts some relief that numbers one to ten were found wanting). 'Samantha Smith' is perhaps the most satisfying of his features, but his soprano solo on 'Walk To The Mountain (And Tell The Story Of Love's Thunderclapping Eyes)' suggests he may have been taking harmony lessons from the maverick and wildly prolific West Coast composer, Alan Hovhaness. There again, though, the pairing of saxophone and harmonium is typically distinctive. 'Grounding', which follows, sounds remarkably like Jack Bruce's 'Make Love' but features a bassoon solo of real grit and substance, belying Thomas Mann's much-quoted sneer about the instrument's weak-bassed bleating; only Illinois Jacquet has given the least mettlesome of the reed instruments as much conviction in a jazz context.

Fascinating and straightforwardly enjoyable, it's a difficult one to call. *Signs Of Life* could be a happy one-off, or it could be a preface to a new configuration of popular music in the 1990s.

PETER APPLEYARD (born 1928)
VIBES

**   **Barbados Heat** Concord CCD 4436 CD/MC
       Appleyard; Rick Wilkins (*ts*); Bucky Pizzarelli (*g*); Major Holley (*b*); Butch Miles
       (*d*). 2/90.

Appleyard is a veteran who has spent most of his playing life away from any jazz limelight, working in Canada and Bermuda. He played with Benny Goodman in the '70s, and his Hampton-derived style obviously stood him in good stead there. This is the only record under his own name in print, recorded at a Barbados concert, and its uncomplicated swing makes for a typical Concord date. The sound-mix favours Miles, which is an advantage, since his rather noisy style gives the music some extra kick. Hackneyed material throughout, although Wilkins gives a good account of 'Body And Soul'.

(*)   **Barbados Cool Concord CCD 4475 CD/MC
       As above. 2/90.

More from the same session. Pleasing versions of Strayhorn's 'Passion Flower', a feature for Pizzarelli, and John Lewis's 'Django' give this programme a slight edge over its predecessor.

ARCADO
GROUP

(*) **Arcado** JMT 8344239 CD/LP

***(*) **Behind The Myth** JMT 834441 CD/LP
Mark Dresser (*b*); Hank Roberts (*clo*); Mark Feldman (*vn*). 2/89, 3/90.

Arcado follow in the path of Billy Bang's String Trio of New York (and, by no means incidentally, new music prodigies, the Kronos Quartet) in exploring a range of instrumentation still considered problematic in small-group jazz. The debut album oozed promise, but it was with *Behind The Myth* that Arcado established themselves as something quite exceptional. The long title-track has moments of breathtaking beauty, with Feldman stretching above the lower strings. Though all the tracks are self-written, along the way they touch on influences as various as Django Reinhardt, Charles Mingus and, on the closing 'Somewhere', hints of Jimi Hendrix (for which they may well be indebted to the Kronos). Jazz with no horns? . . . no piano? . . . no drums? Purists will whisper anathemas, and will be the losers. Highly recommended.

*** **For Three Strings And Orchestra** JMT 849 152 2 CD
Mark Dresser (*b*); Mark Feldman (*vn*); Hank Roberts (*clo*); Kölner
Rundfunkorchester. 6/91.

Not strictly a jazz album at all, but a fascinating experiment in large-scale writing by this adventurous group. There's no sense in which it's even an *un*orthodox triple concerto. The three principals seem to develop material unrelated to the background of each composition (one apiece and one, 'In Cold Moonlight', credited to Manfred Niehaus), with the exception of Feldman's long 'Naked Singularities' which has a persuasively cumulative logic that makes more effective use of (presumably) free elements than the other pieces. Perhaps a little too close to squeaky-door music for some tastes, but undeniably challenging.

JULIAN ARGUELLES
TENOR SAXOPHONE

*** **Phaedrus** Ah Um 010 CD
Arguelles; John Taylor (*p*); Mick Hutton (*b*); Martin France (*d*). 91.

An encouragingly personal sax-and-rhythm date for the young British saxophonist. Abjuring obvious role-models has apparently led him in the direction of such players as Warne Marsh and some of the modern European masters, but he tempers that danger of humourless expertise with some typically off-kilter melodies which Taylor, in particular, lines with great harmonic and textural strength. While there are hints of deliberate foolishness in some of the writing – a trait that continues to be a besetting sin among many British players – it livens up the sometimes portentous Taylor no end, and Hutton and France play with plenty of enjoyment too.

LIL ARMSTRONG (1898–1971)
PIANO, VOCAL

(*) **Lil Armstrong Born To Swing 1936–37** Harlequin HQ 2069 LP
Armstrong; Joe Thomas, Shirley Clay (*t*); Buster Bailey (*cl*); Prince Robinson, Robert Carroll (*ts*); Chu Berry, James Sherman, Teddy Cole (*p*); Arnold Adams, Huey Long (*g*); John Frazier, Wellman Braud (*b*); Pops Foster, Manzie Johnson (*d*). 10/36–7/37.

*** **Lil Hardin Armstrong And Her Swing Orchestra 1936–1940** Classics 564 CD
As above, plus Ralph Muzillo, Johnny McGee, Reunald Jones, Jonah Jones (*t*); Al Philburn, J. C. Higginbotham (*tb*); Tony Zimmers (*cl*); Don Stovall (*as*); Russell Johns (*ts*); Frank Froeba (*p*); Dave Barbour (*g*); Haig Stephens (*b*); O'Neil Spencer, Sam Weiss (*d*); Midge Williams, Hilda Rogers (*v*). 10/36–3/40.

The former Mrs Armstrong was never much of a piano player, which may be why keyboard duties were entrusted to others on most of these sessions. But her vocal talents were more likeable, and on these now-obscure sides she comes on like a precursor of Nellie Lutcher and other, vaguely racy, post-war singers. The accompaniments offer a rough distillation of small-band swing and rather older styles, suggested by the presence of such veterans of the '20s as Robinson and Clay alongside the more modernistic Thomas and Berry. Titles such as '(I'm On A) Sit-down Strike For Rhythm' have a self-explanatory charm, and there's a more distinctive jazz content in the typically hot and fluent playing of Bailey.

For a long time, the Harlequin LP was the only edition of this music available. But the Classics CD offers a full roster of 26 tracks, covering later sessions up to 1940; on the final date, Ms Armstrong returns to the piano and leaves the singing to others. The sound has been conscientiously handled by the company.

LOUIS ARMSTRONG (1900–71)
TRUMPET, CORNET, VOCAL

*** **Louis Armstrong 1923–1931** BBC REB/CD/ZEF 597 CD/LP/MC
Armstrong; Zilmer Randolph, Otis Johnson, Henry Allen (*t*); King Oliver (*c*); John Thomas, Honoré Dutrey, Preston Jackson, Jack Teagarden, J. C. Higginbotham, Fred Robinson (*tb*); Johnny Dodds (*cl*); Albert Nicholas, Charlie Holmes, Don Redman (*cl, as*); Jimmy Strong (*cl, ts*); Bert Curry, Crawford Wethington (*as*); Teddy Hill, Happy Caldwell (*ts*); George James, Albert Washington, Lester Boone (*reeds*); Lil Armstrong, Earl Hines, Joe Sullivan, Luis Russell, Charlie Alexander (*p*); Lonnie Johnson, Eddie Lang, Will Johnson (*g*); Bud Scott, Johnny St Cyr, Mancy Cara, Mike McKendrick (*bj*); Pete Briggs (*bb*); Joe Lindsay, Pops Foster (*b*); Baby Dodds, Zutty Singleton, Kaiser Marshall, Paul Barbarin, Tubby Hall (*d*). 6/23–11/31.

Knowing where to start with Armstrong's music on record is something of a problem for newcomers to jazz, since his vast output has now been comprehensively reissued but, alas, in a far from coherent manner. This compilation isn't a bad introduction to his early work, although Robert Parker's stereo remastering techniques were at an early stage of development when he prepared this set and it is consequently not as fine as his later efforts. However, it's the only compilation which starts with Armstrong in the King Oliver band and goes through to his big band work of the early 1930s. The 16 tracks are almost uniformly magnificent: three of the finest Hot Seven sides, six Hot Fives including 'West End Blues' and 'Muggles', 'Symphonic Raps' with the Carroll Dickerson band and 'Knockin' A Jug' from a 1929 all-star small-group date. But the arbitrary nature of the record overall emphasizes that Armstrong's 1920s records are too consistently valuable to be scattered across compilations.

**** **Louis Armstrong And The Blues Singers 1924–1930** Affinity AFS 1018-6 6CD
Armstrong; Charlie Green, Aaron Thompson, Charlie Irvis, Kid Ory, Tommy Dorsey (*tb*); Sidney Bechet (*cl, ss*); Don Redman (*cl, as*); Jimmy Strong (*cl, ts*); Buster Bailey, Jimmie Noone, Artie Starks, Jimmy Dorsey (*cl*); Coleman Hawkins (*ts*); Fred Longshaw (*harm, p*); Justin Ring (*p, cel*); Fletcher Henderson, Lil Armstrong, James P. Johnson, Richard M. Jones, Earl Hines, Hersal Thomas, Clarence Williams, Gene Anderson (*p*); Harry Hoffman, Joe Venuti (*vn*); Eddie Lang (*g*); Charlie Dixon, Buddy Christian, Johnny St Cyr, Mancy Cara (*bj*); Kaiser Marshall, Zutty Singleton (*d*); Ma Rainey, Virginia Liston, Eva Taylor, Alberta Hunter, Margaret Johnson, Sippie Wallace, Maggie Jones, Clara Smith, Bessie Smith, Trixie Smith, Billy Jones, Coot Grant, Wesley Wilson, Perry Bradford, Bertha 'Chippie' Hill, Blanche Calloway, Hociel Thomas, Baby Mack, Nolan Welsh, Butterbeans And Susie, Lillie Delk Christian, Seger Ellis, Victoria Spivey, Clarence Todd, Jimmie Rodgers (*v*). 10/24–7/30.

An astonishing collection. Armstrong worked as an accompanist to a number of singers in the 1920s, and although his records with Bessie Smith are well known, most of the others are familiar only to experienced Armstrong collectors. Yet there is enough material to fill six CDs, and this handsomely mounted set includes all of it. There are sessions with some of the greatest of the 'classic' blues singers, including Clara Smith, Trixie Smith, Chippie Hill, Alberta Hunter and Ma Rainey, as well as with more vaudeville-orientated singers such as Butterbeans And

Susie, Eva Taylor and Lillie Delk Christian (who is backed by what was basically the Hot Five). Affinity have also rounded up oddities such as the beautiful 'Blue Yodel No 9', where Armstrong plays a gorgeous accompaniment to country singer Jimmie Rodgers, and the amazing 'I Miss My Swiss', where the Fletcher Henderson orchestra backs Billy Jones on a novelty tune which Armstrong utterly transforms with a glittering solo. The trumpeter often provides the only interest on many of the recordings and it's his ability to create parts of almost offhand radiance which sustains a listener even through six entire CDs. The remastering has been done using the CEDAR process, and while this has sometimes mixed results on recordings of varying original quality, there must be few complaints about the overall ambience of the sound. For specialists rather than general listeners, perhaps, but we give this the highest recommendation to anyone interested in Armstrong's work away from his most renowned sessions.

*** **Louis Armstrong With Red Onion Jazz Babies** Fountain FJ-107 LP
Armstrong; Charlie Irvis, Aaron Thompson (*tb*); Sidney Bechet (*cl, ss*); Buster Bailey (*cl*); Lil Armstrong (*p*); Buddy Christian (*bj*); Alberta Hunter (*v*). 11/12/24.

The LP is shared with nine tracks featuring Freddie Keppard, but otherwise this collects Armstrong's eight sides with the Red Onion Jazz Babies, all of which are also included on the Affinity set listed above. Fair remastering from sometimes rough originals, though Armstrong shines through as always, as does Bechet.

(****) **The Hot Fives Vol. 1** CBS 460821-2 CD
Armstrong; Kid Ory (*tb*); Johnny Dodds (*cl*); Lil Armstrong (*p*); Johnny St Cyr (*bj*). 11/25–6/26.

(****) **The Hot Fives And Hot Sevens Vol. II** CBS 463052-2 CD
As above, except add John Thomas (*tb*), Pete Briggs (*bb*); Baby Dodds (*d*), May Alix (*v*). 6/26–5/27.

***** **Hot Fives And Sevens Vol. 1** JSP 312 CD
As above. 11/25–11/26.

(****) **The Hot Fives And Hot Sevens Vol. III** Columbia CK 44422 CD
As above, except add Lonnie Johnson (*g*). 5–12/27.

***** **Hot Fives And Sevens Vol. 2** JSP 313 CD
As above. 5–12/27.

**** **Louis Armstrong & His Hot Five & Hot Seven** Classics 585 CD
As above. 5–12/27.

(****) **Louis Armstrong And Earl Hines Vol. IV** Columbia CK 45142 CD
Armstrong; Fred Robinson (*tb*); Jimmy Strong (*cl, ts*); Don Redman (*cl, as, v*); Earl Hines (*p, cel, v*); Mancy Cara (*bj, v*); Zutty Singleton (*d*). 6–12/28.

***** **Hot Fives And Sevens Vol. 3** JSP 314 CD
Armstrong; Homer Hobson (*t*); Fred Robinson, Jack Teagarden (*tb*); Bert Curry, Crawford Wethington (*as*); Jimmy Strong (*cl, ts*); Happy Caldwell (*ts*); Earl Hines (*p, cel, v*); Joe Sullivan (*p*); Carroll Dickerson (*vn*); Eddie Lang (*g*); Dave Wilborn (*bj, g*); Mancy Cara (*bj, v*); Pete Briggs (*bb*); Zutty Singleton, Kaiser Marshall (*d*). 6/28–2/29.

These are some of the most famous of all jazz recordings, and their power to astonish and invigorate listeners is undimished, even after more than six decades. One is envious of those who hear masterpieces such as 'Potato Head Blues' or 'Hotter Than That' for the first time, for their beauty and intensity provide the most thrilling experiences to anyone who comes fresh to jazz. Countless listeners must have been converted into jazz fans by these tracks. The Hot Five and the subsequent larger group the Hot Seven were units which existed only in the recording studios, and their sessions were hurriedly arranged, but they showcase Armstrong's blossoming genius with brilliant clarity. His improvisations, ensemble parts and vocals are all imbued with an iconoclastic majesty which is sustained through almost all of their individual records. While the early sides feature a rough exuberance, Armstrong still finding his way but superbly creative on the likes of 'Cornet Chop Suey' and 'Jazz Lips', the Hot Seven tracks move with an almost furious power, exemplified in the overwhelming solo on 'Wild Man Blues', which in turn leads to the poetic, perhaps mollified grandeur of 'West End Blues', 'Muggles' and 'Tight Like This'. A detailed summary is beyond the scope of this book, but we must insist that any who are still unaware of these records make their acquaintance as soon as possible.

They have been reissued many times over the years, and OKeh's excellent studio sound has been faithfully transferred to a number of LP editions from the 1960s onwards. But we have to express disappointment with Columbia's transfers, which render some parts of the ensembles with poor clarity and generally lose much of the original life in the music (the disclaimer that 'it has been impossible to find clean copies of the 78rpm discs' is preposterous: as jazz 78s go, these are not rare records). John R. T. Davies's remastering of the material for JSP is, however, a superior effort which shames the Columbia engineering, and it's to these which we award our five-star commendation. The third volume includes the two tracks by Carroll Dickerson's Savoyagers, a sort of augmented Hot Five, and ends with the meeting of Armstrong with Teagarden, Eddie Lang and Joe Sullivan in the beautiful 'Knockin' A Jug'. Again, the transfers – though wholly unafraid of surface hiss – are marvellously clear and lifelike. The Classics CD, part of a comprehensive overview of all of Armstrong's pre-war work under his own leadership, is a good single-disc representation of the 1927 records, but again the sound is inferior to the JSP discs.

****   **Louis In New York Vol. V** Columbia CK 46148 CD
Armstrong; Homer Hobson (*t*); Fred Robinson, Jack Teagarden, J. C. Higginbotham (*tb*); Jimmy Strong (*cl, ts*); Albert Nicholas, Charlie Holmes, Bert Curry, William Blue, Crawford Wethington (*as*); Happy Caldwell (*ts*); Joe Sullivan, Luis Russell, Buck Washington (*p*); Eddie Lang, Lonnie Johnson (*g*); Eddie Condon (*bj*); Pops Foster (*b*); Paul Barbarin, Kaiser Marshall (*d*); Hoagy Carmichael (*v*). 3/29–4/30.

****   **Big Bands Vol. 1** JSP 305 CD
Armstrong; Ed Anderson, Leon Elkins, George Orendorff, Harold Scott (*t*); Henry Hicks, Lawrence Brown, Luther Graven (*tb*); Bobby Holmes (*cl, as*); Castor McCord, Charlie Jones (*cl, ts*); Les Hite (*as, bs*); Theodore McCord, Leon Herriford, Willie Stark, Marvin Johnson (*as*); William Franz (*ts*); Joe Turner, Buck Washington, L Z Turner, Henry Prince (*p*); Bernard Addison, Bernard Prince (*g*); Ceele Burke (*bj*); Lavert Hutchinson, Reggie Jones (*bb*); Joe Bailey (*b*); Lionel Hampton (*d, vib*); Willie Lynch (*d*). 4/30–4/31.

****   **Louis Armstrong Vol. VI** Columbia CK 46996 CD
As above. 4/30–3/31.

****   **Big Bands Vol. 2** JSP 306 CD
Armstrong; Zilmer Randolph (*t*); Preston Jackson (*tb*); George James (*cl, ss, as*); Lester Boone (*cl, as*); Albert Washington (*cl, ts*); Charlie Alexander (*p*); Mike McKendrick (*g, bj*); John Lindsay (*b*); Tubby Hall (*d*). 4/31–3/32.

****   **Louis Armstrong & His Orchestra 1928–1929** Classics 570 CD
Personnel as listed under appropriate dates above. 6/28–3/29.

****   **Louis Armstrong & His Orchestra 1929–1930** Classics 557 CD
Personnel as listed under appropriate dates above. 3/29–5/30.

****   **Louis Armstrong & His Orchestra 1930–31** Classics 547 CD
Personnel as listed under appropriate dates above. 5/30–4/31.

****   **Louis Armstrong & His Orchestra 1931–32** Classics 536 CD
Personnel as listed under appropriate dates above. 11/31–3/32.

Following the final Hot Five records, Armstrong recorded almost exclusively as a soloist in front of big bands, at least until the formation of the All Stars in the 1940s. Although the records became much more formal in shape – most of them are recordings of contemporary pop tunes, opened by an Armstrong vocal and climaxing in a stratospheric solo – the finest of them showcase Louis as grandly as anything he'd already recorded. The Columbia *Louis In New York* is a close duplicate of Classics 557, though with fewer titles, and mostly covers the period where Armstrong was fronting the Luis Russell band. 'Black And Blue', 'Dallas Blues' and 'After You've Gone' offer superb improvisations against bland but functional backdrops, and while some of the sheer daring has gone out of Armstrong's playing, he's become more poised, more serenely powerful than before. Finer still, though, are the records made in Los Angeles in

1930 with, among others, the young Lionel Hampton. There are few superior Armstrong performances to 'Body And Soul', 'I'm A Ding Dong Daddy From Dumas' and 'Memories Of You', where his singing is as integral and inventive as his trumpet-playing, and the sequence culminates in the moving and transcendent playing of 'Sweethearts On Parade'. The 1931–32 sessions find him in front of another anonymous orchestra, and although arrangements and performances are again merely competent, they serve to throw the leader's own contributions into a sharper relief, with 'Star Dust', 'Lawd, You Made The Night Too Long' and 'Chinatown, My Chinatown' among the outstanding tracks. These were his final recordings for OKeh before a move to Victor in 1933.

While the Columbia engineers have generally been a little more successful with these later records, we must again primarily recommend the excellent JSP transfers, although their packaging is less substantial. The Classics sequence, though, has the merit of uninterrupted chronological presentation at an attractive price, and while their transfers aren't always of the finest, there are no serious problems with the overall sound.

***(*) **Laughin' Louis 1932–1933** Bluebird NL/ND/NK 90404 CD/LP/MC
Armstrong; Louis Bacon, Louis Hunt, Billy Hicks, Charlie Gaines, Elmer Whitlock, Zilmer Randolph (*t*); Charlie Green, Keg Johnson (*tb*); Pete Clark, Scoville Brown, George Oldham (*cl, as*); Edgar Sampson (*as, vn*); Louis Jordan, Arthur Davey (*as*); Budd Johnson (*cl, ts*); Elmer Williams, Ellsworth Blake (*ts*); Don Kirkpatrick, Wesley Robinson, Teddy Wilson (*p*); Mike McKendrick (*bj, g*); John Trueheart (*g*); Ed Hayes, Bill Oldham (*bb, b*); Elmer James (*b*); Chick Webb, Benny Hill, Yank Porter (*d*). 12/32–4/33.

**** **Louis Armstrong & His Orchestra 1932–33** Classics 529 CD
As above. 12/32–4/33.

Armstrong's Victor records of 1932–33 are among his most majestic statements. If he had simplified his style, the breadth of his tone and seeming inevitability of timing and attack had been fashioned into an invincible creation: the way he handles 'I Gotta Right To Sing The Blues' or 'Basin Street Blues' makes them seem like conclusive offerings from jazz's greatest virtuoso. Even so, weaker material was already starting to creep into his repertoire, and even the title-track of *Laughin' Louis* gives some indication of what was happening to his music. The Bluebird collection is incomplete in terms of dealing with this period, but it's the best possible cross-section and the sound, although the NoNoise process won't be to all tastes, is dry but substantial. The Classics series continues apace and gathers in most of the Victor material on to one CD.

**** **Louis Armstrong & His Orchestra 1934–36** Classics 509 CD
Armstrong; Jack Hamilton, Leslie Thompson, Leonard Davis, Gus Aiken, Louis Bacon, Bunny Berigan, Bob Mayhew (*t*); Lionel Guimaraes, Harry White, Jimmy Archey, Al Philburn (*tb*); Pete Duconge (*cl, as*); Sid Trucker (*cl, bs*); Henry Tyre, Henry Jones, Charlie Holmes, Phil Waltzer (*as*); Alfred Pratt, Bingie Madison, Greely Walton, Paul Ricci (*ts*); Herman Chittison, Luis Russell, Fulton McGrath (*p*); Maceo Jefferson, Lee Blair, Dave Barbour (*g*); German Artango, Pops Foster, Pete Peterson (*b*); Oliver Tynes, Paul Barbarin, Stan King (*d*). 10/34–2/36.

***(*) **Rhythm Saved The World** MCA GRP 16022 CD
Largely as above. 10/35–2/36.

***(*) **Louis Armstrong & His Orchestra 1936–37** Classics 512 CD
As above, except add Snub Mosley, Bobby Byrne, Joe Yuki, Don Mattison (*tb*); Jimmy Dorsey, Jack Stacey (*cl, as*); Fud Livingston, Skeets Herfurt (*cl, ts*); Bobby van Eps (*p*); George Archer, Harry Baty (*g, v*); Roscoe Hillman (*g*); Sam Koki (*stg*); Andy Iona (*uke, v*); Jim Taft, Joe Nawahi (*b*); Ray McKinley, Lionel Hampton (*d*); Bing Crosby, Frances Langford, The Mills Brothers (*v*). 2/36–4/37.

**** **Louis Armstrong & His Orchestra 1937–38** Classics 515 CD
Armstrong; Shelton Hemphill, Louis Bacon, Henry Allen (*t*); George Matthews, George Washington, J. C. Higginbotham, Wilbur De Paris (*tb*); Pete Clark, Charlie Holmes, Rupert Cole (*as*); Albert Nicholas, Bingie Madison (*cl, ts*); Luis Russell (*p*); Lee Blair (*g*); Pops Foster, Red Callender (*b*); Paul Barbarin (*d*); The Mills Brothers (*v*). 6/37–5/38.

***(*)   **Louis Armstrong & His Orchestra 1938–39** Classics 523 CD
As above, except add Bob Cusamano, Johnny McGee, Otis Johnson, Frank Zullo, Grady Watts, Sonny Dunham (*t*); Al Philburn, Murray McEachern, Russell Rauch, Pee Wee Hunt (*tb*); Sid Stoneburn (*cl*); Art Ralston, Clarence Hutchinrider (*as*); Pat Davis, Dan D'Andrea, Joe Garland (*ts*); Kenny Sargent (*bs*); Nat Jaffe, Howard Hall (*p*); Jack Blanchette, Dave Barbour (*g*); Haig Stephens, Stan Dennis (*b*); Sam Weiss, Sid Catlett, Tony Briglia (*d*). 5/38–4/39.

Armstrong's Decca recordings in the 1930s have been a maligned and undervalued group, seldom reissued and often written off as a disastrous pop period. While there are many throwaway songs and plain bad ideas – even Louis couldn't do much with 'She's The Daughter Of A Planter From Havana' and its sorry ilk – he does rise above the circumstances much as Fats Waller and Billie Holiday do in the same period: the sheer *sound* of Armstrong, whether singing or playing trumpet, is exhilarating. The sequential Classics issues are therefore very welcome. The 1934–35 disc includes a memorable session made in Paris with a local band including the very fine pianist Herman Chittison, with a terrific 'St Louis Blues'; from there, Armstrong is backed mostly by a Luis Russell band, and it performs very creditably, with some members stepping forward for occasional solos. 1936–37 includes two tremendous pieces in 'Swing That Music' and 'Mahogany Hall Stomp' as well as a peculiar meeting with a Hawaiian group and two dates with The Mills Brothers. The fine session from January 1938 is on the next disc, with Albert Nicholas almost stealing the occasion on 'Struttin' With Some Barbecue' until Louis's own solo. The 1938–39 record has a session with the Casa Loma Orchestra, another with a rather white-toned gospel group, the lovely 'My Walking Stick' with The Mills Brothers and a concluding date which remakes 'West End Blues' and Don Redman's 'Save It, Pretty Mama'. We must award all these high marks if only for the occasions when the material, music and Armstrong himself are all strong. The transfers are mostly very good. The MCA compilation takes a look at one of the most enjoyable of this run of sessions, from 1935–36, with 'I've Got My Fingers Crossed', 'Solitude' and 'I'm Putting All My Eggs In One Basket' among the standouts. Some may prefer the highly cleaned-up sound of these transfers, using the NoNOISE system, although the liveliness of some of the tracks has been slightly diminished.

***   **On The Sunny Side Of The Street** Jazz J-CD-19 CD
Armstrong; Shelton Hemphill, Frank Galbreath, Bernard Flood, Robert Butler, Louis Gray, Fats Ford (*t*); George Washington, Henderson Chambers, James Whitney, Russell Moore, Waddet Williams, Nat Allen, James Whitney (*tb*); Don Hill, Amos Gordon, Rupert Coile (*as*); Dexter Gordon, Budd Johnson, John Sparrow (*ts*); Earnest Thompson (*bs*); Prince Robinson, Joe Garland, Carl Frye (*saxes*); Luis Russell, Earl Mason, Gerald Wiggins (*p*); Elmer Warner, Lawrence Lucie (*g*); Art Simmons, Arvell Shaw (*b*); Chick Morrison, Edmond McConney, Jesse Price (*d*); The Mills Brothers, Velma Middleton, Jimmy Anderson, Ann Baker, Bea Booze (*v*). 6/38–8/46.

A very entertaining compilation of broadcast and soundtrack material. Three shows for forces radio feature plenty of mugging and a degree of great trumpet, though a soundtrack reading of 'Jeepers Creepers' also has a strong solo, and a closing and very frantic 'Hot Chestnuts' is surprisingly wild. Sound-quality is very clean for all except two tracks, which suffer from some distortion.

***(*)   **Pops: The 1940s Small Band Sides** Bluebird ND 86378 CD
Armstrong; Bobby Hackett (*t*); Jack Teagarden (*tb, v*); Kid Ory (*tb*); Barney Bigard (*cl*); Peanuts Hucko (*cl, ts*); Ernie Caceres (*cl, bs*); Johnny Guarnieri (*p, cel*); Dick Cary, Charlie Beal (*p*); Bud Scott, Al Casey (*g*); Bob Haggart, Red Callender, Al Hall (*b*); George Wettling, Minor Hall, Cozy Cole (*d*). 10/46–5/47.

***(*)   **Sugar** Bluebird ND 90634 CD
As above. 9/46–7/47.

After some years of comparative neglect, Armstrong bounced back via the film *New Orleans*, which was made during the period covered by the earliest tracks here, and the formation of the All Stars, a move initiated by the 1947 New York Town Hall concert, much of which is included here, along with some other studio sides with Teagarden. With vintage jazz undergoing something of a revival, Armstrong sounded like a pillar: his playing here on 'Back O'Town

Blues', 'Jack-Armstrong Blues' and another 'Mahogany Hall Stomp' has riveting intensity. Teagarden matches him with his own playing, and the small bands generally have the lightness of touch which the later All Stars records miss. An important collection, capably remastered. *Sugar* is a pocket edition of the same material, carrying ten of the best tracks at a bargain price.

***   **All Stars At Symphony Hall** Giants Of Jazz 235 CD
Armstrong; Jack Teagarden (*tb, v*); Barney Bigard (*cl*); Dick Cary (*p*); Arvell Shaw (*b*); Sid Catlett (*d*); Velma Middleton (*v*). 10/47.

(*)   **Live At The Exhibition Garden, Vancouver Instant INS 5046 CD
Armstrong; Jack Teagarden (*tb, v*); Barney Bigard (*cl*); Earl Hines (*p*); Arvell Shaw (*b*); Cozy Cole (*d*); Velma Middleton (*v*). 1/51.

(*)   **The Great Concert Of Louis Armstrong Accord 401542 CD
As above. 51.

Following the great success at New York's Town Hall, Armstrong formed the All Stars as a regular touring band, and with the eventual arrival of Hines it should have lived up to its name. But the shows quickly fell into routine. The Symphony Hall set finds them still fresh enough to make the music exciting, but by the 1951 shows the set list has grown predictable and the routines routine. Yet Armstrong himself still lights up much of the music. The Giants Of Jazz session features average sound but the band are clearly enjoying themselves; the Vancouver set offers some 55 minutes of Bigard, Velma Middleton and not nearly enough Armstrong, who sounds wonderful on the blues 'Where Did You Stay Last Night' and does an uproarious 'Baby It's Cold Outside' with Middleton; and the Accord set features a similar programme with some extra tracks. Neither of these discs is exactly hi-fi, with the balance on the Vancouver set a hopeless muddle and Shaw and Hines virtually inaudible throughout. Armstrong admirers, though, will enjoy them regardless.

***(*)   **Plays W. C. Handy** Columbia CK 40242 CD
Armstrong; Trummy Young (*tb*); Barney Bigard (*cl*); Billy Kyle (*p*); Arvell Shaw (*b*); Barrett Deems (*d*); Velma Middleton (*v*). 6/54.

***   **Satch Plays Fats** Columbia CK 40378 CD
As above. 4-5/55.

Two of Louis's best records of the 1950s. When granted an intelligent choice of programme, Armstrong still sounded in imperious command, and the Handy collection in particular sounds like a master delivering a definitive interpretation of a sequence of standards. While he sounds more comfortable on the slower numbers – such as a stately 'Hesitating Blues' – his singing is eloquent throughout, and just as fine on the Waller collection, although here the showbiz characteristics which stick to many of the tunes renege on their jazz content. The All Stars were playing well enough, but Young is scarcely a strong replacement for Teagarden, no matter how lax the latter might become, and the ratings for almost all the All Stars records from this point refer only to Louis himself: without him, the band would amount to nothing at all. Remastering of both discs is good.

(*)   **Greatest Hits CBS 21058 CD
Armstrong; Trummy Young (*tb, v*); Tyree Glenn (*tb*); Barney Bigard, Edmond Hall, Buster Bailey (*cl*); Billy Kyle, Marty Napoleon (*p*); Arvell Shaw, Dale Jones, Buddy Catlett (*b*); Barrett Deems, Danny Barcelona (*d*). 4/55–66.

Aside from the inclusion of 'Cabaret' from 1966, this is a sensible collection from the earlier Columbia period, although there's nothing from the Handy collection. Many of the tracks are otherwise unavailable.

(*)   **Porgy And Bess Verve 827475-2 CD
Armstrong; Ella Fitzgerald (*v*); Russell Garcia Orchestra. 8/57.

(*)   **Louis Armstrong: The Silver Collection Verve 823446-2 CD
Armstrong; Russell Garcia Orchestra. 8/57.

***   **Louis Armstrong Meets Oscar Peterson** Verve 825713-2 CD
Armstrong; Oscar Peterson (*p*); Herb Ellis (*g*); Ray Brown (*b*); Louie Bellson (*d*). 7–10/57.

***   **Compact Jazz: Louis Armstrong** Verve 833293-2 CD
Armstrong; Oscar Peterson (*p*); Herb Ellis (*g*); Ray Brown (*b*); Louie Bellson (*d*);
Russell Garcia Orchestra. 7–10/57.

***   **Jazz Around Midnight: Louis Armstrong** Verve 843422-2 CD
As above, except add Tyree Glenn (*tb*), Buster Bailey (*cl*), Marty Napoleon (*p*),
Alfred Di Lernia (*bj*), Buddy Catlett (*b*), Danny Barcelona (*d*). 7/57–5/66.

Verve recorded Armstrong with a little more initiative as regards concepts, but it didn't always
work out. The two-handed version of *Porgy And Bess* didn't suit either Ella or Louis very well:
it's too stiff and formalized for either one to loosen up either vocally or instrumentally, some
nice moments notwithstanding. *The Silver Collection* finds Armstrong fronting Russell Garcia's
hearty though not graceless orchestra with his usual aplomb, and comparing, say, 'I Gotta Right
To Sing The Blues' with his version of some 25 years earlier isolates the maturity of
Armstrong's later art: he hasn't the chops for grandstand improvisations any more, but his
sense of timing and treatment of pure melody are almost as gratifying. Yet some of the songs
end up as merely dull. The meeting with Oscar Peterson's trio is another very mixed success: not
because Peterson is too modern for Armstrong, but because he can't avoid his besetting
pushiness. On the slower tunes, though, especially 'Sweet Lorraine' and 'Let's Fall In Love',
the chemistry works, and Louis is certainly never intimidated. Both of the two compilations are
quite thoughtfully chosen – they actually duplicate three tracks – and aside from a throwaway
1966 'Tin Roof Blues' the *Jazz Around Midnight* disc, which has a brighter sound, is a good
sampler of the period.

(*)   **Pasadena Civic Auditorium Giants Of Jazz 53032 CD
Armstrong; Trummy Young (*tb, v*); Edmond Hall (*cl*); Billy Kyle (*p*); Squire Gersback
(*b*); Barrett Deems (*d*). 6/56.

***   **Mack The Knife** Pablo 2310941 CD/LP
As above, except Squire Gersback (*b*) replaces Shaw. 7/57.

(*)   **Basin Street Blues Black Lion BLCD 760128 CD
As above, except add Dale Jones (*b*). 8/56–10/57.

There seem to be many, many All Stars concerts which have survived on tape, and these three
are no better or worse than any for the period. They're also all pretty much the same, songwise
and treatment-wise. But the Pablo set, which includes a slightly more concentrated amount of
jazz material, is marginally the best, with certainly the best sound.

(*)   **Ella And Louis Again Vol. 1 Verve 825373-2 CD
Armstrong; Oscar Peterson (*p*); Herb Ellis (*g*); Ray Brown (*b*); Louis Bellson (*d*);
Ella Fitzgerald (*v*). 57.

(*)   **Ella And Louis Again Vol. 2 Verve 825374-2 CD
As above. 57.

There's something too respectful about the various meetings of these great singers on record:
Fitzgerald never gets ripe the way Velma Middleton does, and while that may be asking too
much of such a stately singer, there's only the slightest sense of interaction during this lengthy
session. There are felicitous moments and, indeed, tracks, but it hardly lives up to potential.

*(*)   **Singin' 'N' Playin'** LRC CDC 7685 CD
Armstrong; Trummy Young, Tyree Glenn (*tb*); Edmond Hall, Joe Muranyi (*cl*); Billy
Kyle, Marty Napoleon (*p*); Dale Jones, Buddy Catlett (*b*); Barrett Deems, Danny
Barcelona (*d*). 59–67.

(*)   **Americans In Sweden Tax CD 3712-2 CD
Armstrong; Trummy Young (*tb, v*); Peanuts Hucko (*cl*); Billy Kyle (*p*); Mort Herbert
(*b*); Danny Barcelona (*d*); Velma Middleton (*v*). 1/59.

The Stockholm concert is an unusually crisp and forthright example of a latter-day All Stars
performance: the sound is clear and well balanced, and Louis's singing is impeccable, although
most of the instrumental spots are given over to the band. The LRC disc is a mishmash of two
sessions, the second dispensable, and isn't recommended.

****   **Louis Armstrong & Duke Ellington: The Complete Sessions** Roulette CDP 793844-2
CD
Armstrong; Trummy Young (*tb*); Barney Bigard (*cl*); Duke Ellington (*p*); Mort
Herbert (*b*); Danny Barcelona (*d*). 4/61.

These sessions have never been highly regarded: Ellington is more or less slumming it with the
All Stars, and some of his piano parts do sound eccentrically isolated. Yet this is Armstrong's
date, not his, even with all the material composed by Duke: Louis stamps his imprimatur on it
from the first vocal on 'Duke's Place'. His occasional frailties and the sometimes tired tempos
only personalize further his single opportunity to interpret his greatest contemporary at length.
On the extraordinarily affecting 'I Got It Bad And That Ain't Good' or the superbly paced 'It
Don't Mean A Thing', Louis reflects on a parallel heritage of tunes which his traditional
proclivities perhaps denied him; and the results are both moving and quietly eloquent. The
sound is excellent on CD, although the music is also spread across two LPs, *Together For The
First Time* (Roulette ROU 1007) and *The Great Reunion* (Roulette ROU 1008).

**   **Masters Of Jazz: Louis Armstrong** Storyville SLP 4101 LP
Armstrong; Trummy Young (*tb*); Joe Darensbourg (*cl*); Billy Kyle (*p*); Billy Cronk
(*b*); Danny Barcelona (*d*). 8/62.

*   **Louis Armstrong & The All Stars 1965** EPM Musique FDC 5100 CD
As above, except Eddie Shu (*cl*) and Arvell Shaw (*b*) replace Darensbourg and Cronk,
add Jewel Brown (*v*). 3/65.

(*)   **The Great Performer Traditional Line TL 1304 CD
As above. 3/65.

By the mid-1960s, Armstrong's powers as a trumpeter were finally in serious decline, and there
are sad moments among the glimmers of greatness which remain. The Storyville date isn't bad,
but the band sound overcome by ennui, while the other disc, recorded at concerts in Prague and
East Berlin, is poorly recorded and, aside from a moving version of Fats Waller's 'Black And
Blue', scarcely worth hearing. Another edition of the Prague concert, though, turns up on *The
Great Performer*, and this time the sound is superb and puts Louis in a much better light,
particularly as a singer.

**   **What A Wonderful World** Bluebird ND 88310 CD
Armstrong; studio orchestra. 70.

The final studio recordings have little to do with jazz but much to do with Armstrong, since his
voice is by now so inimitable that it transcends any material which could be put before it.
Nevertheless, it is in other respects a record of few pleasures.
    We should point out that Louis Armstrong has been more widely anthologized and subjected
to spurious budget-label reissues than any jazz musician aside from Duke Ellington. We have
omitted several such compilations, most of which are inferior live sessions or clumsy instances
of repackaging, and recommend that the reader seeks out the records listed above ahead of such
other discs.

ART ENSEMBLE OF CHICAGO
GROUP

(*)   **A Jackson In Your House/Message To Our Folks Affinity AFF 752 CD
Lester Bowie (*t, flhn, perc*); Joseph Jarman, Roscoe Mitchell (*saxes, perc*); Malachi
Favors (*b, perc*). 6–8/69.

****   **People In Sorrow** Nessa N-3 LP
As above. 8/69.

***   **Eda Wobu** JMY 1008-2 CD
As above. 10/69.

Those who know the Art Ensemble of Chicago only by their considerable reputation may be
disappointed by their work as it's been documented on record. Bowie, Jarman, Favors and
Mitchell, later joined by percussionist Famoudou Don Moye, have been celebrated as among
the most radical and innovative musicians in the intensely creative environment which was

centred on Chicago's AACM movement in the 1960s. Unsurprisingly, they had to uproot and head for Europe in order to find work and recording opportunities at the time, and most of their music remains on European labels. As a mix of personalities, the Ensemble has always been in a crisis of temperament, with Bowie's arsenal of sardonic inflections pitched against Mitchell's schematic constructions, Jarman's fierce and elegant improvising and Favors's other-worldly commentaries from the bass. Satire, both musical and literal, has sustained much of their music; long-and short-form pieces have broken jazz structure down into areas of sound and silence. At their best, they are as uncompromisingly abstract as the most severe European players, yet their materials are cut from the heart of the traditions of black music in Chicago and St Louis.

A spate of recording in France in 1969 is currently out of print, aside from the albums listed above. The Affinity CD unfortunately couples the two weakest records of the period, fuzzily recorded and beset by passages of low-level inspiration, although it does include Jarman's lovely 'Ericka' and Mitchell's intense 'Song For Charles'. The Nessa album is also indifferently recorded, but this is the Ensemble at their best, building a long piece over two sides which slowly intensifies, a schizophrenic alto solo from Jarman leading to a scathing final improvisation. With this LP edition now hard to find, we would also note that there is a Japanese CD release of the same session on EMI Odeon CJ32-5013. *Eda Wobu* is a single 48-minute improvisation with an interesting concentration on the lower registers by Jarman and Mitchell and some particularly fine passages by Bowie, and though the recording is less than ideal it's an agreeably mysterious piece of music, though the 'naturalistic' percussion in the freak-out passage at the half-way mark emphasizes how badly they needed a proper drummer.

***   **Live** Delmark DE-432 CD
As above, plus Famoudou Don Moye (*d*). 1/72.

***   **Nice Guys** ECM 1126 CD/LP
As above. 5/78.

***   **Live In Berlin** West Wind WW 2051 2CD
As above. 3/79.

***   **Full Force** ECM 1167 CD/LP
As above. 1/80.

****   **Urban Bushmen** ECM 1211/1212 CD/LP
As above. 5/80.

The Ensemble made only a handful of discs in the 1970s, all now hard to find. But the live session recorded at Chicago's Mandel Hall in 1972 has recently been remastered for CD. This was something of a homecoming affair and there is much jubilation in the playing, but the recording remains imperfect, the detail skimped, and in a continuous 76-minute performance there are inevitable dead spots which the Ensemble have never truly found a way of avoiding. It wasn't until they secured a deal with ECM that they were finally given the opportunity to record in the sonic detail which their work has always demanded. Even so, the two studio albums were good yet unexceptional instances of the group at work. *Nice Guys* has two absorbing Jarman pieces in '597-59' and 'Dreaming Of The Master' but the attempt at a ska beat in 'JA' is unconvincing and much of the music seems almost formulaic, the improvisation proscribed. *Full Force* is a little more outgoing without cutting loose, and the lengthy 'Magg Zelma' seems long-winded rather than epic in its movement. The Ensemble's concert appearances could still generate music of blistering power, which made their apparently desultory records all the more frustrating. So the live *Urban Bushmen*, while still somewhat muted and inevitably deprived of the theatrical impact of the Ensemble's in-person charisma, proved to be their most worthwhile record for many years. Spread over 90 minutes, the group displayed their virtuosity on a vast panoply of devices (Jarman alone is credited with playing 14 different wind instruments, along with sundry items of percussion) and the patchwork of musics adds up to a tying together of their many endeavours in form and content. Certainly the best introduction to their work. Completists will also want the West Wind double-CD, which is essentially a similar set to the ECM double, though in less proficient sound; anyone else should make do with *Urban Bushmen*.

(*)   **The Third Decade ECM 1273 CD/LP
As above. 6/84.

A dispiriting continuation after another longish absence from the studios. Embarking on their third decade together suggested nothing so much as the atrophy of a once-radical band. The horn players are as spikily creative as ever in the moments where the Ensemble parts to reveal them, but the crucial decline is in the quality of interaction: several of these pieces dispel the collective identity of the group rather than binding it together.

***   **Live In Japan** DIW 8005 CD/LP
    As above. 4/84.

***   **The Complete Live In Japan** DIW 8021/2 2CD/2LP
    As above. 4/84.

The AEOC commenced a new contract with the Japanese DIW company with this worthwhile though hardly enthralling live set (the first record is a distillation of the concert, which appears in its completeness on the subsequent double-album and CD). Some of the earlier ECM material appears in concert form: the differences in emphasis are interesting, if little more. Acceptable rather than outstanding sound.

***   **Naked** DIW 8011 CD/LP
    As above. 11/85–7/86.

(*)   **Vol. I: Ancient To The Future DIW 8014 CD/LP
    As above, plus Bahnamous Lee Bowie (*ky*). 3/87.

The group's recording for DIW continued with records which, because of their limited distribution, caused little excitement. But the music continued to be a revisiting of old haunts rather than anything strikingly new. Mitchell and Bowie were, in any case, more active elsewhere. A taste for fancifiul, zig-zagging hard bop lightens some of *Naked*, and the impeccable recording affords some pleasure in just listening to the sound of Jarman, Mitchell and Favors in particular. But the attempts at rounding up 'the tradition' on DIW 8014 include poorly conceived stabs at 'Purple Haze' and 'No Woman No Cry' which mock their mastery.

****   **The Alternate Express** DIW 8033 CD/LP
    As above, except omit Bowie. 1/89.

When it seemed the AEOC was all but spent, they pulled out this tremendously powerful session. The huge, blustering 'Kush' rekindles the wildness of their best improvising; 'Imaginary Situations' is a ghostly collective sketch; 'Whatever Happens' catches Bowie at his melancholy best, while Mitchell's title piece is a fine tribute to the group's inbred spirit. A valuable and welcome document that might be called a comeback.

(*)   **Art Ensemble Of Soweto DIW 837 CD/LP
    As above, plus Elliot Ngubane (*v, ky, perc*); Joe Leguabe (*v, perc*); Zacheuus Nyoni, Welcome Max Bhe Bhe, Kay Ngwazene (*v*). 12/89–1/90.

This might have seemed like a logical collaboration, between the Ensemble and the African male chorus Amabutho, but the results tend to declare the differences betwen the two groups rather than their allegiances. The harmonic dignity of Amabutho stands alone on the three tracks which they're featured on, while the best instrumental music comes on Mitchell's 'Fresh Start', an invigorating blast of free bop. Worth hearing, but not the grand encounter which must have been intended.

***   **Live At The Eighth Tokyo Music Joy 1990** DIW 842 CD
    Lester Bowie, Stanton Davis, E. J. Allen, Gerald Brazel (*t*); Vincent Chancey (*frhn*); Steve Turre, Clifton Anderson (*tb*); Roscoe Mitchell, Joseph Jarman (*reeds*); Bob Stewart (*tba*); Malachi Favors (*b*); Famoudou Don Moye, Vinnie Johnson (*d*). 2/90.

A meeting between two great ensembles, the AEOC and Bowie's Brass Fantasy. Each has three tracks of their own and there are four collective pieces, of which Steve Turre's arrangement of 'The Emperor' seems to prove the idea that he is the real leader of Brass Fantasy – or, at least, the one who knows how to make it work for the best. A celebratory meeting but not an altogether successful one.

***   **Dreaming Of The Masters Vol. 2: Thelonious Sphere Monk** DIW 846 CD
    Lester Bowie (*t*); Roscoe Mitchell, Joseph Jarman (*reeds*); Cecil Taylor (*p*); Malachi Favors (*b*); Famoudou Don Moye (*d*). 1–3/90.

***   **Dreaming Of The Masters Suite** DIW 854 CD
As above, except omit Taylor. 1–3/90.

It seems a curiously neoclassic device for the Ensemble to be so specifically paying tribute to senior spirits, which is on the face of it the kind of laborious dues-paying which Bowie in particular has been critical of in many of today's younger players. Their approach is, of course, different: the colouristic interchanges between Mitchell and Jarman, Bowie's now inimitable irreverence and the patient, otherworldly bass of Favors all ensure that. But neither of these records is anything much more than a reminder that the AEOC are still here and still playing; certainly no specific new ground is broken, and in that sense the encounter with Cecil Taylor is a disappointment, although Taylor's singing is actually a fascinating embellishment of the Ensemble's own tradition. When he plays piano, the two sides – perhaps inevitably – don't really meet. Oddly, neither record is much about its respective dedicatees: there are only two Monk tunes and three by Coltrane here, though 'Impressions' is a fine repertory performance. Both are excellently recorded.

HAROLD ASHBY (born 1925)
TENOR SAXOPHONE

***   **The Viking** Gemini GM 60 CD/LP
Ashby; Norman Simmons (*p*); Paul West (*b*); Gerryck King (*d*). 8/88.

***   **What Am I Here For?** Criss Cross Jazz Criss 1054 CD
Ashby; Mulgrew Miller (*p*); Rufus Reid (*b*); Ben Riley (*d*). 11/90.

***   **I'm Old Fashioned** Stash ST-CD-545 CD
Ashby; Richard Wyands (*p*); Aaron Bell (*b*); Connie Kay (*d*). 7/91.

A late arrival in the Duke Ellington orchestra, Harold Ashby was really Ben Webster's replacement: he still has the Webster huff on ballads and the grouchy, just-woke-up timbre on uptempo tunes. Quicker tempos don't bother him as much as they did Ben, but he likes to take his own time, and fashions storytelling solos which can freshen up the material: on both these discs, some of the songs are very old indeed. There's little to choose between the two records. *What Am I Here For?* is an ideal programme of Ellingtonia, and though the disc is a little too long to sustain interest, the playing is jauntily assured from track to track. The Gemini set sounds a little perkier, perhaps because the rhythm section is less of a signed-up star group, and because Ashby sounds expansive and happy with the four original lines he came up with for the date ('Hash' sounds unsurprisingly like 'Dash', which is on the Stash record). Solidly enjoyable jazz.

LOVIE AUSTIN (1887–1972)
PIANO

***   **Lovie Austin And Her Blues Serenaders** Fountain FJ105 LP
Austin; Tommy Ladnier, Bob Shoffner, Shirley Clay (*c*); Kid Ory (*tb*); Johnny Dodds, Jimmy O'Bryant (*cl*); Eustern Woodfork (*bj*); W. E. Burton (*d*); Priscilla Stewart, Henry Williams (*v*). 24–26.

Austin, née Cora Calhoun, was an extraordinary figure whose status as one of the first women to make a contribution to jazz remains undervalued. She was born in Tennessee and had a formal musical training which stood her in good stead for the job of house pianist at Paramount in the early 1920s. She eventually settled in Chicago at the end of the decade and scarcely recorded again until the '60s. The 17 surviving sides by her Blues Serenaders are collected on this indispensable LP. Though it will sound primitive to contemporary ears, Austin's music was a sophisticated variation on the barrelhouse music that was played in Chicago at the time. The two earliest sides here are by a trio of Austin, Ladnier and O'Bryant, performing a densely plaited counterpoint that seems amazingly advanced for its time. The quartet and quintet sides are harsher, with Burton's clumping drumming on what sounds like a military side-drum a distraction; but the simple breaks and stop-time passages have a rough poetry about them that is good enough for the music to transcend the typically poor Paramount recording. Austin was not an improviser herself but her piano parts are a driving and integral part of the music.

In 1961, when in her seventies, she was persuaded to record again in accompaniment to the blues singer Alberta Hunter, and the results were recently reissued on Original Blues Classics OBC-510.

ALBERT AYLER (1936–70)
TENOR SAXOPHONE, ALTO SAXOPHONE, SOPRANO SAXOPHONE

*** **The First Recordings** Sonet SNTCD 604 CD
Ayler; Torbjörn Hultcrants (*b*); Sune Spånberg (*d*). 10/62.

*** **Vibrations** Freedom (7)41000 CD/LP

*** **The Hilversum Session** Coppens CCD 6001 CD
Ayler; Don Cherry (*t*); Gary Peacock (*d*); Sunny Murray (*d*). 9/64, 11/64.

There is an almost Aeschylean inevitability to Albert Ayler's life and death, a downward trajectory of neglect and misprision. The final tragedy has been dressed up as almost everything from murder to recall by the planet Zog, but is now known to have been plain, exhausted suicide. Ayler's style has been subjected to just as many conspiracy theories, but is now generally considered to be a highly personal amalgam of New Orleans brass, rhythm and blues (to which Ayler unapologetically returned in his last two years), and some of the more extreme timbral innovations of the '60s New Thing.

The first recordings are astonishingly sparse. With no harmony instrument and a concentration on stark melodic variations in and out of tempo, they sound influenced by early Ornette Coleman, but what is immediately distinctive about Ayler is the almost hypnotic depth of his concentration on a single motif, which he repeats, worries, splinters into constituent harmonics, until 'I'll Remember April', the first track and a long-standing bebop staple, is virtually unrecognizable. Ayler's impatience with bop is evident throughout, and for all their unrelieved starkness, these rather solitary experiments are still remarkably refreshing. Not called on to keep time, Hultcrants and Spånberg occasionally resort to marking it, but they seem mostly unfazed by Ayler's primitivism.

The chief problem with the Ayler discography – quite apart from the record companies' unwillingness until recently to keep it up to date – is his remarkably slender basic repertoire; there was not much of it, and what there was tended to be melodically skeletal, almost folkish. Versions of 'Ghosts' turn up on both the latter pair, played pretty much straight and in line with his growing sense that the exact notes mattered considerably less than the amount of emotional charge that could be put across the poles of a melody.

Cherry was, as with Ornette, his most sympathetic interpreter, a more responsive and clear-sighted musician than the saxophonist's brother, trumpeter Donald Ayler, with whom he was to form his next band, this time in the USA. Both 1964 sessions are well recorded and transfer well to CD (the shift of medium is particularly advantageous to Peacock, whose critical contribution tends to get lost on vinyl).

*** **In Memory Of Albert Ayler** Jazz Door 1203 CD
Ayler; Donald Ayler (*t*); Michael Sampson (*vn*); Lewis Worrell (*b*); Ronald Shannon Jackson (*d*). 5/66.

*** **Lörrach/Paris 1966** hat Art 6039 CD
Ayler; Don Ayler (*t*); Michel Sampson (*vn*); William Folwell (*b*); Beaver Harris (*d*). 11/66.

The 1966 band was probably Ayler's most dramatic move in the direction of complete abstraction, and was an uneasy affair. Ayler was visibly battling to reconcile the demands of arhythmic and atonal free jazz with traditional black music and was succeeding only partially.

The nature of the material left from this time makes a full assessment rather difficult. The live registration is muzzy in both cases, with little clear sense of what the rhythm section is being asked to do. Most of the queries, though, relate to Ayler's treatment of his themes. The live versions of 'Bells', which had just appeared on ESP-Disk are mostly unproblematic, but the addition of a second string instrument only contributes to an often-remarked sense of incompleteness in Ayler's work. 'Spirits' (*Lörrach/Paris* only) and the three versions of

'Ghosts' – or 'Ghost' as it is given on the hat Art, which has two of them – are unquestionably performances of great power by Ayler but again the recording quality makes it difficult to assess the pieces as a whole.

(*)   **Albert Ayler Philology W 88 LP
As above. 11/64, 11/66.

The Ayler discography may well become a more and more confusing place as tapes are dusted down, edited and repackaged. So small is the studio output that Ayler students are more than usually dependent on archaeological artefacts like this. Inevitably, the product itself, issued to mark the twentieth anniversary of the saxophonist's death, is a little dusty and cracked.

Side one was recorded less than a week before the *Hilversum Session* (and sensibly covering different material, no small plus with Ayler records), is OK-ish in sound quality and absolutely sterling in performance. 'Mothers' and 'Children', ostensibly showing Ayler's less haunted side, are lovingly and sensitively (*sic*.) done, with Cherry and Murray in brilliant, contained form.

The rest of the material comes from the same long swing through Europe that yielded the only marginally better *Lörrach/Paris* album. Some of the material on *Albert Ayler* was previously released on *The Berlin Concerts* (also from an Italian label). The Ayler brothers and the patchy Samson confront their demons in the city that, as Dolphy found, seemed to focus the contradictions of the modern world, and of its most passionate music.

****   **In Greenwich Village** Impulse AS 9155/254635 CD/LP
Ayler; Donald Ayler (*t*); Michel Sampson (*vn*); Joel Friedman (*clo*); Alan Silva (*b*); William Folwell, Henry Grimes, (*b*); Beaver Harris (*d*). 2/67, 12/67.

Whatever technical and aesthetic shortcomings the Lörrach and Paris sessions may have had (there is a nihilistic, fragmentary quality to the latter) the Village Theater and Village Vanguard sessions are hugely affirmative and satisfyingly complete without losing a jot of Ayler's angry and premonitory force. *In Greenwich Village* is one of the essential post-war jazz albums, and features some of Ayler's best playing on both alto ('For John Coltrane', ironically or self-protectively), and tenor (the apocalyptic 'Truth is Marching In'). For comparison, try the closing version of 'Our Prayer' here, with the version recorded in Germany above. The addition of a second bass, in addition to either violin or cello, actually sharpens the sound considerably, producing a rock-solid foundation for Ayler's raw witness. If his reputation hangs on any single recording, it is this one.

(*)   **Love Cry Impulse GRP 11082 CD
Ayler; Don Ayler (*t*); Call Cobbs (*hpd*); Alan Silva (*b*); Milford Graves (*d*). 8/67, 2/68.

***(*)   **Fondation Maeght Nights: Volume 1** Jazz View COD 004 CD

***   **Fondation Maeght Nights: Volume 2** Jazz View COD 005 CD
Ayler; Call Cobbs (*p*); Steve Tintweiss (*b*); Allen Blairman (*d*); Mary Maria (*v*, *ss*). 7/70.

Recording of *Love Cry* began six weeks after John Coltrane's painful death from liver cancer. Ayler had been quick to identify himself with the Holy Ghost in Coltrane's Trinity. In the time left to him, he moved with unnerving swiftness from the torrential outpourings of *Bells* and *Spirits Rejoice* towards the irredeemably banal R&B of *New Grass*. What was wrong with the last studio album (a point amply proven by Ayler's superb playing on the limited edition Fondation Maeght sessions, which marked a late return to jazz playing) was the pinched, inelastic beat. Though Blairman, who has also recorded superbly with Mal Waldron, is absolutely on the case, he is no match for the extraordinary polystylistic work of Milford Graves. Graves is one of the heroes of the New Thing, a percussionist of inexhaustible resource, who could call up anything from huge tribal calls-to-arms to quiet, filigreed patterns. He sounds restless, but also completely contained. A word, too, for Silva, who plays magnificently.

Though of only very qualified brilliance, *Love Cry* is an important reissue. Not only is 'Universal Indians', with its odd whooping vocal, restored to its full nine and three-quarter minutes, the set contains alternate takes of it and the gospelly 'Zion Hill', the clearest indication on the set of where Ayler was headed next. It also includes a confusingly titled 'Love Cry II', which is a different composition from the original piece. 'Love Cry' features another vocal, in a disturbing Spanish-Moorish wail. Only on it and the issued take of 'Zion Hill' does Ayler play his alto saxophone. Listening to the fierce tenor line on 'Ghosts', played unusually fast, and the tender protestations on 'Dancing Flowers' and 'Love Flower', it's easier to see what Ayler's most distinguished disciple David Murray took and what he chose to leave behind.

AZIMUTH
GROUP

***　　**Azimuth** ECM 1099 LP
Norma Winstone (*v*); John Taylor (*p, org, synth*); Kenny Wheeler (*t, flhn*). 3/77.

***　　**The Touchstone** ECM 1130 LP
As above. 6/78.

***　　**Depart** ECM 1163 LP
As above, except add Ralph Towner (*g, 12-string g*). 12/79.

**　　**Azimuth '85** ECM 1298 LP
As above. 3/85.

The players could hardly have a better pedigree. Kenny Wheeler is considered by many to be the finest trumpet player currently working, with a flugelhorn technique that belies the slackness of tone often associated with its lower registers. Norma Winstone's vocal range is quite remarkable. No one who has ever heard it will ever forget her entrance on Mike Westbrook's large-scale *Metropolis*, where she sounds like some freshly invented woodwind lent speech, like a scene from Ovid in reverse. John Taylor has a rock-solid technique and, if he has often tended to hide his light under bushels of visiting Americans – who say he's the best keyboard player in Europe – he is nevertheless a solo artist of considerable standing.

Taylor's music for Azimuth is appropriately angular and not at all as gently filigreed as sceptics usually assume to be typical of ECM productions. Wheeler and Winstone float on a carpet of keyboard textures with sufficient harmonic irregularities built in to let the music out of the New Age category into which it occasionally – damagingly on the disappointing *Azimuth '85* – seems inclined to lapse, and lending it a genuinely improvisatory edge. Guitarist Towner, who favours firm ostinati in the middle register and flowing top and bass lines, was an ideal guest and seemed to free Taylor a little. Winstone's *vocalise* is magnificent, but so too is her much underrated sense of form (she is a fine standards singer).

With the fourth album, Azimuth – who mustn't, incidentally, be confused with the spell-it-with-a-y bunch below – fell into the trap Towner's Oregon have always avoided: that of letting a style become a manner. There is no fixed requirement that musicians or bands 'develop' stylistically but, for all the quality of writing and performance, *Azimuth '85* did seem to be an unconfident step back.

AZYMUTH
GROUP

**　　**Light As A Feather** Black Sun 15006-2 CD
Jose Roberto Bertrami (*ky, v, perc*); Alex Malheiros (*b, v*); Ivan Conte (*d, ky*);
Aleuda (*perc*). 79–80.

*(*)　　**Telecommunication** Milestone M-9101 CD/LP/MC
As above, except omit Aleuda. 81.

*(*)　　**Cascades** Milestone M-9109 LP/MC
As above, except add Jose Carlos Bigorna (*f*); Maurice Einhorn (*hca*); Sidney Moreira,
Carlinhos de Mocidade (*perc*). 8/82.

**　　**Rapid Transit** Milestone M-9118 LP/MC
As above, except omit Einhorn. 83.

*(*)　　**Flame** Milestone M-9118 LP/MC
As above. 84.

*(*)　　**Spectrum** Milestone M-9134 LP/MC
As above. 85.

* **Tightrope Walker** Milestone M-9143 CD/LP/MC
  As above. 86.

*(*) **Crazy Rhythm** Milestone M-9156 CD/LP/MC
  As above. 87.

*(*) **Carioca** Milestone M-9169 CD/LP/MC
  As above, plus Paulo Russo (*b*); Jurim Moreira (*d*). 12/88.

While this chattering, lightweight music might serve as a temperate background to some mindless activity, it is barely worth paying any attention to. Azymuth are basically the core trio of Bertrami, Conti and Malheiros; in another time and place they might have ended up as just another cocktail-lounge trio. But their Brazilian background meant that a synthesis of samba and bossa nova rhythms with the simplest kind of jazz feel (one can scarcely call it improvisation) has brought about a bland blend that is obviously successful enough to let them continue making much the same kind of record every year. The earlier records are just the tiniest amount more abrasive, and the Black Sun CD features 'Jazz Carnival', once a major pop hit in the UK. Everything else is bright, fluffy and Brazilian enough to appease any who would prefer to investigate the compelling rhythms of that country's music at a very remote and very safe distance.

BENNY BAILEY (born 1925)
TRUMPET, FLUGELHORN

*** **Big Brass** Candid CS 9011 CD/LP
  Bailey; Julius Watkins (*hrn*); Phil Woods (*as, b cl*); Les Spann (*f, g*); Tommy Flanagan
  (*p*); Buddy Catlett (*b*); Art Taylor (*d*). 11/60.

** **Islands** Enja 2082 LP
  Bailey; Sigi Schwab (*g, sitar*); Eberhard Weber (*b*); Lala Kovacev (*d*). 5/76.

*** **Grand Slam** Storyville JC 8 LP
  Bailey; Charlie Rouse (*ts*); Richard Wyands (*p*); Sam Jones (*b*); Billy Hart (*d*). 10/78.

Bailey is probably best known as first trumpet in the Kenny Clarke/Francy Boland big bands of the '60s, but he is also an impressive and entertaining soloist, with a number of distinguishing marks on his musical passport, noticeably his much-commented octave plummets and his attraction to enigmatic lines that seem from moment to moment to have neither melodic nor harmonic significance, just a strangely specific logic all their own.

His bebop background is still evident on *Big Brass*, perhaps his finest available record (though the deleted *Serenade To The Planet* is considered essential documentation). The themes have begun to stretch out, though, into long, quasi-modal strings that contain any number of potential resolutions. Flanagan is a sympathetic accompanist, though Wyands on the later set seems in tune rather with Bailey's more extravagant gestures. Woods and Rouse could hardly be more different, but Bailey responds magnanimously to the challenge posed by each. Only *Islands* seems a little vacuous. Weber's bass is not quite right, and Schwab's guitar and sitar seem almost surplus to the more straightforward themes.

***(*) **While My Lady Sleeps** Gemini GMCD 69 CD
  Bailey; Harald Gundhus (*ts*); Emil Viklický (*p*); František Uhlír (*b*); Ole-Jacob
  Hansen (*d*). 4/90.

The quartet are completely attuned to Bailey's music, combining an attractive obliqueness with some wonderfully concentrated ballad playing on 'While My Lady Sleeps'; Gundhus solos impressively and the rhythm section sustain a long, throbbing accompaniment. Two originals by Viklický (the disappointing opening 'Vino, Oh Vino!') and Uhlir ('Expectation') are redeemed by Bailey's thoughtful commentaries; but the meat of the album is kept for last with the long version of the title-track and a tight reading of Benny Golson's 'Along Came Betty'. Recording was done at the Rainbow Studio in Oslo by Jan Erik Kongshaug, both associated with ECM; the quality is exactly what you'd expect. Recommended.

DEREK BAILEY (born 1930)
GUITAR

***   **Notes** Incus LP48 LP
4–7/85.

***   **Solo Guitar: Volume 1** Incus CD 10 CD

***(*) **Solo Guitar: Volume 2** Incus CD 11 CD
Bailey (*g* solo).

***   **Time** Incus LP34 LP
Bailey; Tony Coe (*cl*). 4/79.

****   **Dart Drug** Incus LP41 LP
Bailey; Jamie Muir (*perc*). 8/81.

***   **Royal: Volume 1** Incus LP43 LP

***   **Moments Précieux** Victo 02 LP
Bailey; Anthony Braxton (*reeds*).

****   **Compatibles** Incus LP50 LP
Bailey; Evan Parker (*ss*).

***   **Cyro** Incus CD01 CD
Bailey; Cyro Baptista (*perc*).

***(*) **Han** Incus CD02 CD
Bailey; Han Bennink (*perc*).

****   **Figuring** Incus CD05 CD
Bailey; Barre Phillips (*b*). 5/87, 9/88.

***(*) **Village Life** Incus CD09 CD
Bailey; Thebe Lipere (*perc, v*); Louis Moholo (*d, perc, v*). 9/91.

Though scarcely a household name (or likely to become one) Derek Bailey has won almost universal acclaim from fellow improvising musicians on both sides of the Atlantic. His sometimes forbidding but always challenging music, premised on the avoidance of any groove (whether rhythmic, harmonic or melodic), illuminates certain important differences between European and American improvisers. Whereas American free jazz and improvisation have tended to remain individualistic – the most convenient image is the soloist stepping forward from the ensemble – European improvisers have tended to follow a broadly collectivist philosophy which downplays personal expression in favour of a highly objectified or process-dominated music.

Perhaps the best concrete illustration of the difference can be found in Bailey's duo performances with the multi-instrumentalist Anthony Braxton (q.v.). Despite considerable mutual admiration, these confirm the old saw about Europeans and Americans being divided by a common language; Braxton's formulations are still conditioned by the deep structures of jazz, Bailey's according to a mysterious metalanguage by which a performance offers few guidelines as to its presumed origins and underlying processes. (The guitarist did once record a splendidly ironic version of 'The Lost Chord'.)

Like a good many European improvisers, Bailey underwent an accelerated and virtually seamless transition from jazz to free-jazz to free music. He has performed with such innovative groups as Josef Holbrooke and Iskra 1903 (see the eponymous and excellent Incus LP 3/4), but since 1976 his activities have centred on solo and duo work (where is he most influential as a performer) and on his loosely affiliated collective Company (q.v.), locus of some of the most challenging musical and para-musical performance of recent years. Company has been sufficiently unlimited to draw in musicians from a 'straight' jazz background (most strikingly Lee Konitz), avant-garde composer-performers such as trombonist Vinko Globokar, and even dancer Katie Duck, as well as long-standing associates Evan Parker, Jamie Muir, Barre Phillips, Han Bennink, Tristan Honsinger, with all of whom Bailey has made significant duo recordings.

It has always been a matter of some controversy whether music conceived as Bailey's is belongs in the repeatable, reified grooves of a record (and now CD, *mutatis mutandis*). Against the argument that improvisation belongs to the moment of creation only is Bailey's own conviction that it should be documented. Incus records was co-founded with saxophonist Evan Parker to do just that. Its output is non-commercial and uncompromising, but the surviving releases above are far from ephemeral. Bailey's music inevitably resists exact description and evaluation. Eschewing special effects (apart from a swell pedal on his amplified performances), he plays intensely and abstractly, a musical discourse that is far removed from the chatty 'conversational' style of much duo jazz. Given certain reservations about his collaborations with Braxton, and allowing that his relationship with Parker (now no longer directly involved with Incus) is exceptional, he has generally preferred to work in the company of percussionists and a quick comparison of his recordings with the elegant Baptista, the forceful and witty Bennink, the pulseless trances conjured by Jamie Muir on *Dart Drug*, and on the recent *Village Life* with African modernists Thebe Lipere and Louis Moholo demonstrates how thoughtfully contextualized all his work is. Dialogue in the conventional musical sense rarely occurs (with Braxton it sounds like a dialogue of the deaf), but with Phillips on the excellent *Figuring* there is evidence of a to-and-fro of ideas which makes it perhaps the most accessible of the duos.

Bailey's solo performances afford the clearest impression of his pitchless, metreless playing, but these are extremely forbidding and are perhaps best approached only when *Figuring*, *Han* and *Dart Drug* have been absorbed and Bailey's initially unfriendly tongue assimilated. As a crib and consolation, his 1980 book *Improvisation* is indispensable.

VICTOR BAILEY
BASS, KEYBOARDS

(*)   Bottoms Up Atlantic 781978-2 CD/MC
Bailey; Terence Blanchard (*t*); Mark Ledford (*picc-t, v*); Wayne Shorter, Branford Marsalis (*ss*); Donald Harrison (*as*); Michael Brecker, Alex Foster, Najee, Bill Evans (*ts*); Jim Beard, Clyde Criner (*ky*); Richard Tee (*org*); Wayne Krantz, Kevin Eubanks, Mike 'Dino' Campbell, Jon Herington (*g*); Lonnie Plaxico (*b*); Omar Hakim, Dennis Chambers, Richie Morales (*d*); Mino Cinelu, Steve Thornton, Jeff Watts (*perc*). 89.

Given that solo albums by fusion-associated bassists are often hopelessly anonymous, as with contemporaries Charnett Moffett and Lonnie Plaxico, Bailey's record isn't at all bad, bolstered with some engaging tunes along with the expected freight of major-name guests and plenty of his own rapid-fire electric playing. The singing on three tracks is entirely dispensable and a certain hip cuteness gets the better of the music from time to time, but it's a clever and occasionally passionate record too. Shorter contributes one of his startling cameos to 'Miles Wows (Live)', and 'Round Midnight' is given a humid treatment. Bright but warm studio sound.

CHET BAKER (1929–88)
TRUMPET, FLUGELHORN, VOCAL

**   Live At The Trade Winds 1952** Fresh Sound FSCD-1001 CD
Baker; Ted Ottison (*t*); Sonny Criss (*as*); Wardell Gray, Jack Montrose, Dave Pell (*ts*); Les Thompson (*hca*); Jerry Mandell, Al Haig (*p*); Harry Babasin (*clo*); Bob Whitlock, Dave Bryant (*b*); Lawrence Marable, Larry Bunker (*d*). 3–8/52.

***   Witch Doctor** Original Jazz Classics OJC 609 CD/LP/MC
Baker; Rolf Ericson (*t*); Bud Shank (*as, bs*); Jimmy Giuffre, Bob Cooper (*ts*); Russ Freeman, Claude Williamson (*p*); Howard Rumsey (*b*); Max Roach, Shelly Manne (*d*). 9/53.

Chet Baker's most crucial years came right at the beginning of his career, 1952–53, when he played with Charlie Parker (undocumented in the studios) and in Gerry Mulligan's pianoless quartet. Some of the Monday night jam sessions at the Trade Winds Club in Inglewood, California, produced the music collected on the Fresh Sound CD: scrappily recorded, it doesn't make much of an album, but Baker already sounds like himself – cool, restrained, diffidently lyrical – and Criss is very much himself, a fire engine next to Baker's roadster. Gray, Montrose and the mysterious Les Thompson garner other features, but it's nothing special. *Witch Doctor* was recorded at the Lighthouse and sounds superior, though again the diffuseness of the jam-session atmosphere tends to militate against it standing up as a record in its own right.

***   **Grey December** Pacific Jazz CDP 79710602 CD
Baker; Herb Geller (*as*); Jack Montrose (*ts*); Bud Shank (*f*); Bob Gordon (*bs*); Russ Freeman (*p*); Corky Hale (*hp*); Joe Mondragon, Red Mitchell (*b*); Shelly Manne, Bob Neel (*d*). 12/53–2/55.

***(*)   **The Best Of Chet Baker Plays** Pacific Jazz CDP 7971612 CD
Baker; Conte Candoli, Norman Faye (*t*); Frank Rosolino (*tb*); Bob Brookmeyer (*vtb*); Bud Shank (*as, bs*); Herb Geller, Art Pepper (*as*); Richie Kamuca, Jack Montrose, Phil Urso, Bill Perkins (*ts*); Russ Freeman, Bobby Timmons, Pete Jolly, Carl Perkins (*p*); Carson Smith, Joe Mondragon, Curtis Counce, Leroy Vinnegar, Jimmy Bond (*b*); Larry Bunker, Lawrence Marable, Shelly Manne, Stan Levey, Peter Littman (*d*); Bill Loughborough (*perc*). 7/53–10/56.

****   **Let's Get Lost: The Best Of Chet Baker Sings** Pacific Jazz CDP 79299322 CD
Baker; Russ Freeman (*p*); Carson Smith, Jimmy Bond, Joe Mondragon (*b*); Shelly Manne, Bob Neel, Lawrence Marable, Peter Littman (*d*). 2/53–10/56.

***   **The Route** Pacific Jazz CDP 7929312 CD
Baker; Art Pepper (*as*); Richie Kamuca (*ts*); Pete Jolly (*p*); Leroy Vinnegar (*b*); Stan Levey (*d*). 7/56.

***   **Playboys** Pacific Jazz CDP 7944742 CD
Baker; Art Pepper (*as*); Phil Urso (*ts*); Carl Perkins (*p*); Curtis Counce (*b*); Lawrence Marable (*d*). 10/56.

***   **At the Forum Theater** Fresh Sound FSRCD-168 CD
Baker; Phil Urso (*ts*); Bobby Timmons (*p*); Jimmy Bond (*b*); Peter Littman (*d*). 7/56.

***   **Chet Baker Cools Out** Boplicity CDBOP 013 CD
As above, except add Art Pepper (*as*); Richie Kamuca (*ts*); Pete Jolly (*p*), Leroy Vinnegar (*b*), Stan Levey (*d*). 7/56.

Richard Bock began recording Baker as a leader when the quartet with Mulligan began attracting rave notices and even a popular audience, and the records the trumpeter made for Pacific Jazz remain among his freshest and most appealing work. The material is currently a little scattered across the seven releases listed above, two of which are best-of's, and one – *The Route* – which was subsequently put together from tracks strewn across various compilations over the years. *Playboys*, co-credited to Pepper and Baker, is good if under-powered: somehow the results never quite match up to what were the ingredients for a superb band, with Jimmy Heath's tunes offering apparently no more than workmanlike inspiration for the soloists. *The Route* is stronger: Kamuca is strong enough to match the other horns, and the rhythm section does a surprisingly better job on what are mostly standards. On *Forum Theater* and *Cools Out*, Urso's almost mentholated tenor is an apposite foil, but the music is rather under-achieved, and all too similar to many of the sessions being cut in the city in this period. A couple of tracks duplicate each other on these two CDs (not all the tracks were made for Pacific), and the Boplicity disc includes a single item from the *Route* band. To hear the best of Baker himself, one must turn to the other records. Controversy has simmered over the extent of Baker's powers: a poor reader, a restrained technician, he sticks to the horn's middle range and picks at bebop lines as if they were something that might do him harm, yet he can play with sometimes amazing accomplishment. The blues 'Bea's Flat' (on *The Best Of Chet Baker Plays*), a scintillating line by Russ Freeman, provokes a solo of agility enough to dismiss charges of Baker's incompetence as ludicrous. It was on the various quartet sessions with Freeman that Baker did most of his best work for Pacific, and it's a pity that they are currently only available only in the excellent Mosaic boxed-set (see Introduction). The five tracks on *Plays* will have to suffice. The rest of the compilation makes an intelligent choice from the trumpeter's other sessions, and – as the title suggests – it's all trumpet and no vocals. *Grey December* covers five somewhat maudlin trumpet and vocal tracks with strings from 1955 and an earlier session organized around a series of arrangements by Jack Montrose: it's more a trim, lightly engaging

West Coast session than a real Baker date, but it's sparkily played. The fidelity on this particular date sounds a little faded, but the others appear fine.

The other disc contains what are still Baker's most popular recordings, his first vocal sessions for Pacific. The 20 tracks include all of the original *Chet Baker Sings* LP, which is a modest classic in its way. Baker's soft, pallidly intimate voice retained its blond timbre to the end of his life, but here – with his phrasing and tone uncreased by any trace of hard living – it sounds as charming as it ever would, and a song such as 'There Will Never Be Another You' is so deftly organized for voice, trumpet and rhythm section (Freeman's role here is as crucial as it is on the instrumental sessions) that it is very hard not to enjoy the music, even if it has become as buttressed by glamorous legend as much of Billie Holiday's later output.

***(*) Chet Baker In Paris Volume 1 EmArcy 837474-2 CD
Baker; Richard Twardzik, Gerard Gustin (*p*); Jimmy Bond (*b*); Peter Littman, Bert Dale (*d*).10/55.

***(*) Chet Baker In Paris Volume 2 EmArcy 837475-2 CD
As above, except add Benny Vasseur (*tb*), Jean Aldegon (*as*), Armand Migiani (*ts*), William Boucaya (*bs*), Rene Urtreger (*p*). 10/55.

***(*) Chet Baker In Paris Volume 3 EmArcy 837476-2 CD
Baker; Benny Vasseur (*tb*); Reddy Ameline (*as*); Bobby Jaspar, Jean-Louis Chautemps, Armand Migiani (*ts*); William Boucaya (*bs*); Rene Urtreger, Francy Boland (*p*); Eddie de Haas, Benoit Quersin (*b*); Jean-Louis Viale, Charles Saudrais, Pierre Lemarchand (*d*). 12/55–3/56.

*** Chet Baker In Paris Volume 4 EmArcy 837477-2 CD
As above three discs. 10/55–3/56.

Baker's Parisian sessions are among his finest and most considered work. The celebrated association with Richard Twardzik – abruptly terminated by the latter's ugly narcotics death – is followed on volume one, with tantalizing Twardzik originals such as 'The Girl From Greenland' and almost equally interesting writing from Bob Zieff to engage Baker's interest. The drift of the sessions varies from spare and introspective quartet music to more swinging larger groups, and it's by no means all pale and melancholic: what's striking is the firmness of Baker's lines and his almost Tristano-like logic on occasion. There is some very downcast music in the session immediately following Twardzik's death, but otherwise lyricism and energy usually combine to high effect. Of the four discs, only the last, which is a supplemental set of alternative takes, is comparatively inessential.

(***) In Europe 1955 Philology W 42-2
Baker; Rolf Shneebiegel (*t*); Jean Louis Chautemps (*ts*); Richard Twardzik, Ralph Schecroun (*p*); Eddie de Haas, Jimmy Bond (*b*); Charles Saudrais, Peter Littman (*d*). 9–11/55.

An interesting addenda to Baker's European sojourn, these concert tapes find him with the Twardzik quartet in Mainz and with a French group in Copenhagen. Baker sounds in good form and the sound, though rather rough in Mainz, is quite clear in Copenhagen; but it also sounds as though there is a slight speed problem with the original tapes, which may be running too fast. We can't offer a clear-cut recommendation in consequence.

*** It Could Happen To You Original Jazz Classics OJC 303 CD/LP/MC
Baker; Kenny Drew (*p*); George Morrow, Sam Jones (*b*); Dannie Richmond, Philly Joe Jones (*d*). 8/58.

*** Chet Baker In New York Original Jazz Classics OJC 207 CD/LP/MC
Baker; Johnny Griffin (*ts*); Al Haig (*p*); Paul Chambers (*b*); Philly Joe Jones (*d*). 9/58.

*** Chet Original Jazz Classics OJC 087 CD/LP/MC
Baker; Herbie Mann (*ts, f*); Pepper Adams (*bs*); Bill Evans (*p*); Kenny Burrell (*g*); Paul Chambers (*b*); Connie Kay, Philly Joe Jones (*d*). 3/59.

*** Plays The Best Of Lerner & Loewe Original Jazz Classics OJC 137 CD/LP/MC
Baker; Herbie Mann (*ts, f*); Zoot Sims (*ts, as*); Pepper Adams (*bs*); Bill Evans, Bob Corwin (*p*); Earl May (*b*); Cliford Jarvis (*d*). 7/59.

Perhaps Baker wanted nothing more than to be a part of the modern jazz mainstream; certainly, after his earlier adventures, his records were taking on the appearance of another bebop trumpeter wandering from session to session. These are all worthwhile records, but without any regular cast of players Chet sounds like a man trying to be one of the boys. He has no problem with the assertiveness of the group on *In New York*, which shows how far he'd come from the supposed early fumblings (never very apparent from the actual records). But this set, and the Lerner and Loewe collection and the similarly directed *Chet*, aren't very different to the standard bop outings of the time; good, but working off a solid routine. *It Could Happen To You* is more of a singing record, and includes a couple of his most charming efforts on 'Do It The Hard Way' and 'I'm Old Fashioned'.

*** **With Fifty Italian Strings** Original Jazz Classics OJC 492 CD/LP/MC
 Baker; Mario Pezzotta (*tb*); Glauco Masetti (*as*); Gianni Basso (*ts*); Fausto Papetti
 (*bs*); Giulio Libano (*p, cel*); Franco Cerri (*b*); Gene Victory (*d*). 9/59.

(*) **In Milan Original Jazz Classics OJC 370 CD/LP/MC
 Baker; Glauco Masetti (*as*); Gianni Basso (*ts*); Renato Sellani (*p*); Franco Cerri (*b*);
 Gene Victory (*d*). 9–10/59.

Back in Europe, Baker lived in Italy, where he eventually ended up in jail. The strings album is a rather good one of its kind: it was inevitable that Baker would go with this treatment eventually, and by now he was assured enough not to let the horn solos blow away on the orchestral breeze. 'Violets For Your Furs', for instance, makes the most of both the melody and the changes. *In Milan* features a good band – Basso was one of the leading Italians of the day – but it's an uneventful session.

*** **The Italian Sessions** RCA Bluebird 82001 CD/LP/MC
 Baker; Bobby Jaspar (*ts, f*); Amadeo Tommasi (*p*); René Thomas (*g*); Benoit Quersin
 (*b*); Daniel Humair (*d*). 62.

*** **Somewhere Over The Rainbow** RCA Bluebird 90640 CD
 As above. 62.

A fine group – it was mostly Bobby Jaspar's, with local man Tommasi sitting in – and Baker has to work hard to get some room. Quersin and Humair are a grooving rhythm section, Thomas gets in some voluble solos, and Jaspar is his usual mix of detachment and intensity; Baker, though, seems undecided whether to play hot or cool. *Somewhere Over The Rainbow* offers a budget-price version of the same music, minus two tracks.

*** **You Can't Go Home Again** A&M 396997 CD
 Baker; Paul Desmond (*as*); Michael Brecker (*ts*); Hubert Laws (*f, bf, picc*); John
 Scofield (*g*); Richard Beirach (*p, ky*); Kenny Barron, Don Sebesky (*ky*); Ron Carter
 (*b*); Alphonso Johnson, Tony Williams (*d*); Ralph McDonald (*perc*); strings. 5/72.

(****) **My Funny Valentine** Philology W 30 2 CD
 Baker; Stan Getz (*ts*); Nicola Stilo (*f*); Philip Catherine (*g*); Nino Bisceglie, Kenny
 Drew, Gil Goldstein, Michel Graillier, Mike Melillo, Enrico Pieranunzi (*p*); Furio Di
 Castri, George Mraz, Edy Olivieri, Jean-Louis Rassinfosse, Larry Ridley (*b*); David
 Lee, Victor Lewis, Ilario De Marinis (*d*). 80–87.

In 1968, having moved to San Francisco, Chet was attacked and severely beaten, suffering the kind of injuries to his mouth that horn players dread. The incident has been explained as a random mugging, and as a 'reminder' of defaulted drug payments by a local supplier. Whatever the explanation, the loss of several teeth and a nearly unbreakable narcotics habit gave his face that caved-in, despairing look that it wears on a score of album covers from the 1980s. If Chet began as a golden youth, he ended his days as a death's head.

 F. Scott Fitzgerald wrote that there were no second acts in American lives. To an extent, Chet bore that out. The years between 1970 and his rather mysterious death in 1988 were a prolonged curtain. What they did confirm was the truth of another literary tag, Thomas Wolfe's 'You can't go home again', which was used for a wonderful quartet piece recorded by the slowly rehabilitating trumpeter in 1972 with Paul Desmond, by far the best thing on the A&M album, though by no means representative of its rather slick, fusion-tinged product. America really didn't know what to do with him, other than wrap him up in no-substance parcels like this, and he left for Europe again in 1975.

For the remainder of his life, Chet lived out of a suitcase. He enjoyed cult status in Europe and followed an exhausting and seemingly futile itinerary, 'going single' with local musicians. Having moved over to flugelhorn after his beating, he gradually restored his lip. The late sound is frail, airy, almost ethereal. Usually assumed to be a development of Miles Davis's style (and Chet followed a similar repertoire of standards), it was actually more reminiscent of Fats Navarro at his most delicate and attenuated. Unlike Miles, Chet did not favour mutes but developed a quiet, breathy delivery that made such accessories irrelevant.

His singing voice, which took on an increasingly significant role in his work was a perfect match for his playing, a slight, hurt tenor, with a wistful vibrato. Though his singing was valued out of all proportion to its real worth, it served as reminder of how important an understanding of the lyrics was to Chet, who often sounds as if he is softly enunciating the words through his horn. No song characterized his last years more fully than 'My Funny Valentine', another Miles-associated tune that he played and sang at almost every concert he gave. It appears with absolute predictability on the majority of the live albums, and was the encore to the last full-scale concert he gave.

The Philology compilation brings together seven different performances of the song and illustrates a significant point about 'late Chet'. Though the material was increasingly repetitive, Chet's treatment of it was rarely formulaic, but adapted to the demands of particular contexts and moods. There is, then, a dramatic difference between the all-star confrontation with Stan Getz at the Jazzhus Montmartre in 1983 and the very long version recorded with a drummerless quartet in Senigallia the year before he died. In contrast to its nearly 16 minutes, a July 1975 performance with Kenny Drew and a bebop-based rhythm section at Pescara is untypically boiled down. Performances range from the straightforward and melodic to the near-abstract, and this is characteristic of the late years. There is a huge mass of material, but it is more various than initially appears. There is almost always something of interest and only patient sampling will separate the corn from the chaff, and the tough-minded music from the sentimental corn.

***   **In Concert** India Navigation IN 1052 LP
Baker; Lee Konitz (*as*); Michael Moore (*b*); Beaver Harris (*d*). 74.

Not a label on which one would expect to find either of the two front men, concentrating as it did largely on avant-garde music. This set, apparently Chet's first in America for some time, was recorded at Ornette Coleman's New York City loft. It's standard bop fare, freeze-dried and then set to the quite demanding rhythm set up by Moore and Harris. Sonny Rollins's 'Airegin' gets things moving and a long 'Au Privave' completes the first side. Later tracks are more representative of Chet's style, and he shapes some lovely solos on 'Body And Soul' (demonstrating that it's not just a tenor saxophonist's number), 'Willow Weep For Me' and 'Walkin''. The sound is rather poor, and there's quite a lot of surface noise on the LPs, but the music is interesting enough and fills in an awkward gap in the current discography.

***   **Live In Paris, 1960–3 & Nice, 1975** France's Concert FCD 123 CD
Baker; Bob Mover (*as*); George Arvanitas (*p*); Guy Pedersen, Larry Ridley (*b*);
Daniel Humair, David Lee, Ray Mosca Jr (*d*); Radio Orchestra Baden-Baden. 10/60,
6/63, 7/75.

***(*)   **In Paris: Volume 2** West Wind 2059 CD
Baker; Phil Markovitz (*p*); Jean-François Jenny-Clark (*b*); Jeff Brillinger (*d*). 6/78.

(*)   **Live In Chateauvallon, 1978 France's Concert FCD 128 CD
Baker; Phil Markovitz (*p*); Scott Lee (*b*); Jeff Brillinger (*d*). 11/78.

The earlier set is a useful bridging compilation that brings together live material from before and after the enforced sabbatical. Though none of the recordings are particularly good, they're enough to establish that Chet's tone hasn't changed dramatically. The big-band 'Autumn In New York' from 1960 has him sounding confident and full-voiced, but how much of that is in response to quite buoyant arrangements and how much it reflects a younger, relatively unchastened man isn't clear. The 1963 material with Arvanitas has him at his most Miles-like, with the pianist bringing a hint of Red Garland to 'Milestones' and 'Porgy And Bess'.

The 1975 stuff from Nice is nowhere near as good, and though Baker was well used to playing in pianoless groups, he sounds unmercifully exposed on 'Stella By Starlight' with just Ridley and Mosca, and only slightly happier with the colourless Bob Mover on hand for a breezy 'Dear Old Stockholm' and 'Mister B'.

The 1978 band with Markovitz, Jenny-Clark and Brillinger was a fine one and probably the most modernist in outlook that Chet assembled. Richie Beirach's theme 'Broken Wing', written for the trumpeter, kicks off the set and establishes a standard for some daringly unconventional arrangements that always seem on the verge of abandoning conventional tonality altogether. Jenny-Clark is a giant on the bass and the recording catches him just left of centre in a remarkably spacious live mix. Despite interesting material, the Chateauvallon set never quite grabs the attention. There's a much stronger version of Wayne Shorter's 'House Of Jade', a favourite of Chet's, on the last studio album, *Little Girl Blue*, below, and once or twice there seem to be breakdowns of communication between the drummer and a competent, but hardly inspired, group.

***(*) **Once Upon A Summertime** Original Jazz Classics OJC 405 CD/LP
     Baker; Greg Herbert (*ts*); Harold Danko (*p*); Ron Carter (*b*); Mel Lewis (*d*). 2/77.

Originally released on Galaxy, this is a fine, straightforward jazz session. Herbert isn't particularly well known, but acquits himself with honour in a no-frills ballad style with occasional glimpses of a tougher hard-bop diction peeking through. Chet plays very cleanly and sounds in better lip than at any time for the previous ten years. The rhythm section can't be faulted. Good versions of 'E.S.P.' and 'The Song Is You', with Danko well to the fore on the latter.

**** **Live At Nick's** Criss Cross Jazz Criss 1027 CD/LP
     Baker; Phil Markowitz (*p*); Scott Lee (*b*); Jeff Brillinger (*d*). 11/78.

Distinguished by a notably fresh choice of material, this is another fine jazz set. Richie Beirach's 'Broken Wing' was written specially for Chet, but the long version of Wayne Shorter's 'Beautiful Black Eyes' (it can also be heard on the later France's Concert session) is the product of an unexpected enthusiasm that fed the trumpeter with new and relatively untried material. Markowitz is an admirably responsive accompanist and fully merits 'featured' billing on the sleeve. The Shorter track is by far the longest thing on the session, though two CD bonuses, the relatively predictable standards 'I Remember You' and 'Love For Sale', are both over ten minutes. Gerry Teekens is too sophisticated and demanding a producer to have settled for just another ballad album and with the exception of the two last tracks, this is extremely well modulated, one of a mere handful of records from the last two decades of Chet's career that have to be considered essential.

*** **Ballads For Two** Inak 8561 CD
     Baker; Wolfgang Lackerschmid (*vib*). 1/79.

***(*) **Chet Baker/Wolfgang Lackerschmid** Inak 8571 CD
     Baker; Wolfgang Lackerschmid (*vib*); Larry Coryell (*g*); Buster Williams (*b*); Tony Williams (*d*). 11/79.

The duo session is pretty and not much more. The group set, though, has to be considered exceptional on the strength of the line-up alone. Tony Williams is surprisingly just right for Chet's non-directional approach, and he reduces his strike-rate to an appropriate level, allowing the vibes and guitar to make their presence felt. Lackerschmid, as co-leader, is given plenty to do and sounds a lot more committed and Hutcherson-like than on *Ballads For Two*. Buster Williams has a relatively free role and plays delightful counter-melodies a couple of octaves below the trumpeter on a number of tracks. Coryell, who contributes 'Toku Do', is over-delicate and is least favoured by a complicated mix which makes a remarkably good job of what must have been very difficult music to balance.

***(*) **The Touch Of Your Lips** Steeplechase 1122 CD/LP/MC

*** **Daybreak** Steeplechase 1142 CD/LP/MC

*** **This Is Always** Steeplechase 1168 CD/LP

*** **Someday My Prince Will Come** Steeplechase 1180 CD/LP
     Baker; Doug Raney (*g*); Niels-Henning Ørsted-Pedersen (*b*). 6/79, 10/79, 10/79, 10/79.

Chet greatly relished this format (and returned to it to even greater effect with Philip Catherine and Jean-Louis Rasinfosse in the mid-1980s). The absence of a drummer allowed him to develop long, out of tempo lines that were reminiscent of Miles Davis's ballad experiments in the 1950s in which bar-lines were largely ignored and phrases were overlapped or elided. This broke down the conventional development of a solo, replacing it with a relatively unstructured sequence of musical incidents, all of them directly or more obliquely related to the main theme. This was easier to do on ballads and Chet's dynamics became increasingly restrictive in the last few years. *Chet's Choice*, below, is more varied in pace, but in 1979 Chet was still suffering some intonation problems, presumably as a result of losing teeth, and he fluffs some of the faster transitions. On slower material, he sounds masterful, and is ably accompanied by Raney's soft-bop guitar and NHØP's towering bass (a studio duo album with the big Dane would have been something to hear). Steeplechase are often guilty of issuing poorly recorded *audio verité* sessions with little adjustment of balance or volume. This, though, is admirably done, though there's more than an element of overkill in the other three sessions, apparently from later that same year, where there really isn't enough good material for more than one carefully edited CD, a double at most.

***   **All Blues** Arco 3 ARC 102 CD
       Baker; Jean-Paul Florence (*g*); Henri Florence (*p*); James Richardson (*b*); Tony
       Mann (*d*); Rachel Gould (*v*). 9/79.

Chet recorded surprisingly rarely with other singers. The tracks with Rachel Gould would be more interesting if she had a more appealing voice. There are two versions of 'Valentine' and two takes of 'Round About Midnight', a tune he tackled only rather rarely despite a considerable affection for the more lyrical side of Monk. The Florences play effectively, but are not kindly served by a very dry acoustic. Generally good.

***   **No Problem** Steeplechase 1131 CD/LP/MC
       Baker; Duke Jordan (*p*); Niels-Henning Ørsted-Pedersen (*b*); Norman Fearrington
       (*d*). 10/79.

A more than usually boppish set for this vintage. Though none of the material is orthodox bebop, there is something about Chet's phrasing, and Jordan's tight, unelaborate comping, that looks back to a much earlier period. That may recommend the session to those who find the later material too far removed from the blues. Others may feel Chet had moved too far beyond this kind of approach to be able to return to it comfortably.

***(*)   **Live At Fat Tuesday's** Fresh Sound FSR CD 131 CD
       Baker; Bud Shank (*as*); Hal Galper, Phil Markovitz (*p*); Ron Carter (*b*); Ben Riley
       (*d*). 4/81.

A great shame that Shank wasn't able to sit in on 'You Can't Go Home Again', thus wakening memories of the superb Baker–Desmond version, but there's no doubt that the altoist gives Chet a shot in the arm on their two tracks together. 'In Your Own Sweet Way' is handled with more fire than normal. Shank's tone (well captured on CD) is clear and bright and Chet sounds more pungent and full-bodied than usual. Warmly recommended.

***   **Live At The Paris Festival** DIW 339 CD
       Baker; René Urtreger (*p*); Pierre Michelot (*b*); Aldo Romano (*d*). 11/81.

A romping version of 'Chasin' The Bird' reasserts Chet's place in the later history of bebop. The chord structure appears to have been simplified slightly, or at least rationalized, which is fair enough for a festival gig, but it's still clear that Chet has something to offer in a blues-derived idiom. A couple of tracks later, he's tackling Miles Davis's 'Down', which in the event proves to be more of an obstacle. The other material includes Jimmy Heath's 'For Minors Only', a favourite at that time, a mournful 'But Not For Me' and the inevitable 'Valentine'. A good session, but not an essential one.

****   **Peace** Enja CD 4016 CD/LP
       Baker; David Friedman (*vib, mar*); Buster Williams (*b*); Joe Chambers (*d*). 82.

By far the most interesting of the later studio sessions, *Peace* consists largely of David Friedman originals. The exceptions are 'The Song Is You' and a feeling interpretation of the title piece, a Horace Silver composition. 'Lament For Thelonious' has an elaborate-sounding melody, built up out of very simple elements. As on 'Peace', it's Williams rather than Friedman who takes responsibility for sustaining the chord progression, leaving the vibraharpist to elaborate the theme. His response to Chet's first couple of choruses is softly ambiguous. Chambers also takes a simple but effective solo. The CD has an alternate take of the opening '3 + 1 = 5', a confident post-bop structure that deserves to be covered more frequently. Remixed in 1987, the album sounds sharp and uncluttered.

*** **Everything Happens To Me** Timeless SJP 176 CD
Baker; Kirk Lightsey (*p*); David Eubanks (*b*); Eddie Gladden (*b*). 3/83.

Stars for Lightsey, who has a good proportion of the album to himself and his characteristically respectful readings of Wayne Shorter themes. Chet comes in for 'Ray's Idea' and the title piece, making more of an impact than he does on many a longer set. Worth buying for Lightsey alone, but collectors will welcome Chet's trumpet and vocal contributions.

*** **Mister B** Timeless SJP 192 CD
Baker; Michel Graillier (*p*); Philip Catherine (*g*); Riccardo Del Frà (*b*).

*** **Sings Again** Timeless SJP 238 CD
As above, except omit Catherine; add John Engels (*d*). 5/83.

Catherine unfortunately shows up only on a single track, the far from typical 'Father Christmas'. However, the trio sessions on *Mister B* are good enough. Graillier was a sympathetic pianist in the lush, romantic manner (Danko, Beirach, Galper, Lightsey) which Chet preferred and which one associates with pianists who accompany singers.The absence of a drummer on the first album is more than made up for by Del Frà, who is brought through very strongly on this remixed issue, which also includes the bonus 'White Blues' and the Catherine track. All the same points apply to the *Sings Again* session, except that Del Frà has been relegated to the background in favour of Engels's notably soft touch, largely on brushes.

(*) **Live In Sweden Dragon DRLP 56 LP
Baker; Ake Johansson (*p*); Kjell Jansson (*b*); Göran Levin (*d*). 9/83.

Unremarkable vinyl-only set with a stiffly accomplished local rhythm section. The closing 'You Can't Go Home Again' is quite moving.

*** **Deep In A Dream Of You** Moon MCD 026 CD
Baker; Jacques Peltzer (*f*); Harold Danko (*p*); Isla Eckinger (*b*).

*** **Night Bird** West Wind 2037 CD

*** **Tune Up** West Wind 2038 CD
Baker; Nicola Stilo (*f*); Karl Ratzer (*g*); Riccardo Del Frà (*b*); Al Levitt (*d*). 6/80.

***(*) **Chet Baker At Capolinea** Red CD 123206 CD
Baker; Diane Varvra (*ss*); Nicola Stilo (*f*); Michel Graillier (*p*); Riccardo Del Frà (*b*); Leo Mitchell (*d*). 10/83.

*** **A Night At The Shalimar** Philology W 59 2 CD
Baker; Nicola Stilo (*f*); Mike Melillo (*p*); Furio Di Castri (*b*). 5/87.

Flute was an integral feature of many of the 1980s groups and Stilo had a particular facility for the long, slightly shapeless lines that the trumpeter was looking for. These are all attractive sets in a rather lightweight way, but only the Red offers much challenge. Varvra's soprano is used, like the flute, to filigree the backgrounds, allowing Graillier to play slightly more percussively than usual, much as the guitarist plays on the rather good West Winds. The first of these includes material by Richie Beirach, Jimmy Heath, Enrico Pieranunzi, Bud Powell and Miles Davis, which gives a measure of how far afield Chet was searching at the time.

The Moon set is undated and again includes relatively enterprising material. Danko's thematic variations on 'If You Could See Me Now' almost steal the show, but Eckinger seems to be doing interesting things, if only the recording permitted them to be heard clearly. Peltzer doesn't quite reach Stilo's high standard, but is a simpler, less linear player, and concentrates rather more on the chordal structure than on weaving elaborate countermelodies.

Of the group, the Red is the one to go for. The opening 'Estate' is one of the most imaginative available readings of the Bruno Martino tune and (typical of Chet's unflagging ability to pull out unexpected themes) there is an excellent version of J. J. Johnson's little heard 'Lament'.

***   **Let's Get Lost** RCA PL 83054 CD/LP/MC
Baker; Nicola Stilo (*f, g*); Frank Strazzeri (*p*); John Leftwich (*b*); Ralph Penland (*d, perc*).

Stilo unfortunately appears on only one track here, the evocative 'Zingaro'. Most of the titles are for drummerless trio and are slightly uncertain in register. Things are a little sharper when Penland is playing and 'Every Time We Say Goodbye' and 'I Don't Stand A Ghost Of A Chance With You' are done without undue sentimentality.

****   **Blues For A Reason** Criss Cross Jazz Criss 1010 CD
Baker; Warne Marsh (*ts*); Hod O'Brien (*p*); Cecil McBee (*b*); Eddie Gladden (*d*). 9/84.

It has always been a matter of considerable debate whether or not Chet belongs in the 'Cool School', is a Tristano disciple, or has the authentic 'West Coast sound'. Just as it's now recognized in most quarters that Tristano was a much more forceful and swinging player than the conventional image allows, so it's clear that the near-abstraction and extreme chromaticism of Chet's last years was a perfectly logical outgrowth of bebop. Warne Marsh's style has been seen as equally problematic, 'cold', 'dry', 'academic', the apparent antithesis of Chet's romantic expressionism. When the two are put together, as on this remarkable session, it's clear that unsubstantiated generalizations and categorizations quickly fall flat.

While Chet is quite clearly no longer an orthodox changes player, having followed Miles's course out of bop, he's still able to live with Marsh's complex harmonic developments. *Blues For A Reason* stands out from much of the work of the period in including relatively unfamiliar original charts, including three by Chet himself. The best of these, 'Looking Good Tonight', is heard in two versions on the CD option, demonstrating how the trumpeter doesn't so much rethink his whole strategy on a solo as allow very small textural changes dictate a different development. Marsh, by contrast, sounds much more of a *thinking* player, and to that extent, just a little less spontaneous. The saxophonist's 'Well Spoken', with which the set begins, is perhaps the most challenging single item Chet tackled in his final decade and he sounds as confident with it as with the well-worn 'If You Could See Me Now' and 'Imagination'. This is an important and quietly salutary album that confounds the more casual dismissals of the trumeter's latter-day work.

**   **My Foolish Heart** IRD TDM 002 CD/LP
Baker; Fred Raulston (*vib*); Floyd Darling (*p*); Kirby Stewart (*b*); Paul Guerrero (*d*); Martha Burks (*v*).

**   **Misty** IRD TDM 003 CD/LP
As above.

**   **Time After Time** IRD TDM 004 CD/LP
As above. 1/85.

Exhaustive and mostly futile documentation of two nights in Dallas. The performances are well below par and the group sounds self-conscious and slightly contrived. Almost all of the material is familiar and Martha Burks is merely dull. IRD don't currently list any other titles.

***(*)   **Diane** Steeplechase 1207 CD/LP/MC
Baker; Paul Bley (*p*). 2/85.

Considerably undervalued as a standards player, Bley is exactly the right duo partner for Chet. His accompaniments frequently dispense with the chords altogether, holding on to the theme with the lightest of touches, and allowing the basic rhythm to stretch out and dismantle itself. Typically of this period, the material is quite straightforward, but the treatments are far from orthodox and *Diane* would certainly merit an unqualified fourth star were it not for rather murky sound.

****   **Chet's Choice** Criss Cross Jazz Criss 1016 CD/LP

***(*)   **Strollin'** Enja 5005 CD
Baker; Philip Catherine (*g*); Jean-Louis Rassinfosse (*b*); Hein Van De Geijn (*b* on *Chet's Choice* only). 6/85.

This was the most productive year of Chet's last decade and in the association with Catherine he hit a purple patch. It was a format he liked and had used to great effect in the 1979 sessions with Doug Raney and NHØP. The Criss Cross session is the most completely satisfying studio record of the period. Playing a basic standards set, he sounds refocused and clear-voiced, with a strength and fullness of tone that is undoubtedly helped by Gerry Teeken's typically professional production job. All three players are recorded in tight close-up, but with excellent separation. Three long tracks – 'My Foolish Heart', 'Pettiford's 'Blues In The Closet' and 'Stella Starlight' – are not on the LP.

The Enja performances are equally good, but the live sound isn't quite as distinct and it's a very much shorter set. One interesting link reflects Baker's outwardly unlikely enthusiasm for Horace Silver compositions, 'Doodlin' on *Choice*, the title piece on *Strollin'*. Their built-in rhythmic quality is ideal for players like Baker and Catherine who tend to drift out of metre very quickly, developing long, carefully textured improvisations with only a very basic pulse. Both of these sessions are strongly recommended.

** **Symphonically** Soul Note SN 1134 CD/LP
Baker; Mike Melilo (*p*); Massimo Moriconi (*b*); Giampaolo Ascolese (*d*); Orchestra Filarmonica Marchigiana. 7/85.

Baker often performed well in front of big orchestras, but this was an over-produced and rather heavy-handed session and contains little of interest. The sound is very slushy and Chet is made to sound rather cavernous.

(*) **Hazy Hugs Limetree MLP 198601 LP
Baker; Edu Ninck Blok (*c*); Evert Hekkema (*bhn*); Kees Van Lier (*as*); Dick De Graaff (*ts*); Jan Vennik (*bs*); Bert Van Den Brink (*p*); Hein Van De Geijn (*b*); John Engels (*d*). 9/85.

Credited to the Amstel Octet, Chet guests on four out of six tracks, floating with insouciant ease over slightly stiff horn arrangements. Like Charlie Parker, the trumpeter had the gift of not appearing to be constrained by relatively unswinging settings. Here, he trots out some one-size-fits-all solos which, apart from the unusual 'Tergiversation', won't excite much interest.

***(*) **Live From The Moonlight** Philology W 10/11 2 2CD/2LP
Baker; Michel Graillier (*p*); Massimo Moriconi (*b*). 11/85.

More than two and a half hours (on CD) from a single night at the Moonlight Club, Macerata. The extra material comprises three tracks from a third, presumably later set, and a long rehearsal performance of 'Polka Dots And Moonbeams'. Chet is in good lip and reasonable voice. There isn't a track under ten minutes and most are longer than a quarter of an hour. This, depending on the trumpeter's state of mind, was either his most serious vice or, as here, his most underrated virtue, for he was capable of remarkable concentration and, ironically, compression of ideas, and his up-close examination of themes like 'Estate' and Richie Beirach's 'Night Bird' (CD only) is extremely impressive. As an insight into how Chet worked over an entire evening, this is hard to beat. Without a drummer, the music can start to sound a little rarefied, and Moriconi often isn't clearly audible. A fine document, nevertheless. For a change the liner document includes something more useful than the usual over-emotional '*ciao*, Chet, *mille grazie*', a discography from 1952 to 1988 that lists a sobering 198 items; specialists will doubtless be able to add more to that.

***(*) **When Sunny Gets Blue** Steeplechase 1221 CD/LP/MC
Baker; Butch Lacy (*p*); Jesper Lundgaard (*b*); Jukkis Uotila (*d*). 2/86.

A rather melancholic session, but one of the better ones from the period. Lacy is a much underrated piano player. He gives Chet a great deal of room, leaving chords suspended in unexpected places and rarely resorting to predetermined structures even on very familiar tunes. Indeed, he sets up conventional expectations on 'Here's That Rainy Day' and 'You'd Be So Nice To Come Home To' and then confounds them utterly with altered tonalities and out of tempo figures. Lundgaard and Uotila are both thoroughly professional and contribute to a fine, unpredictable set.

(*) **As Time Goes By Timeless SJP 251/2 CD

(*)   **Cool Cat Timeless SJP 262 CD/LP
Baker; Harold Danko (*p*); Jon Burr (*b*); Ben Riley (*d*). 12/86.

**   **Heartbreak** Timeless SJP 366 CD
As above; with Michel Graillier (*p*); Riccardo Del Frà (*b*); John Engels (*d*); strings.
86–88, 91.

The first two were recorded at a single session, with considerable emphasis on Chet's singing. Given that his chops sound in very poor shape, this may not have been a matter of choice. Posthumously adding strings to a selection of tunes from the Timeless catalogue clearly was. The editing on *Heartbreak* hasn't been well done and there are joins all over the place, particularly obvious to anyone who knows the original sessions. These are slight enough, though Danko is a fine, lyrical player. Further sweetening doesn't redeem or enliven some very weary material.

***(*)   **Memories: Chet Baker In Tokyo** Paddle Wheel K32Y 6270 CD

***   **Four: Live In Tokyo – Volume 2** Paddle Wheel K32Y 6495 CD
Baker; Harold Danko (*p*); Hein Van Der Geyn (*b*); John Engels (*d*). 6/87.

Despite crowd-pleasing versions of 'Stella By Starlight' and 'Valentine', the material and arrangements are by no means as predictable as on similar live sets. On Volume 1, there is a brisk reading of Jimmy Heath's staple 'For Minors Only', a long, long version of Jobim's 'Portrait In Black And White', with Danko eating up the soft bossa rhythm, and then there's a surprise. Like Miles, Chet kept his eyes open for new pop standards and had enjoyed a brief association with Elvis Costello, playing an unforgettable, delay-laden solo on Costello's own version of his anti-Falklands War anthem 'Shipbuilding'. Chet returns the compliment with a sharp, well thought out version of Costello's 'Almost Blue', a song that offers a combination of romantic sentiment and hard-edged melody. This is an excellent set, slightly remote but very true and the inclusion of a drummer, as so often, gives Chet a much needed impetus. Volume 2 strongly suggests that the best of the material has already been heard, but anyone who feels enthusiastic about the first set will also want the second, which includes Richie Beirach's lovely 'Broken Wing' and a slightly unusual arrangement of 'Seven Steps To Heaven'. Recommended.

***   **Naima** Philology W 52 2 CD
Baker; Mario Concetto Andriulli, Pino Caldarola, Martino Chiarulli, Tom Harrell, Mino Lacirignola (*t*); Nino Besceglie, Nucci Guerra, Giovanni Pellegrini, Muzio Petrella (*tb*); Giovanni Congedo, Franco Lorusso, Silvano Martina, Nicola Nitti, Pino Pichierri (*reeds*); Hal Galper, Hank Jones, Kirk Lightsey, Edy Olivieri, Enrico Pieranunzi (*p*); Steve Gilmore, Rocky Knower, Ilario de Marinis, Red Mitchell, Massimo Moriconi (*b*); John Arnold, Bill Goodwin, Shelly Manne, Vicenzo Mazzone (*d*). 6/83, 9/85, 7, 8 & 11/87.

Billed as Volume 1 of a sequence called 'Unusual Chet', this certainly has some unusual discographical quirks. Two tracks, valuable big-band readings of Benny Golson's 'Killer Joe', 'Lover Man' and Thad Jones's 'A Child Is Born' from 1985 are identified as 'never on record'. Two others, though, including a long version of the Coltrane title piece with Lightsey, are described as 'never recorded', which presents a philosophical problem or suggests that they're coming from the Other Side.

Essentially, this grab-bag set brings together live tapes of compositions that Chet rarely played or hadn't put on official releases. The big-band tracks are surprisingly strong, though the tone suggests he might be playing a flugelhorn. Much of the rest, like the opening blues scat with Jones, Mitchell and Manne, is rather scrappy. Despite its length, 'Naima' seems rather attenuated. A collector's set, but an interesting sidelight on Chet for non-specialists as well.

***   **The Heart Of The Ballad** Philology W 20 2 CD/LP
Baker; Enrico Pieranunzi (*p*). 2/88.

***(*)   **Little Girl Blue** Philology W 21 2 CD/LP
Baker; Enrico Pieranunzi (*p*); Enzo Pietropaoli (*b*); Fabrizio Sferra (*d*). 3/88.

Billed as Chet's last studio recordings, these encounters with Pieranunzi and his thoroughly professional Space Jazz Trio were recorded less than a week apart. Predictably, there are no late reversals or epiphanies, just a straightforward reading of some uncontroversial charts. On the group session, Chet counts each tune in, but slows up progress after the theme in almost every case, not so much out of hesitancy as an apparent desire to linger over the melody. There are exceptions. 'Old Devil Moon' is quite upbeat and Wayne Shorter's 'House Of Jade', which had been a regular item in Chet's book for a long time, is given a smoothly swinging reading. Pieranunzi brings a crisp formality to his solos. The CD bonus is a long (presumably rehearsal) meditation on 'I Thought About You', which is placed first. It's slightly shapeless but includes some fine passages from Chet that one wouldn't have liked to have missed. The duos aren't particularly compelling, but Pieranunzi is a careful, quietly challenging accompanist and leaves a sufficient number of chords hanging or incompletely resolved to generate a measure of tension that's largely missing on the group set. It's unfortunate there are no tunes in common with the Paul Bley duets, above. Pieranunzi certainly lacks the Canadian's brittle sensitivity and rarely risks anything like Bley's departures from conventional tonality. Generally, though, he shapes up pretty well.

(*)   **Live In Rosenheim Timeless SJP 233 CD/LP
Baker; Nicola Stilo (g, f); Marc Abrams (b); Luca Flores (d). 4/88.

There's a slightly distasteful but commercially understandable desire among record labels to be able to release the last word from a great artist. This, following the final studio session, was billed as the last *quartet* recording. It's pretty thin stuff. Chet takes a turn at the piano, quite inconsequentially, and though the material is reasonably enterprising ('Funk In Deep Freeze', 'Arborway', 'Portait In Black And White'), it's played with an almost total lack of conviction. The sound is respectable, though Stilo's flute, long a feature of Chet's groups, is sometimes overpoweringly vibrant.

***   **My Favourite Songs** Enja 5097 CD/LP
Baker; L. Axelsson, H. Habermann, B. Lanese, M. Moch (t); W. Ahlers, E. Christmann, M. Grossman, P. Plato (tb); Herb Geller (as); A. Boether, H. Ende, K. Nagurski, E. Wurster, John Schröder (g); Walter Norris (p); W. Schlüter (vib); Lucas Lindholm (b); Aage Tanggaard (d); Radio Orchestra Hannover.

***   **Straight From The Heart** Enja 6020 CD/LP
As above. 4/88.

Billed as 'The last great concert' (Volume 1) and 'The great last concert' and only quibbles about one word. This was certainly something more than just another small-group recording, but by no stretch of the imagination does it merit any imputation of greatness. The photograph on the sleeve, repeated in reverse on Volume 2, is quite ghastly, a shrunken, pucker-mouthed shell of a man who looks ten years older than his actual 59 everywhere but the eyes which still have the soft, faraway look they had back in the 1950s when Chet seemed like the freshest thing out. The horn with the big mouthpiece (pictured dewed with water on the cover of *Naima*, above) still looks burnished and pristine but it only takes a track or two to realize that by the last year of his life Chet was trading on nothing more than pure sound and reputation. There are no new ideas any more and the old ones lack the morning freshness that was their greatest lasting stock in trade.

There are small-group, big-band and orchestra tracks. There isn't much to choose between them, but for the fact that on the few quintet sessions one listens more attentively to Geller and Walter Norris than to Chet. The run of material is pretty standard, with Miles's 'All Blues', John Lewis's 'Django', 'Summertime', Brubeck's 'In Your Own Sweet Way', Monk's 'Well, You Needn't' and the inevitable 'Valentine' all on Volume 1; the sequel covers slightly less familiar ground, but, yes, the encore is 'My Funny Valentine' again. Two weeks after the Hannover concert, Chet Baker fell to his death from an Amsterdam hotel window. The exact circumstances have never been fully explained.

GINGER BAKER (born 1939)
DRUMS, PERCUSSION

(*)   **African Force ITM 1417 CD/LP
      Baker; Ludwig Gotz (*tb*); Wolfgang Schmidtke (*ss, ts, bs*); Jan Kazda (*b, g, ky*); J. C.
      Commodore (*perc, v*); Ampofo Acquah (*perc, g, v*); Ansoumana Bangoura (*perc*);
      Francis Kwaku A Mensah (*perc, v*).

***   **Palanquin's Pole** ITM 1433 CD/LP
      Baker; Ampofo Acquah (*perc, g, v*); Ansoumana Bangoura (*perc*); Thomas Akuru
      Dyani (*perc*); Francis Kwaku A. Mensah (*perc, v*). 5/87.

***   **No Material** ITM 1435 CD/LP
      Baker; Peter Brötzmann (*reeds*); Sonny Sharrock, Nicky Skopelitis (*g*); Jan Kazda (*b*).
      3/87.

When the 1960s 'supergroup' Cream split up in 1969, there were dark mutterings from the two members who were still talking that it had always 'really' been a jazz group, and not really their thing at all. Eric Clapton and Ginger Baker went on to form Blind Faith, and after its brief (one album, one massive gig) career, Baker found himself tired of supergrouping, formed a percussion-laden outfit called Airforce, which included the still-viable Phil Seamen, and then found he was tired of the whole bloody business and went off to open a studio in Nigeria.

Whatever the internal stresses and stated objectives of Cream, Baker has always seemed a jazzer *manqué*, a Charlie Watts figure under whose relentless 4/4s beat a heart tuned to something else entirely. Baker's *African Force* is a percussion band of formidable energy, occasional sophistication and considerable charm. Whether what they play is 'really' jazz or not is a metaphysical question.

In addition to the African drummers, the original *African Force* featured all but the drummer (naturally) of the German band Das Pferd. The polyrhythms bog down a little in the Europeans' more linear approach, and the potential for a genuinely creative synthesis is largely missed. *Palanquin's Pole* repeats two of the tracks – 'Brain Damage' and 'Ansoumania' (a punning eponym for one of the drummers) – but the treatment is altogether brighter and more inventive. 'Ginger's Solo' is overlong but, God knows, a lot shorter than the notorious 'Toad' of Cream days, which allowed punters to go for a pint, a three-course dinner and a haircut before Clapton and Bruce picked up their guitars again.

Second track in, Baker gravely informs the audience that, at this juncture, he and his colleagues would like to administer brain damage. Those interested should skip briskly on to *No Material*, so named as a nod to Bill Laswell's band, Material, and because there was no set list for the concert documented. Baker's project, which lasted for exactly one week in 1987, was the rump of an ambitious three-way collaboration between African Force, Last Exit and Material. Laswell's absence on more lucrative chores meant the recruitment of Skopelitis and, from Das Pferd again, bassist Jan Kazda.

Fans of Last Exit shouldn't bother listening for anything like Shannon Jackson's polydirectional drumming. Baker plays it unwaveringly straight. Sharrock and Skopelitis crunch and clang away, and Brötzmann squeals furiously. More than just a fluke, it probably sounded absolutely great at the time. It wears a little thin on subsequent hearings, but it does confirm Baker's often unrecognized sense of artistic challenge.

(*)   **Middle Passage Axiom AXCD 3001 CD
      Baker; Bernie Worrell (*org*); Nicky Skopelitis (*g, electric bj, syn, sitar*); Jonas
      Hellborg, Bill Laswell, Jah Wobble (*b*); Faruk Takbilek (*ney, zurna*); Aiyb Dieng,
      Magette Fall, Mar Gueye (*perc*). 90.

In overall impact, *Middle Passage* is reminiscent of bassist Jah Wobble's original Invaders of the Heart project: big dub basslines, North African *ney* effects, acoustic and processed guitar, and PlayMe organ chords. Baker's relentlessly unwavering patterns get on the nerves long before the opening 'Metoub' is halfway done; and his solo feature, 'Basil', is a major, but mercifully brief, trial of patience. After that, the set peters out with the bland 1970s jazz-pop of 'South To The Dust', a soft swirl of Tim-Buckley-meets-The-Doors. The earlier tracks are better, but this isn't a particularly compelling record and the interplay of electric and MIDI basses with ethnic percussion is rarely crisp enough to fight through a bottom-heavy mix.

KENNY BAKER (born 1921)
TRUMPET, CORNET, FLUGELHORN

**   **Baker's Dozen** Dormouse DM9 LP
Baker; Freddie Clayton, Tommy McQuator (*t*); George Chisholm, Jacky Armstrong (*tb*); E. O. 'Poggy' Pogson (*reeds*); Harry Hayes (*cl, as, ts*); Keith Bird (*cl, bcl, ts*); Derek Collins (*ts*); Harry Klein (*bs*); Freddie Ballerini (*cl, ts, vn*); Bill McGuffie (*p, cel*); Norman Stenfalt (*p*); Bill Le Sage (*vib, acc*); Martin Slavin (*vib*); Joe Muddel, Lennie Bush (*b*); Eric Delaney, Phil Seamen (*d*). 5/55–5/57.

***   **Presents The Half-Dozen** Dormouse DM19 LP
Baker; George Chisholm (*tb*); Derek Collins (*cl, ts*); Harry Smith (*p*); Jack Fallon, Eric Dawson (*b*); Lennie Hastings (*d*). 3–4/57.

An Armstrong disciple much admired by the British mainstream fraternity, Baker's superb technique and absolute security in all registers of the trumpet are undeniable. These albums date from the period when he was leading a regular band for a BBC programme. *Baker's Dozen* certainly has a Light Programme ambience to it, and the 16 arrangements are so tightly nailed down that the music is frankly impersonal. When Baker gives himself some space, as in the beautiful break on 'Mean Dog Blues', one can hear what command he has; but the feeling remains that these tracks have worn far less well than most British trad of the period. Pogson, a dance-band veteran, contributes some of the quirkier moments, since he plays bass sax and serpent along with the usual reeds. The smaller band on *Presents The Half Dozen* is more successful. Chisholm, whose career on record has often misrepresented his major talent, delivers pointed and richly toned solos throughout, and Baker's Berigan-like low-register playing is a strong balance to his sometimes overlit high-note work. But the rhythm section is as penny-plain as always in British jazz of the period. Excellent remastering, although the unsuitably reverberant production on the second record is something of a drawback.

IAIN BALLAMY (born 1965)
SAXOPHONES

***   **Balloon Man** Editions EG EEG 63 CD/LP
Ballamy; Django Bates (*ky, thn*); Steve Watts (*b*); Martin France (*d*). 12/88.

Ballamy is one of the generation of young musicians who have crested the wave of fresh popularity which has invigorated British jazz in recent years. Although closely associated with the Loose Tubes big band, his debut as a leader suggests that he is very much his own man. Rather than pursuing a particular style on one of the saxophones, he plays with a light-toned fluency on both alto and tenor; and instead of featuring himself, he prefers to work closely with his comrade Bates – many of the tracks here are almost like contrapuntal duets with rhythm accompaniment. Ballamy likes to subvert expectations: 'Albert', for Albert Ayler, is speedy and cartoon-like, while the tango structure of 'Rahsaan' pulls between its very pretty melody and Bates's mocking sound-effects. In fact the pianist plays with rare accomplishment and has a splendid solo on the title piece, while 'Mode Forbode' and 'Remember' are models of Tristano-like counterpoint. The playful tone of much of the record sets it apart from the neo-classic approach of Ballamy's American contemporaries without sacrificing substance.

JON BALLANTYNE (born 1964)
PIANO

***   **Sky Dance** Justin Time JUST-30 CD
Ballantyne; Joe Henderson (*ts*); Neil Swainson (*b*); Jery Fuller (*d*). 12/88.

***   **A Musing** Justin Time JUST 39-2 CD
Ballantyne; Paul Bley (*p*); Dave Laing (*d*). 2/91.

Ballantyne is an accomplished Canadian pianist, but he's also rather chameleonic: the major stylistic trait of these two rather good records is his ability to sound like whoever else he fancies, though luckily there's enough good humour about it to make him stand aside from many of the post-Tyner pianists. The meeting with Henderson is distinguished by the saxophonist's now almost predictable inventiveness and lustrous solos, with a good blues in 'BYO Blues' and a nicely sonorous ballad performance of the title-track. Ballantyne is a rather more outward-looking pianist than Henderson normally works with, and there's some piquancy in the contrast. With Bley, who sits in on five tunes – there are two solos and two duets with Laing – Ballantyne finds that his mischievous streak is rather akin to Bley's own, and there is some suitably elliptical playing by both men, though Ballantyne's solo 'Question' seems almost slavishly Bley-like. The best things happen on the two duos with Laing, whose rather circumspect and deftly stroked playing adds subtle rhythmic colour rather than impetus to Ballantyne's own playing.

BILLY BANG (born 1947)
VIOLIN

****   **Rainbow Gladiator** Soul Note SN 1016 LP

**   **Invitation** Soul Note SN 1036 LP
         Bang, Charles Tyler (*as, bs*); Michele Rosewoman (*p*, on *Gladiator*); Curtis Clark (*p*, on *Invitation*); Wilber Morris (*b*); Dennis Charles (*d*). 6/81, 4/82.

Titular head of the unfortunately-named Bang Gang, the most significant jazz violinist of his day reverses the old cliché about Chicago gangsters going round with Thomson machine-guns in their fiddle cases. Bang's rapid-fire approach stems partly from the work Ramsey Ameen did with Cecil Taylor, approaching strings much as Taylor approaches piano: as a percussion instrument.

Rainbow Gladiator is one of the finest records of the 1980s, and is certainly Bang's most convincing recording. Rhythmic and polycultural, it has a highly distinctive instrumental coloration (echoed somewhat more artificially on his later albums) and an urgency that is somewhat tamed on the subsequent *Invitation*, a more immediately appealing set that palls with repeated hearings. Rosewoman plays superbly and is better recorded than on some of her own sessions; as always, Soul Note's Giovanni Bonandrini gets an evenly democratic final mix.

***   **The Fire From Within** Soul Note SN 1086 CD/LP
         Bang; Ahmed Abdullah (*t*); Oscar Sanders (*g*); William Parker (*b*); Thurman Barker (*mar, perc*); John Betsch (*d*); Charles Bobo Shaw (*perc*).

***   **Live At Carlos 1** Soul Note SN 1136 CD/LP/MC
         As above, except omit Abdullah, Betsch and Shaw; add Roy Campbell (*t*); Zen Matsuura (*d*); Eddie Conde (*congas*). 11/86.

The horn/guitar/marimba combination is highly unusual and very effective as a setting for Bang's skittering lines. An even more noticeable swing here towards African – or, more strictly, Middle Eastern and North African – rhythms and cells. Abdullah's keying is faintly reminiscent of Leo Smith's but much more limber and somewhat less sure of tone. Betsch, who played with Bang on Marilyn Crispell's fine *Spirit Music*, is a tighter and more traditional player than Matsuura, but there's little to choose between them, or between the albums.

No point looking for 'Live At Carlos Volume 2'. Carlos 1 was a club in Greenwich Village.

***(*)   **Valve No. 10** Soul Note 121186 CD/LP
         Bang; Frank Lowe (*ts*); Sirone (*b*); Dennis Charles (*d*). 2/88.

Without question Bang's best work of recent years, *Valve No. 10* has a balance and precision equal to its intensity. It is certainly one of the violinist's most deeply felt recordings. 'Bien-Hoa Blues' is named after the army post where Bang served in Vietnam; the music suggests Southern fields and rice paddies, Spanish moss and monkey jungle by dizzying turns. Even more intense are the two tributes to Coltrane, recorded to commemorate the twentieth anniversary of the saxophonist's death. 'September 23rd' (Coltrane's birth-date) is less successful, a combination of music and spoken verse that drifts toward banality and does little more than name-check Trane and rerun the 'Love Supreme' chant. The long, concluding 'Lonnie's Lament' is more heart-felt. The tune adapts well to Bang's violin and Sirone – too rarely in a recording studio these days – plays beautifully underneath him. Lowe's breathy delivery stems from a generation or two before Coltrane, but sounds quite in keeping.

The other tracks are rather more abstract. 'Improvisation For Four' has awkward moments when Charles comes unstuck trying not to play the obvious cadence, but he is absolutely on the case on the opening 'P. M.', where solos are deployed irregularly and asymmetrically, starting in the middle of one chorus and leaking over into the middle of a later one, overlapping or leaving oddly syncopated gaps. It's an impressive start to a throughly intriguing album.

PAUL BARBARIN (1899–1969)
DRUMS

***(*)   Streets Of The City** 504 LP9 LP
     Barbarin; Ernest Cagnolatti (*t, v*); Alvin Alcorn (*t*); Eddie Pierson, Bob Thomas (*tb*); Albert Burbank (*cl*); Lester Santiago (*p*); Johnny St Cyr (*bj, v*); Richard McLean (*b*). 50.

***   Paul Barbarin And His Band** Storyville SLP 6008 CD/LP
     As above, except omit Alcorn and Thomas. 51.

One of the major New Orleans drummers, Paul Barbarin was most visibly active in the 1930s, when he played and toured with such leaders as Louis Armstrong and Luis Russell; but it was the revival of interest in New Orleans jazz which let him record as a leader. He had a hard yet restless manner of playing the beat, and his bands swing with a kind of relentlessness that can be very exciting. Both these albums catch his groups at a peak: the horns are all excellent soloists as well as vivid ensemble players, with Pierson a shouting trombonist, Burbank terrifically agile and Cagnolatti making light work of sounding tough and imaginative at the same time. The 504 disc is slightly preferred because the band, which varies slightly across three sessions, gets the entire record to itself (the Storyville album is shared with a jam session led by Percy Humphrey): remastered from rehearsal acetates by Charlie Crump, the sound is imperfect (and 'Milenburg Joys' comes from a damaged disc) but lively enough, and the group sound loose and full of energy. But the Storyville album is scarcely less enjoyable: there's an uproarious version of 'Clarinet Marmalade' and, though all the material is staple Dixieland repertoire, they play it all with seasoned rather than hackneyed dedication. The sound is a little flat but perfectly acceptable.

***   Paul Barbarin And His New Orleans Band** Atlantic 90977 CD
     Barbarin; John Brunious (*t*); Bob Thomas (*tb*); Willie Humphreys (*cl*); Lester Santiago (*p*); Danny Barker (*bj*); Milt Hinton (*b*). 55.

It's good to have something by a Barbarin band on CD, although this edition of the group – which includes some major New Orleanians – is perhaps less exciting than the one which made the 1951 sessions. The music is otherwise much as before, though Hinton's flexible bass gives the underlying rhythms a more varied sense of swing, and this is certainly the clearest sound of Barbarin's available music.

CHRIS BARBER (born 1930)
TROMBONE, BASS TRUMPET, VOCALS

***(*)   Live In 1954/5** London 820878-2 CD
     Barber; Pat Halcox (*c*); Monty Sunshine (*cl*); Lonnie Donegan (*bj*); Jim Bray (*b, bb*); Ron Bowden (*d*); Ottilie Patterson (*v*). 10/54, 1/55.

***(*)   Echoes Of Harlem** Dormouse DM 8 LP
     As above, except add Micky Ashman (*b*). 9/55.

****   30 Years Chris Barber** Timeless TTD 517/8 CD/2LP
     Barber; Pat Halcox (*t, v*); Monty Sunshine, Ian Wheeler (*cl*); John Crocker (*ts*); Dr John (Mac Rebennack) (*p, v*); Eddie Smith (*bj*); Roger Hill (*g*); Dick Smith (*b*); Vic Pitt (*tba*); Ron Bowden, Norman Emberson, Johnny McCallum (*d*). 12/56–11/84.

****   Chris Barber In Concert: Volumes 1 & 2** Dormouse 23CD/24CD 2CD
     Barber; Pat Halcox (*t*); Monty Sunshine (*cl*); Eddie Smith (*bj*); Dick Smith (*b*); Graham Burbidge (*d*); Ottilie Patterson (*v*). 1 & 3/58.

***(*) **The Classic Concerts: 1959/1961** Chris Barber Collection CBJBCD 4002 CD
Barber; Pat Halcox (*t*); Monty Sunshine (*cl*); Joe Harriott (*as*); Eddie Smith (*bj*); Dick
Smith (*b*); Graham Burbidge (*d*); Ottilie Patterson (*v*). 5/59, 3/61.

***(*) **Trad Tavern** Philips 838397-2 CD
Barber; Pat Halcox (*t*); Ian Wheeler (*cl, as, ss*); Eddie Smith (*bj*); Dick Smith (*b*);
Graham Burbidge (*d*); Ottilie Patterson, Ted Wood (*v*). 60–62.

***(*) **Live In East Berlin** Black Lion BLCD 760502 CD
Barber; Pat Halcox (*t*); John Crocker (*as, cl*); John Slaughter (*g*); Stu Morrison (*bj*);
Jackie Flavelle (*b, v*); Graham Burbidge (*d*). 11/68.

*** **The Grand Reunion Concert** Timeless TTD 553 CD/LP
Barber; Pat Halcox (*t, flhn, v*); Monty Sunshine (*cl*); John Crocker (*cl, as, v*); Lonnie
Donegan (*bj, g, v*); Johnny McCallum (*bj, g*); John Slaughter (*g*); Jim Bray (*b*); Ron
Bowden, Graham Burbidge (*d*). 6/75.

*** **Jazz Zounds: Chris Barber** Zounds 2720008 2CD/2LP
Barber; Pat Halcox (*t, v*); John Crocker (*cl, as, ts*); Ian Wheeler (*cl, as*); John
Slaughter (*g*); Johnny McCallum (*bj, g*); Vic Pitt (*b*); Norman Emberson (*d*);
Rundfunkorchester Berlin. ?

***(*) **Creole Love Call** Timeless TTD 502/3 2LP
As above, except omit Slaughter and Rundfunkorchester Berlin; add Roger Hill (*g*).
10/79 & 3/81.

*** **Live In '85** Timeless TTD 527 CD/LP
As above. 11/85.

***(*) **Chris Barber Meets Rod Mason's Hot Five** Timeless TTD 524 CD
Barber; Rod Mason (*c, v*); Klaus Dau (*tb*); Helm Renz (*cl, as*); Ansgar Bergmann (*p*);
Udo Jagers (*bj*). 8/85.

In his memoir, *Owning Up*, George Melly describes how Chris Barber 'prettified' the
fundamentalist jazz of the 'holy fool', Ken Colyer. Colyer had been jailed in New Orleans,
actually for overstaying his permit, but in the eyes of his acolytes for having dared to play with
black musicians. In Melly's view, Colyer alone could never have brought about the British trad
boom that lasted from the mid-1950s until rock and pop took a solid hold of the music industry
a decade later. Melly presented the trad revolution as if it were the Reformation, purging jazz of
solos and arrangements, bringing it back to the primitive collectivism of the Delta. 'It was
[Ken] who established the totems and taboos, the piano-less rhythm section, the relentless
four-to-the-bar banjo, the loud but soggy thump of the bass drum. Ken invented British
traditional jazz. It wasn't exactly ugly' – as Picasso's primitivist canvases were thought to be
ugly – 'on the contrary, it was quite often touchingly beautiful, but it was clumsy. It needed
prettifying before it could catch on. Chris Barber was there to perform the function.'

Barber had been leading bands while still in his teens, but his first serious attempt was a
co-operative group pulled together in 1953 during Colyer's extended 'vacation' in New Orleans.
Colyer, who had some reason to feel that a *coup d'état* had taken place behind his back, was
invited to join, and he did for a time, until he found himself out of tune with Lonnie Donegan's
grandstanding (Donegan was soon to become a star in his own right) and what he thought of as
the (gasp!) bebop mannerisms that were creeping in. Pat Halcox, who had declined the offer
first time around, joined up and has grown in Barber's company from the slightly raw voice
heard on *Echoes Of Harlem* and *Live In 1954/5* into a first-rate performer with a ringing and
occasionally vocalized tone of some power.

The early live material on London includes two skiffle features for Donegan, whose 'Rock
Island Line' was to become a million-seller. The jazz material (which on *Echoes* takes in a
little-known Ellington tune, 'Doin' The Crazy Walk') is not so much prettified as a 'middle
way' between modern jazz (with accoutrements like solos and formal arrangements) and the
grim nonconformist Protestantism of Colyer's approach. It's hard to over-estimate the
significance of Barber's contribution at this period, or that of Donegan's skiffle, which became
the musical foundation for the Beatles and Herman's Hermits. Melly's description of the music
holds good for *Live In 1954/55* and the Dormouse sessions, which overlap chronologically. It's

awkwardly recorded, the banjo chugs relentlessly and there's a plodding predictability to the bass drum beat.

Things are much better on the other Dormouse compilation (a long concert from Birmingham Town Hall and one from the Dome, Brighton), *The Classic Concerts* and *Trad Tavern*. The Philips is actually shared with material under Pat Halcox's and Ottilie Patterson's leadership, but Barber is the dominant presence; 'Revival' and 'We Shall Walk Through The Streets Of The City' are essential performances, marked by his generously toned tailgating style. A 1962 trio version of 'Body And Soul', not usually thought to be a trad anthem, offers a measure of one of Barber's greatest qualities: his shrewd adaptability. When rock and the British blues scene took off, he added electric basses and guitars to his band, rechristened it the Chris Barber Jazz & Blues Band and secured a haven between what already seemed to be irreconcilable musical tendencies. In the 1980s he has recorded very successfully with the New Orleans legend, Dr John, who (as 'The Night Tripper') was an icon of psychedelic blues in the later '60s; *Take Me Back To New Orleans* [Black Lion BLCD 760163 CD], with Dr John and bass drummer Freddie Kohlman, is not currently in the catalogue, but Dr John can be heard on 'Good Queen Bess' on *30 Years Chris Barber*, a slightly misleading compilation that brings together material from 1956 (a film soundtrack for *Holiday*) and from 1984, but not from the intervening period; so it isn't a handy sampler.

Barber's groups were at their peak in the late 1950s. At the end of the decade they became the first British group to play the blue riband Ed Sullivan Show. 'Bill Bailey', 'Sweet Sue' and 'Georgia Grind' from the Brighton concert (Dormouse) are slightly gentler in outline than the rougher Birmingham material, but there's no mistaking the raw authenticity of the May 1959 sell-out concert at the Deutschhalle in Berlin. There were allegedly 3,000 East Germans in the audience, and it's important to recognize with what respect and seriousness Barber's brand of jazz was regarded in the Eastern bloc; a measure of that respect is the collaboration with the Rundfunkorchester Berlin on the rather overcooked *Jazz Zounds*. In the communist countries, traditional jazz was the spontaneous music of an oppressed proletariat, uncomplicated by formalism or individualism, created collectively. Barber's later *Live In East Berlin* rarely reaches the heights of Ottilie Patterson's unaccompanied intro to 'Easy, Easy, Baby' or the rocking optimism of 'Gotta Travel On', but 'Royal Garden Blues' and 'Sweet As Bear Meat' have an authentic energy that highlights the leader's unironic populism. The East Berlin set also features a superb version of 'Revival' by Joe Harriott, the West Indian-born saxophonist who seemed able to play in any context from trad to free. Harriott guests on 'Revival' at the 1961 London Palladium concert (Classic Concerts), which was a celebration of *Jazz News* poll winners. By 1968, Harriott was a forgotten figure, 'going single' round Britain, a reminder of the kind of suffering and neglect out of which jazz came.

Just because he was successful, Barber never forgot the origins of the music he loved. He has become an important practical historian of early 'hot' music in Britain and has constantly purified his own style. In important essentials, it has not changed in nearly four decades; adaptability has never meant compromise. The later material, notably *Reunion* and *Live In 85*, albeit recorded a decade apart, betrays some signs of rote playing from some of the band, but Sunshine (who went off to make a career of his own on the back of 'Petite Fleur', a 1959 clarinet feature on which Barber did not solo, but which became a major band hit) is an elegant and often moving performer, and Halcox has grown in stature with the years. *Creole Love Call*, though hardly 'fundamentalist', is marvellous, especially 'St Louis Blues' and 'South Rampart Street Parade', and the record with Rod Mason's drummerless but piano'd Hot Five is well worth checking out.

Barber is one of the major figures in British popular music. His longevity is not that of a survivor but of a man whose roots go too deep to be disturbed by mere fashion.

****   **Panama!** Timeless CD TTD 568 CD
       Barber; Wendell Brunious (*t, v*); Pat Halcox (*t*); Ian Wheeler (*cl, as*); John Crocker (*cl, ts*); Johnny McCallum (*bj, g*); Vic Pitt (*b*); John Slaughter (*g*); Russell Gilbrook (*d*). 1/91.

Really a showcase for the young New Orleansian trumpeter, who supplants the long-serving Halcox on most of the solo slots. Brunious builds a lovely solo on the extended 'Georgia On My Mind' and sings in a mournful, wavery mid-tenor. 'Careless Love' features clarinet before the vocal, and then continues with a soft, cry-baby wah-wah chorus on trumpet (presumably from Brunious) that drops behind a delicate banjo and bass accompaniment; McCallum doubles the time on his own intriguingly jittery solo line. Typically well crafted and intelligent, Barber's arrangements of 'Oh! Lady Be Good' and William Tyers's title tune reflect traditional jazz at its best. Barber fans shouldn't miss it and trad enthusiasts should jump at the opportunity to hear Brunious in sympathetic company.

LEANDRO 'GATO' BARBIERI (born 1934)
TENOR SAXOPHONE, FLUTE, PERCUSSION, VOICE

***   **Confluence** Affinity AFF 39 CD
         Barbieri; Dollar Brand (*clo, p*). 3/68.

Barbieri is a classic victim of what is known as Rodin's Syndrome: being best known for your least representative work. Bernardo Bertolucci's *Last Tango In Paris*, as well as working some pretty farfetched variations on 'The Kiss', was graced by one of the most remarkable soundtrack scores of recent times, performed by Barbieri with orchestra. A staple ever since, despite long deletion, *Last Tango* has tended to cloud Barbieri's significance and doubtless helped push him towards the tiresome disco vein of the later '70s.

Two decades before he had been one of the most innovative young horn players working in Europe, where he cut a classic set with Don Cherry (*Complete Communion* – Blue Note (A) BST 84226) and the intermittently available *Obsession* (originally on ESP) under his own name, before establishing himself in the Jazz Composers' Orchestra.

Confluence is an improbable classic, a meeting on neutral ground of two exiles with strong musical roots and, let's say, assertive musical personalities. In the event, the only track that sounds unambiguously like one or the other is the tiny, hymnic 'Hamba Khale!' in which Barbieri patiently follows Brand's abecedarian melody. The rest of the set is freer and more raucous, with Barbieri working in his favourite 'false' upper register and Brand pounding the Fonorama Studio piano into submission. This is what they mean when they talk about World Music; a genuine confluence.

(*)   **Bolivia RCA PD 89559 CD/LP
         Barbieri; Lonnie Liston Smith (*p*); George Dalto (*ky*); John Abercrombie, Paul
         Metzke (*g*); Jean-François Jenny-Clark, Stanley Clark, Chuck Rainey, Ron Carter (*b*);
         Bernard Purdie (*d*); James M'tume, Gene Golden, Sonny Morgan, Babafemi (*congas*);
         Ray Mantilla, Airto Moreira (*perc*); Nana Vasconcelos (*berimbau, perc*); Moulay Ali
         Hafid (*dumbeg*). 71–74.

Symbolic of the state of the Barbieri catalogue, this is a grab-bag of bits from the early '70s. Since it is Barbieri, the bits are better than average, but one yearns for longer sets from each of the three constituent bands. He combines well with the guitarists, the hugely undervalued Metzke in particular, and with his long-standing pianist Smith. Barbieri has an intuitive feel for percussion, as he showed on the now-deleted *Chapter One*, and Moreira is a master at giving quite minimal effects maximum dramatic impact.

Barbieri's own playing is a little off the mark on some of the tracks. For the real 'wind off the pampas' stuff, it's important to get hold of the live Flying Dutchman set *El Pampero* (the track of that name is included here) or Impulse's 1974 live recording at the Bottom Line, New York.

***(*)   **Chapter Three: Viva Emiliano Zapata** Impulse GRP 11112 CD
         Barbieri; Randy Brecker, Bob McCoy, Victor Paz, Alan Rubin (*t, flhn*); Ray Alonge,
         Jimmy Buffington (*frhn*); Buddy Morrow (*tb*); Alan Raph (*btb*); Howard Johnson
         (*tba, flhn, bcl*); Seldon Powell (*f, picc, af, as, bs*); Eddie Martinez (*p, ky*); George
         Davis, Paul Metzke (*g*); Ron Carter (*b*); Grady Tate (*d*); Ray Armando, Luis
         Mangual, Ray Mantilla, Portinho (*perc*). 6/74.

In the early 1970s, Barbieri steadily turned his back on abstraction in an effort to reacquaint himself with his own cultural roots. The breakthrough albums were *The Third World* and *El Pampero*, but then – with *Last Tango In Paris* briefly and lucratively intervening – the saxophonist recorded a sequence of four 'Chapters', the albums that are collectively his most significant. The first, *Latin America*, had an almost wholly 'ethnic' feel, with Barbieri roaring and wailing over a swarming carpet of unusual percussion effects. *Chapters Two* and *Four* are, in their way, much more mainstream; the latter, *Alive In New York*, is one of the great jazz albums of the mid-1970s, alas deleted. Its best moments were a reworking of 'La China

Leoncia' from *Chapter One* and 'Milonga Triste' from *Viva Emiliano Zapata*. The latter is a Cuban-derived *habanera*, thematically very simple. Barbieri builds up the emotion steadily, shifting key and rhythm in relentlessly logical stages, climaxing with one of his false upper-register flag-wavers. The softer cha-cha rhythm of 'Lluvia Azul' allows the subtle orchestration to show through. 'El Sublime' is in Barbieri's favourite double waltz time, a metre that permits the most flexible phrasing and occasional syncopation of notes. It's unusual to find Barbieri playing a standard, but the arrangement of 'What A Difference A Day Makes' goes under the unfamiliar title 'Cuando Vuelva A Tu Lado' and does so without a trace of an accent. The closing title-track has no explicit programme, but it's clear from Barbieri's burning solo that he isn't just spraying slogans on walls for the hell of it.

JEROME BARDE (born 1963)
GUITAR

**   **Feliz** Sunnyside SSC 1042 CD/LP
      Barde; Kirk Lightsey (*p*); Rufus Reid (*b*); Billy Hart (*d*). 9/89.

The Frenchman is obviously a capable player, but this debut session is poorly characterized: nine of the ten tracks are originals and most of them lack real interest, while Barde struggles to find common ground with his accompanists. If it falls agreeably on the ear, this slice of modern mainstream offers little more than that and, at 75 minutes, has too much music for its own good.

A. SPENCER BAREFIELD
GUITAR, 12-STRING GUITAR, SYNTHESIZER

**   **Live At Nickelsdorf Konfrontation** sound aspects 007 LP
      Barefield; Anthony Holland (*as, ss*); Tani Tabbal (*d, perc*). 6/84.

**   **After The End** sound aspects 030 LP
      Barefield; Hugh Ragin (*t*); Oliver Lake (*as*); Richard Davis (*b*); Andrew Cyrille (*d*);
      Ballade String Quartet. 10/87.

These are slightly tentative sets, full of good ideas and fine playing, but ultimately a little diffuse. Barefield, perhaps best known for his work with Roscoe Mitchell's Sound/Space Ensembles, is a fine guitarist who works at the opposite pole from the Sonny Sharrock/James 'Blood' Ulmer *Sturm und Drang* school. His acoustic figures are almost classical in execution, and the appearance of a string quartet – albeit in hectically improvisatory mode – on the title-track of *After The End* only reinforces the impression. He combines well with both Lake and Holland, saxophonists of like persuasion, while Tabbal, Davis and Cyrille knock out the kind of metre he appears to prefer. Perhaps the most striking thing on either album is Ragin's bat-squeak trumpet. Barefield is someone to watch; but these are for converts only.

GUY BARKER
TRUMPET

(*)   **Holly J Miles Music MM078 LP
      Barker; Nigel Hitchcock (*as, ts*); Jason Rebello (*p*); Frank Ricotti (*vib*); Chris
      Laurence (*b*); Clark Tracey (*d*). 3/89.

A characteristic statement from the modern British mainstream: Barker's trumpet pays homage by implication to Hubbard, Morgan and Brown, Hitchcock plays the kind of second-fiddle role associated with James Spaulding at Blue Note, and the rhythm section – even with the more experienced Laurence and Ricotti on hand – is similarly neo-classic. The results are as capable and predictable as one might expect.

JOHN BARNES (born 1932)
CLARINET, SOPRANO, ALTO, TENOR AND BARITONE SAXOPHONES

(*)   **Fancy Our Meeting! Calligraph CLG 019 LP/MC
Barnes; Alan Barnes (*ss, as, cl*); Colin Bates (*p*); Ian Scott Taylor (*b*); Eddie Taylor (*d*). 9/88.

Barnes the elder has been a familiar voice in British jazz for decades, but this is the only album under his own leadership: most of his best work on record is with either Alex Welsh or Humphrey Lyttelton. He plays with consummate authority here and sets down a definitive 'Stardust' on baritone (probably his most distinctive horn), along with shrewd meditations on 'Moonlight Becomes You', 'It Happened In Monterey' and a couple of inoffensive originals, Barnes the younger assisting here and there. It's a pity, though, that the record is largely let down by the rhythm section, which has perhaps grown so used to this sort of guileful mainstream that it forgets to inject any real drive or finesse into the music, and the production, which is smooth and anodyne enough to lend an air of elevator music to a set that deserves better. Consult the Lyttelton and Welsh sections to hear more of Barnes.

WALTER BARNES (1905–40)
TENOR SAX, BANDLEADER

***   **Walter Barnes And George E. Lee** Retrieval FJ-125 LP
Barnes; Cicero Thomas, George Thigpen (*t*); Ed Bruke, William 'Bullett' Bradley (*tb*); Irby Gage, Wilson Underwood (*cl, as*); Lucius Wilson (*ts*); Paul Johnson (*p*); Plunker Hall (*bj*); Louis Thompson (*bb*); Billy Winston (*d*). 12/28–7/29.

Barnes led his Royal Creolians for many years, but the ten tracks collected here are the only records he ever made. His own playing is undistinguished, but the music is a pleasing if often ragged example of a second-division black band of the day setting down the best of their repertoire for posterity. Thomas is the one outstanding soloist: although the recording suggests a rather thin tone, he plays with real flair and no lack of zip. The reeds are unfortunately sloppy on occasion, a defect made more pronounced by the intricacy of some of the scores, but the rhythm section plays with great drive and Hall and Thompson are both outstandingly good in their roles. Their most famous piece, 'Third Rail', appears in two takes, and it still sounds like an exciting set-piece. The remastering is well up to Retrieval's high standards. The rest of the LP is devoted to various bands led by George E. Lee. Barnes never recorded again, and he came to a sad end when he and most of his band perished in a ballroom fire in Natchez in 1940.

CHARLIE BARNET (1913–91)
TENOR, ALTO AND SOPRANO SAXOPHONES

***(*)   **Cherokee** RCA Bluebird ND 90632 CD
Barnet; Charles Huffine, Bobby Burnet, Marshall Mendel, Johnny Owens, Billy May, Lyman Vunk, George Esposito (*t*); Ben Hall, Don Ruppersberg, Bill Roberston, Spud Murphy, Ford Leary (*tb*); Don McCook (*cl, as*); Gene Kinsey, Skippy Martin, Leo White, Conn Humphries (*as*); Kurt Bloom (*ts*); Jimmy Lamare (*bs*); Bill Miller, Nat Jaffe (*p*); Bus Etri (*g*); Phil Stephens (*b*); Wesley Dean, Ray Michaels, Cliff Leeman (*d*). 1/39–1/41.

****   **Drop Me Off In Harlem** MCA GRP 16122 CD
Barnet; Peanuts Holland, Irving Berger, Joe Ferrante, Chuck Zimmerman, Al Killian, Jimmy Pupa, Lyman Vunk, Roy Eldridge, Art House, Johnny Martel, Jack Mootz, Everett McDonald, George Seaberg, Ed Stress, Paul Webster, Art Robey (*t*); Russ Brown, Kahn Keene, Wally Baron, Bill Robertson, Eddie Bert, Ed Fromm, Spud Murphy, Bob Swift, Porky Cohen, Tommy Pedersen, Ben Pickering, Charles Coolidge, Gerald Foster, Dave Hallett, Burt Johnson, Frank Bradley, Lawrence Brown (*tb*); George Bone, Conn Humphries, Murray Williams, Buddy DeFranco, Ray DeGeer, Harold Herzon, Joe Meisner, Gene Kinsey, Les Robinson (*as*); Kurt Bloom, Mike Goldberg, Ed Pripps, Kenny Dehlin, Dave Mathews (*ts*); James Lamare, Danny Bank,

Bob Poland, Bob Dawes (*bs*); Bill Miller, Dodo Marmarosa, Al Haig, Sheldon Smith (*p*); Tommy Moore, Turk Van Lake, Barney Kessel, Dennis Sandole (*g*); Jack Jarvis, Russ Wagner, Andy Riccardi, Howard Rumsey, John Chance, Morris Rayman, Irv Lang (*b*); Cliff Leeman, Harold Hahn, Mickey Scrima (*d*); Frances Wayne, Kay Starr (*v*). 4/42–6/46.

Although a handful of Barnet's records – especially his big hits 'Cherokee' and 'Skyliner' – stand as staples of the big-band era, he's generally been less than well served critically and by jazz collectors: only these two albums remain easily available, and all his later work for Capitol is out of print. His own playing – which always points to Johnny Hodges as a first influence, and splendidly so – is usually restricted to a few telling bars, but he was an enthusiastic advocate of other, greater players, and remains one of the few bandleaders to have virtually ignored racial distinctions. It may have cost him dear in career terms, too, though Barnet (of a very wealthy background) never seems to have cared very much.

The Bluebird set (an earlier, more comprehensive disc of his Bluebird period has recently been deleted, though copies may still be in circulation) is a fine introduction: the 11 tracks are more like skilful patchworks of other orchestras, especially those of Basie and Ellington, than original frameworks, but the sparkle of 'Redskin Rumba', 'The Count's Idea' and the original hit reading of 'Cherokee' have weathered the years very well. Maybe his 'Rockin' In Rhythm' sounds mechanized next to the natural swing of any Ellington version, but Barnet's admiration for his contemporary was genuine, and it makes the band sound at a level a long way ahead of such commercial rivals as Glenn Miller.

The tracks collected on the MCA compilation are, though, better still. Arranger Andy Gibson (ex-Basie) turned in charts such as that for 'Shady Lady', which find new tone colours for the sections; key soloists included Roy Eldridge and Dodo Marmarosa, and lead trumpeter Al Killian gave the brass a stratospheric punch which would only be equalled only in the next decade by the young Maynard Ferguson. Of the 20 tracks collected here, the pick include the still-glorious hit 'Skyliner', Eldridge's murderous romp through 'Drop Me Off In Harlem', Barnet's own not undistinguished playing on 'West End Blues', the tongue-in-cheek menace of 'Pow-Wow', and above all Ralph Burns's astonishing arrangement to feature Marmarosa on 'The Moose', a chart that anticipates so much of bebop (both men were still only teenagers at the time, which gives the lie to the 'modern' movement of jazz masters barely involved in manhood). Many of Barnet's records still lacked the last shred of individuality which would have allotted him a place right next to Ellington or Basie, but he was already starting to sound more riskily modern than either of those leaders. The remastering of both records has been capably done: there is no scratch on the MCA tracks, though some of the reproduction is a little muffled, and the Bluebird music, while cheerfully radiating a little crackle, is perhaps a shade more lively.

JOEY BARON
DRUMS, ELECTRONICS

*** **Miniature** JMT 834423 CD/LP
Baron; Tim Berne (*as*); Hank Roberts (*clo, elec, v*). 3/88.

(**) **Tongue In Groove JMT 849158 CD
Baron; Steve Swell (*tb*); Ellery Eskelin (*ts*). 5/91.

Baron has an interesting list of credits, taking in sessions for Jim Hall and Toots Thielemans, as well as most of the leading lights of the downtown, post-Ornette school of noise-orientated sophisticates who record for JMT. *Miniature* is strongly influenced by Coleman's harmolodic revolution, but it's also a melodists' album that takes in elements of Bill Frisell's fractured country sound ('Circular Prairie Song' is dedicated to the guitarist) as well as black, hip-hop and free elements. Co-credited to Berne and Roberts, both excellent writers, it's accessible and well recorded.

Tongue In Groove – or, more plausibly, in cheek – is characterized as an 'all-acoustic, all-live, no mix, no edit, gutbucket digital recording', which is pretty much how it sounds, all sharp, splintery edges and untrimmed takes with a lot of fuzz and dirt in all the places where one might like to hear the detail unimpeded. Baron sounds thrashier than usual and the unusual instrumentation makes very few compromises. Sixteen tracks and only two topping five minutes, so the pace is quite ferocious. Fascinating music, but a cleaned-up mix wouldn't have hurt.

DAN BARRETT
TROMBONE

*** **Strictly Instrumental** Concord CCD 4331 CD/MC
Barrett; Warren Vaché (c); Chuck Wilson (as); Ken Peplowski (cl, ts); Howard Alden (g); Dick Wellstood (p); Jack Lesberg (b); Jackie Williams (d). 6/87.

Dan Barrett is a formidably talented technician on the most problematic of jazz instruments, but he has a shrewd musical mind too. This session is perhaps a little too smoothly mainstream, in the accredited Concord manner but, by mixing standards with surprise choices ('Quasimodo' and 'Minor Infraction'), Barrett tips one off that he doesn't think everything stops with swing. The band is a blend of youth and experience, too, with the leader, Vaché and Peplowski a strong front line and the dependable Wellstood underscoring the variations in texture. Barrett will surely have more adventurous records ahead of him.

BILL BARRON (1932–90)
TENOR AND SOPRANO SAXOPHONE

*** **Jazz Caper** Muse MR 5235 LP
Barron; Jimmy Owens (t); Kenny Barron (p); Buster Williams (b); Ed Blackwell (d). 8/78.

*** **Variations In Blue** Muse MR 5306 LP
Barron; Jimmy Owens (t); Kenny Barron (p); Ray Drummond (b); Ben Riley (d). 8/83.

*** **The Next Plateau** Muse M 5368 CD/LP
Barron; Kenny Barron (p); Ray Drummond (b); Ben Riley (d). 3/87.

Less renowned than his pianist brother Kenny, Bill Barron was a hard bop tenorman with a grouchy tone and a broad vocabulary of short, legato phrases that made him resemble a less amiable Dexter Gordon. He appeared on Cecil Taylor's 1959 *Love For Sale* session but seldom recorded in the years prior to his death. All the same, these three sessions for Muse are a fine memorial to his carefully wrought methods. Both *Jazz Caper* and *Variations In Blue* offer a stack of thoughtfully arranged material, nothing especially adventurous but all of it slightly off-centre from the customary hard bop blowing date. Owens plays smart and ingratiating trumpet and the rhythm players respond with interest.

The Next Plateau, his final record, is a fine, mature statement of modern hard bop, with six interesting original tunes and the fluent support of a rhythm section that knew the leader well. Barron invests his material with considerable intellectual fire without sacrificing the excitement or swing. It's to be hoped that his important 1962 *Modern Windows* set will appear on CD in due course.

KENNY BARRON (born 1943)
PIANO

***(*) **Sunset To Dawn** Muse MCD 5018 CD/LP/MC
Barron; Warren Smith (vib, perc); Bob Cranshaw (b); Freddie Waits (d); Richard Landrum (perc). 73.

**** **Peruvian Blue** Muse MR 5044 LP/MC
Barron; Ted Dunbar (g); David Williams (b); Albert Heath (d); Richard Landrum, Sonny Morgan (perc). 3/74.

*** **Lucifer** Muse MR 5070 LP/MC
Barron; Charles Sullivan (t); Bill Barron (ss); James Spaulding (as, bf); Carlos Alomar (g); Chris White (b); Billy Hart (d). 4/75.

***(*)   **In Tandem** Muse MR 5140 LP/MC
Barron; Ted Dunbar (*g*).

***(*)   **Golden Lotus** Muse MR 5220 LP/MC
Barron; John Stubblefield (*ts*); Steve Nelson (*vib*); Buster Williams (*b*); Ben Riley
(*d*).

****   **Green Chimneys** Criss Cross Jazz Criss 1008 CD
Barron; Buster Williams (*b*); Ben Riley (*d*). 7/83.

***(*)   **1 + 1 + 1** Black-Hawk 50601 LP/MC
Barron; Ron Carter, Michael Moore (*b*). 4/84.

***   **Landscape** Limetree MLP 0020 CD/LP
Barron; Cecil McBee (*b*); Al Foster (*d*). 10/84.

***(*)   **Scratch** Enja 4092 CD/LP/MC
Barron; Dave Holland (*b*); Daniel Humair (*d*). 3/85.

***   **What If** Enja 5013 CD/LP/MC
Barron; Wallace Roney (*t*); John Stubblefield (*ts*); Cecil McBee (*b*); Victor Lewis (*d*).
2/86.

***   **Live At Fat Tuesday's** Enja 5071 CD/LP
Barron; Eddie Henderson (*t*); John Stubblefield (*ts*); Cecil McBee (*b*); Victor Lewis
(*d*). 1/88.

(*)   **Rhythm-A-Ning Candid CCD 79044 CD
Barron; John Hicks (*p*); Walter Booker (*b*); Jimmy Cobb (*d*). 9/89.

Barron came to notice during a short stint with multi-instrumentalist Yusef Lateef in 1961, having previously played in R&B bands with his elder brother, Bill Barron. At nineteen, he replaced Lalo Schifrin in Dizzy Gillespie's group and worked with the trumpeter for nearly five years, subsequently rejoining Lateef and playing with Freddie Hubbard and Yusef Lateef.

Barron has a funky, angular style that owes something to Monk, but is highly adept at lighter samba lines, romantic ballads and orthodox minor blues. His versatility is well attested in over 70 recordings, mostly as sideman but with a substantial number under his own name. The Muses are consistently good, with fine, inventive programmes and excellent sound. Barron fans may feel that *Sunset To Dawn*, the only item from the catalogue to have been transferred to CD, still sounds rather better on vinyl, minus the rather brittle edge that digitalization sometimes brings. It's a fine album, if a little less adventurous than later trio sessions with Dave Holland and Daniel Humair, Cecil McBee and Al Foster, Buster Williams and Ben Riley.

Of the Muses, by far the best is the rather dubiously titled *Peruvian Blue*. Barron's additional debt to Bud Powell is evident on his unaccompanied exposition and development of 'Here's That Rainy Day', but the real stand-out track is a reading of 'Blue Monk' that involves him in some astonishing interplay with the much underrated guitarist Ted Dunbar (compare the pianist's work with Larry Coryell on *Shining Hour*, MR 5360) which anticipates their collaboration on *In Tandem*.

The later work is mostly disappointing in comparison, but only the misconceived *Rhythm-A-Ning* is a real clunker, with the two-piano front line never sounding remotely convincing. There are good things on almost all of these records, though, and Barron, who has suffered the kind of critical invisibility that comes with ubiquity, shouldn't be overlooked.

GARY BARTZ (born 1940)
ALTO SAXOPHONE; ALSO SOPRANO SAXOPHONE, CLARINET, FLUTE, WOOD FLUTE

(*)   **Monsoon SteepleChase SCS 1234 CD/LP
Bartz; Butch Lacy (*p*); Clint Houston (*b*); Billy Hart (*d*). 4/88.

**   **Reflections Of Monk** SteepleChase SCS 1248 CD/LP
Bartz; Eddie Henderson (*t*); Bob Butta (*p*); Geoff Harper (*b*); Billy Hart (*d*); Jenelle
Fisher, Mekea Keith (*v*). 11/88.

In 1972, Bartz was collecting poll wins like beer mats. By the end of the decade he was playing, er, disco, a shift of idiom perhaps blessed by his one-time boss Miles Davis and one by no means out of keeping with the tenor – or, in this case, alto – of the times.

What was galling was that Bartz had quickly been identified, by Max Roach and Art Blakey before Miles, as one of the finest young saxophone voices of the time, perhaps the best since Jackie McLean. These recent sets mark a partial return to form. Whether at near-fifty he still cuts it like he used to remains more or less non-proven. Both albums seems slightly tentative, a little uncertain in register and far from instantly compelling. There is a fine 'Soul Eyes' on *Monsoon*, but the Monk covers are slightly robotic despite Eddie Henderson's fine contribution. The superadded vocals on 'Monk's Mood' and 'Reflections' were a mistake (Jenelle Fisher's no Abbey Lincoln). Enough of the Wunderkind survives in Bartz to guarantee listenability, but not much more than that.

***(*) **West 42nd Street** Candid CCD79049 CD
Bartz; Claudio Roditi (*t, flhn*); John Hicks (*p*); Ray Drummond (*b*); Al Foster (*d*). 3/90.

Sometimes, just sometimes, when a saxophone player climbs the stand at Birdland and lays a reed on his tongue, a tubby ghost wobbles unsteadily out of the shadows and whispers in his ear. Bartz plays like a man inspired, turning 'It's Easy To Remember' into a huge romantic edifice, from which he soars into 'Cousins' and a surprisingly Coltraneish 'The Night Has A Thousand Eyes'. Hicks is the best piano player Bartz has come across in years, and Al Foster sends little whiplash flicks down the line of the metre, coaxing the three main soloists on to even better things. Slightly exhausting, in the way a hot club set teeters between euphoria and growing weariness, but a more than welcome confirmation of Bartz's long-latent qualities. Strongly recommended.

**** **There Goes The Neighbourhood!** Candid CCD79506 CD
Bartz; Kenny Barron (*p*); Ray Drummond (*b*); Ben Riley (*d*). 11/90.

Bartz's finest hour. The opening 'Racism' is a boiling blues in double B flat minor, an original played with an increasingly noticeable Coltrane inflexion. The first of two Tadd Dameron compositions, 'On A Misty Night', was originally recorded in the mid-1950s by a band that included Coltrane; the mid-point of the set is a severe interpretation of 'Impressions'. Bartz's homage isn't limited to a growing repertoire of anguished cries and dissonant transpositions. He has also paid attention to how the younger Coltrane framed a solo; working against the trajectory of Dameron's theme, he constructs an ascending line that culminates each time in a beautifully placed false note.

Johnny Mercer's 'Laura' receives a serene and stately reading, with Drummond featured. Bartz's coda restatement is masterful. He tackles 'Impressions' in the most boiled-down way, with only minimal rhythmic support, concentrating on the basic musical information. Barron returns to the foreground for 'I've Never Been In Love' and the closing 'Flight Path', his own composition. Throughout, his touch is light but definite, freeing his accompaniments of any excess baggage.

Though previously Charles McPherson and Bobby Watson have laid claim to Parker's alto crown, Bartz appears to have come into his kingdom at last. A superb album that will grace any collection; recorded live at Birdland, it's beautifully balanced and free from extraneous noise.

COUNT BASIE (1904–84)
PIANO, ORGAN

***** **The Original American Decca Recordings** MCA GRP 36112 3CD/3MC
Basie; Buck Clayton, Joe Keyes, Carl Smith, Ed Lewis, Bobby Moore, Kar⎪
Harry Edison, Shad Collins (*t*); Eddie Durham (*tb, g*); George Hunt, Da⎪
Benny Morton, Dicky Wells (*tb*); Jack Washington (*as, bs*); Caughey ⎪
Warren (*as*); Lester Young, Herschel Evans (*cl, ts*); Chu Berry (*ts*); ⎪
Freddie Green (*g*); Walter Page (*b*); Jo Jones (*d*); Jimmy Rushing⎪
1/37–2/39.

**** **Listen . . . You Shall Hear** Hep CD 1025 CD
As above. 1–10/37.

****   **Do You Wanna Jump . . . ?** Hep CD 1027 CD
As above. 1–11/38.

****   **Count Basie Volume One 1932–1938** BBC RP 785 CD/MC
As above, except add Hot Lips Page, Dee Stewart (*t*), Ben Webster (*ts*), Leroy Berry
(*g*), Willie McWashington (*d*). 12/32–6/38.

***   **Jive At Five** ASV AJA 5089 CD
As above. 12/32–2/39.

****   **Count Basie 1936–1938** Classics 503 CD
As MCA disc, except omit Collins, Edison, Wells, Berry and Humes. 10/36–1/38.

****   **Count Basie 1938–39** Classics 504 CD
As above, except omit Keyes, Smith, Hunt, Roberts and Williams, add Harry Edison,
Shad Collins (*t*), Dicky Wells (*tb*) and Helen Humes (*v*). 1/38–1/39.

The arrival of the Count Basie band – on an East Coast scene dominated by Ellington,
Lunceford and Henderson – set up a new force in the swing era, and hearing their records from
the late 1930s is still a marvellous, enthralling experience. Basie's Kansas City band was a
rough-and-ready outfit compared with the immaculate drive of Lunceford or Ellington's urbane
mastery, but rhythmically it might have been the most swinging band of its time, based around
the perfectly interlocking team of Basie, Green, Page and Jones, but also in the freedom of
soloists such as Lester Young, Buck Clayton and Herschel Evans, in the intuitive momentum
created within the sections (famously, Basie had relatively few written-out arrangements and
would instead evolve head arrangements on the stand) and in the best singing team of any
working with the big bands, Helen Humes and the incomparable Jimmy Rushing. There are
paradoxical elements – the minimalism of the leader's piano solos that is nevertheless as
invigorating as any chunk of fast stride piano, Green's invisible yet indispensable chording, the
power of the band which still seems to drift rather than punch its way off the record. Yet they all
go to make up an orchestra unique in jazz.

There are too many great individual records to cite here, and instead we shall note only that
there are two significant early periods covered by reissues, the Decca tracks (1937–39) and the
subsequent recordings for Vocalion, Okeh and Columbia (1939–42). A contractual oddity is
that Basie's first session – credited to Jones-Smith Inc, and marking the astonishing debut of
Lester Young on record – was made for Columbia rather than Decca, yet the Columbia reissues
haven't even put the four tracks together. Two of them are on the hotchpotch *Jive At Five*, but
the first Classics CD has them all together. For a definitive study of the Decca sides, one must
look to either the Hep or the MCA CDs. The Hep discs only go as far as the 1939 'Panassie
Stomp', while the MCA is complete to 1939 on three CDs. There is actually very little to choose
between the transfers: the Hep remastering is sometimes a little more full-bodied, but the MCA
is mostly smoother and often a little brighter. But given the completeness and the handsome
packaging on the MCA discs (a contrast to the misleadingly amateurish-looking Hep CDs), we
have awarded them top marks for what is desert-island music.

The Classics CDs, as usual, ignore any 'label' boundaries and simply go through all the music
chronologically, although no alternative takes are included. The transfers here are
unpredictable. Some seem to have a lot of reverberation, which suggests second-hand tape
transfers, and while all the discs sound good enough they can't compete with the Hep or MCA
sets. A fourth CD issue has also been commenced by the French EPM label but as we go to
press we have not been able to examine copies.

(***)   **The Essential Count Basie Vol. 1** CBS 460061 CD/MC
As above. 10/36–6/39.

(***)   **The Essential Count Basie Vol. 2** Columbia CK 40835 CD/MC
Similar to above. 8/39–5/40.

(***)   **The Essential Count Basie Vol. 3** Columbia CK 44150 CD/MC
Similar to above. 8/40–4/41.

***(*)   **Count Basie 1939** Classics 513 CD
Basie; Buck Clayton, Ed Lewis, Harry Edison, Shad Collins (*t*); Dicky Wells, Benny
Morton, Dan Minor (*tb*); Earl Warren (*as*); Jack Washington (*as, bs*); Chu Berry,

Buddy Tate, Lester Young (*cl, ts*); Freddie Green (*g*); Walter Page (*b*); Jo Jones (*d*); Jimmy Rushing, Helen Humes (*v*). 1–4/39.

***(*)   **Count Basie 1939 Vol. 2** Classics 533 CD
As above, except omit Berry. 5–11/39.

***   **Count Basie 1939–1940** Classics 563 CD
As above, except add Al Killian (*t*), Tab Smith (*ss, as*), omit Collins. 11/39–10/40.

***   **Count Basie 1940–1941** Classics 623 CD
As above, except add Ed Cuffee (*tb*), Paul Bascomb, Coleman Hawkins (*ts*). 11/40–4/41.

It's a pity that Basie's second wave hasn't been as well served by Columbia as his first has been by other companies. The three volumes of 'Essential' Basie haven't been treated with the kind of care which the 'essential' should merit: muddy, lifeless transfers do a disservice to the music, which is almost but irritatingly not quite chronological or complete. The Classics CDs are again uneven but are surely a better bet.

The great change which commenced this Basie era was the sad death of Herschel Evans, 'the greatest jazz musician I ever played with in my life', as Jo Jones remembered him. In many ways, the band was never the same again. Evans's partnership with Lester Young had given the reed section its idiosyncratic fluency, and in a way his death marked the end of the original Basie era, when the band relied on its individual players to combine and create the instinctive Basie sound. That said, Chu Berry was a more than capable replacement for Evans, and the orchestra was still approaching a technical peak. Other arrivals – Shad Collins, Tab Smith – who also did some strong arrangements – and later Buddy Tate, when Berry also departed, also had an impact on the band, and emerging arrangers (Andy Gibson, Buck Clayton) had a beneficial effect. But Basie was already steeped in a routine of riffs, conventional harmonies and familiar patterns, which even the soloists (including the finally disenfranchised Young) couldn't really transcend, let alone transform. Taken a few at a time, these tracks are fine, but all together they can be sometimes dull as full-length records.

Highlights to listen for are 'Evil Blues', a memorable band performance, Lester Young's solo on 'Taxi War Dance' (both Classics 513), 'Clap Hands, Here Comes Charlie' and the Kansas City Seven date of September 1939 (all Classics 533), 'Blow Top' (Classics 563), Clayton's 'Love Jumped Out' and Helen Humes's delightful vocal on 'My Wanderin' Man' (both Classics 623). There are plenty of other interludes and solos to savour: this was too good a band to lack interest. Coleman Hawkins also makes a guest appearance on two tracks on Classics 623. But the paucity of genuinely memorable compositions and Basie's own leaning towards ensemble punch and exactness over personal flair sows the seeds of the band's decline.

There are also Basie's own piano 'solos' (actually with the rhythm section), ten of which were recorded in 1938–39 (they are split between Classics 503, 504 and 513). Basie had long since started to pare away the more florid and excitable elements of his early stride style, and by now was cutting down to the bone. It works best on the elegance of 'How Long' and the almost playful feel accorded to 'Fare Thee Well, Honey, Fare Thee Well'. They also let the great rhythm section display itself away from the confines of the band, and one can hear how perfectly the team interlocks. But they also expose something of the repetitiousness and sometimes false economies of Basie's playing, even at the curtailed 78rpm length.

***(*)   **The Jubilee Alternatives** Hep CD 38 CD
Basie; Harry Edison, Al Killian, Ed Lewis, Snooky Young (*t*); Eli Robinson, Robert Scott, Louis Taylor, Dicky Wells (*tb*); Jimmy Powell, Earl Warren (*as*); Buddy Tate, Lester Young, Illinois Jacquet (*ts*); Rudy Rutherford (*bs, cl*); Freddie Green (*g*); Rodney Richardson (*b*); Jo Jones, Buddy Rich (*d*); Thelma Carpenter, Jimmy Rushing (*v*). 12/43–10/44.

Splendidly remastered in very crisp sound, these studio 'alternatives' to AFRS Jubilee show broadcasts give a useful impression of a transitional Basie band. Buddy Rich and Illinois Jacquet replace Jones and Young on some tracks, and the brass section is largely different to the previous commercial studio tracks. There are some good charts here – Andy Gibson's freshly paced 'Andy's Blues', Clayton's excellent 'Avenue C', and Tab Smith's 'Harvard Blues', one of the best of the later Columbias, with a repeat performance of the tour de force vocal by Jimmy Rushing – and many of the soloists sound in unusually lively form.

***(*) **Beaver Junction** Vintage Jazz Classics VJC-CD-1018 CD
As above, except add Buck Clayton, Karl George (*t*), J. J. Johnson (*tb*), Lucky Thompson (*ts*), Shadow Wilson, Joe Marshall (*d*). 44–46.

More Jubilee and V-Disc material, in excellent shape and featuring all the strengths of the mid-1940s band. Similar material to the above, but there are one or two previously unavailable tracks, and with all the remastering done from clean glass acetates, the sound is uncommonly bright and clear.

*** **Count Basie And His Orchestra – 1944** Circle CCD-60 CD
Similar to above. 1/44.

Cut in a single three-hour session, these are 16 transcriptions from the Lang-Worth service. Another solid Basie session with staples from his then-current book, three rather gooey ballads sung by Earl Warren and only two features for Rushing. Hardly essential but the sound of the transcriptions is exceptionally clear and fresh.

*** **Brand New Wagon** RCA Bluebird ND 82292 CD/LP/MC
Basie; Harry Edison, Ed Lewis, Emmett Berry, Snooky Young (*t*); Bill Johnson, Ted Donnelly, George Matthews, Dickie Wells, George Simon, George Washington, Eli Robinson (*tb*); Preston Love, Rudy Rutherford, C. Q. Price (*as*); Paul Gonsalves, Buddy Tate (*ts*); Jack Washington (*bs*); Freddie Green (*g*); Walter Page (*b*); Jo Jones (*d*); Jimmy Rushing (*v*). 1–12/47.

*** **Basie's Basement** RCA Bluebird ND 90630 CD
As above, except add Clark Terry, Gerald Wilson, Jimmy Nottingham (*t*), Earl Warren, W Parker (*as*), S Palmer (*b*), Butch Ballard (*d*). 1/47–7/49.

Basie signed a three-year contract with Victor in 1947, and the results have usually been regarded as something of a low point in his discography. But this set of 21 tracks from that intitial year present a good set of Basie performances, even if they show little sign of any marked change from the formula which had been enveloping the orchestra over the previous seven years. Gonsalves, seldom remembered as a Basieite, turns in some strong solos, 'Swingin' The Blues' and 'Basie's Basement' trim the band down to a small group without losing any impact, and there is the usual ration of features for Jimmy Rushing, always worth hearing. The sound hasn't been best served by the NoNOISE process of remastering but will suffice. The subsequent *Basie's Basement* takes ten tracks from the earlier CD and adds a single 1949 recording. The sound is bigger but also seems over-resonant and booms in the bass.

*** **Americans In Sweden Vol. 1** Tax CD 3701-2 CD
Basie; Reunald Jones, Joe Wilder, Wendell Culley, Joe Newman (*t*); Bill Hughes, Henry Coker, Benny Powell (*tb*); Marshall Royal (*as, cl*); Ernie Wilkins (*as, ts*); Frank Wess (*ts, f*); Frank Foster (*ts*); Charlie Fowlkes (*bs*); Freddie Green (*g*); Eddie Jones (*b*); Gus Johnson (*d*). 3/54.

*** **Americans In Sweden Vol. 2** Tax CD 3702-2 CD
As above. 3/54.

** **Class Of '54** Black Lion BLCD CD
As above, except Thad Jones (*t*) replaces Wilder. 9/54.

Basie had been obliged to work with an octet rather than a full band in 1950–51, but he put a new orchestra together the following year, and from then on he always remained in charge of a big band. It was the start of the 'modern' Basie era. By taking arrangements from a new team, of which the most important was Neal Hefti, Basie made the most of a formidable new reed section, trumpets that streamlined the old Basie fire with absolute precision, and the first of a line of effusive drummers, Gus Johnson. The new soloists were showstoppers, but in a rather hard, sometimes brittle way, and Basie's belief in the primacy of the riff now led inexorably to arrangements which had screaming brass piled on top of crooning reeds on top of thunderous drums: it was a fearsome and in its way very exciting effect.

The two Tax CDs come from what was Basie's first European tour, and the sound is very good for the period, with only a few balance problems for the rhythm section: the brass and reeds come through very strikingly. In set-pieces like Foster's flag-waving solo on 'Jumpin' At The Woodside', Hefti's glittering charts for 'Fancy Meeting You' and 'Two Franks', and similarly punchy efforts by John Mandel and Buster Harding, all the gusto of the new Basie band comes powering through. The Black Lion CD mixed tracks by a nonet drawn from the band and others from a 1954 radio concert, though the sound is much less attractive on this disc, and the Tax CDs give a much better impression of the band as it then was.

***   **April In Paris** Verve 825575-2 CD
Basie; Reunald Jones, Thad Jones, Joe Newman, Wendell Culley (*t*); Benny Powell, Henry Coker, Matthew Gee (*tb*); Marshall Royal (*cl, as*); Bill Graham (*as*); Frank Wess (*ts, f*); Frank Foster (*ts*); Charlie Fowlkes (*bs*); Freddie Green (*b*); Eddie Jones (*b*); Sonny Payne (*d*); Joe Williams (*v*). 1/56.

***   **Basie In London** Verve 833805-2 CD
As above. 9/56.

***   **Live In Basel 1956** Jazz Helvet JH 05 2CD
As above. 9/56.

***   **Compact Jazz: Count Basie And Joe Williams** Verve 835329-2 CD
As above, except add Ella Fitzgerald (*v*). 55–56.

(*)   **Count Basie At Newport Verve 833776-2 CD
As above, except add Roy Eldridge (*t*), Illinois Jacquet, Lester Young (*ts*), Jo Jones (*d*), Jimmy Rushing (*v*). 7/57.

Facsimile editions of some of the most significant of Basie's Verve albums from the 1950s – *Dance Session No 1* and *No 2*, and *The Band Of Distinction* – have yet to appear. Of the three originals now on CD, *April In Paris* and *Basie In London* are typical Basie fare of the period, bustling charts, leathery solos and pinpoint timing. *At Newport* is a fun reunion with some of Basie's old sidemen (though Young sounds as wayward as he usually then was) and features Eldridge going several miles over the top on 'One O'Clock Jump'. The compilation of material with Joe Williams spotlights Basie's new singer: rich-toned, as oleaginous as Billy Eckstine could be, yet with a feeling for the blues which at least came some way near the irreplaceable Rushing, Williams's smoothness and debonair manner fitted the new Basie band almost perfectly. The compilation includes 'Alright, Okay, You Win' and 'Every Day I Have The Blues' among several of his best-known songs. The Jazz Helvet double-CD catches the band on tour in this period, and chronicles a typical set with all the favourites intact in quite listenable sound.

****   **The Atomic Mr Basie** Roulette CDP 7932732 CD
Basie; Joe Newman, Thad Jones, Wendell Culley, Snooky Young (*t*); Benny Powell, Henry Coker, Al Grey (*tb*); Marshall Royal, Frank Wess (*as*); Eddie Lockjaw Davis, Frank Foster (*ts*); Charlie Fowlkes (*bs*); Freddie Green (*g*); Eddie Jones (*b*); Sonny Payne (*d*). 10/57.

***   **Sing Along With Basie** Roulette CDP 7953322 CD
As above, except add Dave Lambert, Jon Hendricks, Annie Ross, Joe Williams (*v*). 5–9/58.

(*)   **One More Time Roulette CDP 7972712 CD
As above, except Billy Mitchell (*ts*) replaces Davis. 12/58–1/59.

***   **Basie Swings Bennett Sings** Roulette CDP 7938992 CD
As above, except add Ralph Sharon (*p*), Tony Bennett (*v*). 1/59.

(*)   **Kansas City Suite Roulette CDP 7947972 CD
As above. 9/60.

***(*)   **The Best Of The Roulette Years** Roulette CDP 7979692 CD
As above Roulette discs, except add Jimmy Nottingham (*t*), Benny Carter (*as*), Budd Johnson (*ts*), Sam Herman (*g*). 57–62.

Basie opened his contract for Roulette with the great showstopping album that this band had in it, *The Atomic Mr Basie* (complete with mushroom cloud on the cover, a cold war classic). It might be the last great Basie album. He had Neal Hefti, who already had scored most of the hottest numbers in the band's recent book, do the whole record, and Hefti's zesty, machine-tooled scoring reached its apogee in 'The Kid From Red Bank', 'Flight Of The Foo

Birds', 'Splanky' and the rest. But it also had a guest soloist in the great Lockjaw Davis, whose splenetic outbursts gave just the right fillip to what might otherwise have been a too cut-and-dried effort. Collectors should note that some early pressings of the CD issue have flawed, incomplete masters.

Thereafter, the Roulette albums become as prosaic and sensible as the rest of Basie's latter-day output. The meeting with Tony Bennett will please Bennett fans more than Basie admirers, but it's a very enjoyable record. *Kansas City Suite* is a disappointingly plain group of Benny Carter charts, which the band stubbornly fail to bring to life, and *One More Time* brings in ten Quincy Jones arrangements. Jones's faceless professionalism seems all too suitable for this edition of the band. *Sing Along With Basie* is perhaps the one occasion where the band has sounded good with singers other than their regulars: Lambert, Hendricks and Ross swing infectiously through ten Basie staples, with Ross's work on 'Lil' Darlin'' particularly delightful. Given that the playing times on these Roulette discs are rather short, the 20-track compilation is a good way to acquire a decent cross-section of this period of the band. Remastering of this series is excellent.

***(*) Count On The Coast Vol. 1 Phontastic PHONT CD 7574 CD
Basie; Snooky Young, Thad Jones, Wendell Culley, Joe Newman (*t*); Benny Powell, Henry Coker, Al Grey (*tb*); Frank Wess (*as, f*); Billy Mitchell, Frank Foster (*ts*); Charlie Fowlkes (*bs*); Freddie Green (*g*); Eddie Jones (*b*); Sonny Payne (*d*); Joe Williams (*v*). 6–7/58.

***(*) Count On The Coast Vol. 2 Phontastic PHONT CD 7575 CD
As above. 6–7/58.

*** The 'Atomic' Band In Concert Bandstand BDCD 1525 CD
As above, except add Marshall Royal (*as*). 58.

***(*) Live 1958–59 Status STCD 110 CD
As above, except add John Anderson (*t*), Marshall Royal (*as, cl*). 6/58–11/59.

These are exceptionally strong live recordings. The two Phontastic CDs and the Status disc are all in such clear and powerful sound that the recordings belie their age; and Basie's men sound in particularly muscular and good-humoured form, especially on the Status set, which includes a few uncommon parts of the Basie repertoire and some dry runs for the Roulette sessions that were coming up. Foster is a titan among the soloists, but Powell, Wess and Newman also have their moments, and Williams is very good on the Phontastic discs. Although not clearly identified and shoddily packaged, the Bandstand CD seems to be from the same period and is also in very good sound.

***(*) Live Sequel NXT CD 182 3CD
As appropriate Verve and Roulette discs above, except add Harry Edison, Gene Coe, Oscar Brashear (*t*), Grover Mitchell, Richard Boone, Bill Hughes, Frank Hooks (*tb*), Bobby Plater, Eddie 'Lockjaw' Davis, Eric Dixon, Budd Johnson (*reeds*), Norman Keenan (*b*), Harold Jones (*d*). 9/56–1/59.

A smartly assembled collection of five different Basie live sets over a period of some 13 years. Eleven numbers cut in Sweden in 1956 are followed by the Newport set from *Count Basie At Newport* and two session from the Roulette years, including the superior material from *Basie At Birdland*, where Budd Johnson plays a memorable role and the band practically lift off on 'Blee Blop Blues'. Finally, there's a much later Las Vegas set from 1969, once released as *Standing Ovation*: the orchestra sound in healthy spirits, although the material is practically all drawn from the 1950s period. As a single representation of Basie in concert, this is as strong as any, and the sound is consistently good.

*** Basie In Sweden Roulette CDP 7959742 CD
Basie; Thad Jones, Sonny Cohn, Fip Ricard, Al Aarons, Benny Bailey (*t*); Benny Powell, Ake Persson, Henry Coker, Quentin Jackson (*tb*); Marshall Royal, Frank Wess, Frank Foster, Eric Dixon, Charlie Fowlkes (*reeds*); Freddie Green (*g*); Ike Isaacs (*b*); Louie Bellson (*d*); Irene Reid (*v*). 8/62.

***   **Lil' Ol' Groovemaker ... Basie!** Verve 821799-2 CD
As above, except add Don Rader (*t*), Grover Mitchell, Urbie Green (*tb*), Buddy Catlett (*b*), Sonny Payne (*d*), omit Jones, Bailey, Persson, Jackson, Isaacs, Bellson, Reid. 4/63.

**   **Basie's Bounce** Affinity AFS 1001 CD
Basie; Sam Noto, Wallace Davenport, Sonny Cohn, Phil Guilbeau, Al Aarons (*t*); Al Grey, Henderson Chambers, Grover Mitchell, Bill Hughes (*tb*); Bobby Plater, Marshall Royal (*as*); Eric Dixon, Sal Nistico, Eddie 'Lockjaw' Davis (*ts*); Charlie Fowlkes (*bs*); Freddie Green (*g*); Wyatt Reuther, Al Lucas (*b*); Rufus Jones, Sonny Payne (*d*); Leon Thomas (*v*). 64–65.

***   **Our Shining Hour** Verve 837446-2 CD
Probably similar to above, except add Sammy Davis Jr (*v*). 65.

(*)   **Count Basie 1966 Jazz Archives 90.106-2 CD
Basie; Gene Coe, Al Aarons, Sonny Cohn, Roy Eldridge (*t*); Richard Boone (*tb*, *v*); Bill Hughes, Grover Mitchell, Harlan Floyd (*tb*); Marshall Royal, Bobby Plater (*as*); Eric Dixon, Eddie 'Lockjaw' Davis (*ts*); Charlie Fowlkes (*bs*); Freddie Green (*g*); Norman Keenan (*b*); Ed Shaughnessy (*d*), Richard Boone (*v*). 66.

**   **Live At Antibes 1968** France's Concert FC 112 CD/LP
As above, except Oscar Brashear (*t*) replaces Eldridge. 7/68

Basie was at a low ebb in the mid-1960s and his studio albums (thankfully unreissued) were dedicated to Beatles tunes, among others. *Our Shining Hour* is more showbiz in a collaboration with Sammy Davis, but the singer plays up to the occasion so much – and elevates the band in doing so – that it's hard not to enjoy. *Basie In Sweden* is a late Roulette disc and quite a good one, although most of the best live Basie recordings for the label are in the Mosaic deluxe edition (see Introduction). *Lil' Ol' Groovemaker* is another, and this time rather better, set of Quincy Jones charts, with 'Pleasingly Plump' turning out to be a rather gracious ballad and the swingers taking off effectively. *Basie's Bounce* includes two broadcast sets, in scratchy and congested sound that suggests a vintage of at least 20 years earlier; nevertheless, the band is at battle stations throughout, with an almost overpowering charge through 'This Could Be The Start Of Something Big' at the beginning. The Jazz Archives disc is in a somewhat better fidelity, but suffers from an odd balance whereby Freddie Green is occasionally louder than the rest of the band put together. Superior treatments of 'I'm Beginning To See The Light', 'Hayburner' and some respectable blues sustain a programme that runs for nearly 70 minutes. The sound on *Antibes 1968* is much clearer but there are again balance problems, with the brass sometimes disappearing and the odd soloist standing a half-mile away. This set starts with the seemingly hypermodern 'A Night In Tunisia' – not very well handled – but soon settles down into a familiar Basie set.

***   **Compact Jazz: Count Basie** Verve 831364 CD
As appropriate discs above. 8/54–10/65.

**   **Compact Jazz: Count Basie – The Standards** Verve 841197 CD
Basie; Joe Newman, Gene Coe, George Cohn, Snooky Young, Al Aarons, Don Rader, Rickie Fortunatas, Waymon Reed (*t*); Buddy Morrow, Grover Mitchell, Henry Coker, Benny Powell, Frank Hooks, Bill Hughes, Mel Wanzo (*tb*); Jerry Dodgion, Eric Dixon, Bill Adkins, Eddie 'Lockjaw' Davis, Marshall Royal, Bobby Plater, Charlie Fowlkes, Cecil Payne, Frank Foster, Frank Wess (*reeds*); Freddie Green (*g*); Buddy Catlett, George Duvivier, Norman Keenan (*b*); Harold Jones, Sonny Payne (*d*). 4/63–2/70.

The first *Compact Jazz* compilation includes six tracks from the 1950s and six more from Basie's next Verve period: a predictable choice, and not bad. The *Standards* set is a programme of mostly rote performances of the likes of 'Chicago' and 'Blues In My Heart' and has little to offer beyond the tunes and a pack of functional Basie performances of them.

***   **The Bosses** Pablo 2310-709 MC
Basie; Harry Edison (*t*); J. J. Johnson (*tb*); Eddie 'Lockjaw' Davis (*ts*); Zoot Sims (*ts*); Irving Ashby (*g*); Ray Brown (*b*); Louie Bellson (*d*); Joe Turner (*v*). 12/73.

***   **Basie Jam** Pablo 2310-718 CD
As above, except omit Turner. 12/73.

***   **For The First Time** Pablo 2310-712 CD/LP/MC
Basie; Ray Brown (*b*); Louie Bellson (*d*). 5/74.

***   **For The Second Time** Original Jazz Classics OJC 600 CD/LP/MC
Basie; Ray Brown (*b*); Louie Bellson (*d*). 8/75.

(*)   **Satch And Josh Pablo 2310-722 CD/LP/MC
Basie; Oscar Peterson (*p*); Freddie Green (*g*); Ray Brown (*b*); Louie Bellson (*d*).
12/74.

***   **Basie And Zoot** Pablo 2310-745 MC
Basie; Zoot Sims (*ts*); John Heard (*b*); Louie Bellson (*d*). 4/75.

**   **Jam Session At Montreux 1975** Pablo 2310-750 CD
Basie; Roy Eldridge (*t*); Johnny Griffin (*ts*); Milt Jackson (*vib*); Niels-Henning
Ørsted-Pedersen (*b*); Louie Bellson (*d*). 7/75.

***   **Basie Big Band** Pablo 2310-756 CD
Basie; Pete Minger, Frank Szabo, Dave Stahl, Bob Mitchell, Sonny Cohn (*t*); Al Grey,
Curtis Fuller, Bill Hughes, Mel Wanzo (*tb*); Bobby Plater (*as, f*); Danny Turner (*as*);
Eric Dixon, Jimmy Forrest (*ts*); Charlie Fowlkes (*bs*); Freddie Green (*g*); John Duke
(*b*); Butch Miles (*d*). 8/75.

(*)   **Basie And Friends Pablo 2310-925 CD/LP/MC
Basie; Oscar Peterson (*p*); Freddie Green (*g*); Ray Brown, John Heard,
Niels-Henning Ørsted-Pedersen (*b*); Louie Bellson (*d*). 12/74–11/81.

It hardly seemed likely that, at 70, Basie would embark on a new career; but that was more or less what happened, when Norman Granz signed him to his new Pablo label and began taking down Basie albums more prolifically than ever before, some three dozen in the last ten years of the bandleader's life. Eight of them were set down in the first 18 months. *The Bosses*, which has yet to make it to CD, was a fine beginning, setting Basie alongside Joe Turner, who is in mellow but not reticent mood: there are too many remakes of his old hits here, but Turner and Basie make a magisterial combination, and the horns aren't too intrusive. *Basie Jam* was the first and perhaps the best of a series of studio jam sessions. The formula is, let it be said, predictable: fast blues, slow blues, fast blues, slow blues . . . sort-of-fast blues. Basie plays as minimally as he ever has, but presides grandly from the rear, and there are entertaining cameos from Johnson, Sims and Davis. *Basie And Zoot* is another good meeting, Sims as reliably swinging as always and getting Basie to perk up on the quicker tunes. The *Montreux Jam* is a bore, with Eldridge past his best and the others simply going on too long, while *Basie Big Band* was his first set for Pablo with the regular orchestra. This was a more than encouraging start. Sam Nestico, who wrote all nine charts, offered no radical departures from the Basie method, but at least he looked for more interesting harmonies and section colours, and there were some fine players in the band again: Jimmy Forrest, Bobby Mitchell, Curtis Fuller. Butch Morris, the least self-effacing of Basie's drummers, had also arrived, but was so far behaving, and Granz's dry studio sound suited the clean and direct lines rather well.

As far as Basie the pianist went, he made his first trio album in *For The First Time* (a formula repeated on *For the Second Time*) and traded licks with Oscar Peterson, his stylistic opposite, in the amusing *Satch And Josh*. Neither record was exactly a revelation, since Basie basically carried on in the style he'd played in for the last 40 years, but as fresh areas of work after 25 years of making the same kind of record, it must have been invigorating; and he plays as if it was. *Basie And Friends* is a collection of outtakes from various sessions, mostly made in this period, though a couple date from later on.

***   **I Told You So** Pablo 2310-767 CD/LP/MC
As above, except John Thomas, Jack Feierman (*t*) replace Sazbo and Stahl. 1/76.

***   **Basie Jam No. 2** Original Jazz Classics OJC 631 CD/LP/MC
Basie; Clark Terry (*t*); Al Grey (*tb*); Benny Carter (*as*); Eddie 'Lockjaw' Davis (*ts*);
Joe Pass (*g*); John Heard (*b*); Louie Bellson (*d*). 5/76.

(*)   **Basie Jam No. 3 Original Jazz Classics OJC 687 CD
As above. 5/76.

(*)   **Prime Time Pablo 2310-797 CD/LP/MC
Basie; Pete Minger, Lyn Biviano, Bob Mitchell, Sonny Cohn (*t*); Al Grey, Curtis
Fuller, Bill Hughes, Mel Wanzo (*tb*); Danny Turner, Bobby Plater (*as*); Jimmy
Forrest, Eric Dixon (*ts*); Charlie Fowlkes (*bs*); Nat Pierce (*p*); Freddie Green (*g*);
John Duke (*b*); Butch Miles (*d*). 1/77.

**   **Montreux '77** Original Jazz Classics OJC 377 CD/LP/MC
As above, except Waymon Reed (*t*), Dennis Wilson (*tb*) replace Minger and Fuller.
7/77.

***   **Jam Montreux '77** Original Jazz Classics OJC 379 CD/LP/MC
Basie; Roy Eldridge (*t*); Vic Dickenson, Al Grey (*tb*); Benny Carter (*as*); Zoot Sims
(*ts*); Ray Brown (*b*); Jimmie Smith (*d*). 7/77.

***   **Satch And Josh ... Again** Pablo 2310-802 CD
Basie; Oscar Peterson (*p*); John Heard (*b*); Louie Bellson (*d*). 9/77.

If Basie hadn't made too many records in the early 1970s, he was certainly making up for lost
time now. The two further *Basie Jam* albums are lesser editions of the previous set, though, like
all such records, they have a moment or two when things start happening. Carter and Davis are
the most reliable soloists on hand. *I Told You So* and *Prime Time* were the second and third full
orchestra albums for Pablo, and while the first one is solid, the second misfires a few times:
'Bundle O'Funk' was exactly the kind of modishness which Basie's return to traditionalism
should have eschewed, and some of the soloists sound tired. But it's better than the desperately
routine live set from Montreux which wanders joylessly through a stale Basie set. The
small-band jam from the same year is much better: Carter's gorgeous solo on 'These Foolish
Things', Sims wherever he plays, and even the by-now-unreliable Eldridge all make something
good out of it. The second *Satch And Josh* album follows the same sort of pattern as the first
and takes much of its energy from the grooving beat laid down by Heard and Bellson: 'Home
Run', for instance, is deliciously spry and merry.

***   **Live In Japan '78** Pablo 2308-246 CD/LP/MC
Basie; Pete Minger, Sonny Cohn, Noland Smith, Waymon Reed (*t*); Mel Wanzo, Bill
Hughes, Dennis Wilson, Alonzo Wesley (*tb*); Bobby Plater, Danny Turner (*as*); Eric
Dixon (*ts, f*); Kenny Hing (*ts*); Charlie Fowlkes (*bs*); Freddie Green (*g*); John Clayton
(*b*); Butch Miles (*d*). 5/78.

***   **Night Rider** Original Jazz Classics OJC 688 CD
Basie; Oscar Peterson (*p*); John Heard (*bb*); Louie Bellson (*d*). 2/78.

***   **The Timekeepers** Pablo 2310-896 CD/LP
Basie; Oscar Peterson (*p*); John Heard (*b*); Louie Bellson (*d*). 2/78.

(*)   **Yessir, That's My Baby Pablo 2310-923 CD/LP/MC
As above. 2/78.

***   **On The Road** Pablo 2312-112 LP/MC
Basie; Pete Minger, Sonny Cohn, Paul Cohen, Raymond Brown (*t*); Booty Wood, Bill
Hughes, Mel Wanzo, Dennis Wilson (*tb*); Charlie Fowlkes, Eric Dixon, Bobby Plater,
Danny Turner, Kenny Hing (*reeds*); Freddie Green (*g*); Keter Betts (*b*); Mickey
Roker (*d*). 7/79.

***   **Get Together** Pablo 2310-924 CD/LP/MC
Basie; Clark Terry (*t, flhn*); Harry Edison (*t*); Budd Johnson (*ts, bs*); Eddie 'Lockjaw'
Davis (*ts*); Freddie Green (*g*); John Clayton (*b*); Gus Johnson (*d*). 9/79.

The Japanese concert must have been a happy experience for the band since they sound in
excellent spirits, and familiar charts take on a springier life. The sound is unfortunately slightly
constricted and certainly isn't as wide-bodied as the punchy crescendos secured on *On The
Road*, which is another of the better live albums from this stage of Basie's career. The sheer
wallop of 'Wind Machine' and 'Splanky' sums up the kind of unhindered and creaseless power
which Basie's orchestra worked to secure and, while it says little of any personal nature, taken a

few tracks at a time it certainly knocks the listener over. So far, though, this one has yet to make it to CD. The three albums with Peterson are good enough on their own terms but anyone who has either of the earlier discs won't find anything different here. Peterson carries most of the weight, and Basie answers with his patented right-hand fills and occasional brow-furrowing left-hand chords. If anything makes the music happen, though, it's again the exemplary swing of Heard and Belson. *Get Together* is yet another small-group jam on a few old favourites, but the presence of the great Budd Johnson adds a few more felicitous moments than usual.

***   **Kansas City 7** Original Jazz Classics OJC 690 CD
Basie; Freddie Hubbard (*t*); J. J. Johnson (*tb*); Eddie 'Lockjaw' Davis (*ts*); Joe Pass (*g*); John Heard (*b*); Jake Hanna (*d*). 4/80.

(*)   **Kansas City Shout Pablo 2310-859 CD/LP/MC
Basie; Pete Minger, Sonny Cohn, Dale Carley, Dave Stahl (*t*); Booty Wood, Bill Hughes, Dennis Wilson, Grover Mitchell, Dennis Rowland (*tb*); Eddie Vinson (*as, v*); Eric Dixon, Bobby Plater (*as*); Danny Turner, Kenny Hing (*ts*); John Williams (*bs*); Freddie Green (*g*); Cleveland Eaton (*b*); Duffy Jackson (*d*); Joe Turner (*v*). 4/80.

***   **Warm Breeze** Pablo 2312-131 CD
As above, except add Bob Summers, Willie Cook, Harry Edison, Frank Szabo (*t*), Harold Jones, Gregg Field (*d*), omit Rowland, Stahl, Minger. 9/81.

***   **Farmers Market Barbecue** Pablo 2310-874 LP/MC
As above, except Chris Albert (*t*), James Leary (*b*), replace Eaton, Jackson, Vinson, Jones and Turner. 5/82.

***   **Me And You** Pablo 2310-891 CD
As above, except Steve Furtado, Frank Szabo (*t*), Eric Schneider (*ts*), Chris Woods (*as*), Dennis Mackrel (*d*) replace Albert, Rowland, Hing, Dixon, Plater, Field. 2/83.

(*)   **88 Basie Street Pablo 2310-901 CD/LP/MC
As above. 5/83.

(*)   **Fancy Pants Pablo 2310-920 CD/LP/MC
As above, except Jim Crawford (*t*) replaces Furtado. 12/83.

***   **Kansas City Six** Original Jazz Classics OJC 449 CD/LP/MC
Basie; Willie Cook (*t*); Eddie Vinson (*as, v*); Joe Pass (*g*); Niels-Henning Ørsted-Pedersen (*b*); Louie Bellson (*d*). 11/81.

***   **Mostly Blues . . . And Some Others** Pablo 2310-919 CD/LP/MC
Basie; Snooky Young (*t*); Eddie 'Lockjaw' Davis (*ts*); Joe Pass (*g*); Freddie Green (*g*); John Heard (*b*); Roy McCurdy (*d*). 6/83.

Basie carried on, regardless of encroaching arthritis, eventually working the stage from a wheelchair. The big-band records from this patch are some of his best Pablos, for the simple reason that Granz was recording the band to a more telling effect: studio mixes had improved, the weight and balance of the orchestra came through more smoothly and arrived with a bigger punch and, since those virtues counted for more with Basie than did individual solos or any other idiosyncrasy, the band just sounded bigger and better. The arrangements on the final albums are shared between a number of hands. Sam Nestico was again responsible for most of *Warm Breeze* and *Fancy Pants*, while other band-members contributed to the other three discs, which also featured numbers by Ernie Wilkins and Basie himself. *Warm Breeze* is a particularly shapely album, with Willie Cook featured on a couple of tunes, Harry Edison guesting on 'How Sweet It Is' and the themes standing among Nestico's more melodic efforts. *Me And You* and *Farmers Market Barbecue* are both split between full-band and some tracks by a smaller edition of the orchstra: the latter has a splendid 'Blues For The Barbecue' and fine tenor by Kenny Hing on 'St Louis Blues', while the former includes an overripe Booty Wood solo on a dead slow 'She's Funny That Way' as well as a look all the way back to 'Moten Swing'. *88 Basie Street* and *Fancy Pants* are a little more routine, but the slickness and precision are unfaltering. *Kansas City Shout* and *Six* are fun albums with Vinson and Turner vying for attention and Basie refereeing with stately calm at the piano. But the two best records from this closing period are probably *Kansas City 7* and *Mostly Blues . . . And Some Others*. The former features a cracking line-up and, though Hubbard sometims goes too far and Hanna's cymbals are annoyingly over-busy, it makes for some steaming music. The latter is as slow, full-flavoured and hefty as Basie seemed to want his blues to be: Pass and the imperturbable Green make a memorable combination, and Young and Davis blow things that turn out just fine. The pianist, of course, does his usual.

*** **Fun Time** Pablo 2310-945 CD/MC
Basie; Sonny Cohn, Frank Szabo, Pete Minger, Dave Stahl, Bob Mitchell (*t*); Al Grey, Curtis Fuller, Mel Wanzo, Bill Hughes (*tb*); Eric Dixon, Danny Turner, Bobby Plater, Jimmy Forrest, Charlie Fowlkes (*reeds*); Freddie Green (*g*); John Duke (*b*); Butch Miles (*d*); Bill Caffey (*v*). 7/75.

The first of what could be many more Basie records yet, depending on what Pablo has in its unreleased stockpile. This is the orchestra at Montreux in 1975, a very grand edition of the band, and delivering on all cylinders. Big and clear concert sound.

*** **The Best Of Count Basie** Pablo 2405-408 CD/LP/MC

*** **The Best Of The Count Basie Big Band** Pablo 2405-422 CD/LP/MC

Two solid compilations from a vast trove of recordings. The first concentrates on the small groups, the second on the orchestra, and either will serve as a sampler of the later Basie.

GIANNI BASSO (born 1931)
TENOR SAXOPHONE

*** **Lunet** Splasc(h) H101 LP
Basso; Klaus Koenig (*p*); Isla Eckinger (*b*); Peter Schmidlin (*d*). 3/82

*** **Maestro + Maestro = Exciting Duo** Splasc(h) H.103 LP
Basso; Guido Manusardi (*p*). 2/83.

Basso is rather older than many of the Italian youngsters who record for Splasc(h), but he has no need to give them any ground. His playing has settled into a likeable amalgam of cool and hot post-bop saxophone, and his occasional forays into freer territory lend an anticipatory air of surprise to his music. *Lunet* displays his more conventional side, a relaxed and outgoing tenor-and-rhythm date, while his meeting with Manusardi is a little more excitable, sometimes recalling the punch and counter-punch of Stan Tracey and Art Themen.

DJANGO BATES (born 1960)
PIANO, KEYBOARDS, HORN, TRUMPET, COMPOSER

** **Music For The Third Policeman** Ah Um 003 CD
Bates; Powder Room Collapse: Steve Buckley (*as, cl, whistles, bell*); Steve Berry (*clo, b*); Martin France (*d, perc, etc.*); Stuart Hall (*bjo, vn, 12-str g; mnd*); Sarah Harrison (*vn, hooter*); Robert Juritz (*bsn*); Dai Pritchard (*cl, bcl*); Eddie Parker (*bf*); Dave Pattman (*bongos*); Ashley Slater (*tb*). 1–2/90.

Bates always seemed to stand slightly apart from the laddishness that afflicted the putatively talented Loose Tubes, a quiet, reflective figure absorbed in his chords. There was early evidence of his ability as a composer/arranger and then, more surprisingly, of his willingness to play cooking jazz, as half (later a third) of the excellent First House.
    Not so here. The music, inspired by Flann O'Brien's over-praised novel, seems curiously uninspired, and the playing has lapsed back into mere gestures with little logic or sense. What it does have, on occasion, is a modicum of energy and humour. Pared down to a quartet and given leave to dispense with at least five of the thirteen 'movements' – none longer than six minutes – there might have been a bit more mileage in it.

STEFANO BATTAGLIA (born 1966)
PIANO

***   **Things Ain't What They Used To Be** Splasc(h) H131 LP.
Battaglia; Piero Leveratto (*b*); Gianni Cazzola (*d*). 2 & 4/87.

***   **Auryn** Splasc(h) H161 CD/LP.
Battaglia; Paolino Dalla Porta (*b*); Manhu Roche (*d*). 5/88.

Like many of the younger generation of Italian jazzmen, Battaglia is a superb executant in the
throes of developing a personal style. Both of these records offer an imposing display of
pianism without convincing that he has anything especially individual to say. *Things Ain't What
They Used To Be* is a recital of standards: some played dutifully, others with a certain
impatience, as if he would rather be dealing with his own material; and *Auryn*, correspondingly,
is a programme of Battaglia originals. The rubato structure of 'The Real Meaning (Of The
Blues)' and the Jarrett-like melodies elsewhere are vehicles for full-blooded solos which
nevertheless don't lead anywhere in particular. Both rhythm sections offer alert support.

***(*)   **Explore** Splasc(h) H 304-2 CD
Battaglia; Tony Oxley (*d*). 2/90.

***(*)   **Confession** Splasc(h) H 344-2 CD
Battaglia; Paolino Dalla Porta (*b*); Roberto Gatto (*d*). 3/91.

Two records which affirm that Battaglia must be monitored further. Most of the duo pieces on
Explore are quite brief and contained, and structurally there's little sense of anything but
careful preparation; yet spontaneity runs all through the music, whether in full-tilt, crashing
interplay with the drummer or in small-voiced dialogue which shows great sensitivity.
Confession is a much more closely developed trio music than that of his earlier releases, all
three men taking a virtually equal role in a triologue that they sustain with few problems over
the course of several very long tracks. These are distinctive and worth seeking out.

SIDNEY BECHET (1897–1959)
SOPRANO SAXOPHONE, CLARINET; ALSO TENOR SAXOPHONE, BASS SAXOPHONE, PIANO, BASS, DRUMS

***   **Sidney Bechet: Complete Edition – Volume 1, 1923** Media 7 MJCD 5 CD

***   **The Complete 1923–6 Clarence Williams Sessions: 1** EPM Musique FDC 5197 CD
Bechet; Thomas Morris (*c*); Charlie Irvis, John Mayfield (*tb*); Clarence Williams (*p*);
Narcisse Buddy Christian (*d, bjo*); Rosetta Crawford, Margaret Johnson, Sara Martin,
Mamie Smith, Eva Taylor (*v*). 7, 8, 9 & 10/23.

***   **The Chronological Sidney Bechet, 1923–1926** Classics 583 CD
Bechet; Clarence Brereton, Wendell Culley, Demas Dean, Tommy Ladnier (*t*); Billy
Burns, Chester Burrill, Teddy Nixon (*tb*); Chauncey Haughton (*cl, as*); Ralph
Duquesne, Rudy Jackson (*cl, as, ss*); Ramon Usera (*cl, ts*); Jerome Pasqual, Gil White
(*ts*); Harry Brooks, Henry Duncan, Lloyd Pinckney, Clarence Williams (*p*); Oscar
Madera (*vn*); Buddy Christian, Frank Ethridge (*bj*); Jimmy Miller (*g*); Wilson Myers
(*b, v*); Edward Coles (*bb*); Jimmy Jones (*b*); Jack Carter, Wilbert Kirk, Morris
Morland (*d*); Billy Banks, Lena Horne, Billy Maxey, Noble Sissle (*v*). 10/23, 2 & 4/31,
9/32, 34, 3/36.

***(*)   **The Chronological Sidney Bechet, 1937–1938** Classics 593 CD
Bechet; Clarence Brereton, Wendell Culley, Demas Dean, Charlie Shavers (*t*); Chester
Burrill (*tb*); Chauncey Haughton (*cl, as*); Jerome Pasquall, Gil White (*ts*); Ernie
Caceres (*bs*); Oscar Madera (*vn*); Dave Bowman, Harry Brooks, Erskine Butterfield,
Sam Price (*p*); Teddy Bunn, Jimmy Miller, Leonard Ware (*g*); Richard Fulbright,
Jimmy Jones, Henry Turner (*b*); Wilbert Kirk, Zutty Singleton (*d*); O'Neil Spencer (*d,
v*); Billy Banks, The Two Fishmongers (*v*). 4/37, 2, 5 & 11/38.

'When one has tried so hard and so often in the past to discover one of the figures to whom we
owe the advent of an art . . . what a moving thing it is to meet this very black, fat boy with white
teeth and that narrow forehead who is very glad one likes what he does, but who can say

nothing of his art save that it follows his "own way" and then one thinks his "own way" is perhaps the highway the world will swing along tomorrow.' Thus the Swiss conductor Ernest Ansermet recorded his first impressions of the Southern Syncopated Orchestra and their clarinet player in an essay entitled 'On a Negro Orchestra' in the October 1919 issue of *Revue Romande*. Ansermet's article has become one of the central reference points of Bechet's early career, and it helped establish his increasingly extravagant European reputation. Even so, it's fraught with oddities: was Bechet 'very black'? (he was actually a light-skinned Creole); why insist on the narrowness of his forehead (over in Munich a frustrated house-painter was putting together a theory based on such 'observations'); and was Bechet really as naïve and untutored in his approach to music as Ansermet implies?

On the last point, Bechet himself contributed to the heav'n-taught image. His auto-biography, *Treat it Gentle*, is a masterpiece of contrived ingenuousness – the opposite, one might say, of Charles Mingus's ruthlessly disingenuous rants in *Beneath the Underdog*. The fact is that Bechet was an exceptionally gifted and formally aware musician whose compositional skills greatly outshine those of Louis Armstrong, his rival for canonization as the first great jazz improviser. Armstrong's enormous popularity – abetted by his sky-writing top Cs and vocal performance – tended to eclipse Bechet everywhere except in France. Yet the musical evidence is that Bechet was an artist of equal and parallel standing. His melodic sense and ability to structure a solo round the harmonic sequence of the original theme (or with no theme whatsoever) has been of immense significance in the development of modern jazz. Bechet made a pioneering switch to the soprano saxophone (a stronger-voiced and more projective instrument than the clarinet) in the same year as Ansermet's essay, having found a second-hand horn in a London shop. Within a few years his biting tone and dramatic tremolo were among the most distinctive sounds in jazz.

Bechet made a relatively slow start to his recording career. His first cuts as 'leader' are as accompanist on two tracks made in New York in October and credited to Rosetta Crawford & the King Bechet Trio. The early sessions with Clarence Williams and a variety of modestly talented singers (also available under Williams's name) include carefully annotated breaks and solos from Bechet, largely on soprano saxophone; but these sessions are of specialist interest in the main. His clarinet style (on tracks with Eva Tyalor) is still strongly coloured by that of Alphonse Picou and Lorenzo Tio, who gave the precocious Bechet lessons, and is markedly less individual than his saxophone playing.

The *Chronological* compilation is less detailed, but included material with Noble Sissle's orchestra not included on either of the other available options. In fact, only the two Rosetta Crawford tracks are in common. The sound is rather abrasive and these early sessions are only essential for a brief, brilliant soprano solo on 'Loveless Love'. According to John Chilton, Bechet is also responsible on this and two other tracks (he solos only on the initially rejected 'In A Café On The Road To Calais') for the bass saxophone parts, which are not credited in the Classics notes. The session of 15 September 1932 is one of Bechet's best yet, with superb solos on 'I Want You Tonight' and 'Maple Leaf Rag'. The later disc is generally more professional and every bit as compelling musically. Bechet reached a new high with two quintet tracks credited to Noble Sissle's Swingsters, an offshoot of the main band. His solos on 'Okey-Doke' and 'Characteristic Blues' are classic performances, full of extravagantly bent notes, trills and time changes. Using both clarinet and soprano saxophone, Bechet creates an atmosphere of considerable tension that is discharged only during a phenomenal solo on 'Characteristic Blues'. Later, in 1938, there was controversy over the exact authorship of 'Hold Me Tight', which Bechet claimed was based on his earlier 'I Want Some Seafood, Mama', but which was declared obscene and withdrawn from radio stations. The real controversy, however, was directed towards what seemed to be a new way of playing jazz, and in that context the session of April 1937 is absolutely critical, not just to Bechet's development but to that of jazz itself.

****   **Sidney Bechet, 1932–43: The Bluebird Sessions** BMG/Bluebird ND 90317 5CD
Bechet; Gus Aiken, Henry Red Allen, Henry Goodwin, Tommy Ladnier, Henry Levine, Sidney De Paris, Charlie Shavers (*t*); Rex Stewart (*c*); Vic Dickenson (*tb, v*); Jack Epstein, J. C. Higginbotham, Teddy Nixon, Sandy Williams (*tb*); Claude Jones (*tb, v*); Alfie Evans, Albert Nicholas (*cl*); Mezz Mezzrow (*cl, ts*); Rudolph Adler, Happy Caldwell, Lem Johnson (*ts*); Don Donaldson, Henry Duncan, Earl Hines, Cliff Jackson, Mario Janarro, Willie 'The Lion' Smith, James Tolliver, Sonny White (*p*); Jelly Roll Morton (*p, v*); Teddy Bunn, Tommy Collucci, Lawrence Lucie, Everett Barksdale, Charlie Howard (*g*); Wellman Braud, Elmer James, John Lindsay, Wilson Myers, Harry Patent, Ernest Williamson (*b*); Wilson Myers (*b, v*); Big Sid Catlett,

Kenny Clarke, Warren Baby Dodds, J. C. Heard, Arthur Herbert, Manzie Johnson, Wilbert Kirk, Nat Levine, Morris Morland, Zutty Singleton (*d*); Herb Jeffries, William Maxey (*v*).

Nothing more clearly establishes Bechet's credentials as a harmonic improviser in the modern sense than his remarkable excursion on 'Shag', an athematic exploration from 1932 of the 'I Got Rhythm' chords. Bechet's tearing, urgent solo has to be seen as one of the earliest foretastes of what was to be standard bebop practice (and many of the bop standards were also based on the Gershwin tune). Even when dealing with a relatively conventional structure like 'Maple Leaf Rag', also with Tommy Ladnier and the 1932 Feetwarmers, he busts the harmonic code wide open, and it's useful-to-valuable to compare his treatment of the Joplin tune with avant-gardist Anthony Braxton's approach on *Duets 1976* [Arista AL 4101 LP].

The 1939 sessions really belong in the Jelly Roll Morton discography, but they feature some fine Bechet accompaniments and two intriguing comparative studies in alternative takes of 'O Didn't He Ramble' and 'Winin' Boy Blues'. A 1940 trio, 'Blues In Thirds', with Earl Hines (the composer) and Baby Dodds is by far the best track from a curiously up-and-down session that features cornetist Rex Stewart, bassist John Lindsay and vocalist Herb Jeffries (who makes William Maxey's abstract scatting on 'Shag' and 'Maple Leaf Rag' sound even better).

In April 1941 Bechet fulfilled the logic of his increasingly self-reliant musical conception (Hines suggested that his quietly 'evil' mood on the day of the 1940 sessions was characteristic of New Orleans players at the time when dealing with Northerners) by recording two unprecedented 'one-man-band' tracks, overdubbing up to six instruments. 'Sheik of Araby' is for the full 'band' of soprano and tenor saxophones, clarinet, piano, bass and drums; so time-consuming was the process that a second item, 'Blues For Bechet', had to be completed without bass or drums, leaving a fascinating fragment for RCA to release.

In September of the same year, Bechet made another classic trio recording, this time with Willie 'The Lion' Smith and the relative unknown, Everett Barksdale, on electric guitar. Though the two sidemen provide no more than incidental distractions, the trio sessions are more compelling than the full band assembled on that day (Charlie Shavers plays monster lines on 'I'm Coming Virginia' as on the October 'Mood Indigo', but is otherwise ill-suited); 'Strange Fruit' is one of Bechet's most calmly magisterial performances, and the two takes of 'You're The Limit' seem too good to have been dumped in the 'unreleased' bin, though perhaps the absence on either of a commanding solo from Bechet (who may not have liked Smith's uncomplicated tune) put the label off.

But what did they know? A month later, in the same session that realized 'Mood Indigo', Bechet cut the utterly awful 'Laughin' In Rhythm', a New Orleans version of 'The Laughing Policeman' that, despite a taut soprano solo, hardly merits revival. Dickenson, whose humour was usually reliable, also plays beautifully on 'Blue In The Air', one of the finest of Bechet's recorded solos and one that merits the closest attention.

CD transfer has in some cases improved the sound-balance (Tommy Ladnier had been disappointed by his position in the early mixes but he is largely restored here) and in some cases has wiped out elements of the background. Understandably, the major emphasis always falls on the main subject. Though there is, inevitably, some dross, these invaluable mid-period documents contain more than 80 tracks from a score of sessions. Essential Bechet material that no serious fan should be without.

***(*) **Sidney Bechet Sessions** Storyville 4028 LP
   Bechet; Mezz Mezzrow (*cl*); Vernon Brown (*tb*); James P. Johnson, Joe Sullivan (*p*); Bernard Addison (*g*); George Pops Foster (*b*); Warren Baby Dodds, George Wettling (*d*). 12/45, 9/46, 2/47.

An excellent compilation of post-war material, bringing together the 1947 'Wax Shop' sides by the Bechet–Mezzrow Feetwarmers, two fine concert tracks ('China Boy' and 'Dear Old Southland') from the previous year by a quartet featuring Johnson, Foster and Dodds, with some less successful material recorded in 1945 under Joe Sullivan's not altogether certain leadership. The 'Royal Garden', 'Fast' and 'Slow' blues from the sessions with Mezzrow are among Bechet's best of the period, and there's a fluency and spontaneity about his solo construction that he was beginning to lose at the time in favour of pre-programmed cadenzas that left the rhythm section far behind.

*** **In The Groove** Jazz Society (Vogue) 670506 CD
Bechet; Claude Luter (*cl*); Pierre Dervaux (*t*); Claude Philippe (*cl, bjo*); Mowgli
Jospin, Guy Longnon, Bernard Zacharias (*tb*); Christian Azzi (*p*); Roland Bianchini
(*b*); François Moustache Galepides (*d*). 10 & 11/49, 10/50, 5/51, 1/52.

***(*) **Salle Pleyel: 31 January 52** Vogue 655001 CD
Bechet; Claude Luter (*cl*); Claude Rabanit (*t*); Guy Longnon, Bernard Zacharias (*tb*);
Christian Azzi (*p*); Claude Philippe (*bjo*); Roland Bianchini (*b*); François Moustache
Galepides (*d*). 1/52.

*** **In Concert** Vogue 655625 CD
Bechet; Claude Luter (*cl*); Pierre Dervaux, Giles Thibaut (*t*); Benny Vasseur (*tb*);
Yannick Singery (*p*); Claude Phillipe (*bjo*); Roland Bianchini (*b*); Marcel Blanche
(*d*). 12/54.

Luter was a surprisingly confident and self-assured partner for the newly emigrated Bechet, who
regarded his move to France as the fulfilment of racial destiny rather than as escape from an
unfeeling and unappreciative environment. Even so, Bechet's reputation in America never
matched the adulation he received in France. With the exception of the leader, the French band
give him an easy ride, offering *carte blanche* for either relatively pat solos or more developed
excursions, as the mood took him. 'Ghost Of The Blues' and 'Patte De Mouche' (with Bechet
taking over at the piano) are rare gems and 'Les Oignons' is a delight. Generally, though, quite
low-key.

The Salle Pleyel concert was a noisy, vociferous affair but also surprisingly inward-looking
and musicianly. Introduced by Charles Delaunay, it features favourites like 'Les Oignons'
again, 'Petite Fleur', 'St Louis Blues', 'Frankie And Johnny', 'Maryland My Maryland' and
alternative versions of both 'Sweet Georgia Brown' and 'Royal Garden Blues' that are of more
than incidental documentary interest. Recommended.

The later concert record has some interesting elements (Bechet's solos on 'Buddy Bolden
Stomp' and 'On The Sunny Side Of The Street' are contrastingly good) but with a slightly bland
air which isn't helped by a very skew-whiff recording that makes everyone sound as if they're
moving around onstage.

***(*) **Sidney Bechet At Storyville** Black Lion 60902 CD/LP/MC
Bechet; Vic Dickenson (*tb*); George Wein (*p*); Jimmy Woode (*b*); Buzzy Drootin (*d*).
10/53.

A tight and professional set from mid-way through a residency at George Wein's Boston club.
There is a slight sense of motions being gone through on some of Bechet's briefer breaks, but
every now and then, as on 'Crazy Rhythm', he will make subtle changes of direction that Wein,
for one, doesn't seem to have noticed. Sound-balances are erratic in places, but everyone can be
heard and Woode in particular gains over his showing on the original Storyville LP release.
Recommended.

**** **Brussels World Fair Concert 1958** Vogue 500203 LP
Bechet; Buck Clayton (*t*); Vic Dickenson (*tb*); George Wein (*p*); Arvell Shaw (*b*);
Kansas Fields (*d*); Sarah Vaughan (*v*). 7 & 8/58.

When asked for an explanation of his increasingly strong vibrato, Bechet is alleged to have
replied, 'Senility, old boy, senility.' Even by the most generous calculation (one unlikely theory
sets Bechet's birth-date as 1891), the saxophonist was still a relatively young man in 1958 when
these marvellous concert sessions were recorded. Yet, though there was no sign of a serious
breakdown in his health, he would be dead within the year. Bechet first visited Brussels in 1925
as a member of *La revue nègre*. A subsequent visit with Claude Luter was far from happy, but
the success of these splendid sides must largely be attributed to George Wein's sharp
recruitment of a genuinely sympathetic band. Clayton in particular is superb and takes a fine
solo feature on 'All Of Me'. Bechet's own playing is assured and strong, if a little predictable;
his finest moment is an extraordinary 'St Louis Blues', on which he punches out the melody
with fervid expression, holding notes long enough to confound any suspicion that his fatal
pulmonary problems had already taken hold. There is a rather drab 'Ad Lib Blues' with Sarah
Vaughan and a perfunctory 'When The Saints Go Marching In', which is the only sign of
physical or artistic exhaustion. Though not yet on CD, this fine recording is thoroughly
recommended.

GORDON BECK (born 1938)
PIANO, ELECTRIC PIANO, SYNTHESIZERS

*(*)   **Dreams** JMS 049-2 CD
         Beck; Rowanne Mark (v). 5–6/89.

For all his extravagant talent – his acuity as a composer has been acknowledged on record by the finicky Gary Burton – Gordon Beck has never broken through to the wider audience he deserves. In recent years, after shifting his centre of operations to the French jazz scene, he has undergone a revival of fortunes, producing excellent records on JMS and Owl with guitarist Allan Holdsworth and singer Helen Merrill (for whom, see the relevant entries), which perfectly highlighted his remarkable technique and facility for complex melodic invention, coupled with an inner metronome programmed by Horace Silver and the ghost of Art Tatum.

Dreams, though, is a rather disappointing set, far too involuted and personal to communicate fully its unashamedly sentimental vision. Keyboard-generated bass and drum effects are never entirely satisfactory and there is a stiffness in the pulse which mars some fascinating and adventurous writing which is occasionally reminiscent of Chick Corea in style-switching mood. Rowanne Mark's vocal contributions are attractive but could, for the most part, just as easily have been created by a sampling keyboard. Holdsworth's production is impeccable.

****   **For Evans Sake** JMS 059 CD
         Beck; Didier Lockwood (vn); Dave Holland (b); Jack DeJohnette (d). 9/91.

At last, a band and a session commensurate with Beck's remarkable talents. If the excitement of the opening 'You Are All The Things', with Lockwood's violin squealing away like a row of saxophones, isn't maintained, it primes the listener for a thoughtful and often very moving tribute to Bill Evans. Interestingly, Beck uses nothing by Evans himself. Miles Davis's 'Blue In Green' is the only familiar piece, and that is an unaccompanied bass solo from the marvellous Holland. Beck has been accumulating this material for many years. 'Trio Type Tune Two?' was written as long ago as 1966. As Evans's example has sunk in and assimilated, Beck has become ever more sophisticated as a composer. 'Re: Mister E', far from pastiche, is a virtuosic performance with a complex harmonic and rhythmic profile to which all three performers contribute in full measure, and there's no mistaking the certainty of the closing 'He Is With Us Still'. DeJohnette is now so completely in command of his drums that he can appear to be playing strict time when the basic metre is changing bar to bar. Beck responds very forcefully to that and one sees why in the past decade he has felt obliged to experiment with solo multi-tracked recording; the average bassist or drummer simply isn't fleet and agile enough for music of this level of sophistication. Lockwood is an intermittent presence (and it was sensible not to use him on every track); when he does play, he often surprises with the grace and precision of his ravelling, intricate lines. Most strongly recommended.

HARRY BECKETT (born 1935)
TRUMPET, FLUGELHORN

***   **Bremen Concert** West Wind 0007 CD/LP

***   **Live: Volume 2** West Wind 0030 CD/LP
         Beckett; Chris McGregor (p); Courtney Pine (ts, ss on *Live: Volume 2* only); Fred
         Thelonious Baker (b); Clifford Jarvis (d). 5/87.

***(*)   **Passion And Possession** ITM 1456 CD
         Beckett; Django Bates, Joachim Kühn, Keith Tippett (p). 4/91.

Too vital a presence to be merely a father-figure, Beckett lent a rugged avuncular blessing to the re-integration of young black musicians into post-free British jazz. New star Courtney Pine's appearance on the second – but marginally earlier – of the West Winds may be seen as a gesture of recognition and thanks, but also as an object lesson in not teaching your uncle to suck eggs, for Beckett good-naturedly blows him out of sight. Though, like many of the African-and-Caribbean-born musicians who fell within the circle of Chris McGregor's Brotherhood of Breath, Beckett moved without strain between free and mainstream improvisation, his essential qualities are an untroubled romanticism and a brightly lyrical tone (to which he adds gruff asides and occasionally startling rhythmic punctuations).

Though some of the best of Beckett's work is on sessions for other leaders, his re-emergence as a recording artist (no more than his deserts, albeit on small labels) finds him consolidating his strengths as an improviser. The four long tracks on the German concert sessions allow the group to develop typically simple thematic materials in directions that are unexpectedly searching and complex, with Beckett's flugelhorn in particular providing timbral nuances which have been explored by few players of his generation. Technical shortcomings mean that interplay within the group – from Baker particularly – is not always discernible, and the addition of an extra horn on *Volume 2* strains the reproduction at higher volumes.

No such problems with *Passion And Possession*, a set of nine brass and keyboard duets with three leading pianists. Predictably, Keith Tippett isn't content to restrict himself merely to the keyboard, reaching inside the piano body to strum out zither and koto effects on 'Floating Crystals'. Nothing else on the record is quite so experimentally inclined. Kühn's rippling romanticism inspires some of Beckett's most nakedly emotional playing, but even that is marked by a needling scepticism that prevents the music from running away with itself. The pieces with Bates are, predictably, the most problematic and in some regards the most challenging. Weaned on British free bop, the pianist brings an engaging structural awkwardness to 'Almost Unchanged', significantly the longest track, never allowing it to settle into a waiting groove. Beckett teases and cajoles and, for a moment or two, floats off into reminiscence. A difficult album to categorize, but perhaps the best available example of Beckett's sterling virtues.

BIX BEIDERBECKE (1903-1931)
CORNET

*** **Bix Beiderbecke** Milestone M 47019 2 LP
Beiderbecke; Jimmy McPartland, Muggsy Spanier (*c*); Miff Mole, Tommy Dorsey, Guy Carey, George Brunies, Al Gandee (*tb*); Don Murray, Volly De Faut (*cl*); Jimmy Hartwell (*cl, as*); Frankie Trumbauer (*Cmel*); George Johnson (*ts*); Dick Voynow, Rube Bloom, Paul Mertz (*p*); Mel Stitzel (*p, bj*); Bob Gillette, Howdy Quicksell (*bj*); Min Leibrook (*tba*); Vic Moore, Tom Gargano (*d*). 2–12/24.

Bix Beiderbecke, the cornetist from Davenport, Iowa, remains among the most lionized and romanticized of jazz figures, sixty years after his death. Beiderbecke's understated mastery, his cool eloquence and precise improvising, were long cherished as the major alternative to Louis Armstrong's clarion leadership in the original jazz age, and his records have endured remarkably well – even though comparatively few of them were in the uncompromised jazz vein of Armstrong's studio work. This double-LP collects virtually everything he made in his first year in the studios, with the Wolverine Orchestra, the Sioux City Six and Bix's Rhythm Jugglers. With no vocalists to hinder them, these young white bands were following in the steps of the Original Dixieland Jazz Band and, although they seem rather stiff and unswinging, the ensembles are as daring as almost anything that was being recorded at the time. Yet despite the presence of such players as Mole, Dorsey and Murray, only Beiderbecke's solos have retained an independent life: the beautiful little contribution to 'Royal Garden Blues', for instance, shines through the dull recording and staid surroundings. The record also includes two tracks made after McPartland had replaced Bix in the Wolverines, and seven sides by the rough Chicagoan group led by Muggsy Spanier, The Bucktown Five. First released in the early '70s, the set could certainly stand remastering with more modern techniques.

*** **Bix Beiderbecke 1924–1930** BBC REB/ZEF 601 LP/MC
Beiderbecke; Ray Lodwig, Eddie Pinder, Charles Margulis, Bubber Miley (*t*); Andy Secrest (*c*); Jack Teagarden, Bill Rank, Tommy Dorsey (*tb*); Don Murray (*cl*); Benny Goodman, Jimmy Dorsey, Jimmy Hartwell, Irving Friedman, Frankie Trumbauer (*cl, saxes*); Arnold Brilhart (*as*); Bud Freeman, George Johnson, Charles Strickfadden (*ts*); Ardian Rollini (*bsx*); Irving Brodsky, Frank Signorelli, Lennie Hayton, Hoagy Carmichael, Roy Bargy, Tommy Satterfield (*p*); Joe Venuti, Matty Malneck (*vn*); Eddie Lang (*g*); Min Leibrook (*tba, bsx*); Harry Goodman (*tba*); Mike Trafficante (*b*); Chauncey Morehouse, Hal McDonald, Stan King, Gene Krupa, Harry Gale, Vic Moore (*d*); Irene Taylor, Hoagy Carmichael, The Rhythm Boys (*v*). 24–30.

***   **Bix Lives!** Bluebird ND 86845 CD/LP/MC
Personnel largely as above; others present include Fred Farrar, Henry Busse (*t*); Boyce
Cullen (*tb*); Pee Wee Russell (*cl, as*); Wes Vaughan, Jack Fulton (*v*). 27–30.

***   **Bix'N'Bing** ASV AJA 5005 CD/MC
Personnel largely as above; all tracks by Paul Whiteman Orchestra featuring
Beiderbecke, Bing Crosby (*v*). 27–30.

With Beiderbecke's recordings now out of copyright, reissues have recently emerged from
several sources. Robert Parker's compilation was one of the first releases in his 'Jazz Classics In
Digital Stereo' series for the BBC, and as such lacks a little of the finesse he has brought to
more recent remasterings; nevertheless, working from very fine originals, Parker secures an
admirable clarity of sound. The 16 tracks offer a somewhat hotch-potch collection of
Beiderbecke, from the Wolverines up to his very last session with Hoagy Carmichael; it's a
strong single-disc compilation, but it lacks such important sides as 'Singing The Blues' and 'I'm
Coming Virginia'. The Bluebird collection, numbering 23 tracks, covers only his Victor sides
with the Jean Goldkette and Paul Whiteman orchestras, along with the final date under his own
name. Bix was rather buried amidst dance-band arrangements of pop tunes of the day and has
to be enjoyed in eight-and sixteen-bar solos, but the record does collect virtually everything
important that he did with Whiteman, bar the 'Show Boat' medley which has yet to appear on
CD. The sound is very clean, using BMG's NoNoise technique, although some may find the
timbres a little too dry.

ASV's compilation duplicates much of the Bluebird disc while adding a number of features
for Crosby (then a member of Whiteman's Rhythm Boys) among its 20 tracks. The sound has a
fraction more body but less clarity at top and bottom, and preference between the two is likely
to be a matter of personal taste.

****   **Bix Beiderbecke Vol. 1 Singin' The Blues** CBS 466309 CD/LP/MC
Beiderbecke; Hymie Farberman (*t*); Bill Rank (*tb*); Don Murray (*cl, bs*); Jimmy
Dorsey (*cl, as*); Frankie Trumbauer (*Cmel*); Red Ingle, Bobby Davis (*as*); Adrian
Rollini (*bsx*); Paul Mertz, Itzy Riskin, Frank Signorelli (*p*); Eddie Lang (*g*); Joe
Venuti (*vn*); John Cali (*bj*); Joe Tarto (*tba*); Chauncey Morehouse, Vic Berton (*d*);
Sam Lanin (*perc*); Irving Kaufman, Seger Ellis (*v*). 2–9/27.

****   **Bix & Tram Vol. 1** JSP CD 316 CD
As above. 2–9/27.

Both these compilations follow Beiderbecke chronologically through 1927, arguably his greatest
year in the studios, and both include precisely the same tracks, although the CBS discs includes
an extra in the form of his curious piano solo, 'In A Mist'. Most of them are under Frankie
Trumbauer's leadership, and his own slippery, imaginative solos are often as inventive as Bix's,
demonstrating why Lester Young named him as a primary influence. But most listeners will be
waiting for the shining, affecting cornet improvisations on 'Singin' The Blues', 'Clarinet
Marmalade', 'For No Reason At All In C' and the rest. The contributions of Lang and Dorsey
are a further bonus. The CBS sound is lighter and clearer than the JSP, which some listeners
may prefer, but John R. T. Davies's remastering on the latter certainly has a fuller presence.

****   **Bix Beiderbecke Vol. II At The Jazz Band Ball** CBS 460825 CD/LP/MC
Beiderbecke; Charlie Margulis (*t*); Bill Rank (*tb*); Pee Wee Russell (*cl*); Jimmy
Dorsey, Izzy Friedman, Charles Strickfadden (*cl, as*); Don Murray (*cl, bs*); Frankie
Trumbauer (*Cmel*); Adrian Rollini, Min Leibrook (*bsx*); Frank Signorelli, Arthur
Schutt (*p*); Tom Satterfield (*p, cel*); Joe Venuti, Matty Malneck (*vn*); Carl Kress,
Eddie Lang (*g*); Chauncey Morehouse, Harold MacDonald (*d*); Bing Crosby; Jimmy
Miller, Charlie Farrell (*v*). 10/27–4/28.

The survey of Beiderbecke's OKeh recordings has the advantage of eliminating the Whiteman
material and concentrating on his most jazz-directed music; this volume includes some of the
best of the Bix & His Gang sides, including the title-piece, 'Jazz Me Blues' and 'Sorry', plus
further dates with Trumbauer. As a leader, Beiderbecke wasn't exactly a progressive – some of
the material harks back to the arrangements used by the Original Dixieland Jazz Band – but his
own playing is consistently gripping. Clear and gratifying sound.

RICHARD BEIRACH (born 1947)
PIANO, KEYBOARDS

**   Emerald City Core COCD 9.00522 0 CD
Beirach; John Abercrombie (*g syn*). 2/87.

**(*)   Common Heart Owl 048 CD/LP
Beirach (*p solo*). 9/87.

Entirely successful in the context of bands like Lookout Farm and Quest, Beirach's liquescent keyboard style (partially derived from his experiments with electric piano) cloys dreadfully in solo performance. The logic is all there, but the lines are cluttered with grace-notes and over-ripe sustains. Generally an impressive duo player – as he has proved with Dave Liebman, Frank Tusa and others – he fails utterly to gel with Abercrombie, leaving a sense of discontinuous textures and undeveloped ideas. There are far better things in the second-hand racks.

***   Some Other Time Triloka 180 2 CD
Beirach; Randy Brecker (*t, flh*); Michael Brecker (*ts*); John Scofield (*g*); George Mraz (*b*); Adam Nussbaum (*d*). 4/89.

A tribute to Chet Baker, who hired Beirach in the early 1970s and recorded two of his compositions, 'Broken Wing' and 'Leaving', both recorded here. The group is as good as the affection for Chet's music is patently sincere, but the real star is Mraz (who also contributed 'For B.C.' – impresario Bradley Cunningham – to *Convergence*). He anchors the music brilliantly with a technique that is ageless and individual. Apart from the Beirach originals, the material is fairly predictable, with a final flourish on 'My Funny Valentine'. No mush; just a thoroughly professional performance all round.

***(*)   Convergence Triloka 185 2 CD
Beirach; George Coleman (*ts, ss*). 11/90.

An outwardly improbable partnership, which actually works wonderfully well. It opens with a first glimpse of Coleman on soprano, a complex, polyrhythmic arrangement of Gordon Parish's 'The Lamp Is Low' that feeds both players' considerable harmonic daring. They alternate four-bar sequences on an unusual and highly effective reading of Miles Davis's 'Flamenco Sketches', from *Kind Of Blue*. There are three fine Beirach originals, of which the best is the blues 'Rectilinear', on which Coleman again plays his soprano. He completes the set on the higher horn, appropriately on a version of Wayne Shorter's 'Infant Eyes'.

Beirach uses typically dense textures, but seems to have lost some of the heavy lushness that he brought to duos with Dave Liebman. Coleman is a revelation on the straight horn and nine out of ten people won't guess who it is. The recording itself is immaculate, a tribute to Paul Sloman's loving attention to detail at Triloka/Living Proof.

BOB BELDEN (born 1958)
TENOR SAXOPHONE, KEYBOARDS

**(*)   Treasure Island Sunnyside SSC 1041D CD/MC
Belden; Jim Powell, Tim Hagans (*t, flhn*); John Fedchock (*tb*); George Moran (*btb*); Peter Reit (*frhn*); Tim Ries, Craig Handy (*ss, ts*); Chuck Wilson (*cl, f*); Mike Migliore (*as, f, picc*); Ron Kozak (*bcl, f*); Glenn Wilson (*bs*); Marc Cohen (*ky*); Carl Kleinsteuber (*tba*); Jay Anderson (*b*); Jeff Hirshfield (*d*). 8/89.

A young arranger from Illinois, Belden has gone the accustomed route from college schooling to big-band experience (with Woody Herman) to being an active sideman in New York. His first record as a leader may be belated, but it's not terribly exciting. His own 'Treasure Island Suite' is a cumbersome piece of scoring without anything thematically interesting, and the rest of this well-recorded CD (which runs for nearly 80 minutes) offers an eclectic bunch of modern big-band workouts. Migliore and Wilson, at least, add purposeful improvising.

***   Straight To My Heart Blue Note CDP 7951372 CD/MC
Belden; Jim Powell (*t, flhn*); Tony Kadlek, Tim Hagans (*t*); John Fedchock (*tb*); George Moran (*btb*); Peter Reit (*frhn*); Tim Ries (*ss, ts, bf*); Mike Migliore (*as, f, bf,*

picc); Chuck Wilson (*cl, f, af*); Bobby Watson (*as*); Rick Margitza, Kirk Whalum (*ts*); Glenn Wilson (*bs*); Joey Calderazzo, Marc Copland, Benny Green, Kevin Hays (*p*); Doug Hall, Adam Holzman (*ky*); Pat Rebillot (*org*); Jim Tunnell (*g, v*); John Hart, John Scofield, Fareed Haque (*g*); Darryl Jones, Jay Anderson (*b*); Dennis Chambers, Jeff Hirshfield (*d*); Abraham Adzeneya, Ladji Camara, Jerry Gonzalez, David Earle Johnson (*perc*); Dianne Reeves, Phil Perry, Mark Ledford (*v*). 12/89–5/91.

Eleven compositions by Sting arranged by Belden and performed by an all-star cast drawn from the current Blue Note roster. The material is steeped in what might be called pop sophistication: simple tunes and constructions with underlying harmonic detail to make it interesting for superior players, and Belden utilizes the original structures in interesting ways. 'Roxanne', for instance, has its melody deconstructed and turned into a haunting concerto for Hagans, repetition used with mesmerizing effectiveness. But airplay-orientated touches let down parts of the project: the vocal tracks are tedious, and of the soloists, only Hagans and the superb Margitza – on 'They Dance Alone', easily the best track – make an individual impression.

LOUIE BELLSON (born 1924)
DRUMS

**(*)   Cool Cool Blue Pablo 2310 899 LP/MC
Bellson; Ted Nash (*ss, ts*); Matt Catingub (*ss, as*); Frank Strazzeri (*p*); George Duvivier (*b*). 11/82.

**(*)   The Best Of Louie Bellson Pablo 2405-407 CD/LP/MC
Bellson; Blue Mitchell, Snooky Young, Bobby Shew, Dick Mitchell, Dick Cooper, Cat Anderson, Conte Candoli, Walter Johnson, Ron King (*t*); Nick Dimaio, Gil Falco, Ernie Tack, Mayo Tiana, Bob Payne, Alan Kaplan, Dana Hughes (*tb*); Don Menza, Pete Christlieb, Dick Spencer, Larry Covelli, Bill Byrne, Ted Nash, Andy Macintosh (*reeds*); Nat Pierce, Ross Tompkins (*p*); Emil Richards (*vib, perc*); Mitch Holder, Grant Geissman, Bob Bain (*g*); John Williams, Joel Dibartolo, Gary Pratt (*b*); Paulo Magalhaes, Dave Levine, John Arnold, Gene Estes (*perc*). 5/75–9/78.

Louie Bellson is among the most meritorious of swing drummers, one of the last survivors of a breed of tough and tirelesly energetic men who powered big bands and small groups with the same mix of showmanship and sheer muscle. His comprehensive work with the big-band elite – including Goodman, Basie, James and especially Ellington – gave him a nearly unrivalled experience, and his own groups are marked out by an authority which is often masked by Bellson's comparatively restrained style: virtuoso player that he is, he always plays for the band and seldom overwhelms in the manner of Buddy Rich.

That said, many of his records from the 1970s and '80s are blemished by a shallow attempt at crossover and unhappy eclecticism. In that case, it's lucky that most of his Pablo albums have been deleted; the surviving *Best Of* is no great shakes, but it distils some of the superior moments from what were otherwise dispensable records. The 1982 small group on *Cool, Cool Blue* is a useful outfit, but Nash and Catingub are an efficient rather than a distinctive front line. Nash, then a young alto prodigy, is the interesting one, but it's Bellson who gives the music identity with his own playing.

***   Dynamite! Concord CCD 4105 CD/MC
Bellson; Nelson Hatt, Bobby Shew, John Thomas, Walter Johnson, Ron King (*t, flhn*); Nick Dimaio, Alan Kaplan, Dana Hughes, Bob Payne (*tb*); Dick Spencer, Matt Catingub, Andrew Mackintosh, Gordon Goodwin, Don Menza (*saxes*); Frank Collett (*p*); John Chiodini (*g*); John Williams Jr (*b*); Jack Arnold (*vib, perc*). 8/79.

**(*)   Live At Joe Segal's Jazz Showcase Concord CCD 4350 CD/MC
Bellson; Don Menza (*f, ts*); Larry Novak (*p*); John Heard (*b*). 10/87.

Of Bellson's eight albums for Concord, a much more consistent sequence than his Pablo records, these two are currently the only ones in the catalogue. The big-band date is solidly satisfying without living up to its title, and the main interest probably lies in the gripping section-work by the brass and reeds. The quartet date finds Louie with his trusted sideman and arranger, Don Menza, a hard-swinging and gruff tenor soloist whose amiable drive finds decent if unspectacular assignment here. Both are very cleanly recorded, as is usual with the company.

****   **Hot** Musicmasters/Limelight 5008-2 CD
Bellson; Robert Millikan, Larry Lunetta, Danny Cahn, Glenn Drewes (*t*); Clark Terry
(*flhn*); Don Mikkelsen, Hale Rood, Clinton Sharman, Keith O'Quinn (*tb*); Joe
Roccisano (*as, f*);, George Young (*ss, as, f*); Don Menza (*ts*); Jack Stuckey (*bs, bcl*);
Kenny Hitchcock (*ts, cl, f*); John Bunch (*p*); Jay Leonhart (*b*). 12/87.

***(*)   **East Side Suite** Musicmasters/Limelight 5009-2 CD
As above. 12/87.

A delightful pair of records which revitalize Bellson in the studios. Superbly engineered and
produced, the sound gives the band both warmth and a sheen of top-class professionalism, and
the arrangements – by Menza, Rood, Roccisano and Tommy Newsom – return the favour.
There are storming features for the leader – 'Blues For Uncommon Kids', the opener on *East
Side Suite*, is an absolute knockout – but just as memorable are the smooth changes of gear, the
lovely section-work on 'Peaceful Poet' (*Hot*), the spots allotted to guest horn Clark Terry, the
sense that the band always has something extra in its pocket. A must for big-band admirers.

***(*)   **Jazz Giants** Musicmasters/Limelight 820822-2 CD
Bellson; Conte Candoli (*t*); Buddy DeFranco (*cl*); Don Menza (*ts*); Hank Jones (*p*);
Keter Betts (*b*). 4/89.

Bellson's records have taken such a turn for the better that it's annoying to think of wasted
opportunities in the last two decades. Here he's leading a top-flight sextet on a European tour at
their Swiss stopover, and as a festival blowing date this is about as good as it gets. The soloists
make a nicely contrasting front-line – DeFranco's punctiliousness, Candoli's light fire, Menza's
muscularity – and Louie fires them up with superb and never overbearing drumming.

SATHIMA BEA BENJAMIN
VOCAL

*(*)   **Love Light** Enja 6022 CD
Benjamin; Ricky Ford (*ts*); Larry Willis (*p*); Buster Williams (*b*); Billy Higgins (*d*).
9/87.

**   **Southern Touch** Enja 7015-2 CD
Benjamin; Kenny Barron (*p*); Buster Williams (*b*); Billy Higgins (*d*). 12/89.

Benjamin is Abdullah Ibrahim's wife and is a competent rather than gratifying singer. Her nasal
voice is caught with unflattering clarity on *Love Light*, a programme of standards and modest
originals, although the accompaniments are as well wrought as one would expect from such a
fine backing group. Another impressive team is on hand to support on *Southern Touch*, but the
singer's own efforts are only marginally more impressive. An apparently endless 'Loveless
Love/Careless Love' seems like a completely false start, but matters improve a little from there.

HAN BENNINK (born 1942)
DRUMS, PERCUSSION, ALLSORTS

***   **Solo** FMP SAJ 21 LP
Bennink (*perc*, etc., solo). 10/78.

Though he has a reputation as a showman whose solo performances, as here, are exuberantly
tongue in cheek, it's as well to remember that Bennink is rather different from the 'pots and
pans' school of percussionists with its obsessive concern for novel sonorities. Bennink is above
all a *drummer*, and a very swinging one, whose track record includes stints with some of the
leading bop and mainstream players; he made a notable appearance on Eric Dolphy's not quite
accurately titled *Last Date*. Like Dolphy, no matter how 'free' he plays, he remains wedded to
the basic metres and harmonies of American jazz and all through *Solo* (on which he also plays
viola, clarinet, trombone, banjo and harmonica) there are fractured glimpses of the
one-man-bandmanship that was an important feature of early jazz. Though it's disappointing
that Bennink isn't better represented as a leader, he's always worth looking out for and his
name among the credits is a virtual guarantee of inventive and intelligently rooted

improvisation. (A duo performance with Derek Bailey, called simply *Han* (Incus CD3), is well worth having.)

DAVID BENOIT
PIANO

*(*) **Every Step Of The Way** GRP GRD-9558 CD/MC
Benoit; Jerry Hey, Gary Grant (*t, flhn*); Bill Reichenbach (*tb*); Eric Marienthal (*as*); Sam Riney (*ts*); Dave Valentin (*f*); Chris Smith (*hca*); Randy Waldman, Tom Ranier (*ky*); Russ Freeman, Michael Landau, Neil Stubenhaus, Stanley Clarke, Bob Feldman (*b*); John Robinson, Tony Morales, Harvey Mason (*d*); Michael Fisher, Brad Dutz (*perc*); David Pack, Jeff Pescetto, Philip Ingram, Chuck Sabatino (*v*); Warfield Avenue Symphony Orchestra. 87.

*(*) **Urban Daydreams** GRP GRD-9587 CD/MC
Personnel largely as above, except add Dave Grusin (*ky*); Jimmy Johnson (*b*); Carlos Vega (*d*); Jennifer Warnes (*v*). 88.

** **Waiting For Spring** GRP GRD-9595 CD/MC
Benoit; Emily Remler, Bob Benoit (*g*); Luther Hughes, John Patitucci (*b*); Peter Erskine (*d*). 2–5/89.

*(*) **Inner Motion** GRP GRD-9621 CD/MC
Benoit; Eric Marienthal (*as*); Brandon Fields (*as*); Gary Herbig (*cl*); Pat Kelly, Paul Jackson Jr, Grant Geissman (*g*); Steve Bailey, Neil Stubenhaus (*b*); Vinnie Colaiuta, John Robinson, David Derge (*d*); Michael Fisher, Steve Forman (*perc*); David Pack (*v*); Warfield Avenue Symphony Orchestra. 4–5/90.

*(*) **Shadows** GRPO GRD-9654 CD/MC
Personnel largely as above. 91.

Benoit's jazz-flavoured music may provoke as many savage breasts as it soothes. He is a perfectly secure technician with an agreeable touch and, as the decent interpretation of 'My Romance' on *Waiting For Spring* suggests, he can pass muster as a lightweight interpreter. But these records are uniformly insubstantial and apparently directed at comatose listeners. As in-car entertainment or semi-audible dinner music, they provide an interchangeable service. *Waiting For Spring*, conceived as a 'roots' exercise with a small group, is marginally more involving, but this is scarcely the point of Benoit's music. Our complaint is not that the music is too glossy or that it lacks a jazz 'authenticity', but that its melodic content is so thin. Pop-jazz which fails to engage the ear with hummable melodies or insidious rhythms – as the music of, for example, David Sanborn or Joe Sample consistently does – must surely be accounted a failure. Benoit's pleasantries aren't strong enough for that.

GEORGE BENSON (born 1943)
GUITAR, VOCAL

(*) **The New Boss Guitar OJC 460 LP/CD/MC
Benson; Red Holloway (*ts*); Jack McDuff (*org*); Ronnie Boykins (*b*); Montego Joe (*d*). 5/64.

The huge success he earned in the 1970s and '80s as a light soul vocalist has obscured some of the impact of Benson's guitar playing. He is a brilliant musician. His first records were recorded when Wes Montgomery was alive and the acknowledged master of the style which Benson developed for his own ends: a rich, liquid tone, chunky chording which evolved from Montgomery's octave technique, and a careful sense of construction which makes each chorus tell its own story. At his best, he can fire off beautiful lines and ride on a 4/4 rhythm almost insolent ease; strain is never a part of his playing. Almost any record that he plays guitar on has its share of great moments, although this early date with his then-boss McDuff is comparatively routine, its short tracks and meagre playing-time very much in the organ-combo genre which churned out scores of records in the early and middle '60s. But it's still very good.

***   **Compact Jazz: George Benson** Verve 833292-2 CD

Benson; Jimmy Owens (*t, flhn*); Clark Terry, Ernie Royal, Snooky Young (*t*); Garnett Brown (*tb*); Alan Raph (*btb*); Arthur Clarke, George Marge (*ts, f*); Pepper Adams (*bs*); Buddy Lucas (*hca*); Herbie Hancock, Paul Griffin (*p*); Jimmy Smith (*org*); Eric Gale (*g*); Jack Jennings (*vib, perc*); Bob Cranshaw, Ron Carter, Chuck Rainey (*b*); Billy Cobham, Jimmy Johnson Jr, Idris Muhammad, Donald Bailey (*d*); Johnny Pacheco (*perc*); strings. 1/67–11/68.

After leaving McDuff, Benson cast around for success without really breaking through. His clean, funky but restrained style was hardly the thing in Hendrix's era, and the easy-listening option which Montgomery fell prey to had yet to envelop him while at Columbia and Verve. The *Compact Jazz* compilation is an intelligent cross-section of Benson's small number of recordings in the period: a hot quintet with Hancock, Carter and Cobham glide through 'Billie's Bounce' and 'Thunder Walk', 'I Remember Wes' is a sensitive tribute to the lately deceased Montgomery, and there's a single live track with Jimmy Smith where they pile through 'Tuxedo Junction'. The tracks with a larger band are ordinary; but it hints at Benson's growing versatility, and suggests that he was already seen as Montgomery's natural successor.

*(*)   **Shape Of Things To Come** A&M CD-0803 CD

Benson; Joe Shepley, Marvin Stamm (*t, flhn*); Burt Collins (*t*); Wayne Andre (*tb, bhn*); Alan Raph (*tb, vtb, tba*); Buddy Lucas (*ts, hca*); George Marge, Romeo Penque, Stan Webb (*f*); Herbie Hancock, Hank Jones (*p*); Charles Covington (*org*); Jack Jennings (*vib*); Bernard Eichen, Charles Libove (*vn*); David Markowitz (*vla*); George Ricci (*clo*); Richard Davis, Ron Carter (*b*); Leo Morris (*d*); Johny Pacheco (*perc*). 8/67–10/68.

***   **Beyond The Blue Horizon** CTI ZK-40810 CD

Benson; Clarence Palmer (*org*); Ron Carter (*b*); Jack DeJohnette (*d*); Michael Cameron, Albert Nicholson (*perc*). 2/71.

**   **White Rabbit** CTI ZK-40685 CD

Benson; John Frosk, Alan Rubin (*t, flhn*); Wayne Andre (*tb, bhn*); Jim Buffington (*frhn*); Hubert Laws (*f, picc*); Phil Bodner (*f, ob, cor*); George Marge (*f, cl, ob, cor*); Romeo Penque (*cl, bcl, ob, cor, f*); Jane Taylor (*bsn*); Herbie Hancock (*p*); Gloria Agostini (*hp*); Phil Kraus (*vib, perc*); Jay Berliner, Earl Klugh (*g*); Ron Carter (*b*); Billy Cobham (*d*); Airto Moreira (*perc, v*). 11/71.

**   **Body Talk** CTI ZK-45222 CD

Benson; Jon Faddis, John Gatchell, Waymon Reed (*t, flhn*); Gerald Chamberlain, Dick Griffin (*tb*); Frank Foster (*ts*); Harold Mabern (*p*); Earl Klugh (*g*); Ron Carter, Gary King (*b*); Jack DeJohnette (*d*); Mobutu (*perc*). 7/73.

**   **Bad Benson** CTI ZK-40926 CD

Benson; Jon Frosk, Alan Rubin, Joe Shepley (*t*); Wayne Andre, Garnett Brown, Warren Covington (*tb*); Paul Faulise (*btb*); Jim Buffington, Brooks Tillotson (*frhn*); Phil Bodner (*cl, f, cor*); George Marge (*f, picc, cor*); Al Regni (*cl, f*); Kenny Barron (*p*); Margaret Ross (*hp*); Phil Upchurch (*g, b*); Ron Carter (*b*); Steve Gadd (*d*); strings. 5/74.

(*)   **In Concert At Carnegie Hall CTI ZK-44167 CD

Benson; Hubert Laws (*f*); Ronnie Foster (*ky*); Wayne Dockery, Will Lee (*b*); Marvin Chappell, Steve Gadd, Andy Newmark (*d*); Ray Armando, Johnny Griggs (*v*). 1/75.

(*)   **Benson & Farrell CTI ZK-44169 CD

Benson; Joe Farrell (*ss, f*); Eddie Daniels, David Tofani (*f*); Don Grolnick, Sonny Bravo (*p*); Eric Gale, Steve Khan (*g*); Will Lee, Gary King (*b*); Andy Newmark (*d*); Nicky Marrero (*perc*). 3–9/76.

Creed Taylor, who ran things at CTI, certainly thought Benson should carry on where Montgomery had left off. The A&M album, which quickly bogs down in Don Sebesky's typically ponderous arrangements, is a wet run for what came next, a sequence of strong-selling albums which found Benson gamely making the best of a near-hopeless situation. Given Taylor's proclivities for stupefying charts and tick-tock rhythms, it's surprising that there's as much decent music as there is here. *Beyond The Blue Horizon* is an attractive, smoochy session with Carter and DeJohnette surrounding the guitarist with shrewdly paced rhythms; 'So What' and a very pretty 'The Gentle Rain' are among the high points of Benson's CTI work. *White Rabbit*, *Body Talk* and *Bad Benson* find him ambling through the likes of 'California Dreaming' and 'Top Of The World' while reeds pipe soothingly behind him. Benson still finds interesting fills, but it's a terribly weak assignment for a man who was playing on *Miles In The Sky* a few years earlier. The live album is inevitably livelier, and the date with Joe Farrell, although the latter is confined mostly to the flute, has some spunky playing; yet it scarcely adds up to a strong manifesto for the man who might have been the premier straight-ahead jazz guitarist of the moment. *Beyond The Blue Horizon* will do for anyone who wants to hear the pick of Benson's CTI work.

*** **Breezin'** Warner Bros 256199 CD/MC
Benson; Ronnie Foster, Jorge Dalto (*ky*); Phil Upchurch (*g*); Stanley Banks (*b*); Harvey Mason (*d*); Ralph McDonald (*perc*); strings. 1/76.

** **In Flight** Warner Bros 256327 CD/MC
As above. 8–11/76.

*** **Weekend In L.A.** Warner Bros 3139-2 2CD/2MC
As above, except omit strings. 2/77.

Breezin' was the first jazz album to go platinum and sell a million copies, but more important for the listener was its reconciliation of Taylor's pop-jazz approach with a small-group backing which Benson could feel genuinely at home in: Claus Ogerman's arrangements are still fluffy, and the tunes are thin if not quite anodyne, but Benson and his tightly effective band get the most out of them. It's a very pleasurable listen. *In Flight* reintroduces Benson as vocalist (he actually began as a singer in the 1950s), and 'Nature Boy' blueprints the direction he would take next, but the record is too patently a retread of the previous one. *Weekend In L.A.* is a live set that shows how the band can hit a groove outside the studio. Benson's treatment of 'On Broadway' is an infectious classic because he lives out the song; the session as a whole is a bit deodorized, but smoothness is the guitarist's trademark, and his solos are full of singing melodies, tied to their own imperturbable groove.

** **Tenderly** Warner Bros 25907 CD/LP/MC
Benson; McCoy Tyner (*p*); Ron Carter (*b*); Louis Hayes, Al Foster (*d*). 89.

** **Big Boss Band** Warner Bros 26295 CD/LP/MC
Benson; Bob Ojeda, Byron Stripling, Randy Brecker, Jon Faddis, Lew Soloff, Larry Farrell (*t*); Paul Faulise, Earl Gardner, Keith O'Quinn, James Pugh (*tb*); David Glasser (*as*); Frank Foster (*ts*); Barry Eastmond, Richard Tee, Terry Burrus, David Witham (*ky*); Ron Carter (*b*); Carmen Bradford (*v*); Count Basie Orchestra; Robert Farnon Orchestra. 90.

Most of Benson's records after *Weekend In L.A.* fall outside the scope of this book, although many rate as high-calibre light-soul. But of late he's been investigating a return to more orientated material, possibly as a result of a somewhat waning general popularity. Guest appearances as a sideman with such friends as Earl Klugh and Jimmy Smith haven't yielded much, though, and these two sets must be counted great disappointments. *Tenderly* is far too relaxed: Benson's singing sounds tired, and his playing is as uneventful as that of the others involved, although such seasoned pros always deliver a few worthwhile touches. Weaker still is *Big Boss Band*, a collaboration with Frank Foster's Count Basie band that runs aground on fussy arrangements, material Basie himself wouldn't have touched (the soporific 'How Do You Keep The Music Playing'), and one track with Robert Farnon's band ('Portrait Of Jennie') which suggests a shot at Nat Cole's repertoire may be the next thing on George's agenda. His guitar playing plays an entirely minor role.

BOB BERG (born 1951)
TENOR SAXOPHONE, SOPRANO SAXOPHONE

** **Short Stories** Denon 33CY 1768 CD
Berg; Mike Stern (*g*); Don Grolnick (*p, org, syn*); Jeff Andrews (*b*); Will Lee (*b*); Robby Kilgore (*syn*); David Sanborn (*as*); Peter Erskine (*d*).

**   **Cycles** Sound Planet IN 804 LP
As above, except omit Lee, Kilgore, Sanborn, Erskine; add David Kikowski (*p, syn*); Jerry O'Sullivan (*pipes*); Dennis Chambers (*d*).

***   **In The Shadows** Denon CY 76210 CD
Berg; Randy Brecker (*t*); Mike Stern (*g*); Jim Beard (*ky*); Lincoln Goines, Will Lee (*b*); Dennis Chambers (*d*).

A stint with Miles Davis, far from pushing Berg into the limelight, set his always-promising solo career back a good album or two. Miles, for reasons obvious from his earlier CV, has been less than generous to his latter-day reedmen, obviously looking on the sax as a regressive instrument *vis-à-vis* happening things like 'lead' bass guitars, synths and drum machines.

Berg is a hugely talented mainstream player, with a well-assimilated Coltrane influence who could never realistically have been expected to fit into Miles's avant-disco conception. What he was expected to put in is now history, but what did he take away with him? On the strength of *Short Stories*, not a great deal. The electronic input is fairly conventional, dominated by Don Grolnick's lightish organ lines and regular partner (and fellow Prince of Darkness escapee) Stern's finely modulated guitar. There is less urgent pursuit of exotic timbral effects here than on *Cycles*, which features the, ahem, skirl of the pipes on one, and just one, track. David Sanborn adds a measure of fusion cred to 'Kalimba', by far the weakest of the *Short Stories*: no punch-line, no 'twist', just a rather lamely over-programmed Afro-Caribbean excursion.

By far the most impressive of the three is *In The Shadows*. Berg's enunciation seems just a notch tauter, and Stern plays with a degree more authority than he has of late. The band is much better balanced, and 'Autumn Leaves' is well worth the wait. Again, though, there is a nagging sense that Berg in particular is playing well within himself rather than taking chances, an impression that is ironically reinforced by his avoidance of standards. Even 'letting go', as he does on the ironically titled 'The Search' on *Short Stories*, he still sounds too contained and guarded. Time, perhaps, to come out of the shadows.

(*)   **Back Roads Denon CY 79042 CD
Berg; Jim Beard (*p, ky*); Mike Stern (*g*); Lincoln Goines (*b*); Dennis Chambers, Ben Perowsky (*d*); Manolo Badrena (*perc*). 91.

Discouragingly similar in approach and content to the smoothed-out jazz fusion that Sadao Watanabe has made such a colossal money-spinner for Denon. The title-track, which opens the set, is no more than variations up and down the scale of a sweet, brief theme reminiscent of Watanabe's 'My Dear Life'. Most of the rest is played with a bland, jeans-advert feel that only lifts briefly on 'When I Fall In Love' (which is convincingly romantic) and the closing 'Nighthawks', by which time the harm has been done. Very disappointing.

NATHAN BERG (born 1972)
BASS

***   **Fish With No Fins** Time Is TI9803 CD
Berg; Bob Shephard (*ts*); Alan Broadbent (*p*); Carl Burnett (*d*). 8/90.

Compared with some of the recent leadership debuts of many young players, this is an enterprisingly strong and well-rounded date. Berg's facility is up to the norm for the contemporary crop of teenage virtuosos, but, as prominent as he sounds here, displaying a very big and full tone, he eschews rapid-fire solos in favour of following a very fluid pulse. His interplay with Broadbent and Burnett, on trio versions of 'Monk's Dream' and Horace Silver's 'Lonely Woman', is especially fine, and the duet with Shephard on 'Hey Joe' shows off an almost indecently plummy resonance on the bass. The saxophonist sounds a little less detached than he does on some of his studio dates, too. A name worth remembering.

GUSTAVO BERGALLI
TRUMPET, FLUGELHORN

(*)   **Gustavo Bergalli Quintet Dragon DRLP 119 LP
Bergalli; Hakan Broström (ss, as); Stefan Blomqvist (p); Olle Steinholtz (b); Leif
Fredriksson (d). 5/86.

Bergalli is an expatriate Argentinian who has settled in Sweden, and he made this enjoyable,
lightweight set with a youngish band of Stockholmites. Brostrom is certainly the most striking
soloist here, although some may find his tart alto manner a little too edgy for what is essentially
good-natured hard bop: he seems to be emulating McLean in his own 'Conversation With
Jackie', for instance. The material is short on memorable themes, but Bergalli's sunny playing
results in some attractive solos.

JOHN BERGAMO
PERCUSSION

***(*)   **On The Edge** CMP 27 CD/LP
Bergamo (perc solo). 5/86.

Bergamo, along with Gerry Hemingway, Glen Velez and Edward Vesala, is one of the few
percussionists from outside the Afro-American tradition who is worth listening to in solo
performance. He numbers among his instruments such exotica as engine nacelles from jumbo
jets, and he plays with all the power and reliability that implies. 'Nideggen Uthan', 'Piru Bole'
and 'On The Edge' are tremendously powerful and affecting, balancing technical curiosity (just
how is such-and-such a sound made?) with an involving acceptance of Bergamo's logic. He can
also be heard on a remarkable Coltrane tribute with *Bracha*, CMP 34 CD/LP/MC, a guitar-led
percussion group that failed to garner very much critical attention at the time.

ANDERS BERGCRANTZ
TRUMPET, FLUGELHORN

***   **Opinions** Dragon DRLP 97 LP
Bergcrantz; Ove Ingmarsson (ts); Anders Persson (p); Stefan Bellnas (b); Lennart
Gruvstedt (d). 1/85.

***(*)   **Touch** Dragon DRLP 133 LP
As above. 9/86.

Bergcrantz is a gifted hard bop trumpeter with a popping attack and a penchant for short,
pecked-off phrases. His band is a tight, unfancy group that creates an intense, skilfully
personalized kind of post-bop: it's a band where everyone seems to be pushing to stay at the
top of their game. The studio album, *Opinions*, is a bit formal and contained in parts, although
'Sinuhe' and 'Stan And Oliver' are originals that bring the best out of both horns, and Horace
Silver's 'Peace' gets a blue-chip reading. But the live *Touch* holds the attention throughout: 'A
Little Message For Bu' and 'Depressions' show that the leader can write constructively, and
the labyrinthine investigation of Wayne Shorter's 'Footprints' starts with a gripping Bergcrantz
solo and moves into even darker waters with Ingmarsson's granitic tenor outburst. Highly
recommended, and the location recording is excellent.

JERRY BERGONZI
TENOR AND SOPRANO SAXOPHONE

(*)   **Jerry On Red Red 123224 CD/LP/MC
Bergonzi; Salvatore Bonafede (p); Dodo Goya (b); Salvatore Tranchini (d). 5/88.

Bergonzi is a player of sweeping accomplishment, but he sounds so in thrall to Sonny Rollins as
an influence that it's hard to hear anything individual in his music. On its own terms, this session
is enjoyable, although the rhythm section don't push him hard enough. But the leader's

mannerisms – retarding and rushing the beat, a grey, granitic tone and a penchant for thematic improvising – are so comprehensively borrowed from Rollins that one's reaction is to put on a record by the original instead.

(*)   **Lineage Red 123237 CD
      Bergonzi; Mulgrew Miller (*p*); Dave Santoro (*b*); Adam Nussbaum (*d*). 10/89.

(*)   **Standard Gonz Blue Note 7962562 CD
      Bergonzi; Joey Calderazzo (*p*); Dave Santoro (*b*); Adam Nussbaum (*d*). 10/89–5/90.

Recorded very close together, these two records tell a little more about Bergonzi's powers: *Lineage* keeps up a high level of energy and inventiveness on its own terms, and the more considered studio setting for *Standard Gonz* shows no lack of intensity either. Moment by moment these are fine efforts, but the busyness of each session and the saxophonist's frequently ugly and strangulated tone make them rather wearying too.

BUNNY BERIGAN (1908–42)
TRUMPET

(*)   **Bunny Berigan Atlantis ATS 7 LP
      Berigan; Irving Goodman, Steve Lipkins (*t*); Ray Conniff, Red Jessup or Jack Lacey (*tb*); Gus Bivona, George Bohn, Joe Dixon, Mike Doty, Paul Ricci (*cl, as*); Georgie Auld, Clyde Rounds, Babe Russin or Forrest Crawford (*ts*); Joe Bushkin or Walter Gross (*p*); Dick Wharton (*g*); Mort Stuhlmaker, Hank Wayland (*b*); Henry Adler or Stan King, Johnny Blowers, Buddy Rich (*d*); other personnel unidentified. 3, 6 & 8/38.

***(*)   **Bunny Berigan And The Rhythm Makers: Volume 1 – Sing! Sing! Sing!** Jass J-CD 627 CD
      Berigan; Irv Goodman, Steve Lipkins, Ralph Muzzillo, Harry Preble (*t*); Ray Conniff, Nat Lobovsky, George Mazza, Artie Foster (*tb*); Artie Shaw (*cl*); Joe Dixon, Mike Doty, Carl Swift (*cl, as*); Georgie Auld, Artie Drelinger, Clyde Rounds (*ts*); Joe Bushkin, Joe Lipman (*p*); Dick Wharton (*g*); Morty Stuhlmaker, Hank Wayland (*b*); Johnny Blowers, Bill Flanagan (*d*); Ruth Gaylor, Peggy Lawson, Bernie Mackey (*v*); other personnel unidentified. 7/36, 6/38.

***   **The Complete Bunny Berigan Volume III** Bluebird NL 90439 2CD/2LP/2MC
      Berigan; Irving Goodman, Steve Lipkins (*t*); Ray Conniff, Al George, Sonny Lee, Nat Lovobsky (*tb*); Georgie Auld, Mike Doty, Joe Dixon, Clyde Rounds (*reeds*); Joe Lippman (*p*); Tom Morgan, Dick Wharton (*g*); Hank Wayland (*b*); Johnny Blowers, George Wettling (*d*); Ruth Gaylor, Gail Reese (*v*). 10/37–6/38.

Bunny Berigan's only flaw, in Louis Armstrong's opinion, was that he didn't live long enough. At the height of his career as an independent bandleader, he was making impossible demands on an uncertain constitution. As a leader, he was wildly exciting, cutting solos like 'I Can't Get Started' (there are two versions, but the 1937 one is the classic), one of the lads, but utterly inept as an organizer. Stints with disciplinarians like Goodman and Tommy Dorsey (who valued his genius too much to pitch him out) didn't change his ways.

Though he died prematurely burnt out, Berigan left a legacy of wonderful music. His tone was huge and 'fat', a far cry from the tinny squawk with which he started out. The 1936 material on Jass was recorded for NBC's Thesaurus series of 16-inch electrical transcriptions. The arrangements are mostly very bland and the only thing that holds the attention is Berigan's horn, either open or muted, cutting through the pap with almost indecent ease. Typical devices are his use of 'ghost' notes and rapid chromatic runs that inject a degree of tension into music that often sounds ready to fall asleep. That Berigan's time-sense and ability to play instant countermelodies were god-given, there is no doubt, but it's also clear that he studied Armstrong closely and learned a great deal from him. That's evident from the solos on 'Sing! Sing! Sing!' and 'On Your Toes'. Sound restoration is good and not too vivid.

There's a conventional wisdom that Berigan's best work bloomed unseen in the desert air of Hal Kemp's and Paul Whiteman's orchestras, and that he was already a spent force by the time he recorded on his own account. The later of the sessions on the Jass compilation suggests that that is a hasty judgement. There's an angular quality to the solos on 'Wacky Dust' and 'And So

Forth' (where he growls alarmingly) which may be camouflaged on a first hearing by his sheer timbral inventiveness and resource, but which is none the less impressive.

There's minimal overlap on the Atlantis, but it isn't a particularly exciting compilation, and fans and newcomers alike would be well advised to hold out for the Bluebird set. Three stars, let it be said, for Berigan only. Wading through these four sides is a little like the heron-patient waiting that Bix buffs willingly undergo for occasional glimmers of the man himself. The arrangements are generally better than those Bix had to suffer, but the material is pretty lame (Berigan eased himself out of the Paul Whiteman orchestra, where he had replaced Beiderbecke, in disgust at the band-book and distribution of solos) and much of the supporting play is nothing to write home about. Berigan, though, is remarkably fresh and a lot closer to Miles's minimal approach than anyone else dared attempt in those furiously competitive days. Berigan's ability to sustain power throughout his impressive range was one of his most durable characteristics and he retains the ability to say more in fewer notes than any of his rivals. His development is logical, and impressively simple; he tackles 'Russian Lullaby' without the onion-y emotion most players of the time brought to Irving Berlin's tune, and his deep-toned solo on 'A Serenade To The Stars' is as moving as trumpet gets before Miles Davis came along.

These days, certainly among younger listeners and recent jazz converts, Berigan is little known. It's a pity that Bluebird, having set up a 'complete' and taken the trouble to commission a long and intelligent essay from Richard Sudhalter, should have let the first two volumes lapse.

BERLIN CONTEMPORARY JAZZ ORCHESTRA
GROUP

**** **Berlin Contemporary Jazz Orchestra** ECM 1409 CD
Benny Bailey, Thomas Heberer, Henry Lowther (*t*); Kenny Wheeler (*t, flhn*);
Henning Berg, Hermann Breuer, Hubert Katzenbeier (*tb*); Ute Zimmermann (*btb*);
Paul van Kamenade, Felix Wahnschaffe (*as*); Gerd Dudek (*ts, ss, cl, f*); Walter Gauchel (*ts*); Ernst Ludwig Petrowsky (*bs*); Willem Breuker (*bs, bcl*); Misha Mengelberg, Aki Takase (*p*); Günter Lenz (*b*); Ed Thigpen (*d*); Alex von Schlippenbach (*cond*). 5/89.

Much as Barry Guy's London Jazz Composer's Orchestra (*q.v.*) has turned in recent years to large-scale composition, the Berlin Contemporary Jazz Orchestra presents its conductor/organizer with a more formal and structured resource for presentation of large-scale scored pieces with marked tempi for improvising orchestra. One outwardly surprising inclusion in the line-up is drummer Ed Thigpen, normally associated with conventional mainstream jazz. This superb set, as yet the only recorded output of the BCJO, features one long piece by Canadian trumpeter Kenny Wheeler and two rather less melancholy pieces by Misha Mengelberg.

Wheeler's 'Ana' is a long, almost hymnic, piece whose mournful aspect nevertheless doesn't soften some powerful soloing; Thomas Heberer, Aki Takase and Gerd Dudek are just the most notable contributors, and the piece is held together as much by Thigpen's robust swing as by Wheeler's detailed score.

Mengelberg's 'Reef Und Kneebus' and 'Salz' are very much in the line of a post-war Dutch style in which jazz is almost as dominant an element as serial procedures. Mengelberg's music is frequently satirical, then unexpectedly melancholy. Benny Bailey's bursting solo on 'Salz' prepares the way for some determined over-blowing on the second piece, which fits jazz themes into a 'Minuet', 'Rigaudon', 'Bourrée' matrix. (If the middle element is less familiar, it relates to another seventeenth-century dance-form with a sharp rhythmic hop at the opening and a central bridge passage which sharply changes the direction of both music and dancers. Of such turns are both of Mengelberg's compositions made.) Outstanding solos from Dudek again and Van Kamenade, while on 'Salz' Breuker almost matches Bailey for sheer brass – or, in this case, woodwind. Thoroughly enjoyable and thought-provoking music.

TIM BERNE
ALTO SAXOPHONE, VOICE

*** **The Ancestors** Soul Note 1061 CD/LP/MC
Berne; Clarence Herb Robertson (*t, pocket t, c, flhn*); Ray Anderson (*tb, tba*); Mack
Goldsbury (*ts, ss*); Ed Schuller (*b*); Paul Motian (*d, perc*). 2/83.

*** **Mutant Variations** Soul Note 1091 LP
As above, except omit Anderson, Goldsbury. 3/83.

** **Fractured Fairy Tales** JMT 834 431-1
Berne; Herb Robertson (*t, c, laryngeal crowbar*); Mark Feldman (*vn, baritone vn*);
Hank Roberts (*clo, electric clo, v*); Mark Dresser (*b, giffus, bungy*); Joey Baron (*d,
CZ-101, shacktronics*). 6/89

Tim Berne called his first album *The Five Year Plan*. He released it himself, apparently
unwilling to wait around for the bigger labels to get their heads together and totally unwilling to
spend five or ten years hacking it as a sideman. *The Ancestors* is his fifth album, and a first sign
that he was willing to slow down, look about him and take stock. Recorded live, it's a measured,
authoritative set, rhythmically more coherent than previous and later sessions, with passages of
almost Asiatic beauty from Berne and some classic trombone from the still-developing
Anderson. Berne's charts are increasingly adventurous and ensemble passages are well played
and registered in a typically professional Soul Note production.

The set's coherence might be credited to the veteran Motian (he takes a fine solo on side
two and holds together the excellent *Mutant Variations*, with its leaner, punchier line-up), who
makes a very effective rhythmic anchor with Schuller, a veteran of Berne albums. Dresser, by
contrast, is a less rhythmic, stringier player and is called on to play a very different role on
Fractured Fairy Tales, collaging textures with Roberts and Feldman (the three fiddlers have
recorded recently as Arcado). Unfortunately, though, the sound is muddied and the interplay
imprecise. The electronic input is uneasy and largely superfluous, clogging Berne's logic to the
point of thrombosis at a couple of points. Opt for *Mutant Variations* as a first port of call.

WARREN BERNHARDT
PIANO

(*) **Warren Bernhardt Trio DMP CD 441 CD
Bernhardt; Eddie Gomez (*b*); Peter Erskine (*d*). 1/83.

** **Hands On** DMP CD 457 CD
Bernhardt; Kenny Asher, Robbie Condor, Rick Tuttobene (*ky*); John Tropea (*g*);
Anthony Jackson, Marc Johnson (*b*); Peter Erskine (*d*). 10/86.

** **Heat Of The Moment** DMP CD 457 CD
Bernhardt; Mike DiMicco (*g*); Jay Anderson (*b*); Peter Erskine (*d*); Gordon Gottlieb
(*perc*). 3/89.

*** **Ain't Life Grand** DMP CD 478 CD
Bernhardt; Jay Anderson (*b*); Danny Gottlieb (*d*). 4/90.

A sometime sideman with Gerry Mulligan and Jack DeJohnette among others, Bernhardt has
an uneasy time about establishing individual credentials. He has the harmonic vocabulary
common to all post-Evans pianists but prefers to dig in a little harder than most; nevertheless
his records suffer from a sameness and a modesty of melodic imagination which make them
pleasing but finally unremarkable. The *Trio* set is firmed up by the typically punchy support of
Gomez and Erskine, but the next two records are troubled by the unnecessary embellishment of
guitars and electronics. His latest release, however, finds him at his best: 'Blue Lake' and
'Balanca' are strong originals, and standards such as 'Days Of Wine And Roses' are given brisk
and purposeful attention. The DMP recording is uniformly bright and well balanced.

BILL BERRY (born 1930)
TRUMPET, CORNET

(*)   **Hello Rev Concord CCD-4027 CD/MC
Berry; Cat Anderson, Gene Goe, Blue Mitchell, Jack Sheldon (*t*); Britt Woodman,
Jimmy Cleveland, Benny Powell, Tricky Lofton (*tb*); Marshall Royal, Lanny Morgan,
Richie Kamuca, Don Menza, Jack Nimnitz (*saxes*); Dave Frishberg (*p*); Monty
Budwig (*b*); Frank Capp (*d*). 8/76.

Berry, a journeyman mainstream trumpeter who once worked with Ellington, presides over a
big-band record that searches for an Ellingtonian feel and gets some of the way there. The
group performs with cheerful swing on an effectively chosen programme, including such
lesser-known Ducal pieces as 'Tulip Or Turnip', and the live recording is quite kind, but it's
finally too much like many another midstream big-band date to demand much attention. Berry
himself did much better with the engaging small-group record *Shortcake*, but so far Concord
have left that one out of their reissue programme.

CHU BERRY (1910–41)
TENOR SAXOPHONE

***   **Chu Berry Story** Zeta ZET 738 CD
Berry; no personnel details. 37, 38.

***   **A Giant Of The Tenor Sax** Commodore Classics 8-24293 LP
Berry; Roy Eldridge, Hot Lips Page (*t*); Clyde Hart (*p*); Danny Barker, Al Casey (*g*);
Al Morgan, Artie Shapiro (*b*); Big Sid Catlett, Harry Yeager (*d*). 11/38, 8/41.

Half a century after his premature death, Berry's reputation is still in eclipse. He died just a
little too soon for the extraordinary revolution in saxophone playing that followed the end of
the war. He had a big sound, not unlike that of Coleman Hawkins – who considered him an
equal – with a curiously fey inflexion that was entirely his own and which appealed strongly to
Young Turks like Frank Lowe, who began to listen to Berry again in the 1970s.

For someone who recorded a good deal, the catalogue is depressingly and shamefully sparse.
There are a dozen Jazz Orchestra tracks for 1937–8 on the slightly odd Zeta compilation, which
is nevertheless a valuable addition to the CD catalogue. The Commodore sessions – the later
ones from within a couple of months of Berry's death following an auto accident – have him in
rumbustious form, combining jovially with Eldridge and Page. There is a lovely 'Body And
Soul' from 1938 which sits very well alongside even the canonical versions, and two lovely cuts
of 'On The Sunny Side Of The Street'. Alternate takes expose a rather attenuated structural
sense – solos always seemed to follow much the same trajectory – but he was a wonderfully
complete player in all other regards and repays close attention. When he died, they left his
chair in the Cab Calloway band sitting empty.

STEVE BERRY
DOUBLE BASS

(*)   **Steve Berry Trio Loose Tubes Records LTLP 007 LP
Berry; Mark Lockheart (*saxophones*); Peter Fairclough (*d*). 88.

Steve Berry enjoyed junior prefect status in the Loose Tubes common room, a sober presence
who got on with the serious business without unctuous compromise. His skills as a writer and
soloist remained largely unacknowledged, until the release of this, his debut solo album.

Berry's bass-playing is curiously reminiscent of Oscar Pettiford, with the same blend of
lyricism and fury and the same cello-influenced higher register effects. It combines evocatively
with Mark Lockheart's habitual lump-in-the-throat sax on 'Take Your Time' and a piece called
'After Midnight', which is closer in spirit to J. J. Cale than to Thelonious Monk.

The writing is rhythmically inventive but a little lacking in harmonic interest, which may be
due to Lockheart's unpaid debts to Ornette Coleman. There are also some misgivings about the
recording; Peter Fairclough isn't well registered at all and there is a persistent, inelegant

separation of sound which may simply reflect the loosely discursive nature of the music but which is nevertheless very distracting.

GENE BERTONCINI (born 1937)
GUITAR

**   **The Art Of The Duo** Stash ST-CD-6 CD
Bertoncini; Michael Moore (*b*); Edison Machado (*d*). 86/87.

An enjoyable if lightweight collection. Bertoncini's extensive experience as a sideman has been mainly as an electric guitarist, but here he plays a nylon-strung instrument for some pretty meditations on a broad range of material. Some themes become unlikely medley partners: Puccini's 'Un Bel Dì' with 'Poor Butterfly', Ray Bryant's 'Li'l Suzie' with 'Blue Monk'. Moore is typically sympathetic, but Machado's percussion (he is on four of the 13 tracks) is rather splashy. The CD is a compilation from three earlier LPs.

BEN BESIAKOV (born 1956)
PIANO

**   **You Stepped Out Of A Dream** Steeplechase SCCD-31265 CD/LP
Besiakov; Ron McClure (*b*); Keith Copeland (*d*). 3/90.

Besiakov is a Dane who has recorded as a sideman with Doug Raney. His style is a familiar mixture of post-bop pianists, unemphatic for the most part and agreeable without suggesting much depth. At 72 minutes, the CD is perhaps over-generous. McClure, in fact, has almost as much space as the leader to improvise, and actually sounds more in command.

ED BICKERT (born 1932)
GUITAR

***   **Ed Bickert/Don Thompson** Sackville 4005 LP
Bickert; Don Thompson (*b*). 1/78.

Bickert is a Canadian whose self-effacing style masks a keen intelligence. He has a deceptively soft tone, notes coming demurely off his fingers, but he can muster the whipcrack speed of Tal Farlow when he wants to, and he's as comfortable in group situations as he is in this more exposed setting. His partnership with the equally unassuming Thompson is perhaps a shade too acquiescent, but their empathy is absorbing in itself, and on such as 'You Are Too Beautiful', where the initiative passes to and fro with seamless insight, the duo can be compelling. The live recording is a little unfocused, but it suits the music.

***   **At Toronto's Bourbon Street** Concord CJ 216 MC
Bickert; Warren Vaché (*c*); Scott Hamilton (*ts*); Steve Wallace (*b*); Jake Hanna (*d*). 1/83.

(*)   **Bye Bye Baby Concord CJ 232 MC
Bickert; Dave McKenna (*p*); Steve Wallace (*b*); Jake Hanna (*d*). 8/83.

(*)   **I Wished On The Moon Concord CCD 4284 CD/MC
Bickert; Rick Wilkins (*ts*); Steve Wallace (*b*); Terry Clarke (*d*). 6/85.

Bickert's Concord albums marry his lyric skills with a more propulsive setting: McKenna supplies the drive on *Bye Bye Baby*, while Clarke and Wilkins are the useful foils on *I Wished On The Moon*. Although the music is rather too evenly modulated to sustain attention, Bickert adds interest by choosing unhackneyed material, and CCD 4284 in particular has a fine programme of rare standards. But the most engaging set is the *Bourbon Street* session, where the Concord house horns of Vaché and Hamilton cook their way through a delightful session and Bickert is at his most swinging.

***   **Third Floor Richard** Concord CCD 4380 CD/MC
Bickert; Dave McKenna (*p*); Neil Swainson (*b*); Terry Clarke (*d*). 1/89.

***   **This Is New** Concord CCD 4414 CD/MC
Bickert; Lorne Lofksy (*g*); Neil Swainson (*b*); Jerry Fuller (*d*). 12/89.

Bickert's most recent records continue the formula, but like so many other Concord artists he's inhabiting the style so completely that the records are taking on a special elegance and grace. *Third Floor Richard* returns McKenna to a Bickert date, though he is in for him a quiescent mood, and the playing is sumptuously refined. the quartet with Lofksy, though, is a little sharper, with 'Ah-Leu-Cha' pacifying the contrapuntalism of the playing without surrendering all of the bebop fizz which underlines it. Very agreeable.

ACKER BILK (born 1929)
CLARINET

****   **That's My Home** Philips 830778 CD
Bilk; Ken Sims, Colin Smith (*t*); John Mortimer (*tb*); Bruce Turner (*as*); Colin Bates, Stan Greig (*p*); Tony Pitt (*g*); Roy James (*bj*); Tucker Finlayson, Ernest Price (*b*); Ron McKay, Johnny Richardson (*d*). 4/60–3/70.

*(**)   **Stranger On The Shore** Philips 830779 CD
Bilk; Leon Young String Chorale. 62.

****   **Acker Bilk In Holland** Timeless TTD 506/7 CD/2LP
Bilk; Mike Cotton (*t*); Campbell Burnap (*tb*, *v*); Colin Wood (*p*); Tucker Finlayson (*b*); Richie Bryant (*d*). 2/83.

***(*)   **Blaze Away** Timeless TTD 943/4 CD/2LP
As above. 1/87.

Barber, Ball and Bilk – the 'Three Bs' – were the heirs of Ken Colyer's trad revolution. If Barber 'prettified' Colyer's rough-edged approach, Bilk brought an element of showmanship and humour, speaking in a disconcerting Zummerzet accent, dressing his Paramount Jazz Band in Edwardian waistcoats and bowlers, notching two enormous hits with 'Summer Set' (a further punning reference to the county of his birth) and 'Stranger On The Shore', a tune still much requested at autumnal wedding receptions.

The idea had come from producer Dennis Preston, who wanted Bilk to record with strings. The clarinettist reworked a theme that was originally dedicated to his daughter, recorded it with the Leon Young String Chorale, saw it picked up as the signature to a similarly titled television serial, and counted the royalties. Bilk's success – 'Stranger' sold more than two million copies – and photogenic presentation attracted an inevitable mixture of envy and disdain and it's often forgotten how accomplished and 'authentic' a musician he actually is. Working with Colyer in the mid-1950s, he played in a raw-edged George Lewis style very different from the silky, evocative vibrato he cultivated in later years. The schmaltz of *Stranger* (other tracks include 'I Left My Heart In San Francisco', 'Greensleeves' and 'Petite Fleur') is as comfortably addictive as buttered toast but doesn't provide much in the way of improvisational nourishment and resolute jazz exclusivists may find it a little hard to take.

That's My Home is a valuable compilation of a decade's worth of material and traces his progress from doctrinaire trad (with the banjo going *chung, chung, chung* exactly on the beat, as George Melly describes in *Owning Up*) to a more varied instrumental spectrum that found room for a piano and even (horrors!) a saxophone. Bruce Turner, the 'dirty bopper' who attracted such hostility from the trad lobby in the 1950s, played with Bilk ('Jazz Me Blues' and 'Savoy Blues' here) towards the end of the '60s; his departure was welcomed like the passing of a plague by Bilk's occasionally too vociferous fans, but he added a certain mainstream punch to a band that was in some risk of dead-ending itself.

The excellent Colin Smith was replaced first by Rod Mason (whose Hot Five was a fine revivalist outfit) and later by Mike Cotton, a more intense and subtle player who wasn't content to do Bunk Johnson impressions all night. The two Timeless sets highlight his talents and those of Campbell Burnap, who replaced John Mortimer. Bilk likens 'Stranger' to a pension plan and willingly keeps up payments on it. It appears on both Timeless sets, but that shouldn't detract from some rather less predictable fare, including 'Mood Indigo', 'St Thomas', 'Take The "A" Train' (*In Holland*) and 'Black And Tan Fantasy' (*Blaze Away*), all of which are played with impressive freshness and enough jazz 'feel' for anyone.

Bilk is an impressive middle-register player who seldom uses the coloratura range for spurious effect, preferring to work melodic variations on a given theme. Though he repeats certain formulae, he tends to do so with timbral and rhythmic variations that stop them going stale. A major figure in British jazz, Bilk has to be separated from a carefully nurtured image. On record, he's consistently impressive.

WALTER BISHOP Jr (born 1927)
PIANO

(*)   **Milestones** Black Lion BLCD 760109 CD
Bishop; Jimmy Garrison (b); G. T. Hogan (d). 3/61.

Bishop's dad composed 'Swing, Brother, Swing', but it was W. B. Junior who gave many of the classic bebop sessions their vigorous chordal propulsion and a duly radicalized version of Errol Garner's distinctive right-hand effects. Oddly for a man so well thought of in the counsels of bop, it was not until 1961 that Bishop made a record as leader. The results are finely crafted rather than startling, though alternative takes of 'Sometimes I'm Happy', Pettiford's 'Blues In The Closet' and 'Speak Low' suggest a subtle imagination at work. There is a long take of 'On Green Dolphin Street' that is as good as anything in the piano literature on that overworked subject, and a fine title-track, in which Garrison and the underrated Hogan display a sophisticated understanding of Miles's theme. Recording quality is approximately par for the course, with a slight dulling in the bass, but otherwise bright and clear.

***   **Bish Bash** Xanadu 114 LP
Bishop; Frank Haynes (ts); Reggie Johnson, Eddie Khan (b); Dick Berk, Leo Morris (d). 8/64, 5/68.

Two long tracks – and a rather briefer 'Summertime' – from an August 1964 residency at the Half Note, followed by a later set mostly dominated by originals. Bishop establishes his class with a fine, improvised introduction to 'Days Of Wine And Roses', building Monk quotes into his solo. 'Willow Weep For Me' is taken at a faster clip than usual and works extremely well, with Haynes powering through his choruses. The saxophonist sits it out for 'Summertime', the first of two Gershwin pieces on the album. Again, Bishop laces his development with references to three or four other standards, a typical device which he always handled with great subtlety.

The later sessions are not quite so forceful, but they're a useful introduction to Bishop as a writer. 'Minor Motive' is the most sophisticated, if a little formulaic in places, but 'Party Time' and 'Viva!' are more characteristic of his enthusiastically upbeat approach. Both rhythm sections work well, with particular plaudits to Johnson and Morris on the 1968 trio session. (Morris will be better known to jazz fans by his later, Muslim name, Idris Muhammed.)

MICHAEL BISIO
BASS

***   **In Seattle** Silkheart SHLP-107 LP
Bisio; Ron Söderström (t); Rick Mandyck (as); Teo Sutton (d). 4/87.

An exemplary instance of the kind of contemporary jazz being created away from the principal American centres of the music. Bisio is from Seattle, the group is a local one, and they play a post-bop jazz of conservative, gentle freedom. 'For Harry Carney' floats three thoughtful solos over a drifting, simple vamp; 'Blues For Melodious T' is roisterous without turning to bluster; and 'For Pamela' shows fine melodic and rhythmic ingenuity in its changes of direction. It reminds one of Coleman's and Mingus's music without surrendering its flag to either. Recorded with fine clarity and texture.

CINDY BLACKMAN
DRUMS

**   **Arcane** Muse MR/MCD 5341 CD/LP/MC
Blackman: Wallace Roney (*t*); Kenny Garrett (*as*); Joe Henderson (*ts*); Larry Willis
(*p*); Buster Williams (*b*). 8–12/87.

In terms of sheer ferocity, Blackman is among the most powerful drummers of today: she plays
with stunning forthrightness and her work as a sideperson – on, say, Wallace Roney's *Obsession*
– is thrilling. Her debut album as a leader is a little more reserved (the drum solo track,
'Incindyari', is surprisingly cautious) and is troubled by the material, which emerges as a
faceless set of blowing themes. The horns all have full-blooded statements to make, and
Williams's 'Dual Force' is a thoughtful piece, but there's nothing special here.

***   **Trio + Two** Free Lance FRL CD 015 CD
Blackman; Greg Osby (*as*); Dave Fiuczynski (*g*); Santi Debriano (*b*); Jerry Gonzalez
(*perc*). 8/90.

Much more interesting. A free-flowing jam between Blackman, Debriano and Fiuczynski – the
latter two much more interesting than on Debriano's thin *Soldiers Of Fortune* date – and,
though the guitarist sometimes turns up his amplifier and heads for freak-out, the drummer's
ruthless precision and round after round of press rolls keep time and order in equal measure.
Osby blows a few spools of melody on three tracks.

JOHN BLAKE
VIOLIN

**   **Maiden Dance** Gramavision GRP 8309 CD/LP
Blake; McCoy Tyner, Kenny Barron (*p*); Cecil McBee (*b*); Wilby Fletcher (*d*);
Leonard Gibbs (*perc*); Alan Blake, Lita Blake (*v*). 12/83.

*(*)   **Twinkling Of An Eye** Gramavision GRP 8501 CD/LP
Blake; James Simmons, Onaje Allan Gumbs (*p*); Michael Raye (*syn*); Gerald Veasley,
Avery Sharpe (*b*); Millard Vinson, Wilby Fletcher (*d*); Leonard Gibbs (*perc*); Alan
Blake, Lita Blake (*v*). 1/85.

John Blake's most significant work prior to these records was created under the leadership of
McCoy Tyner, who used his rough-edged virtuosity to telling effect. But the outings under his
own name imply that Blake is prone to faddism and unsure of himself as a composer. *Maiden
Dance* has its enjoyable moments, but the lack of a second front-line soloist places too much
weight on the leader, and several pieces are mere exhibitions of technique. *Twinkling Of An
Eye* takes a polite fusion tack that reduces Blake to fairly hapless showmanship. The vocal
presence of other members of the Blake family add little to the proceedings.

RAN BLAKE (born 1935)
PIANO, KEYBOARDS, COMPOSER

***   **Duke Dreams** Soul Note SN 1027 LP
Blake (*p* solo). 5/81.

(*)   **Suffield Gothic Soul Note SN 1077 CD/LP
Blake (*p* solo); Houston Person (*ts*). 6/81.

***   **Painted Rhythms Vol. II** GM 3008 CD
Blake (*p* solo). 9/83.

Since 1973, Blake has headed the Third Stream music department at the New England
Conservatory. Cynics will say that only in the quieter backwaters of New England is Third
Stream still considered a viable synthesis. Arguably only Blake and NEC president Gunther
Schuller remain strict-constructionists.

Blake is a scholar, and something of a gentleman, with an approach to the music very far removed from the seat-of-the-pants gigging mentality of most jazz musicians. His solo performances – and he has generally preferred to work without sidemen – are thoughtful, precisely articulated, but always intriguingly varied, combining jazz standards, original compositions of great interest, ethnic musics from all over the world (though Blake has a special interest in Spanish/Castilian Sephardic themes, as on *Painted Rhythms*). If he has a single influence from within jazz, it is Monk (though they seem temperamentally quite different) and something of Monk's method of improvising on surprisingly limited motives can be heard even when Blake is working with standards, as on *Suffield Gothic*. His collaboration there with saxophonist Houston Person is intriguing but a little detached. Since his days with Arthur Blythe, though no one's suggesting any conection, Blake has tended to steer clear of saxophonists, and only his ex-NEC student Ricky Ford has worked out a viable *modus operandi*.

The Ellington/Strayhorn pieces are wonderful and Blake's readings of Spanish music (plus 'Blue Monk' and 'Maple Leaf Rag') are among the best things he has put on record.

***   **Improvisations** Soul Note SN 1022 LP
    Blake, Jaki Byard (*p*). 6/81.

Piano duos can be messily unsatisfactory affairs; one thinks of the Cecil Taylor/Mary Lou Williams imbroglio in particular. This, though, is exceptional. Blake and Byard don't so much share a common conception as an ecumenical willingness to meet one another half-way, a characteristic noted on Byard's remarkable Festival Hall, London, encounter with the British improviser Howard Riley. The formalism of 'Sonata For Two Pianos' is mostly in the title; it's a limber, well-spaced piece with considerable harmonic interest. Almost inevitably, there is a taut, academic undercurrent to 'Tea For Two' and 'On Green Dolphin Street'. The pianos don't register quite as well as they might in some of the more exuberant passages but the sound is generally good, given the difficulties of recording this kind of music; a little more crispness in the bass might have helped; but the music is good enough to merit a sprinkle of stars.

****   **Short Life Of Barbara Monk** Soul Note SN 1127 CD/LP
    Blake; Ricky Ford (*ts*); Ed Felson (*b*), Jon Hazilla (*d*). 8/86.

This is a truly marvellous album, which makes Blake's apparent unwillingness to work in ensemble settings all the more galling. The first side ends with the title piece, dedicated to Thelonious Monk's daughter, Barbara, who died of cancer in 1984. It's a complex and moving composition that shifts effortlessly between a bright lyricism and an edgy premonition; Blake plays quite beautifully, and his interplay with the young but supremely confident rhythm section is a revelation.

A death also lies behind the closing track on side two. 'Pourquoi Laurent?' expresses both a hurt need to understand and a calm desire to heal, written in the face of French jazz critic Laurent Goddet's suicide. 'Impresario Of Death' is equally disturbing but so intelligently constructed as to resolve its inner contradiction perfectly. 'Vradiazi' by the Greek composer Theodorakis is a favourite of Blake's, as is the Sephardic melody 'Una Matica De Ruda' (two eye-blink takes), which also features on *Painted Rhythms II* (above).

To lighten the mix a little, there are astonishing versions of Stan Kenton's theme, 'Artistry In Rhythm', and, as an entirely unexpected opener, 'I Got You Under My Skin'. Blake's Falcone Concert Grand sounds in perfect shape and the session – a single day of concentrated music-making – is superbly recorded and pressed.

***   **You Stepped Out Of A Cloud** Owl 055 CD
    Blake; Jeanne Lee (*v*). 8/89.

Jeanne Lee also holds professorial rank at the New England Conservatory, but they manage to keep this rather remarkable album free of academicism. Lee's voice has a sweet indistinctness that really does suggest she has only recently descended with Blake from some great stack of cumulo-nimbus far above what we'd normally call 'jazz'.

'You Stepped Out Of A Dream' has an eerily disembodied quality that is taken up again in 'You Go To My Head'. 'Kristallnacht' suggests a whole different raft of values and priorities, while 'Mysterioso Rose' attempts a macaronic combination of Thelonious Monk and Gertrude Stein, two American originals interpreted by two American originals. Third Stream? Fourth dimension.

***(*) **That Certain Feeling** hat Art 6077 CD
  Blake; Steve Lacy (*ss*); Ricky Ford (*ts*). 90.

The *real* distorters of Gershwin are those who reduce him to a sticky harmonic paste. Blake keeps the *shape* of the songs, if not intact, then at least plastically viable. The 'Overture', played twice, bears no obvious relationship to the rest of the material, except in that it underlines the pianist's highly original and unquantifiable use of non-standard, almost Moroccan intervals. 'Strike Up The Band' brings in both saxophonists, who also duet with Blake elsewhere. It's a noisy and initially off-putting performance, but it yields great prizes, as does the *faux-naïf* 'I Got Rhythm' (Ford may not be faking, but Blake certainly is, and he gets away with it majestically). The music is full of oblique, inverted and sometimes probably imaginary references to Gershwin's corpus. It's a record to be swallowed whole, then nibbled at and digested over time.

ART BLAKEY (1919–90)
DRUMS

**   **New Sounds** Blue Note CDP 784436-2 CD
  Blakey; Kenny Dorham (*t*); Howard Bowe (*tb*); Sahib Shihab (*as*); Musa Kaleem (*ts*); Ernie Thompson (*bs*); Walter Bishop (*p*); Laverne Barker (*b*). 12/47.

A strange start to Blakey's career under his own name, this 1947 session produced four titles (with one alternative take) by a band of very mixed qualities. Dorham and Shihab at least get off some decent ideas in what is otherwise undistinguished bop. The rest of the record is devoted to James Moody material; Blakey admirers should wait for the later records.

****   **A Night At Birdland Vol. 1** Blue Note CDP 746519-2 CD
  Blakey; Clifford Brown (*t*); Lou Donaldson (*as*); Horace Silver (*p*); Curly Russell (*b*). 2/54.

****   **A Night At Birdland Vol. 2** Blue Note CDP 746520-2 CD
  As above. 2/54.

It was still called the 'Art Blakey Quintet', but this was the nexus of the band that became The Jazz Messengers, one of the most durable bywords in jazz, even if the name was first used on a Horace Silver album cover. Blakey wasn't as widely acknowledged as Max Roach or Kenny Clarke as one of the leaders in establishing bop drumming, and in the end he was credited with working out the rhythms for what came after original bebop, first heard to significant effect on these records. Much of it is based on sheer muscle: Blakey played very loud and very hard, accenting the off-beat with a hi-hat snap that had a thunderous abruptness, and developing a snare roll that possessed a high drama all of its own. As much as he dominates the music, though, he always plays for the band, and inspirational leadership is as apparent on these early records as it is on his final ones. Both horn players benefit: Donaldson makes his Parkerisms sound pointed and vivacious, while Brown is marvellously mercurial, as well as sensitive on his ballad feature 'Once In A While' from Volume 1 (Donaldson's comes on 'If I Had You' on the second record). Silver, too, lays down some of the tenets of hard bop, with his poundingly funky solos and hints of gospel melody. The sound has been capably transferred to CD, although owners of original vinyl needn't fear that they're missing anything extra.

***(*) **At The Café Bohemia Vol. 1** Blue Note CDP 746521-2 CD
  Blakey; Kenny Dorham (*t*); Hank Mobley (*ts*); Horace Silver (*p*); Doug Watkins (*b*). 11/55.

***(*) **At The Café Bohemia Vol. 2** Blue Note CDP 746522-2 CD
  As above. 11/55.

A very different band but results of equal interest to the Birdland session (the second volume of the Bohemia date was made twelve days after Volume 1). Hank Mobley is a somewhat unfocused stylist, and nothing quite matches the intensity which the Quintet secured at Birdland, yet the playing is finally just as absorbing. Dorham's elusive brilliance was seldom so extensively captured, his 'Yesterdays' ballad feature displaying a rare tenderness which faces off against the contentious dynamism of his fast solos, which seem to forge a link between Dizzy Gillespie and Miles Davis. Long, midtempo pieces such as 'Soft Winds' and 'Like Someone In

Love' find Silver and Blakey in reflective competition but the drummer never slackens his grip: listen to what he does behind Dorham on 'Minor's Holiday'. The recording captures the atmosphere very truthfully, and there's some added charm in the announcements by Mobley and Dorham before their features.

***   **The Jazz Messenger** Columbia 467920-2 CD
    Blakey; Donald Byrd, Bill Hardman (*t*); Jackie McLean (*as*); Ira Sullivan, Hank
    Mobley (*ts*); Horace Silver, Sam Dockery, Kenny Drew (*p*); Spanky DeBrest, Doug
    Watkins, Wilbur Ware (*b*). 5–12/56.

Compiled from three Columbia albums, this finds Blakey's band in transition. The impact McLean had on the group is clearly illustrated by the first two tracks: after the elegant, rather dapper 'Ecaroh', with Byrd and Mobley in the front line, McLean and Hardman tear things up on 'Cranky Spanky'. That sort of yin and yang is maintained through the first seven tracks, with a measured debut for McLean's standard 'Little Melonae', before a third edition of the band appears at the end, with Byrd and Sullivan in the front line on 'The New Message'. Shrewdly compiled, this makes the best of three sometimes routine original records. The remastering is very clean.

(*)   **Theory Of Art Bluebird ND 86286 CD
    Blakey; Bill Hardman, Lee Morgan (*t*); Melba Liston (*tb*); Jackie McLean, Sahib
    Shihab (*as*); Johnny Griffin (*ts*); Cecil Payne (*bs*); Sam Dockery, Wynton Kelly (*p*);
    Spanky DeBrest (*b*). 8/57.

***   **Ritual** Blue Note B21Y-46858 CD
    Blakey; Bill Hardman (*t*); Jackie Mclean (*as*); Sam Dockery (*p*); Spanky DeBrest (*b*).
    1–2/57.

***   **The Hard Bop Academy** Affinity AFF 773 CD
    As above. 57.

***   **For Minors Only** Charly CD 23 CD
    As above, except add Junior Mance (*p*). 10/57.

The Bluebird album features the only-ever meeting of McLean and Griffin on record in the next edition of The Messengers, and while it doesn't exactly burn the studio down, these five tracks are fiercely characteristic of the kind of bravado Blakey was looking for in his bands. There's also his first extended version of 'A Night In Tunisia', only slightly cooler than the extraordinary Blue Note reading listed below. Two previously unreleased tracks featuring an augmented Messengers are unremarkable stuff, though. *The Hard Bop Academy* is split between bands led by Blakey and Max Roach, and the five tracks by The Messengers feature two terse readings of Duke Jordan's 'Scotch Blues' and 'Flight To Jordan'. The CD sound is rather harsh and trebly. *Ritual*, now available only as a US import, has some similar material as well as the somewhat tedious title piece, a percussion workout of little real interest, although the remastering has been well done. *For Minors Only* is perhaps a notch less interesting but the gutsiness of the playing is hardly less evident.

*****   **Art Blakey's Jazz Messengers With Thelonious Monk** Atlantic 781332-2 CD
    As above, except Thelonious Monk (*p*) replaces Dockery and Mance. 5/57.

Blakey appeared on several of Monk's seminal Blue Note sessions, and he had a seemingly intuitive knowledge of what the pianist wanted from a drummer. Griffin, volatile yet almost serene in his mastery of the horn, was another almost ideal yet very different interpreter of Monk's music. This set of five Monk tunes and one by Griffin is a masterpiece. If Hardman wasn't on the same exalted level as the other three, he does nothing to disgrace himself, and DeBrest keeps calm, unobtrusive time. The continuous dialogue between Blakey and Monk comes out most clearly in passages such as Monk's solo on 'In Walked Bud', but almost any moment on the session illustrates their unique empathy. Both use simple materials, which makes the music unusually clear in its layout, yet the inner complexities are aston   d as a result the music retains an uncanny freshness 35 years later; no passage is lik some of the tempos, such as the those chosen for 'Evidence' and 'I Mean Y unique in the annals of Monk interpretations. The CD remastering is mostl DeBrest seems very remote in the mix. Absolutely indispensable jazz.

***(*)   **Moanin'** Blue Note CDP 746516-2 CD
Blakey; Lee Morgan (*t*); Benny Golson (*ts*); Bobby Timmons (*p*); Jymie Merritt (*b*).
10/58.

***   **Live In Holland 1958** Bandstand BDCD 1532 CD
As above. 11/58.

Benny Golson wasn't a Jazz Messenger for very long – this was his only American album with
the band – but he still contributed three of the most enduring themes to their book, all of them
on *Moanin'*: the title-track, 'Blues March' and 'Along Came Betty'. These versions might seem
almost prosaic next to some of the grandstand readings which other Blakey bands would later
create, but Golson's own playing shows great toughness, and the ebullient Morgan, also making
his Messengers debut, is a splendid foil. The live recording comes from a radio broadcast and
the sound is a little pale, but the soloists come through very clearly, with Golson hitting an
almost outlandish intensity in his fast solos. Timmons, by contrast, is irritatingly rinky-dink in
his playing.

***   **The Big Beat** Blue Note B21Y-46400 CD
Blakey; Lee Morgan (*t*); Wayne Shorter (*ts*); Bobby Timmons (*p*); Jymie Merritt (*b*).
3/60.

***   **Like Someone In Love** Blue Note B21Y-84245 CD
As above. 8/60.

***(*)   **A Night In Tunisia** Blue Note CDP 784949-2 CD
As above. 8/60.

After Golson came Shorter, the most individual of composers and an invaluable source for The
Messengers. Of the seven Blue Note albums with Morgan and Shorter in the front line, only the
above are available, and only *A Night In Tunisia* is still in the UK catalogue. Luckily, it's
perhaps the best of the three: besides the wildly over-the-top version of the title tune, there's
Shorter's lovely 'Sincerely Diana' and two charming Lee Morgan themes. Shorter's playing had
a dark, corrosive edge to it that turned softly beseeching when he played ballads, but some of
his solos don't come off: that on 'The Chess Players' from the patchy *The Big Beat* never gets
started. *Like Someone In Love*, made at the same sessions as *Tunisia*, includes two takes of the
haunting 'Sleeping Dancer Sleep On', and the other themes are attractive but more
conventional. The CD remastering is very good.

***(*)   **Live In Copenhagen 1959** Royal RJD 516 CD
Blakey; Lee Morgan (*t*); Wayne Shorter (*ts*); Walter Bishop Jr (*p*); Jymie Merritt (*b*).
11/59.

***   **Live In Stockholm 1959** DIW 313 CD
As above. 11/59.

***   **Live In Stockholm 1959** Dragon DRLP 182 CD/LP
As above. 11/59.

***   **Live In Stockholm 1960** Dragon DRLP 160 LP
As above, except Bobby Timmons (*p*) replaces Bishop. 12/60.

***   **Unforgettable Lee!** Fresh Sound FSCD-1020 CD
As above. 4–6/60.

Though one might imagine live Messengers recordings to be hotter than their studio
counterparts, the band was able to generate the same intensity in both locations. Still, these live
sessions from a couple of European visits are useful supplements to the Blue Note albums.
There is little variation between the three Stockholm sets – although the 1959 Dragon issue
includes some more interesting themes, recorded on the same day as the DIW disc but
apparently using some different material – but the Royal session includes a couple of rarer
items in Shorter's 'Nelly Bly' and 'The Midgets'. With the recordings probably emanating from
radio tapes, the sound is consistently clear, if not as full-bodied as the studio sessions; and
Morgan and Shorter are in any event always worth hearing as a youthful partnership, creating
the kind of idiosyncratic front line which seems lost among today's more faceless technicians.
The Fresh Sound disc sorts together nine tracks from various Birdland sessions in the spring of

1960 (it is nominally credited to Morgan and has his picture on the CD sleeve) and although anyone who has the other discs listed here will have the material in other versions, this catches the Messengers in very hot form. A brief 'Justice' finds Morgan in explosive form on his solo, and he sounds particularly exciting on most of the tracks on a generously packed CD. The sound, though, is rather grainy and suffers from some drop-outs.

**   **Jazz Messengers** MCA/Impulse! 33103 CD
        Blakey; Freddie Hubbard (*t*); Curtis Fuller (*tb*); Wayne Shorter (*ts*); Cedar Walton
        (*p*); Jymie Merritt (*b*). 6/61.

****   **Mosaic** Blue Note CDP 746523-2 CD
        As above. 10/61.

***   **Caravan** Original Jazz Classics OJC 038 CD/LP/MC
        As above, except Reggie Workman (*b*) replaces Merritt. 10/62.

***(*)   **Ugetsu** Original Jazz Classics OJC 090 CD/LP/MC
        As above. 6/63.

****   **Free For All** Blue Note BCT-84170 CD
        As above. 2/64.

***   **Kyoto** Original Jazz Classics OJC 145 CD/LP/MC
        As above. 2/64.

***(*)   **Indestructible!** Blue Note B21Y-46429 CD
        As above, except Lee Morgan (*t*) replaces Hubbard. 4–5/64.

Exit Morgan, enter Hubbard and Fuller. By now it was clear that Blakey's Jazz Messengers were becoming a dynasty unto themselves, with the drummer driving from the rear. As musical director, Shorter was still providing some startling material, which Hubbard and Fuller, outstanding players but undercharacterized personalities, could use to fashion directions of their own. Cedar Walton was another significant new man: after the lightweight work of Bobby Timmons, Walton's deeper but no less buoyant themes added extra weight to the band's impact.

In some ways, this was the most adventurous of all Messengers line-ups. The two masterpieces are the amazingly intense *Free For All*, which reasserts Blakey's polyrhythmic firepower as never before and finds Shorter at his most ferocious on the title tune and 'Hammer Head', and *Mosaic*, where the complex title-piece (by Walton) shows how the expanded voicings of the band added orchestral sonority to rhythmic power. Hubbard's feisty brightness and Fuller's sober, quickfire solos are a memorable counterweight to Shorter's private, dark improvisations. The tenorman is less evident on *Kyoto*, a breezier session dominated by Fuller and Hubbard, and although the live-at-Birdland *Ugetsu* is fine, it doesn't catch fire in quite the way the band might have been expected to in concert, though Shorter's feature on 'I Didn't Know What Time It Was' is ponderously impressive. *Caravan* is another solid though slightly less imposing set. *Indestructible!* featured Morgan's return and was Shorter's final Messengers album: his solos on 'Sortie', 'When Love Is New' and his own 'Mr Jin' suggest the different pastures he must have been seeking, full of ironic twists and played in a disturbingly mordant tone. Fuller and Morgan are contrastingly sharp and energetic on a very good session. The earliest date, for Impulse!, seems to have been organized more by the producer than the musicians, since it consists almost entirely of standards, and though capably done it's not what this edition of the band was about. All of these dates have been well remastered. Unfortunately, *Free For All* and *Indestructible!* are available only as US imports.

***   **A Jazz Message** MCA/Impulse! MCAD-5648 CD
        Blakey; Sonny Stitt (*as, ts*); McCoy Tyner (*p*); Art Davis (*b*). 6/63.

A rare instance of Blakey as a leader away from the Messengers, but it's basically a Stitt-plus-rhythm date, as characteristically as the drummer plays. A couple of blues and some standards, with Tyner strolling through the date and Stitt playing hard and well.

****   **The Best Of Art Blakey And The Jazz Messengers** Blue Note CDP 793205-2 CD

***   **The Best Of Art Blakey** EmArcy 848245-2 CD
        Blakey; Lee Morgan, Chuck Mangione, Valery Ponomarev (*t*); Bobby Watson (*as*);
        Benny Golson, Barney Wilen, Wayne Shorter, Frank Mitchell, David Schnitter (*ts*);

Bobby Timmons, Walter Davis Jr, Keith Jarrett, James Williams (*p*); Jymie Merritt, Reggie Johnson, Dennis Irwin (*b*). 12/58–2/79.

The Blue Note compilation is well chosen, with 'Moanin'', 'Blues March' and 'Dat Dere' covering the most popular Messengers tunes and 'Mosaic', 'Free For All' and 'Lester Left Town' their most challenging. 'A Night In Tunisia' is also here. EmArcy's collection includes four tracks with Barney Wilen opposite Morgan in the 1958–59 band, a 1966 reading of 'My Romance' which is included mainly for the presence of Keith Jarrett, and a somewhat desultory 1979 version of 'Blues March' by a less than distinguished line-up; a patchwork but worthwhile disc.

(***)   Mellow Blues Moon MCD 032-2 CD
Blakey; Woody Shaw (*t*); Carlos Garnett (*ts*); George Cables (*p*); Scott Holt (*b*). 4/69.

The only Blakey recording from this period is almost spoiled by the sound, which is of bootleg quality and declines into the almost-unlistenable when the drummer starts punishing his kit. It's a pity, because this was a fine edition of the band: Shaw is a volatile and attacking trumpeter, Cables a cooler counterweight, and Garnett is the most Coltrane-like of all Blakey's tenormen: his two long, blistering solos (there are only two tracks on the disc, 'A Night In Tunisia' and an unidentified original) are explosively effective.

**   In My Prime Vol. 1 Timeless SJP 114 LP
Blakey; Valery Ponomarev (*t*); Curtis Fuller (*tb*); Bobby Watson (*as*); David Schnitter (*ts*); James Williams (*p*); Dennis Irwin (*b*); Ray Mantilla (*perc*). 12/77.

**(*)   Jazzbühne Berlin '80 Repertoire REPCD-409CC CD
Blakey; Valery Ponomarev (*t*); Bobby Watson (*as*); Bill Pierce (*ts*); James Williams (*p*); Charles Fambrough (*b*). 5/80.

The long gap in Blakey's discography is symptomatic of the commercial decline of jazz in the 1960s and '70s. Some good Messengers line-ups, featuring Chuck Mangione, Woody Shaw, Bill Hardman and others, made only a few records in the period, and no studio dates are currently in print. This 1977 band was workmanlike rather than outstanding, although the redoubtable Fuller lends class and Watson lends firepower. The music, though, seems to have fallen into routine. The set from Berlin shows a little more spirit, but 'Blues March' and 'I Remember Clifford' sound stale next to the older versions, and Watson and Williams provide the only solos of interest. Respectable live recording.

***   Live At Montreux And Northsea Timeless SJP 150 CD
Blakey; Valeri Ponomarev, Wynton Marsalis (*t*); Robin Eubanks (*tb*); Branford Marsalis (*as, bs*); Bobby Watson (*as*); Bill Pierce (*ts*); James Williams (*p*); Kevin Eubanks (*g*); Charles Fambrough (*b*); John Ramsey (*d*). 7/80.

***(*) Live Kingdom Jazz CDGATE 7003 CD
Blakey; Wynton Marsalis (*t*); Bobby Watson (*as*); Bill Pierce (*ts*); James Williams (*p*); Charles Fambrough (*b*). 10/80.

***   Album Of The Year Timeless SJP 155 CD/LP
As above. 4/81.

***(*) Straight Ahead Concord CJ 168/CCD 4168 CD/LP/MC
As above. 6/81.

***(*) Keystone 3 Concord CJ 196/CCD 4196 CD/LP/MC
As above, except Branford Marsalis (*as*) replaces Watson, Donald Brown (*p*) replaces Williams. 1/82.

Wynton Marsalis's arrival was a turning point for both Blakey and jazz in the 1980s. His peculiar assurance and whipcrack precision, at the age of nineteen, heralded a new school of Messengers graduates of rare confidence and ability. He plays only a minor role in the big-band album, which is devoted mainly to Watson's themes and is an exuberant round-robin of solos and blustering theme statements, with Eubanks appearing as the first guitarist in a Messengers line-up. Once Marsalis took over as MD, the ensembles took on a fresh bite and the soloists sound leaner, more pointed. The live album on Kingdom is a fine document of what Marsalis brought to the band: 'Moanin'' sounds revitalized, 'Au Privave' is crackling. It just edges ahead of *Album Of The Year*. Both *Straight Ahead* and *Keystone 3* were recorded live at San Francisco's Keystone Korner (though on separate occasions), and both find a renewed involvement from Blakey himself, who's well served by the crisp recording. Watson's departure was a shade disappointing, given the tickle of creative confrontation between himself and Marsalis, but brother Branford's arrival, though he sounds as yet unformed, lends another edge of anxiety-to-please to the ensembles.

***   **Oh – By The Way** Timeless SJP 165 LP
    Blakey; Terence Blanchard (*t*); Donald Harrison (*as*); Bill Pierce (*ts*); Johnny O'Neal (*p*); Charles Fambrough (*b*). 5/82.

***(*)   **New York Scene** Concord CCD 4256 CD/MC
    Blakey; Terence Blanchard (*t*); Donald Harrison (*as*); Jean Toussaint (*ts*); Mulgrew Miller (*p*); Lonnie Plaxico (*b*). 4/84.

(*)   **Blue Night Timeless SJP 217 CD/LP/MC
    As above. 3/85.

***   **Live At Sweet Basil** Paddle Wheel K28P 6357 CD/LP
    As above. 3/85.

***   **Live At Kimball's** Concord CJ 307/CCD 4307 CD/LP/MC
    As above. 4/85.

***(*)   **New Year's Eve At Sweet Basil** Paddle Wheel K28P 6426 CD/LP
    As above, except add Tim Williams (*tb*). 12/85.

***   **Dr Jeckyl** Paddle Wheel K28P 6462 CD/LP
    As above. 12/85.

***   **Farewell** Paddle Wheel KICJ 41/41 2CD
    As above. 3–12/85.

***(*)   **Art Collection** Concord CCD 4495 CD/MC
    As Concord albums above. 78–85.

Even after Marsalis departed the band, The Messengers continued their winning streak. Blanchard, whom one might call the first post-Marsalis trumpeter, proved another inspiring MD and his partnership with Harrison made the front line sizzle. Two trumpet solos on the *New York Scene* set, on 'Oh By The Way' and 'Tenderly', show off intelligence, fire and perfectly calculated risk in some abundance. Miller and Plaxico renewed the rhythm section with superlative technique, and the old man sounds as aggressive as ever. Only *Blue Night* is routine. Although all the live sessions are good, *New York Scene* and the first *New Year's Eve* set are particularly hot, with the band sounding very rich and full on the last Paddle Wheel albums. Toussaint's brawny solos are closely in the Messengers tradition, and only Williams sounds a little out of his depth. *Farewell* was released after Blakey's death, and although these are clearly leftovers from the previously released live sets, there is at least one performance to match with the best of those records, a tempestuous reading of Bill Pierce's attractive 'Sudan Blue'. The playing time, at about 85 minutes, is rather short for a double-CD, though. *Art Collection* is a best-of culled from five of the Concord albums, and the shrewd programming and sensible choice of tracks makes this a useful one-disc introduction to what Blakey was doing in the early 1980s.

***   **Hard Champion** Paddle Wheel K28P 6472 CD/LP
    As above, except add Philip Harper (*t*), Kenny Garrett (*as*), Javon Jackson (*ts*), Benny Green (*p*), Peter Washington (*b*), omit Williams. 3/85–5/87.

(*)   **Blue Moon Zounds CD 2720010 CD
    Blakey; Philip Harper (*t*); Robin Eubanks (*tb*); Javon Jackson (*ts*); Benny Green (*p*); Peter Washington (*b*). 11/87.

(*)   **Not Yet Soul Note SN 1105 CD/LP
    As above. 3/88.

(*)   **Standards Paddle Wheel 292 E 6026 CD
    As above. 9/88.

**   **I Get A Kick Out Of Bu** Soul Note SN 12155 CD/LP
As above, except Leon Dorsey (*b*) replaces Washington. 11/88.

The Blanchard/Harrison edition of The Messengers is responsible for most of *Hard Champion*, which includes a scrupulously intense reading of Shorter's 'Witch Hunt', but the new team arrive in time for one track, and are responsible for the next four albums. Blakey's status as a bandmaster for all seasons was now as widely celebrated as anything in jazz, and taking a place in The Messengers was one of the most widespread ambitions among young players. Of those in this edition, only Jackson seems less than outstanding, with Eubanks splendidly peppery, Harper another Marsalis type with a silvery tone, and Green one of the funkiest pianists since the band's earlier days. Yet they never made a truly outstanding Messengers record together. By this time, much of the excitement about neoclassic jazz had subsided, and the players had a hard time escaping the scent of technique-over-feeling which was beginning to invade a lot of precision-orientated young bands. Blakey's own playing remains thunderously powerful, and he makes a lot of things happen which might otherwise have slipped away, yet the Soul Note records seem made by rote, the *Standards* set is focused only by the familiar material, and there's an overall feeling of transition which Blakey himself was too late in his career to move forward.

**   **One For All** A&M 395329-2 CD
Blakey; Brian Lynch (*t*); Steve Davis (*tb*); Dale Barlow, Javon Jackson (*ts*); Geoff Keezer (*p*); Essiet Okon Essiet (*b*). 4/90.

(*)   **Chippin' In Timeless SJP 340 CD
As above, except Frank Lacy (*tb*) replaces Davis.

Keezer aside, the final Messengers line-up is a bit disappointing: Lynch, Barlow and Jackson are all in the front of the second division, but they can't strike sparks the way the best Messenger bands could. It's hard to evade the feeling that Blakey, too, is slowing down, though he's trying his damndest not to let anyone know it. Nevertheless, the Timeless session includes some strong new themes and Lacy and Keezer have energy enough to stake places in the Messengers lineage. These are decent rather than exceptional farewell records from a master.

PIERRE BLANCHARD (born 1956)
VIOLIN

***   **Music For String Quartet, Jazz Trio, Violin And Lee Konitz** Sunnyside SSC 1023 CD/LP
Blanchard; Lee Konitz (*ss, as*); Alain Hatot (*ss*); Alain Jean-Marie (*p*); Vincent Pagliarin, Hervé Cavalier (*vn*); Michel Michalakakos (*vla*); Hervé Derrien (*clo*); Césarius Alvim (*b*); André Ceccarelli (*d*). 11–12/86.

Blanchard's writing for the string players results in ripe and sometimes indulgently rhapsodic textures, for which the more sour notes and tones of Konitz are a welcome antidote. The two long pieces, 'Mani-Pulsations' and 'XVIII Brumaire', come on as too much of an inventive thing, but a reworking of Coltrane's 'Moment's Notice' finds a sharp balance between severity and lushness, and the more conventional shapes of Konitz's 'Chick Came Around' are easier to grasp. Blanchard's own playing is full of cavalier virtuosity and gallantry, and he infuses plenty of life into the other players. A word, too, for Hatot, who is barely credited yet takes a neat little solo on 'Mani-Pulsations'.

BLAUER HIRSCH
GROUP

***   **Cyberpunk** FMP 1240 LP
Mich Gerber (*t*); Werner Lüdi (*as*); Waedi Gysi (*g*); Mani Neumeier (*d*). 10/88.

This seems something like a free music 'repertory' record, since the quartet run through a number of styles: the opening 'Shurike Sprawl' is reminiscent of a free-jazz blow-out of 15 years earlier, while 'Enzyme Valley' takes a more discrete course through several kinds of interplay. But the group is essentially a collision between four dissident voices who are nevertheless keen to co-operate in making some constructive noise. Luedi's fractured squawk pairs up with the reserved Gerber who's often content to mumble to himself under what's otherwise an avalanche of sound from the others. They can be amazingly detailed, as in the four-way chatter of 'Fool In Plasma', or combustible at a moment's notice. Gysi chooses notes or noise as the mood strikes him, but the key figure is probably Neumeier, who often turns on a free-rock beat to contextualize and focus the otherwise disparate improvising of the others. The recording, although done in a radio studio, is a little confused.

CARLA BLEY (born 1938)
PIANO, ORGAN, SYNTHESIZERS, COMPOSER

**(**)   Escalator Over The Hill JCOA/ECM 839 310 2 2CD/3LP
Bley; Michael Mantler (*t, vtb, p*); Enrico Rava, Michael Snow (*t*); Don Cherry (*t, f, perc, v*); Sam Burtis, Jimmy Knepper, Roswell Rudd (*tb*); Jack Jeffers (*btb*); Bob Carlisle, Sharon Freeman (*frhn*); John Buckingham, Howard Johnson (*tba*); Peggy Imig, Perry Robinson (*cl*); Souren Baronian (*cl, dumbec*); Jimmy Lyons, Dewey Redman (*as*); Gato Barbieri (*ts*); Chris Woods (*bs*); Sam Brown, John McLaughlin (*g*); Karl Berger (*vib*); Don Preston (*syn, v*); Jack Bruce (*b, solo v*); Charlie Haden, Ron McClure, Richard Youngstein (*b*); Leroy Jenkins (*vn*); Nancy Newton (*vla*); Calo Scott (*clo*); Bill Morimando (*bells*); Paul Motian (*d*); Roger Dawson (*perc*); Jane Blackstone, Paul Jones, Sheila Jordan, Jeanne Lee, Timothy Marquand, Tod Papageorge, Linda Ronstadt, Bob Stewart, Viva (*solo v*); Jonathan Cott, Steve Gebhardt, Tyrus Gerlach, Eileen Hale, Rosalind Hupp (*v*). 11/68, 11/70, 3 & 6/71.

***   Tropic Appetites Watt/1 LP
Bley; Gato Barbieri (*ts, perc*); Michael Mantler (*t, vtb*); Howard Johnson (*cl, bcl, bs, bsx, tba, v*); Toni Marcus (*vn, vla*); David Holland (*clo, b*); Paul Motian (*d, perc*); Julie Tippetts (*v*). 7/73.

*(*)   13 For Piano And Two Orchestras & 3/4 For Piano And Orchestra Watt/3 LP
Bley; Michael Mantler (*comp*); unknown personnel. 8/75.

***   Dinner Music Watt/6 LP
Bley; Michael Mantler (*t*); Roswell Rudd (*tb*); Bob Stewart (*tba*); Carlos Ward (*as, ts*); Richard Tee (*p*); Eric Gale (*g*); Cornell Dupree (*g*); Gordon Edwards (*b*); Steve Gadd (*d*). 7–9/76.

**   European Tour 1977 Watt/8 LP
Bley; Michael Mantler (*t*); Roswell Rudd (*tb*); Bob Stewart (*tba*); John Clark (*frhn*); Elton Dean (*as*); Gary Windo (*ts*); Terry Adams (*p*); Hugh Hopper (*b, perc*); Andrew Cyrille (*d, perc*). 9/77.

**(*)   Musique Mécanique Watt/9 CD/LP
Bley; Michael Mantler (*t*); Roswell Rudd (*tb*); John Clark (*frhn*); Bob Stewart (*tba*); Alan Braufman (*f, cl, as*); Gary Windo (*bcl, ts*); Terry Adams (*p, org*); Eugene Chadbourne (*g, walkie-talkie*); Charlie Haden, Steve Swallow (*b*); D. Sharpe (*d*); Karen Mantler (*glock*). 8–11/78.

Though she was initially influenced by the likes of Monk and Miles, with all that implies, Carla Bley's imagination seems to have been heavily conditioned by European models. She quickly became disenchanted with free-form improvisation and, from the late 1960s onwards, began experimenting with large-scale composition. No jazz composition – except perhaps Mingus's 'Epitaph' – is as large and ungainly as her massive 'chronotransduction' *Escalator Over The Hill*, which is more wonderful to have heard than to listen to. A surreal, shambolic work, to an impenetrable libretto by Paul Haines, it is more closely related to the non-linear, associative cinema of avant-garde film makers Kenneth Anger, Stan Brakhage, Maya Deren and Jonas Mekas (at whose Cinematheque some of the sessions were recorded) than to any musical parallel. The repetitious dialogue – 'again' is repeated *ad infinitum* – is largely derived from Gertrude Stein and it's perhaps best to take Stein's Alice-in-Wonderland advice and treat everything as meaning precisely what one chooses it to mean. Musically, it's a patchwork of raucous big-band themes like the opening 'Hotel Overture' (many of the events take place in Cecil Clark's Hotel with its pastiche Palm Court band), which has fine solos from Barbieri,

Robinson, Haden and Rudd, heavy rock numbers like the apocalyptic 'Rawalpindi Blues' (McLaughlin, Bruce, Motian), ethnic themes from Don Cherry's Desert Band, and mysterious, ring-modulated 'dream sequences'. There is an element of recitative that, as with most opera recordings, most listeners will prefer to skip, since it doesn't advance understanding of the 'plot' one millimetre, and it's probably best to treat *Escalator* as a compilation of individual pieces with dispensable continuity. The slightly earlier *A Genuine Tong Funeral* is a genuine masterpiece on a slightly less ambitious scale and it, rather than *Escalator* (which was as much Paul Haines's work as Bley's), established her musical idiom of the 1970s.

Tropic Appetites is an acerbic work, with some problems of resolution. Barbieri had been a stalwart of the Jazz Composers' Orchestra and his rather hyperthyroid approach works remarkably well against Bley's haunting tonal backgrounds. If there is a portmanteau term for the work of this period, it is 'operatic'. Solos step forward from the harmonic development rather than emerging seamlessly out of it; frequently, as on the uneasy *European Tour 1977*, they forget to step back again.

There are elements of whimsy about both *Musique Mécanique* and *Dinner Music* and an awkward pretentiousness about Mantler's piano concerti. Nevertheless these are the records that established Bley – and the label she co-runs with Mantler – as an important presence in progressive jazz. Production values have been high throughout Watt's catalogue, with echoes of ECM's 'classical' ambience and the same collegiate approach to recording.

**(*)   Social Studies Watt/11 LP
Bley; Michael Mantler (*t*); Gary Valente (*tb*); Joe Daley (*euph*); Earl McIntyre (*tba*); Carlos Ward (*as, ss*); Tony Dagradi (*cl, ts*); Steve Swallow (*b*); D. Sharpe (*d*). 12/80.

***(*)   Live! Watt/12 CD/LP
Bley; Michael Mantler (*t*); Gary Valente (*tb*); Vincent Chancey (*frhn*); Earl McIntyre (*tba, btb*); Steve Slagle (*as*); Tony Dagradi (*ts*); Arturo O'Farrill (*p, org*); Steve Swallow (*b*); D. Sharpe (*d*). 8/81.

It's at this point that Bley's imagination makes a sharp left away from the European art-music models that haunted her throughout the 1970s and towards a more recognizable jazz idiom, which may be less authentically individual but which gains immeasurably in sheer energy. *Live!* is a treat, representing one of the finest performances by her and Mantler on record. *Social Studies* shouldn't be missed; a bookish cover masks some wonderfully wry music.

**   I Hate To Sing Watt/12½ LP
Bley; Michael Mantler (*t*); Gary Valente (*tb*); Vincent Chancey (*frhn*); Earl McIntyre (*tba, btb, v*); Steve Slagle (*as*); Tony Dagradi (*ts*); Arturo O'Farrill (*p, org, v*); Steve Swallow (*b, d*); D. Sharpe (*d, v*). 8/81–1/83.

**   Heavy Heart Watt/14 CD/LP
Bley; Michael Mantler (*t*); Gary Valente (*tb*); Earl McIntyre (*tba*); Steve Slagle (*f, as, bs*); Hiram Bullock (*g*); Kenny Kirkland (*p*); Steve Swallow (*b*); Victor Lewis (*d*); Manolo Badrena (*perc*). 9–10/83.

**(*)   Night-Glo Watt/16 (827640) CD/LP
Bley; Randy Brecker (*t, flhn*); Tom Malone (*tb*); Dave Taylor (*btb*); John Clark (*frhn*); Paul McCandless (*ob, eng hrn, ss, ts, bcl*); Hiram Bullock (*g*); Larry Willis (*p*); Steve Swallow (*b*); Victor Lewis (*d*); Manolo Badrena (*perc*). 6–8/85.

This is a disappointing vintage in Bley's music. Despite the undoubted popularity of *I Hate To Sing*, it is one of her least imaginative small-group albums, heavily reliant on a limited range of ideas that are far more heavily embellished than usual, with camouflaging percussion and timbral effects. *Heavy Heart* is similarly disappointing, though the arrangements and voicings are beautiful and transfer well to CD. *Night-Glo* is by far the best of the trio; Oregon's Paul McCandless produces some striking woodwind effects and Hiram Bullock's guitar, not yet promoted beyond NCO status, is used more sensibly than on the first item below. Completists – and there must be lots – will be happy enough. New listeners would do better elsewhere.

**(*)   Sextet Watt/17 CD/LP
Bley; Hiram Bullock (*g*); Larry Willis (*p*); Steve Swallow (*b*); Victor Lewis (*d*); Don Alias (*perc*). 12/86–1/87.

***   **Duets** Watt/20 CD/LP
       Bley; Steve Swallow (*b*). 7–8/88.

Towards the end of the 1980s, Bley's emphasis shifted towards smaller and more intimate units. Though never a virtuosic soloist, she grew in stature as a performer. *Sextet* was unusual in having no horns, but Bley's chords are so voiced as to suggest whole areas of harmonic interest that here and in the *Duets* with Swallow remain implicit rather than fully worked out. Bullock is perhaps too insistent a spokesman, though he takes his more promising cues from the veteran bass man. By this time there is an almost telepathic understanding between Bley and Swallow (the compliment is returned in *Carla* [xtra Watt/2], recorded under his name); the duets make an ironic but uncynical commentary on the cocktail-lounge conventions of piano-and-bass duos. It's an entertaining album and an ideal primer on Bley's compositional and improvising techniques.

***(*)   **Fleur Carnivore** Watt/21 839 662 CD/LP
       Bley; Lew Soloff, Jens Winther (*t*); Frank Lacy (*frhn, flhn*); Gary Valente (*tb*); Bob
       Stewart (*tba*); Daniel Beaussier (*ob, f*); Wolfgang Pusching (*as, f*); Andy Sheppard (*ts,
       cl*); Christof Lauer (*ts, ss*); Roberto Ottini (*bs, ss*); Karen Mantler (*hca, org, vib,
       chimes*); Steve Swallow (*b*); Buddy Williams (*d*); Don Alias (*perc*). 11/88.

This is something like a masterpiece. Having concentrated pretty much on small bands during the 1980s, Bley returned wholeheartedly to large-scale scoring and arranging, touring with a Big Band and a Very Big Band, working in an idiom that was not only unmistakably jazz but also plain unmistakable. The relation of parts to whole is far more confident than in times gone by and the solos are uniformly imaginative, with Lauer, Soloff and Mantler, K., deserving special commendation. The writing is acute and the concert recording manages to balance 'live' energy with studio precision and fullness of sound.

***   **The Very Big Carla Bley Band** Watt/23 CD
       Bley; Guy Barker, Steven Bernstein, Claude Deppa, Lew Soloff (*t*); Richard Edwards,
       Gary Valente, Fayyaz Virji (*tb*); Ashley Slater (*btb*); Roger Janotta (*ob, f, cl, ss*);
       Wolfgang Puschnig (*as, f*); Andy Sheppard (*ts, ss*); Pete Hurt (*ts, cl*); Pablo Calogero
       (*bs*); Karen Mantler (*org*); Steve Swallow (*b*); Victor Lewis (*d*); Don Alias (*perc*).
       10/90.

A stirring live outfit, the Very Big Band translate well to record, with plenty of emphasis on straightforward blowing from featured soloists Soloff, Valente, Puschnig and Sheppard. 'United States' opens with splashy percussion, low, threatening brass figures, with the theme only really hinted at in Lew Soloff's sensuous growl solo. The riff and horn voicings that follow are unmistakably Bley's, as is the sudden, swinging interpolation of an entirely new theme. 'Strange Arrangement' opens with an almost childish piano figure, which gives way to huge, shimmering harmonics that instantly explain its logic. 'Who Will Rescue You?' grows out of an almost gospelly vamp, but by this time the album has lost at least some of its initial impetus, and 'Lo Ultimo' is a rather limping curtain-piece.

PAUL BLEY (born 1932)
PIANO

***   **Introducing Paul Bley** Original Jazz Classics OJC 201 CD/LP/MC
       Bley; Charles Mingus (*b*); Art Blakey (*d*). 11/53.

***   **Paul Bley With Gary Peacock** ECM 1003 LP
       Bley; Gary Peacock (*b*); Paul Motian or Billy Elgart (*d*). 4/63.

***   **Open, To Love** ECM 1023 CD/LP

***   **Tango Palace** Soul Note SN 1090

***   **Solo Piano** SteepleChase SCS 1236
       Bley (*p* solo) 9/72, 5/83, 4/88.

There is probably no other pianist currently active with a stylistic signature as distinctively inscribed as Paul Bley's – which is ironic, for he is a restless experimenter with an inbuilt resistance to stopping long in any one place. It is difficult to formulate exactly what unifies his remarkable body of work, beyond a vague sense that Bley's enunciation and accent are different from other people's, almost as if he strikes the keyboard differently. He favours curiously ambiguous diminuendo effects, tightly pedalled chords and sparse right-hand figures, often in challengingly different metre; working solo, he creates variety and dramatic interest by gradually changing note-lengths within a steady pulse (a device introduced to keyboard literature by a minor German improviser called Ludwig van Something), and generates considerable dramatic tension by unexpectedly augmenting chords, shifting the harmonic centre constantly.

Though he has played in a number of classic groups – notably with Jimmy Giuffre and Steve Swallow, that astonishing debut with Mingus and Blakey, and, more recently, with John Surman and Bill Frisell – Bley is still perhaps best heard as a solo performer; a decade apart, the two earlier solo sets neatly overstep the most uncomfortably eclectic phase of Bley's career, when he turned to electronics in a largely unsuccessful bid to increase his tonal vocabulary.

There are fine things on the Soul Note session, but it is a mellow, after-dinner affair compared to the iced-vodka shocks of *Open, To Love*, one of Bley's finest-ever performances and the beginning of a productive relationship with ECM that only really flowered much later. Stand-out track is a fresh reading of ex-wife Carla Bley's uneasy 'Ida Lupino'. The 1988 SteepleChase has excellent sound and features the pianist in meditative mood; his reading of 'You Go To My Head' is so oblique as to suggest another tune entirely. Nevertheless, there is little of the vapid meandering that afflicts so much piano improvisation; Bley is a tremendously disciplined improviser and this is one of his most intellectually rigorous albums.

The 1953 sessions had marked a wonderfully confident debut – including three fine originals, a beautiful 'Like Someone In Love' and a powerful cover of Horace Silver's 'Split Kick' – and convincing confirmation of the old adage about never settling for less than the best in tradesmen. Charles Mingus and Art Blakey seem a reasonable enough coming-of-age present for a 21-year-old from Montreal. Great things, too, from what was to be Bley's established trio. ECM's third release – following a superb Mal Waldron session and a throughly forgettable band led by the enigmatic Alfred Harth – highlighted 'When Will The Blues Leave', a version that bears careful comparison with the petrol-injected, steroid-laden reading on . . .

***   **Footloose** Savoy SV 0149 CD
       Bley; Steve Swallow (*b*); Pete LaRoca (*d*). 8/62 & 9/63.

A valuable reissue of an important session, and it's hard, listening to it after nearly twenty years, to understand why there was so very much excitement about Bill Evans when Bley was producing far more interesting and challenging piano trio music, sometimes only a couple of blocks away. Swallow is every bit as interesting as Scott LaFaro and LaRoca was simply one of the best drummers around.

(*)   **Alone Again DIW 319 / 25019 CD/LP
       Bley (*p* solo). 8/74.

Bley claims that he only listens to his own records nowadays. Tongue in cheek or not, there are certainly enough of them on the backlist to occupy the bulk of his non-playing time (if bulk is the right word for a musician so promiscuously active). There are also signs that Bley listens to his past records in a quite constructive sense, constantly revising and modifying his thematic development (as in these intense reveries), constantly alluding to other melodies and performances. There is, perhaps, inevitably a hint of *déjà vu* here and there, but the terrain is always much too interesting for that to become a problem.

(*)   **The Paul Bley Group Soul Note SN 1140 CD/LP
       Bley; John Scofield (*g*); Steve Swallow (*b*); Barry Altschul (*d*). 3/85.

***   **Fragments** ECM 1320 CD/LP

***   **The Paul Bley Quartet** ECM 1365 CD/LP
       Bley; John Surman (*ss, b cl, bs*); Bill Frisell (*g*); Paul Motian (*d*). 1/86, n. d.

Fragments stands with the best things Bley has done, denied a further star only by the width of the band-book. As on the Soul Note session, recorded a year before, the writing and arranging are surprisingly below par and the recording isn't quite as clean as it might be. The Soul Note features a fine reading of Bley's staple 'Mazatlan', but little else of really compelling interest; Scofield and Swallow blend almost seamlessly, and Altschul has always been the perfect conduit for Bley's more advanced rhythmic cues. By contrast, the ECM band seems all texture, and much less structure; Frisell's almost apologetically discordant lines and reverberations blend unexpectedly well with Surman's almost equally introspective lines and Motian – with whom Bley has duo-ed to great effect – varies his emphases almost by the bar to accommodate whoever is to the forefront. The long 'Interplay' on the later, eponymous set, is disappointing enough to ease that album back a stellar notch. All three, though, are fine examples of a remarkable musician at work without preconceptions, doctrinaire stylistic theories or ego.

***   **Paul Bley / NHØP** Steeplechase SCCD 31005 CD/LP
Bley; Niels-Henning Ørsted-Pedersen (*b*).

***   **Notes** Soul Note SN 1190 CD/LP/MC
Bley; Paul Motian (*d*). 7/87.

Years of standing behind Oscar Peterson did nothing to blunt NHØP's appetite for the job. He complements Bley's haunting chords perfectly, and on the inaugural 'Meeting' constructs an arco solo of great beauty over huge, ringing piano pedals (played on the electric instrument which reappears to good effect on the closing 'Gesture Without Plot' by Annette Peacock). 'Later' is perhaps the best-balanced duo performance; followed by the lively and intriguingly oblique 'Summer', it underlines once again Bley's sensitivity to his fellow-players and the emotional range of his playing.

He is, nevertheless, absolutely distinctive. The opening notes of 'Meeting' could not be by anyone else, and a random sampling of any track uncovers his signature within half a dozen bars. The piano is appropriately well recorded and the bass is well forward with no flattening of the bottom notes (which is where NHØP works best) and no teeth-jangling distortion of his bridgework.

Motian is always wonderful, seeming to work in a time-scale all his own, conjuring tissues of sound from the kit that seem to have nothing to do with metal or skin. Their interplay in the most demanding of all improvisational settings is intuitive and perfectly weighted.

***   **Partners** Owl 058 CD
Bley; Gary Peacock (*b*). 12/89.

Peacock's pedigree is astonishing and his responsiveness undimmed by years of promiscuous gigging, usually without his due of attention. This is another marvellous record (Bley's star rating is worryingly undifferentiated) featuring some remarkably subtle improvisation. The obvious comparison would be with Steve Swallow, except that Swallow has long since shifted permanently to electric bass and a sharper, more percussive articulation than Peacock's remarkably stately delivery.

****   **Bebop** SteepleChase SCCD 31259 CD
Bley; Bob Cranshaw (*b*); Keith Copeland (*d*). 12/89.

The two most distinctive performances in recent times of Charlie Parker's classic 'Now's The Time' have been by Prince (a diminutive, purple-obsessed rock person) and Paul Bley. There's a certain irony in the fact that the man who headed the palace coup that overthrew bebop at the Hillcrest Club in 1958 (the date is often credited to Ornette Coleman, but Bley was the nominal leader) should be the one to produce the most exacting and forward-looking variations on bop language in the last decade.

Far from a nostalgia album, or an easy ride for soloist and sidemen, *Bebop* is a taxingly inventive and constantly surprising run through a dozen kenspeckle bop tunes, including (a circular tribute to the label) 'Steeplechase'. Bley's chording and lower-keyboard runs on 'My Little Suede Shoes' pull that rather banal theme apart; Cranshaw's solo is superb. 'Ornithology' and 'The Theme' receive equally extended attention; the closing '52nd Street Theme' is a suitably elliptical commentary on the whole era.

This is one of the finest piano trio records of the last ten years – or the next, depending on how you view its revisionism.

***   **The Nearness Of You** SteepleChase SCS 1246 CD/LP
Bley; Ron McLure (*b*); Billy Hart (*d*). 11/88.

For those who find Bley a shade too dry, 'Take The A Train' rousts along like it was trying to make up time between stops. By sharp contrast, the title-track is a long reverie punctuated by angry interpolations, almost as if a whole relationship is replaying on some inner screen. Compelling music as always, with an uncharacteristically laid-back rhythm section that on a couple of cuts might just as well have sat out and left the pianist to do his own remarkable thing. Good, well-rounded sound.

(*)   **12 (+6) In A Row hat Art 6081 CD
Bley; Hans Koch (*reeds*); Franz Koglmann (*flhn*). 5/90.

Arnold Schoenberg was once told that composers everywhere were adopting his twelve-tone method: 'Ah, but do they make music with it?' Most jazz musicians are highly resistant to systems and have found Schoenberg's lack of rhythmic nous distinctly off-putting; as a consequence, orthodox serialism has remained only a rather peripheral experimental temptation for eclectics like Gunther Schuller and Don Ellis. Only among jazz pianists – perhaps inevitably, given the conformation of the instrument – have serial procedures taken hold.

It's clear that even Cecil Taylor's celebrated 'atonality' is only episodic, part of a determined expansion of traditional jazz harmony. Roland Hanna, Jaki Byard and Ran Blake have nodded towards Schoenberg in much the same spirit. Paul Bley's remarkable album has to be seen in the context of a current rehabilitation of the so-called Third Stream, and of such marginalized jazz experimenters as Jimmy Giuffre. Drawing on tone-rows (non-repeating sequences of the entire chromatic scale) by Schoenberg and Anton Webern, Bley has created structures for trio improvisation that are as challenging as Anthony Braxton's, and as clearly hooked into jazz tradition.

The 18 tracks – none of which is over five minutes – are divided into Bley solos, together with duos and trios in all the available permutations. The music combines highly abstract improvisation in minimalist (but, again, non-repeating) patterns with sudden blues figures, stride and boogie left-hand lines and snatches of melody, somewhat in the manner of the latter-day Giuffre/Bley/Swallow trio. The two horns have more immediate access to microtones and high harmonics, but Bley has devised a number of techniques (not all of them discernible from listening, but including currently *de rigueur* activity inside his instrument) to overcome the well-tempered resistance of the piano. It's challenging and important music. It's also highly listenable and strongly recommended.

***(*) **Solo** Justin Time Just 28 CD

***(*) **Changing Hands** Justin Time Just 40 CD
Bley (*p* solo). 87, 2/91.

Uniquely thoughtful piano solos recorded back home in Montreal on a beautifully tempered instrument (and producer Jim West has to be congratulated for the immediacy and precision of the sound). Any suspicion that Bley may have become one-dimensionally meditative is allayed by the vigorous 'Boogie' on *Solo* and *Changing Hands*' remarkable interpretation of 'Summertime'. If it came down to a hard choice, the earlier album is marginally to be preferred; don't be seduced by the prettier cover.

****   **Memoirs** Soul Note 121240 CD/LP
Bley; Charlie Haden (*b*); Paul Motian (*d*). 7/90.

A dream line-up that promises much and delivers royally. If anything pricks the bubble of the concurrent trio featuring Geri Allen, it is this fine set. Bley's finely spun chromatic developments are now so finely judged as to give an impression of being quite conventionally resolved. Given the title and the strategically placed 'Monk's Dream' and Ornette's 'Latin Genetics', it's tempting to read the set as an attempt to summarize Bley's career over the past three decades. Haden's 'Dark Victory' and 'New Flame' and Bley's own 'Insanity' suggest how far Bley, Haden and Motian have pushed the conventional piano trio. Tremendous stuff.

***   **Lyrics** Splasc(h) CD H 348-2 CD
Bley; Tiziana Ghiglioni (*p*). 3/91.

Ghiglioni's rather strained delivery does little more than point out the melody on the vocal tracks. These are interspersed by instrumental originals, which are a commentary (though recorded prior to the vocal track) on five otherwise uneventful standards. It's these re-readings which lift this rather low-key set. They're further testimony to Bley's remarkable harmonic imagination and it may that Ghiglioni felt constrained rather than inspired by them. The idea is an intriguing one, but one would like to hear him try it with a more sophisticated vocal artist, like Sheila Jordan.

URS BLOCHLINGER
SAXOPHONES, REEDS

***   **(Aesth)eti(c)k Als Widerstand** Plainisphare PL 1267-3/4 LP
         Blochlinger; Thomas Durst (*b*); Thomas Hiestand (*d*). 10/82.

***   **Cinema Invisible** Plainisphare PL 1267-24/25 LP
         Blochlinger; Hans Kennel (*t*); Peter Hablutzel (*sno, perc*); Jurg Ammann (*p*); Martin
         Schutz (*clo*); Thomas Durst (*b*); Dieter Ulrich (*d*); Daniel Mouthon, Kornelia
         Brugmann (*v*). 6–11/85.

Although Swiss musicians have scarcely made an international mark on jazz to date, it's not for
want of Blochlinger trying it on. His interests lie in the noise-making of the American avant
garde, while his roots in European composition lead to a tug-of-war between the two areas. On
these two double-albums for Plainisphare, there are mixed rewards in the approach.
Blochlinger's own style is an energetic mélange of free licks and tortuous, Braxtonian logic, but
his fellow-players aren't always so self-confident. The trio of the earlier date plays some fine
ensemble parts, but the music eventually bogs down in complexity and Hiestand isn't supple
enough to raise the rhythms. Quartet and octet tracks on the later session are more
encouraging, but still sound as if some of the players are puzzled by the leader's intentions.
Each disc has a share of solos by Blochlinger, five of them on a curmudgeonly bass sax which
again recalls Braxton's adventures in low frequencies.

JANE IRA BLOOM (born 1953)
SOPRANO SAXOPHONE

**   **As One** JMT 834403-1 LP
         Bloom; Fred Hersch (*p*). 9/84.

***   **Mighty Lights** Enja 4044 807519 CD/LP
         Bloom; Fred Hersch (*p*); Charlie Haden (*b*); Ed Blackwell (*d*). 11/82.

Ms Bloom is one of the handful of musicians who play exclusively on the soprano sax, more
frequently used as a secondary instrument by tenor or baritone sax players. Recent recordings –
two quickly deleted albums for Columbia, which found her dabbling with electronics –
suggested she was becoming disenchanted with the possibilities of the instrument in a
straight-ahead jazz format; but these two earlier discs suggest a valuable talent. The duo record
with Hersch is a bit dry – aside from a nicely austere version of Wayne Shorter's 'Miyako', the
lack of strong thematic material tends to encourage the two players to doodle – but *Mighty
Lights* is a fine display of Bloom's powers. She has a sparse, considered delivery, eschewing
vibrato and sentimentality: Leroy Anderson's 'Lost In The Stars' is awarded an attractively tart
reading. Particularly impressive are two tracks in which Hersch sits out and Bloom, Haden and
Blackwell hit a propulsive groove.

BLUE BOX
GROUP

(*)   **Sweet Machine Enja 5001 CD/LP

(*)   **Stambul Boogie Enja 5025 CD/LP

***   **Captured Dance Floor** Tiptoe 807101/888101 CD/LP
         Reiner Winterschladen (*t*); Alois Kott (*b, ky*); Peter Eisold (*d, ky*). 6/85, 7/86,
         6–10/88.

These delightful records sketch a deft satire on some of the more robotic aspects of
contemporary fusion. Kott seems to be the mastermind behind the music, composing most of
the tunes, although there are some which appear to be spontaneous studio turns. *Sweet
Machine* and *Stambul Boogie* are relatively straightforward in their layout: Winterschladen's icy
trumpet skates on the snapping rhythms of Kott and Eisold, and acoustic tracks mingle with
more abstract mood pieces. *Captured Dance Floor*, though, finds Kott reaching for more

remote territory. As the title suggests, the trio annexe what might be bare, stripped-down disco backing-tracks and trace an improvisatory skin over their surface. With its hard, gleaming studio sound, the music acquires an eerie intensity. Winterschladen gets a better hearing on the earlier discs, but the third is their best.

HAMIET BLUIETT (born 1940)
BARITONE SAXOPHONE, ALTO CLARINET

***(*) **Resolution** Black Saint BSR 0014 CD/LP
Bluiett; Don Pullen (*p*); Fred Hopkins (*b*); Famondou Don Moye (*perc*). 11/77.

*** **EBU** Soul Note SN 1088 CD/LP
Bluiett; John Hicks (*p*); Fred Hopkins (*b*); Marvin Smith (*d*). 2/84.

The baritone saxophone enjoyed a brief but historically unspecific boom in the 1950s. Why then? Harry Carney had turned it into a viable solo instrument; there were probably more good ensemble players around, conscious equally of the run-down on paying gigs with big bands and of the attractions of a little solo spotlight; lastly, the prevailing role-models on alto and tenor were, perhaps, a little too dominant. By contrast, no established baritone style developed; Gerry Mulligan was as different from Serge Chaloff as Chaloff was from Pepper Adams; and round the fringes there were players like Sahib Shihab and Nick Brignola doing very different things indeed.

Currently, the situation is much the same. The three most interesting baritonists all play in markedly different styles. The young Amerasian Fred Houn is very much a Carney disciple; Britain's John Surman blows baritone as if it were a scaled-up alto (which by and large it is); Hamiet Bluiett, on the other hand, gives the big horn and his 'double', alto clarinet, a dark, Mephistophelian inflexion, concentrating on their lower registers. A fine section player – and his work with the World Saxophone Quartet is an extension of that – he is a highly distinctive soloist.

Compared to the clutter (or exuberance – tastes vary) of the later, Africanized albums, the earlier recordings are stripped down (or downright sparse – ditto), muscular and sometimes chillingly abrasive. The *Resolution* quartet are perhaps heard to better effect on the deleted *SOS* (India Navigation IN 1039), a live New York set of near-identical vintage, but the studio cuts are still absolutely compelling. Bluiett, on baritone only, is in sterling form, relaxed in perhaps the most conducive company he has assembled on record. Pullen and Hopkins are masters of this idiom, and Moye curbs his occasionally foolish excesses. Production values aren't as hot as on the Soul Note sessions, but the music is way out in front.

A generous mix and better-than-average registration of the lead horn (the CD is first class) redeems *EBU*'s rather slack execution and raises it to front rank. Hicks is a much lighter player than Pullen and is perhaps too much of an instinctive lyricist to combine well with Bluiett's increasingly declamatory responses. The rhythm section sometimes lacks incisiveness, fatally so on a rather odd 'Night In Tunisia'.

*** **Dangerously Suite** Soul Note SN 1018 LP
Bluiett; Bob Nelluns (*p*); Buster Williams (*b*); Billy Hart (*d*); Chief Bey (*African perc*); Irene Datcher (*v*). 4/81.

*** **Nali Kola** Soul Note SN 1188 CD/LP/MC
Bluiett; Hugh Masekela (*t, flhn*); James Plunky Branch (*ss*); Billy Spaceman Patterson (*g*); Donald Smith (*b*); Okyerema Asante, Chief Bey, Titos Sompa, Seku Tonge (*perc*); Quincy Troup (*poet*). 7/87.

Bluiett's pan-Africanism of the early 1980s opened up for him a whole book of new rhythmic codes that helped ease him out of the still impressive but palpably finite resources of his original post-bop orientation. *Dangerously* is a transitional exercise in that it merely grafts African percussion and voice only to the basic horn/piano/rhythm quartet. It is a fine album none the less, neither tentative nor blandly 'experimental'. *Nali Kola* is certainly not tentative, but it lacks the clearly methodological premises someone like Marion Brown brings to projects of this type. The awkward instrumentation is intriguingly handled and well recorded – though the channel separation is a little crude – and Bluiett seems comfortable in his interplay with the still-adventurous Masekela and the little-known Branch and Smith, who are casual additions to the long title-track. It also features the 'verse' of Quincy Troup, now better known for his ghosting of Miles's autobiography. As a whole, it is somewhat reminiscent of Archie Shepp's remarkable 1969 collaboration with Philly Joe Jones (America 30 AM 6102). And none the worse for that!

**** **The Clarinet Family** Black Saint BSR 0097 CD/LP
Bluiett; Dwight Andrews (*sno cl, s cl*); Don Byron, Gene Ghee, John Purcell (*s cl, bcl*); Buddy Collette (*s cl, acl*); J. D. Parran (*sno cl, s cl, acl, contralto cl*); Sir Kidd Jordan (*cbcl*); Fred Hopkins (*b*); Ronnie Burrage (*d*). 11/84.

Utterly remarkable. The ten-minute egg of hard-boiled clarinet revivalism. Bluiett's inspired project may initially sound like a discursive guide to the woodwinds; in practice, it's a deeply celebratory, almost pentecostal rediscovery of the clarinet – once the jazz voice *par excellence* – and its preterite cousins and second cousins. Kidd Jordan's hefty contrabass instrument, hitherto associated only with Anthony Braxton, must count as a second cousin, twice removed; pitched at double B flat, it has an extraordinary tonality, as on 'River Niger', a Jordan composition that conjures up oddly disconnected echoes of Paul Robeson in *Sanders Of The River*.

There's a strong sense of tradition through this fine live set, recorded in Berlin: two long tributes to Machito – a very different 'Macho' from the one credited to Steve Turre on the Brass Fantasy's ECM *Avant Pop* – and Duke Ellington, well shared-out compositional credits, a startling bass solo from Hopkins, and, following it, a beautifully judged climax. After *Resolution* and the better of the WSQ albums, this is the essential Bluiett album, albeit one in which he plays a collective and slightly understated role.

*** **You Don't Need To Know … If You Have To Ask** Tutu CD 888 128 CD
Bluiett; Thomas Ebow Ansah (*g, v*); Fred Hopkins (*b*); Michael Carvin (*d*); Okyerema Asante (*perc, v*). 2/91.

The title refers to a celebrated riposte of Louis Armstrong's when asked by a white lady what jazz really was. In the context of that his quotation of the celebrated waltz theme at the beginning of 'Black Danube', a tune described by drummer Carvin as 'James Brown in 3/4 time', has to be seen as slightly ironic in the context of Bluiett's now thoroughly Africanized approach to jazz performance. The rhythmic base, whether by Carvin or Asante, is in most cases the essence of the piece, over which Bluiett improvises with considerable freedom. His alto flute makes an effective opening to 'If Only We Knew' and Asante's percussion line bridges the piece with 'T. S. Monk, Sir' on which the baritone and bass punch out a respectful pastiche of the great pianist. Guitarist Thomas Ebow Ansah's vocal 'Ei Owora Befame-Ko' is built on a syncopated chord sequence of the sort Bluiett instinctively heads for in his own compositions, and the two voices harmonize superbly with Bluiett punctuating the melody with great bull-roar effects.

The last but one track of the session is perhaps the most straightforward and the most conventionally jazz-oriented. 'The Gift: One Shot From The Hip' has the kind of headlong, thunderous urgency that Bluiett can generate as a soloist, with Hopkins and Carvin tucked in behind like a three-man bob team. The bassist gets his big feature on 'Goodbye Pork Pie Hat', but it's on 'The Gift' that his long-standing commitment to Bluiett's music pays its most generous dividends.

ARTHUR BLYTHE (born 1940)
ALTO SAXOPHONE

** **Basic Blythe** CBS 4606771 CD/LP
Blythe; John Hicks (*p*); Anthony Cox (*b*); Bobby Battle (*d*); small string section. 88.

Arthur Blythe has attracted almost as much 'what went wrong' copy as Desert Orchid and Barry McGuigan. His India Navigation sets of the late 1970s were breathtakingly original and his form-sheet included demanding and chops-quickening stints with Gil Evans and Horace Tapscott. In 1979, he signed with Columbia. *Lenox Avenue Breakdown* was a masterpiece of imaginative instrumentation; there were two more fine albums and then Blythe's wind went.

It is hard to see what is 'basic' about this 1988 set other than its aesthetic misjudgements. A yearning to play with string sections is something that overtakes alto saxophonists at a particular point in their careers, and while Blythe does manage to follow Bird's example here in largely ignoring undynamic settings, the effect is still disappointingly indistinct, muddying an interesting enough quartet in which the excellent John Hicks more than holds his own. Students of what goes wrong might usefully begin with the cover of 'Lenox Avenue Breakdown'. All the technique is there but, as they say about racehorses and boxers, much of the heart has gone.

*** **Hipmotism** Enja 6088 CD
Blythe; Hamiet Bluiett (*bs*); Kelvin Bell (*g*); Gust William Tsilis (*vib, mar*); Bob Stewart (*tba*); Arto Tuncboyaci (*perc, v*); Famoudou Don Moye (*d*). 3/91.

For all the personal references and dedications, Blythe still betrays a lack of essential spirit. There are also signs, most seriously on the opening trio and the concluding, unaccompanied 'My Son Ra', that his articulation problems are becoming more evident. However, the blend of instrumental voices on *Hipmotism* is intriguing enough to carry the day. There are only three all-in tracks, 'Matter Of Fact' and 'Bush Baby', both of them notably abstract, and the title-piece, which is simple and roistering. Blythe sounds good on them all, feeding off the deeper, darker sounds of Stewart's tuba and guest Bluiett's brassy baritone. The sparser settings expose him mercilessly and 'Miss Eugie', for alto saxophone, tuba and Tuncboyaci's percussion and voice, requires a more forceful performance.

A partial return to form, well conceived and produced. And there's a bonus for CD purchasers who loathe those brittle plastic boxes and yearn for old-style album sleeves: the new Enjas come in attractive fold-out laminated card with a plastic insert for the disc. Almost like the real thing again.

JIMMY BLYTHE (c. 1901–31)
PIANO

***(*) **Stomp Your Stuff** Swaggie S1324 LP
Blythe; Natty Dominique, Punch Miller (*c*); Johnny Dodds, Darnell Howard (*cl*); unknown (*as*); Alfred Bell (*kz, wbd, v*); Bud Scott, Ed Hudson (*bj*); Baby Dodds, W. E. Burton, Jimmy Bertrand (*wbd*).

Little is known of Blythe's life: he was born in Louisville, Kentucky, but spent most of his working life in Chicago, specifically as the house pianist for several labels, including Paramount, Vocalion and Gennett. The one LP easily available under his own name includes sides by several of the pick-up groups which he organized: four by Jimmy Blythe's Owls, three by Blythe's Blue Boys, one by the State Street Ramblers, two apiece by The Chicago Stompers, The Midnight Rounders and Jimmy Bertrand's Washboard Wizards, plus two typically steady-rolling piano solos.

Blythe's work is usually characterized as unpretentious, knockabout music, heavily redolent of the barrelhouse atmosphere of some of the less 'respectable' areas of Chicago jazz, but he was a more thoughtful musician than he's often given credit for. His occasional improvisations in the group sides, and the confident, unfussy blues-playing in the two solos, are as strong as those of any other pre-Hines pianist. But his great talent, as Martin Williams points out in his sleeve-notes, may have been to coax his companions into playing above themselves. Most of the musicians in Blythe's groups were no more than competent technicians; it is the leader's sturdy playing that binds the music together and persuades each band to swing. Tracks such as 'Pleasure Mad' or the kazoo-driven 'Wild Man Stomp' have a giddy, endearing lilt to them. Of course, the presence of Dodds on several of the sides raises the game somewhat. The clarinettist plays at his most abandoned on the four sides by Blythe's Owls, less elaborately than with Armstrong but with no less energy. A very fine record in mostly excellently remastered sound, although some of the dubbing is rather reverberant.

SHARKEY BONANO (1904–72)
TRUMPET, VOCAL

***　**Sharkey Bonano At Lenfant's Lounge** Storyville SLP 6015 CD/LP
Bonano; Jack Delaney (*tb*); Bujie Centobie (*cl*); Stanley Mendelson (*p*); Arnold
'Deacon' Loyacano (*b*); Abbie Brunies, Monk Hazel (*d*); Lizzie Miles (*v*). 8–9/52.

***　**Sharkey Bonano And His Band** Storyville SLP 6011 CD/LP
As above, except omit Hazel and Miles. 12/52.

Although he worked in New York during the 1930s, Sharkey Bonano was a New Orleans
trumpeter who seldom strayed far from the city, and he worked and recorded frequently in the
aftermath of the New Orleans revival of the 1940s and '50s. Location recordings catch his able
band in lively form. The leader's own playing suggests that he was more convincing as a front
man than as a soloist: if he tries to push too hard, his tone thins out and his phrases buckle. But
Delany and Centobie are both perfectly assured soloists, and Bonano sensibly gives them the
lion's share of the attention. Lizzie Miles sings a couple of vocals on the first record and shouts
encouragement too. The recordings are clear enough, though they don't have much sparkle, but
the swing of the band stands up well: another valuable document of a genuine New Orleans
outfit, playing to orders – the material is very familiar – but making the most of it.

BONE STRUCTURE
GROUP

(*)　**Bone Structure Calligraph CLG 020 CD/LP/MC
Mark Nightingale, Richard Edwards, Colin Hill, Andy Hutchinson (*tb*); Nigel Barr
(*btb*); Pete Murray (*p*); Mike Eaves (*g*); Don Richardson (*b*); Chris Barron (*d*);
Lorraine Craig (*v*). 4–5/88.

There have been all-trombone front lines before, courtesy of J. J. Johnson, Slide Hampton and
others, but this British group approach the task with a flair and nicely deadpan wit which
alleviate the built-in blandness of their sound. It's hard to make trombones sound interesting
across the length of a record if they set out to avoid the expressionist approach, and
Nightingale's team tend to impress through dexterity and timing. Nor do they truly sidestep the
novelty aspects of the group, a trait which has plagued British trad and mainstream: Horace
Silver's 'Doodlin'' is taken at a silly, ambling pace, and the sonorous treatment of 'Lush Life'
seems designed more to elicit gee-whiz reactions than anything else. But their up-tempo pieces
are delivered with a punch that overcomes doubts about musical integrity: if, at times, one longs
to hear them loosen up, that may have more to do with the metronomic feel of the rhythm
section.

JOE BONNER (born 1948)
PIANO

****　**Parade** Steeplechase SCCD 31116 CD/LP
Bonner; Johnny Dyani (*b*); Billy Higgins (*d*). 2/79.

***　**Devotion** Steeplechase SCS 1182 LP
Bonner (*p* solo). 2/83.

***　**Suburban Fantasies** Steeplechase SCS 1176 LP
Bonner; Johnny Dyani (*b*). 2/83.

***(*)　**Suite For Chocolate** Steeplechase SCCD 31215 CD/LP
Bonner; Khan Jamal (*vib*); Jesper Lundgaard (*b*); Leroy Lowe (*d*). 11/85.

***　**New Life** Steeplechase SCCD 31239 CD/LP
Bonner; Hugo Rasmussen (*b*); Aage Tanggaard (*d*). 8/86.

****　**The Lost Melody** Steeplechase SCCD 31227 CD/LP
Bonner; Bob Rockwell (*ts*); Jesper Lundgaard (*b*); Jukkis Uotila (*d*). 3/87.

*** **New Beginnings** Theresa TR 125 CD
Bonner; Laurie Antonioli (*v*).

*** **Impressions Of Copenhagen** Theresa TR 114 LP
Bonner; Eddie Shu (*t*); Gary Olson (*tb*); Holly Hoffman (*f*); Paul Warburton (*b*); J.
Thomas Tilton (*d*); Carol Michalowski (*vl*); Carol Garrett (*vla*); Beverley Woolery
(*clo*).

Bonner is an impressive modernist whose occasional resemblance to Thelonious Monk probably
stems from the fact that he has listened and paid attention to the same swing-era players that
Monk did. He has a surprisingly light touch (too light on some of the Steeplechases, where the
miking sounds a bit remote) and he can seem a little diffident. He is, though, a fine solo
performer and an adventurous group leader. His most distinctive work to date is the early trio
with Dyani and Higgins and the slightly later duo with the bassist, on which they develop a
tremendous rapport that seems to cement ever more strongly as they move outwards from
settled bop progressions and into freer territory. The African elements also emerge in the
lovely *Suite For Chocolate*, which shouldn't be overlooked or dismissed as a soundtrack album.

   The solo records (Antonioli makes only a limited contribution to *New Beginnings*) are rather
intense and inward looking, with little of the rolling, almost gospelly intensity that Bonner has
brought to Billy Harper and Pharoah Sanders sessions. *The Lost Melody* is a good group
session, marked by strong charts and just the right element of freedom for Rockwell, a fine
soloist within his own square of turf, but apt to flounder beyond it. The other Theresa has some
effectively impressionistic moments and the use of strings is quite original and uncluttered, but
it's a bit of a by-blow and not really consistent in either tone or quality with Bonner's
increasingly impressive jazz output.

BORBETOMAGUS
GROUP

*(*) **Borbeto Jam** Cadence CJR 1026 LP
Toshinori Kondo (*t*); Jim Sauter, Don Dietrich (*saxes*); Milo Fine (*cl*); Jim Miller (*g*);
Tristan Honsinger (*clo*); Peter Kowald (*b*). 85.

Spectacularly ugly sounds from the celebrated trio of Dietrich, Sauter and Miller, here joined by
four comrades in improvisation. The group's relentless assault on saxes and guitar is an early
example of the kind of hardcore noise-making which such groups as Last Exit and Blind Idiot
God turned to in the 1980s, although the presence of four guests tends to confuse the pointed
charge which the group delivered on their superior earlier releases for Agaric, which are
unfortunately very difficult to find. Soupy, monochromatic recording doesn't help, yet
something of the group's terrifying power does abide in the record.

ALLAN BOTSCHINSKY (born 1940)
TRUMPET, FLUGELHORN, ARRANGER

*** **The Night** MA Music NU 6761/2/4 CD/LP/MC
Botschinsky; Ove Ingmarsson (*ss, ts*); Thomas Clausen (*p*); Lars Danielsson (*b*);
Victor Lewis (*d*). n.d.

*** **Duologue** MA Music NU 2060/CD 2063/MC 2064 CD/LP/MC
Botschinsky; Niels-Henning Ørsted-Pedersen (*b*).

Botschinsky, a veteran Danish trumpeter, is an accomplished if somewhat solid arranger: some
of his projects in that capacity for MA have been fussily eclectic and overworked, but these two
less ambitious records cast him in a more effective playing role. The quintet album features an
excellent group: Ingmarsson and Clausen are unflashy but personal post-bop stylists, and the
rhythm section is splendid. But the duo album with Pedersen is a more convincing showcase for
Botschinsky's own playing. He has a rather precise and strait-laced manner, but in this exposed
setting it counterpoints the bassist's virtuosity to great effect and, whether they're doing
'Subconscious-Lee' or 'Jeanie With The Light Brown Hair' it turns out fine.

CHRISTER BOUSTEDT
ALTO SAX

***   **Body And Soul** Dragon DRLP 2 LP
Boustedt; Lasse Werner (*p*).

Veteran Swedish modernist meets a longtime companion in a light and pleasing programme of swing-to-bop standards. Worth hearing.

LESTER BOWIE (born 1940)
TRUMPET, MISCELLANEOUS INSTRUMENTS

***   **Numbers 1 & 2** Nessa N-1 LP
Bowie; Joseph Jarman, Roscoe Mitchell (*reeds, perc*); Malachi Favors (*b, kz*). 8/67.

Bowie was raised in St Louis but his arrival in Chicago in the mid-1960s coincided with the burgeoning new music scene which black musicians were creating at the time. This is one of the seminal early recordings by what came to be the nucleus of the Art Ensemble Of Chicago, and while not as immediately striking as, say, Roscoe Mitchell's *Sound*, the record is an important and surprisingly durable glimpse of what these remarkable players were working on. 'Number 1' is essentially a dialogue between Bowie's horn and the flux of Mitchell's rackful of saxophones, with an elliptical undertow provided by Favors; Jarman joins in on 'Number 2', which is organized mostly by Mitchell. The vividness of the music is unfortunately undercut by the cloudy recording, but in its fragmentary way it offers a sometimes disturbing experience.

***   **The Fifth Power** Black Saint BSR 0020 CD/LP
Bowie; Arthur Blythe (*as*); Amina Myers (*p, v*); Malachi Favors (*b*); Phillip Wilson (*d*). 4/78.

Bowie's 1970s band provides a more straightforward kind of post-Chicago jazz, but this quintet is loaded with expressive talent. Blythe and Myers are the outsiders here, yet their different kinds of playing – Blythe is swaggeringly verbose, Myers a gospellish spirit – add new flavours to Bowie's sardonic music. The 18 minutes of 'God Has Smiled On Me' are several too many, although the ferocious free-for-all in the middle is very excitingly done, while '3 In 1' finds a beautiful balance between freedom and form.

(*)   **The Great Pretender ECM 1209 CD/LP
Bowie; Hamiet Bluiett (*bs*); Donald Smith (*ky*); Fred Wilson (*b*); Phillip Wilson (*d*); Fontella Bass, David Peaston (*v*). 6/81.

(*)   **All The Magic! ECM 1246/7 2CD/2LP
As above, except Ari Brown (*ss, ts*), Art Matthews (*p*) replace Bluiett and Smith. 6/82.

This was a disappointing band, at least on record: in concert, David Peaston's rendition of 'Everything Must Change' was astonishingly uplifting, but the version on *All The Magic!* is disarmingly tame. *The Great Pretender* began Bowie's exploration of pop standards as vehicles for extended free jazz satire, but it tends to go on for too long. Perhaps the typically resplendent ECM recording didn't suit the group, although 'Rios Negros' is a fine feature for the leader. The second half of *All The Magic!*, though, multitracks Bowie's trumpet into a gallery of grotesques: his style has matured into a lexicon of smears, growls, chirrups and other effects, and here he uses it as an expressionist cartoon.

***(*)   **Duet** Paddlewheel K28P-6367 CD/LP
Bowie; Nobuyoshi Ino (*b, ky*). 8/85.

A one-off meeting in Tokyo which spurs Bowie into some of his best playing on record. Ino plays determinedly straight-ahead bass and compels the trumpeter into observing line and length, so that the melodies survive all of Bowie's cracked notes and crying commentaries. Themes such as Sting's 'Moon Over Bourbon Street' and Charlie Haden's 'Ellen David' become moving laments, and the Japanese engineers capture every nuance in the music.

(*)   **I Only Have Eyes For You ECM 1296
Bowie; Stanton Davis, Malachi Thompson, Bruce Purse (*t*); Steve Turre, Craig Harris
(*tb*); Vincent Chancey (*frhn*); Bob Stewart (*tba*); Phillip Wilson (*d*). 2/85.

**   **Avant Pop** ECM 1326 CD/LP
As above, except Rasul Siddik (*t*) and Frank Lacy (*tb*) replace Purse and Harris. 3/86.

**   **Twilight Dreams** Venture CDV E 2 CD
As above. 4/87.

***   **Serious Fun** DIW 834/8035 CD/LP
Bowie; Stanton Davis, E. J. Allen, Gerald Brezel (*t*); Steve Turre, Frank Lacy (*tb*);
Vincent Chancey (*frhn*); Bob Stewart (*tba*); Vinnie Johnson, Ken Cruchfield (*d*);
Famoudou Don Moye (*perc*). 4/89.

These records are by Bowie's group Brass Fantasy, a band with an unprecedented
instrumentation – at least, in modern jazz. The brass-heavy line-up has obvious echoes of
marching bands and the oldest kinds of jazz, however, and one expects a provocative kind of
neo-traditionalism with Bowie at the helm. But Brass Fantasy seldom delivers much more than
a lightweight irreverence on record. The first three albums have some surprising choices of
covers, including Whitney Houston's 'Saving All My Love For You' and Lloyd Price's
'Personality', but the studio seems to stifle some of the freewheeling bravado of the ensemble,
and Bowie himself resorts to a disappointing self-parody. Just as one thinks it can go no further,
though, the DIW disc displays a fresh maturity: the brass voicing acquires a broader resonance,
the section-work sounds funkier, and although the improvising is still too predictable, it suggests
altogether that the group still has plenty left to play.

***   **Works** ECM 837 274 CD/LP

A respectable compilation from Bowie's four ECM records, plus one track ('Charlie M') from
the AEOC's *Full Force*.

***   **The Organizer** DIW 821 CD
Bowie; Steve Turre (*tb*); James Carter (*ts*); Amina Claudine Myers (*org*); Famoudou
Don Moye, Phillip Wilson (*d*). 1/91.

Bowie strips out the horns and adds Amina Myers on organ: it's really an update of his Fifth
Power band of the 1970s, and it works out fine, though the music trades the visceral punch of
organ-soul jazz for a more rambling and discursive impact. Turre, as usual, gets in some of the
best shots on trombone.

CHARLES BRACKEEN (born 1940)
TENOR SAXOPHONE, SOPRANO SAXOPHONE

***   **Bannar** Silkheart SH 105 CD/LP
Brackeen; Dennis Gonzalez (*t*); Malachi Favors (*b*); Alvin Fielder (*d*). 2/87.

***   **Attainment** Silkheart SH 110 CD/LP

****   **Worshippers Come Nigh** Silkheart SH 111 CD/LP
Brackeen; Olu Dara (*co*); Fred Hopkins (*b*); Andrew Cyrille (*d, perc*); Dennis
Gonzalez (*perc*). Both 11/87.

In 1986 the managing director of the recently founded Silkheart Records tracked down the
reclusive Brackeen and persuaded him to record again. Over the following year, the saxophonist
cut three astonishing albums for the label that are as fine as anything released in the late 1980s.
   If Coltrane was the overdetermining presence for most saxophonists of the period, Brackeen
seems virtually untouched, working instead in a vein reminiscent alternately of Ornette
Coleman (as in the stop-start melodic stutter of 'Three Monks Suite' on *Bannar*) and Albert
Ayler ('Allah' on the same album). He favours a high, slightly pinched tone; his soprano
frequently resembles clarinet, and his tenor work is punctuated by Aylerish sallies into the
'false' upper register. The 'Three Monks Suite' is wholly composed and Brackeen really lets go
as a soloist on *Bannar* only with 'Story', a limping melody with enough tightly packed musical
information to fuel two superb solos from the horns.

The two November 1987 sessions are even more remarkable. Gonzalez is a fine, emotive trumpeter, but he lacks the blowtorch urgency of Dara's more hotly pitched cornet. 'Worshippers Come Nigh' is as exciting a jazz piece as any in the catalogue, underpinned by Hopkins's fine touch (less spacious than Favors but generously responsive) and Cyrille's percussion. 'Bannar' confusingly finds its way on to this album rather than the one named after it, but all three have to be seen as a unit. *Attainment* is the least satisfying, but only because there are no solos on a par with 'Worshippers' and 'Story'. However, it does include the fascinating sax/bass/drums trio 'House Of Gold'.

Silkheart's small catalogue is patiently rehearsed and recorded, and flawlessly mastered. In less than five years the label has made a considerable mark on the American jazz scene, shifting the centre of gravity south from New York and California to the Dallas–New Orleans axis celebrated in Gonzalez's *Debenge Debenge* (SHLP 112), which also features Brackeen.

BOBBY BRADFORD (born 1934)
TRUMPET, CORNET

**   **Lost In LA** Soul Note SN 1068 CD/LP
Bradford; James Kousakis (*as*); Roberto Miguel Miranda (*b*); Mark Dresser (*b*); Sherman Ferguson (*d*). 6/83.

**   **One Night Stand** Soul Note SN 1168 CD/LP
Bradford; Frank Sullivan (*p*); Scott Walton (*b*) Billy Bowker (*d*). 11/86.

**   **Comin' On** hat Art 6016 CD
Bradford; John Carter (*cl*); Don Preston (*p, synth*); Richard Davis (*b*); Andrew Cyrille (*d*). 5/88.

Twenty years ago, Bradford was recording with Ornette Coleman (he appears on *Broken Shadows* and the underrated *Science Fiction*), having replaced Don Cherry in the regular quartet ten years earlier. Ironically, he is now probably most often cited as a 'guest' improviser with the British-based Spontaneous Music Ensemble, where he fitted in not quite seamlessly.

His best work with Ornette is supposed to have gone the way of desert flowers, and the recordings made under his own name are curiously unsatisfactory, full of good things (like his superbly constructed solos) but ultimately underachieved. Don Preston seems a wildly improbable choice for the 1988 hat Art session and combines only poorly with Davis and Cyrille, both of whom are uncharacteristically bland. Bradford's interplay with clarinettist Carter falls a long way short of their long-deleted mid-1960s collaborations and his tone seems muffled and indistinct.

Lost In LA has some striking moments and the single-horn format of *One Night Stand* prompts some more of his bravura and his most thoughtful solos. An important and adventurous player, Bradford has yet to recapture the brilliance of the 1973 *Secrets* with Carter; even the live sets seem to lose something of their burnish at the mixing desk.

WILL BRADLEY (born 1912)
TROMBONE

(*)   **Will Bradley 1940 Tax 3713-2 CD
Bradley; Steve Lipkins, Joe Wiedman, Herbie Dell (*t*); Jimmy Emmert, Bill Corti (*tb*); Artie Mendelsohn, Joe Huffman (*as*); Peanuts Hucko (*ts, cl*); Sam Sachelle (*ts*); Freddy Slack (*p*); Steve Jordan (*g, v*); Felix Giobbe (*b*); Ray McKinley (*d, v*); Carlotta Dale (*v*). 2–3/40.

Will Bradley, 'The Boy With The Horn', joined forces with Ray McKinley to form a band in 1939. This CD collects two of their radio broadcasts in clear and very listenable sound. There weren't many outstanding soloists in the band – Hucko, Slack and the thin-toned but lively Lipkins are the only prominent ones – and there's a streak of sweetness which takes some of the punch out of even their grittiest charts, such as 'Flying Home', which appears twice and only just gets off the ground. Bradley's own manner was similar to Tommy Dorsey's, and McKinley was as prominent a singer as he was a drummer; an interesting document, but of secondary importance except to serious big-band collectors. Bradley and McKinley split up in

1942, and the former's next band included Shorty Rogers and Shelly Manne; but it never recorded. The trombonist himself later took up composing.

TINY BRADSHAW (1905-58)
VOCAL, LEADER

**(*)   Tiny Bradshaw / Teddy Hill Harlequin HQ 2053 LP
Bradshaw; Lincoln Mills, Lawrence 'Max' Maddox, Shad Collins (*t*); George Matthews, Eugene Green or Eugene Simon (*tb*); Bobby Holmes (*cl, as*); Eddie Williams (*as*); Edgar Courance (*cl, ts, bs*); Happy Caldwell (*ts*); Clarence Johnson (*p*); Bob Lessey (*g*); Ernest Williamson (*b*); Scrippy Boling (*d*). 9–10/34.

Bradshaw is best remembered as the maker of a large number of R&B sides in the 1940s and '50s. But he began as a dance band vocalist and took to leading his own orchestra in the early 1930s. It's a pity that the band made only eight sides, all collected here, since it had good soloists in Shad Collins, Eddie Williams and Happy Caldwell, and Bradshaw's Calloway-like vocals lend a fine – if occasionally tiresome – exuberance to the sound. They are excellently transferred on this LP, which is shared with three important sessions by Teddy Hill's band.

TIM BRADY
GUITAR, SYNTHESIZER

***   Visions Justin Time JTR 8413-2 CD
Brady; Kenny Wheeler (*t, c, flhn*); Montreal Chamber Orchestra. 11/85–6/88.

**   Double Variations Justin Time JTR-8415-2 CD
Brady; John Abercrombie (*g, g-syn*). 11/87–12/89.

**(*)   Bradyworks Justin Time JTR 8433-2 CD
Brady; John Surman (*ss, bs*); Simon Stone (*saxes, f*); Christopher Best (*clo*); Barre Phillips (*b*); Marie Josée Simard, Pierre Tanguay (*perc*). 11/88–4/91.

Brady is a Montreal-based guitarist and composer whose jazz affiliations are only a part of a wide-ranging schemata. *Visions* consists of a five-movement work for orchestra, with Wheeler as soloist, plus two duets by Wheeler and Brady and four solos by the guitarist. The orchestral piece doesn't instil much impression beyond the familiar one when faced by such an effort – that here is an orchestral piece by an occasional 'serious' composer – but Wheeler gives it his full attention and creates some passages of striking empathy with the material. Certainly anyone who likes a Keith Jarrett record such as *Luminescence* will want to explore this. The solos and duos suggest a more stop-motion approach to improvising, with Brady exploring textures and sound-barriers a step at a time. *Double Variations* is a sort of combination of both approaches, with Abercrombie pressed into the 'traditional' soloist's role while Brady sets up banks of electronic sound. Comparisons with Abercrombie's records with Ralph Towner are misleading, for this is much less of a yin–yang situation, and the continuously blurred articulation and use of multi-tracking create an overlapping of sound which is finally rather wearisome. *Bradyworks* continues what is a four-part sequence (based on ideas in Jacques Attali's *Bruit*) in much the same style, with a grander cast but a similar dependence on synthesizer samples. It's a thoughtful and scrupulously prepared piece of work, but there seems little here which – since they're both present – Surman and Phillips haven't done better on their own forays into this area.

RUBY BRAFF (born 1927)
CORNET, TRUMPET

**(*)   Hustlin' And Bustlin' Black Lion BL (7)60908 CD/LP
Braff; Vic Dickenson (*tb, v*); Dick LeFave (*tb*); Buzzy Drootin (*cl, ts*); Edmond Hall (*cl*); Kenneth Kersey, Sam Margolis (*ts*); George Wein (*p*); John Field, Milton Hinton (*b*); Bobby Donaldson, Jo Jones (*d*). Summer 51, 5/54, 6/54.

***(*) **The Mighty Braff** Affinity AFF 757 CD
Braff; Eddie Hubble (*tb*); Bob Wilber (*cl, ts*); Hymie Schertzer (*as*); Al Klink, Sam
Margolis, Boomie Richman (*ts*); Sol Schlinger (*bs*); Johnny Guarnieri, Dick Katz, Ellis
Larkins (*p*); Art Ryerson, Mundell Lowe (*g*); Walter Page, Gene Ramey (*b*); Bobby
Donaldson, Izzy Sklar (*d*). 54–55.

Braff was born a generation too late and spent much of what should have been his most
productive years in the 1950s with a great deal less to do than his talent deserved. His cornet
playing has an almost vocal agility that balances delicacy of detail with a strong underlying
pulse and harmonic richness. There's hardly a fault to be registered, beyond the uneasy sense
that Braff didn't always have sidemen who were equal to his gifts. The opening 'Hustlin' And
Bustlin" is associated with Louis Armstrong and binds Braff inextricably to the jazz mainstream
that went underground with Dizzy Gillespie and Clifford Brown. 'Shoe Shine Boy' has a bright
polish and the self-written 'Flaky' an intriguingly ironic edge.

   The Affinity compilation – much of it available for some time – is, if anything, even stronger
and features eight marvellous tracks setting Braff, on trumpet, against a saxophone section
(little known, except for Wilber), an unusual combination for him. This is perhaps his most
virtuosic representation on record (where he tends to be more restrained than in clubs or
concerts) and some of the lower register work is quite remarkable. Newcomers should look no
further.

***(*) **Hear Me Talkin'** Black Lion BLCD 760161 CD
Braff; Alex Welsh (*t*); Roy Williams (*tb*); Al Gay (*ts*); Johnny Barnes (*bs*); Jim
Douglas (*g*); Fred Hunt (*p*); Ron Rae (*b*); Lennie Hastings (*d*). 11/67.

Recorded in London at the tail end of a mouth-watering 'Jazz Expo' package which introduced
British players to some of their American idols. The Welsh band had been playing with Wild
Bill Davison at the 100 Club before these sessions were recorded and something of Davison's
brisk attack creeps into the brass chase that ends 'No One Else But You'. Though Welsh mostly
defers to Braff as far as solo space is concerned, the real star of the set is trombonist Roy
Williams, who plays a marvellous solo on 'Ruby Got Rhythm' and even more outstandingly on
'Smart Alex Blues', both originals put together by Braff for the set. His own finest moment is
on the long 'Between The Devil And The Deep Blue Sea', where he plays in his equally
distinctive lower register.

   The Welsh band was probably the finest mainstream unit of its time and had recently had an
opportunity to prove its quality in international company at Antibes (Newport beckoned for
1968). It offers Braff spirited company, with sparks of real class from both Williams and Welsh;
the music is faithfully reproduced on this valuable reissue.

(*) **Plays Gershwin Concord CCD 6005 CD

(*) **Plays Rodgers & Hart Concord CCD 6007 CD
Braff; George Barnes, Wayne Wright (*g*); Michael Moore (*b*). 7/74, n. d.

In the end, they couldn't get along together, but while they were playing (rather than
squabbling), Braff and Barnes produced some of the best small-group jazz of the day. Needless
to say, the critics were looking in the other direction at the time. This isn't just another
'Goishwin' route-march, but a genuine attempt to get inside the tunes and unpick their still far
too little understood progressions. Unfortunately, if Braff is on his usual plateau of excellence,
there is something slightly unresolved about Wayne Wright's rhythm guitar and Moore's bass.

   The mix is perhaps better on the Rodgers/Hart set. 'Spring Is Here' is completely masterly
and Barnes seems happier with this material than with the Gershwin. On a toss-up, though,
Gershwin's writing breaks the deadlock.

*** **America The Beautiful** Concord GW 3003 CD
Braff; Dick Hyman (*org*). n. d.

No question of tongues in cheeks here. The first is a warmly engaging tribute to America and
her song, an example of what Braff once called 'adoration of the melody'. His exquisite tone is
ideally suited to Braff favourites like 'When It's Sleepy Time Down South' (compare the band
version on *Hustlin' And Bustlin'*) and Hyman's slightly emphysemic pipe-organ sound is a
perfect complement. A lovely record, highly recommended.

The later duo with Hyman steers even nearer to the wind of pure sentiment and carves a brilliant tack out of danger. 'I've Grown Accustomed To Her Face' and 'On The Street Where You Live' have had their moments in jazz, but not, surely, the 'Ascot Gavotte' or 'Wouldn't It Be Luvverly', two melodies that under normal circumstances it would be quite difficult to adore. The fast and slow versions of 'With A Little Bit Of Luck' offer intriguing insights into Braff's thinking. Hyman's piano playing is excellent as always.

(*)   **A First Concord CCD 4274 CD/MC

(*)   **A Sailboat In The Moonlight Concord CCD 4296 CD/MC
     Braff; Scott Hamilton (*ts*); John Bunch (*p*); Chris Flory (*g*); Phil Flanigan (*b*); Chuck Riggs (*d*). 2/85.

Two fine albums from the same 1985 sessions. Hamilton, a generation younger, is a co-religionist in his refusal to accept the orthodoxy of bop or its aftermath. He and Braff blend as effectively as any one reed player he has partnered over the years, and the two albums move with an unstinted eloquence, punctuated by moments of real fire.

***   **Me, Myself And I** Concord CCD 4381 CD/MC

***   **Bravura Eloquence** Concord CCD 4423 CD/MC
     Braff; Howard Alden (*g*); Jack Lesberg (*b*). 6/88.

These are probably the finest things Braff has done in recent years. His tone is still ringingly strong, the allusions and melodic palimpsests as thought-provoking as ever; particularly effective are the segues from 'Smile' to 'Who'll Buy My Violets?' and in the long, superb 'Judy [Garland] Medley', which contains not just the inevitable 'Rainbow' but 'If I Only Had A Brain'. On *Me, Myself And I*, he even takes a shot at the big toon from *Swan Lake*. Lesberg and Alden provide sterling support. Two of those 'nice warm feeling' records that don't starve the grey cells.

***(*)   **And His New England Songhounds: Volume 1** Concord CCD 4478 CD
     Braff; Scott Hamilton (*ts*); Dave McKenna (*p*); Frank Tate (*b*); Alan Dawson (*d*). 4/91.

Braff and McKenna last did a studio session together in 1956, when the cornettist cut the fine *Braff!* for Epic. The chemistry still works. The hand-picked band offers Braff a warmly swinging background for one of his best performances of recent years. The original 'Shŏ-Time' is dedicated to Scott Hamilton's son, a relatively rare writing credit for Braff but further evidence of his skill as a melodist. Stand-out tracks have to be 'My Shining Hour', Billie's 'Tell Me More', and the brief closing 'Every Time We Say Goodbye'. Mainstream jazz at its best; Volume 2 will be worth the wait.

DOLLAR BRAND – see ABDULLAH IBRAHIM

ANTHONY BRAXTON (born 1945)
ALTO SAXOPHONE, ALL OTHER SAXOPHONES AND CLARINETS, FLUTE, ELECTRONICS, PERCUSSION

****   **Seven Compositions (Trio) 1989** hat Art CD 6025 CD
     Braxton; Adelhard Roidinger (*b*); Tony Oxley (*d*). 89.

Anthony Braxton records are a little like No. 12 buses. There's always another one along in a moment. He is, perhaps, the most extensively documented contemporary improviser – remarkably so, given the dauntingly cerebral character of at least some of his output. There is a further problem: is Braxton's music jazz at all, since a large proportion of his work, solos and all, is – gasp! – scored? The 1989 trio settles the second of these at least. Whatever the prevailing definition of jazz (and, as the man said, if you have to ask . . .), this music conforms majestically: rhythmic, virtuosic, powerfully emotive, constantly reinventing itself. Tony Oxley, a veteran of the British free jazz movement of the 1960s, plays superbly and is beautifully recorded. Braxton runs through his usual gamut of horns, including the antiquated C-melody saxophone, and sounds assured and confident. There's even a standard, a powerful 'All The

134

Things You Are'. If you've room for only one Braxton, or are about to do 'Desert Island Discs', look no further; no question at all as to the validity of this particular release.

** **Live At Moers Festival** Moers 01002 LP

*** **Composition 113** sound aspects 003 LP

** **19 (Solo) Improvisations 1988** New Albion Records NA023 CD
Braxton (*saxophone* solo). 6/74, 12/83, 4/88.

In 1968 Braxton set the jazz world back on its heels with an album of solo saxophone improvisations entitled *For Alto*. There was nothing fundamentally new about unaccompanied saxophone – Coleman Hawkins had done it years before with the intriguingly abstract 'Picasso' – but *For Alto* was stingingly powerful, abstract and daring. It was, perhaps, Braxton's finest hour.

By comparison, the Moers set is disappointing: hectic and slightly incoherent, as if Braxton is special-pleading rather than playing from conviction. There are problems with the sound register, too – not uncommon on live Moers recordings, but definitively intrusive here; Braxton surely never sounds quite that acid?

Composition 113, which is scored for soprano saxophone and a couple of props, is one of Braxton's most effective conceptual pieces. Suprisingly moving in a live setting – the soloist stands beside a photograph of a deserted railway station with a train lantern suspended above him – it transfers well to record and has a meditative calm which is rare with Braxton.

The recent New Albion set, product of yet another new recording deal, is thin stuff indeed, almost as if that remarkable technique has become a polished manner which can be taken on and off at will. 'Compositions' they may be; pointlessly enigmatic they certainly are.

(*) **In The Tradition Steeplechase 1015 CD/LP

(*) **In The Tradition Steeplechase 1045 CD/LP
Braxton; Tete Montoliu (*p*); Niels-Henning Ørsted-Pedersen (*b*); Albert Heath (*d*).
5/74.

***(*) **Eight (+3) Tristano Compositions 1989** hat Art 6052 CD
Braxton; John Raskin (*bs*); Dred Scott (*p*); Cecil McBee (*b*); Andrew Cyrille (*d*).
12/89.

Braxton more than most had eventually to prove himself as a performer of standards. The Monk sessions (below) are a triumph, but *In The Tradition*, his first sustained essay in revisionism, was less successful, partly because the piano player, the blind Catalan Tete Montoliu, so patently misunderstood his intentions. Braxton's lyrical lines – on shibboleths like 'Ornithology' and 'Goodbye Pork Pie Hat' – are so clearly drawn as to render the chords and Montoliu's embellishments almost redundant. The bass and drums are by contrast almost ideally adapted to Braxton's needs, a particular tribute to NHØP's resilience and catholicity of taste.

If *In The Tradition* remains a collectable curiosity with occasional flashes of brilliance, as in Braxton's statements on 'Marshmallow', *Eight (+3) Tristano Compositions* is another small masterpiece in the same mould as the Monk set. Intended as a tribute to the late Warne Marsh, a less than immediately obvious influence on Braxton, it adds Marsh's 'Sax Of A Kind', Irving Berlin's 'How Deep Is The Ocean' and Vincent Youmans's 'Time On My Hands' – all Cool School standbys – to a roster of Tristano originals. Though Braxton (restricted to alto and sopranino saxophones and flute) manages to get inside the tunes, it's not clear that the second saxophonist, John Raskin, fully understands the idiom. No hesitancy, though, from Dred Scott (whose historical namesake enjoys a significant libertarian niche in American history), or from a marvellously adaptive veteran rhythm section. If Braxton's own compositions have started to recentre our definitions of jazz scoring and structure, his treatment of standards is no less radical. Recommended.

*** **Three Compositions Of New Jazz** Delmark DS 423 CD/LP
Braxton; Leo Smith (*t, perc*); Leroy Jenkins (*vn, vla, perc*); Muhal Richard Abrams (*p, clo, cl*). 68.

***(*) **Dortmund (Quartet) 1976** hat Art 6075 CD
Braxton; George Lewis (*tb*); Dave Holland (*b*); Barry Altschul (*d*). 76.

***   **Performance (Quartet) 1979** hat Art 6044 CD
Braxton; Ray Anderson (*tb*); John Lindberg (*b*); Thurman Barker (*b*). 9/79.

***   **Four Compositions (Quartet) 1983** Black Saint BSR 0066 LP
Braxton; George Lewis (*tb*); John Lindberg (*b*); Gerry Hemingway (*d*). 3/83.

***   **Four Compositions (Quartet) 1984** Black Saint BSR 0086 CD/LP
Braxton; Marilyn Crispell (*p*); John Lindberg (*b*); Gerry Hemingway (*d*). 9/84.

****   **Quartet (London) 1985** Leo LR 2CD 200/201
As above, except add Mark Dresser (*b*). 11/85.

****   **Quartet (Birmingham) 1985** Leo CD LR 202/3 2CD
Braxton; David Rosenboom (*p*); Mark Dresser (*b*); Gerry Hemingway (*d*).

(*)   **Five Compositions (Quartet) 1986 Black Saint BSR 0106 CD/LP
As above. 7/86.

****   **Six Monk's Compositions (1987)** Black Saint 120 116 1 CD
Braxton; Mal Waldron (*p*); Buell Neidlinger (*b*); Bill Osborne (*d*). 7/87.

For all his compositions for amplified shovels, 100 tubas and galactically dispersed orchestras, the core of Braxton's conception remains the recognizably four-square jazz quartet. This, along with the 1989 trio, is where he has been seen to best advantage in the 1980s. The minimally varied album-titles are confusing perhaps, but there is a straightforward rule of thumb. If Marilyn Crispell is on it, buy it. The Braxton Quartet of 1984–5 was of remarkable vintage and Crispell's Cecil Taylor-inspired but increasingly individual piano playing was one of its outstanding features. There are unauthorized recordings of this band in circulation, but the Leo sets are absolutely legitimate, and pretty nearly exhaustive; the CDs offer good-quality transfers of the original boxed set, six sides of quite remarkable music that, in conjunction with the other quartet sessions, confirm Braxton's often-stated but outwardly improbable interest in the Lennie Tristano school and in particular the superb harmonic improvisation of Warne Marsh. Those who followed the 1985 British tour may argue about the respective merits of different nights and locations, but there really isn't much to separate the London and Birmingham sets for the non-specialist, though the latter reaches a hectic climax with an encore performance of 'Kelvin 40(O)' that does further damage to Braxton's undeserved reputation as a po-faced number-cruncher.

Rosenboom is a poor substitute for Crispell on the 1986 set, but the rhythm section of Dresser or Lindberg and Hemingway was beginning to sound custom-made by this stage, perfectly attuned to the music. Compare the looser, drummerless concept of the 1968 AACM graduation exercises (Braxton, on his recording debut, and his fellow-alumni enjoying a relaxed hour in the studio with old Professor Abrams) and you realize how much he has written and played his way back – which in this context is forward – into the jazz tradition. That is exactly what he is doing on the curiously but appropriately titled *Six Monk's Compositions*. Far from the usual pastiche, these are reinvented versions of a half-dozen obscurer items from the monastic oeuvre. Pianist Mal Waldron is there to confirm the apostolic succession, but Braxton's readings are thoroughly apostate, furiously paced and unapologetically maximal.

In one significant sense, Braxton is an almost archetypal CD artist. This is less a matter of sound-quality *per se* than of durations, for it is increasingly important to hear how an entire concert set develops. *Performance (Quartet) 1979* is, as Graham Lock discusses in his highly informed liner note, very much a transitional stage in Braxton's career, linking the more oppositional work of the 1970s to the composer's increasing interest in collage forms and 'pulse track structures' (which alternate notated sequences with freely improvised 'spaces' which radically shift the axes of bebop and post-bop improvisation). The 1979 group is one of the funkiest Braxton ever assmbled, but it is also, paradoxically, one of the most cerebral. 'Composition 40F' is generically part of the sequence consolidated on *Three Compositions (Trio) 1989* and should be heard in conjunction with that remarkable record.

The Dortmund set finds Braxton at the top of his form and it prompts a nagging doubt as to whether his playing – as opposed to his still-remarkable compositional and conceptual strides – has ever been better. Braxton's 'other' trombonist, Lewis, is a notoriously capricious player in a free context (though it's often forgotten how much he owes to the likes of Vic Dickenson and Dicky Wells) but capable of quite extraordinarily beautiful lines, especially on the thumping 'Composition 40B', which also highlights the superb rhythm section. Alongside this, Braxton's 'standards' and 'in the tradition' work almost seems like redundant special pleading. By the mid-1970s, he *is* the tradition, and those unforgivingly numbered compositions, perhaps destined never to be repertoire pieces, are the contemporary standards.

Never expect an easy ride with Braxton. A little patience with the Leo set is repaid many times over, and the Monk session is near-essential.

***   **Composition 99, 101, 107 and 138** hat Art 6019 CD
    Braxton; Garrett List (*tb*); Marianne Schroeder (*p*).

Not by any means a classic Braxton album, but distinguished by some fine solo and duo performances from the classically leaning Schroeder, who has a lighter and more diffuse touch than Crispell but is nevertheless an effective performer in this idiom. The trio music doesn't entirely convince, but there is some fine solo Braxton on 'Composition 99B' which, Cage-like, incorporates simultaneous elements of four other compositions.

***   **Elements Of Surprise** Moers 01036 LP
    Braxton; George Lewis (*tb*). 6/76.

(*)   **Six Duets (1982) Cecma 1005 LP
    Braxton; John Lindberg (*b*). 7/82.

***   **Duets Vancouver 1989** Music & Arts 611 CD
    Braxton; Marilyn Crispell (*p*). 6/89.

**   **Kol Nidre** sound aspects SAS 031 CD
    Braxton; Andrew Voigt (*saxophones, f*). 12/88.

Duetting with Braxton must be a daunting gig. His London appearances in the 1970s with Derek Bailey (*mutatis mutandis*) were frankly disappointing, largely again because Braxton's idiom is still jazz and Bailey's is something else; the saxophonist's 1976 partnership with Muhal Richard Abrams, a living conduit of the black musical tradition, makes for telling comparison. In that regard Crispell and Lewis more than hold their own, she with a sympathetic awareness, he with a kind of arrogant insouciance. The Vancouver duets are as warmly approachable as anything Braxton has done. There is no soft-pedalling from Crispell, and she may even be the more compelling voice. There are some signs, minor here, fatal to *Kol Nidre*, that Braxton is settling into an uneasy alternation between a relatively fixed style and sudden, nihilistic eruptions. The two-saxophone format doesn't work – Voigt is a member of ROVA, for which, see below – and the sax-and-bass album just seems incomplete, despite some wonderful playing on both parts.

*(*)   **The Aggregate** sound aspects SAS 023 CD
    Braxton; ROVA Saxophone Quartet. 88.

A well-intentioned but rather desiccated collaboration with the ground-breaking saxophone quartet. Too much horning in on each other's space, perhaps, though Braxton seems surprisingly comfortable in the setting. One for completists only.

(***(*))   **8KN-(B-12)IR10 For String Quartet** sound aspects SAS 009 CD/LP
    Braxton; Robert Schumann String Quartet. 11/79.

A tricky one, this, for much of the music emphatically isn't in the jazz idiom or anything close to it. It is, however, quite remarkable musically and does include some very fine solo Braxton, as well as alternative versions – with and without saxophone – of his densely conceived string quartet. Recommended (with caution).

***   **Composition No. 96** Leo Records LR 169 LP
    Braxton conducting Composers and Improvisers Orchestra. 5/81.

Braxton's earlier experiments with large-scale orchestral 'composition' – difficult to hear any of it as uniformly scored – were not particularly happy. It's ironic that while one of the routine criticisms levelled at his small-group work is that it is too rigidly formalized, his orchestral works can sound unproductively chaotic. *Composition 96*, which comes from a particularly fruitful phase in Braxton's career, is a huge, apocalyptic thing that might serve as a soundtrack for some post-creationist epic of the Next Frontier.

**** **Eugene (1989)** Black Saint 120137 CD
Braxton; Rob Blakeslee, Ernie Carbajal, John Jensen (*t*); Mike Heffley, Tom Hill, Ed
Kammerer (*tb*); Thom Bergeron, Jeff Homan, Carl Woideck (*reeds*); Mike Vannice
(*reeds, p*); Toddy Barton (*syn*); Joe Robinson (*g*); Forrest Moyer (*b*); Charles Dowd
(*vib, perc*); Tom Kelly (*perc*). 1/89.

One of Braxton's finest records, and certainly the most accessible of the larger-group
recordings, this features eight compositions dating from 1975 to the present day, and was
recorded in Eugene, Oregon, during a 'creative orchestra' tour of the Pacific North-West.
Much of the credit for the project has to go to trombonist Mike Heffley, who originally
proposed and subsequently organized the tour.

The earliest of the pieces, 'Composition No. 45', was written for a free jazz festival in
Baden-Baden and is defined by Braxton in his *Composition Notes C* as 'an extended platform
for the challenge of post-Coltrane/Ayler functionalism'. A march, it anticipates the more
complex 'Composition No. 58' (not included here) but demonstrates how creatively Braxton
has been able to use the large-scale 'outdoor' structures he draws from Henry Brant, Sun Ra
and traditional marching music, to open up unsuspected areas of improvisatory freedom; the
link with Ayler's apocalyptic 'Truth Is Marching In' is immediately obvious. 'Composition No.
91' is a delicately pointillistic piece with a much more abstract configuration. Less propulsive
than 'No. 45' or the more conventional ensemble-and-soloists outline of 'No. 71', it underlines
the composer's brilliant grasp of instrumental colour; synthesizer and electric guitar provide
some unfamiliar tonalities in the context of Braxton's work and, perhaps in reaction, he limits
his own playing to alto saxophone.

Braxton's work has taken on an increasingly ritualistic quality, as in the processional opening
and steady two-beat pulse of the most recent piece, 'Composition No. 134'. As such, it stands
beside the work of Stockhausen and the composers mentioned above. If its underlying
philosophy is millennial, its significance is commensurate with that.

**** **London (Solo) 1988** Impetus IMP 18818 LP
Braxton solo. 88.

. . . but it all boils down in the end to a man alone with his saxophone centre stage. Braxton's
solo concert at London's Institue of Contemporary Arts marks an important turning-point in
British perception and acceptance of his music. It is an uncompromising set, compounded of
original material and (though it shouldn't have been a surprise) standards. What was
momentarily surprising was the use of Coltrane, the apparent antithesis to Braxton's sometimes
chilly formalism, as a historical benchmark. His performances of 'Naima' and 'Impressions' on
that occasion were reference points in themselves, urgent reminders of Braxton's continual
re-examination of Afro-American music. A valuable documentation whose vinyl-only format
somehow underlines its complementary differences from the item above. Like it, though,
essential.

BRAZZ BROS
GROUP

*** **Brazzy Landscapes** Odin 4020 LP
Phil Minton (*t, v*); Jarle Førde, Jan Magne Førde (*t*); Helge Førde (*tb*); Runar Tafjörd
(*frhn*); Stien Erik Tafjörd (*tba*); Egil Johansen (*d*). 12/86.

Lip-splitting pyrotechnics from two teams of brothers, with Minton making a guest appearance
and Johansen supplying the drum parts. Jarle and Helge do most of the arranging and, as on
their carousing version of 'Blue Rondo A La Turk', the group stroll effortlessly down a thin
line between satire and serious blowing. British groups tend to sound merely po-faced when
attempting this kind of serio-comic jazz, but Brazz Bros deliver with much more aplomb. They
don't draw especial attention to their virtuosity, but any tuba player will marvel at Stien Erik
Tafjörd's tuba tongueing.

THE BRECKER BROTHERS
GROUP

**   **Collection Vol. 1** RCA Novus 90442 CD
Randy Brecker (*t, flhn, ky*); David Sanborn (*as*); Michael Brecker (*ts*); Don Grolnick,
Mark Gray, George Duke, Doug Riley, Paul Schaeffer (*ky*); Barry Finnerty, David
Spinozza, Hiram Bullock, Steve Khan (*g*); Neil Jason, Marcus Miller, Will Lee (*b*);
Harvey Mason, Terry Bozzio, Steve Jordan, Richie Morales, Steve Gadd, Alan
Schwartzberg (*d*); Sammy Figueroa, Rafael Cruz, Manolo Badrena, Ralph MacDonald
(*perc*). 75–81.

**   **Collection Vol. 2** RCA Novus 83076 CD
As above, except omit Riley, Schaeffer, Khan, Miller, Morales, Gadd, Schwartzberg
and Badrena. 75–81.

Aside from their individual exploits, the two Brecker brothers made some commercially
successful records as co-leaders in the mid-1970s, and these two best-ofs give a clear picture of
what they did: jazz-funk rhythms streamlined with guitars and keyboards, sometimes as settings
for grandstand solos by either of the two principals but equally often as grooving ensemble
pieces. It's very hard to agree with Michael Cuscuna's sleevenote to Volume 1, though, when he
avers that 'any of this material could easily have been recorded yesterday'. It may say more
about the ephemerality of the group that it actually sounds more dated – or, at least, more
timelocked – than any hard bop session. The bouncing, constricted rhythms, existential
meanderings of the soloists and dinky-sounding keyboards and guitars sound irresistibly like the
least enlightened music of the 1970s. But it has its following, and either compilation will do to
sample the music.

MICHAEL BRECKER (born 1949)
TENOR SAXOPHONE, EWI

***   **Michael Brecker** Impulse! MCA 5980 CD/MC
Brecker; Kenny Kirkland (*ky*); Pat Metheny (*g*); Charlie Haden (*b*); Jack DeJohnette
(*d*). 87.

**   **Don't Try This At Home** Impulse! MCA 42229-2 CD/MC

The sax-playing one of the Brecker brothers has appeared on more than 400 record dates but
has made only a handful of discs as sole leader. He is, nevertheless, one of the most admired and
emulated saxophonists of the day. He began playing in rock and soul bands in the late 1960s,
worked with Horace Silver and Billy Cobham in the '70s and put together the very successful
Steps Ahead group in 1979. His tenure as a sessionman has polished his style into something
superbly confident and muscular, a Coltrane without the questing inner turmoil. His steely,
brilliant sense of structure ensures that almost every solo he plays is impressive; whether he is
emotionally involving may depend on the listener's willingness to believe.

Michael Brecker, his 1987 debut, suggested that he had been unreasonably shy about
recording as a leader: his own compositions, 'Sea Glass' and 'Syzygy', are attractive if not
exactly haunting, while producer Don Grolnick's tunes elicit some suitably herculean solos. The
interplay with DeJohnette inevitably recalls something of the Coltrane–Elvin Jones
partnership, while Kirkland, Haden and the unusually restrained Metheny combine to create a
super-session of genuine commitment. But *Don't Try This At Home* seemed like a too casual
follow-up, with several of the pieces sounding like left-overs from the first session and Brecker
cruising through the record in his sessionman identity rather than imposing a leader's presence.

***   **Now You See It . . . (Now You Don't)** GRP GR-9622 CD/MC
Brecker; Jim Beard, Joey Calderazzo (*ky*); Jon Herington (*g*); Victor Bailey, Jay
Anderson (*b*); Adam Nussbaum, Omar Hakim (*d*); Don Alias, Steve Berrios, Milton
Cardona (*perc*). 90.

Brecker's third record as a leader is a mixed success. Too few of the eight themes are truly
memorable or demanding on anything other than a technical level, and some of the synthesizer
orchestration is a distraction rather than a benefit. The best jazz comes in the tracks where the
saxophonist gets a clear run at the listener: on 'Peep', which turns into a kind of abstract funk,

and 'The Meaning Of The Blues', which is unadorned tenor-plus-rhythm. The slow intensification of the saxophonist's improvisation on 'Minsk' is the one moment where Brecker best displays his mastery: it's staggeringly well played. Don Grolnick's production is snappy and clean without being as glaring as many fusion records.

RANDY BRECKER (born 1945)
TRUMPET

**   **In The Idiom** Denon 33CY 1483 CD/LP
Brecker; Joe Henderson (*ts*); David Kikoski (*p*); Ron Carter (*b*); Al Foster (*d*). 10/86.

*(*)   **Live At Sweet Basil** Sonet SNTF 1011 CD/LP
Brecker; Bob Berg (*ts*); David Kikoski (*p, synth*); Dieter Ilg (*b*); Joey Baron (*d*).
11/88.

Brecker is less generously talented than his saxophone-playing younger sibling, but he is still an impressive soloist whose style has mellowed and matured since the barnstorming fusion days of the Brecker Brothers. *In The Idiom*'s top-drawer line-up suggested a strong desire to move back into the jazz mainstream, and the chops to pull it off. Henderson and the pedigree rhythm section give him lots of time and room, and Brecker plays two or three strongly authentic solos, marked by an unhurried exploration of basic (but by no means banal) harmonic ideas.

The later, live recording is altogether more hectic and in some respects more 'contemporary', whatever that means, with Berg and a plugged-in Kikoski egging the trumpeter on to the kind of stunting bravura he appeared briefly to have left behind. Both are perfectly enjoyable sets and the two drummers give particular cause for pleasure, but the Denon has an odd sound-balance which afflicts Henderson most seriously.

DAVE BRENNAN
BANJO, GUITAR

(*)   **Take Me To The Mardi Gras Lake LACD 20 CD
Brennan; Pat O'Brien (*t, v*); Dave Vickers (*tb*); Frank Brooker (*cl, as, ts*); Mick Kennedy (*b*); Terry Kennedy (*d*). 4/90–2/91.

Dave Brennan has been leading his Jubilee Jazz Band for 30 years, though records have been very few. This anniversary set is scarcely a milestone in British trad, but it sums up both the pros and cons of the genre. The material is determinedly unhackneyed and includes Henry Allen's 'Ride Red Ride', 'Rip 'Em Up Joe', 'Eccentric Rag' and 'Dauphine Street Blues'; the playing ranges from rumbustious energy to a surprisingly delicate touch on the filigree treatment of 'Mood Indigo'; the echoes of George Lewis and Bunk Johnson are integrated into a home-grown spirit which is by now just as 'authentic'; and the best of the individual contributions, particularly Dave Vickers's trombone solos, are impressive. On the other side of the coin are the vocals (still the least appealing aspect of British trad); the frequently flat dynamics; and a sense of ennui which the restrictive practices of the genre encourage rather than exonerate. But it would be churlish to deny the best of this music. The recording is truthful and lifelike.

JOHN WOLF BRENNAN
PIANO, KEYBOARDS, ELECTRONICS, COMPOSER

(*)   **The Beauty Of Fractals Creative Works CW 1017 1 CD

(*)   **Iritations Creative Works CW 1021 CD
Brennan (*ky* solo). 12/88, 4/90.

***   **Henceforward** Core COCD 900871 0 CD
Brennan; Christy Doran (*g*). 5/88.

**   **Entupadas** Creative Works CW 1013 MC
Brennan; Corina Curschellas (*v, dulcimer, kalimba, acc, f, police siren, perc*). 11/85.

(*)   **Mountain Hymn L + R 45002 CD/LP
Brennan; Urs Leimgruber (*ts, ss, bs s, bamboo f, etc.*). 9/85.

***   **An Chara** L + R 45007 CD/LP
As above. 1/86.

*(*)   **Polyphyllum** L+R 45013 CD
As above. 5/89.

(*)   **MAP (Music For Another Planet) L+R 45021 CD
As above, except add Norma Winstone (*v*). 8/88 & 5/89.

John Wolf Brennan was born and raised in Ireland, lives and works in Switzerland, and bears a startling resemblance from certain angles to Gene Pitney. This is, as they say, a complex fate.

His music combines the romanticism of the one place with the watchmaker exactness of the other. It is approachable but somehow also irreducible and manages to avoid a fatal descent into New Age blandness only by the thickness of Brennan's remarkable aptitude for the unexpected. The solo *Beauty Of Fractals*, which combines studio and live recordings, and the 'nonsolopiano' *Iritations* (which combines standard and prepared piano with Martin Spuhler's environmental sound objects), are perhaps the best introduction to his style, but the duos with Leimgruber and with Doran particularly are powerful and affecting; Leimgruber's extreme tonal range fits in perfectly both with the folkish material of the earlier sets and with the increasing abstraction of *Polyphyllum* and *MAP*. The addition of Norma Winstone's remarkable voice adds a dimension to a handful of cuts on *MAP*; by contrast, Corina Curschallas tends to overpower. (Brennan has also recently composed a cycle of art songs called *Bestiarium* – Swiss Pan 510 046 CD – to be performed by other players. These are certainly neither jazz nor improvised pieces but they merit a listen.)

Brennan is a thoughtful composer, not merely a slick executor. Where some of the solo pieces are over-intellectualized, his collaborations tend to steer him in the welcome direction of a simpler lyricism, which is convincing, entire and very beautiful . . . but is it jazz? Pass.

WILLEM BREUKER
SAXOPHONES, CLARINETS, RECORDER

****   **De Onderste Steen** Entr'acte CD 2 CD
Breuker; Andy Altenfelder, Kees Klaver, Boy Raaymakers (*t*); Iman Soetemann, Jan Wolff (*frhn*); Bernard Hunekink (*tb, tba*); Gregg Moore (*tb*); Willem Van Manen (*tb, v*); Dil Engelhardt (*f*); André Goodbeek (*as*); Peter Barkema (*ts, bs*); Emil Keijzer, Reinbert de Leeuw, Bert van Dijk (*p*); Leo Cuypers (*p, mca*); Henk De Jonge (*p, acc, ky*); Louis Andriessen (*p, org, hpd*); Johnny Meyer (*acc*); Michael Waisvisz (*syn*); Sytze Smit (*vn*); Maarten van Regteren Altena, Arjen Gorter (*b*); Han Bennink, Martin van Duynhoven, Rob Verdurmen (*perc*); Frits Lambrechts, Olga Zuiderhoek (*gamelan*); Mondriaan Strings; Ernö Ola String Quartet; Daniël Otten String Group. 74–91.

****   **Live In Berlin** FMP SAJ 06/BVHAAST 008 LP
Breuker; Boy Raaymakers (*t*); Bernhard Hunnekink, Willem Van Manen (*tb*); Jan Wolff (*frhn*); Leo Cuypers (*p*); Arjen Gorter (*b*); Rob Verdurmen (*d*). 11/75.

***(*)   **. . . Superstars** FMP SAJ 017 LP
Breuker; Leo Cuypers (*p*). 3/78.

***(*)   **In Holland** BVHAAST 041/042 2LP
Breuker; Andreas Altenfelder, Boy Raaymakers (*t*); Bernard Hunnekink, Willem Van Maanen (*tb*); Bob Driessen (*as, bs*); Maarten Van Norden (*as, ts*); Henk De Jonge (*p, acc*); Arjen Gorter (*b*); Rob Verdurmen (*d*). 4 & 5/81.

***   **Driesbergen-Zeist** BVHAAST 050 LP
Breuker; Andreas Altenfelder, Boy Raaymakers (*t*); Bernard Hunnekink, Garrett List (*tb*); Michiel De Ruyter (*cl*); Andre Goudbeek (*as, cl*); Maarten Van Norden (*ts, cl*); Henk De Jonge (*p, ky, Hawaiian g*); Arjen Gorter (*b*); Rob Verdurmen (*d*); Dick Swidde (*v*). 9 & 11/83.

***(*)   **To Remain** BVHAAST CD 8904 CD
Breuker; Andreas Altenfleder, Boy Raaymakers (*t*); Chris Abelen, Bernard
Hunnekink, Garrett List, Gregg Moore (*tb*); Andre Goudbeek (*as*); Peter Barkema,
Maarten Van Norden (*ts*); Henk De Jonge (*p, ky*); Arjen Gorter (*b*); Rob Verdurmen
(*d, perc*). 9/83, 12/84, 1–4/89.

****   **De Klap** BVHAAST 068 LP
Breuker; Andreas Altenfelder, Boy Raaymakers (*t*); Chris Abelen, Bernard
Hunnekink (*tb*); Andre Goudbeek (*as*); Peter Barkema (*ts*); Henk De Jonge (*p, ky*);
Arjen Gorter (*b*); Rob Verdurmen (*d*). 12/85.

Joachim Berendt likens Breuker's use of Dutch and Low German folk music to Roland Kirk's
unironic and loving use of the less elevated music of the black tradition. Eclecticism of this sort
has been a feature of post-war Dutch music; composers like Louis Andriessen (who appears on
De Onderste Steen) and Misha Mengelberg have made extensive use of jazz and rock forms as a
way of breaking down the tyranny of serialism and of rigid formal structures.

Breuker has also frequently been likened to Kurt Weill (he includes 'Pirate Jenny's Song'
from *Die Dreigroschenoper* on *Driesburgen-Zeist*) and is as likely to use harmonic devices,
structural principles, and occasionally straight quotes, from concert music ('Prokof' on *In
Holland* is a good example) as from popular sources; he is also a fundamentally theatrical
composer, whose Kollektief is a performance band in the fullest sense.

Superstars is useful in allowing a glimpse of Breuker in an challenging, intimate context. He
begins in free mode, blaring forcefully and then interrupting himself with a brief tag from
'Come To The Big Top'; Cuypers then joins him in a cheesy little tune which they play virtually
unembellished. Very much in the Brötzmann mode as a saxophonist, Breuker plays the clarinets
with surprising delicacy; his bass clarinet work is reminiscent of John Surman's, essentially
melodic despite the gruffness of tone.

Of the Kollektief albums, by far the best known (and probably the best initial bet) is the
FMP/BVHAAST co-release *Live In Berlin*. The obvious model is Ellington; Breuker uses his
soloists in the same individualistic but still disciplined way (one wonders how 'anarchic' these
bands *really* are) and this early set is only bettered by *De Klap*, which includes a first version of
'Duke Edwards-Misere' and the wonderful 'Casablanca Suite'. 'Creole Love Call', like the
Gershwin arrangements on a currently unavailable 1987–8 tribute, is played remarkably
straight, though such is the imaginative tension that the Kollektief generates that one finds
onesself listening more intently than usual in constant expectation of a sudden chorus of
raspberries or dramatic swerve of tone. It's possible that critics and even Breuker have
overplayed the comic hand; *To Remain*'s 11 movements suggest that his reputation as a *farceur*
is (like Roland Kirk's) emphasized at the expense of understanding his remarkable technical
and structural abilities.

To Remain, which also takes in 'Driesbergen-Zeist', is a welcome CD in a not entirely
modernized catalogue, but *De Onderste Steen* is a truly indispensable sampling of Breuker's
improvised and compositional work over a decade and a half. The opening piece is a traditional
Indian melody; the next is the magnificent threnody for Duke Ellington, marked by an
emotional growl solo by Raaymakers (who hâs obviously absorbed Rex Stewart and Cootie
Williams) over a throbbing, dead-march ostinato. There are two tangos, a gamelan, some cod
Vivaldi, and a bizarre swing blues called 'My Baby Has Gone To The Schouwburg', which
eventually collapses in harmonic(a) chaos, a Satie-influenced composition for Reinbert de
Leeuw (a distinguished interpreter of Satie piano pieces), and two theatre pieces. Musically, it's
the best available profile of Breuker's work over nearly twenty years, but availability may very
well be a moot point. Ask around.

NICK BRIGNOLA (born 1936)
BARITONE, SOPRANO AND ALTO SAXOPHONES, CLARINET

***   **L.A. Bound** Night Life SB 2003/CDNLR 3007 CD/LP
Brignola; Bill Watrous (*tb*); Dwight Dickerson (*p*); John Heard (*b*); Dick Berk (*d*).
10/79.

Opening on Horace Silver's 'Quicksilver', delivered at a hurricane tempo, this is a good way to get to know the playing of a journeyman who's never had a clear shot at the major league, recording almost exclusively for small labels. Though he doubles on all the reeds – and plays some soprano here – Brignola's key horn is the baritone, and he gets an unusually lambent tone from it which allows him to create fast-moving solos with no loss of coherence. The programme here could be straight off a Blue Note session and it's played with admirable panache by the quintet, Watrous as agile as Brignola is.

***   **Raincheck** Reservoir RSR CD 108 CD
       Brignola; Kenny Barron (*p*); George Mraz (*b*); Billy Hart (*d*). 9/88.

****   **On A Different Level** Reservoir RSR CD 112 CD
       Brignola; Kenny Barron (*p*); Dave Holland (*b*); Jack DeJohnette (*d*). 9/89.

***   **What It Takes** Reservoir RSR CD 117 CD
       Brignola; Randy Brecker (*t*); Kenny Barron (*p*); Rufus Reid (*b*); Dick Berk (*d*).
       10/90.

Three good records. Brignola's facility goes hand in hand with a consistently imposing sound – as fluently as he plays, he always makes the baritone sound like the big horn that it is – and the flat-out burners are as tonally effective as the big-bodied ballads which are dotted through these sessions. *Raincheck* is a trifle diffuse, since Brignola turns to clarinet and soprano every so often, and *What It Takes* brings on Randy Brecker for a little variation in the front line, which is bought at the expense of the music's more personal feel (and the leader again doubles on the other reeds). *On A Different Level*, though, is suitably head-and-shoulders above the others. Brignola sticks to baritone as his sole horn here, and the solos on 'Tears Inside', 'Hot House' and 'Duke Ellington's Sound Of Love' are sustained with fantastic strength, mirrored in the playing of the rhythm section, which is the kind of team that makes any horn player sound good. Brignola's shrewd choice of tunes here encapsulates a pocket history of jazz baritone – from Carney on 'Sophisticated Lady' to Adams on the Mingus tune – but he puts it all under his own flag, with DeJohnette and Holland marking superb time behind him. A great modern baritone set.

GORDON BRISKER
TENOR SAX, FLUTE

(*)   **About Charlie Discovery DSCD-923 CD
       Brisker; Tom Harrell (*t, flhn*); Cedar Walton (*p*); Eddie Gomez (*b*); Victor Lewis (*d*);
       Monique & Louis Aldebert (*v*). 2/85.

***   **New Beginning** Discovery DSCD-938 CD
       Brisker; Bob Summers, Steve Huffsteter, Carl Saunders (*t, flhn*); Eric Culver, Randall
       Aldcroft (*tb*); Bob Sheppard (*ss, as, f*); Kim Richmond (*as, cl*); Doug Webb (*ts, f*);
       James Germann (*bs, bcl*); John Beasley (*p*); Robert Bowman (*b*); Victor Lewis (*d*);
       Dave Black (*perc*). 4/87.

Although the small-group album is well enough done, one can tell from the meticulous way he harmonizes the horns on 'Maui', the outstanding track, that Brisker is really a big-band man. In the 1960s and '70s he went the familiar Californian route of section work (in Woody Herman's band), teaching, studio chores and odd-job arranging. These two discs are an attractive portfolio of some satisfying if not especially distinctive music. *About Charlie* features a credential-laden quintet of which Brisker, as a player, is the least impressive member. Aside from the charmless title-track, a moribund sung tribute to the record's dedicatee, *About Charlie* is light but engaging post-bop. The big-band record is more lively: Brisker tries too hard to cram incident into some of the scores, including the messily elaborate 'In The Land Of The Snake People' and a rather too bumptious 'Just One Of Those Things', but the hard-bitten handling of Wayne Shorter's 'Prince Of Darkness' is impressive and Kim Richmond's tart alto improvisation on a very bright 'Be My Love' is just right. Crystal-clear recording for this session, too.

ALAN BROADBENT (born 1947)
PIANO

***   **Another Time** Trend TRCD-546 CD
Broadbent; Putter Smith (*b*); Frank Gibson Jr (*d*).

***   **Everything I Love** Discovery DSCD-929 CD
As above.

****   **Live At Maybeck Recital Hall Vol. 14** Concord CCD
Broadbent (*p* solo). 5/91.

There's a great clarity of thought about Alan Broadbent's playing: his interpretations of jazz and show standards seem thought-through and entire; while that may suggest a lack of spontaneity, he also manages to make the music sound fresh. These are all very satisfying records. Broadbent, who is a native of New Zealand, studied at Berkeley in the 1960s and then joined Woody Herman's band, before leading groups of his own; he hasn't recorded much, and the two trio albums have nothing routine on them: each mixes standards and a very few originals, and there is enough in each treatment to vary it slightly from the norm. Broadbent takes his first cues from Parker and Powell, yet one seldom thinks of bop while listening to him: there is much interplay between the hands, a sly but considerate cunning and a striking concern to develop melodies which are entirely faithful to the material. Good as the trio albums are, though, it's the Maybeck Hall setting which brings out the best in the pianist: Broadbent's internal rhythms are springy enough to keep even his ballads on a simmering heat, and the neatly tucked readings of such as 'Oleo' (most of the pieces run out to only three or four minutes each) or the cleverly shaded 'Sweet And Lovely' are genuinely fascinating. The sound is as fine as is customary for this series.

BOB BROOKMEYER (born 1929)
VALVE TROMBONE, PIANO

***(*)   **The Dual Role Of Bob Brookmeyer** Original Jazz Classics OJC 1729 CD/LP
Brookmeyer; Jimmy Raney (*g*); Teddy Charles (*vib*); Teddy Kotick (*b*); Mel Lewis, Ed Shaughnessy (*d*); Nancy Overton (*v*). 1/54, 6/55.

****   **Back Again** Sonet SNTCD 778 CD/LP
Brookmeyer; Thad Jones (*t*); Jimmy Rowles (*p*); George Mraz (*b*); Mel Lewis (*d*).

***   **Oslo** Concord CCD 4312 CD/LP/MC
Brookmeyer; Alan Broadbent (*p, ky*); Eric Von Essen (*b*); Michael Stephans (*d*).

(*)   **Dreams Dragon DRCD 169 CD
Brookmeyer; Gustavo Bargalli, Jan Kohlin, Lars Lindgren, Fredrik Norén, Stig Persson (*t, flh*); Mats Hermansson, Mikael Raberg, Bertil Strandberg (*tb*); Sven Larsson (*btb*); Dave Castle (*as, ss, cl*); Hakan Broström (*as, ss, f*); Johan Alenius, Ulf Andersson (*ts, ss, cl*); Hans Arktoft (*bs, bcl*); Anders Widmark (*p, ky*); Jan Adefeldt (*b*); Johan Diedelmans (*d*). 8/88.

Almost the first sounds to be heard on the classic *Jazz On A Summer's Day* soundtrack are the mellow tones of Bob Brookmeyer's valve trombone interweaving with Jimmy Giuffre's clarinet on 'The Train And The River'. It's a curiously formal sound, almost academic, and initially difficult to place. Valve trombone has a more clipped, drier sound than the slide variety and Brookmeyer is probably its leading exponent, though Maynard Ferguson, Stu Williamson and Bob Enevoldsen have all made effective use of it.

Late '50s recordings, like his own *Traditionalism Revisited*, saw Brookmeyer exploring classic material with an augmented version of Giuffre's Newport trio and in an idiom the clarinetist was to christen 'folk jazz'. On 'Honeysuckle Rose' there are some choruses where he accompanies himself on piano without double tracking, a rather extreme example of the 'dual role' he has adopted throughout his performing career. Brookmeyer was a founding member and arranger for the influential Thad Jones–Mel Lewis band (the Sonet reunion is the most upbeat and dynamic of the available records), and played with both Clark Terry and Gerry Mulligan. He shared piano duties with the latter and is a very considerable keyboard player, as he proves on the OJC. 'Rocky Scotch' and 'Under The Lilacs' are both readily categorized as 'cool' jazz, but there is a surprising degree of variation in Brookmeyer's tone. In legato passages (inevitably harder to execute on a valve instrument) he can sound almost like an alto saxophonist, Lee Konitz say, at the lower end of his range, but he mingles this with sly growls and purrs (as on 'With The Wind And The Rain In Your Hair' on *Oslo*) and austere, almost toneless equations that sound more like a formula for music than a realized performance. He is also capable of quite broad humour, and isn't above adding the odd Dicky Wells effect to an otherwise straightforward solo. Perhaps the biggest criticism and irony of Brookmeyer's *later* work, is that it has become humourless as his tone has relaxed and broadened. *Dreams* is best seen as an example, and not a particularly inspiring one, of his work as an arranger. It's a dull piece, lifted by one or two passages on 'Cats' and 'Missing Monk'. By far the best available is the charging, wry interplay of *Back Again*, made after a longish stint as a session player and writer.

CECIL BROOKS III
DRUMS

***   **The Collective** Muse MCD 5377 CD/MC
Brooks; Greg Osby (*as*); Gary Thomas (*ts*); Geri Allen (*p*); Lonnie Plaxico (*b*). 3/89.

It's interesting to conjecture how sessions like this will be evaluated by future jazz followers: if they sound to be balanced on a cutting edge of today's modern jazz, they may come to seem as everyday as, say, a Prestige blowing session of 30 years earlier. Brooks has certainly assembled a roster of the most highly reputed young talent on the New York scene of the day, with Osby and Thomas running their complex and acerbic lines against the sharply defined harmonic fills of Allen. The tunes, aside from a couple of standards, are also in the contemporary manner: jolting melodic parts, abstruse counterpart, polyrhythmic aggression from Brooks underneath. As such, it's a fine effort, with the saxophonists and Allen all adding to their standing.

PETER BRÖTZMANN (born 1941)
ALL SAXOPHONES AND CLARINETS, TAROGATO

***   **For Adolphe Sax** FMP 0080 LP
Brötzmann; Peter Kowald (*b*); Sven Ake Johansson (*d*). 6/67.

*****   **Machine Gun** FMP 0090/CD 24 CD/LP
Brötzmann; Willem Breuker, Evan Parker (*ts*); Fred Van Hove (*p*); Buschi Niebergall, Peter Kowald (*b*); Han Bennink, Sven Ake Johansson (*d*). 5/68.

Brötzmann's influence over the European free music scene is enormous, and many of his pioneering achievements have only recently been acknowledged in the wider domain. He was playing free jazz in the early 1960s and by the time of these first two LPs – originally pressed and distributed by the saxophonist himself – was a stylist whose intensity and sureness of focus was already established. The huge, screaming sound he makes is among the most exhilarating things in the music, and while he has often been typecast as a kind of sonic terrorist, that does insufficient justice to his mastery of the entire reed family. The only precedents for his early work are to be found in the contemporary records of Albert Ayler, but Brötzmann arrived at his methods independently of the American. The trio record is of a similar cast to, say, Ayler's *Spiritual Unity*, a raw, ferocious three-way assault, yet it is surpassed by the astounding *Machine Gun*, one of the most significant documents of the European free-jazz underground. The three saxophonists fire off a ceaseless round of blasting, overblown noise, built on the continuous crescendo managed by Bennink and Johansson, and as chaotic as it sounds, the music is informed by an iron purpose and control. Although the recording of both discs is crude, the grainy timbre is a fitting medium for the music. In 1990, *Machine Gun* was reissued on CD with two alternative takes which match the original versions in their fearsome power.

***   **Balls** FMP 0020 LP
Brötzmann; Fred Van Hove (*p*); Han Bennink (*cl, d, perc*). 8/70.

***   **Brötzmann, Van Hove, Bennink** FMP 0130 LP
        As above. 2/73.

The trio with Van Hove and Bennink became a staple group of its time. Although these were recorded under superior studio conditions, the sound is still less than exemplary. 0020 has longer, more discursive pieces with a variety of moods within each one, while the briefer episodes of 0130 tend to explore singular ideas. Humorous touches ('Wir Haben Uns Folgendes Uberlegt' opens with Van Hove playing boogie piano) are folded in with dark cacophony, such as the whining 'Konzert Fur 2 Clarinettes').

***   **Elements** FMP 0030 LP

***   **Couscouss De La Mauresque** FMP 0040 LP

***(*) **The End** FMP 0050 LP
        Brötzmann; Albert Mangelsdorff (*tb*); Fred van Hove (*p*); Han Bennink (*cl, d, perc*).
        8/71.

***   **Outspan No. 1** FMP 0180 LP
        As above. 4/74.

The three 1971 albums were culled from two days of performance at the Berlin Free Music Market, where the trio was augmented by trombonist Albert Mangelsdorff, whose experience in many other areas of jazz left him unintimidated by the demands of this group. Sound is again only average, but the vigour and earthy bravado of the quartet sustains the listener through the unglamorous circumstances of the music-making. There's little to choose between the three records, but *The End* has a compelling feature for Mangelsdorff in 'Alberts' as well as the long, sprawling title-track. The title piece of *Couscouss De La Mauresque* includes some finely detailed playing by van Hove, even though his piano is often obscured. He is similarly distant on the 1974 disc, which has more exceptionally strong work from the trombonist. The first three albums above have now been reissued on *The Berlin Concert* (FMP 34/35 2CD).

(*)   **Outspan No. 2 FMP 0200 LP
        As above, without Mangelsdorff. 5/74.

(*)   **Tschüs FMP 0230 LP
        As above. 9/75.

The trio's final recordings offer, basically, more of the same. *Outspan No. 2* is another live set, offering a coda to the previous discs, while *Tschüs* collects a group of studio miniatures of sometimes desultory quality.

***   **Solo** FMP 0360 LP
        Brötzmann (solo). 5/76.

Such kindred spirits as Anthony Braxton and Evan Parker had already made solo records, so Brötzmann's session came as no surprise. The 12 pieces include an enjoyably galumphing bass sax outing in 'Humpty Dumpty' and shrill, hair-raising clarinet and alto scribbles. The improvisations range from a few seconds to nearly ten minutes in length, and the shrewd programming and raw sound ensure a consistent level of interest.

(*)   **Ein Halber Hund Kann Nicht FMP 0420 LP
        Brötzmann; Han Bennink (*bcl, p, vla, bj, d, perc*). 3–4/77.

**   **Schwarzwaldfahrt** FMP 0440 LP
        As above. 5/77.

Brötzmann's duo records with Bennink are a blend of madcap exuberance and a more pointed intensity. The music is cut up into staccato outbursts of frenzied expression or ominous rattlings; in small doses it's stimulating enough, but at LP length the sessions tend to pall, especially FMP 0440, which was recorded alfresco in the Black Forest and is as indulgent as Brötzmann ever gets.

(*)   **Three Points And A Mountain FMP 0670 LP
        Brötzmann; Misha Mengelberg (*p*); Han Bennink (*cl, ts, d, v*). 2/79.

***(*)   **The Nearer The Bone, The Sweeter The Meat** FMP 0690 LP
Brötzmann; Harry Miller (*b*); Louis Moholo (*d*). 8/79.

***(*)   **Opened, But Hardly Touched** FMP 0840/0850 2LP
As above. 11/80.

These contrasting trio situations bring out some of Brötzmann's best playing. the session with Mengelberg and Bennink is still subject to the Dutch pair's eccentricities of form, although there are two bristling longer pieces. The records with Miler and Moholo, however, are big and brawling encounters which realign the saxophonist's playing with a 'mainstream' free-jazz approach, and the recording's punchier sound does the music more justice.

(*)   **Maar Helaas! FMP 0800
Brötzmann; Willi Kellars (*vib, d*). 11/80.

***   **Andrew Cyrille Meets Peter Brötzmann In Berlin** FMP 1000 LP
Brötzmann; Andrew Cyrille (*d*). 3/82.

Brötzmann meets two percussionists. Kellars is sometimes pernickety, a mixture of Bennink and the polyrhythmic American free drummers, but he strikes some impassioned sparks with the saxophonist. The encounter with Cyrille, though not quite as cataclysmic as one might have expected, traces a long form of dialogue similar to the American's exchanges with Jimmy Lyons in the Cecil Taylor group, and is splendidly powerful.

***   **Alarm** FMP 1030 LP
Brötzmann; Toshinori Kondo (*t*); Johannes Bauer (*tb*); Willem Breuker, Frank Wright (*ts*); Alex Von Schlippenbach (*p*); Harry Miller (*b*); Louis Moholo (*d*). 11/81.

(*)   **Pica Pica FMP 1050 LP
Brötzmann; Albert Mangelsdorff (*tb*); Günter Sommer (*d*). 9/82.

Alarm is a 40-minute concert performance by a group of improvisers from several disciplines, but it's stamped by Brötzmann's outsize conception, a dynamic which deepens from loud to very loud. Kondo's cartoon of the trumpet adds an hysterical edge which is underscored by Wright's unrelieved shriek, a sonic brother to the leader's own playing. In the circumstances, the engineers secured a remarkably decent sound. *Pica Pica* is something of a letdown after the previous meetings with Mangelsdorff, a tolerable blow with the less than resourceful Sommer on hand.

***(*)   **14 Love Poems** FMP 1060 LP
Brötzmann (solo). 8/84.

***   **Go-No-Go** FMP 1150 LP
Brötzmann; Alfred Harth (*as, ts*). 1–2/87.

The streams of melody in his second solo album suggest not so much a mellowing of Brötzmann's muse as a reconciliation with the possibilities of song: he opens the recital with a snatch of Ornette Coleman's 'Lonely Woman', which threads a little more of free-jazz convention into an uncompromised vision. Recorded with good clarity, it's a fine introduction to the saxophonist's music. The meeting with Harth stops and starts just as its title suggests, with some of the pieces frustratingly short, but there is some crackling interplay among the 12 tracks.

***   **Berlin Djungle** FMP 1120 LP
Brötzmann; Toshinori Kondo (*t*); Johannes Bauer, Alan Tomlinson (*tb*); Tony Coe, J. D. Parran, Ernst-Ludwig Petrowsky, Louis Sclavis, John Zorn (*cl*); William Parker (*b*); Tony Oxley (*d*). 11/84.

Another two-sides-long concert set, by Brötzmann's 'Clarinet Project'. The piercing fusillade of clarinets is anchored by the superb rhythm work of Parker and Oxley and if it's all a bit of a scramble, it's a very enjoyable one.

***(*)   **Low Life** Celluloid CELL 5016 CD/LP
Brötzmann; Bill Laswell (*b*). 1/87.

An extraordinary session, even by Brötzmann's standards. He plays only bass saxophone (a 1923 Conn model) against the earthquake rumble of Laswell's electric basses. While some may find an entire disc of such music hard to take, the guttural intensity is almost as overwhelming as *Machine Gun* was in its day.

***   **Reserve** FMP CD 17 CD
Brötzmann; Barre Phillips (*b*); Gunter Sommer (*d*). 11/88.

Back on relatively conventional turf, with the more gently inclined Phillips at the bass, Brötzmann digs through three long improvisations. Even on CD, sound is still only reasonable in fidelity, but the music has some attractive empathy, particularly between the leader and Phillips.

***   **Last Home** Pathological CD/LP
Brötzmann; Caspar Brötzmann (*g*). 90.

This is a remorseless meeting between father and son, the younger Brötzmann emulating his elder's ferocity on a distortion-drenched electric guitar. There's no real 'interplay', more a collision between two elemental forces; even with amplification at his disposal, the younger man can't overpower his partner, though. Whether one hears it as energizing or tedious, it's quite devastating. There are several extra tracks on the CD.

***   **Wie Das Leben So Spielt** FMP CD 22 CD
Brötzmann; Werner Lüdi (*as*). 9/89.

Lüdi has drifted in and out of free playing for many years, but he sounds enthusiastic enough about being added to Brötzmann's pack of sparring partners on record. Playing only alto, while Brotz runs through his whole arsenal of reeds, Lüdi concocts a stuttery romanticism (of sorts) to set against his companion's fields of fire. Highly invigorating, as usual.

***(*)   **No Nothing** FMP CD 34
Brötzmann. 8/90.

The saxophonist still has plenty of new things to say on his third solo album, perhaps the most quiescent of the three yet often exploding into a logical catharsis. He changes between various saxes and clarinets during the 14-track programme and manages to sustain close to 75 minutes of music, all of it faithfully recorded by Jost Gebers.

***(*)   **Dare Devil** DIW 857 CD
Brötzmann; Haruhiko Gotsu (*g*); Tetsu Yahauchi (*b*); Shoji Hano (*d*). 10/91.

Yet another sensational – and sensationally effective – blow-out. Recorded live in Tokyo with what sounds like some kind of Japanese hardcore band, Brötzmann sounds completely at home and enjoying every second of the challenge. Hano, who produced the record, beats out minimal but brazenly effective tattoos and Gotsu is a modest master at making riffs into feasible compositions. Brötzmann just goes at it head first.

CLIFFORD BROWN (1930–56)
TRUMPET

***   **Clifford Brown Memorial** Original Jazz Classics OJC 017 CD/LP
Brown; Art Farmer, Idries Sulieman (*t*); Herb Mullins, Ake Persson (*tb*); Arne Domnérus, Gigi Gryce (*as*); Benny Golson (*ts*); Oscar Estell, Lars Gullin (*bs*); Tadd Dameron, Bengt Hallberg (*p*); Percy Heath, Gunnar Johnson (*b*); Philly Joe Jones, Jack Noren (*d*); collective personnel. 6 & 9/53.

***(*)   **Clifford Brown Memorial Album** Blue Note CDP 781526 2CD
Brown; Lou Donaldson (*as*); Gigi Gryce (*as, f*); Charlie Rouse (*ts*); Elmo Hope, John Lewis (*p*); Percy Heath (*b*); Art Blakey, Philly Joe Jones (*d*); collective personnel. 6 & 8/53.

***(*)   **Clifford Brown Quartet In Paris** Original Jazz Classics OJC 357 CD/LP/MC
Brown; Henri Renaud (*p*); Pierre Michelot (*b*); Benny Bennett (*d*). 10/53.

***(*)   **Clifford Brown Sextet In Paris** Original Jazz Classics OJC 358 CD/LP/MC
Brown; Gigi Gryce (*as*); Henri Renaud (*p*); Jimmy Gourley (*g*); Pierre Michelot (*b*);
Jean-Louis Viale (*d*). 10/53.

****   **Clifford Brown Big Band In Paris** Original Jazz Classics OJC 359 CD/LP/MC
Brown; Art Farmer, Fred Gerard, Quincy Jones, Fred Verstraete, Walter Williams (*t*);
Jimmy Cleveland, Alvin Hayes, Bill Tamper (*tb*); Anthony Ortega (*as*); Henri
Bernard, André Dabonneville, Clifford Solomon (*ts*); William Boucaya, Henri Jouot
(*bs*); Henri Renaud (*p*); Pierre Michelot (*b*); Alan Dawson, Jean-Louis Viale (*d*). 9 &
10/53.

***(*)   **Blue and Brown** Jazz Society (Vogue) 670505 CD
Brown; Gigi Gryce (*as, ld*); Art Farmer, Fred Gerard, Quincy Jones, Fernand
Verstraete, Walter Williams (*t*); Jimmy Cleveland, Alvin Hayes, Bill Tamper (*tb*);
Anthony Ortega (*as*); André Dabonneville, Teddy Edwards, Harold Land, Clifford
Solomon (*ts*); William Boucaya (*bs*); Carl Perkins, Richie Powell, Henri Renaud (*p*);
Jimmy Gourley (*g*); George Bledsoe, Pierre Michelot, George Morrow (*b*); Benny
Bennett, Alan Dawson, Max Roach, Jean-Louis Viale (*d*); collective personnel. 9 &
10/53, 4/54.

In the days after Clifford Brown died – Richie Powell with him – and as the news filtered
through to clubs and studios up and down the country, hardened jazz musicians put away their
horns and quietly went home to grieve. Only 26, Brown was almost universally liked and
admired. Free of the self-destructive 'personal problems' that haunted jazz at the time, he had
seemed destined for ever greater things when his car skidded off the turnpike.

To this day, his influence on trumpeters is immense, less audibly than Miles Davis's, perhaps,
because more pervasive. Though most of his technical devices – long burnished phrases,
enormous melodic and harmonic compression within a chorus, internal divisions of the metre –
were introduced by Dizzy Gillespie and Fats Navarro, his two most significant models, it was
Brownie who melded them into a distinctive and coherent personal style of great expressive
power. Almost every trumpeter who followed, including present-day figures like Wynton
Marsalis, has drawn heavily on his example; few though have managed to reproduce the
powerful singing grace he took from the ill-starred Navarro.

After a first, near-fatal car accident, Brown gigged in R&B bands and then worked briefly
with Tadd Dameron, before touring Europe with Lionel Hampton towards the end of 1953, on
which he enjoyed a good-natured and stage-managed rivalry with Art Farmer, and recorded the
excellent quartet, sextet and big band sides now reissued on OJC and sampled on *Blue And
Brown*. By this time, he had already recorded the session on the confusingly titled *Memorial*
(OJC) and *Memorial Album* (Blue Note). The former combined European and American
sessions and isn't the most compelling of his recordings, though Dameron's arrangements are as
challenging as always, and there are some fine moments from the Scandinavians on the
September date.

Blue and Brown is full of interesting material, but nowhere does the trumpeter really knock
sparks off any of the themes, and he seems hampered by busy or hesitant arrangements.
Perhaps the best of the tracks are the two sextet takes of *All The Things You Are* and the three
quartet versions, each subtly different, of 'I Can Dream, Can't I?'. *Blue And Brown* doesn't
offer either, but it might seem an attractive alternative, if only for the fact that its selection of
tracks from the 1953 Paris sessions is so determinedly perverse. There have to be some doubts
about the French rhythm section, experienced as it was, but it shapes up pretty well in
comparison to the Scandinavian players on *Memorial*.

The Blue Note is essential. Brown still sounds slightly blurred on 'Cherokee', but his solo on
Gryce's 'Hymn of the Orient' and his medium-paced delivery on 'Minor Mood' are
exceptional. The original second side featured a session with Lou Donaldson and then rising
star Elmo Hope. The opening 'Brownie Speaks' is (along with 'Hymn') perhaps the most
accessible introduction to the trumpeter's style and method. Quarter and eighth notes are
played square to the very vigorous rhythm without any loss of lyrical force and without any
hesitation. 'You Go to My Head' underlines his sensitivity as a ballad player. Much of this
material was supplemented by a valuable collection of *Alternate Takes* [Blue Note BST 84428
LP] which so far hasn't made the transition from vinyl. Good as most of these masters are (and
they also include a single track, 'Get Happy', from a J. J. Johnson date) they do also indicate

how inexperienced and occasionally callow 1954's *downbeat* 'New Star' could still be. Fortunately, Brown's best work was still to come.

****   Jazz Immortal Pacific Jazz CDP 7468502 CD

Brown; Stu Williamson (*vtb*); Zoot Sims (*ts*); Bob Gordon (*bs*); Russ Freeman (*p*); Joe Mondragon, Carson Smith (*b*); Shelly Manne (*d*). 7 & 8/54.

While playing with Max Roach on the West Coast, Brown was asked to record a session for Dick Bock's Pacific Jazz. The arrangements are all by Jack Montrose, and though they're slighter, less demanding harmonically, more 'West Coast' than what Brownie was used to with Roach, they brought out some of his most relaxed and mellow playing. His solo on Montrose's 'Finders Keepers' is a model of uncomplicated and mellifluous invention. Zoot Sims slides in next with some lovely choruses in a drier than usual tone. 'Joy Spring', like the opening 'Daahoud', underlines how resilient and adaptable Brown's themes could be; a third, 'Bones For Jones', is a rarity, perhaps a dedication to Quincy Jones, but not recorded elsewhere, and there are two takes of the ironically formal 'Tiny Capers', another little-known Brown composition. Perhaps his best solo is reserved for 'Blueberry Hill', from the August session.

****   Brownie EmArCy 838 306-16 10CD

Brown; Maynard Ferguson, Clark Terry (*t*); Herbie Mann (*f*); Danny Bank (*f, bs*); Herb Geller, Joe Maini (*as*); Walter Benton, Harold Land, Paul Quinichette, Sonny Rollins (*ts*); Kenny Drew, Jimmy Jones, Junior Mance, Richie Powell (*p*); Barry Galbraith (*g*); Joe Benjamin, Keter Betts, Curtis Counce, Milt Hinton, George Morrow (*b*); Oscar Pettiford (*b, clo*); Bobby Donaldson, Roy Haynes, Osie Johnson, Max Roach (*d*); Helen Merrill, Dinah Washington, Sarah Vaughan (*v*); strings arranged and conducted by Neal Hefti; collective personnels. 8/54, 12/54, 1/55, 2/55, 1/56, 2/56.

****   Compact Jazz: Clifford Brown EmArCy 842933 CD

Brown; as above. 2, 8 & 12/54, 1/55, 2/56.

***   Clifford Brown & The Neal Hefti Orchestra West Wind WW 0032 CD/LP

Brown; Richie Powell (*p*); Barry Galbraith (*g*); George Morrow (*b*); Max Roach (*d*); Neal Hefti Orchestra; strings. 1/55.

****   In Concert Vogue 655602 CD

Brown; Max Roach (*d*); Teddy Edwards, Harold Land (*ts*); Carl Perkins, Richie Powell (*p*); George Bledsoe, George Morrow (*b*). 4 & 8/54.

Brownie gathers together all the material Brown recorded for EmArCy between 2 August 1954 and 16 February 1956. It includes no fewer than nine previously unreleased takes, together with a number of alternative takes that have appeared in other contexts. The research was done by the indefatigable Kiyoshi Koyama and the recordings remastered digitally from the originals, held at the PolyGram Tape Facility at Edison, New Jersey. The liner notes are by Dan Morgenstern and are impeccably detailed.

Inevitably, the best of the music is in the Roach–Brown sessions. The drummer's generosity in making the younger man co-leader is instantly and awesomely repaid. On the earliest of the sessions (Discs 1 and 2, originally released as *Brown and Roach Incorporated* and elsewhere as EmArCy MG36036 and 36008), there is a brilliantly impressionistic arrangement of Bud Powell's 'Parisian Thoroughfare' (whose onomatopoeic effects are echoed on a 'Take the "A" Train' from February 1955, Disc 9), a superb 'Jordu', and an offcut of Brown soloing on 'Sweet Clifford', a reworking of the 'Sweet Georgia Brown' changes. Whether cup-muted or open, he sounds relaxed and completely confident. Land plays a more than supportive role and is generously featured on 'Darn That Dream'.

The next session (Discs 3 and 4) was a studio jam recorded a week or so later, with Herb Geller, the un-chancey Joe Maini and Walter Benton all on saxophones, and Kenny Drew, Curtis Counce and Roach filling out the band. There are three takes (the first incomplete) of a blues called 'Coronado' (Disc 3), then extended versions of 'You Go To My Head', 'Caravan' – and a fragmentary variant, 'Boss Man' – and 'Autumn In New York'. Posthumously released as *Best Coast Jazz* and *Clifford Brown All Stars*, they contain some of the trumpeter's weakest and most diffuse playing. Always eminently disciplined, his solos lost much of their shape in this context. However, it's worth it for Maini's contribution.

The 14 August jam with Dinah Washingon (Discs 5 and 6) includes over-long versions of 'What Is This Thing Called Love', 'Move' and 'I'll Remember April', but there are two fine medleys and Brown is superb on 'It Might As Well Be Spring', which extends his accompanist's role. He has less space round Sarah Vaughan (Disc 7, eponymously released as [EmArCy MG 36004]), but he compresses his responses to the vocal line into beautifully polished choruses and half-choruses; Paul Quinichette is magnificent. Brown also accompanies Helen Merrill (Disc 8) on her debut recording; this is slighter, even prettified, and Quincy Jones's arrangements are definitely overcooked, but the trumpeter's contributions are gently effective.

The *Clifford Brown With Strings* sessions (Disc 8, originally released as [EmArCy MG36005]) are very much in the Bird mould. Brown sounds almost philosophically calm on a range of ballads, tightened up by Hefti's firmly organized string backings and the Brown–Roach Quintet rhythm section, somewhat unnecessarily beefed up by guitarist Barry Galbraith. This session is also available as a West Wind CD, but the remastering doesn't sound as clean or true.

The first quintet sessions for six months (Disc 9) find the group in rattling form. *Study in Brown* [originally EmArCy MG36037, then on CD as 814646] marks the trumpeter's emergence as an individual star of formidable magnitude. He takes 'Cherokee' at a dangerous pace and doesn't fudge a single note (there are bootleg recordings of him doggedly alternating and inverting practice phrases). Throughout the album, his entries have real *presence* and his delivery floats over the rhythm section without ever losing contact with Roach's compelling metres. 'Jacqui' is relatively unusual fare, and it may be significant that Land, with his West Coast roots, handles it most comfortably. This was the saxophonist's last studio date with the band, though he appears again on the fine *In Concert*, alternated with Teddy Edwards. His replacement, Sonny Rollins, has at this point in his career a slightly crude approach. He is nevertheless bursting with ideas that push the group's capabilities to the utmost and his first statement on 'Gertrude's Bounce' may suggest recourse to the review button, so daring is it in conception and execution. Brown himself sounds as though he must be reading off prearranged sequences, firing out eight-, four- and two-bar statements that seem to contain more and more musical information the shorter they get. This is the material released as *At Basin Street* [EmArCy MG36070 and on CD as 814 648].

Koyama has dug out previously unsuspected masters of 'Love Is A Many Splendored Thing' (taken at a distinctly unslushy pace) and of 'Flossie Lou' (which re-works 'Jeepers Creepers'). A rehearsal fragment of the latter is included on a 3-inch bonus CD single, like the cherry on top of the cake. *Brownie* is a bulky, and inevitably expensive, work of documentation. The trumpeter has scarcely a bad moment, but there is a lot of material to digest, and newcomers might prefer to begin with the excellent *Compact Jazz* compilation, which draws from all but the unfeasibly long jam sessions and consists of 'The Blues Walk', 'I Get A Kick Out Of You', 'Jordu', 'Parisian Thoroughfare', 'Daahoud', 'It's Crazy', 'Stardust', 'I'll Remember April', 'I've Got You Under My Skin', 'Yesterdays' and the original release of 'Flossie Lou'. For accessibility and sheer value, it could hardly be bettered. At least some of those who invest will want to move on to the Complete Works. Brown's qualities ring out on every bar.

DONALD BROWN
PIANO

***   **Early Bird** Sunnyside SSC 1025D CD
      Brown; Bill Mobley (*t, flhn*); Donald Harrison (*f*); Steve Nelson (*vib*); Bob Hurst (*b*);
      Jeff Watts (*d*). 87.

***   **The Sweetest Sounds** Jazz City 660.53.008 CD
      Brown; Steve Nelson (*vib*); Charnett Moffett (*b*); Alan Dawson (*d*). 6/88.

(*)   **Sources Of Inspiration Muse MR/MCD 5385 CD/LP/MC
      Brown; Eddie Henderson (*t, flhn*); Gary Bartz (*as*); Buster Williams (*b*); Carl Allen
      (*d*). 89.

Donald Brown followed James Williams into the piano chair for the Jazz Messengers in 1981 but he has made comparatively few recordings since, owing to problems with arthritis. Each of these sessions, though, is rewarding, and they seldom get stuck in the sometimes over-zealous groove which many later Messengers graduates fall prey to. *Early Bird* is a little careful and civilized, but it's interesting to hear Harrison dealing primarily with the flute, and Brown reveals a very mature grasp of Tadd Dameron's 'If You Could See Me Now', which he takes as a piano solo. *Sources Of Inspiration* sounds more hastily prepared, and Henderson and Bartz are only intermittently persuasive as improvisers. But Brown's best to date is the excellent quartet date for Jazz City. The piano sound is very bright and clear, and Nelson's vibes are complementary rather than contradictory on the four tracks he appears on. Moffett curbs his occasional tendency to overplay – he hits a perfect groove on 'I Used To Think She Was Quiet' – and the rarely sighted Dawson makes a convincing return to the studios. But it's two solo ballads – 'Betcha By Golly Wow' and a dramatic reshaping of 'Killing Me Softly With His Song' – which prove Brown's personal evaluations of rhythm and harmony to best effect.

***   **People Music** Muse MCD 5406 CD/MC
Brown; Tom Harrell (*t, flhn*); Vincent Herring (*as, f*); Steve Nelson (*vib*); Bob Hurst (*b*); Samarai Celestial (*d, v*); Daniel Sadownick (*perc*); Lenora Helm (*v*). 3/90.

Brown's music continues to diversify: his intention here, according to the sleeve-notes, was to reflect the many rhythmic styles of black music, and the clipped, funky 'The Biscuit Man' and Latin-flavoured pop of 'I Love It When You Dance That Way' display range at least. Harrell and Herring are a cleverly chosen front line, the former coolly vigorous, the latter blues-drenched and irresistibly colourful. Nelson, too, adds some deft remarks. But the impression remains that Brown's own playing isn't well served by a group that features so many others who are eager to play: his one feature, 'Booker T', is a marvellous, sanctified piano solo that makes one ache to hear a Brown solo record. The recording quality is superb throughout.

MARION BROWN (born 1935)
ALTO SAXOPHONE

****   **Recollections – Ballads And Blues For Saxophone** Creative Works CW 1001 LP
Brown (*as* solo). 87.

(*)   **La Placita – Live In Willisau Timeless SJP 108 LP
Brown; Brandon Ross (*g*); Jack Gregg (*b*); Steve McCraven (*d*). 3/77.

(*)   **Afternoon Of A Georgia Faun ECM 1004 LP
Brown; Anthony Braxton (*as, ss, cl, cbcl, Chinese musette, f, perc*); Chick Corea (*p, bells, gong, perc*); Andrew Cyrille (*perc*); Larry Curtis (*p*); William Green (*Top O'Lin, perc*); Jack Gregg (*b, perc*); Jeanne Lee (*v, perc*); Billy Malone (*d*); Bennie Maupin (*ts, af, bcl, acorn, bells, wood f, perc*); Gayle Palmore (*v, p, perc*). 8/70.

**   **Gemini** Birth 0037 LP
Brown; Gunter Hampel (*vib, b cl*). 6/83.

Possessed of a sweet, slightly fragile tone and a seemingly limitless melodic resource, Brown is nevertheless one of the most undervalued of contemporary saxophonists. There is a certain poignant irony in the fact that his finest recorded work should be solo saxophone, for he is a dedicated educator with a long-standing commitment to collective – and often untrained or amateur – music-making. *Afternoon Of A Georgia Faun* comes out of that ethos, performed by six instrumentalists and three 'assistants' on 'little instruments' like Brown's invented Top O'Lin (pot lids affixed to a board and bowed like a fiddle). All the performers permutate their instruments at work-stations in fulfilment of Brown's ideal of 'interchangeable discourse'. The results, predictably, are uneven, but there is some very affecting music on the album. Chick Corea's solo on the long title-piece is near perfect, and both Braxton and Maupin produce passages of great beauty.

Working with a more conventional quartet, Brown emerges as an unassertive but calmly confident soloist, moving through ideas logically but unstuffily. The live recording is good and the band sounds well rehearsed on the originals. *Gemini*, on Gunther Hampel's Birth label, is slightly odd, but the contrasting timbre of vibes and bass clarinet produces a stimulating setting for some of Brown's most interesting playing. Easily overlooked, it's well worth a listen.

Recollections shouldn't be overlooked at any price. A near-perfect set of standards – ranging from 'Angel Eyes' and 'Black And Tan Fantasy' to 'Blue Monk' and 'After The Rain' – it poignantly exposes Brown in reverie. His blues are technically watertight and, though the tempo is varied only minimally, the whole set communicates a wide range of emotions. Very warmly recommended indeed.

***(*)   **Back To Paris** Freelance FRL CD 002 CD
Brown; Hilton Ruiz (*p*); Jack Gregg (*b*); Freddie Waits (*d, perc*). 2/80.

This Valentine's Day gig is an exact and loving re-creation of the material in Brown's fine (but rather thinly recorded) studio album, *November Cotton Flower* [Baystate RJL 2679 LP]. The performances are in practice no more extended on the live version, but they have an immediacy and presence (a little too uprfront so far as the drummer is concerned). One misses guitarist Karl Rausch's lovely introduction to 'Sweet Earth Flying', but Gregg is a firmer and more lyrical bassist than Earl May and Ruiz is almost as good as the 'Hilton Luiz' credited on the original Japanese issue; one wonders if they are by chance related. A long version of 'Body And Soul' features the pianist to good effect but is otherwise disappointing. Brown fans will continue to treasure *November Cotton Flower* (not least for a gorgeous sleeve), but the Freelance has very much to recommend it.

(*)   **Native Land ITM 1471 CD/LP
Brown; Udo Hagen Zempel (*as*); Michael Möhring (*g, perc*); Peter Krug (*b*); Mathias Reh (*d, perc*); Wolfgang Kropp (*perc*). 3/91.

An uneasily eclectic collaboration with the slightly Teutonic Latin sound of Jazz Cussion, an alto-and guitar-led group with whom Brown first-jammed in 1989. The problem with *Native Land* is that he doesn't sound any better integrated with the band's repertoire and approach than he must have done then. Though he lacks Brown's emotional urgency on pieces like 'I Can't Get Started' or Horace Silver's *Nica's Dream*, Zempel is a lighter and rhythmically more buoyant player. He may need some help in the ensembles but none as a soloist, and Brown's contributions, pushed very far forward in the mix, seem superadded rather than integral. The title-track, spun out over African drum, highlights the differences between them. The bonus tracks on CD are nothing much, though Michael Möhring's guitar solo on 'Bahamian Street Dance' is probably his most distinctive of the session.

RAY BROWN (born 1926)
DOUBLE BASS

(*)   **Brown's Bag Concord CCD 4019 CD
Brown; Blue Mitchell (*t*); Richie Kamuca (*ts*); Dave Grusin, Art Hillery (*p*); John Guerin, Jimmie Smith (*d*).

As with Paul Chambers and Ron Carter, the Brown discography is enormous; bassists seem to job quite promiscuously, and bassists of Brown's calibre are hard to find. Unlike the other two, however, Brown's output as a leader is proportionately and qualitatively substantial.

He is almost certainly best heard in any of the trios featuring pianist Gene Harris, his most sympathetic collaborator, but this relaxed session features some fine moments from the still-undervalued Kamuca and the lamented Blue Mitchell. The sound is a shade flat, but the music is well up to Brown's impressive standard.

**   **Live At The Concord Jazz Festival** Concord CCD 4102 CD
Brown; Monty Alexander (*p*); Jeff Hamilton (*d*); Ernestine Anderson (*v*). 79.

With his foot off the gas, Brown can be as ordinary as the next guy. Most of the running here seems to come from the interplay between Alexander and the impressive Hamilton, but that impression may be unfairly compounded by an uneasy sound mix. Ernestine Anderson is an acquired taste which not everyone may have the patience to acquire. She shares something of the great Al Hibbler's surrealist diction, but little of his latterly wacky charm. The stars are mostly for Hamilton.

(*)   **A Ray Brown 3 Concord CJ 213 MC
Brown; Sam Most (*f*); Monty Alexander (*p*). 2/82.

The indefinite article underlines the fact that this isn't the Ray Brown Trio, but a somewhat quirkier affair, drummerless and with the addition of Most's piquant flute. The whole is only slightly more than the sum of its parts, but it is an intriguing sidestep that opens up new areas of sound-colour for the bassist and confirms his adventurous responsiveness to new stimuli. Well worth a listen.

***   **Soular Energy** Concord CCD 4268 CD/MC
       Brown; Gene Harris (*p*); Gerryck King (*d*); Red Holloway (*ts*); Emily Remler (*g*).
       8/84.

A really fine album which only needs Jeff Hamilton in his usual slot behind the drums to lift it into minor classic status. King is a fine drummer but lacks sparkle and is inclined to hurry the pulse unnecessarily.

Perhaps in retaliation, Brown takes the '"A" Train' at a pace that suggests privatization may be around the corner. Slowed down to an almost terminal grind, it uncovers all manner of harmonic quirks which Brown and the attentive Harris exploit with great imagination. Red Holloway and – rather more anonymously – the late Emily Remler sign up for a shortish and slightly inconsequential 'Mistreated But Undefeated Blues'. Brown's counter-melody figures on 'Cry Me A River', and, especially, the closing 'Sweet Georgia Brown' could almost be taped as his calling card. Exemplary.

**   **Don't Forget The Blues** Concord CCD 4293 CD/MC
       Brown; Al Grey (*tb*); Ron Eschete (*g*); Gene Harris (*p*); Grady Tate (*d*). 5/85.

*   **Bye Bye Blackbird** Paddle Wheel K28P 6303 LP
       Brown; Ichiro Masuda (*vib*); Cedar Walton (*p*); Mickey Roker (*d*); Emi Nakajima
       (*v*). 4/85.

The first is a cheery 'all-star' – so why Eschete? – session that never really amounts to much. Tate is another in a line of first-class drummers to have recorded under Brown's leadership. In some regards he is the most conventional, though Tate is no revolutionary either, and there is a slightly stilted quality to some of the medium-tempo tracks.

Blackbird never gets off its stilts and totters badly as a result. This is probably Brown's least impressive work as leader.

***(*)   **Bam Bam Bam** Concord CCD 4375 CD/MC

***   **Summer Wind** Concord CCD 4426 CD/MC
       Brown; Gene Harris (*p*); Jeff Hamilton (*d*). 7/88, 12/88.

Two superb live sets from an excellent working trio who interweave seamlessly and earn their solo spaces many times over. Brown's writing and arranging have been much more confident of late. The version of 'A Night In Tunisia' on *Bam Bam Bam* is quite remarkable, featuring hand percussion from Hamilton, and the tributes on both albums to Sonny Rollins ('T. S. R.'), Victor Feldman ('Rio'), and Art Blakey ('Buhaina Buhaina') are intelligent reinventions of some unexpected stylistic associations. Brown's blues stylings get more assured with each passing year. Originals like 'The Real Blues', the eponymous 'Bam Bam Bam' and Milt Jackson's oblique, bebop-flavoured 'Bluesology' all repay careful attention. 'If I Loved You', 'Summertime' and 'Days Of Wine And Roses' all comfortably fit the former Mr Ella Fitzgerald, while 'It Don't Mean A Thing', 'Mona Lisa' and 'Put Your Little Foot Right Out' uncover quite different aspects of Brown's increasingly complex musical persona.

***(*)   **Moore Makes 4** Concord CCD 4477 CD/MC
       Brown; Ralph Moore (*ts*); Gene Harris (*p*); Jeff Hamilton (*d*). 91.

But does Moore make more? On balance, yes. The cover depicts a saxophone standing in as fourth leg of a tea table. The Brown trio has stood up on its own for years now and scarcely needs the help. On the other hand, Moore's forceful tenor adds such an effective element to 'My Romance' and the superb 'Stars Fell On Alabama' that one wonders what filled those spaces before. Brown's bass lines are still among the best in the business, and the desk-slide was pushed well up to catch them. A return fixture seems inevitable.

ROB BROWN (born 1962)
ALTO SAXOPHONE

***   **Breath Rhyme** Silkheart SHCD-122 CD
       Brown (*as*); William Parker (*b*); Dennis Charles (*d*). 4/89.

Brown's allegiances are with the free jazz of the 1960s, of Ayler and Jimmy Lyons, although he demurs at the mention of both names as influences. This trio does, nevertheless, offer a powerful reminder of the kind of skirling declamations which those musicians would deploy against a rhythm section which works in rhythmic waves: Charles especially rolls out a beat that derives from Sunny Murray. Brown's own playing is a litany of overblown wails and long, anguished cries, although he is more temperate on the slower pieces. The sense of disorder is deceptive, for closer listening reveals subtle differentiations between pieces and a shrewd sense of detail – but that doesn't prevent some of the longer pieces from becoming monotonous. Slower, briefer episodes such as 'Stillness' may be more convincing for some. Parker is immensely interesting, but unfortunately the sound-balance does him few favours.

SANDY BROWN (1929–75)
CLARINET, VOCAL

***   **McJazz** Dormouse DM6 LP
       Brown; Al Fairweather (*t*); Jeremy French (*tb*): Ian Armit (*p*); Diz Disley (*g, bj*); Tim
       Mahn (*b*); Graham Burbidge (*d*). 3/57.

This fondly remembered Scotsman didn't make many records, and this is the only one of his studio sets currently available, but it reveals something of Brown's inquiring mind and fruitful embellishment of the trad ensemble. His partnership with Fairweather – both came to London from Edinburgh – created an unusually sympathetic frontline, and the ensemble playing here is lucid, colourful and swinging in a way that British trad seldom managed, partly through Brown's interest in high-life rhythms, which feature on a number of tracks. Disley, who takes a few Reinhardt-like solos, is the key member of the rhythm section, but Armit does well at the piano. The main interest, though, is in Fairweather's and Brown's solos: their blues improvisations strive to avoid cliché, and the clarinettist's pungent attack is close to inimitable. The remastering of the original LP is bright and clear.

(*)   **Splanky Spotlite SPJ 901 LP
       Brown; Ray Crane (*t*); Brian Lemon (*p*); Phil Bates (*b*); Mike Scott (*d*). 3/66.

A Nottingham club recording salvaged as a memorial to Sandy Brown. The material is a typically catholic programme; Neal Hefti's 'Splanky', Ellington's 'I Got It Bad', Pete Johnson's 'Roll 'Em Pete' and a brief sally through 'Royal Garden Blues'. On a purely musical level this is about as scrappy as might be expected, and the recording isn't outstandingly good, but Brown's clarinet keeps coming up with striking things, whether on a blues or out of the crevices of some other chord sequence: weird, whistling high notes mix with gurgling sounds in an unidentified register, yet the solo always seems to come out right. His singing is perhaps a bit more of an acquired taste.

TED BROWN (born 1927)
TENOR SAX

**   **In Good Company** Criss Cross Jazz Criss 1020 LP
       Brown; Hod O'Brien (*p*); Jimmy Raney (*g*); Buster Williams (*b*); Ben Riley (*d*).
       12/85.

**   **Free Spirit** Criss Cross Jazz Criss 1021 CD/LP
       Brown; Hod O'Brien (*p*); Jacques Schols (*b*). 10/87.

Criss Cross Jazz have made a speciality of rekindling the careers of some forgotten players, but in the case of Ted Brown the new records don't do much justice to a semi-legendary figure. He recorded with Warne Marsh and Art Pepper in the 1950s but has seldom been heard from since; these dates reveal a musician whose loyalty to Lester Young has been unswerving for an entire career. Some of his solos come together in just the way that Young's successful later ones do: rhythmically suspended on the brink of disaster, the melodic ideas sew the improvisation together. His tone is also much like Young's hesitant, half-formed timbre. But without Lester's tragic mystique, the music doesn't add up to very much. The other players on *In Good Company* lend strong support, but it tends to point up Brown's own comparative frailty, while his temperamental reserve means that the trio date of *Free Spirit* is sorely under-characterized.

DAVE BRUBECK (born 1920)
PIANO

***(*)   **The Dave Brubeck Octet** Original Jazz Classics OJC 101 CD/LP/MC
Brubeck; Dick Collins (*t*); Bob Collins (*tb*); Paul Desmond (*as*); Dave Van Kriedt (*ts*); Bill Smith (*cl, bs*); Ron Crotty (*b*); Cal Tjader (*d*). 48–49.

***   **The Dave Brubeck Trio** Fantasy F 24726 CD/2LP/2MC
Brubeck; Ron Crotty (*b*); Cal Tjader (*d, perc*).

***(*)   **Dave Brubeck – Paul Desmond** Fantasy F 24727 CD/MC
Brubeck; Paul Desmond (*as*); Ron Crotty, Wyatt Ruther (*b*); Herb Barman, Lloyd Davis, Joe Dodge (*d*). 52, 53, 54.

***   **Stardust** Fantasy F 24728 CD/LP/MC
As above; with Norman Bates, Fred Dutton (*b*).

****   **Jazz At Oberlin** Original Jazz Classics OJC 046 CD/LP/MC
Brubeck; Paul Desmond (*as*); Ron Crotty (*b*); Lloyd Davis (*d*). 3/53.

***   **Jazz At The College Of The Pacific** Original Jazz Classics OJC 047 CD/LP/MC
Brubeck; Paul Desmond (*as*); Ron Crotty (*b*); Joe Dodge (*d*).

***   **In Concert** Fantasy 60-013 CD
As above. 6/53.

Often derided as a white, middle-class formalist with a rather buttoned-down image and an unhealthy obsession with classical parallels and clever-clever time signatures, Brubeck is actually one of the most significant composer-leaders in modern jazz. Tunes like 'Blue Rondo A La Turk', 'Kathy's Waltz' and Paul Desmond's 'Take Five' (which Brubeck made an enormous hit) insinuated their way into the unconscious of a whole generation of American college students. Though he has contributed very little to the 'standards' gene-pool ('In Your Own Sweet Way' is probably the only Brubeck original that is regularly covered), he has created a remarkable body of jazz and formal music, including orchestral pieces, oratorios and ballet scores. The Brubecks constitute something of a musical dynasty. His elder brother Howard is a 'straight' composer in a rather old-fashioned Francophile vein, while his sons, bassist and trombonist Chris, drummer Danny, and keyboard player Darius, have all played with him.

It used to be conventional wisdom that the only Brubeck records that mattered were those that featured the liquid alto of Paul Desmond. Such was the closeness – and, one might say, jealousy – of the relationship that it was stated in Desmond's contract that his own recordings had to be pianoless. What no one seemed to notice was that Desmond's best playing was almost always with the Brubeck group. Brubeck himself was not a particularly accomplished soloist, with a rather heavy touch and an unfailing attachment to block chords, but his sense of what could be accomplished within the bounds of a conventional jazz quartet allowed him to create an impressive and often startling body of music that demands urgent reassessment.

The early Octet catches Brubeck at the height of his interest in an advanced harmonic language (which he would have learned from Darius Milhaud, his teacher at Mills College); there are also rhythmic transpositions of a sort that popped up in classic jazz and were subsequently taken as read by the 1960s avant-garde, but which in the '50s had been explored thoroughly only by Max Roach. Relative to Gerry Mulligan, Brubeck has been not been widely regarded as a writer-arranger for larger groups but the better material on this rather indifferently recorded set underline how confidently he approached the synthesis of jazz with other forms. Tracks like 'Serenades Suite' and 'Schizophrenic Scherzo' are a great deal more swinging than most products of the Third Stream, a movement one doesn't automatically associate with Brubeck's name.

The trios are bubbly and smoothly competent, but lack the luminous quality that Desmond brought. The saxophonist joined in 1951 and immediately transformed the group. His duos with Brubeck on the later Fantasy are a measure of their immediate mutual understanding; 'Over The Rainbow' is one of the loveliest improvisations of the period, caught in a whispery close-up. Tjader is still an interestingly varied player at this period, far from the bland stylist he was to become later.

The quartets with Crotty (he succeeded Norman Bates; no, not that one) and Davis aren't considered to be the classic Brubeck groups; that was the later line-up with Wright and Morello, but they were excellent on their own less ambitious terms. There's an intriguing rehearsal version of the 'Trolley Song' on Fantasy 24727 that suggests something of what went into this music. *Stardust* is more of a grab-bag and is perhaps the dullest compilation from this early period; there are, though, fine Desmond performances throughout, and Brubeck fans will want to have some less familiar material collected there.

Jazz At Oberlin was an enormous success on its first release and is still durable 40 years later, with some of Brubeck's and Desmond's finest interaction; one of the pianist's innovations was in getting two musicians to improvise at the same time, and there are good examples of that on the Oberlin College set. It's all standard material, and there are excellent performances of 'Perdido', 'Stardust' and 'How High The Moon' which adumbrate Brubeck's later interest in unconventional time signatures. The other 1953 set (and the location underlines what Brubeck's constituency was) and the CD-only *In Concert* are less compelling at first glance. Desmond is having a slightly quieter night on the first, but Brubeck is in exceptional form, playing well within himself but showing all his class and sophistication. Repeats of 'Stardust' and 'All The Things You Are' on *In Concert* confound the notion that this was a 'reading' band, too stiff to improvise. The sound on all three is a bit remote and Crotty isn't always clearly audible.

***   **Reunion** Original Jazz Classics OJC 150 CD/LP/MC
Brubeck; Paul Desmond (*as*); Dave Van Kriedt (*ts*); Norman Bates (*b*); Joe Morello (*d*). 2/57.

***   **Brubeck A La Mode** Original Jazz Classics OJC 200 CD/LP
Brubeck; Bill Smith (*cl*); Eugene Wright (*b*); Joe Morello (*d*). 5 & 6/60.

(*)   **Near-Myth Original Jazz Classics OJC 236 LP/MC
As above. 3/61.

From the end of his association with Fantasy (he'd signed for Columbia in 1954) *Reunion* brings back the full-voiced Van Kriedt and Bates from the early bands. There's a greater preponderance of 'classical' tags – 'Pieta', 'Prelude', 'Divertimento', 'Chorale' – most of them interpreted rather loosely. *A La Mode* introduced another regular associate, fellow-Californian Smith, who has a lumpier touch than Desmond and a far less sophisticated improvisational sense. Interesting writing on the vinyl-only *Near-Myth*, but both the playing and the reproduction are a shade muted. None of these should be considered essential, though Van Kriedt is worth checking out.

***   **Newport '58: Brubeck Plays Ellington** CBS 450317 LP
Brubeck; Paul Desmond (*as*); Joe Benjamin (*b*); Joe Morello (*d*). 7/58.

From the same year as the classic movie *Jazz On A Summer's Day*, Brubeck confronts the giant form that still lies athwart the jazz composer's path, shows he understood what Ellington was all about, and chips in with a couple of tribute compositions of his own, notably 'The Duke'. Desmond's playing on 'Perdido' (which is actually a Juan Tizol tune, but Ellington-associated) is flawless, and Brubeck himself pounds out a cheerful counter-statement on 'Things Ain't What They Used To Be'.

Like Duke, Brubeck plays more than merely 'composer's piano', but this set exposes some of his technical shortcomings as a concert performer, not least a tendency to telegraph changes of key and time-signature by at least a couple of bars. Because of that, it is rarely dramatic music and seldom betrays much tension, but it's entertaining none the less.

****   **Time Out** CBS 62068 CD
Brubeck; Paul Desmond (*as*); Eugene Wright (*b*); Joe Morello (*d*). 6, 7 & 8/59.

Catalogued as a 'Historic Reissue' (industry-speak for a golden egg), this is the music everyone associates with Brubeck. So familiar is it that no one actually hears what's going on any more. As the title suggests, Brubeck wanted to explore ways of playing jazz that went a step beyond the basic 4/4 that had remained the norm long after jazz threw off the relentless predictability of B flat. The opening 'Blue Rondo A La Turk' (with its Mozart echoes) opens in an oddly distributed 9/8, with the count rearranged as 2-2-2-3. It's a relatively conventional classical *rondo* but with an almost racuous blues interior. 'Take Five' is in the most awkward of all key signatures, but what is remarkable about this almost iconic slice of modern jazz is the extent to which it constantly escapes the 5/4 count and swings. Morello's drum solo is perhaps his best work on record (though his brief 'Everybody's Jumpin'' solo is also excellent) and Brubeck's heavy vamp has tremendous force. Though it's almost always identified as a Brubeck tune, 'Take Five' was actually written by Desmond.

Most of the other material is in waltz and double-waltz time. Max Roach had explored the idea thoroughly on *Jazz In 3/4 Time*, but not even Roach had attempted anything as daring and sophisticated as the alternations of beat on 'Three To Get Ready' and 'Kathy's Waltz', which is perhaps the finest single thing on the album. Desmond tends to normalize the count in his solo line and it's easy to miss what is going on in the rhythm section if one concentrates too exclusively on the saxophone. The Desmond cult may be fading slightly and as it does it may be possible to re-establish the Brubeck Quartet's claim *as a unit* to be considered among the most innovative and adventurous of modern jazz groups.

***   **St Louis Blues** Moon M 028 CD/LP
       Brubeck; Paul Desmond (*as*); Eugene Wright (*b*); Joe Morello (*d*). 7/59, 1/62.

Good live material from the same period as *Time Out* and a little later. The recording is a little remote and there's an unaccustomed brusqueness to some of Desmond's work. Otherwise unexceptional, and the title piece alone will be meat and drink to Brubeck connoisseurs.

***(*)   **At Carnegie Hall** CBS 66234 2LP
       Brubeck; Paul Desmond (*as*); Eugene Wright (*b*); Joe Morello (*d*). 2/63.

***   **25th Anniversary Reunion** A & M 396998 CD
       As above. 3/76.

Brubeck and Desmond teamed up again for one-shot tours all through the early 1970s and played to huge crowds. Something of the magic had gone out, though, and despite some masterful high-harmonic runs and beautifully crafted solos from Desmond (who only had another year before his death from cancer) this reunion set sounds a bit contrived and stilted. Much of the space is taken up with the long 'African Times Suite', a loose configuration of themes that tend to cut Desmond adrift from the trio. The sound is good, however, and there's a bright, crowd-pleasing 'St Louis Blues'.

***   **The Quartet** LRC CDC 7681 CD
       Brubeck; Paul Desmond (*as*); Darius Brubeck (*ky*); Eugene Wright (*b*); Joe Morello
       (*d*).

Very routine material – 'Three To Get Ready', 'St Louis Blues', 'Someday My Prince Will Come' – but above average recording. The two tracks with the younger Brubeck are attractive enough without adding anything of any real substance. 'In Your Own Sweet Way' coaxes some mellifluous choruses out of Desmond. Second-order stuff for real collectors only.

(*)   **Greatest Hits CBS 32046 CD/MC
       Brubeck; Paul Desmond (*as*); Eugene Wright (*b*); Joe Morello (*d*).

***   **All Time Greatest Hits** CBS 68288 2LP
       As above, except add Norman Bates, Joe Benjamin (*b*); Joe Dodge (*d*).

Fairly predictable packaging of standard fare. For the record: the single album set includes 'Take Five', 'It's A Raggy Waltz', 'Camptown Races', 'Unsquare Dance', 'Mister Broadway', 'I'm In A Dancing Mood', 'The Trolley Song', 'In Your Own Sweet Way' and 'Blue Rondo A La Turk'. The final apotheosis omits 'Mister Broadway' but throws in 'Two Part Contention' from 1956 with Bates and Dodge, 'The Duke' from '58 with Joe Benjamin, and throws in eight other tracks (most of them well-worn standards). The first is probably more representative of

Brubeck the composer, but *All Time Greatest Hits* is certainly rather better value for money and offers a tantalizing sample of the earlier material.

**   **Back Home** Concord CJ 103 LP
Brubeck; Jerry Bergonzi (*ts, b*); Chris Brubeck (*b, tb*); Butch Miles (*d*). 8/79.

(*)   **Concord On A Summer Night Concord CCD 4198 CD/MC
Brubeck; Bill Smith (*cl*); Chris Brubeck (*b, tb*); Randy Jones (*d*). 8/82.

(*)   **For Iola Concord CCD 4259 CD/MC
As above. 8/84.

***   **Reflections** Concord CCD 4299 CD/MC
As above. 12/85.

(*)   **Blue Rondo Concord CCD 4317 CD/MC
As above. 11/86.

***   **Moscow Night** Concord CCD 4353 CD/MC
As above. 3/87.

The Concord years suggest that whatever Brubeck once had has now been thoroughly run to ground. Only the most dedicated fans will find much to get excited about on these albums. 'We Will All Remember Paul' on *Reflections* is a heartfelt tribute to Desmond (who died in 1977) and the surrounding material seems to be lifted by it. *Moscow Night* also seems to be up a gear and the versions there of 'Three To Get Ready', 'Unsquare Dance' and 'St Louis Blues' are the best for years. Otherwise non-essential. Brubeck *fils* and Jones are curiously stiff and unswinging and Smith's initial promise seems to have evaporated; he is probably a less sophisticated player now than he was in 1960.

ALAIN BRUNET
TRUMPET

(*)   **Rominus Label Bleu LBLC 6541 CD
Brunet; Denis Badault (*p*); Didier Lockwood (*vn*); Patrick Rollin (*g*); Yves Torchinsky (*b*); Francis Lassus (*d*). 91.

This is basically a quartet album, with Lockwood making only two appearances and Rollin confined to accompanying the trumpeter on a minute-and-a-half reading of 'Caravan'. The most striking thing is a version of 'Ode To Billie Joe', which recasts Bobbie Gentry's song as a medium-tempo shuffle and makes the most of the tune. If anything, it shows up the rest of the material as merely clever exercises in sort-of-bebop writing, and Brunet, who has a tone much akin to Chet Baker's and a deadpan line in humour which he slips into his playing – there is a tick-tock version of 'St Thomas' which some will find intensely irritating – sounds like a character player in search of a good leader. 'Rominus' itself, though, initiates a striking partnership with the mercurial Lockwood and makes one wish he'd been more involved in the rest of the record.

MERRITT BRUNIES (1895–1973)
CORNET

**   **Merritt Brunies And His Friars Inn Orchestra** Retrieval FJ-124 LP
Brunies; Henry Brunies (*tb*); Volly De Faut (*cl, as*); Bill Cregar (*cl, as, bsn*); Clarence Piper (*as, bj*); Sumner 'Rip' Logan (*ts, Cmel*); Dudley Mecum, Maurie Friedman (*p*); Gordon Pouliot (*vn*); Norman Van Hook (*bb*); Bill Paley (*d*); Lew King (*v*).
9/24–3/26.

The Brunies brothers are footnotes in jazz history, although their brother George made a rather greater renown for himself as a trombonist (Henry's trombone-playing is less than a highlight here, despite a reputation as 'the world's greatest trombonist'). The music of Merritt's band, which played at Chicago's Friars Inn for two years while these records were made, is stolid jazz-dance music typical of the day: they make a game attempt at the likes of 'Sugar Foot

Stomp', 'Clarinet Marmalade' and 'Angry', which the brothers actually co-wrote, but these are lumbering performances. De Faut has some of the better solos on clarinet, although Merritt takes a few worthwhile spots, including a fierce one on 'Flamin' Mamie'. Jelly Roll Morton's alleged presence on 'Clarinet Marmalade' seems plausible enough from what can be heard of the pianist, but that isn't saying a great deal. The remastering of what are extremely rare 78s has been achieved with typical diligence by John R. T. Davies.

RAINER BRUNINGHAUS
KEYBOARDS

**   **Freigeweht** ECM 1187 LP
Bruninghaus; Kenny Wheeler (*flhn*); Brynjar Hoff (*ob, cor*); Jon Christensen (*d*). 8/80.

***   **Continuum** ECM 1266 LP
Bruninghaus; Markus Stockhausen (*t, picc-t, flhn*); Fredy Studer (*d*). 9/83.

Bruninghaus first made an impression as the keyboard player in Eberhard Weber's superb series of ECM albums. His own two records as leader aren't quite so distinctive, although each has its moments. *Freigeweht* suffers from a lack of Weber's melodic ingenuity; Bruninghaus uses the same deployment of overlapping keyboard riffs that he used with the bassist but, aside from the title-track, most of the themes sound a little thin. Wheeler performs a cameo role and sounds relatively uninvolved, although Christensen is as fine as usual.

    Continuum is more successful on several counts. Stockhausen sounds completely at ease with the dancing parts he's required to play, and there are moments in 'Continuum' and 'Schattenfrei' when the group create a glittering trio jazz. The keyboard orchestration is subtler and the use of electronics more refined, while the leader's own playing sounds more decisive.

JOHN BRUNIOUS
TRUMPET

(*)   **Bye And Bye 504 LP13 LP
Brunious; Eddie King (*tb*); Paul Barnes (*cl*); Lester Santiago (*p*); Charles Easley (*b*); Emil Maurice (*d*); Wendell Brunious (*v*). 10/64.

The Brunious family aren't well known outside New Orleans circles, but Chief John 'Pickey' Brunious was a hot and swinging trumpeter who also led the Eagle Brass Band, and this memento from a group he fronted at the Royal Orleans Hotel makes a vigorous job of interpreting the customary standards and a few enterprising originals, including 'Dwight Breaux Blues' and 'Hot Sausage Rag'. Brunious and Noble handle their duties with righteous aplomb, but trombonist King is more troublesome, his ragged solos and blowsy intonation scuppering some of the flair of the horns. Wendell Brunious makes a fair job of singing 'That Old Green River' – at least as nine-year-old vocalists go – and thankfully is a mere bystander elsewhere. The sound is boxy and poorly balanced, but frequent listeners to this kind of record won't find it too troubling.

RAY BRYANT (born 1931)
PIANO

***(*)   **Alone With The Blues** Original Jazz Classics OJC 249 LP

***(*)   **Montreux 77** Original Jazz Classics OJC 371 CD/LP/MC
Bryant (*p* solo). 12/58, 12/76, 7/77.

Noted for an imaginative and influential alteration of the basic 12-bar blues sequence on his 'Blues Changes', Bryant is a distinctive pianist who superficially resembles Hampton Hawes. Unlike Hawes, though, he prefers to play solo, and his Pablo trios are much less interesting than the solo work. Bryant is not an orthodox bopper in the way Hawes once was, and his solo performances are even further away from the predominant Bud Powell model of bop piano.

Bryant's reputation has been undeservedly limited to a smallish circle of jazz-piano aficionados and he's poorly represented on CD. Fortunately, the Montreux set, recorded in a vintage year, catches him very nearly at his best. There are excellent versions of 'Georgia On My Mind', 'Take The "A" Train' and John Lewis's 'Django', all three of which demonstrate Bryant's ability to invest even quite small harmonic changes with considerable dramatic significance. There are also fine blues performances and a typical gospelly reading of 'Sometimes I Feel Like A Motherless Child'. Bryant has written a sequence of numbered blues originals. 'Blues No. 6' is on *Montreux 77*, 'Blues No. 3' on the earlier OJC, which shouldn't be missed either, particularly for a fine version of 'Lover Man', which demonstrates the pianist's astonishingly expansive left-hand chords.

RUSTY BRYANT
ALTO SAXOPHONE

**(*) Rusty Bryant Returns! Prestige OJC-331 LP
   Bryant (*ts*); Sonny Phillips (*org*); Grant Green (*g*); Bob Bushnell (*b*); Herbie Lovelle (*d*). 8/69.

This hard-hitting soul-sax player has been ill-served by the catalogues in recent times. Most of his unsubtle but exciting sessions from the 1960s and early '70s are long out of print, and the single OJC reissue is a little marred by an eager but finesse-free rhythm section, Green excluded. Bryant's occasional use of the varitone attachment on his alto dates the record, but it's energetic stuff all the same.

MILTON BUCKNER (1915–77)
PIANO, ORGAN, ARRANGER

*(*) Play, Milt, Play France's Concert 103 CD
   Buckner; Roy Eldridge (*t*); Illinois Jacquet (*ts*); Jimmy Woode, Slam Stewart (*b*); Jo Jones (*d*). 11/66, 7/69, 4/71.

Milt Buckner's musical roots lay in the broad-brush band arrangements of the 1920s and '30s, rather than in small-group jazz. His father Ted had played alto saxophone with Jimmie Lunceford, and Buckner Junior held two campaign medals from gruelling stints with Lionel Hampton in the 1940s (most of them) and early '50s.

His pioneering use of electric organ was in part an attempt to bring some of the energy and power of a full horn section to small-group playing. Though the trios with Jo Jones and Slam Stewart are cluttered and rather undifferentiated, the five organ/drum duos with Jones are surprisingly effective. Buckner seems far less restrained and a great deal more imaginative on the electric keyboard than on piano (which is virtually inaudible in any case). His old skills as an arranger are more in evidence on the quartet/quintet tracks than any technical virtuosity. Eldridge and Jacquet (the saxophonist was a long-standing associate) contribute pointedly good solos that stand out, and not just qualitatively, from a thin background.

The crowd seems to enjoy it, though there are one or two disconcerting jeers, but then they were there and were presumably spared a curious, tinnitus effect, much like listening to music from the flat next door, all top and bottom tones and no middle. Which might explain how '(On A Clear Day) You Can See Forever', comes out as 'I Can't See Fever'.

JANE BUNNETT
SOPRANO SAXOPHONE, FLUTE

*** In Dew Time Dark Light DL 9001 LP
   Bunnett; Larry Cramer (*t, flhn*); Vincent Chancey (*frhn*); Dewey Redman (*ts*); Brian Dickinson, Don Pullen (*p*); Scott Alexander (*b*); Claude Ranger (*d*). 2/88.

Like Steve Lacy, her acknowledged model on soprano saxophone, Canadian Jane Bunnett leads a band almost wholly dedicated to Monk themes. This isn't it, but this one has Don Pullen and Dewey Redman guesting, plus the not inconsiderable talent of horn player Chancey. Don

Pullen, who clearly recognizes talent when he hears it, gives her the quirky harmonies and off-centre count that she hears in Monk's tunes. On the duets, he coaxes and provokes, encouraging Bunnett's unstuffy progressions. He takes a much smaller role on *In Dew Time*, but the flute–piano duet of 'Big Alice' is gorgeous, with a hint of Dolphy there and on Carla Bley's oblique 'Utviklingssang' in the sharply puffed top notes. Early days yet, presumably, so well worth watching.

**(*)   Live At Sweet Basil Denon CAN 9009 CD
Bunnett; Larry Cramer (*t*); Don Pullen (*p*); Kieran Overs (*b*); Billy Hart (*d*).

There are some signs here that Bunnett still doesn't quite hack it as an improvising player. The opening is stunning (if a little contrived), but the long set tends to break down into its constituents and the writing isn't quite strong enough to carry some very untogether playing. Bunnett's chill soprano is better suited to more abstract duet settings than to a relatively straightforward blowing session. She concentrates largely on textures, leaving the piece to plod its own way home. Pullen's deliciously unexpected outbursts keep the ingredients stirring and the pace unpredictable, but there's nothing more than the odd off-centre voicing coming from the trumpeter, and the rhythm section sounds oddly mechanized.

Bunnett's 'In Dew Time' gets an airing and she does some lovely flute work on 'You Don't Know What Love Is', but she's trying to make silk purses when she needs to concentrate on the basic fabric which simply isn't robust enough. Perhaps the most teasingly original new saxophone voice on the scene, but no one's written her a good script yet.

***   Spirits Of Havana Denon CAN 9011 CD
Bunnett; Larry Kramer (*t, flhn*); Frank Emilio, Flynn Rodríques, Gonzala Rubalcaba, Hilario Durán Torres (*p*); Ahmed Barroso (*g*); Kieran Overs (*b*); Oqduardo Díaz Anaya, Justo M. Garcia Arango, Orlando Lage Bozva, Guillermo Barreto Brown, Ignacio Ubicio Castillo, Jacinto Soull Castillo, Ernesto Rodríquez Guzman, Francisco Hernández Mora, Roberto García Valdes (*perc*); Merceditas Valdés, Grupo Yoruba Andabo (*v*). 9 & 10/91.

Jane Bunnett is adamant that this isn't just another Latin jazz date, but a genuine attempt to bring Cuban music within her own constantly widening purview. She was already listening to and playing salsa before making her all-important first trip to Havana and seems immediately at ease in an idiom which puts conventional (that is, jazz-and bop-derived) soloing at a premium, shifting emphasis towards the overall sound of the group. The opening 'Hymn' is a flute tribute to the spirit of Miles Davis, who had just died. There is a searing version of 'Epistrophy' with Cuban percussion not so much added as incorporated into the fabric of the composition. For the rest, the material is nearly all traditional Afro-Caribbean or written in collaboration with the late Guillermo Barreto Brown, who masterminded the project.

Bunnett's soprano and flute figures are haunting on 'La Luna Arriba', by her close associate Larry Kramer, who is superb on the Monk tune. Frank Emilio's 'G.M.S.' opens with pan-American flute but gets lost in a thicket of percussion. Merceditas Valdés's vocals will not be to everyone's taste, but they're integral to a fascinating project. It would be interesting to hear Bunnett extend the 'Epistrophy' experiment, taking in compositions by the Caribbean-born Andrew Hill and by her sometime associate Don Pullen, who has also recently worked in a parallel idiom.

ALBERT BURBANK (1902–76)
CLARINET

***   Albert Burbank With Kid Ory And His Creole Jazzband Storyville SLP 6010 CD/LP
Burbank; Alvin Alcorn (*t*); Kid Ory (*tb*); Don Ewell (*p*); Ed Garland (*b*); Minor Hall (*d*). 5–7/54.

Burbank scarcely ever left New Orleans, and it's an irony that the only disc currently under his own name should have been recorded elsewhere (he toured briefly with Ory's band and returned home the same year). These tracks, culled from six different 1954 concerts at San Francisco's Club Hangover, were made under Ory's leadership and it's rather a matter of paying respects that they appear under Burbank's name: Ory and Alcorn have just as major a role in the music. But the clarinettist has much to say, too. He was a dramatic player, switching between long and short phrases and possessing an odd, shrimpy vibrato which gives his high notes a peculiarly affecting quality. There are fine solos on 'Fidgety Feet' and the rest of a frankly ordinary set of material, but the epic 'Blues For Jimmie Noone', which runs for 11 minutes, has a funereal grandeur that is only finally undercut by Garland's disastrous arco passage. Alcorn is, as ever, in rousing form, too. Fair recording, given the source material.

DAVE BURRELL (born 1940)
PIANO, KEYBOARDS

***(*)   **In: Sanity** Black Saint BSR 0006/7 2LP
Burrell; Beaver Harris (*d*); Keith Marks (*f*); Hamiet Bluiett (*bs, cl, f*); Azar Lawrence (*ts*); Cecil McBee (*b*); Sunil Garg (*sitar*); Jack Alston, Coleridge Barbour, Lawrence McCarthy, Roger Sardinha, Titos Sompa, Michael Sorzano (*steel d*). 3/76.

****   **In Concert** Victor CD016 CD
Burrell; David Murray (*ts*). 10/91.

Burrell's best record, *Windward Passages* [hat Art 2025 2LP], was a solo version of a large-scale jazz opera co-written with his wife, Monika Larsson. It was an autobiographical account of a young musician growing up, as Burrell had done, in Hawaii and suffering all the dispossession that haunts non-white Americans. An intensely private work, it communicated well as a solo piano performance, showing off Burrell's remarkable syncretism of black musics. He combines bop, rag, stride, blues and free elements with complete ease and is a figure of unacknowledged importance in recent attempts to recolonize the earlier history of jazz after the scorched-earth policy of the 1960s radicals. He has worked with Marion Brown, Giuseppi Logan, Archie Shepp and Sonny Sharrock, among many others.

In: Sanity includes another large-scale composition, scored for an orchestra co-led with Beaver Harris. The opening 'Tradewinds' and the atmospheric 'Sahara' give a fine sense of Burrell's disciplined impressionism, but the real meat of the set is the three-part 'In: Sanity Suite', a powerful composition that uses multi-ethnic instrumentation and world music references to explore a rather dark mindscape that nevertheless coincides at significant points with the themes of *Windward Passages*. Burrell also plays organ and celeste in some sections.

The 1991 Victoriaville duo was widely and perhaps inevitably received as another David Murray album. While it is a collective performance, there's some justification in claiming it for Burrell's unfortunately thin discography. The pianist contributes three out of five compositions (including 'Punaluu Peter' and the threnody to Coltrane's bassist, Jimmy Garrison, from *Windward Passages*). It's also clear that Murray's revisionist approach to the black music tradition has been much influenced by the man who plays on many of his best records. The stride accompaniments on 'Punaluu Peter' suddenly erupt into volcanic outbursts of sound that suggest something of the pressure that always comes up from below in Burrell's work. Murray's well-worked 'Hope Scope' almost becomes a feature for the pianist, but on 'Ballad For The Black Man' that is reversed, with Burrell patiently comping for Murray's calm statement of his own theme and then sustaining a harmonic base for some incredibly sustained upper-register whistles. 'Intuitively' and 'Teardrops For Jimmy' bring the performance to a moving and effective close. The sound is excellent for a live recording, with no distortion or drop-out at either end of the dynamic scale. Strongly recommended as an introduction to either man.

KENNY BURRELL (born 1931)
GUITAR

***   **All Night Long** Original Jazz Classics OJC 427 CD/LP/MC
Burrell; Donald Byrd (*t*); Hank Mobley (*ts*); Jerome Richardson (*ts, f*); Mal Waldron (*p*); Doug Watkins (*b*); Art Taylor (*d*). 12/56.

***   **All Day Long** Original Jazz Classics OJC 456 CD/LP/MC
Burrell; Donald Byrd (*t*); Frank Foster (*ts*); Tommy Flanagan (*p*); Doug Watkins (*b*); Art Taylor (*d*). 1/57.

***   **Blue Moods** Original Jazz Classics OJC 019 LP/MC
Burrell; Cecil Payne (*bs*); Tommy Flanagan (*p*); Doug Watkins (*b*); Elvin Jones (*d*).
2/57.

***   **The Cats** Original Jazz Classics OJC 079 CD/LP
Burrell; Idrees Sulieman (*t*); John Coltrane (*ts*); Tommy Flanagan (*p*); Doug Watkins
(*b*); Louis Hayes (*d*). 4/57

***   **Kenny Burrell & John Coltrane** Original Jazz Classics OJC 300 CD/LP/MC
Burrell; John Coltrane (*ts*); Tommy Flanagan (*p*); Paul Chambers (*b*); Jimmy Cobb
(*d*). 3/58.

Burrell's playing is tied to bebop and rhythm-and-blues, yet he's the most gentlemanly of
musicians, never losing his grip on a playing situation and in command of a seemingly
inexhaustible supply of interesting licks. He has a tone as lulling as that of Joe Pass, but shies
away from that player's rococo extravagances. It's difficult to pick out the best of Burrell, for his
earliest sessions are as maturely formed as his later ones, and while he's played with a vast
number of musicians, he manages to fit seamlessly into whatever the context happens to be. In
the 1950s he was a popular man to have on blowing dates, and his early work for Prestige is
mostly in that mould. The sessions that were designated as all-day and all-night don't actually
go on that long, but some of the solos seem to, and there's little to recommend them beyond a
few livelier moments. *Blue Moods* is a reflective canter through a typical programme of blues
and standards, with a feature for Jones on 'Drum Boogie'. OJC 300 finds Coltrane in his
restless early period, but Burrell seems to be a calming influence, and they have a beautifully
shaded duet on 'Why Was I Born?'. *The Cats* benefits from Flanagan's leadership, and the
pianist's shapely contributions add further lustre to the music, all of it very well engineered.

***(*)   **On View At The Five Spot Café Vol. I** Blue Note B21Y-46538 CD
Burrell; Tina Brooks (*ts*); Bobby Timmons, Roland Hanna (*p*); Ben Tucker (*b*); Art
Blakey (*d*). 8/59.

***   **Blue Lights Vol. 1** Blue Note B21Y-81596 CD
Burrell; Louis Smith (*t*); Tina Brooks (*ts*); Duke Jordan, Bobby Timmons (*p*); Sam
Jones (*b*); Art Blakey (*d*). 5/58.

***   **Blue Lights Vol. 2** Blue Note B21Y-81597 CD
As above. 5/58.

Burrell's live recordings, unusually, don't fan the flames any more brightly than his studio
sessions. But the Five Spot date is a particularly strong one for the presence of the
seldom-recorded Brooks, whose solos strike a truce between urgency and relaxation, and the
exhortative Blakey. The two *Blue Lights* records are at a slightly lesser temperature, although
the soloists still create feelingful music, especially on 'The Man I Love' from the second
volume. These are now US-only releases.

***   **Midnight Blue** Blue Note B21Y-46399 CD
Burrell; Stanley Turrentine (*ts*); Major Holley (*b*); Bill English (*d*); Ray Barretto
(*perc*). 1/63.

Just what the title says, and a sketch for a quiet classic in its way. Turrentine breezes over the
changes as if he's trying to huff out a flame flickering somewhere across the room, and Burrell
simply pads around him. Kenny's solo 'Soul Lament' makes a nice party-piece.

***(*)   **Guitar Forms** Verve 825576-2 CD
Burrell; Johnny Coles, Louis Mucci (*t*); Jimmy Cleveland, Jimmy Knepper (*tb*); Andy
Fitzgerald, George Marge (*cor, f*); Ray Alonge, Julius Watkins (*frhn*); Steve Lacy (*ss*);
Ray Beckenstein (*as, f*); Lee Konitz (*as*); Richie Kamuca (*ts, ob*); Bob Tricarico (*bsn,
f*); Roger Kellaway (*p*); Bill Barber (*tba*); Ron Carter, Joe Benjamin (*b*); Elvin Jones,
Charli Persip, Grady Tate (*d*); Willie Rodriguez (*perc*). 12/64–4/65.

The closest Burrell has come to a singular masterpiece, even if it is more by association with Gil
Evans, who arranged it. Burrell's tonal pallor and sanguine approach might make him a less
characterful soloist than those who've handled other of Evans's concerto set-pieces, but in
some ways that works to the music's advantage: without misleading emotional resonances of the

kind associated with, say, Miles Davis cracking notes, the purity of Evans's veils of sound emerges the more clearly in the likes of 'Lotus Land'.

**   **Handcrafted** Muse MR 5144 LP
      Burrell; Reggie Johnson (*b*); Sherman Ferguson (*d*). 2–3/78.

***   **Live At The Village Vanguard** Muse MR 5216 LP
      Burrell; Larry Gales (*b*); Sherman Ferguson (*d*). 12/78.

***   **In New York** Muse MR 5241 LP
      As above. 12/78.

**   **Listen To The Dawn** Muse MR 5264 LP
      Burrell; Rufus Reid (*b*); Ben Riley (*d*). 12/80.

Burrell worked patiently through the 1970s and '80s. These are decent if mostly unexciting records: the two sets cut at the Vanguard have a bit more fizz, but Burrell is otherwise to work his unambitious way through each session.

(*)   **Guiding Spirit Contemporary 14065 CD
      Burrell; Jay Hoggard (*vib*); Marcus McLaurine (*b*); Yoron Israel (*d*). 8/89.

Still pretty, still bebop, still no trouble, still fine; still not that great unless one needs a late-night painkiller.

GARY BURTON (born 1943)
VIBRAPHONE

***   **Green Apple** Moon MPL 013 CD/LP
      Burton; David Pritchard (*g*); Steve Swallow (*b*); Bill Goodwin (*d*). 69.

***   **The New Quartet** ECM 1030 CD/LP
      Burton; Michael Goodrick (*g*); Abraham Laboriel (*b*); Harry Blazer (*d*). 3/73

***   **Times Square** ECM 1111 LP
      Burton; Tiger Okoshi (*t*); Steve Swallow (*b*); Roy Haynes (*d*). 1/78.

**   **Picture This** ECM 1226 LP
      Burton; Jim Odgren (*as*); Steve Swallow (*b*); Mike Hyman (*d*). 6/80.

***   **Real Life Hits** ECM 1293 CD/LP
      As above, except Makoto Ozone (*p*) replaces Odgren. 1/82, 11/84.

Ever since the late 1960s, and the band that established his name and mature style, Burton has shown a marked preference for the quartet format, and for working with guitarists. The 1967 band included Larry Coryell, Steve Swallow and Bob Moses and remains perhaps his most consistently inventive unit. Swallow has been a steady presence, and provides a consistent but imaginative bottom line for Burton's occasionally flyaway approach. The New Quartet was a more or less self-conscious attempt to synthesize the earlier band; the newcomers are by no means faceless epigoni (neither was the quartet captured live in Nice on *Green Apple*), and the resulting album is robustly conceived and performed, and marked by some of the best writing Burton had to work with. There are pieces by Carla Bley, Gordon Beck and Michael Gibbs; 'Olhos de Gato' and Beck's 'Mallet Man' are masterly.

Real Life Hits is understated almost to the point of blandness, but it is also one of Burton's most interesting set of compositions, and merits close attention. Back in 1978, trumpeter Tiger Okoshi helped make *Times Square* one of the vibist's most completely satisfying sessions, complementing his instinctive delicacy with some much-needed fire and force. It's a pity, though, that there isn't more reliable live recording, like the Moon set, on which Pritchard is very impressive and the edges attractively roughened.

***   **Ring** ECM 1051 CD
      Burton; Mick Goodrick, Pat Metheny (*g*); Steve Swallow (*b*); Bob Moses (*d*). 74.

(*)   **Dreams So Real ECM 1072 CD
      As above, except add Eberhard Weber (*b*). 75.

***   **Passengers** ECM 1092 CD/LP
Burton; Pat Metheny (*g*); Steve Swallow, Eberhard Weber (*b*); Dan Gottlieb (*d*).
11/76.

***   **Reunion** GRP 95982 CD/MC
Burton; Pat Metheny (*g*); Mitch Forman (*p, ky*); Will Lee (*b*); Peter Erskine (*d*).

Burton's mid-1970s albums with rising star Metheny and the distinctive Weber now sound a little tarnished but their blend of country softness and Weber's slightly eldritch melody lines still make for interesting listening, even if the group never sounds quite as enterprising as it did live. The three ECMs are pretty much of a piece, but *Passengers*, actually co-credited to Weber, is probably the one to go for initially.

Burton makes a considerable virtue out of what might have become an awful clutter of strings and percussion. The themes are open and clearly stated, even when they are relatively complex, as on 'The Whopper', and Weber's forceful, wailing sound is strongly contrasted to those of the two guitarists; Swallow as usual plays bass guitar with a pick, getting a clean, exact sound whose colouration is totally different from Metheny's rock-influenced sustains. Weber's own composition 'Yellow Fields' (see ECM 1066) undergoes an attractive variation.

The Burton–Metheny *Reunion* is rather good, too, but marred by a very ripe mix and the rather compromising introduction of Forman.

(*)   **Whiz Kids ECM 1329 CD/LP
Burton; Tommy Smith (*ts*); Makoto Ozone (*p*); Steve Swallow (*b*); Martin Richards
(*d*). 6/86.

Though Ozone (who has a fine CBS album to his credit) resurfaced to great effect on *Whiz Kids*, all the buzz was about the Scottish *Wunderkind* Smith, another pupil of Burton's at Berklee, and just at this time beginning to receive serious critical attention on the other side of the Atlantic. The results, perhaps inevitably given all the hype, are a shade disappointing. Burton has never been easy with saxophone players (see his two tracks with Michael Brecker on *Times Like These*), and the lead voices clutter and compete furiously, without any logic or drama. Ozone keeps things more or less tidy, but it is an uncomfortable set and definitely missable.

***   **Matchbook** ECM 1056 CD/LP
Burton; Ralph Towner (*g*). 7/74.

(*)   **Duet ECM 1140 CD
Burton; Chick Corea (*p*). 10/78.

At first blush, the Burton/Corea partnership looked like a marriage made in heaven, and they toured extensively. In practice, and at least on record, the collaboration fell foul of the inevitable similarity between piano and vibraphone and of the performers' out-of-synch musical personalities. An earlier set, *Crystal Silence*, is more properly credited to Corea, since he is the chief writer. On *Duet*, the pianist never seems far from whimsicality, and it is interesting to see how much more positively and forcefully Burton responds to Towner's light but well-anchored style. *Matchbook* is surprisingly disciplined and coherent for all its lacey textures and delicate, almost directionless transitions; *Slide Show* (ECM 1306) reversed the performers' names on the cover and so – by our ruthlessly alphabetical rubric – stops for T. Disappointing, though. Equally disappointing is the (temporary, one hopes) disappearance of *Hotel Hello* [ECM 1055 LP], a marvellous duet with Steve Swallow, which is by far the most impressive of Burton's two-handers.

(*)   **Times Like These GRP 95069 CD/LP
Burton; Michael Brecker (*ts*); John Scofield (*g*); Marc Johnson (*b*); Peter Erskine (*d*).

(*)   **Cool Nights GRP 9643 2 CD
Burton; Bob Berg (*ts*); Bob James (*ky*); Wolfgang Muthspiel (*g*); Will Lee (*b, perc*);
Peter Erskine (*d, perc*). 91.

For all the sophistication of Burton's writing, these are drab, middle-of-the-road sets. *Cool Nights* is too laid-back by half and further blurred by a muzzy, rock-album mix, out of which Brecker, Berg, Scofield and, less often, the Australian-born Muthspiel occasionally emerge to do rather self-conscious solo spots and twiddles. *Times Like These* is marginally better, as the line-up would suggest, but it's still very disappointing.

***   **Artist's Choice** Bluebird ND86280 CD
Burton; various line-ups, 1963–8.

**   **Works** ECM 823267-2 CD/LP
Burton; Chick Corea, Steve Swallow (*p*); Mick Goodrick, Pat Metheny, Ralph Towner (*g*); Abe Laboriel, Steve Swallow, Eberhard Weber (*b*); Harry Blazer (*d*); Bobby Moses (*perc*); orchestra. 72–80.

Works is one of the better balanced of ECM's 15th anniversary artist samplers, with a good range of material from what some would consider his vintage years. Virtually all the material is readily available elsewhere, though, and what makes *Artist's Choice* so valuable is, well, that most of the material isn't available elsewhere. The earlier stuff also reveals an altogether tougher harmonic thinker, much less concerned with the finely woven textures that became his trademark under the aegis of ECM. Titles like 'Norwegian Wood' and Dylan's 'I Want You' (from the deleted *Time Machine* and *Tennessee Firebird* respectively) underline a well-assimilated rock influence that took an intriguing new turn with the brilliant 'Country Roads', co-written with Steve Swallow. There are also valuable tracks from Carla Bley's *A Genuine Tong Funeral*, which is a far more significant work than the overblown *Escalator Over The Hill*.

As a pair, they represent the best possible introduction to Burton's work.

JOHN BUTCHER
TENOR, SOPRANO AND BARITONE SAXOPHONES

****   **Thirteen Friendly Numbers** Acta 6 CD
Butcher (*ss, ts, bs* solo). 3–12/91.

A British improviser whose playing is highly accomplished and strikingly individual, Butcher's recital is unlike any other solo saxophone record. Nine of the 13 tracks are real-time solos on either tenor or soprano, while the other four create some unprecedented sounds and textures through overdubbing: 'Bells And Clapers', for instance, piles up four tenors into a brittle choir of humming overtones that has a chilling, sheet-metal sound, while the amplification introduced into the very brief 'Mackle Music' is peculiarly disturbing. On the more conventional solo tracks, Butcher's mastery of the instrument creates a vocabulary which can accommodate pieces as disparate as 'Notelet', which is like a single flow of melody, and the explorations of single aspects of performing technique, as on 'Humours And Vapours' and 'Buccinator's Outing'. Assisted by a very clear and suitably neutral recording, this is a masterful record which should be investigated by anyone interested in the latest steps in free playing.

BILLY BUTLER (1924–91)
GUITAR

*(*)   **Guitar Soul!** Original Jazz Classics OJC 334 CD/LP
Butler; Seldon Powell (*f, varisx*); Sonny Phillips (*org*); Bob Bushnell (*b*); Specs Powell (*d*). 9/69.

Typically brisk, unambitious soul-jazz date, led by a guitarist whose claim to fame is perhaps known only to himself. Nothing here that wasn't done better by Grant Green or Wes Montgomery, and the cheap electronic treatment of Powell's sax buries that fine player under a useless gimmick.

JAKI BYARD (born 1922)
PIANO

***   **Blues For Smoke** Candid 9018 CD/LP
         Byard (*p* solo). 12/60.

(*)   **To Them, To Us Soul Note SN 1025 CD/LP
         Byard (*p* solo). 5/81.

Byard's enormous power and versatility were grounded on a thorough knowledge of brass, reeds, drums and guitar, as well as piano, and there are passages in solos which suggest some attempt to replicate the phrasing of a horn rather than a keyboard instrument. On a straight comparison between two solo sets two decades apart, it seems that Byard does now play more pianistically, though the distinctive left-and right-hand articulation of themes – based on a highly personal synthesis of ragtime and stride, bop and free jazz – is still strongly evident in 1981. The earlier album is a minor classic, with the wonderful 'Aluminium Baby', originally written for trumpeter/bandleader Herb Pomeroy, and 'Diane's Melody'. There is a more generous register (perhaps down to a more responsive piano) on the Soul Note set, but it lacks some of the percussive energy of the Candid. Both are recommended.

***   **Giant Steps** Prestige P24086 2LP
         Byard; Ron Carter (*b*); Roy Haynes or Pete La Roca (*d*). 3/61–1/62.

***   **Foolin' Myself** Soul Note 121 125 CD/LP
         Byard; Ralph Hamperian (*b*); Richard Allen (*d*). 8/88.

Byard's solo performances are perhaps his best and most characteristic. An expansive and eclectic player, he is inclined to swamp sidemen with weather-changes of idiom or mood. No such problems with either of these trio sets. Carter and Haynes are more than equal to the challenge, and there's a hint of willing compromise in Byard's attack which suggests a measured respect all round. No great revelations in his alto sax doublings on the Prestige, beyond renewed surprise at his adaptability. The later set is full of oblique harmonies and wonderfully off-centre themes; the CD offers a big sound with a lot of warmth, typical of Giovanni Bonandrini's in-house production at Soul Note. Prestige albums of the earlier vintage were of equally high quality and *Giant Steps* is well up to scratch. What's a scratch, daddy?

***(*)   **Live At The Royal Festival Hall** Leo LR 133 LP
         Byard; Howard Riley (*p*). 83.

A remarkable encounter with one of the most austere and formal of the European free players. Byard's approach is, oddly, even less conventionally swinging than Riley's, breaking up Monkish phrase-lengths into shorter and shorter rhythmic cells and then spinning them all together into long bop lines that have everything but a settled key centre. The separation of sound is very much better than at the original concert and the music is consistently fascinating. Highly recommended.

*(*)   **Phantasies** Soul Note SN 1075 CD/LP
         Byard; The Apollo Stompers. 9/84.

Working with Maynard Ferguson and then Mingus gave Byard some insight into how to steer at high speed. Without any doubt his excellence as a section player fed into his solo and small-group playing as well. *Phantasies* is an uncomfortable big-band excursion with vocals from Byard's Denyce and Diane (she of the melody – see above); though well produced and more than adequately executed, the album runs pastiche a little too close for comfort and lands somewhere among at least three stylistic stools.

DON BYAS (1912–72)
TENOR SAXOPHONE

***   **Living My Life** Vogue/Savoy VG 650122 CD
         Byas; Benny Harris (*t*); Teddy Brannon, Sanford Gold, Jimmy Jones (*p*); Leonard Gaskin, John Levy, Frank Skeete (*b*); Fred Radcliffe, Max Roach (*d*). 5/45, 11/45, 8/46.

***   **Tenderly** Vogue/Savoy VG 655620 CD
Byas; Christian Chevallier, Martial Solal, Maurice Vander, Mary Lou Williams (*p*);
George Daly, Sadi (*vib*); Marcel Bianchi (*g*); Buddy Banks, Pierre Michelot (*b*);
Benny Bennett, Richie Frost, Pierre Lemarchand, Gerard Pochonnet (*d*). 11/51, 5/52,
7/52, 11/53, 12/53, 5/55.

*(*)   **A Night In Tunisia** Black Lion BLCD 760136
Byas; Bent Axen (*p*); Niels-Henning Ørsted-Pedersen (*b*); William Schiopffe (*d*). 1/63.

Somewhat in eclipse these days, Byas was regarded as the foremost tenor player of the late war
years and immediate post-war period. He had a broad, chocolatey tone that collapsed when the
tempo exceeded a canter, so he preferred, as in most of the above, to stick to a late-night stroll,
never stepping on the cracks (his on-the-beat articulation made some impact later on John
Coltrane), less aimless and more purposeful than at first appears. It's said that Byas transposed
some of Tatum's harmonic language to the saxophone; he is undoubtedly a wonderfully
intelligent player.

Living My Life is culled from a Savoy double (WL 70512 809315) which includes superb 1944
sessions with Charlie Shavers, Clyde Hart and Slam Stewart. The remainder is still exceptional,
though one misses Shavers's bite. The autobiographical 'Donby' and 'Byas A Drink', relatively
conventional changes on a well-worn chord structure, expose his limitations as a composer,
though Byas's genius is clearly directed elsewhere.

As was the remainder of his life. In 1946, having toured Europe with Don Redman, the first
American jazz musicians to visit after the war, he emigrated first to France, then Holland. He
died in Amsterdam in 1972. There were plenty of respectful young locals eager to play with
him. Few had the innate talent of Martial Solal, but the Paris sessions included on *Tenderly* have
a patina of freshness that is gone by the time of the Copenhagen sessions compiled on *A Night
In Tunisia*. He sounds strained much of the time and there are articulation problems in some of
the faster passages. Nevertheless he demonstrates a broad understanding of the bebop classics
and produces a fine solo on 'Loverman' (compare it with the 1953 Paris version on *Tenderly*).

For Byas, beauty of sound was everything, which is why he could get away with something as
dangerously schmaltzy as a straight run-through – on *Living My Life* – of 'Danny Boy' or, more
properly, 'The Londonderry Air'. Once that beauty had faded, there wasn't a great deal left.
Roll last three reels of *Round Midnight* . . .

(*)   **Yesterdays Moon Records MPL 009 CD/LP
Byas; Dizzy Gillespie (*t, v*); Bill Tamper (*tb*); Hubert Fol (*as*); Raymond Fol (*p*);
Pierre Michelot (*b*); Pierre Lemarchand (*d*). 4/52.

Recorded live in Milan, this is probably better seen as a piece of Gillespie marginalia than as a
representative Byas set. The saxophonist is poorly recorded and sounds very brittle on CD, with
the rhythm section very homogenized and indistinct. Fun versions of 'Lady Be Good', 'Birks'
Works' and 'Groovin' High' lift the second half, but it isn't an urgent purchase.

CHARLIE BYRD (born 1925)
GUITAR

(*)   **Latin Byrd Milestone M 47005 LP
Byrd with various groups. 61–3.

**   **Byrd At The Gate** Original Jazz Classics OJC 262 LP
Byrd; Clark Terry (*t*); Seldon Powell (*ts*); Keter Betts (*b*); Bill Reichenbach (*d*). 5/63.

The release in 1962 of the evergreen *Jazz Samba* with Stan Getz and the legal kerfuffle that
followed put Charlie Byrd firmly on the map. Like all hugely successful products, there was an
element of ersatz about it and Byrd's Latin stylings have never sounded entirely authentic and
are often quite rheumaticky in articulation. Here, though, are three valuable historical albums,
full of that characteristically American syndrome that John Aldridge called 'the energy of new
success' and which comes just before what the French call the *crise de quarante*. Byrd sounds
full-toned and quick-fingered, and the themes still have a bloom they were to lose all too
quickly in the years that followed.

**   **Blue Byrd** Concord CCD 4082 CD/MC

**   **Sugarloaf Suite** Concord CCD 4114 CD

**   **Isn't It Romantic** Concord CJ 252 MC
Byrd; Joe Byrd (*b*, *v*); Wayne Phillips (*d* except on *Isn't It Romantic*); Chuck Riggs (*d* on *Isn't It Romantic* only). 8/78, 8/79.

Byrd had a dull time for much of the 1970s. These discs find him less becalmed than usual and, on *Blue Byrd*, occasionally inspired. He handles mainstream standards well, surprising now and again with a figure completely out of left field; but the trio format leaves him much too exposed for comfort, and the up-close recording almost parades his stiffness.

(*)   **Brazilville Concord CCD 4173 CD/MC
Byrd; Bud Shank (*as*); Joe Byrd (*b*); Charles Redd (*d*). 5/81.

(*)   **It's A Wonderful World Concord CCD 4374 CD/MC
Byrd; Scott Hamilton (*ts*); John Goldsby (*b*); Chuck Redd (*d*). 8/88.

Byrd's quality in a horn-led band suggests that he was done only economic favours by having greatness thrust upon him so suddenly, 30 years ago. With both Shank and Hamilton he plays elegantly and with considerable taste. Both albums show a marked centring of Byrd's stylistic range; by no means everything is automatically Latinized and on *Wonderful World* in particular he displays an improvisational confidence that seemed to have deserted him in the 1970s. Nobody looks to Byrd for fire and brimstone, but there's an edgy, slightly restless quality to both of these that belies their bland packaging and suggests a genuinely improvisatory spirit at work. The Ellington and Arlen pieces are particularly fine.

(*)   **Byrd & Brass Concord CCD 4304 CD/MC
Byrd; Joe Byrd (*b*); Chuck Redd (*d*); Annapolis Brass Quintet. 4/86.

A surprisingly sharp and swinging set from an offbeat and unpromising line-up. Byrd pushes things along with unwonted enthusiasm; the brass is generously voiced and the rhythm work tighter than Byrd normally favours. Well recorded, too.

*   **The Charlie Byrd Christmas Album** Concord CCD 42004 CD
Byrd (*g* solo). 6/82.

This is fine for those that like this sort of thing, as Jean Brodie might say. Almost everyone else will hate it with a passion.

DONALD BYRD (born 1932)
TRUMPET, FLUGELHORN

**   **First Flight** Delmark 407 CD/LP
Byrd; Yusef Lateef (*ts*); Barry Harris (*p*); Bernard McKinney (*euph*); Alvin Jackson (*b*); Frank Gant (*d*). 8/55.

(*)   **Byrd's Word Savoy SV-0132 CD
Byrd; Frank Foster (*ts*); Hank Jones (*p*); Paul Chambers (*b*); Kenny Clarke (*d*). 9/55.

First Flight is the first album under Byrd's own name, recorded at a concert in Detroit, and, while it gave a smart indication of his own promise, it's Lateef's more commanding solos that take the attention. Harris, perhaps the quintessential Detroit pianist, is also imposing, although he has to contend with a poor piano, and the location sound is disappointingly muddy. *Byrd's Word* comes in fine remastered sound, but it adds up to another routine Savoy blowing date: Foster plays with intermittent enthusiasm and the rhythm section show some sparkle, but one feels that some of them were watching the clock.

***   **Byrd In Hand** Blue Note B21Y-84019 CD
Byrd: Charlie Rouse (*ts*); Pepper Adams (*bs*); Walter Davis (*p*); Sam Jones (*b*); Art Taylor (*d*). 12/58.

(*)   **Fuego Blue Note B21Y-46534 CD
Byrd; Jackie McLean (*as*); Duke Pearson (*p*); Sam Jones (*b*); Lex Humphries (*d*). 10/59.

***   **At The Half Note Vol. 1** Blue Note B21Y-46539 CD
Byrd; Pepper Adams (*bs*); Duke Pearson (*p*); Laymon Jackson (*b*); Lex Humphries (*d*). 11/60.

***   **At The Half Note Vol. 2** Blue Note B21Y-46540 CD
As above. 11/60.

***   **Free Form** Blue Note B21Y-84118 CD
Byrd; Wayne Shorter (*ts*); Herbie Hancock (*p*); Butch Warren (*b*); Billy Higgins (*d*). 12/61.

By the time he signed a deal with Blue Note in 1958, Byrd had already made more records than any of the other up-and-coming trumpeters of the day. It was his easy-going proficiency which made him sought-after: like Freddie Hubbard, who was to the early 1960s what Byrd had been to the previous five years, he could sound good under any contemporary leader without entirely dominating the situation. His solos were valuable but not disconcertingly personal, dependably elegant but not strikingly memorable. His records as a leader emerged in much the same way: refined and crisp hard bop which seems to look neither forwards nor backwards. Choosing from the above selection – all of them available only as US releases at present – is more a matter of which of the accompanying musicians is most appealing, since Byrd's own performances are regularly polished – almost to the point of tedium, some might say. *Byrd In Hand* and *Fuego* are typical Blue Note blowing sessions, the latter slightly more rewarding thanks to the reliable Adams, a frequent partner of the trumpeter; *Fuego* has some good McLean, but the tunes are dull. The live sessions at New York's Half Note are impeccably played and atmospherically recorded, but they tend to show the best and worst of Byrd: on the first number on Volume 1, 'My Girl Shirl', he peels off chorus after chorus of manicured licks, and this process gets repeated throughout. One is impressed but dissatisfied, and Humphries's less than outstanding drumming is another problem, although Adams is again splendid. *Free Form* puts Byrd among altogether more difficult company, and there's an unflattering contrast between his prim solo on the gospel cadences of 'Pentecostal Feeling' and Shorter's bluff intensity. But he plays very prettily on Herbie Hancock's 'Night Flower' (which sounds like 'I Left My Heart In San Francisco') and the more severe leanings of the title-track suit Byrd's punctilious manner well.

***(*)   **Groovin' For Nat** Black Lion BL 760132 CD/MC
Byrd; Johnny Coles (*t*); Duke Pearson (*p*); Bob Cranshaw (*b*); Walter Perkins (*d*). 1/62.

**   **A New Perspective** Blue Note 7841242 CD
Byrd; Hank Mobley (*ts*); Herbie Hancock (*p*); Donald Best (*vib*); Kenny Burrell (*g*); Butch Warren (*b*); Lex Humphries (*d*); choir. 12/63.

**   **I'm Tryin' To Get Home** Blue Note B21Y-84188 CD
Byrd; Ernie Royal, Snooky Young, Jimmy Owens, Clark Terry, Joe Ferrante (*t*); J. J. Johnson, Jimmy Cleveland, Henry Coker, Benny Powell (*tb*); Jim Buffington, Bob Northern (*frhn*); Stanley Turrentine (*ts*); Freddie Roach (*org*); Herbie Hancock (*p*); Grant Green (*g*); Don Butterfield (*tba*); Bob Cranshaw (*b*); Grady Tate (*d*); choir. 12/64.

After dozens of straightforward hard bop dates, Byrd branched out with mixed success. *Groovin' For Nat* is measure for measure one of his most enjoyable records: Coles, a splashier but characterful player, spars with him through a dozen duets, and the unusual combination of two trumpets and rhythm proves to be a joyous rather than a one-dimensional setting. Nevertheless, it's Coles who steals the record with a very expressive turn through 'Friday's Child'. The Black Lion CD includes three previously unavailable alternative takes, and the sound is very persuasive.

The Blue Note albums have remained popular and they contain the seeds of Byrd's wider success in the 1970s: his own playing is set against large-scale scoring and the use of a choir and, while there was talk at the time of gospel-inspired fusions, it seems clear that the music aimed for an easy-listening crevice somewhere between soul-jazz and mood music. Set against the stricter tenets of the records which came before them, they're both dispensable.

(*)   **Harlem Blues Landmark LCD-1516 CD/MC
Byrd; Kenny Garrett (*as*); Mulgrew Miller (*p*); Mike Daugherty (*ky*); Rufus Reid (*b*);
Marvin 'Smitty' Smith (*d*). 9/87.

(*)   **Gettin' Down To Business Landmark LCD-1523 CD/MC
Byrd; Kenny Garrett (*as*); Joe Henderson (*ts*); Donald Brown (*p*); Peter Washington
(*b*); Al Foster (*d*). 10/89.

(*)   **A City Called Heaven Landmark LCD-1530 CD/MC
Byrd; Joe Henderson (*ts*); Bobby Hutcherson (*vib*); Donald Brown (*p*); Rufus Reid
(*b*); Carl Allen (*d*); Lorice Stevens (*v*). 1/91.

Byrd's 1970s albums for Blue Note and Elektra, in which he scored crossover hits and fronted
the Blackbyrds group, have disappeared from the catalogue, and his return to the studios for
Orrin Keepnews's Landmark operation has been inauspicious. A cloudier tone, unsure vibrato
and intonation problems mar all of these records and, on the evidence of the latest, *A City
Called Heaven*, matters seem to be getting worse rather than better. Frustratingly, everyone
else on these sessions plays particularly well as if to compensate. The new-generation outfit on
Harlem Blues play with typical button-down drive; Garrett and Henderson mesh with purpose
and take some fine solos on *Gettin' Down To Business* and, despite a couple of intrusive vocals
by Stevens, the sextet on the latest record seems to have power to spare: Hutcherson continues
his Indian summer in the studios with swarming, harmonically dense lines and Henderson's
profoundly cast solos evince all the grand maturity which seems to have eluded Byrd.

CABAZZ
GROUP

**   **Chinese Garden** Dragon DRLP 150 LP
Jonas Knutsson (*ss, as*); Per Westerlund (*g, g-syn*); Anders Forsberg (*ky*); Mikael
Berglund (*b*); Morgan Agren (*d*); Robert Torne (*perc*); Lars Johansson (*v*). 5–8/87.

(*)   **Far Away Dragon DRCD 194 CD
As above, except omit Torne and Johansson.

Fusion is as international a genre as hard bop or trad now, and this energetic Swedish group
have no difficulties in delivering the trademark electric wallop which fusion demands.
Unfortunately they also fall prey to the excesses of the style: heavy-handed drumming, riffs
worked to death, keyboards used as textural flab, noisy guitar solos. Knutsson is an
accomplished soloist, though, and while they don't come up with a great variety of tunes, there
are moments – 'Rails' on the first record, and several tracks on *Far Away* – which suggest the
lyricism most closely associated with Pat Metheny. *Far Away*, although too long at 74 minutes, is
the more diverse offering, with 'Slash Romantic' and the title tune exploiting the harder and
softer sides of the group to full effect.

GEORGE CABLES (born 1944)
PIANO

***   **Circles** Contemporary C 14015 LP/MC
Cables; Joe Farrell (*f*); Ernie Watts (*ts*); Rufus Reid (*b*); Eddie Gladden (*d*). 3/79.

***   **Cables Visions** Contemporary C 14001 LP
Cables; Freddie Hubbard (*t, flhn*); Ernie Watts (*ts, ss*); Bobby Hutcherson (*vib*); Tony
Dumas (*b*); Peter Erskine (*d*); Vince Charles (*perc*). 12/79.

(**)   **Phantom Of The City Contemporary C 14014 LP/MC
Cables; John Heard (*b*); Tony Williams (*d*). 5/85.

***(*)   **By George** Contemporary C 14030 CD/LP
Cables; John Heard (*b*); Ralph Penland (*d*). 2/87.

***(*)   **Night And Day** DIW 606 CD
Cables; Cecil McBee (*b*); Billy Hart (*d*). 5/91.

Still probably best known for his duo performances with the late Art Pepper on the marvellous Galaxy *Goin' Home* (a role he has since resumed with Frank Morgan on *Double Image*, Contemporary C 14035 CD/LP, and on Morgan's more recent Antilles sets), Cables is a fine accompanist who has been consistently underrated as a soloist. His touch can be rather sharp and there is sometimes an awkward bounce to his chording at fast tempi, but he is a fine solo and trio performer.

Cables also saw service with Dexter Gordon on the saxophonist's return to the United States and can be heard with Rufus Reid and Eddie Gladden, his rhythm section on *Circles*, on Gordon's exactly contemporary Keystone Korner sets (Blue Note CDP 794848/49/50 2 3CD). The trio tracks on *Circles* are preferable to the three quartet numbers, though Farrell plays beautifully on 'The Phantom'. On 'Thank You, Thank You', Cables plays electric piano and clavinet, using the latter with surprising taste and economy. The recording is very one-dimensional, though, and that failing of touch is very evident even on the excellent 'I Remember Clifford'. He plays an electric instrument throughout *Cables Visions* with the exception of a single acoustic duo with Bobby Hutcherson called 'The Stroll', which deserves to be more widely known.

Phantom Of The City is an excellent record, marred only by a very splashy sound that loses a lot of Williams's lower-pitched work and blurs some of Cables's faster runs. 'Dark Side, Light Side', 'You Stepped Out Of A Dream' and 'Blue Nights' are, however, some of his finest performances on record and, in default of a CD reissue, well worth purchasing; a very noisy cassette version should be avoided like the plague. The 1987 Gershwin tribute is perhaps the most sophisticated set Cables has put together and the solo performances of 'Embraceable You' and 'Someone To Watch Over Me' are an excellent example of his innate rhythmic sense, a quality that has been valued by an impressive range of employers over the years. The only other CD on offer also marks a switch of label. DIW's production flatters him no more than his due and the selection of material is much more imaginative than usual, mixing well-worn standards like 'Night And Day' (given a little twist in the middle chorus), 'I Love You' and 'I Thought About You', with more enterprising numbers like Rollins's 'Doxy', Bill Evans's 'Very Early' (another possible source for Cables's keyboard approach), and Jaco Pastorius's misterioso funk 'Three Views Of A Secret'. An able composer, Cables has tended to keep this side of his work under wraps, writing for others but sticking to standards on his own records; 'Ebony Moonbeams' on *Night And Day* suggests that this is a pity.

CADENCE ALL STARS
GROUP

***   **Lee's Keys Please** Timeless SJP 284 CD/LP
Ernie Krivda (*ts*); Glenn Wilson (*bs*); Rory Stuart (*p*); Alan Simon (*p*); Jeff Halsey (*b*); Jon Hazilla (*d*). 11/87.

Although it's a little surprising to find a band of company favourites on a different company's label, the music is fine: six bright originals with the excellent front line of Krivda and Wilson, two saxophonists whose own albums for Cadence aren't much known to a general audience. The rhythm section, although capable, work on a slightly lower flame, but the main point of the record is to hear the locking of two vigorous horns.

MIKE CAIN (born 1966)
PIANO

**   **Strange Omen** Candid CCD 79505 CD
Cain; Bruce Saunders (*g*); Glen Velez (*perc*). 11/90.

Cain is currently working with Jack DeJohnette's band, and his pensive playing gets a respectable showing here; but the music is rather slow to unfold and make its mark, and the responsibility for what energy there is rests mainly with Saunders and Velez. Cain's interest in world music and composition makes Velez's appearance less of a surprise than it might be with most of today's younger pianists; and Saunders, while rather subliminally placed, contributes the two most focused compositions in 'Follow Through' and 'The Way Things Work'. Cain himself has a precise and fine touch, but too many of the pieces here – particularly the four solo 'Piano

Sketch' themes, which offer a slight recall of Chick Corea's ECM records – sound like home exercises rather than real compositions. Only on 'Bestido Al Cielo De Noche', where the trio work up a real interplay, are expectations fulfilled.

JOEY CALDERAZZO (born 1966)
PIANO, KEYBOARDS

**   **In The Door** Blue Note CDP 7951382 CD/MC
    Calderazzo; Branford Marsalis (ss, ts); Jerry Bergonzi, Michael Brecker (ts); Jay
    Anderson (b); Peter Erskine, Adam Nussbaum (d); Don Alias (perc). 90.

**   **To Know One** Blue Note CDP 7981652 CD/MC
    Calderazzo; Branford Marsalis (ss, ts); Jerry Bergonzi (ts); Dave Holland (b); Jack
    DeJohnette (d). 91.

Calderazzo came to prominence as a Michael Brecker sideman, and he has an effusive command of the piano. Brecker also returns the favour by playing a huge, blustering solo on 'Pest' on the first album, which is speckled with star cameos by the three saxophone players. But there's nothing very flavoursome about either of these records, which come out as glossy pieces of contemporary jazz product. His original themes are all style and little substance, and as deliberately energetic as the playing is on both records – with a real cast of heavyweights in support – each is disarmingly forgettable.

CALIFORNIA RAMBLERS
GROUP

***   **California Ramblers With Adrian Rollini** Village VILCD 011-2 CD
    Frank Cush, Chelsea Quealey, Roy Johnston (t); Red Nichols (c); Lloyd 'Ole' Olsen,
    Tommy Dorsey, Abe Lincoln, Ed Lappe (tb); Bobby Davis (ss, as, cl); Arnold
    Brilhart, Jimmy Dorsey, Pete Pumiglio (cl, as); Sam Ruby, Freddy Cusick (ts); Adrian
    Rollini (bsx, gfs, xy); Irving Brodsky, Jack Russin (p); Arthur Hand (vn); Ray
    Kitchingman, Tommy Felline (bj); Stan King (d, kazoo); Herb Weil (d); Arthur
    Fields, Ed Kirkeby (v). 8/23–7/27.

They rambled from Ohio, rather than California, to New York in 1921, and took up residency at the California Ramblers Inn at Pelham Bay Park. This was one of the best white dance bands of the 1920s, and they continued to record under this name – as well as countless pseudonyms for other labels – for 10 years. While men such as Nichols and the Dorseys turned up as guests from time to time, the nucleus of the band – Cush, Quealey, Davis and Rollini – gave it a distinctive, agile and sometimes slightly ironic sound: musicians as knowing as Rollini must have realized how much dross was coming out of Tin Pan Alley and, while they reserved their best energies for the superior hot tunes such as 'Stockholm Stomp', there's a tartness to their novelty tunes which raises them a notch above most of the other dance orchestras of the period. They really could swing, too: the 1924 record of 'Copenhagen', one of the first tracks here, can stand with any version of the day, and is at least as good as Fletcher Henderson's efforts at the tune. The reed players were the most interesting: Davis is erratic, but he had a lean, sinuous alto style which is actually heard to better advantage on records missed out of this compilation. Rollini is consistently superb, as powerful and hard-hitting on the earlier tracks as he is on the later ones, and he makes the bass saxophone into as big a sonic presence as it deserves.

To some extent, this compilation is a missed opportunity: the tracks seem to have been chosen almost at random from their huge discography, and the selection of many sides recorded for Edison and in the acoustic period means that the sound-quality will strike contemporary ears as more archaic than it should be. It also seems pointless to have included alternative takes of 'Sidewalk Blues' and the feeble 'Collegiate' when such fine records as 'T.N.T.', 'Pardon The Glove' and 'Jelly Roll Blues' have been passed over. These 18 tracks, though, are a useful introduction and will have to do until a superior disc comes along. The remastering is mostly good enough, although (as elsewhere in the Village series) some of the originals have uncorrected blemishes.

CAB CALLOWAY (born 1907)

VOCAL

***(*)   Cab Calloway & The Missourians 1929–1930 JSP CD 328 CD
Calloway; R. Q. Dickerson, Lammar Wright, Reuben Reeves (*t*); De Priest Wheeler
(*tb*); George Scott, Thornton Blue (*cl, as*); Andrew Brown (*cl, ts*); Walter Thomas (*cl,
ts, bs*); Earres Prince (*p*); Morris White (*bj*); Jimmy Smith (*bb, b*); Leroy Maxey (*d*);
Lockwood Lewis (*v*). 6/29–12/30.

The rough, almost violent playing of The Missourians, a black dance band recording in New
York but drawing most of its talent from the Mid-West, is as impassioned as any band of the
day, and their thinly disguised blues constructions, freakishly wild ensembles and occasional
snarling solos (by Wheeler and Dickerson especially) are still exciting to listen to. Their dozen
records are splendidly remastered here, along with two alternative takes, as well as the first ten
tracks featuring the man who took the band over, Cab Calloway. At his very first session – July,
1930, with an astonishingly virtuoso vocal on 'St Louis Blues' – he served notice that a major
jazz singer was ready to challenge Armstrong with an entirely different style.

***   Cab Calloway 1930–1931 Classics 516 CD
Calloway; R. Q. Dickerson, Lammar Wright, Reuben Reeves, Wendell Culley (*t*); De
Priest Wheeler (*tb*); Thornton Blue, Arville Harris (*cl, as*); Andrew Brown (*bcl, ts*);
Walter Thomas (*as, ts, bs, f*); Earres Prince, Bennie Payne (*p*); Morris White (*bj*);
Jimmy Smith (*bb, b*); Leroy Maxey (*d*). 7/30–6/31.

***(*)   Cab Calloway 1931–1932 Classics 526 CD
As above, except add Edwin Swayzee, Doc Cheatham (*t*), Harry White (*tb*), Eddie
Barefield (*cl, as, bs*), Al Morgan (*b*), omit Dickerson, Culley, Prince and Blue.
7/31–6/32.

***(*)   Cab Calloway 1932 Classics 537 CD
As above, except add Roy Smeck (*g*), Chick Bullock (*v*), omit Reeves and Smith.
6/32–12/32.

***   Cab Calloway 1932–1934 Classics 544 CD
As above, except omit Smeck and Bullock. 12/32–9/34.

It didn't take long for Calloway to sharpen up the band, even though he did it with
comparatively few personnel changes. Unlike the already-tested format of a vocal feature within
an instrumental record, Calloway's arrangers varied detail from record to record, Cab
appearing throughout some discs, briefly on others, and usually finding space for a fine team of
soloists. Some of the discs are eventful to an extraordinary extent: listen, for instance, to the
1935 'I Ain't Got Nobody' or the dazzling 1930 'Some Of These Days' to hear how
enthusiastically the band tackled its charts. The lexicon of reefers, Minnie the Moocher and
Smokey Joe, kicking gongs around and – of course – the fabulous language of hi-de-ho would
have soon become tiresome if it hadn't been for the leader's boundless energy and ingenious
invention: his vast range, from a convincing bass to a shrieking falsetto, has remained
unsurpassed by any male jazz singer, and he transforms material that isn't so much trite as
empty without the investment of his personality. This was a very popular band, long resident at
the Cotton Club, and the stability of the personnel says much about the good pay and working
conditions. The prodigious number of records they made both during and after the depression
was scarcely matched by any other bandleader, and it has taken the Classics operation no less
than ten well-filled CDs to cover them all. Unfortunately, reproduction is rather a mixed bag.
The earlier sides were made for Banner and other budget labels and suffer from some booming
recording; but there is a fair amount of surface noise, too. The first volume duplicates the last
ten tracks on the JSP CD and reproduction is clearly inferior on the Classics issue. However,
there's nothing unlistenable here, and since Calloway's music is at its freshest, casual listeners
may choose one of these earlier discs as representative.

(***)   Cab Calloway 1934–1937 Classics 554 CD
As above, except add Shad Collins, Irving Randolph (*t*), Claude Jones, Keg Johnson
(*tb*), Garvin Bushell, Thornton Blue (*cl, as*), Ben Webster (*ts*), Milt Hinton (*b*).
9/34–3/37.

***(*) **Cab Calloway 1937–1938** Classics 568 CD
As above, except add Chu Berry (*ts*), Chauncey Haughton (*cl, as*), Danny Barker (*g*),
omit Swayzee, Culley, Cheatham and Morgan. 3/37–3/38.

*** **Cab Calloway 1938–1939** Classics 576 CD
As above, except add June Richmond (*v*), Cozy Cole (*d*), omit Webster and White.
3/38–2/39.

***(*) **Cab Calloway 1939–1940** Classics 595 CD
As above, except add Dizzy Gillespie, Mario Bauza (*t*), Tyree Glenn (*tb, vib*), Quentin
Jackson (*tb*), Jerry Blake (*cl, as*), omit Maxey, Bushell and Richmond. 3/39–3/40.

***(*) **Cab Calloway 1940** Classics 614 CD
As above, except omit Collins, Randolph, Jones and Blue. 3–8/40.

*** **Cab Calloway 1940–1941** Classics 625 CD
As above, except add Jonah Jones (*t*). 3/40–7/41.

Calloway progressed through the 1930s with unquenchable enthusiasm. He took fewer risks on
his vocals and chose to set down some more straightforward ballad interpretations on several of
the later sides, but the singing is still exceptional, and there are new points of interest among
the soloists: Ben Webster appears on several tracks on the 1934–37 disc, and Chu Berry follows
him in as a regular soloist, while Gillespie, Jackson and Jefferson emerge too. The 1940 disc
features some arrangements by Benny Carter and the bizarre 'Cupid's Nightmare' score by
Don Redman, a mystifying mood piece. Jonah Jones, the last great soloist to arrive in this era,
sparks several of the 1941 tracks. Reproduction is mostly clean if sometimes lacking in sparkle
on the later discs, but the 1934–37 disc is marred by preposterously heavy surface noise on the
opening tracks and we must issue a caveat in this regard.

(*) **Jazz Off The Air Vol. 4 Spotlite SPJ148 LP
Calloway; Shad Collins, Jonah Jones, Lammar Wright, Russell Smith (*t*); Keg Johnson,
Tyree Glenn, Quentin Jackson, Fred Robinson (*tb*); Andy Brown (*cl, as*); Benny
Carter, Hilton Jefferson (*as*); Al Gibson, Illinois Jacquet, Ike Quebec (*ts*); Greely
Walton (*bs*); Benny Payne (*p*); Danny Barker (*g*); Milt Hinton (*b*); J. C. Heard (*d*).
43–46.

** **Cab Calloway '44** Magnetic MRCD 123 CD
Probably as above. 9/44.

(*) **Get With Cab West Wind 2403 CD
Probably similar to above. 44–50.

Cab Calloway continues performing to this day, but more recent records have been few and far
between. These airshots give some idea of the vitality of the group away from the studios. The
Spotlite LP draws together three different broadcasts: the second seems to have a speed
problem, but the other tunes feature some feisty playing, especially from new tenor Ike Quebec.
The Magnetic airshots are poorly recorded and give only a glimpse of some good workouts. The
West Wind set is a hotch-potch from hard-to-identify sources, but the sound is surprisingly full
and strong on most of the tracks and it gives some impression of the band in full flow.

MICHEL CAMILO
PIANO

(*) **Why Not? Electric Bird K28P 6371
Camilo; Lew Soloff (*t*); Chris Hunter (*as, ts*); Anthony Jackson (*b*); Dave Weckl (*d*);
Sammy Figueroa, Guarionex Aquino (*perc*). 2/85.

*** **In Trio** Electric Bird K28P 6445 CD/LP
Camilo; Anthony Jackson (*b*); Joel Rosenblaff, Dave Weckl (*d*). 6/86.

***(*) **Michel Camilo** CBS Portrait PRT 463330 1 CD
Camilo; Marc Johnson, Lincoln Jones (*b*); Joel Rosenblatt, Dave Weckl (*d*); Mongo
Santamaria (*perc*). 1–2/88.

Camilo grins broadly as he plays, almost palpably enjoying the music he makes. Born in the Dominican Republic and formally schooled, he had been a fixture on the New York club scene and a word-of-mouth star long before he won a major record deal. He is possessed of a formidable technique with very few traces of the conservatory left in it, beyond his fondness for occasional Bartók-isms in his folkier themes. Hurricane-fast, he sings along with himself, not in Bud Powell's anguished cry or with Jarrett's exaggerated passion, but in sheer exuberance.

The CBS Portrait is perhaps his best showing to date on record, a headlong set mainly of originals, but with an intriguing piano/conga version of Kenny Dorham's 'Blue Bossa', which confirms Camilo's jazz credentials and his impressive individuality at a stroke. 'Caribe' is also particularly strong, and evidence of Camilo's ability to mix vintages as well as genres.

The earlier trio recording is a little less sure of itself and certainly not so well produced, with a slight hazing of the top notes and percussion accents. The Latin component is also more prominent, which will please some and repel others.

An accomplished big band and orchestral arranger, Camilo sounds quite easy round horns. He has worked with Soloff and his regular Jackson/Weckl rhythm section before, under the name *French Toast* (Electric Bird K28P 6314). It's a fine album, but *Why Not?* is the one to look out for.

***(*) **On The Other Hand** Epic 466937 CD/LP/MC
Camilo; Michael Phillip Mossman (*t*); Ralph Bowen, Chris Hunter (*as*); Michael
Bowie (*b*); Cliff Almond (*d*); Sammy Figueroa (*perc*); D. K. Dyson (*v*).

Camilo attempts something more ambitious on the long 'Suite Sandrine: Part 3', which occupies nearly nine minutes of the second side, but the really impressive tracks are a version of Jaco Pastorius's 'City Of Angels' and Camilo's own thundering 'Impressions', which would have made an excellent climax, but is buried in the middle of the CD and towards the end of the LP's first side. There are, perhaps inevitably, some dullish fusion elements to negotiate, and D. K. Dyson's late-nite vocal on 'Forbidden Fruit' seems a touch *ersatz*. Otherwise, though, beyond reproach musically, and marred only by a rather loud, cranky sound-mix, which might sound good through a club system, but isn't easy to adjust on home stereo.

FRANK CAPP (born 1931)
DRUMS

(*) **Juggernaut Concord CCD 4040 CD/MC
Capp; Blue Mitchell, Gary Grant, Bobby Shew (*t*); Buster Cooper, Britt Woodman,
Alan Kaplan (*tb*); Bill Green, Marshall Royal (*as*); Richie Kamuca, Plas Johnson (*ts*);
Quin Davis (*bs*); Nat Pierce (*p*); Al Hendrickson (*g*); Chuck Berghofer (*b*); Ernie
Andrews (*v*). 79.

** **Juggernaut Strikes Again!** Concord CD 4183 CD/MC
Capp; Bill Berry, Snooky Young, Johnny Audino, Frank Szabo, Al Aarons, Warren
Luening (*t*); Alan Kaplan, Buster Cooper, George Bohannon, Mel Wanzo (*tb*);
Marshall Royal, Joe Roccisano, Jackie Kelso (*as*); Pete Christlieb, Bob Cooper, Bob
Efford (*ts*); Bill Green (*ss, bs*); Nat Pierce (*p*); Bob Maize (*b*); Ernie Andrews (*v*).
10–11/81.

(*) **Live At The Alley Cat Concord CCD 4336 CD/MC
Capp; Bill Berry, Snooky Young, Frank Szabo, Conte Candoli (*t*); Charles Loper,
Garnett Brown, Buster Cooper (*tb*); Dave Edwards, Joe Romano (*as*); Red Holloway,
Bob Cooper (*ts*); Bill Green (*bs*); Nat Pierce (*p*); Ken Pohlman (*g*); Chuck Berghofer
(*b*); Ernestine Anderson (*v*). 6/87.

Co-led by Capp, a drummer loaded with big-band experience, and Pierce, *Juggernaut* is essentially a troupe of sessionmen out for a good time on the stand. Because they're such proficient players, there's nothing casual about the music; but that also means that it never becomes quite as freewheeling as the musicians might imagine. Too many of the arrangements rely on stock devices pulled from the Basie and Herman books, while the section playing is sometimes overwound, especially on *Strikes Again!*. Nevertheless, so many good players are on hand that the results are seldom less than enjoyable, and when somebody cuts loose – as, say, Buster Cooper does on 'Things Ain't What They Used To Be', on Concord CCD 4183 – it's as thrilling as they intend. The live record features Anderson as guest vocalist and she is in fair voice, and never as fulsome as Andrews is on the other two discs.

IAN CARR (born 1933)
TRUMPET, FLUGELHORN

***   **Belladonna** Core 9.006784 CD
Carr; Brian Smith (*ts, ss, af, bamboo f*); Gordon Beck, Dave Macrae (*ky*); Allan Holdsworth (*g*); Roy Babbington (*b*); Clive Thacker (*d*); Trevor Tomkins (*perc*). 7/72.

Reissued in line with a broad re-evaluation of British jazz-rock of the 1970s, *Belladonna* comes across as a rather soft-focus version of Carr's pioneering work with Nucleus. The release of their *Elastic Rock* in 1970 was a significant moment in British jazz, opening it up to an audience for whom jazz meant Kenny Ball and Acker Bilk. *Belladonna* seems to fall in a slight lull between the sometimes explosive energy of the first two Nucleus albums (*Solar Plexus* left some listeners winded) and the more ambitious large-scale structures of *Labyrinth*, toured and recorded in 1973, heralding Carr's emergence as a major jazz composer. (In the same year, he published *Music Outside*, a significant study of contemporary jazz in Britain.)

In keeping with the rather vacuous original artwork, *Belladonna* is impressionistic and slightly soft-centred. Production values (the original deskwork was done by Jon Hiseman) were good for the time and are sharpened considerably by digital transfer, but this tends to do no more than throw into even sharper relief a vague feeling that tracks like 'Belladonna' and 'Suspension' are little more than a watered-down version of Miles Davis (Carr has also written a fine biography of his fellow-trumpeter). This is unfair, for it's clear that, whatever Miles's impact on Carr's playing (the soft harmonic slurs, dramatic stabs, out-of-tempo fills), Carr and Nucleus evolved independently out of contradictions and unfulfilled potentialities in the British music scene.

New Zealander Smith (who has since returned to the Southern Hemisphere) contributes two good compositions, rawer than Carr's but more straightforwardly argued, and some excellent saxophone and flute fills. Macrae (another Antipodean) is rather sliding and indistinct in this small-group context (compare his big-band work with Mike Westbrook), and it's Gordon Beck on his three tracks who gives the music the cohesion it seems to lack.

(*)   **Old Heartland MMC MMC 1016 CD
Carr; Phil Todd (*ss, bcl*); Mark Wood (*g*); Geoff Castle (*ky*); Steve Berry, Mo Foster, Dill Katz (*b*); John Marshall (*d*); Kreisler String Orchestra. 4–5/88.

They say it's a bad moment in a horn player's life when he contracts a desire to play with strings; look at Charlie Parker and Chet Baker. Carr and the Kreisler String Orchestra confound all doubts that this is an armchair gig. The composition is taut and full of incident, Carr is playing well again and the youthful Mancunian orchestra have an abundant energy that breaks through even this rather muzzy recording.

TERRI LYNE CARRINGTON (born 1962)
DRUMS, PERCUSSION

*(*)   **Real Life Story** Verve Forecast 837 697 CD/LP
Carrington (*d, perc, v*); Greg Osby (*as, ss*); Gerald Albright (*as*); Grover Washington Jr (*ts*); Wayne Shorter (*ts*); Patrice Rushen (*ky*); John Scofield, Carlos Santana, Hiram Bullock (*g*); Keith Jones (*b*); Don Alias (*perc*); Dianne Reeves (*v*). 89.

The American drummer who made a great impression with Wayne Shorter's group in the late 1980s made a disappointing stab at a solo project with this record. A cast of guest stars groups round the solid rhythm section of Jones, Rushen and Carrington, but the material takes a miserable bath in the clichés of light-fusion, made wetter by Carrington's misguided attempts at singing. The one exception is Rushen's oddly compelling mood piece 'Shh', which makes one wish that the leader had turned the task of musical direction over to the keyboard player.

BAIKIDA CARROLL
TRUMPET, FLUGELHORN

*(*)   Shadows And Reflections Soul Note SN 1023 LP
Carroll; Julius Hemphill (*as, ts*); Anthony Davis (*p*); Dave Holland (*b*); Pheeroan
AkLaff (*d*). 1/82.

A more or less perfect example of a sum amounting to considerably less than its parts, a
fabulously talented quintet producing nothing of any real moment. Davis's gait is perhaps a
little too stiff for a band with akLaff as pacemaker, and though Holland is as generously
adaptive as ever, there are signs of unease even from him. Carroll plays well, with a pleasantly
mordant tone, but, aside from a few arresting moments between him and Hemphill, there is
little meat on the bones of a truly spectacular band.

BENNY CARTER (born 1907)
ALTO SAXOPHONE, TRUMPET, CLARINET, VOCALS

***(*)   The Chronological Benny Carter, 1929–1933 Classics 522 CD
Carter; Louis Bacon, Shad Collins, Leonard Davis, Bill Dillard, Frank Newton,
Howard Scott, Bobby Stark, Rex Stewart (*t*); J. C. Higginbotham, Wilbur De Paris,
George Washington, Dicky Wells (*tb*); Jimmy Harrison (*tb, v*); Howard Johnson (*as*);
Don Redman (*as, v*); Wayman Carver (*as, f*); Chu Berry, Coleman Hawkins (*ts*);
Horace Henderson, Red Rodriguez, Luis Russell, Fats Waller, Teddy Wilson (*p*);
Benny Jackson, Lawrence Lucie (*g*); Richard Fulbright, Ernest Hill (*b*); John Kirby
(*b, bb*); Cyrus St Clair (*bb*); Sid Catlett (*d, vib*); Kaiser Marshall, George Stafford (*d*);
other personnel unidentified. 9/29, 12/30, 6/32, 3, 4 & 5/33.

***(*)   The Chronological Benny Carter, 1933–1936 Classics 530 CD
Carter; Henry Allen (*t, v*); Dick Clark, Leonard Davis, Bill Dillard, Max Goldberg,
Otis Johnson, Max Kaminsky, Eddie Mallory, Tommy McQuater, Irving Randolph,
Howard Scott, Russell Smith, Duncan Whyte (*t*); Ted Heath, Keg Johnson, Benny
Morton, Bill Mulraney, Floyd O'Brien, Wilbur De Paris, Fred Robinson, George
Washington, Dick Wells (*tb*); Howard Johnson, Andy McDevitt (*cl, as*); Wayman
Carver (*cl, as, f*); Glyn Paque, E. O. Pogson, Russell Procope, Ben Smith (*as*);
Coleman Hawkins (*cl, ts*); Chu Berry, Buddy Featherstonhaugh, Johnny Russell, Ben
Webster (*ts*); Pat Dodd, Red Rodriguez, Teddy Wilson (*p*); George Elliott, Clarence
Holiday, Lawrence Lucie (*g*); Al Burke, Ernest Hill, Elmer James (*b*); Sid Catlett,
Ronnie Gubertini, Walter Johnson (*d*); Charles Holland (*v*). 5 & 10/33, 12/34, 4/36.

***(*)   The Chronological Benny Carter, 1936 Classics 541 CD
Carter; Max Goldberg, Tommy McQuater, Duncan Whyte (*t*); Leslie Thompson (*t,
tb*); Lew Davis, Ted Heath, Bill Mulraney (*tb*); Freddie Gardner, Andy McDevitt (*cl,
as*); E. O. Pogson (*as*); Buddy Featherstonhaugh (*ts*); Pat Dodd, Billy Munn, Gene
Rodgers (*p*); George Elliott, Albert Harris, Ivor Mairants (*g*); Al Burke, Wally Morris
(*b*); George Elrick, Ronnie Gubertini (*d*). 4, 6 & 10/36.

***(*)   The Chronological Benny Carter, 1937–1939 Classics 552 CD
Carter; Jack Bulterman, Sam Dasberg, Rolf Goldstein, Tommy McQuater, Lincoln
Mills, Joe Thomas, Leslie Thompson, George Van Helvoirt, George Woodlen, Cliff
Woodridge (*t*); Jimmy Archey, Lew Davis, George Chisholm, Vic Dickenson, Bill
Mulraney, Harry van Oven, Marcel Thielemans (*tb*); Tyree Glenn (*tb, vib*); Freddie
Gardner, Andy McDevitt, Andre van der Ouderaa, Wim Poppink, Jimmy Williams (*cl,
as*); Fletcher Allen, Carl Frye, James Powell, Louis Stephenson (*as*); Alix Combelle,
Sal Doof, George Evans, Buddy Featherstonhaugh, Coleman Hawkins, Bertie King,
Castor McCord, Ernie Powell, Jimmy Williams (*ts*); Eddie Heywood Jr, Freddy
Johnson, Eddie Macauley, Nich de Roy, York de Souza (*p*); Albert Harris, Ulysses
Livingstone, Django Reinhardt, Ray Webb (*g*); Len Harrison, Hayes Alvis, Wally
Morris, Jack Pet (*b*); Al Craig, Kees Kranenburg, Robert Montmarche, Henry
Morrison (*d*). 1, 3 & 8/37, 3/38, 6/39.

**** The Chronological Benny Carter, 1940–1941 Classics 631 CD
Carter; Emmett Berry, Doc Cheatham, Bill Coleman, Roy Eldridge, Jonah Jones, Lincoln Mills, Sidney De Paris, Rostelle Reese, Russell Smith, Nathaniel Williams (*t*); Jimmy Archey, Joe Britton, Vic Dickenson, John McConnell, Benny Morton, Milton Robinson, Madison Vaughan (*tb*); Eddie Barefield, George Dorsey, Chauncey Haughton, Ernie Purce, Bill White (*as*); George James (*as, bs*); George Auld, Alfred Gibson, Coleman Hawkins, George Irish, Fred Mitchell, Ernie Powell, Stafford Simon, Fred Williams (*ts*); Sonny White (*p*); Bernard Addison, Everett Barksdale, William Lewis, Ulysses Livingstone, Herb Thomas (*g*); Hayes Alvis, Charles Drayton, John Kirby, Wilson Myers, Ted Sturgis (*b*); Sidney Catlett, J. C. Heard, Yank Porter, Keg Purnell, Berisford Shepherd, Al Taylor (*d*); Roy Felton, Maxine Sullivan, Joe Turner, The Mills Brothers (*d*). 5, 10 & 11/40, 1, 4 & 10/41.

**** The Complete Recordings: 1930–40 – Volume 1 Charly CD AFS 1022 3CD
Carter; Rune Ander, Louis Bacon, Jack Bulterman, Olaf Carlson, Doc Cheatham, Dick Clark, Shad Collins, Leonard Davis, Bill Dillard, Thore Ehrling, Max Goldberg, J. C. Higginbotham, George van Helvoirt, Keg Johnson, Otis Johnson, Max Kaminsky, Eddie Mallory, Tommy McQuater, Frank Newton, Kurt Pederson, Gosta Peterson, Irving Randolph, Fred Robinson, Axel Skouby, Joe Smith, Russell Smith, Bobby Stark, Rex Stewart, Leslie Thompson, Duncan Whyte (*t*); Ed Cuffee, Lew Davis, Uno Gorling, Jimmy Harrison, Ted Heath, Benny Morton, Bill Mulraney, Floyd O'Brien, Wilbur De Paris, Peder Rasmunsen, Marcel Thielemans, Leslie Thompson, Palmer Traulsen, George Vernon, George Washington, Dicky Wells (*tb*); Quentin Jackson (*tb, v*); Charles Redland (*cl*); Freddie Gardner, Hilton Jefferson, Andy McDevitt, Joe Moxley, Andre van der Ouderaa, Wim Poppink, Aage Voss (*cl, as*); Prince Robinson (*cl, ts*); Kai Ewans, Howard Johnson, Tony Mason, Glyn Paque, E. O. Pogson, Russell Procope, Ben Smith, Ole Thallen (*as*); Wayman Carver (*as, f*); Chu Berry, Sal Doof, George Evans, Buddy Featherstonhaugh, Zilas Gorling, Henry Larsen, Coleman Hawkins, Knut Knutsson, Johnny Russell, Anker Skjoldborg, Ben Webster (*ts*); Pat Dodd, Everett Haden, Horace Henderson, Stig Holm, Christian Jensen, Eddie McAuley, Gerry Moore, Billy Munn, Gene Rodgers, Rod Rodrigues, Nico de Rooy, Teddy Wilson (*p*); Todd Rhodes (*p, cel*); Bernard Addison, George Elliott, Albert Harris, Clarence Holiday, Benny Jackson, Lawrence Lucie, Ivor Mairants, Ulrik Neumann, Olle Sahlin (*g*); Dave Wilborn (*bj, g*); Al Burke, Richard Fulbright, Ernest Hill, Elmer James, Wally Morris, Kelof Nielsen, Jack Pet, Thore Sederby (*b*); John Kirby (*b, bb*); Billy Taylor (*bb*); Sture Aberg, Cuba Austin, Al Craig, George Elrick, Ronnie Gubertini, Gosta Haden, Walter Johnson, Eric Kragh, Kees Kranenburg (*d*); Sid Catlett (*d, vib*); Charles Holland, Elisabeth Welch (*v*); collective personnel; some identifications uncertain. 12/30, 9/31, 6/32, 3 & 10/33, 12/34, 4, 6, 8, 9 & 10/36, 1 & 3/37.

By 1930, Carter was being widely recognized as a gifted young arranger and multi-instrumentalist. Carter's charts, like his playing, are characteristically open-textured and softly bouncing, but seldom lightweight; though he had a particular feel for the saxophone section, as is often noted, and he pioneered a more modern approach to big-band reeds, his gifts extend throughout the orchestra. As a soloist, he developed in a direction rather different from that of Johnny Hodges, who explored a darker register and a less buoyant sensibility.

Carter's earliest recordings with the Chocolate Dandies (the band included Coleman Hawkins) and with McKinney's Cotton Pickers put considerable emphasis on his multi-instrumentalism. Set against trombonist Quentin Jackson's suprisingly effective vocals, he sounds poised and elegant – the essential Carter qualities – whatever his horn, and two takes each of 'Do You Believe In Love At First Sight' and 'Wrap Your Troubles In Dreams' demonstrate how beautifully crafted and custom-made his choruses habitually were.

None of these performances is included on the Classics *Chronological* format which is, on the face of it, rather surprising, since Volumes 1 and 2 include sides Carter recorded with Spike Hughes's Negro Orchestra. Apart from that, the two series are the same, but for the fact that Affinity's first volume stops in March 1937 with a Ramblers session cut for Decca, and the *Chronological* pushes on to the high spots of Carter's career just before Pearl Harbor, when he had the likes of Doc Cheatham, Vic Dickenson and Jonah Jones in his band and was sounding completely mature. As far as comparisons of sound are concerned, the Affinity is richer and more atmospheric than the Classics sets, which tend to sound rather tinny. There's certainly no strong advantage in the choice of material (Djangologists may jump at a March 1938 Paris session on the fourth *Chronological* that included the guitarist); the few variations have a roundabouts-and-swings feel. Affinity's three-CD box and booklet is neat and attractive, but discs can't be bought individually. You pays your money . . .

In the early 1930s, Carter's band had been increasingly identified as a proving ground for young talent, and the number of subsequently eminent names appearing in Carter sections increases as the decade advances. In 1936, the urbane young American took up a post as staff arranger for the BBC Dance Orchestra, then under Henry Hall. The London period saw some excellent recording with the local talent, including 'Swingin' At Maida Vale', and there are two separate Vocalion sessions with Elisabeth Welch, the first yielding the classic 'When Lights Are Low', the later and better superb arrangements of 'Poor Butterfly' and 'The Man I Love'.

Later sets with Kai Ewans' orchestra (not on *Chronological*) and a variety of European bands are less striking, perhaps because after five (or Affinity's three) well-filled discs, Carter's particular mastery does, unjustifiably, begin to pall. There is little tension in a Carter solo, which is presented bright and fresh like a polished apple, and his seemingly effortless approach is rather hard to square with a new construction of jazz improvisation which came in with bebop. However, these sides and those following on in the early 1940s are significant because, for much of the next two and a half decades, Carter concentrated on lucrative film music and small groups.

*** **When Lights Are Low** Conifer/Happy Days CDHD 131 CD
Carter; Max Goldberg, Tommy McQuater, Duncan Whyte (*t*); Leslie Thompson (*t, tb*); Lew Davis, Ted Heath, Bill Mulraney (*tb*); Freddie Gardner, Andy McDevitt (*cl, as*); E. O. Pogson (*as*); Buddy Featherstonhaugh (*ts*); Pat Dodd, Billy Munn, Gene Rodgers (*p*); George Elliott, Albert Harris, Ivor Mairants (*g*); Al Burke, Wally Morris (*b*); George Elrick, Ronnie Gubertini (*d*). 4, 6 & 10/36.

A useful abstract of the London sessions Carter made for Vocalion. Conifer have even managed to unearth one track – a rejected take of 'Gin And Jive' – not covered by Affinity's completism. Oddly, though, they skip two better tracks, 'Scandal In A Flat' and 'Accent On Swing', from the same session. Carter returned to 'Gin And Jive' in January 1937 and cut a vastly superior version with essentially the same band. Swings and roundabouts again, but the Conifer reissue will appeal to anyone who doesn't want to fork out for the three-CD set (with a volume to come) or who has a particular interest in the development of hot music in Britain in the 1930s.

*** **Devil's Holiday** JSP JSPCD 331 CD
Carter; Dick Clark, Shad Collins, Leonard Davis, Bill Dillard, Freddie Goodman, Ben Gusick, Otis Johnson, Reunald Jones, Max Kaminsky, Eddie Mallory, Chelsea Quealey, Irving Randolph, Russell Smith (*t*); J. C. Higginbotham, Floyd O'Brien, Wilbur De Paris, Keg Johnson, Benny Morton, Fred Robinson, George Washington (*tb*); Mezz Mezzrow (*cl, as*); Howard Johnson, Glyn Paque, Russell Procope, Ben Smith (*as*); Wayman Carver (*as, f*); Chu Berry, Bud Freeman, Johnny Russell, Ben Webster (*ts*); Nicholas Rodriguez, Willie 'The Lion' Smith', Teddy Wilson (*p*); Clayton Duerr, Clarence Holiday, Lawrence Lucie (*g*); Pops Foster, Ernest Hill, Elmer James, John Kirby (*b*); Walter Johnson, Jack Maisel, Chick Webb (*d*); Sid Catlett (*d, vib*); Charles Holland (*v*). 3, 10 & 11/33, 5 & 12/34.

The excellent 1933 sessions with the Chocolate Dandies and Carter's own orchestra are already available on Classics and Charly, as are the December 1934 sessions. A useful addition to these well-transferred sides are the tracks recorded in May 1934 with Mezz Mezzrow (who is alleged to have played drums on the earlier 'Krazy Kapers'). These represent a third of the album and will be useful for collectors, with fine performances on 'Dissonance' and 'Old Fashioned Love'. Otherwise, nothing to recommend this over the items discussed above.

*** **On The Air** Nueva JU 327 CD
Carter; Miles Davis, Lincoln Mills, Ira Pettiford, Calvin Strickland, Joe Thomas, Freddie Trainer, Walter Williams, Bob Woodlen (*t*); Tyree Glenn (*tb, vib*); Jimmy Archey, Vic Dickenson, Al Grey, Charles Johnson, John Morris, Candy Ross (*tb*); Bob Graettinger (*sax*); Joe Epps, Carl Frey, Jimmy Powell (*as*); Harold Clark, Castor McCord, Ernie Powell (*ts*); Willard Brown (*bs, ts*); Eddie Heywood, Sonny White (*p*);

James Cannady, Ulysses Livingstone (*g*); Hayes Alvis, Thomas Moultrie (*b*); Percy Briced, Ted Fields, Henry Morrison (*d*); Dell St John (*v*); collective personnel; some identifications uncertain. 7/39, 46.

[***(*) **Coleman Hawkins/Benny Carter** Forlane UCD 19011 CD]
Carter; Freddie Webster (*t*); Claude Dunson, Jake Porter, Gerald Wilson, Eugene Snooky Young (*t*); Shorty Haughton, J. J. Johnson, Alton Moore (*tb*); Porter Kilbert (*as*); Bumps Myers, Gene Porter (*ts*); Willard Brown (*bs*); Teddy Brannon, Sonny White (*p*); Ulysses Livingstone (*g*); Curley Russell (*b*); Oscar Bradley, Max Roach (*d*); collective personnel; some identifications uncertain. 43.

***(*) **Benny Carter And His Orchestra** Jazz Door 1206 CD
Carter; Paul Cohen, Miles Davis, Irving Lewis, Gerald Wilson (*t*); Rex Stewart (*c*); Al Grey, J. J. Johnson, Alan Moore, Candy Ross (*tb*); Barney Bigard (*cl*); Porter Kilbert (*as*); Dexter Gordon, Bumps Myers, Lyle Parker, Lucky Thompson (*ts*); Willard Brown (*bs*); Sonny White, Mary Lou Williams (*p*); James Cannady (*g*); Charlie Drayton, Thomas Moultrie (*b*); Percy Brice, Max Roach (*d*); The Pied Pipers (*v*). 45–48.

Carter returned to the United States in 1938, by which time the big-band era was well under way. His sterling talents seem to have appealed more to other musicians than to the public at large and, as the war progressed, he switched coasts. The Forlane material, which shoulders for space with some fine Coleman Hawkins tracks, features one of Carter's best bands, one that included Gerald Wilson (soon himself to be an influential big-band modernist), the trumpet talents of Snooky Young and the 18-year-old J. J. Johnson, making his professional debut.

Metronome concluded around this time that Carter's bands died so slowly that *rigor mortis* had no chance to set in. From the point of view of the dance floor, he offered little enough, but his arrangements have more than survived transfer to unforgiving CD and there is some astonishing musicianship on the slightly later Jazz Door material. Miles Davis plays on 'Just You, Just Me', 'Jump Call' and an untitled original; but the highlight is a version of Mary Lou Williams's 'Roll 'Em', with the composer at the piano in an arrangement that rivals the Clouds of Joy original.

The Nueva material is scrappier than the other two and of less robust provenance. Split over a seven-year period, it's also much less consistent in tone. The Jazz Door disc probably remains the best bet, and it's nice to imagine one can hear future careers in embryo.

**** **3, 4, 5: The Verve Small Group Sessions** Verve 849395 CD
Carter; Don Abney, Oscar Peterson, Teddy Wilson (*p*); Herb Ellis (*g*); Ray Brown, George Duvivier (*b*); Louie Bellson, Jo Jones, Bobby White (*d*).

Irritatingly, no exact dates are provided for these sterling sessions for Norman Granz's label. The trio sides with Teddy Wilson and Jo Jones are seeing the light of day only after 40 years in the vaults; mysteriously, because a similar session with Art Tatum and Louie Bellson *was* released. Far from wondering at the absence of a bass player (and Wilson wasn't one of the big left-hand men), one might almost wish that the under-recorded Jones had been left out altogether, so bright is the interplay between alto and piano. Wilson is supreme on 'June In January' and the Parker/Sanicola/Sinatra 'This Love Of Mine', a perfect vehicle for Carter's sinuous para-bop phrasing.

An 'audio disclaimer' pointing out 22 seconds of 'slight wow and warbling' on 'Moonglow' has to be considered somewhat diversionary, for the music on the middle quartet section really isn't up to the rest of the album. Originally released as *Moonglow: Love Songs By Benny Carter And His Orchestra* (*sic*.), the material is a bit lame, however beautifully played.

The final three tracks, also unreleased, come from a super-session with rising star, Oscar Peterson. Again, the drummer – added for the date – makes very little mark on the music, which includes the intriguing 'Don't You Think', written by Stuff Smith.

Despite some reservations about the middle tracks, this makes a superb introduction to Carter the player (there's not a single writing credit) at a fine stage in his distinguished career.

**** **Jazz Giant** Original Jazz Classics OJC 167 CD/LP/MC
Carter; Frank Rosolino (*tb*); Ben Webster (*ts*); André Previn, Jimmy Rowles (*p*); Barney Kessel (*g*); Leroy Vinnegar (*b*); Shelly Manne (*d*). 6, 7 & 10/57, 4/58.

***   **Swingin' The Twenties** Original Jazz Classics OJC 339 CD/LP
       Carter; Earl Hines (*p*); Leroy Vinnegar (*b*); Shelly Manne (*d*). 11/58.

Carter was still playing trumpet (and piano on the later album) in addition to alto saxophone at this stage, and sounding remarkably adept. The material on *Swingin'* is generally pretty bland, though 'A Monday Date' and 'Laugh, Clown, Laugh' uncover some interesting harmonic wrinkles. The rhythm section was one of the best money could buy at the time, nicely balancing old and new. *Jazz Giant* is one of Carter's best small-group records, full of imagination and invention, and the interchanges with Webster are classic. Originally released on Contemporary, it's very much in line with that label's philosophy of easy swing. The CD of *Swingin'* includes some interesting alternative takes.

****   **The King** Pablo 2310768 CD/LP
       Carter; Milt Jackson (*vib*); Joe Pass (*g*); Tommy Flanagan (*p*); John B. Williams (*b*);
       Jake Hanna (*d*). 2/76.

Jackson is another brilliant improviser whose mellifluous approach has led detractors to suspect him of giving short weight. Here again, he underlines his genius with a dozen blues choruses of immense sophistication. The closing D flat blues opens up the kind of harmonic territory on which Carter and Flanagan both thrive, and the set ends with a ringing affirmation. Williams is rather anonymous and Pass seems to miscue slightly on a couple of faster ensembles. Otherwise hard to fault.

***(*)   **Wonderland** Pablo 2310922 CD/LP/MC
       Carter; Harry Edison (*t*); Eddie 'Lockjaw' Davis (*ts*); Ray Bryant (*p*); Milt Hinton
       (*b*); Grady Tate (*d*). 11/76.

Remarkable to think that as long ago as 1976 Carter was approaching his seventieth birthday. He sounds in good form on this relaxed set, ably accompanied by Edison (Carter let others handle the brass duties by this stage) and an uncharacteristically cool Lockjaw Davis. 'Misty' was to remain a favourite, played with curious emphases and a wry unsentimentality.

***(*)   **Montreux '77** Original Jazz Classics OJC 374 CD/LP/MC
       Carter; Ray Bryant (*p*); Niels-Henning Ørsted-Pedersen (*b*); Jimmie Smith (*d*). 7/77.

1977 was a monster year at Montreux, and a good deal of the music performed over the main weekend has been preserved on live Pablo releases (and subsequently on OJC). The Carter set is one of the best of them. Though his soloing here doesn't quite match up to some choruses on a Count Basie Jam from the following day, 'Three Little Words', 'Body And Soul' and 'On Green Dolphin Street' are absolutely sterling. The band swings comfortably and NHØP plays delightful countermelodies on 'In A Mellow Tone'.

***   **Summer Serenade** Storyville SLP 4047 LP
       Carter; Kenny Drew (*p*); Jesper Lundgaard (*b*); Ed Thigpen (*d*); Richard Boone (*d*).
       8/80.

Carter's small-group encounters, like this Scandinavian session, were a well-polished act; but it takes a certain genius to make the umpteenth version of quite banal tunes like 'Back Home In Indiana' and 'When Lights Are Low' sound quite as freshly minted as Carter does here. The rhythm section is admirably professional and Boone holds his wheesht for all but one track, which is all to the good.

***(*)   **A Gentleman And His Music** Concord CCD 4285 CD/MC
       Carter; Joe Wilder (*t, flhn*); Scott Hamilton (*ts*); Ed Bickert (*g*); Gene Harris (*p*);
       John Clayton Jr (*b*); Jimmie Smith (*d*). 8/85.

A wonderfully urbane set which puts Carter in the company of the young traditionalist, Scott Hamilton, whose tone and relaxed inventiveness are perfectly in keeping with Carter's own. No real surprises; just a generously proportioned album of first-rate jazz music, professionally performed and recorded.

***(*)   **Meets Oscar Peterson** Pablo 2310926 CD/LP/MC
       Carter; Oscar Peterson (*p*); Joe Pass (*g*); Dave Young (*b*); Martin Drew (*d*).

How much more interesting this might have been as a duo. Even allowing for some melodic breaks from Pass, the rhythm backings are bland and undynamic enough to seem superfluous. 'Baubles, Bangles And Beads' moves at the gentle lope both men seem to prefer nowadays, and Peterson's statement of the theme is about as straightforward as he's ever been.

***   **My Kind Of Trouble** Pablo 2310935 Cd/LP/MC
        Carter; Art Hillery (*p*); Joe Pass (*g*); Andy Simpkins (*b*); Ronnie Bedford (*d*). 88.

Disappointing only because the band is. The rhythms never quite cohere and on 'Berkeley Bounce' and 'Gee, Baby, Ain't I Good To You', Carter appears to be leading the count rather than playing on top of it. Nevertheless, he is in finer voice than seems decent for a man entering his eighties and well past his fiftieth year of climbing on and off bandstands.

***(*)   **All That Jazz – Live At Princeton** Limelight 820841 CD
        Carter; Clark Terry (*t, flhn, v*); Kenny Barron (*p*); Rufus Reid (*b*); Kenny Washington
        (*d*); Billy Hill (*v*). 11/90.

Carter first played at Princeton University in 1928, as a member of the Fletcher Henderson Orchestra. In the late 1970s, he became a visiting professor and was awarded an honorary doctorate. This 1990 concert was treated as a triumphant homecoming. Thelonious Monk's 'Hackensack' was played cold, after Clark Terry hummed the melody to Carter as they walked onstage. The band get in behind and off they all go. 'I'm Beginning To See The Light' and 'Misty' were more familiar themes to the saxophonist, but he gives the Garner/Burke tune a curious off-balance feel that is unexpectedly witty. 'Now's The Time' is renowned as a Parker tune, though the theme is known to be much older. Carter delves down into its roots and comes up with something that seems to unite swing and bop approaches. Terry growls round him like a friendly dog pretending to be tough. Most Carter enthusiasts would have willingly dispensed with the services of Billy Hill, who comes on for the last four tunes. The title-track has some vocals from the two horn men but the charm is strictly limited.

BETTY CARTER (born 1930)
VOCALS

****   **Finally – Betty Carter** Roulette EMI CDP 795333 CD
        Carter; Norman Simmons (*p*); Lisle Atkinson (*b*); Al Harewood (*d*). 12/69.

*****   **The Audience with Betty Carter** Verve 835684 2CD
        Carter; John Hicks (*p*); Curtis Lundy (*b*); Kenny Washington (*d*). 79.

****   **Jazzbuhne Berlin '85** Repertoire REPCD 4901 CC CD
        Carter; Benny Green (*p*); Tarik Sha (*b*); Lewis Nash (*d*). 6/85.

***(*)   **Compact Jazz: Betty Carter** Verve 843274 CD
        Carter; Jerry Dodgion (*as*); Don Braden (*ts*); Benny Green, Onaje Allan Gumbs, John
        Hicks, Danny Mixon, Khalid Moss, Stephen Scott (*p*); Michael Bowie, Ira Coleman,
        Curtis Lundy, Buster Williams (*b*); Troy Davis, Winard Harper, Louis Hayes, Chip
        Lyle, Lewis Nash, Kenny Washington (*d*); strings. 76–87.

****   **Droppin' Things** Verve 843991 CD
        Carter; Freddie Hubbard (*t*); Craig Handy (*ts*); Geri Allen, Marc Cary (*p*); Tarus
        Mateen (*b*); Gregory Hutchinson (*d*). 5 & 6/90.

Billie Holiday once said that she didn't feel like she was singin', she felt like she was playin' a horn. So, too, with Betty Carter, who transcended the reductive tag 'bop vocalist' and created a style that combined the fluent improvisational grace of an alto saxophone with an uncanny ⸺⸺ of diction. Even when her weighting of a lyric is almost surreal, its significance is ⸺⸺ sarcastically subversive. The latter quality has allowed her to skate on ⸺⸺ nal standard material, much of which has acquired a veneer of ⸺⸺ days being heard only as instrumentals; 'Body And Soul' is the ⸺⸺ yed with 'Heart And Soul' on *Finally*, it has an almost discursive ⸺⸺ the familiar melody to the point of virtual breakdown (a device ⸺⸺ ing). 'Blue Moon' is almost unrecognizable in its staccato, deliberately ⸺⸺ almost, but not quite. Like all her best work, this 1969 reissue was recorded live. Carter can sound remarkably dead in a studio, as on the ballad duet with Geri Allen on the recent *Droppin' Things*. Because she needs a crowd to bounce off, just as much as she needs rhythmically and harmonically subtle accompanists (and she recruits only the best) the title of *The Audience With Betty Carter* is a multiple pun. She works the room with consummate skill, sliding from the slightly squeaky *faux naïf* mannerisms that prompted Lionel Hampton to call her 'Betty Bebop' (a less condescending and more accurate nickname than she liked to acknowledge) to soaring climbs up off the bottom that wouldn't disgrace Sarah Vaughan. Her feminism is not so much explicit in the choice or creation of material ('30 Years' on *Droppin' Things* is a relatively untypical original) as in the way she subverts all expectations about female singers, and about women in the bebop business, where they occupied a notoriously marginal and subservient role.

It's clear that the East German audience on *Jazzbuhne '85* are less responsive than on the Verves and Roulette. 'My Favourite Things' loses its ditsy send-up quality and becomes a much straighter performance. Some of the responsibility for that is down to the presence of Benny Green rather than the more sympathetic Hicks. Carter's trio are always vital to her conception, and the wild opening to 'Girl Talk' on *Finally* is a perfect example of how she breaks up the accepted conventions of singer-and-accompaniment. The arrival of Hubbard and Handy on *Droppin' Things* whistles a whole new ball game, and her diction changes yet again, probably subconsciously.

Audience and (a short nose behind) *Finally* are among the finest vocal jazz albums ever made, and everyone should give at least the first a whirl. The Verve compilation isn't too bad, but nothing matches Carter in her proper context.

JOHN CARTER (1929–91)
CLARINET, ALTO SAXOPHONE

***   **Variations On Selected Themes For Jazz Quintet** Moers 01056 LP
     Carter; Bobby Bradford (*t*); James Newton (*f*); Bob Stewart (*tba*); Phillip Wilson (*d*).

(*)   **A Suite Of American Folk Pieces For Solo Clarinet Moers 02014 LP
     Carter (*cl* solo). 8/79.

John Carter emerged from the Fort Worth community, which also spawned Ornette Coleman and Ed Blackwell, and his playing is certainly as free and inquiring as Coleman's own. But Carter has preferred to concentrate on the clarinet rather than the alto, and his music offers a refraction of that instrument's jazz history while remaining essentially modern: few contemporary players can match Carter's combination of old, woodsy timbre with sharply modern conceptions. The records under his own name, though, achieve a somewhat mixed success. Nothing on the quintet LP surpasses the two excellent discs made for Revelation in the late 1960s, where Carter and Bradford created some of the most inventive variations on the 'classic' free-jazz setting: Newton's presence softens rather than adds to the music. The solo record is a promising notebook on black music history, yet its academicism is perhaps too proudly self-conscious: the cakewalk, blues and funk impressions finally sound contrived, for all Carter's instrumental mastery.

***   **Dauwhe** Black Saint BSR 0057 CD/LP
     Carter; Bobby Bradford (*c*); Charles Owens (*ss, cl, ob*); James Newton (*f*); Red Callender (*tba*); Roberto Miguel Miranda (*b*); William Jeffrey (*d*); Luis Peralta (*perc*). 2–3/82.

***   **Castles Of Ghana** Gramavision 18-8603-1 LP
     Carter; Bobby Bradford (*c*); Baikida Carroll (*t, v*); Benny Powell (*tb*); Marty Ehrlich (*bcl, perc*); Terry Jenoure (*vn, v*); Richard Davis (*b*); Andrew Cyrille (*d*). 11/85.

***(*)   **Fields** Gramavision 18-8809-1 LP
     As above, except Don Preston (*ky*) replaces Carroll, Fred Hopkins (*b*) replaces Davis. 3/88.

***(*)   **Shadows On A Wall** Gramavision R2 79422 CD
     As above. 3/89.

These four records are part of a set of five by Carter, entitled 'Roots And Folklore', which purports to create an episodic history of native American music as the composer sees and hears it. Unfortunately, at least the third instalment, *Dance Of The Love Ghosts*, is currently out of print. But each disc stands in its own right as a history lesson-cum-celebration of black Americana as Carter has it, creating a sense of repertory with their evocations of folk tunes, blues and gospel strains and their contemporary parallel in the expert free improvising of the differing groups.

The final two discs in the sequence are the most convincing, perhaps because the band is especially in tune with Carter's intentions. Bradford is always a sympathetic collaborator, but more surprising is the shrewd keyboard commentary by Preston – who acts as both colourist and improviser – and Jenoure, whose vocal parts narrate some of the music and whose violin is strikingly apt. Carter's own playing is his finest on record: *Fields* includes a number of extemporizations that take in every part of the clarinet's range while holding to an authentically countrified sound.

RON CARTER (born 1937)
DOUBLE BASS, BASS GUITAR, CELLO; OTHER INSTRUMENTS

***   **Where?** Original Jazz Classics OJC 432 CD/LP/MC
Carter; Eric Dolphy (*as, bcl, f*); Mal Waldron (*p*); George Duvivier (*b*); Charles Persip (*d*). 6/61.

**   **Spanish Blue** CTI EPC 45093 2 CD
Carter; Hubert Laws (*f*); Jay Berliner (*g*); Roland Hanna, Leon Pendarvis (*p*); Billy Cobham (*d*); Ralph McDonald (*perc*). 11/74.

***   **Peg Leg** Original Jazz Classics OJC 621 CD//LP/MC
Carter; Jerry Dodgion, Walter Kane, George Marge (*reeds*); Jay Berliner (*g*); Kenny Barron (*p*); Buster Williams (*b*); Ben Riley (*d*). 11/77.

**   **Pastels** Original Jazz Classics OJC 665 CD/MC
Carter; Kenny Barron (*p*); Hugh McCracken (*g, hca*); Harvey Mason (*d*); strings. 10/76.

If 'piccolo bass' isn't a contradiction in terms, then it probably ought to be. As befits perhaps the most technically adept bassist of recent times, the Carter discography is colossal, well in excess of 500 albums. Though the greater bulk of these is, of course, as sideman, Carter has also made a respectable number of albums as leader. It's a pity that these should be of such mixed quality, marred by Carter's flirtation with electric bass guitar (on which he is a surprisingly indifferent player) and the aforementioned octave-divided instrument which allows a bassist to mimic a lead guitarist. The irony is that Carter, such a fleet and resonant player on the acoustic instrument, becomes very anonymous when electricity is involved.

Spanish Blue is a good, collectable set, featuring some of the bassist's most melodic work. The rock influences seem better assimilated and in return Carter shows how maddeningly plodding and abecedarian most rock bass actually is. The later *New York Slick*, which revives much of the *Spanish Blue* line-up, is also well worth tracking down, though the sound-quality is, by contrast, a lot less distinct.

Peg Leg is excellent, with a first-rate version of Monk's 'Epistrophy' (piccolo bass and all), though the overall sound is a little floaty and indistinct in register. The quality set is *Where?*, which must also count as a significant item in the Dolphy discography. It's dominated by a brilliant bass/clarinet duet of the sort Dolphy worked many times with Charles Mingus, and by a fine, unsentimental reading of 'Softly As In A Morning Sunrise'. Carter plays cello on 'Really' and 'Saucer Eyes' as he had on Dolphy's second album, *Out There*, also originally released on New Jazz. Waldron and (on the two cello tracks) Duvivier give firm support and Persip once again displays the skills that should have guaranteed him a higher rating than he currently receives in histories of the music.

History will doubtless draw a discreet veil over *Pastels* and, while there is nothing inherently suspect about a 'with strings' album (Charlie Parker made some, after all), a strings album entitled *Pastels* should ring a warning bell somewhere.

***   **Heart And Soul** Timeless SJP 158 LP
Carter; Cedar Walton (*p*). 12/81.

***   **Live at Village West** Concord CJ 245 MC

***   **Telephone** Concord CCD 4270 CD/MC
Carter; Jim Hall (*g*). 11/82, 8/84.

Carter's bass is unmistakably a *string* instrument. That is made clear on his unexpected and thoroughly impressive collaboration with the Kronos Quartet (Landmark LLP 1505) and by these fine duos. The Hall sets are absolutely top-drawer, with superb standard performances of 'All The Things You Are', 'Embraceable You', 'Bag's Groove', 'Baubles, Bangles and Beads', and Sonny Rollins's 'St Thomas', while *Telephone* includes a lovely 'Stardust' and the obligatory duo, 'Alone Together'.

Walton doesn't quite achieve Hall's rapport, but *Heart And Soul* is none the less exemplary, with the pianist's long melodic lines sparking some of Carter's most interestingly lateral play.

MICHAEL CARVIN (born 1944)
DRUMS

***   **The Camel** Steeplechase SCS 1038 LP
Carvin; Cecil Bridgewater (*t, flhn*); Sonny Fortune (*ss, as, f*); Ron Burton (*p*); Calvin Hill (*b*). 7/75.

**   **First Time** Muse MR 5352 LP
Carvin; Cecil Bridgewater, Claudio Roditi (*t, flhn*); Frank Lacy (*tb*); Ron Bridgewater, John Stubblefield (*ts*); Onaje Allan Gumbs (*ky*); David Williams (*b*). 10/86.

(*)   **Between Me And You Muse MR 5370 CD/LP
As above, except Cyrus Chestnut (*p*) and Calvin Hill (*b*) replace Lacy, Williams and Gumbs. 9/89.

***   **Revelation** Muse MCD 5399 CD/MC
As above, except add Sonny Fortune (*as*); John Hicks (*p*). 12/89.

Carvin's pinpoint technique and easeful approach to a wide variety of settings have granted him a valued if somewhat anonymous position among contemporary drummers. He played plenty of jazz-rock in the 1970s, but his one date as a leader from that era, the Steeplechase album, is straight ahead and made characterful by the presence of the excitable Fortune, who always lends extra fire to a session. In the 1980s he involved himself heavily in teaching, but his occasional albums for Muse have resulted in some enjoyable if rather carelessly focused music. Rudy Van Gelder's engineering rarely serves the band's drummer as well as it might, and the sound sometimes reduces Carvin to a splashy noisemaker. But he enthuses his sidemen, and there are some fine improvisations scattered through the three records. *First Time* and *Between Me And You* are a bit diffuse, and each suffers from a lack of either strong originals or interesting standards; the Bridgewaters too are a less than challenging front line. But *Revelation* is a good deal stronger. Fortune returns and immediately raises the general game, blazing through the title-track (and inspiring Roditi to his best work) and smouldering on a very fetching 'Body And Soul', while the contrasts between Bridgewater's nervy horn and Roditi's confident brilliance result in useful creative tension.

AL CASEY (born 1915)
GUITAR

(*)   **Jumpin' With Al Black & Blue 233056 CD
Casey; Arnett Cobb, Candy Johnson (*ts*); Jay McShann (*p*); Milt Buckner (*org*); Roland Lobligeois (*b*); Paul Gunther, Michael Silva (*d*). 7–8/73.

The former Fats Waller sideman worked busily in the 1980s, but these sides were recorded at a rather quiet point in his career. The quartet sides with McShann, an old *compadre*, are the most successful, with Casey humming along à la Slam Stewart to his crustily picked solos; he plays acoustic for most of the record, but there are three bouncing work-outs on electric with Buckner and Johnson in simmering fettle. Cobb sits in for two tracks and sounds even more cantankerous than usual. Dry, closely miked recording which suits the music quite well.

PHILIP CATHERINE (born 1942)
GUITAR, ELECTRIC GUITAR, GUITAR SYNTHESIZER

***(*)   Sleep, My Love CMP CD 5
Catherine; Charlie Mariano (*ss, as, f, nagaswaram*); Jasper van't Hof (*ky, kalimba*).
12/78 & 2/79.

Catherine is of mixed English/Belgian parentage. His first guitar influence, apart from the unavoidable Django Reinhardt, was the brilliant Belgian René Thomas (who died prematurely in 1975), but he was quick to respond to the jazz-rock techniques of both John McLaughlin and Larry Coryell, duetting with the latter to great effect on Elektra ELK K 52086 and 52232 (see Coryell).

Sleep, My Love is absolutely gorgeous, a near-perfect blend of instrumental voices. Catherine had still not emerged as a fully mature composer at this point; his 'Janet' (repeated on Elektra ELK K 5244, below) is very personal and slightly guarded, and his most significant compositional input is a remarkable arrangement of Schönberg's expressionistic *Verklärte Nacht*. Mariano, as always, is superb.

***   Babel Elektra ELK K 5244 CD
Catherine; Jean-Claude Petit (*ky, syn*); Jannick Top (*b*); André Ceccarelli (*d, perc*); Isabelle Catherine, Janet Catherine (*v*); string quartet. 80.

Catherine's larger ensemble work has never had quite the same impact as his duos and trios (surprisingly, he is a not altogether confident solo performer), but *Babel* manages largely to belie the suggestion of chaotic cross-talk in the title. Well arranged by keyboard player Petit, it has some of the impetus that Catherine is often tempted – not for want of rhythmic sense – to abandon in favour of sheer texture.

***   Transparence Inak 8701 CD
Catherine; Hein van de Geyn (*b*); Aldo Romano (*d*); Michael Herr (*ky*); Diederik Wissels (*p*). 11/86.

***   September Sky September 5106 CD
As above, except omit Herr and Wissels. 9/88.

'René Thomas' repays an early debt, and *Transparence* (originally released as Timeless SJP 242) is an album of often moving *hommages*. 'Father Christmas' is dedicated to Charles Mingus and 'Galeries St Hubert' to the ghost of Django Reinhardt; there is also an unexpected tribute to the British multi-instrumentalist, Victor Feldman, which opens up another putative line of descent for the guitarist.

September Sky is an album of (mainly) standards, but what is immediately obvious in both these backward-looking sets is how confidently in possession of his own voice and interpretative skill Catherine now is. On the earlier album, 'L'Eternel Désir' may bear a more than striking thematic resemblance to Ralph Towner's 'Silence Of A Candle', but it is far more deeply suffused with the blues than Towner has ever been, and far more dramatically modulated. Of the standards, 'Body And Soul', 'Stella By Starlight' and 'All Blues' stand out.

***(*)   I Remember You Criss Cross Criss 1048 CD
Catherine; Tom Harrell (*flhn*); Hein Van De Geyn (*b*). 10/90.

Recorded as a tribute to the late Chet Baker, *I Remember You* reunites the line-up that made *Chet's Choice* (Criss Cross Criss 1016 CD/LP) in 1985, with Tom Harrell's floating melancholic flugelhorn steering dangerously close to Baker's weary, self-denying diction. Harrell contributes two fine originals – the softly swinging 'From This Time, From That Time' and 'Songflower' – De Geyn one and Catherine two. The opening 'Nardis' serves as an unintended farewell to Miles. Hank Mobley's 'Funk In Deep Freeze' and the closing 'Blues For G. T.' are slightly unexpected in this context but, drummerless, take on the same slightly enervated quality that is raised only by Catherine's astonishingly accurate rhythm guitar. 'My Funny Valentine'? Well, yes, of course; they could hardly have got away without it. Harrell's statement and subsequent solo are pretty much in the Baker vein, and again it's the guitarist who lifts the performance a notch, using his pedals imaginatively. A beautiful album.

SANDRO CERINO
SAXOPHONES

***   **Tom Thumb In The Magic Castle** Splasc(h) HP 03 LP
Cerino; Renato Rivolta (*f*); Claudio Angeleri (*ky*); Bernardino Penazzi (*clo*); Ares Tavolazzi (*b*); Federico Monti (*d*). 7/87.

***   **Che Fine Fanno I Personaggi Dei Sogni** Splasc(h) H 190 LP.
Riccardo Lupi (*f*) replaces Rivolta; Penazzi absent; others as above. 6/89.

Cerino is both a splendidly capable player and a shrewd organizer of his music: although both these records are portentously cast as suites, the compositions become airy frameworks for some excellent improvising, especially by the leader and Angeleri. Cerino plays virtually the entire reed family but is perhaps at his best on soprano sax, which he imbues with graceful agility without merely turning cartwheels on the horn, as many saxophonists do. There is a beautifully pointed episode on bass clarinet, too, on 'Occhi Che Ridono' on *Tom Thumb*. Tavolazzi is another in the seemingly inexhaustible line of fine Italian bassists, and both discs are scrupulously engineered.

HENRI CHAIX (born 1925)
PIANO

***   **Jumpin' Punkins** Sackville CD2-2020 CD
Chaix; Alain Du Bois (*b*); Romano Cavicchiolo (*d*). 10/90.

'A listener could close his eyes and never believe that this is a Swiss playing in Geneva' – thus did Rex Stewart commend Henri Chaix's playing in 1967. Chaix became Switzerland's mainstream leader in the 1940s, and he backed many American visitors. But his own circumstances have seldom taken him to international audiences. This recent recording finds him in vigorous form, touching few intensities but taking a satisfyingly personal route through jazz-piano tradition. His favourite manner is a medium-tempo stride, a variation which is faithful to James P. Johnson's methods, and he makes 'Yesterdays' and 'All God's Chillun Got Rhythm' into believable stride vehicles. Yet his unassumingly romantic treatment of 'Ruby My Dear' suggests that more demanding jazz material holds few terrors for him. Du Bois and Cavicchiolo stay out of his way, and the recording pays handsome regard to the Bösendorfer piano.

SERGE CHALOFF (1923–57)
BARITONE SAXOPHONE

***(*)   **The Fable Of Mabel** Black Lion BLCD 760923 CD
Chaloff; Capazutto, Herb Pomeroy (*t*); Gene DiStachio (*tb*); Charlie Mariano, Boots Mussulli (*as*); Varty Haritounian (*ts*); Russ Freeman, Dick Twardzik (*p*); Ray Oliver, Jimmy Woode (*b*); Buzzy Drootin, Jimmy Zitano (*d*). 6 & 9/54.

Hugely talented, but the career was riven by 'personal problems' and the end was dreadful. Chaloff's approach to the unwieldy baritone was restrained rather than virtuosic (the result of an extended apprenticeship with Jimmy Dorsey, Georgie Auld and Woody Herman), and concentrated on the distinctive timbre of the instrument rather than on outpacing all opposition. Nevertheless, he was an agile improviser who could suddenly transform a sleepy-sounding phrase with a single overblown note.

Astonishingly, very little of Chaloff's work is currently available. *Boston Blow Up!* and the later, classic *Blue Serge* have not yet been reissued on CD by Affinity (but surely will be soon) and all that remains of a highly compressed career is the item above. Recorded before the onset of a final decline which was only interrupted by the brilliance of *Blue Serge*, it reflects the blocked intensity of his playing. A Chaloff solo, as on the three takes of 'The Fable Of Mabel', two of 'Eenie Meenie Minor Mode', always seems about to tear its own smooth fabric and erupt into something quite violent. Harmonically and rhythmically subtle they also seem to represent a triumph of self-control. The later, All Stars, sessions, from which these tracks come, are in every way superior to the quintet tracks recorded in June, which are rather bland. Though his phrasing is quite conventional, Mariano's alto sound is wild and penetrating and Dick Twardzik's crabby piano is perfect for the setting. With the exception of the Pomeroy, the rest of the band are virtually unknown.

Gerry Mulligan once walked into a studio while Chaloff was recording. Seeing the younger baritonist in the listening booth, Chaloff executed a perfect imitation of his fledgling style and then savagely reduced it to a heap of down and feathers. Relative to the enormous Mulligan discography, the older man, who gave the baritone saxophone its greatest impetus since Harry Carney, is seriously neglected.

JOE CHAMBERS (born 1942)
DRUMS

***(*)   **Phantom Of the City** Candid CCD 79517 CD
Chambers; Philip Harper (*t*); Bob Berg (*ts*); George Cables (*p*); Santi Debriano (*b*).
3/91.

Joe Chambers has featured in post-bop jazz mostly as a drummer, but he is a gifted composer as well, and several of his earlier themes – particularly the four he wrote for Bobby Hutcherson's *Components* (Blue Note) – deserve to be better known than they are. He numbers Jimmy Giuffre as a crucial influence, and there's certainly a parallel between the thinking of both men regarding free and formal structures. That said, only two of the themes on this recent date are Chambers compositions: 'For Miles Davis', a serene yet vaguely ominous *in memoriam*, and the brighter 'Nuevo Mundo'. Chambers the drummer has become a thoughtful, interactive performer, seldom taking a driving-seat initiative and preferring a careful balancing of tonal weights and measures. He has a near-perfect band for his needs here: Berg's tenor is habitually analytical, Cables is a romantic with a terse streak of intelligence, and Harper's Berigan-like low notes and dryly-spun lyricism – featured on an extended reading of 'You've Changed' – add further spice. The live recording, from New York's Birdland, is clear and full-bodied.

PAUL CHAMBERS (1935–69)
DOUBLE BASS

(*)   **The East/West Controversy Xanadu 104 LP
Chambers; Jack Montrose (*ts*); Bill Perkins (*ts, bs*); Paul Moer (*p*); Philly Joe Jones, Mel Lewis (*d*). 1/57.

***   **Bass On Top** Blue Note B21Y 46533 CD
Chambers; Hank Jones (*p*); Kenny Burrell (*g*); Art Taylor (*d*). 7/57.

***(*)   **Paul Chambers Stars** Jazz View COD 014 CD
Chambers; Donald Byrd, Freddie Hubbard (*t*); Curtis Fuller (*tb*); Cannonball Adderley (*as*); Yusef Lateef (*ts, f*); Wynton Kelly (*p*); Jimmy Cobb, Philly Joe Jones (*d*). 60.

Bass solos weren't issued as of right until Mr P.C. was around. That he was around only briefly is one of the saddest of ironies, since his high-register fills and contrapuntal lines are now firmly part of every bass player's available discourse.

The discography is awesome, though the number of albums as leader is sadly limited. The Xanadu session is shared with Hampton Hawes, one of a number of records from around that time reflecting a critical furore about the respective merits of jazz from opposite coasts. His bowed solos are lean and articulate at almost any speed and particularly brilliant (in the proper sense) on 'The Mouse Hop'. The Blue Note was recorded later the same year. There are fine things from the (increasingly prominent) leader and a tighter and more coherent feel to the arrangements. The best of the available sessions may only be available rather briefly. Jazz View is a limited issue label, releasing only 2,000 copies of each title. Unlike many of the others, the Chambers set, recorded in New York, is an essential item in the discography, not just a completist's tick. The sound is slightly wavering and the bassist (typical of the time) not particularly well registered, but the groups and the music are first rate.

THOMAS CHAPIN
ALTO SAXOPHONE, FLUTE, SOPRANO SAXOPHONE

***(*)   **Radius** Mu MUCD 1005 CD
      Chapin; Ronnie Mathews (*p*); Ara Dinkjian (*oud*); Ray Drummond (*b*); John Betsch
      (*d*); Sam Turner (*perc*). 90.

***   **Third Force** Enemy EMCD 123 CD
      Chapin; Mario Pavone (*b*); Steve Johns (*d*). 11/90, 1/91.

Lively, inventive post-bop from a well-respected figure on the 'downtown' New York scene who has not yet completely hit stride as a recording artist. In addition to the *Radius* quartet, Chapin has also worked with Lionel Hampton and Chico Hamilton. His flute playing on 'Forgotten Game' recalls another Hamilton graduate, Eric Dolphy, and the following 'Jitterbug Waltz' (played on what is described as 'mezzo-soprano sax') sounds like a cross between Dolphy and Cannonball Adderley. The addition of an oud to 'Forgotten Game' recalls the world music interests developed on Chapin's *Spirits Rebellious* (Alacra, worth finding).

The Enemy set is gruffer and in some respects less adventurous, adhering to a narrower groove, often trading on rather limited ideas. 'Ahab's Leg', perhaps the best track, can also be heard on a useful Knitting Factory European tour compilation (Enemy EMCD 121) that includes James Blood Ulmer, the impenetrable Samm Bennett and guitarist Gary Lucas. *Radius* is the one to look out for, though.

TEDDY CHARLES (born 1928)
VIBES, PIANO

***(*)   **Collaboration: West** Original Jazz Classics OJC 122 LP
      Charles; Shorty Rogers (*t*); Jimmy Giuffre (*ts, bs*); Curtis Counce (*b*); Shelly Manne
      (*d*). 8/53

***   **Evolution** Original Jazz Classics OJC 1731 CD/LP
      As above, plus J. R. Monterose (*ts*); Charles Mingus (*b*); Gerry Segal (*d*). 8/53–1/55.

When remembered at all – he has scarcely been a popular figure in post-war jazz – Charles is usually respected as a harbinger of Coleman's free music: these two records aim for an independence of bebop structure which still sounds remarkably fresh. The two 1953 sessions, spread across the two discs, explore contrapuntal textures in a way which only Lennie Tristano had already tried, and there is a wonderful sense of interplay with Rogers and Manne especially. 'Variations On A Theme By Bud' from *Collaboration: West*, is a small classic of anticipatory freedom, the music played around key centres rather than a framework of chords. But Charles's interest in harmony and arrangement required larger groups than these, and the quartet session with Mingus, Monterose and Segal is less impressive. The flat sound doesn't do the music any favours.

****   **The Teddy Charles Tentet** Atlantic 790983-2 CD
      Charles; Art Farmer (*t*); Eddie Bert (*tb*); Gigi Gryce, Hal Stein (*as*); Robert Newman,
      J. R. Monterose (*ts*); George Barrow, Sol Schlesinger (*bs*); Jim Buffington (*frhn*);
      Hall Overton, Mal Waldron (*p*); Jimmy Raney (*g*); Don Butterfield (*tba*); Addison
      Farmer, Teddy Kotick, Charles Mingus (*b*); Joe Harris, Ed Shaughnessy (*d*). 1–11/56.

Charles's masterpiece has been truthfully transferred to CD with the bonus of three tracks from the comparably fine *Word From Bird* album, made the same year – although that one should be made available in its entirety. Besides Charles's own scores, including the stunning 'The Emperor' and a bizarre transformation of 'Nature Boy', there are arrangements by Jimmy Giuffre, Brookmeyer, Waldron, Gil Evans and George Russell, whose heated 'Lydian M-1' is one of his sharpest pieces of the era. With its density of incident, acute solos and arresting textures, this music relates closely to Russell's Jazz Workshop recordings of the same period.

Yet Charles is more than a Svengali, taking an important instrumental part in several of the themes.

**   **On Campus!** Fresh Sound FSR-CD 43 CD
      Charles; Zoot Sims (*ts*); Sam Most (*f*); Jimmy Raney (*g*); Dave McKenna (*p*); Bill Crow (*b*); Ed Shaughnessy (*d*). 60.

The original liner notes on this reissue reveal that Charles had 'n.d.' painted on his vibes, standing for 'new directions'. If anything, though, this kind of disc was a step backward. It's little more than a blowing date, and while Sims is in reliably good shape and Raney and McKenna make the best of it, this is scarcely Charles's ideal forte, and the poor sound – it was recorded in what sounds like the gymnasium at Yale University – detracts further.

**   **Live At The Verona Jazz Festival 1988** Soul Note SN 121183 CD/LP
      Charles; Harold Danko (*p*); Ray Drummond (*b*); Tony Reedus (*d*). 6/88.

An indifferent comeback by Charles, who had effectively retired from music for many years. He plays well with an imposing rhythm section, but, as noted above, this kind of casual blowing session is hardly his forte, and the live recording isn't distinguished.

TOMMY CHASE (born 1947)
DRUMS

(*)   **Rebel Fire Moles MRILD 002 CD/LP
      Chase; Ben Waghorn (*as*); Gary Baldwin (*org*); Arnie Somogyi (*b*). 90.

Uptight, no-frills hard bop and soul-jazz from one of the most determined champions of the music on the British scene. Chase's insistence on this music as a one true way may narrow its power to transcend what is a closely cropped genre, but the spiky delivery of the quartet, bounced off Chase's almost ruthless 4/4, makes it work from track to track, although an album's worth lacks staying poower. The weakest thing is the studio sound, which rather inevitably diminishes the band (Baldwin is a particular sufferer on *Rebel Fire*). Heard live, Chase's group are a far more formidable experience, and perhaps only a live set would do them justice.

DOC CHEATHAM (born 1905)
TRUMPET, VOCALS

***(*)   **It's A Good Life!** Parkwood PW 101 LP
      Cheatham; Chuck Folds (*p*); Al Hall (*b*); Jackie Williams (*d*). 12/82.

***   **The Fabulous Doc Cheatham** Parkwood PW 104 LP
      Cheatham; Dick Wellstood (*p*); Bill Pemberton (*b*); Jackie Williams (*d*). 10/83.

Adolphus 'Doc' Cheatham has surely been the most enduring of all living jazz musicians. He was effectively rediscovered in the 1970s after many years of society band work, having been among the most esteemed of lead trumpeters in the big-band era. He was recording in the late 1920s and his studio work of some 60 years later shows amazingly little deterioration in the quality of his technique, while the ideas and appetite for playing remain wholly unaffected by the passage of time. It's not so much that one feels a sentimental attachment to such a veteran, but that Cheatham's sound represents an art which has literally died out of modern jazz: the sweet, lyrically hot style of a swing-era man. Prior to his records in the 1980s, Cheatham's main work was with Cab Calloway in the 1930s, Eddie Heywood in the '40s (often backing Billie Holiday), and in various settings in the 1950s and '60s; but it wasn't until these albums that he was heard at length as a leader. *It's A Good Life!* features the band which began backing him at his regular Sunday afternon gigs in New York and, although Hall and Williams play with square resilience rather than exuberance, the rhythm is exactly what Doc needs to swing on. His solos have a classical economy and a courageous spring to them, and the tiny shakes and inflexions in his sound only help to make it uniquely his own, with a songful high register and choruses which, after 60 years of playing, he knows exactly how to pace. Of the two Parkwood albums (both unfortunately rather difficult to find in the UK), the second benefits a little from Wellstood's attacking piano, but the first includes a couple of gems which nobody else does any more: 'Struttin' With Some Barbecue' and 'Peggy'. Cheatham's dapper, delicate vocals on several tracks only add to the fun. Excellent recording.

***(*)   **Doc & Sammy** Sackville 3013 LP
Cheatham; Sam Price (*p*). 82.

****   **Black Beauty** Sackville 3029 LP
As above.

***(*)   **At The Bern Festival** Sackville 2-3045 CD
Cheatham; Roy Williams (*tb*); Jim Galloway (*ss*); Ian Bargh (*p*); Neil Swainson (*b*); Terry Clarke (*d*). 4/83–1/85.

Good though the Parkwood albums are, these are even better. The live session finds Cheatham unfazed by a hard-swinging and quite modern-sounding band, with Roy Williams sitting in on the first six tracks – he has a delightful feature on 'Polka Dots And Moonbeams' – and Galloway's soprano measuring the distance between Sidney Bechet and Steve Lacy. Three later tracks were taped on more local ground in Toronto. If the rhythm section sometimes crashes rather more than it might for Cheatham's taste, he still sounds invigorated by the setting, and his hand-muted playing on 'Creole Love Call' or the firm, silvery solos on 'Cherry' and 'Love Is Just Around The Corner' are commanding examples of his best work. The two duet albums with Price are, though, surely his finest latter-day achievements. Trumpet–piano duets are rarities in the jazz literature, and one might almost think back to Louis Armstrong and Earl Hines: except that Cheatham, whose favourite model from the early years was Ellington's trumpeter, Arthur Whetsol, makes one think of Armstrong only at a certain remove. *Doc & Sammy* is a relatively loose affair, but *Black Beauty* is rather more pointed, programmed as a tribute to early black songwriters and offering such material as 'Memphis Blues', 'I've Got A Feeling I'm Falling' and 'I'm Coming Virginia'. Price's blues (or blues-inflected) playing is relatively unsubtle and rehearsed next to Cheatham's variety of phrasings; but they bring out the best in each other, swinging with little apparent effort through the tunes and suggesting something of a history lesson in jazz roots and evolution. Very highly recommended.

JEANNIE CHEATHAM
PIANO, VOCAL

and

JIMMY CHEATHAM
BASS-TROMBONE, VOCAL

***   **Sweet Baby Blues** Concord CCD 4258 CD/MC
Jimmy Cheatham; Jeannie Cheatham; Snooky Young (*t, v*); Jimmie Noone (*ss, cl*); Charles McPherson (*as*); Curtis Peagler (*as, ts*); Red Callender (*b, tba*); John 'Ironman' Harris (*d*); Danice Tracey, Chris Long (*v*). 9/84.

***   **Midnight Mama** Concord CJ 297 MC
As above, except Dinky Morris (*ss, ts, bs*) and Eddie 'Lockjaw' Davis (*ts*) replace McPherson, Tracey and Long omitted. 11/85.

***   **Homeward Bound** Concord CCD 4321 CD/MC
As above, except Eddie Vinson (*as, v*) replaces Davis. 1/87.

These are charming records by a husband-and-wife team whose music is a contemporary variation on jump-band blues (the group is now known as the Sweet Baby Blues Band, after the first album). Rather than striving for authenticity, hardly possible in the 1980s and in Concord's pristine sound, they play the music as well-loved repertory; in many hands it wouldn't work, but Jeannie's voice has the right mix of girlishness and blues-mama maturity, and the arrangements take in looseness as well as precision. There's little to choose between the three records. Admirers of Vinson or Davis may like to investigate the discs which they guest on.

***   **Basket Full Of Blues** Concord CCD 4501 CD/MC
Jimmy Cheatham; Jeannie Cheatham; Nolan Smith, Snooky Young (*t, flhn*); Rickey
Woodard (*as, ts, cl*); Frank Wess (*ts, f*); Curtis Peagler (*as, ss, ts, bs*); Dinky Moris (*bs,
ts*); Red Callender (*b*); John 'Ironman' Harris (*d*). 11/91.

Like many of their somewhat younger counterparts on Concord, the Cheathams have now been
doing this kind of record for the label long enough to create their own little genre. Some may
find the ultra-smooth recording not much in keeping with the greasier spirits of the music, but
the horns are perfectly cast to get the most out of this fetching bunch of jump and trad blues
pieces, and Woodard is an inspired addition to the group. Almost certainly Red Callender's last
recording, since he died a few weeks after it was completed.

DON CHERRY (born 1936)
POCKET TRUMPET, WOODEN FLUTES, DOUSSN'GOUNI, MISCELLANEOUS INSTRUMENTS AND PERCUSSION,
VOICE

***(*)   **Live At The Montmartre: Volume 1** Magnetic MRCD 111 CD

****   **Live At The Montmartre: Volume 2** Magnetic MRCD 112 CD
Cherry; Gato Barbieri (*ts*); Karl Berger (*vib*); Bo Stief (*b*); Aldo Romano (*d*). 65 or
66.

A musical gypsy, Cherry has defined his art as that of people 'listening and travelling'. Like
many travellers, he has been treated with suspicion, and record companies have been notably
reluctant to cross his palm with silver. His unconventional choice of instruments makes him an
easy mark as a temporary recruit for 'colour' – Cherry favours a tiny pocket trumpet, bamboo
flutes, and the Malian *doussn'gouni*, a calabash guitar with rattles attached – but the errant
lifestyle seems to suit his world-view and there is something about his staccato, declamatory
style that lends itself to brief interjection rather than to developed 'performance'. Cherry
conspicuously lacks the self-consciousness of most improvisers.

His impact on the development of Ornette Coleman's revolutionary new synthesis may now
never be clearly identified; their work together at the Lenox School of Music in Massachusetts is
caught on a valuable concert compilation (Royal Jazz RJD 513 CD) and suggests the
partnership may have been more equal than is sometimes thought. On the classic Coleman
records, though, Cherry sounds thin and slightly plaintive, the saxophonist's echo rather than an
independent voice, but this may be a function of contemporary recording techniques and
Cherry's status as 'sideman', and it's clear that his squealing, undisciplined sound is rather hard
to catch and adjust on pre-modern technology. Cherry left Coleman in 1961, co-founded the
New York Contemporary Five with Archie Shepp and John Tchicai, then moved to Europe
with Albert Ayler, where he formed a group with the Ayler-influenced Argentinian shouter,
Gato Barbieri. They recorded the much-admired *Complete Communion* [Blue Note BST 84226
LP] and the less successful *Symphony For Improvisers* [Blue Note BST 82427 LP] with a larger
group that included Pharoah Sanders.

Both albums featured the drumming talents of Ed Blackwell (who later played in Cherry's
Old and New Dreams band (q.v.)), who is rather missed on the live dates, above. Stief and
Romano work away manfully, but seem to be missing the point of some of the music.
Organized like the studio albums in large collective improvisations in which individual
compositions are only meeting places, Cherry's performance ethos is already close to the folk
and ritual roots that were to become so important later in his career. The sound is wobbly and
not much assisted by digital processing, but as documentation (and in the continued absence of
Complete Communion) these are valuable records.

***(*)   **Mu (The Complete Session)** Affinity AFF 774 CD

***   **El Corazon** ECM 1230 CD/LP
Cherry; Ed Blackwell (*d*). 8/69, 2/82.

After Coleman and the ill-fated Collin Walcott in later years, Cherry's closest and longer-lasting
artistic association has been with Ed Blackwell. *Mu* was a remarkable exploration of relatively
untried territory; the New Thing had freed percussionists from mere time-keeping and
reminded Afro-Americans of their heritage in percussion-based music. The reconstructed
session probably contains some extraneous material, but a perfectly coherent performance can

be programmed on the CD and the music holds up very well, prefiguring some of Cherry's folksy work with Codona (q.v.).

The later album is much more obviously lyrical, as one might expect from the label, and includes what by that time had become a rare Cherry performance of a jazz staple, 'Bemsha Swing', a Thelonious Monk/Denzil Best tune which Cherry returned to on his jazz and big label comeback, *Art Deco*, below. Though the material is somewhat different from the later Old and New Dreams group (which specialized very largely in Ornette Coleman material), the approach is broadly similar and *El Corazon* may be read as a germ or distillation of what the quartet were to do later in the 1980s.

****   **Art Deco** A & M 395258 CD
       Cherry; James Clay (*ts*); Charlie Haden (*b*); Billy Higgins (*d*). 8/88.

Cherry was a pioneer of world music before the term acquired capital letters, market-niche status, and a weight of opprobrium that even Cherry has found it hard to shake off. Recent years have seen him working with 'ethnic' and pop musicians, including Ian Dury and the Blockheads, Lou Reed and his own stepdaughter Neneh, and thus by critical inference further and further removed from jazz (Old and New Dreams can be conveniently dismissed as a 'nostalgic' reconstruction of the original Ornette Coleman Quartet).

It was, though, surprising to find Cherry, recently signed to his first major label contract in many years, recording a relatively conventional jazz album that sees him concentrate on trumpet playing opposite a remarkably straightforward 'Texas tenor'. Alongside Coleman tunes like 'The Blessing' and 'Compute' which invite a freer approach, there are standards like 'When Will The Blues Leave', 'Body And Soul', and a further, rather indifferent, version of 'Bemsha Swing'. Clay has had a quiet career since the 1950s and has only recently garnered much critical notice; he plays beautifully, sounding like an ancestor of Ornette-on-tenor. Cherry, mostly playing muted, seems to have reverted to a cross between his old, rather tentative self and mid-period Miles Davis.

***(*)   **Multi Kulti** A & M 395323 CD
       Cherry; Bill Ortiz (*t, v*); James Harvey (*tb*); Jeff Cressman (*tb, v*); Bob Stewart (*tba*);
       Carlos Ward (*as*); Jessica Jones, Tony Jones (*ts*); Peter Apfelbaum (*ts, kys, perc*);
       Peck Allmond (*bs*); Will Bernard, Stan Franks (*g*); David Cherry, Frank Serafine
       (*syn*); Karl Berger (*mar*); Bo Freeman, Mark Loudon Sims (*b*); Ed Blackwell, Deszon
       X. Claiborne (*d*); Joshua Jones V (*d, perc, v*); John L. Price (*d programming*); Frank
       Ekeh, Robert Buddha Huffman, Nana Vasconcelos (*perc*); Anthony Hamilton, Ingrid
       Sertso (*v*); collective personnel. 12/88, 1/89, 1, 2/90.

Very much closer to what one has come to expect of a Don Cherry album, perhaps too self-consciously so. Yet Cherry's eclecticism is confident enough to rid this poly-stylistic collection of any suspicion of mere artistic tourism. In Carlos Ward he finds a particularly sympathetic partner and he has clearly drawn considerable sustenance from his stepdaughter's street-wise and commercially successful hip-hop and rap styles. User-friendly and thoroughly enjoyable.

ELLEN CHRISTI
VOCAL

(*)   **Senza Parole Splasc(h) H 201 LP
       Christi; Carlo Actis Dato (*ts, bs, bcl*); Enrico Fazio (*b*); Fiorenzo Sordini (*d*). 8/89.

**   **Dreamers** Splasc(h) H 311 CD
       Christi; Claudio Lodati (*g*). 4/90.

Born in Chicago, Christi made these records in Italy, where she seems to be a more popular figure. She's an improvising vocalist in the manner of Jeanne Lee and Urszula Dudziak, and she hovers between words and sounds in a confident but sometimes unappealing manner: neither a committed improviser like Maggie Nicols nor a convincing bop-scat singer, she doesn't characterize her material with enough certainty to persuade a listener that she really knows what she's doing. The first record has some fine moments through the participation of the reliably absorbing work of Dato and Fazio and, while Christi rambles through the music with little directional pulse, she creates a surprisingly effective coda to Dato's 'Dogon' in particular.

The duet session with Lodati seems dated, relying on overdubs and cooing textures which suggest a throwback to some of the improvising experiments of the 1970s.

CHARLIE CHRISTIAN (1916–42)
GUITAR

***   **Live Sessions At Minton's Playhouse** Jazz Anthology 550012 CD
Christian; Victor Coulson, Joe Guy, Hot Lips Page (*t*); Rudy Williams (*as*); Don Byas (*ts*); Thelonious Monk, Alan Tinney (*p*); Paul Ebenezer, Nick Fenton (*b*); Kenny Clarke, Taps Miller (*d*). 5/41.

Who actually invented bebop? Parker and Gillespie seemed to arrive at near-identical solutions to the blind alley of jazz harmony. Thelonious Monk was never an orthodox bopper, but he had his two-cents' worth. And then there was Charlie Christian, who in some accounts was the first to develop the long lines and ambitious harmonic progressions of bop. Christian's appetite for booze and girls was only ever overtaken by his thirst for music. He once improvised 'Rose Room' for nearly an hour and a half, a feat that prompted Benny Goodman to hire him.

Christian's greatest contributions, however, were at the historic jams at Minton's in New York, out of which the bebop revolution came about. He was already seriously ill with tuberculosis, but the graceful flowing music he creates on these sessions (the album is shared with three Dizzy Gillespie tracks) is of considerable historical importance. Christian was the first guitarist to make completely convincing use of an electric instrument and his solos on 'Stompin' At The Savoy' and 'Up On Teddy's Hill' demonstrate his ability to steer a path away from the usual saxophone-dominated idiom and towards something that established guitar as an improvising instrument in its own right. The recordings are noisy, lo-fi, but undeniably atmospheric and by far the best available evidence for Christian's importance. There's also a reasonable selection of material on a budget compilation called *Genius Of The Electric Guitar* [Giants of Jazz GOJCD 53049] which takes in his work with Goodman.

GUNTER CHRISTMANN (born 1942)
TROMBONE, BASS, CELLO

***(*)   **We Play** FMP 0120 LP
Christmann; Detlef Schonenberg (*d*). 2/73.

***   **Remarks** FMP 0260 LP
As above, plus Harald Bojé (*syn*). 3–8/75.

No one has mastered a wider vocabulary of sounds for the trombone than this Polish-born German free improviser, whose expressionist exuberance is comical, passionate, lyrical, disturbing. Although he has often performed in a solo context, his best music has been in collaboration with more earthbound souls who can provide a context for his wildness. The long-standing duo with Schonenberg is represented only by these two discs: *We Play* is a forgotten gem, sharply recorded to leave all the abrasiveness of their interplay intact, and though there are occasional slow patches, with Schonenberg lumbering a little here and there, the illogical momentum is mostly well sustained. *Remarks* includes the prehistoric electronics of Bojé on some tracks and three bizarre little solos by the trombonist.

***   **Earmeals** Moers Music 01040 LP
Christmann; Tristan Honsinger (*clo*). 5/78.

**   **Off** Moers Music 01070 LP
Christmann (solo). 76–78.

The solo album, a scrapbook of odds and ends including a composition for typewriters, is disappointing; away from other players, Christmann's nutty sensibility can seem merely trivial. Honsinger's madcap temperament could have been too much of a good thing too, but their series of duets offers much pithy improvising.

***   **Weavers** Po Torch PTR/JWD 7 LP
Christmann; Maarten Altena (*b*); Paul Lovens (*d*). 79–80.

In the company of two other masters, Christmann creates a compelling recital, h
at its most abstract at some moments and jazz-like at others. Altena's grinding
peculiarly appropriate, as are Lovens's parts. Unglamorous but effective recording.

(*)   **Vario II Moers Music 01084 LP
    As above, plus John Russell (*g*), Maggie Nicols (*v*). 6/80.

(*)   **Vario Moers Music 02048 LP
    Christmann; Wolfgang Fuchs (*sno*); John Russell, Jo Sachse, Davey Williams (*g*); Jon
    Rose (*vn*); LaDonna Smith (*vla*); Gyde Knebusch (*hp*); Torsten Muller, Maarten
    Altena (*b*); Gerd Glasmer, Paul Lovens, Roger Turner (*d*); Shelley Hirsch; Phil
    Minton (*v*). 83–85.

Christmann's two *Vario* projects are similar in scope to Derek Bailey's Company collectives. It's
just a pity that neither of their two records amount to very much, the first sounding a little
slack, the second too piecemeal in its make-up, though both have their moments.

(*)   **Carte Blanche FMP 1100 LP
    Christmann; Torsten Muller (*b*). 8/85.

His only record of recent years finds Christmann in another unlikely combination, trombone
and bass. A bassist himself, the trombonist makes the most of the sonic affinities between the
two instruments, creating a music composed mostly of low-register scrapes and snarls. Muller is
a sympathetic partner. But they find it hard to sustain a creative dynamic over an entire record,
and most will find it hard going after the half-way mark.

JUNE CHRISTY (1926–90)
VOCAL

****   **Something Cool** Capitol CDP 796329-2 CD
    Christy; Pete Rugolo Orchestra. 53–55.

June Christy's solo recordings, following her stint with the Stan Kenton orchestra, have been
reissued in various forms over the years, but this compilation from two albums, several
uncollected singles and two previously unreleased tracks is – if not a wholly satisfactory
substitute for albums which should be reissued in their entirety on individual discs – a beautiful
celebration of one of the most undervalued singers of the post-swing era. Christy's wholesome
but peculiarly sensuous voice is less an improviser's vehicle than an instrument for long,
controlled lines and the shading of a fine vibrato. Her greatest moments – the breathtaking
title-track, 'Midnight Sun', 'I Should Care' – are as close to creating definitive interpretations
as any singer can come. Rugolo's arrangements are nicely inventive without getting in her way,
and although some of the tracks are more like collectable items – the cooing male vocals on
'Why Do You Have To Go Home', for instance – than essential ones, there are very few less
than exceptional moments on the record, which includes all of the original *Something Cool* LP
among its 24 tracks. The remastering is bright and well defined.

(*)   **A Lovely Way To Spend An Evening Jasmine JASMCD 2528 CD
    Christy; Stu Williamson (*t*); Herb Geller (*as*); Russ Freeman (*p*); Monty Budwig (*b*);
    Shelly Manne (*d*); Jerry Gray Orchestra. 57–59.

Poor documentation and thin packaging makes this collection of Christy's late-1950s
performances look cheaply presented. The sound is thin and weakly spread, too; but the
performances find the singer in inventive and bright form, and both those tracks with Manne's
group and with the Jerry Gray band are hip and swinging affairs.

***(*)   **Impromptu** Discovery DSCD 836 CD
    Christy; Jack Sheldon (*t*); Frank Rosolino (*tb*); Bob Cooper (*ts*); Lou Levy (*p*); Bob
    Daugherty (*b*); Shelly Manne (*d*). 6/77.

Christy's only late record is a lovely and often moving session. Her voice has inevitably declined
– it's heavier, deeper, the vibrato wider and less sure – but it's still instantly recognizable, and
she sings these ten songs with enormous dedication. Because of the vulnerability of her voice,
the ballads – especially 'Once Upon A Summertime' and an almost mystically thoughtful
'Angel Eyes' – are the most affecting, but the way she swings through 'My Shining Hour' suits

the excellent accompaniment by many old friends from her West Coast days. Remastered for CD but no noticeable improvement over the LP.

MASSIMO CIOLLI
GUITAR

***   **Cronopios** Splasc(h) H 171 LP
Ciolli; Sergio Gistri (*t, flhn*); Nicola Vernuccio (*b*); Stefano Bambini (*d*).

Admirably terse and probing music from this Italian quartet. Although Ciolli is the leader, and wrote all the tunes, Gistri is at least an equal influence on the music, his thin, piping tone effective in less ambitious solos, more troubling in a long extemporization such as that on 'Metamorfosi'. Ciolli's tunes encourage a state of sour romanticism, and the clear, slightly trebly recording is entirely suitable.

ROBERTO CIPELLI
KEYBOARDS

***   **Moona Moore** Splasc(h) H 173 LP
Cipelli; Paolo Fresu (*t, flhn*); Tino Tracanna (*ts*); Marco Micheli (*b*); Manhu Roche (*d*). 11–12/88.

Cipelli is a keyboard player who plays with quiet restraint as often as he does with quickfire exuberance. The horn players appear on a few tracks – Fresu is typically lyrical on the lovely 'Black Orchids' – but the trio pieces are even finer, 'The Island' securing a distinctive group interplay. Recorded with Splasc(h)'s customary finesse.

CIRCLE
GROUP

****   **Paris Concert** ECM 1018/1019 2CD
Anthony Braxton (*reeds, perc*); Chick Corea (*p*); Dave Holland (*b, clo*); Barry Altschul (*d, perc*). 2/71.

A hardy perennial of new music, perhaps remembered and treasured more for the opening and closing ensemble numbers – Wayne Shorter's complex 'Nefertiti' and a surprisingly straight reading of Isham Jones's 'There Is No Greater Love' – than for the more rarefied solo and duet pieces in between. Of these, Holland's 'Song For The Newborn' is the most intense, though an improvised duet between Corea and Braxton runs it close for sheer intensity.

Altschul and Corea gain most from CD transfer. The pianist's staccato and almost atonal punctuations behind Braxton's solo on 'Nefertiti' were almost lost on the original LP. As live recordings of the period go, though, it is pretty good, and the music has stood up remarkably well, though some of its appeal is undoubtedly related to the four players' subsequent and separate success as bandleaders in their own right. Corea's sleeve-note is embarrassingly breathless, but it's clear that something special did happen on a February night in Paris.

CURTIS CLARK
PIANO

***   **Phantasmagoria** Nimbus NS 3368 LP
Clark; Roberto Miranda (*b*); Son Ship Theus (*d*). 1/84.

***   **Self Trait** FMP SAJ 52 LP

***   **Dedications** Freelance FRL003 LP
Clark (*p* solo). 11/84, ?.

***(*) **Amsterdam Sunshine** Nimbus NS 3691 LP
    Clark; Michael Moore (*as*); Ernst Reijseger (*clo*); Ernst Glerum (*b*); Don Mumford
    (*d*). 11/84.

*** **Deep Sea River** Nimbus NS 3580 LP
    Clark; Merlene Holsey (*v*). 3/85.

A West Coast figure who has yet to make a significant impact with a wider audience, Clark has been an invigorating sideman with Billy Bang, Julian Priester, David Murray and Butch Morris, a roster of names that offers some hint as to his playing strategies. Clark is a radical traditionalist, drawing on elements of swing and popular song and seems increasingly untouched by the dominant piano style derived from bebop. The two solo recordings (Holsey only performs on one track of *Deep Sea River*) suggest a rugged individualist in the Horace Tapscott lineage who can assimilate free procedures with extended song forms and come up with something that is genuinely individual. 'Bouquet (For Dorien Van Stokkom)', which appears on both *Phantasmagoria* and the FMP set, develops logically and attractively. The group versions on *Amsterdam Sunshine* of two more excellent originals, 'Peu De Sentiment' (from the contemporaneous *Self Trait*) and 'Thought Of One' (*Phantasmagoria*), suggest that Clark is a performer/composer to be closely watched, currently restricted only by small label status. The CD audience is going to have to wait a while longer.

MIKE CLARK
DRUMS

*** **Give The Drummer Some** Stash ST-CD 22 CD
    Clark; Jack Walrath (*t*); Ricky Ford (*ts*); Neal Kirkwood (*p*); Jack Wilkins (*g*); Chip
    Jackson (*b*). 89.

While this is ostensibly Clark's album – and the title-track is indeed a drum solo – it's hard to take the attention away from Walrath and Ford, the former one of the wittiest and most unpredictable of post-bop trumpeters, the latter a tenorman who makes up in drive and opulent sound what he lacks in signature individuality. The horns sit out on two other tracks, including a nice 'If You Could See Me Now', but it's on burners like 'Baghdad By The Sea' that the music happens.

SONNY CLARK (1931–63)
PIANO

(**) **The Sonny Clark Memorial Album Xanadu 121 LP
    Clark; Simon Brehm (*b*); Bobby White (*d*). 1/54.

*** **Sonny Clark Trio** Blue Note B21Y 46547 CD
    Clark; Paul Chambers (*b*); Philly Joe Jones (*d*). 1/57.

*** **Sonny's Crib** Blue Note B21Y 46819 CD
    Clark; Donald Byrd (*t*); Curtis Fuller (*tb*); John Coltrane (*ts*); Paul Chambers (*b*);
    Arthur Taylor (*d*). 10/57.

*** **Sonny Clark** Bainbridge Time BCD 1044 CD
    Clark; George Duvivier (*b*); Max Roach (*d*). 3/60.

**** **Leapin' And Lopin'** Blue Note 784091 CD
    Clark; Tommy Turrentine (*t*); Ike Quebec, Charlie Rouse (*ts*); Butch Warren (*b*);
    Billy Higgins (*d*). 11/61.

It's slightly difficult now to remember that Clark was once the piano player of choice in the Blue Note studios. He debuted on record with Wardell Gray, for Prestige this time, played with Dexter Gordon, Sonny Rollins and Charles Mingus, and worked on Serge Chaloff's classic *Blue Serge* date for Capitol. His short career was punctuated by lapses all too familiar from the period and his last few years were spent on an awful pendulum back and forth between heroin addiction and alcoholism (the latter contracted in a failed bid to cure himself of the first).

Perhaps surprisingly, Clark's music betrays very little sign of the darkness of his life. In sharp contrast to Bud Powell, who was still the dominant model for post-bop piano players, Clark gave off a sense of effortless ease. Original melodies and variations on standards seemed to flow from his fingers and the only player one might possibly confuse him with is Hampton Hawes. Like Hawes, Clark very rarely performed solo and there is no 'official' studio album. The Xanadu *Memorial* was privately recorded at a party in Oslo, after Clark and Bobby White had finished their regular gig with the Buddy DeFranco group. There are only two, albeit long, trio tracks, of which 'After You've Gone' is the better. The meat of the session is in Clark's two untitled improvisations, the second of which leads him through some familiar Charlie Parker changes to a reading of 'Over The Rainbow'. 'All God's Chillun Got Rhythm' is the most Bud-like performance on record, almost self-consciously so, but the Hawes likeness is evident on a spontaneous progression from 'Body And Soul' to 'Jeepers Creepers'. The sound quality is horrendous, but the performances represent an important modern jazz document.

The best of the Blue Notes is unquestionably *Leapin' And Lopin'*, which has him in the sympathetic company of Turrentine and Rouse, and, for one track only, Ike Quebec. Though 'Voodoo' stands out as a brilliant original composition, 'Deep In A Dream' is Clark's classic performance, choruses of beautifully inventive piano following one another without the slightest hint of strain. Nothing else quite comes up that standard, though 'Speak Low' and 'With A Song In My Heart' on the sextet *Sonny's Crib* make a contender for second choice with *Trio*, which has exuberant performances of 'I Didn't Know About You', 'Two Bass Hit' and 'Softly, As In A Morning Sunrise'. The Bainbridge CD is of excellent quality and typical of the relaxed approach of the Time series. Those were the settings that suited Clark best. For all his exuberant self-confidence, he never quite seemed a convincing professional, but rather an inspired amateur, happy when there was a piano in the corner, a bottle open on top, and some business to be attended to in a back room.

THOMAS CLAUSEN (born 1949)
PIANO

***   **Piano Music** M. A. Music A.801 CD
       Clausen (*p* solo). 89.

Like many of the younger European pianists, Clausen's methods are informed by twentieth-century composition as much by the jazz tradition, but there's nothing remotely academic about the music on this splendid disc. Four of the 14 themes are Clausen originals, including an enchanting 'Lullaby' and the expertly voiced 'Pomona', yet his treatment of standards is even more absorbing: 'What Is This Thing Called Love' is entirely restructured, passing in and out of tempo in Tatum-like manner, while a refreshingly simple 'Liza' displays an inherent affection for melody which is the touchstone of Clausen's playing. Superbly engineered and packaged with good sleeve-notes by the pianist, this is an excellent record.

JAMES CLAY
TENOR SAXOPHONE

***   **The Sound Of The Wide Open Spaces** Original Jazz Classics OJC 257 CD/LP
       Clay; David Newman (*ts*); Wynton Kelly (*p*); Sam Jones (*b*); Art Taylor (*d*). 4/60.

Clay is a semi-legendary figure whose reported influence on Ornette Coleman is interesting but scarcely borne out by this early record. It gets into the brawling spirit typical of such two-tenor encounters, but offers only a glimpses of Clay as a distinctive force. His return to the studios with Don Cherry in the 1980s offers the best evidence of his plangent yet oddly reluctant manner.

(*)   **I Let A Song Go Out Of My Heart Antilles 422848279 CD/MC
       Clay; Cedar Walton (*p*); David Williams (*b*); Billy Higgins (*d*). 1/89.

Clay's first album under his own name for nearly 30 years is distinctly mixed. The blend of jazz and show standards which makes up the programme might be unsuitable for a maverick player such as he: the saxophonist seems to struggle to stay in tune and keep up with some of the tempos, and unwonted fluffs are made more significant by the rhythm section, which comprises three of the most failsafe pros on the scene. Rudy Van Gelder's studio sound is also rather trebly. There are felicitous moments but one feels the session might have been profitably remade.

BUCK CLAYTON (1911–91)
TRUMPET

***(*)   **The Classic Swing Of Buck Clayton** Original Jazz Classics OJC 1709 CD
Clayton; Dickie Wells, Trummy Young (*tb*); Buster Bailey, Scoville Brown (*cl*); George Johnson (*as*); Jimmy Jones, Billy Taylor (*p*); Brick Fleagle, Tiny Grimes (*g*); John Levy, Al McKibbon, Sid Weiss (*b*); Cozy Cole, Jimmy Crawford (*d*). 46.

***   **Copenhagen Concert** Steeplechase SCC 6006/7 2CD/2LP
Clayton; Emmett Berry (*t*); Dickie Wells (*tb*); Earl Warren (*as, cl*); Buddy Tate (*ts*); Al Williams (*p*); Gene Ramey (*b*); Herbie Lovelle (*d*); Jimmy Rushing (*v*). 9/59.

(*)   **Jammin' At Eddie Condon's: Volume 1 Jazz Up JU 311 CD

(*)   **Jammin' At Eddie Condon's: Volume 2 Jazz Up JU 312 CD
Clayton; Cutty Cutshall, Benny Morton (*tb*); Peanuts Hucko (*cl*); Dave McKenna (*p*); Bob Haggart (*b*); Buzzy Drootin (*d*). 60.

***(*)   **A Buck Clayton Jam Session** Chiaroscuro CRD 132 CD
Clayton; Doc Cheatham, Joe Newman (*t*); Urbie Green (*tb*); Earl Warren (*as*); Budd Johnson, Zoot Sims (*ts*); Joe Temperley (*bs*); Earl Hines (*p*); Milt Hinton (*b*); Gus Johnson (*d*).

Clayton is one of the great players of mainstream jazz. Responsible for no particular stylistic innovation, he managed to synthesize much of the history of jazz trumpet up to his time with a bright, brass tone and an apparently limitless facility for melodic improvisation, which made him equally ideal in open-ended jams like the Condon's sessions (and the rather better one on Chiaroscuro) and as a vocal accompanist. He played with Basie until 1946, the year of the fine *Classic Swing* sessions, and after a stint in the army struck off on his own again, forming a productive association with shouter Jimmy Rushing which survived long enough for the European tour featured on the Steeplechase set. Clayton's fills and subtle responses are always tasteful, but he's heard to better effect on the instrumental All Stars tracks from the same occasion, tackling 'Moonglow' with consummate artistry and taste.

A hint of vulgarity creeps into some of the Condon's sessions and the ideas have become rather repetitive and formulaic. Since a rather poor transfer even gets to Clayton's normally unassailable tone (and wipes out McKenna completely), these aren't particularly desirable sets and the best option, in default of the great CBS jams of the early 1950s, is the OJC. 'Harlem Cradle Song', with Young and Wells, has a lovely, easy swing, and there is a fine instrumental version of 'I Want A Little Girl' that avoids the slightly crass quality of the Rushing version.

CLAYTON–HAMILTON JAZZ ORCHESTRA
GROUP

***   **Groove Shop** Capri 74021 CD/MC
Bobby Bryant, Snooky Young, Oscar Brashear, Clay Jenkins (*t, flhn*); George Bohannon, Ira Nepus, Thurman Green (*tb*); Maurice Spears (*btb*); Jeff Clayton (*ss, as, ts, ob, f*); Bill Green (*as, cl, f*); Ricky Woodard (*ts, cl*); CHarles Owens (*ts, cl*); Lee Callett (*bs, bcl*); Bill Cunliffe (*p*); Doug MacDonald (*g*); John Clayton (*b*); Jeff Hamilton (*d*). 4/89.

***   **Heart And Soul** Capri 74028 CD/MC
As above, except Jim Hershman (*g*) replaces MacDonald. 2/91.

It's the arranging, by ex-Basieite John Clayton which gives this blithe orchestra its character: there are some good soloists here, especially Snooky Young and the emerging Woodard, but the integration and polish of the sections is what makes the music come alive. Clayton seeks little more than grooving rhythms and call-and-response measures, and they all figure dutifully enough in the arrangements, though occasionally – as on the very slow and piecemeal variation on 'Take The "A" Train' on *Heart And Soul* – the band have something more out-of-the-ordinary to play. Detailed and full-blooded recording lets one hear how all the wheels go round.

ALEX CLINE (born 1956)
DRUMS, PERCUSSION

*** **The Lamp And The Star** ECM 1372 CD/LP
Cline; Aina Kemanis, Nels Cline (*v*); Jeff Gauthier (*vn, vla, v*); Hank Roberts (*clo, v*); Wayne Peet (*p, org*); Eric von Essen (*b*); Susan Rawcliffe (*didjeridu*). 9/87.

The Clines – Alex and guitarist Nels – used to trade under the name Quartet Music, partnered by Gauthier and von Essen. The music they make with an augmented line-up is even further from academia, full of lush textures and strange transitions that don't conform to any recognizable logic. *The Lamp And The Star* has an unspecifically devotional programme, characterized by Cline's imagistic titles – 'A Blue Robe In The Distance', 'Emerald Light', 'Accepting The Chalice' – but there is nothing mushy or New Age-ish about the music, which has a strong and very individual resonance. Well worth checking out.

NELS CLINE (born 1956)
GUITAR, ELECTRIC GUITAR

*** **Angelica** Enja 5063-47 CD
Cline; Stacy Rowles (*t, flhn*); Tim Berne (*as*); Eric von Essen (*b*); Alex Cline (*d*). 8/87.

This could almost be a Charlie Haden band of the early 1970s, with Cline picking as gently and fluently as Sam Brown and Berne summoning up something close to Carlos Ward's muezzin quaver. To continue the parallel, twin brother Alex Cline, who has gigged and recorded with Haden, works in a seam originally opened up by Paul Motian, but with a far heavier accent.

Worth searching out, *Angelica* is a series of dedications – to Maria Farandouri, the Chilean martyr Victor Jara, bandoneon virtuoso Dino Saluzzi, to Vinny Golia (who does a superb production job) and, on the superb long 'Fives And Sixes', to trumpeter Booker Little.

*** **Silencer** Enja 60982 CD
Cline; Mark London Sims (*b*); Michael Preussner (*d*). 12/90.

Two years after *Angelica* and with a regularly working band, Cline seems to have found the balance he wants between rock'n'roll pyrotechnics and a much more atmospheric and minimalist guitar trio sound. Set alongside some of Terje Rypdal's recent trios, *Silencer* seems much more thoughtful and considered, examining textures and slow transitions rather than heading straight for Rypdal's all-out ferocity. The opening 'Las Vegas Tango' (a Gil Evans composition) and the two-part 'Lapsing' are the most evocative, the latter suggesting something of Cline's growing stature as a composer. The sound is slightly muzzy, like a picture taken through a Vaselined lens, but that suits the progress of the music rather well.

ROSEMARY CLOONEY (b. 1928)
VOCAL

*** **Blue Rose** Mobile Fidelity MFCD-850 CD
Clooney; Willie Cook, Ray Nance, Clark Terry, Cat Anderson (*t*); Gordon Jackson, Britt Woodman, John Sanders (*tb*); Johnny Hodges (*as*); Russell Procope (*as, cl*); Jimmy Hamilton (*cl, ts*); Paul Gonsalves (*ts*); Harry Carney (*bs*); Duke Ellington (*p*); Jimmy Woode (*b*); Sam Woodyard (*d*). 56.

Ellington's collaborations with singers were few, and the pairing with Rosemary Clooney was, on the face of it, surprising. In fact, she overdubbed her parts on to already-recorded Ellington tracks. Yet it works very well: as a pop stylist who recognized rather than courted jazz-singing principles, she handles Ellington's often difficult (for a singer) songs with attentive finesse, and it culminates in one of the most gracious and thought-through versions of 'Sophisticated Lady' on record.

*** **Everything's Coming Up Rosie** Concord CCD 4047 CD/MC
Clooney; Bill Berry (*t*); Scott Hamilton (*ts*); Nat Pierce (*p*); Monty Budwig (*b*); Jake Hanna (*d*). 77.

*** **Rosie Sings Bing** Concord CJ 60 MC
As above, except Cal Collins (*g*) replaces Berry. 78.

*** **Here's To My Lady** Concord CJ 81 MC
As above, except add Warren Vaché (*c*). 79.

***(*) **Sings The Lyrics Of Ira Gershwin** Concord CCD 4112 CD/MC
Clooney; Warren Vaché (*c, flhn*); Scott Hamilton (*ts*); Roger Glenn (*f*); Nat Pierce (*p*); Cal Collins (*g*); Chris Amberger (*b*); Jeff Hamilton (*d*). 10/79.

*** **With Love** Concord CCD 4144 CD/MC
Clooney; Warren Vaché (*c, flhn*); Scott Hamilton (*ts*); Nat Pierce (*p*); Cal Tjader (*vib*); Cal Collins (*g*); Bob Maize (*b*); Jake Hanna (*d*). 11/80.

*** **Sings The Music Of Cole Porter** Concord CCD 4185 CD/MC
As above, except add David Ladd (*f*). 1/82.

***(*) **Sings The Music Of Harold Arlen** Concord CJ 210 MC
Clooney; Warren Vaché (*c*); Scott Hamilton (*ts*); Dave McKenna (*p*); Ed Bickert (*g*); Steve Wallace (*b*); Jake Hanna (*d*). 1/83.

Clooney virtually quit music in the 1960s and went through some difficult personal times, but her re-emergence with Concord in the 1970s and '80s has been one of the most gratifying returns of recent years. Not all of her 16 albums for the label have yet made it to CD, but the best of them – and they're a very consistent run – set a very high standard. If she is not, at her own insistence, a jazz singer, she responds to the in-house team with warm informality, and the breadth of her voice smooths over any difficulties with some of the more intractable songs. Her voice has a more matronly and less flexible timbre than before, but pacing things suits her style, and good choices of tempo are one of the hallmarks of this series. The 'Songbook' sequence is one of the best of its kind: the Arlen and Gershwin records are particularly fine, and *Sings Bing* makes the best of some occasionally creaky material. *With Love* has some indifferent 'contemporary' tunes from the likes of Billy Joel, but the rest of it more than matches up. Countless cameos from Hamilton, Vache and the others lend further class.

*** **My Buddy** Concord CCD 4226 CD/MC
Clooney; Scott Wagstaff, Mark Lewis, Paul Mazzio, Bill Byrne, Dan Fornero (*t, flhn*); Gene Smith, John Fedchock (*tb*); Randy Hawes (*btb*); Woody Herman (*cl, as*); Frank Tiberi (*ts*); Mark Vinci, Jim Carroll (*ts, f*); Nick Brignola (*bs*); John Oddo (*p*); John Chiodini (*g*); John Adams (*b*); Jeff Hamilton (*d*). 8/83.

*** **Sings The Music Of Irving Berlin** Concord CCD 4255 CD/MC
Clooney; Warren Vaché (*c, flhn*); Scott Hamilton (*ts*); John Oddo (*p*); Ed Bickert, Chris Flory (*g*); Phil Flanigan (*b*); Gus Johnson (*d*). 6/84.

***(*) **Rosemary Clooney Sings Ballads** Concord CCD 4282 CD/MC
As above, except Chuck Israels (*b*) and Jake Hanna (*d*) replace Flory, Flanigan and Johnson. 4/85.

*** **Sings The Music Of Jimmy Van Heusen** Concord CCD 4308 CD/MC
As above, except Michael Moore (*b*) and Joe Cocuzzo (*d*) replace Israels and Hanna, add Emily Remler (*g*). 8/86.

**** **Sings The Lyrics Of Johnny Mercer** Concord CCD 4333 CD/MC
As above, except Dan Barrett (*tb*) replaces Remler. 8/87.

***(*) **Show Tunes** Concord CCD 4364 CD/MC
Clooney; Warren Vaché (*c*); Scott Hamilton (*ts*); John Oddo (*p*); John Clayton (*b*); Jeff Hamilton (*d*). 8–11/88.

203

***	**Sings Rodgers, Hart And Hammerstein** Concord CCD 4405 CD/MC
	Clooney; Jack Sheldon (*t, v*); Chauncey Welsh (*tb*); Scott Hamilton (*ts*); John Oddo
	(*p*); John Clayton (*b*); Joe LaBarbera (*d*); The L.A. Jazz Choir (*v*). 10/89.

John Oddo began working regularly with Clooney with the Woody Herman album, and has
been MD of most of the records since. But the steady, articulate feel of the records is a
continuation of what came before. The Johnny Mercer is perhaps the single best record Clooney
has ever done: the choice of songs is peerless, and she has the measure of every one. *Show
Tunes*, though something of a mixture, is another very good one, and the *Ballads* and Jimmy
Van Heusen are full of top-rank songs. Very little to choose between any of these sets, though
the Mercer would be our first choice for anyone who wants just a taste of what Rosie can do.

**(*)	**For The Duration** Concord CCD 4444 CD/MC
	Clooney; Warren Vaché (*c*); Scott Hamilton (*ts*); John Oddo (*p*); Chuck Berghofer,
	Jim Hughart (*b*); Jake Hanna (*d*); strings. 10/90.

***	**Girl Singer** Concord CCD 4496 CD/MC
	Clooney; Warren Luening, George Graham, Larry Hall, Bob Summers (*t, flhn*);
	Chauncey Welsh, Bill Booth, Bill Elton, George Roberts (*tb*); Brad Warnaar (*frhn*);
	Dan Higgins (*c, as, ts, f*); Joe Soldo (*cl, as, f*); Gary Foster (*as, af, f*); Pete Christlieb
	(*cl, ts, f*); Bob Cooper (*ts, f*); Bob Tricarico (*bs, bcl, f*); John Oddo (*ky*); Tim May (*g*);
	Tom Warrington (*b*); Joe LaBarbera (*d*); Joe Porcaro (*perc*); Monica Mancini, Ann
	White, Mitchel Moore, Earl Brown, Mitch Gordon (*v*). 11–12/91.

If anything, these are slightly disappointing. *For The Duration* is a set of wartime songs similar
to one attempted by Mel Torme and George Shearing, and Clooney belabours what is
occasionally trite (or at least over-exposed) material. *Girl Singer* features an orchestra which
has one thinking about the small group of the earlier records: if that formula had perhaps been
used to the point of diminishing returns, this one is a top-heavy alternative which suits
Clooney's voice less well. Still, Oddo's arrangements leave room for some solos from the horns,
and the singer moves from Dave Frishberg to Duke Ellington to Cy Coleman songs with her
customary resilience.

ARNETT COBB (born 1918)
TENOR SAXOPHONE

**(*)	**Party Time** Original Jazz Classics OJC 219 LP
	Cobb; Ray Bryant (*p*); Wendell Marshall (*b*); Art Taylor (*d*). 5/59.

*(*)	**Live In Paris 1974** France's Concert FC 133 CD/LP
	Cobb; Tiny Grimes (*g*); Lloyd Glenn (*p*); Roland Lobligeois (*b*); Panama Francis (*d*).
	4/74.

**	**Live** Timeless SJP 174 LP
	Cobb; Rein de Graaf (*p*); Jacques Schols (*b*); John Engels (*d*). 11/82.

Cobb overcame serious illness and a (literally) crippling motor accident to keep his career afloat
in the 1960s and after. A powerful player in the so-called 'Texas tenor' tradition, he was an
ideal big-band player – with Lionel Hampton mostly – who never scaled down quite enough for
small-group work. *Party Time* just predates the accident; it's a lively, slightly hectic set with an
adequate rhythm section and a serious shortage of good material. The Paris date, co-led with
Tiny Grimes, is pleasantly shambolic and the French crowd clearly had a ball. Grimes, though,
had never entirely recovered from the great days with Tatum and is inclined to go his own way
regardless. Going Dutch suits Cobb somewhat better. De Graaf is a fine, responsive
accompanist who will go to his grave with a bent back from having carried so many visiting
'singles' over the years. Cobb plays well, if a little fruitily, and the sound is mostly adequate,
given the provenance.

BILLY COBHAM (born 1944)
DRUMS, PERCUSSION, ELECTRONICS

** **A Funky Thide Of Sings** Atlantic 7567 81434 1 LP
Cobham; John Scofield (*g*); Randy Brecker, Walter Fowler (*t*); Glen Ferris, Tom
Malone (*tb*); Michael Brecker (*sax*); Milcho Leviev (*ky*); Alex Blake (*b*).

** **Flight Time** Inak 8616 CD
Cobham; Barry Finerty (*g*); Don Grolnick (*ky*); Tim Landers (*b*). 6/80.

** **Stratus** Inak 813 CD
Cobham; Michal Urbaniak (*electric vn*); Mike Stern (*g*); Gil Goldstein (*ky*); Tim
Landers (*b*). 3/81.

*(*) **Observations** Elektra MUS K 52386 LP
Cobham; Dean Brown (*g*); Gil Goldstein (*ky*); Tim Landers (*b*).

** **Life And Times** Atlantic 7567 81558 1 CD/LP
Cobham; Phil Bodner (*bcl, f*); John Scofield (*g*); Dawilli Gonga (*ky*); Allan Zavod
(*org*); Richard Davis, Doug Rauch (*b*); string trio.

** **Warning** GRP D 9528 CD/LP
Cobham; Dean Brown (*g, g syn*); Gerry Etkins (*ky*); Baron Browne (*b*); Sa Davis
(*perc*). 85.

(*) **Power Play GRP D 9536 CD
As above, except add Onaje Allan Gumbs (*ky*). 86.

*** **Picture This** GRP GRD 9551 CD
Cobham; Randy Brecker (*flhn*); Grover Washington (*saxes*); Michael Abene (*p*);
Gerry Etkins (*ky*); Tom Scott (*lyricon*); Ron Carter (*b*); Victor Bailey, Abraham
Laboriel (*b*); Sa Davis (*congas*). 87.

To some extent, the jury is still out on Billy Cobham. A superb technician and clearly a man of
great musical intelligence and resource, he has nevertheless committed some awful clunkers to
record. Whereas *Spectrum*, his debut as leader, was one of the finest records of the jazz-rock
era, much of what has followed has been remarkably hazy. The cliché about Cobham, that he is
all fire and fury and 20-minute drum solos, has never stood up to scrutiny. In actuality, he is a
somewhat introspective drummer whose compositions are often blurry and unmemorable.

Of the available albums, the best by far are the three late-1980s sets dominated by Gerry
Etkins's fine, robust keyboards and, in the case of *Picture This* (perhaps the best of the bunch),
Grover Washington's very underrated saxophone playing. Washington contributes a plangent
but anger-edged solo line to the beautiful 'Same Ole Love' and Prince's 'Sign O' The Times',
and the old 'Taurian Matador' seems to remember most of his most extravagant passes.

The sad truth remains, though, that Cobham is much too good a drummer for most of the
material he is working with. The self-written things are full of interesting ideas (and the solo
percussion 'Danse For Noh Masque', again on *Picture This*, is highly inventive). The cross-over
gestures of *Funky Thide*, *Flight Time* and *Stratus* now seem wildly dated and Cobham unable to
develop the dialect that had seemed so fresh and strong with Miles Davis and the Mahavishnu
Orchestra. *Observations* is particularly limp, and *Life And Times* a small masterpiece of
miscasting.

** **Billy's Best Hits** GRP 95075 CD/LP
Cobham; as for GRD 9551 and GRP D 9528, above.

There can't be many 'best of . . .' albums that really are. Culled from just two previous releases
– *Warning* and *Picture This* – this compilation puts together a very acceptable package of
latter-day Cobham funk-jazz that should do very well for all but dedicated completists.

MICHAEL COCHRANE
PIANO

***(*) **Elements** Soul Note SN 1151 LP
Cochrane; Tom Harrell (*t*); Bob Malach (*ts*); Dennis Irwin (*b*); James Madison (*d*).
9/85.

The ensembles are keenly pointed, the solos have great contextual power, and Cochrane's tunes are all just slightly out of the ordinary: this is in sum a very interesting post-bop record by a leader looking hard for new ground. 'Tone Row Piece No. 2' is the most surprising theme, the melody organized with strict adherence to 12-tone technique, and, although it's a little less fluid than the other pieces, one can't fault Cochrane's ambitions. Or his own playing – he has a terse, improvisational flair tempered by a romantic streak. Harrell and the fine and underrated Malach sound in very good shape, and the contrast between the boisterous 'Reunion' and the steadily darkening 'Waltz No. 1' shows the extent of the range on offer here. Recommended.

CODONA
GROUP

***(*) **Codona** ECM 1132 CD/LP
Don Cherry (*t, f, doussn'gouni, v*); Collin Walcott (*sitar, tabla, hammered dulcimer, sanza, v*); Nana Vasconcelos (*berimbau, perc, v*). 9/78.

*** **Codona 2** ECM 1177 CD/LP
As above. 5/80.

*** **Codona 3** ECM 1243 CD/LP
As above. 9/82.

In 1978, at Collin Walcott's behest, three musicians gathered in Tonstudio Bauer, Ludwigsburg, and recorded one of the iconic episodes in so-called (but never better called) 'world music'. Any tendency to regard Codona's music, or Walcott's compositions, as floating impressionism is sheer prejudice, for all these performances are deeply rooted in modern jazz (Coltrane's harmonies and rhythms, Ornette Coleman's melodic and rhythmic primitivism) and in another great and related improvisational tradition from Brazil.

Nothing done subsequently quite matches the impact of the original *Codona*. It featured three long Walcott pieces (most notably the closing 'New Light'), the collectively composed title-track, and a brief, witty medley of Ornette Coleman tunes and Stevie Wonder's 'Sir Duke'. The permutations of instrumental sound are astonishing, but rooted in a basic jazz-trio format of horn, harmony and percussion. All three men contribute string accompaniment: Walcott on his sitar, Vasconcelos on the 'bow-and-arrow' berimbau, Cherry on the Malian *doussn'gouni*. The interplay is precise and often intense.

The members' developing interests and careers created a centrifugal spin on the later albums, which are by no means as coherent or satisfying. At their best, though, which is usually when Walcott's writing is at its best, they are still compelling. 'Walking On Eggs' on *Codona 3* is one of his and their best performances.

TONY COE (born 1934)
TENOR SAXOPHONE, CLARINET, SOPRANO SAXOPHONE, BASS CLARINET

*** **Coe, Oxley & Co: Nutty On Willisau** hat Art 6046 CD
Coe; Chris Laurence (*b*); Tony Oxley (*d*). 8/83.

***(*) **Canterbury Song** Hot House HHCD 1005 CD/LP
Coe; Benny Bailey (*t*); Horace Parlan (*p*); Jimmy Woode (*b*); Idris Muhammad (*d*).
88.

These discs confirm what fellow-players have been saying about Tony Coe for years. One of the finest saxophonists/clarinettists ever to grace these shores, he must also be one of the most ubiquitous (he played the lead saxophone part on Henry Mancini's 'Pink Panther' theme) and stylistically the most adaptable. *Canterbury Song* is a relaxed – sometimes deceptively relaxed –

session, combining a near-perfect choice of material with a well-pedigree'd band of Americans, with some of whom Coe had previously worked in Europe (where his standing is even higher than at home) and in the Clarke–Boland Band. There are two fine originals, 'Canterbury Song' and 'Lagos'. The closing 'Morning Vehicle' is a valuable bonus on the CD, an intriguing theme highlighting Coe's superb clarinet. Parlan's taut chording (a childhood bout of polio allegedly, but only allegedly, restricts his right-hand play) opens out on a duo 'Blue 'N' Green' that re-invents some of the harmonic terrain and on 'Re: Person I Knew' (another theme with Bill Evans's hand on it; compare the trio version on *Nutty On Willisau*) where Coe's distinctive soprano tones are perfectly deployed.

Like all the hyphenate reed players – Sidney Bechet, Barney Bigard, Jimmy Giuffre – Coe assimilates the qualities of one horn to another; his clarinet punchy and full-throated, his soprano and tenor making complex legato runs with no loss of breath. He is equally adept at switching idioms, always in a recognizably personal accent. The 1983 double album links him with perhaps the finest improvising percussionist in Europe. Oxley's contribution to the standards is breathtaking, introducing an element of abstraction to 'Re: Person I Knew' and to a majestically simple 'Body And Soul'. Chris Laurence is undoubtedly the junior partner but plays as if he's looking for a seat on the board.

Both albums, different as they are, come warmly recommended.

AL COHN (born 1925)
TENOR SAXOPHONE

(*)   **From A To Z And Beyond Bluebird ND 86469 CD
Cohn; Zoot Sims (*ts*); Dick Sherman (*t*); Hank Jones or Dave McKenna (*p*); Milt Hinton (*b*); Osie Johnson (*d*). 1/56.

Virtually all one needs to know about Al and Zoot's long-standing association can be found on the sober-sounding 'Improvisation For Two Unaccompanied Saxophones' on the less than sober-sounding *Hot Tracks For Cool Cats*, Volume 2 already (Polydor 816380). All the virtues – elegant interplay, silk-smooth textures – and all the vices – inconsequentiality and a tendency to blandness – are firmly in place. A and Z were apt to cover the whole expressive gamut from A to B, as Dorothy Parker once memorably said about Miss Hepburn.

The 1950s set, replete with alternative takes that prove the wrong point, is a workmanlike mixture of originals and slightly off-beat jazz tunes. Sherman's contributions are impressive, but the two lead players lock horns in the politest possible way.

***   **Body And Soul** Muse MCD 5356 CD/LP
Cohn; Zoot Sims (*ts, ss*); Jaki Byard (*p*); George Duvivier (*b*); Mel Lewis (*d*). 3/73.

The later *Body And Soul* is much more striking, largely because the supporting cast is so good. Byard has all his big-band instincts on show and plays superbly. Duvivier and Lewis hold the tempo up well and the main soloists are occasionally goaded into something slightly more acid than usual. Certainly the best thing that partnership ever put on record.

***   **Play It Now** Xanadu 110 LP
Cohn; Barry Harris (*p*); Larry Ridley (*b*); Alan Dawson (*d*). 6/75.

***(*)   **Al Cohn's America** Xanadu 138 LP
Cohn; Barry Harris (*p*); Sam Jones (*b*); Leroy Williams (*d*). 12/76.

***(*)   **Heavy Love** Xanadu 145 LP
Cohn; Jimmy Rowles (*p*). 3/77.

***(*)   **No Problem** Xanadu 179 LP
Cohn; Barry Harris (*p*); Steve Gilmore (*b*); Walter Bolden (*d*). 12/79.

***(*)   **True Blue** Xanadu 136 LP
Cohn; Blue Mitchell, Sam Noto (*t*); Dexter Gordon (*ts*); Barry Harris (*p*); Sam Jones (*b*); Louis Hayes (*d*). 10/76.

***   **Silver Blue** Xanadu 137 LP
As above. 10/76.

Cohn's Xanadu recordings mark something of a purple patch. The sound is rather shaky, with a bad loss of resolution in the bass, but Cohn is miked very close, giving the music an immediacy and intimacy that work particularly well on *Heavy Love*. Duet playing had become something of a forte; he and Harris give exemplary readings of Hoagy Carmichael tunes on the other two albums – 'Georgia On My Mind' on *Play It Now* and 'Skylark' on *America* – which must count among his most sensitive ballad performances. Though the Rowles set is superb, Harris is a wonderfully instinctive partner and it's a shame they didn't cut a whole album of duets. 'America The Beautiful' makes an unusual and effective opening to the later quartet disc, but again it's Harris's softly swinging solo that lifts the track; followed by 'Night And Day' and 'My Shining Hour', it makes for a beautifully constructed *side*, a creative unit that has now mostly surrendered to the much longer, continuous run of CD but which is still affectionately remembered and preserved on these three fine albums. Harris also makes some fine, boppish interventions on *No Problem*, a set distinguished by a rapid-fire 'All The Things You Are' that takes the classic Parker opening as read and belts through the changes, and by sensitive readings of 'Mood Indigo' and 'Sophisticated Lady', the former treated as a medium-pace waltz, the latter almost abstract in its meditative drift round the tune. *True Blue* and *Silver Blue* come from a single session, recorded in October 1976. The two trumpeters come in for the long title-pieces but the outstanding track is a beautifully crafted 'How Deep Is The Ocean' on Xanadu 136, and that alone makes it the album of choice and a must for Dexter Gordon completists.

***   **Nonpareil** Concord CJ 155 MC
Cohn; Lou Levy (*p*); Monty Budwig (*b*); Jake Hanna (*d*). 4/81.

***   **Standards Of Excellence** Concord CCD 4241 CD/MC
Cohn; Herb Ellis (*g*); Monty Budwig (*b*); Jimmie Smith (*d*). 11/83.

A brilliant arranger, Cohn hasn't always been the most convincing soloist, leaving his own most compelling ideas rather hanging in the air. This latter-day set has him in fine voice, with a tougher, more segmented delivery than previously. The *bossa nova* stylings bear comparison with the rather muffled versions recorded with Zoot Sims.

Ellis is a less satisfactory foil than Levy, and overcooks some of the simpler transitions. Generally, though, standards of excellence are well up to form and Cohn sounds deliciously relaxed on 'Embraceable You', a wonderful tune with a consistency somewhere between marshmallow and quicksand that has lured and lost many a soloist.

(*)   **Tour De Force Concord CCD 4172 CD/MC
Cohn; Scott Hamilton, Buddy Tate (*ts*); Cal Collins (*g*); Dave McKenna (*p*); Bob Maize (*b*); Jake Hanna (*d*). 8/81.

Something of a throwback to the multi-tenor sessions Cohn made with Zoot, Brew Moore, Allen Eager and Stan Getz back in 1949, it's engaging enough stuff, but not surely not sufficiently compelling to merit the critical raves it received on its appearance in 1981. Ten years on, it definitely sounds a bit thin.

***   **The Final Performance Volume 1** RAZmTAZ Jazz 44003 CD/LP
Cohn; Frank Beyerer, Al Porcino, Claus Reichstaller, Peter Tuscher (*t*); Gerd Fink, Erwin Gregg, Jon Welch (*tb*); Auwi Geyer (*btb*); Thomas Faist, Otto Staniloy (*as*); Petri Kral, Herman Martlreiter (*ts*); Thomas Zoller (*bs*); Roberto Di Goia (*p*); Paulo Cardoso (*b*); Wolfgang Haffner (*d*). 3/87.

The European – mostly German – big band does him proud on this, though it's Al Porcino's inspired leadership that gives the set its taut energy. The quartet 'Body And Soul' is one of the best Cohn has recorded; the Lester Young influences seem ever more recessive and irrelevant. He sounds like a man who has recovered his own diction. Docked a star for very disappointing sound, even on the CD, which is very harsh and flat.

***(*)   **Rifftide** Timeless SJP 259 LP
Cohn; Rein de Graaff (*p*); Koos Serierse (*b*); Eric Ineke (*d*). 6/87.

An absolutely marvellous set, with Cohn's brooding tone working an unhurried magic over 'Speak Low', 'Blue Monk' and 'Hot House', as surprising and moving a side as he's ever recorded. The three tracks on side 2 are less familiar but, if anything, better played, with 'We'll

Be Together Again' and the title-tune underlining how subtle an accompanist de Graaff can be. Further proof, if any were needed, of Cohn's creative stamina.

GEORGE 'KID SHEIK' COLAR (born 1908)
TRUMPET, VOCAL

**(*)   The Sheik Of Araby 504 LPS 1 LP
Colar; Louis Nelson (*tb*); Clarence Ford (*cl, ts*); Jeanette Kimball (*p*); Les Muscutt (*bj, g*); Stewart Davis (*b*); Chester Jones (*d*). 8/81.

A great New Orleans trumpet man. But he sounds frankly some way past his best on this session, the fierce phrasing and barking accents of his earlier work softened into something that's more like hesitancy, or shortness of breath. Still, it's an engaging record at its best: the set-list includes some material one rarely encounters in trad programmes, and the rumbustious, barrelling motion of the band makes a rough-and-ready music of it all. Ford's clarinet is weak, but his tenor playing, on a splendid '823 Blues', is much more enterprising; and Nelson was by then as *sui generis* as any of the New Orleans masters. Odd man out: Les Muscutt, a mere forty years old, whose birthplace was Barrow-in-Furness. Wait for Kid Sheik's 1960s recordings to turn up on CD to hear him at his best.

COZY COLE (1909–81)
DRUMS

**   Earl's Backroom And Cozy's Caravan Affinity AFF 167 CD/LP
Cole; Lou Jones (*t*); Phatz Morris (*tb, hca*); Boe McCain (*ts*); June Cole (*p*); Dicky Thompson (*g, v*); Pete Compo (*b*). 2/58.

One of the very great pre-modern drummers, Cole was an intelligent player who constantly redefined and finessed his technique. Predictably, given the hierarchies of the day, he is not well represented as a leader (though there is an extensive discography of work as a sideman with Louis Armstrong, Stuff Smith and Teddy Wilson).

On *Earl's Backroom And Cozy's Caravan* Cole shares the space with a fine Earl Hines quartet, also from February 1958. Only three tracks, but enough to establish Cole's quality; 'Caravan' is beautifully done, and 'Phatz's Blues' lets the undeservedly forgotten trombonist have his head. Worth looking out for.

NAT COLE (1917–65)
PIANO, VOCAL

***(*)   Hit That Jive Jack: The Earliest Recordings MCA MCAD-42350 CD/MC
Cole; Oscar Moore (*g*); Wesley Prince (*b*). 12/40–10/41.

The discographer Brian Rust has pointed out that while Nat 'King' Cole made many records between 1943 and 1966, 'there is virtually no jazz music on any of them'. This kind of slight has been conferred on Cole's output for literally decades. While we have omitted most of his later, vocal records from this book, there should be no doubt that this great pianist never really left jazz behind. He began with the records collected here, deceptively lightweight, jiving music (sample titles: 'Scotchin' With The Soda', 'Stop, The Red Light's On') which masked the intensity of his piano style to a large extent. Smooth, glittering, skating over melodies, Cole's right-hand lines were breaking free of his original Earl Hines influence and looking towards a dashing improvisational freedom which other players – Powell, Haig, Marmarosa – would turn into the language of bebop. Cole was less inclined towards that jagged-edge approach and preferred the hip constrictions of songs and good-natured jive. With pulsing interjections from Moore and Prince, this was a surprisingly compelling music, and the remastering of these tracks has been brightly done.

****   The Best Of The Nat King Cole Trio Capitol CDP 7982882 CD
Cole; Oscar Moore, Irving Ashby (*g*); Johnny Miller, Joe Comfort (*b*); Jack Costanza (*perc*). 11/43–3/49.

***(*)   **The Early Forties** Fresh Sound FSR-CD 139 CD
Cole; Oscar Moore (*g*); Wesley Prince, Johnny Miller (*b*). 40–44.

***(*)   **Nat King Cole The Trio Recordings Vol. 1** Laserlight 15746 CD
As above, except omit Prince. 41.

***(*)   **Nat King Cole The Trio Recordings Vol. 2** Laserlight 15747 CD
As above. 42.

***(*)   **Nat King Cole The Trio Recordings Vol. 3** Laserlight 15748 CD
As above. 42–43.

****   **Nat King Cole The Trio Recordings Vol. 4** Laserlight 15749 CD
As above, except add Anita O'Day (*v*). 44–45.

***(*)   **Nat King Cole The Trio Recordings Vol. 5** Laserlight 15750 CD
As above, except omit O'Day. 45.

Cole made a tremendous number of recordings with his trio, and the definitive collection is the awe-inspiring collection of 18CDs or 27LPs issued by Mosaic, which covers his entire output for Capitol with the group. Capitol's *Best Of*, though, is a fine introduction which covers instrumental-only tracks and highlights Cole's swing, dextrous touch, intelligently varied arrangements for the Trio and their wonderfully responsive following of his leads. Moore is, indeed, almost Cole's equal on an executive level, and their best playing often runs in dazzling, parallel lines. The Laserlight collection (available at budget price) is a fine alternative to the Mosaic set, though: these are transcription recordings which emerge in excellent sound and which feature performances that are usually at least as good as the studio tracks. Volume 4 is especially entertaining since Anita O'Day guests on four tracks, and there's also the best song title Cole (always a hip mind in these situations) ever came up with: 'A Trio Grooves In Brooklyn'. This and several other tracks are also not included in any versions in the Mosaic set, which remains, nevertheless, unsurpassable as a portrait of Cole's work (it also includes his complete *After Midnight* session, listed below). The Fresh Sound disc offers a cross-section of the same transcription material and includes 22 tracks.

***   **Anatomy Of A Jam Session** Black Lion BLCD 760137 CD
Cole; Charlie Shavers (*t*); Herbie Haymer (*ts*); John Simmons (*b*); Buddy Rich (*d*).
6/45.

Not a great deal of music here – 38 minutes, and that includes six alternative takes – but it's a swinging interlude in the normal run of Cole's records of the time, with Haymer and Shavers in knockabout form and Rich at his most brusque. Cole himself is unperturbed by the surrounding racket and makes cool, elegant space for himself. The sound is mostly good with only some surface noise present.

(*)   **The King Cole Trios Live: 1947–48 Vintage Jazz Classics VJC-1011-2 CD
Cole; Duke Ellington (*p*); Oscar Moore, Irving Ashby (*g*); Johnny Miller (*b*); Clark
Dennis, The Dinning Sisters, Pearl Bailey, Woody Herman (*v*). 3/47–3/48.

Taken from *King Cole Time* broadcasts, the routine here is that each guest on the show chats with Nat, 'chooses' songs, and does one number with the Trio. Main interest, inevitably, is on Ellington, who sounds under-rehearsed but does a neat solo on 'Mood Indigo', while the other singers offer slighter stuff. The rest is no more or less than Cole and the trio on their regular form, though several of the tunes are despatched very quickly. Sound quality varies from fairly terrible on the Pearl Bailey and Dinning Sisters shows to quite good with Herman and Ellington. For dedicated Cole fans only.

***   **After Midnight** Capitol 7483282 CD
Cole; Harry Edison (*t*); Juan Tizol (*vtb*); Willie Smith (*as*); Stuff Smith (*vn*); John
Collins (*g*); Charlie Harris (*b*); Lee Young (*d*); Jack Costanza (*perc*). 8–9/56.

Cole's most famous latter-day album still sounds terrific, and the remastering is rather impressive. The only problem with what should have been a dream session – Cole reunited with his regular trio and four star guest soloists – is that it falls into a pattern of routine: the hipness of the 1940s sessions has been traded for a sometimes stultifying back-to-my-roots feeling that can sound like a man trying too hard to be faithful to his old self. By now, Cole was a major vocal star, and this date – though it has many marvellous moments – simply came to late.

***(*)   **Big Band Cole** Capitol CDP 7962592 CD
　　　Cole; Count Basie, Stan Kenton Orchestras. 50–58.

A compilation of sessions with Basie's band (minus Basie) and two tracks with the Kenton orchestra, plus two other songs with a top-flight studio band. Cole should have made more big-band jazz records than he did – for all the beauty and warmth of his 'straight' records – and this compilation shows the missed opportunity. Cole doesn't swing noticeably harder here than he does normally, but set-pieces such as 'The Blues Don't Care' and 'Wee Baby Blues' establish a very different mood to his normal regimen, and he sounds as comfortable and good-humoured as he ever did elsewhere. Beautifully remastered, this is highly recommended.

· As fine as Nat Cole's many albums for Capitol are, we have chosen to include only the above two discs here, our disagreement with Brian Rust notwithstanding.

RICHIE COLE (born 1948)
ALTO AND TENOR SAXOPHONES

**   **New York Afternoon** Muse M 5119 CD/LP
　　　Cole; Mickey Tucker (p); Vic Juris (g); Rick Laird (b); Eddie Gladden (d); Ray
　　　Mantilla (perc); Eddie Jefferson (v). 10/76.

(*)   **Alto Madness Muse M 5155 CD/LP
　　　As above, except Harold Mabern (p) replaces Tucker, add Steve Gilmore (b). 12/77.

**   **Keeper Of The Flame** Muse MR 5192 LP
　　　As above, except omit Gilmore. 9/78.

**   **Hollywood Madness** Muse M 5207 CD/LP
　　　Cole; Dick Hindman (p); Marshall Hawkins, Bob Magnusson (b); Les Demerle (d);
　　　Michael Spiro (perc); Eddie Jefferson, Manhattan Transfer (v). 4/79.

(*)   **Side By Side Muse M 5237 CD/LP
　　　Cole; Phil Woods (as); Eddie 'Lockjaw' Davis (ts); John Hicks (p); Walter Booker
　　　(b); Jimmy Cobb (d). 7/80.

**   **Some Things Speak For Themselves** Muse MR 5295 LP
　　　Cole; Smith Dobson (p); Bruce Forman (g); Marshall Hawkins (b); Scott Morris (d).
　　　2/81.

**   **Cool 'C'** Muse MR 5245 LP
　　　Cole; Shin Kazuhara, Yoshikazu Kishl, Hitoshi Yokoyama, Masahiro Kobayashi (t);
　　　Michio Kagiwada, Hitomi Uchida, Toshinobu Iwasaki, Shigeru Kawashima (tb);
　　　Himicho Kikuchi (p); Nobuyoshi Ino (b); Motohiko Hino (d); Tadaomi Anai, Masato
　　　Kawase (perc). 2/81.

***   **Alive!** Muse MR 5270 LP
　　　Cole; Bobby Enriquez (p); Bruce Forman (g); Marshall Hawkins (b); Scott Morris
　　　(d). 6/81.

***   **Pure Imagination** Concord CCD 4314 CD/MC
　　　Cole; Vic Juris (g); Ed Howard (b); Victor Jones (d); Ray Mantilla (perc). 11/86.

*(*)   **Popbop** Milestone 9152 CD/LP/MC
　　　Cole; Dick Hindman (p); Vic Juris (g); Marshall Hawkins, Eddie Howard (b); Victor
　　　Jones (d); Kenneth Nash, Tim Hauser (perc). 87.

**   **Signature** Milestone 9162 CD/LP/MC
　　　Cole; Ben Sidran (ky); Tee Carson (p); Vic Juris (g); Keith Jones, Marshall Hawkins
　　　(b); Mel Brown (d); Andy Narell, Babatunde Olatunji (perc). 88.

(*)   **Bossa Nova International Milestone 9180 CD/LP/MC
　　　Cole; Hank Crawford (as); Emily Remler (g); Marshall Hawkins (b); Victor Jones
　　　(d). 6/87.

There was a time when Richie Cole seemed on the verge of some kind of international jazz stardom, but his impact has waned a bit since the late 1970s and early '80s, when most of these records were made. A former student of Phil Woods, at his best he sounds like a good version of Woods, which – when the original has so many records available – tends to raise the question as to whether it's worth listening to a good copy. A little unfair, perhaps, but none of these records has the kind of sustained interest that makes one want to return to them very often. *Side By Side*, where he actually plays with Woods, is a barnstorming encounter, but it's wearisome over the full stretch, and it's the studio sessions which usually work out for the best, particularly *Alto Madness*, although Eddie Jefferson's singing is another acquired taste. The best of the location recordings is *Alive!*, where Cole and pianist Bobby Enriquez work up an overpowering head of steam without the aid of any guest stars: for showmanship alone this merits a listen. A move to Milestone hasn't reaped any greater artistic rewards – *Popbop* is as disastrous as its title suggests, and *Signature* forsakes bebop heat for damp soul-jazz – but *Bossa Nova International* benefits from the felicitous presence of Emily Remler, whose comping binds the music together.

EARL COLEMAN (born 1925)
VOCAL

**   **Earl Coleman Returns** Original Jazz Classics OJC 187 LP
Coleman; Art Farmer (*t*); Gigi Gryce (*as*); Hank Jones (*p*); Wendell Marshall or Oscar Pettiford (*b*); Wilbert Hogan or Shadow Wilson (*d*). 3–6/56.

A less dramatic vocalist than King Pleasure, Coleman still got closer to the fountainhead of bebop. Perhaps his best-known recordings are 'This Is Always' and the aptly titled 'Dark Days' from the 1947 Charlie Parker Dial sessions. This 1956 'comeback' is surprisingly effective. The Farmer quartet/quintet plays superbly, with Gryce in unusually good-natured form, and the rhythm section noticeably tolerant of Coleman's slight hesitancy. The Parker sessions are still exemplary, but this is well worth checking out.

GEORGE COLEMAN (born 1935)
TENOR SAXOPHONE, ALTO SAXOPHONE

***   **Big George** Charly 83 CD
Coleman; Danny Moore (*t, flhn*); Frank Strozier (*as*); Junior Cook (*ts*); Mario Rivera (*bs*); Harold Mabern (*p*); Lisle Atkinson (*b*); Idris Muhammad (*d*); Azzedin Weston (*perc*). 11/77.

Like his near-namesake of the boxing ring, George Coleman plays a little weight-bound but gets in the odd spectacular punch. On *Big George* he sticks to the basics with flexible ensemble readings of 'Body And Soul' and 'On Green Dolphin Street', and the kind of muscular soloing that has influenced some of the younger generation of British tenor players who heard him at Ronnie Scott's in 1978 on the same European stint as Timeless SJP 129, below.

This is well recorded, though the horns tend to crowd one another like tiring heavyweights and the piano moves in and out of view like a nervous ref. Perhaps he could do with a little more 'Joggin'', a hard-edged theme which recalls Miles's trimmed-down harmonies, but there's nothing flabby anywhere on the set. Fine stuff, and strongly recommended.

***   **Amsterdam After Dark** Timeless SJP 129 CD/LP
Coleman; Hilton Ruiz (*p*); Sam Jones (*b*); Billy Higgins (*d*). 12/78.

(*)   **Manhattan Panorama Theresa TR 120 CD/LP
Coleman; Harold Mabern (*p*); Jamil Nasser (*b*); Idris Muhammad (*d*). 82 or 83.

Hard to tell how sincere Coleman's love affair with the Big Apple really is. Woody Allen turned the same skyline into a wry, Gershwin-drenched poem. Coleman, with an eye on 'El Barrio' and the 'New York Housing Blues', is by no means so dewy-eyed; the inevitable 'Manhattan' and 'I Love New York' are both in place, but there's also a vocal tribute to 'Mayor Koch' that suggests a much tougher perspective, and there's a chill wind blowing through 'Autumn In New York' on the Timeless album. The Mabern/Muhammad rhythm axis fuels some fine solos from

Coleman, who also plays his alto on this date, with a fleet diction that belies any charges of ponderousness.

The Dutch cityscape is even finer, with an absolutely superb rhythm section and a beautiful registration that picks up all the tiny, grainy resonances Coleman gets across his reed. Ruiz and Higgins play with perfect understanding and Sam Jones must be one of the best slow-tempo players on the scene.

** **Meditation** Timeless SJP 110 CD/LP
Coleman; Tete Montoliu (*p*). 4/77.

A not entirely successful collaboration. Coleman's meditative mode is still a little tense and, without the backing of a section, he seems uncertain about metres. Montoliou is a much less linear player, and there are moments when the two seem to be occupying different musical spaces. Coleman fans will find it intriguing, though.

*** **Playing Changes** Ronnie Scott's Jazz House JHCD 002 CD
Coleman; Hilton Ruiz (*p*); Ray Drummond (*b*); Billy Higgins (*d*). 4/79.

For anyone who has worn smooth their copy of the old *Ronnie Scott Presents George Coleman 'Live'* [Pye N 121 LP] mentioned above, this could be a fair substitute. Recorded during the same 1979 residency at Frith Street, *Playing Changes* consists of just three – two *long*, one shorter – takes. Coleman's attack is typically robust and veined with unexpected harmonic ore. However, anyone whose copy of the original LP survives may feel that they already have the best of the deal. The long 'Laura' is, at 23 minutes plus, a tad *too* long, and slightly overgenerous to both Ruiz and the still-inexperienced Drummond; by contrast, 'Stella By Starlight', which occupies a whole side of the Pye, is a much more coherent performance. The second track, 'Siorra', is an unconvincing Coleman original, and the best of the saxophonist's work occurs when he moves sideways of the given changes and into his inventive high harmonic mode. There are either misfingerings or symptoms of a weary reed in the closing ensembles of the end-of-set 'Moment's Notice' which detract a little from an intriguing variation on the Coltrane original. On balance, it might have been better to put together a stronger 65-minute CD integrating the best of the two sessions. Scratches aside, most listeners will be returning to the Pye a lot more often than to this.

ORNETTE COLEMAN (born 1930)
ALTO SAXOPHONE, TRUMPET, VIOLIN, TENOR SAXOPHONE

*** **Something Else!!** Original Jazz Classics OJC 163 CD/LP/MC
Coleman; Don Cherry (*t*); Walter Norris (*p*); Don Payne (*b*); Billy Higgins (*d*). 2/58.

*** **Tomorrow Is The Question** Original Jazz Classics OJC 342 CD/LP/MC
Coleman; Don Cherry (*t*); Percy Heath or Red Mitchell (*b*); Shelly Manne (*d*). 1, 2, 3/59.

Though the 1958 Hillcrest Club sessions under Paul Bley's nominal leadership represent something of a crux in Coleman's development, it is still startling to hear him work with a pianist. He got the first of these sessions at Red Mitchell's behest and it suffers from all the vices of a hasty pick-up; problems that were largely ironed out on the more thoughtful *Tomorrow Is The Question*, a set which includes 'Tears Inside', perhaps the most beautiful single item in the whole Coleman canon – and sucks to all the critics who considered him a raucous circus act. *Tomorrow* is also notable for Shelly Manne's impeccably hip contribution; an unlikely recruitment on the face of it, even given his tenure at Contemporary, but absolutely bang up to the moment.

**** **The Shape Of Jazz To Come** Atlantic 781339-2 CD
Coleman; Don Cherry (*pocket t*); Charlie Haden (*b*); Billy Higgins (*d*). 10/59, 10/59, 7/60.

**** **Change Of The Century** Atlantic SD 1327 LP
As above. 10/59.

**** **This Is Our Music** Atlantic SD 1353 LP
As above, except omit Higgins, add Ed Blackwell (*d*). 10/59.

***(*)   **The Art Of The Improvisers** Atlantic 90978 2 CD
          As above, except add Jimmy Garrison, Scott LaFaro (*b*). 7/60.

These are the classic Coleman quartet sessions. It is slightly hard to quantify their 'influence'. There were a score and more of dime-store Coltranes for every one alto player with Coleman's sharp harmonic astigmatism. The slightly hectoring and apocalyptic tone of the album titles isn't entirely borne out by the music inside, which is far more introspective and thoughtful than is often suggested. The first two were released slightly out of chronological sequence; if 'progress' and 'development' can show inside a month, then *The Shape Of Jazz To Come* really is a major step forward.

CD transfer is slowly changing perceptions of these and later sets, uncovering the extent to which the bands worked collectively and from the bottom up, never entirely dominated by the two horns. On vinyl, Haden in particular has to be listened for very carefully indeed.

Most of the essential Coleman pieces are to be found here: 'Lonely Woman' and 'Congeniality' on *Shape*, 'Una Muy Bonita' on *Change*, 'Blues Connotation' on *Our Music*, with a wonderful revisionist 'Embraceable You' on the last of the three which underlines its consolidating place in Coleman's output.

Hard to think that any of these is less than essential. Like *Twins*, *Art Of The Improvisers* is a useful piece of documentation from a particularly fertile period. First released in 1970 as a fill-in, it stands up quite respectably and offers a useful running check on how Coleman reacts to changing line-ups.

****   **Free Jazz** Atlantic SD 1364 CD
          Coleman; Don Cherry (*pocket t*); Freddie Hubbard (*t*); Eric Dolphy (*bcl*); Charlie
          Haden, Scott LaFaro (*b*); Ed Blackwell, Billy Higgins (*d*). 12/60.

(*)   **Twins Atlantic SD8810 LP
          As above.

The original Jackson Pollock cover to *Free Jazz* was a fairly accurate summation of a common *Zeitgeist*. It's gestural music, splashing instrumental colour about with a total indifference to accurate figuration. Coleman's huge double quartet, with its blandly generic title, set a course for large-scale 'comprovisation' over the next decade, and notably Coltrane's grandly metaphysical *Ascension* (Impulse GRD 21132). Free it may have been harmonically, but it was still locked into an oddly mechanical theme-and-solos format which, with eight sturdy egos to massage, takes a bit of time. The much briefer 'First Take' on the useful *Twins* compilation has its proponents, and the album makes useful documentation of an artist who has been rather poorly served by the big labels.

What redeems *Free Jazz* and elevates it to senior status in the modern canon is the extraordinary variety of sound-colour that comes from the twinned soloists. Dolphy's fruity bass clarinet is a perfect specific to Coleman's thin, slightly flat tone. Hubbard and Cherry could hardly be less alike. LaFaro's out-of-tempo play contrasts well with Haden's Ware-influenced, long-legged gait. Separating Blackwell and Higgins requires an almost ornithological attention to detail and is, in any case, largely for the birds. Both are superb.

***(*)   **Ornette On Tenor** Atlantic SD 1394 LP
          Coleman; Don Cherry (*pocket t*); Jimmy Garrison (*b*); Ed Blackwell (*d*). 3/61.

Charlie Parker on tenor sounded like, well, Charlie Parker. Coleman sounds a little different on his original horn, with the Old Adam, Texas R&B peeping through. The tonality is very much the same, but there is a narrative quality to his soloing on the B flat instrument that is entirely missing from his angular, abstract alto work. Not a classic, but certainly more than a curiosity.

****   **At The Golden Circle, Stockholm: Volume 1** Blue Note BCT 84224 CD
          Coleman; David Izenzon (*b*); Charles Moffett (*d*). 65.

****   **At The Golden Circle, Stockholm: Volume 2** Blue Note BCT 84225 CD
          As above.

Marvellous live sessions from Coleman's most stripped-down touring band. Moffett is a thrasher, but Izenzon's cantorial cries, already heavily laced with the tragedy that was to dog his life, provides a perfect grounding for some of Coleman's best solo work on record. Guess-the-next-note pieces like 'European Echoes' work less well than 'Morning Song' and

'The Riddle', and the obligatory fiddle and trumpet feature, 'Snowflakes And Sunshine', is unusually bland. Otherwise, the material is excellent.

The sound is surprisingly good for a club recording and for Coleman's spare, almost minimalist music, certainly better balanced than some of the classic Atlantics. CD underscores Izenzon's merits and Moffett's defaults in roughly equal measure, and long-standing fans may prefer to hang on to pristine vinyl, which softens the shriller overtones of the leader's alto.

One of the slight myths of Coleman's career is that he 'hears' changes and progressions according to some inner logic and doesn't require the conventional supports of piano accompaniment or pedal notes on the bass. In fact, as with Dewey Redman in years to come, Coleman here relies heavily on Izenzon, working along pathways laid out by the bassist's deep-rooted chords, often quite conventionally.

** **New York Is Now** Blue Note CDP 7 84287 CD
Coleman; Dewey Redman (*ts*); Jimmy Garrison (*b*); Elvin Jones (*d*). 4–5/68.

** **Love Call** Blue Note CDP 7 84356 CD
As above.

A thin and somewhat directionless point in Coleman's career. This is perhaps his least familiar band and something of a misalliance. Recording with the recently deceased Coltrane's rhythm section, Coleman is nudged in the direction of some uncharacteristic vertical improvisation on largely implicit chords. Whereas Cherry had followed him almost anywhere, Redman seems content here (as on the New York University gig recorded as *Crisis*) to play an anchor role, offering capacious pedal points and comfortably contoured lower-register figures which reduce the dynamism of Coleman's solos significantly, spinning them out into long, frantic noodles.

Long opening tracks – 'The Garden Of Souls' on *New York Is Now* and 'Airborne' on *Love Call* – would have made the basis of a respectable single album. Much of the rest is makeweight. An alternative take of the already tedious R&B 'Broad Way Blues' constitutes a rather ambiguous 'bonus', and 'We Now Interrupt For A Commercial', a hectic cityscape not dissimilar to Redman's later 'Funcitydues', is plain silly. Completists only.

** **Live In Milano, 1968** Jazz Up JU 310 CD
Coleman; Charlie Haden, David Izenzon (*b*); Ed Blackwell (*d*). 2/68.

*** **Broken Shadows** Moon M 022 CD/LP
Coleman; Dewey Redman (*ts, musette*); Charlie Haden (*b*); Ed Blackwell (*d*). 8/69.

Two poorly recorded live dates, the first of which will appeal only to completists able to separate the material identified as 'Tutti', 'Three Wisemen And The Saint' and 'New York' from an aural blur that reduces the twinned basses to a largely indistinguishable rumble (a shame, for some of the duet parts are more interesting than Haden's rather predictable soloing) and which makes Blackwell's opening percussion sound like crickets.

The jungle noises are a little clearer on *Broken Shadows*, and particularly on 'Space Jungle', but the sound quality is still poor and the performances (with the exception of Blackwell's) lack the impact of the nearly contemporary and similarly programmed *Crisis* (long since deleted on Impulse!), which was recorded at New York University with Don Cherry also in attendance. Without his high, sharp sound, 'Song For Che' and the dirge 'Broken Shadows' (with which *Crisis* unforgettably opens) are pretty thin. All but the most dedicated collectors would be well advised to consider the pair above inessential.

** **Jazzbuhne Berlin '88** Repertoire RR 4905 CD
Coleman; Chris Rosenberg, Ken Wessel (*g*); Al McDowell, Chris Walker (*b*);
Denardo Coleman (*d*); Badal Roy (*tablas*); probable personnel, and not as listed on sleeve. 6/88.

Eagle-eyed fans were quick to point out the inconsistency between the liner photo and the putative line-up (the sleeve listing is in keeping with Coleman's more familiar Prime Time personnel). Acceptance of the revised roll-call is pretty much an act of faith, for this is a messy, congested performance that reduces 'Song X' to adolescent 'heaviness', 'Dancing In Your Head' to drearily repetitive techno-jazz-funk. It's also near impossible to determine what any tabla player who may have been present is actually doing. Coleman sounds more engaged and convincing on his trumpet than on his first horn, and the brief 'Chanting' is quietly affecting. Otherwise very much a record for fans of a 'you had to be there' persuasion.

** **Virgin Beauty** Columbia/Portrait 44301 CD
Coleman; Charles Ellerbee, Jerry Garcia, Bern Nix (*g*); Al McDowell, Chris Walker
Calvin Weston (*d*); Denardo Coleman (*d, ky*). 88.

Dull, MOR jazz-funk in which the outlines of tougher material ('3 Wishes', 'Desert Players', 'Healing The Feeling') are smothered in a clotted rock mix and further compromised by Denardo's bland keyboard washes. Grateful Dead man Garcia was a controversial inclusion, but does nothing to merit all the fuss, spinning out inoffensively countrified figures that merely take their place in the queue. Only the haunting title-track wakens memories of what Ornette was once capable of as a pure melodist.

STEVE COLEMAN
ALTO SAXOPHONE, SOPRANO SAXOPHONE, VOCALS

***(*) **Motherland Pulse** JMT 834401 CD/LP
Coleman; Graham Haynes (*t*); Geri Allen (*p*); Lonnie Plaxico (*b*); Marvin Smitty
Smith (*d*). 3/85.

*** **Five Elements** JMT 834405 CD/LP
Coleman; Graham Haynes (*t*); Kelvyn Bell (*g, v*); Kevin Bruce Harris (*b, v*); Geri
Allen (*ky*); Mark Johnson, Marvin Smitty Smith (*d, perc*); Cassandra Wilson (*v*). 1 &
2/86.

*** **World Expansion** JMT 834410 CD/LP
Coleman; Graham Haynes (*t*); Robin Eubanks (*tb, v*); Geri Allen (*p, ky*); Kelvyn Bell
(*g*); Kevin Bruce Harris (*b*); Mark Johnson (*d*); D. K. Dyson, Cassandra Wilson (*v*).
11/86.

Coleman's most interesting work to date has been with bassist Dave Holland's band on a group of interesting ECMs, recorded after these rather erratic and tentative sessions. Coleman has a crisp diction with an attractive sourness of tone, and he is a surer technician than his label-mate, tenorist Gary Thomas.

Thomas shares a broad commitment to M-Base's syncretism of jazz, funk, hip-hop, beatbox and other black urban musics, but he makes his approach from the opposite angle, as it were. Coleman is unmistakably a jazz player whose harmonic developments on *Motherland Pulse*, by far the best album of the three, suggest a sophisticated musical intelligence. This has become slightly mannered on the two later albums, which are credited to Coleman and his band, Five Elements. Smith is an able accompanist in all branches of black music, but Allen's keyboard figures are maddeningly inconsistent, brightly inventive one moment, bland enough for an MOR pop album the next. Cassandra Wilson's vocals have a joyous, soaring quality and the band always sounds best when it falls in behind her.

Purely as entertainment, all three are attractive propositions, but anyone interested in what Coleman has to offer should get hold of Dave Holland's *Extensions*, *The Razor's Edge* and the fine trio *Triplicate* (ECM 1410, 1353, 1373 CD/LP).

JOHN COLIANNI (born 1963)
PIANO

*** **John Colianni** Concord CJ-309 CD/LP/MC
Colianni; Joe Wilder (*t*); Emily Remler (*g*); Bob Field (*b*); Connie Kay (*d*). 8/86.

(*) **Blues-O-Matic Concord CJ-367 CD/LP/MC
Colianni; Lew Tabackin (*ts, f*); Lynn Seaton (*b*); Mel Lewis (*d*). 8/88.

Younger than he plays, Colianni learned his trade in Washington piano bars and with Lionel Hampton's big band. The most impressive thing about this youthful mainstreamer is his rock-steady rhythm: that confidence means he can take a slow-to-mid-tempo tune such as Ray Brown's engaging 'Soft Shoe', on *John Colianni*, and make it swing. The first record is divided into solo, trio and quartet tracks, with Wilder sitting in for one tune, and it's all bright and affectionate music. The second session is a fraction less appealing, since Tabackin seems a vaguely distracted participant, and the pianist is a tad less decisive.

BUDDY COLLETTE (born 1921)
REEDS AND WOODWINDS

(*)   **Man Of Many Parts Original Jazz Classics OJC 239 LP
Collette; Gerald Wilson (*t*); Dave Wells (*bt*); Bill Green (*as*); Jewel Grant (*bs*);
Gerald Wiggins, Ernie Freeman (*p*); Barney Kessel (*g*); Gene Wright, Red Callender,
Joe Comfort (*b*); Max Alright, Bill Richmond, Larry Bunker (*d*). 2–4/56.

Buddy Collette had the misfortune to be a pioneer on an instrument whose jazz credentials
remain in doubt: though he was a capable performer on alto, tenor and clarinet, he became
renowned as a flautist and consequently got stuck in the role of novelty sessionman in the West
Coast scene of the mid-1950s. The few remaining records under his own name are no stronger
than the ones he made as a sideman, principally with Chico Hamilton. The OJC reissue,
originally issued on Contemporary, is gimcracked around his multi-instrumentalism and is
mildly enjoyable without catching much fire.

***   **Flute Talk** Soul Note SN 1165 CD/LP
Collette; James Newton (*f*); Geri Allen (*p*); Jaribu Shaind (*b*); Gianpiero Prina (*d*).
7/88.

Collette's return to the studios, recorded on an Italian tour, is hurried but agreeable enough,
and this is probably the best group he's ever led on record. The meeting with Newton is more
respectful than combative, and Allen is her usual unpredictable self, alert in places, asleep in
others. The recording could be sharper.

MAX COLLIE (born 1931)
TROMBONE, VOCALS

**   **Frontline** Timeless TTD 504 LP
Collie; Phil Mason (*t*); Jack Gilbert (*cl*); Jim McIntosh (*bjo*); Trefor Williams (*b*); Ron
McKay (*d*). 12/82.

**   **Backline** Timeless TTD 508 LP
As above.

This sort of music doesn't really sound right on a CD and if there is such an entity as the 'CD
generation', they probably don't buy it anyway. Collie works at the blue-collar, Transit van end
of the Bilk–Ball–Barber spectrum, a rough-diamond revivalist with a big strong tone, notably
tight and well-schooled bands and an entertainment potential that goes off the scale. From a
single 1982 session, these albums do little more than provide tasters of the live act.

(*)   **20 Years Jubilee Timeless TTD 519 LP
Collie; Denny Ilett (*c*); Paul Harrison (*cl*); Jim McIntosh (*bjo*); T. J. Johnson (*p, v*);
Trefor Williams (*b*); Peter Cotterill (*d*). 12/84.

**   **Sensation** Timeless TTD 530 CD/LP
As above, except Mason (*c*) replaces Ilett. 7/86.

Far from awarding himself a sabbatical, Collie has been working harder than ever. This band
has a rather more 'authentic' feel, whatever that means, than its predecessor; Ilett's sharp,
brassy cornet may be one reason. Fine performances, better material and a clearer pick-up on
the rhythm section.

CAL COLLINS (born 1933)
GUITAR

(*)   **Ohio Style Concord CCD 4447 CD/MC
Collins; Jerry Van Blair (*flhn*); Lou Lausche (*b*); Tony Sweet (*d*). 11/90.

None of the previous six albums for Concord by Cal Collins remains in the catalogue. Of the
many swing-styled guitarists which the company has recorded, Collins is rather more exciting
than most: a former bluegrass player and a rather late developer, his manner owes much to

Django Reinhardt although he follows Tal Farlow's lead more closely. What comes out is a kind of down-home swing-to-bop, a manner that lets him create some crackling improvisations at fast tempos, although he tends towards sleepy gentility on a ballad. This recent session pairs him with cornetist Van Blair in a setting which sounds much like a Ruby Braff–George Barnes date or something involving Bobby Hackett. There isn't that level of class here, but it's well done in its way.

LOU COLOMBO
TRUMPET

**   **I Remember Bobby** Concord CCD 4435 CD
Colombo; Dave McKenna (*p*); Gray Sargent (*g*); Phil Flanigan (*b*); Keith Copeland (*d*). 6/90.

The 'Bobby' is Bobby Hackett, but Colombo isn't much like that master, nor is he especially interesting as a leader-soloist. A proficient player, but there's nothing in this pleasant mainstream session which couldn't have been done as well by many other section trumpeters. McKenna and the others offer their customary capable support.

MASSIMO COLOMBO
KEYBOARDS

*(*)   **Alexander** Splasc(h) H 177 LP
Colombo (*ky*); Marco Micheli (*b*); Francesco Sotgu (*d*). 1–2/89.

An unappetizing batch of impressionist doodles from this accomplished pianist: Colombo has the technique, but his tunes are low on interest, and the use of electric keyboards as colour is merely a distraction. The outstanding player here is probably Micheli, who has a fine tone and some useful ideas. Impeccably recorded in the Splasc(h) manner.

COLSON UNITY TROUP
GROUP

(*)   **No Reservation Black Saint BSR 0043 LP
Adegoke Steve Colson (*ts, p*); Wallace MacMillan (*ss, as, ts, picc, perc*); Reggie Willis (*b*); Dushun Mosley (*perc*); Iqua Colson (*v*). 7/80.

Something of a one-off, but none the worse for the absence of recognizable star names. The ethos is somewhat to the Tamla Motown side of the Art Ensemble of Chicago, but the results are modestly impressive. Worth a try.

JOHN COLTRANE (1926–67)
TENOR, ALTO AND SOPRANO SAXOPHONES, FLUTE

***   **Dakar** Original Jazz Classics OJC 393 CD/LP/MC
Coltrane; Cecil Payne, Pepper Adams (*bs*); Mal Waldron (*p*); Doug Watkins (*b*); Art Taylor (*d*). 4/57.

***   **Coltrane** Original Jazz Classics OJC 020 CD/LP/MC
Coltrane; Johnny Splawn (*t*); Sahib Shihab (*bs*); Mal Waldron (*p*); Paul Chambers (*b*); Albert 'Tootie' Heath (*d*). 5/57.

***   **Lush Life** Original Jazz Classics OJC 131 CD/LP/MC
Coltrane; Donald Byrd (*t*); Red Garland (*p*); Earl May (*b*); Art Taylor, Louis Hayes, Albert 'Tootie' Heath (*d*). 5/57–1/58.

***   **Traneing In** Original Jazz Classics OJC 189 CD/LP/MC
Coltrane; Red Garland (*p*); Paul Chambers (*b*); Art Taylor (*d*). 8/57.

***(*)   **Blue Train** Blue Note CDP 7460952 CD/MC
Coltrane; Lee Morgan (*t*); Curtis Fuller (*tb*); Kenny Drew (*p*); Paul Chambers (*b*);
Philly Joe Jones (*d*). 9/57.

Coltrane had moved from obscurity to front-ranking stardom in a matter of two years. When he joined the Miles Davis quintet, he rapidly asserted a primal voice on the tenor saxophone: a hard, iron tone, a ceaseless, tumbling flow of phrases, a sense of some great architecture in the making. He had already played big-band section-work for years, and his work with Davis now sounds transitional – although, in a sense, so does all of his music. His early sessions as a leader for Prestige are mere stopovers on the journey, expansive, prolific, but never finally achieved in the way that his great later works would be. In 1957, the year he also worked with Thelonious Monk, whose influence on him is important but hard to pin down, he made these five sessions under his own name. All of the OJC reissues (from Prestige originals) are enjoyable without leaving a lasting impression. *Dakar* is timbrally unusual, with its rumbling two-baritone front line (in the excellent remastering the music emerges as quite a feast of low-register grumbling and growling), but Coltrane sounds out of place, even on the three interesting originals by session superviser Teddy Charles. *Coltrane* and *Lush Life* are full of pwerful tenor: the latter is interesting for three tracks with just bass and drums support, but Trane never uses this as the challenge which Sonny Rollins took up at the Village Vanguard in the same year (it only came about, in any case, because the pianist never showed up). *Traneing In*, with the Davis rhythm section, features a tumultuous solo on the title-track and the lovely, deep-set ballad playing on 'You Leave Me Breathless' which is the untarnished virtue of the Prestige sessions and one of the things which attracts many to Coltrane in the first place. More significant, though, is his sole date for Blue Note, *Blue Train*, which has one of his most coherent early solos on the title-track. The rest of the band are inappropriate players for the occasion, though Fuller tears off a great outburst on 'Locomotion': the underlying strength of 'Moment's Notice', which has since become a standard, is reduced to hard bop cliché here. But there is always a sense of Coltrane having something tremendous almost within sight. *Coltrane* and *Lush Life* have also been combined on a single UK-issue CD (Prestige CDJZD-001).

(*)   **Tenor Conclave Original Jazz Classics OJC 127 CD/LP/MC
Coltrane; Paul Quinichette, Hank Mobley, Al Cohn, Zoot Sims (*ts*); Red Garland (*p*);
Paul Chambers (*b*); Art Taylor (*d*). 9/56.

***   **Cattin' With Coltrane And Quinichette** Original Jazz Classics OJC 460 CD/LP/MC
Coltrane; Paul Quinichette (*ts*); Mal Waldron (*p*); Julian Euell (*b*); Ed Thigpen (*d*).
5/57.

***   **Wheelin' And Dealin'** Original Jazz Classics OJC 672 CD/MC
Coltrane; Frank Wess, Paul Quinichette (*ts*); Mal Waldron (*p*); Doug Watkins (*b*); Art
Taylor (*d*). 57.

One of Coltrane's chores for Prestige was to blow his way through sundry encounters with other tenors. The *Tenor Conclave* album is moderately good fun, but the essential pointlessness of the exercise is shown up by the looseness of the material and arrangements, even if professionalism does win out. The meeting with Quinichette is rather better, Trane's intensity making a good match for Quinichette's lighter and more carefree (but still bluesy) mannerisms. 'Cattin' itself is a great uptempo swinger. *Wheelin' And Dealin'* returns to the tenors-all-out formula, and is respectable enough.

***(*)   **Soultrane** Original Jazz Classics 021 CD/LP/MC
Coltrane; Red Garland (*p*); Paul Chambers (*b*); Art Taylor (*d*). 2/58.

***(*)   **Settin' The Pace** Original Jazz Classics OJC 078 CD/LP/MC
As above. 3/58.

(*)   **Black Pearls Original Jazz Classics OJC 352 CD/LP/MC
As above, except add Donald Byrd (*t*). 5/58.

***   **The Standard Coltrane** Original Jazz Classics OJC 246 CD/LP/MC
As above, except Wilbur Harden (*t, flhn*), Jimmy Cobb (*d*) replace Byrd and Taylor.
7/58.

***   **The Stardust Session** Prestige 24056 CD
As above. 7/58.

***   **Bahia** Original Jazz Clasics OJC 415 CD/LP/MC
As above, except add Art Taylor (*d*). 12/58.

***   **The Last Trane** Original Jazz Classics OJC 394 CD/LP/MC
Coltrane; Donald Byrd (*t*); Red Garland (*p*); Paul Chambers, Earl May (*b*); Art
Taylor, Louis Hayes (*d*). 8/57–3/58.

***(*)   **John Coltrane And The Jazz Giants** Prestige 60104 CD
Coltrane; Donald Byrd, Miles Davis, Wilbur Harden (*t*); Tadd Dameron, Red
Garland, Thelonious Monk (*p*); Paul Chambers, Jamil Nasser, Wilbur Ware, John
Simmons (*b*); Shadow Wilson, Jimmy Cobb, Philly Joe Jones, Louis Hayes, Art Taylor
(*d*). 56–58.

Even as Coltrane grew in stature, with the celebrated 'sheets of sound' – covering every
possible permutation of one chord before the next arrived – as the dominant part of his sound
and delivery, the circumstances of his recording tenure at Prestige stubbornly refused to open
up to him, with the casual nature of the sessions reinforced by sole use of standards and blues as
the blowing material. *Soultrane*, with its first version of a later favourite, 'I Want To Talk
About You', and *Settin' The Pace*, featuring a spearing assault on Jackie Mclean's 'Little
Melonae' and a glowing 'If There Is Someone Lovelier Than You', are both outstanding
tenor-and-rhythm dates where Coltrane gives himself as much rope as he feels he can find.
Black Pearls is let down by the overlong and tedious 'Sweet Sapphire Blues', and *Bahia* –
though it has a couple more excellent Coltrane ballad treatments – is also routine. *The Standard
Coltrane* dwells on ballads and will please any who prefer the more tractable side of Coltrane's
music, while *The Last Trane* pulls together four outtakes from earlier sessions, 'Come Rain Or
Come Shine' standing up particularly well. *The Stardust Session* includes all of *Standard
Coltrane*, two tracks from *Bahia* and 'Stardust' and 'Love Thy Neighbour'. There is little in
these records of genuinely outstanding calibre, and the compilation *John Coltrane And The Jazz
Giants* – which includes tracks with Davis and Monk – is as good a way as any of geting to know
this period without toiling through what are mostly verbose and disorganized records. But
Coltrane's sound, of course, endures.

****   **Giant Steps** Atlantic 781337-2 CD/MC
Coltrane; Tommy Flanagan (*p*); Paul Chambers (*b*); Art Taylor (*d*). 5/59.

A fresh start – almost a debut album – and perhaps Coltrane's most playable, memorable and
best-sustained record. The tunes are uniformly marvellous, riffs or steps or even melodies which
have all – except for 'Spiral' – become integral parts of the modern jazz book. Coltrane's tone
has lost some of its remorselessness, and it gives the ballad 'Naima' a movingly simple lyrical
intent. It's almost like an interlude on Coltrane's journey, this record, a summing up of past
achievements in sparer, easier forms, before the great steps forward of the next few years.
'Giant Steps' itself has a sunny quality which its rising theme embodies; 'Mr P.C.' is a blowing
blues which is idiomatic enough to have become the most frequently blown blues in the
repertory. 'Syeeda's Song Flute' explores the possibilities of a single long line. There is very
able support from Flanagan, Chambers and Taylor and the CD edition includes four alternative
takes.

****   **Coltrane Jazz** Atlantic 1354-2 CD/MC
Coltrane; Wynton Kelly, McCoy Tyner (*p*); Paul Chambers, Steve Davis (*b*); Jimmy
Cobb, Elvin Jones (*d*). 11–12/59.

***   **The Avant-Garde** Atlantic 90041-2 CD
Coltrane; Don Cherry (*t*); Charlie Haden, Percy Heath (*b*); Ed Blackwell (*d*). 6–7/60.

Coltrane had had some important dental work done and had to redevelop his embouchure:
'Harmonique' on *Coltrane Jazz* features split tones that suggest the saxophonist testing out
what he could do. On the same record he began doubling on soprano. *Coltrane Jazz* is largely a
continuation of the spirit of *Giant Steps* without quite securing the same consistency of result,
and there is a stray track, 'Village Blues', from a session by the later quartet. Nevertheless,
there is some magnificent tenor playing. *The Avant Garde* found him meeting Don Cherry in an
approximation of the freedoms of the Coleman quartet, but Coltrane's responses are tentative,

and he sounds too bulky and grandiose to fly around as easily as Cherry does in this situation. He sounds happiest on Monk's 'Bemsha Swing'.

**** **My Favorite Things** Atlantic 782346-2 CD
Coltrane; McCoy Tyner (*p*); Steve Davis (*b*); Elvin Jones (*d*). 10/60.

**** **Coltrane's Sound** Atlantic 1419-2 CD/MC
As above. 10/60.

**** **Coltrane Plays The Blues** Atlantic 1382-2 CD
As above. 10/60.

**** **Olé Coltrane** Atlantic 1373-2 CD
Coltrane; Freddie Hubbard (*t*); Eric Dolphy (*as, f*); McCoy Tyner (*p*); Art Davis, Reggie Workman (*b*); Elvin Jones (*d*). 5/61.

The new quartet – Davis didn't last long, and would soon be replaced by Jimmy Garrison – pitched Coltrane into his next phase, but the last four albums for Atlantic are in some ways transitional, with Elvin Jones not yet embarking on the great polyrhythmic dialogues he would later conduct with the leader. *My Favorite Things* is dominated by the leader's soprano sax improvisation on the title-track, a theme he would return to over and over again: the important thing here is that both Coltrane and McCoy Tyner reduce the material to a couple of scales and ignore the changes, without forgetting to return to the theme. This gives the music a suitably endless feel, helps Coltrane push far beyond the normal performance durations, and sustains him into what would eventually be marathon performances (this one is a mere 13 minutes or so). The music also echoes the joyfulness of the lyric, and points towards the searching for ecstasy that would also come to characterize some parts of later Coltrane.

Plays The Blues is six versions of the blues, split between tenor and soprano; *Coltrane's Sound* includes a crushingly intense tenor solo on 'Liberia' and a very dark 'The Night Has A Thousand Eyes'. These are forbiddingly powerful records (both records were cut in two very long days in the studio). Jones has begun to develop his singular role at the drums and Tyner, his thumpingly overdriven block chords and flurries of right-hand figures.

Olé Coltrane includes just three pieces, and was cut two days after one of the sessions for *Africa/Brass*. By comparison with that date, this is a lesser affair, but the title theme and 'Dahomey Dance' evoke some of the orchestral swirl which Coltrane (and Dolphy) were aiming to secure in these bigger works. The CD issues of all these records sound faithful to the mastertapes, though they present no noticeable improvement over original vinyl.

***(*) **Africa / Brass: Volumes 1 & 2** MCA MCAD 42001 CD
Coltrane; Freddie Hubbard, Booker Little (*t*); Charles Greenlee, Julian Priester, Britt Woodman (*tb*); Donald Corrado, Bob Northern, Robert Swissel, Julius Watkins (*frhn*); Bill Barber (*tba*); Carl Bowman (*euph*); Eric Dolphy (*as, bcl*); Pat Patrick (*reeds*); McCoy Tyner (*p*); Paul Chambers, Art Davis (*b*); Reggie Workman (*b*); Elvin Jones (*d*). 5 & 6/61.

This was Coltrane's first recording for Impulse! Eric Dolphy has long been credited with the brass arrangements (which are of an unprecedented scale in Coltrane's work), but it's clear that most of the structures were fully worked by Coltrane and Tyner, leaving the other saxophonist little to do but straightforward orchestration for the baritone horns and conducting the take. Coltrane's desire to experiment with rhythm (most of his work had been in basic 4/4, with occasional waltz-time pieces like 'My Favorite Things') was fostered by an interest in African music and the 16-minute 'Africa' is an experiment with altered signatures and an implied chord structure. This remains very much in the background, freeing the saxophonist for some of his most powerful and unfettered solo work to date. The second tune could hardly be more different. 'Greensleeves' is played pretty straight as a 3/4 arrangement for soprano saxophone, much like 'My Favorite Things' and the later 'Chim Chim Cheree' (*Plays*, below). 'Blues Minor' is an uncomplicated blowing theme, with an easy swing and some attractively altered chords.

Volume 2 of *Africa/Brass*, consisting mainly of alternative takes, was released only in the mid-1970s. The traditional 'Song Of The Underground Railroad', recorded in a single take, hadn't been issued before, but there were significant variant performances of 'Greensleeves' (a slightly longer second take) and 'Africa' (a preliminary take with a rather tentative solo from

Coltrane). The reissue – and subsequent CD compilation – have refocused attention on what is increasingly seen as one of Coltrane's most adventurous experiments.

****   Live At The Village Vanguard MCA MCAD 39136 CD
Coltrane; Eric Dolphy (*bcl*); McCoy Tyner (*p*); Reggie Workman (*b*); Elvin Jones (*d*). 11/61.

***(*)   Impressions MCA MCAD 5887 CD
As above, except add Jimmy Garrison (*b*). 11/61, 9/62, 4/63.

Coltrane told Impulse! producer Bob Thiele that he liked the intimacy and human contact of a club setting, where direct communication with an audience was possible. The opening 'Spiritual' has a preaching immediacy that Dolphy picks up in his extraordinary, vocalized bass clarinet solo. He follows Coltrane on soprano, who returns to finish off a number he based on an actual spiritual heard many years before and stored away. There were only three tracks on the original album. After the relatively conventional 'Softly As In A Morning Sunrise' (Dolphy drops out, but Coltrane remains on soprano), the scorching blues of 'Chasin' The Trane' comes as an almost physical shock. There had been nothing quite like this in jazz; no one had dared to create a solo as freely stressed, polytonal, downright ugly, as this since the days of the early blues men. The difference was that Coltrane was able to sustain inventiveness in that genre for nearly 16 minutes, an achievement that became the immediate target of hostile criticism. There is a hint of Philip Larkin's celebrated feeling (directed at the *Live In Birdland* record, which he confessed to liking) that Coltrane spends too much time 'rocking backwards and forwards as if in pain between two chords', but there is little doubt that the pain is genuine.

Further material from Coltrane's Village Vanguard residency is included on *Impressions*, which like the first album features Dolphy on bass clarinet for just one fine track ('Indiana') and like the later *Live At Birdland* also includes studio material. 'After The Rain', recorded with Garrison on bass in April 1963, is a hymnic ballad with a repetitive structure that builds up emotion to an almost unbearable extent and then dies away into nothing. (Purchasers should be aware that *Live At The Village Vanguard Again*, currently available on a European CD reissue, relates to a 1966 session by the later group that included Alice Coltrane, Pharoah Sanders and Rashied Ali. Other material from the classic 1961 Vanguard sessions is scattered around; no sign yet of any attempt to bring it all together on a single CD set.)

****   European Impressions Bandstand BD 1514 CD/LP
Coltrane; Eric Dolphy (*as, bcl, f*); McCoy Tyner (*p*); Reggie Workman (*b*); Elvin Jones (*d*). 11/61.

***(*)   Live In Stockholm, 1961 Charly CD 117 CD
As above.

There are indications that Dolphy's presence as 'fifth man' generated tensions in the group that occasionally spilled over into the music. It isn't evident from these overlapping compilations of material, much of which was previously issued on vinyl on the small Beppo label. His flute solo on 'My Favorite Things' is quite magical and his bass clarinet interjection on 'Naima' completely transforms the rather billowy expressionism of a track that was otherwise becoming a feature for Tyner. The session is also valuable for a rare live version of 'Blue Train'. Recommended. The Bandstand is probably marginally better value for money.

***(*)   Coltrane MCA MCAD 5883 CD
Coltrane; McCoy Tyner (*p*); Jimmy Garrison (*b*); Elvin Jones (*d*). 4 & 6/62.

Less well known than its immediate predecessors, this was the first full-scale studio record by the classic Coltrane quartet. It's a curious album, led off by the magnificent 'Out Of This World', one of Coltrane's greatest achievements. This was followed by Mal Waldron's lovely 'Soul Eyes' and then the album slips. How many even enthusiastic Coltrane listeners would list 'Tunji' amd 'Miles' Mode' in the front rank of the saxophonist's work? 'The Inch Worm', an irritating Frank Loesser theme from *Hans Christian Andersen*, is the regulation show-tune arrangement for soprano. The album stands and falls, though, on that magnificent reading of the old Harold Arlen/Johnny Mercer tune and is well worth having on the strength of that alone.

***(*)   From The Original Master Tapes MCA MCAD 5541 CD
As for *Coltrane* and *Africa/Brass*; with Garvin Bushell (*ob*); Ahmed Abdul-Malik (*oud*); Reggie Workman (*b*); Roy Haynes (*d*). 61–62.

Digitally remastered from first generation stereo masters, this is as much a tribute to Bob Thiele as to Coltrane himself. 'Song Of The Underground Railroad', from the *Africa/Brass* sessions, is included, along with 'Soul Eyes', 'Dear Lord', 'Big Nick' and 'Vilia', one of Coltrane's less well known subversions of pop material. There are also previously unreleased performances of 'Spiritual' and of 'India' with Dolphy, Bushell and Abdul-Malik lending the latter theme an exotic sound-palette. The reproduction is predictably good (which mostly means that Garrison and Workman can be heard properly) and it stands as a fine reminder of Thiele's very considerable contribution to Coltrane's most dramatic years.

***(*) **Live At Birdland** Charly CD 68 CD
Coltrane; McCoy Tyner (*p*); Jimmy Garrison (*b*); Elvin Jones (*d*). 62.

***(*) **The European Tour** Pablo Live 2308222 CD
As above. 62.

*** **Bye Bye Blackbird** Original Jazz Classics OJC 681 CD
As above. 62.

*** **The Complete Graz Concert: Volume 1** Magnetic MRCD 104 CD
As above. 62.

*** **The Complete Graz Concert: Volume 2** Magnetic MRCD 105 CD
As above. 62.

***(*) **The Complete 1962 Stockholm Concert: Volume 1** Magnetic MRCD 108 CD
As above. 62.

***(*) **The Complete 1962 Stockholm Concert: Volume 2** Magnetic MRCD 109 CD
As above. 62.

*** **On Stage, 1962** Accord 556632 CD
As above, except add Eric Dolphy (*as*). 62.

A comprehensive documentation of live material from a rather troubled year, which nevertheless saw unprecedented public exposure. The first of the Charlys mustn't be confused with the very important Impulse! recording of the same name, below. Much of *Live At Birdland* is contemporary with the later sessions on *Coltrane* and reflects the same unfettered outpouring of ideas. The Pablo Live *European Tour* is a good choice from this vintage, with 'The Promise' unrepresented elsewhere. The other Pablo session, subsequently reissued by OJC, consists of just two mammoth performances, 'Bye Bye Blackbird' and 'Traneing In'. Though the Graz performances were certainly bettered elsewhere on the autumn 1962 tour, the two-volume Magnetic sets are a useful reminder of what an overwhelming experience a Coltrane concert must have been at that time. A staple mixture of originals and ballad standards, it's probably the best buy alongside the much more compact Pablo. The Accord material is distinguished by a fine 'Improvisation' featuring Dolphy. Even so, anyone building a CD collection from scratch would be well advised to concentrate on Impulse! releases only for the time being.

*** **Live At Birdland And The Half Note** Cool & Blue C&B CD 101 CD
Coltrane; McCoy Tyner (*p*); Jimmy Garrison (*b*); Elvin Jones (*d*). 5/62, 2/63, 5/65.

***(*) **Coltrane Live At Birdland** MCA MCAD 33109 CD
As above. 10, 11/63.

To gain a sense of how rapidly Coltrane developed in the early 1960s, the main focus of comparison here should be 'I Want To Talk About You', originally recorded on *Soul Trane*, above. There are versions on both the Birdland sets, recorded eight months apart in 1963. Though Coltrane's sound on the 1963 recordings is harsher, restless, unsettlingly sombre, far from the Getz-like ballad phrasing of the Prestige sessions, the real, structural differences relate every bit as much to the rest of the band. Compare Jones's shredded rhythms, Garrison's drones and Tyner's every-which-way polytonality with the relatively conventional accompaniments of Garland, Chambers and Taylor, and it's again clear that the Coltrane *Quartet* should be studied as a whole not as a secondary aspect of the saxophonist's lonely struggle.

He sounds isolated enough on the unaccompanied coda, and it's clear that there's no end to the turbulence. The album is actually slightly mis-titled for two of the tracks, one of them of considerable stylistic importance, were recorded in the studio just over a month after the club sesions. 'Alabama' was inspired by the murder of four black children in a church bombing. Fuelled by an almost militaristic pulse from Jones, it's a sad, stately ballad theme that rides at an angle to the basic tempo. Where a player like Archie Shepp might have turned such inspiration into a scream of pain, Coltrane attempts to find a route to transcendence, a way up out of the vicious mire of the modern South. Set opposite the long 'Afro-Blue', a soprano feature built up out of eerily unfamiliar intervals and a repetitive, almost *raga*-like theme, and 'The Promise', it makes this one of the most emotionally satisfying records of the period. Only the final track, 'Your Lady', seems rather slight, though it features some very telling unaccompanied exchanges between Coltrane and Jones that in some respects set a precedent for the later *Interstellar Space* with Rashied Ali.

The Cool & Blue set is a mixed bag, with New York performances ranging over nearly three years. The long 'Song Of Praise' (May 1965) is perhaps the most valuable single track, unmistakably in the 'late' style, but 'My Favorite Things' and 'Body And Soul' (June 1962) are very welcome as well and the sound is quite respectable for a club recording.

***(*)   **Ballads** MCA MCAD 5885 CD
         Coltrane; McCoy Tyner (*p*); Jimmy Garrison (*b*); Elvin Jones (*d*).

***   **John Coltrane And Johnny Hartman** MCA MCAD 5661 CD
         As above, except add Johnny Hartman (*v*). 12/61, 9 & 11/62, 3/63.

***(*)   **The Gentle Side Of John Coltrane** Impulse! GRD 107 CD
         As above, except add Duke Ellington (*p*); Aaron Bell (*b*); Roy Haynes, Sam
         Woodyard (*d*); Johnny Hartman (*d*).

It was apparently producer Bob Thiele who suggested the *Ballads* and Hartman projects to Coltrane, who had been experiencing articulation problems and was unable to play as accurately at speed as he wished. It was certainly Thiele who set up the historic encounter with Duke which is recorded on Impulse! MCAD 39103 (reviewed elsewhere), which is marked by a superb reading of 'In A Sentimental Mood'. Coltrane had always been an affecting ballad player and there was a sound market logic in an album of this type. He was less experienced working with a singer, but the sessions with Hartman have a satisfaction all of their own and it's a shame that with the exception of 'Lush Life', which Coltrane had recorded with Donald Byrd and Red Garland in 1958, the set doesn't include a vocal version of one of the standard songs in Trane's regular repertoire.

Most of the songs on *Ballads* are relatively little used as jazz standards, though 'Nancy (With The Laughing Face)', 'You Don't Know What Love Is' and 'Too Young To Go Steady' have all been favoured at one time or another. To some extent, this is Tyner's session. He floods the tunes with chords and lush flurries of single notes, with Garrison placing long, cello-like tones underneath him. Jones is inevitably at something of a premium, but plays very tunefully, with a hint of Max Roach in his stick-work on the the cymbals.

The Gentle Side is a reasonable option for anyone who really can't take Coltrane's flat-out style. Apart from the Ellington and Hartman tracks, it includes 'Soul Eyes' (also on *The Original Master Tapes*, below), 'Wise One' from *Crescent*, 'After The Rain' from *Impressions*, 'Dear Lord' from the currently unavailable *Transition*. Thirteen tracks in all, and good value if you don't mind duplications.

***   **Live In Stockholm, 1963** Charly CD 33 CD
         Coltrane; McCoy Tyner (*p*); Jimmy Garrison (*b*); Elvin Jones (*d*).

****   **Afro Blue Impressions** Pablo Live 2620101 CD/2LP
         As above. 10/63.

The 1963 tour was slightly anti-climactic compared to those of the previous two years. Though Coltrane's solos on 'Spiritual' and 'I Want To Talk About You' are exceptional, even by the standards of the Birdland session, the Charly is for serious collectors in the main. The other set comes close to being essential. Coltrane and (somewhat less audibly) Garrison plays powerfully on 'Lonnie's Lament' (a foretaste of the *Crescent* sessions the following spring), there's a good version of 'Cousin Mary', and staple fare like 'My Favorite Things', 'Naima' and 'Impressions'. Strongly recommended.

(*)   **Coast To Coast Moon MCD 035 CD/LP
         Coltrane; McCoy Tyner (*p*); Jimmy Garrison (*b*); Elvin Jones (*d*). 2/64, 4/65.

'Alabama', 'Impressions' and 'Creation', all material previously available on vinyl as *Creation* on Blue Parrot Records, a label whose title strongly confirms the possibility that the Monty Python team were in charge of production and quality control. 'Creation' is an important piece, but there's an inordinate amount of hiss on the tapes and much of the rhythm section is lost.

***(*) **Crescent** MCA MCAD 5889 CD
  Coltrane; McCoy Tyner (*p*); Jimmy Garrison (*b*); Elvin Jones (*d*). 4, 6/64.

In the spiritual odyssey of Coltrane's last years, *Crescent* has always been cast as the dark night of the soul, coming before the triumphant affirmation of *A Love Supreme*, below. It is certainly Coltrane's most melancholy record, dominated by the mournful 'Wise One' and the haunting blues ballad 'Lonnie's Lament'. If 'Crescent' was meant to suggest growth, it's a hesitant, almost blindfolded progress, with little of the soaring joy that Coltrane usually brought to such themes. 'Bessie's Blues' is a brightly bubbling three and a half minutes that seems almost out of place on an album so sombre but it served as a brief feature for the unsettled Tyner. 'Lonnie's Lament' contains one of Garrison's best solos on record, and the closing 'Drum Thing' is largely devoted to Elvin Jones, who plays a less than usually prominent part elsewhere.

***** **A Love Supreme** MCA DMCL 1648 CD/LP/MC
  Coltrane; McCoy Tyner (*p*); Jimmy Garrison (*b*); Elvin Jones (*d*). 12/64.

***(*) **A Love Supreme** [live] France's Concert FCD 106 CD
  As above. 7/65.

*** **A Love Supreme** [live] Crusader Jazz CJZLP 1 LP
  As above. 65.

Great albums are usually made by groups who have attained a certain measure of mutual understanding. Very great albums are almost always made by groups on the brink of splitting asunder. By the autumn of 1964, the quartet had reached a point where further development along the free-modal path they had been exploring since the November 1961 Village Vanguard dates seemed impossible.

A Love Supreme was Coltrane's most profoundly spiritual statement and cannot (despite at least one generation of text-free sleeves) be separated from a passionate statement of belief on the gatefold and the free-verse text that accompanies. The fourth movement, 'Psalm', was intended as a 'musical narration' of this text and is the point towards which the whole sequence gravitates.

Coltrane's spirituality was more than usually hard won. A mere seven years before, he had been seriously addicted to heroin and alcohol, and in a very real sense *A Love Supreme*, coming at the end of a cycle of years, is a document of his struggle to extricate himself from that slough. Coltrane suffered agonizing dental problems and had considerable difficulty with his mouthpiece in 1961 and 1962. The pure, vibrato-less tone of earlier years has gone, to be replaced with a tearing, rather brutal delivery replete with false notes, splintery harmonics and harsh, almost toneless breath-noises. The vocal parallels to parts of *A Love Supreme* are in keeping with his desire (already evident on *Live At The Village Vanguard*) to recapture something of the highly vocalized sound of the blues, field shouts, and the unaccompanied psalms of the primitive Black Church.

The sequence begins with a calmly untroubled fanfare of 'Acknowledgement'. This gives way to a stately 8-bar theme which serves as background for one of the short motifs out of which Coltrane constructed much of his music at this period. The four notes stated and restated by Jimmy Garrison and then echoed by Coltrane in a questioning variation of keys are probably the best known in the whole of modern jazz. They create much of the material for Coltrane's shifting, gradually ascending solo and then for the famous, husky iteration of 'a love supreme' by the four players. Jones's drumming is absolutely extraordinary, using double-tim̄ figures of considerable complexity, while Garrison and Tyner sustain a background ostinato   vents the whole piece from falling apart.

'Resolution' increases the emotional temperature very considerably, with
the rhythm somewhat and stoking up the dynamics mercilessly. Coltrane, aga
cuts loose with a scalding solo that brought the first half of the origina
unsurpassable climax. 'Pursuance' is a dark blues, with a nervously fragm
carried by Coltrane himself but resolved into a fantastic duet with

performance, FCD 106), which becomes increasingly untenable as the piece develops. This paves the way for the extraordinary final movement.

The final movement has always been seen as continuing a line established by 'Alabama' on the Birdland album. 'Psalm' is an out of tempo ballad with the most beautiful saxophone playing on the album. Coltrane's sound is still rather acerbic, but his non-verbal narration of a deeply felt credo is expressed in tones of great majesty. At the very end, in an episode much discussed by Coltrane fans, a second saxophone (perhaps Archie Shepp's) joins with a two-note figure corresponding to the final 'amen' of Coltrane's text. Coltrane responds with a fragment of the opening fanfare, bringing the music full circle.

The live versions greatly subordinate affirmation and transcendence to a spirit of painful quest by a group, not an individual and this is another reason why their top-heavy, sibilant sound-balances are so unsatisfactory. The France's Concert performance is well over LP length and the final 'amen' seems to last for ever, soaring off into the high harmonic range, as if it isn't after all the final word.

The greatest jazz album of the modern period? Or the most overrated? *A Love Supreme* is certainly one of the best known and among the most personal, factors that make objective assessment rather problematic. On that account, it may be forgivable that the album was credited to Coltrane alone rather than to the quartet (whose full names and instruments are not even given on the original sleeve). However, it's vital to appreciate the contribution that they made to the music. Though he was much more prominently featured elsewhere, *A Love Supreme* was arguably Garrison's finest hour with Coltrane, and it was certainly one of Jones's. If anyone showed slight signs of dissatisfaction with the way the music was progressing, it was Tyner, a feeling reinforced on the European tour of summer 1965, which has to be seen as a kind of denouement for perhaps the most influential single jazz group of the post-war period.

****   The John Coltrane Quartet Plays MCA MCAD 3310 CD
As for *Coltrane*; with Art Davis (*b*). 65.

The title should strictly read . . . *Plays 'Chim Chim Cheree', 'Song Of Praise', 'Nature Boy', 'Brazilia'*, all of which was printed on the original sleeve in inch-high letters, but the album has always been known as *Plays* and there is something appropriate in that, for after the sky-scraping affirmations of *A Love Supreme*, it sounds as if the group have got down to some basic jazz playing again, themes, choruses, standard tunes. There are, of course, clear signs of Coltrane's growing concerns. 'Song Of Praise', actually played last, is a towering hymn in the line of 'Psalm', and the addition of a second bassist for the well-worn 'Nature Boy' is an often overlooked indication of Coltrane's desire to break down the conventional time-keeping role of the rhythm section.

The most interesting track, though, is the *Mary Poppins* tune, another of Coltrane's soprano features. The poet and critic LeRoi Jones (now known as Amiri Baraka) has persuasively shown how Coltrane's subversive aesthetic is based on the deceptive co-option of mass-cultural materials, followed by their complete subversion. It's possible to argue, along Jones's lines, that 'My Favorite Things', which begins this particular line of inquiry, 'The Inch Worm' and 'Chim Chim Cheree' are Coltrane's *most* radical improvisations. The last of the three is certainly the most ferociously deconstructed. The weird, slightly off-pitch sound of the soprano turns the familiar tune into something more closely resembling an Indian *raga* or a Korean court theme and the rhythm section piles up an enormous flurry of sound behind him. Despite the apparently conventional division of themes and solos, the quartet is playing as a whole in a way that points unambiguously forward to the collective experiments of the last years. This is an often overlooked item in the Coltrane discography, but it's a very important one.

*****   The Major Works Of John Coltrane Impulse! GRD 21132 2CD
As for *Coltrane*, with Freddie Hubbard, Dewey Johnson (*t*); Marion Brown, John Tchicai (*as*); Pharoah Sanders, Archie Shepp (*ts*); Donald Garrett (*bcl, b*); Joe Brazil (*f, perc*); Frank Butler (*d*); Juno Lewis (*perc, v*). 6/65, 10/65.

The short pattern of notes played by Coltrane at the beginning of 'Ascension' was a clear reference to the fanfare that opened 'Acknowledgement' on *A Love Supreme*. To those who had asked where Coltrane might go after the December 1964 album, the two versions of *Ascension* were the answer. The circumstances of their release are now hopelessly muddied and at one point MCA actually got the liner notes reversed. Coltrane had originally ok'd release of first, forty minute take and this was issued as *Ascension* Impulse A-95 in late 1965. Then the saxophonist decided that the 'wrong' master had been issued and the second take was substituted, leaving *Ascension – Edition I* as a piece of discographical apocrypha until GRP put the two together on this important, but still oddly named compilation.

The oddity stems only from the fact that however significant *Ascension* is, the other items included, 'Om', 'Kulu Se Mama' (both of which once fronted albums of those names) and 'Selflessness', would not initially seem to belong in the same league, and are unlikely to spring first to mind when asked to set out Coltrane's 'major works'. However, 'Om', with its initial chant again recalling *A Love Supreme*, is clearly derived from the complex sound-world of *Ascension*, with two bassists weaving complementary and sometimes overlapping lines and Joe Brazil's flute adding a mysterious quality to structures of great 'plasticity' (the term was Coltrane's).

'Kulu Se Mama' was recorded on the West Coast as a musical objectification of Juno Lewis's Afro-Creole poem. The chanting is slightly offputting and Coltrane is rather muted, and it's something of a relief to turn to the relatively familiar outline of 'Selflessness'.

What they all share, with the partial and instructive exception of the last track, is a developing commitment to collective improvisation. In a very real sense, *Ascension* was alien to the American spirit of individualistic performance in improvised music; even Ornette Coleman's *Free Jazz* resolved very rapidly into a sequence of separate solo features. *Ascension*, though, was much closer to a European aesthetic of collective improvisation (which drew sustenance, of course, from early jazz). Coltrane organized his augmented group (similarly constituted to Coleman's) in such a way that he was able to give signals for switches of mode that implied new scalar and harmonic patterns. These were sketched out by Hubbard and Tyner respectively, but left individual players to develop their own material in an apparently chaotic field of sound that sometimes sounds like a dense canvas of pointillist gestures, sometimes like a huge wall of rhythmic sound, pushing ever forwards, sometimes like enormous blocks of static noise with no obvious structural rationale. The success of the piece lay quite explicitly in Coltrane's ability to steer the individual freedoms of his players in accordance with the code established in the first few bars.

There are, of course, solos, but these serve a very different purpose to those on *Free Jazz*. There, soloists emerge out of the ensemble and impose a rather normative structure on the collective improvisations. Here, the soloists create internal commentaries on the progress of the music, which is genuinely transcendent. The main obvious difference between the two versions of *Ascension* lies in the sequence of solos: the revised release Edition II runs Coltrane, Johnson, Sanders, Hubbard, Brown, Shepp, Tchicai, Tyner, and a bass duet; Edition 1 relocates Shepp and Tchicai in front of Brown and adds an Elvin Jones solo at the end. On purely aesthetic grounds there is remarkably little to separate them and over time they come to resemble the same piece of landscape from a subtly adjusted viewing point.

If Coltrane had never recorded another note of music, he would be guaranteed greatness on the strength of *Ascension* alone. Compiling the two versions with the slightly later material from 1965 makes considerable sense, certainly more so than the original location of the later pieces. Though *Ascension*, an admittedly demanding, even 'difficult', work, has tended to be eclipsed in popularity by *A Love Supreme*, its importance has long been recognized and this version comes without the ludicrous fade-edits on the first European CD that marked the end of the original LP sides. The sound is surprisingly good, though it must have been a nightmare to record. What is needed now is a full-scale reassessment of 'Om', 'Kulu Se Mama' and 'Selflessness' in the light of an entirely new construction of what a jazz group was capable of.

***   **New Thing At Newport** Impulse! GRD 105 CD
Coltrane; McCoy Tyner (*p*); Jimmy Garrison (*b*); Elvin Jones (*d*).

(**)   **Live In Antibes, 1965 France's Concert FCD 119 CD
As above.

***(*)   **Live In Paris** Charly CD 80 CD
As above. 7/65.

July 1965 saw the quartet performing at two major festivals. The Newport sessi
with Archie Shepp and originally contained only 12 minutes of Coltrane ('One I
is the same theme as 'One Up And One Down' on the Cool & Blue compilat'
adds a brutal reading of 'My Favorite Things' which was formerly available on
Mastery Of John Coltrane series. The MC identifies Elvin Jones as 'a newcor

228

seems a quite incredible piece on condescension, and may explain some of the rhythmic fury that follows.

The Antibes session is the same as that which yielded the live version of *A Love Supreme*, above. The sound quality is again rather poor, with a good deal of tinkering to disguise the sound of Coltrane's bell striking the microphone, but the performances are very good indeed. 'My Favorite Things' is somewhat more relaxed and there are fine readings of 'Naima', 'Blue Waltz/Valse' (its only recorded appearance), 'Impressions' and 'Afro Blue', the last two of which were actually recorded the following day in Paris. The Charly is identical to FCD 119 and is probably to be preferred on the strength of a more rational projection of the sound.

***(*)   **Live In Seattle** Impulse! WMC5 116 CD
Coltrane; Pharoah Sanders (*ts*); Donald Garrett (*bcl*); McCoy Tyner (*p*); Jimmy Garrison (*b*); Elvin Jones (*d*). 9/65.

Apocalyptic and just verging on the preposterous. 'Evolution' clocks in at 36 minutes and takes in some of the worst and some of the most innovative Coltrane on record. For much of its length, the piece is marking time in the curiously uninvolving flat-out register that became the norm after *A Love Supreme*. Then, before the chanting begins, there's a marvellous passage for all three horns and Garrison (who can just about be heard clearly), improvising the interweaving lines that had been the essence of *Ascension*. 'Cosmos' gets things going at an extraordinary altitude; Tyner sounds lost from the word go and, for a change, Jones doesn't dominate proceedings. Though he's far back in the mix, he's also quieter than on many a session and Coltrane's main dialogues are with Sanders.

This is a Japanese issue, but there are some Coltrane imports worth re-mortgaging the house for, and the 2LP original issue is still floating around in the second-hand bins.

***(*)   **Meditations** MCA MCAD 39139 CD
As for *Coltrane*; with Pharoah Sanders (*ts*); Rashied Ali (*d*). 11/65.

****   **First Meditations** Impulse! GRP 11182 CD
As for *Coltrane*. 2/65.

These two sessions, covering essentially the same material, bridge the end of the classic quartet and the opening phase of the new, augmented group with Sanders and Ali. In February 1965, Coltrane and the quartet recorded a preliminary version of a new five-part suite consisting of 'Love', 'Compassion', 'Joy', 'Consequences', 'Serenity'. When he returned to the studio in November, the saxophonist substituted the unbelievably turbulent 'The Father And The Son And The Holy Ghost' for the original opening movement, and moved 'Love' to what was the start of the continuous second side on the released LP. The most immediate difference between the two versions, apart from the extraordinary change in the rhythm section wrought by the introduction of Ali's pure-sound percussion, is that the movements are run together almost seamlessly, with quite long transitional sections, whereas on *First Meditations* the breaks are distinct though played through without a pause. On grounds of simple beauty, the first version is still to be preferred, though it clearly no longer represented what Coltrane wanted to do with his group and would experiment with on the critical *Ascension*, below.

Set alongside *A Love Supreme*, it becomes more obvious how formulaic and predetermined some of Coltrane's large-scale composition was becoming. Much as *Ascension* develops out of a a simple fanfare figure like that on the December 1964 album, so, too, does the original *Meditations* seem to develop out of coded harmonic and rhythmic patterns set out by Garrison and Jones, which have become far more deeply embedded in the ensembles of the release version.

The CD of the February session includes an alternative version of 'Joy', the piece that sets in motion the final, multi-art movement. It's obvious that Coltrane is already trying to escape the sticky webs that Jones weaves for him. Had the old and new drummers been able to play together (there is evidence of considerable tension), 'Father/Son/Holy Ghost' suggests that something quite out of the ordinary might have developed. As it is, Ali was closer to Coltrane's new conception of pure sound and a haunted, runaway rhythm sustained by the horns, not by the bass and drums, and the shift between the two versions is a first dramatization of his final break with bop idiom and its descendants.

****   Live At The Village Vanguard Again! Impulse! 254647 2 CD
Coltrane; Pharoah Sanders (*ts*); Alice Coltrane (*p*); Jimmy Garrison (*b*); Rashied Ali
(*d*); Emmanual Rahid (*perc*). 5/66.

Back at the Vanguard with a new band and the only weak link is the one survivor from the 1961 sessions. Garrison's long unaccompanied intro to 'My Favorite Things' is prosaic in the extreme, but what follows is the most comprehensively dissected version Coltrane ever put on record (and that includes the marathon version below). The real high spot of the set is a wonderful, roiling 'Naima', originally dedicated to Trane's first wife, not the lady comping spacily behind him, but gradually transformed into a billowing expression of love *per se*. The addition of a percussionist greatly increases the rhythmic shimmer, but it also ironically pushes Ali back towards something like the old duelling style associated with Jones. This is sometimes thought to be from the same sessions as the 1961 album. The briefest of samples underlines how far Coltrane had come in the five years in between. That sense of intimacy and communication with the audience had certainly not been lost, but was continuing at an ever higher and more invasive level. If the first album was subject to hostile misprision, the reception accorded this one frequently went off the scale: arch-conservative Philip Larkin thought it the quintessence of the 'blended insolence and ugliness' of the New Wave and it does for the first time seem to have taken a full step off the classic jazz tradition which was Larkin's absolute standard and into an unexplored void.

***   Live In Japan Impulse! GRP 4102 2 4CD
Coltrane; Pharoah Sanders (*ts*); Alice Coltrane (*p*); Jimmy Garrison (*b*); Rashied Ali
(*d*). 7/66.

Three and a half hours of music. It was quickly clear that the recruitment of Ali allowed Coltrane to break his last ties to bebop phrasing and chorus structure (however elongated both had become). His performances here, with or without Sanders in close proximity, are essentially duets with the drummer of the sort he developed in the studio for *Interstellar Space* and it's easy to see why cosmic titles and analogies sprang to mind, so little tied to earth does it all seem. There is an *hour-long* version of 'My Favorite Things', which takes it as far from the original song as seems conceivable. An interesting development is Coltrane's first documented use of alto saxophone (apparently a plastic model like Ornette Coleman's or the one Bird used at Massey Hall) since the late 1950s. Garrison contributes very little, even when he *is* completely audible, and Alice arpeggiates furiously, but adds nothing essential to the music. There must be some niggles of doubt about the viability of music as unflaggingly humourless and god-bothering as this. *Live In Japan* could hardly have been much more tiring to play than it is to listen to.

****   Interstellar Space Impulse! GRP 11102 CD
Coltrane; Rashied Ali (*d*). 2/67.

The final masterpiece. It's now conventional wisdom that Coltrane took the harmonic development of post-bop jazz as far as it could be taken, and then some. What is often forgotten is the attention the saxophonist paid to *rhythm* and the Impulse! years – from *Africa/Brass* to *Interstellar Space* – are very largely devoted to a search for the time beyond time, an uncountable pulse which would represent a pure musical experience not chopped up into bars and choruses. Though Ali is more than just a sound-effects man on this extraordinary set, it's clear that Coltrane is leading from the front. With no bass and piano in competition (as it increasingly seemed), he's recorded in dramatic close-up and with none of the off-mike wavers that afflicted the Seattle and Tokyo concerts.

'Mars', first of the planetary sequence, is characterized as the 'battlefield of the cosmic giants' and that is exactly how it sounds, with huge, clashing brass tones and a thunderous clangour from the drum kit. 'Venus,' by contrast, is delicate, amorous and almost fragile, with Ali barely skiffing his cymbals with wire brushes. 'Jupiter (Variation)' was known to Coltrane fans even when *Interstellar Space* was out of catalogue, from being included on one of the *Mastery Of John Coltrane* compilations of out-takes and ephemera. The release version is the shortest item on the set, a stately expression of 'supreme wisdom', coming immediately before the climactic evocation of joy on 'Saturn'. 'Leo' is known in a live version from the Tokyo concerts, but wasn't on the original album.

Interestingly, Coltrane sticks with his tenor saxophone throughout, eschewing soprano for the first time in very many years and not following up the alto experiments of *Live In Japan*.

***   **Expression** Impulse! MCA 254646 CD
As for *Live In Japan*. 2 & 3/67.

It would be wonderfully neat if the last studio album really had represented the final wisdom of the greatest saxophonist since Parker, but *Expression* is a murky, often undistinguished work. There's some interest in hearing Coltrane on flute ('To Be') , but what little of the music really convinces occurs on 'Offering' and 'Expression' itself, both of which represent elements of Trane's calm-after-storm lyricism.

Oddly, and quite unlike the much improved *Interstellar Space*, the sound is if anything worse on the CD, with long passages quite indistinct. The recording sessions bracket the session with Ali and the contrast between the two strongly suggests that Coltrane had finally exhausted the horn–piano–rhythm format that had totally dominated jazz since the advent of bebop. Where he might have gone next is anyone's guess.

KEN COLYER (1928–88)
CORNET, TRUMPET, GUITAR, VOCAL

(*)   **The Crane River Jazz Band 1950–53 Dormouse DM18 LP
Colyer; Sonny Morris (*c*); John R. T. Davies, Ray Orpwood (*tb*); Monty Sunshine (*cl*); Pat Hawes (*p*); Ben Marshall (*bj*); Julian Davies (*b*); unknown (*d*); Bill Colyer (*v*). 3/50–5/53.

***   **In The Beginning** Lake LA5014 LP/MC
Colyer; Chris Barber, Ed O'Donnell (*tb*); Monty Sunshine, Acker Bilk (*cl*); Lonnie Donegan, Diz Disley (*bj*); Jim Bray (*tba, b*); Dick Smith (*b*); Ron Bowden, Stan Greig (*d*). 11/53–9/54.

**   **Tuxedo Rag** Lake LA5004 LP/MC
Colyer; Mac Duncan (*tb, v*); Ed O'Donnell (*tb*); Acker Bilk, Ian Wheeler (*cl*); Ray Foxley (*p*); Johnny Bastable, Diz Disley (*bj*); Dick Smith, Ron Ward (*b*); Stan Greig, Colin Bowden (*d*). 10/54–3/58.

***   **Sensation!** Lake LA5001 LP/MC
Colyer; Mac Duncan (*tb*); Ian Wheeler (*cl*); Ray Foxley (*p*); Johnny Bastable (*bj*); Dick Smith, Ron Ward (*b*); Stan Greig, Colin Bowden (*d*). 4/55–5/59.

(*)   **Club Session With Colyer Lake LA5006 LP/MC
As above, except omit Greig and Ward. 56.

***   **Marching Back To New Orleans** Lake LACD 21 CD
As above, except add Bob Wallis, Sunny Murray (*t*), Mick Clift (*tb*), Dave Keir (*as*), Derek Easton (*ts*), Maurice Benn (*tba*), Neil Millet, Stan Greig (*d*). 4/55–9/57.

(**)   **The Decca Skiffle Sessions 1954–1957** Lake LA5007 LP/MC
Colyer; Bob Kelly (*p*); Alexis Korner (*g, mand*); Johnny Bastable (*g, bj*); Mickey Ashman, Ron Ward (*b*); Bill Colyer, Colin Bowden (*wbd*). 6/54–11/57.

(*)   **Ken Colyer's Skiffle Group And Ken Colyer's Jazzmen KC Records KC.2 LP
Colyer; Mac Duncan (*tb*); Ian Wheeler (*cl*); Bob Kelly (*p*); Johnny Bastable (*bj*); Ron Ward (*b*); Colin Bowden (*d, wbd*). 5/57.

***   **Lonesome Road** Lake LA5010 LP/MC
Colyer: Mac Duncan (*tb*); Ian Wheeler (*cl*); Ray Foxley (*p*); Johnny Bastable (*bj*); Ron Ward (*b*); Colin Bowden (*d*). 6–8/58.

Colyer was one of the most interesting figures British jazz ever produced. At a time when the trad boom of the 1950s was just getting under way, he abjured such 'modern' role models as Armstrong and Morton and insisted on the earlier New Orleans methods of George Lewis and Bunk Johnson. Colyer's records from the period emerge as an intriguing muddle of stiff British orthodoxy and something that finds a genuine if limited accord with the music that obsessed him. Before leading his own groups he worked with the Crane River Jazz Band, which, after innumerable reunions, finally called it a day in 1992. The Dormouse LP of their early recordings – mostly remastered from acetates by John R. T. Davies, who appears in this book more often as an engineer than as a trombonist – is about as prehistoric as British trad gets, and despite the occasionally unbalanced sound and frequently ragged playing, it's full of gumption and shaky panache. *In the Beginning* must go down as a crucial document of British jazz if only for the musicians involved – Barber, whose subsequent disagreements with the trumpeter led him to assume command of a different edition of the band; Bilk, whose somewhat hamfisted clarinet had yet to assume the distinctive glow of his later records; Sunshine, who stayed with Barber and has since enjoyed an immortal reputation among European trad audiences; and Donegan, the major name of the skiffle movement. The album is compiled from two ten-inch LPs, and while the music is comparatively stilted, its formal strictness pays off in the music's terseness, never falling foul of ragged ensembles or windy solos.

Having established the blueprint, Colyer worked hard at refining it during the 1950s. *Tuxedo Rag* documents two concerts – Royal Festival Hall 1954 and Hamburg 1958 – which demonstrate not so much a progression as a varying concentration: tired stuff such as 'Bill Bailey' is inevitably less interesting, but 'When The Saints' shows how Colyer could evade trad bombast, and the jaunty swing of the ensemble is as redolent of British jazz in the 1950s as the pick of Lyttelton or Dankworth. *Club Session With Colyer*, perhaps his most famous record, is a peculiar mixture, from the cod-gospel 'Walking With The King' to 'Home Sweet Home', but 'Chrysanthemum Rag' and 'Thriller Rag' suggest how far afield Colyer was prepared to look for material. The most useful reissues, though, are *Lonesome Road*, *Marching Back To New Orleans* and *Sensation*. The latter is effectively an alternative live version of the unavailable *Colyer Plays Standards*, although much of the material – 'Underneath The Bamboo Tree' and 'Bluebells Goodbye', to name two – would hardly be classed as standards in most band books. *Marching Back To New Orleans* opens with seven tracks from the session which produced *Sensation* – including an uproarious 'Red Wing' – and then includes the entire date by the Omega Brass Band, where Colyer tried his hand at an 'authentic' New Orleans parade band: shambling, stentorian, it's a bizarre sound, and actually surprisingly close to the genuine article. Typically, Colyer refused to pick obvious tunes, and chose 'Isle Of Capri', 'Tiger Rag' and 'Gettysburg March' as some of the tunes, which occasionally rise in an almost hysterical crescendo. *Sensation* collects various single and EP tracks, including all four from the sought-after *They All Played Ragtime* EP, which is in some ways Colyer's most distinctive achievement: it includes such rarities as 'Kinklets' (recorded by Bunk Johnson at his final session), 'Fig Leaf Rag' and what might be the first jazz version of 'The Entertainer', many years before Joshua Rifkin and *The Sting*. This is an ensemble music: Colyer wasn't a great soloist, and although Wheeler and Duncan are lively they struggle a bit when left on their own. Foxley is actually the most impressive improviser on the basis of *Lonesome Road*. But Colyer's steady, unflashy lead, and the four-square but oddly hypnotic beat of the rhythm section (using a banjo to the end), add their own character. Paul Adams has done a fine job in assembling and remastering all these records. The 1957 date split between the Skiffle group and the Jazzmen is tarnished by reverberant and amateurish sound, and the jazzmen performances sound ragged: for fanatics only.

This leaves only the Colyer Skiffle Group. Colyer's interest in skiffle appears to have been heartfelt enough, although it seems a bizarre accompaniment to his jazz-directed performances, with the group hammering through material like 'Streamline Train' and 'How Long Blues'. Colyer was an unexceptional vocalist and he played steel guitar with a machine-like drive; despite the presence of Korner, who at least knew how to play feasible blues, the group seems like a quaint aberration now. *The Decca Skiffle Sessions* tells the story as well as anything will.

(*) **When I Leave The World Behind Lake LACD 19 CD
Colyer; Geoff Cole (*tb*); Sammy Rimington (*cl*); Johnny Bastable (*bj*); Ron Ward (*b*); Pete Ridge (*d*). 3/63.

If everything here was as good as a terrifically swinging account of J. C. Higginbotham's 'Give Me Your Telephone Number', this would be a classic record. As it is, it's an interesting memento of Colyer's 1960s band, playing a broad range of rags, King Oliver tunes, and other odds and ends. Rimington weaves interesting lines all through the music, Cole is a strong, hard-bitten trombonist, only the rhythm section, bothered by the pedestrian Ridge, is weaker. The recording, salvaged by Paul Adams from some private tapes, is variable and rather boomy, but it's listenable enough.

** **One For My Baby** Joy JOY-CD-1 CD
Colyer; Geoff Cole (*tb*); Tony Pyke (*cl*); Johnny Bastable (*bj*); Bill Cole (*b*); Malcolm Murphy (*d*). 1–2/69.

** **Spirituals Vol. 1** Joy JOY-CD-5 CD
As above, except Ken Ames (*b*) replaces Cole. 69.

** **Spirituals Vol. 2** Joy JOY-CD-6 CD
As above. 69.

** **Watch That Dirty Tone Of Yours – There Are Ladies Present** Joy JOY-CD-3 CD
As above. 5/70.

** **At the Thames Hotel** Joy JOY-CD-4 CD
As above. 5/70.

(*) **Ragtime Revisited Joy JOY-CD-2 CD
As above, except add Ray Smith (*p*). 70.

These are solid examples of Colyer at work, and there's little here to detain any but the fanatic: the 1950s music is fresher, and the band with Rimington had a superior front line. Even Colyer himself lacks the stamina to sustain an album's worth of material. Still, there are better moments on most of the records. The first *Spirituals* has a firmer grip, the *Thames Hotel* live set has a neat set-list, and the *Ragtime Revisited* disc continues Colyer's grappling with the rag form to create a viable bridge between styles. The sound is much as it was on the original LPs and, for those who were there, the two live sets (*Thames Hotel* and *One For My Baby*) will rekindle the atmosphere.

*** **Ken Colyer And His Handpicked Jazzmen** Ken Colyer Trust KCT 2R LP
Colyer; Mike Sherbourne (*tb*); Jack Gilbert (*cl*); Jim McIntosh (*bj*); Ray Holland (*b*); Tony Scriven (*d*). 1/72.

*(*) **Painting The Clouds With Sunshine** Black Lion 760501 CD
Colyer; Mike Sherbourne (*tb*); Bruce Bakewell (*cl*); Ray Smith (*p*); Bill Stotesbury (*bj*); Alyn Shipton (*b*); Colin Bowden (*d*). 10/79.

Colyer disbanded his regular group in 1971, partly due to illness, and these are two of the pick-up bands he occasionally fronted after that. The 1972 session is probably the best latter-day Colyer on record, in clear, detailed live sound. His own playing is erratic, but the sextet play with uncanny empathy together, and the even gait of the rhythm section binds together Sherbourne's noisy trombone parts and Gilbert's would-be Doddsian clarinet. The 1979 date is nothing like as good. The rhythm section provides Colyer's favoured chugging momentum, but the horns are frankly unmemorable.

** **Too Busy** CMJ 008 CD
Colyer; Les Hanscombe (*tb*); Dave Bailey (*cl*); Tim Phillips (*bj*); Keith Donald (*b*); John Petters (*d*). 2/85.

Colyer guests with the John Petters group, and is clearly taking things very gingerly. The band plays decent, fat-free trad, but the trumpeter's own contribution is unexceptional.

COMPANY
FLEXIBLE IMPROVISING ENSEMBLE

*** **Music Improvisation Company, 1968/70** Incus LP17 LP
Derek Bailey (*g*); Evan Parker (*ss*); Hugh Davies (*elec, org*); Jamie Muir (*perc*).

*** **Company 2** Incus LP23 LP
Derek Bailey (*g*); Evan Parker (*ss, ts*); Anthony Braxton (*ss, as, cl, cbcl*). 8/76.

***(*) **Company 3** Incus LP25 LP
Derek Bailey (*g*); Han Bennink (*perc*). 9/76.

***(*) **Company 4** Incus LP26 LP
Derek Bailey (*g*); Steve Lacy (*ss*). 11/76.

***(*) **Company 5** Incus LP28 LP
Derek Bailey (*g*); Leo Smith (*t*); Steve Lacy (*ss*); Anthony Braxton (*reeds*); Evan Parker (*ss, ts*); Tristan Honsinger (*clo*); Maarten Altena (*b*). 5/77.

**** **Fables** Incus LP36 LP
Derek Bailey (*g*); George Lewis (*tb*); Evan Parker (*ss, ts*); Dave Holland (*b*). 5.80.

(*) **Fictions Incus LP38 LP
Derek Bailey (*g, v*); Lol Coxhill (*ss, v*); Misha Mengelberg (*p, v*); Steve Beresford (*v, toy instruments*); Ian Croal (*v*). 8/77.

**** **Trios** Incus LP51 LP
Derek Bailey (*g*); Jon Corbett (*t*); Vinko Globokar (*tb*); Peter Brötzmann, Evan Parker, J. D. Parran (*reeds*); Joëlle Léandre (*b*); Hugh Davies (*elec*); Jamie Muir (*perc*). 5/83.

**** **Once** Incus CD04 CD
Derek Bailey (*g*); Lee Konitz (*as, ss*); Richard Teitelbaum (*ky*); Carlos Zingaro (*vn*); Tristan Honsinger (*clo*); Barre Phillips (*b*); Steve Noble (*perc, bugle*). 5/87.

At the end of his very important book, *Improvisation: Its Nature And Practice In Music*, Derek Bailey collages a number of quotations that might be said to hold the key to what his improvising collective, Company, is about: for Leo Smith, improvisation is an individual's 'ability to instantaneously organize sound, silence and rhythm with the whole of his or her creative intelligence'; Peter Riley defines the process much more crisply as 'the exploration of occasion'.

Incus, the label Bailey co-founded in 1970 with saxophonist Evan Parker and drummer Tony Oxley, has dedicated much of its catalogue to the documentation of those explorations and those occasions (once annual, otherwise as occasion demanded) when Bailey brought together groups of British and international improvisers for a weekend or week of unstructured improvisation. Company was founded in 1976 (the first item, above, explores its pre-history) and has been the most important locus of free improvisation in Britain since then. It is, of course, moot whether existential performances which admit of no gap between conception and execution and which are completely conditioned by intuition really belong on record. What is remarkable about the above records is the extent to which they remain compellingly listenable long after the occasion of their performance is past; newcomers are directed particularly to *Fables*, *Trios* and *Once* (only the last of which is on CD), which seem to encapsulate the challenges and beauties of Company in equal measure.

The music is extremely difficult to quantify or categorize. It was clear from the earlier encounters that it was necessary to negotiate a divide between free music which owned to no generic ties and a deep structure drawn from jazz. Visiting Americans (notably Braxton) appeared to find the radical and collective freedom on which Bailey quietly insisted rather unsettling; against that, both Steve Lacy and, much more suprisingly, former Tristano disciple Lee Konitz (who took part in the 1987 Company) have managed to assimilate their notably dry approach to Bailey's. Lacy's intensely disciplined, almost clinical playing is a feature of *Company 4* and *5*, but there is no doubt that it is Evan Parker in the earlier years who best represents the group's channelled, ego-less virtuosity.

Given that the Company ethos (like that of Bailey's own work, *q.v.*) is a ruthless resistance to any settled groove, drummers occupy a difficult position. After Oxley, Bailey has found only a handful of percussionists with whom he is sympathetic. Han Bennink is certainly one, but their encounter on the more recent *Han* (Incus CD02 CD) is to be preferred to the rather chaotic *Company 3*. Likewise, Jamie Muir's best work with Bailey is to be found on *Dart Drug* (Incus LP41 LP). The young Steve Noble (*q.v.*) is a more recent discovery, a percussionist of immense resource and humour.

Company has consistently avoided whimsy. Tristan Honsinger (whose dancer wife, Katie Duck, contributed greatly, but silently, to the 1987 Company Week) is occasionally guilty of pointless histrionics (he can be heard calling, 'We better get out of here,' on *Once*) and only the drab *Fictions* falls foul of a deliberate whimsicality. Equally, though, Company has rarely been po-faced. The participation of improvisers with 'straight' backgrounds on *Trios* (Globokar, Léandre, Parran), alongside supposed 'terrorists' like Brötzmann, far from leading to excessive seriousness, yields one of the more lyrical albums in the group.

Though demanding, Company performances are uniquely rewarding. *Once* seems an ideal place to pick up the story.

CONCORD ALL STARS
GROUP

***   **Tour De Force** Concord CCD 4172 CD/2MC
Al Cohn, Scott Hamilton, Buddy Tate (*ts*); Dave McKenna (*p*); Cal Collins (*g*); Bob Mate (*b*); Jake Hanna (*d*). 8/81.

***   **Take 8** Concord CCD 4347 CD/MC
Warren Vaché (*c*); Dan Barrett (*tb*); Red Holloway (*as*); Scott Hamilton (*ts*); Dave McKenna (*p*); Steve Wallace (*b*); Jimmie Smith (*d*). 11/87.

***   **Ow!** Concord CCD 4348 CD/MC
As above, except add Ed Bickert (*g*); Ernestine Anderson (*v*). 11/87.

Casually organized but informed by the innate discipline of some of the best-focused players in the mainstream, these civilized jam sessions may lack the brawling excitement of Jazz At the Philharmonic, but they also expunge the excessive solos and ragged ensembles in that kind of jazz. *Tour De Force* concentrates on the three tenors, and Hamilton holds his own with Cohn and Tate without problems: 'Tickle Toe', 'Broadway' and 'Rifftide' are classic tenors-all-out features, but the slower moments let them wear hearts on sleeves too. The other session is basically the Vaché–Hamilton band with Holloway as an extra front-line guest, and this unit's suave manner with standards and swing staples is effortlessly maintained. Anderson joins in for three tracks of *Ow!*, finishing on 'Down Home Blues'.

EDDIE CONDON (1905–73)
GUITAR

***   **The Definitive Eddie Condon And His Jazz Concert All Stars: Volume 1** Stash ST-CD-530 CD
Condon; Bobby Hackett, Muggsy Spanier (*c*); Billy Butterfield, Max Kaminsky (*t*); Hot Lips Page (*t, v*); Lou McGarity, Benny Morton (*tb*); Ernie Caceres (*cl, bs*); Edmond Hall, Pee Wee Russell (*cl*); Gene Schroeder, Jess Stacy (*p*); Bob Haggart (*b*); Joe Grauso, George Wettling (*d*); Liza Morrow, Lee Wiley (*v*). 6 & 10/44.

***   **Eddie Condon Floor Show: Jazz On The Air** Jazzline JL 20803 CD
Condon; Wild Bill Davison (*c*); Louis Armstrong (*t, v*); Cutty Cutshall (*tb*); Jack Teagarden (*tb, v*); Peanuts Hucko (*cl*); Ernie Caceres (*bs*); Joe Bushkin, Gene Schroeder (*p*); Jack Lesberg (*b*); Big Sid Catlett (*d*). 6 & 7/49.

***   **Dixieland Jam** CBS 465680 2 CD
Condon; Wild Bill Davison (*c*); Billy Butterfield (*t*); Cutty Cutshall, Vic Dickenson (*tb*); Bob Wilber (*cl*); Gene Schroeder (*p*); Leonard Gaskin (*b*); George Wettling (*d*). 8 & 9/57

***(*)   **Eddie Condon In Japan** Chiaroscuro GRD 154 CD
Condon; Buck Clayton (*t*); Vic Dickenson (*tb*); Bud Freeman (*ts*); Pee Wee Russell (*cl*); Dick Cary (*p, ahn*); Jack Lesberg (*b*); Cliff Leeman (*d*); Jimmy Rushing (*v*).

A brilliant entrepreneur and colourful raconteur with a good head for whisky, Condon was the focus of Chicago jazz from the 1920s to the 1940s, garnering a personal reputation that far exceeds his actual musical significance. Condon is now best seen as a catalyst, a man who made things happen and in the process significantly heightened the profile of Dixieland jazz in America.

Despite his fame, which was supported by a television show and several fine books, there are very few records available. Condon was rarely anything more than a straightforward rhythm guitarist, generally avoiding solos, but he had a very clear sense of what his role ought to be and frequently 'laid out' to give the piano player more room. His chords have a rather melancholy ring, but are always played dead centre.

The 1944 transcriptions on Stash are straightforward Condon fare, played with considerable professionalism, and marked by some fine solos from Russell, Page, Morton (with his vintage-style trills on 'Royal Garden Blues') and the lyrical Hackett, but with a slight chill about them, too. There are some first takes and breakdowns, but three of the latter amount to less than five seconds apiece and really don't merit inclusion in a compilation of this type.

In 1948, Condon was given his own television show, the first time a major network had recognized jazz in this way, and a considerable accolade, even for a white musician. The Jazzline material is all taken from two star-studded Floor Show performances. Armstrong is already past his best and Teagarden sounds rather pat, but the mainly Dixieland material is played with gusto. The bluesier tunes from the 9 July broadcast are rather better, with some fine front-line work from Davison, Cutshall and Hucko.

Condon enjoyed a long and very successful association with Columbia, who released a substantial body of work in the 1950s. *Dixieland Jam*, featuring two different bands a month apart, is a relaxed, joyous affair, on which Condon can be heard encouraging the players, ordering drinks, wisecracking, doing everything in fact except playing very much guitar. He's rather lost in the digital remix, which greatly favours the horns, putting a polish on Billy Butterfield's solos on 'When A Woman Loves A Man' and 'Why Was I Born?'. The live set from Japan is poorly balanced and some of the playing sounds a little makeshift. However, it's generally up to scratch and a good buy for anyone who doesn't have the multi-disc Jazzology sessions, which are only rather intermittently available.

HARRY CONNICK Jr (born 1968)
VOCAL, PIANO

**   **Harry Connick** CBS CK 40702 CD/MC
Connick. 87.

(*)   **20 CBS 462996 CD/LP/MC
Connick; Dr John (*org, v*); Robert Hurst (*b*); Carmen McRae (*v*). 5–6/88.

***   **We Are In Love** CBS 466736 CD/LP/MC
Connick; Branford Marsalis (*ss, ts*); Russell Malone (*g*); Ben Wolfe (*b*); Shannon Powell (*d*); strings. 3–5/90.

**   **Lofty's Roach Souffle** CBS CD/LP/MC
Connick; Ben Wolfe (*b*); Shannon Powell (*d*).

(*)   **Blue Light, Red Light Columbia 469087 CD/LP/MC
Connick; Jeremy Davenport, Leroy Jones, Dan Miller, Roger Ingram (*t*); Mark Mullins, Craig Klein (*tb*); Lucien Barbarin (*tb, sou*); Joe Barati (*btb*); Louis Ford (*cl*); Brad Leali, Will Campbell (*as*); Jerry Welden, Ned Goold (*ts*); David Schumacher (*bs, bcl, f*); Russell Malone (*g*); Ben Wolfe (*b*); Shannon Powell (*d*). 6–7/91.

Barely out of his teens, this New Orleans singer and pianist has become the most commercially successful jazz musician of his generation in a whirlwind romance with the public. Cannily promoted around a hit soundtrack (*When Harry Met Sally*), matinee idol looks and a vicarious appeal to an audience too young to remember demob suits and pre-rock crooning, Connick has cleaned up with a flair and showmanship which are actually – given his marketing-man's-dream aura – surprisingly hard to dislike. He is a gifted if rather pointlessly eclectic pianist, his solos an amiable but formless amalgam of Monk, Garner and Hines influences; and his real talent (reversing the jazz norm) is surely his singing, which is rather affected and overloaded with mannerisms on *20*, the first record he sang on, but is still good enough to deliver an unexpectedly poignant treatment of 'Imagination'. *Lofty's Roach Souffle* wasn't so much premature – it was released, more or less simultaneously with *We Are In Love*, as a 'jazz' instrumental album paired with the songs collection – as half-baked. Any good piano trio record will outdo this one. But *We Are In Love* is much better, a neat blend of copycat originals and carefully pitched standards, with Marsalis taking a couple of guest solos. Connick's voice is maturing all the time, as *Blue Light, Red Light* shows, and, although this set of all-original songs is pretty thin fare, the arrangements for a young big band are encouragingly untypical of middle-of-the-road big-band scoring, even if some of the charts sound a little wilfully odd. And Connick sings even the tritest of the lyrics with care.

CHRIS CONNOR (born 1929)

VOCAL

***   **Cool Chris** Charly 117 CD
    Connor; J. J. Johnson, Kai Winding (*tb*); Ronnie Ordich (*f, cl*); Herbie Mann (*f*); Don
    Burns (*acc*); Ralph Sharon, Ellis Larkins (*p*); Everett Barksdale, Joe Puma, Joe
    Cinderella (*g*); Milt Hinton (*b*); Osie Johnson, Beverley Peer, Art Mardigan (*d*).
    54–55.

One of the premier cool vocalists of the 1950s, Connor's best work was made for Atlantic, but
her earliest solo records – she was formerly the featured vocalist with Stan Kenton's Orchestra –
have their own rewards. The accompaniments suggest a rather affected, chamber-jazz style,
with their flutes and trombones, but the singing is both refined and direct on a fine set of
standards. The Charly CD brings together various sides recorded for Bethlehem, and the
wonderfully clear recording has been maintained in the reissue; the one disappointment is the
concentration on 'cool' as 'laid-back', since the disc includes almost none of the up-tempo
songs which Connor made for Bethlehem.

****   **Sings The George Gershwin Almanac Of Song** Atlantic 2-601 2CD
    Connor; Joe Newman, Doc Severinson (*t*); Eddie Bert, Jimmy Cleveland, Jim
    Thompson, Warren Covington (*tb*); Sam Most, Peanuts Hucko (*cl*); Herbie Mann (*f*);
    Eddie Wasserman, Al Cohn (*ts*); Danny Bank (*bs*); Ralph Sharon, Stan Free, Hank
    Jones (*p*); Barry Galbraith, Joe Puma, Mundell Lowe (*g*); Milt Jackson (*vib*); Wendell
    Marshall, Milt Hinton, Oscar Pettiford, Vinnie Burke (*b*); Osie Johnson, Ed
    Shaughnessy, Ronnie Free (*d*); Johnny Rodriguez (*perc*).

Most of Connor's marvellous series of Atlantic albums are (disgracefully) out of print, but at
least this superb collection has been reissued on a double-CD, with previously unreleased sides
as a bonus. The vocalist works comprehensively through the Gershwin songbook in the
company of seven different instrumental groups, and the results are probably superior even to
Ella Fitzgerald's similar recordings of the period. Trifles such as 'Bla Bla Bla' or 'I Can't Be
Bothered Now' are graced with thoughtful readings, the swingers despatched unhurriedly, the
ballads lingered over; despite the size of the project, there's no sense of routine. The
remastering has been admirably done.

***(*)   **Classic** Contemporary C-14023 CD/LP/MC
    Connor; Claudio Roditi (*t, flhn*); Paquito D'Rivera (*as*); Michael Abene, Richard
    Rodney Bennett (*ky*); Rufus Reid (*b*); Akira Tana (*d*). 8/86.

A fine return to the studios for Connor. Although some of the accompaniments are a shade too
bright, the material is a refined choice of standards, and the vocalist shows few signs of
advancing years. She revisits 'Blame It On My Youth' with poignant sincerity and elsewhere
handles the pulse of Bennett's arrangements with undiminished skill.

(*)   **New Again Contemporary C-14038 CD/LP/MC
    Connor; Claudio Roditi (*t, flhn*); Bill Kirschner (*ss, as, ts, f, cl*); Dave Valentin (*f*);
    Michael Abene, Richard Rodney Bennett (*ky*); Michael Moore (*b*); Buddy Williams
    (*d*); Sammy Figueroa (*perc*). 8/87.

Something of a let-down after the sublime *Classic*. The band is a little too pushy and loud for
the singer to come through clearly, and some of the songs are inappropriate choices for a
vocalist whose strengths lie in more traditional interpretation. But a handful of tunes, especially
'I Wish I'd Met You', approach Connor's best form.

BILL CONNORS (born 1949)

GUITAR

***   **Theme To The Guardian** ECM 1057 CD/LP
    Connors (*g solo*). 11/74.

***   **Swimming With A Hole In My Body** ECM 1158 CD/LP
    As above. 8/79.

(*)   **Step It Core COCD 9.00818 CD
Connors; Tom Kennedy (*b*); Dave Weckl (*d*). 6 & 10/84.

(*)   **Double Up Core COCD 9.00826 CD
Connors; Tom Kennedy (*b*); Kim Plainfield (*d*). 85.

*(*)   **Assembler** Core COCD 9.00519 CD
As above. 6/87.

Once Chick Corea's guitarist in Return to Forever, Connors shares his old boss's galling tendency to short-change exceptional technical ability with rather bland and self-indulgent ideas. The later trios have a certain energy and immediacy but they're crude in comparison with the Corea-influenced solo projects. Connors's acoustic work is finely detailed and there are some interesting things on *Swimming*, albeit worked out in a shut-off, self-absorbed away that may appeal to guitar technicians but which can be curiously off-putting for everyone else. *Theme*, long in the tooth now, is probably the most satisfactory of the bunch; 'Song For A Crow', 'Frantic Desire' and 'My Favorite Fantasy' are tense, atmospheric pieces with a solid underlying pulse. It may be, though, that Connors has yet to find a sympathetic group setting that will allow him to play more simply without descending to the awful banalities of *Assembler*.

CONTRABAND
GROUP

***(*)   **Live At The Bimhuis** Bvhaast CD 8906 CD
Toon De Gouw, Louis Lanzing, Ad Gruter (*t*); Willem Van Manen, Hans Sparla, Hans Visser (*tb*); Theo Jorgensmann, Paul Van Kemenade, Rutger Van Otterloo, Maarten Van Norden, Eckard Koltermann (*reeds*); Ron Van Rossum (*p*); Hein Offermans (*b*); Martin Van Duynhoven (*d*). 11/88.

***(*)   **De Ruyter Suite** Bvhaast CD 9104 CD
As above, except Chris Abelen (*tb*), Jeroen Van Vliet (*p*) and Eric Van der Westen (*b*) replace Sparla, Van Rossum and Offermans. 4/91.

Contraband is Willem van Manen's 'occasional' big band. The trombonist and veteran of Holland's post-bop and free-music scene is a skilled and dynamic composer–arranger, and these records – one live, one studio, and both written almost entirely by van Manen – are packed with incident. If, as both sleeve-notes suggest, the idea is to prove the big-band tradition is alive by blending conventional forms with new ideas and structures, van Manen almost proves his point: the group swings and shouts with all the power and finesse of the great big bands, and it glories in soloists who crackle their way out of complex charts. But sometimes there are hints of strain or of over-familiar effects – clustering muted trumpets or high reeds, for instance, or fast cutting from passages of rigid orthodoxy to all-out freedom – which suggest that it's a best of both worlds which the band can't quite grasp. It would be churlish, though, to deny the vividness, sweep and panache of a band which ought to be far better known than it is. 'Contra-Suit' from the live record, and the three-part title-piece of *De Ruyter Suite*, dedicated to Dutch critic Michiel de Ruyter, are grand yet wholly coherent big-scale structures, and the soloists – especially Jorgensmann on clarinet and van Kemenade on alto – refuse to dilute the intensity of the whole band. Both discs are sumptuously recorded.

JUNIOR COOK (1934–92)
TENOR SAX

(*)   **Stablemates Affinity 766 CD
Cook; Mickey Tucker (*p*); Cecil McBee, Junior Booth (*b*); Leroy Williams (*d*). 11/77.

**   **Something's Cookin'** Muse MR 5218 LP
Cook; Cedar Walton (*p*); Buster Williams (*b*); Billy Higgins (*d*). 6/81.

Junior Cook was one of the most reliable sidemen in Horace Silver's groups of the early and middle 1960s, never a great original but a first-class soloist who could play with insuperable finesse. The price for this was a certain impersonality: it's hard to spot his playing in a blindfold test and, perhaps for that reason, he's never had much success as a leader in his own right. The Affinity CD, which is shared with a session by George Coleman and which offers excellent value at nearly 80 minutes' playing time, is solid, though short of a single above-average performance to take it into the top category. Of Cook's two albums for Muse, *Something's Cookin'* is the second and the only one currently available, even if only on vinyl. It's not bad, and the rhythm section play well up to their credentials, but Cook can't evade the feeling that he's doing no more than shadowing other, greater records.

*** **The Place To Be** Steeplechase SCS 1240/SCCD 31240 CD/LP
Cook; Mickey Tucker (*p*); Wayne Dockery (*b*); Leroy Williams (*d*). 11/88.

*** **On A Misty Night** Steeplechase SCCD 31266 CD
As above, except Walter Booker (*b*) replaces Dockery. 6/89.

Steeplechase has been a profitable home for many a journeyman hard bopper, with the label's comfortable house sound and familiar menus making plenty of otherwise disenfranchised musicians feel at home. Junior Cook's two records for the company have both worked out rather well. If Cook's dependability is his strongest suit, he nevertheless manages to find enough in the way of ear-catching ideas to give his uptempo workouts an edge of involvement, which grants even something as simple as 'Cedar's Blues' on *The Place To Be* a tough credibility. His powers were also in decline to some extent, but that tends to lend such a professional player a further challenge: how does he deal with it? Cook's answer seems to be to shy away from over-familiar material and to turn to more timbral variation than he would have bothered with as a younger man. *On A Misty Night* is marked by a considered choice of material – 'By Myself', 'Make The Girl Love Me', 'My Sweet Pumpkin' – and the leader's thoughts on the title-tune, once associated with Coltrane, stake his place in the grand tenor lineage. Both records are greatly assisted by the presence of Tucker, sympathetic, and driving when he has to be.

MARTY COOK
TROMBONE

*** **Nightwork** Enja 5033 LP
Cook; Jim Pepper (*ts*); Essiet Okon Esiet (*b*); John Betsch (*d*). 10/86–1/87.

*** **Red White Black And Blue** Enja 5067 CD/LP
Cook; Jim Pepper (*ts*); Mal Waldron (*p*); Ed Schuller (*b*); John Betsch (*d*). 11/87.

If Ray Anderson is way out on his own, Cook must be leading the contemporary trombone pack. Whatever their respective merits, there is certainly no quantitative comparison to their respective outputs. Anderson is everywhere, while Cook's most noted recorded work before the mid-1980s was a too-brief appearance on *Out From Under*, a typically enigmatic Gunther Hampel release from the fissiparous Birth label.

The Enja sets show that he has considerable qualities as both soloist and leader: bright articulation, inexhaustible ideas, sharp arrangements, and an impressive structural awareness. In Jim Pepper, the Amerindian composer of 'Witchi Tai To', he has the perfect instrumental complement; Betsch drums with great control and rigour and Waldron, on *Red White . . .*, is a virtual guarantee of quality. Worth checking out.

BOB COOPER (born 1925)
TENOR SAXOPHONE, OBOE

(*) **Coop! The Music Of Bob Cooper Original Jazz Classics OJC-161 CD/LP
Cooper; Conte Candoli, Pete Candoli, Don Fagerquist (*t*); Frank Rosolino, John Halliburton (*tb*); Lou Levy (*p*); Victor Feldman (*vib*); Max Bennett (*b*); Mel Lewis (*d*). 8/57.

Because he chose to spend much of his career away from any leadership role, Cooper's light has been a little dim next to many of the West Coast players of the 1950s, especially as he often worked as an accompanist to his wife, vocalist June Christy. His flute-and-oboe sessions with Bud Shank are out of print, but this sole feature album, recorded for Contemporary, displays a light, appealing tenor style and arrangements which match rather than surpass the West Coast conventions of the day. The drily effective recording is typical of the studios of the period.

***   **Milano Blues** Fresh Soundd FSR-CD 179 CD
Cooper; Hans Hammerschmid, Pim Jacobs (*p*); Rudolf Hansen, Ruud Jacobs (*b*);
Victor Plasil, Wessel Ilcken (*d*). 3–4/57.

Two sessions from a European visit, both with local rhythm sections, a studio date in Milan and a live show in Holland. Cooper sounds a little over-relaxed on the Italian date but the livelier 'Cappucino Time' is sinuously done, and the live tracks feature a fine tenor blow on 'Indiana'. A couple of oboe features don't assert a great jazz role for the instrument. Goodish sound throughout, though the drums are a bit thin on the studio date.

***   **Plays The Music Of Michel Legrand** Discovery DSCD 935 CD
Cooper; Mike Wofford, Russ Tompkins (*p*); Chuck Berghofer, Tom Azarello (*b*);
John Guerin, Jim Plank (*d*). 80.

**   **In A Mellotone** Contemporary C-14017 LP/MC
Cooper; Snooky Young (*t, flhn*); Ross Tompkins (*p*); Doug MacDonald (*g*); Monty
Budwig (*b*); Jeff Hamilton (*d*); Ernie Andrews (*v*). 10/85.

***   **For All We Know** Fresh Sound FSR-CD 167 CD
Cooper; Lou Levy (*p*); Monty Budwig (*b*); Ralph Penland (*d*). 8/90.

Cooper has made rather sporadic returns to the studios in the 1980s and '90s, but he remains a guileful player, his tone deceptively languid: when the tempo picks up, the mastery of the horn asserts itself, and he gets the same kind of even-handed swing which the more demonstrative Zoot Sims or Al Cohn could muster. The Discovery CD puts together two albums of Legrand tunes, with exemplary support from Mike Wofford on one of the sessions. *In A Mellotone* finds Cooper paired with Young's rather faded swing-styled playing and some desultory light blues from Andrews, who sings on four of the ten tracks. Budwig and Hamilton do their best to put a little more life into the music. Better to turn to the wistful *For All We Know*, which benefits from typically thoughtful preparation by Cooper and Levy, on good and unhackneyed standards and with quartet arrangements that make the most of the various combinations of players.

LINDSAY COOPER (born 1951)
SOPRANINO SAXOPHONE, BASSOON

****   **Oh Moscow** Victor CD 015 CD
Cooper; Phil Minton (*t, v*); Alfred '23' Harth (*ts*); Elvira Plenar (*p*); Hugh Hopper
(*b*); Marilyn Mazur (*d, perc*); Sally Potter (*v*). 10/89.

(*)   **Schrödinger's Cat Femme/Line FECD 9.01093 CD
Cooper; Stuart Jones (*t, clo, b*); Peter Whyman (*as, ss, bcl*); Dean Brodrick (*ky, p, acc,
bsn*). 9/90.

Coming first in categories of one usually either guarantees spurious eminence or virtual neglect. Cooper's skills as a bassoonist and on the treacherously pitched and virtually unexploited sopranino saxophone are highly regarded by fellow musicians (she has played with the advanced rock group, Henry Cow, David Thomas's Pedestrians, the Mike Westbrook band, the Feminist Improvising Group and the Maarten Altena Octet) but have made little public impact as yet. Her output as leader has until recently been rather small and her best work before the two items above was probably done in the company of Maggie Nicols and Joëlle Léandre on *Live At The Bastille* (Sync Pulse).

The two available records are, in keeping with much of her output, strongly dramatic in conception. *Schrödinger's Cat* is a set of short and rather brittle dance-pieces written for a piece of choreography called *Edge*. The instrumentation is highly unusual and effective, but the music is lacklustre in the extreme, tied up in a series of metaphors and analogies drawn from quantum mechanics, like the bizarre and rather sadistic uncertainty experiment which gives the set its title. Any temptation to open the CD box to see if the music is alive or dead is profoundly resistible. The wind-dominated band whirls uncertainly without charm and with only the most superficial strangeness.

Oh Moscow is very much closer to Mike Westbrook's brand of music-theatre and recalls Eisler's fetishization of musical 'objects', which are dotted through the music like reference points. Sally Potter's texts follow a compelling but painful course through modern European history, culminating in the horrors wrought by German nationalism; the shattering 'On German Soil' comes half-way through. Musically it's very forceful, with Cooper's snake-charming sopranino coiling through some beautifully complex charts. The band is terrific, with Minton magnificent in all his voices, and Hugh Hopper, Marilyn Mazur and Elvira Plenar involved in interchanges which are not so hyper-subtle as to lose the inexorable progress of the music. Recorded live at Victoriaville, the performance draws additional emphasis from events at the time in Central Europe. Sobering and grand.

CHICK COREA (born 1941)
PIANO, KEYBOARDS, COMPOSER

***   **Piano Improvisations Vols 1 & 2** ECM 1014/1020 CD/LP
       Corea (*p* solo); Ida Kavafian (*vn*); Fred Sherry (*clo*). 4/71.

*(*)   **Children's Songs** ECM 1267 CD/LP
       As above. 7/83.

Corea is a pianist and composer of remarkable range and energy, combining a free-ish jazz idiom with a heavy Latin component and an interest in more formal structures. The obvious parallel is with his ECM stable-mate Keith Jarrett, an even more prolific keyboard improviser with a similar facility for melodic invention within relatively conventional popular forms or in more loosely conceived improvisatory settings; they also share a certain ambivalences about audiences. Corea's stated ambition is to assimilate the 'dancing' qualities of jazz and folk musics to the more disciplined structures of classical music. He has written a half-dozen classic melodies, notably the much-covered 'La Fiesta', 'Return To Forever' and 'Tones For Joan's Bones'.

There is certainly a world of difference between the miniatures on *Piano Improvisations* and Jarrett's hugely rambling excursions. Corea is superficially less demanding, but still repays detailed attention. If his taste was to lapse in the following years, he was surely never more decorously apt than in these 1971 sessions, which after 20 years are still wearing well. *Children's Songs* is a much less compelling set.

**   **Now He Sings, Now He Sobs** Blue Note CDP 790 055 CD
       Corea; Miroslav Vitous (*b*); Roy Haynes (*d*). 68.

**   **Trio Music** ECM 1232/33 CD/LP
       As above. 11/81.

**   **Trio Music, Live In Europe** ECM 1310 CD/LP
       As above. 9/84.

***(*)   **The Song Of Singing** Blue Note B21Y 84353 CD/LP/MC
       Corea; Dave Holland (*b*); Barry Altschul (*d*). 70.

***   **A.R.C.** ECM 1009 CD/LP
       As above. 1/71.

The trios offer the best internal evidence of Corea's musical and philosophical trajectory. The early *Sings/Sobs* is a fine, solid jazz set with some intelligently handled standard material. A bare three years later, Corea, falling under the influence of the Scientology movement, was playing altogether more experimentally. *The Song Of Singing* (arguably Corea's best record) is marked by fine melodic invention and some remarkably sophisticated group interplay which demands that the record be seen as a trio performance, not just as Corea plus rhythm. The two 'Ballads', numbered I and III, are credited to the three musicians and are presumably improvised over predetermined structures; one wonders how many were left on the editing-room floor. Corea's two compositions, 'Rhymes' and 'Flesh', are slightly vapid but sharpen up on familiarity. *A.R.C.* isn't entirely successful, but the quality of Holland and

Altschul renders it a credible essay that Corea was never fully to develop. He left the demanding Circle (whose single record contained versions of Holland's 'Toy Room' and Wayne Shorter's 'Nefertiti', both covered on *The Song Of Singing*) later in 1971, convinced that the music was losing touch with its audience. This is the beginning of the pianist's awkward populism, which was to lead him to a commercially successful but artistically null flirtation with fusion music of various sorts.

The later trio perfectly underscores his change in attitude. Vitous and Haynes are both superbly gifted players, but they take no discernible chances, sticking close to a conception laden with Corea's increasingly vapid philosophizing. By 1984, there isn't much left on Old Mother Hubbard's shelves.

**(*) Early Days Denon CD 33C38 7969 CD
Corea; Woody Shaw (*t*); Hubert Laws (*f, picc*); Bennie Maupin (*ts*); Dave Holland (*b*); Horace Arnold, Jack DeJohnette (*d*). 69.

Fine stuff from an unexpected and largely forgotten line-up that bears every sign of being influenced by Miles Davis's new cross-over style (Corea had joined the Miles band the previous year). Good things from the late Woody Shaw, then still a viable performer, and from the estimable DeJohnette. Well worth looking for.

** Compact Jazz: Chick Corea Polydor 831365 2 CD
Corea; Joe Farrell (*f, ts*); Bill Connors, Al diMeola (*g*); Jean-Luc Ponty (*v*); Stanley Clarke (*b*); Steve Gadd, Lenny White (*d*); Narada Michael Walden (*perc*); Gayle Moran (*v*). 72–76.

*** Works ECM 825426-2 CD
Corea (*p* solo and with various bands). 71–83.

A well-selected sample of the pianist's decade-plus with ECM. Not many surprises, though it's interesting how thin the short piano improvisations from ECM 1014 and 1020 sound when heard out of context.

*** Light As A Feather Polydor 2310247 CD/LP
Corea; Joe Farrell (*f, ts*); Stanley Clarke (*b*); Airto Moreira (*perc*); Flora Purim (*v, perc*). 10/72.

*(*) Where Have I Known You Before Polydor 2310354 CD/LP
Corea; Al DiMeola (*g*); Stanley Clarke (*b*); Lenny White (*d, perc*). 7–8/74.

Lightweight perhaps, but the 1972 album is a perennial favourite, with Corea bouncing joyously and unselfconsciously over themes like '500 Miles High', 'Captain Marvel' and the ubiquitous 'Children's Song'. Purim's voice was never better and Clarke keeps his lead guitarist ambitions to himself for the present.

There's something very, um, 1974 about *Where Have I Known You Before*. It does, though, retain some of the freshness and energy of the earlier, acoustic band and it's perfectly possible to shut one's eyes to Corea's quasi-mystical titles. Wears rather better than ever seemed possible, and the CD burnishes up some of the duller components.

** Corea Hancock Polydor 835360 CD
Corea; Herbie Hancock (*p*). 2/78.

*** Crystal Silence ECM 1024 CD/LP
Corea; Burton (*vib*). 10/79.

** In Concert, Zurich, October 28, 1978 ECM 1182/3 CD/LP
As above.

* Lyric Suite For Sextet ECM 1260 CD/LP
As above, except add string quartet. 9/82.

Interesting duo performances of 'La Fiesta' and 'Maiden Voyage' on *Corea Hancock* (a compositional credit apiece), but by no means a compelling album, with some of Hancock's notions baffling in the extreme. *Crystal Silence* is a lot more substantial than it initially sounds and the music holds up well on the subsequent concert performance, which for a time was a worthwhile substitute, though CD has given the sound a cleaner and more distinctive edge.

'Senor Mouse' and 'Crystal Silence' reappear from the studio disc and there is a fine eponymous Bud Powell tribute that is well worth the admission price.

The *Lyric Suite* recalls Ravel more readily than Alban Berg, which is no bad thing. It's delicate, attractive music, sensibly limited in scope, firmly executed and, as always, beautifully executed. Less baroquely ambitious than Jarrett's classical compositions, it comes across as something of a by-blow.

*   **Voyage** ECM 1282 CD/LP
Corea; Steve Kujala (*f*). 7/84.

*(*)   **Septet** ECM 1297 CD/LP
As above, except add strings and French horn. 7/84, 10/84.

Voyage is a flimsy confection that is very difficult to take entirely seriously. Part of the problem is that the two players take it very seriously indeed, when what it cries out for is a little lightness of touch. *Septet* is no more pulse-quickening, but it has the benefit of a certain variation of register and timbre that is episodically quite interesting.

*   **My Spanish Heart** Polydor 2669034 CD/LP
Corea; 17-piece band, including strings; Jean-Luc Ponty (*vn*); one track of Corea; Stanley Clarke (*b*); Narada Michael Walden (*perc*). 10/76.

A rare instance of Corea working with a large band. It gives every impression of having been got up for the tourists. It's a rather ersatz Latin concoction that never seems to earn its climaxes or justify the band's rather strained enthusiasm. The quartet 'Armando's Rhumba' can also be found, should you want it, on Polydor 831365 2, below.

(*)   **Light Years** GRP 91036 CD/LP
Corea; Eric Marienthal (*sax*); Frank Gambale (*g*); John Patitucci (*b*); Dave Weckl (*d*).

(*)   **Eye Of The Beholder** GRP 94053 CD/LP
As above.

*   **Beneath The Mask** GRP 96492 CD
Corea; John Patitucci (*b*); Dave Weckl (*d*).

Product of a rush of blood to the head known as the Elektrik Band (yes, the Akoustik Band was not far behind) and deeply horrid.

(*) **Alive GRP 96272 CD
Corea; John Patitucci (*b*); Dave Weckl (*d*).

From the very first notes of 'On Green Dolphin Street', Corea is unmistakable. For better or worse he has perhaps the most distinctive stylistic signature in contemporary jazz piano, a rippling fullness of sound that cloys very quickly. Here, then, the promised Akoustic Band and a mainly standards set. Compared to what Keith Jarrett has done with similar repertoire, the thinness of Corea's conception becomes clearer. This is, though, an uncomplicated, entertaining set; the piano sounds first rate and the production is spot-on.

LARRY CORYELL (born 1943)
GUITAR

***   **Spaces** Start VMCD 7305.
Coryell; John McLaughlin (*g*); Chick Corea (*p*); Miroslav Vitous (*b*); Billy Cobham (*d*).

This is the sort of thing that might have got fusion a good name. Coryell and McLaughlin stay just this side of pipe-and-slippers and leave it to the excitable rhythm section to keep the adrenalin flowing. The much-maligned Cobham shows how good a drummer he was and Vitous carves out muscular lines that suggest a range of influences from Wilbur Ware to Jimmy Garrison. The 1970s weren't all bad.

***   **Tributaries** Novus PD83072 CD
Coryell; Joe Beck, John Scofield (*g*). 8/78, 8 & 9/79.

Coryell's fascination with the Hendrix legacy was passing by the late 1970s. Even so, it was still a faintly self-conscious act to sit down and record a wholly acoustic set. Five solo tracks (one with a second 12-string overdub), a duo apiece with Beck and the emerging Scofield (who allegedly didn't even own an acoustic guitar at this time), and five rather busy trios. 'The File' is perhaps the best of these. 'Zimbabwe' is a more freewheeling jam, with quotes and stylistic allusions patchworked rather uneasily together. What's interesting about the set (given its dateline) is how consciously it's inscribed in orthodox jazz terms. Wes Montgomery (and for Beck, Charlie Christian) is the most obvious influence on the playing. There's a good solo medley of Horace Silver's 'Song For My Father' and 'Sister Sadie', and a thoroughly unexpected version of Coltrane's 'Equinox'. Novus are doing sterling work in their Series '70, recovering so much half-forgotten material from what was supposed to have been jazz's bleakest decade.

(*) **Bolero String 233850 CD
Coryell; Brian Keane (*g*). 4/81, 1/82, 11/83.

Coryell had already tackled Ravel (and Robert de Visée) on *The Restful Mind* [Vanguard] and it was inevitable that he would add 'Bolero' to 'Pavane For A Dead Princess'. Ravel was a perfectly logical focus for Coryell and he also tackles the prelude from 'Le Tombeau De Couperin', lending it an elaborate contrapuntal feel that almost buries the intriguing modal progression that links it to the gypsy and flamenco traditions that intrigue both men. The rest of the set is typical of Coryell's intriguing blend of styles, incorporating country strums, fast gut-strung lines, amplified sustains and huge, complicated arpeggios on his magnificently toned Ho 12-string. 'Blues In Madrid' is a good example of the way he compresses idioms, skirting tourist flamenco with cheeky insouciance and then chucking in a quote from 'Buttons And Bows' just to show he's still thinking like a jazz man. Keane joins in for the last half dozen tracks but serves better as a guest composer than as an accompanist. His 'Piece For Larry' is a straightforward picking theme, but 'At The Airport' and 'Patty's Song' bespeak a more sophisticated awareness.

*** **Together** Concord CJ 289 CD/LP/MC
Coryell; Emily Remler (*g*). 8/85.

Emily Remler's death from a heart attack, aged only 32, robbed America of one of its foremost instrumental voices and a jazz musician of considerable stature. *Together* delivers fulsomely, a warm, approachable album which does not lack for subtleties. Recommended.

*** **Toku Du** Muse MCD 5350 CD/LP
Coryell; Stanley Cowell (*p*); Buster Williams (*b*); Beaver Harris (*d*). 9/87.

'Schizophrenic' is a wildly misused critical adjective, but if there were ever a split musical personality, it is Coryell. The guitarist never seemed able to make up his mind whether he wanted to be Chet Atkins, Jimi Hendrix or Segovia; and there were always doubts about his chops as an improviser. *Toku Du*, named after a fine Buster Williams piece, represents Coryell's rapprochement with The Tradition. Versions of 'My Funny Valentine', 'Round Midnight', 'Sophisticated Lady' and Coltrane's 'Moment's Notice' seem convincing enough proof of his credentials. Brilliantly engineered by Rudy van Gelder, the band sounds in top form, with Cowell particularly effective.

GIUSEPPE COSTA
BASS

(*) **Picture Number One Splasc(h) H 141 LP
Costa; Vito Giordano (*t, flhn*); Salvatore Pizzo, Fabio Palacino (*tb*); Agostino Cirrito (*as*); Salvatore Bonafede (*p*); Pippo Cataldo (*d, marim*). 8/87.

(*) **Picture Number Two Splasc(h) H 325-2 CD
Costa; Flavio Boltro (*t, flhn*); Danilo Terenzi, Stefano Scalzi (*tb*); Sandro Satta (*as*); Andrea Beneventano (*p*); Pippo Cataldo (*d*). 5/90.

Two records co-led by the bass and drums partnership of Giuseppe Costa and Pippo Cataldo. While both use the odd instrumentation of trumpet, two trombones, alto and rhythm section, they're quite different from each other: the first, using an all-Sicilian cast, is slightly more ragged and more exciting, with the careering 'Luce Nascente' getting the record off to a cracking start which the rest of the programme occasionally lives up to: this is lively post-bop jazz with plenty of rough edges and enthusiasm taking precedence over finesse. *Picture Number Two*, which has a more familiar cast of new Italian jazzmen, is much smoother and, while it's better played all through, some of the impetuousness has been disadvantageously lost. Boltro's lovely playing on 'To Gil' makes up for what's gone missing, though. Decent and entertaining records.

CURTIS COUNCE (born 1926)
BASS

***   **You Get More Bounce** Original Jazz Classics OJC 159 CD/LP
Counce; Jack Sheldon or Gerald Wilson (*t*); Harold Land (*ts*); Carl Perkins (*p*); Frank Butler (*d*). 10/56.

***   **Landslide** Original Jazz Classics OJC 606 CD/LP
As above. 4/57.

**   **Carl's Blues** Original Jazz Classics OJC 423 CD/LP
As above. 8/57.

*(*)   **Sonority** Contemporary C 7655 CD
As above. 1/58.

'More bounce' promised, more bounce delivered. Elasticity aplenty in Counce's late-1950s quintet, one of the better and more resilient bands working the West Coast scene at the time. Perhaps the best of the albums, *Exploring The Future*, appeared on Dooto/Boplicity and is currently unavailable, but *Landslide* is a fine substitute, showcasing Land's beefy tenor and Sheldon's very underrated soloing. Perkins, remembered best for his weird, crab-wise technique, was probably on better form with this band than anywhere else on record, but the real star – a point recognized by the drum solo 'The Butler Did It' on *Carl's Blues* and 'A Drum Conversation' on the bin-end *Sonority* – was Frank Butler, a powerful technician who shared Counce's own instinctive swing. Most of the material stems from the same half dozen sessions, but is none the worse for that.

STANLEY COWELL (born 1941)
PIANO, ELECTRIC PIANO

***   **Equipoise** Galaxy GXY 5125 LP
Cowell; Cecil McBee (*b*); Roy Haynes (*d*). 11/78.

****   **Sienna** Steeplechase SCCD 31253 CD
Cowell; Ron McClure (*b*); Keith Copeland (*d*). 7/89.

The two opening tracks – a passionate tribute to trumpeter/composer 'Cal Massey' (which also appears on the solo Maybeck Hall recital below), and the gentle ballad 'I Think It's Time To Say Goodbye' – take the measure of Cowell's extraordinary range. Copeland seems a little out of place on slower tracks, which might well have been done as duos, but his abrupt unison accents on 'Evidence' are startlingly effective. This is quite the best version of Monk's tune since the master's own and it represents a peak from which the album can only decline, in relative terms at least. A long 'I Concentrate On You' adds nothing in particular to the hundreds that have gone before and it's only with the title piece and the last-but-one track 'Dis Place' that Cowell lets loose his remarkable harmonic and rhythmic intelligence. An excellent album, recorded in slightly uncomfortable close-up.

***(*)   **Live at Maybeck Recital Hall** Concord CCD 4431 CD/MC
Cowell solo. 6/90.

A supremely gifted player who bridges Bud Powell with the free movement of the 1960s, Cowell has received far less than his due of critical attention. Perhaps as a result, his recorded output has been somewhat restricted to jobbing sideman for Galaxy, working with Art Pepper, John Klemmer, Johnny Griffin and, returning the compliment here, Roy Haynes.

Like Haynes, Cowell has an almost chameleon facility for widely differing musical contexts. Never an out-and-out modernist, he seems easiest in the eclectic, cross-over trio charts suggested by *Equipoise*. McBee is another highly adaptive player and has seldom been better on record than here. There are better Cowell moments in the vaults, but this is very well worth having.

Live is the fifth and one of the best of Concord's series of piano recitals in the beautiful acoustic of a small hall in Berkeley, California. Cowell features himself as a composer only sparingly – 'I Am Waiting', 'Little Sunny' and the concluding 'Cal Massey', a dedication to the neglected trumpeter/composer (*q.v.*) – concentrating instead on demanding reinterpretations of standards and bebop staples. 'Softly, As In a Morning Sunrise' opens the set in a uncontroversially pianistic C minor, but then undergoes an astonishing *twelve* changes of key; the effect is not just blandly virtuosic but offers considerable insight into Cowell's harmonic imagination and way of approaching the subsequent programme. 'Stella By Starlight' and 'I'll Remember April', 'Out Of This World', 'Autumn Leaves' and 'Django' receive subtly off-centre readings. Wayne Shorter's 'Nefertiti' is a *tour de force*, rarely attempted by an unaccompanied pianist, and Charlie Parker's 'Big Foot' (or 'Air Conditioning') is a finger-breaker. An excellent set by a master at the height of his considerable powers.

****   **Close To You Alone** DIW 603E CD
Cowell; Cecil McBee (*b*); Ronnie Burrage (*d*). 8/90.

No sense of anti-climax with this one, which catches the pianist in the middle of a purple streak. It begins with dramatic bass chords from McBee on his own ''D' Bass-ic Blues'. Cowell's entry is reminiscent of 1950s Cecil Taylor but ripples off in his characteristic Bud Powell vein. McBee and Burrage account for four of the seven tracks between them, and with 'Stella By Starlight' finishing the set, it's another example of Cowell's apparent unwillingness to foreground his own material. 'Equipoise' makes a welcome reappearance, its curiously balanced, rather static initial theme sounding almost as if it is built out of some five-note Chinese scale (and Cowell's stiff-fingered, chopsticks attack increases the effect) but then breaking out into a good-natured funk roll. Few current pianists are more interesting to listen to; Cowell seems quite genuinely to be expanding the improvising vocabulary of his instrument while remaining within relatively conventional jazz structures. High marks for McBee and Burrage, too, though the drummer's compositional skills are not yet fine-tuned.

LOL COXHILL (born 1932)
SOPRANO SAXOPHONE

***   **Johnny Rondo Duo Plus Mike Cooper** FMP SAJ 29 LP
Coxhill; Dave Holland (*b*); Mike Cooper (*g*). 5/80.

An original. Coxhill is a well-known figure on the British festival scene, valued as a drily funny MC and a cheap-and-cheerful opening act. As a result, his busking solo performances have been considerably undervalued. It's perhaps more accurate to think of Coxhill as an 'instant composer' than as a jazz player *per se*. Though he is an adventurous changes player when the mood takes him, his real forte is as a melodist, chancing across attractive folksy patterns in the midst of long, outwardly shapeless monologues on his attractively thin-toned soprano. And he is often impressive in a totally free context, such as Derek Bailey's Company project, where he can sound like a direct hybrid of his two most obvious influences on the straight horn, Evan Parker and Steve Lacy.

The Johnny Rondo Duo falls mid-way between Coxhill's free-form playing and the folksier approach. Holland is an ideal partner. His career is equally multi-faceted and he typically balances free playing with folk forms. The Duo offers a cod dance-band programme, terspichorean nightmares like 'Russian Dance' and Coxhill's staple 'Frog Dance', interspersed with a set of 'Flöz Variations' which are an excellent example of the saxophonist's 'instant composition'. Cooper doesn't add a great deal to the music, and the sound engineer even less, but it's a worthwhile acquisition in the absence of anything else.

PAUL CRAM
ALTO AND TENOR SAXOPHONES

*** **Blue Tales In Time** Onari/Sackville 006 LP
Cram; Ken Newby (*ss, bsn*); Karen Oliver (*vn*); Paul Plimley (*vib, p*); Lyle
Lansall-Ellis (*b*); Gregg Simpson (*d*). 4/81.

Part of Vancouver's modestly-documented improvising movement, Paul Cram is an energetic
player but is probably more interesting as a musical organizer: his tenor solo piece 'Nebula' is
no more than an exercise here. The other tracks, arranged for trio and quartet combinations,
purvey a keen sense of rhythmic and harmonic detail, written passages burst open by
improvisation. Two compositions by Lansall-Ellis are less engaging, but three pieces for a
chamber trio of Cram, Newby and Oliver are scintillating, and Charlie Parker's 'Au Privave' is
given a brusque hosing-down. Cram has a slithery legato style which suits his twisting writing,
and the recording, while unglamorous, does the players no injustice.

HANK CRAWFORD (born 1934)
ALTO SAXOPHONE

*** **Midnight Ramble** Milestone M9112 CD/LP/MC
Crawford; Waymon Reed, Charlie Miller (*t*); Dick Griffin (*tb*); David Newman (*ts*);
Howard Johnson (*bs*); Dr John (*ky*); Calvin Newborne (*g*); Charles Greene (*b*);
Bernard Purdie (*d*). 11/82.

(*) **Indigo Blue Milestone M9119 CD/LP/MC
Crawford; Martin Banks, Danny Moore (*t*); David Newman (*ts*); Howard Johnson
(*bs*); Melvin Sparks (*g*); Wilbur Bascomb (*b*); Bernard Purdie (*d*). 8/83.

(*) **Down On The Deuce Milestone M9129 LP/MC
Cedar Walton (*p*); Jimmy Ponder (*g*); others as above. 6/84.

** **Mr Chips** Milestone M9149 CD/LP/MC
Crawford; Randy Brecker, Alan Rubin (*t*); David Newman (*ts*); Howard Johnson
(*bs*); Richard Tee (*ky*); Cornell Dupree (*g*); Wilbur Bascomb (*b*); Bernard Purdie (*d*).
11/86.

*** **Night Beat** Milestone M9168 LP/MC/CD
Crawford; Lew Soloff, Alan Rubin (*t*); David Newman (*ts, f*); Howard Johnson (*bs*);
Dr John (*ky*); Melvin Sparks (*g*); Wilbur Bascomb (*b*); Bernard Purdie (*d*). 9–10/88.

*** **Groove Master** Milestone M9182 LP/MC/CD
Lou Marini (*ts*) replaces Newman, add Gloria Coleman (*org*), others as above. 2–3/90.

Hank Crawford says that he tries 'to keep the melody so far in front that you can almost sing
along', and that irresistibly vocal style lends his simple approach to the alto a deep-rooted
conviction. His records are swinging parties built on the blues, southern R&B – Crawford
apprenticed in the bands of Ike and Tina Turner and Ray Charles – and enough bebop to keep
a more hardened jazz listener involved. He recorded 12 albums for Atlantic in the 1960s, but
none of them is currently in the catalogue, and his renewed career has been thanks to the
initiative of Milestone, who have provided him with consistently sympathetic settings. There's
little to choose between the albums listed above, all of them smartly organized around
Crawford's libidinous wail: *Mr Chips* gets lower marks for a mundane choice of material, while
Midnight Ramble, *Night Beat* and *Groove Master* are enlivened by the inspiring presence of Dr
John on piano and organ. Typical of Crawford's mature command is the way he empowers
Whitney Houston's 'Saving All My Love For You' on *Groove Master* with a real authority.

*** **Soul Survivors** Milestone M9142 LP/MC/CD
Crawford; Jimmy McGriff (*ky*); George Benson, Jim Pittsburg (*g*); Mel Lewis,
Bernard Purdie (*d*). 1/86.

(*) **Steppin' Up Milestone M9153 LP/MC/CD
Crawford; Jimmy McGriff (*ky*); Billy Preston (*p*); Jimmy Ponder (*g*); Vance James
(*d*). 6/87.

(*)   **On The Blue Side Milestone M9177 CD/LP/MC
As above. 7/89.

Crawford shares leadership duties with McGriff on these small-group albums, and between them they update the sound of the 1960s organ combo without surrendering the juice and fire of the original music. *Soul Survivors* is the best of the three because the renewed partnership is at its freshest, and Benson is for once employed in a worthwhile jazz context; but, taken a few tracks at a time, all three discs are exhilarating.

(*)   **Portrait Milestone 9192 CD/MC
Crawford; David 'Fathead' Newman (*ts*); Johnny Hammond (*org*); Jimmy Ponder (*g*); Vance James (*d*). 90.

Crawford soldiers on with another album out of the same locker. While there's little danger of his delivering a duff record in this style, there's nothing in this set that will be required listening for any who've heard one or two out of the previous half-dozen.

CLYDE CRINER
KEYBOARDS

**   **Behind The Sun** RCA Novus PL 83029 CD/MC
Criner; Craig Rivers (*ss*); Carlos Santana (*g*); Marcus Miller (*b*); Omar Hakim, Rodney Holmes (*d*); Steve Thornton, Kevin Jones, Ocasio (*perc*). 10/87.

Criner is a sessionman whose own music lacks much distinction, but he at least assembles an interesting line-up here, with Santana making a rare appearance away from his own records, and with Miller and Hakim handling most of the rhythm tracks. A minor diversion.

MARILYN CRISPELL
PIANO

***   **Spirit Music** Cadence CJR 1015 LP

**   **Live In Berlin** Black Saint BSR 0069 LP
Crispell; Billy Bang (*vn*); Peter Kowald (*b*, on *Live In Berlin*); John Betsch (*d*); Wes Brown (*g*, on *Spirit Music*). 5/81–1/82, 1/82.

One of the most remarkable talents of the 1980s, Crispell seems destined to become a major presence in the '90s. In retrospect, the Coltrane and Cecil Taylor influences weigh much less heavily on her earliest recordings than was routinely thought of them. 'Spirit Music' is dedicated to Coltrane and represents some sort of coming-to-terms with her 'overwhelming' introduction to 'A Love Supreme'. It is a powerful piece, well recorded, live, at New York University and dominates an album of long tracks; Wes Brown's guitar fits in surprisingly well, seldom clashing with Bang's furiously scrabbled violin.

    It is a measure of Crispell's quality and strength of personality that she has no palpable difficulty keeping her head above water in this company. The *Berlin* set, of almost identical vintage, is less directly appealing. As with Taylor, it's questionable whether a bass player was strictly required; Kowald has a firm voice but, unlike Brown, he seems to conflict with the violin and sounds hyperactive in freer passages.

(*)   **Rhythms Hung In Undrawn Sky Leo Records LR 118 LP
Crispell (*p* solo). 5/83.

***   **A Concert In Berlin** FMP SAJ 46 LP
As above. 5/83.

***   **Labyrinths** Les Disques Victo 06 LP
As above. 10/87.

***(*)   **Live In San Francisco** Music & Arts 633 CD
As above. 10/89.

***   **And Your Ivory Voice Sings** Leo Records LR 126 LP
        Crispell; Doug James (*perc*). 3/85.

Solo performances by Crispell are dramatic, harmonically tense and wholly absorbing. *Rhythms* is a shade tentative and surprisingly introverted, and is perhaps best returned to after the excellent *Labyrinths*, a fine live set recorded in Canada. (The air above the 49th parallel obviously agrees with Crispell: see her *Vancouver Duets* with Anthony Braxton.) The 1983 Berlin concert is initially rather more academic – there is even a dedication to Olivier Messiaen – but develops into a powerful emotional statement that culminates, deliberately or not, with an 'America' that has nothing to do with either Leonard Bernstein or Paul Simon, but which is Crispell's own. (A CD might enhance the dramatic flow and coherence of the performance; the vinyl sound isn't exactly crystalline either.) The 1987 set seems largely dedicated to exploring Coltrane's harmonic and rhythmic legacy; Crispell's version of 'After The Rain' has long been a show-stopper, and this one makes an interesting point of comparison with the earlier version on *And Your Ivory Voice Sings*. Doug James's embellishments there are not always entirely satisfying, not always necessary at all; there is certainly no sense that he adds anything to her always robust rhythmic drive. 'And Your Ivory Voice Sings' is dedicated to Cecil Taylor, as is the altogether tougher 'Au Chanteur Qui Danse' on *Labyrinths*, and captures something of Taylor's furious percussive poetry.

Recorded shortly after the Californian earthquake of 1989, *Live In San Francisco* alternates the subdued aftershocks and beatific restorations of her own 'Tromos' and Coltrane's 'Dear Lord', with some unexpectedly light and romantic touches. 'When I Fall In Love' has a hesitant shyness that makes the theme statement all the more moving; the same applies to the humour of Monk's 'Ruby, My Dear', which underlines Crispell's impressive rhythmic awareness. (Interestingly, the CD also contains two 'sampler' tracks from other Music & Arts titles featuring Crispell: the long 'Composition 136' with Anthony Braxton from the Vancouver duets record mentioned above (CD 611) and a shorter group track with another senior collaborator, Reggie Workman, and his highly inventive ensemble (CD 634).)

Four very special albums, then, and one that should be kept in reserve until Crispell's particular magic takes hold.

***   **The Kitchen Concerts** Leo LR 178 CD
        Crispell; Mark Dresser (*b*); Gerry Hemingway (*d*). 2/89.

This marks a slight but significant change of direction for Crispell. In place of free or structured improvisation, *The Kitchen Concerts* documents a first, rather tentative, confrontation with written forms of her own. Her own recorded misgivings are reflected to some degree in the music itself, which exposes areas of hesitancy rarely encountered in her improvised performances. The tonalities are a little forced, in sharp contrast to her normal instinctive 'centring' of a piece. By her own remarkable standards a less than wholly successful album, it still merits close attention, not least for the contributions of Dresser and of Hemingway, whose insistent (if rather similar) solos on 'Ahmadu/Sierra Leone' and the Tristano-dedicated 'For L. T.' lend the music a much-needed impulse.

****   **Overlapping Hands: Eight Segments** FMP CD30 CD
        Crispell; Schweizer (*p*). 90.

Like much of Crispell's best work this is a concert performance, and a duo at that. There are moments when it might almost be one person playing, so close is the understanding between the two women, but for the fact that they do sound very different. Schweizer's sound is sharper and more Europeanized; Crispell's draws deeper on an American tradition and constantly refers to tonal centres that her collaborator wants to push away to the very boundaries of the music. The recording is near perfect, and a tremendous advance on some of FMP's more Heath Robinsonish concert efforts; the music is a joy.

****   **Gaia** Leo Records LR 152 CD/LP
        Crispell; Reggie Workman (*b*); Doug James (*d, perc,*). 3/87.

***   **Live In Zurich** Leo Records LR CDLR 122 CD
        As above, except omit James; add Paul Motian (*d, perc*). 4/89.

Gaia is one of the finest composition/improvisation records of the 1980s, a hymn to the planet that is neither mawkish nor sentimental, but tough-minded, coherent and entire. Spared conventional rhythm section duties, Workman and James combine extremely well, producing both a dense ripieno for Crispell's dramatic concertante effects and a powerful drama of their own. *Live In Zurich* finds her working against a much more conventional rhythm (though Motian shares James's delicacy of touch). Though it consists of individual pieces (including the obligatory Coltrane, 'Dear Lord'), the Zurich set comes to resemble a single suite, opening with some haunting North African *vocalise* (an equally obligatory nod in Taylor's direction), and developing strongly into one of her finest recorded piano performances.

SONNY CRISS (1927–77)
ALTO SAXOPHONE, SOPRANO SAXOPHONE

***   **California Boppin'** Fresh Sound FSR CD 156 CD
Criss; Al Killian, Howard McGhee (*t*); Teddy Edwards, Wardell Gray (*ts*); Charlie Fox, Russ Freeman, Hampton Hawes, Dodo Marmarosa (*p*); Barney Kessel (*g*); Harry Babasin, Red Callender, Addison Farmer (*b*); Tim Kennedy, Jackie Mills, Roy Porter (*d*). 4, 6, 7 & 10/47.

***   **Intermission Riff** Pablo 2310-929 LP/MC
Criss; Joe Newman (*t*); Bennie Green (*tb*); Eddie Davis (*ts*); Bobby Tucker (*p*); Tommy Potter (*b*); Kenny Clarke (*d*). 10/51.

Criss was perhaps a little too tightly wrapped for the destiny that seemed to await him. Though it was the altogether more robust Sonny Stitt – with whom Criss is occasionally confused – to whom Charlie Parker promised 'the keys of the Kingdom', it was Criss out on the West Coast who inherited most of the ambiguities of Parker's legacy.

California wasn't a happy place for Bird, by and large, and there's something hectic, almost desperate, in Criss's super-fast runs and soaring, high-register figures. The earliest of material is rather derivative but provides several excellent opportunities to hear Criss's pure, urgent tone and delivery; he comes in behind Wardell Gray on 'Groovin' High' almost impatiently with a little flurry of notes before stretching out and shaping those distinctive wailing passages and held notes. The June 1947 material, with the rhythm section that backed Parker at the Hi-De-Ho in Los Angeles earlier that year (Hawes, Farmer, Porter) is probably the best on the disc, with a particularly fine version of 'The Man I Love' that also features Teddy Edwards and Howard McGhee. Two long jam sessions have lots of episodic interest, but are marred by Al Killian's dreary high note work.

It's clear, though, that Parker wasn't the only influence and that there's more thought going into the development of solos than first appears. The Jazz at the Philharmonic band is good, with 'Lockjaw' Davis and the underrated Green of particular interest. There are also elements drawn from Benny Carter and Johnny Hodges in Criss's solo on 'Body And Soul'. Clarke's boppish drumming is always right on the button and there's little of that sense one had later in Criss's career that the saxophonist was outpacing his rhythm section. The sound is no better or worse than it should be on a recording four decades old; no CD, though.

***(*)   **This Is Criss!** Original Jazz Classics OJC 430 CD/LP/MC
Criss; Walter Davis (*p*); Paul Chambers (*b*); Alan Dawson (*d*). 66.

****   **Portrait Of Sonny Criss** Original Jazz Classics OJC 655 CD/LP/MC
As above. 67.

These are probably the two best Criss albums currently available. His ability to invest banal tunes with real feeling (see *I'll Catch The Sun!*, below, for real alchemy) is evident on 'Sunrise, Sunset', a tune from *Fiddler On The Roof* given a brief but intense reading on *This Is Criss!*. Criss does something similar, though at greater length, to 'Days Of Wine And Roses', adjusting his timbre subtly throughout the opening choruses.

'Wee' on *Portrait* takes him back to bop days, an astonishing performance that manages to skate over a lack of solid ideas with sheer virtuosity. 'Smile' bears comparison with Jackie McLean's readings, but the real stand-out tracks are 'On A Clear Day', which is hugely emotional, and 'God Bless The Child'. The CD also offers a bonus 'Love For Sale', which probably deserved to be left out first time round. The band is good and Davis (who wrote 'Greasy' on *This Is Criss!* and 'A Million Or More Times' on *Portrait*) is the mainstay.

****   **Sonny's Dream** Original Jazz Classics OJC 707 CD
Criss; Conte Candoli (*t*); Dick Nash (*tb*); Ray Draper (*tba*); David Sherr (*as*); Teddy Edwards (*ts*); Peter Christlieb (*bs*); Tommy Flanagan (*p*); Al McKibbon (*b*); Everett Brown Jr (*d*). 68.

This is a most welcome CD reissue of a project subtitled 'Birth Of The New Cool' and featuring six Horace Tapscott compositions and arrangements. Though he has only recently begun to receive wider recognition, Tapscott's influence on the West Coast has been enormous and this was a rare chance for Criss to play in front of a carefully orchestrated mid-size band.

'Sonny's Dream' is an astonishing opener, with luminous solos from both Criss and Tommy Flanagan. Criss switches to soprano for the brief 'Ballad For Samuel', dedicated to a respected teacher, but profoundly marked by Coltrane (who had recently died). Tapscott's inventiveness and political sensibilities are equally engaged on 'Daughter Of Cochise' (a unusually relaxed solo from Criss) and 'Black Apostles', originally dedicated to Arthur Blythe (another Angelean saxophonist who made a personal accommodation with Bird's idiom) but transformed into a brooding and ferocious lament for the three martyrs of the black liberationist movement.

A remarkable album that lapses only to the extent that the band is sometimes reduced to providing highly coloured backdrops for Tapscott's American history lessons and Criss's soloing (which bears comparison with Parker's on the 'With Strings' sessions).

***(*)   **I'll Catch The Sun!** Prestige PR 7628 CD
Criss; Hampton Hawes (*p*); Monty Budwig (*b*); Shelly Manne (*d*). 1/69.

Something of a comeback for Criss and perhaps the most amenable and sympathetic band he ever had, reuniting him with Hawes. The material is vile, but players like these made a living out of turning sows' ears into silken purses and both 'California Dreaming' and 'Cry Me A River' have a genuine depth of focus. Criss sounds composed and confident in this company, and solos with impressive logic and considerable emotion.

***   **Saturday Morning** Xanadu 105 LP
Criss; Barry Harris (*p*); Leroy Vinnegar (*b*); Lenny McBrowne (*d*). 3/75.

During the early 1970s, Criss tried to bury his own troubles, working with juvenile alcoholics in the Watts ghetto. His return to playing finds his tone unimpaired and more and more marked by Coltrane devices. Long, harmonically dense lines pile up on top of one another, but the tone is unexpectedly buoyant on the Harris original 'Saturday Morning', which opens the second side in very different mood from the first, which begins with a dark-hued 'Angel Eyes' that finds Criss bursting with sombre melodic notions. 'Until The Real Thing Comes Along' is an ironic closing item, bluesy but softly upbeat. The shadows were gathering, though; in 1977, brought to the brink yet again, Sonny Criss shot himself dead.

BOB CROSBY (born 1913)
VOCAL, LEADER

****   **Bob Crosby 1937 To 1938** BBC REB/CD/ZCF 688 CD/LP/MC
Yank Lawson, Charlie Spivak, Billy Butterfield, Zeke Zarchy, Sterling Bose, Andy Ferretti (*t*); Ward Silloway, Mark Bennett, Warren Smith (*tb*); Irving Fazola (*cl*); Matty Matlock (*cl, as*); Noni Bernardi, Joe Kearns (*as*); Eddie Miller (*cl, ts*); Gil Rodin, Dean Kincaide (*ts*); Bob Zurke (*p*); Nappy Lamare (*g*); Bob Haggart, Haig Stephens (*b*); Ray Bauduc (*d*). 37–38.

***(*)   **Bob Crosby** Zeta/Jazz Archives ZET 766 CD
As above. 36–38.

Powerfully remastered by Robert Parker, whose 'jazz classics in digital stereo' process usually works at its best on discs from the 1930s, this shrewdly assembled compilation makes a good case for reassessing Crosby's contribution to the big-band jazz of the decade. The vocalist was only the nominal leader of a group directed musically by Matlock, Kincaide and Haggart: they steered the band's output between an old-fashioned allegiance to the New Orleans past (yet to be customarily tagged as 'dixieland'), via the small group known as the Bobcats, to a modern, fluidly stomping big-band sound that was quite different from Goodman's emerging swing manifesto. Haggart's impeccable work lent the rhythm section a contemporary swing, while such outstanding individuals as Miller, Lawson, Fazola and the excitable Zurke gave the records a distinctive cast of soloists. They surrendered to popular novelty at times, as in 'The Big Crash From China' or 'The Big Noise From Winnetka', but their best sides have an enduring zest. Eleven of these eighteen sides are by the Bobcats and there are only three vocals, ironically none of them by Crosby, who is nowhere to be heard on the collection. The Zeta collection comes in more 'traditional' remastered sound, but duplicates many of the same tracks on the BBC collection. In purely musical terms, there's very little to choose between either disc.

RONNIE CUBER (born 1941)
BARITONE SAX

**   **Cuber Libre** Xanadu 135 LP
Cuber; Barry Harris (*p*); Sam Jones (*b*); Albert Heath (*d*). 8/76.

***   **The Eleventh Day Of Aquarius** Xanadu 156 LP
Cuber; Tom Harrell (*t, flhn*); Mickey Tucker (*p*); Dennis Irwin (*b*); Eddie Gladden (*d*). 1/78.

**   **Passion Fruit** Electric Bird K 28P 6347 CD/LP
Cuber; Richard Tee (*p*); Rob Mounsey (*ky*); George Wadenius, George Benson (*g*); Will Lee (*b*); Dave Weckl (*d*); Sammy Figueroa, Manolo Badrena (*perc*). 2–3/85.

**   **Pin Point** Electric Bird K 28P 6415 CD/LP
Cuber; David Sanborn (*ts*); Rob Mounsey (*ky*); George Wadenius (*g*); Will Lee (*b*); Steve Gadd (*d*); Steve Thornton (*perc*). 11–12/85.

It seems as if Cuber is a spunky musician, since he sets out to ignore the lumbering status of the baritone and play as if he had an alto in his hands. But he sounds more like an executant of other people's ideas rather than an especially distinctive voice, and the records under his own name are playable but uneventful. He can't sustain enough interest as the sole horn to make *Cuber Libre* into a strong enough session, despite a convincingly felt reading of 'Misty', and the other Xanadu album is recommended primarily for the fine work by Harrell and Tucker. Cuber turns to a palatable kind of fusion on the other records, but not enough happens to lift the music out of a well-played but dull set of grooves.

GIL CUPPINI (born 1924)
DRUMS

(*)   **A New Day Red VPA 123154 LP
Cuppini; Emilio Soana, Fermo Lini, Franco Corvini, Luciano Biasutti, Bruno Moretti, Sergio Fanni, Oscar Valdambrini (*t*); Rudy Migliardi, Nicola Castriota, Palmiro Mautino, Claudio Barbieri, Cesare Gagliardi, Beppe Bergamasco (*tb*); Glauco Masetti, Giancarlo Barigozzi, Gianluigi Trovesi, Nando Nebuloni, Cesare Bergonzi, Eraldo Volente, Gianni Basso, Leandro Prete, Athos Poletti, Stelio Licudi, Sergio Rigon (*saxes*); Ettore Righello (*p*); Piero Gosio (*ky*); Mario Bosi (*vib*); Alberto Pizzigoni (*g*); Giorgio Azzolini, Carlo Milano (*b*); Carlo Sola (*perc*). 10/69–10/77.

Gilberto Cuppini is a drummer who came up in the swing idiom, but this sprawling record – made across three sessions over eight years – finds him leading a Don Ellis-like hotchpotch of incident. Useful to hear so many relatively unfamiliar names from the Italian jazz scene prior to its great resurgence in the 1980s, although ensembles dominate over soloists.

TED CURSON (born 1935)
TRUMPET

***(*)   **Plays Fire Down Below** Original Jazz Classics OJC 1744 CD/LP
Curson; Gildo Mahones (*p*); George Tucker (*b*); Roy Haynes (*d*); Montego Joe
(*perc*). 12/62.

Thin representation for a highly significant innovator who came to prominence with Mingus, wrote the beautiful 'Tears For Dolphy' and then spent much of his time in Europe. A radical with a strong interest in classic jazz, Curson's work on piccolo trumpet often resembles Rex Stewart, though he's closer to Fats Navarro on the concert horn. *Fire Down Below* is a reasonable representation of his pungent, unsentimental style. Mahones laces a basically conventional approach with figures reminiscent of Carl Perkins. Tucker and Haynes might explain a resemblance to Eric Dolphy's debut album on New Jazz, on which they played, and they're equally impressive here. The drummer is quietly forceful on the two quartet tracks, 'The Very Young' and 'Only Forever', but he sounds slightly cramped by the addition of congas on the remainder. Enthusiasts for Curson need to get hold of *Blue Piccolo And Fireball* from 1976 and *The Ted Curson Trio* from 1979 (both currently deleted); there is also a fine tribute to Mingus and a rare 1962 live set from La Tete de l'Art in Toronto, originally released on Trans World and briefly reissued on Can-Am.

CUTTING EDGE
GROUP

***   **Cutting Edge** Odin 04 LP/MC
Morten Halle (*ts, f*); Rune Klakegg (*ky*); Knut Vaernes (*g*); Edvard Askeland (*b*);
Frank Jakobsen (*d*). 4/82.

***   **Our Man In Paradise** Odin 10 LP/MC
As above, except Stein Inge Braekhaus (*d*) replaces Jakobsen. 9–10/83.

Cheerful light-fusion from Norway, with a few distinguishing marks: Halle has the chilly, wailing timbre that Norwegian saxophonists seem to have a patent on, Klakegg works to get pleasing sounds from his keyboards rather than stunning pyrotechnics, and the tunes (mostly by Klakegg) have melodic substance without resorting to pop–jazz hooks. The first record is a little short on memorability, but *Our Man In Paradise* is a fine effort.

ANDREW CYRILLE (born 1939)
DRUMS

***(*)   **Nuba** Black Saint BSR 0030 LP
Cyrille; Jimmy Lyons (*as*); Jeanne Lee (*v*). 6/79.

***   **Special People** Soul Note SN 1012 LP
Cyrille; Ted Daniel (*t, flhn*); David S. Ware (*ts*); Nick DiGeronimo (*perc*). 10/80.

***   **The Navigator** Soul Note SN 1062 LP
Cyrille; Ted Daniel (*t, flhn*); Sonelius Smith (*p*); Nick DiGeronimo (*d*). 9/82.

Cyrille was a mainstay of what was probably Cecil Taylor's most influential group. Together, they explored a significant redefinition of jazz as a non-Western music, one largely based on percussive techniques and sonorities. 'Whence I Came' on *What About?* (an Affinity set that marked his debut as leader but which is now, sadly, deleted) had him using vocal techniques, mostly sighs evocative of loss and enslavement, to convey his sense of place in the wider spectrum of Afro-American history and culture; 'mouth percussion' has become a staple of his solo work since then (and can be heard to excellent effect on Geri Allen's fine trio album, *The Printmakers*. Cyrille has steadily moved back from the free/abstract idiom he originally espoused (and to which he partially returned in the encounter with Brötzmann, below), towards an outwardly more conventional music that draws on orthodox jazz structures, as in the two fine Soul Notes (which, unfortunately, remain LP only).

Pieces like 'High Priest' (*Special People*) and 'The Navigator' and the linked 'Circumfusion' and 'The Magnificent Bimbo' represent a significant extension of 1960s radicalism into a more formal and tradition-aware context. In that regard, Daniel is an ideal collaborator. Unfortunately, the sound still reflects difficulties in capturing percussion, a shortcoming that has dogged drummers from the word go but which is particularly critical in this context. It's rather better on the Black Saint, and the combination of Lyons (another former Taylor collaborator) and Jeanne Lee is extremely potent. Recommended.

*** **Andrew Cyrille Meets Peter Brötzmann In Berlin** FMP 1000 LP
Cyrille; Peter Brötzmann (*ts, ss, bs, cl, tarogato*). 3/82.

If the title sounds like the first line in a game of Consequences, the results are almost as unpredictable and frequently as bizarre. One does not normally think of the saxophonist as a lyrical player and, while much of his tenor and baritone work is entirely consistent with past form, he also produces gentle, almost folksy, sounds on the second of two extended improvisations, getting a particularly interesting tone with the wooden tarogato. Cyrille's ability to create a whole orchestra of effects from a relatively standard kit is undiminished, and the album as a whole is surprisingly entire and satisfying for such an uncompromising format.

***(*) **Galaxies** Music & Arts CD 672 CD
Cyrille; Vladimir Tarasov (*d, perc, elec*). 6/90.

The California-based Music & Arts label is acquiring a growing reputation, not least for programming challenging duos of this sort, mainly recorded at the Vancouver Jazz Festival. Tarasov, formerly the drummer with the Ganelin Trio and an often overlooked influence on that important group's sound, offers three significant compositions. 'Galaxies' and 'Action V' are performed together, with unobtrusive electronic washes and ostinati filling in the background. Cyrille's own 'No. 11' seems to represent an autobiographical statement, tracing his own re-accommodation to the jazz tradition, a stance that is undoubtedly also problematic for Tarasov. Perhaps the place to start, though, is the final track, disproportionately shorter than the two main performances and still only half the length of Tarasov's short 'Summit'; it's a version of John Coltrane's 'One Up, One Down', reflecting Cyrille's detailed study of Coltrane's late experiments in metre, an aspect of the saxophonist's work that has only recently begun to be fully recognized. *Galaxies* is a dense, detailed album that may well tax the attention of listeners not entirely persuaded of the merits of solo percussion. It should, perhaps, be listened to track-by-track rather than as an uninterrupted whole.

TONY DAGRADI
TENOR AND SOPRANO SAXOPHONE

*** **Lunar Eclipse** Gramavision GR 8103 LP
Dagradi; David Torkanowsky (*ky*); Jim Singleton (*b*); John Vidacovich (*d*); Mark Sanders (*perc*). 81.

A tenorman from New Orleans, Dagradi plays with massive authority and big-toned drive, blending some of the rollicking power of R&B saxophonists with a keener architectural sense. This record is slightly inferior to an earlier Gramavision date, *Oasis*, currently unavailable: there, matched with some Carla Bley sidemen, his music took on a rasping vitality. This session is a little more conventional, but it clears the way for his own solos and establishes on record his rapport with fellow New Orleanians Singleton and Vidacovich.

*** **Dreams Of Love** Core COCD 9.00798 O CD
As above, except Steve Masakowski (*g*) replaces Sanders. 9/87–1/88.

This is well played but a little conformist: Dagradi sounds like someone who wants to break out, but these pieces are too pat and sensible to let him go. The rhythm section, though, is excellent again, and all are very well recorded.

***(*) **Images From The Floating World** Core COCD 9.00727 CD
As above, except omit Torkanowsky and Masakowski. 90.

Slimming the group down to a trio affords Dagradi the space and freedom to turn this into a terrific blowing session. 'Parading', which was also on the last record, becomes a boastful New Orleans march, 'O. F. O.' is a convincing tribute to Ornette Coleman, and there's nothing wasted in the long and impassioned exchanges between the leader and his partners on the other pieces.

ALBERT DAILEY (1938–84)
PIANO

***   **That Old Feeling** Steeplechase SCS 1107 LP
Dailey; Buster Williams (b); Billy Hart (d). 7/78.

***   **Textures** Muse MR 5256 LP
Dailey; Arthur Rhames (ts); Rufus Reid (b); Eddie Gladden (d). 6/81.

These are the only surviving albums made by Albert Dailey as a leader. Valued as an accompanist by Stan Getz among others, his trio recordings suggest a man who liked a locked, three-way groove between piano, bass and drums, and both these bands create some exhilarating examples of the style, which recalls the feel of a Junior Mance or Horace Silver set-up. Dailey can be fulsome and many-noted when he wants, as in the slightly too built-up version of Dameron's 'If You Could See Me Now' on the Muse session, but the driving 'Textures' is a better instance of what he can do. The Steeplechase date is standard material and the Muse record gives us four Dailey originals, including one in which Rhames sits in to no special purpose; but *Textures* suffers a little from idiosyncratic sound – the bass is very loud, and Gladden's cymbals seem to have been recorded at the expense of his snare – while *That Old Feeling* is better balanced.

DEL DAKO (born 1955)
BARITONE AND ALTO SAXOPHONES

(*)   **Balancing Act Sackville SKCD2-2021 CD
Dako; Richard Whiteman (p); Dick Felix (b); Mike McClelland (d). 3–11/90.

A Canadian known only to local audiences, Dako waited until he was 35 before making his debut album. Although he plays alto in places, notably on the thoughtful original 'Steve The Weave' which opens the record, Dako's primary horn is the baritone, which he employs with a gruff, bull-headed swing: he loves the grouchiness of baritone timbre, and his solo on 'Just Don't Slip With That Axe' is a memorable string of complaints. But the music is rhythmically less assured, Dako not quite authoritative enough to command the best from a so-so rhythm section, and it results in a bit of a potboiler.

MEREDITH D'AMBROSIO
VOCAL, PIANO

***   **Another Time** Sunnyside SSC 1017D CD
D'Ambrosio. 2/81.

***(*)   **Little Jazz Bird** Sunnyside SSC 1040D CD
D'Ambrosio; Phil Woods (cl, as); Hank Jones (p); Gene Orloff, Fred Buldrini (vn); Julian Barber (vla); Fred Slatkin (clo); Steve Gilmore (b); Bill Goodwin (d). 3/82.

****   **It's Your Dance** Sunnyside SSC 1011 CD
D'Ambrosio; Harold Danko (p); Kevin Eubanks (g). 3/85.

(*)   **The Cove Sunnyside SSC 1028D CD
D'Ambrosio; Lee Konitz (as); Fred Hersch (p); Michael Formanek (b); Keith Copeland (d).

***(*) **South To A Warmer Place** Sunnyside SSC 1039D CD
       D'Ambrosio; Lou Colombo (*t*); Eddie Higgins (*p*); Don Coffman (*b*); Danny Berger
       (*d*). 2/89.

Literate, polished singing from a vocalist whose approach is so soft and unemphatic that
sometimes she barely seems to be present at all. But her choice of songs is so creative and the
treatments so consistently refined that the records assume a peculiarly compelling power.
Another Time is a reissue of a privately produced session, and its bare-bones approach is
perhaps a little too austere, but it's still an impressive recital of 18 songs. *Little Jazz Bird*,
despite an eccentric studio production by Rudy Van Gelder, is ingeniously programmed to
accommodate Woods and the string quartet, and the songs encompass Dave Frishberg, Gene
Lees, Loonis McGloohan and two exceptional pieces by Deborah Henson-Conant, 'How Is
Your Wife' and 'When The End Comes'. *It's Your Dance* is arguably D'Ambrosio's most fully
realized record: with only Danko and Eubanks (who's never played better) in support,
D'Ambrosio maintains a supernal glow throughout the record. Almost all the songs are unusual,
from her own lyrics to 'Giant Steps' and Dave Brubeck's 'Strange Meadowlark' to Al Cohn's
'The Underdog', the title-track's reworking of John Carisi's 'Israel' and the lovely Burke–Van
Heusen rarity, 'Humpty Dumpty Heart'. The vocalist's choice of material and the hip
understatement of her singing create the core of her work. Her voice is too small and
unambitious to make any play for jazz virtuosity, but she achieves a different authenticity
through economies of scale.

    That said, it goes a little wrong on *The Cove*, which is too composed and sleepy, the playing
sounding fatigued rather than laid-back. But *South To A Warmer Place* restores her run:
Colombo plays a Bobby Hackett-like role and, since many of the songs are relatively familiar,
this may be the best place to start hearing D'Ambrosio's enchanting work.

TADD DAMERON (1917–65)
COMPOSER, BANDLEADER, PIANO

*** **Fats Navarro Featured** Milestone M 47041 CD/LP/MC
       Dameron; Fats Navarro (*t*); Kai Winding (*tb*); Rudy Williams (*as*); Allen Eager (*ts*);
       Milt Jackson (*vib*); Curly Russell (*b*); Kenny Clarke (*d*). 48.

*** **Fontainebleau** Original Jazz Classics OJC 055 CD/LP/MC
       Dameron; Kenny Dorham (*t*); Henry Coker (*tb*); Sahib Shihab (*as*); Joe Alexander
       (*ts*); Cecil Payne (*bs*); John Simmons (*b*); Shadow Wilson (*d*). 3/56.

It's Dameron's fate to be remembered now largely for a handful of compositions – 'Hot House'
and 'Lady Bird' pre-eminently – which became standards. As such, Dameron is a
much-underrated performer who stands at the fulcrum of modern jazz, midway between swing
and bebop. Combining the broad-brush arrangements of the big-band and the advanced
harmonic language of bop, his own recordings are difficult to date blind.

    Fats Navarro played as well with Dameron as he did with anyone; the Blue Note sets issued
as *The Fabulous Fats Navarro* (781531/2) should strictly be credited to the Tadd Dameron
Sextet/Septet and to Bud Powell's Modernists, but became known as a posthumous tribute to
the brilliant young trumpeter who died in 1950. Navarro's big, ringing brass-tone is superb on a
second take of 'Anthropology' (Dameron features on the first), two takes of 'Good Bait' and a
witty 'Oh! Lady Be Good'. The overall sound is a little too muzzy to catch some of Dameron's
more sophisticated voicings – but then 1948 was a rather uncertain year for everyone in the
music, and Navarro peals out of the fog quite beautifully.

    Fontainebleau originates from Dameron's last full year of freedom before the term of
imprisonment that more or less ended his career. It's a fine set, with no clutter in the horns. The
title-piece is wholly written out, with no scope for improvising, but there is plenty of fine
individual work elsewhere, notably from Dorham. Never a virtuoso soloist, Dameron prefers to
work within the very distinct chord progressions of his tunes, big, lush confections that are too
sharp-edged ever to cloy.

(*) **The Magic Touch Original Jazz Classics OJC 143 LP/MC
       Dameron; Ernie Royal, Charlie Shavers, Clark Terry, Joe Wilder (*t*); Jimmy
       Cleveland, Britt Woodman (*tb*); Julius Watkins (*hn*); Jerry Dodgion, Leo Wright (*as*,

f); Jerome Richardson (*ts, f*); Johnny Griffin (*ts*); Tate Houston (*bs*); Bill Evans (*p*);
Ron Carter (*b*); Philly Joe Jones (*d*); Barbara Winfield (*v*). 2–3–4/62.

Dameron's final recordings betrayed little sign of weariness or of the illness that was to kill him
less than three years later. The band charts are as cleanly drawn as ever and the treatment of
familiar material like 'Our Delight' and 'Fontainebleau' is far from perfunctory. The solos,
particularly from the reeds, are of the highest quality, but – hence the reservation – don't sit at
all comfortably in the mix. Reservations apart, it's time Dameron's recordings were better
known.

PAOLO DAMIANI
BASS, CELLO

***   **Poor Memory** Splasc(h) HP 07 LP
Damiani; Paolo Fresu (*t, flhn*); Gianluigi Trovesi (*ss, as, bcl*); Claude Barthelemy (*g*);
Aldo Romano (*d*). 7/87.

A very enjoyable concert recording, featuring several of the brightest young talents in Italian
jazz. Fresu continues to impress as a lyrical voice, but Trovesi's hard-hitting reed solos and
Barthelemy's harsh, rock-directed guitar provide piquant contrast. Damiani's compositions find
a suitable middle ground between hard bop and freer modes, and the live recording is agreeably
rough-edged and human-sounding.

FRANCO D'ANDREA (born 1941)
PIANO, KEYBOARDS

***   **Dialogues With Superego** Red 123157 LP
D'Andrea (*p* solo). 3/80.

***   **Es** Red 123158 LP
D'Andrea (*p* solo). 6/80.

***   **My One And Only Love** Red 123201 LP
D'Andrea; Mark Helias (*b*); Barry Altschul (*d*). 5/83.

***   **No Idea Of Time** Red 123202 LP
D'Andrea; Tino Tracanna (*ss, ts*); Mark Helias (*b*); Barry Altschul (*d*). 5/83.

***   **Made In Italy** Red 123200 LP
D'Andrea; Tino Tracanna (*ss, ts*); Attilo Zanchi (*b*); Gianni Cazzola (*d*). 2/82.

***   **Live** Red 123195 LP
As above. 11/85.

(*)   **My Shuffle Red 123199 LP
As above. 11/85.

D'Andrea is a senior figure among Italy's post-bop musicians and, by the time these records
were made, he'd been through jazz-rock and free playing and emerged with his own sly
variations on contemporary methods. There's a certain attractive irony to his compositions,
which can function as blowing vehicles or structural set-pieces: the title piece of *My Shuffle* is an
example of how he combines the two. There's a Monk-like deliberation about his own playing
which lends weight to his freer explorations: the two solo albums have a whiff of academicism
about them, but D'Andrea takes his studies with large doses of good humour, and rhythmically
he can be as ebullient as he is inventive. *No Idea Of Time* and *My One And Only Love* are
perhaps the pick of these Red albums, since Helias and Altschul are highly responsive; the
former is especially adventurous, with two quite different takes of the title tune, a humorous
minor blues which D'Andrea delivers a solo reading of on *Es*, and the long and impressive
'Globetrotter'. The all-Italian quartet aren't quite as strong since his companions don't always
share his flair: Tracanna can sound like a middleweight Rollins disciple, and Cazzola is
sometimes heavy-handed. The 1985 live recordings could be more full-bodied.

***   **Volte** Owl 052 CD/LP
D'Andrea; Hein Van De Geyn (*b*); Aldo Romano (*d*). 3/89.

A satisfying set of miniatures by the pianist, with watchful accompaniment from Van De Geyn and the excellent Romano, whose own record with D'Andrea is also worth hearing. 'Norwegian Wood' is a bit willowy, but the original pieces keep the attention. Superior recording.

***   **Earthcake** Label Bleu LBLC 6539 CD
D'Andrea; Enrico Rava (*t, bugle*); Miroslav Vitous (*b*); Daniel Humair (*d*). 1/91.

*(*)   **Enrosadira** Red 123243-2 CD
D'Andrea; Luis Agudo (*perc*). 91.

The Label Bleu disc is something of an all-star session, and while nothing extraordinary happens it's a significantly democratic affair, with compositions from each man and the title piece standing as a highly articulate and detailed improvisation. The latest Red disc, though, is eminently avoidable, a muddle of electronic keyboards pitched against Agudo's splashy percussion: good therapy for D'Andrea, perhaps, but tedious to listen to.

PETER DANEMO
DRUMS

***   **Baraban** Dragon DRCD 206 CD
Danemo; Inge Petersson (*ts*); Esbjorn Svensson (*ky*); Klavs Hovman (*b*). 5/91.

A session very much in the house style of the company – drifting, modal jazz with a hard centre, expertly recorded. Danemo wrote most of the 11 themes here and, while they start with simple materials, the quartet transmute them into frequently intense explorations of a motif or a mood. The opening 'Below The Surface', for instance, is built into an impressively intense ensemble piece. Solos tend to emerge as part of the overall fabric: Petersson, another in the line of fine Sewdish tenors, plays a co-operative rather than a front-line role, and Svensson, who contributes two charming compositions, is a thoughtful source of support. There are almost 67 minutes of music on the CD.

EDDIE DANIELS (born 1941)
CLARINET, TENOR SAXOPHONE

**   **Breakthrough** GRP GRD-9533 CD/MC
Daniels; London Philharmonia Orchestra, Ettore Strata (*cond*). 86.

(*)   **To Bird With Love GRP GRD-9544 CD/MC
Daniels; Fred Hirsch, Roger Kellaway (*ky*); John Patitucci (*b*); Al Foster (*d*); Steve Thornton (*perc*). 87.

**   **Memos From Paradise** GRP GRD-9561 CD/MC
Daniels; Roger Kellaway (*ky*); David Nadien, Elena Barbere (*vn*); Lamar Alsop (*vla*); Beverly Lauridsen (*clo*); Eddie Gomez (*b*); Al Foster, Terry Clarke (*d*); Glen Velez (*perc*). 12/87–1/88.

Flawless technician that he is, Daniels seems happiest when creating the most trivial kind of light chamber-jazz. His early work on tenor sax in the 1960s and '70s was undistinguished, and his clarinet playing would be too if it weren't for the mastery of the instrument which he displays. On these intermittently playable records, Daniels creates various acceptable faces on ideas that might have called for more stringent resources. *To Bird With Love* is bebop without any teeth, and the two albums with strings pander to saccharine values while pretending to a sterner virtuosity. A dreary sequence, made more so by the plush recording.

**   **Nepenthe** GRP GRD-9607 CD/MC
Daniels; Chuck Loeb (*g*); John Patitucci (*b*); Dave Weckl, Adam Nussbaum (*d*); Sammy Figueroa (*perc*). 12/89.

Daniels finally becomes an innovator: the first clarinettist fully to embrace fusion, though it's no more significant than any of Herbie Mann's similarly perky records. The sessionmen in support play with their usual exhausting aplomb, but Daniels's original material is forgettable.

** **This Is Now** GRP GRD-9635 CD/MC
Daniels; Billy Childs (*p*); Tony Dumas, Jimmy Johnson (*b*); Ralph Penland, Vinnie Colaiuta (*d*). 90.

Daniels in a traditional, acoustic setting, but there's nothing to trouble anyone's slumbers here. There is a mildly galling comparison between his version of 'Body And Soul' with the Coleman Hawkins classic, but otherwise there's nothing offensive in this clean and spotlessly delivered set. Nothing very interesting, either.

LARS DANIELSSON
BASS, KEYBOARDS

***(*) **New Hands** Dragon DRLP/DRCD 125 LP/CD
Danielsson; David Liebman (*ss*); Bobo Stenson (*p*); Goran Klinghagen (*g, ky*); Jon Christensen (*d*). 12/85.

**** **Poems** Dragon DRCD 209 CD
As above, except omit Klinghagen. 4/91.

This is a very fine group, and *New Hands* is certainly the equal of any of Liebman's records with Quest. The bassist's six compositions range from a mysterious electronic lament on 'Chrass' to the memorable ballads of 'It's Your Choice' and 'Johan', the former featuring a bass solo of astonishing virtuosity. Stenson and Christensen live up to their standing as two of the most outstanding Europeans on their respective instruments, and Liebman's work is typically broad in its sympathies, from gnarled volleys of notes to long-breathed lines of high lyrical beauty.

Poems, recorded after a brief 'reunion' tour by the band, is a degree finer even than *New Hands*. Liebman contributes the funky, brittle 'Little Peanut' and two other tunes, while the bassist turns in some of his best writing for the haunting 'Crystalline' and 'Suite'; but it's the interaction of four master musicians which engenders the magic here: there really are no joins to be seen and, with Christensen at his most robustly inventive, the rhythmic layers are as songful as those created by Liebman and Stenson. Richly recorded and highly recommended.

HAROLD DANKO
PIANO

(*) **The First Love Song Jazz City 660 53 011 CD
Danko; Tom Harrell (*t, flhn*); Rufus Reid (*b*); Mel Lewis (*d*). 3/88.

Though there is also a duo album released under Lee Konitz's name (Musidisc 500162) and another under Kirk Lightsey's leadership (Sunnyside SSC 1004 D), there's still much too little Danko in the catalogue and this, his debut for the label, never quite peaks. The opening version of Bob Brookmeyer's gently oblique 'The First Love Song', with Harrell floating muted (and Miles Davis-influenced) whole-note progressions above a bare statement of the chords, underlines Danko's ability to build solos of genuine significance and considerable beauty out of relatively limited resources; there is also a lovely bowed solo by Lewis. Originals like 'Swift Shifting' and the contrasting slow 'To Start Again' allow him to work against the basic pulse to good effect. 'Eleanor Rigby', like most jazz transcriptions of Lennon–McCartney tunes, is a schmaltzy lost cause.

Danko was pianist with the Thad Jones–Mel Lewis big band and returns the compliment with a gig for the underused Lewis, who plays tidily but without much fire.

*** **Alone But Not Forgotten** Sunnyside SSC 1033 CD/LP
Danko; Marc Johnson, Michael Moore (*b*); Joe LaBarbera (*d*); Bob Dorough (*v*); strings arranged by John LaBarbera. 11/85, 2 & 5/86.

A softly romantic session with a good deal more musical substance than initially appears. Danko's interest in Brazilian music – Jobim, the percussionist Edison Machado, and singer Elis Regina – is reflected in the title piece and Edu Lobo's 'O Circo Mistico', his European roots in the lovely ballad 'Martina'. His admiration for Bill Evans is reflected in almost every note but more specifically in a vocal version of 'Laurie', while the opening 'Wayne Shorter' points to another, less obvious source for Danko's unique phrasing and harmonic sense. The string arrangements – by the drummer's brother – are a model of their kind and should be studied by all producers who want to orchestrate ballad albums.

JOHN DANKWORTH (born 1927)
ALTO SAXOPHONE

*** **The Vintage Years 1953–1959** Sepia RSCD2014; RSK2014 CD/MC
Dankworth; Derrick Abbott, Dickie Hawdon, Bill Metcalfe, Eddie Blair, George Boocock, Charlie Evans, Tommy McQuater, Stan Palmer, Colin Wright, Dougie Roberts (t); Maurice Pratt, Keith Christie, Eddie Harvey, Bill Geldard, Laurie Monk, Gary Brown, Harry Puckles, Danny Elwood, Tony Russell, Gib Wallis (tb); Geoff Cole, Maurice Owen, Rex Rutley, Lew Smith (as); Tommy Whittle, Rex Morris, Pete Warner, John Xerri, Freddie Courteney (ts); Alex Leslie (bs); Dave Lee, Derek Smith, Bill Le Sage (p); Jack Seymour, Bill Sutcliffe, Eric Dawson (b); Allan Ganley, Kenny Clare (d). 53–59.

An excellent compilation of material recorded by the big band Dankworth formed after disbanding the John Dankworth Seven in 1953 – although, in giving an accurate picture of the band's development, it does portray how much Dankworth's ambitions were compromised by British jazz surroundings at the time. Most of the earlier material is akin to dance-band arrangements with a jazz leaning and only the later sides, such as the vivid reworking of 'How High The Moon' and 'Jive At Five', achieve the more purposeful jazz feel of the Seven recordings. None of the soloists betters Dankworth's own creamy contributions and it's a point of mild regret that he didn't feature himself more. The CD remastering is very good.

DAVID DARLING
CELLO, ELECTRIC CELLO, PERCUSSION

(*) **Journal October ECM 1161 CD/LP
Darling (clo solo). 10/79.

Sir Thomas Beecham once snapped in fury at a woman cellist: 'You have between your legs the most sensitive instrument known to man and all you can do is sit there and scratch it.' At first blush, there isn't much more to David Darling's music than rather haphazard scratchings that border on self-absorption if not self-abuse. Repeated hearings confirm that, far from abusing his enormous technical talent, Darling is striving for a music commensurate with it.

There is, of course, already a substantial body of jazz cello: Oscar Pettiford, Ron Carter, Dollar Brand, Dave Holland, Tristan Honsinger. Perhaps inevitably, Darling's basic conception, particularly when he uses his 8-string solid-bodied amplified instrument, is closest to that of ECM stablemate Eberhard Weber, who has considerably extended the timbral and tonal range of amplified bass playing. Darling's music is less dynamic and more textural; it is certainly more 'classical' in structure and may prove a little too evanescent for tastes conditioned by jazz rhythms and structures. Journal October shouldn't be dismissed unheard, though, and Darling's sessions with Ralph Towner (ECM 1153, and on the Towner sampler, ECM 823268) and with Terje Rypdal (ECM 1263) are well worth a try.

CARLO ACTIS DATO
REEDS

*** **Noblesse Oblige** Splasc(h) H 118 LP
Dato; Piero Ponzo (cl, bcl, as, bs, f); Enrico Fazio (b); Fiorenzo Sordini (d). 7/86.

***   **Oltremare** Splasch H 153 LP
         As above. 10/87.

***(*) **Ankara Twist** Splasc(h) H 302 CD
         As above. 10/89.

Though Dato plays some tenor, he is most at home on baritone and bass clarinet, and he's a volatile and unpredictable player with a compensating brilliance of timing: just when one thinks he's gone too far in a solo, he pulls it around and returns to the structure. As a composer, he writes themes that suggest some bridging-point between jazz and Balkan folk music, and the bucolic air of, say, 'Moonlight In Budapest' on *Oltremare* is counterpointed by the very next tune on the record, 'Portorico Smog'. The tracks on these quartet albums are rather brief and have a programmatic feel to them, but they're played with great verve and enthusiasm by the group: Ponzo is a useful foil to the leader, Fazio is authoritative, Sordini full of bustle. *Ankara Twist* gets a slightly higher rating for the complete assurance of form which the quartet has mastered.

***(*) **Zig Zag** Splasc(h) H 186 LP
         Dato; Laura Culver (*ss, clo, berim*). 3/89.

A witty and cleverly varied programme of duets. The two players take it in turns to improvise over vamps set up by the other musician, and it gives Dato the space to let off some of his fieriest solos: 'Summer In Bucharest' is explosive in its use of multiphonics. Excellent sound projects the music with all the character it needs. Culver, primarily a cellist, is by no means overshadowed by her ebullient partner.

***(*) **Dune** Splasc(h) H 354-2 CD
         As above, except add Alex Rolle (*xy, perc*), Massimo Barbiero (*d, marim*). 2/91.

Rolle and Barbiero join in the fun and the quartet take some aspects of 'world music' to the cleaners: march and tango rhythms are mischievously undercut by Carlo's tendency to jump into bawling improvisations – he lets off another almost brutal baritone assault on 'Ketchup' – and by Laura's deadpan drones and vamps on the cello. The two percussionists are pressed into subsidiary roles, leavening the sometimes sparse arrangements, and sometimes the action seems a little too contrived on a very long (74 minutes) CD: 'Mar Del Plata' is rather stiffly delivered. But the crackerjack liveliness of the best playing is a delight.

WOLFGANG DAUNER (born 1935)
PIANO, KEYBOARDS

***   **Dream Talk** L & R 41004 LP
         Dauner; Eberhard Weber (*b*); Fred Braceful (*d*). 9/64.

Dauner's wider reputation among a record-buying public scarcely reflects his significance. Founder of the influential United Jazz and Rock Ensemble and of Mood Records, he was a major presence on the European free music scene in the 1960s; he is a composer and educator.

His own trio reflected a more inward and constrained side to his personality, as the medium to a large extent dictates. *Dream Talk* has a slightly obscure, night-side feel (not altogether unconnected to a very odd mix), replete with fleeting images and sudden changes of tense that look back and forward in the history of the music. Weber's eldritch bass is the perfect second voice, and the little-known Braceful's drumming helps sustain a deep inner pulse. A good ECM [1006] is currently missing in action.

KENNY DAVERN (born 1935)
CLARINET

***(*) **Stretchin' Out** Jazzology JCD-187 CD
         Davern; Dick Wellstood (*p*); Chuck Riggs (*d*). 12/83.

***(*) **Playing For Kicks** Jazzology JCD-197 CD
         Davern; Martin Litton (*p*); John Petters (*d*). 11/85.

***(*)   **I'll See You In My Dreams** Limelight/Musicmasters 60212 CD
Davern; Howard Alden (*g*); Phil Flanigan (*b*); Giampaolo Biagi (*d*). 1/88.

Kenny Davern has recorded infrequently as a leader, and his records are the more valuable and surprising because of it: there's no waste in his execution, as garrulous as his playing often is, and he succeeds in playing in what is essentially a swing-based clarinet style while suggesting that he's also perfectly aware of every jazz development that has taken place since (he once recorded with Steve Lacy, Steve Swallow and Paul Motian on the now-deleted *Unexpected*, Kharma PK-7). He plays soprano with Bob Wilber in the Soprano Summit group but on these three records he sticks to the clarinet. *Stretchin' Out* is perhaps the single best showcase for his own playing, starting with a mellifluous and perfectly paced 'The Man I Love' and proceeding through five more standards with unflagging inventiveness. Wellstood is a superb partner, harrying and supporting him in equal measure, but the drawback is the presence of Riggs, who's not only too loud in the mix but superfluous to what should have been a duo session. *Playing For Kicks* uses the same instrumentation, and while Litton isn't remotely up to Wellstood's standard, it's another great clarinet set, with the ancient ('Willie The Weeper') and the comparatively modern ('Lullaby Of The Leaves') on the agenda. Much the same happens on *I'll See You In My Dreams*, though with Alden on hand rather than a pianist the music has a lighter, more fluid feel to it, and the treatment of some of the older pieces – especially 'Riverboat Shuffle' – strikes up something of the chamber-jazz feel of a Venuti–Lang group. Again, Davern himself is irreproachable.

ANTHONY DAVIS (born 1951)
PIANO, KEYBOARDS, COMPOSER

(*)   **I've Known Rivers Gramavision 8201 CD
Davis; James Newton (*f*); Abdul Wadud (*clo*). 4/82.

***   **Hemispheres** Gramavision 8303 CD
Davis; Leo Smith (*t, steelophone, perc*); George Lewis (*tb*); Dwight Andrews (*f, picc, ss, cl*); J. D. Parran (*cl, cb cl*); Dave Samuels (*vib, mar*); Shem Guibbory (*v*); Eugene Friesen (*clo*); Rick Rozie (*b*); Pheeroan AkLaff (*d, perc*). 7/83.

(*)   **Middle Passage Gramavision 8401 CD
Davis (*p* solo. 84.

Inclined to be slightly abstract and structure-bound in his solo performances (a legacy of his work with the new-music outfit Episteme), Davis loosens up considerably in freer company. Newton's Dolphyish flute contrasts very sharply with Davis's mannerly runs and long, discursive progressions in and out of harmony. Wadud combines bass and left-hand piano functions on his cello, using heavy bow pressure, and a percussive, resonant attack in more rhythmic passages.

Hemispheres brings together the two sides (!) of Davis's approach more successfully than anything else he has done to date. In overall impact, it resembles a user-friendly version of Anthony Braxton's explorations of post-bop and post-serial language. AkLaff's drumming is powerfully idiomatic, and the horns are dominated by Smith's extraordinary diction; Parran's contrabass clarinet boldly goes where only Braxton had gone before, and Davis himself plays with great intelligence and control, as he does on *Middle Passage*.

The solo album represents his not-too-programmatic account of the Africans' coming to America and their uneasy confrontation with a new and alien culture. Resonantly recorded and beautifully played, it suffers only from an occasional lapse back into discursiveness (which may well be the fault of composers Ursula Oppens and Earle Howard). Not for all tastes by any means, but Davis is a powerfully individual voice at the more formal end of contemporary jazz.

ART DAVIS (born 1934)
BASS

***   **Life** Soul Note SN 1143 CD/LP
      Davis; Pharoah Sanders (*ts*); John Hicks (*b*); Idris Muhammad (*d*). 10/85.

The sole album under the leadership of this hugely experienced bassist belongs primarily to Sanders, whose gruffly magisterial sound tends to conquer any surroundings it finds itself in. The spare, modal structures open the music out, and there is an extract from Davis's large-scale 'Concertpiece For Bass', but it's Sanders (and the powerful Hicks) that one remembers.

DANNY DAVIS
ALTO SAXOPHONE

***   **Global Village Suite** FMP SAJ 60
      Davis; Takehisa Kosugi (*vn*); Peter Kowald (*b*). 10/86.

A one-off concert meeting between a Sun Ra sideman, a Japanese violinist and the leading German free bassist. It sounds like the recipe for incoherence, perhaps, but Davis's voice is a lyrical one, and his curling lines never give up on melody at the expense of drive and free swing: he bonds the music together, while the scrapes and scratches of the other two provide counterpoint and textural mystery. Clear if unglamorous recording.

EDDIE 'LOCKJAW' DAVIS (1922–86)
TENOR SAXOPHONE

(*)   **Jaws And Stitt At Birdland Roulette CDP 797507 CD
      Davis; Sonny Stitt (*ts*); Doc Bagby (*org*); Charlie Rice (*d*). 54.

(*)   **Eddie Davis . . . Uptown Swingtime ST 1021 LP
      Davis; Doc Bagby, Shirley Scott (*org*); Bill Pemberton (*b*); Charlie Rice (*d*).
      4/55–6/58.

***   **The Cookbook Vol. 1** Original Jazz Classics OJC 652 CD/LP/MC
      Davis; Jerome Richardson (*ts, f*); Shirley Scott (*org*); George Duvivier (*b*); Arthur
      Edgehill (*d*). 6/58.

***   **The Cookbook Vol. 2** Original Jazz Classics OJC 653 CD/LP/MC
      As above. 12/58.

***   **Jaws With Shirley Scott** Original Jazz Classics OJC 218 LP/MC
      As above, except Richardson omitted. 9/58.

***   **Jaws In Orbit** Original Jazz Classics OJC 322 LP/MC
      As above, plus Steve Pulliam (*tb*). 5/59.

One of the great saxophone pugilists, Eddie Davis made more or less the same record as a leader for 30 years. His apprenticeship in New York big bands in the 1940s led him towards rhythm-and-blues rather than bebop, but it was as either a section soloist (notably with Count Basie, where he starred on several 1950s sessions) or a jazz combo leader that Jaws functioned best. He spent the late '50s leading the group which made the Prestige and OJC reissues listed above. The records are formulaic – blustering solos over bluesy organ riffs – but endowed with a no-nonsense spirit that makes the discs highly enjoyable, taken one at a time. The two *Cookbook* albums are the most entertaining, with the food theme followed through in all the titles ('The Chef', 'Skillet', 'In The Kitchen' and so on) and Jaws taking the lid off on 'Have Horn, Will Blow'. Richardson's flute is a needless cooling-off device on most of the tracks but these are fun records. The Swingtime album collects various tracks from the same period in rather less gratifying sound. The meeting with Sonny Stitt offers a prototype of the two-tenor battles Jaws would later enjoy with Johnny Griffin, although the sound is rather foggy and the music lacks some of the suaveness of later such encounters.

****   **Very Saxy** Original Jazz Classics OJC 458 CD/LP/MC
Davis; Coleman Hawkins, Arnett Cobb, Buddy Tate (*ts*); Shirley Scott (*org*); George
Duvivier (*b*); Arthur Edgehill (*d*). 4/59.

Prestige called in three other tenormen on their books to sit in with the Davis–Scott combo,
and the results were barnstorming. The programme is all simple blues, but the flat-out
exuberance of the playing is so exhilarating that it would be churlish to give it anything less
than top marks, particularly in the excellent remastered sound. As competitive as it might
appear, nobody is bested, and the clout of Davis and Cobb is matched by the suaver Tate and
the grandiloquent Hawkins. Their 'Lester Leaps In' is a peerless display of saxophone sound.

(*)   **Afro-Jaws Original Jazz Classics OJC 403 CD/LP/MC
Davis; Clark Terry, Ernie Royal, Phil Sunkel, John Bello (*t*); Lloyd Mayers (*p*); Larry
Gales (*b*); Ben Riley (*d*); Ray Barretto (*perc*).

***   **Trane Whistle** Original Jazz Classics OJC 429 CD/LP/MC
Davis; Clark Terry, Richard Williams, Bob Bryant (*t*); Melba Liston, Jimmy Cleveland
(*tb*); Jerome Richardson, Oliver Nelson, Eric Dolphy, George Barrow, Bob Ashton
(*reeds*); Richard Wyands (*p*); Wendell Marshall (*b*); Roy Haynes (*d*). 9/60.

Afro-Jaws puts the saxophonist in front of brass and percussion to no very telling effect. But
Trane Whistle, a set of Oliver Nelson arrangements for a cracking big band, puts him in his
element, and though the charts are perhaps too functional to make the record a classic, the
knock-out power of Davis's blowing is thrilling. An Ernie Wilkins arrangement of 'You Are
Too Beautiful' shows off his skills with a ballad, too. The recording has been well remastered.

***   **Griff And Lock** Original Jazz Classics OJC 264 LP/MC
Davis; Johnny Griffin (*ts*); Junior Mance (*p*); Larry Gales (*b*); Ben Riley (*d*). 11/60.

Davis's recordings with fellow saxophonist Johnny Griffin have been characterized as mere
blowing dates, but both men were too inquiring to settle for simply trading licks. These sessions
are marked out for their interest in saxophone sound – Davis sounds at his most speechlike in
tone, and his phrasing borrows freely from both swing and bop parlance – and the varying
inflections which the line-up of two tenors and rhythm section allows. The energy level, of
course, is consistently high, hard and fast, but that doesn't obliterate subtlety or eloquence. The
material is a mix of standards and bop themes, with a special interest in Thelonious Monk
tunes: unfortunately, their *Lookin' At Monk* session, perhaps their best disc together, is
currently unavailable, but we hope it will be reissued in time for our next edition.

(*)   **Save Your Love For Me RCA Bluebird NL 86363 CD/LP
Davis; Ernie Royal, Joe Newman, Snooky Young, Burt Collins, Thad Jones (*t*); Urbie
Green, Jimmy Cleveland, Wayne Andre, J. J. Johnson (*tb*); Tony Studd (*b-tb*);
Jerome Richardson, Bobby Plater (*as*); Frank Wess, Billy Mitchell, Paul Gonsalves,
Frank Foster (*ts*); Danny Bank (*bs*); Hank Jones, Roland Hanna, Ross Tompkins (*p*);
Les Spann, Gene Bertoncini, Everett Barksdale (*g*); George Duvivier, Ben Tucker,
Russell George (*b*); Grady Tate , Chuck Lampkin (*d*); Ray Barretto (*perc*). 6/66–8/67.

This usefully brings together six sessions when Jaws was under contract to RCA in the
mid-1960s. A date with a vague Latin feel to it seems self-consciously restrained, and the
big-band tracks do nothing that *Trane Whistle* didn't do better, but the tenorman gusts through
all the same. A potentially intriguing meeting with Paul Gonsalves is interesting but not much
more.

***   **Jaws Strikes Again** Black & Blue 59.004 2 CD
Davis; Wild Bill Davis (*org*); Billy Butler (*g*); Oliver Jackson (*d*). 1/76.

(*)   **Swingin' Till The Girls Come Home Steeplechase SCS 1058 CD/LP
Davis; Thomas Clausen (*p*); Bo Stief (*b*); Alex Riel (*d*). 3/76.

***   **Montreux '77** Original Jazz Classics OJC 384 CD/LP/MC
Davis; Oscar Peterson (*p*); Ray Brown (*b*); Jimmie Smith (*d*). 7/77.

***   **The Heavy Hitter** Muse MR 5202 LP
Davis; Albert Dailey (*p*); George Duvivier (*b*); Victor Lewis (*d*). 1/79.

Davis went the journeyman route of wandering freelance through the 1970s and '80s. Of the two European records, the Black & Blue session is superior through the reunion with Davis, whose energy is as infectious as the leader's. The Steeplechase session is a little routine. The real stars of the Montreux concert recording are Peterson and Brown, whose hard clarity creates a formidable platform for the nominal leader; but Davis himself sounds somewhat below par, his solos overwrought, and the music is only inconsistently exciting.

The Heavy Hitter is abetted by the splendid rhythm section: a medley of 'Old Folks' and 'Out Of Nowhere' strikes a consummate balance between tenderness and a tougher declamation.

*** **Eddie Lockjaw Davis** Enja 3097 CD/LP
Davis; Horace Parlan (*p*); Reggie Johnson (*b*); Oliver Queen (*d*). 2/81.

*** **Live At The Widder Vol. 1** Divox CDX 48701 CD
Davis; Gustav Csik (*p*); Isla Eckinger (*b*); Oliver Jackson (*d*). 3/82.

(*) **That's All Kingdom Jazz Gate 7019 LP
Davis; Lou Bennett (*org*); George Collier (*d*); Teddy Martin (*v*). 2/83.

*** **All Of Me** Steeplechase SCS 1181 LP
Davis; Kenny Drew (*p*); Jesper Lundgaard (*b*); Svend-Erik Norregaard (*d*). 8/83.

Davis was still a commanding player up until his unexpected death in 1986. His recording regimen was a casual one, and his later discs have a pot-luck quality, but the leader himself secures an unusual level of commitment: all of these sessions are recommendable for his own tenor playing. The Enja date matches him with a fine trio, and is excellently recorded, as is the Steeplechase set, which opens with an exceptionally hard-bitten treatment of 'I Only Have Eyes For You'. *That's All* is rather more desultory, with indifferent contributions from the other players.

The most revealing session, though, is the live set captured on the Divox CD. There are 11 tunes in just over an hour of music, which shows how Davis had little time for open-ended blowing: there are a couple of throwaway blues, but most of the tunes are thoughtfully paced and prepared. Compare, for instance, the difference in his approach to two ballads – 'I Can't Get Started' offers Hawkins-like rising drama, while 'If I Had You' moves evenly to a beautifully shaped cadenza. The other players aren't very helpful but Jaws is reason enough to have the record.

MILES DAVIS (1926–91)
TRUMPET, FLUGELHORN

don't even look "Ina Silent Way"!

**** **Birth Of The Cool** Capitol CDP 792862 CD
Davis; Kai Winding, J. J. Johnson (*tb*); Junior Collins, Sandy Siegelstein, Gunther Schuller (*frhn*); Lee Konitz (*as*); Gerry Mulligan (*bs*); John Barber (*tba*); John Lewis, Al Haig (*p*); Joe Shulman, Al McKibbon, Nelson Boyd (*b*); Max Roach, Kenny Clarke (*d*); Kenny Hagood (*v*). 1/49–3/50.

***(*) **The Real Birth Of The Cool** Bandstand BDCD 1512 CD
As above, except Mike Zwerin (*tb*) replaces Winding and Johnson, Curley Russell (*b*) replaces Shulman and Boyd, Siegelstein, Schuller, Haig and Clarke absent. 9/48.

***(*) **Cool Boppin'** Fresh Sound FSCD-1008 CD
As above, except add Kai Winding (*tb*), Sahib Shihab (*as*), Benjamin Lundy (*ts*), Cecil Payne (*bs*), Tadd Dameron (*p*), John Collins (*g*), Kenny Clarke (*d*), Carlos Vidal (*perc*). 9/48–2/49.

Davis's first records under his own name, in 1947, can be located in Charlie Parker's entry. The groundbreaking *Birth Of The Cool* band – the record actually consists of three sessions recorded over the period of a year – was strikingly new to bebop listeners at the time, and still sounds particularly fresh. Davis at the time presided over a group of young explorers based in New York, and the music by this nine-piece band (though a commercial failure) included some of the pioneering efforts by arrangers Mulligan and Gil Evans and composer John Carisi: the results were allusive, magical scores that channelled the irresistible energy of bop into surprising textures and piquant settings for improvisation. Davis and Konitz played as if a new world were almost within their grasp. The availability of the original LP has fluctuated over the years, but the capable if no more than adequate remastering for CD should ensure its current catalogue life. The Bandstand record brings to CD airshot recordings from the Royal Roost club, where Davis's band made a brief engagement: the sound is comparatively poor, but it's a valuable look at how these arrangements came alive in person, and the soloists are spontaneously exciting, especially the leader. Nine of the same tracks open *Cool Boppin'*, but the remaining six are by a ten-piece Tadd Dameron group which makes an interesting addendum to the Davis sessions: 'Focus', 'Webb's Delight' and 'Casbah' display Dameron's askew lyricism to sometimes ponderous effect, but Davis's own improvisations hit some daringly high notes for him, and it makes for an interesting contrast to the Nonet tracks. Sound is about the same as on the Bandstand disc.

*** **Quintet With Lee Konitz; Sextet With Jackie McLean** Fresh Sound FSCD-1000 CD
Davis; Don Elliott (*mel, vib*); Lee Konitz, Jackie McLean (*as*); John Lewis, Gil Coggins (*p*); Curley Russell, Connie Henry (*b*); Max Roach, Connie Kay (*d*); Kenny Hagood (*v*). 9/48–5/52.

Useful glimpses of Davis in action away from the studios, at a period when he wasn't getting much done on legitimate recordings. The 1948 session features him with Konitz on four titles, and aside from a lugubrious 'You Go To My Head' all are fast and exciting. Davis hits some improbable high notes and is in ebullient mood, while Konitz's serpentine elegance is already individual, if attuned to a more straight-ahead bop vision than he would later apply. The sextet date is a bit cluttered but still offers some strong bop-styled playing: the best performance is a Davis original, 'Out Of The Blue', with an impassioned and agile trumpet solo and the young McLean in eager form. Sound for both sessions is typically muddy but listenable enough.

** **Miles Davis With Horns** Original Jazz Classics OJC 053 CD/LP/MC
Davis; Bennie Green, Sonny Truitt (*tb*); Sonny Rollins, Al Cohn, Zoot Sims (*ts*); John Lewis (*p*); Leonard Gaskin, Percy Heath (*b*); Roy Haynes, Kenny Clarke (*d*). 1/51–2/53.

*** **Dig** Original Jazz Classics OJC 005 CD/LP/MC
Davis; Jackie McLean (*as*); Sonny Rollins (*ts*); Walter Bishop Jr (*p*); Tommy Potter (*b*); Art Blakey (*d*). 10/51.

Davis's first sessions for Prestige are scarcely harbingers of what was to come: the earliest is doleful and undistinguished, and while there are a couple of challenging trumpet solos on 'My Old Flame' and 'Blueing', the second isn't a great deal better; sound balance favours the horns at the expense of the rhythm section. The 1953 date, arranged by Cohn, finds Davis in atypical but obviously enjoyable surroundings, since he plays brightly alongside the two-tenor partnership; on their own terms, these four tracks offer slight but exuberant entertainment. The contents of both the above records may still be available on the double-LP *Dig* (Prestige P 24054).

*** **Collectors' Items** Original Jazz Classics OJC 071 CD/LP/MC
Davis; Sonny Rollins, Charlie Parker (*ts*); Walter Bishop Jr, Tommy Flanagan (*p*); Percy Heath, Paul Chambers (*b*); Philly Joe Jones, Art Taylor (*d*). 1/53–3/56.

*(*) **At Last! Miles Davis And The Lighthouse All Stars** Original Jazz Classics OJC 480 CD/LP/MC.
Davis; Rolf Ericson, Chet Baker (*t*); Bud Shank (*as*); Bob Cooper (*ts*); Lorraine Geller, Russ Freeman (*p*); Howard Rumsey (*b*); Max Roach (*d*). 9/53.

The 1953 session with Parker on tenor is a curio, and it makes an odd makeweight for the accompanying, later quintet date with Rollins, which includes a skilful solo by the saxophonist on 'Vierd Blues' and a fine investigation of Brubeck's 'In Your Own Sweet Way' by Davis. This session, along with *Blue Moods* (OJC 043, see below), may also still be available as the double-LP *Collectors' Items* (Prestige P 24022). The live jam session recorded at the Lighthouse is best forgotten by admirers of the trumpeter, whose desultory playing was hardly worth preserving on ponderous versions of 'Infinity Promenade' and 'Round Midnight'; the others do better, but not much. Surprisingly well-recorded under the circumstances.

***(*) **Miles Davis Vol. 1** Blue Note CDP 7815012 CD

265

***(*)   **Miles Davis Vol. 2** Blue Note CDP 78150122 CD
Davis; J. J. Johnson (*tb*); Jackie McLean (*as*); Jimmy Heath (*ts*); Gil Coggins, Horace
Silver (*p*); Oscar Pettiford, Percy Heath (*b*); Kenny Clarke, Art Blakey (*d*). 5/52–3/54.

***   **The Best Of Miles Davis** Blue Note CDP 7982872 CD
As above Blue Note and Capitol sessions, except add Cannonball Adderley (*as*), Hank
Jones (*p*), Sam Jones (*b*). 1/49–3/58.

While these are inconsistent records, they're also Davis's most personal and clear-sighted
statements up to this point, both as a soloist and as an emerging small-group leader. Although
still suffering heroin addiction when the first two sessions were made, and with his professional
life in considerable disarray, Davis was beginning to move beyond the confines of small-group
bop. The tracks on the earlier dates are still brief in duration with pithy and well-turned solos,
but the emotional timbre is different to bop – intense yet restrained, cool yet plangent. The first
date seems comparatively hurried, but the second, with fine compositions from Johnson, Heath
and Bud Powell included, is indispensable. The third, featuring Davis as sole horn, includes
some of his best playing to date, with fast, eventful solos on 'Take Off' and 'The Leap' and a
potent reading of Monk's 'Well You Needn't'.

The jumbled sequencing of the original LPs has been corrected for CD release: the first and
third sessions are complete on the first volume and the second is on Volume 2. The sound is a
little fresher if not noticeably superior in the remastering.

The Best Of collection covers the Blue Note albums, *Birth Of The Cool* and 20 minutes of
material from Cannonball Adderley's *Somethin' Else* session from 1958. A fine selection, but
the original discs are all but indispensable.

***   **Blue Haze** Original Jazz Classics OJC 093 CD/LP/MC
Davis; Dave Schildkraut (*as*); John Lewis, Charles Mingus, Horace Silver (*p*); Percy
Heath (*b*); Kenny Clarke, Art Blakey, Max Roach (*d*). 5/53–4/54.

****   **Walkin'** Original Jazz Classics OJC 213 CD/LP/MC
Davis; J. J. Johnson (*tb*); Dave Schildkraut (*as*); Lucky Thompson (*ts*); Horace Silver
(*p*); Percy Heath (*b*); Kenny Clarke (*d*). 4/54.

***(*)   **Bags' Groove** Original Jazz Classics OJC 245 CD/LP/MC
Davis; Sonny Rollins (*ts*); Milt Jackson (*vib*); Thelonious Monk, Horace Silver (*p*);
Percy Heath (*b*); Kenny Clarke (*d*). 6/54.

****   **Miles Davis And The Modern Jazz Giants** Original Jazz Classics OJC 347 CD/LP/MC
Davis; John Coltrane (*ts*); Milt Jackson (*vib*); Thelonious Monk, Red Garland (*p*);
Percy Heath, Paul Chambers (*b*); Kenny Clarke, Philly Joe Jones (*d*). 12/54–10/56.

The *Blue Haze* set is split between a merely good quartet date from 1953 and three altogether
excellent tracks from the following March, by the same quartet that cut the final date for Blue
Note. Plus a single track from the April 1954 session with the undervalued Schildkraut on alto.
Walkin' and *Bags' Groove* find the great leader of post-bop jazz hitting his stride. The former
session includes two clear-cut masterpieces in the title-track and 'Blue 'N' Boogie': the solos
here are brilliantly sharp, dazzlingly inventive. Most of the *Bags' Groove* set is by a quintet with
Rollins, which produced fine if slightly less enthralling music, though the trumpeter uses the
harmon mute sound which was to become a trademark for the first time on 'Oleo'. Two
compelling takes of the title-track round off the record, but these come from the Christmas Eve
date which is otherwise contained on OJC 347, the only official meeting between Davis, Monk
and Jackson. The clash between Jackson's typically fleet lines and the different kinds of
astringency represented by Monk and Davis made for a tense and compelling situation. This
disc is, in turn, completed by a very fine 'Round Midnight' by the quintet with John Coltrane.

The original recordings of all this material were very faithfully done, and the CD remastering
sounds well. Most of OJC 245 and 347 is also available on the double-LP *Tallest Trees* (Prestige
P 24012), while the contents of OJC 093 and 213 are also on the double-LP *Tune Up* (Prestige P
24077).

(*)   **The Musings Of Miles Original Jazz Classics OJC 004 CD/LP/MC
Davis; Red Garland (*p*); Oscar Pettiford (*b*); Philly Joe Jones (*d*). 6/55.

***   **Blue Moods** Original Jazz Classics OJC 043 CD/LP/MC
       Davis; Britt Woodman (*tb*); Teddy Charles (*vib*); Charles Mingus (*b*); Elvin Jones (*d*).
       7/55.

***(*)   **Quintet/Sextet** Original Jazz Classics OJC 012 CD/LP/MC
       Davis; Jackie McLean (*as*); Milt Jackson (*vib*); Ray Bryant (*p*); Percy Heath (*b*); Art
       Taylor (*d*). 8/55.

Davis's final quartet session prior to the formation of his famous quintet is a surprisingly lacklustre affair (Jones and Pettiford were allegedly exhausted or, in Pettiford's case, drunk). Davis holds the music together but sounds rather sour.The brief *Blue Moods* session, though poor value on a single CD, offers an instrumentation which Davis never tried again, and has a desolate version of 'Nature Boy' that prepares one for the melancholy poetry of his later ballads. The August 1955 session is something of a farewell to Davis's most carefree music, with four pacy and involving workouts on mostly blues material, though at little more than 30 minutes this is poor value for a single CD.

***(*)   **Miles** Original Jazz Classics OJC 006 CD/LP/MC
       Davis; John Coltrane (*ts*); Red Garland (*p*); Paul Chambers (*b*); Philly Joe Jones (*d*).
       11/55.

****   **Cookin'** Original Jazz Classics OJC 128 CD/LP/MC
       As above. 10/56.

****   **Relaxin'** Original Jazz Classics OJC 190 CD/LP/MC
       As above. 5/56–10/56.

****   **Workin'** Original Jazz Classics OJC 296 CD/LP/MC
       As above. 5/56–10/56.

****   **Steamin'** Original Jazz Classics OJC 391 CD/LP/MC
       As above. 5/56–10/56.

Despite an initially unfavourable reaction from musicians and listeners, Davis's 1956 quintet quickly established a major following, and their five albums for Prestige (actually recorded to fulfill a contract before Davis could move to Columbia) have endured as some of the most famous documents of the music as it stood in the mid-1950s. They are uneven in inspiration and there is no single standout record, but the sense of spontaneity and of a combative group in brilliant creative flux is surpassed by no other jazz records. The greatest contrast is between Davis – spare, introspective, guileful – and the leonine, blustering Coltrane, who was still at a somewhat chaotic stage of his development. But equally telling are the members of the rhythm section, who contrive to create a different climate behind each soloist and sustain the logical flow of the tunes. Recorded at a handful of marathon sessions, the records each have their own special rewards: a slow, pierced 'My Funny Valentine' on *Cookin'*, the supple swing of 'I Could Write A Book' and revitalized bebop in 'Woody'n You' from *Relaxin'*, a haunted trumpet reading of 'It Never Entered My Mind' on *Workin'*. All five, however, should be a part of any significant jazz collection.

     Rudy van Gelder's splendid engineering and Bob Weinstock's production have ensured that the music has survived in excellent condition, and the CD reissues – although the individual OJC editions are all rather short measure – sound well enough, if a little compressed. The English company Ace has, however, coupled *Cookin'* and *Relaxin'* on a single CD (Ace/Prestige CDJZD 003), a considerable bargain. Some double-LP sets may also still be in circulation, as follows: *Green Haze* (Prestige P-24054), coupling *The Musings Of Miles* and *Miles*; and *Miles Davis* (Prestige P-24001), coupling *Cookin'* and *Relaxin'*.

***(*)   **Round About Midnight** CBS 460605 CD/MC
       As above. 10/55–9/56.

A Columbia footnote to the Prestige sessions, with six tracks culled from three sessions, cut in the middle of the Prestige tenure. The playing is probably as fine, but somehow the music doesn't cast quite the consistent spell which the Prestige records do.

(****)   **Miles Ahead** CBS 460606 CD/MC
       Davis; Bernie Glow, Ernie Royal, Louis Mucci, Taft Jordan, John Carisi (*t*); Frank
       Rehak, Jimmy Cleveland, Joe Bennett (*tb*); Tom Mitchell (*btb*); Willie Ruff, Tony

Miranda (*frhn*); Lee Konitz (*as*); Romeo Penque, Sid Cooper (*woodwinds*); Danny Bank (*bcl*); Bill Barber (*tba*); Paul Chambers (*b*); Art Taylor (*d*); Gil Evans (*cond*). 5/57.

Davis's first full-length collaboration with arranger Gil Evans remains the best, if not the best known of their recordings. While the ensemble as directed by Evans isn't always note-perfect – a failing even more obvious on the later *Porgy And Bess* – the interlinking of the tracks with written bridge passages and subsequent splicing is impeccably done, and Davis the soloist provides continuity and spontaneous illumination of the scores, which make manifest the neo-classical leanings of such previous ensembles as the 'Birth Of The Cool' nonet. The excitement which the record created – as a long-playing record, a 'concerto', and a vehicle for Davis's lyric side, spotlit by his use of flugelhorn throughout the album – survives the passage of time. Unfortunately, we have to include a serious caveat, in that the remastered CD version appears to consist of a series of alternative takes (most of them of secondary quality) to the original album. We must hope that Columbia rectify this disgrace as soon as possible.

**** **Milestones** CBS 460827 CD/MC
Davis; Cannonball Adderley (*as*); John Coltrane (*ts*); Red Garland (*p*); Paul Chambers (*b*); Philly Joe Jones (*d*). 4/58.

Milestones is as essential as any Miles Davis of the period. While usually considered a transitional album, between the quintet period and the modal jazz initiated fully in *Kind Of Blue*, it stands as a superb record by itself. Davis's contrasting solos on 'Sid's Ahead' – a brooding, coolly mournful improvisation – and 'Milestones' itself – a sharply ambiguous and dancing treatment – are enough to make the record important, but the standard of writing and playing by everyone involved makes this an outstanding group record as well as one of Davis's strongest sessions.

***(*) **Miles And Coltrane** CBS 460824 CD/MC
Davis; John Coltrane (*ts*); Cannonball Adderley (*as*); Bill Evans, Red Garland (*p*); Paul Chambers (*b*); Jimmy Cobb, Philly Joe Jones (*d*). 10/55–7/58.

(*) **Live In New York Bandstand BD 1501 CD/LP
Davis; John Coltrane (*ts*); Bill Evans, Wynton Kelly, Red Garland (*p*); Paul Chambers (*b*); Jimmy Cobb, Philly Joe Jones, Art Taylor (*d*). 57–59.

The two 1955 tracks, 'Little Melonae' and 'Budo', are leftovers from an earlier session. Most of the other material on the CBS record is from a live set at the 1958 Newport Festival. There is much effervescence in the live setting and Coltrane, especially, is in tremendous form on 'Ah-Leu-Cha' and 'Bye Bye Blackbird'; the contrasts with Davis's spareness were seldom as striking as here. Evans and Adderley also play well, the former taking a fine solo on 'Straight No Chaser', but it's the two principal protagonists who make the record.

The Bandstand record is a hotch-potch of tracks from this period, mostly in fair rather than good sound. Desultory though it may be – and there is a version of 'Milestones' which is clearly more recent, probably by the later band with Shorter – there is a fine, simmering version of 'So What' and some sharp uptempo playing on 'Four' and 'Walkin''.

**** **Porgy And Bess** CBS 450985 CD/MC
Davis; Louis Mucci, Ernie Royal, John Coles, Bernie Glow (*t*); Jimmy Cleveland, Joseph Bennett, Richard Hixon, Frank Rehak (*tb*); Daniel Banks, Cannonball Adderley (*as*); Willie Ruff, Julius Watkins, Gunther Schuller (*frhn*); Philip Bodner, Romeo Penque, Jerome Richardson (*f*); Bill Barber (*tba*); Paul Chambers (*b*); Philly Joe Jones, Jimmy Cobb (*d*). 7–8/58.

Gil Evans scored Gershwin's masterpiece in glowing terms, using flutes and horns in place of saxes to create a palette of delicacy as well as toughness. Davis rose to the occasion, sounding at his most majestic in the contemplative improvisations on 'Summertime' and even making the brief passages such as 'Gone, Gone, Gone' into something singular and memorable. If the record falls a trifle short, it's in the imperfections of the ensemble, which mar some of the more difficult passages. The remastering is well enough done but adds little to the clarity of the original LP.

*****   **Kind Of Blue** CBS 32109 CD/MC
       Davis; Cannonball Adderley (*as*); John Coltrane (*ts*); Bill Evans, Wynton Kelly (*p*);
       Paul Chambers (*b*); Jimmy Cobb (*d*). 3–4/59.

One of the two or three most celebrated albums in jazz history still lives up to its reputation, especially in this fine remastering for CD. The key presence may be that of Bill Evans (Kelly plays only on the blues 'Freddie Freeloader') whose allusive, almost impressionist accompaniments are the ideal platform for the spacious solos created by the horns, in what was the first widely acknowledged 'modal jazz' date. Tension is consistently established within the ensembles, only for Davis and Coltrane especially to resolve it in songful, declamatory solos. The steady mid-tempos and plaintive voicings on 'So What' and 'All Blues' establish further the weightless, haunting qualities of the music, which no collection, serious or casual, should be without.

***(*)   **Sketches Of Spain** CBS 460604 CD/MC
       Davis; Bernie Glow, Ernie Royal, John Coles, Louis Mucci, Taft Jordan (*t*); Frank
       Rehak, Dick Hixon (*tb*); John Barrows, Jim Buffington, Earl Chapin, Joe Singer, Tony
       Miranda (*frhn*); Albert Block, Eddie Caine, Harold Feldman, Romeo Penque
       (*woodwinds*); Jack Knitzer (*bsn*); Danny Bank (*bcl*); Bill Barber (*tba*); Janet Putnam
       (*hp*); Paul Chambers (*b*); Jimmy Cobb, Elvin Jones (*d*). 11/59–3/60.

Though it has many moments of luminous beauty, it's hard to evade the feeling that this is an overrated record. Despite – or perhaps because of – far more time in the studios than was used on the earlier collaborations with Gil Evans, the feel of the record seems ill-focused, with the ambitious 'Concierto De Aranjuez' sounding sometimes like inflated light music, with only Davis's occasional intensities driving energy into the whole. The dialogue between trumpet and ensemble in 'Solea' is the best sequence on the session. Although the trumpeter is giving of his best throughout, the sometimes haphazard percussion tracks and muzzy ensembles suggest a harbinger of some of the electric trance music which Davis would later delve into in the 1970s. The original sound – never very good, as far as the orchestra was concerned – receives a rather dry remastering for CD.

****   **Live In Stockholm 1960** Dragon DRLP 90/91 2LP
       Davis; John Coltrane (*ts*); Wynton Kelly (*p*); Paul Chambers (*b*); Jimmy Cobb (*d*).
       3/60.

***   **Copenhagen 1960** Royal Jazz RJD 501 CD
       As above. 3/60.

***(*)   **Live In Stockholm 1960** Dragon DRLP 129/130. 2LP
       As above, except add Sonny Stitt (*as, ts*); 10/60.

(*)   **Live In Stockholm 1960 Royal Jazz RJD 509 CD
       As above. 10/60.

A number of live recordings exist from this period, away from Davis's officially sanctioned releases, and the above two – both excellently recorded by Swedish Radio – are valuable glimpses of two European sojourns in 1960. The concert with Coltrane (which includes a six-minute interview with the saxophonist) suggests a battle of giants: Trane piles in with all his most abandoned lines, while Davis remains – especially in a nearly anguished 'All Blues' – aloof. The rhythm section play with impervious jauntiness and it adds up to a tremendous concert recording. The Royal Jazz CD offers three tracks from a subsequent concert in rather less acceptable sound.

    The session with Stitt is only slightly less effective. Stitt, admittedly, wrestles with no dark demons, but his plangency and itch to play are scarcely less powerful than Coltrane's, and his switching between alto and tenor offers more light and shade. Davis is again bitingly inver   e, even on material which he must already have played many times over.

    The Royal Jazz disc includes some extra material from the same concert with Sti   rhythm section alone, and goes on to duplicate three tracks with the Dragon LPs recommendable alternative.

***   **Some Day My Prince Will Come** Columbia CK 40947 CD
       Davis; Hank Mobley, John Coltrane (*ts*); Wynton Kelly (*p*); Paul C
       Joe Jones, Jimmy Cobb (*d*). 3/61.

***(*)   **Friday Night At The Blackhawk Vol. 1** Columbia CK 44257 CD/MC
As above, except omit Coltrane and Jones. 4/61.

***(*)   **Saturday Night At The Blackhawk Vol. 2** Columbia CK 44425 CD/MC
As above. 4/61.

Although a fine, individual tenor player, Hank Mobley never sounded right in the Davis band – at least, not after Coltrane, whose 'guest' appearance on the somewhat lethargic *Some Day My Prince Will Come* is astonishing: he plays two solos, on the title-track and on 'Teo', which put everything else in the shade. The live sessions from The Blackhawk were Davis's first attempts at an official live album, and although Mobley plays well – he negotiates the tempo of a rocketing 'Walkin'' without any bother – he sounds at some remove from the rest of the group, which was sparking with Miles. The leader's solos, both muted and open, mix a spitting intensity with thoughtful, circling phrases, at both fast and medium tempos. The outstanding recording of the original albums has been capably transferred to CD.

***(*)   **At Carnegie Hall 1961** CBS 460064 CD/MC
Davis; Bernie Glow, Ernie Royal, Louis Mucci, Johnny Coles (*t*); Frank Rehak, Dick Hixon, Jimmy Knepper (*tb*); Julius Watkins, Paul Ingraham, Bob Swisshelm (*frhn*); Bill Barber (*tba*); Hank Mobley (*ts*); Jerome Richardson, Romeo Penque, Eddie Caine, Bob Tricarico, Danny Bank (*reeds, woodwinds*); Wynton Kelly (*p*); Paul Chambers (*b*); Janet Putnam (*hp*); Bobby Rosengarden (*perc*). 5/61.

***   **Live Miles: More Music From The Legendary Carnegie Hall Concert** Columbia CK 40609 CD/MC
As above. 5/61.

Davis's Carnegie Hall concert of 1961 set the seal on his emergence as a jazz superstar during the previous five years. Split between music by the quintet and Evans's arrangements of some of the material from their albums together, the two records are distinguished by the leader's own playing – he plays with more incisiveness on the Evans material than he does on the studio versions, and 'Teo' and 'No Blues' feature compelling solos – but Mobley is again no match for what Coltrane might have done, and 'Concierto De Aranjuez' sounds no more convincing in this setting.

****   **Miles In Antibes** CBS CD
Davis; George Coleman (*ts*); Herbie Hancock (*p*); Ron Carter (*b*); Tony Williams (*d*). 7/63.

***(*)   **Cote Blues** JMY 1010-2 CD
As above. 7/63.

A very fine concert set from a generally undervalued period in Davis's discography. Some of the excellent albums with Coleman on tenor have yet to appear on CD, but this one, recorded only a few weeks after the band had been formed, is unpredictable and exciting. Coleman's muscular, scouring style proves surprisingly effective and the new, young rhythm section, powered by the thunderous rhythm of Williams, draws Davis into taking fresh risks. Even though the material is much the same as it had been for the last five years, the treatments are newly abstract or expressionist by turns. The JMY set appears to consist of further tracks from the same programme, and is in mostly excellent sound.

***(*)   **Miles In Berlin** Columbia CD
As above, except Wayne Shorter (*ts*) replaces Coleman. 9/64.

***(*)   **Live In Paris 1964** Moon 021 CD/LP
As above. 10/64.

***(*)   **Davisiana** Moon 033 CD
As above. 10/64.

Wayne Shorter's arrival stabilized the new group, since Shorter was a major composer as well as soloist. Although the set in Berlin is the standard one of 'So What' and so on, the pungency of Davis's solos is matched by a new depth of interplay with the rhythm section, as well as by Shorter's phenomenally harsh-sounding parts. The highlight is a superbly intense reading of 'Autumn Leaves'. The Moon set was recorded a month later; taken apparently from radio tapes, the sound is second-rate, but the playing continues to unfold compellingly. Much the same may be said of *Davisiana*, recorded in Sindelfingen a few days shy of the Paris concert; imperfect sound, but everything comes through clearly, and the band sound marvellous.

****   **E.S.P.** CBS 467899 CD/MC
     As above. 1/65.

****   **Cookin' At The Plugged Nickel** Columbia CK 40645 CD/MC
     As above. 12/65.

***(*)   **Nefertiti** CBS 467089 CD/MC
     As above. 6–7/67.

***   **No Blues** JMY 1003 CD
     As above. 11/67.

***   **Filles De Kilimanjaro** CBS 467088 CD/MC
     As above, except add Chick Corea (*ky*), Dave Holland (*b*). 6–9/68.

***   **Circle In The Round** Columbia C2T 46862 2CD/2MC
     Davis; Cannonball Adderley (*as*); John Coltrane, Hank Mobley, Wayne Shorter (*ts*); Herbie Hancock, Chick Corea, Red Garland, Wynton Kelly, Joe Zawinul, Bill Evans (*p*); George Benson, Joe Beck (*g*); Paul Chambers, Ron Carter, Dave Holland (*b*); Philly Joe Jones, Jimmy Cobb, Tony Williams (*d*). 10/55–1/70.

Several good records from this period (*Miles Smiles*, *Sorceror*) are currently out of print, but the five Columbia/CBS albums listed above chart the extraordinary progress of the most mysterious of all of Davis's bands. The trumpeter returns to his tactic with Coltrane, of paring away: sometimes he doesn't even take a solo, as on the slowly simmering 'Nefertiti', which the horns pace out over Williams's boiling rhythms. *E.S.P.* is probably the best album, with seven excellent original themes and the players building a huge creative tension between Shorter's oblique, churning solos and the leader's private musings, and within a rhythm section that is bursting to fly free while still playing time. *Nefertiti* is nearly as strong, if a little too cool, but *Filles De Kilimanjaro* is a little stiffer, with the quintet at the point of break-up (Corea and Holland arrive for two tracks).

The live albums are different – the programmes continue to look back to standard Davis sets, and the long, exhaustive treatments of the likes of 'Stella By Starlight' and 'All Blues' sometimes ramble yet seem to have a different subtext for every player. There is always something happening. The JMY session is probably as good as the Plugged Nickel date but offers somewhat shorter measure.

Circle In The Round is an interesting if seldom compelling set of outtakes from Davis's Columbia albums over a 25-year period. The long title-track is an attempt at a mesmerizing mood piece which works for some of the time but tends to fade in and out of the listener's attention. Earlier pieces with the great quintet, plus a marvellous 'Love For Sale' from 1958, are more vital. The CD omits some of the music from the original double-LP.

***(*)   **Get Up With It** Core/Line CLCD 9.009827/8 2CD
     Davis; Sonny Fortune (*as, f*); Carlos Garnett, John Stubblefield (*as*); Steve Grossman (*ss*); David Liebman (*f*); Wally Chambers (*hca*); Cedric Lawson (*p, org*); Herbie Hancock, Keith Jarrett (*ky*); Pete Cosey, Cornell Dupree, Dominique Gaumont, Reggie Lucas, John McLaughlin (*g*); Khalil Balakrishna (*sitar*); Michael Henderson (*b*); Billy Cobham, Al Foster, Bernard Purdie (*d*); Airto Moreira, Mtume, Badal Roy (*perc*); additional brass and rhythm arrangements by Wade Jarcus and Billy Jackson. 70–74.

Miles's first attempt to make Ellington dance with Stockhausen. Dedicated to the recently deceased Duke and dominated by a huge, mournful tribute, *Get Up With It* is more coherent than its immediate predecessors and very much more challenging. Recorded over a period of four years, it traces Miles's growing interest in a whole range of apparently irreconcilable musics. In his ghosted autobiography, he explains his growing attachment to Sly Stone's technologized Afro-funk on the one hand and Stockhausen's brooding music-as-process on the other. What united the two, beyond an obvious conclusion that pieces no longer needed to end or be resolved, was the idea that instrumental sound could be transformed and mutated almost infinitely and that the interest of a performance could be relocated from harmonic 'changes' and settled on the manipulation of sound textures over a moving carpet of rhythm. Since *Bitches Brew*, and very noticeably on an album like *Jack Johnson*, Miles had been willing to consider the studio and the editing room a further instrumental resource. With *Get Up With It* and the two live albums that follow, Miles went a step further, putting together bands that create similar phases and process-dominated 'improvisations' in real time.

There is a conventional wisdom that Miles's trumpet playing was at a low ebb during this period; health problems are adduced to shore up the myth of a tortured genius robbed of his truest talent, clutching at even the most minimal musical opportunities. Even those who *had* heard the mid-1970s albums, which acquired an added mystique by being the last before Miles's five-year 'retirement', were apt to say that he 'no longer played any trumpet'. Though distorted by wah-wah pedals and constantly treading water in its own echo, Miles's horn was still doing precisely what the music required of it; the same applied to his resort to organ ('Rated X') and piano ('Calypso Frelimo'). The poorer tracks ('Maishya' and 'Red China Blues' start off very late-nite) give only a misleading representation of how finely balanced Miles's radical populism actually was; a live version of 'Maishya' from the infamous Osaka gig is altogether tougher.

The essence of the 'new' Miles is to be found on the Duke tribute, 'He Loved Him Madly', a swarthy theme that sounds spontaneously developed, only gradually establishing a common pulse and tone-centre, but replete with semi-conscious, almost dreamed references to Ellington's work. 'Honky Tonk', by contrast, is an actual throwback to the style and personnel of *Jack Johnson* (which, like *Lift For The Scaffold* before it, greatly exceeded its occasion in musical significance, even if that was recognized only retrospectively). Though put together piecemeal and with Miles apparently willing to let Teo Macero edit greater or lesser chunks out of extended performances, *Get Up With It* is of considerable historical importance, looking forward not just to the apocalyptic live performances of 1975 but to the more polished and ironic pop-jazz of the comeback years.

***(*)   **Agharta** Columbia 467897 CD
Davis; Sonny Fortune (*as, ss, f*); Pete Cosey (*g, syn, perc*); Reggie Lucas (*g*); Michael Henderson (*b*); Al Foster (*d*); Mtume (*perc*). 2/75.

****   **Pangaea** Columbia C2K 46115 CD
As above.

It bears repeating: Miles's trumpet playing on these astonishing records is of the highest and most adventurous order, not the desperate posturing of a sick and cynical man. The use of a wah-wah pedal – routinely interpreted as part of the same turn towards a pop market signalled by Corky McCoy's much sneered-at cover art for *On The Corner* – is often fantastically subtle, creating surges and ebbs in a harmonically static line, allowing Miles to build huge melismatic variations on a single note. The truth is that the band, Fortune apart, aren't fully understanding of the leader's conception; Henderson in particular tends to plod, and the two guitarists are inclined to get off on long spotlit solos that are almost laughably tame and blustery when set alongside Miles's knifefighter's reserve and reticence.

A re-run 'Maishya' and a long edit from the *Jack Johnson* theme (miscredited on the original release of *Agharta*) underlines the importance of two underestimated earlier albums. The music scarcely touches any longer on European norms, adding Stockhausen's conception of a 'world music' that moves like creeping tectonic plates (*Pangaea* and 'Gondwana' are the names palaeo-geographers give to the primeval super-continents) to Afro-American popular forms. 'Gondwana' is the most consistent performance on either album. It opens on Fortune's surprisingly delicate flute and proceeds trance-like, with Miles's central trumpet episode bracketed by shimmering organ outlines and sullen, percussive stabs. It is difficult music to divide. Key centres are only notional and deceptive; most of the rhythmic activity – unlike Ornette Coleman's Prime Time bands – takes place along a single axis, but with considerable variation in the intensity and colouration of the pulse; the solos – like Weather Report's – are constant but also inseparable from the main thrust of the music. There is a growing appreciation of these admittedly problematic recordings (which were originally released only in Japan) but time will tell how significant they are in the overall trajectory of Miles's music.

**   **The Man With The Horn** Columbia COL 4687012 CD
     Davis; Bill Evans (*ss*); Barry Finnerty (*g*); Rod Hill (*g, v, ky*); Robert Irving III (*p, ky*); Felton Crews, Marcus Miller (*b*); Al Foster, Vince Wilburn (*d*); Sammy Figueroa (*perc*). 81.

Glittery, mechano-funk, and one of the trumpeter's tiredest performances on record. 'Back Seat Betty' was a concert favourite (see the live double set, *We Want Miles*, Columbia, which awaits reissue). There's also a bravura pastiche on a theme from *Aida*. It was never possible to dismiss Miles, but this is one record that can safely be overlooked.

***(*)   **You're Under Arrest** Columbia COL 4687032 CD
     Davis; Bob Berg (*ss*); Robert Irving III (*ky*); John McLaughlin, John Scofield (*g*); Darryl Jones (*b*); Al Foster (*d*); Steve Thornton (*perc*); Marek Olko, Sting (*v*). 85.

The final studio release with Columbia (issued with a preposterous cover-picture of a sick-looking Miles posing grouchily with what looks like a toy longstock pistol) has acquired classic status on the strength of two of his best latterday transformations of pop material. His version of Cyndi Lauper's 'Time After Time', a medium-tempo waltz, is straightforwardly lovely, etched in melting top notes and passionate soars; but the finest performance on the record is the version of Michael Jackson's 'Human Nature'. The title-track is set up with some engaging 'read him his rights' / 'you got one phone-call' nonsense from the guest 'vocalists' and there's some steaming funk on 'Katia'. McLaughlin and Scofield vie for attention, but the dominant sound is the solid whoomph of Darryl 'The Munch' Jones's thumb-slap bass. Entertainment-wise, perhaps the best of the late albums.

***   **Tutu** Warner Brothers 925 490 CD/LP/MC
     Davis; George Duke (*ky, etc.*); Adam Holzman, Bernard Wright (*ky*); Michael Urbaniak (*vn*); Marcus Miller (*b, ky*); Omar Hakim (*d, perc*); Paulinho Da Costa, Steve Reid (*perc*). 86.

***(*)   **Amandla** Warner Brothers 925 873 CD/LP/MC
     Davis; Kenny Garrett (*as*); Rick Margitza (*ts*); Jean-Paul Bourelly, Michael Landau, Foley McCreary, Billy Spaceman Watson (*g*); Joe Sample (*p*); Joey DeFrancesco, George Duke (*ky*); Marcus Miller (*ky, b, etc.*); Al Foster, Omar Hakim, Ricky Wellman (*d*); Don Alias, John Bigham, Mino Cinelu, Paulinho Da Costa, Bashiri Johnson (*perc*). 89.

Miles's first post-CBS albums were an uneasy blend of exquisite trumpet miniaturism and drab cop-show funk, put together with a high production gloss that camouflaged a lack of real musical substance. Though he was acutely sensitive to any perceived put-down by middle-class whites, little was known about Miles's specific political beliefs at this or any previous time. Talking to a French interviewer, he said that naming albums for Bishop Tutu and after the ANC battle-cry was the only contribution he could make to the liberation struggle in South Africa; Miles also namechecks Mandela on 'Full Nelson', though this also relates back to an earlier 'Half Nelson', and simultaneously signals a reawakening interest in blues and bop harmonies which was to be interrupted only by his death.

     The horn sounds as deceptively fragile as ever, but it's made to dance in front of shifting sonic backdrops put together in a cut-and-paste way that succeeds very much better on *Amandla* than on the earlier set. 'Big Time' and 'Jilli' have a hectic, thudding energy, while at the other end of the spectrum, Miles's dedication to the late 'Mr Pastorius' catches him in convincingly lyrical form. There's no mistaking the ultimate provenance of Marcus Miller's vivid techno-arranging. In particular, his use of synthesized percussion on 'Hannibal' recalls 'La Nevada' on Gil Evans's *Out Of The Cool*, an influence that became explicit to the point of pastiche on the item below.

(*)   **Music From Siesta Warner Brothers 925 655 CD/LP/MC
     Davis; Marcus Miller (*ky, b, etc.*).

By this time, Marcus Miller had taken over writing and arranging duties and Miles was beginning to take on an unaccustomed Grand Old Man demeanour and a series of guest appearances. *Siesta*, based on a Patrice Chaplin novel, was a flop as a movie, and Miles's free-hand Spanish sketches have subsequently taken on a life of their own. However they related to the film's imagery, they are now appealingly abstract, if a little undemanding. By no means an essential item in the discography, but pleasant enough.

****   Aura Columbia 463351 CD/LP

Davis; Palle Bolvig, Perry Knudsen, Palle Mikkelborg, Benny Rosenfeld, Idrees Sulieman, Jens Winther (*t, flhn*); Jens Engel, Ture Larsen, Vincent Nilsson (*tb*); Ole Kurt Jensen (*btb*); Axel Windfeld (*tba, btb*); Niels Eje (*ob, eng hn*); Per Carsten, Bent Jaedig, Uffe Karskov, Flemming Madsen, Jesper Thilo (*reeds*); Thomas Clausen, Ole Koch-Hansen, Kenneth Knudsen (*ky*); John McLaughlin, Bjarne Rouypé (*g*); Lillian Tbernqvist (*hp*); Niels-Henning Ørsted-Pedersen, Bo Stief (*b*); Lennart Gruvstedt, Vince Wilburn (*d*); Marilyn Mazur, Ethan Weisgaard (*perc*); Eva Thaysen (*v*). 85.

Miles's first big-band record since the Gil Evans albums in the late 1950s. In 1984, he was awarded the prestigious Sonning Prize by the Danish government, an accolade normally accorded only to 'straight' composers. In recognition, and as a personal tribute to the influence of Miles's music, Palle Mikkelborg composed 'Aura' and persuaded the trumpeter to appear as soloist. CBS promptly sat on it for three years.

The piece, a suite of eight 'colour poems' with an introduction and a wonderful variation on 'Red', is built up out of a slightly bizarre 10-tone scale – stated by John McLaughlin in a brief 'Intro' – derived from the letters of Miles's name. This in turn yields a chord and a basic theme, which is then transformed by all the usual processes of serial composition, and by Miles's familiar alchemy.

Miles's inclusion clearly lent the music a considerable fillip and cachet, and Mikkelborg (a gifted trumpeter with a particular expertise in electronic shadings and transformations) might just as readily have taken the lead role himself. It is, though, marvellous to have Miles ranged against a large group again, and Mikkelborg's arrangements (particularly on 'Green', which is an explicit tribute) are clearly influenced by Gil Evans's grouping of instruments and interest in non-standard sonorities.

Miles's duet with NHØP on 'Green' is one of the finest moments on the record, spacious and delicately executed. He's almost as good on 'Orange', which makes explicit references to the *Bitches Brew* period, and on the two versions of 'Red' / 'Electric Red', where he tries out the theme a second time, muted, and moves outside the structure entirely to lay bright watercolour washes over the insistent riff. Mikkelborg's intention seems to have been to inscribe Davis and his music yet more firmly into the history of American music. The solitary musings of 'White' are repeated with Mikkelborg's carefully stacked horns on 'Yellow' (which also restates the M.I.L.E.S. D.A.V.I.S. row), drawing the trumpeter into the musical community that he helped to create. There are more-or-less explicit references to such touchstones as *Kind Of Blue* and *Sketches Of Spain*. There are also plenty of generic references: hints of bebop harmony, subtle modes and, on 'Blue', reggae. The closing 'Violet' is a blues, an idiom to which Miles returned more and more frequently in his last years. It's also, though, a tribute to two former Sonning winners, Igor Stravinsky and Olivier Messiaen (whose colour mysticism Mikkelborg adapts). In referring to them, and to Charles Ives on the pivotal 'Green', Mikkelborg also allows Miles to take his place in a broader musical continuum, not just in the condescending by-way that came to be known (though not by Miles) as 'jazz'.

Unique among his later records, *Aura* has an unexpected power to move.

***(*)   Mellow Miles Columbia 469440 2 CD

Davis; various personnels as above.

When Norman Mailer was asked if he thought he was getting mellower with age, he replied, 'Well, I guess I'm about as mellow as old camembert.' There's still a sharp whiff of risk and enterprise coming up off this outwardly bland, life-style packaging of late-night Davis hits, but it's unlikely in itself to send anyone hitherto unfamiliar with the trumpeter's work scuttling out for a copy of *Milestones* or *Agharta*. There is, needless to say, nothing from the latter included here, but it does kick off with 'Miles' (aka 'Milestones') and runs a reasonably predictable course from there: 'So What' and 'Freddie Freeloader' from *Kind Of Blue*, 'Summertime' and 'It Ain't Necessarily So' from *Porgy And Bess*, the title-tune of *Miles Ahead*, ''Round Midnight' and 'Bye Bye Blackbird' from *Round About Midnight*, 'Pfrancing' from *Someday My Prince Will Come* and, jumping a whole generation, 'Human Nature' and 'Time After Time' from the currently deleted *You're Under Arrest*. Reasonable value, but most true believers will still prefer their own mental compilation of 'Hostile Miles'.

***   **Dingo** Warner Brothers 7599 264382 CD
Davis; Chuck Findley, Oscar Brashear, Raymond Brown, George Graham (*t*); George
Bohannon, Thurman Green, Jimmy Cleveland, Lew McGreary, Dick Nash (*tb*); David
Duke, Marnie Johnson, Vince De Rosa, Richard Todd (*frhn*); Buddy Collette, Kenny
Garrett, Bill Green, Jackie Kelso, Marty Krystall, Charles Owens, John Stephens
(*reeds*); Kei Akagi, Michel Legrand, Alan Oldfield (*ky*); Mark Rivett (*g*); Foley,
Abraham Laboriel, Benny Rietveld (*b*); John Bigham, Harvey Mason, Alphonse
Mouzon, Ricky Wellman (*d, perc*). 91

Though Rolf De Heer's movie will undoubtedly draw a little extra resonance from the casting of
Miles as trumpeter/shaman 'Billy Cross', the music may again be a little more vital than the
images it was written to accompany, as with *Siesta*. Michel Legrand's scores and orchestrations
are predictably slick and rather empty, but there are some nice touches and a couple of sly
echoes (presumably intentional) to Miles's work for Louis Malle's *L'ascenseur pour l'échafaud*.
Lest anyone be alarmed at what has happened to Miles's lip on the opening 'Kimberley
Trumpet', solo duties are shared with Chuck Findley, in the role of 'Dingo Anderson'.
Attractive, but a slightly sad memorial of a dying man.

***   **Doo-Bop** Warner Brothers 7599 26938 2 CD
Davis; Easy Mo Bee, J. R., A. B. Money (*v*); other personnel not specified. 91.

His last bow. Perhaps inevitably, it isn't of earth-shaking significance but, equally predictably, it
finds Miles taking another ostensibly rejuvenating stylistic turn. Unfortunately, Easy Mo Bee's
doo-wop/rap stylings are so soft-centred and lyrically banal – 'Let's kick a verse for my man
called Miles / Seems to me his music's gonna be around for a long while / 'Cuz he's a
multi-talented and gifted musician / Who can play any position' – as to deny 'The Doo-Bop
Song', 'Blow' and the 'posthumous' 'Fantasy' any credibility. Miles brought in material
recorded in the late 1980s and known as the RubberBand session, and this final set might be
likened to the grab-bag approach of *Get Up With It*, though without its retrospective promise of
fresh fields to explore.

Miles plays well, sometimes with surprising aggression, but the backgrounds are uniformly
trite and the samples (from Kool & The Gang, James Brown, Donald Byrd's 'Street Lady',
Gene Ammons's 'Jungle Strut', among others) are unimaginatively used. As a curtain call, it's
a severe disappointment. Best, perhaps, to wait for an all-star big-band live set from Montreux,
recorded in the last summer of the trumpeter's life, but not yet released as we go to press.

NATHAN DAVIS (born 1937)
TENOR SAXOPHONE, SOPRANO SAXOPHONE

**   **London By Night** DIW 813 / 8019 CD/LP
Davis; Dusko Goykovich (*t, flhn*); Jean Toussaint, Stan Robinson (*ts*); Kenny Drew
(*p*); Jimmy Woode (*b*); Al Levitt (*d*). 8/87.

The same session yielded Dusko Goykovich's own *Celebration* (DIW 806 / 8016) and, again, it's
the quality of the largely Europe-based rhythm section that really makes the difference. The
two quartet performances – 'I Thought About You' and 'But Beautiful' – are relaxed and
free-swinging, with Drew's extended and almost unbarred right-hand lines rightly forward in the
mix. 'Shades', arranged for three saxophones and rhythm, is far less successful, but the quintet
tracks could almost be from an undiscovered Jazz Messengers tape. Goykovich's flugelhorn has
a fat, luxuriant quality that blends well with Davis, and there are fine, controlled solos all
round, notably on 'Dr Bu', where the Blakey/Messengers debt is most openly acknowledged.

RICHARD DAVIS (born 1930)
DOUBLE BASS

***(*)   **Persia My Dear** DIW 805 CD
Davis; Sir Roland Hanna (*p*); Frederick Waits (*d*). 8/87.

***(*)   **One For Frederick** Hep CD 2047 CD
      Davis; Cecil Bridgewater (*t*); Ricky Ford (*ts*); Sir Roland Hanna (*p*); Frederick Waits
      (*d*). 7/89.

Stravinsky's favourite bass player, Davis draws heavily on the example of fellow-Chicagoan
Wilbur Ware, bringing considerable rhythmic virtuosity and a tremendous range of pitches and
timbres to solo performances. Whatever the merits of his pizzicato work (and there are those
who find him much too mannered, relative to Ray Brown and Ron Carter), there is no one to
touch him as a soloist with the bow. His arco statements on 'Manhattan Safari', the opening
track of the excellent studio *Persia My Dear*, rather take the sting out of Hanna's funky lines,
but Hanna too shares an ability to mix dark-toned swing with a sort of classical propriety, as he
shows on three compositions.

On the later set, recorded live at Sweet Basil, bass and piano combine particularly well for
'Misako', a Monk-influenced Davis original which also appears on the excellent *Four Play*
(DIW 836 CD), with Clifford Jordan, James Williams, Ronnie Burrage and Davis. The same
influence is even more explicit on 'De Javu Monk', which offers probably the best
representation on record of Davis's unaccompanied style, all weird intervals and changes of
metre. As on the closing 'Strange Vibes' (a Horace Silver tune), Hanna comes in to balance the
bassist's tendency to abstraction. The Hep album is dedicated to drummer Waits, who died four
months after the recording. His introduction to 'City Bound' (and to the album) is very strong,
and he turns in a fine accelerated solo on 'Brownie Speaks', one of the stronger tracks on *Persia
My Dear*.

WILD BILL DAVIS (born 1918)
ORGAN, PIANO

(*)   **Impulsions Black & Blue 590372 CD
      Davis; Floyd Smith (*g*); Chris Columbo (*d*). 5/72.

Most of Davis's work on record has been with other leaders. He had twenty years of arranging
behind him when he began to attract serious attention as an organist, his most celebrated
association being the partnership with Johnny Hodges in the early 1960s. Though he made
several records as a sideman in Europe in the early '70s, this is the only one under his own
name. The 14 tracks take a solid, unadventurous course through swing and blues and are a
conservative variation on the more hard-hitting manner of organists of the Jimmy Smith school.
Floyd Smith is generously featured, along with the leader. The recording is clear, if a little
lacking in crispness.

WILD BILL DAVISON (1906–90)
CORNET

**   **Plays The Greatest Of The Greats** Dixieland Jubilee 508 LP
      Davison; Stan Wrightsman (*p*); George Van Eps (*g*); Morty Corb (*b*); Nick Fatool
      (*d*). 58.

***   **Wild Bill Davison** Storyville SLP 4005 LP
      Davison; Eddie Condon (*g*); Cutty Cutshall (*tb*); Peanuts Hucko (*cl*); Johnny Varro
      (*p*); John B. Williams (*b*); Buzzy Drootin; and with unknown musicians. 61, unknown.

Recorded towards the end of Davison's full-time stint under Condon – guest appearances
continued more or less until Condon's death in 1973 – this is an excellent representation of
Davison's tough, middle-register approach and armoury of aggressive effects. Less concerned
than Armstrong (he had the critical misfortune to be only six years younger than Satchmo) with
trying to clear top C, he spent much of his younger career buried under negative comparisons
which, however amply justified, ignored the fact that he was a very different player indeed.
Highlights of these 1961 sessions are a bouncy 'Muskrat Ramble' and an aching 'Blue And
Broken Hearted'. The unknown (but presumably later) sessions feature a glorious 'Sheikh Of
Araby'.

There is some interesting material on the earlier set – including a fine 'Embraceable You'
and 'Mood Indigo' – but, apart from Fatool, the band isn't up to much.

(*) **And Papa Bue Storyville SLP 250 LP
Davison; Arne Bue Jensen (*tb*); Jorgen Svare (*cl*); Bent Jedig (*ts*); Jorn Jensen (*p*);
Lars Blach (*g*); Jens Solund (*b*); Knud Ryskov Madsen (*d*). 2/74.

(*) **All-Stars Timeless TTD 545 CD/LP
Davison; Tom Saunders (*t, v*); Bill Allred (*tb*); Chuck Hedges (*cl*); Danny Moss (*ts*);
Johnny Varro (*p*); Isla Eckinger (*b*); Butch Miles (*d*); Banu Gibson (*v*). 10/86.

Born in Defiance, Ohio, Wild Bill Davison looks to have slung the town sign round his neck as a
badge of identity. In the 1970s, and well into his seventh decade, he went to live and work in
Scandinavia. The local talent was immediately responsive to his only slightly mellowing
approach and the sessions with Papa Bue are, if not vintage, well worth checking out.

With the *All Stars* album, Davison marks his arrival in the CD era. Like Armstrong, he had
suffered serious lip problems, allegedly caused by a blow from a Schlitz bottle (this is the only
known instance of an empty bottle touching Davison's lips). At eighty, and with an unforgiving
playback, his articulation isn't all it used to be (!), and the line-up and repertoire not entirely in
his usual line. His energy and raw humour are nevertheless undiminished. The singing is very
so-so indeed.

ELTON DEAN (born 1945)
ALTO SAXOPHONE, SAXELLO

***(*) **Duos** ED Tapes no number MC
Dean; Howard Riley, Keith Tippett (*p*); Mark Hewins (*g*); Marcio Mattos, Paul
Rogers (*b*). n.d.

*** **Trios** ED Tapes 02 MC
As above, with John Etheridge (*g*); Fred Thelonious Baker (*b*). n.d.

***(*) **EDQ Live** ED Tapes 03
Dean; Paul Dunmall (*ts*); Paul Rogers (*b*); Tony Levin (*d*). 8/89.

*** **Unlimited Saxophone Company** Ogun OGCD 002 CD
As above, with Trevor Watts (*as*); Simon Picard (*ts*); Paul Rogers (*b*); Tony Levin (*d*).
89.

The man – believe it or not – from whom Elton John borrowed his stage moniker, Dean is a
powerful free-jazz player who gets a Roland Kirk-like tone out of the curved saxello and
maintains an individual dialogue with tenor heavyweights like Coltrane, Pharoah Sanders and
Joe Henderson. Dean's Ninesense big band was one of the most exciting units of the desiccated
late '70s in Britain. In recent years, despite an enthusiastic following for his smaller groups, he
has been heard less often. He has also begun to release his music on a privately run tape-only
label (available from ED Tapes, 7 Farleigh Road, London N16 7TB), a lo-fi operation whose
unfussy production and packaging disguises some highly impressive music.

The duos (and *Trios* includes two more, with pianist Tippett) are consistently inventive and
exciting, underlining Dean's ability to communicate with other instrumentalists and still take
charge of the overall direction of the music. With Hewins he nudges great blocks of guitar
sound into shape, moving round each episode as if it were a physical object. With Riley, he
reacts to the pianist's complex figurings by throwing in occasional quotes to ' 'Round Midnight'
(incidentally suggested by one of Riley's patterns) and to the much-lamented British alto
saxophonist, Mike Osborne, no longer active in music. It's with Tippett and with Rogers (who
unfortunately doesn't reappear on the *Trios* session, where he is replaced by the unimpressive
Baker) that he sounds most at ease. The partnership with Tippett is long-established and almost
telepathic. Rogers, a member of Tippett's Mujician band, perhaps offers a greater challenge,
refusing to remain still and constantly varying the pace and intensity. *Trios* is more accessible
but also blander.

Paul Dunmall is also a Mujician member. On *EDQ Live* (a substantial stylistic shift from the
old Ogun live session of 1976, *They All Be On This Old Road*), he powers the music with
open-shouldered intensity, almost cutting Dean in the process. Drummer Levin sounds as if *he*
is trying to keep up and Rogers is uncharacteristically subdued. There are only two long tracks,
'The Duke' and 'The Haus', so called for the Jazzhaus club at the Duke of Wellington pub, but
there are hints of Ellington's small-group organization on both *Live* and the augmented

Unlimited Saxophone Company. Watts and Dean run no risk of cancelling one another out; they are very different players, and Dean's tight-sounding saxello broadens the timbral spectrum considerably. Picard is largely supernumerary, but Rogers and Levin are at their best on 'Small Strides' and 'One Three Nine'. Just because you won't find them on the High Street doesn't mean you shouldn't try them.

***(*)   **All The Tradition** Slam 201 CD
Dean; Howard Riley (*p*); Paul Rogers (*b*); Mark Sanders (*d*). 6/90.

This one may be even harder to find, but it's more than worth the effort. Co-led with pianist Riley, this uncovers Dean's often unacknowledged standards side. *They All Be On This Old Road* had included a wonderful long version of 'Naima'; the Coltrane of choice here is the yet more demanding 'Crescent', which sits comfortably enough alongside 'Darn That Dream', 'I Remember Clifford' and long free passages to confirm Dean's claims on 'the tradition'. He plays with complete authority and Riley (not normally associated with standards repertoire) approaches each number with untroubled assurance and a beautiful romantic touch.

JOHN D'EARTH
TRUMPET

(*)   **One Bright Glance Enja 6040 CD
D'Earth; John Abercrombie (*g*); Marc Johnson (*b*); Howard Curtis (*d*). 7/89.

D'Earth is a thoughtful trumpeter whose list of credits suggests a wide range of interests – Gunter Hampel, Emily Remler and Bob Moses are some of the leaders he's recorded with. This session has some pleasing moments, and the leader's lucid tone and agile phrasing mesh well with Abercrombie's more soft-edged lines. But the music lacks a deeper character: it slips unassumingly by.

SANTI DEBRIANO
BASS

**   **Soldiers Of Fortune** Freelance FRL-CD 012 CD
Debriano; John Furcell (*ts, bcl, f*); Kenny Werner (*ky*); Joe Locke (*vib*); Dave Fiuczynski (*g*); Ronnie Burrage (*d*). 7/89.

Debriano has been a solid sideman with Archie Shepp and Kirk Lightsey, among other leaders, but his own record is a busy yet uneventful affair. Purcell and Locke are given some solo space, but it's Fluczynski's fusion-orientated guitar which gets the lion's share of the attention, along with the leader, who seems unable to resist giving himself more space than he would merit under any other leader. The material is no more than serviceable.

DECEMBER JAZZ TRIO
GROUP

***   **The Street One Year After** Splasc(h) H 329-2 CD
Giorgio Occhipinti (*p*); Guiseppe Guarrella (*b*); Francesco Branciamore (*d*). 8/90.

***   **Concert For Ibla** Splasc(h) H 359-2 CD
As above, except add Pino Minafra (*t, flhn*). 1/91.

It's appropriate that the trio is democratically named, for this is genuine group music, a highly accomplished and detailed mixture of form and improvisation, touching on jazz and avant-garde elements alike. The key player is, in many ways, Branciamore, whose propulsive and momentous playing suggests an orchestral concept, and who never lets the music settle into random doodling. Occhipinti varies his contributions from locked-hands passages to long, meandering lines, but seldom seems at a loss for an idea, even over some very long tracks on both records; and Guarrella plays with unassuming virtuosity. Minafra's guest role on the live recording is sometimes a little remotely-recorded, and the overall sound on the studio disc is significantly superior, but both feature a great deal of interesting music.

BRIAN DEE
PIANO

**   **Homeing In** Spotlite SPJ539 CD/LP/MC
        Dee; Mario Castronari (*b*); Bobby Worth (*d*). 5/88-2/89.

A workmanlike set by a stalwart of the British mainstream, this isn't really strong enough to pass muster in an overcrowded genre. Dee's treatments of 'Little Rootie Tootie' or 'Daahoud' are solid and sincerely meant, but without anything more distinctive about it this hasn't the stature to compete with the countless piano trio records in the contemporary field. It's an impeccably recorded set, though.

JOEY DeFRANCESCO (born 1971)
ORGAN, PIANO, SYNTHESIZER, TRUMPET

(*)   **All Of Me Columbia CK 44463 CD/MC
        DeFrancesco; Houston Person (*ts*); Lou Volpe (*g*); Alex Blake (*b*); Buddy Williams
        (*d*); Bashuri Johnson (*perc*). 89.

***   **Where Were You?** Columbia CK 45443 CD/MC
        DeFrancesco; Wallace Roney, Virgil Jones, Spanky Davis, Victor Paz, Art Baron (*t,*
        flhn); Grover Mitchell, Warren Covington, Dick Griffin (*tb*); Garfield Fobbs (*btb*);
        Kirk Whalum (*ss, ts*); Jerome Richardson, Chuck Wilson (*as*); Illinois Jacquet,
        Patience Higgins, Bill Easley, Bob Ackerman (*ts*); Babe Clark (*bs*); Harvey Estrin,
        Billy Kerr, Phil Bodner, John Campo (*f, reeds*); Lou Volpe, John Scofield (*g*); Milt
        Hinton, Wilbur Bascomb (*b*); Eugene Jackson, Billy Hart, Denis Mackrel (*d*); Sammy
        Figueroa, Steve Thornton (*perc*). 90.

(*)   **Part III Columbia CK 47063 CD/MC
        DeFrancesco; J. R. 'Big Jim' Henry (*t*); Robert Landham (*as*); Glenn Guidone (*ts*);
        John DeFrancesco (*org*); Paul Bollenback (*g*); Byron 'Wookie' Landham (*d*); Ted
        Moore (*perc*). 91.

Organ players are a rarer breed than before, although the Hammond B-3 has made a surprise comeback in the age of synthesizers and samplers, and DeFrancesco might be the youngest of the new tribe. He plays respectable trumpet, too, and handles piano with equal facility, but it's his organ playing (he actually uses a modified C-3) which is his calling card. Barely into his twenties, he already has three major-label albums under his belt. These are enjoyable sessions that miss the substance which would make them anything more than that. Interestingly, DeFrancesco seems to have grasped the element of schmaltz which is a significant part of jazz organ playing: his versons of 'All Of Me' and 'Close To You' on the first record are as gratifyingly corny as the best (or worst, according to taste) of Jimmy Smith or Jack McDuff. Smith, inevitably, is the principal shaping force on DeFrancesco's playing, and 'Blues For J', the opening track on *All Of Me*, is a Smith tribute which is a ringer for the older man's work. Modish funk and pop touches on the first album betray the dead hand of 'crossover potential', though, and the superior second record, which is split between big-band charts, quartet pieces with Illinois Jacquet, Kirk Whalum or John Scofield, and a rousing two-tenor bout with 'Red Top', is the one to get if you want to hear what DeFrancesco can do. He's a dextrous player, can get up to speed in the space of a couple of bars, and swings as well as any of his older peers; but he lacks the kind of outside ambitions which make Barbara Dennerlein's work exciting, and none of these dates can stand beside her *Hot Stuff* or *Straight Ahead*. The third record suggests, indeed, that DeFrancesco is already stuck for a useful direction: though it features him on trumpet and in another variety of settings, with his father sitting in on the double-organ duel of 'Gut Bucket Blues', the prosaic back-ups and routine material are disheartening.

BUDDY DeFRANCO (born 1923)
CLARINET

****   **The Complete Verve Buddy DeFranco / Sonny Clark** Mosaic MR 117 CD/LP
DeFranco; Sonny Clark (*p*, *org*); Tal Farlow (*g*); Gene Wright (*b*); Bobby White (*d*).
4/54–8/55.

Nobody has seriously challenged DeFranco's status as the greatest post-swing clarinettist, although the instrument's desertion by reed players has tended to disenfranchise its few exponents. Only Benny Goodman and Artie Shaw matched DeFranco in terms of technical virtuosity: his incredibly smooth phrasing and seemingly effortless command are unfailingly impressive on all his records. But his taste for the challenge of translating this virtuosity into a relevant, post-bop environment has left his career on record somewhat unfulfilled.

His Verve albums with pianist Clark are among his finest achievements. The Mosaic boxed set collects the results of six sessions, mostly of standard material but with a few tantalizingly direct nods to bop, including an electrifying version of Parker's 'Now's The Time'. DeFranco's playing is a model of elegance and civilized debate with the chordal frameworks, yet the common charge of coldness and clinical expression falls before the unbroken stream of invention he displays at every tempo. It's telling that Clark, usually praised as a gutsy and soulful performer, sounds far less characterful than the leader. The recordings have been faithfully remastered to Mosaic's usual high standards in what is an indispensable set.

(*)   **Mr Lucky Pablo 2310-906 LP/MC
DeFranco; Albert Dailey (*p*); Joe Cohn (*g*); George Duvivier (*b*); Ronnie Bedford
(*d*). 82.

***   **Holiday For Swing** Contemporary 14047 CD/LP/MC
DeFranco; Terry Gibbs (*vib*); John Campbell (*p*); Todd Coolman (*b*); Gerry Gibbs
(*d*). 8/88.

DeFranco recorded little in the 1960s and '70s, while teaching and bandleading, but he has made something of a comeback in recent years. The Pablo album shows all his facility is still present, but the session is too workmanlike and never catches fire. His association with the exuberant Terry Gibbs, though, has given him a better focus and, although there are better things listed under Gibbs's own name, *Holiday For Swing* bounces through a well-chosen programme where the clarinettist creates some febrile improvisations.

JACK DeJOHNETTE (born 1942)
DRUMS, PIANO, KEYBOARDS, MELODICA

***   **New Directions** ECM 1128 CD/LP

***(*)   **New Directions In Europe** ECM 1157 CD/LP
DeJohnette; Lester Bowie (*t*); John Abercrombie (*g*, *mand g*); Eddie Gomez (*b*). 6/78,
6/79.

In Europe is perhaps DeJohnette's finest album, and there may be a message in the live provenance. DeJohnette never seems to play his own material with this amount of conviction in the studio and there's a noticeable contrast in the basic dynamic of the two albums. The thinnish air of Willisau hasn't cut his wind or Bowie's, though Abercrombie sounds a little cyanosed and plays a relatively modest background role, reserving his energy for the final, group-devised 'Multo Spiliagio', where he stutters out a nervous cross-beat to DeJohnette's hissing cymbals and free-ish tom-tom accents; his solos are caught a lot more cleanly in the studio. DeJohnette opens the long and very beautiful 'Bayou Fever' on piano, building up the temperature much more effectively than on the original version.

***   **Special Edition** ECM 1152 CD/LP
DeJohnette; David Murray (*ts*, *bcl*); Arthur Blythe (*as*); Peter Warren (*b*, *clo*). 3/79.

(*)   **Inflation Blues ECM 1244 LP
DeJohnette; Baikida Carroll (*t*); John Purcell (*picc*, *af*, *acl*, *cl*, *bcl*, *as*, *bs*); Chico
Freeman (*ss*, *ts*, *bcl*); Rufus Reid (*b*). 9/82.

***   **Tin Can Alley** ECM 1189 LP
DeJohnette; Chico Freeman (*ts, f, bcl*); John Purcell (*as, bs, f*); Peter Warren (*b, clo*).

***   **Album Album** ECM 1280 CD/LP
DeJohnette; David Murray (*ts*); John Purcell (*as, ss*); Howard Johnson (*tba*); Rufus Reid (*b*). 6/84.

(*)   **Audio Visualscapes Impulse MCA 8029 CD/LP/MC

****   **Earth Walk** Blue Note CDP 7 96690 CD
DeJohnette; Gary Thomas (*ts, f, bcl*); Greg Osby (*as, ss*); Michael Cain (*p, electric p, syn on Earth Walk only*); Mick Goodrick (*g on Audio Visualscapes only*); Lonnie Plaxico (*b*); Joan Henry (*animal noises on Earth Walk*). 2/88, 6/91.

After 1979 and ECM 1152, Special Edition became DeJohnette's name for a series of markedly different working bands, united by his growing interest in quite extreme instrumental sonorities – tuba, bass clarinet, baritone saxophone – and by quite complex charts. The original *Special Edition* featured some of Arthur Blythe's last decent playing before his mysterious decline; the opening tribute, 'One For Eric' (which can also be found on the *Works* compilation (ECM 825427)) foregrounds Murray's surprisingly Dolphyish bass clarinet.

John Purcell's multi-instrumentalism, kept in check on the two later recordings, works well in the context of the more experimental and less achieved *Inflation Blues*, softening Carroll's rather acidulous attack and complementing Chico Freeman's linear approach. One of the least known of DeJohnette's albums, *Tin Can Alley* is certainly one of the very best, with Freeman's increasingly rock-and funk-coloured approach balancing Purcell's rather more abstract styling and Warren's imaginative, off-line patterns and rich timbre. DeJohnette's solo spot – a peril of drummer-led albums – is the vivid 'Gri Gri Man'.

The band featured on *Audio Visualscapes* is probably the most road-hardened DeJohnette has been able to take into the studio (with *New Directions* it worked the other way round). If anything, it's the material that is at fault. Greg Osby's M-Base approach to composition doesn't suit DeJohnette's more complex multi-dimensional style. There is a long, perhaps overlong, reading of Ornette's 'The Sphinx' and a re-run of 'One For Eric' that adds nothing to the original recording. The closing title-track (a skimpy fourth side on the audiophile LP format) is a mish-mash.

It's difficult to judge whether *Earth Walk* has benefited most from the move to Blue Note or simply from the additional couple of years that this version of Special Edition has had together. The band sounds tighter and the soloing more confidently grounded; the production, by DeJohnette himself, is impeccable. Having handed over keyboard duties to the solidly imaginative Michael Cain, DeJohnette concentrates on some of the best drumming of his recording career, and certainly the best on any album under his own name. His figuring on 'Where Or Wayne' and the long title-track has an almost algebraic precision; throughout the album he alternates a powerful, straightforward count with hiddens and unknowns. DeJohnette is credited with all nine full-length compositions (there is a brief coda) and seems to have better assimilated the funk and rap influences that pervaded *Audio Visualscapes*. 'Earth Walk', with its slightly stale *Zebra*-droppings (see below; animal sounds really are a bit hackneyed), is over-long and a shade repetitive at 13 minutes but, with four of the tracks nearing or topping 10 minutes, there are remarkably few compositional longueurs. DeJohnette has emerged as a rounded and successful performer/composer/leader.

**   **Pictures** ECM 1079 LP
DeJohnette; John Abercrombie (*g*). 2/76.

Attractive, but strictly minor. Abercrombie's guitar playing has rarely seemed so inconsequential, and there's little interest in the material.

(*)   **The Piano Album Landmark LLP 1504 CD/LP/MC
DeJohnette; Eddie Gomez (*b*); Freddie Waits (*d*). 1/85.

Not as dreadful as it sounds (and DeJohnette has an unhappy propensity for naff or just plain diffident album-titles), this more or less confirms DeJohnette's entitlement to equal consideration as a keyboard player. Two versions – trio and solo – of 'Quiet Now' demonstrate his remarkable intuitions about musical space. Surprisingly or not, his keyboard attack is anything but 'percussive'. In style, it comes from somewhere in the basically lyrical territory marked out by Bill Evans, Keith Jarrett and (another ECM polymath) Ralph Towner. Well worth checking out, though it will be harder to find than the ECMs.

*(*)   **Parallel Realities** MCAD 42313 CD
DeJohnette; Pat Metheny (*g, synclavier*); Herbie Hancock (*p, ky*).

This one really doesn't work at all, though it's bound to sustain a better-than-deserved sale index because of Metheny. His presence lifted Ornette Coleman's *Song X* firmly into the cross-over market. DeJohnette also worked on that session and deserves more credit for the album's almost dangerously accelerated pulse than the ludicrously overrated Denardo Coleman.

The problem with parallel realities is that it's rather difficult to communicate between them. Where *Song X* succeeded on happy chance and a basic agreement to differ, there is too much compromise here. Hancock prowls a twilight zone and DeJohnette's keyboard bass is horribly stiff. Too much artifice, and not enough music.

*(*)   **The DeJohnette Complex** Original Jazz Classics OJC 617 CD/LP/MC
DeJohnette; Bennie Maupin (*ts, f*); Stanley Cowell (*electric p*); Eddie Gomez, Miroslav Vitous (*b*); Roy Haynes (*d*). 12/68.

Playing with Charles Lloyd had thrown DeJohnette very suddenly into the spotlight. Recording under his own name a month after his first studio shift with Miles Davis, DeJohnette still sounds a bit up in the air. His melodica is rather too heavily featured and has an uneasy, slightly ersatz tone. The second day's music-making – minus Haynes – put DeJohnette back on the drum stool, where he sounds considerably more together and offers intriguing hints of the work that was to come. Otherwise rather forgettable.

(*)   **Zebra Pan PMC 1104 CD
DeJohnette; Lester Bowie (*t*). 5/85.

DeJohnette's intelligent synth patterns make an effective incidental soundtrack to Tadayuki Naito's video. The music catches light on its own terms only on the opening closing 'Ntoro I/II', when Lester Bowie's high, swaying horn-cries lift the dynamic a shade. Not usually a techno-freak, DeJohnette seems curiously complacent with the Siel DK 600's plodding percussion tracks; a little live percussion would have made all the difference. Not really a jazz album at all, but well worth having for some striking atmospheric music.

***   **Works** ECM 825427 CD/LP
DeJohnette with various line-ups. 1975–80.

'Gri Gri Man' and the long, piano-led 'Bayou Fever' from ECM 1157 highlight this intelligently representative cull of DeJohnette's decade and a half with the label. A more than worthy sampling from a slightly undifferentiated output, and an excellent point of entry for anyone who doesn't know the original discs.

RICCARDO DEL FRÀ
BASS

**   **A Sip Of Your Touch** IDA 021 LP/CD
Del Frà; Art Farmer (*flhn*); Dave Liebman (*ss*); Enrico Pieranunzi, Michel Graillier (*p*); Rachel Gould (*v*). 89.

The description that springs to mind here is 'spare' – but then a series of duets between a bassist and various other instrumentalists couldn't be much else. Del Frà is a good listener and a sympathetic partner and, aside from the title-piece (a straightforward bass solo), he takes only a small space for himself. So the qualities in the pieces depend very much on his collaborators, and they're rather mixed: Liebman's spiky dialogue is the most rewarding, but Gould and Pieranunzi and Farmer don't seem interested in bringing very much to the occasion. Insubstantial.

BARBARA DENNERLEIN (born 1964)
ORGAN, KEYBOARDS

***   **Orgelspiele** Bebab 003 CD/LP
Dennerlein; Jorg Widmoser (*vn*); Peter Wolpl (*g*); Harald Ruschenbaum (*d*). 5/84.

***   **Bebab** Bebab 250964 CD/LP
Dennerlein; Hermann Breuer (*tb*); Allan Praskin (*as*); Jurgen Seefelder (*ts*); Joe Nay
(*d*). 7/85.

(*)   **Plays Classics Redken BD 1188 CD/LP
Dennerlein; Christophe Widmoser (*g*); Andreas Witte (*d*). 11/88.

**   **'Live' On Tour!** Bebab 250965 CD/LP
Dennerlein; Oscar Klein (*t, cl, g*); Charly Antolini (*d*). 1/89.

Her first four releases marked Dennerlein out as a compelling, surprising performer. It's rare
enough to find anyone taking up the organ as their main keyboard – and she doesn't even sound
like any of the acknowledged masters of the Hammond – but her interest in different settings is
just as unusual. *Orgelspiele* has its novelty elements, including rather kitschy versions of
Chopin's Prelude No. 4 and Bach's 'Jesu, Joy Of Man's Desiring', but the unusually thoughtful
reading of Chick Corea's 'Spain' is intriguing, and Wolpl and Widmoser have plenty of their
own to say. *Bebab* offers more conventional organ-band hard bop, chirpily performed with
infectious enthusiasm, but *Plays Classics* is a little more constricted, with Witte's stiff rhythms
tying the trio down; even so, Dennerlein piles into material like 'How High The Moon' and
'Take The "A" Train'. The live session with Klein and Antolini, two veterans of the German
scene, is a rather queer meeting, since Dennerlein's bristling energy on the likes of 'Au Privave'
sounds in a different world from that of her companions' more mainstream thinking.

***(*)   **Straight Ahead!** Enja 5077 CD/LP
Dennerlein; Ray Anderson (*tb*); Mitch Watkins (*g*); Ronnie Burrage (*d*). 7/88.

***(*)   **Hot Stuff** Enja 6050 CD
Dennerlein; Andy Sheppard (*ts*); Mitch Watkins (*g*); Mark Mondesir (*d*). 6/90.

Straight Ahead! belies its title with some unexpectedly adventurous music: the blues accounts
for three of the compositions, but they're blues blown open by Anderson's yawning trombone
expressionism, Watkins's post-modernist funk and Burrage's wide range of rhythms. Dennerlein
sounds happiest on the uptempo numbers, such as the heroically delivered title-piece, but her
use of organ colour maximizes the potential of a cumbrous instrument.

   Hot Stuff is in some ways more conventional, with Sheppard a less wayward spirit than
Anderson, but the band cooks harder than before and the compositions – especially 'Wow!',
'Birthday Blues' and 'Polar Lights' – take organ-band clichés and turn them on their head.
Mondesir's excitable drumming adds to the intensity.

PHILIPPE DESCHEPPER (born 1949)
GUITAR

(*)   **Sad Novi Sad IDA 008 CD
Deschepper; Martin Fredebeul (*ss*); Michel Godard (*tba*); Gérard Marais (*g*); Steve
Swallow, Jean-Luc Ponthieux, Henri Texier (*b*); Jacques Mahieux (*d, v*). 4/86.

The intense interest in the guitar as a renewed jazz instrument centres broadly on two
directions: the destructive, post-rock attack of players such as Sonny Sharrock and Caspar
Brötzmann, and the modified classicism of Pat Metheny and John Scofield. Deschepper clearly
comes from the latter area, and his combination of a clean, open tone with lots of sustain and an
underlying regard for blues and rock licks is certainly very like Scofield's. This is an intelligently
paced and varied album, with the central trio of the leader, Swallow and Mahieux embellished
by various guests. The two versions of 'Wildrose Avenue' explore the quick fingering and
lyrical twists in Deschepper's playing, while the terser 'Little Nemo' pits him against
Fredebeul's soprano to quietly exciting effect. It's not a distinctive record, but it's hard not to
enjoy the calibre of the playing by all involved.

***   **Impossible Trio** Thelonious THE 0101 CD
      Deschepper; Michel Godard (*tba, serpent*); Youval Micenmacher (*perc*). 3–11/90.

Not quite impossible, but this is certainly an idiosyncratic line-up. Micenmacher plays sparse percussive lines and Deschepper works through his full range of pedals and effects; but the interesting man here is Godard, whose use of tuba is as melodically warm and sensitive as Bob Stewart's: he creates moving laments against the textural finesse of the others. Well worth seeking out.

PAUL DESMOND (1924–77)
ALTO SAXOPHONE

**   **Featuring Don Elliott** Original Jazz Classics OJC 119 LP/MC
      Desmond; Don Elliott (*t, mellophone*); Norman Bates (*b*); Joe Dodge (*d*). 2/56.

***   **East Of The Sun** Discovery 840 LP
      Desmond; Jim Hall (*g*); Percy Heath (*b*); Connie Kay (*d*). 9/59.

(*)   **Pure Desmond CTI EPC 450572 CD
      Desmond; Ed Bickert (*g*); Ron Carter (*b*); Connie Kay (*d*). 7/74.

***(*)   **Polka Dots And Moonbeams** Bluebird ND 90637 CD
      Desmond; Jim Hall (*g*); Eugene Cherico, Percy Heath, Eugene Wright (*b*); Connie Kay (*d*). 63–64.

It's still fashionable among the more categorical sort of jazz enthusiast to anathematize anything committed to record by Dave Brubeck *unless* it also features Paul Desmond. In addition to downplaying Brubeck's considerable significance, this rather overplays Desmond's occasionally self-conscious style and rather begs the question why most of his better performances tended to be with Brubeck in any case.

    Desmond's own-name outings were, by verbal agreement with Brubeck, always made without piano. There are hints on both *East Of The Sun* and the earlier sessions with Don Elliott of Gerry Mulligan's pianoless quartets. There was also the added plus of Jim Hall, who perfectly fitted Desmond's legato approach and interest in top harmonics (an approach that improbably influenced Anthony Braxton). Bickert is, almost needless to say, no match for Hall, but the later album has a warmth and regained confidence that recalls Desmond's finest performances. New listeners certainly shouldn't pass *East Of The Sun*. The Bluebird compilation was formerly available as *Easy Living*, but has been reissued shorn of four tracks, but fully remastered and it, too, makes a fine introduction to Desmond's limpid work.

LAURENT DE WILDE
PIANO

***   **Off The Boat** IDA 015 LP/CD
      De Wilde; Eddie Henderson (*t, flhn*); Ralph Moore (*ss, ts*); Ira Coleman (*b*); Billy Hart (*d*). 87.

**   **Odd And Blue** IDA 023 LP/CD
      De Wilde; Ira Coleman (*b*); Jack DeJohnette (*d*). 89.

On his own, or at least with the support of just Coleman and DeJohnette, this technically dazzling pianist sounds gifted but dull: he makes themes by Shorter and Monk into conservatory exercises, and his own tunes have little to say. The album with horns is much better, though, due in no small measure to Moore's incantatory power even on contained solos and straightforward themes. Henderson is less sure of himself, but De Wilde, Coleman and Hart spur the group on with full-flushing power. The playing time is rather short at some 38 minutes.

GARRY DIAL
KEYBOARDS

(*)   **Dial And Oatts DMP 465 CD
          Dial; Dick Oatts (*ss, as, ts, f*); Jay Anderson (*b*); Joey Baron (*d*); string orchestra.
          9–10/88.

Dial and Oatts have recorded together in the smart neo-bop band led by Red Rodney and recorded by Steeplechase. This project uses a few bop licks in passing, but it's a rather different matter overall: Dial's writing for strings ties the 14 tracks together into a kind of suite, with Oatts cast as a concerto-like lead voice and the rhythm section, somewhat peculiarly, behaving as if the orchestra weren't there (which they presumably weren't when the record was made). The result is a not disagreeable blend of mood music and modern bop, though it's hardly a significant fusion. Glossy digital sound that's characteristic of DMP.

FURIO DI CASTRI
BASS, PIANO

**   **Solo** Splasch HP 04 LP
          Di Castri; E. Ruffinengo (*ky*). 4/87.

Di Castri is primarily a bassist, and a very acomplished one; but here he takes a solo turn (Ruffinengo adds electric embellishment to a couple of tracks) on piano. There's some sensitive and mildly engaging playing, but this scarcely counts as anything more than an indulgence.

***   **What Colour For A Tale** Splasch H 351-2 CD
          Di Castri; Stefano Cantini (*ss, perc*); Ramberto Ciammarughi (*ky*); Manhu Roche (*d*).
          4/91.

A far superior record. Across a very long, 15-track programme, Di Castri displays a fine ear for nuance and interplay in a quartet that features the most delicate electronic additions from the mainly acoustic Ciammarughi and pert, fiery soprano from Cantini. One standard, Jimmy Van Heusen's 'Nancy', turns up in the middle, but otherwise the tunes are mostly penned by the leader. Beautifully recorded.

VIC DICKENSON (1906–84)
TROMBONE

***   **Just Friends** Sackville 2015 LP
          Dickenson; Red Richards (*p, v*); John Williams (*b*). 10/81–3/85.

He seldom recorded as a leader, and this solitary date from almost the end of his life is a charming reminder of his music and a valuable example of the unencumbered Dickenson, playing a typically offbeat set of tunes – including 'Once And Only Once', 'Bye Bye Pretty Baby' and 'Me And My Shadow' – with helpful and unobtrusive support from bass and piano. Though less agile than of yore, the trombonist had lost none of his wit and knack for the unexpected continuation, even in his mid-seventies. He also takes a couple of vocals. Two tunes were recorded by Richards and Williams after Dickenson's death.

WALT DICKERSON (born 1931)
VIBRAPHONE

***   **Peace** Steeplechase SCS 1042 LP
          Dickerson; Lisle Atkinson (*b*); Andrew Cyrille (*d*).

(*)   **Serendipity Steeplechase SCS 1070 LP
          Dickerson; Rudy McDaniels (*b*); Edgar Bateman (*d*). 8/76.

**   **To My Queen Revisited** Steeplechase SCS 1112 CD/LP
          Dickerson; Albert Dailey (*p*); Andy McKee (*b*); Jimmy Johnson (*d*). 7/78.

(*)   **To My Son Steeplechase SCS 1130 LP
As above, except omit Dailey. 9/78.

Despite a recent revival of enthusiasm for his vividly original vibes approach, Walt Dickerson has never enjoyed the kind of critical praise heaped on Bobby Hutcherson's head. While Hutcherson is unquestionably the more innovative player, with a direction that diverges sharply from the orthodoxy laid down in the late 1940s and early '50s by Milt Jackson, Dickerson is arguably the more interesting player, with a style that combines something of Jackson's piano-based approach with Lionel Hampton's exuberantly percussive sound. Never an easy sideman, Dickerson's quite well represented as a leader, and much of his best work is again available.

Though the earliest, *Peace* is probably the best of this group, lifted into a new dimension altogether by Cyrille's brilliantly contained drumming; Cyrille was joined by bassist Sirone on the fine *Life Rays* [Soul Note SN 1028], which has sadly disappeared from the catalogue. Though *Serendipity* repeats what was to be Dickerson's favoured formula of extended trio improvisations on (mostly) original themes, it lacks both the power and the control of the earlier record. The addition of Albert Dailey, a pianist of severely limited conceptual range, to another successful trio was a tactical error. Vibes and piano are apt to cancel each other out; when they don't on *To My Queen Revisited*, they merely sound mismatched. *To My Son* is more satisfactory and Dickerson sounds more confident, but one feels a need for a more forcefully voiced instrument.

***   **Divine Gemini** Steeplechase SCS 1089 CD/LP
Dickerson; Richard Davis. 2/77.

***   **Tenderness** Steeplechase SCS 1213 LP
As above.

***   **Landscape With Open Door** Steeplechase SCS 1115 LP
Dickerson; Pierre Dørge (*g, perc*). 8/78.

(*)   **Visions Steeplechase SCS 1126 CD/LP
Dickerson; Sun Ra (*p*). 7/78.

(*)   **I Hear You John Steeplechase SCS 1146 LP
Dickerson; Jimmy Johnson (*d*). 10/78.

The duo was probably Dickerson's ideal performing context. A busy player, he nevertheless revelled in space (and not always the kind of space that a collaboration with Sun Ra implies). For all its cosmic subtexts, *Visions* is remarkably restrained, with Ra playing some of his most intimate and earthbound piano. Once considered a minor classic (and certainly Dickerson's most playlisted recording), it has lost a lot of its original sheen. By contrast, the sets with Johnson and Dørge have both gained in impact. The guitarist is an awkward player to categorize but produces a lovely tone which chimes perfectly with the cleaner vibes lines the context seems to impose; Dickerson also weathers the shorter format very well, compressing his ideas into a tighter compass with no sign of strain. By contrast, *I Hear You John* is flabby and rather prosaic, but it is perhaps Dickerson's most deeply felt recording, and, if the instrumental line-up sounds unpromising, it actually succeeds very well.

Richard Davis is a well-practised duo improviser – most notably with Eric Dolphy – and he falls in at once with Dickerson's conception, giving the tracks a rich, almost symphonic depth of tone and breadth of development. Along with *Peace*, these are the Dickerson albums that should prevail. For the moment, though, he remains a rather 'outside' presence.

DIRTY DOZEN BRASS BAND
GROUP

***   **My Feet Can't Fail Me Now** Concord 3005 CD/LP/MC
Gregory Davis, Efrem Towns (*t*); Charles Joseph (*tb*); Roger Lewis (*ss, bs*); Kevin Harris (*ts*); Kirk Joseph (*tba*); Jenell Marshall, Benny Jones (*d*). 84.

***   **Live: Mardi Gras In Montreux** Rounder RR 2052 CD/LP
As above, except Lionel Batiste (*d*) replaces Jones. 7/85.

Positioned between novelty group, authentic revivalists and neoconservative brass masters, this New Orleans ensemble make exciting and funny and clever records without finally convincing the listener that they're delivering as much as they seem to promise. The playing is too slick to approximate the unaffected character of the great New Orleans bands of the past, but the individual players don't suggest that they have anything important to say away from the voicings and the spirited beats and bass lines of the arrangements. Their first two albums, both recorded live, are surely the best ones to get, because this isn't a music – or at least a band – that was meant to 'develop' itself very far. Each disc captures much of the fun which their concerts provide.

(*)   **Voodoo CBS CK 45042 CD/MC
As above, plus Dizzy Gillespie (*t, v*); Branford Marsalis (*ts*); Dr John (*p, v*). 8–9/87.

The addition of three guest stars, plus the muscle of a major-label contract, actually do little to suggest that the DDBB is anything more than an engaging distraction. They cover Charlie Parker and Stevie Wonder here, but it seems merely cute, not a revision of the tradition. Excellent and suitably brassy recording, however.

***   **The New Orleans Album** Columbia CK 45414 CD/MC
As above, except omit Gillespie, Marsalis and John, add Eddie Bo (*p*), Elvis Costello (*v*). 12/89.

***   **Open Up (Whatcha Gonna Do For The Rest Of Your Life?)** Columbia 468365 CD/MC
As above, except add Raymond Webber (*d*). 1–4/91.

The New Orleans set finally goes the full way and has the band paying a specific homage – not to old New Orleans, though, so much as to the rhythm-and-blues of the city in the post-war period. Guest spots by Bo and Costello enliven things: this is still a good partyband, and though their records will always be secondary to their live efforts, the sheer wallop of 'The Monkey' makes an excellent case for them.

Open Up opens them up to procedural music: Raymond Webber's 'conventional' drum parts anchor the rolling rhythms of the band to a steadier beat, and there's some tension between the parping eccentricities of the solo horns and the straighter beats below. It's not especially better or worse than any earlier DDBB session, though.

BILL DIXON (born 1925)
TRUMPET, FLUGELHORN, PIANO

*(*)   **Thoughts** Soul Note SN 1111 CD
Dixon; Marco Eneidl (*as*); John Buckingham (*tba*); Peter Kowald, William Parker, Mario Pavone (*b*); Laurence Cook (*d*). 5/85.

***   **Son Of Sisyphus** Soul Note 121138 CD/LP/MC
As above, except omit Eneidl, Kowald and Parker. 6/88.

Disappointingly, Soul Note's valuable documentation of one of the more thoughtful figures in contemporary jazz is now rather thin. Still best known for his work with Cecil Taylor – notably on *Conquistador* – Dixon's own work languished in a backwater in the later 1970s and '80s. Pavone and Cook survive from the excellent *November 1981* [Soul Note SN 1037/8], but *Thoughts* lacks its impact and drifts off into inconsequential and even slightly pretentious ramblings (for which, see 'For Nelson And Winnie: A Suite In Four Parts'!).

Son Of Sisyphus is superior in almost every regard. It opens with a brooding duo for bass and Dixon on piano. 'Silences For Jack Moore' is a threnody for a dancer friend, cast in the bass tones Dixon favours. The sonorities are even darker on the long title-track, where Buckingham's tuba fills the role accorded a trio of string bassists on *Thoughts*, but the overriding impression is of tremendous space and movement, and there's a sense in which Dixon's melancholically graceful soloing conforms to Cecil Taylor's much-quoted assertion concerning his own work: that it imitates the leaps that a dancer makes in space. A much underrated soloist who developed late and more or less bypassed the bebop generation, Dixon is capable of extraordinary beauty and, on 'Vecctor', some exuberance.

'Son Of Sisyphus' relates to an earlier, large-scale composition. Behind almost all of Dixon's small-group performances there is a sort of dark, inner pressure, like the imprint of a much larger conception that has been denied expression. For much of his long career, that was Dixon's unfortunate fate. He is one of the most significant figures in contemporary jazz and *Son Of Sisyphus*, beautifully recorded and packaged with examples of Dixon's painting on front and back covers (CD/LP), is an ideal introduction that should send at least some listeners hurrying to the second-hand bins to catch up on earlier material.

JOHNNY DODDS (1892–1940)
CLARINET, ALTO SAXOPHONE

***(*)** **Johnny Dodds, 1926–40: Part One** Affinity CD AFS 1023 3CD
Dodds; Louis Armstrong, Natty Dominique, Freddie Keppard, George Mitchell, King Oliver, Bob Shoffner (*c*); Eddie Ellis, Kid Ory, Roy Palmer, Eddie Vincent (*tb*); Junie Cobb (*cl*); Stump Evans, Barney Bigard (*cl, ss, ts*); Darnell Howard (*cl, as*); Joe Clark (*as*); Lockwood Lewis (*as, v*); Lil Hardin Armstrong, Lovie Austin, Jimmy Blythe, Arthur Campbell, Earl Hines, Jelly Roll Morton, Tiny Parham, Luis Russell (*p*); Curtis Hayes, Bud Scott, Cal Smith, Freddy Smith, Eustern Woodfork (*bj*); Johnny St Cyr (*bj, v*); Clifford Hayes (*vn*); Bert Cobb (*tba*); Baby Dodds (*d, wbd*); W. E. Burton (*wbd*); Henry Clifford (*jug*); Earl McDonald (*jug, v*); Paul Barbarin (*d*); Jimmy Bertrand, Jasper Taylor (*perc*); Edmonia Henderson, Papa Charlie Jackson, Teddy Peters, Trixie Smith (*v*); others unknown. 26–28.

**** **The Chronological Johnny Dodds, 1926** Classics 589 CD
Dodds; Freddie Keppard, George Mitchell (*c*); Kid Ory, Eddie Vincent (*tb*); Junie Cobb (*cl*); Joe Clark (*as*); Lockwood Lewis (*as, v*); Lil Hardin Armstrong, Jimmy Blythe, Arthur Campbell, Tiny Parham (*p*); Curtis Hayes, Cal Smith, Freddy Smith (*bj*); Eustern Woodfork, Johnny St Cyr (*bj, v*); Clifford Hayes (*vn*); W. E. Burton (*wbd, v*); Earl McDonald (*jug, v*); Jimmy Bertrand, Jasper Taylor (*d, perc*); Papa Charlie Jackson, Trixie Smith (*v*). 5, 7, 8, 9, 10 & 12/26.

**** **The Chronological Johnny Dodds, 1927** Classics 603 CD
Dodds; Freddy Keppard (*c*); Eddie Ellis (*tb*); Lil Hardin Armstrong, Jimmy Blythe, Tiny Parham (*p*); Jasper Taylor (*d*); Warren Baby Dodds (*wbd*). 1, 3, 3, 8 & 10/27.

**** **The Chronological Johnny Dodds, 1927–8** Classics 617 CD
Dodds; Natty Dominique, George Mitchell (*c*); R. Q. Dickerson (*t*); Honore Dautrey, Kid Ory, John Thomas (*tb*); Charlie Alexander, Jimmy Blythe (*p*); Bud Scott (*bj*); Bill Johnson (*b*); Warren Baby Dodds (*d*); W. E. Burton (*wbd, v*); Julia Davis (*v*). 10 & 12/27, 3, 6 & 7/28.

Johnny Dodds was the model professional musician. He rehearsed his men, frowned on alcohol and drugs, and watched the cents. In 1922 he was a member of King Oliver's Creole Jazz Band at Lincoln's Garden in Chicago, a band that included Louis Armstrong, Lil Hardin Armstrong, trombonist Honore Dautrey, and Dodd's wayward younger brother, Warren Baby Dodds. The clarinettist left in 1924, after a quarrel about money, and set out on a highly successful recording career of his own that faltered only with the beginnings of the swing boom. Dodds died in 1940 and was promptly canonized by the revivalists.

His tone was intense and sometimes fierce, rather removed from the soft introspections of Jimmie Noone or George Lewis's folksy wobble. Like Jimmy Giuffre two generations later, Dodds favoured the lower – *chalumeau* – register of the instrument in preference to the piercing *coloratura*. He doubles briefly on alto saxophone on July 1926 cuts (CD2 above) with Jimmy Blythe. The switch may have been an attempt to get some change out of Paramount's insensitive microphones for, unlike Sidney Bechet, Dodds never seriously considered a full turn to the saxophones.

Though much of his best work was with Louis Armstrong's Hot Five and Seven (*q. v.*), the Affinity and Classics compilations are (or will be when the former is complete) the essential Dodds documents. They contain work for Brunswick, Columbia, Gennet, the ropey Paramount, Victor and Vocalion. The three earliest tracks on Affinity (not included on *Chronological*) are dismal vocal pieces, with Dodds accompanying manfully. The real classics are the cuts made for Columbia with the New Orleans Wanderers/Bootblacks, a line-up that included George

Mitchell, Kid Ory, Joe Clark, Johnny St Cyr and Lil Hardin Armstrong. There are fine clarinet duets with Junie Cobb (and without brass) from 26 August which have been rather overlooked in the rush of enthusiasm for the Wanderers/Bootblacks performances of the previous month.

Inevitably, very little matches up to these classics, but Dodds's reconciliation with King Oliver in September for a single track ('Someday Sweetheart'; not on *Chronological*) underlines the great might-have-been of their interrupted association. Dodds by this time was making too much regular money in Burt Kelly's Stables, a South Side club much frequented by Italian businessmen (if you follow), to pursue or accept a longer recruitment. A pity, because there's a definite falling-off after 1926. The duets with Tiny Parham are interesting, and there are excellent things on the Vocalion trios of April 1927; too many pick-up bands, though, and on a lot of the material Dodds is overpowered by other voices, notably Louis Armstrong (in for a Black Bottom Stompers session that also included Barney Bigard and Earl Hines) and Jelly Roll Morton. The Classics format omits the two Morton tracks but does reinstate a number, 'Cootie Stomp', from the State Street Ramblers session of August 1927 and includes a rare June 1928 session with the vocalist Julia Davis (allegedly half her entire recorded output) and trumpeter R. Q. Dickerson.

The 1927–8 *Chronological* does, though, include some of the material excerpted on *Blue Clarinet Stomp*, below, omitting an alternative take of the title-track. This is a no-nonsense feature of the Classics series as a whole and one that may recommend it to more casual listeners.

There is considerable controversy over the remastering of early jazz, and the CEDAR system used by Affinity has come in for considerable flak. Though clean, the sound is a little harsh, with not much nuance. On this occasion, the Classics *Chronological* is very much to be preferred, with a considerably warmer sound. However, the NoNoise system used by Bluebird (see below) certainly carries the day. Non-specialists may – for the time being, at any rate – opt for the perfectly acceptable Bluebird compilation, which overlaps on only a few tracks and which has a slightly sweeter delivery.

***(*) **South Side Chicago Jazz** MCA 42326 CD
       Dodds; Louis Armstrong, Natty Dominique, Herb Morand (*c*); Roy Palmer, John
       Thomas (*tb*); Barney Bigard (*ts*); Charlie Alexander, Lil Hardin Armstrong, Jimmy
       Blythe, Earl Hines, Frank Melrose (*p*); Bud Scott (*g, bj*); Jimmy Bertrand, W. E.
       Burton (*wbd*); Warren Baby Dodds (*d, wbd*). 4 & 10/27, 3/28. 7/29.

**** **Blue Clarinet Stomp** Bluebird ND 82293 CD/LP
       Dodds; Natty Dominique (*c*); Honoré Dutrey (*tb*); Lockwood Lewis (*as*); Charlie
       Alexander, Lil Hardin Armstrong, Jelly Roll Morton (*p*); Clifford Hayes (*vn*); Curtis
       Hayes, Emmitt Perkins, Cal Smith (*bjo*); Bill Johnson (*b*); Baby Dodds (*d, wbd*); H.
       Clifford, Earl McDonald (*jugs*). 12/26, 6/27, 7/28, 1 & 2/29.

Though nominally a thematic compilation, *South Side Chicago Jazz* is in effect a useful Dodds anthology, since he plays on every track. It reduplicates a good deal of material from the more detailed compilations above, notably 1927 material by Dodds's Trio and Black Bottom Stompers, Jimmy Blythe's Owls and Blythe's and Jimmy Bertrand's Washboard Wizards, but it is attractive as an across-the-board sample of early Dodds work with a variety of bands, though there's only one item, a 1929 'Forty And Tight' with Herb Morand, not (yet) covered by either of the fuller documents. *Blue Clarinet Stomp* may be the better buy. Processed by the computerized NoNoise system, it lets the musical information come through almost without interference and, if there's a suspiciously 'modern' extra dimension to the bass, it's neither intrusive nor excessively overdone. The vintage trio tracks with Jelly Roll Morton from 1927 are another plus; these are on Affinity but not *Chronological*, as stated above. MCA have a good holding of Dodds material right through to his death in 1940, and they have scoured the archive quite intelligently, with a good mix of styles, from the appealingly raucous Beale Street Washboard Band to the slightly earlier sets with Louis Armstrong and Lil Hardin Armstrong. These are some of the most significant cuts in pre-war jazz and it is good to have them in a respectable single-CD format.

CHRISTIAN MINH DOKY
DOUBLE BASS

***   **Appreciation** Storyville STCD 4169 CD/LP
Doky; Thomas Schneider (*ts*); Thomas Clausen (*ky*); Larry Petrowsky (*d*). 1/89.

***   **The Sequel** Storyville STCD 4175 CD/LP
Doky; Ulf Wakenius (*t*); Bill Evans (*sax*); Niels Lan Doky (*p, ky*); Adam Nussbaum
(*d*). 90.

***(*) **Letters** Storyville STCD 4177 CD/LP
Doky; Randy Brecker (*t, ky*); Niels Lan Doky (*p, ky*); Hans Oxmond (*g*); Adam
Nussbaum (*d*). 2 & 4/91.

Brother of and frequent collaborator with the brilliant young piano player, Niels Lan Doky, Minh Doky has a firm, controlled tone on the bass and the kind of popping smoothness in faster runs that is derived from the better bass guitarists. Like his fellow-Dane, the great NHØP, Minh Doky favours the lower register of his instrument and moves down the bridge only for occasional dramatic accents. The opening album is polished but not particularly inspired and the later, Shorter-tinged writing hasn't yet made much impact. In fact the best things on *Appreciation* are a lilting but unsentimental version of 'When You Wish Upon A Star' and an original version of the bassist's warhorse, 'Alone Together'. The second album is a disappointment but is also clearly transitional, placing greater emphasis on collective skills. In mood and structure, it is fleetingly reminiscent of similar projects by Ron McClure.

With *Letters*, Minh Doky really comes into his own. Brecker's spare lines are effectively used on the opening, title-track and thereafter and the bassist's brother plays crisply and with his now familiar ability to work quite abstractly within the confines of a melody. Oxmond provides Scofield-derived guitar touches on two tracks and the closing traditional 'Lullaby' is a bass solo with just washes of synthesizer for accompaniment. The finest track, however, is the gentle ballad 'Please, Don't Leave Me', on which Minh Doky develops a minimal idea at length over a shifting, steadily changing background. As producer, he has given himself a resonant acoustic, with a strong touch of echo, which suits his tone very well indeed.

NIELS LAN DOKY (born 1963)
PIANO

***(*) **Here Or There** Storyville SLP 4117 LP
Doky; Niels-Henning Ørsted-Pedersen (*b*); Alvin Queen (*d*). 1/86.

***   **The Target** Storyville SLP 4140 LP
Doky; Niels-Henning Ørsted-Pedersen (*b*); Jack DeJohnette (*d*). 11/86.

(*) **The Truth Storyville SLP 4144 LP
Doky; Bob Berg (*ts*); Bo Stief (*b*); Terri Lyne Carrington (*d*). 6/87.

***   **Daybreak** Storyville SLP/STCD 4160 CD/LP
Doky; John Scofield (*g*); Niels-Henning Ørsted-Pedersen (*b*); Terri Lyne Carrington
(*d*). 9/88.

***   **Close Encounter** Storyville SLP/STCD 4173 CD/LP
Doky; Gary Peacock (*b*); Alex Riel (*d*). 7/89.

Doky seems set to be the next Danishman to carve an international jazz reputation after NHØP. He plays with dazzling fluency, has a biting, percussive touch, relishes fast tempos and has a decisive, linear manner. He writes terrific riff tunes, too. Storyville's five albums are all strong examples of what he can do, brusquely recorded to show off his sound. While there's little to choose between the three trio dates, all of which are made up of originals plus a favourite standard or two, we've given the edge to the debut record for the sheer excitement that seems to energize every minute of the music. *The Truth*, a live session, loses some immediacy over the course of four long pieces, but it's an accomplished quartet, even if Berg's occasionally faceless tenor isn't an ideal match. *Daybreak* adds Scofield's dependably handsome guitar to the proceedings and 'Jet Lag' and 'Natural' find Doky's writing at its wittiest.

***   **Dreams** Milestone M 9178 CD/LP/MC
Doky; Randy Brecker (*t*); Bob Berg (*ts*); John Scofield (*g*); Christian Minh Doky (*b*);
Adam Nussbaum (*d*). 8/89.

***(*)   **Friendship** Milestone M 9183 CD/LP/MC
Doky; Randy Brecker (*t*); Bill Evans (*ss*); Rick Margitza (*ts*); John Abercrombie, Ulf
Wakenius (*g*); Christian Minh Doky, Niels-Henning Ørsted-Pedersen (*b*); Adam
Nussbaum, Alex Riel (*d*). 8–9/90.

Doky had already graduated from Berklee in 1984 and moved to New York in the mid-1980s.
So his 'American' albums are scarcely a departure from his earlier work. *Dreams* has two of his
catchiest themes in 'That's It' and 'Faxed', and the writing is generally good enough to
overcome any hint of *ennui* which the star sidemen might have introduced. But *Friendship* is
even better, split between sessions in Copenhagen and New York, with Doky's native crew
outdoing the New Yorkers for bravura and unity and the album produced (by Doky himself) in
stunningly upfront sound.

ERIC DOLPHY (1928–64)
ALTO SAXOPHONE, FLUTE, BASS CLARINET, CLARINET

***   **Outward Bound** Original Jazz Classics OJC 022 CD/LP/MC
Dolphy; Freddie Hubbard (*t*); Jaki Byard (*p*); George Tucker (*b*); Roy Haynes (*d*).
4/60.

Eric Dolphy's recording debut was with the Roy Porter band in California in early 1949. The
session afforded him an almost apostolic contact with the roots of bebop. Thereafter, though,
the desert. It was to be nearly a decade before he was asked to record again, when he joined the
Chico Hamilton band. After leaving Hamilton at the end of 1959, he did some sessions with
Sammy Davis Jr ('no solos', as the discographies laconically put it) where he met the bassist,
George Tucker. It's thought that Tucker used his contacts to sign Dolphy up for his first session
as leader.

Outward Bound was recorded on All Fools' Day, 1960. Issued with a murkily surreal sleeve,
it is immediately and unsettlingly different from anything Dolphy had attempted before. If it
lacks the sudden, alienating wallop of an equivalent dose of Ornette Coleman or Cecil Taylor,
it's no less challenging. Though his alto playing was still marked by occasional Parkerisms, his
work on bass clarinet pointed in an entirely new direction, as on an introspective ramble down
'Green Dolphin Street'.

***   **Out There** Original Jazz Classics OJC 023 CD/LP/MC
Dolphy; Ron Carter (*clo*); George Duvivier (*b*); Roy Haynes (*d*). 8/60.

The rest of 1960 was almost absurdly overbooked: Dolphy was to play on a staggering 18 albums
before the year's end. His own second album as leader was recorded in August. Still far more
conventionally tonal than most New Wave jazz, Dolphy was already hearing dimensions to
chords few other musicians and very few critics were attuned to hear. *Out There* marked a
significant stage in his exploration of timbre and sonority; this time he dispensed with piano,
replacing it with Ron Carter's eerily effective cello. If the disturbing example of Ornette
Coleman – a nemesis Dolphy had yet to confront – lay behind the jagged rhythms of the first
album, *Out There* was very much a tribute to Charles Mingus, with whom Dolphy enjoyed
probably his closest, if least disputable, artistic partnership.

Disguised, like its predecessor, behind an ersatz, Dali-and-water sleeve-design, *Out There*
really did sound different. The blues-based 'Serene' is one of his finest compositions and the
Mingus-inspired 'Eclipse' affords a rare and intriguing glimpse of his work on a normal,
concert-pitched clarinet.

(*)   **Other Aspects Blue Note B21Y 48041 CD/MC
Dolphy; Ron Carter (*b*); Gina Lalli (*tabla*); Roger Mason (*tamboura*); other musicians
unidentified. 7 & 11/60, 62.

Dolphy's only other Blue Note album, *Out To Lunch*, is a masterpiece, but this is a collection of
oddments, not released until the 1980s, fascinating for the light it casts on Dolphy's restless
experimentalism but not entirely satisfying in itself. The long 'Jim Crow', whose personnel is

not known, is a powerful piece that has Dolphy on all three of his horns, carving something positive out of protest. The two 'Inner Flight's are highly personal flute meditations that don't communicate quite convincingly; there is also some distortion of sound on the original tapes. 'Dolphy-N' is a fine alto/double-bass duet with Ron Carter. The Indian-influenced 'Improvisation And Tukras' contains some fascinating music, as Dolphy anticipates some of Joe Harriot's work on *Indo-Jazz Fusions*. Despite the title, much of the music sounds as if it has been worked out in advance. Essential for serious Dolphy collectors, this will otherwise be of limited interest.

****   **Far Cry** Original Jazz Classics OJC 400 CD/LP/MC
       Dolphy; Booker Little (*t*); Jaki Byard (*p*); Ron Carter (*b*); Roy Haynes (*d*). 12/60.

***   **At the Five Spot: Volume 1** Original Jazz Classics OJC 133 CD/LP/MC
       Dolphy; Booker Little (*t*); Mal Waldron (*p*); Richard Davis (*b*); Ed Blackwell (*d*).

(*)   **At The Five Spot: Volume 2 Original Jazz Classics OJC 247 LP/MC
       As above.

***   **Memorial Album** Original Jazz Classics OJC 353 CD/LP/MC
       As above. 7/61.

When trumpeter Booker Little died in October 1961, Dolphy was robbed of one of his most promising and sympathetic artistic partnerships. All the same, it's somehow rather telling that the most striking track on *Far Cry*, his only studio album as leader with Little (there was a return bout the following March, released as *Out Front* (Candid 9027)), should be for unaccompanied alto saxophone. 'Tenderly' is one of the truly remarkable performances in modern jazz; it draws a firm line from Coleman Hawkins's 'Picasso' to Anthony Braxton's innovative *For Alto*.

Side one sees Dolphy paying respectful but now more distant homage to Charlie Parker, a suite of three loosely connected tracks culminating in the title-piece. By the end of 1960, Dolphy had long left the nest and was tempting altitudes that Parker wouldn't have dreamt of, as on a re-run of the blues, 'Serene', which wasn't included on the original release but only on the interesting but now unavailable label compilation, *25 Years Of Prestige* [P 24046].

Nor would Parker have felt easy with the sustained harmonic invention of Dolphy's live sets with Little. The skittering 'Fire Waltz' and 'Bee Vamp' show what Dolphy was capable of with a top-of-the-range rhythm section; Waldron's chords are just ambiguous enough, and Davis's orchestral-sounding bass opens up the harmonic texture even more. For once a 'memorial album' really does merit the title, though it serves as a more immediate epitaph to Little. By no means a pound-of-flesh release, the two long tracks are of consistently high quality (as, more surprisingly, is the sound-quality), with Dolphy exploring some of his most intriguing harmonic ideas and Little playing exquisitely. Unaccountably, the second volume of *At The Five Spot* is unavailable on CD, but Volume 1 has a valuable alternative of 'Bee Vamp'. This material was formerly also available on a three-LP Prestige set called *The Great Concert Of Eric Dolphy*.

(*)   **Berlin Concerts Enja 3007 9 807605 & 882960 CD/LP
       Dolphy; Benny Bailey (*t*); Pepsi Auer (*p*); Jamil Nasser (*b*); Buster Smith (*d*). 8/61.

Dolphy in the city where he died, dying only occasionally in the arms of a willing but short-winded rhythm section. Benny Bailey's contributions to the long opening 'Hot House' and the closing 'I'll Remember April' are characteristically impressive, but once again the highlights come only when Dolphy's magnificent bass clarinet is picked out solo, as in the by then *de rigueur* 'God Bless The Child' and a long trio version of Benny Carter's 'When Lights Are Low', with just bass and drums in support.

(*)   **In Europe: Volume 1 Original Jazz Classics OJC 413 CD/LP
       Dolphy; Erik Moseholm (*b*); Bent Axen (*p*); Jorn Elniff (*d*); Chuck Israels (*b*). 9/61.

(*)   **In Europe: Volume 2 Original Jazz Classics OJC 414 CD/LP
       As above.

(*)   **In Europe: Volume 3 Original Jazz Classics OJC 415 CD/LP
       As above.

*(*)   **Stockholm Sessions** Enja 3055 CD/LP
        Dolphy; Idries Sulieman (*t*); Knud Jorgensen, Rune Ofwerman (*p*); Jimmy Woode
        (*b*); Sture Kalin (*d*). 9/61.

Recorded less than a month after the *Berlin Concerts* and an object lesson in the perils of 'going single'. The first and second are overlapping releases. The OJC sets (which sound tinnier on CD) include versions of 'Miss Ann' and 'Don't Blame Me' and 'Glad To Be Unhappy'. They also include a rather inconsequential three-parter called 'In The Blues'.

The Danish rhythm section, nominally led by Moseholm but bearing all the symptoms of advanced rhythmic and harmonic disorientation, flounder in Dolphy's increasingly insouciant wake. By this time, he had – like Charlie Parker before him – learned to ignore inadequate settings and go his own way. There is another wonderful 'God Bless The Child', less terse and stripped down, but gamier in articulation, and a fine duo with bassist Chuck Israels – where did he spring from? – on 'Hi-Fly', another intriguing point of comparison with the Berlin set, where it gets a trio reading. Collectable, and for completists self-evidently essential, but by no manner of means classic performances. In value-for-money terms, the OJC CDs are a better bet, though they lack the warmth of the old Prestige *Copenhagen Concert* on vinyl.

The Swedes are a little more adventurous and Jorgensen's chording in particular suggests greater familiarity with the idiom, but Dolphy appears to be having some articulation problems and there is a tiredness even in familiar themes like 'Miss Ann', 'G.W.' and, yes, 'God Bless The Child'. On balance, though, not least with the advantage of nicely fronted CD sound, the Swedish sessions are the ones to plump for.

*****   **Out To Lunch!** Blue Note CDP 746522 CD
        Dolphy; Freddie Hubbard (*t*); Bobby Hutcherson (*vib*); Richard Davis (*b*); Tony
        Williams (*d*). 2/64.

Out to Lunch! is one of the handful of absolutely essential post-war jazz records. Perhaps predictably, the conjunction of Dolphy and Blue Note (and the only one, apart from the indifferent *Other Aspects*) resulted in something extraordinary.

Though Dolphy had played better, he had never had a more cohesive or responsive band. His control on the opening 'Hat And Beard', dedicated to Thelonious Monk, is extraordinary, but the real power of the track comes from the wonderfully fragmented rhythm section: Tony Williams's broken-field drumming, Richard Davis's big, freely pulsed bass and, where once there would have been a piano, Bobby Hutcherson's furiously percussive vibes. 'Something Sweet, Something Tender' is marked by a wonderful unison between Dolphy (on bass clarinet) and Richard Davis. On 'Out To Lunch', all semblance of a fixed metre breaks down; Williams plays almost entirely 'free' (though the basic count appears to be a taxing 5/4) and Davis ignores the bar-lines altogether, allowing the group to improvise unrestrictedly around a brief, staccato theme. 'Straight Up And Down' has a lop-sided, knockabout feel that isn't entirely successful. If Dolphy's flute-playing was the last of his three instrumental disciplines to mature, then 'Gazelloni' is its apotheosis, a wonderful performance after which jazz flute could never be the same again.

The album is a near-perfect example of 'pure' invention on a remarkably slight foundation of melodic ideas that have only implicit harmonic support and which are not governed by strict time-signatures. *Out To Lunch!* seems to reorganize modern jazz around itself: Charlie Parker's vertical take-offs from the top of the chord; Ornette Coleman's morse-code melody; John Coltrane's hugely expansive harmonic reach; even a touch of Cecil Taylor's all-out atonality. Yet it resists anything as drearily repetitive as a personal 'style'. Rudy Van Gelder's engineering is inch-perfect and, of all Dolphy's recordings, *Out to Lunch!* is the most coherently conceived and packaged (right down to Reid Miles's distinctive art-work). It almost doesn't look or sound like Dolphy's record at all. It was always hard to locate Dolphy in his music, almost as if it really wasn't his but an item of unclaimed property which reverts to us each time it goes on the turntable. As it should at very regular intervals.

(*)   **Candid Dolphy Candid 9033 CD/LP
        Dolphy; Benny Bailey, Ted Curson, Roy Eldridge, Lonnie Hillyer, Booker Little (*t*);
        Jimmy Knepper, Julian Priester (*tb*); Charles McPherson (*as*); Walter Benton,
        Coleman Hawkins (*ts*); Nico Bunink, Kenny Dorham, Tommy Flanagan, Don
        Friedman, Mal Waldron (*p*); Ron Carter, Art Davis, Charles Mingus, Peck Morrison

(*b*); Jo Jones, Dannie Richmond, Max Roach (*d*); Roger Sanders, Robert Whitley (*perc*); Abbey Lincoln (*v*). 10 & 11/60, 2, 3 & 4/61.

This is how curates like their eggs done. Parts of it – like the first take of 'Stormy Weather' with Mingus – are excellent; the Abbey Lincoln parts are horrid. The long solo opening to 'Stormy Weather' is one of the best things Dolphy ever did, and the sessions with Little helpfully represent his next most fruitful artistic partnership. As an index of the extremes to which Dolphy's playing career was subjected, it's a useful compilation.

**   **Vintage Dolphy** Enja 5045 CD/LP
    Dolphy; Edward Amour, Don Ellis, Nick Travis (*t*); Jimmy Knepper (*tb*); Phil Woods (*as*); Benny Golson (*ts*); Lalo Schifrin (*p*); Barry Galbraith, Jim Hall (*g*); Warren Chiasson (*vib*); Art Davis, Richard Davis, Chuck Israels, Barre Phillips (*b*); Gloria Agostini (*hp*); Sticks Evans, J. C. Moses, Charlie Persip (*d*); string quartet. 3/62, 3/63, 4/63

By no possible stretch of the imagination 'vintage' anything. The first – jazz – side has some fine solo material from Dolphy, notably on 'Iron Man', but nothing that re-centres the original, 'official' discography. Side two, but for a so-so 'Donna Lee' (notable only for Dolphy's confrontation with the radical Don Ellis), documents his involvement with Gunther Schuller's Third Stream movement, a jazz-meets-serialism *rapprochement* that was always slightly more interesting as an idea than in actuality. The recording quality has an *audio vérité* shakiness, and, though some of the pieces have a clever, palindromic logic, Dolphy never sounds entirely easy with Schuller's atonal scores. Though now considered a relatively important way-station in Dolphy's progress, this shouldn't be considered an urgent acquisition.

(*)   **Here & There Original Jazz Classics OJC 673 CD/MC
    Dolphy; as for OJC 22; Prestige 34002; OJC 413.

A useful if slightly raggedy collection of out-takes. 'Status Seeking' and (yet) another 'God Bless The Child', slightly below par, round out the *Great Concert* sessions without adding significantly to their stature. There is a second bash at 'Don't Blame Me' from the Copenhagen sessions, with another fine effort from Dolphy on flute, and the same manful struggle from the local rhythm section.

Most intriguing is a quartet track (i.e. no Freddie Hubbard) from Dolphy's debut as leader, *Outward Bound*. Under the title-of-convenience 'April Fool', a reference to the day in 1960 when the album was recorded, it's the equal of anything on the original release and, but for Hubbard's absence, might well have been included. Worth having.

***   **The Essential Eric Dolphy** Prestige 60-022 CD
    Dolphy; Freddie Hubbard, Booker Little, Richard Williams (*t*); Oliver Nelson (*as, ts, cl*); Booker Ervin (*ts*); Jaki Byard, Mal Waldron, Richard Wyands (*p*); Ron Carter (*clo*); Joe Benjamin, George Duvivier, George Tucker (*b*); Roy Haynes, Charlie Persip (*d*). 4, 5, 8 & 12/60, 1 & 6/61.

'Les' from *Outward Bound*, 'Feathers' from *Out There*, 'Ode To Charlie Parker' and 'Bird's Mother' from *Far Cry*, 'Status Seeking' from Mal Waldron's *The Quest*, and 'The Meetin'' and 'Ralph's New Blues' from Oliver Nelson's *Screamin' The Blues* and *Straight Ahead* respectively. A worthwhile collation of material that might appeal to a newcomer.

(*)   **Unrealized Tapes West Wind 0016 CD/LP [also released as *Last Recordings* DIW 25020 CD/LP]
    Dolphy; Donald Byrd (*t*); Nathan Davis (*ts*); Jack Dieval (*p*); Jacques B. Hess (*b*); Franco Monzecci (*d*); Jacky Bambou (*congas*).

(*)   **Naima West Wind 2063 CD
    As above, except omit Byrd. 6/64.

(*)   **Iron Man West Wind 2057 CD [originally released as Douglas International SD785]
    Dolphy; Woody Shaw (*t*); Clifford Jordan (*ss*); Sonny Simmons (*as*); Prince Lasha (*f*); Garvin Bushell (*bsn*); Bobby Hutcherson (*vib*); Richard Davis, Eddie Khan (*b*); J. C. Moses (*d*). 7/63.

There are almost as many Dolphy 'Last Dates' and 'Final Sessions' as there were 'last' interviews with Roy Orbison. Just as every music magazine had to have one, every independent label was at one time vying to put their own prefix on Dolphy's last message to the world.

There has been controversy in the past over some of West Wind's contractual idiosyncrasies, but this is the authentic article; musically at least – the hula-hooping female on the cover is a further instance of producer/proprietor Uli Blobel's rather, ahem, *individual* symbology. More than just another pick-up band, the Champs Elysees All-Stars sound well versed in the Dolphy literature. Davis and Byrd are not the front line any wide-awake promoter would have picked, but they blossom generously through a long 'Springtime' (which has just a hint of a better-known 'Summertime' buried in its changes) and on reworkings of two of Dolphy's most resilient compositions, 'G.W.' (from *Outward Bound*) and 'Serene' (from *Out There*). The rhythm section plays more than adequately, and the *Unrealized Tapes* (which is at least a relatively honest title) make a welcome addition to the Dolphy catalogue. Much the same goes for *Naima*, not least the title-track, and there is a useful version of 'Ode To Charlie Parker', first recorded on *Far Cry*.

Iron Man is less compelling but valuable for two fine duets with Richard Davis and for glimpses of Dolphy playing with the ill-fated Woody Shaw, a desperately underrated but unforgivably prodigal trumpeter whose recorded legacy is only a fraction of what it ought to be.

***   **Last Date** EmArCy 5101242 CD
Dolphy; Misha Mengelberg (*p*); Jacques Schols (*b*); Han Bennink (*d*). 6/64.

A welcome reappearance. Though the items above were actually recorded later, this long-deleted disc has entered the mythology as Dolphy's last word to the world, a feeling sustained by the words he speaks as the final notes of 'Miss Ann' die away: 'When you hear music, after it's over, it's gone in the air. You can never recapture it again.' Dolphy's reading of 'Epistrophy' is typically angular and devastatingly precise, and for once on his European travels he has a rhythm section who are with him almost all the way. Bennink in particular is highly responsive and puts in some lovely fills and accents on 'South Street Exit' and 'Miss Ann'. Not his greatest performance ever, but one to cherish nevertheless.

ARNE DOMNÉRUS (born 1924)
ALTO SAXOPHONE, CLARINET, BARITONE SAXOPHONE

***   **Arne Domnérus And His Favourite Groups** Dragon DRLP 111 LP
Domnérus; Leppe Sundewall (*t, bt*); Bengt Hallberg, Gösta Theselius (*p*); Ulf Linde (*vib*); Yngve Akerberg, Gunnar Almstedt, Thore Jederby (*b*); Sven Bollhem, Anders Burman, Jack Noren (*d*). 8, 9 & 10/49, 2 & 3 50.

(***)   **Blåtoner Fra Troldhaugen** FXCD 65 CD
Domnérus; Rune Gustafsson (*g*); Bengt Hallberg (*p*); Georg Riedel (*b*). 9/86.

One of the finest Scandinavian jazz musicians of his generation, Domnérus oversaw a shift away from the heavily bop-influenced Scandinavian idiom of the early 1950s and towards something more straightforwardly romantic and impressionistic. The early sessions are clearly marked by bebop, and the opening 'Conversation' is a familiar-sounding variation on 'Cherokee', but Domnérus himself sounds closer to Benny Carter than to Parker in his phrasing and has a wan, meditative quality that frequently refers to diatonic folk themes and hymn tunes. (It may be Domnérus that the ageing bopper is thinking about in the great jazz movie *Sven Klangs Kvintett* when he says that the only places you could hear jazz in Norway in the 1970s are churches. For a time at least, Domnérus performed in 'sacred concerts' that combined jazz and liturgical materials.)

His typical sound, even on the alto and clarinet, is low, soft and somewhat undynamic. However, he does turn this to interesting advantage in a quiet clarinet version of 'Body And Soul', on which trumpeter Sundewall is credited as bassist. Elsewhere, as on a dark-toned 'Everything But You', where he partners Domnérus's baritone saxophone, he plays very effective bass trumpet, a little-used horn with a dark-blue sonority not unlike valve trombone that is particularly effective in slow ballads. Of the piano players, Theselius is highly lyrical, but lacks the bop-inspired rhythmic flexibility one hears in the later sessions with Hallberg.

With *Blåtoner*, Domnérus has tackled a figure almost as sacrosanct in Scandinavia as the liturgical themes he was examining at the end of the 1970s. This beautiful chamber session, recorded without a drummer, is based entirely on compositions by Edvard Grieg, mostly the *Lyric Pieces*, the *Nordic Dances*, the inevitable *Peer Gynt Suite* (which yields the lovely 'Solveig's Song') and *Norwegian Folk Tunes*. It's light, delicate, with only a rather attenuated jazz content and most of Domnérus's improvisations are along the lines of conventional Romantic variations, with little vertical-harmonic inventiveness. Worth trying, though it gives only a rather poor account of the Swede's skills as a jazzman. For that, the Dragon is the best resource.

BARBARA DONALD (born 1942)
TRUMPET

** **Olympia Live** Cadence CJR1011 LP
Donald; Carter Jefferson (*ss, ts*); Steve Munger (*as*); Cookie Morenco (*p*); Steve Jacobson (*g*); Jay Maibin (*b*); Irvin Lovilette (*d*). 3/81.

(*) **The Past And Tomorrows Cadence CJR1017 LP
Donald; Carter Jefferson, Gary Hammon (*ts*); Peggy Stern (*b*); Mike Bissio (*b*); Irvin Lovilette (*d*). 4/82.

Barbara Donald played with Sonny Simmons's group for many years and, although their recordings are currently out of print, at least these sessions with bands of her own are available. Her work with Simmons displayed a free, harmonically open player whose buzzing sound and long lines suggested she was playing Donald Ayler to Simmons's Albert. An exhilarating sound, yet these two dates are more in a freebop vein and are arguably far less distinctive. The earlier, live, session suffers from tattered organization and a less than capable ensemble; but the more sensitively organized themes and playing on the second date are more rewarding. Sound is no more than adequate on both discs.

LOU DONALDSON (born 1926)
ALTO SAXOPHONE

*** **Quartet/Quintet/Sextet** Blue Note CDP 7815372 CD
Donaldson; Blue Mitchell, Kenny Dorham (*t*); Matthew Gee (*tb*); Horace Silver, Elmo Hope (*p*); Gene Ramey, Percy Heath (*b*); Arthur Taylor, Art Blakey (*d*). 6/52–8/54.

Lou Donaldson was and has remained among the most diligent of Charlie Parker's disciples. His playing has hardly altered in 40 years of work: the fierce tone, quickfire phrasing and blues colourings remain constant, and if he's as unadventurous as he is assured, at least his records guarantee a solid level of well-executed improvising. He replaces Parker's acidity with a certain sweetness, which can make his work pall over extended listening, but it's an engaging sound. Some of his best work was made with Art Blakey and Clifford Brown in this period, but these first quartet dates, with a blue-chip Blue Note team, are happy and energetic sessions with splendid sound for the time.

(*) **Blues Walk Blue Note B21Y-46525 CD
Donaldson; Herman Foster (*p*); Peck Morrison (*b*); Dave Bailey (*d*); Ray Barretto (*perc*). 7/58.

** **Alligator Boogaloo** Blue Note BC7-84263 CD
Donaldson; Melvin Lastie Sr (*c*); Lonnie Liston Smith (*org*); George Benson (*g*); Leo Morris (*d*).

(*) **Lush Life Blue Note B21Y-84254 CD
Donaldson; Freddie Hubbard (*t*); Garnett Brown (*tb*); Jerry Dodgion (*as, f*); Wayne Shorter (*ts*); Pepper Adams (*bs*); McCoy Tyner (*p*); Ron Carter (*b*); Al Harewood (*d*). 1/67.

Donaldson's stack of Blue Note albums have drifted in and out of circulation; those listed above are the ones easiest to find on CD, although what is possibly his best, *Wailing With Lou*, is currently unavailable in the UK at least. *Blues Walk*, true to its title, is Donaldson at his bluesiest, and Bailey and Barretto make a propulsive combination; the material, though, is rather dull. *Alligator Boogaloo* comes from the period when the saxophonist was trying to make the best of the soul-jazz trend, without much success on this occasion – routine playing on lightweight, back-beat music. The stellar cast of *Lush Life* do no more than enunciate Duke Pearson's arrangements in support of Donaldson's ballad solos, but it's enough to make this undemanding set cast a modest spell, especially on such pretty themes as 'Sweet Slumber' and 'The Good Life'.

(*) Sweet Poppa Lou Muse MR 5247 LP
Donaldson; Herman Foster (*p*); Calvin Hill (*b*); Idris Muhammad (*d*); Ralph Dorsey (*perc*). 1/81.

** Back Street** Muse MR 5292 LP
Donaldson; Herman Foster (*p*); Geoff Fuller (*b*); Victor Jones (*d*). 82.

** Forgotten Man** Timeless SJP 153 CD/LP
As above. 7/81.

** Live In Bologna** Timeless SJP 202 CD/LP
As above. 1/84.

The title of the earlier Timeless record is a little indulgent, since Donaldson is more widely represented in the catalogue than many of his peers. All of these sessions, with the faithful Herman Foster still on the piano bench, have nothing surprising in them, from the material to Lou's favourite licks, but they probably say as much for the survival of original bebop mannerism in the 1980s as anything else recorded at the time. The first Muse set is slightly more vivid than the others.

(*) Play The Right Thing Milestone MCD 9190 CD/MC
Donaldson; Lonnie Smith (*org*); Peter Bernstein (*g*); Bernard Purdie (*d*); Ralph Dorsey (*perc*). 90.

Lou's flame burns a little more brightly here, but he's still sounding a little worn out after 40 years of bebop. Smith is a feeble prop and Bernstein plays many of the best licks. Nice studio sound, but it's for dedicated fans only.

ARMEN DONELIAN (born 1949)
KEYBOARDS

(*) Trio '87 Odin 4024-2 CD
Donelian; Carl Morten Iversen (*b*); Audun Klieve (*d*). 7/87.

(*) Secrets Sunnyside SSC 1031 CD/LP
Donelian; Barry Danielian (*t, flhn*); Dick Oatts (*ss, ts*); Anthony Cox (*b*); Bill Stewart (*d*); Arto Tuncboyaci (*perc*). 2/88.

Donelian makes elaborate work of some of his chosen themes on the trio record, and while it sometimes pays off – as in the bright, finely judged treatment of Dave Brubeck's 'In Your Own Sweet Way' – his admittedly considerable technique masks the feeling that it's hard to discern the point of some of his ideas. Iversen and Klieve, though, add a muscular third dimension to the music.

While *Secrets* is a difficult record to warm to – Donelian's themes can sound pointlessly tricky, and he sacrifices melodic warmth for textural density – the musicians perform the music with a lot of heart. Danielian and Oatts move from in to out with believable fluency, Oatts in particular using the material to forge some wiry improvisations, and Cox and Stewart (along with the excitable Tuncboyaci on two tracks) deliver their parts with fine crispness. Danielian's long-phrased solo on 'New Blues' is nearly worth the admission price. Bright and full-bodied recording.

CHRISTY DORAN (born 1949)
GUITARS, EFFECTS

**   **Red Twist & Tuned Arrow** ECM 1342 CD/LP
         Doran; Stephan Wittwer (*g, syn, elec*); Freddy Studer (*d*). 11/86.

**   **Henceforward** Core COCD 9.00871 0 CD
         Doran; John Wolf Brennan (*p, prepared strings*). 5/88.

(*)   **Phoenix hat Art 6074 CD
         Doran; Ray Anderson (*tb*); Marty Ehrlich (*cl, ts, as*); Urs Leimgruber (*ss*); Hank
         Roberts (*clo*). 12/89–4/90.

A superb technician with considerable imaginative range, Doran has, like his Irish compatriot
and fellow exile, John Wolf Brennan, come uncomfortably close on occasion to an awkward
New Ageism. There are moments on *Henceforward*, notably the opening bars of 'Waltz For
Erik Satie', when he appears to be bent on nothing more than ersatz 'Gymnopédies' for the
1990s. But Doran is too uncompromising an improviser for lassitude and complacency. He has a
fierce and occasionally biting tone which complements Brennan's complex arpeggiations (the
opening track is nothing but) and is unembarrassed about placing plain, folksy strums in open
tunings among all the effects.

Grouped with Wittwer and Studer, he sounds a little less adventurous. ECM production is
invariably faultless, though, and the album survives some rather indifferent material. Doran
seems to work best in dialogue rather than in more obviously hierarchical conformations. The
Phoenix duets are intelligently conceived and beautifully played. It's rather a pity there can't be
an all-in jam at the end, in the spirit of Derek Bailey's improvising collective Company, for
individual contributions seem to be itching towards some higher principle of organization. Ray
Anderson is superb, worth the price of admission alone.

***(*) **Corporate Art** JMT 849155 2 CD
         Doran; Gary Thomas (*ts, f*); Mark Helias (*b*); Bobby Previte (*d*). 4, 5 & 6/91.

Doran seems more than usually effectual as a member of a hard-hitting modern jazz outfit. He's
still the dominant voice, though Thomas makes some powerful statements on saxophone and
(particularly) flute, and his dark, school-of-Hendrix feedback storm on 'Chiaroscuro' is the
single most impressive thing on the record. Helias and Previte are a top-drawer rhythm section,
lifted well to the front of Stefan Winter's hard-edged mix. Strong stuff, *Corporate Art* makes
some of Doran's solo work seem rather inconsequential.

**   **Musik Für Zwei Kontrabasse, Elektrische Gitarre Und Schlagzeug** ECM 1436 CD
         Doran; Bobby Burri, Oliver Magnenat (*b*); Freddy Studer (*d*). 5/90.

Doran's second ECM album is an uncomfortable and ultimately unsatisfactory affair which
veers between hard, almost industrial sound and a nervous, algebraic discourse. The formal,
'new music' title isn't really reflected in the eight tracks (one of which is by Burri and only two
of which, 'Chemistries I/II', are related – by name only). Doran's sound is as pumped up as
usual, and it's tempting to speculate whether the music would have had greater impact had the
zwei Kontrabasse been stood down for the afternoon. Recording twin basses is an engineer's
nightmare; but for a rather crude channel separation, they are virtually indistinguishable.
Production is credited to the band; one wonders how ECM chief Manfred Eicher might have
handled it.

***(*) **What A Band** hat Art CD 6105 CD
         Doran (*g* solo). 6/91.

Using delay devices in real time, Doran is able to improvise over ostinati or simply chords,
thereby creating an impression of many simultaneous voices. The opening 'Solomutations'
whirls off into the kind of flamenco-coloured territory John McLaughlin has been exploring in
recent years, but the real highlight of the set is the second track, a cranked-up electric version of
'She Moved Through The Fair', which is more explicitly drawn from Hendrix's feedback
anthems.

Technical virtuosity at this level is inclined to pall rather quickly and *What A Band* is perhaps
best sampled a track at a time than listened to continuously. It certainly shouldn't be missed.

PIERRE DØRGE (born 1946)
GUITAR

(*)   **Landscape With Open Door Steeplechase SCS 1115 LP
Dørge; Walt Dickerson (*vib*). 79.

**   **Ballad Round The Left Corner** Steeplechase 1132 LP
Dørge; John Tchicai (*ss, as*); Niels-Henning Ørsted-Pedersen (*b*); Billy Hart (*d*). 10/79.

The Dane is an experienced performer in jazz-rock and free settings, although his guitar tone is bright and clear, almost in a mainstream jazz tradition. But these small-group settings don't suit him very well. The duo session with Dickerson blends counterpoint almost too cleanly and tends to pall rather quickly; while the quartet date, despite the promising line-up – Tchicai has been a frequent collaborator with the guitarist – is depressingly low in vitality, the compositions given only a perfunctory treatment.

***(*)   **Very Hot – Even The Moon Is Dancing** Steeplechase SCS 1208/SCCD 31208 CD/LP
Dørge; Harry Beckett (*t, flhn*); Kenneth Agerholm, Niels Neergaard (*tb*); Soren Eriksen, Doudou Gouirand (*ss, as*); Jesper Zeuthen (*as*); John Tchicai (*ts, v*); Morten Carlsen (*ts, bsx, f, tara, cl, zurna*); Irene Becker (*ky, perc, v*); Bent Clausen (*vib, perc*); Johnny Dyani (*b, p, v*); Hugo Rasmussen (*b*); Marilyn Mazur (*d*); Ahmadu Jarr (*perc*). 7/85.

***(*)   **Johnny Lives** Steeplechase SCS 1228/SCCD 31228 CD/LP
As above, except omit Neergaard, Eriksen, Gouirand, Dyani and Jarr, add Hamid Drake (*d*), Thomas Dyani (*perc*). 4/87.

These albums are by New Jungle Orchestra, the nearly-big band under Dørge's leadership which is among the most enterprising and unpredictable outfits of its kind. Dørge explores the idea of a global jazz village by pushing what is basically a post-bop orchestra into African, European and any other climes he can assimilate: roistering horn parts might emerge from a lush percussive undergrowth, or heartbreaking ballads may be brightened by Dørge's own sparkling high-life guitar solos. Inevitably, there are moments on the records that sound misconceived, or cluttered, but these are surprisingly few: what one remembers is the joyful swing of the ensembles, the swirling tone colours and rhythmic pep. There are fine soloists too in Tchicai, Carlsen and Beckett. The earlier of the above pair of discs is slightly fresher, with a winning reworking of Ellington's 'The Mooche' and two very long yet convincing pan-global jams; but it would be unwise to pass up *Johnny Lives*, dedicated to the late John Dyani, which has some beautiful writing and playing in such as 'Lilli Goes To Town' and 'Mbizo Mbizo'. The CD issues of both records include extra material, and each is expansively recorded, while retaining a lively feel.

(*)   **Live In Denmark Olufsen DOC 5077 CD/LP
Dørge; Jan Kaspersen (*p, picc*). 9/87.

A surprisingly sober and careful meeting between two of the more madcap spirits in Danish jazz. They work as a kind of chamber duo on a selection of self-composed and standard material, with three variations on Satie's 'Gnossiennes' typical of the sort of feel of the programme. The best things are a reflective piece by Kaspersen called 'Snail Trail' and a bittersweet reading of 'Blue Monk', though the oddball duets on altohorn and piccolo at the end of the record bring the most applause! The sound is a little chilly and recessed.

***(*)   **Different Places, Different Bananas** Olufsen DOC 5079 CD/LP
As previous Steeplechase session, except Aage Tanggaard (*d*), Gert Mortensen and Ivan Hansen (*perc*) replace Mazur and Drake. 11/88.

Further rollicking adventures from the New Jungle Orchestra. The compositions are the accustomed rag-bag of riffs, African rhythms and jazz in-jokes, which some of the titles suggest: 'Fats Waller In The Busch Of Leipzig', for instance, or 'Sun Ra Over La Luna'. The latter includes some deliciously grumpy bass sax from Clausen, but singling out soloists is unfair – everybody plays well. Tchicai's 'Largo Lapidarius' may be the most memorable theme they've been given to play, too. The Olufsen recording is quite as good as that for Steeplechase.

***   **Live In Chicago** Olufsen DOC 5122 CD/LP
Dørge; Harry Beckett (*t*); John Tchicai (*ss, ts*); Jesper Zeuthen (*as, bcl, f*); Irene
Becker (*ky*); Harrison Bankhead (*b*); Hamid Drake (*d*). 7/90.

As boisterous as ever, but this is a mildly disappointing session: the live versions of 'The
Mooche' and 'Mbizo Mbizo' add little to the studio treatments, and the sound quality is
bottom-heavy and missing in essential detail. A nice souvenir for any who saw this edition of the
band, but not important in its own right.

KENNY DORHAM (1924–72)
TRUMPET

***(*)   **Kenny Dorham Quintet** Original Jazz Classics OJC 113 LP
Dorham; Jimmy Heath (*as, bs*); Walter Bishop Jr (*p*); Percy Heath (*b*); Kenny Clarke
(*d*). 12/53.

(*)   **Afro-Cuban Blue Note 7468152 CD
Dorham; J. J. Johnson (*tb*); Hank Mobley (*ts*); Cecil Payne (*bs*); Horace Silver (*p*);
Oscar Pettiford (*b*); Art Blakey (*d*); Carlos Patato Valdez (*congas*). 1/55, 3/55.

Dorham never sounded more like Dizzy Gillespie than on *Afro-Cuban*, punching out single-note
statements across the rhythm. The marvellous 1953 quintet features gulping blues passages that
manage to thrive on the thinnest harmonic oxygen; never a mere showman, it is Dorham's
mental stamina that impresses, a concentration and attention to detail that make him one of the
most coherent and structurally-aware of the bebop players. He is also one of the better
composers, a fact – 'Blue Bossa' apart – which is generally overlooked.

(*)   **Jazz Contrast Original Jazz Classics OJC 028 LP/MC
Dorham; Sonny Rollins (*ts*); Hank Jones (*p*); Oscar Pettiford (*b*); Max Roach (*d*);
Betty Glamman (*hp*). 5/57.

***   **Two Horns / Two Rhythm** Original Jazz Classics OJC 463 CD/LP/MC
Dorham; Ernie Henry (*as*); Wilbur Ware (*b*); Granville T. Hogan (*d*). 11/57, 12/57.

The piano-less horn-and-rhythm experiment posed interesting problems for Dorham. Ware's
big bass almost fills in the gap; but what is interesting about the set as a whole is how Dorham
adjusts his delivery, counting rests much more carefully, filling in with a broader intonation on
ensemble passages. Henry and Hogan are by no means passengers, but the real drama of the
recording is played out across the three octaves that divide trumpet and bass on some of the
bridging passages.
  Rollins wasn't at first glance the ideal partner for Dorham, but he began to steer him in the
direction of an altogether different approach to thematic variation which really became evident
only towards the end of the decade. *Horns/Rhythm* gains a star for boldness; *Jazz Contrast*
drops back one for the wishy-washy sound.

***   **Blue Spring** Original Jazz Classics OJC 134 CD/LP/MC
Dorham; David Amram (*frhn*); Julian Cannonball Adderley (*as*); Cecil Payne (*bs*);
Cedar Walton (*p*); Paul Chambers (*b*); Jimmy Cobb or Philly Joe Jones (*d*). 1/59, 2/59.

***   **Quiet Kenny** Original Jazz Classics OJC 250 LP/MC
Dorham; Tommy Flanagan (*p*); Paul Chambers (*b*); Art Taylor (*d*). 11/59.

(*)   **West 42nd Street Black Lion 60119 CD/LP
Dorham; Rocky Boyd (*ts*); Walter Bishop Jr (*p*); Ron Carter (*b*); Pete La Roca (*d*).
3/61.

***   **Osmosis** Black Lion 760146 CD
Dorham; Curtis Fuller (*tb*); Frank Haynes (*ts*); Tommy Flanagan (*p*); Ben Tucker (*b*);
Dave Bailey (*d*). 10/61.

Dorham enjoyed a brief resurgence towards the end of the 1950s, and any of the four above
would serve as a reasonable introduction to his more deliberate, Miles-influenced approach of
that period. *Quiet Kenny* is a minor masterpiece. The blues-playing is still as emotional as ever,
but there is a more relaxed approach to the basic metres, and Tommy Flanagan in particular

invites a quieter and more sustained articulation of themes. *West 42nd Street*, good as it is, isn't a Dorham album. It was recorded and originally released on Jazztime under the leadership of tenor player Rocky Boyd, which rather explains the order and emphasis of the solos. The two takes each of 'Stella By Starlight' and of 'Why Not?' soon dispel a faint aroma of marketing cynicism.

***(*) **Jazz Contemporary** Time BCD 1048 CD
Dorham; Charles Davis (*bs*); Steve Kuhn (*p*); Jimmy Garrison, Butch Warren (*b*); Buddy Enlow (*d*). 2/60.

Bob Shad's A&R work for Time yielded some strikingly innovative and polished sessions, and trumpeters seem to have been particularly favoured; there are excellent things in the catalogue by both Booker Little and Tommy Turrentine. On *Jazz Contemporary*, Dorham plays with great technical daring, attempting dramatic upward sweeps on 'Monk's Mood', staccato bursts of sound on 'Horn Salute' and the inventive ensemble composition 'Tonica', another jazz dedication to the Baroness Nica de Koenigswarter, which reveals Dorham as a fine melodist. On Brubeck's 'In Your Own Sweet Way' and the Sinatra song, 'This Love Of Mine', he cleaves very close to the melody line, and it's interesting to compare Dorham's version of the Brubeck with Miles Davis's (which he apparently hadn't heard).

The band is young and slightly moody, with the sound anchored round Warren's baritone sound (refreshingly independent of all the likely role-models) and the bass, creating charts in which much of the drama comes from extremes of pitch. As with other items in the series, digital transfer has done a little violence to the trumpet sound but with the pay-back of a better ensemble feel; that's a considerable bonus on the sololess 'Tonica' which, in contrast to the LP version, suddenly leaps into focus.

***(*) **Matador/Inta Somethin'** Blue Note CDP 7844602 CD
Dorham; Jackie McLean (*as*); Walter Bishop, Bobby Timmons (*p*); Teddy Smith, Leroy Vinnegar (*b*); J. C. Moses, Art Taylor (*d*). 1/61, 4/62.

(*) **Una Mas Blue Note 746515 CD
Dorham; Joe Henderson (*ts*); Herbie Hancock (*p*); Butch Warren (*b*); Tony Williams (*d*). 4/63.

*** **Trompeta Toccata** Blue Note B21Y 84181 CD
Dorham; Joe Henderson (*ts*); Tommy Flanagan (*p*); Richard Davis (*b*); Albert Heath (*d*). 9/64.

** **Short Story** Steeplechase SCC 6010 LP
Dorham; Allan Botschinsky (*flhn*); Tete Montoliu (*p*); Niels-Henning Ørsted-Pedersen (*b*); Alex Riel (*d*). 12/63.

*(*) **Scandia Skies** Steeplechase SCC 6011 LP
As above, but Rolf Ericson (*t, flhn*) replaces Botschinsky. 12/63.

Despite the sustained energy of *Una Mas* and *Trompeta Toccata* (both of which paired the trumpeter's brightly burnished tone with the muscular tenor of Joe Henderson), Dorham seemed to be running out of steam in 1963; 'one more time' was beginning to sound like once too often. The Steeplechases are essentially footnote albums to a remarkable career which still had nearly a decade to run. In themselves perfectly respectable and always eminently listenable, they lack the profound emotional urgency that was Dorham's trademark whether he was playing fast, high-register runs or sustained blues cadences. The writing is good but increasingly precise and Dorham's occasional 'classical' experiments, the beautifully cadenced 'Trompeta Toccata' and, on the Latin-influenced *Matador*, a Villa-Lobos prelude for Dorham and the unsuitable Timmons, don't quite effect the kind of syntheses he managed in Henderson's company. Produced in the wake of a South American tour, *Matador* (originally released on United Artists) is touched by Brazilian rather than Afro-Cuban rhythms. McLean plays beautifully and plays an anguished introduction to 'Lover Man' that recalls Parker's disastrous Dial recording of the tune.

JIMMY DORSEY (1904–56)
ALTO AND BARITONE SAXOPHONES, CLARINET, TRUMPET

(*)   **Pennies From Heaven ASV AJA 5052 CD
Dorsey; George Thow, Toots Camarata, Joe Meyer (*t*); Don Mattison (*tb, v*); Bobby
Byrne, Joe Yuki, Bruce Squires (*tb*); Fud Livingston (*as, ts*); Jack Stacey, Len Whitney
(*as*); Skeets Herfurt, Charles Frazier (*ts*); Bobby Van Eps, Freddie Slack (*p*); Roc
Hillman (*g, v*); Slim Taft, Jack Ryan (*b*); Ray McKinley (*d, v*); Bob Eberle, Frances
Langford (*v*). 3/36–6/37.

(*)   **At The 400 Restaurant 1946 Hep CD 41 CD
Dorsey; Bob Alexy, Claude Bowen, Ray Linn, Tonny Picciotto, Nathan Solomon,
Seymour Baker, Irving Goodman, Louis Mucci (*t*); Simon Zentner, Thomas Lee,
Nicholas DiMaio, Anthony Russo, Fred Mancusi, Don Mattison, Bob Alexander (*tb*);
Jack Aiken, Frank Langone, Bill Covey, Cliff Jackson (*as*); Bobby Dukoff, Charles
Frazier, Charles Travis, Gill Koerner (*ts*); Bob Lawson, Johnny Dee (*bs*); Marvin
Wright, Lou Carter (*p*); Herb Ellis, Teddy Walters (*g*); Jimmy Middleton, Norman
Bates (*b*); Adolf Shutz, Karl Kiffe (*d*); Dee Parker, Paul Chapman (*v*). 1/46.

The elder Dorsey brother was a saxophonist of the highest technical accomplishment, though it
tended to lead him to merely show off on many of the records he made as a sessionman in the
1920s, such as 'Beebe' and 'I'm Prayin' Humble', which have yet to make it to CD. The band
he formed in 1935 after splitting up with his brother was a commercial dance band rather than
any kind of jazz orchestra, but the group could swing when Dorsey wanted it to, and there was
some impeccable section-playing, particularly from the trombones. The ASV disc pulls together
18 tracks from this period and, though there is a genuinely fine best-of waiting to be compiled
from Dorsey's pre-war band, this mixture of vocal features for Eberle, Langford and McKinley
and more jazz-orientated titles will have to do for now. 'Dorsey Dervish' harks back to the
leader's technical exercises of the decade before, but 'Stompin' At The Savoy' is creditable
enough, and Bobby Byrne's beautiful lead trombone on 'In A Sentimental Mood' (contrary to
the sleevenotes, Byrne doesn't sing on this tune) outdoes even Tommy Dorsey for
mellifluousness. It's a pity, though, that titles such as 'Swamp Fire', 'Major And Minor Stomp'
and 'Cherokee' are omitted. The remastering is rather lifeless.

The Hep CD is a lot more modernistic: among the opening four tracks, which date from 1944,
is a Dizzy Gillespie arrangement of 'Grand Central Getaway'. The remainder are airshots taken
from a New York engagement two years later, and while the band has nothing very outstanding
about it there are one or two worthwhile solos from Bob Avery and the leader, whose attractive
score 'Contrasts' hints at directions which he never really followed. Generally, though, there is
rather more jazz-inflected material here than on the earlier CD, and remastering makes the best
of the broadcast recording.

TOMMY DORSEY (1905–56)
TROMBONE, TRUMPET

***   **Yes, Indeed!** Bluebird ND 904499 CD/LP/MC
Dorsey; Yank Lawson, Pee Wee Irwin, Andy Ferretti, Mickey Bloom, Jimmy Blake,
Ray Linn, Clyde Hurley, Ziggy Elman, Chuck Peterson, Al Stearns, Manny Klein,
Jimmy Zito, Roger Ellick, Mickey Mangano, Dale Pierce, George Seaberg, Charlie
Shavers, Gerald Goff (*t*); Dave Jacobs, Elmer Smithers, Ward Silloway, Lowell
Martin, George Arus, Les Jenkins, Walter Mercurio, James Skiles, Walt Benson,
Nelson Riddle, Tex Satterwhite, Karle De Karske, William Haller, Richard Noel (*tb*);
Johnny Mince, Fred Stulce, Skeets Herfurt, Dean Kincaide, Babe Russin, Hymie
Schertzer, Paul Mason, Don Lodice, Heinie Beau, Manny Gershman, Bruce Snyder,
Harry Schuchman, Buddy DeFranco, Sid Cooper, Gale Curtis, Al Klink, Bruce
Branson, Babe Fresk, Dave Harris, Gus Bivona, Vido Musso (*saxes*); Howard Smith,
Joe Bushkin, Milt Raskin, Milt Golden, John Potoker, Duke Ellington (*p*); Carmen
Mastren, Clark Yocum, Bob Bain, Sam Herman (*g*); Joe Park (*tba*); Gene Traxler, Sid
Weiss, Phil Stevens, Sid Block (*b*); Dave Tough, Cliff Leeman, Buddy Rich (*d*);
Edythe Wright, Sy Oliver, Jo Stafford (*v*). 6/39–5/45.

The one currently available compilation of Tommy Dorsey's big-band recordings for Victor only hints at the surprisingly consistent excellence of the trombonist's groups. Orrin Keepnews' compilation chooses a sequence of mostly instrumental, mostly jazz-orientated tracks, with a cross-section of work by arrangers Paul Weston, Sy Oliver and Bill Finnegan, and there are such hits as 'Opus No 1', 'Swing High' and Oliver's remarkable transformation of 'Swanee River' alongside adventurous charts like 'Stomp It Off' and 'Loose Lid Special'. There are but few glimpses of the 'sentimental' style which buttered Dorsey's bread for most of the swing era, and his somewhat underrated skills as a soloist emerge best on 'Mandy, Make Up Your Mind'. But a single disc can't hope to include a proper representation of this prolific bandleader's work, and we hope that more adequate representation of the orchestra's studio sides will come up on future Dorsey compilations, especially now that the complete Bluebird edition on American RCA and French RCA's four excellent *Indispensable Tommy Dorsey* double-albums are now out of general circulation. The sound is as clean as the NoNOISE process allows, though some may prefer the occasionally more sprightly sound of earlier LP reissues, as patchy as they often were.

**(*) The Music Goes Round And Round Bluebird ND 83140 CD/LP
Dorsey; Sterling Bose, Max Kaminsky, Pee Wee Irwin, Yank Lawson, Jimmy Blake, Charlie Shavers, Ziggy Elman (*t*); Joe Dixon, Johnny Mince, Buddy DeFranco (*cl*); Bud Freeman, Sid Block, Babe Russin, Boomie Richman (*ts*); Dick Jones, Howard Smith, John Potoker, Teddy Wilson (*p*); Bill Schaeffer, Carmen Mastren, Sam Herman, Billy Bauer (*g*); Gene Traxler, Sid Block (*b*); Dave Tough, Maurice Purtill, Graham Stevenson, Cliff Leeman, Alvin Stoller (*d*); Edythe Wright, Hughie Prince, Sy Oliver, Hanna Williams (*v*). 12/35–2/47.

While there are a few marvellous sides here – including the instrumentals 'The Sheik Of Araby' and 'Chinatown, My Chinatown' – too many numbers in this collection by Dorsey's small group, The Clambake Seven, fall victim to corny material and time-wasting vocals, although Edythe Wright's singing has a lot of charm. Some of the kitsch numbers, especially 'Rhythm Saved The World', with its irresistible sign-off, and the heated 'At The Codfish Ball', are elevated by what were even then old-fashioned hot treatments of the kind Dorsey graduated on in the 1920s. If it's a period piece, it still includes plenty of compelling moments from soloists such as Freeman, Kaminsky and Dorsey himself. The CD remastering will sound muffled to those who've heard the original 78s, but will probably satisfy everybody else.

*** The Carnegie Hall V-Disc Session April 1944 Hep CD 40 CD
Dorsey; Pete Candoli, George Seaburg, Sal La Perche, Dale Pearce, Bob Price, Ralph Santangelo, Mickey Mangano (*t*); Walter Benson, Tommy Pedersen, Tex Satterwhite, Nelson Riddle (*tb*); Budy DeFranco, Hank D'Amico (*cl, as*); Sid Cooper, Leonard Kaye (*as*); Gail Curtis, Al Klink, Don Lodice, Mickey Sabol (*ts*); Bruce Branson, Manny Gershman (*bs*); Dodo Marmarosa, Milt Raskin (*p*); Dennis Sandole, Bob Bain (*g*); Joe Park (*tba*); Sid Block (*b*); Gene Krupa, Maurice Purtill, Buddy Rich (*d*); Bing Crosby, Frances Langford, Georgia Gibbs, Bob Allen, The Sentimentalists, Bonnie Lou Williams (*v*). Plus string section. 10/43–9/44.

**(*) The All Time Hit Parade Rehearsals Hep CD 39 CD
As above, except omit Candoli, Price, Santangelo, D'Amico, Kaye, Klink, Gershman, Raskin, Sandole, Krupa and Purtill, Crosby and Gibbs, add Judy Garland, Frank Sinatra (*v*). 6–9/44.

Although there isn't a great deal of jazz on these records, they give a clearer idea of the sound of Dorsey's band, since John R. T. Davies's superb remastering puts the Bluebird records to shame. *All Time Hit Parade* is drawn from acetate transcriptions of rehearsals for a radio show of that name, and while they tend to display the sweeter side of Dorsey's band, the smooth power of the sections is smartly put across by the sound. Sinatra has a couple of fine features in 'I'll Walk Alone' and 'If You Are But A Dream' and there's a showcase for Marmarosa on 'Boogie Woogie'. The V-Disc material, again in splendid restoration, is rather more exciting, with a number of spots for La Perche, DeFranco and Klink. Crosby and Langford deliver a couple of messages to the troops as a bonus.

**   **Tommy Dorsey Plays Sweet And Hot** Tax CD 3705-2 CD
Dorsey; Zeke Zarchey, Lee Castaldo, Jimmy Blake (*t*); Ward Silloway, Lowell Martin
(*tb*); Johnny Mince (*cl, as*); Fred Stulce, Les Robinson (*as*); Babe Russin, Paul Mason
(*ts*); Bob Kitsis (*p*); Bob Heller (*g*); Gene Traxler (*b*); Buddy Rich (*d*); Frank Sinatra,
Jo Stafford, The Pied Pipers (*v*). 2/40.

***(*)   **Well, Git It!** Jass J-CD-14 CD
Dorsey; Pete Candoli, Bob Price, George Seaberg, Sal La Perche, Vito Mangano, Dale
Pierce, Gerald Goff, Charlie Shavers, Paul McCoy, Mickey Mangano, Cy Baker, Chuck
Genduso (*t*); Walter Benson, Tommy Pedersen, Tex Satterwhite, Nelson Riddle,
Richard Noel, Karl DeKarske, Al Esposito, William Siegel, Bill Schallen, Sam Levine
(*tb*); Hank D'Amico, Buddy DeFranco, Gus Bivona (*cl, as*); Sid Cooper, Leonard
Kaye (*as*); Bruce Branson (*ts, as, bs*); Hank Lodice, Gail Curtis, Mickey Sabol, Al
Klink, Babe Fresk, Boomie Richman (*ts*); Manny Gershman (*bs*); Milt Raskin, Jess
Stacy, Dodo Marmarosa, Johnny Potoker (*p*); Sam Herman, Danny Sandoli (*g*); Sid
Block, Joe Park (*b*); Alvin Stoller, Buddy Rich, Gene Krupa (*d*); Skip Nelson, Stuart
Foster, Bonnie Lou Williams, The Sentimentalists (*v*). 43–46.

There could hardly be a more striking contrast than there is between these two discs of airshots.
The Tax CD offers a complete show from the Meadowbrook Ballroom in New Jersey from
February 1940, and it's all sweet and not very hot: there are corny arrangements of college
songs, novelty tunes and a few worthwhile ballads – with Sinatra and Jo Stafford being perhaps
the main points of interest in the broadcast. There isn't much jazz, but the sound of the band is
caught very clearly by Jack Towers's fine remastering of the material. The Jass collection is a
little rougher, but it's infinitely more exciting, opening on a wildly over-the-top 'Well, Git It!'
featuring guest Gene Krupa (Buddy Rich has his own turn on another version at the end of the
disc). In between are new versions of many of Dorsey's better hits, a few of the superior sweet
items, and solo spots for DeFranco, Shavers, Candoli and more. A first-class compilation of its
kind.

DORSEY BROTHERS ORCHESTRA
GROUP

***   **Harlem Lullaby** Hep CD 1006 CD
Manny Klein, Sterling Bose, Bunny Berigan (*t*); Tommy Dorsey (*tb*); Larry Binyon
(*cl, as, ts*); Jimmy Dorsey (*cl, as*); Joe Venuti, Harry Hoffman, Walter Edelstein, Lou
Kosloff (*vn*); Joe Meresco, Fulton McGrath (*p*); Dick McDonough (*g*); Artie
Bernstein (*b*); Stan King, Chauncey Morehouse, Larry Gomar (*d*); Bing Crosby, Mae
West, Ethel Waters, Mildred Bailey, Lee Wiley 2–7/33.

The Dorsey brothers co-led a band before making separate careers as swing-era bandleaders,
and while many of their 78s are still awaited on CD, this compilation offers the chance to hear
them backing four vocalists of the day. Mae West's pair of titles are little more than a not
especially tuneful extension of her man-eating persona, and Wiley's session shows the singer still
in raw shape, but the four tracks with Crosby show how much the singer had learned from jazz
players and the eight featuring Mildred Bailey are delightful, her light and limber voice gliding
over the music with little effort. There are brief solos for the Dorseys and Berigan here and
there, but the record belongs mostly to the singers. First-class remastering throughout.

**   **'Live' In The Big Apple 1954/5** Magic DAWE44 CD
Charlie Shavers (*t*); Tommy Dorsey, Jimmy Henderson (*tb*); Jimmy Dorsey (*cl, as*);
Buddy Rich (*d*); Johnny Amorosa, Billy Raymond, Dick Haymes, Kitty Kallen, Lynn
Roberts (*v*); rest unknown.1/54–10/55.

While the brothers were famous for quarrelling, they patched up their differences and joined
forces again in the 1950s, although the orchestra here was principally Tommy's. Neither man
was long for this world, and the jazz content here is low: a swinging 'Puddlewump' and 'Skirts
And Sweaters' have to fight for space with some feeble vocals (aside from Dick Haymes's
beautiful 'Our Love Is Here To Stay') and dining and dancing music. Most of the band is
appropriately anonymous. Culled from various radio broadcasts, the sound is low-fi but
listenable.

KENNY DREW (born 1928)
PIANO

**(*)   The Kenny Drew Trio Original Jazz Classics OJC 065 LP
Drew; Paul Chambers (b); Philly Joe Jones (d). 9/56.

Drew's earliest-available album as a leader is no better or worse than many another piano trio date of the day: light, bluesy variations on a flock of standards. Chambers and Jones are typically strong in support, but the material is under-characterized.

**(*)   This Is New Original Jazz Classics OJC 483 CD/LP/MC
Drew; Donald Byrd (t); Hank Mobley (ts); Wilbur Ware (b); G. T. Hogan (d). 3–4/57.

Nothing very new here, despite both the title and the period: this sort of hard-bop fare was already becoming a standard repast in 1957. It may say something for the principals involved that the most interesting presence appears to be Ware, who is constantly inventive. The recording is somewhat reticent in dealing with the horns. There is also a compilation LP, *Trio/Quartet/Quintet* (OJC 6007, CD/LP/MC), which selects tracks from both the above discs.

***   Duo Steeplechase SCS 1002 LP
Drew; Niels-Henning Ørsted-Pedersen (b); Ole Molin (g). 4/73.

***   Duo 2 Steeplechase SCS 1010 LP/MC
As above, except omit Molin. 2/74.

***   Duo Live In Concert Steeplechase SCS 1031 LP/MC
As above. 6/74.

**(*)   Everything I Love Steeplechase SCS 1007 LP
Drew (p solo). 10–12/73.

Drew left America for Europe in 1961 and has worked and recorded there ever since. His numerous records for Steeplechase are modest successes, but the pianist's very consistency is perhaps his undoing: it's frequently hard to tell one disc – or even one performance – from another. The three duo sessions with Pedersen are the best, if only because there is a fine clarity of interplay and the bassist doesn't settle for Drew's plainer modes of expression. The solo date is rather too quiescent.

**   If You Could See Me Now Steeplechase SCS 1034 LP
Drew; Niels-Henning Ørsted-Pedersen (b); Albert Heath (d). 5/74.

**   Morning Steeplechase SCS 1048/SCCD 31048 CD/LP
As above, except Philip Catherine (g) replaces Heath. 9/75.

**(*)   Lite Flite Steeplechase SCS 1077 LP
Drew; Thad Jones (c); Bob Berg (ts); George Mraz (b); Jimmy Cobb (d). 2/77.

**(*)   In Concert Steeplechase SCS 1106 CD/LP/MC
Drew; Niels-Henning Ørsted-Pedersen (b); Philip Catherine (g). 2/77.

**   Ruby My Dear Steeplechase SCS 1129 CD/LP/MC
Drew; David Friesen (b); Clifford Jarvis (d). 8/77.

Although Drew recorded in a variety of settings for Steeplechase, a certain blandness continued to detract from his sessions as a leader. The quintet date with Jones and Berg is amiable but no more exciting than the trio records, of which *In Concert* is the best, benefiting from the in-person atmosphere. Drew's powers as an accompanist are best demonstrated elsewhere, in his sessions with Dexter Gordon.

**   Home Is Where The Soul Is Xanadu 166 LP
Drew; Leroy Vinnegar (b); Frank Butler (d). 10/78.

***   For Sure! Xanadu 167 LP
As above, plus Sam Noto (t); Charles McPherson (as). 10/78.

A return visit to the US resulted in two albums for Don Schlitten's Xanadu label. The trio date is no different from the Steeplechase albums, but the meeting with two of Schlitten's favourite horn players has an extra burst of energy and is very good of its kind, including a fine version of Drew's attractive 'Dark Beauty'. Close, crisp sound-quality.

**   **Your Soft Eyes** Soul Note SN 1040 LP
Drew; Mads Vinding (*b*); Ed Thigpen (*d*). 11/81.

(*)   **And Far Away Soul Note SN 1081 LP
Drew; Philip Catherine (*g*); Niels-Henning Ørsted-Pedersen (*b*); Barry Altschul (*d*). 2/83.

Drew made several records for the Japanese Baystate company in the early 1980s, as well as these two sessions for Soul Note: his compositions continue to work a slight, pretty seam to rather soporific ends, but the second record benefits from the presence of Altschul, whose ear for texture helps to create a more integrated and purposeful sound to such Drew originals as 'Rianne'.

***   **Recollections** Timeless SJP 333 CD/LP
Drew; Niels-Henning Ørsted-Pedersen (*b*); Alvin Queen (*d*). 5/89.

It might be thanks to digital sound of tremendous impact, but this set sounds like a revitalization of Drew's music. Whether tackling standards or originals, he digs in with a verve and a decisive attack which will surprise anyone familar with the earlier trio dates. Pedersen and Queen respond with appropriate vigour of their own.

KENNY DREW Jr
PIANO

***(*)   **The Flame Within** Jazz City 660 53 017 CD
Drew; Bob Berg (*ts*); Charnett Moffett (*b*); Al Foster (*d*). 11/87.

****   **Third Phase** Jazz City 660 53 002 CD
Drew; Buster Williams (*b*); Marvin 'Smitty' Smith (*d*). 6/89.

Kenny Jr doesn't really sound in the least like his father. Classically trained, he uses non-blues intervals to a far greater extent and has a less percussive attack. His opening statement on an unaccompanied 'Lush Life' (*Third Phase*) is wonderfully out of kilter in every department and scarcely prepares the listener for the gently swinging performance that follows; elsewhere, he manages to arrest attention in an otherwise conventional standards performance with soft dissonances and startling out-of-tempo melodic interpolations where it sound almost as if he's lost it for a bar or two.

Drew's debut on Jazz City, *Rainbow Connection* [D28Y 0203], also featured Charnett Moffett, another distinguished 'son of'. On *The Flame Within*, he's a little more muted, but his solo on Chick Corea's 'Matrix' is a model of invention and control, as is his intro to fellow-bassist Jaco Pastorius's marvellous 'Three Views Of A Secret'. It's interesting to look at Drew's choice of material. The debut album was dominated by two Monk tunes, 'Rhythm-A-Ning' and 'Boo Boo's Birthday'. He's equally adventurous on the second album, doing the little known 'We See' in addition to a quartet 'Criss Cross', with Berg dropping a couple of Charlie Rouse references into his first chorus. The pianist's big solo spot on *The Flame Within* is a very fulsome version of 'A House Is Not A Home', which pulls up just short of self-indulgence.

Drew's ear for a tune is tested on 'Heather On The Hill', an improbable theme drawn from *Brigadoon*. His own compositional resources, modestly represented on both albums, suggest that he's worked his way through the Blue Note back catalogue. 'Third Phase' and 'The Flame Within' could have come from any one of half a dozen Hancock/Shorter sets from the early 1960s, and that's presumably the music Drew Jr came up with, rather than the bop revolution, in which his dad had a part. At first glance, Monk's 'I Mean You' aside, the third album looks like a more conventional standards set. But Drew's treatments are notably imaginative and he has the backing of two of the best sidemen in the business; Williams's solo on the warhorse 'Alone Together' should be a model for bass players and Smith's changes of pace (and of sticks) on 'Falling In Love With Love' are equally exemplary. 'Autumn Leaves' follows that wanly delicate 'Lush Life' with a breath-taking Latin romp that substantially rearranges the tune and points to another of Drew's characteristics, the ability to invest internal divisions of a melody with unexpected rhythmic weight. Both albums are well worth having.

PAQUITO D'RIVERA (born 1948)
ALTO, SOPRANO AND TENOR SAXOPHONES, CLARINET

*** **Tico! Tico!** Chesky 034 CD
D'Rivera; Danilo Perez (*p*); Fareed Haque, Romero Lobambo, Tibero Nascimiento (*g*); David Finck, Nilsson Matta (*b*); Portinho, Mark Walker (*d*). 7–8/89.

D'Rivera was the first of the recent wave of Cuban musicians to defect to the US (in 1980), and his intensely hot, infectiously runaway style on alto has enlivened quite a number of sessions. He has the same difficulty which besets his compadre, Arturo Sandoval: finding a consistently productive context for a talent which is liable to blow away on the winds of its own virtuosity. D'Rivera is never short of a string of firecracker phrases, but they can often be as enervating to a listener as the most laid-back of jazz easy-listening dates. His Columbia albums, which seem to have drifted quickly out of the catalogue and which weren't in any case issued in the UK, tend to end up as Latinized hard bop, no better or worse than a typical neo-classical session if a little more sparky than most. But this Chesky album suggests ways that D'Rivera can make a more convincing kind of fusion. The bolero, waltz and *bossa nova* rhythms are integrated into a setting which sifts bebop into an authentic South American stew, and the leader turns to the clarinet as well as the alto (and a little tenor) to decorate the pulse. Chesky's brilliant sound only heightens the sunny qualities of Paquito's music.

*** **Havana Café** Chesky JD 80 CD
D'Rivera; Danilo Perez (*p*); Fareed Haque, Ed Cherry (*g*); David Finck (*b*); Jorge Rossy (*d*); Sammy Figueroa (*perc*).

More of the same, really. But the very quick tempos tend to underline D'Rivera's difficulty in finding a context: he can handle these rapid-fire speeds, but other members of the band – Perez and Haque in particular – find it difficult both to sustain the pace and to have anything interesting to say. Two classical pieces, 'Improvisation' and 'Contradanza', offer a little more variety, and this time D'Rivera brings out his soprano rather than his tenor.

RAY DRUMMOND
BASS

*** **Camera In A Bag** Criss Cross Jazz 1040 CD
Drummond; David Newman (*ts, f*); Kenny Barron (*p*); Steve Nelson (*vib*); Marvin 'Smitty' Smith (*d*). 12/89.

A sideman of high repute, Drummond has appeared as a leader on few occasions. This session works out very well, although nothing exactly arrives with a bang. Newman plays as much flute as tenor and sounds full and funky on both instruments, while Nelson functions peripherally; the strongest music, though, comes from the rhythm section, which develops a tremendously assured momentum across the nine compositions, four of them by Drummond.

MARC DUCRET
GUITAR, GUITAR-SYNTHESIZER

*** **La Théorie Du Pilier** Label Bleu LBL 6508 LP
Ducret; Michel Benita (*b*); Aaron Scott (*d*). 87.

***(*) **Le Kodo** Label Bleu LBL 6519 CD/LP
Ducret; Larry Schneider (*ss, ts*); Michel Benita (*b*); Adam Nussbaum (*d*). 12/88.

*** **Gris** Label Bleu LBLC 6531 CD
Ducret; Enrico Rava (*t*); Yves Robert (*tb*); François Jeanneau (*ss*); Andy Emler (*p*); Michel Benita, Renaud Garcia Fons (*b*); Joel Allouche (*d*). 5/90.

Ducret should be in the forefront of those guitarists who've fused rock, jazz and blues accents into an accessible new genre, but, hidden away on small European labels, his work lags far behind that of Scofield or Frisell in terms of reputation. *La Théorie Du Pilier* is a temperate trio record, concentrating on the interplay of the group, with Ducret sticking mostly to a clean, traditional guitar tone; but *Le Kodo* is a far tougher and more exciting session, the underrated Schneider piling through his solos and Ducret upping the ante on his own playing by several notches. Nussbaum plays with all the requisite energy, but sometimes one wishes for a drummer with a little more finesse. *Gris* varies the pace again: 'Elephanta' is a guitar–drums duet, Rava, Emler, Jeanneau and Robert drift in and out of the other tracks, and both bassists appear on 'Danser'. All three records have their share of good tunes as well as intelligent solos: Ducret pens a pleasing melody.

***   **News From The Front** JMT 849148-2 CD
Ducret; Herb Robertson (*t, flhn*); Yves Robert (*tb*); François Verly (*d*). 6–7/91.

A surprising step forward, although the record is finally let down by some questionable judgements. After the straight 'jazz guitar' of the previous discs, this first for a new company finds Ducret choosing a range of different guitar sounds and a dispersal of the jazz/rock time which had governed his previous discs. Verly is employed for percussive colour (via a drum machine) as much as for timekeeping, and the most serious relationship here is between Ducret's guitars and Robertson's mocking, splintery trumpet and flugelhorn. Their opening duet on 'Pour Agnes', with Ducret on acoustic 12-string, sounds eerily like an echo of some old Ralph Towner meditation, but the bigger pieces such as the title-track and the long – perhaps too long – 'Fanfare' splay electric solos against a background of brass noise in still space. Robert doesn't have much to do, but his trombone chords on 'Wren Is Such A Strange Name' (the titles suggest an, er, concept) add another note of mystery. It isn't fully sustained, and passages such as the closing 'Golden Wren' sound more like an elevated kind of art-rock than anything, but Ducret is taking a courageous shot at the outside.

GERD DUDEK (born 1938)
SOPRANO SAXOPHONE, TENOR SAXOPHONE, FLUTE

(*)   **Open FMP 0570 LP
Dudek; Buschi Niebergall (*b*); Edward Vesala (*d*). 4/77.

By no means an orthodox sax–bass–drums trio, *Open* is a free-ish collaboration on half a dozen markedly angular titles which give the greatest scope to Vesala's inspirational and utterly individual drumming. Dudek sounds a trifle small-voiced in places, which may be down to the engineering; but this is certainly not on a par with his work with trumpeter Manfred Schoof or the Globe Unity Orchestra. A fudged extra half-star for Vesala.

***(*)   **After All** Konnex KCD 5022 CD
Dudek; Ali Haurand (*b*); Rob Van Den Broeck (*p*).

This is more like it. Dudek's tenor sound has become one of the most distinctive of the 1980s (with an individualized Coltrane influence evident on the superb 'Alabama') and it's rather shocking that he remains so little known and so poorly represented as a leader. The remaining material is more ambitious for a drummerless trio, but all three players contribute to the maintenance of a solid but elastic pulse. Surely there's a major label watching from the wings?

TED DUNBAR (born 1937)
GUITAR

**   **Opening Remarks** Xanadu 155 LP
Dunbar; Tommy Flanagan (*p*); Sam Jones (*b*); Leroy Williams (*d*). 1/78.

(*)   **Secundum Artem Xanadu 181 LP
Dunbar; Kenny Barron (*p*); Steve Nelson (*vib*); Rufus Reid (*b*); Al Foster (*d*). 6/80.

***   **Jazz Guitarist** Xanadu 196 LP
Dunbar (*g* solo). 7/82.

Anyone hearing Dunbar for the first time and expecting to encounter a characteristic soul–jazz guitarist will find these records a surprise. He's a very thoughtful and deliberate player, his improvising moving to an exceptionally even dynamic, his tone solid and grey (he plays with his thumb, rather than using a pick) – he takes an almost Tristano-like approach to his solos. His interest in George Russell's Lydian theories adds a further dimension to a compositional style which is intensely cultivated. But the records for Xanadu don't serve him as well as they might. *Opening Remarks* is too cautious: his debut as a leader has a preponderance of slow tempos and, while 'Hang In There' and 'Tonal Search' follow interesting lines, the slack rhythmic content lets the music sag. *Secundum Artem* is a little sharper. Barron, Reid and Foster are fine by themselves, and Nelson, in his first appearance on record, is energetic if somewhat sidelined; 'It's About Everything' is an abstruse yet warm-blooded ballad. But both records are troubled by a very flat, ungracious studio sound. Since Dunbar's music relies on finely tuned interplay, it's a damaging weakness.

The solo album is his most satisfying statement. He chooses several themes by pianists, and they're rarely heard as guitar solos: 'Hi-Fly', 'Epistrophy', 'Nica's Dream'. The latter especially is a solo of fine cumulative power. Dunbar's unemphatic manner tends to disguise the subtlety of his ideas: the rhythms of 'Hi-Fly', for instance, are varied with particular inventiveness, and his recasting of 'Body And Soul' as 'Total Conversion' snakes around the melody without ever quite referring to it. The studio sound is again too dull, but it's a refreshingly unusual solo album.

PAUL DUNMALL
SAXOPHONES, CLARINET

***(*) **Soliloquy** Matchless MR 15 CD
Dunmall (solo *reeds*). 10 & 12/86.

A powerful soloist with Spirit Level and with Keith Tippett's Mujician, Dunmall here explores territory normally associated with John Surman, coaxing a fierce poetry out of his saxophones. Multi-tracking allows him to build contrapuntal lines and stark harmonic intervals, but perhaps the most striking effects are created when, as on 'Human Atmospheres' he plays a long unaccompanied bridge using Ayler's or Peter Brötzmann's extremes of pitch. On the much shorter 'Elementals' he swaps his long, developed lines for a dense, pointillistic effect; 'Holocaust' opens with anguished 'unison' blares before opening out into an intense tenor soliloquy that is both anguished and admirably controlled. 'Clarinet And Ocarina' is not as slight as its resources might suggest, but the real star piece is 'Voyage', which nine out of ten blindfold-tested listeners would guess was Surman until the long *a capella* soprano solo pushes the music in a very different direction. Intelligently conceived and performed, *Soliloquy* is well worth having.

EDDIE DURAN (born 1925)
GUITAR

(*) **Jazz Guitarist Original Jazz Classics OJC 120 LP
Duran; Howard Dundune (*cl, ts*); Dean Riley (*b*); John Markham (*d*). 57.

A veteran of the San Francisco scene from the 1940s onwards, Duran's unfussy, swinging playing has been a useful component of groups led by Cal Tjader and Tania Maria, to name the leaders he's been most productively featured with. A 1979 Concord album is currently out of print, which leaves only this OJC reissue of a Fantasy album. Sunny playing on a set of mostly standard tunes.

BRAD DUTZ
PERCUSSION, KEYBOARDS

** **Brad Dutz** Nine Winds NWCD 0141 CD
Dutz; Tom McMoran (*p*); Bernie Dressel, Chet McCracken (*d*). 2–8/90.

Coolly pleasant percussion music, based around hand drums and MIDI-mallet controlled samples, where Dutz creates chinking soundscapes that percolate nicely for a few minutes before disappearing again. The only jazz element arrives in McMoran's two appearances, where the piano solos strike an oddly jarring note. Harmless, aimless music.

JOHNNY MBIZO DYANI (1945–86)
DOUBLE BASS

***   **Witchdoctor's Son** Steeplechase SCS 1098 CD/LP/MC
Dyani; John Tchicai (*as, ss*); Dudu Pukwana (*as, ts*); Alfredo Do Nascimento (*g*); Luiz Carlos de Sequeira (*d*); Mohamed Al-Jabry (*perc*). 3/78.

***   **Song For Biko** Steeplechase SCS 1109 CD/LP/MC
Dyani; Dudu Pukwana (*as*); Don Cherry (*co*); Makaya Ntoshko (*d*). 7/78.

(*)   **Mbizo Steeplechase SCS 1163 LP/MC
Dyani; Dudu Pukwana (*as, ss*); Ed Epstein (*as, bs*); Churchill Jolobe (*d*). 2/81.

(*)   **Afrika Steeplechase SCS 1186 LP
Dyani; Ed Epstein (*as, bs*); Charles Davis (*as*); Thomas Ostergren (*b*); Gilbert Matthews (*d*); Rudy Smith (*steel d*); Thomas Akuru Dyani (*congas*). 10/83.

(*)   **Born Under The Heat Dragon DRLP 68 LP
Dyani; Ulf Adaker (*t*); Mosa Gwangwa (*tb*); Charles Davis (*as*); Peter Shimi Radise (*ts*); Krister Andersson (*ts*); Thomas Ostergren (*b*); Gilbert Matthews (*d*). 11/83.

***   **Angolian Cry** Steeplechase SCS 1209 CD/LP
Dyani; Harry Beckett (*t, flhn*); John Tchicai (*ts, bcl*); Billy Hart (*d*). 7/85.

The solo 'Wish You Sunshine' on *Born Under The Heat* is the perfect encapsulation of what the late Johnny Dyani was about: calmly visionary, with a deep swelling of anger and irony underneath; technically robust; stylistically various. More than any of the South African exiles, Dyani absorbed and assimilated a wide variety of styles and procedures. He spent much of his active life in Scandinavia where he forged close artistic relationships with John Tchicai, Don Cherry and with Dollar Brand (Abdullah Ibrahim), with whom he shared a particular vision of Africa.

The music is strongly politicized but never programmatic. *Witchdoctor's Son* and *Song For Biko* come from Dyani's most consistently inventive period. Some of the early 1980s material is a little more diffuse and, though Pukwana – another who has since re-entered Azania beyond life – is a powerfully compelling solo voice, he always seemed to mute Dyani's more inventive progressions.

Afrika is probably the weakest of Dyani's records, marred by an ill-matched rhythm section and out-of-character horns. *Mbizo* is much less cluttered in execution, but it has a starkness that may have been deliberate and circumstantial, but which is rather alienating. Dyani never found another drummer with Ntoshko's instincts and empathy, but he came briefly close with Churchill Jolobe and then again towards the end of his life with Billy Hart. *Angolian Cry* is a marvellous record, brimming with the pathos and joy that marked *Song For Biko*. Beckett is an uncut national treasure and it's interesting to hear Tchicai on the less familiar tenor.

JON EARDLEY (born 1928)
TRUMPET, FLUGELHORN

(*)   **From Hollywood To New York Original Jazz Classics OJC 1746 CD/LP

***   **The Jon Eardley Seven** Original Jazz Classics OJC 123 LP
Eardley; Milt Gold (*tb on Seven* only); Phil Woods (*as on Seven* only); Zoot Sims (*ts on Seven* only); J. R. Monterose (*ts on From Hollywood* only); George Syran (*p*); Teddy Kotick (*b*); Nick Stabulas (*d*). 12/54, 1/56.

Uncontroversial swing from the sometime Chet Baker doppelgänger. The arrangements and voicings for septet are actually rather closer to those of another of Eardley's occasional employers, Gerry Mulligan, but something of Baker's fragile diction and vulnerable emotionalism creeps through even in the stronger passages.

From Hollywood To New York is from an earlier quintet fronted by Eardley and the ever-about-to-be-rediscovered Monterose, who is one of the more adventurous of the middle-generation tenor players; the rhythm section is robust, and turned out to be durable, producing a near-identical groove on the later recording.

It's hard to be categorical about Eardley because he doesn't make categorical music. On its own unambitious terms, unexceptionable.

CHARLES EARLAND (born 1941)
ORGAN, SOPRANO SAXOPHONE

***(*)   **Black Talk!** Original Jazz Classics OJC 335 LP/MC
Earland; Virgil Jones (*t*); Houston Person (*ts*); Melvin Sparks (*g*); Idris Muhammad (*d*); Buddy Caldwell (*perc*). 12/69.

Earland began as a tenor saxophonist in organ combos, but switched sides in the late 1960s and moved over to the keyboard. *Black Talk!* comes close to being a genre classic: Earland updated the heavier style of players such as Jack McDuff and Jimmy Smith, chose more pop-orientated material and delivered it with a snappier, almost percussive attack. The other musicians on the date are useful supports, with Sparks prominently featured, but Earland's leadership drives the music. The unpromising choice of 'Aquarius', for instance, is transformed into a convincing, bluesy groove piece.

***   **Front Burner** Milestone M 9165 CD/LP/MC
Earland; Virgil Jones (*t*); Bill Easley (*ts*); Bobby Broom (*g*); Rudy Williams (*d*); Frank Colon (*perc*). 6/88.

The recent revival of interest in 'traditional' jazz organ has rekindled Earland's career. There's some fluff on this date – the theme to *Moonlighting*, for example – but the organist, who plays straight-ahead Hammond throughout, sounds at his happiest and most relaxed fronting a band that has all the right moves down cold. The recording is glossier than it used to be, but the feel comes through.

BILL EASLEY
REEDS

(*)   **Wind Inventions Sunnyside SSC 1022 CD/LP
Easley; Mulgrew Miller (*p*); Victor Gaskin (*b*); Tony Reedus (*d*). 9/86.

This talented multi-instrumentalist is a proven asset as a sideman, but his debut as a leader is a trifle colourless. He performs most of this programme on clarinet and, while it's a welcome change from hearing yet another prodigious saxophonist, his improvisations are facile rather than compelling. The sleeve-note compares the date to Buddy DeFranco's '50s records, but Easley doesn't approach DeFranco's piercing insight, and his swing-into-bop manner sounds bland across the length of an album. The soft-edged sound doesn't assist him.

JON EBERSON
GUITAR

**   **Stash** Odin 19 CD/LP
Eberson; Bjorn Kjellemyr (*b*); Audun Klieve (*d*). 8/86.

Jon Eberson has the problem of being Norway's 'other' guitarist after Terje Rypdal, and it's likely to be compounded by his decision to use Rypdal's Chasers rhythm section for this brawny but not especially distinctive set. The 13 compositions often boil down to decorated riffs and, while their brevity at least prevents stasis setting in, it means that nothing gets developed very far either.

BILLY ECKSTINE (born 1914)
VOCAL, TRUMPET

**** I Want To Talk About You Xanadu 207 LP
Eckstine; Walter Fuller, Milton Fletcher, Ed Sims, George Dixon, Shirley Clay, Harry Jackson, Rostelle Reese, Leroy White, Tommy Enoch, Benny Harris, Freddy Webster, Jesse Miller, Shorty McConnell, Gail Brockman, Boonie Hazel, Fats Navarro (*t*); Ed Burke, John Ewing, Joe McLewis, Ed Fant, George Hunt, Nat Atkinson, Jerry Valentine, Taswell Baird, Chippy Outcalt, Howard Scott (*tb*); Leroy Harris, Scoops Carry, John Jackson, Bill Frazier (*as*); Bob Crowder, Jimmy Mundy, Budd Johnson, Franz Jackson, Willie Randall, Gene Ammons (*ts*); Omer Simeon, Leo Parker (*bs*); Earl Hines, John Malachi (*p*); Claude Robertson, Hurley Ramey, Clifton Best, Connie Wainwright (*g*); Quinn Wilson, Truck Parham, Tommy Potter (*b*); Alvin Burroughs, Rudy Traylor, Art Blakey (*d*); Madeline Green (*v*). 2/40–3/45.

The ripest, most luxuriant baritone voice in black music – but Billy Eckstine wasn't the conservative that description might suggest. In the 1940s he led the most challenging of modern big bands which included most of the important young boppers at some point, and his own singing, while fundamentally lavish and romantic, offered subtle musical hints about tempo and inflexion that were picked up by many jazz musicians. The sides his orchestra made for Savoy are currently awaiting reissue on CD, but this glorious compilation collects many of the key sides he made with the Earl Hines Orchestra of 1940–41, along with three transcriptions of his own big band from 1945. Some might not take to the idea of a record of what are basically slow, elegant ballads sung by a baritone who's more concerned with resonance than with improvisational flow, but Eckstine's singing here is, as Don Schlitten's note points out, truly radical: if blacks were meant to sing about worry and strife, Eckstine's romantic power booms magnificently past expectations. Although he liked to disdain claims of being a blues singer, there are two superb blues performances in 'Jelly Jelly' and 'Stormy Monday Blues', both arranged by Budd Johnson. The ballads are nevertheless consistently affecting in the sheer sumptuousness of Eckstine's voice. The final tracks include Blakey, Navarro, Ammons and other young gladiators, but it's Eckstine, his voice now fully mature, who dominates: 'If That's The Way You Feel' and 'I Want To Talk About You' are marvels of control and strength. The remastering is respectable if a little dull, and it suggests that the singer was too close to the microphone on some tracks; but it scarcely blunts the enjoyment of a restorative record.

*** Once More With Feeling Fresh Sounds FSR-CD 24 CD
Eckstine; Billy May Orchestra. 60.

*** At Basin Street East Emarcy 832592 CD
Eckstine; Benny Bailey, Clark Terry, Ernie Royal (*t*); Curtis Fuller (*tb*); Julius Watkins (*frhn*); Phil Woods (*as*); Jerome Richardson, Eric Dixon (*ts, f*); Sahib Shihab (*bs*); Patti Bown (*p*); Don Elliott (*vib*); Don Arnone (*g*); Stu Martin (*d*). 61.

Eckstine's many records for Mercury from the 1950s and '60s are seriously neglected. Both of these sessions are rousing encounters with big bands. Billy May, following his records with Sinatra, arranges a dozen staple standards for Eckstine to amble through and, while there's a hint of routine about the project, both voice and orchestra sound in excellent fettle. More interesting, though, is the meeting with Jones's big band. The contrast here is between Eckstine's opulent, take-my-time delivery and the scintillating punch of what was a fierce, slick, note-perfect organization. We hope that one of his finest Mercury albums, *Billy's Best*, will appear on CD in due course.

**** No Cover No Minimum Roulette CDP 7985832 CD
Eckstine; Charlie Walp (*t*); Bucky Manieri (*tb*); Charlie McLean, Buddy Balboa (*saxes*); Bobby Tucker (*p*); Buddy Grievey (*d*). 8/60.

A superlative example of Eckstine's art, and unquestionably his best record in print. Recorded at a Las Vegas lounge, the 21 tracks (12 of them previously unissued) luxuriate in Bobby Tucker's simple arrangements and bask in the grandeur of Eckstine's voice and phrasing.

'Moonlight In Vermont' has never sounded more richly expansive, 'Lush Life' is a proper ode to barfly poetry, and the swingers are delivered with an insouciance and a perfect mastery of metre which creates shivers of delight. A few trumpet solos are the least we can forgive him for, although actually they're not bad. The remastering is very full and vivid on what is an indispensable issue.

HARRY EDISON (born 1915)
TRUMPET

***   **Jawbreakers** Original Jazz Classics OJC 487 CD/LP/MC
        Edison; Eddie 'Lockjaw' Davis (ts); Hugh Lawson (p); Ike Isaacs (b); Clarence
        Johnston (d). 4/62.

**   **Opus Funk** Storyville SLP 4025 LP
        Edison; Eddie 'Lockjaw' Davis (ts); John Darville (tb); Kenny Drew (p); Hugo
        Rasmussen (b); Svend Erik Norregaard (d). 6/76.

(*)   **Sweets And Jaws Black & Blue 233106 CD
        Edison; Eddie 'Lockjaw' Davis (ts); Gerald Wiggins (p); Major Holley (b); Oliver
        Jackson (d). 2/77.

(*)   **Simply Sweets Pablo 2310806 CD
        Edison; Eddie 'Lockjaw' Davis (ts); Dolo Coker (p); Harvey Newmark (b); Jimmie
        Smith (d). 9/77.

Ubiquitous as a accompanist/soloist, Edison has made surprisingly few records of his own. The 1970s association with Lockjaw Davis produced some of the best and *Jawbreakers* comes highly recommended, with a big, raw sound and a lovely version of 'A Gal In Calico' that contrasts well with the tough funk of 'Oo-ee!'. The Pablos have a good, full sound and there's no great bonus in the Black & Blue CD transfer, though it does have the best of several available readings of 'There Is No Greater Love', an Edison staple. *Opus Funk* is disappointingly woolly.

***   **Can't Get Out Of This Mood** Orange Blue OB 006 CD
        Edison; Kenny Drew (p); Jimmy Woode (b); Oliver Jackson (d). 10–11/88.

***(*) **For My Pals** Pablo 2310934 CD/LP/MC
        Edison; Buster Cooper (tb); Curtis Peagler (as, ts); Art Hillery (p, org); Andrew
        Simpkins (b); Albert 'Tootie' Heath (d). 12/88.

***   **Swing Summit** Candid CCD 79050 CD
        Edison; Buddy Tate (cl, ts); Frank Wess (ts, f); Hugh Lawson (p); Ray Drummond
        (b); Bobby Durham (d). 4/90.

Edison's artistic longevity has been remarkable; his ability and willingness continually to develop is nothing short of miraculous. The very recent *For My Pals*, with a larger than usual group, marks a welcome return to form for a player who often performs better under other leaders; 'Lover Man' and 'There Is No Greater Love' are both top-notch performances and the sound is immaculate. *Can't Get Out Of This Mood* and *Swing Summit* contain less interesting material, but both are brightly and faithfully recorded and both CDs are excellent value.

CLIFF EDWARDS (1895–1971)
VOCAL, UKULELE

***(*) **Cliff Edwards And His Hot Combination 1925–26** Retrieval FV-203 LP
        Edwards; Red Nichols (c); Miff Mole (tb); Bobby Davis, Frankie Trumbauer (as);
        Fred Morrow (ts); Adrian Rollini (bsx); Arthur Schutt, Irving Brodsky (p); Dick
        McDonough, Nick Lucas (bj); Vic Berton (d). 2/25–10/26.

The voice of Jiminy Cricket was, as American critic Will Friedwald has pointed out, a great unsung figure in the development of jazz singing. His 1920s recordings as 'Ukulele Ike' show how amazingly prescient Edwards was in his singing, which uses scatting (or 'eefing', as Edwards called it) with as much rhythmical abandonment as Louis Armstrong. Edwards was more of a novelty singer – he sends up Irving Berlin's 'Remember' mercilessly, by entering into a dialogue with his own falsetto voice – and most of the tunes here are throwaway pop songs of the day. But his interplay with The Red Heads, the band that provides most of the backing, is genuinely improvisational, and his chase chorus with Nichols on 'Dinah' proves that he could hold his own with the smartest figures on the New York studio scene. Indeed, Edwards is more free-spirited and inventive than anybody else on these sides. The original records were made for Pathé Actuelle, and the surfaces have a lot of hiss, but the remastering is still a mostly fine job.

TEDDY EDWARDS (born 1924)
TENOR SAXOPHONE

****   **Together Again!** Original Jazz Classics OJC 424 CD/LP/MC
Edwards; Howard McGhee (t); Phineas Newborn Jr (p); Ray Brown (b); Ed Thigpen (d). 5/61.

**   **Heart And Soul** Original Jazz Classics OJC 177 LP
Edwards; Gerald Wiggins (org); Leroy Vinnegar (b); Milton Turner (d). 62.

***   **Out Of This World** Steeplechase SCS 1147 CD/LP
Edwards; Kenny Drew (p); Jesper Lundgaard (b); Billy Hart (d). 12/80.

**   **Good Gravy** Timeless SJP 139 CD/LP
Edwards; Rein de Graaff (p); Henk Haverhoek (b); John Engels (d). 12/81.

Unrated as a soloist, Edwards is still one of the most influential voices around. His reunion with a cleaned-up Howard McGhee in 1962 led to one of the best mainstream albums of the post-war years. *Together Again!* is beautifully and almost effortlessly crafted. The ultra-straight 'Misty' showcases Edwards's moody ballad approach and there is a fine 'You Stepped Out Of A Dream'.

Nothing else quite compares, though the unfortunately deleted *Teddy's Ready* on Contemporary had a timeless vigour that should soon restore it to the catalogue. The 1980s material is pretty much of a piece, but Edwards isn't on form for *Good Gravy*. He also lacks a convincing bass player. Spoilt by Leroy Vinnegar, Edwards never again found someone who could put so much relaxed spring into his solo gait. Haverhoek copes manfully but hasn't the lyricism to match the firmly accented pulse.

There's no point by-passing *Together Again!*. Subsequent ports of call should be *Teddy's Ready* and *Out Of This World*, in that order.

**   **Mississippi Lad** Antilles 314 511 411 CD
Edwards; Nolan Smith (t); Jimmy Cleveland (tb); Art Hillery (p); Leroy Vinnegar (b); Billy Higgins (d); Ray Armando (d); Tom Waits (v). 3/91.

Tom Waits is much like olives. People either love him or *really* dislike him. He actually appears on only two songs, the disconcerting opener 'Little Man' and the later 'I'm Not Your Fool Anymore', both with music and lyrics by Edwards. It's also clear, by way of a further consolation to the olive-haters, that Edwards, denied his share of recording opportunities in recent years, probably couldn't have made *Mississippi Lad* without Waits's enthusiastic imprimatur and crossover marketability.

In practice, the album is a sorry mish-mash of up-tempo Latino dance-numbers, oozing ballads, and a couple of good straightforward jazz pieces. 'Symphony On Central' opens promisingly with Vinnegar's instantly recognizable walking bass and Higgins's incisive cymbal pattern; both later solo, and Higgins fans will be reassured to think he had nothing to do with the idiotic percussion solo on 'Safari Walk'. By and large, though, 'Symphony' and the following 'Ballad For A Bronze Beauty' are features for the leader and rhythm, with the other horns and Señor Armando out. A disappointing album, but, as the man said, parts of it are excellent.

MARK EGAN (born 1951)
BASS

**   **A Touch Of Light** GRP 9572 CD/MC
Egan; Bill Evans (*ss*); Clifford Carter, Gil Goldstein (*ky*); Danny Gottlieb (*d*); Cafe (*perc*). 4–5/88.

Mark Egan, who once studied with Jaco Pastorius, might have emerged as Pastorius's successor to the title of leading electric bassist, but his solo projects – usually in the group Elements with Danny Gottlieb – have settled for niceness over depth and weight. This GRP session has its moments, with Evans a useful player to have on hand, but the usual flavourless production damps down the initiative, and titles like 'Ocean Child' and 'Waterfall Cafe' tell the story.

MARTY EHRLICH
REEDS, FLUTES

***   **The Welcome** Sound Aspects sas 002 LP
Ehrlich; Anthony Cox (*b*); Pheeroan AkLaff (*d*). 3/84.

Ehrlich maintains a consistent level of excellence on all his instruments – he's a pungent improviser with a colourful imagination – but it's his work on B-flat and bass-clarinets which is most striking, since he uses them as often as he does the more familiarly contemporary alto sax and flute. An interest in collective improvisation and a taste for folkish melodies gives this trio a feel comparable to Ornette Coleman's mid-1960s group, and Ehrlich, Cox and AkLaff respond keenly to each other's playing. The recording is a little dry.

****   **Pliant Plaint** Enja 5065 CD/LP
Ehrlich; Stan Strickland (*ss, ts, f*); Anthony Cox (*b*); Robert Previte (*d*). 4/87.

***(*)   **The Traveller's Tale** Enja 6024 CD/LP
As above, except Lindsey Horner (*b*) replaces Cox. 5–6/89.

Ehrlich's Enja albums provide entertaining samplers for the breadth of contemporary jazz. His compositions are eclectic in the best way, drawing on different rhythmic and formal backgrounds but impressed with his own spirited playing. Strickland, a gutsy and agile tenor player, is an excellent foil for the leader, and both rhythm sections are fine, though Cox is marginally more responsive than Horner. We prefer *Pliant Plaint* for its sense of variety: there's an impeccable composed piece, 'After After All', played by Ehrlich alone in a series of overdubs, and an enchanting flute duet on 'What I Know Now', along with more familiar thematic improvising on the other pieces. *The Traveller's Tale* is, though, nearly as good, with Ehrlich sounding strong on four different reeds.

***(*)   **Side By Side** Enja 5065-2 CD
Ehrlich; Frank Lacy (*tb*); Wayne Horvitz (*p*); Anthony Cox (*b*); Andrew Cyrille (*d*). 1/91.

***   **Falling Man** Muse MCD 5398 CD
Ehrlich; Anthony Cox (*b*). 90.

Side By Side continues an exceptionally rewarding sequence of records. Ehrlich's instinct for good tunes accompanies ensemble playing and direction which go about as far out from hard bop orthodoxy as they can: it's highly melodic and rhythmically liberated free playing, with enough arranged detail to keep a composer's sensibility happy. Lacy and Ehrlich are all over their horns, and the rhythm section play just as strongly. *Falling Man* reduces the cast to two, with a certain loss of individuality as a result: by himself, Ehrlich isn't so interesting a soloist, and there's only so much that he can find to say in tandem with Cox, though 'You Don't Know What Love Is' – a retrospective nod at Mingus and Dolphy, two very kindred influences – is very good.

EIGHT BOLD SOULS
GROUP

**   **Eight Bold Souls** Sessoms 0002 LP

Robert Griffin (*t, flhn*); Isaiah Jackson (*tb*); Edward Wilkerson (*as, ts, bs, cl*); Mwata
Bowden (*ts, bs, cl*); Aaron Dodd (*tba*); Naomi Millender (*clo*); Richard Brown (*b*);
Dushun Mosley (*d*). 86.

This has its moments, but it's an octet – led by the highly regarded Chicagoan, Wilkerson – with
little of the collective integrity and purpose of, say, David Murray's similarly sized group.
Wilkerson's writing is more a matter of juxtaposition – sometimes fortuitous, sometimes not –
than coherent composing and, though there are some impassioned solos (especially,
surprisingly, from Dodd) the record seems under-prepared and is perhaps an unjust reflection of
the group's capabilities.

ROY ELDRIDGE (1911–88)
TRUMPET

***   **Little Jazz** CBS 465684 CD

Eldridge; Bill Coleman, Bill Dillard, Joe Thomas, Dick Vance (*t*); Fernando Arbello,
Ed Cuffee, Dicky Wells (*tb*); Eddie Powell (*f*); Buster Bailey, Robert Burns, Jimmy
Carroll (*cl*); Carl Prager (*bcl*); Russell Procope (*cl, as*); Scoops Carry, Carl Frye,
Howard Johnson, Jimmy Powell (*as*); Chu Berry, Teddy Hill, Elmer Williams, Dave
Young (*ts*); Sam Allen, Teddy Cole, Horace Henderson, Sonny White, Teddy Wilson
(*p*); Putney Dandridge (*p, v*); John Collins, Hilton Lamare, Bob Lessey, Lawrence
Lucie, John Smith (*g*); Artie Bernstein, Israel Crosby, Richard Fulbright, John Kirby,
Truck Parham, Pete Peterson (*b*); Bill Beason, Sid Catlett, Hal West (*d*). 2 & 6/35, 3 &
5/36, 1/37, 1, 2 & 4/40.

***(*)   **After You've Gone** GRP Decca 16052 CD

Eldridge; Gus Aiken, Henry Clay, Paul Cohen, Sidney De Paris, Andy Ferretti, Bill
Graham, Tom Grider, John 'Bugs' Hamilton, Marion Hazel, Elton Hill, Yank Lawson,
Sylvester Lewis, Robert Mason, Jimmy Maxwell, Dave Page, Pinky Savitt, Jim
Thomas, Clarence Wheeler, Elmon Wright (*t*); Nat Atkins, Will Bradley, Wilbur
De Paris, Vic Dickenson, Richard Dunlap, Charles Greenlea, Ted Kelly, John
McConnell, Hal Matthews, Fred Ohms, Albert Riding, Fred Robinson, George
Robinson, Ward Silloway, George Stevenson, Sandy Watson, Sandy Williams, Gerald
Wilson (*tb*); Buster Bailey (*c*); Curby Alexander, Mike Doty, Ray Eckstrand, Joe
Eldridge, Andrew Gardner, Edmond Gregory (Sahib Shihab), Chris Johnson, Porter
Kilbert, Sam Lee (*as*); Tom Archia, Chu Berry, Charles Bowen, Al Green, Franz
Jackson, George Lawson, Walt Lockhart, Don Purviance, Ike Quebec, Mike Ross, Hal
Singer, Harold Webster (*ts*); Ernie Caceres, Dave McRae, Cecil Payne, Al Townsend
(*bs*); Dave Bowman, Ted Brannon, Tony D'Amore, Teddy Cole, Rozelle Gayle,
Buster Harding, Duke Jordan (*p*); Sam Allen, Mike Bryan, John Collins, Luke Fowler
(*g*); Louis Carrington, John Kirby, Carl Pruitt, Rodney Richardson, Ted Sturgis, Billy
Taylor, Carl Wilson (*b*); Lee Abrams, Sid Catlett, Cozy Cole, Les Erskine, Earl
Phillips, Mel Saunders, Harold West (*d*). 2/36, 11/43, 6 & 10/44, 3/45, 1, 7 & 9/46.

Roy Eldridge has been widely acknowledged as the bridge between swing and bebop trumpet.
Listening to Dizzy Gillespie at the (in)famous Massey Hall concert with Charlie Parker, Charles
Mingus, Bud Powell and Max Roach, there is very little doubt about the ancestry of the
trumpeter's high-register accents. However, Eldridge can't just be seen as Moses who led his
people out of the desert of late swing and up to the borders of bop's promised land. Eldridge did
his thing longer and more consistently than the modernists' version of the story would have you
believe.

Eldridge moved to New York in 1934 and was quickly recognized as a new star. The
introductory bars of '(Lookie, Lookie) Here Comes Cookie', first item on the valuable *Little
Jazz*, offers a glimpse of the excitement the youngster must have caused. His ability to displace
accents and plays questionable intervals with perfect confidence and logic is immediately
evident. More than just a high-note man, Eldridge combined remarkable rhythmic intuition

with an ability to play intensely exciting music in the middle and lower register, often the acid test that separates the musicians from the instrumentalists. His solo on 'Blue Lou', recorded with the Fletcher Henderson band in March 1936 is a perfect case in point. He does the same kind of thing with the Teddy Wilson band on 'Blues In C Sharp Minor', fitting his improvisation perfectly to the moody key; Chu Berry's follow-up and Israel Crosby's tensely throbbing bass complete a masterful performance. At the other end of the emotional spectrum, there are the starburst top Cs (and beyond) of 'Heckler's Hop', highpoint of an excellent set as leader with a band anchored on Zutty Singleton's tight drumming. The vocal tracks with Mildred Bailey are often quite appealing, and show how responsive an accompanist Eldridge was, again able to play quietly and in contralto range when called upon. A solitary Billie Holiday track – 'Falling In Love Again' – gives a flavour only of that association, which is more fully documented under her name.

After You've Gone is a valuable compilation of 'Little Jazz''s American Decca recordings of the late war years, with one brief glimpse back at the sessions with clarinettist Buster Bailey and tenor saxophonist Chu Berry two years before the more familiar Little Jazz Ensemble dates on Commodore Classics' valuable Chu Berry compilation *A Giant of the Tenor Sax* (Commodore 8.24293). The set includes some material never commercially released before, like a 'St Louis Blues' used on a 1965 Decca promotional for *Life* magazine (doubtless pitched in *Life*'s inimitably condescending way). The transfers are done on the Sonic Solutions NoNOISE system which leaves the masters clean but a little bleached-out in some areas. Eldridge occupies most of the foreground, whacking out top notes like Satchmo had never been heard of; the opening of (an unissued) 'I Surrender, Dear' is almost absurdly skyscraping. Unfortunately, Eldridge has been saddled with the reputation of being a high-note man. His muted 'stroll' opening to his own composition, 'The Gasser', is equally typical, giving way to a fine soulful solo from Ike Quebec, and then Eldridge again in more familiar mode on open horn.

Long before he became known as a JATP stalwart and itinerant sitter-in, Eldridge had sounded comfortable in front of big bands where his reaching tone and simple phrasing sounded less forced than they can in smaller groups. There is a lovely 'Body And Soul' (compare the version with Berry, above) and a fine 'I Can't Get Started' with the October 1944 line-up that yields the teasing, stop-start 'After You've Gone' (it's the only piece with an alternative take, though there are a couple of incompletes). 'Embraceable You' from the following year is equally fine; but the quality thins badly around this point in the compilation. None of the later tracks matches up to the astonishing ripping intensity of his tone on 'Star Dust' with the 1943 group, which counts as one of his finest performances ever, studded in the middle chorus with a single high note.

Given the dominance of Dizzy and the alternative direction opened up by Miles, Eldridge's work has been at something of a premium in recent years. These, though, are essential – and usefully complementary – documents of modern jazz and offer a salutary lesson for anyone who still tends to think of the music as a sequence of upper-case historical styles.

(*)   **Frenchie Roy Vogue 655009 CD
Eldridge; Benny Vasseur (*tb*); Don Byas, Albert Ferreri (*ts*); William Boucaya (*bs*); Claude Bolling, Raymond Fol, Gerald Wiggins (*p*); Guy de Fatto, Pierre Michelot, Barney Spieler (*b*); Robert Barney, Kenny Clarke, Armand Molinetti (*d*). 50–51.

***   **Just You, Just Me – Live In '59** Stash 531 CD
Eldridge; Coleman Hawkins (*ts*); Don Wilson (*p*); Bob Decker (*b*); Buddy Dean (*d*). 59.

(*)   **Montreux '77 Original Jazz Classics OJC 373 CD/LP/MC
Eldridge; Oscar Peterson (*p*); Niels-Henning Ørsted-Pedersen (*b*); Bobby Durham (*d*). 7/77.

***   **Happy Time** Original Jazz Classics OJC 628 CD/LP/MC
Eldridge; Oscar Peterson (p); Joe Pass (*g*); Ray Brown (*g*); Eddie Locke (*d*).

***   **Jazz Maturity ... Where It's Coming From** Pablo 2310928 CD
Eldridge; Dizzy Gillespie (*t*); Oscar Peterson (*p*); Ray Brown (*b*); Mickey Roker (*d*).

Much of Eldridge's recorded output is tucked away on trumpet compilations and festival albums. Perhaps the best of the latter is the Montreux set, part of a good series. The trumpeter appears to have regained some of his fire and sparkle and doesn't seem to require much notice for the upper-register stabs.

The CDs flatter his tight, fleet tone. The French compilation catches him in his first year-and-a-bit of exile, insulated from the virtual gang-warfare of big-band jazz Stateside in which Eldridge – as brittle as he was aggressive – got badly cut. The sessions with Don Byas and Claude Bolling are excellent, and there are two fascinating duos – 'Fireworks' and 'Wild Man Blues' – with the pianist.

Hawkins was a less adaptable second horn than Byas and tends to crowd a little in ensembles. The rhythm section obviously find some of the sharper angled ascents too tough, but generally it's a fine album, not too histrionic, catching both men in a period of renewed confidence. Eldridge collectors will still need to do some digging around in the 'Various Artists (Trumpet)' bin, though.

ELIANE ELIAS
PIANO

(*)   **Illusions Denon 33CY-1569 CD
Elias; Toots Thielemans (*hca*); Stanley Clarke, Eddie Gomez (*b*); Lenny White, Steve Gadd, Al Foster (*d*). 10/86.

(*)   **Crosscurrents Denon CY-2180-EX CD
Elias; Barry Finnerty (*g*); Eddie Gomez (*b*); Jack DeJohnette (*d*). 3/87.

Elias, who came first came to prominence in the group of her husband, Randy Brecker, is a capable if scarcely outstanding pianist, who works most comfortably in a light Latin genre not unlike that of, say, Vince Guaraldi. She keeps heavy company on both these dates, most of the tracks in a trio format; and *Crosscurrents* especially includes some worthwhile variations on standards. But one shouldn't expect gripping music.

(*)   **Plays Jobim Blue Note CDP 7930892 CD
Elias; Eddie Gomez (*b*); Jack DeJohnette (*d*); Nana Vasconcelos (*perc*). 12/89.

The material here suits Elias much better, and there is heavyweight support in the bass and drum roles; also some singing by the pianist. Very pleasant, and perhaps a slight step forward, but nothing too exciting.

DUKE ELLINGTON (1899–1974)
PIANO

(*)   **Complete Edition Vol. 1 1924–1926 Masters Of Jazz MJCD 8 CD
Ellington; Bubber Miley, Pike Davis, Harry Cooper, Leroy Rutledge, Louis Metcalf (*t*); Jimmy Harrison (*tb, v*); Charlie Irvis, Joe 'Tricky Sam' Nanton (*tb*); Don Redman (*cl, as*); Otto Hardwick (*Cmel, as, ss, bs*); George Thomas (*as, v*); Edgar Sampson (*as*); Prince Robinson (*ts, cl*); George Francis, Fred Guy (*bj*); Mack Shaw, Henry 'Bass' Edwards (*bb*); Sonny Greer (*d, v*); Alberta Prime, Jo Trent, Alberta Jones, Florence Bristol, Irving Mills (*v*). 11/24–11/26.

***   **Complete Edition Vol. 2 1926–1927** Masters Of Jazz MJCD 9 CD
Ellington; Bubber Miley, Louis Metcalf, June Clark (*t*), Joe Nanton (*tb*); Otto Hardwick (*ss, as, bs*); Prince Robinson, Rudy Jackson (*cl, ts*), Harry Carney (*bs, as, cl*); Fred Guy (*bj*); Henry 'Bass' Edwards, Wellman Braud (*b*); Sonny Greer (*d*); Adelaide Hall (*v*). 12/26–10/27.

***   **Duke Ellington 1924–1927** Classics 542 CD
As above two discs, except omit Prime, Bristol, Trent. 11/24–10/27.

Ellington's story on record remains the most commanding legacy in the music, impossible to surpass, and the current state of reissues of material from the 78 era is a transitional one. After the enormous and comprehensive LP reissues of the 1970s – specifically the multiple-disc sets issued by French RCA and CBS, as well as numerous and lengthy sequences of broadcast material from private labels – the industry has been rather slow to transfer much of this material to CD. With the copyright now lapsed on all the pre-1940 records, smaller labels are now taking up the challenge of chronological reissues. The Masters Of Jazz operation (based in France) boasts of a 'complete edition', although as we go to press only the above two discs covering the earliest material have been released. The Classics sequence, meanwhile, currently stands at ten discs, covering the period up to 1933.

The first two Masters Of Jazz discs certainly secure a comprehensive track listing, with all of Ellington's rarest early appearances including the accompaniments to Alberta Prime, Jo Trent and Florence Bristol and the 1925 duet with Irving Mills, while Classics are content to stick to the band sides leading up to the Victor version of 'Black And Tan Fantasy' in 1927. However, the very early material will be of interest only to scholars and the merely curious. Poor recording – the mastering of several tracks is rough, and in the absence of hearing high-quality originals ourselves, we're unsure as to how good a job has been done on some of the items – and a primitive, clumsy ensemble will be almost shocking to any who've never been acquainted with the earliest Ellington. Certainly the stiff rhythms and feeble attempts at solos on all the pre-1926 records are sometimes painful to hear, and if it weren't for Bubber Miley, the man who made Ellington 'forget all about the sweet music', there'd be nothing to detain anyone here. Yet Miley is already distinctive and powerful on his solo on The Washingtonians's 'Choo Choo', from November 1924. But the first volume ends with 'East St Louis Toodle-Oo', from the first important Ellington session, and from there the music demands the attention. Volume 2 of the MJ series includes two more versions of that tune, which points up how Ellington spread himself around different record labels: he recorded for Broadway, Vocalion, Gennett, Columbia, Harmony, Pathé, Brunswick, Okeh and Victor in the space of a little over three years. It also includes the first two versions of 'Black And Tan Fantasy', Ellington's first masterpiece, and Adelaide Hall's vocal on 'Creole Love Call'. The Classics disc sails past alternative takes, and is perhaps more listenable than either of the MJ discs, but remastering is again occasionally indifferent.

***(*)   **Duke Ellington 1927–1928** Classics 542 CD
Ellington; Bubber Miley, Jabbo Smith, Louis Metcalf, Arthur Whetsol (*t*); Joe 'Tricky Sam' Nanton (*tb*); Otto Hardwick (*ss, as, bs, bsx*); Rudy Jackson, Barney Bigard (*cl, ts*); Harry Carney (*bs, as, ss, cl*); Fred Guy (*bj*); Wellman Braud (*b*); Sonny Greer (*d*); Adelaide Hall (*v*). 10/27–3/28.

***(*)   **Duke Ellington 1928** Classics 550 CD
As above, except add Lonnie Johnson (*g*), Baby Cox, The Palmer Brothers (*v*), omit Jackson, Smith. 3–10/28.

***   **Duke Ellington 1928–29** Classics 559 CD
As above, except add Freddy Jenkins (*t*), Johnny Hodges (*cl, ss, as*), Ozie Ware, Irving Mills (*v*), omit Metcalf, Cox and Palmers. 10/28–3/29.

***(*)   **The Complete Brunswick Recordings Vol. 1** MCA MCAD 42325 CD
As above three discs. 3/27–1/29.

Ellington progressed quickly from routine hot dance records to sophisticated and complex three-minute works which showed a rare grasp of the possibilities of the 78-r.p.m. disc, a trait which he developed and exemplified better than anyone else in jazz from then until the 1950s. Yet during these years both Ellington and his band were still seeking a style that would turn them into a genuinely distinctive band. Having set down one or two individual pieces such as 'Black And Tan Fantasy' didn't mean that Duke was fully on his way. The 1926–28 records are still dominated to a high degree by the playing of Bubber Miley, and on a track such as 'Flaming Youth' (Classics 559), which was made as late as 1929, it is only Miley's superb work which makes the record of much interest. Arthur Whetsol made an intriguing contrast to Miley, his style being far more wistful and fragile: the way he plays 'The Mooche', on the 1928 Victor version, is a striking contrast to Miley's delivery (all versions are on Classics 550), and his treatment of the theme to 'Black Beauty' (also on Classics 550) is similarly poignant. Joe Nanton was a shouting trombonist with a limited stock of phrases, but he was already starting to work on the muted technique which would make him into one of Duke's most indispensable players. It was already a great brass team. But the reeds were weaker, with Carney taking a low-key role (not always literally: he played as much alto and clarinet as baritone in this era), and until Bigard's arrival in 1928 it lacked a distinctive soloist. Hodges also didn't arrive until October 1928. When the Ellington band went into the Cotton Club at the end of 1927, the theatricality which had begun asserting itself with 'Black And Tan Fantasy' became a more important asset, and though most of the 'Jungle' scores were to emerge on record around 1929–30, 'The Mooche' and 'East St Louis Toodle-Oo' show how set-piece effects were becoming important to Ellington. The best and most 'Ellingtonian' records of the period would include 'Blue Bubbles' (Classics 542), 'Take It Easy' and 'Jubilee Stomp' (1928 versions, on Classics 550), and 'Misty Mornin' and 'Doin' The Voom Voom' (both Classics 559), but even on the lesser tunes or those tracks where Ellington seems to be doing little more than copying Fletcher Henderson, there are usually fine moments from Miley or one of the others. The Classics CDs offer admirable coverage, with a fairly consistent standard of remastering, and though they ignore alternative takes, Ellington's promiscuous attitude towards the various record companies means that there are often several versions of a single theme on one disc (Classics 542, for instance, has three versions of 'Take It Easy'). MCA's Brunswick disc has the merit of conscientious if not always very lively remastering, while it covers only the tracks made for that label in the period.

***(*) **Duke Ellington 1929** Classics 569 CD
Ellington; Cootie Williams (*t, v*); Arthur Whetsol, Freddy Jenkins (*t*); Joe 'Tricky Sam' Nanton (*tb*); Barney Bigard (*cl, ts*); Johnny Hodges (*ss, as, cl*); Harry Carney (*bs, cl, as*); Fred Guy (*bj*); Wellman Braud (*b*); Sonny Greer (*d, v*); Ozie Ware (*v*). 3–7/29.

*** **Duke Ellington 1929–1930** Classics 577 CD
As above, except add Juan Tizol (*vtb*), Teddy Bunn (*g*), Bruce Johnson (*wbd*), Harold Randolph, Irving Mills (*v*), omit Ware. 8/29–1/30.

*** **Duke Ellington 1930** Classics 586 CD
As above, except add Cornell Smelser (*acc*), Dick Roberston (*v*), omit Bunn, Johnson and Randolph. 1–6/30.

*** **Duke Ellington 1930 Vol. 2** Classics 596 CD
As above, except add Charlie Barnet (*chimes*), Sid Garry, Jimmy Miller, Emmanuel Paul (*v*), omit Smelser. 6–11/30.

*** **Duke Ellington 1930–1931** Classics 605 CD
As above, except add Benny Paine (*v, p*), Chick Bullock, Frank Marvin, Smith Ballew (*v*), omit Barnet, Roberston, Miller and Paul. 11/30–1/31.

*** **The Brunswick Recordings Vol. 2** MCA MCAD 42348 CD
Similar to above Classics discs. 1/29–1/31.

***(*) **The OKeh Ellington** Columbia 4669644-2 2CD
As appropriate discs above. 3/27–11/30.

The replacement of Bubber Miley by Cootie Williams was the key personnel change in this period: Williams was a leaner, less outwardly expressive but equally fiery version of Miley, his scat singing was a fast development of Armstrong's vocal style, and he gave the brass section a new bite and brightness, even if he lacked Miley's ability to growl quite so intently. Hodges and Carney, too, were coming into their own, and along with the increasing mastery of Ellington's handling of his players, the band was now growing in assurance almost from session to session. The Victor date of 7 March 1929 (Classics 569) exemplifies many of the new powers of the orchestra. 'Hot Feet' includes a superb Hodges solo, Williams singing and playing with great authority, and the band moving out of the older hot style without sacrificing any drive. It was the now extraordinarily powerful swing of the rhythm section that was responsible for much of this advance: the same session is a fine instance of what they could do, from Braud's subtly propulsive drive on the excellently scored 'The Dicty Glide' to his outright stomping line on 'Hot Feet', with Greer taking a showman's role on his cymbals and traps and the remarkable Guy strumming a quick-witted counterpoint that made the banjo seem far from outdated (he would, though, soon switch to guitar). The two important Victor sessions on this disc (a third, two parts of a Cotton Club medley, is less substantial) make this a valuable issue, and there are two fascinatingly different versions of the small group blues 'Saratoga Swing' as well as

little-known Ellington attempts at 'I Must Have That Man' and an accompaniment to singer
Ozie Ware.

Ellington was recording at a prodigious pace, surprisingly so given the state of the industry at
that time, and there are some three CDs' worth of material from 1930. Classics 586 includes
some tunes that reek of Cotton Club set-pieces – 'Jungle Nights In Harlem', 'Jungle Blues' –
and some thin novelty tunes, but new versions of 'The Mooche' and 'East St Louis Toodle-Oo'
and new originals like 'Shout 'Em Aunt Tillie', 'Hot And Bothered' and 'Cotton Club Stomp'
are more substantial. Classics 596 has three different versions of 'Ring Dem Bells', each with
outstanding solos by Williams, three of 'Old Man Blues', and a first try at 'Mood Indigo'.
Classics 605 has three versions of 'Rockin' In Rhythm', each showing a slight advance on the
other, the tempo brightening and the reeds becoming smarter, and a slightly ironic reading of
'Twelfth Street Rag' which hints at Duke's later treatment of other people's jazz standards. But
the record closes with his first lengthy work, the two-part 'Creole Rhapsody', where for perhaps
the first time the soloists have to take a firm second place to the arrangement (this is the
ten-inch 78 version; the subsequent 12-inch version is on the next disc in the Classics sequence).
Remastering is mostly good and full-bodied: some of the records from more obscure companies
sound a little rougher, there are some tracks where bass boom overcomes mid-range brightness,
and frequent hints that these are not first-hand dubbings. Still, only more demanding ears may
be particularly troubled by the mixed transfer quality. The second volume of MCA's Brunswick
series is generally cleaner, and takes the story up to 'Creole Rhapsody', the same place where
Classics 605 stops. Columbia's OKeh set includes 49 titles ranging from 'East St Louis
Toodle-Oo' up to 'Rockin' In Rhythm' in a comprehensive account of the OKeh series. It's
capably remastered. Whether one wants to isolate the recordings by company in this way must
be a matter for the individual collector.

***   **Duke Elligton 1931–1932** Classics 616 CD
Ellington; Arthur Whetsol, Freddy Jenkins, Cootie Williams (*t*); Joe 'Tricky Sam'
Nanton, Lawrence Brown (*tb*); Juan Tizol (*vtb*); Johnny Hodges (*as, ss, cl*); Barney
Bigard (*cl, ts*); Harry Carney (*bs, cl*); Fred Guy (*bj, g*); Wellman Braud (*b*); Sonny
Greer (*d*); Frank Marvin, Ivie Anderson, Bing Crosby (*v*). 1/31–2/32.

***   **The Brunswick Sessions 1932–1935 Vol. 1** Jazz Information CAH 3001 CD/LP
As above, except add Otto Hardwick (*as, bsx*), omit Marvin. 2–5/32.

***   **Duke Ellington 1932–1933** Classics 626 CD
As above, except add Ray Mitchell, Adelaide Hall, The Mills Brothers, Ethel Waters
(*v*), omit Crosby. 5/32–1/33.

***   **The Brunswick Sessions 1932–1935 Vol. 2** Jazz Information CAH 3002 CD/LP
As above, except add Joe Garland (*ts*), omit Mitchell, Hall, Mills Bros, Waters.
5/32–5/33.

****   **The Brunswick Sessions 1932–1935 Vol. 3** Jazz Information CAH 3003 CD/LP
As above, except add Rex Stewart, Charlie Allen (*t*), Billy Taylor Sr (*b, bb*), Hayes
Alvis (*b*). 5/33–3/35.

The second 'Creole Rhapsody' opens Classics 616, a longer and better-played though still
imperfect version, but the rest of the disc is more conventional Ellington, with 'It Don't Mean
A Thing' and 'Lazy Rhpasody' the highlights in a programme which is mostly made up of other
writers' songs. The arrival of both Lawrence Brown and Ivie Anderson is more important:
Brown gave the brass section a new mellifluousness, and Anderson was probably the best
regular singer Duke ever employed. Classics 626 has ten Ellington themes out of 23 tracks, and
loses impetus at the end with sundry accompaniments to singers, but there are four substantial
pieces in 'Slippery Horn', 'Blue Harlem', 'Ducky Wucky' and especially 'Lightnin'', though
the orchestra often sounds sloppy here.

The three Jazz Information albums, with fine remastering from original 78s and excellent
sleevenotes, cover all of Duke's work for Brunswick (he was still also recording for Columbia
and Victor in the same period, though to a lesser extent) up to 1935. Most of the first two discs
are also on the final two Classics discs, but remastering here is rather better. The third volume,
though, is essential. Two Ellington standards make their debut here – 'Sophisticated Lady' and
'Solitude' – and there are at least four more major pieces in 'Bundle Of Blues', 'Harlem

Speaks', 'Saddest Tale' and 'Sump'n 'Bout Rhythm'. Stewart and Allen arrive in time for four tracks and Stewart already makes a mark on the brass sound of the orchestra on 'Margie'.

***(*) **Early Ellington 1927–1934** RCA Bluebird 86852 CD/LP/MC
As appropriate discs above. 27–34.

***(*) **Jungle Nights In Harlem** RCA Bluebird 82499 CD/LP/MC
As appropriate discs above. 12/27–2/32.

*** **Jazz Cocktail** ASV AJA 5024 CD
As appropriate discs above. 10/28–9/32.

(*) **Rockin' In Rhythm ASV AJA 5057 CD
As appropriate discs above. 3/27–7/36.

**** **Swing 1930 To 1938** BBC CD/REB/ZDF 686 CD/LP/MC
As appropriate discs above, except add Wallace Jones, Harold Baker (t), Ben Webster
(ts). 11/30–1/38.

Of the various compilations of early Ellington, we have examined the above five discs. The two ASV discs aren't really competitive since the remastering is rather grey and undefined, especially on ASV AJA 5057. Both of the Bluebird compilations, though, are shrewdly chosen from Duke's Victor output: the first is a mixed bag of mostly better-known material, while the second concentrates more on the 'threatrical' Ellington and includes several Cotton Club set-pieces such as the title-track, 'Haunted Nights' and two medleys. Both are among the better examples of the NoNOISE system of remastering. Robert Parker's BBC compilation uses the finest original 78s for remastering, and while we must include the usual reminder that Parker's use of a very slight reverberation to simulate concert-hall conditions may be unpleasing to some ears, these are exceptionally fine, clear and full-bodied transfers, one of his finest efforts to date. The tracks are a well-chosen selection from Duke's 1930s output and also include the otherwise-unavailable 'In A Jam' and 'Stepping Into Swing Society'.

**** **The Duke's Men: Small Groups Vol. 1** Columbia 468618 2CD/2MC
Ellington; Cootie Williams, Freddy Jenkins (t); Rex Stewart (c, v); Lawrence Brown,
Joe 'Tricky Sam' Nanton, Sandy Williams George Stevenson (tb); Juan Tizol (vtb);
Johnny Hodges (ss, as); Rudy Powell (cl, as); Otto Hardwick (as); Barney Bigard,
Bingie Madison (cl, ts); Harry Carney (bs); Roger 'Ram' Ramirez, Tommy Fulford
(p); Fred Guy, Bernard Addison, Brick Fleagle, Ceele Burke (g); Billy Taylor Sr,
Hayes Alvis, Wellman Braud (b); Sonny Greer, Chick Webb, Jack Maisel (d); Charlie
Barnet (perc); Sue Mitchell (v). 12/34–1/38.

Ellington's sidemen recorded a number of small-group dates under the nominal leadership of one or other of them during the late 1930s, and this superb compilation brings many of these dates together. There are a few undistinguished arrangements of pop tunes here, but for the most part this is inventive and skilful small-group jazz of the period. Duke is at the piano as often as not and there are a number of scarce Ellington tunes here, but many of the sides are features for Stewart, Bigard or Williams, who are the three main leaders (Hodges is credited with only two tracks, but his great work comes later, for Victor). 'Caravan', 'Stompy Jones', 'Back Room Romp', 'Tea And Trumpets', 'Love In My Heart' and 'Echoes Of Harlem' are all essential slices of Ellingtonia, but all 45 tracks have at least something of interest. Columbia have done one of their better eforts at remastering and there is an excellent accompanying essay by Helen Oakley Dance, who was involved with producing many of the records. This set completely supersedes the earlier one-disc compilation *Back Room Romp* (CBS Portrait 465021-2).

***(*) **Braggin' In Brass – The Immortal 1938 Year** CBS Portrait 465464 2CD/2MC
Ellington; Harold 'Shorty' Baker, Wallace Jones, Cootie Williams (t); Rex Stewart
(c); Lawrence Brown, Joe 'Tricky Sam' Nanton (tb); Juan Tizol (vtb); Barney Bigard
(cl, ts); Johnny Hodges (ss, as, cl); Otto Hardwick (as); Harry Carney (bs, as, cl); Fred
Guy (g); Hayes Alvis, Billy Taylor Sr (b); Sonny Greer (d). 1–12/38.

A valuable set from a very good, if not quite great (let alone immortal) year. The really outstanding Ellington themes here number only a few – 'Boy Meets Horn', a scintillating feature for Rex Stewart, 'Dinah's In A Jam', 'T.T. On Toast', 'I Let A Song Go Out Of My

Heart' – and many of the others get by on orchestral twists or quality solos. But there are a good number of those. The remastering is good if not quite as lively as it might have been.

***** **The Blanton–Webster Years** RCA Bluebird 85659 3CD/4MC
Ellington; Wallace Jones, Cootie Williams, Ray Nance (*t*); Rex Stewart (*c*); Joe 'Tricky Sam' Nanton, Lawrence Brown (*tb*); Juan Tizol (*vtb*); Barney Bigard, Chauncey Haughton (*cl*); Johnny Hodges (*ss, as, cl*); Harry Carney (*bs, cl, as*); Otto Hardwick (*as, bsx*); Ben Webster (*ts*); Billy Strayhorn (*p*); Fred Guy (*g*); Jimmy Blanton, Junior Raglin (*b*); Sonny Greer (*d*); Ivie Anderson, Herb Jeffries (*v*). 3/40–7/42.

With much late 1930s Ellington currently out of print, the advance to this astounding 1940 orchestra seems more sudden than it actually was. Ellington had been building a matchless team of soloists, his own composing was taking on a finer degree of personal creativity and sophistication, and with the arrival of bassist Jimmy Blanton, who gave the rhythm section an unparalleled eloquence in the way it swung, the final piece fell into place. The 6 May 1940 session, which opens this three-disc set, is one of the great occasions in jazz history, when Ellington recorded both 'Jack The Bear' (a feature for Blanton) and the unqualified masterpiece 'Ko Ko'. From there, literally dozens of masterpieces tumbled out of the band, from originals such as 'Harlem Air Shaft' and 'Main Stem' and 'Take The "A" Train' to brilliant Ellingtonizations of standard material such as 'The Sidewalks Of New York' and 'Clementine'. The arrival of Billy Strayhorn, Ellington's closest collaborator until Strayhorn's death in 1967, is another important element in the music's success. This set collects 66 tracks over a two-year period, which many hold as Ellington's greatest on record, and it's certainly the summation of his work within the three-minute confines of the 78rpm record. There are one or two minor errors in the set, and the remastering, though fine enough, may yet be improved on in future editions. But we cannot feasibly withhold a five-star recommendation for some of the finest twentieth-century music on record.

**** **Fargo, ND 11/7/40** Vintage Jazz Classics VJC-1019/20 2CD
As above, except omit Haughton, Strayhorn and Raglin. 11/40.

**** **Fargo 1940 Vol. 1** Tax CD 3720-2 CD
As above. 11/40.

**** **Fargo 1940 Vol. 2** Tax CD 3721-2 CD
As above. 11/40.

Of the many surviving location recordings of the Ellington band, this is one of the best, catching over two hours of material from a single dance date in North Dakota, part of it broadcast but most of it simply taken down by some amateur enthusiasts. The sound has been extensively cleaned up by both VJC and Tax and there is little to choose between the two editions, though the VJC version is available only as a double-set. Here is the great Ellington orchestra on a typical night, with many of the best numbers in the band's book and the most rousing version of 'St Louis Blues' to climax the evening. The sound is inevitably well below the quality of the studio sessions, but it's a very fine supplement to them.

***(*) **Take The 'A' Train** Vintage Jazz Classics VJC-1003-2 CD
As above, except omit Williams, add Junior Raglin (*b*). 1–12/41.

A fascinating set of studio transcriptions. There are eight tunes which Duke never recorded in the studio again, including 'Madame Will Drop Her Shawl' and Strayhorn's 'Love Like This Can't Last', a pretty feature for Webster on 'Until Tonight' and unexpected things like a boisterous 'Frenesi', a Rex Stewart feature called 'Easy Street' and debut recordings of 'West Indian Stomp', 'Moon Mist' and 'Stomp Caprice'. The sound is mostly clear ~~~~~, if a fraction below first-class.

**** **The Great Ellington Units** RCA Bluebird ND86751 CD
Ellington; Cootie Williams, Ray Nance (*t*); Rex Stewart (*c*); Lawre~
Juan Tizol (*vtb*); Johnny Hodges (*ss, as*); Ben Webster (*ts*); Harr~
Billy Strayhorn (*p*); Jimmy Blanton (*b*); Sonny Greer (*d*). 11/40~

These small-group dates aren't far behind the full orchestra sides of the same period. The sessions led by Rex Stewart and Barney Bigard are slighter stuff, but the eight tracks led by Johnny Hodges are superlative features for his own playing, immensely swinging on 'Squatty Roo', suitably passionate on 'Passion Flower'. Ellington and Strayhorn add little touches of their own and the remastering is firm and clear.

****   **Black, Brown And Beige** RCA Bluebird 86641 3CD/4MC
Ellington; Taft Jordan, Cat Anderson, Shelton Hemphill, Ray Nance, Rex Stewart, Francis Williams, Harold 'Shorty' Baker (*t*); Claude Jones, Lawrence Brown, Joe 'Tricky Sam' Nanton, Tommy Dorsey, Wilbur De Paris (*tb*); Jimmy Hamilton (*cl, ts*); Otto Hardwick (*as*); Johnny Hodges (*as*); Al Sears (*ts*); Russell Procope (*cl, ts*); Harry Carney (*bs*); Fred Guy (*g*); Junior Raglin, Sid Weiss, Oscar Pettiford, Al Lucas, Bob Haggart (*b*); Sonny Greer, Sid Catlett (*d*); Al Hibbler, Joya Sherrill, Kay Davis, Marie Ellington, Marian Cox (*v*). 12/44–9/46.

While this ultimately stands a notch below the music on *The Blanton–Webster Years* it is still an essential Ellington collection. Besides numerous further examples of the composer's mastery of the three-minute form, there are the first of his suites to make it to the studios, including most of 'Black, Brown And Beige' – which was never finally recorded in its entirety in the studio – and 'The Perfume Suite'. New Ellingtonians include Cat Anderson and Taft Jordan – two brilliantly individual members of the brass section – as well as the lyrical Shorty Baker, Al Sears and Russell Procope. Ellington's confidence may have been sagging a little from the loss of major soloists – Webster, Williams – and the indifference to some of his higher ambitions as a composer, but the orchestra itself is still inimitable. Remastering is kind enough even if not always wholly respectful of the music, but most will find it acceptable.

***   **Sophisticated Lady** RCA Bluebird ND 90625 CD
As above Bluebird discs. 2/41–9/46.

Eleven tracks filched from the two big sets for a snapshot hits collection. Unanswerably great music, but docked a star for a few mundane choices: it wouldn't have hurt to have had 'Harlem Air Shaft' or 'Ko Ko' in here instead of 'Just Squeeze Me' or 'Caravan'.

***(*)   **The Duke Ellington Carnegie Hall Concerts January 1943** Prestige 34004 2CD
Ellington; Rex Stewart, Harold 'Shorty' Baker, Wallace Jones (*t*); Ray Nance (*t, vn*); Joe 'Tricky Sam' Nanton, Lawrence Brown (*tb*); Juan Tizol (*vtb*); Johnny Hodges, Ben Webster, Harry Carney, Otto Hardwicke, Chauncey Haughton (*reeds*); Fred Guy (*g*); Junior Raglin (*b*); Sonny Greer (*d*); Betty Roche (*v*). 1/43.

***(*)   **The Duke Ellington Carnegie Hall Concerts December 1944** Prestige 24073 2CD
As above, except add Shelton Hemphill, Taft Jordan, Cat Anderson (*t*), Claude Jones (*tb*), Al Sears, Jimmy Hamilton (*reeds*), Hillard Brown (*d*), Kay Davis, Marie Ellington, Al Hibbler (*v*), omit Baker, Wallace Jones, Webster, Haughton, Greer, Roche. 12/44.

***(*)   **The Duke Ellington Carnegie Hall Concerts January 1946** Prestige 24074 2CD
As above, except add Francis Williams (*t*), Wilbur De Paris (*tb*), Al Lucas (*g*), Oscar Pettiford (*b*), Sonny Greer (*d*), Joya Sherrill (*v*), omit Stewart, Nanton, Guy, Raglin, Brown, Marie Ellington. 1/46.

***(*)   **The Duke Ellington Carnegie Hall Concerts December 1947** Prestige 24075 2CD
As above, except add Harold 'Shorty' Baker, Al Killian (*t*), Tyree Glenn (*tb, vib*), Russell Procope (*reeds*), Fred Guy (*g*), Junior Raglin (*b*), omit Jordan, Anderson, De Paris, Hamilton, Lucas, Sherrill. 12/47.

***(*)   **Carnegie Hall November 1948** Vintage Jazz Classics VJC-1024/25 2CD
As above, except add Quentin Jackson (*tb*), Ben Webster (*ts*), omit Jones. 11/48.

Ellington's Carnegie Hall appearances began in 1943 and continued on an annual basis. The only surviving recordings are mostly in indifferent condition and none of the Prestige CDs can really be called hi-fi, despite extensive remastering work. Nevertheless, Ellington scholars will find them essential and even casual listeners should find much to enjoy. The 1943 concert premiered 'Black, Brown And Beige' and its lukewarm reception became a notorious snub that ̄ nated Ellington's confidence in the work. These surviving extracts are fascinating but inconclusive. The rest of the programme includes many greatest hits and one or two scarcer pieces. The 1944 concert includes many less familar tunes – 'Blutopia', 'Suddenly It Jumped', 'Blue Cellophane' – plus more 'Black, Brown And Beige' and the debut of 'The Perfume Suite', as well as a glorious finale showcase for Nanton on 'Frankie And Johnny'. Notable in the next concert were a reworking of 'Diminuendo And Crescendo In Blue' and some fine miniatures including 'Magenta Haze', Joya Sherrill's fine interpretation of 'The Blues' and a euphoric treatment of 'Solid Old Man'. The 'Liberian Suite' is one of the principal items of the 1947 set, but the Ray Nance feature in 'Bakiff', Duke's own spot on 'The Clothed Woman' and Carney on 'Mella Brava' are of equal interest. While all the concerts have their weak spots, each has enough fine Ellington to make it more than worthwhile. The recently released 1948 concert features a guest return by Ben Webster and a rare recording of 'Lush Life'; sound quality is again imperfect but listenable.

***(*)   **The Complete Duke Ellington Vol. 1** CBS 462985 CD/MC
Ellington; Shelton Hemphill, Francis Williams, Harold 'Shorty' Baker, Ray Nance, Dud Bascomb (*t*); Lawrence Brown, Claude Jones, Tyree Glenn (*tb*); Russell Procope, Johnny Hodges, Jimmy Hamilton, Al Sears, Harry Carney (*reeds*); Billy Strayhorn (*p*); Fred Guy (*g*); Oscar Pettiford (*b*); Sonny Greer (*d*); Kay Davis, Al Hibbler, Dolores Parker (*v*). 8/10/47.

***(*)   **The Complete Duke Ellington 1947–52 Vol. 2** CBS 462986 CD/MC
As above, except add Al Killian, Herman Grimes (*t*), Wilbur De Paris (*tb*), Edgar Brown, Junior Raglin (*b*). 11–12/47.

***   **The Complete Duke Ellington 1947–52 Vol. 3** CBS 462987 CD/MC
As above, except add Nelson Williams, Dave Burns, Fats Ford, Cat Anderson (*t*), Quentin Jackson (*tb*), Charlie Rouse, Jimmy Forrest (*ts*), Wendell Marshall (*b*), Willie Smith (*as*), Paul Gonsalves (*ts*), Louie Bellson (*d*), Lu Elliott, Yvonne Lanauze (*v*), omit Hemphill, Francis Williams, Bascomb, Pettiford, De Paris. 1/49–5/51.

***   **The Complete Duke Ellington 1947–52 Vol. 4** CBS 462988 CD/MC
As above, except add Willie Cook, Clark Terry, Dick Vance, John Hunt, John Carroll (*t*), Britt Woodman (*tb*), Porter Kilbert, Hilton Jefferson (*reeds*), Lloyd Oldham, Jimmy Grissom, Betty Roche (*v*), omit Elliott, Hibbler, Lanauze. 5/51–12/52.

***(*)   **The Complete Duke Ellington Vol. 5** CBS 462989 CD/MC
Ellington; Shelton Hemphill, Francis Williams, Harold 'Shorty' Baker, Al Killian, Ray Nance, Nelson Williams, Fats Ford (*t*); Quentin Jackson, Lawrence Brown, Tyree Glenn, Claude Jones (*tb*); Mercer Ellington (*frhn*); Jimmy Hamilton, Johnny Hodges, Russell Procope, Al Sears, Harry Carney, Paul Gonsalves (*reeds*); Billy Strayhorn (*p*); Fred Guy (*g*); Wendell Marshall, Oscar Pettiford, Junior Raglin (*b*); Sonny Greer (*d*); Al Hibbler, Yvonne Lanauze (*v*). 12/47–12/50.

Perhaps the least well-known period of Ellington on record, though that's scarcely a fair judgement on the music. These were leaner times for the band, and with a higher turnover of personnel and fewer hit tunes coming from Ellington himself, much of the music from this period has been overlooked. Any Ellington admirer will find much fine music here. There are still appealing little concertos for the great soloists, smart new works and fragments from longer pieces; as well as better-forgotten pieces. Among new arrivals, the most notable is Paul Gonsalves in 1950, but Clark Terry, Louie Bellson and Willie Cook are also fresh faces in this period. Rather than choose highlights, we ask readers to make their own way though these five discs, but Volume 2 includes a particularly felicitous programme, and the final disc – which includes all of the 'Liberian Suite' and the album once issued as *Masterpieces By Ellington*, consisting of extended variations on four of his most successful tunes – rounds up two sessions particularly neatly. Remastering is a little lacking in brightness on the two earliest discs, but the later ones are superior.

(*)   **Great Times! Original Jazz Classics OJC 108 CD/LP
Ellington; Billy Strayhorn (*p, celeste*); Wendell Marshall, Lloyd Trottman (*b*); Oscar Pettiford (*clo*); Jo Jones (*d*). 9, 11/50.

A curiosity, but a valuable one. Ellington duets on the overworked '"A" Train' with its creator, Strayhorn, who plays celeste; Pettiford saws away in the near background over bass and drums. There are eight two-piano tracks of mixed success, and an odd pair – 'Perdido' and 'Blues For Blanton' – minus Strayhorn. A chance recording, maybe, it conveys something quite profound about the chemistry at work between the two pianist/composers. Aspects of a single self?

***   **Live At the Blue Note** Bandstand BDCD 1523 CD
Ellington; Clark Terry, Willie Cook, Ray Nance, Cat Anderson (*t*); Quentin Jackson, Britt Woodman (*tb*); Juan Tizol (*vtb*); Hilton Jefferson, Jimmy Hamilton, Russell Procope, Harry Carney (*reeds*); Wendell Marshall (*b*); Louie Bellson (*d*). 7–8/52.

Unexceptional concert material, but distinguished by a benchmark performance of Tizol's 'Bakiff', which will be remembered from the Carnegie Hall concerts of 1943 and 1947. Otherwise little of interest to any but serious collectors.

***(*)   **Piano Reflections** Capitol CDP 7928632 CD
Ellington; Wendell Marshall (*b*); Butch Ballard, Dave Black (*d*); Ralph Colier (*perc*). 4–12/53.

Ellington's apparent reluctance to document himself extensively as a pianist must be a source of regret, but these 1953 sessions find him pondering on 14 of his own tunes (and Mercer's 'Things Ain't What They Used To Be'). Most of them are too short to show any great development from the original themes, and Duke's habitual cat-and-mouse with the listener takes some of the pith out of the session; but it shows how distinctive his touch had become, how mannerism could become even more inimitable than Basie's minimalism, and how Ellington could fashion moving little episodes out of mere fragments.

(*)   **Sophisticated Lady Jazz Society 670502 CD
Ellington; Cat Anderson, Harold Baker, Willie Cook, Shelton Hemphill, Taft Jordan, Clark Terry, Francis Williams (*t*); Ray Nance (*t, vn*); Quentin Jackson, Lawrence Brown, Claude Jones, Wilbur De Paris, John Sanders, Juan Tizol, Britt Woodman (*tb*); Russell Procope (*as, cl*); Rick Henderson, Johnny Hodges (*as*); Jimmy Hamilton (*ts, cl*); Paul Gonsalves, Al Sears (*ts*); Harry Carney (*bs*); Fred Guy (*g*); Wendell Marshall, Oscar Pettiford, Jimmy Woode (*b*); Dave Black, Sonny Greer, Jimmy Johnson (*d*); Jimmy Grissom (*v*). 3/53, 4/54, 10/56, 12/58, 3/59.

A range of five years, and one or two significant personnel changes, such as the appearance of bassist Oscar Pettiford, drummer Sonny Greer and some unfamiliar horns on the solitary 1956 track. Jimmy Grissom's vocals are eminently dispensable but there's enough unusual material on the remainder to justify the purchase. The CD reproduction is good and sharp.

***   **Ellington '56** Charly CD 20 CD
Ellington; Cat Anderson, Willie Cook, Clark Terry (*t*); Ray Nance (*t, vn*); Quentin Jackson, Britt Woodman (*tb*); John Sanders (*vtb*); Johnny Hodges (*as*); Russell Procope (*as, cl*); Paul Gonsalves (*ts*); Jimmy Hamilton (*cl, ts*); Harry Carney (*bs, bcl*); Jimmy Woode (*b*); Sam Woodyard (*d*). 2/56.

Product of a single two-day session in 1956. The sound is good, if a little bright, and the performances (which are mainly of familiar material) are pretty much up to standard. Though it isn't a vintage set, it has good broad appeal and some fine soloing.

****   **At Newport** Columbia 40587 CD/MC
Ellington; Cat Anderson, Willie Cook, Ray Nance, Clark Terry (*t*); Quentin Jackson, John Sanders, Britt Woodman (*tb*); Johnny Hodges, Russell Procope (*as*); Paul Gonsalves, Jimmy Hamilton (*ts*); Harry Carney (*bs*); Jimmy Woode (*b*); Sam Woodyard (*d*). 7/56.

The 1956 Newport Festival marked a significant upswing in Duke's critical and commercial fortunes. In large part, the triumph can be laid to Paul Gonsalves's extraordinary 27 blues choruses on 'Diminuendo And Crescendo In Blue', which CBS producer George Avakian placed out of sequence at the end of what was to be Ellington's best-selling record.

Gonsalves's unprecedented improvisation (which opened up possibilities and set standards for later tenor saxophonists from John Coltrane to David Murray) was clearly spontaneous. There were two theories at the time as to how he had managed to play so long and so well. One was that the veteran drummer Jo Jones, sitting sidestage, had egged him on by slapping out the rhythm with a rolled-up magazine, further fuelling the crowd's enthusiastic shouts. Another was that Gonsalves was serenading a beautiful blonde in a black dress who had got up to dance uninhibitedly to his solo. Since the saxophonist's eyes were clamped shut in the near-ecstasy, that has become the image of the improvising genius.

Gonsalves himself has suggested that a particularly competitive edge to the band that night was the real reason. Johnny Hodges had just returned to the fold after a brief stint as an independent bandleader. His beautiful, almost stately solo on 'Jeep's Blues' was intended as the climax to the concert, but Hodges found himself upstaged in the subsequent notices (and by Avakian's reprogramming) and the concert firmly established Gonsalves as one of the leading soloists in jazz.

Unfortunately, much of the solo was played badly off-mike and it's slightly difficult to get a complete sense of its extraordinary impact. It does, nevertheless, dominate the album, overshadowing Hodges and, more significantly, the three-part 'Festival Suite' which Ellington and Strayhorn had put together for the occasion. The first part, 'Festival Junction' is more or less a blowing theme for a parade of soloists, including an incisive first excursion by Gonsalves, who gives notice of what's to come with some blistering choruses (though not 27) on the third part, 'Newport Up'.

An essential Ellington album, *At Newport* documents a rejuvenating experience for the band and the impetus for the experiments of the 1960s.

***   **Duke 56/62: Volume 1** CBS 88653 2LP

(*)   **Duke 56/62: Volume 2 CBS 88654 2LP
Ellington; Cat Anderson, Harold Baker, Bill Berry, Sonny Cohen, Willie Cook, Fats Ford, Lennie Johnson, Thad Jones, Taft Jordan, Eddie Mullens, Ray Nance, Clark Terry, Francis Williams, Gerald Wilson, Eugene Snooky Young (*t*); Lou Blackburn, Henry Coker, Chuck Connors, Matthew Gee, Quentin Jackson, Benny Powell, John Sanders, Juan Tizol, Booty Wood, Britt Woodman (*tb*); Rick Henderson, Johnny Hodges, Marshall Royal (*as*); Russell Procope (*as, cl*); Jimmy Hamilton (*ts, cl*); Frank Wess (*ts, f*); Frank Foster, Paul Gonsalves, Budd Johnson (*ts*); Harry Carney, Charlie Fowlkes (*bs*); Count Basie, Billy Strayhorn (*p*); Freddie Green (*g*); Aaron Bell, Al McKibbon, Oscar Pettiford, Jimmy Woode (*b*); Oliver Jackson, Jimmy Johnson, Sonny Payne, Sam Woodyard (*d*). 7, 8 & 12/56, 3, 9, 10 & 12/57, 2, 4, 7 & 8/58, 2 & 6/59; 12/59, 6 & 7/60, 3, 6, 7 & 10/61, 1 & 6/62.

The four-disc vinyl format may prove unacceptably cumbersome in CD times, but the sound is good and the material better, though Volume 2 of *Duke* gets a little diffuse (finding space for a 'Jingle Bells' recorded in June). It's difficult to generalize about the fruits of 25 separate recording sessions and as many often only slightly varying bands, but this does now seem to be a period of consolidation, the innovative years past, the main soloists settling down to a job. It comes across as a little passionless, but then Ellington was mightily suspicious of conviction music. There are some valuable small-group improvisations on Volume 1, most notably two 1957 takes of 'All The Things You Are' with Woode and Woodyard. Nothing much of that sort on the second volume, which includes a collaboration with the Basie band and both parts of the *Asphalt Jungle* theme.

***(*)   **Live At The 1957 Stratford Festival** Music & Arts 616 CD
Ellington; Cat Anderson, Willie Cook, Clark Terry (*t*); Ray Nance, (*t, vn*); Quentin Jackson, Britt Woodman (*tb*); John Sanders (*tb, vtb*); Russell Procope (*as, cl*); Johnny Hodges (*as*); Jimmy Hamilton (*ts, cl*); Paul Gonsalves (*ts*); Harry Carney (*bs, bcl*); Jimmy Woode (*b*); Sam Woodyard (*d*). 57.

Unusual and highly inventive material, beautifully remastered for CD with a bright, clear mono sound that puts space round individual voices in the ensembles and gives the rhythm section a better-than-average profile. A slightly larger band than its immediate predecessor, it produces a denser sound, with a lot more resolution in the bass and a shade more colour in the horns. Tracks include 'Harlem Air Shaft' and 'La Virgin De La Macarena'.

***(*) **Newport 58** Sony/Columbia COL 4684362 CD
Ellington; Cat Anderson, Harold Baker, Ray Nance, Clark Terry (*t*); Quentin Jackson, John Sanders, Britt Woodman (*tb*); Harry Carney, Paul Gonsalves, Jimmy Hamilton, Johnny Hodges, Gerry Mulligan, Russell Procope (*reeds*); Jimmy Woode (*b*); Sam Woodyard (*d*); Ozzie Bailey (*v*). 58.

Not quite the triumph of two years before, but a fine set nevertheless. 'Jazz Festival Jazz' may have its tongue in its cheek, but for the most part the set is as straightforward as one ever hears an Ellington band. The crowd-pleasers, 'El Gato' and 'Hi Fi Fo Fum', traditionally a Woodyard feature, are given big licks, but the real highlight is a guest appearance by Mulligan and a marvellous duet with fellow-baritonist Carney on 'Prima Bara Dubla'. A good-value set, carefully transferred and with a more reliable sound-mix than its illustrious 1956 predecessor.

***   **In Concert At The Pleyel Paris, 1958 – Part 1** Magic DAWE 39 CD
Ellington; Harold Baker, Clark Terry, Nelson Williams (*t*); Ray Nance (*t, v*); Quentin Jackson, John Sanders, Britt Woodman (*tb*); Harry Carney, Paul Gonslaves, Jimmy Hamilton, Johnny Hodges, Russell Procope (*reeds*); Jimmy Woode (*b*); Sam Woodyard, Ozzie Bailey (*d*). 58.

***(*) **In Concert At The Pleyel Paris, 1958 – Part 2** Magic DAWE 40 CD
As above.

Bluff mono recordings that manage to preserve a good deal of detail. Volume 2 is very much better than the rather diffident first half. It kicks off with a rousing version of 'El Gato'; Ellington's acknowledgement of 'our five trumpeters' casts a little doubt on the liner notes, which make no mention of the non-soloing Williams. The next track is outrageously wonderful, with Ray Nance doing a wildly over the top vocal version of 'Take The "A" Train', namechecking a dozen other jazz tunes along the way; the track then breaks, drops to half-tempo for Paul Gonsalves's rhapsodic 'extension', a feature that confirms his standing as Most Favoured Soloist at that time. Sam Woodyard's long excursion on 'Hi Fi Fo Fum' is a model of what drum solos could be. A good value set, available separately.

****   **Back To Back** Verve 8236372 2 CD
Ellington; Johnny Hodges (*as*); Harry Edison (*t*); Les Spann (*g*); Al Hall, Sam Jones (*b*); Jo Jones (*d*). 2/59.

Welcome reissue of a marvellous 'play the blues' session jointly credited to Ellington and Hodges. The opening 'Wabash Blues' sets an attractive 32-bar theme over an initially disconcerting Latin rhythm that goes all the way back to W. C. Handy's experiments with tango measures in a blues context. Hodges and Edison take contrasting approaches on their solos, with the trumpeter working the changes in fairly orthodox fashion, Hodges sticking very much closer to the melody. 'Basin Street Blues' features Spann in a slightly wavering but completely authentic solo, after which Hodges comes in with two delightfully varied choruses. Ellington's own solo is a curious affair, with a slightly wistful quality but also marked by repeated references to his own youthful style, in particular the descending arpeggios that became something of a tic.

The varied 12-bar form of 'St Louis Blues' is further developed in Ellington's fast, accurate introduction. The two horns do a call-and-response routine that further underlines their different approaches. Duke is the featured soloist again on 'Loveless Love' ('Careless Love'), a traditional tune with some kinship to the blues, but not a strict blues at all. Fittingly, though, the set ends with 'Royal Garden Blues', an orthodox 12-bar structure given a deliberately basic (Basie-like?) treatment. Digital remastering has done a little violence to Hodges's tone, which sounds far tinnier than on the not altogether satisfactory original LP. Musically, though, it's a more than worthwhile set, and it's an important document in understanding Ellington's approach to the blues.

**   **The Duke D.J. Special** Fresh Sound 141 CD
Ellington; Cat Anderson, Shorty Baker, Clark Terry (*t*); Ray Nance (*t, vn*); Quentin Jackson, John Sanders, Britt Woodman (*tb*); Jimmy Hamilton (*cl,ts*); Russell Procope (*cl, as*); Johnny Hodges (*as*); Paul Gonsalves (*ts*); Harry Carney (*bs*); Jimmy Woode (*b*); Jimmy Johnson (*d*). 3/59.

***   **Live!** EmArCy 840271 CD
    Ellington; Cat Anderson, Shorty Baker, Fats Ford, Clark Terry (*t*); Ray Nance (*t, vn*);
    Quentin Jackson, John Sanders, Britt Woodman (*tb*); Jimmy Hamilton (*cl, ts*); Russell
    Procope (*cl, as*); Johnny Hodges (*as*); Paul Gonsalves (*ts*); Harry Carney (*bs*); Jimmy
    Woode (*b*); Sam Woodyard (*d*). 7/59.

The EmArCy is a lively concert performance with the trumpets in particularly good throat. Juan
Tizol's 'Perdido' makes a welcome return to the band-book. The CD transfers are good, with
very little dirt. The slightly earlier *Special* has a near-identical band in lower gear and with an
occasionally slipping clutch. While it's comforting to know that Homer nods, there's no need to
have him doing it on your stereo.

****   **Blues In Orbit** CBS 460823 CD
    Ellington; Cat Anderson, Shorty Baker, Clark Terry (*t*); Ray Nance (*t, vn*); Quentin
    Jackson, John Sanders, Britt Woodman (*tb*); Matthew Gee (*bhn*); Harry Carney, Paul
    Gonsalves, Bill Graham, Jimmy Hamilton, Johnny Hodges, Russell Procope (*reeds*);
    Billy Strayhorn (*p*); Jimmy Woode (*b*); Jimmy Johnson, Sam Woodyard (*d*). 2/58,
    2/59.

Teo Macero took control of the sound booth for the first time on an Ellington session for the
bulk of these stratospheric studio sessions. It would be convenient to argue that the huge
separation between Ellington's chips-of-ice piano and the chesty, distant horns on the
title-track was a typical Macero touch but for the fact that the first two items were produced by
the Duke's old friend and collaborator, Irving Townshend. If 'Blues In Orbit' was some sort of
Ducal welcome to the age of Sputnik, the previously unreleased 'Track 360' is an elegant
train-ride, Pullman class and with a nod in the direction of Honegger's popular concert-opener
'Pacific 351', swaying over a track laid down by Sam Woodyard; the drummer fell ill shortly
afterwards and isn't heard on the rest of the album.

    There are two more tracks which weren't on the original release. 'Brown Penny' is a
state-of-the-art Hodges solo, played in imitation of Kay Davis's earlier vocal version and
sounding as if it is being poured out of a bottle. The other also features Hodges, on a slightly
too syrupy reading of 'Sentimental Lady' (aka 'I Didn't Know About You'). Hodges rather
dominates the album, even being featured on 'Smada', which was usually a Hamilton spot.
Hamilton himself has mixed fortunes, sounding anonymous on tenor on his own 'Three J's
Blues' and 'Pie Eye's Blues', a rackety 12-bar that compares badly with the subsequent 'C Jam
Blues', where he goes back to clarinet, rounding off a sequence of solos that includes excellent
work by Gonsalves, the little-known Matthew Gee and Bootie Wood. Wood's plunger solo on
'Sweet And Pungent' is technically adept and even moving; Stanley Dance relays the story that
Wood was nevertheless disgusted with its tricksiness, presumably uneasy at being cast as
Quentin Jackson's substitute.

    A very fine album, with just enough new compositional input – 'Blues In Blueprint' and
'The Swinger's Jump' – to vary a slightly predictable profile. Strongly recommended.

***(*)   **Live In Paris, 1959** Affinity CD AFF 777 CD
    Ellington; Cat Anderson, Andres Meringuito, Clark Terry (*t*); Ray Nance (*t, v*);
    Quentin Jackson, Booty Wood, Britt Woodman (*tb*); Jimmy Hamilton, Russell
    Procope (*cl, as*); Johnny Hodges (*as*); Paul Gonsalves (*ts*); Harry Carney (*bs, cl*);
    Jimmy Woode (*b*); Jimmy Johnson (*d*); Lil Greenwoon (*v*). 9/59.

Recorded without much depth of focus (Cat Anderson sounds as if he could be out on the roof
of the Salle Pleyel on 'Jam With Sam'), but distinguished by some superfine soloing. The
clarinettists score particularly highly, Procope on the opening medley, Hamilton on 'VIP
Boogie', coming in behind Carney's fine opening cadenza. Hodges is in top form on 'All Of
Me', with the hooded elegance that he increasingly brought to featured spots, almost as if he
wished he were somewhere else, but . . . *noblesse oblige*. Two vocals by Lil Greenwood – on
'Won't You Come Home, Bill Bailey' and 'Walkin' and Singin' The Blues' – don't add very
much to the value of the set, but Nance is marvellously urbane on 'Just Squeeze Me', bringing
a whisper of Don Redman or Noble Sissle to what is already a very polished and largely
mainstream performance. Recommended.

***   **The Ellington Suites** Original Jazz Classics OJC 446 CD/LP
Ellington; Cat Anderson, Harold Baker, Mercer Ellington, Money Johnson, Eddie
Preston, Clark Terry (*t*); Ray Nance (*t, vn*); Quentin Jackson, Vince Prudente, John
Sanders, Malcolm Taylor, Booty Wood, Britt Woodman (*tb*); Johnny Hodges, Harold
Minerve, Norris Turney (*as*); Russell Procope (*as, cl*); Jimmy Hamilton (*ts, cl*); Russ
Andrews, Harold Ashby, Paul Gonsalves (*ts*); Harry Carney (*bs, bcl*); Joe Benjamin,
Wulf Freedman, Jimmy Woode (*b*); Jimmy Johnson, Rufus Jones (*d*). 2, 4/59, 4/71,
10/72.

An interesting collection of extended and medley pieces from the 1959 'Queen's Suite' to the
late and indifferent 'Uwis Suite'. Significantly or not, the most arresting track on the whole
album, which has good sound-quality throughout, is 'The Single Petal Of A Rose', a duo for
Ellington and bassist Jimmy Woode.

***   **Hot Summer Dance** Red Baron AK 498631 CD
Ellington; Willie Cook, Fats Ford, Eddie Mullens (*t*); Ray Nance (*c, v*); Lawrence
Brown, Booty Wood, Britt Woodman (*tb*); Russell Procope (*as, cl*); Johnny Hodges
(*as*); Jimmy Hamilton (*ts, cl*); Paul Gonsalves (*ts*); Harry Carney (*bs, bcl*); Aaron Bell
(*b*); Sam Woodyard (*d*). 7/60.

Recorded at the Mather Air Force Base in California, this is very immediate stuff, with an
entirely convincing live feel. After the obligatory '"A" Train', Ellington tries out a new 'Paris
Blues', a couple of arrangements from *The Nutcracker Suite*, 'Such Sweet Thunder', and, for a
climax, Paul Gonsalves's party piece, which on this occasion gets a slightly strained reading.
Being a dance gig, most of the tracks are taken at a brisk clip and the band squeeze in 16 tunes
(or 15 and a medley) in just over an hour. The tapes have been decently handled and the soloists
all come across strongly, with Jimmy Hamilton in particularly strong form on 'Tenderly'.

**   **S.R.O.** LRC CDC 7680 CD
Ellington; Cat Anderson, Roy Burrowes, Cootie Williams (*t, perc*); Ray Nance (*c, vn*);
Lawrence Brown, Buster Cooper, Britt Woodman (*tb*); Chuck Connors (*btb*); Russell
Procope (*as, cl*); Johnny Hodges (*as*); Jimmy Hamilton (*cl, ts*); Paul Gonsalves (*ts*);
Harry Carney (*bs, bcl, cl*); Billy Strayhorn (*p, perc*); Aaron Bell, John Lamb, Jimmy
Woode (*b*); Sam Woodyard (*d*). 61.

(*)   **Afro Bossa Discovery DS 871 LP
Ellington; Cat Anderson, Roy Burrowes, Cootie Williams (*t, perc*); Ray Nance (*c, vn*);
Lawrence Brown, Buster Cooper (*tb*); Chuck Connors (*b tb*); Russell Procope (*as, cl*);
Johnny Hodges (*as*); Jimmy Hamilton (*cl, ts*); Paul Gonsalves (*ts*); Harry Carney (*bs,
bcl, cl*); Billy Strayhorn (*p, perc*); Ernie Shepard (*b*); Sam Woodyard (*d*). 11 & 12/63,
1/63.

Afro Bossa is not the best known of the 1960s Ellingtons but one of the more interesting. The
band don't always seem entirely easy with the more roistering tempos and the extra percussion
is all over the place, but the material is imaginative and there are fine solo passages from
Hodges, Carney and Brown. *S.R.O.* is merely dullish, with no Hodges in a significant percentage
of the tracks, and an unhelpful sound-mix that doesn't work on CD. Another point for vinyl!

(*)   **The Feeling Of Jazz Black Lion BLCD 760123 CD/LP
Ellington; Cat Anderson, Harold Baker, Bill Berry, Roy Burrowes, Ray Nance (*t*);
Lawrence Brown, Chuck Connors, Leon Cox (*tb*); Jimmy Hamilton (*cl, ts*); Johnny
Hodges, Russell Procope (*as*); Paul Gonsalves (*ts*); Harry Carney (*bs*); Aaron Bell
(*b*); Sam Woodyard (*d*). 2, 5 & 7/62.

A very unexceptional mixed programme of old and newer material. Even at third or fourth
hearing, it seems indistinguishable from half a dozen early 1960s concert recordings and even
the solos come straight off the peg. Serious collectors only.

***(*)   **Duke Ellington And John Coltrane** MCA MCAD 39103 CD
Ellington; John Coltrane (*ts, ss*); Aaron Bell, Jimmy Garrison (*b*); Elvin Jones, Sam
Woodyard (*d*). 9/62.

It's known that Coltrane was going through a difficult, transitional phase when this remarkable opportunity was presented him. Six months before, he had recorded the simply titled *Coltrane* with what was to be the classic quartet. He was, though, stretching for something beyond its surprisingly relaxed lyricism and had managed to wreck his mouthpiece (no minor loss for a saxophonist) trying to improve its lay. His work around this time is, in retrospect, quite conventional, certainly in relation to what was to follow, and it's often Ellington, as so often in the past, who sounds the 'younger' and more adventurous player. It is, for all that, a slightly disappointing record, which peaks early with a brilliant reading of 'In A Sentimental Mood', but never reaches such heights again.

***(*) **Money Jungle** Blue Note B21Y 46398 CD/LP/MC
Ellington; Charles Mingus (*b*); Max Roach (*d*). 9/62.

Set up by United Artists, this was intended to put Duke in the company of two modernists of the next generation, both of whom (Mingus particularly) had drawn particular sustenance from his example. It was the first trio recording the bassist had done since the 1957 Jubilee sessions with Hampton Hawes and Dannie Richmond and, despite his apparent misgivings before and during the session, he completely steals the show, playing complicated countermelodies and dizzying, out-of-tempo runs in every register. Much of the material seems to have been put together at speed and inevitably relies quite heavily on the blues. 'Money Jungle' itself and 'Very Special' are both reasonably orthodox 12-bars and both sound improvised. 'La Fleurette Africaine' is clearly developed from a very simple melodic conception, stated at the beginning by the piano. Long-standing Ellington staples 'Warm Valley' and 'Caravan' are rather less successful and it isn't clear on the former whether a rather agitated Mingus is unfamiliar with the changes or whether he is suffering one of the minor huffs Ellington recounted later. Throughout, Roach plays with the kind of ordered freedom that is characteristic of him. Unfortunately, he is poorly served by the recording and even on CD sounds rather tinny. A fascinating set, though, which will be of particular interest to Mingus fans and collectors.

*** **Recollections Of The Big Band Era** Atlantic 7 90043 2 CD
Ellington; Cat Anderson, Bill Berry, Roy Burrowes, Eddie Preston, Cootie Williams (*t*); Ray Nance (*t, vn*); Lawrence Brown, Chuck Connors, Buster Cooper (*tb*); Russell Procope (*cl, as*); Jimmy Hamilton (*cl, ts*); Johnny Hodges (*as*); Paul Gonsalves (*ts*); Harry Carney (*bs, cl, bcl*); Ernie Shephard (*b*); Sam Woodyard (*d*). 11/62.

Something of a novelty set, bringing together some of the most famous theme and signature tunes of the pre-and immediately post-war bands. Billy Strayhorn's arrangement of Don Redman's 'The Chant Of The Weed' and piano part on the Harry James-associated 'Ciribiribin' are noteworthy, but there are also namechecks for Woody Herman ('The Woodchopper's Ball'), Erskine Hawkins ('Tuxedo Junction'), Louis Armstrong ('When It's Sleepy Time Down South'), Paul Whiteman (Gershwin's 'Rhapsody In Blue') and, inevitably, Basie's 'One O'Clock Jump' and Cab Calloway's 'Minnie The Moocher'. Thoroughly enjoyable, and something more than just a nostalgic wallow. Some of Ellington's own arrangements are strikingly original, virtually reconceiving the material.

(*) **Masters Of Jazz – Volume 6 Storyville SLP 4106 LP
Ellington; Cat Anderson, Shorty Baker, Bill Berry, Eddie Mullen, Ray Nance (*t*); Lawrence Brown, Chuck Connors, Leon Cox (*tb*); Jimmy Hamilton (*cl, ts*); Russell Procope (*as, cl*); Johnny Hodges (*as*); Paul Gonsalves (*ts*); Harry Carney (*bs, cl, bcl*); Aaron Bell (*b*); Sam Woodyard (*d*). 62, 66.

The *Masters of Jazz* series is generally quite sound, though there have been question marks about pressings in the past. The performances here are pretty much *comme il faut*, but again it's Ellington's solo medley, recorded somewhat later than the rest, which really catches the ear. The complexity of his delivery is quite astonishing, even when it is clearly calculated to beguile. Not a great album, but enthusiasts will want the solo spot.

***(*) **The Great Paris Concert** Atlantic SD 2-304 CD
Ellington; Cat Anderson, Roy Burrowes, Cootie Williams (*t*); Ray Nance (*co, v*); Lawrence Brown, Chuck Connors, Buster Cooper (*tb*); Johnny Hodges (*as*); Russ Procope (*cl, as*); Jimmy Hamilton (*cl, ts*); Paul Gonsalves (*ts*); Harry Carney (*b Ernie Shepard (*b*); Sam Woodyard (*d*). 2/63

Great? Very nearly. Oddly, perhaps, the quality of this set doesn't lie so much in the solos as in the ensembles, which are rousing to an almost unprecedented degree. 'Suite Thursday' is an unexpected gem for anyone who hasn't encountered it before, and there are lovely settings of 'Rose Of The Rio Grande' and the *Asphalt Jungle* theme. The sound is big and resonant, as it presumably was in the hall and, more than almost any of the live recordings of the time, conveys something of the excitement of a concert performance.

(*) **Live At Carnegie Hall 1964 – 1 Nueva/Jazz Up JU 322 CD
Ellington; Cat Anderson, Rolf Ericson, Herbie Jones, Cootie Williams (*t*); Lawrence Brown, Buster Cooper, Chuck Connors (*tb*); Russell Procope (*as, cl*); Johnny Hodges (*as*); Jimmy Hamilton (*cl, ts*); Paul Gonslaves (*ts*); Harry Carney (*bs, bcl, cl*); Major Holley, Jimmy Woode (*b*); Sam Woodyard (*d*). 64.

(*) **Live At Carnegie Hall 1964 – 2 Nueva/Jazz Up JU 323 CD
As above.

*** **Harlem** Pablo Live 2308245 CD/LP/MC
As above.

In 1964, Ellington made a triumphal return to Carnegie Hall, scene of the famous (and slightly overblown) wartime concerts. The two latterday sets, respectably transferred, include the marvellous 'Harlem', a concert selection from *The Far East Suite*, see below, including 'Depk', 'Amad', 'Agra', 'Bluebird Of Delhi' and, on Volume 2, a lovely 'Isfahan', a tune made in heaven for Johnny Hodges. The similarly vintaged Pablo material is better ordered and more sharply transferred and, but for archival purposes, is the one to go for.

*** **Jazz Group 1964** Jazz Anthology 550192 CD
Ellington; Rolf Ericson (*t*); Lawrence Brown (*tb*); Johnny Hodges (*as*); Paul Gonsalves (*ts*); Harry Carney (*bs*); John Lamb (*b*); Sam Woodyard (*d*). 64.

***(*) **'65 Revisited** Affinity AFS 1000 CD
Ellington; Cat Anderson, Mercer Ellington, Herbie Jones, Cootie Williams (*t*); Lawrence Brown, Chuck Connors, Buster Cooper (*tb*); Johnny Hodges, Russell Procope (*as*); Jimmy Hamilton (*cl, ts*); Harry Carney (*bs*); John Lamb (*b*); Sam Woodyard (*d*). 65.

These are probably as good an introduction to Ellington studies as there is for a CD generation with no pile of vinyl in the cupboard. The big show-stoppers are all there, a ration of affecting ballads, and a fair sampling of the star soloists. Hodges isn't on best form on the earlier of the pair, but he plays with characteristic grace and precision, enough to whet an appetite for more. The small-group arrangements are tight and the sound-quality very good, if a bit tinny round the horns.

The 1965 date is inevitably fuller in sound and the transfer is more polished. Though some of the material is slightly dubious – 'Supercalifragilsticexpialidocious' might have been left well alone – the arrangements on their own, leaving aside some quality solos from the horns, justify its inclusion.

*** **Featuring Paul Gonsalves** Original Jazz Classics OJC 623 CD/LP/MC
Ellington; Cat Anderson, Bill Berry, Roy Burrowes, Ray Nance (*t*); Lawrence Brown, Chuck Connors, Leon Cox (*tb*); Russell Procope (*cl, as*); Johnny Hodges (*as*); Jimmy Hamilton (*cl, ts*); Harry Carney (*bs*); Aaron Bell (*b*); Sam Woodyard (*d*).

A deserved album feature for a saxophonist who contributed enormously to the Ellington sound and who has m̲a̲d̲... ...rable impact on contemporary players like David Murray, but ...newhat eclipsed by that of Johnny Hodges. The tenorist's solo ...and supremely logical, and his tone, sometimes a little muffled ...is razor sharp. Whether the 'name' ranking was planned ...nition of particularly inspired playing isn't clear, but this this is a ...sung geniuses of the saxophone, who joins Warne Marsh and ...ose who have been passed over by noisier talents.

...se Original Jazz Classics OJC 645 CD/LP/MC
...ton, Money Johnson, Eddie Preston, Cootie Williams (*t*);
... Taylor, Booty Wood (*tb*); Russell Procope (*cl, as*); Norris

Turney (*as*); Harold Ashby, Paul Gonsalves (*ts*); Harry Carney (*bs*); Joe Benjamin (*b*); Rufus Jones (*d*).

'World music' of a very high order. Ellington's grasp of non-Western forms was often limited to a grasp of unusual tone-colours, but here, on 'Chinoiserie', 'Didjeridoo' and 'Afrique', he produces something that sounds genuinely alien. The original Fantasy release sounded veiled and mysterious, but the CD reissue is quite bright, perhaps too much so for music of this sort. However, sharper resolution does confirm a strong impression that, far from being a by-blow, these pieces are essential items in the Ellington canon.

**   **Concert In The Virgin Islands** Discovery DS 841 LP
Ellington; Cat Anderson, Herbie Jones, Cootie Williams, Richard Williams (*t*); Ray Nance (*t, vn*); Lawrence Brown, Chuck Connors, Buster Cooper (*tb*); Russell Procope (*as, cl*); Johnny Hodges (*as*); Jimmy Hamilton (*ts, cl*); Paul Gonsalves (*ts*); Harry Carney (*bs*); John Lamb (*b*); Sam Woodyard (*d*). 4/65.

(*)   **Yale Concert Original Jazz Classics OJC 664 CD/MC
Ellington; Cat Anderson, Herbie Jones, Cootie Williams, Mercer Ellington (*t*); Lawrence Brown, Chuck Connors, Buster Cooper (*tb*); Russell Procope (*as, cl*); Johnny Hodges (*as*); Jimmy Hamilton (*ts, cl*); Paul Gonsalves (*ts*); Harry Carney (*bs*); Jeff Castleman (*b*); Sam Woodyard (*d*). 4/65.

Relatively unfamiliar and one-off repertoire – 'Big Fat Alice's Blues', 'Island Virgin', 'Virgin Jungle' – lifts the first of these inexpertly engineered sets up out of the 'serious collectors only' category. By no means a classic, all the same. The *Yale Concert* is rather better behaved aurally but, apart from 'A Chromatic Love Affair' and a beautiful Hodges medley, there's nothing worth cutting classes for.

****   **The Far East Suite** Bluebird ND 87640 CD
Ellington; Cat Anderson, Mercer Ellington, Herbie Jones, Cootie Williams (*t*); Lawrence Brown, Chuck Connors, Buster Cooper (*tb*); Harry Carney, Paul Gonsalves, Jimmy Hamilton, Johnny Hodges, Russell Procope (*reeds*); John Lamb (*b*); Rufus Jones (*d*). 12/66.

As people always point out, it should really have been *The Near East Suite*. In 1963, the State Department sent the Ellington band on a tour that took in Ceylon, India and Pakistan, most of the Middle East, and Persia. The tour was eventually interrupted by the assassination of JFK, but Duke and co-writer Strayhorn slowly absorbed the sights and tone-colours of those weeks, and nearly three years later went into the studio to record the suite. Typical of Ellington's interpretation of the genre, it is really little more than a well-balanced programme of individual songs but with a greater-than-usual degree of overall coherence, summed up at the end by 'Amad'. 'The Tourist Point Of View' serves as overture and reminder of the Duke's characteristic sound, and introduces two of the most important solo voices, Anderson and Gonsalves. 'Bluebird Of Delhi' relates to a mynah that mocked Billy Strayhorn with a beautiful song (played by Jimmy Hamilton) and then brought him down with the resounding raspberry one hears at the end of the piece.

What follows is perhaps the most beautiful single item in Ellington's and Strayhorn's entire output. Hodges's solo on 'Isfahan' is like attar of roses, almost (but not quite) *too* sweet and, once smelt, impossible to forget. Critical attention has almost always focused on Hodges, but it's important to be aware of the role of the backing arrangements, a line for the saxophones that seems as monumental as the place it celebrates. The other unquestionable masterpiece of the set is 'Mount Harissa', a soft, almost spiritual opening from Ellington, building up into a sinuous Gonsalves solo over a compulsive drum and cymbal pattern and huge orchestral interjections. An evocation of Agra, location of the Taj Mahal, is quite properly assigned to Harry Carney, in superb voice.

'Amad' is strictly the end of the suite, but there is one additional track (which ironically justifies the title). 'Ad Lib On Nippon' was devised (it's not absolutely clear where credit for the composition should lie) in the wake of a later tour to Japan. Attributed to Ellington alone, it may have derived from a Jimmy Hamilton idea. Certainly, the clarinettist's monumental solo puts a stamp of authority on the music.

Ellington's ability to communicate points of contact and conflict between cultures, assimilating the blues to Eastern modes in tracks like 'Blue Pepper (Far East Of The Blues)' never sounds editorialized or excessively self-conscious. This remains one of the peaks of post-war Ellington.

***(*)   **The Intimacy Of The Blues** Original Jazz Classics OJC 624 CD/LP/MC
Ellington; Cat Anderson, Willie Cook (*t*); Lawrence Brown (*tb*); Norris Turney (*f*); Johnny Hodges (*as*); Harold Ashby, Paul Gonsalves (*ts*); Harry Carney (*bs*); Wild Bill Davis (*org*); Joe Benjamin, Victor Gaskin, Paul Kondziela, John Lamb (*b*); Rufus Jones (*d*). 3/67, 1 & 6/70.

Delightful small-group settings of which the 1967 'Combo Suite', incorporating the title-piece, 'Out South', 'Near North' and 'Soul Country', is far and away the best. Even in restricted settings like this, Ellington still manages to get a tremendous depth of sound, and the disposition of horns is such that Carney's line often suggests that a whole section is at work. The tenor is contrastingly quieter and less forceful, which has the same effect.

***   **Live In Italy: Volume 1** Jazz Up JU 305 CD

(*)   **Live In Italy: Volume 2 Jazz Up JU 306 CD
Ellington; Cat Anderson, Mercer Ellington, Money Johnson, Herbie Jones, Cootie Williams (*t*); Lawrence Brown, Chuck Connors, Buster Cooper (*tb*); Jimmy Hamilton (*cl, ts*); Russell Procope (*cl, as*); Johnny Hodges (*as*); Paul Gonsalves (*ts*); Harry Carney (*bs*); Joe Benjamin (*b*); Sam Woodyard (*d*). 67.

Indifferently recorded, but Volume 1 is packed with fine performances of unusual material. 'Mount Harissa', from *The Far East Suite*, is of exceptional quality. Volume 2 is much more diffuse, but 'Tootie For Cootie' and 'The Shepherd' are worth having in an Ellington collection.

(*)   **... And His Mother Called Him Bill Bluebird ND 86287 CD
Ellington; Cat Anderson, Mercer Ellington, Herbie Jones, Cootie Williams (*t*); Clark Terry (*flhn*); Lawrence Brown, Chuck Connors, Buster Cooper, John Sanders (*tb*); Harry Carney, Johnny Hodges, Paul Gonsalves, Jimmy Hamilton, Russell Procope (*reeds*); Aaron Bell, Jeff Castleman (*b*); Steve Little, Sam Woodyard (*d*). 8, 9 & 11/67.

This is Ellington's tribute to Billy Strayhorn, who died in May 1967. The mood is primarily one of loss and yearning, and Strayhorn titles like 'U.M.M.G.', standing for 'Upper Manhattan Medical Group', and 'Blood Count' bear poignant witness to his prolonged final illness. Hodges's solo on the latter is almost unbearable, and is surpassed in creative terms only by the later 'Day-Dream'. 'U.M.M.G.' has an urgent, ambulance-ride quality, largely conveyed by Ellington's clattering piano that sets it in sharp opposition to the easy swing of the opening 'Boo-Dah'.

The CD has four previously unreleased tracks, including 'Smada', 'My Little Brown Book' and (another Hodges feature) 'Lotus Blossom'; but the main interest focuses on the tracks mentioned above and on the astonishing 'All Day Long', which counts as one of Duke's most devastating orchestral conceptions, as daring as anything in the modern movement.

In a brief written tribute, dated on the day of Strayhorn's death, Ellington states that his collaborator's 'listening-hearing self was totally intolerant of his writing-playing self when, or if, any compromise was expected or considered expedient'. Fortunately, Ellington's notion of expedience was arrogance itself where music was concerned. Strayhorn couldn't have hoped for a finer memorial.

***   **The English Concerts, 1969 And 1971** Sequel Jazz CD 183 2CD
Ellington; Cat Anderson, Johnny Coles, Mercer Ellington, Rolf Ericson, Harold Johnson, Cootie Williams (*t*); Lawrence Brown, Chuck Connors, Malcolm Taylor, Mitchell 'Booty' Wood (*tb*); Harold Ashby, Harry Carney, Paul Gonsalves, Johnny Hodges, Harold Minerve, Russell Procope, Norris Turney (*reeds*); Wild Bill Davis (*org*); Joe Benjamin, Victor Gaskin (*b*); Rufus Jones (*d*). 11/69, 10/71.

The tours are fondly remembered by British fans, but the music is nothing exceptional, pretty much standard fare served up without a great sense of adventure or enterprise. 'El Gato' and 'Black Butterfly', features for Anderson and Hodges respectively in 1969, almost sound done by rote and the band often seems tired and uninventive. Hodges died in 1970 and, though his limpid voice is much missed, the 1971 sessions (recorded in Bristol and Birmingham) have a degree more bite than the earlier material. A nice souvenir for Brits whose first or last encounter with the Duke coincided with one or other visit. Otherwise a bit flat.

(*)   **The Intimate Ellington Pablo 2310787 CD
      Ellington; various line-ups, 1969–71.

Definitions of intimacy must vary. This isn't an obvious choice for last thing at night with a glass of malt and the dimmer turned down. Apart from the horrendous 'Moon Maiden', on which Ellington plays celeste, it's an averagely appealing album with some assured big-band playing and a useful sample of Ellington's still underrated trio performances (which may yet come to seem more significant than essays on the scale of 'Symphonette').

The sound wobbles a bit from track to track, an almost inevitable problem on compilations for quite various forces, and there is a problem with the bass register. Otherwise good.

***   **Second Sacred Concert** Prestige P 24045 CD/LP
      Ellington; Cat Anderson, Mercer Ellington, Cootie Williams (*t*); Lawrence Brown,
      Buster Cooper (*tb*); Harry Carney, Paul Gonsalves, Johnny Hodges, Russell Procope
      (*reeds*); Jeff Castleman (*b*); Sam Woodyard (*d*); voices. 68.

Ellington's last few years were largely spent writing liturgical music. The first of the sacred concerts, based on the piece *In The Beginning, God*, was performed in Grace Cathedral, San Francisco. The second is equally moving, its blend of jazz, classical and black gospel materials profoundly influenced by the large-scale Masses and praises of Mary Lou Williams, Ellington's only serious rival in jazz composition on the large scale. Despite the dimensions of the piece and the joyous, ringing concords, it is a surprisingly dark work, with a tragic sub-theme that constantly threatens to break through. Non-believers will still appreciate the extraordinary part-writing; for Christians of whatever persuasion, it remains an overwhelming musical experience.

***(*)   **In The Uncommon Market** Pablo 2308247 CD/LP/MC
      Ellington; Cat Anderson, Roy Burrowes, Cootie Williams (*t*); Ray Nance (*t, vn*);
      Lawrence Brown, Chuck Connors, Buster Cooper (*tb*); Johnny Hodges (*as*); Russell
      Procope (*as, cl*); Jimmy Hamilton (*ts, cl*); Paul Gonsalves (*ts*); Harry Carney (*bs*);
      Ernie Shephard (*b*); Sam Woodyard (*d*).

Challengingly unfamiliar scores – 'Bula', 'E.S.P.', 'Silk Lace' – and trio performances of two concepts of 'The Shepherd' make this a valauble session. The soloing is not so much below par as clearly subordinated to collective values, and the ensembles repay the closest attention. The CD is very good indeed.

(*)   **Up In Duke's Workshop Pablo 2310815 LP
      Ellington; Johnny Coles, Willie Cook, Mercer Ellington, Money Johnson, Jimmie
      Owens, Eddie Preston, Alan Rubin, Fred Stone, Cootie Williams (*t*); Tyree Glenn,
      Bennie Green, Benny Powell, Julian Priester, Vince Prudente, Malcolm Taylor, Booty
      Wood (*tb*); Russell Procope (*as, cl*); Johnny Hodges, Harold Minerve, Buddy Pearson,
      Norris Turney (*as*); Harold Ashby, Paul Gonsalves (*ts*); Harry Carney (*bs*); Joe
      Benjamin, Victor Gaskin, Paul Kondziela (*b*); Rufus Jones (*d*). 4, 5 & 6/69, 6 & 12/70,
      2 & 6/71, 12/72.

The line-ups don't actually vary very much, but there are a number of relatively unfamiliar names, notably those trying to fill Johnny Hodges's shoes, for which they should have been assigned rabbit's feet). As the title implies, these are working sessions – and slightly tentative ones at that. The early 'Black Butterfly' and the interesting 'Neo-Creole' are significant pieces, but in only eight cuts there's a fair bit of slack.

***   **Standards: Live At The Salle Pleyel** JMY 1011 2 CD
      Ellington; Cat Anderson, Mercer Ellington, Cootie Williams (*t*); Lawrence Brown,
      Chuck Connors (*tb*); Harry Carney, Paul Gonsalves, Johnny Hodges, Russell Procope,
      Norris Turney (*reeds*); Victor Gaskin (*b*); Rufus Jones (*d*). 11/69.

Not strictly a standards set at all but a concert collection of Ellington favourites. It opens with 'Black And Tan Fantasy', which is give a slightly acid reading, a little faster than normal. There are good (and generally well-recorded) versions of '"A" Train', 'Perdido', 'Caravan', 'El

Gato' and the Hodges feature 'Black Butterfly'. Attractive, well-balanced set, but a little more abrasive in places than some will like.

[**** **Duke Ellington: The Private Collection** Saja 10CD]

**** **Volume 1: Studio Sessions, Chicago 1956** Saja 7 91041 2 CD
Ellington; Cat Anderson, Willie Cook, Ray Nance, Clark Terry (*t*); Quentin Jackson, John Sanders, Britt Woodman (*tb*); Johnny Hodges (*as*); Russell Procope (*cl, as*); Jimmy Hamilton (*cl, ts*); Paul Gonsalves (*ts*); Harry Carney (*bs, cl*); Jimmy Woode (*b*); Sam Woodyard (*d*). 3 & 12/56.

*** **Volume 2: Dance Concerts, California, 1958** Saja 7 91042 2 CD

*** **Volume 6: Dance Dates, California, 1958** Saja 7 91230 2 CD
Ellington; Harold Baker, Clark Terry (*t*); Ray Nance (*t, v, vn*); Quentin Jackson, John Sanders, Britt Woodman (*tb*); Russell Procope (*as, cl*); Bill Graham (*as*); Paul Gonsalves (*ts*); Jimmy Hamilton (*ts, cl*); Harry Carney (*bs, cl, bcl*); Jimmy Woode (*b*); Sam Woodyard (*d*); Ozzie Bailey (*v*). 3/58.

*** **Volume 3: Studio Sessions, New York, 1962** Saja 7 91043 2 CD
Ellington; Cat Anderson, Bill Berry, Roy Burrowes, Ray Nance, Cootie Williams (*t*); Lawrence Brown, Chuck Connors, Buster Cooper, Britt Woodman (*tb*); Johnny Hodges, Russell Procope (*as*); Paul Gonsalves (*ts*); Jimmy Hamilton (*ts, cl*); Harry Carney (*bs*); Aaron Bell (*b*); Sam Woodyard (*d*); Milt Grayson (*v*). 7 & 9/62.

*** **Volume 4: Studio Sessions, New York, 1963** Saja 7 91044 2 CD
Ellington; Ray Nance (*c*); Cat Anderson, Rolf Ericson, Eddie Preston, Cootie Williams (*t*); Lawrence Brown, Chuck Connors, Buster Cooper (*tb*); Johnny Hodges, Russell Procope (*as*); Jimmy Hamilton (*cl, ts*); Paul Gonsalves (*ts*); Harry Carney (*bs*); Ernie Shepard (*b*); Sam Woodyard (*d*). 4, 5 & 7/63.

***(*) **Volume 5: The Suites, New York, 1968 & 1970** Saja 7 91045 2 CD
Ellington; Cat Anderson, Dave Burns, Willie Cook, Mercer Ellington, Al Rubin, Fred Stone, Cootie Williams (*t*); Chuck Connors, Cliff Heathers, Julian Priester, Booty Wood (*tb*); Johnny Hodges (*as*); Russell Procope (*as, cl*); Norris Turney (*as, f*); Harold Ashby, Paul Gonsalves (*ts*); Harry Carney (*bs*); Joe Benjamin, Jeff Castleman (*b*); Rufus Jones (*d*); Dave Fitz, Elayne Jones, Walter Rosenberg (*perc*). 11 & 12/68, 5 & 6/70.

*** **Volume 7: Studio Sessions, 1957 & 1962** Saja 7 91231 2 CD
Ellington; Cat Anderson, Bill Berry, Roy Burrowes, Willie Cook, Ray Nance, Clark Terry (*t*); Lawrence Brown, Chuck Connors, Leon Cox, Quentin Jackson, John Sanders, Britt Woodman (*tb*); Harold Ashby, Harry Carney, Paul Gonsalves, Jimmy Hamilton, Johnny Hodges, Russell Procope (*reeds*); Billy Strayhorn (*p*); Aaron Bell, Jimmy Woode (*b*); Sonny Greer, Sam Woodyard (*d*); Milt Grayson (*v*). 1/57, 3, 5 & 6/62.

*** **Volume 8: Studio Sessions, 1957, 1965–7, San Francisco, Chicago, New York** Saja 7 91232 2 CD
Ellington; Nat Adderley, Cat Anderson, Willie Cook, Mercer Ellington, Herbie Jones, Howard McGhee, Ray Nance, Clark Terry, Cootie Williams (*t*); Lawrence Brown, Chuck Connors, Buster Cooper, Quentin Jackson, John Sanders, Britt Woodman (*tb*); Harry Carney, Paul Gonsalves, Jimmy Hamilton, Johnny Hodges, Russell Procope (*reeds*); John Lamb, Jimmy Woode (*b*); Louie Bellson, Chris Columbus, Rufus Jones, Steve Little, Sam Woodyard (*d*). 1/57, 3, 4 & 8/65, 8 & 12/66, 7/67.

***(*) **Volume 9: Studio Sessions, New York, 1968** Saja 7 91233 2 CD
Ellington; Cat Anderson, Willie Cook, Money Johnson, Cootie Williams (*t*); Lawrence Brown, Chuck Connors, Buster Cooper (*tb*); Harold Ashby, Harry Carney, Paul Gonsalves, Johnny Hodges, Russell Procope (*reeds*); Jeff Castleman (*b*); Rufus Jones (*d*); Trish Turner (*v*). 11 & 12/68.

*** **Volume 10: Studio Sessions, New York & Chicago, 1965, 1966 & 1971** Saja 7 91234 2 CD
Ellington; Cat Anderson, Mercer Ellington, Money Johnson, Herbie Jones, Eddie

Preston, Paul Serrano, Cootie Williams, Richard Williams (*t*); Ray Nance (*c, v*);
Lawrence Brown, Chuck Connors, Buster Cooper, Malcolm Taylor, Booty Wood (*tb*);
Harold Ashby, Harry Carney, Jimmy Hamilton, Johnny Hodges, Buddy Pearson,
Russell Procope, Norris Turney (*reeds*); Joe Benjamin, John Lamb (*b*); Rufus Jones,
Sam Woodyard (*d*); Tony Watkins (*v*). 3 & 5/65, 8/66, 5/71.

Duke Ellington was one of the first composers – in any field – to recognize the aesthetic
implications of recording. His own forays into the industry were not marked with unqualified
success; his investment in both Musicraft and Sunrise (a gamble prompted by the post-war
recording ban) was largely lost and the later Mercer label, administered by his son, was a flop.

It did, though, become Ellington's practice to document his work on tape and this
remarkable 10CD set represents the Duke's personal archive of compositions and
arrangements. Given its bulk and the availability elsewhere of most of the compositions
covered, it's chiefly for serious Ellington scholars. However, discs can be purchased individually
and the best of them have sufficient intrinsic merit to be attractive to more casual listeners.

Best of all, perhaps, is Volume 1, devoted to a vintage year for the Ellington band. Johnny
Hodges had just returned to the band after his solo foray and Newport in the summer was to be
the scene of Ellington's greatest triumph. At the festival, Paul Gonsalves played one of the
historic solos of modern jazz, a staggering 27 choruses on 'Diminuendo And Crescendo In
Blue'. Appropriately, it's Gonsalves, rather than the returned prodigal Hodges, who dominates
the Chicago *Studio Sessions*. He is brilliant on 'Satin Doll' and 'In A Sentimental Mood' and
takes over from Ray Nance on Mercer's 'Moon Mist', a theme originally composed for Ben
Webster, but which became inextricably associated with the fiddle-playing trumpeter. Hodges
stakes his claim with a beautiful chorus on 'Prelude To A Kiss'.

Hodges and Cat Anderson don't appear on the 1958 dance concerts, which are spread across
Volumes 2 and 6, the latter disc covering a second night at the Travis Air Force base in
California. Both are jolly, rather shambolic affairs, beautifully recorded by Wally Heider, but
somewhat lacking in substance. On the first of the pair, Nance sings a second version of 'Take
The "A" Train' and there's a wild, impromptu arangement of 'Oh! Lady Be Good'. Perhaps
the best track, ironically, is an arrangement of Basie's 'One O'Clock Jump' theme, with
Ellington taking off his friendly rival in the opening statement and the ensembles rocking along
in good Kansas City fashion. Baker's solo on 'Willow Weep For Me' looks like being the
highpoint of Volume 6, until Ray Nance steps in with a perfectly crafted solo on 'Caravan'. The
version of 'Blues In Orbit' is longer and more open-textured than the issued version, above,
and Ellington's piano work is supreme.

'E.S.P.' was written as a feature for Gonsalves, who tries it out on Volume 3 with
characteristic self-confidence and speed of thought. In the same way, Johnny Hodges's reading
of the classic 'Isfahan' on the 1963 New York sessions (Volume 4) is a try-out for the
magnificent *Far East Suite*. The great satisfaction of these recordings is in being able to hear
Duke work out new and challenging arrangements. 'Take It Slow', again from New York in
1962 is scored for three trombones, three saxophones and rhythm and steers a wistful course
under Gonsalves's fine solo. 'Cordon Bleu' is interesting in that Ellington and Strayhorn
alternate at the piano and duet briefly when Duke arrives back from a spot of conducting.
Cootie Williams had just returned to the fold and was welcomed back with a 'New Concerto'
and with a ranking solo on 'September 12th Blues'.

'The Degas Suite' on Volume 5 was written for the soundtrack of a film about the French
Impressionist painter. When the project ran out of money, Ellington was given back the score in
recompense. It's a brightly lit work, scored for a much smaller band than usual, with a lot of
humour and dabbed with detail that close up or on a score would make no sense, but which
contributes perfectly to the overall impact. Volume 5 is completed with a run-down of an
original danced score *The River*, commissioned for the American Ballet Theater. It's a
meditative, rather inward piece, bubbling up from the 'The Spring', a solo piece by the piano
player, and then flowing down towards Carney's deep, dark solo on 'Her Majesty The Sea',
taking in obvious geographical features on the way, but also touching human settlements like
'The Neo-Hip-Hot Kiddies Communities' and the contrasting 'Village Of The Virgins' along
the way. It's hard to judge which community Duke would have felt most at home in.

Like Volume 6, the last four discs jump back in time somewhat, taking in a decade's worth of
studio material, leading up to the death of Billy Strayhorn in 1967. Some of the tapes have
deteriorated rather badly and the sound is somewhat unreliable, but they give a fascinating
glimpse of Ellington in a workshop setting and represent a valuable checklist of Ellington's

compositional output right through his career. Highlights? Hodges's 'Sophisticated Lady' with just rhythm on Volume 9 and his rather inward 'Something Sexual' on 7, Anderson's blood'n'sand 'El Viti' on 8, and the sections from *Black, Brown And Beige* on the final volume.

No one had ever or has since done more with the jazz orchestra, and these recordings (some of them merely torsos, some of commercially unacceptable sound quality) are a fitting monument to Ellington's genius. They are also something more important: a living laboratory for musicians, composers and arrangers, which was Ellington's other purpose. The 'stockpile', as he called it, was expected to pay dividends of one sort or another.

***(*)   **Latin American Suite** Original Jazz Classics OJC 469 CD/LP/MC
Ellington; Lawrence Brown, Buster Cooper (*tb*); Johnny Hodges (*as*); Paul Gonsalves (*ts*); Harry Carney (*bs*); only soloists identified. 72.

Typically, this late suite is not an attempt to reduplicate the sounds and rhythms Ellington and his band heard on their first trans-equatorial trip in 1968 (surprisingly late in his career, on the face of it). Rather, it records the very personal impressions the southern half of the Americas made on a mind so fine that it was never violated by anything so vulgar as a new influence, and never so closed-off as to reject any new stimulus. Where most composer/bandleaders would have packed the rhythm section with congas, shakers and timbales, as Stanley Dance points out, Ellington conveys a strong Latin feel with his regular rhythm section. On the short 'Tina', an impression of the Argentine, he uses a small rhythm group with two bassists and works a bluesy variation on the tango. (Elsewhere on the album, the bass is so heavily recorded that it sounds very much like an electric instrument; unfortunately, the personnel are not identified.) The bass is again important on the jovial 'Latin American Sunshine', paired with Ellington on a rather untypical theme statement. The opening 'Oclupaca', a title that follows the jazz cliché of reversing names, is a bright, danceable theme that recalls the Latin-influenced big bands of the 1930s and '40s. And that is the overall impression of the set. Perhaps fittingly, there is a nostalgic feel underneath its typically adventurous arrangements and voicings. There's a wistful quality to 'The Sleeping Lady And The Giant Who Watches Over Her', ostensibly the two mountains overlooking Mexico City, but one wonders if Ellington wasn't thinking about Latin America and the neo-colonial United States, with its cultural dominance and magpie eclecticism, and expressing a tinge of regret that he hadn't plunged into the music of the southern continent earlier in his career.

***   **This One's For Blanton** Pablo 2310721 CD/MC
Ellington; Ray Brown (*b*). 12/72.

The main event here is a four-part 'Fragmented Suite For Piano And Bass', which has a lot of humour it it, along with the serious aspects of this tribute to the father of modern bass playing. Brown, a disciple, has much of Jimmy Blanton's rapid, melodic delivery and the older man – who died in 1942 – would have envied the clarity with which the bass comes across in these fine transfers. The remaining material is pretty safe Ellington, but the duo readings are not particularly stirring.

*(*)   **Duke's Big 4** Pablo 2310703 CD
Ellington; Joe Pass (*g*); Ray Brown (*b*); Louie Bellson (*d*). 73.

A jolly, matey sort of set that put little demand on the improvisational instincts of any of the participants. This was the sort of stuff they could all do blindfold at festivals and, apart from some of Duke's chording, which is typically unpredictable, there's not much to listen to.

***(*)   **Digital Duke** GRP GRD 9548 CD
Mercer Ellington (*cond*); Kamau Adilefu, Barry Lee Hall, Lew Soloff, Clark Terry, Ron Tooley (*t, flh*); Al Grey, Britt Woodman (*tb*); Chuck Connors (*btb*); Norris Turney (*as*); Jerry Dodgion (*as, cl*); Branford Marsalis (*ts*); Eddie Daniels, Herman Riley (*ts, cl*); Charles Owens (*bs, cl, bcl*); Roland Hanna, Gerry Wiggins (*p*); Bucky Pizzareli (*g*); J. J. Wiggins (*b*); Louie Bellson, Rocky White (*d*). 87.

Like most of the great big bands, the Ellington orchestra continued to perform after the leader's death. Frank Foster carried on the Basie band with great success, but Ellington had a literal heir among his musicians. Mercer Ellington took up the most daunting mantle in jazz with great professionalism. *Digital Duke* is perhaps the finest tribute to his work, and though some potential (or even actual) purchasers may feel let down when they realize the eponymous Duke is no longer present in the flesh, these latterday performances of absolutely standard Ellington fare are not to be sneezed at.

Roland Hanna clearly isn't Ellington, but he mimics enough of the master's approach to the opening bars of 'Satin Doll' to more than pass muster. Elsewhere, he shares the solo space with Wiggins. Soloff makes a convincing high-note man ('Cottontail') but Clark Terry is the real thing on '22 Cent Stomp' (the US postage stamp of that denomination, celebrating Ellington, is on the cover) and 'Perdido'. Turney is another who had worked with the Duke in life and he sounds poised and reflective in the Hodges role. Herman Riley and Branford Marsalis stand in for Gonsalves.

Michael Abene's 32-track production is cracklingly precise, sometimes a little too up-front, ironically exposing just a hint of one-dimensionality in the arrangements, which completely lack Duke's mysterious ambiguities and daringly voiced chords. But it's a perfectly valid set. Those versed in Duke's music will enjoy the solos (or at least enjoy making invidious comparisons with the band now playing in heaven), those who have not yet got to grips with big bands may well be attracted by some of the younger names on show. Either way, a worthwhile purchase.

DON ELLIS (1934–78)
TRUMPET

***   **... How Time Passes ...** Candid 9004 CD/LP
Ellis; Jaki Byard (*p, as*); Ron Carter (*b*); Charles Persip (*d*). 10/60.

***   **Out Of Nowhere** Candid 9032 CD/LP
Ellis; Paul Bley (*p*); Steve Swallow (*b*). 4/61.

How Time Passes was made before the Third Stream finally ran dry. Half the album is devoted to 'Improvisational Suite No. 1', in which the soloists are asked to extemporize, not on chord progressions or standard melodies, but on a relatively orthodox twelve-tone row, distributed among the instruments and out of which chords can be built. The material is less reminiscent of Arnold Schoenberg, who'd spent his last years in Ellis's native California, than of Ernst Krenek, another European exile to the West Coast. Miraculously, it still swings.

The title-track is loosely inspired by Stockhausen's views on musical duration. The extraordinary accelerations and decelerations of tempo are initially almost laughable; but it's a highly significant piece, and Ellis's own solo (with Byard following less convincingly on his alto saxophone 'double') is superbly structured. The ballad 'Sallie' has a more straightforward modal theme.

Out Of Nowhere is outwardly much more conventional and standards-based, but Ellis plays lines and melodic inversions of considerable inventiveness, always striking out for the microtonal terrain he was to colonize later in the 1960s when he began to work on a four-valve quarter-tone trumpet. 'All The Things You Are' – a fifth take, incidentally – is quite extraordinary, running from free abstract patterns round the subdominant to fast, almost Delta-ish runs in quadruple time. The two versions of 'I Love You' show how he miscues occasionally here – but always in pursuit of metrical accents no one else was attempting at the time. Bley plays superbly, though unfortunately Swallow is a bit recessed in the mix.

Ellis's magnificent *Electric Bath* [CBS] has long since vanished and, apart from a solitary take of 'Whiplash' on a Verve 'Jazz Club' trumpet compilation (840038 2), there is nothing of his innovative big-band music in the catalogue. The two Candids, though, are essential for anyone interested in the technical development of modern jazz.

***   **New Ideas** Original Jazz Classics OJC 431 CD/LP/MC
Ellis; Al Francis (*vib*); Jaki Byard (*p*); Ron Carter (*b*); Charlie Persip (*d*). 6/61.

'I believe in making use of as wide a range of expressive techniques as possible.' That's palpably true on this fine quintet session, where Ellis moves effortlessly between the D72 blues of 'Uh Huh', the atonal 'Tragedy', the strict canon of 'Imitation', and the stark improvisational approach of 'Despair To Hope' and a piece for unaccompanied trumpet. Even with a more conventional jazz context, the opening 'Natural H' and 'Cock And Bull' are strikingly original, with Ellis demonstrating an ability to assimilate advanced harmonic ideas to jazz. Challenging, provocative music, sympathetically recorded by Rudy Van Gelder. The band are on the case from start to finish, with a particular word of praise for Francis, who has a demanding role. Ellis's own liner-notes are very informative about his methods.

HERB ELLIS (born 1921)

GUITAR

***	**Jazz/Concord** Concord CCD 6001 CD/MC	

***   **Jazz/Concord** Concord CCD 6001 CD/MC
Ellis; Joe Pass (*g*); Ray Brown (*b*); Jake Hanna (*d*). 72.

(*)   **Seven Come Eleven Concord CCD 6002 CD/MC
As above. 7/73.

***   **Soft Shoe** Concord CCD 6003 CD/MC
Ellis; Harry Edison (*t*); George Duke (*p*); Ray Brown (*b*); Jake Hanna (*d*). 74.

**   **Rhythm Willie** Concord CCD 6010 CD/MC
Ellis; Ross Tompkins (*p*); Freddie Greene (*g*); Ray Brown (*b*); Jake Hanna (*d*). 75

***   **Hot Tracks** Concord CCD 6012 CD/MC
Ellis; Harry Edison (*t*); Plas Johnson (*ts*); Mike Melvoin (*ky*); Ray Brown (*b*); Jake Hanna (*d*). 76.

(*)   **Soft And Mellow Concord CCD 4077 CD/MC
Ellis; Ross Tompkins (*p*); Monty Budwig (*b*); Jake Hanna (*d*). 8/78.

***   **Doggin' Around** Cncord CCD 4372 CD/MC
Ellis; Red Mitchell (*b, v*). 3/88.

Herb Ellis was with Oscar Peterson in the 1950s, and then made some fine records (*Nothin' But The Blues*, *Midnight Roll*, *Thank You Charlie Christian*) for Columbia and Verve, which could certainly stand reissue. But what's in the catalogue at present is this sequence of amiable and not very enthralling records for Concord. Ellis was one of the early members of the Concord stable, and his first discs for the label set something of the house style: tempos at an easy jog, standard programmes with one or two eccentric choices ('Inka Dinka Doo' on *Soft Shoe*, 'Squatty Roo' on *Hot Tracks*), and bands that are like an assembly of old rogues joshing each other about old glories. The two albums with Edison and Brown are probably the best, with Ellis digging in a little harder than usual, the trumpeter turning in some of his wryest solos, and Brown insuperably masterful as always. The discs with Pass and Green tend to go the way of all such encounters, the pleasantness of the sound cancelling out most of the musical challenges, and the disc with Green is almost somnambulistic in parts. *Soft And Mellow* is another one that tends to live up to its title. But *Doggin' Around*, made after Ellis had been away from the label for some time, is probably the most engaging album of the lot. Red Mitchell thrives in this kind of open and relaxed situation, which gives him the chance to unearth some of his ripest licks, and Ellis sounds keen-witted in a way that he perhaps disguises on the earlier records. His playing at its best is as swinging and hard-hitting as that of more modern guitarists such as Farlow and Raney, but he can send himself to sleep at times. Still, any of these sessions will go down well as a late-night palliative after a hard day.

KAHIL EL'ZABAR

DRUMS, PERCUSSION, FLUTE

****   **Three Gentlemen From Chikago** Moers Music 01076 LP
El'Zabar; Edward Wilkerson (*as, ts, cl, f*); Henry Huff (*ss, ts, bs, bcl*). 82.

El'Zabar is a percussionist with a knack for creating exciting musical situations out of few materials. This session, credited to Ethnic Heritage Ensemble, is typical of the absorbing music which some of the younger Chicago musicians have been developing in the wake of the AACM, though opportunities to document it have been unfortunately few in number. The four pieces are simply structured, often no more than a folk melody over a rhythm struck from a single drum, but they become vehicles for superb counterpoint and improvisation by Huff and Wilkerson, as vivid and expressive as Jarman and Mitchell at their best.

(*)   **The Ritual sound aspects sas 011 LP
El'Zabar; Lester Bowie (*t*); Malachi Favors (*b*). 11/85.

***   **Sacred Love** sound aspects sas 021 LP
As above, plus Raphael Garrett (*cl, perc*). 11/85.

El'Zabar's meeting with two more senior Chicagoans is a mixed success. Recorded in the city itself, the first record is a 42-minute improvisation based around Favors's 'Magg Zelma', and it contains inevitable dead spots along with some intriguing music. For all these musicians' commitment to freedom, the most uplifting music results when they play together in something like a post-bop trio. When joined by Garrett, in a session recorded on the same occasion, the music takes on a more satisfying consistency, and the two horn players play expressively; there is even a rendition of 'There Is No Greater Love' at the end.

***   **Another Kind Of Groove** sound aspects sas 016 LP
El'Zabar; Billy Bang (*vn, bells*); Malachi Favors (*b, perc*). 5/86.

Billy Bang isn't the sort of musician who operates in meandering situations, and his terseness sits well with El'Zabar's sparse rhythms and Favors's familiarly elemental bass parts. The music is a little unfocused, but there is some fetching, swinging interplay among the members of the trio.

***   **Ancestral Song** Silkheart SH 108 CD/LP
El'Zabar; Joseph Bowie (*tb, marim, perc*); Edward Wilkerson (*ts, cl, perc*). 5/87.

Credited once again to Ethnic Heritage Ensemble, this is a slightly disappointing follow-up to the earlier release. The in-concert date suffers from the substitution of Huff by the less imaginative Bowie, whose trombone parts are relatively conservative, and a general lowering of voltage between the players. Wilkerson, though, remains a forthright improviser.

RENATO EMANUELE (born 1935)
GUITAR

(*)   **To Meet Again Olufsen DOC 5111 LP
Emanuele; Thomas Agergaard (*ts, f*); Nikolaj Hess (*p*); Ole Rasmussen (*b*); Toni Cigna (*d*). 12/90.

This veteran Belgian guitarist has been sighted only rarely in recent times, but this album with a young Danish band is amiable, boppish music with the occasional modish tinge, as in the lightly funky 'Black Out'. Agergaard's gruff and sombre tenor is the counterpoint to the leader's gently articulated solos. Pleasant though unexceptional.

JAMES EMERY
GUITAR

***   **Artlife** Lumina L007 LP
Emery; Leroy Jenkins (*vn*). 12/82.

**   **Exo Eso** FMP SAJ 59
Emery (*g* solo). 10/87.

The guitarist from String Trio Of New York has been a little overlooked among the spate of new performers on the instrument. Admittedly, these solo recordings are under-characterized, but Emery obviously has as much technique as any of the post-modern guitarists who are making records by the lorryload. He favours a high yet damped-down sound, and his frequent use of the soprano guitar often gives the impression that he's using some sort of toy instrument; the lightning runs and effortless picking, though, are unarguably the work of a fine musician. The Lumina record features one side of electric solos and one of acoustic work: the electric material is more concerned with formal experimentation and tends towards novelty at times, but other pieces such as the brief 'Ruminations' tie Emery's free playing to a more conventional jazz tradition and make both ends work. Two duets with Leroy Jenkins seem surprisingly stiff. The recording is very dry.

    The FMP set is perhaps a more obviously virtuoso performance, ten acoustic solos which interpolate a lot of lightning-fast picking and furious strumming into otherwise lyrical structures, but a certain emptiness of concept wears down the listener after a few of these: there doesn't seem to be much more than a great deal of fancy fretwork here when all's said and done. Truthful if unglamorous recording.

GIUSEPPE EMMANUELE
PIANO

***   **A Waltz For Debby** Splasc(h) H 200 CD/LP
Emmanuele; Paolo Fresu (*t, flhn*); Pietro Tonolo (*ss, ts*); Nello Toscano (*b*); Pucci Nicosia (*d*). 1/90.

A lovely record. Emmanuele is a Bill Evans admirer, and the quintet's version of 'Waltz For Debby' pays suitable homage to its composer, but the four originals by the pianist show a light but clear watermark of his own, and he plays with strength as well as delicacy: the solo on an unusually sunny reading of Lennie Tristano's 'Wow' even suggests some of the energy of the young Tristano himself. Fresu and Tonolo, though, are probably the most accomplished players here, and both have plenty of chances to shine.

SIDSEL ENDRESEN
VOCALS

***(*)   **So I Write** ECM 1048 CD/LP
Endresen; Nils Petter Molvaer (*t, flhn, perc*); Django Bates (*p*); Jon Christensen (*d*). 6/90.

Working rather obliquely outwards from a jazz/folk/improvised idiom, Endresen sings with a deceptive range that pushes her up into the lyric-soprano register and down into contralto accents on the more sombre songs. Jon Balke's settings, to 'So I Write', 'This Is The Movie' and 'Dreamland', perfectly suit her slightly prosaic lyrics. There are no up-tempo tracks but, whether singing exactly on the beat or drawing out the words without any pretext of verse-metre, Endresen seems completely confident, and the accompanying group is superb though often minimal in gesture. Bates – who's credited with the two weakest compositions – plays beautifully: no electronics, no horn, no additional percussion, just beautifully modulated stylings which accord with the accompanist's duty to point up the words without swamping them.

ENTEN ELLER
GROUP

(*)   **Cassandra Splasc(h) H 176 LP
Mario Simeoni (*ts, f*); Carlo Actis Dato (*ts, bs, bcl*); Ugo Boscain (*p*); Giovanni Maier (*b*); Massimo Barbiero (*d*); Jolanda Romano (*v*). 2/89.

***   **Antigone** Splasc(h) H 352-2 CD
As above, except add Alex Rolle, Andrea Stracuzzi (*perc*), omit Romano. 1/91.

This band is from Piedmont, which has spawned several of the best new Italian groups (Enrico Fazio, Claudio Lodati, Carlo Actis Dato). *Cassandra* is a rough-and-ready set which has too many ragged edges to convince that the group has its potential under control, but in at least one piece – the graphically intense 'La Mademoiselle Rouge', with its explosion of a bass clarinet solo by guest Actis Dato – the group hint at much greater things, and even where they lack finesse there's plenty of excitement in the playing. *Antigone* is, if anything, even more brawling, with the opening tracks 'Il Mago' and 'Pragma' blown open by Actis Dato and Simeoni, but a lengthy set includes ballads too, and the basic quintet know each other's moves to make this blend of modal, bop and fusion leanings into an entertaining whole. The CD brings out much more detail in the band's sound.

ED EPSTEIN (born 1946)
BARITONE, TENOR AND SOPRANO SAXOPHONES

***   **The Art Of Survival** Olufsen DOCD 5131 CD
Epstein; Erling Kroner (*tb*); Peter Epstein (*ss, as*); Jan Lundgren, (*p*); Thomas Oveson (*b*); Jonas Johansen (*d*); Lisbeth Diers (*perc*). 6–7/90.

Epstein is a Texan saxophonist who decamped for Sweden at the end of the 1960s. This recent session reveals a conservative but energetic stylist who harks back to swing and mainstream tenor as well as to the familiar post-bop models. His son, Peter, is a happy choice as front-line partner (Kroner plays on only three tracks) and Epstein Sr's most distinctive horn proves to be the baritone, which he solos on with as much gusto as he does tenor. The all-original material is no great shakes but there's plenty of good-humoured blowing here.

PETER ERSKINE (born 1954)
DRUMS

*** **Peter Erskine** Original Jazz Classics OJC 610 CD/LP/MC
Erskine; Randy Brecker (*t, flhn*); Michael Brecker (*ts*); Bob Mintzer (*ts, bcl*); Don Grolnick, Kenny Kirkland (*p*); Mike Mainieri (*vib*); Eddie Gomez (*b*); Don Alias (*perc*). 6/82.

Erskine is (justifiably) among the most sought-after drummers of the contemporary American circuit: besides his formidable technique, he's gregarious enough to handle virtually any musical situation and is a thoughtful composer to boot. His first record as a leader found him in charge of a relatively straightforward post-bop session; but, with such a heavyweight gathering of studio craftsmen all on their toes, the results are impressive if a little too brawny here and there.

**** **Transition** Denon 33CY-1484 CD
Erskine; Joe Lovano (*ss, ts*); Bob Mintzer (*ts*); Peter Gordon (*frhn*); Kenny Werner, Don Grolnick (*ky*); John Abercrombie (*g, g-syn*); Marc Johnson (*b*). 10/86.

*** **Motion Poet** Denon CY 72582 CD
Erskine; Randy Brecker, Lew Soloff, Joe Mosello (*t, flhn*); Dave Bargeron (*tb, tba*); Matt Finders (*btb*); Peter Gordon, Jerry Peel, John Clark (*frhn*); Lawrence Feldman (*ss, as, f*); Bob Mintzer (*ts, f*); Michael Brecker (*ts*); Roger Rosenberg (*bs*); Jim Beard, Eliane Elias (*ky*); John Abercrombie (*g, gsyn*); Jeff Mironov (*g*); Will Lee, Marc Johnson (*b*). 4–5/88.

Erskine outdid his leadership potential with these very fine records. He achieves the seemingly impossible task of diversifying the music without making it seem eclectic, giving himself considerable space without turning the sessions into mere 'drummer's records'. *Transition* is outstanding: richly melodic and detailed compositions by Erskine and Vince Mendoza, intensely committed playing by all hands, a lovely reading of 'My Foolish Heart' by the Erskine/Abercrombie/Johnson trio, and quite stunning digital sound. By comparison, *Motion Poet* is slightly less interesting, with a brass section used to no very telling effect, but there's an impeccable revision of Joe Zawinul's 'Dream Clock' and a fine Erskine ballad in 'Not A Word'. Both records prove what New York's finest studio players can do when they have a challenging assignment before them.

(*) **Big Theatre Ah Um 004 CD
Erskine; Vince Mendoza (*t, flhn*); Peter Gordon French (*horn*); Jerry Peel (*frhn*); Don Grolnick (*ky*); Will Lee (*b, v*); Paulinho Da Costa (*perc*). 86–89.

Erskine has been commissioned to do a number of theatre scores, and this is the music from three different Shakespeare plays. Harmless, pretty putterings from the workshop, with sweet synthesizer dances and other fragments, most of them no more than a moment or two long; only Will Lee's vocal on 'O Mistress Mine' (no Elizabethan, he!) is unpalatable. But it's hardly much more than a distraction, or light background music.

***(*) **Sweet Soul** RCA Novus PD 90616 CD/MC
Erskine; Randy Brecker (*t*); Joe Lovano (*ss, ts*); Bob Mintzer (*ts*); Kenny Werner (*p*); John Scofield (*g*); Marc Johnson (*b*); Peter Erskine (*d*). 3/91.

On his regular sessions, Erskine continues to set a formidable standard. The lovely rearrangement of William Walton's 'Touch Her Soft Lips And Part' is another Shakespearean borrowing, and a more practical one: Lovano's bewitching drift is as haunting as anything he's done. Other credits are split between Erskine, Werner and Vince Mendoza, and there's not a weak tune in the pack. Improvisations grow naturally from their surroundings, and even such over-exposed players as Brecker and Scofield function at their best.

BOOKER ERVIN (1930–70)
TENOR SAXOPHONE

***(*)   **That's It** Candid 9014 CD/LP
Ervin; Horace Parlan (*p*); George Tucker (*b*); Al Harewood (*d*). 1/61.

(*)   **Lament For Booker Ervin Enja 2054 LP
Ervin; Kenny Drew (*p*); Niels-Henning Ørsted-Pedersen (*b*); Alan Dawson (*d*);
Horace Parlan (*p solo*). 10/65, 5/75.

It's slightly hard to credit that 'The Trolley Song' on the now deleted *Down In The Dumps* and
the sessions for the magnificent *That's It* were recorded on successive days. On the Candid
album, Ervin is in full, fierce voice, blending elements of Don Byas and John Coltrane into a
typical Texan shout. 'Uranus' is his finest ballad performance. George Tucker's deliberate
introduction to 'Booker's Blues' takes the music down into some South-western storm cellar,
where it spins out its unhurried message. To avoid contractual problems, Parlan was originally
credited (with rather arcane literary humour) as 'Felix Krull', but there is nothing fraudulent
about his playing on the album. He was always Ervin's most sympathetic sideman, and it is
Parlan who spins out the 'Lament' for Ervin on Enja 2054, adding a sad, posthumous
afterthought to a 1965 European session which doesn't quite come off.

**   **Soulful Saxes** (Affinity AFF 758 CD)
Ervin; Zoot Sims, Tommy Turrentine (*ts*); Tommy Flanagan (*p*); George Tucker (*b*);
Dannie Richmond (*d*). 6/60 – album also includes material by Roland Kirk (q. v.).

Ervin combines well on 'Largo' with Flanagan (who shares Parlan's virtues and adds an extra
shade on lyricism). The tenor-pursuit on the other tracks is by no means as appealing, and the
recording is a touch hard.

***   **Cookin'** Savoy SV 0150 CD
Ervin; Richard Williams (*t*); Horace Parlan (*p*); George Tucker (*b*); Dannie
Richmond (*d*). 11/60.

Just about as 'straight-ahead' as it comes. There's not much subtlety to the arrangements, which
are played with a jumpy regularity, but Ervin and Williams both solo strongly, and the
saxophonist's long meditation with rhythm only on 'You Don't Know What Love Is' is perhaps
the most affecting extended performance on the record. A welcome reissue.

DAVE ESHELMAN
TROMBONE

***   **The Jazz Garden** Jazz Mind 1002 LP
Eshelman; Carl Leach, Bill Resch, Dave Bendigkeit, Steve Campos (*t, flhn*); John
Russell, Mike Humphrey, Ken Wirt, Phil Zahorsky (*tb*); Mary Park (*as, f*); Rory
Snyder (*as, f, cl*); Bennett Friedman (*ts, f, cl*); Glenn Richardson (*ts, f, cl, picc*); Bob
Farrington (*bs, f, cl, bcl*); Smith Dobson (*p*); Tim Volp (*g*); Jon Ward (*b*); Russ
Tincher (*d*). 6–7/82.

***(*)   **Deep Voices** Sea Breeze SB 2039 CD/LP
As above, except Rich Theurer (*t, flhn*), Chris Braymen (*tb*), Daniel Zinn (*ts, f*), Joe
Henderson (*ts*), Bruce Forman (*g*) and Seward McCain (*b*) replace Leach, Wirt,
Richardson, Volp and Ward. 10/88.

Southern California has been a spawning ground for a number of interesting bands in the past
20 years, with such West Coast hold-outs as Gerald Wilson maintaining a West Coast tradition,
which groups like Eshelman's Jazz Garden Big Band – a San Francisco fixture through the late
1970s and '80s – have amplified further. These are unflashy, thoughtful sessions which are
beautifully performed without resorting to slickness or facile racing. A trombonist himself,
Eshelman gets a fine, singing timbre out of his 'bone section, and he pitches it to scintillating
effect against the trumpets and woodwinds: sample the fascinating arrangement of 'Softly As
In A Morning Sunrise' on *Deep Voices*. The latter album takes the lead for a couple of guest
spots by Joe Henderson and Bruce Forman, whose guitar solo on 'To Catch A Rainbow' is a

thrilling beat-the-clock feat. Even the title-work on *Deep Voices*, which tackles the favourite Californian topic of whale-song, sidesteps bathos. Excellent, expansive sound.

ELLERY ESKELIN (born 1959)
TENOR SAX

(*)   **Setting The Standard Cadence CJR 1044 LP
          Eskelin; Drew Gress (*b*); Phil Haynes (*d*). 2/88.

***   **Forms** Open Mind 2403 CD
          As above. 3/90.

While there are countless young tenor players making records, Eskelin is one who deserves more than a single glance. Gress and Haynes are regular working partners with Eskelin; as a unit, the trio creates with unusual empathy. The saxophonist has a querulous tone and likes to stretch phrases into elongated shapes that push against what are otherwise fairly conventional parameters: he chooses standards or simple thematic constructions to play on, and sounds to be good at moving in and out of familiar tonalities. Gress and Haynes don't so much follow as run along parallel paths, commenting and abstracting ideas of their own: Haynes can be rather carefree with his cymbals, but it's a trio in which everybody talks. *Setting The Standard* uses seven show tunes as the programme and, while some are a little unformed – 'East Of The Sun' becomes a clumsy blow-out, and 'I Want To Talk About You' is a self-consciously strained tenor solo – there are some grittily evocative variations, including a surprisingly effective reading of the unpromising 'Jitterbug Waltz'.

    Forms, though, is a superior set – better played, better recorded, with five originals plus Ellington's 'African Flower' and Gillespie's 'Bebop'. The trio's collective intensity is best caught on 'Blues' and 'In Three', while 'Ballad' has Eskelin exploring the horn with plangent authority. It's still redolent of sketchwork in parts, and a couple of the tracks are simply too long, but these are clearly musicians with something to say.

KEVIN EUBANKS (born 1957)
GUITAR, ELECTRIC GUITAR

(*)   **Face To Face GRP D 9539 / 91029 CD/MC
          Eubanks; Dave Grusin (*DX 7*); Ron Carter, Marcus Miller (*b*); Buddy Williams (*d*);
          Crusher Bennett, Paulinho Braga, Ralph McDonald (*perc*). 86.

**   **The Heat Of Heat** GRD 9552/91041 CD/MC
          Eubanks; Onaje Allan Gumbs, Patrice Rushen (*ky*); Ron Carter, Rael Wesley Grant
          (*b*); Gene Jackson (*d*); Don Alias (*perc*). 87.

*   **Shadow Prophets** GRP 9565/91054 CD/MC
          Eubanks; Victor Bailey, Rael Wesley Grant (*b*); Tommy Campbell, Gene Jackson (*d*);
          Mark Ledford (*v*); Onaje Allan Gumbs (*syn strings*). 1/88.

*(*)   **The Searcher** GRP 9580 CD/MC
          Eubanks; Edward Simon (*p*); Victor Bailey, Kenny Davis (*b*); Dennis Chambers,
          Gene Jackson (*d*); Mark Ledford (*v, v perc*); Duane Cook Broadnax (*beatbox drum
          v*). 11/88.

(*)   **Promise Of Tomorrow GRP 9604 CD/MC
          Eubanks; Edward Simon (*p, ky*); Kenny Davis (*b*); Gene Jackson or Marvin Smitty
          Smith (*d*). 11/89.

Dripping with talent and technique, Kevin Eubanks has yet to produce anything on record genuinely commensurate with either. All too often the albums drift off into soft elevator funk, laced with mawkish dedications (notably to Krishnamurti) and superadded 'effects'.

    The earliest of the group is by far the best, and there are adventurous duos with Ron Carter on 'Relaxin' at Camarillo' and the Krishnamurti-inspired 'Silent Waltz'. There is virtually no other opportunity to hear Eubanks 'straight'; 'Poem For A Sleeping Child', which closes *The Searcher*, is a piece of New Age thistledown. The glycerined-bicep guitar hero cover-shot to *The*

Heat Of Heat (Eubanks is a big sports and iron-pumping enthusiast) is coupled with dire warnings of a 'rock guitar solo' among the credits. In reality, and in body-building parlance, the solo has very poor def indeed, a lot of posing and fake-sweat, no stamina or lasting muscle.

Eubanks is a more than competent composer, understands advanced harmony and has pushed through and beyond his initial dedication to George Benson. Even so, he suffers recurrent lapses of judgement. *Shadow Prophets* is certainly the nadir, opening with sampled voices and the unrelieved keyboard surf that constantly swamps Eubanks's fleet lines. 'Cookin'', on *The Searcher*, treads basically the same path with sub-McFerrin vocal percussion and ultra-bland octave guitar effects.

Promise Of Tomorrow brings some relief. The guitar gets back on top of the wave again, and there is A Standard (!), 'In A Sentimental Mood', played with gentle conviction, acoustic piano well up. If this represents promise of a future simplification of means or the kind of straightforwardness he has brought to his brother Robin Eubanks's recordings, so much the better.

ROBIN EUBANKS (born 1959)
TROMBONE, BASS TROMBONE, KEYBOARDS

**(*)   Different Perspectives JMT 834424 CD/LP
Eubanks; Michael Phillip Mossman (*flhn*); Clifton Anderson, Slide Hampton (*tb*); Douglas Purviance (*b tb*); Steve Coleman (*as*); Kevin Eubanks (*g*); James Weidman (*p, syn*); Peter Washington, Rael Wesley Grant (*b*); Teri Lyne Carrington, Jeff Tain Watts (*d*).

Harder-edged and much more clearly conceived than any of his brother Kevin's albums to date, *Different Perspectives* is an impressive effort, well worth checking. The title-track is the straightest performance of the set, with a good mix of horns and no electronics. 'Walkin'' brings in Hampton and Anderson for a big trombone revivalist meeting. The veteran's clean delivery is immediately distinguishable from the leader's more legato and slurred approach. Very much a studio session, with instrumentations tailored exactly for each track, it continually poses the question of what any one grouping might have sounded like live. Which is probably a good sign.

**(*)   Dedication JMT 834433 CD/LP/MC
Eubanks; Steve Turre (*tb*); Mulgrew Miller (*p, syn*); Francesca Tanksley (*syn*); Charnet Moffett (*b*); Tommy Campbell, Tony Reedus (*d*); Jimmy Delgado (*congas, perc*). 4/89.

Co-led with fellow-trombonist Steve Turre, this looks almost like an attempt at Jay and Kai for the early 1990s. The two horns lock firmly on 'Trance Dance' and 'Perpetual Groove', not always easy to separate. The synthesizer backgrounds are somewhat elided and spare, and Campbell's distinctive drumming sounds very sure and straightforward. A lot of the bass is lost on the cassette, which may disappoint potential Walkman users.

**   Karma JMT 834446 CD/LP/MC
Eubanks; Earl Gardner (*t*); Greg Osby (*as*); Branford Marsalis (*ts*); Kevin Eubanks (*g*); Renee Rosnes, Ken Werner (*ky*); Dave Holland (*b, v*); Lonnie Plaxico (*b*); Marvin Smitty Smith (*d*); Mino Cinelu (*perc, v*); Kimson Kism Albert, Cassandra Wilson, Stefan Winter (*v*). 5/90.

A little heavier on the vocals, with raps all round on the title-track, and a somewhat raggedy chorus behind Eubanks's trombone on 'Minoat'. The trios with Holland and Smith are excellent, and the Art Blakey tribute, 'Remember When', strikes just the right chord, an M-Base response to the Jazz Messengers' great example. A fine album, with a few rough corners.

WENDELL EUGENE (born 1923)
TROMBONE, VOCAL

***   **West Indies Blues** 504 LPS 8 LP
      Eugene; Albert Walters (*c*); Raymond Burke (*cl*); Jeannette Kimball (*p*); Les Muscutt
      (*bj, g*); Emanuel Sayles (*bj, v*); Chester Zardis (*b*); Chester Jones (*d*). 9/78.

Aside from Barrow-born Les Muscutt, Eugene is the youngest member of this band of
Louisiana veterans, and their music is old-time even by New Orleans traditionalist standards.
The sparse rhythms supplied by Zardis, Sayles and Jones leave a very open canvas for the
soloists, and the impression is of the clear, simple music suggested by the earliest New Orleans
records rather than the tourist Dixieland which has come to plague the genre. Walters and
Burke, though both well into their seventies when the record was made, play firm, stiffly
graceful lines, and if Eugene's trombone lacks any timbral finesse, he has his own peculiar
momentum. Jones is a swinging drummer, too: he makes the most of both 'Bourbon Street
Parade' and the unexpected 'Pagan Love Song'. The recording is suitably clean and dry.

EUROPEAN JAZZ ENSEMBLE
GROUP

(*)   **Live Ear-Rational 1011 CD
      Manfred Schoof, Allan Botschinsky (*t, flhn*); Steve Galloway (*tb*); Ernst Ludwig
      Petrowsky (*as, cl*); Gerd Dudek (*ss, ts, f*); Rob van den Broeck (*p*); Ali Haurand (*b*);
      Tony Oxley (*d*); Uschi Bruning (*v*). 8/87.

***   **At The Philharmonic Cologne** MA Music A-800 CD/LP/MC
      As above, except Enrico Rava (*t, flhn*), Stan Sulzmann (*ss, ts*), Philip Catherine (*g*)
      and Tony Levin (*d*) replace Galloway and Oxley. 4/89.

While this isn't a genuinely pan-European band, it's an unusual cross-section of players, and any
idea that they would aim for an MOR modernism is quickly dispelled by the first track on *Live*,
Petrowsky's bizarre exercise in extremities of register, 'Skizzen', which features Bruning's only
vocal on the disc. Petrowsky and Dudek are certainly given free rein: even on a relatively
conventional theme such as Botschinsky's 'Folkmusic Nr', Petrowsky's howling clarinet solo
ruptures the seams. Oxley's diffuse rhythms never let matters settle down, and the Ensemble
tend to split up into smaller groupings rather than playing as an entirety: it's an altogether very
free set, although the concert recording is rather remote and unfocused. The second session
offers more of the same, though the new players temper some of the freedoms, and the larger
group has a bigger sound.

BILL EVANS (1929–80)
PIANO

***   **New Jazz Conceptions** Original Jazz Classics OJC 035 CD/LP/MC
      Evans; Teddy Kotick (*b*); Paul Motian (*d*). 9/56.

The most influential pianist of modern times began with a fine, comfortable set of boppish trio
performances which created little stir at the time (the record sold some 800 copies over the
course of one year). Orrin Keepnews, the producer, was convinced to record Evans by hearing
a demo tape played over the telephone, and the pianist's distinctive touch and lovely tone is
already apparent: he makes bop material such as Tadd Dameron's 'Our Delight' into
comprehensive structures, and the three tiny solos – including the very first 'Waltz For Debby',
his most renowned original – hint at what was to come. But it's clearly a talent in its early
stages.

****   **Everybody Digs Bill Evans** Original Jazz Classics OJC 068 CD/LP/MC
      Evans; Sam Jones (*b*); Philly Joe Jones (*d*). 12/58.

Perennially reluctant, busy with the Miles Davis group, Evans didn't record as a lead
another two years. This superb record was worth the wait, though. Jones and Jones
with enough spirit to bring out his most energetic delivery, and the assertivenes

with Davis lent Evans an assurance which makes 'Night And Day' and 'Oleo' into driving performances. But 'Peace Piece', a translucent reshaping of the opening phrases of 'Some Other Time', which Evans came up with in the studio, is one of his most affecting soliloquies, and the ballad reading of 'Young And Foolish' is an almost astonishing contrast to the uptempo pieces. 'Some Other Time', which was omitted from the original LP, is present on the CD version of the reissue.

****   **Portrait In Jazz** Original Jazz Classics OJC 088 CD/LP/MC
           Evans; Scott LaFaro (b); Paul Motian (d). 12/59.

****   **Explorations** Original Jazz Classics OJC 037 CD/LP/MC
           As above. 2/61.

*****   **Sunday At The Village Vanguard** Original Jazz Classics OJC 140 CD/LP/MC
           As above. 6/61.

*****   **Waltz For Debby** Original Jazz Classics OJC 210 CD/LP/MC
           As above. 6/61.

Evans was having trouble finding good bassists, but LaFaro's arrival precipitated the advent of one of the finest piano trios jazz has ever documented. The bassist's melodic sensitivity and insinuating sound flowed between Evans and Motian like water, and while notions of group empathy have sometimes been exaggerated in discussion of this music – it was still very much directed by Evans himself – the playing of the three men is so sympathetic that it set a universal standard for the piano–bass–drums set-up which has persisted to this day. Both *Portrait In Jazz* and *Explorations* have their small imperfections: there's an occasional brittleness in the latter, possibly a result of the quarrel which LaFaro and Evans had had just before the session, and the recording of both does less justice to LaFaro's tone and delivery than it might. But 'Autumn Leaves', 'Blue In Green', 'Beautiful Love' and the transformation of John Carisi's 'Israel' to the trio format are as sublimely integrated and inspiring as this kind of jazz can be. Yet the two records culled from a day's work at the Village Vanguard are even finer. Evans's own playing is elevated by the immediacy of the occasion: all his contributions seem all of a piece, lines spreading through and across the melodies and harmonies of the tune, pointing the way towards modality yet retaining the singing, rapturous qualities which the pianist heard in his material (Evans retained a relatively small repertoire of favourite pieces throughout his career). All of the Vanguard music is informed by an extra sense of discovery, as if the musicians were suddenly aware of what they were on to and were celebrating the achievement. They didn't have much time: LaFaro was killed in a car accident ten days later. There are extra tracks and alternative takes on the CD editions of all the above, and because the trio finally left very little music behind them, they are indispensable.

***(*)   **Moon Beams** Original Jazz Classics OJC 434 CD/LP/MC
           Evans; Chuck Israels (b); Paul Motian (d). 5–6/62.

****   **How My Heart Sings!** Original Jazz Classics OJC 369 CD/LP/MC
           As above. 5–6/62.

Chuck Israels replaced LaFaro, although Evans was at first so upset by the bassist's death that he stopped playing for a while. After some months of work, the pianist felt they were ready to record, and Keepnews, who'd wanted to get an all-ballad album out of Evans, cut both of the above discs at the same sessions, alternating slow and up-tempo pieces and saving the ballads for *Moon Beams*. There are five Evans originals – 'Very Early' and 'Re: Person I Knew' on *Moon Beams*, 'Walking Up', 'Show-Type Tune' and '34 Skidoo' on *How My Heart Sings!* – and the slightly unfoc̶u̶s̶e̶d̶ readings by the trio can be accounted for by the fact that the pianist re̶t̶u̶r̶n̶e̶d̶ only at the dates. But this was otherwise a superb continuation of
Evans's work. Israel plays p̶ushy, hard-bitten lines and meshes very capably with Motian, and it a̶ ̶s̶o̶m̶e̶times pugnacious mood: 'Summertime' numbers among the more s̶t̶andard, and 'In Your Own Sweet Way', present on the CD of *How* d̶i̶f̶f̶erent takes, negotiates Brubeck's theme with a hint of asperity. Not S̶tairway To The Stars', for instance, is a model of firm melodic

te CDP 7905382 CD
5/62.

***   **Interplay** Original Jazz Classics OJC 308 CD/LP/MC
    Evans; Freddie Hubbard (*t*); Jim Hall (*g*); Percy Heath (*b*); Philly Joe Jones (*d*). 7/62.

Temperamentally, Evans and Hall hit it off perfectly in the studios. Their duet album is a masterpiece of quiet shadings, drifting melancholy and – perhaps surprisingly – hard swinging, the latter quality emerging on a particularly full-blooded 'I'm Getting Sentimental Over You'. But it's the nearly hallucinatory ballads 'Dream Gypsy' and 'Romain' which stick in the mind, where harp-like tones and gently fingered refrains establish a rare climate of introspection. The *Interplay* session, organized by Keepnews to keep Evans in funds, is comparatively desultory, but Hubbard plays rather well, and 'When You Wish Upon A Star' retains its powdery charm.

***(*)   **At Shelly's Manne Hole** Original Jazz Classics OJC 263 CD/LP/MC
    Evans; Chuck Israels (*b*); Larry Bunker (*d*). 5/63.

An understated yet tremendously intense 'Round Midnight' is among the highlights of this considerable club recording. Bunker and Israels were again given sight of some of the material only on the night of the recording, and their concentration adds to the tense lyricism which Evans was spinning out at the piano. A couple of rare excursions into the major blues, 'Swedish Pastry' and 'Blues in F/Five', complete a very strong programme, and the recording is particularly fine and well balanced.

****   **The Solo Sessions Vol. 1** Milestone M 9170 CD/LP/MC
    Evans. 1/63.

***(*)   **The Solo Sessions Vol. 2** Milestone M 9195 CD/LP/MC
    Evans. 1/63.

Both of these solo records were made on the same evening, as part of a contract-fulfilling exercise, and they lay unreleased for over 20 years. The music finds Evans at his most exposed (the tunes include 'Why Was I Born?' and 'What Kind Of Fool Am I?'), and there's an underlying tone of aggressive disquiet – which has to be set against some deliriously lyrical passages. Two medleys, of 'My Favourite Things / Easy To Love / Baubles, Bangles And Beads' and 'Love Theme From Spartacus / Nardis', are particularly revealing (both are on *Volume 1*) and there's a reading of 'Ornithology' on the second disc which sounds as vital and energized as anything which Evans recorded for Riverside.

****   **The Complete Riverside Recordings** Riverside 018 18LP/12CD
    Personnel collected from all above-listed OJC records. 56–63.

This huge collection is certainly a breathtaking monument to Evans's art, and it would earn a fifth star if the individual albums weren't so easily available. It includes all the music listed on the OJC albums above, as well as the two solo discs on Milestone, which originally made their first appearance in this boxed set.

***(*)   **Empathy / A Simple Matter Of Conviction** Verve 837757-2 CD
    Evans; Monty Budwig, Eddie Gomez (*b*); Shelly Manne (*d*). 8/62–10/66.

Although Budwig is excellent, and Gomez, making his debut with Evans, is superb, it's the partnership with Manne which is the most interesting thing about these records. Evans seldom responded to a hard-driving drummer – a meeting with Tony Oxley in the 1970s was fairly disastrous – but Manne's canny momentum creates sparks of interplay without disturbing the pianist's equilibrium. That said, the high spontaneity of these sessions sometimes misses the clarity of thought which is at the core of Evans's music, and although there's a flashing ingenuity on their playing on, say, 'With A Song In My Heart', with its mischievious coda, the more considered strengths of the pianist's regular trios are finally more satisfying. But Evans fans mustn't miss it.

***(*)   **Conversations With Myself** Verve 8219884-2 CD
    Evans (*p* solo). 1–2/63.

***(*)   **Trio '64** Verve 815057-2 CD
    Evans; Gary Peacock (*b*); Paul Motian (*d*). 12/63.

Currently available only as US releases, these discs show how much music Evans was coming up with in this period: an entire album of overdubbed three-way piano, something only Tristano had tried before, and another new trio taking on a striking set of fresh material. *Conversations* has aroused sometimes fierce views both for and against its approach, but in an age where overdubbing is more or less the norm in record-making, its musicality is more important. Carefully graded, each line sifted against the others, this is occasionally too studied a record, and the follow-up *Further Conversations With Myself* (currently missing from print) is arguably more graciously realized; but 'Theme From Spartacus' and a fine-grained 'Round Midnight' are pieces where Evans seems to gaze at his own work and find it compelling. The trio record features Peacock's only official appearance with Evans, and the empathy is stunningly adventurous: on 'Little Lulu', for instance, the reach of the bassist's lines and his almost flamenco-like rhythms score brilliant points against the pianist's own energetic choruses. Motian, for once, seems subdued.

*** **Compact Jazz** Verve 831366-2 CD
Evans; Monty Budwig, Chuck Israels, Eddie Gomez, Gary Peacock (*b*); Larry Bunker, Jack DeJohnette, Shelly Manne, Paul Motian, Arnold Wise (*d*); strings. 8/62–6/68.

An excellent compilation from Bill's Verve sessions, including something from all the above discs as well as a couple of less important tracks with strings arranged by Claus Ogerman.

*** **Paris 1965** Royal Jazz RJD 503 CD
Evans; Eddie Gomez (*b*); Marty Morell (*d*). 2/65 (?).

*** **Live In Stockholm 1965** Royal Jazz RJD 519 CD
Evans; Palle Danielsson (*b*); Rune Carlsson (*d*). 11/65.

The date listed for the Paris session at least must be wrong, since Gomez and Morell joined Evans much later. Both concerts offer standard Evans programmes, and each is typical of the many excellent sets recorded and released elsewhere: for that reason, and the less than perfect sound, both will appeal only to real Evans completists, though it's interesting to hear him with the Scandinavians.

*** **Alone** Verve 833801-2 CD
Evans (*p* solo). 9–10/68.

This was Evans's first officially released solo record, aside from the multi-tracked albums, and although some of the pieces sound low-voltage, even for him, the very long (over 14 minutes) exploration of 'Never Let Me Go' explores what would become Keith Jarrett territory with both prowess and resource to spare. The CD includes alternative takes of three of the pieces.

*** **You're Gonna Hear From Me** Milestone 9164 CD/LP/MC
Evans; Eddie Gomez (*b*); Marty Morell (*d*). 11/69.

*** **Montreux II** Columbia ZK 45219 CD
As above. 6/70.

(*) **The Bill Evans Album Columbia CK 30855 CD
As above. 5/71.

*** **Live In Paris Vol. 1** Frances Concert FC 107 CD/LP
As above. 2/72.

*** **Live In Paris Vol. 2** Frances Concert FC 114 CD/LP
As above. 2/72.

*** **Live In Paris Vol. 3** Frances Concert FC CD/LP
As above. 2/72.

*** **Yesterday I Heard The Rain** Bandstand BDCD 1535 CD
As above. *c.* 72.

*** **The Tokyo Concert** Original Jazz Classics OJC 345 CD/LP/MC
As above. 1/73.

(*) **Live In Buenos Aires Vol. 1 Jazz Lab JLCD 1 CD
As above. 6/73.

(*) **Live In Europe Vol. 1 EPM FDC 5712 CD
As above. 74.

**(*)   Live In Europe Vol. II EPM FDC 5713 CD
As above. 74.

Some of the steam had gone out of Evans's career on record at this point, after the astonishing consistency of his first ten years in the studio. Gomez, a great technician, has an immediately identifiable, 'soulful' sound which tends to colour his lines a mite too highly: his interplay with the leader assumes a routine excellence, which Morell, a fine if self-effacing drummer, tends to play alongside rather than inside, and bass and piano take more conspicuously solo turns rather than seeking out the three-way interplay of the earlier trios. On their own terms, the individual albums are still usually very good and highly enjoyable. *You're Gonna Hear From Me*, cut live at Copenhagen's Montmartre, is a lively date, with 'Waltz For Debby' taken at possibly its fastest-ever tempo, a surprisingly light-hearted 'Round Midnight' and an excellent 'Nardis' in a generally bountiful session. The Montreux session is a mixture of older tunes and the pieces which Evans would play over and over again in the years ahead. He dabbles with a little electric piano on *Album*, but the Japanese concert is straight-ahead and flows with ideas: 'Up With The Lark' is a marvellous piece. Excellent live recording. The three *Live In Paris* discs also benefit from good sound, which gives them the edge over many of the concert recordings from this period: Evans tended to play a very similar set from stage to stage, and the many live recordings which date from this period feature only slight variations on the same programme. The French discs offer a complete concert, including such staples as 'Very Early', '34 Skidoo', 'Turn Out the Stars', 'Time Remembered' and 'Two Lonely People'; Gomez's bass tone is a trifle flat, but otherwise the fidelity is fine. No details are given about the likely date and location of the Bandstand session: fidelity is quite good, and the trio plays very well, especially on a very vigorous 'What Are You Doing The Rest Of Your Life?' and an extended treatment of 'My Romance'. The Buenos Aires session is a decent if unexceptional set of the expected tunes, in sometimes wayward sound (Morell is the sufferer this time), while the problem with the two EPM discs seems to be an erratic speed level: many of the tracks sound as if they're playing back too fast.

***   Since We Met Original Jazz Classics OJC 622 CD/LP/MC
As above. 1/74.

***   Re: Person I Knew Fantasy F-9608 LP
As above. 1/74.

***   Jazzhouse Milestone M 9151 CD/LP/MC
As above. 74.

***   Blue In Green Milestone M 9185 CD/LP/MC
As above. 74.

***   Intuition Original Jazz Classics OJC 470 CD/LP/MC
As above, except omit Morell. 11/74.

***   Montreux III Original Jazz Classics OJC 644 CD/LP/MC
As above. 7/75.

***   Eloquence Fantasy F-9618 LP
As above. 11/73–12/75.

Evans signed to Fantasy (the source of the OJC material listed above) and with his assiduous producer, Helen Keane, created a big body of work that lasted through the 1970s. *Since We Met* and *Re: Person I Knew* both come from a single Village Vanguard engagement, and though Gomez and Morell don't erode memories of LaFaro and Motian, the music speaks with as much eloquence as this trio could muster. *Jazzhouse* and *Blue In Green* are more recent 'discoveries' of Evans concerts, which tell us nothing new about him and must be considered for collectors only, even if the playing is mostly impeccable. Consistency had become Evans's long suit, and he seemed content to tinker endlessly with his favourite pieces, disclosing little beyond the beauty of his touch, which by now was one of the most admired and imitated methods in piano jazz. The three albums with Gomez as sole partner explore a wider range of material – *Montreux III* is a particularly well-turned concert set – but one still misses the extra impetus of a drummer. *Eloquence* collects bits and pieces from a number of sessions and includes six solos, some from the otherwise unavailable *Alone (Again)* date.

(*)   **Quintessence Original Jazz Classics OJC 698 CD
Evans; Harold Land (*ts*); Kenny Burrell (*g*); Ray Brown (*b*); Philly Joe Jones (*d*).
5/76.

***   **The Complete Fantasy Recordings** Fantasy 1012 9CD
As all Fantasy/OJC sessions listed above. 73–79.

The Fantasy material isn't on a par with the magnificent complete Riverside set, but it has many
rewards, and includes two otherwise-unavailable bonuses: an interview with Marian McPartland
from her *Piano Jazz* radio series, and a 1976 date in Paris, as well as the *Alone (Again)* session.
Quintessence provided some answer as to what Evans would have done if he'd recorded more
frequently with a bigger group in his later years: he would have made an amiable and not
especially interesting Evans-plus-horns date.

****   **The Tony Bennett/Bill Evans Album** Original Jazz Classics OJC 439 CD/LP/MC
Evans; Tony Bennett (*v*). 6/75.

***   **Together Again** Nelson SIV 1122 CD
As above. 9/76.

Pairing Evans with Tony Bennett was an inspired idea, which pays off in a session which has an
illustrious kind of after-hours feel to it. Bennett, as big-hearted as always, lives out the
helpless-Romeo lyrics of such as 'When In Rome', and sounds filled with wonder when working
through a gorgeous 'The Touch Of Your Lips'. He also sings what's surely the definitive vocal
version of 'Waltz For Debby', where the corn of Gene Lees's lyric suddenly sounds entirely
right. Evans plays deferentially but creates some lovely accompaniments and seems to read
every mood with complete accuracy. *Together Again* is, alas, a merely very good successor.

***   **Live In Switzerland 1975** Jazz Helvet JH 01 CD
Evans; Eddie Gomez (*b*); Eliot Zigmund (*d*). 2/75.

*(*)   **Bill Evans & Monica Zetterlund** West Wind 2073 CD
As above, except add Monica Zetterlund (*v*). 2/75.

***   **In Buenos Aires Vol. 2** Jazz Lab JLCD-2 CD
Evans; Marc Johnson (*b*); Joe LaBarbera (*d*). 9/79.

***(*)   **The Brilliant** Timeless CDSJP 329 CD
As above. 8–9/80.

***(*)   **Consecration 1** Timeless SJP 331 CD/LP
As above. 8–9/80.

***(*)   **Consecration 2** Timeless SJP 332 CD/LP
As above. 8–9/80.

Evans's final years were full of personal problems, yet his music seemed set on fresh paths of
discovery. The trio with Zigmund made only a few recordings, and the live Swiss session is a
typical one, but with Gomez becoming restless he had to build a new group. The other date
from the same month, issued on West Wind, finds Zetterlund guesting on six tracks to
sometimes desultory effect, and the poor sound (several tracks are marred by bad distortion)
rules this one out except for the curious. Several months with Philly Joe Jones at the drums
seem to have gone undocumented, but Johnson and LaBarbera eventually proved to be a
challenging team which propelled the pianist through a remarkable burst of creativity. He
compared this group to his original band with LaFaro and Motian, and there's certainly a sense
of an evolving music, with the three men playing as a close-knit ensemble and Evans stretching
out in improvisations which were roaming much more freely than before. Even long solos had
hitherto kept a relatively tight hold of the thematic material underpinning them, but in all of the
concerts which these discs cover, Evans sounds unencumbered by frameworks, and such pieces
as 'Gary's Theme' (*Buenos Aires Vol. 2*) and 'Letter To Evan' (*The Brilliant*) are as close to
clear freedom as he ever came. The Timeless records all come from an engagement at San
Francisco's Keystone Korner, and chart a very high level of playing, with Johnson especially
challenging memories of the many great bassmen who had worked with Evans. Fine recording
on most of the discs, although the Buenos Aires session is a shade less vivid.

BILL EVANS (born 1958)
TENOR AND SOPRANO SAXOPHONES

****   **Moods Unlimited** Paddle Wheel KICJ 65 CD
       Evans; Hank Jones (*p*); Red Mitchell (*b*). 10/82.

Evans – the third Bill Evans to make a name for himself in jazz, after Bill Evan.
Evans (alias Yusef Lateef, saxes) – was the saxophonist in the Miles Davis 'c
around the time of this session. With Miles, he always seemed frozen-off
mysteriously ignored by the leader, yet he was surely among the best sidemen t. ⌐eter
had in the 1980s: in possession of a hard, piercing tone and a compelling rhythmic assurance,
Evans cut through fusion backbeats with little trouble. Here, he sounds superb in an entirely
different situation, an immaculately recorded after-hours session with two masters of an earlier
generation. The three of them mull over five standards at their leisure, but there's nothing
undercooked here: the long, ruminative trawl through 'In A Sentimental Mood' must be
accounted one of the greatest on record, with Jones creating a peerless improvisation and
Evans's soprano underscoring every heartfelt step of the melody. Mitchell's wonderfully
idiosyncratic bass marks out all the other lines. Highly recommended.

***   **The Alternative Man** Blue Note B21Y 46336 CD
       Evans; Lew Soloff (*t*); Hiram Bullock, Jeff Golub, Chuck Loeb, Sid McGinnis, John
       McLaughlin (*g*); Clifford Carter, Mitch Forman (*ky*); Mark Egan, Marcus Miller (*b*);
       Al Foster, Dan Gottlieb (*d*); Manolo Badrena (*perc*). 1–5/85.

The Alternative Man was very much in the line of the debut, marked by a hard-edged electric
sound (and by Evans's apparent preference for programmed in addition to acoustic drums) and
a heavy, rock-funk beat with strong boppish overtones in the distribution of off-accents. 'Miles
Away' was an explicit tribute to Evans's former boss, but 'The Cry In Her Eyes' was much
more the kind of fragile theme that Miles might have covered and given a lot more space and
light than in this rather anxious reading. 'The Alternative Man' itself is a shiny modern theme,
marked by unusual time-switches and chord progressions which seem to happen out of synch
with one another. Of the remainder, only 'Flight Of The Falcon' and 'Survival Of The Fittest'
restore the promise of the debut set, and Evans has been disappointingly quiet since, despite a
fine stint in the re-vamped Mahavishnu Orchestra, under John McLaughlin (who is the leaven
on the two tracks last mentioned). A fine, exuberant talent, Evans appears not so much to have
lost his way as not quite to have found it yet.

***   **Summertime** Jazz City 66053018 CD
       Evans; Gil Goldstein (*ky*); Chuck Loeb (*g*); Marc Johnson (*b*); Danny Gottlieb (*d*).
       2–4/89.

(*)   **Let The Juice Loose Jazz City 66053001 CD
       Evans; Jim Beard (*ky*); Chuck Loeb (*g*); Darryl Jones (*b*); Dennis Chambers (*d*). 9/89.

(*)   **The Gambler Jazz City 66053025 CD
       Evans; Mitch Forman (*ky*); Victor Bailey (*b*); Richie Morales (*d*). 9/90.

After leaving Davis, Evans worked with John McLaughlin and Herbie Hancock and cut a
couple of now deleted records of his own. The Jazz City albums are entertaining examples of
Evans in action – the later two were both recorded live in Tokyo – but none of them suggest a
particularly commanding leadership, and without the saxophonist these would be very bland
records indeed. *Summertime* suggests a variation on Pat Metheny's lyrical-pastoral fusion bent,
and 'Chatterton Falls' might be a ringer for anything off a mid-period Metheny record. But the
leader keeps his own playing at a high level of invention, concentrating mostly on soprano on a
mainly acoustic record. The two Tokyo sessions feature much flexing of muscles: Jones and
Chambers have some jaw-dropping moments on the first disc, and Evans takes some long,
calculatedly impassioned solos, but the record is too long and the live sound, while clear, is
somewhat recessed. *The Gambler* has a bigger soundstage and the music sounds more pointed,
perhaps as a result. Forman, though, is too much of a doodler to make Evans work very hard,
and it's Bailey's showstopping 'Kid Logic' that will appease fusion fans the most.

(*)   **Gil Evans And Ten Original Jazz Classics OJC 346 CD/LP/MC
Evans; John Carisi, Jack Loven, Louis Mucci (*t*); Jimmy Cleveland, Bart Varsalona
(*tb*); Willie Ruff (*hn*); Lee Konitz (*as*); Steve Lacy (*ss*); Dave Kurtzer (*bn*); Paul
Chambers (*b*); Jo Jones, Nick Stabulas (*d*); collective personnel.

****   **Out Of The Cool** MCA MCACD 9653 CD
Evans; Johnny Coles , Phil Sunkel (*t*); Keg Johnson, Jimmy Knepper (*tb*); Tony Studd
(*btb*); Bill Barber (*tba*); Ray Beckenstein, Eddie Cane (*as, f, picc*); Budd Johnson (*ts,
ss*); Bob Tricarico (*f, picc, bsn*); Ray Crawford (*g*); Ron Carter (*b*); Elvin Jones,
Charlie Persip (*d*). 12/60.

***   **Into The Hot** Impulse MCAD 39104 CD
Evans; John Carisi, John Glasel, Clark Terry, Joe Wilder (*t*); Bob Brookmeyer, Urbie
Green (*tb*); Jimmy Buffington (*hn*); Gene Quill, Phil Woods (*as*); Eddie Costa (*p,
vib*); Barry Galbraith (*g*); Art Davis, Milt Hinton (*b*); Osie Johnson (*d*); and Cecil
Taylor (*p*); Ted Curson, Roswell Rudd (*tb*); Jimmy Lyons (*as*); Archie Shepp (*ts*);
Henry Grimes (*b*); Sunny Murray (*d*); collective personnel. 9–10/61.

***(*)   **The Individualism Of Gil Evans** Verve 833804 CD
Evans; Ernie Royal, Johnny Coles, Bernie Glow, Louis Mucci (*t*); Jimmy Cleveland,
Tony Studd (*tb*); Ray Alonge, Jim Buffington, Gil Cohen, Don Corado, Robert
Northern, Julius Watkins (*frhn*); Bill Barber (*tba*); Al Block, Garvin Bushell, Eric
Dolphy, Andy Fitzgerald, Steve Lacy, George Marge, Jerome Richardson, Wayne
Shorter, Bob Tricarico (*reeds*); Kenny Burrell, Barry Galbraith (*g*); Bob Maxwell,
Margaret Ross (*hp*); Paul Chambers, Richard Davis, Milt Hinton, Gary Peacock, Ben
Tucker (*b*); Osie Johnson, Elvin Jones (*d*). 9/63, 4 & 7/64.

They used to say it was an anagram of Svengali. Certainly, Evans's influence on other musicians
(the notoriously solipsistic Miles only most obviously) was quite remarkable. The sessions on
Gil Evans and Ten, recorded four months after his epochal arrangements for *Miles Ahead*, are
oblique, intelligent, modern jazz, with Carisi's trumpet prominent, Lee Konitz and Steve Lacy
lending the reed parts the floating feel typical of an Evans chart. *Into The Hot* is a slightly odd
album, credited to the Gil Evans Orchestra and then to its individual constituents, a large and a
smaller band led by John Carisi and Cecil Taylor respectively. The compositions are also by
Carisi and Taylor. What Evans brings is a kind of tutelary genius with the harmonic structure of
a theme (and Carisi's 12-note materials become tonal only by a kind of undogmatic sleight) and
a brilliant grasp of instrumentation.

As was to be typical of his own later bands, Evans welds disparate materials into a single,
absolutely solid structure which maintains an *appearance* of freedom. Taylor's atonal
commentaries on bebop are demanding even after 30 years of more extreme revisions, but
they're so absolutely self-consistent and achieved that they become totally absorbing rather
than alienating.

Out Of The Cool is Evans's masterpiece under his own name (some might want to claim the
accolade for some of his work with Miles) and one of the best examples of jazz orchestration
since the early Ellington bands. It's the soloists – Coles on the eerie 'Sunken Treasure', a
lonely-sounding Knepper on 'Where Flamingoes Fly' – that most immediately catch the ear, but
repeated hearings reveal the relaxed sophistication of Evans's settings, which give a hefty band
the immediacy and elasticity of a quintet. Evans's time-sense allows Coles to double the metre
on George Russell's 'Stratusphunk', which ends palindromically, with a clever inversion of the
opening measures. 'La Nevada' is one of his best and most neglected (but see *Rhythm-A-Ning*,
below) scores, typically built up out of quite simple materials. The sound, already good, has
been enhanced by digital transfer revealing yet more timbral detail.

Individualism is a looser album, made with a pool of overlapping ensembles, perfectly
tailored to the compositions, and all securely grounded in the bass. The solos are now mainly
improvised rather than written, and stray more freely from the original composition, in
anticipation of the 1980s bands. 'Hotel Me' is an extraordinary performance, basically very
simple but marked by throaty shouts from the brass that set up Evans's own churchy solo. 'El
Toreador' again features Coles, less certain-sounding than on *Out Of The Cool*, but still a soloist

of considerable imagination. Remarkable as the music is, there's an oddly unfinished feel to the record, as if it has been put together out of previously rejected bits and pieces. It isn't just a CD round-up, though.

** **Blues In Orbit** Enja 3069 CD/LP
Evans; Johnny Coles, Mike Lawrence, Ernie Royal, Snooky Young (*t*); Garnett Brown, Jimmy Cleveland, Jimmy Knepper (*tb*); Ray Alonge, Julius Watkins (*hn*); Howard Johnson (*bs, tba*); Hubert Laws (*f*); George Marge (*f, ss*); Billy Harper (*f, ts*); Joe Beck (*g*); Gene Bianco (*hrp*); Herb Bushler (*b*); Elvin Jones, Alphonse Mouzon (*d*); Sue Evans, Donald McDonald (*perc*); collective personnel. 69, 71.

Highly regarded, but now wearing rather badly. Evans's instincts seem for once to have deserted him. The arrangements are a touch ragged and the solos have a centrifugal energy that leaves the ensembles firmly earthbound. A rather bright register kills a lot of interesting activity down in the bass.

** **Tokyo Concert** West Wind 2056 CD
Evans; Lew Soloff, Kunitoshi Shinohara (*t*); Tom Malone (*tb, syn*); Pete Levin (*hn, syn, org*); Bob Stewart (*tba*); George Adams (*ts, f*); Koshuke Mine (*ts*); Ryo Kawasaki, Keith Loving (*g*); Jeff Berlin (*b*); Sue Evans, Warren Smith (*d, perc*). 6/76.

** **Live '76** Zeta 714 CD
Evans; Ernie Royal, Lew Soloff (*t*); Tom Malone (*tb*); Pete Levin (*hn, syn*); Bob Stewart (*tba*); Arthur Blythe (*as*); George Adams (*ts*); John Clark (*g, hn*); Mike Richmond (*b*); Sue Evans (*d, perc*). 76.

(*) **Little Wing DIW 329 / 25029 CD
Evans; Lew Soloff (*t, picc t*); Terumasa Hino (*t*); Gerry Niewood (*as, ss, f*); George Adams (*ts, f, perc*); Bob Stewart (*tba*); Pete Levin (*syn*); Don Pate (*b*); Bob Crowder (*d*). 10/78.

Evans's wish to record with Jimi Hendrix was thwarted by the guitarist's death. His interest in the music continued, and 'Stone Free' and 'Little Wing' became staple items in his concert performances. None of these sets should be considered essential, but they do underline Evans's growing commitment to a more open improvisational approach. Of the 1976 live performances, the Zeta (if you can find it) is probably marginally preferable. The recordings are all reasonably good and the solos modestly adventurous; Adams is in full, not to say vociferous, voice throughout.

***(*) **Priestess** Antilles ANCD 8717 CD
Evans; Hannibal Marvin Peterson, Ernie Royal, Lew Soloff (*t*); Jimmy Knepper (*tb*); John Clark (*frhn*); Howard Johnson, Bob Stewart (*tba*); Arthur Blythe, David Sanborn (*as*); George Adams (*ts*); Pete Levin (*ky*); Keith Loving (*g*); Steve Neil (*b*); Susan Evans (*d*). 5/77.

Priestess stands a little apart from the other live recordings of the later 1970s. Rightly or wrongly, it has attained cult status for cross-over star David Sanborn's aching alto solo on 'Short Visit' (he also plays opposite Blythe on the title-track). The only other featured soloists are George Adams, not in the best form on a brief version of Mingus's 'Orange Was The Color Of Her Dress, Then Blue Silk', and the scorching Lew Soloff on 'Priestess' itself, which was written by Billy Harper. No Evans originals, no Hendrix, and one oddity, 'Lunar Eclipse' by Masabumi Kikuchi. But everyone remembers it for Sanborn, who established his jazz credentials beyond query.

(*) **Live At The Public Theater Volume 1 Black Hawk BKH 525 CD/LP

(*) **Live At The Public Theater Volume 2 Black Hawk BKH 526 CD/LP
Evans; Jon Faddis, Hannibal Marvin Peterson, Lew Soloff (*t*); George Lewis (*tb*); Dave Bargeron (*tb, tba*); Arthur Blythe (*as, ss*); Hamiet Bluiett (*bs, a f*); John Clark (*hn*); Masabumi Kikuchi, Pete Levin (*syn*); Tim Landers (*b*); Billy Cobham (*d*). 2/80.

A transitional band in most regards, with all the lags and hesitancies that implies. Individual performances are generally good, but there's a lack of excitement about the music and a greater abstraction than in preceding and later line-ups. Hendrix sits very comfortably alongside Evans's favourite Mingus, 'Orange was the Color of her Dress . . .'

***   **Live At Sweet Basil** Electric Bird K23P 6355/6 CD/LP

***   **Live At Sweet Basil – Volume 2** Electric Bird K19P 6421/2 CD/LP
Evans; Miles Evans, Shunzo O'no, Hannibal Marvin Peterson, Lew Soloff (*t*); Tom
Malone (*tb*); Chris Hunter (*as*); George Adams (*ts*); Howard Johnson (*bs, bcl, tuba*);
Hiram Bullock (*g*); Pete Levin (*syn*); Mark Egan (*b*); Adam Nussbaum (*d*); Mino
Cinelu (*perc*). 8/84.

***   **Farewell** Electric Bird K28P 6486 CD/LP
Evans; Johnny Coles, Miles Evans, Shunzo O'no, Lew Soloff (*t*); Dave Bargeron (*tb*);
Dave Taylor (*btb*); John Clark (*hn, hornette*); Chris Hunter (*as, ss, f*); Bill Evans (*ts,
ss, f*); Hamiet Bluiett (*bs, cl, bcl*); Gil Goldstein, Peter Levin (*syn*); Hiram Bullock (*g*);
Mark Egan (*b*); Danny Gottlieb (*d*).

***   **Bud And Bird** Electric Bird K19P 6455/6 CD/LP
As above, except omit Coles. 12/86.

For a man who didn't lead a regular band until he was nearly 50, Evans has stuck with it pretty
well. The 1980s bands, and notably the Monday Night Orchestra at Sweet Basil, play
open-textured music, drawn from basic melodic structures. They are inescapably linked to
Miles's new conception, with its rock and pop themes, deceptive orderliness, and renewed blues
orientation. The tracks are long but logically developed. The only repetition in up to 20 minutes
is a basic ostinato that slowly changes as the piece progresses. 'Little Wing', on the *Farewell*
album, receives a strong, rock-flavoured interpretation, laced with Hiram Bullock's
choke-chords and high sustains; it's quite the best of a number of competing versions. All the
horns play to the highest standard. All three can be recommended unreservedly.

***(*)   **Rhythm-A-Ning** EmArCy 836401 CD
Evans; Laurent Cugny (*ky*); Stéphane Belmondo, François Chassagnite, Christian
Martinez (*t, flhn*); Gilles Salommez (*tb*); Bernard François (*frhn*); Pierre Legris (*tba*);
Denis Barbier (*f, af, picc*); Pierre-Olivier Govin, Bobby Rangell (*as, ss*); Charles
Schneider, Andy Sheppard (*ts*); Manuel Rocheman (*p*); Benoit De Mesmay (*ky*);
Lionel Benhamou (*g*); Dominique Di Piazza (*b*); Stéphane Huchard (*d*); Xavier
Desandre, Marilyn Mazur (*perc*). 11/87.

Dream-come-true stuff for the young French arranger Laurent Cugny and his Lumière Big
Band. Despite initial resistance, Evans accepted the invitation. Working bands are often harder
to work with than pick-up ensembles, but Cugny's dedication to Evans's work (best expressed
in his patient transcription and re-creation of the original 'La Nevada') palpably warmed the
old guy's heart and Evans, never a very confident or forthright soloist, plays wonderful,
Ellingtonian exchanges with the band on 'London'. The Monk title tune gets a vivid, brassy
run-through with a sharp Andy Sheppard solo. Hendrix's 'Stone Free' isn't as good as it might
be (the solos by Barbier and Schneider don't amount to much), but Cugny's own 'Charles
Mingus's Sound Of Love', centred on the 'Goodbye, Pork Pie Hat' theme, is an unexpected
bonus, even without a contribution from Evans. A lovely album, with a useful synoptic range of
Evans material.

***   **Paris Blues** Owl 049 CD/LP
Evans; Steve Lacy (*ss*). 12/87.

A good example of Owl's staple: intimate, and generally quite abstract, improvisations in a
reflective mode. Evans is no virtuoso, Lacy one of the few unquestioned instrumental geniuses
in modern jazz, so there's a certain disproportion written in from the outset; but the two takes
of 'Esteem' are nicely varied and well developed on both parts. Another reading of 'Orange
Was the Color of her Dress . . . ' merely reconfirms Evans's obsession with its ambiguously
open, slightly blurted theme. An oddity, without the essential status of Ellington's small group
and solo projects, but bearing much the same relation to the main body of work.

***   **Heroes** Verve 511 621 2 CD
Evans; Lee Konitz (*as, ss*). 1/80.

Though Evans's name comes first, this is very much a Konitz-plus-accompaniment set. They run
through a brisk club set, marked by an enterprising choice of material that takes in Wayne
Shorter's 'Prince Of Darkness', Mingus's 'Reincarnation Of A Lovebird', 'All The Things You
Are', 'Lover Man', a blues improvisation and an arrangement of Chopin's 'C minor Prelude
No. 20, Opus 28'. The sound is nice and Konitz is in excellent voice.

EVERYMAN BAND
GROUP

***   **Everyman Band** ECM 1234 CD/LP
        Marty Fogel (*ss, ts*); David Torn (*g*); Bruce Yaw (*b*); Michael Suchovsky (*d*). 3/82.

***   **Without Warning** ECM 1290 CD/LP
        As above. 12/84.

A couple of strong records in the sparse field of impressionist jazz-rock: the spare textures of the quartet, blessedly free of keyboards, are thickened by Torn's occasional recourse to an orchestral palette; but there is an interesting emphasis on group form and improvisation, and Fogel is a determined force, even when restrained by the tasteful engineering. The compositions are tuneful, too, though nothing is as strong as some of the pieces Fogel composed for his CMP recording.

EXCELSIOR BRASS BAND
GROUP

***(*) **Jolly Reeds And Steamin' Horns** GHB BCD-290 CD
        Teddy Riley, James May (*t*); Gregory Stafford (*c*); Fred Lonzo, Clement Tervalon
        (*tb*); Michael White (*cl*); Oscar Rouzan (*as*); David Grillier (*ts*); Walter Payton (*bb*);
        Freddie Kohlman, Calvin Spears, Stanley Stephens (*d*). 10/83.

The rich yet highly restricted tradition of New Orleans brass bands is slowly getting through to CD, and this disc by perhaps the oldest institution in the genre – the EBB was originally formed in 1880 – is a very fine example of the tradition as it stands today (or, at least, in 1983). The digital sound allows one to hear all the detail which scrappy old recordings eliminated, and the ineffable bounce of the drummers (two on snare, one on bass), the old-fashioned tremble of the reeds and the sheer brassiness of the brass create some sense of a living tradition, on material which is profoundly historical ('Just A Closer Walk With Thee', 'Amazing Grace', 'Down In Honky Tonk Town', 'Just A Little While To Stay Here' and so on). At the same time, the primitivism of the band can only be affected: players such as White, Lonzo and Riley can probably go bebop if they wanted to, which one could never say about original brass band stalwarts. Whether that matters may be up to the ear of the behearer. It still makes for a very spirited and enjoyable session, adding four tracks to the earlier LP issue.

JON FADDIS (born 1953)
TRUMPET, FLUGELHORN

(*)   **Jon & Billy Black Hawk BKH 532 CD/LP
        Faddis; Billy Harper (*ts*); Roland Hanna (*p, electric p*); George Mraz (*b*); Motohiko
        Hino (*d*); Cecil Bridgewater (*kalimba*). 3/74.

***   **Youngblood** Pablo 2310765 LP
        Faddis; Kenny Barron (*p*); George Mraz (*b*); Mickey Roker (*d*). 1/76.

(*)   **Legacy Concord CJ 291 CD/LP/MC
        Faddis; Harold Land (*ts*); Kenny Barron (*p*); Ray Brown (*b*); Mel Lewis (*d*). 8/85.

Three out of four blind-tested subjects will tell you that Jon Faddis is Dizzy Gillespie. The influence is still transparent, but in the near-decade that separates the precocious *Youngblood* from the more measured *Legacy*, the technique has become far more individual and, though the 'A Night On Tunisia' solo on the later session makes explicit (though possibly unconscious) allusions to Gillespie at the legendary Massey Hall concert, Faddis seems to have steered a new course somewhere between Miles and Clark Terry.

Musically, the Concord is every bit as good, but the CD sound is rather harsh, particularly on an over-miked saxophone. The early *Jon & Billy*, though stylistically the most derivative in terms of the 21-year-old's trumpet approach, is also the most ambitious musically. 'Seventeen Bar Blues' has a witty theme and structure, and 'Ballad' stretches its dedicatee to the limit of his expressive resources; two tracks augment the basic quintet with Cecil Bridgewater's alien-sounding kalimba, the Bantu ancestor of the more familiar marimba.

MASSIMO FARAO
PIANO

***   **For Me** Splasc(h) H 337-2 CD
       Farao; Flavio Boltro (*t, flhn*); Aldo Zunino, Dado Moroni (*b*); Gianni Cazzola (*d*).
       12/90.

A boisterous and pleasing display of piano which starts out like a grooving Junior Mance or Bobby Timmons session on 'That's How We Like It!' then softens up with a long, languorous treatment of 'It's Easy To Remember'. Boltro sits in on a blues and an original called 'The Flea', but it's Farao's record, elegant in an Italian way (he even does a version of Lehár's 'Yours Is My Heart Alone') but keenly characterized throughout.

TAL FARLOW (born 1921)
GUITAR

***(*)   **First Set** Xanadu 109 CD/LP
       Farlow; Eddie Costa (*p*); Vinnie Burke (*b*); Gene Williams (*v*). 12/56.

***(*)   **Second Set** Xanadu 119 CD/LP
       As above, except omit Williams. 12/56.

***(*)   **The Return Of Tal Farlow** Original Jazz Classics OJC 356 CD/LP/MC
       Farlow; John Scully (*p*); Jack Six (*b*); Alan Dawson (*d*). 9/69.

One would hardly know from the catalogue that Farlow is one of the major jazz guitarists, since most of his records – as both leader and sideman – are currently out of print. His reticence as a performer – he has been semi-retired for nearly 35 years – belies his breathtaking speed, melodic inventiveness and pleasingly gentle touch as a bop-orientated improviser. The two sessions above are separated by 14 years yet show no appreciable change in Farlow's approach. The Xanadu albums were recorded privately by Ed Fuerst and find all three players in bristling form. The sound isn't quite perfect but should give few problems, and the playing – on standards stretched out as long as the performers please – is top-notch. *The Return* is no less fine, and Farlow plays even more quickly, yet with even greater insight: try the lovely variations on 'My Romance'.

***   **A Sign Of The Times** Concord CCD 4026 CD/MC
       Farlow; Hank Jones (*p*); Ray Brown (*b*). 77.

This is the only one of several Concord albums to make it to CD so far. The music's delivered with pristine accuracy and brightness by these infallible pros, but somehow there's a spark missing. Even though they've gone to the trouble of arranging a dark contrapuntal framework for 'You Don't Know What Love is', for instance, or treat 'Stompin' At The Savoy' in a unique way, one misses the sizzle of Farlow's older work. Sumptuously recorded and balanced between the three players, though, and hard not to enjoy.

ART FARMER (born 1928)
FLUGELHORN, TRUMPET

***   **Art Farmer Septet** Original Jazz Classics OJC 054 LP/MC
       Farmer; Jimmy Cleveland (*tb*); Clifford Solomon, Charlie Rouse (*ts*); Oscar Estell,
       Danny Bank (*bs*); Quincy Jones, Horace Silver (*p*); Monk Montgomery, Percy Heath
       (*b*); Art Taylor, Sonny Johnson (*d*). 7/53–6/54.

***(*)   **When Farmer Met Gryce** Original Jazz Classics OJC 072 LP
       Farmer; Gigi Gryce (*as*); Freddie Redd, Horace Silver (*p*); Addison Farmer, Percy
       Heath (*b*); Kenny Clarke, Art Taylor (*d*). 5/54–5/55.

**** **The Art Farmer Quintet** Original Jazz Classics OJC 241 LP/MC
Farmer; Gigi Gryce (*as*); Duke Jordan (*p*); Addison Farmer (*b*); Philly Joe Jon⌐
10/55.

(*) **Two Trumpets Original Jazz Classics OJC 018 LP/MC
Farmer; Donald Byrd (*t*); Jackie Mclean (*as*); Barry Harris (*p*); Doug Watkins (*b*),
Art Taylor (*d*). 8/56.

*** **Farmer's Market** Original Jazz Classics OJC 398 CD/LP/MC
Farmer; Hank Mobley (*ts*); Kenny Drew (*p*); Addison Farmer (*b*); Elvin Jones (*d*).
11/56.

Art Farmer began his recording career with the ten-inch album *Work Of Art*, the contents of which are on OJC 018. Although pitched around Farmer's trumpet solos, the music is as much in debt to the composing and arranging of Jones and Gryce, and witty originals such as 'Elephant Walk', 'The Little Band Master' and 'Wildwood' make up the programme. Yet Farmer's skilful contributions elevate the scores and it's clear that his style was already firmly in place: a pensive restraint on ballads, a fleet yet soberly controlled attack on uptempo tunes, and a concern for tonal manipulation within a small range of inflexions. If he was comparatively unadventurous, then as later, it didn't stop him from developing an individual style.

This begins to come clear in the small-group work of the mid-1950s. The group he led with Gigi Gryce has been somewhat forgotten in recent years, but the two OJC reissues are both impeccable examples of a more considered approach to hard bop forms. While *When Farmer Met Gryce* is the better known, it's slightly the lesser of the two: *Art Farmer Quintet* has some of Gryce's best writing in the unusual structures of 'Evening In Casablanca' and 'Satellite', while 'Nica's Tempo', constructed more from key centres than from chords, might be his masterpiece; in the sequence of long solos, Farmer turns in an improvisation good enough to stand with the best of Miles Davis from the same period. The rhythm section, too, is the most sympathetic of the three involved.

The two-trumpet meeting with Byrd is capable but routine, a typical Prestige blowing session of the period, while *Farmer's Market* suffers slightly from unexpectedly heavy tempos and an erratic performance from Mobley, although Kenny Drew takes some crisp solos. The remastering of all these reissues is cleanly done.

**** **Modern Art** Blue Note CDP 784459 CD
Farmer; Benny Golson (*ts*); Bill Evans (*p*); Addison Farmer (*b*); Dave Bailey (*d*).
9/58.

*** **Meet The Jazztet** Chess CHD 91550 CD
Farmer; Curtis Fuller (*tb*); Benny Golson (*ts*); McCoy Tyner (*p*); Addison Farmer (*b*);
Lex Humphries (*d*). 2/60.

***(*) **Live At The Half Note** Atlantic 90666 CD
Farmer; Jim Hall (*g*); Steve Swallow (*b*); Walter Perkins (*d*). 12/63.

*** **To Sweden With Love** Atlantic AMCY 1016 CD
As above, except Pete La Roca replaces Perkins. 4/64.

(*) **Art Worker Moon 014 CD/LP
Farmer; Ernie Royal (*t*); Jimmy Cleveland (*tb*); Oscar Estell (*as, ts, bs*); Harold
Mabern (*p*); Jimmy Woode (*b*); Roy McCurdy (*d*). 68.

The Blue Note album, originally on United Artists and finely remastered, is one of Farmer's most successful records of the period. Golson contributes one excellent theme, 'Fair Weather', but most of the others involve subtle reworkings of familiar standards: a surprisingly jaunty 'The Touch Of Your Lips', a beguilingly smooth reading of Junior Mance's 'Jubilation', a stately 'Like Someone In Love'. The presence of Evans makes a telling difference: his solos are so finely thought out that it makes one wish he'd become the regular man in the Jazztet.

Not much of Farmer's work as a leader in the 1960s remains easy to find. The European Chess CD is the only available disc by the original Jazztet, the group co-led by Farmer and Golson to fine effect: the brief, first-time treatments of such staple fare as 'Killer Joe', 'I Remember Clifford' and 'Blues March' lack the expansiveness of other versions but have a compensating freshness, and the more suave approach of this talented band makes a powerful contrast with the contemporary Blakey and Silver groups. The empathy between Farmer and

Jim Hall makes the live Half Note session a compelling occasion: long and unflagging renditions of 'I Want To Be Happy' and 'Stompin' At The Savoy' feature both men in vibrant improvisations, and each has an engaging ballad feature. The record of Swedish themes is something of a curio, but again both men approach the session with customary dedication, even if a certain unfamiliarity with the music renders the playing a little careful. The Moon record finds Farmer fronting a motley group of players: the cloudy recording doesn't assist, but the leader turns in some typically erudite improvisations all the same.

(*) **Gentle Eyes Mainstream MDCD 716 CD
Farmer; Jimmy Heath (ss); Cedar Walton (p); Sam Jones (b); Billy Higgins (d); Mtume (perc); string orchestra directed by Johannes Fehring. 71–72.

The arrangements are so deliberate and the tempos so ponderously slow that this session with strings is somnolent stuff and even Farmer sounds bored, as prettily as he plays. The one small-group track stuck on the end of the record, with most of the personnel listed above, does far better by 'Some Other Time'.

*** **On The Road** Original Jazz Classics OJC 478 CD/LP/MC
Farmer; Art Pepper (as); Hampton Hawes (p); Ray Brown (b); Shelly Manne, Steve Ellington (d). 7–8/76.

An exceptional band, although the music is not quite as good as one might have hoped. The sole outstanding group performance is 'Namely You', where Farmer and Pepper both turn in superb solos, while 'Will You Still Be Mine?' and 'What Am I Here For?' are merely very good. Pepper, entering his Indian summer in the studios, was still a little unfocused, and Hawes is not quite at his best. But Farmer is as consistently fine as ever, by now using the flugelhorn almost exclusively, and the recording captures much of the quality of his tone.

(*) **Foolish Memories L+R 45008 CD/LP
Farmer; Harry Sokal (ts); Fritz Pauer (p); Heiri Keinzig (b); Joris Dudli (d). 8/81.

***(*) **Manhattan** Soul Note SN 1026 LP
Farmer; Sahib Shihab (ss, bs); Kenny Drew (p); Mads Vinding (b); Ed Thigpen (d). 11/81.

***(*) **Mirage** Soul Note SN 1046 CD/LP
Farmer; Clifford Jordan (ts); Fred Hersch (p); Ray Drummond (b); Akira Tana (d). 9/82.

*** **Warm Valley** Concord CCD 4212 CD/MC
As above, except omit Jordan. 9/82.

Farmer spent the early part of the 1980s recording, like so many of his colleagues, for European rather than American companies. The L+R date would be very routine if it weren't for his presence, but the leader turns in his usual conscientious performance. The two Soul Note dates are much more interesting. *Manhattan* blends excellent original material from Drew, Horace Parlan and Bennie Wallace, with a jaunty reading of Parker's 'Passport', and Shihab is an unexpected but rumbustious partner in the front line; *Mirage* is perhaps a shade better, with Jordan at his most fluent, Hersch numbering among Farmer's most sympathetic accompanists and another Parker tune, 'Barbados', taken at an ideal tempo. Drummond and Tana are also splendid. The Concord date misses only the stimulation of another front-line horn to set off against Farmer's most introspective playing, although Hersch's finely wrought ballad 'And Now There's You' is the kind of track which makes any record worth keeping for that alone. All three discs are recorded with great presence and very sharp clarity.

*** **Maiden Voyage** Denon 38C38-7071 CD
Farmer; Sato Masahiko (p); Ron Carter (b); Jack DeJohnette (d); strings conducted by David Nadien. 4/83.

(*) **In Concert Enja 4088 LP
Farmer; Slide Hampton (tb); Jim McNeely (p); Ron McClure (b); Adam Nussbaum (d). 8/84.

*** **You Make Me Smile** Soul Note SN 1076 CD
Farmer; Clifford Jordan (ts); Fred Hersch (p); Rufus Reid (b); Akira Tana (d). 12/84.

It was inevitable that Farmer's beautiful tone would again bedeck a record with strings, and
Denon session (a CD reissue) is as well done as this sort of thing can be, favouring strong
material – 'Ruby My Dear', 'Goodbye Pork Pie Hat' – over standards. The Enja conc
recording from the following year is inauspicious, a less than scintillating day in the players'
lifetimes, although Farmer turns on his ballad mode for 'Darn That Dream' to agreeable effect.
The music on *You Make Me Smile* is a mite disappointing after the exemplary earlier Soul Notes
– but only by those standards, since Farmer and Jordan are basically their usual pedigree selves.

*** **The Jazztet: Moment To Moment** Soul Note SN 1066 CD/LP
Farmer; Curtis Fuller (*tb*); Benny Golson (*ts*); Mickey Tucker (*p*); Ray Drummond
(*b*); Albert 'Tootie' Heath (*d*). 5/83.

***(*) **Back To The City** Contemporary C 14020 LP/MC
As above, except Marvin 'Smitty' Smith (*d*) replaces Heath. 2/86.

***(*) **Real Time** Contemporary C 14034 CD/LP/MC
As above. 2/86.

The occasionally re-formed Jazztet is rather more of a showcase for Golson – as both composer
and performer – than it is for Farmer. Their Soul Note session is a somewhat perfunctory return,
with the six themes passing in proscribed fashion, but the two Contemporary albums, both
recorded live at a single residency at New York's Sweet Basil, give a vivid idea of the group's
continued spirit. *Back To The City* features lesser-known items from the band's book, including
such Golson orginals as 'Vas Simeon' and 'From Dream To Dream', along with a rare outing
for Farmer as a composer, 'Write Soon', while *Real Time* offers lengthy readings of Golson
staples such as 'Whisper Not' and 'Are You Real'. There's also an expansive treatment of
'Autumn Leaves' which finds all the soloists at their best. Coltrane's influence on Golson is
arguably never more clear than in this music; Farmer is keenly incisive with the muted horn,
romantically ebullient with it open; and Tucker emerges as a considerable soloist and
accompanist: his solo on 'Autumn Leaves' is sweepingly inventive. Smith, the most audacious
drummer of his generation, is the ideal occupant of the drum stool. Admirable location
recording and production by Helen Keane.

(*) **Azure Soul Note SN 1126 CD/LP
Farmer; Fritz Pauer (*p*). 9/87.

Although Farmer clearly enjoys the company of Pauer, these nine duets are not very compelling
listening. One can't avoid the feeling that Farmer relaxes more in the company of a full rhythm
section and, adept as Pauer is at filling the rhythmic and harmonic backdrops, the results seem
a little stiff here and there, despite showcasing Farmer's flugelhorn tone at its most beguiling.

**** **Something To Live For** Contemporary C 14029 CD/LP/MC
Farmer; Clifford Jordan (*ts*); James Williams (*p*); Rufus Reid (*b*); Marvin 'Smitty'
Smith (*d*). 1/87.

***** **Blame It On My Youth** Contemporary C 14042 CD/LP/MC
As above, except Victor Lewis (*d*) replaces Smith. 2/88.

**** **Ph. D** Contemporary C 14055 CD/LP/MC
As above, except Marvin 'Smitty' Smith (*d*) replaces Lewis, add Kenny Burrell (*g*).
4/89.

As he entered his sixties, Art Farmer was playing better than ever. The three albums by this
wonderful group speak as eloquently as any record can on behalf of the generation of players
who followed the first boppers (Farmer, Jordan) yet can still make modern music with a
contemporary rhythm section (Williams, Reid, Lewis, Smith). The first record, dedicated to
Billy Strayhorn's music, is a little doleful on the ballads but is otherwise perfectly pitched.
Blame It On My Youth, though, is a discreet masterpiece. Art's reading of the title-track is one
of his very finest ballad interpretations, even by his standards; Jordan plays with outstanding
subtlety and guarded power throughout and has a memorable feature of his own in 'I'll Be
Around'; Williams leads the rhythm section with consummate craft and decisiveness. But it's
Lewis who, like Smith, shows amazing versatility and who really makes the music
finding an extra ounce of power and crispness in every rhythm he has to mark

doesn't quite maintain this exalted level but, with Burrell guesting in jovial mood, it's as good-humoured and fluent as the others. Outstanding production work from Helen Keane.

*** **Central Avenue Reunion** Contemporary C 14057 CD/LP/MC
Farmer; Frank Morgan (*as*); Lou Levy (*p*); Eric Von Essen (*b*); Albert 'Tootie' Heath (*d*). 5/89.

The reunion is between Farmer and Morgan, friends from the Los Angeles scene of the early 1950s, yet never together on record before. The music, from a live engagement at Kimball's East in California, is finally disappointing: Morgan's keening and late-flowering interest in what extremes he can reach on his horn isn't a very apposite partner for Farmer's unflappable flugelhorn, and the rhythm section have few ambitions beyond comping. Some fine moments amidst a generally routine record.

JOE FARRELL (1937–86)
TENOR SAXOPHONE, SOPRANO SAXOPHONE, FLUTE

(*) **Vim 'n' Vigor Timeless SJP 197 CD
Farrell; Louis Hayes (*d*); Rob Van Den Broeck (*p*); Harry Emmery (*d*). 11/83.

Farrell's painful death in 1986 silenced a voice probably best known for the life-raft it threw Chick Corea's original 'Return To Forever', and consistently undervalued ever since. To rub in the affront, Farrell's best album, *Sonic Text* [Contemporary 14002], has (temporarily, one hopes) slipped out of the catalogue.
Vim 'n' Vigor is co-led by Louis Hayes, who toured with Farrell for two years before moving on to the McCoy Tyner Trio. Farrell's Rollins debts are still audible in the phrasing on 'Miles Mode', but the intonation is very much his own, and his flute style (occasionally reminiscent of Prince Lasha) is quite individual. This is a fine album that might have been improved by the addition of a more sympathetic drummer.

CLAUDIO FASOLI
TENOR AND SOPRANO SAX

(*) **Lido Soul Note SN 1071 LP
Fasoli; Kenny Drew (*p*); Niels-Henning Ørsted-Pedersen (*b*); Barry Altschul (*d*). 2/83.

Fasoli is one of the most prominent of the contemporary Italian saxophonists. Like many of his countrymen, he takes American models and imbues them with a recognizably Italian melodicism: a Rollinsesque swagger and brusqueness work alongside an unpredictable, tender lyricism. This programme of originals is beguiling but not quite strongly enough characterized by the leader to suggest that he was fully in command of the music. The rhythm section play with professional aplomb.

(*) **For Once Splasc(h) H 126 LP
Fasoli; Hilaria Kramer (*t, flhn*); Marco Vaggi, Piero Leveratto (*b*); Gianni Cazzola (*d*). 5/87.

(*) **Egotrip Splasc(h) H 161 LP
Fasoli. 2–6/88.

Both records show Fasoli looking for free-form credentials, but since he sounds more of a post-bopper at heart they're both a little uncomfortable. The quintet works through a series of somewhat doleful minor-key themes by the leader which occasionally break open into freer passages: the two bassists work an almost continuous dialogue through the session, and Kramer is a tentative but courageous player. It hangs together, but only just. The solo date is a confusing mix of short pieces, some of them with overdubbed piano or voice, some merely throwaway, others of more substance, such as the soprano-and-ticking-metronome of 'Cha' and the gnarled tenor oratory of 'Off'. Heavy dashes of ECM-like reverberation do little to clarify Fasoli's intentions.

RICCARDO FASSI
KEYBOARDS

***   **Riccardo Fassi Tankio Band** Splasc(h) H 107 LP
Fassi; Massimo Nunzi, Enrico Fineschi (*t, flhn*); Danilo Terenzi (*tb*); Sandro Satta
(*as*); Michel Audisso (*ss, as, bcl*); Torquato Sdrucia (*bs*); Francesco Puglisi, Enzo
Pietropaoli (*b*); Massimo D'Agostino (*d*). 3/85.

***   **Il Principe** Splasc(h) H 180 LP
Fassi; Claudio Corvini, Aldo Bassi (*t*); Mario Corvini (*tb*); Giancarlo Schiaffini (*tb,
tba*); Michel Audisso (*ss, as*); Steve Grossman (*ss, ts*); Sandro Satta (*as*); Torquatro
Sdrucia (*bs*); Fabio Zeppetella (*g*); Massimo Moriconi (*b*); Massimo D'Agostino (*d*);
Alfredo Minotti (*perc*); Joy Garrison (*v*). 2/89.

Fassi is an enthusiastic organizer of sound, and his Tankio Band, which made both of these
records, is a colourful orchestra full of good players: Terenzi and Satta play well on the earlier
date, while Grossman stars on the second. There's nothing strikingly original or imaginative on
either session, perhaps, but, in aiming comparatively low, Fassi directs some quite purposeful
music. The rather more ambitious miniatures of *Il Principe* are brought off with some aplomb.

**   **Joining** Splasc(h) H 113 LP
Fassi; Antonello Salis (*p, acc, perc, v*). 2/86.

A series of duets with moments of Italianate charm and a certain lyrical flow, but Fassi and Salis
change instruments and directions frequently enough to give the session a flippant air rather
than a sensitive basis for interaction.

(*)   **Toast Man Splasc(h) H 307 CD
Fassi; Flavio Boltro (*t, flhn*); Dario La Penna (*g*); Massimo Moriconi (*b*); Alberto
D'Anna (*d*); Massimo Rocci, Alfredo Minotti (*perc*). 2–4/90.

British readers will be reminded of Kenny Wheeler with John Taylor when they hear 'Octopus'
and 'La Foresta'. Some of the other tracks here, though, aim for a studious kind of fusion, Fassi
turning to synthesizer over piano, and his lyrical bent is obscured by those settings, although
Boltro is attractively elegant throughout.

ZUSAAN KALI FASTEAU
SOPRANO SAXOPHONE, FLUTES, PIANO, PERCUSSION, VOICE

***   **Worlds Beyond Words** Flying Note FNCD 9001 CD
Fasteau; James C. Jamison II (*g*); Elizabeth Panzer (*hp*); Bob Cunningham (*b*);
Rashied Ali (*d*); Paul Leake (*tabla*); David Cornick (*perc*). 89.

A New Yorker, Fasteau spent much of her early career abroad, absorbing a huge range of
musics and refining her quite remarkable multi-instrumentalism. On *World Within Worlds* she
alternates tough, Coltrane-influenced trio performances with Ali and Cunningham (of which
the long 'From Above' is the most coherent) and 'world music' pieces that use multitracking to
suggest ensemble performance. She's a fine flautist, with an authentic-sounding tone on the
difficult shakuhachi ('Dolphin Meditation'), and has a strong, grainy voice ('Appreciating
People', 'Spiritual Kinship'). Flying Note also released three cassettes of Fasteau's music in the
late 1980s – *Bliss* (6001), *Beyond Words* (7003), and *Affinity* (6003) – and while these may be
difficult to track down, all are worth hearing.

PIERRE FAVRE (born 1937)
DRUMS, PERCUSSION

***   **Santana** FMP 0630 LP
Favre; Irene Schweizer (*p*); Peter Kowald (*b*). 10/68.

One of the most innovative percussionists in Europe, Favre hasn't always been heard to best
advantage on his own recordings. This 1968 trio is the exception, a powerful but contained
performance that differs in significant respects from the main thrust of European improvisation

at the time. Schweizer's playing is every bit as impressive as on *Early Tapes* (FMP 0590), made a year before with a different trio, and Kowald is solidly intelligent. Warmly recommended for anyone unfamiliar with any of the players.

** **Singing Drums** ECM 1274 CD/LP
Favre; Paul Motian (*d, gongs, crotales, calabashes, rodbrushes*); Freddy Studer (*d, gongs, log d, cym*); Nana Vasconcelos (*berimbau, tmp, congas, water pot, shakers, bells, voice*). 5/84.

All-percussion albums are always a problem. This one rapidly degenerates into an acoustically near-perfect sampling of effects and devices with no sense of centre and very little coherent development. Ironically, on such a crowded canvas, the music seems to call out for horns or strings to draw the various strands together. For converts only.

ENRICO FAZIO

BASS

*** **Mirabilia!** CMC 107 LP
Fazio; Alberto Mandarini (*t*); Lauro Rossi (*tb*); Francesco Aroni Vigone (*ss, as*); Carlo Actis Dato (*ts, bs, bcl*); Giorgio Girotto (*ob*); Andrea Bressan (*bsn*); Fiorenzo Sordini (*d, vib, marim*). 4/88.

***(*) **Euphoria** Splasc(h) H 327-2 CD
As above, except add Franca Silveri (*v*); omit Girotto and Bressan. 7/89.

This is a fizzing band, full of carnival colours and offbeat energies. Fazio, Actis Dato and Sordini all work together in the reed player's group, but here the bassist's themes are equally full of surprise and prime improvisational flair. While the longest section of *Euphoria* is a tribute to Charles Mingus, which incorporates four Mingus themes, it doesn't sound much like a Mingus band: trombone, bassoon and oboe make only fleeting appearances, but the central unit of three horns, bass and drums swarms all over Fazio's pleasing melodies enough to convince that there's a bigger band at work here than the numbers suggest. Mandarini is very different from the cool trumpeters who set today's brass norm: notes seem to topple out of his horn, and long, barely controlled lines spiral crazily over the ensemble. Actis Dato's typically zesty ripostes and Vigone's brusque, pinchy alto lines fill in the rest. The CMC LP is dryly recorded and confines itself to short, punchy pieces, but *Euphoria* is both more expansive and more ambitious in its scope: a long piece such as 'Gardel' is impressively written, developed and sustained.

LEONARD FEATHER (born 1914)

COMPOSER, ARRANGER, PIANO

*** **Night Blooming** Mainstream MDCD 719 CD
Feather; Blue Mitchell (*t*); Lew Tabackin (*ts, f*); Ernie Watts (*as, ts, f*); George Shearing (*p*); Charles Kynard (*org*); Joe Pass, Fred Robinson (*g*); Andy Simpkins, Max Bennett, Al McKibbon (*b*); Stix Hooper, Paul Humphrey (*d*); Willie Bobo, Chino Valdes (*perc*); Kitty Doswell (*v*). 71–72.

Feather is renowned more as a critic and supporter of jazz than as an active musician, but he's proved a useful catalyst at many recording sessions, and these sessions feature a number of studio pros in good fettle. Latin percussion adds an extra spice to the rhythm sections, while 12 of the 14 tracks are Feather originals which, while scarcely memorable, act as unobtrusive springboards for solos from such dependables as Watts and Tabackin. There is also a surprisingly tough reading of 'Freedom Jazz Dance', which suggests some of the directions jazz-funk would take later in the 1970s. CD remastering has slightly brightened the rather terse original sound.

BUDDY FEATHERSTONHAUGH(1909–76)

TENOR SAXOPHONE, CLARINET

***   **Vic Lewis Jam Sessions: Volume 4 – 1942–3** Harlequin HQ 3011 LP
Featherstonhaugh; Don Macaffer (*tb*); Harry Rayner (*p*); Vic Lewis (*g, v*); Frank
Clarke (*b*); Jack Parnell (*d*). 12/42–6/43.

Featherstonhaugh – pronounced as 'Fanshawe' – was a fine mainstream-traditional player
with a clear, swinging delivery. He first came to wider notice early in the Second World War
when he succeeded fellow-clarinettist Harry Parry on the BBC's token jazz slot *Radio Rhythm
Club*. The sessions above were recorded just before Featherstonhaugh and his RAF Sextet
began a successful association with HMV, but they embody much the same virtues. The
material is pretty unsurprising – 'Stardust', 'Soft Winds', 'Cotton Tail', 'Body And Soul' – but
is briskly and unpretentiously despatched and Featherstonhaugh shows himself to be a fine
soloist. Vocalist Lewis had pretensions as the 'British Kenton' and later went on to found a
modernist super-band which flopped badly. Jack Parnell became an influential bandleader and,
latterly, television personality.

VICTOR FELDMAN (1934–87)

PIANO, VIBRAPHONE, DRUMS

***(*)   **Suite Sixteen** Original Jazz Classics OJC 1768 CD/LP
Feldman; Jimmy Deuchar, Dizzy Reece, Jimmy Watson (*t*); Ken Wray (*t, bt*); John
Burden (*frhn*); Jim Powell (*tba*); Derek Humble (*as*); Tubby Hayes, Ronnie Scott (*ts*);
Harry Klein (*bs*); Tommy Pollard, Norman Stenfalt (*p*); Lenny Bush, Eric Peter (*b*);
Tony Crombie (*d, p*). 8 & 9/55.

It was probably inevitable that Feldman would move to America, but there's enough fine
musicianship on *Suite Sixteen* to suggest he might just as easily have stayed and played at home
had London just offered enough adventurous paying gigs. Divided into big-band, septet and
quartet tracks, *Suite Sixteen* was cut just prior to his first American trip. As a cross-section of the
local talent – Deuchar, Scott, Hayes, Crombie, Seamen, Reece – it's a remarkable document.
Musically, it doesn't come up to some of the later, American sessions, but it features four
excellent Feldman originals (the ambitious title piece was actually written by Tony Crombie),
Allan Ganley's 'Duffle Coat', Dizzy Reece's exuberant 'Maenya', which makes a fine closer,
and Kenny Clarke's and Gerald Wiggins's 'Sonar'.

    Feldman plays all three of his instruments, but concentrates on vibes, with excellent solos on
his own brief 'Elegy', where he follows the fiercely melancholic Deuchar, and on 'Maenya'. It's
an interesting aspect of his solo work that its quality always seems to be in inverse proportion to
its length. Feldman was a master of compression who often lost his way beyond a couple of
choruses. The septet and quartet tracks are less buoyant, though 'Brawl For All', which
features the leader's only piano contribution, is excellent. The sound is good but needs to be
adjusted according to personnel.

****   **The Arrival Of Victor Feldman** Original Jazz Classics OJC 268 LP
Feldman; Scott LaFaro (*b*); Stan Levey (*d*). 1/58.

A marvellous record, completed just after the multi-instrumentalist – 'Victor Feldman Plays
Everything in Sight!' one album cover shouted – had settled in Los Angeles. LaFaro's role in
extending the vocabulary of the piano trio is well documented in his association with Bill Evans
and elsewhere in his tragically foreshortened career. His work with Feldman is an aspect that is
often overlooked.

    Though on a less equal footing than in the Evans groups, bass and piano construct long,
highly wrought lines round a basic bop figuration; Levey's accents are quietly insistent and the
whole recording seems to have been miked very close, as was the practice at the time.
'Serpent's Tooth', 'There is no Greater Love' and 'Satin Doll' are the outstanding tracks. This
one should certainly be in the collection of anyone interested in the evolution of the piano trio
in jazz.

***   **Merry Olde Soul** Original Jazz Classics OJC 402 CD/LP/MC
Feldman; Hank Jones (*p*); Sam Jones, Andy Simpkins (*b*); Louis Hayes (*d*).

Altogether more predictable and perhaps an indication of the toll exacted by Feldman's time as an in-demand session player. 'Bloke's Blues' contains flashes of originality (though Hank Jones didn't seem to know what it was all about) and there's a wonderful shimmering quality to the vibes on 'Serenity'. Otherwise, it's rather bland standards fare.

(*) The Artful Dodger Concord CCD 4351 CD
Feldman; Jack Sheldon (*t, v*); Monty Budwig, Chuck Domanico (*b*); Colin Bailey (*d*).

As with Hampton Hawes, the switch to electric piano at the end of the 1960s did Feldman no favours, robbing him of that characteristically percussive touch and blurring the edges of his lines. This is an agreeable and sometimes surprising set, but apart from a very direct 'Limehouse Blues' and the title piece, it errs on the fussy side and isn't helped by a soft-focus mix which is very much of its time.

** **To Chopin With Love** TBA Records 8053 CD
Feldman; John Patitucci (*b*); Trevor Feldman (*d*). 5/83.

* **Fiesta** TBA Records 8066 CD
Feldman; Chuck Mangione (*flhn, t*); Chick Corea (*ky*); Diane Reeves (*v*). 6–8/84.

Thin fare for Feldman's 50th birthday and unlikely to sustain a revival of interest. The Chopin tribute contains some interesting moments, mostly when Feldman and Patitucci get on to the same wavelength, and there is a beautiful waltz-time threnody to Scott LaFaro. *Fiesta* is astonishingly feeble, full of predictable harmonies and pointless embellishment. Strange to say, Mangione is probably the main attraction.

SIMON H. FELL
BASS

***(*) **Compilation 1** Bruce's Fingers BF 1/BFC 5 LP/MC
Fell; Martin Jones (*t, flhn*); Charle Wharf (*ss, ts*); Shay McIntyre (*tb*); Andy Street (*p*); Ray Harborne (*g*); Tony Shepherd, Neil Bates, Peter Fairclough (*d*). 11/85.

*** **Pride And Prejudice** Bruce's Fingers BF3/BFC 10 LP/MC
Fell; Charles Wharf (*ss, bcl, perc*). 7/87.

*** **Two Steps To Easier Breathing** Bruce's Fingers BF2/BFC 12 LP/MC
Fell; Martin Jones (*t, flhn, perc*); Pete Minns (*ss, ts, bs, perc*); Tony Shepherd (*d, perc*).

*** **Termite One** Bruce's Fingers BFC 24 MC
Fell; Lol Coxhill (*ss*); George Haslam (*bs*); Paul Rutherford (*tb*); Paul Hession (*d*). 11/89.

***(*) **Termite Two** Bruce's Fingers BFC 25 MC
Fell; Alan Wilkinson (*as*); Paul Buckton (*g*); John McMillan (*elec*); Paul Hession (*d*). 11/89.

**** **Compilation II** Bruce's Fingers BF4/BFC 27 LP/MC
Fell; Alan Leggett (*t*); Martin Jones (*flhn*); Charles Wharf (*ss, cl, bcl*); Alan Wilkinson (*as, bs*); Tim Brooks (*tb*); Bruce Godfrey (*vn*); Pete Minns (*ts*); Helen Godfrey (*clo*); Paul Hession (*d*). 3–7/90.

*** **Eight Classic Jazz Originals You Can Play** Bruce's Fingers BFC 33 MC
Fell; Jeffrey Morgan (*as*); Paul Hession (*d*). 5/91.

***(*) **Max** Bruce's Fingers BFC 35 MC
Fell (*b* solo). 6/91.

**** **Bogey's** Bruce's Fingers BFC 36 MC
Fell; Alan Wilkinson (*as, bs*); Paul Hession (*d*). 6/91.

Working quietly – or, more often, very noisily – in the peaceful surroundings of Haverhill, Suffolk, Simon Fell has been creating some of the most vivid and creative improvisation/composition fusions in recent times. His own Bruce's Fingers operation is a determinedly home-made outfit, but it has been assiduously documenting some superb music in the last few years. The two *Compilation* albums are the places to start ('catastrophically creative', one critic called them), wholly individual mixtures of real-time improvisation, writing that cheerfully filches from all post-bop and compositional areas yet which depends as much on the colour and intensity of the individual improvisations as it does on Fell's witty and often bewilderingly complex structures. His partnerships with Hession and Wharf are tersely confrontational, the former an explosive, sometimes demented percussionist, the latter working through arid, bleak registers of his chosen horns or tearing across structural boundaries. *Two Steps To Easier Breathing* is a somewhat more conventional free-into-bop album, but none the worse for that. The two sets recorded live at Leeds' Termite Club are rough, often crazy, all-out slugfests, but even these pale beside the thrillingly intense *Bogey's* recording by the inflammatory Hession–Wilkinson–Fell trio, a band that outdoes the old Brotzmann groups for sheer firepower. *Eight Classic Jazz Originals You Can Play* is, naturally, nothing like its title and is unplayable by anyone else, and the solo bass cassette is just the latest in Fell's series: he is a very fine instrumentalist himself, and titles such as 'On Meeting Barry Guy In Sainsbury's' disguise a fine technique and a great flow of ideas. Fell has more tapes available, some of them of environmental recordings (Bruce's Fingers, 24 Chauntry Road, Haverhill, Suffolk CB9 8BE).

LIONEL FERBOS (born 1911)
TRUMPET, VOCAL

** **At The Jazz Band Ball** 504 LPS 18 LP
Ferbos; David Griller (*cl, ts*); Les Muscutt (*g*); McNeal Breaux (*b*); John Robichaux (*d, v*). 11/87.

A very gently paced and frankly rather tired session by a group of New Orleans veterans (aside from the ubiquitous Muscutt). Lionel Ferbos is more of a strict-tempo musician than an improviser, and his sound here is shaky and tentatively directed, but there's a certain charm about the music, especially on the likes of 'Cherry Pink And Apple Blossom White', while 'Bogalusa Strut' tackles a New Orleans anthem with some aplomb. Robichaux, another veteran from a famous musical family in the city, keeps firm time but delivers a surprisingly tough vocal on 'My Blue Heaven'.

MAYNARD FERGUSON (born 1928)
TRUMPET, FLUGELHORN, VALVE TROMBONE, BARITONE HORN, BANDLEADER

**** **The Birdland Dreamband** Bluebird ND 86455 CD
Ferguson; Al Derisi, Joe Ferrante, Jimmy Nottingham, Ernie Royal, Al Stewart, Nick Travis (*t*); Eddie Bert, Jimmy Cleveland, Sonny Russo (*tb*); Herb Geller (*as*); Al Cohn, Budd Johnson, Frank Socolow (*ts*); Ernie Wilkins (*bs*); Hank Jones (*p*); Arnold Fishkin, Milt Hinton (*b*); Jimmy Campbell, Osie Johnson, Don Lamond (*d*); collective personnel. 9/56.

(*) **A Message From Newport Roulette CDP 7932722 CD
Ferguson; Bill Chase, Clyde Reasinger, Tom Slyney (*t*); Slide Hampton, Don Sebesky (*tb*); Jimmy Ford (*as*); Carmen Leggio, Willie Maiden (*ts*); Jay Cameron (*bs*); John Bunch (*p*); Jimmy Rowser (*b*); Jake Hanna (*d*). 5/58.

There are few sights more impressive in animal physiology than the muscles in Maynard Ferguson's upper thorax straining for a top C. Unfortunately, on record there are no such distractions; putting a Ferguson disc on the turntable evokes sensations ranging from walking into a high wind to being run down by a truck.

What's impressive about the (excellently) remastered 1956 sessions is the quality of the arrangements. These are essentially still swing charts, but with some of the polychordal sophistication introduced by people like Bob Brookmeyer ('Still Water Stomp') and Jimmy Giuffre ('Say It With Trumpets'); the other arrangers are Manny Albam, Al Cohn, Herb Geller (after Ferguson, the most impressive soloist), Bill Holman, Willie Maiden, Johnny Mandel, Marty Paich, Ernie Wilkins, and are consistently excellent. The latter track introduces a sequence of three – 'You Said It' and 'Everybody Moan' – on which the leader's high notes reach almost absurd levels. For sheer excitement, 'You Said It' is hard to beat.

The message from Newport seems to be: stand further back. (In the rough year of 1958, that might even have been justified in the interests of band safety.) Ferguson's upper-register runs are technically dazzling, at moments almost uncannily sustained, but such effects pall very quickly. The band bellow and roar like college jocks after a big game, Hampton and Sebesky well to the fore.

For anyone enthusiastic about Ferguson's pumped-up style, this is a pretty good vintage.

*** **Two's Company** Fresh Sound FSR 30/Roulette 52068 CD/LP
Ferguson; Bill Berry, Rolf Ericson, Chet Feretti (*t*); Kenny Rupp, Ray Winslow (*tb*); Lanny Morgan (*as, f*); Willie Maiden (*ts, cl*); Joe Farrell (*ts, ss, f*); Frank Hittner (*bs, bcl*); Jaki Byard (*p*); John Neves (*b*); Rufus Reid (*d*); Chris Connor (*v*). 6/61.

It's always been known that Ferguson can also play pretty. His middle register work is often remarkably subtle, with unexpected inflections reminiscent of his apparent opposite Don Ellis (whose big-band experiments nevertheless betray a reciprocal Ferguson influence). Chris Connor is the finest band singer of her generation, and the band are duly respectful, leading her through a typically unhackneyed programme with some finesse.

***(*) **Maynard '61** Roulette CDP 7939002 CD
Ferguson; Bill Berry, Rolf Ericson, Chris Ferretti, Rick Kiefer, Jerry Tyree (*t*); Slide Hampton, Kenny Rupp (*tb*); Joe Farrell, Frank Hittner, Lanny Morgan, Willie Maiden (*reeds*); Jaki Byard (*p*); Charlie Sanders (*b*); Rufus Jones (*d*). 10 & 12/60, 1/61.

*** **Si! Si! – M.F.** Roulette CDP 7953342 CD
Ferguson; Gene Coe, Nat Pavone, Don Rader (*t*); John Gale, Kenny Rupp (*tb*); Lanny Morgan (*as*); Frank Hittner (*bs*); Willie Maiden, Don Menza (*ts, ss, cl, f*); Mike Abene (*p*); Linc Milliman (*b*); Rufus Jones (*d*). 62.

For those who find Ferguson's conveyor belt climaxing a bit hard to swallow, parts of *Si! Si!* are surprisingly gentle and considered. As a piece of material, 'Mimi' isn't the most demanding thing he's ever tackled, but it's beautifully played and serves as reminder of the considerable artistry that goes into Ferguson's arrangements. Material from both these sessions originally appeared on *Maynard '64*, but is restored to its original context here and considerably brightened in the transfer to CD. Perhaps the outstanding track on either session is 'Morgan's Organ' on *Si! Si!*, written by Ernie Wilkins and featuring saxophonist Morgan against a background of sharply percussive brasses. 'Go East, Young Man' on *Maynard '61* is one of three bonus tracks and alongside Joe Farrell's 'Ultimate Rejection' and Marty Paich's moody arrangement of 'Cold Water Canyon Blues' the most impressive piece of the set; Ferguson's own solo is as powerful and thoughtful as any since he left Kenton and his playing throughout is of conistently high standard.

*** **The Blues Roar** Mainstream MDCD 717 CD
Ferguson; Bernie Glow (*t*); John Bello, August Ferretti, Jimmy Nottingham, Don Rader (*t, flhn*); Wayne Andre, Paul Faulise, Urbie Green, John Mesner, William Watous (*tb*); Ray Alonge, Jimmy Buffington (*frhn*); Don Butterfield (*tba*); Charlie Mariano (*as, cl*); Lanny Morgan (*as, cl, f*); Willie Maiden, Frank Vicari (*ts*); Romeo Penque (*ts, f, af*); Phil Bodner, Stan Webb (*reeds*); Roger Pemberton (*bs*); Mike Abene (*p*); Barry Galbraith (*g*); Margaret Ross (*hp*); Richard Davis (*b*); Mel Lewis (*d*); George Devens (*perc*). 71.

**** **Magnitude** Mainstream MDCD 712 CD
Ferguson; Lanny Morgan (*as, f*); Willie Maiden (*ts, bs*); Mike Abene (*p, cel*); Ron McClure (*b*); Tony Inzalaco (*d*). 71.

Pretty much state-of-the-art Ferguson, beautifully transferred from 1971 releases. The big-band set takes no prisoners, but is still open to the same adventurous textural devices as the smaller-scale *Magnitude*. Butterfield's tuba lends a powerful, low-register locomotion to 'Night Train', and Bodner's and Webb's remarkable range of horns (no less impressive than Ferguson's own multi-instrumentalism; he uses his valve trombone on *Blues Roar*) keep the colours shifting in an attractive and suggestive way.

Of the small-group tracks, the 'Love Theme From "The Sandpiper"' (better known as 'The Shadow Of Your Smile') is scored for flugelhorn, flute, arco bass and celeste, a combination which isn't merely cosmetic. *Magnitude* also includes three unreleased tracks,

'The Clef', 'Mike's Mike' and 'Slide By Slide', which are a valuable addition to the Ferguson discography from this period.

*(*) **Storm** TBA TBCD 8052 CD
Ferguson; no personnel or recording details.

*(*) **Live From San Francisco** TBA TBCD 8077 CD
Ferguson; Hoby Freeman, Hugh Ragin, Alan Wise (*t*); Chris Braymen, Steve Wiest (*tb*); Tim Ries (*as*); Daniel Jordan (*ts, f*); Denis Di Blasio (*bs, f*); Rod Pedley (*ky*); Matt Bissonette (*b*); Greg Bissonette (*d*). 5/83.

*(*) **Body And Soul** Black Hawk 50101 CD/LP/MC
Ferguson; Wayne Bergeron, Alan Wise (*t, flhn*); Alex Iles (*tb*); Tim Ries (*as, ts, ss, f*); Rick Margitza (*ts, ss*); Denis Di Blasio (*f*); Todd Carlon (*ky*); Michael Higgins (*g*); Dave Carpenter (*b*); Dave Miller (*d*); Steve Fisher (*d*); Chad Wackerman (*d machine prog*); collective personnel. 1/86.

Ferguson's revival in the 1980s has been interesting to watch. There's no less reliance on bruising volume, but Ferguson has slowly been revising the basic textures. The charts are more solidly ground in large-scale bass patterns and the textures are no longer merely passive launching pads for stratospheric solos. Difficult to pick between the three, but on balance *Body and Soul* is marginally the most stimulating and inventive.

** **Big Bop Nouveau** Intima 773390 LP
Ferguson; Wayne Bergeron, Roger Ingram, Peter Olstad (*t, flhn*); Alex Iles (*tb*); Rich Berkeley (*btb, ttb*); Christopher Hollyday (*as*); Matt Wallace (*ts*); Gene Burkert (*ts, ss*); Glenn Kostur (*bs*); John Toomey (*ky*); Tom Bevan (*g*); Jim Donica (*b*); David Tull (*d*); Billy Hulting (*perc*). 89.

A rather dreary run-through of greatest hits lightened and lifted by Hollyday's spirited solo on 'Cherokee'. For the rest, it sounds pretty much like a stage-managed celebration. Ferguson's flugelhorn solo on 'But Beautiful' has a lovely tone but virtually no creative content and the 'Hit Medley' (which includes the inevitable 'MacArthur Park' and a dull version of former staff arranger Joe Zawinul's 'Birdland') is almost painfully contrived. Very brightly recorded (on vintage mikes), it will please fans and leave sceptics unconverted.

BOULOU FERRE
GUITAR

and

ELIOS FERRE
GUITAR

(*) **For Django Steeplechase SC 1120 CD/LP/MC
Ferre (*g*); Ferre (*g*). 6–9/79.

(*) **Gypsy Dreams Steeplechase SC 1140 CD/LP/MC
Ferre (*g*); Ferre (*g*). 6/80.

(*) **Relax And Enjoy Steeplechase SC 1210 CD/LP
Ferre (*g*); Ferre(*g*); Jesper Lundgaard (*b*); Ed Thigpen (*d*). 4/85.

(*) **Nuages Steeplechase SC 1222 CD/LP
As above, except omit Thigpen. 5/86.

The Ferre brothers continue the gypsy guitar tradition of Django Reinhardt with all the requisite dazzle and panache. The two duo albums naturally offer them the most space, but Lundgaard and Thigpen round out the sound without becoming intrusive on the later records. Although they tackle a couple of bebop themes on *Gypsy Dreams*, the music is essentially a display of showmanship that is occasionally pointless or enervating, but usually proffers the prepared excitement which will appeal to those who enjoy this kind of playing. The four records are essentially much like one another.

MATELO FERRET (born 1918)
GUITAR, BANJO

***   **Tziganskaia And Other Rare Recordings 1960–78** Hot Club HCRCD 46 CD
Ferret; Jacques Montagne, Boulou Ferret, Sarane Ferret (g); Michel Villach
(cymbalom); Ernst Pseffer (b). 60, 78.

(*)   **Tribute To Django France's Concert 124 CD
Ferret; Sarane Ferret, Auguste Malla, Pierre-Jean Marre (g); Jean Tordo (cl); Viviane
Villerstein (vn); Patrick Greussay (p); Bernard Isselin, Alf Masselier (b); Claude
Delcloo, Roger Paraboschi (d). 4/67, 5/73.

One frequently forgotten aspect of the Nazi convulsion was its destruction of a vital and
Europe-wide Gypsy culture. Apart from Django Reinhardt, who is in every regard a special
case, Gypsy music has entered the wider culture only as a kind of synthetic location music in
films and on television. Matelo Ferret and an impressive dynasty of Ferrets have helped to keep
the tradition alive in France. The traditional 'Tsiganskaia' is perhaps the best link to a musical
style that has roots from the Adriatic to the Atlantic and as far north as the Baltic. Hot Club's
generous anthology – 27 tracks and 73 minutes of music, somewhat misleadingly taken from two
sessions in 1960 and 1978, rather than continuously over that period – groups it with a strong
selection of melodies from within that tradition, and with four unissued waltzes written by
Django Reinhardt.

Inevitably, perhaps, Ferret has largely built his reputation on an association with the
near-legendary Django. In comparison, he is a cruder and more interventionist performer,
ladling out arpeggios and trills, where his great predecessor would have been content to hold a
chord. Surprisingly, perhaps, the *Tribute To Django* (on which Ferret shares top billing with his
brother, Sarane) makes no attempt to reconstruct or pastiche the great Hot Club de France
performances. 'Out Of Nowhere', 'The Man I Love' and 'What Is This Thing Called Love' are
very much in the jazz mainstream, and the instrumentation is more conventionally adapted to a
jazz style than the percussionless tracks on Hot Club with their vivid cymbalom settings.
Recommended.

MARY FETTIG
ALTO SAXOPHONE, FLUTE

(*)   **In Good Company Concord CJ 273 LP
Fettig; Peter Sprague (g); Marian McPartland (p); Ray Brown; Jeff Hamilton (d).
1/85.

The company is indeed top class (though Sprague is surely included only on sufferance) for a
distinctive soloist with a track record that takes in Stan Kenton and Tito Puente. This is a more
varied and less Latinized set, with good versions of 'Scrapple From The Apple' and 'Secret
Love'. The rhythm section coaxes and cajoles gently and Marian McPartland lays out a fine
basis for Fettig's fresh mainstream sound. Recommended.

FIREHOUSE FIVE PLUS TWO
GROUP

**   **The Firehouse Five Plus Two Story** Good Time Jazz 27055 2CD
Johnny Lucas, Danny Alguire (t); Ward Kimball (tb); Clark Mallory, Tom Sharpsteen,
George Probert (cl); Ed Penner (bs, tba); Frank Thomas (p); Dick Roberts (g, bj);
Harper Goff (bj); Jim McDonald, Monte Mountjoy, Jerry Hamm (d). 5/49–2/50,
10/50–7/51, 3/51–3/54.

(*)   **Goes South! Good Time Jazz 12018 CD/LP
As above, except omit Mallory, Sharpsteen and Hamm. 1/54–10/56.

**   **Goes To Sea** Good Time Jazz 10028 LP
As above, except Ralph Ball, George Bruns (tba, b) replace Penner; Eddie Forrest (d)
replaces McDonald. 2/57–11/57.

| ** | **Around The World** Good Time Jazz 10044 LP |
| | As above, except Don Kinch (*b, tba*) replaces Ball. 11/57–3/60. |

| ** | **Crashes A Party** Good Time Jazz 10038 LP |
| | As above. 11/58–9/59. |

| **(*) | **Dixieland Favourites** Good Time Jazz 10040 CD/LP |
| | As above. 9/59–3/60. |

| ** | **At Disneyland** Good Time Jazz 10049 LP |
| | As above. 7/62. |

| ** | **Goes To A Fire** Good Time Jazz LP |
| | As above. 4–6/64. |

| ** | **Twenty Years Later** Good Time Jazz 10054 LP |
| | As above, except K.O. Eckland (*p*) replaces Thomas; Bill Newman (*bj*) replaces Roberts; add George Bruns (*tba*). 10/69. |

It's difficult to offer a serious criticism of this group, which was always a semiprofessional band: it was formed by Ward Kimball and its personnel was originally drawn from the staff at Walt Disney's animation studios. The music seldom varies from record to record, even from track to track – it's Dixieland done with vigorous enthusiasm rather than panache, and it's as formulaic as anything done by British trad groups. Yet there's a certain degree of authenticity which the group conferred on itself, largely through sheer persistence. The earlier versions of the band play with clockwork momentum, and there is an almost Spike Jones-like feel to their music, occasionally underlined by Kimball's use of sirens and washboards to point up what was already a kitsch act. The personnel which settled down in the later 1950s, though, made some rather more personal and quite successful records, notably the *Dixieland Favourites* set and *Goes South!*. The brass players were often rather reticent about taking solos, and it was mainly left to Probert to be the chief improviser: his playing is often sour and he can't sustain solos for very long, but there's an interestingly quirky edge to his best moments . . . which tends to go for the band as a whole, too.

Not easy, then, to recommend any of these discs, even though all are well recorded and still pack a surprising punch. It's just that if you want to hear this kind of jazz, there are usually better places to find it. Still, the popularity of this pro-am group is attested by the fact that they still have no fewer than nine records in the catalogue.

FIRST AVENUE
GROUP

| ** | **First Avenue** ECM 1194 LP |
| | James Knapp (*t, flhn*); Denney Goodhew (*as, f, bcl*); Eric Jensen (*clo*). 11/80. |

Although the chamber-jazz aspects of the ECM operation have been overstated through the years, it must be admitted that this is the sort of tasteful, low-key and ultimately boring record which detractors of the company have usually cited as cause for derision. The eight tracks have little to distinguish them on any jazz or compositional basis. Impeccably recorded.

FIRST HOUSE
GROUP

| ** | **Erendira** ECM 1307 CD/LP |
| | Ken Stubbs (*as, ss*); Django Bates (*p, tenor hn*); Mick Hutton (*b*); Martin France (*d*). 7/85. |

| **(*) | **Cantilena** ECM 1393 CD/LP |
| | As above. 3/89. |

First House were always a very different proposition from Human Chain, Bates's other extracurricular sortie from the surprisingly demanding keyboard and writing/arranging desk at Loose Tubes. It's a more thoughtful band, relying less on sheer energy and more on Bates's

by no means a charismatic player, but the results are adequate to
...ce combine well.

...re thoroughly achieved and lacks some of the pretentiousness and
...d of Bates's subsequent recording and concert band, Powder Room

R (born 1928)

***   ...overy DSCD 948 CD
Fisc... ...onte Candoli, John Audino, Larry McGuire, James Zito, Buddy Childers,
Steve Huffsteter, Stewart Fischer (*t*); Gil Falco, Roy Main, Ronnie Smith, Phil Teele,
Charley Loper, David Sanchez, Morris Repass (*tb*); Louis Cotti, Bill Perkins, John Lowe,
Gary Foster, Bud Shank, David O'Rourk, Warne Marsh, Kim Richmond (*reeds*);
Bobby West, Chuck Domanico (*b*); Larry Bunker (*d*). 69.

****   **Blues Trilogy** Discovery DSCD 936 CD
Fischer; Gary Foster (*as, f, cl*); Joe Soldo, Gene Cipriano (*f, cl*); Bob Tricarico (*cl,
bcl*); Jack Nimitz (*cbcl*); John Patitucci (*b*); Vinnie Colaiuta (*d*). 11/82.

***(*)   **By And With Himself** Discovery DSCD 934 CD
Fischer; John Patitucci (*b*); Walfredo Reyes (*d*). 5/85–3/86.

The disappearance of the Revelation catalogue from general circulation has meant the loss of
many of Fischer's important recordings, which offer a unique variation on Bill Evans's piano
methods. While Fischer shared Evans's delicacy of touch and harmonic insights, he added an
obliqueness and an interest in deliberately slow tempos which gave his solo playing a special
gravity without sacrificing its gentler associations. Fischer also has a particular interest in Latin
rhythms, and his amalgamation of salsa and bossa nova forms with a stricter jazz pedigree was a
pioneering effort.

Discovery has restored at least the *Waltz* collection to circulation. If not Fischer's finest hour
as an arranger–composer, there are some distinctive charts here. A charming reworking of Cal
Tjader's 'Liz Anne' is better than anything Tjader himself ever did, and there are a couple of
strong revisions of jazz standards in 'Come Sunday' and 'Lennie's Pennies'. But it's a pity that
the solo space is rather restricted, with only a few spots for Perkins, Foster, Marsh and Candoli
apart from the leader.

Blues Trilogy is much stronger, with a lovely sequence of woodwind arrangements and
Fischer and Foster as the two soloists. 'A Long Time Ago' is a gorgeous original waltz, and
even David Gates's lachrymose 'If' emerges as tolerable. Four other tracks are reissued from
part of a fine duo session by Foster and Fischer alone. The solo album (bass and drums appear
on one track only) isn't quite one of Fischer's best: a few inconsequential originals don't attain
his usual absorbing standard, and 'Giant Steps' is reworked in a rather gimmicky way. But
intensely felt readings of 'Turn Out The Stars' and 'Last Night When We Were Young' are
enough to raise the record above the usual standard of solo piano albums.

***   **Tjaderama** Trend TRCD 551 CD
Fischer; Dick Mitchell (*ss, f, af*); Brent Fischer, Andy Simpkins (*b*); Walfredo Reyes
(*d*); Michito Sanchez, Luis Conte (*perc*). 6/87.

**   **Lembrancas** Concord CCD 4404 CD/MC
Fischer; Dick Mitchell (*reeds*); Brent Fischer (*b*); Tris Imboden (*d*); Michito Sanchez,
Luis Conte (*perc*). 6/89.

Fischer's interest in Latin rhythms has been important in his career, but it's also encouraged a
populist streak which has resulted in some more recent records being as fluffy and
inconsequential as his earlier ones were lean and intense. The Concord session is unfortunately
typical: Fischer plays only synthesizer, and the music is a pretty concoction of light Latin fusion
styles, pleasant and forgettable. But *Tjaderama* is a rather more engaging effort. As lightweight
as the music is, Fischer uses his electric keyboards with a delicacy which suits the music
perfectly, and the springiness of his rhythms – abetted by some exceptionally deft percussion
work from Reyes, Sanchez and Conte – is infectiously happy and invigorating. A glittering
revision of 'Woody 'N You' is especially attractive.

ELLA FITZGERALD (born 1918)

VOCAL

(***)   **Ella Fitzgerald** ASV AJD 055 2CD
Fitzgerald; Taft Jordan, Mario Bauza, Bobby Stark, Gordon Griffin, Zeke Zarchey, Ziggy Elman (*t*); Sandy Williams, Nat Story, Claude Jones, Murray McEachern, Red Ballard (*tb*); Benny Goodman (*cl*); Teddy McRae, Louis Jordan, Pete Clark, Edgar Sampson, Elmer Williams, Wayman Carver, Garvin Bushell, Chauncey Haughton, Hymie Schertzer, Bill De Pew, Arthur Rollini, Vido Musso (*reeds*); Tommy Fulford, Joe Steele, Jess Stacy (*p*); John Trueheart, Allan Reuss, Bobby Johnson (*g*); Beverly Peer, Bill Thomas, Harry Goodman (*b*); Chick Webb, Gene Krupa (*d*). 10/35–12/37.

(*)   **Ella Fitzgerald 1935–1937 Classics 500 CD
As above, plus Frankie Newton (*t*), Benny Morton (*tb*), Chu Berry (*ts*), Teddy Wilson (*p*), Leemie Stanfield (*b*), Cozy Cole (*d*). 6/35–1/37.

(*)   **Ella Fitzgerald 1937–1938 Classics 506 CD
As above, except omit Griffin, Zarchey, Elman, McEachern, Ballard, Goodman, Schertzer, De Pew, Rollini, Musso, Stacy, Reuss, Goodman, Newton, Morton, Berry, Wilson, Stanfield and Cole, add George Matthews (*tb*), The Mills Brothers (*v*). 1/37–5/38.

***   **Ella Fitzgerald 1938–1939** Classics 518 CD
As above, except add Dick Vance (*t*) and Hilton Jefferson (*as*), omit The Mills Brothers. 5/38–239.

**   **Ella Fitzgerald 1939** Classics 525 CD
As above, except add Bill Beason (*d*). 2–6/39.

***   **Ella Fitzgerald 1939–1940** Classics 566 CD
As above, except add Irving Randolph (*t*), John Haughton, Jimmy Archey, Floyd Brady, John McConnell (*tb*), Sam Simmons (*ts*), Roger Ramirez (*p*), omit Webb. 8/39–5/40.

**   **Live From The Roseland Ballroom New York 1940** Jazz Anthology 550032 CD
Fitzgerald; Dick Vance, Taft Jordan, Bobby Stark (*t*); George Matthews, Nat Story, Sandy Williams (*tb*); Garvin Bushell (*cl, ss*); Hilton Jefferson (*as*); Wayman Carver (*as, ts, f*); Teddy McRae (*ts, bs*); Tommy Fulford (*p*); John Trueheart (*g*); Beverly Peer (*b*); Bill Beason (*d*). 40.

Fitzgerald's fabled break came when she won an Apollo Theatre talent contest in 1934, still only 16, and by the following year she was singing for Chick Webb's band. When Webb died in 1939, the singer inherited leadership of his band, for by this time she was its undoubted star. But her recordings of the period are often hard to take because the material is sometimes insufferably trite: after Ella had a major hit with the nursery rhyme tune 'A Tisket A Tasket' she was doomed – at least, until the break-up of the band – to seek out similar songs. The Classics CDs offer a chronological survey of her work up to 1940, and while the calibre of her singing is consistent enough – the voice at its freshest, her phrasing straightforward but sincerely dedicated to making the most of the melody – the tracks seem to spell the decline of what was, in the mid-1930s, one of the most swinging of big bands. The arrangements are often blandly supportive of the singer rather than creating any kind of partnership, and when the material is of the standard of 'Swinging On The Reservation' it's difficult to summon much enthusiasm. But there are perhaps many minor successes. The 1937–38 CD includes the session which produced Webb's only 12-inch 78, 'I Want To Be Happy' and 'Halleleujah', arranged by Turk Van Lake, and 'Rock It For Me' and 'Bei Mir Bist Du Schoen' look forward to the authority which Fitzgerald would bestow on her later records. The 1939–40 disc, although it sports 'My Wubba Dolly', has a number of swinging features such as 'After I Say I'm Sorry', 'I'm Not Complainin'' and a fine 'Baby, Won't You Please Come Home?' Fitzgerald tends to treat all the songs the same – there's little of Billie Holiday's creative approach to the beat – but the lightness of her voice lets her float a lyric without losing her grip on it.

The remastering of all these discs is very mixed. The earlier discs vary almost from track to track, some laden with hiss, some foggy, others crisp. 'A Tisket A Tasket'. on the 1937–38 volume, is dreadfully brassy. Only the 1939–40 set has consistently clear transfers. The ASV two-disc set offers a cross-section from Ella's earliest sessions but the remastering is bass-heavy and listening isn't much fun. The Jazz Anthology set captures a 1940 airshot which mixes superior material – 'Royal Garden Blues', 'Sugar Blues' – with tunes of the order of 'Chewin' Gum', but it's not without period charm, though the sound is indifferent.

****   **Ella Sings Arlen Vol. 1** Polydor 817527-2 CD
Fitzgerald; Billy May Orchestra. 8/60–1/61.

****   **Ella Sings Arlen Vol. 2** Polydor 817528-2 CD
Fitzgerald; Billy May Orchestra. 8/60–1/61.

****   **The George & Ira Gershwin Songbook** Verve 821024-2 3CD
Fitzgerald; Nelson Riddle Orchestra. 1–3/59.

***   **The Johnny Mercer Songbook** Verve 821247-2 CD
Fitzgerald; Nelson Riddle Orchestra. 10/64.

***(*)   **The Rogers And Hart Songbook Vol. 1** Verve 821579-2/3112014 CD/MC
Fitzgerald; Buddy Bregman Orchestra. 8/56.

***   **The Rogers And Hart Songbook Vol. 2** Verve 821580-2 CD
Fitzgerald; Buddy Bregman Orchestra. 8/56.

***   **The Jerome Kern Songbook** Verve 821669-2 CD
Fitzgerald; Nelson Riddle Orchestra. 63.

****   **The Cole Porter Songbook Vol. 1** Verve 821989-2/3112054 CD/MC
Fitzgerald; Buddy Bregman Orchestra. 2/56.

***(*)   **The Cole Porter Songbook Vol. 2** Verve 821990-2/3112055 CD/MC
Fitzgerald; Buddy Bregman Orchestra. 2–3/56.

***(*)   **The Irving Berlin Songbook Vol. 1** Verve 829534-2 CD
Fitzgerald; Paul Weston Orchestra. 3/58.

***(*)   **The Irving Berlin Songbook Vol. 2** Verve 829535-2 CD
Fitzgerald; Paul Weston Orchestra. 3/58.

****   **Sings The Duke Ellington Songbook** Verve 837035-2 2CD
Fitzgerald; Cat Anderson, Willie Cook, Clark Terry, Harold Baker (*t*); Quentin Jackson, Britt Woodman, John Sanders (*tb*); Jimmy Hamilton (*cl, ts*); Johnny Hodges (*as*); Russell Procope (*cl, as*); Ben Webster, Paul Gonsalves, Frank Foster (*ts*); Harry Carney (*bs, bcl, cl*); Duke Ellington, Paul Smith, Oscar Peterson (*p*); Stuff Smith (*vn*); Barney Kessel, Herb Ellis (*g*); Jimmy Woode, Joe Mondragon, Ray Brown (*b*); Alvin Stoller, Sam Woodyard (*d*). 9/56–10/57.

***   **The Songbooks** Verve 823445-2 CD
As above discs. 56–64.

Somewhat astonishingly, there is virtually nothing available from Ella's tenure with Decca in the 1940s and early '50s, although MCA's ongoing reissue programme may have dealt with this situation by the time we are in print with this edition. In January 1956, she began recording for Norman Granz's Verve label, and the first release, *The Cole Porter Songbook*, became the commercial rock on which Verve was built. It was so successful that Granz set Ella to work on all the great American songwriters, and her series of 'songbook' albums are an unrivalled sequence of their kind. The records work consistently well for a number of reasons: Fitzgerald herself was at a vocal peak, strong yet flexible, and her position as a lyric interpreter was perfectly in tune with records dense with lyrical detail; each disc carefully programmes familiar with lesser-known material; the arrangers each work to their strengths, Bregman and May delivering hard-hitting big-band sounds, Riddle the suavest of grown-up orchestrations; and the quality of the studio recordings was and remains outstandingly lifelike and wide-ranging on most of the discs, although some of the earlier sessions are more constricted in scope.

The single most awe-inspiring piece is the Gershwin set, once a five-LP box, now a resplendent three-CD set (though currently only available as an import in the U.K.) which works patiently through 53 songs without any suspicion of going through the motions. The delight in hearing these discs one after another is in hearing some almost forgotten tunes –

'The Half Of It, Dearie Blues', 'You've Got What Gets Me', even 'Just Another Rhumba' – alongside the premier Gershwin melodies, and Fitzgerald's concentration is such that a formidable standard is maintained. The Harold Arlen and Cole Porter sets are, though, barely a step behind, although the much-loved Porter discs now sound less profound through the sometimes perfunctory arangements. Arlen's songs are among a jazz singer's most challenging material, though, and Fitzgerald is ebulliently partnered by Billy May, who sounds more pertinent here than he did on some of the sessions he did with Sinatra. The Mercer record is slightly disappointing after the previous Gershwin triumph with Riddle, and the Kern collection, though fine enough, is also a secondary choice. The two discs dedicated to Berlin are a bit patchy, but the first volume starts off with a quite unsurpassable reading of 'Let's Face The Music And Dance', where Ella negotiates all the changes in backdrop without the slightest hint of discomfort, and goes on to wonderfully tender versions of 'Russian Lullaby' and 'How Deep Is The Ocean'. The second disc works further wonders with 'Isn't This A Lovely Day' and 'Heat Wave'. The discs dedicated to Rogers and Hart are also slightly behind the others: Fitzgerald's plain speaking doesn't always touch on the ingenuity of Hart's lyrics. But the first disc is virtually unmissable for the famous readings of 'Manhattan' and 'With A Song In My Heart'.

The collection made with Duke Ellington is a somewhat different matter, with the composer himself working with the singer. It's been an undervalued record in the past, with charges of under-rehearsal, and there's certainly a major difference between these sessions and the others: Riddle would surely have never tolerated the looseness of some of the playing, or Sam Woodyard in any circumstances. Yet the best of the disc finds Ellington inspired, with such as 'Caravan' evoking entirely new treatments and swingers like 'Drop Me Off In Harlem' fusing Ella's imperturbable time with the rough-and-ready movement of the band in full cry. Some of the tracks feature her with a small group, and there is an 'I Got It Bad And That Ain't Good' which finds Ben Webster almost oozing out of the speakers. Highly recommended.

The best-of pick on *The Songbooks* isn't bad, with 19 tracks and a little over an hour of music, but it emphasizes how little fat there is in the original albums.

***   **At The Opera House** Verve 831269-2 CD
Fitzgerald; Roy Eldridge (*t*); J. J. Johnson (*tb*); Sonny Stitt (*as*); Coleman Hawkins, Stan Getz, Flip Phillips (*ts*); Oscar Peterson (*p*); Herb Ellis (*g*); Ray Brown (*b*); Connie Kay (*d*). 9–10/57.

***   **Clap Hands, Here Comes Charlie!** Verve 835646-2 CD
Fitzgerald; Lou Levy (*p*); Herb Ellis (*g*); Joe Mondragon, Wilfred Middlebrooks (*b*); Stan Levey, Gus Johnson (*d*). 1-6/61.

***   **Mack The Knife (Ella In Berlin)** Verve 825670-2 CD
Fitzgerald; Paul Smith (*p*); Jim Hall (*g*); Wilfred Middlebrooks (*b*); Gus Johnson (*d*). 2/60.

***   **Ella Returns To Berlin** Verve 837758-2 CD
Fitzgerald; Lou Levy, Oscar Peterson (*p*); Herb Ellis (*g*); Wilfred Middlebrooks, Ray Brown (*b*); Gus Johnson, Ed Thigpen (*d*). 2/61.

***(*)   **Ella Wishes You A Swinging Christmas** Verve 827150-2 CD
Fitzgerald; Frank DeVol Orchestra. 60.

***   **These Are The Blues** Verve 829536-2 CD
Fitzgerald; Roy Eldridge (*t*); Wild Bill Davis (*org*); Herb Ellis (*g*); Ray Brown (*b*); Gus Johnson (*d*). 10/63.

***(*)   **The Intimate Ella** Verve 829838-2 CD
Fitzgerald; Paul Smith (*p*). 60.

***   **Ella In Rome (The Birthday Concert)** Verve 835454-2 CD
Fitzgerald; Oscar Peterson, Lou Levy (*p*); Herb Ellis (*g*); Ray Brown, Max Bennett (*b*); Gus Johnson (*d*). 4/58.

***(*)   **Ella And Basie** Verve 821576-2 CD
Fitzgerald; Joe Newman, Al Aarons, Sonny Cohn, Don Rader, Fip Ricard (*t*); Henry Coker, Grover Mitchell, Benny Powell, Urbie Green (*tb*); Marshall Royal (*as, cl*); Eric

Dixon (*ts, f*); Frank Wess (*ts, as, f*); Frank Foster (*ts*); Charlie Fowlkes (*bs*); Freddie Green (*g*); Buddy Catlett (*b*); Sonny Payne (*d*). 7/63.

***(*)   **Compact Jazz: Ella Fitzgerald** Verve 831367-2 CD
As above Verve discs, plus Bill Doggett, Marty Paich, Nelson Riddle Orchestra. 7/57–10/65.

***(*)   **Compact Jazz: Ella Fitzgerald Live** Verve 833294-2 CD
Fitzgerald; Roy Eldridge, Cootie Williams, Cat Anderson, Herbie Jones, Mercer Ellington (*t*); J. J. Johnson, Lawrence Brown, Buster Cooper (*tb*); Chuck Connors (*btb*); Johnny Hodges, Russell Procope (*as*); Jimmy Hamilton (*cl, ts*); Sonny Stitt, Stan Getz, Illinois Jacquet, Coleman Hawkins (*ts*); Harry Carney (*bs*); Duke Ellington, Jimmy Jones, Lou Levy, Tommy Flanagan, Paul Smith, Oscar Peterson (*p*); Herb Ellis, Barney Kessel, Jim Hall (*g*); Ray Brown, Wilfred Middlebrooks, Bill Yancey, John Lamb, Jim Hughart (*b*); Connie Kay, Gus Johnson, Jo Jones, Sam Woodyard, Grady Tate, Alvin Stoller (*d*). 8/56–7/66.

The 'songbook' albums may be Fitzgerald's best-remembered at Verve, but there were many more good ones, and a fair number of them are still in print. Essential: the meeting with Basie, which is a little more fun than her encounters with Ellington, brash and exciting but tempered by the invulnerable machine that was Basie's band; *The Intimate Ella*, a one-on-one meeting with underrated pianist Paul Smith, and a good instance of the big voice being shaded down; and the Christmas album, the least affected and most swinging seasonal jazz album ever made. Good ones: *At The Opera House*, which is a bit of a typical JATP rave-up but has its moments; *Clap Hands, Here Comes Charlie!*, a swinging small-group encounter, and something of a rarity in her record dates from this period; and the recently issued *Returns To Berlin*, which comes in excellent sound and is rather better than the original *Berlin* set. Disappointing, but still worth hearing, are *These Are The Blues*, which tends to prove that Ella is no great queen of the blues, despite the nicely simmering back-ups from Davis and Eldridge, and the Rome concert. The two Compact Jazz compilations are both full of good things for those who don't want to trawl through the whole Verve catalogue. Her albums with Louis Armstrong are listed under his name.

(*)   **30 By Ella Capitol CDP 7483332 CD
Fitzgerald; Harry Edison (*t*); Benny Carter (*as*); George Auld (*ts*); Jimmy Jones (*p*); John Collins (*g*); Bob West (*b*); Panama Francis (*d*).

*(*)   **Ella Fitzgerald's Christmas** Capitol CDP 7944522 CD
Fitzgerald; studio orchestra. 67.

**   **Brighten The Corner** Capitol CDP 7951512 CD
Fitzgerald; Ralph Carmichael Choir and Orchestra.

**   **Misty Blue** Capitol CDP 7951222 CD
Fitzgerald; Sid Feller Orchestra.

Fitzgerald's Capitol albums are surely the bleakest period of her discography. *Misty Blue* is torpedoed by shockingly poor material (sample titles: 'Don't Let That Doorknob Hit You', 'This Gun Don't Care'); *Brighten The Corner* is a flyweight sacred album, and the Christmas set isn't a patch on the secular version for Verve. the most seriously disappointing, though, is probably the meeting with Benny Carter, which is made up entirely of medleys and never lets anybody settle down. These discs can be happily left alone.

***   **Take Love Easy** Pablo 2310-702 CD
Fitzgerald; Joe Pass (*g*). 73.

(*)   **Fine And Mellow Pablo 2310-829 CD/LP/MC
Fitzgerald; Clark Terry (*t, flhn*); Harry Edison (*t*); Eddie 'Lockjaw' Davis, Zoot Sims (*ts*); Tommy Flanagan (*p*); Joe Pass (*g*); Ray Brown (*b*); Louie Bellson (*d*). 1/74.

***(*)   **Ella In London** Pablo 2310-711 CD
Fitzgerald; Tommy Flanagan (*p*); Joe Pass (*g*); Keter Betts (*b*); Bobby Durham (*d*). 4/74.

***   **Montreux 1975** Pablo 2310-751 CD/LP/MC
        As above, except omit Pass. 7/75.

***(*)   **Ella And Oscar** Pablo 2310-759 CD/LP/MC
        Fitzgerald; Oscar Peterson (*p*); Ray Brown (*b*). 5/75.

***   **Fitzgerald And Pass . . . Again** Pablo 2310-772 CD/MC
        Fitzgerald; Joe Pass (*g*). 1–2/76.

**   **Dream Dancing** Pablo 2310-814 CD/MC
        Fitzgerald; Nelson Riddle Orchestra. 6/72–2/78.

(*)   **Lady Time Pablo 2310-825 CD
        Fitzgerald; Jackie Davis (*org*); Louie Bellson (*d*). 6/78.

***   **A Perfect Match** Pablo 231-2110 CD
        Fitzgerald; Pete Minger, Sonny Cohn, Paul Cohen, Raymond Brown (*t*); Booty Wood,
        Bill Hughes, Mel Wanzo, Dennis Wilson (*tb*); Kenny Hing, Danny Turner (*ts*); Eric
        Dixon, Bobby Plater (*as*); Charlie Fowlkes (*bs*); Count Basie (*p*); Freddie Green (*g*);
        Keter Betts (*b*); Mickey Roker (*d*). 7/79.

***   **A Classy Pair** Pablo 2310 132 CD/MC
        As above, except add Nolan Smith (*t*), John Clayton (*b*); Butch Miles (*d*), omit
        Cohen, Betts and Roker. 2/79.

Back with Norman Granz again, Ella recorded steadily through the 1970s; but there was little to
suggest that she would either repeat or surpass the best of her earlier music. If encroaching age
is supposed to impart a greater wisdom to a singer of songs, and hence into the interpretation of
those songs, it's a more complex matter with Fitzgerald, who has never been much of a purveyor
of lyrics, more a musician who happens to sing. Her scatting has grown less fluent and more
exaggerated, but no less creative in its construction; her manipulation of time and melody has
become more obvious because she has to push herself harder to make it happen. There are still
many good records here, but no really great ones, and all of them miss a little of the grace and
instinctive improvisation which float off all her older records.

   Granz recorded her in several settings. With Joe Pass, the bare-strings accompaniment is
initially intimate but finally dull: Pass can't devise enough variation to make the music stay
awake, and Fitzgerald isn't always sure how strongly she's able to come on. Their duet albums
are nice enough, but one is enough. *Fine And Mellow* is a rather noisy and brash session, but the
title-track is a very good version of the Holiday favourite, which sounds just as good in Ella's
hands. The Montreux and Nice live sets are merely OK, and much better is the London date
from 1974: probably the final chance to hear Ella in a club setting, and it's a racy and sometimes
virtuosic display by the singer, a fine souvenir of what was a memorable visit. Of the big-band
dates, *Dream Dancing* features Nelson Riddle at his sententious worst, and is missable, while
the two sets with Basie are boisterous if comparatively uneventful. *Lady Time* is an unusual
setting which tries Ella out as a kind of club-class blueswoman; she makes a game go of it. The
other must-hear record, though, is the duet (almost – Ray Brown offers discreet support) with
Oscar Peterson, *Ella And Oscar*. The pianist plays as hard as usual, but instrumentalist and
vocalist bring out the best in each other, and there are at least three near-classics in 'Mean To
Me', 'How Long Has This Been Going On?' and 'Midnight Sun'.

(*)   **Ella Abraça Jobim Pablo 2630-201 CD/MC
        Fitzgerald; Clark Terry (*t*); Zoot Sims (*ts*); Toots Thielemans (*hmca*); Mike Lang,
        Clarence McDonald, Terry Trotter (*ky*); Joe Pass, Oscar Castro-Neves, Paul Jackson,
        Mitch Holder, Roland Bautista (*g*); Abe Laboriel (*b*); Alex Acuna (*d*); Paulinho Da
        Costa (*perc*). 9/80.

(*)   **The Best Is Yet To Come Pablo 2312-138 CD/LP
        Fitzgerald; Al Aarons (*t*); Bill Watrous (*tb*); Marshall Royal (*as*); Bob Cooper (*ts*);
        Jimmy Rowles (*p*); Art Hillery (*org*); Joe Pass, Tommy Tedesco (*g*); Jim Hughart (*b*);
        Shelly Manne (*d*); strings and woodwinds. 2/82.

(*)   **Let's Call The Whole Thing Off Pablo 2312-140 CD/LP/MC
        Fitzgerald; André Previn (*p*). 5/83.

***   **Speak Love** Pablo 2310-888 CD/LP
Fitzgerald; Joe Pass (*g*). 3/83.

***   **Easy Living** Pablo 2310-921 CD/LP/MC
As above.

**   **All That Jazz** Pablo 2310-938 CD/LP/MC
Fitzgerald; Clark Terry, Harry Edison (*t*); Al Grey (*tb*); Benny Carter (*as*); Mike
Wofford, Kenny Barron (*p*); Ray Brown (*b*); Bobby Durham (*d*). 3/89.

***   **The Best Of Ella Fitzgerald** Pablo 2405-421 CD/LP/MC

The 1980s saw Fitzgerald slackening off her workload as illness and perhaps sheer tiredness
intervened. The Jobim collection came too late, since every other singer had already had their
shot at this kind of thing; *The Best* was another tiresome set of Nelson Riddle arrangements;
and the duo album with Previn was a pointless bit of star-matching. Which left two more albums
with Pass and what may prove to be a farewell set in the strained and unconvincing *All That
Jazz*. At least the best-of is a good selection from the pick of the above.

PAUL FLAHERTY
ALTO AND SOPRANO SAXOPHONES

(*)   **Impact Cadence CJR 1046 LP
Flaherty; Stephen Scholz (*vn*); Randall Colbourne (*d*). 1/90.

**   **Primal Burn** Tulpa TP 016 LP
As above, except Richard Downs (*b*) replaces Scholz. 11/90.

Paul Flaherty is in some ways an old-fashioned player: as an improviser he sticks close to the
tenets of free playing as it stood in the 1970s, with long, lacerating blow-outs as the norm and
unrelieved energy playing ('The results could probably be categorized as free energy jazz', he
says in the notes to *Impact*) as the *modus operandi*. But while it's a therapeutic exercise for the
players, listeners may need a little more variation in design, and both records suffer from a
sameness of approach as well as occasionally pedestrian ideas. Flaherty is a repetitive player,
but he lacks the sheer visceral power which allows a musician such as Peter Brötzmann to get
away with it. The best music on *Impact* comes with the addition of violinist Scholz to the duo on
four tracks: his agile, gnawing lines are a useful liniment for the wounded roar of the music.
Primal Burn is a nearly non-stop slugfest and, while it has its cathartic moments, Colbourne's
rhythms tend to batter down the music rather than raising it up.

TOMMY FLANAGAN (born 1930)
PIANO

***   **The Complete 'Overseas'** DIW 305/25004 CD/LP
Flanagan; Wilbur Little (*b*); Elvin Jones (*d*). 8/57.

***   **In Stockholm 1957** Dragon DRLP 87 LP
As above.

***   **The Tommy Flanagan Trio** Original Jazz Classics OJC 182 LP
Flanagan; Tommy Potter (*b*); Roy Haynes (*d*). 5/60.

(*)   **The Tokyo Recital Pablo 2310724 CD
Flanagan; Keter Betts (*b*); Bobby Durham (*d*). 2/75.

(*)   **Montreux '77 Original Jazz Classics OJC 371 CD/LP/MC
As above. 7/77.

(*)   **The Best Of Tommy Flanagan Pablo PACD 2405 410 CD/LP/MC
As above. 2/75 & 7/77.

**   **Something Borrowed, Something Blue** Original Jazz Classics OJC 473 CD/LP/MC
As above, except Jimmie Smith (*d*) replaces Durham. 1/78.

***   **Eclipso** Enja 2088 LP
          Flanagan; George Mraz (*b*); Elvin Jones (*d*). 2/77.

(*)   **Confirmation Enja 4014 LP
          Flanagan; George Mraz (*b*); Elvin Jones (*d*). 2/77 & 11/78.

***   **Ballads And Blues** Enja 3031 LP
          Flanagan; George Mraz (*b*, duo). 11/78.

****   **Giant Steps: In Memory Of John Coltrane** Enja 4022 CD/LP
          Flanagan; George Mraz (*b*); Al Foster (*d*). 2/82.

(*)   **Thelonica Enja 4052 CD/LP
          Flanagan; George Mraz (*b*); Art Taylor (*d*). 12/82.

(*)   **Plays The Music Of Harold Arlen DIW 328 / 25030 CD/LP
          Flanagan; George Mraz (*b*); Connie Kay (*d*); Helen Merrill (*v*). n.d.

****   **Jazz Poet** Timeless SJP 301 CD/LP
          Flanagan; George Mraz (*b*); Kenny Washington (*d*). 1/89.

***(*) **Super Session** Enja 3059 CD/LP
          Flanagan; Red Mitchell (*b*); Elvin Jones. 2/80.

(*)   **The Music Of Rodgers And Hammerstein Savoy 650116 CD
          Flanagan; Wilbur Harden (*t, flhn*); George Duvivier (*b*); Granville T. Hogan (*d*). 9/58.

If it's difficult to make fine qualitative distinctions within Tommy Flanagan's discography, it isn't difficult to distinguish his output from the average piano trio of the last 30 years. The earlier albums date from a period before he became known as one of the finest accompanists in the business, backing Tony Bennett and, more memorably, Ella Fitzgerald in her great late-1960s resurgence; Flanagan's touch lacks the delicacy that it acquired later, but he has a fine boppish attack that is complemented by Jones on the excellent European sessions, and by the adaptable Roy Haynes.

Jones's presence and multidirectional approach are always a plus on the later dates. *Eclipso* (and *Confirmation*, which uses up some unreleased masters from the February 1977 session) develops the relationship further; *Super Session* brings it to a peak. Increasingly, though, it is the partnership of Flanagan and bassist Mraz which dominates and Jones who tends to follow. *Ballads And Blues* is a piano–bass duo, and again the residual material is on *Confirmation*; only Red Mitchell has managed to equal Mraz's superb harmonic response to Flanagan's long, almost unsupported lines (Betts, by contrast, is very much a rhythm player). Mraz is also a fine soloist.

The live sessions on Pablo 2310724 and OJC 371 have been usefully compressed (with one or two unfortunate omissions) on to a single CD called *The Best Of* . . . It might more usefully have been labelled a Strayhorn tribute, since he is the main composer represented. Flanagan sounds bright and airy, but also a little empty of ideas.

It's often forgotten that it was Flanagan who accompanied John Coltrane on (most of) the original *Giant Steps* (Atlantic 7567 81337). The quartet sessions with Harden occasionally recall those days, but not particularly memorably; the homage to Coltrane, though, is one of the finest piano trio albums of the last 20 years. Flanagan repeats several of the tracks from *Giant Steps*, adds 'Central Park West', and tackles 'Naima', which Coltrane had entrusted to Wynton Kelly on a later session. Flanagan's reinterpretations are emotive, often harmonically clearer, and very beautiful. As is the most recent of these records: featuring Mraz again and the brightly swinging Kenny Washington. 'Jazz poet' would be a fair passport entry for Flanagan; he is a wonderfully lyrical performer, with the widest imaginable range of diction and association. There is not a dull or fudged set in the bunch, but it's hard to go past *Giant Steps* or *Jazz Poet*.

***(*) **Beyond The Bluebird** Timeless SJP 350 CD
          Flanagan; Kenny Burrell (*g*); George Mraz (*b*); Lewis Nash (*d*). 4/90.

After concert and recorded tributes to Ellington and Coltrane, Flanagan turns back to bebop and the spirit of Charlie Parker. The pianist, though, has always been conscious that music is very precisely mediated by time and place, specific contexts. The Bluebird Inn in Detroit was a significant bop locus; Flanagan and Elvin Jones both played in the house band there, as did Barry Harris, whose 'Nascimento' anchors the second half of the disc. The first half of the set is dedicated to it and the music played there: two (relatively unfamiliar) Parker compositions, 'Bluebird' and 'Barbados', a long 'Yesterdays' featuring Burrell at his most contemplative, Benny Carter's 'Blues In My Heart' and '50-21' (the Bluebird's address) by trumpeter/bandleader Thad Jones, like his brother a stalwart of the club.

The second half of the set is, in the words of Flanagan's title-piece 'Beyond The Bluebird', dispelling any imputation of mere nostalgia, and further bracketed by Burrell's closing 'Bluebird After Dark'. 'Something Borrowed, Something Blue' reappears from the old Galaxy session reissued on OJC 473, above, a fine reinvention. Typical of Flanagan's eclectic approach is the inclusion of Dizzy Reece's rarely played 'The Con Man', whose unusual blues tonality provides a vivid setting for remarkable solos by Flanagan and George Mraz.

JAY C. FLIPPEN (1898–1971)
VOCAL

(*)   **Jay C. Flippen And His Gang Fountain FV-204 LP
Flippen; Tommy Gott, Chelsea Quealey (*t*); Earl Oliver, Red Nichols (*c*); Sammy Lewis, Brad Gowans, Miff Mole, Abe Lincoln (*tb*); Jimmy Lytell, Bobby Davis (*cl, as*); Larry Abbott, Jimmy Dorsey, Dick Johnson (*cl*); Sam Ruby (*ts*); Jimmy Johnston, Adrian Rollini (*bsx*); Bill Wirges, Arthur Schutt, Bill Haid, Irving Brodsky (*p*); Dick McDonough (*g, bj*); Harry Reser, John Cali, Tommy Felline (*bj*); Joe Tarto (*bb*); Vic Berton (*d*). 6/26–8/27.

Flippen became a character actor in Hollywood later in life, but he was a vaudeville singer with a southern twang (he was born in Little Rock, Arkansas) in the 1920s. The singing is rather irritating after two or three songs, as is his habit of saying 'Turn it over!' at the end of every tune, but the accompaniments used the pick of the New York sessionmen, and they have some strong moments: Nichols, who takes an entire chorus on 'For My Sweetheart' and 'Short And Sweet', sounds especially fine, and it's good to find Quealey, whose work hasn't been reissued much, on four of the tracks. The jazz content here is more subliminal than stated, but it's interesting to hear how improvising of some thoughtfulness was even creeping into otherwise routine pop material of the day. The remastering has been done impeccably, although the indistinct sound of the original Pathé recordings may trouble some ears.

CHRIS FLORY
GUITAR

***   **For All We Know** Concord CCD 4403 CD/MC
Flory; Mike LeDonne (*p, org*); Phil Flanigan (*b*); Chuck Riggs (*d*). 1/88.

Another in the Concord repertory of young mainstreamers, Flory's cool phrasing and ambiguous tone (soft when you expect a hardness, and vice versa) lends an attractive piquancy to his improvisations. This is a very good rhythm section, too. But the material – swing standards and a couple of blues – is a shade too ordinary; Flory should be given a more challenging brief to bring out his best.

RICKY FORD (born 1954)
TENOR SAXOPHONE

(*)   **Saxotic Stomp Muse MCD 5373 CD
Ford; James Spaulding (*as, f*); Charles Davis (*bs*); Kirk Lightsey (*p*); Ray Drummond (*b*); Jimmy Cobb (*d*). 9/87.

***   **Manhattan Blues** Candid 9036 CD/LP

***(*)   **Ebony Rhapsody** Candid 9053 CD/LP
Ford; Jaki Byard (*p*); Milt Hinton (*b*); Ben Riley (*d*). 3/89, 6/90.

An erratic but occasionally brilliant player, Ford is best known for his work with Ran Blake and Abdullah Ibrahim. His own records are ambitious in range, covering a range of idioms from bop, modal-to-free harmony, and back to a broad swing style. On the 1989 *Manhattan Blues* his breadth of reference is instantaneously answered by the eclectic Byard, and by the bassist and drummer; Ford's soloing is thoughtful but still curiously uninvolving. *Ebony Rhapsody*, with the same line-up, irons out the occasional awkwardnesses and finds Ford with a band that seems increasingly responsive to his changes of direction; 'Mirror Man', a duet with Milt 'The Judge' Hinton, has an authority worthy of Coleman Hawkins, and the other originals bespeak a growing compositional talent.

Saxotic Stomp has little of its successors' bite and polish. The three horns lock rather inconsequentially, and Spaulding in particular sounds slightly off, a far cry from his own *Brilliant Corners* (Muse 600610). Cobb is wonderfully at ease, but Lightsey sounds constrained at times, noticeably on 'For Mary Lou' (which may be no surprise, given the dedication).

***   **Hard Groovin'** Muse MCD 5373 CD
        Ford; Roy Hargrove (*t*); Geoff Keezer (*p*); Bob Hurst (*b*); Jeff Watts (*d*). 89.

Arnold Schoenberg freely conceded that, despite the advent of serialism, there was still a lot of good music to be written in C major. One might say much the same sort of thing about hard bop. If there's an element of young-fogeyism to the generation of musicians who've abandoned the avant-garde to rally under a banner inscribed 'Forward to the 1950s', Ford gives his revivalism a curiously magisterial gravitas, almost as if he were giving a lecture on the evolution of jazz saxophone.

There are some symptoms of reinvention of the wheel on *Hard Groovin'*, a title clearly intended to leave potential purchasers with no misgivings that they're going to be foisted off with any experimental nonsense. This is so straight-ahead that it has creases in its jeans. Keezer keeps the stew simmering and contributes the most intriguing composition in 'Masaman' (one would like to hear it covered by older-generation players), and Hargrove belts out impressive Hubbard-influenced lines that just occasionally work themselves under an overhang and have to inch shamefacedly back the way they came. Can't say it's an 'advance' on past performances, since advance doesn't seem to be the point.

BRUCE FORMAN (born 1956)
GUITAR

(*)   **Dynamics Concord CJ 279 MC
        Forman; George Cables (*p*). 2/85.

***   **There Are Times** Concord CCD 4332 CD/MC
        Forman; Bobby Hutcherson (*vib*); George Cables (*p*); Jeff Carney (*b*); Eddie Marshall (*d*). 8/86.

(*)   **Pardon Me Concord CCD 4368 CD/MC
        Forman; Billy Childs (*p*); Jeff Carney (*b*); Eddie Marshall (*d*). 10/88.

All the guitarists who record for Concord seem to come from the same brotherhood: a clean, modulated tone, quick attack and a detailed fluency in their solos; a swing-based style with a streak of bebop complexity running through it. It's appropriate that the company released the later records of Tal Farlow, who is the exemplar of the style. Bruce Forman, a much younger guitarist, is nevertheless entirely of the same persuasion and, as capable as he is, it's hard to glean much excitement or consistent interest from these records. The date with Hutcherson is the best, simply because the vibesman is such a great-hearted musician; but most of the music on all three records is well turned out and not much more.

MITCH FORMAN
KEYBOARDS

**   **Childhood Dreams** Soul Note SN 1050 LP
        Forman (*p* solo). 2/82.

**   **Only A Memory** Soul Note SN 1070 LP
         Forman (*p* solo). 8/82.

Forman's credentials as a sessionman and fusion-band keyboardist don't seem to have prepared
him adequately for these unfocused and doodling solo albums. The first is all done on acoustic
piano, the second adds some organ washes, and neither makes any impression on an already
overcrowded area of endeavour, the solo piano record.

MICHAEL FORMANEK
BASS

***(*)   **Wide Open Space** Enja 6032-2 CD
         Formanek; Greg Osby (*ss, as*); Wayne Krantz (*g*); Mark Feldman (*vn*); Jeff Hirshfield
         (*d*). 1/90.

Formanek has a list of interesting credits to his name as a sideman, but this debut appearance as
a leader is even more impressive. Form and instrumentation are cleverly varied through the
seven tunes; modal pieces are interspersed with drifting, abstract mood-settings; and there are
striking individual parts from Osby, Krantz and Feldman. Osby in particular sounds more
unaffectedly lively and focused than he does on some of his own records. Excellent recording.

JIMMY FORREST (1920–80)
TENOR SAXOPHONE

(*)   **Forrest Fire Original Jazz Classics OJC 199 LP
         Forrest; Larry Young (*org*); Thornel Schwartz (*g*); Jimmie Smith (*d*). 8/60.

***   **Out Of The Forrest** Original Jazz Classics OJC 097 LP
         Forrest; Joe Zawinul (*p*); Tommy Potter (*b*); Clarence Johnson (*d*). 4/61.

Understandably, much of the interest of these centres on a pre-Weather Report Joe Zawinul and
the late, great Larry Young, but Forrest is an intriguing performer. For reasons never
satisfactorily explained, there weren't that many tenor saxophonists in the bebop revolutions.
Like Big Nick Nicholas and Lucky Thompson, Forrest was something of a players' player, with
only a rather marginal following now. That's a pity for, as these two sets amply demonstrate, his
playing was full of character, a little rough-hewn in places, but capable of greater subtlety than
his big hit, 'Night Train', might suggest. Forrest is the mid-point, stylistically if not quite
geographically, between Charlie Parker and Ornette Coleman.
     Forrest Fire pits him against the brimstone stomp of Young's Hammond; between them, they
roll up the floor. The best of the three is undoubtedly *Out Of The Forrest*, also originally from
Prestige. Zawinul's writing has always been anchored round a firm left hand; here, as on his
work with Ben Webster, he gives the music an unambiguous tonal centre, allowing Tommy
Potter a springier stance and freeing Forrest for some of his best solos on record.

***   **Most Much!** Original Jazz Classics OJC 350 CD/LP/MC
         Forrest; Hugh Lawson (*p*); Tommy Potter (*b*); Clarendon Johnson (*d*); Ray Barretto
         (*perc*). 10/61.

A fine set, restoring two tracks from the same session previously released only as part of *Soul
Street* on New Jazz. More than anything, *Most Much!* demonstrates what a developed time-feel
Forrest had. The first three tracks could hardly be more different in emphasis. 'Matilda' is a
traditional calypso, given a forceful reading, with the saxophonist closely backed by the unsung
Hugh Lawson. 'Annie Laurie' is similarly upbeat but seldom departs from the melody.
'Autumn Leaves' is full of glassy harmonies and a first taste of the curious rhythmic
displacements and imaginative harmonic inflexions that make him such a significant way-station
between bop and the New Thing. The closing 'Most Much' is a tough rocker, with strong
upper-register effects. The recording isn't really up to standard but, as usual, it's 'only' Tommy
Potter who suffers unduly.

FRANK FOSTER (born 1928)

TENOR AND SOPRANO SAX

*** **The House That Love Built** Steeplechase SCS 1170 CD/LP
Foster; Horace Parlan (*p*); Jesper Lundgaard (*b*); Aage Tanggaard (*d*). 9/82.

*** **Two For The Blues** Pablo 2310905 LP/MC
Foster; Frank Wess (*as, ts, f*); Kenny Barron (*p*); Rufus Reid (*b*); Marvin 'Smitty'
Smith (*d*). 10/83.

(*) **Frankly Speaking Concord CCD 4276 CD/LP/MC
As above. 12/84.

Although Frank Foster made his name with Count Basie's orchestra in the 1950s – and a less
bop-orientated band one couldn't wish to find – he had assimilated enough of the music of
Charlie Parker into his playing to make him stand out as a particularly vivid soloist in that
tightly integrated unit. Since he has assumed leadership of the Basie band following the Count's
death, small-group recording under his own name has recently taken a back seat. These three
sessions from the early 1980s are entertaining examples of Foster's mighty swing and
full-blooded improvising, yet the settings somehow don't demand enough of him to make him
give of his absolute best. Despite comprising mostly original material, the Steeplechase quartet
date emerges as much like any other modern tenor-plus-rhythm session, although 'I Remember
Sonny Stitt' is an imposing tribute to the then recently-departed saxophonist. The meetings with
Frank Wess, another Basie colleague, are rather carefully conceived, as if the players were
trying too hard to avoid the blowing clichés which sometimes dominate such records. The
title-track of *Two For The Blues* is a wonderfully swaggering way to start the record, but most
of the remaining tunes sound curtailed, although Foster gets off a bruising ballad feature in 'A
Time For Love'. Much the same thing happens on the Concord session, and here the studio
sound is too smooth and even to make the saxophones register with enough weight.

RONNIE FOSTER

KEYBOARDS, VOCALS

** **The Racer** Electric Bird K28P 6441 CD/LP
Foster; Mike O'Neal, Phil Upchurch (*g*); Harvey Mason, Ndugu (*d*); Paulinho Da
Costa (*perc*).

Undistinguished fusion from a technology addict who knows how to beat a good idea to death.
The settings and production are slick enough, but there's no real substance to the music.

TOMAS FRANCK (born 1958)

TENOR SAXOPHONE

*** **Tomas Franck In New York** Criss Cross Jazz Criss 1052 CD
Franck; Mulgrew Miller (*p*); Kenny Washington (*b*); Billy Drummond (*d*). 12/90.

A stalwart of the Danish Radio Big Band, Franck sounds much like many another hard-bop
tenorman, heavily in hock to Coltrane, Gordon and so forth. But it must be admitted that he has
the style down as well as most, and the prospect of recording this quartet date on a first trip to
New York seems to have held no terrors for him at all. Miller is his usual courteous and
thoughtful self, and Washington and Drummond keep good time. Four Franck originals suggest
nothing special in the way of composing, but he knows how to get the best out of himself as an
improviser: the long solo on the opening 'Triton' shows no lack of ideas. The playing time is a
little long, though, at 68 minutes.

FREE JAZZ QUARTET
GROUP

****   **Premonitions** Matchless MR18 CD
Paul Rutherford (*tb*); Harrison Smith (*ts, ss, bcl*); Tony Moore (*clo*); Eddie Prévost
(*d*). 7/89.

If the group's title is a wry reference to the Modern Jazz Quartet (see also Prévost's punning
Supersession), it takes in Ornette Coleman's seminal *Free Jazz* as well. The terminology is used
advisedly, for this superb recording is more obviously rooted in one of the dialects of post-bop
than, say, the process-dominated free improvisation of AMM. The underlying motif of
Premonitions is warning: 'Red Flags', 'Roman Geese', 'Gathering Clouds', 'Cry Wolf',
'Tocsin' and even 'Old Moore's' (an oblique reference to the trombonist's *Old Moore's
Almanack* album). The music is tense and often powerfully dramatic, strung along highly
attenuated motivic threads. Prévost's drumming is as good as he has ever been on record and
Rutherford is, as always, good enough to listen to on his own. Just as politically Prévost and his
circle have tended to reject the bland triumphalism of the doctrinaire left, so musically he
clearly rejects the anything-goes attitude that gives free improvisation a bad name. This is
intense and concentrated music. A warning: please do not 'understand' it too quickly.

BUD FREEMAN (1906–91)
TENOR SAXOPHONE, CLARINET

***   **The Bud Freeman All Stars** Original Jazz Classics OJC 183 LP
Freeman; Shorty Baker (*t*); Claude Hopkins (*p*); George Duvivier (*b*); J. C. Heard
(*d*). 5/60.

One far from exceptional recording from relatively late in his career (though he plugged on
right through the 1980s) is hardly an adequate trawl. Fortunately, it's a fine album. Freeman was
perhaps the first truly significant white tenor player. If he looked, and chose to behave, like the
secretary of some golf club in the Home Counties – episode one of his autobiography was called
You Don't Look Like A Musician – his saxophone walked all over the carpets in spikes, a rawer
sound than Lester Young's (to which it is often likened) and with a tougher articulation.

Freeman developed late, worked in some unpromising contexts, and ended up one of the
most distinctive tenorists of all time (and any colour). In 1960, he sounds confident, even
arrogant, sweeping through 'I Let A Song Go Out Of My Heart' and 'But Not For Me' with
consummate skill.

CHICO FREEMAN (born 1949)
TENOR SAXOPHONE, SOPRANO SAXOPHONE, BASS CLARINET, CLARINET, FLUTE

***   **Beyond The Rain** Original Jazz Classics OJC 479 CD/LP/MC
Freeman; Hilton Ruiz (*p*); Jooney Booth (*b*); Elvin Jones (*d*). 6/77.

***(*)   **Spirit Sensitive** India Navigation IN 1070 CD
Freeman; John Hicks (*p*); Jay Hoggard (*vib*); Cecil McBee (*b*); Billy Hart, Famoudou
Don Moye (*d*). 78.

***(*)   **No Time Left** Black Saint BSR 0036 CD/LP
Freeman; Jay Hoggard (*vib*); Rick Rozie (*b*); Famoudou Don Moye (*d*). 6/79.

****   **The Pied Piper** Black Hawk BKH 50801 CD/LP/MC
Freeman; John Purcell (*as, bs, ob, af, picc*); Kenny Kirkland, Mark Thompson (*p*);
Cecil McBee (*b*); Elvin Jones (*d*). 4/84.

***   **Tales Of Ellington** Black Hawk BKH 537 CD/LP
Freeman; Johnny Coles (*t*); John Purcell (*bs, as, cl*); George Cables, Mark Thompson
(*p*); Larry Willis (*syn*); Herbie Lewis, Cecil McBee (*b*); Elvin Jones, Eddie Moore,
Freddie Waits (*d*). 4/84, 6/85, 11/86, 3/87.

**   **You'll Know When You Get There** Black Saint BSR 0128 CD/LP
Freeman; Eddie E. J. Allen (*t, flhn*); Von Freeman (*ts, p*); Geri Allen (*p, ky*); Don
Pate (*b*); Victor Jones (*d*); Norman Hedman (*perc*); Joel Brandon (*whistling*). 8/88.

For a radical, Chico Freeman has a highly developed sense of tradition. In the late 1970s, when
most of his contemporaries were highly resistant to the notion, he recorded a set of standards
(*Spirit Sensitive*) and he has continually resorted to the tradition since then, often with a
strange, Doppler-shift effect that is also evident on two other India Navigation titles – *Chico*,
1034, and *The Search*, 1059 – which are intermittently available on vinyl. The Ellington album is
a fine and sensitive effort, with a reading of 'Sophisticated Lady' on unaccompanied tenor
saxophone to put alongside more conventional ensemble pieces.

Despite an impressive line-up that includes his father, Von Freeman, and Geri Allen, *You'll
Know . . .* is curiously muted. *Pied Piper*, on the other hand, is one of the essential jazz albums
of the 1980s, building on the foundation of the earlier sets. Not always the most rhythmically
subtle of players, Freeman leans heavily on Elvin Jones's powerful drumming. The range of
instrumentation is remarkable, with Freeman and Purcell calling on a dozen horns between
them; however, the effect is not bland versatility and virtuosity, but genuine musical
intelligence.

***   **Freeman & Freeman** India Navigation IN 1070 CD
Freeman; Von Freeman (*ts*); Muhal Richard Abrams, Kenny Barron, Cecil McBee (*b*);
Jack DeJohnette (*d*).

The family firm. The Freemans play well together, with Von's sliding tonalities closing the gap
between his more mainstream blues approach and Chico's pure-toned modernism. Their gruff
partnership on 'The Shadow Of Your Smile' invests a hokey tune with considerable dignity,
and 'I Can't Get Started' is an excellent performance from both. A fascinating band, held
together by DeJohnette's endlessly interesting figures and powerful surges; the two keyboard
men undertake a concise exercise in comparative pianistics, Chicago *v.* Philly, with Barron
coming out fractionally ahead on points.

**   **The Mystical Dreamer** In + Out 7006 CD/LP
Freeman; Brainstorm: Delmar Brown (*ky, v*); Chris Walker (*b, ky, v*); Archie Walker
(*d, ky*); Norman Hedman (*perc*). 5/89.

**   **Sweet Explosion** In + Out 7010 CD/LP
Freeman; Brainstorm: Delmar Brown (*ky, p, v*); Norman Hedman (*perc*); Alex Blake
(*b*); Tommy Campbell (*d*). 4/90.

For all his professed hostility to 'compromise' music, Freeman has long wiggled his toes in a
rather dismal funk idiom that gives his extraordinary talent precious little room for manoeuvre.
The Mystical Dreamer by his Brainstorm group has a refreshing crispness – and eye-catching
cover art. If Freeman is rather wasted, the synthesizer stabs and racketing percussion maintain
interest. The live performances that make up *Sweet Explosion* were recorded at Ronnie Scott's
club in London. There is a long version of 'On The Nile' from the first album, which gives
Freeman a chance to stretch out, but there is also a vocal track so banal as to defy description
or categorization and which makes 'I'll Be There' from *Mystical Dreamer* sound like
Winterreise.

RUSS FREEMAN (born 1926)
PIANO

***(*)   **Trio** Pacific Jazz CDP 746861 CD
Freeman; Joe Mondragon, Monty Budwig (*b*); Shelly Manne (*d*). 10/53–8/57.

Although Russ Freeman was among the most popular pianists in Los Angeles during the 1950s,
he seems to have had few ambitions as a leader, and the 12 tracks here (the remaining eight are
by Richard Twardzik) are among his very few recordings in this capacity (and even these were
originally recorded as makeweights at two Chet Baker sessions). With only three numbers
straying over three minutes in length, Freeman doesn't dawdle. He has a punchy, boppish style
that was grittier than some of his West Coast contemporaries, and his five original themes have
an epigrammatic feel – as if each were a snatch of an idea which Freeman tosses at us with a wry

insouciance. If never as original as Twardzik, his music is compelling in its offhand immediacy. Good sound for the period.

VON FREEMAN (born 1922)
TENOR SAXOPHONE

***   **Serenade And Blues** Chief CD 3 CD
Freeman; John Young (*p*); David Shipp (*b*); Wilbur Campbell (*d*). 6/75.

Opening with Glenn Miller quotes may be, as the fashion advisers say, 'very ageing', but Von Freeman has never been impressed by trends. While his son and fellow-tenorist Chico has explored sometimes baffling extremes of free jazz and neo-funk, Von Freeman has stuck with a curious down-home style that occasionally makes his saxophone sound as if it is held together with rubber bands and sealing wax. Stylistically it is closer to Ornette Coleman than to Lester Young (and it fitted quite seamlessly into Chico's band in the 1980s), but in the sense that Ornette is himself a maverick traditionalist.

Serenade And Blues is a relaxed and wholly untroubled set of standards, cut with a friendly rhythm section; the session was originally released, shorn of a track, on the parent Nessa as *Have No Fear*. It's also 15 years old; the decision to stay back in Chicago did nothing for Freeman's recording schedule. The best track – perhaps oddly, perhaps significantly – is the shortest. 'Time After Time', younger listeners, shouldn't be confused with the Cyndi Lauper weepie, transmogrified by Miles Davis. The Styne-Cahn classic actually has a tune.

'Von Freeman's Blues' and the strong closing 'I'll Close My Eyes' are, for now, the closest thing on record to a Freeman set at the Enterprise Lounge. In 1975.

FRENCH TOAST
GROUP

(*)   **French Toast Electric Bird K28P 6032 LP
Lew Soloff (*t*); Peter Gordon (*hrn*); Jerry Dodgion (*as*); Michel Camilo (*p*); Anthony Jackson (*b*); Steve Gadd or Dave Weckl (*d*); Sammy Figueroa, Gordon Gottlieb (*perc*). 4/84.

A jolly, unassuming record led by the good-natured Camilo and featuring Lew Soloff's huge trumpet range. The arrangements are quite subtle, with interesting parts for Gordon's horn on all but a couple of the tracks. No romantic agonies, no long God-bothering solos, just good contemporary jazz.

PAOLO FRESU
TRUMPET, FLUGELHORN

***   **Ostinato** Splasc(h) H 106 LP
Fresu; Tino Tracanna (*ss, ts*); Roberto Cipelli (*p*); Attilo Zanchi (*b*); Ettore Fioravanti (*d*). 1/85.

***   **Inner Voices** Splasc(h) H 110 CD/LP
As above, plus David Liebman (*ss, f*). 4/86.

***(*)   **Mamut: Music For A Mime** Splasc(h) H 127 LP
As above, except omit Liebman, add Mimmo Cafiero (*perc*). 11/85–5/86.

***   **Quatro** Splasc(h) H 160 CD/LP
As above, except omit Cafiero. 4–6/88.

***   **Live In Montpellier** Splasc(h) H 301 CD
As above. 7/88.

An outstanding exponent of the new Italian jazz, Fresu is in much demand as a sideman but his records as a leader offer the best views of his music. Fresu's quintet includes the agile Tracanna and the expert bassist Zanchi, and together they follow an energetic yet introspective kind of jazz that suggests a remote modern echo of an early Miles Davis group – the trumpeter does, indeed, sound like the Davis of the mid-1950s at times. Most of the time the resulting music is engaging rather than compelling: the soloists have more to say than the compositions, and although the group works together very sympathetically, the records never quite take off. Liebman is soon at home on the session he guests on; the live record from Montpellier is scrappy yet often more exciting than the others; and *Quatro* has some bright originals. *Mamut*, though, is the best of these records: although the programme is a collection of fragments for the theatre, the miniatures include some of Fresu's most vivid writing, and the title piece and 'Pa' are themes which hang in the memory. Fresu even finds something new to say on a solo reading of 'Round Midnight'.

DAVE FRIEDMAN (born 1944)
VIBES, MARIMBA

**   **Futures Passed** Enja 2068 LP
    Friedman; Pat Rebillot (*p*); Harvie Swartz (*b*); Bruce Ditmas (*d*); Rimona Francis (*v*). 1/76.

***   **Of The Wind's Eye** Enja 3089 LP
    Friedman; Jane Ira Bloom (*ss*); Harvie Swartz (*b*); Daniel Humair (*d*). 7/81.

(*)   **Shades Of Change Enja 5017 CD/LP
    Friedman; Geri Allen (*p*); Anthony Cox (*b*); Ronnie Burrage (*d*). 4/86.

Friedman's methods are unusual among vibes players in that he seems as interested in the percussive and rhythmic qualities of the instrument as he is in harmony and melody. He also uses the marimba as often as he does the vibraphone. It adds up to a purposeful style that deglamourizes the often shallow prettiness which the vibes can settle into, although Friedman's own romantic streak can allow his playing to meander to nowhere in particular.

His work as a leader in the 1970s and '80s – he also co-led the group Double Image with Dave Samuels – is interesting rather than especially memorable. The first Enja session provides little more than bright cocktail music, but the second, *Of The Wind's Eye*, is probably his best single record. The quartet respond well to the programme, with Humair outstandingly vivid on 'A Swiss Celebration' and Bloom in piquant form. There's a brisk reading of Monk's 'Four In One' and a couple of thoughtful originals in 'Fonque' and 'For Now'.

Allen, Cox and Burrage are a close-knit trio, and Friedman sounds as if he's decorating their lines rather than integrating with them on the 1986 session: tonally this is a rather bland group, although the Enja recording is as resonant as usual.

BILL FRISELL (born 1951)
GUITAR, ELECTRIC GUITAR, BANJO, GUITAR SYNTHESIZER, EFFECTS

***(*)   **In Line** ECM 1241 LP
    Frisell; Arild Andersen (*b*). 8/82.

***   **Smash And Scatteration** Minor Music 005 CD/LP
    Frisell; Vernon Reid (*g, syn*); duos, solos. 12/84.

There are always murmurs of 'Hendrix, Hendrix' whenever a new electric guitarist of more than modest inventiveness hits the scene, and they're usually inaccurate. However warmly he may have responded to Jimi Hendrix as an example, Bill Frisell's playing is much closer to Frank Zappa's licks-based and treatment-heavy style. However concerned he appears to be with textures, Frisell concentrates on the exact figuration of brief but often quite complex melodic shapes, out of which a whole piece grows. With repeated hearings, it is these shapes that insist.

The process is more evident on the solo album, which is the best place to start. The basic ideas could be jotted down on a couple of sides of stave paper, but the developments open up whole ranges of musical language; the best track, 'Throughout', so appealed to the British composer, Gavin Bryars, that he turned it into an atmospheric concert-piece called 'Sub Rosa'. For the most part, though, Frisell's free modal themes are geared to open improvisation. Paired with Vernon Reid (with whom the 'Hendrix' labels make a deal of sense), he sounds brawnier and the ideas, presumably cooked up quickly for the session, are left just on the raw side of underdone. Good cross-over appeal, though; Living Color fans might take note.

*** **Rambler** ECM 1287 CD/LP
Frisell; Kenny Wheeler (*t, c, flhn*); Bob Stewart (*tba*); Jerome Harris (*b*); Paul Motian (*d*). 8/84.

***(*) **Lookout For Hope** ECM 1351 CD/LP
Frisell; Hank Roberts (*clo, v*); Kermit Driscoll (*b*); Joey Baron (*d*). 3/87.

*** **Before We Were Born** Elektra Musician 960843 CD/LP
Frisell; Billy Drewers, Julius Hemphill (*as*); Doug Wieselman (bs); Arto Lindsay (*g, v*); Peter Scherer (*ky*); Hank Roberts (*clo, v*); Kermit Driscoll (*b*); Joey Baron (*d, perc*); Cyro Baptista (*perc*);

*** **Is That You?** Elektra Musician 960956 CD
Frisell; Dave Hofstra (*t, tba*); Wayne Horvitz (*ky, b*); Joey Baron (*d*). 8/89.

(*) **Where In The World? Elektra Nonesuch 7559 61181 CD
As above. 91.

Rambler doesn't succeed at every level – it has a disconcertingly soft centre – but it is a beautifully structured album with a fascinating instrumental blend. Frisell's experiments in that direction continue with *Lookout For Hope*, his best album to date. Rough samples of a wide variety of styles (including a previously unexploited enthusiasm for Country and Western) recall the emergence of Larry Coryell, but where Coryell was a quick-change artiste rather than a genuine synthesizer, Frisell boils every resource down to usable basics. His is a completely individual voice, without a hint of pastiche.

Until, that is, *Where In The World?* which, despite an identical line-up, sounds curiously self-absorbed and anything but interactive. All the usual infusion of country and folk themes (though these are turned head over heels on 'Rob Roy'), bludgeoning blues and abstractionist devices, but there's a polymorophous New Age quality to much of the music that from a player of Frisell's gifts seems downright perverse.

It worked better on *Is That You?*, which was a rather self-conscious dive down into the guitarist's roots, taking in country trashings, big generous sweeps of abstract sound, jazz and free structures. The programming is almost as random as that on Frisell's Elektra debut, *Before We Were Born*, which gives his gentle eclecticism and occasional bad-boy tantrums an almost postmodern sheen. The second album might just as well have been a solo set, so incidental does the 'band' appear; the musicians are better used on *Born*, if only because Lindsay's contributions are so utterly no-shit and apposite. The switch of labels doesn't seem to have done the guitarist any non-fiscal favours. ECM's occasionally absolutist purity constrained him very little; Elektra's market trufflings are, on this showing, doing him no good at all.

*(*) **Works** ECM 8372732/1 CD/LP
Frisell; various line-ups.

Premature, and by no means adequately representative.

DAVID FRISHBERG (born 1933)
PIANO, VOCAL

**** **Classics** Concord CCD 4462 CD
Frishberg; Steve Gilmore (*b*); Bill Goodwin (*d*). 12/82–3/83.

***(*) **Live At Vine Street** Fantasy F 9638 LP/MC
Frishberg (*p* solo). 10/84.

*** **Can't Take You Nowhere** Fantasy F 9651 CD/LP/MC
Frishberg (*p* solo). 87.

*** **Let's Eat Home** Concord CCD 4402 CD/MC
Frishberg; Snooky Young (*t*); Rob McConnell (*vtb*); Jim Hughart (*b*); Jeff Hamilton (*d*). 1/89.

Although Frishberg himself notes that a supply sergeant once told him that 'Jazz is OK, but it ain't got no words', he has done his best to deliver hip songwriting in a form that fits with his individual brand of mainstream piano. If he's become best known as a cabaret recitalist, Frishberg nevertheless has a strong, swinging keyboard style that borrows from the swing masters without making him seem like a slavish copyist. He has worked extensively as a sideman and seems most suited to swing-styled groups with enough space for him to let loose his favourite, rolling, two-fisted solos. Of those recordings under his own name currently in print, *Classics* is the best, since it gathers all his best-known songs together on a single CD (which is a reissue of two LPs made for Omnisound). Sparsely but crisply presented by the trio, here are the prototype versions of such Frishberg favourites as 'My Attorney Bernie', 'Dodger Blue' and 'Do You Miss New York?', bittersweet odes which he is very good at investing with both warmth and wryness. The sound has been dried out by CD remastering but isn't disagreeable.

The *Vine Street* set is a characteristic example of one of his live shows, including 'Blizzard Of Lies' and 'The Dear Departed Past', notebooks of Americana. They're sung in a small and cracking voice which somehow suits them well; and there is an eight-minute medley of Johnny Hodges tunes which shows off his piano expertise. *Can't Take You Nowhere* is mostly more of the same, as is the recent Concord set, although the horns are more of a distraction than a bonus. The spotlight is best left on Frishberg on his own records.

TONY FRUSCELLA (1927–69)
TRUMPET

**   **Debut** Spotlite SPJ 126 LP
       Fruscella; Chick Maures (*as*); Bill Triglia (*p*); Red Mitchell, Teddy Kotick (*b*); Dave
       Troy, Art Mardigan (*d*). 12/48–53.

**   **Fru 'N Brew** Spotlite SPJ 126 LP
       Fruscella; Brew Moore (*ts*); Bill Triglia (*p*); Teddy Kotick (*b*); Art Mardigan (*d*). 53.

Despite a formidable reputation among some collectors, Fruscella has remained an obscure figure and, of his very few recordings, these don't show him in a very flattering light. The studio session on the first side of *Debut* was never released until 1981, and it's also the only recording by altoist Chick Maures. Together they make a pale and winsome front line, Fruscella hinting at the directions Chet Baker would take, and the carefully spun solos have some idiomatic charm – bop on a very cool day. But the wan rhythms let the music down. The session with Moore, which dates from a similar vintage to the second side of the earlier Spotlite LP, is an interesting glimpse of minor-league bebop in its day, but the hesitations and plain fumbling which affect much of the music – attributed to alcohol by the sleeve-notes – make for painful listening, and the sound is bootleg-quality. Fruscella made one decent record for Atlantic which has yet to be reissued. He died a melancholy death, many years wasted through addiction.

WOLFGANG FUCHS
SOPRANINO SAX, CLARINET, BASS CLARINET, CONTRABASS CLARINET

(*)   **Momente FMP 0610 LP
       Fuchs; Hans Schneider (*b*); Klaus Huber (*d*). 10/78.

(*)   **FinkFarker FMP CD 26 CD
       Fuchs; Georg Katzer (*elec*). 6/89.

Fuchs is an improviser who's especially interested – as his choice of instruments suggests – in timbral extremes. He gets squalling, hysterical sounds out of the sopranino and the clarinet, phrases diced into the smallest fragments, and, while one can construe lines out of the sonic splinters, deconstruction is Fuchs's speciality. *Momente* has sympathetic partners in Schneider and Huber, but the brief, rhythmically static improvisations build and never release tension, and it's a frustrating music to hear. *FinkFarker* operates across wider soundscapes, the reed player combating Katzer's electronics in pieces entitled 'Vicious', 'Confrontation' and so on. Interesting but rarefied: Fuchs works best with more challenging partners, such as Fred Van Hove (on the two 'Berliner Begegnug' albums) and Evan Parker on FMP's *Duets*.

CURTIS FULLER (born 1934)
TROMBONE

**   **New Trombone** Original Jazz Classics OJC 077 LP
     Fuller; Sonny Red (*as*); Hank Jones (*p*); Doug Watkins (*b*); Louis Hayes (*d*). 5/57.

***   **Blues-ette** Savoy SV 0127 CD
     Fuller; Benny Golson (*ts*); Tommy Flanagan (*p*); Jimmy Garrison (*b*); Al Harewood
     (*d*). 5/59.

Curtis Fuller made his mark on one of the most memorable intros in modern jazz, the opening
bars of Coltrane's 'Blue Train', and, for many, the story stops there. Fuller's contribution to
that rather over-rated album was well below par. Possessed of an excellent technique, if slightly
derivative of J. J. Johnson, he occasionally found it difficult to develop ideas at speed and
tended to lapse back (as on 'Blue Train') into either repetition or sequences of bitten-off
phrases that sounded either diffident or aggressive, depending on the context.

    Blues-ette is far and away his finest available album (three good Blue Notes are currently
missing in action). Fuller sounds much more confident than on the early – and honestly titled –
New Trombone, which has promise rather than finish. Golson is a strong and supportive player
and Flanagan's quick fills more than make up for any residual shortcomings in the longer solos.

***   **The Curtis Fuller Jazztet** Savoy SV 0134 CD
     Fuller; Lee Morgan (*tb*); Benny Golson (*ts*); Wynton Kelly (*p*); Paul Chambers (*b*);
     Charlie Persip (*d*). 8/59.

***   **Imagination** Savoy SL 0128 CD
     Fuller; Thad Jones (*t*); Benny Golson (*ts*); McCoy Tyner (*p*); Jimmy Garrison (*b*);
     Dave Bailey (*d*). 12/59.

***   **Images of Curtis Fuller** Savoy SL 0129 CD
     Fuller; Wilbur Harden, Lee Morgan (*t*); Yusef Lateef (*ts, fl*); McCoy Tyner (*p*);
     Jimmy Garrison, Milt Hinton (*b*); Bobby Donaldson, Clifford Jarvis (*d*). 6/60.

For those familiar with Fuller's work on *Blue Train*, his introductory solo on 'Accident', first
track on *Images*, will strike an immediate chord. Its big, vocalized blues tonalities are typical of
his work of the period, and these reissues (along with *Blues-ette*) represent the trombonist's
most coherent and successful playing. Golson is a particularly sympathetic partner, as are the
trumpeters, and Lateef produces a beautiful intro and solo on flute (not credited on the
re-packaging) to 'Darryl's Minor'.

    What emerges most strongly from these albums is the strength and individuality of the
trombonist's writing. Numbers such as the mysterious 'Lido Road' (*Imagination*) and the
impressionistic 'Arabia' (*Jazztet*) bespeak a remarkable talent. The remasterings are rather
'dead' and unresonant, but in that regard do little more than reproduce the shortcomings of the
original releases, which completely lacked the vibrancy one associates with Blue Note. The
liner-notes – with original art-work included – are unreliable and occasionally inconsistent.

**   **Four On The Outside** Timeless SJP 124 CD
     Fuller; Pepper Adams (*bs*); James Williams (*p*); Dennis Irwin (*b*); John Yarling (*d*).
     9/78.

(*)   **Meets Roma Jazz Trio Timeless SJP 204 CD/LP
     Fuller; Danilo Rea (*p*); Enzo Pietropaoli (*b*); Roberto Gatto (*d*). 12/82.

Fuller's career drifted into the doldrums after the mid-1960s and took some time to recover.
Though the band is unexceptionable, *Four On The Outside* is curiously uncommunicative and
Fuller's normally reliable medium blues phrasing sounds slightly off. The later Italian job is
really much more interesting; Fuller has a lot of time to play with and judges his solo passages
with greater ease.

JOHN FUMO
TRUMPET

**   **After The Fact** Nine Winds 0116 LP
         Fumo; Dan Fornero, Sal Cracchiolo, Dave Norman (*t*); Fred Simmons, Claude Cailliet
         (*tb*); Wayne Peet (*ky*); Nels Cline (*g*); Steubig (*b*); Chris Mancinelli (*d*); Rudy
         Regalado, Mitchito Sanchez (*perc*). 7/86.

A surprising record to emerge from the normally demanding Nine Winds operation, this is a
rock-based fusion band with Fumo's trumpet as its principal voice. The best piece, 'Reveal', sets
his high, clear sound against a sparse and slow rhythm with suitable interjections from Cline
and Peet; but most of the record gets impaled on Mancinelli's plodding rock beat, and themes
such as 'Body Wrap' sound as if they date from the late 1970s rather than 1986. Fumo's
limitations are apparent enough: he has a nice sound but has little to say as an improviser. The
extra horns appear on two tracks only.

JOEL FUTTERMAN
PIANO

*(*)   **Moments** Ear-Rational 882 456 909 CD
         Futterman; Jimmy Lyons (*as*); Karen Borca (*bsn*); Robert Adkins (*d*). 7/81–6/83.

**   **In-Between Positions** Bellaphon 45018 CD
         As above, except omit Borca. 5/82.

**   **Inner Conversations** Ear-Rational 1019 CD
         Futterman; Jimmy Lyons (*as*); Richard Davis (*b*); Robert Adkins (*d*). 10/84–6/88.

Energy music without a centre. It might seem unjust to align Futterman with Cecil Taylor, but
he does almost beg the comparison. Over three very long tracks on *Moments* he duets with
Adkins much as Taylor duels with his drummers, and inviting Lyons to arrive for the 34-minute
'Future State' suggests a pointless duplication of the senior pianist's approach. Futterman
resembles Taylor at half-speed, though: if his rate of execution isn't so far behind Cecil's, he
articulates and develops ideas at about half the rate of velocity which Taylor treats as normal.
Lyons and Borca are both somewhat remote in the sound-mix and, if they sound committed
enough, there's little here which isn't better revealed by Taylor's music. *In-Between Positions* is
superior, if only because of better studio sound, and *Inner Conversations* offers both a solo set
by the pianist and a quartet date with Lyons, Davis and Adkins. But the feeling remains that
Futterman is using a powerful technique to no particular ends and, though any opportunity to
hear Lyons is welcome, these are more like elevated blowing sessions than constructive
encounters.

STEVE GADD (born 1945)
DRUMS

***   **Gaddabout** Electric Bird K28P 6314 CD/LP
         Gadd; Lew Soloff (*t*); George Young (*ss, ts*); Ronnie Cuber (*bs*); Richard Tee (*ky*);
         Jeff Mironov (*g*); Neil Jason (*b*). 7/84.

Gadd's breathtaking virtuosity at the kit might have placed him in the vanguard of
contemporary jazz drummers, but he has seldom appeared in straight-ahead jazz situations; his
most public work has come as a session drummer in rock contexts and with fusion-orientated
groups, where his penchant for kinetic energy finds its most natural release. His principal
trademarks – an exacting precision of line, discernible even at the fastest tempos, and a linear
approach to the individual drums – are integral to a style that is somehow superabundant in
technique without seeming too flashy.

     He is not, however, a particularly distinctive leader and has seldom recorded in this capacity.
The Electric Bird session matches him with some of his colleagues from the Manhattan Jazz
Quintet plus a lite-fusion rhythm section for a spry series of workouts, hard bop horns grafted

on to the taut pulse of players more accustomed to rock. It's lively enough, and brightly recorded.

SLIM GAILLARD (1916–90)
PIANO, GUITAR, VOCAL

** **Slim And Slam – Volume 1** Tax m 8028 LP
Gaillard; Slam Stewart (*b, v*); various line-ups. 1938–41.

** **Slim And Slam – Volume 2** Tax m 8043 LP
As above.

** **Slim And Slam – Volume 3** Tax m 8044 LP
As above.

(*) **Original 1938 Recordings – Volume 1 Tax S 1-2 CD
As above.

(*) **Original 1938–9 Recordings – Volume 2 Tax S 2-2 CD
As above.

*** **The Legendary McVouty** Hep CD 6 CD
Gaillard; Jay Thomas (*t*); Digby Fairweather (*co*); Buddy Tate, Jay Thomas (*ts*); Jay McShann (*p*); Peter Ind (*b*); Alan Ganley (*d*). 10/82.

Gaillard must be the only jazz musician ever quoted in public by Ronald Reagan. Which gives Democrats an easy out. Gaillard's presence on the Savoy Parkers makes it harder for the purists, much as they may prefer, to ignore him. An element of sheer capriciousness – verbal, musical, personal – was always at the heart of the bebop movement and the hipster lifestyle it purported to distil and reflect. Gaillard was probably the last and most unreconstructed survivor of that era, a reminder of its lighter side. His brand of humour, centred largely on a hip dialect known as 'vout', either tickles you or it doesn't, but it's hard to maintain reserve in the face of 'Laughin' In Rhythm', and it's clear that Gaillard's more purely musical output, and particularly the highly popular sessions with Slam Stewart, deserve and have recently received a posthumous rethink.

The 1982 Hep sessions reintroduced Gaillard to a younger audience. His energy is extraordinary and his mind constantly, laterally inventive. His mainly British sidemen (Gaillard eventually settled in London) are not too po-faced about the whole thing, and it chugs along splendidly. The Tax CDs are identical with the earlier LP, *Slim And Slam*, give or take an alternate take-oroonie, but they stop short at the end of 1939, excluding such delights as 'Sploghm' and 'Hit That Mess'. You picks your licks.

RICCARDO GALARDINI
GUITAR

*** **Insolitudine** Splasc(h) H 155 LP
Galardini; Klaus Lessmann (*ss, ts, cl*); Carlo Morena (*p*). 4/88.

An unambitious yet peculiarly satisfying trio session. The ten themes – all originals, save for 'Some Other Time' – offer simple, folk-like frameworks for rather quiet and tidy solos, yet the pleasing empathy among the musicians is uncommonly graceful and uplifting. Lessmann is a thick-toned saxophonist whose parts never overwhelm the Italianate textures blended by Galardini and Morena, and the charming tunes are shared among the trio in terms of composer credits. A surprising and delightful discovery. The dry recording and very close miking may not be to everyone's taste, but it tends to enhance the sense of eavesdropping on some private music-making.

LARRY GALES (born 1936)
BASS, VOCAL

**(*)   A Message From Monk Candid CCD 79503 CD
Gales; Claudio Roditi (*t*); Steve Turre (*tb*); Junior Cook (*ts*); Benny Green (*p*); Ben Riley (*d*). 6/90.

There could hardly be a more appropriate rhythm section for a tribute to Monk than this one, since both Gales and Riley were veterans from the master's own quartet. It's a pity, then, that this otherwise quite spirited set, recorded live at New York's Birdland, has a few crucial failings. Cook in particular sounds tired and ill-prepared, and yet he is the most featured of the horns: 'Off Minor' and 'Ruby My Dear' sound ragged as a result. Turre is easily the most characterful soloist, with pungent improvisations on 'Straight No Chaser' and the one Gales original, 'A Message From The High Priest'; and Roditi takes some pleasing risks on the latter tune, too. Green tries to work his way out of seeming like the Monk substitute and does well enough, and Gales and Riley play dependably; but Larry's vocal on ''Round Midnight' wasn't the best idea in the world. The location recording is well managed.

HAL GALPER (born 1938)
PIANO, KEYBOARDS

***(*)   Reach Out Steeplechase 1067 CD/LP
Galper; Randy Brecker (*t*); Mike Brecker (*ts, f*); Wayne Dockery (*b*); Billy Hart (*d*). 11/76.

***   Speak With A Single Voice Enja 4006 LP
As above, except Bob Moses (*d*) replaces Hart. 2/78.

***   Now Hear This Enja 2090 LP
Galper; Terumasa Hino (*t, flhn*); Cecil McBee (*b*); Tony Williams (*d*). 2/77.

Reach Out is a vivid, hard-hitting set. The Brecker brothers have seldom combined so effectively under anyone else's leadership, and the arrangements are razor-fine. The later *Speak With A Single Voice* lacks tension and sounds slightly slack on vinyl. Though Hino is a limited soloist with a narrow improvisational range, McBee and Williams lift *Now Hear This* all on their own.

**(*)   Ivory Forest Enja 3053 CD/LP
Galper; John Scofield (*g*); Wayne Dockery (*b*); Adam Nussbaum (*d*). 10–11/79.

The star of this fine set is Scofield, who plays a brilliant, unaccompanied 'Monk's Mood'. Galper plays a duo with the guitarist ('Continuity') and with Dockery ('Yellow Days'), and there are three strong quartet tracks.

***   Naturally Black Hawk BKH 529 CD/LP
Galper; Rufus Reid (*b*); Victor Lewis (*d*). 1/82.

**(*)   Dreamsville Enja 5029 LP
Galper; Steve Gilmore (*b*); Bill Goodwin (*d*). 3/86.

****   Portrait Concord CJ 383 CD/LP/MC
Galper; Ray Drummond (*b*); Billy Hart (*d*). 2/89.

**(*)   Live At Maybeck Recital Hall Concord CCD 4438 CD/MC
Galper (*p* solo). 7/90.

Galper's wide, sweeping keyboard style needs bass and drums to salt a touch of sugariness that creeps in from time to time. The solo Maybeck Hall set is unusually self-sufficient in this regard. Galper's touch is exact; the ideas come unimpeded but rarely glibly. There is, though, a lack of any real drama, and the set doesn't repay repeated hearings.

Of the trios, *Naturally* and *Portrait* stand out, the latter for a wonderfully profound 'Giant Steps' that rivals 'Tommy Flanagan''s, the earlier for a beautiful 'Star Eyes' and an energetic 'Hi Fly'. The Randy Weston tune is also worked over on *Dreamsville*, but the drummer sounds slightly off and the vinyl-only format is a bit lacking in resonance and bounce.

For anyone unfamiliar with Galper's work, *Portrait*, *Reach Out* and a duo recorded under Lee Konitz's name (Steeplechase 1057) are the ideal starting-points.

GANELIN TRIO
GROUP

***** **Catalogue: Live In East Germany** Leo LR 102 LP
Vyacheslav Ganelin (*p, basset, g, perc*); Vladimir Chekasin (*as, ts, basset cl, cl, ob, v, perc*); Vladimir Tarasov (*d, perc*). 77–82.

**** **Poco A Poco** Leo CD LR 101 CD
As above.

*** **Ancora Da Capo: Part 1** Leo LR 108 LP
As above.

*** **Ancora Da Capo: Part 2** Leo LR 109 LP
As above.

***(*) **New Wine** ... Leo LR 112 LP
As above.

***(*) **Con Affetto** Leo LR 137 LP
As above.

***(*) **Non Troppo** hat Art CD 6059 CD
As above.

One of the genuinely significant moments in recent jazz history occurred on March 1984 at the Bloomsbury Theatre in London, when the Ganelin Trio, an improvising group from the Soviet Union played a concert organized under the auspices of the Arts Council Contemporary Music Network and attended by an unprecedented claque of musicians (whose expectations were, in the event, confounded and disappointed), arts administrators, journalists and mysterious raincoats from the Soviet Embassy. The Ganelin Trio's work was already known in Britain through the good offices of Leo Feigin, who had released smuggled tapes of the group on his Leo Records, and acquired a certain *samizdat* mystique which almost outweighed the impact of what was certainly the most dramatic development in jazz performance since the New Thing of the 1960s.

The Trio had been performing together for nearly thirteen years when the London performance took place but had only received Soviet release in 1976, following a successful appearance at the Jazz Jamboree in Warsaw. *Con Anima* was the fifth of the Trio's suites, all of them bearing similarly neutral titles mostly drawn from classical music performance but developed in a way which diverges sharply both from orthodox 'classical' performance and from the surprisingly restrictive conventions of jazz. In the first place, it is clear that underlying the work of the Ganelin Trio – as of Sergey Kuryokhin and other Russian musicians released by Leo Feigin – is a strong element of theatricality, a tradition of licensed foolery that (carried to pretty severe lengths it has to be admitted) alienated much of the audience at the Bloomsbury Theatre in 1984. Chekasin's outbursts of lunacy and Tarasov's deliberately undynamic drumming opened the Trio to charges of wilful perversity and aesthetic nihilism that are wholly contradicted by the body of music now available on record, which is densely structured (though not according to orthodox Western principles) and expressive.

For all its evident dependence on bebop as a basic musical language, the Ganelin Trio is probably closer in spirit to the multi-instrumentalism and competitively tinged collectivism of the earliest jazz groups. There are, though, obvious parallels with figures such as Rahsaan Roland Kirk (Chekasin has adopted the simultaneous performance of two horns as a stage ... ...emble of Chicago, and even the Dave Brubeck Quartet (whose 'classical' ... impact on Soviet jazz fans). What one sees in a Trio performance is an ... history of jazz compressed into brief spans, each of which relates to the ... process. Its apparent freedoms are relatively circumscribed and the group ... ded performances as expositions of a composed work rather than ... ; there are now alternative performance recordings of several important ... er understanding of the group's working methods.

The first of Feigin's Ganelin Trio releases was the very important *Catalogue*, created in 1981 as a summation of their first decade. This is one of the very important jazz records of recent times, even despite the inadequacies of the recording; it was brought to the West clandestinely and released with a disclaimer intended to protect the Trio from any association with a Western recording. The piece is performed in a continuous cycle and alternates quiet, remarkably formal sections using what sounds like a formal, serial construction and only occasional eruptions of improvisational frenzy, with intense outbursts of sound in which Chekasin's saxophone is the main component. Like almost all the Trio's work, and most notably 'Non Troppo' (see *New Wine* and the hat Art CD for significant performances), the music is dark and almost tragic and makes only a very specialized use of the traditional theme and variation format of jazz performance.

This technique *does*, however, play an important part in the second parts of both 'Non Troppo' and 'Ancora Da Capo', both of them profoundly healing pieces in which the presentation of a melodic theme (in the case of 'Non Troppo' a standard, 'Too Close For Comfort') is seen as the culmination rather than the starting point of performance and may even have been done as a slap in the face of critics who criticized the group for their 'inability' to play standards-derived jazz. 'Non Troppo' was also the basis of the 1984 Bloomsbury performace (a second piece, entitled 'Old Bottles' and related to 'New Wine' from the concert is available on Leo's encyclopaedic *Document: New Music From Russia – The 80s*, see below under Various Artists). It's a sombre, mournful piece, marked by notably desolate playing from Ganelin and some remarkably restrained work by Chekasin. Its dynamism, like that of 'Ancora Da Capo' and the minutely detailed 'Concerto Grosso', is intellectual rather than metrical and this is certainly one of the sticking points in appreciation of the Trio's music. Tarasov's drumming, which hits an occasional groove on *Con Affetto*, is much more usually rhythmically static and unpropulsive. There is no conventional bass either, though Ganelin makes very individual use of the basset. This is not to be confused with the basset-horn or basset-clarinet, played by Chekasin; it is in fact a small keyboard instrument which mimics the sound of a double bass, but which lacks the rhythymic bounce that a string bass has, giving the Trio's 'bass line' a curiously lifeless initial impact that requires to be unpacked and rethought for listeners weaned on jazz bass.

In purely instrumental terms, the group probably never again reached the heights of *Catalogue: Live In East Germany*, where Chekasin's saxophone and bass clarinet playing is stunning. One doesn't want to draw attention and recognition away from Leo Feigin's achievement in bringing this music to the West, but hat Art's *Non Troppo* CD was a major technical step forward, containing both parts of both 'Ancora Da Capo' (issued separately by Leo) and 'Non Troppo' (which is certainly the Trio's most significant single suite). Anyone interested in this remarkable music should certainly also be directed to three currently deleted items on Leo [*Con Fuoco*, LR 106, *Vide* LR 117, *Strictly For Our Friends*, LR 120, *Baltic Triangle*, LR 125, all LP] and to associated items such as *Inverso* (Leo LR 140) which pairs Vyacheslav Ganelin with the saxophonist Pyatras Vishnyauskas, and the relatively explanatory *1 + 1 = 3* (Leo 160 LP), recorded by Chekasin and Tarasov alone at Le Mans, and *3 − 1 = 3* (Leo LR 410/411 2LP), a set of Ganelin duos. Both reflect the breakdown of the original trio . . .

***   **Jerusalem February Cantabile** Leo LR 168 LP
Vyacheslav Ganelin (*p, f, syn, gamelan*); Victor Fonarev (*b, clo, gamelan*); Mika Markovich (*d*). 2/89.

***(*)   **Opuses** Leo CD LR 171 CD
As above, except add Uri Abramovitch (*v*). 12/89.

In the mid-1980s, 'Slava' Ganelin defected to the West and took up residence in Israel. The music from this period is markedly different from the predominantly tragic and highly theatrical music of the original Trio. It is austere, sometimes to the point of frostiness, a development that is perhaps reflected in Ganelin's acquisition of a synthesizer, which he utilizes with notable restraint and to largely abstract effect. The singing tones of 'Cantabile' and 'Cantus', Opus 3 of the excellent CD are immediately less alien than any of the Russian-period pieces and a certain tension seems to have gone out of the music (in keeping, perhaps, with Sergey Kuryokhin's view that the lifting of cultural repression in the Soviet Union was a mixed blessing from a purely artistic point of view). On their own terms, though, these are both beautiful records and some of the playing on *Opuses* equals anything in the earlier catalogue. If *Catalogue*, *New Wine* or *Non Troppo* remain impenetrable, it is probably worth trying the CD, which has a user-friendliness that one doesn't find on the earlier material. It lacks the humour, too, unfortunately, but that is one of the prices one pays for freedom.

JAN GARBAREK (born 1947)
TENOR SAXOPHONE, SOPRANO SAXOPHONE, BASS SAXOPHONE, FLUTES, KEYBOARDS, PERCUSSION

***(*)   **Afric Pepperbird** ECM 1007 CD/LP
Garbarek; Terje Rypdal (*g, bugle*); Arild Andersen (*b*); Jon Christensen (*d*). 9/70.

(*)   **Sart ECM 1015 CD
As above, except add Bobo Stenson (*p*). 4/71.

Jan Garbarek's high, keening saxophone is perhaps the most readily universalized instrumental sound in contemporary music, regularly pressed into service on documentary soundtracks to evoke almost anything from the Chernobyl-blighted Lappish tundra to the African desert.

Afric Pepperbird was an astonishing label debut. By far his most 'out' recording, it exposes Garbarek's early Coltrane obsession at its most extreme, but also as it collides with other influences, notably Ayler's multiphonic intensity and Dexter Gordon's phrasing; his flute has a thin, folky timbre that is particularly effective when overblown. The rhythm partnership of Andersen and Christensen was hard to beat at the time (though Eberhard Weber and Palle Danielsson became the bassists of choice in future), and Rypdal's abstract, unmetrical chime-chords are more or less perfect. Production, as with virtually all that follows, can't be faulted.

Sart suffers considerably by comparison. On its own terms, it's a strong set. Garbarek again uses flute and bass saxophone in addition to his more familiar tenor (but at this stage, not the Wayne Shorter-inspired soprano that was to make such an impact on *Dansere* and *Dis*).

**   **Red Lanta** ECM 1038 CD/LP
Garbarek; Art Lande (*p*). 11/73.

Garbarek's least-known ECM recording is an odd, dimly speculative affair that seems to go in no particular direction. Lande's keyboard style is quite abstract and only intermittently effective.

(*)   **Witchi-Tai-To ECM 1041 CD/LP
Garbarek; Bobo Stenson (*p*); Palle Danielsson (*b*); Jon Christensen (*d*). 11/73.

(*)   **Dansere ECM 1075 / 8291932 CD/LP
As above. 11/75.

Recorded at the same time as *Red Lanta*, *Witchi-Tai-To* is a more satisfactory album in almost every respect. Garbarek's intonation is much more relaxed, with a less pressurized embouchure and more sense of playing in distinct breath-groups or verses. Jim Pepper's surprise hit makes an appealing centre-piece to the album.

Dansere is as much Stenson's album as Garbarek's, and it would be good to hear more of the trio, which moves restlessly and often out of metre under some of Garbarek's most plaintive lines.

**   **Luminessence** ECM 1049 CD/LP
Garbarek; strings of the Sudfunk Symphony Orchestra. 7/74.

Logical in label – if not artistic – terms that Garbarek should attempt something of the sort at this point in his career. Keith Jarrett's scoring is quite beautiful but, on repeated hearings, completely one-dimensional. By no means a vital item in the Garbarek canon.

****   **Belonging** ECM 1050 CD/LP/MC
Garbarek; Keith Jarrett (*p*); Palle Danielsson (*b*); Jon Christensen (*d*). 4/74.

***(*)   **My Song** ECM 1115 CD/LP/MC
As above. 11/77.

Though ludicrously overpraised by Ian Carr in his biography of Keith Jarrett, *Belonging* is still one of the finest albums of the 1970s and contributed no little in helping to bring a rock-weaned audience around to jazz. Jarrett plays with superb control throughout this and *My Song* and Garbarek, restricting himself to tenor and soprano saxophones, plays some of his most directly enunciated solos, proof – if such were needed – that he was capable of playing within the broader Euro-American jazz tradition, and not just off on his nomadic own. (Both these albums are more properly credited to Keith Jarrett and can also be found under his heading.) Needless to add, both are strongly recommended.

***   **Dis** ECM 1093 CD/LP
        Garbarek; Ralph Towner (*g, 12 str g*); wind harp; brass sextet. 12/76.

***   **Places** ECM 1118 CD/LP
        Garbarek; Bill Connors (*g*); John Taylor (*org*); Jack DeJohnette (*d*). 12/77.

(*)   **Photo With Blue Sky ECM 1135 CD
        Garbarek; Bill Connors (*g*); Eberhard Weber (*b*); Jon Christensen (*d*). 12/78.

(*)   **Eventyr ECM 1200 CD/LP
        Garbarek; John Abercrombie (*g, 12 str g, mand*); Nana Vasconcelos (*talking d, perc, v*). 12/80.

***   **Paths, Prints** ECM 1223 CD/LP
        Garbarek; Bill Frisell (*g*); Eberhard Weber (*b*); Jon Christensen (*d*). 12/81.

(*)   **Wayfarer ECM 1259 CD/LP
        As above, except omit Christensen, add Michael DiPasqua (*d, perc*). 3/83.

The end of the 1970s saw a pattern established whereby Garbarek went into the studio at each year's end to consolidate and capture what had been learnt in performance and to send out new feelers for the year ahead. One constant aspect of these albums (which are otherwise quite unalike) is Garbarek's use of a guitarist; the beautiful *Folk Songs* [ECM 1170] with Charlie Haden and guitarist Egberto Gismonti is currently out of the catalogue. The early sessions with Rypdal were unrepeatable, and perhaps only Bill Frisell comes close; Towner and Abercrombie are strongly atmospheric players, but Connors is a trifle prosaic for this music.

Places is a small masterpiece, again dominated by one long track (a pattern that recurs throughout Garbarek's output). 'Passing' begins with misterioso organ from Taylor, tense drum rips from DeJohnette, and an unresolved questioning figure on the guitar. Garbarek's entry picks it up without variation. There was by this point almost no linear argument in a Garbarek solo, just a static and very occasionally ponderous meditation on a figure of runic simplicity and mystery. Much of the power of *Dis*, Garbarek's most plundered album, works in a similar way, with a windharp and a brass group offering unstructured Aeolian backgrounds for plangent spells and riddles on soprano saxophone and wood flute.

**   **Aftenland** ECM 1169 CD/LP
        Garbarek; Kjell Johnsen (*org*). 12/79.

On a checklist of ECM and Garbarek clichés, this scores quite highly. Nordic? Unmistakably. Moody? Certainly. Atmospheric? Definitely. But funky and swinging it surely isn't. Reminiscent of similar experiments by Keith Jarrett, it conspicuously lacks Jarrett's arrogant and insouciant self-confidence.

***   **It's OK To Listen To The Gray Voice** ECM 1294 CD/LP
        Garbarek. /84.

By this point in his career, Garbarek is possessed of an unmistakably individual voice. The weirdly titled *It's OK* (the reference is to a poem by Tomas Tranströmer) represents a consolidation rather than a new initiative. There are decided longueurs, but in sum it's classic Garbarek.

**   **All Those Born With Wings** ECM 1324 / 8313942 CD/LP
        Garbarek (*saxes* solo). 8/86.

As with *Luminessence*, it was probably inevitable that Garbarek would attempt something like this. It is probably his weakest album since *Red Lanta*, with a dull aftertaste of introversion that is conspicuously missing from even his most meditative work elsewhere.

(*)   **Legend Of The Seven Dreams ECM 1381 CD/LP/MC
        Garbarek; Rainer Bruninghaus (*ky*); Nana Vasconcelos (*perc, v*). 7/88.

**(*)   Rosensfole ECM 1402 CD/LP/MC
Garbarek; Agnes Buen Garnas (*v*). 88.

***   I Took Up The Runes ECM 1419 CD/LP/MC
Garbarek; Rainer Bruninghaus (*p*); Eberhard Weber (*b*); Manu Katche (*d*); Nana
Vasconcelos (*perc*); Bugge Wesseltoft (*syn*); Annte Ailu Gaup (*v*). 8/90.

Towards the end of the 1980s, Garbarek began to explore Nordic folk musics and myth in a
more structured way, thus turning the casually unsubstantiated generalizations about his
'Nordic' style into a conveniently self-fulfilling critical prophecy. *Rosensfole* is really Garnas's
album and is none the worse for that, Garbarek limited in the main to providing a shifting,
minimal stage set for her rather dramatic singing. The opening 'He Comes From The North' on
Legend is based on a Lappish *joik*, converted into state-of-the-art 'world music' by
Vasconcelos's unplaceable percussion and vocal. There are also three brief, unaccompanied
tracks, two on soprano saxophone, one on flute, to demonstrate how Garbarek has pared down
his harmonic conception.

Runes is in very much the same vein, but the experiment of adding a rock drummer and
synthesizer player to the basic core trio of saxophone, piano and drums was an inspired one, and
the long central track is one of Garbarek's most ambitious works to date. The energy of the live
performances doesn't quite come across on the record, but there is more than enough of interest
to bridge occasional repetitive lapses. The cassette format is above average throughout the
ECM catalogue.

***(*)   Star ECM 1444 CD/LP/MC
Garbarek; Miroslav Vitous (*b*); Peter Erskine (*d*). 1/91.

Initial expectations of a welcome return to serious jazz playing are slightly confounded by the
disappointingly woolly opening track, the sole Garbarek composition, which does little more
than lay out a palette of tone-colours. These, though, are imaginatively employed in a
democratic trio session whose stripped-down configuration suits the saxophonist perfectly. The
tone is still pristine, and Garbarek manages to infuse his tenor playing with the sort of
brittle-edged fragility one normally associates with soprano. There is still a slight tendency to
place long notes like monograms, but the signature is in a new, bolder sans-serif which reads as
freshly as *Triptykon* did 20 years ago (twenty years!). Vitous's playing has become much more
purposive and surely grounded; it's interesting to note that the clouds are in the mountains now,
not vice versa. Erskine doesn't at first seem the obvious choice for this session, but the obvious
alternative – Jon Christensen – hasn't the simplicity and directness the session seems to call for.
The (presumably) improvised 'Snowman' is indicative of how far Garbarek has progressed
during his folksy sabbatical from blowing jazz, and it may even be a satirical response to all the
editorial blah about his 'Nordic' cool and stiffness. It hardly seems necessary to say that the
sound is superb; bass and drums well to the front.

**   Works ECM 823266 CD/LP
Garbarek; various line-ups. 1970–80.

This is perhaps the least successful of ECM's generally useful résumés, largely because in the
decade it covers, Garbarek's music developed in so many directions that a representative
sample, let alone an inclusive synopsis, seems out of reach. The collection is dominated, quite
rightly, by 'Beast Of Kommodo' from *Afric Pepperbird*; 'Passing' from *Places* is a further
eleven minutes, and the six remaining tracks betray slight hints of having been chosen for
length, not quality.

RED GARLAND (1923–84)
PIANO

***   A Garland Of Red Original Jazz Classics OJC 126 CD/LP/MC
Garland; Paul Chambers (*b*); Art Taylor (*d*). 8/56.

***   Groovy Original Jazz Classics OJC 061 CD/LP/MC
As above. 12/56–8/57.

***   Red Garland's Piano Original Jazz Classics OJC 073 CD/LP/MC
As above. 3/57.

***   **Manteca** Original Jazz Classics OJC 428 CD/LP/MC
As above, plus Ray Barretto (*perc*). 4/58.

***   **All Kinds Of Weather** Original Jazz Classics OJC 193 CD/LP/MC
As above. 11/58.

(*)   **The Red Garland Trio Original Jazz Classics OJC 224 LP/MC
As above. 11/58.

***   **Red In Bluesville** Original Jazz Classics OJC 295 LP/MC
As above, except Sam Jones (*b*) replaces Chambers. 4/59.

Unassuming, graceful, yet authentically bluesy, Red Garland's manner was flexible enough to accommodate the contrasting styles of both Miles Davis and John Coltrane in the Davis quintet of the mid-1950s. His many records as a leader, beginning at about the same period, display exactly the same qualities. His confessed influences of Tatum, Powell and Nat Cole seem less obvious than his debts to Errol Garner and Ahmad Jamal, whose hit recording of 'Billy Boy' from the early 1950s seems to sum up everything that Garland would later go on to explore. All of the above trio sessions feature the same virtues: deftly fingered left-hand runs over bouncy rhythms, coupled with block-chord phrasing which coloured melodies in such a way that Garland saw no need to depart from them. Medium-uptempo treatments alternate with sometimes sluggish ballads, and Chambers and Taylor are unfailingly swinging partners. The later sessions feature a slightly greater empathy, but there is very little to choose among any of the records, and favourite choices may depend on the tunes on each record, some of which are presented thematically (*All Kinds Of Weather*, for instance, is made up of 'Rain', 'Summertime', and so on). The guest role for Barretto on *Manteca* is a mostly peripheral one, although he's given a couple of lively features with Taylor on the title-tune and 'Lady Be Good'. The remastering is clean, although Chambers, while conspicuously present, is seldom awarded anything better than a dull bass sound.

***   **All Mornin' Long** Original Jazz Classics OJC 293 CD/LP/MC
Garland; Donald Byrd (*t*); John Coltrane (*ts*); George Joyner (*b*); Art Taylor (*d*). 11/57.

***(*)   **Soul Junction** Original Jazz Classics OJC 481 CD/LP/MC
As above. 11/57.

***(*)   **High Pressure** Original Jazz Classics OJC 349 CD/LP/MC
As above. 11–12/57.

(*)   **Dig It! Original Jazz Classics OJC 392 CD/LP/MC
As above, plus Paul Chambers (*b*). 3/57–2/58.

Garland's recordings with Coltrane are typical of the long, relaxed blowing sessions which Prestige were recording at the time, and some of the tracks are very long indeed: 'All Mornin' Long' runs for 20 minutes, 'Soul Junction' and 'Lazy Mae' from *Dig It!* for 16 apiece. There are inevitable longueurs in this approach, and Byrd, though accomplished, lacks the greater authority which he would bring to his later Blue Note albums. But there are some solos of immense power from the tenor saxophonist, and the playing on *Soul Junction* and *High Pressure* especially is as purposeful as the format allows (all the recordings from November 1957 were made on the same day). *Dig It!*, patched together from three sessions and including a fairly routine trio version of 'Crazy Rhythm', is slightly inferior. All four records have been remastered well. *Soul Junction* and *All Mornin' Long* have also been available as a double-LP, *Jazz Junction* (Prestige 24023). *High Pressure* has also been reissued with all the quintet tracks from *Dig It!* and two tracks from 1961 by a quintet with Oliver Nelson, Richard Williams, Peck Morrison and Charlie Persip, on the double-LP *Saying Something* (Prestige P 24090).

***   **Red Garland Trio With Eddie 'Lockjaw' Davis Vol. 1** Original Jazz Classics OJC 360 CD/LP/MC
Garland; Eddie 'Lockjaw' Davis (*ts*); Sam Jones (*b*); Art Taylor (*d*). 12/59.

***   **Bright And Breezy** Original Jazz Classics OJC 265 LP/MC
Garland; Sam Jones (*b*); Charlie Persip (*d*). 7/61.

Davis appears on only three tracks of OJC 360, but it's enough to enliven an otherwise somnolent LP of ballads, originally issued in Prestige's Moodsville series; a stentorian reading of 'When Your Lover Has Gone' works especially well. *Bright And Breezy* returns to Garland's accustomed trio setting.

***   **Crossings** Original Jazz Classics OJC 472 CD/LP/MC
          Garland; Ron Carter (*b*); Philly Joe Jones (*d*). 12/77.

(*)   **Feelin' Red Muse MR 5130 LP
          Garland; Sam Jones (*b*); Al Foster (*d*). 5/78.

**   **Misty Red** Timeless SJP 179 LP
          Garland; Jamil Nasser (*b*); Frank Gant (*d*).

Most of the few records Garland made in the 1970s and '80s have been deleted, and those that remain show his style unchanged, although some of the litheness went out of his touch. *Crossings* and *Feelin' Red* feature such fine support from the respective rhythm sections that the music gathers its own momentum, but the Timeless album is eventually rather dull.

ERROL GARNER (1926–77)
PIANO

*(*)   **Historical First Recording 1944** Jazz Anthology 550042 CD
          Garner (*p* solo). 44.

Garner's style was already in place when he made these private recordings, but the poor fidelity means that they lack much interest.

***   **The Elf** Savoy 650113 CD
          Garner; John Levy, John Simmons (*b*); George De Hart, Alvin Stoller (*d*). 9/45–49.

(*)   **Yesterdays Savoy 650148 CD
          Garner; Mike Bryan (*g*); Slam Stewart, John Simmons, Leonard Gaskin (*b*); Harold
          West, Alvin Stoller, Charlie Smith (*d*). 1/45–6/49.

***   **Relaxin'** Vogue 500117 CD
          Garner; Leonard Gaskin, John Simmons (*b*); Charlie Smith, Harold West (*d*).
          9/49–4/50.

Garner's position in jazz legend as an untutored genius is a romantic one, but it's true that he never read music and his tumbling, percussive, humorous style was entirely his own. Although he recorded with Charlie Parker and other leading boppers, bebop was alien to him: his orchestral manner at the keyboard and the undiluted romanticism of his approach suggest Waller and Ellington as his forebears. His 1940s recordings for Savoy predate the great popularity he would acquire in the next decade, but as a series of miniatures they hold a charm which can transcend the apparent triviality of Garner's readings. The three LPs which collected all the Savoy sides in sequence have been deleted, but the best of them are on *Yesterdays*, while *The Elf* includes a long (1949) session with the unobtrusive support of Simmons and Stoller. The sound is average for the period. *Relaxin'* includes a number of originals and lesser-known songs and is of slightly greater interest.

***   **Gems** CBS 21062 LP/MC
          Garner; John Simmons, Wyatt Ruther (*b*); Shadow Wilson, Eugene 'Fats' Heard (d).
          1/51–3/53.

***   **Too Marvellous For Words** EmArcy 824419-2 CD
          Garner; Wyatt Ruther (*b*); Eugene 'Fats' Heard (*d*). 5/54.

***   **Plays Misty** Fresh Sounds FSR-CD 158 CD
          As above, plus Candido Camero (*perc*). 7/54.

By this period Garner had settled into his format as well as his style – swashbuckling trios which plundered standards with blowsy abandon. Bass and drums have only to keep up with Garner, but they provide a deceptively important anchor, for otherwise his treatments might simply wander off. Garner's heartiness, his fondness for extravagantly arpeggiated ballads and knockabout transformations of standards can grow wearisome over the length of an album, and his favourite mannerisms become irritating. Track by track, though, all these records are entertaining enough. The best things happen when Garner encounters an unlikely tune – 'Kitten On The Keys' on *Too Marvellous For Words*, 'I Wanna Be A Rug Cutter' on *Plays Misty*, which gains an extra degree of vitality from Candido's presence.

***   **Concert By The Sea** CBS 451042 CD/LP
Garner; Eddie Calhoun (*b*); Denzil Best (*d*). 9/55.

(*)   **The Most Happy Piano CBS 450306 LP
Garner; Al Hall (*b*); Specs Powell (*d*). 56.

Garner's most famous LP, and one of the biggest-selling jazz records ever made, *Concert By The Sea* is essentially no more or less than a characteristic set by the trio in an amenable setting. Moments such as the teasing introduction to 'I'll Remember April', the flippant blues of 'Red Top' and the pell-mell 'Where Or When' find Garner at his most buoyant; but rather more interesting is his well-shaped treatment of 'How Could You Do A Thing Like That To Me'. The recording was never outstanding but the reissue serves it well enough. The later trio session is rather less interesting.

(*)   **Plays Gershwin & Kern Mercury 826224 CD
Garner; Eddie Calhoun, Ike Isaacs (*b*); Kelly Martin, Jimmie Smith (*d*). 8/64–2/68.

***(*)   **Compact Jazz: Erroll Garner** Mercury 830695 CD
Garner; Wyatt Ruther (*b*); Eugene 'Fats' Heard (*d*); Candido Camero (*perc*). 6/54–3/55.

***   **Jazz Around Midnight – Erroll Garner** Verve 846191 CD
Garner; Red Callender, John Simmons, Leonard Gaskin, Wyatt Ruther (*b*); Lou Singer, Harold West, Charlie Smith, Eugene 'Fats' Heard (*d*). 12/45–3/55.

Most of Garner's many albums from the late 1950s and '60s have been lost from the catalogue, and the Gershwin and Kern set is typical and unremarkable of the period. But Garner is well served by the above compilations. The excellent survey on the Mercury CD includes a wildly swinging 'Russian Lullaby', the first version of 'Misty' and a genuinely inventive and finely resolved solo reading of 'Sleep', along with four other solo pieces. The piano sound is rather hard on the CD but the music comes through very cleanly. There is slight duplication with the tracks on the Verve set, which is a little more ordinary in its programme, although it closes with a very long and unpredictable 'Over The Rainbow'. Well-remastered sound.

KENNY GARRETT
ALTO SAXOPHONE, FLUTE

***   **Introducing Kenny Garrett** Criss Cross 1014 CD/LP
Garrett; Woody Shaw (*t, flhn*); Mulgrew Miller (*p*); Nat Reeves (*b*); Tony Reedus (*d*). 12/84.

(*)   **Garrett 5 Paddle Wheel K32Y 6280 / K28P 6494 CD/LP
Garrett; Wallace Roney (*t*); Mulgrew Miller (*p*); Charnett Moffett (*b*); Tony Reedus (*d*); Rudy Bird (*perc*). 9/88.

It was in Garrett's company that Miles Davis felt most inclined of late to return to the blues. The young saxophonist has a warm, vibrant delivery that works best in short, fairly discontinuous passages. Woody Shaw plays wonderfully on the debut album, a far more amenable partner than the younger and gruffer Roney. Miller sounds particularly good on the later album, though he's apt to sink into the mix. Garrett's own bluesy phrasing is consistently interesting throughout. Promising stuff from a saxophonist and flautist who hasn't yet reached his peak.

GIORGIO GASLINI (born 1929)
PIANO, KEYBOARDS

****   **Gaslini Plays Monk** Soul Note 1020 CD/LP
Gaslini (*p* solo). 5/81.

***   **Schumann Reflections** Soul Note 1120 CD/LP
Gaslini; Piero Leveratto (*b*); Paolo Pellegatti (*d*).

***   **Multiple** Soul Note 1220 CD/LP
Gaslini; Roberto Ottaviano (*as, ss, sno s, bcl*); Claudio Fasoli (*ts, ss*); Bruno Tommaso (*b*); Gianpiero Prina (*d*). 10/87.

***(*)   **Ayler's Wings** Soul Note 1270 CD/LP
Gaslini (*p* solo). 7/90.

Monk has received no more sensitive and intelligent reading than Gaslini's remarkable 1981 homage. He makes no attempt to mimic the style, just to get inside those mysterious and deceptive tunes. Schumann would seem to be a more intractable subject, but Gaslini exploits considerable harmonic and contrapuntal ingenuity to bring it off. The quintet session has a better rhythm section and progress is a little brisker. Transcribing Albert Ayler, the most anti-pianistic of improvisers, would seem to be an almost absurdly quixotic task. Gaslini converts Ayler's fierce microtonality into ripples and arpeggios that are as provocative as they are unexpectedly appealing. Superimposing 'Omega Is The Alpha' over 'Bells' is the only slight oddity (but it works), and the versions of 'Ghosts' and 'Truth Is Marching In' acquire a Bachian simplicity and exactness. Gaslini's is a quite astonishing output that urgently deserves wider coverage.

ROBERTO GATTO (born 1958)
DRUMS

***   **Ask** Inak 8802 CD
Gatto; Danilo Rea (*ky*); John Scofield, Battista Lena (*g*); Enzo Pietropaoli, Massimo Bottini (*b*). 7–9/87.

**   **Notes** Inak 8805 CD
Gatto; Flavio Boltro (*t*); Maurizio Giammarco (*ss, ts*); Michael Brecker (*ts*); Rita Marcotulli, Danilo Rea (*ky*); Umberto Fiorentino (*g*); Enzo Pietropaolo, Furio Di Castri, Francesco Puglisi (*b*). 1–3/87.

Gatto heads two fusion records full of flourish and bravado but lacking a little in substance. Each is pitched around the playing of their respective American guests, but the disc with Scofield is superior on several counts: he sounds as if he's actually playing with the band, there are one or two good themes and a fine duet version of 'There Will Never Be Another You' with Gatto, and the music is generally a little more considered. Brecker sounds as though he might simply be overdubbing solos on to ready-made backgrounds, and it's all anonymously energetic.

CHARLES GAYLE (born 1939)
TENOR SAXOPHONE

(*)   **Always Born Silkheart 115 CD
Gayle; John Tchicai (*as, ts*); Sirone (*b*); Reggie Nicholson (*d*). 4/88.

***   **Homeless** Silkheart 116 CD
Gayle; Sirone (*b*); Dave Pleasant (*d*). 4/88.

***(*)   **Spirits Before** Silkheart 117 CD
As above. 4/88.

Gayle has lived the life of a street musician in Manhattan for some years, and these three records were all recorded in the same week on what was effectively a field trip by Silkheart. Gayle is like a folk musician in other ways, too: he harks back to unreconstructed energy music of the 1960s, blowing wild, themeless lines with an abandon that sometimes sounds neurotic, sometimes pleading, occasionally euphoric. He seems oblivious to all 'fashions' in jazz, keeps faith with only a few players – drummmer Pleasant, whose fractured and weirdly illogical time is a prime feature of the two records he appears on, and bassist Sirone appear to be two of them – and questions the status quo with unblinking certainty. *Always Born* is a well-meaning failure through Tchicai's efforts: Gayle wasn't really meant to play with another saxophonist, even a venerable veteran of the wave which he harks back to. *Homeless* and especially *Spirits Before* are the real, hard stuff, with 'Give' a particularly knotty and troubling performance. If and when Gayle records again seems open to question, but *Spirits Before* should certainly be heard now.

GIANNI GEBBIA
SOPRANO SAX

**(*)   Arabesques Splasc(h) H 147 LP
Gebbia; Pino Minafra (*t*); Pino Greco (*g*); Lelio Giannetto (*b, v*); Giovanni Lo Cascio (*d*). 1/88.

Gebbia is an enterprising musician who had already recorded an all-solo programme for his own Sound Event label before embarking on this small-group disc for Splasc(h). The leader's soprano playing is agile rather than especially distinctive, but the best tracks here – 'La Caduta Di J Pless' and the virtuoso showmanship of 'Saudades Du Sud' – make the most of the compositions, the former a fine example of a simple figure developed into a shapely improvisation. But the very long 'Shamal', where Minafra guests and studio trickery embellishes the music, is tedious. The digital recording tends to over-brightness.

HERB GELLER (born 1928)
ALTO SAXOPHONE, SOPRANO SAXOPHONE, FLUTE

****   That Geller Feller Fresh Sound FSR CD 91 CD
Geller; Kenny Dorham (*t*); Harold Land (*ts*); Lou Levy (*p*); Ray Brown (*b*); Lawrence Marable (*d*). 3/57.

**(*)   Birdland Stomp Enja 5019 LP
Geller; Michael Melzer (*g*); Red Mitchell (*b*); Harold Smith (*v*). 1/86.

**   A Jazz Songbook Meeting Enja 6006 CD/LP
Geller; Walter Norris (*p*); John Schroeder (*g*); Mike Richmond (*b*); Adam Nussbaum (*d*). 7/88.

Relatively untroubled by fashion, Geller set out as an orthodox, Parker-influenced bopper – *rara avis* on the West Coast in those days – before turning towards a more broadly based and decidedly cooler style which incorporated elements of Paul Desmond, Johnny Hodges and even Benny Goodman, with whom he worked in the later 1950s. Until recent years, he's been hard to spot, buried in a German radio big band and other groups.

That Geller Feller is the best of the available sets. The originals – 'S'Pacific View', 'Marable Eyes', 'An Air For The Heir', and 'Melrose And Sam' – are tightly organized and demand considerable inventiveness from a group that frequently sounds much bigger than a sextet. Dorham plays a lovely, crackling solo on the opening track, but is otherwise rather anonymous when out on his own. Geller's own introduction to 'Jitterbug Waltz' is wonderfully delicate, with more than a hint of Benny Carter in the tone and phrasing. He also does a fine version of the Arlen–Gershwin rarity 'Here's What I'm Here For', which John Williams picked up on later in 1957 on the excellent *Plays The Music Of Harold Arlen* (Discovery DSCD 891 CD).

With some of his better sessions deleted, it's good to have two more recent recordings. *Birdland Stomp* is from a capable and sometimes quite energetic drummerless trio anchored on Red Mitchell's magnificently capable bass-playing. Harold Smith's characterless vocals are mercifully limited to a single track. Mitchell also figures prominently on the interesting compilation *Jazz Club – Bass* (Verve 840037), playing in 1955 with Geller and his wife, pianist Lorraine Geller, who tragically died three years later, aged only thirty. The quintet sessions are slightly disappointing, largely because Geller's soloing is just off-line. The CD format presents no evident advantages.

***(*)   **Birdland Stomp** Fresh Sound FSRCD 174 CD
Geller; Kenny Drew (p); Niels-Henning Ørsted-Pedersen (b); Mark Taylor (d). 5/90.

Confusingly titled, given the Enja above, but way ahead on quality. At 62, Geller has a beautiful tone and the Ellington–Strayhorn medley with which the Spanish-recorded session ends suggests he has renewed his debt to Hodges. His articulation on Parker's 'Cheryl' isn't all it might be, and even the capable Drew sounds a bit sticky, but both are magnificent on the title-tune and 'Autumn Nocturne'. Recorded very strongly, with a heavy emphasis on NHØP's bass. An excellent introduction to an interesting figure who charted his own course out of orthodox bebop.

THE GEORGIA MELODIANS
GROUP

(*)   **The Georgia Melodians Volume 1 Fountain FG 402 LP
Ernie Intlehouse (c); Herb Winfield (tb); Merritt Kenworthy (cl, as, bsx); Clarence Hutchins (cl, ts, bs); Oscar Young (p); Elmer Merry (bj); unknown (bb); Carl Gerold (d). 4–9/24.

(*)   **The Georgia Melodians Volume 2 Fountain FG 405 LP
As above, except add Vernon Dalhart (v). 10/24–4/26.

This was a house band for the Edison Company, which went on using the hill-and-dale recording process when others had abandoned it in the 1920s: as a result, the records are rather longer than was normal for the period, averaging around four minutes each, and the original studio sound is outstandingly good for acoustic recording. The music isn't terribly exciting: they run through many of the more promising tunes in the hot-dance field of the day, and there are generous spaces left for solos, with Intlehouse and Winfield proving to have a few worthwhile ideas to hand. 'Tea Pot Dome Blues' makes interesting comparison with the Fletcher Henderson version, made not long before this one; and, by the later sessions, the group had loosened up sufficiently to make light of some of the more demanding passages. But the listener is worn down by the sheer routine of the records. Nobody is characterful enough to raise the music beyond mere competence, and it's significant that these players – aside from Winfield – never made records for anyone else. Excellent remastering, as usual, from Fountain/Retrieval.

STAN GETZ (1927–91)
TENOR, SOPRANO AND BARITONE SAXOPHONES

***   **Early Stan** Original Jazz Classics 654 CD/LP/MC
Getz; Shorty Rogers (t); Earl Swope (tb); George Wallington, Hall Overton (p); Jimmy Raney (g); Curley Russell, Red Mitchell (b); Shadow Wilson, Frank Isola (d). 3/49–4/53.

(*)   **The Brothers Original Jazz Classics OJC 008 CD/LP/MC
Getz; Zoot Sims, Al Cohn, Allen Eager, Brew Moore (ts); Walter Bishop Jr (p); Gene Ramey (b); Charlie Perry (d). 4/49.

***   **Prezervation** Original Jazz Classics OJC 706 CD
Getz; Kai Winding (tb); Al Haig (p); Gene Ramey, Tommy Potter (b); Roy Haynes, Stan Levey (d); Junior Parker, Blossom Dearie (v). 6/49–2/50.

***   **Stan Getz Quartets** Original Jazz Classics OJC 121 CD/LP/MC
Getz; Al Haig, Tony Aless (p); Gene Ramey, Tommy Potter, Percy Heath (b); Stan Levey, Roy Haynes, Don Lamond (d). 6/49–4/50.

After starring as one of Woody Herman's 'Four Brothers' sax section, and delivering a luminous ballad solo on the 1948 'Early Autumn', Getz went out on his own and at first seemed much like the rest of the Lester Young-influenced tenormen: a fast, cool stylist with a sleek tone and a delivery that soothed nerves jangled by bebop. The 'Brothers' idea was pursued in the session on OJC 008 (the rest of the disc is devoted to a Zoot Sims–Al Cohn date): the five tenors trade punches with panache, and it's a fun session if hardly an important one (the CD includes three alternative takes not on the LP issue). *Early Stan* finds Getz as a sideman with a septet led by Terry Gibbs and a quartet under Jimmy Raney's direction. Bright, appealing cool-bop on the Gibbs date, but the Raney session, from 1953, is more substantial, the quartet whisking through four stretching exercises including 'Round Midnight'.

Prezervation rounds up some odds and ends, including an improbable alliance with Junior Parker on two tracks and a Haig sextet date with Winding and two vocal duets by Jimmy Raney and Blossom Dearie! Not very important. But the *Quartets* set is an attractive dry run for the upcoming four-piece sessions for Roost, and features the tenorman in very lithe form. The sound on most of these issues was fairly indifferent to start with and these latest editions emerge well enough.

****   **The Roost Quartets 1950–1951** Roulette CDP 7960522 CD
     Getz; Horace Silver, Al Haig (*p*); Jimmy Raney (*g*); Joe Calloway, Tommy Potter (*b*);
     Walter Bolden, Roy Haynes (*d*). 5/50–8/51.

****   **The Best Of The Roost Years** Roulette CDP 7981142 CD
     As above, except add Sanford Gold, Duke Jordan (*p*); Johnny Smith (*g*); Eddie
     Safranski, Teddy Kotick, Bill Crow, Leonard Gaskin, Bob Carter (*b*); Frank Isola,
     Tiny Kahn, Roy Haynes, Don Lamond, Morty Feld (*d*). 5/50–12/52.

****   **At Storyville** Blue Note B21Y-94507 CD
     Getz; Al Haig (*p*); Jimmy Raney (*g*); Teddy Kotick (*b*); Tiny Kahn (*d*). 10/51.

It's a moot point as to when Getz did his finest work on record, but it's possible to argue that these are his best records. The side-length of 78 rpm discs lent a terseness and conviction to his improvisations which perhaps drifted away in the LP era, and even on club dates – as those at Boston's Storyville show, four tracks of which are on the best-of disc – Getz kept himself on a tighter rein. The lovely, mottled tone which he displays blinks through even the sometimes indifferent Roost recording, although the engineers have done an excellent job in making the music come up bright and clear; and bebop energy and surprise inform all the up-tempo pieces, some of which go off at a fearful pace. Haig and Silver both play splendidly. The *Quartets* disc rounds up all the piano four-piece sides from 1950–51, while the *Storyville* disc is a classic club session cut in Boston. The best-of samples from both of them, and adds tracks from a quartet session with Jimmy Raney. It also includes the gorgeous 'Moonlight In Vermont' from a session with guitarist Johnny Smith. All command the highest recommendation.

(***)   **At Carnegie Hall** Fresh Sound FSCD 1003 CD
     Getz; Kai Winding (*tb*); Al Haig, Duke Jordan (*p*); Jimmy Raney (*g*); Bill Crow,
     Tommy Potter (*b*); Frank Isola, Roy Haynes (*d*). 12/49–11/52.

(***)   **Birdland Sessions** Fresh Sound FSR-CD 149 CD
     Getz; Horace Silver, Duke Jordan (*p*); Jimmy Raney (*g*); Nelson Boyd, Charles
     Mingus, Gene Ramey (*b*); Phil Brown, Connie Kay (*d*). 4–8/52.

There's some excellent Getz on both these discs – but we have to withhold a firm recommendation because of the sound-quality. He sounds in prime form at both of the two Carnegie Hall concerts on FSCD 1003, but the sound deteriorates (frustratingly, after a good start) to complete muddiness by the end of the 1952 show. Jordan tends to toss out clichés, but the interplay with Raney is as subtle as usual. The Birdland recordings have been available on various pirate LPs over the years, and this edition is about as listenable as the others. For Getz addicts only.

***   **Together For The First Time** Fresh Sound FSCD-1022 CD
     Getz; Chet Baker (*t*); Russ Freeman, Donn Trenner (*p*); Carson Smith, Joe
     Mondragon, Gene Englund (*b*); Larry Bunker, Shelly Manne, Jimmy Pratt (*d*).
     9/52–12/53.

An interesting discovery: the Mulligan quartet at the Haig with Getz subbing for the leader. He sounds perfectly at home with Baker, Smith and Bunker, and there are some forthright variations on six tunes including 'Half Nelson' and 'Yardbird Suite'. A subsequent quintet version of 'All the Things You Are' is a lot more dispirited, and there are four quartet airshots from 1952 to fill up the disc, which is in surprisingly good sound for the most part, the Haig titles having been apparently recorded by Richard Bock.

***(*)   **Stan Getz Plays** Verve 833535-2 CD
Getz; Jimmy Rowles, Duke Jordan (*p*); Jimmy Raney (*g*); Bob Whitlock, Bill Crow (*b*); Frank Isola, Max Roach (*d*). 12/52–1/54.

Getz's long association with Norman Granz and Verve starts here. Some of the best recording he was given in the period, and much of the playing is as fine as it is on the Roost dates, with the 1954 quartet session with Rowles particularly pretty.

***   **Stan Getz And The Oscar Peterson Trio** Verve 827826 CD/MC
Getz; Oscar Peterson (*p*); Herb Ellis (*g*); Ray Brown (*b*). 10/57.

***   **At The Opera House** Verve 831272 CD/MC
Getz; J. J. Johnson (*tb*); Oscar Peterson (*p*); Herb Ellis (*g*); Ray Brown (*b*); Connie Kay (*d*). 10/57.

***   **Getz Meets Mulligan In Hi-Fi** Verve 849392-2 CD
Getz; Gerry Mulligan (*bs, ts*); Lou Levy (*p*); Ray Brown (*b*); Stan Levey (*d*). 10/57.

***   **Compact/Walkman Jazz: Stan Getz And Friends** Verve 835317-2 CD/MC
As above three Verve discs, plus Bob Brookmeyer (*vtb*), Lionel Hampton (*vib*), Chick Corea (*p*), Leroy Vinnegar, Ron Carter, Bill Anthony, Gene Cherico (*b*), Shelly Manne, Art Mardigan, Elvin Jones, Joe Hunt, Grady Tate (*d*). 12/53–3/67.

Getz's 1950s tracks for Verve aren't yet on CD as comprehensively as they might be, with at least two classic sessions – *West Coast Jazz* and *More West Coast Jazz* – as yet unavailable. The session with Peterson is as ebullient as expected, and the Opera House concert with J. J. Johnson includes some extrovert playing from everyone, especially on a snorting romp through Bud Powell's 'Blues In The Closet'. Listening to this kind of playing makes one wonder at Getz's reputation for being a featherlight stylist (he preferred 'stomping tenor-man'). The session with Mulligan is beautifully dovetailed: although, somewhat notoriously, they chose to swap instruments for part of the session, the sound of the two horns speaks of a tonal fraternity which sounds rare and entrancing. In the circumstances, the Compact Jazz compilation becomes the more useful, with tracks from all these dates and others with Ella, Dizzy, Brookmeyer, Hampton and (from the 1960s) Burton and Corea.

***(*)   **In Stockholm** Dragon DRLP 157/8 / DIW 317/8 2LP/2CD
Getz; Benny Bailey (*t*); Åke Persson (*tb*); Erik Norstrom, Bjarne Nerem (*ts*); Lars Gullin (*bs*); Jan Johansson, Bengt Hallberg (*p*); Gunnar Johnson (*b*); William Sciöppfe (*d*). 8–9/58.

A spell in Stockholm led to some recording with Swedish musicians, and these admirable sessions were the result, a Swedish variation on the cool manner with Getz sounding perfectly comfortable in Hallberg's and Johansson's charts. Gullin and Hallberg himself shine too. The recording sounds equally fine on either the Dragon LP edition or on the DIW double-CD.

***   **Stan Getz With Cal Tjader** Original Jazz Classics OJC 275 CD/LP/MC
Getz; Cal Tjader (*vib*); Vince Guaraldi (*p*); Eddie Duran (*g*); Scott LaFaro (*b*); Billy Higgins (*d*). 2/58.

A one-off session with Cal Tjader which looks forward with some prescience to the bossa nova records that were to come: certainly the coolly pleasant backings of Tjader's rhythm section make up a cordial meeting ground for tenor and vibes to play lightly appealing solos, and the charming version of 'I've Grown Accustomed To Her Face' is a winner.

***   **Stan Getz With European Friends** LRC CDC 7679 CD
Getz; Eddie Louiss (*org*); Martial Solal, Rene Urtreger (*p*); Jimmy Gourley, René Thomas (*g*); Pierre Michelot, Jean-Marie Ingrand (*b*); Kenny Clarke, Bernard Lubat (*d*). 58–71.

Scruffy documentation makes it hard to determine the origin of these tracks, and two of them are much later than as dated here, since they're apparently outtakes from the *Dynasty* sessions listed below. The other tracks feature Getz with French rhythm sections (Kenny Clarke aside) and there is actually some good mid-period Getz on them. Variable recording.

***(*) **Jazz Samba** Polydor 810061-2 CD
Getz; Charlie Byrd (*g*); Keter Betts (*b*); Gene Byrd (*g, b*); Buddy Deppenschmidt, Bill Reichenbach (*d*). 2/62.

*** **Big Band Bossa Nova** Verve 825771-2 CD
Getz; Doc Severinsen, Bernie Glow, Joe Ferrante, Clark Terry (*t*); Tony Studd, Bob Brookmeyer, Willie Dennis (*tb*); Ray Alonge (*frhn*); Gerald Sanfino, Ray Beckenstein (*f*); Eddie Caine (*af*); Babe Clark, Walt Levinsky (*cl*); Romeo Penque (*bcl*); Hank Jones (*p*); Jim Hall (*g*); Tommy Williams (*b*); Johnny Rae (*d*); Jose Paulo, Carmen Costa (*perc*). 8/62.

***(*) **Jazz Samba Encore** Verve 823613-2 CD
Getz; Antonio Carlos Jobim (*g, p*); Luiz Bonfa (*g*); George Duvivier, Tommy Williams, Don Payne (*b*); Paulo Ferreira, Jose Carlos, Dave Bailey (*d*); Maria Toledo (*v*).2/63.

*** **Getz And Gilberto** Verve 810048-2 CD
Getz; Antonio Carlos Jobim (*p*); Joao Gilberto (*g, v*); Tommy Williams (*b*); Milton Banana (*d*); Astrud Gilberto (*v*). 3/63.

*** **Getz Au Go Go** Verve 821725-2 CD
Getz; Gary Burton (*vib*); Kenny Burrell (*g*); Gene Cherico (*b*); Joe Hunt, Helcio Milito (*d*); Astrud Gilberto (*v*). 64.

***(*) **The Girl From Ipanema** Verve 823611-2 4CD
As above discs, except add Steve Kuhn (*p*); Laurindo Almeida (*g*), Edison Macahdo, Jose Soorez, Luiz Parga (*perc*). 62–64.

***(*) **Round Midnight: Stan Getz** Verve 841445 CD
As above. 62–64.

Getz's big commercial break. However much he protested that he played other stuff besides the bossa nova in later years, his most lucrative records – and some of his best playing – were triggered by the hit versions of first 'Desafinado' from the first album and then 'The Girl From Ipanema' with Gilberto, the tune which a thousand wine-bar bands have had to play nightly ever since. The original albums still hold up very well. Getz actually plays with as much pungency and alertness as anywhere else, and even though the backings sometimes threaten to slip into a sleepwalk, there's always an interesting tickle from the guitar or the bass to keep the music alive; and the melodies, by Bonfa, Gilberto and Jobim, have proved their quality by how well they've endured. The first and third albums are the best: the big band set has some clever arrangements by Gary McFarland, but sundering the intimacy of these whispery settings seems a fairly pointless exercise. And *Getz Au Go Go*, which had the vocals by Gilberto dubbed in subsequently, sounds just a mite too forceful, as though Getz were hurrying to push on to something else. Astrud Gilberto's singing isn't so much an acquired taste as a languid, ghostly sound on the breeze; many will prefer Maria Toledo on the third record listed. *The Girl From Ipanema* collects all the music plus the session for *Stan Getz / Laurindo Almeida*. The *Round Midnight* disc is a functional one-volume sampler with all the hits.

**** **Focus** Verve 821982-2 CD
Getz; Eddie Sauter Orchestra. 4–6/65.

Nobody ever arranged for Getz as well as this, and Sauter's luminous and shimmering scores continue to bewitch. This isn't art-jazz scoring: Sauter had little of Gil Evans's mysterioso power, and he was shameless about tugging at heartstrings. But within those parameters – and Getz, the most pragmatic of soloists, was only too happy to work within them – he made up the most emotive of frameworks. It doesn't make much sense as a suite, or a concerto; just as a series of episodes with the tenor gliding over and across them. In 'Her', the tune dedicated to Getz's mother, the soloist describes a pattern which is resolved in the most heartstopping of codas. This was surely Getz's finest hour. The CD remastering hasn't eliminated much of the tape hiss, but it sounds good enough.

*** **A Song After Sundown** RCA Bluebird ND 86284 CD
Getz; Gary Burton (*vib*); Jim Hall (*g*); Steve Swallow (*b*); Roy Haynes (*d*); Boston Pops Orchestra. 8/66.

Almost a rerun – in a live setting – of *Focus*, but with nothing like the refinement of result. David Raksin, Alec Wilder and Eddie Sauter all contributed material to the project but, aside from small moments of real beauty, too much of it ends up as mere kitsch, failing to transcend the way that *Focus* so consistently does.

***   **Sweet Rain** Verve 815054-2 CD
      Getz; Chick Corea (*p*); Ron Carter (*b*); Grady Tate (*d*). 3/67.

Bland but occasionally beautiful, this was one of the more willowy of Getz's quartets, with Corea the probable culprit and Carter failing to save the situation. Getz's tone still sings its way through the cod-Spanish material with much elegance.

***(*)   **Dynasty** Verve 839117-2 2CD
      Getz; Eddie Louiss (*org*); René Thomas (*g*); Bernard Lubat (*d*). 1–3/71.

Recorded at a live engagement in London, Getz was in happy and swinging form here, and the quartet stretch out as far as they want on the material. Louiss is far more flexible and discreet than most jazz organists and Getz is untroubled by anything the instrument produces, while the reliable Thomas takes some excellent solos.

***   **But Beautiful** Jazz Door 1208 CD
      Getz; Bill Evans (*p*); Eddie Gomez (*b*); Marty Morell (*d*). 8/74.

**   **Best Of Two Worlds** Columbia CK 33703 CD
      Getz; Albert Dailey (*p*); Joao Gilberto (*g. perc, v*); Oscar Neves (*g*); Clint Houston,
      Steve Swallow (*b*); Billy Hart, Grady Tate (*d*); Airto Moreira, Ruben Bassini, Ray
      Armando, Sonny Carr (*perc*); Heloisa Buarque de Hollanda (*v*). 5/75.

***   **The Master** Columbia 467138-2 CD
      Getz; Albert Dailey (*p*); Clint Houston (*b*); Billy Hart (*d*). 10/75.

***   **Live At Montmartre** Steeplechase SCS 1073 2CD/2LP/2MC
      Getz; Joanne Brackeen (*p*); Niels-Henning Ørsted-Pedersen (*b*); Billy Hart (*d*). 1/77.

This wasn't a vintage period for Getz. The Columbia albums range from perfunctory to mildly engaging: nothing very wrong with the settings (aside from *Best Of Two Worlds*, which is a very pallid rerun of the *bossa nova* years), but Getz's own playing has taken on a wayward, purposeless quality, and the licks he sometimes fell back on when bored recur frequently enough to be troublesome. The Montmartre set suffers from a rhythm section that don't really work with him, and the missing *Another World* found him drifting towards easy listening, a turn that would become disastrous with the thankfully deleted *Children Of The World*. *The Master*, though, is a better record, which doesn't shake the earth but finds the leader very comfortable on the bed of rich chords which Albert Dailey lays down. The live set with Bill Evans is a recently released concert session: while one might expect two such leading lyricists to provide a superabundance of beauty, their respective styles actually move somewhat blandly alongside each other. 'Lover Man', for instance, is beautiful, yet disarmingly over-polished. Better things happen on the few faster moments, such as 'Funkallero'. Sound quality is quite good, if a notch below excellent.

**   **Autumn Leaves** West Wind 2046 CD
      Getz; Joe Farrell (*ts*); Andy Laverne (*p*); Chuck Loeb (*g*); Brian Bromberg (*b*);
      Victor Jones (*d*). 1/80.

***(*)   **Billy Highstreet Samba** Emarcy 838771 CD
      Getz; Mitch Forman (*ky*); Chuck Loeb (*g*); Mark Egan (*b*); Victor Lewis (*d*); Bobby
      Thomas (*perc*).

***(*)   **The Dolphin** Concord CCD 4158 CD/LP/MC
      Getz; Lou Levy (*p*); Monty Budwig (*b*); Victor Lewis (*d*). 5/81.

***(*)   **Spring Is Here** Concord CCD 4500 CD/MC
      As above. 5/81.

****   **Pure Getz** Concord CCD 4188 CD/MC
      Getz; Jim McNeely (*bp*); Marc Johnson (*b*); Victor Lewis (*d*). 1/82.

*** **Line For Lyons** Sonet SNTCD 899 CD
Getz; Chet Baker (*t*); Jimmy McNeely (*p*); George Mraz (*b*); Victor Lewis (*d*). 2/83.

Not so much a miraculous return to form as an artist reasserting his artistry. Getz passed fusion leanings by and moved back to his greatest strength, tenor and rhythm section, of which the Concord albums are triumphant illustrations. *The Dolphin* and its recently issued companion *Spring is Here* offer live sessions with a first-class band: Getz is at his most expansive here, reeling off very long but consistently expressive and well-argued solos, his tone a shade harder but still with a misty elegance that softens phrases at key moments. *Pure Getz*, recorded in the studio, is perhaps even better: there is a celebrated version of Billy Strayhorn's 'Blood Count', which alternates between harsh cries and soft murmurings, and which became a staple part of Getz's live set at the time, but the variations on 'Come Rain Or Come Shine' and a terse 'Sippin' At Bells' are probably even more masterful. But *Billy Highstreet Samba* is by no means a second-rate Getz album: here, for once, he adapted well to what could have been a fusion-led project. The material (by Loeb and Forman) is unusually perspicacious, and Getz responds with bright and committed playing against a group more concerned with playing music than licks. There is also a strong 'Body And Soul', and a couple of rare outings for Getz on soprano. *Line For Lyons* suffers from a certain lack of interest between the two horns – Getz seemed to lose interest in jamming, and he preferred the challenge of a good rhythm section to another front-line horn – and while it's agreeable enough, it scarcely matches up to the Concord discs. *Autumn Leaves* is a stray live album with the unlikely presence of Farrell making up a mismatched front line.

***(*) **The Stockholm Concert** Sonet SNTCD 1019 CD
Getz; Jim McNeely (*p*); George Mraz (*b*); Victor Lewis (*d*). 2/83.

**** **Anniversary** EmArcy 838769 CD/MC
Getz; Kenny Barron (*p*); Rufus Reid (*b*); Victor Lewis (*d*). 7/87.

**** **Serenity** EmArcy 838770 CD/MC
As above. 7/87.

Getz's last great records are pristine examples of his art. Sometimes it seems as if there is nothing there but his sound, the 'incredibly lovely sound', as he once murmured to himself, and it's possible to find an emptiness at the heart of this music. Certainly he had no pretence to playing anything but long, self-regarding lines that had little to do with anything going on around him: as impeccably as both of these rhythm sections play, their function is purely to sketch in as painless a backdrop as possible for the unfurling of Getz's sound. But it is such a breathtaking beauty that he creates that these might be the most sheerly pretty jazz albums of their day. The two EmArcy sets are the definitive ones, splendidly recorded and letting the listener bathe in the rapturous sound of the tenor.

*** **Apasionado** A&M 395297 CD/MC
Getz; orchestra. 89.

Though already troubled by his terminal illness, Getz still plays handsomely on this superior example of mood music. His earlier records with strings wait to be reissued, so this one – with keyboards substituting for the string parts and a mélange of soft rhythms and whispering brass in support – will serve to illustrate this most soothing side of his art.

***(*) **People Time** EmArcy 510134-2 2CD
Getz; Kenny Barron (*p*). 3/91.

Cut not long before his death, Getz has his moments of struggle on this imposing, double-length series of duets with Kenny Barron, his last keyboard partner. Some of the butter has run out of his tone, and unlike many valedictory recordings there isn't a compensating ardour of delivery to go with it: he sounds as if he's just trying to be the same old Getz. But knowledge of his impending death still, inevitably, lends a poignancy to this music which even those previously unmoved by the saxophonist's work may find themselves responding to. And Barron is as imperturbably sound as always.

TIZIANA GHIGLIONI
VOCAL

(*)   **Streams Splasc(h) H 104 LP
Ghiglioni; Luca Bonvini (*tb*); Maurizio Caldura Nunez (*ss, ts*); Luca Flores (*p*); Franco Nesti (*b*); Alessandro Fabbri (*d*). 12/84.

***   **Well, Actually** Splasc(h) H 117 LP
Ghiglioni; Giancarlo Schiaffini (*tb, eu, tba*). 1–3/87.

***   **Onde** Splasc(h) H 133 CD/LP
Ghiglioni; Carlo Actis Dato (*ts, bs, bcl*); Claudio Lodati (*g*); Enrico Fazio (*b*); Fiorenzo Sordini (*d, perc, marim*). 6/87.

***   **Yet Time** Splasc(h) H 150 CD/LP
Ghiglioni; Roberto Ottaviano (*ss*); Stefano Battaglia (*p*); Paolino Dalla Porta (*b*); Tiziano Tononi (*d*). 3/88.

Since she seems to appear in a quite different setting almost from record to record, it's a little difficult to focus on the merits of Tiziana Ghiglioni's singing. Her albums for Splasc(h) find her both fronting groups and working as an integral element within them: she is almost peripheral to *Onde*, where she guests with Actis Dato's Art Studio band, yet her singing on 'Rosso Di Sera' and 'Voci' is a striking wordless invention. *Streams* and *Yet Time* find her taking a Norma Winstone-like role of alternating pastoral scat with cool readings of lyrics. She has a big, rangy voice which she's reluctant to use in a big way, so many of her vocal improvisations sound restrained; fluency doesn't come easy to her, either. Yet the improvisation on Ornette Coleman's 'Round Trip' on *Yet Time* is sustained with great skill, and her meeting with Schiaffini, which includes bare-bones readings of 'When I Fall In Love' and 'All Blues' as well as more outré material, shows her unfazed by working alone with an improvising trombonist. Her enunciation always makes one aware that she's not singing in a native language, and her self-written lyrics are awkward, but she's a charismatic performer.

(*)   **Sounds Of Love Soul Note 1056 LP
Ghiglioni; Kenny Drew (*p*); Niels-Henning Ørsted-Pedersen (*b*); Barry Altschul (*d*). 2/83.

***   **Somebody Special** Soul Note SN 1156 CD/LP
Ghiglioni; Steve Lacy (*ss*); Franco D'Andrea (*p*); Jean-Jacques Avenel (*b*); Oliver Johnson (*d*). 4/86.

***   **I'll Be Around** Soul Note 121256 CD/LP
Ghiglioni; Enrico Rava (*t*); Mal Waldron (*p*). 7–8/89.

Ghiglioni's albums for Soul Note seek out a more conservative context, with mixed results. The collection of standards and jazz themes with Drew's trio requires her to compete with the finest jazz singers and she makes heavy work of some of the tunes, although her occasionally wayward phrasing has its own charm in such as 'I Remember You'. Steve Lacy's iron presence is the dominant feature of *Somebody Special*, and while Ghiglioni is a better singer than Irene Aebi, and the quartet are in excellent form, the vocalist doesn't make a strong case for besting Lacy's sometimes intractable forms. *I'll Be Around* is dedicated to Billie Holiday, an inspiration rather than an influence, and in this collection of deathly slow ballads the singer does surprisingly well with Waldron and Rava, the latter especially at his most hauntingly poignant.

(*)   **Goodbye, Chet Philology W 22-2 CD
Ghiglioni; Chet Baker (*t*); Mike Melillo, E Olivieri (*p*); M Moriconi, Ilario De Marinis (*b*); Giovanni Ascolese, V Mazzone (*d*). 7/85–3/88.

A pretty strange record, even by the often oddball standards of Philology. Ghiglioni was to make a record with Baker but never did, and here instead is a set of eight standards by the singer with Melillo, followed by a rehearsal tape of Baker with Melillo's trio and an orchestra, which then leads into two versions of J. J. Johnson's 'Lament' by Baker with Ghigiloni's quartet at Bari harbour, taped in offhand circumstances by Paolo Piangiarelli. The songs with Melillo are well done by the singer, but whether one wants to go through the rest of it – Baker sounds as weary as usual in his final years – is another matter.

MICHAEL GIBBS (born 1937)
BANDLEADER, COMPOSER, TROMBONE, PIANO

***(*) **Big Music** Venture CDVE 27 CD
Gibbs; Lew Soloff, Alan Rubin, Earl Gardner, Ian Carr (*t*); Dave Bargeron, David
Taylor (*tb*); John Clark (*frhn*); Chris Hunter (*ss, as, ts, f*); Lou Marini (*ss, ts, f*); Jim
Odgren (*as*); Bob Mintzer (*ts, f, bcl*); Dave Tofani (*f, picc*); Brad Hatfield, David
Bristow (*ky*); John Scofield, Kevin Eubanks, Bill Frisell, Duke Levine, Dave
Fiuczynski (*g*); Kai Eckhardt (*b*); Bob Moses (*d*); Ben Wittman (*perc*). 89.

Thanks to such patrons as Stan Getz and Gary Burton, some of this Rhodesian-born composer's
themes have achieved a wider currency. But his infrequent records are almost all out of the
catalogue. Gibbs was early interested in the possibilities of jazz with rock, and there's no
discomfort in his use of drum machines, funk rhythms and the guitars of Eubanks, Scofield and
Frisell; yet this is very much a big band at work, rumbling forward rather than swinging, and
dealing in great blocks of sound rather than textural contrast. Vivid rhythm arrangements stop
the music from congealing, and features for Scofield and Hunter recall Gil Evans's way of
letting soloists emerge naturally from their surroundings. The record is a little shapeless as a
whole but offers many rewards. It sounds as if there was plenty of post-production on the sound,
although it's atmospherically mixed.

TERRY GIBBS (born 1924)
VIBRAPHONE, DRUMS

*** **Dream Band** Contemporary CCD 7647 CD/LP/MC

(*) **The Sundown Sessions Contemporary CCD 7562 CD/LP/MC

*** **Flying Home** Contemporary CCD 7654 CD/LP/MC
Gibbs; Conte Candoli, Al Porcino, Ray Triscari, Stu Williamson (*t*); Johnny Audino (*t*
on *Sundown Sessions*); Frank Higgins (*t* on *Flying Home*); Bob Enevoldsen (*vtb*);
Vernon Friley (*tb*); Bob Burgess (*tb* on *Sundown Sessions*); Joe Cadena, Med Flory,
Bill Holman (*ts*); Joe Maini, Charlie Kennedy (*as*); Jack Schwartz (*bs*); Pete Jolly (*p*);
Lou Levy (*p* on *Flying Home*); Max Bennett (*b*); Buddy Clark (*b* on *Flying Home*);
Mel Lewis (*d*). 3/59, 11/59, 3 & 11/59.

***(*) **Main Stem** Contemporary CCD 7656 CD/LP/MC
Gibbs; Conte Candoli, Frank Huggins, Al Porcino, Ray Triscari, Stu Williamson (*t*);
Bob Edmondson, Vernon Friley, Frank Rosolino (*tb*); Charlie Kennedy, Joe Maini (*as*);
Richie Kamuca, Bill Perkins (*ts*); Jack Nimitz (*bs*); Pat Moran (*p*); Buddy Clark (*b*);
Mel Lewis (*d*). 1/61.

*** **The Big Cat** Contemporary CCD 7657 CD/LP/MC
As above.

The Gibbs bands combined the high-energy swing of Lionel Hampton with the sophistication of
the Thad Jones/Mel Lewis outfits (Mel Lewis straddled the drum stool during Gibbs's most
productive period). The arrangements, by Marty Paich, Lennie Niehaus and others, are all
good, but with an emphasis on the higher horns that sounds mushy on LP. Gibbs's playing is
closer to Hampton's percussive bounce than to any of the competing influences (*Jazz Club –
Vibraphone* (Verve 840034) sets it in longer stylistic perspective) and he solos with considerable
verve; the two later sets are perhaps to be preferred and Gibbs's choruses on 'Ja-Da' (with
Candoli) and 'Sweet Georgia Brown' (with Triscari) are the highlights of *Main Stem*. Even so,
it's a style that draws a great deal from bop and it's no less well adapted to the small-group
performances on . . .

***(*) **Bopstacle Course** Xanadu 210 LP
Gibbs; Barry Harris (*p*); Sam Jones (*b*); Alan Dawson (*d*). 7/74.

*** **The Latin Connection** Contemporary C 14022 LP
Gibbs; Frank Morgan (*as*); Sonny Bravo (*p*); Bobby Rodriguez (*b*); Tito Puente,
Orestes Vilato (*timbales*); Jose Madera Jr, Johnny Rodriguez (*perc*). 5/86.

***   **Chicago Fire** Contemporary 14036 CD/LP/MC

***   **Holiday For Swing** Contemporary 14047 CD/LP/MC
Gibbs; Buddy DeFranco (*cl*); John Campbell II (*p*); Todd Coolman (*b*); Gerry Gibbs (*d*). 7/87, 8/88.

***   **Air Mail Special** Contemporary 14056 CD/LP/MC
Gibbs; Buddy DeFranco (*cl*); Frank Collett (*p*); Andy Simpkins (*b*); Jimmie Smith (*d*). 10/81.

***(*)   **Memories Of You** Contemporary 14066 CD
Gibbs; Buddy DeFranco (*cl*); Herb Ellis (*g*); Larry Novak (*p*); Milt Hinton (*b*); Butch Miles (*d*).

Lively latter-day sets from a player who must be taking multi-vitamins. *Bopstacle Course* might be the best of the bunch, but for the absence of a CD option and some problems with volume. The original 'Do You Mind?' is full of harmonic interest and the theme is developed in intriguing directions by Gibbs and Jones. The standards are better still, with a remarkably cool and abstract reading of 'Body And Soul' (a tune he returns to on *Air Mail Special*) and an equally bold interpretation of 'Softly As In A Morning Sunrise' that parcels out the melody round the band. The Latin sessions are particularly well suited to Gibbs's approach, and some of the rhythmic interplay is quite dazzling, with Morgan well to the fore in one of the best of his comeback performances.

The remainder of this batch team him with fellow New Jerseyan DeFranco in a series of friendly but competitive sets, which were also repeated with the clarinettist as (strictly nominal) leader, but what's a credit among friends? The CD-only *Memories Of You* is perhaps the best all-round set, with an excellent reading of 'Flying Home' and a romantic but un-schmaltzy 'Poor Butterfly'. Of the remainder, *Air Mail Special* ('Love For Sale', 'Blues For Brody', 'Body And Soul') is particularly recommended, with *Chicago Fire* (unexpected versions of 'Giant Steps' and the '52nd Street Theme'). The big-band stuff is the most wholly authentic, but Gibbs's small groups are perhaps more in tune with prevailing tastes.

DIZZY GILLESPIE (born 1917)
TRUMPET, PERCUSSION, PIANO, VOCAL

****   **Shaw 'Nuff** Musicraft MVSCD-53 CD
Gillespie; Dave Burns, Ray Orr, Talib Daawud, John Lynch, Kenny Dorham, Elmon Wright, Matthew McKay (*t*); Al Moore, Leon Comeghys, Charles Greenlea, Gordon Thomas, Taswell Baird (*tb*); Charlie Parker, Sonny Stitt (*as*); Dexter Gordon (*ts*); Howard Johnson, John Brown, Ray Abrams, Warren Luckey, Pee Wee Moore, Scoops Carey, James Moody, Billy Frazier, Leo Parker (*saxes*); Frank Paparelli, Clyde Hart, Al Haig, John Lewis (*p*); Milt Jackson (*vib*); Chuck Wayne, Remo Palmieri (*g*); Murray Shipinsky, Ray Brown, Curly Russell, Slam Stewart (*b*); Shelly Manne, Cozy Cole, Sid Catlett, Kenny Clarke, Joe Harris (*d*); Sarah Vaughan, Alice Roberts, Gil Fuller (*v*). 2/45–11/46.

***(*)   **Groovin' High** Savoy SV-0152 CD
As above, except omit Vaughan, Roberts. 2/45–11/46.

John Birks Gillespie had already been recording for almost a decade when he made the earliest of these tracks, and in the Cab Calloway and Teddy Hill bands he cut the outline of a promising Roy Eldridge disciple. His associations with Thelonious Monk and Charlie Parker, though, took him into hitherto uncharted realms. While he continues to credit Parker as the real inspirational force behind bebop, Gillespie was the movement's scholar, straw boss, sartorial figurehead and organizer: his love of big band sound led him into attempts to orchestrate the new music which resulted in some of the most towering jazz records, particularly (among those here) 'Things To Come' and (among those on the essential supplement to this disc, RCA Bluebird's *The Bebop Revolution* compilation) 'Cubano Be-Cubano Bop'. But his own playing is at least as powerful a reason to listen to these tracks. Gillespie brought a new virtuosity to jazz trumpet just as Parker created a matchless vocabulary for the alto sax. It scarcely seems possible that the music could have moved on from Louis Armstrong's 'Cornet Chop Suey' to Gillespie's astonishing flight on 'Dizzy Atmosphere' in only 20 years. A dazzling tone, solo construction that was as logical as it was unremittingly daring, and an harmonic grasp which was built out of countless nights of study and experimentation: Gillespie showed the way for every trumpeter in post-war jazz. His Musicraft recordings include a single sextet track with Dexter Gordon ('Blue 'N' Boogie'), seven with Parker, four with Sonny Stitt and Milt Jackson, and the balance with his big band. There are what amount to novelty vocals (such as 'He Beeped When He Shoulda Bopped') which slow the pace down to some extent, but even these underline the good humour and sly bravado which have equally informed Gillespie's art, and without which no portrait of him would be complete. The transfers are good, though one feels that those on the Savoy reissue are rather brighter; however, this edition leaves out six of the tracks included on the Musicraft disc.

(***) **Live 1946** Bandstand BDCD 1534 CD
Gillespie; Dave Burns, Talib Daawood, Kenny Dorham, John Lynch, Elmon Wright (*t*); Leon Comegeys, Charles Greenlea, Alton 'Slim' Moore (*tb*); Howard Johnson, Sonny Stitt (*as*); Ray Abrams, Warren Luckey (*ts*); Leo Parker (*bs*); Milt Jackson (*vib*); Thelonious Monk, John Lewis (*p*); Ray Brown (*b*); Kenny Clarke (*d*). 6–11/46.

*** **Bebop Enters Sweden** Dragon DRLP 34 LP
Gillespie, Benny Bailey, Dave Burns, Lamar Wright Jr, Elmon Wright, Conte Candoli, Gosta Torner, Arnold Johansson (*t*); William Shepherd, Ted Kelly (*tb*); John Brown, Howard Johnson, Arne Domnérus (*as*); Joe Gayles, George Nicholas, Frank Socolow, Lennart Kohlin (*ts*); Cecil Payne (*bs*); John Lewis, Lou Levy, Gosta Theselius (*p*); Terry Gibbs (*vib*); Chubby Jackson, Al McKibbon, Leppe Sundewall (*b*); Denzil Best, Kenny Clarke, Sven Bollhem, Jack Noren (*d*); Chano Pozo (*perc*). 12/47–10/49.

Although the big band made only a small number of studio records, it was caught on the wing at a number of concerts, even if seldom in hi-fi conditions. The Bandstand set is typical: three New York gigs, all with the band sounding in good spirits, but only the very last track – an ominous-sounding reading of 'Emanon' – approaching a truthful recording. The Dragon LP is in comparatively fine sound: it's shared between Gillespie's band, a sextet led by Chubby Jackson, with Terry Gibbs and Conte Candoli, and James Moody guesting with a Swedish band. The Gillespie session, though, is the most important: they rarely stray from familiar arrangements of 'Ool-Ya-Koo' or 'Ray's Idea', and none of the performances breaks what would have been the regular 78-side barrier, but the frisson of a live set adds some extra pep to the playing (even though this was reportedly an unhappy tour away from the bandstand). Four (unidentified) tracks from the same period are tacked on to the end of the LRC album listed below. A classic session recorded in Pasadena in August 1948 is currently unavailable.

*** **Pleyel Concert 1953** Vogue 655608 CD
Gillespie; Bill Graham (*bs*); Wade Legge (*p*); Lou Hackney (*b*); Al Jones (*d*); Joe Carroll (*v*). 2/53.

When economics required Gillespie to dissolve the big band, he carried on with small groups. Operating at something of a tangent to bop – he still performed with Parker on a few occasions, and there is a superb session for Verve with Monk and Bird, as well as the famous Massey Hall concert of 1953 – his playing began to take on a grandeur which sounded even more ravishing than Parker's alto did when confronted with strings. At the same time, he continued to delight in on-stage horseplay, and this record of a French concert includes plenty of interplay with Joe Carroll on the likes of 'Oo-Shoo-Be-Doo-Be'. What's missing is anyone to challenge him the way Parker or Powell could.

*** **Diz And Getz** Verve 833559-2 CD
Gillespie; Stan Getz (*ts*); Oscar Peterson (*p*); Herb Ellis (*g*); Ray Brown (*b*); Max Roach (*d*). 12/53.

(*) **For Musicians Only Verve 837435-2 CD
As above, except add Sonny Stitt (*as*), John Lewis (*p*), Stan Levey (*d*), omit Peterson and Roach. 10/56.

These all-star encounters have perhaps been overrated. It's interesting to hear Gillespie on what was effectively mainstream material on *Diz And Getz* – two Ellington tunes, three standards and a single Latin theme – but the group strike a surprisingly shambolic note in places, seldom managing to play together, and the superfast blues 'Impromptu' is a virtual disaster. Worth salvaging are a lovely trumpet treatment of 'It's The Talk Of The Town', some moments from the otherwise audibly ruffled Getz, and a version of 'It Don't Mean A Thing' where the tempo is actually matched by the intensity of the playing. The music has never sounded like a great feat of engineering, and the latest CD transfer improves little on previous editions. *For Musicians Only* is even more of a blow-out, with 'Be-Bop' and 'Dark Eyes' running over 12 minutes each and Stitt treating it as a carving session: the tempos are almost uniformly hell-for-leather. Exhilarating in small doses, but it's hardly as significant a date as it might have been with a little preparation.

*** **Groovin' High** Bandstand BDCD 1513 CD
Gillespie; Joe Gordon, Ermet Perry, Carl Warwick, Quincy Jones (*t*); Melba Liston, Frank Rehak, Rod Levitt (*tb*); Phil Woods, Jimmy Powell, Ernie Henry (*as*); Benny Golson, Billy Mitchell, Ernie Wilkins (*ts*); Marty Flax (*bs*); Walter Bishop (*p*); Nelson Boyd (*b*); Charlie Persip (*d*). 8–12/56.

Gillespie was sponsored by the State Department to take a big band on a world tour, and it was a fine orchestra: but their few studio sessions are mostly out of print, and Dizzy had to break the band up again for lack of work by the end of 1957. This disc couples two live sessions: the first is rather mustily recorded, but the cleaner, tighter sound of the second gives some indication of the crispness of the sections and the calibre of the arrangements (by Melba Liston and others). Dizzy himself sounds Olympian in many places: try the astonishing, vaulting coda to 'Tangorine' as one example.

*** **A Portrait Of Duke Ellington** Verve 817107-2 CD
Gillespie; Bennie Green (*tb*); Robert de Dominica (*f*); Stan Webb, Paul Richie, John Murtaugh, Ernest Bright (*woodwinds*); Richard Berg, Ray Alonge, Joe Singer (*frhn*); George Devens (*vib*); Hank Jones (*p*); Jay McAllister (*tba*); George Duvivier (*b*); Charlie Persip (*d*). 4/60.

*** **Compact/Walkman Jazz: Dizzy Gillespie** Mercury 832574 CD/MC
Gillespie; Lee Morgan, Ermet Perry, Carl Warwick, Talib Dawud (*t*); Melba Liston, Al Grey, Chuck Connors, (*tb*); Leo Wright (*as*, *f*); Jimmy Powell, Ernie Henry (*as*); James Moody (*ts*, *f*); Billy Mitchell, Sonny Stitt, Benny Golson (*ts*); Pee Wee Moore, Charlie Ventura (*bs*); Gilberto Valdes (*f*); Alejandro Hernandez, Wynton Kelly, Kenny Barron, Lalo Schifrin, Junior Mance, Ray Bryant (*p*); Elec Basik (*g*); Roberto Rodriguez, Paul West, Tommy Bryant, Chris White, Sam Jones (*b*); Lex Humphries, Charlie Persip, Rudy Collins (*d*); Candido Camero, Rafael Miranda, Jose Mangual, Ubaldo Nieto, Kansas Fields (*perc*). 6/54–11/64.

*** **Round Midnight: Dizzy Gillespie** Verve 510088-2 CD
As above, except add Quincy Jones, Jimmy Nottingham, Ernie Royal (*t*); Jimmy Cleveland, Rod Levitt, Henry Coker, Frank Rehak, Leon Comegys, J. J. Johnson, George Matthews (*tb*); George Dawson, Gigi Gryce, Hilton Jefferson (*as*); Hank Mobley, Lucky Thompson, Ernie Wilkins (*ts*); Billy Root, Danny Bank, Marty Flax (*bs*); Wade Legge, Walter Davis Jr (*p*); Lou Hackney (*b*); Carlos Valdes (*perc*); omit Connors, Stitt, Moore, Hernandez, Kelly, Rodriguez, Candido, Miranda, Mangual, Nieto. 6/54–11/64.

Gillespie's Verve contract was finally disappointing in that it produced no single indispensable record. The big-and small-band dates were pot-pourris of dazzling breaks and solos which never quite gelled into the long-playing masterpiece Gillespie surely had in him at this time. Having already outlived many of his key contemporaries in bebop, he was beginning to be a player in search of a context. The Ellington album, skilfully if sometimes blandly arranged by Clare Fischer, is a fine showpiece-set but not a very meaningful meditation on the composer's music: it's no more profound than Richards's scores had been ten years earlier, and perhaps a bit less exciting. Best to turn to the two compilations, though one could blend the best of each of them for a single greater record. After a 'Night In Tunisia' with Latin musicians, the *Compact Jazz* disc meanders through mostly small-band dates, and often misses some good material: the fine *Have Trumpet, Will Excite!* session, for instance, is plundered only for 'Lorraine', a pretty but not very exciting ballad. That track also appears on the *Round Midnight* set, which starts with a series of calypso features for Dizzy's early-1960s group and then drifts back through some of the 1950s big band music. In keeping with the rest of this series, it concentrates on ballads over up-tempo tunes, but there is a fine 'There Is No Greater Love' and the touring big band working over 'Whisper Not' and 'I Can't Get Started'. Sound on both discs is very bright, occasionally harsh but clear.

**   **Angel City** Moon 025 CD/LP
Gillespie; Harry Edison, Melvin Moore, Fred Hill, Johnny Audino (*t*); Lester Robinson, Francis Fitzpatrick, Jim Amlotte (*tb*); Herman Lebow, Sam Cassano, David Burke, Alan Robinson (*frhn*); Buddy Collette, Gabe Baltazar, Bill Green, Carrington sor Jr, Jack Nimitz (*reeds*); Phil Moore (*p*); Bobby Hutcherson (*vib*); Dennis Budimir (*g*); Jimmy Bond (*b*); Earl Palmer (*d*). 65.

It must have been a fine band, but you can't tell much from this sloppy recording. Gil Fuller's score on 'Fuller's Idea' is fairly decimated by the low-fi. There are also two quintet tracks.

**   **Dizzy Gillespie & Mitchell-Ruff Duo** Mainstream MDCD 721 CD
Gillespie; Dwight Mitchell (*p*); Willie Ruff (*b*, *frhn*). 71.

Dizzy seems to have been a surprise guest at a concert by the Mitchell-Ruff duo. In the circumstances, he plays a couple of Gillespian solos, but this is hardly an important part of his discography.

***(*)   **Dizzy Gillespie's Big 4** Original Jazz Classics OJC 443 CD/LP/MC
Gillespie; Joe Pass (*g*); Ray Brown (*b*); Mickey Roker (*d*). 9/74.

(*)   **The Trumpet Kings Meet Joe Turner Original Jazz Classics OJC 497 CD/LP/MC
Gillespie; Roy Eldridge, Clark Terry, Harry Edison (*t*); Connie Crayton (*g*); Jimmy Robbins (*b*); Washington Rucker (*d*); Joe Turner (*v*). 9/74.

**   **The Trumpet Kings At Montreux '75** Original Jazz Classics OJC 445 CD/LP/MC
Gillespie; Roy Eldridge, Clark Terry (*t*); Oscar Peterson (*p*); Niels-Henning Ørsted-Pedersen (*b*); Louie Bellson (*d*). 7/75.

(*)   **Montreux '77 Original Jazz Classics OJC 381 CD/LP/MC
Gillespie; Jan Faddis (*t*); Milt Jackson (*vib*); Monty Alexander (*p*); Ray Brown (*b*); Jimmie Smith (*d*). 7/77.

(*)   **The Trumpet Summit Meets The Oscar Peterson Big 4 Original Jazz Classics OJC 603 CD/LP/MC
Gillespie; Freddie Hubbard, Clark Terry (*t*); Oscar Peterson (*p*); Joe Pass (*g*); Ray Brown (*b*); Bobby Durham (*d*). 3/80.

**   **The Best Of Dizzy Gillespie** Pablo 2405-411 CD/LP/MC

Gillespie's Pablo period marked a return to regular recording of some years of neglect in the studios. The *Big 4* album was the first session he did and it remains perhaps the best. There is a superb display of trumpet chops in 'Be Bop', a very good ballad in 'Hurry Home' and an intriguing revision of 'Jitterbug Waltz' where Pass and Gillespie push each other into their best form. The other records seem to betray Norman Granz's indecision as to how best to employ Dizzy's talents. The three Trumpet Kings/Summit encounters are typical of their kind: brilliant flashes of virtuosity interspersed with rhetoric and mere showing-off. The best is probably the Joe Turner meeting, where the great R&B singer puts everyone through their paces. *Montreux '77* is Gillespie featuring his young protégé, Jon Faddis, who xeroxes the young Gillespie style but comes up with a remark or two of his own. The best-of set is weak, picking some tracks off records that have thankfully disappeared, including a hopeless collaboration with Lalo Schifrin. A pity, though, that one of the better Pablo albums, *Bahiana*, has yet to make it to CD.

***   **Jazzbühne Berlin 1981** Repertoire REP 4913 CD
Gillespie; Curtis Fuller (*tb*); Ed Cherry (*g*); Michael Howell (*b*); Tommy Campbell (*d*). 5/81.

**   **New Faces** GRP 91012 CD/MC
Gillespie; Branford Marsalis (*ss*, *ts*); Kenny Kirkland (*p*); Lonnie Plaxico, Lincoln Goines (*b*); Robert Ameen (*d*); Steve Thornton (*perc*). 84.

***   **Dizzy Gillespie Meets Phil Woods Quintet** Timeless SJP 250 CD/LP
Gillespie; Tom Harrell (*t*); Phil Woods (*as*); Hal Galper (*p*); Steve Gilmore (*b*); Bill Goodwin (*d*). 12/86.

*   **Endlessly** MCA MCAD 42153 CD/MC
Gillespie; Arthur Blythe (*as*); Manny Boyd (*ts, f*); Barry Eastmond (*ky*); Vesta Maxey (*vib*); Steve Kelly, Steve Love, Bobby Broom (*g*); Lonnie Plaxico, Alex Blake, John Lee (*b*); Robert Ameen, Buddy Williams, Victor Jones (*d*); Marya Casales (*perc*). 2–5/87.

(*)   **Live At the Royal Festival Hall Enja 6044 CD/LP/MC
Gillespie; Arturo Sandoval, Claudio Roditi (*t*); Slide Hampton (*tb*); Steve Turre (*tb, conch*); Paquito D'Rivera (*as, cl*); James Moody (*ts, f, as*); Mario Rivera (*ss, ts, perc*); Danilo Perez (*p*); Ed Cherry (*g*); John Lee (*b*); Ignacio Berroa (*d*); Airto Moreira, Giovanni Hidalgo (*perc*); Flora Purim (*v*). 6/89.

The haphazard nature of Gillespie's recording regimen in the 1980s brings home how much the industry has wasted the opportunity to provide a meaningful context for such a creative musician. Perpetually on the road, perhaps Dizzy simply hasn't been so interested in making records; but the point remains that his legacy of genuinely great records is disappointingly small, and mostly concentrated at the other end of his career. The Berlin concert catches one of his touring bands in good fettle, with the leader sonding still in very creative mind, even on material which he'd played over and over down the years. Fuller has a pleasing if over-extended feature of his own on 'Lover Man', and the sound is surprisingly sharp and clear. His guest appearance with the Phil Woods band is respectable fare as such things go: there is yet another ''Round Midnight' of little interest, and Tom Harrell (uncredited) takes all the really strong trumpet parts, but it's a goodish Woods album with Dizzy making a few remarks. The two GRP albums are missable. *New Faces* pits Dizzy against various young turks: their chops are in better shape, and he paces things to suit himself, the result being an awkward encounter. *Endlessly*, elevator music with strings, is junk, and the least credible album he's made. The Festival Hall concert catches something of the exuberance which continues to attend this kind of global-summit band, and though it's best approached as a souvenir for anyone who heard the group in concert, there are felicitous moments from a band very eager to please their boss.

***(*)   **Max + Dizzy, Paris 1989** A&M 6404 2CD
Gillespie; Max Roach (*d*). 3/89.

A unique, moving, exciting experience. Bop's most eminent surviving champions reflect on close to 50 years of their music in an encounter which is as free as either man will ever play. Across some 90 minutes of music (the final section features the two of them talking it over), Roach sometimes pushes Dizzy a shade uncaringly, for the trumpeter's powers aren't what they were; but most of the horn playing is astonishingly clean and unmarked for a man in his seventies. As a kind of living history lesson, or a record of two of jazz's great personalities having a final exchange of ideas, it's a singular and generously entertaining occasion. Excellent sound.

(*)   **Bebop And Beyond Plays Dizzy Gillespie Blue Moon 917072 CD
Gillespie; Warren Gale (*t, flhn*); Mel Martin (*ss, as, ts, f*); George Cables (*p*); Randy Vincent (*g*); Jeff Chambers (*b*); Donald Bailey (*d*); Vince Lateano, John Santos (*perc*). 5/91.

Bebop And Beyond are a good bop repertory group, and they create an affectionate backdrop for the old man here. With his articulation and delivery now blurred, Gillespie's work has to stand on the innate class of his musical ideas, and harmonically he's still thinking up new turns on the old steps.

GEORGE GIRARD (1930–57)
TRUMPET, VOCAL

***   **George Girard** Storyville SLP 6013 LP
    Girard; Santo Pecora, Bob Havens (*tb*); Raymond Burke, Harry Shields (*cl*); Lester
    Bouchon (*ts*); Jeff Riddick (*p, v*); Bob Discon (*p*); Emile Christian, Chink Martin (*b*);
    Monk Hazel, Paul Edwards (*d*). 9/54–7/56.

Girard, who died young after contracting cancer, was a very fine trumpeter. He made his name
in the Basin Street Six with Pete Fountain, but these recordings – one session made at the
Municipal Auditorium in 1954, the other at the Parisian Room in 1956, only a few months
before his death – offer formidable evidence of a great, idiosyncratic New Orleans hornman,
somewhat in the manner (if not the style) of Henry Allen. Girard's firm lead is countered by his
unpredictable solos, which may suddenly flare up into wild high notes or stay in a sober middle
range: he's hard to second-guess, even on warhorse material such as the tunes played at the 1956
session, which also has excellent work from Havens and Shields. The earlier date is marred by
the recording, which is poorly balanced and muffled, and by the feeble tenor work of Bouchon;
but Girard and Pecora are both very good: the trumpeter's brilliant solo on 'A Good Man Is
Hard To Find' is a small masterpiece of controlled tension. The 1956 recordings are more than
adequate, and it's hard to believe that Girard's playing is the work of a man who was already
very ill.

JIMMY GIUFFRE (born 1921)
CLARINET, TENOR SAXOPHONE, SOPRANO SAXOPHONE, FLUTE, BASS FLUTE

***(*)   **The Jimmy Giuffre 3** Atlantic 90981 CD
    Giuffre; Jim Hall (*g*); Jim Atlas, Ralph Pena (*b*). 12/56.

***   **Princess** Fini Jazz 8803 CD/LP
    Giuffre; Jim Hall (*g*); Buddy Clark (*b*). 6/59.

****   **1961** ECM 1438/9 2CD/2LP
    Giuffre; Paul Bley (*p*); Steve Swallow (*b*). 3 & 8/61.

Cultivating a brown *chalumeau* register on his clarinet and defending the aesthetic benefits of
simple quietness, Giuffre created what he liked to call 'folk jazz'. *The Jimmy Giuffre Clarinet*
and *Music Man*, recorded for Atlantic in the 1950s, evoked a middle-America which had
hitherto played little part in jazz. Giuffre's soft meditations and homely foot-tapping on the
earlier album suggested a man playing out on his front porch, sufficiently solitary and
unselfconscious to forget the rules and try out unfamiliar tonalities. Giuffre's subsequent
drummerless trios and cool, almost abstract tonality created almost as much stir as Gerry
Mulligan's pianoless quintets and encountered considerable critical resistance at the end of the
1950s.

    The Jimmy Giuffre 3 contains some of the essential early material, notably a fine version of
'The Train and the River', on which Giuffre moves between baritone and tenor saxophones and
clarinet, and the long 'Crawdad Suite', which intelligently combines blues and folk materials.
Giuffre's out-of-tempo playing recalls the great jazz singers. Jim Hall was his longest-standing
and most sympathetic cohort; they were partnered either by trombonist Bob Brookmeyer or a
bassist, most successfully Ralph Pena or Buddy Clark (Jim Atlas only plays on two bonus tracks
on the Atlantic CD).

    Princess is a live set, recorded in Europe. The sound isn't pristine, but the music is lovely.
The routine charges of abstraction and 'no swing' seem entirely absurd in the face of music so
perfectly oriented that every track seems to balance like a compass needle. Strongly
recommended.

    Nothing, though, quite prepares us for the astonishing work that Giuffre created with Paul
Bley and Steve Swallow in two 1961 albums called *Fusion* (a term which hadn't yet taken on its
1970s associations) and *Thesis* (which seemed equally unpromising as the title of a jazz album).
Paired and remastered as *1961* they constitute ECM's first ever reissue and it's interesting, first,
how modern the music sounds after thirty years (compare it with the Owl sets below) and then
how closely it seems to conform to ECM's familiar aesthetics of great formal precision and
limpid sound. Herb Snitzer's session photographs have often been commented on. In deeply

shadowed and evocatively focused black and white, they say something about the music. It's arguable that Giuffre's playing is equally monochrome and its basic orientation uncomfortably abstract, but again one notices its sometimes urgent but always compelling swing. The slightly earlier *Fusion* is perhaps the more daring of the two sets, balancing starkly simple ideas, as on 'Jesus Maria' and 'Scootin' About' with some complex harmonic conceptions (to which all three contribute). *Thesis*, though, is tighter and more fully realized and tunes like 'Ictus' and 'Carla' (the former written by the dedicatee of the latter, Bley's then wife, Carla Bley) have been an inexhaustible element of the pianist's concert improvisations ever since. By contrast, the music on *Fusion* seems fixed in and of its moment.

These are essential documents in the development of a broader jazz idiom that refused to see bop as the only recourse. Giuffre's pioneering has only slowly been recognized and it's valuable to jump straight from these sessions to *Diary Of A Trio*, below. Almost nothing has changed, except that Giuffre's tone has lost its slightly discursive quality, an effect underlined by his use of soprano saxophone, and Steve Swallow has renounced upright bass, on which he creates throbbing lines and interjections (these are, perhaps, the most dramatic sounds on *1961*) in favour of bass guitar.

***   **Quasar** Soul Note 1108 CD/LP
Giuffre; Pete Levin (*ky*); Bob Nieske (*b*); Randy Kaye (*d*). 5/85.

***   **Liquid Dancers** Soul Note 1158 CD/LP
As above. 4/89.

For much of the later 1960s and '70s, the most intuitive improviser of his generation was obliged to teach improvisation to college students, gigging only in relative obscurity. Randy Kaye was a loyal and dependable supporter in those days, and adds just the right kind of softly enunciated percussion to Giuffre's 1980s quartet albums (a third Soul Note, *Dragonfly*, is currently unavailable).

Bob Nieske's 'The Teacher', on *Liquid Dancers*, pays no less a tribute. Scored for Giuffre's bass flute, it has a crepuscular, meditative quality that isn't altogether typical of a lively and almost self-consciously ('Move With the Times') contemporary set. Levin's keyboard stylings are perhaps a little too blandly atmospheric, but they open up the texture for Giuffre's familiar chalumeau clarinet and a surprisingly agile soprano saxophone.

The earlier *Quasar* is equally fine and the writing may even be a little better.

***(*)   **Eiffel** CELP C6 CD
Giuffre; André Jaume (*bcl, sax*). 11/87.

The best of these thoughtful, often delicate duos recall the best of Giuffre's work with Bookmeyer. Jaume has the same intensity and dry wit and the register of his bass clarinet is not so far from that of the trombone. Recorded in concert, *Eiffel* consists of scored and improvised duets, none longer than five and a half minutes, most around three. Jaume's saxophone on 'Stand Point' tends to break the mood a little but the studied, contemplative tone remains otherwise intact and Giuffre's articulation and tone have seldom been more compelling.

****   **Diary Of A Trio: Saturday** Owl 059 CD

****   **Diary Of A Trio: Sunday** Owl 060 CD
Giuffre; Paul Bley (*p*); Steve Swallow (*b*); solos, duos and trio. 12/89.

When Jimmy Giuffre went back into the studio with Paul Bley and Steve Swallow in December 1989, the first notes he improvised were identical to a figure he had played on their last meeting nearly thirty years before. Whether conscious or not, the gesture helps underline not just the intevening period of (for Giuffre) relative neglect, but also the tremendous understanding that developed in the trio that produced *Free Fall*, *Fusion* and *Thesis*.

Diary of a Trio is an astonishing achievement, whatever the chronology. A series of solos, duos and trio pieces, it has considerable spontaneity and freedom. There are, of course, significant changes from the early records. Swallow is now wholly converted to electric bass, and is perhaps the leading bass guitarist in improvised music; Bley, though, has passed through his romance with electronics, and now concentrates almost exclusively on acoustic piano. Giuffre, who was always a formidable tenor player as well as clarinettist, has added soprano saxophone, relishing both its directness and its untamable 'wildness' of pitch. Not least of the differences is a willingness to play standards, which they do with a characteristically oblique touch. Most highly recommended.

GLOBE UNITY ORCHESTRA
GROUP

***   **Live In Wuppertal 73** FMP 0160 LP
Manfred Schoof, Kenny Wheeler (*t*); Paul Rutherford, Gunter Christmann (*tb*); Evan Parker (*ss, ts*); Peter Bennink (*as, bagpipes*); Peter Brötzmann (*as, ts, bsx*); Gerd Dudek, Michel Pilz (*bs, bcl, f*); Peter Kowald (*tba, alphorn*); Alex Von Schlippenbach (*p*); Buschi Niebergall (*b*); Paul Lovens (*d*).

***   **Evidence Vol. 1** FMP 0220 LP
As above, except Albert Mangelsdorff (*tb*) replaces Christmann, Steve Lacy (*ss*) replaces Bennink, omit Schoof, Brötzmann, Pilz and Niebergall. 3/75.

***   **Into The Valley Vol. 2** FMP 0270 LP
As above. 3/75.

***(*) **Rumbling** FMP CD 40 CD
As above. 3/75.

Formed in 1966, the Globe Unity Orchestra has had to sustain itself with rare concerts and even rarer records, an unworthy fate for arguably the finest group to attempt to reconcile big-band forms with free improvisation. Although there has been a revolving cast of players throughout the group's existence, a few hardy spirits – notably Alex Schlippenbach, the original organizer – act as a point of reference. The *Wuppertal* LP is divided into a section of short pieces and a long work-out credited to Kowald and, while the fragments of 'Wolverine Blues' and Eisler's 'Solidaritatslied' are rumbustiously done and suggest an interest in repertory which is an early precursor of much of today's jazz activity, it's the long 'Maniacs' which has the real creative energy. The second and third records are credited to 'Globe Unity Special' and are more like a contingent from the orchestra. *Evidence* offers Monk's title-tune, a march by Misha Mengelberg and a tune by Lacy, while *Into The Valley* is a nearly continuous, 38-minute piece. The latter is the best demonstration of the group's powers, moving through solo and duet passages between the horns to thunderous all-in tussles. Problematically, all three records are inadequately recorded, the 1975 concerts sounding grey and boxy, with all detail lost at loud moments. However, the appearance of *Rumbling*, which collects the music from the second and third albums on to a single remastered CD, has alleviated this difficulty to some extent: it's still a less-than-perfect recording, but the sound is much bigger and more convincing here.

***(*) **Hamburg '74** FMP 0650 LP
Manfred Schoof, Kenny Wheeler (*t*); Gunter Christmann, Paul Rutherford (*tb*); Peter Brötzmann, Rudiger Carl, Gerd Dudek, Evan Parker, Michel Pilz (*reeds*); Alex Von Schlippenbach (*p*); Derek Bailey (*g*); Peter Kowald (*b, tba*); Han Bennink (*d, perc, cl*); Paul Lovens (*d*); Choir of the NDR-Broadcast, Helmut Franz (*cond*).

****   **Pearls** FMP 0380 LP
As above, except add Enrico Rava (*t*), Albert Mangelsdorff (*tb*), Anthony Braxton (*reeds*), Buschi Niebergall (*b*), omit Bennink and Bailey. 11/76.

The collaboration with the NDR Choir is an unprecedented fusion and, as chaotic and unresolved as it sometimes sounds, the music – a long construction by Schlippenbach and another by Schoof – is wild, funny and unique. The contrast between the superbly drilled outbursts of the choir and the spontaneous bluster of the orchestra makes for an odd kind of creative tension and, while it's probably a failure, it's an extraordinary one. Greatly superior recording to the previous records, as is also the case for *Pearls*, the finest record by the Orchestra. A long Evan Parker construction contains a series of duets between members of the Orchestra; Schlippenbach's 'Kunstmusik II' is a stunning evocation of a composed improvisation; and a lugubrious 'Ruby My Dear' takes sudden life with a scathing alto solo by guest Braxton.

***   **Compositions** JAPO 60027 LP
As above, except Steve Lacy (*ss*) replaces Braxton, Bob Stewart (*tba*) replaces Kowald, omit Carl. 1/79.

***   **Intergalactic Blow** JAPO 60039 LP
Toshinori Kondo, Kenny Wheeler (*t*); Gunter Christmann, Albert Mangelsdorff, George Lewis (*tb*); Gerd Dudek (*ss, ts, f*); Evan Parker (*ss, ts*); Ernst Ludwig Petrowsky (*as, bs, f*); Alex Von Schlippenbach (*p*); Bob Stewart (*tba*); Alan Silva (*b*); Paul Lovens (*d*). 6/82.

Compositions is a sequence of mostly brief themes contributed by members of the Orchestra, and some are more suitable than others: Lacy's 'Worms' crawls almost unbearably, but Schoof's 'Reflections' and Wheeler's 'Nodagoo' are satisfying set-pieces. Excellent studio sound. The companion record from this period, *Improvisations*, is out of print. *Intergalactic Blow* provides four improvisations by a new edition of the Orchestra. Some of the music is a little sluggish – 'Quasar' sounds as if it's trying to get started for nearly ten minutes – and the somehat recessed sound isn't helpful, but the cumulative power of 'Mond Im Skorpion' is impressive and there is the usual dusting of scintillating moments.

GIL GOLDSTEIN
KEYBOARDS

***   **City Of Dreams** Blue Note CDP 793893 CD
Goldstein; John Clark (*frhn*); John Patitucci (*b*); Lenny White (*d*); Don Alias, Bruce Martin (*perc*). 3–7/89.

Goldstein's sideman work with Billy Cobham and Gil Evans suggests a personality comfortable in brawny fusion and more impressionistic music alike, and it's fitting that his solo record touches both bases. Some of his own tunes lack distinction, but he also covers Egberto Gismonti, Jaco Pastorious, Richard Rodgers and Lennon and McCartney here and makes it into a plausible, enjoyable sort of pop-jazz, modish but not without substance – in his thoughtful piano solos – and a certain charm.

BENNY GOLSON (born 1929)
TENOR SAXOPHONE

***   **Benny Golson's New York Scene** Original Jazz Classics OJC 164 CD/LP
Golson; Art Farmer (*t*); Jimmy Cleveland (*tb*); Julius Watkins (*frhn*); Gigi Gryce (*as*); Sahib Shihab (*bs*); Wynton Kelly (*p*); Paul Chambers (*b*); Charlie Persip (*d*). 10/57.

****   **Groovin' With Golson** Original Jazz Classics OJC 226 LP
Golson; Curtis Fuller (*tb*); Ray Bryant (*p*); Paul Chambers (*b*); Art Blakey (*d*). 8/59.

***   **The Other Side Of Benny Golson** Original Jazz Classics OJC 1750 CD/LP
Golson; Curtis Fuller (*tb*); Barry Harris (*p*); Jymie Merritt (*b*); Philly Joe Jones (*d*). 11/58.

He is still best known as an arranger and composer – of such standards as 'I Remember Clifford', 'Whisper Not' and 'Stablemates' – so Benny Golson's powers as a saxophonist have been somewhat undervalued as a result. Although he has contributed several of the staple pieces in the hard-bop repertoire, his own playing style originally owed rather more to such swing masters as Hawkins and Lucky Thompson: a big, crusty tone and a fierce momentum sustain his solos, and they can take surprising and exciting turns, even if the unpredictability sometimes leads to a loss of focus. The 1957 session concentrates on the more reflective side of his work, with three tracks by a nonet, three by a quintet with Farmer, and a ballad interpretation of 'You're Mine You' with the rhythm section alone: all well played but comparatively reserved. The later discs are by the group which would, when joined full-time by Farmer, become the Jazztet. *Groovin'* is titled appropriately since the band hit a splendid pace from the start, and Golson and Fuller turn in inspired solos. *The Other Side* is at a lower temperature but is still very worthwhile. We hope that two more sessions with Fuller from the same period, *Gettin' With It* and *Gone With Golson*, will be reissued soon.

*** **California Message** Timeless SJP 177 CD/LP
Golson; Oscar Brashear (*t*); Curtis Fuller, Thurman Green (*tb*); Bill Mays (*p*); Bob
Magnusson (*b*); Roy McCurdy (*d*). 10/80.

*** **Time Speaks** Timeless SJP 187 LP
Golson; Freddie Hubbard, Woody Shaw (*t*); Kenny Barron (*p*); Cecil McBee (*b*); Ben
Riley (*d*). 12/84.

(*) **This Is For You, John Timeless SJP 235 CD/LP
Golson; Pharoah Sanders (*ts*); Cedar Walton (*p*); Ron Carter (*b*); Jack DeJohnette
(*d*). 12/83.

Golson aged in an interesting way. Though his tone has weakened and taken on a querulous
edge, his playing hasn't so much declined in stature as changed its impact. He had traded his
swing influences for Coltrane 20 years earlier and, by the 1980s – after a sabbatical in film and
TV scoring – it had resulted in the kind of introspective passion which marks out some of
Coltrane's music, even if Golson chose a more conservative set of aims. These three Timeless
albums include some top-drawer sidemen, but Golson is invariably the most interesting
presence on each session. *California Message* is a good if rather routine date; *Time Speaks* is
better, with the stellar line-up clearly enjoying itself. Golson's solo on the opening 'I'll
Remember April' is a textbook example of how he adapted Coltrane's methods to his own ends.
Unfortunately, the interplay between Hubbard and Shaw is rather splashy, and the piano is too
remote in the mix (a characteristic Rudy Van Gelder trait). *This Is For You, John* should have
been a classic meeting with Sanders, with Golson confronting Coltrane's influence to the full,
yet the session too often degenerates into rambling solos to maintain real interest.

*** **Stardust** Denon 33CY-1838 CD
Golson; Freddie Hubbard (*t, flhn*); Mulgrew Miller (*p*); Ron Carter (*b*); Marvin
'Smitty' Smith (*d*). 6/87.

*** **Benny Golson Quartet** LRC CDC 9018 CD
Golson; Mulgrew Miller (*p*); Rufus Reid (*b*); Tony Reedus (*d*). 6/90.

Golson's latest recordings find him in confident if sometimes discursive form. *Stardust* has him
co-leading a blue-chip group with Hubbard, and originals such as 'Gypsy Jingle-Jangle' (which
also appears on the LRC record) are strong enough to put the band on its mettle; the session is
finally a little ordinary, though, if only because Hubbard lacks front-line substance on this
occasion. Golson's saxophone has probably never been closer to a microphone than it is on the
LRC date: again, the Coltrane streak keeps breaking through, and Golson's latest thoughts on
'Stablemates' are surprisingly fresh and compelling. Only at ballad tempo, as on 'Goodbye',
does he sound sedentary. The rhythm section is respectful yet assertive when it has to be.

EDDIE GOMEZ (born 1944)
BASS

(*) **Down Stretch Black Hawk BKH 531 CD/LP
Gomez; Takehiro Honda (*p*); Elliott Zigmund (*d*). 1/76.

*** **Gomez** Denon DC 8562 CD
Gomez; Chick Corea (*p, syn*); Steve Gadd (*d*); Yasuaki Shimizu (*ts*); Kazumi
Watanabe (*g*). 1–2/84.

A veteran of the Bill Evans Trio and a staggering roster of free(ish)-modern to fusion line-ups
since then, Gomez hasn't been extensively recorded as leader. *Down Stretch* suggests that this is
a pity. He has a fine, rounded tone that never loses resolution even at breakneck speed and is
capable of the sweetest lyricism and grace. His confederates aren't entirely commensurate with
his talents, but Zigmund in particular is a capable and sometimes inventive player.

Gomez moves closer to the company (and production values) he deserves. Corea is
immediately responsive, notably on the two duo tracks, and Gomez also duets effectively with
Gadd. The Japanese saxophonist and guitarist are responsible for some mildly interesting
aesthetic mismatches, but neither is sufficiently individual to carry it off regardless. An
unqualified three stars for the best of it; mild reservations about the remainder.

NAT GONELLA (born 1908)
TRUMPET, VOICE

***   **Mister Rhythm Man** EMI EG 2601881 LP
Gonella; Bruts Gonella, Johnny Morrison (*t*); George Evans (*as*); Pat Smuts, Albert
Torrance (*cl, as*); Don Barrigo (*ts*); Harold Hood, Monia Liter (*p*); Arthur Baker,
Jimmy Messini (*g*); Will Hemmings, Charlie Winter, Tiny Winters (*b*); Bob Dryden
(*d*). 1/34, 2–3/35.

The classic Gonella album, with a band that can still mist the eye of anyone who remembers the
pre-war scene, when bop was yet to be and the theatres were crowded eight houses a week.
Gonella was still playing (and re-recording) 'Oh Monah' 40 years later with undiminished
enthusiasm, and there's a good interim version of it on *The Best Of British Traditional Jazz*
(Philips 81865 CD), featuring Tony Skidmore, Jimmy Skidmore, Stan Tracey and Phil Seamen.
Stars of the 1934–5 sessions are pianist 'Babe' Hood and reeds players Albert Torrance and
Pat Smuts. Gonella's records were, in effect, British counterparts to Louis Armstrong's sides
from the same period: vocal and trumpet features on jazz-directed popular material, although
Gonella worked with somewhat smaller backings. The group was known as The Georgians
(following Gonella's popular version of 'Georgia On My Mind') and their records endure as
bright and pleasing, though formulaic music which Gonella's own playing is not quite strong
enough to transcend, although such titles as 'Basin Street Blues' and 'Rhythm Is Our Business'
display the leader's brisk phrasing and idiosyncratic swing. There is a vaudeville element which
was as inescapable for him as it was for Armstrong, and his ease as a showman explains why he
forged ahead of such (otherwise equally gifted) players as Max Goldberg. The sound comes
through strongly and with surprisingly little dirt. A key figure in trad, Gonella's influence on
three generations of British players (many of whom he outlived) is immeasurable.

PAUL GONSALVES (1920–74)
TENOR SAXOPHONE

****   **Gettin' Together** Original Jazz Classics OJC 203 CD/LP/MC
Gonsalves; Nat Adderley (*t*); Wynton Kelly (*p*); Sam Jones (*p*); Jimmy Cobb (*d*).
12/60.

A staggeringly underrated player, who stands in a direct line with earlier masters like Chu Berry
and Don Byas, and Young Turks like Frank Lowe and David Murray. It would be absurd to
compare his influence with Coltrane's, but it's now clear that he was experimenting with
tonalities remarkably similar to Coltrane's famous – and usually mislocated – 'sheets of sound'
long before Coltrane; it's also unarguably true that more people heard Gonsalves (albeit in his
more straight-ahead role as an Ellington stalwart). His fabled 27 choruses on 'Diminuendo And
Crescendo In Blue' at the Newport Jazz Festival in 1956 can be considered the first important
extended saxophone solo in modern jazz. Whatever the impulse (and one version suggests that
the presence of an enthusiastic young female fan dancing onstage had something to do with it)
its impact was very considerable.

Gettin' Together is a remarkable album, beautifully played and recorded. Wynton Kelly's
piano playing on 'Walkin'' and 'I Cover the Waterfront' is of the highest quality, and
Adderley's slightly fragile, over-confident tone fits in perfectly. Most strongly recommended.

***   **Just A-Sittin' And A-Rockin'** Black Lion BLCD 760148 CD
Gonsalves; Ray Nance (*t, vn, v*); Norris Turney (*as, cl*); Raimond Fol, Hank Jones (*p*);
Al Hall (*b*); Oliver Jackson (*d*); collective personnel. 8/70.

'I Cover the Waterfront' is again the stand-out track on Black Lion's relaxed old pals reunion.
Nance is a less dramatic soloist than Gonsalves's more familiar foil, Cat Anderson, and his
singing and fiddle-playing are less than compelling, but he blends beautifully in the ensembles
and is imaginative enough to essay out-of-tempo sequences and slurred rounds around the
saxophonists. Turney, a not quite time-served Ellington employee, plays exceedingly well.

DENNIS GONZALEZ
TRUMPET, POCKET TRUMPET, FLUGELHORN, OTHER INSTRUMENTS

****   **Stefan** Silkheart 101 CD/LP
Gonzelez; John Purcell (*bcl, bf, enghn, syn, v*); Henry Franklii
Richardson (*d*). 4/86.

***(*)   **Namesake** Silkheart 106 CD/LP
Gonzalez; Ahmed Abdullah (*t, flhn, balafon*); Charles Brackeen
Ewart (*bcl, as, f*); Malachi Favors (*b*); Alvin Fielder (*d*). 2/87.

***(*)   **Catechism** Daagnim CD 1 CD
Gonzalez; Rob Blakeslee (*t*); Kim Corbet (*tb*); Elton Dean (*as, sa⌐ ⌐, ⌐eith* Tippett
(*p*); Marcio Mattos (*b*); Louis Moholo (*d*). 7/87.

****   **Debenge, Debenge** Silkheart 112 CD/LP
Gonzalez; Marlon Jordan (*t*); Charles Brackeen (*ts*); Kidd Jordan (*sno s, as, bcl*);
Malachi Favors, Henry Franklin (*b*); Alvin Fiedler, W. A. Richardson (*d*). 2/88.

The three Silkhearts are central texts in Gonzalez's attempt to wrest initiative back from New York and the West Coast and restore the South's, and particularly the Delta's, slightly marginal standing in the new jazz. The band assembled for *Debenge, Debenge* goes under the uncomfortably agglutinative name New Dallasorleanssippi, which gives no sense at all of its coherence and directness of statement. Gonzalez's other great achievement was to have tempted the great tenor player, Charles Brackeen, out of a self-imposed semi-retirement.

Stefan is probably Gonzalez's masterpiece. The opening 'Enrico', dedicated to the Italian trumpeter, Enrico Rava, opens a path for magnificent flugelhorn figurations over a bass/bass clarinet accompaniment. 'Fortuity' is calm and enigmatic, like the title-track (a dedication to Gonzalez's son) a simple theme on open chords, but with a strange, dramatic interlude for voices. 'Hymn For Don Cherry' is based on 'At The Cross' and reflects two more of Gonzalez's influences. 'Boi Fuba', the briefest and least successful track, explores Brazilian materials, while John Purcell's closing 'Deacon John Ray' features his Dolphyish alto, and the trumpeter's superbly instinctive on the borders of total harmonic abstraction. A masterful record.

Namesake only suffers by comparison, but it shouldn't be missed. The long title-piece is a complex 7/4 figure that manages to sound completely coherent and also as if it were being played by a very much larger band, as if Gonzalez had been listening to Mingus's appropriations of Ellington on *The Black Saint And The Sinner Lady*. 'Separation Of Stones' is tranced and dreamy, and the solos are softly enunciated, with Gonzalez muted and the Armstrong-influenced Abdullah on flugelhorn. A percussion overture sets up a mood of combined grief and triumph in anticipation of 'Hymn For Mbizo', a threnody for South African bassist Johnny Dyani, but is interrupted by the lightweight 'Four Pigs And A Bird's Nest', on which Gonzalez plays his Cherry-patented pocket trumpet, muted on this occasion.

Debenge, Debenge, along with Brackeen's own *Banaar* and *Worshippers Come Nigh* (Silkheart 105 & 111), quickly consolidated the label's quality and confirmed Gonzalez's considerable musical intelligence. The multi-talented Kidd Jordan builds a bridge between Gonzalez's ringing, sometimes slightly sharp-toned trumpet and Brackeen's powerful tenor; his son, Marlon Jordan, is a fresh new voice and the Art Ensemble of Chicago veteran Favors shows more of his formidable technique than for some time. A superb record, beautifully engineered and produced.

The earlier *Catechism*, recorded in London, is rawer and the British free-scene players dictate a greater emphasis on collective improvisation. Dean and Tippett are the most prominent as soloists. The writing (two *kwelas* dedicated to the trumpeter's wife, Gerard Bendiks's delightfully titled 'The Sunny Murray–Cecil Taylor Dancing Lesson', and 'Catechism', written for the Creative Opportunity Orchestra in Austin, Texas) is of consistently high quality, and only a rather flat sound and the likelihood of limited availability keeps this one down to three and a half stars.

Ya Yo Me Cure American Clave AMCL 1001 LP
Gonzalez; Steve Turre (*tb, conch, perc*); Papo Vasquez (*tb*); Mario Rivera (*ts*); Hilton
Ruiz (*p*); Edgardo Miranda (*g*); Andy Gonzalez (*b*); Don Alias (*d*); Frankie
Rodriguez, Carlos Mestre, Vincent George, Nicky Marrero, Gene Golden (*perc*);
Milton Cardona (*v*). 7–8/80.

*** **The River Is Deep** Enja 4040 CD/LP
Gonzalez; Steve Turre (*tb, btb*); Papo Vasquez (*tb*); Wilfredo Velez (*as*); Jorge Dalto
(*p*); Edgardo Miranda (*g*); Andy Gonzalez (*b,v*); Steve Berrios (*d, v*); Gene Golden,
Hector 'Flaco' Hernandez, Nicky Marrero, Frankie Rodriguez (*perc*). 11/82.

*** **Obalata** Enja 5095 CD/LP
Gonzalez; John Stubblefield (*ts*); Larry Willis (*p*); Edgardo Miranda (*g*); Andy
Gonzalez (*b*); Steve Berrios (*d*); Nicky Marrero, Milton Cardona, Angel 'Papa'
Vacquez (*perc*). 11/88.

Jerry Gonzalez has been surpassed in popularity by Arturo Sandoval but he is a trumpeter of
comparable gifts, whose efforts at blending jazz and Latin genres have all the necessary
ingredients: zesty, explosive rhythm sections, pellucid brass breaks, sunny melodies and an
element of kitsch: the first record listed above includes a version of the *I Love Lucy* theme. But
Gonzalez likes to interpret Thelonious Monk and Wayne Shorter and, though he sometimes
turns their compositions into unsuitably happy-go-lucky vehicles, there's a sensitive streak in his
treatment of 'Footsteps' (*Obalata*) and 'Nefertiti' (*Ya Yo Me Cure*). The two earlier records
are the more energetic, while *Obalata* benefits from the considerable presence of Stubblefield
and the thoughtful Willis in a slightly smaller band.

BENNY GOODMAN (1909–86)
CLARINET

***(*) **B.G. And Big Tea In NYC** MCA GRP 16092 CD
Goodman; Red Nichols, Leo McConville, Ruby Weinstein, Charlie Teagarden, Manny
Klein, Dave Klein, Ray Lodwig (*t*); Bix Beiderbecke (*c*); Jack Teagarden, Glenn
Miller, Bill Trone (*tb*); Benny Goodman (*cl, as*); Arthur Rollini, Larry Binyon, Babe
Russin (*ts*); Sid Stoneburn (*as*); Adrian Rollini (*bsx*); Ed Bergman, Wladimir
Solinsky, Matty Malneck, Joe Venuti (*vn*); Arthur Schutt, Joe Sullivan, Jack Russin,
Frank Signorelli, Howard Smith (*p*); Eddie Lang, George Van Eps, Carl Kress (*g*);
Treg Brown (*bj*); Ward Lay, Art Miller, Artie Bernstein (*b*); Stan King, Neil Marshall,
Gene Krupa (*d*). 4/29–10/34.

None of these sides were recorded under either Goodman's or Teagarden's leadership: but they
dominate much of the record, in bands led by Nichols, Rollini and Irving Mills. The great
exception is the superb Lang–Venuti All Star Orchestra date of 1931, which the nominal
leaders play their tails off in, though Goodman has a fine solo on 'Farewell Blues'. This is all
polished New York Dixieland of its day, and well worth reviving.

*** **Benny Goodman 1935 Vol. 1** Tax CD 3708-2 CD
Goodman; George Erwin, Nathan Kazebier, Jerry Neary (*t*); Red Ballard, Jack Lacey
(*tb*); Toots Mondello, Hymie Schertzer (*as*); Arthur Rollini, Dick Clark (*ts*); Frank
Froeba (*p*); Allan Reuss (*g*); Harry Goodman (*b*); Gene Krupa (*d*). 6/35.

*** **Benny Goodman 1935 Vol. 2** Tax CD 3709-2 CD
As above. 6/35.

(****) **The Birth Of Swing (1935–1936)** RCA Bluebird ND90601 3CD
Goodman; Bunny Berigan, Pee Wee Erwin, Ralph Muzillo, Jerry Neary, Nathan
Kazebier, Harry Geller, Chris Griffin, Manny Klein, Sterling Bose, Ziggy Elman, Zeke
Zarchey (*t*); Red Ballard, Jack Lacey, Jack Teagarden, Murray McEachern (*tb*); Toots
Mondelo, Bill DePew, Hymie Schertzer (*as*); Arthur Rollini, Dick Clark, Vido Musso
(*ts*); Frank Froeba, Jess Stacy (*p*); George Van Eps, Allan Reuss (*g*); Harry Goodman

(*b*); Gene Krupa (*d*); Helen Ward, Ella Fitzgerald, Joe Harris, Buddy Clark (*v*).
4/35–11/36.

Goodman was struggling as a bandleader until the mystical night of 21 August 1935, when the swing era apparently began following his broadcast from Los Angeles. He already had a good band: the reed section was skilful, the trumpets – boosted by the arrival of Bunny Berigan, who had a terrific impact on Goodman himself – strong, and the book was bulging with material. The two Tax CDs, of transcriptions for radio, contain 50 numbers yet were recorded in a single day's work. There were Fletcher Henderson arrangements which would help to make Goodman's fortune – 'Blue Skies', 'King Porter Stomp', 'Basin Street Blues' – and Jimmy Mundy and Edgar Sampson charts of a similar calibre. There was Gene Krupa at the drums; and Goodman, perhaps the first great virtuoso of the swing era himself.

It may surprise some, at this distance, to hear how Goodman actually played more of an ensemble role than that of a star leader – at least in terms of the sound of his clarinet and its place on the records. Solos are usually quite short and pithy, and though he takes the lion's share, that was only right and proper – he was far and away the best improviser (Berigan aside, who didn't last very long) in his own band. What one notes about the records is their smooth, almost ineluctable power and fleetness: Krupa's drumming energized the orchestra, but its brass and reed sections were such fine executants (only Lunceford's band could have matched them) that they generated their own kind of inner swing. Henderson, Mundy and Sampson all supplied arrangements which, in a gesture that has dominated big-band writing to this day, pointed up those strengths without looking for fancy textures or subtleties.

The Tax CDs are in excellent sound, and though there are plenty of second-rate tunes and occasional dead passages, the standard stays surprisingly high, with Goodman in good to inspirational form. The Bluebird three-CD set should be the definitive document of the start of the swing era, but it's badly let down by inconsistent remastering: a handful of tracks (including 'Blue Skies') sound as if they were recorded under water, and the general standard, though listenable enough, is varied almost from track to track. That said, it's of consistent musical interest and Loren Schoenberg's excellent notes add to the impact of the set.

***   **Stompin' At The Savoy** RCA Bluebird ND 90631 CD
As above, except add Harry James (*t*). 7/35–2/38.

Ten tracks from Goodman's Victor era in this budget-price sampler, including the 1937 'Sing Sing Sing' with Harry James. Superior remastering to the above set, at least.

***   **Airplay** Columbia AGK 40350 CD
Goodman; Ziggy Elman, Harry James, Irving Goodman, Chris Griffin (*t*); Red Ballard, Murray McEachern, Vernon Brown (*tb*); Bill DePew, Hymie Schertzer, Noni Bernardi, George Koenig, Dave Matthews (*as*); Vido Musso, Arthur Rolini, Bud Freeman (*ts*); Jess Stacy, Teddy Wilson (*p*); Lionel Hampton (*vib*); Allan Reuss, Ben Heller (*g*); Harry Goodman (*b*); Dave Tough, Gene Krupa (*d*). 36–38.

Airshots from unidentified sources, though full dates and personnel are supplied. The sound is often rather clunky and not as good as, say, the VJC issues listed below; but the music finds the Goodman crew in virile and swinging form throughout, with speciality numbers for Jess Stacy (a solo on Beiderbecke's 'In A Mist') and the quartet.

***(*)   **Roll 'Em** CBS 460062-2 CD
Goodman; Harry James, Ziggy Elman, Chris Griffin, Corky Cornelius, Jimmy Maxwell, Johnny Martell (*t*); Red Ballard, Murray McEachern, Vernon Brown, Bruce Squires, Will Bradley, Ted Vesely (*tb*); Hymie Schertzer, George Koenig, Toots Mondello, Buff Estes (*as*); Arthur Rollini, Vido Musso, Bus Bassey, Jerry Jerome, Babe Russin (*ts*); Fletcher Henderson, Jess Stacy (*p*); Allan Reuss, Arnold Covey (*g*); Artie Bernstein, Harry Goodman (*b*); Gene Krupa, Nick Fatool (*d*); Helen Ward, Louise Tobin, Mildred Bailey (*v*). 3/37–11/39.

A fine cross-section of Columbia material. The first six tracks are all airshots, and include an almost delirious version of Mary Lou Williams's great 'Roll 'Em' and a tingling sequence of exchanges between Goodman and Harry James on 'Ridin' High', a tune the band never put down in the studios. The remaining 10 tracks are all from studio dates, and are a mix of standard dance fare and a few more adventurous pieces: even on a fairly plain 'Night And Day', though, there's the pleasure of hearing a beautifully shaped treatment of the theme by the leader.

Remastering is, as seems usual from this source, a mixed bag, but is on the whole quite listenable.

****   **After You've Gone** RCA Bluebird ND 85631 CD
    Goodman; Lionel Hampton (*vib*); Teddy Wilson (*p*); Gene Krupa (*d*). 7/35–2/37.

***(*)   **Avalon** RCA Bluebird ND 82273 CD
    As above, except add Jess Stacy (*p*); John Kirby (*b*); Buddy Schutz, Dave Tough (*d*). 7/37–4/39.

Goodman's small groups set a new standard for 'chamber jazz', the kind of thing Red Nichols had tried in the 1920s, but informed with a more disciplined – and blacker – sensibility. That said, Goodman's own playing, for all its fineness of line and tonal elegance, could be blisteringly hot, and he is by far the strongest personality on all their records, the presence of domineering figures like Hampton and Krupa notwithstanding. The earliest sides are among the best, but both these Bluebird compilations come highly recommended. Perhaps the Trio sessions, made before Hampton's arrival, are the most satisfying, since the brilliant empathy between Goodman and Wilson – one of the great unspoken jazz partnerships – is allowed its clearest expression. Certainly the likes of 'After You've Gone' and 'Body And Soul' express a smooth yet spontaneously refined kind of improvisation. Hampton made the music 'swing' a little more obtrusively, yet he often plays a rather quiet and contained ensemble role, the vibes shimmering alongside Wilson's playing, and it created a fascinating platform for Goodman's lithest playing. While this quickly became formulaic jazz, it was a very good formula. The NoNOISE remastering isn't ideal, but it lets all the players stand clearly in the mix.

***(*)   **Carnegie Hall Concert** Columbia C2K-40244 2CD
    Goodman; Ziggy Elman, Buck Clayton, Harry James, Gordon Griffin (*t*); Bobby Hackett (*c*); Red Ballard, Vernon Brown (*tb*); Hymie Schertzer, George Koenig, Johnny Hodges (*as*); Arthur Rollini, Lester Young, Babe Russin (*ts*); Harry Carney (*bs*); Jess Stacy, Teddy Wilson, Count Basie (*p*); Lionel Hampton (*vib*); Allan Reuss, Freddie Green (*g*); Harry Goodman, Walter Page (*b*); Gene Krupa (*d*). 1/38.

A very famous occasion indeed, and the music still stands up extraordinarily well. This was one of those events – like Ellington at Newport nearly two decades later – where jazz history is spontaneously changed, even if Goodman had clearly planned the whole thing as a crowning manoeuvre. Unmissable points: Krupa's fantastically energetic drumming throughout, leading to the roof coming off on 'Sing, Sing, Sing', an Ellington tribute and a jam on 'Honeysuckle Rose' with various guests from other bands (George Simon called it 'ineffectual', but it's very exciting), Ziggy Elman powering through 'Swingtime In The Rockies' and the original quartet going through their best paces. But the whole affair is atmospheric with the sense of a man and a band taking hold of their moment.

****   **Solo Flight** Vintage Jazz Classics VJC-1021-2 CD
    Goodman; Cootie Williams (*t*); George Auld (*ts*); Lionel Hampton (*vib*); Fletcher Henderson, Johnny Guarnieri, Count Basie (*p*); Charlie Christian, Freddie Green (*g*); Artie Bernstein, Walter Page (*b*); Jo Jones, Gene Krupa, Nick Fatool (*d*). 8/39–6/41.

****   **Roll 'Em!** Vintage Jazz Classics VJC 1032-2 CD
    Goodman; Jimmy Maxwell, Billy Butterfield, Cootie Williams, Slim Davis (*t*); Lou McGarity, Cutty Cutshall (*tb*); Gene Kinsey, Clint Neagley (*as*); George Berg, Vido Musso, Pete Mondello (*ts*); Skip Martin, Chuck Gentry (*bs*); Mel Powell (*p*); Tommy Morganelli (*g*); Walter Iooss, Johnny Simmons, Marty Blitz (*b*); Sid Catlett (*d*). 7–10/41.

Two fabulous collections of airshots and V-Discs. Various breakdowns and alternative takes sunder the flow on *Roll 'Em!* to some extent, but the band sound absolutely mercurial, careering through a sensational 'Henderson Stomp' and coming through loud and clear in excellent remastering. The collection with Christian features the guitarist in wonderful extended solos, but Goodman himself matches him blow for blow and, though the sound is dustier, it's perfectly listenable. Essential supplements to a Goodman collection.

****   Sextet Featuring Charlie Christian Columbia CK 45144 CD
Goodman; Cootie Williams (*t*); George Auld (*ts*); Fletcher Henderson, Johnny
Guarnieri, Count Basie (*p*); Lionel Hampton (*vib*); Artie Bernstein (*b*); Nick Fatool,
Jo Jones, Dave Tough (*d*). 39–41.

***   Small Groups 1941–1945 Columbia 44437 CD
Goodman; Lou McGarity, Cutty Cutshall (*tb*); Red Norvo (*vib*); Teddy Wilson, Mel
Powell (*p*); Tom Morgan, Mike Bryan (*g*); Slam Stewart, Sid Weiss (*b*); Morey Feld,
Ralph Collier (*d*); Peggy Lee (*v*). 10/41–2/45.

Christian was a once-in-a-lifetime collaborator with Goodman, who had bad luck with some of
his best sidemen (Christian, Berigan, Hasselgard – all of whom came to untimely ends). The first
Sextet compilation is full of finely pointed small-group jazz, hinting every now and then at bop,
but not so much as to give anyone any trouble. Equally interesting is the mixture of
personalities – Williams, Goodman, Christian, Auld, Basie – which gives thge sextet
performances a blend of coolness and resilience which seems to be a direct extension of the
leader's own ambitions. Goodman had led a nearly perfect double-life with the small groups and
the big band, balancing dance material and 'listening' jazz and making both commercially and
artistically successful; and part of that freshness which the small groups created may be due to
the fact that several participants – Wilson, Hampton, Christian – weren't regular members of
the big band. But after a reorganization in 1941 he started using regular band-members, who
turn up on the *Small Groups 1941–45* compilation. While this is a less impressive set than the
earlier small-band discs, with Cutshall and McGarity standing as curious choices and the timbre
of most of the tracks sounding like a slightly paler echo of what had gone before, Goodman still
plays very well. Respectable remastering on both discs.

***(*)   'Way Down Yonder Vintage Jazz Classics VJC-1001-2 CD
Goodman; Lee Castle, Frank Muzzillo, Charlie Frankhauser, Johnny Dee, Frank
Berardi, Mickey Mangano (*t*); Bill Harris, H. Collins, Al Mastren (*tb*); Heinie Beau,
Eddie Rosa, Hymie Schertzer, Leonard Kaye (*as*); Al Klink, Zoot Sims (*ts*); Ernie
Caceres, Eddie Beau (*bs*); Jess Stacy, Mel Powell, Teddy Wilson (*p*); Red Norvo
(*vib*); Sid Weiss (*b*); Morey Feld, Gene Krupa, Johnny DeSoto (*d*); Lorraine Elliott
(*v*). 12/43–1/46.

More broadcast material. Goodman hadn't lost the keys to the kingdom, but his popularity was
past its peak and the big bands were starting to enter their steep decline. Nevertheless, this
collection of V-Discs includes some very impressive and hard-hitting performances, and some
new faces – Zoot Sims, for one – add further interest. Very good transfers, considering the
source of the material.

***(*)   Slipped Disc 1945–46 CBS 463337-2 CD
Goodman; Joe Bushkin, Teddy Wilson, Mel Powell (*p*); Red Norvo, Johnny White
(*vib*); Barney Kessel, Mike Bryan (*g*); Harry Babasin, Slam Stewart (*b*); Louie
Bellson, Morey Feld, Cozy Cole (*d*); Jane Harvey, Art Lund (*v*). 2/45–10/46.

There is some excellent music here and it stands a fresh evaluation, even if this was a largely
ignored area of Goodman's discography. Goodman was on the verge of abandoning his big
band altogether and the vibrancy of his playing on 'After You've Gone' and the two versions
of 'I Got Rhythm' hits an exultant peak in his small-group work. The music runs along less
provocative rails than it did with Christian on guitar, and Stewart is an irritation on some
tracks, but the best of it is very fine. Two previously unreleased tracks will add extra
collector-appeal, and the remastering is cleanly done.

***   Sextet Columbia CK 40379 CD
Goodman; Teddy Wilson (*p*); Terry Gibbs (*vib*); Johnny Smith (*g*); Bob Carter (*b*);
Charles Smith (*d*). 50–52.

More latterday sextet sessions. Goodman was at a rather low ebb, like every other fallen giant
of the decade before, and Wilson and Gibbs play with professional calm rather than passion, but
there's the usual quota of neatly swinging music.

****   B.G. In Hi-Fi Capitol CDP 7926842 CD
Goodman; Ruby Braff, Charlie Shavers, Chris Griffin, Carl Poole, Bernie Privin (*t*);
Will Bradley, Vernon Brown, Cutty Cutshall (*tb*); Al Klink, Paul Ricci, Boomie

Richman, Hymie Schertzer, Sol Schlinger (*saxes*); Mel Powell (*p*); Steve Jordan (*g*); George Duvivier (*b*); Bobby Donaldson, Jo Jones (*d*). 11/54.

Goodman left the big-band era with his finances and his technique intact and, although this was a more or less anachronistic programme of trio, quintet and big-band sides in 1954, the playing is so good that it's a resounding success. A few Goodman staples are mixed with Basie material such as 'Jumpin' At The Woodside' and Benny's readings are by no means outdone by the original's. Shavers, Braff, Richman and Powell all have fine moments, but Goodman himself is peerless. The sound is a trifle dry but otherwise excellent, and the CD reissue adds four tracks – including a beautiful trio version of 'Rose Room' – to the original LP.

***   **Yale Archives Vol. 2: Live At Basin Street** Limelight 820803 CD
Goodman; Ruby Braff (*t*); Urbie Green (*tb*); Paul Quinichette (*ts*); Teddy Wilson (*p*); Perry Lopez (*g*); Milt Hinton (*b*); Bobby Donaldson (*d*). 3/55.

This recording, from Goodman's personal collection now in Yale University, catches a characteristic club engagement by a typical Goodman band, only eight in number but big enough to suggest the swing of the leader's orchestras. The material is old hat, even for Goodman, but the unusual gathering of names lends a fresh twist, and Braff and Green sound in particularly good shape. Well recorded and remastered.

***   **Live At The International World Exhibition Brussels: The Unissued Recordings** Magic DAWE 36 CD
Goodman; Billy Hodges, Taft Jordan, John Frosk, Ermit Perry (*t*); Vernon Brown, Willie Dennis, Rex Peer (*tb*); Al Block, Ernie Mauro (*as*); Zoot Sims, Seldon Powell (*ts*); Gene Allen (*bs*); Roland Hanna (*p*); Billy Bauer (*g*); Arvell Shaw (*b*); Ray Burns (*d*); Ethel Ennis, Jimmy Rushing (*v*). 5/58.

***   **Yale Archives Vol. 3** Limelight 820814 CD
As above. 5/58.

The band is a bit of a ragtag troupe, lacking the kind of punctilious precision one expects of a Goodman ensemble, and they can't finesse their way through some of the more risky moments in the scores. But it's still an interesting orchestra, and on what are familar Goodman programmes the leader summons enough spirit of his own to see them through. Little to choose between these discs, though the Limelight set is the best-sounding.

(*)   **Yale Archives Vol. 4: Big Band Recordings Limelight MSTR-5017-2 CD
Goodman; John Frosk, Allen Smith, E. V. Perry, Benny Ventura, Jimmy Maxwell, Mel Davis, Al Mairoca, Fern Caron, Joe Wilkder, Joe Newman, Tony Terrar, Ray Triscari, Jimmy Zito, Taft Jordan, Billy Butterfield, Buck Clayton (*t*); Rex Peer, Harry DeViuto, Vernon Friley, Bob Edmondson, Jimmy Knepper, Willie Dennis, Wayne Andrew, Hale Rood, Buster Cooper, Vernon Brown, Eddie Bert (*tb*); Herb Geller, Jimmy Santucci, Bob Wilber, Babe Clark, Pepper Adams, Gene Allen, Walt Levinsky, Al Block, Budd Johnson, Bill Slapin, Phil Woods, Jerry Dodgion, Zoot Sims, Tommy Newsom, Skeets Furfurt, Herbie Steward, Teddy Edwards, Bob Hardaway (*reeds*); Pete Jolly, Russ Freeman, Roland Hanna, Hank Jones, John Bunch (*p*); Kenny Burell, Turk Van Lake, Benny Garcia, Steve Jordan (*g*); Milt Hinton, Henry Grimes, Irv Manning, Bill Crow, Monty Budwig (*b*); Mousie Alexander, Shelly Manne, Roy Burns, Mel Lewis, Colin Bailey (*d*); Martha Tilton, Mitzi Cottle (*v*). 11/58–6/64.

There's some dreary stuff – including a terrible version of 'People' – on this hotchpotch of leftovers from bands that Goodman led in the late 1950s and early '60s. Many major players involved here, and some of them take the odd solo, but Goodman is at centre stage and main interest remains on his own solos. For Goodman collectors only, who'll have to salvage bits and pieces.

***   **In Stockholm 1959** Phontastic NCD 8801 CD
Goodman; Jack Sheldon (*t*); Bill Harris (*tb*); Jerry Dodgion (*as, f*); Flip Phillips (*ts*); Red Norvo (*vib*); Russ Freeman (*p*); Jimmy Wyble (*g*); Red Wootten (*b*); John Markham, John Poole (*d*); Anita O'Day (*v*).10/59.

Although the leader plays very well on this souvenir of a European tour which Goodman scholars credit as a peak period in his later work, the rather desultory presentation of the music – too many offhand introductions by Benny, and the inclusion of crowd-pleasing pieces like 'Sing Sing Sing' and the hits medley – take some of the fizz out of the record. The band aren't granted too much individual space – which is frustrating, since Sheldon, Norvo and Freeman all sound excellent – and Goodman's habit of whistling through other people's solos is caught by the mostly very clear recording, which suffers from only occasional drop-outs.

***(*)   **Benny Goodman Vol. 5** Limelight 820827-2 2CD
Goodman; Jack Sheldon, Bobby Hackett (*t*); Bill Harris, Urbie Green (*tb*); Jerry Dodgion (*as, f*); Flip Phillips (*ts*); Modesto Bresano (*ts, f*); Red Norvo (*vib*); Gene DiNovi, John Bunch (*p*); Jimmy Wyble (*g*); Steve Swallow, Red Wooten, Jimmy Rowser (*b*); John Markham, Ray Mosca (*d*). 11/59–6/63.

More from Goodman's own archive. There is some happy and spirited playing by these sometimes improbably constituted small groups. The first band features Phillips, Norvo and Sheldon, and creates some agreeable swing re-creations, but the second is graced by the lovely trumpet-playing of Bobby Hackett and merits an extra notch on the ratings. Clear sound, capably remastered.

***(*)   **Together Again** RCA Bluebird ND 86283 CD
Goodman; Teddy Wilson (*p*); Lionel Hampton (*vib*); Gene Krupa (*d*). 63.

A reunion of the old quartet and, with everyone playing well, this is a surprisingly fresh and uncliché'd encounter, with little of the old repertory brought into the programme. Goodman himself sounds spikily involved and the other three seem happy to be there. Recommended.

(*)   **Recorded Live In Stockholm 1970 Verve 820471 2CD
Goodman; John McLevy, Derek Watkins, Gregg Bowen (*t*); Keith Christie, Nat Peck, Jimmy Wilson (*tb*), Bob Burns, Don Honeywell (*as*); Frank Reidy, Bob Efford (*ts*), Bill McGuffie (*p*); Bucky Pizzarelli, Louis Stewart (*g*); Lenny Bush (*b*); Bobby Orr (*d*). 2/70.

***   **40th Anniversary Concert – Live At Carnegie Hall** London 820349 2CD
Goodman; Victor Paz, Warren Vaché, Jack Sheldon (*t*); Wayne André, George Masso, John Messner (*tb*); George Young, Mel Rodnon (*as*); Buddy Tate, Frank Wess (*ts*); Sol Schlinger (*bs*); Mary Lou Williams, Jimmy Rowles, John Bunch (*p*); Lionel Hampton (*vib*); Cal Collins, Wayne Wright (*g*); Michael Moore (*b*); Connie Kay (*d*); Martha Tilton, Debi Craig (*v*). 1/78.

***   **Compact Jazz: Benny Goodman** Verve 820543 CD
As above two discs, plus Zoot Sims (*ts*), Peter Appleyard (*vib*), Hal Gaylord (*b*). 2/70–1/78.

Goodman's enduring facility as a clarinettist is the most absorbing thing about these sessions. The bands play a functional rather than challenging role, the job being to replicate standard scores as flawlessly as the leader wished, and, although there are many fine players involved, Goodman's iron hand stifles anything freewheeling which might have emerged. The Stockholm performance lacks the star names present for the Carnegie Hall session, but both orchestras sound practically identical. The Compact Jazz collection includes tracks from both dates, as well as some numbers from a deleted small-group session from 1972 with Zoot Sims, and is probably the best buy if one wants Goodman in this period.

(*)   **The King BBC/Century CJC 835 CD/MC
Goodman; Jack Sheldon (*t*); Wayne André (*tb*); Buddy Tate (*ts*); John Bunch (*p*); Cal Collins (*g*); Major Holley (*b*); Connie Kay (*d*). 6/78.

A surprisingly brash-sounding session, although it's partly due to the aggressive and closely miked studio sound. Some tracks feature Goodman and the rhythm section alone, but Sheldon and Tate add spice and humour with their appearances, and the set ends with an uproarious 'Limehouse Blues' which is almost worth the price of purchase. Ungenerous playing time of a mere 35 minutes.

***(*)   **Yale Archives Vol. 1** Limelight 82080 CD
Goodman; Ermit Perry, Taft Jordan, Buzz King, John Frosk, Joe Newman, Ruby
Braff, Allan Smith, Benny Ventura, Jack Sheldon, Joe Mosello, Randy Sandke, John
Eckert (*t*); Vernon Brown, Eddie Bert, Harry DeVito, Urbie Green, Bill Harris,
Buster Cooper, Rex Peer, Hale Rood, Mat Finders, Dan Barrett (*tb*); Ernie Mauro,
Skippy Colluchio, Jerry Dodgion, Herb Geller, Jimmy Sands, Jack Stuckey, Chuck
Wilson (*as*); Zoot Sims, Buddy Tate, Dick Hafer, Flip Phillips, Bob Wilber, Babe
Clark, Paul Quinichette, Ken Peplowski, Ted Nash (*ts*); Gene Allen, Pepper Adams
(*bs*); Bernie Leighton, Roland Hanna, Dave McKenna, Martin Harris, Gene DiNovi,
Russ Freeman, Teddy Wilson, Ben Aronov (*p*); Red Norvo (*vib*); Attila Zoller, Chuck
Wayne, Steve Jordan, Leo Robinson, Jimmy Wyble, Turn Van Lake, Perry Lopez,
Billy Bauer, James Chirillo (*g*); George Duvivier, Henry Grimes, Tommy Potter, Al
Simi, Red Wootten, Milt Hinton, Arvell Shaw, Murray Wall (*b*); Joe Marshall, Roy
Burns, Bobby Donaldson, Bob Binnix, John Markham, Shelly Manne, Don Lamond,
Louie Bellson (*d*). 9/55–1/86.

What was the first collection from Goodman's personal archive is a fascinating cross-section of
work, most of it from the 1950s, but with two tracks by a 1967 septet featuring Joe Newman and
Zoot Sims and one by the 1986 big band that must be among his final testaments. That his
playing on that last session is as impeccable as ever says much for Goodman's tireless devotion
both to the clarinet and to the rigorous, swinging music which he believed was his métier. Small
groups of five, seven and eight predominate in this selection, and although there's little which
can be called surprising, the themes chosen – including 'Macedonia Lullaby', 'Marching And
Swinging' and 'Diga Diga Doo' – are at least unfamiliar Goodman fare. A delightful
'Broadway' with Bill Harris and Flip Phillips is one highlight, and shrewd programming makes
the CD consistently interesting, with all the recordings, despite their differing vintage, sounding
well.

MICK GOODRICK (born 1945)
GUITAR

***   **In Passing** ECM 1139 LP
Goodrick; John Surman (*ss, bs, bcl*); Eddie Gomez (*b*); Jack DeJohnette (*d*). 11/78.

***(*)   **Biorhythms** CMP CD 46 CD
Goodrick; Harvie Swartz (*b*); Gary Chaffee (*d*). 10/90.

Goodrick's brand of electric guitar impressionism has been slow to make an impact, at least in
comparison with that of such peers as Frisell and Metheny (Goodrick worked with Metheny in
Gary Burton's mid-1970s band). He seems to have fewer ambitions as a leader; but both these
records reveal an intelligent grasp of form and a shrewd management of resources. The earlier
session is a little more diffuse: Surman is a more dominant voice than Goodrick, and the music
aspires to the pastel tones of a typical ECM session. *Biorhythms* is a follow-up that took a long
time to emerge, but it's a feast of guitar playing, with excellent support from Swartz and
Chaffee, who can play jazz or funk time with equal aplomb. Goodrick's themes range from the
peppy groove of the title-tune and 'Groove Test' through to a reflective sequence for Emily
Remler, 'Bl'ize Medley', and the lavish farewell of '(I'll) Never Forget'. Restrained use of
overdubs and crystal-clear sound by engineer Walter Quintus ensure that the music holds the
interest even across generous CD length.

BOB GORDON (1928–55)
BARITONE SAXOPHONE

***   **Bob Gordon Memorial** Fresh Sound FSR-CD 180 CD
Gordon; Herbie Harper (*tb*); Jack Montrose (*ts*); Jimmy Rowles, Paul Moer (*p*);
Harry Babasin, Joe Mondragon (*b*); Roy Harte, Billy Schneider (*d*). 12/53–5/54.

Bob Gordon was killed in a freeway accident, and the few records where he's featured are the
only testimony to a very strong and gifted player. Always swinging, never encumbered by the
baritone, he is easily the dominant personality on the two sessions collected here, one by a

quintet with Harper sharing front-line duties, the other with Jack Montrose – whom Cooper shared a special affinity with – on tenor. The quintet tracks offer only some straight-ahead west coast blowing, but those with Montrose (who wrote most of the material) are of a different order: 'Two Can Play' sounds like a precursor of some of George Russell's material of later in the decade, and the oblique harmonies of 'For Sue' and wry treatment of 'What A Difference A Day Made' suggest that these players should have done much more together. Gordon's solos aren't especially affecting in the way that Serge Chaloff's are, but he can play with fine poise and freshness. The recordings are, unfortunately, rather dusty, and CD remastering has done little to assist.

DEXTER GORDON (1923–89)
TENOR SAXOPHONE, SOPRANO SAXOPHONE

***   **Long Tall Dexter** Savoy 650117 CD/LP
Gordon; Leonard Hawkins, Fats Navarro (t); Tadd Dameron, Sadik Hakim, Bud Powell (p); Nelson Boyd, Gene Ramey, Curly Russell (b); Art Mardigan, Eddie Nicholson, Max Roach (d). 10/45, 1/46, 12/47.

***   **Dexter Rides Again** Savoy SV 0120 CD
Gordon; Leonard Hawkins (t); Leo Parker (bs); Tadd Dameron, Sadik Hakim, Bud Powell (p); Gene Ramey, Curly Russell (b); Art Blakey, Eddie Nicholson, Max Roach (d). 10/45, 1/46, 12/47.

One of the giants (literally) of modern jazz, Gordon made an impact on such players as unlike as Sonny Rollins and John Coltrane, but himself remained comparatively unrecognized until a comeback in the 1960s (Gordon had lived and worked in Scandinavia in the early half of the decade), by which time many of the post-Lester Young stylistic devices he had introduced were firmly in place under others' patents.

Gordon's on-off partnership with fellow-tenorist Wardell Gray was consistently productive, pairing him for much of the late 1940s with another Lester Young disciple who had taken on board most of the modernist idiom without abandoning Young's mellifluously extended solo style. Most of the Gray material, including a fine Savoy 2-LP set called *The Hunt*, is currently unavailable and is some way down-line on Denon's CD reissue programme. For the time being, there is only the rather mixed compilation of sessions on *Dexter Rides Again*. The saxophonist's signature-theme, 'Long Tall Dexter', and the equally well-known '. . . Rides Again' and '. . . Digs In' are from a fine session with Bud Powell and Max Roach, which also featured the little-known Leonard Hawkins. Best of all, though, is a rousing 'Settin' The Pace', where Gordon repeats the 'chase' sequences of the sets with Gray, but this time in the company of Leo Parker, whose jaunty baritone-sound is a good foil. The still underrated Tadd Dameron comps impressively and Blakey stokes up the engines. The last of the three sessions is slightly muted. Argonne Thornton, later known as Sadik Hakim, was supposedly present at Charlie Parker's classic Savoy recordings. On the strength of these four sides with Gordon, one can see why Dizzy Gillespie (sic!) was called in as a pianist. Denon have redistributed their Savoy holdings somewhat, and the first of these reissues is less attractive than its immediate predecessor on CD, which also included material with Fats Navarro. Some masking of the sound has been eliminated, though, and the new Savoys are released at an attractive price.

***(*)   **The Dial Sessions** Storyville SLP 814 LP
Gordon; Melba Liston (tb); Teddy Edwards, Wardell Gray (ts); Jimmy Bunn, Charles Fox, Jimmy Rowles (p); Red Callender (b); Roy Porter, Chuck Thompson (d). 6–12/47.

A critical document in Gordon's great early period. 'The Chase' (with Gray) and 'The Duel' (with Edwards) cast him in two-tenor action with like-minded soloists who prefer fencing to the usual howitzer barrage. 'Chromatic Aberration' with Jimmy Bunn, Red Callender and Chuck Thompson is a token of Gordon's technical intelligence and Bunn's deceptive adaptability; the other pianists are every bit as responsive. Inevitable warts on the sound, but nothing that can't be explained by the dateline.

***   **Daddy Plays The Horn** Charly 57 CD

*** **The Bethlehem Years** Fresh Sound FSR 152 CD
    Gordon; Conte Candoli (*t* on *Bethlehem*); Frank Rosolino (*tb*); Kenny Drew (*p*);
    Leroy Vinnegar (*b*); Lawrence Marable (*d*). 9/55.

Daddy would be worth the purchase for 'Confirmation' and 'Autumn In New York' alone, but
for the fact that *The Bethlehem Years* compilation is rather better value for money. Neither
Candoli nor Rosolino are charismatic soloists, but they spur Gordon on and lend 'Ruby My
Dear' a beefy resonance. Drew and Vinnegar play exceptionally well, and the CD transfer is
generally good. In 1955, the year of Charlie Parker's death, Gordon has already cemented the
style he was to utilize virtually to the end of his career, but he was playing in the interim
between two drug-related prison sentences that more or less wound up the 1950s, which should
have been his decade.

**** **Doin' Alright** Blue Note CDP 784077 2CD
     Gordon; Freddie Hubbard (*t*); Horace Parlan (*p*); George Tucker (*b*); Al Harewood
     (*d*). 5/61.

Back in the world and doing all right. Gordon's first recording after a long and painful break is
one of his best. Critics divide on whether Gordon was influenced by Coltrane at this period or
whether it was simply a case of the original being obscured by his followers. Gordon's phrasing
on *Doin' Alright* certainly suggests a connection of some sort, but the opening statement of 'I
Was Doin' Alright' is completely individual and quite distinct, and Gordon's solo development
is nothing like the younger man's.
    This is one of Gordon's best records and should on no account be missed. There is a useful
sample on a Blue Note *Best of . . .* (791139 CD – below).

*** **Dexter Calling** Blue Note B21Y 46544 CD
    Gordon; Kenny Drew (*p*); Paul Chambers (*b*); Philly Joe Jones (*d*). 5/61.

Recorded three days later and reflecting the same virtues. With a better-drilled but slightly
more conventional band, Gordon is pushed a little wider on the solos, ranging much further
away from the stated key (as on a memorable mid-chorus break on 'Ernie's Tune') and varying
his timbre much more than he used to. As indicators of how his harmonic language and
distinctive accent were to develop, the two 1961 Blue Notes are particularly valuable. The sound
is a little better on the later record.

*** **Go!** Blue Note CDP 7460942 CD
    Gordon; Sonny Clark (*p*); Butch Warren (*b*); Billy Higgins (*d*). 8/62.

*** **A Swingin' Affair** Blue Note CDP 7841332 CD
    As above.

Typically good husbandry on the part of Blue Note to get two albums from this not altogether
riveting date, one of the first since his return to normal circulation. *Swingin' Affair* stands and
falls on a lovely version of 'You Stepped Out Of A Dream'. *Go!* includes Gordon's simplest
and finest reading of 'Where Are You', a relatively little-used standard with interesting changes
and a strong turn in the middle. The hipsters' motto (pinched from novelist John Clellon
Holmes) was meant to suggest relentless improvisatory progress. Gordon was to play better, but
rarely with such directness, and it's not entirely idle to ask whether he felt himself hampered by
a rhythm section that was not always responsive.

(*) **The Best Of Dexter Gordon Blue Note CDP 791139 2CD
     Gordon; Freddie Hubbard (*t*); Sonny Clark, Kenny Drew, Horace Parlan (*p*); Paul
     Chambers, George Tucker, Butch Warren (*b*); Al Harewood, Billy Higgins, Philly Joe
     Jones (*d*); 5/61, 8/62.

It isn't, of course, and wasn't then, but it did reproduce some good material from *Go!* and *A
Swinging Affair* (and there was probably one really good album between them), and a superb
'Smile' from the 1961 sessions with Drew, Chambers and Jones. The material with Hubbard
and the Horace Parlan trio was originally released on the Blue Note *Doin' Alright* and is the
most significant on this compilation, marking as it does Gordon's slightly gate-fevered return to
the fold after a second stint breaking rocks for The Man. His tone is big but acutely balanced,
and his sense of timing is impeccable.

*(*)   Cry Me A River Steeplechase 6004 CD/LP
Gordon; Atli Bjorn (*p*); Benny Nielsen, Marcel Rigot (*b*); Finn Frederiksen, William Schiopfe (*d*). 11/62, 6/64.

A pretty dismal album by any standard, much of it is given over to Bjorn's own trio. The title-track receives a predictably fulsome and emotive reading but Bjorn seems to be all over his keyboard in contrast to Gordon's discipline and reserve. Not an album for the A-list.

****   Our Man In Paris Blue Note CDP 7463942 CD
Gordon; Bud Powell (*p*); Pierre Michelot (*b*); Kenny Clarke (*d*). 5/63.

Gordon's 'purest' bebop album since the early 1950s, *Our Man* also shows how much he had continued to absorb of the pre-bop sound of Lester Young and Johnny Hodges. There are hints of both in his ballad playing, and in the winding, almost incantatory solo on 'Night In Tunisia', which is one of his finest performances on record. A classic.

***(*)   One Flight Up Blue Note B21Y 84176 CD
Gordon; Donald Byrd (*t*); Kenny Drew (*p*); Niels-Henning Ørsted-Pedersen (*b*); Art Taylor (*d*). 6/64.

Three extended performances, dominated by 'Darn That Dream' (see also *Ballads*, below) and the turned-sideways 'Coppin' The Haven' theme. Byrd was still an impressive player at this period, though he's rarely as adventurous as Hubbard, and Drew is a brilliant accompanist. It's easy to see, particularly on 'Darn', how Gordon continued to influence John Coltrane's harmonic development.

***   Clubhouse Blue Note B21Y 84445 CD
Gordon; Freddie Hubbard (*t*); Barry Harris (*p*); Butch Warren (*b*); Billy Higgins (*d*). 5/65.

***(*)   Gettin' Around Blue Note B21Y 46681 CD
Gordon; Bobby Hutcherson (*vib*); Barry Harris (*p*); Bob Cranshaw (*b*); Billy Higgins (*d*). 5/65.

By no means the best-known of Gordon's Blue Notes, there are still fine things on both. *Clubhouse* is mainly remarkable for the ease of his playing and for some dramatic exchanges of mood with Hubbard. The opening of the trumpeter's solo on 'I'm A Fool To Want You' (following Gordon's Byas-and-Berry-tinged opening statement) sends a tingle up and down the back every time it's heard. Though rather muffled in the mix, Harris comps beautifully, tying his heavy left-hand chords into Warren's rather deliberate lines. Listen for the sensuous growl in the middle of Gordon's second solo; it's unbelievably sexy.

Gettin' Around benefits enormously from the inclusion of Hutcherson. He makes Gordon play more simply, in the sense of going for fewer notes, but he provides a far more challenging harmonic background than Harris, and the big man has to negotiate some intriguingly non-standard changes on 'Who Can I Turn To' and 'Everybody's Somebody's Fool'.

***   The Tower Of Power! Original Jazz Classics OJC 299 LP/MC
Gordon; James Moody (*ts*); Barry Harris (*p*); Buster Williams (*b*); Albert Heath (*d*). 4/69.

Moody's single contribution to this rather overlooked set is pretty facile but there are three good quartet numbers, including a thumping version of 'Stanley The Steamer' that is marvellous stand-up jazz. Unfortunately only available on vinyl and cassette (and the latter certainly can't be recommended), with no sign of a CD reissue in the wings. Not a priority purchase.

***   At Montreux Prestige 7861 CD/LP
Gordon; Junior Mance (*p*); Martin Rivera (*b*); Oliver Jackson (*d*).

Mance isn't the obvious man for the job, but he sounds great on the CD bonus track, 'The Panther', and he powers through 'Rhythm-A-Ning' and 'Blue Monk' with a blissful disregard for their supposed 'complexities'. One suspects that Monk might have approved. Gordon is in good voice and hits a rich, deep tone on 'Sophisticated Lady' that one heard more and more often in the last years; untroubled by 'changes' and content to colour in the tune, he produces a solo of gentle washes and tiny details that is the antithesis of the harmonic complications and agonies Coltrane bequeathed to jazz.

(**)   **Nights At The Keystone: Volume 1 Blue Note CDP 794848 2 CD

(**)   **Nights At The Keystone: Volume 2 Blue Note CDP 794849 2 CD

(**)   **Nights At The Keystone: Volume 3 Blue Note CDP 794850 2 CD
Gordon; George Cables (p); Rufus Reid (b); Eddie Gladden (d). 5 & 9/78, 3/79.

Indifferent recordings, but utterly magisterial performances from three stints at the Keystone Korner in San Francisco. All but those on Volume 3 (dominated by a magnificent 'Body And Soul', which is also on *Ballads*, below) have been available before, but the CD format gives a far better impression of how a club date might have progressed.

This was one of the best groups Gordon had had since the 1950s and, though Gladden is over-loud, he introduces just enough urgency and control to sustain a very long blues like 'The Panther' (Volume 2) or the relaxed swing of 'Easy Living'. Cables's solos are surprisingly pointed on the March 1979 material and sound as if they're played on a different, brighter piano. Reid is consistently excellent, often leaving a strict beat to echo a lazy phrase of Gordon's or to invert one of his calmly adventurous progressions.

Volume 1 kicks off with a 'Scotch snap' intro to 'It's You Or No One', which is dedicated to the Loch Ness Monster, and there are flashes of humour throughout. There are a couple of moments in his solo on 'Backstairs'/'LTD' (final number and theme of Volume 2) when Gordon pretends to be drunk, and elsewhere he does convincing impressions of a man nodding off to sleep with the reed still in his mouth. But generally his control is remarkable and the horn almost seems incidental to the music coming out of him in that husky, laid-back tone.

***   **Ballads** Blue Note CDP 7 96579 2 CD
Gordon; Donald Byrd, Freddie Hubbard (t); George Cables, Sonny Clark, Kenny Drew, Barry Harris, Horace Parlan, Bud Powell (p); Paul Chambers, Bob Cranshaw, Pierre Michelot, Niels-Henning Ørsted-Pedersen, Rufus Reid, George Tucker, Butch Warren (b); Kenny Clarke, Eddie Gladden, Al Harewood, Billy Higgins, Philly Joe Jones, Art Taylor (d). 61–65, 78.

Very much in line with a recent rash of 'mellow' and 'gentle side' compilations, which have been reviving the fortunes of the once-popular but latterly despised ballad set. Mostly early-1960s material and thus likely to be very familiar to Gordon enthusiasts, it does also include a live performance of 'Body And Soul' that surfaced on a third disc of previously unreleased material on *Nights At The Keystone*. For newcomers, the highlights are 'I'm A Fool To Want You' (from *Clubhouse*, see above), 'Willow Weep For Me' with Bud Powell (*Our Man In Paris*, ditto) and 'You've Changed' from *Doin' Alright*. There's also material from *Dexter Calling*, *Go*, *A Swingin' Affair* and *One Flight Up*.

(*)   **Cheese Cake Steeplechase 6008 CD/LP
Gordon; Tete Montoliu (p); Benny Nielsen, Niels-Henning Ørsted-Pedersen (b); Alex Riel (d). 6/64.

***   **King Neptune** Steeplechase 6012 CD/LP
As above. 6/64.

***   **I Want More** Steeplechase 6015 CD/LP
As above. 7/64.

***   **Love For Sale** Steeplechase 6018 CD/LP
As above. 7/64.

(*)   **It's You Or No One Steeplechase 6022 CD/LP
As above. 8/64.

(*)   **Billie's Bounce Steeplechase 6028 CD/LP
As above. 8/64.

***   **Stable Mable** Steeplechase 1040 CD/LP
Gordon; Tete Montoliu, Horace Parlan (p); Benny Nielsen, Niels-Henning Ørsted-Pedersen (b); Alex Riel, Tony Inzalaco (d). 11/74.

(*)   **Bouncing With Dex Steeplechase 1060 CD/LP
Gordon; Tete Montoliu (*p*); Benny Nielsen, Niels-Henning Ørsted-Pedersen (*b*); Alex Riel, Billy Higgins (*d*). 3/75, 9/75.

Newly settled in Scandinavia, Gordon turns the tap on full. There's still the emotional equivalent of an airlock, slightly spluttering hesitations alternating with sudden scalding flows, but it all starts to fit together as this fascinating sequence of albums progresses. A more comprehensive pianist, Parlan or Flanagan, might have varied the structures a little, but Montoliou is sympathetic and very lyrical.

The touchstone 'Body And Soul' is beautifully enunciated on *King Neptune* and the band gels in the ensemble passages, with little of the slightly mechanistic pulse that afflicted the earlier *Cheese Cake* session. *I Want More* and *Love For Sale* are the best of this group. Gordon's understanding with the players seems increasingly telepathic and his approach to themes correspondingly inventive. Considered as a set, this is some of Gordon's best work, documented at close quarters on good pressings and CD transfers.

Bouncin' With Dex takes essentially the same band forward a decade. By the time of *Swiss Nights*, the act is consummately polished. Montoliou sounds relaxed and confident and plays with considerable authority.

***   **Both Sides Of Midnight** Black Lion 60103 CD/LP

***(*)   **Body And Soul** Black Lion 60118 CD/LP/MC

(*)   **Take The 'A' Train Black Lion 60133 CD/MC

**   **The Apartment** Steeplechase 1025 CD/LP

***   **Swiss Nights – Volume 1** Steeplechase 1050 CD/LP

***   **Swiss Nights – Volume 2** Steeplechase 1090 CD/LP/MC

(*)   **Swiss Nights – Volume 3 Steeplechase 1110 CD/LP/MC

(*)   **Lullaby For A Monster Steeplechase 1156 LP/MC
Gordon; Kenny Drew (*p*; not on *Lullaby*); Niels-Henning Ørsted-Pedersen (*b*); Albert Heath (*d* on 7/67, 11/74) or Alex Riel (*d* on 8/75, 6/76). 7/67, 7/67, 11/74, 8/75, 8/75, 8/75, 6/76.

Both Sides and *Body And Soul* are vintage albums from a two-shift session in July 1967. '"A" Train' uses up some of the alternate takes ('For All We Know' from the former, and 'Blues Walk' from the second) and is a little dilute as a consequence. Drew is a more rhythmic pianist than Montoliou, and the metre of Gordon's solos tends to stretch, fragment, re-integrate at great speed when in his company. *Lullaby*, a piano-less trio and thus unusual for Gordon, sees him trying rather unsuccessfully to bridge the gaps that Drew's absence leaves. It contains some of his freest solos, notably 'On Green Dolphin Street', but there's an element of constancy lacking.

There's a slight break in the continuity between 1967 and 1974. *The Apartment* isn't one of Gordon's best records; it sounds curiously timebound now, far more than anything else he did, and there's a flatness to some of the solo work. Whatever the reason, the three volumes of *Swiss Nights* sound vigorous, pumped-up and highly coherent. There probably wasn't enough material for three albums, though the last is justified by 'Sophisticated Lady'. Together, they make a fine set and a good summation of what this quartet was about.

**   **Live At The Amsterdam Paradiso** Affinity 751 CD
Gordon; Cees Slinger (*p*); Jacques Schols (*b*); Han Bennink (*d*). 2/69.

Bennink proves to be an able and intelligent accompanist, but there must be doubts about Slinger and Schols, neither of whom seems willing to adapt to Gordon's conception. The sound is rather unstable and marred by jolting top notes. For serious collectors – of Gordon or Bennink – only.

**   **At Montreux** Prestige 7861 CD/LP
Gordon; Junior Mance (*p*); Martin Rivera (*b*); Oliver Jackson (*d*). 7/70.

Gordon plays a slightly routinized set with Mance's trio, incorporating two Monk tunes and the *de rigueur* 'Body And Soul'. For once, the Swiss air doesn't seem to have got him high.

**   **Tower Of Power** Original Jazz Classics OJC 299 LP
Gordon; James Moody (*ts*); Barry Harris (*p*); Buster Williams (*b*); Albert Heath (*d*).
4/69.

The 'battle of the tenors' format never suited Gordon's extended delivery. Though this is subtler than an old-fashioned cutting contest, Moody tends to impede rather than spur Gordon; fortunately his contribution is restricted to a single track, 'Mon Maestre'. The quartet numbers are better, but Gordon isn't firing on all cylinders.

(*)   **Body And Soul Arco 3 ARC 109 CD
Gordon; George Cables (*p*); Rufus Reid (*b*); Eddie Gladden (*d*). 10/71.

Long and highly developed solos of the highest calibre, but set against a rather dull and acoustically wooden background. For students of Gordon's method, *Body And Soul* (not to be confused with its Black Lion namesake) might prove a more accessible text than his better albums, where the joins and welds are kept out of sight. For casual listeners, non-essential.

**   **The Shadow Of Your Smile** Steeplechase 1206 LP
Gordon; Lars Sjösten (*p*); Sture Nordin (*b*); Fredrik Norén (*d*). 4/71.

(*)   **After Hours Steeplechase 1226 LP
As above, except add Rolf Ericson (*t*).

Apparently not bound for the CD catalogue, these are weak performances by Gordon's high and consistent standard. 'Polka Dots And Moonbeams' on *Shadow* suffers some difficulties in the first dozen measures, mostly down to the Danish rhythm section. Not usually lacking in proportion, Gordon sounds merely grandstanding on 'Secret Love' and never quite gets hold of 'Shadow Of Your Smile'; there's a much better (1961) version of the latter with Dizzy Reece, Slide Hampton and Kenny Drew on the Verve sampler *Jazz Club – Tenor Sax* (840031 CD). Ericson has a bold, swinging tone, but it cuts across Gordon's development on 'All The Things You Are' quite disconcertingly. Two to miss with a clear conscience.

***(*)   **Biting The Apple** Steeplechase 1080 CD/LP/MC
Gordon; Barry Harris (*p*); Sam Jones (*b*); Al Foster (*d*). 11/76.

Prodigal comes home. Hugs and forgiveness on all sides, and then the party. In 1976, Gordon made a rare return visit to the States. The response was so overwhelmingly positive that he decided to end his exile permanently. 'Apple Jump' is a joyous homecoming and 'I'll Remember April' one of his loveliest performances. Harris, Jones and Foster fit in comfortably, and the sound is good.

****   **More Than You Know** Steeplechase 1030 CD/LP/MC
Gordon; Palle Mikkelborg, Allan Botschinsky, Benny Rosenfeld, Idries Sulieman (*t, flhn*); Richard Boone, Vincent Nilsson (*tb*); Axel Windfeld (*btb*); Ole Molin (*g*); Thomas Clausen (*p, electric p*); Kenneth Knudsen (*syn*); Niels-Henning Ørsted-Pedersen (*b*); Alex Riel, Ed Thigpen (*d*); Klaus Nordsoe (*perc*); chamber winds and strings. 2–3/75.

**   **Strings And Things** Steeplechase 1145 LP
Gordon; Allan Botschinsky, Markku Johansson (*t*); Eero Koivistoinen, Pekka Poyry (*reeds*); George Wadenius, Ole Molin (*g*); Niels-Henning Ørsted-Pedersen (*b*); unknown ensemble. 2/65, 5/76.

***   **Something Different** Steeplechase 1136 CD/LP/MC
Gordon; Philip Catherine (*g*); Niels-Henning Ørsted-Pedersen (*b*); Billy Hart (*d*). 9/75.

(*)   **Sophisticated Giant CBS 450316 CD/LP
Gordon; Benny Bailey, Woody Shaw (*t, flhn*); Wayne Andre, Slide Hampton (*tb*); Frank Wess (*f, as, picc*); Howard Johnson (*tba, bs*); Bobby Hutcherson (*vib*); George Cables (*p*); Rufus Reid (*b*); Victor Lewis (*d*). 6/77.

Beautifully arranged and orchestrated (by Mikkelborg), *More Than You Know* sets Gordon in the middle – as it sounds – of a rich ensemble of textures which are every bit as creatively unresolved and undogmatic as his solo approach. 'Naima' rarely works with a large band, but this is near-perfect and Gordon responds with considerable emotion and inventiveness. The cassette sound is a little flat, but the CD shouldn't be missed.

Gordon rarely played with a guitarist, but Catherine was an inspired choice for the September 1975 session, alternating warm, flowing lines with more staccato, accented figures towards the top of his range. NHØP responds with firmly plucked and strummed figures and Gordon rides on top in a relatively unfamiliar programme for him – Miles's 'Freddie Freeloader', 'When Sunny Gets Blue', 'Polka Dots And Moonbeams'.

Sophisticated Giant is an energetic but occasionally oblique album that shows off more of Gordon's Coltrane mannerisms. The arrangements – by Slide Hampton – and the typically overmixed CBS sound mask some of the subtlety of Gordon's soloing, and the true sound of his soprano. The trumpets are a trifle brittle and, with no CD in immediate prospect, this might be considered a later gap-filler rather than an essential buy.

Strings And Things is a diffident, rather shapeless compilation of material with none of the bite of Mikkelborg's usually intelligent orchestration.

**(*)   Midnight Dream West Wind 2040 CD
Gordon; Lionel Hampton (*vib*); Roland Hanna, Hank Jones (*p*); Vincent Bell (*g*); George Duvivier, George Mraz (*b*); Oliver Jackson, Sammy Turner (*d*); Candido Camero (*congas*). 77.

Two unusual sessions from 1977. It's a pity that Gordon didn't play more with Roland Hanna, who clearly understands his idiom and plays superbly. The partnership with Hampton was an interesting one-off but never quite sparked. Some good solos from all the principals. Respectable sound.

**(*)   Round Midnight CBS 70300 CD/LP
Gordon; various line-ups. 85.

**(*)   The Other Side Of Round Midnight Blue Note 746397 CD
As above. 86.

Soundtrack material from French movie director Bernard Tavernier's sentimentalized treatment of a composite black musician (played with Methodical conviction by Gordon) slowly unwinding his life. The music, curiously, is far more atmospheric on its own. Good contributions from Bobby Hutcherson, John McLaughlin and Herbie Hancock; very up-close, how you say? intimate sound. *The Other Side* is pretty much the same as this one.

JOE GORDON (1928–63)
TRUMPET

***   Lookin' Good Original Jazz Classics OJC 174 LP
Gordon; Jimmy Woods (*as*); Dick Whittington (*p*); Jimmy Bond (*b*); Milton Turner (*d*). 7/61.

A minor hard bopper from Boston, Gordon made few records and only two as leader. This date, originally for Contemporary, is a notch below his 1955 Emarcy session, if only because the company – previously including Art Blakey, Junior Mance and Charlie Rouse – is less stimulating. The fiery and excitable alto of Woods makes an interesting foil for Gordon's cleanly articulated, romantically inclined playing, and the originals in the programme pique the interest of the players. But the rhythm section is no more than adequate, and the music is finally much like any other West Coast hard-bop date.

DANNY GOTTLIEB (born 1953)
DRUMS

***(*)   Whirlwind Atlantic 781958 CD/LP/MC
Gottlieb; Lew Soloff (*t*); Bill Evans (*ts*); Doug Hall, Mitch Forman, Gregory Smith, Steve Sauber (*ky*); John Abercrombie, Chuck Loeb, Jon Herington (*g*); Mark Egan, Chip Jackson (*b*); Cafe, Nana Vasconcelos, Trilok Gurtu (*perc*). 89.

Gottlieb's work with Pat Metheny and Elements is strong and brusque in the manner of the contemporary fusion drummer, but it doesn't prepare one for the consistent beauty and brightness of this record. The compositions are simple rather than cluttered, leaving the players to work with surprising clarity around Gottlieb's punchy yet unflashy rhythms, and even if such as 'Tropic Heat' and 'Twilight Drive' aim to be little more than pop-jazz sketches, they emerge as gracefully as anything in the genre. Abercrombie, the principal soloist, has some terrific moments, and there is a remarkable rhythm improvisation where Gottlieb is joined by Vasconcelos and Gurtu. Superbly crisp and clear recording throughout.

DUSKO GOYKOVICH (born 1931)
TRUMPET, FLUGELHORN

***(*) **Swinging Macedonia** Enja 4048 CD/LP
Goykovich; Eddie Busnello (*as*); Nathan Davis (*ts, ss, f*); Mal Waldron (*p*); Peter Trunk (*b*); Cees See (*d*). 8/66.

One of the most convincing attempts to synthesize jazz and the curious scalar progressions of Balkan folk music. Born in Yugoslavia, Goykovich studied at Berklee and saw action with Maynard Ferguson, Woody Herman and with the Clarke–Boland big band. His most characteristic work, though, has been with smaller groups. He is a bright, rhythmic player, with a full, rather folksy sound that draws somewhat selectively on the bop trumpet tradition.

Swinging Macedonia was a bold stroke, with an impact akin to that of Ivo Papasov's much-hyped Bulgarian Wedding Band. Goykovich, though, is more purely a jazz player, and a more adventurous improviser. He's ably supported by an international line-up that hinges on the two American exiles. Waldron deals splendidly with some unfamiliar chord changes, Davis sounds authentically Slavonic (indeed, much like Papasov) and the little-known Busnello makes three or four very effective interventions. More than just an oddity, this deserves to be known more widely.

(*)   **After Hours Enja 2020 LP
Goykovich; Tete Montoliu (*p*); Rob Langereis (*b*); Joe Nay (*d*). 11/71.

'Old Fisherman's Daughter' reappears from *Swinging Macedonia*, but with little of her maidenly freshness and just a whiff of the red herrings. This is one of Goykovich's poorer performances; solos follow false trails, the underlying pulse is unsteady, and the band consistently plays safe.

Montoliu has established a considerable pedigree as a solo and small-group player, but is less than convincing here. Langereis has recorded with Peter Herbolzheimer and Toots Thielmanns and is a fine, adaptable player. Nay is rather more diffident; the drum sound is also slightly harsh.

***(*) **Celebration** DIW 806/8016 CD/LP
Goykovich; Kenny Drew (*p*); Jimmy Woode (*b*); Al Levitt (*d*). 8/87.

There weren't many better mainstream-to-modern rhythm sections doing the rounds in the later 1980s than Drew, Woode and Levitt. Behind Goykovich, they are seamless and sympathetically responsive to his still occasionally surprising harmonic shifts. This, though, is his most Western album (one can't strictly say 'American'), with hints of everything from the Ellington small groups to the Jazz Messengers. Goykovich negotiates 'Blues In The Closet' and 'The Touch Of Your Lips' with admirable self-confidence. The originals have a clean bop edge. All in all, an impressive way of marking a third decade in the biz. *Nazdravie.*

FRIEDMANN GRAEF
SOPRANO SAXOPHONE, TENOR SAXOPHONE, CLARINET, BARITONE SAXOPHONE

**   **Daily New Paradox** FMP 0450 LP
Graef; Thomas Wiedermann (*tb*); Thomas Wegel (*b*); Albrecht Riermeier (*vib, perc*); Lutz Halfter (*d*). 6/77.

(*)   **Exit FMP 0820 LP
Graef; Albrecht Riermeier (*vib, mar, d, perc*). 1/81.

There must be a Central Casting file for Euro-free saxophonists of this stamp. Graef has touches of Braxton and (in his baritone work) Brötzmann in his make-up but consistently manages to sound like less than the sum of his technically impressive parts. The duos with percussionist Riermeier are episodically interesting; otherwise these show no individuality whatsoever.

STÉPHANE GRAPPELLI (born 1908)
VIOLIN

***   **Special** Jazztime 251286 2 CD
Grappelli; Roger Chaput, Henri Crolla, Jimmy Gourley, Georges Megalos, Joseph Reinhardt (g); Jack Dieval (p); Pierre Spiers; (hrp); Pierre Michelot, Benoit Quersin, Emmanuel Soudieux (b); Armand Molinetti, Baptiste Reilles (d). 47–61.

An excellent and well-transferred sampler of non-Django material, covering the period from their post-war reunion to the great guitarist's death in 1953 and beyond. Grappelli once said somewhat wearily that he would rather play with lesser musicians than ever again have to suffer Django's 'monkey business'. There's enough evidence here to confirm both the violinist's independent stature as an improviser and the plentiful supply of like-minded players.

Half a dozen tracks locate Grappelli in harpist Spiers's fine standards-based quartet. Earlier – 1954 – sets find him alongside the excellent pianist Dieval, yielding a lovely 'The World Is Waiting For The Sunrise', and the guitarist Henri Crolla, who plays in an idiom intriguingly removed from Django's. A single track from the immediately post-war Hot Four, which included Hot Club veterans Chaput and Django's brother Joseph Reinhardt, marks it unmistakably as Grappelli's band, with a less ambitious improvisatory focus than the great original. 'Tea For Two' is a charmingly slight piano solo from Grappelli.

***   **Meets Barney Kessel** Black Lion BLCD 760150 CD
Grappelli; Barney Kessel (g); Nino Rosso (g); Michel Gaudry (b); Jean-Louis Viale (d). 6/69.

(*)   **Limehouse Blues Black Lion BLCD 760158 CD
As above.

(*)   **Venupelli Blues Charly CD 73
Grappelli; Joe Venuti (vn); Barney Kessel (g); George Wein (p); Larry Ridley (b); Don Lamond (d). 10/69.

It might have been better had they restricted both of these to a duo. The second guitar, though it follows a sanctified precedent, really adds nothing to the overall sound of the Black Lion, and Grappelli scarcely needs a drummer as prosy as Viale to keep him to the mark. Kessel, who is a disciple of Charlie Christian rather than a practising Djangologist, sounds bluesier than most of Grappelli's usual cohorts, but the combination works surprisingly well on a roster of unexceptionable standards.

Limehouse Blues scrapes together more material from the same Paris studio sessions. There are previously unreleased readings of Kessel's 'Copa Cola' and 'Blues For Georges', 'I Got Rhythm', and a fine 'Perdido', together with an alternative take of 'Honeysuckle Rose'.

Kessel turns up again on *Venupelli Blues*. As a stylistic hybrid, the title-track sums up the divide between the two fiddlers. Venuti had just hauled himself up out of the swamp of alcoholism and was making a succesful comeback. 'The Mad Fiddler From Phillie', as an album-title once styled him, combines better than anyone might have expected with the Urban Virtuoso from Paris and, though the rhythm section is once again less than compelling, the music coheres well.

***   **Compact Jazz** MPS 831370-2 IMS CD
Grappelli; Mark Hemeler, George Shearing (p); Philip Catherine, Larry Coryell, Diz Disley, Ike Isaacs (g); Isla Eckinger, Niels-Henning Ørsted-Pedersen, Andrew Simpkins, Eberhard Weber (b); Kenny Clare, Rusty Jones (d). 71–9.

A useful and generally high-quality sampler of 1970s' material. Pairing Grappelli with the Shearing trio worked less well than might have been expected; the collaboration with Coryell and Catherine, both of them admittedly adaptable and Catherine in particular loyal to the memory of Django, works rather better, including an excellent run through Grappelli's favourite 'Minor Swing'.

More material from the same sessions can be found on two other MPS Compact Jazz compilations, MPS 833284 2 IMS, dedicated to Shearing, and MPS 835320 2 IMS, which includes Violin Summit performances with Jean-Luc Ponty who, in purely artistic terms, is Grappelli's grand-nephew. Worth having all three.

***(*) To Django Accord 401202 CD
> Grappelli; Alan Clare, Marc Hemmeler (*p*); Ernie Cranenburgh, Lennie Bush (*b*); Chris Karan (*d*). 6/72.

*** Joue George Gershwin Et Cole Porter Accord 402052 CD
> Grappelli; Marc Hemmeler, Maurice Vandair (*p*); Eddie Louiss (*org*); Jimmy Gourley, Ike Isaacs (*g*); Guy Pedersen, Luigi Trussardi (*b*); Daniel Humair (*d*).

The Gershwin/Porter material is fairly predictable and played with either jaunty insouciance or syrupy romanticism, neither of which does much credit to Grappelli or the composers he is honouring. Despite sounding as if it were recorded in a cathedral, *To Django* is much preferable. The opening version of 'Djangology' is one of the best available, and there are lovely versions of 'Manoir De Mes Rêves' and 'Nuages' (featuring Hemmeler and Clare respectively on electric piano). There's a warmth and richness to Grappelli's tone that suggest viola rather than orthodox fiddle. That's particularly noticeable on the longest track, an extended 'Blues' co-written with Django before the war, as was 'Minor Swing', which receives a particularly sensitive reading.

*** Stardust Black Lion BLP 60117 CD/LP/MC
> Grappelli; Alan Clare (*p, cel*). 3/73.

There aren't too many 'alternate takes' of Grappelli performances available. The *Stardust* CD affords a valuable opportunity to study how the violinist thinks and rethinks his way through a theme, subtly roughening textures and sharpening the basic metre on a second take of 'Tournesol' (the original is also sampled on a good label compilation *Artistry In Jazz* – BLCD 760100) and rescuing two rather schmaltzy 'Greensleeves' with firm bow-work.

***(*) Parisian Thoroughfare Black Lion BLP 60132 CD/LP/MC
> Grappelli; Roland Hanna (*p, electric p*); George Mraz (*b*); Mel Lewis (*d*). 9/73.

A further counter to the persistent canard that Grappelli is an MOR entertainer with no real jazz credibility. Working with a first-class mainstream rhythm section, he sounds fantastically assured but also probingly sceptical about the broader and better-trodden melodic thoroughfares. Hanna's electric piano is a little over-bright and loses some of the firmness he invests in left-hand chords, but Mraz and Lewis combine superbly.

***(*) To Django Accord 401202 CD
> Grappelli; Alan Clare, Marc Hemmeler (*p*); Ernie Cranenburgh, Lennie Bush (*b*); Chris Karan (*d*). 6/72.

*** Joue George Gershwin Et Cole Porter Accord 402052 CD
> Grappelli; Marc Hemmeler, Maurice Vandair (*p*); Eddie Louiss (*org*); Jimmy Gourley, Ike Isaacs (*g*); Guy Pedersen, Luigi Trussardi (*b*); Daniel Humair (*d*).

The Gershwin/Porter material is fairly predictable and played with either jaunty insouciance or syrupy romanticism, neither of which does much credit to Grappelli or the composers he is honouring. Despite sounding as if it were recorded in a cathedral, *To Django* is much preferable. The opening version of 'Djangology' is one of the best available, and there are lovely versions of 'Manoir De Mes Rêves' and 'Nuages' (featuring Hemmeler and Clare respectively on electric piano). There's a warmth and richness to Grappelli's tone that suggests viola rather than orthodox fiddle. That's particularly noticeable on the longest track, an extended 'Blues' co-written with Django before the war, as was 'Minor Swing', which receives a particularly sensitive reading.

*** Live In London Black Lion BLCD 760139 CD
> Grappelli; Diz Disley; Denny Wright (*g*); Len Skeat (*b*). 11/73.

'Not jazz', the promoters muttered and Grappelli's ultim[...]
a round of folk clubs and small theatres, thereby reinforcin[...]
much more effectively than if he had remained on the jazz ci[...]
London aren't quite vintage, but they represent a more th[...]
sensibly weighted nostalgia of the Hot Club of London. [...]
Grappelli appears to have rationed since, and a lovely 'Manoir De[...]

**

Steff And Slam Black & Blue 233076 CD
Grappelli; Bucky Pizzarelli, Jimmy Shirley (*g*); Johnny Guarn[...]
George Duvivier, Slam Stewart (*b*, *v*); Oliver Jackson, Jackie W[...]

***(*) **London Meeting** String 233852 CD
Grappelli; Bucky Pizzarelli (*g*); Roland Hanna, Hank Jones (*p*); Ge[...]
Jimmy Woode (*b*); Alan Dawson, Oliver Jackson (*d*). 7/78, 7/79.

The Black & Blue is an attempt – neither altogether successful nor well judged – to capitalize on the popularity of the old Slim and Slam partnership of Gaillard and Stewart. Significantly, perhaps, the best track is a lovely 'Sweet And Lovely', solitary representative of a much later session with Pizzarelli, Hanna, Duvivier and Jackson, players equal to the violinist's innate seriousness and intelligence.

That session – minus 'Sweet And Lovely' – occupies half of *London Meeting*, one of the straightest recordings of Grappelli's career, and one of the best. The Hank Jones Quartet, with Jimmy Woode particularly responsive, give him acres of room for manoeuvre, but it's Pizzarelli's and Hanna's tight, intelligent chording that draws out his most extravagant and daring lines. *London Meeting* is a must.

****

Tivoli Gardens, Copenhagen, Denmark Original Jazz Classics OJC 441 CD/LP/MC
Grappelli; Joe Pass (*g*); Niels-Henning Ørsted-Pedersen (*b*). 7/79.

A superb set, marred only slightly by variable sound. Grappelli's interpretations of 'Paper Moon', 'I Can't Get Started', 'I'll Remember April', 'Crazy Rhythm', 'How Deep Is The Ocean', 'Let's Fall In Love', 'I Get A Kick Out Of You' reaffirm his genius as an improviser and also his ability to counter slightly saccharine themes with the right hint of tartness. Pass, who occasionally errs on the side of sweetness, plays beautifully, and NHØP is, as always, both monumental and delicate.

***

Satin Doll Musidisc 440162 CD
Grappelli; Eddie Louiss (*org*); Marc Hemmeler (*p*); Jimmy Gourley (*g*); Guy Pedersen (*b*); Kenny Clarke (*d*).

(*) **Plays Jerome Kern GRP 91032 CD/LP
Grappelli; Marc Fosset (*g*, *v*); Martin Taylor (*g*); Jack Sewing (*b*); Alf Bigden, Martin Drew, Jean-Louis Viale, Graham Ward (*d*); strings.

Two above-average standards sessions, of which the first, on CD only, is superior by virtue of a much tighter rhythm section and the absence of a superfluous string garnish. As always, Grappelli's improvisations have a tightly coherent logic, interspersed with occasional rhapsodic flights that recall the coloratura clarinet players of New Orleans.

***

At The Winery Concord CCD 4139 CD/MC
Grappelli; John Etheridge (*g*); Martin Taylor (*g*); Jack Sewing. 9/80.

***

Live In San Francisco Black Hawk BKH 51601 LP
Grappelli; Martin Taylor, Diz Disley (*g*); Jack Sewing (*d*). 7/82.

Taylor and Disley have been Grappelli's two most sympathetic latter-day collaborators (the latter organized Grappelli's highly successful 1972 British tour) and they complement each other near-perfectly on the live set recorded in the States exactly a decade later. Taylor's amplified sound adds a little sting to Grappelli's playing, which is always more robust live than in an acoustically 'dead' and feedback-free studio situation. The Beatles' 'Here, There And Everywhere' was a mistake (as if Charles Lloyd hadn't already proved that), but the rest of the material is lively and well-judged.

Better known as a jazz-rock player in one of the many later versions of the protean Soft Machine, Etheridge nevertheless fits in well with Grappelli's conception on *At The Winery*. Hard to choose between the two sets, though enthusiasts will want both.

Gerard Gustin (*g*); Jack Sewing (*b*); Armand Cavallero (*d*).

om a CD-only label with a small but oddly eclectic catalogue (that includes a good session on Arco 3 ARC 110). The title here, though, is slightly misleading, since this is a collection of tributes to a number of musicians who might claim some influence on Grappelli's career, however remote: Jobim, Basie, Ray Brown, Bird, Joao Gilberto, Duke, Dizzy Gillespie, Errol Garner, and so on.

It's an oddly mixed group but serves as a salutary – and doubtless deliberate – reminder that Grappelli's style wasn't fixed for ever in a smoky Left Bank *boîte* in the far-off 1930s, but has been developing and refining itself ever since. Not far enough to demand a bow in the direction of Leroy Jenkins or Billy Bang (now wouldn't that be a more interesting collaboration than the over-hyped Grappelli–Menuin tête-à-tête?) but far enough to shake off the fogey tag for good.

***   **Happy Reunion** Owl 021 CD
       Grappelli; Martial Solal (*p*). 2/80.

France's two most distinguished living jazz players in a friendly, but by no means undemanding collaboration. 'Nuages' and 'Parisian Thoroughfare' attract slightly clinical readings, 'God Bless The Child' a genuinely moving one; 'Grandeur Et Cadence' and 'Et Si L'On Improvisait' bear further witness to Grappelli's now well-attested intelligence. It would have been good to hear them play one of André Jolivet's or Henri Tomasi's small-scale chamber pieces, 'legitimate' works with a folkish, improvisatory feel and ideally suited to both men's style.

***   **Stephanova** Concord CCD 4225 CD/MC
       Grappelli; Marc Fosset (*g*). 6/83.

The relatively unfamiliar material suggests either momentary impatience with his usual regimen of personalized standards, or else a genuine desire to branch out into new areas. Fosset is a more interesting player in this more sharply focused context than in a group setting (see below), and the two trade a range of interesting and occasionally adventurous ideas.

(*)   **In Tokyo Denon Compact Disc CY 77130
       Grappelli; Marc Fosset (*g*); Jean-Philippe Viret (*b*); Marcel Azzola (*acc*). 10/90.

***   **One On One** Milestone M 9181 CD/LP/MC
       Grappelli; McCoy Tyner (*p*). 4/90.

At 82, some signs of ageing may well be inevitable. *In Tokyo* is a slightly jaded set, not so much in execution (Grappelli's playing is as zestful as ever), but in conception. Themes are medleyed rather too slickly and with occasional minor violence to taste. Azzola adds a little Gallic bounce (a shade too self-consciously?) to a rather static rhythm section.

By contrast, the outwardly improbable duo with McCoy Tyner works astonishingly well, including Coltrane's 'Mr P. C.' and the Coltrane-associated 'I Want To Talk About You', alongside more familiar repertoire like 'I Got Rhythm' and 'St Louis Blues'. Ever the romantic stylist, Tyner plays with impeccable taste, never losing contact with the basic structure of a tune. Recommended.

GEORG GRÄWE
PIANO, BANDLEADER, COMPOSER

(*)   **Songs And Variations hat Art CD 6028
       Gräwe; Phil Minton (*v*); Horst Grabosch (*t*); Radu Malfatti (*tb*); Michael Reissler (*cl*);
       Roberto Ottaviano (*as*); Phil Wachsmann (*vn*); Dieter Manderscheid (*b*); Thomas
       Witzmann (*vib*); Achim Kramer (*d*). 12/88, 5/89.

Gräwe the composer may prove a little too hard-boiled for the average jazz enthusiast, though if *Songs And Variations* proves too daunting, the more approachable *Six Studies For Piano Solo* [West Wind CD 012; currently deleted] would be well worth hunting out. The long and rather fraught 'Variations For Chamber Ensemble', with which *Songs And Variations* ends, is Webernian not just in some of its structures but also in the refreshing directness of its articulation, a model for contemporary chamber and improvising players. Gräwe's

GrubenKlangOrchester attempts a bold synthesis between the two idioms, and much of the time it succeeds.

The two longish 'song' pieces are settings of T. S. Eliot's 'East Coker' – 'In my end is my beginning' and all that stuff – and of 'Lookin' for Work' by Manfred Karge, which develops the line of enquiry established in Gräwe's *Industrial Folk Songs* and Brecht scores. Phil Minton's voice is one of the most remarkable instruments in jazz but it's oddly querulous when confronted by an English text, and it's a rather strained version of Eliot's inherently musical measures that comes across. To be approached with (some) caution.

***   **Sonic Fiction** hat Art CD 6043 CD
     Gräwe; Ernst Reijseger (*clo*); Gerry Hemingway (*d, perc*). 3/89.

In addition to a duo with the drummer Willi Kellers, Gräwe has worked regularly with two very different improvising trios: apparently unrecorded but well-received work with tubaist Melvyn Poore and GrubenKlangOrchester member Phil Wachsmann; and the trio captured in striking form on *Sonic Fiction*. Much like the larger group, it features three players of markedly different temperament, united by a resistance to the fixed resolutions of both 'jazz' and 'New Music'. They play undogmatically and with great exactness, as if they have been rehearsing these pieces for years. Like Eddie Prévost, Hemingway manages to swing even when playing completely free, and his range of articulation is quite extraordinary.

The long 'Fangled Talk' is slightly disappointing, a solitary lapse into what is usually called self-indulgence but which is probably merely inattention. Gräwe, one of the most enterprising of the post-Schlippenbach pianists, is apt to dissolve his own most acute observations in a flood of repetitions and curious evasions, but the ideas are strong enough to resist corrosion. Reijseger, by contrast, knows how to enjoy an idea and when to dispense with it. Thoroughly recommended.

WARDELL GRAY (1921–55)
TENOR SAXOPHONE

(*)   **One For Prez Black Lion 60106 CD/LP
     Gray; Dodo Marmarosa (*p*); Red Callender (*b*); Chuck Thompson or Doc West (*d*). 11/46.

Like his friend and collaborator, Dexter Gordon, Wardell Gray had to look to Europe for recognition. His first recordings, made just after the war, were not released in the United States. There were not to be very many more, for Gray died of an apparent heroin overdose in 1955, three months after Charlie Parker, and the shadow cast by Bird's passing largely shrouded Gray's no less untimely departure.

Unlike Gordon, Gray was less than wholly convinced by orthodox bebop, and continued to explore the swing style of bop's immediate ancestor, Lester Young. *One For Prez* is, as it sounds, an extended tribute to Young. Heavy on alternate takes, but sufficiently inventive to merit the inclusion of all but a few. Gray is in firm voice and Marmarosa, who has since vanished from sight, plays brilliantly.

(*)   **Way Out Wardell Crown CDBOP 014 CD
     Gray; Howard McGhee, Ernie Royal (*t*); Vic Dickenson (*tb*); Vido Musso (*ts*); Errol Garner, Arnold Ross (*p*); Irving Ashby, Barney Kessel (*g*); Harry Barbison, Red Callender, Don Lamond, Jackie Mills (*d*). 48.

There is some confusion – and the liner notes are giving nothing away – about the exact line-ups on this superb 1948 concert reissue; Benny Carter is mentioned in the liner notes but not among the formal personnel. The album is jointly credited to Gray and the inimitable Errol Garner, whose solo on 'Tenderly' is one of the highlights; the ensembles are fine, if spatially a little displaced, and the bass comes through quite strongly. Only discographers and hard-case audiophiles will baulk at either the dearth of reliable information or the steady tape-hiss. The music is very fine and Gray sounds in fine, occasionally antagonistic voice throughout.

***   **Easy Swing** Swingtime ST 1 CD
     Gray; Gene Phipps (*t*); Tate Houston (*bs*); Jimmy Raney (*g*); Al Haig, Dodo Marmarosa, Norman Simmons (*p*); Red Callender, Tommy Potter, Victor Sproles (*b*);

Vernell Fournier, Charlie Perry, Doc West (*d*); Ivory Joe Hunter, Little Willie Littlefield (*p, v*); other/collective personnel. 1949–55.

There also seems to be some doubt about the dating of the earliest – and best – of these sessions. Gray was essentially a consolidator rather than a revolutionary and, even with the most exuberant revisionist intention, it would seem improbable at this late date to find that he was the source and Charlie Parker the later recipient of some of the most significant structural alterations in jazz.

Gray sounds ever more like a man desperate to straddle the generations (with R&B men Hunter and Littlefield, he simply sounds desperate); the two takes of 'One For Prez' find him slipping in and out of character, and the second (and better) run of 'The Man I Love' is closer both to Young's conception and to the essential harmonic shifts of bop. The best of the material here is very good indeed, with Gray up and managing most of his contradictions. The tail-off, to the record as to the life, was depressing indeed.

***   **Live At The Haig 1952** Fresh Sound FSR CD 157
Gray; Art Farmer (*t*); Hampton Hawes, Amos Trice (*p*); Howard Roberts (*g*); Joe Mondragon (*b*); Shelly Manne (*d*). 9/52.

He was no less fortunate in having the gloriously expressive Hampton Hawes on all but one track of this fine 1952 date (one Amos Trice, better known for his work with Harold Land, plays on 'Lady Bird'). Gray had been working with Count Basie before these sessions and his conception is significantly pared down, even from the uncluttered approach of *One For Prez*. There is, though, a creeping weariness and inwardness in the voice, sadly reminiscent of Young's own rather paranoid decline, and it's left to Hawes and a pre-flugelhorn Art Farmer to keep spirits up. The mix of styles is just about right and the sound perfectly respectable for material nearly four decades old.

***   **Memorial – Volume 1** Original Jazz Classics OJC 050 CD/LP
Gray; Frank Morgan (*as*); Sonny Clark, Al Haig, Phil Hill (*p*); Teddy Charles (*vib*); Dick Nivison, Tommy Potter, Johnny Richardson (*b*); Roy Haynes, Lawrence Marable, Art Mardigan (*d*). 11/49, 4/50, 2/53.

***   **Memorial – Volume 2** Original Jazz Classics OJC 051 CD/LP
Gray; Art Farmer, Clark Terry (*t*); Sonny Criss (*as*); Dexter Gordon (*ts*); Jimmy Bunn, Hampton Hawes (*p*); Harper Crosby, Billy Hadnott (*b*); Lawrence Marable, Chuck Thompson (*d*). 8/50, 1/52.

The earliest of these sessions, a quartet consisting of Haig, Potter and Haynes, includes Gray's best-known composition, the oddly atmospheric 'Twisted' (which has since been covered by Annie Ross and Joni Mitchell, among others). Co-led with Haig (a single track, 'Easy Living', is sampled on the rather good Prestige *First Sessions* compilation), this is an altogether more impressive line-up than that of April 1950, with Phil Hill leading an uneasy rhythm section, only partially redeemed by Art Mardigan's forceful drumming; that apart, it's unlikely anyone will remember this April.

All the other sessions, on both volumes of the set, feature Gray with other horns. He can sound frail around brass, though Farmer's softly enunciated solos complement his perfectly (certainly better than Terry's, which, on the long jams 'Scrapple From The Apple' and 'Move', are too metallic), while among the reeds Sonny Criss's slightly querulous emotional urgency. By 1950, he and Gordon have already moved apart, following different stars.

BENNIE GREEN (1923–77)
TROMBONE

***   **Blows His Horn** Original Jazz Classics OJC 1728 CD/LP
Green; Charlie Rouse (*ts*); Cliff Smalls (*p*); Paul Chambers (*b*); Osie Johnson (*d*); Candido Camero (*perc*). 6–9/55.

(*) **Walking Down Original Jazz Classics OJC 1752 CD/LP
Green; Eric Dixon (*ts*); Lloyd Mayers (*p*); Sonny Wellesley (*b*); Bill English (*d*). 6/56

While these are good records, they rate some way below the excellent discs Green made for Blue Note in 1958–9. Albums For Time, Bethelehem and Jazzland, all from the early 1960s, would also be welcome in reissue form. For now, these are enjoyable if unremarkable hard-bop sessions with a penchant for blues and swing forms underscoring Green's cautious modernism. Although he was one of the first trombonists to fraternize with bop – as a teenager, he was in the Earl Hines orchestra that included Parker and Gillespie – his personal allegiance remained with a less demanding approach. The 1955 session highlights his singing tone and straightforward phrasing on attractive versions of 'Travellin' Light' and 'Body And Soul'. The band is a congenial one and Rouse's solos are an ounce more interesting than the leader's. *Walking Down* features a less impressive group and is slightly less interesting as a result, though Green is again in swinging form. OJC remastering is quite clean in both cases.

BENNY GREEN (born 1965)
PIANO

***   **Prelude** Criss Cross 1036 CD/LP
Green; Terence Blanchard (t); Javon Jackson (ts); Peter Washington (b); Tony Reedus (d). 2/88

***   **In This Direction** Criss Cross 1038 CD/LP
Green; Buster Williams (b); Lewis Nash (d). 12/88–1/89.

Green came to prominence as pianist with Betty Carter's group, and his mastery of bebop piano – particularly the chunky rhythms of Horace Silver – was leavened by an apparent interest in swing styles as well: Green hits the keyboard hard on uptempo tunes, and his preference for beefy chords and straight-ahead swing can make him sound like a more 'modern' Dave McKenna. These albums for Criss Cross feature a lot of piano, but there's nothing particularly outstanding about them: the quintet date sounds too much like a mere blowing session for any of the players to make a distinctive mark, and the trio set seems hastily prepared, although the rhythm section lend impressive support.

***(*)   **Lineage** Blue Note CDP 793670 CD/MC
Green; Ray Drummond (b); Victor Lewis (d). 1–2/90.

***(*)   **Greens** Blue Note CDP 796485 CD/MC
Green; Christian McBride (b); Carl Allen (d). 3/91.

Handsomely recorded, impeccably organized and programmed, delivered with panache and full-blooded commitment, these are exemplars of the contemporary piano trio record. Green has few pretences to innovation, and his composing is persuasive rather than absorbing, but these sessions are so full of brio and certainty of intention that such shortcomings are made to seem like mere details. *Lineage* is the more concentrated of the two, with a surprising list of compositions – from Monk, Ma Rainey, Neil Hefti and Bobby Timmons – dealt with in crisp, attacking terms; originals such as 'Debo's Theme' and the swinging 'Phoebe's Samba' introduce Green the composer almost shyly. He restricts himself to four credits on *Greens*, including the haunting title blues, and allows the trio a greater freedom with form.

BUNKY GREEN
ALTO AND SOPRANO SAXOPHONES

***   **Healing The Pain** Delos DE 4020 CD
Green; Billy Childs (p); Ralph Penland (b); Art Davis (d). 12/89.

There's nothing in print from Green's earlier stint with Argo and Vanguard, which leaves about a dozen albums in the cold. This set for Delos concentrates on ballads and has a rather forlorn air (the title reflects on his own situation since both Green's parents were recently dead at the time of the session). 'Who Can I Turn To' and 'Goodbye' are particularly downcast. But Green's severe tone and legato phrasing give the melodies real power, and on an up-tempo piece like 'I Concentrate On You' he runs through the changes with a finely controlled abandon. The rhythm section are reserved but attentive.

GRANT GREEN (1931–79)
GUITAR

**(*)   Reaching Out Black Lion BLCD 760129 CD
Green; Frank Haynes (*ts*); Billy Gardner (*org*); Ben Tucker (*b*); Dave Bailey (*d*).
3/61.

***   Grantstand Blue Note B21Y 46430 CD/MC
Green; Yusef Lateef (*ts, f*); Jack McDuff (*org*); Al Harewood (*d*). 8/61.

This is Green's most familiar setting. He started out in the early 1960s playing in organ groups
led by Jack McDuff and others, an association that de-emphasized his remarkable delicacy
(almost fragility) of tone and highlighted his harder, bluesier side. Recorded less than six
months before his fine Blue Note debut, *Reaching Out* is a disappointing portent of the bland
funk he chugged out in the post-detox early 1970s. Haynes, who plays beautifully on Kenny
Dorham's *Osmosis* (Black Lion 760146 CD), sounds curiously messy here and certainly fogs
some of Green's more thoughtful ideas. *Grantstand* is in every respect much better, though the
format is still rather unsubtle, and McDuff's swirling lines and sudden, choked-off probings are
often too loud to hear Green's subtler movements. Lateef has a lovely flute tone and his
straightforward tenor style, on 'Old Folks' and 'My Funny Valentine', sets up some of the best
playing on the album.

***(*)   Born To Be Blue Blue Note B21Y 84432 CD
Green; Ike Quebec (*ts*); Sonny Clark (*p*); Sam Jones (*b*); Louis Hayes (*d*). 12/61, 3/62.

The delicacy of Green's playing is highlighted by Ike Quebec's booting tenor on 'Someday My
Prince Will Come', but the very fact that Green is in evidence at all suggests that he's a tougher
customer than at first appears. His solos on 'My One And Only Love' and 'If I Should Lose
You' are among his most directly emotional on record and 'Count Every Star', taken from a
slightly earlier date, is judged to perfection, letting down just before it threatens to turn
schmaltzy. Sonny Clark contributes enormously to the overall sound, a talent still in the throes
of rediscovery.

***(*)   Feelin' The Spirit Blue Note B21Y 46822 CD
Green; Herbie Hancock (*p*); Butch Warren (*b*); Billy Higgins (*d*); Garvin Maseaux
(*tambourine*). 12/62.

A remarkable set of gospel tunes given thoroughly contemporary readings by a fine house band.
'Just A Closer Walk With Thee' sounds momentarily as if it's about to break into a closer
jogtrot and 'Go Down Moses' is a little *too* withers-wringing, but these are excellent
performances and Green gets better service from Hancock than from any subsequent piano
player, with the possible (and, on the face of it, surprising) exception of McCoy Tyner.

****   Idle Moments Blue Note B21Y 84154 CD/MC
Green; Joe Henderson (*ts*); Bobby Hutcherson (*vib*); Duke Pearson (*p*); Bob
Cranshaw (*b*); Al Harewood (*d*). 11/63.

Probably Green's best record and the clearest measure of his subsequent decline. The addition
of Hutcherson to the date was a vital stroke. The vibist brings a typically adventurous rhythmic
sense, knows how to play softly, and seems to spur the leader on to better and better things,
culminating in a sterling performance of John Lewis's 'Django'. Green's soloing is brightly
lyrical, with notes picked cleanly and exactly, rather than lazily approximated. Henderson is in
fine voice and the rhythm section is more than competent, though rather distantly recorded.

***   Matador Blue Note 784442 CD
Green; McCoy Tyner (*p*); Bob Cranshaw (*b*); Elvin Jones (*d*). 5/64.

It took pretty robust *cojones* to tackle 'My Favorite Things' with two-thirds of John Coltrane's
rhythm section while Trane still walked the earth, but Green's performance merits an *ole!* and a
couple of ears, even if he does get a little overheated and executes one pass too many. As does
the album as a whole. Tyner, perhaps unexpectedly, is the perfect partner, an exact pianistic
echo of Green's combination of delicacy, structural awareness and sheer power; Jones he
already knew from Chicago and a 1959 Jimmy Forrest session, which was Green's recording
debut.

Sadly, this is all that currently exists of Green's work. It would be well worth searching the second-hand and import bins for the marvellous *Solid*, which is *rara avis* nowadays.

HAZE GREENFIELD (born 1955)
ALTO AND SOPRANO SAXOPHONE

**(*)   Five For The City Owl 3819052 CD
Greenfield; Tom Harrell (*t, flhn*); Ted Lo (*ky*); Wayne Krantz (*g*); Paul Socolow (*b*); John Riley (*d*). 12/87.

Though on the surface this looks like another hard-bop date, Greenfield is actually seeking more tranquil and allusive ground. The sound of the record is often alarmingly close to some late-1970s ECM date, with Harrell coming on as Kenny Wheeler and the leader skirling mournfully in the middle distance. Lo's keyboard effects and Krantz's guitar-whine add further to the sense of some urban desolation and, while this finally sounds like a pretentious kind of mood-jazz, in its way it's astutely done.

MICHAEL GREGORY
GUITAR, VOCAL

**   The Way We Used To Do Tiptoe 888806 CD
Gregory (solo). 5/82.

Gregory is a talented guitarist with no luck on record. In the 1970s he secured an association with some of the music being made in New York lofts, and appeared with Oliver Lake in the studios, but this reissue of a 1982 album highlights his unsure affiliations: an interesting fusion of rock, jazz and free styles on the guitar is augmented by a decent soul voice, yet he can't sustain a solo album like this, and his subsequent foray into soul fusion for Novus disappeared very quickly.

STAN GREIG (born 1930)
PIANO

**(*)   Blues Every Time Calligraph CLG 004 LP
Greig; Pete Skivington (*b*); Johnny Richardson (*d*). 3/85.

Like the great clarinettist Sandy Brown, Greig was an alumnus of the strikingly jazzy Royal High School in Edinburgh. Much of Greig's best work was with Brown's imaginatively revivalist band in the late 1960s, then with Acker Bilk for most of the next decade, and then with the much-missed (and scandalously unrecorded) London Jazz Big Band.
   A warm, clubby player, Greig communicates less well on disc, but *Blues Every Time* is a valuable documentation and contains some highly impressive moments. The ghost of Sandy Brown hangs over 'Willow Weep For Me' and 'Love For Sale', but how about 'A Little Three Quarter For God & Co.' as a track listing? How could you resist?

AL GREY (born 1925)
TROMBONE

***   Al Grey Featuring Arnett Cobb And Jimmy Forrest Black & Blue 233143 CD
Grey; Xavier Chambon, Claude Gousset (*tb*); Michel Attenoux (*as*); Arnett Cobb, Jimmy Forrest, Hal Singer (*ts*); Ray Bryant, Tommy Flanagan (*p*); Stan Hunter (*b*); Clarence Gatemouth Brown (*g*); John Duke (*b*); J. C. Heard, Bobby Durham, Chris Columbo (*d*). 4/73–7/77.

***   Al Grey–Jesper Thilo Quintet Storyville SLP 4136 LP
Grey; Jesper Thilo (*ts*); Ole Kock Hansen (*p*); Hugo Rasmussen (*b*); Alex Riel (*d*). 8/86.

Al Grey will always be remembered as a Basie sideman, even though he spent more years away from the Count's band than with it. His humorous, fierce style of improvising is more in the tradition of such colleagues as saxophonist Lockjaw Davis than in the rather more restained trombone lineage, although Grey is especially accomplished with the plunger mute. He has only infrequently recorded as a leader. The Black & Blue CD collects material from three different sessions, most of the tracks coming from a rousing meeting with the rambunctious Arnett Cobb: unambitious blues material, but it's impossible not to feel better after hearing the likes of 'Ain't That Funk For You'. Two tracks with a quintet including Forrest and Flanagan are gentler, and two more with a mostly French group are fillers. The Storyville session, made on another of his many European sojourns, is typical of his usual manner: brisk mainstream with some sterling blues playing, although Thilo and the rhythm section accomodate rather than compel Grey into his best form.

***   **The New Al Grey Quintet** Chiaroscuro CD 305 CD
Grey; Mike Grey (*tb*); Joe Cohn (*t, g*); J. J. Wiggins (*b*); Bobby Durham (*d*). 5/88.

***(*)   **Al Meets Bjarne** Gemini GM 62 CD/LP
Grey; Bjarne Nerem (*ts*); Norman Simmons (*p*); Paul West (*b*); Gerryck King (*d*). 8/88.

The quintet date for Chiaroscuro features a 'family band': Mike is Al's son, Joe is Al Cohn's son, and J. J. Wiggins is pianist Gerald's offspring. Although the group sound a little rough-and-ready at times, and the absence of a pianist is probably not quite as useful a freedom as it might have been, it works out to be a very entertaining record. Mike is almost as ripe a soloist as his father, and the sound of the two trombones together leads to a few agreeably toe-curling moments; but Joe Cohn's playing is equally spirited, and Wiggins and Durham sound fine. The set-list includes some standards and a few pleasingly obscure choices, such as Hank Mobley's 'Syrup And Bisquits' and Art Farmer's 'Rue Prevail'.
    The session with Nerem was cut on a visit to Norway. The title blues is almost indecently ripe, and 'I'm In The Mood For Love' is taken at a surely the slowest tempo on record, but there are meaty blowing tunes as well and Nerem, a player in the kind of swaggering swing tradition which Grey enjoys, has the measure of the trombonist. Outstandingly good studio sound.

JOHNNY GRIFFIN (born 1928)
TENOR SAXOPHONE

***(*)   **Introducing Johnny Griffin** Blue Note B21Y 46536 CD
Griffin; Wynton Kelly (*p*); Curley Russell (*b*); Max Roach (*d*). 4/56.

***   **A Blowing Session** Blue Note 781559 CD
Griffin; Lee Morgan (*t*); John Coltrane, Hank Mobley (*ts*); Wynton Kelly (*p*); Paul Chambers (*b*); Art Blakey (*d*). 5/57.

These are where Griffin's youthful rep as the fastest tenor on the block was made official. In the company of Coltrane and Mobley, neither of them slouches, he rattles through 'The Way You Look Tonight' like some love-on-the-run hustler with his mates waiting out in the car. Only Trane seems inclined to serenade, and it's interesting to speculate how the track might have sounded had they taken it at conventional ballad tempo; 'All The Things You Are' begins with what sounds like Reveille from Wynton Kelly and then lopes off with almost adolescent awkwardness. This was a typical Griffin strategy. For much of his most productive period, Griffin more or less bypassed ballad-playing and only really adjusted his idiom to the medium and slower tempos as he aged; 'The Boy Next Door' on *Introducing* is given a bright swing that runs counter to the usual mournful treatment and even 'Lover Man' has a defiant quality. 'It's All Right With Me' is way over the speed limit, as if Griffin is trying to erase all memory of Sonny Rollins's magisterial reading of a deceptively difficult tune. There's a slight confusion over the title of the earlier album, which is given on the back of the original sleeve as *Chicago Calling*. Either way, it's a fine introductory set, establishing Griffin's sound and method. *Blowing Session* is oddly unsettling and by no means the most appealing thing Griffin put his name to. (Lovers of two-tenor duels should certainly look into Griffin's albums with Eddie

Lockjaw Davis, of which *Live at Minton's* (Prestige P 24099) and the eponymous *Griff and Lock* (OJC 264) are currently available.)

***   **The Little Giant** Original Jazz Classics OJC 136 LP
        Griffin; Blue Mitchell (*t*); Julian Priester (*tb*); Wynton Kelly (*p*); Sam Jones (*b*);
        Albert Heath (*d*). 8/59.

This isn't the only album bearing this title (which refers to the diminutive saxophonist's nickname), so it might be worth checking that you're getting the right one. Heath finds it harder than Blakey to keep up, but the rhythm section get it just about right, opening up the throttle for Griffin and two rather underrated brass soloists with just the right amount of brassiness in their tone to match the leader's. Recommended, though the absence of a CD is a pity.

***   **Salt Peanuts** Black Lion BLP 60121 CD/LP
        Griffin; Bud Powell (*p*); Guy Hyat (*b*); Jacques Gervais (*d*). 8/64.

Strictly speaking a Bud Powell set, recorded in France during the last productive period of his life. There's a lot of the old fire left and he and Griffin trade powerful choruses on 'Wee', 'Hot House' and 'Straight, No Chaser'. Neither the piano nor the rhythm section are anything to write home about, but those were the settings in which Powell found himself towards the end, and Griffin seems to have decided If it's good enough for him . . .

***   **The Big Soul Band** Original Jazz Classics OJC 485 CD/LP/MC
        Griffin; Bob Bryant, Clark Terry (*t*); Matthew Gee, Julian Priester (*tb*); Charlie Davis,
        Pat Patrick, Frank Strozier, Edwin Williams (*reeds*); Harold Mabern, Bobby Timmons
        (*p*); Bob Cranshaw, Vic Sproles (*b*); Charlie Persip (*d*).

Solid, blues-based charts and a big, raw sound would seem guaranteed to egg Griffin on to ever greater feats of speed and endurance. In point of fact, this rather overlooked session contains some of his most affecting solo work. The tempos are a shade more relaxed and his phrasing seems just slightly more spacious on traditional themes like 'Nobody Knows The Trouble I've Seen' and 'Deep River'. The band is hard to fault.

***   **The Man I Love** Black Lion BLP 60107 CD/LP
        Griffin; Kenny Drew (*p*); Niels-Henning Ørsted-Pedersen (*b*); Albert Heath (*d*). 3/67.

In the Black Lion catalogue, this immediately follows Wardell Gray's *One for Prez* (BLP 60106), which includes three takes of 'The Man I Love'. There could hardly be a sharper contrast. Where Gray's tone and delivery drew heavily on Lester Young's pre-bop idiom, Griffin swoops on the same material with and almost delinquent energy that comes direct from Charlie Parker. It isn't the most settling of sounds, but the technical control is superb and only a rhythm section of the quality of this one could keep the tune on the road.

**   **Blues For Harvey** Steeplechase SCS 1004 CD/LP
        Griffin; Kenny Drew (*p*); Mads Vinding (*b*); Ed Thigpen (*d*). 7/73.

**   **The Jamfs Are Coming** Timeless SJP 121 CD/LP
        Griffin; Rein De Graaff (*p*); Henk Haverhoek or Koos Serierse (*b*); Art Taylor (*d*).
        12/75, 10/77.

Both these sessions mark something of a low point in Griffin's generally even output. There's something slightly numbed about the solos on *Blues for Harvey* (compare the title-track with the lovely version on *The Man I Love* [above]), and some questionable material, which includes a mercifully rare jazz reading of Gilbert O'Sullivan's 'Alone Again (Naturally)'). Griffin takes the theme at his natural clip, but makes nothing significant of it. He constantly overshoots the measure on 'Rhythm-a-Ning', another slightly surprising choice which wrong-foots the band on a couple of measures. De Graaff is an interesting player with a steady supply of unhackneyed ideas, but he's only a questionable partner for Griffin and the two never catch light on *The Jamfs are Coming*.

    Griffin fans with some practice in mentally editing out dodgy backgrounds might well want to have both of these, but everyone else might as well hang on to their cash.

***   **The Cat** Antilles 422 848 421 CD
        Griffin; Curtis Fuller (*tb*); Steve Nelson (*vib*); Michael Weiss (*p*); Dennis Irwin (*b*);
        Kenny Washington (*d*). 10/90.

At 60-plus, Griffin has lifted his foot and eased back to cruising speed, revealing a tender balladeer underneath the furious munchkin of the 1950s and '60s. 'Hot Sake' still belts along, but '63rd Street Theme', dedicated to the clubs and bars of Chicago's South Side, has more of a melancholy ring these days (compare the version on *The Little Giant*, above, where he rampages through it like a latter-day Chicago Fire), its minor blues tonality milked shamelessly. Uncontroversial stuff, it's hard to imagine objecting violently, or being wildly converted to Griffin on the strength of it, but well worth the admission fee all the same.

TINY GRIMES (born 1916)
PIANO, VOCAL

(*)   **Callin' The Blues Original Jazz Classics OJC 191 LP
Grimes; J. C. Higginbotham (*tb*); Eddie 'Lockjaw' Davis (*ts*); Ray Bryant (*p*); Wendell Marshall (*b*); Osie Johnson (*d*). 7/58.

At one time, Grimes's standing with fans and fellow-musicians utterly confounded his diminutive nickname. One of the midwives of popular music, he attended bebop's first contractions (the earliest of the legendary Charlie Parker Savoy sessions were under Grimes's leadership – Savoy 70520 LP/650107 CD/886421 CD, complete) and then, in the early 1950s, slapped rock and roll firmly on the bottom with his bizarrely kilted (*sic*!) Rockin' Highlanders, who can be heard on the now deleted *Rock The House* [Swingtime 1016 LP].

That album contains some of the best of Grimes's work on record (though his work with Tatum and Slam Stewart – Black Lion 60114, all formats – shouldn't be missed). By contrast, the later *Callin' The Blues* is less than inspirational. Grimes's chunky, blues-based guitar still communicates enormous energy, but the band lacks the extraordinary interplay he enjoyed with Tatum. An important figure, but perhaps you had to be there.

NIKOLAJ GROMIN (born 1938)
GUITAR

***   **Blues For Thad** Olufsen DOCLP 5130 LP
Gromin; Jesper Lundgaard (*b*). 90.

A Muscovite who now lives in Copenhagen, Gromin's bland tone and apologetic manner don't detract from an agreeably melodic style which acknowledges Wes Montgomery and Jim Hall without planting his flag in any particular camp. This straightforward but warmly sustained set of standards, a blues and a traditonal Danish tune passes an enjoyable 50 minutes or so. Lundgaard is actually a more powerful presence than the guitarist, and his authoritative lines and succinctly delivered solos put the real stamp on the session.

STEVE GROSSMAN (born 1951)
SOPRANO AND TENOR SAX

***   **Way Out East Vol. 1** Red 123176 LP
Grossman; Juni Booth (*b*); Joe Chambers (*d*). 7/84.

***   **Way Out East Vol. 2** Red 123183 LP
As above. 7/84.

***   **Love Is The Thing** Red 123189 LP
Grossman; Cedar Walton (*p*); David Williams (*b*); Billy Higgins (*d*). 5/85.

(*)   **Steve Grossman Quartet Vol. 1 DIW 8007 LP
Grossman; Fred Henke (*p*); Walter Booker (*b*); Masahiro Yoshida (*d*). 11/85.

(*)   **Steve Grossman Quartet Vol. 2 DIW 8008 LP
As above. 11/85.

***   **Reflections** Musidisc 500212 CD
Grossman; Alby Cullaz (*b*); Simon Goubert (*d*). 9/90.

Grossman was working with Miles Davis when still only a teenager, and it's tempting to suggest that his career peaked too early. He has a prodigious command of the saxophone and a fearless energy, which puts him in the same class as Michael Brecker and Bill Evans. But Grossman's unlovely tone and sometimes faceless facility can also make him appear as just another Coltrane/Rollins disciple. The records under his own name make no attempt to evade the appropriate comparisons, since they all stand as quickly prepared blowing dates, Grossman peeling off suitably muscular solos against a conventional post-bop rhythm section. The two trio sessions for Red offer perhaps the most exciting music, since Grossman gets more space to work in, and *Vol. 1* provides some impressively characterized standards. *Love Is The Thing*, though, has the players setting themselves a few challenges by turning a ballad recital upside down in a couple of places with, for instance, an almost brutal 'I Didn't Know What Time It Was'. A later return to the trio format in *Reflections* is also a shade more interesting than the somewhat plain dates for DIW, but Grossman's undoubted talent may work best either with another leader or with a firm producer.

***   **Moon Train** Phrases ZD 74868 CD
Grossman; Flavio Boltro (*t, flhn*); Piero Odorici (*as*); Riccardo Fassi (*p*); Massimo Moriconi (*b*); Giampaolo Ascolese (*d*). 4/90.

Smartly organized, with Fassi's strong regular group in support, this is probably the best album Grossman has made under his own leadership. The title-piece and 'Fred In The Swimming Pool' are vivid originals which aren't eclipsed by the presence of 'Reflections' and 'Soul Eyes'. Boltro's canny playing is a nice counterweight to Grossman's torrential style, and the comparatively short tracks sustain the attention.

MARTY GROSZ (born 1930)
GUITAR, BANJO, VOCAL

***(*)   **Swing It!** Jazzology JCD-180 CD
Grosz; Peter Ecklund (*t*); Dan Barrett (*tb*); Bob Gordon (*cl*); Loren Schoenberg (*ts*); Keith Ingham (*p*); Murray Wall (*b*); Hal Smith (*d*). 6–7/88.

***   **Extra!** Jazzology JCD-190 CD
Grosz; Peter Ecklund (*c*); Bob Gordon (*cl, v*); Ken Peplowski (*cl, as*); Murray wall, Greg Cohen (*b*). 8–9/89.

Anyone who's heard this transplanted Berliner in concert will know that these very entertaining studio records are only half his story: a laconic, merciless wit, Grosz comes on like the spirit of Cliff Edwards inside a political satirist's shell. The humour here isn't deadpan or mocking, though: it's natural, and there's nothing of the sense of overworked labour which can attend, say, Leon Redbone's records. *Swing It!* (credited to the band 'Destiny's Tots') and *Extra!* (credited to 'The Orphan Newsboys') fish around in ancient pools and come up with songs that don't seem to have been recorded for decades: Louis Armstrong's 1926 'The last Time', for instance, or 'A High Hat, A Piccolo And A Cane', or even Glenn Miller's 'Sunrise Serenade'. The earlier disc is preferable because the tunes are more surprising, the band is a degree hotter – Barrett, Gordon, Schoenberg and Ecklund are all keen voices – and the presence of a drummer gives it an extra lift. On both, Grosz rips through the songs in a voice that should probably belong to a non-singer but which he gets by with anyway. His rhythm guitar is a bit livelier than Eddie Condon's ever was.

GRP ALL STARS
GROUP

**   **GRP Live In Session** GRP 91023 CD/MC
Dave Valentine (*f*); Larry Williams (*ts, syn*); David Grusin (*ky*); Lee Ritenour (*g, syn*); Abe Laboriel (*b*); Carlos Vega (*d*); Diane Schuur (*v*).

A routine meeting of some of the leading names on the GRP roster. Ritenour comes off best among the soloists – but, since Valentine and Williams are fluent, faceless players, that's not saying a great deal. Typically glossy GRP sound serves mainly to underline the pointlessness of the music.

GIGI GRYCE (1927–83)
ALTO SAXOPHONE, FLUTE

[***   **Blue And Brown** Jazz Society (Vogue) 670505 CD]
Gryce; Clifford Brown, Art Farmer, Fred Gerard; Quincy Jones, Walter Williams, Fernand Verstraete (*t*); Jimmy Cleveland, Alvin Hayse, Bill Tamper, Benny Vasseur (*tb*); Anthony Ortega (*as*); Henri Bernard, André Dabonneville Clifford Solomon (*ts*); William Boucaya, Henri Jouot (*bs*); Henri Renaud (*p*); Jimmy Gourley (*g*); Pierre Michelot (*b*); Alan Dawson, Jean Louis Viale (*d*). 9–10/53; other material 53 & 54.

A slightly mixed compilation of big-band material recorded under Gryce's name and demonstrating his skills as a composer-arranger (the 20-year-old Quincy Jones took note from the trumpet bench), together with small-group material co-led with Clifford Brown and under Brown's and Max Roach's own names. The rationale for putting them all together is perfectly logical (it is in effect yet another Brown tribute) but doesn't necessarily make for a very coherent album. The best of the Gryce-led cuts is the tough 'Keeping Up With Jones', which is curiously reminiscent of the Lionel Hampton Band, where Gryce, Brown and Jones had all previously worked (see *European Tour 1953* – Royal Jazz RJD 517 CD).

[**(*)   **Bird Calls 2** Savoy 650111 CD]
Gryce; Duke Jordan (*p*); Oscar Pettiford (*b*); Kenny Clarke (*d*). 3/55.

It seemed to be Gryce's destiny to share albums with others rather than have them to himself. This is the second of two similarly named sets which don't, appearances to the contrary, seem to have too much to do with Charlie Parker (who actually died nine days after Gryce's session), other than in airing Bird's followers on the alto saxophone. The first of the pair – Savoy 65010 – is given over to Phil Woods, the remainder of this album to a clean-sounding Frank Morgan. Gryce's 'Embraceable You' is unmistakably his own reading, rather than a pastiche of Parker; but the real key to his sound comes in his favourite 'Jordu', monogrammed by its composer Duke Jordan. Here, Gryce sounds exact and impatient, hurried and confident in almost equal measure. The album is something of an oddity, but it may after all give a better impression of Parker's putative lineage than the conventional claimants' union of McLean, Stitt and Criss.

***   **The Rat Race Blues** Original Jazz Classics OJC 081 LP
Gryce; Richard Williams (*t*); Richard Wyands (*p*); Julian Euell (*b*); Mickey Roker (*d*). 6/60.

Gryce's success as a writer – 'Capri' for J. J. Johnson, 'Nica's Tempo' for Art Farmer and the Jazz Messengers – rather overshadowed his abilities as a boppish altoist, who in all but instrumental timbre sounds like a cross between Jackie McLean and Sonny Criss. *The Rat Race Blues* is certainly his best album, full of vivid originals and marked by Williams's and Wyands's distinctive phrasings.

VINCE GUARALDI (1928–76)
PIANO

(*)   **Vince Guaraldi Trio Original Jazz Classics OJC 149 CD/LP/MC
Guaraldi; Eddie Duran (*g*); Dean Reilly (*b*). 4/56.

(*)   **A Flower Is A Lovesome Thing Original Jazz Classics OJC 235 LP/MC
As above. 4/57.

***   **Modern Jazz From San Francisco** Original Jazz Classics OJC 272 LP
Guaraldi; Jerry Dodgion (*as*); Sonny Clark (*p*); Eddie Duran (*g*); Gene Wright, Ron Crotty (*b*); John Markham (*d*). 8/55.

(*)   **Jazz Impressions Original Jazz Classics OJC 287 LP/MC
         Guaraldi; Eddie Duran (*g*).

(*)   **Live At El Matador Original Jazz Classics OJC 289 LP/MC
         Guaraldi; Bola Sete (*g*); unknown (*b*), (*d*). 66.

**   **Jazz Impressions Of Black Orpheus** Original Jazz Classics OJC 437 LP/MC/CD
         Guaraldi; Monty Budwig (*b*); Colin Bailey (*d*). 62.

***   **Greatest Hits** Fantasy MPF-4505/FCD 8431 CD/LP/MC

***   **A Boy Named Charlie Brown** Fantasy F 8430 CD/LP/MC
         Guaraldi (*p* solo).

**   **A Charlie Brown Christmas** Fantasy F 8431 CD/LP/MC
         As above.

Guaraldi was a harmless pop-jazz pianist, not as profound as Dave Brubeck, not as swinging as Ramsey Lewis, but capable of fashioning catchy tunes from favourite licks; the most famous example remains his Grammy-winning 'Cast Your Fate To The Wind'. If this kind of music appeals, the best way to sample it is through the *Greatest Hits* collection. The earlier trio dates offer mild, unambitious variations on standards, with Eddie Duran figuring rather more strongly than Guaraldi himself, while the live set with guitarist Bola Sete isn't very exciting. The *Black Orpheus* set is marked by the seemingly relentless triviality of the material.

As a composer, though, Guaraldi is best represented by his music for the Charlie Brown TV/cartoon series. The first record in particular includes some charming miniatures, performed with surprising delicacy. The second is merely more of the same with less of the freshness.

GUIDO GUIDOBONI
TRUMPET

(*)   **Xoanon Splasc(h) H 145 LP
         Guidoboni; Roberto Rossi (*tb*); Ico Manno (*p*); Stefano Travaglini (*b*); Glauco Oleandri (*d*). 11/87.

Some may find Guidoboni's manner unappealing: he has a big, graceless sound on trumpet that lends some of his solos and lead playing a rather clumsy air. But he writes strong post-bop material that this plain-speaking group negotiates quite well. Rossi is a bland front-line partner, but Manno takes some pert solos and the title-tune at least is one that sticks in the mind. Smartly recorded in the style of the house.

LARS GULLIN (1928–76)
BARITONE SAXOPHONE

***   **The Great Lars Gullin Vol. 1** Dragon DRLP 36 LP
         Gullin; Chet Baker (*t*); George Olsson (*tb*); Arne Domnérus (*cl*, *as*); Rolf Berg, Bjarne Nerem (*ts*); Lennart Jansson (*bs*); Dick Twardzik, Gunnar Svensson (*p*); George Riedel, Jimmy Bond (*b*); Peter Littman, Bosse Stoor, Egil Johansen (*d*). 4/55–5/56.

****   **The Great Lars Gullin Vol. 2** Dragon DRLP 75 LP
         Gullin; Weine Renliden (*t*); Kettil Ohlsson (*bs*); Putte Lindblom, Bob Laine, Mats Olsson (*p*); Yngve Åkerberg, Georg Riedel, Simon Brehm, Lars Petersson, Tauno Suojärvi (*b*); Jack Noren, Boose Stoor (*d*). 3–12/53.

***   **The Great Lars Gullin Vol. 3** Dragon DRLP 127 LP
         Gullin; Leppe Sundewall (*bt*); Richard Johansson, Kurt Järnberg (*tb*); Rolf Billberg (*ts*); Bengt Hallberg (*p*); Rolf Berg (*g*); Georg Riedel (*b*); William Schiöppfe, Bosse Stoor (*d*); The Moretone Singers (*v*). 9/54–6/55.

***(*)   **The Great Lars Gullin Vol. 4** Dragon DRLP 156 LP
         Gullin; Bengt-Arne Wallin (*t*, *flhn*); George Vernon, Andreas Skjold, Eje Thelin (*tb*); Putte Wickman (*cl*); Rolf Billberg (*as*); Harry Backlund (*ts*); Lars Bagge (*p*); Sune

Larsson (*g*); Lars Petersson, Claes Lindroth, Erik Lundborg (*b*); Sture Kallin, Bosse Skoglund, Bob Edman (*d*). 1/59–9/60.

*****   **The Great Lars Gullin Vol. 5** Dragon DRLP 181
Gullin; Rolf Berg (*g*); George Riedel (*b*); Bob Edman, Bo Stoor (*d*). 5/54–1/55.

It's sad that such a major figure as Gullin should be so underrepresented in the catalogues, and all the more welcome that the Swedish company Dragon has sought to reissue all of Gullin's most important recordings. After working in big bands as an alto player, he took up the baritone at the age of 21, and his utterly distinctive sound – delicate, wistful, pensively controlled – is the linchpin of his music: when he wrote for six or eight or more instruments, he made the band sound like a direct extension of that big, tender tone. He seems like neither a bopper nor a swing stylist. The first volume includes a meeting with Baker's quartet, with a few precious glimpses of Twardzik, a very melancholy 'Lover Man' and Catherina Valente vocalizing on 'I'll Remember April'; there are also three charming octet scores. The second disc opens with the tracks that were issued as a ten-inch album by Contemporary in the US: Gullin sustains a steady, effortless flow of ideas on all his solos and plays alto on two tunes. The rest of the disc is taken up with various rarities, including two scruffy airshots, a wistful 'Love Me Or Leave Me' with Bob Paine and two tracks with drummer Jack Norén's band cut on a Finnish tour: all good value. The third volume includes alternative takes of 'Lars Meets Jeff' and 'Manchester Fog' (see *Volume 5*, below), two fine sextet tracks – 'Late Summer' is a characteristic piece of Gullin's most folk-like writing – and six tracks with The Moretone Singers. Their cooing delivery is inevitably more of a distraction than a positive contribution, and it's the more frustrating since Gullin's own playing is especially inspired: his improvisation on 'Lover Man', for instance, is a beautiful variation on the melody.

Volume 4 collects the results of four EPs made by Gullin in 1959–60, inlcuding twelve original scores, two standards and a crabby-sounding 'Birk's Works'. Though the musicians involved garner some solo spots, the music is essentially a sequence of miniatures that purvey Gullin's idiosyncratic sort of jazz impressionism – dense harmonies over plain rhythms, a bittersweet enjoyment pervading such themes as 'The Black Rose' and 'Nightshade'. The first nine tracks were available only in mono form, but like the stereo half of the record the quality is clear and truthful.

The masterpiece of the series is *Volume 5*. The two sessions feature Gullin alone with guitar, bass and drums, and in this exposed setting he unfurls streams of melody which make clear his affinities with Lee Konitz. Yet the music is as personal as Serge Chaloff's on *Blue Serge*, avoiding Chaloff's overt expressionism and choosing a more even dynamic which makes 'Danny's Dream', 'Manchester Fog' (present in two takes) and 'Igloo' into compelling experiences. His companions are by no means outclassed – Berg contributes some beautiful solos – but the music here constitutes Gullin's finest legacy. There were many more sessions to come, almost until his death in 1976, but all the later ones have yet to make a reappearance.

BARRY GUY (born 1947)
DOUBLE BASS, COMPOSER

and

LONDON JAZZ COMPOSERS ORCHESTRA (founded 1970)
GROUP

****   **Harmos** Intakt 013 CD

***(*)   **Double Trouble** Intakt 019 CD
Guy; Jon Corbett, Henry Lowther (*t*); Marc Charig (*co*); Radu Malfatti, Paul Rutherford, Alan Tomlinson (*tb*); Steve Wick (*tba*); Paul Dunmall, Peter McPhail, Evan Parker, Simon Picard, Trevor Watts (*reeds*); Phil Wachsmann (*vn*); Howard Riley (*p*); Barre Phillips (*b*); Paul Lytton (*d*). 4/89, 4/89.

In an age of hyper-specialization and carefully compartmentalized musical styles, it's encouraging to find someone like Barry Guy. Classically trained in both composition and double-bass, Guy has combined a passionate commitment to free improvisation with a long-standing interest in large-scale composition for improvising ensembles, and a far from incidental interest in Baroque music, an area of music-making which, for a time at least, he considered every bit as radical and experimental as free improvisation. Needless to say, eclecticism as untroubled as this has tended to alienate those of his more dogmatic brethren who regard anything older than yesterday as dead and buried and who subject anything as authoritarian as a score to the purest anathema.

What unites these apparently disparate interests is Guy's concern for the articulation of musical language, learning how it is that music speaks to us. In recent years, Guy has been concentrating on improvisation and on writing for and directing the London Jazz Composers Orchestra, the remarkable group he first formed two decades ago.

The orchestra was inspired by the example of the American trumpeter and composer Michael Mantler's Jazz Composers' Orchestra, which afforded improvising players a rare opportunity to work outside the small-group circuit and to experiment with enlarged structures that went a little beyond the 8-and 16-bar tunes that were the basic jazz staple. Inevitably, given the European commitment to collective improvisation, the LJCO quickly developed a more radical – some thought chaotic – language which was most clearly represented in a hefty piece called *Ode*. *Ode* proved to be a little hard-boiled for most of the critics, and for some of the players, and represented something of a blind alley in Guy's attempt to maximize soloists' freedom in such a way as not to blur or compromise an overall and very coherent musical argument.

In the years that followed the LJCO changed somewhat in ethos, opening up its repertoire to compositions other than those by Guy. These included challenging graphic scores by drummer Tony Oxley, intricately structured pieces by pianist Howard Riley, looser structures from trombonist Paul Rutherford, and, from outside the band, challenging works from 'straight' composers with an interest in improvisation. *Harmos* marks what Guy considers a third stage in the band's progress. Guy intends the title to be understood in its original sense of a coming together. It opens sharply enough with a kind of broken fanfare from the trombones that has the jagged authority typical of the best of British improvisation, followed by a stately chorale that calls to mind Guy's other enthusiasms. But if the piece has a centre, it is the long, winding melody played by saxophonist Trevor Watts, a veteran of the band and in this composition its first mate and pilot. Coming quite early (it's a long piece), Watts's solo nevertheless shapes the whole composition around itself and marks Guy's re-awakened and always adventurous interest in harmonic language. Everyone in the 17-strong line-up has at least some solo space, so *Harmos* fits very closely Guy's ideal of a large scale musical argument which nevertheless leaves its participants considerable personal freedom. Even if 45 minutes isn't considered tip-top value on CD, *Harmos* should be in every serious, contemporary jazz collection.

Double Trouble is a slightly tougher nut. Originally intended as a two-piano project for Howard Riley and Alex Von Schlippenbach, the recorded version is anchored on Riley alone, with a sequence of carefully marshalled instrumental groupings (notably two trios, the first consisting of Guy, Evan Parker and Paul Lytton, and the second of Riley, Marc Charig and Barre Phillips) not so much following in his wake as orbiting. As a whole the piece has a strong centrifugal coherence that balances the apparently anarchic, but often tightly scored, behaviour of soloists and section players. If it's down a degree of stellar magnitude on *Harmos*, that's simply because it seems much less immediately available. On the other hand, it may pay a longer dividend.

**** **Arcus** Maya MCD 9101 CD
Guy; Barre Phillips (*b*). 90.

Though recorded as if on the other side of the veil of Maya, this is improvised music of the very highest order. Guy's productive trade-off of freedom against more formal structures is constantly in evidence, and there is enough music of straightforward, digestible beauty to sustain listeners who might otherwise find an hour and a quarter of contrabass duos more than a little taxing.

It ends, appropriately enough, on the quiet majesty of 'New Earth', where Phillips's purged simplicity and dancer's grace sound out ahead of Guy's more formal and sculpted delivery. Twice wonderful, but may call for patience.

JOE GUY (1920–62)
TRUMPET

** **Trumpet Battle At Minton's** Xanadu 107 LP
Guy; Hot Lips Page (*t*); Kermit Scott, Herbie Fields (*ts*); Thelonious Monk, Clyde
Hart (*p*); Charlie Christian (*g*); Ebenezer Paul, Nick Fenton (*b*); Kenny Clarke (*d*).
41.

Joe Guy is probably best (or worst) remembered as one of Billie Holiday's companions. As a
trumpeter, he remained in thrall to Roy Eldridge and, although these sessions found him
pitching in with some of the turks who were working towards bebop, it was more of a historical
accident than anything. The music comes from private recordings made by student Jerry Field at
New York's Minton's, and the main feature is the way Guy and Lips Page trade punches. Page
was no more a bop sympathizer than Guy, but his range and feel were far greater than the
younger man's, and there are scattered moments of greatness among the generally desultory
results which Field captured here. There are tantalizing glimpses of Monk on two tracks and of
Christian on a prototype 'Rhythm-A-Ning', but the large number of unknown players also
involved and the straggling, impromptu routines affirm that much of this stuff was more fun to
be playing than to listen to 50 years later. Guy's best moments come in 'Sweet Lorraine' and
'Sweet Georgia Brown', but noting that even an offhand Page outdoes him throughout tells
more about Joe's footnote status than his own playing. Considering the source of the music, the
sound has survived pretty well in this issue, but don't expect hi-fi.

BOBBY HACKETT (1915–76)
CORNET, TRUMPET

(*) **Gotham Jazz Scene Dormouse DMI CDX 03 CD
Hackett; Dick Cary (*a hn*); John Dengler (*tba*); Ernie Caceres (*cl, bs*); Tommy
Gwaltney (*cl, vib*); Mickey Crane (*p*); Al Hall or Milt Hinton (*b*); Nat Ray (*d*). 3 &
4/57.

***(*) **Jazz Ultimate** Pathé 1566181 (Capitol T 933) LP
Hackett; Jack Teagarden (*tb*); Peanuts Hucko (*cl, ts*); Ernie Caceres (*cl, bs*); Gene
Schroeder (*p*); Billy Bauer (*g*); Jack Lesberg (*b*); Buzzy Drootin (*d*). 9/57.

**** **Coast Concert/Jazz Ultimate** Dormouse International DMI CDX 02 CD
As for *Jazz Ultimate*; and with Matty Matlock (*cl*); Abe Lincoln (*tb*); Nappy Lamare
(*g*); Dick Owens (*p*); Phil Stephens (*b, bb*); Nick Fatool (*d*). 10/55, 9/57.

Louis Armstrong liked to keep the opposition under the closest observation and so, for much of
the 1940s, Bobby Hackett played second cornet under the wing of the man who had influenced
his style more than any other. The best of Hackett was yet to come, though. His association in
the 1950s with trombonist Jack Teagarden produced some of the best traditional/mainstream
jazz of the post-war years with Hackett's supremely elegant legato and deceptive force perfectly
matched by the man who virtually patented modern jazz trombone.

The earlier Dormouse compilation is actually a two-header, featuring 11 tracks each from
Hackett and from a 1958 Teagarden quintet. It's a useful CD introduction to both, well
transferred and produced and affording comparative readings of 'Wolverine Blues' which show
how much Hackett was content to stay within the confines of a tune, while Teagarden nudges
uneasily at its edges.

Jazz Ultimate isn't quite the album that 1955's epic *Coast To Coast* is, but it still ranks as one
of the finest traditional albums of the period. As a monument to two drinking men who eked
out their pain in brief, intense distillations, it's hard to over-rate. Hucko and Caceres take
essentially supportive roles but still contribute mightily to the sum. The rhythm section,
anchored on Drootin's deceptively relaxed lines, is fine, and the material – which includes
'Back Home Again In Indiana' and a marvellous '55th And Broadway' – is top-drawer. A
classic and, for all except those with acute sensitivity to vinyl, a must.

Coast Concert features Hackett on cornet, which he later abandoned. His break on 'Muskrat
Ramble' is one of the best examples of his spontaneous gifts and the whole set is of the highest
quality. A classic compilation.

(*)   **Melody Is A Must: Live At The Roosevelt Grill** Phontastic PHONT 7571/2 LP
     Hackett; Vic Dickenson (*tb*); Dave McKenna (*p*); Jack Lesberg (*b*); Cliff Leeman (*d*).
     3 & 4/69.

Switching from Jack Teagarden to Vic Dickenson must have felt a little like dating Liza Minnelli after Judy Garland. Unmistakable kinship, same eyes and voice, same raw edges, but somehow not quite, a little safer and more humane. Dickenson's very limited technique was carefully husbanded and put in the service of a warm, humorous approach which drew something from Dickie Wells, but which worked most comfortably alongside someone like Hackett who shared his untroubled preference for a quiet good time.

     Melody Is A Must is a perfect example of Hackett's grace-without-pressure. There are no steam-valve emotional tantrums underlying a mixed and rather more contemporary repertoire than usual. Nor is there any casual verbosity. As Whitney Balliett relates, Duke Ellington once spoke, apparently approvingly, of Dickenson's 'three tones'. Like Dickenson, Hackett keeps his music simple and direct, remarkably uncluttered by ego.

***   **Live At The Roosevelt Grill** Chiaroscuro CRD 105 CD
     Hackett; Vic Dickenson (*tb*); Dave McKenna (*p*); Jack Lesberg (*b*); Cliff Leeman (*d*).

Reasonable quality live recordings that find Hackett slightly eclipsed by the ebullient Dickenson and the whole set frequently hijacked by an in-form McKenna.

CHARLIE HADEN (born 1937)
DOUBLE BASS

***(*)   **Liberation Music Orchestra** Impulse MCAD 39125 CD
     Haden; Michael Mantler (*t*); Don Cherry (*c*); Roswell Rudd (*tb*); Bob Northern (*frhn*); Howard Johnson (*tba*); Perry Robinson (*cl*); Gato Barbieri (*ts, cl*); Dewey Redman (*ts, as*); Carla Bley (*org, p*); Sam Brown (*g, Tanganyikan g, thumb p*); Paul Motian (*d, perc*); Andrew Cyrille (*perc*). 4/70.

***   **The Ballad Of The Fallen** ECM 1248 CD/LP
     Haden; Don Cherry (*pocket t*); Michael Mantler (*t*); Gary Valente (*tb*); Sharon Freeman (*frhn*); Jack Jeffers (*tba*); Jim Pepper (*ts, ss, f*); Dewey Redman (*ts*); Steve Slagle (*as, ss, cl, f*); Mick Goodrick (*g*); Carla Bley (*p, glock*); Paul Motian (*d*). 11/82.

(*)   **Dream Keeper** Polydor 847876-2 CD
     Haden; Tom Harrell (*t, flhn*); Earl Gardner (*t*); Ray Anderson (*tb*); Sharon Freeman (*frhn*); Joe Daley (*tba*); Ken McIntyre (*as*); Joe Lovano (*ts, f*); Branford Marsalis, Dewey Redman (*ts*); Juan Lazaro Mendolas (*wooden f, pan pipes*); Mick Goodrick (*g*); Amina Claudine Myers (*p*); Paul Motian (*d*); Don Alias (*perc*); Carla Bley (*cond*); Oakland Youth Chorus. 4/90.

The inclusion of 'Hymn Of The Anarchist Women's Movement' on *Dream Keeper* may help explain the performance ethos of the revived Liberation Music Orchestra, whose live sets in 1982 and afterwards entirely confounded any expectations based on the excellent *Ballad Of The Fallen* or, more nostalgically, on the original 1970 record. No great arranger himself (his compositional talents are restricted to outwardly slight melodies of remarkable emotional power), Haden has relied heavily throughout on Carla Bley's fine structural sense, which deserts her only on the shambolic *Dream Keeper*.

     Her efforts aside, the LMO remains essentially an augmented small group, centred on the insistently low-pitched voices of Haden, Bley and Redman, with one or more of the lower register brasses, and with Motian keeping the surface textures variable and interesting. That basic foundation provides launching pads for stratospheric soloists like Barbieri.

     Much of the material is drawn from songs of the Spanish Civil War (with a broader mix of liberationist anthems from the Latin Third World on the latter pair), but the classic cut is, of course, Haden's own 'Song For Che' on the original *Liberation Music Orchestra*. After two decades it survives triumphantly, and significantly longer than the doomed praxis of its dedicatee.

     'Dream Keeper' is a long suite by Carla Bley which intersperses the Latin-American and Spanish anarchist songs familiar from earlier Haden/Liberation Music Orchestra records with a poem by the Harlem Renaissance writer, Langston Hughes. Sung by the Oakland Youth

457

Chorus, it has a sombre, almost apocalyptic quality, like a '*Dies Irae*', that matches Haden's own brooding statements, whose apparent hesitancy allows each note to resonate on into the silence. His introduction to a later track, 'Sandino', so strongly recalls 'Song For Che' that one wonders if Haden's melodic sense isn't beginning to recycle. There is a slightly too familiar aspect to much of the music on the album. Soloists like Dewey Redman and Mick Goodrick (who does a good Sam Brown impression on 'Sandino') seem to have less to say than their talents would suggest, and *Dream Keeper* as a whole is more surface than substance. Only the palimpsest of (a South African) choir and band on 'Nkosi Sikelel'i Afrika', the anthem of the African National Congress, reflects the passion Haden used to bring to this music. By contrast, Carla Bley's arrangement of the 'Hymn of the Anarchist Women's Movement' sounds like tourist folk. Disappointing.

**   **Silence** Soul Note SN 1172 CD/LP
      Haden; Chet Baker (*t, v*); Enrico Pieranunzi (*p*); Billy Higgins (*d*). 11/87.

An oddity, really, which without the presence of Billy Higgins would be quite conscionably ignorable. Baker's chops were irreparably busted by this point (a fact which certainly isn't reflected in one of the most overcooked discographies of recent times) and the solos are incredibly enervated. Haden paradoxically thrives in that kind of environment – and it is, after all, his album. The little-known Pieranunzi has made some impressive records of his own, and if *Silence* has one overriding merit, it is that it might introduce an excellent pianist to listeners who haven't caught up with his previous work with Baker or with the Space Jazz Trio.

***   **Magico** ECM 1151 CD/LP
      Haden; Jan Garbarek (*ts, ss*); Egberto Gismonti (*g, p*). 6/79.

***(*)   **Folk Songs** ECM 1170 CD/LP
      As above. 11/79.

Though released under Haden's name, the dominant voice on both of these splendid albums is, perhaps inevitably, Garbarek's. The saxophonist swoops and wheels over Gismonti's rippling patterns (interesting to compare with Ralph Towner's more abstract approach) and the deep swell of Haden's rather sombre approach. The slightly later *Folk Songs* (usefully sampled on Garbarek's *Works* – ECM 823266) is a classic, one of the finest records of the late 1970s.

**   **In Angel City** Verve 837031 CD/LP
      Haden; Ernie Watts (*ts, syn*); Alan Broadbent (*p*); Lawrence Marable or Alex Cline
      (*d*). 6/88.

A companion to Haden's original *Quartet West* album [Verve 831673, currently missing in action], and by no means as appealing. Once again dedicated to the bassist's adopted home, the Chandlerish evocation of Los Angeles is more diffuse and the range of material less convincing. Watts is a surprisingly effective foil and Marable, who drums on all but one of the tracks, marvellously precise without being dogmatic about the exact count. Less than compelling, though.

***   **First Song** Soul Note 1222 CD/LP
      Haden; Enrico Pieranunzi (*p*); Billy Higgins (*d*). 4/90.

Credited to Haden, but interesting primarily for the stately lyricism Pieranunzi brings to the music. In approach, he is much like the bassist, combining a deep-toned, romantic approach with a clipped swing at faster tempos. Higgins has little to do on the quiet opening track, but contributes crisp, uncountable metres elsewhere, with his characteristic throbbing pulse. The session really only gets into top gear with the fourth track, Tristano's 'Lennie's Pennies', a thoughtful essay by the bassist, and may be a little too understated for some tastes.

***   **Haunted Heart** Verve 513078 CD
      Haden; Ernie Watts (*ts, ss*); Alan Broadbent (*p*); Lawrence Marable (*d*); Billie
      Holiday, Jeri Southern, Jo Stafford (*v* on records). 90.

A nostalgic, 'radio days' reconstruction by Haden's Quartet West, this time making use of old recordings: Billie Holiday singing 'Deep Song', Jeri Southern on 'Every Time We Say Goodbye' and Jo Stafford's haunting title piece. If it's a wallow, it's a remarkably disciplined one, with well-organized arrangements and some fine playing from all concerned.

AL HAIG (1924–82)
PIANO

***   **Al Haig Meets The Master Saxes Vol. 1** Spotlite SPJ 139 LP
Haig; Eddie Bert, Kai Winding (*tb*); Coleman Hawkins, John Hardee, Wardell Gray,
Al Epstein (*ts*); Buddy Greco (*p*); Clyde Lombardi, Tommy Potter (*b*); Tiny Kahn,
J. C. Heard, Sonny Igoe, Charlie Perry (*d*); Buddy Stewart (*v*). 48.

***   **Al Haig Meets The Master Saxes Vol. 2** Spotlite SPJ 140 LP
Haig; Bennie Green (*vtb*); Allen Eager, Stan Getz, Zoot Sims (*ts*); Gene Di Novi (*p*);
Jimmy Raney (*g*); Clyde Lombardi (*b*); Charlie Perry (*d*); Dave Stewart, Buddy
Lambert, Blossom Dearie (*v*). 48.

**   **Al Haig Meets The Master Saxes Vol. 3** Spotlite SPJ 143 LP
Haig; Red Rodney (*t*); Kai Winding (*tb*); Stan Getz, Zoot Sims, Herbie Steward (*ts*);
Jimmy Raney (*g*, *v*); Clyde Lombardi, Tommy Potter, Curley Russell, Don Russo (*b*);
Charlie Perry, Roy Haynes, Tiny Kahn (*d*). 48–51.

Al Haig's mastery of bebop piano was so comprehensive that he was, paradoxically, a figure of
some reticence: unlike such a self-destructive character as Bud Powell, Haig could retain an
inner calm at even the quickest tempo, and he can sound self-effacing as a result. While this
may account for the decline in his prominence as a jazz performer, it's certainly true that Haig
was unlucky with recording: he was never signed as a leader to any major label, and scarcely
recorded at all after the bebop era until his career was revitalized in the mid-1970s. These three
Spotlite albums chronicle some of Haig's work during the 1948 recording ban: the sound is
consistently troublesome, often heavy with distortion, and the piano frequently suffers in the
mix; but there is some top-class late bop here, even if the saxophonists often take precedence
over Haig himself. Volume 1 includes five urbane flights by Wardell Gray, four pieces by John
Hardee – where Haig at least gets a fine solo into 'Prelude To A Kiss' – and three with
Hawkins, the tempo flagging a bit on a long concert version of 'Stuffy' but the solos holding
inventively together. Volume 2 is probably the most interesting, with some very rare items by
Getz – 'Pardon My Bop' and 'As I Live And Bop' especially – and three brief but scintillating
showcases for Allan Eager. Four pallid ballads by Buddy Stewart are less appetizing. The third
LP has Kai Winding's sextet at Birdland, Getz's quintet at Carnegie Hall, four tunes with
Herbie Steward, the most lightweight of the Four Brothers, and a tedious quartet session
featuring Terry Swope's vocals – rather a mixed bag. Haig seldom plays more than a subsidiary
role on all three LPs but they're interesting bebop scatterings.

***   **Live In Hollywood** Xanadu 206 CD/LP
Haig; Chet Baker (*t*); Sonny Criss (*as*); Jack Montrose (*ts*). 8/52.

***   **Al Haig Quartet** Fresh Sound FSR CD 12 CD
Haig; Benny Weeks (*g*); Teddy Kotick (*b*); Phil Brown (*d*). 9/54.

The Fresh Sound reissue is a valuable one, offering one of Haig's few dates from the period, and
although his accompanists are no more than adequate, the pianist's subtle touch on a typical
programme of standards is impeccable. The sound is fair enough for the source. The Xanadu
session finds Baker at his most adolescent and Criss is in typically incendiary form, but the
sound is unkind to most of the players.

****   **Invitation** Spotlite AH 4 LP
Haig; Gilbert Rovere (*b*); Kenny Clarke (*d*). 1/74.

***   **Special Brew** Spotlite LP 8 LP
Haig; Jimmy Raney (*g*); Wilbur Little (*b*); Frank Gant (*d*). 11/74.

***(*)   **Solitaire** Spotlite SPJ LP 14 LP
Haig (*p* solo). 2–6/76.

***   **Stablemates** Spotlite SPJ LP 11 LP
Haig; Jon Eardley (*t*); Art Themen (*ts*); Daryl Runswick (*b*); Alan Ganley (*d*). 9/77.

***   **Manhattan Memories** Seabreeze SB 1008 LP
Haig; Eddie Diehl (*g*); Jamil Nasser (*b*); Jimmy Wormsworth, Frank Gant (*d*).
2/77–7/77.

***   **Expressly Ellington** Spotlite SPJ LP 20 LP
        Haig; Art Themen (*ts*); Jamil Nasser (*b*); Tony Mann (*d*). 10/78.

**   **Bebop Live** Spotlite SPJ LP 23 LP
        Haig; Art Themen (*ss, ts*); Peter King (*as*); Kenny Baldock (*b*); Alan Ganley (*d*). 5/82.

Many of Haig's latterday albums have become rather hard to find, and have yet to make their way to CD. The Spotlites still map out a splendid Indian summer in the studios. The masterpiece is *Invitation*, a remarkably finished and dedicated recital of tunes by Cedar Walton, Tadd Dameron (a quite marvellous 'If You Could See Me Now'), Billy Strayhorn and J. J. Johnson. Haig's understanding of bop has broadened into a significantly comprehensive knowledge of jazz piano styles, and while his grasp remains most firm on the music he apprenticed on, there is a breadth of keyboard practice here which is timeless in quality. Touch, intonation and timing have classical shape and intensity. Clarke drums in perfect accord, and the lack of empathy on some of the other dates here is the problem with latterday Haig. The session with Jimmy Raney is just a bit too laid-back and thoughtful, with Little and Gant almost slumbering at their posts, while the Seabreeze set is a relatively ordinary compilation from two sessions in 1977. There are a couple of fine Ellington transformations, and a thoughtful solo reading of 'I'll Keep Loving You', but the pianist receives only cursory accompaniment, and much the same thing happens on the *Expressly Ellington* disc: as urbane as Haig is, he responds better to a bass-drums duo who make him work hard. *Stablemates* trudges along on too many ballads, and Eardley sounds perfunctory, but Haig's own solos and accompaniments – there are model lessons for aspiring pianists in some of his comps and fills here – are impeccable. The solo album avoids all this sort of interference from lesser players, and is a shrewdly delivered if slightly detached session. *Bebop Live* was made not long before Haig's sudden death, and isn't a distinguished farewell: some worthwhile playing, but the conglomeration of bebop standards are despatched with messy fervour by the mismatched band, and the recording makes them sound very far away.

EDMOND HALL (1901–67)
CLARINET

(*)   **This Is Jazz Vol. 3 Storyville SLP 5069 LP
        Hall; Wild Bill Davison (*c*); Jimmy Archey (*tb*); Ralph Sutton (*p*); Danny Barker (*g*);
        Pops Foster (*b*); Baby Dodds (*d*). 9–10/47.

Hall was one of the most popular musicians in the Eddie Condon circle, but his experience – with big bands in the 1920s and '30s and with Louis Armstrong's All Stars – was much wider than that. He played in a driving manner that married the character of his New Orleans background with the more fleet methods of the swing clarinettists. His Blue Note sides from the 1940s are currently available only in a Mosaic compilation , but Hall seldom recorded as a leader in any event. This session, compiled from some *This Is Jazz* broadcasts, includes much excellent work by the leader in an impassioned Dixieland context, but the rough recording quality, poor even for the period, spoils much of the enjoyment.

****   **Edmond Hall In Copenhagen** Storyville STCD 6022 CD
        Hall; Finn Otto Hansen (*t*); Arne Bue Jensen (*tb*); Jørgen Svare (*cl*); Jørn Jensen (*p*);
        Bjarne 'Liller' Petersen (*bj*); Jens Sølund (*b*); Knud Ryskov Madsen (*d*). 12/66.

'I like to work in different contexts, but I can only play one style.' Hot, fluent, swinging, pinching the odd note here and there but mostly displaying a remarkably clean and supple line, here is Ed Hall at his best, only a few weeks before he died. The Papa Bue band play on two tracks, the rhythm section and Hall on most of the others, and while the Swedish players are no great masters they know how to respect a player who is. Hall even turns in a lovely acapella treatment of 'It Ain't Necessarily So'. Splendid remastering of a beautiful record.

JIM HALL (born 1930)
GUITAR

(*)   **Alone Together Original Jazz Classics OJC 467 CD/LP
Hall; Ron Carter (*b*). 8/72.

A live set without a single rough edge or corner, and with almost no improvisational tension either. The slight surprise of Rollins's 'St Thomas' quickly evaporates as Hall negotiates its contours with almost cynical ease – is there really no more to it than that? The rest is more caressingly familiar. There are moments of genuine beauty, notably on 'Softly As In A Morning Sunrise' and 'Autumn Leaves', but there's something fatally lacking in the conception. All of which is just a curmudgeonly, jazz-critic way of saying this is a lovely record which a lot of people are going to like.

(*)   **These Roots Denon CY 30002 EX CD
Hall; Tom Harrell (*t, flhn*); Steve LaSpina (*b*); Joey Baron (*d*). 2/88.

A solo 'All Too Soon', a couple of intriguing duos with Harrell and LaSpina respectively on 'Something Tells Me' and 'Darn That Dream', a trio 'My Funny Valentine' that draws all the remaining marrow out of the tune, and a generally effective quartet set hinged on 'Where Or When' and 'With A Song In My Heart'. Typically uncontroversial stuff from Hall, but Harrell is much too diffident in the group setting; it's a shame the duo format wasn't observed throughout.

***(*)   **All Across The City** Concord 384 CD/LP/MC
Hall; Gil Goldstein (*p, ky*); Steve LaSpina (*b*); Terry Clarke (*d*). 5/89.

This contains some of Hall's most innovatively 'contemporary' playing. Certainly, no one thrown into the deep end of 'R. E. M. Movement' – a Gil Goldstein composition with free passages from all the players – would suspect the provenance. Elsewhere the material is more familiar. 'Young One (For Debra)' consciously recalls Bill Evans and 'Waltz For Debbie'. Of the other originals, the gentle 'Jane' is dedicated to Mrs Hall, composer in turn of 'Something Tells Me'; 'Drop Shot' and 'Big Blues' are tougher but also more humorous in conception, the former featuring Goldstein's electronic keyboards to good effect, the latter an unexpected tribute to Stanley Turrentine. The title-track, a gentle and slightly wondering cityscape, also recalls Hall's association with Bill Evans.

Hall, though, is much more than an impressionistic colourist. His reading of Monk's 'Bemsha Swing' confirms his stature as one of the most significant harmonic improvisers on his instrument. Good sound on all three formats. Strongly recommended.

BENGT HALLBERG (born 1932)
PIANO

***(*)   **Kiddin' On The Keys** Dragon DRLP 170 LP
Hallberg; Gunnar Johnson (*b*); Anders Burman (*d*). 12/59.

***(*)   **At Gyllene Cirkeln** Dragon DRLP 107 LP
Hallberg; Lars Pettersson (*b*); Sture Kallin (*d*). 12/62.

Hallberg was making records before he'd even turned sixteen, and early partners on record included Stan Getz and Lee Konitz on their Swedish tours. *Kiddin' On The Keys* was his second 5full-length album; its reissue by Dragon restores a valuable record to circulation. Hallberg's manner is dry without being arid, his touch is very subtle on ballads, but he has an impish sense of humour which turns 'Kitten On The Keys' into something very far from Zez Confrey's original. If at this stage he recalls such influences as Lennie Tristano (in the methodical unfolding of a solo) and Teddy Wilson (in the genial voicings and spry rhythms) more than he does later, he's still impressively his own man, working in isolation from most modern piano currents. Johnson and Burman are more derivative accompanists, and one wishes for a more challenging setting, but Hallberg's own playing is a delight, with the meditations on 'Moonlight In Vermont' and 'Along Together' especially fine.

The sleeve-notes to the 1962 session, recorded live at Stockholm's Golden Circle, reveal that Hallberg hadn't heard 'So What' or Bill Evans at the time, which makes his growing affinities with both modality and Evans-like voicings the more interesting. The latter comes through particularly on a glowing 'Willow Weep For Me', but this is an attacking set: a couple of impromptu blues suggest formidable reserves of invention, and a bizarre reading of 'Dinah' dismembers the tune completely. Pettersson and Kallin keep out of the way more than they get involved, and it's a memorable record which results.

***   **Hallberg's Happiness** Phontastic PHONT 7544 LP
Hallberg (p solo). 3/77.

***   **The Hallberg Touch** Phontastic PHONT 7525 LP
Hallberg (p solo). 8/79.

The pianist made only a few albums under his own name in the 1960s and '70s, and most of those have disappeared, but these two solo sessions are engaging if a little lightweight compared to the earlier discs. *Happiness* is a packed collection of miniatures, some dispatched in a few breaths, others lingered over: there is a measured look at 'Sophisticated Lady' as well as a couple of jolly, faintly ludicrous ragtime pieces. the presence of the traditional 'Herdesa/ng' reminds that Hallberg looked into the possibilities of improvising on native Scandinavian tunes before many more publicized attempts. *Touch* is another mix of unpredictable choices – 'In A Little Spanish Town', 'Charleston' – but plays out with a more thoughtful elan overall.

***   **Bengt Hallberg In New York** Phontastic PHONT 7550 LP
Hallberg; Tom Harrell (t, flhn); Jan Allan (t); Jimmy Knepper (tb); Arne Domnérus (cl); Jerry Dodgion, Gerry Niewood (as); Rune Gustafsson (g); Georg Riedel (b); Magnus Persson (d). 9/82.

Cut on a brief visit with a troupe of comrades in tow, Hallberg shepherded several variations on the above personnel through a pleasing mainstream-to-bop date. Disappointingly, perhaps, there is far more from the horns than there is from the piano, and Persson is a more pedestrian drummer than the occasion demanded. But Harrell and Allan – in their quite different ways – have absorbing points to make, and Dodgion is about the most reliable altoman one could have on hand.

***   **Hallberg's Yellow Blues** Phontastic PHONT CD/LP
Hallberg (p solo). 84.

***   **Hallberg's Surprise** Phontastic PHONT 7581 CD/LP
Hallberg (p solo). 3–5/87.

Few would credit Hallberg with leading the march from jazz to any kind of 'world music'. Yet the sleeve-note author for *Surprise* opines that it 'is not a jazz record', and the other disc consists of traditional folk material. Hallberg has studied and composed in the European tradition, and he moves through non-jazz mediums with the same ease with which he slips from swing to bop and after. These records feature him improvising on music remote from conventional jazz repertory, but they sound unequivocally comfortable, the familiar songful touch brought to bear on a surprising range of themes. The folk pieces are dealt with a little more discreetly, and the pianist trusts the inner lights of the material rather than imposing too much of himself on it; but the *Surprise* record is considerably more adventurous, with 'Take The "A" Train' sandwiched between Paganini's 'Caprice No. 24' and Handel's 'Sarabande', and Neal Hefti lining up with Corelli and Chopin. Hallberg plays on and around each of the pieces, never unduly respectful but sticking to his essential thriftiness and grace as an improviser: some pieces work superbly, others sound curiously abstracted, yet it's an altogether intriguing record.

***   **Spring On The Air** Phono Suecia PSCD 51 CD
Hallberg; Jan Allan, Gustavo Bergalli, Bertil Lövgren, Magnus Johansson (t, flhn); Lars Olofsson, Olle Holmqvist, Ulf Johansson (tb); Sven Larsson (btb); Arne Domnérus, Krister Andersson (cl, as); Lennart Åberg (ss, ts, af); Jan Kling (ts, f); Erik Nilsson (bs, bcl, f); Stefan Nilsson (p); Rune Gustafsson (g); Sture Åkerberg (b); Egil Johansen (d). 5/87.

Hallberg's writing for big band hasn't been widely documented on record, which makes this CD the more welcome. Nearly an hour of music is devoted to a sequence of impressionist themes meant to evoke aspects of his country and, while it's hard to know if the sax writing for 'Göta River' is any kind of accurate picture, there's a vividness in the writing which the players respond to with the kind of sober relish that's characteristic of them. Old friends such as Jan Allan and Arne Domnérus are provided with features which suggest either Ellington or Gil Evans, but a piece such as 'Night In The Harbour', with its virtuoso trombone part by Ulf Johansson, sounds like Hallberg through and through. The recording lacks a little punch, but the clarity illuminates all the strands of the writing.

RICH HALLEY
TENOR SAX

***(*) **Cracked Sidewalks** Avocet P 105 LP
Halley; Tom Hill (*tb*); Gary Harris (*as*); Geoff Lee (*p*); Phil Sparks (*b*); William Thomas (*d*). 7/86.

*** **Saxophone Animals** Nine Winds NWCD 0139 CD
As above, plus Rob Blakeslee (*t, flhn, perc*). 7/88–8/90.

Halley, who lives and works in Portland, Oregon, has asserted a firm and engaging identity on his records. His band, The Lizard Brothers, perform his charts with great enthusiasm: on *Cracked Sidewalks* he melds blues, bop and more outré forms with a naturalness that's a little surprising for a band that operates far from the customary centres of jazz. Halley's 'A View Of The World From 3rd And Burnside' is a small-town view of big-world jazz that works superbly, and the muscular charge of 'Threok' is genuinely thrilling.

Working in a straight-ahead context with the occasional nod towards freedom seems to be Halley's best routine, for he reaches further out on *Saxophone Animals* to somewhat lesser effect. While there are some striking things here – an interesting reworking of Miles Davis's 'The Serpent's Tooth', for instance – the long pieces struggle a little to balance the free and formal ingredients, and Hill and Harris sound less at ease than they were on the earlier record. Halley himself, though, remains a formidable improviser in the Rollins mould.

LIN HALLIDAY (born 1936)
TENOR SAXOPHONE

*** **Delayed Exposure** Delmark DE 449 CD
Halliday; Ira Sullivan (*t, flhn, f*); Jodie Christian (*p*); Dennis Carroll (*b*); George Fludas (*d*). 6/91.

The title is suitably pointed, since this was Halliday's debut as a leader: 'An extremely likeable tenor saxophonist,' says the sleeve-note writer, and there's little here to make one disagree. Halliday emerges as a well-practised Rollins disciple. He's been living and working in Chicago for a little over a decade, and Delmark's minor crusade to record the city's less sensational but worthy constituents pays off with a muscular, well-fashioned blowing date. Some standards and a blues give everyone a chance to hold down some choruses and, if Sullivan's trumpet turns are the most distinctive things here, Halliday acquits himself with the comfortable assurance of a veteran player. Extremely likeable.

CHICO HAMILTON (born 1921)
DRUMS

(*) **Gongs East Discovery DSCD 831 CD

(*) **Featuring Eric Dolphy Fresh Sound FSCD 1004 CD
Hamilton; Eric Dolphy (*as, f, bcl*); Dennis Budimir (*g*); Nathan Gershman (*clo*); Wyatt Ruther (*b* on both); Ralph Pena (*b* on *Featuring Eric Dolphy* only). 12/58, 5/59.

Hamilton poses rather self-consciously on the cover like a pre-Charles Atlas, 110-lb weakling version of J. Arthur Rank's trademark gong-beater. By 1958, though, nobody was kicking sand in the face of this band, which was commercially one of the most successful modern jazz units of its day. The recruitment of Dolphy in place of previous multi-reedmen Buddy Colette and Paul Horn came just in time for the Newport Jazz Festival appearances, captured in the evergreen movie, *Jazz On A Summer's Day*, and gave the album, his second with Hamilton, the kind of unexpectedly pointed resonance that has always characterized the drummer's slightly Europeanized chamber jazz.

Dolphy's later enthusiasm for cello in place of piano may have been inspired by Gershman's distinctive passage-work, but the album is now primarily of interest for his own increasingly confident soloing; check out 'Passion Flower'. His bass clarinet work on the title-track and the alto-led ensembles on 'Tuesday At Two' are particularly distinctive. Budimir makes a few successful interventions and Hamilton's drumming is as adventurous as always.

The May 1959 session – previously released as *That Hamilton Man* – is darker and more angular. On his last studio appearance with the Quintet, Dolphy chips in with his first recorded composition; the moody 'Lady E' largely avoids the folkish sentimentality of parts of *Gongs East* and helps sustain the later album's prevailing air of appealing melancholy.

*** **Reunion** Soul Note 121 191 CD/LP
Hamilton; Buddy Collette (*f, cl, as*); Fred Katz (*clo*); John Pisano (*g*); Carson Smith (*b*). 6/89.

No longer 110 lb, the latter-day Hamilton packs a beefy and impressive punch. After spelling out the personnel – a brief album-and-tour reunion of the original Hamilton Quintet, with Pisano in for the otherwise-engaged Jim Hall – the liner note announces rather enigmatically: 'Chico Hamilton plays [large blank space] drums'. Though a maker's name or logo has presumably dropped off the final proof, it's tempting to follow up the cue, for *Reunion* reveals Hamilton as one of the most underrated and possibly influential jazz percussionists of recent times. Rather than keeping up with any of the Joneses, he sustains a highly original idiom which is retrospectively reminiscent of Paul Motian's but is altogether more abstract. The spontaneously improvised 'Five Friends' might have worked better as a duet with Colette (like 'Brushing With B' and 'Conversation'), but the immediately preceding 'Dreams Of Youth', dedicated by its composer, Fred Katz, to the dead and betrayed of Tiananmen Square, is one of the most moving jazz pieces of recent years, drawing out Hamilton's non-Western accents.

By no means a cosy 'old pals' act, *Reunion* is confidently exploratory and powerfully effective. Recommended.

***(*) **Arroyo** Soul Note 121241 CD/LP
Hamilton; Eric Person (*as, ss*); Cary DeNigris (*g*); Reggie Washington (*b*). 12/90.

That Hamilton should christen his latest band Euphoria is testimony to his continued appetite for music-making. Though it's as far in style as it is in years from the 1950s Quintet, there are clear lines of continuity. Hamilton's preference for a guitarist over a piano player helps free up the drums, allowing Hamilton to experiment with melodic improvisation. Typically, DeNigris is given considerable prominence – much as Jim Hall, Larry Coryell and John Abercrombie were at different times – with Person assigned a colourist's role.

The long opening 'Alone Together' is a vibrantly inventive version of a wearying warhorse. Hamilton's polyrhythms open the tune to half a dozen new directions and Washington produces some of his best work of the set. The other standard, Lester Young's and Jon Hendricks's 'Tickle Toe', has the drummer scatting with the same relaxed abandon he applies to his kit. His writing on 'Sorta New', 'Cosa Succede?' and the intriguingly titled 'Taunts Of An Indian Maiden' is still full of ideas, exploiting band textures to the full. DeNigris and Person both claim at least one writing credit, and the guitarist's 'Stop' is ambitious and unsettling.

The mix doesn't favour the leader unduly, but Washington is slightly submerged on some of the up-tempo numbers. Hamilton's inventiveness seems unstinted; this is impressive stuff.

SCOTT HAMILTON (born 1954)
TENOR SAXOPHONE

***(*) **Tenorshoes** Concord CCD 4127 CD/MC
Hamilton; Dave McKenna (*p*); Phil Flanigan (*b*); Jeff Hamilton (*d*). 12/79.

When the disturbingly young Scott Hamilton signed up with Concord in 1977, his arrival was greeted with much the same mixture of uncritical excitement and patronizing cavil as the boy Jesus's disputation with the Elders. The fact was that Hamilton was playing in an idiom two generations old, and playing so superbly as to render favourable comparison with his putative forebears – Coleman Hawkins, Chu Berry, Lester Young, Don Byas and Zoot Sims – more than mere rhetoric.

The cover of *Tenorshoes* features a pair of basketball boots bronzed like a baby's first shoes, and beside them a dish of chocolates. However tired he was of references to his age – a veteran 25 in 1979 – he should certainly have sued over the sweets, for Hamilton's tenor playing is fat-free, low-cholesterol jazz of a very high order. However saccharin the themes – here 'I Should Care', 'The Shadow Of Your Smile' and 'The Nearness Of You' are perhaps the most filling-threatening – Hamilton explores the changes with a fine, probing intelligence that is every bit as satisfying intellectually as it is emotionally fulsome.

The unaccompanied intro to 'I Should Care' and an energetic reading of 'How High The Moon' bespeak considerable formal control which is fully matched by the band, with McKenna soloing beautifully and succinctly on both of the above. The album as a whole is brightly recorded, though the saxophone is occasionally a shade over-miked.

***   **In Concert** Concord CCD 4233 CD/MC
Hamilton; Eiji Kitamura (*cl* – 1 track); John Bunch (*p*); Chris Flory (*g*); Phil Flanigan (*b*); Chuck Riggs (*d*). 6/83.

***   **The Second Set** Concord CCD 4254 CD/MC
As above, except omit Kitamura. 6/83.

***(*)   **Plays Ballads** Concord CCD 4386 CD/MC
As above. 3/89.

Setting aside the irritation of a relentlessly self-congratulatory Japanese audience (who applaud themselves every time they recognize a standard), the two Tokyo sets are absolutely marvellous. It's not often that a label can cull two top-flight discs from a single concert, but there's nothing shopsoiled or second-rate about *The Second Set*, which opens with a reading of 'All The Things You Are' that within a few bars confirms Hamilton as a highly individual improviser and not just a mellow stylist. The band play briskly and intelligently. Guitarist Flory's contributions to big-band flag-wavers like Basie's 'Taps Miller' (*Second Set*) and 'One O'Clock Jump' (*In Concert*) are impeccably judged, and Bunch turns in half a dozen exceptional choruses between the two sets. The *In Concert* CD has a bonus encore featuring the Japanese clarinetist Eiji Kitamura (who has a worthwhile album of his own on Concord CJ 152).

Ballads was Hamilton's best record to date; the recent *Race Point* just beats it to the line. Though he handles faster numbers with consummate skill and without an awkward excess of notes, this is his natural tempo. 'Round Midnight' and 'In A Sentimental Mood' are read with an intriguing slant which considerably mitigates the former's recent over-exposure. 'Two Eighteen', dedicated to Hamilton's wife, is his first recorded composition; it doesn't suggest a writing talent commensurate with his playing, but it's an engaging enough piece.

The Don Byas-associated 'Laura' and an oblique 'Body And Soul' are CD-only. If Byas and Coleman Hawkins have clubbed together in Jazz Heaven to buy a compact disc player, they'll like what they hear. Ballad albums are not as fashionable as they were. This is an impeccable example and certainly the best way to start a Hamilton collection (there are now 35 albums in the discography, as leader and sideman).

(*)   **Major League Concord CCD 4305 CD/MC
Hamilton; Dave McKenna (*p*); Jake Hanna (*d*). 5/86.

In comparison to Hamilton's consistently high standard, and more specifically in comparison to the same trio's earlier baseball-inspired *No Bass Hit* [Concord CJ 97], this is slightly disappointing. Hanna is a more propulsive drummer than Riggs or Jeff Hamilton, and the extra bounce doesn't seem to suit the saxophonist, though Connie Kay's spring-wristed metre on *Radio City* (below) serves him very well indeed. Top credit really goes to Dave McKenna, the more than nominal leader on *No Bass Hit* as well. The pianist's solo on 'It All Depends On You' is masterly, with a powerful low-register left-hand line that, as on all the tracks, more than compensates for the absence of a string bassist. Disappointing, but only slightly.

***(*)   **Radio City** Concord CCD 4428 CD/MC
Hamilton; Gerry Wiggins (*p*); Dennis Irwin (*b*); Connie Kay (*d*). 2/90.

Excellent. The material is the usual mix of familiar – 'Yesterdays', 'My Ideal', 'The Touch Of Your Lips' – and less familiar – Duke and Mercer Ellington's lovely 'Tonight I Shall Sleep With A Smile On My Face' and Woody Herman's 'Apple Honey' – together with a couple of originals. The title-track is the best of these to date, a vigorous, bouncing theme with an appealing rawness of tone. Wiggins is a superb piano player with a big, friendly delivery; right on top of Kay's rimshots and sharp cymbal accents, he pushes Hamilton up a further gear without the least hint of strain. The future is going to be interesting.

****   Race Point Concord CCD 4492 CD
Hamilton; Gerry Wiggins (*p*); Howard Alden (*g*); Andy Simpkins (*b*); Jeff Hamilton (*d*). 9/91.

Carl Perkins's 'Groove Yard' is an intriguing choice of opener and sets the tone for Hamilton's best and most inventive set to date. Interspersed with the quartet tracks are four duets with guitarist Alden; 'Chelsea Bridge' is outstanding, and so is 'The Song Is You', which closes the set. Alden's bass figures and Hamilton's squeezed harmonics give the duos a tremendous range. Of the quartets, Hamilton's own 'Race Point' is notable; Wiggins opens up the middle section with a wild, intervallic ladder that feeds a storming solo. Jeff Hamilton plays immaculately, if a little stiffly in places. The sound is crisp but rather bunched towards the centre, which gives a good 'live' feel but tends to spoil some of the louder ensembles.

GUNTER HAMPEL (born 1937)
COMPOSER, VIBRAPHONE, PIANO, REEDS

**   Dances Birth 002 LP
Hampel (solo). 1/70.

***   Wellen-Waves: Berlin Soloflight FMP 0770 LP
As above. 5/80.

Virtually all of Hampel's work since 1969 has appeared on the fissiparous Birth label (and virtually the whole Birth catalogue consists of Hampel's work, in small groups and in various versions of his Galaxie Dream Band; the only two exceptions are duos nominally led by singer Jeanne Lee, who is Mrs Hampel, and by the alto saxophonist Marion Brown). Birth is still vinyl only, but new releases will be on CD, and once stocks are exhausted there are plans to transfer some if not all of the back catalogue to the new format.

There are obvious and misleading parallels between Hampel's work and that of the similarly cosmically obsessed Sun Ra, but Hampel is typically saturnine rather than Saturnian and he lacks the ripping, swinging joy of Ra's various Intergalactic Arkestras. *Dances* is – suprisingly – the only solo recording in the home catalogue, a sequence of intermittently imaginative choreographies for Hampel's unusual range of instruments. There is also a rare repertoire piece, Coltrane's 'Naima', segued into a vibraphone dance. Despite the significant artistic success of Joachim Berendt's programme of unaccompanied solo concerts at the Munich Olympics, in which Hampel took part (an association which may still carry a certain traumatic resonance), he has appeared disinclined to release solo material since. The Berlin solo concert (a rare appearance on another label, though there are duos with Cecil Taylor in the offing) is better recorded and much more coherent in execution.

**(*)   The 8th July 1969 Birth 001 LP
Hampel; Anthony Braxton (*as, ss, sno, f, cbcl*); Willem Breuker (*ss, as, ts, b cl*); Arjen Gorter (*b*); Steve McCall (*d*); Jeanne Lee (*v*). 7/69.

**(*)   Familie Birth 008 LP
As above, except omit Breuker, Gorter and McCall. 4/72.

However deeply absorbed he has appeared to be in Afro-American music, multi-instrumentalist composer Anthony Braxton learned a great deal from the European collective/free movement of the late 1960s, and particularly at that time from Hampel, who has written pieces with numbered and coded titles reminiscent of Braxton's own later practice. Braxton is also the only other contemporary player to make convincing music on the brutally unfeasible contrabass clarinet and, if much of Hampel's endeavour in this rather tortured register resembles a modern

Laocoön, it's none the less impressive for that, and his work on the vibraphone, his main instrument, is wonderfully light and evocative.

The earlier, larger group, *8th July 1969*, is not quite as timewarped as the free-form *Familie*, but it isn't quite as individual. Lee's voice is one of the most significant in contemporary improvisation; only Linda Sharrock, Diamanda Galas and Joan La Barbara match her for sheer strength and adaptability. Willem Breuker is already an imaginative and powerful soloist. Braxton, who in 1969 had just completed the epochal solo *For Alto* (which then had to wait three years for commercial release), still sounds as if he's fishing for a music commensurate with his remarkable talent. It's not at all clear that he found it with Hampel, but there is fine music on both albums, and on a later Braxton association with Hampel's Galaxie Dream Band (Birth 0025, below).

(*)   **Ballet-Symphony Birth 003 LP
Hampel; Maxine Gregg (*clo*); Jack Gregg (*b*); Bobby Moses (*d*); Jeanne Lee (*v*); Michel Waifisz (*syn*). 1/70.

***   **People Symphony** Birth 005 LP
Hampel; Willem Breuker (*ss, as, ts, bcl*); Willem Van Maanen (*tb*); Maxine Gregg (*clo*); Jack Gregg (*b*); Arjen Gorter (*b*); Jeanne Lee (*v*). 2/70.

***   **Escape** Birth 006 LP
Hampel; Boulou Ferre (*g*). 8–10/70.

***   **Spirits** Birth 007 LP
Hampel; Perry Robinson (*cl*); Jeanne Lee (*v*). 8/71.

***   **Waltz For Three Universes In A Corridor** Birth 0010 LP
Hampel; Toni Marcus (*v, va*); Jeanne Lee (*v*). 6/72.

[**(*)   **Out From Under** Birth 0016 LP]
Hampel; John D'Earth (*tp*); Marty Cook, John Wolf (*tb*); Perry Robinson (*cl*); Thomas Keyserling, Allan Praskin (*as, f*); Mark Whitecage (*f, acl*); Jonathan Kline (*vn*); Jeanne Lee (*v*). 1/74.

(*)   **Cosmic Dancer Birth 0024 LP
Hampel; Perry Robinson (*cl*); Steve McCall (*dc*); Jeanne Lee (*v*). 9/75.

***   **Freedom Of The Universe** Birth 0030 LP
Hampel; Jeanne Lee (*v*). 6/79.

(*)   **Companions Birth 0036 LP
Hampel; Thomas Keyserling (*f, as*); Jeanne Lee (*v*). 11/82.

Often overlooked in favour of the Galaxie Dream Band, Hampel's informal small groups registered some of his best, and certainly most approachable, music. *Waltz* is a particularly fine album and, along with *Cosmic Dancer* and the much later *Companions*, a good point of entry to this aspect of Hampel's work. As well as the airy title-piece – which is echoed or continued in 'Waltz For Eleven Universes In A Corridor' on the later *Journey to the Song Within* (Birth 0017) – there is a dedication to guitarist Boulou Ferre, his improbable but rather effective collaborator on *Escape*, an example of Hampel's more folkish style.

Hampel, like Sun Ra or Duke Ellington (to whom there are clear references on *Enfant Terrible*, below [9]), has commanded extraordinary loyalty from his regular sideman. Perry Robinson is a more or less constant member of the Galaxie Dream Band, and Keyserling a regular. Both have highly individual voices well suited to Hampel's brand of freely associative improvisation. Toni Marcus's distinctive fiddle and viola lines are an important element on *Waltz*, and Robinson plays beautiful concert clarinet lines in opposition to the leader's dark mutterings on the bass reeds. The key figure, though, is Jeanne Lee, to whom *Freedom Of The Universe* should more strictly be credited. It's a fine and occasionally moving album.

Ballet-Symphony and *People Symphony* contain examples of Hampel's quirkily miniaturist 'symphonic' writing. 'Symphony No. 6' on the former, though far removed from pastoral intent, is scored for a folksy combination of soprano saxophone, vibraphone and ocarina (all played by Hampel) and Michel Waifisz's slightly cumbersome Putney synth-system. But then it's usually more satisfactory to ignore the exact components of Hampel's sound and to accept it as an occasionally magnificent, often unconscionable *fait accompli* which never quite resolves the tension between avant-gardist hostility and a much gentler lyricism. *People Symphony* is the most prodigally free-form of the albums.

(Though nominally a Galaxie Dream Band release, the most effective tracks on *Out From Under* are small-group, duo and trio interactions between Hampel and some of his most trusted lieutenants. 'Intimate', a duo with flautist Keyserling, is particularly effective, while the two-clarinet and percussion 'Celebration Portrait For Mr Robinson' is warmly humorous, neither adjective automatically applicable to Hampel's work.)

***   **Angel** [1] Birth 009 LP

(*)   **Broadway [2] Birth 0011 LP

(*)   **I Love Being With You [3] Birth 0012 LP

***   **Unity Dance – European Concert** [4] Birth 0013 LP

[**   **[GDB] Out From Under** [5] Birth 0016 LP]

***   **Journey To The Song Within** [6] Birth 0017 LP

***   **Celebrations** [7] Birth 0021/22 LP

**   **Ruomi** [8] Birth 0023 LP

***   **Enfant Terrible** [9] Birth 0025 LP

**   **Transformation** [10] Birth 0026 LP

(*)   **Live At The Berlin Jazz Festival [11] Birth 0027 LP

(*)   **All Is Real [12] Birth 0028 LP

**   **Vogelfrei** [13] Birth 0029 LP

(*)   **All The Things You Could Be If Charles Mingus Was Your Daddy [14] Birth 0031 LP

(*)   **A Place To Be With Us [15] Birth 0032 LP

(*)   **Life On This Planet 1981 [16] Birth 0033 LP

***   **Celestial Harmony** [17] Birth 0040 CD
Hampel; Galaxie Dream Bands of varying personnel: John D'Earth (*t* on 5); Fredric Rabold (*t, flhn* on 7, 8, 10); Enrico Rava (*t* on 1); Manfred Schoof (*t* on 10); Marty Cook (*tb* on 5, 6); John Wolf (*tb* on 5, 6); Perry Robinson (*cl, perc* on all except 4, 8, 15); Thomas Keyserling (*f, ts, as, perc* on 5–10, 12–16); Daniel Carter (*ts, as, f* on 1); Mark Whitecage (*as, acl, f* on 1–6, 9, 11, 12, 14); Allan Praskin (*as, cl, f, rec* on 2–8); Anthony Braxton (*as, ss, cbcl, cl, f* on 9); Toni Marcus (*vn* on 2, 3); Jonathan Kline (*vn* on 4–6); David Eyges (*clo* on 2–4); Paul Bouillet (*g* on 1, 2); Jack Gregg (*b, wooden f, African d* on 2–4, 6–9); John Shea (*b* on 1–3); Murugar (*d, perc* on 1); Martin Bues (*d, perc* on 9–16); Sunny Murray (*d* on 6); Jeanne Lee (*v, perc* on all except 8, 13); specific instrumentations are not differentiated – performers may not use all instruments indicated on every record. 5/72, 7/72, 72 or 73, 6/73, 1/74, 2/74, 6/74, 10/74, 9/75, 9/76, 11/78, 11/78, 10/76, 7/80, 1/81, 9/81, 9/91.

A hefty and sometimes bewildering catalogue of material which, though the quality is remarkably consistent, only the most committed of enthusiasts – and quite possibly only members of the Hampel family – will want to possess in its entirety. The early recordings, particularly *Angel* and *Broadway*, are, for the moment, the best. And only for the moment; there are signs of a major resurgence in Hampel's remarkably hermetic career, increased exposure in the United States and, on the evidence of *Celestial Harmony*, a much more approachable and jazz-tinged style. The ambitiously large-scale structures of the early sets, though, afford considerable space for individual and collective improvisation, and Mark Whitecage's Dolphy-influenced alto becomes increasingly influential.

After the mid-1970s, there is a noticeable falling-off in coherence and intensity, though the difference between the Berlin Jazz Festival set and the studio *All Is Real*, recorded within a fortnight in November 1978, is very striking. The band was always dependent to some extent on 'star' or guest performers. Braxton certainly lifts *Enfant Terrible*, as does Enrico Rava *Angel*.

Sunny Murray's considerable presence on *Journey To The Song Within* clearly underlines the band's single endemic fault: the lack of a powerful rhythmic centre.

Where to begin (and, just possibly, end)? *Angel*, for certain; *Broadway*, if possible; the Berlin concert, for a taste of the later 1970s; then perm any one or two from the remaining dozen or so, and put a note in the files to keep an ear open. Sound-quality isn't always top-notch – particularly on the live recordings – but the music usually more than makes up for any merely technical shortcomings.

***   **Cavana** Birth 0034 LP

Hampel; Rudiger Mettenbrink (*t*); Joachim Guckel (*tb*); Jens Frahm, Perry Robinson (*cl*); Thomas Keyserling (*as, f*); Otto Jansen (*as, ts*); Charles Walker (*ts*); Ove Vollquartz (*ts, ss, bcl*); Ingo Marmulla (*g*); Jurgen Attig (*b*); Martin Bues (*d*); Klaus Mages (*perc*); Jeanne Lee (*v*). 12/81.

**   **Generator** Birth 0035 LP

As above. 12/81.

This single session was released under a 'big-band' rubric and introduced one or two unfamiliar names into the almost family atmosphere of the Hampel bands. There are some beautiful moments on 'Serenade For Marion Brown', a piece which appears on the duo *Gemini* (Birth 0037) with the saxophonist, and the title-track of *Cavana*. All the better eggs were certainly put into that basket; *Generator* is unaccountably thinner and less assured.

***   **Jubilation** Birth 0038 LP

Hampel; Manfred Schoof (*t*); Albert Mangelsdorff (*tb*); Perry Robinson (*cl*); Marion Brown (*as*); Thomas Keyserling (*as, f, af*); Barre Phillips (*b*); Steve McCall (*d*); Jeanne Lee (*v*). 11/83.

***   **Fresh Heat – Live At Sweet Basil** Birth 0039 LP

Hampel; Stephen Haynes, Vance R. Provey (*t*); Curtis Fowlkes (*tb*); Bob Stewart (*tba*); Perry Robinson (*cl*); Thomas Keyserling, Mark Whitecage (*as, f*); Bob Hanlon (*ts, f*); Lucky Ennett (*ts*); Bill Frisell (*g*); Kyoto Fujiwara (*b*); Marvin Smitty Smith (*d*); Arthur Jenkins, Jeanne Lee (*v*). 2/85.

Promising signs that Hampel, now in his mid-fifties, is branching out in new directions and at the same time attracting a wider following. *Jubilation* is an excellent album – 'Little Bird' is particularly strong – which lacks some of the instinctive empathy of the Galaxie Dream Band but also some of its increasingly hermetic inwardness. The live New York City set smacks of no one more forcibly than Charles Mingus, who was at the very least a conscious presence in Hampel's thinking as far back as 1980 and the double reference of *All The Things You Could Be* . . . (Birth 0031). Mingus's legacy is still largely unexplored and Hampel, now that he has abandoned the more indulgent aspects of free music, may be the man to do it.

LIONEL HAMPTON (born 1909)
VIBES, PIANO, DRUMS, VOCAL

***   **Lionel Hampton 1929 To 1940** BBC RPCD/ZCRP 852 CD/MC

Hampton; Benny Carter (*t, as*); Ziggy Elman, George Orendorff, Jonah Jones, Cootie Williams, Walter Fuller, Dizzy Gillespie, Henry Red Allen (*t*); Bobby Hackett (*c*); J. C. Higginbotham, Lawrence Brown, Vernon Brown (*tb*); Benny Goodman, Eddie Barefield, Pee Wee Russell, Buster Bailey, Edmond Hall, Mezz Mezzrow (*cl*); Marshall Royal, Omer Simeon (*cl, as*); Vido Musso (*cl, ts*); Johnny Hodges, Earl Bostic, Toots Mondello, Buff Estes, George Oldham (*as*); Arthur Rollini, Paul Howard, Bud Freeman, Budd Johnson, Robert Crowder, Ben Webster, Chu Berry, Coleman Hawkins, Jerry Jerome (*ts*); Edgar Sampson (*bs*); Jess Stacy, Joe Bushkin, Clyde Hart, Harvey Brooks, Dudley Brooks, Sir Charles Thompson, Nat Cole, Spencer Odun (*p*); Ray Perry (*vn*); Allan Reuss, Charlie Christian, Freddie Green, Ernest Ashley, Oscar Moore, Irving Ashby, Eddie Condon (*g*); Thomas Valentine (*bj*); James Jackson (*bb*); Billy Taylor, Artie Shapiro, Jesse Simpkins, Milt Hinton, Artie Bernstein, Vernon Alley, Mack Walker, Johnny Miller, John Kirby, Wesley Prince (*b*); Cozy Cole, Alvin Burroughs, Sid Catlett, Zutty Singleton, Sonny Greer, Gene Krupa, Lee Young, Nick Fatool, Al Spieldock (*d*). 4/29–12/40.

***(*)   **Lionel Hampton 1937–1938** Classics 524 CD
Hampton; Ziggy Elman, Cootie Williams, Jonah Jones (*t*); Lawrence Brown (*tb*); Vido
Musso (*cl, ts*); Mezz Mezzrow, Eddie Barefield (*cl*); Johnny Hodges, Hymie Schertzer,
George Koenig (*as*), Arthur Rollini (*ts*); Edgar Sampson (*bs*); Jess Stacy, Clyde Hart
(*p*); Bobby Bennett (*g*) Allan Reuss (*g*); Harry Goodman, John Kirby, Mack Walker,
Johnny Miller, Billy Taylor (*b*); Gene Krupa, Cozy Cole, Sonny Greer (*d*). 2/37–1/38.

***(*)   **Lionel Hampton 1938–1939** Classics 534 CD
Hampton; Cootie Williams, Harry James, Walter Fuller, Irving Randolph, Ziggy
Elman (*t*); Rex Stewart (*c*); Lawrence Brown (*tb*); Benny Carter, Omer Simeon (*cl,
as*); Russell Procope (*ss, as*); Hymie Schertzer (*as, bcl*); Johnny Hodges, Dave
Matthews, George Oldham (*as*); Herschel Evans, Babe Russin, Jerry Jerome, Chu
Berry (*ts*); Edgar Sampson, Harry Carney (*bs*); Jess Stacy, Billy Kyle, Spencer Odun,
Clyde Hart (*p*); Allan Reuss, Danny Barker (*g*); Billy Taylor, John Kirby, Jesse
Simpkins, Milt Hinton (*b*); Sonny Greer, Jo Jones, Alvin Burroughs, Cozy Cole (*d*).
1/38–6/39.

***(*)   **Lionel Hampton 1939–1940** Classics 562 CD
Hampton; Dizzy Gillespie, Henry Allen, Ziggy Elman (*t*); Benny Carter (*t, as*); Rex
Stewart (*c*); Lawrence Brown, (*tb*); Edmond Hall (*cl*); Toots Mondello (*cl, as*); Earl
Bostic, Buff Estes (*as*); Coleman Hawkins, Ben Webster, Chu Berry, Jerry Jerome,
Budd Johnson (*ts*); Harry Carney (*bs*); Clyde Hart, Nat Cole, Joe Sullivan, Spencer
Odun (*p*); Allan Reuss, Charlie Christian, Al Casey, Ernest Ashley, Oscar Moore (*g*);
Billy Taylor, Milt Hinton, Artie Bernstein, Wesley Prince (*b*); Sonny Greer, Cozy
Cole, Sid Catlett, Slick Jones, Zutty Singleton, Nick Fatool, Al Spieldock (*d*).
6/39–5/40.

(****)   **Hot Mallets Vol. 1** Bluebird ND 86458 CD/LP/MC
Personnel basically as above three records. 4/37–9/39.

(***)   **The Jumpin' Jive Vol. 2** Bluebird ND 82433 CD/LP/MC
Personnel basically as above four records. 2/37–10/39.

Lionel Hampton's Victor sessions of the 1930s offer a glimpse of many of the finest big-band
players of the day away from their usual chores: Hampton creamed off the pick of whichever
band was in town at the time of the session and, although most of the tracks were hastily
organized, the music is consistently entertaining. If one has a reservation, it's to do with
Hampton himself: if you don't enjoy what he does, these discs are a write-off, because nobody at
any of the dates can have been under any illusion as to who the leader was; Hampton
dominates everything. He'd already worked with Louis Armstrong in Les Hite's band as far
back as the late 1920s, and he came to New York in 1936 following an offer from Benny
Goodman. The Victor dates began at the same time, and Hampton cut a total of 23 sessions
between 1936 and 1941. The personnel varies substantially from date to date: some are like
small-band sessions drawn from the Ellington or Goodman or Basie orchestras, others – such as
the extraordinary 1939 date with Gillespie, Carter, Berry, Webster and Hawkins – are genuine
all-star jams. Carter wrote the charts for one session, but mostly Hampton used head
arrangements or sketchy frameworks. The bonding agent is his own enthusiasm: whether
playing vibes – and incidentally establishing the dominant style on the instrument with his
abrasive accents, percussive intensity and quickfire alternation of long and short lines – or piano
or drums, or taking an amusing, Armstrong-influenced vocal, Hamp makes everything swing.

In the end, surprisingly few tracks stand out: what one remembers are individual solos and
the general climate of hot, hip good humour which prevails. One might mention Benny Carter
on 'I'm In The Mood For Swing', Chu Berry on 'Shufflin' At The Hollywood', Dizzy Gillespie
on 'Hot Mallets', J. C. Higginbotham on 'I'm On My Way From You' or Buster Bailey on
'Rhythm, Rhythm'; but there are few disappointments amid an air of democratic enterprise.
Hamp's drum and piano features are less than enthralling after one has heard them once, but
they don't occupy a great deal of space. The availability of this fine jazz is less than outstanding
at present. While the Classics CDs take a full chronological look up to May 1940, the sound is
inconsistent: some tracks field too much surface noise, others seem unnecessarily dull. That said,
they do at least offer a comprehensive survey: the Bluebird CDs include a total of 43 tracks,
including two alternative takes, and while they are intelligently chosen (the first volume was
selected by Hampton himself) it seems pointless that a third CD wasn't made available for a

comprehensive chronological survey. The sound is again variable: some tracks have noticeable distortion, others seem thin and, while the best exude the fine ringing tone of the original Victor recording, it seems a disappointingly slapdash effort by the compilers. We commend *Hot Mallets* as a good introduction to Hampton's work, with the above proviso.

Robert Parker's BBC compilation goes further in looking at Hampton on record over the entire decade and including tracks by the Goodman small groups, an Eddie Condon band and one piece by Paul Howard's Quality Serenaders, with Hampton making his debut on record. The choice of Victor tracks is a trifle eccentric, but the sound is the liveliest of all these reissues, although Parker's use of reverb is occasionally irritating.

**(*)   The Mess Is Here Magic AWE 18 CD
Hampton; Snooky Young, Wendell Culley, Al Killian, Joe Morris, Dave Page, Lammar Wright (*t*); Booty Wood, Vernon Porter, Andrew Penn, Fred Beckett, Sonny Carven, Allen Durham, Alvin Hayse (*tb*); Herbie Fields, (*cl, as*); Gus Evans, George Dorsey (*as*); Arnett Cobb, Fred Simon, Jay Peters (*ts*); Charlie Fowlkes (*bs*); Milt Buckner (*p*); Billy Mackel (*g*); Charles Harris, Ted Sinclair (*b*); George Jenkins, Fred Radcliffe (*d*); Dinah Washington (*v*). 44–45.

(***)   Lionel Hampton Orchestra Jazz Archives 90.506 CD
As above, except omit Killian, Wood, Hayse, Fields, Simon, Peters, Harris, Jenkins. 44.

****   Just Jazz MCA 42329 CD
Hampton; Charlie Shavers (*t*); Willie Smith (*as*); Corky Corcoran (*ts*); Tommy Todd (*p*); Barney Kessel (*g*); Slam Stewart (*b*); Lee Young (*d*). 8/47.

Hampton's big bands of the 1940s were relentlessly entertaining outfits, their live shows a feast of raving showstoppers which Hampton somehow found the energy to replenish time and again. He tended to rely on a repertoire – including 'Flying Home', 'Hamp's Boogie Woogie' and a few others – which he has stuck by to this day, but his ability to ignite both a band and an audience prevailed over any doubts concerning staleness. The band actually made a number of fine studio records during the period, and notable soloists included Arnett Cobb, Dexter Gordon and even Charles Mingus; but the Decca recordings have been mysteriously neglected by reissues, even during the LP era. We expect MCA to offer a comprehensive reissue within the life of this volume, but in the meantime the Jazz Archives and Magic discs of airshots give some impression of the Hampton band's hard-hitting excitement on the likes of 'Slide Hamp Slide' and 'Lady Be Good'. Neither disc offers very good fidelity, and the Jazz Archives set is wildly erratic in sound: with top-notch remastering this band would sound breathtaking, but in low-fi its poorer qualities tend to dominate. Still, they're useful documents.

The *Just Jazz* album features Hampton on only a single track – but it's one of his greatest performances on record, a stunningly vivid and impassioned improvisation on 'Stardust' which sums up his art as a player. Here are the double-time runs, riff variations and joyous, humorous swing which Hamp has dedicated his playing life to, crystallized in a single great solo. The rest of the record offers a bombastic set by the other participants in what was a concert organized by Gene Norman.

***   European Tour 1953 Royal Jazz RJD 517 CD
Hampton; Clifford Brown, Art Farmer, Quincy Jones, Walter Williams (*t*); Jimmy Cleveland, George Cooper, Alvin Hayse (*tb*); Gigi Gryce, Anthony Ortega (*as*); Clifford Solomon, Clifford Scott (*ts*); Oscar Estell (*bs*); George Wallington (*p*); Billy Mackel (*g*); Monk Montgomery (*b*); Alan Dawson, Curley Hamner (*d*). 9–12/53.

***   The Complete Paris Session 1953 Vogue 655609 CD
Hampton; Walter Williams (*t*); Alvin Hayse, Jimmy Cleveland (*tb*); Mezz Mezzrow (*cl*); Clifford Scott, Alix Combelle (*ts*); Claude Bolling (*p*); Billy Mackel (*g*); Monk Montgomery (*b*); Curley Hamner (*d*). 2–9/53.

****   Chicago Jazz Concert CBS 21107 CD
Hampton; Billy Brooks, Wallace Davenport, Eddie Mullens, Roy Slaughter (*t*); George Cooper, Al Hayes, Harold Roberts (*tb*); Bobby Playter (*cl, as*); Jay Dennis (*as*); Edwin Frazier, Jay Peters (*ts*); Oscar Estell (*bs*); Dwight Mitchell (*p*); Billy Mackel (*g*); Peter Bradie (*b*); Bill Eddleton (*d*). 7/54.

*** **Lionel Hampton In Vienna Vol. 1** RST 9032925 LP
Hampton; Wallace Davenport, Julius Brooks, Ed Mullens, Nat Adderley (*t*); Harold
Roberts, Al Hayes, George Cooper (*tb*); Robert Plater, Jay Dennis (*as*); Elwyn
Frasier, Jay Peters (*ts*); Joe Evans (*bs*); Dwight Mitchell (*p*); Billy Mackel (*g*); Peter
Badie (*b*); Bill Eddleton, Curley Hamner (*d*); Bertice Reading, Sonny Parker (*v*).
11/54.

*** **Lionel Hampton In Vienna Vol. 2** RST 9032926 LP
As above. 11/54.

**** **Compact Jazz: Lionel Hampton** Verve 833 287-2 CD
Hampton; Buddy DeFranco (*cl*); Stan Getz (*ts*); Oscar Peterson, Teddy Wilson (*p*);
Ray Brown, Red Callender, Leroy Vinnegar (*b*); Gene Krupa, Buddy Rich (*d*).
4/54–8/55.

*** **Live In Paris** Accord 401052 CD
Hampton; Billy Brooks, Dave Gonsalves, Eddie Mullens, Eddie Preston (*t*); Al Hayse,
Walter Morris, Larry Wilson (*tb*); Scoville Brown (*cl, as*); Bobby Plater (*as, f*); Eddie
Chamblee, Ricky Brauer (*ts*); Curtis Lowe (*bs*); Oscar Dennard (*p*); Billy Mackel (*g*);
Peter Badie (*b*); Albert 'June' Gardner (*d*); Robert Mosley (*v*). 1/56.

*** **Paris Session 1956** EMI Jazztime 251274-2 CD
Hampton; Guy Lafitte (*ts*); Claude Bolling (*p*); Billy Mackel (*g*); Paul Rovere (*b*);
Curley Hamner (*d*). 5/56.

*** **Lionel Hampton And His All Stars 1956** Jazz Anthology 550172 CD
Hampton; Ray Copeland (*t*); Jimmy Cleveland (*tb*); Lucky Thompson (*ts*); Oscar
Dennard (*p*); Oscar Pettiford (*b*); Gus Johnson (*d*). 8/56.

The big band which Hampton took to Europe in 1953 was a star-studded one; despite his refusal
to let them moonlight on other dates, Brown and others made records behind his back in Paris
(Hampton filed charges against them when the band returned!). The Royal Jazz CD captures
various concert performances from the tour, and though the quality is variable – and the
material doesn't give the players much chance for anything but flag-waving playing – it gives
some idea of the band's impact. The Vogue CD patches together Hampton and some of his
sidemen with local players, and there are three superb trio performances of 'September In The
Rain', 'Always' and 'I Only Have Eyes For You', as well as the increasingly unhinged 'Real
Crazy', 'More Crazy', 'More And More Crazy' and 'Completely Crazy', which do their best to
live up to the titles. The Chicago concert, though by a less formidable orchestra, might be
Hamp's single best in-person record: there is another marvellous version of 'Stardust', along
with a typically fervent series of up-tempo pieces, with tenorist Jay Peters and altoist Jay Dennis
striking sparks on 'How High The Moon'. The recording is more atmospheric than hi-fi in
quality but it feels like the most authentic record of a Hampton concert. The two RST albums
document a privately recorded Viennese concert and, while it seems like an average night for
Hampton's band, there's plenty of exciting music. Little to choose between the two LPs: the
second winds up with crowd-pleasers that don't translate to record but it also includes three fine
vibes ballads, including a very pretty 'Our Love Is Here To Stay'. The sound, considering it was
taped off the radio (on a 'Stuzzi' tape recorder, the sleeve-notes attest!), is quite good, though
climaxes tend to be noisy.

 Hamp's own playing was at its finest in the 1950s, and the superior recording of the period
allowed the first clear hearing of the nuances of his style. The Compact Jazz sampler offers a
splendid cross-section of his studio work for the label, including several tracks with Oscar
Peterson, one with Stan Getz, two effusive partnerships with Buddy DeFranco and three
magnificent efforts with Teddy Wilson: as capably as Hampton plays, it's Wilson's solos on
'The Man I Love' and 'Moonglow' that one remembers, perfectly shaped and executed
improvisations. The sound on the CD is excellent.

 The big-band session made at the Paris Olympia in 1956 is weighted with one rave-up too
many to be a particularly enjoyable set, and the sound is just adequate; but the later Paris studio
session features the vibraphonist in very fluent form, perhaps too much so for the others: Lafitte
sounds very stodgy and unswinging, and Bolling is blandly supportive. But Hamp's own playing
carries the band.

(*)   **Hamp's Blues LRC CD 7973 CD
Hampton; Joe Romano (ss); Zoot Sims, Sal Nistico (ts); Kenny Barron, Teddy Wilson
(p); George Duvivier, Anthony Jackson, Bob Cranshaw (b); Buddy Rich (d); Ted
Sommer, Stanley Kay (perc). 74

(*)   **Lionel Hampton And His Jazz Giants Black & Blue 59107-2 CD
Hampton; Cat Anderson (t); Eddie Chamblee (as, ts); Paul Moen (ts); Milt Buckner
(org); Billy Mackel (g); Barry Smith (b); Frankie Dunlop (d). 5/77.

***   **As Time Goes By** Sonet SNTCD 779 CD
Hampton; Svend Asmussen (vn); Rune Ofwerman (p); Niels-Henning
Ørsted-Pedersen (b); Ed Thigpen (d). 5/78.

Like many another swing-era giant, Hampton's discography features a gap in the 1960s, at least
so far as currently available material is concerned; we hope that records such as the fine
Newport Uproar from 1967 will appear on CD in due course. Hamp carried on his exhaustive
touring and playing regimen with undiminished energy as he entered his sixties. If he stuck
mostly to his trusted routines with the big bands, occasional record dates in other circumstances
produced entertaining if not enlightening music. *Hamp's Blues*, while it has the anonymous feel
of many of the sessions issued under the LRC label, has three strong quintet tracks with Sims
and Wilson, although the remainder of the record is given over to a bigger group playing modish
early-1970s material, overloaded with percussion. The Black & Blue disc is patchy and sounds
dull when the leader chooses to play drums rather than vibes, but there is some lovely interplay
with Buckner on 'Limehouse Blues' especially, and Anderson gets off a couple of mocking
muted solos. *As Time Goes By* pairs Hampton with the similarly mischievous Asmussen and,
although the material features yet another 'Flying Home' and 'Airmail Special', the band play
with no trace of sloppiness or fatigue. Good sound on both discs.

**   **Live** MCA 33101 CD
Hampton; Joe Newman, Victor Paz (t); Eddie Chamblee (as, ts); Paul Moer (ts); Wild
Bill Davis (p, org); Billy Mackel (g); Barry Smith (b); Frankie Dunlop (d). 78.

**   **Live At The Muzevaal** Timeless SJP 120 CD
As above. 5/78.

**   **All Star Band At Newport '78** Timeless SJP 142 CD
Hampton; Cat Anderson, Jimmie Maxwell, Joe Newman (t, flhn); Doc Cheatham (t);
Eddie Bert, John Gordon, Benny Powell (tb); Earle Warren (cl, as, f); Bob Wilber
(cl); Charles McPherson (as); Arnett Cobb, Paul Moen (ts); Pepper Adams (bs); Ray
Bryant (p); Billy Mackel (g); Chubby Jackson (b); Panama Francis (d). 7/78.

**   **Hamp In Harlem** Timeless SJP 133 CD
Hampton; Joe Newman, Wallace Davenport (t); Curtis Fuller (tb); Steve Slagle (as);
Paul Moen (ts); Paul Jeffrey (bs); Wild Bill Davis (p, org); Billy Mackel (g); Garry
Mazzaroppi (b); Richie Pratt (d). 5/79.

This is a disappointing batch of records. The three albums by smaller bands set only a functional
setting for Hampton and, although there's some interesting material – 'Giant Steps', 'Moment's
Notice' and Joe Henderson's 'No Me Esqueca' on *Muzevaal*, for instance – the arrangements
are stolid and the playing routine. Nor is the recording very good, poor in balance and detail.
It's worse on the *All Star Band* record, though, which is a weak souvenir of what must have been
a fine tribute concert. Panama Francis is too far upfront – his hi-hat sounds louder than the
brass section – and some instrumentalists disappear altogether, while the final 'Flying Home' is
a mess. There are some good moments from the soloists – especially Cheatham's pointed
improvisation on 'Stompin' At The Savoy' – but only hardcore Hampton enthusiasts will get
much out of it.

***   **Made In Japan** Timeless SJP 175 CD
Hampton; Vince Cutro, John Marshall, Barry Ries, Johnny Walker (t); John Gordon,
Chris Gulhaugen, Charles Stephens (tb); Tom Chapin, Ricky Ford, Paul Jeffrey, Yoshi
Malta, Glenn Wilson (saxes); John Colianni (p); Todd Coolman (b); Duffy Jackson (d);
Sam Turner (perc). 6/82.

The opening charge through 'Air Mail Special' makes it clear that this was one of the best of Hampton's latter-day big bands: accurate, attacking section-work, a set of virile soloists and a hard-hitting rhythm section fronted by the useful Colianni. The choice of material spotlights the interesting paradox in the leader's direction – while he seems content at one moment to rely on the most familiar warhorses in his repertoire, uncompromising 'modern' scores such as Ricky Ford's 'Interpretations Opus 5' and James Williams's 'Minor Thesis' sit just as comfortably in the programme, and Hampton takes to them with the same enthusiasm. Ford stands out on his own tune, and there are worthy efforts from Jeffrey, Wilson and others. The sound is big and strong, although the vibes have a less attractive dryness in their timbre.

** **Mostly Blues** Limelight/Decca 820805-2 CD
    Hampton; Bobby Scott (*p*); Joe Beck (*g*); Bob Cranshaw, Anthony Jackson (*b*);
    Grady Tate, Chris Parker (*d*). 3–4/88.

*(*) **Mostly Ballads** Limelight/Decca 820834-2 CD
    Hampton; Lew Soloff (*t*); Harold Danko, John Colianni (*p*); Philip Markowitz,
    Richard Haynes (*ky*); Bill Moring, Milt Hinton (*b*); James Madison, James D. Ford
    (*d*). 9–11/89.

** **Live At The Blue Note** Telarc Jazz CD-83308 CD
    Hampton; Clark Terry (*t, flhn*); Harry Edison (*t*); Al Grey (*tb*); James Moody, Buddy
    Tate (*ts*); Hank Jones (*p*); Milt Hinton (*b*); Grady Tate (*d*). 6/91.

Hampton's recent recordings are, with the best will in the world, echoes of a major talent. Since he isn't the kind of artist to indulge in autumnal reflections, one has to use his earlier records as a yardstick, and these sessions inevitably fall short in energy and invention. At this stage in his career, Hamp is taking things steady and, while no one can blame him for that, one can only recommend these discs to Hampton completists. The *Blues* and *Ballads* collections are both taken at an undemanding tempo throughout, and both – particularly the soporific *Ballads* – sound as if they'd prefer to stay well in the background. The session recorded at New York's Blue Note is an expansive all-star session by musicians whose best work is, frankly, some way behind them: only the seemingly ageless Terry and the exuberant Grey defy the circumstances and muster a sense of commitment. Everyone else, including Hampton, falls back on simple ideas and tempos which give no cause for alarm.

SLIDE HAMPTON (born 1932)
TROMBONE

(*) **World Of Trombones Black Lion 60113 CD
    Hampton; Clifford Adams Jr, Clarence Banks, Curtis Fuller, Earl McIntyre, Douglas
    Purviance, Janice Robinson, Steve Turre, Papo Vasquez (*tb*); Albert Dailey (*p*); Ray
    Drummond (*b*); Leroy Williams (*d*). 1/79.

This kind of band is a logical development for Hampton, who has always loved trombone sound, has developed a rare fluency in his own playing, yet has made his significant mark as an arranger. An arranger's band featuring an all-trombone front line is, not surprisingly, long on texture and short on much excitement or flexibility. The massed horns gliding through 'Round Midnight' and 'Chorale' are impressive, but the record isn't very involving overall.

**** **Roots** Criss Cross Jazz Criss 1015 CD/LP
    Hampton; Clifford Jordan (*ts*); Cedar Walton (*p*); David Williams (*b*); Billy Higgins
    (*d*). 4/85.

A session where everything worked out right. Hampton and Jordan are perfectly paired, the trombonist fleet yet punchy, Jordan putting a hint of dishevelment into otherwise finely tailored improvisations; and Walton has seldom played with as much vitality, yet without surrendering his customary aristocratic touch. Williams and Higgins are asked to play hard throughout the four long titles, and they oblige without flagging. Although a very fast 'Solar' is arguably the highlight, it's a fine record altogether.

HERBIE HANCOCK (born 1940)
PIANO, KEYBOARDS

***   **Takin' Off** Blue Note 746506 CD
Hancock; Freddie Hubbard (*t*); Dexter Gordon (*ts*); Butch Warren (*b*); Billy Higgins
(*d*). 63.

Takin' Off was a pretty remarkable debut by any standards and lifted Hancock straight into the front rank of contemporary jazz pianists. It also established him as a composer with a God-given instinct for the line that separates good taste from kitsch. 'Watermelon Man' alone must have earned Hancock more in BMI copyright returns than most jazz composers see in a whole career.

Gordon – at the peak of his comeback powers – was the perfect collaborator, and the intimacy of the relationship was more than fleetingly reflected in the movie *Round Midnight*, where Hancock played accompanist to Gordon's ageing 'Dale Turner' (CBS 70300).

****   **Maiden Voyage** Blue Note 743392 CD
Hancock; Freddie Hubbard (*t, c*); George Coleman (*ts*); Ron Carter (*b*); Tony
Williams (*d*). ?.

***   **Empyrean Isles** Blue Note 784175 CD
As above, except omit Coleman. 6/64.

Joachim Berendt likens both albums to Debussy's *La Mer* and considers them to contain the best jazz tone-poems since Ellington. That is, as they say, a fairly heavy number to lay on anyone. *Maiden Voyage* is, though, by any standards one of the finest albums in post-war jazz, keeping its freshness through all the dramatic stylistic changes that the music has undergone (not least at Hancock's own nimble hands).

The playing, from a line-up that is effectively the Blue Note house band, is fleet and utterly confident, and the writing and arranging are sophisticated without sounding mannered or contrived. 'Maiden Voyage', the lovely 'Dolphin Dance' and 'Canteloupe Island' from *Empyrean Isles* have become highly successful repertoire pieces. The ensembles are both expansive and uncluttered (and thus far worthy of the Ellington parallel), and there's a fullness to Hancock's unpacking of the harmonic and melodic information that makes Berendt's even grander parallel not completely preposterous.

Maiden Voyage should be in every self-respecting collection. Most will want to find room for the slightly tauter *Empyrean Isles* as well.

(*)   **Speak Like A Child Blue Note 746136 CD
Hancock; Thad Jones (*flhn*); Jerry Dodgion (*af*); Peter Phillips (*btb*); Ron Carter (*b*);
Mickey Roker (*d*). 3/68.

Hancock makes effective use of a trio of unusually pitched winds to create another almost suite-like album that, 'The Sorcerer' apart, conspicuously lacks the melodic spontaneity and immediacy of its predecessors. Not to be overlooked, though.

(*)   **The Best Of Blue Note 791142 CD
Hancock; Freddie Hubbard (*t*); Thad Jones (*flhn*); Peter Phillips (*btb*); Jerry Dodgion
(*af*); George Coleman, Dexter Gordon (*ts*); Ron Carter, Butch Warren (*b*); Billy
Higgins, Mickey Roker, Tony Williams (*d*). 5/62, 6/64, 3/65, 3/68.

'Watermelon Man' from *Takin' Off*, 'Dolphin Dance' and the eponymous 'Maiden Voyage', 'One Finger Snap' and 'Canteloupe Island' from *Empyrean Isles*, and 'Riot' and 'Speak Like A Child'. No complaints about the selection or old-fashioned VFM. Ideal for a tight budget or for the car.

(*)   **Sound-System CBS 26062 CD/LP/MC
Hancock; Wayne Shorter (*lyricon*); Henry Kaiser, Nicky Skopelitis (*g*); Bill Laswell
(*b, syn, elec*); Johnny St Cyr (*turntables*); Will Alexander, Bob Stevens (*elec*); Anton
Fier (*d, perc*); Hamid Drake, Daniel Ponce (*perc*); Aiyb Dieng (*perc*); Jali Foday
Musa Suso (*dusunguni, balafon*); Bernard Fowler, Toshinori Kondo (*v*). 84.

Hancock's mid-1980s work has little of the freshness and impact of the original *Headhunters* album and the best of those that followed (all of which have now mysteriously disappeared into CBS's roomy Dead Platter Office, though not before *Headhunters* became the best-selling jazz album of all time). *Sound-System* has its moments – notably 'Hardrock' and the title-track – but its synthesis of Afro-funk with New Wave gestures and relatively straight jazz voicings never quite gels.

JOHN HANDY (born 1933)
ALTO SAXOPHONE, FLUTE, OTHER REEDS

*(*)   **Where Go The Boats** Inak 861 CD
        Handy; Lee Ritenour (*g*); Nolan Smith (*t*); Hermann Riley (*ts*); Donald Cooke (*ts, b tb*); Bill King (*p, electric p*); Steve Erquiaga (*g*); Ian Underwood (*syn*); Abe Laboriel (*b*); James Leary III (*b*); James Gadson, Eddie Marshall (*d*); Eddie Brown (*perc*); Ashish Kahn (*sarod*).

*   **Handy Dandy Man** Inak 8618 CD
        Handy; Benorce Blackman, Bobby Eli, Steve Erquiaga (*g*); Ron Kersey, Frank Martin (*p*); Henry Davis, Joy Julks (*b*); James Gadson, Scott Morris (*d*); Eddie Brown, Melvin Webb (*perc*); Clyde Jackson, Marti McCall, Julia Tillman Waters, Maxine Willard Waters, Michelle Wiley (*v*); strings.

Not to be confused with the much older alto saxophonist, 'Captain' John Handy, the Texan is one of the few contemporary players who sounded as though he had listened carefully to Eric Dolphy. He shares Dolphy's ability to adapt his multi-instrumentalism to almost any setting without losing its individuality and character and, like Dolphy, he has shown a particular interest in Indian music. A decade ago, Handy was active with the Indo-jazz group Rainbow, where he adapted some of the techniques he had learned with Charles Mingus to a new and striking group format.

Though recent years have seen a partial return to the jazz mainstream, *Where Go The Boats* is rather disappointing. There are still some largely incidental traces of Handy's Indian interests – most obviously in his use of Ashish Kahn's sarod, an upright rhythm guitar, not a percussion instrument as is sometimes assumed – but the harmonically static structures are now overlaid with an awful textural clutter and the more straightforward boogie tracks simply overladen. Even on a piece as sympathetically arranged as Joni Mitchell's 'The Hissing Of Summer Lawns' (returning the compliment she has consistently paid modern jazz), Handy sounds unengaged, and co-leader Ritenour equally fails to impress. The singing might have been dispensed with, too, though the title-track (to words by that old jazzer, Robert Louis Stevenson) is rather beautiful.

Much the same applies to the equally disappointing *Handy Dandy Man*, which features more of the saxophonist's forgettable vocals, with backing singers, strings and a wilderness of guitars. Handy enthusiasts will find themselves hurrying back to *Mingus Ah Um* or one of Handy's own deleted CBS or Impulse albums.

JAKE HANNA (born 1931)
DRUMS

***   **Live At Concord** Concord CCD 6011 CD/MC
        Hanna; Bill Berry (*t*); Carl Fontana (*tb*); Plas Johnson (*as, ts*); Dave McKenna (*p*); Herb Ellis (*g*); Herb Mickman (*b*). 75.

This imperturbable sessionman and late-swing veteran seldom heads up records of his own, but this reissue of one of the earliest Concord albums restores to the catalogue the band he co-led with Carl Fontana. It's what one would expect – simple charts taking a swinging route through a bunch of tunes anyone can whistle – but Hanna's resolute professionalism acts as a tonic on Berry and Johnson, who play with no suspicion of boredom. Full and crisp sound.

ROLAND HANNA (born 1932)
PIANO

***(*)   **Perugia** Freedom 41007 CD/LP
Hanna (*p* solo). 7/74.

***   **Piano Soliloquy** L + R 40003 LP
As above. 6/79.

Sir Roland Hanna, as he should more properly be addressed (he was knighted by the President of Liberia in 1970), is one of the finest living piano improvisers. Though Bud Powell remains the single most important influence on his playing style, he has also taken careful note of Tommy Flanagan and Teddy Wilson. In these superb solo performances, there are also echoes of Tatum's tightly pedalled rapid-fire runs and crisply arpeggiated chords. *Perugia* begins with a superb rendition of Strayhorn's 'Take The "A" Train' and a clever 'I Got It Bad And That Ain't Good', before moving off into original material.

Sound-quality on the 1979 *Soliloquy* is not as good as it might be, and there are a couple of points where the piano sounds inexplicably off (it may be a tape problem), but the music is penetratingly beautiful, notably 'Back In Your Own Loveyard' and the two cuts (one brief) of 'Interloper'.

Anyone unfamiliar with Hanna's work should begin with *Perugia*.

***   **Impressions** Black & Blue 59.753 2 CD
Hanna; George Duvivier or Major Holley (*b*); Alan Dawson (*d*). 7/78, 7/79.

***   **Romanesque** Black Hawk BKH 527 LP
Hanna; George Mraz (*b*).

(*)   **Glove Black Hawk BKH 530 CD/LP
As above, except add Motohiko Hino (*d*).

(*)   **Persia My Dear DIW 8015 CD
Hanna; Richard Davis (*b*); Freddie Waits (*d*). 8/87.

A brilliant accompanist – he worked for Sarah Vaughan from 1960 – Hanna has well-developed instincts for the dynamic of a rhythm section. He's content and able to let his left hand pick out a walking bass-line while the double-bass goes 'out' for a measure or two, or to punch in sharply damped tom-tom accents while the drummer concentrates on ride and splash cymbals, all the time developing a constantly shifting top line.

He sounds most obviously like Flanagan when duetting with the excellent Mraz. Of the two, *Romanesque* is the more interesting album and it's a pity that a CD is not (yet) available; some of the bassist's more intense figures are somewhat lost. The material is largely in Hanna's classicist vein, including a snatch of Tchaikovsky that confounds the old syllogism about all swans being white. There's also a startlingly lovely *Clair De Lune*, without a hint of schmaltz about it.

Surprisingly, perhaps, with Richard Davis, normally the most classically inclined of bassists, Hanna opts to groove. The title, 'Persia My Dear', has a Monkish quality, but the stand-out tracks are 'Summer In Central Park' and 'Manhattan Safari', tributes to the city that has been the Detroit-born Hanna's working home for many years and focus of his long-standing New York Jazz Quartet . . .

***   **Surge** Enja 2094 LP

(*)   **Blues For Sarka Enja 3025 LP

(*)   **Oasis Enja 3083 LP
Hanna; New York Jazz Quartet; Frank Wess (*ts, ss, f, bf*); George Mraz (*b*); Sam Jones (*b*, one track on *Oasis*); Richie Pratt (*d* on *Surge*); Grady Tate (*d* on *Blues For Sarka*); Ben Riley (*d* on *Oasis*). 6/77, 5/78, 2/81.

The original NYJQ, founded in 1974, consisted of Hanna and Wess, with drummer Ben Riley (who reappeared to some effect on the 1981 *Oasis*) and the brilliant Ron Carter. Probably only Mraz or Richard Davis could have replaced him, and even the redoubtable Sam Jones tends to off-balance the unit as a whole, which was one of the best and most underrated on the late-1970s scene.

Hanna's ensemble work, particularly on the excellent *Surge*, is impeccable and, though his solo space is slightly more restricted, he gains in compression what he might have lost in linear development. A wonderfully fluent and thought-provoking performer, he deserves to be better known.

KIP HANRAHAN (born 1937)
COMPOSER, ARRANGER, VOCAL, PERCUSSION

***   **Coup De Tete** American Clave AMCL 1007 CD/LP
Hanrahan; Michael Mantler (*t*); John Clark (*frhn*); David Liebman (*ss*); Chico Freeman (*ts, cl*); Byard Lancaster (*ts, f*); John Stubblefield, Teo Macero (*ts*); George Cartwright (*as, picc, f*); Carlos Ward (*as*); Carla Bley (*p, v*); Orlando DiGirolamo (*acc*); Billy Bang (*vn*); Arto Lindsay, Bern Nix, Fred Frith, George Naha (*g*); Bill Laswell, Cecil McBee (*b*); Anton Fiuer, Victor Lewis, Ignacio Berroa (*d*); Daniel Ponce, Nicky Marrerro, Jerry Gonzalez, Dom Um Romao, Carlos Mestre, Angel Perez (*perc*); Lisa Herman (*v*). 7/79–1/80.

(*)   **Desire Develops An Edge American Clave AMCL 1008/9 LP(2)/CD
Hanrahan; Dave Liebman (*ss*); Carlos Ward (*as*); George Cartwright (*as, f*); Chico Freeman (*ts*); Byard Lancaster (*ts, f*); John Clark (*frhn*); Orlando DiGirolamo (*acc*); Arto Lindsay, George Naha (*g*); Billy Bang (*vn*); Bill Laswell, Jamaaladeen Tacuma (*b*); Ignacio Berroa, Anton Fier (*d*); Daniel Ponce, Jerry Gonzalez, Angel Perez, Nicky Marrero (*perc*); Lisa Herman (*v*). 7–9/82.

***   **Conjure** American Clave AMCL 1006 CD/LP
Olu Dara (*t*); Lester Bowie (*t, v*); David Murray (*ts*); Allen Toussaint (*p, org*); Kenny Kirkland, Peter Scherer (*p*); Taj Mahal (*g, v*); Jean-Paul Bourelly, Elysee Pyronneau, Arto Lindsay (*g*); Steve Swallow, Jamaaladeen Tacuma, Sal Cuevas (*b*); Billy Hart (*d*); Puntilla Orlando Rios, Milton Cardona, Frisner Augustin, Olufemi Claudette Mitchell (*perc*); Ejaye Tracey, Don Jay, Ishmael Reed, Molly Farley, Brenda Norton, Robert Jason (*v*). 8–10/83.

**   **A Few Short Notes From The End Run** American Clave AMCL 1011 EP LP
Hanrahan; Allen Toussaint (*p*); Clem Clempson (*g*); Jack Bruce (*b, v*); Andy Gonzalez, Steve Swallow (*b*); Ignacio Berroa, Anton Fier, Bruce Gary (*d*); Milton Cardona, Manenquito Giovanni Hidalgo, Daniel Ponce, Charles Neville (*perc*). 7/84–10/85.

***   **Cab Calloway Stands In For The Moon** American Clave AMCL 1015 CD/LP
Olu Dara (*t, hca, v*); Eddie Harris, David Murray (*ts, v*); Lennie Pickett (*ts*); Hamiet Bluiett (*bs*); Allen Toussaint (*p*); Don Pullen (*org, v*); Leo Noventelli, Elysee Pyronneau, Johnny Watkins (*g*); Fernando Saunders (*b, v*); Steve Swallow (*b*); Ignacio Berroa (*d*); Milton Cardona, Manenquito Giovanni Hidalgo, Frisner Augustin (*perc*); Diahnne Abbott, Tennessee Reed, Shaunice Harris, Carla Blank, Ishmael Reed, Bobby Womack, Calire Bathe, Robert Jason, Grayson Hugh (*v*). 9/87–3/88.

The main mystery surrounding these records is Kip Hanrahan's own contribution: though credited as chief composer, he seldom plays anything much, sings in a tired, half-speaking voice, and otherwise seems to 'direct' proceedings like some *auteur* of New York's avant-garde jazz and Latin communities. Luckily, formerly involved in record distribution himself, he founded his own record label to get these discs out. *Coup De Tete* has an amazing cast of players, scattered into disparate groupings: the music emerges as a prickly series of enigmatic songs set to Latinesque rhythms, offering a vague recall of *Escalator Over The Hill* – and, suitably enough, Carla Bley and Michael Mantler appear on a couple of tracks – yet energized by outbursts from such performers as Lancaster, Ward and Freeman.

Having set this pattern, Hanrahan's records have followed it ever since, with sundry variations on a dissolute theme. *Desire Develops An Edge* turned the singing duties over to Bruce, but the album (originally released as one LP and one EP) is too long for its own good. *Conjure*, the title of which came to be used for a Hanrahan touring group, found him slipping further into the background, directing music to texts by Ishmael Reed, with the addition of Taj Mahal involving another strain of roots music. In peculiar fusions such as 'Untitled II', played by a quartet of Mahal, Murray, Swallow and Hart, Hanrahan was certainly overseeing a departure, blending a blues set with a jazz one; but despite greater use of the studio, the record again seemed too disparate to create a consistent impression. The brief collection of odds and ends on *A Few Short Notes* was little more than an interlude before *Cab Calloway Stands In For The Moon*, which included the tracks 'The Author Reflects On His 35th Birthday' and 'Beware: Don't Listen To This Song'. At least there was another stellar cast of players. Hanrahan's interest in Latin percussion endures, and all his music musters a rhythmic thrust to carry it over the more pretentious spots. But it usually requires a sympathetic ear.

WILBUR HARDEN (born 1925)
TRUMPET, FLUGELHORN

***(*)   **Countdown** Savoy 650102 CD
      Harden; John Coltrane (*ts*); Tommy Flanagan (*p*); Doug Watkins; Louis Hayes (*d*). 3/58.

***   **Africa** Savoy 650129 CD
      Harden; Curtis Fuller (*tb*); John Coltrane (*ts*); Tommy Flanagan, Howard Williams (*p*); Al Jackson (*b*); Art Jaylor (*d*). 5–6/58.

He made so few jazz recordings that Harden has been perpetually undervalued – it was both good luck and a misfortune that his important records all featured John Coltrane for, while they have kept the music in print, Coltrane's contributions have entirely overshadowed Harden's own. *Africa* also seems to have both Harden and Fuller further back in the sound-mix than the strongly miked Coltrane. The two sessions on that disc are a little overstretched, with a long piece such as 'Gold Coast' failing to sustain interest; yet both here and on the more successful earlier session, Harden's burnished tone (he was one of the first trumpeters to make extensive use of doubling on flugelhorn) and circumspect phrasing help him establish a quiet corner next to the massive sound of the saxophonist. While it's true that Coltrane does provide the principal interest – there are towering blues solos on the two takes of 'Count Down', and similarly bursting solos on 'West 42nd Street' and 'Wells Fargo' – Harden makes a tacit foil in the manner, if not quite the character, of Miles Davis. The dapper Flanagan also finds some fine moments. Solid CD remastering.

BILL HARDMAN (1933–90)
TRUMPET

***(*)   **Jackie's Pal** Original Jazz Classics OJC 1714 LP
      Hardman; Jackie McLean (*as*); Mal Waldron (*p*); Paul Chambers (*b*); Philly Joe Jones (*d*). 8/56.

Hardman's earliest records – he was with McLean in the Jazz Messengers at this time – sound immature because of his raw, unformed tone and jittery delivery. But he was a trumpeter of surprising originality. In a performance here such as 'Dee's Dilemma' his ideas are already moving out of a pure bebop mould and into more varied kinds of expression, a facility he would later find useful in several stints with Blakey and Charles Mingus. On its own terms, this is a tough, absorbing hard bop date with Hardman and Mclean setting a fierce standard. Slightly brittle but otherwise good sound.

***   **Politely** Muse MR 5184 LP
      Hardman; Junior Cook (*ts*); Walter Bishop Jr (*p*); Paul Brown (*b*); Leroy Williams (*d*). 7/81.

This is the only one of three fine Muse albums still in the catalogue, all of them featuring Hardman with his old friend, Junior Cook. The six tunes include a standard, a Tadd Dameron theme and some of Hardman's own attractive writing. By now, his playing had settled into a genial middle age, and if urgency has been replaced by a more casual energy, his solos still move with some flair, and Cook's bustling playing is a fine second. Bishop, Brown and Williams aren't the most exciting of rhythm sections, but they know the right moves.

*** **What's Up** Steeplechase SCS 1254 CD/LP
Hardman; Robin Eubanks (*tb*); Junior Cook (*ts*); Mickey Tucker (*p*); Paul Brown (*b*); Leroy Williams (*d*). 7/89.

Hardman's final album, made not long before his sudden death, is another likeable statement. Eubanks, who can play in almost any kind of modern setting, fits in comfortably alongside Hardman's regular colleagues and, as well as the customary hard bop and blues, there are a couple of sober ballads in 'I Should Care' and 'Like Someone In Love' which, in the circumstances, suggest a poignant farewell to the trumpeter's art. Exceptionally well recorded by the Steeplechase team: Hardman's sound was probably never captured better.

ROY HARGROVE (born 1970)
TRUMPET

*** **Diamond In The Rough** Novus PD 90471 CD
Hargrove; Antonio Hart (*as*); Geoff Keezer, John Hicks (*p*); Charles Fambrough, Scott Colley (*b*); Ralph Peterson Jr, Al Foster (*d*). 12/89.

*** **Public Eye** Novus PD 83113 CD
Hargrove; Antonio Hart (*as*); Stephen Scott (*p*); Christian McBride (*b*); Billy Higgins (*d*). 10/90.

While much of the new jazz of the 1990s has attracted criticism for excessive orthodoxy or mere executive showmanship, it's less often remarked that many of today's younger players exhibit a rhythmic bravado and harmonic lucidity which are a natural step forward from (and within) the tradition. After the sideways evolutionary paths of fusion, the so-called 'neo-classicism' which players like Hargrove represent offers a dramatic refocusing, if not any particular radicalism. Hargrove is a highly gifted trumpeter whose facility and bright, sweet tone bring a sense of dancing fun to his music: there's no strict sobriety in either of these dates, which bubble with good spirits, as controlled as they are. Antonio Hart, a friend and college colleague, is equally impressive, his searingly pure tone placed at the service of a canny understanding of bebop alto. The earlier set, *Diamond In The Rough*, is slightly stronger for a couple of reasons: the two different groups involved create a greater variety, with Peterson's aggression a vigorous spur on the five tracks on which he appears, and the original material is superior – there are three satisfying themes by Geoff Keezer; whereas *Public Eye* relies on Hargrove for four of its tunes, and as yet he isn't a very telling composer. But the *Public Eye* band – all very young, apart from the comparatively ancient Higgins – is still very good, and there's a delightful reading of 'September In The Rain'. Hargrove takes a solo on his own 'Lada' which sums up his appeal: snappy, button-bright, and daring enough to suggest a man who wants to push himself hard.

HARLEM HAMFATS
GROUP

*** **Harlem Hamfats 1936–1939** Document DLP 547 LP
Herb Morand (*t, v*); Odell Rand, Buster Bailey (*cl*); Chris Regell (*ts, cl*); Horace Malcolm, Black Bob Hudson (*p*); Joe McCoy (*g, v*); Charlie McCoy (*g, mand*); Ransom Knowling, John Lindsay (*b*); Pearlis Williams, Fred Flynn (*d*); Lil Allen (*v*). 10/36–9/39.

*** **Keep It Swinging Round And Round** Blues Documents BD 2045 LP
As above, except add Rosetta Howard, Alberta Smith (*v*). 12/36–9/39.

***(*) **Hot Chicago Jazz, Blues & Jive 1936–1937** Folklyric 9039 LP
As above, except omit Howard and Smith. 36–37.

They were led by Herb Morand, whose trumpet playing lent the New Orleans jazz element, and Joe McCoy, who, with his brother Charlie, added a blues feel which made the Hamfats an early fusion band. Their music fell somewhere between the good-time music of Jimmy Blythe's groups and the more sophisticated rhythm and blues which Louis Jordan would pioneer in the following decade. Morand, Rand and whoever else was on hand in the horn section played roistering solos, while Joe McCoy, who did most of the singing, led the rhythm section through the knockabout tunes. Their material was racy rather than risqué, and their best songs have titles like 'The Garbage Man', 'Don't Start No Stuff', 'You Can't Win In Here' and 'What Was You Doing'. Lighthearted though the music is, the group could pull off some fine playing, and Morand's trumpet especially is always worth hearing. These three albums include virtually all their many records, and the Folklyric emerges just ahead through superior transfers – some of the tracks on the other discs are necessarily dubbed from lesser copies of rare originals. But any one offers a very enjoyable 50 minutes or so.

BILLY HARPER (born 1943)
TENOR SAXOPHONE, ALTO SAXOPHONE

***(*)   **Black Saint** Black Saint BSR 0001 CD
    Harper; Virgil Jones (*t*); Joe Bonner (*p*); David Friesen (*b*); Malcolm Pinson (*d*). 7/75.

***   **In Europe** Soul Note SN 1001 CD
    Harper; Everett Hollins (*t*); Fred Hersch (*p*); Louis Spears (*b*); Horace Arnold (*d*); d). 1/79.

(*)   **Destiny Is Yours Steeplechase 1260 CD/LP/MC
    Harper; Eddie Henderson (*t*); Francesca Tanksley (*p*); Clarence Seay (*b*); Newman Baker (*d*). 12/89.

'They told me all the hymns were born / Out of the saxophone,' rock-jazz musician Tim Buckley used to sing. Saxophonist Billy Harper's very personal and distinctive style combines elements of bebop and of John Coltrane's harmony with a passionate interest in gospel music. He creates on saxophone a highly emotional, almost hymnic sound, and his compositions (such as 'Thoroughbred' and 'Priestess', which were recorded by Gil Evans) are similarly rooted in big, strophic patterns.

Harper currently kicks off two important contemporary jazz labels. The eponymous Black Saint album is still perhaps his best and Joe Bonner is the key to its success, constantly building up the fervour. The sound is excellent, a benchmark for the label as a whole. By contrast, the Soul Note is slightly disappointing, but full of good things. The less than generously exposed Everett Hollins, who has also recorded with Archie Shepp, lays joyous top lines over Harper's Old Testament preaching and Latter-Day inflexions. There are three long tracks, of which 'Calvary' is outstanding. The most recent of the sets, recorded a full decade after *In Europe*, *Destiny Is Yours*, is marred by an awkwardly mechanical rhythm section. However, the excellent Henderson (who combines a musical career with work as a physician and a psychiatric practice) combines with Harper in a way occasionally reminiscent of the Ayler brothers' brief but intense performing relationship. Strongly recommended; start with *Black Saint*.

TOM HARRELL (born 1946)
TRUMPET, FLUGELHORN

***(*)   **Play Of Light** Black Hawk BKH 50901 LP/MC
    Harrell; Ricky Ford (*ts*); Bruce Forman (*g*); Albert Dailey (*p*); Eddie Gomez (*b*); Billy Hart (*d*). 2/82.

***   **Moon Alley** Criss Cross 1018 CD/LP
    Harrell; Kenny Garrett (*as, f*); Kenny Barron (*p*); Ray Drummond (*b*); Ralph Peterson (*d*). 12/85.

(*)   **Open Air Steeplechase SCS 1220 CD/LP
    Harrell; Bob Rockwell (*ts*); Hal Galper (*p*); Steve Gilmore (*b*); Bill Goodwin (*d*). 5/86.

***(*)   **Stories** Contemporary C 14043 CD/LP/MC
    Harrell; Bob Berg (*ts*); Niels Lan Doky (*p*); John Scofield (*g*); Ray Drummond (*b*); Billy Hart (*d*). 1/88.

***(*)   **Form** Contemporary C 14059 CD/LP
    Harrell; Joe Lovano (*ts*); Danilo Perez (*p*); Charlie Haden (*b*); Paul Motian (*d*). 4/90.

Though Harrell's output has been notoriously uneven, it is still difficult to pick one outstanding album from the current catalogue. Persistent psychological problems of a more than incidental nature (though why is it that self-doubt assails trumpeters more than almost any other musicians?) have sometimes led him to cultivate an artificial evenness of tone which is rather off-putting. But it's worth listening hard to Harrell, for the tiny shifts of harmony and rhythmic emphasis with which he punctuates the eggshell finish of a solo.

Of the above, only *Open Air* falls more or less flat as an album, though it's worth hearing for the fine lyrical interplay between the trumpeter and Galper. *Play Of Light* is on balance probably the best of the bunch, though the cassette format is to be avoided. Ricky Ford, another patchy performer, is on fine form, and Harrell didn't find a more sympathetic reed man until falling in with the gently bearish Joe Lovano, who may sometimes sound as if he's drowsing, only to show his claws, and who knows where to find honey in the most improbable places. *Form* is an exceptionally fine album. With the anchor of Haden and Motian – not one of your cut-price rhythm sections – Harrell sounds very secure.

The earlier *Moon Alley* has a slightly morose quality in places, but it's probably the most-rounded of the performances, showing off Harrell's technical range to best advantage. On open trumpet, he sounds most like Kenny Dorham, but, alongside Art Farmer and Freddie Hubbard, he is among the best contemporary exponents of the reverse-action flugelhorn, avoiding the 'fat' sound many doubling players slip into. Harrell's natural sound has an almost keening quality that seems to come from somewhere between Clifford Brown and Miles, two men who dealt with self-doubt in their own, very different ways. Teamed with Kenny Garrett – one of the last of Miles's saxophone players – he sounds uncannily like a younger Miles, slightly out of synch with the rapid progressions of 'Scrapple From The Apple'. Berg comes from the same academy, and comes across beefy and strong on *Stories*, with Scofield adding his class to the three strongest tracks. 'Story' is a long minor-key campfire, round which all the soloists tell their tales; Harrell's only solo is strikingly original.

JOE HARRIOT (1928–73)
ALTO SAXOPHONE

(**)   **Swings High Cadillac SGC/MLP 12-150 LP
Harriot; Stuart Hamer (*t*); Pat Smythe (*p*); Coleridge Goode (*b*); Phil Seamen (*d*). 67.

One of the legendary (and ultimately tragic) figures of British jazz, Harriot was a fine, expansive bopper who also took on trad (guesting with Chris Barber, who regularly featured Harriot's 'Revival'), collaborated with violinist/composer John Mayer on the remarkable *Indo-Jazz Fusions*, and experimented with free music. Harriot's *Free Form* album (Jazzland) was almost exactly contemporaneous with Ornette Coleman's *Free Jazz*, and thus can't be said to have been influenced by it. The notion of simultaneous evolution is always a tricky one, but it seems that Harriot derived his ideas (and those on the later *Abstract* (CBS)) quite independently. Where Coleman still relied on a firm pulse, Harriot was looking for a metre-less music, with no identifiably harmonic progression, but which derived something of its underlying philosophy and much of its scorching energy from Afro-Caribbean forms.

Born in Jamaica, Harriot moving to London in his early twenties. Despite initial success, recognition and the artistic opportunities that go with it were only rather intermittent and Harriot died in poverty and isolation. Recorded around the same time as the second and less successful *Indo-Jazz Fusions*, *Swings High* (originally released on Melodisc) is much less adventurous technically. On the other hand, it's immediately clear that 'Polka Dots And Moonbeams' isn't simply a piece of fluff. Harriot's melodic resource was unquenchable, and his hot, driving lines cut through a dismal recording. Perhaps even better is his reading of Dizzy Reece's seldom-covered 'The Rake', on which one can hear a trickledown from the earlier, experimental phase with its suspension of bar-lines and free-for-all harmonics. Here, as throughout the set, Stuart Hamer plays well, though it would have been good to hear Harriot's fellow-West Indian Shake Keane back in to complete the band that made *Free Form*. (Keane moved to the continent before returning to St Vincent, where he served a term as Minister for Culture.) 'Shepherd's Serenade' explores some unfamiliar and challenging tonalities, but is largely defeated by the sound mix.

Technical shortcomings and the absence of a CD will put off some potential purchasers, but this is a rare and valuable opportunity to sample the last British jazz 'boom' and the work of near-mythical figures like Seamen.

BARRY HARRIS (born 1929)
PIANO

***   **At The Jazz Workshop** Original Jazz Classics OJC 208 LP
Harris; Sam Jones (b); Louis Hayes (d). 5/60.

***   **Preminado** Original Jazz Classics OJC 486 CD/LP/MC
Harris; Joe Benjamin (b); Elvin Jones (d). 12/60–1/61.

The career of Barry Harris suggests a self-effacing man, for although he is among the most accomplished and authentic of second-generation bebop pianists, his name has never excited much more than quiet respect among followers of the music. Musicians and students – Harris is a noted teacher – hold him in higher esteem. One of the Detroit school of pianists, which includes Tommy Flanagan and Hank Jones, Harris's style suggests Bud Powell as an original mentor, yet a slowed-down, considered version of Powell's tumultuous manner. Despite the tempos, Harris gets the same dark timbres from the keyboard. He cut several records for Prestige and Riverside in the 1960s, but the above two are the only ones left in the catalogue. The live date from 1960 finds him with the ebullient rhythm section of Cannonball Adderley, and the music is swinging if not especially absorbing. Rather better is the date with Elvin Jones, which features some fiery interplay between piano and drums, although the highlight is probably an uncommonly thoughtful solo reading of 'I Should Care'. Both records have been smartly remastered.

***   **Plays Tadd Dameron** Xanadu 113 LP
Harris; Gene Taylor (b); Leroy Williams (d). 6/75.

***(*)   **Live In Tokyo** Xanadu 130 CD/LP
Harris; Sam Jones (b); Leroy Williams (d). 4/76.

***   **Tokyo 1976** Xanadu 177 LP
As above, but add Charles MacPherson (as), Jimmy Raney (g). 4/76.

***   **Plays Barry Harris** Xanadu 154 CD/LP
Harris; George Duvivier (b); Leroy Williams (d). 1/78.

***   **The Bird Of Red And Gold** Xanadu 213 LP
Harris. 9/89.

Harris's five albums for Xanadu provide a fine portrait of a refined bebop mind. The 1989 session is as fluent and concisely delivered as the earlier discs, and while Harris can suggest a detached, workmanlike inspiration, somewhat akin to that of such fellow bop survivors as Kenny Drew and Duke Jordan, there is an unusual weight and strength to his improvisations on classic bop themes. The Tokyo concert set is arguably the best instance of his work, for here he plays material such as 'Dance Of The Infidels' and 'Un Poco Loco' in as unaffected and fresh a way as it is possible to play them, thirty years after the bop era. Raney and MacPherson arrive for a few tracks on the companion record from the same concerts, but Harris takes the honours.

The Dameron record is nearly as good, but the disc comprising his own themes seems to be cast at a lower voltage, and several of the tunes – as the sleeve-notes suggest – have a discursive quality, although there is a fine reading of 'Father Flanagan'.

****   **Live At Maybeck Recital Hall Vol. 12** Concord CCD 4476 CD/MC
Harris (p solo). 3/90.

Very fine, and a prime example of why this series is working so well. Harris has sometimes sounded too hurried or too desultory on his solo records, but here he finds just the right pace and programme: a leisurely but not indolent stroll through bop and after, with Powell and Parker represented as composers and influences, and a lovely choice of tunes including 'Gone Again', 'Lucky Day' and 'Would You Like To Take A Walk'.

BEAVER HARRIS (1936–92)
DRUMS

(*)   **Beaver Is My Name Timeless SJP 196 LP
Harris; Andrew White (*ts*); Juney Booth (*b*); Francis Haynes (*steel d*). 11/83.

Probably still best-known for his work with Albert Ayler (see *Live In Lörrach And Paris*, hat Art CD 6039), Harris is a powerful drummer in the Sunny Murray mould, who belies his Pennsylvania origins with a style that is pure latter-day New Orleans. As well as Ayler, Harris has played alongside some of the most aggressively forceful jazz players, accompanying Pharoah Sanders, Dexter Gordon, Archie Shepp and Gato Barbieri. In the late 1960s, he co-founded the 360 Degree Experience with trombonist Grachan Moncur III (an association best documented in two currently deleted albums, both recorded in June 1979 – *Safe* [Red VPA 151] and *Beautiful Africa* [Soul Note SN 1002]).

Disappointingly little is currently available, but *Beaver Is My Name* is a more than adequate introduction to Harris's work. It contains an African drum feature that is worth comparing with some of Andrew Cyrille's explorations in the idiom; there's also a version of 'J. C. Moses', a composition also covered on *Safe* and dedicated to Eric Dolphy's and Archie Shepp's one-time drummer.

BILL HARRIS (1916–73)
TROMBONE

****   **Bill Harris And Friends** Original Jazz Classics OJC 083 LP
Harris; Ben Webster (*ts*); Jimmy Rowles (*p*); Red Mitchell (*b*); Stan Levey (*d*). 9/57.

Harris was always among the most distinctive and sometimes among the greatest of jazz trombonists. His style was based firmly on swing-era principles, yet he seemed to look both forward and back – his slurred notes and shouting phrases recalled a primitive jazz period, yet his knowing juxtapositions and almost macabre sense of humour were entirely modern. But he made few appearances on record away from Woody Herman's orchestra and is now a largely forgotten figure. This splendid session should be far more widely known. Both Harris and Webster are in admirable form and make a surprisingly effective partnership: Ben is at his ripest on 'I Surrender, Dear' and 'Where Are You', and Harris stops the show in solo after solo, whether playing short, bemused phrases or barking out high notes. A fairly hilarious reading of 'Just One More Chance' caps everything. The remastering favours the horns, but the sound is warmly effective.

CRAIG HARRIS (born 1954)
TROMBONE

***(*)   **Black Bone** Soul Note 1055 CD
Harris; George Adams (*ts*); Donald Smith (*p*); Fred Hopkins (*b*); Charles Persip (*d*). 1/83.

The trombone is by no means as prominent an instrument in contemporary jazz as it was in the 1940s. Nevertheless players as distinctive as Albert Mangelsdorff and Paul Rutherford in Europe, Ray Anderson, George Lewis and Craig Harris in the United States are keeping the tradition alive.

Harris plays in a strong, highly vocalized style which draws directly on the innovations of former Mingus sideman Jimmy Knepper and on players like Grachan Moncur III and Roswell Rudd who, in reaction to the trombone's recent desuetude, have gone back to the New Orleans and Dixieland traditions in an attempt to restore and revise the instrument's 'natural' idiom.

Adams is the perfect partner in any modern/traditional synthesis and the rhythm section (Smith occasionally excepted) is rock solid on such pieces as 'Conjure Man' and 'Song For Psychedelic Souls', which could almost have been by Roland Kirk. Excellent.

***   **Shelter** JMT 834408 CD/LP

(*)   **Blackout In The Square Root Of Soul JMT 834415 CD/LP
Harris; Tailgater's Tales: Eddie E. J. Allen (*t*); Don Byron (*c, b cl*); Rod Williams (*p*
on *Shelter* only); Clyde Criner (*ky* on *Blackout* only); Jean-Paul Bourelly (*g* on
Blackout only); Anthony Cox (*b*); Pheeroan AkLaff (*d* on *Shelter* only); Ralph Peterson
(*d* on *Blackout* only); Tunde Samuel (*v* on *Shelter* only). 12/86, 11/87.

(*)   **4 Play JMT 834444 CD/LP
Harris; Cold Sweat: Eddie E. J. Allen (*t*); Sam Furnace (*as, bs, f*); George Adams,
Booker T. Williams (*ts*); Brandon Ross, Fred Wells (*g*); Douglas Booth (*ky*); James
Calloway, Melvin Gibbs (*b*); Damon Mendes (*d*); Kweyao Agyapon (*perc*); Andy
Bey, Sekou Sundaita (*v*). 8/90.

The first two are credited to Harris's band, Tailgater's Tales, *4 Play* to a more recent and
somewhat funkier line-up known as Cold Sweat, on which some tracks again feature George
Adams's big, bawling tenor. 'Tailgating' was a trombone style popularized by Kid Ory and
named after the fact that on a New Orleans bandwagon the trombonist had to sit on the back
running-board to accommodate the extension of his slide. No longer limited to mere bass
phrasing, Ory 'filled' round the other horns, often creating long, slithering runs up through the
scale. Harris's latter-day revisions of that style take note of all sorts of other putative influences,
from the European free movement to Fred Wesley's brass arrangements for James Brown.
    Tailgater's Tales are a superb live band who have never quite lived up to promise on disc.
AkLaff's drumming is as good as always, but there's a slight vagueness of conception
(particularly on *Blackout*) which is hard to shake off.

EDDIE HARRIS (born 1934)
TENOR SAX, KEYBOARDS, TRUMPET

***   **The Best Of Eddie Harris** Atlantic 1545-2 CD
Harris; Ray Codrington, Mal Lastie, Joe Newman, Snooky Young, Jimmy Owens (*t*);
Tom McIntosh, Bennie Powell (*tb*); King Curtis, David Newman (*ts*); Heywood
Henry, Seldon Powell (*bs*); Cedar Walton, Jodie Christian, Muhal Richard Abrams
(*p*); Ronald Muldrow (*g*); Ron Carter, Melvin Jackson, Rufus Reid, Charles Rainey,
Louis Spears (*b*); Billy Higgins, Richard Smith, Grady Tate, Billy Hart, William
James (*d*); Joe Wohletz, Ray Barretto (*perc*). 9/65–12/73.

**   **A Tale Of Two Cities** Night VN 3 CD/LP/MC
Harris; Jack Wilson, Rob Schneiderman (*p*); Louis Spears, Herbie Lewis (*b*); Eddie
Marshall, Tootie Heath (*d*). 78–83.

There's nothing amiss with Harris's command of the tenor saxophone. But he spent most of his
first ten years on record experimenting with electric saxes, trumpets played with sax
mouthpieces and other gimmicks, with varying levels of success. The Atlantic compilation is a
useful way of getting to know the extravagant range of Harris's music, including straight-ahead
post-bop in 'Freedom Jazz Dance', pretty pop-jazz with 'The Shadow Of Your Smile', a
growling big-band chart in '1974 Blues' and some exciting if patchy live tracks. 'Is It In', the
title-track of one of Harris's best albums of the period, is a funky display of tricks. But one is
frustrated by the novelty feel of much of the music. With all the albums from the period deleted,
it's the only way to get to hear most of Harris's work from the time. But the Night compilation
of live tracks may offer an equally truthful picture, including a lot of tedious banter with the
audiences as well as some gritty tenor playing. With tighter editing, this would have been a
strong souvenir of what Harris can do on a stage.

**   **People Get Funny ...** Timeless SJP 228 CD/LP
Harris; William S. Henderson III (*ky, perc*); Larry Gales (*b*); Carl Burnett (*d*).

**   **Eddie Who?** Timeless SJP 244 CD/LP
Harris; Ralph Armstrong (*b, v*); Sherman Ferguson (*d, v*). 2/86.

Harris's career got off to such an explosive start in commercial terms – his 'Theme From
Exodus' sold in the millions in 1961 – that the subtext of much of his later work seems to be of
the order of why-can't-I-sell-more? At least on the title-track of *Eddie Who?* he gets some fun
out of it. Both these records suffer from the leader's modest attention-span: on the earlier disc,

he switches from alto to tenor to electric sax to piano to clavinet and then sings a little, and on the 1986 session he works through some strong material with the same diffuse results. Frankly, these are hardly worth bothering with.

***   **There Was A Time (Echo Of Harlem)** Enja 6068 CD
        Harris; Kenny Barron (*p*); Cecil McBee (*b*); Ben Riley (*d*). 5/90.

At last, Harris produces a concentrated tenor-and-rhythm date, and the results are good enough to make you wonder why he wastes his time on the other music. There's a courageous solo reading of 'The Song Is You', but the rest is adeptly supported by the no-nonsense rhythm team and, although Harris's rubbery tone and pinched expressiveness won't be to all tastes, there's no denying his energy.

GENE HARRIS (born 1933)
PIANO

***   **Gene Harris Trio Plus One** Concord CJ/CCD 303/4303 CD/LP/MC
        Harris; Stanley Turrentine (*ts*); Ray Brown (*b*); Mickey Roker (*d*). 11–12/85.

***   **Listen Here!** Concord CJ/CCD 385/4385 CD/LP/MC
        Harris; Ron Eschete (*g*); Ray Brown (*b*); Jeff Hamilton (*d*). 3/89.

After many years with The Three Sounds, Gene Harris has assumed a wider reputation in the last 10 years via his work for Concord, specifically with big bands. These small-band dates are good in their way – simply resolved light blues on the second record, a handful of standards on the first with Turrentine sitting in – but polish and good taste tend to stand in for genuine excitement, without a compensating depth of ideas. Brown, Tucker and Hamilton can certainly cover their tasks here without having to try very hard. Turrentine sounds like his now sensible, middle-aged self on *Trio Plus One*.

***   **Tribute To Count Basie** Concord CCD 4337 CD/MC
        Harris; Jon Faddis, Snooky Young, Conte Candoli, Frank Szabo, Bobby Bryant (*t*);
        Charles Loper, Bill Watrous, Thurman Green, Garnett Brown (*tb*); Bill Reichenbach
        (*btb*); Marshall Royal, Bill Green, Jack Kelso (*as*); Bob Cooper, Plas Johnson (*ts*);
        Jack Nimitz (*bs*); Herb Ellis (*g*); James Leary III, Ray Brown (*b*); Jeff Hamilton (*d*).
        3–6/87.

***   **Live At Town Hall, N.Y.C.** Concord CCD 4397 CD/MC
        Harris; Joe Mosello, Harry Edison, Michael Philip Mossman, Johnny Coles (*t*); Eddie
        Bert, Urbie Green, James Morrison (*tb*); Paul Faulise (*btb*); Jerry Dodgion, Frank
        Wess (*as, f*); James Moody (*ts, cl, f*); Ralph Moore (*ts*); Herb Ellis (*g*); Ray Brown
        (*b*); Jeff Hamilton (*d*); Ernestine Anderson, Ernie Andrews (*v*). 9/89.

***   **World Tour 1990** Concord CCD 4443 CD/MC
        Harris; Johnny Morrison (*t, flhn*); Harry Edison, Joe Mosello, Glenn Drewes (*t*);
        Urbie Green, George Bohannon, Robin Eubanks (*tb*); Paul Faulise (*btb*); Jeff
        Clayton, Jerry Dodgion (*as, f*); Plas Johnson (*ts, f*); Ralph Moore (*ts*); Gary Smulyan
        (*bs*); Kenny Burrell (*g*); Ray Brown (*b*); Harold Jones (*d*). 10/90.

Like the latter-day records of such bandleaders as Basie and Herman, these discs tend to be enjoyable more for their gold-plated class and precision than for any special inventiveness. The first session, credited to Gene Harris and The All Star Big Band, is, in those circumstances, a very truthful kind of tribute to Basie's band, the eight charts offering a fair approximation of the familiar sound. The two discs by the later bands – now known as The Philip Morris Superband – are, we find, rather more entertaining. The *Town Hall* set boasts a vast digital presence, the brass particularly bright and all the soloists well catered for, but some may find its showbiz atmosphere less than ingratiating. Andrews and Anderson have some enjoyable vehicles and there are appropriately outgoing solos from Edison, Ellis, Dodgion and others. *World Tour 1990* reprises the situation, with a somewhat different cast but much the same atmosphere.

***   **At Last** Concord CCD/CJC 4434/434 CD/MC
        Harris; Scott Hamilton (*ts*); Herb Ellis (*g*); Ray Brown (*b*); Harold Jones (*d*). 5/90.

Scott Hamilton's unwavering consistency is somewhat akin to Harris's own, but the tenorman has a slightly greater capacity to surprise and, while the material could have stood a couple of less familiar inclusions, the quintet plays with great gusto. Even 'You Are My Sunshine' is listenable.

KEVIN BRUCE HARRIS
BASS

(*)   **Kevin Harris & Militia TipToe 807102 CD/LP
Harris; Rod Williamson (*ky*); David Gilmore (*g*); Victor Jones (*d, v*); David Silliman (*perc*); D. K. Dyson (*v*). 1/89.

Harris has worked frequently with Cassandra Wilson and Steve Coleman and he sounds well versed in the emerging M-Base genre which their music represents. His own offering is an oddball gathering of ideas and, like so many other such records, is more a sampler of his interests than a coherent set. But there are humorous, clever pieces such as 'Revenge Of The Elephants' along with bruising funk and the kind of dreamy mood pieces which end up as ballad substitutes.

DONALD HARRISON (born 1960)
ALTO SAXOPHONE, SOPRANO SAXOPHONE, BASS CLARINET

**   **Eric Dolphy & Booker Little Remembered** Paddle Wheel K28P 6450 CD/LP

**   **Eric Dolphy & Booker Little Remembered** Paddle Wheel K28P 6476 CD/LP
Harrison; Terence Blanchard (*t*); Mal Waldron (*p*); Richard Davis (*b*); Ed Blackwell (*d*). 10/86.

There's an old Russian proverb about water and vodka: appearance-wise, not much to choose between them . . . but who'd be fobbed off with water? 25 years on, ex-Messengers Harrison and Blanchard rerun the classic Eric Dolphy–Booker Little Five Spot sessions with the original and now grizzled rhythm section. It's a bold and eye-catching stroke, but it doesn't really come off and both men have played more impressively than this. Harrison has always had Dolphy's colours firmly nailed to his mast, and his grasp of the outer harmonics on 'Fire Waltz' and 'Number Eight' is quite impressive, but he lacks Dolphy's astonishing formal accuracy, much as Blanchard lacks Little's fire and bite. No flute. No 'Bee Vamp'. And very little of the tension of the 1961 sets.

On their own terms, though? Well it's difficult, if not redundant, to listen to these two albums entirely on their own terms. Dolphy fans will know every note of Original Jazz Classics OJC 133 (with CD option) and may find they never leave. Reconstructions of this sort are a worthy effort by younger generation players to get in touch with a so far neglected heritage and push it a step further. The results are occasionally refreshing but hardly intoxicating.

***   **For Art's Sake** Candid CCD 79501 CD
Harrison; Marlon Jordan (*t*); Cyrus Chestnut (*p*); Christian McBride (*b*); Carl Allen (*d*). 11/90.

This is a classic instance of a leader being upstaged by his sidemen. Harrison has assembled a powerful young band (bassist McBride was only eighteen) who know the tradition inside out and are ready to chip in with their own contributions. Chestnut's semi-eponymous 'Nut' follows on from the opening 'So What'; the pianist turns in a beautifully sculpted and quite formal solo, prising apart the rhythm (as Allen does in his short, staccato interlude) and laying out the workings to see. Harrison gives most of the opening statements to the nineteen-year-old Jordan, a rawer version of Wynton Marsalis, and really comes into his own only on his featured 'In A Sentimental Mood', which he gradually cranks up from a melancholy ballad into a funky swinger. Offered as 'proof' that 'hard bop is the basis of '90s jazz' *For Art's Sake* does no more than confirm that there are still lots of youngsters around who are willing to take it on. Which isn't quite the same thing.

***   **Indian Blues** Candid CCD 79514 CD
Harrison; Cyrus Chestnut, Mac Rebennack (Dr John) (*p, v*); Phil Bowler (*b, v*); Carl
Allen (*d, v*); Bruce Cox, Howard Smiley Ricks (*perc, v*); Donald Harrison Sr (*v*). 5/91.

A startling mixture of direct hard bop and Fat Tuesday vocal histrionics. Harrison Sr has been
Big Chief of four Mardi Gras Indian 'tribes' and is currently leader of Guardians of the Flame,
who also feature on the album. 'Hiko Hiko' and 'Two-Way-Pocky-Way' are traditional chants
(the former is credited to the legendary Black Johnny); 'Ja-Ki-Mo-Fi-Na-Hay' and the opening
'Hu-Ta-Nay' are credited to the Harrisons. Dr John sings and plays piano on the two originals,
sings on Professor Longhair's 'Big Chief' and plays piano on 'Walkin' Home' and Big Chief
Jolly's 'Shave 'Em Dry'.

If it's part of Harrison's intention to reflect the continuity of the black music tradition, he
does so very convincingly, and there's no sense of a break between the densely rhythmic
N'w'Orleans numbers with their chattering percussion, and the more orthodox 'jazz' tracks. He
plays 'Indian Red' pretty much as a straight alto feature, but then adds a rhythmic line to the
prototypical standard 'Cherokee' that gives it an entirely new dimension. His own 'Indian
Blues' and 'Uptown Ruler' reflect a decision in 1989 to 'mask Indian' once again and joined the
feathered throngs that march on Mardi Gras. In touching his roots, he's brought them
something new as well.

ALFRED '23' HARTH
TENOR SAXOPHONE, ALTO SAXOPHONE, SOPRANO SAXOPHONE, BASS CLARINET

**   **This Earth!** ECM 1264 LP
Harth; Paul Bley (*p*); Barre Phillips (*b*); Trilok Gurtu (*perc*); Maggie Nicols (*v*). 5/83.

Harth acquired his curious numerical nickname from his alleged ability to play 23 instruments.
It's tempting to suggest that he might have been better employed cutting back to one or two.
Though he is capable of quite powerful lines on all his horns, he seems most at ease on the alto
saxophone; when his tone decides to settle, he sounds almost like a cross between American
avant-gardists like Oliver Lake and the British experimenters of the 1970s, Elton Dean, the
now sadly inactive Mike Osborne, and Trevor Watts.

Given the line-up, this is a terribly disappointing album. There are wonderful moments from
Bley and Phillips, and from Nicols's marvellously fluting voice (which, when unembarrassed by
Vicky Scrivener's awful lyrics, acts as a further horn) but these come as isolated glimpses only.
Harth's cosmic-scientist ideas and titles – 'Relation To Light Colour And Feeling', 'Female Is
The Sun', 'Transformate Transcend Tones And Images' – sound quaintly dated, like pamphlets
from a Rudolf Steiner bookshop, and the playing is all curiously diffuse. Enthusiasts only.

*(*)   **Gestalt Et Jive** Moers Music 02038 LP
Harth; Steve Beresford (*ky, elec, tb, pkt-t, g*); Ferdinand Richard (*b*); Uwe Schmitt (*d,
perc*); Anton Fier (*d*). 1/85.

There are moments of (almost incidental) beauty dotted amongst these miniatures, but for the
most part it's archly sophomoric stuff from a group of musicians demonstrably capable of much
better.

(*)   **Red Art Creative Works CW 1004 LP
Harth; Mani Neumeier (*d, perc*).

(*)   **Anything Goes Creative Works CW 1005 LP
Harth (*reeds, ky, v* solo).

Anything Goes strongly suggests that Harth's main creative problem has been finding
like-minded musicians prepared to join him in his sometimes enigmatic explorations. Where the
equally multi-talented Gunter Hampel is able to communicate his intentions to an admittedly
circumscribed but steadily changing group of interpreters, Harth's ideas often seem to be
short-circuited by his fellow-players.

Here he has the luxury of a completely blank page; the results, though still by no means
crystal-clear in conception or execution, have a satisfying consistency quite lacking in most of
his other work. On *Red Art* he seems to use percussionist Neumeier as an extension of his own

idiolect. It works rather well. Together, these are perhaps the best introduction to Harth's unusual sound-world.

** **Gestalt Et Jive** Creative Works CW 1006/7 2LP
Harth; Ferdinand Richard (*b, 6-string b*); Peter Hollinger (*d, etc.*). 10/86.

Confusingly titled, given the above, but a far preferable product in every respect. The album appears to be in part at least a subversion of the conventional horn–bass–drums jazz trio. There are fleeting echoes of standards and repertoire pieces, but nothing to get a reliable hold of. Intriguing, but slightly frustrating – and certainly too long.

(***) **Plan Eden** Creative Works CW 1008 LP
Harth; Hans Antiker (*tb*); John Zorn (*as*); Lindsay Cooper (*bsn, sno s*); Gunther Muller (*d, zither, elec*); Andreas Bosshart (*elec*); Phil Minton (*v*). 6/86, 2/87.

More than slightly frustrating. The best of this – such as the saxophone duets with Zorn and Cooper – are quite excellent, and 'Aleister And Alice' demonstrates that Harth does know what to do with voices when they are as adaptable as Minton's. The rest, though, consisting of solo tenor saxophone essays, merits nothing more than a testy 'See me' from the spirit of Adolphe Sax.

MICHAEL HASHIM
ALTO AND SOPRANO SAX

**** **Lotus Blossom** Stash ST-CD-533 CD
Hashim; Mike LeDonne (*p*); Dennis Irwin (*b*); Kenny Washington (*d*). 90.

*** **A Blue Streak** Stash ST-CD-546 CD
Hashim; Mike LeDonne (*org*); Peter Bernstein (*g*); Kenny Washington (*d*). 91.

Hashim is that rarity, a passionate, humorous and quick-witted repertory player. His alto recalls Hodges, Carter and Willie Smith without placing himself entirely in anybody's debt, and his sound and phrasing have a mercurial, breezy assurance. From the opening measures of 'Grievin'', from *Lotus Blossom*, which is entirely dedicated to Billy Strayhorn themes, it's clear that the material is at Hashim's service rather than the other way around. He has often worked with the Widespread Depression/Jazz Orchestra and sounds entirely at home with pre-bop material: the excellently produced first record captures his rich timbre with eloquent clarity, and his quartet – especially the oustanding Washington – shadow him with exact aplomb. Since *Lotus Blossom* is so consistently delivered, honouring Strayhorn's familiar pieces and refurbishing such lesser-known ones as 'Juniflip' and 'Sunset And The Mockingbird', it's easily the superior record. *A Blue Streak* is slightly disappointing, with Hashim turning to more bop-directed music on some tracks: Le Donne's switch to organ, on which he doesn't have much to say, is another drawback, as is the somewhat bass-heavy sound. But tracks such as a fine soprano reading of 'Brother, Can You Spare A Dime?' are still substantial.

ÅKE 'STAN' HASSELGÅRD (1922–48)
CLARINET

*** **Åke 'Stan' Hasselgård 1945–1948** Dragon DRLP 25 LP
Hasselgård; Rolf Ericson, Gösta Törner (*t*); Sven Hedberg (*tb*); Kjeld Bonfils, Bob Laine, Barbara Carroll (*p*); Sven Stiberg, Folke Eriksson, Chuck Wayne (*g*); Thore Jederby, Simon Brehm, Clyde Lombardi (*b*); Pedro Biker, Bertil Fryhlmark, Mel Zelnick (*d*); Britta Mårtensson (*v*). 10/45–11/48.

*** **Jammin' At Jubilee** Dragon DRLP 29 LP
Hasselgård; Billy Eckstine (*vtb, v*); Benny Goodman (*cl*); Wardell Gray (*ts*); Teddy Wilson, Arnold Ross, Mary Lou Williams, Jimmy Rowles, Dodo Marmarosa (*p*); Barney Kessel, Al Hendrickson, Billy Bauer (*g*); Harry Babasin, Arnold Fishkind, Clyde Lombardi (*b*); Jackie Mills, Frank Bode, Mel Zelnick (*d*). 1–7/48.

***   **At Click 1948** Dragon DRCD 183 CD
Hasselgård; Benny Goodman (*cl*); Wardell Gray (*ts*); Teddy Wilson (*p*); Billy Bauer
(*g*); Arnold Fishkind (*b*); Mel Zelnick (*d*). 5–6/48.

***(*)   **The Permanent Hasselgård** Phontastic NCD 8802 CD
As above three discs, except add Tyree Glenn (*tb*), Red Norvo, Allen Johansson (*vib*),
Thore Swanerud (*p, vib*), Hasse Eriksson, Lyman Gandee (*p*), Sten Carlberg (*g*),
Rollo Garberg, Jud De Naut (*b*), Uffe Baadh, Nick Fatool (*d*); Louis Tobin (*v*).
10/45–11/48.

Stan Hasselgård left only a handful of legitimate recordings at the time of his death – he was
killed in a car accident while driving to California – but the diligence of Lars Westin of Dragon
Records in Sweden has ensured that his legacy has been enriched by many airshots and private
records. There is something like five CD's worth of material to be issued. So far, Dragon has
issued four LPs which are now disappearing from print, but the new *At Click* CD begins a
programme of CD transfers, and the Phontastic release covers the broad spectrum of the
clarinettist's work.

His precocious talent and early death have made Hasselgård something of a folk hero in
Swedish jazz circles, and the evidence of the surviving tracks is that he was an outstanding
player. He worshipped Goodman, and never tried to evade comparisons with his guru, but the
traces of bebop in his playing hint at a stylistic truce which he never had the opportunity to
develop further. The two remaining Dragon LPs chronicle early work in Sweden and tracks he
made on moving to the US in 1947. The Swedish records feature another young talent in Rolf
Ericson, as well as the veteran trumpeter Törner and the surprising pianist Bonfils, and the
music is smart, energetic small-group swing. But the American performances on DRLP 29 are
altogether more imposing, including an all-star band with Gray and Marmarosa, airshots with
Arnold Ross and Billy Eckstine (mostly on valve trombone), a quintet with Rowles and Kessel
and some of the Goodman septet recordings which are comprehensively covered on *At Click*,
where Hasselgård worked with his idol in a two-week engagement. The contrast between the
two players isn't as interesting as the similarity: often it's quite hard to tell them apart, and
whatever Hasselgård is reputed to have taught Goodman about bop isn't clear from this music.
In fact, Hasselgård often gets short shrift in these tracks, with Goodman getting the lion's share
of the solos, and Gray and Wilson taking their share. But it's surprising to hear Goodman
playing on the likes of 'Mary's Idea' and even 'Donna Lee'. The sound on all four discs varies
from clean and clear to quite rough, but the meticulous remastering has done the best possible
job, and they are scholarly and engaging records.

Anyone wanting a one-disc primer on Hasselgård, though, is directed to the Phontastic
compilation, which includes many of the tracks on the Dragon releases as well as four fine
quintet tracks led by the clarinettist (in excellent sound), a feature for Tyree Glenn and a sextet
track with Red Norvo. A generously filled and respectful memorial to a fine player.

FRITZ HAUSER
DRUMS, PERCUSSION

***(*)   **Zwei** hat Art 6010 CD
Hauser; duos with Christy Doran (*g*); Stephan Grieder (*p*); Rob Kloet (*perc*); Rene
Krebs (*stereo flhn, seashell*); Lauren Newton (*v*); Pauline Oliveros (*acc, elec
environment*). 12/87.

***   **Die Trommel/Die Welle** hat Art 6017 CD
Hauser (*d* solo) and with: Michel Erni, Roli Fischer, Barbara Frey, Martin Andre
Grutter, Fran Lorkovic, Cyril Lutzelschwab, Lukas Rohner, Severin Steinhauser, Hans
Ulrich, Ruud Weiner (*perc*). 11/87, 11/88.

***   **Solodrumming** hat Art 6023 2CD
Hauser (*d* solo). 4/85.

(*)   **The Mirror hat Art 6037 CD
Hauser; Stephan Grieder (*org*). 3/89.

Percussion-only and even percussion-led albums often make excessive demands on the listener. There are probably only a handful of drummer-percussionists active today – Andrew Cyrille, Edward Vesala, John Bergamo, Gerry Hemingway, Tony Oxley – who really are worth listening to on their own. Hauser is certainly one of that number.

His music is unapologetically abstract, but it is by no means undynamic. 'Dog's Night', his long duo with fellow-percussionist Rob Kloet on *Zwei*, is one of the most exciting improvisatory performances of recent years. Indeed, *Zwei* as a whole can't be recommended too strongly. Hauser has selected his partners with care. Guitarist Doran and flugelhorn-player Krebs are in places a little too light in touch, but in general all the participants are wonderfully complementary. Pauline Oliveros – along with the Australian Eric Gross the most significant composer of accordion music in the West – is at her very best on 'La Chambre Obscure', playing 'in' an electro-acoustic environment devised by Peter Ward.

The most conventional structures are those devised with pianist Grieder, whose church organ-figures on *The Mirror* would be more compelling had they been more sympathetically recorded. Otherwise an excellent album.

Hauser's solo work is uniquely impressive. The massive double CD *Solodrumming* is an exhausting experience but affords the best available representation of his technical range. Those unfamiliar with his work might do better to start with '*Die Trommel*' and its remarkable percussion-choir partner, '*Die Welle*' – 'The Drum' and 'The Wave'. The latter features tympani, cymbals and tam-tam in an extraordinary exploration of resonance that equals the best percussion pieces by 'serious' composers like Xenakis.

Almost needless to repeat, Hauser comes highly recommended, and shouldn't on any account be missed.

HAMPTON HAWES (1928–77)
PIANO

***   **The Challenge** Storyville SLP 1013 LP
       Hawes (*p* solo). 5/68.

Hampton Hawes's *Raise Up Off Me* is one of the most moving and authentic autobiographical documents ever written by a jazz musician, full of valuable insights into the bebop movement. In it he briefly mentions *The Challenge*, his first and only solo album, recorded in Tokyo as a result of a Japanese producer's enthusiasm for Hawes's music.

Towards the end of his life he looked back at the album and said, 'There's a space between me and the piano.' If it's audible at all to us, it's only in the unusual control with which the normally emotive Hawes deploys carefully contrapuntal left-hand lines, doubtless compen-sating for the absence of bass and drums.

With the exception of a finely swinging 'Bag's Groove', where he digs deep into blues tonalities, the pieces are generally short, sometimes even enigmatic. '(My Darling) Clementine' doesn't really work at all but, as a methodological sketch, it reveals a good deal about Hawes's harmonic instincts and his fine structural intelligence.

Coloured by his recent enthusiasm for Bill Evans and foreshadowing his 1970s flirtation with electricity, it's not the best album in the pianist's output, but it remains the only one on which he is heard unaccompanied and, considerable intrinsic merit apart, its main importance lies in that.

****   **The Trio** Original Jazz Classics OJC 316 CD/LP
       Hawes; Red Mitchell (*b*); Chuck Thompson (*d*). 6/55.

****   **The Trio** Original Jazz Classics OJC 318 CD/LP
       As above. 12/55.

***(*)   **Everybody Likes** Original Jazz Classics OJC 421 CD/LP/MC
       As above. 1/56.

***(*)   **The Green Leaves Of Summer** Original Jazz Classics OJC 476 CD/LP/MC
       Hawes; Monk Montgomery (*b*); Steve Ellington (*d*). 2/64.

(*)   **Here And Now Original Jazz Classics OJC 178 CD/LP
       Hawes; Chuck Israels (*b*); Donald Bailey (*d*). 5/65.

***   **I'm All Smiles** Contemporary C 7631 LP
         Hawes; Red Mitchell (*b*); Donald Bailey (*d*). 4/66.

***   **The Seance** Original Jazz Classics OJC 455 CD/LP/MC
         As above. 5/66.

(*)   **Blues For Bud Black Lion BLCD 760126 CD
         Hawes; Jimmy Woode (*b*); Art Taylor (*d*). 3/68.

(*)   **Live In Montreux, '71 Fresh Sound FSR 133 CD
         Hawes; Henry Franklin (*b*); Michael Carvin (*d*). 6/71.

(*)   **Plays Movie Musicals Fresh Sound FSR 65 CD
         Hawes; Bobby West (*b*); Larry Bunker (*d*); strings.

(*)   **Live At The Jazz Showcase, Chicago: Volume 1 Enja 3099 LP

(*)   **Live At The Jazz Showcase, Chicago: Volume 2 Enja 6028 CD/LP
         Hawes; Cecil McBee (*b*); Roy Haynes (*d*). 6/73.

(*)   **At The Piano Contemporary C 7637 LP
         Hawes; Ray Brown (*b*); Shelly Manne (*d*). 8/76.

If the trio was Hawes's natural territory, there are few better places to explore it than on the first three of these, which represent a reorganization of material from his first LP as leader and from subsequent Contemporary sessions with the same line-up. Brilliant up-tempo performances from an almost telepathic group who show a fine sensitivity in ballad playing as well.

The best of the rest are undoubtedly the sessions recorded, again with Mitchell, but with the slightly tougher Donald Bailey on the drum stool, in 1966, when the pianist had been back in circulation only a couple of years; the slightly earlier *Green Leaves Of Summer*, with Wes Montgomery's elder brother on bass, and *Here And Now* still betray occasional shades of the prison-house (Hawes spent the early 1960s in jail). On *The Seance*, 'Oleo' almost perfectly reconstructs the bridge between Parker's bebop and Miles Davis's cool, modal explorations; 'For Heaven's Sake' and 'My Romance' are classic performances.

Though he had always explored unusual melodic configurations and unfamiliar repertoire, later in his career Hawes tried to compensate for the roughening edges of his once instinctive lyricism by delving into some slightly questionable material; the forgettable *Plays Movie Musicals* was fortunately an aberration, the strings quietly murdering Hawes's songful lines. 'Killing Me Softly With His Song' on the late *At The Piano* is one of his poorest released performances. On the other hand, the first version of 'The Shadow Of Your Smile' on *I'm All Smiles* has a tact and discipline lacking in the later Chicago recording on Enja (Volume 2) which is dangerously schmaltzy. Why only the poorer of the two sets, with Hawes drifting into late Chet Baker mode, should have been transferred to CD is slightly mysterious, though it's useful and overdue recognition in that format. Unfortunately, the Fresh Sound performances don't match up to their sound-quality, verbose, over-long and strangely crude in execution, but the Black Lion sets suddenly lift his remarkable and very 'classical' touch back up into focus; it's ironic that a tribute album to Bud Powell should be the clearest testimony to how *little* Hawes was influenced by Powell's approach and seemed instead to anticipate – most noticeably on *The Trio* – some of Horace Silver's 'funky' blues approach.

***   **The East/West Controversy** Xanadu 104 LP
         Hawes; Harper Cosby (*b*); Lawrence Marable (*d*). 9/51.

**   **Piano: East/West** Original Jazz Classics OJC 1705 LP
         Hawes; Larry Bunker (*vib*); Clarence Jones (*b*); Lawrence Marable (*d*). 12/52.

***(*)   **All Night Session: Volume 1** Original Jazz Classics OJC 638 CD/LP/MC

***(*)   **All Night Session: Volume 2** Original Jazz Classics OJC 639 CD/LP/MC

***   **All Night Session: Volume 3** Original Jazz Classics OJC 640 CD/LP/MC
         Hawes; Jim Hall (*g*); Red Mitchell (*b*); Bruz Freeman (*d*). 11/56.

(*)   **Four! Original Jazz Classics OJC 165 CD/LP
         Hawes; Barney Kessel (*g*); Red Mitchell (*b*); Shelly Manne (*d*). 1/58.

Hawes's session of the night of 12/13 November 1956 remains one of his best. The material was mainly familiar bop fare – 'Groovin' High', 'I'll Remember April', 'Woody'n'You' – but cuts like 'Hampton's Pulpit' are a reminder of the pianist's church background and the curious underswell of gospel, Bach and Rachmaninov that keeps freshening the top-waters of his harmony. Hall is magnificent, comparing very favourably with Barney Kessel's more conventional approach on *Four!*. The combination of Mitchell (whose legato soloing was the most immediate influence on Scott LaFaro, below) with Manne was inspired, and it's no disgrace to Bruz Freeman that his Max Roach-influenced approach doesn't compare.

Piano: East/West was a double-header album shared with Freddie Redd, much as the similarly titled and conceived *East/West Controversy* was with bassist Paul Chambers, who represents the opposite seaboard on side two. Though Hawes gets off good solos on 'Hamp's Paws' and, again, 'I'll Remember April', the combination with vibraphonist Bunker isn't all that successful. The 1951 trio with Cosby and Marable is mostly Parker-based and much more horn-like than usual, even on 'Bud's Blues', a Sonny Stitt theme written in tribute to Bud Powell. One reason, perhaps, is the rather echo-y sound, which introduces a 'chime' to Hamp's rapid right-hand lines.

*** **Live At Memory Lane** Fresh Sound FSR CD 406
Hawes; Harry Edison (*t*); Sonny Criss (*as*); Teddy Edwards (*ts*); Leroy Vinnegar (*b*); Bobby Thompson (*d*); Joe Turner (*v*). 70.

Jazz has never been well served by television on either side of the Atlantic, but this record stands as reminder of what could be done. Hawes and his group were captured at a beat-up old club in Los Angeles as part of a series of short films made by Jack Lewerke. The combination of Criss and Hawes is irresistible (see also the saxophonist's entry) and their blues interpretations are impeccable. The entry of Joe Turner dilutes the musical content a little, but the audience love it and the sound of cheering must have attracted Teddy Edwards, who sits in for a final extended blues jam on which only Edison is rather disappointing. Good, clubby sound.

COLEMAN HAWKINS (1901–69)
TENOR SAXOPHONE, VOCAL

**** **Coleman Hawkins 1929–1934** Classics 587 CD
Hawkins; Henry Allen, Jack Purvis (*t, v*); Russell Smith, Bobby Stark (*t*); Muggsy Spanier (*c*); Glenn Miller, J. C. Higginbotham, Claude Jones, Dickie Wells (*tb*); Russell Procope, Hilton Jefferson, Jimmy Dorsey (*cl, as*); Pee Wee Russell (*cl*); Adrian Rollini (*bsx*); Red McKenzie (*comb, v*); Frank Froeba, Jack Russin, Horace Henderson, Buck Washington (*p*); Bernard Addison, Jack Bland, Will Johnson (*g*); Pops Foster, Al Morgan, John Kirby (*b*); Gene Krupa, Charles Kegley, Josh Billings, Walter Johnson (*d*). 11/29–3/34.

The first great role model for all saxophonists began recording in 1922, but compilations of his earlier work usually start with his European sojourn in 1934. This valuable cross-section of the preceding five years shows Hawkins reaching an almost sudden maturity. He was taking solos with Fletcher Henderson in 1923, and was already recognizably Hawkins, but the big sound and freewheeling rhythmic command wasn't really evident until later. By 1929 he was one of the star soloists in the Henderson band – which he remained faithful to for over ten years – and the blazing improvisation on the first track here, 'Hello Lola' by Red McKenzie's Mound City Blue Blowers, indicates the extent of his confidence. But he still sounds a little tied to the underlying beat, and it isn't until the octet session of September 1933 that Hawkins establishes the gliding but muscular manner of his 1930s music. The ensuing Horace Henderson date of October 1933 has a feast of great Hawkins, culminating in the astonishing extended solo on 'I've Got To Sing A Torch Song', with its baleful low honks and daring manipulation of the time. Three final duets with Buck Washington round out the disc, but an earlier session under the leadership of the trumpeter Jack Purvis must also be mentioned: in a curious line-up including Adrian Rollini and J. C. Higginbotham, Hawkins plays a dark, serious role. Fine transfers throughout.

*** **The Hawk In Europe** ASV AJA 5054 CD
Hawkins; Arthur Briggs, Noel Chiboust, Pierre Allier, Jack Bulterman, George van
Helvoirt (*t*); Benny Carter (*t, as*); Guy Paquinet, Marcel Thielemans, George
Chisholm (*tb*); Andre Ekyan, Charles Lisee, Alix Combelle, Wim Poppink, Sal Doof,
Andre van den Ouderaa, Jimmy Williams (*saxes*); Stanley Black, Stephane Grappelli,
Nico de Rooy, Freddy Johnson (*p*); Albert Harris, Django Reinhardt, Jacques Pet,
Frits Reinders, Ray Webb (*g*); Tiny Winters, Len Harrison, Eugene d'Hellemmes,
Toon Diepenbroek (*b*); Maurice Chaillou, Kees Kranenburg, Tommy Benford, Robert
Montmarche (*d*). 11/34–5/37.

***(*) **Coleman Hawkins 1934–1937** Classics 602 CD
As above, except add Henk Hinrichs (*t*), Ernst Hoellerhagen (*cl, as*), Hugo Peritz,
Omer de Cock (*ts*), Ernest Berner, Theo Uden Masman (*p*), Billy Toffel (*g*), James
Gobalet (*b*), Benny Peritz (*d*), Annie de Reuver (*v*), omit Carter, Williams, Johnson
and Webb. 11/34–37.

Hawkins arrived in England in March 1934 and stayed in the old world for five years. Most of
his records from the period have him as featured soloist with otherwise strictly directed
orchestras, and while this might have been occasionally dicomforting – the routines on such as
'What Harlem Is To Me' with the Dutch group The Ramblers aren't much better than a suave
variation on Armstrong's contemporary struggles – Hawkins was polishing a sophisticated,
rhapsodic style into something as powerful as his more aggressive earlier manner. Two sessions
with Benny Carter, including the four tumultuous titles made by the All Star Jam Band, are
included on the ASV set, while the Classics sticks to the chronology; but the ASV sound is
much more mixed. Classics begin with four titles made in London with Stanley Black at the
piano, continue with dates in The Hague, Paris and Laren, and add the little-known Zurich
session which finds Hawkins singing on the fairly awful 'Love Cries'! A spirited 'Tiger Rag'
makes amends, and there's a curiosity in an unidentified acetate (in very poor sound) to close
the disc. 'I Wish I Were Twins', 'What A Difference A Day Made' and 'Netcha's Dream' are
three examples of the lush but shrewdly handled and often risky solos which Hawkins creates
on an instrument which had still only recently come of age.

**** **Coleman Hawkins 1937–1939** Classics 613 CD
Hawkins; Jack Bulterman, George van Helvoirt (*t*); Benny Carter (*t, as*); Maurice
Thielmans (*tb*); Wim Poppink (*cl, as*); Alix Combelle, Andre van der Ouderaa (*cl, ts*);
Sal Doof (*as*); Nico de Rooy, Stéphane Grappelli, Freddy Johnson (*p*); Fritz Reinders,
Django Reinhardt (*g*); Jack Pet, Eugene d'Hellemmes (*b*); Kees Kranenburg, Tommy
Benford, Maurice van Cleef (*d*). 4/37–6/38.

The last of Hawk's European recordings. The All Star Jam Band titles turn up here again, as
well as a further session with The Ramblers, but otherwise the main interest is in ten titles with
just Freddy Johnson (and Maurice van Cleef on the final six). 'Lamentation', 'Devotion' and
'Star Dust' are masterclasses in horn technique, Hawkins exploring the registers and feeling
through the harmonies with complete control. The sound is good, although the engineers aren't
bothered about surface hiss. Vinyl followers should be aware of *Dutch Treat* (Xanadu 189, LP),
which includes all the tracks with Johnson and van Cleef (including two alternative takes) and
the 1936 Zurich session, in respectable transfers.

***(*) **Coleman Hawkins 1939–1940** Classics 634 CD
Hawkins; Tommy Lindsay, Joe Guy, Tommy Stevenson, Nelson Bryant (*t*); Benny
Carter (*t, as*); Earl Hardy, J. C. Higginbotham, William Cato, Sandy Williams, Claude
Jones (*tb*); Danny Polo (*cl*); Eustis Moore, Jackie Fields, Ernie Powell (*as*); Kermit
Scott (*ts*); Gene Rodgers, Joe Sullivan (*p*); Ulysses Livingstone (*g, v*); Lawrence Lucie,
Bernard Addison, Gene Fields (*g*); William Oscar Smith, Artie Shapiro, Johnny
Williams, Billy Taylor (*b*); Arthur Herbert, George Wetling, Walter Johnson, Sid
Catlett, J. C. Heard (*d*); Thelma Carpenter, Jeanne Burns, Joe Turner, Gladys
Madden (*v*). 10/39–8/40.

**** **Body And Soul** RCSA Bluebird ND 85717 CD/LP/MC
As above, except omit Bryant, Cato, Williams, Powell, Scott, Fields, Taylor, Turner,
Madden and Burns, add Fats Navarro, Jimmy Nottingham, Bernie Glow, Lou Oles,
Ernie Royal, Charlie Shavers, Nick Travis (*t*); J. J. Johnson, Urbie Green, Jack

Satterfield, Fred Ohms, Tom Mitchell, Chauncey Walsh (*tb*); Jimmy Buffington (*frhn*); Budd Johnson, Hal McKusick, Sam Marowitz (*as*); Zoot Sims, Al Cohn (*ts*); Marion De Veta, Sol Schlinger (*bs*); Phil Bodner Ob); Julius Baker, Sid Jekowsky (*f*); Hank Jones (*p*); Marty Wilson (*vib*); Chuck Wayne, Barry Galbraith (*g*); Jack Lesberg, Milt Hinton (*b*); Max Roach, Osie Johnson (*d*). 10/39–1/56.

**** **April In Paris** RCA Bluebird ND 90636 CD
As above. 10/39–1/56.

Hawkins didn't exactly return to the U.S. in triumph, but his eminence was almost immediately reestablished with the astounding 'Body And Soul', which still sounds like the most spontaneously perfect of all jazz records. Fitted into the session as an afterthought (they had already cut 12 previous takes of 'Fine Dinner' and eight of 'Meet Doctor Foo'), this one-take, two-chorus improvisation is so completely realized, every note meaningful, the tempo ideal, the rhapsodic swing irresistible, and the sense of rising drama sustained to the final coda, that it still has the capacity to amaze new listeners, just like Armstrong's 'West End Blues' or Parker's 'Bird Gets The Worm'. A later track on the Classics CD, the little-known 'Dedication', revisits the same setting, and although masterful in its way it points up how genuinely immediate the greatest jazz is: it can't finally compare to the original. If the same holds good for the many later versions of the tune which Hawkins set down – there is one from 1956 on *Body And Soul* – his enduring variations on the structure (and it's intriguing to note that he only refers to the original melody in the opening bars of the 1939 reading – which didn't stop it from becoming a huge hit) say something about his own powers of renewal.

The Classics CD is let down by dubbing from some very surfacey originals, even though it includes some strong material – two Varsity Seven sessions with Carter and Polo, the aforementioned 'Dedication' and a 1940 date for Okeh which features some excellent tenor on 'Rocky Comfort' and 'Passin' It Around' – and those who want a superior-sounding 'Body And Soul' should turn to either of the two Bluebird CDs. *Body And Soul* also includes the full, remarkable date with Fats Navarro and J. J. Johnson, who are superb on 'Half Step Down, Please' and 'Jumping For Jane', as well as the 1956 tracks, which suffer from schmaltz-driven arrangements but feature the Hawkins tone in the grand manner. *April In Paris* offers (at budget price) only ten of the tracks on the earlier set, and misses the best of the Navarro/Johnson date, but it's a pleasing introduction, and the remastering (abjuring the NoNOISE system, though there's actually little to choose between the two discs) is very full and forward. Both deserve four stars on the basis of the best of the material included.

*** **Bean And Ben 1944–1945** Harlequin HQ 2004 CD/LP
Hawkins; Emmett Berry, Jonah Jones, Charlie Shavers (*t*); Eddie Barefield (*cl, as*); Budd Johnson (*cl, ts*); Ernie Caceres (*cl, bs*); Walter Thomas (*as, ts*); Hilton Jefferson, Milt Yaner (*as*); Ben Webster (*ts*); Clyde Hart, Thelonious Monk, Billy Taylor (*p*); Oscar Pettiford, Milt Hinton, Edward Robinson, Slam Stewart (*b*); Cozy Cole, Denzil Best (*d*). 4/44–3/45.

**** **Hollywood Stampede** Capitol 793201-2 CD
Hawkins; Howard McGhee (*t*); Vic Dickenson (*tb*); Sir Charles Thompson (*p*); Allan Reuss (*g*); Oscar Pettiford, John Simmons (*b*); Denzil Best (*d*). 2–3/45.

Hawkins's 1944 sessions for Keynote aren't currently available on separate CDs, but these dates for Capitol and for independent label boss Joe Davis contain some top-flight Hawk. *Bean And Ben* is split between sessions with Hawkins and Ben Webster: Hawkins appears on four enjoyable jump-band pieces with Jonah Jones on trumpet, but the most interesting tracks are four by a quartet with Thelonious Monk on piano: 'Recollections' and 'Drifting On A Reed' are pure Hawkins rhapsody, but the others feature Monk solos which are already tantalizingly close to his future course (and it's worth remembering that Hawkins himself chose the musicians for this date). *Hollywood Stampede* includes the results of a recording trip to Los Angeles, with McGhee an ebullient and simpatico partner: 'Rifftide' and 'Stuffy' show the older man relishing the challenge of McGhee's almost-bop pyrotechnics, although the sly intrusions of Vic Dickenson on four other titles are just as effective, and Pettiford and Best are a crackling rhythm section. The remastering makes the most of the dry but very immediate recording.

*(*)   **Bean And The Boys Vol. 1** Bean 01 LP
Hawkins; Roy Eldridge, Bunny Berigan, Harry James, Nelson Bryant, Joe Guy,
Tommy Lindsay, Tommy Stevenson (*t*); Tommy Dorsey, Jack Jenney, William Cato,
Claude Jones, Sandy Williams (*tb*); Jackie Fields, Eustis Moore, Ernie Powell (*as*);
Kermit Scott (*ts*); Count Basie, Gene Rodgers (*p*); Gene Fields (*g*); John Kirby, Billy
Taylor (*b*); Gene Krupa, J. C. Heard (*d*). 6–8/40.

(*)   **Bean And The Boys Volume 2 Bean 02 LP
As above, except add Gladys Madden (*v*), omit Eldridge, Berigan, James, Dorsey,
Jenney, Basie, Kirby, Krupa. 7–8/40.

***   **Bean And the Boys Vol. 3** Bean 03 LP
Hawkins; Louis Armstrong (*t, v*); Roy Eldridge, Billy Butterfield, Jimmy Maxwell,
Irving Goodman (*t*); Jack Teagarden (*tb, v*); Lou McGarity, Cutty Cutshall (*tb*);
Barney Bigard (*cl*); Les Robinson, Gus Bivona (*as*); Georgie Auld, Pete Mondello
(*ts*); Skippy Martin (*bs*); Art Tatum, Johnny Guarnieri, Frank Froeba (*p*); Red Norvo
(*xy, vib*); Lionel Hampton (*vib, d*); Terry Snyder (*vib*); Mike Bryan, Al Casey (*g*);
Artie Bernstein, Dick Kissinger, Oscar Pettiford (*b*); Dave Tough, Sid Catlett
(*d*).4/41–1/44.

***   **Bean And The Boys Volume 4** Bean 04 LP
Hawkins; Roy Eldridge (*t*); Jack Teagarden (*tb, v*); Barney Bigard (*cl*); Art Tatum
(*p*); Red Norvo (*xy, vib*); Lionel Hampton (*vib, d*); Al Casey (*g*); Oscar Pettiford (*b*);
Sid Catlett (*d*); unknown big band. 1–8/44.

***(*)   **Bean And The Boys Volume 5** Bean O5 LP
Hawkins; Howard McGhee, Buck Clayton (*t*); Lester Young (*ts*); Kenny Kersey, Sir
Charles Thompson (*p*); Oscar Pettiford, Billy Hadnott (*b*); Denzil Best, Shadow
Wilson (*d*); Helen Humes (*v*); unknown big band. 8/44–4/46.

**   **Bean And The Boys Volume 6** Bean 06 LP
Hawkins; Buck Clayton, Roy Eldridge (*t*); Charlie Parker (*as*); Illinois Jacquet, Lester
Young (*ts*); Kenny Kersey, Hank Jones, Al Haig, Erroll Garner (*p*); Al McKibbon,
Percy Heath, Tommy Potter, Eddie Safranski (*b*); J. C. Heard, Jackie Mills, Kenny
Clarke, Buddy Rich (*d*). 4/46–49.

Originally part of a major boxed-set covering live and broadcast material going up to 1965,
these six LPs have been made available separately. Volume 1 is almost a write-off due to the
appalling sound on the first side, an otherwise promising all-star jam session, but the broadcast
by Hawkins's big band is a little better and there is more from the same source of Volume 2. Joe
Guy and Sandy Williams take a few decent if irrelevant solos, but the function of the band is to
act as a backdrop to Hawkins, and he plays with great commitment, as if worried about getting
bored: even perfunctory fragments of 'Body And Soul', which had quickly become a theme
song for him, are treated without diffidence, and although there are weak ballad features for
the vocalists, Hawkins's solos are always worth the wait. The sound is listenable if still rough on
Volume 2. The third disc opens with a brief 'Georgia On My Mind' with Benny Goodman's
Orchestra before moving into a sequence of broadcasts and concerts with an all-star Esquire
award winners line-up. The sound here is rather better than the other tracks to date, and despite
various signs of jam session confusion, there's some excellent jazz, too: 'Mop Mop' and 'Sweet
Georgia Brown' are full-blooded jams with Eldridge and Teagarden, while Armstrong,
Hampton and Norvo all have guest spots. 'Esquire Bounce' is a modernistic-sounding piece but
otherwise the material is trad-orientated. Whatever Hawkins thought about the occasion, he
sounds in high spirits. The final session continues through most of Volume 4 and ends on a less
inspiring bash through 'Flying Home', a Hampton warhorse already, even in 1944. The rest of
this disc includes two ballads with unknown big bands behind Hawk on 'Body And Soul' and
'The Man I Love', and both are fine readings.

Volume 5 is easily the pick of the series. It starts with two 'Mildred Bailey Show' broadcasts
featuring another 'The Man I Love' and 'Yesterdays', and Hawkins spins beautiful variations
out of each, before moving into two exciting tracks by the West Coast quintet with Howard
McGhee, 'Hollywood Stampede' and 'Mop Mop'. Then two more readings of 'Body And
Soul': the second, from an AFRS transcription, is in excellent sound, and shows how far
Hawkins was prepared to step away from his original version of the song. The first 32 bars in

most of his subsequent versions follow a similar pattern to the studio cut, but thereafter he opens up fresh paths, dramatic and romantic alike. The rest of the album features another AFRS session with Buck Clayton and Lester Young, the latter in a rare meeting with Hawkins, and both tenormen jam oustanding solos on 'I Got Rhythm' and 'Sweet Georgia Brown'. Volume 6 is a letdown in comparison, despite having two promising JATP All-Stars dates, one with Young and Illinois Jacquet and the other with Parker and Eldridge. The sound on both is so atrocious that they can scarcely be enjoyed. Much better are three tracks by a quartet with Al Haig and a single version of 'Cocktails For Two' made in Paris with Erroll Garner, although these too are in imperfect fidelity. Overall, this is an intriguing series which Hawkins specialists will be interested to work their way through, but only the splendid fifth volume can be called essential.

***(*) **Jazz Tones** Xanadu FDC 5156 CD
    Hawkins; Emmett Berry (t); Eddie Bert (tb); Billy Taylor (p); Milt Hinton (b); Jo Jones (d). 11/54.

Hawkins didn't make many records under his own name in the early 1950s, and this date – originally isssued on Jazztone – is something of an exception. It finds him in good fettle nonetheless: the opening 'Cheek To Cheek' features chorus after chorus of ideas, and the excellent rhythm section keep fast, flexible time. Berry and the boppish but still swing-directed trombone of Bert join in on six tracks. The only drawback is the original sound, which is heavily reverberant, somewhat in the manner of the Dial and Savoy sessions of the 1940s.

***(*) **Coleman Hawkins & Ben Webster** Verve 833296 CD/MC
    Hawkins; Roy Eldridge, Harry Edison (t); Benny Carter (as); Budd Johnson, Ben Webster (ts); Oscar Peterson, Jimmy Jones (p); Les Spann, Herb Ellis (g); Ray Brown (b); Alvin Stoller, Jo Jones (d). 12/53–4/59.

Something of a missed opportunity, since it includes only half of *Blue Saxophones*, the brilliant 1957 meeting of Hawkins and Webster. While both men seem to be vying to see who could sound first more nasty and second more charming, there's an undercurrent of mutual feeling that makes 'It Never Entered My Mind' and 'Yolanda' as moving as anything in Hawkins's discography. But the rest of the disc includes two tracks by Webster, Edison and Carter, two by Hawkins with Peterson's band and a three-tenor jam with Budd Johnson and Roy Eldridge – all fine, but it saps the impact of the Hawkins–Webster tracks.

***(*) **Standards And Warhorses** Jass J-CD-2 CD
    Hawkins; Henry 'Red' Allen (t); J. C. Higginbotham (tb); Sol Yaged, Earl Warren (cl); Lou Stein, Marty Napoleon (p); Milt Hinton, Chubby Jackson (b); Cozy Cole, George Wettling (d). 57.

These two sessions were – along with the Henry Allen date which produced *World On A String* (RCA Bluebird) – effectively Hawkins's final nod back to a 'traditional' jazz. The music here is a hectic, sometimes almost hysterical Dixieland, though such histrionics derive mostly from the backing group, which accompany in such a one-dimensional way that they try and copy the more outlandish flights of Allen and end up sounding cartoonish. It's still a remarkable effort by both leading lights, with Allen's bludgeoning solos carrying their own peculiar elegance and Hawkins sounding as immediately explosive as he did in his Fletcher Henderson days.

**** **The Hawk Flies High** Original Jazz Classics OJC 027 CD/LP/MC
    Hawkins; Idrees Sulieman (t); J. J. Johnson (tb); Hank Jones (p); Barry Galbraith (g); Oscar Pettiford (b); Jo Jones (d). 3/57.

***(*) **Soul** Original Jazz Classics OJC 096 CD/LP/MC
    Hawkins; Ray Bryant (p); Kenny Burrell (g); Wendell Marshall (b); Osie Johnson (d). 1/58.

*** **Hawk Eyes** Original Jazz Classics OJC 294 CD/LP/MC
    Hawkins; Charlie Shavers (t); Ray Bryant (p); Tiny Grimes (g); George Duvivier (b); Osie Johnson (d). 4/59.

***(*) **Coleman Hawkins With The Red Garland Trio** Original Jazz Classics OJC 418 CD/LP/MC
    Hawkins; Red Garland (p); Doug Watkins (b); Charles 'Specs' Wright (d).

***(*) **At Ease With Coleman Hawkins** Original Jazz Classics OJC 181 LP/MC
Hawkins; Tommy Flanagan (p); Wendell Marshall (b); Osie Johnson (d). 1/60.

*** **Coleman Hawkins All Stars** Original Jazz Classics OJC 225 LP/MC
Hawkins; Joe Thomas (t); Vic Dickenson (tb); Tommy Flanagan (p); Wendell
Marshall (b); Osie Johnson (d). 1/60.

*** **Night Hawk** Original Jazz Classics OJC 420 CD/LP/MC
Hawkins; Eddie Lockjaw Davis (ts); Tommy Flanagan (p); Ron Carter (b); Gus
Johnson (d). 12/60.

*** **The Hawk Relaxes** Original Jazz Classics OJC 709 CD
Hawkins; Ronnell Bright (p); Kenny Burrell (g); Ron Carter (b); Andrew Cyrille (d).
2/61.

(*) **In A Mellow Tone Original Jazz Classics OJC 6001 CD/LP/MC
As above eight discs. 58–61.

Hawkins's records for Riverside and Prestige revived a career that was in decline, and
reasserted his authority at a time when many of the older tenor voices – Lester Young, Don
Byas – were dying out or in eclipse. Hawkins could still feel at home with his immediate
contemporaries – the same year he made *The Hawk Flies High*, he cut tracks with Henry Red
Allen and a Fletcher Henderson reunion band – but the younger players represented by J. J.
Johnson and Idrees Sulieman on *Flies High* were a greater challenge, and the tenorman
responds not by updating his style but shaping it to fit the context. The rhythm sections on these
records are crucial, particularly the drummers: Jo Jones, Osie Johnson and Gus Johnson were
men after Hawk's own heart when it came to the beat, and their bass-drum accents underscore
the saxophonist's own rhythmical language.

Hawkins keeps abreast of the times, but he doesn't really change to suit them. *The Hawk Flies
High* was an astonishingly intense beginning, almost a comeback record and one where
Hawkins plays with ferocious spirit. The notes claim that he picked all his companions on the
date, and Sulieman and Johnson were intriguing choices: it brings out the bluesman in each of
them rather than the bopper, and both seldom played with this kind of bite. 'Laura' is a peerless
ballad, but it's the blues on 'Juicy Fruit' and 'Blue Light' which really dig in. *Soul*, though
sometimes rattling uneasily over prototypical soul-jazz grooves courtesy of Burrell and Bryant,
isn't much less intense, and 'Soul Blues' and the bewilderingly harsh 'I Hadn't Anyone Till
You' are classic set-pieces. Unfortunately, the similar *Blues Groove* with Tiny Grimes is
currently deleted, but *Hawk Eyes* brings in Grimes and Charlie Shavers, though to sometimes
hysterical effect: Hawkins's opening solo on 'C'mon In' seems to be carved out of solid rock,
but Shavers's preposterous bawling soon takes the pith out of the music. Still an exciting session
overall, though.

The trio sessions with Garland and Flanagan are hot and cool, respectively, and prove that
Hawkins could fill all the frontline space a producer could give him. The force he puts into his
phrasing in this period sometimes undoes the flawless grip he once had over vibrato and line,
but these are living sessions of improvised jazz. *Night Hawk* is a good-natured five-round
contest with Lockjaw Davis, who was virtually suckled on the sound of Hawkins's tenor, and
there's plenty of fun if no great revelations and little of the intuitive empathy with Webster (see
above). *The Hawk Relaxes* puts him back with Kenny Burrell on a more peaceable programme,
and there are no problems here. As a sequence of tenor albums, there aren't many this strong,
in whatever jazz school one can name. But the best-of, *In A Mellow Tone*, gets only moderate
marks for an imbalance of ballads: there are already two fine ballad records listed above, and a
classic compilation from these eight discs has yet to be made.

*** **Just You, Just Me** Stash ST-CD 531 CD
Hawkins; Roy Eldridge (t); Don Wilson (p); Bob Decker (b); Buddy Dean (d). 59.

** **Live In Concert** Bandstand BD 1510 CD/LP
Hawkins; Roy Eldridge (t); Ray Bryant, Tommy Flanagan (p); Tommy Bryant, Major
Holley (b); Oliver Jackson, Eddie Locke (d). 59–62.

*** **Bean Stalkin'** Pablo 2310-933 CD/LP/MC
Hawkins; Roy Eldridge (t); Benny Carter (as); Don Byas (ts); Lou Levy, Lalo Schifrin
(p); Herb Ellis (g); Max Bennett, Art Davis (b); Gus Johnson, Jo Jones (d). 10-11/60.

***   **Blowin' Up A Breeze** Spotlite SPJ 137 LP
Hawkins; Eddie Higgins, Tommy Flanagan (*p*); Bob Cranshaw, Major Holley (*b*);
Walter Perkins, Eddie Locke (*d*). 8/59–6/63.

***   **Masters Of Jazz Vol. 12: Coleman Hawkins** Storyville SL4112 CD/LP
Hawkins; Billy Taylor, Bud Powell, Kenny Drew (*p*); Oscar Pettiford, Niels-Henning
Ørsted-Pedersen (*b*); Kenny Clarke, Albert 'Tootie' Heath, Jo Jones (*d*). 11/54–2/68.

***   **Lover Man** France's Concert FCD 104 CD/LP
Hawkins; Roy Eldridge, Harry Edison (*t*); Vic Dickenson (*tb*); Hubert Rostaing (*cl*);
Michel De Villiers (*ts*); Sir Charles Thompson, Lou Levy (*p*); Arvell Shaw, Jimmy
Woode (*b*); Jo Jones, J. C. Heard (*d*). 58–64.

***(*)   **Bean And The Boys** Fresh Sound FSCD-1013 CD
Hawkins; Jimmy Cleveland (*tb*); Benny Golson (*ts*); Eddie Costa, Bobby Scott (*p*);
Billy Bauer (*g*); George Tucker, Major Holley (*b*); Eddie Campbell, Eddie Locke (*d*).
9/59–9/62.

Live recordings from this period find Hawkins in variable but usually imposing form. His tone
had hardened, and much of his old fluency had been traded for a hard-bitten, irascible delivery
that placed force over finesse. But he was still Hawkins, and still a great improviser,
weatherbeaten but defiant. The meeting with Bud Powell found him in flag-waving form (the
rest of the Storyville album is made up of odds and ends), and the two European sets on *Bean
Stalkin'* are strong sessions, as are the two somewhat foggy dates on the Spotlite LP: the second
set, with Flanagan, and dating from 1963, finds him wreathing lovely lines around 'I Can't Get
Started' in particular. Roy Eldridge was one of his favourite jamming partners, and they made
several sets together: *Just You, Just Me* comes from a Washington club set, and the remastering
has been well done, leaving the music sounding clear and quite bright: a good set, though the
material is sometimes a bit too well thumbed. The Bandstand set is let down by poor sound, and
Eldridge in any case sounds as if he can't think of anything interesting to play. *Lover Man* has
two tracks from Cannes, 1958 and five from Paris, 1964: there is a glorious Hawkins ballad solo
on 'Lover Man' itself, and a briefer one on 'Indian Summer', but otherwise much of the disc is
given over to the other players, with a somewhat tedious feature for Woode and Jones in
'Caravan'. Excellent sound throughout. *Bean And The Boys* catches Hawk in imperious form
on two club shows. Most of the music comes from a Rhode Island date of 1959, with three blues
workouts and a 'Perdido' where Hawk invites Jimmy Cleveland and Benny Golson to join him
and subsequently turns his own playing up by a couple of notches (there is also a long 'Blues'
without Hawkins but featuring the other two horns). Eddie Costa is the pianist, and he does
very well. The other four tracks come from a 1962 broadcast and Hawkins shows no loss of
attention, storming through 'Disorder At the Border' and characterizing 'If I Had You' with
the best of his high drama. Quite good sound, though a little boxy on both dates.

**   **Hawk Talk** Fresh Sound FSR-CD 130 CD
Hawkins; Hank Jones, Dick Hyman (*p*); Milt Hinton, George Duvivier (*b*); Jimmy
Crawford, Osie Johnson (*d*); Frank Hunter Orchestra. 3/63.

***   **Desafinado** MCA MCAD-33118 CD
Hawkins; Tommy Flanagan (*p*); Barry Galbraith, Howard Collins (*g*); Major Holley
(*b*); Eddie Locke (*d*); Willie Rodriguez (*perc*). 10/62.

(*)   **Wrapped Tight Impulse! GRP 11092 CD/MC
Hawkins; Bill Berry, Snooky Young (*t*); Urbie Green (*tb*); Barry Harris (*p*); Buddy
Catlett (*b*); Eddie Locke (*d*). 2–3/65.

There was probably a great Hawkins-with-strings album to be made, but *Hawk Talk* wasn't
really it. The pieces are trimmed too short to give the tenorman much space to rhapsodize, and
too many of them sound foreshortened. Nor are Hunter's strings particularly well handled.
Desafinado and *Wrapped Tight* are also disappointing in their way. Manny Albam's
arrangements for *Wrapped Tight* plod through the material, and Hawkins can't muster a great
deal of interest. There's a readier warmth and lustre on *Desafinado*, where Hawkins gets a
sympathetic setting and a sense of time passing at just the pace he wants; still, like most such
records of the period, it's finally little more than an easy-listening set with the saxophonist
adding a few characteristic doodles of his own.

(*)   **Coleman Hawkins Vs Oscar Peterson Moon M 018 CD/LP
Hawkins; Oscar Peterson (*p*); Sam Jones (*b*); Bobby Durham (*d*). 10/67.

Not quite the fisticuffs the title suggests, but the old man had plenty of fight left in him even if the articulation is slurred and the spirits are audibly sagging. Hawkins mostly has to fall back on favourite arpeggios and riffs, and the shadow on his playing is disheartening, but so much of the man is kept in the sound that the results are predictably moving. The recording is of good broadcast quality.

ERSKINE HAWKINS (born 1914)
TRUMPET

***   **The Original Tuxedo Junction** Bluebird ND 90363 CD/LP
Hawkins; Dam Lowe, Wilbur Bascomb, Marcellus Green, James Harris, Charles Jones, Willie Moore, Robert Johnson (*t*); Edward Sims, Robert Range, Richard Harris, Norman Greene, David James, Donald Cole (*tb*); William Johnson, Jimmy Mitchelle, Bobby Smith (*cl, as*); Julian Dash, Paul Bascomb, Aaron Maxwell (*ts*); Heywood Henry (*cl, bs*); Avery Parrish, Ace Harris (*p*); William McLemore, Leroy Kirkland (*g*); Leemie Stanfield (*b*); James Morrison, Edward McConney, Kelly Martin (*d*). 9/38–1/45.

They called him 'The Twentieth Century Gabriel' and, although Erskine Hawkins was at heart only a Louis Armstrong disciple, his big band's records stand up remarkably well, considering their comparative neglect since the orchestra's heyday. They were certainly very popular with black audiences in the 1930s and '40s, staying in residence at Harlem's Savoy Ballroom for close to 10 years and delivering a smooth and gently swinging music that was ideal for dancing. Hawkins's rhapsodic high-note style has been criticized for excess, but his was a strain of black romanticism which, interestingly, predates the work of later Romeos such as Billy Eckstine, even if he did sing with his trumpet. Besides, the band had a number of good soloists, including Julian Dash, Paul Bascomb and Avery Parrish, who, with Sam Lowe, arranged most of the material. The 16 tracks here are a valuable cross-section of the band's work, with swingers such as 'Rockin' Rollers' Jubilee' and 'Swing Out' balancing the sweetness of 'Nona' and 'Don't Cry Baby'. If the character of the music is comparatively bland, it was absolutely reliable. The transfers are, for the most part, clean and full-blooded, but a couple of tracks (notably the 1945 'Tippin' In') sound harsh.

LOUIS HAYES (born 1937)
DRUMS

***   **Ichi-Ban** Timeless SJP 102 CD
Hayes; Woody Shaw (*t*); Junior Cook (*ts*); Ronnie Mathews (*p*); Stafford James (*b*); Guilherme Franco (*perc*). 5/76.

Having drummed for Cannonball Adderley throughout that leader's most successful period, Louis Hayes has gone on to become a leader of some authority himself. He plays hard and fast and without unnecessary complexities, but he likes to nudge a soloist along with surprising fills, and his partnership with Junior Cook – they co-led the group that made this Timeless album – was a brief but interesting one (Woody Shaw shared leadership duties when Cook left). In the end this is perhaps just another hard bop record, but the quality of the playing means that it's a good one.

(*)   **Light And Lively Steeplechase SCS/SCCD 31245 CD/LP
Hayes; Charles Tolliver (*t*); Bobby Watson (*as*); Kenny Barron (*p*); Clint Houston (*b*). 4/89.

***   **Una Max** Steeplechase SCCD 31263 CD
Hayes; Charles Tolliver (*t*); Gerald Hayes (*as*); John Stubblefield (*ts*); Kenny Barron (*p*); Clint Houston (*b*). 12/89.

***   **The Crawl** Candid CCD 79045 CD
Hayes; Charles Tolliver (*t*); Gary Bartz (*as*); John Stubblefield (*ss, ts*); Mickey Tucker
(*p*); Clint Houston (*b*). 10/89.

These are good, hard-headed records which are disappointing only in that there's little to
remember them by: everyone plays well, but the bands lack a purposeful identity. Besides
Hayes's own playing – and he is probably the star performer overall – the main source of
interest is the return of Tolliver to active duty after a number of years away. He sounds in need
of some further woodshedding on *Light And Lively*, but the two later records are better
showcases for him. Watson sounds a shade too slick for the company on the first record, too,
and Stubblefield and Bartz are a much more equable pairing, though Bartz's alto sounds
decidedly sour at some moments. The Candid set, recorded live, could use a little editing, but
it's an atmospheric occasion; while the studio session for Steeplechase is the best evidence of the
band's expertise – accomplished but rough and immediate solos from all the players, with even
Barron loosening up here and there. Each record is clearly balanced and recorded.

TUBBY HAYES (1935–73)
TENOR AND SOPRANO SAXOPHONES

***(*)   **The New York Sessions** Columbia CK 45446 CD/MC
Hayes; Clark Terry (*t*); Horace Parlan (*p*); Eddie Costa (*vib*); George Duvivier (*b*);
Dave Bailey (*d*). 10/61.

***(*)   **For Members Only** Mastermix CDCHE 10 CD
Hayes; Mick Pyne (*p*); Ron Mathewson (*b*); Tony Levin (*d*). 1–10/67.

When Hayes went to New York in 1961 he had no problem holding his own with a stellar cast of
the city's finest: the original *Tubbs In New York* has been amplified with four extra tracks to
make a CD running over 70 minutes in length, though it's currently only an American release.
Tubby Hayes has often been lionized as the greatest saxophonist Britain ever produced, and
while his facility on the horn (and both soprano and vibes) is as formidable and muscular as
that of, say, George Coleman, there is a question mark over his ability to make his solos fall into
place. Having put together a big, rumbustious tone and a delivery that features sixteenth notes
spilling impetuously out of the horn, Hayes often left a solo full of brilliant loose ends and
ingenious runs that led nowhere in particular. Both these discs, while highly entertaining as
blow-outs of sustained energy, tend to wobble on the axis of Hayes's creative impasse: having
got this facility together, he never seemed sure of what to do with it in the studio, which may be
why none of his original records (all currently missing in action) seem to ultimately fall short of
the masterpiece he never came to make. Still, both the New York album – which has plenty of
lively jousting between Hayes and Terry – and the Mastermix CD – culled from three radio
broadcasts, and featuring some shapely ballads as well as the expected breakneck workouts –
are imposing reminders of a talent that is still much missed by those who heard him play in
person. The Columbia remastering is fine; the Mastermix CD suffers from some occasional
blinks and drop-outs, but nothing too distracting.

GRAHAM HAYNES
CORNET

***   **What Time It Be** Muse MCD 5402 CD
Haynes; Lance Bryant (*ts, f*); M. Fergu (*ky*); David Gilmore, Andy Bassford (*g*);
Marque Gilmore (*b, perc*); Kevin Bruce Harris (*b*); Gregory Lany (*d*).3/90.

An impressive and warm-blooded exploration of the synthesis which New York musicians are
currently investigating, between jazz and funk, rap and various points on the 'world music'
graph. Haynes is a player who enjoys contrast: while the rhythms stagger along in a variety of
complex times, he likes to decorate the pulse with comparatively laid-back lines, utilizing the
classical possibilities of jazz cornet playing. Bryant is agile without finding a great deal to say,
and the rhythm players seem to have furrowed brows from following the time, but it's often
surprisingly approachable and entertainingly diverse.

ROY HAYNES (born 1926)
DRUMS

***   **We Three** Original Jazz Classics OJC 196 LP
       Haynes; Phineas Newborn Jr (*p*); Paul Chambers (*b*). 11/58.

Relative to his enormous contribution to post-war jazz, Haynes's output as leader has been disappointingly small. Few contemporary drummers have been so precise in execution, and what Haynes lacks in sheer power – he is a small man and has generally worked with a scaled-down kit – he gains in clarity, playing long, open lines that are deceptively relaxed but full of small rhythmic tensions.

In 1958, his work still clearly bears the mark of stints with Thelonious Monk and Miles Davis. Bar lines shift confidently or else are dispensed with altogether, without violence to the underlying pulse. Phineas Newborn's recent association with Charles Mingus had helped pare down his slightly extravagant style; he plays very differently against Haynes's slightly staccato delivery than with, say, Elvin Jones much later in his career (Contemporary C 7622 and C 7634) or Philly Joe Jones in 1961 (Original Jazz Classics OJC 175) where Chambers again provided the harmonic substructure. Haynes himself sounds wonderful on 'Sugar Ray' and the romping 'Our Delight', where he is almost tuneful.

***   **True Or False** Freelance FRLCD 007 CD
       Haynes; Ralph Moore (*ts*); David Kikoski (*p*); Ed Howard (*b*).

A bright, breezy set, without much personality. Moore plays some interesting stuff, but never sounds entirely relaxed. The mix is overloud, with some distortion at the top end.

JIMMY HEATH (born 1926)
TENOR SAXOPHONE, ALTO SAXOPHONE, SOPRANO SAXOPHONE

***   **The Riverside Collection: Nice People** Original Jazz Classics OJC 6006 CD/LP/MC
       Heath; Donald Byrd, Freddie Hubbard, Clark Terry (*t*); Nat Adderley (*c*); Curtis
       Fuller, Tom McIntosh (*tb*); Dick Berg, Jimmy Buffington, Don Butterfield (*tba*);
       Julius Watkins (*frhn*); Cannonball Adderley (*as*); Pat Patrick (*bs*); Herbie Hancock,
       Wynton Kelly, Cedar Walton (*p*); Kenny Burrell (*g*); Paul Chambers, Percy Heath
       (*b*); Albert Heath, Connie Kay (*d*). 12/59–64.

The middle of the three Heath brothers is perhaps and quite undeservedly now the least known. Jimmy Heath's reputation as a player has been partly overshadowed by his gifts as a composer ('C. T. A.', 'Gemini', 'Gingerbread Boy') and arranger. The Riverside compilation is an ideal introduction to the man who was once known as 'Little Bird' but who later largely abandoned alto saxophone and its associated Parkerisms in favour of a bold, confident tenor style that is immediately distinctive.

Heath's arrangements often favour deep brass pedestals for the higher horns, which explains his emphasis on trombone and french horn parts. The earliest of these sessions, though, is a relatively stripped-down blowing session ('Nice People' and 'Who Needs It') for Nat Adderley, Curtis Fuller and a rhythm section anchored on youngest brother Albert, who reappears with Percy Heath, the eldest of the three, on the ambitous 1960 'Picture Of Heath'. Like Connie Kay, who was to join Percy in the Modern Jazz Quartet, Albert is an unassuming player, combining Kay's subtlety with the drive of Kenny Clarke (original drummer for the MJQ).

More than once in these sessions (and most noticeably on the 1964 'All The Things You Are' with Kenny Burrell and the brilliant Wynton Kelly) it's Albert who fuels his brother's better solos. This is a fine set, though chronological balance occasionally dictates a less than ideal selection of material. Well worth investigating.

***(*)   **Picture Of Heath** Xanadu 118 LP
       Heath; Barry Harris (*p*); Sam Jones (*b*); Billy Higgins (*d*). 9/75.

This fine, mid-period session kicks off with a version of 'For Minors Only', a minor-key theme whose childish simplicity helps spring the pun in the title. It was originally recorded for Riverside but isn't included in the compilation above. It's followed by what is perhaps Heath's best standard performance, a magnificent 'Body And Soul', stated on soprano saxophone and then, following Harris's well-judged variations on the basic theme, developed on tenor. Heath uses his soprano again for 'All Members', giving it a smooth, clarinet feel, which he sustains right through the register and at speed. The other originals are 'CTA', liberally sprinkled with quotes by the name-dropping Harris, the long, perhaps over-long 'Bruh' Slim', which drifts into Caribbean mode, and the title-track, an ironic self-portrait of the jazz man just beginning to feel his years, mumbling, getting repetitive, pretending to lose his way. Vinyl reproduction is above average and Don Schlitten's production is, as usual, impeccable, letting Sam Jones come through clearly in the ensembles as well as on his brief, telling solos. A CD would be welcome, of course.

*** **New Picture** Landmark LM 1506 CD/LP
Heath; Benny Powell (*tb*); Bob Boutch, John Clark (*frhn*); Howard Johnson (*tba*); Tommy Flanagan (*p, electric p*); Tony Purrone (*g*); Rufus Reid (*b*); Al Foster (*d*). 6/85.

(*) **Peer Pleasure Landmark LM 1514 CD/LP
Heath; Tom Williams (*t, flhn*); Larry Willis (*p*); Tony Purrone (*g*); Stafford James (*b*); Akira Tana (*d*). 2/87.

Heath's playing career has been marked by a number of hiatuses, usually when he was busy writing and arranging. The sabbaticals have if anything increased his appetite for performance. He clearly relished the sibling challenges of the Heath Brothers, and in the later 1980s has produced some strong solo material. *New Picture* is beautifully conceived and arranged (French horns again), with sweetly deft piano lines from Tommy Flanagan (undimmed by the switch to a Fender instrument) and effective guitar by Purrone, who reappears among the younger line-up on *Peer Pleasure*, a less appealing album but testimony to Heath's resilience and adaptability.

CHRISTOPH HEBERER (born 1965)
TRUMPET, KEYBOARDS

*** **The Heroic Millipede** ITM 1443 CD
Heberer; Frank Kollges (*d*). 3–8/88.

**** **Chicago Breakdown** Jazzhaus Musik JHM 38 CD
Heberer; Dieter Manderschied (*b*). 10/89.

Heberer is an outstandingly gifted young trumpeter. The music on the ITM disc occasionally slips into the kind of cerebral mood-music of which Mark Isham is a particular exponent, devoted mostly to trumpet lines that plume over an insistent keyboard throb, with Kollges restricted to only two tracks. It's attractive music all the same, and a pleasing showcase for Heberer's golden tone on the horn.

Far better, though, is the essential *Chicago Breakdown*. An album of trumpet and bass duets sounds like a forbidding exercise, but the material puts everything on much more familiar ground: they perform variations on six Jelly Roll Morton themes. Miraculously, the music succeeds in honouring Morton and letting the identity of his melodies endure while at the same time deconstructing them entirely and subjecting the themes to the most outlandish of variations. Heberer can play anything he thinks of on the horn: freakish (and they do play 'Freakish' here) effects and tonal grotesqueries intermingle with lovely voluntaries and lip-splitting exercises in virtuosity. He sounds alert to all the free-playing innovations of the last 30 years yet brings insights and sensibilities which suggest a post-modern bite and snap. Manderschied is by no means outclassed; though performing an essentially subsidiary role, he is a full duet partner, and comes up with voicings and counterweights of his own. Highly recommended.

DICK HECKSTALL-SMITH (born 1934)
TENOR SAXOPHONE, SOPRANO SAXOPHONE, BARITONE SAXOPHONE

***   **Woza Nasu** Aura Records AU 737 CD

aka

***   **Where One Is** Mainstream MDCD 201 CD
    Heckstall-Smith; Claude Deppa (*t*); Ed Jones (*ts*); Ashley Slater (*tb*); Dave Moore
    (*ky*); Malcolm Bruce, Alan Weekes (*g*); Ike Leo, Paul Rogers (*b*); Julian Bahula, Pete
    Brown, Jim Drummond, Kenrick Rowe, Frank Tontoh (*d*); Tina Lyle (*perc*). 90.

Remarkably, this is Heckstall-Smith's first record as leader since *Dust In The Air Suspended Marks The Place Where A Story Ended* was released nearly two decades ago. The lesson may be never to borrow an album title from T. S. Eliot, or never to use a dozen words when you can get away with four syllables. The music has changed remarkably little and is as distinctive as ever, combining a tough, bluesy distillation of Hank Mobley and Wayne Shorter with Roland Kirk's simul-instrumentalism (younger British players like Barbara Thompson took the notion of playing two saxophones at once from Heckstall-Smith). Some of his more extreme acoustic effects border on abstraction, but in a manner which recalls the typically British but Afro-tinged avant-populism of Dudu Pukwana and Harry Beckett.

'A Knite In Whoneedsya?' is a witty and thematically elegant bop pastiche; unfortunately it serves only to establish the album's rather second-hand quality. To some extent, *Woza Nasu* is a compression of much of the music that has passed under the bridge since Heckstall-Smith last recorded. As he has not been inactive in the intervening period (working *in* DHSS, his own band, rather than *on* the DHSS), he has kept confidently abreast of everything from neo-abstraction to funk and has always been a sufficiently eclectic stylist not to sound breathless away from base camp.

He scales some impressive heights on the title-track and on the lovely 'Il Cinghiale' – 'the wild boar' – where his stately pronouncements seem to belong to a different jazz generation again. The (mostly young) band are thoroughly professional, if a bit off-hand in places, and nothing else on the record quite reaches Heckstall-Smith's level of concentration. A most welcome return for a figure even some of his one-time fans had forgotten about.

MARK HELIAS (born 1950)
DOUBLE BASS, ELECTRIC BASS

***(*)   **Split Image** Enja 4086 LP
    Helias; Herb Robertson (*c, t, vtb*); Tim Berne (*as*); Dewey Redman (*ts*); Gerry
    Hemingway (*d*). 8/84.

(*)   **The Current Set Enja 5041 CD/LP
    Helias; Herb Robertson (*t, c, flhn*); Robin Eubanks (*tb*); Tim Berne (*as*); Greg Osby
    (*ss*); Victor Lewis (*d*); Nana Vasconcelos (*perc, v*). 3/87.

***   **Desert Blue** Enja 6016 CD/LP
    Helias; Herb Robertson (*t, c*); Ray Anderson (*tb*); Marty Ehrlich (*as, ts, cl, b cl*);
    Anthony Davis (*p, syn*); Pheeroan AkLaff (*d*). 4/89.

There is now a fully fledged generation of jazz musicians for whom rock is a simple fact, part of the undifferentiated background of contemporary music, and not a hard place to be defiantly or submissively negotiated. Helias is one of the more influential of the Young Turks; as well as his own impressive work, he has recorded with Barry Altschul and with Ray Anderson, who makes a welcome appearance on *Desert Blue*.

Helias is capable of boiling intensity or an almost desolate abstraction. The contrast is most evident on the superb *Split Image*, which is the most tightly structured and arranged of the three, largely due to Hemingway's inspirational drumming. The combination of Tim Berne, who is much less effective on *The Current Set*, with the veteran Dewey Redman, currently enjoying a welcome rejuvenation, is particularly effective.

Helias is rhythmically not the most sophisticated of players and seems to rely quite heavily on his drummers. Lewis is in some respects too oblique and elided and it's AkLaff's every-which-way explosions around a solid beat which lift *Desert Blue*. Helias is, though, constantly aware of texture and resonance, and of his own technical limitations, deploying instrumental voices with great subtlety. Regular cohort Robertson is a less than virtuosic player but makes up for any purely mechanical shortcomings with a clever disposition of brasses. Good husbandry all round, but *Split Image* is the one to go for.

GERRY HEMINGWAY
DRUMS, PERCUSSION

***   **Tubworks** Sound Aspects sas 022 LP
       Hemingway (solo). 12/83, 7 & 8/85, 8/87.

Gerry Hemingway is still a little weighed down in critical terms by his part in what for a significant number of listeners remains *the* Anthony Braxton group, the 1985 quartet with Marilyn Crispell and Mark Dresser (for which, see Leo LR 200/201 CD). A lot of water, as Sam Goldwyn used to say, has been passed since then. Hemingway has gone on to assert himself as a fine individual talent with a strong sense of tradition, incidentally revealing in the process, one suspects, that his attunement to Braxton's vibrational philosophy was an act of will rather than of instinct and conviction.

Tubworks is excellent, conviction playing to the final clatter. The 'Four Studies For Single Instruments' (namely snare drum, hi-hat, bass drum and cymbal) are more than merely virtuosic essays; each has a fine and satisfying musical logic, something rather lacking in 'Dance Of The Sphygmoids', which was recorded earlier than the other tracks. But for documentary interest, it might have been left out. A CD version might have had room for more in the vein of 'Tub Etudes' and the remarkable 'Trance Tracks', but the sound is more than respectable on vinyl, resonant in the bass and with no obvious problems in the higher registers. Solo percussion records are difficult to handle, both technically and commercially, and rarely succeed artistically. This scores on the first and third counts and, in an ideal world, ought to also on the second. Take the plunge.

(*)   **Outerbridge Crossing Sound Aspects sas 017 CD
       Hemingway; Ray Anderson (*tb, tba*); David Mott (*bs*); Ernst Reijseger (*clo*); Mark
       Helias (*b*). 9/85.

***   **Special Detail** hat Art 6084 CD
       Hemingway; Don Byron (*reeds*); Wolter Wierbos (*tb*); Ernst Reijseger (*clo*).

Despite Ray Anderson's typically exuberant contributions, *Outerbridge Crossing* is slightly disappointing – especially for anyone familiar with Hemingway's work for Anthony Braxton – and gives a less than ideal impression of Hemingway's consistent intelligence as a group player. *Special Detail* is much more representative of Hemingway's sophisticated harmonic awareness, and it's interesting how much more of the earlier album reveals itself in the context of the later one. Reijseger is superb on both and if Wierbos isn't another Ray Anderson – and there's probably only room on the planet for one Ray Anderson at a time – he's still a wonderfully effective player.

JULIUS HEMPHILL (born 1940)
ALTO SAXOPHONE, SOPRANO SAXOPHONE

***(*)   **Flat-Out Jump Suite** Black Saint 120040 CD/LP
       Hemphill; Olu Dara (*t*); Abdul Wadud (*clo*); Warren Smith (*perc*). 6/80.

Initially a rather more abstract session that Hemphill's more recent output, the four-part suite builds to a rousing funk climax on 'Body'. Hemphill intones the title to each part as it begins, starting with the soft, percussion-led figures of 'Ear', plunging into the complexities of 'Mind' (which is dominated by Wadud's Ron Carter-influenced cello) and then picking up a more continuous rhythm with 'Heart', on which Hemphill begins to string together his light, slightly floating textures into a more continuous, jazz-based improvisation.

On the original LP, 'Mind, Part 2' opened the second side with a brief coda to the long central piece. It makes more sense as an integral drum solo, typically understated. It is, until the very end, a remarkably quiet album that requires some concentration. Dara uses his mute a good deal and otherwise plays quite softly. Hemphill seems to play a wooden flute and gives his saxophone a soft-edged quality that is very attractive. An excellent record, easily overlooked.

(*) **Georgia Blue Minor Music 003 LP
     Hemphill; Nels Cline (*g*); Alex Cline (*d, perc*); Jumma Santos (*p*). 8/84.

Hemphill is certainly better known as a (now former) member of the pioneering World Saxophone Quartet, but he has also been an influential band leader and composer, with a particular interest in theatrical and mixed-media presentations. Culminating in the much admired *Kawaida*, a large-scale collage piece that reflected the aesthetics of BAG, the Black Artists Group, Hemphill's vigorously populist approach (which has influenced fellow-BAG members like Lester Bowie) drew on stints with Ike Turner's rock and roll revue and later on Kool and the Gang's funk-soul Hustler's Convention. *Georgia Blue* is credited to the JAH Band, a title that refers to the leader's full moniker, Julius Arthur Hemphill, rather than to the Almighty. Much less compelling than the mid-1970s *'Coon Bid'ness* [Arista/Freedom AL 1012], it nevertheless oozes with Hemphill's usual vigour and directness of approach. 'Dogon 2' refers back to another important early album, *Dogon A. D.*, on his own Mbari Records. The Cline brothers concede him most of the foreground, but as a unit they work closely and well, with a good modulation of pace and attack. Enthusiasts are still going to have to pick him out of the mix on WSQ albums.

***(*) **Julius Hemphill Big Band** Elektra Musician 960831 2 CD
     Hemphill; David Hines, Rasul Siddik (*t*); Frank Lacy (*tb*); David Taylor (*btb*);
     Vincent Chancey, John Clark (*frhn*); Marty Ehrlich (*as, ss, f*); J. D. Parran (*bs, f*);
     John Purcell (*ts, ss, f*); John Stubblefield (*ts, ss, f*); Bill Frisell, Jack Wilkins (*g*);
     Jerome Harris (*b*); Ronnie Burrage (*d*); Gordon Gottlieb (*perc*). 2/88.

Though Hemphill's keening alto (astonishingly beautiful on 'Leora' and 'For Billie') is only one of several outstanding instrumental voices (Lacy, Ehrlich, Burrage and Wilkins all play fine individual passages), the striking quality of the set as a whole is the leader's growing sophistication as a composer and arranger. The set opens with ambiguous, threatening chords that seem to contradict the track's title, 'At Harmony'; in fact, it's the soloists who restore a degree of concord. 'Leora' is a solo feature, with only nervously see-sawing pedals from the band. Oddly, the image recurs in the hotly swinging 'C/Saw', the most straightforward and upfront track, but with a curious coda break that gives it an uneasy balance. The long 'Drunk On God' is set to a poem by K. Curtis Lyle, a shamanistic fantasy in that curiously grad school visionary style that overtook American writers in the late 1960s. Hemphill's soft brass voicings are full of unexpected cadences and bizarre turnings that carry over into the final tune, as if the whole sequence has been unconsciously conceived as a suite. On the closing 'Bordertown' Hemphill manages to sound like Hodges on soprano, dancing over a 4/4 that doesn't seem sure of its progress until the climax of Frisell's solo and Hemphill's reprise, when it turns into a straight blowing number.

Intriguing, provocative music. Top marks, too, to the two horn players (Chancey and Clark have made great strides in assimilating the horn to jazz) and to percussionist Gottlieb for some striking background effects.

***(*) **Fat Man And The Hard Blues** Black Saint 1201152 CD
     Hemphill; Marty Ehrlich (*as, ss, f*); Carl Grubbs (*as, ss*); James Carter, Andrew White
     (*ts*); Sam Furnace (*bs, f*). 7/91.

'The Hard Blues', the last and longest track on Hemphill's first post-WSQ recording, is an old tune (it also appears on *Georgia Blue*, above) which seems finally to have found its appropriate setting. These rhythmless sextets are an obvious extension of his work with the WSQ, but they put still greater emphasis on Hemphill's considerable compositional and arranging skills and his highly distinctive variation on conventional theme-and-solo jazz; often the group will improvise round a theme stated quite simply and directly by the 'soloist'. This has quite a profound impact on the overall sound, which does tend to become rather heavy round the middle. Hemphill tends to avoid extremes of pitch, scoring blocks of sound in which rather small variations of register and timbre take on considerable significance. That's particularly noticeable on the sinuous 'Tendrils', which features the two flautists in one of the more linear themes. The piece actually seems to unravel, in contrast to the melting, blurry quality of most of the other tracks. Unwise to review an album by recourse to its sleeve, but the deceptively liquescent lines of ceramic artist Jeff Schlanger's blue stoneware saxophone suggests something of Hemphill's hard centre. *Fat Man And The Hard Blues* is both an intelligent continuation of the last decade's work and a challenging new departure. Future projects should be watched with interest.

FLETCHER HENDERSON (1897–1952)
PIANO, BANDLEADER

***   **The Henderson Pathés** Fountain FJ 112 LP
Henderson; Elmer Chambers, Howard Scott, Louis Armstrong (*c*); Teddy Nixon, Charlie Green (*tb*); Don Redman (*cl, as*); Buster Bailey (*cl*); Coleman Hawkins (*ts, Cmel, cl*); Billy Fowler (*bsx*); Charlie Dixon (*bj*); Ralph Escudero (*bb*); Kaiser Marshall (*d*). 11/23–2/25.

***   **Fletcher Henderson 1924–1925** Classics 633 CD
Henderson; Louis Armstrong, Elmer Chambers, Howard Scott, Joe Smith, Russell Smith (*t, c*); Charlie Green (*tb*); Don Redman (*cl, as, v*); Buster Bailey (*cl, as*); Coleman Hawkins (*cl, Cmel, ts, bsx*); Charlie Dixon (*bj*); Ralph Escudero (*bb*); Kaiser Marshall (*d*); Billy Jones (*v*). 11/24–11/25.

***(*)   **Fletcher Henderson With Louis Armstrong** EPM FDC 5702 CD
As above. 24–25.

***(*)   **Fletcher Henderson 1924–1927** Zeta ZET 753 CD
As above, except add Tommy Ladnier (*t*), Jimmy Harrison (*tb*), June Cole (*bb*). 24–27.

Henderson drifted into both music and bandleading, after casually working for the Black Swan record label, and his first records as a leader (in 1923, yet to appear on CD) are frequently no more than routine dance music. The arrival of Louis Armstrong – whom Henderson first heard in New Orleans at the turn of the decade – apparently galvanized everyone in the band and, eventually, every musician in New York. But it's hard to make assumptions about Henderson's band. He already had Don Redman and Coleman Hawkins working for him prior to Armstrong's arrival, and there are too many good records prior to Louis's first session of October 1924 to dismiss the group as jazz ignoramuses. The Fountain LP tells some of the story: it's a stiffer and less adventurous band, but these were skilful if not particularly outward-looking musicians, and even as early as 1923 – on 'Shake Your Feet' or '31st Street Blues' – there are fragments of solos which work out. Nevertheless, Armstrong still stands out like a beacon on many of the tracks here: he arrives for the last two sessions on the Fountain LP, and is present on most of Classics 633, which is (so far) the first volume in the chronological survey by Classics of Henderson's large and valuable discography. Luckily, the cornetist is given solo space on almost every track of the 21 he appears on here, and the improvisations – often set against Marshall hitting the off-beat to heighten the dramatic effect – are breathtaking, especially on what would otherwise be dreary tunes, such as 'I'll See You In My Dreams' or the amazing 'I Miss My Swiss', where he electrifies the whole band. But some of the other musicians were getting into their stride, too: Redman delivers some strong early arrangements, Hawkins and Bailey sneak through some breaks, and the best of the material – 'TNT', 'Money Blues', 'Carolina Stomp' and above all their hit version of 'Sugar Foot Stomp' – lets the best black band in New York play to their strengths.

Transfer quality is unfortunately often indifferent. The originals are a mixture of acoustic and electric recording, and while the tracks from Columbia masters sound good, those from Banner, Vocalion and Pathé are surfacey, and the pair of titles from 12 January 1925 are full of reverb, which suggests a tape source. The two alternative CDs present in some ways a stronger case. The Zeta Jazz Archives collection has a considerably cleaner sound for the most part, but this is more of a cross-section of henderson material going up to 1927 and includes 16 of the tracks with Armstrong in a programme of 22 tracks in all. The EPM set also includes 16 tracks with Armstrong, and the sound is also largely superior to the Classics CD, which remains the most all-inclusive set. Readers will have to judge on the basis of which tracks they most want, though for a one-disc representation of Henderson's early period, we recommend the Zeta CD.

***   **Fletcher Henderson 1925–1926** Classics 610 CD
As above, except Rex Stewart (*c*) replaces Armstrong, Scott and Chambers.
11/25–4/26.

***(*)   **Fletcher Henderson 1926–1927** Classics 597 CD
As above, except add Tommy Ladnier (*t*), Jimmy Harrison (*tb*), Fats Waller (*p, org*),
June Cole (*bb, v*), Evelyn Thompson (*v*). 4/26–1/27.

***(*)   **Fletcher Henderson 1927** Classics 580 CD
As above, except add Jerome Pasquall (*cl, as*); omit Escudero, Thompson. 1–5/27.

***(*)   **Fletcher Henderson 1927–1931** Classics 572 CD
Bobby Stark, Tommy Ladnier, Russell Smith, Rex Stewart, Cootie Williams (*t, c*);
Jimmy Harrison (*tb, v*); Charlie Green, Claude Jones, Benny Morton (*tb*); Jerome
Pasquall, Benny Carter, Harvey Boone (*cl, as*); Coleman Hawkins (*cl, ts*); Fletcher
Henderson (*p*); Charlie Dixon, Clarence Holiday (*bj, g*); John Kirby, June Cole (*bb,
b*); Kaiser Marshall, Walter Thompson (*d*); Lois Deppe, Andy Razaf (*v*). 11/27–2/31.

****   **Fletcher Henderson 1925–1929** JSP CD 311 CD
As above four discs. 25–29.

***(*)   **Fletcher Henderson 1925–1928** BBC CD/REB/ZCF 720 CD/LP/MC
As above. 5/25–12/28.

By the mid-1920s, Henderson was leading the most consistently interesting big band on record.
That doesn't mean all the records are of equal calibre, and the title of a famous earlier
retrospective of Henderson's work – 'A Study In Frustration' – gives some idea of the
inconsistencies and problems of a band that failed to secure any hit records and never sounded
on record the way it could in person (at least, according to many witnesses). But Henderson's
best records are classics of the period. Don Redman was coming into his own, and his scores
assumed a quality which no other orchestral arranger was matching in 1926–27 (though it is
tantalizing to ponder on what Jelly Roll Morton could have done with the same band): 'The
Stampede', 'The Chant', 'Henderson Stomp', the remarkable 'Tozo' and above all the truly
astonishing 'Whiteman Stomp' find him using the colours of reeds and brass to complex yet
swinging ends. Luckily, Henderson had the players who could make the scores happen: though
Armstrong had departed, Hawkins, Ladnier, Joe Smith, Jimmy Harrison and Buster Bailey all
had the stature of major soloists as well as good section-players. The brass sections were,
indeed, the best any band in New York could boast – the softer focus of Smith contrasting with
the bluesy attack of Ladnier, the rasp of Rex Stewart, the lithe lines of Harrison – and any
group with Hawkins (who was loyal enough to stay for ten years) had the man who created jazz
saxophone. Henderson's own playing was capable rather than outstanding, and the rhythm
section lumbered a bit, though string bass and guitar lightened up the feel from 1928 onwards. It
took Henderson many records to attain a real consistency: in 1925, he was still making sides like
'Pensacola' (for Columbia, and on the JSP disc), which starts with a duet between Hawkins and
Redman on bass sax and goofus! But there weren't many vocals, which let the band drive
through their three-minute allocation without interruption, and if Henderson never figured out
the best use of that timespan (unlike Ellington, who grew to be his most serious rival among
New York's black bands) his team of players made sure that something interesting happens on
almost every record.

    Those who want to sample Henderson's music should go straight to the JSP CD. This collects
all of his records for Columbia (where he invariably received the best studio sound) and
includes 'Jackass Blues', 'Tozo', 'Whiteman Stomp', 'A Rhythmic Dream', 'King Porter
Stomp' and several other near-masterpieces. The remastering is mostly superbly done by John
R. T. Davies, although there still seems to be a hint of distortion on some loud passages. The
Classics CDs offer chronological surveys which Henderson specialists will welcome, although
no alternative takes are included (there are actually relatively few in existence). We would
single out the 1926–27 and 1927 discs as the most important, but there are so many fine
moments scattered through even second-rate pieces that any who sample the series may well
find that they want them all. Remastering is again variable: the tracks made under the name
'The Dixie Stompers' were made for Harmony, which continued to use acoustic recording even
after most other companies switched over to the electric process in 1925, and some may find
these tracks a little archaic in timbre. Mostly, we find that the transfers are acceptable, though

they don't measure up to the relentlessly high standards of JSP. The 1927–31 disc marks the departure of Redman, the first steps by Henderson himself as arranger, guest appearances by Fats Waller (who reportedly gave Henderson a dozen tunes in trade for a plate of hamburgers at a Harlem eaterie) and Benny Carter, and the arrival of the fine and undervalued trumpeter Bobby Stark, whose solos on 'Blazin'' and 'Sweet And Hot' find a lyrical streak somewhere between Joe Smith and Rex Stewart. But the band was already in decline, especially following Henderson's car accident in 1928, after which he was never the same man. They cut only three record dates in 1929 and three in 1930 (compared with 17 in 1927).

The BBC compilation has been impeccably remastered by Robert Parker, though his digital-stereo process may displease some ears. It's a cross-section of some of the best of the late-1920s tracks.

***   **Fletcher Henderson 1931** Classics 555 CD
As above, except add Sandy Williams (*tb*); Russell Procope (*cl, as*); Edgar Sampson (*cl, as, vn*); Horace Henderson (*p*); George Bias, Dick Robertson (*v*); omit Ladnier, Green, Pasquall, Dixon, Cole, Marshall, Deppe, Razaf. 2–7/31.

(*)   **Fletcher Henderson 1931–1932 Classics 546 CD
Henderson; Russell Smith, Bobby Stark (*t*); Rex Stewart (*c*); Sandy Williams, J. C. Higginbotham (*tb*); Russell Procope (*cl, ss, as*); Edgar Sampson (*cl, as, vn*); Coleman Hawkins (*cl, ts*); Clarence Holiday, Ikey Robinson (*bj, g*); John Kirby (*bb, b*); Walter Johnson (*d*); John Dickens, Harlan Lattimore, Baby Rose Marie, Les Reis, Dick Robertson (*v*). 7/31–3/32.

***(*)   **Fletcher Henderson 1932–1934** Classics 535 CD
As above, except add Henry Allen, Joe Thomas, Irving Randolph (*t*); Keg Johnson, Claude Jones, Dicky Wells (*tb*); Buster Bailey (*cl*); Hilton Jefferson (*cl, as*); Ben Webster (*ts*); Horace Henderson (*p*); Bernard Addison, Lawrence Lucie (*g*); Elmer James (*b*); Vic Engle (*d*); Charles Holland (*v*); omit Robinson, Holiday, Lattimore, Marie, Reis and Robertson. 12/32–9/34.

***   **Fletcher Henderson 1934–1937** Classics 527 CD
Henderson; Russell Smith, Irving Randolph, Henry Allen, Dick Vance, Roy Eldridge, Joe Thomas, Emmett Berry (*t*); Ed Cuffee (*tb, v*); Keg Johnson, Claude Jones, Fernando Arbello, George Washington, J. C. Higginbotham (*tb*); Omer Simeon (*cl, as, bs*); Jerry Blake (*cl, as, v*); Buster Bailey, Hilton Jefferson, Russell Procope, Jerome Pasquall (*cl, as*); Benny Carter, Scoops Carey (*as*); Ben Webster, Elmer Williams, Chu Berry (*ts*); Horace Henderson (*p*); Bob Lessey, Lawrence Lucie (*g*); Elmer James, John Kirby, Israel Crosby (*b*); Walter Johnson, Sid Catlett (*d*); Teddy Lewis, Georgia Boy Simpkins, Dorothy Derrick (*v*). 9/34–3/37.

***   **Fletcher Henderson 1929–1937** BBC CD/REB/ZDF 682 CD/LP/MC
As above four discs. 5/29–9/37.

(*)   **Under The Harlem Moon ASV 5067 CD
As above two discs. 12/32–6/37.

**   **Fletcher Henderson 1937–1938** Classics 519 CD
Henderson; Russell Smith, Emmett Berry, Dick Vance (*t*); George Washington, Ed Cuffee, Milt Robinson, George Hunt, J. C. Higginbotham, Albert Wynn, John McConnell (*tb*); Jerry Blake (*cl, as, v*); Eddie Barefield (*cl, as*); Hilton Jefferson (*as*); Chu Berry, Elmer Williams, Ben Webster (*ts*); Lawrence Lucie (*g*); Israel Crosby (*b*); Walter Johnson, Cozy Cole, Pete Suggs (*d*); Chuck Richards (*v*). 3/37–5/38.

Henderson's music was already in decline when the 1930s began, and by the end of the decade – as illustrated on the rather sad final disc in the Classics sequence – the orchestra was a shadow of what it was in its glory days. Ironically, it was Henderson's own work as an arranger in this period which set off the swing era, via the charts he did for Benny Goodman. The 1931 and 1931–32 discs offer sometimes bewildering juxtapositions of corn (Henderson employed some excruciating singers at this time) and real jazz: the extraordinary 'Strangers', on Classics 546, includes an amazing Coleman Hawkins solo in the middle of an otherwise feeble record, while some of the tunes which the Hendersonians might have been expected to handle well – 'Casa Loma Stomp' (Classics 546) and 'Radio Rhythm' (Classics 555) – turn out poorly. Yet the band was still full of fine ensemble players and soloists alike, and some of the Horace Henderson arrangements from this time – especially 'Queer Notions', 'Yeah Man' and 'Wrappin' It Up' (all on Classics 535) – are as well managed as any band of the period could do. Besides, while players of the calibre of Hawkins, Allen and (subsequently) Webster, Berry and Eldridge were on hand, there can't help but be fine moments on many of the records. Classics 535 is certainly the pick of these later discs, with a dozen excellent tracks included. Classics 527 and 519, which were mostly recorded after Henderson temporarily disbanded for a while in 1934 and worked with Goodman, show the vitality of the band sagging, and the final dozen sides they made might have been done by any competent dance orchestra. Transfers are usually reasonably good and clear, although as usual it's the later discs which sound cleaner and less prone to track-to-track fluctuations in quality. The ASV disc compiles 23 of the better tracks from the 1932–37 period, but the sound appears muddier than on the Classics issues. The BBC disc goes through the whole era, and is inevitably a little skimpy, but the 16 tracks all have their virtues and it's a strong start for anyone wanting to hear Henderson's music of the 1930s.

HORACE HENDERSON (born 1904)
PIANO

****   **Horace Henderson 1940** Tax M-8013 LP
Henderson; Emmett Berry, Harry 'Pee Wee' Jackson, Gail Brockman, Nat Bates (*t*); Harold 'Money' Johnson (*t, v*); Ray Nance (*t, vn*); Edward Fant, Nat Atkins, Joe McLewis, Leo Williams, Archie Brown (*tb*); Delbert Bright (*cl, as*); Willie Randall, Howard Johnson, Charles Q. Price (*as*); Elmer Williams, Dave Young, Mosey Gant, Bob Dorsey, Lee Pope (*ts*); Leonard Talley (*bs*); Hurley Ramey, Leroy Harris (*g*); Jesse Simpkins, Israel Crosby (*b*); Oliver Coleman, Debo Williams (*d*); Viola Jefferson (*v*). 2–10/40.

'One of the most talented yet most neglected and enigmatic figures in all of jazz' – Gunther Schuller's verdict on Horace Henderson sounds over-enthusiastic, but the 1940 tracks collected on this important LP go a long way towards bearing out his verdict. Fletcher's brother was a fine, Hines-like pianist, but it was his arranging that was outstanding: the 16 themes collected here include charts by both brothers, and the contrasts between Fletcher's stylized call-and-reponse figures and the fluid, overlapping ideas of Horace are remarkable. Horace's band was full of fine soloists who received sometimes unprecedented space: Nance has two full choruses of violin on the engaging 'Kitty On Toast', and Berry is generously featured throughout: his 'Ain't Misbehavin'' melody is beautifully sustained. But it's the section-work, the saxes full and rich, the brass outstandingly punchy, which brings complex charts to life: 'Shufflin' Joe', the very first track here, is a little masterpiece of varied dynamics and interwoven tone-colours. The rhythm players – including the young Israel Crosby on some of the later sides – are as good as their colleagues. The remastering for LP is effective rather than outstanding, but the force of the music comes through clearly enough.

JOE HENDERSON (born 1937)
TENOR SAXOPHONE

****   **Page One** Blue Note CDP 784140-2
Henderson; Kenny Dorham (*t*); McCoy Tyner (*p*); Butch Warren (*b*); Pete La Roca (*d*). 6/63.

Joe Henderson is always in the middle of a great solo. He's a thematic player, working his way round the structure of a composition with methodical intensity, but he's a masterful licks player too, with a seemingly limitless stock of phrases that he can turn to the advantage of any post-bop setting: this gives his best improvisations a balance of surprise, immediacy and coherence which few other saxophonists can surpass. His lovely tone, which combines softness and plangency in a similar way, is another pleasing aspect of his music. *Page One* was his first date as a leader, and it still stands as one of the most popular Blue Notes of the early 1960s. Henderson had not long since arrived in New York after being discharged from the army, and this six-theme set is very much the work of a new star on the scene. 'Recorda-Me', whose latinate lilt has made it a staple blowing vehicle for hard bop bands, had its debut here, and the very fine tenor solo on Dorham's 'Blue Bossa' explains much of why Henderson was creating excitement. But everything here, even the throwaway blues 'Homestretch', is impressively handled. Tyner, Warren and La Roca are a rhythm section who seldom played together, but they do very well here, as does the erratic Dorham.

****   **Our Thing** Blue Note B21Y-84152 CD
As above, except Andrew Hill (*p*) and Eddie Khan (*b*) replace Tyner and Warren. 9/63.

****   **Inner Urge** Blue Note B21Y-84189 CD
Henderson; McCoy Tyner (*p*); Bob Cranshaw (*b*); Elvin Jones (*d*). 11/64.

***(*)   **Mode For Joe** Blue Note B21Y-84227 CD
Henderson; Lee Morgan (*t*); Curtis Fuller (*tb*); Bobby Hutcherson (*vib, mar*); Cedar Walton (*p*); Ron Carter (*b*); Louis Hayes (*d*). 1/66.

These three discs are now only available as US releases. *Our Thing* was an intriguing meeting with Andrew Hill: Henderson had already worked on the pianist's *Point Of Departure*, and while Hill doesn't contribute anything as a composer here, his sparse and oblique comping and angular solos help to assert the dark qualities which Henderson's records were becoming imbued with. The preponderance of minor-key themes here – even Dorham's three tunes are surprisingly bleak – and the intensity of the improvising create a sombre but compelling climate. *Inner Urge*, which features Henderson as sole horn, is if anything even darker: the title tune, commemorating Henderson's experiences of trying to make a living in New York, is a blistering effort at a medium tempo, and it's interesting to compare Tyner and Jones as they are with Henderson rather than with Coltrane. While the atmosphere isn't as teeth-grittingly intense, it's scarcely less visceral music. Even the sunny reading of 'Night And Day' musters a terrific urgency via Jones's continuously glittering cymbals.

Mode For Joe plants Henderson in a bigger environment, and at times he sounds to be forcing his way out: the solos on the title-track and 'A Shade Of Jade' make a baroque contrast with the otherwise tempered surroundings. Chambers drums with piledriving intensity in places, and though the large number of players tends to constrict the soloists at a time when Henderson could handle all the stretching out he was given, it's still a fine record.

***   **The Best Of Joe Henderson** Blue Note CDP 7956272 CD
As above four discs, plus Richard Davis, Ron Carter (*b*), Al Foster (*d*). 6/63–11/85.

An attractive compilation from the Blue Note period, with two tracks from the otherwise-unavailable *In 'N Out* and one from the latter-day *State Of The Tenor Vol. One*. But there's so much good music on the originals that most will want to hear all of them.

(*)   **The Kicker Original Jazz Classics OJC 465 CD/LP/MC
Henderson; Mike Lawrence (*t*); Grachan Moncur III (*tb*); Kenny Barron (*p*); Ron Carter (*b*); Louis Hayes (*d*). 8/67.

A disheartening step after the Blue Note albums, Henderson's debut for Milestone, now reissued as an OJC, is respectable but prosaic stuff, with Lawrence and Moncur adding little of interest and the tracks sounding short and 'produced'. Much better was to come on Milestone – including a fine live session with Woody Shaw and *In Japan*, a magisterial blowing date with a Tokyo rhythm section – but it all awaits reissue.

****   **The State Of The Tenor Volume One** Blue Note CDP 7462962 CD
Henderson; Ron Carter (*b*); Al Foster (*d*). 11/85.

****   **The State Of The Tenor Volume Two** Blue Note CDP 7464262 CD
As above. 11/85.

Although they had a mixed reception on their release, these records now sound as authoritative as their titles suggest. Henderson hadn't recorded as a leader for some time, and this was his return to the label where he commenced his career, but there is nothing hesitant or routine about the playing here. Carter and Foster provide detailed support – the dates were carefully prepared, the themes meticulously chosen and rehearsed, before the recordings were made at New York's Village Vanguard – and the bassist in particular is as inventive as the nominal leader. Henderson takes an occasional wrong turning, noted perhaps in a recourse to a favourite lick or two, but mostly he functions at the highest level. The intelligent choice of themes – from

Silver, Monk, Mingus, Parker and others, none of them over-familiar – prises a rare multiplicity of phrase-shapes and rhythmical variations out of the tenorman: as a single instance, listen to his manipulations of the beat on Mingus's 'Portrait' (on *Volume Two*), with their accompanying subtleties of tone and attack. Both discs are highly recommended.

***   **An Evening With Joe Henderson** Red 123215-2 CD
Henderson; Charlie Haden (*b*); Al Foster (*d*). 7/87.

More of the same, with Haden substituting for Carter, and the four longish tracks opening out a little further. The music isn't as comprehensively prepared, and Haden's flatter sound and less flexible rhythms make him no match for Carter, but Henderson himself plays with majestic power. Decent concert recording, from the Genoa Jazz Festival of 1987.

***   **Punjab** Arco ARC 104 CD
Henderson; Renée Rosnes (*p*); Marlene Rosenberg (*b*); Sylvia Quenca (*d*). 11/86.

***(*)   **The Standard Joe** Red RR 123248-2 CD
Henderson; Rufus Reid (*b*); Al Foster (*d*). 3/91.

***(*)   **Lush Life** Verve 511 779-2 CD/MC
Henderson; Wynton Marsalis (*t*); Stephen Scott (*p*); Christian McBride (*b*); Gregory Hutchinson (*d*).

There are no studio recordings by the band Henderson formed with an all-female rhythm section, but the Arco release catches the quartet in a club performance from 1986. The one-dimensional sound tells against the music, but the band play with high energy and intensity on three long tunes, with a brief sortie on Monk's 'Friday The Thirteenth' to end on, and the leader's determined playing sets a particular standard. There is very little to choose between the two 1991 recordings, though they're very different from each other. The trio session for Red is an off-the-cuff blowing date, but it's obvious from the first measures of 'Blue Bossa' that all three players are in peak form, and the matching sonorities of Reid and Henderson create a startlingly close level of empathy. There is almost 70 minutes of music, including two long but quite different takes of 'Body And Soul', and the invention never flags. *Lush Life* is a programme of Billy Strayhorn compositions, done as one solo ('Lush Life'), three duos (one with each member of the rhythm section), a lovely quartet reading of 'Blood Count' and three pieces with Marsalis joining the front line, of which 'Johnny Come Lately' is especially spirited. If Henderson's delivery sounds a fraction less assured than he does at his best, the quality of his thinking is as outstanding as always, and though there is the odd tiny blemish – Scott's treatment of 'Lotus Blossom' seems too irritatingly clever – it's a splendid record.

MICHELE HENDRICKS
VOCAL

(*)   **Carryin' On Muse MR/MCD 5336 CD/LP/MC
Hendricks; Stan Getz, Ralph Moore (*ts*); David Leonhardt (*p*); Ray Drummond, Anthony Jackson (*b*); Marvin 'Smitty' Smith (*d*); Kenyate Rahman (*perc*).

(*)   **Keepin' Me Satisfied Muse MR/MCD 5363 CD/LP/MC
Hendricks; Claudio Roditi (*t*); Slide Hampton (*tb*); David Newman (*ss, ts*); David Leonhardt (*p*); Anthony Jackson, Ray Drummond (*b*); Marvin 'Smitty' Smith (*d*); Jon Hendricks (*v*). 5/88.

Jon Hendricks's daughter has a powerful voice of her own, but these scrappy records present her in the endless search for context. Like every singer with mixed jazz and pop ambitions, she can't settle down in either genre. The backings are consistently fine: Leonhardt is a rather moony pianist, but the rhythm sections are otherwise sharp and swinging, and Moore and Getz turn in useful guest-star spots on *Carryin' On*. The biggest problem is with the material: *Carryin' On* is respectably chosen, with a charming 'Dream A Little Dream Of Me' and a well-judged 'Old Devil Moon', but the attempt at funking up 'I Feel The Earth Move' has few planetary virtues. *Keepin' Me Satisfied* is very erratic: Marvin Gaye's 'What's Going On' is a disastrous start, and the duet with her father is pure indulgence; but a virtuoso dash through 'Just In Time' is genuinely clever and exciting. Hendricks has a good voice, but she can't seem to do more than toy with her material and wander between bases. She may have a great record in her yet.

ERNIE HENRY (1926–57)
ALTO SAX

(*)   **Presenting Ernie Henry Original Jazz Classics OJC 102 LP
Henry; Kenny Dorham (*t*); Kenny Drew (*p*); Wilbur Ware (*b*); Art Taylor (*d*). 8/56.

(*)   **Last Chorus Original Jazz Classics OJC 086 LP
As above, plus Lee Morgan (*t*); Melba Liston (*tb*); Benny Golson, Sonny Rollins (*ts*); Cecil Payne (*bs*); Wynton Kelly, Thelonious Monk (*p*); Eddie Mathias, Paul Chambers, Oscar Pettiford (*b*); Philly Joe Jones, Max Roach, Granville T. Hogan (*d*). 8/56–11/57.

Henry left few records in a very brief career, but those he did make reveal a limited but vividly creative post-Parker altoist. His intense tone points towards Jackie McLean, even as his phrasing mixes the wistfulness of Tadd Dameron (with whom he made some of his early records) and Parker's high drama. *Presenting Ernie Henry* is a bit plain, with Dorham an efficient rather than a bountiful partner for Henry, and *Last Chorus*, put together after Henry's death, is a patchwork of bits of various sessions: four tracks by an octet, an out-take from *Presenting*, a quartet with Dorham and an excerpt from Monk's 'Ba-Lue-Bolivar Ba-Lues-Are', which features what's arguably the altoist's best solo on record. His sessions with Monk are perhaps his best memorial, but it's a pity that his other album, the fine *Seven Standards And A Blues*, is currently unavailable.

PETER HERBOLZHEIMER (born 1935)
BANDLEADER, ARRANGER, TROMBONE

(*)   **Bandfire [1] Koala Records Panda 1 CD/2LP

**   **Fat Man Boogie** [2] Koala Records Panda 2 CD/LP

**   **Fatman 2: Tribute To Swing** [3] Koala Records Panda 3 CD/LP

***   **Bigband Bebop** [4] Koala Records Panda 5 CD/LP

***   **More Bebop** [5] Koala Records Panda 6 LP

**   **Music For Swinging Dancers: Volume 1** [6] Koala Records Panda 8

(*)   **Music For Swinging Dancers: Volume 2 [7] Koala Records Panda 9

**   **Music For Swinging Dancers: Volume 3** [8] Koala Records Panda 10

**   **Music For Swinging Dancers: Volume 4** [9] Koala Records Panda 12

***   **Latin Groove** [10] Koala Records Panda 13 CD/LP
Peter Herbolzheimer Rhythm Combination and Brass; Allan Botschinsky (*t, flhn* on 1, 2, 3, 4, 5, 9, 10); Gregg Bowen (*t* on 4, 10); Bob Coassin (*t* on 1, 9, 10); Alan Downey (*t* on 3, 4, 9); Chuck Findley (*t* on 1); Gary Grant (*t* on 2); Andreas Haderer (*t* on 10); Larry McGuire (*t* on 3); Jan Oosthof (*t* on 1, 2, 3, 4, 5, 9, 10); Don Rader (*t* on 1); Ack Van Rooyen (*t, flhn* on 1, 2, 3, 4, 5, 9, 10); Greg Ruvolo (*t* on 9); Derek Watkins (*t* on 3, 5, 10); Otto Bredl (*tb* on 1, 2, 3, 4, 5, 9); Bob Burgess (*tb* on 2); Roy Deuvall (*tb* on 4, 9); Joe Gallardo (*tb* on 10); Torolf Molgaard Kristensen (*tb* on 1); Ulli Launhardt (*tb* on 1); Seep Romeis (*tb* on 10); Bart Van Lier (*tb* on 1, 2, 3, 4, 5, 9, 10); Erik Van Lier (*tb* on 2, 3, 5, 9, 10); Kies Van Den Dolder (*tb* on 9); Barry Ross (*tb* on 1); Jiggs Whigham (*tb* on 2, 3, 4, 5, 9, 10); Karl Drevo (*as, ts* on 2, 3, 4, 5, 9, 10); James Towsey (*as* on 1, 2, 3, 4, 9, 10); Ray Warleigh (*as* on 9); Ferdinand Povel (*ts, ss, f* on 1, 2, 3, 5); John Ruocco (*sax* on 5, 9, 10); Heinz von Hermann (*ts* on 1, 2, 3, 4, 5, 9, 10); Karl Heinz Wiberny (*sax* on 4); Bubi Aderhold (*bs* on 2, 3, 5, 9, 10); Heinz Kretschmar (*b cl* on 5); Thomas Clausen (*p* on 5, 9); Rob Franken (*p, ky* on 1, 2, 3, 4); Jorg Reiter (*p* on 10); Eef Albers (*g* on 1); Stefan Diez (*g* on 9); Peter Tiehuis (*g* on 2, 3, 4, 5, 9, 10); Michael

Hertin (*syn* on 5); Wolfgang Schlüter (*vib*); John Clayton Jr (*b* on 3); Theo De Jong (*b* on 4); Dave King (*b* on 9, 10); Bob Langereis (*b* on 5); Bo Stief (*b* on 1, 2); Mads Vinding (*b* on 10); Bruno Castellucci (*d, perc* on 1, 2, 3, 4, 5, 9, 10); Freddie Santiago (*perc* on 2, 4, 5, 9, 10); Dom Um Romao (*perc* on 10); collective personnel; exact personnel for 6, 7, 8 unknown. 3 & 8/81, 11/81, 1/82, 10 & 12/83, 8/84, 84, 84, 84, 5, 6 & 9/84, 86.

*** **Jazz Gala Concert '79** Rare Bid BID 156501 2LP
Herbolzheimer; Allan Botschinsky, Art Farmer, Chuck Findley, Palle Mikkelborg, Jan Oosthof (*t*); Erich Kleinschuster, Nat Peck, Bart Van Lier, Jiggs Whigham (*tb*); Herb Geller (*as, f*); Tony Coe, Don Menza, Ferdinand Povel (*ts*); Heinz Von Hermann (*bs*); Fritz Pauer (*p, electric p*); Eef Albers (*g*); Niels-Henning Ørsted-Pedersen (*b*); Alex Riel, Grady Tate (*d*); Leata Galloway (*v*). 11/79.

Peter Herbolzheimer's Rhythm Combination and Brass is a superbly schooled and utterly professional big band with a well-deserved reputation among musicians and fans alike. It has retained a remarkably consistent line-up throughout the 1980s and, perhaps as result, can sound on occasions about as exciting as a well-tuned auto engine. On the other hand, Herbolzheimer's charts can generate intense excitment. His handling of trumpets is particularly vivid and it's this aspect that lifts the heavily guest-starred *Jazz Gala Concert* of 1979 right out of the ordinary; alongside such intriguingly named originals as 'The Age Of Prominence' and 'The Mixolydian Highlander' (a reference to one of the modes of medieval music), there are superb readings of 'Giant Steps', 'Stormy Monday' and 'Bluesette'.
  Of the Rhythm Combination albums, by far the best are the two bebop collections (the first has a wonderfully tight version of Charlie Parker's 'Au Privave', the second fine readings of 'Jordu', 'Straight, No Chaser' and 'Goodbye, Pork Pie Hat') though there are excellent things to be found on the more recent *Latin Groove*. The *Music For Swinging Dancers* albums are strictly consumption items, professionally done in the manner of the early dance bands, but with little or no 'hot' material.
  Herbolzheimer's first love is the blues and he is probably the best large-scale arranger of blues themes working outside the United States, where his reputation is still somewhat and unfairly restricted. One doesn't turn to these albums for stratospheric soloing or for collective abstract improvisation (though there are nods here and there to contemporary innovations) but rather for the sheer exhilaration of Herbolzheimer's brass and woodwind voicings.

WOODY HERMAN (1913–87)
CLARINET, ALTO SAXOPHONE, VOCAL

*** **Blues On Parade** MCA GRP 16062 CD
Herman; Clarence Willard, Kermit Simmons, Steady Nelson, Mac MacQuordale, Bob Price, John Owens, Ray Linn, Cappy Lewis, George Seaberg, Billie Rogers, Charles Peterson (*t*); Joe Bishop (*flhn*); Neal Reid, Toby Tyler, Bud Smith, Vic Hamann, Tommy Farr, Walter Nimms (*tb*); Murray Williams, Don Watt, Joe Estrin, Ray Hopfner, Herb Tompkins, Joe Denton, Eddie Scalzi, Jimmy Horvath, Sam Rubinowich (*as*); Saxie Mansfield, Bruce Wilkins, Pete Johns, Ronnie Perry, Nick Caiazza, Sammy Armato, Mickey Folus, Herbie Haymer, Pete Mondello (*ts*); Skippy DeSair (*bs*); Horace Diaz, Tommy Linehan (*p*); Nick Hupfer (*vn*); Chick Reeves, Hy White (*g*); Walter Yoder (*b*); Frank Carlson (*d*). 4/37–7/42.

Woody Herman didn't secure his principal fame until after these early tracks were made, but as an instrumentalist and vocalist he was already a characterful performer, and the pre-war sides – by a band that came together out of the Isham Jones Orchestra in 1936 – were centred mainly around him. There was some light pop fodder in among them but this compilation concentrates on the better material, and while the band is short on strong soloists – trombonist Reid and flugelhorn player Bishop, who also contributed several of the charts, are about the best of them – the arrangements make the most of simple blues resources, one reason why the orchestra was called 'The Band That Plays The Blues'. By the 1940s, though, Herman was seeking out superior material and hiring sharper musicians. Lowell Martin contributed a fine 'Blues In The Night' to the band's book, and the final tune on this disc, 'Down Under', was penned by J⌐ ⌐ Birks Gillespie. Woody himself was a clarinettist whose easy-going playing lacked the ⌐ ⌐

of Goodman or Shaw but made up in affable, on-the-beat timing. A few tracks are by the small band of The Four Chips and the immortal 'Woodchoppers' Ball' is here in its original version, a Joe Bishop head arrangement. The transfers here are mostly superior examples of the NoNOISE system of remastering.

**** **The Thundering Herds 1945–1947** CBS 460825 CD
Herman; Sonny Berman, Shorty Rogers, Conrad Gozzo, Cappy Lewis, Bob Peck, Chuck Petersch, Al Porcino, Pete Candoli, Conte Candoli, Chuck Frankhauser, Carl Warwick, Ray Wetzel, Neal Hefti, Irv Lewis, Ray Linn, Ernie Royal, Bernie Glow, Stan Fisheison, Marky Markowitz (*t*); Bill Harris, Ed Kiefer, Ralph Pfiffner, Neal Reid, Earl Swope, Ollie Wilson, Bob Swift (*tb*); Sam Marowitz, John La Porta (*as*); Herbie Steward (*as, ts*); Mickey Folus, Flip Phillips, Pete Mondello, Stan Getz, Zoot Sims (*ts*); Sam Rubinowich, Skippy Desair, Serge Chaloff (*bs*); Ralph Burns, Jimmy Rowles, Fred Otis, Tony Aless (*p*); Margie Hyams, Red Norvo (*vib*); Chuck Wayne, Billy Bauer, Gene Sargent (*g*); Joe Mondragon, Chubby Jackson, Walt Yoder (*b*); Dave Tough, Don Lamond, Buddy Rich (*d*). 2/45–12/47.

A brilliant rhythm section, a brass team that could top any big band section on either coast and arrangements that crackled with spontaneity and wit: Herman's 1945 band was both a commercial and an artistic triumph. With Burns, Bauer, Tough and Jackson spurring the horns on, the band handled head arrangements and slicker charts such as Neal Hefti's 'Wild Root' with the same mixture of innate enthusiasm and craft. There was a modern edge to the group that suggested something of the transition from swing to bop, even though it was the Second Herd (represented by only two tracks here, with Getz and Sims in the reed section) that threw in its lot with bop spirit if not letter. What endures is the flying wildness of the First Herd: flag-wavers such as 'Northwest Passage' and 'Apple Honey' remain hugely exciting, and the soloists – including Berman, the Candolis, Harris and Phillips – take cameo roles as distinctive as anything that Ellington's or Basie's men were coming up with. Bill Harris, especially, created a niche of his own. There's scarcely a less than outstanding track among the 16 on offer here, even though the sound is thinner than it might have been and the playing time, when there is still much more to reissue, is finally ungenerous.

*** **Woodchoppers' Ball Live 1944 Vol. 1** Jass 621 CD
Herman; Neal Hefti, Billy Robbins, Ray Wetzel, Pete Candoli, Conte Candoli, Charlie Frankhouser, Carl 'Bama' Warwick (*t*); Ralph Pfeffner, Bill Harris, Ed Kiefer (*tb*); Sam Marowitz, Bill Shine, John LaPorta (*as*); Flip Phillips, Pete Mondello (*ts*); Skippy Desair (*bs*); Ralph Burns (*p*); Margie Hyams (*vib*); Billy Bauer (*g*); Chubby Jackson (*b*); Dave Tough (*d*); Frances Wayne (*v*). 8–10/44.

***(*) **Northwest Passage Live 1945 Vol. 2** Jass 625 CD
As above, except add Sonny Berman, Ray Linn (*t*), Tony Aless (*p*), omit Robbins and Shine. 7–8/45.

Live material by Herman was reissued in a somewhat haphazard way in the LP era, and these two CDs sort out a few broadcasts with good sound and sensible programming. The first includes a V-Disc version of 'Flying Home' and two broadcast sessions. Herman, Harris, Phillips and Pete Candoli take the lion's share of the solo features and the band sound in exuberant form. But the second disc, with this edition of the Herd really getting into its stride, is even better: Frances Wayne has two of her best features in 'Saturday Night' and 'Happiness Is A Thing Called Joe' and the band rocket through 'Apple Honey', 'Bijou' and 'Red Top'. A valuable supplement to the studio sessions.

*** **Early Autumn** Discovery DSCD-944 CD
Herman; Don Fagerquist, John Howell, Roy Caton, Stu Williamson, Tommy DiCarlo, Joe Brunette, Ernie Royal, Bernie Glow, Harold Wegbreit, Bobby Styles, Doug Mettome, Chris Griffin, Phil Cook, Dick Collins, Al Porcino, Reuben McFall, Bill Gastagnino, Arno Marsh, Bill Perkins, Charlie Walp (*t*); Cy Touff (*bt*); Carl Fontana, Urbie Green, Jack Green, Will Bradley, Frank Rehak, Vernon Friley, Kai Winding, Dick Kenney, Keith Moon (*tb*); Arno Marsh, Dick Hafer, Bill Perkins, Bill Trujillo, Jerry Coker, Dave Madden (*ts*); Sam Staff (*bs, f*); Jack Nimitz (*bs*); Nat Pierce (*p, cel*); Chubby Jackson, Red Kelly (*b*); Sonny Igoe, Art Mardigan, Chuck Flores (*d*); Candido Camero, Jose Manguel (*perc*). 5/52–7/54.

Frustratingly, almost nothing by Woody's Second Herd (with the Four Brothers rhythm section) is generally available at present. The 'Early Autumn' here is primarily a feature for Herman as a vocalist (and a fine one, too). This CD collects 17 performances by the Third Herd: it may have lacked the starry quality of the previous band, and in the aftermath of the big band era charts such as 'Four Others' (a 'Four Brothers' revision for the trombone section) and the light hokum of 'Mother Goose Jumps' sound anachronistic at a time when, for instance, Shorty Rogers was streamlining big band practice. But the orchestra still had a lot of very good players, and a piece such as 'Men From Mars' finds the Herd adjusting to cooler conditions with a fair degree of success. The remastering has been carefully done and the band sound big and strong.

****   **Live Featuring Bill Harris Vol. 1** Status STCD 107 CD
Herman; Bill Berry, John Cappola, Bill Castagnino, Andy Peele, Danny Styles (*t*); Bill Harris, Bobby Lamb, Willie Dennis (*tb*); Jay Migliori, Jimmie Cooke, Bob Newman (*ts*); Roger Pemberton (*bs*); John Bunch (*p*); Jimmy Gannon (*b*); Don Michaels (*d*). 6/57.

****   **Live Featuring Bill Harris Vol. 2** Status STCD 110 CD
As above. 6/57.

***(*)   **Live At Peacock Lane Hollywood 1958** Bandstand BD 1508 CD/LP
Herman; Danny Stiles, Bobby Clark, John Cappola, Andy Peele, Hal Posey (*t*); Bill Harris, Archie Martin, Roy Weigand (*tb*); Joe Romano, Jay Migliori, Arno Marsh (*ts*); Roger Pemberton (*bs*); Pete Jolly (*p*); Jimmy Gannon (*b*); Jake Hanna (*d*). 1/58.

Superbly remastered by Dave Kay, the Status CDs are wonderful souvenirs of the Herman band as it sounded on a typical dance date in Omaha in 1957. While Woody's records for Capitol and Verve from the 1950s have nearly all slipped from circulation, these live sets are a glowing testimony to how fine the band could be. The ballads have a smooth, perfectly cooked texture, the brass almost gliding from piano to forte, but the swingers hit home with astonishing precision, and the arrangements – mostly by Ralph Burns or Gene Roland – play to all the strengths of the band and give them enough to chew on to keep everybody interested. The simple notion of Roland's 'Stairway To The Blues' is almost a textbook exercise, but the band make it into a classic performance, finding just the right tempo and leavening with half-a-dozen solos that lead to Bill Harris's climactic statement. Harris had already been with Herman for many years, but only now was he genuinely asserting himself as the band's major soloist, his playing utterly unpredictable and individual from phrase to phrase. Both discs are full of great music, and so is the Peacock Lane session, which is also in fine sound: there is a spellbinding feature for Harris in Ralph Burns's arrangement of 'Gloomy Sunday', but the reeds have a very good night of it as well. The best of Herman's Capitol records from the period, meanwhile, languish in neglect. The Peacock Lane music can also be found on Jazz Hour 1004.

***   **Compact/Walkman Jazz: Woody Herman** Verve 835319 CD/MC
Herman; John Bello, Doug Mettome, Roy Caton, Don Ferrara, Nick Travis, John Coppola, Bill Castagnino, Billy Berry, Andrew Peele, Danny Stiles, John Macombe, Harry Edison, Billy Hunt, Dave Gale, Bill Chase, Gerald Lamy, Paul Fontaine, Ziggy Harrell (*t*); Urbie Green, Jerry Dorn, Herb Randel, Bill Harris, Willie Dennis, Bob Lamb, Jerry Dorn, Fred Lewis, Bob Rudolph, Phil Wilson, Henry Southall, Eddie Morgan (*tb*); Kenny Pinson, Phil Urso, Jack Dulong, Bill Perkins, Sal Nistico, Gordon Brisker, Larry Covelli, Bobby Jones, Ben Webster, Jimmy Cooke, Jay Migliori, Bob Newman (*ts*); Sam Staff, Gene Allen, Frank Hittner, Roger Pemberton (*bs*); Nat Pierce, Dave McKenna, Jimmy Rowles, John Bunch (*p*); Red Wooten, Chuck Andrus, Joe Mondragon, Jimmy Gannon (*b*); Sonny Igoe, Larry Bunker, Don Michaels, Jake Hanna (*d*). 3/51–5/63.

A spirited if erratic cross-section of Herman's work for Verve. There is better Herman elsewhere: the earliest (1951) tracks are unexceptional, and some of the six 1963 tracks (recorded live) are played almost for laughs, especially a kitsch treatment of 'Bijou' and a version of 'Caldonia' taken at such a fast tempo that Sal Nistico's tenor solo barely touches the ground. Better are a boisterous arrangement of 'Camel Walk' featuring Phil Wilson, and a couple of somewhat out-of-place small-group tracks, a 1957 'Makin' Whoopee' with Harry Edison and Ben Webster, and a quartet reading of 'Pee Wee Blues' featuring Herman's clarinet.

***   **1963 Summer Tour** Jazz Hour 1006 CD
Herman; Bill Hunt, Dave Gale, Bill Chase, Gerald Lamy, Paul Fontaine (*t*); Bob
Rudolph, Phil Wilson, Henry Southall (*tb*); Sal Nistico, Bobby Jones, Carmen Leggio,
Jack Stevens (*ts*); Frank Hittner, Marvin Holladay (*bs*); Nat Pierce (*p*); Chuck Andrus
(*b*); Jake Hanna (*d*). 63.

***(*)   **Live In Antibes 1965** France's Concert FC 117 CD/LP
Herman; Bill Chase, Don Rader, Dusko Goykovich, Gerald Lamy, Bobby Shew (*t*);
Ron Myers, Don Doane, Henry Southall (*tb*); Sal Nistico, Andy McGhee, Gary Klein
(*ts*); Tom Anastas (*bs*); Nat Pierce (*p*); Anthony Leonardi (*b*); Ronnie Zito (*d*). 7/65.

An incessant roadworker, Herman kept going through what were supposed to be very lean
years for traditional big bands: only Basie and Ellington could pace him so far as continuous
gigging was concerned. He sharpened the band with younger players: the trumpet section
especially had hit a rare peak by 1965, and arrangements by Don Rader and Bill Chase were a
blend of familiar Herman virtues – bright, brassy swing and soloists who characterized rather
than slotted into scores – with leaner, more subtly paced scoring. The showstoppers – like the
amazing all-trumpet chase of '23 Red', or the deep-set funky swing of Horace Silver's 'The
Preacher' – were what still galvanized audiences, though. Nor did Herman's own clarinet and
alto take any lesser a role: even if almost everyone else had abandoned the clarinet, Herman –
hardly thought of as the equal of either Shaw or Goodman – still made it sound sharply
effective without ever altering his style in the slightest. Both of these live albums capture much
of the sheer clout which the best Herman Herds could turn on seemingly every night. The Jazz
Hour set features a few surprising choices – 'Jazz Me Blues', 'Days Of Wine And Roses' –
alongside current staple such as 'Watermelon Man' and Sal Nistico's barnstorming tear-up on
'Sister Sadie'. The Antibes set covers much of the same ground as the classic out-of-print
album *Woody's Winners* (Columbia), in what is good sound for the source; the Jazz Hour set is
slightly paler. But both are highly entertaining records.

***   **Live In Seattle** Moon M 002 CD/LP
Herman; Richard Cooper, John Madrid, Harry Hall, Bill Chase (*t*); Vincent Prudente,
Bob Burgess (*tb*); Frank Vicari, Sal Nistico, Steve Lederer (*ts*); Ronnie Cuber (*bs*);
John Hicks (*p*); Michael Moore (*b*); Jack Ranelli (*d*). 67.

***   **Somewhere** Moon 030 CD/LP
As above, except add Bill Byrne (*t*), Bruce Fowler (*tb*). 5/69.

Herman wasn't just trying to keep up. He interpolated pop material into his sets to keep the
band interested – after all, he was still playing 'Woodchoppers Ball' in Rome in 1969, where
Somewhere was made, and a band can't survive on 30-year-old material alone – and while some
may wince at hearing him tackle 'Hush' (on *Live In Seattle*) or 'I Say A Little Prayer' and
'Light My Fire', as he did in Rome, the band swing harder, if anything, than they do on the
more deliberate jazz material. 'Light My Fire' remains a useless song, and it seems a trifle
bizarre when 'I Say A Little Prayer' segues into first 'Woodchoppers Ball' and then an
Ellington medley, but the orchestra makes the transition work. This was still a very strong
Herman Herd: the tenor section romp through an updated 'Four Brothers' on the earlier disc,
Cuber is a forthright and winning soloist, and Hicks and Moore direct the rhythm section with
canny intensity: it's a pity that Hicks is often lost in the mix on the earlier disc, and his feature
on 'Greasy Sack Blues' is dispersed as a result. Otherwise the sound-quality is quite full-bodied
and reasonably transparent on both sessions, the second having the brass more upfront. Flawed,
perhaps, but these are both highly enjoyable sessions: Herman's band refused to stop swinging.

***   **The 40th Anniversary Carnegie Hall Concert** RCA Bluebird ND 86878 CD/MC
Herman; Pete Candoli, Conte Candoli, Alan Vizutti, Nelson Hatt, John Hoffman,
Dennis Dotson, Bill Byrne, Danny Styles (*t*); Phil Wilson, Jim Pugh, Dale Kirkland
(*tb*); Jim Daniels (*btb*); Stan Getz, Flip Phillips, Zoot Sims, Jimmy Giuffre, Sam
Marowitz, Frank Tiberi, Gary Anderson, Joe Lovano, John Oslawski (*reeds*); Jimmy
Rowles, Nat Pierce, Ralph Burns, Pat Coil (*p, ky*); Billy Bauer (*g*); Chubby jackson,
Rusty Holloway (*b*); Don Lamond, Jake Hanna, Dan D'Imperio (*d*); Mary Ann
McCall (*v*). 11/76.

***   **Early Autumn** RCA Bluebird ND 90629 CD
As above. 11/76.

A star-studded occasion for sure: most of the original Four Brothers deliver the famous set-piece (with composer Giuffre and Al Cohn subbing for the departed Herbie Steward and Serge Chaloff), 'Apple Honey' and 'Bijou' roll back the years, and the huge augmented Herd steam through the programme. Not much genuinely memorable jazz, perhaps, and more of a grand party than anything, but Herman fans will enjoy it. *Early Autumn* trims the programme down to a bargain-price six choice numbers from the dozen on the full-length CD.

**(*)   Road Father BBC Century CJ 829 CD/MC
Herman; Jay Sollenburger, Allen Vizutti, Nelson Hatt, Glenn Drewes, Dennis Dotson, Bill Byrne (*t, flhn*); Birch Johnson, Larry Farrell (*tb*); Jim Daniels (*btb*); Frank Tiberi, Gary Anderson, Joe Lovano, Bruce Johnstone (*reeds*); Pat Coil (*p*); Marc Johnson (*b*); Jeff Hamilton (*d*); Jack Arnold (*perc*). 1/78.

*   Plays Chick, Donald, Walter And Woodrow BBC Century CJ 830 CD/MC
As above, except add Tom Scott (*ts*), Victor Feldman (*ky, perc*), Mitch Holder (*g*).

Two albums originally recorded for direct-to-disc: great sound, but the music is a terrible decline. *Road Father* at least asserts some of Herman's traditional values, with a version of Charles Mingus's 'Duke Ellington's Sound Of Love' that's powerful in its melancholy; Lovano is good here, and on 'Isn't She Lovely', which suggests something of the joy Sonny Rollins found in the tune. But the second album is a disaster. Chick Corea contributes a preposterously overblown 20-minute suite, and the rest is Steely Dan material which sounds absurdly pretentious away from the pop-irony of the composers' versions.

***   La Fiesta West Wind WW 2400 2CD
Herman; Bill Byrne, Glenn Drewes, Dave Kennedy, Jim Powell (*t, flhn*); Timothy Burke (*t*); Birch Johnson, Nelson Hinds (*tb*); Larry Shunk (*btb*); Bill Ross, Frank Tiberi, Joe Lovano (*ts, f*); Gary Smulyan (*bs*); Dava Lalama (*p*); Jay Andersen (*b*); John Riley (*d*). 11/78.

A typical late-period Herman concert, cut in the DDR in 1978. The gamut runs from 'Caldonia' through to two fine new scores by Alan Broadbent, a modish but not unfortunate take on 'Fanfare For The Common Man' and Woody's vocal on 'Laura' – despite his gangsterish speaking voice, his singing style still sounds remarkably light and romantic. Good sound, and although the best of the music could probably have been better edited down to a single CD, Herman followers will want this one.

***   Woody And Friends Concord CCD 4170 CD/MC
Herman; Dizzy Gillespie, Joe Rodriguez, Tim Burke, Kitt Reid, Jim Powell, Bill Byrne, Woody Shaw (*t*); Birch Johnson, Nelson Hinds, Larry Shunk, Slide Hampton (*tb*); Frank Tiberi (*ts, f, bsn*); Dick Mitchell (*ts, f, af, ob, picc*); Bob Belden, Stan Getz (*ts*); Gary Smulyan (*bs*); Dava Lalama (*p*); Dave LaRocca (*b*); Ed Soph (*d*). 9/79.

***   Woody Herman Presents . . . Vol. 1: A Concord Jam Conord CCD 4142 CD/MC
Herman; Warren Vaché (*c*); Eiji Kitamura (*cl*); Dick Johnson (*as, f*); Scott Hamilton (*ts*); Dave McKenna (*p*); Cal Tjader (*vib*); Cal Collins (*g*); Bob Maize (*b*); Jake Hanna (*d*). 8/80.

***   Woody Herman Presents . . . Vol. 2: Four Others Concord CK 180 MC
Herman; Al Cohn, Sal Nistico, Flip Philips, Bill Perkins (*ts*); John Bunch (*p*); George Duvivier (*b*); Don Lamond (*d*). 7/81.

**(*)   Live At The Concord Jazz Festival Concord CCD 4191 CD/MC
Herman; Brian O'Flaherty, Scott Wagstaff, Mark Lewis, George Rabbai, Bill Stapleton (*t, flhn*); Gene Smith, John Fedchock, Larry Shunk (*tb*); Bill Ross (*ts, f, af, picc*); Paul McGinley (*ts, f*); Randy Russell (*ts, f*); Al Cohn, Zoot Sims (*ts*); Nick Brignola (*bs, bcl*); John Oddo (*p*); Mike Hall (*b*); Dave Ratajczak (*d*). 8/81.

***   Live In Chicago Status 105 CD
As above. 3/81.

**(*)   World Class Concord CCD 4240 CD/MC
As above, except Bill Byrne (*t, flhn*), Randy Hawes (*tb*), Sal Nistico, Jim Carroll, Med Flory, Flip Phillips, Frank Tiberi (*ts*), Dave Shapiro (*b*), Jeff Hamilton (*perc*) replace Stapleton, Shunk, Ross, Russell, Sims and Hall. 9/82.

518

(*)   **Woody Herman Presents . . . Vol. 3: A Great American Evening** Concord CJ 220 MC
Herman; Jack Sheldon (*t, v*); George Masso (*tb*); Eiji Kitamura (*cl*); Scott Hamilton
(*ts*); Nat Pierce (*p*); Cal Collins (*g*); Bob Maize (*b*); Jake Hanna (*d*). 4/83.

***   **50th Anniversary Tour** Concord CCD 4302 CD/MC
Herman; Roger Ingram, Les Lovitt, Mark Lewis, Ron Stout, Bill Byrne (*t*); John
Fedchock, Paul McKee (*tb*); Mark Lusk (*btb*); Dave Riekenberg (*ts, f*); Frank Tiberi,
Jerry Pinter (*ts*); Nick Brignola (*bs*); Brad Williams (*p*); Lynn Seaton (*b*); Jim Rupp
(*d*). 3/86.

(*)   **Woody's Gold Star** Concord CCD 4330 CD/MC
As above, except George Baker, Jim Powell (*t, flhn*), Joe Barati (*btb*), Joel Weiskopf
(*p*), Nick Carpenter (*b*), Dave Miller (*d*), Pete Escovedo, Poncho Sanchez, Ramon
Banda (*perc*) replace Lovitt, Lewis, Lusk, Williams, Seaton and Rupp. 3/87.

Herman's final years were capably documented by Concord, and although there are no truly
outstanding records in this stint there are good standards of big-band playing on the orchestral
records and plenty of characteristic Herman dudgeon on the small-group discs. Though his final
years were tragically marred by problems with the IRS he somehow found the spirit to play jazz
with much of his old fire. What had changed – as it did for Ellington, Basie and Goodman, his
fellow survivors from a bygone era – was the traditional big band's place in the music. As a
repertory orchestra, filled with good idiomatic players but few real characters, Herman's last
Herd had no more going for it than precision and automatic punch. *Woody And Friends* finds
them at the 1979 Monterey Festival, with Gillespie, Hampton, Shaw and Getz (doing a lovely
'What Are You Doing The Rest Of Your Life') as guest stars, and the occasion is
atmospherically recalled by the record. The *Concord Jam* session mixes young and older players
and everyone is in strong voice, with features for everybody. *Four Others* lines up four tenor
stalwarts to so-so effect, while the *Great American Evening* re-runs the earlier jam session to
slightly lesser effect. The remaining big band records all have their moments without securing
any serious candidacy for a collection that already has plenty of vintage Herman in it.

HEROINES
GROUP

**   **She's Back** Cadence CJR 1040 LP
Jan Labate (*as, vla*); Victoria Trent (*b, v*); Sybl Joan Glebow (*d, hca, v*). 11/84–4/88.

This Californian trio create a sparse, reflective kind of free jazz: all eight pieces are improvised
and depend on interplay rather than melodic or rhythmic impetus. The best player is Labate,
who studied with Jimmy Lyons and has some interesting ideas on alto, although her viola
playing was ill-advised. So, unfortunately, is Trent's desultory vocalizing. Unglamorous but
truthful recording.

FRED HERSCH
PIANO

***   **Horizons** Concord CJ 267 MC
Hersch; Marc Johnson (*b*); Joey Baron (*d*). 10/84.

***   **Sarabande** Sunnyside SSC 1024 CD
Hersch; Charlie Haden (*b*); Joey Baron (*d*). 12/86.

***   **Heartsongs** Sunnyside SSC 1047 CD
Hersch; Mike Formanek (*b*); Jeff Hirshfield (*d*). 12/89.

Even though he denies the closeness of the affinity, Fred Hersch is one of the guardians of Bill
Evans's light. He's rhythmically more varied in his approach than Evans but, in terms of touch
and harmonic sensibility, there's a very close parallel. Originals such as 'Lullabye'
(*Heartsongs*) and 'Child's Song' (*Sarabande*) are close kin to Evans's ballads, too. But Hersch
has an energy of his own, and these are three very gratifying trio records. *Heartsongs* is the
best-integrated, since it's by a regular trio: Haden is a little too stodgy to make *Sarabande*'s

liveliest tunes break out, and *Horizons* is good though a trifle routine. *Heartsongs* has the most individual approach to the material, and Hersch chooses good covers: Wayne Shorter's 'Fall' is done in *passacaglia* form, and Ornette Coleman's 'The Sphinx' casts the composer in an impish light. But a few of the freer pieces sound more effortful than they should: Hersch may be an impressive conservative, but he's a conservative all the same.

ANDREW HILL (born 1937)
PIANO

***   **Live At Montreux** Freedom 41023 CD/LP
Hill (*p* solo). 7/75.

(*)   **Faces Of Hope Soul Note 1010 CD/LP
As above. 6/80.

***(*)   **Verona Rag** Soul Note 1110 CD/LP
As above. 7/86.

Hill's whole career has been marked by the silences that punctuate his compositions. Of the important bop and post-bop pianists – Bud Powell, Horace Silver, Mal Waldron, Paul Bley, Cecil Taylor – he is the least known and most erratically documented; even Herbie Nichols enjoys a certain posthumous cachet. And if Hill's primary influence is Thelonious Monk, the connection is more a matter of spirit and personality than of direct technical inheritance. He is in every respect an original.

Born in Haiti, Hill's work has been marked by the same emotional and spiritual ambivalence one associates with that divided island. Marked by a forceful dissonance, unusual and unsettling harmonic intervals, its dark, incantatory manner sometimes obscures a lighter, folksy side. Like Monk's, his gammy melodic patterns work better either solo or with horns; conventional trio playing represents only a suprisingly small proportion of his output.

Of the solo albums, the latest and best is *Verona Rag*, a gloriously joyous set full of romping vamps, gentle ballad interludes and Hill's characteristic harmonic ambiguities. Not recognized as a standards player, he invests 'Darn That Dream' with an almost troubling subtext in the bass that stops just short of reinventing the tune.

The Montreux set is marred by some unevenness of tone and *Faces Of Hope* by some of his least compelling charts. However, both are essential purchases for Hill enthusiasts and only disappoint relative to an astonishingly high career standard.

****   **Black Fire** Blue Note BCT 84151 CD
Hill; Richard Davis (*b*); Roy Haynes (*d*). 63.

Hill's debut was a startling blend of unfamiliar harmonics and a driving but asymmetrical beat, both carried right across the trio and given further impetus by Hill's imaginative adaptation of non-jazz intervals and melodic materials. 'Subterfuge' is probably the quintessential Hill performance of the time, all awkward corners and unresolvable dilemmas, but dancing self-confidently over Haynes's multi-directional line.

*****   **Point Of Departure** B11E 81467 CD/LP/MC
Hill; Kenny Dorham (*t*); Eric Dolphy (*as, f, bcl*); Joe Henderson (*ts*); Richard Davis (*b*); Tony Williams (*d*). 3/64.

One of the very great jazz albums of the 1960s. Nowhere is Hill's determination to build on the example of Monk clearer than on the punningly titled 'New Monastery'. Hill's solo, like that on the long previous track 'Refuge', is constructed out of literally dozens of subtle shifts in the time-signature, most of them too subliminal to be strictly counted. Typically, Hill is prepared to hold the basic beat himself and to allow Williams to range very freely. 'Spectrum' is the one disappointment, too self-conscious an attempt to run a gamut of emotions and instrumental colours; an extraordinary 5/4 passage for the horns almost saves the day. Henderson at first glance doesn't quite fit, but his solos on 'Spectrum' and 'Refuge' are exemplary and in the first case superior to Dolphy's rather insubstantial delivery. The mood of the session switches dramatically on the final 'Dedication', a dirge with a beautiful structure that represents the sharpest contrast to the rattling progress of the previous 'Flight 19' and brings the set full circle.

Hill's writing and arranging skills matured dramatically with *Point Of Departure*. Unfortunately, he had the opportunity to record with similar forces only occasionally in years to come and suffered long neglect, pigeon-holed with the awkward squad. The original sound was so good that little sweetening seems to have been required for the CD. Unfortunately, digital processing gives a rather brittle quality to Dolphy's and Hill's contributions, overstates the drums to a degree, and gives Davis's fine, almost pianistic lines a whumphing sonority that kills their subtlety. An essential purchase, even so.

***   **Spiral** Freedom 41007 CD/LP
     Hill; Ted Curson (*t, flhn, picc t*); Robin Kenyatta (*as*); Lee Konitz (*as, ts, ss*); Stafford James, Cecil McBee (*b*); Barry Altschul, Art Lewis (*d*). 12/74, 1/75.

Spiral is a slightly mixed album, featuring two rather different bands. The sessions with Konitz, Curson, McBee and Lewis are smoother and outwardly less oblique, but without cost to the harmonic interest. The disposition of Curson's and Konitz's three horns apiece (it's often now forgotten how adept Konitz was on tenor and even baritone saxophones) invest 'Laverne', 'The Message' and the title-track with maximum variety, and the solos are extremely effective. By no means an afterthought on this session, there is a duo 'Invitation' by Hill and Konitz, spontaneously done and strongly recalling Hill's Waldron-like talents as an accompanist. (The performance compares very favourably with the trio version Hill was to make the following year on a fine album of that name [*Invitation*, Inner City 2026].)

In contrast to the variety he achieves with Konitz, the sessions with alto saxophonist Robin Kenyatta, another adoptive New Yorker with a highly individual musical background, are much more direct and to the point, with less self-conscious manipulation of mood. Kenyatta is a fine and restless player, who nevertheless prefers to get down to business, doing most of his soul-searching and experimentation on his own time.

***   **Divine Revelation** Steeplechase 1044 LP
     Hill; Jimmy Vass (*as, ss, f*); Chris White (*b*); Leroy Williams (*d*). 7/75.

Recorded in the same month as *Live At Montreux*, *Divine Revelation* shares not only 'Snake Hip Waltz' but the solo album's strengths and vices in almost equal parts. Oddly for a player as percussive as Hill, and one with such a good right hand, he has proven to be surprisingly dependent on a sympathetic drummer and bassist, Tony Williams and Richard Davis on the classic *Point Of Departure*, Ben Riley and Rufus Reid in recent years. Williams and White clearly understand what Hill is about and mesh convincingly with his more elaborately extended metres. However 'pianistic' a player Hill is, he has a great understanding of horn, and it's a pity that Vass should be so light of touch, occasionally almost lost in a too-resonant mix (a CD transfer might help out).

The quartet version of 'Snake Hip Waltz' is tough and abrasive (and a lot more direct than the Montreux version) but it rides over a pattern that belies the title and sets up interference patterns that demand the nimblest footwork. At a full 25 minutes, 'Divine Revelation' itself is too self-conscious a choreography of slow-slow-quick-quick-slow. Like 'Spectrum' on *Point Of Departure*, Hill is clearly anxious to exploit the fullest dynamic range, but he does so here to the detriment of any dramatic or emotional logic.

Hill's isn't an anti-climactic music, but it is sufficiently abstract to rule out any conventional excitation: theme, repetition, climax. On the little-known *Lift Every Voice* [Blue Note BST 84330] Hill tried to get round the problem by using a small, gospelly choir. On 'Divine Revelation' he gets mixed up, climax before foreplay, a moody solo genesis followed too abruptly by a noisy apocalypse, followed out of turn by a long, tedious piano genealogy. Half a good album. Or a good half-album, depending on how you look at it.

****   **Shades** Soul Note 1113 CD/LP
     Hill; Clifford Jordan (*ts*); Rufus Reid (*b*); Ben Riley (*d*). 7/86.

***(*)   **Eternal Spirit** Blue Note 792051 CD
     Hill; Greg Osby (*as*); Bobby Hutcherson (*vib*); Rufus Reid (*b*); Ben Riley (*d*). 1/89.

***   **But Not Farewell** Blue Note 7949712 CD
     Hill; Greg Osby (*as, ss*); Robin Eubanks (*tb*); Lonnie Plaxico (*b*); Cecil Brooks III (*d*).

Far from settling back into a comfortable accommodation with a 'personal style', Hill's work of the later 1980s has been as adventurous as anything he has done since *Point Of Departure*. Reid and Riley create exactly the right background for him, taut but undogmatic, elastic around the end of phrases, constantly propulsive without becoming predictable.

Shades is one of the very best jazz albums of the decade. The two trio tracks – that is, with the pungent Jordan absent – are probably the finest since his debut on *Black Fire*. Hill has been inclined to avoid the conventional trio format. Like Monk, he operates better either solo or with horns, but on 'Tripping' and 'Ball Square' he is absolutely on top of things, trading bass lines with Reid and constantly stabbing in alternative accents. 'Monk's Glimpse' pays not altogether submissive homage to Hill's spiritual ancestor.

The one slight misgiving about the album is its sound, which is a trifle dark, even on CD. In that regard particularly, the move back to Blue Note was rather significant. On *Eternal Spirit*, Rudy Van Gelder gives Hill a much brighter mien, accentuating the bounce in his playing. The material, too, is sunnier than one normally associates with him. That's especially obvious in the up-tempo 'Tail Feather', with Hutcherson and Osby better attuned to these speeds than to the ballad form of 'Bobby's Tune'. Osby recalls the urgency of Jimmy Vass on *Divine Revelation* but with a firmer tone. Hutcherson has seldom sounded this good in recent years on his own albums; the approach is gentler and less percussive now but still powerful.

But Not Farewell is a slightly disappointing follow-up. Hill's group-playing is by now an almost perfect inversion of a common practice among the Old Master painters, assigning students and apprentices the big, easy washes and unimportant background detail while the Master concentrates on the foreground portraiture or the salient parts of the landscape. By contrast, Hill assigns the foreground to his sidemen and then distracts attention totally by creating backgrounds of such ambiguous and shifting fascination that the foreground becomes almost a distraction. Which is a pity, because Osby and Eubanks play well, particularly on the title-track. 'Gone' – with a whisper of a quote from 'My Man's Gone Now' – is vintage Hill. *Eternal Spirit* remains Hill's friendliest and most accessible recording. As such, it's an excellent place to start, by which time some more of the 1960s classics might be restored to their rightful place in the catalogue.

EARL HINES (1905–89)
PIANO, VOCAL

***(*)   Earl Hines 1928–1932 Classics 545 CD
Hines; Shirley Clay, George Mitchell, Charlie Allen, George Dixon, Walter Fuller (*t*); William Franklin (*tb, v*); Lester Boone, Omer Simeon (*cl, as, bs*); Darnell Howard (*cl, as, vn*); Toby Turner (*cl, as*); Cecil Irwin (*cl, ts*); Claude Roberts (*bj, g*); Lawrence Dixon (*g*); Quinn Wilson (*bb, b*); Hayes Alvis (*bb*); Wallace Bishop (*d*). 12/28–6/32.

****   Earl Hines 1932–1934 Classics 514 CD
As above, except add Louis Taylor, Trummy Young, Kenneth Stuart (*tb*); Jimmy Mundy (*cl, ts*); Herb Jeffries (*v*); omit Clay, Mitchell, Boone, Turner, Roberts and Alvis. 7/32–3/34.

***(*)   Earl Hines 1934–1937 Classics 528 CD
As above, except add Milton Fletcher (*t*); Budd Johnson (*ts*); The Palmer Brothers, Ida Mae James (*v*); omit Franklin. 9/34–2/37.

Earl Hines had already played on some of the greatest of all jazz records – with Louis Armstrong's Hot Five – before he made any sessions under his own name. The piano solos he made in Long Island and Chicago, one day apart in December 1928, are collected on the first Classics CD – a youthful display of brilliance which has seldom been surpassed. His ambidexterity, enabling him to finger runs and break up and supplant rhythms at will, is still breathtaking, and his range of pianistic devices is equalled only by Tatum and Taylor. But these dozen pieces were a preamble to a career which, in the 1930s, was concerned primarily with bandleading. The remainder of the first Classics disc is filled with the first recordings by the orchestra which Hines led at Chicago's Grand Terrace Club for 10 years, from December 1928. Their 1929 sessions struggle to find an identity, and only the leader cuts any impressive figures.

The 1932–4 sessions on the second record are better played, better organized and full of brilliant Hines. The surprising thing may be Hines's relatively subordinate role within the band: he had few aspirations to compose or arrange, entrusting those duties to several other hands (including Fuller, Mundy, Johnson, Crowder and Wilson); he revelled instead in the role of star soloist within what were increasingly inventive frameworks. By 1934, the band was at its first peak, with fine Mundy arrangements like 'Cavernism' (including a startling violin solo by Darnell Howard) and 'Fat Babes' and Wilson's vigorous revisions of older material such as 'Maple Leaf Rag' and 'Wolverine Blues'. It's a pity that the chronology has split the 1934 sessions between the second and third Classics volumes. Hines is a wonder throughout, both in solo and in the commentaries with which he counters the arrangements. The other prinicpal soloist is Walter Fuller, a spare, cool-to-hot stylist whose occasional vocals are agreeable copies of Armstrong. The 1934–7 disc shows an unfortunate decline in the consistency of the material, and their move to Vocalion to record coincided with a dissipation of the band's energy.

All three records feature transfers which are respectable rather than notably effervescent, which is disappointing – the sound of the original recordings is excellent, as John R. T. Davies had shown on some earlier LP transfers for Hep, currently yet to emerge on CD.

***   **Earl Hines 1937–1939** Classics 538 CD
Hines; Walter Fuller (*t, v*); Milton Fletcher, Charlie Allen, Freddy Webster, George Dixon, Edward Sims (*t*); Louis Taylor, Trummy Young, Kenneth Stuart, Joe McLewis, Edward Bruke, John Ewing (*tb*); Omer Simeon (*cl, as, bs*); Leroy Harris (*cl, as, v*); Darnell Howard (*cl, as*); Budd Johnson (*cl, as, ts*); William Randall, Leon Washington (*cl, ts*); Robert Crowder (*ts*); Lawrence Dixon, Claude Roberts (*g*); Quinn Wilson (*b*); Wallace Bishop, Alvin Burroughs, Oliver Coleman (*d*); Ida Mae James (*v*). 37–39.

***   **Earl Hines 1939–1940** Classics 567 CD
As above, except add Shirley Clay, Harry Jackson, Rostelle Reese, Leroy White (*t*); Edward Fant (*tb*); Scoops Carey (*as*); Franz Jackson, Jimmy Mundy (*ts*); Hurley Ramey (*g*); Truck Parham (*b*); Billy Eckstine, Laura Rucker, Madeline Green (*v*); omit Allen, Taylor, Young, Stuart, Howard, Randall, Washington, Dixon, Bishop and James. 10/39–12/40.

***   **Piano Man** RCA Bluebird NK/ND/NL 86750 CD/LP/MC
Similar to above. 10/37–3/42.

It wasn't until the emergence of Budd Johnson as an arranging force that the Hines band recovered some of its flair and spirit. The most renowned of the later pieces – 'Grand Terrace Shuffle' and 'G. T. Stomp' – are both on the 1937–9 CD, which follows the band as it tries to recapture its earlier zip. Johnson himself is a significant soloist, and Hines softens into a more amiable version of his daredevil self. The important thing about the 1940 tracks, on the final Classics CD, is the arrival of Billy Eckstine, who would influence the band's move towards modernism and first provide it with a couple of major hits, starting with the 1940 'Jelly, Jelly'.

Some of these sides also turn up on the Bluebird compilation, which covers 1939–42.

***   **At The Village Vanguard** Xanadu 106/FDC 5165 CD/LP
Hines; Roy Eldridge (*t*); George Tucker (*b*); Oliver Jackson (*d*). 3/65.

****   **Blues In Thirds** Black Lion CLCD 760120 CD
Hines (*p* solo). 4/65.

***   **Live At The Village Vanguard** CBS 462401 CD
Hines; Budd Johnson (*ss, ts*); Gene Ramey (*b*); Eddie Locke (*d*). 6/65.

**   **Hine's Tune** France's Concert FC 101 CD/LP
Hines; Roy Eldridge (*t*); Don Byas, Ben Webster (*ts*); Stuff Smith (*vn*); Jimmy Woode (*b*); Kenny Clarke (*d*). 11/65.

***(*)   **A Night At Johnnie's** Black & Blue 59.300-2 CD
Hines; Budd Johnson (*ss, ts*); Bill Pemberton (*b*); Oliver Jackson (*d*). 11/68.

Hines's career on record is something of a mess, at least as far as his sessions from the 1950s onward are concerned. He joined Louis Armstrong's All Stars in 1948, but he worked as a soloist or leader from 1951 until his death, and the host of records he made are now only spottily available. There is virtually nothing left from the 1950s – a couple of fine albums for

Fantasy await CD reissue – and these 1960s albums are all that survive from the next decade. Hines made a strong transition to the LP era, even though it happened rather slowly. He was able to unleash all the rococo elements in his methods at whatever length he chose, and the so-called 'trumpet style' – using tremolo to suggest a horn player's vibrato and taking a linear path even when playing an ensemble role – began to sound modern by dint of its individuality. Nobody played like Hines, as influential as he had been. He was more or less rediscovered in 1964, following New York concerts that were greeted as a sensation, and thereafter embarked on regular tours and records. For some reason, 1965 is particularly well represented at present. The Xanadu disc is scrappily recorded – Tucker's bass is often inaudible and Jackson's cymbals are uncomfortably loud – but it opens with an extraordinary medley by Hines and ends with another of similar extravagance (Hines liked medleys, and most of his live records from this point feature tunes in clutches). Eldridge has two tunes to himself and the rhythm section, and he sounds in good humour if not quite great form. The album includes marvellous notes by Don Schlitten.

The France's Concert disc comes in very fine sound but, despite the top-class personnel, there are slim pickings here. Half the record is spent on warm-up routines for the band; though Webster is at his sleepy best on 'Sweet Lorraine', and the final blues is sprightly enough, there's not much else to talk about. The two sessions with Budd Johnson, who remained a favourite partner of Hines's, work better. The CBS Vanguard set isn't very well recorded, but he and Johnson strike some very bright sparks. *A Night At Johnnie's* is a generously filled CD and opens with half an hour of Hines with bass and drums, before Johnson joins in for 'Body And Soul' and a whirlwind 'Lester Leaps In'. A number of tunes are duplicated among these records – 'Tea For Two' keeps turning up, as do 'Black Coffee' and 'Sweet Lorraine' – but the pianist's enthusiasm is undimmed. The best portrait is provided by, inevitably, the one solo set, *Blues In Thirds*, which adds three extra tracks to the original LP release. The 'Tea For Two' here is an overwhelming *tour de force* and the blues playing on 'Black Lion Blues' and 'Blues After Midnight' is even more luxuriant than Art Tatum's essays in the method.

***   **Live At The New School** Chiaroscuro CRD 157 CD
Hines (*p* solo). 3/73.

***   **Live** Black & Blue 59/305.2 CD
Hines (*p* solo). 7/74.

It's hard to go wrong with Hines on record, but one should be a trifle cautious in approaching some of his live records: the fondness for medleys and a weakness for an overextended right-hand tremolo betray a hankering for applause which, as merited as it may be, occasionally tips his style into excess. The 16-minute Fats Waller medley on *New School* and other flag-wavers let down the superior aspects of the set, while the Ellington medley on *Live* misses the intensity of the set listed below. But both still have a share of Hines in regal form: he liked to play for people, and some of the pyrotechnics are *echt*-Hines.

***   **Hines Plays Hines** Swaggie S1320 LP
Hines (*p* solo). 7/72.

****   **Tour De Force** Black Lion BLCD 760140 CD
Hines (*p* solo). 11/72.

****   **Tour De Force Encore** Black Lion BLCD 760157 CD
Hines (*p* solo). 11/72.

***   **Plays George Gershwin** Swaggie S1339 LP
Hines (*p* solo). 8/73.

***   **Hines 74** Black & Blue 59.073.2 CD
Hines; Jimmy Leary (*b*); Panama Francis (*d*). 7/74.

***   **Piano Portraits Of Australia** Swaggie S1350 LP
Hines (*p* solo). 8/74.

A spate of solo recording meant that, in his old age, Hines was being comprehensively documented at last, and he rose to the challenge with consistent inspirational force. The two *Tour De Force* discs are perhaps the best records to get, since the studio sound is fine, if a little hard, and Hines seems completely relaxed and under his own orders (although Stanley Dance's discreet supervision must have assisted). The CD versions include previously unheard tracks, but since alternative takes are spread across the pair of discs, most will choose one or the other. The single take of 'Mack The Knife' on each disc is, though, Hines at his most extraordinary – his variation of time, ranging from superfast stride to wholly unexpected suspensions, is bemusing enough, but the range of dynamics he pushes through each solo is more so. He seldom lingers in thought – one of the things he bequeathed to later players such as Oscar Peterson and Cecil Taylor was the bruising speed of the process by which ideas are executed – but the essentially tuneful stamp he puts on every improvisation (and the different takes underline his spontaneity) humanizes what might be an otherwise relentless, percussive attack.

The Swaggie albums – hard to find but apparently still available on vinyl – are concept records of sometimes mixed success. The oddest set, the Australian album, consists of themes by Aussie composer Dave Dallwitz, and is a rare example of Hines sounding less than familiar with his material: an interesting but frankly subduing idea. There is a sprawling reading of 'The Man I Love', stretching from a gently fingered statement to a stride hurricane, on the Gershwin set, which tends to dwarf the rest of the material: nevertheless, Earl sounds in fine humour. *Hines Plays Hines* repeats an earlier idea of having the pianist record only his own material and, although these are songs which he had probably done too often, it's handsomely done. *Hines 74* restores him to a rhythm section.

**** **Earl Hines Plays Duke Ellington** New World NW 361/2 2CD/2LP
Hines (*p* solo). 12/71–4/75.

Made over a period of four years, this is much more than a casual one-giant-nods-to-another record. Hines was cajoled by Stanley Dance into looking into many unfamiliar Ellington tunes and creating a memorial (Ellington died around the time of the final sessions) which is surely among the best tributes to the composer on record. Since Hines's more aristocratic touches are close in feeling to Ellington's own, there is an immediate affinity in such pieces as 'Love You Madly' and 'Black And Tan Fantasy'. But Hines finds a wealth of new incident in warhorses such as 'Mood Indigo' and 'Sophisticated Lady' and turns 'The Shepherd' and 'Black Butterfly' into extravagant fantasies which go far beyond any of Ellington's own revisionist approaches. Even a simple piece such as 'C Jam Blues' receives a fascinating, rhythmic treatment, and the voicings conjured up for 'I'm Beginning To See The Light' upset conventional wisdom about Ellingtonian interpretation. In his variety of resource, Hines also points up all the devices he passed on to Powell, Monk and virtually every other post-swing pianist. A memorable lesson, and a fine tribute to two great piano players, spread over two hours of music on both CD and LP.

TERUMASA HINO (born 1942)
TRUMPET, FLUGELHORN, CORNET

*** **Vibrations** Enja 2010 LP
Hino; Heinz Sauer (*ts*); Peter Warren (*b*); Pierre Favre (*d*). 11/71.

(*) **Taro's Mood Enja 2028 LP
Hino; Mikio Masuda (*p*); Yoshio Ikeda (*b*); Motohiko Hino (*d*); Yuji Imamura (*perc*). 6/73.

Japanese jazz musicians were still something of a novelty to western audiences when Hino started making waves in Europe and the US. Like so many of his classical contemporaries, he displayed a terrific technique – faultless intonation and a fat, glossy tone – and these early Enja albums remain interesting for the ambiguity of his direction, leaning close to hard bop on the date with a Japanese rhythm section, hinting at freer paths on the session with Sauer, Warren and Favre. But the rather long tracks and less than perfectly disciplined solos predicted something of Hino's next move, which was to immerse himself in the modal jazz-rock of the mid-1970s, partly as a result of his intense devotion to Miles Davis.

(*) **Bluestruck Blue Note CDP 7936712 CD
Hino; Bobby Watson (*as*); Rob Scheps (*ts*); Onaje Allan Gumbs (*p*); John Scofield (*g*); Bob Hurst, Michael Formanek (*b*); Victor Lewis (*d*). 9/89.

This is a pretty and accomplished album, and Hino plays extremely well – he uses cornet throughout, gets a sweet and lyrical tone, and delivers a gorgeous reworking of his ballad 'Alone, Alone And Alone', which first featured on *Taro's Mood*. But it feels so much like another stylized 'new Blue Note' album – with Watson, Scofield and Scheps running off clean and unblemished solos – that whatever individuality that Hino seeks is caught up in the smooth-running works.

*** **From The Heart** Blue Note CDP 7966882 CD
Hino; Roger Byam (*ts*); Onaje Allan Gumbs (*p*); John Hart (*g*); Michael Formanek (*b*); Billy Hart (*d*). 1/91.

A superior example of Hino on record. Partly because his companions are less given to keynote mannerisms this time, and also through a more open-ended set of themes, there's a more free-flowing feel to the date, and the fierceness of 'Free Mandela' and 'Kimiko' sustain interest where the last record flagged. Worth investigating for those who don't know Hino's work.

MILT HINTON (born 1910)
DOUBLE BASS

*** **Old Man Time** Chiaroscuro CRD 310 2CD
Hinton; Doc Cheatham (*t*); Eddie Barefield (*as, ts*); Buddy Tate (*ts*); Red Richards (*p*); Al Casey (*g*); Gus Johnson (*d*).

Hinton is a great entertainer, playing, singing and rapping about the good old days with undiminished vigour into his eighties. Like a great many rhythm players, the discography is huge but very little is credited to him, so this slightly overcooked two-volume set has to be seen as some kind of long-service award. The band, arranged and conducted by Buck Clayton, gives Old Man Time plenty of room for his party pieces on the big bull fiddle, while the Mississippi voice spins its yarns. Entertaining, but lightweight.

PAUL HOCK
GUITAR, GUITAR SYNTHESIZER

*** **Fresh Fruit** Timeless SJP 343 CD
Hock; Ben Van den Dungen (*ts*); Harry Emmery (*b*); Cees Kranenburg (*d*). 2/91.

After two tracks it sounds as if the record will be nothing but a straight steal from John Scofield, with Hock affecting a carbon of Sco's tone and the rest of the group functioning much as the players on the Blue Note albums do. But then comes a spare and surprisingly evocative reading of Jacques Brel's 'Voir Un Ami Pleurer', and the music opens out and moves to a different plane. Hock's improvising still owes much to the American, although touches of guitar-synth add a further colour, and Van den Dungen's lines aren't notably individual, but a theme such as 'Samba For Johan Cruyff' creates a distinctive climate for improvisation, and bassist and drummer work with the same intensity as the front line. A name worth watching.

ART HODES (born 1904)
PIANO

** **Blues To Save The Trees** L + R 40015 LP
Hodes solo and with Reimer Von Essen (*cl*); Trevor Richards (*d*). 11/81.

*** **South Side Memories** Sackville 3032 LP
Hodes (*p* solo). 11/83.

*** **Blues In The Night** Sackville 3039 LP
As above. 6/85.

***(*) **Pagin' Mr Jelly** Candid 9037 CD/LP
As above. 11/88.

Born in Russia and raised in Chicago, Hodes combines a blues-drenched South Side piano style with a passionate articulacy which turned him into one of jazz's most significant ambassadors and educators, working as a disc jockey, journalist (on *The Jazz Record*) and lecturer.

If consistency and regularity are the keys to longevity, Hodes seems to have survived by *not* bending to the winds of fashion. Though little of his hefty output is currently available, his records – solos in particular – tend to be comfortably interchangeable and only real enthusiasts for his rather throwaway style or for the South Side pianists in general will want shelf-loads.

Though often less interesting as a solo performer than in a group context, Hodes conjures some interesting variations on Jelly Roll Morton, his greatest single influence, on *Pagin' Mr Jelly*, and this is perhaps the place for fans of either to start; there are further Morton covers by Hodes on the patchy *Tribute to Jelly Roll Morton* (Storyville SLP 4050). Easily the best of *Blues to Save the Trees* is in the two solo numbers; the rest, with the sterling exception of a strangely moving 'Old Rugged Cross' for trio, is rather forgettable, further marred by a curiously slushy sound.

There are fine things on *South Side Memories*, but comparing Hodes's version of Morton's 'The Pearls' with Mary Lou Williams's suggests that he is a rather superficial player, a stylist rather than a re-inventor. It's rather galling that his liner note should be more compelling than the music inside. *Blues In The Night* features a more mainstream repertoire (including Hoagy Carmichael's 'Lazybones' and the under-recorded 'Snowball') but it's a light, fluffy set played on the same rather unresonant piano (it may be that Hodes prefers instruments that echo the sharper sound of the old nightclub uprights) he uses on the earlier Sackville.

***(*) **Sessions At Blue Note** Dormouse International DMI CDX04 CD
Hodes; Max Kaminsky, Oliver Mesheux (*t*); Ray Conniff, Vic Dickenson, George Lugg, Sandy Williams (*tb*); Leonard Centobie, Rod Cless, Edmond Hall, Mezz Mezzrow, Omer Simeon (*cl*); Jack Bland, Chick Robertson, Jimmy Shirley (*g*); Israel Crosby, Pops Foster, Bob Haggart, Sid Jacobs, Jack Lesberg, Al Lucas, Fred Moore, Sid Weiss (*b*); Danny Alvin, Fred Moore (*d*). 3/44.

Hodes signed to the pre-bop Blue Note in 1944 and immediately recorded two sessions with a group of Chicagoans. The material was straight out of his usual bag, Joplin, Handy, Oliver, Morton, one original and a fine version of 'There'll Be Some Changes Made'. The band has a loud, roistering quality that comes through clearly on the original 78 masters despite a little crackle here and there. Max Kaminsky was an ideal associate and Hodes was equally lucky with trombonists throughout his Blue Note period, using Vic Dickenson, the underrated Sandy Williams (excellent on 'Jug Head Boogie' from the third, April 1944, session) and the pre-MOR Ray Conniff. By far the most interesting sessions, though, are the three trio sides cut a year later with the unusual instrumentation of trumpet (Kaminsky again), piano and drums. An 'Eccentric Rag', and Hodes's own 'KMH Drag' and 'Blues'N'Booze', all invested with a remarkably desolate blues feel. Of the three oddments at the end, 'Mr Jelly Lord' is the best, with New Orleansian clarinetist Leonard 'Bujie' Centobie bringing a rawly authentic sound to the Morton tune. A valuable collection of material, decently handled and packaged.

(*)   **Live From Toronto's Café Des Copains Music & Arts 610 CD
Hodes; Jim Galloway (*ss, bs*).

Music & Arts have a slightly odd approach to matchmaking on disc, alternating avant-garde couplings Anthony Braxton and Marilyn Crispell, Jane Bunnett and Don Pullen with the likes of this decidedly Odd Couple set. Though the material doesn't always seem to suit Hodes, he responds imaginatively to some of Galloway's more probing cues and plays like a man on monkey glands. Worth checking out.

JOHNNY HODGES (1907–70)
ALTO SAXOPHONE, SOPRANO SAXOPHONE

*(*)   **The Complete Johnny Hodges And His Orchestra, 1937–8** Le Jazz 8103 CD
Hodges; Cootie Williams (*t*); Lawrence Brown (*tb*); Barney Bigard (*cl*); Otto Hardwick (*as*); Harry Carney (*bs*); Duke Ellington (*p*); Fred Guy (*g*); Hayes Alvis, Billy Taylor (*b*); Sonny Greer (*d*); Buddy Clark, Leon LaFell, Mary McHugh (*v*). 5/37, 1, 3, 6, 8/38.

***   **A Man And His Music** Storyville SLP 4073 LP
        Hodges; Harold Shorty Baker, Charlie Shavers (*t*); Lawrence Brown (*tb*); Buster
        Bailey (*cl*); Russell Procope (*as*); John Coltrane (*ts*); Billy Kyle, Al Walshon (*p*); Joe
        Schmalz (*b*); Ed Knil, Specs Powell, O'Neil Spencer (*d*). 54 & unknown dates.

***(*)   **Used To Be Duke** Verve 849 394 CD
        Hodges; Harold Shorty Baker (*t*); Lawrence Brown (*tb*); John Coltrane (*ts*); Jimmy
        Hamilton (*ts, cl*); Harry Carney (*bs*); Call Cobbs, Richard Powell (*p*); John Williams
        (*b*); Louie Bellson (*d*). 7 & 8/54.

***   **Side By Side** Verve 821578 CD
        Hodges; Harry Edison, Roy Eldridge (*t*); Lawrence Brown (*tb*); Ben Webster (*ts*);
        Duke Ellington, Billy Strayhorn (*p*); Les Spann (*g, f*); Al Hall, Wendell Marshall (*b*);
        Jo Jones (*d*). 8/58, 2/59.

(*)   **Masters Of Jazz: Volume 9 Storyville SLP 4109 CD/LP
        Hodges; Ray Nance (*t*); Lawrence Brown (*tb*); Harry Carney (*bs*); Ben Webster (*ts*);
        Herb Ellis (*g*); Lou Levy, Al Williams (*p*); Aaron Bell, Wilfred Middlebrooks (*b*);
        Gus Johnson, Sam Woodyard (*d*). 11/60, 3/61.

**   **Compact Jazz: Johnny Hodges – Wild Bill Davis** Verve 839288 CD
        Hodges; Wild Bill Davis (*org*); Lawrence Brown (*tb*); Jimmy Hamilton (*cl*); Hank
        Jones (*p*); Kenny Burrell, Billy Butler, Grant Green, Mundell Lowe (*g*); Les Spann (*g,
        f*); Bob Cranshaw, Richard Davis, Sam Jones, Bob Bushnell (*b*); Ben Dixon, Louis
        Hayes, Osie Johnson, Ed Shaughnessy, Grady Tate (*d*). 8/61, 9/63, 4/64, 1/65, 1/66,
        7/65.

****   **Everybody Knows Johnny Hodges** Impulse! GRP 11162 CD
        Hodges; Cat Anderson, Rolf Ericson, Herbie Jones, Ray Nance (*t*); Lawrence Brown,
        Buster Cooper, Britt Woodman (*tb*); Harry Carney, Paul Gonsalves, Jimmy Hamilton,
        Russell Procope (*reeds*); Jimmy Jones (*p*); Ernie Shepard (*b*); Grady Tate (*d*). 2/64.

(*)   **In A Mellotone Bluebird ND 82305 CD
        Hodges; Wild Bill Davis (*org*); Lawrence Brown (*tb*); Robert Brown (*ts, f*); James
        Thompson (*g*); Robert Durham (*g*). 9/66.

***(*)   **Triple Play** Bluebird ND 90208 CD
        Hodges; Ray Nance (*c*); Cat Anderson, Roy Eldridge (*t*); Lawrence Brown, Buster
        Cooper, Benny Powell (*tb*); Paul Gonsalves, Jimmy Hamilton (*ts*); Harry Carney (*bs*);
        Hank Jones, Jimmy Jones (*p*); Bill Berry (*vib*); Billy Butler, Tiny Grimes, Les Spann
        (*g*); Aaron Bell, Joe Benjamin, Milt Hinton (*b*); Oliver Jackson, Gus Johnson, Rufus
        Jones (*d*). 1/67.

When Johnny Hodges gave up playing like an angel and went to heaven in person, Adolphe Sax
beat St Peter to a handshake at the gates. 'Thank you, my friend', he cried, 'That is the way my
saxophone was meant to sound.' There are still few voices in jazz more purely sensuous.
Subtract Hodges's solos from Duke Ellington's recorded output and it shrinks
disproportionately. Sadly, perhaps, for all his pricklish dislike of sideman status in the Ellington
orchestra (he frequently mimed counting bills in the Duke's direction when receiving his usual
ovation for yet another perfectly crafted solo), Hodges was a rather unassertive leader and his
own recordings under-represent his extraordinary qualities which only began to dim with the
onset of the 1960s.

Perhaps the best-known of those records, the lovely *Everybody Knows Johnny Hodges* has
only recently reappeared, in a bright CD issue that captures the saxophonist's distinctive
combination of tough jump tunes and aching ballads. Billy Strayhorn composed '310 Blues'
specially for the session (Hodges is somewhat upstaged by both Gonsalves and the on-form
Brown), but has the final word. Strayhorn's other credit is the evergreen 'A Flower Is A
Lovesome Thing', given a brief and tender reading. It's one of four small-group pieces from
within the full band. 'Papa Knows' and 'Everybody Knows' represent a pair; the first is
something of a ragbag of familiar Hodges materials, the latter a fine opening blues. Other tracks
include a big band 'Main Stem' and a medleyed 'I Let A Song Go Out Of My Heart'/'Don't
Get Around Much Anymore'.

There's a good back-up version of 'The Jeep is Jumpin'' on the Hodges volume of *Masters of Jazz* with both Lawrence Brown and the great Harry Carney. The earlier material with Shorty Baker has more bite, but is still unrepresentative of the best of that association which can be sampled on the otherwise ignorable *Ellingtonians in Paris* CD (Jazztime 251275) or the rather later, though much better, single cut on *Compact Jazz: Duke Ellington and Friends* (Verve 833291). Available in some territories is a valuable Prestige compilation called *Caravan* (24103 CD) bringing together material under Ellington's, Strayhorn's and Hodges's leadership.

Otherwise only Verve and Bluebird have done much to bring Hodges into the CD era, even if in the rather improbable company of organist Wild Bill Davis, a *mésalliance* of spectacular proportions that nonetheless survived a half dozen recorded encounters during the early 1960s. The inclusion of guitar, for which Hodges had contracted an inexplicable dependence and liking, on most of the tracks muddies the sound still further and tracks like 'Wings and Things' and the lovely 'Peg o'My Heart' on *Hodges/Davis* combine organ, trombone, piano and guitar (albeit the excellent Grant Green's) in an arrangement that not even Hodges's limpid alto can redeem. *In A Mellotone*, from a later live session, is better, with four fine Hodges originals (including 'Good Queen Bess' and 'Rockville') and good versions of 'It's Only A Paper Moon' and the co-written (with Ellington Jr) 'Belle Of The Belmont'. The sound is uneven, but Hodges comes across well.

Of the other Verves, *Side by Side*, is much better, with glimpses of the saxophonist working close to his good and bad angels, Duke Ellington and Billy Strayhorn. If Strayhorn ultimately won the battle for the saxophonist's soul, there was usually enough of Duke's nature in his playing to keep it from cloying, and so it is here. Certainly the only CD that could be unreservedly recommended until the reissue of *Used to Be Duke*. Repackaged with three further tracks from the same session – including the slightly poppy 'Skokiaan' – this is from the later stages of Hodges's solo foray from the Ellington band. Even when his own man, though, Duke was never far from mind, and there is a strong Ellingtonian cast to the arrangements. In addition to the powerful title number, there is a reading of Ellington's 'Warm Valley'. The bulk of the album is a long, beautifully modulated ballad medley, which parcels out the solos and theme statements, with Carney and Richard Powell deservedly prominent. Baker plays beautifully, with more attention to the middle register than usual. Coltrane completists should be aware that he only fills out the backings on 'Used to Be Duke' and the additional 'All of Me'; no solos.

Hodges's own modest diffidence and subtle mainstream approach failed to start any critical or contractual fires. In little over a year, he was back with Ellington. As an instance of what he was capable of on his own account, *Used to Be Duke* is an essential acquisition. The later *Triple Play* is not so immediately attractive, but there's a fine line-up of Ellingtonians (called in in three groups over two days) and there are three previously unreleased tracks which will please collectors who can get over the weird remastering. Surprisingly, Hodges and Tiny Grimes seem to get along famously; 'A Tiny Bit Of Blues' and the two parts of a gospel-laden 'Take 'Em Off, Take 'Em Off' are about the best things on an otherwise pretty average set. From the other end of his career, the Le Jazz compilation consists of well-intentioned but forgettable transfers of early Vocalion and Variety masters which are all but fatally marred by Vocalion's song-plugging insistence on a vocal component for most of the tracks. Nonetheless, Hodges's alto (and, on some tracks, his soprano) saxophone cuts across some indifferent commercial singing, and there are fine early versions of 'I Let a Song Go Out of My Heart' and 'The Jeep is Jumping' which he was to play, the latter at least, to the end of his life.

***   **Rarities And Private Recordings** Suisa JZCD 361 CD
Hodges; Cat Anderson, Harold Baker, Wilbur Bascomb, Emmett Berry, Willie Cook, Mercer Ellington, Fats Ford, Shelton Hemphill, Eddie Jones, Jonah Jones, Taft Jordan, Al Killian, Eddie Mullens, Rex Stewart, Cootie Williams, Francis Williams (*t*); Ray Nance (*t, co, vl*); Lawrence Brown, Chuck Connors, Buster Cooper, Tyree Glenn, Quentin Jackson, Claude Jones, Joe Nanton, Wilbur De Paris (*tb*); Otto Hardwicke, Russell Procope (*as*); Paul Gonsalves, Jimmy Hamilton, Flip Phillips, Al Sears, Ben Webster (*ts*); Harry Carney (*bs*); Duke Ellington, Earl Hines, Leroy Lovett, Teddy Wilson (*p*); Al Casey, Fred Guy, Lawrence Lucie (*g*); Lionel Hampton (*vib, v*); Aaron Bell, Jimmy Blanton, John Kirby, John Lamb, Wendell Marshall, Oscar Pettiford, Junior Raglin, Billy Taylor, Lloyd Trotman (*b*); Sid Catlett, Cozy Cole, Sonny Greer, Joe Marshall, Sam Woodyard (*d*); Billie Holiday (*v*). 6/36, 4/37, 8/38, 2/39, 11/40, 7/41, 4/44, 4/45, 6/47, 49, 10/51, 7/60, 1/65.

This is mainly for serious collectors, as might be expected, and doesn't always highlight the saxophonist as prominently as might be hoped. The opening 'I Cried For You' is a Billie Holiday feature with the Teddy Wilson orchestra and though Hodges plays a suitably wounded introduction, he doesn't play much part in the rest. 'On The Sunny Side Of The Street' is a Lionel Hampton recording from the following year, with the leader singing as well as playing vibes. Hodges accompaniments and fill are unmistakable, but it's still rather thin fare and he doesn't really receive much airing until two Ellington cuts from 1938 and 1939 which perfectly illustrate the saxophonist's jump style of the time. A very much later version of 'Jeep's Blues', recorded privately at a USAF base concert in 1960 makes for a useful comparison of early and later approaches. The whole of that dance concert is available as *Hot Summer Dance* on Red Baron AK 48631, an above average live Ellington produced by Bob Thiele.

The material recorded under Hodges's own name isn't necessarily the best of the material, but it does feature him most strongly, and his solos on Strayhorn's 'Day Dream' (1940) and 'A Little Taste', which Hodges co-wrote with Ellington, are exceptional. The sound, predictably, isn't. Worth having, nonetheless, particularly at Suisa's bargain price.

ALLAN HOLDSWORTH (born 1946)
GUITAR, ELECTRIC GUITAR, GUITAR SYNTHESIZER

**(*)   With A Heart In My Song JMS 044 CD/LP
Holdsworth (*g* solo) and with Gordon Beck (*p, p* solo). 5 & 6/88.

In the 1970s, Holdsworth built up a considerable reputation as a fusion guitarist with the likes of Jon Hiseman's Colosseum, Soft Machine, Jean-Luc Ponty, and a later version of Tony Williams's seminal jazz-rock band Lifetime, where he succeeded John McLaughlin, one of his own main influences. In recent years, he has largely sunk from view in his native Britain but still enjoys an enviable following in the United States, Japan and continental Europe. Perhaps his most significant contribution to jazz in the 1980s has been as producer and associate of the scandalously under-valued Gordon Beck, with whom he shares *With A Heart In My Song*.

Somewhat like Beck himself (who contributes a fine solo piano feature, '999') but certainly reminiscent of McLaughlin, Holdsworth plays tense, tightly organized clusters of notes, sometimes only obliquely related to the underlying key. The acquisition of a MIDI guitar synthesizer, known as the SynthAxe, has considerably expanded his range, most obviously in solo performances like '54 Duncan Terrace' and 'Sundays'.

The duets with Beck are among the most impressive work either man has recorded in some years. 'Equus' is a powerful and imaginative performance that repays close attention, and the title-track is very beautiful in a curiously callow way.

BILLIE HOLIDAY (1915–59)
VOCAL

***   The Quintessential Billie Holiday Vol. 1 1933–35 CBS 450987 CD
Holiday; Charlie Teagarden, Shirley Clay, Roy Eldridge, Dick Clark (*t*); Benny Morton, Jack Teagarden (*tb*); Cecil Scott, Benny Goodman, Tom Macey (*cl*); Johnny Hodges (*as*); Art Karle, Ben Webster, Chu Berry (*ts*); Joe Sullivan, Teddy Wilson (*p*); Dick McDonough, Lawrence Lucie, John Trueheart, Dave Barbour (*g*); Artie Bernstein, Grachan Moncur, John Kirby (*b*); Cozy Cole, Gene Krupa (*d*). 11/33–12/35.

***(*)   The Quintessential Billie Holiday Vol. 2 1936 CBS 460060 CD
Holiday; Chris Griffin, Jonah Jones, Bunny Berigan, Irving Randolph (*t*); Rudy Powell, Artie Shaw, Irving Fazola, Vido Musso (*cl*); Harry Carney (*cl, bs*); Johnny Hodges (*as*); Ted McCrae, Ben Webster (*ts*); Teddy Wilson (*p*); John Trueheart, Allan Reuss, Dick McDonough (*g*); Grachan Moncur, John Kirby, Pete Peterson, Artie Bernstein, Milt Hinton (*b*); Cozy Cole, Gene Krupa (*d*). 1–10/36.

****   The Quintessential Billie Holiday Vol. 3 1936–37 CBS 460820 CD
Holiday; Irving Randolph, Jonah Jones, Buck Clayton, Henry 'Red' Allen (*t*); Vido Musso, Benny Goodman (*cl*); Cecil Scott (*cl, as, ts*); Edgar Sampson (*cl, as*); Ben

Webster, Lester Young, Prince Robinson (*ts*); Teddy Wilson (*p*); Allan Reuss, Jimmy McLin (*g*); Milt Hinton, John Kirby, Walter Page (*b*); Gene Krupa, Cozy Cole, Jo Jones (*d*). 10/36–2/37.

***   **Billie Holiday 1933–37** Classics 582 CD
As above three discs. 33/37.

Ø ****   **The Quintessential Billie Holiday Vol. 4 1937** CBS 463333 CD
Holiday; Cootie Williams, Eddie Tompkins, Buck Clayton (*t*); Buster Bailey, Edmond Hall (*cl*); Johnny Hodges (*as*); Joe Thomas, Lester Young (*ts*); Harry Carney (*bs*); Teddy Wilson, James Sherman (*p*); Carmen Mastren, Freddie Greene, Allan Reuss (*g*); Artie Bernstein, Walter Page, John Kirby (*b*); Cozy Cole, Alphonse Steele, Jo Jones (*d*). 2–6/37.

***(*)   **The Quintessential Billie Holiday Vol. 5 1937–38** CBS 465190 CD
Holiday; Buck Clayton (*t*); Benny Morton (*tb*); Buster Bailey (*cl*); Prince Robinson, Vido Musso (*cl, ts*); Lester Young (*ts*); Claude Thornhill, Teddy Wilson (*p*); Allan Reuss, Freddie Greene (*g*); Walter Page (*b*); Jo Jones (*d*). 6/37–1/38.

***(*)   **The Quintessential Billie Holiday Vol. 6 1938** CBS 466313 CD
Holiday; Bernard Anderson, Buck Clayton, Harry James (*t*); Dickie Wells, Benny Morton (*tb*); Buster Bailey (*cl*); Edgar Sampson, Benny Carter (*as*); Lester Young (*cl, ts*); Babe Russin, Herschel Evans (*ts*); Claude Thornhill, Margaret 'Queenie' Johnson, Teddy Wilson (*p*); Al Casey, Freddie Greene (*g*); John Kirby, Walter Page (*b*); Cozy Cole, Jo Jones (*d*). 5–11/38.

(*)   **The Quintessential Billie Holiday Vol. 7 1938–39 CBS 466966 CD
Holiday; Charlie Shavers, Roy Eldridge, Hot Lips Page, Frankie Newton (*t*); Bobby Hackett (*c*); Trummy Young, Tyree Glenn (*tb*); Tab Smith (*ss, as*); Benny Carter, Toots Mondello (*cl, as*); Teddy Buckner (*as*); Kenneth Hollon, Ernie Powell, Bud Freeman, Chu Berry, Stanley Payne (*ts*); Teddy Wilson, Sonny Payne, Kenny Kersey (*p*); Danny Barker, Al Casey, Jimmy McLin, Bernard Addison (*g*); Milt Hinton, John Williams (*b*); Cozy Cole, Eddie Dougherty (*d*). 11/38–7/39.

***   **Billie Holiday 1937–1939** Classics 592 CD
As above four discs. 37–39.

***   **The Quintessential Billie Holiday Vol. 8 1939–1940** Sony 467914 CD
Holiday; Charlie Shavers, Buck Clayton, Roy Eldridge, Harry Edison (*t*); Tab Smith, Earl Warren, Jimmy Powell, Carl Frye, Don Redman, George Auld (*as*); Kenneth Hollon, Stanley Payne, Lester Young, Kermit Scott, Jimmy Hamilton, Don Byas (*ts*); Jack Washington (*bs*); Sonny White, Teddy Wilson, Joe Sullivan (*p*); Bernard Addison, Freddie Greene, John Collins, Lawrence Lucie (*g*); John Williams, Water Page, Al Hall (*b*); Eddie Dougherty, Jo Jones, Harold 'Doc' West, Kenny Clarke (*d*). 7/39–9/40.

***   **Billie Holiday 1939–1940** Classics 601 CD
As above two Columbia discs. 39–40.

Ø ****   **Billie Holiday – The Voice Of Jazz: The Complete Recordings 1933–1940** Affinity AFS 1019 8CD
Collective personnel as above Columbia records. 11/33–10/40.

***   **The Quintessential Billie Holiday Vol. 9 1940–42** Columbia 47031 CD
Holiday; Bill Coleman, Shad Collins, Emmett Berry, Roy Eldridge (*t*); Benny Morton (*tb*); Jimmy Hamilton (*cl*); Benny Carter (*cl, as*); Leslie Johnakins, Hymie Schertzer, Eddie Barefield, Ernie Powell, Lester Boone, Jimmy Powell (*as*); Lester Young, George Auld, Babe Russin (*ts*); Sonny White, Teddy Wilson, Eddie Heywood (*p*); Ulysses Livingstone, John Collins, Paul Chapman, Gene Fields, Al Casey (*g*); Wilson Meyers, Grachan Moncur, John Williams, Ted Sturgis (*b*); Yank Porter, Kenny Clarke, J. C. Heard, Herbert Cowens (*d*). 10/40–2/42.

Billie Holiday has become so surrounded by hagiography that it's now almost impossible to hear and treat her music on its own terms: the legendary suffering and mythopoeic pain which countless admirers have sought out in her work make it difficult for the merely curious to warm to a singer who was uneven and sometimes content to coast. There is occasionally a troubling detachment in Holiday's singing which is quite the opposite of the living-every-line virtue which some have impressed on her records; and those that she made in her later years often demand a voyeuristic role of any listener determined to enjoy her interpretations. Nevertheless, Holiday was a singular and unrepeatable talent, whose finest hours are remarkably revealing and often surprisingly – given her generally morose reputation as an artist – joyful. New listeners may find the accumulated weight of the Holiday myth discouraging and they may be equally surprised at how much fun many of the earlier records are. Part of the difficulty in approaching her lies in the way her music has been repackaged. All of her pre-war music is now available on CD: the nine-record sequence on CBS and Columbia is perhaps the most desirable way to collect it, since the handsome packaging offers comprehensive documentation. The Affinity set includes many alternative takes and is lavishly spread across eight packed CDs. But both projects are let down by the transfers, which don't have much sparkle but homogenize the often superb accompaniments into a dull blend that lacks dynamics. Some of the dubbings sound crisp while others are beset by surface noise (this particularly applies to the alternative masters heard on the Affinity set). The sheer weight of both sets also tells against music which is best heard session by session: the casual nature of the original dates invites one to listen to a few songs at a time, and – as with many such reissue projects – some listeners may find the bulkiness of the presentation intimidating.

We must not, however, carp too much! The standard of these records – particularly considering how many tracks were made – is finally very high, and the best of them are as poised and finely crafted as any small-group jazz of the period. One of Holiday's innovations was to suggest a role for the singer which blended in with the rest of the musicians, improvising a line and taking a 'solo' which was as integrated as anything else on the record. On her earlier sides with Wilson as leader, she was still credited as responsible for the 'vocal refrain', but the later titles feature 'Billie Holiday and her Orchestra'. She starts some records and slips into the middle of others, but always there's a feeling of a musician at ease with the rest of the band and aware of the importance of fitting into the performance as a whole. Her tone, on the earliest sides, is still a little raw and unformed, and the trademark rasp at the edge of her voice – which she uses to canny effect on the later titles – is used less pointedly; but the unaffected styling is already present, and there are indications of her mastery of time even in the tracks on *Quintessential* Volume 1. While the most obvious characteristic of her singing is the lagging behind the beat, she seldom sounds tired or slow to respond, and the deeper impression is of a vocalist who knows exactly how much time she can take. She never scats, rarely drifts far from the melody, and respects structure and lyrical nuance, even where – as has often been remarked – the material is less than blue-chip. But her best singing invests the words with shades of meaning which vocalists until that point had barely looked at: she creates an ambiguity between what the words say and what she might be thinking which is very hard to distil. And that is the core of Holiday's mystique. Coupled with the foggy, baleful, sombre quality of her tone, it creates a vocal jazz which is as absorbing as it is enduring.

Like her fellow musicians, she had good and bad days, and that's one reason why it's difficult to pinpoint the best of the records listed above. Some may prefer to have those albums featuring the best-known songs; but one peculiarity of these sessions is that her attention seldom depends on the quality of the material: an otherwise forgotten Tin Pan Alley novelty may give rise to as great a performance as any of the best-known standards. The constantly changing personnel is also a variable. The tracks with Lester Young on tenor (and occasionally clarinet) have been acclaimed as the greatest of her collaborations, and those on Volumes 3 and 4 of the Columbia sequence are certainly among the best tracks: but some may find them occasionally lachrymose rather than moving. 'This Year's Kisses' (Volume 3), for instance, may be a serenely involving treatment of the song, with Holiday and Young seemingly reading each other's minds, but it points towards the bathos which blights much of her later work. Other accompanists do equally fine work in their way: Roy Eldridge, who suppresses his wildest side to surprisingly controlled effect on his appearances; Ben Webster, whose solo on 'With Thee I Swing' (Volume 2) is memorably sustained; Bunny Berigan, who plays superbly on Volume 2 and contributes (along with Artie Shaw) a classic solo to 'Billie's Blues', one of the greatest performances in the series; Irving Fazola, Buck Clayton, Tab Smith and Hot Lips Page, who all play with knowing insight; and, above all, Teddy Wilson, who organized many of the sessions, and who finesses his playing into little masterpieces of economy and apposite counterpoint, whether in solo or ensemble terms.

Holiday herself is at her freshest and most inspirational in these pre-war recordings and, whatever one may think about the later albums, these sessions surrender nothing in gravitas and communicate a good humour which is all their own. The session producers – John Hammond or Bernie Hanighen – encouraged an atmosphere of mutual creativity which the singer seldom fails to respond to and, even on the less immortal songs, Holiday makes something of the situation: there is no sense of her fighting against the material, as there often is with Armstrong or Waller in the same period. On some sessions she sounds less interested: much of the music on Volume 7 fails; and elsewhere she reacts against a tempo or simply lets her interest flag, sometimes within the parameters of a single tune. If we single out Volumes 3, 4 and 5 of the CBS series, it's purely because some of the tracks – such as 'I Must Have That Man', 'My Last Affair' (3), 'Foolin' Myself', 'Mean To Me' (4), 'Trav'lin' All Alone' and 'I Can't Believe That You're In Love With Me' (5) – reach a special peak of creativity from all involved. The Classics CDs cover all the material which isn't also included on their Teddy Wilson series: a useful way to fill gaps if the other discs are already in the collection, but splitting the music between Wilson and Holiday separates much of the best material. The transfer quality is mixed. The Affinity set is at least comprehensive and, given the quality of the material, it would be churlish to award it any less than four stars; only scholars will find the alternative-take material of much interest, though.

Other compilations from the period include *The Early Classics 1935–40* (Flapper CD-9756 CD), a decent cross-section in bright if sometimes thin sound; and *Billie Holiday & Her Orchestra* (Giants Of Jazz 53038 CD), a somewhat aimless selection. An absolutely definitive selection from the series has yet to be delivered and may indeed be near-impossible to compile, given the evenly high standard of the best material.

*** **The Legacy (1933–1958)** Columbia 47724 3CD/3MC
As above Columbia discs, plus Duke Ellington Orchestra, Benny Goodman Orchestra, Martha Tilton, Johnny Mercer, Leo Watson (*v*). 33–58.

An unsatisfactory mixture of Columbia's pick from the nine-volume 'Quintessential' series and various obscure airshots, including 'Saddest Tale' with Ellington and two pieces with Goodman's band. There are 70 tracks, and most of them come from the 1936–41 period; only a few from her final years are here, and they sound wretched in comparison. Ornately packaged in an oversize box, this seems awkward and unnecessarily overbearing as a compilation, but the best of the music is, of course, splendid.

***(*) **The Complete Original American Decca Recordings** MCA GRP 26012 2CD
Holiday; Russ Case, Joe Guy, Gordon Griffin, Rostelle Reese, Billy Butterfield, Jimmy Nottingham, Emmett Berry, Buck Clayton, Bernie Privin, Tony Faso, Dick Vance, Shad Collins, Bobby Williams, Bobby Hackett (*t*); Dickie Wells, George Matthews, Henderson Chambers, Mort Bullman, George Stevenson (*tb*); Milter Yaner, Bill Stegmeyer (*cl, as*); Hymie Schertzer, Jack Cressey, Lem Davis, Toots Mondello, Al Klink, Rudy Powell, George Dorsey, Johnny Mince, Pete Clark, Sid Cooper (*as*); John Fulton (*ts, cl, f*); Dick Eckles (*ts, f*); Larry Binyon, Paul Ricci, Dave Harris, Hank Ross, Armand Camgros, Bob Dorsey, Artie Drelinger, Lester Young, Joe Thomas, Budd Johnson, Freddie Williams, Pat Nizza (*ts*); Eddie Barefield (*bs, cl*); Stan Webb, Sol Moore, Dave McRae (*bs*); Dave Bowman, Sammy Benskin, Joe Springer, Charles LaVere, Bobby Tucker, Billy Kyle, Horace Henderson, Bernie Leighton (*p*); Carl Kress, Tony Mottola, Everett Barksdale, Bob Bain, Mundell Lowe, Tiny Grimes, Jimmy Shirley, Dan Perry (*g*); Haig Stephens, Bob Haggart, Billy Taylor, John Simmons, Thomas Barney, George Duvivier, Joe Benjamin, Jack Lesberg, Lou Butterman (*b*); Johnny Blowers, George Wettling, Specs Powell, Sid Catlett, Kelly Martin, Denzil Best, Kenny Clarke, Norris 'Bunny' Shawker, Shadow Wilson, Cozy Cole, Wallace Bishop, Jimmy Crawford, Nick Fatool (*d*); Louis Armstrong (*v*); strings and choir. 10/44–3/50.

Holiday's Decca sessions have been impeccably presented here, in a double-CD set which has been remastered to make the music sound as big and clear as possible. Some may prefer a warmer and less boomy sound, but the timbre of the records is impressively full and strong. These sessions were made when Holiday had established a wider reputation, and their feel is very different to the Columbia records: carefully orchestrated by a multitude of hands, including Sy Oliver and Gordon Jenkins, the best of them are as good as anything Holiday did. Many listeners may, indeed, find this the single most entertaining set of Holiday reissues on the market, for the polish and class of the singing and playing – while less spontaneously improvisational in feel – is hard to deny. Her own songs 'Don't Explain' and 'God Bless The Child' are obvious highlights, even if they mark the beginning of Holiday's 'victim' image, and here is the original reading of the subsequently famous 'That Ole Devil Called Love', two duets with Louis Armstrong, slow and emotionally draining readings of 'Porgy' and 'My Man' (from the one session with the sole accompaniment of a rhythm section), and a lot of pleasing, brightly-paced readings of superior standards. Few players stand out the way Young and Wilson do on the pre-war sides, but these aren't the same kind of records.

***   **Songs For Distingué Lovers** Verve 815055-2 CD
Holiday; Harry Edison (*t*); Ben Webster (*ts*); Jimmy Rowles (*p*); Barney Kessel (*g*); Joe Mondragon (*b*); Alvin Stoller, Larry Bunker (*d*). 7/56.

***   **Lady Sings The Blues** Verve 833770 CD/MC
Holiday; Charlie Shavers, Harry Edison (*t*); Tony Scott (*cl*); Willie Smith (*as*); Paul Quinichette (*ts*); Bobby Tucker, Wynton Kelly (*p*); Kenny Burrell, Barney Kessel (*g*); Red Callender, John Simmons (*b*); Larry Bunker, Chico Hamilton (*d*). 54-56.

***(*) **The Billie Holiday Songbook** Verve 823246-2 CD/MC
Holiday; Joe Newman, Charlie Shavers, Roy Eldridge, Buck Clayton, Harry Edison (*t*); Tony Scott (*cl*); Willie Smith (*as*); Paul Quinichette, Al Cohn, Coleman Hawkins (*ts*); Wynton Kelly, Carl Drinkard, Mal Waldron, Oscar Peterson, Bobby Tucker (*p*); Kenny Burrell, Herb Ellis, Freddie Green, Barney Kessel (*g*); Aaron Bell, Ray Brown, Carson Smith, Milt Hinton, Red Callender (*b*); Gus Johnson, Chico Hamilton, Ed Shaughnessy, Don Lamond, Lenny McBrowne (*d*). 7/52-9/58.

***   **Compact Jazz: Billie Holiday** Verve 831371-2 CD
Holiday; Harry Edison (*t*); Benny Carter (*as*); Ben Webster (*ts*); Jimmy Rowles (*p*); Barney Kessel (*g*); John Simmons, Joe Mondragon (*b*); Larry Bunker, Alvin Stoller (*d*). 8/55-8/56.

***(*) **Lady In Autumn** Verve 849434 2CD/2MC
Holiday; Buck Clayton, Joe Guy, Charlie Shavers, Joe Newman, Harry Edison, Roy Eldridge (*t*); Tommy Turk (*tb*); Tony Scott (*cl*); Romeo Penque (*as, bcl*); Willie Smith, Gene Quill, Benny Carter (*as*); Ben Webster, Lester Young, Coleman Hawkins, Al Cohn, Paul Quinichette, Budd Johnson (*ts*); Oscar Peterson (*p, org*); Milt Raskin, Bobby Tucker, Mal Waldron, Carl Drinkard, Jimmy Rowles, Hank Jones, Wynton Kelly (*p*); Irving Ashby, Barney Kessel, Kenny Burrell, Barry Galbraith, Freddie Greene (*g*); Janet Putnam (*hp*); Milt Hinton, Carson Smith, Joe Mondragon, Red Mitchell, Red Callender, Aaron Bell, Leonard Gaskin, John Simmons, Ray Brown (*b*); Dave Coleman, Alvin Stoller, J. C. Heard, Ed Shaughnessy, Chico Hamilton, Larry Bunker, Lenny McBrowne, Osie Johnson (*d*); strings. 4/46-3/59.

Holiday's last period in the studios was with Verve in the 1950s, and this is the best-known and most problematical music she made. Her voice has already lost most of its youthful shine and ebullience – even a genuine up-tempo piece like 'What A Little Moonlight Can Do', where Oscar Peterson does his best to rouse the singer, is something she only has the energy to glide over. Whether this makes her music more revealing or affecting or profound is something the listener will have to decide for him-or herself. There are songs where the pace and the timbre of her voice are so funereal as to induce nothing but acute depression; others have a persuasive inner lilt which insists that her greatness has endured. And the best of the interpretations, scattered as they are through all these records, show how compelling Holiday could be, even when apparently enfeebled by her own circumstances. The only surviving 'original' albums are *Lady Sings The Blues* and *Songs For Distingué Lovers*, and both are good if patchy sessions: the former includes a superb 'I Thought About You', and the latter has Harry Edison and Ben Webster in particularly astute form as accompanists (whatever Holiday's own state, producer Norman Granz always put top-flight bands behind her). Superior, though, are the compilations: *Songbook* is a single-disc representation which includes most of her more renowned songs, while *Lady In Autumn* is a generous spread of two discs' worth of material, opening with a few so-so JATP live tracks and moving through some of her best studio tracks, although some of the better efforts – 'I Thought About You' and 'Embraceable You' – have been omitted.

Remastering on all the records has been pretty well done: the singer's voice is very forward (occasionally opppressively so), and the backing groups emerge clearly.

*(*)   **Miss Brown To You** Magic DATOM 6 CD
Holiday; Louis Armstrong (*t, v*); Jack Teagarden (*tb*); Coleman Hawkins (*ts*); Art Tatum, Count Basie (*p*); Al Casey (*g*); Oscar Pettiford (*b*); Sid Catlett (*d*); rest unknown. 37-49.

(*)   **Masters Of Jazz Vol. 3: Billie Holiday Storyville 4103 CD/LP
Holiday; Hot Lips Page, Roy Eldridge, Neal Hefti (*t*); Herbie Harper, Jack Teagarden (*tb*); Barney Bigard (*cl*); Herbie Steward (*cl, ts*); Coleman Hawkins (*ts*); Teddy Wilson, Jimmy Rowles, Art Tatum (*p*); Al Casey (*g*); Iggy Shevak, Oscar Pettiford (*b*); Blinkie Garner, Sid Catlett (*d*). 44/49.

***   **Summer Of '49** Bandstand BDCD1511 CD
Holiday; Neal Hefti, Hot Lips Page, Wild Bill Davison (*t*); Bobby Hackett (*c*); Herbie Harper, Cutty Cutshall (*tb*); Herbie Steward (*cl, ts*); Peanuts Hucko (*cl*); Ernie Caceres (*p*); Horace Henderson, Jimmy Rowles (*p*); Red Norvo (*vib*); Eddie Condon (*bj, g*); Iggy Shevak, Jack Lesberg (*b*); Blinkie Garner, George Wettling (*d*). 6–9/49.

(*)   **Billie Holiday 1948–1959 Royal RJD 508 CD
Holiday; Neal Hefti (*t*); Herbie Harper (*tb*); Buddy DeFranco, Tony Scott (*cl*); Herbie Steward (*cl, ts*); Jimmy Rowles, Buster Harding, Mal Waldron, Sonny Clark, Carl Drinkard (*p*); Red Norvo (*vib*); Jimmy Raney (*g*); Iggy Shevak, Red Mitchell, Gilbert Rovere, John Fields (*b*); Blinkie Garner, Kansas Fields, Elaine Leighton, Marquis Foster (*d*). 48-59.

**   **The Complete 1951 Storyville Club Sessions** Fresh Sound FSR-CD 151 CD
Holiday; Stan Getz (*ts*); Buster Harding (*p*); John Fields (*b*); Marquis Foster (*d*). 10/51.

(*)   **At Storyville Black Lion BLCD 760921 CD
As above, except add Carl Drinkard (*p*); Jimmy Woode (*b*); Peter Littman (*d*). 10/51-10/53.

***   **Billie's Blues** Blue Note CDP 7487862 CD
Holiday; Monty Kelly, Larry Neill, Don Waddilove (*t*); Skip Layton, Murray McEachern (*tb*); Buddy DeFranco (*cl*); Alvy West, Dan D'Andre, Lennie Hartman (*reeds*); Heywood Henry (*ts, bs*); Carl Drinkard, Bobby Tucker, Buddy Weed, Sonny Clark, Beryl Booker (*p*); Jimmy Raney, Mike Pingitore, Tiny Grimes (*g*); Red Mitchell, Artie Shapiro (*b*); Elaine Leighton, Willie Rodriguez (*d*). 42-54.

**   **The Essential Billie Holiday Carnegie Hall Concert** Verve 833767-2 CD/MC
Holiday; Buck Clayton, Roy Eldridge (*t*); Tony Scott (*cl*); Al Cohn, Coleman Hawkins (*ts*); Carl Drinkard (*p*); Kenny Burrell (*g*); Carson Smith (*b*); Chico Hamilton (*d*). 11/56.

**   **At Monterey 1958** Black-Hawk BKH 50101 CD/LP/MC
Holiday; Buddy DeFranco (*cl*); Benny Carter (*as*); Gerry Mulligan (*bs*); Mal Waldron (*p*); Eddie Khan (*b*); Dick Berk (*d*). 10/58.

Holiday left a vast number of live recordings, most of them unauthorised at the time, and they make a rather depressing lot to sort through. Unlike, say, Charlie Parker's live music, this presents a less than fascinating portrait, mostly of a musician in adversity. Club recordings such as the two Storyville discs find her in wildly varying voice, almost from song to song: truly affecting performances may sit next to ragged, throwaway ones. *Miss Brown To You* includes airshots with Count Basie and concert tracks with Louis Armstrong, but all but the last few are in appalling sound, and this can't be recommended. The 'Masters Of Jazz' series disc includes some good material from the 1940s, but better is the Bandstand disc, which includes some excellent tracks with a trio and some surprisingly spirited blues singing with (of all people) Eddie Condon, from a 1949 TV show. Sound here is good for the period. *Billie's Blues* is an interesting cross-section of tracks: several from a European tour which was a mixed success, including three with Buddy DeFranco's group that feature some fine clarinet by the leader, and four from an obscure session for Aladdin with a group that puts the singer into a jump-band blue situation. She handles it unexpectedly well. Much weaker are the Carnegie Hall concert of 1956 (which featured readings from her *Lady Sings The Blues* book) and the trudging Monterey appearance of 1958. These may cause pain to those who admire the young Holiday.

(***)   **Lady In Satin** Columbia CK-40247 CD/MC
         Holiday; strings. 58.

(***)   **Last Recordings** Polydor 835370 CD/MC
         Holiday; Harry Edison, Joe Wilder (*t*); Jimmy Cleveland, Bill Byers (*tb*); Romeo
         Penque (*as, ts, bcl*); Gene Quill (*as*); Al Cohn (*ts*); Danny Bank (*bs*); Hank Jones (*p*);
         Kenny Burrell, Barry Galbraith (*g*); Milt Hinton, Joe Benjamin b); Osie Johnson (*d*);
         strings. 3/59.

A troubling farewell which, nevertheless, has a certain macabre fascination. The croaking voice which barely gets through *Lady In Satin* has its admirers, and there is arguably some of the tormented revelation which distinguishes such earlier works as Parker's 'Lover Man', but we suggest that it is approached with care. *Last Recordings* emerges in much the same way, if it is in sum rather less harrowing.

DAVE HOLLAND (born 1946)
DOUBLE BASS, CELLO

(*)   **Emerald Tears ECM 1109 LP
         Holland (*clo* solo). 8/77.

***   **Life Cycle** ECM 1238 CD/LP
         As above. 11/82.

Miles smiled when he first saw and heard Holland. The premier British bass player of his generation has the quality, rare among rhythm players, of drawing attention to what he is doing, almost irrespective of whatever else is going on in the band. Even more remarkably, he does so entirely without histrionics; he is always a seamless part of any group of which he is a member. Even so, given his formidable technique on both cello and bass fiddle, solo recording was always likely.

Though both *Emerald Tears* and the more personal *Life Cycle* are demanding in their absolute concentration of resources, neither is forbiddingly so. The cello phrasings on the latter conjure echos of just about everyone from Bach to Zoltán Kodály, and then onward to Oscar Pettiford and Ron Carter. *Emerald Tears* suffers the same longueurs as Barre Phillips's similarly stabled *Call Me When You Get There* [ECM 1257 LP], but not fatally. Both should be investigated.

****   **Conference Of The Birds** ECM 1027 CD/LP
         Holland; Anthony Braxton, Sam Rivers (*reeds, f*); Barry Altschul (*d, perc, marimba*).
         11/72.

Twenty years old and one of the classics of modern jazz. The title-track has less to do with Attar than with the dawn chorus outside Holland's London flat, and there's a shifting, edge-of-sleep quality to each of Holland's six compositions. Braxton and Rivers intermesh more or less indistinguishably on flutes, but their saxophone voicings are almost antagonistic, which works fine. Time and again attention is quite properly diverted to Holland's astonishingly musical bass lines which illustrate his near-perfect tone and timing. Altschul is superb throughout, but his marimba figure on the title-piece is achingly beautiful, setting the listener up for the bite and bustle of 'Interception'. Indispensable.

***(*)   **Jumpin' In** ECM 1269 CD/LP

***   **Seeds Of Time** ECM 1292 CD/LP

***   **The Razor's Edge** ECM 1353 CD/LP
         Holland; Kenny Wheeler (*t, pkt-t, c, flhn*); Julian Priester (*tb on Jumpin' In and Seeds
         Of Time*); Robin Eubanks (*tb on The Razor's Edge*); Steve Coleman (*as*); Steve
         Ellington (*d on Jumpin' In*); Marvin Smitty Smith (*d on Seeds Of Time and The
         Razor's Edge*). 10/83, 11/84, 2/87.

***   **Extensions** ECM 1410 CD/LP
      Holland; Steve Coleman (*as*); Kevin Eubanks (*g*); Marvin Smitty Smith (*d*). 9/89.

Hard to choose between them. State-of-the-art modern jazz pivoted on the interplay between Coleman (who miraculously combines the qualities of his two saxophonic namesakes) and Holland's beautifully tempered bass playing. As on *Conference*, the individuality of the music stems from a tension between modernist freedoms and old-fashioned melodic susceptibilities. 'Blues For C. M.' on *Razor's Edge* is a tribute to Charles Mingus, who may be a greater influence on Holland's theme-writing than on his actual playing, which hovers between Scott LaFaro and early Ron Carter. The ground-breaking *Jumpin' In* should be considered essential, but it's hard to envisage a well-rounded collection without at least one of the others.

(*)   **Triplicate ECM 1373 CD/LP
      Holland; Steve Coleman (*as*); Jack DeJohnette (*d*). 3/88.

An album that hovers uneasily between wonderful and galling, almost like a *nouvelle cuisine* meal that, dammit, looks too good to eat. One of the rare occasions where the much-blathered-about 'ECM sound' actually does seem a hindrance rather than a virtue. Much as you might scuttle out of a trendy restaurant and devour a hamburger at the corner, *Triplicate* creates a hunger for the sort of after-hours brilliance the trio could doubtless conjure up when a trifle less self-conscious than this.

RICK HOLLANDER
DRUMS

(*)   **Private Ear yvp 3013 LP
      Hollander; Tim Armacost (*ts*); Walter Lang (*p*); Jos Machtel (*d*). 12/88.

Hollander leads a post-bop session with few frills: smartly delivered by a good quartet, the original material isn't especially absorbing but does its duty.

MAJOR HOLLEY (1924–90)
BASS, VOCAL

***   **Mule** Black & Blue 59.002 CD
      Holley; Gerry Wiggins (*p*); Ed Thigpen, Oliver Jackson (*d*). 3/74–2/77.

A great deal of fun. This was Major Holley's sole effort as a leader and, although Gerry Wiggins provides much of the strictly musical interest, Holley's loping bass parts and singalong arco work (in the manner pioneered by Slam Stewart) give the likes of 'Mack The Knife' a fresh spirit. As solid a mainstream bassist as one could find, Holley deserved at least one showcase on his own – and here it is, although over full CD length it may pall with some listeners.

RED HOLLOWAY
ALTO AND TENOR SAXOPHONE

**   **Cookin' Together** Original Jazz Classics OJC 327 CD/LP
      Holloway; Jack McDuff (*org, p*); George Benson (*g*); Wilfred Middlebrooks (*b*); Joe Dukes (*d*). 2/64.

Holloway, a Chicagoan tenorman with all the characteristics of that city's saxophonists – burly tone, swaggering drive – was already a veteran R&B player when he began recording in a jazz context. But this is a dull session: too many ordinary blues themes, flat sound and a generally drooping sense of momentum, in an area where high spirits count for nearly everything. Benson is the most interesting soloist here.

***   **Nica's Dream** Steeplechase SCS 1192 LP
      Holloway; Horace Parlan (*p*); Jesper Lundgaard (*b*); Aage Tanggaard (*d*). 7/84.

A pleasant tenor and rhythm date, with a solid rhythm section supporting Holloway on standards and blues; the pick is a fine 'Georgia On My Mind'.

** **Blues In The Night Vol. 1: The Early Show** Fantasy F 9647 CD/LP

(*) **The Late Show – Live At Maria's Memory Lane Supper Club Vol. 2 Fantasy F 9655 CD/LP
Holloway; Eddie 'Cleanhead' Vinson (*as, v*); Jack McDuff (*org*); Shuggie Otis (*g*); Richard Reid (*b*); Paul Humphrey (*d*); Etta James (*v*). 5/86.

These records are billed under James's and Vinson's names, but Holloway is in some ways the most authoritative presence here: he leads the band with aplomb, gets off a few blustering solos and firms up an occasion which the rather ailing Vinson and the often wayward James would have had difficulty sustaining by themselves. The first disc is rather tired, but the second, with a mischievous duet on 'Teach Me Tonight' and a mighty 'I'd Rather Go Blind' from James, has plenty of atmosphere.

(*) **Red Holloway & Company Concord CJ 322 CD/LP/MC
Holloway; Cedar Walton (*p*); Richard Reid (*b*); Jimmie Smith (*d*). 1/87.

***(*) **Locksmith Blues** Concord CCD 4392 CD/MC
Holloway; Clark Terry (*t, flhn, v*); Gerald Wiggins (*p*); Phil Upchurch (*g*); Richard Reid (*b*); Paul Humphrey (*d*). 6/89.

Although the 1987 session is a pleasing enough collection, Holloway sounds perfunctory in the company of players who are content to perform to order. With nobody pushing him much and with a pro's pro like Walton at the piano, the music is just another set of standards and blues. But the meeting with Clark Terry is very different, suggesting that Hollloway is always happier with another horn to joust with. The title blues is lavishly done, 'Red Top' is a terrific swinger, and the Ellington tunes are delivered with a finesse which normally eludes Holloway's records.

CHRISTOPHER HOLLYDAY (born 1970)
ALTO SAXOPHONE

*** **Christopher Hollyday** RCA Novus PL 83055 CD/LP/MC
Hollyday; Wallace Roney (*t*); Cedar Walton (*p*); David Williams (*b*); Billy Higgins (*d*). 1/89.

(*) **On Course RCA Novus PD 83087 CD/LP
Hollyday; Larry Goldings (*p*); John Lockwood (*b*); Ron Savage (*d*). 1/90.

(*) **The Natural Moment RCA Novus PD 83118 CD/LP/MC
Hollyday; Brad Mehldau (*p*); John Webber (*b*); Ron Savage (*d*). 1/91.

Hollyday emerged as a *wunderkind* some years before the debut record for Novus, which was actually his fourth album. He has a formidable technique, but the striking thing about him is his tone: he has the sour, fractious sound which is a stock-in-trade of his idol, Jackie McLean – so much so, in fact, that some have dismissed him as a McLean imitator. Since Hollyday recorded two McLean themes on *Christopher Hollyday*, it seemed as if he was scarcely trying to avoid the comparisons. But that first session is a highly enjoyable slice of contemporary bop. The uptempo charges through 'Bebop' and 'Ko-Ko' are so handsomely led by Hollyday that his more experienced sidemen have to play hard to keep up, and the McLean tunes, 'Omega' and 'Appointment In Ghana', are a refreshing change from the customary hard-bop fare of Silver, Shorter et al.

The subsequent records, unfortunately, emerge as rather less impressive. *On Course* offers eight originals by the leader plus one by Goldings, along with 'Memories Of You': it's all well played, and the group read each other's moves well enough, but the music misses the edge of excitement which distinguished the first record, and Hollyday's writing is all bits and pieces. He contributes five further tunes to *The Natural Moment*, and there are four pieces from other hands, including a reading of 'Every Time We Say Goodbye' which is so tart that it strikes a note of parody. This time the music seems over-intense, as if Hollyday were reacting to the usual charges of neo-conservatism by trying to prove how impolite he can be. He does sound more like McLean than ever, but the fierceness of the title-track, for instance, seems like a hurried miscalculation. Nevertheless, this is characterful work from a player who will surely do greater things.

BILL HOLMAN (born 1927)
TENOR SAXOPHONE, ARRANGER

***   **Satin Nights** Black Hawk BKH 536 CD/LP
Carl Saunders, Don Rader (*t, flhn*); Andy Martin (*tb*); Pete Beltran (*btb*); Ron
Loufbourrow (*frhn*); Ted Nash (*ss, as, ts, f*); Phil Woods (*as, cl*); Bob Cooper (*ts, f*);
Charlie Shoemake (*vib*); Alan Broadbent (*p*); Monty Budwig (*b*); Jeff Hamilton (*d*);
Sandu Shoemake (*v*). 9/86.

***   **Bill Holman Band** JVC JLP 3308 CD/LP
Holman; Carl Sanders, Frank Szabo, Don Rader, Bob Summers (*t, flhn*); Jack
Redmonds, Bob Enevoldsen, Eric Culver (*tb*); Pete Beltran (*btb*); Bob Melitello (*ss,
as, cl, f*); Lanny Morgan (*ss, as, f*); Bob Cooper, Dick Mitchell (*ss, ts, f*); Bob Efford
(*bs, bcl*); Rich Eames (*p*); Barry Zweig (*g*); Bruce Lett (*b*); Jeff Hamilton (*d*).
11–12/87.

Holman qualifies as an unsung giant. Although he's a well-known arranger, he seems to have
acquired a merely workmanlike reputation with the jazz audience, based on his prolific scoring
for Stan Kenton, Shorty Rogers and Maynard Ferguson. Yet his best work suggests a knack for
sitting comfortably in an established band-style while creating material which provides a
challenge to go one step further. His best work for Kenton, for instance, streamlined that
orchestra's sometimes ponderous lines into something much tougher and sleeker.

He has led his own big bands on record only occasionally, and his early records – including *In
A Jazz Orbit*, *Bill Holman's Great Big Band* and *The Fabulous Bill Holman* – are all now hard
to find. The 1986 session for Black Hawk offers a group of Holman originals played by a band
that knows the leader well and, while there's an occasional trace of sessionman ennui about
some of the playing, it explores the arranger's scores with the right kind of finesse.

The record for JVC is rather more exciting. Holman leads this band when he can in the Los
Angeles area, and it seems to have inspired him to take up playing again (he had previously laid
down the saxophone in the 1960s, to concentrate on writing). Although there are one or two
pop-orchestral trifles, such as the ingratiating version of Stevie Wonder's 'Isn't She Lovely',
there are surprising scores such as 'The Real You' and 'Primrose Path', while 'Goodbye Pork
Pie Hat' is an excellent feature for the perennially undervalued Bob Cooper – even if Holman
does rearrange Charles Mingus's harmonies.

RICHARD 'GROOVE' HOLMES (1931–91)
ORGAN

***   **Groovin' With Jug** Pacific Jazz CDP 792930-2 CD
Holmes; Gene Ammons (*ts*); Gene Edwards (*g*); Leroy Henderson (*d*). 8/61.

**   **Soul Message** Original Jazz Classics OJC 329 LP/MC
Holmes; Gene Edwards (*g*); Jimmie Smith (*d*). 8/65.

Holmes was one of the most swinging of organists. A sometime bassist, he liked earthy,
elemental bass lines and he decorated melodies with something like reluctance: he made the
organ sound massive and implacable. He recorded most prolifically in the 1960s, but most of
those records are now long out of print. The above reissues give some idea of his music: the
Pacific Jazz set catches him at a Los Angeles club, with Ammons is typically bustling mood, and
the quartet working up a strong head of steam on most of the tunes (a nine-minute 'Exactly
Like You' is a newly issued track to add to the original LP). *Soul Message* is a fine instance of
Holmes in straight-ahead style, and includes his hit version of 'Misty', but it suffers from the
dependence on formula and repetition which make most jazz organ albums boring over the long
haul.

(*)   **Hot Tat Muse M 5395 CD/LP
Holmes; Cecil Bridgewater (*t*); Houston Person (*ts*); Jimmy Ponder (*g*); Wilbur
Bascomb (*b*); Greg Bandy (*d*); Ralph Dorsey (*perc*). 9/89.

Groove passed away in 1991 and this might have been his last album. Sadly, it's not much good. Modish soul licks from Ponder and Person playing his umpteenth hollering blues solo don't give the organ man much company, and some of the tunes are feeble. Better to remember him via one of the reissues from the 1960s – which was, when all's said and done, his real era.

TRISTAN HONSINGER
CELLO

***   **Live Performances** FMP SAJ 10 LP
Honsinger (*clo* solo) [& Maarten Van Regteren (*b* solo)]. 11/76.

(*)   **Earmeals Moers 01040 LP
Honsinger; Gunter Christmann (*tb, b*). 5/78.

After Derek Bailey, Honsinger is by far the most uncompromising of the European free players. At times this has led him into both pointless obduracy and irritating whimsy. At his best, though, as on *Live Performances*, he is immensely powerful, dramatic and abstract at the same time. It is a shame that the album (which is not particularly well recorded) has had to be shared between two such interesting players, both of whom amply merit the full stretch, but Regteren is less well-known and should gain some adherents by virtue of the association. In contrast to the oddly balanced diet of *Earmeals*, where Honsinger seems alternately tentative and hostile towards his partner, the November 1976 set is beautifully balanced; 'Garlic And The Fever' and 'She' are among the most riveting free-music performances of the 1970s and, in sharp contrast to a good deal of music in that genre, fully repay repeated hearings.

WILLIAM HOOKER
DRUMS, VOCAL

**   **Lifeline** Silkheart SH 119 CD/LP
Hooker; Masahiko Kono (*tb*); Alan Michael, Claude Lawrence (*as*); Charles Compo (*ts*); Mark Hennen (*p*); William Parker (*b*). 8-12/88.

***   **The Firmament / Fury** Silkheart SH 123 CD
As above, except add Donald Miller (*g*), omit Hennen and Parker. 4/89.

Drummer, scholar and poet, Hooker has a hard time making these records work. Both are couched as free jazz rave-ups, with the drummer's own recitation setting the tone of the long piece which dominates *Lifeline* (the other two pieces are on the CD edition only). While the first record is intermittently exciting, the music seems wastefully indulgent. The best moments of *Lifeline* could have been edited down into a single piece of 15 minutes or so, with the intertwining altos of Michael and Lawrence lending a certain coherence, but Compo's overblowing is merely fatiguing, the interesting Kono is overwhelmed in the mix, and the sound is rough and poorly-defined. *The Firmament / Fury*, though, is rather better, and shows how important it is to record this kind of music properly: Hooker's drums are miked with much better clarity, and his basically simple methods – long, cumulative rolls spiked by abrupt cymbal explosions – grant a wrathful but controlled atmosphere to improvisations which benefit from a less chaotic direction. The duet with Lawrence is quite thoughtfully done, Compo and Kono work rather better on 'Lustre' and 'The Coming One', and Borbetomagus's Miller adds suitably gothic scrawls of guitar to 'Pralaya' and 'Radiance'. If anything, it's Hooker himself who doesn't find enough diversity in his responses, tying the music to a single rhythmic roll. Worth investigating to followers of freedom.

ELMO HOPE (1923–67)
PIANO

***(*)   **Trio And Quintet** Blue Note CDP 784438 2 CD
Hope; Freeman Lee, Stu Williamson (*t*); Frank Foster, Harold Land (*ts*); Percy Heath, Leroy Vinnegar (*b*); Frank Butler, Philly Joe Jones (*d*). 6/53, 5/54, 10/57.

***(*)   **Meditations** Original Jazz Classics OJC 1751 CD/LP/MC
         Hope; John Ore (*b*); Willie Jones (*d*). 6/55.

***   **Hope Meets Foster** Original Jazz Classics OJC 1703 CD/LP/MC
         Hope; Freeman Lee (*t*); Frank Foster (*ts*); John Ore (*b*); Art Taylor (*d*). 10/55.

***   **The All Star Sessions** Milestone M 47037 CD
         Hope; Donald Byrd, Blue Mitchell (*t*); John Coltrane, Jimmy Heath, Hank Mobley,
         Frank Wess (*ts*); Paul Chambers, Percy Heath (*b*); Philly Joe Jones (*d*). 5/56, 6/61.

***   **Elmo Hope Trio** Original Jazz Classics OJC 477 CD/LP/MC
         Hope; Jimmy Bond (*b*); Frank Butler (*d*). 2/59.

***(*)   **Plays His Own Original Compositions** Fresh Sound FSR CD 181 CD
         Hope; Paul Chambers, Butch Warren (*b*); Granville Hogan, Philly Joe Jones (*d*). 61.

***(*)   **The Final Sessions: Volume 1** Original Jazz Classics OJC 1765 CD
         Hope; John Ore (*b*); Clifford Jarvis, Philly Joe Jones (*d*). 66.

***(*)   **The Final Sessions: Volume 2** Original Jazz Classics OJC 1766 CD
         Hope; John Ore (*b*); Clifford Jarvis (*d*). 66.

Hope managed to sound sufficiently different from both his main influences, Bud Powell (with whom he went to school) and Thelonious Monk, to retain a highly individual sound. His reputation as a composer is now surprisingly slight, but he had a strong gift for melody, enunciating themes very clearly, and was comfortable enough with classical and modern concert music to introduce elements of fugue and canon, though always with a firm blues underpinning.

Like a good many pianists of his generation, he seems to have been uneasy about solo performance (though he duetted regularly with his wife Bertha) and is heard to greatest effect in trio settings. The early *Meditations* sounds remarkably Monk-like in places and John Ore's slightly limping lines confirm the resemblance (Ore was a long-standing member of the Thelonious Monk quartet and Jones was one of Monk's favourite drummers, a rating passed on to Charles Mingus). 'Elmo's Fire' and 'Blue Mo' are deft originals. The Blue Note sessions are taut and well disciplined, and the trios are generally better organized than the quintet tracks, where the sequence of solos begins to seem rather mechanical and Hope progressively loses interest in varying his accompaniments of others. Originals like 'Freffie' and 'Hot Sauce' come across well, though.

Hope responded well to the challenge of Coltrane's developing harmonic language and the Milestone sessions contain some provocative indications of Trane's early willingness to deconstruct standard material, in this case a bold reading of 'Polka Dots And Moonbeams'. The sessions with Foster are rather more conventional, but 'Georgia On My Mind' demonstrates Hope's original and uncompromising approach to standard ballad material, and Foster is only able to embellish a very strong conception. The 1959 trio, which was for Contemporary, is rather disappointing, but Hope had by this stage moved to the West Coast (which he found professionally conducive – i.e. more gigs – but artistically a little sterile) and had become further involved in drugs, for which he was eventually gaoled. His fortunes were on a roller-coaster from then until his untimely death, aged only 43. The Fresh Sound is an excellent way of getting Hope's most interesting compositions on one disc, though the Blue Note should be the item of first choice. *The Final Sessions*, released in 1966, are a fitting tribute to a much underrated musician. Jones, who had played on the later Milestone date, including four fine trio tracks with Hope and Heath, is marvellous on Volume 1, but Jarvis is highly accomplished and has a finely developed instinct for when to make use of space and silence. In the final analysis, it's a quite substantial legacy of material. Hope deserves still wider recognition.

PAUL HORN (born 1930)
FLUTE, ALTO SAX

(*)   **The Jazz Years Black Sun 15015 CD
        Horn; Emil Richards (*vib*); Victor Feldman, Paul Moer (*p*); Chuck Israels, Jimmy
        Bond, Vic Gaskin, Bill Plummer (*b*); Milt Turner, Maurice Miller, Colin Bailey (*d*);
        Larry Bunker (*perc*). 61–63.

Paul Horn first secured attention in Chico Hamilton's group, when Hamilton was adopting a chamber-jazz approach, and his subsequent career has all been pitched at that sort of level. This is a useful compilation of three albums from the early 1960s. Although Horn could play with a scurrying, mildly exciting facility on the alto sax, he favoured the flute as his first instrument and, even though he varies the textures in these tracks – sometimes using alto or bass flute for contrast – all of them are pretty and little more. Richards plays a major role in the music, but his own contributions are as insubstantial as the leader's. Some of the tracks appear more interesting than they prove, with much variation in metre and form; but the music is melodically drab and rhythmically square. As the 1960s progressed, Horn went to play his flute in the Taj Mahal and the Pyramids and worked on music which anticipated, alas, much of what now goes under the heading of New Age.

**   **The Altitude Of The Sun** Black Sun 15002 CD
Horn; Don Salvador (*p*); Egberto Gismonti (*p, g, f*); Ron Carter (*b*); Roberto Silva (*d*); Dom Um Romao (*perc*). 75–76.

A compilation of two CBS albums from the mid-1970s. These tracks have a little more bite to them, since Gismonti provides a touch of authenticity and lyric energy, but the thin tunes and Horn's own dilettante-ish playing betray too much of the music as an unconvincing fusion.

**   **500 Miles High** West Wind 2043 CD
Horn; Stan Getz, Joe Farrell (*ts*); Mike Gerson (*p*); Vincent Bell (*g*); George Mraz (*b*); Patrick Artero (*d*); Sugar Blue (*v*). 1/80.

**   **Live At Palm Beach Casino, Cannes 1980** Rare Bid BID 15505 CD/LP
Horn; Stan Getz (*ts*); Mike Garson (*p*); Mark Michel (*b*); Umberto Pagnini (*d*). 1/80.

These desultory live recordings seem all too typical of Horn's later output: doodling, inconsequential music which doesn't so much struggle to find an identity as contentedly slip into oblivion. Getz's sole appearance on the Rare Bid record is in a duet with Horn on 'Nature Boy'. On the other set, he and Farrell make up the numbers in an odd group, but Horn's bland conceptions, even on jazz material, set the irritatingly blissful tone.

SHIRLEY HORN
PIANO, VOCAL

***   **Loads Of Love/Shirley Horn With Horns** Merccury 843454-2 CD
Horn; Jimmy Cleveland (*tb*); Hank Jones, Bobby Scott (*p*); Kenny Burrell (*g*); Milt Hinton (*b*); Osie Johnson (*d*); rest unknown. 63.

A reissue of the two albums Horn made for Mercury in 1963. They're modest, pleasing records, much like many another light-jazz vocal record of the period, and while Horn's voice is transparently clear and warm, she was used to accompanying herself, and placed in the studios with a stellar but unfamiliar band she occasionally sounds stilted. Nor was she allowed to work at her favourite dead-slow tempos on ballads. Fine remastering.

***(*)   **A Lazy Afternoon** Steeplechase SCS 1111 CD/LP
Horn; Buster Williams,(*b*); Billy Hart (*d*). 7/78.

***(*)   **All Night Long** Steeplechase SCS 1157 LP/MC
Horn; Charles Ables (*b*); Billy Hart (*d*). 7/81.

***   **Violets For Your Furs** Steeplechase SCS 1164 LP
As above. 7/81.

***   **The Garden Of The Blues** Steeplechase SCS 1203 CD/LP
Horn; Charles Ables (*b*); Steve Williams (*d*). 11/84.

Horn's first Steeplechase set broke a long silence; if anything, it was effectively a debut album. The manner here, and throughout these four fine and under-recognized records, is reflective and sparsely evocative. Horn establishes her liking for intensely slow tempos with a compelling treatment of 'There's No You', but feels able to immediately contrast that with the hipsterish reading of 'New York's My Home', and the long trio instrumental on 'Gentle Rain' displays a piano method that works with the simplest materials and makes something distinctive. Williams and Hart – the latter an old friend who might understand Horn's music better than anyone – play with complete empathy. If anything, the three remaining discs are a slight letdown after *A Lazy Afternoon*, since Horn had already made a nearly definitive statement in this context, although each has its valuable interpretations.

***   **Softly** Audiophile 224 CD
            Horn; Charles Ables (*b*); Steve Williams (*d*). 10/87.

***   **I Thought About You** Verve 833235 CD/MC
            As above. 87.

***(*)   **Close Enough For Love** Verve 837933 CD/MC
            Horn; Buck Hill (*ts*); Charles Ables (*b*); Steve Williams (*d*). 11/88.

***(*)   **You Won't Forget Me** Verve 847482 CD/MC
            Horn; Miles Davis, Wynton Marsalis (*t*); Buck Hill, Branford Marsalis (*ts*); Toots Thielemans (*hmca, g*); Charles Ables (*b, g*); Buster Williams (*b*); Billy Hart, Steve Williams (*d*).6–8/90.

***   **Shirley Horn With Strings** Verve 314 511 879 CD/MC
            Horn; Wynton Marsalis (*t*); Steve Kujala, James Walker (*f*); Alan Broadbent (*p*); John Chiodini (*g*); Charles Ables, Chuck Domanico (*b*); Steve Williams, Harvey Mason (*d*); strings. 91.

What amounts to Horn's second comeback has been distinguished by a perfect touch and luxury-class production values. Actually, in terms of her own performances or those of her trio – Ables and Williams have been faithful and diligent disciples – there's no special advance on her Steeplechase albums, or on the single Audiophile set, which is an especially slow and thoughtful disc. The first two Verves continue to work at favourite standards, and Hill's presence adds a useful touch of salt to proceedings that may sound a little too sweetly sensuous for some listeners. But *You Won't Forget Me* is a step forward in its pristine attention to detail, awesome array of guest-star soloists – Davis was a great Horn admirer, and he sounds like himself, if well below his best – and the faithfulness with which Horn's voice is recorded. Marsalis turns up again on two tracks on *Here's To Life*, which is otherwise dedicated to arangements by Johnny Mandel, and again there's a hint of overdoing the sentiment: some may find the title-track far too wobbly in its emotional appeal. But the particular qualities of Horn's singing – the eschewal of vibrato, the even dynamic weight – are given full rein.

LARS HORNFELDT (born 1940)
ALTO SAX

(*)   **Jazz Portrait Dragon DRLP 83
            Hornfeldt; Jan Allan (*t*); Lars Sjösten (*p*); Soren Bo Addemos (*g*); Sture Nordin (*b*); Leif Wennerstrom (*d*). 10/84.

A refreshingly unslick and hard-fought session. Hornfeldt, who has played semi-professionally for many years on the local Swedish scene, emerges here as a Lee Konitz disciple whose stammering delivery and lack of rhythmic finesse create a surprisingly affecting climate on, say, 'My Foolish Heart'. Tristano's '317 East 32nd Street' sets the tone for the date, although it must be admitted that the music's lack of natural grace sometimes wears on the ears. Allan sounds a shade below his best, but Sjösten and the less familiar Addemos play well. Good, natural studio sound.

HORNWEB
GROUP

***   **Kinesis** Cadillac SGC 1014 LP
            Martin Archer (*ss*); Derek Saw (*sno, as, ts, bs*); Nigel Manning (*as, ts, f, cl*); Vic Middleton (*bs, f*). 5–8/86.

(*)   **Sixteen Ladder Rung 001 LP
As above, except add Tom Spears (*t*), Pete Lyons (*ts*), Charlie Collins (*picc, bcl, bsx*), John Jasnoch, Neil Carver, John Hanlon (*g*); Mary Schwarz (*vla*), Jo Cammack (*xy, perc*), Tim Cole (*clo*), Paul Shaft (*b*), Pete Infanti (*d*). 84–87.

***(*)   **Universe Works** Discus 2 LP
Martin Archer (*ss*); Pete Lyons (*ts*); Derek Saw (*sno, as*); Vic Middleton (*bs*). 2–3/89.

Of the many sax-only groups now working in post-bop improvisation, Hornweb are the most demanding and in many ways the most satisfying. While standing remote from any of the tradition aspirations of 29th Street or WSQ, their avant-garde techniques seem far less affected than those of ROVA or Your Neighbourhood Sax Quartet, even when much of the music – as covered by these three records – courts and occasionally slips into disaster. *Kinesis* and *Sixteen* contain some of their early work. The bluff, rough-and-ready textures of *Kinesis* betray a certain rhythmic stodginess in the quartet but, since they don't really set out to swing, the likes of 'Surfing At Windscale', 'Osculator' and the intense vocalizations on 'Jukejoint' take their place in the British improvising tradition with great aplomb. *Sixteen*, which involves a number of other friends and colleagues in expanded instrumentations, is something of a notebook on the Sheffield improvising scene of the mid-1980s, an exceptionally fertile and challenging situation. The music embodies clichés about northern grit and dourness, but it has to be admitted that some of the seven tracks sound too blunderingly grim to sustain interest, and a piece such as the wood flute solo 'Zircon Over Shanghai' fragments the flow to no useful purpose. Archer's 'Cardinals', though, with its scratchy intrusions by the three guitarists, is a memorable battle between form and improvisation, a struggle which moves through all of Hornweb's music. While none of the saxophonists is a significant virtuoso, their co-operative intensity moves towards a triumphant assertion of the group spirit over individual ego, a sense that pervades all of the splendid *Universe Works* (named after the studio where it was recorded). Derek Saw's compositions 'Nina' and 'Freedom Road' have a celebratory melodicism which commingles with Martin Archer's splintery 'Wild Pathway Favourites' and the piledriving four-way commotion of 'Sucker MC'. All three albums are slightly held back by greyish documentary recording, but the character of the music comes through untarnished, and they make up an important document of a particular strand in the British improvising scene of recent years.

WAYNE HORVITZ
PIANO, KEYBOARDS

(*)   **Some Order Long Understood Black Saint BSR 0059 CD/LP
Horvitz; Butch Morris (*c, mar syn*); William Parker (*b*). 2/82.

***   **Nine Below Zero** Sound Aspects sas 014 CD/LP
As above, except omit Parker, add Robert Previte (*d, mar, syn*). 1/86.

[**(*) **Todos Santos** Sound Aspects sas 019 CD/LP]
As above. 1/88.

Nine Below Zero is named after a Brett Easton Ellis novel, and seems compounded of much the same volatile mix of sharply self-conscious style and furious, half-suppressed violence. Whether or not 'Three Places In Suburban California' is intended to echo Charles Ives's American classic *Three Places In New England*, the syncretism of high and low styles is very much the same in spirit. A marvellous, effective album.

Nothing is more fearsome than intelligence suffused with anger (or vice versa). These are the qualities Morris brings to all three records, a dramatic counterpoise to Previte's tranced drums-and-effects and Horvitz's tense, Gestalt-therapy keyboard patterns. The longer and more developed improvisational structures on *Some Order Long Understood* cue some of the most interesting episodic material, but the album doesn't entirely cohere as a whole, and there's little of the compression that excites the shorter pieces on *Nine Below*. It's slightly difficult to set *Todos Santos* against the same measure, since the disc is shared with a group of fine duo performances from Doug Wieselman and Bill Frisell, which fans of the guitarist will want to have in any case; all the material, though, is written (or comprovised, to work changes on Butch Morris's macaronic 'conduction') by Horvitz's wife, Robin Holcomb, who has had an occasionally rough ride from jazz critics. Rather too filigreed for most tastes, it rarely settles into anything appealingly tangible.

***(*)   **Miracle Mile** Elektra Nonesuch 7559 79278 2 CD
Horvitz; J. A. Deane (*tb, elec*); Denny Goodhew (*sax*); Doug Wieselman (*ts, cl*); Stew Cutler, Bill Frisell, Elliott Sharp (*g*); Ben Steele (*g syn*); Kermit Driscoll (*b*); Bobby Previte (*d*). 91.

Moody and slightly threatening music from Horvitz's band, The President. Horvitz is an impressive melodist, but tunes are constantly set in front of rather sinister guitar and synth backgrounds as if to suggest that the 'kinder, gentler America' of George Bush, apostrophized in an interesting 'Open Letter', merely caps the kind of violence implied by the dramatic smoke-pall on the cover. The horns don't do much of interest, but Previte is absolutely superb, giving one of his best performances on record.

CLINT HOUSTON (born 1946)
BASS

(*)   **Inside The Plain Of The Elliptic Timeless SJP 132 LP
Houston; Joanne Brackeen (*g*); Ryo Kawasaki (*g*); Rubens Bassini (*perc*). 4/79.

Houston is something of a journeyman. He's played in countless sideman roles with a wide variety of leaders, and although he has dabbled in free playing he sounds most content in a straightforward, post-bop situation. This single entry as a leader isn't very impressive: the compositions are melodically threadbare and the playing, despite Houston's customary busyness, offers frugal rewards, most of them coming from the dependable Brackeen.

JIM HOWARD
ARRANGER

***   **No Compromise** Sea Breeze SB 2005 LP
Randy Brown, Ken Tinnish, Mike Malone, Tom Bourke (*t*); John Bebbington, John Botari, George Behr (*tb*); Colin Murray (*btb*); Darcy Hepner, Leo Sullivan, Paul Augustyn, Doug Warrick, Don Englert (*reeds*); Jim Reechia (*p*); Brian Legere (*g*); Shelley Berger (*b*); Anthony Terpstra (*d*). 6/78.

Jim Howard and Pat Sullivan are writers and arrangers who direct this punchy Canadian big band. The main work here is a five-part piece, 'Gordon's Studio Suite', arranged by Sullivan and performed with much enthusiasm by the orchestra. Admirers of, say, the Thad Jones–Mel Lewis band will enjoy the record, although a lack of truly distinctive soloists means that it falls short of any special identity, since the writing is well organized rather than inspired.

NOAH HOWARD (born 1943)
ALTO SAXOPHONE

***(*)   **Berlin Concert** FMP SAJ 07 LP
Howard; Takashi Kako (*p*); Kent Carter (*b*); Oliver Johnson (*d*); Lamont Hampton (*perc*). 1/75.

***   **Schizophrenic Blues** FMP SAJ 13 LP
Howard; Itaru Oki (*t*); Jean-Jacques Avenel (*b*); Oliver Johnson (*d*). 5/77.

Howard's playing in the 1970s bears the tribal scars of his association with Archie Shepp, a music that blends political and aesthetic radicalism with a straightforward desire to entertain – schizophrenic blues, indeed. Typically, a Howard concert was an almost too self-conscious alternation of styles, tempos and treatments. The earlier of these two live sets (both from Berlin, where Eric Dolphy's ghost still occasionally pops up in the clubs) is perhaps the best-balanced performance he ever committed to record, though the long-gone *At Judson Hall* [ESP 1064], which featured Dave Burrell and the tragic young British trumpeter, Ric Colbeck, who subsequently took his own life, remains his best record.

Berlin Concert is bracketed by two of Howard's keening, incantatory compositions, taken at a steady tempo, lapped with floods of notes from Takashi Kako. Of the two, the latter and longer 'Marie Laveau' is the more convincing. 'New York Subway' is a rather literal tone-poem, bustling, aggressive and exciting. 'Mardi Gras' is an early and still viable example of the funk style that, considerably diluted, drowns Howard's considerable talents on *Migration* (below).

The final track is a surprisingly rare cover of Coltrane's 'Olé'; much like the 'Homage To Coltrane' on *At Judson Hall*, Howard makes no attempt to pastiche the master's style or delivery, cleaving to the slightly sharp Dolphyish tones he evokes on *Schizophrenic Blues*. There he rides on the same singing accompaniment from Jean-Jacques Avenel and Oliver Johnson that Steve Lacy has so often relied upon. It's by no means as coherent a record, though, and Itaru Oki's trumpet playing sits slightly awkwardly with the leader's basically direct approach.

*   **Migration** Altsax 9009 CD
Howard; Lode Gansen (*t*); Tammy Hall (*ky, syn*); Marty Townsend, Jan Verheysen (*g*); LC, Curt Hanson (*b*); Cesare, Walter Metz (*d*); Danny Dhont (*electric perc*); Hildegarde Koning, Els DeSchepper; Christine De Vos, Walter Metz, Peter Van Den Heuvel (*v*).

Archie Shepp's career and reputation survived the fleeting illusion that he was also possessed of a good singing voice. Noah Howard's may not. However well intentioned and sincere, 'African Man' is one of the most embarrassing performances ever committed to record. Much of the rest of *Migration* consists of tired funk riffs with vapid electric backgrounds. 'Nairobi' is just about passable but might just as easily have been tossed off by Carlos Garnett on a day off as by one of the most genuinely original of contemporary players. Dismal.

FREDDIE HUBBARD (born 1938)
TRUMPET, FLUGELHORN

****   **Open Sesame** Blue Note CDP 784040 2CD
Hubbard; Tina Brooks (*ts*); McCoy Tyner (*p*); Sam Jones (*b*); Clifford Jarvis (*d*). 7/60.

***(*)   **Here To Stay** Blue Note CDP 784135 2CD
Hubbard; Wayne Shorter (*ts*); Cedar Walton (*p*); Reggie Workman (*b*); Philly Joe Jones (*d*). 12/62.

***(*)   **Breaking Point** Blue Note CDP 784172 2CD
Hubbard; James Spaulding (*as*); Ronnie Mathews (*p*); Eddie Khan (*b*); Joe Chambers (*d*). 5/64.

Freddie Hubbard's career on record has been a frustrating one, since his great technique and beautiful tone have so often been deployed in chanceless settings and on dismal material. As a young giant of hard bop, he was among the most admired and sought after of musicians and, although several of his best Blue Note albums remain unreissued – including *Goin' Up* and *Ready For Freddie* – these three show something of his early flair. Made when he had just turned 22, the year before he joined the Jazz Messengers, *Open Sesame* is full of the characteristic sparkle and punch of the young Hubbard. If he wasn't quite as incendiary as his contemporary, Lee Morgan, there is a compensating logic and shapeliness to his phrases which makes his solos consistently satisfying. Brooks, who wrote several of the themes, sounds at his best, and the very young Tyner and Jarvis play with great verve. The CD includes two previously unreleased versions of two of the original tracks.

Here To Stay is a little more reserved, but the opening 'Philly Mignon' includes an astonishing solo by Hubbard; there is a rapturous 'Body And Soul', and 'Nostrand And Fulton' is one of Freddie's smartest originals. Wayne Shorter, then Hubbard's front-line partner in the Messengers, plays with equal intensity. *Breaking Point* reflects some of Hubbard's adventures with the likes of Ornette Coleman and Eric Dolphy: the writing includes many shifting meters, unexpected harmonies and the like. If it is always going to sound like uncomfortable territory for the trumpeter, this record is one of his most convincing efforts at looking outside his normal hard-bop parameters. The long 'Far Away' is a complex yet smoothly delivered theme, and 'D Minor Mint' is an admirable bop swinger. James Spaulding, the unsung hero of many a Blue

Note session, matches the leader's drive. Essentially, any record from this period by Hubbard is going to be worth hearing.

***(*)   **Hub Cap** Blue Note B21Y 84073 CD
Hubbard; Julian Priester (*tb*); Jimmy Heath (*ts*); Cedar Walton (*p*); Larry Ridley (*b*); Philly Joe Jones (*d*). 4/61.

****   **Hub-Tones** Blue Note B21Y 84115 CD
Hubbard; James Spaulding (*as, f*); Herbie Hancock (*p*); Reggie Workman (*b*); Clifford Jarvis (*d*). 10/62.

Although available only as American imports, these fine Hubbard Blue Notes shouldn't go unremarked. The band on *Hub Cap* is sometimes blandly professional in the manner of much hard bop, but Hubbard himself plays some smouldering improvisations, and the splendid *Hub-Tones* is a classic meeting with Spaulding, including an affecting tribute to Booker Little and a couple of strong originals in 'Hub-Tones' and 'Prophet Jennings'. Blue Note's usual excellent sound transfers well to the CD reissues. *The Best Of Freddie Hubbard* (Blue Note CDP 793202 CD) is a well-chosen compilation, mostly from his early Blue Note years.

***   **Minor Mishap** Black Lion BL 60122 CD/LP
Hubbard; Willie Wilson (*tb*); Pepper Adams (*bs*); Duke Pearson (*p*); Thomas Howard (*b*); Lex Humphries (*d*). 8/61.

This doesn't burn as brightly as the contemporary Blue Notes, perhaps because the band is less enthusiastic than Hubbard who plays well, if a little within himself. Extra takes of all but one of the seven titles pad it out to CD length, but to no special advantage.

(*)   **Backlash Atlantic 7567-90466-2 CD
Hubbard; James Spaulding (*as, f*); Albert Dailey (*p*); Bob Cunningham (*b*); Ray Appleton (*d*); Ray Barretto (*perc*). 10/66.

A good enough session, but the emphasis on backbeats, riff tunes and squared-off solos is a broad hint at the lighter direction Hubbard was already looking towards, as jazz faced its slump in popularity. Perhaps he can't be blamed. A likeable 'Up Jumped Spring', the most enduring of the trumpeter's compositions, adds a little extra weight.

***(*)   **The Artistry Of Freddie Hubbard** MCA 33111 CD
Hubbard; Curtis Fuller (*tb*); John Gilmore (*ts*); Tommy Flanagan (*p*); Art Davis (*b*); Louis Hayes (*d*). 7/62.

Hubbard made two appearances as a leader for Impulse. The 1962 sextet session is unusual for Gilmore's presence, one of the few small-group albums he made away from Sun Ra in the early 1960s. The music offers a slightly more expansive setting than Hubbard was used to at Blue Note and, though Fuller and Gilmore are perhaps at less than their best, the music has a forceful presence, with Flanagan offering a dapper counterpoint to the horns.

***(*)   **Red Clay** CTI EPC ZK 40809 CD
Hubbard; Joe Henderson (*ts, f*); Herbie Hancock (*p, org*); Ron Carter (*b*); Lenny White (*d*). 1/70.

**   **First Light** CTI EPC 450562 CD
Hubbard; George Marge (*cl, f*); Romeo Penque (*ob, c, f*); Walter Kane (*bsn, f*); Hubert Laws (*f*); Jane Taylor (*bsn*); Ray Alonge, Jimmy Buffington (*frhn*); Richard Wyands (*p*); Phil Kraus (*vib*); George Benson (*g*); Ron Carter (*b*); Jack DeJohnette (*d*); Airto Moreira (*perc*); strings arr. Don Sebesky. 9/71.

**   **Sky Dive** CTI EPC 460838 CD
Hubbard; Alan Rubin, Marvin Stamm (*t, flhn*); Wayne Andre, Garnett Brown (*tb*); Paul Faulise (*btb*); Hubert Laws (*f*); Phil Bodner (*f, bcl, picc*); George Marge (*cl, bcl, f*); Wally Kane (*bcl, picc*); Romeo Penque (*cl, ob, c, f*); Keith Jarrett (*p*); George Benson (*g*); Ron Carter (*b*); Billy Cobham (*d*); Ray Barretto, Airto Moreira (*perc*). 10/72.

***   **In Concert Vol. 1 & 2** CTI ZGR 40688 CD
Hubbard; Stanley Turrentine (*ts*); Herbie Hancock (*p*); Eric Gale (*g*); Ron Carter (*b*); Jack DeJohnette (*d*). 3/73.

(*)   **Keep Your Soul Together CTI EPC 460417 CD
Hubbard; Junior Cook (*ts*); George Cables (*p*); Aurell Ray (*g*); Kent Brinkley, Ron
Carter (*b*); Ralph Penland (*d*); Juno Lewis (*perc*). 10/73.

These were successful albums for Hubbard, at a time when jazz trumpeters faced unpalatable
artistic and commercial choices, and they have worn perhaps slightly better than one might have
imagined. *Red Clay* is a fine instance of an updated blowing session, with everybody playing
hard within a shiny-sounding context that suggested a possible fresh direction for the traditional
hard-bop mien. But CTI production values instead stuck Hubbard in front of large orchestras
and in the middle of ponderous arrangements, where the only thing worth listening to is the
beauty of Hubbard's tone. It's a tribute to his innate powers that that is sometimes enough.
Keep Your Soul Together, despite a less than perfect rhythm section, takes on Cook as a useful
partner, and the *In Concert* sessions, while no masterpieces, at least reassert Hubbard in a
relatively challenging situation, even if the similarly restrained Turrentine isn't a very exciting
partner. All the albums have been suitably remastered for CD, and there is some unremarkable
extra music on both *Red Clay* and *First Light*.

(*)   **Live At Northsea Jazz Festival 1980 Pablo 2620-113 2LP
Hubbard; David Schnitter (*ts*); Billy Childs (*ky*); Larry Klein (*b*); Sinclair Lott (*d*).
7/80.

**   **Born To Be Blue** Pablo 2312-134 LP/MC
Hubbard; Harold Land (*ts*); Billy Childs (*ky*); Larry Klein (*b*); Steve Houghton (*d*);
Buck Clark (*perc*). 12/81.

***   **Outpost** Enja 3095 CD/LP
Hubbard; Kenny Barron (*p*); Buster Williams (*b*); Al Foster (*d*). 2–3/81.

(*)   **Face To Face Pablo 2310-876 CD
Hubbard; Oscar Peterson (*p*); Joe Pass (*g*); Niels-Henning Ørsted-Pedersen (*b*);
Martin Drew (*d*). 5/82.

All of Hubbard's 1970s albums for Columbia are currently out of print. These records for Pablo
are a disappointing lot. The two earlier sessions were both recorded live on European tours and,
while the leader plays with much of his old energy, neither group musters much distinction:
Schnitter is a faceless foil and Land sounds largely uninterested, while Childs adds nothing
special of his own. While there is the usual quota of virtuoso fireworks on the meeting with
Peterson, the session is, like so many involving Peterson's group, built on technical bravura
rather than specific communication. The quartet session for Enja, though, is much more
worthwhile. Hubbard sometimes sounds bland, and, as talented as the rhythm section, is they
don't ask him to be demonstrative; but there are some glowingly executed solos and a
particularly rapt flugelhorn treatment of 'You Don't Know What Love Is'. Excellent recording.

***(*)   **Double Take** Blue Note CDP 7462942 CD
Hubbard; Woody Shaw (*t*); Kenny Garrett (*as, f*); Mulgrew Miller (*p*); Cecil McBee
(*b*); Carl Allen (*d*). 11/85.

***(*)   **The Eternal Triangle** Blue Note CDP 7480172 CD
As above, except Ray Drummond (*b*) replaces McBee. 6/87.

Hubbard's return to Blue Note (he has since left the label again) was best realized on these two
records, where he was set in inspired partnership with Woody Shaw. Although Shaw's playing
had by now become somewhat unpredictable, both sessions mustered many creative sparks,
with Garrett taking an occasional solo and the rhythm section in prime form on both dates. As
an example of two-horn lead playing both records are celebratory in nature, and the brassy
brilliance of the unison passages is enough to make up for any shortfall in some of the solos.
Another plus is the choice of material, an unusual collection of jazz themes associated with
trumpeters: *Double Take* includes Clifford Brown's 'Sandu' and the Navarro–McGhee
'Boperation', while *The Eternal Triangle* features themes by Little Benny Harris, Kenny
Dorham and Lee Morgan. Both are recommended.

***   **Feel The Wind** Timeless SJP 307 CD
Hubbard; Javon Jackson (*ts*); Benny Green, Mulgrew Miller (*p*); Lonnie Plaxico, Leon
Dorsey (*b*); Art Blakey (*d*). 11/88.

**(*)   Times Are Changing Blue Note CDP 790905 CD
Hubbard; Todd Cochran (*ky*); Stanley Clarke (*b*); Michael Shrieve, Stix Hooper (*d*);
Munyango Jackson (*perc*); Phil Perry (*v*). 89.

The Timeless session reunites Hubbard with Blakey for one last time, in the company of some
younger Jazz Messengers. Nothing terribly exciting happens, but the now-senior trumpeter
proves with his solo on 'Off Minor' that he can improvise on difficult tunes with as much
aplomb as any Young Turk. Todd Cochran plays most of the instruments, mainly keyboards, on
the final Blue Note date, and the result is a glossy pop-jazz which updates Hubbard's CTI sound
of the 1970s. Disposable, perhaps, but it must be admitted that the prettiness of Hubbard's
playing in this kind of context is still hard to resist. 'Back To Lovin' Again', for instance, might
have been lifted off any of Miles Davis's recent records.

***(*)   Bolivia Musicmasters/Limelight 820837-2 CD
Hubbard; Ralph Moore (*ss, ts*); Vincent Herring (*ss, as*); Cedar Walton (*p*); David
Williams (*b*); Billy Higgins (*d*); Giovanni Hidalgo (*perc*). 12/90–1/91.

Every so often Hubbard does a session like this and all his old virtues fall back into place. The
major props here are Cedar Walton and Billy Higgins, two men who've little time for frippery,
and they play with such class that it obliges Hubbard to work hard and return the favour.
Moore is a little in shadow (and Herring makes only one appearance) but the weight rests on
Hubbard and he seems to be feeling good about it.

PEANUTS HUCKO (born 1918)
CLARINET, TENOR SAXOPHONE, VOCALS

***   Tribute To Louis Armstrong / Benny Goodman Timeless TTD 512/3 CD/LP
Hucko; Billy Butterfield (*t*); Trummy Young (*tb*); Marty Napoleon (*p*); Lars Erstrand
(*vib*); Jack Lesberg (*b*); Gus Johnson (*d*); Louise Tobin (*v*). 10/83.

**(*)   Tribute To Louis Armstrong / Benny Goodman Timeless TTD 541/2 LP
Hucko; Randy Sandke (*t*); Al Grey (*tb*); John Bunch (*p*); Frits Landesbergen (*vib*);
Jack Lesberg (*b*); Jake Hanna (*d*). 7/86.

It's not really so very difficult to understand the rationale behind these two (or four) confusingly
titled sessions. Hucko's association with both Armstrong and Goodman (for whom he tactically
shifted to tenor saxophone) affords him the best possible background for this kind of material.
In tone, he combines something of Goodman's sinuous grace with the blacker, biting sound of
Edmond Hall. On the Armstrong numbers, notably 'Basin Street Blues' on TTD 512, 'Royal
Garden Blues' and 'The Sheik of Araby' on TTD 541, he favours a grittier, grainier vibrato, but
there's a slight tendency these days to squeal in the upper register. The smoother chalumeau
appropriate for much of the Goodman material suits the seventy-plus Hucko a little better.
Beginners and the yet-to-be-converted will want the slightly earlier set; the horns are clearer
and more varied, and there's a fine, if slightly faded, version of Hucko's signature, 'Stealin'
Apples', a classic of traditional jazz. (The existence of a CD shouldn't affect any decision either
way; the transfer isn't particularly generous and something seems to have happened to the
rhythm section in the process.)

SPIKE HUGHES (1908–87)
BASS

***   Spike Hughes, His Decca-dents & His Dance Orchestra 1930 Retrieval FG 407 LP
Hughes; Sylvester Ahola, Jack Jackson, Max Goldberg (*t*); Max Farley (*cl, as*); Danny
Polo, Rex Owen (*cl*); Bobby Davis (*as, bs*); Philip Buchel (*as*); Eddie Carroll, Claude
Ivy (*p*); Stan Andrews (*vn*); Leslie Smith (*g*); Val Rosing (*d, v*); Bill Harty (*d*).
3–4/30.

***   Spike Hughes & His Dance Orchestra & His Three Blind Mice 1930 Vol. 2 Retrieval
FG 409 LP
Hughes; Jack Jackson, Norman Payne, Bill Gaskin (*t*); Jock Fleming (*tb*); Max Farley
(*cl, as, f*); Philip Buchel, Jimmy Dorsey (*cl, as*); Bobby Davis, Harry Hines (*cl, bs*);

Eddie Carroll, Claude Ivy, Gerry Moore (*p*); George Hurley (*vn*); Leslie Smith, Alan Ferguson (*g*); Bill Harty (*d*), Val Rosing (*v*). 4/30–7/30.

*** **Spike Hughes & His Dance Orchestra 1930 Vol. 3** Retrieval FG 411 LP
Hughes; Leslie Thompson (*t, tb*); Norman Payne, Arthur Niblo (*t*); Muggsy Spanier (*c*); Jock Fleming, Lew Davis, Bernard Tipping (*tb*); Jimmy Dorsey, Max Farley, Harry Hines (*cl, as*); Philip Buchel (*as*); Buddy Featherstonhaugh (*cl, ts*); Eddie Carroll (*p*); Stan Andrews (*vn*); Leslie Smith, Alan Ferguson (*g*); Bill Harty (*d*). 5–12/30.

*** **Spike Hughes & His Dance Orchestra & His Three Blind Mice 1931** Retrieval FG 413 LP
Hughes; Leslie Thompson (*t, tb*); Norman Payne, Arthur Niblo, Jimmy Macaffer, Chuck Smith, Billy Higgs (*t*); Lew Davis, Bill Mulraney (*tb*); Harry Hines, Billy Amstell, Harry Hayes (*cl, as*); Sid Owen (*as*); Buddy Featherstonhaugh (*ts*); Eddie Carroll, Billy Mason (*p*); Alan Ferguson (*g*); Bill Harty, Ronny Gubertini (*d*); Betty Bolton, Joey Shields, Val Rosing (*v*). 1–11/31.

Spike Hughes quit while he was ahead: one of the most forward-looking musicians in the British dance-band world of the 1930s, by 1934 he had virtually finished with the music, and he subsequently became a major figure in the classical establishment. This was after creating many of the most striking hot-dance records to come out of Britain at the time, as well as masterminding an extraordinary session in New York in 1933 with many of the best musicians of the day (Hawkins, Allen, Wells and others). While these later records are still awaited on a single CD, the four Retrieval LPs contain some of the most sought-after original records of their kind. The first two sessions were by 'Spike Hughes And His Decca-dents', but thereafter it was mostly the Hughes Orchestra which took the label credits, conglomerations of some of the best studio musicians of the day. Even in the earliest sessions, Hughes was looking for hot material – 'Zonky', 'The Man From The South' – and by the time of the sessions at the end of Volume 2, he was arranging the likes of 'Harlem Madness', 'Blue Turning Grey Over You' and – for guest soloist Jimmy Dorsey – 'Tiger Rag' and 'St Louis Blues'. Nor was this any kind of throwback to 1920s hot-dance playing. The 'weird ending', as trumpeter Norman Payne remembers it, on 'Everything Is Peaches Down In Georgia', or the Ellington covers 'Misty Mornin'' (Volume 3) and 'High Life' (Volume 4), suggest a mind inquiring beyond the formulaic music of the Five Pennies, which was the dominant influence on this kind of music in the previous decade. The striking rearrangement of Joe Venuti's 'Doing Things' (Volume 3) and especially Spike's own two-part 'A Harlem Symphony' (Volume 4) are tracks to seek out, but throughout there is much fine solo work from Ahola, Payne, Featherstonhaugh and Davis, while Hughes's own bass playing is functional rather than inspiring. These are fascinating pointers to jazz developing away from the USA before 1939, and the excellent transfers make them very listenable.

DANIEL HUMAIR (born 1938)
DRUMS

**** **9–11 p.m. Town Hall** Label Bleu LBLC 6517 CD
Humair; Michel Portal (*sax, bcl, bandoneon*); Joachim Kuhn, Martial Solal (*p*); François Jenny-Clark (*d*). 6/88.

It's often a little difficult when Gato Barbieri is playing in his characteristic hyperthyroid manner, to hear much else that is going on in the band. But sometime try to follow the drumming behind Barbieri on the classic *Last Tango In Paris*, for it illustrates in convenient miniature the qualities that have made Humair one of the finest European drummers. He has all the rhythmic subtlety and inventiveness one associates with Philly Joe Jones, but also some of the inherent tunefulness of Roy Haynes.

Humair's own records have the same thoroughgoing musicality that he brings to work with artists as different as Anthony Braxton, Stéphane Grappelli and Lee Konitz. *Town Hall* is a superb introduction to all the participants, and if the veteran Solal's part isn't as large as one might wish for, it's none the less significant as an exercise in the genealogy of the 'new' French jazz, whose roots actually strike a lot deeper than first appears. That is nowhere more evident than here and on . . .

***   **Up Date 3.3** Label Bleu LBLC 6530 CD
        Humair; François Jeanneau (*as, ss, ts, f*); Henri Texier (*b*). 2/90.

. . . where Humair teams up with Texier (a bassist with a more folkish and st.
than the more freely orientated Jenny-Clark) in an album of looser c
improvisations. Jeanneau more than makes up for any slight technical shor
intelligent disposition of his four horns, but the real foundation of the music is th
the bass and drums. Both come highly recommended.

***(*)   **Edges** Label Bleu LBLC 6545 CD
        Humair; Jerry Bergonzi (*saxes*); Aydin Esen (*p*); Miroslav Vitous (*b*). 5/91.

Much of the interest here settles again on the interplay between Humair and another great
European bassist. Vitous's own 'Monitor' is a strange stop–start theme that downplays Esen's
rippling accompaniments and Bergonzi's full-ahead Coltranism in order to explore the complex
times and sonorities that are meat and drink to both 'rhythm' players. Something of the same
goes on throughout the very long 'Genevamalgame' (co-written by Joachim Kuhn and the
drummer, his only compositional credit on the album).

    The title suggests a much more exploratory, risk-taking endeavour. Humair's out-of-tempo
sequences and dramatic *rallentando* passages must be extremely challenging to his players.
There may be a hint of compromise to the market in Bergonzi's and Esen's dramatic soloing,
but they are both capable of abstraction, too, and the net effect of their more obvious strategies
is to concentrate attention on the drummer and bassist. The mix is nicely horizontal, though
Vitous could have done with a slight lift, particularly on the early tracks.

HELEN HUMES (1913–81)
VOCAL

****   **'Tain't Nobody's Biz-ness If I Do** Original Jazz Classics OJC 453 CD/LP/MC
        Humes; Benny Carter (*t*); Frank Rosolino (*tb*); Teddy Edwards (*ts*); André Previn
        (*p*); Leroy Vinnegar (*b*); Shelly Manne, Mel Lewis (*d*). 1–2/59.

****   **Songs I Like To Sing** Original Jazz Classics OJC 171 CD/LP/MC
        Humes; Al Porcino, Ray Triscari, Stu Williamson, Jack Sheldon (*t*); Harry Betts, Bob
        Fitzpatrick (*tb*); Art Pepper (*cl, as*); Ben Webster, Teddy Edwards (*ts*); Bill Hood
        (*bs*); André Previn (*p*); Barney Kessel (*g*); Leroy Vinnegar (*b*); Shelly Manne (*d*).
        9/60.

***(*)   **Swingin' With Helen** Original Jazz Classics OJC 608 CD/LP/MC
        Humes; Joe Gordon (*t*); Teddy Edwards (*ts*); Wynton Kelly (*p*); Al Viola (*g*); Leroy
        Vinnegar (*b*); Frank Butler (*d*). 7/61.

Helen Humes made her first records as far back as 1927, when she was 14, but her sessions with
Count Basie in the 1930s established her career. Her three albums for Contemporary have
luckily all been reissued in the OJC series, and they make a powerful argument for her standing
as one of the finest – and most overlooked – jazz vocalists of the swing era and after. Recorded
in stereo for the first time, her voice's natural mix of light, girlish timbre and hard-hitting attack
creates a curiously exhilarating impact. She's like a less matronly Ella Fitzgerald, yet she can
phrase and change dynamics with more inventiveness than Ella. The 1960 session, organized
almost as a jam session by Benny Carter, has a rare grip and immediacy, and although almost
everything on its is fine, special mention should be made of a superbly structured 'Stardust' and
'I Got It Bad And That Ain't Good' and a perfectly paced 'You Can Depend On Me'. The
band, a strange mix of players, work unexpectedly well together, with the rhythm section's
modern grooving offsetting terrific solos by Carter, Rosolino and Edwards.

    Swingin' With Helen is just a shade less impressive, but the twelve standards here are all
delivered with great charm and aplomb. The pick of the three, though, is *Songs I Like To Sing*,
which arranger Marty Paich built very specifically around Humes's talents. The singer has no
problem dealing with scores which would have taxed such a modernist as Mel Torme, and these
eight tracks define a modern approach to swing singing. But the other four, with Humes set
against a rhythm section and the sole horn of Ben Webster, are equally beautiful, particularly a
glorious reading of 'Imagination'. Although Humes's voice isn't as forward in the sound
balance as it might be, the remastering of all three records is very crisp and strong.

Sneakin' Around Black & Blue 233083 CD

Humes; Arnett Cobb, Gerard Bardini (*ts*); Gerald Wiggins, Jay McShann (*p*); Milt Buckner (*org*); Clarence Gatemouth Brown (*g*); Major Holley, Roland Lobligeois (*b*); Paul Gunther, Ed Thigpen (*d*). 8/73–5/74.

Humes is in good voice, and the band, although a motley bunch of players on both sessions, sounds enthusiastic. But the material is no more than a run-through of Helen's greatest hits, all available in better versions elsewhere. Her later albums for Muse and Columbia are currently out of print.

***   The New Year's Eve Le Chant Du Monde LDJ 274914 CD

Humes; Gerald Wiggins (*p*); Deon Rieley (*b*); Benny Barth (*d*). 80.

These two live sets from 1980 may have been Helen's last recordings. It's a pity that the sound is imperfect – in fact, it's pretty disgraceful for a record made in 1980 – and that the slightly superior second show accounts for only three of the 20 tracks. But otherwise Humes is in spirited and beguiling voice, only a little breathless here and there, with the timbre and sweetness of her voice disarmingly intact on a very good programme of material, ranging from Fats Waller's 'If You're A Viper' to 'Sunday, Monday Or Always'. The trio give smiling support.

PERCY HUMPHREY (born 1905)
TRUMPET

**(*)   Sounds Of New Orleans Vol. 1: Paul Barbarin & His Band/Percy Humphrey's Jam Session Storyville SLP 6008 CD/LP

Humphrey; Joe Avery (*tb*); Ray Burke (*cl*); Sweet Emma Barrett (*p*); Billy Huntington (*bj*); Ricard Alexis (*b*); Cie Frazier (*d*). 5/54.

**   A Portrait Of Percy Humphrey Storyville SLP 231 LP

Humphrey; Louis Nelson (*tb*); Orange Kellin (*cl*); Lars Edegran (*p*); Al Lewis (*bj, v*); Chester Zardis (*b*); Louis Barbarin (*d*). 9/72.

**   New Orleans To Scandinavia Storyville SLP 232 LP

As above, except add Jorgen Svare (*cl*); Soren Sorenson (*ts*) and Jorn Jensen (*p*). 9/72.

The youngest of the three Humphrey brothers is a substantial figure in New Orleans jazz. His most significant playing was usually done with the city's brass bands, and he became leader of the Eureka Brass Band in the early 1950s until its disbandment some 20 years later. The 1954 jam session, one half of an LP shared with a Paul Barbarin set, is relatively slight music, but Humphrey plays with the characteristically curt, short-breathed phrasing of the New Orleans brassman and makes all of his notes count: his solo on 'Everybody Loves My Baby', decorated with the familiar wobble which is the New Orleans vibrato, sums up his style, a mixture of abrasiveness and raw melody. The sound is quite good, although Sweet Emma Barrett, a minor legend who wore bells on her hat and around her ankles, is almost inaudible at the piano.

Most of Humphrey's later records are hard to locate, but these two Storyvilles, cut in Copenhagen on a visit by Humphrey's New Orleans Joy Makers, are still in circulation. They're disappointingly thin, cut-and-dried music, with Humphrey, Nelson and their fellow Americans assisted by local players to no great effect and the sessions weighted with tired trad standards.

BOBBY HUTCHERSON (born 1941)
VIBRAPHONE, MARIMBA, PERCUSSION

*****   Dialogue Blue Note B21Y 46537 CD

Hutcherson; Freddie Hubbard (*t, flhn*); Sam Rivers (*ts, ss, bcl, f*); Andrew Hill (*p*); Richard Davis (*b*); Joe Chambers (*d*). 4/65.

****   Happenings Blue Note B21Y 46530 CD

Hutcherson; Herbie Hancock (*p*); Bob Cranshaw (*b*); Joe Chambers (*d*).

****   Oblique Blue Note B21Y 84444 CD

Hutcherson; Herbie Hancock (*p*); Albert Stinson (*b*); Joe Chambers (*d*). 7/67.

***(*) **Total Eclipse** Blue Note B21Y 84291 CD
Hutcherson; Harold Land (*ts, f*); Chick Corea (*p*); Reggie Johnson (*b*); Joe Chambers (*d*). 68.

If Bobby Hutcherson had been a horn player, or even a pianist, he would certainly be regarded as one of the major figures of the past 25 years. Unfortunately, the vibraphone is still seen as something of a novelty instrument, suitable for showbizzy histrionics (Lionel Hampton's doing) or else as too soft in tone for serious improvisation. There is, of course, a lively tradition of vibraharp playing with both traditionalist and radical wings, but few have developed such a consistently challenging language for the instrument as Hutcherson. In the 1960s he made a series of superb albums for Blue Note, the equal of any of the classic dates from that label. Though an early work, *Dialogue* stands head and shoulders above them all. Drawing on some of the free-harmonic and -rhythmic innovations developed on Eric Dolphy's *Out To Lunch* (on which Hutcherson played), he began to develop a complex contrapuntal style that involved parallel melodies rather than unisons and complex rhythm patterns which he conceived (much as Mingus conceived key centres) as focal points round which the musicians operated. Hutcherson probably never ventured further down the freedom road than on this album, and 'Les Noirs Marchent' is his most unfettered and abrasive composition, marking a sharp contrast with the more formal counterpoint of 'Idle While' and the title-piece.

Happenings is not quite so impressive, but it does represent an important showcase for Hutcherson's rapidly developing harmonic awareness. 'Bouquet' is one of the most underrated jazz compositions of the 1960s, and there is an excellent version of Herbie Hancock's 'Maiden Voyage', which some might place a notch ahead of the original. *Oblique* is perhaps the least known of the Blue Notes but deserves wider exposure. Hutcherson's 'free counterpoint' is not quite as daring as it was on *Dialogue*, but here he blends it with samba rhythm (on 'Til Then' and 'Subtle Neptune'), and in a difficult 12/8 on 'My Joy', which also features a fine solo from the ill-fated Stinson. Hutcherson plays drums on 'Bi-Sectional' briefly sidelining the faithful Chambers, who provides exactly the right mixture of firmness and freedom throughout the Blue Note period.

In 1968, Hutcherson formed a regular group with Harold Land, recording under alternative names for Blue Note and Mainstream. *Total Eclipse* is a fine record by any standard and, if it doesn't quite come up to the standard of *Dialogue*, that's no disgrace. Hutcherson was willing to play prettier (very obviously so on the closing 'Pompeian', with its tinkling bell sounds) and to communicate rather dark and complex ideas, as on the mysterious 'Total Eclipse' with a refreshingly light touch and not a hint of sententiousness. Corea is a swinging, very melodic partner and his own 'Matrix' sounds well made for this line-up. Land's solos, notably on the opening 'Herzog' and the Corea tune, are firm-voiced and logical, with barely a wasted note. Two other fine Blue Notes – *Components* [84213 LP] and *Stick-Up* [84244 LP] have been out of print for some time, more's the pity, since they round out an extraordinary decade of achievement.

By contrast, the 1970s were a bleak time for Hutcherson's music. Too complex a harmonic imagination to fit easily into the relatively packaged harmonies of fusion music, he frittered away what might have been his most productive decade in less than challenging projects.

*** **Solos/Quartet** Original Jazz Classics OJC 425 CD/LP/MC
Hutcherson solo and with McCoy Tyner (*p*); Herbie Lewis (*b*); Billy Higgins (*d*); John Koenig (*bells*). 9 & 10/81, 3/82.

***(*) **Farewell Keystone** Theresa TR 124 CD/LP/MC
Hutcherson; Oscar Brashear (*t, flhn*); Harold Land (*ts*); Cedar Walton (*p*); Buster Williams (*b*); Billy Higgins (*d*). 7/82.

The 1980s have seen something of a revival in his fortunes: uncompromised recording opportunities, sympathetic collaborators, and, one suspects, a consequently renewed faith in his own abilities. *Farewell Keystone* reunites him with Harold Land and the encounter still sounds pretty incisive 10 years on, with a truly fantastic rhythm section propelling the front men. Hutcherson's multi-directional contrapuntal imagination, with melodic, harmonic and rhythmic parameters all intelligently controlled, makes solo performance more than commonly feasible, particularly with the use of multi-tracking; where Lionel Hampton required a great surfer's wave of chords and riffs piled up behind him, Hutcherson creates his own internal impetus. The tone is by no means as percussive as it was on *Out To Lunch*, though ironically Hutcherson has put increasing emphasis on xylorimbas at the same time as smoothing out his vibraphone lines in what looks like a degree of accommodation with Milt Jackson.

The quartet sessions, which include a sparkling 'Old Devil Moon' and 'My Foolish Heart', simply underline Tyner's astonishing eclecticism and adaptability. Those with longer memories will automatically track back to Hampton's interplay with Teddy Wilson in the classic Benny Goodman Quartets of 1936 and 1937. That good.

***   **Good Bait** Landmark LM 1501 CD/LP/MC
Hutcherson; Branford Marsalis (*ts, ss*); George Cables (*p*); Ray Drummond (*b*); Philly Joe Jones (*d*). 8/84.

Marsalis, B., doesn't seem right for this gig. He has a slithery, almost lackadaisical approach to phrasing, as if he'd try to get away with fewer notes if only he could be bothered riding the spaces. In the event, you get a lazy-man's-load of sound, bits falling off it all over the place. It's engaging stuff, though, and the rest of the band are great. By far the best track is a quartet 'Spring Is Here', with Hutcherson and Cables nudging slightly cautiously at one another, and explicit references to Miles's more emotional approach in the modes and voicings. Like almost all the Landmark catalogue, impressively well recorded, with just the right miking for the drum kit.

***(*)   **Color Schemes** Landmark LM 1508 CD/LP/MC
Hutcherson; Mulgrew Miller (*p*); John Heard (*b*); Billy Higgins (*d*); Airto Moreira (*perc*). 10/85.

A marvellous record. The duos with Miller and Airto drift into occasional redundancies and embellishments, but Hutcherson sustains the overall direction with impressive ease. Miller really comes into his own on a quintet reading of 'Bemsha Swing' that dis-assembles the chord structure rather than merely improvising with it. Though Jones's contribution to *Good Bait* is enormous, Higgins would seem to be *the* drummer for Hutcherson. As on *Solos/Quartet* (above) and in marked contrast to Victor Lewis (below), who likes to play by the book, he scythes through the bar-lines, keeping the pulse and the metre in view with the odd, accurately placed accent or simply with the sheer impetus of his playing. Very highly recommended.

****   **In The Vanguard** Landmark LM 1513 CD/LP/MC
Hutcherson; Kenny Barron (*p*); Buster Williams (*b*); Al Foster (*d*). 12/86.

Take the title any way you like – it refers, of course, to the one in the Village – Hutcherson is still at the forefront on contemporary jazz. This, a surprisingly rare live recording, is one of the very best things he has ever committed to disc. The setting – with no horns – develops his interest in the interaction of piano and vibes, with the enormous harmonic and contrapuntal possibilities that implies. Standards-based, the emphasis is on improvisation, rather than on tightly organized charts (and producer Orrin Keepnews has described the album as a deliberate tactic in reaction to the very controlled, and occasionally contrived, feel of its predecessors).

As it turns out, the band's harmonic centre is the bassist; Buster Williams has a huge tone and, with his wonderfully controlled pedal passages on the likes of 'Some Day My Prince Will Come' (which needs to be compared with Miles's version), pushes the rest of the band in the direction of freedom; his introduction to Bruno Martino's 'Estate', an underexploited theme which has also caught Herbie Hancock's eye, is the perfect cue for Hutcherson at his most romantic. The set opens with Randy Weston's 'Little Niles', then blows the fluff off 'Young And Foolish' and 'Witchcraft', and tackles Monk's 'Well, You Needn't' like it was already overtime. Al Foster does the work of three men and Barron could almost be Hutcherson's third instrument. Superb; high in the top 50 albums of the decade.

***(*)   **Cruisin' The 'Bird** Landmark LM 1517 CD/LP
Hutcherson; Ralph Moore (*ts, ss*); Buddy Montgomery (*p*); Rufus Reid (*b*); Victor Lewis (*d*). 4/88.

By no means just a straight-ahead blowing session and not, as one American reviewer glibly assumed (did he *listen* to it?), a tribute to Charlie Parker. The second apostrophe gives it away; Hutcherson's 'Bird is a 1964 convertible the size of a swimming pool, and a fair image of the classic aerodynamics and effortless acceleration that had reappeared in the vibist's playing two decades later.

Hutcherson's ability to work on several levels simultaneously opens up this fine set of originals. The three rhythm players (Montgomery, himself normally a vibist, here fulfils a largely supportive role) provide a footsure platform for some fine solo work from both Hutcherson and Moore, whose soprano figures on the ballad, 'Sierra', are noticeably individual; Hutcherson doubles marimba on the same track, and in a curious way it's the wooden instrument that now more often reflects his familiar, firmly struck style. *Cruisin' the 'Bird* is a deceptively demanding album; its immediate pay-off doesn't last long, but there's so much incident, so much evidence of pure improvisational *thinking*, that tracks – let alone sides – call for the repeat button.

(*)   **Ambos Mundos (Both Worlds) Landmark LM 1522 CD/LP
Hutcherson; James Spaulding (*f*); Bruce Forman, Randy Vincent (*g*); Smith Dobson
(*p*); Jeff Chambers (*b*); Eddie Marshall (*d*); Francisco Aguabella, Orestes Vilato,
Roger Glenn (*perc*). 8–9/89.

Disappointing in the light of recent strides back to full performing and compositional form. The Latin structures and metres do clearly appeal to Hutcherson, but his treatment of them, and his obvious unwillingness to eschew the vibraharp for even one session, weakens the impact slightly; it's a little too light and floating. Bruce Forman plays well on 'Besame Mucho' and 'Tin Tin Deo', returning the compliment of his own *There Are Times* (Concord CJ 332) on which Hutcherson guested.

***(*)   **Mirage** Landmark LM 1529 CD/LP
Hutcherson; Tommy Flanagan (*p*); Peter Washington (*b*); Billy Drummond (*d*). 2/91.

This doesn't quite reach the heights of the Village Vanguard sessions, but it's close. Hutcherson and Flanagan had never played together previously, so there's a certain tentative respect on the three originals. The set catches light with Monk once again. 'Pannonica' was Keepnews's idea and is played as a duet, as is 'Love Letters'. The latter illustrates once again Hutcherson's enthusiasm for taking the ribbon off unread standards. Antonio Carlos Jobim's 'Zingaro' is little performed in a jazz context and Cole Porter's 'I Am In Love' is a surprising rarity. Cedar Walton's 'Groundwork' becomes a feature for Billy Drummond; originally written for his namesake Higgins, the comparison by no means disgraces the younger man. Hutcherson enters another decade in the top flight.

DICK HYMAN (born 1927)
PIANO, ORGAN, SYNTHESIZER

***   **14 Jazz Piano Favourites** Music & Arts CD 622 CD
Hyman (*p* solo). 6/88.

***(*)   **Music Of 1937** Concord CCD 4415 CD/MC
Hyman (*p* solo). 2/90.

Dick Hyman has had a pretty paradoxical career in many ways. In the 1940s he was playing with both Charlie Parker and Benny Goodman. Working as a studio musician through much of the 1950s and '60s, he also recorded novelty tunes under various pseudonyms, as well as Scott Joplin's complete works. He loves early jazz, is an expert on the jazz piano tradition, can re-create pit-band orchestrations or ragtime arrangements to order – yet he was also one of the first to record an album of tunes played on prototype synthesizers.

Unsurprisingly, perhaps, he has seldom made 'straight' jazz albums under his own name. But these amusing records validate his findings with their exuberance as well as their attention to detail. He goes back as far as ragtime and Jelly Roll Morton on the Café Des Copains recital, making light of any rhythmical squareness in the likes of 'Frog-I-More Rag' and freshening up 'Blue Skies' until it sings. *Music Of 1937*, an early entry in the Maybeck Recital Hall series, concentrates on a single year in songwriting: by no means exceptional, but the best of these pre-war hits – 'The Folks Who Live On The Hill', 'Some Day My Prince Will Come', 'Thanks For The Memory' – tend to prove the subtext that they don't write 'em like that any more, which would be a curmudgeonly verdict if it weren't for the sprightly and glowing readings which Hyman gets. Unfortunately, some excellent Hyman records for Musicmasters/Limelight have already been deleted from the UK catalogue.

ABDULLAH IBRAHIM (formerly known as DOLLAR BRAND) (born 1934)
PIANO, SOPRANO SAXOPHONE, CELLO, VOICE

***   **Reflections** Black Lion 760127 CD
          Ibrahim (*p* solo). 3/65.

****   **African Piano** Japo 60002 CD/LP
          As above. 10/69.

***   **Ancient Africa** Japo 60005 LP
          As above. 6/72.

***   **Sangoma** Sackville 3006 LP
          As above. 2/73.

***   **African Portraits** Sackville 3009 LP
          As above. 2/73.

***(*) **Ode To Duke Ellington** West Wind 2020 CD/LP
          As above. 12/73.

***   **. . . Memories** West Wind 2029 CD/LP
          As above. ?.

(*)   **African Sketchbook Enja 2026 LP
          As above. ?.

***(*) **African Dawn** Enja 4030 CD/LP
          As above. 6/82.

***   **Jazzbühne Berlin '82** Repertoire REPCD 4907 CD
          As above. 6/82.

Ibrahim left his native South Africa in the aftermath of the Sharpeville massacre, settling first in Europe, latterly in the United States. He adopted his Islamic name on his conversion in 1968, but his given name, Dollar Brand, still has considerable currency and, however improperly, is still apt to be used interchangeably.

Brand came to the attention of Duke Ellington in the United States and it was Ellington who gave him the opportunity to make his first American recordings. He repays the debt on *Ode To Duke Ellington*, stringing together a number of favourite compositions – 'In A Sentimental Mood', 'Single Petal Of A Rose' both make frequent reappearances throughout his career – with a couple of spirituals and imaginative variations, which include 'Caravan' and the astonishingly titled 'What Really Happened In The Cornfields Is That The Birds Made Music All Day And So I Let A Song Go Out Of My Heart At Duke's Place'. Ellington had been his greatest single influence, though there are perhaps stronger traces of black church music, African folk themes and hints of Thelonious Monk and the 1960s free movement in his solo performances. These have a hypnotic intensity and a surprising level of formality, which lends an often-repeated tune like 'Bra Joe From Kilimanjaro' (the two Japos, *African Portraits*) an almost ritual quality. Some of that is reflected on . . . *Memories*, where the central tribute is a much more personal one, to his wife, singer Sathima Bea Benjamin, who made a considerable impact on Ibrahim's career.

African Piano is certainly still the best of the solo records, even though the CD robs the music of some of its full-hearted resonance. The later Enja (*Sketchbook* is as bitty as it sounds) offers valuable insights into some of Ibrahim's stylistic debts, with tributes to Ellington, Coltrane (just one of a rash of memorials marking the 15th anniversary of the saxophonist's death) and Monk. He plays 'A Flower Is A Lovesome Thing', 'Blue Monk' and an inventive, firmly contoured 'Round About Midnight' that strips the tune down to more authentically Monkish basics. The early *Reflections* develops a similar range of material, applying Brand's drumming lyricism to 'Don't Get Around Much Any More' (an astonishing performance), 'Mood Indigo', 'Take The "A" Train' and 'Monk's Mood'. The two Sackville LPs come from a single recording session. Like the Japos, they're recorded in dramatic close-up. The live session from East Berlin on Repertoire is the opposite: tinny, echoing and timbrally rather flat. It's difficult to judge whether the fault lies with the acoustic, the piano itself (which doesn't sound that responsive) or the recording technology, for the 'Liberation Suite' medley is in every other regard an absolutely characteristic performance.

*** **Round Midnight At The Montmartre** Black Lion 760111 CD/LP
Ibrahim; Johnny Gertze (*b*); Makaya Ntoshko (*d*). 1/65.

'Round About Midnight' takes on a more conventional outline in this trio performance, recorded at the Cafe Montmartre. There's a short version of 'Tintiyana', developed by a large band on Enja 2032, below, and two solo tracks, which are much jazzier than usual and don't initially sound typical of Brand's work of the time. Ntoshko plays in the post-Elvin Jones idiom favoured by Billys Higgins and Hart. Like his fellow-countryman Louis Moholo, he has the ability to range between freedom and strict (but complex) time and can blur the line between poly-rhythmic playing and complete abstraction so much that it often sounds as though Brand is keeping time for the drummer. The mix is rather uneven and the bass is often lost altogether (less so on CD), though what one can hear isn't that interesting.

*** **African Space Program** Enja 2032 LP
Ibrahim; Cecil Bridgewater, Enrico Rava, Charles Sullivan (*t*); Kiane Zawadi (*tb*);
Sonny Fortune, Carlos Ward (*fl, as*); Roland Alexander (*ts, hca*); John Stubblefield
(*ts*); Hamiet Bluiett (*bs*); Cecil McBee (*b*); Roy Brooks (*d*). 11/73.

A rare opportunity to hear Ibrahim fronting a substantial, hand-picked band. Six months before Duke's death, the parallels are once again strongly evident, with Ward sounding like an Africanized Hodges, and Hamiet Bluiett slipping easily into the Harry Carney role. 'Tintinyana' falls into two parts, its progress clarified by the leader's piano statements and percussive breaks. The sound is rather poor and nips off a lot of the higher notes.

***(*) **Good News From Africa** Enja 2048 CD/LP
Ibrahim; Johnny Mbizo Dyani (*b, bells, v*). 12/73.

**** **Echoes From Africa** Enja 3047 CD/LP
As above. 9/79.

Dyani towers on these fascinating and often moving duos, which move between a dark, almost tragic pessimism to a shouting, joyous climax. 'Saud' is a dedication to McCoy Tyner (the title reflects the other pianist's more briefly adopted Islamic name) and interestingly suggest how some of Ellington's modal explorations of the 1960s filtered into the vernacular via younger piano players. Ibrahim adds some flute colours to the earlier album and the two voices entwine in celebration of the homeland. *Echoes* was originally released as an audiophile direct-to-disc recording. CD makes the music even more immediate and penetrative.

*** **The Children Of Africa** Enja 2070 CD/LP
Ibrahim; Cecil McBee (*b*); Roy Brooks (*d*). 1/76.

A set of strongly coloured African themes, containing the germ of Ibrahim's 1980s work with Carlos Ward and Ekaya. In fact, what the set seems to call for is a full-time horn player. The pianist's limited contribution on soprano saxophone does little more than point to its lack elsewhere and there's a touch of thinness to the overall sound that can't entirely be blamed on a poor mix, though McBee's middle register does collide awkwardly with the piano.

(*) **Africa Tears And Laughter Enja 3039 LP
Ibrahim; Talib Qadar (*ss, as, v*); Greg Brown (*b*); John Betsch (*d*). 3/79.

One of the slightest of Ibrahim's records, with a slightly mushy feel that even comes across in 'tone-poem' titles like 'The Perfumed Forest Wet With Rain' (it gets a much tighter reading by a far superior band on *Montreux '80*, below). Betsch is a fine drummer, and it's a pity he hasn't recorded more extensively with the pianist. This one is for committed fans only.

***(*) **Montreux '80** Enja 3079 CD/LP/MC
Ibrahim; Carlos Ward (*as, f*); Craig Harris (*tb*); Alonzo Gardner (*b*); Andre Strobert
(*d*). 7/80.

***(*) **Duke's Memories** String 233853 CD
Ibrahim; Carlos Ward (*as*); Rachim Ausur Sahu (*b*); Andre Strobert (*d*). 6/81.

***   **Zimbabwe** Enja 4056 CD/LP
Ibrahim; Carlos Ward (f, as); Essiet Okon Essiet (b); Don Mumford (d). 5/83.

***   **Abdullah Ibrahim/Dollar Brand** Enja 5007 CD/LP
As above, except add Johnny Classens (v). 7/83.

***(*)   **Live At Sweet Basil: Volume 1** Black-Hawk 50204 LP
Ibrahim; Carlos Ward (as, f). 10/83.

***(*)   **Ekaya** Black-Hawk 50205 CD/LP
Ibrahim; Dick Griffin (tb); Carlos Ward (as, f); Ricky Ford (ts); Charles Davis (bs); Cecil McBee (b); Ben Riley (d). 11/83.

****   **Water From An Ancient Well** Black-Hawk 50207 CD/LP/MC
As above, except David Williams (b) replaces McBee. 10/85.

***(*)   **The Mountain** Kaz Records KAZ CD 7 CD
As above, except omit Williams. ?.

The association with Carlos Ward has been the most productive and sympathetic of Ibrahim's career. The saxophonist has a high, exotic tone (superficially reminiscent of Sonny Fortune's, but much less raucous) that is ideally suited to his leader's conception. Working with Ward has reinforced Ibrahim's preference for song-like forms built over harmonically unvarying ostinati but has allowed him to develop a more abstract improvisational feel, which reaches its peak on *Water From An Ancient Well*.

This was made by Ibrahim's band Ekaya (the word means 'home'), who are also responsible for the other, eponymous Black-Hawk, and for the live Kaz set; *Water* is a carefully structured album with something of the feel of Ellington's *Far East Suite*, and most of the drama comes from the interplay between Ibrahim and the horns. It includes another heartfelt tribute to Sathima Bea Benjamin, 'Daughter Of Cape Town'. It's a pity that the fine *Live At Sweet Basil* hasn't been favoured with a CD format, for despite a rather shaky sound it's a fine representation of his work with Ward. They play both parts of 'For Coltrane' (the second is taken from 'Zimbabwe') in a programme that steers clear of standard material. The String CD shouldn't be mistaken for an 'Ellington Songbook' production; it's actually a highly individualized homage that considers 'In A Sentimental Mood' and 'Virgin Jungle' along with a number of Ibrahim compositions that bear the mark of the Ellington who after 1963 took an increasing interest in 'world music'. There's also another version of 'For Coltrane'.

In their rather earlier encounters, Ward seemed willing to play Charlie Rouse to Ibrahim's Monk, but increasingly he develops his own approach, and by 1983 is putting his own stamp on the music. *Ibrahim/Brand* is the most self-consciously African of the group, an impression heightened by Classens's effective vocal contributions. *Zimbabwe* is less original in either content or treatment, but it contains some of Ibrahim's best group work on record and Essiet's bass work (clearly drawn from the example of Johnny Dyani) is very fine.

***   **Mindif** Enja 5073 CD/LP
Ibrahim; Benny Powell (tb); Ricky Ford (ts, ss); Craig Handy (f, ts); David Williams (b); Billy Higgins (d, perc). 3/88.

****   **African River** Enja 6018 CD/LP
Ibrahim; Robin Eubanks (tb); John Stubblefield (fl, ts); Horace Alexander Young (ss, as, picc); Howard Johnson (bs, tba); Buster Williams (b); Brian Adams (d). 6/89.

Ward is immediately missed on *Mindif*, but Powell and Handy are both exciting players and Higgins's drumming is so imaginative as often to become the focus of a piece like 'African Market' or 'Thema [sic] For Monk'. The later album is absolutely superb and a vivid extension of the kind of arrangements Ibrahim had attempted on *African Space Program*. 'The Wedding' reappears from 1980 (*Montreux* and *Duke's Memories*) and receives a definitive performance, with Eubanks to the fore. Stubblefield and Young more than make up for the departure of Ricky Ford, and Howard Johnson does his usual patented stuff in the bottom half of the chart. Williams is a rather significant addition, playing big, singing lines that are occasionally reminiscent of Ibrahim's own early experiments on cello. Anyone with the solo *African Piano* and *African River* in their possession (the titles are uniquely repetitive and rather unimaginative) can feel confident of a reasonable purchase on his best work.

ICP ORCHESTRA
GROUP

***   **Herbie Nichols/Thelonious Monk** BVhaast 026 CD
Toon de Gouw (*t*); Wolter Wierbos, George Lewis (*tb*); Steve Lacy (*ss*); Michael
Moore (*cl, as*); Paul Termos (*as*); Ab Baars (*ts, ss, cl*); Sean Bergin (*ts*); Misha
Mengelberg (*p*); Ernst Reijseger (*clo*); Maurice Horsthuis (*vla*); Larry Fishkind (*tba*);
Han Bennink (*d*). 84–87.

A larger-scale version of the tributes which Mengelberg, Lacy and others recorded for Soul
Note at much the same time, this highly coloured and generous programme makes light of the
difficulties in both composers' work. Monk tributes have become commonplace, but Baars,
Moore and Wierbos are soloists with an idiosyncratic accent, and Lewis appears on a few tracks
for an extra brassiness. Mengelberg and Bennink, the most practised of in-to-out rhythm
sections, make Monk's rhythmic eccentricities their own property, too. But the Nichols tracks
are more interesting, since his tunes are less familiar and the larger group – which includes
Termos, Horsthuis, Bergin and Lacy – lends a firmer substance to music which is difficult to
characterize.

KLAUS IGNATZEK
PIANO

***   **Magic Secret** Nabel 4617 CD/LP
Ignatzek (*p* solo). 1/85.

(*)   **Gershwin Songs Nabel 4631 CD/LP
As above. 7/88.

**   **Plays Beatles Songs** Nabel 4643 CD/LP
As above. 8/90.

Ignatzek has immersed himself so completely in the idiom (shouldn't that be idiom*s*?) of Horace
Silver, Bill Evans, Sonny Clark and Wynton Kelly as to claim almost apostolic understanding of
the roots of hard bop. Like some clairvoyant transcriber of 'posthumous' Mozart symphonies,
he has produced a steady stream of rather unconvincing pastiche that may sound good in a club
setting but which seems a thoroughly dull option when set against a random sample of
late-1950s Blue Notes.

Technically, Ignatzek is hard to fault, but compositions like the ubiquitous 'Monk's Visit'
(heard in its most po-faced form on *Magic Secret*, the best of the solo albums) carry little more
than a whisper of the dedicatee's divine simplicity and humour. The Gershwin and Beatles sets
seriously miscalculate the robustness and durability of the original material. The average
Lennon–McCartney song played 'straight' would sound much more impressive than these
earnest stylings which flood the tunes with irrelevance.

***   **The Spell** Nabel 4612 CD/LP
Ignatzek; Dave Liebman (*ss*); Dieter Ilg (*b*); Uwe Ecker (*d*). 4 & 5/84.

(*)   **Tender Mercies Nabel 46211 LP
As above. 3/85.

***   **Live In Switzerland** Nabel 4627 LP
Ignatzek; Steve Wagner (*t*); Bobby Watson (*as, ss*); Dieter Ilg (*b*); Joe Pulice (*d*).
11/85.

***   **Live At Leverkusener Jazztage** Nabel 4630 LP
As above, except omit Wagner, add Roman Schwaller (*ts*). 11/86.

**   **Blue Energy** Red RR 217 LP
Ignatzek; Roman Schwaller (*ts*); Dieter Ilg (*b*); Joris Dudli (*d*). 7/87.

(*)   **Don't Stop It Timeless SJP 271 CD/LP

***(*) **Jacaranda** Timeless SJP 292 CD/LP
Ignatzek; Claudio Roditi (*t, flhn*); Paulo Cardoso (*b*); Mario Gonzi (*d*). 5/87.

(*)   **The Klaus Ignatzek Trio** yvp 3020 CD
Ignatzek; Jean-Louis Rassinfosse (*b*); John Engels (*d*). 7/89.

***   **Day For Night** Nabel 4639 CD/LP
Ignatzek; Joe Henderson (*ts*); Jean-Louis Rasinfosse (*b*); Joris Dudli (*d*). 10/89.

Ignatzek has been singularly fortunate in his access to saxophone players of the quality of Bobby Watson, Dave Liebman and Joe Henderson. Watson's recording career, post-Messengers, really took off in Europe and he took his opportunities wherever and whenever they presented themselves. He soars above the band on his three credits, not without a certain callowness. Ignatzek's comping gives him little to work on. This is less of a problem for Liebman, who gives the music an uncharacteristically abstract cast. *The Spell* is rather good. Henderson, perhaps inevitably, treats the gig much more functionally and good-humouredly, with no obvious anxiety to get inside Ignatzek's bland modalities. 'Blue Energy' and 'Monk's Visit' are dispatched with untroubled understanding.

If the saxophonists are the measure of the music, that explains the dim confusions of *Blue Energy* and also the remarkably intermittent quality of Ignatzek's regular band of the late 1980s. *Jacaranda* is remarkably good, with trumpeter Roditi leading a Messengers line on standards such as 'Softly As In A Morning Sunrise' and 'There Is No Greater Love', along with an original 'Blues for Lee M.' and a take of 'Day For Night'. Neither the earlier *Don't Stop It* (with the same group) nor the ghastly and mercifully deleted *New Surprise* [Timeless SJP 324 CD], which adds Tim Armacost's inept tenor, sounds like the same band at all, and the charges of bland revivalism, to which Ignatzek has always hotly replied, very definitely stick. Just as clichés are clichés because they communicate some pretty basic truths, standards are standards because they contain something over and above the normal run of songs. Even the most ambitious of the boppers knew that they had to negotiate the standards first.

COSMO INTINI (born 1958)
PIANO

***   **Seeing The Cosmic** Splasc(h) H 121 LP
Intini; Paolo Fresu (*t, flhn*); Fabio Tullio (*as*); Enrico Ghelardi (*bs*); Francesco Puglisi (*b*); John Arnold (*d*). 11/86.

(*)   **My Favourite Roots** Timeless SJP 339 CD
Intini; Paolo Fresu (*t, flhn*); Gary Bartz (*ss, as*); Carroll Dashiell (*b*); Victor Lewis (*d*). 5/89.

Intini is a strong if unambitious executant whose music suggests a player keen to make the most of a conservative setting. The Splasc(h) album is essentially a set of trio performances, with a few guest shots by the hornmen: the opening piece, 'They Made Me Latin', is a real head-turner, sunny yet grippingly intense, with the trio evolving a group ID immediately. Since the rest of the record is merely very good – Fresu makes 'Oh, Fantasie!' into one of his charming flugelhorn ballads – the level drops somewhat. The Timeless session is clearly a pick-up date, with Bartz sounding prosaic and the rhythm section impersonally alert; yet one of the two originals, 'Powerful Warrior', is a striking theme, and a leisurely stroll through 'When Sunny Gets Blue' is sustained gracefully, with Fresu at his most Milesian. Well recorded, aside from Dashiell's bass, which has a disagreeably buzzing timbre.

ISKRA
GROUP

**   **Luft** Dragon DRCD 200 CD
Jorgen Adolfson (*sno, ss, as, g, syn, etc.*); Tuomo Haapala (*b, v, etc.*); Sune Spangberg (*d, perc, etc.*). 5/90.

This release coincided with the twentieth anniversary of Iskra, probably Sweden's leading free-improvisation group, and it's a pity that a relatively undistinguished set was the result. Most of the record is episodic and unconvincing, the three musicians moving between instruments somewhat aimlessly and often resorting to novelty, as in '*Luft*' ('Air') and '*Minnesforlustens*

Tid', which appear to be searching for a naïve prettiness. Only when they move to their primary instruments – sax, bass and drums – does the music aspire to a result.

MILT JACKSON (born 1923)

****   Milt Jackson Blue Note CDP 7815092 CD
Jackson; Lou Donaldson, Sahib Shihab (*as*); Thelonious Monk, John Lewis (*p*); Percy Heath, John Simmons, Al McKibbon (*b*); Shadow Wilson, Art Blakey, Kenny Clarke (*d*). 6/48–4/52.

Six of these tracks are also found on records under Thelonious Monk's name, while the quintet date with Donaldson and what was to become the Modern Jazz Quartet was first issued on a single ten-inch LP. The music is quite marvellous. Jackson had made few appearances on record up to this point but his style was entirely established already: flawlessly paced solos, perfectly contrapuntal thinking, lines delivered without a hint of waste. The tracks with Monk are classics which are discussed under the pianist's name, while the other session, though at lower voltage, includes a couple of pretty ballads for the quartet and some fluid but unhurried bop that Donaldson is entirely at home with. CD remastering has done little for the original sound, which was always rather dull, but the quality of the music shines through.

***   MJQ Original Jazz Classics OJC 125 CD/LP
Jackson; Henry Boozier (*t*); Horace Silver (*p*); Percy Heath (*b*); Kenny Clarke (*d*). 6/54.

***   Milt Jackson Original Jazz Classics OJC 001 CD/LP/MC
Jackson; Horace Silver (*p*); Percy Heath (*b*); Connie Kay (*d*). 5/55.

***   Opus De Funk Prestige P 24048 2LP
Jackson; Henry Boozier, Kenny Dorham, Virgil Jones (*t*); Jimmy Heath (*ts*); Horace Silver, Tommy Flanagan (*p*); Ron Carter, Percy Heath (*b*); Connie Kay, Kenny Clarke (*d*). 6/54–11/62.

***   From Opus De Jazz To Jazz Skyline Savoy 650103 CD
Jackson; Frank Wess (*ts, f*); Lucky Thompson (*ts*); Hank Jones (*p*); Eddie Jones, Wendell Marshall (*b*); Kenny Clarke (*d*). 10/55–1/56.

***(*)   Second Nature Savoy 650149 CD
As above, except omit Wess and Jones, add Wade Legge (*p*). 1/56.

MJQ features four titles by the personnel listed (the remainder are by a first-generation MJQ). Though no more than a pick-up date, all concerned play well. *Milt Jackson* is more substantial, but the preponderance of slow tempos lends a rather sleepy air to the date: the exception is 'Stonewall', a blues with a 13-chorus vibes solos that effectively defines the principles of Jackson's art. Remastering up to the strong OJC standard.

The Savoy reissues offer some of Jackson's best work away from the MJQ. The earlier set combines two original LPs: *Opus De Jazz* is a languorous date of four long tracks, with Wess content to play an undemonstrative role, but *Jazz Skyline* offers some of the music made in a magisterial series of dates with Lucky Thompson, the rest of which are on the second CD. The level of playing is consistently inspired across both discs: Jackson takes pellucid improvisations at up-tempo and is severely lyrical on the ballads, while Thompson offers some of his clearest and most decisive playing, his tone attractively mottled, his phrasing tilting at bop while staying committed to his original Hawkins influence. Clarke's pulse swings without upsetting the inner delicacy of the music. Only the occasionally tame original material – mostly simple Jackson blues lines – is faintly disappointing. Attractive CD remastering.

***   Plenty, Plenty Soul Atlantic 1269-2 CD
Jackson; Joe Newman (*t*); Jimmy Cleveland (*tb*); Cannonball Adderley (*as*); Frank Foster, Lucky Thompson (*ts*); Sahib Shihab (*bs*); Horace Silver (*p*); Oscar Pettiford, Percy Heath (*b*); Art Blakey, Connie Kay (*d*). 1/57.

*** **Soul Brothers/Soul Meeting** Atlantic 781951-2 CD
Jackson; Ray Charles (*as, p*); Billy Mitchell (*ts*); Kenny Burrell, Skeeter Best (*g*);
Percy Heath, Oscar Pettiford (*b*); Connie Kay, Art Taylor (*d*). 9/57–4/58.

*** **Bags' Opus** Blue Note CDP 784458-2 CD
Jackson; Art Farmer (*t*); Benny Golson (*ts*); Tommy Flanagan (*p*); Paul Chambers
(*b*); Connie Kay (*d*). 12/58.

*** **Bags Meets Trane** Atlantic 1553-2 CD
Jackson; John Coltrane (*ts*); Hank Jones (*p*); Paul Chambers (*b*); Connie Kay (*d*).
1/59.

Jackson's Atlantic records pitched him into some interesting situations. *Plenty, Plenty Soul*
features him with both a large group and a sextet, and though Quincy Jones's charts are
desperately dull, the nominal leader takes some admirable solos; and Thompson shines again
on three tracks. When he met Trane, Charles and the fellows on *Opus*, they all played the blues:
the Charles session is a bit modish (with electric piano!), and Coltrane is hardly an ideal
partner, but all three dates work up some simmering blowing, and Jackson, the most
unprejudiced of collaborators, simply goes ahead and jams.

*** **At The Village Gate** Original Jazz Classics OJC 309 CD/LP/MC
Jackson; Jimmy Heath (*ts*); Hank Jones (*p*); Bob Cranshaw (*b*); Albert 'Tootie'
Heath (*d*). 12/63.

Jackson was firmly ensconced in the MJQ by this time, but occasional blowing dates were
something he obviously enjoyed. This is one such: Heath is a resourceful man to have in the
front line, and there's nothing fancy here, just a good bluster through the blues.

*** **The Big Three** Pablo 2310-757 LP/MC
Jackson; Ray Brown (*b*); Joe Pass (*g*). 8/75.

*** **Montreux '77** Original Jazz Classics OJC 375 CD/LP/MC
Jackson; Clark Terry (*t*); Eddie 'Lockjaw' Davis (*ts*); Monty Alexander (*p*); Ray
Brown (*b*); Jimmie Smith (*d*). 7/77.

** **Feelings** Original Jazz Classics OJC 448 CD/LP/MC
Jackson; Hubert Laws, Jerome Richardson (*f*); Tommy Flanagan (*p*); Dennis Budimir
(*g*); Ray Brown (*b*); Jimmie Smith (*d*); strings. 4/76.

*** **All Too Soon** Original Jazz Classics OJC 450 CD/LP/MC
Jackson; Joe Pass (*g*); Ray Brown (*b*); Mickey Roker (*d*). 1/80.

*** **Jackson, Johnson, Brown And Company** Pablo 2310-897 LP/MC
Jackson; J. J. Johnson (*tb*); John Collins (*g*); Tom Ranier (*p*); Ray Brown (*b*); Roy
McCurdy (*d*). 5/83.

*** **It Don't Mean A Thing If You Can't Tap Your Foot To It** Original Jazz Classics OJC
601 CD/LP/MC
Jackson; Cedar Walton (*p*); Ray Brown (*b*); Mickey Roker (*d*). 7/84.

*(*) **Soul Believer** Original Jazz Classics OJC 686 CD
Jackson; Plas Johnson (*ts*); Cedar Walton (*p*); Dennis Budimir (*g*); Ray Brown (*b*);
Billy Higgins (*d*). 9/78

(*) **Bags' Bag Pablo 2310-842 CD/LP/MC
Jackson; Cedar Walton (*p*); Vaughan Andre, John Collins (*g*); Ray Brown (*b*); Billy
Higgins, Frank Severino (*d*).

*** **Soul Route** Pablo 2310-900 CD/MC
Jackson; Gene Harris (*p*); Ray Brown (*b*); Mickey Roker (*d*). 11–12/83.

*** **Brother Jim** Pablo 2310-916 CD/LP/MC
Jackson; Jimmy Heath, Harold Vick (*ss, ts*); Cedar Walton (*p*); Joe Pass (*g*); Bob
Cranshaw (*b*); Mickey Roker (*d*). 5/85.

*** **A London Bridge** Pablo 2310-932 CD/LP/MC
Jackson; Monty Alexander (*p*); Ray Brown (*b*); Mickey Roker (*d*). 4/82.

***   **Mostly Duke** Pablo 2310-944 CD/MC
As above. 4/82.

***   **Memories Of Thelonious Sphere Monk** Pablo 2308-235 LP/MC
As above. 4/82.

Jackson's signing to Pablo – which snared the MJQ for a time too – brought forth a flood of albums, of which these are still available. Just as he did with Count Basie, Granz basically set Milt up in the studio and let him go, which means that all these records are solidly entertaining without ever seeming like either an essential date or a particular step forward for Jackson's art. The only croppers come up with *Soul Believer*, where Jackson sings, on advice; mysteriously, this has made it to CD, whereas the fine *The Big Three* and *Jackson, Johnson, Brown And Company* haven't, as yet. *Feelings*, with strings, is pretty but disposable. The pick here, aside from the two mentioned above, are the irresistibly swinging *It Don't Mean A Thing* and *Soul Route*, and any of the three final albums, all cut at a single live engagement in London, with Alexander proving a fine companion for Jackson.

OLIVER JACKSON (born 1933)
DRUMS

**   **Billie's Bounce** Black & Blue 59.183-2 CD
Jackson; Irvin Stokes (*t*); Norris Turney (*as*); Claude Blake (*p*); Ali Jackson (*b*).
10/84.

Despite his nickname (Bops Junior), Oliver Jackson has spent more time in the company of swing stylists than with boppers. This rare item under his own leadership is an unpretentious programme of jazz standards played by a profoundly unassuming quintet: nothing wrong, but nothing special.

RONALD SHANNON JACKSON (born 1940)
DRUMS, PERCUSSION, OTHER INSTRUMENTS

***(*)   **Decode Yourself** Island ILPS 9827 LP
Jackson; David Gordon (*t*); Robin Eubanks (*tb*); Eric Person (*as, ss, v*); Vernon Reid (*g, bj, g syn*); Akbar Ali (*vn, v*); Onaje Allan Gumbs (*ky*); Melvin Gibbs, Bruce Johnson (*b, v*); Bill Laswell (*elec*); Abel Domingues, Jim Grant, David Hershkovits (*v*). ?.

***(*)   **Nasty** Moers 01086 LP
Jackson; David Gordon (*t*); Charles Brackeen (*ts, ss*); Lee Rozie (*ts, ss*); Vernon Reid (*g, bj, g syn*); Khan Jamal (*vib*); Melvin Gibbs, Bruce Johnson (*b, v*); Abel Domingues, Jim Grant (*v*). 3/81.

***   **Street Priest** Moers 01096 LP
Jackson; David Gordon, Lee Rozie (*ts, ss*); Zane Massey (*ts, ss*); Vernon Reid (*g, bj, g syn*); Melvin Gibbs, Bruce Johnson (*b, v*); Abel Domingues, Jim Grant (*v*). 6/81.

***(*)   **Taboo** Virgin CDVE 47 CD
Jackson; David Gordon, Henri Scott (*t*); Robin Eubanks (*tb*); Eric Person (*as, ss, v*); Lee Rozie (*ts, ss*); Vernon Reid (*g, bj, g syn*); Akbar Ali (*vn, v*); Onaje Allan Gumbs (*ky*); Melvin Gibbs, Bruce Johnson (*b, v*); Abel Domingues, Jim Grant (*v*). ?.

The sound of Shannon Jackson's Decoding Society is characteristically an unsettling amalgam of dark, swampy vamps, huge, distorted chorales, and sudden outbursts of urban noise. Decoded, it yields up a huge range of putative influences, from Albert Ayler's increasingly abstract and fissile music (Shannon played with the saxophonist in the early 1960s), to Mingus's open-ended compositional style, to Ornette Coleman's harmolodics, to black and white thrash-metal music; it was James Blood Ulmer's brutal funk *Are You Glad To Be In America?* that established the drummer's reputation in Europe. He in turn has had a powerful impact on such currently fashionable outfits as Decoding Society guitarist Vernon Reid's Living Colour and the Black

Rock Coalition, while his work with the heavyweight Last Exit has spawned a shoal of imitators.

Decode Yourself enjoyed considerable popular success. Jackson had spent much of the 1970s in obscurity, slowly absorbing the innovations and implications of New Thing revolutionaries like Sunny Murray and Milford Graves. The album represents a careful synthesis of avant-garde explorations and more generic popular music with a degree of success Jackson hasn't managed elsewhere (or perhaps except under the auspices of Last Exit). By virtue of their provenance, *Nasty* and *Street Priest* are perhaps closer to jazz proper and develop an impressive improvisatory diction; Brackeen's presence on the former helps give it its dark power, though Jackson has generally preferred to work with a regular line-up of younger and more rock-orientated players. *Taboo* is a marvellous record, all the things Charles Mingus might have done if Charles Mingus had been born just a little later. There are big-band accents from an unusually large array of horns (previously Jackson had favoured just saxes with Robin Eubank's blarting slide), coupled with virtually free passages that explore a variety of instrumental and electronic landscapes. Jackson's drumming throughout is a revelation and a joy. An essential voice of the 1980s.

WILLIS JACKSON (1928–87)

TENOR SAXOPHONE

(*)   **Cool Gator** Original Jazz Classics OJC 220 LP
Jackson; Jack McDuff (*org*); Bill Jennings (*g*); Tommy Potter, Milt Hinton, Wendell Marshall (*b*); Al Johnson (*d*); Buck Clark (*perc*). 5/59–2/60.

***   **Please Mr Jackson** Original Jazz Classics OJC 321 LP/MC
Jackson; Jack McDuff (*org*); Bill Jennings (*g*); Tommy Potter (*b*); Alvin Johnson (*d*). 5/59.

Willis 'Gator' Jackson made many records for Prestige, most of them in the tenor-and-organ format. They sound rather dull today, although Jackson could huff his way through such a date quite as well as such similarly inclined colleagues as Rusty Bryant. When required to do more than growl and swagger through such tunes as 'Cool Grits', though, he tends to run short of steam. Both of these reissues are decent enough, but neither will impress a listener looking for more than stock instrumental R&B.

(*)   **Headed And Gutted** Muse MR 5048 LP
Jackson; Mickey Tucker (*ky*); Pat Martino (*g*); Bob Cranshaw (*b*); Freddie Waits (*d*); Richard Landrum, Sonny Morgan (*perc*). 5/74.

**   **In The Alley** Muse MR 5100 LP
Jackson; Sonny Phillips (*p*); Carl Wilson (*org*); Jimmy Ponder (*g*); Jimmy Lewis (*b*); Yusef Ali (*d*); Buddy Caldwell (*perc*). 76.

(*)   **Bar Wars** Muse MR 5162 CD/LP
Jackson; Charles Earland (*org*); Pat Martino (*g*); Idris Muhammad (*d*); Buddy Caldwell (*perc*). 12/77

**   **Single Action** Muse MR 5179 LP
Jackson; Carl Wilson (*org*); Pat Martino (*g*); Jimmy Lewis (*b*); Yusef Ali (*d*); Ralph Dorsey (*perc*). 4/78.

**   **Lockin' Horns** Muse MR 5200 LP
Jackson; Von Freeman (*ts*); Carl Wilson (*org*); Joe Jones (*g*); Yusef Ali (*perc*). 8/78.

(*)   **Nothing Butt ...** Muse MR 5294 LP
Jackson; Charles Earland (*org*); Pat Martino (*g*); Grady Tate (*d*); Buddy Caldwell (*perc*). 6/80.

(*)   **Ya Understand Me?** Muse MR 5316 LP
Jackson; Richard 'Groove' Holmes (*org*).

All but two of Jackson's albums for Muse remain available, although they are rather hard to find. All of them continue Jackson's trusted formula of hard blowing over simple organ blues and shuffles, with most of the records sounding like one another. The meeting with Freeman, recorded live at a European festival, offers something different, but unfortunately the occasion seemed to bring out the least appealing aspects of each man's playing, and it ends up as a series of ragged blow-outs. Dreary pop tunes crowd on to too many of the records, but *Bar Wars* features a good programme and a hard-hitting band, and the final meetings with Earland (*Nothing Butt . . .*) and Holmes (*Ya Understand Me?*) also fare slightly better.

ILLINOIS JACQUET (born 1922)
TENOR SAXOPHONE, ALSO BASSOON

***   **Flying Home** Bluebird ND 90638 CD
Jacquet; Russell Jacquet (*t, v*); Joe Newman (*t*); J. J. Johnson (*tb*); Ray Perry (*as*); Leo Parker, Maurice Simon (*bs*); Milt Buckner, Cedric Haywood, Sir Charles Thompson (*p*); Lionel Hampton (*vib*); John Collins (*g*); George Duvivier, Al Lucas (*b*); Alan Dawson, Jo Jones, Shadow Wilson (*d*). 12/47, 4/49, 5/50, 7/67.

Despite the apparent chronological spread, this is essentially a sampling of Jacquet's late-1940s work, with a single track, the concluding 'Flying Home', from the Newport Festival in 1967 on which the tune's co-author Lionel Hampton is the main attraction. The rest of the material is typical high-energy Jacquet. Not much sophistication, compared to what he was capable of in other contexts, but jolly, soulful jazz all the same. The bands are always rather distanced in the mix (with the distinctive baritones too far back for proper effect), and there's a good deal of tape hiss, but the sound quality is generally very faithful to the original and there has been no obvious attempt to clear Jacquet's distinctive tone, which always sounds as if it should have Vick rubbed on it. For sheer grandstanding, it's hard to beat his manically repeated two-note figure on the opening 'Jet Propulsion'. It seems to go on forever. With the exception of the above-mentioned title piece, all the material is by Jacquet (Russell Jacquet sings and wins a co-credit on 'Try Me One More Time') and offers a valuable introduction to his less recognized talent.

***   **How High The Moon** Prestige P 24057 2LP
Jacquet; Russell Jacquet, Joe Newman, Ernie Royal (*t*); Matthew Gee (*tb*); Frank Foster (*ts*); Cecil Payne (*bs*); Milt Buckner (*p, org*); Barry Harris, Wynton Kelly (*p*); Billy Butler, Tiny Grimes, Wally Richardson (*g*); Al Lucas, Ben Tucker, Buster Williams (*b*); Alan Dawson, Oliver Jackson, Jo Jones (*d*); Montego Joe (*congas*). 3/68, 8/68, 3/69, 9/69.

Born in Broussard, Louisiana, and raised in Houston, Texas, you somehow just know how Illinois Jacquet is going to sound. It's a big blues tone, edged with a kind of desperate loneliness that somehow underlines Jacquet's status as a permanent guest star, an unbreakable mustang of a player who was never really given either the right amount of room or genuinely sympathetic sidemen. He learned his showmanship in the Lionel Hampton band of the early 1940s, trading on his remarkable facility in the 'false' upper register and sheer energy.

Jacquet seems permanently saddled with the largely meaningless 'Texas tenor' tag. In fact, his playing can show remarkable sensitivity (as on many of these late-1960s sessions) and he is one of the fastest thinkers in the business (as witness his remarkable 'Flying Home' solo for the Hampton band, not currently available). *How High The Moon* is, *faute de mieux*, a good introduction to his work. Vinyl only, but the quality is more than acceptable and the performances well up to scratch. There are three big(gish) band tracks where he's able to paw the dirt ahead of a good array of horns, reeds and Milt Buckner, but the best of the material, including the title-track, is for smaller groupings. On 'How High The Moon', Buckner proves himself an equally interesting pianist, and Barry Harris creates some interesting textures on Dameron's classic 'Our Delight'; but the best of the material is from a September 1969 session with Tiny Grimes, the masterful Wynton Kelly and Buster Williams. Listen to 'Round About Midnight'. Jacquet had recently learnt to play bassoon, and its melancholy, steer-like lowing adds an intriguing new dimension to one of jazz's underrated voices.

***   **Bottoms Up** Original Jazz Classics OJC 417 CD/LP/MC
Jacquet; Barry Harris (*p*); Ben Tucker (*b*); Alan Dawson (*d*)

***   **The Blues, That's Me!** Original Jazz Classics OJC 614 CD/LP/MC
Jacquet; Wynton Kelly (*p*); Tiny Grimes (*g*); Buster Williams (*b*); Oliver Jackson (*d*).

***   **The Soul Explosion** Original Jazz Classics OJC 674 CD/LP/MC
         Jacquet; Russell Jacquet, Joe Newman, Ernie Royal (*t*); Matthew Gee (*tb*); Frank
         Foster (*ts*); Cecil Payne (*bs*); Milt Buckner (*org*); Wally Richardson (*g*); Al Lucas (*b*);
         Al Foster (*d*).

Jacquet seldom played the blues better than on these three good sets, all originally released on
Prestige. Not much to be said about the music, except that the large-group material on *The Soul
Explosion* is more sophisticated than might be supposed. Fine versions of 'Our Delight' and the
CD only 'Don't Blame Me' (*Bottoms Up*), 'Still King' (*The Blues, That's Me!*; there's also a
CD bonus version on *Soul Explosion*) and a romping 'St Louis Blues' on the third album.
None will disappoint.

(*)   **Illinois Jacquet And Wild Bill Davis Black & Blue 233044 CD
         Jacquet; Wild Bill Davis (*org*); Al Bartee. 1/73.

[***   **Midnight Shows: Volume 8** Black & Blue 193582 CD]
         Jacquet; Hank Jones (*p*); George Duvivier (*b*); J. C. Heard (*d*). 3/78.

Typical of Black & Blue's rather jolly catalogue, these are friendly and pleasurable records,
clearly and faithfully transferred to CD. The earlier has Jacquet in familiar organ and drums
setting; not as sympathetic a collaboration as the very successful trio with Milt Buckner (a
Black & Blue stalwart) and Jo Jones, but there are some rousing performances, notably 'Blue
Skies (Trumpets No End)' and a gentler 'The Man I Love'. The later album (shared with the Sir
Charles Thompson trio) features Jacquet in yet quieter and more introspective mood. He still
knows how to take a tune apart – 'Someone To Watch Over Me' undergoes a few interesting
shifts in the later choruses – while remaining basically faithful to its mood. Jacquet always
sounds best with a really good rhythm section, and this one is hard to fault, though Heard rushes
some of his tempi. Well transferred and clean-sounding, a worthwhile addition to the catalogue
which (but for a few compilation items, notably 'Soft Winds' and 'Sweet Georgia Brown' with
George Freeman on *The Best Of The Jazz Saxophones, Volume 2* and *Volume 3*, LRC CDC
8529 and 9009 CD, and three tracks from Jimmy McGriff featuring Hank Crawford (LRC CDC
9001 – see below) is still desperately thin.

(*)   **Loot To Boot LRC CDC 9034 CD
         Jacquet; Jimmy McGriff, Wild Bill Davis (*org*); Kenny Barron (*electric p*); George
         Freeman (*g*); Bob Cranshaw (*b*); Buddy Rich (*d*).

Restores the (undated) sessions sampled on *The Best Of The Jazz Saxophones*, with three tracks
also issued under organist McGriff's leadership (see above) and three with Wild Bill Davis and
the uncredited Al Bartee which were formerly released on Black & Blue 233044. The highlights
are the long 'Blues From/For New Orleans' (there is some doubt about the preposition) with
Davis, and a superb Rich/McGriff original called 'Racquet Club'; the latter is no means one of
the saxophonist's better outings, drawing its power from the interplay of tight organ-chords,
insistent guitar, firm bass and drums. A respectable compilation of material from Sonny Lester's
capacious archive, but Jacquet fans are likely to have most of it already.

AHMAD JAMAL (born 1930)
PIANO

***   **Ahmad's Blues** Jazz Society (Vogue) 670507 CD
         Jamal; Israel Crosby (*b*); Vernell Fournier (*d*). 1/58, 9/58, 6/61.

***   **Live At The Alhambra** Vogue 655002 CD
         As above. 6/61.

**   **Digital Works** Atlantic 781258 CD
         Jamal; Larry Ball (*b*); Herlin Riley (*d*); Iraj Lashkary (*perc*). 85.

**   **Rossiter Road** Atlantic 781645 CD
         Jamal; James Cammack (*b*); Herlin Riley (*d*); Manolo Badrena (*perc*). 85.

(*)   **Live At The Montreux Jazz Festival Atlantic 781699 CD
         As above, except Seldon Newton (*perc*) replaces Badrena. 2/86.

(*)   **Crystal Atlantic 781793 CD
          Jamal; James Cammack (*b*); David Bowler (*d*); Willie White (*perc*); orchestra.

*(*)   **Pittsburgh** Atlantic 782029 CD
          As above, except omit White, orchestra.

But for his enormous influence on Miles Davis and especially on Miles's conception of rhythm, Ahmad Jamal might by now have fallen into the pit dug for him by tin-eared critics, dismissed as an inventive cocktail pianist, or (still more invidiously) as an entertainer rather than an artist.

Sadly, the trio recordings of the late 1950s are only patchily available. The Jazz Society compilation of work with bassist Israel Crosby and drummer Vernell Fournier (who had replaced an earlier guitarist) contains some fine, inventive jazz, mostly of a romantic inclination. There's no overlap between the two discs, though the June 1961 tracks on *Ahmad's Blues* appear to come from the same sessions as *Live At The Alhambra* (Jamal's own club); either would make a good introduction to his work. The CD transfers are clear and generally faithful, though they perhaps favour the pianist a shade. Crosby is a good player with a surprisingly lean approach and deserves more prominence.

Jamal's own technique – which is probably closer to Errol Garner than to anyone else – has remained absolutely pristine, concentrating on fragile textures and almost calligraphic melodic statements, rather than the propulsive logic of bebop piano. There is, though, a slackness and repetitiousness in his soloing in the 1980s which quickly wear off the chrome-bright delivery. The addition of electric and electronic keyboards on *Digital Works* creates some interesting colorations, reminiscent of his better work with orchestras. *Pittsburgh*, alas, doesn't fall into that category. Most of the recent recordings sound as if they need a little cigarette smoke blown through the tape gates.

The *Montreux* set contains some fine moments. There is a fine version of Wayne Shorter's 'Footprints', which extends Jamal's reading on *Digital Works* in a way that suggests his jazz brain still functions when called upon. Equally, his reading of Roland Hanna's 'Perugia' on *Crystal* shows an imaginative approach to a challenging theme. On the other hand, the *Montreux* version of 'Rossiter Road' shows how readily the pianist lapses back into prefabricated figures and patterns.

KHAN JAMAL (born 1946)
VIBRAPHONE, MARIMBA

(*)   **Infinity Stash ST 278 LP
          Jamal; Byard Lancaster (*as, f*); Clifton Burton (*hca*); Bernard Sammul (*p*); Reggie Curry (*b*); Dwight James or Sunny Murray (*d*); Omar Hill (*African d, perc*). 12/82, 3/84.

***(*)   **Dark Warrior** Steeplechase SCS 1196 LP
          Jamal; Charles Tyler (*as, bs*); Johnny Dyani (*b*); Leroy Lowe (*d*). 9/84.

***   **Three** Steeplechase SCS 1201 LP
          Jamal; Pierre Dørge (*g*); Johnny Dyani (*b*). 10/84.

***   **The Traveller** Steeplechase SCS 1217 LP
          Jamal; Johnny Dyani (*b*); Leroy Lowe (*d*). 10/85.

***   **Thinking Of You** Storyville SLP 4138 LP
          Jamal; Byard Lancaster (*as, f, cl, b cl*); Oliver Collins (*p, syn*); Tim Motzer (*syn prog*); Jamaaladeen Tacuma (*b*); Billy Hart (*d*); Omar Hill (*perc*). 10/86.

The dedication to Cal Tjader on *Three* suggests one (outwardly improbable) lineage for Jamal's firmly rhythmic but freely pulsed vibraphone style. Almost all the albums, which are difficult to distinguish by merit, have a dark freedom and surge which is curiously Europeanized, the kind of thing one hears when passing an African-frequented tea-house or café in the Paris Zone, in Hamburg or Copenhagen. The albums with the late Johnny Dyani are the best to start with, and *Dark Warrior* is probably the finest of all, with Charles Tyler's sweet-and-sour alto and bossy baritone fitting the leader's time feel much better than Byard Lancaster, who seems nevertheless first choice for the phone call.

There is just a hint of Tjader's pattering approach, and vibes fans may hear echoes of just about everyone from Bobby Hutcherson, Steeplechase stablemate Walt Dickerson, to Karl Berger. Though his approach to a standard, like the usually saxophonic 'Body And Soul' on *The Traveller*, is reminiscent of Hutcherson's free counterpoint, in terms of diction it is even less horn-like, closer to Dickerson's abstract theme formulations. Enthusiasts will also want to hear Jamal's contribution to pianist Joe Bonner's *Suite For Chocolate* (Steeplechase 1215), which is available on CD.

DWIGHT JAMES
DRUMS

(*)   Inner Heat Cadence CJR 1014 LP
James; Clarence Bradlkey (*t*); Byard Lancaster (*as*); Middie Middleton (*ts*); Khan Jamal (*vib*); Howard Cooper (*b*). 5–11/81.

Sturdy free-bop from a mixture of familiar and lesser-known names. James himself has led a small number of obscure sessions, and the playing here is energetic but not particularly inspiring; Lancaster, usually a galvanizing presence, is unfortunately present on only one track. Functional rather than especially good recording.

HARRY JAMES (1916–83)
TRUMPET

***(*)   Jazz Live And Rare: All-Time Standards** Jazzline JL 20814 CD/LP
James; Nick Buono, Claude Bowen, Buck Clayton, Phil Cook, Alexander Cuozzo, Art DePew, Tommy Gonsoulin, Everett McDonald, Jack Palmer, Jack Schaeffer (*t*); Hoyt Bohannon, Russell Brown, Vernon Brown, Ziggy Elmer, Truett Jones, Lew McCreary, Lee O'Connor, Ralph Osborn, Dalton Rizzotto, David Robbins, Harry Rodgers, Bruce Squires, Juan Tizol (*tb*); Claude Lakey, Sam Marowitz, Dave Matthews, Willie Smith, Earl Warren (*as*); Jack Washington (*as, bs*); James Cook, Corky Corcoran, Clint Davis, Herschel Evans, Bill Luther, Bill Massingill, Drew Page, Bob Poland (*ts*); Musko Ruffo (*as, ts*); Herbie Steward (*as, ts, cl*); Francis Polifroni (*bs*); Jack Gardner, Al Lerner, Bruce McDonald, Jess Stacy, Tommy Todd (*p*); Ben Heller, Bryan Kent, Francis Lee, Jack Marshall (*g*); Theo Hays, Walter Page, Robert Stone, Thurman Teague (*b*); Ralph Hawkins, Jo Jones, Jackie Mills, Buddy Rich, Mickey Scrima (*d*). 1938–54.

In January 1939, Harry James left the Benny Goodman band and struck out on his own (though still under B. G.'s canny financial wing). He had already recorded as leader by this time but he confronted freedom with the greatest enthusiasm. This essential set straddles that early period and then hops rather awkwardly to 1950 and then to 1953–4. Pre-war, the James band was one of the hottest things going. Indentured to Goodman, the young trumpeter had learnt to pack a lot of kinetic energy into 16 scant bars. On his own, he sounds more relaxed but also able to develop ideas at his own pace, and the range of tones he goes for is ever greater; singer Helen Forrest, who later became his girlfriend, talked about his 'Jewish phrasing', an unfortunate tag for those times, but strangely accurate. In 1940, *Metronome* voted him top trumpet. By the end of the war, the energy and appetite with which he had started out seemed to have dissipated. Marriage to Betty Grable was widely considered the culprit.

Even so, the later material is much better than average from that period. There is a wonderful 'Lush Life' from October 1953, impelled by Buddy Rich's drumming, and a sensuous version of 'These Foolish Things' that recalls the origins of James's hot butterscotch 'sweet style'.

(*)   Saturday Night Swing Giants of Jazz GOJ 1016 LP
James; Nick Buono; (*t*); Juan Tizol (*tb*); Herb Lorden (*cl, as*); Willie Smith (*as*); Herbie Steward (*ts*); Larry Kinamon (*p*); Floyd Blanton (*b*); Buddy Rich (*d*). 12/53, 1/54.

James's smaller post-war bands were less an aesthetic preference – as seems to have been the case with his former boss, Benny Goodman – than a reaction to tougher climatic conditions for big groups. Most at ease as a soloing section head, James never sounds quite so convincing in this setting, though in Tizol, yo-yoing back and forth between James and the Ellington orchestra, and the loyal Willie Smith he had like-minded players who understood his requirements.

The opening 'Ciribiribin' theme is strongly stated, but there's much less fire in what follows, and a rather bitty eclecticism, a tame descendant of James's bums-on-seats 'sweet style', prevails throughout. Tizol's 'Caravan', though, is lovely, as is 'Moonglow'. Sound-levels aren't quite right in the quieter passages, as if someone at the desk has been overcompensating, but the ensembles are admirably clear and distinct.

*** **More Harry James In HiFi** Capitol EMS 1148 LP
James; Nick Buono, Art DePew, Joe Dolny, Conrad Gozzo, Don Smith (t); Roy Main, Dick Nash, George Roberts, Juan Tizol (tb); Herb Lorden, Willie Smith (as); Corky Corcoran, Jeff Massingill, Bob Poland (ts); Larry Kinnamon (p); Tiny Timbrell (g); Joe Comfort (b); Buddy Combine (d); strings; vocalists. 11/55, 12/55, 1/56.

Part of a series – Kenton and Goodman are also marked – to celebrate star names' output. Some of it is not so much high fidelity as moderately perfidious, with the sound slipping in and out of definition; but the material is more than enough to make up for technical shortcomings. James liked to work his orchestras in big overlapping blocks of sound, sometimes setting his reeds (or strings if they were available, as they are on four good tracks here) cater-corner to the main blast of the horns. The results are very powerful and numbers like 'The Mole' and 'Street Scene' get a big lift-off. The Goodmanish 'Melancholy Rhapsody' isn't a patch on the big 1941 'Trumpet Rhapsody', but it still has a warmth and power that no other current player could achieve. Recommended.

***(*) **The Best Of Harry James: The Capitol Years** Capitol CDP 798952 2 CD
James; Nick Buono, Phil Cook, Art Depew, Joe Dolny, Conrad Gozzo, Mickey Mangano, Everett McDonald, Ralph Osborne, Don Smith (t); Hoyt Bohannon, Roy Main, Lew McCreary, Dick Nash (tb); Juan Tizol (vtb); George Roberts (btb); Herb Lorden, Willie Smith (as); Pat Chartrand, Bill Massingill, Herbie Stewart (ts); Bob Poland, Tom Suthers (bs); Larry Kinnamon, Doug Parker (p); Allen Reuss, Tiny Timbrell (g); Joe Comfort, Rob Stone (b); Buddy Combine, Gene Estes, Jackie Mills (d). 55–56.

After leaving Columbia, James signed to Capitol and benefited immediately from the label's up to the minute recording technology and exacting production standards. With arrangements by Ray Conniff, Ernie Wilkins, Neal Hefti, Billy May and others, the trumpeter could hardly go wrong and this is an ideal introduction to his work, opening and closing with a brief thematic statement of 'Ciribiribin' and including trademark pieces like 'Trumpet Blues And Cantabile', 'Sleepy Lagoons' (better known in Britain with added gull cries as the theme to *Desert Island Discs*), Helen Forrest's lovely, wry 'I'm Beginning To See The Light' and, also from the Ellington book, a fine version of 'In A Sentimental Mood' that puts altoist Willie Smith in the spotlight. Ron Hill's digital transfers sound as if they were done yesterday.

** **Compact Jazz: Harry James** Verve 833285 CD
James; Johnny Audino, Harold Billings, Nick Buono; Dick Cathcart, Mike Conn, Sam Conte, Vern Guerlin, Fred Koyen, Larry McGuire, Ollie Mitchell, Bob Rolfe, Bob Turk (t); Joe Cadena, Vince Diaz, Bob Edmondson, Dick Hyde, Dick McQuary, Ray Sims, Ernie Tack, Juan Tizol (tb); Matty Matlock (cl); Pat Chartrand, Herb Lorden, Joe Riggs, Willie Smith (as); Modesto Brisano, Corky Corcoran, Jay Corre, Sam Firmature, Dave Madden, Eddie Miller (ts); Bob Poland, Ernie Small (ts, bs); Jack Perciful (p); Dave Koonce, Terry Rosen, Dempsey Wright (g); Joe Comfort, Red Kelly, Russ Phillips (b); Tony DiNicola, Jake Hanna, Jackie Mills, Buddy Rich (d). 1959–62.

Though enormously popular right up until his final illness, James's post-war work inevitably lacked the impact of his earlier material. This is a particularly tired selection. Some of the playing is first class, but even Neal Hefti's and Ernie Wilkins's arrangements can't lift the charts much above a dullish, middle-of-the-road swing with occasional Dixieland and modernist inflexions. 'Weather Bird', arranged by clarinettist Matlock, is the most interesting performance, but not so much as to justify urgent purchase.

**   **The Hits** Capitol CDP 7912202 CD/M 1515 LP

**   **The Golden Trumpet** London 820178 CD
James and orchestra; no details.

Unexceptionable trawl of material – 'Ciribiribin', 'Two O'Clock Jump' on both, 'Trumpet Blues And Cantabile' and 'Music Makers' on *Hits*, and the show-stopping 'You Made Me Love You' on *Golden Trumpet* – but *Hits* in particular is harshly and inconsistently transferred. The CD, with no bonus tracks, may be useful for anyone unfamiliar with the James trumpet, but it's by no means a reliable collector's item. *The Golden Trumpet* is a poppier selection with less overt jazz content.

STAFFORD JAMES (born 1946)
BASS

***   **Stafford James Ensemble** Red VPA 142 LP
James; Frank Strozier (*as*); Harold Mabern (*p*); Louis Hayes (*d*). 78.

A rare outing for this fine, contemporary bassist as a leader. He exerts no greater influence on the music than anyone else in the quartet, which proves to be primarily a feature for the impassioned alto of Frank Strozier, on standard post-bop material such as 'Impressions' and 'Soul Eyes'. Strozier's bitter sound and sweeping attack make quite an impact, but the more sober pleasures of the rhythm section – James and Hayes work beautifully together – are as effective.

LARS JANSSON
PIANO, KEYBOARDS

***   **A Window Towards Being** Imogena IGCD 019 CD
Jansson; Brynjar Hoff (*ob*); Lars Danielsson (*b*); Anders Kjellberg (*d*). 2/91.

Jansson is an excellent post-bop pianist whose affection for Bill Evans's manner is wedded to an attractive way with melody in his writing: it means that his music comes out with a little more brightness than that of the typical Evans disciple. The fine *Trio 84* on Dragon is currently out of print, but this sensitive programme is played with some flair by the trio: Danielsson is the most reliable of bassists, and Kjellberg has a very good touch. Hoff is used for instrumental colour on three atypically lightweight tracks; but the main interest is in the piano improvisations on Jansson's own originals. The recording is a little soft-edged, although it suits the music.

JOSEPH JARMAN (born 1937)
SAXOPHONES, OTHER REEDS, FLUTE

(*)   **Song For Delmark DD 410 CD
Jarman; Bill Brimfield (*t*); Fred Anderson (*ts*); Christopher Gaddy (*p, mar*); Charles Clark (*b*); Thurman Barker, Steve McCall (*d*). 10 & 12/66.

(*)   **As If It Were The Seasons Delmark DFS 417 LP
Jarman; John Jackson (*t*); Lester Lashley (*tb*); Joel Brandon (*f*); Fred Anderson, John Stubblefield (*ts*); Richard Abrams (*p, ob*); Charles Clark (*b, clo, koto*); Thurman Barker (*d, perc*); Sherri Scott (*v*).

***   **The Magic Triangle** Black Saint BSR 0038 LP
Jarman; Famoudou Don Moye (*d, perc*); Don Pullen (*p, v*). 7/79.

(*)   **Black Paladins Black Saint BSR 0042 LP
As above, except omit Pullen, add Johnny Dyani (*b, p*). 12/79.

Art Ensemble of Chicago fans are apt to regard record projects by Joseph Jarman or Roscoe Mitchell much as Rolling Stones fans might regard a new solo record by Mick Jagger or Charlie Watts: worthy of notice and support, but essentially a distraction from the main matter at hand. In the former case, at least, they're quite wrong. Whether or not the Art Ensemble members feel disinclined to record or tour together, there's no doubt that most of their interesting work since 1975 has been apart.

This is particularly true of Jarman who, depending on your viewpoint, is either the quintessential voice of the AEC or else its squarest peg. Recording under his own name – and the *nom de studio* Magic Triangle – Jarman sounds poised and intense. The reissued *Song For* is relatively standard AACM fare, intercut with neo-Dada recitations and characterized by a lack of formal shape. The supporting performers, with the exception of the two drummers, are not always up to scratch, though Clark produces some wonderfully sonorous bass on 'Adam's Rib', which certainly benefits considerably from CD transfer. The long tracks – 'Non-Cognitive Aspects Of The City', 'Song For' and a second and longer unissued take of Fred Anderson's 'Little Fox Run' with its skittering marimba patterns – pall slightly on repeated hearings. Of great documentary and historical significance, it's unlikely to effect any dramatic conversions. Clark is also important on *As If It Were*, where he anchors the two connected quartet pieces that make up side one of the LP; the augmented group plays rather predictable AACM stuff, with lots of 'additional' percussion, gongs, harps and bells, giving 'Song For Christopher' an unattractive traffic-jam feel which tends to bury Jarman.

By contrast, the title-track of *Black Paladins*, recorded a dozen years later, contains some of Jarman's best work on record, and one suspects that Johnny Dyani gives him the sort of firm harmonic support that Malachi Favors seems disinclined to contribute to the Art Ensemble. Don Moye's contribution to the album can't be underestimated (he is nominal co-leader), but Dyani and Jarman are the dominant voices. 'Humility In The Face Of The Creator' and 'Ode To Wilbur Ware', dedicated to the great bassist, are valuable performances.

The Magic Triangle is, on balance, a more coherent and satisfying record. The contribution of Don Pullen is enormous, but Jarman is utterly at ease, flinging out everything in his satchel from Hodges swoons on 'Lonely Child' to faster passages evocative of Ornette Coleman and Anthony Braxton by turns. No CD, unfortunately, but no problems with Black Saint's typically good production and pressings.

KEITH JARRETT (born 1945)
PIANO, ORGAN, SOPRANO SAXOPHONE, OTHER INSTRUMENTS

***(*)   **Facing You** ECM 1017 CD/LP
Jarrett (*p* solo). 11/71.

***(*)   **Solo Concerts** ECM 1035/6/7 2CD/3LP
As above. 3 & 7/73.

****   **The Köln Concert** ECM 1064/5 CD/2LP/MC
As above. 1/75.

***(*)   **Hymns Spheres** ECM 1086/7 2LP
Jarrett (*org* solo). 9/76.

***   **Spheres** ECM 8274632 CD
As above. 5/76.

(*)   **Staircase ECM 1090/1 CD/LP
Jarrett (*p* solo). 11/76.

***   **Sun Bear Concerts** ECM 1100 6CD/10LP
As above. 3/80.

**   **Sacred Hymns Of G. I. Gurdjieff** ECM 1174 CD/LP
As above. 11/79.

**   **Invocations** ECM 1201/2 2CD/2LP
Jarrett (*p, pipe org, ss* solo). 7–10/80.

***   **Concerts** ECM 1227 CD/LP
        Jarrett (*p* solo). 5 & 6/81.

(*)   **Keith Jarrett Concerts ECM 1227/9 3LP
        As above. 7/85.

*   **Spirits** ECM 1333/4 2CD/2LP
        Jarrett (assorted instruments). 4/87.

**   **Dark Intervals** ECM 1379 CD/LP
        Jarrett (*p* solo). 10/88.

**   **Paris Concert** ECM 1401 CD/LP/MC
        As above.

'Cult status' is a long way behind. Keith Jarrett is now a major world religion, commanding a mixture of unthinking critical persecution and equally unthinking idolatry. He is perhaps the most sophisticated technician working today outside the 'straight' repertoire (and he has, of course, made his own incursions into classical and new music, tackling Bach's *Goldberg Variations* and *The Well-tempered Clavier* (ECM 1362 & 1395 CD/LP) and premiering important work by the contemporary composer, Lou Harrison). His piano style is as much influenced by rock and country music as by the jazz mainstream, and he is one of the finest 'instant composers' on the scene, a process subtly different from improvisation in the conventional jazz sense. In his extended performances – and, boy, are some of them extended! – Jarrett alternates tightly constructed vamps and sure-footed harmonic and melodic progressions with curious, abecedarian themes and huge, rapturous chorales that are completely individual and *sui generis*. Like all great artists, he is wildly inconsistent.

Though recently Jarrett's output has been more contained (a shift also reflected in his highly successful 'Standards' trio, below), there was an uneasy giantism in his work of the later 1970s, culminating in the release of the infamous *Sun Bear Concerts*, a 10-LP box, and only slightly less cumbersome on CD, of densely personal piano improvisations. It's clear that these episodically remarkable performances occupied a very significant, slightly chastened place in Jarrett's rather lonely and dogged self-exploration, but that doesn't automatically make for good music. Without being excessively Dr Johnsonish ('It is not done well; but you are surprised to find it done at all') about music so naked and questing, one wonders how much of the critical excitement it garnered was simply a response to its size and to Jarrett's brass neck in releasing product on a scale usually only accorded the great dead. The jury needn't stay out quite so long on the preposterous *Spirits*, a double (of course) album of overdubs on a bizarre variety of ethnic insruments. For the record, the album has its serious proponents but, for all its healing and restorative intent (and apparent impact on the music that followed), it occupies only a marginal place in Jarrett's output. Other offences to be taken briefly into consideration are the thin *Gurdjieff* essays and the dismal *Invocations*, executed in part on the same organ as *Hymns Spheres*, but lacking that album's extraordinary experimental intensity and concentration.

Hymns Spheres (and the single-CD excerpt, *Spheres*) is by no stretch of the imagination a jazz record, but it does belong to another great improvisatory tradition, that of European organ music; it may be significant that, in contrast to the critical spanking it received in the United States, the album was favourably reviewed in Europe. Jarrett's approach to the unfamiliar keyboards and their associated pedals and stops is quite remarkable and generates one of his finest ever performances, easily the equal in conception and intelligence of the best-selling *Köln Concert*.

This is perhaps Jarrett's best and certainly his most popular record. ECM has been dining out or, to be fairer, recording others on the proceeds for over a decade. Made in conditions of exceptional difficulty – not least an audibly unsatisfactory piano – Jarrett not for the first time makes a virtue of adversity, carving out huge slabs of music with a rare intensity. His instrument does sound off-puttingly bad-tempered, but his concentration on the middle register throughout the performance has been a characteristic of his work throughout his career.

The Bremen and Lausanne sets on *Solo Concerts* are almost equally good. Jarrett's first multi-volume set was extraordinarily well received on its release and stands up particularly well now (by contrast, *Facing You* seems slightly time-locked for some reason). These are friendlier, less intense performances than the *Köln* sides, but no less inventive for that, exploring Jarrett's characteristic blend of popular and 'high' forms. The 1981 *Concerts/Keith Jarrett Concerts* were also recorded in Germany and in slightly easier circumstances (Jarrett suffered agonizing back pain throughout the Bremen *Solo Concert*); perhaps as a consequence there's far less tension in the music, a quality noticeable in both *Facing You*, the earliest of the solo recordings and the best place to get a feel of Jarrett's characteristic method before tackling the multi-volume sets, and *Staircase*, where he seems to range across a multiplicity of idioms (many of them identifiably classical rather than popular) with no apparent urgency.

Much has been made of the cohesion and unity of Jarrett's solo performances. They are often likened to multi-movement suites rather than collections of discontinuous tunes or numbers. This is certainly true of *Facing You*, which shares with the *Köln Concert* a satisfying roundness; it certainly isn't true of *Staircase* or of the recent *Dark Intervals* and *Paris Concert*. The former is a moody, sonorous affair, recorded live in Tokyo and interspersed with thunderously disciplined applause. As a whole, it's reminiscent of the ageing musician's plaint in the great jazz movie *Sven Klangs Kvintett* that the only place young Scandinavians of the 1970s could hear jazz was in church. Apart from 'Fire Dance' – track titles are rare or *ex post facto* in the improvised performances – the music has a very formal, concertizing solemnity. The *Paris Concert*, by contrast, is lively at least but is also disturbingly predictable. The idiomatic shifts have become mannered almost to the point of self-parody, and there's a slightly cynical quality to Jarrett's apparent manipulation of audience expectations. The notorious grunting and moaning, with which he signals ecstasy and effort, have never been more intrusive.

**(*)   Somewhere Before Atlantic 7567 81455 CD
Jarrett; Charlie Haden (*b*); Paul Motian (*d*). 8/68.

**(*)   Fort Yawuh Impulse MCAD 33122 CD
Jarrett; Dewey Redman (*ts, perc*); Charlie Haden (*b*); Paul Motian (*d*); Danny Johnson (*perc*). 2/73.

Ⅎ⅃Sparreasure Island Impulse MCA 39106 CD/LP
Jarrett; Dewey Redman (*ts, perc*); Sam Brown (*g*); Charlie Haden (*b*); Paul Motian (*d*); Guilherme Franco (*perc*); Danny Johnson (*perc*). 2/74.

***(*)   The Survivor's Suite ECM 1085 CD/LP
Jarrett; Dewey Redman (*ts, perc*); Charlie Haden (*b*); Paul Motian (*d*). 4/76.

*(*)   Eyes Of The Heart ECM 1150 CD/2LP
Jarrett; Dewey Redman (*ts, perc*); Charlie Haden (*b*); Paul Motian (*d*). 5/76.

Jarrett's American quartet probably never reached the heights or achieved the almost telepathic understanding of the European group responsible for the classic *Belonging*, below. The early *Somewhere Before* is for trio, reuniting the line-up that made *Life Between The Exit Signs* (two tracks survive on an Atlantic piano trio compilation shared with McCoy Tyner, Herbie Hancock and Chick Corea – 81402 CD). Heavily rock influenced and still reminiscent of the methodology of the Charles Lloyd Quartet, of which Jarrett had been a member, it includes a version of Bob Dylan's 'My Back Pages' and two delightfully cadenced rags. Recorded live and slightly rough in texture, it has a freshness of approach that Jarrett quickly lost and was slow to regain.

The addition of Dewey Redman on *Fort Yawuh* (another of Jarrett's irritating pun-anagrams, this time of 'Fourth Way') gives that album a dark power that re-emerges on *Treasure Island*. Recorded a matter of weeks before *Belonging*, *Treasure Island* has most of the virtues of the 'European' album in embryo, but there is little doubt that Haden and Motian were either uncertain of Jarrett's direction or else were simply too forceful to fall in with his increasingly eclectic approach.

With the appearance of *Belonging*, Jarrett was able to operate a highly creative trade-off between two working bands. *Survivor's Suite* is a masterpiece, with the quartet pulling together on an ambitiously large-scale piece, each member contributing whole-heartedly and passionately. By the sharpest of contrasts, *Eyes Of The Heart*, a live exploration of much the same material, is a near-disaster. The original release was as a double LP with one blank side. What it documents – and the format is in every way symbolic – is the final break-up of a rather fissile band; Dewey Redman contributes scarcely anything, and the album ends with Jarrett playing alone.

***   Silence Impulse! GRP 11172 CD
Jarrett; Dewey Redman (*ts*); Charlie Haden (*b*); Paul Motian (*d*). 75.

A sensible compilation of two previous Impulse! LPs, *Bop-Be* and *Byablue*, dropping 'Pyramids Moving' from the former, and concentrating on those tracks on *Byablue* that featured the whole group, with the exception of a piano solo reading of 'Byablue' itself. This was the last of Jarrett's records for the label and it's a slightly uneasy affair, reflecting not just a measure of strain that had grown up within the group but also (a matter of months after the Cologne concert) Jarrett's increasing interest in solo performance. As such, it's of considerable historical importance, but can't be considered one of the more important albums.

****   **Expectations** Columbia 467902 CD
       Jarrett; Dewey Redman (*ts*); Sam Brown (*g*); Charlie Haden (*b*); Paul Motian (*d*);
       Airto Moreira (*perc*); strings and brass. 10/71.

Only recently restored from Columbia's capacious back-catalogue, this is one of Jarrett's best group-sessions and his only one for the label; predictably they claim it as his breakthrough, and it's possible to argue that line rather more disinterestedly by pointing to the pianist's increasingly confident synthesis of jazz ('Circular Letter'), rock ('Sundance'), gospel ('There Is A Road') and Latin ('Common Mama') themes into a passionate, occasionally ecstatic mix, which all comes together on the closing 'Nomads'. Some of the more extravagant freedoms relate closely to his work with a man who stayed with Columbia a while longer. Jarrett learned – or allowed himself – to play free on Miles Davis's *Live–Evil* and there is ample evidence of that here. Redman plays on only half the tracks, Brown on six; a piano-and-strings track has been dropped and the running order revised, but with perfect logic. Jarrett plays soprano saxophone in addition to piano, but also, and despite Columbia's silence on the matter, organ and percussion. A fine record from a vintage period.

****   **Belonging** ECM 1050 CD/LP/MC
       Jarrett; Jan Garbarek (*ts, ss*); Palle Danielsson (*b*); Jon Christensen (*d*). 4/74.

***(*)   **My Song** ECM 1115 CD/LP/MC
       As above. 1/77.

***   **Nude Ants** ECM 1171/2 CD
       As above. 5/79.

Both *Belonging* and *My Song* have also been covered in the entry on Jan Garbarek, because the saxophonist's contribution to both albums seems particularly significant. The 'European Quartet' was probably the most sympathetic grouping Jarrett ever assembled and *Belonging* in particular is a superb album, characterized by some of the pianist's most open and joyous playing on record; his double-time solo on 'The Windup' is almost Tatum-like in its exuberance and fluency. The country-blues feel of 'Long As You Know You're Living Yours' is a confident reflection of his music roots. The ballads 'Blossom', 'Solstice' and the title-piece – the first two powerfully extended, the last uncharacteristically brief – are remarkable by any standards; Garbarek's slightly out-of-tune opening statement on 'Solstice' and Danielsson's subsequent solo are masterful, while Jarrett's own split chords accentuate the mystery and ambiguity of the piece.

     Nude Ants is a live set from New York City (the title is a metathesis of the bouncing 'New Dance'). It's a valuable documentation of the European Quartet outside the studio, but the performances are somewhat below par and Garbarek (who admits dissatisfaction with the performances) sounds alternately forced and diffident. Recording quality is also disappointing and well below ECM's usual standard.

(*)   **Rutya And Daitya ECM 1021 LP
       Jarrett; Jack DeJohnette (*d*). 5/71.

***(*)   **Standards: Volume 1** ECM 1255 CD/LP/MC
       As above, except add Gary Peacock (*b*). 1/83.

***   **Changes** ECM 1276 CD/LP
       As above. 1/83.

****   **Standards: Volume 2** ECM 1289 CD/LP
       As above. 7/85.

***   **Standards Live** ECM 1317 CD/LP
       As above. 7/86.

***(*)   **Still Live** ECM 1360/1 2CD/2LP
As above. 10/89.

***(*)   **Changeless** ECM 1392 CD/LP
As above. 4/90.

(*)   **Tribute ECM 1420/1 2CD/2LP/2MC
As above.

****   **The Cure** ECM 1440 CD/LP/MC
As above.

One of the less fair subtexts to the widespread critical acclaim for Jarrett's 'Standards Trio' is the implication that he is at last toeing the line, conforming to an established repertoire, finally renouncing the extravagances of the *Köln Concert* and the other multi-volume sets.

In practice, nothing could be much further from the truth. Jarrett's approach to standards is nothing if not individual; for all his obvious respect and affection for the material, he consistently goes his own way. The main difference from the solo performances is the obvious one: Peacock's firmly harmonic bass and DeJohnette's astonishingly imaginative drumming (which Jarrett failed fully to appreciate on the early and little-known *Rutya And Daitya*) adjust his improvisatory instincts to the degree that they simplify his articulation and attack and redirect his attention to the chords and the figuration of melody.

It doesn't always come off. There are moments on *Standards: Volume 1* which are simply flat and uninspired, as on 'God Bless The Child'. *Volume 2* immediately feels more confident. The themes, which are less familiar anyway, are no longer an embarrassment; Jarrett clearly feels able to leave them implicit a little longer. That is even more obvious on the fine *Standards Live* and *Still Live*, though it's a pity – from the point of view of comparison – that Jarrett hasn't repeated any of the studio titles. The only occasion where this is possible is on the strangely patchy *Tribute*, which repeats 'All The Things You Are' from *Standards: Volume 1*. The later version is more oblique, but also simpler. Like the rest of the tracks, it is intended as a *hommage*, in this case to Sonny Rollins, which is pretty typical of the curious but doubtless very conscious matching of standards and dedicatees. Typically, perhaps, Jarrett adds two of his own compositions to an already rather overblown and diffuse set, as if to inscribe himself more legibly into the tradition he is exploring and rediscovering.

In that same vein, the 'Standards Trio' hasn't limited itself to existing repertoire. *Changes* and *Changeless* contain original material which is deeply subversive, though also respectfully aware, of the whole tradition of jazz as a system of improvisation on 'the changes'. Typically, Jarrett invests the term with quite new aesthetic and philosophical considerations. On *Changeless*, there are no chord progressions at all; the trio improvises each section in a single key, somewhat in the manner of an Indian *raga*. The results are impressive and thought-provoking, like everything Jarrett has attempted. Even his failures, of which two more are listed below, are never less than interesting.

(As a footnote, the same trio has also recorded under Gary Peacock's leadership. The fine *Tales Of Another* (ECM 101 CD/LP) is reviewed more fully under the appropriate heading.)

(*)   **In The Light ECM 1033/4 2CD/2LP
Jarrett; Ralph Towner (*g*); string quartet; brass quintet; strings. 73.

(*)   **Luminessence ECM 1049 CD/LP
Jarrett; Jan Garbarek (*ts, ss*); strings. 4/74.

(*)   **Arbour Zena ECM 1070 CD/LP
Jarrett; Jan Garbarek (*ts, ss*); Charlie Haden (*b*); strings. 10/75.

*(*)   **The Celestial Hawk** ECM 1175 CD/LP
Jarrett; symphony orchestra. 3/80.

If it's every jazzer's dream (it was certainly Charlie Parker's) to play with strings, then it seems hard to deny Jarrett his moment. Hard, but not impossible. These mostly sound like the indulgences of a star figure unchecked by sensible aesthetic criteria and doubtless encouraged by sheer bankability. Jarrett and the Dagenham Girl Pipers? Why not? The *Köln Concert* is still shifting units like a life-jacket sale before the Flood.

Jarrett would doubtless argue that critical sniffiness about these albums is the result of sheer prejudice, the jazz community's snotty, elbows-out attitude to anything scored or on the grand scale and, on the other hand, the sheer exclusivism of the 'straight' music cartel. *Arbour Zena* and *Luminessence* contain some beautiful moments, but what an opportunity missed for a stripped-down duo with Garbarek. The overall mood of *Arbour Zena* is elegiac and slightly lorn, and the strings melt like marshmallows over some of the sharper flavours; the later album has simply been left cooking too long.

The earlier *In The Light* was a composer's showcase and, as such, a forerunner of ECM's much-admired New Series. The individual works struggle to stay in focus, but as a whole the album has surprising consistency. *The Celestial Hawk* is pure tosh . . . with some nice bits.

**   **Works** ECM 825425 CD/LP
       Jarrett (solo) and with Jan Garbarek (*ts*); Palle Danielsson (*b*); Jon Christensen (*d*);
       string quartet.

There was once a joke that in the year 2045 someone brought out a 'Best of Keith Jarrett' set in the currently fashionable laser-hologram/virtual reality format. It consisted of 87 LHVR diskettes. (There was an audiophile vinyl option, but you needed your own truck to take it home.) Selecting a Jarrett compilation must have been a thankless task. The results – 'Ritooria' from *Facing You*, part of the eponymous 'Staircase', 'Country' and 'Journey Home' from *My Song*, selections from the *Sun Bear Concerts*, *Invocations* and *In The Light* – are anything but predictable; nothing from *Belonging*, not so much as a quick edit-and-fade from the *Köln Concert*, too early in the shops for the 'Standards' stuff. Taken cold as a first introduction to Jarrett, it's no more misleading than any other logistical sample, but it's hardly an inspired choice.

***(*)   **Vienna Concert** ECM 1481 CD/MC
          Jarrett (*p* solo). 91.

Jarrett's solo concerts have by now established their own terms of reference and seem to exist completely *sui generis*. This is at once more formal and more coherent than the disappointing *Paris Concert*. If there is a dominant influence it is Bach, who is explicitly (though possibly unconsciously) quoted at a number of points, as is Shostakovitch, whom Jarrett has also been recording. It opens with a quiet, almost hymnic theme which develops very slowly over sombre pedals for just over twenty minutes, before opening out into a broken-tempo country theme that still preserves the original material in inverted form. The second and third pieces seem to develop material from the first, but in such a way that one wonders if they have been released in the order of the original concert. Long-standing Jarrett fans will find all the required elements in place; newcomers may find this more approachable than *Köln* or *Sun Bear*, but only if they're not put off by the classical resonances of the opening movement.

BOBBY JASPAR (1926–63)
TENOR SAXOPHONE, FLUTE

***   **Memory Of Dick** EmArcy 837208-2 CD
        Jaspar; Rene Urtreger (*p*); Sacha Distel (*g*); Benoit Quersin (*b*); Jean-Louis Viale (*d*).
        12/55.

***   **Bobby Jaspar With Friends** Fresh Sound FSR-CD 166 CD
        Jaspar; Mundell Lowe, René Thomas (*g*); George Duvivier, Monty Budwig,
        Jean-Marie Ingrand (*b*); Ed Shaughnessy, Nick Ceroli, Jean-Louis Viale (*d*). 58–62.

Jaspar, who was born in Liege, sounded like Lester Young might have done if Lester had been Belgian. His pale tone and amorphous phrasing on tenor were matched with an agile and exceptionally pointed flute style, abjuring the mere prettiness which normally attends that instrument. It's mostly tenor on *Memory Of Dick*, which features a band that was a regular unit for Jaspar: Quersin and Viale are often so pedestrian that the beat hardly picks itself off the floor, but it hardly seems to bother Jaspar, whose solos take a wispy but surprising path which, on 'Milestones', for instance, creates some of the leanest and most enigmatic of bebop improvisations. In this context, the plainness of Distel (actually quite a fair Jimmy Raney disciple at this stage) and Urtreger throws Jaspar's ideas into fuller relief. *Bobby Jaspar With Friends* collects material from four sessions, and the spread of material – including Hawkins's

'Stuffy', Parker's 'Now's The Time', and the charming original 'Suite For A Clown' – hints at Jaspar's breadth of sympathies. Fluency is prized over attack, and although the music is sometimes a little too restrained, it makes a refreshing alternative to the gruffer tenor-and-rhythm dates which were then the norm, thanks in part to the presence of Lowe or Thomas instead of a pianist.

***(*)   **Phenil Isopropl Amine** EmArcy 837207 CD
Jaspar; Michel Hausser (*vib, xy*); Sadi Lallemand (*vib*); Paul Rovere, Jimmy Merritt (*b*); Kenny Clarke (*d*); Humberto Canto (*perc*). 12/58.

Arguably the best single representation of Jaspar's work, since it presents him exclusively on flute, in a dozen tracks of brief length, where the interplay with the vibes players is particularly sharp and pertinent. Clarke provides understated yet perfectly propulsive drums. There are two takes of a previously unreleased tune, 'Jeu De Quarte', to add to the original LP issue. CD sound is beautifully fresh and clear.

***   **The Bobby Jaspar Quartet At Ronnie Scott's 1962** Mole 11 CD
Jaspar; René Thomas (*g*); Benoit Quersin (*b*); Daniel Humair (*d*). 1/62.

This private recording features a rather flat and grey sound, but the music has plenty of colour. Jaspar frequently takes second place to the exceptionally energetic Thomas: any hint that this might be like the Rollins–Jim Hall partnership, especially with three Rollins themes in the set, is dispelled by Thomas's sometimes helter-skelter playing. Jaspar performs well, although he sometimes falters in longer solos, and the set – while excellent value at 75 minutes in length – includes some lesser material. A charming flute version of 'Stella By Starlight', though, recalls Jaspar's other talent.

ANDRÉ JAUME (born 1940)
TENOR SAXOPHONE, FLUTE, CLARINET, BASS CLARINET

***   **L'Oc** hat Art CD 6058 CD
Jaume; Jean-François Canape (*t, flhn*); Yves Robert (*tb*); Jacques Veille (*btb*); Michael Overhage, Heiner Thym (*clo*); François Mechali (*b*); Gérard Siracusa (*perc*). 10/81.

After beginning with Dixieland groups, Jaume sought out more modern company in the 1960s, and since then his work on record has been rather unpredictable, with solo and duo recordings (with Joe McPhee, a long-time associate) sequenced with more large-scale efforts. This 1981 session puts an octet through Jaume's paces for seven tunes, with a further two pieces rendered by smaller editions of the same band. What emerges is a rather crabby sort of impressionism. There are some good improvisers in the group – Robert is a master, full of unexpected sounds, and Jaume himself has filtered his experience into a lean and questing solo style – but the sometimes fragmentary nature of the music can distract the listener. Still well worth hearing for admirers of European free jazz.

***   **Standards** CELP C12 CD
Jaume; Jean-Sebastien Simonoviez (*p*); François Mechali (*b*); Olivier Clerc (*d*). 4/89.

(*)   **Something . . . CELP C15 CD
Jaume; Joe McPhee (*ss, vtb*); Clyde Criner (*p*); Anthony Cox (*b*); Bill Stewart (*d*). 4/90.

The *Standards* collection sets Jaume off on a new midstream course. Aside from a single original, 'Escapade', the programme offers nine familiar songs to work with, and Jaume's querulous tone and slightly tortuous phrasing make deliberately unsettled work of the music. He takes out the bass clarinet as often as the tenor and soprano, and it lends a mooching air to 'Nancy'. Jaume's first recording with an American rhythm section is a little disappointing. Criner, Cox and Stewart play as if this were just another post-bop date, and that's how it ends up sounding: with compositions by Jackie McLean and Grachan Moncur in the programme, as well as four Jaume originals, the feel is reminiscent of Blue Note's experimental mid-1960s period. But Jaume and McPhee give the impression of being tranquillized by the setting. An austere reworking of Moncur's 'Love And Hate' is rather effective, and Jaume's terseness works well with the splashier playing of McPhee, but the record is slack overall.

***(*)   **Peace/Pace/Paix** CELP C19 CD
Jaume; Charlie Haden (*b*); Olivier Clerc (*d*). 3/91.

***(*)   **Abbaye De L'Épau** CELP C20 CD
Jaume; Charlie Mariano (*as, f*). 5/90.

Jaume sounds as if he's growing ever more quiet and introspective. He seldom raises his saxophone voice on either of these two records, yet both make a firmer impression than the earlier discs. The trio session establishes a line of descent from Ornette Coleman, which 'Peace' and 'Blue Connotation' make manifest, but Jaume's playing has little of Coleman in it: he's too quirkily himself, and the steady-rolling pulses devised by Haden and Clerc support what's now a very personal kind of melodic improvisation. *Abbaye De L'Épau* is more soberly reflective, a little akin to his programme of duets with Jimmy Giuffre (Eiffel), and the very even pacing of the music makes this sequence all-of-a-piece, with Mariano turning his own light down a little to remain in keeping with the occasion. Both discs are well recorded (the second is from a concert session) and gently absorbing.

JAZZ COMPOSERS ORCHESTRA (founded 1967)
GROUP

***(*)   **Communications** JCOA 1001/2 CD/2LP
Michael Mantler (*dir*); Don Cherry (*c*); Randy Brecker, Steve Furtado, Lloyd Michaels (*flhn*); Bob Northern, Julius Watkins (*frhn*); Jimmy Knepper, Roswell Rudd (*tb*); Jack Jeffers (*btb*); Howard Johnson (*tba*); Al Gibbons, Steve Lacy, Steve Marcus (*ss*); Bob Donovan, Gene Hull, Frank Wess (*as*); Gato Barbieri, George Barrow, Pharoah Sanders, Lew Tabackin (*ts*); Charles Davis (*bs*); Carla Bley, Cecil Taylor (*p*); Kent Carter, Ron Carter, Bob Cunningham, Richard Davis, Eddie Gomez, Charlie Haden, Reggie Johnson, Alan Silva, Steve Swallow, Reggie Workman (*b*); Andrew Cyrille, Beaver Harris (*d*). 1/68, 5/68, 6/68.

The JCO was formed to give improvising musicians an opportunity to play extended structures in larger formations than were normally considered either economic or artistically viable. Its best-known product is still the massive opera – or 'chronotransduction' – *Escalator Over The Hill* remembered with affection by crossword puzzlers, proto-*Twin Peaks* fans and the odd adventurous rocker, but, alas, not in the current catalogue.

Communications is, if anything, a more ambitious work. It consists of four enormous slabs of orchestrated sound and a brief 'Preview' (which comes fourth of five), each with a featured soloist. Or, in the case of the opening 'Communications No. 8', two soloists: Don Cherry and Gato Barbieri. Mantler's scoring is interesting in itself. Cherry's squeaky cornet is the only high-pitched brass instrument; the sections are weighted towards french horns and trombones, with flugelhorn accents generally located in the middle register and the higher-pitched parts assigned to soprano saxophones. In addition, Mantler scores for five double-basses on each track (perm from the list above), which gives each piece a complex tonal rootedness for the soloists' (mostly) unrestrained excursions.

Restraining Gato Barbieri would be pointless. He tends to begin a solo where most saxophonists climax. It's redundant to say he sounds strained on 'Communications No. 8' but, tone apart, he seems to be straining for ideas. By contrast, Pharoah Sanders has to squeeze everything into a brief three and a half minutes on 'Preview' and nearly achieves meltdown in the process.

On 'Communications No. 9' Larry Coryell is used as a sound-effects department. If Barbieri seems slightly short of ideas, Coryell is a *tabula rasa*. Fortunately, the best is still to come. Roswell Rudd's playing on the longer 'No. 10' is some of the best he has committed to record; Steve Swallow's bass introduction establishes its parameters with great exactness, and again the dark scoring works superbly.

The final, two-part section fully justifies Cecil Taylor's top billing. His solo part is full of huge, keyboard-long runs and pounded chords and arpeggios that leave Andrew Cyrille sounding winded and concussed. Very much of its time, and betraying occasional signs of a dialogue of the deaf, *Communications* is still a vitally important historical document. However demanding its headlong progress may be on the intellect and the emotions, Mantler – like

Barry Guy, who followed his example in the United Kingdom – has a considerable musical intelligence and shapes performances that have logic, form and a sort of chastening beauty.

JAZZ GROUP ARKHANGELSK
GROUP

***(*)   **Pilgrims** Leo LR 412/413 2LP
Vladimir Rezitsky (*as, f, vargan, hca, v*); Vladimir Turov (*p, ky*); Nikolai Klishin (*b, vn*); Oleg Yudanov (*d, f*); Nikolai Yudanov (*perc*).

On the downside of the 'liberation' of Eastern Europe and Russia is a dramatic change in the status of creative artists in the former people's democracies. The Jazz Group Arkhangelsk is a perfect instance of a creatively adventurous ensemble that won official sanction, playing regular 'workers' concerts' in and around the northern port of Arkhangel. Typical of Russian new music – see entries on the Ganelin Trio and Sergey Kuryokhin – the JGA combined an accelerated historiography of jazz (the opening piece is called 'Arkhangelsk-Trad', complete with chunking banjo) and a welter of native and imported popular musics. Singer Valentina Ponomareva is of gypsy origin and sings in a curious blend of styles that is almost incantatory and usually unsettling; she can also be heard elsewhere in the Leo catalogue. Leader Rezitsky on the other hand is a deceptively smooth player, sounding almost as if he is still doing the restaurant gigs that supported the band until they received state backing. The overall blend is headlong, buoyant and joyous, even in the rather more abstract bell and percussion section that opens a two-side live performance from October 1985. A bit different.

JAZZ INC.
GROUP

***   **Live At Fasching** Caprice CAP 1217 LP
Bertil Lövgren (*t*); Krister Andersson (*ss, as, ts, cl*); Nisse Sandström (*ts*); Lars Sjösten (*p*); Sture Nordin (*b*); Egil Johansen (*d*). 2/80.

***   **Be-Bop Is Beautiful** Dragon DRLP 37 LP
As above. 10/81.

A conclave of veteran Swedish boppers delivering 'expressionistic, romantic bebop' on two live sessions. While none of these players is perhaps quite strong enough to challenge the very finest of hard bop standards, the two dates create a meaty, satisfying stack of improvisations on material that stretches from crafted originals (Sjösten's 'The Day The Stranger Felt At Home' on *Be-Bop Is Beautiful*) to personalized bop standards. As with so much European post-bop, there's a repertorial feel which the musicians can't entirely evade, but their arrangements – as in the two-tenor version of 'In A Sentimental Mood' on the Caprice disc, or in Lövgren's chart for 'Lazy Bird' on the Dragon set – make the most of their distance from American procedures, and in Sandström at least they have a stylist who can stand apart. The other horns are less individual, but there's nothing here that lacks entertainment. Both sessions have good location recording.

ALAIN JEAN-MARIE
PIANO

(*)   **Latin Alley IDA 015 CD/LP
Jean-Marie; Niels-Henning Ørsted-Pedersen (*b*). 87.

Jean-Marie has an attractive touch, and is well recorded on this occasion; but, while some of the pieces have a certain authority – mostly the standard repertoire of 'Nica's Dream', 'Barbados' and 'Old Folks' – his original tunes have a curiously naïve quality. 'On Ti Berceuse', for instance, makes no attempt to go beyond its simple strain, even if it is rather boisterous for a lullaby. It might have been a more distinctive record if he'd chosen an all-original programme. Pedersen is his usual massive-sounding self.

EDDIE JEFFERSON (1918–79)
VOCALS

***   **Letter From Home** Original Jazz Classics OJC 307 CD/LP/MC
Jefferson; Ernie Royal, Clark Terry (*t*); Jimmy Cleveland (*tb*); James Moody (*as, f*);
Johnny Griffin (*ts*); Arthur Clarke (*bs*); Junior Mance, Joe Zawinul (*p*); Barry
Galbraith (*b*); Louis Hayes, Osie Johnson, Sam Jones (*d*). 12/61.

***   **There I Go Again** Prestige P 24095 MC
Jefferson; as above, plus Dave Burns, Bill Hardman, Joe Newman (*t*); Jimmy
Cleveland, Bill Shepherd (*tb*); Charles McPherson (*as*); James Moody (*as, ts, f*);
Seldon Powell (*ts*); Numa Moore (*bs*); Sadik Hakim, Barry Harris, Wynton Kelly, Ed
Swanston (*p*); Steve Davis, Sam Jones, John Latham, Peck Morrison, Gene Taylor
(*b*); Bill English, Clarence Johnston, Herbie Lovelle (*d*); Pablo Sanchez, Irv Taylor
(*v*). 2/53, 1/54, 1/55, 8/55, 12/61, 1/62, 2/62, 9/68, 8/69.

***(*)   **Body And Soul** Original Jazz Classics OJC 396 CD/LP/MC
Jefferson; Dave Burns (*t*); James Moody (*ts, f*); Barry Harris (*p*); Steve Davis (*b*); Bill
English (*d*). 9/68.

***(*)   **Come Along With Me** Original Jazz Classics OJC 613 CD/LP/MC
Jefferson; Bill Hardman (*t*); Charles McPherson (*as*); Barry Harris (*p*); Gene Taylor
(*b*); Bill English (*d*). 8/69.

A death sentence is a pretty harsh review, as Ralph Ellison wrote of Salman Rushdie. In 1979,
the sixty-year-old Jefferson was shot dead outside the Detroit club in which he'd been
appearing. Like most of the bebop vocalists – and despite a brief recent revival in the critical
fortunes of King Pleasure, who successfully co-opted Jefferson's style – he is little known among
younger jazz fans. There is though a widespread belief that Pleasure wrote the lyrics to
'Moody's Mood For Love', a vocalized transcription of James Moody's alto saxophone solo on
'I'm In The Mood For Love'; Pleasure certainly made it a monster hit, but the song was
Jefferson's. Perhaps his best track, an intelligent and inventive 'Body And Soul' (later revived
by Manhattan Transfer as a tribute to Jefferson), is revived on the fine 1968 session, which also
features Moody and a brilliant version of 'Filthy McNasty'.

There I Go Again, now apparently available only on cassette, incorporates some of the same
material as *Letter From Home* and incorporates an earlier *Body And Soul* album [Prestige P
7619]. *Letter* boasts a heavyweight line-up and some sure-footed – Jefferson was also a dancer –
vocal arrangements. Four of the tracks are for sextet, but the better pieces use the full breadth
of the band, with Jefferson high-wiring it over the 29-year-old Joe Zawinul's spry comping;
check out Jefferson's version of the pianist's 'Mercy, Mercy, Mercy' on the 1968 *Body And
Soul*. The singer's longest-standing partnership with saxophonist Moody is reflected in a dozen
cuts, one of the best of which is a lively 'So What' (again on *Body And Soul*). Their
relationship had rekindled in the 1960s, when Jefferson, who had been eclipsed by smoother
talents like Jon Hendricks, staged something of a comeback; the later sessions (*Come Along
With Me*) with Bill Hardman and Charles McPherson on staples like 'Yardbird Suite' and
'Dexter Digs In' are well worth catching, though the voice has lost some of its elasticity and
bounce. Like King Pleasure, Jefferson improvised and wrote lyrics to some of the classic bop
solos; precisely because they worked such similar turf, there was a constant risk of copyright
wrangles, which explains why 'Body And Soul' is sometimes retitled 'I Feel So Good' and
'Parker's Mood' 'Bless My Soul'. Not to everyone's taste, but vocal jazz of Jefferson's sort is a
significant and currently neglected aspect of jazz history that needs to be taken account of in any
comprehensive collection.

BILLY JENKINS (born 1954)
GUITAR, PIANO, VOICE

(*)   **Piano Sketches: 1973–84 Wood Wharf WWR 841 LP
Jenkins (*p* solo). 73–84.

***(*)   **In The Nude: Standards Volume 1** VOTP VOCA 904 MC
Jenkins (*g* solo). 88.

***(*)   **In The Nude** West Wind WW 010 CD
        As above.

Billy Jenkins is a musical anarchist. Notably resistant to ideology, he espouses a version of the kitchen-sink Situationism which lay behind the British punk movement. If music has become business (an equation he rejects), then the only refuge is a kind of unselfconscious anti-technique Jenkins has christened 'Spazz', which encourages the retention of 'wrong' notes and false starts, and the propagation of lo-fi recordings on the least sophisticated of formats.

Jenkins is uniquely concerned with the packaging of music, not just in the cardboard-and-laminate sense, but in terms of its perceived contours and limits. The 'Big Fights' sequence, below, restricts duo improvisation to 12 three-minute 'rounds' (a predetermination that represents the antithesis of the open-ended approach of most 'free' improvisers, but which also levels pertinent comment at their tacit belief that sheer duration is an end in itself). More satirically, Jenkins has mimicked the ubiquitous 'Nice Price' cover to Miles Davis's *Sketches Of Spain* on his unfortunately deleted group record, *Scratches Of Spain*. The furious *Motorway At Night*, below, is labelled 'real New Age music' and made to resemble an album by the New Age label, Windham Hill, while the disc label (DCM) is made to resemble that of the hi-tech German label, ECM. The reissued *Uncommerciality* sampler tapes are made to resemble bars and boxes of Cadbury's chocolate, a rather more obvious comment on music's consumable nature.

Jenkins calls his own compilation of *Piano Sketches* 'the result of musical suppression', a response to certain assumptions about 'professionalism' and marketability. The themes are simple, unoblique, stripped of irony. Technique is stripped even further on *In The Nude*, a collection of standards (plus some of his own material) played according to orthodox 'Spazz' principles. Jenkins 'sings' the opening line of 'Food, Glorious Food' as he launches into one of the most enshrined of all jazz standards, 'On Green Dolphin Street'. The effect is unsettling, but also quite logical. This material has also been released as a CD on the German label, West Wind; good sound, but somehow Jenkins doesn't seem to lend himself to digital output.

***   **Beyond E Major** Allmusic ALMS 1 LP
        Jenkins; John Eacott (*t*); John Harbone (*tb*); Steve Buckley (*ts*); Steve Berry (*b*); Roy Dodds (*d*).

Cast in 'Rockschool' format in four generic chunks – 'Country And Western', 'The Blues', 'Heavy Metal', 'Rock And Roll' – the performances treat genres as if they were 'standards' in themselves, bases for improvisation. To call the results unpredictable is to miss the point somewhat.

***(*)   **Sounds Like Bromley** Plymouth Sounds LBB1 LP
        Jenkins; Simon Etchell (*t*); Dave Jago (*tb*); Ian Trimmer (*ts*); Neill MacColl (*g*); Tim Matthewman (*b*); Roy Dodds, Dawson (*d*). 82.

****   **Greenwich** Wood Wharf WWR 852 LP
        Jenkins; Skid Solo (*t*); Dave Jago (*tb*); Dai Pritchard (*as, bs, bcl*); Iain Ballamy (*as, ts*); Steve Berry (*b, clo*); Roy Dodds (*d*); Dawson (*perc*); Andy McFarlane (*vn*); Patrick White (*vla*). 85.

***(*)   **Motorway At Night** De Core Music DCM 108 LP
        Jenkins; Dai Pritchard (*t, bs, cl*); Chris Batchelor (*slide t*); Dave Jago (*tb, t*); Frank Mead (*as*); Iain Ballamy (*as, ts*); Mark Lockheart, Andy Sheppard (*ts*); Django Bates (*ky, thn*); Neill MacColl, Nick Page (*g*); Simon Edwards (*b*); Steve Berry (*clo*); Steve Arguëlles, Roy Dodds (*d*); Andy McFarlane (*vn*); Patrick White (*vla*). 88.

Jenkins as tone-poet. The aural imagery on *Greenwich* is magnificent, asthmatic bass clarinet on 'Dreadnought Seamen's Hospital', yammering confusion on 'Greenwich One-Way System', irritant ensembles on 'Arrival Of The Tourists' and 'Discoboats At Two O'Clock', two good examples of social realism in jazz. Jenkins's tribute to Bromley, 'a place straining to be mediocre' (but also H. G. Wells's birthplace) is futurist-populist in equal proportions, full of nearly whistleable tunes and sudden eruptions into 'free jazz'. The 'real New Age' sounds of *Motorway At Night* throb to a decidedly unrelaxing metronome setting and chaotic instrumental mixes. Jenkins's Voice of God Collective draws on the work of his earlier Burlesque band (which included Ian Trimmer) and on its successor, Trimmer & Jenkins; *Motorway At Night* also draws on the laddish jazz big band, Loose Tubes, who rehearsed at Wood Wharf Studios,

Greenwich, centre of Jenkins's operations. All questions about the guitarist's 'seriousness' (in the sense of viability) as a musician are settled by *Greenwich*, which remains one of the most distinctive British albums of the 1980s.

The others require a pinch of salt, which will usefully disrecommend them to anyone with high blood pressure and on a low sodium regimen.

***   **Round Midnight Cowboy** VOTP VOCA 905 MC
Jenkins; Dai Pritchard (*cl, bcl, t*). 6/88.

***(*)   **Blue Moon In A Function Room** VOTP VOCA 906 MC
Jenkins; Stuart Hall (*g, vn*); Steve Watts (*b*); Steve Arguëlles (*d*). 5/90.

Billed as 'Standards: Volumes 2 & 3', these extend *In The Nude*'s generous interpretation of what consititutes a standard. Jenkins opuses like 'Sade's Lips' and 'Dreadnought Seamen's Hospital' jostle 'Lullaby Of Birdland' and 'Stranger On The Shore' on *Round Midnight Cowboy*, while *Blue Moon* (a fair representation of what Jenkins can do at your wedding, 21st, bar mitzvah) includes the only known jazz reading of the theme from *Vision On*, a TV programme for deaf children.

****   **Uncommerciality: Volume 1** VOTP VOCA 912 MC
Jenkins; Iain Ballamy (*as, ts*); Dai Pritchard (*as, bs, bcl*); Tim Matthewman (*b*); Roy Dodds (*d*); Dawson (*perc*). 1 & 2/86.

***   **Uncommerciality: Volume 2** VOTP VOCA 913 MC
Jenkins; Chris Batchelor (*t*); Mark Lockheart (*ts*); Iain Ballamy (*ss, as, ts*); Dai Pritchard (*cl, bcl, as, t*); Ashley Slater (*tba, btb, perc*); Django Bates (*org*); Steve Berry (*b, clo*); Charlie Hart (*b, acc, vn*); Roy Dodds (*d*); Martin France (*perc*); VOGC Junior League Vocal Chorus. 6–8/88.

***   **Wiesen '87** VOTP VOCA 901 MC
Jenkins; Dave Jago (*tb*); Ashley Slater (*btb, tba, v*); Mark Lockheart (*ts*); Dai Pritchard (*as*); Steve Berry (*b*); Roy Dodds (*d*); Dawson (*perc*). 7/87.

***(*)   **Jazz Café Concerts: Volume 1** VOTP VOCA 902 MC

***(*)   **Jazz Café Concerts: Volume 2** VOTP VOCA 903 MC
Jenkins; Iain Ballamy (*as, ts*); Steve Watts (*b*); Roy Dodds (*d*). 7, 10, 11 & 12/89.

The Voice of God Collective live in Austria and Camden Town, and aren't the acoustics better in N 16. *Wiesen '87* is pretty much a predictable selection of Jenkins's most grating hits – 'Exodus From Bromley', 'Donkey Droppings', the warcry 'Brilliant', 'Parking Meters', 'Discoboats At Two O'Clock' – ropily recorded off the p.a. and determinedly unsweetened thereafter. Tunes and performances are better on the Jazz Café sessions (product of a regular gig there), with 'Sade's Lips', 'Greenwich One-Way System' and 'Rock And Roll' on *Volume 1*, 'Spastics Dancing', 'Fat People' from *Bromley*, 'Motorway At Night', more evidence of incontinent donkeys, and an indifferent 'Country And Western' all on *Volume 2*. The sound is a bit sweeter and, though he might not think that was the point, it does recommend the two home-grown sets.

LEROY JENKINS (born 1932)
VIOLIN, VIOLA

***   **Space Minds, New Worlds, Survival America** Tomato 2696512 CD
Jenkins; George Lewis (*tb*); Anthony Davis (*p*); Andrew Cyrille (*d*). 8 & 9/78.

***   **Mixed Quintet** Black Saint 0060 LP
Jenkins; John Clark (*frhn*); James Newton (*f*); J. D. Parran (*cl*); Marty Ehrlich (*b cl*). 3/79.

(*)   **Urban Blues Black Saint 0083 LP
Jenkins; Terry Jenoure (*vn, v*); James Emery, Brandon Ross (*g*); Alonzo Gardner (*b*); Kamal Sabir (*d*). 1/84.

Leroy Jenkins and George Lewis share one often-forgotten characteristic that makes them ideal improvising partners. Though both are given to very forceful and even violent gestures, they are also capable of great lyricism; the same has to be said of Andrew Cyrille. In a period where Billy Bang is, rightly or wrongly, the benchmark jazz violinist, critics have often missed the fact that Jenkins's percussive, rasping delivery rarely departs from an identifiable tonal centre or melodic logic. His preference is for looping statements, punctuated with abrupt rhythmic snaps; the most obvious influence is Stuff Smith, but there are also parallels with the way saxophonist Anthony Braxton used to deliver improvised lines. Like pianist Anthony Davis, Jenkins has an almost 'legitimate' technique and a tone that one can imagine negotiating with Bartók or Stravinsky.

Space Minds is still reminiscent of Jenkins's AACM-influenced Revolutionary Ensemble. It has the intensity – one might almost say moral intensity – of the RE's powerful but long-deleted ESP recording *Vietnam*. Davis and Cyrille act as a twin centre of gravity to which the others make repeated reference. To that extent Jenkins is a traditionalist rather than a radical. His interests, though, reach well beyond jazz. The *Mixed Quintet* is a fascinating exploration of timbres and countervailing rhythmic possibilities; it is best seen on the long and off-puttingly titled 'Shapes, Textures, Rhythms, Moods', which isn't nearly as schematic as some of the briefer cuts on *Urban Blues*. Without a drummer or orthodox rhythm player, the band relies on cues distributed among the different voices. The results are well worth investigating, and the sound is rather better than on the badly balanced Tomato CD. Parran is one of the unsung heroes of contemporary jazz-meets-composition, a superb technician with a flawless tone.

Jenkins's working band Sting were capable of great things in a live setting, an impact not unlike that of Ornette Coleman's Prime Time. The instrumentation is strongly reminiscent – Ornette even scrapes a fiddle of his own – but Jenkins redeploys the harmonic and rhythmic emphases differently. Where Prime Time can be bludgeoningly illogical, Sting can sound, as here, perversely rational. *Urban Blues* is a less than representative account of a contemporary master.

BJORN JOHANSEN (born 1940)
TENOR SAX

***   **Dear Henrik** Gemini GMLP 52 LP
Johansen; Erling Aksdal (*p*); Carl Morten Iversen (*b*); Ole Jacob Hansen (*d*). 2–5/86.

***   **Take One** Odin 21 CD/LP/MC
Johansen; Cedar Walton (*p*); David Williams (*b*); Billy Higgins (*d*).

A Norwegian with much local experience but with little exposure overseas, Johansen is one of the many cases of European jazz musicians who ought to be better known outside their local base. His leathery tone and sometimes gnarled phrasing remind one of Clifford Jordan, and it's no surprise to find a tune on the Gemini album dedicated to the American saxophonist. Johansen works a furrow which is much like other post-bop – but, as conventional as it may be, the music never quite settles into cliché or routine. 'Beside', on *Dear Henrik*, opens as a ballad yet gathers power and momentum in a surprising way, with Aksdal proving a match for Walton on the 'American' session. Higgins gives an ounce or two of extra lift to the Odin record, but there is really little to choose between them, although the Gemini is recorded a little more modestly in terms of sonic punch.

AKE JOHANSSON
PIANO

***   **Live At Nefertiti** Dragon DRLP 42 LP
Johansson; Kjell Jansson (*b*); Göran Levin (*d*). 2/83.

***   **Born To Be Blue** Dragon DRLP 114 LP
As above, except Rune Carlsson (*d*) replaces Levin. 8/85.

***   **Encore** Dragon DRLP 159 LP
As above. 8/87.

This is a trio that produces a good result, whether working by themselves or with visiting horn players: they work splendidly behind Chet Baker, for instance, on the latter's *Live At Sweden* (Dragon DRLP 56). Johansson is a swinging and lyrical post-bop player with few pretensions to greatness but a clear-headed and generous approach to his group; his partnership with Carlsson, who shares the writing credits on all three albums listed above, is a fruitful one. On the serene slow waltz, 'Vals Till Goran', on *Born To Be Blue*, their empathy is strong enough to make a potentially gloomy piece into something translucent, and both men write melodies which have a way of returning to the mind. Levin and, subsequently, Carlsson are attentive, but the focus is on the piano–bass interplay. The two live records, *Nefertiti* and *Encore*, have an extra kick to them, and *Encore* has perhaps the best selection of originals.

BUDD JOHNSON (1910–84)
TENOR, SOPRANO AND ALTO SAX, CLARINET

***   **Blues A La Mode** Limelight 820602 CD
Johnson; Charlie Shavers (*t*); Vic Dickenson (*tb*); Al Sears (*bs*); Bert Keyes (*p, org*); Ray Bryant (*p*); Joe Benjamin (*b*); Jo Jones (*d*). 2/58.

***(*)   **Budd Johnson & The Four Brass Giants** Original Jazz Classics OJC 209 LP
Johnson; Nat Adderley (*c*); Harry Edison (*t*); Clark Terry (*t, flhn*); Ray Nance (*t, vn*); Tommy Flanagan, Jimmy Jones (*p*); Joe Benjamin (*b*); Herbie Lovelle (*d*). 8–9/60.

***(*)   **Let's Swing** Original Jazz Classics OJC 1720 LP
Johnson; Keg Johnson (*tb*); Tommy Flanagan (*p*); George Duvivier (*b*); Charles Persip (*d*). 12/60.

Budd Johnson was a jazz giant for over five decades, yet he made comparatively few recordings under his own leadership; some of the best of them – three tremendously swinging albums for Argo – are out of print. These OJC reissues at least restore two fine sessions to wider availability, even if they have yet to reach CD. Johnson was a veteran when he made these, having been an arranger for big bands throughout the 1930s and '40s, involving himself in many of the pioneering bebop gatherings and generally slotting comfortably into almost any setting. His tone was in the classic Hawkins mould – big, broad, soaked in blues feeling. 'Blues By Budd', on *Let's Swing*, is an inimitable example of Johnson at his best. There is a certain dry humour in his playing which never spills over into parody or flippancy: listen to the way he opens his solo on 'Uptown Manhattan' on the quintet album, and hear how he intensifies his playing from that point.

The two sessions with the larger groups offer a good opportunity to sample Johnson's writing, including a long tribute to Lester Young on OJC 209. The Limelight album, originally issued on Felsted, is split between septet tracks and a quintet session and, although Shavers's usual excesses won't be to all tastes, Johnson's own playing is impeccable. Perhaps the only disappointing thing about the meeting with the four trumpet masters is that it gives Johnson himself less room – he is such a mobile, authoritative soloist that one yearns to hear him in this period with just a rhythm section. His brother, Keg, on *Let's Swing*, plays some cheerful solos, but again it's Budd's record – try the lovely reading of 'Someone To Watch Over Me', where the saxophonist composed a unison passage for himself and Duvivier. All three sessions are in good and truthful sound.

***   **In Memory Of A Very Dear Friend** Dragon DRLP 94 LP
Johnson; Palle Thomsen (*p*); Roman Dylag (*b*); Rune Carlsson (*d*). 3/78.

Johnson spent much of the 1970s and '80s teaching, and the handful of fine records which he made with the JPJ Quartet have been deleted. This set was issued posthumously, hence the title, but was recorded in 1978 with a sympathetic rhythm section. Johnson's playing is inevitably less lithe than it had been in his prime, but there's still some fine and sometimes bristling work on 'Lester Leaps In' and 'I Want To Be Happy'. Respectful rather than challenging support from the rhythm section.

BUNK JOHNSON (1889–1949)

TRUMPET

***   **Bunk Johnson And His Superior Jazz Band** Good Time Jazz 12048 CD
Johnson; Jim Robinson (*tb*); George Lewis (*cl*); Walter Decou (*p*); Lawrence Marrero
(*bj*); Austin Young (*b*); Ernest Rogers (*d*). 6/42.

***   **Bunk And Lou** Good Time Jazz 12024 CD
Johnson; Lu Watters, Bob Scobey (*c*); Turk Murphy (*tb*); Ellis Horne (*cl*); Wally
Rose, Burt Bales (*p*); Clancy Hayes, Russ Bennett, Pat Patton (*bj*); Dick Lammi (*bb*);
Squire Gersback (*b*); Bill Dart (*d*). 2/44.

A difficult and contentious man, Bunk Johnson remains mysterious and fascinating, still the
figurehead of 'revivalist' jazz even though his records remain difficult to find and have been
marginalized where those by, say, George Lewis have kept their reputation. Deceitful about his
age – he was long thought to have been born in 1879, which would have made him even older
than Buddy Bolden – Johnson was rediscovered in 1942 and, after being fitted out with new
teeth, began making records. He had never recorded before, even though he'd played in
Bolden's band, had moved on from New Orleans sometime in the mid-teens and gone on to
play all over the South. But many records came out of the next five years. Those for Good
Time Jazz were among the earliest. *Bunk Johnson And His Superior Jazz Band* establishes the
best-remembered Johnson line-up, with fellow veterans Robinson, Lewis and Marrero, and the
material is a mostly New Orleans staples such as 'Down By The Riverside'. *Bunk And Lou* pits
him against the Lu Watters band, who mix 'modern' items such as 'Ory's Creole Trombone'
with a number of truly ancient ragtime pieces like 'Smokey Mokes', although frustatingly
Johnson only plays on the more recent material. While neither is a really satisfactory record –
Watters and company sound too slickly amateur to suit an original like Johnson, and the other
record lacks the awareness which Johnson would quickly develop – both establish the tenets of
his own trumpet style: a polished, almost courtly sort of phrasing, the elimination of 'hot' tricks
such as growls or shakes or needless vibrato, a bright and optimistic open tone and a way of
swinging which sounds like a development out of ragtime and older brass traditions than jazz.
Something, perhaps, between swing and syncopation.

***   **Bunk Johnson In San Francisco** American Music AMCD-16 CD
Johnson; Mutt Carey (*t*); Jim Robinson, Kid Ory, Turk Murphy (*tb*); Wade Whaley,
Ellis Horne (*cl*); George Lewis (*cl*); Buster Wilson, Burt Bales, Bertha Gonsoulin (*p*);
Frank Pasley (*g*); Lawrence Marrero, Pat Patton (*bj*); Sidney Brown (*bb*); Ed
Garland, Squire Gersback (*b*); Everett Walsh, Clancy Hayes, Edgar Moseley (*d*).
9/43–1/44.

***   **The King Of The Blues** American Music AMCD-1 CD
Johnson; Jim Robinson (*tb*); George Lewis (*cl*); Lawrence Marrero (*bj*); Sidney 'Jim
Little' Brown (*b, bb*); Alcide 'Slow Drag' Pavageau (*b*); Baby Dodds (*d*). 44-45.

***   **Spicy Advice** GHB 101 LP
Johnson; Floyd O'Brien (*tb*); Wade Whaley (*cl*); Fred Washington (*p*); Frank Pasley
(*g*); Red Callender (*b*); Lee Young (*d*). 7/44.

***   **Bunk Johnson 1944** American Music AMCD-3 CD
Johnson; Jim Robinson (*tb*); George Lewis (*cl*); Sidney Brown (*bb*); Lawrence
Marrero (*bj*); Alcide 'Slow Drag' Pavageau (*b*); Baby Dodds (*d*). 44.

Johnson's American Music recordings, of which there are now three CD versions available, are
his most substantial legacy, but they were plagued by indifferent sound quality and various
incompatabilities with sidemen and material. Robinson and Lewis may have been New
Orleans's finest, but Johnson didn't seem to like them all that much, and he certainly plays
much better than Lewis on these sessions. Nevertheless, both *The King Of The Blues* and *1944*
feature much fine music, the first all on blues themes, the second a mix of the obvious
('Panama' and so forth) and tunes which show Johnson's weakness for popular novelties, such
as 'There's Yes Yes In Your Eyes'. It is mostly an ensemble music, leads being passed around
the front line, and small inflections making each performance unique to itself; but the sound and
the occasional raggedness, even amidst what is always a ragged music, ensures that one needs a
patient ear.

In many ways, the other two (less typical) discs are the more interesting. *In San Francisco* includes a This Is Jazz broadcast with an all-star band including, intriguingly, Johnson's trumpet contemporary Mutt Carey, and though Johnson sounds unhappy on 'Dipper Mouth Blues', it's absorbing music. Even better, though, are the six trumpet–piano duets with Bertha Gonsoulin. Nowhere else can one hear Johnson's silvery tone and proper phrasing so clearly. The 1944 date with a much younger band than Johnson was used to might seem unfeasible to New Orleans purists, but the fact is that the sound is some of the best Johnson was ever served with, the material seems to suit him very well – the title-track was an old pop tune of his own – and the easy roll of the rhythm section, abetted by Callender's knowing tuba parts, gives the music a swing which many of his other records miss.

There is much more Johnson yet to be made available on CD. Even if he can often seem like an unenlightened figure, whose example has possibly been regressive to many seeking a true way in New Orleans jazz, his own playing remains personal and oddly moving. Fifty years after his comeback turned on the revivalist tap, he's still worth listening to.

J. J. JOHNSON (born 1924)
TROMBONE

*****   **The Eminent Jay Jay Johnson: Volume 1** Blue Note B21Y 81505 CD

****   **The Eminent Jay Jay Johnson: Volume 2** Blue Note B21Y 81506 CD
Johnson; Clifford Brown (*t*); Hank Mobley (*ts*); Jimmy Heath (*ts, bs*); Wynton Kelly, John Lewis, Horace Silver (*p*); Paul Chambers, Percy Heath, Charles Mingus (*b*); Kenny Clarke (*d*); Sabu Martinez (*perc*). 6/53, 9/54, 6/55.

***   **The Bebop Legends** Jazz Up JU 302 CD/LP
Johnson; Howard McGhee (*t*); Sonny Stitt (*as*); Walter Bishop (*p*); Tommy Potter (*b*); Kenny Clarke (*d*).

J. J. Johnson is one of the most important figures in modern jazz. Once voguish, the trombone, like the clarinet, largely fell from favour with younger players with the faster articulations of bebop. Johnson's unworthily low standing nowadays (his partnership with Kai Winding, as 'Jay and Kai' was once resonantly popular) is largely due to a perceived absence of trombone players with whom to compare him. In fact, Johnson turned an occasionally unwieldy instrument into an agile and pure-toned bop voice; so good was his articulation that single-note runs in the higher register often sounded like trumpet. He frequently hung an old beret over the bell of his horn to soften his tone and bring it into line with the sound of the saxophones around him. He sounds softly muted on a couple of tracks on *Bebop Legends*, a useful but poorly transferred set that he shares with the classic Monk quartet.

The first volume of the Blue Note set is one of the central documents of post-war jazz and should on no account be missed. Johnson – who was working as a blueprint checker at the time of the earliest sessions recorded, apparently dissatisfied with his output to date – sounds fleet and confident, and has a marvellous band round him, including a young Clifford Brown. 'Turnpike' and 'Capri' exist in two versions each and show Johnson's ability to rethink his phraseology, adjusting his attack on the original release versions to accommodate Clarke's powerful but unemphatic swing (which is rather swamped on the sessions of September 1954 by Mingus's chiming bass and the slap-happy Martinez); even on the slow-tempo 'Turnpike', Clarke provides an irresistible moving force underneath the melody. 'Get Happy' is appropriately up-beat and joyous, with notes picked off like clay pipes at a shooting stall. In contrast, 'Lover Man' is given a mournful, drawn-out statement that squeezes out every drop of emotion the melody has to offer. The 1954 session yields some fine exchanges between Johnson and Kelly, notably on 'It's You Or No One' and 'Too Marvellous For Words', where the leader's tone and attack are almost as perfect as on 'Turnpike'. Volume 2 is filled out with a less than inspiring 1955 date featuring Hank Mobley and Horace Silver, neither of whom seem attuned to Johnson's taxing idiom.

***   **Four Trombones: The Debut Recordings** Prestige P 24097 CD
Johnson; Willie Dennis, Bennie Green, Kai Winding (*tb*); John Lewis (*p*); Charles Mingus (*b*); Arthur Taylor (*d*).

Originally recorded for the short-lived independent label co-run by Mingus and Max Roach, this suffers slightly from its own ungainly format, which buries Johnson a little. There are, though, fine and fresh performances all round, including a stirring acount of 'Now's The Time'. Mingus takes charge more than once. The sound is a shade too bright on the transfer and the top notes are inclined to be a bit vinegary. All but Dennis can also be heard on the vinyl-only *Trombone By Three* (Original Jazz Classics OJC 091), which includes fine 1949 material from Johnson in the company of Kenny Dorham and Sonny Rollins, and on *Early Bones* (Prestige P 24067 LP).

***(*)   **The Birdlanders** Fresh Sound FSRCD 170 CD
Johnson; Jerry Lloyd (*t*); Al Cohn (*ts*); Gigi Gryce (*bs*); Milt Jackson (*vib, p*); Henri Renaud (*p*); Percy Heath, Curley Russell (*b*); Walter Bolden, Charlie Smith (*d*). 2 & 3/54.

***(*)   **Live At The Café Bohemia** Fresh Sound FSRCD 143 CD
Johnson; Bobby Jaspar (*ts, f*); Tommy Flanagan (*p*); Wilbur Little (*b*); Elvin Jones (*d*). 2/57.

Among the best of the surviving albums, both are beautifully transferred to CD, avoiding the awkward chiming effect that plagues much trombone of the period, particularly on live recordings. The first is very nearly hi-jacked by the vibraharpist, whose soloing on another supposedly cumbersome instrument is dazzlingly self-confident. Cohn is actually rather muted and the later sessions with Gryce and trumpeter Jerry Lloyd aren't up to standard. Despite Jaspar's shortcomings as a soloist (he's still a block ahead of Henri Renaud), and a degree of unease in the ensembles, the Café Bohemia sessions provide an ideal blowing context for Johnson; he lets go joyously on 'Angel Eyes', 'Old Devil Moon' (see also *Eminent*, Volume 1) and, a favourite, 'Solar'. Flanagan's chording and fills are as near perfect as they could be. A constant delight.

***(*)   **The Trombone Master** Columbia 44443 CD/MC
Johnson; Nat Adderley (*c*); Victor Feldman (*p, vib*); Tommy Flanagan (*p*); Paul Chambers, Sam Jones, Wilbur Little (*b*); Louis Hayes, Albert Heath, Max Roach (*d*). 4 & 5/57, 2/58, 12/60.

A marvellous compilation with the accent on ballads and easy-swinging numbers. It's interesting to compare Johnson's approach to Monk's 'misterioso', the opening cut, with the version he recorded with Sonny Rollins on the saxophonist's eponymous 1957 Blue Note. It's smoother, but also more sophisticated rhythmically, with that wonderful french horn sound. On 'Laura', Johnson sticks to a slightly faster than usual tempo and builds a solo of near perfect melodic invention. The long 'Blue Trombone' is gutsier and closer to an orthodox blowing theme, but 'My Old Flame' and 'Cry Me A River' stay very close to the basic song-form, and the closing 'Goodbye' is a small masterpiece of compression.

Perhaps a little too laid back to be completely representative of Johnson's skills, but a valuable introduction to his gentler side.

***(*)   **Say When** Bluebird ND 86277 CD
Johnson; Bert Collins, Art Farmer, Thad Jones, Jimmy Maxwell, Ernie Royal, Danny Stiles, Clark Terry, Joe Wilder, Eugene Young (*t*); Jimmy Cleveland, Paul Faulise, Tommy Mitchell, Benny Powell, Tony Studd (*tb*); Ray Alonge, Jim Buffington (*frhn*); Bill Stanley (*tba*); Ray Beckenstein, Phil Bodner, Jerry Dodgion, Harvey Estrin, Budd Johnson, Oliver Nelson, Jerome Richardson, Tommy Newsom, Frank Wess (*reeds*); Hank Jones (*p*); Ron Carter, Bob Cranshaw (*b*); Grady Tate (*d*); Bobby Rosengarten (*perc*). 12/64, 11 & 12/66.

Johnson's pre-eminence as an instrumentalist has tended to eclipse his skills as a composer and arranger. These sessions are highly imaginative and often very subtle, with a sophisticated and very exciting arrangement of George Russell's 'Stratusphunk' and one of the best ever recordings of Miles Davis's much over-used 'So What'. Oliver Nelson arranged his own fine 'Stolen Moments', but for the most part the charts are all by Johnson and are marked by sophisticated brass voicings and some fine solos. Very warmly recommended.

***(*)   **We'll Be Together Again** Pablo 2310911 CD/LP
Johnson; Joe Pass (*g*). 10/83.

***   **Things Are Getting Better All The Time** Pablo Today 2312141 CD
Johnson; Al Grey (*tb*); Kenny Barron (*p, ky*); Ray Brown (*b*); Mickey Roker (*d*).
11/83.

Johnson kept out of sight for most of the 1970s, composing and arranging for the movies and television. Within five weeks in 1983, however, he made two sterling albums that belied the full-stop some critics had put after his name. The sanguinely titled *Things* looks suspiciously like another attempt to reduplicate the Jay and Kai sound, but it comes across much more individually. Grey, a year younger than Johnson, is a more traditional stylist; a genius with the plunger mute, he has a big, belting tone that goes well with Johnson's increasingly delicate fills and recapitulations. 'Soft Winds', 'Paper Moon' and 'Softly As In A Morning Sunrise' are particularly good. Pianist Barron is contained and exact, but Brown and Roker are uncharacteristically listless, perhaps recognizing that the two principals (who shared the billing) play to their own inner metre. Good stuff.

Like Johnson, Joe Pass represents an extraordinary cross-section of modern jazz idiom, all carefully assimilated and absorbed. His constant lower-string pulse makes him particularly adaptable to solo and duo performance, and *Together Again* has the fullness of texture that might be expected of a larger group. The performances – 'Nature Boy', 'Bud's Blues', 'Solar', 'When Lights Are Low', six others – have a fresh-minted sparkle and immediate currency. Strongly recommended.

JAMES P. JOHNSON (1894–1955)
PIANO, COMPOSER

****   **Snowy Morning Blues** MCA/GRP 16042 CD
Johnson (*p* solo) and with Eddie Dougherty (*d*). 30, 44.

Too little is known now about James P. Johnson's orchestral music (of which much has been lost) to make any settled judgement about his significance as a 'straight' composer. Ironically, though, his enormous importance as a synthesizer of many strands of black music – ragtime, blues, popular and sacred song – with his own stride style has been rather eclipsed by the tendency to see him first and only as Fats Waller's teacher.

Johnson was in almost every respect a better musician than Waller, and perhaps the main reason for his relative invisibility has been the dearth of reliable recorded material. There is a fine solo 'Arkansas Blues' on the Jazzline *Esquire Concerts* compilation (JL 95810-14 5LP/CD), but there wasn't much else until GRP's release of these excellent American Decca sessions. Only the first four tracks come from 1930, but they include 'You've Got To Be Modernistic' and 'Jingles', which were originally released together as a Brunswick 78. Unfortunately, the version of the title 'Snowy Morning Blues', one of Johnson's most beautiful compositions, is a later one. Some of the 1944 cuts already betray signs of the ill-health that, as a series of mild but progressively debilitating cerebral haemorrhages, was to overtake Johnson later in the decade, finally incapacitating him in 1951.

The basic elements of the style are still in place, though. The subtly varied bass figures and forward motion of his sophisticated melodic variations place him closer to later jazz than to the increasingly basic syncopations and repetitions of ragtime. For that reason alone, and for his incorporation of jazz and blues tonalities, Johnson sounds much more 'modern' than many of his contemporaries, and a far more compelling musician than the overrated Waller.

These CD transfers are taken either from original metal masters, from safety copies (or, in the case of the four 1930 tracks, from shellac 78s) and remastered using the NoNoise system. Absolutely no complaints about the sound, though Dougherty's irritatingly under-recorded percussion does at faster tempi blur into a background crackle. It's worth looking out for *The Symphonic Jazz of James P. Johnson* [Musicmasters 20066 LP], with an intelligent liner note by Johnson scholar, Willa Rouder.

MARC JOHNSON
DOUBLE BASS, ELECTRIC BASS

***   **Bass Desires** ECM 1299 CD/LP
Johnson; Bill Frisell (*g, g synth*); John Scofield (*g*); Peter Erskine (*d*). 5/85.

**   **Second Sight** ECM 1351 CD/LP
As above. 3/87.

The original *Bass Desires* was a vibrantly exciting album which used Bill Frisell's disciplined surrealism in an imaginative textural counterpoint to Scofield's more logically organized play. 'Samurai Hee-Haw' and the remarkable arrangement of 'Black Is The Color Of My True Love's Hair' (compare 'straight' composer Luciano Berio's version in *Folk Songs*) were among the freshest sounds heard in 1985–6. The backgrounds are all big and stately, perhaps too much influenced by the prevailing (deny it as they may) house style at ECM. By contrast, *Second Sight* is less than visonary, swapping the bite and humour of the first album for a wishy-washy product, alternating saccharine high-note twiddles with a sort of apologetic deutero-rock that sounds disconcertingly like the way Sonny Sharrock might if he were put on probation.

PETE JOHNSON (1904–67)
PIANO

****   **Boogie Woogie Trio** Storyville SLP 4094 LP
Johnson; Albert Ammons, Meade Lux Lewis (*p*). 9–10/39.

****   **The Boogie Woogie Boys** Storyville SLP 229 LP
As above, except add Smokey Stover (*d*); Joe Turner (*v*). 2/39–1/53.

***   **Boogie Woogie Trio Vol. 3** Storyville SLP 4006 LP
As above, except add Sonny Rogers (*g*), Johnny Parker (*b*), Roy Milton (*d*) and omit Turner. 10/39–9/54.

Of the three great boogie-woogie pianists who recorded as The Boogie Woogie Trio, a kind of summit meeting of masters of that style, Pete Johnson was perhaps the least formidable as a soloist. Yet his contributions to the above recordings, which constitute some of the classic boogie sessions, are impressive. On SLP 4094 he creates three rather reflective solos in 'G Flat Blues', 'Pete's Blues' and 'Mama's Blues' and plays a fine duet with Ammons on 'St Louis Blues'. There are some more impressive duets with Ammons on the second record, as well as two driving blues with Joe Turner: 'Roll 'Em' and 'Goin' Away'. The third record is less good overall; but Johnson's 1947 session with a full rhythm section, though sometimes a little hackneyed, includes a gripping treatment of 'Yancey Special'. His Blue Note recordings are (unfortunately) currently out of print.

ELVIN JONES (born 1927)
DRUMS

***   **Elvin!** Original Jazz Classics OJC 259 LP
Jones; Thad Jones (*c*); Frank Wess (*f*); Frank Foster (*ts*); Hank Jones (*p*); Art Davis (*b*). 7 & 12/61, 1/62.

***(*)   **Live At The Village Vanguard** Enja 2036 CD
Jones; Hannibal Marvin Peterson (*t*); George Coleman (*ts*); Wilbur Little (*b*).

If one were to make a list of the dozen most influential jazz musicians in the period since 1945, Elvin Jones would *have* to be upsides with Miles Davis, Ornette Coleman and the drummer's former boss and mentor, John Coltrane. His whirlwind style and famous 'polyrhythmic' delivery (frequently name-checked but still not clearly understood) are of lasting significance and, if Coltrane lies across the history of saxophone playing like the Great Wall of China (as Keats said of Milton), then it's equally hard for drummers to avoid a confrontation with Elvin Jones.

Elvin! is noisy, heated hard bop with some good interplay between Jones and a naughty-boy front rank that won't stay in line. The trio tracks with Jones and Davis are particularly good, but the best of the album can be had on an above-average drummers' sampler, *The Big Beat* (Milestone M 47016 CD/2LP), which also includes Art Blakey, Max Roach and Philly Joe Jones (who's no blood kin, but a kind of artistic Dutch uncle to the Mr Jones under discussion).

Imagine the Coltrane Quartet as a (pianoless) trio, with the drummer playing 'chords' and counter-melodies behind the saxophone. That is approximately the effect of Jones's Village Vanguard sessions. At first blush George Coleman sounds unlikely to trouble John Coltrane's ghost, but he is a more sophisticated harmonic thinker than at first appears, let down only by a Brillo-pad tone. Much as in the 1960s when Jones and Coltrane seemed to be in astral communication to the virtual exclusion of Garrison or Workman and Tyner, the drums and saxophone leave little for bassist Little to do, and he contents himself with steady figuring and occasional keep-awake flurries. Hannibal Peterson gatecrashes on 'Mr Jones', taking the shine off another perfectly good trumpet. Good, enjoyable stuff all through.

*** **Poly-Currents** Blue Note B21Y 84331 CD/LP
Jones; Joe Farrell (*ts, enghn, f*); Fred Tomkins (*f*); George Coleman (*ts*); Pepper Adams (*bs*); Wilbur Little (*b*); Candido Camero (*perc*). 9/69.

Jones has always held the flute in particular affection and features it prominently in both the quartet and sextet settings represented here. Farrell is still a desperately underrated figure and his wind colours are well judged to Jones's busy arrangements. Coleman is again in good form, but the addition of a third saxophone on 'Agenda', 'Mr Jones' and 'Agape Love' rather overloads the sound on both formats. The quartets are better balanced and 'Yes', which features flautist Tomkins for a single track, is particularly well favoured. Musically good, but marked down on production values.

*(*) **Heavy Sounds** Impulse MCAD 33114 CD
Jones; Richard Davis (*b*); Frank Foster (*ts*); Billy Green (*p*). 68.

** **Reunited** Black Hawk BKH 521 CD/LP
Jones; McCoy Tyner (*p*); Jean-Paul Bourelly (*g*); Richard Davis (*b*). 4/82.

Put the piano back into the mix and . . . it doesn't really work. Tyner is such an adaptive musician that he can recentre his idiom many times over without strain, but on this one hears little more than one of the wobbles on the axle of the Coltrane Quartet, a slight but basic incompatibility of vision and timing. Bourelly seems extraneous and gets in the way of some of Davis's more inventive moves and progressions. 'Little Rock's Blues' is great; 'Sweet And Lovely' falls apart. A draw.

Heavy Sounds is a pretty horrible record. Billed as a Jones–Davis co-effort, it breaks down into a series of individual 'features' – like Davis's misconceived out-of-tempo breaks on the overlong opening 'Raunchy Rita' – stitched together with rather suspect ensemble play. Foster's compositions, 'Rita' and the classic 'Shiny Stockings', are actually rather good, and there's a good but unexploited number from pianist Greene. Jones's one composition credit is the dismal 'Elvin's Guitar Blues', on which he strums the opening choruses like a teenager with a teach-yourself book. 'Summertime' is left an unrecognizable corpse, but 'Here's That Rainy Day' is quite nice. Too late, though.

(*) **The Elvin Jones Jazz Machine In Europe Enja 7009 2 CD
Jones; Sonny Fortune (*ts, f*); Ravi Coltrane (*ts, ss*); Willie Pickens (*p*); Chip Jackson (*b*). 6/91.

Lest anyone get overexcited at the thought of Jones playing with a Coltrane again, it has to be said that Ravi, born only a year before his father's death, is not an altogether convincing chip off the block. His tone is painfully uncertain and his solos virtually devoid of ideas. Almost all the emphasis falls on Fortune, a wonderfully atmospheric player who doesn't worry overmuch about complex harmonic relationships; his flute introduction to 'Doll Of The Bride', a traditional Japanese tune arranged by Jones's wife, Keiko, is one of the best things on a thinly recorded album that clocks in at just over an hour and feels like twice that.

ETTA JONES (born 1928)
VOCAL

***(*) **Don't Go To Strangers** Original Jazz Classics OJC 298 LP/MC
Jones; Frank Wess (ts, f); Richard Wyands (p); Skeeter Best (g);
Roy Haynes (d). 6/60.

(*) **Something Nice Original Jazz Classics OJC 221 LP/MC
Jones; Lem Winchester (vib); Richard Wyands, Jimmy Neely (p); Ge⌐
Michael Mulia (b); Roy Haynes, Rudy Lawless (d). 9/60–3/61.

Jones began recording as a teenager in the 1940s, and by the time she came to r⌐ ⌐on't Go
To Strangers she was already a veteran. But the title song from the LP became a gold record,
and she subsequently made several albums for Prestige. In its modest way, the LP remains a
fine achievement, with Jones's heavy, blues-directed voice piling extra substance on to fluff such
as 'Yes Sir, That's My Baby', with rolling support from an excellent band. The subsequent
Something Nice is more quiescent, the eleven songs despatched matter-of-factly, although
Jones's regal delivery makes such as 'Through A Long And Sleepless Night' into sometimes
heady stuff. The usual good remastering from OJC.

*** **I'll Be Seeing You** Muse M 5351 CD/LP/MC
Jones; Houston Person (ts); George Devens (vib); Stan Hope (p); Milt Hinton (b);
Vernell Fournier (b); Ralph Dorsey (d). 9/87.

(*) **Sugar Muse M 5379 CD/LP/MC
Jones; Houston Person (ts); Horace Ott (ky); Stan Hope (p); Randy Johnson (g);
Wilbur Bascomb, Peter Martin Weiss (b); Cecil Brooks III, Bertel Knox (d); Ralph
Dorsey (perc); Della Griffin, Earl Coleman (v). 10/89.

(*) **Christmas With Etta Jones Muse M 5411 CD/LP/MC
Jones; Johnny Coles (flhn); Bill Easley (ts, f); Houston Person (ts); Horace Ott, Stan
Hope (p); Randy Johnson (g); Wilbur Bascomb, Peter Martin Weiss (b); Bertel Knox,
Cecil Brooks III (d); Sammy Figueroa (perc). 6/90.

Jones has been in considerable voice of late, and this fruitful sequence of albums is, taken a disc
at a time, very enjoyable. Person has become her keeper of the flame, producing and playing on
all these sessions with an authority that matches Etta's own singing, and while some of the
albums strain a bit to stay together, they're finished with wise authority. I'll be Seeing You is
probably the best for the magisterial treatment of 'Jim' and 'Etta's Blues', but Sugar is nice
enough, though the guest shots by Coleman and Griffin are decidedly hammy. The Christmas
album is about as friendly as these things can be, but it ends on an unspeakably dreary 'I'll Be
Home For Christmas', and tolerance will depend on how many seasonal greetings one is
prepared to receive over the course of a CD.

HANK JONES (born 1918)
PIANO

**** **Hank** All Art AAJ 11003 CD
Jones (p solo). 1/76.

*** **Tiptoe Tapdance** Galaxy 5108 LP
As above. 6/77 & 1/78.

The eldest of the three brothers, Hank Jones is as quiet and unassuming as drummer Elvin is
extrovert, but he shares something of the late Thad Jones's deceptive sophistication, often lost
in outsize arrangements or group settings. An early Savoy, Have You Met Hank Jones? is
currently out of catalogue but is worth pursuing. Never much of a composer, a fact often
adduced to downplay his significance, Jones is not given to wholesale reassessment of standard
progression, but concentrates very largely on the sound of a tune. Hank is certainly the place to
start; the songs are all very brief – and there are 14 of them squeezed into less than 45 minutes –
but it's worth listening closely to the way Jones colours every chord and fine-brushes his own
solo contributions. As a title Tiptoe Tapdance gives some impression of his delicacy and
balance, qualities that have enhanced and prolonged his reputation as a great accompanist, but

... a rather lightweight soloist. The album is full of gospel and hymn tunes, which ... ensitive and sometimes quite oblique interpretations. There are some inconsistencies ... ound, but nothing untoward. Though neither has the inventive fire of the Savoy, the 1970s ... ets are to be preferred for their almost magisterial calm and command.

(*)   **Jones–Brown–Smith** Concord CCD 4032 CD
       Jones; Ray Brown (b); Jimmie Smith (d).

***   **I Remember You** Black & Blue 233122 CD
       Jones; George Duvivier (b); Alan Dawson, Oliver Jackson (d). 7/77 & 7/78.

***(*)   **Bluesette** Black & Blue 233168 CD
       As above, except omit Jackson. 7/78 & 7/79.

****   **The Oracle** EmArCy 846376 IMS CD
       Jones; Dave Holland (b); Billy Higgins (b). 3 & 4/89.

Perhaps untypically of players of his type, the trio is not always Jones's 'natural' format. He often sounds better with a whisper of brass or flute. The Black & Blues have a soft and occasionally plangent quality which is highly appealing; Jones's inventiveness as a bluesman is much underrated. The Concord is nowhere as impressive, perhaps because the material is more mixed, but there are wonderful versions of 'Spring is Here' and 'Bag's Groove'.

Holland has worked comfortably with Jones for some time, with no sign that he finds the material too routine. Higgins, as always, is a wonder, pacy and lyrical. *The Oracle* is a small masterpiece, certainly Jones's most inventive and adventurous album for a great many years; they sound as well harmonized and individualized as a great vocal trio. 'Trane Connections' is certainly marked by Tommy Flanagan's approach to Coltrane and there is enough elsewhere – 'Blood Count', 'Maya's Dance', 'Beautiful Love' – to suggest that Jones has kept his ears pinned back for new wrinkles. Old pianists don't die; they just get better.

***(*)   **Quartet/Quintet** Savoy 0147 CD
       Jones; Donald Byrd, Matty Dice (t); Eddie Jones (b); Kenny Clarke (d). 11/55.

***   **Bluebird** Savoy 0138 CD
       As above; with Joe Wilder (t); Jerome Richardson (ts, f); Herbie Mann (f); Wendell Marshall (b). 8 & 11/55.

(*)   **Just For Fun Original Jazz Classics OJC 471 CD/LP
       Jones; Howard Roberts (g); Ray Brown (b); Shelly Manne (d). 6/77.

****   **Lazy Afternoon** Concord CCD 4391 CD/MC
       Jones; Ken Peplowski (as, cl); Dave Holland (b); Keith Copeland (d). 7/89.

Well transferred, the two Savoys represent an attractive investment in Jones's mid-1950s. *Quartet/Quintet* is marginally the better of the two. Working without a saxophone and using the two trumpets (mostly in thirds on unison themes) gives the band a bright, hard-edged sound that is enhanced by a faithful, hiss-free reproduction. A hint of echo in the acoustic adds some depth to spacious uncomplicated arrangements. The formula works best on the long 'An Evening At Papa Joe's', where the slow blues theme encourages Byrd to stretch out a bit, and introduces Dice for three good choruses. The young Newarkian has a slightly raucous tone that is an effective foil to Byrd's saxophone-influenced phrasing and roughens up the ensemble textures. 'Hank's Pranks' on *Bluebird* follows the same configuration but falls a little short.

Jones's interest in new and unusual textures is also evident on the deleted *Relaxin' At Camarillo*, and on *Bluebird* he again relies quite heavily on flute in preference to saxophone, using either Jerome Richardson or the 25-year-old Herbie Mann, whose articulation on the title-track is typically beautiful and a salutary reminder of what he was capable of before fusion settings overwhelmed his impeccable sound; the title piece is another extended form, but this time it palls as it approaches a rather inconsequential conclusion.

Just for Fun should probably have been left that way. Despite the presence of Manne (the players actually split into two – drummerless and guitarless respectively – trios) the results are consistently disappointing. Jones is too straightforward an executor to be able to rely on irony, and pieces like 'A Very Hip Rock and Roll Tune' and 'Kids Are Pretty People' fall flat on that account.

Lazy Afternoon is a peach: warm, vibrant jazz wit[...]
date. Jones is generous with solo space for his sideme[...]
Weill's 'Speak Low', a striking choice for openers, is [...]
Holland and Copeland had acted as the pianist's perfor[...]
quite properly, the bassist is strongly featured, with parti[...]
Johnson composition 'Lament' and the succeeding 'Comin' F[...]
a colourist is evident on the title-track, where a hint of [...]
Peplowski's smooth clarinet spices a slightly bland approach. War[...]

***(*) 'Bop Redux Muse MCD 5444 CD/MC
Jones; George Duvivier (*b*); Ben Riley (*d*). 1/77.

For Jones's first Muse recording, he deliberately restricted himself [...] and
Thelonious Monk compositions, a decision that still left him spoilt for ch[...] ch to
Monk is especially interesting, in that he tends to even out the jagged e[...] e original
themes and turn them into something altogether more polished and entire[...]onk's Mood',
treated rather briefly at the end, loses much of its lumpiness (and some of its blues tonality) and
sounds like a different piece. The Parker pieces are more faithful to the originals, and work
rather better in trio arrangements; the Monk material would almost all sound better as solo
performances. Recording quality is reasonably good for the mid-1970s.

***(*) Duo Timeless SJP 283 CD/LP
Jones; Red Mitchell (*b*). 12/87.

Two master craftsmen left to their own devices with a pile of music. Mitchell's singing tone
fulfils the same function as Holland's slightly more robust approach. Jones works around and
under the bassist's lines like the great accompanist he is. 'Wee' and 'I'll Remember April' are
almost consciously misremembered returns to bebop, freshly and inventively conceived. 'Like
Someone in Love' draws freely on Coltrane's reading. Gorgeous.

JO JONES (1911–85)
DRUMS

*** Jo Jones Trio Fresh Sounds FSR-CD 40 CD
Jones; Ray Bryant (*p*); Tommy Bryant (*b*). 3/59.

*** Jo Jones Sextet Fresh Sounds FSR-CD 144 CD
Jones; Harry Edison (*t*); Bennie Green (*tb*); Jimmy Forrest (*ts*); Tommy Flanagan (*p*);
Tommy Potter (*b*). 4/60.

The master drummer of the swing era became widely celebrated after he left Count Basie in
1948, but thereafter he seldom found the best contexts for his work, at least on record. There
were some splendid sessions for Vanguard in the 1950s, which have so far not been issued
domestically on CD. The two Fresh Sounds CDs are pleasant and relaxed, but somewhat
lacking in a pressing need to exist. The session with the Bryant brothers is a little masterclass in
trio playing – deft, swinging, loose and tight at once – but Jones's companions don't have a
great deal to offer beyond familiar turns of phrase. The sextet date is a rerun of the earlier
Vanguard sessions, and while the 12 tunes receive economical, good-natured treatments, the
music is formulaic mainstream.

OLIVER JONES (born 1934)
PIANO

**(*) The Many Moods Of Oliver Jones Justin Time JUST 3 CD/LP
Jones (*p* solo). 2–3/84.

** Lights Of Burgundy Justin Time JUST 6 CD/LP/MC
Jones; Fraser McPherson (*ts*); Reg Schwager (*g*); Michel Donato (*b*); Jim Hillman (*d*).
4/85.

**(*) Requestfully Yours Justin Time JUST 11 CD/LP/MC
Jones; Skip Beckwith (*b*); Anil Sharma (*d*). 11/85.

Hard Justin Time JUST 17 CD/LP
eckwith (b); Jim Hillman (d). 7–9/85.

n' At Sweet Basil Justin Time JUST 25 CD/LP
ones; Dave Young (b); Terry Clarke (d). 9/87.

(*)   **Just Friends** Justin Time JUST 31 CD/LP
Jones; Clark Terry (t); Dave Young (b); Nasyr Abdul Al-Khabyyr (d). 1/89.

**   **Northern Summit** Justin Time JUST 34 CD/LP
Jones; Herb Ellis (g); Red Mitchell (b). 6–9/90.

***   **A Class Act** Justin Time JUST 41 CD/LP
Jones; Steve Wallace (b); Ed Thigpen (d). 4–5/91.

Oliver Jones is destined to be always the second most famous piano export from Canada, after Oscar Peterson. His style is heavily indebted to Peterson's too, and his original tunes – such as 'Blues For Helene' (*Just Friends*) or 'Fulford Street Maul' (*Lights Of Burgundy*) – are exactly the kind of uptempo blues which Peterson himself writes. Jones is nevertheless a frequently engaging soloist, filling his records with good-hearted, swinging music. His ballads are glossy rather than introspective, but one listens to Jones for his generous virtuosity, not his tenderness. He worked away from any limelight as an accompanist until the 1980s, but since then he has recorded regularly for Justin Time.

Since his playing scarcely varies in intensity or prowess from record to record, preferred sessions are more a matter of the setting. The solo set is slightly less interesting since, like Peterson, Jones thrives on a propulsive rhythm section. Both *Speak Low Swing Hard* and the *Sweet Basil* concert set find everyone playing with huge enthusiasm, and the earlier of these sessions is distinguished by some interesting material, including Ferdie Grofé's 'On The Trail' and a reading of 'I'm An Old Cowhand' that sounds as if it was played on tiptoes. *Lights Of Burgundy* is let down by the unattractive studio-sound. Clark Terry sparks a few tracks on *Just Friends*, although he's not quite at his best; but the meeting with Mitchell and Ellis takes a ponderous course, with so much space allotted to each man that the music lacks Jones's usual ebullience. *A Class Act*, though, might be his best record to date, with two of his best originals in 'Mark My Time' and 'Peaceful Time', and a couple of mature embllishments on Kenny Wheeler's 'Everybody's Song But My Own' and Bill Evans's 'Very Early'. Thigpen and Wallace offer seamless support.

PHILLY JOE JONES (1923–85)
DRUMS

***   **Blues For Dracula** Original Jazz Classics OJC 230 CD/LP/MC
Jones; Nat Adderley (co); Julian Priester (tb); Johnny Griffin (ts); Tommy Flanagan (p); Jimmy Garrison (b). 9/58.

(*)   **Mo'Joe Black Lion BLCD 760154 CD
Jones; Les Condon, Kenny Wheeler (t); Chris Pyne (tb); Pete King (as); Harold McNair (ts, f); Mike Pyne (p); John Hart, Ron Mathewson (b). 10/68.

(*)   **Drum Song Galaxy GXY 5153 LP
Jones; Blue Mitchell (t); Slide Hampton (tb); Charles Bowen (ts, ss); Harold Land (ts); Cedar Walton (p); Marc Johnson (b). 10/78.

***   **Mean What You Say** Sonet SNT 735 CD/LP
Jones; Tommy Turrentine (t); Charles Bowen (ts, ss); Mickey Tucker (p); Mickey Bass (b).

The first three are neatly spaced with exactly a decade between them. *Blues for Dracula* was recorded towards the end of the drummer's main association with Miles Davis's touring band, a period in which he was much in demand musically, but also making absurd demands on himself by means of a well-developed habit. There are some signs of strain on a mainly good-natured blowing album, with Jones well up in the mix and his characteristic rimshots slightly overloud; 'Two Bass Hit', which inspired some of Philly Joe's best moments on Davis's *Milestones*, is particularly strong. The three horns were well chosen but sound ragged in some of the less frenetic ensembles. Parts of *Drum Song* come close to the energetic highs of the earlier album, but the most effective tracks are the two with either just Hampton ('I Waited For You') or Bowen (an excellent 'Hi-Fly' that matches his contribution to Cedar Walton's 'Ugetsu' on *Mean What You Say*) and rhythm. 'Dameronia' is a tribute – by a beautifully arranged septet – to the composer whose work Jones did so much to keep in an increasingly indifferent public eye in the early 1980s. The 'European' sessions sound altogether less certain, though Wheeler and King in particular produce an acceptable synthesis of their own slightly abstract idiom with Jones's whacking verve and oblique intelligence. The Sonet is a fine album with two excellent guest spots from the patchy Tommy Turrentine. Again, though, the sound isn't up to much. There was to be no 1988 record; Jones died three years earlier, more or less worn out.

None of the three can be said to be absolutely essential to a good modern· collection; nonetheless, Philly Joe was a significant presence for three decades, and his influence can be heard today in the likes of Andrew Cyrille.

*** **Showcase** Original Jazz Classics OJC 484 CD/LP/MC
Jones; Blue Mitchell (*t*); Julian Priester (*tb*); Bill Barron (*ts*); Pepper Adams (*bs*); Sonny Clark, Dolo Coker (*p*); Jimmy Garrison (*b*). 59.

*** **Drums Around The World** Original Jazz Classics OJC 1792 CD
Jones; Lee Morgan, Blue Mitchell (*t*); Curtis Fuller (*tb*); Cannonball Adderley (*as*); Benny Golson (*ts*); Herbie Mann (*f, picc*); Wynton Kelly (*p*); Jimmy Garrison, Sam Jones (*b*). 5/59.

Some of this material – 'Battery Blues' and 'Gone Gone Gone' from *Showcase*, 'Stablemates', 'El Tambores', and the solo percussion 'Tribal Message' from OJC 1792, which is subtitled *Big Band Sounds* – may be familiar from a good Milestone compilation of drummers' bands called *The Big Beat* (Milestone M 47016 CD/2LP). It's all good stuff, with imaginative horn arrangements and carefully disciplined solo stretches from the leader. 'Cherokee' on the latter album is a good example of how positively Jones responds to the challenge of overworked changes. Recording quality is still far short of what contemporary percussionists would expect as of right, but it's better than most.

SAM JONES (1924–81)
BASS, CELLO

*** **The Riverside Collection: Sam Jones – Right Down Front** Original Jazz Classics OJC 6008 CD/LP/MC
Jones; Blue Mitchell, Clark Terry, Snooky Young (*t*); Nat Adderley (*c*); Melba Liston, Jimmy Cleveland (*tb*); Cannonball Adderley, Frank Strozier (*as*); Jimmy Heath, Jimmy Smith (*ts*); Charles Davis, Tate Houston, Pat Patrick (*bs*); Bobby Timmons, Victor Feldman, Joe Zawinul, Wynton Kelly (*p*); Les Spann (*g, f*); Keter Betts, Ron Carter, Israel Crosby (*b*); Louis Hayes, Ben Riley, Vernell Fournier (*d*). 3/60–6/62.

Sam Jones had a beautiful sound on bass – fat, resonant, fluid without any loss of body – and he was among the first to make the cello sound plausible in post-bop jazz. This compilation is chosen from five sessions he made during his time with Cannonball Adderley and, although the settings are mostly rather ordinary – two tracks by a big band with Melba Liston charts are more challenging – Jones's quiet good humour gives as much buoyancy as his bass to the music. A quintet reading of 'Round Midnight' with Jones on cello is a little fluffy, and 'Some Kinda Mean' gives a better idea of his powers on that instrument.

** **Cello Again** Xanadu 129 LP
Jones; Charles McPherson (*as*); Barry Harris (*p*); David Williams (*b*); Billy Higgins (*d*). 1/76.

*** **Something In Common** Muse MR 5149 LP
Jones; Blue Mitchell (*t*); Slide Hampton (*tb*); Bob Berg (*ts*); Cedar Walton (*p*); Billy Higgins (*d*). 9/77.

(*) **Changes And Things Xanadu 150 LP
As above, except Louis Hayes (*d*) replaces Higgins. 9/77.

(*)   Visitation Steeplechase SCS 1097 CD/LP/MC
Jones; Terumasa Hino (*c*); Bob Berg (*ts*); Ronnie Mathews (*p*); Al Foster (*d*). 3/78.

Sam's few sessions as a leader in the 1970s found him pursuing a lyrical kind of hard bop. *Cello Again* is another example of jazz cello not really adding up to anything much, but the 1977 band is a grooving one. It's a pity that the horns are rather unremarkable – Mitchell sounds thin and past his best, Berg was as yet unfocused, and Hampton sounds the best of the three – but both rhythm sections swing effortlessly, and the treatment of Walton's 'Bolivia' on the Muse album is a modest classic. *Visitation* is, again, dependable rather than especially exciting, although Hino's peculiar mix of rhapsody and restlessness is as engaging as usual. The Steeplechase offers the best recording, too.

THAD JONES (1923–86)
TRUMPET, CORNET, FLUGELHORN, VALVE TROMBONE, BANDLEADER, ARRANGER

***   **Paris 1969** Royal RJD 519 CD
Jones; Mel Lewis (*d*); Danny Moore, Al Porcino, Richard Williams, Snooky Young (*t*); Eddie Bert, Ashley Fannell, Jimmy Knepper (*tb*); Cliff Heather (*btb*); Eddie Daniels, Jerry Dodgion, Joe Henderson, Jerome Richardson (*reeds*); Pepper Adams (*bs*); Roland Hanna (*p*); Richard Davis (*b*). 9/76.

***(*)   **Thad Jones / Mel Lewis** LRC CDC 9004 CD
Jones; Mel Lewis (*d, co-leader*); Danny Moore, Jimmy Nottingham, Al Porcino, Marvin Stamm, Richard Williams, Snooky Young (*t*); Eddie Bert, Jimmy Knepper, Benny Powell (*tb*); Cliff Heather (*btb*); Dick Berg, Jimmy Buffington, Earl Chapin, Julius Watkins (*frhn*); Howard Johnson (*tba*); Jerome Richardson (*cl, as, ss, picc*); Jerry Dodgion (*as, f*); Eddie Daniels (*ts, f*); Joe Farrell (*ts, ss*); Billy Harper (*f, as, ss*); Richie Kamuca, Joe Temperley (*bs*), Pepper Adams (*bs, cl*); Roland Hanna (*p*); Sam Brown, Barry Galbraith (*g*); Richard Davis (*b*). 7/69, 1/70, 5/70.

***   **The Orchestra** West Wind 2044 CD
Jones; Mel Lewis (*d, co-leader*); Larry Moses, Simo Slaminen, Irving Stokes, Ron Tooley (*t, flhn*); Dick Bienenfeld, Lollie Bienenfeld, John Mosca, Don Purviance, Lee Robertson (*tb*); Steve Coleman (*as, cl, f*); Dick Oatts (*ss, as, cl, f*); Richard Perry, Bob Rockwell (*ts, f*); Charles Davis (*bs, cl, bcl*); Jim McNeely (*p*); Jesper Lundgaard (*b*). 10/78.

***   **Body And Soul** West Wind 2048 CD
as above.

Though better known than the quiet Hank, the middle Jones brother has been consistently underrated as a soloist, recognized mainly as an arranger for the band he co-led with drummer Mel Lewis and which sustained a Monday night residency at the Village Vanguard for longer than either of the principals could remember on some occasions. The early, eponymous LRC and the near-contemporary *Paris* set are both good-quality representations of an absolutely top-notch band. Jones's arrangements are as adventurous as always, with a plentiful in-put of latter-day idiom to spice up the powerful swing he adopted from Basie. 'Dedication' on *Jones/Lewis* is a little too heavy on the French horns, but the backgrounds are a perfect vehicle for Jones, who throughout sticks to a flugelhorn (with an intonation reminiscent of French horn). The two West Winds are later, (inexplicably) poorer in register and with a less adventurous band. By 1978, Jones's last months with the orchestra, some of the fire and commitment had perhaps been extinguished or exhausted; it was, after all, a punishing schedule. *Thad Jones/Mel Lewis* should be in most collections; the other pair are mainly for fans and elegiasts, though *Body And Soul* includes a beautiful version of Jones's classic composition 'A Child Is Born'.

***(*)   **The Fabulous Thad Jones** Original Jazz Classics OJC 625 CD/LP/MC
Jones; Frank Wess (*ts, f*); John Dennis, Hank Jones (*p*); Charles Mingus (*b*); Kenny Clarke, Max Roach (*d*). 54.

***   **After Hours** Original Jazz Classics OJC 1782 CD
    Jones; Frank Wess (*ts, f*); Kenny Burrell (*g*); Mal Waldron (*p*); Paul Chambers (*b*);
    Arthur Taylor (*d*).

The first of these is a bit of a mixed bag, but the sessions done for Mingus's and Roach's Debut label are very good indeed. Mingus admired the trumpeter inordinately and Jones was the only artist to record twice under his own name for Debut. Their duo on 'I Can't Get Started' is interesting first of all for Mingus's restructuring of the harmony, but Jones's response to this bare-boned setting and to the quasi-modal 'Get Out Of Town' is full confirmation of his ability to improvise at the highest level. Wess's flute makes a fine contrast on 'Sombre Intrusion'. The slighter *After Hours* has nothing quite so daring, but it's a solidly inventive session nonetheless and the CD sound on both is very good.

***   **Village Vanguard Live Sessions** LRC CDC 9013 CD
    Jones; Mel Lewis (*d, co-leader*); Jimmy Nottingham, Richard Williams, Snooky Young
    (*t*); Garnett Brown, Tom McIntosh (*tb*); Bob Brookmeyer (*vtb*); Cliff Heather (*btb*);
    Jerry Dodgion, Jerome Richardson (*as*); Eddie Daniels, Joe Farrell (*ts*); Pepper
    Adams (*bs*); Roland Hanna (*p*); Richard Davis (*b*). 11/70.

The arrangements – by Jones, Brookmeyer and, on his own feature 'Baca Feelin'', Garnett Brown – are consistently good, and it's a shame that the recording is so uncertain. There's a lot of disruptive noise and the top brass notes are subject to a good deal of distortion; that's particularly unfortunate because the contributions by Jimmy Nottingham ('Gettin' Sassy') and Richard Williams ('The Second Place') are so spirited. The woodwinds fare a little better and Joe Farrell's fine solo on the second half of 'Little Pixie' is one of his best on record. Brookmeyer is responsible for the arrangement of Fats Waller's 'Willow Tree' and makes a characteristically cool and inventive job of it. Valuable as a record of the Jones–Lewis band, this isn't always comfortable listening and may require considerable knob-twiddling to get the treble sorted out.

***   **Eclipse** Storyville SLP 4089 CD/LP
    Jones; Jan Glasesel, Tim Hagans, Egon Petersen, Lars Togeby, Erik Tschentscher (*t*);
    Richard Boone, Ture Larsen, Niels Neergaard, Bjarne Thanning, Axel Windfeld (*tb*);
    Michael Hove, Bent Jaedig, Ole Thoger Nielsen, Jorgen Nilsson, Sahib Shihab (*sax*);
    Horace Parlan (*p*); Jesper Lundgaard (*b*); Ed Thigpen (*d*). 9/79.

After leaving Mel Lewis in 1978, Jones spent most of his remaining years in Scandinavia, where he formed and led the Eclipse big band, an outfit which reflected some of the old partnership's combination of power and complexity. For all his virtues, Thigpen is no Lewis, but the band sounds well drilled and the charts are razor-sharp. In the late 1970s, Jones took up valve trombone as an alternative horn. It sounds fleet and subtle, and lends him a breadth of tone he could not have achieved with trumpet. The LP sound doesn't hold up to current digital standards, but it's big and warm and preserves enough of the grain in the ensembles to afford a hint of what this band was like in concert.

***(*)   **Mad Thad** Fresh Sound FSR CD 117 CD
    Jones; Henry Coker (*tb*); Frank Foster (*ts*); Frank Wess (*ts, f*); Tommy Flanagan,
    Jimmy Jones (*p*); Eddie Jones, Doug Watkins (*b*); Elvin Jones, Jo Jones (*d*). 12/56.

[**(*)   **First Recordings** Jazz Anthology 550142 CD]
    As above. 1/57.

(*)   **Mean What You Say Original Jazz Classics OJC 464 CD/LP
    Jones; Pepper Adams (*bs*); Duke Pearson (*p*); Ron Carter (*b*); Mel Lewis (*d*). 4 &
    5/66.

***   **Three And One** Steeplechase SCS 1197 CD/LP
    Jones; Ole Kock Hansen (*p*); Jesper Lundgaard (*b*); Ed Thigpen (*d*). 10/84.

Not usually considered a small-group player, or even a soloist of any unusual interest, Jones's recorded explorations on this scale are few and far between. On the measure of *Three And One* alone, this is a pity. He's a subtle and vibrant player with a cornet tone reminiscent of Nat Adderley but able to sustain big transitions of pitch with absolute confidence, much as he demands of his big bands. 'But Not For Me' is marred by a slightly tentative accompaniment, but Thigpen splashes in sensuous slo-mo, almost tuneful. Recommended.

Though keeping up with all the Joneses is far from easy, *Mad Thad* is even better. The trumpeter was signed to Basie for most of the late 1950s and early '60s, a period that firmed up his reputation as an arranger but afforded regrettably few solo flights. He'd recorded on Mingus's demanding *Jazz Experiment* and won the bassist's heart for ever with his bustling, opportunistic runs and confident entanglements in and and around the theme. On *Mad Thad*, playing trumpet only, he sounds full-throated and sure of himself; there are what appear to be very minor articulation problems on a couple of tracks, but these are incidental stammers in some beautifully crafted ('Whisper Not' especially) solos. *First Recordings* (shared with some slightly uncertain Sonny Rollins tracks) consists of far from second-rate material from the *Mad Thad* sessions. There's a fine 'Lust For Life' with Foster, Jimmy Jones, Watkins and Jo Jones, and a beautifully sculpted ballad medley with Coker, Wess, Flanagan, Eddie Jones and Elvin Jones.

Mean What You Say comes just after the formation of the Jones–Lewis big band. Though it casts the trumpeter in what should be completely sympathetic company, it's a rather uncertain affair, with most of the honours going to baritonist Pepper Adams, named as co-leader on the session. The sound is exemplary, though, with a representation of bass and percussion that was better than average for the time, even on the very acceptable vinyl.

Fans of the underrated Jones trumpet might sample him alongside Howard McGhee and Kenny Dorham on *The Best Of The Jazz Trumpet* (LRC CDC 8516 CD), playing 'The Theme': a duff collection, but a fine track.

HERBERT JOOS (born 1940)
TRUMPET, FLUGELHORN, ARRANGER

*** **Daybreak** Japo 60015 CD
     Joos; strings. 10/76.

*** **Cracked Mirrors** ECM 1356 CD/LP
     Joos; Harry Pepl (*g, g synth*); Jon Christensen (*d*). 2/87.

Joos has been a member of the Vienna Art Orchestra since the end of the 1970s, an association that reflects his equal interest in improvisation and more formal structures. The music of *Cracked Mirrors* offers back a splintered version of his Miles-influenced quasi-modality, but with a hard and brilliant tone that is all his own. Christensen is responsive to every parameter of the music, and the production establishes a fine balance between the three players, with Pepl's guitar synthesizer acting as colour and condiment in one. If *Daybreak* then reflects Joos's interest in Miles Davis, it is a Miles refracted by Gil Evans. The Stuttgart Radio Symphony strings sound slightly muffled in places, but Joos plays with a deceptively hard edge to his romanticism. This is a further intriguing example of the impact Miles has made on classically influenced European composers, to be set alongside the best of Palle Mikkelborg's work.

CLIFFORD JORDAN (born 1931)
TENOR SAXOPHONE

***(*) **Starting Time** Original Jazz Classics OJC 147 LP
       Jordan; Kenny Dorham (*t*); Cedar Walton (*p*); Wilbur Ware (*b*); Albert Heath (*d*).
       61.

Jordan's Blue Note debut, *Blowin' In From Chicago* [BLP 1549], is currently in limbo. Thirty years ago his style was much closer to the tempestuous approach associated with such natives of the Windy City as Johnny Griffin (whom he momentarily resembles on 'Sunrise In Mexico' here) and – in timbre particularly – Von Freeman. The *Starting Time* band is an early sign of Jordan's genius for putting together players of similar disposition or for so arranging more contingent line-ups that his particular signature stays legible down through the layers. Dorham is almost liquid, though the vinyl doesn't flatter him. Ware gave Jordan the kind of big legato that he got later from Sam Jones and Richard Davis. His friend, Tootie Heath, balanced drive and unobtrusive precision with an undogmatic approach to the basic metre. Walton sounds like his superego, a constant reminder that there are chords in there, demanding their due. A marvellous record, and an ideal starting point.

***   **Bearcat** Original Jazz Classics OJC 494 CD/LP/MC
      Jordan; Cedar Walton (*p*); Teddy Smith (*b*); J. C. Moses (*d*).

The perfect characterization of Jordan's sound, sometimes growling, sometimes purring. This old Jazzland set isn't especially well recorded and the bassist seems prone to sudden surges towards the mike, but the music is fine and Jordan is in fine voice on 'How Deep Is The Ocean?' and the original 'Middle Of The Block'. A word of praise, too, for Walton and Moses.

***   **Half Note** Steeplechase SCS 1198 LP
      Jordan; Cedar Walton (*p*); Sam Jones (*b*); Albert Heath (*d*). 4/74.

***   **On Stage: Volume 1** Steeplechase SCS 1071 CD/LP
      As above, except Billy Higgins (*d*) replaces Heath. 3/75.

***   **On Stage: Volume 2** Steeplechase SCS 1092 LP/MC
      As above. 3/75.

***   **On Stage: Volume 3** Steeplechase SCS 1104 LP
      As above. 3/75.

***   **The Highest Mountain** Steeplechase SCS 1047 CD/LP
      As above. 4/75.

***   **Firm Roots** Steeplechase SCS 1033 CD/LP
      As above. 4/75.

It's having those firm roots that allows Jordan to drift through the theme as cavalierly as he does. Throughout the highly productive mid-1970s, he was probably playing more 'legitimately' than at any other time in his career, but there are constant reminders of his Mingus-influenced tendency to regard the note as a dartboard (which, of course, you don't always want to hit dead centre) and a progression as a series of mentally totted-up scores that always come out right in the end. Compare the version of old pal Sonny Rollins's 'St Thomas' on *Half Note* and the third *On Stage* to hear how that works. This isn't Jordan's best clip; he's a consummate ballad player (see 'Stella By Starlight' on *On Stage: Volume 2*) with the kind of articulation and presence that suggests unused gears.

In the 1970s, Jordan was playing regularly with Cedar Walton, Sam Jones and Billy Higgins under the name The Magic Triangle; the first and last of the above albums were more prosaically designated, but the evocative title captures something like the equidistance and responsiveness that Jordan, a great arranger, achieved with his colleagues. They work hard for each other, creating spaces and textures, laying off chords that lead whoever is soloing out into new territory, then gently pulling on the strings.

It's very difficult to choose from among these records. The quality is consistently high, and none will disappoint.

***(*)   **Highest Mountain** Muse MCD 5445 CD
      Jordan; Cedar Walton (*p*); Sam Jones (*b*); Billy Higgins (*d*). 3/75.

A remarkable live set, recorded in France. The title piece is a complex, irregular theme divided into two passages of 23 bars each. Walton takes a prominent solo, then Higgins, and the piece closes with a sequence of ambiguous resolutions that so closely recall those on 'Psalm' at the end of *A Love Supreme* that 'Highest Mountain' almost sounds like the culmination of a suite begun with the opening 'John Coltrane'. Written by Bill Lee, the father of movie director Spike Lee, this is a stately, multi-part theme which develops in a manner very similar to Coltrane's epic, and over very much the same kind of propulsive cymbal accent. Half way through, as if to rubber-stamp the resemblance, the group chant 'John Coltrane, black spirit, first new-born' in an echo of the *Love Supreme* mantra.

After these two tracks, on which Jordan maintains a keening, restless tone, 'Blue Monk' seems quite conventional, and Jordan's delivery immediately simplifies, shedding the overtones and harmonics in favour of a conventional blues shout. Walton's solo suddenly accelerates into double time, a bravura performance that confirms the responsiveness of the whole rhythm section. The pianist's 'Midnight Waltz' is one of his loveliest compositions and features low-register interplay between piano and bass. Jones again features strongly on his own composition 'One For Amos', sharing the main statement with Jordan. Thoroughly recommended.

***   **Repetition** Soul Note SN 1084 CD/LP
Jordan; Barry Harris (*p*); Walter Booker (*b*); Vernell Fournier (*d*). 2/84.

***   **Royal Ballads** Criss Cross Criss 1025 CD/LP
Jordan; Kevin O'Connell (*p*); Ed Howard (*b*); Vernell Fournier (*b*). 12/86.

In recent years, Jordan has perfected a ballad style that is strikingly reminiscent of Wardell Gray's. *Royal Ballads* is a lovely record; if it steers close to easy listening on occasion, a more attentive hearing uncovers all manner of subtleties and harmonic shifts. The opening 'Lush Life' is almost lost in Fournier's constant cymbal-spray, but the drummer – who has worked to great effect with Ahmad Jamal – is a great ballad player and every bit as adept as Jordan at varying an apparently sleepy beat with odd, out-of-synch metres and quiet paradiddles. As Jordan quotes 'Goodbye Pork Pie Hat' on the original 'Royal Blues', Fournier squeezes the tempo almost subliminally, so that the reference evades identification as the mind subconsciously readjusts to the beat. Subtle and intelligent jazz, and a sure sign that ballads albums are not just the preserve of MOR acts.

The slightly earlier *Repetition* has more variation of pace (though no less inventive a trawl of material). Fournier doesn't seem quite so much at ease, but Harris is a much subtler player than O'Connell, who tends toward literalism.

Once again, nothing to choose between them. Late-nighters might prefer the ballads.

(*)   **Two Tenor Winner Criss Cross Criss 1011 CD
Jordan; Junior Cook (*ts*); Kirk Lightsey (*p*); Cecil McBee (*b*); Eddie Gladden (*d*). 10/84.

Blowin' In From Chicago was a classic session. This falls significantly short of the 1957 album's powerful two-stroke front-line, with John Gilmore's sturdy hard-bop manner complementing Jordan's already capricious placing of notes. The rhythm section couldn't be a lot better, and 'Groovin' High' has terrific energy and controlled pace, but each track seems to flag as if from a dearth of ideas; the obvious culprit is Cook, who seems a mass of unassimilated influences, at least some of them palpably hampering him.

***(*)   **Four Play** DIW 836 CD
Jordan; James Williams (*p*); Richard Davis (*b*); Ronnie Burrage (*d*).

It's not quite clear who's supposed to be leader here. A companion DIW set, *sans* Jordan, and either deliberately or misleadingly entitled *I Remember Clifford*, is reviewed under Richard Davis's name. Jordan contributes two fine compositions to *Four Play* and kicks off the session on his 'Tokyo Road' with a dark, Coltranish wail that lightens steadily as the set progresses. There's an excellent reading of Monk's 'I Mean You', one of the less exploited items in the canon, and a superb long version of Randy Weston's 'Hi-Fly', which leads in to Richard Davis's moving 'Misako – Beautiful Shore', a theme that brings back some of the sombre quality to Jordan's voice. Impeccably recorded, and laurels for the unsung Williams and the prodigious Burrage. Well worth what might seem a pricey investment.

DUKE JORDAN (born 1922)
PIANO

***(*)   **Jor-Du** Vogue 655010 CD
Jordan; Gene Ramey (*b*); Lee Abrams (*d*). 1/54.

****   **Flight To Jordan** Savoy 650118 CD
Jordan; Eddie Bert (*tb*); Cecil Payne (*bs*); Percy Heath (*b*); Art Blakey (*d*). 10/55.

(*)   **Midnight Moonlight Steeplechase SCS 1143 LP
Jordan (*p* solo). 79.

Duke Jordan's career has an odd trajectory. At 25, with an apprenticeship under Coleman Hawkins behind him, he was thrust into the limelight with Charlie Parker and proved himself an able and frequently imaginative accompanist. Thereafter, though, his progress has been curiously elided, with long disappearances from the scene. Perhaps as a consequence, he is by far the least well-known of the bebop pianists, surprisingly diffident in performing manner, and little given to solo performance. Though he is a fine standards player (*Flight To Denmark*, *Two Loves*, *Tivoli*, below), he has from time to time preferred to rework a sizeable but tightly organized body of original compositions. These have been documented by the Danish Steeplechase label with a thoroughness which borders on redundancy and which seems quite inconsistent with the pianist's rather marginal reputation. There are very many recorded versions of some of the pianist's most successful themes. 'Jordu', in particular, has become a popular repertoire piece, not just for piano-led groups; it's disguised in 'Minor Encamp' on the eponymous Vogue, a good-quality documentation of early sessions with an average rhythm section but with some valuable alternative takes. His themes tend to be brief, tightly melodic rather than just a launching-pad of chords, and disconcertingly unmemorable, in the positive sense that they resist being hummed.

Midnight Moonlight is a rare solo excursion, though there are solo tracks on *Thinking Of You* and *Time On My Hands*, below, which repay close attention. Jordan's delivery is quiet, unshowy, and almost intellectual. There are no familiar standards, as there are on the masterful *Flight To Jordan*, to establish reference points, and it's sometimes difficult to get a bearing on Jordan's intentions. His long lines are essentially segments of melody, and his rhythm surprisingly staccato and uncountable, like a milder and more 'legitimate' version of Thelonious Monk.

The trio tracks on *Flight* are as good as he has ever played. 'Summertime' and 'Night In Tunisia' recall his musical background and document his divergence from it. The sound is good and clear. It muddies a little with the addition of trombone and baritone saxophone, and Jordan himself tends to disappear, but 'Flight To Jordan' and 'Two Loves' – the latter has an imaginative structure – are particularly strong, and 'Yesterdays', a rhapsodic swirl of chords and melodic fragments. Jordan almost always sounds better in a group context.

(*) **Flight To Denmark Steeplechase SCS 1011 CD/LP
Jordan; Mads Vinding (*b*); Ed Thigpen (*d*). 11/73.

***   **Two Loves** Steeplechase SCS 1024 CD/LP
As above. 12/73.

(*) **Truth Steeplechase SCS 1175 LP
As above. 3/75.

Unlike his later work for Steeplechase, the first two of these are essentially albums of standards, and in some sense an attempt to come to terms with the legacy of bebop. There are finely judged readings of 'Here's That Rainy Day', 'On Green Dolphin Street' and 'How Deep Is The Ocean' on *Flight*, 'I'll Remember April' and 'Embraceable You', 'Blue Monk' and 'My Old Flame' on *Two Loves*, which also includes the ubiquitous 'Jordu' and 'Lady Dingbat', an unaccountably popular original. *Truth* includes two of his best themes, 'Night Train To Snekkersten' and 'Misty Thursday', but is otherwise unremarkable. Jordan's career had been rather stop-start since the mid-1950s and there are occasional rust-spots on his faster runs and a slight stiffness in his octaves. The CD transfers aren't perfect, and most listeners will find the vinyl quite acceptable. There are alternative takes of several tracks; newcomers might find *Two Loves* preferable.

(*) **Tivoli One Steeplechase SCS 1189 LP
Jordan; Wilbur Little (*b*); Dannie Richmond (*d*).

***   **Tivoli Two** Steeplechase SCS 1193 LP
As above.

(*) **Wait And See Steeplechase SCS 1211 CD/LP
As above.

(*) **Change A Pace Steeplechase SCS 1135 LP/MC
Jordan; Niels-Henning Ørsted-Pedersen (*b*); Billy Hart (*d*). 7 & 10/79.

***   **Thinking Of You** Steeplechase SCS 1165 LP
As above. 10/79.

(*) **Time On My Hands Steeplechase SCS 1232 CD/LP
Jordan; Jesper Lundgaard (*b*); Billy Hart (*d*). 79.

(*)   As Time Goes By Steeplechase SCS 1247 CD/LP
As above. 7/85.

The late 1970s were a remarkably productive time for Jordan. In Billy Hart and Dannie Richmond he found drummers with the kind of rhythmic tension he required on which to sound his taut melodic figures. The mix of material is much as usual, but some mention should be made of 'Light Foot' and 'The Queen Is Home To Stay' on *Thinking Of You*, which averages out as the best of this group.

The two *Tivoli* sessions with Richmond are again standards-based, with an accent on bebop-associated themes. *Volume Two* is the more compelling, despite or because of its relative slackness of delivery. *Wait And See* is available on compact disc, but any implicit advantage is offset by the better material on SCS 1189 and 1193.

Jordan's vocals on *Time On My Hands* and *As Ditto Goes By* can't be considered an advantage. Much as Ahmad Jamal is popularly supposed to, Jordan occasionally skirts a Vegas-style 'entertainment' approach that obscures his more interesting ideas to all but the most attentive listeners.

(*)   Misty Thursday Steeplechase SCS 1053 LP
Jordan; Chuck Wayne (*g*); Sam Jones (*b*); Roy Haynes (*d*). 6/75.

Compare these studio versions of 'Night Train To Snekkersten' and 'Misty Thursday' with the live versions recorded in Osaka fifteen months later (below). Jones has a more contained approach and lacks Little's strength, but he is absolutely right for the lovely 'Hymn To Peace'. The sound is a little flat.

***(*)   Duke's Delight** Steeplechase SCS 1046 LP
Jordan; Richard Williams (*t*); Charlie Rouse (*ts*); Sam Jones (*b*); Al Foster (*d*). 11/75.

***   Lover Man** Steeplechase SCS 1127 LP/MC
As above, except omit Williams, Rouse. 8/79.

Delight is simply that, a marvellous record with fine, vibrant performances from Rouse and the still-unfancied Williams. The rhythm axis is absolutely on the case from the first bar, and throughout the fine trio, *Lover Man*. Strongly recommended.

***   Live In Japan** Steeplechase SCCD 1063/4 2CD/2LP
Jordan; Wilbur Little (*b*); Roy Haynes (*d*). 9/76.

***   Osaka Concert: Volume 1** Steeplechase SCCD 31271 CD
As above.

***   Osaka Concert: Volume 2** Steeplechase SCCD 31272 CD
As above.

(*)   Flight To Japan Steeplechase SCS 1088 CD/MC
As above.

The Osaka concert is a confident and lively recording and, though *Volume One* possesses a snap and professionalism that seem to drift on the sequel, it amply justifies the double release, which reprocesses the same material as *Live In Japan*, which was apparently recorded two nights earlier. Steeplechase's obsessive documentation continued with the briefer *Flight* from the following week, but this need trouble only completists. Since favourites like 'Misty Thursday', 'Jordu' and 'Flight To Jordan' are all included, it might make a sensible introduction to the pianist's work. The CD quality is excellent, with good atmosphere.

***   Duke's Artistry** Steeplechase SCS 1103 CD/LP/MC
Jordan; Art Farmer (*flhn*); David Friesen (*b*); Philly Joe Jones (*d*). 6/78.

(*)   The Great Session Steeplechase SCS 1150 CD/LP/MC
As above, except omit Farmer, add Paul Jeffrey (*bells*). 6/78.

'Lady Bird' on *The Great Session* helpfully points to Tadd Dameron as a further factor in the development of Jordan's approach (Lennie Tristano, at the opposite pole from bebop, is another). These are unexceptionable sessions; Philly Joe plays with his incomparable verve and exactness, and Friesen sounds confident and aware.

LOUIS JORDAN (1908–75)
ALTO SAXOPHONE, VOCAL

***   **At the Swing Cats' Ball** JSP CD 330 CD
Jordan; Mario Bauza, Bobby Stark, Taft Jordan, Courtney Williams (*t*); Sandy
Williams, Nat Story (*tb*); Pete Clark (*cl, as, bs*); Lem Johnson (*cl, ts*); Ted McRae,
Stafford 'Pazuza' Simon (*ts*); Wayman Carver (*ts, f*); Stafford Simon (*ts*); Tommy
Fulford, Clarence Johnson (*p*); John Trueheart (*g*); Beverley Peer, Charlie Drayton
(*b*); Chick Webb, Walter Martin (*d*); Rodney Sturgis (*v*). 1/37–11/39.

***   **Somebody Done Hoodooed The Hoodoo Man** Jukebox Lil JB 619 CD/LP
Jordan; Courtney Williams, Freddy Webster, Eddie Roane (*t*); Lem Johnson, Kenneth
Hollon, Stafford 'Pazuza' Simon (*ts*); Clarence Johnson, Arnold Thomas (*p*); Charlie
Drayton, Dallas Bartley, Henry Turner (*b*); Walter Martin (*d*); Mabel Johnson,
Rodney Sturgis (*v*). 12/38–7/42.

***(*)   **Best Of Louis Jordan** MCA MCAD-4079 CD
Jordan; Eddie Roane (*t*); Arnold Thomas (*p*); Dallas Bartley, Al Morgan (*b*); Walter
Martin, Shadow Wilson (*d*). 42–45.

**   **Live Jive** Magic DATOM-4 CD
Jordan; rest unknown. No date.

***   **Cole Slaw** Jukebox Lil JB 605 CD/LP
Jordan; Aaron Izenhall, Bob Mitchell, Hal Mitchell (*t*); Josh Jackson (*ts*); Bill Doggett
(*p*); Carl Hogan, Bill Jennings (*g*); Bob Bushnell, Billy Hadnott (*b*); Joseph Chris,
Columbo Morris, Charlie Rice (*d*). 12/47–5/52.

***   **Five Guys Named Moe** Bandstand BDCD 1531 CD
Jordan; Aaron Izenhall (*t*); Josh Jackson, Eddie Johnson (*ts*); Bill Davis, Bill Doggett
(*p*); Bill Jennings (*g*); Bob Bushnell, Dallas Bartley (*b*); Joe Morriss, Christopher
Columbus (*d*), Peggy Thomas, Bixie Crawford (*v*). 48–49.

(*)   **The Complete Aladdin Sessions EMI CDP 7965672 CD
Jordan; Bob Mitchell (*t*); Count Hastings (*ts*); Chester Lane (*p*): Bert Payne (*g*);
Sammy Guy (*b*); Johnny Kirkwood (*d*). 1/54.

Jordan, who came from Arkansas and had a father in vaudeville, quit playing in big bands in the
early 1940s to form his Tympany Five, one of the most successful small bands in jazz history:
their hit records, 'Five Guys Named Moe', 'Choo Choo Ch'Boogie', 'Caldonia' and many
more, established the idea of the jump band as a jiving, irrepressible outfit which persists to this
day. Rightly so: Jordan was a pro's pro, tirelessly seeking out fresh songs and constantly
touring. But, surprisingly, the music seldom suffered, which is why his best sides still sound
fresh. Most of the hits – which mixed comic lyrics with spirited swing-style playing and paved
the way for R&B – are collected on the MCA record. The JSP disc tells the beginning of the
story, opening with three tracks with the Chick Webb band and then going into a sequence of
1937–9 tracks, none of them quite as outlandish as some of the later jive would become. The
two Jukebox Lil discs are excellent compilations of lesser-known titles, including 'Two Little
Squirrels (Nuts To You)' and 'Is My Pop In There?', and ending on the 'we're coming in on the
swing ticket' of 'Jordan For President' ('I promise that every living American will get his
portion – after I've had mine'). *The Complete Aladdin Sessions* dates from after his peak years
and the material is sounding tired, but the excellent remastering gives the band a real kick.
Jordan's salty alto – which was loved by everyone from Sonny Rollins to Van Morrison –
doesn't get much space, but he makes eight bars count for a lot. The Magic record offers some
dusty-sounding airshots – atmospheric, but nothing that you can't hear better on the studio
records. The Bandstand record offers similar material, but in superior sound, and this time the
exuberance of Jordan's stage show comes fizzing through on knockabout stuff such as 'Safe,
Sane And Single' and 'I Like 'Em Fat Like That'.

(*)   **I Believe In Music Black & Blue 59.059-2 CD
Jordan; Irv Cox (*ts*); Duke Burrell (*p*); Louis Myers (*g*); John Duke, Dave Myers (*b*);
Archie Taylor, Fred Below (*d*). 11/73.

A bunch of Louis's old hits, some standards and a few blues, all done with few signs of Jordan slowing up. He sings with the same elan, if not quite with the old abandonment, and his alto playing remains attractively greasy. Good fun.

** **Louis Jordan And Chris Barber** Black Lion BLCD 760156 CD
Jordan; Pat Halcox (*t*); Chris Barber (*tb, v*); Ian Wheeler, John Crocker (*cl, as*); Steve Hammond, Johnny McCallum (*g, bj*); John Slaughter (*g*); Eddie Smith (*bj*); Dick Smith, Jackie Flavelle (*b*); Graham Burbidge (*d*). 12/62–12/74.

Nine tracks with the 1962 Barber band and five more by Barber's men without Louis. Jordan does his best but these Englishmen aren't much good at jiving.

MARLON JORDAN (born 1970)
TRUMPET

*** **For You Only** CBS 466895-2 CD/MC
Jordan; Branford Marsalis (*ts*); Kent Jordan (*f*); Daryl Grant, Darrell Lavigne (*p*); Elton Heron (*b, p*); Ira Coleman (*b*); Jeff Watts, Troy Davis (*d*). 12/88.

** **Learson's Return** Columbia CK 46930 CD/MC
Jordan; Tim Warfield (*ts*); Peter Martin (*p*); Tarus Mateen (*b*); Troy Davis (*d*). 90.

Another trumpet prodigy from New Orleans – after Wynton Marsalis and Terence Blanchard – Marlon Jordan is Kent Jordan's younger brother and sounds impressed enough by Marsalis's progress to have emulated much of his sound and manner. *Learson's Return* in particular could almost be a Marsalis session, with Delfeayo Marsalis producing and Jordan's set of originals sounding just the kind of abstract, knowing note which the older trumpeter enjoys. But it's immature, uninvolving music: the solos here sound like exercises of the most introverted kind, with Jordan's undoubted gifts directed towards a kind of pointless virtuosity. *For You Only* is actually much better: the studio sound is brighter and clearer than Marsalis's muddy mix, brother Kent gets a chance to show how assertively he can play away from his usual fusion context, and Branford has just the right sort of authority that Warfield lacks on the second date. Jordan's cautious, slowly revolving solos are shapelier and far more convincing. At his age, though, his future prospects are wide open.

SHEILA JORDAN (born 1928)
VOICE

**** **Portrait Of Sheila** Blue Note CDP 789902 CD
Jordan; Barry Galbraith (*g*); Steve Swallow (*b*); Denzil Best (*d*). 9 & 10/62.

*** **Sheila** Steeplechase SCS 1081 CD/LP/MC
Jordan; Arild Andersen (*b*). 8/77.

(*) **Old Time Feeling Muse MCD 5366 CD
Jordan; Harvie Swartz (*b*). 10/82.

*** **The Crossing** Black-Hawk BKH 50501 CD/LP
Jordan; Tom Harrell (*flhn*); Kenny Barron (*p*); Harvie Swartz (*b*); Ben Riley (*d*). 10/84.

Sheila Jordan owes her stage name and something of her distinctive delivery to a marriage, since dissolved, to the bebop pianist, Duke Jordan. She has all her former husband's concentration on the melodic progress of a song (and pays notable attention to the semantics of a lyric) and much of his intelligent, unhistrionic and almost diffident delivery. Like the truly great instrumentalists, Sheila Jordan is content to explore all the potential of the middle register, where words are more likely to remain intact (with lesser talent, prosaically so), rather than over-reach a range which is nevertheless greater than sometimes appears. At the end of phrases, she deploys a superbly controlled vibrato.

On *Portrait*, her most complete artistic statement, she ranges between the rapid and slightly alienating 'Let's Face The Music And Dance' (which anticipates the surrealism of her contributions to Roswell Rudd's remarkable *Flexible Flyer* [Affinity/Freedom]) to the fragile beauty of 'I'm A Fool To Want You' and 'When The World Was Young' with its extraordinary, ambiguous ending.

The instrumentation is highly subtle. Bobby Timmons's 'Dat Dere' is given just to voice and bass (and Swallow is superb), 'Who Can I Turn To?' to voice and guitar; while 'Hum Drum Blues' and 'Baltimore Oriole' are set against rhythm only, as if she were a horn.

If one is looking for an exact instrumental analogy for Sheila Jordan's voice, it's probably the round, precariously controlled wobble of the reverse-action flugelhorn. Tom Harrell is a near-perfect foil on *The Crossing*, but the more conventional arrangements suit her less well and there are moments when she seems to be straining uncharacteristically for effects.

The sparser landscape of *Sheila* and *Old Time Feeling*, where she is accompanied only by double bass, suits her much better. Andersen is a much more interesting player, and appears more responsive, than Swartz, but the Muse is well worth having. Few singers have been as consistently inventive and challenging in an era dominated by horns and guitars; few, predictably, have been so little appreciated. Sheila Jordan is an essential figure in modern jazz and *Portrait* should be in every collection.

****   **Lost And Found** Muse 5390 CD/LP/MC
Jordan; Kenny Barron (*p*); Harvie Swartz (*b*); Ben Riley (*d*). 90.

This is the first product of Sheila Jordan's first mutually acceptable recording contract. To underline just how disgraceful the industry's default has been, it's her best record yet and a surprise winner in *The Wire* magazine's 1991 album of the year poll.

Her voice is in superb form and the band know what they're about. She's a daring performer, switching from 'Lost In The Stars' to the Jacobite plaint 'The Water Is Wide' to 'My Shining Hour' and 'We'll Be Together Again'. The understanding with Barron is particularly close, but she likes the lift of bass and drums as well. Urgently recommended. If you 'don't like' jazz singing, this is as good a way as any to take the cure.

STANLEY JORDAN (born 1959)
GUITAR

(*)   **Magic Touch Blue Note CDP 7460922 CD
Jordan; Onaje Allan Gumbs (*ky*); Wayne Braithwaite, Charnett Moffett (*b*); Omar Hakim, Peter Erskine (*d*); Sammy Figueroa, Bugsy Moore (*perc*). 84.

**   **Standards Vol. 1** Blue Note 7463332 CD
Jordan (*g* solo). 86.

*   **Flying Home** Blue Note 7486822 CD
Jordan; Bernard Wright (*ky*); Yossi Fine (*b*); Kenwood Dennard (*d*). 88.

**   **Cornucopia** Blue Note 7923562 CD
Jordan; Kenny Kirkland (*p*); Bernard Wright (*ky*); Charnett Moffett, Yossi Fine (*b*); Jeff Watts, J. T. Lewis, Michael Flythe, Kenwood Dennard, Flare Funston (*d*). 8/86–3/89.

Jordan's emergence in the early 1980s was greeted with some excitement because of his technique – tapping on the guitar strings at both ends to create playing of dazzling speed and precision. Several lesser-known players had already used the method, Hans Reichel in particular, but Jordan was the one who got the attention. Unfortunately, it was clear from the beginning that his powers lacked any useful focus, and while *Magic Touch* and *Standards Vol. 1* have some pretty moments – especially his crowd-pleasing version of 'Eleanor Rigby' from the first album – the original material is mundane, the backings stuck in a soft-fusion rut. Matters worsen on *Flying Home*, which gets noisier and busier to no special purpose, as if Jordan were trying to flatten an audience with bombast, a discredited path at best. But *Cornucopia* readjusted his direction. While some tracks were mere electric slush looking for airplay, a live solo piece called 'Fundance' is an amusing display of acrobatics, two tracks with Kirkland, Moffett and Watts are credible midstream showpieces, and the concluding solo title-track, while rambling, sustains at least some interest for its 22-minute length.

ANDERS JORMIN
BASS

***   **Eight Pieces** Dragon DRLP 165 LP
Jormin; Staffan Svensson (*t*); Thomas Gustafsson, Dave Wilczewski (*ss, ts*); Thomas
Jäderlund (*as*); Harald Svensson (*ky*); Bobo Stenson (*p*); Göran Klinghagen (*g*);
Audun Klieve (*d*). 3/88.

Typically thoughtful and well-prepared music from some of the leading Swedish contemporary
players. Jormin has done sideman work on many fine Dragon records, and this outing as a
leader features a commissioned suite and three trio pieces which disclose an inquiring, alert
mind: he positions Svensson's keyboards to bind the pieces together, while the writing strays
into more remote modal areas and the soloists take an often starkly contrasting course:
Jäderlund's asthmatic-sounding alto in 'Burkina', for instance. Klieve and Jormin himself make
a useful rhythm section, too, patiently exploiting the simple pulses for maximum effect.
Excellent and truthful studio sound throughout.

JULIAN JOSEPH (born 1967)
PIANO

***   **The Language Of Truth** East West 75122-2 CD/MC
Joseph; Jean Toussaint (*ts*); Alec Dankworth (*b*); Mark Mondesir (*d*); Sharon
Musgrave (*v*). 91.

A strong and completely assured debut by this impressive British pianist. He has a very sure
touch at all tempos, and though the writing shows nothing very profound – his best hooks sound
like variations on old soul-jazz material – the grippingly intense playing by Toussaint,
Dankworth and Mondesir puts a stamp of class on the occasion. Two vocal appearances by
Sharon Musgrave, one on a Curtis Mayfield tune that sounds like it drifted in from another
record altogether, break up the flow of the record to no useful purpose: it's Joseph and the
others one remembers.

HASSE KAHN (born 1923)
VIOLIN, VIOLA, VOCAL

***   **Royal Export** Dragon DRLP 86 LP
Kahn; Kenneth Arnström (*cl, as, bcl*); Bernt Rosengren (*ts, f*); Thore Swanerud, Knud
Jörgensen, Rolf Larsson (*p*); Rune Gustafsson (*g*); Sture Åkerberg (*b*); Pelle Hultén,
Rune Carlsson (*d*). 4–5/85.

Vague expectations that this Swedish fiddler would sound like a chilly likeness of Stéphane
Grappelli are quickly confounded by the music here. Kahn has been bandleading since he was
13 (he had to give up the cornet at the age of ten after a spell of bronchitis) and is master of a
swing-violin style which owes its greatest debt to Stuff Smith rather than to anyone of the
European tradition. His viola playing is suitably dark and almost throaty-sounding, and on the
lighter instrument he gets the kind of earthy drive which characterized Smith's best records.
This LP puts him alongside various generations of Swedish players, and Kahn doesn't defer to
any of them. 'Taking A Walk' features Rosengren at his most spirited on tenor, while all three
pianists have their moments elsewhere on the record. Even Kahn's vocal on 'Is It True What
They Say About Dixie?' causes no pain. A lot of fun.

RICHIE KAMUCA (1930–77)
TENOR SAXOPHONE

***(*)   **Jazz Erotica** Fresh Sound FSR 500 CD
Kamuca; Conte Candoli, Ed Leddy (*t*); Frank Rosolino (*tb*); Bill Holman (*bs*); Vince
Guaraldi (*p*); Monty Budwig (*b*); Stan Levey (*d*). 59.

***(*) **West Coast Jazz In Hi-Fi** Original Jazz Classics OJC 1760 CD/LP
As above.

The title (not the jazz part) is perhaps a shade misleading, though Kamuca favoured an intimate, close-to-the-ear murmur which comes direct from Lester Young, seductive with little hint of Pres's native ambivalence. The 'jazz' part in the title is important because there isn't much sign either of the gimmicky Kenton approach in which much of the band was schooled. Kamuca's approach to standards – 'Star Eyes', 'Angel Eyes', 'Stella By Starlight' – is direct and unsentimental, and for combined impact and sophistication there's little to choose between the four quartet tracks and Holman's arrangements for the larger group. There are one or two minor technical quibbles about the transfer and the identical OJC sounds a little brighter and cleaner, but in the absence of three excellent Concords, *Drop Me Off In Harlem* [CJ 39], *Richie* [CJ 41], and *Richie Kamuca's Charlie* [CJ 96] (where he explores the Parker legacy), makes for a highly desirable introduction to the saxophonist's work.

JAN KASPERSEN
PIANO

***(*) **Space And Rhythm Jazz** Olufsen DOCD 5060 CD
Kaspersen; Anders Bergcrantz (*t*); Simon Cato Spang-Hanssen (*ss, ts*); Frederik Lundin (*ss, ts*); Michael Hove (*as, bs*); Peter Danstrup (*b*); Ole Romer (*d*). 10/87.

*** **Ten By Two** Olufsen DOCD 5053 CD
Kaspersen; Simon Cato Spang-Hanssen (*ss, ts*). 7/87.

***(*) **Special Occasion** Olufsen DOCD 5111 CD
Kaspersen; Peter Danstrup (*b*); Ole Romer (*d*). 9/90.

**** **Live In Sofie's Cellar** Olufsen DOCD 5136 CD
Kaspersen; Anders Bergcrantz (*t*); Bob Rockwell (*ts*); Peter Danstrup (*b*); Ole Romer (*d*). 8/91.

Marvellous records from a Dane whose music is a beautifully personal, inventive and humorous response to the particular influence of Thelonious Monk. *Space And Rhythm Jazz* is a skilful all-original programme that makes the music of a quirkily expressive cast of horn players and creates consistently abosrbing ideas within what is broadly a post-bop framework. *Ten By Two* relies in the main on Monk and Ellington and is a bit po-faced, perhaps because Spang-Hanssen is a little stolid in places, but there are still some pleasing variations on the material. The pianist gets a fuller rein on the trio set, which has some mischievous originals ('Bird Goes Cuckoo') and a couple of nicely reflective ballads. Kaspersen's heavily rolling manner will strike a chord of recognition in British listeners who've heard Stan Tracey, but his sense of humour is a little more impish than our man's. The masterpiece here is the glorious live session: Bergcrantz reveals himself as a major (and so far shamefully under-recognized) soloist, Rockwell is only a beat behind, and Kaspersen directs with great exuberance from the piano. There is the third version of his favourite 'I Mean Monk' and this is surely the best. Warmly recommended.

GEORGE KAWAGUCHI (born 1927)
DRUMS

(*) **Plays Herbie Hancock Paddle Wheel K28P 6469 CD/LP
Kawaguchi; Terence Blanchard (*t*); Donald Harrison (*as, ts, bs*); Hideo Ichikawa, Cyrus Chestnut (*p*); Takashi Mizuhashi (*b*). 7/87.

The Japanese Art Blakey is scarcely known outside his own country, and none of the albums by Big Four, which he led for some 30 years, are available in the West. This meeting with three young Blakey graduates affirms everybody's credentials, without extending matters any further. Blanchard and Harrison are customarily vigorous and detailed, while their Japanese colleagues provide enthusiastic support.

GEOFF KEEZER (born 1970)
PIANO

***(*)   **Waiting In The Wings** Sunnyside SSC 1035D CD
Keezer; Bill Mobley (*t*); Billy Pierce (*ss, ts*); Steve Nelson (*vib*); Rufus Reid (*b*); Tony
Reedus (*d*). 9/88.

***   **Curveball** Sunnyside SSC 1045D CD
Keezer; Steve Nelson (*vib*); Charnett Moffett (*b*); Victor Lewis (*d*). 6/89.

***   **Here And Now** Blue Note CDP 796691-2 CD
Keezer; Donald Harrison (*as*); Steve Nelson (*vib*); Peter Washington (*b*); Billy
Higgins (*d*). 10/90.

Geoff Keezer is a formidable prodigy, even in a generation in which youthful endeavour is
nothing out of the ordinary. All these records were made before he was twenty. While he's a
vivid executant, synthesizing such influences as Ahmad Jamal and Phineas Newborn into the
kind of broad post-bop style which is the contemporary norm, he's also an unusually thoughtful
composer, organizing a small band into a distinctive ensemble and building rhythmic licks into
convincing melodies. Examples here include the title-tunes of *Waiting In The Wings* and
Curveball, 'Accra', a blistering waltz-tune, and *Here And Now*'s 'Headed Off At The Pass'; but
Keezer's thoughtful programming of rare Ellington and Monk themes adds a piquant variety to
his own writing. He greatly admires Steve Nelson's playing, and the vibes player in turn does
some of his best work on record on all three sessions. While there is an occasional shortfall of
ideas and an inevitable assumption that Keezer has greater music in him still to come, these are
all highly enjoyable records, with perhaps the first Sunnyside release edging through on the
sheer enthusiasm displayed by all the players.

ROGER KELLAWAY (born 1939)
PIANO

****   **A Portrait Of Roger Kellaway** Fresh Sound FSR-CD 147 CD
Kellaway; Jim Hall (*p*); Steve Swallow, Ben Tucker (*b*); Dave Bailey, Tony Inzalaco
(*d*). 63.

Kellaway made only four albums in the 1960s, and only this one has been restored to
circulation. It's good enough to make one wish that he'd done much more in the studios. He has
a scholar's approach to jazz history, bundling together stride, boogie and swing devices into a
manner which is otherwise entirely modern. 'Double Fault' calls to mind such contemporaries
as Andrew Hill, yet the off-centre lyricism and abstracting of melody mark Kellaway as very
much his own man. Tucker and Bailey offer prime, swinging support on four tracks, which
keeps the composer's ideas in accessible domain, while the trio of Hall, Swallow and Inzalaco
create a contrapuntal music of sometimes bemusing intricacy to go with the pianist's work. Two
solos are equally rich and detailed, and there is a brilliant transformation of 'Crazy She Calls
Me'. Slightly brittle sound doesn't mar a very fine record.

(*)   **Alone Together Dragon DRCD 168 CD
Kellaway; Red Mitchell (*b*). 7/88.

***(*)   **Live At Maybeck Recital Hall Vol. 11** Concord CCD-4470 CD
Kellaway (*p* solo). 3/91.

Kellaway's career has kept him away from jazz more often than not, working in the classical and
film-score fields, but his few more recent recordings show no loss of inspiration. The duo session
with Red Mitchell is all standards, but Kellaway is too deferential to his partner, whose
indulgence in looking for the lowest bass notes he can find is finally irritating, and several of the
tunes ramble rather than develop. The solo set is far more satisfying. Perhaps the pianist is
sometimes a little too relaxed, with three tunes running around nine minutes and the tempos
more often stately than up, but there is much marvellous pianism here. He takes three minutes
over the first chorus of 'How Deep Is The Ocean' before moving into an intense, labyrinthine
exploration, and his bitonal ventures are so completely assimilated that the most outré gestures
become a plausible part of his flow. Especially fine is the resplendent version of Hoagy

Carmichael's 'New Orleans'. As with the rest of this series, impeccable sound and an attentive crowd.

***   **That Was That** Dragon DRCD 201 CD
       Kellaway; Jan Allan (*t*); Red Mitchell (*b*). 1/91.

While this is something of a rerun of the earlier session with Mitchell, the presence of Jan Allen seems to focus the music much more, and though most of the tracks run to seven or eight minutes in length there's no sense of excessive meandering. Mitchell's amusing vocals on 'Leavin' Blues' and the title-track add to the fun and there are some very pleasing solos by Allan, whose unassuming and rather frail playing suits this context very well.

WYNTON KELLY (1931–71)
PIANO

(*)   **Piano Interpretations Blue Note CDP 784456 CD
       Kelly; Oscar Pettiford or Franklin Skeete (*b*); Lee Abrams (*d*). 7 & 8/51.

****   **Kelly Blue** Original Jazz Classics OJC 033 CD/LP
       Kelly; Nat Adderley (*c*); Bobby Jaspar (*f*); Benny Golson (*ts*); Paul Chambers (*b*); Jimmy Cobb (*d*). 2 & 3/59.

****   **Stockholm 1960** Royal Jazz RJD 509 CD
       As above, except omit Adderley, Jaspar, Golson. 10/60.

***(*)   **Piano** Original Jazz Classics OJC 401 CD/LP/MC
       Kelly; Kenny Burrell (*g*); Paul Chambers (*b*); Philly Joe Jones (*d*).

On the face of it, Kelly didn't seem the most obvious replacement for Bill Evans and Red Garland in the Miles Davis group, but he had a lyrical simplicity and uncomplicated touch that appealed enormously to the trumpeter, who hired him in 1959; Kelly only played on one track on the classic *Kind of Blue*, but 'Freddie Freeloader' is enough to show what distinguished him from Evans's more earnestly romantic style and to establish his quality.

Stockholm 1960 was, understandably, pushed as a Miles Davis/Sonny Stitt album, but it's Kelly who dominates, whether as leader – on 'Makin' Whoopee', 'June In Night' and 'Softly As In A Morning Sunrise' – or as sideman. There is a gentle bounce to his chording that is nonetheless highly dynamic. It comes to the fore on the marvellous *Kelly Blue* (which also reunites the *Kind of Blue* rhythm section). On the title-track and 'Keep It Moving', the addition of Adderley and Jaspar makes perfect sense, but Benny Golson's robust contributions tend to unbalance the delicate strength of Kelly's arrangements. As on *Stockholm 1960* the trio cuts are far superior.

This was Kelly's natural turf. *Piano Interpretations* catches the 20 year old in transition from the blues and R&B network to the mature post-bop of *Kelly Blue* and the other Riverside, *Piano*. In some respects it's a very callow album. Skeete and Abrams are inelastic, Pettiford impatient, and the accompaniment seldom flatters Kelly's liquid triplets and confident Horace Silver-like vamps; two alternate takes, and particularly the second, slower attempt at 'Goodbye', discover him adjusting his ambitions downward, squaring up the edges of the metre and disambiguating some of the progressions. The overall sound is unspoiled by a few gremlins. Uncluttered by horns, *Piano* is perhaps the best place to hear Kelly in his most natural setting. He trades tough, percussive phrases with Burrell, leaves spaces for Mr PC's slightly sombre passing notes and fills, and clatters out figures which mimic Philly Joe's quieter than usual playing. It is, in every way, a very responsive album, a musicians' album, with none of the inwardness that normally suggests. 'Whisper Not' is communicative, questioning jazz of a high order and the two takes of 'Dark Eyes' (CD only) suggest something of Kelly's dissatisfaction with formulaic responses. His death at only 40 robbed jazz of one of its most inventive and hard-working figures. He deserves wider recognition.

STAN KENTON (1911–79)
PIANO, VOCAL, BANDLEADER

***   **Summer Of '51** Garland GRZ006 CD
Kenton; Maynard Ferguson, John Howell, Chico Alvarez, Ray Wetzel, Shorty Rogers
(*t*); Milt Bernhart, Harry Betts, Bob Fitzpatrick, Dick Kenney, Bart Varsalona (*tb*);
Bud Shank, Art Pepper (*as*); Bob Cooper, Bart Calderall (*ts*); Bob Gioga (*bs*); Ralph
Blaze (*g*); Don Bagley (*b*); Shelly Manne (*d*); Jay Johnson (*v*). 51.

A vast band, a colossal legacy, and an outsize personality at the helm: Kenton's achievement is
possibly the 'biggest' which jazz has ever seen or will see. How much of it is truly worth
listening to is harder to evaluate. Kenton seemed to believe in principles which often had little
to do with musical substance: volume, power, weight, noise. Nobody ever had bigger-sounding
big bands, and nobody ever went to such pretentious lengths as Kenton could, with his espousal
of 'progressive' ideas and arrangements which owed more to half-assimilated ideas of
twentieth-century orchestral composition than to jazz scoring. Later editions of the band
pilfered from rock and soul idioms without loosening the stiffness of Kenton's stays. Yet his
best music swung mightily, was brilliantly played, and went to exhilarating extremes of both
musicianship and showmanship.
  One could best start with the earliest music, but frustratingly there is very little of Kenton's
first decade as a bandleader (he began in 1940, with a band that owed much to Jimmie
Lunceford) currently available. Now that the Creative World label – Kenton's own, which
acquired virtually all of his back catalogue from Capitol and reissued it over a series of some 80
LPs – is only slowly transferring its vinyl backlog to CD, we must assume that the early material
will be made available in the fullness of time. A start can be made, though, with this enjoyable
broadcast session from 1951. A glance at the personnel will reveal the extent of Kenton's
sidemen, and Cooper, Rogers, Ferguson and especially the unpredictable and volatile Milt
Bernhart play some exciting solos on what are swing charts brassed over by blaring horn volleys.
Highlights include a couple of Pete Rugolo charts, 'Minor Riff' and 'Collaboration', the Cuban
feel accorded to 'Love For Sale' – Kenton was quick to endorse and follow-up Dizzy Gillespie's
experiments – and a frenetically overblown 'Lover' to end on. The sound is quite good, if
occasionally scuffed by age and inclement broadcasting weather.

***(*)   **New Concepts Of Artistry In Rhythm** Capitol CDP 7928652 CD
Kenton; Conte Candoli, Buddy Childers, Maynard Ferguson, Don Dennis, Ruben
McFall (*t*); Bob Fitzpatrick, Keith Moon, Frank Rosolino, Bill Russo (*tb*); George
Roberts (*btb*); Lee Konitz, Vinnie Dean (*as*); Richie Kamuca, Bill Holman (*ts*); Bob
Gioga (*bs*); Sal Salvador (*g*); Don Bagley (*b*); Stan Levey (*d*); Derek Walton (*perc*);
Kay Brown (*v*); 9/52.

Laden with top-flight musicians, this was another of Kenton's best bands. There is one
arrangement by Bill Holman – the intriguing 'Invention For Guitar And Trumpet' – but most
of the scores were penned by Bill Russo, including the glorious kitsch of the opening
'Prologue: This Is An Orchestra!', a kind of Young Person's Guide with Kenton himself
narrating and characterizing each member of the band (considering the personalities he's
describing, it's both funny and oddly moving at this distance, especially when he calls Frank
Rosolino – who would later take his own life – 'this fellow who has few if any moody
moments'). The brass section is top-heavy and blows all else before it, but the rhythm section
swings hard, and there are some wonderful interjections on almost every piece by the major
soloists, especially Salvador on 'Invention', Konitz on 'Young Blood' and 'My Lady', Rosolino
on 'Swing House'. The remastering is bright and just a little harsh in places, but it makes the
band sound grandly impressive, which is as it should be.

(*)   **Paris 1953 Royal RJD 504 CD
Kenton; Conte Candoli, Buddy Childers, Don Dennis, Ziggy Minichelli, Don Smith
(*t*); Bob Burgess, Keith Moon, Frank Rosolino (*tb*); Bill Smiley (*btb*); Dave
Schildkraut, Lee Konitz (*as*); Bill Holman, Tony Ferina (*bs*); Barry Galbraith (*g*);
Don Bagley (*b*); Stan Levey (*d*). 9/53.

***(*)   **The Concerts In Miniature Broadcasts 1952–53** Artistry CD 001 CD
Kenton; Conte Candoli, Buddy Childers, Ernie Royal, Don Dennis, Don Smith,
Maynard Ferguson, Ruben McFall, Vinnie Dean, Ziggy Minchelli (*t*); Frank Rosolino,

Bill Russo, Keith Moon, Tommy Shepard, Milt Gold (*tb*); George Roberts, Bill Smiley (*btb*); Lee Konitz, Don Carone, Dave Schildkraut (*as*); Zoot Sims, Ed Wasserman, Richie Kamuca (*ts*); Tony Ferina (*bs*); Sal Salvador, Barry Galbraith (*g*); Don Bagley (*b*); Stan Levey (*d*).

*** **Stan Kenton Orchestra Vol. 1** Vogue/Sigla 655905 CD
Kenton; Buddy Childers, Ernie Royal, Conte Candoli, Don Denis, Don Smith, Ziggy Minichelli, Sam Noto, Stu Williamson, Ed Leddy, Al Porcino, Bob Clark, Dizzy Gillespie (*t*); Frank Rosolino, Tommy Shepard, Keith Moon, George Roberts, Milt Gold, Bill Russo, Carl Fontana, Gus Chappell, Don Kelly, Joe Ciavardone (*tb*); Bob Dockstader, Bob Smiley, Buddy Burgess, Kent Larsen, Bob Fitzpatrick (*btb*); Don Carone, Lee Konitz, Charlie Mariano, Lennie Niehaus, Dave Schildkraut, Charlie Parker (*as*); Bill Holman, Zoot Sims, Ed Wasserman, Bill Perkins, Mike Cicchetti, Dave Van Kriedt (*ts*); Tony Ferina, Lorraine Ragon, Don Davidson (*bs*); Bob Lesher, Sal Salvador, Ralph Blaze, Barry Galbraith (*g*); Don Bagley, Max Bennett (*b*); Stan Levey, Mel Lewis (*d*). 6/53–11/55.

*** **Stan Kenton Orchestra Vol. 2** Vogue/Sigla 655906 CD
As above. 6/53–11/55.

These are all broadcast performances and there's some duplication between the Artistry CD and the two Vogue/Sigla sets: sound on both varies from good to fair, although anyone accustomed to radio airshots from the period will find them quite listenable. The Royal performance offers a single concert set, with a typical Kenton programme: 'Opus In Pastels', 'Intermission Riff', 'Frank Speaking'. The interesting thing about the Vogue/Sigla discs is the guest presence of Parker and Gillespie on a few tracks: Bird sounds very below par, but Gillespie is his usual high-spirited self, even though Kenton's men do little more than offer subdued accompaniment. Elsewhere there are good features for Konitz and Sims and a few strong Holman scores: nothing that isn't handled at least as well on the studio dates, but the flavour of the period comes through. The Artistry CD is the best value at over 70 minutes, while the other two offer shorter measure: minus a couple of tracks, all the music could have fitted on to a single CD.

*** **Festival Of Modern American Jazz** Status CD 101 CD
Kenton; Bobby Clark, Johnny Capolo, Sam Noto, Herb Pomeroy, Norman Prentice, Conte Candoli (*t*); Bob Fitzpatrick, Frank Rosolino, Kent Larsen, Frank Strong (*tb*); Norman Bartold (*btb*); Lennie Niehaus, Charlie Mariano (*as*); Boots Mussulli (*as, bs*); Bill Holman, Jack Montrose (*ts*); Ralph Blaze (*g*); Gene Englund (*tba*); Max Bennett (*b*); Mel Lewis (*d*). 9/54.

(*) **In Stockholm 1956 Swedish Radio Jazz Years SRJCD-104 CD
Kenton; Vinnie Tano, Sam Noto, Phil Gilbert, Lee Katzman (*t*); Bob Fitzpatrick, Carl Fontana, Kent Larsen, Don Kelly (*tb*); Fred Fox, Irving Rosenthal (*frhn*); Lennie Niehaus (*as*); Bill Perkins, Don Rendell (*ts*); Harry Klein (*bs*); Ralph Blaze (*g*); Curtis Counce (*b*); Mel Lewis (*d*). 4/56.

*** **Kenton '56** Artistry CD 002 CD
Kenton; Ed Leddy, Dennis Grillo, Lee Katzman, Phil Gilbert, Tom Slaney (*t*); Archie LeCocque, Kent Larsen, Jim Amlotte (*tb*); Ken Shroyer (*btb*); Irving Rosenthal, Joe Mariani (*frhn*); Lennie Niehaus (*as*); Bill Perkins, Richie Kamuca (*ts*); Pepper Adams (*bs*); Ralph Blaze (*g*); Jay McAllister (*tba*); Don Bagley (*b*); Mel Lewis (*d*). 11/56.

(*) **Live At The Macumba Club Vol. 1 Magic DAWE CD
As above. 11/56.

(*) **Live At The Macumba Club Vol. 2 Magic DAWE CD
As above. 11/56.

*** **Cuban Fire** Capitol CDP 7962602 CD
Kenton; Ed Leddy, Sam Noto, Phil Gilbert, Al Mattaliano, Bud Brisbois, Dalton Smith, Bob Rolfe, John Audino, Steve Hofsteter (*t*); Bob Fitzpatrick, Carl Fontana, Kent Larsen, Don Kelly, Dick Hyde, Ray Sikora (*tb*); Jim Amlotte, Bob Knight (*btb*); Dwight Carver, Joe Burnett, Bill Horan, Tom Wirtel, Gene Roland (*mel*); Gabe Baltazar, Lennie Niehaus (*as*); Bill Perkins, Lucky Thompson, Sam Donahue, Paul

Renzi (*ts*); Wayne Dunstan (*bs, bsx*); Billy Root, Marvin Holladay (*bs*); Ralph Blaze (*g*); Jay McAllister, Albert Pollan (*tba*); Curtis Counce, Pete Chivily (*b*); Mel Lewis, Art Anton (*d*); Saul Gubin, George Gaber, Tommy Lopez, George Laguna, Roger Mozian, Maro Alvarez, George Acevedo (*perc*). 5/56–9/60.

The mid-1950s found Kenton somewhat in transition, from the more stylized West Coast touches of the early '50s band to another kind of progressive-orchestral music which he had tried in the 1940s with mixed results. Live sessions were customarily a blend of straight-ahead swing variations on standards, the Afro-Cuban element, and Kenton's penchant for orchestral bombast. All three turn up on *Festival Of Modern American Jazz*, an enjoyable live set in excellent sound (although there are a few balance problems with some of the soloists). Candoli features on two tracks (and makes a belated appearance while an embarrassed Kenton has to fill in!) but the main body of music is made up of charts by Holman and Russo; the latter's 'Improvisation' and 'A Theme Of Four Values' typify the kind of pop-complexity which Kenton seemed to admire. Excellent playing, though, and Niehaus and Mussulli make sure the brass don't have things all their own way. The 1956 albums are a patchy lot. The Swedish issue works out sometimes a little blearily on material that was starting to sound too familiar ('Concerto To End All Concertos', 'Intermission Riff'), although Rendell and Klein, who were in as substitutes, can't have known it that well. The sound is quite acceptable. The three discs from the Mocamba Club use some of the same material and the best choice is probably the Artistry CD, which runs for over 70 minutes and includes some of the best music. A new trumpet section and Adams on baritone lend some variation to the sound, but otherwise it's standard Kenton fare, in respectable if not terrific sound. *Cuban Fire* chronicles the arrival of arranger Johnny Richards, who had been studying Latin rhythms and came up with a series of charts which incorporated a six-man percussion team. The results catch much of the undertow of explosive kitsch which Latin bands love, although how 'authentic' it is in other ways is harder to judge. The six later tracks, from 1960, document one of Kenton's so-called 'mellophonium' bands, with five men playing that instrument among what is incredibly a band with 16 brass. Much of it sounds like mood or movie music, taken at tempos which tend towards trudging. The remastering is strong on the brass, but the bass frequencies are less well handled and the percussion section is mixed well off-mike on the earlier session.

*** **At The Rendezvous Vol. 1** Status CD 106 CD
Kenton; Sam Noto, Jules Chaikin, Billy Catalano, Lee Katzman, Phil Gilbert (*t*); Kent Larsen, Archie LeCocque, Don Reed, Jim Amlotte (*tb*); Kenny Shroyer (*btb*); Lennie Niehaus (*as*); Bill Perkins, Wayne Dunstan (*ts*); Billy Robinson (*bs, as*); Steve Perlow (*bs*); Red Kelly (*b*); Jerry McKenzie (*d*); Ann Richards (*v*). 1/58.

*** **At The Rendezvous Vol. 2** Status STCD 108 CD
As above. 1/58.

***(*) **At Ukiah** Status STCD 109 CD
Kenton; Frank Huggins, Bud Brisbois, Rolf Ericson, Joe Burnett, Roger Middleton (*t*); Archie LeCocque, Kent Larsen, Jimmy Knepper (*tb*); Jim Amlotte, Bill Smiley (*btb*); Lennie Niehaus (*as*); Bill Trujillo, John Bonnie (*ts*); Billy Root, Sture Swenson (*bs*); Scott LaFaro (*b*); Jerry McKenzie (*d*). 2/59.

***(*) **In New Jersey** Status STCD 104 CD
As above, except add Bobby Knight (*btb*), Charlie Mariano (*as*), Jack Nimitz (*bs*), Carson Smith (*b*), Billy Stuart (*d*), Mike Pacheco (*perc*), omit Niehaus, Swenson, LaFaro, McKenzie and Smiley. 6/59.

*** **Road Show** Capitol CDP 7963282 CD
Kenton; Bud Brisbois, Rolf Ericson, Bill Mathieu, Roger Middleton, Dalton Smith (*t*); Kent Larsen, Archie LeCocque, Don Sebesky (*tb*); Jim Amlotte, Bob Knight (*btb*); Charlie Mariano (*as*); Ronnie Rubin, Bill Trujillo (*ts*); Marvin Holladay, Jack Nimitz (*bs*); Pete Chivily (*b*); Jimmy Campbell (*d*); Mike Pacheco (*perc*); June Christy, The Four Freshmen (*v*). 10/59.

(*) **Live In Biloxi Magic DAWE 30 CD
Kenton; Frank Huggins, Bud Brisbois, Jack Sheldon, Billy Catalano, Bob Ojeda (*t*); Archie LeCocque, Kent Larsen, Jim Amlotte (*tb*); Bob Olsen, Bill Smiley (*btb*);

Lennie Niehaus (*as*); Bill Perkins, Bill Trujillo (*ts*); Bill Robinson, Steve Perlow (*bs*); Red Kelly (*b*); Jerry McKenzie (*d*). c.60.

**(*)   Return To Biloxi Magic DAWE 35 CD
As above. *c.* 60.

This recently issued crop of live CDs has given Kenton's 1958–59 period a comprehensive documentation. The Status CDs are superb feats of remastering, giving the band real presence and a transparent clarity on most of these discs. The two *Rendezvous* discs both feature programmes of standards – in person, Kenton was usually playing dance or dinner dates, and seldom got to fire out all his most progressive material – and display a top-class big band in a period where there weren't many of them left. The *Ukiah* and *New Jersey* discs are similarly inclined, and casual listeners might try the New Jersey performance as the best introduction: there are some immaculately crafted little variations on the likes of 'Bernie's Tune', 'Laura' and 'Frenesi', and Jimmy Knepper – not much remembered as a Kentonian – takes some splendid solos. Only Kenton himself sounds a bit grumpy in his introductions, and his piano is a little remote in the mix. *Ukiah* has an almost entirely different set, with good work from Ericson, Root and Niehaus and the surprise appearance of Scott LaFaro in the rhythm section. The two Biloxi sets – the first is the more progressive material, the second a more standards-orientated session – are mistily recorded and the orchestra comes over rather waywardly. The 'official' *Road Show* session is rather showbiz-inflected, with the pointless intrusion of The Four Freshmen and Kenton's band sounding tightened-up on some of their familiar fare; but June Christy's segment of the programme is a welcome reminder of her role as the best of Kenton's singers.

***(*)   Mellophonium Magic Status CD 103 CD
Kenton; Dalton Smith, Bob Behrendt, Marvin Stamm, Bob Rolfe, Phil Grossman (*t*); Dwight Carver, Gene Roland, Carl Saunders, Keith LaMotte (*mel*); Bob Fitzpatrick, Jack Spurlock, Bud Parker (*tb*); Jim Amlotte (*btb*); Dave Wheeler (*btb, tba*); Gabe Baltazar (*as*); Sam Donahue, Paul Renzi (*ts*); Wayne Dunstan (*bs, bsx*); Marvin Holladay (*bs*); Pierre Josephs (*b*); Jerry McKenzie (*d*); George Acevedo (*perc*). 6/61.

***(*)   Mellophonium Moods Status STCD 106 CD
Kenton; Dalton Smith, Marvin Stamm, Bob Behrendt, Keith Lamotte, Bob Rolfe (*t*); Gene Roland, Ray Starling, Dwight Carver, Carl Saunders (*mel*); Bob Fitzpatrick, Dee Barton, Bud Parker (*tb*); Jim Amlotte (*btb*); Dave Wheeler (*btb, tba*); Gabe Baltazar (*as*); Charlie Mariano, Ray Florian (*ts*); Allan Beutler (*bs*); Joel Kaye (*bsx*); Val Kolar (*b*); Jerry McKenzie (*d*). 3/62.

Kenton's 'mellophonium' band took his fascination with brass to new lengths: there are 14 brass players in both of these bands. the leader's verdict was that the band represented 'the New Era in Modern American Music', but it actually sounds like a beefier, more metallic edition of the old Kentonian machine. By this time Kenton had become entirely *sui generis*, and the prevailing winds of jazz fashion had little effect on the orchestra's direction. But he was still usually on the dinner-dance circuit, and both these discs contain somewhat rueful admissions from the leader that they'll play something people can dance to, but he wouldn't mind if people wanted to listen too. No false pride: this was a great, swinging band, and if Kenton had lost most of his best soloists, the features for Baltazar, Mariano and some of the brassmen are handled with great aplomb. The *Mellophonium Moods* set is the better one in terms of fidelity – the sound is quite superb for a supposedly private recording – and with a higher degree of original material, including a number of Kenton rarities, it's marginally more intersting musically, too. But either disc will surprise even those who may think Kenton is merely bombastic and tedious.

**(*)   Live At Redlands University Creative World STD 1015 CD
Kenton; Joe Ellis (*t, v*); Mike Vax, Jim Kartchner, Dennis Noday, Warren Gale (*t*); Dick Shearer, Mike Jamieson, Fred Carter, Tom Bridges (*tb*); Graham Ellis (*btb, tba*); Quin Davis (*as*); Richard Torres, Norm Smith, Jim Timlin (*ts*); Willie Maiden (*bs*); Gary Todd (*b*); John Von Ohlen (*d*); Efraim Logreira (*perc*). 10/70.

**(*)   Live At Brigham Young University Creative World STD 1039 CD
Kenton; Mike Vax, Gary Pack, Jay Saunders, Joe Marcinkiewicz (*t*); Dick Shearer, Fred Carter, Mike Jamieson, Mike Wallace, Graham Ellis (*tb*); Quin Davis, Kim

Frizell (*as*); Willie Maiden (*ts, bs*); Richard Torres (*ts*); Chuck Carter (*bs*); Gary Todd (*b*); John Von Ohlen (*d*); Ramon Lopez (*perc*). 8/71.

**   **Live At Butler University** Creative World STD 1059 CD
Kenton; Jay Saunders, Dennis Noday, Mike Vax, Mike Snustead, Raymond Brown (*t*); Dick Shearer, Mike Jamieson, Fred Carter, Mike Wallace (*tb*); Phil Herring (*btb, tba*); Quin Davis (*as, f*); Richard Torres, Chris Galuman (*ts, f*); Chuck Carter (*bs, ss, f*); Willie Maiden (*bs*); John Worster (*b*); Jerry McKenzie (*d*); The Four Freshmen (*v*). 6/72.

***   **Birthday In Britain** Creative World STD 1065 CD
Kenton; Denis Noday, Paul Adamson, Frank Minear, Mike Snustead, Robert Winiker (*t*); Dick Shearer, Harvey Coonin, Lloyd Spoon (*tb*); John Park (*as*); Chris Galuman (*ts, f*); Richard Torres, Willie Maiden (*ts*); Roy Reynolds (*bs*); John Worster (*b*); Peter Erskine (*d*); Ramon Lopez (*perc*). 2/73.

(*)   **7.5 On The Richter Scale Creative World STD 1070 CD
As above, except add Mike Barrowman (*t*), Gary Pack, Dale Devoe, Bill Hartman, Mike Wallace (*tb*), Mary Fettig (*ts*), Kim Park (*ts, as*), Kirby Stewart (*b*), omit Minear, Winiker, Coonin, Maiden and Worster. 8/73.

(*)   **Kenton '76 Creative World STD 1076 CD
Kenton; John Harner, Jay Sollenberger, Steve Campos, Jim Oatts, Tim Hagans (*t*); Dick Shearer, Dave Keim, Mike Egan (*tb*); Alan Morrissey (*btb*); Douglas Purviance (*btb, tba*); Terry Layne (*as, f*); Roy Reynolds, Dan Salmasian (*ts, f*); Alan Yankee, Gregg Smith (*bs, f*); Dave Stone (*b*); Gary Hobbs (*d*); Ramon Lopez (*perc*). 12/75.

Like any bandleader working through this period, Kenton had to change and compromise to survive, and the orchestra he worked with through the 1970s became as modish and subject to fads as any big band survivor. But at least Kenton had always stood by his 'progressivenes', and as subject to trashy material and clockwork charts as many of the later records are, the orchestra is no less predictable or bombastic than, say, the Basie band in the same period. Kenton had no great array of soloists but, as with the Buddy Rich band, he valued precision and overall effect, and all of the surviving records (on CD – presumably there is much more that will be reissued) have virtues of their own.

The various university concerts (where Kenton was always in favour, it seems) are sometimes bizarre mixtures of old and new: at Redlands he plays 'Hey Jude' and 'Macarthur Park' alongside 'Here's That Rainy Day' and 'Artistry In Rhythm'. At Brigham Young, it's 'Theme From Love Story' and 'Rhapsody In Blue'. Most peculiar of all is the Butler University set, where the band play 'Surfer Girl' (in 1972?) and 'Brand New Key' and then have The Four Freshmen join them! But the usual assertiveness of the brass section introduces moments of both grandeur and genuine excitement into all of these sets. *Birthday In Britain* has a better set of charts (with the young Peter Erskine driving them), and *7.5 On The Richter Scale*, despite opening with the theme from *Live And Let Die* and going on to 'It's Not Easy Being Green', isn't a bad set of punch-ups for the sections. *'76*, with another new band, is merely OK big-band fare. Ultimately, there is still a lot of Kenton to choose from, even with a vast proportion of his work currently out of print.

ROBIN KENYATTA (born 1942)
ALTO SAXOPHONE, TENOR SAXOPHONE, SOPRANO SAXOPHONE, FLUTE

*   **Take The Heat Off Me** ITM Pacific ITMP 970069 CD
Kenyatta; Lew Soloff (*t*); Pat Coil, Masao Nakajima, Mike Nox, Dom Salvadore, Peter Solomon (*p*); Cornell Dupree, Marcus Fiorillo, Darryl Thompson (*g*); Ed Montiero (*acc, v*); Sal Cuevas, David Eubanks, John Lee (*b*); Leroy Clouden, Brian Janszen, John Susswell (*d*); Crusher Bennett, Mike Pomier (*perc*); Chuck Hudson (*v*); Chuck Green (*dancer*); strings. 79.

Printing the wrong track order on the liner may have been a feeble attempt to put hostile critics off the scent. This is the weakest work Kenyatta ever put on record, a bland, MOR set in a version of Chick Corea's latinized *Return To Forever* idiom, but marred by excruciating vocals, skittering percussion and bland 'soul' arrangements that would embarrass any hourly-rate producer worthy of the name. Low points – as if they were needed – include an arrangement of 'The Sheik Of Araby' that is quite spectacularly bad, and, God help us, a tap-dancer. Avoid.

(*) **Live At Cully – Blues For Mama Doll Jazz Dance 1989 CD
Kenyatta; François Couturier (*p*); Reggie Johnson or François Laizeau (*b*);
Jean-Pierre Arnaud or Jean-Paul Celea (*d*). 1/87 & 3/89.

*** **Ghost Stories** ITM ITMP 970060 CD
Kenyatta; Morten Gronvad (*vib*); Reggie Johnson (*b*); Ronnie Burrage (*d*). 2/91.

Something of a musical gypsy, Robin Kenyatta has absorbed a huge range of modern jazz idiom – everything from Afro-Latin to free form – without ever taking on the embarrassment of a personal 'style'. *Ghost Stories* appears to be some attempt to appease and keep his ancestors at a distance. 'Lullaby Of The Leaves' and 'The Breeze And I' are good examples of Kenyatta's funked-up mainstream approach. 'My Favorite Things' is sufficiently original and integral not merely to seem a farewell to the abiding presence of John Coltrane. Perhaps oddly, Trane's impact on the New Yorker is more obvious in his earlier alto work than in his off-on interest in tenor saxophone (enthusiasts should look out for *Beggars And Stealers* [Muse MR 5095], a record of Kenyatta's 1969 'Tenor Concert'); on the most recent showing, it still isn't his natural horn; the comparison between the two is best caught on the compilation of 1987 and 1989 sets on *Blues For Mama Doll*, named after a jaunty original also covered on *Ghost Stories*. Kenyatta once partnered vibraharpist Karl Berger in a free-jazz line-up; Gronvad's soft but propulsive approach is more conventional but also more effective than Couturier's off-the-peg lines; Burrage lives up to his billing as 'featured' artist with fine, unshowy percussion; Reggie Johnson is probably the most sympathetic bassist he has worked with since Walter Booker and Arild Andersen and is the mainstay of both sets.

Kenyatta's best-known record probably remains the deleted 1970 ECM *Girl From Martinique* [ECM 1008 LP], but these are both attractive introductions, and the ITM is vividly recorded.

FREDDIE KEPPARD (1890–1933)
CORNET

*** **Red Onion Jazz Babies/Cook's Dreamland Orchestra/Freddie Keppard's Jazz Cardinals** Fountain FJ-107 LP
Keppard; Elwood Graham (*c*); Fred Garland, Eddie Vincent (*tb*); Jimmie Noone, Clifford King (*cl, as*); Johnny Dodds (*cl*); Joe Poston (*as*); Jerome Pasquall (*ts*); Arthur Campbell, Antonia Spaulding (*p*); Jimmy Bell (*vn*); Stan Wilson (*bj*); Bill Newton (*bb*); Bert Green, Jasper Taylor (*d*); Papa Charlie Jackson (*v*). 1/24–9/26.

'The greatest hot trumpeter in existence . . . the best ear, the best tone and the most marvellous execution I ever heard.' Jelly Roll Morton remembered Freddie Keppard that way, and it's one of the enduring disappointments in early jazz that his surviving records don't live up to this assessment. The second 'King' of New Orleans horn, after Buddy Bolden and before Joe Oliver, Keppard passed up offers to record even before the ODJB – allegedly because he didn't want other people hearing and stealing his ideas – and by the time he did come to make records he was surely past his best. His half of the above LP (the rest is by the Red Onion Jazz Babies with Armstrong and Bechet) collects many of the few discs he left behind. The six titles by Cook's Dreamland Orchestra have him hidden in a 12-piece band, and the courtly arrangements and novelty effects sink most of the efforts at jazz which the band can muster: but here and there, as in the very last measures of 'So This Is Venice' or the muted solos on 'Moanful Man', Keppard asserts himself. His two-cornet partnership with Graham seems to be modelled on the front line of Oliver's Creole Jazz Band, and it's tantalizing to wonder what they could have done, away from such constricting arrangements.

The two tracks (plus one alternative take) by the Jazz Cardinals are the best evidence of Keppard's worth. In what is probably a unique partnership with the country blues master, Papa Charlie Jackson, the band play a driving, harsh kind of jazz–blues, with Dodds in the ascendant and Keppard piling into the role of lead horn. His fluttering vibrato and staccato phrasing are clearly the work of a man from another era, even to the jazz of the 1920s, and it makes his bursting manner all the more fascinating. Alas, the tracks, which were recorded for the Paramount company, share the atrocious qualities of all their recordings, but the remastering has made the most of them and the band certainly power through the surroundings. If this is ultimately a frustrating record, it's a very important document of a player whose true worth we'll never really know.

BARNEY KESSEL (born 1923)
GUITAR

(*) **Easy Like Original Jazz Classics OJC 153 CD/LP/MC
Kessel; Bud Shank, Buddy Collette (*as, f*); Harold Ross, Claude Williamson (*p*);
Harry Babasin (*b*); Shelly Manne (*d*). 11/53–2/56.

*** **Plays Standards** Original Jazz Classics OJC 238 CD/LP/MC
Kessel; Bob Cooper (*ts, ob*); Claude Williamson, Hampton Hawes (*p*); Monty Budwig,
Red Mitchell (*b*); Shelly Manne, Chuck Thompson (*d*). 6–7/54.

*** **To Swing Or Not To Swing** Original Jazz Classics OJC 317 CD/LP/MC
Kessel; Harry Edison (*t*); Georgie Auld, Bill Perkins (*ts*); Jimmy Rowles (*p*); Al
Hendrickson (*g*); Red Mitchell (*b*); Irv Cottler (*d*). 6/55.

'The blues he heard as a boy in Oklahoma, the swing he learned on his first band job and the modern sounds of the West Coast school': Nesuhi Ertegun's summary of Kessel, written in 1954, still holds as good as any description. Kessel has been undervalued as a soloist in recent years: the smoothness and accuracy of his playing tends to disguise the underlying weight of the blues which informs his improvising, and his albums from the 1950s endure with surprising consistency. *Easy Like*, with flute by Shank and Collette, is a little too feathery, but the guitarist's clean lines spare little in attack, and the terrific 'Vicky's Dream' emerges as furious bop. The two subsequent albums suggest a firm truce between Basie-like small-band swing – hardly surprising with Edison on hand – and the classic West Coast appraisal of bop. The inclusion of such ancient themes as 'Louisiana', 'Twelfth Street Rag' and 'Indiana' suggests the breadth of Kessel's interests, and although most of the tracks are short, nothing seems particularly rushed. Lester Koenig's superb production has been faithfully maintained for the reissues: Manne, especially, is well served by the engineering.

*** **The Poll Winners** Original Jazz Classics OJC 156 CD/LP/MC
Kessel; Ray Brown (*b*); Shelly Manne (*d*). 3/57.

(*) **The Poll Winners Ride Again Original Jazz Classics OJC 607 CD/LP/MC
As above. 8/58.

*** **Poll Winners Three** Contemporary C 7576 LP
As above. 11/59.

***(*) **Exploring The Scene** Contemporary C 7581 LP
As above. 8–9/60.

Since Kessel, Brown and Manne regularly scored high in jazz fans' polls of the day, Contemporary's decision to record them as a trio was commercially impeccable. But they were a committed musical group too. *The Poll Winners* includes jamming on 'Satin Doll' and 'Mean To Me' which is sophisticated enough to imply a telepathy between Kessel and Manne. But the group push harder on the remaining records, although *Ride Again* includes some weak material. By the time of *Exploring The Scene*, the trio were comfortable with greater challenges, and this set of contemporary themes from such as Davis, Coleman and John Lewis displays a rare concern to go forward even within a comparatively conservative format. The superb studio sound highlights inner detail.

** **Plays Carmen** Original Jazz Classics OJC 269 CD/LP/MC
Kessel; Ray Linn (*t*); Harry Betts (*tb*); Buddy Collette (*cl, f*); Bill Smith (*cl, bcl*); Jules
Jacobs (*cl, ob*); Pete Terry (*bcl, bsn*); Herb Geller (*as*); Justin Gordon (*ts, f*); Chuck
Gentry (*bs*); André Previn (*p*); Victor Feldman (*vinb*); Joe Mondragon (*b*); Shelly
Manne (*d*). 12/58.

*** **Some Like It Hot** Original Jazz Classics OJC 168 CD/LP/MC
Kessel; Joe Gordon (*t*); Art Pepper (*cl, as, ts*); Jimmy Rowles (*p*); Jack Marshall (*g*);
Monty Budwig (*b*); Shelly Manne (*d*). 3–4/59.

The *Carmen* album was a cute idea that might best have stayed as no more than that, although Kessel gives it enough dedication to create some typical swinging blues out of the likes of 'Carmen's Cool'. *Some Like It Hot* works much better, since this set of tunes from the then-hit film offered the kind of new-lamps-for-old which Kessel had already been trying on earlier records. Pepper shines on all three horns, Gordon contributes some acrid solos on one of his rare appearances on record, and Kessel experiments with three different guitars and a couple of duo-only tunes. 'Runnin' Wild', taken at a blistering pace, is a tiny gem.

(*)   **Autumn Leaves Black Lion BL 60112 CD/LP
Kessel; Teddy Edwards (*ts*); Jimmy Rowles (*p*); Kenny Napper (*b*); John Marshall (*d*). 10/68–9/69.

***   **Feeling Free** Original Jazz Classics OJC 179 LP/MC
Kessel; Bobby Hutcherson (*vib*); Chuck Domanico (*b*); Elvin Jones (*d*). 2/69.

**   **Just Friends** Sonet SNT 685 CD/MC
Kessel; Sture Nordin (*b*); Pelle Hulten (*d*). 9/73.

***   **The Poll Winners/Straight Ahead** Original Jazz Classics OJC 409 CD/LP/MC
Kessel; Ray Brown (*b*); Shelly Manne (*d*).7/75.

Kessel spent most of the 1960s as a studio session guitarist, but when he did return to a jazz setting his playing was scarcely impaired. Most of the music on *Autumn Leaves* is with the sole support of Napper and Marshall, who play perfunctorily, which leaves Kessel to toy with ideas; it's still a pretty record, with three odd tracks with Edwards and Rowles as makeweight. Despite a couple of pop tunes, *Feeling Free* finds the guitarist in tough company, and the blues pieces receive intense treatment, especially 'Blues Up, Down And All Around'. The Poll Winners reunion is as good as their earlier records, yet looser, less drilled. 'Caravan' and 'Laura' become springboards for playing as freely as they ever could together. *Just Friends* is a club date recorded in Stockholm, and although one misses the kind of support that Brown and Manne can provide, Kessel's own improvisations sustain the music.

**   **Three Guitars** Concord CCD 6004 CD/MC
Kessel; Herb Ellis, Charlie Byrd (*g*); Joe Byrd (*b*); Johnny Rae (*d*). 7/74.

**   **Barney Plays Kessel** Concord CCD 6009 CD/MC
Kessel; Herbie Steward (*ss, as, f*); Victor Feldman (*vib*); Jimmy Rowles (*p*); Chuck Domanico (*b*); Jake Hanna (*d*); Milt Holland (*perc*). 4/75.

**   **Soaring** Concord CCD 6033 CD/MC
Kessel; Monty Budwig (*b*); Jake Hanna (*d*). 77.

Kessel doesn't sit very comfortably in Concord's cosy setting. The duos and trios with Byrd and Ellis offer only routine virtuosity, and his first programme of originals isn't much of an event when the accompanying band play them as politely as they do here. *Soaring* creates some pretty music, but is laid-back enough to scarcely raise itself above the horizontal. He fares better on his meeting with Monty Alexander, *Spontaneous Combustion*.

STEVE KHAN (born 1947)
GUITAR

**   **Local Color** Denon 33CY-1840 CD
Khan; Rob Mounsey (*ky, v*). 4–5/87.

(*)   **Public Access GRP GRD-9599 CD/MC
Khan; Anthony Jackson (*b*); Dave Weckl (*d*); Manolo Badrena (*p, v*). 1/89.

A talented guitarist in search of a context, Steve Khan's records succumb to introversion. He's far from the expected merchant of bombast which so many fusion-orientated guitarists become, his improvisations often interestingly fragmented and concerned with tonal variation as much as with racing up and down complex scales. He apprenticed as a rock session musician through most of the 1970s, but his interest in jazz playing led him to form Eyewitness, the band which is responsible for *Public Access*. The album of duets, *Local Color*, is sensitively done, but dull: the seven tunes miss the melodic fillip which might compensate for the rhythmic languor, and

Mounsey's playing is faceless. Eyewitness are inward-looking in another way: Khan seems reluctant to take command, and it's Weckl's irritatingly busy rhythms which dominate their work. As a result, the group sounds as if it's playing only for itself, with Jackson's fast-fingered bass parts low in the mix and Badrena contributing a lot of tiresome distractions as both vocalist and percussionist. When Khan gets to take charge – on the interesting 'Blue Zone 41', where he patiently builds a thoughtful solo in the midst of a torrent of other noise – matters look up. The best moment by far is his gentle reading of 'Dedicated To You', co-written by his father, Sammy Cahn; here Weckl plays relatively straight time and Khan's vibrant tone is distinctly affecting.

DAVID KIKOSKI
KEYBOARDS

(*)   **Presage Freelance FRL 011 CD
Kikoski; Eddie Gomez (*b*); Al Foster (*d*). 7–8/89.

Like so many younger pianists, David Kikoski stands in the shadows of McCoy Tyner and Herbie Hancock. At fast tempos he approximates Tyner's grand sense of attack, while at the steadier pace of, say, the title-tune, the one memorable original in this batch, he insinuates the chords and strokes his way through in a manner which is very reminiscent of Hancock. It's a good record in its way: Gomez and Foster play with respectful interest, the bassist's voluminous sound lining every harmonic movement, and a couple of standard treatments – 'In The Still Of The Night', which is dismantled and recast in a mildly striking way, and a slow and pensive 'A Nightingale Sang In Berkeley Square' – find the pianist at his most creative. But one feels that this kind of contemporary jazz date has already been made many times over.

PETER KING (born 1940)
ALTO AND TENOR SAXOPHONES

***   **New Beginning** Spotlite SPJ520 LP
King; Dick Pearce (*t*); John Horler, Pat Smythe (*p*); Ron Mathewson, Dave Green (*b*); Spike Wells (*d*). 82.

***   **East 34th Street** Spotlite SPJ524 LP
As above, except omit Pearce, Smythe and Mathewson. 1/83.

***   **Hi-Fly** Spotlite SPJ527 LP
King; Pete Jacobsen, Brian Dee (*p*); Riccardo Del Frà (*b*); 84.

***   **Live: 90% Of 1%** Spotlite SPJ 529 LP
King; Henry Lowther (*t*); John Horler (*p*).

***(*) **Brother Bernard** Miles Music MM 076 LP
King; Guy Barker (*t*); Alan Skidmore (*ts*); John Horler (*p*); Dave Green (*b*); Tony Levin (*d*). 4/88.

Peter King's admirers despair that he will ever get the recognition he deserves: on the other hand, what plaudits await a British saxophonist who has mastered the bop vocabulary so thoroughly and entertainingly? Session-work and star sideman roles seem to be King's destiny, and it's to his credit that his playing has never shown any hints of discouragement, at least as far as records are concerned: only these small-label albums remain in the catalogue, so far there is nothing on CD, and *Crusade*, a one-shot crossover album for a Warner Brothers subsidiary, made no impact at all. King has been a first-call altoman for 30 years and, while his manner has outwardly changed very little, he's intensified rather than refined away the elements of his style. He was a poised, inventive soloist from the start, and his tone and phrasing – an Anglophile tempering of Parker's virtuosity, although the man he sounds most like is Phil Woods – have become as inimitable as a bop saxophonist can be. All these records give him all the space and support he needs, but only on a few occasions does it seem that King is truly transcending the situation. Like Woods, or Sonny Stitt, he can make it sound so easy that the music drifts into automatic.

East 34th Street, by King's regular quartet, is the best of these
thoughtful set of originals by King, Horler and Dick Walters, and the
the pace and attack of the group rather than leaving the rhythm sectio
the leader. The other Spotlites are all good and generously filled with
but only the live set, with Henry Lowther adding his own post-bop lyric
extra edge to it. *Brother Bernard* is nothing more nor less than a continua
Wonder's 'Overjoyed' was an excellent choice, and 'But Beautif
comprehensive skill at ballad playing; but the three tracks with Barker and
horns add little but extra weight.

ANDY KIRK (born 1898)
BANDLEADER, BASS SAXOPHONE, TUBA

**** The Chronological Andy Kirk, 1936–1937 Classics 573 CD
Kirk; Paul King, Harry Lawson, Earl Thomson, Clarence Trice (*t*); Ted Donnelly,
Henry Wells (*tb*); John Harrington (*cl, as, bs*); John Williams (*as, bs*); Earl Miller (*as*);
Dick Wilson (*ts*); Claude Williams (*vn*); Mary Lou Williams (*p*); Ted Brinson, Ted
Robinson (*g*); Booker Collins (*b*); Ben Thigpen (*d*); O'Neil Spencer, Pha Terrell (*v*).
3, 4 & 12/36.

***(*) The Chronological Andy Kirk, 1937 Classics 581 CD
As above. 2, 4, 7 & 12/37.

***(*) The Chronological Andy Kirk, 1937–1938 Classics 598 CD
As above. 2, 9, 10 & 12/38.

*** The Uncollected Andy Kirk Hindsight HSR 227 LP
Kirk; Art Capehart, Harry Lawson, Howard McGhee, Fats Navarro (*t*); John Baird,
Bobby Murray, Wayne Richardson (*tb*); John Harrington (*cl, as, bs*); Jimmy Forrest
(*ts*); James D. King, Eddie Loving (*saxes*); John Young (*p*); Booker Collins (*b*); Ben
Thigpen (*d*); June Richmond (*v*); probable personnel. 44.

Though he was often out front for photo opportunities, Andy Kirk ran the Clouds of Joy strictly
from the back row. The limelight was usually left to singer June Richmond or vocalist/conductor
Pha Terrell; the best of the arrangements were done by Mary Lou Williams, who left the band
in 1942; as a bass saxophonist, Kirk wasn't called on to take a solo. All the same, he turned the
Clouds of Joy – which he inherited bloodlessly from Terrence Holder's Dark Clouds of Joy in
1929 and ran successfully and then intermittently for the next five decades – into one of the
most inventive swing bands. His disposition was sunny and practical and he was a competent
organizer (who in later life ran a Harlem hotel, the legendary Theresa, and organized a
Musicians' Union local in New York City.)
     Inevitably, given Kirk's low musical profile, critical attention is more usually directed to
other members of the band. The classic Clouds of Joy cuts are those that feature Mary Lou
Williams's arrangements and performances, and for these the three Classics compilations are
essential, though many of the best tracks can be found on compilations under Williams's own
name. The earlier material is still the best, with 'Moten Swing', 'Until The Real Thing Comes
Along' and the hit 'Froggy Bottom' prominent. There are, though, fine performances from 1937
and 1938, most notably 'Mary's Idea' from December 1938. Sound-reproduction is reasonably
good. Still missing from the catalogue are the sessions recorded between 1939 and Mary Lou
Williams's departure, and which include such classic tracks as 'Floyd's Guitar Blues', 'McGhee
Special', a feature for young trumpeter Howard McGhee. This will be rectified in subsequent
Classics releases. The weaker 1944 band is of historical interest mainly for the emergence of
McGhee, fellow-trumpeter Fats Navarro and tenor saxophonist Jimmy Forrest. 'Roll 'Em' was
a big hit for Benny Goodman; the Clouds' version is simpler and more choppy, but still
engaging. 'St Louis Blues' and 'Seven Come Eleven' are well worth the entrance money but, to
avoid disappointment, newcomers will have to look elsewhere.

ROLAND KIRK (1936–77)

SAXOPHONE, MANZELLO, STRITCH, FLUTE, ASSORTED INSTRUMENTS

[*   **Soulful Saxes** Affinity AFF 758 CD]
       Kirk; Jimmy Madison (*p*); Carl Pruitt (*b*); Henry Duncan (*d*). 11/56.

(*)   **Introducing Roland Kirk Chess CHD 91551 CD
       Kirk; Ira Sullivan (*t, ts*); William Burton (*org, p*); Donald Garrett (*b*); Sonny Brown
       (*d*). 6/60.

Jazz purists were quick to dismiss Roland Kirk as a mere showman. Blinded as an infant, he built his music on a vivid dream-life, using false fingerings and one or two blatant tricks to enable him to play up to three saxophones at a time. The saxophones themselves were non-standard. In a music-shop basement Kirk discovered a manzello and a stritch, rare horns apparently used in Spanish marching bands. The manzello approximated the pitch of the soprano saxophone – close, as they said in the booths, but no cigar – and the stritch was an off-pitch alto saxophone. By playing them together and breezily circumventing some of the harmonic anomalies, Kirk could mimic a whole saxophone section. His flute was heavily vocalized and he punctuated performances with blasts from whistles and sirens.

His first recordings were more or less ignored. The earliest material is preserved on *Soulful Saxes*, a compilation that also features Booker Ervin, another heterodox saxophonist who would catch Charles Mingus's eye. The sound is raw and slightly off-putting, and Kirk hasn't yet achieved the astonishing contrapuntal effects of the later live sets, below, and there is some overdubbing of saxophone 'ensembles'. 'The Nearness Of You' offers some pointers to greatness and the Ervin tracks are well worth having.

The later Chess is already more assured. Kirk's conception of his art as 'Black classical music' depended on the exclusion of virtually all references to the European tradition. *Introducing* is as utterly American as Walt Whitman's verse: stripped, contradictory, occasionally perverse, and compelling. The addition of flute in no way softens the sound. The recording quality is fine for the vintage, though there are slight problems with the organ.

(*)   **Kirk's Work Original Jazz Classics OJC 459 CD/LP
       Kirk; Jack McDuff (*org*); Joe Benjamin (*b*); Art Taylor (*d*). 7/61.

'Skater's Waltz' is one of Kirk's best bits of surreal kitsch, combined with his familiar inventive ambiguity. He clearly enjoys the big, bruising sound of McDuff's electric organ and boots furiously on all three saxophones and flute. On 'Three For Dizzy' he executes difficult tempos with quite astonishing dexterity. A largely forgotten Kirk album, but one which largely deserves the classic reissue billing.

****   **Rahsaan** Mercury 846630 10CD + bonus CD
       Kirk; Nat Adderley, Al Derisi, Freddie Hubbard, Virgil Jones, Jimmie Maxwell, Joe Newman, Jimmy Nottingham, Ernie Royal, Clark Terry, Richard Williams, Snooky Young (*t*); Martin Banks (*flhn*); Garnett Brown, Billy Byers, Jimmy Cleveland, Paul Faulise, Curtis Fuller, Charles Greenlea, Dick Hixon, Quentin Jackson, J. J. Johnson, Melba Liston, Tom McIntosh, Tom Mitchell, Santo Russo, Tony Studd, Kai Winding (*tb*); Ray Alonge, Jimmy Buffington, Earl Chapin, Paul Ingraham, Fred Klein, Tony Miranda, Bob Northern, Willie Ruff, Julius Watkins (*frhn*); Don Butterfield, Jay McAllister, Henry Phillips, Bill Stanley (*tba*); Benny Golson, Lucky Thompson (*ts*); Tubby Hayes (*ts, vib*); James Moody (*ts, f;* as 'Jimmy Gloomy'); Pepper Adams (*bs*); Al Cohn, Jerry Dodgion, Budd Johnson, Walt Levinsky, Romeo Penque, Seldon Powell, Jerome Richardson, Zoot Sims, Stan Webb, Frank Wess, Phil Woods (*reeds*); Walter Bishop Jr, Jaki Byard, Hank Jones, Wynton Kelly, Harold Mabern, Tete Montoliu, Bobby Scott, Horace Parlan, Richard Wyands (*p*); Andrew Hill (*p, cel*); Patti Brown, Lalo Schifrin, Bobby Scott (*p, org*); Eddie Baccus (*org*); Gary Burton, Milt Jackson, Bobby Moses (*vib*); Vincent Bell, Kenny Burrell, Mose Fowler, Jim Hall, Wayne Wright (*g*); Sonny Boy Williamson (*hca;* as 'Big Skol'); Charles McCoy (*hca*); Bob Cranshaw, Art Davis, Richard Davis, George Duvivier, Michael Fleming, Milt Hinton, Sam Jones, Wendell Marshall, Vernon Martin, Eddie Mathias, Don Moore, Niels-Henning Ørsted-Pedersen, Major Holley, Abdullah Rafik, Ben Tucker, Chris White (*b*); Art Blakey, Sonny Brown, George Cook, Rudy Collins, Charles Crosby, Henry Duncan, Steve Ellington, Louis Hayes, Roy Haynes, Albert Heath,

Osie Johnson, Elvin Jones, J. C. Moses, Walter Perkins, Charlie Persip, Ed Shaughnessy (*d*); Bill Costa, Jack Del Rio, George Devens, Charles Gomez, Phil Kraus, Montego Joe, Jose Paula, Manuel Ramos (*perc*); Miss C. J. Albert (*v*); others unidentified. 61–64.

Potential purchasers shouldn't be misled into thinking that this is a 'Complete' or 'Collected' Kirk. It represents only the – admittedly marvellous – recordings he made for the Mercury label during five of his most productive years. Serious collectors will also want to have later material like *The Inflated Tear*, and a group of unpredictable Atlantics, *Volunteered Slavery* [ATL 40042 LP], *Rahsaan Rahsaan* [ATL 40127 LP], *Natural Black Invention: Roots Strata* [ATL 40185 LP], *Left And Right* [ATL 40235 LP] and *Here Comes The Whistleman* [ATL 40389 LP].

Disc 1 of the Mercury set is a repackaging of the popular *We Free Kings* [formerly Polydor 846455] with a good alternative take of Parker's 'Blues For Alice' and an unissued 'Spring Will Be A Little Late This Year'. This is roughly the pattern observed throughout the set: alternatives have been included on merit, not (as with some Parker compilations) merely for the sake of checking matrix numbers. The other original releases are *Domino* [MG 20748, now disc 2], *Reeds And Deeds* [MG 20800, discs 3–4], *The Roland Kirk Quartet Meets The Benny Golson Orchestra* [MG 20844, now 4] where Kirk sounds quite at home in Golson's rich, Gil Evans-like arrangements; there is the live *Kirk In Copenhagen* [MG 20894, now discs 5–6, with nine unissued tracks] featuring Sonny Boy Williamson, *Gifts And Messages* [MG 20939, now disc 7], *I Talk With The Spirits* [LM 82008, now disc 8], *Rip, Rig And Panic* [LM 82027, now disc 9 – but see below], and *Slightly Latin* [LM 82033, now disc 9]. In addition to an uncredited and mostly unissued 1964 session on disc 7, there are also cuts made under the leadership of Tubby Hayes, organist Eddie Baccus (one track only) and Quincy Jones.

The Jones tracks bear much the same relation to the better material as the Bird-with-strings sessions to the classic Verve small groups. Jones's advocacy – like Ramsey Lewis's – was critical to the hornman's career and helped overcome a deadweight of industry suspicion, but the mid-market pitch was unfortunate. Eminently professional, the arrangements smooth out Kirk's eldritch sound in a way that Golson's imaginative charts don't.

Of the small groups, the *We Free Kings* session is still as fresh as paint; Kirk's mildly irreverent reworking of the Christmas carol sounds hokey at first hearing but makes increasing sense on repeated exposure, much like Thelonious Monk's 'straight' 'Abide With Me'. 'Three For The Festival' became one of his most frequently performed compositions. There are marvellous things, too, on the 1962 and 1963 sessions with Andrew Hill (his first working group) and Harold Mabern slip-anchoring sympathetic rhythm sections. Some of the real surprises come in the one-off collaboration with Tubby Hayes. Also featuring James Moody (under the contractual *nom de studio*, 'Jimmy Gloomy'), the pairing of flutes over Hayes's vibes on 'Lady "E"' is masterful. The tenor chase effects recall 'Three For The Festival'. Elsewhere, Kirk and Moody play off against the visitor's less abstract bop style. During a superb ballad medley, Kirk attacks 'For Heaven's Sake' without a reed in his tenor saxophone; the sound is both startling and beautiful.

The live Copenhagen sessions with bluesman Williamson are credited with two bassists, Don Moore and the ubiquitous NHØP. They don't seem to play together, but it isn't always easy to pick detail out of a raucous, clubby recording which has Montoliu optimistically bashing an out-of-tune and tinny piano much as his model Bud Powell had to do in later years. Needless to say, Kirk remains triumphantly unfazed.

Inevitably expensive but beautifully packaged, and with an intelligently detailed booklet by critic Don Morgenstern. *Rahsaan* nevertheless affords unparalleled detail on perhaps the most significant single phase of Kirk's career. Newcomers should certainly start elsewhere, but enthusiasts will find these ten discs (and the brief bonus 'Stritch In Time' from the 1962 Newport Festival) essential acquisitions.

***   **Now Please Don't You Cry, Beautiful Edith** Verve 2304519 LP
Kirk; Lonnie Liston Smith (*p*); Ronnie Boykins (*b*); Grady Tate (*d*). 4/67.

***(*)   **Rip, Rig And Panic / Now Please Don't You Cry, Beautiful Edith** EmArCy 832164 IMS CD
Kirk; as above, plus Jaki Byard (*p*); Richard Davis (*b*); Elvin Jones (*d*). 1/65, 4/67.

Now superseded by the EmArCy CD twofer, the single LP re-release of *Now Please Don't You Cry, Beautiful Edith* revives one of Kirk's unaccountably least-known recordings; it was his only record for Verve, made between contracts. Kirk's usual approach to schmaltz was to pepper it furiously. Brief as it is, 'Alfie' is given a half-ironic, half-respectful reading that is genuinely moving, with a typically ambiguous coda. Elsewhere, Kirk ranges from big Ellingtonian themes to out-and-out rock'n'roll.

Rip, Rig And Panic justifies single-CD release in this packaging (it's also to be found on the *Rahsaan* compilation, above) by its sheer energy and popularity (a British-based funk band named themselves after the album). The opening 'No Tonic Pres' is a tribute to Lester Young developed without definite key resolution. Like the succeeding 'From Bechet, Fats And Byas', it underlines Kirk's allusive invention and ability to make music with the most attenuated materials. Both 'Slippery, Hippery, Flippery' and the furious title-track develop Kirk's interest in 'found' or chance effects; Byard's piano playing switches between Bud Powell, the rhythmic fractures of Monk and the uncentred tonality of Cecil Taylor. Elvin Jones's drum solo on 'Rip, Rig And Panic' is one of his very best on record. On the final 'Mystical Dream', Kirk plays stritch, tenor and, incredibly, oboe at the same time, posing articulation and harmonic problems that would have sunk a less complete musician.

Fine as it is, there seems little point in going for the vinyl *Now Please Don't You Cry* unless you've already invested in the ten-CD *Rahsaan*. If not, *Rip, Rig And Panic* is a must.

***(*) **The Inflated Tear** Atlantic 7567 81396 CD
Kirk; Ron Burton (*p*); Steve Novosel (*b*); Jimmy Hopps (*d*). 5/68.

One of the finest of all Kirk's albums, it is also one of the most contained and straightforward, establishing his gifts as an improviser beyond all contradiction. The title-track relates to his blindness and conveys the dreamlike oddity and human passion of his music to perfection. The band are by no means top-drawer, but Kirk had a happy knack not just of getting the best out of players but also of subtly adapting his own delivery to the men round him. An ideal place to begin if you've never heard a note of Kirk; but prepare for surprises elsewhere. The CD sound is pretty good.

** **The Case Of The Three-sided Dream In Audio Color** Atlantic 1674 CD
Kirk; Pat Patrick (*bs*); Cornell Dupree, Keith Loving, Hugh McCracken (*g*); Arthur Jenkins, Hilton Ruiz, Richard Tee (*ky*); Francisco Centeno, Matthias Pearson, Bill Salter (*b*); Sonny Brown, Steve Gadd, John Goldsmith (*d*); Lawrence Killian; Ralph McDonald (*perc*).

** **The Man Who Cried Fire** Night VNLP 1 CD/LP/MC
Kirk; Steve Turre (*tb*); Kenny Rogers (*bs*); Ron Burton, Hilton Ruiz (*p*); Henry Metathius Pearson (*b*); Sonny Brown, John Goldsmith, Robert Shy (*d*); Todd Barkan, Joe Habad Texidor (*perc*).

These later albums are both disappointing. The much-hyped *Three-sided Dream* was a self-conscious bid to bring Kirk to the attention of rock audiences. The cover art was a good match for his surrealist approach, but the arrangements are too flabby for the imaginative suite-like approach, and the performance as a whole tumbles between two stools. Given that Kirk could almost always levitate in exactly that position, its failure is all the more galling. *The Man Who Cried Fire* suffers from a similarly over-egged production, but the New Orleans passages are strong and effective, and the version of Coltrane's 'Mr P. C.' is completely convincing, elisions and all.

*** **Live In Paris: Volume 1** France's Concert FCD 109 CD
Kirk; Ron Burton (*p*); Vernon Martin (*b*); Jerome Cooper (*d*); Joe Texidor (*perc*).
2/70.

*** **Live In Paris: Volume 2** France's Concert FCD 115 CD
As above.

*** **Petite Fleur** Moon Records 027 CD/LP
As above.

(*) **Paris 1976 Royal Jazz RJD 510 CD
Kirk; Steve Turre (*tb*); Hilton Ruiz (*p*); Phil Bowler (*b*); John Goldsmith (*d*); Michael Hill (*v, perc*). 11/76.

French air suited Kirk and he liked the crowd. These are valuable concert documents from the last phase of his career. By 1970, the busking one-man-band was more or less transformed into a sophisticated and subtle jazz player. The later Kirk showed more interest in playing standards but was typically eager to enlarge the catchment by including pieces like Stevie Wonder's 'beautiful African American beautiful French' 'Ma Chérie Amour' (which appears on the first *Live In Paris* and more convincingly four days later on *Petite Fleur*).

Kirk's interest in Sidney Bechet, one of the great idols of the French jazz scene, had been evident as early as 'From Bechet, Byas And Fats'. Including 'Petite Fleur' in a set was a guaranteed crowd-pleaser; again, it also appears in a different version on *Live In Paris: Volume 1*. The second of the France's Concert sets continues Kirk's running engagement with jazz tradition. The imaginatively constructed 'Parker Medley' is among the best live recordings of Kirk in existence and 'Satin Doll' isn't far behind. The sound on the France's Concerts is pretty ropey, with disconcertingly abrupt cut-offs on the applause, but, as with *Petite Fleur*, which is technically slightly better, the real significance is documentary and musical.

The Kirk who revisited France in 1976 had already been stricken with the first of the cerebral haemorrhages which were to kill him a year later. Severely paralysed, Kirk had largely to abandon his multi-instrumental approach in favour of single horns and concentrating the greater part of his effort on the more familiar sound of the tenor saxophone, adapting his fingering as always. Almost miraculously, he now played some of the best music of his career, quashing at the last hurdle the persistent canard that he was not 'really' a jazz musician at all but a kind of street entertainer. *Paris 1976* is by no means the best of the later concerts, but it is a more than worthwhile record; 'A Night In Tunisia' is marvellous and the retake of 'The Man Who Cried Fire' is a gem.

JOHN KLEMMER (born 1946)
TENOR AND SOPRANO SAX, FLUTE

**   **Waterfalls** MCA MCAD 33123 CD
Klemmer; Mike Nock (*p*); Wilton Felder (*b*); Eddie Marshall (*d*); Victor Feldman (*perc*); Diana Lee (*v*). 6/72.

**   **Barefoot Ballet** MCA MCAD 1583 CD
Klemmer; Bernie Fleischer (*f*); Dave Grusin (*p*); Larry Carlton (*g*); Chuck Domanico (*b*); John Guerin (*d*); Joe Porcaro (*perc*). 4–5/76.

*(*)   **Lifestyle** MCA MCAD 31351 CD
Klemmer; Bernie Fleischer (*f*); Milcho Leviev (*p*); Chuck Domanico (*b*); Harvey Mason (*d*); Chino Valdes (*perc*). 77.

*(*)   **Arabesque** MCA MCAD 5858 CD
Klemmer; Pat Rebillot (*p*); Oscar Castro-Neves (*g*); Abe Laboriel (*b*); Lenny White (*d*); Alex Acuna, Airto Moreira (*perc*). 77.

Klemmer's had a strange career on record. He made his first mark as one of the leading soloists in Don Ellis's band in the 1960s, and some subsequent albums for Cadet (long out of print) saw him searching for a psychedelic jazz-fusion, fairly uneventfully. But he found a much bigger audience in the 1970s for a stack of records that toyed with a vaguely experimental light-fusion concept, based mostly round the use of an echoplex attachment on his horn. These four at least have been remastered for CD and, while none of them amounts to much, with the electronic effects now sounding quaintly dated and the rhythm sections either fussy or faceless, at least Klemmer himself comes across as a far more baroque stylist than the crowd of saxophonists making the wallpaper fusion of today. *Waterfalls*, the earliest, is, not surprisingly, the freshest.

ERIC KLOSS (born 1949)
ALTO SAX

(*)   **One, Two, Free Muse MR 5019 LP
Kloss; Ron Thomas (*p, perc*); Pat Martino (*g*); Dave Holland (*b*); Ron Krasinski (*d*). 8/72.

**   **Battle Of The Saxes Vol. 1** Muse MR 5082 LP
        Kloss; Richie Cole (*as*); Mickey Tucker (*p*); Rick Laird (*b*); Eddie Gladden (*d*). 3/76.

Since this is all there is by Kloss in the catalogue at present, it's hard to square the excitement his arrival caused in the late 1960s with these two middleweight records. No less than ten albums for Prestige, all of them at least very good, are out of print. His scouring, acerbic attack on the alto is demonstrated to some effect on *One, Two, Free*, but the material is (a little self-consciously) in a progressive vein and hasn't worn as well as most of the unavailable records. The meeting with Cole is fleetingly exciting, but soon falls into Cole's customary routine of flag-waving solos which eventually wear the listener down. At least Mickey Tucker keeps some order at the piano. Kloss has been heard from scarcely at all in recent years.

JIMMY KNEPPER (born 1927)
TROMBONE

(*)   **Cunningbird Steeplechase SCS 1061 CD/LP
        Knepper; Al Cohn (*ts*); Roland Hanna (*p*); George Mraz (*b*); Dannie Richmond (*d*).
        11/76.

***   **First Place** Black-Hawk BKH 51001 LP
        Knepper; Bruce Forman (*g*); Mike Richmond (*b*); Billy Hart (*d*). 2/82.

***(*)   **I Dream Too Much** Soul Note SN 1092 CD/LP
        Knepper; John Eckert (*t*); John Clark (*frhn*); Roland Hanna (*p*); George Mraz (*b*);
        Billy Hart (*d*). 2 & 3/84.

***   **Dream Dancing** Criss Cross Jazz Criss 1024 LP
        Knepper; Ralph Moore (*ts*); Dick Katz (*p*); George Mraz (*b*); Mel Lewis (*d*). 4/86.

Long associated with Charles Mingus, Knepper has an astonishingly agile technique (based on altered slide positions) which allows him to play extremely fast lines with considerable legato, more like a saxophonist than a brass player. Doing so has allowed him to avoid the dominant J. J. Johnson style and to develop the swing idiom in a direction that is thoroughly modern and contemporary with a bright, punchy tone.

A dramatic contretemps with Mingus drove him out of active jazz performance for some time, and much of the next decade was spent in the relative obscurity of recording sections and theatre work. *Cunningbird* effectively marked his renaissance as a soloist and leader. It's a fine, strong album, though Knepper's tone isn't quite as assured here as it became in the 1980s, and Al Cohn is below par.

Mraz's firm melodic sense makes him the ideal accompanist, but Knepper has also been shrewd or lucky in his choice of drummers. Hart has the right kind of swing and Richmond is endlessly adaptable; an initial question mark about Lewis's big sound on *Dream Dancing* resolves into an ignorable quirk of the mix, which could be rectified on what would be a welcome CD transfer. It's not quite the best of the bunch, but it's still a fine album. Ralph Moore still had some growing to do, but he didn't make the mistake of doing it in the studio, concentrating on playing within his perfectly respectable limits.

The beautifully arranged brass tonalities of *I Dream Too Much* make it Knepper's most ambitious and fulfilling album. Less of a blowing session than *First Place*, where the backgrounds – by Forman and, unusually, with no piano – are relatively passive and open-ended. Hanna's comping is first rate throughout, though he isn't very generously placed in the mix on *Cunningbird*.

KENNETH KNUDSEN
PIANO, KEYBOARDS

***   **Bombay Hotel** Stunt Records 18903 CD
        Knudsen; Mikkel Nordsoe (*g, pipa*); Ole Theill (*tablas*). 10/88.

Knudsen's best work on record has, unfortunately, all been under other leaders, notably with Palle Mikkelborg and Niels-Henning Ørsted-Pedersen on the trumpeter's beautifully crafted Miles pastiche *Heart To Heart* (Storyville SLP 4114, see below), where his highly textured keyboard palette was the key to the album's success.

Bombay Hotel is a strange, seductive album, virtually uncategorizable but drawing more on orthodox jazz procedures than either instrumentation or immediate impact might suggest. Knudsen plays with great sureness, eschewing flashy runs in favour of straightforward melodic argument and, again, a rich texture. Nordsoe doubles on the pipa, a short-necked fretted Chinese lute with an oddly winsome timbre. Unusual, but worth seeking out.

HANS KOCH
TENOR AND SOPRANO SAXOPHONES, CLARINET, BASS CLARINET

**   **Acceleration** ECM 1357 CD/LP
         Koch; Martin Schutz (*b, clo*); Marco Käppeli (*d*). 6/87.

(*)   **The Art Of The Staccato Sound Aspects sas CD 033 CD
         As above. 1/90.

Koch is perhaps heard to better advantage on the *Duets, Dithyrambisch* (FMP) set with Evan Parker and Louis Sclavis, but there is some harsh, interesting music on both these records. Schutz and Käppeli play a subsidiary but highly interactive role: on the ECM album, against some ponderous improvising by Koch on a variety of horns, they work up a vivid rhythm partnership. But the programming of that album, with dreary interludes such as the clarinet solo on 'Loisada', lets it down. The Sound Aspects disc is rather better, the trio working more cohesively and Koch's improvisations breathing more freely in the air surrounding cello and drums, but finally nothing too special. Interested parties may also be able to seek out an all-solo cassette which Koch has produced.

FRANZ KOGLMANN
TRUMPET, FLUGELHORN

***(*)   **Trio KoKoKo: Good Night** Creative Works CW 1002 LP
         Koglmann; Eckard Koltermann (*bci, bs*); Klaus Koch (*b*). 11/85.

****   **About Yesterday's Ezzthetics** hat Art 6003 CD
         Koglmann; Steve Lacy (*ss*); Mario Arcadi (*ob*); Klaus Koch (*b*); Fritz Hauser (*d, perc*). 4/87.

***   **Orte Der Geometrie** hat Art 6018 CD
         Koglmann; Rudolf Ruschel (*tb*); Jean-Christoph Mastnak (*frhn*); Raoul Herget (*tba*); Mario Arcadi (*ob*); Martin Schelling (*cl*); Roberto Ottaviano (*ss*); Guillerno Gregorio (*as*); Ran Blake, Robert Michel Weiss (*p*); Burkhard Stangl (*g*); Klaus Koch (*b*); Fritz Hauser (*d*). 11/88.

***   **Ich** hat Art 6033 CD
         Koglmann; Rudolf Ruschel (*tb*); Martin Mayes (*frhn*); Raoul Herget (*tba*); Mario Arcadi (*ob*); Martin Schelling (*cl*); Roberto Ottaviano (*ss*); Robert Michel Weiss (*p*); Klaus Koch (*b*); Peter Barborik (*d*). 10/86.

****   **A White Line** hat Art 6048 CD
         Koglmann; Jean-Christoph Mastnak (*frhn*); Raoul Herget (*tba*); Mario Arcadi (*ob*); Tony Coe (*cl, ts*); Helmut Federle (*acc*); Paul Bley (*p*); Burkhard Stangl (*g*); Klaus Koch (*b*); Gerry Hemingway (*d*); Gustav Bauer (*cond*). 11/89.

****   **The Use Of Memory** hat Art 6078 CD
         Koglmann Pipetet. 90

****   **L'Heure Bleue** hat Art 6093 CD
         Koglmann; Tony Coe (*cl, ts*); Burkhard Stangl (*g*); Klaus Koch (*b*); Misha Mengelberg (*p*). 4/91.

With important recent recordings by Anthony Braxton, Steve Lacy, Cecil Taylor, David Murray, Georg Grawe, Joe McPhee and the late Warne Marsh in its catalogue, the Swiss-based hat Art label has become the locus of one of the most comprehensive re-examinations of the jazz and improvisation tradition currently in progress. In contrast to the others, Austrian flugelhorn player Franz Koglmann is a label discovery. He may yet turn out to be one of the most significant jazz revisionists of the new decade.

It's clear that he is undertaking that revision from outside the jazz tradition proper; given that, he almost inevitably picks on the work of jazz outsiders – Richard Twardzik on *A White Line*, George Russell extensively on the manifesto-like *About Yesterday's Ezzthetics*; he also makes frequent reference to literary and plastic artists. Koglmann is not primarily an improviser and his bleakly sentimental attachment to Bix is, on the face of it, rather strange. His charts are meticulously detailed and increasingly (a dead giveaway) scored without drums; Gerry Hemingway makes only sporadic and rather abstract contributions to *A White Line* and Koglmann doesn't seem to know what to do with Barborik or even the splendidly inventive Hauser on earlier albums. His models are primarily 'cool' and 'progressive'; *White Line* – cited again because it seems to have been his breakthrough record – includes Shorty Rogers, Gerry Mulligan and Stan Kenton materials; earlier, Johnny Carisi's newborn-cool 'Israel' was included on *Orte der Geometrie*. However, recent evidence is that he is working through from the almost Webernian sparseness and stillness of the earlier records to a richer (and, dare one say it, more humane) feel.

Ich and *Orte der Geometrie* are not quite satisfactory, marking a significant step backwards from the remarkable compression and intelligence of *About Yesterday's Ezzthetics* and the inventive early trio. Ran Blake, who has done similar work to Koglmann on the Gershwin songbook (*That Certain Feeling*, hat Art CD 6077), appears as a guest on a new and yet more melancholy version of his own 'Short Life Of Barbara Monk'. There's much less overt standard material here, and a good deal of the music could be updated Third Stream. 'My Funny Valentine', with nods to both Chet Baker and Miles Davis, sets *Ich* back on a jazz parallel, but the cue isn't really followed and the record slowly evaporates in a series of precise but insubstantial meditations.

The Use Of Memory could have been put together only by a European of a particular age. A shoring of jazz fragments against the ruins of the European tradition, it begs the question, how some of the themes came to be broken in the first place. Listening to it is rather like sifting through a rich but chaotic archaeological dig or trying to solve two or three jigsaw puzzles whose pieces have been mixed in a single box. Koglmann's flugelhorn has an almost valedictory air, poised as if prepared to fade on any of the tiny thematic segments it handles. *L'Heure Bleue*, his finest record to date, to a large extent puts the pieces back together. New and old themes are recalled at twilight. Coe's clarinet carries the title-piece almost single-handed, and there are extraordinarily beautiful duet performances with Misha Mengelberg of 'My Old Flame', Tony Fruscella's 'Baite', and the originals, 'Slow Fox' and 'Nachts'. The guitarist's four-note encodement of the opening 'Leopard Lady' is the most obvious insight yet into Koglmann's method. Also included are 'Night And Day', Ellington's 'Black Beauty', and Ralph Richardson's 'It Ain't Easy'; and there is a further dedication 'For Bix', which gets ever closer to the spirit of thing. Jazz? Very nearly, but something else besides.

EERO KOIVISTOINEN
TENOR SAXOPHONE

***   **Picture In Three Colors** Core Records/Line COCD 9.00515 CD
Koivistoinen; Tom Harrell (*t, flhn*); John Scofield (*g*); Jim McNeely (*p*); Ron McClure (*b*); Jack DeJohnette (*d*). 10/83.

The line-up is a virtual guarantee of quality. DeJohnette is relaxed and attentive to the spaces in Koivistoinen's impressive charts, creating abstract figurations within the basic sequence. Harrell has rarely sounded more haunted but is in excellent voice, as is the saxophonist, who has yet to make much of a mark on the international scene. Koivistoinen has a pungent, spicy tone that is deceptively 'American' in accent; certainly, his kinship with the dominant Garbarek approach is rather fleeting.

The only quibble is the co-presence of both McNeely and Scofield. Given the nature of the music, it might have been preferable to dispense with a keyboard instrument and rely more heavily on the less formalized chording and high accents of the guitarist who is replacing John Abercrombie as the player of choice for this kind of gig.

HANS KOLLER (born 1921)
TENOR SAXOPHONE, SOPRANO SAXOPHONE, SOPRANINO SAXOPHONE

[**   **Hello, Baden Baden** Jazzline JL 20828 CD/2LP]
Koller; Joki Freund, Don Menza (*ts*); Willie Sanner (*bs*); Pepsi Auer (*p*); Gary Peacock (*b*); Rudi Sehring (*d*). 6/57.

[**(*)   **The Concert: 23 June 1958** Jazzline JL 20829 CD/2LP]
Koller; Roland Kovac (*p*); Peter Trunk (*b*); Kenny Clarke (*d*).

[**(*)   **The K & K In New York** L + R 40010 LP]
Koller; Attila Zoller; George Mraz (*b*). 6/79.

***   **The Horses** L + R 40008 LP
Koller; Robert Demmer, Karl Fian, Hannes Kottek, Ernst Lamprecht (*t*); Lee Harper (*t, flhn*); Robert Politzer, Ack Van Rooyen (*flhn*); Herbert Joos (*flhn, bar hn, cor*); Robert Dodge, Ilter Jenisen, Albert Mangelsdorff (*tb*); Christian Radovan (*tb, btb*); Roy Deuvall (*btb*); Paul Schwarz (*p*); Jurgen Wuchner (*b*); Janusz Stefanski (*d*). 12/79.

***   **Live At The Jazz Festival Frankfurt** L + R 40014 LP
As above, except add Kenny Wheeler (*t*); Erich Kleinschuster (*tb*); Fritz Pauer (*p*) replaces Schwarz. 10/80.

***(*)   **Multiple Koller** L + R 41003 LP
Koller; Fritz Pauer (*p*); Hans Rettenbacher (*b*); Victor Plasil (*d*). 12/62.

One of the most remarkable figures in modern jazz, Koller's career began under the shadow of Nazism. Hitler's *Anschluss* had swallowed the saxophonist's native Austria and proscribed jazz as 'Judaeo–Negroid' degeneracy. Koller played on regardless and became one of the beacons of post-war American jazz, playing in a personalized Cool School manner that increasingly took on modernist inflexions, the most notable of which was John Coltrane's impact on Koller's tenor saxophone playing.

The two Jazzlines are concert recordings and feature Koller with two of his own groups and in company with Don Byas, Lee Konitz, Willie Dennis, Lars Gullin and Zoot Sims, good indication of the trajectory of his work at the time. The three-tenor (and baritone) lumber through 'Minor Conversation' on *Hello* is slightly tiresome, and the most interesting tracks are those under other flags; best of all is Konitz's All Stars 'Zoot' with Gullin and Willie Sanner.

The K & K In New York is ostensibly an Attila Zoller Trio album, but Koller's duet with bassist George Mraz on 'The Clown Down And Upstairs' is the highlight of a fascinating album, marred only by a rather flat sound. The same problem afflicts the big-band International Brass Company sessions on the same label. These find Koller, who has added soprano and the snake-charming sopranino saxophones to his impressive repertoire, at the head of an essentially modernist line-up. 'The Horses' evokes Koller's activity in abstract painting; his playing is increasingly unreferential, scooting round the tonality with an easy freedom that suggests a younger player – or, rather, one wholly schooled in the post-bop era.

The best of the group, and one of the most intriguing European albums of its time, is *Multiple Koller*, a series of dedications, like 'Norma Jean' on *The Horses*, but on this occasion to a mixture of jazz men (Mingus, Dolphy), artists and poets. It's a taut, evocative record, almost overstuffed with ideas, with a disturbing *mise-en-abîme* effect, almost as if every track suggests a whole album, every line a new composition. Koller is one of the quietly heroic figures of contemporary jazz whose reputation as a composer and performer is high among his fellow-musicians yet still somewhat muted among listeners. *Multiple Koller* makes a fine point of redress.

TOSHINORI KONDO
TRUMPET, ELECTRONICS

*(*)   **This, That And The Other** ITM 0021 CD/LP
Kondo; Tristan Honsinger (*clo*); Sean Bergin (*ts, mca*); Michael Moore (*cl*);
Jean-Jacques Avenel (*b*); Steve Noble (*d*); Tiziana Simona (*v*).

Rarely has an album been better named. There is a fine, imaginative duet with Honsinger, who is co-leader, but for the most part the music is scatty, fatuous and bordering on the ill-tempered, with poorly distributed sound that disfavours the excellent Steve Noble. Kondo's work with Peter Brötzmann is streets ahead of this. Or That And The Other.

LEE KONITZ (born 1927)
ALTO SAXOPHONE, SOPRANO SAXOPHONE

***(*)   **Lone-Lee** Steeplechase SCS 1035 CD/LP
Konitz solo. 8/74.

Most of the more casual generalizations about Lee Konitz – cool, abstract, passionless, untouched by bebop – were last true about 40 years ago. A stint in the Stan Kenton band, the musical equivalent of Marine Corps boot camp, toughened up his articulation and led him steadily away from the long, rather diffuse lines of his early years under the influence of Lennie Tristano towards an altogether more pluralistic and emotionally cadenced approach.

Astonishingly, Konitz spent a good many of what should have been his most productive years in relative limbo, teaching when he should have been playing, unrecognized by critics, unsigned by all but small European labels (on which he is, admittedly, prodigal). Despite (or because of) his isolation, Konitz has routinely exposed himself over the years in the most ruthlessly unpredictable musical settings, thriving on any challenge, constantly modifying his direction.

Even three years after the release (also on a Danish label) of Anthony Braxton's ground-breaking *For Alto*, solo saxophone performance was still considered a radical strategy. Konitz's unaccompanied treatment of just two standards – 'Cherokee' and 'The Song Is You' – contains some of his very best playing. Smooth legato passages are interspersed with harsher, almost percussive sections in which his pads snap down impatiently on the note. There are few if any hints of the free playing he essayed during a thoroughly unexpected collaboration with Derek Bailey's improvising collective Company in 1987; but there is a further dimension of freedom in his playing on the record that is rarely encountered elsewhere in his work. Even so, nowhere does he lose contact with the source material, which is transformed with a robust logic that never degenerates into pointless noodling. Recording quality is unexceptional and the CD sounds rather metallic.

***(*)   **Subconscious-Lee** Original Jazz Classics OJC 186 CD/LP/MC
Konitz; Warne Marsh (*ts*); Sal Mosca. Lennie Tristano (*p*); Billy Bauer (*g*); Arnold Fishkin (*b*); Denzil Best, Shelly Manne, Jeff Morton (*d*). 1/49, 6/49, 9/49, 4/50.

[***(*)   **First Sessions 1949–50** Prestige P 24081 2LP]
As above.

***   **Jazz At Storyville** Black Lion BLP 60901 LP
Konitz; Ronnie Ball (*p*); Percy Heath (*b*); Al Leavitt (*d*). 1/54.

(*)   **Konitz Black Lion BLCD 760922 CD
Konitz; Ronnie Ball (*p*); Peter Ind (*b*); Jeff Morton (*d*). 8/54.

Subconscious-Lee brings together material made under Lennie Tristano's leadership in January 1949, with quartet and quintet tracks made a few months later, featuring the wonderful Warne Marsh on the anything but redundant 'Tautology' and four other numbers. The remaining group material with Mosca and Bauer is less compelling (and certainly not as good as the 1951 sessions with Miles Davis on the deleted *Ezz-thetic*), but there is a fine duo with the guitarist on 'Rebecca' which anticipates some of the saxophonist's later intimacies. *First Sessions* omits 'Progression', 'Ice Cream Konitz', 'Palo Alto', 'You Go To My Head' and 'Rebecca', but is filled out with useful introductory material from Eddie Lockjaw Davis, Wardell Gray, Al Haig,

J. J. Johnson, Don Lanphere, Fats Navarro, Leo Parker, Sonny Stitt, Kai Winding and, there being no CD option, might be considered more desirable on that basis.

The rather later Teddy Charles sessions must seem a bit of an afterthought. Now little mentioned, the vibist had much of Milt Jackson's thoughtful fluency and arranging skills that recall some of the more challenging Modern Jazz Quartet records. But for Raney's softly enunciated guitar, 'Nocturne' might almost be the MJQ. The hints of Chopin are no more than subliminal; nor is 'Composition For Four Pieces' any more long-hair than the Konitz–Bauer 'Duet'. It's very beautiful music that probably deserves space of its own.

Konitz is a useful CD-only reminder of how the saxophonist sounded on demob from the Kenton orchestra (though it's difficult to see why it, and not the better *Storyville*, was deemed worthy of a CD transfer). Multiple cuts of 'Mean To Me', 'Bop Goes The Leesel' (ouch!) and 'Nursery Rhyme' show to what extent he'd already reached an accommodation with some of the more intractable lessons of bebop and how far behind he'd left his initial thrall to Lennie Tristano. Morton and Ind are too mannerly even for this company. The *Storyville* band has some of the edge Konitz thrives on. 'Lee' puns abound in the track titles but 'These Foolish Things' and 'Foolin' Myself' are both first rate.

(There's an interesting Konitz track from the same period, but in the improbable company of Charles Mingus on an intriguing compilation called *Autobiography In Jazz*, Original Jazz Classics OJC 115 LP; how self-revealing the saxophonist actually is remains a matter for conjecture.)

***   **Together Again** Moon MLP 024 CD/LP
Konitz; Bill Evans (*p*); Niels-Henning Ørsted-Pedersen (*b*); Alan Dawson (*d*). 10 & 11/65.

***   **Trio And Quartet** Magnetic MRCD 107 CD
As above.

Though Konitz always appeared to share and even anticipate some of Bill Evans's blurring of the harmonic sequence, their association on these nearly interchangeable sets from the autumn of 1965 isn't altogether successful. 'How Deep Is The Ocean' and 'My Melancholy Baby' perhaps weren't instinctive choices for Evans, though he makes sufficient concession to allow the latter to work. The (Konitz) trio tracks, versions of 'All The Things You Are' and 'What's New', are more confidently crafted, though the sound is a little too pinched at the top end to do justice to fine playing. The Moon adds two Evans trio tracks (the lunar sleeve-notes are oddly shy on personnel, but it sounds like the same session) which are worth having.

***(*)   **The Lee Konitz Duets** Original Jazz Classics OJC 466 CD/LP
Konitz, with Marshall Brown (*vtb, euph*); Joe Henderson, Richie Kamuca (*ts*); Dick Katz (*p*); Karl Berger (*vib*); Jim Hall (*g*); Ray Nance (*vn*); Eddie Gomez (*b*); Elvin Jones (*d*). 9/67.

****   **I Concentrate On You** Steeplechase SCS 1018 CD/LP
Konitz; Red Mitchell (*b, p*). 6/74.

***(*)   **Windows** Steeplechase SCS 1057 CD/LP
Konitz; Hal Galper (*p*). 77.

***   **Toot Sweet** Owl 028 CD/LP
Konitz; Michel Petrucciani (*p*). 5/82.

***(*)   **Art Of The Duo** Enja 5059 LP
Konitz; Albert Mangelsdorff (*tb*). 6/83.

(*)   **Once Upon A Live Musidisc 500162 CD
Konitz; Harold Danko (*p*). 6/90.

Improvising duets fall somewhere between the intimacies of a private dinner and the disciplines of the boxing ring. If there are minor embarrassments in being overheard with, so to speak, the emotional gloves off, that's nothing to being caught out by a sudden rhythmic jab or harmonic cross from your partner; there's no band waiting in the corner. In a very real sense, the duo is Konitz's natural constituency. Perhaps only fellow alto saxophonist Marion Brown gets near him for sheer quality in a demanding setting that perfectly suits Konitz's balancing of almost conversational affability with a gimlet sharpness of thought.

On the 1967 record, Konitz comes on like a cross between an all-comers' booth boxer and a taxi dancer: a lover, not a fighter. The album pivots on five versions of the classic duo piece 'Alone Together'; the first is solo, the next three duets with Karl Berger, Eddie Gomez, and with Elvin Jones (with whom he made the marvellous *Motion* [Verve 821553]), culminating in a fine quartet reading.

The pairings with saxophonists Joe Henderson ('You Don't Know What Love Is') and Richie Kamuca ('Tickle Toe'), and with trombonist Marshall Brown are astonishing, as far as possible from the comforting horn-plus-rhythm options, most of them refused, of the tracks with Dick Katz, Jim Hall, and even Ellingtonian Ray Nance (who plays his 'second' instrument). It all culminates in a fine, all-in nonet, an intriguing numerical anticipation of one of Konitz's best later bands.

Hal Galper's lush, velvety backgrounds inspire some of Konitz's most lapidary performances. There is very little harmonic tension in the pianist's approach, in contrast to Red Mitchell (either on double bass or piano), and the result is to focus Konitz very much on the tune rather than on its changes. That is particularly noticeable on 'Stella By Starlight'. Each man has one (improvised) solo slot; Konitz's 'Soliloquy' is a lean, un-self-indulgent exercise in low-fat improvisation and, as such, an illustration of the album's considerable strengths; Galper's 'Villainesque' is exactly the opposite, clotted like some multi-layered Viennese confection.

By the sharpest contrast, Petrucciani's approach is as sharp as citrus. One of a string of (mostly solo) early-1980s albums for Owl, *Toot Sweet* reveals the young Frenchman as a rather more raggedy technician than the supremely confident player who moved over and up to Blue Note shortly thereafter. The piano sounds as if one of the mikes is out or badly positioned and Konitz himself is slightly recessed. The material – 'I Hear A Rhapsody', 'Lover Man', ''Round About Midnight', a couple of originals – is unsurprising, but played with great verve and considerable warmth. The duos with Harold Danko are more assured – and the CD recording is better – but they suggest a polished concert performance, rather than the exploratory intrigues of *Toot Sweet*. 'Hi, Beck', based on the chords of 'Pennies From Heaven', has become an established set-opener, perhaps too familiar now to Konitz-watchers to reveal all the finessing he does on the top line. Danko is an adequate partner, but a desperately unexciting one; it's by no means the only instance of Konitz playing brilliantly in less than challenging contexts.

The Cole Porter readings with Red Mitchell explore equally familiar territory, but as if by night. Konitz clearly enjoys this kind of dead-reckoning performance and steers through the chords with finely tuned instinct. He also seems to like the extremes of pitch he gets opposite the notoriously straight-backed Mitchell, a man who prefers to play bass-as-bass, and it's a pity that the saxophonist wasn't currently toting a soprano instrument as well. Minor quibbles can't detract from the unfailing quality of the performances, which are absolutely top-notch. An essential Konitz album.

The 1967 partnership with Marshall Brown proved that the saxophone–trombone duo partnership could work. The Enja set substantially develops the idiom. Mangelsdorff, like George Lewis, is an avant-garde player with a deep understanding and abiding affection for the more lyrical aspect of mainstream playing. *Art Of The Duo* is a marvellous, unexpected album that repays frequent repeats; the sound isn't great but the music is endlessly challenging.

***(*)   **Jazz A Juan** Steeplechase SCS 1072 CD/LP
Konitz; Martial Solal (*p*); Niels-Henning Ørsted-Pedersen (*b*); Daniel Humair (*d*).
7/74.

Top-of-the-range standards jazz by a marvellously Esperantist quartet. Solal is one of the great harmonists, with the ability to find anomalous areas of space within the most restrictively familiar themes; his statement and subsequent excursions on ''Round About Midnight' are typical of his innate resistance to cliché. NHOP is the Terry Waite of jazz: big and bearded; willing to go anywhere; able to communicate in almost any company; a reconciler of opposites, gentle, but with a hard centre. His low notes behind 'Autumn Leaves' merit at least one listen with the 125-Hz slide on the graphic equalizer up at +10 and the rest zeroed. Konitz sounds relaxed and easy, flurrying breathy top notes and leaving space round the brighter middle register.

***(*)   **Oleo** Sonet SNT 690 CD/LP
Konitz; Dick Katz (*b*); Wilbur Little (*b*). 1/75.

Konitz's reading of 'Lush Life' is one of his finest recorded performances. The drummerless trio allows him to stretch out the tempi much more than he does usually and here, as on 'I Remember Clifford', he stretches and compresses measures with real inventiveness, packing in an extraordinary amount of musical information. Sound isn't spectacular on the vinyl format, but on musical ground alone, *Oleo* is thoroughly recommended.

**   Chicago 'N' All That Jazz LRC 7971 CD
Konitz; Richard Hurwitz, Lloyd Michaels (*t*); Barry Maur, Alan Ralph (*tb*); Joe Farrell, Don Palmer (*ts*); Dick Katz (*p, electric p*); Michael Longo (*ky, syn*); George Davis (*g*); Major Holley (*b, v*); Eddie Locke (*d*); Ray Armando (*perc*). 5/75.

A disappointing and rather time-locked set from one of Konitz's medium-size orchestras. The rhythm tracks rarely approach the exact resolutions the saxophonist usually requires, and the mix is thickened by the electronic keyboards, guitar and percussion to the point where the music loses direction.

***(*)   Pyramid Improvising Artists Inc 123845 2 CD
Konitz; Paul Bley (*p*); Bill Connors (*g*). 77.

A welcome reissue from the influential IAI label, which specialized in this kind of Third Stream-ish abstraction. Konitz's dry, papery sound of the time blends well with the other two, both of whom use amplified instruments as well as acoustic. Konitz also doubles on soprano saxophone, most effectively on the duet with Connors, 'Tavia'. Cool, slightly academic music, of a sort one associates with Jimmy Giuffre, but with an unmistakable, deep rooted swing. Connors is mainly used as a colourist. The sound is rather remote, but perfectly acceptable.

***   Yes Yes Nonet Steeplechase SCS 1119 CD/LP/MC
Konitz; Tom Harrell (*t, flhn*); John Eckert (*t, picc t, flhn*); Jimmy Knepper (*tb*); Sam Burtis (*btb, tba*); Ronnie Cuber (*bs, cl*); Harold Danko (*p*); Buster Williams (*b*); Billy Hart (*d*). 8/79.

**(*)   Live At Laren Soul Note 1069 CD/LP
Konitz; Red Rodney (*t, flhn*); John Eckert (*t, picc t, flhn*); Jimmy Knepper (*tb*); Sam Burtis (*btb, tba*); Ronnie Cuber (*bs, cl*); Ben Aronov (*p, electric p*); Harold Danko (*p*); Ray Drummond (*b*); Billy Hart (*d*). 8/79.

The *Nonet* was one of Konitz's more successful larger groups. The brass settings were well ventilated and open-textured and Konitz soloed confidently, often oblivious to the constraints of metre. The Steeplechase is the better of the two (though the title is unforgivable), largely because Harrell sounds more sympathetic to Konitz's own conception; Wayne Shorter's 'Footprints' is the outstanding cut. On *Live At Laren*, generally a good concert rendering, the saxophonist rather too generously accommodates Rodney's rather backward-looking bop manner with what occasionally sound – on 'April' and 'Moon Dreams' – like pastiches of himself.

**(*)   Dedicated To Lee Dragon DRLP 66 LP
Konitz; Lars Sjøsten (*p*); Jan Allan (*t*); Gustavo Bergalli (*t, flhn*); Torgny Nilsson (*tb*); Hector Bingert (*ts*); Gunnar Bergsten (*bs*); Lars Lundstrom (*b*); Egil Johansen (*d*). 11/83.

Slightly misleading, for the dedication is really to the music of the great Swedish baritone saxophonist Lars Gullin, with Konitz as featured soloist. Sjøsten is nominal leader, and his arrangements on the septet and octet tracks are a sensitive tribute to Gullin, who died in 1976. The Swede had a notably delicate tone on the big horn; consequently he was often likened to Konitz, who responds warmly and intelligently to the folkish elements in 'Peter Of April' (arranged for quintet) and the cool structures of 'Dedicated To Lee', which clarify Gullin's much-debated Tristano influence. Though the vinyl-only recording is nothing to write home about, particularly on the larger ensembles, the music is well worth having and provides a valuable starting-point for reconsideration of Gullin's still undervalued contribution.

***   Ideal Scene Soul Note SN 1119 CD/LP
Konitz; Harold Danko (*p*); Rufus Reid (*b*); Al Harewood (*d*). 7/86.

***   The New York Album Soul Note SN 1169 CD/LP
Konitz; Harold Danko (*p*); Marc Johnson (*b*); Adam Nussbaum (*d*). 8/87.

Two of the best of the more recent quartet albums. Danko's exact chording and fine grasp of durations on *Ideal Scene* open up the challenging spaces of George Russell's 'Ezz-thetic' and the more familiar, but inexhaustible, 'Stella By Starlight'. He is more conventional but no less inventive on *The New York Album*. Constant duo performance tended to reinforce Konitz's early preference for very long, unpunctuated lines. Working with a band as closely attentive as both of these allows him to break up his development and give it an emotional directness which is reminiscent – in mood if not always in tonality – of the blues. Johnson's and Reid's moody delivery, and Nussbaum's almost casual two-fours on the later album, reinforce the slightly darker sound – 'Limehouse Blues' included! Hard to choose between them.

***   **Medium Rare** Label Bleu LBLC 6501 CD
Konitz; Dominique Cravic (*g*); Francis Varis (*acc*); Hélène Labarrière (*b*);
Jean-Claude Jouy (*d*). 86.

Positively undercooked in places, but there's enough juicy substance from the mid-point 'Monk's Mood' onward to keep eyes on the plate. 'Ezz-thetic' is marvellous again, one of the most imaginative covers the piece has ever received; 'Chick Came Round' also reappears from *Ideal Scene* (and is worth a brief comparison); and Dominique Kravic's three originals (notably the namechecking 'Blue Label', with its fine intro from Hélène Labarrière) are all excellent. The accordion functions very differently from a piano or even a vibraphone in the mix, keeping the harmonies from tightening up, laying on areas of colour, accentuating a softly shuffling rhythm. Konitz ranges between alto and soprano saxophones, with a tight clarinet sound in the higher registers which is exactly right for this company. Unusual and fine.

***(*)   **Round And Round** Limelight 820804 CD
Konitz; Fred Hersch (*p*); Mike Richmond (*b*); Adam Nussbaum (*d*). 88.

At sixty-plus, Konitz sounds relaxed and confident, using a broader embouchure for dramatic contrast, touching icons like Miles ('Someday My Prince Will Come') and Coltrane ('Giant Steps') with sureness and a hint of wry humour. With the exception of a fine 'Bluesette', there still isn't enough variation of tone; this would have seemed an ideal opportunity for some of Konitz's still-undervalued soprano saxophone.

***   **Blew** Philology W26-2 CD
Konitz; Enrico Pieranunzi (*p*); Enzo Pietropaoli (*b*); Alfred Kramer (*d*). 3/88.

A studio recording by the have-sax-will-travel Konitz and the highly professional Space Jazz Trio. The set has the feel of one put together in rather a hurry, though it seems to have followed a short residency at Rome's Big Mama club. Pieranunzi's 'From E To C' sounds a little like a back-of-envelope run-down (though the pianist plays it with great conviction and development) and the two standards at the end sound as if they have been tacked on *faute de mieux*. Konitz's tone is sharp and resonant, and very well captured by producer Piangiarelli.

****   **Zounds** Soul Note 121219-2 CD
Konitz: Kenny Werner (*p, ky*); Ron McClure (*b*); Bill Stewart (*d*). 5/90.

Konitz continues to surprise with three remarkable free improvisations on which he abandons chord changes, conventional melody and straightforward rhythmic computations in favour of an exploration of pure sound. These tracks are interspersed with two staple items ('Prelude To A Kiss' and 'Taking A Chance On Love'), an original samba and the astonishing 14-minute 'All Things Considered', which sounds like a summation of what Konitz has been doing for the last 25 years. The whole set has a freewheeling, spontaneous feel that confirms the saxophonist's status as one of the most original players on the scene.

As a free player, Konitz has well-attested credentials, having worked in unscripted formats with Lennie Tristano, four decades before his surprise inclusion in Derek Bailey's Company collective for 1987. 'Synthesthetics' is a set of duets over Werner's highly individual synthesizer lines (an individual player, he brings a doom-laden atmosphere even to the Ellington tune); Konitz vocalizes with surprising self-confidence. His soprano saxophone playing on 'Soft Lee' is probably the best he's yet committed to record. Werner and McClure are both magnificent, but there has to be a slight hesitation over Bill Stewart, who seems to fall in and out of synch with the music, overcompensating furiously when a more regular groove is re-established. Otherwise absolutely sterling.

***   **Solitudes** Philology W28-2 CD
         Konitz; Enrico Pieranunzi (*p*).

In contrast with his earlier performances with Pieranunzi's Space Jazz Trio, Konitz plays with a rather thin detachment that doesn't quite fit in with the Italian's very proper phrasing and tight rhythmic control. Konitz almost sounds as if he has gone back to a version of the Lester Young-influenced cool he espoused at the beginning of his career. It would be interesting to hear him do it in a rather more promising context than this.

(*)   **Lee Konitz In Rio M.A. Music International A 737 CD/LP/MC
         Konitz; Luiz Avellar (*ky*); Victor Biglione (*g*); Nico Assumpcao (*b*); Carlos Gomez
         (*d*); Armando Marcal (*perc*). 89.

Where the French sessions assiduously avoided cliché – even the movie soundtrack formula of 'accordion + guitar = Paris' – this Latin session betrays an unfortunate willingness to take exactly the next step that even the most casual listener might expect. Except, that is, for Konitz himself, who remains aloof from the sticky entanglements of the accompaniment and skywrites enigmatic messages with his delicate alto and soprano saxophone lines. Converts and completists will love it, but it takes an effort of attention to edit out the backgrounds.

(*)   **S'Nice Nabel 4641 CD/LP
         Konitz; Frank Wunsch (*p*); Gunnar Plumer (*b*); Christoph Heberer (*d*). 9/90.

Just before this was recorded, a British cabinet minister, hostile to the idea of European union, opined that the Germans were constitutionally bent on world domination. On this showing, it won't be with their native rhythm sections. Konitz plays with typical grace and detachment, largely ignoring the awkward lockstep behind him. A very middling album, again only for real enthusiasts.

TOMMY KOVERHULT
TENOR SAXOPHONE AND FLUTE

***(*)   **Live At Nefertiti** Dragon DRLP 110 LP
         Koverhult; Gunnar Bergsten (*bs*); Bobo Stenson (*p*); Bjorn Alke (*b*); Leroy Lowe
         (*d*). 3/85.

Koverhult is a veteran modernist whose command of the tenor is nearly as bracing and muscular as that of his obvious idol, John Coltrane. His cavalry charge through the closing 'Tingle Tangle' is monumentally powerful and the striking thing is how little waste there is, even in such a voluble solo as this one. Elsewhere, his ballad, 'Ilsebil', recalls the Coltrane of 'Alabama', and his flute on 'Gisela' makes a nice, piping contrast to his other parts. His quintet play with suitably flying fervour: Bergsten's baritone, fat and lumbering but not without agility, makes clever opposition to the leader, and Stenson and Alke are masters of their craft. Only Lowe, who splashes around with sometimes aimless force, lets things down, and he's less than ideally served by the concert recording. A little disappointing, too, to find that – judging by the applause at the close of the record – there were only about ten people in the audience.

PETER KOWALD (born 1944)
DOUBLE BASS

***   **Open Secrets** FMP 1190 LP
         Kowald (*b* solo). 1/88.

***   **Paintings** FMP 0960 LP
         Kowald; Barry Guy (*b*). 10/81.

(*)   **Two Making A Triangle FMP 0990 LP
         Kowald; Maarten Altena (*b, clo*). 3/82.

Solo bass and bass duet albums may have too forbidding an aspect to tempt many casual listeners. It would be a pity if these three fine records were passed over untasted. Kowald is one of the finest and most accessible of the European free players, combining the firm rhythmic awareness of conventional jazz bass with a strong musical philosophy that comes out best in the visual arts parallels of his 1981 collaboration with Briton Barry Guy. The most striking of these is instigated by Marcel Duchamps' 'Large Glass', more raunchily known as 'The Bride Stripped Bare By Her Batchelors, Even'. Though cracked and illogical, the music is yet capable of the same philosophical depth and convulsive beauty Kowald achieves in solo performance.

Open Secrets is a remarkable record. Though the technical range is impressive – triple stopping, high harmonics, full chords – it never draws attention to itself (as does the technical finessing of *Two Making A Triangle*) but makes a steady progress through areas that sound predetermined but which are encountered according to a chance-driven logic that throws up challenging transitions and juxtapositions.

The duo with Altena is altogether more mannered and lacks the innate sympathies of *Paintings*. The cello helps vary surface textures but makes little impact on the music's direction. *Open Secrets* has the best sound, but no complaints about the others.

***   **If You Want The Kernels, You Have To Break The Shells** FMP 0920 LP
Kowald; Leo Smith (*t, flhn*) Günter 'Baby' Sommer (*d*). 1 & 5/81.

Further nutritional advice from FMP (carnivores will welcome a high-protein trio by Peter Brötzmann, the late Harry Miller, and Louis Moholo called *The Nearer The Bone, The Sweeter The Meat*, FMP 0690) and from a trio alphabetically credited to the bassist, but which has also recorded as the Leo Smith Trio on the excellent *Touch The Earth* (FMP 0730) from 1979.

The earlier album is marginally the better only because Smith is in more convincing voice. The longer cuts on *Kernels* allow the players – Kowald most obviously – to stretch out and explore their interactions. Smith's Rastafarian commitment is clearly evident, but the overriding sense is of ego-less improvisation unburdened by ideology or by musical preconceptions.

****   **Duos Europa** FMP 1260 LP
Kowald; Floris Floridis (*cl*); Derek Bailey (*g*); Peter Brötzmann (*ts*); Marilyn Mazur (*perc*); Joëlle Léandre (*b, v*); Evan Parker (*ss*); Irene Schweizer (*p*); Han Bennink (*d*); Conrad Bauer (*tb*); Fred Frith (*g*). 3/86–8/89.

****   **Duos America** FMP 1270 LP
Kowald; Diamanda Galas (*v*); Butch Morris (*c*); Anne Le Baron (*hp*); Danny Davis (*as*); Andrew Cyrille (*d, v*); Vincent Chancey (*fr hn*); Tom Cora (*clo*); Jeanne Lee (*v*); Zeena Parkins (*hp*); Julius Hemphill (*as*). 3/86–6/90.

***(*)   **Duos Japan** FMP 1280 LP
Kowald; Seizan Matsuda (*shakuhachi*); Junko Handa (*biwa, v*); Yoshisaburo Toyozumi (*d*); Michihiro Sato (*shamisen*); Tadapo Sawai (*koto*); Keiki Midorikawa (*clo*); Masahiko Kono (*tb*); Akira Sakata (*as*); Takehisa Kosugi (*vn*); Toshinori Kondo (*t, elec*). 2/84–10/86.

****   **Duos: Europa America Japan** FMP CD 21 CD
Kowald; with Derek Bailey, Conrad Bauer, Han Bennink, Peter Brötzmann, Tom Cora, Andrew Cyrille, Danny Davis, Floris Floridis, Diamanda Galas, Junko Handa, Masahiko Kono, Jeanne Lee, Joëlle Léandre, Seizan Matsuda, Keiki Midorikawa, Akira Sakata, Irene Schweizer, Tadao Sawai, Evan Parker. 86–90.

These are marvellous records, and an ideal introduction to contemporary improvised music. They're also historically important, because the three LPs are to be FMP's last releases on vinyl, bringing to an end a first (one hopes) important chapter in the label's dedicated advocacy of free improvisation. The CD affords a very acceptable sampler, but it's important to realize that all but three of the tracks are *alternative* versions of the pieces. Where the pieces differ markedly between versions, they have been given different titles.

Though not quite as formulaic as Billy Jenkins's twelve-by-three-minute bouts, Kowald's approach is neatly and accessibly organized: five improvisations per side, ten partners per album, no piece clocking in at more than seven minutes and many of them very much shorter than that. By no means all of them are purely spontaneous free improvisation; the pieces with Evan Parker, Conny Bauer, Andrew Cyrille, Akira Sakata, Peter Brötzmann and some others were developed on the basis of a predetermined idea, the piece with Vincent Chancey segues into a brief, very moving version of Horace Silver's 'Peace', and that with the traditional *biwa* player Junko Handa is based on a traditional lyric. Nor is the usual improvising convention of absolute democracy and equality among instruments strictly observed. In quite a number of cases, Kowald takes an accompanist's role, backing Diamanda Galas's typically fraught vocal with doomy pedals, Andrew Cyrille's increasingly complex body language with quite conventional octaves and a vocal drone.

The instrumental combinations are of particular interest and it's fascinating to hear Kowald adapt his attack accordingly. As if to prove the point he plays near-identical figures (albeit in very different register, but recorded two years apart) behind Zeena Parkins and Anne Le Baron, two players who have between them created a very significant role for the harp in improvised music. Le Baron is also a 'straight' composer, who prominently features improvisation in her work, but 'Minimally Fleshy' is one of the less obviously structured pieces. The same is true of Léandre's 'Frerebet Soeurboise', which is disappointing by her high standard, but illustrates the problem (only partially mitigated on Cora's piece by his rather higher register) of improvising with identical instruments. Butch Morris's 'Burden Of Choice Suite' is only sampled and thus might be expected to sound incomplete, but Kowald takes a much more prominent role with the horn players, building countermelodies and little retrograde progressions as he does alongside Hemphill on 'Balances & Cloves', sometimes developing his own abstract line as with Parker and Brötzmann, sometimes almost palpably listening to and reinventing a melody as he does on 'Maria's Black' with clarinettist Floros Floridis, who may be a new name even to seasoned improvisation fans. He has a gorgeous tone (better still on CD) and a patient, absorbed manner that's very appealing.

There are inevitable difficulties with the Japanese performances. The problem isn't by any means one of sonority (Derek Bailey's guitar frequently sounds like *shamisen* or *biwa*) but of basic aesthetic philosophies. Though Sakata and Kondo are well versed in jazz and formal harmony from the West (and they play orthodox improvising instruments), most of the others espouse a kind of violent synthesis between great formality of diction and very disruptive abstraction. Though this is also typical of Bailey's music (his 'Found Bits' is one of the few real disappointments, incidentally), the poles are reversed with attention diverted to the *form* rather than the aural substance of the piece. A question-mark over the fourth star, then, shouldn't be seen as too negative. This is a remarkable sequence of music, which deserves careful study as much as it invites repeated enjoyment.

KARIN KROG (born 1937)
VOCALS

(*)   **Some Other Spring Storyville SLP 5045 LP
Krog; Dexter Gordon (*ts, v*); Kenny Drew (*p*); Niels-Henning Ørsted-Pedersen (*b*); Epsen Rud (*d*). 5/70.

Disappointingly, some of Krog's best recorded work – with fellow Norwegians Jan Garbarek and Arild Andersen, Red Mitchell and Archie Shepp – has drifted into the back file. Her best-known recent work has been with saxophonist John Surman, who permits only rare visitors to his musical hermitage, and in particular the fine album *Such Winters Of Memory* (ECM 1254 LP).

As if spring isn't quite her season, the sessions with Gordon are a little diffident and more than a little light-weight. 'Blue Monk' stretches the voice a bit, and there are good things about 'Jelly Jelly' and 'Everybody's Somebody's Fool', but the finer modulations are lost on a rather unfriendly recording. Enthusiasts should look up the compilation *Live At The Festival* (Enja 2030 LP) from 1973, where she duets with bassist Arild Andersen on ''Round About Midnight'; less adventurous or assured than Sheila Jordan in the same company (see Steeplechase SCS 1081), she is nevertheless highly impressive, combining 'straight' jazz singing in the tradition of Ella Fitzgerald with some understanding of the 'extended vocal technique' of composer-performers like Joan La Barbara and Cathy Berberian.

GENE KRUPA (1909–73)
DRUMS

[***   **Lionel Hampton / Gene Krupa** Forlane UCD 19008 CD]
Krupa; John Bello, Gordon Boswell, Roy Eldridge, Don Fagerquist, Ray Triscari (*t*);
Herb Randel, Frank Rehak, Walter Robertson, Frank Rosolino (*tb*); Joe Cohen (*p*);
Ralph Blaze (*g*); Don Simpson (*b*); Hernando Bravo, Ramon Rivera (*perc*); Dolores
Hawkins (*v*). 49.

***(*)   **Compact Jazz: Gene Krupa** Verve 833286 IMS CD
Krupa; Roy Eldridge (*t, v*); Al DeRisi, Joe Ferrante, Bernie Glow, Marky Markowitz,
Charlie Shavers, Ernie Royal, Doc Severinsen, Al Stewart, Nick Travis (*t*); Eddie Bert,
Billy Byers, Jimmy Cleveland, Willie Dennis, Urbie Green, Bill Harris, J. J. Johnson,
Freddie Ohms, Frank Rehak, Kai Winding (*tb*); Hal McKusick, Sam Marowitz, Willie
Smith, Phil Woods (*as*); Al Cohn, Eddie Lockjaw Davis, Illinois Jacquet, Flip Phillips,
Aaron Sachs, Eddie Shu, Frank Socolow, Eddie Wasserman, Ben Webster (*ts*); Danny
Bank (*bs*); Ronnie Ball, Hank Jones, Dave McKenna, Oscar Peterson, Bobby Scott,
Teddy Wilson (*p*); Lionel Hampton (*vib*); Herb Ellis, Barry Galbraith, Steve Jordan
(*g*); Ray Brown, Red Callender, Israel Crosby, Johnny Drew, Jimmy Gannon,
Wendell Marshall (*b*); Anita O'Day (*v*). 4, 9 & 11/53, 12/54, 2, 7 & 11/55, 2/56, 6/57,
11/58.

[***   **Compact Jazz: Gene Krupa & Buddy Rich** Verve 835314 IMS CD]
Krupa; Buddy Rich (*d*); Roy Eldridge, Dizzy Gillespie, Don Goldie, Al Stewart, Nick
Travis, Joe Wilder (*t*); Jimmy Cleveland, Frank Rehak (*tb*); Illinois Jacquet, Flip
Phillips (*ts*); Danny Bank, Sam Marowitz, Jerry Sanfino, Eddie Wasserman (*reeds*);
Oscar Peterson (*p*); George Barnes, Howard Collins, Herb Ellis (*g*); Trigger Albert,
Ray Brown (*b*). 1 & 11/55, 1/62.

***(*)   **The Exciting Gene Krupa** Enoch's Music 839773 CD
Krupa; Charlie Shavers (*t*); Bill Harris (*tb*); Willie Smith (*as*); Ben Webster (*ts*);
Teddy Wilson (*p*); Herb Ellis, Steve Jordan (*g*); Ray Brown, Israel Crosby (*b*). 5 &
9/53.

There is a memorable photograph of the young Gene Krupa at the kit, hair slick, tux sleeves
and collar soaked with sweat, mouth and eyes wide and hungry, his brushes blurred to smoke
with the pace of his playing. Received wisdom has Krupa down as a showman who traded in
subtlety for histrionic power. George T. Simon, in the hopped-up prose that was almost *de
rigueur* in the *Metronome* of the late 1930s, referred to the drummer's 'quadruple "f" musical
attacks'; it's interesting to speculate how many people read that as 4F (that is, unfit for military
service) rather than as some battering dynamic above *molto fortissimo*, for there is no doubt
that Krupa's film-star looks and superb technique also made him a target. During the war,
which he spent as a very combative non-combatant, he was twice set up for police arrest and
spent part of his thirty-fifth year waiting on remand until a witness contracted amnesia. The
critics have taken much the same route, sniping, then forgetting.

Even in neglect, Krupa's impact on the jazz rhythm section is incalculable. He himself said, 'I
made the drummer a high-priced guy.' Though black percussionists who had worked for years in
the shadow of the front men had some cause to be resentful, Krupa's respectful investigation of
the African and Afro-American drumming tradition was of tremendous signficance, opening the
way for later figures as diverse as Max Roach, Elvin Jones, Andrew Cyrille and Milford Graves.

Sharing a compilation with the consummately professional Hampton band of 1948 serves to
show how callow Krupa could still be after nearly a decade of leadership. Where Hampton's
horns sting and caress by turns, Krupa's brass seems locked in a single gear. 'Disc Jockey
Jump', though, arranged for Krupa by the twenty-year old Gerry Mulligan, is a classic, much
ahead of the other arrangements by Mulligan and George Williams; 'Pennies From Heaven'
offers no more than a frustrating hint of what could be done with those chords.

The Verve Compact Jazz dedicated to Krupa alone brings together some valuable material
from the 1950s, leading up to the hiatus of Krupa's seemingly inevitable heart attack of 1960.
There are fine small-group tracks featuring Charlie Shavers, a much less impressive 1954/5
quartet with Eddie Shu and Bobby Scott, and an attempt to recapture some of the successes of
the Benny Goodman Quartet (from whom Krupa had split, not terminally as it turned out, in

1938), reuniting the drummer with Lionel Hampton and Teddy Wilson and bringing in bassist Red Callender. Quincy Jones's arrangement on the well-known 'Drummin' Man' is a little slack, but Roy Eldridge leads the brass with considerable power. There is also a reasonable later version of 'Disc Jockey Jump' which brings out more of its energy than the original 1949 recording.

The Exciting Gene Krupa on the small Enoch's Music label fills out the septet session featuring Shavers, Harris, Webster, Wilson, Ellis and Brown that yielded 'Imagination' and 'Swedish Schnapps' on the Verve compilation. Both tracks are repeated, with half a dozen others of compararble quality. The remainder of this good-quality CD is a further sample of the sextet that played 'Paradise' on the Verve, with Willie Smith, Israel Crosby and Steve Jordan joining Shavers and Wilson. 'Overtime' and 'Coronation Hop' are among the best of Krupa's underrated small-group performances and further testimony to the surprisingly subtle musicality he brought to even quite high dynamics.

While it's unfair to make Buddy Rich a receptacle for all of Krupa's less desirable qualities, it's clear from the Verve compilation shared between the two that Rich is a much less talented performer with a stiff, thudding style in marked contrast to Krupa's forceful swing. The two-kit 'Duo' is rather like listening to calisthenics, but there are good things from both Rich and the two drummers together (on the session of November 1955 that yielded 'Gene's Blues' on Verve 833286 IMS) fronting a high-quality band consisting of Eldridge, Gillespie, Jacquet, Phillips, Peterson, Ellis and Brown. The drum partnership works better with these forces than with the larger bands, partly because Rich is less competitive; his 'Buddy's Blues', recorded without Krupa, is surprisingly good.

TOM KUBIS
SAXOPHONES

***   **Slightly Off The Ground** Sea Breeze SB 109 CD/MC
Kubis; Jack Sheldon (*t, v*); George Graham, Wayne Bergeron, Dan McGurn, Stan Martin, Charlie Peterson (*t*); Charlie Moralis, Andy Martin, Alex Iles, Rich Bullock, Bill Watrous (*tb*); Dan Higgins, Greg Huckins, Gordon Goodwin, Bill Liston, Paul Baker (*saxes*); Matt Catingub (*p, as*); Mike Higgins (*g*); Kevin Axt (*b*); Matt Johnson (*d*). 1/89.

Southern California is full of skilful big-band players, and this ensemble headed by Kubis is accomplished enough to make his demanding charts seem like simplicity itself. The style is late Basie in terms of the section-work, with drilled brass trading licks with the reed section over the kind of clipped rhythms that dominate modern mainstream orchestras, but there's enough good humour to give it an extra fillip. Sheldon's vocal on 'Play It Again, Sam' will become tiresome after a few listens, but he takes a couple of superior solos elsewhere, and Watrous plays a trombone part on the title-track which will have most trombonists in despair. The material is a mix of derivative originals – 'Purple Porpoise Parkway' is 'On Green Dolphin Street', 'Exactly Like This' is 'Exactly Like You', and so on – and a handful of standards.

JOACHIM KÜHN (born 1944)
PIANO, KEYBOARDS

***   **Distance** CMP CD 26 CD
Kühn (*p* solo). 5/84.

***   **Wandlungen/Transformations** CMP CD 29 CD
As above. 5/86.

(*)   **Ambiance AMB 1 CD
Kühn; Walter Quintus (*digital sound-board*). 88.

***(*)   **Get Up Early** Ambiance AMB 2 CD
As above. 91.

(*)   **Kiel/Stuttgart Live! Inak 868 CD
Kühn; Jan Akkerman (*g, el g, syn*). 79.

***(*)   **Nightline New York** Inak 869 CD
    Kühn; Michael Brecker, Bob Mintzer (*ts*); Eddie Gomez (*b*); Billy Hart (*d*); Mark
    Nauseef (*perc*); collective personnel. 4/81.

***   **I'm Not Dreaming** CMP 22 LP
    Kühn; George Lewis (*tbn*); Ottomar Borwitzky (*clo*); Mark Nauseef (*picc, ts, perc*);
    Herbert Forsch (*perc*). 3/83.

***(*)   **Easy To Read** Owl 043 CD/LP
    Kühn; Jean-François Jenny-Clark (*b*); Daniel Humair (*d*). 6/85.

****   **From Time To Time Free** CMP 35 CD/LP/MC
    As above. 4/88.

***(*)   **Let's Be Generous** CMP CD 53 CD
    Kühn; Miroslav Tadic (*g*); Tony Newton (*b*); Mark Nauseef (*d, perc*). 8/90.

Joachim Kühn has a prodigious, rather 'legitimate' technique that reflects a solid grounding in classical practices and sometimes cramps his improvisational instincts. These, though, are considerable and they're perhaps better heard in a group or duo context than in solo performance. *Distance* is a beautifully inflected album as is the subsequent solo *Transformations*, and much of the credit for their success goes to CMP supremo Walter Quintus, who also figures as live electronics man on the experimental *Ambiance* and its rather better and more achieved sequel *Get Up Early*. This is not strictly a duo performance at all. Quintus operates a digital soundboard which transforms the sound of Kühn's piano (huge, Weather Report-like gongs at the start of *Get Up Early*, harpsichord trills, thunder, massed strings); despite a set-up which allows each man to react to the movements of the other, Quintus's acoustic environments on the first album do not sound particularly responsive.

Nor, unfortunately, are Jan Akkerman's. Star of the once-fashionable progressive rock band Focus, Akkerman manages to sound both fleet and stiff, not at all an instinctive improviser, and is best at colouring backdrops for Kühn's lavishly voiced chord structures and thoughtful lines. Some of the same limitations affect the self-named 1983 CMP session, though Lewis adds a significant dimension to the rather crowded foreground of percussion and instrumental effects, working in his characteristic free-lyrical vein.

To gauge Kühn as an improviser in the Euro-American contemporary mainstream, one needs to turn to *Nightline New York*, where he sounds quite at ease with a quick-witted two-tenor front line, and in particular to the superb trios with Jenny-Clark and Humair. These are of the highest quality. The Owl sessions may be slightly under-rehearsed, but there is a rawness of texture which balances Kühn very well indeed, and which is evident again in the choice of material on the later set, where 'India' and 'Spy Vs Spy' are the outstanding tracks.

The recent *Let's Be Generous* is a powerful – and, judging by the chatter of studio noise at the beginning, largely improvised – set that brings a heavy, Mahavishnu Orchestra sound largely compounded of guitar, synthesizer and drums to Eric Dolphy's 'The Prophet' and 'Something Sweet, Something Tender', and to some fine Kühn originals. The final track is wholly improvised and points a new way forward for Kühn, perhaps into the territory softened up by Last Exit.

ROLF KUHN (born 1929)
CLARINET, SYNTHESIZER

***(*)   **Rolf Kuhn** Blue Flame 40162 CD
    Kuhn; Joachim Kuhn (*p, syn*); Klaus Blodau, Larry Elam, Paul Kubatsch, Mannie
    Moch (*t*); Wolfgang Ahlers, Egon Christmann (*tb*); Ronald Piesarkiewicz (*tba*); Herb
    Geller, Charlie Mariano (*reeds*); Klaus-Robert Kruse, Thilo Von Westernhagen (*ky*);
    Philip Catherine, Peter Weihe (*g*); Niels-Henning Ørsted-Pedersen (*b*); Alphonse
    Mouzon (*d*); strings. 78, 80.

***   **Don't Split** L + R 40016 LP
    Kuhn; Bob Mintzer (*ts*); Joachim Kuhn (*p*); Peter Wiehe (*g*); Detlev Beier (*b*); Mark
    Nauseef (*d, perc*). 6/82.

***(*)   **As Time Goes By** Blue Flame 40292 CD
   Kuhn; Joachim Kuhn (*p*); Detlev Beier (*b*). 4/89.

Clarinet is still sufficiently rare an item in contemporary jazz to render exact location of Rolf Kuhn's style rather difficult. Leonard Feather, though, was in no doubt when he called the young German the 'new Benny Goodman'. Like his pianist brother, Joachim Kuhn, who makes intelligent contributions to all three albums, and, of course, much like Goodman, Rolf Kuhn has a well-schooled and sophisticated approach that suits both small groups and larger orchestral settings. In 1959 he played some memorable sessions with the great American bassist Oscar Pettiford, which can still be found on a good Jazzline CD and double LP called *Jazz Legacy – Baden-Baden Unreleased Radio Tapes* (JL 20827).

The fusion impulse that underlines much of the music on *Don't Split* and the earlier big-band album is handled with considerable intelligence and a fine grasp of dynamics and textures, but it's encouraging to find Kuhn making a more direct approach to jazz in the late 1980s. *As Time Goes By* is a fine combination of standard material – 'When I Fall In Love' and the title-track – with originals and some elements of free-form playing. Not plugging in his once-ubiquitous synthesizer allows him to develop a much more direct discourse, which is extremely impressive and well worth the effort of discovery.

STEVE KUHN (born 1938)
PIANO, KEYBOARDS

***   **Ecstasy** ECM 1058 LP
   Kuhn (*p* solo). 11/74.

***   **Life's Magic** Black Hawk BKH 522 LP
   Kuhn; Ron Carter (*b*); Al Foster (*d*). 3/86.

***   **Porgy** Jazz City 66053012 CD
   Kuhn; Eddie Gomez or Buster Williams (*b*); Al Foster (*d*); Laura Ann Taylor (*v*).
   12/88.

***(*)   **Looking Back** Concord CCD 4446 CD/MC
   Kuhn; David Finck (*b*); Lewis Nash (*d*). 10/90.

Unrelated to Rolf and Joachim Kuhn – though occasionally confused with the latter – Steve Kuhn is an older and more traditionally minded player whose roots reach back as far as Tatum and Waller, but who most immediately recalls Bill Evans. Kuhn has worked with Kenny Dorham [Bainbridge BT 1048], Stan Getz (Verve 831368) and Sheila Jordan [ECM 1159], and is often at his best comping for a very lyrical player or singer. With a left hand that is less than sturdy, he is more than usually dependent on a strong bass player and has tended to recruit very dominant bass fiddlers to his trios; his solo work, as on *Ecstasy*, can sound a little ungrounded, and it is fascinating to compare the versions of 'The Saga Of Harrison Crabfeathers' on that album with the voice and bass duet recorded by Jordan and Arild Andersen (Steeplechase 1981).

Of the available trios – the fine *Trance* with Steve Swallow and Jack DeJohnette is deleted [ECM 1052] – by far the best is the recent *Looking Back* where, perhaps ironically, the pianist is working with a much less dominant rhythm section and gives signs of having broadened his own intonation and sharpened his attack. On the very beautiful *Porgy*, he alternates Eddie Gomez, who shines on the title Gershwin piece with a superbly controlled solo, and Buster Williams, who propels numbers like the Ellington/Gaines 'Just Squeeze Me' and the Joe Henderson tune 'Isotope' with a rapid, clever lyric by Laura Ann Taylor. On Steve Swallow's 'Ladies With Mercedes', it's the left hand that develops the tune, over Foster's quietly inventive patterns.

'Looking Back', Kuhn appears increasingly to be taking stock of huge areas of modern jazz composition, refining his technique, opening up his imagination far more than when dealing with relatively limiting originals. Foster also contributes substantially to *Life's Magic*, but there is far less impetus in the music and Kuhn seems to lean more heavily on his rhythm players than he does in the later, more democratically balanced and straightforwardly better albums.

***(*)   **Live At Maybeck Recital Hall: Volume 13** Concord CCD 4484 CD
   Kuhn (*p* solo). 11/90.

Recorded a month after *Looking Back*, this solo recital underlines once again the differences between Kuhn's solo and trio work. Where the latter is increasingly a partnership of equals, the solo work opens up a remarkable amount of space in the middle of the music. The Maybeck Hall series, recorded in a warm but uncomplicated acoustic in Berkeley, California, has tended to feature meditative and/or lyrical piano music rather than the wilder shores of improv, and this is no exception.

Kuhn's sometimes extreme opposition of left and right hands (if you like, the exact antithesis of Keith Jarrett's normal strategy) still betrays a certain crudity towards the bass end. The marvellous, Bird-influenced melodic figures on 'Old Folks', the opening cut, are made over an almost childishly simple left-hand alternation that very quickly palls (if it isn't intended to make a satirical comment about the song). Much the same happens on an otherwise beautiful and very thoughtful 'I Remember You', where a rumbling bass-line suddenly and disconcertingly gives way to an abstract passage over the basic chords.

Kuhn has rarely confronted the blues so straightforwardly. The closing 'Meaning Of The Blues' is perhaps the rawest he's ever allowed himself to be, and even the 12-bar but non-blues 'Solar' is infused with an intensity of feeling that belies its structural diffidence. Impressive and worthwhile.

SERGEY KURYOKHIN (born 1954)
PIANO, OTHER INSTRUMENTS

***   The Ways Of Freedom Leo LR 107 LP
Kuryokhin (*p* solo). 81.

***(*)   Some Combinations Of Fingers And Passion Leo LRCD 178 CD
As above. 91.

Classically trained, and capable of playing quite legitimately in the midst of an otherwise chaotic performance, Kuryokhin is easily the most charismatic of the younger Russian players. He fronts his own 'Pop Mechanics' performances, mixed-media pieces that ape Western forms in a deliberately exaggerated, 'Martian' fashion that is not so much satirical as clownishly respectful. *An Introduction To Pop Mechanics* and *Pop Mechanics No 17*, a performance of the variable piece, may still be found on Leo LR 146 and 158 and Kuryokhin can also be heard on his own *Piano Zoological Elements* (Leo LR 148), with guitarist Boris Grebenschchikov, the first of the Russian new wave to be accorded major-label status in the West, on *Mad Nightingales In The Russian Forest* (Leo LR 167) and the double *Subway Culture* (LR 402/3), and with Grenshchikov and saxophonist Vladimir Chekasin on *Exercises* (LR 115). However, Leo's vinyl stocks are running down and it is in any case as a piano player that Kuryokhin is most interesting on record. (The 'Pop Mechanics' projects, recently sampled on Leo Feigin's television documentaries about the new Russian music, were probably best heard and seen live and translate to record only rather partially.)

Kuryokhin is more likely to refer to Rachmaninov than to Art Tatum in his solo performances, and seems to make it a point of principle to avoid direct reference from the jazz tradition. 'Blue Rondo A La Russ – A Tribute to Dave Brubeck' on *Some Combinations* is an apparent exception; Brubeck is perceived in a very different way in Russia than in his native United States, and enjoys honorific status as one of the first major jazzmen to appear there, but Kuryokhin's tribute is typically oblique.

Technically, his technique is interesting largely for its avoidance of the usual jazz-piano dichotomy between the left hand, with its rhythmic chording, and the right, which carries the melody and the subsequent improvisation. In addition, Kyrokhin is a virtuosic user of the pedals (a sharp contrast to Cecil Taylor, who uses them very sparingly indeed), creating some quite remarkable two-piano illusions. Rapidly pedalling also creates an occasional sense, as on the long 'Passion And Feelings' section of the later session, that tiny segments of music are being edited together at very high speed, creating the studied artificiality of tone that one hears throughout *The Ways Of Freedom*, an apparent refutation of conventional pianistic 'passion', whether of the Horowitz or Taylor variety.

Kuryokhin's is very difficult music to characterize, because it consistently undermines its own premises. Pieces like 'No Exit' and 'Archipelago' on the earlier album are discernibly in the line of Euro-free jazz, but 'Rules Of The Game' and the opening 'Theory And Practice' (another problematic 'combination') draw on a set of aesthetic principles which are quite alien to Western ears and whose satirical thrust is weirdly overstated by some oddities of the original tape, which seems to accelerate at various points during the performance. Kuryokhin is on record as believing that the end of state suppression of improvised music is an aesthetic disaster on a par with the death of Satan. There is certainly a slackness of purpose to the later record that one does not associate with Kuryokhin and which dilutes its considerable technical achievements.

CHARLES KYNARD
ORGAN

**   **Reelin' With The Feelin'** Original Jazz Classics OJC 333 LP
      Kynard; Wilton Felder (*ts*); Joe Pass (*g*); Carol Kaye (*b*); Paul Humphrey (*d*). 8/69.

Kynard, who is from Kansas City, was perhaps the last of the jazz organists to emerge in the 1960s. This is the only one of his five Prestige albums to be reissued and, while it has its moments, it's not a record to be listened to closely, since both tunes and solos are laden with clichés and Humphrey is a pedestrian drummer. The much hotter *Afro-Disiac*, with Grant Green and Houston Person, would make a better choice for reissue.

L.A.4 (founded 1974)
GROUP

(*)   **Just Friends Concord CJ 199 CD/MC

***   **The L.A.4** Concord CCD 4018 CD/MC

***   **Watch What Happens** Concord CCD 4063 CD/MC

(*)   **The L.A.4 Scores! Concord CCD 6008 CD
      Bud Shank (*as, f*); Laurindo Almeida (*g*); Ray Brown (*b*); Jeff Hamilton or Shelly Manne (CCD 4018 and 6008 only) (*d*).

Though with a broader palette and dynamic range, the L.A.4 shares something of the Modern Jazz Quartet's intelligent conflation of jazz with classical forms. Almeida's presence also guarantees a hefty infusion of Latin-American themes and rhythms, and the two influences come together on CCD 4018 with a fine excerpt from Rodrigo's *Concierto De Aranjuez*, a piece which it is now difficult to hear unmediated by either Segovia or Miles Davis and Gil Evans, but which is performed with intelligence and some fire. Some of these experiments, like 'Prelude Opus 28, No. 4' on *The L.A. Four Scores!* and 'Nouveau Bach' on *Just Friends*, the two most disappointing of the albums, drift towards pretentiousness. By and large, though, the quartet has a strong jazz feel and is capable of playing, as on the excellent *Montreux* set, with a robust swing; the Ellington medley – or 'melange' – is beautifully done.

    As well as a few residual Parkerisms, Shank has something of the tendency of his next model, Art Pepper, to float free of the rhythm section, which in this context permits some interesting counterpoint with Almeida. Shank's flute playing is usually more challenging but tends to accentuate a vapidity which overtakes Almeida on slower ballads, as on his mostly forgettable Concord albums with Charlie Byrd. The rhythm section are unimpeachable and, though Manne was a more interesting drummer, Hamilton is a better blend with the overall sound. *Watch What Happens* is a good alternative to a currently deleted *Montreux* set, with sensitive readings of 'Summertime', 'Mona Lisa', 'Nuages' and 'Misty'.

PAT LABARBERA (born 1944)
SOPRANO, ALTO AND TENOR SAX

***   **Virgo Dance** Justin Time Just 24 LP
      LaBarbera; George McFetridge (*p*); Neil Swainson (*b*); Greg Pilo (*d*). 4/87.

Though he grew up in New York State, LaBarbera moved to Canada many years ago and is now seldom heard from on record. His most renowned stint was with Buddy Rich in the 1960s and '70s. This programme – originals, a standard ballad, Shorter's 'Footprints' – tests him without really extending him, but his Coltraneish drive gives the right propulsion to a set done mostly on alto and soprano.

WOLFGANG LACKERSCHMIDT
VIBES

**   **Live Conversation** Inak 8521 CD
Lackerschmidt; Gunter Lenz (*b*). 10/84.

Best known for his recordings with Chet Baker, Lackerschmidt is an accomplished player who has rather little to say on an instrument not known for its intensity of expression. Where they have a decent theme to work on – 'You Took Advantage Of Me' is the only really good one here – the melody wins out; but mostly this is nice and dull.

STEVE LACY (born 1934)
SOPRANO SAXOPHONE

***   **Stabs** FMP SAJ 05 LP
Lacy (*ss* solo). 4/75.

***(*)   **Only Monk** Soul Note 1160 CD/LP
As above. 7/85.

(*)   **Solo In Situ 590051 CD
As above. 85.

****   **More Monk** Soul Note 121210 CD/LP
As above. 4/89.

There are, at a conservative estimate, more than 100 recordings in the Lacy discography, with a substantial proportion of those as leader or solo performer. His prolific output anticipates that of Anthony Braxton, consisting as it does of group performances with a relatively conventional – if Thelonious Monk can ever be considered conventional – 'standards' repertoire, large-scale compositions for ensembles and mixed-media groups, right down to solo improvisation. In one significant respect, though, the two part company utterly. Where Braxton has been promiscuously eclectic in his multi-instrumentalism, tackling all the saxophones from sopranino to contrabass, and all the clarinets as well, Lacy has concentrated his considerable energies throughout his career on the soprano saxophone.

Drawing his initial inspiration from Sidney Bechet, he has combined a profound interest in Dixieland jazz with an occasionally extreme modernism. In a typical performance there may be short, almost abecedarian melodic episodes, repeated many times with minimal variation; there will be passages of free, abstract sound, often produced by sucking through the reed (see *High, Low And Order*, below); there may even be strange onomatopoeic effects, like the quacking cries with which Lacy, anticipating John Zorn, opens 'The Duck' on *Stabs*. Lacy also favours tremendously long lines with no obvious developmental logic, which might be reminiscent of Lee Konitz's work but for Lacy's insistence on long, sustained notes and modestly paced whole-note series. The weakness of *Solo*, caught live in the mid-1980s and perhaps best left in the vaults, is that such devices do untypically seem to be in default of anything larger. A melodist rather than an orthodox changes player – those unfamiliar with his music can find it deceptively simplistic, almost naïve, on first exposure – Lacy has been obsessed with the compositions of Thelonious Monk for more than 30 years and has become perhaps the foremost interpreter of Monk's music.

The two solo Monk albums are among the finest of Lacy's multifarious and often interchangeable recordings. If the earlier of the pair is less immediately appealing, it is also more challenging and requires a closer acquaintance with the source material; with the exception of 'Pannonica' and 'Misterioso', the pieces are less well known than those established favourites on *More Monk*: 'Ruby My Dear', 'Straight No Chaser', 'Trinkle Tinkle', 'Crepuscule With Nellie'.

Something of Monk's approach is discernible in the monosyllabic utterances of *Stabs* (single-word titles are characteristic of Lacy's output), where he accelerates essentially simple twelve-tone figures to the point of disintegration, allowing each piece to end unresolved. The antithesis of bebop expressionism or the huge inscapes of John Coltrane (whose use of soprano saxophone was directly inspired by Lacy's example), the solos are cold and impersonal but not – witness 'The Duck' – without a certain broad humour that skirts burlesque. There are perhaps more completely achieved recordings than these, but there's no better place to make acquaintance with one – or perhaps two – of the music's great originals.

***   **Soprano Sax** Original Jazz Classics OJC 130 CD/LP
Lacy; Wynton Kelly (*p*); Buell Neidlinger (*b*); Dennis Charles (*d*). 11/57.

****   **Reflections** Original Jazz Classics OJC 063 CD/LP
Lacy; Mal Waldron (*p*); Buell Neidlinger (*b*); Elvin Jones (*d*). 10/58.

As with *The Straight Horn*, below, there was some attempt at the end of the 1950s to market Lacy as the soprano saxophone specialist, trading on the instrument's relative unfamiliarity. *Soprano Sax* is somewhat atypical in that it consists of rather more developed harmonic improvisations on open-ended standards. Kelly's time-feel and exuberant chording aren't obviously suited to Lacy's method and 'Rockin' In Rhythm' sounds much as if a lion were playing see-saw with a swan. There is, though, an excellent, slightly off-beat reading of 'Alone Together'. Some hints still of the problems recording engineers faced in miking Lacy's horn.

Reflections was the first of Lacy's all-Monk recordings. Waldron was one of the few piano players who understood how such intractable material could be approached, and there are hints already of what he and Lacy were capable of in duo performance. Neidlinger has an attractively firm sound on both records, but Jones sounds slightly out of place, reinforcing Lacy's characteristic tendency to ignore the explicit metre. The sound is not altogether well balanced, and Neidlinger's lower-register fills are lost on the vinyl format. Lacy, on the other hand, sounds rather acid on the CD, but the performances more than make up for minor cosmetic defects.

***   **The Straight Horn Of Steve Lacy** Candid 9007 CD/LP
Lacy; Charles Davis (*bs*); John Ore (*b*); Roy Haynes (*d*). 60.

One of the best-known and certainly most accessible of Lacy's records, *The Straight Horn* sounds rather muted and tentative after the passage of three decades. In conception, it marks a bridge between bebop (which was never Lacy's natural constituency) to the New Thing, as represented by two Cecil Taylor compositions. Monk again provides the keystone, but whereas the saxophonist sounds in complete sympathy with this material – 'Introspection', 'Played Twice' and 'Criss Cross' – his approach to Charlie Parker's 'Donna Lee' sounds remarkably hesitant, all the more so given Roy Haynes's palpable delight in the accelerated metre. Nor is it certain that Lacy or his sidemen have got a firm purchase on Taylor's 'Louise' and 'Air'; compare Archie Shepp's handling of the latter on *The World of Cecil Taylor* (Candid CS 9006).

Nevertheless, this is a significant and not unattractive record. Davis's throaty baritone fulfils much the same timbral function as Roswell Rudd's or George Lewis's trombone on later recordings, and the piano-less rhythm section generates a more sympathetic context than Elvin Jones's wilder rush. Recommended, but with reservations.

***(*)   **Evidence** Original Jazz Classics OJC 1755 CD/LP
Lacy; Don Cherry (*t*); Carl Brown (*b*); Billy Higgins (*d*). 11/61.

Lacy's associations with Monk and Cecil Taylor are well known, and there was an intriguing attraction-of-opposites in his impact on John Coltrane. Rarely, though, is he ever mentioned in the same breath as the other great modernist, Ornette Coleman. In part, this is because they worked on parallel tracks, rarely intersecting but concentrating on a similar redistribution of melody and rhythm. *Evidence* is the closest Lacy comes to the sound if not the substance of Coleman's great quartets. On 'The Mystery Song' and 'Evidence', he achieves something like Ornette's lonely stillness. Cherry, on trumpet rather than one of his squeaky miniatures, provides a strong tonal contrast (but wouldn't it have been interesting to pair Lacy's soprano with cornet or pocket trumpet?) and the rhythm section, piano-less again and with the little-known Carl Brown standing as acceptable substitute for Charlie Haden, plays with good understanding.

***   **Trickles** Black Saint 0008 CD
       Lacy; Roswell Rudd (*tb, chimes*); Kent Carter (*b*); Beaver Harris (*d*). 3/76.

With his brief substantive titles, Lacy almost seems to be attempting a new generic definition with each succeeding album. There is certainly a sense in which *Trickles* works by the slowest accumulation, like the slow accretions of limestone. There is also, unfortunately, an obduracy and resistance in this music that one doesn't often find elsewhere. The fault is not with the band. Rudd plays wonderfully, carving big abstract shapes that are shaded in by Carter and Harris, coaxing a more intense sound from the saxophonist. It's Lacy who seems unyielding. On sabbatical from his lifelong study of Monk, he seems at something of a loss, stating ideas without rationale or conviction, redeeming them only by the absolute consistency of his playing. Utterly fascinating, like all of Lacy's work, and perhaps all the more significant for being less entire and achieved, but certainly not his most successful recording.

***   **High, Low And Order** hat Art 6069 CD
       Lacy; Maarten Altena (*b*). 12/77.

***   **Company 4** Incus 26 LP
       Lacy; Derek Bailey (*g*).

****   **Chirps** FMP CD 29 CD
       Lacy; Evan Parker (*ss*). 7/85.

By the turn of the 1980s, Lacy appears to have regarded total improvisational abstraction as a way-station rather than a long-term direction in his work. Nevertheless, in *Chirps* he and fellow soprano saxophonist Evan Parker produced one of the best and most significant free albums of the decade. Concentrating on high, brief sounds that are more like insect-twitter than bird-song, the two players interleave minimalist episodes with a level of concentration that seems almost superhuman. Endlessly demanding – and a quarter of an hour longer on CD reissue – it's unlikely to appeal to anyone primed for hummable melody or more than usually susceptible to sounds at the dog-whistle end of the spectrum. It is, though, curiously involving and has considerably more accessible charm than the duos with British guitarist Derek Bailey, who by contrast has managed to sustain a total commitment to freedom. Recorded as part of one of Bailey's Company collectives, it's a record of sere whisperings and occasional violence, less disturbing for the impression it gives (augmented by the low-tech recording) of taking place at some distance or under glass.

    The Altena duos, on the other hand, are in an intimate close-up. At first hearing, the spectrum seems altogether wider, ranging from the total abstraction of 'Inconsistent Shuffle' (on which Lacy doesn't blow a single note) to freely harmonic passages with a discernible beat. This good-quality CD reissue puts back together what sounds like an altogether less fragmented performance, a relationship whose moods may seem initially paradoxical to outsiders, while remaining perfectly logical to the participants.

    Lacy doesn't sound like any of these any more, but all three open up significant aspects of his technique and musical vision, and *Chirps* at least shouldn't be ignored.

***   **Follies** FMP SAJ 18 LP
       Lacy; Steve Potts (*as, ss*); Irène Aebi (*vl, clo, v*); Kent Carter (*b, clo*); Oliver Johnson (*d*). 4/77.

(*)   **Troubles Black Saint BSR 0035 CD
       As above. 5/79.

This was the period when Lacy characterized his music as 'poly-free', an attempt to categorize his still rather ramshackle combination of unfettered group improvisation with scored or predetermined passages. One of the problems with both albums is that they sound precisely like that: uneasy alternations with little coherence or flow other than the sidewinding motion of Lacy's own lines.

***(*)   **Songs** hat Art 6045 CD
       Lacy; Steve Potts (*as, ss*); Bobby Few (*p*); Irène Aebi (*vn, v*); Jean-Jacques Avenel (*b*); Oliver Johnson (*d*); Brion Gysin (*v*). 1/81.

****   **Futurities** hat Art 6031/2 2CD
        Lacy; George Lewis (*tb*); Steve Potts (*as, ss*); Gyde Knebusch (*hp*); Barry Wedgle (*g*);
        Jef Gardner (*p*); Jean-Jacques Avenel (*b*); Oliver Johnson (*d*); Irène Aebi (*v*). 11/84,
        1/85.

Two relatively ambitious examples of Lacy's interest in multi-media encounters (the latter embraces abstract plastic images and movement, in addition to text). Robert Creeley's verse has the same fractured immediacy as Lacy's music; like all the Black Mountain poets, his work is much concerned with 'rhymes', not in the sense of precise aural consonance, but rather sympathetic semantic vibrations which lead the reader out of the text. In much the same way, Lacy has composed a group of what he was to call 'instant standards', brief, unflustered patterns which are not so much melodies as potentialities of melody and certainly a strong invitation to improvisation other than on chord progressions. The earlier *Songs*, to texts by the late Brion Gysin, co-inventor of the 'cut-up' method associated with William Burroughs, is less successful, largely because Gysin's words are too forthright to remain part of the musical fabric. Irène Aebi's voice has a flat, almost discursive quality that is far removed from conventional jazz singing and which takes some getting used to, but her expressive range is considerable. George Lewis plays beautifully as always on *Futurities* and, like Roswell Rudd (see above) would seem a perfect duo partner for Lacy, should the opportunity present itself again. Though full marks are awarded to both albums for sheer adventurousness, it's the later set that commands attention.

***(*)   **The Flame** Soul Note SN 1035 CD/LP
        Lacy; Bobby Few (*p*); Dennis Charles (*d*). 1/82.

Whenever he plays, Few emerges as the fulcrum of Lacy's groups. His composition 'Wet Spot', is the briefest and the only non-Lacy number on the album, but it's a particularly clear example of how Lacy and his loyal group of collaborators have rationalized the stretched-out improvisations of Cecil Taylor and the tautness of Monk. In timbre and tonality, these sessions strongly resemble Taylor's 'bassless' trios, but with the emphasis switched unequivocally to the saxophone. Lacy's four compositions form part of an ongoing series of dedications to 'eminent source figures', or what Lacy calls his 'Luminaries'; 'The Match' is for the surrealist Man Ray, 'Gusts, 'Licks', and 'The Flame' for an assortment of instrumentalists from around the world whose music has inspired him.
    In the trio context, Lacy sounds much more rhythmic than usual and appears to adapt his line to the drummer's beat, punching his own little toneless accents at appropriate moments.

***   **The Condor** Soul Note SN 1135 CD/LP
        Lacy; as for *Songs*, but without Gysin. 6/85.

****   **Morning Joy: Live At Sunset Paris** hat Art 6014 CD
        Lacy; Steve Potts (*as, ss*); Jean-Jacques Avenel (*b*); Oliver Johnson (*d*). 2/86.

***(*)   **Flim-Flam** hat Art 6087 CD

****   **Live In Budapest** West Wind 0011 CD/LP
        Lacy; Steve Potts (*as, ss*). 12/86, 10/87.

***(*)   **The Window** Soul Note SN 1185 CD/LP
        Lacy; Jean-Jacques Avenel (*b*); Oliver Johnson (*d*). 7/87.

Morning Joy is perhaps the best single Lacy album, and certainly one of the most straightforward; like much of his recorded work of this period, it reworks material to be found on the excellent *Blinks* [hat Art 2006 2LP] which is unfortunately deleted. The line-up on *Morning Joy* is a stripped-down version of his long-standing sextet (pianist Bobby Few and Lacy's cellist wife, Irène Aebi, weren't on the gig) for a one-night club date. As always, the material is a mixture of originals and Monk tunes, with 'In Walked Bud' receiving a notably bouncy reading which contrasts sharply with the slightly melancholy version on *More Monk*, above. Throughout, Lacy pitches himself against Potts's throatier and more expressive delivery, as he does in duo performance.
    The channel separation on *Flim-Flam* is a little too complete and exact to allow the two voices to merge and interact. A long track like '3 Points' begins to sound like a chance overlap rather than a coherent performance, certainly the opposite effect to the developed discourse of

'Wickets' (all 16 minutes of it) on *Morning Joy*, which ranks as one of the finest jazz performances of the later 1980s.

The off-centre swing of 'Prospectus' and the almost Turkish inflexions of 'Morning Joy' reappear on *Live In Budapest*, pared down to those two uneasily twinned reeds. 'Morning Joy' also kicks off the fine 1985 *The Condor*, where the balance of written-out passages and freer improvisation seems almost ideal; it also features some of the best interplay between the two saxophones, with Potts in exceptionally good form. If one of the great pleasures of investigating Lacy's mammoth output is the comparison of (sometimes drastically, sometimes only minimally) different versions of the same repertoire piece or 'instant standard' (his term), then these are critical performances for an understanding of how unconventionally he relates to a 'rhythm section'.

Stripped down to just saxophone, bass and drums on *The Window*, he reveals just how unconventional a player he actually is, refusing all the obvious rhythmic and chordal clues, playing lines so oblique as almost to belong to another piece altogether. 'Flakes' is another of those apparently self-descriptive compositions that resist all external reference. Again, very fine.

***(*)   The Gleam Silkheart SHLP 102 LP
Lacy; Steve Potts (*as, ss, perc*); Bobby Few (*p*); Irène Aebi (*vl, clo, v*); Jean-Jacques Avenel (*b*); Oliver Johnson (*d*). 7/86.

***(*)   Momentum Novus 3021-1-N LP
As above. 5/87.

In the sleeve-notes to *The Gleam*, Lacy suggests that 'the voice had almost gone out of jazz in the fifties', and that it was swamped by the turbulence of the 1960s. He credits Irène Aebi with showing him how the music could be re-centred on the voice and these two records – along with *Futurities* – arguably represent the peak of her contribution to the group. Again, Brion Gysin provides lyrics for her, one a dedication to Dizzy Gillespie, 'Gay Paree Bop', while two others are taken from similarly gnomic Oriental sources. The two best tunes, though, are settings of poems by Anne Waldman ('Napping') and Bob Kaufman ('As Usual'). Both reflect the cool, almost emotionless timbre and paradoxical intensity that Aebi brings to a lyric. Potts is in superb form, twinning the leader on soprano and then breaking out into boppish, almost funky, lines on his alto. Few leads a rhythm section that has become perhaps the most distinctive and individual in contemporary jazz.

Momentum consists of four splendid tracks, dedicated to four more of Lacy's luminaries: Herman Melville (from whom the stoical text to 'Art' is taken), Henry Miller ('The Bath'), drummer Kenny Clarke ('Momentum') and Brion Gysin and Oum Kalsoum ('The Song'). The last of these shows how strongly Lacy has been influenced by Eastern modes and tonalities, needling round the theme with characteristic precision. Only this and 'Art' actually involve texts, but almost of Lacy's work of the period (see *Anthem*, below) seems to involve verbal cues which are used to establish a melodic cell and a rhythmic cadence on which the composition and subsequent improvisations steadily build. One of the best of the 1980s albums.

***(*)   Anthem Novus PD 83079 CD
Lacy; Glenn Ferris (*tb*); Steve Potts (*as*); Bobby Few (*p*); Jean-Jacques Avenel (*b*); John Betsch (*d*); Sam Kelly (*perc*); Irène Aebi, La Velle (*v*). 6/89.

This group has a slightly unfamiliar aspect, but an utterly distinctive sound. The only significant difference is the introduction of Glen Ferris's trombone, who recreates for Lacy the whole battery of slide and mute effects that were so characteristic of the Ellington trombone benches (the saxophonist has suggested that his musical model for 'The Bath' on *Momentum* was the great Ellingtonian Lawrence Brown). John Betsch similarly draws much of his highly idiomatic approach from the great swing drummers, posing a sharp contrast with the Africanized diction of Sam Kelly. La Velle joins Aebi on the very moving 'Prayer', which is dedicated to Monk's veteran saxophonist Charlie Rouse. Lacy himself can't be said to be in top form, but he is less prominent than on some of the preceding albums and seems to have devoted more of his energies to a more collective, almost orchestral, sound. That's evident on the title piece, 'Prelude And Anthem', written to celebrate the 200th anniversary of the French Revolution. A setting of Osip Mandelstam's 'Twilight Of Liberty', it's as far away as possible from the troubled funk of the opening 'Number One', creating a contrast that makes this one of Lacy's most satisfying records, even if his own contribution is surprisingly muted.

(*)   **Image Ah Um 001 CD
         Lacy; Steve Arguelles (*d*). 10/87.

Arguelles may be outclassed; Lacy may have done just one gig too many of this sort. The effect is of two players conversing politely over slightly too great a distance, like friends spotting each other by chance at opposite corners of a restaurant and refusing to get up and walk over to the other's table, thus spending the evening mouthing deafly over the gap. Lacy generally takes the lead, easing his way through Monk's 'Evidence' with almost magisterial calm, leaving the drummer to patter out completely autonomous lines and figures (how might Steve Noble have faced the same challenge?). Only towards the end of the set, which goes up a gear after the second track and then over-revs in it until almost too late, is there any real dialectic. Lacy has some fine moments, like the solo intro to 'Art', but it's not a classic.

***(*)   **Deadline** sound aspects sas 013 CD
         Lacy; Ulrich Gumpert (*p*). 3/85.

[****(*) **Sempre Amore** Soul Note SN 1170 CD/LP]
         Lacy; Mal Waldron (*p*). 2/86.

***   **Hot House** Novus PD 83098 CD
         As above. 90.

Gumpert is a classically schooled player with an instinctive understanding of the whole range of modern piano repertoire from Schoenberg through Satie to Cage and beyond. *Deadline* is lighter in touch than one might expect, with an intellectually playful approach to fixed intervals. By way of homage, it includes one early version of 'I Feel A Draft' (orchestrated on *Itinerary*, below; there are other versions on deleted records), a rippling theme dedicated to Lacy's long-time associate Mal Waldron. It's by far the most affecting piece on a notably cool album, which nevertheless repays careful and repeated attention.

Waldron's name comes first on the wonderful *Sempre Amore*, but the honours are strictly shared. The pianist's big, dark left-hand chords and single-note statements take some of the acid out of Lacy's frail and thinly voiced takes on a bag of Ellington and Strayhorn themes. This is very different material from the free-hand shapes of the 1981 *Let's Call This* [hat Art 6112]. The opening 'Johnny Come Lately' is appealingly off-centre and 'Prelude To A Kiss' sounds at the edge of sleep. It's worth comparing 'A Flower Is A Lovesome Thing' to the version Waldron recorded with Marion Brown the previous year on *Songs Of Love And Regret* (Freelance FRL CD 006), where his accompaniment is little more than a sequence of moodily recessed pedals. With the undemonstative Lacy, he's all over the place, arpeggiating and trilling furiously, like Wordsworth trying to explain to Newton what a flower really is.

Though the material is more varied, the later *Hot House* is something of a disappointment, exposing the narrowness of Lacy's emotional range rather cruelly, leaving even more of the work to the pianist who, for his pains, gets second billing on this occasion.

***(*)   **The Door** RCA/Novus 83049 CD/LP/MC
         Lacy; collective personnel as for *Songs*, but without Gysin, and add Sam Woodyard (*d*). 7/88.

A marvellously concentrated set of performances from internal permutations of Lacy's (by now almost telepathically responsive) regular band. The addition of a second drummer on 'Virgin Jungle' follows no obvious rationale but works remarkably well, and there are intriguing Ellington touches in the distribution of voices. The duos and trio with Few, Avenel, and Avenel and Johnson are completely confident, highlighting Lacy's searching ricercars and 'found' melodies. 'Clichés' – again from *Blinks* – sets him against Avenel on African thumb piano, odd but quite beautiful and far from hackneyed.

(*)   **Itinerary hat Art 6079 CD
         Lacy; Klaus Peham (*t*); Franz Koglmann (*flhn*); Glenn Ferris, Radu Malfatti (*tb*); Raoul Herget (*tba*); Andreas Kolbe (*f, picc*); Steve Potts (*as, ss*); Urs Leimgruber (*ss, ts*); Hans Steiner (*bcl*); Bobby Few (*p*); Burkhard Stangl (*g*); Gyde Knebusch (*hp*); Irène Aebi (*clo, vn, v*); Jean-Jacques Avenel (*b*); John Betsch (*d*); Sam Kelly (*perc*). 11/90.

Surprise that this is Steve Lacy's first recording with a large group of his own may be tempered somewhat by the recognition that some of the material is more than 20 years old. (The liner art is lovingly produced, but might have gone with a free-jazz record c. 1975.) The second track, 'Cloudy' (part of a triptych called 'Precipitation Suite' which has been played by the Rova Saxophone Quartet and the Kronos String Quartet), and the later 'Moon' both appear in solo performance on the 1975 album, Stabs. It's not immediately clear what the music gains from orchestration, for its essence remains as simple as raindrops, and it's tempting to see the tune's history as a piece of reverse-action natural history, a bright condensation reversing course and turning into a murky cloud.

Itinerary as a whole is dedicated to Gil Evans and betrays more than a few touches of the master's hand, notably in the handling of the saxophones. Individual items are also dedicated: 'I Feel A Draft' (which was previewed on Deadline, above) to Mal Waldron, 'Cloudy' to the conceptualist Giuseppe Chiari, 'Rain' to Cecil Taylor (who provides its informing scale) and the title-track to 'Juan Louis Borges' (who might have enjoyed being told of the mistaken version of his name). Through-composed, the pieces seem a little stiff, but in the way that Borges's prose is stiff, resistant to critical enquiry. But there's little flexibility in the playing, which sounds like a sight-read rehearsal. It's easy to be put off by surfaces: Irène Aebi's flat recitation of a Buckminster Fuller text on 'Sun' is calculatedly odd and not intended to sound lyrical. Some of the voicings are deliberately wayward. The problems lie deeper. This does not sound like music that was written for these forces. Working outside his natural territory, Lacy looks to have 'worked up' existing material with very little sense of the inherent problems of idiom and scale. With all the 'anxiety of influence', he seems to have misread Gil Evans's example.

***(*)   **Remains** hat Art CD 6102 CD
Lacy (ss solo). 4/91.

Dominated by two long pieces, this is Lacy's most accomplished solo performance for some time, and a close-up, attentive recording catches every gritty little resonance and breath noise. This is particularly appropriate to the opening piece, actually a suite of shorter tracks inspired by the Tao Te Ching and very much concerned with what might be thought of as the interface between the physical and the spiritual: 'Bone', 'The Breath', 'Name', 'Life On Its Way'. This is an abiding concern of Lacy's and it comes through again in the 18-minute 'Remains', a piece inspired by Belgian artist James Ensor's bizarre 1880 self-portrait of his own skeleton as it would appear in 1960. Originally a dance piece, it explores ideas of decay and disintegration by making virtuosic use of repetitions with a progressively diminished body of material. Largely scored, it also includes three improvised sections.

Lacy's work is often thought to be desiccated and intellectual, fatally unfunky. As if to quash that one, Lacy follows 'Tao' and 'Remains' with an Kansas City blues, 'Afterglow', dedicated to Jay McShann, and a brief take of Monk's 'Epistrophy', which is typically quite unlike any other performance he has recorded.

****   **Spirit Of Mingus** Freelance FRLCD 016 CD
Lacy; Eric Watson (p). 12/91.

Could this be the beginning of a fruitful association with another great compositional output? Lacy sounds uncharacteristically effusive throughout this delightful set. He's noticeably fuller-toned and more developed harmonically on the opening 'Peggy's Blue Skylight', on which Watson restricts himself to staccato, Monk-like phrases. Later, though, both men revert to type, with Watson restoring his usual romantic breadth and Lacy moving back into the dry, familiar tones of earlier sets. Only with Waldron has he ever attempted anything as fulsome as this, and it works extremely well with Watson. 'Reincarnation Of A Lovebird' is more characteristic, and the harsh animal sounds with which 'Pithecanthropus Erectus' begins are further in the direction of pure noise than even Mingus ever attempted. The Lester Young threnody 'Goodbye, Pork Pie Hat' is more conventionally lyrical, which is slightly disappointing. Isn't it time someone tried to rethink it? And who is more capable than Lacy? Quibbles apart, a fine set, recorded live in Paris. The sound is clear and authentic and the hour-plus programme develops Mingus's work in a valid and promising direction.

LADD'S BLACK ACES
GROUP

***   **Ladd's Black Aces Volume 1** Fountain FJ 102 LP
Phil Napoleon, Benny Bloom (*c*); Moe Gappell, Miff Mole (*tb*); Doc Behrendson, Jimmy Lytell (*cl*); Loring McMurray (*as*); Cliff Edwards (*kazoo*); Jimmy Durante, Frank Signorelli (*p*); John Cali (*bj*); Jack Roth (*d*); Billy de Rex (*v*). 8/21–8/22.

***   **Ladd's Black Aces Volume 2** Fountain FJ 106 LP
Phil Napoleon (*c*); Miff Mole, Charles Panelli (*tb*); Jimmy Lytell (*cl*); Frank Signorelli (*p*); Jack Roth (*d*); Mandy Lee (*v*). 8/22–4/23.

***   **Ladd's Black Aces Volume 3** Fountain FJ 111 LP
Phil Napoleon, Harry Gluck (*c*); Vincent Grande, Miff Mole, Charles Panelli, Sammy Lewis (*tb*); Ken 'Goof' Moyer (*cl, as*); Jimmy Lytell (*cl*); Frank Signorelli, Rube Bloom (*p*); John Cali, Ray Kitchingman (*bj*); Joe Tarto (*bb*); Jack Roth (*d*); Mandy Lee, Vernon Dalhart, Arthur Fields (*v*). 4/23–8/24.

Ladd's Black Aces were actually the Original Memphis Five, one of the first white bands to follow up the success of the Original Dixieland Jazz Band. Phil Napoleon formed the initial incarnation of the group as far back as 1919, but their first records emerged in 1921, and the group used 'Ladd's Black Aces' as their recording name for some three years. These Fountain LPs collect 48 tracks from the period. Like every such band of the period, they modelled themselves on the Original Dixieland Jazz Band, but the Aces were a leaner, more streamlined outfit. Roth's drumming was simpler than Tony Sbarbo's; the rhythms were less relentless but no less driving. Solos were still few in number, Lytell being the outstanding improviser, and breaks based around stop-time routines were more the norm. Napoleon played a firm lead and Grande and Panelli were serviceable trombonists, but the most advanced musician by far was Miff Mole: when he's present, which is on nine of the 26 sessions, the front-line swings as it never does elsewhere.

Yet this was a remarkably consistent band. It grew looser and more daring as it went on, but even the earliest sides here have their own giddy momentum: the very first track, a spirited shaking of 'Aunt Hagar's Children Blues', already sounds like a band that knew what had to be done. Jimmy Durante, in his first and, alas, last real jazz records, can just be heard stomping away on the piano on the first eight tracks. There's a curiously addictive quality about the music: although any one of the three LPs will suffice for all but the dedicated follower of this kind of jazz, it's as likely that one purchase will lead to another. The acoustic recording, originally for the Gennett company, has been handsomely remastered.

BIRELI LAGRENE (born 1966)
GUITAR

***   **Routes To Django** Jazzpoint JP 1003 CD
Lagrene; Jorg Reiter (*p*); Wolfgang Lackerschmidt (*vib*); Gaiti Lagrene, Tschirglo Loeffler (*g*); Scmitto Kling (*vn*); Jan Jankeje (*b*). 5/80.

***   **Bireli Swing '81** Jazzpoint JP 1009 CD/LP
As above, except omit Reiter, Lackerschmidt and Kling, add Bernd Rabe (*ss*), Allen Blairman (*d*). 4/81.

**   **Ensemble** Inak 865 CD
Lagrene; Vic Juris, Gaiti Lagrene, Diz Disley (*g*); Jan Jankeje (*b*). 6/85.

***   **And Special Guests** Inak 8610 CD
Lagrene, Larry Coryell (*g*); Miroslav Vitous (*b*). 5/86.

If Django Reinhardt were to have a spiritual heir, it would surely be Lagrene, who emerged from a gypsy community in the 1980s to stun European and American audiences with his virtuosity. All the above were recorded in concert, with Lagrene's electrifying improvisations (all done on acoustic guitar) conducted on a range of material which includes swing, blues, bop and original themes, all of it mastered with effortless aplomb, even when it sounds as if the guitarist isn't sure of his ground.

That hint of flying blind gives the greatest excitement to the debut album, *Routes To Django*, which includes a nerve-racking romp through the tune identified as 'Night And Day' (actually 'Don't Worry 'Bout Me'). The 1981 session is nearly as good, although Rabe is an irrelevance, but from this point Lagrene began to fall foul of seeming like a novelty act. *Ensemble* pits him against Juris in a lot of twin-lead lines that go nowhere, an excuse merely to show off; while the meeting with Coryell, though often very exciting, has occasional flaws of tuning and intonation that blemish Lagrene's necessary clarity of expression.

(*)   **Stuttgart Aria Jazzpoint JP 1019 CD/LP/MC
Lagrene; Vladislaw Sendecki (*ky*); Jaco Pastorius (*b, p, v*); Jan Jankeje (*syn, v*); Peter Lubke (*d*); Serge Bringolf (*perc, v*). 3/86.

Lagrene meets Pastorius. This souvenir of a European tour is good-humoured but tends to go the way of all live fusion albums: a noisy dead-end. Salvaged by flashes of brilliance by both front-men, including a ferocious 'Donna Lee', it doesn't amount to very much.

*(*)   **Foreign Affairs** Blue Note CDP 790967 CD
Lagrene; Koono (*ky*); Jeff Andrews, Jurgen Attig (*b*); Dennis Chambers (*d*); Cafe (*perc*). 8/88.

(*)   **Acoustic Moments Blue Note CDP 795263 CD
Lagrene; Koono (*ky*); Michel Camilo (*p*); Loic Pontieux (*d*); Simon Pomara (*perc*). 7/90.

Nothing much wrong with Lagrene's Blue Note debut, except that it seems a fatuous waste to have this natural master of the guitar blustering through what's (for the most part) a soundalike fusion programme, with only a couple of pretty originals to commend it. *Acoustic Moments* is almost a masterpiece in comparison. Lagrene returns to foregrounding his prowess as an acoustic soloist: there's a dazzling set-piece to start, 'Made In France', and a headlong sweep through Coltrane's 'Impressions'. Irritating fills by the uninteresting Koono take up too much space, but at least Lagrene seems to be finding more room for his own personality in music which is still aimed primarily at radio-play.

OLIVER LAKE (born 1944)
ALTO SAXOPHONE, OTHER SAXOPHONES, FLUTE

***   **Prophet** Black Saint BSR 0044 LP
Lake; Baikida Carroll (*t, flhn*); Donald Smith (*p*); Jerry Harris (*b*); Pheeroan AkLaff (*d*). 8/80.

***   **Clevont Fitzhubert (A Good Friend Of Mine)** Black Saint BSR 0054 LP
As above. 4/81.

***   **Expandable Language** Black Saint BSR 0074 LP
Lake; Geri Allen (*p*); Kevin Eubanks (*g*); Fred Hopkins (*b*); Pheeroan AkLaff (*d*). 9/84.

***(*)   **Gallery** GR 8609 CD
As above, except omit Eubanks, add Rasul Siddik (*t*). 6/86.

A founding member of the pioneering World Saxophone Quartet, Lake has been rather neglected in the rush to sanctify his WSQ partner David Murray. A player of great power who touches bases in funk and free improvisation, Lake is also capable of great sophistication and a sort of convulsive beauty that requires a little time to assimilate.

Gallery is the later and better of two impressive sets involving pianist Geri Allen (who has since largely dissociated herself from this aesthetic). Less impressive than *Otherside*, it is nevertheless an impressive performance. Siddik's contributions to 'The Sport Suite' add a further dimension to Lake's multi-instrumentalism. The tunes are all compact and rather intense and much is required of the three rhythm players.

Lake shares with Allen a powerful enthusiasm for the work of Eric Dolphy, and on *Prophet* includes two of Dolphy's most vibrant compositions, 'Hat and Beard' and 'Something Sweet, Something Tender', both from the classic *Out to Lunch!* (Blue Note CDP 746524 CD). They're imaginative re-readings, not just pastiches. The slightly later *Clevont Fitzhubert* (the name is an imaginary one, suggested by a friend for the Lakes' unborn child) was recorded with the same group, but sounds a much tighter unit, with far greater integration between the two horns. 'Sop', a soprano feature, and 'November 80' are the most distinctive tracks and both have a quality of Thelonious Monk in the writing. AkLaff uses his brushes on 'Tap Dancer', another track that recalls Lake's interest in classic jazz. Retaining a piano might seem to be a restrictive move, given Lake's increasing use of free tonality, but Smith is such an open-minded and inventive player that he never seems to be tying the music down.

As so often, Kevin Eubanks is more impressive as a sideman than on his own records. His contributions to *Expandable Language* are sharp, exact and inventive, complementing Geri Allen's robustly unpredictable lines. *Gallery* may be a more coherent piece of work, but the earlier album is better representative of Lake's able synthesis of styles.

**** **Compilation** Gramavision GV 79458 CD
Lake; Frank Abel, Geri Allen (*p*); Anthony Peterson, Alphonia Tims (*g*); Santi Debriano, Billy Grant, Fred Hopkins (*b*); Andrew Cyrille, Pheeroan AkLaff, Gene Lake, Brandon Ross (*d*); Jawara (*perc*). 82, 86, 87, 88.

A valuable collection of material from *Gallery* (above), and the no longer available *Impala* and *Otherside*, with a solitary track from the much earlier *Jump Up*. It hangs together well, with the bands organized like latter-day Dolphy units. Lake's keening intensity somehow never palls and Geri Allen comps and solos with imagination and grace. Together with *Prophet* and *Expandable Language*, covers much of what you might need and ever so slightly supersedes the excellent *Gallery*.

***(*) **Again And Again** Gramavision GRV 74682 CD
Lake; John Hicks (*p*); Reggie Workman (*b*); Pheeroan AkLaff (*d*). 4/91.

An uncommonly lyrical and mainstream performance from Lake. Only 'Aztec' and 'Re-cre-ate' approach the angularity one normally expects of his soloing. There's no doubt that Hicks contributes substantially to the romantic atmosphere and the closing 'M.I.L.D.' (apparently Lake's wife's initials) is the most nakedly emotional he has allowed himself to be on record.

LAMBERT, HENDRICKS & ROSS
GROUP

***(*) **Sing A Song Of Basie** Impulse GRP 11122 CD
Dave Lambert, Jon Hendricks, Annie Ross (*v*); Freddie Green (*g*); Nat Pierce (*p*); Eddie Jones (*b*); Sonny Payne (*d*). 8 & 9/57.

Stanley Dance's liner-note (originally written in 1965) provides some useful background to the relatively brief fashion of jazz vocalese. One thing that he doesn't make clear is an important distinction with a classical technique known as *vocalise*, whereby the singer fits wordless syllables and phonemes to the music, sometimes ad lib., often in accordance with a strict score. Jazz vocalese, which may have begun as a version of the classical form with the Mills Brothers' vocal mimicry of brass and saxophone sections, developed along very different lines when Eddie Jefferson and then King Pleasure and Annie Ross began to fit words to famous jazz solos; Jefferson's vocalization of James Moody's solo on 'I'm In The Mood For Love' was perhaps better known in the King Pleasure version; Ross's virtuoso interpretation of Wardell Gray's 'Twisted' was a huge hit (and was revived nearly 40 years later by soul singer Crystal Waters on a chart album). Perhaps the finest exponent of vocalese, though, was Jon Hendricks, who seemed to have an unfailing facility for words to fit particular instrumental effects and for glib rhymes to link lines together. Whatever the weather.

On *Sing A Song Of Basie* Creed Taylor and Irv Greenbaum used multi-tracking, enabling the vocal trio to mimic with extraordinary precision the instrumental parts in 10 Basie big-band arrangements. The liner-notes reproduce the words used and the sections and solos copied. Ross had a particular genius for the timbre of trumpets. Her section-work is remarkable, full of growls, 'shakes' and sudden, percussive blasts; her versions of Buck Clayton's solo on 'Fiesta In Blue' and Joe Newman's on 'Blues Backstage' are quite remarkable, as is her 'tenor saxophone' duet with Hendricks on 'Two For The Blues' (which had originally featured Frank Foster and Frank Wess).

Though a relatively short-lived phenomenon in this (with due apology to Hendricks) 'white' form, vocalese called on a long-standing black tradition of rapid-fire, hip improvisation, and it reappears in its purest form in contemporary rap, perhaps the most influential popular music of the late 1980s and early '90s.

LAMMAS
GROUP

***(*)   **Lammas** Future Music FMR CD04-0791 CD
Kenny Wheeler (*t*); Tim Garland (*ss, ts, f, ky*); Don Paterson (*g*); Mark Fletcher (*d*);
Mike Donaghy (*perc*); Norma Winstone, Christine Tobin (*v*). 12/90–3/91.

A striking attempt at bringing jazz and Celtic folk musics together, with traditional Irish reels gliding into original themes with surprisingly few qualms. Part of the success lies in the stripped-away instrumentation, with a starkness of timbre attending all the music, and a sense that much has been pared down before the final cut. Garland sounds like a fine if sometimes cautious stylist, very much in the manner of Jan Garbarek, and there's an unavoidable recall of such sessions as *Dis* and *Eventyr* here, although Paterson's guitars and Fletcher's rhythms ensure that nothing drifts off into mere atmospherics for very long. Cameo appearances by Wheeler, Winstone and Tobin add some piquancy to what could have been a dreary effort and, if one sometimes wishes for one or two more abandoned pieces – they have the mystery but not much of the joy of the folk strains in here – it's still a strong effort.

HAROLD LAND (born 1928)
TENOR SAXOPHONE, FLUTE, OBOE

***   **Harold In The Land Of Jazz** Original Jazz Classics OJC 162 CD/LP
Land; Rolf Ericson (*t*); Carl Perkins (*p*); Leroy Vinnegar (*b*); Frank Butler (*d*). 1/58.

Made towards the end of his stint with bassist Curtis Counce's band, this is the first of a series of fine Land records. A still underrated player, hampered by a rather dour tone, Land favoured – or happened across – unusual piano players, giving more than one of his albums a harmonic unease that is more disconcerting that genuinely attractive. Perkins's crab-wise gait across the keyboard is mitigated by the vibrant rhythm work of Vinnegar and Butler, and the best track on the album is the quartet 'You Don't Know What Love Is', which the showy Ericson sits out (Land made some interesting brass appointments as well).

***(*)   **The Fox** Original Jazz Classics OJC 343 CD/LP/MC
Land; Dupree Bolton (*t*); Elmo Hope (*p*); Herbie Lewis (*b*); Frank Butler (*d*). 8/59.

Jazz history has drawn something of a veil over the subsequent career of trumpeter Dupree Bolton. Though this is his solitary appearance in the current catalogue, he plays with confidence and some fire, seemingly at ease at the accelerated tempo of 'The Fox' and the easier flow of 'Mirror-Mind Rose'. If Carl Perkins recalls a crab, then Elmo Hope has to be, yes, a butterfly. His touch was as light as his ideas and colours were fleeting. One of the least dynamic of players (and singularly dependent on drummers of Butler's kidney), he was nevertheless able to keep track with a rhythm line he wasn't actually playing, laying out astonishing melody figures on 'One Down' in what is probably his best recorded performance, certainly a step ahead of *Harold In The Land Of Jazz*.

Land is an underrated composer with a deep feeling for the blues, who never quite translated his most compelling ideas into practice. *The Fox*, tricky and fugitive as much of it is, must be thought his finest moment.

***   **Westcoast Blues** Original Jazz Classics OJC 146 LP
Land; Joe Gordon (*t*); Wes Montgomery (*g*); Barry Harris (*p*); Sam Jones (*b*); Louis Hayes (*d*). 5/60.

This was a fine band that should have recorded more. Montgomery and Gordon sugar Land's rather sardonic theme statements with some beautifully light touches that in no way trivialize the dark, blues feeling that wells up under the music. Parker's 'Klactoveesedstene' is enigmatic and strong. No CD in the offing, but the LP is well worth the search.

(*)   **Eastward Ho! Original Jazz Classics OJC 493 CD/LP/MC
        Land; Kenny Dorham (*t*); Amos Trice (*p*); Joe Peters (*d*). 7/60.

Pianist Trice was briefly known for his work with Wardell Gray and, heard blindfold, this rather unusual session might well suggest Gray's work. Land and Dorham are both in fine voice but rarely seem to be thinking along the same lines. 'Slowly' and 'On A Little Street In Singapore' (the latter well known to Glenn Miller fans) are both engagingly handled. Not one of Land's best records, though.

**** **Damisi** Mainstream MDCD 714 CD
        Land; Oscar Brashear (*t, flhn*); Harold Land Jr (*p*); Bill Henderson (*p, electric p*); Bobby Hutcherson (*vib*); Reggie Johnson, Buster Williams (*b*); Billy Hart, Ndugu, Woody Theus (*d*); Mtume (*perc*). 71, 72, 74.

Damisi is a compilation of material from a period when Land was examining the implications of John Coltrane's harmonic shifts and also the rhythmic potential of rock (as on 'In The Back, In The Corner, In The Dark') and Eastern music. 'Pakistan' is a remarkable performance, pairing Land's Lateef-influenced oboe (which he keeps admirably in pitch) and Brashear's high, muted trumpet. The ensembles have an eerie quality, underpinned by Williams's rolling bass lines and Ndugu's marvellously varied percussion. Most of the material is from 1972, but there is a track apiece from sessions recorded in 1971 and 1974. Both feature vibraharpist Hutcherson (of whom more below) and suggest that Land's Coltrane explorations had also led him to examine Wayne Shorter's work. The idiom is bang up to date, and a good deal more challenging than most of the stuff that came out under this stylistic flag in the 1980s. Strongly recommended.

***(*) **Xocia's Dance** Muse M 5272 CD/LP/MC
        Land; Oscar Brashear (*t, flhn*); George Cables (*p*); Bobby Hutcherson (*vib*); John Heard (*b*); Billy Higgins (*d*); Ray Armando (*perc*). 10/81.

***   **Mapanzi** Concord 4044 CD
        Land; Blue Mitchell (*t, flhn*); Kirk Lightsey (*p*); Reggie Johnson (*b*); Albert Heath (*d*). 77.

The association with Hutcherson was a much-needed shot in the arm for Land. The two-decade gap in the current catalogue sees the saxophonist emerging from a long and not always coherent examination of John Coltrane's harmonics with a new, mature style that retains much of the temper of his late 1950s work, but with added strength in the upper register. The cuts with Hutcherson are more interesting than those with Cables alone; the pianist is apt to be a rather stultifying player in groups of this size but, pitched against the vibes, he damps notes more sharply and cleans up the edges of his chords. Brashear has a lovely tone, with an unapologetic wobble round the 'break'. The overall sound is very good indeed.

The earlier *Mapanzi* is *almost* a terrific record, but Mitchell seems ill at ease with the saxophonist's new-found modernism and catches light only on his own 'Blue Silver'. Land and Lightsey work well together, and the leader's 'Rapture' is a finely etched confessional that pitches his adapted 'sheets of sound' approach against the pianist's highly wrought but never overwrought chords.

ART LANDE (born 1947)
PIANO

(*)   **Rubisa Patrol ECM 1081 LP
        Lande; Mark Isham (*t, flhn, ss*); Bill Douglas (*b, f*); Glenn Cronkhite (*d*). 5/76.

Lande's two albums for ECM with this band (the second record is deleted) are charming examples of the house style near its discreet best. The music is slight – Lande emerges here as a minor Keith Jarrett disciple – but the ambience and drift of the sound suggest a sequence of nocturnes, distilled by Isham's customarily bright trumpet and the playing of Douglas, who performs a beautiful bamboo flute solo at the very beginning.

**   **Hardball!** Great American Music Hall 2702 CD
        Lande (*p* solo).

Lande has made solo recordings before, but this is the only one easily available. By himself the pianist is slightly more individual, suggesting a sense of folksy Americana in his melodies and pared-down structures. But his rhythmic indolence tends to mislay what spark the music has to start with.

EDDIE LANG (1904–33)
GUITAR

***(*) **A Handful Of Riffs** ASV AJA 5061 CD
Lang; King Oliver (c); Leo McConville, Andy Secrest, Bill Margulis (t); Tommy Dorsey , Bill Rank (tb); Jimmy Dorsey (cl, as); Charlie Strickfadden, Bernard Daly (as); Izzy Friedman (cl, ts); J. C. Johnson, Frank Signorelli, Arthur Schutt (p); Hoagy Carmichael (p, cel); Henry Whiteman (vn); Lonnie Johnson (g); Joe Tarto, Mike Trafficante (b); George Marsh, San King (d); Justin Ring (perc). 4/27–10/29.

*** **Jazz Guitar Virtuoso** Yazoo 1059 CD
Lang; Frank Signorelli, Rube Bloom, Arthur Schutt (p); Lonnie Johnson, Carl Kress (g); Justin Ring (chimes). 27–29.

Eddie Lang was the first guitarist to make a major impact on jazz away from the blues, and even there he took a hand by recording many duets with the 'authentic' bluesman, Lonnie Johnson. Lang's polished, civilized art was worked out in dance bands and as an accompanist – after joining Paul Whiteman in the late 1920s, the guitarist struck up a professional kinship with Bing Crosby, who hired him until his early death. He was an important member of the white New York school of the period and can be found on records by Beiderbecke, Joe Venuti and the Dorseys, but the sides made under his own name were also plentiful. We still await a truly comprehensive CD collection, but the two discs above provide a useful if finally inadequate representation of his work.

Exasperatingly, eight of the Yazoo tracks are also included on the ASV set. Yazoo concentrate on Lang the soloist, including all eight of the sides he made in that context, plus two tracks with Carl Kress and three with Johnson. There isn't much jazz in Rachmaninov's 'Prelude' or 'April Kisses', but showpieces like 'Eddie's Twister' and the luxuriant duet with Johnson on 'Blue Guitars' show all of Lang's beauty of touch, harmonic shrewdness and rhythmical dexterity. A couple more spirited tracks wouldn't have come amiss here, and the ration of 14 tracks is somewhat short measure.

The ASV issue offers a wider choice of 21 pieces, including the famous session with King Oliver on cornet and the five tracks by an orchestra led nominally by Lang. Sound on both issues is generally very good: the Yazoo is a little livelier but has a higher level of surface hiss. A comprehensive edition of Lang's solo and duet work was issued by Swaggie on two LPs (S1276, S1229) which may still be available: these 32 tracks also include the 1929 'Knockin' A Jug' session with Louis Armstrong, as well as such beautiful duets as 'Guitar Blues', omitted from the above. His tracks with violinist Joe Venuti are discussed under Venuti's name.

DON LANPHERE (born 1928)
TENOR SAXOPHONE, SOPRANO SAXOPHONE

[*** **First Sessions 1949/50** Prestige P 24081 2LP]
Lanphere; Fats Navarro (t); Al Haig, Duke Jordan (p); Tubby Phillips, Tommy Potter (b); Roy Hall, Max Roach (d). 7 & 9/49.

*** **From Out Of Nowhere** Hep 2019 LP
Lanphere; Jon Pugh (t); Paul Scea (ts); Marc Seales (p, electric p); Glen Gurnard (mar); Chuck Deardorff (b); Dean Hodges (d). 6/82.

*** **Into Somewhere** Hep 2022 LP
Lanphere; Jon Pugh (t); Don Friedman (p); Geoff Fuller (b); Dave Peterson (g); Glen Gurnard (mar); Ignacio Berroa (d). 12/83.

Hailing from the far north-west of the United States, Lanphere made a momentous decision in 1947 when he moved to New York rather than down the long coast to Los Angeles. His fiddly, off-beat phrasing and inimitable tone might well have been rationalized away in warmer climes and among cooler jazz; on the other hand, his playing career might have been more continuous. In 1948 and 1949 he recorded promising sets with trumpeter Fats Navarro and some debut sides with his own quartet, which featured Duke Jordan. The Navarro cuts are better, largely because the rhythm section of Haig, Potter and Roach is more accomplished than Lanphere's own.

It's interesting to listen to the saxophonist in close proximity to sessions from Cool exponents Lennie Tristano and Lee Konitz; the kinship is immediately evident, even amid the boppish phrases. *First Sessions* is not simply a chronicle of early promise; more than one of the tyros featured on it came to a sticky end. Lanphere's at least wasn't terminal. Introduced to heroin in New York, he was charged with possession and fled home to Washington State, where he sold rather than made records for most of the next 20 years, playing rather intermittently. He managed to outride the nightmare, though, and re-emerged, with a robust, Born Again faith, in the 1980s.

From Out Of Nowhere is both aptly and ironically named. As far as most listeners were concerned, Lanphere was a newcomer in 1982, but he seemed remarkably 'finished' in tone and method, not at all like a beginner. *Into Somewhere*, on the other hand, seemed merely ironical, for there was virtually nowhere for Lanphere to go with a time-capsule style and an almost solipsistic approach. In place of the relatively straightforward music of the first album, which concluded with a fine Parker-tinged 'Out Of Nowhere' and a surprisingly moving 'Lord's Prayer', the second set, made a year later with broadly similar instrumentation, sounds both tentative and restless, filling in gaps rather than moving forward. It's not clear how the second part of 'Noble Indian Song' relates to the first, and 'Take The "A" Train' is dismal. The use of marimba was an intelligent stroke, extended from a single track on *From Out Of Nowhere*. Pugh, credited as 'featured' artist, is effective co-leader and fills some of the most interesting solo space. Lanphere is one of those isolated and rather peripheral figures who refuses to occupy the pre-stressed critical compartments. He is nevertheless worth hearing.

***(*)   **Go . . . Again** Hep 2040 CD

***(*)   **Don Lanphere/Larry Coryell** Hep 2048 CD
Lanphere; Larry Coryell (*g* on *Lanphere/Coryell* only); Jon Pugh (*t* on *Go . . . Again* only); Jeff Hay (*tb*); Marc Seales (*p, syn*); Chuck Deardorff (*b*); Dean Hodges (*d*); Jay Clayton (*v* on *Go . . . Again* only). 1/87 & 3/88, 4/90.

'*Go . . . Again*' harks back to Lanphere's 1949 sessions with Fats Navarro, a free blow round the chords of 'The Way You Look Tonight'. Trumpet and trombone accompany the saxophone at opposite ends of the register. 'What Are You Doing The Rest Of Your Life' is for soprano saxophone and synthesizer; Lanphere plays it straight, with a delivery reminiscent of Ronnie Scott. Jay Clayton's vocal on 'Darn That Dream' is pitched somewhere between Sheila Jordan and Carmen McRae. A beautiful album, resolutely performed.

It's a pity there isn't more duo material with Coryell. Horace Silver's 'Peace' was chosen as a brief 'Amen' to the 1990 session, a scant minute that retrospectively promises much. At the opposite end, the opening 'Dragon Gate' leaves Lanphere on the outskirts of a trombone–guitar unison statement until he comes in with a smoothly burnished soprano solo. Bill Evans's 'Very Early' has him shift to a less familiar or effective alto. Coryell takes the lead on a duet 'Spring Can Really Hang You Up The Most' with keyboard man Seales, who's an impressive writer too on the strength of 'Ascending Truth'. Coryell's busy action and pure diction fit remarkably well with Lanphere's, and the album has an engaging sweetness of tone. Recommended.

ELLIS LARKINS (born 1923)
PIANO

(*)   **Duologue Black Lion BLCD 760911 CD
Larkins (*p* solo). 54.

(*)   **A Smooth One Black & Blue 591232 CD
Larkins; George Duvivier (*b*); J. C. Heard (*d*). 7/77.

Larkins's mastery is so understated that one despairs of him ever making the recorded masterpiece that may be in him. Although he has been active for over half a century – he was a child prodigy in his native Baltimore and worked in New York clubs through the 1940s – Larkins has made few records, and then usually as an accompanist, to singers such as Ella Fitzgerald and Anita Ellis. *Duologue* offers four brief solos from 1954 (the rest of the record features Lee Wiley with a Ruby Braff group). *A Smooth One* is Larkins's only available trio date. Several of the eight pieces remind one of his judgement that with some songs 'you just play them and get out'; but there are some bewitching moments hidden behind his professional excellence.

PRINCE LASHA (born 1929)
ALTO SAXOPHONE, FLUTE

****   **Journey To Zoar** Enja 4008 LP
   Lasha; Sonny Simmons (*as, ob*); Bobby Hutcherson (*vib*); Buster Williams (*b*);
   Charles Moffett (*d*).

***   **Inside Story** Enja 3073 LP
   Lasha; Herbie Hancock (*p*); Cecil McBee (*b*); Jimmy Lovelace (*d*). 65.

Lasha – pronounced 'Lashay' – was in the same Fort Worth high school band as Ornette Coleman and King Curtis. There are elements of both in his playing, should you wish to look for them, but the dominant influence is Eric Dolphy, with whom Lasha played on *Iron Man* (West Wind 2057 CD). That session also featured Hutcherson and Simmons, who help to make the 'Journey To Zoar' and 'City Of Zoar', the two long takes that make up Enja 4008, such an unforgettable experience; a CD is urgently called for, with any unreleased material from that session.

Lasha has a frail, slightly thin tone on alto saxophone, explained in part by his choice of a plastic instrument (this was inspired not so much by Ornette Coleman as by Charlie Parker's use of a bakelite horn at the famous Massey Hall concert); on *Journey to Zoar*, where his articulation may suggest some of Anthony Braxton's 1970s work, he sounds as if he may be playing a North African or Asian wind instrument of variable pitch. Following the same instinct for unusual colours, he also uses a wooden flute, which gives a softer, slightly 'dead' timbre; though influenced again by Dolphy, it is a markedly individual sound which anticipates the later work of multi-instrumentalists like Oliver Lake, Douglas Ewart and, above all, Henry Threadgill.

Inside Story is rather more conventional in instrumentation and hovers on the brink of dullness. In this context, Lasha's oddities of tone no longer present an aesthetic advantage. Some of the ordinariness, though, stems from the group. Set against Moffett's bashing intensity and Williams's deep throb, McBee and Lovelace seem almost skittish. Lasha had more interesting things to say than this album might suggest, and enthusiasts should dig out the rarely-heard *Insight* [CBS 62409 LP], where he plays opposite a British band numbering Stan Tracey, Jeff Clyne, trumpeter Chris Bateson, one-time Mahavishnu Orchestra bassist Rick Laird and harpist David Snell in its ranks. The album offers two fine examples of Lasha's 'straight' standards playing – 'Out Of Nowhere', a flute-led 'Body And Soul' – and a moving tribute to Dolphy.

LAST EXIT
GROUP

****   **Last Exit** Enemy EMY 101 CD/LP
   Peter Brötzmann (*reeds*); Sonny Sharrock (*g*); Bill Laswell (*b*); Ronald Shannon
   Jackson (*d, v*). 2/86.

***(*)   **Köln** ITM 1446 CD
   As above. 2/86.

****   **The Noise Of Trouble** Enemy EMY 103 CD/LP
   As above, plus Akira Sakata (*cl, as*); Herbie Hancock (*p*). 10/86.

*** **Cassette Recordings 87** Enemy/Celluloid 6147 LP
As above, except omit Sakata and Hancock. 87.

***(*) **Iron Path** Virgin Venture CDVE 38 CD
As above. 88.

Some may feel that the above are generous evaluations for a group which some have dismissed as a noisy rock-jazz band, but the sheer exhilaration which Last Exit can create when they hit their stride is almost incomparable. The group is a meeting of four particularly cussed spirits whose tastes for sonic extremes are competitive: at their wildest, these recordings suggest four men all trying to outdo one another in volume and extravagance. While Jackson's polyrhythmic parts establish a single, ever-evolving drum solo, Laswell anchors the pieces with huge, juddering bass-lines decorated by the wailing Brötzmann and Sharrock, whose guitar parts bridge heavy metal rock and free jazz more cogently than anyone else has ever done.

All the above are live recordings, aside from the Venture set. The mixes inevitably leave much to be desired, but for bludgeoning force there is little to choose between *Last Exit*, *Köln* and *Cassette Recordings 87*. Pieces such as 'Discharge' and 'Hard School' establish an outpouring of sound with few equals among the records in this book, but there are elements of the blues as well as a canny sensitivity to how far to push things, which both vary and intensify the flow. *The Noise Of Trouble* adds the maverick element of guest star Sakata duelling crazily with Brötzmann on 'Blind Willie', as well as a bewildering appearance by Hancock on 'Help Me Mo, I'm Blind'. *Iron Path*, their only studio date, may strike some as being too tame after the onslaught of the previous four: the title-piece is a restrained rumble, and 'Sand Dancer' is nearly terpsichorean. Yet such as 'Marked For Death' and 'Eye For An Eye' introduce detail and concentration into their sound without sacrificing visceral impact. Every collection should contain at least one of these records.

YUSEF LATEEF (born 1921)
TENOR SAXOPHONE, OBOE, FLUTE, OTHER SAXOPHONES, COR ANGLAIS, OTHER INSTRUMENTS

***(*) **Blues For The Orient** Prestige P 24035 2LP
Lateef; Wilbur Harden (*flhn*); Barry Harris (*p*); Ernie Farrow (*b, rabat*); Lex Humphries (*d*); Oliver Jackson (*d, perc*). 10/57, 9/61.

***(*) **Other Sounds** Original Jazz Classics OJC 399 CD/LP/MC
Lateef; Wilbur Harden (*flhn*); Hugh Lawson (*p*); Ernie Farrow (*b*); Oliver Jackson (*d*).

*** **Cry! – Tender** Original Jazz Classics OJC 482 CD/LP/MC
Lateef; Lonnie Hillyer (*t*); Wilbur Harden (*flhn*); Hugh Lawson (*p*); Ernie Farrow, Herman Wright (*b*); Frank Gant, Oliver Jackson (*d*).

***(*) **Eastern Sounds** Original Jazz Classics OJC 612 CD/LP/MC
Lateef; Barry Harris (*p*); Ernie Farrow (*b*); Lex Humphries (*d*).

***(*) **Into Something** Original Jazz Classics OJC 700 CD/LP/MC
Lateef; Barry Harris (*p*); Ernie Farrow (*b*); Elvin Jones (*d*).

***(*) **The Many Faces Of Yusef Lateef** Milestone M 47009 2LP
Lateef; Clark Terry (*t, flhn*); Richard Williams (*t*); Curtis Fuller (*tb*); Tate Houston (*bs*); Josea Taylor (*bsn*); Barry Harris, Hugh Lawson, Joe Zawinul (*p*); Ben Tucker, Herman Wright (*b*); Ron Carter (*clo*); Lex Humphries (*d*); Garvin Masseaux, Roger Sanders (*perc*). 5 & 10/61, 6/61.

*** **The Gentle Giant** Atlantic 1602 CD
Lateef; Bill Campbell (*as*); Ray Bryant (*p*); Kenny Barron (*electric p*); Eric Gale (*g*); Neal Boyer (*vib, chimes*); Sam Jones, Chuck Rainey (*b*); Bob Cunningham, Bill Salter (*b*); Albert Heath, Jimmy Johnson (*d*); Sweet Inspirations (*v*). 74.

Born plain Bill Evans, Lateef avoided the confusion of yet another Evans boy in the catalogue by adopting a Muslim name in response to his growing and eventually life-long infatuation for the musics of the Levant and Asia. One of the few convincing oboists in jazz and an ancestor of East-West outfits like Oregon (whose Paul McCandless has consciously or unconsciously adopted some of Lateef's tonal devices), he has suffered something of Rahsaan Roland Kirk's fate in finding himself dismissed or marginalized as a 'speciality act' working apart from the central dramas of modern jazz. Like Kirk's, Lateef's music underwent a degree of market distortion when he came under Atlantic's enthusiastic but market-led wing, making albums that were enthusiastically promoted and received, but which rarely represented the best of his work.

On the question of his jazz credentials, it's unfortunate that two good Impulse concert recordings – *Live at Pep's* and *Club Date* – are no longer available; but even the most cursory exposure to his powerful oboe solo on 'Blues for the Orient' on the compilation of that name confirms his qualities as an improviser and the four OJCs are full of jazz improvisation (on all three main instruments) of the highest order. Highlights are certainly the sessions with Elvin Jones on *Into Something*, where the drummer's African cross-rhythms help transform a familiar standard like 'I'll Remember April' into something much more dramatic, and the powerful originals on the aptly named *Other Sounds*.

Like Kirk again, the tenor saxophone is Lateef's 'natural' horn, but in his best period he made jazz whatever he was playing. In approach, he is somewhat reminiscent of the pre-bop aspect of Sun Ra's long-time associate John Gilmore, working in a strong, extended swing idiom rather than with the more complex figurations of bebop. This is most obvious on the early sessions on *Blues for the Orient* which fill out what was originally released as *Eastern Sounds*. Playing opposite Harden on 'Take the "A" Train', he sounds perfectly easy with the idiom. The *Eastern Sounds* session also included film music from *The Robe* and *Spartacus*, on flute and oboe respectively, that borders on kitsch, but the tenor-led 'Snafu', a thoroughly Occidental expression of fatalism, has a surging energy that has Lateef's very good band panting.

The Many Faces is almost equally good (though both albums are in need of a CD facelift) and features sterling work from trumpeters Terry and Williams and trombonist Fuller. The tone colours are intelligently varied, with further examples of Lateef's musicological interests. The vocal contributions to 'Jungle Fantasy' don't quite come off and merely anticipate the grosser insult of 'Hey, Jude' on *The Gentle Giant*. In turning Lateef into a marketable, crossover performer, Atlantic took most of the bite out of his playing. There are four good tracks on the mid-1970s album, most notably 'Nubian Lady', but there was an awful thinness to much of the rest that boded ill for the future.

*(*)   **Yusef Lateef's Little Symphony** Atlantic 781757 CD
Lateef (various instruments). 6/87.

*(*)   **Concerto For Yusef Lateef** Atlantic 781863 CD
Lateef; Christopher Salvo (*cl*); Robert Daley (*g*); John Nuhn, George Cooke (*b*); Mulazimuddin S. Rasool (*perc, mar*); Tony Vaca (*perc*). 3/88.

(*)   **Nocturnes Atlantic 781977 CD
Lateef; Hugh Schlick (*flhn*); Patrick Tucker (*fr hn*); Christopher Salvo (*cl*). 2/89.

These are albums of numbing banality and pretentiousness, only redeemed by occasional glimpses of Lateef's old fire. The generic and dynamic labels pasted all over *Concerto* – which isn't – are mostly misapplied. The music luxuriates in exoticism and the latter pair steer an uneasy course between so-called World Music and New Age wallpaper. The solo *Symphony* strongly recalls Keith Jarrett's therapeutic multi-instrumental *Spirits* (ECM 1333/4) and is almost as horrible to listen to.

CHRISTOF LAUER
TENOR SAXOPHONE

***(*)   **Christof Lauer** CMP 39 CD/LP/MC
Lauer; Joachim Kühn (*p*); Palle Danielsson (*b*); Peter Erskine (*d*). 4/89.

One of the younger generation of European players who have stepped beyond the overpowering influence of John Coltrane, Lauer has assimilated such a range of styles – from Stan Getz's smooth legato to Albert Ayler's all-out fury – that he seems derivative only episodically. Taken over the length of this sterling set of originals, he is very much his own man. The emotional range is impressive, covering the adventurous up-tempo post-bop of 'Descent' to the backward glances of 'Harlem Nocturne'. If 'Eva' records a romantic affair, it must have been a doozy; half-way through, after a sensitive interlude from Kuhn, Lauer breaks into an upper-register scream that is almost as impressively controlled as it is emotionally fraught. Danielsson and Erskine are as impressive as ever. Too early yet to make categorical judgements about Lauer's progress, but this is a most impressive record.

ANDY LAVERNE (born 1948)
KEYBOARDS

**   **Another World** Steeplechase SCS 1086 LP
LaVerne; Mike Richmond (*b*); Billy Hart (*d*). 9/77.

(*)   **Frozen Music Steeplechase SCS 1244 CD/LP
LaVerne; Rick Margitza (*ss, ts*); Marc Johnson (*b*); Danny Gottlieb (*d*). 4/89.

**   **Fountainhead** Steeplechase SCCD 31261 CD
LaVerne; Dave Samuels (*vib*). 6/89.

(*)   **Standard Eyes Steeplechase SCCD 31280 CD
LaVerne; Steve LaSpina (*b*); Anton Fig (*d*). 10/90.

LaVerne is a dedicated, accomplished player whose records consistently fail to spark into life. There's no gainsaying his technique and taste, but his music tends to run aground on its own thoughtfulness: rhythmically, he can be a little four-square, without the compensating lightness of touch which adds light and shade to such a style. His Steeplechase albums are worthy rather than absorbing sessions. *Frozen Music* offers a glimpse of the useful young Margitza, but the LaVerne originals are disappointingly unmemorable. The meeting with Samuels creates a lot of pretty music and not much more, while the session of standards at least affords the trio something strong to work with.

(*)   **Liquid Silver dmp CD 449 CD
LaVerne; Sebu Sirinian, Jennifer Cowles (*vn*); Amy Dulsky (*vla*); Patricia Smith (*clo*); John Abercrombie (*g*); Eddie Gomez (*b*); Peter Erskine (*d*). 10–11/84.

**   **Plays Chick Corea** Jazzline 11108 CD
LaVerne; John Abercrombie (*g*); Marc Johnson, Mark Egan (*b*); Danny Gottlieb (*d*). 81–86.

**   **Jazz Piano Lineage** dmp CD 463 CD
LaVerne (*p* solo). 3/88.

Liquid Silver offers an intelligently varied programme of duets, trios and two tracks with a string quartet; Gomez, Abercrombie and Erskine enliven their tracks, and there is a charming reading of 'Turn Out The Stars', a favourite of LaVerne's teacher, Bill Evans. The idea of LaVerne paying tribute to Corea may strike some as a twice-removed project and while it's enthusiastically executed there's not much substance in the results. *Jazz Piano Lineage* features the pianist's thoughts on tunes associated with Monk, Brubeck, Evans and others, and it was probably more important to him than to the listener. There is also a perfectly competent reading of Debussy's Prelude No. 7. Excellent piano sound.

**   **Natural Living** Musidisc 500092 CD
LaVerne; John Abercrombie (*g*). 11/89.

LaVerne and Abercrombie work well together and this should have been a promising collection of standards and originals. But the bass-heavy sound smudges detail and sensitivity, and one tune soon comes to sound like another; only on the title-piece, in which Abercrombie switches to acoustic guitar, does the music achieve a genuine intensity of expression.

HUGH LAWSON (born 1935)
PIANO

***   **Colours** Soul Note SN 1052 CD
Lawson; Calvin Hill (*b*); Louis Hayes (*d*). 1/83.

Better known as a sideman with George Adams–Dannie Richmond, Turk Mauro and Yusef Lateef, Lawson has a strong, slightly dry delivery that lends itself better to the ironies of 'Pictures At An Exhibition' and 'If' than to the more conventional changes of '23rd Street Blues'. Hayes raises the temperature and Hill, who has also recorded with Max Roach and McCoy Tuner, keeps the multilinear feel going. Worth checking out.

THE LEADERS
GROUP

***   **Mudfoot** Black Hawk BKH 52001 CD/LP/MC

***(*)   **Out Here Like This** Black Saint BSR 0119 CD/LP
       Lester Bowie (*t*); Arthur Blythe (*as*); Chico Freeman (*ts, bcl*); Kirk Lightsey (*p*); Cecil McBee (*b*); Famoudou Don Moye (*d*). 6/86, 2/87.

Occupying a mid-point between the now almost parodic anarchy of the Art Ensemble of Chicago and the more professional musical showmanship of Lester Bowie's Brass Fantasy, and offering a left-of-centre balance between Chico Freeman's freer style and the soul-funk of his Brainstorm band, The Leaders also helped redeem Arthur Blythe's skidding career. Never as impressive on record as they have been live, the second album is nevertheless a powerful and varied sampling of contemporary styles. There's a better balance of sound between the front-row voices and a more prominent role for McBee, who shares some of Ron Carter's ability to style-shift while maintaining a basic consistency of tone. Bowie's theatrical approach manages to compress a huge acreage of jazz history, calling in references to Armstrong, Bix Beiderbecke and Miles Davis.
    Mudfoot shouldn't be dismissed, but it is a scrappier performance, still sounding more like a well-starred pick-up band and less like a viable touring unit.

THE LEADERS TRIO

***(*)   **Heaven Dance** Sunnyside SSC 1034 CD
       Lightsey (*p*); McBee (*b*); Moye (*d*). 5/88.

Not the least of *Heaven Dance*'s merits is that it sends us back to the original Leaders sets with a heightened awareness of what was going on in the warp-factor engine room. Which is not to say that *Heaven Dance* is not a substantial achievement on its own terms. Though it may masquerade as a conventional piano trio, the balance of emphasis favours McBee (particularly) and Don Moye. The title-track is an intriguing pattern of melorhythms with some fine piano; 'Cecil to Cecil' and a tribute to the great bassist Wilbur Ware also catch the eye. Recommended.

MIKE LEDONNE
PIANO

(*)   **'Bout Time Criss Cross Jazz Criss 1033 CD/LP
       LeDonne; Tom Harrell (*t, flhn*); Gary Smulyan (*bs*); Dennis Irwin (*b*); Kenny Washington (*d*). 1/88.

(*)   **The Feeling Of Jazz Criss Cross Jazz Criss 1041 CD
       As above. 1/90.

LeDonne leads a very capable group here and, while they deliver two very consistent records, there's little to feel excited about. Tunes, charts and solos all bespeak an unflagging but charmless dedication to hard bop routine. Four of the themes on the second record are handled by the rhythm section alone, but otherwise there's little to tell the two records apart. The CD issue of *'Bout Time* has some extra material over the LP.

URS LEIMGRUBER
TENOR SAXOPHONE, SOPRANO SAXOPHONE, BASS SAXOPHONE, FLUTE

(*) **Reflexionen Timeless SJP 199 LP
Leimgruber; Don Friedman (*p*); Bobby Burri (*b*); Joel Allouche (*d*). 11/83.

*** **Reflexionen Live** Timeless SJP 234 CD/LP
As above. 11/85.

*** **Reflexionen** Enja 5057 CD
Leimgruber; Don Friedman (*p*); Palle Danielsson (*b*); Joel Allouche (*d*). 2/87.

***(*) **Statement Of An Antirider** hat Art 6013 CD
Leimgruber (solo). 3/88.

In tonal range and diversity of concerns, Leimgruber somewhat resembles Briton John Surman. Surman, though, has only rarely ventured into total freedom and utilizes extremes of pitch rather sparingly. Leimgruber's Reflexionen is far from being a conventional horn-and-rhythm unit. The Timeless sessions find him working with space and extended structures – like the 'Rotsee Suite' – while the two later recordings document a shift towards a more abstract and gestural approach, still with occasional folk or traditional references (much as he has developed in duo with John Wolf Brennan).

The solo *Statement* is a quite remarkable performance and has to be seen as the quintessence of Leimgruber's work to date. Even when working with a highly sophisticated band and with players of the calibre of Danielsson and Friedman, he always sounds slightly detached and self-involved, much as Surman frequently sounds alone at the centre of the music. To that extent, solo performance is a logical progression for both of them.

JAY LEONHART (born 1940)
BASS, VOCAL

** **There's Gonna Be Trouble** Sunnyside SSC 1006D CD
Leonhart; Joe Beck (*g*).

** **The Double Cross** Sunnyside SSC 1032D CD
Leonhart; George Young (*ts*); Roger Kellaway (*p*); Grady Tate, Terry Clarke (*d*); Michael Leonhart, Carolyn Leonhart (*v*).

** **Salamander Pie** dmp CD 442
Leonhart; Mike Renzi (*p*). 3/83.

While he's an entirely plausible bassist, Leonhart would rather be known as a singer-songwriter in the manner of Dave Frishberg or Randy Newman, though he misses both Frishberg's wit and Newman's irony. These are song records rather than playing dates, and while *The Double Cross* has a little more grit in it, all will appeal only if Leonhart's hick ingenue stance proves convincing. Some of the songs on *Salamander Pie* at least have nice ideas. In 'Robert Frost' he muses on the poet's financial situation rather than his inspiration – 'Could he go down to the country store and sell a poem saying, Here's a nice one I wrote about the snow?' But his singing, all exaggerated vowels and laboured rhythms, is very hard to take.

STAN LEVEY (born 1925)
DRUMS

** **Stanley The Steamer** Affinity AFF 768 CD
Levey; Conte Candoli (*t*); Frank Rosolino (*tb*); Dexter Gordon, Zoot Sims (*ts*); Jimmy Giuffre (*bs*); Claude Williamson, Lou Levy (*p*); Leroy Vinnegar, Max Bennett (*b*). 12/54–9/55.

Split between two sessions, with only Candoli and Levey common to both, this is potboiler West Coast jazz of its day. The earlier date offers some writing by Bill Holman, Bob Cooper and Giuffre but emerges as a routine blow, the sound less than excellent, even for 1954. The second session offers a rare chance to hear Gordon in the mid-1950s, but he's hardly at his best, and the very quick tempo for 'Max Is Making Wax' defeats him entirely. The best soloist here is the consistently witty Rosolino. Levey himself is a self-effacing leader.

HAKAN LEWIN
ALTO AND SOPRANO SAX

***(*)   **Excursions** Dragon DRLP 98 LP
           Lewin; Gosta Rundqvist (*p*); Lars-Urban Helje (*b*); Mats Hellberg (*d*). 2/85.

A thoughtful and judiciously sustained programme: it's a long LP, running for some 50 minutes, and the compositions – four by Rundqvist, and two by Steve Swallow – unfold with patient inevitability. The quartet is made up of four musicians who live far apart from one another, in remote northern Swedish provinces, but their empathy is surprisingly natural and unforced. Lewin, who plays more soprano than alto here, has an impassive tone and a more tangible interest in casting long notes against the steadily developing manoeuvres of the rhythm section. Both 'Falling Grace' and 'Gostas Vals' are quietly compelling treatments which take an organic course to resolution: the former starts slowly and carefully and builds to a fierce intensity that will catch most listeners by surprise. Rundqvist's themes are melodically simple yet fruitful terrain for individual improvisations – try his swinging, rigorously drawn solo on 'Fasters Motvals' – yet it's the co-operative strength of the group which leaves the deepest impression. Strongly recommended, as another fine document of Swedish jazz from the estimable Dragon operation.

GEORGE LEWIS (born 1952)
TROMBONE, COMPUTER

***(*)   **George Lewis – Douglas Ewart** Black Saint BSR 0026 LP
           Lewis; Douglas Ewart (*as, bcl, cym*). 78.

*****   **Homage To Charles Parker** Black Saint BSR 0029 CD/LP
           As above, except add Anthony Davis (*p*); Richard Teitelbaum (*syn*). 79.

It is significant that, as a trombonist growing up in a period marked by the dominance of the saxophone, George Lewis should have taken saxophone players as his primary models. His rather emotional legato is reminiscent of both Lester Young and, depending on context, virtually all the evolutionary stages of John Coltrane's style. Context is of considerable importance because Lewis has played in a bewildering variety of musical settings, from relatively conventional section-playing (a brief stint with the mid-1970s Basie band) to technically adventurous free playing (as with Douglas Ewart on BSR 0026, and with Derek Bailey's improvising collective Company on *Fables* – Incus 36 LP – and *Epiphany* – Incus 46/7 LP). Lewis habitually plays either with intense and surprisingly gentle lyricism or with a deconstructive fury that has led him to dismantle his trombone in mid-performance, producing non-tempered and abstract tones on mouthpiece and slide. He has also taken a close interest in electronics, using computers with increasing technical assurance to provide backgrounds and to create a much-needed dialectical tension in improvised performances.

Homage to Charles Parker represents a further triumphant extension and synthesis of these interests, combining improvisation with predetermined structures – rather in the manner of Lawrence 'Butch' Morris or pianist-composer Anthony Davis, who plays on the date – and reintroducing a strong programmatic element to abstract music. As he shows in the fine duets with Ewart, using predetermined structures in indeterminate juxtapositions and dynamics can create a music of considerable resonance. 'Homage To Charles Parker' and 'Blues', the two long sides that made up the original LP, are among the most profound and beautiful performances of recent times and certainly rank in the top dozen or so jazz/improvised records made since 1960.

Lewis's rather stilted liner-notes somewhat undersell the emotional impact of both pieces. 'Blues' consists of four independent diatonic 'choruses' of absolute simplicity which are played in shifting configurations by the four musicians. Despite the fact that there are no conventional resolutions and no predictable coincidence of material, the piece evokes order as much as freedom. Although none of the material conforms to the blues, its 'feel' is absolutely unmistakable and authentic.

If 'Blues' is a triumphant extension of the black tradition in music, 'Homage To Charles Parker' concerns itself intimately with the saxophonist's putative afterlife and musical real-presence. There is a long opening section on electronics, synthesizers and cymbals which evoke Parker's 'reality'. Reminiscent of evocations of primeval Chaos by Marilyn Crispell on *Gaia* (Leo Records) and the electronic composer Bernard Parmegiani, it gradually yields place to a series of apparently discontinuous solos on saxophone, piano and finally with no ensemble backing beyond the synthesizer sounds, which recast and project Parker's life and language. There are no explicit bebop references and, indeed, the piece seems to serve as a healing response to the fractures that separated bop from the earlier history of black American music, of which it was also the apotheosis. The music is calm and almost stately, occasionally suggesting a chorale. Lewis's concluding statements are unbearably plangent but also forceful and intelligent. In their refusal of tragedy, they also have to be seen as political statements. This is an essential modern record.

GEORGE LEWIS (1900–68)
CLARINET

****   **George Lewis With Kid Shots** American Music AMCD 2 CD
Lewis; Bunk Johnson, Louis 'Kid Shots' Madison (*t*); Jim Robinson (*tb*); Lawrence Marrero (*bj*); Alcide 'Slow Drag' Pavageau (*b*); Baby Dodds (*d*). 7 & 8/44.

****   **Trios And Bands** American Music AMCD 4 CD
Lewis; Avery 'Kid' Howard, Louis 'Kid Shots' Madison (*t*); Jim Robinson (*tb*); Lawrence Marrero (*bj*); Ricard Alexis, Alcide 'Slow Drag' Pavageau, Chester Zardis (*b*); Baby Dodds, Edgar Moseley (*d*).

***(*)   **The George Lewis Ragtime Band Of New Orleans: The Oxford Series – Volume 1** American Music AMCD 21 CD

***(*)   **The George Lewis Ragtime Band Of New Orleans: The Oxford Series – Volume 2 (Concert First Half)** American Music AMCD 22 CD

***(*)   **The George Lewis Ragtime Band Of New Orleans: The Oxford Series – Volume 3 (Concert Second Half)** American Music AMCD 23 CD
Lewis; Percy G. Humphrey (*t*); Jim Robinson (*tb*); Alton Purnell (*p*); Lawrence Marrero (*bj*); Alcide 'Slow Drag' Pavageau (*b*); Joe Watkins (*d*). 52.

***(*)   **At Club Hangover: Volume 3** Storyville SLP 4061 LP
Lewis; Kid Howard (*t*); Alton Purnell (*p*); Lawrence Marrero (*bjo*); Alcide 'Slow Drag' Pavageau (*b*); Joe Watkins (*d*). 11/53.

***(*)   **Jazz At Vespers** Original Jazz Classics OJC 1721 LP
As above. 2/54.

***(*)   **Jass At Ohio Union** Storyville STCD 6020/1 2CD
As above. 3/54.

***   **Sounds Of New Orleans: Volume 7** Storyville SLP 6014 CD/LP
Lewis; Kid Howard (*t*); Jim Robinson (*tb*); Alton Purnell (*p*); Lawrence Marrero (*bj*); Alcide 'Slow Drag' Pavageau (*b*); Joe Watkins (*d*); Lizzie Miles (*v*). 12/53 & 1/54.

(*)   **George Lewis/Paul Barbarin Storyville SLP 4049 LP
Lewis; Kid Howard (*t*); Percy Humphrey (*t*); Alton Purnell (*p*); Jeanette Kimball (*p*); Johnny St Cyr (*g*); Lawrence Marrero (*bj*); Alcide 'Slow Drag' Pavageau (*b*); Joe Watkins (*d*); Sister Elizabeth Eustis (*v*). 7/57.

***   **Jazz In The Classic New Orleans Tradition** Original Jazz Classics OJC 1736 CD/LP
Lewis; Alvin Alcorn (*t*); Bill Matthews (*tb*); Alton Purnell, Lester Santiago (*p*); Lawrence Marrero (*bj*); Alcide 'Slow Drag' Pavageau (*b*); Paul Barbarin (*d*).

** **George Lewis In Japan** Storyville SLP 514 LP
Lewis; Jack Willis (*t, mellophone*); Louis Nelson (*tb*); Joe Robichaux (*p*); Emmanuel
Sayles (*bjo*); Placide Adams (*b*); Alonzo Stewart (*d*). 6/64.

Rarely has a traditional jazz musician been documented on record in so concentrated a way as
clarinettist George Lewis was in the early 1950s. Having been coaxed out of a 'retirement'
working as a dockhand at the start of the war, Lewis was by the mid-'50s the surviving pillar of
'serious' revivalism, which he'd helped kick off with Bunk Johnson, working what looked like a
politician's itinerary across the United States; Johnson is featured on three tracks of the early
With Kid Shots compilation.

The early material is absolutely pristine and comes across on CD with remarkable freshness.
The *Trios & Band* compilations includes some second takes from the group sessions with
'Shots' (including a marvellous second try on 'San Jacinto Blues' and the first, presumably
rejected take of 'High Society'). He was apparently, unhappy about the quality of some of the
performances and asked to make some more discs with just banjo and bass. These contain some
of his best-ever improvisations, all delivered in that plaintive, singing style that is among the
most imitated of jazz sounds. The bounce and economy of 'Ice Cream' and the brief, gentle
optimism of 'Life Will Be Sweeter' contain in four minutes the essence of Lewis's music, clear
melodic statement, rhythmic simplicity and straightforward emotion.

In 1952, Lewis was recorded by the American Folklore Group of the English department at
Miami University, an institution rather confusingly situated in Oxford, Ohio. The 'Oxford
Series' CDs are well mastered and sound amazingly fresh for recordings four decades. Lewis
made a studio recording of seven quite extended pieces, including a long 'Tin Roof Blues' on
which Humphrey makes his presence felt and a rousing 'Saint' to finish. The subsequent
concert discs are better still, with excellent performances of Lewis staples like 'Over The
Waves', 'Darktown Strutters' Ball', 'Careless Love', closing with a vintage 'Sheikh Of Araby'.

There is remarkably little repetition among the later live material on Storyville (only three
'Saints', for example), though it's unlikely that any but the most dedicated of completists will
want to have all these sets. Nevertheless, Lewis's almost studied primitivism and simplicity of
tone (he used a cheap Albert system metal clarinet) is curiously beguiling and he had the
disconcerting ability to invest almost subliminal changes of emphasis or diction with a
disproportionate significance. It's easy to see why Lewis became the icon and his work the
sacred texts of the revivalist movement, susceptible as both are to myth-making and picayune
analysis.

The *Times-Picayune* in his native city became inclined to harshness about Lewis's technical
shortcomings in succeeding years, and there is no doubt that constant performance of a severely
limited repertoire seriously overstretched his abilities. The Japan set, recorded a decade later, is
very sub-standard and slightly *ersatz*, with none of his characteristic spontaneity. The earlier
recordings, though, stand as a monument to the clarinettist's astonishing and very significant
career. His residency at the Hangover Club in San Francisco was in some respects the
high-water mark of revivalism, but in recording terms is entirely superseded by American
Music's splendid series. The later Storyville serves to introduce bandleader Paul Barbarin, a
nearly exact New Orleans contemporary of Lewis's. Utterly obsessed, where Lewis was
innocently untroubled (and thus manipulable), about the status of black musicians, Barbarin
dropped dead on his first appearance at the hitherto segregated Proteus parade; Lewis beat him
to the farm by a mere two months.

JOHN LEWIS (born 1920)

PIANO

*** **Grand Encounter** Blue Note B21Y-46859 CD
Lewis; Bill Perkins (*ts*); Jim Hall (*g*); Percy Heath (*b*); Chico Hamilton (*d*). 2/56.

***(*) **The Wonderful World Of Jazz** Atlantic 90979-2 CD
Lewis; Herb Pomeroy (*t*); Gunther Schuller (*frhn*); Eric Dolphy (*as, f*); Benny Golson,
Paul Gonsalves (*ts*); Jimmy Giuffre (*bs*); Jim Hall (*g*); George Duvivier (*b*); Connie
Kay (*d*). 7–9/60.

John Lewis's greatest preoccupation has been with the MJQ, but he has been making occasional discs under his own name since the mid-1950s, and this is one of the earliest. Hall and Perkins quickly grasp the refined but deep-set bluesiness of Lewis's preferred settings, and the result is a West Coast album of unusual intimacy and quiet feeling. '2 Degrees East, 3 Degrees West' is the track to remember, but it's a very pretty record. Unfortunately, many of Lewis's later records have yet to make it to CD. But *The Wonderful World Of Jazz* has recently been remastered. It opens with a superb Gonsalves solo on a 15-minute 'Body And Soul' and then works through a short programme of jazz standards, including a new '2 Degrees East, 3 Degres West'. Newly available on the CD are 'The Stranger', precious for Eric Dolphy's solo, and a long quartet version of 'If You Could See Me Now'; but the whole disc is a thoughtful reflection on the jazz tradition as it was standing in 1960.

***(*)   **The Garden Of Delight** EmArcy 834478-2 CD
Lewis; Howard Collins (*g*); Marc Johnson (*b*). 10/87.

***(*)   **Midnight In Paris** EmArcy 838036-2 CD
Lewis; Sasha Lewis (*as*); Christian Escoude (*g*); Pierre Michelot, Michel Gaudry (*b*); Daniel Humair (*d*). 12/88.

Away from the MJQ, Lewis has pursued ambitions which are temperamentally much the same if formally different to his work with the Quartet. A number of albums of Bach Preludes and Fugues have appeared, as well as two discs with his wife Mirjana Lewis. The two excellent discs listed here continue his interest in a literate, highly considered jazz that still keeps one foot in the blues (Lewis will always, if asked, confess to the highest regard for Muddy Waters and the great masters of the Chicago blues). With Johnson and Collins he creates a serpentine, elliptical series of variations on some favourite themes: 'Concorde', 'Django' and 'Delaunay's Dilemma' from his own book, 'Billie's Bounce' and 'Don't Blame Me' from Bird's. There are endlessly subtle sleights of hand, filgree bits of business and a tranquil but firm guiding authority over the whole project. The session recorded in France has his son Sasha on alto on three tracks and the two bassists sharing duties across the seven pieces. 'Django' and 'Delaunay's Dilemma' appear again, utterly different, and the pianist's latest thoughts on 'Round Midnight' and 'Sait-On Jamais' accrue their usual intriguing detail. Highly recommended, even if Lewis's detractors will find nothing here to change their mind about him.

MEL LEWIS (1929–90)
DRUMS

(*)   **Naturally! Telarc 83301 CD
Lewis; Earl Gardner, Ron Tooley, Larry Moses, John Marshall (*t*); John Mosca, Lee Robertson, Lollie Bienenfeld (*tb*); Jim Daniels (*btb*); Dick Oatts, Steve Coleman (*ss, as, f*); Bob Rockwell, Richard Perry (*ts, f*); Gary Brown (*bs*); Jim McNeely (*p*); Bob Bowman (*b*). 3/79.

Lewis was a master of big-band drumming, less relentlessly driving than Buddy Rich but as capable of swinging a big ensemble from the kit. His enduring achievements in that respect were with the band he led for many years with Thad Jones; yet almost nothing from their (admittedly rather sparse) discography is currently available. *Naturally!* is distinguished by the excellent reed section, with Oatts and Coleman sounding young and hungry; and the lacerating punch of the brass is undeniable; but the degree of flair that Jones could interpolate is missed.

*(*)   **The New Mel Lewis Quintet Live** Inak 8611 CD
Lewis; Bill Hardman (*t*); Kai Winding (*tb*); Joe Gallardo (*p*); Wilbur Little (*b*). 9/79.

***(*)   **The Lost Art** Limelight 820815 CD
Lewis; Jim Powell (*flhn*); John Mosca (*tb*); Dick Oatts (*ss, as, ts*); Gary Smulyan (*bs*); Kenny Werner (*p*); Dennis Irwin (*b*). 4/89.

The live record is an unworthy souvenir. The musicians perform well enough, but the clattery sound and poor balance reduce it to a cheerless occasion. The sextet date, one of Lewis's final recordings, is entirely different. The music is skilfully arrranged by the idiosyncratic Werner – who cites such influences here as Andrew Hill and Bob Brookmeyer – into a rounded portrait of the options for small-group jazz in the aftermath of hard bop. On the face of it, Lewis is an unlikely choice as drummer for such an occasion, but he never played better, embellishing march or 4/4 or intensely slow pieces with the same assiduous craft and subtlety. 'The Lost Art' itself refers to his use of the brushes. Mosca is too bland, but Oatts, Smulyan and Werner are an absorbing team of improvisers, and they were all masterfully recorded by producer John Snyder. A fine farewell for Lewis in the studios.

TED LEWIS (1890–1971)
VOCAL, CLARINET, C-MELODY SAXOPHONE

***   **Classic Sessions 1928–1929** JSP CD 326 CD
Lewis; Dave Klein, Walter Klein (*t*); Muggsy Spanier (*c*); George Brunies, Harry Raderman (*tb*); Don Murray (*cl, as, ts, bs*); Frank Teschemacher (*cl, ts*); Frank Ross, Jack Aronson (*p*); Sol Klein, Sam Shapiro (*vn*); Tony Girardi (*g*); Bob Escamilla, Harry Barth (*bb*); John Lucas (*d*). 2/28–8/29.

Lewis was a vaudevillian rather than a jazzman, and his capabilities as a clarinettist were of dubious value: when he takes a solo, he plays in the gaspipe manner which musicians such as Boyd Senter turned into masterpieces of low art. He recognized better players though (he had Benny Goodman in his band for a time, and, on one record, he has the cheek to call out 'Play it, Ted!' during one of Goodman's solos) and many strong players turn in solos on Lewis's records. The leader had actually begun recording as far back as 1917, with Earl Fuller's Famous Jazz Band, but this compilation takes in one of the peaks of the Lewis band, with Spanier, Murray (who was killed in a car accident in the period between the final two recording sessions here) and Brunies all on hand. The 23 tracks vary fairly wildly in quality, and the determining factor seems to be how much Lewis himself is involved. His egregious vocal style will be enough to send many listeners to the track-skip facility, but even a feeble entry like 'Oh, Baby!' features a fine solo by Murray. The straight-ahead jazz titles – including 'Farewell Blues', 'Wabash Blues', 'Clarinet Marmalade' and 'Limehouse Blues', all of which are free of vocals – inevitably emerge as the best, and here the band shows it could play as well as the best of the white New York dance bands of the day. A useful collection, and the sound has been beautifully remastered by John R. T. Davies.

DAVID LIEBMAN (born 1946)
TENOR SAXOPHONE, SOPRANO SAXOPHONE, FLUTES

(*)   **One Of A Kind Core/Line COCD 9.00887 CD
Liebman (*ss* solo). 81–84.

**   **The Loneliness Of A Long Distance Runner** CMP 24 CD/LP
As above. 11 & 12/85.

***   **The Tree** Soul Note 121195 CD/LP
As above. 4/90.

It's one of the paradoxes of David Liebman's career that an improviser who has put such emphasis (in bands such as Lookout Farm and Quest) on collective improvisation and non-hierarchical musical tradition should so frequently evoke solitariness. In 1980 Liebman, perhaps tired of reading about the 'dominant Coltrane influence' on his work, decided to give up tenor saxophone and flute in order to concentrate on the horn that best expressed his individuality. It's interesting that the soprano saxophone (which was always the least Coltrane-accented of his horns) should also be associated, via John Surman and Steve Lacy, with solo performance.

One Of A Kind is a curious act of self-restitution. Multi-tracked, like some of Surman's or Alfred 23 Harth's solo projects or Keith Jarrett's restorative *Spirits*, it has something of the same self-probing intensity; track-titles like 'Ethnic Suite: The Semites', 'Real Self', 'Relentless', 'Words', 'Spirit', 'The Power Of The Cross', and even the Satie 'Trois Gnossiennes', give some sense of Liebman's curiously referential approach to improvisation.

That is even clearer in the 1985 *Loneliness Of A Long Distance Runner*, a 'concept album' of the oddest sort which evokes with surprising literalism the frequent agonies and occasional ecstasies of marathon competition. The album's demerits and joys occur in roughly those proportions, and most listeners will feel cramp setting in before the second half.

In contrast, *The Tree* is for unaugmented soprano saxophone, with none of the overdubs of the previous pair. Liebman solemnly intones, 'Roots – take one,' gradually building up his image of jazz tradition as a vegetative organism with taproots and trunk representing origins and mainstays, giving way to branches and twigs of lesser structural or more individual significance, and finally the transitory leaves of fashion. Palindromic in structure, the second takes occur in mirror order, leading back to the roots. In its lonely oddity and *faux-naïf* simplicities, it's reminiscent of Joyce Kilmer's great-awful poem about trees. In sharp contrast to the creeping pretentiousness of the earlier sets, it's simple and direct, and the mimetic references – wind, mainly – are logical and unintrusive.

Far removed from either Coltrane or Lacy, Liebman's sound is vocalized in a much more straightforwardly humane way, and one can easily reconstruct the impact it has had on the French saxophonist and clarinettist, Louis Sclavis. Remarkable as these albums may be, they're probably best approached via Liebman's more conventional group work.

*** **In Australia** Enja 3065 LP
Liebman; Mike Nock (*p*); Ron McClure (*b*); Ed Soph (*d*). 2/79.

Nock is a more vigorous and spacious pianist than Beirach, and Liebman is coaxed towards a directness and absence of introspection that are now uncharacteristic of his work. There is a rare standard in 'I Concentrate On You', played with something like Lee Konitz's open phrasing. 'The Opal Hearted Aborigine' is rather more typical, though.

***(*) **Doin' It Again** Timeless SJP 140 CD

*** **If They Only Knew** Timeless SJP 151 CD
Liebman; Terumasa Hino (*t, flhn*); John Scofield (*g*); Ron McClure (*b*); Adam Nussbaum (*d*). 80.

This was Liebman's touring band of the late 1970s, and one of his very best. Some of the rhythmic energy of his early rock experience (with the otherwise forgettable *Ten Wheel Drive* and in Miles Davis's fusion experiment) had crept back into his work, and he seems liberated by the absence of piano, playing off and against the high energy pairing of Hino and Scofield. The first of the CDs is marginally the better, but both are worth having; the writing and playing are of high quality and there's one great standard on each, 'Stardust' and a wholly unexpected 'Autumn In New York'.

(*) **Dedications CMP 9 LP
Liebman; Richard Beirach (*p*); Eddie Gomez (*b*); Charles Veal Jr (*d*); Susan Ornstein (*v*); Judy Geist (*clo*). 9/79.

An intermittently successful 'orchestral' album of highly personal music that leads inexorably, via the gnostic 'Code's Secret Code' to the shivering 'Treblinka', like the 'Hiroshima Memorial' on *One Of A Kind*, above, a quiet response to inhumanity and mass destruction.

**** **Double Edge** Storyville SLP 4091 CD/LP
Liebman; Richard Beirach (*p*). 4/85.

At first glance, not at all the kind of set one would expect to find on the rather traditionalist Storyville. At second, Liebman's approach to an obvious-looking set of standards – 'Naima', 'Lover Man', ''Round Midnight', 'On Green Dolphin Street' – is even less likely to attract conservatives.

It's the very lushness of Beirach's chording and the frequent but almost subliminal displacements of the rhythmic pattern that cue Liebman for his more adventurous explorations. On 'Naima', which became a pianist's tune in any case, he moves outside the chords; on 'Green Dolphin Street' he all but ignores them. Throughout, he sounds quizzical, as if reading from an early and much-revised manuscript of the tune. Liebman at his best.

(*) **Homage To John Coltrane Owl 046 CD
Liebman; Caris Visentin (*ob*); Jim McNeely (*p*); Jim Beard (*syn*); Eddie Gomez, Mark Egan (*b*); Bobby Moses, Adam Nussbaum (*d, perc*). 1/87.

One of a rash of tributes timed to the twentieth anniversary of Coltrane's death, this one is marked a little more than most with oedipal hostilities. The amplified sessions with Beard, Egan and Moses – on 'India' (compare the version with Beirach, above), a preposterous 'Dear Lord', and 'Dahomey Dance' – are awkward and anxious, but there are fine things with the better-balanced 'acoustic' quartet, and Liebman seems to have got inside both the difficult 'Crescent' and the potentially swamping 'After The Rain', touching unsuspected elements in both. Liebman's ability to construct extended variations is now closer to Coltrane's for having thrown over most of the tonal and pseudo-Eastern imitations. The faintly hysterical timbre of the oboe fits in perfectly with the leader's now full-time soprano work.

***(*)   **Trio + One** Owl 051 CD/LP
Liebman; Caris Visentin (*ob*); Dave Holland (*b, clo*); Jack DeJohnette (*d*). 5/88.

***(*)   **Quest/Natural Selection** Core/Line 9.00748 CD
Liebman; Richard Beirach (*p*); Ron McClure (*b*); Billy Hart (*d*). 6/88.

The slightly calculated eccentricity of Liebman's standards playing surfaces only peripherally on *Trio + One* with the ironic 'All The Things That . . . '. For the most part, this is an intelligent set of straightforwardly conceived originals, given flesh and complexion by the top-flight rhythm section and a heightened emotional profile by the interplay of the horns. DeJohnette is in powerful form, but it's odd that other leaders don't find room for his outstanding synthesizer work.

Liebman's band, Quest, a more settled outfit with a more exploratory ethos, steered an unsteady course between starchy music logics and inspired nonsense. At their best, as on most of *Natural Selection*, they seemed able to find a reasonable middle ground with a configuration that represented an at least partial return to conventional horn-piano-rhythm hierarchy, with which Liebman – no instinctive radical, one suspects – seems happiest.

***   **Nine Again** Red RR 123234 CD/LP
Liebman; Franco D'Andrea (*p*). 89.

D'Andrea is a less troubled romantic than Richie Beirach, but he's well up to Liebman's by now almost routine respraying of standards. 'Autumn Leaves', a tune that creaks with the weight of bad interpretations, sounds as if it were written yesterday. Repertoire pieces, like the once fashionable 'Freedom Jazz Dance', are given a fresh gloss. The problem is that these brightened-up covers contain absolutely no suggestion of depth. With Beirach, Liebman seemed to reach down into a tune; with D'Andrea, it's all brushwork and no perspective or dimensionality. A lot more interesting than just watching paint dry, all the same.

(*)   **Chant CMP CD 40 CD
Liebman; Richard Beirach (*p*). 7/89.

This has some of the properties of a private conversation, fascinating to the outside precisely because of its implicit freemasonry, but ultimately impenetrable. In freer mode – there are only two tracks, 'Incantation' and 'Invocation' – Liebman and Beirach know each other too well to avoid cancelling out some of the more interesting ideas from each. Improvisation requires a degree of tension, perhaps even antagonism, to work well. This conspicuously lacks both and, though Walter Quintus's admirable production presents the music crisply and balanced well, CD seems a very mixed blessing and not much more than an encouragement to be prolix.

*(*)   **The Blessing Of The Old Long Sound** Nueva IN 810 CD
Liebman; Alberto Mariani (*ts, launeddas*); Carlo Mariani (*launeddas*); Tiziano Tononi (*d, perc*). 11/89.

Afro-Italian oddness. Pass.

***(*)   **West Side Story (Today)** Owl 061 CD
Liebman; Gil Goldstein (*ky*). 9/90.

On the final day of recording, during 'I Feel Pretty', there was some unexplained interference on tape. Liebman subsequently discovered that Leonard Bernstein had just died, some blocks away from the studio. It's an interesting sidelight on an interpretation that restores something of the tragic element to a body of music that has been steadily prettified over the years.

Goldstein's synth patterns are extremely variable, ranging from an irritating rhythm-box loop on 'Tonight, Tonight' to the big, spray-can effects of 'Cool', on which one expects Miles Davis to chip in at any second. The piano intro and synthesized orchestra on 'One Hand, One Heart' – one of the less hackneyed *West Side Story* tunes – are atmospheric, steering Liebman away from his abrupt, Miles-tinged stabs to a more conventionally romantic register. It's important, though, to register that '(Today)' is part of Liebman's title and that his intention is explicitly to bring Bernstein's material up to date. 'Jet Song' is an angrily free-form urban clatter that gives way to the most desolate of Liebman's solos, tracked over a thin backing that carries over into 'Maria', restoring something of the religious overtones Bernstein and Sondheim wrote into the original aria. Interestingly, it's 'Maria' that develops into the most obviously jazz-based arrangement.

An intriguing experiment that succeeds in spite of its occasional banalities.

KIRK LIGHTSEY (born 1937)
PIANO

***(*) **Lightsey Live** Sunnyside 1014 D CD
Lightsey (*p* solo). 6/85.

*** **Shorter By Two** Sunnyside 1004 D CD
Lightsey (*p* solo) and with Harold Danko (*p*). 7/83.

Beginning, middle and end: Lightsey's compositions and solo performances have a well-made, almost narrative quality that is the antithesis of free-form 'blowing'. It's a characteristic he shares with Wayne Shorter, and Lightsey has long shown an interest in the saxophonist's unusually gnomic small-group compositions (which Miles Davis once likened to short stories).

Transcribing Shorter pieces for solo piano presents quite particular difficulties. These are partially overcome in the duos with Danko, whose rich articulation is a softer version of Lightsey's, but a good many of these pieces are over-egged and compare rather poorly with the wonderful 'Fee Fi Fo Fum' on *Live*. The solo album also takes in Monk – a finger-bending 'Trinkle Tinkle' – Cole Porter, Rodgers and Hart, and Tony Williams, whose 'Pee Wee' (from the drummer's 1988 *Angel Street*, Blue Note 748494 CD) gets the album off to a deceptively stately start. Lightsey's delivery is quite formal, and improvisations unfold with an absence of histrionics, which means that tracks often make their full impact only on subsequent hearings.

***(*) **Isotope** Criss Cross Criss 1003 LP
Lightsey; Jesper Lundgaard (*b*); Eddie Gladden (*d*); Jerry Gonzalez (*perc*). 2/83.

*** **First Affairs** Limetree MLP 0015 LP
As above, except add Santi Wilson Debriano (*b*); omit Gladden. 4/86.

*** **Everything Is Changed** Sunnyside SSC 1020 CD
As above, except add Jerry Gonzalez (*t, flhn*); Jerry Routch (*frhn*); Chico Freeman, Famoudou Don Moye (*perc*). 6/86.

(*) **Kirk'n'Marcus Criss Cross Criss 1030 LP
As above, except add Marcus Belgrave (*t, flhn*); Jean Toussaint (*ts*). 12/86.

Only deceptively in opposition to Lightsey's interest in Shorter is a liking for broad vamps over repeated figures, a device strongly reminiscent of Abdullah Ibrahim (*Dollar Brand*), who has something of Shorter's enigmatic brevity. On *First Affairs*, 'Habiba' (given a superior reading on the *Live* solo record) counters a strong African flavour with imaginative Bartók progressions and dramatic shifts of pace.

The quartet version reduces it to rather more of a head-and-solo piece, but the other tracks are, perhaps oddly, much stronger. 'For Albert' has a greater emotional range than the pianist normally strives for, but at the partial expense of accuracy. The LP sound muffles some of his critical middle-and lower-register phrases, but the group are well caught.

They function equally well on the near-contemporary *Everything Is Changed*, but the significant addition of Jerry Gonzalez further restricts Lightsey's multi-linear instincts (as does the 'featured' Marcus Belgrave on the disappointing *Kirk'n'Marcus*, where the writing is a lot more compelling than the playing). Gonzalez's brass lead flatters 'Blues On The Corner' (arranged for piano trio on *First Affairs*) but tends to muffle Lightsey elsewhere. There are, though, interesting experiments in tone-colour, notably the french horn on 'Nandi' and the augmented percussion (featuring, of all people, Chico Freeman, *sans* saxophone, and, another Leader, Don Moye).

Debriano and Gladden serve the pianist no less well than Moye and McBee in the hived-off Leaders Trio (*q. v.*) but with less emphasis on a democracy of voices; the bassist is often a shade recessed and his role is certainly more functional than McBee's. The earlier and excellent *Isotope* is unfortunately not yet available on CD and loses a degree of resolution as a result; the performances, though, are very fine indeed, with an unexpected 'Oleo', some more Monk stylings, and another fine version of Williams's 'Pee Wee'. Newcomers might do well to begin with either this or *Lightsey Live*. Or, ideally, both.

***   **From Kirk To Nat** Criss Cross Criss 1050 CD
       Lightsey; Kevin Eubanks (*g*); Rufus Reid (*b*). 11/90.

The immediate inspiration for this is Nat Cole's wartime piano–guitar–bass trio with Oscar Moore and Johnny Miller (see *The Early Forties*, Fresh Sound FSR CD 139). One of the most copied of piano and vocal stylists, Cole has rarely been imitated successfully, and Lightsey steers well clear of pastiche. His singing on 'Never Let Me Go' and 'Close Enough For Love' is growly and soft, almost spoken, and draws something from late Chet Baker. On piano, he is already individual enough not to risk unconscious echo, and his firm touch on the opening 'You And The Night And The Music' sets the tone for the whole album.

Guitarist Eubanks, always more impressive on other people's albums, presents a useful latter-day version of Oscar Moore's single-note runs and softly strummed counter-melodies; it's Rufus Reid who dominates the longest single track, a subtle 'Sophisticated Lady', with a resonant solo that is mixed too loud but which is as purposeful and strongly outlined as anything by Jimmy Blanton.

ABBEY LINCOLN
VOCALS

(*)   **Straight Ahead Candid CCD 79015 CD/LP
       Lincoln; Booker Little (*t*); Julian Priester (*tb*); Eric Dolphy (*as, b cl, f*); Walter
       Benton, Coleman Hawkins (*ts*); Mal Waldron (*p*); Art Davis (*b*); Max Roach (*d*);
       Roger Sanders, Robert Whitley (*perc*). 2/61.

It would be quite wrong – and at worst deeply patronizing – to suggest that Abbey Lincoln owes her career to her association and marriage with Max Roach. However, it's true that her oddly persistent reputation has been built on her part in Roach's powerful *We Insist! Freedom Now Suite* (Candid 9002 CD/LP), which helped complete her transformation from a rather *ersatz* club 'shan-tooze' into a figure closely associated with the new Black consciousness, and perceived in some quarters as Billie Holiday's matrilineal heir.

Straight Ahead was recorded with basically the same players as *We Insist!*, but with the notable addition of Eric Dolphy, whose dance card for 1961 was almost absurdly over-subscribed. In the event, it's Dolphy's friend and associate Booker Little and the slightly raw-toned Coleman Hawkins who take the majority of the solo slots. The arrangements are mostly excellent and the recording quality stands up very well.

The received wisdom is that Roach allowed Abbey Lincoln to become a more 'natural' and a more feeling singer, but the immediate impression of these tracks is a self-absorption which, however respectful of the words, is seldom responsive to the music. There is certain nothing legitimate about her delivery, but 'expressive' flatting of notes has to be handled with scrupulous care if it isn't to look like incompetence. Three tracks stand out: 'When Malindy Sings', based on a Paul Lawrence Dunbar poem, a vocalization of 'Blue Monk' (with the composer's blessing), and the closing 'Retribution', co-written with Julian Priester, which is forceful in the extreme. Here at least, Lincoln seems willing to confront the music rather than stand upstage of it.

***   **That's Him!** Original Jazz Classics OJC 085 CD/LP
       Lincoln; Kenny Dorham (*t*); Sonny Rollins (*ts*); Wynton Kelly (*p*); Paul Chambers
       (*b*); Max Roach (*d*). 10/57.

***   **It's Magic** Original Jazz Classics OJC 205 CD/LP
Lincoln; Kenny Dorham, Art Farmer (*t*); Curtis Fuller (*tb*); Benny Golson (*ts*); Jerome Richardson, Sahib Shihab (*f, bs*); Wynton Kelly (*p*); Paul Chambers, Sam Jones (*b*); Philly Joe Jones (*d*). 8/58.

***(*)   **Abbey Is Blue** Original Jazz Classics OJC 069 CD/LP
Lincoln; Kenny Dorham, Tommy Turrentine (*t*); Julian Priester (*tb*); Stanley Turrentine (*ts*); Les Spann (*g, f*); Wynton Kelly, Cedar Walton, Philip Wright (*p*); Bobby Boswell, Sam Jones (*b*); Philly Joe Jones, Max Roach (*d*). 59.

If Billie Holiday suggested two diverging means of expressing the black woman's place in American society – the surreal anger of 'Strange Fruit' and the weary-but-assertive deconstructions of conventional romantic modes – Abbey Lincoln made a brave attempt to combine the two; see also Enja 6012, below. It's noticeable, though, that in the late 1950s she was more or less content to work within the available tradition of jazz-show tunes, subverting their original content by shifts of emphasis, displacements of metre and meaning, and downright distortions of intent. It's very much the same method John Coltrane was to bring to 'My Favourite Things' and 'Chim Chim Cheree'.

'Afro Blue', with the Max Roach Sextet on *Abbey is Blue*, is as powerful a performance as anything she recorded, but not without indications of later defaults. The unaccompanied 'Tender as a Rose' on *That's Him* is rather mannered, but very nearly succeeds. Dorham's trumpet is one of the most vocal of the bop trumpeters, and as such an ideal partner. However, it's Kelly's rhythmic approach that always seems to carry the day and it's a shame there are no duo performances in the catalogue.

***   **Painted Lady** ITM 0022 CD/LP
Lincoln; Archie Shepp (*ts*); Roy Burrowes (*ts*); Hilton Ruiz (*p*); Jack Gregg (*b*); Freddie Waits (*d*).

Shepp fits with Lincoln's voice in much the way Coleman Hawkins did, an awkward, heavily vocalized delivery that, aw, shucks, doesn't seem to be able to say what it wants to. There's a plangent quality to what becomes both a tribute to 'Lady Day' – Billie Holiday – but also a record of Lincoln's struggle to maintain a convincing artistic self-conception in the face of an industry that pigeon-holes female singers rigorously and black female singers more rigorously still. An impressive and rather moving record; 'I Know Why the Caged Bird Sings' is one of the most moving vocal performances of the last thirty years.

**   **People In Me** ITM 0039 CD/LP
Lincoln; David Liebman (*ts, ss, f*); Hiromasa Suzuki (*p*); Kunimitsu Inaba (*b*); Al Foster (*d*); James Mtume (*perc*). 6/73.

Lincoln's attempt to recolonize the border regions of pop and soul have consistently foundered on her ultra-self-conscious *negritude* and patent unwillingness to sing a lyric plainly. The 'people in me' might be anyone from Bessie Smith to Diana Ross, which is fine as far as it goes, except that they seem to be jostling for the spotlight. There are two fine tracks on this 1973 album. One, significantly by Max Roach is 'Living Room', which evokes a convincing response; the other is the opening 'You and Me Love' with Lincoln's words to a tune by Johnny Rotalla. A similar job on Coltrane's 'India' is preposterous, and it's fair to ask if her lack of trust in an improvisatory vocalise is less an emotional-political insistence on significant statment than a tacit recognition of technical shortcomings.

**   **Talking To The Sun** Enja 4060 CD/LP
Lincoln; Steve Coleman (*as*); James Weidman (*p*); Bill Johnson (*b*); Mark Johnson (*d*); Jerry Gonzalez (*perc*); Bemshee Shirer, Naima Williams (*v*). 11/83.

A largely empty display of technical prowess in a marketably 'contemporary' setting. Lincoln follows the stage directions scrupulously, but has rarely sounded more passionless. Coleman plays very nicely, as members of the extended Coleman tribe carrying saxes invariably do.

***   **A Tribute To Billie Holiday** Enja 6012 CD/LP
Lincoln; Harold Vick (*ts*); James Widman (*p*); Tarik Shah (*b*); Mark Johnson (*d*). 11/87.

The band here really aren't up to the task, but Lincoln herself seems to be awash with ambivalence, tackling 'Strange Fruit' with a pitch of emotion that almost sounds sarcastic, giving 'Lover Man' the back of her hand. It's a fine, un-obvious set, that generally speaking works well. The recording quality isn't too exciting, but lends a smoky authenticity to what on second hearing sound like slightly fudged settings. Recommended, though. Self-consciousness isn't always a bad thing.

***   **The World Is Falling Down** Verve 843476 CD/LP
        Lincoln; Clark Terry (*t, flhn*); Jerry Dodgion, Jackie McLean (*as*); Alain Jean-Marie (*p*); Charlie Haden (*b*); Billy Higgins (*d*). 2/90.

A whole new audience got a handle on Abbey Lincoln *via* her title-track vocal on Steve Williamson's Verve debut *A Waltz for Grace* (Verve 843088 CD). Her own 1990 set draws on similar stylistic roots, but melds them rather better. With a finely tuned band, and an intelligent book of songs, she does better than for several years. 'How High the Moon' gives the answer almost astronomically, but without losing the romance; 'Hi Fly', still the only universally known composer by her *Straight Ahead* ('African Lady') collaborator, is vibrant and tough. Fine performances all round.

***(*)   **You Gotta Pay The Band** Verve Gitanes 511 110-2 CD
        Lincoln; Stan Getz (*ts*); Hank Jones (*p*); Charlie Haden (*b*); Maxine Roach (*vla*); Mark Johnson (*d*). 2/91.

This is a marked improvement on recent sets. Lincoln still sounds a little too involved in the seen-it-all persona at the expense of straightforward singing and she's still inclined to chop the sense of a lyric. However, she has a band worthy of her talents and the material (with the exception of 'Bird Alone') is immeasurably better than on *People In Me*. The set will be valued every bit as much for a curtain-call from Stan Getz, who played with lyrical grace and feeling to the very end. The best track is undoubtedly 'A Time For Love', where the metre seems to fall just right for that slightly lazy delivery.

GORAN LINDBERG
PIANO

**   **Don't Explain** Dragon DRLP 71 LP
        Lindberg; Krister Andersson (*ts*); Peter Axelsson (*b*); Kurt Roxstrom (*d*). 3/84.

Dragon have recorded a number of significant Scandinavian musicians whose work would otherwise be entirely unknown outside their local haunts: Lindberg is one example, a pianist whose work in Swedish jazz went undocumented – as far as sessions under his own leadership were concerned – for many years. This debut album emerged after some 25 years of live work. He is a fairly conservative post-bop player whose compositions have a modest but well-finished manner, and they certainly aren't disgraced in the company of the standards here, 'Don't Explain' and 'I Wish I Knew'. Andersson's virile tenor makes an imposing lead voice on the four tracks on which he appears, and his duet with Strandberg, 'Christians Ogon', is particularly absorbing. But the record is let down badly by the pedestrian drumming of Roxstrom, and the studio sound is grey and unflattering.

JOHN LINDBERG (born 1959)
DOUBLE BASS

***   **Unison** Cecma 1006 LP

***(*)   **Dimension 5** Black Saint BSR 0062 LP

***(*)   **Team Work** Cecma 1004 LP

***   **Relative Reliability** West Wind WW 0014 CD/LP

(*)   **As Tears Go By ITM 0029 CD/LP
        Lindberg; Hugh Ragin (*t, picc t* on *Dimension 5* and in duo with Lindberg on *Team Work*); Marty Ehrlich (*as, f, cl, bcl;* and in duo with Lindberg on *Unison*); Billy Bang

(*vn* on *Dimension 5* only); Thurman Barker (*d*). 1/81, 2/81, 3 & 4/82, not known, 12/87 & 2/88.

***(*)   **Give And Take** Black Saint BSR 0072 LP
Lindberg; George Lewis (*tb*); Barry Altschul (*d, tym, berimbau, mar*). 11/82.

***(*)   **The East Side Suite** Sound Aspects sas 001 CD/LP
Lindberg; John Carter (*cl*); Eric Watson (*p*). 7/83.

**   **Trilogy Of Works For Eleven Instrumentalists** Black Saint BSR 0082 LP
Lindberg; Hugh Ragin (*t*); Michael Philip Mossman (*t, picc t*); Ray Anderson (*tb*);
Vincent Chancey (*frhn*); Marty Ehrlich (*as, f, picc*); J. D. Parran (*ts, cl*); Pablo
Calogero (*bs*); Allan Jaffe (*g*); Eric Watson (*p*); Thurman Barker (*d, bells, xyl*);
Anthony Braxton (*cond*). 9/84.

It's disappointing that the very fine Black Saints and the two extraordinary Cecmas (a small label which appears to deal only in the highest quality performance) should not be available on CD. It isn't just the outer shadows of Lindberg's dark tone that are lost on vinyl but, more critically, some of the smaller motions of the music itself. Untypically of a bassist, Lindberg is a miniaturist, working best with a restricted canvas and tiny, almost calligraphic musical gestures. On *Trilogy* he has overstretched himself somewhat, but if the draughtsmanship is shaky on 'Holler' and 'Dresden Moods', the individual brushstrokes are highly impressive.

The *Dimension 5* quintet concentrates its power in small, discontinuous quanta that hop excitedly from one member of the group to the next. Ragin – as on the duo, *Team Work* – produces high, almost insect-like figures on his smaller horn. Bang's scurrying trills and quieter, almost toneless susurrations down near the bridge are no less evocative. Thurman Barker, like Barry Altschul on *Give And Take*, is a percussionist in the strict sense rather than an engine-room drummer. Both men prefer to work the music's perimeter, playing melodically and spaciously in a way that shows how, on *East End Suite*, Lindberg is able to dispense with a drummer altogether.

Though he seems generally better disposed to brass players than to the more legato diction of the reeds, the bassist responds superbly to Carter's fragmented lines, developing a long-form piece with the interior logic that is lacking in the *Trilogy*. If 'give and take' is the key to improvisation at any length, that may be why. Certainly, the set with Lewis and Altschul is the one to go for.

FRANÇOIS LINDEMANN
PIANO

(*)   **Piano-Duo Live At Montreux 82 Plainisphare 1267-2 LP
Lindemann; Sebastian Santa Maria (*ky*). 7/82.

***   **Piano-Duo** Plainisphare 1267-8 LP
Lindemann; Antoine Auberson (*ss*); Sebastian Santa Maria (*p*); Patrice Caratini (*b*);
Alvin Queen (*d*). 9/83.

A partnership of acoustic and electric keyboards alone has seldom been explored in jazz, which goes towards making the Montreux meeting of these two gifted players a piquant match. While they both play acoustic on some of the tracks, it's the child-like beauty of 'La Petite Forêt' and interplay of 'Le 63' which show what they can do together. Lindemann is the more accomplished and adventurous improviser, a glittering technique wedded to a mischievous sense of form and melody. On the second record, also made at a concert, the tracks vary in instrumentation, Queen and Auberson appearing on two apiece, Caratini on four. Lindemann's writing is at its most characterful in 'Très Vite' and 'Le Carillon Noir', but Santa Maria's duet with Auberson, 'Cueca Triste', touches a rare vein of melancholy beauty. Decent live recording.

****   **Different Masks** Plainisphare 1267-47 CD
Lindemann; Matthieu Michel (*t, flhn*); Robin Eubanks (*tb*); Yvan Ischer (*as*); Maurice
Magnoni (*ss, ts*); Olivier Rogg (*ky*); Ivor Malherbe (*b*); Marc Erbetta (*d*). 10/89.

This ingeniously prepared and brilliantly executed record is an exemplar of what's currently happening in European jazz. Lindemann's themes manage to be tuneful, funny and deeply felt, using familiar harmonic language yet whirling together new ensemble colours and a rare vitality of improvisation. It's some indication of the quality of the playing that the admirable Eubanks, a famous visitor from New York, has to take his place with the other soloists, all of whom are excellent. The maddeningly catchy lines of 'Ghost Train', lavish textures of 'Forgotten Faces' and 'Different Masks' and the far-from-lugubrious requiem for Woody Shaw, 'Song For Woody', are highlights of a programme that is enormously satisfying. Well recorded and highly recommended.

ERICA LINDSAY (born 1955)
TENOR SAXOPHONE

***(*)   **Dreamer** Candid CCD 79040 CD
Lindsay; Robin Eubanks (*tb*); Howard Johnson (*tba, bs, flhn, penny whistle*); Francesca Tanksley (*p*); Anthony Cox (*b*); Newman Baker (*d*). 3/89.

For a debutant recording, this is tremendously impressive. Born in San Francisco and educated in Europe, Erica Lindsay studied at the Berklee School of Music and under veteran pianist Mal Waldron, from whom she seems to have assimilated a directness of vision and a slightly sombre coloration. She is not (yet) a completely convincing soloist, but it's interesting to hear a young player whose primary influence is Dexter Gordon's rugged swing and not the still dominant Coltrane. What makes *Dreamer* so impressive is rather the quality of her writing and arranging. All but one of the songs and arrangements are Lindsay's (the exception being the old Johnny Hodges feature 'Day Dream', the only track to feature Eubanks, where Howard Johnson did the charts), and they range from the confident vibrancy of 'First Movement' and 'Gratitude' to the more inward 'Walking Together', 'Dreamer' and 'At The Last Moment'.

  The closing 'Gratitude' features an astonishing penny whistle solo from the multi-talented Johnson, who contributes his usual colour-range to the other tracks. Tanksley is a wonderful pianist, well up with the Geri Allens and Michele Rosewomans; she solos with authority and great clarity. Cox and Baker are hard to fault; the bassist in particular combines power with delicacy. Beautifully engineered, this is a record that shouldn't be missed.

LINES
GROUP

***   **Lines** Odin 4026 CD/LP
Tore Brunborg (*ts*); Vigleik Storaas (*p*); Olaf Kamfjord (*b*); Tron Kopperud (*d*). 9/88.

Brunborg is one of the best post-Garbarek saxophonists to emerge from Norway, and away from Masqualero, the group he's best known in, his delivery takes on a more playful, if no less intense, edge. This free-speaking band somehow suggests a very loose gait without surrendering structural power: hear 'Penn' for a fine, multifarious tune that is full of incident and somehow spontaneous in feeling. Brilliantly engineered by the redoubtable Jan Erik Kongshaug.

STAFFAN LINTON (born 1916)
PIANO

**   **Nevergreen** Dragon DRLP 76 LP
Linton; Yasuhito Mori (*b*). 6/84.

***   **Unfinished Affair** Dragon DRCD 193 CD
As above, plus Christian Jormin (*d*). 3/90.

Linton spent some of his formative years in London and actually broadcast for the BBC in the 1940s, cutting a few sides for Decca in 1948. He didn't make another record, though, until *Nevergreen* in 1984, having worked as a semi-pro until 1981. This 'comeback' record is a little too deliberate: Linton's thoughts on standards are cautious, his originals agreeable but slight, and Mori is very unattractively recorded. But these problems were solved by the excellent *Unfinished Affair*. Jormin provides just the right balance of drive and sensitivity, and the session is beautifully recorded. The youthful gaiety of 'Song For Judith' belies Linton's age, and the trio even concoct a reggae-like syncopation for 'Heart Beat'. The leader composes plain but often affecting minor-key melodies, and the music is a refreshing antidote to the busy, overwrought attack of many contemporary pianists.

BOOKER LITTLE (1938–61)
TRUMPET

*** **Booker Little 4 And Max Roach** Blue Note CDP 784457 CD
Little; Louis Smith (*t*); Frank Strozier (*as*); George Coleman (*ts*); Tommy Flanagan, Phineas Newborn (*p*); Calvin Newborn (*g*); Art Davis, George Joyner (Jamil Nasser) (*b*); Charles Crosby, Max Roach (*d*). 58.

***(*) **Booker Little** Time BCD 1041 CD
Little; Tommy Flanagan, Wynton Kelly (*p*); Scott LaFaro (*b*); Roy Haynes (*d*). 4/60.

*** **In New York** Jazz View COD 028 CD
As above.

***(*) **Out Front** Candid 9027 CD/LP
Little; Julian Priester (*tb*); Eric Dolphy (*as, b cl, f*); Don Friedman (*p*); Ron Carter, Art Davis (*b*); Max Roach (*d, tym, vib*). 3 & 4/61.

The arithmetic is depressingly straightforward – 23 scant years. It's very difficult to assess Little's output, for he was only just shaking off the husk of a then-dominant Clifford Brown influence and drying his wings in the early sun of a partnership with Eric Dolphy when he died of uraemia. His tone was bright and resonant, but there were already ambiguities inscribed in his playing which can't be put down to youthful uncertainty but point forward to a new configuration he was never able to articulate.

In face of dearth, small survivals become more valuable. The slightly shapeless jams on 'Blue'n'Boogie' and 'Things Ain't What They Used to Be' (the latter marred by outbreaks of static) on the Blue Note would probably not be considered worth releasing if there were more Little around (like the 1960 group with another doomed youth Scott LaFaro, which has appeared as *The Legendary Quartet Album* on Island and as a valuable Time CD, with the same material covered by the limited edition live series Jazz View). As it is, out-takes assume an even more considerable significance. Little had emerged under Max Roach's patronage, playing on the classic *Freedom Now Suite* (Candid 9002 CD/LP) and on *Straight Ahead* (Candid 9015 CD/LP) by Roach's then wife Abbey Lincoln. The Blue Note reissue pairs him with fellow Memphisite George Coleman in a state-of-the-art '50s front line that on tracks like 'Dungeon Waltz' and 'Jewel's Tempo' – both Little compositions – suggests a development independent of and parallel to Ornette Coleman's voicing experiments. Flanagan's piano, which is rather poorly recorded and inaudible *vis-à-vis* the drums, scarcely gets a look in, and there are moments when the two horns seem break free of the chords.

The larger group that recorded the Ellington and Gillespie jams is inevitably much less inventive, but there are fine moments from Little (who makes the unrated Smith's trumpet sound positively verdigrised) and from both Coleman again and alto player Frank Strozier, who has enough of a foretaste of Dolphy's imaginative harmonics to satisfy.

The Time set is relaxed, almost laid-back, but with a steel-trap precision just beneath the slightly lazy surface. Little's horn is at its most bell-like, though it has lost a little of its richness (particularly on the peaceful original 'Life's A Little Blue') in the transfer from vinyl to CD. The upside of that, though, is that Flanagan comes through much more strongly, and LaFaro's singing lines and virtuosic solo on 'Bee Tee's Minor Plea' are given full prominence. Haynes is impeccable, too, doing the full Max Roach thing on 'The Grand Valse'. Recommended.

Out Front is one of the best albums of the early 1960s. The opening 'We Speak' serves straightforwardly as an introduction to the players. The balance of tonalities, consonant and dissonant harmonies evokes a faint reflection of Ornette's *Free Jazz* experiment, recorded a bare four months before, but the direction is unmistakably Little's and Roach's. The drummer adds tympani and vibraharp to the overall sound, making up for some of the shortcomings of Friedman's piano playing, but tending to interfere with Davis and Carter, who alternated bass duties. The shifting signature of 'Moods in Free Time' stretches Little's phrasing and 'Hazy Hues' explores his interest in tone colour; there are valuable alternate takes of both tracks, and of 'Quiet, Please' on the *Candid Dolphy* compilation (Candid 9033 CD/LP). The closing 'A New Day', with its inbuilt freedoms and fanfare-like annunciations, acquires a certain retro-spective irony given the trumpeter's fate, but is still a wonderfully positive note on which to end.

CHARLES LLOYD (born 1938)
TENOR SAXOPHONE, FLUTE

***   **Dream Weaver** Atlantic AMCY 1010 CD
Lloyd; Keith Jarrett (*p*); Cecil McBee (*b*); Jack DeJohnette (*d*). 3/66.

***   **Fish Out Of Water** ECM 1398 CD/LP/MC
Lloyd; Bobo Stenson (*p*); Palle Danielsson (*b*); Jon Christensen (*d*). 7/89.

Any man who discovers both Keith Jarrett *and* Michel Petrucciani can't be more than half bad. The story and the statistics of Charles Lloyd's astonishing rise to fame as the token jazz presence of the Haight-Ashbury and the Love Generation (a stereotype that pretended to no understanding of the kind of music he was playing) has been told often enough elsewhere. Despite the kind of 'demographics' then enjoyed only by pop musicians, Lloyd turned his back on jazz performance (more gradually than is sometimes supposed) after the end of the 1960s. By the late '70s, the sabbatical was judged to be permanent and Lloyd was largely forgotten.

His return to performance came in 1982, when he made a much-trumpeted, but slightly under-saxed, appearance at the Montreux Jazz Festival, playing in the same diffidently mystical style (which owed something to the 'Eastern' Coltrane) that had marked the highly successful quartet. *Dream Weaver* was probably the best of the 1960s albums. For those who experienced it first time around, it sets off immediate psychic triggers, concepts like 'kaftan', 'grass', 'peace', 'love', mostly experienced vicariously from a safe, suburban distance. For anyone approaching the music for the first time (and forgiving of purely technical shortcomings on the recording; even a sweetened CD still sounds a bit Heath Robinsonish), the music may well resonate rather more straightforwardly. The Lloyd of the 1960s was a fine player, with more blues coloration than was generally acknowledged. 'Sombrero Sam' is lively and the 'Autumn Sequence' (which takes in a low-budget 'Autumn Leaves') has some affecting moments. There's little of the slack one finds on the live-at-Monterey *Forest Flower* [Atlantic SD 1473 LP] and it's interesting to check out the early evolution of both Jarrett, with his gospel and country inflexions, and DeJohnette.

The Petrucciani-inspired comeback inevitably set tape machines whirring. In addition to the Montreux set, there was a live record of *One Night With Blue Note* [BT 85116] and a live concert with Bobby McFerrin in Copenhagen [BT 85104]. But the main fruit of Lloyd's renewed creativity was the studio album *Fish Out Of Water*. Lloyd takes six new but rather samey compositions at an easy pace, unhurried by the ECM house rhythm section, who can do this stuff with pyjamas on. Though there are flashes of increased intensity, it's mostly a rather enervated affair. Lloyd's tone, digitalized, has lost none of its soft burnish and mild Traneisms; his flute-sound on 'Haghia Sophia' is deep and tremulous enough to be an alto instrument. Low-key and late-night.

***(*)   **Notes From Big Sur** ECM 1465 CD/LP
Lloyd; Bobo Stenson (*p*); Anders Jormin (*b*); Ralph Peterson (*d*). 11/91.

A more varied and enterprising set, still dominated by Coltranisms but with a bedrock of solid invention underneath the rather melancholy delivery. It might have been preferable to start with the jolly 'Monk In Paris'. 'Requiem' is probably the weakest thing on the album and certainly shouldn't have come first. 'Sister', which follows, is alarming similar in theme and it's only really with Jormin's plangent introduction to 'Persevere', part one of 'Pilgrimage To The Mountain', that interesting things start to happen. 'Sam Song' is a medium-tempo swinger underpinned by Peterson's gentle but unmistakably firm drumming (he's a more percussive player than Christensen and pushes Lloyd along proportionately harder) and Stenson's impeccable accompaniment. Jormin introduces 'Takur' with horn-like harmonics down near the bridge, but the piece doesn't travel beyond its own opening bars. 'When Miss Jessye Sings', a tribute to opera singer Jessye Norman, begins disconcertingly close to Coltrane's most famous intro and, in the light of 'Pilgrimage To The Mountain: Persevere/Surrender', one almost wonders if Lloyd intends this album to be his *Love Supreme*, a passionate personal statement in suite form rather than a collection of discontinuous pieces. If so, he falls inevitably short, but he has created something rather lovely in the attempt.

JOE LOVANO
TENOR SAXOPHONE, ALTO SAXOPHONE, ALTO CLARINET

***   **Tones, Shapes And Colors** Soul Note SN 1132 CD/LP
     Lovano; Ken Warner (*p*); Dennis Irwin (*b*); Mel Lewis

****   **One Time Out** Soul Note SN 1224 CD/LP
     Lovano; Bill Frisell (*g*); Paul Motian (*d*). 9/87.

***   **Village Rhythm** Soul Note SN 1182 CD/LP
     Lovano; Tom Harrell (*t*); Ken Werner (*p*); Marc Johns

In a club setting, the Lovano–Frisell–Motian trio generated til
there are more subtleties, more opportunities for sophi
straightforward technician, Lovano (who has tended to play better for other leaders than on his
own records) relies on others to embellish his slightly throaty but plain-speaking lines. Long
association with Motian has accustomed him to a very strong pulse embedded in a vibrant
surface; he gets much the same thing from the late Mel Lewis, who is surprisingly reminiscent of
Krupa in a small-group setting, and also from guitarist Frisell, whose chords and single-note
figures are ever more clearly enunciated as his delay-and-distort effects become more dominant.

Village Rhythm is as impressive for the writing as for the playing, and reveals Lovano to be a
surprisingly accomplished bop melodist. 'Sleepy Giant' is particularly memorable. On a couple
of tracks the saxophonist overdubs his own rather World Music-al drumming. An indulgence?
No more so than the ghastly poem to his father on 'T'Was to Me'.

Bearish and slightly withdrawn of aspect, Lovano hadn't yet made a completely individual
impact, but all three of these are worthwhile efforts, steering clear of cliché'd effects and
overworked material.

****   **Landmarks** Blue Note CDP 796108 CD
     Lovano; John Abercrombie (*g*); Ken Werner (*p*); Marc Johnson (*b*); Bill Stewart (*d*).
     8/90.

This is Lovano's breakthrough record, a wholly satisfying set that shouts for the repeat button
before the last raucous notes of 'Dig This' (with its curious, Monkish interruptions) have died
away. Stylistically it's poised midway between Monk and Coltrane, but with a pungent sauce of
latterday urban funk poured over the top, as on the mid-point 'Here And Now', with
Abercrombie's uncharacteristically vocalized guitar well to the fore. The (impeccable)
production is by John Scofield, who might have been a more obvious choice for the guitarist's
role, but Abercrombie seems to take in Scofield's virtues as well as his own, absolutely howling
through 'Dig This'.

Lovano's ballad-playing, as on the tribute to Elvin Jones, is increasingly impressive, with a
virile focus that belies the slightly tremulous delivery. One of the finest jazz albums of 1991 and
a pointer for the decade to come.

****   **Sounds Of Joy** Enja CD 7013 2 CD
     Lovano; Anthony Cox (*b*); Ed Blackwell (*d*). 1/91.

Working without a harmony instrument still places considerable demands on a horn player. The
opening 'Sounds Of Joy' immediately recalls the stark, melodic approach of the classic Ornette
Coleman Atlantics, a jolting, unpredictable saxophone sound that seems to select notes from all
over the scale without reference to anything other than the simplest sequences of melody. There
are clear signs that Lovano is anxious to broaden his sound as much as possible. In addition to
tenor and soprano (the latter given its most thorough and demanding workout to date on the
dedication 'This One's For Lacy'), he has also taken on the alto saxophone (giving it a sonority
somewhere between Bird and Ornette) and the seldom-used alto clarinet, which he unveils on
Judith Silverman's free-tonal 'Bass Space', an almost formal theme executed over a tense 7/8
beat from Blackwell (the actual count varies considerably) and huge, arco effects from the fine
Cox, who solos magnificently on 'Strength And Courage'.

Lovano looks increasingly bound for stardom in the 1990s and this is an album that everyone
interested in the development of the music should try to hear.

...NS (born 1949)
...ON, SAW

...as It Me? Po Torch PTR/JWD 1 LP
Lovens; Paul Lytton (*d, elec*). 1/77.

Moino Da Asneira / A Cerca Da Bela Vista A Graca Po Torch PTR/JWD 5 LP
As above. 12/78–11/79.

*** **The Fetch** Po Torch PTR/JWD 8 LP
As above. 6/80–8/81.

Having worked in conventional post-bop jazz as a teenager, Lovens has become a genuine original, a percussionist whose combination of hyperactivity, arhythmical structure and intense precision have played a crucial role in the European free aesthetic, particularly in his work with Alex Schlippenbach and Globe Unity Orchestra. These all-percussion records, issued by the label which Lovens co-runs with Paul Lytton, are dour affairs and none of them is well recorded, but the unadorned concentration of the players can create a sonic architecture as bewitching as that of, say, Varèse's 'Ionisation' – except that Lovens and Lytton have fashioned their work entirely through improvisation.

The brief episodes of *Was It Me?* give way to the long, live improvisations of *Moino / A Cerca* and *The Fetch*: the latter is the most successful instance of their partnership if only because it's the best-recorded. Lytton's subtle use of electronics shades rather than directs the sound, while Lovens's empoloyment of the singing saw and the high detail of cymbals provide an illumination which is a useful leavening. Minus the in-person focus of the concert experience, these records inevitably have dead spots, but they can be an agreeably discomforting experience.

***(*) **The Ericle Of Delphi** Po Torch PTR/JWD 13/14 2LP
Lovens; Paul Rutherford (*tb*); Evan Parker (*ss, ts*); Dave Holland (*clo, b*). 11/76–4/85.

A double-album containing two sessions recorded nearly 10 years apart. The sometimes dim recording obscures a lot of detail – and that's a serious flaw in this kind of music – but the playing is superbly realized, Parker and Rutherford in uncanny accord at times and the quartet creating high drama as well as almost pointillistic refinements of tone and texture. While the absence of CDs is a problem with this catalogue – although they use fine-quality vinyl – it shouldn't deter anyone from checking out Lovens's almost visionary music.

BERTIL LOVGREN
TRUMPET, FLUGELHORN

(*) **First Time Dragon DRLP 117 LP
Lovgren; Lars Olofsson (*tb*); Krister Andersson (*as, ts*); Bernt Rosengren, Nils Sandstrom (*ts*); Goran Lindberg (*p*); Christer Karlberg (*g*); Sven Larsson (*tba*); Lars Lundstrom, Sture Nordin (*b*); Leif Wennerstrom (*d*). 9/86.

Lovgren has been a fixture in Swedish jazz for 30 years, both in person and on record, and has had something valuable to say in many strong sessions. His one album as a leader suggests that he's something of a natural second banana: this is serviceable hard bop with lots of class but not much in the way of personality. The record varies pace and instrumentation from a duo to an eight-piece band, the latter turning up the most interesting music in a simmering reading of Horace Silver's 'Speculation' that features some fine work from Rosengren. But the playing is otherwise workmanlike rather than inspiring and, though Lovgren handles the quicker numbers with his usual aplomb, he sounds distinctly uneasy in the trumpet–guitar ballad 'I'm Glad There Is You'.

FRANK LOWE (born 1943)
TENOR SAXOPHONE

****   Decision In Paradise Soul Note 1082 CD
Lowe; Don Cherry (*t*); Grachan Moncur III (*tb*); Geri Allen (*p*); Charnett Moffett
(*b*); Charles Moffett (*d*). 9/84.

Memphis-born Lowe has the big, abrasive tone of his fellow-townsman George Coleman,
tempered with a once-unfashionable interest in classic swing players like Chu Berry and, from
slightly later, Don Byas. There is little bop residue in his harmonic thinking, and a cover like
'Cherryco', doubtless suggested by the trumpeter's presence, isn't immediately suited to his
approach. A heavyweight rhythm section, led off by Allen's no less forcefully eclectic chords
and runs, keeps the energy-level high; Moncur, as always, plays superbly, varying his slide
positions and embouchure to stay just this side of multiphonics. Two excellent Lowes are
currently in the limbo file: *The Flam* [Black Saint BSR 0005 LP] with Leo Smith and Joe
Bowie is close in conception to *Decision in Paradise*; *Exotic Heartbreak* [Soul Note SN 1032
LP] features Lawrence Butch Morris and Amina Claudine Myers in excellent form. Both would
be worth reviving.

***   Inappropriate Choices ITM Pacific ITM 970062 CD
Lowe; James Carter, Michael Marcus, Carlos Ward (*saxes*); Phillip Wilson (*d*).

When the World Saxophone Quartet invited drummers to the party, they at least had the grace
to give them something to do. Wilson, a fine technician, is left without a job description on this
boldly interesting but ultimately unsatisfactory sax quartet-plus set. Future releases should be
well worth hearing. On this, though, a raincheck.

JIMMIE LUNCEFORD (1902–47)
ALTO SAXOPHONE, BANDLEADER

****   Jimmie Lunceford 1930–1934 Classics 501 CD
Lunceford; Sy Oliver, Eddie Tompkins, Tommy Stevenson, William 'Sleepy' Tomlin
(*t*); Henry Wells (*tb, v*); Russell Bowles (*tb*); Willie Smith, Earl Carruthers (*cl, as, bs*);
LaForest Dent (*as*); Joe Thomas (*cl, ts*); Edwin Wilcox (*p, cel*); Al Norris (*g*); Moses
Allen (*bb, b*); Jimmy Crawford (*d, vib*). 6/30–11/34.

***(*)   Jimmie Lunceford 1934–1935 Classics 505 CD
As above, except add Paul Webster (*t*), Elmer Crumbley, Eddie Durham (*tb, g*), Dan
Grissom (*cl, as, v*), omit Tomlin. 11/34–9/35.

***   Jimmie Lunceford 1935–1937 Classics 510 CD
As above, except add Ed Brown (*as*), omit Stevenson, Wells. 9/35–6/37.

***(*)   Jimmie Lunceford 1937–1939 Classics 520 CD
As above, except add Trummy Young (*tb*), Ted Buckner (*as*). 6/37-1/39.

***(*)   Jimmie Lunceford 1939 Classics 532 CD
As above, except omit Durham, add Gerald Wilson (*t*). 1–9/39.

***   Jimmie Lunceford 1939–1940 Classics 565 CD
As above, except add Snooky Young (*t*), The Dandridge Sisters (*v*), omit Tompkins.
12/39–6/40.

**(*)   Jimmie Lunceford 1940–1941 Classics 622 CD
As above, except omit Dandridge Sisters. 7/40–12/41.

Lunceford's orchestra is doomed always to be remembered behind Ellington and Basie as the
great also-ran big band of its day. Part of the reason for that is its sheer class: there were no
special idiosyncrasies which lifted the Lunceford orchestra away from the consistent excellence
which it aspired to. Its principal arrangers – Sy Oliver in particular, but also Edwin Wilcox (in
the earlier days) and Willie Smith – built the section-sounds into superbly polished, interlocking
parts which made their records exude a high professional elan. Soloists stepped naturally out of
and back into this precision machine, and there was never much danger of a Rex Stewart or a
Lester Young breaking any rule. Lunceford's virtues were very different to those of the

rough-and-ready (early) Basie band, or to Ellington's unique cast of characters. Still, the records endure very well, even though – as so often with the big bands of the period – the later sides show a dramatic falling-off. The first volume of the Classics chronological survey shows the band coming together – there is a single 1930 session in the discography, followed by an incongruous jump to 1934 – but the important hit coupling of 'Jazznocracy' and 'White Heat' is here, as well as the remarkably nonconformist versions of 'Mood Indigo' and 'Sophisticated Lady'; once underway in earnest, Lunceford turned out some very fine records. The first two CDs feature some of the best of Oliver and Wilcox – there is even the very rare instance of two Ellington compositions, 'Rhapsody Junior' and 'Bird Of Paradise', which were never recorded by Duke, on the 1934–35 disc – and the 1935–37 session includes one of Oliver's masterpieces, the chart for 'Organ Grinder's swing'. But a certain staleness sets in to the band from about 1936 onwards, with the Lunceford precision taking on a formulaic feel that fast tempos and good soloists – Smith was a rival to Hodges and Carter as one of the great alto atylists of the day, and Joe Thomas and Eddie Tompkins were excellent half-chorus players – never quite overcame.

The band continued to develop in minor ways: new players such as Trummy Young and Snooky Young were given tasks which raise the overall game on several of the tracks. Young's extraordinary playing (and singing) on 'Annie Laurie' and 'Margie' (Classics 520) is enough to make one wonder if this is the same man who was such a dullard with Louis Armstrong's All Stars. Nevertheless, the band's records started to sound as if they were being churned out by the end of 1939, although considered track by track there is still much eloquent and occasionally surprising music here. The departure of first Oliver and then Smith (the latter in 1942, after the last of the record here) was a blow that Lunceford's orchestra never recovered from, though to its last records it still sounds like a skilful band, a tribute to Lunceford's meticulous preparations and admiration for Paul Whiteman. There is some dreary material on the last two discs, particularly the 1940–41 set, but even here there are a couple of interesting arrangements by new arrival Gerald Wilson ('Hi Spook' and 'Yard Dog Mazurka') and the closing two-part 'Blues In The Night', though laden with kitsch, is effective in its way. Overall, on musical standards, we recommend the first two discs as the near-essential Lunceford, with the next three still full of interesting music. Transfers are, as usual from this source, rather variable: some of the earliest sides sound scratchy, and some of the later ones have a reverberant feel which suggests dubbings from tape copies at times. For the most part, though, it's been cleanly done.

****   Stomp It Off MCA GRP 16082 CD
As appropriate discs above. 9/34–5/35.

The start of MCA/Decca's own chronological series of Lunceford reissues. They have to miss out the two 1934 sessions for Victor, but the 21 tracks here (including an alternative take of 'Rhythm Is Our Business') make a strong grouping and the NoNOISE restoration has made the music come through very cleanly. A fine way to make Lunceford's acquaintance.

BRIAN LYNCH (born 1955)
TRUMPET, FLUGELHORN

***(*)   Peer Pressure Criss Cross Criss 1029 CD/LP
Lynch; Ralph Moore (ts); Jim Snidero (as); Kirk Lightsey (p); Jay Anderson (b); Victor Lewis (d). 12/86.

**(*)   Back Room Blues Criss Cross Criss 1042 CD
Lynch; Javon Jackson (ts); David Hazeltine (p); Peter Washington (b); Lewis Nash (d). 12/89.

Peer pressure, indeed. One of the occupational horrors of the jazz musician's life is 'going single', travelling from town to town, playing with local rhythm sections. Eric Dolphy suffered profoundly by it, Lee Konitz seems to thrive on it; *Back Room Blues* would seem to put Brian Lynch squarely with the Dolphys. There's nothing amiss about the leader's playing. His bright, brassy sound – particularly vivid on the often smudgy flugelhorn – is well up to scratch. But the band seems entirely devoid of ideas and the sound might just as well be live.

The line-up on *Peer Pressure* makes weight-for-weight comparison of the two albums as uneven as a Don King boxing bill. Where Jackson is sophomoric, the British-born, Berklee-graduated Ralph Moore is right on the case, responding to Lynch's unpretentious hard bop with a mixture of fire and intelligence. Jim Snidero has less to say but says it with unapologetic verve; his own *Mixed Bag* (Criss Cross Criss 1032 CD/LP: the label's titles are always curiously self-revealing!) also features Lynch, and is worth checking out.

Tommy Turrentine's roistering 'Thomasville' gets everybody in and warmed up for the subtler cadence of Benny Golson's 'Park Avenue Petite'. Horace Silver's 'The Outlaw' gets a slightly camp reading but, apart from the low-key CD bonus, 'I Concentrate On You', the rest of the material is by the trumpeter and is generally very impressive, both in conception and in execution. Amazing what a bit of peer pressure can do.

JIMMY LYONS (1932–86)
ALTO SAXOPHONE, FLUTE

***(*)   **Give It Up** Black Saint BSR 0087 CD
Lyons; Enrico Rava (*t, flhn*); Karen Borca (*bsn*); Jay Oliver (*b*); Paul Murphy (*d*).
3/85.

If Charlie Parker had a true heir – in the sense of someone interested in getting interest on the inheritance, rather than merely preserving the principal – it was Jimmy Lyons. Compared to his light-fingered onrush, most of the bop *epigoni* sound deeply conservative. He didn't have the greatest tone in the world, though it seems rather odd to describe a saxophonist's tone as 'reedy' as if that were an insult. Lyons's delivery was always light and remarkably without ego. Years of playing beside Cecil Taylor, in addition to accelerating his hand-speed, probably encouraged a certain self-effacement as well.

On *Give It Up*, he seems quite content to remain within the confines of the group. Significantly pianoless and with only a rather secondary role for the bassist and drummer, it resolves into a series of high, intermeshed lines from the saxophone and horn, with the bassoon tracing a sombre counterpoint. Karen Borca's role might have been clearer were she not so close in timbre to Jay Oliver's bass, but it's worth concentrating for a moment on what she is doing; the effect is broadly similar to what Dewey Redman used to do behind Ornette Coleman and Don Cherry; she also appears to great effect on the earlier and deleted *Wee Sneezawee* [Black Saint BSR 0067 CD/LP], which merits a reissue. Only on the brief, uncharacteristic 'Ballada', with which the album ends, does Lyons occupy the foreground. It's immediately clear that his fey, slightly detached tone doesn't entail an absence of feeling; the closing track is a sad monument to an undervalued career that had little more than a year left to run.

***(*)   **Something In Return** Black Saint BSR 0125 CD/LP
Lyons; Andrew Cyrille (*perc*). 81.

****   **Burnt Offering** Black Saint 120130 CD/LP
As above. 82.

One of the most fruitful encounters of Lyons's sadly under-documented career. Cyrille, a fellow-alumnus of Cecil Taylor Academy, is a one-man orchestra, conjuring layered energies that make a sax and drums 'Take The "A" Train' seem anything but absurd. Cyrille probably doesn't come across as well on the slightly uneven recording of *Burnt Offering* as one hopes he did at the original concert. One of the great modern drummers, Cyrille can play at astonishing volume (at one point almost sounding as if he were trying to re-create a Cecil Taylor trio *à deux*), but also with considerable subtlety and a user-friendly reliability of beat. 'Exotique', on the later session, is a superbly structured and emotionally committed performance. For sheer power and sophistication, this is the equal of Braxton and Roach (*Birth And Rebirth*, Black Saint BSR 0024 CD), with which that great track in particular merits comparison.

JOHNNY LYTLE (born 1932)
VIBES

(*)   **The Village Caller Original Jazz Classics OJC 110 LP
Lytle; Milt Harris (*org*); Bob Cranshaw (*b*); Peppy Hinant (*d*); Willie Rodriguez
(*perc*). 64–65.

(*)   The Loop/New & Groovy BGP CDBGPD 961 CD
          Lytle; unknown *p*, *b* and *d*. 65.

If there is a classic record by this Ohio-born drummer-turned-vibesman, it's surely *The Village Caller*, where he lives out all the clichés of organ–vibes rhythm combos and delivers a perfectly cooked slice of soul-jazz in the title-tune. The rest of the record offers only makeweight variations on some standards, but it passes agreeably enough. The BGP CD couples two very rare albums from the same period, originally issued on Tuba with no personnel details, and the music is even slighter (typical titles include 'The Snapper' and 'Screamin' Loud'). The formula wears thin after a number of tracks but, taken a few at a time, they certainly stir the feet. The pianist sounds very like Wynton Kelly here and there, and the remastering is good if a little overbright.

*(*)   **Everything Must Change** Muse MR 5185 LP
          Lytle; David Schnitter (*ts*); John Patton (*org*); Paul Marshall (*syn*); Robbin Gordon
          (*hp*); George Duvivier (*b*); Al Foster (*d*). 10/77.

(*)   **Fast Hands Muse MR 5185 LP
          Lytle; Houston Person (*ts*); Mickey Tucker (*ky*); Mervyn Bronson (*b*); Idris
          Muhammad (*d*); Larry Killian, Fred Miller (*perc*). 4/80.

**   **Good Vibes** Muse MR 5271 LP
          Lytle; Houston Person (*ts*); Neal Creque (*p*); David Brahan (*ky*); Melvin Sparks (*g*);
          Jimmy Lewis (*b*); Idris Muhammad (*d*); Ralph Dorsey (*perc*). 10/81.

After recording a dozen out-of-print albums for Jazzland, Prestige, Pacific Jazz, Solid State and Milestone, Lytle at least sought out a company that keeps most of its catalogue in print. Unluckily, this was scarcely a vintage period for him. Like so many contemporaries in the soul-jazz boom, Lytle had to mark time through and beyond the disco era with dreary material, tedious vamps and cluttered rhythm sections. *Fast Hands* is slightly ahead for its comfortable blues themes and the reliably gruff Person and Tucker, but there's little to feel excited about on any of the records, and Lytle's own playing sounds enervated.

HUMPHREY LYTTELTON (born 1921)
TRUMPET, CORNET, CLARINET

***   **Delving Back And Forth With Humph** S.O.S. 1160 LP
          Lyttelton; Keith Nichols, Harry Brown (*tb*); Wally Fawkes (*cl*); George Webb, Pat
          Hawes, Stan Greig (*p*); Neville Skrimshire (*g*); Paul Sealey (*bj*); Les Rawlings, Annie
          Hawkins (*b*); Dave Carey, John Robinson, Colin Bowden (*d*). 48–86.

Lyttelton is by now so renowned as a jazz presenter, broadcaster and media wit that it's hard to focus on his talents purely as a musician. His records, though, are evidence enough of a talented player and a shrewd and restless musical mind. Typecast for many as a trad player, he's actually a musician of broad and generous sympathies and, while this first record is untypical, it's revealing of the extent of Lyttelton's self-knowledge. The first half consists of recently discovered acetates by some of the first of his bands: Fawkes and George Webb (whose band the trumpeter basically took over in 1948) are the only players of much substance, aside from the leader, but they play spirited, tightly organized jazz which walks a line between the fashionable revivalism of the day and a homegrown hot music in the tradition of the previous generation of players. The second half features a current Lyttelton band playing in a consciously older style (which Humph mostly eschews today); as a canny piece of repertory playing, it's very artfully done: 'Chatanooga Stomp', for instance, is a fine variation on King Oliver's arrangement, and Lyttelton originals like 'Randolph Turpin Stomp' keep the faith with the music Lyttelton grew up on but which he has since absorbed into a wider view. The remastering on the acetates has been handsomely done, considering the state such tracks usually turn up in.

***   **A Tribute To Humph Volume 1** Dormouse DM1 LP
          Lyttelton; Keith Christie (*tb*); Ian Christie, Wally Fawkes (*cl*); George Webb (*p*);
          Buddy Vallis (*bj*); Micky Ashman, John Wright (*b*); George Hopkinson, Bernard
          Saward (*d*). 11/49–7/50.

***(*) **A Tribute To Humph Volume 2** Dormouse DM2 LP
As above, except omit Wright and Saward. 8/50–1/51.

***(*) **A Tribute To Humph Volume 3** Dormouse DM3 LP
As above, except omit Ian Christie, add Johnny Parker (*p*); Freddy Legon (*g, bj*).
2–10/51.

Lyttelton started recording for Parlophone in 1949, and his entire studio output for the label up to 1957 has been reissued in this admirable series on Dormouse. If Lyttelton was the leader of the British trad movement, it was down to both his authority as a trumpeter and a meticulous approach to material. With a Musicians' Union ban on visiting Americans, the British players had to develop in isolation, and Lyttelton's scholarly investigations – seeking out original discs and preparing arrangements from Oliver, Dodds and Armstrong originals – paid off in sessions which Anglicized the material without paying the price on authenticity. His own playing was firm and crisp without losing the terminal vibrato which was a feature of many 1920s trumpeters: if he doted on Louis Armstrong's manner, he actually didn't sound much like him. A typical solo, on 'Come On And Stomp, Stomp, Stomp' (Volume 1) is assured and wasteless in its use of notes and its perfectly controlled attack. He also played some clarinet, though at this stage it turned up only on the overdubbed 'One Man Went To Blow' (Volume 3). Lyttelton's band, though, was strong enough to ensure that the leader didn't stand apart from the rest of them. Fawkes was the best clarinettist of the day, gifted with a fine low register and an agile step which suggested a real understanding of the New Orleans masters: 'Cakewalkin' Babies From Home' (Volume 2), where the trombone is absent, underlines the empathy between Humph and Fawkes. A piece such as 'It's Over Now' (Volume 3) reveals a delicacy of touch that was also unique to Lyttelton's band. Keith Christie's rather short-breathed style sat well with the front line and, although the rhythm section is seldom asked to do more than play a simple pulse, they avoid the trudging metre which ruined many a trad ensemble. Ian Christie doubled up the clarinet front-line on many of the tracks on the first two volumes and, though the possibilities aren't fully explored, it adds a pungent timbral variation to some of the material. Excellent remastering throughout.

*** **Jazz At The Royal Festival Hall/Jazz At The Conway Hall** Dormouse DM22 CD
Lyttelton; Johnny Picard (*tb*); Wally Fawkes (*cl*); Bruce Turner (*as*); Johnny Parker (*p*); Freddy Legon (*g, bj*); Micky Ashman (*b*); George Hopkinson (*d*). 11/51–11/54.

The 1951 concert, previously unreleased (a reissue of the 1954 *Humph At The Conway* has yet to make it to CD), is a pleasingly tough account of the Lyttelton band as it then stood, with a sound programme of originals and standards. Parker's arrival had strengthened the rhythm section, and the clear (and slightly harsh) sound points up the accuracy of the Lyttelton–Fawkes front line. The RFH concert, from 1954, is a shade disappointing in contrast: Humph was perhaps obliged to pick warhorse material, and the band sound more public and less tightly in harness than on the earlier set.

*** **A Tribute To Humph Volume 4** Dormouse DM4 LP
Lyttelton; Wally Fawkes (*cl, bcl*); Freddy Grant (*cl*); Bertie King (*as*); Johnny Parker, Mike McKenzie (*p*); Freddy Legon (*g, bj*); Fitzroy Coleman, Denny Wright (*g*); Micky Ashman, Norman Boucarut, Jack Fallon (*b*); George Hopkinson (*d, wbd*); George Roberts, Donaldo, Leslie Weeks, George Walker, George Browne (*perc*); Marie Bryant (*v*). 2–10/52.

Lyttelton had played a gig with Cyril Blake's Calypsonians in Holborn and had joined forces with them at the end; out of it came the Grant–Lyttelton Paseo Jazz Band, which cut eight of the tracks on this volume. Humph took the opportunity to set three Jelly Roll Morton tunes in a suitably Caribbean mould, and the combination of Fawkes with the Trinidadian clarinettist, Freddy Grant, gives the music a piping immediacy, although the percussion section is perhaps surprisingly gentle and reserved: the session which produced 'London Blues' and 'Mike's Tangana' also features the excellent alto of Bertie King, a splendid Jamaican-born player who has been neglected by the revival of interest in the players of the era. Besides these, there are two sessions by the regular band, with Lyttelton actually sounding rather shrill and out of sorts on the first, and a very routine date with the trumpeter and Mike McKenzie backing singer Marie Bryant.

*** **A Tribute To Humph Volume 5** Dormouse DM5 LP
As above, except add Al Fairweather (*t*); Bruce Turner (*ss, as, cl*); Sandy Brown (*cl*);
Joe Sampson (*b*); Neva Raphaello, Iris Grimes (*v*); omit Donaldo and Walker.
10/52–9/53.

Two further sessions with Bryant and the Lyttelton Paseo Band, but the main point of interest here is the arrival of Bruce Turner in January 1953. While he plays some clarinet, he delivers mostly alto and soprano, hinting at a mainstream move by Lyttelton which famously outraged trad purists of the time (though at this distance it seems mild enough). Grimes and Raphaello hardly challenge Adelaide Hall and Bessie Smith on their respective chores, but 'Kater Street Rag', 'Maryland My Maryland' and 'Forty And Tight' are sparky efforts, with Fairweather and Brown turning up as guests on the final session. A mixed but entertaining bag.

*** **A Tribute To Humph Volume 6** Dormouse DM12 LP
Lyttelton; John Picard, George Chisholm (*tb*); Wally Fawkes (*cl*); Bruce Turner (*ss, as, cl*); Johnny Parker, Mike McKenzie (*p*); Freddy Legon, Fitzroy Coleman (*g*); Joe Muddel, Micky Ashman (*b*); Eric Delaney, George Hopkinson, Stan Greig (*d*).
10/53–8/55.

***(*) **A Tribute To Humph Volume 7** Dormouse DM13 LP
As above, except add Jim Bray (*b*); omit Chisholm, McKenzie, Coleman, Muddel, Ashman, Delaney, Hopkinson. 8–9/55.

**** **A Tribute To Humph Volume 8** Dormouse DM14 LP
As above, except add Eddie Taylor, Tommy Jones (*d*). 10/55–8/56.

Although Lyttelton had shifted away from the intensely traditional music of his first records, this was still a band dedicated to the original spirit of the music, and 'Shim-Me-Sha-Wobble' (Volume 7) and Ma Rainey's 'Jelly Bean Blues' (Volume 6) are as 'trad' as anything else produced in the period. It was by now an experienced and increasingly sophisticated band, though, and Lyttelton's shrewd variations in material and approach keep the sequence of albums remarkably fresh. Volume 6 has an interesting session with the perennially underrated Chisholm sitting in, as well as Eric Delaney on drums, and the other tracks include spirituals, rags, blues and standards ('The Glory Of Love'). Volume 7 starts with a set cut before a studio audience (originally issued as a 10-inch album called *Jazz Session With Humph*), which concludes with an 11-minute blues and features some excellent playing from the front line. The final three tracks (and the first two on Volume 8) are by a quintet with Lyttelton and Turner as sole horns, and the trumpeter's solos on 'Squeeze Me' and 'Lightly And Politely' are proof of how fine a player he'd become, economical but wonderfully vivid. All of Volume 8, the last in the series, is exemplary stuff: it features Fawkes's final appearance with the band on the Bechet-like 'Close Your Eyes', Humph's solitary hit, 'Bad Penny Blues' ('It climbed, with the help of Jack Jackson and Jack Payne, to number 19 in the Top 20 and then fell back, exhausted'), and a closing session which includes two of the best performances in the entire series, 'Christopher Columbus' and the rousing tribute to Henry Allen, 'Swing Out'. Top-class remastering by John R. T. Davies, as usual, and the premier introduction to Lyttelton's work of the time.

**** **Back To The Sixties** Philips 834458-2 CD
Lyttelton; Buck Clayton (*t*); John Picard (*tb*); Tony Coe (*cl, as*); Jimmy Skidmore, Danny Moss (*ts*); Joe Temperley (*bs*); Ian Armit (*p*); Brian Brocklehurst, Pete Blannin (*b*); Eddie Taylor (*d*); Cab Kaye (*v*). 1/60–7/63.

***(*) **Humphrey Lyttelton & His Band 1960–1963** Philips 838764 CD/LP
As above. 1/60–7/63.

These two compilations will surprise anyone who still considers Lyttelton a trad player. The 1960 sessions scattered through the two discs display a forthright, ambitious band with a three-man sax section and pointed and challenging arrangements of such material as Gillespie's 'The Champ'. The change of impetus from the final Parlophone sessions is close to astonishing: 'Body And Soul', a sumptuous feature for Skidmore, and the later 'Stompy Jones' and even Cannonball Adderley's 'Sack O' Woe' show how quickly Lyttelton had moved on, and his association with Buck Clayton is celebrated in three titles from one of their sessions together. Coe, Skidmore, Moss and Temperley all make a much firmer impression than Turner ever did with the leader (on record at least), and the rhythm section manage a deft middle path between swing and traditional pulses. *Back To the Sixties* has the edge for the more generous choice of material and a higher ratio of superior tracks, but both discs should be mandatory for those interested in British mainstream. Excellent remastering throughout.

***   **Movin' And Groovin'** Black Lion BL 760504 CD/MC
Lyttelton; Roy Williams (*tb*); Bruce Turner (*as*); Kathy Stobart, John Barnes (*ts, bs*); Mick Pyne (*p*); Dave Green (*b*); Adrian Macintosh (*d*). 1/83.

A long gap – although Lyttelton soldiered on with recording through the 1960s and '70s, this is all that's currently available, at the tail-end of a Black Lion contract. Another bridge between trad ('Basin Street Blues', 'Aunt Hagar's Blues') and mainstream ('Never No Lament', 'One For Buck'), this shows Lyttelton had kept faith with a catholic philosophy which few others – anywhere in the music – have cared to maintain. His own chops also sound little weathered by the years.

***   **It Seems Like Yesterday . . .** Calligraph CLG 001 LP/MC
Lyttelton; Pete Strange (*tb*); Bruce Turner (*cl, as*); Wally Fawkes (*cl*); John Barnes (*bs, cl*); Mick Pyne (*p*); Paul Bridge (*b*); Adrian Macintosh (*d*). 9/83.

***   **Humph At The Bull's Head** Calligraph CLG 005 LP/MC
As above, except omit Fawkes. 11/84.

***   **This Old Gang Of Ours** Calligraph CLG 012 LP
Lyttelton; Kenny Davern (*cl*); John Barnes (*ss, as, bs*); Martin Litton (*p*); Mick Hutton (*b*); Colin Bowden (*d*). 12/85.

(*)   **Gonna Call My Children Home Calligraph CLG 013 LP
Lyttelton; Alan Elsdon (*t, c*); Pete Strange (*tb*); Russell Davies (*vtb*); John Barnes, Randy Colville (*cl*); Ron Weatherburn (*p*); Henry Lowther (*vn*); Keith Graville (*g*); Jim Bray (*bb, b*); Colin Bowden (*d*). 7/86.

***   **Gigs** Calligraph CLG 015 LP/MC
Lyttelton; Pete Strange (*tb*); Bruce Turner (*cl, as*); John Barnes (*cl, ss, ts, bs*); Stan Grieg (*p*); Paul Bridge (*p*); Adrian Macintosh (*d*). 8/87.

***(*)   **Beano Boogie** Calligraph CLG 021 CD/LP/MC
As above, except Alan Barnes (*cl, ss, as*) replaces Turner. 3/89.

***   **Rock Me Gently** Calligraph CLG 026 CD/MC
As above, except Kathy Stobart (*cl, ss, ts, bs*) replaces John Barnes, add Dave Cliff (*g*). 7/91.

The formation of Calligraph, his own label, has produced a steady stream of new records from Humph, and they maintain a standard which many jazz musicians should envy. *It Seems Like Yesterday . . .* is a reunion with Wally Fawkes that goes well, if fairly uneventfully, and the place to start is perhaps the rousing live set, caught at the Bull's Head in suburban Barnes. A typically unpredictable programme includes a rip-roaring alto chase for Turner and Barnes on Herschel Evans's 'Doggin' Around', features for Strange, Turner and Barnes on their own, and Lyttelton at his best on an exceptionally vivid take on Ellington's 'Echoes Of Harlem'. Uncovering neglected Ellington is one of the leader's specialities, and there's a fine 'Black Butterfly' on *Gigs* and splendid readings of 'Echoes Of The Jungle' and 'Cop Out' on *Beano Boogie*. The meeting with Kenny Davern is another date distinguished by inventive thinking: 'Jackass Blues' and Lenny Hayton's 'Mood Hollywood' are among the tunes, and the three horns create some nicely tart interplay over a leaner-than-usual rhythm section.

Gigs celebrates (though in the studio) more than 10,000 Lyttelton engagements, and includes jump-band music on 'The Golden Gumboot' and Caribbean and High-Life strains elsewhere. But the ensuing *Beano Boogie* is better, thanks to the arrival of Alan Barnes, whose alto turns add some new fizz to the front line. Though the record gets off to a slow start, when it reaches 'Apple Honey', a nearly explosive reading of the Woody Herman tune, it lifts off. Also worth noting is Alan Macintosh's drumming, which gave the band an extra lift from the Bull's Head session onwards. The elder Barnes departed with *Rock Me Gently*, but Kathy Stobart's return to the fold (35 years after they recorded 'Kath Meets Humph') means there is no drop in authority, and she delivers a grippingly unsentimental version of 'My Funny Valentine' on what's a generously filled CD.

The oddball record in the batch is *Gonna Call My Children Home*, an attempt at suggesting Buddy Bolden's music, using traditional and original material. As carefully conceived as it is, the verdict should be 'interesting failure' – not so much through the playing as the production. The kind of wide-bodied, contemporary-sounding studio mix which is used here makes it sound like little more than a modern band playing old repertory. That said, Lyttelton's own evocations of Bolden, while hardly brassy and untutored enough to be convincing, are curiously moving, especially in the passages intended to evoke Bolden's solitary breakdown.

***(*) At Sundown** Calligraph CLG 027 CD/MC
Lyttelton; Acker Bilk (*cl, v*); Dave Cliff (*g*); Dave Green (*b*); Bobby Worth (*d*). 1/92.

It seems little short of amazing that these two veterans had never recorded together before, but they hadn't. The result is a warmly amiable meeting which holds up throughout CD length. Humph's own interest in the clarinet – there's at least one clarinet feature for him on most of the Calligraphs listed above – makes him a fine match for Bilk here on 'Just A Little While To Stay Here', but it's the easy give-and-take between trumpet and clarinet, over an almost lissom rhythm section, which gives the record its class; even Acker's vocals sound sunny enough, and his clarinet has become as idiosyncratic and engaging as Pee Wee Russell's.

PAUL LYTTON (born 1947)
DRUMS, PERCUSSION, ELECTRONICS

**   The Inclined Stick** Po Torch PTR/JWD 4 LP
Lytton. 6–7/79.

Shabbily recorded, this is not a disc that will make many converts to Lytton's mysterious music, an outcropping of his work that dates back to the London Musicians CoOp of the 1960s. He is at his least convincing when he plays a straightforward free drum solo on 'Brummnummer': the amplified scrapes and groans of 'I Can't Get Started' are more to his taste, and in its discordant way this makes a case for the percussion kit as anything but a purveyor of rhythm. The home-made fidelity, though, is distracting rather than unpretentious.

HAROLD MABERN (born 1936)
PIANO

**   Rakin' And Scrapin'** Original Jazz Classics OJC 330 LP
Mabern; Virgil Jones (*t, flhn*); George Coleman (*ts*); Buster Williams (*b*); Leo Morris (*d*). 12/68.

Mabern's style, notably on the electric piano, may be reminiscent of Kenny Barron's soul-and-funk-tinged work of slightly later date. A good, propulsive sideman, with a strong Bud Powell coloration, Mabern has little of Barron's individuality or flow of ideas. It's Williams, rather than the pianist's left hand, that keeps the music together, and the album is of interest primarily for the off-centre playing of Virgil Jones (who was mainly associated with Roland Kirk and, later, Billy Harper) and, on 'I Heard It Through The Grapevine', a foretaste of saxophonist Coleman's treatment of contemporary pop and soul. Otherwise missable.

***   Joy Spring** Sackville 2016 LP
Mabern (*p* solo). 1/85.

The solo *Joy Spring* underlines Mabern's other close stylistic debts, to Ahmad Jamal and Phineas Newborn Jr, both pianists who made a distinctive use of space. This live set from Toronto's Café des Copains has an ambitious range of material – Wayne Shorter's 'House Of Jade' rubs shoulders with original blues and boogie numbers, Bobby Timmons's 'Dat Dere' with Sonny Rollins's 'Thou Swell'. Not an entirely compelling solo player, Mabern relies heavily on rhythmically subtle chromatic runs that pall a little on repetition and he very much benefits from the company of a decent band. The title piece, a Clifford Brown composition, seems in particular need of underpinning in the bass department. Otherwise a fascinating set by an interesting stylist.

TEO MACERO (born 1925)
TENOR SAX

*** **Teo Macero With The Prestige Jazz Quartet** Original Jazz Classics OJC 1715 LP
Macero; Teddy Charles (*vib*); Mal Waldron (*p*); Addison Farmer (*b*); Jerry Segal (*d*).
4/57.

Prior to his involvement with third-stream composition and long tenure as a record producer for Columbia, Macero made a handful of mildly interesting albums as a saxophonist-leader. As a soloist, he stands as a somewhat pale version of Warne Marsh and, since the music seeks out the off-centre lyricism which suggests Lennie Tristano's groups – they even do a version of Marsh's favourite 'Star Eyes' – the echo at times seems complete. Waldron's typically dark-hearted hard bop strengthens the sound and Charles's quizzical lines add further interest to the five originals, which are uncliché'd yet hard to remember. Macero returned to the studios in the 1980s, but the results are already hard to find.

FRASER MacPHERSON (born 1928)
TENOR SAXOPHONE

*** **Indian Summer** Concord CCD 4224 CD/MC
MacPherson; Oliver Gannon (*p*); Steve Wallace (*b*); Jake Hanna (*d*). 6/83.

*** **Honey And Spice** Justin Time Just 23 LP
MacPherson; Oliver Gannon (*g*); Steve Wallace (*b*); John Sumner (*d*). 3/87.

*** **Encore** Justin Time 8420 CD
As above. 4/90.

He might have been the Canadian Getz, or Sims, or another Lestorian pupil; but Fraser MacPherson's name has seldom been kept much before the wider jazz public, and his decent, graceful sound and sure-footed delivery must be accounted as merely the work of another good tenorman with a couple of records to his name. Anyone checking him out with no greater expectations will find these records good value. The Concord album is a little more refined in studio terms (there are two other deleted albums on the label) but the Justin Time discs benefit from complete understanding between MacPherson and his rhythm team.

BOB MAGNUSSON (born 1947)
BASS

(*) **Revelation Discovery DSCD 927 CD
Magnusson; Joe Farrell (*ss, ts, f*); Bill Mays (*p*); John Guerin (*d*); Jim Plank (*perc*).
4/79.

** **Song For Janet Lee** Discovery DSCD 912 CD
Magnusson; Bobby Shew (*t, flhn*); Hubert Laws (*f*); Peter Sprague (*g*); Billy Mintz
(*d*). 3/84.

Magnusson has enormous reach and all the speed a bassist could want, even if his rubbery sound won't be to the taste of those who like their fiddle to sound fat and slow. As a leader, though, he made a very modest mark with these less than essential records. What lights up *Revelation* is the superb Farrell whose career on and off record never turned out the way it should have: he sneaks in a couple of furious soprano and tenor solos which cut completely against the grain of the writing, yet which still sound plausible. The rest of the music has its subtleties – Magnusson was a horn player for 12 years before he even thought about bass, and there's nothing wrong with his technique – but it can't escape a certain prissiness, which the fussy Guerin can't firm up. Matters get worse on the subsequent record. Laws is an agile, well-meaning player and Shew's elegance is quite telling, even though he only breaks through to the surface a couple of times. Sprague, though, is a dull, conformist spirit, and he tends to set the tone for each track.

RADU MALFATTI
TROMBONE

(*)   **Thrumblin' FMP 0350 LP
Malfatti; Stephan Wittwer (*g, perc*). 5/76.

(*)   **Und? FMP 0470 LP
As above. 2/77.

***   **Zwecknagel** FMP SAJ 34 LP
Malfatti; Harry Miller (*b*). 11/80.

An occasionally suspect technician, Malfatti works somewhat in the shadow of the great Albert Mangelsdorff, whose artistic descendant he is. Lacking Mangelsdorff's immense range – in both stylistic and performing terms – the younger player has tended, as in the work with Wittwer, to find himself bogged down in what can come across as a self-defeating irony. With Miller, as the album title hints, there is a more purposive approach. The impressive battery of effects and accents, ranging from a vocalized tone and the fringes of multiphonics to old-fashioned tailgating phrases in curious rubato measures, is far more effectively deployed. Miller's hoarse, passionate tone hammers home the point. Just as blasphemy isn't the same as atheism, distortion isn't the same as abstraction, and Wittwer always sounds as if he's deliberately scrabbling a conventional resolution, rather than improvising a line on its own terms. He does, though, achieve more obviously attractive effects than, say, Derek Bailey, and these are briefly but unsatisfyingly beguiling.

STEFANO MALTESE (born 1955)
REEDS

**   **Hanging In The Sky** Splasc(h) H139 LP
Maltese; Pino Minafra (*t, flhn*); Luca Bonvini, Sebi Tramontana (*tb*); Eugenio Colombo (*ss, as, f*); Carlo Actis Dato (*bs, bcl*); Martin Joseph (*p*); Enrico Fazio (*b*); Antonio Moncada (*d*); Gioconda Cilio (*v*). 7/87.

**   **Amor Fati** Splasc(h) H 184 LP
Maltese; Sebi Tramontana (*tb*); Carlo Cattano (*ts, f, picc*); Giuseppe Mirra (*b*); Antonio Moncada (*d*); Gioconda Cilio (*v*). 4/89.

Maltese attempts to balance free playing and loose-limbed structures on both of these records, but with only mixed success. The ensembles on the earlier set sound ragged and unformed rather than free-spirited, and only the soloists inject real life – often superbly, as in Minafra's beautiful flugelhorn on 'Dans Les Ciels' and peppery trumpet on 'Miroir Oblique'. A dull and flat studio sound does the music no extra favours.

Amor Fati is better organized, but Tramontana, Cattano and Maltese himself are exposed as soloists of limited powers, and the slow, stuttering tempos add to the air of sluggishness. Cilio can't be counted a virtue on either session.

JUNIOR MANCE (born 1928)
PIANO

***(*)   **Smokey Blues** JSP CD 219 CD
Mance; Marty Rivera (*b*); Walter Bolden (*d*). 6/80.

***   **For Dancers Only** Sackville 3031 LP
Mance; Martin Rivera (*b*). 7/83.

***   **Junior Mance Special** Sackville CD 2-3043 CD
Mance (*p* solo). 9/86, 11/88.

Unmistakable from a random sample of half a dozen bars as a Chicago man, Mance can be a maddeningly predictable player on record, resorting to exactly the figure one expects him to play rather too often to leave any interest for his often adventurous variations and resolutions. There's an immediate lift to the five live tracks on *Special* recorded at Toronto's intimate and much-documented Café des Copains, which suggests that studio performance really isn't Mance's strong suit. Certainly, the opening 'Yancey Special', done on a better-tempered studio piano, is remarkably flat and unvaried; the long interpretations of 'Careless Love', Billy Taylor's 'I Wish I Knew How It Would Feel To Be Free' (a theme known to Barry Norman fans as the sig to *Film '92*) and Ivory Joe Hunter's 'Since I Lost My Baby I Almost Lost My Mind', are characteristically bluesy, but also rather tentative, and it's only among the live tracks – which include 'Blue Monk', Golson's 'Whisper Not' and two Ellington numbers – that Mance really seems to let go, working towards those knotted climaxes for which he is rightly admired.

Rivera is a bassist who fits snugly into the pianist's conception of how the blues should be played: strongly, but with considerable harmonic subtlety. *For Dancers Only* is a fine album, recorded with Phil Sheridan's usual care at McClear Place Studios in Toronto. 'Harlem Lullaby' (title-track of an intriguing Atlantic that featured Mance on harpsichord) gets the set off to a fine start, but the real *tour de force* is an extended improvisation on 'Summertime'. The tune betrays no signs of tiredness or irritation at Mance's sometimes eccentric harmonics. Often likened to the slightly younger Ray Bryant, he sounds here much more like Sonny Clark. The best of the rest is Horace Silver's 'Come On Home'.

The trio album is perhaps the best of the three, despite a rather uncertain sound mix. Mance's ability to suffuse relatively banal ballad material with genuine blues feeling (a characteristic noted by the late Charles Fox in a typically perceptive liner note) is nowhere more obvious than on 'Georgia On My Mind', a melody that can sound footling and drab but which acquires something close to grandeur here. Bolden's 'Deep' is basically a feature for the rhythm players and doesn't add very much to the total impact, but the closing 'Ease On Down The Road' and 'Smokey Blues' are authentic Mance performances.

AUGUSTO MANCINELLI
GUITAR

***(*) **Extreme** Splasc(h) H 303-2 CD
Mancinelli; Roberto Rossi (*tb, shells*); Valerio Signetto (*cl*); Pietro Tonolo (*ts*); Mario Arcari (*ob*); Giulio Visibelli (*f*); Piero Leveratto (*b*); Tony Oxley (*d*). 10/88–3/90.

A fascinating set which will appeal to anyone interested in improvisation. Mancinelli includes three very precise and hair-fine compositions, 'Poiesis' consisting of 23 sounds and a dodecaphonic series, written for oboe, flute and clarinet and designed to go with a display of electronic art. The other 29 tracks are all free improvisations, some lasting less than a minute, none more than five. Some are guitar solos – Mancinelli uses everything from wide, Frisell-like sweeps to hectic fingerpicking and strangled-tone twangs – while others involve Oxley, Leveratto, Rossi and Arcari (but not Tonolo or Signetto) in various combinations. As fragmented as it all is, the even dynamic of the music binds the various pieces together, and several of the improvisations sound so whole and finished that they might as well be compositions in any case. Mancinelli clearly has a challenging mind, and one hopes there will be much more forthcoming from this source.

ALBERT MANGELSDORFF (born 1928)
TROMBONE

***(*) **Purity** Mood 33631 CD
Mangelsdorff (*tb* solo).

(*) **New Jazz Ramwong L + R 41007 LP
Mangelsdorff; Heinz Sauer (*ts, ss*); Gunther Kronberg (*as*); Gunter Lenz (*b*); Ralf Hubner (*d*). 6/64.

*** **Live In Tokyo** Enja 2006 LP
As above, except omit Kronberg. 2/71.

(*) **Two Is Company Mood 33614 CD
Mangelsdorff; Wolfgang Dauner (*p*).

*** **Live In Berlin** FMP 0390 LP
Mangelsdorff; Heinz Sauer (ts); Buschi Niebergall (b); Hans-Peter Giger (d). 1/70.

*** **Spontaneous** Enja 2064 LP
Mangelsdorff; Masahiko Hito (p, ring modulator); Peter Warren (b); Allen Blairman
(d).

Relative to his enormous significance, there is far too little of Mangelsdorff's work currently available; in comparison to saxophonist Peter Brötzmann, a figure of comparable significance albeit in a more heavily subscribed instrumental category, he is all but invisible to younger record buyers. One of the least egocentric of musicians, Mangelsdorff has been a model proponent of collectivist improvisation, both in smaller units nominally under his leadership and in larger combinations like the Globe Unity Orchestra and the United Jazz and Rock Ensemble, with whom he has produced some of his most striking work. He has worked with everyone from Lee Konitz to Barbara Thompson and Jaco Pastorius (joining the cult bassist and drummer Alphonse Mouzon on a single track on the Verve CD bass sampler 840037; he gets a walk-on with Trombone Summit on the 'bone compilation, too – Verve 840040, but that hardly reflects his impact on current practice on the instrument). Whatever the context, Mangelsdorff always manages to sound both absolutely responsive and absolutely himself.

Of the thin current offering, the unaccompanied *Purity* is quite remarkable. Few trombonists of any period could sustain interest over this length, but Mangelsdorff has such a range at his disposal, from caressing, saxophone-like sounds to hard, blatting snaps and vicious, stiletto-thin harmonics, that it is like listening to a whole group of players. The duo with Dauner is much more conventional and actually rather dull, lacking the intelligent interplay of the trombonist's Enja collaboration with Lee Konitz. For the rest, one is left with rather patchy live material that gives only a rather two-dimensional impression of Mangelsdorff's seemingly endless resource. *Spontaneous* is a fine set, and a good place to begin.

EMIL MANGELSDORFF (born 1925)
ALTO SAXOPHONE, FLUTE, CLARINET

*** **Swinging Oildrops 1966** L + R 41002 LP
Mangelsdorff; Gustl Mayer (ts); Fritz Martschuh (vib); Joki Freund (p, ts, ss); Volker
Kriegel (g); Gunter Lenz (b, g); Rafi Luderitz (d, perc). 9/66.

(*) **10 Jahre Interaction Jazz L + R 40021 LP
Mangelsdorff; Jo Flinner (p, electric p); Gerhard Bitter (b); Wolfgang Wusteney
(perc). 12/84.

The suppression of jazz in both Germany and Japan before and during the Second World War resulted in a dramatic acceleration of interest as soon as the war ended. In Germany there was a particularly strong underground jazz movement during the war years. Hans Koller was perhaps its leading light, but Emil Mangelsdorff and his young brother Albert (see above) took part. The brothers share a broad grounding in the swing movement with a highly condensed exposure to bebop and the beginnings of free jazz. Emil retained more of the earlier style, but – as *Interaction Jazz* bears out – achieved a highly intelligent synthesis of older and new techniques. The band are professional in the slightly stiff way one associates with musicians who learned their music copying records.

That is even more true of the much earlier *Swinging Oildrops* line-up, except that they show considerably more enthusiasm for the task and play a mixed repertoire of originals and standards with commendable verve. By no means the towering figure his brother has become, Emil Mangelsdorff is still a considerable musician and well worth tracking down; the vinyl-only recordings are unexceptional but mostly satisfactory.

MANHATTAN JAZZ QUINTET
GROUP

*** **Manhattan Jazz Quintet** Paddle Wheel K28P 6313 CD/LP
Lew Soloff (*t*); George Young (*ts*); David Matthews (*p*); Eddie Gomez (*b*); Steve Gadd (*d*). 7/84.

*** **Autumn Leaves** Paddle Wheel K28P 6350 CD/LP
As above. 3/85.

*** **My Funny Valentine** Paddle Wheel K28P 6410 CD/LP
As above. 11/85.

*** **Live At Pit Inn** Paddle Wheel K20P 6429/30 2CD/2LP
As above. 4/86.

*** **The Sidewinder** Paddle Wheel K28P 6452 CD/LP
As above. 10/86.

*** **My Favourite Things** Paddle Wheel K28P 6465 CD/LP
As above. 4/87.

*** **Plays Blue Note** Paddle Wheel K28P 6480 CD/LP
As above, except John Patitucci (*b*) and Dave Weckl (*d*) replace Gomez and Gadd. 1/88.

*** **Caravan** Paddle Wheel 292 E 6002 CD
As above. 12/88.

*** **Face To Face** Paddle Wheel 292 E 6032 CD
As above. 5/88–3/89.

It may seem over-cautious to award the above records with an identical rating throughout, but such is the consistency of this studio-supergroup that there genuinely is almost nothing to choose among the discs on overall merit. This brand of contemporary jazz is of a sort that creates a love-it-or-hate-it polarity among listeners: the quintet plays a perfectionist hard bop, seamless in its arrangements – rhythmic, harmonic or merely structural – and flawless in its pacing and solo contributions. Whether this strikes one as exciting or tediously conformist will depend upon one's own tastes. There is no edge-of-the-seat excitement such as one might get from a vintage Jazz Messengers record: all here is polish and control. But the skintight virtuosity of the band offers its own rewards: there's none of the empty showmanship that often turns up in fusion, and the variations of approach often display a more inquiring bent than many a more 'authentic' hard-bop session.

Although he provides the group arrangements, Matthews is the weak link as a player, his piano parts a characterless blend of hard-bop references. Soloff and Young, though, are consistently enterprising and graceful, the trumpeter a lean, affable soloist, the tenorman a prodigious aggressor who can turn surprisingly harsh when he wants to. Gomez and Gadd play with magisterial authority, as befits their status as pros' pros, and while their precision tends to streamline rather than propel the horns, it creates the kind of blue-chip ambience which acts as context. Patitucci and Weckl, their replacements on the later records, are a little less interesting but, as the other three have grown even more confident, one scarcely notices.

Most of the music is drawn from the familiar hard-bop repertoire, with only a handful of Matthews originals spread through the records. The live double-set is no less polished than the studio material, although a little more elongated. *Plays Blue Note* offers the band exploring the repertory of the most famous of hard-bop labels, and it's gratifying to note that they choose less obvious tunes, such as 'Cleopatra's Dream' and 'Cheese Cake'. The part-live, part-studio *Face To Face* is a strong introduction to the current edition of the band, with a powerfully sustained version of 'Moanin'', while the six pieces on *Autumn Leaves* characterize the earlier group with perhaps the best distinction. All the discs are recorded with sometimes glaring digital clarity.

(*) **Manhattan Blues Sweet Basil 660.55.001 CD
Lew Soloff (*t*); George Young (*ts*); David Matthews (*p*); John Scofield (*g*); Eddie Gomez (*b*); Steve Gadd (*d*). 2/90.

Billed as a reunion of the original band, with Scofield guesting on three tracks to add a little fresh flavour, the MJQ carry on as if nothing had intervened. Scofield's wry solos on 'Blues March' and 'St Louis Blues' inculcate a little hip insouciance into the music, but otherwise the music is the same brew as before. In the pantheon of MJQ albums, though, it's a low-level achievement: most of the tunes are taken too easy.

HERBIE MANN (born 1930)
FLUTE, ALTO FLUTE, SAXOPHONE

***   **Memphis Underground** Atlantic/WEA 7567 81364 CD/LP
Mann; Roy Ayers (*vib, perc*); Bobby Emmons (*org*); Larry Coryell, Sonny Sharrock, Reggie Young (*g*); Bobby Wood (*p, electric p*); Tommy Coghill, Mike Leach, Miroslav Vitous (*b*); Gene Christman (*d*). 68.

Mann occupies a similar position to Charles Lloyd in recent jazz history. Influential, but cursed by commercial success and an unfashionable choice of instrument, both have been subject to knee-jerk critical put-down. Where Lloyd's flute was his 'double', Mann's concentration slowly evolved a powerful and adaptable technique which gave him access to virtually every mood from a breathy etherealism, down through a smooth, semi-vocalized tone that sounded remarkably like clarinet (his first instrument), to a tough metallic ring that ideally suited the funk contexts he explored in the late 1960s.

Though most of the Atlantics are, for the moment at least, out of the catalogue, the perennial *Memphis Underground*, one of the founding documents of the fusion movement, has made a successful transfer to CD. Though the recording quality would scarcely pass current muster, the music has survived unexpectedly well. The interplay of three guitarists, notably the Cain and Abel opposition of Sonny Sharrock and Larry Coryell, gives it a flavour that from moment to moment gives off a whiff of Ornette Coleman's *Prime Time*; the addition of Roy Ayers's vibes and Bobby Emmons's organ gives the backgrounds a seething quality that adds depth to Mann's slightly unemotional virtuosity. The presence of one-time Weather Report bassist Miroslav Vitous on a single track, the excellent 'Hold On, I'm Comin'', may also attract notice. Head and shoulders with Lloyd above most of the crossover experimenters of the time, Mann deserves to be heard, and it's a pity there isn't more around. A solitary example of his earlier approach, in the 'Californians' band that included Jack Sheldon, Jimmy Rowles and Mel Lewis, can be found on the compilation *Blues For Tomorrow* (Original Jazz Classics OJC 030 2LP). Otherwise, it's the second-hand racks.

***   **Caminho De Casa** Chesky JD 40 CD
Mann; Eduardo Simon or Mark Soskin (*p*); Romero Lubambo (*g*); Paul Socolow (*b*); Ricky Sebastian (*d*); Cafe (*perc*). 3/90.

Mann calls his current *bossa*-influenced band Jasil Brazz; fortunately the synthesis is slightly more elegant than the nomenclature. Like Gato Barbieri's more obviously Latin 'Chapters', this is pan-American music with a vigorous improvisational component, not just a collection of exotic 'stylings'. Guitarist Lubambo is particularly impressive, but it's the drummer who keeps the music rooted in jazz tradition, leaving most of the colour work to percussionist Cafe. Mann himself is in fine voice, particularly on the beautifully toned alto flute. Only one of the nine tracks – the rather weak 'Yesterday's Kisses' – is credited to him; the rest are substantial enough. Recommended.

SHELLY MANNE (1920–84)
DRUMS

****   **The Three And The Two** Original Jazz Classics OJC 172 CD/LP
Manne; Shorty Rogers (*t*); Jimmy Giuffre (*cl, ts, bs*); Russ Freeman (*p*). 9/54.

One of the finest – and shrewdest – musicians in modern jazz, Manne is also one of the most fully documented, playing with everyone from Charlie Parker and Coleman Hawkins to modernists like Ornette Coleman. (A useful wrong-footer for a jazz Trivial Pursuit is: Who played drums on *Tomorrow Is The Question*? Answer on OJC 342 CD/LP.) He combines the classic qualities of reliability and adaptable time with a much more inventive side that has more to do with the *sound* of the drums, an ability to play melodically, than with self-conscious fractures and complications of the basic four-in-a-bar. In the same way, Manne's solos could hardly have been more different from those of important predecessors like Gene Krupa. Where Krupa made the drummer a 'high-price guy', giving him a prominence from which Manne benefited, Manne draws attention to himself not by showmanship but by the sophistication of his playing.

The trios with Rogers and Giuffre find the players working in parallel, not in a horns-and-rhythm hierarchy. On 'Flip', Manne plays in counterpoint with his colleagues. On 'Autumn In New York', the horns diverge almost entirely, giving the standard the same rather abstract feel that pianist Freeman brings to a notably unsentimental duo reading of 'With A Song In My Heart'. 'Three In A Row' is an experiment in serial jazz, giving a tone-row the same status as a 'head' or standard. Cool and almost disengaged it may be, but it's also compellingly inventive.

The duos with Freeman have survived rather less well, but broadly the same instincts are at work. On 'The Sound Effects Manne', Freeman plays a sharply percussive line alongside Manne's 'theme statement'. 'Billie's Bounce' is compact, bluesy and very intense. Strongly recommended.

***   **The West Coast Sound** Original Jazz Classics OJC 152 CD/LP
Manne; Bob Enevoldsen (*vtb*); Joe Maini (*as*); Bob Cooper (*ts*); Jimmy Giuffre (*bs*); Russ Freeman (*p*); Ralph Pena (*b*). 9/55.

***   **Swinging Sounds** Original Jazz Classics OJC 267 LP/MC
Manne; Stu Williamson (*t, vtb*); Charlie Mariano (*as*); Russ Freeman (*p*); Leroy Vinnegar (*b*). 1 & 2/56.

***   **More Swinging Sounds** Original Jazz Classics OJC 320 LP
As above. 7 & 8/56.

The mid-1950s saw Manne turning his back slightly on the experimentalism still evident on *The West Coast Sound* in favour of a more direct idiom which nevertheless incorporated quietly subversive harmonic devices and a much-enhanced role for the drummer. Both the OJCs cry out for a CD reissue, ideally reinstating some further material from these lively sessions. On *More* Williamson, like Enevoldsen, doubles his very West Coast trumpet with the currently fashionable valve trombone; he gets a good, strong sound out of it that helps anchor Mariano's slightly floaty lines. The material on *West Coast Sound* is probably more interesting, but there's that almost academic quality to the delivery which one associates with some of Giuffre's work of the time. 'Grasshopper' and 'Spring Is Here' are worth the money on their own, though.

***(*)   **Shelly Manne And His Friends: Volume 1** Original Jazz Classics OJC 240 LP
Manne; André Previn (*p*); Leroy Vinnegar (*b*). 2/56.

***   **My Fair Lady** Original Jazz Classics OJC 336 LP
As above. 8/56.

***(*)   **My Fair Lady** Original Master Recordings MFCD 809 CD
As above. 8/56.

***(*)   **My Fair Lady/West Side Story** Contemporary CDCOPCD 942 CD
As above. 8/56.

Working as a cinema accompanist, André Previn once got so bored comping his way through D. W. Griffiths' epic *Intolerance* that his attention wavered and he looked up to find himself playing a hot 'Tiger Rag' during the Crucifixion. Probably 75 per cent of the people who know André Previn as a TV-friendly orchestral conductor don't suspect his jazz credentials, which are considerable. The first and probably best of these Contemporary reissues establishes firmly what a fine trio this was. 'Stars Fell On Alabama' and a movingly unhackneyed 'I Cover The Waterfront' see Previn and Manne giving one another lots of room and letting bassist Vinnegar determine the pace. The two-piano *Double Play*, OJC 157 LP, co-led by Previn and Russ Freeman, with Manne on drums, is well worth catching, as is Previn's *West Side Story* covers, originally on OJC 422 CD/LP, and now reissued as a twofer with Manne's outwardly less promising *My Fair Lady*. It has taken on a life of its own. The Original Master Recording CD is, inevitably, to be preferred to the vinyl, but the bonus of the Previn tracks could outweigh the slightly less vivid sound on the Contemporary double set. Manne's handling of 'Get Me To The

Church On Time' and the surprisingly swinging 'I Could Have Danced All Night' is no surprise, but he works a kind of magic on 'Ascot Gavotte' and the reading of the standard 'I've Grown Accustomed To Her Face' is exemplary.

***** **At The Blackhawk** Original Jazz Classics OJC CD 656–660 5CD
     Manne; Joe Gordon (*t*); Richie Kamuca (*ts*); Victor Feldman (*p*); Monty Budwig (*b*).
     9/59.

One of the finest and swingingest mainstream recordings ever made, *At The Blackhawk* benefits immeasurably from CD transfer. Feldman's slightly dark piano sound is lightened, Gordon and Kamuca lose a little of the crackle round the edges, and Budwig reappears out of the vinyl gloom. From the opening 'Our Delight' to the previously unissued material on Volume Five, and taking in a definitive performance of Golson's 'Whisper Not' along the way, this is club jazz at its very best. 'A Gem From Tiffany', heard on *Swinging Sounds*, above, had become Manne's signature theme and is rather indifferently played and repeated. Otherwise, everything sounds as fresh as paint, even the previously rejected 'Wonder Why' and 'Eclipse In Spain'. Utterly enjoyable . . . nay, essential.

***(*) **A Night On The Coast** Moon 008 CD/LP
      Manne; Conte Candoli (*t*); Bob Cooper or Richie Kamuca (*ts*); Russ Freeman or
      Hampton Hawes (*p*); Ray Brown or Monty Budwig (*b*); Irene Kral (*v*). 62, 69/70.

A most acceptable compilation of fine work from opposite ends of Manne's 'forgotten' decade when much of his energy was going into Hollywood scoring, horse-breeding and the administration of Shelly's Manne-Hole. Hawes is wonderful on 'Milestones' and 'Stella By Starlight' at the latter end of the decade, and the slightly tougher sound of Russ Freeman ideally suits 'The Breeze And I' and 'Straight No Chaser', knocked out under Candoli's taut statements. Irene Kral sings 'Forgettable', and she's absolutely right.

*** **Mannekind** Original Master Recordings MFCD 853 CD

aka

*** **Mannekind** Mainstream MDCD 727 CD
    Manne; Gary Barone (*t*); John Gross (*ts, f*); John Morell (*g*); Mike Wofford (*p*); Jeff
    Castleman (*b*); Brian Moffatt (*perc*). 72

One of many attempts in jazz to capture the whole range of human experience under the arc of a loosely organized suite. In effect, it's hyperbolic rather than parabolic. Manne is unusually kitted up, adding berimbau, waterphones, maracas and dakha-de-bellos to his drum set, but these exotica only serve to underline once again how consistently inventive and radical Manne had always been sonically; his influence on percussionists of a more obviously modernist tendency has been considerable, if little acknowledged. Doubled with Moffatt's, the percussion is by far the most interesting thing on the album; the horns range from strict-time passages to relative freedom and hints of 1950s style atonality. Manne intersperses longer jazz compositions that bear more obliquely on his theme with brief sound-effect interludes suggestive of 'Birth', 'Fertility', 'Maturity' and 'Infinity'. Most of the writing ('Scavenger', 'Seance', 'Tomorrow' and 'Mask') is by pianist Wofford, but there are two fine tracks ('Witches' and 'Pink Pearl') from John Morell. Perhaps a little too unsettling to be entirely appealing, but nonetheless a remarkable work by this most adventurous of drummers.

***(*) **Shelly Manne Plays Richard Rodgers: Rex** Discovery DSCD 783 CD
      Manne; Lew Tabackin (*ts, f*); Mike Wofford (*p*); Chuck Domanico (*b*). 5/76.

Richard Rodgers' last-but-one show was not a big success and probably survives most vividly in Manne's imaginative set of variations, which build on the enormous success of the *My Fair Lady* album. Typically, he transforms the material exactly as and how he needs, turning 'As Once I Loved You' into a raunchy blues feature for Tabackin's tenor, a total contrast to the fast, skittering flute figures of the opening 'Christmas At Hampton Court', which began with a Manne solo, snapping out patterns and abstract shapes as brittle as icicles and as complex as frost patterns on glass. Wofford switches to Fender piano for 'So Much You Loved', another remarkably abstract theme developed over quiet cymbal sounds. 'No Song More Pleasing' is, fittingly, the most interesting set of melodic variations, but 'Elizabeth', equally fittingly, is the most striking single track, with Tabackin back on flute. Don't be put off by the show-tune format or unfamiliar material; this is a remarkable modern album that adds significantly to Manne's reputation.

RAY MANTILLA
PERCUSSION

***   **Dark Powers** Red 123221 CD
Mantilla; Bobby Watson (*as*); Dick Oatts (*ts, ss, f*); Eddie Martinez (*p*); Ruben Rodriguez (*b*); Steve Barrios (*d, perc*); Vivien Ara Martinez (*v*). 2/88.

Lifted a little out of the ordinary by the presence of guest star Watson (who is nevertheless a shade below par), *Space Station* is a cool and rather elegant set of Latinate jazz tunes. At first hearing, it might have been made somewhere on the West Coast sometime around the end of the 1950s. Watson's bluesy wail and Oatts's tougher, R&B-influenced tenor are unmistakably contemporary, though, and drummer Berrios/Barrios (who, to be honest, provides most of the rhythmic interest) refuses to let the pace slacken; his 'Dialogue' with sometime Max Roach collaborator Mantilla leaves the honours approximately even. Significantly or not, the best track is a Watson composition, 'Catch Me If You Can', reminiscent of some of the material on his wonderful Red release *Love Remains* (123212 CD/LP). As for this, enjoyable but not earthshaking.

MICHAEL MANTLER (born 1943)
TRUMPET, COMPOSER

***(*)   **No Answer** Watt 2 LP
Mantler; Don Cherry (*t*); Carla Bley (*ky*); Jack Bruce (*b, v*). 7 & 11/73.

***   **The Hapless Child** Watt 4 CD/LP
Mantler; Terje Rypdal (*g*); Carla Bley (*ky*); Steve Swallow (*b*); Jack DeJohnette (*d*); Alfreda Benge, Albert Caulder, Nick Mason, Robert Wyatt (*v*). 7/75 & 1/76.

**   **Silence** Watt 5 LP
Mantler; Carla Bley (*p, org, v*); Chris Spedding (*g*); Ron McClure (*b*); Clare Maher (*clo*); Robert Wyatt (*v, perc*); Kevin Coyne (*v*); strings. 1/76.

***   **Movies** Watt 7 LP
Mantler; Larry Coryell (*g*); Carla Bley (*p, syn*); Steve Swallow (*b*); Tony Williams (*d*). 11/77.

(*)   **More Movies Watt 10 LP
Mantler; Gary Windo (*ts*); Philip Catherine (*g*); Carla Bley (*p, org*); Steve Swallow (*b*); D. Sharpe (*d*). 8/79 & 3/80.

***   **Something There** Watt 13 LP
Mantler; Mike Stern (*g*); Carla Bley (*p*); Steve Swallow (*b*); Nick Mason (*d*); orchestra. 6 & 7/82.

(*)   **Alien Watt 15 CD/LP
Mantler; Don Preston (*syn*). 3 & 7/85.

****   **Live** Watt 18 CD/LP
Mantler; Rick Fenn (*g*); Don Preston (*syn*); John Greaves (*b, p*); Nick Mason (*d*); Jack Bruce (*v*). 2/87.

***(*)   **Many Have No Speech** Watt 19 CD/LP
Mantler; Rick Fenn (*g*); Jack Bruce, Marianne Faithfull, Robert Wyatt (*v*); orchestra. 5–12/87.

If Michael Mantler's world-view can be inferred from the texts he has chosen for setting, it is a dark and occasionally whimsical vista. His improvisational credentials have always been in some doubt and, were it not for the magnificent 'Communications' for his Jazz Composers Orchestra – and particularly No. 11, which featured Cecil Taylor – he might be consignable to an awkward limbo between jazz and art music. Born and raised in Vienna, Mantler appears to have swallowed the elephant of serialism whole, while straining at a 'simple' blues. His avant-gardism is tempered (or else confirmed) by an equal and opposite dependence on the raw, off-key quality of Austrian café music, and his songs hinge on an enervated drone that is deeply unsettling.

The surprisingly excellent *Live* (which is the place to begin) sums up the best of Mantler's music of the preceding decade. By no means a sampler or greatest hits (though it does repeat some of the Edward Gorey material from *The Hapless Child*), it demonstrates his use of a favoured instrumentation: Fenn's souped-up guitar, Preston's 'orchestral' synth programmes, Mason's rock-influenced drumming and, over it all, a voice that combines thorough illegitimacy of tone and diction with enormous emotional resonance.

Jack Bruce, like Robert Wyatt, Kevin Coyne and Marianne Faithfull elsewhere, skins a lyric till it shows the nerves and sinews underneath. Grossly overrated as a bass player (and still sheet-anchored by the stresses of supergroup membership with Cream), he makes a remarkable virtue of his glaring technical faults. On *No Answer* he is scouringly nihilistic in his articulation of Samuel Beckett's words from *How It Is*. The music is equally bare-boned and empty of obvious signifiers; a CD would be more than welcome twenty years on.

Bruce comes into his own again on the wonderful *Many Have No Speech*, which adds Philippe Soupault and Ernst Meister to the lyricists' roster and the gravelly Marianne Faithfull to the singers. Robert Wyatt, for many years Mantler's other vocal standby, is disappointingly little used here but is reserved for homier roles like the Harold Pinter settings on *Silence* and the Gorey whimsies of *The Hapless Child*, which is musically and lyrically one of Mantler's more accessible works. Without histrionics, Wyatt *lives* every word and every line. By contrast, Coyne and Faithfull seem to be contriving vocal or intepretative eccentricities, and Faithfull's French pronunciation on *Many Have No Speech* is truly awful.

Of the non-vocal records, the best is almost certainly *Something There*, in which Mantler seems to have accommodated his more doctrinaire modernisms to an altogether more contemporary (and occasionally almost danceable) idiom. Ex-Miles Davis prat-faller Mike Stern outdoes even Spedding, Coryell and Fenn at high-altitude note-bending without a net, and there is a real orchestra in place of the synthesizer, beautifully arranged by Michael Gibbs. Alongside this, earlier efforts like the two *Movies* sound even more excessively cerebral and shut off, and *Alien* like the work of a man who hasn't seen daylight for twenty years.

Mantler has a strong but anti-virtuosic voice on his instrument and is capable of moments of rather bleak beauty. If you are receiving medication or any other treatment for a depressive condition, you should consult a physician before buying any of these records.

KAREN MANTLER
HARMONICA, ORGAN, VOICE

**(*)   My Cat Arnold XtraWatt 3 CD/LP
Mantler; Eric Mingus (*v*); Steven Bernstein (*t*); Pablo Calogero (*bs, f*); Marc Muller (*g*); Steve Weisberg (*ky, syn*); Jonathan Sanborn (*b*); Ethan Winogrand (*d*). spring 88.

***   Karen Mantler And Her Cat Arnold Get The Flu XtraWatt 5 CD
As above,except add Michael Mantler (*t*); Steve Swallow (*flhn*); Carla Bley (*Cmel*). summer 90.

One of the most evocative sounds on Carla Bley's superb *Fleur Carnivore* (Watt/21 839 662) was daughter Karen's floating harmonica solo on 'Song Of The Sadness Of Canute'. As yet, it's an underexploited voice. Her solo albums are basically song collections, alternately reminiscent of Laurie Anderson's half-spoken narratives and Carla Bley's own free-associating surrealism on *Escalator Over The Hill*, but influenced by 1930s popular song and basic rock rhythms.

The most obviously Anderson-like of the songs is the nightmarish 'Flu', spoken with a wry lack of expression. 'Mean To Me' is pure pastiche, featuring Mom and Dad and 'Uncle' Steve Swallow on decidedly unfamiliar instruments. The instrumental 'Au Lait', which appears to have been recorded live, is the most obviously jazz-based, with beautiful harmonica and trumpet parts.

Otherwise, this is no-category music that stands very sturdily on its own merits. It would only show bad breeding to mention the slightly dodgy liner pictures of Ms Mantler *en déshabille*.

GUIDO MANUSARDI (born 1935)
PIANO

*** **Bridge Into The New Generation** Splasc(h) H102 LP
Manusardi; Fulvio Sisti (*as*): Pietro Tonolo (*ts*); Marco Vaggi (*b*); Alfredo Golino (*d*).
6/81.

*** **Outstanding: Live In Tirano** Splasc(h) H 115 LP
Manusardi; Piero Leveratto (*b*); Luigi Bonafede (*d*). 4/86.

** **Love And Peace: Solo Piano Performance** Splasc(h) HP 02 LP
Manusardi. 4/86.

*** **Bra Session** Splasc(h) H 125 LP
Manusardi; Marco Tamburini (*t*); Aldo Mella (*b*); Paolo Taverna (*d*). 3/87.

(*) **Acqua Fragia Splasc(h) H 178 LP
Manusardi; Marco Tamburini (*t, flhn*); Roberto Rossi (*tb*); Piero Odici (*as, ts*);
Paolino Dalla Porta (*b*); Giancarlo Pillot (*d*). 3/89.

** **Velvet Soul** Splasc(h) HP 14 LP
Manusardi; Lee Konitz (*as, v*); Alessandro Moccia, Corrado Masoni (*vn*); Gaetano
Nasilio, Marco Lombardi (*clo*); Piero Leveratto (*b*); Luigi Bonafede (*d*); Laurenzia G.
D'Amato Chorus (*v*). 86.

Manusardi is one of the elder statesmen of modern Italian jazz, but he surrenders little to the younger musicians in terms of enterprise. He began leading his own recordings in 1967, and there are 16 out-of-print albums prior to the first Splasc(h) release listed above. While there isn't anything in his style to make him immediately identifiable, his decisive touch and trusty swing make him the sort of player who can carry a problematical situation and turn in a solid result. The quintet session sets him up with some of the younger players, and the trio record catches him at his most inventive as an improviser, although the date with trumpeter Tamburini, *Bra Session*, offers the best evidence of his powers as a composer. The episodic *Acqua Fragia*, is 'dedicated to the places I love', but its impressionism is a little too delicate at times, while the solo session tends to ramble: Manusardi works best with a good bass–drums team at his back. *Velvet Soul* is quite a curio, featuring a 33-strong women's choir and Lee Konitz, who sounds a little perplexed himself and even takes a vocal of his own on 'Nature Boy'. Newcomers should start with either *Outstanding* or *Bra Session*.

(*) **Downtown Soul Note SN 1131 LP
Manusardi; Isla Eckinger (*b*); Ed Thigpen (*d*). 5–6/85.

Downtown should have been the ideal introduction to Manusardi's music, with four originals, two good standards, a fine rhythm section and good Soul Note recording. But some of the material isn't his best: 'Alexandria' is a merely doleful ballad, and only the Red Garland-like manoeuvres of 'Downtown' find the pianist at his most resourceful, although the up-tempo chosen for 'My Romance' is at least unusual.

*** **Together Again** Soul Note 121181 CD
Manusardi; Red Mitchell (*b*). 11/88.

*** **So That** Splasc(h) H 328-2 CD
Manusardi; Eddie Gomez (*b*); Gianni Cazzola (*d*). 10/90.

Manusardi meets two distinguished bassists. There's a greater compatability with Mitchell, though the bassist is as wilful as ever, eccentrically dawdling over figures but doing so in such a charming way that the music picks up an idiosyncratic lilt which the pianist also takes note of; 'But Not For Me' is a delightful game of cat and mouse. *So That* is more obviously open-handed, the trio barrelling through most of the tunes at a rapid-fire tempo, but Gomez crowds out Manusardi at times and it's the sly interjections of Cazzola (listen to his fours on 'There Is No Greater Love') which referee the playing. Gomez's singalong bass is irritatingly picked up by the microphones, but recording is otherwise excellent.

GERARD MARAIS
GUITAR, GUITAR-SYNTHESIZER

(*)   **Big Band De Guitares Thelonious THE 0601 CD
Marais; Claude Barthelemy, Raymond Boni, Philippe Deschepper, Philippe Gumplowicz, Jacques Panisset, Benoit Thiebergien, Colin Swinburne, Frédéric Sylvestre (*g*); Jean Luc Ponthieux (*b*); Jacques Mahieux (*d*). 6/84.

***(*)   **Katchinas** Thelonious THE 0501 CD
Marais; Jean-François Canape (*t, bugle*); Yves Robert (*tb*); Michel Godard (*tba*); Henri Texier (*b*); Jacques Mahieux (*d*).

Gerard Marais works in the aftermath of all the Lower East Side experiments of the 1970s and '80s, and these entertaining records suggest that he's an impressive organizer of some surprising music. The earlier set – which sat, unmixed and unreleased, for six years – is rather too much of a good thing in piling up eight guitarists: admittedly, on only a couple of tracks do they seem particularly overbearing, but democratic assignment of parts and solos thins out the project, and the rockier elements sit a little queasily next to the improvisation. *Katchinas* is very different: with high attention given to tonal colourings, solos-with-accompaniments and creative contrast, this is an excellent group, distinctive through the use of Godard's tuba, illuminated by Marais's filigree use of electronics. The best pieces – 'Brain Dance' and 'Cassavetes' – are impeccably varied and sustained.

RICK MARGITZA (born 1963)
TENOR AND SOPRANO SAXOPHONE

(*)   **Colors Blue Note CDP 792279-2 CD/MC
Margitza; Joey Calderazzo (*p*); Jim Beard (*ky*); Steve Masakowski (*g*); Marc Johnson (*b*); Adam Nussbaum (*d*); Airto Moreira (*perc*). 4–5/89.

***(*)   **Hope** Blue Note CDP 794858-2 CD/MC
As above, except Peter Erskine (*d*) replaces Nussbaum, add Jeff Kievit, Danny Cahn (*t*); Charles Pilow (*ob*); Richard Margitza (*vn*), Olivia Koppel (*vla*), Jesse Levy (*clo*). 6/90.

Margitza is a talented player whose problem may be that there are all too many talented young saxophonists. He has a grand, declamatory style reminiscent of the young Rollins, and his solos have an insistent, somewhat clenched quality that can be compelling or wearisome from moment to moment. But he's an unusually prolific and rather gifted writer, too, which suggests that he may stand out from the ranks of younger tenormen. *Colors* is an interesting debut, with eleven Margitza originals performed by a strong band, and the various styles he tries – shifting chords over rhythmic vamps, waltz-time, synthesizer ballads, tenor–bass–drums blow-outs – are all invaded without discomfort. But the record runs out of steam half-way through, a common ailment among new records of the CD era. *Hope* is even longer, but there's a more convincing variety this time. 'The Journey' is a haunting arrangement for soprano and tenor over changing chords – a trick repeated from the first record's 'Widow's Walk', but done much better this time – and several more of the tunes find the same mix of musical acuity and catchiness. The extra instrumentation is used sparingly, voices are added to 'Recess' to create a playful, skipping atmosphere, slightly reminiscent of Pat Metheny at his sunniest, and although some of the themes are a little overstretched, Margitza oversees the record with real authority, as both performer and guiding hand. The rhythm section and Masakowski play with championship heart.

***   **This Is New** Blue Note CDP 7971962 CD/MC
Margitza; Tim Hagans (*t*); Joey Calderazzo (*p*); Robert Hurst (*b*); Jeff Watts (*d*). 5/91.

This sounds like a troubled record, with a preponderance of basically slow speeds and one or two ballads – especially 'On Green Dolphin Street', which has the quality of an ominous dream, and a cracked 'Body And Soul' – that have a faintly disturbing gait. As a record of standards, this seems a disappointing move after the striking qualities of *Hope*, and Margitza saves his most optimistic playing for his own two original themes, one of which – 'Beware Of The Dog', which Hurst and Watts lend a Marsalis band-like feel to – is notable for Hagans's sole appearance on the session. Still, the tenorman (he plays no soprano here) creates some stark and assuredly intense improvisations on the material: he still sounds like a very considerable voice.

TANIA MARIA (born 1948)
PIANO, VOCAL

** **Piquant** Concord CJ/CCD 151/4151 CD/LP/MC
Maria; Eddie Duran (g); Bob Fisher (b); Vince Lateano (d); Willie Colon (perc).
12/80.

*(*) **Taurus** Concord CJ/CCD 175/4175 CD/LP/MC
As above, except add Ken Middleton (perc). 8/81.

** **Come With Me** Concord CJ/CCD 200/4200 CD/LP/MC
Maria; Eddie Duran, Jose Neto (g); Lincoln Goines, John Pena (b); Portinho (d);
Steve Thornton (perc). 8/82.

** **Love Explosion** Concord CJ/CCD 230/4230 CD/LP/MC
Maria; Harry Kim (t, flhn); Art Velasco (tb); Justo Almario (as); John Beasley (ky);
Dan Carillo (g); Abe Laboriel, John Pena (b); Joe Heredia, Alejandro Acuna, Steve
Thornton, Jon Lucien (perc). 9–10/83.

(*) **The Real Tania Maria: Wild! Concord CJ/CCD 264/4264 CD/LP/MC
Maria; John Purcell (ss, as); Dan Carillo (g); John Pena (b); Walfredo Reyes (d);
Frank Colon (perc). 9/84.

Maria's blend of Brazilian rhythms and bebop improvisation is a definitive example of the renowned live performer failing to turn her music into something worthwhile in the studios. There's nothing very wrong with any of these records, but the thinness of the material and the attempts to create studio-bound excitement are at best mildly engaging, at worst woefully flat. The earliest of the Concord albums are little more than light Brazilian muzak, and even with *Love Explosion* the enlarged band does no more than underscore the fluffy material. Maria's primary trait – scatting along with her piano lines – becomes dangerously wearisome even within the context of a single tune; over a whole disc . . . But the live record has enough zest to engender more enthusiasm, even if the music is scarcely enough to create any kind of addiction. Purcell is shamefully under-used, and Pena's popping bass parts point up the leader's next direction, into light funk. Her other records hardly qualify for inclusion here.

CHARLIE MARIANO (born 1923)
ALTO SAXOPHONE, SOPRANO SAXOPHONE, FLUTE, NAGASWARAM

*** **Boston All Stars/New Sound From Boston** Original Jazz Classics OJC 1745 CD/LP
Mariano; Joe Gordon, Herb Pomeroy (t); Sonny Truitt (tb); Jim Clark (ts); George
Myers (bs); Roy Frazee, Richard Twardzik (p); Bernie Griggs, Jack Lawlor (b); Gene
Glennon, Carl Goodwin, Jimmy Weiner (d); Ira Gitler (bells). 12/51, 1/53.

(*) **Charlie Mariano Sextet Original Jazz Classics OJC 118 LP
Mariano; Dick Collins (t); Sonny Truitt (tb, bs); Richard Wyands (p); Vernon Alley
(b); Joe McDonald (d). 3/53.

*** **Swinging With Mariano** Affinity 767 CD
Mariano; Stu Williamson (t); Frank Rosolino (tb); Claude Williamson (p); Max
Bennett (b); Stan Levey, Mel Lewis (d). 12/53.

(*) **Charlie Mariano Plays Fresh Sound FSR CD 115 CD
As above, except add John Williams (p). 7/54.

Mariano is a consistently underrated performer, largely because some of his best recorded work has been under other leaders. He worked with Mingus on *Black Saint And The Sinner Lady* (MCA MCAD 5649 CD) and with his (now ex-) wife Toshiko Akiyoshi on the excellent *Toshiko Mariano Quartet* (Candid 9012 CD/LP); he has also worked with bassist Eberhard

Weber (ECM 1066, 1107, 1186 LPs), Shelly Manne (OJC 267 LP, 320 LP), and on a wilderness of Stan Kenton sessions.

Critics were quick to locate Mariano in the gaggle of post-Bird alto players, a categorization that has been reinforced by the curious foreshortening early death brings. Mariano was born only three years after Parker, and his first and greatest influence remains Johnny Hodges. His studies in Indian music, and on the wooden, oboe-like *nagaswaram*, have helped emphasize the exotic overtones he absorbed from Hodges and which are already evident in these early bop-inspired sessions.

The wrenching intensity of later years is not yet apparent, though Mariano invests 'Stella By Starlight' on *New Sound From Boston* with entirely convincing and personal feeling. It's interesting to compare this performance with that on the Fresh Sound *It's Standard Time* (below), made after a long break from standards repertoire. In the 1950s, Mariano is still playing in a very linear way, without the three-dimensional solidity and textural variation that he developed later; he was also still more or less rooted in conventional bop harmonics, an attachment that weakened as he came to understand Indian music.

Of these albums, *New Sound From Boston* is excellent, if a little raw; *Sextet* is shared with some Nat Pierce–Dick Collins tracks, and the latter pair contain essentially the same material, though *Swingin'* has more material.

**(*)   Crystal Bells CMP 10 LP
Mariano; Stu Goldberg (*electric p, syn*); Gene Perla (*b*); Don Alias (*d, perc*). 12/79.

Endlessly responsive to new directions in music, Mariano seemed less than certain of his course in the fusion-dominated 1970s. This is a disappointing record, redeemed by the saxophonist's consistent ability to construct solos of almost perfect self-sufficiency. Influenced by Coltrane's 'Eastern sound' on soprano saxophone, Mariano carried that line of enquiry even further; on *Crystal Bells*, he also uses bamboo flute and *nagaswaram*.

***   Jyothi ECM 1256 CD
Mariano; Karnataka College of Percussion: R. A. Ramamani (*v, tamboura, konakkol*); T. A. S. Mani (*mridamgam*); R. A. Rajagopal (*ghantam, morsing, konnakol*); T. N. Shashikumar (*kanjira, konakkol*). 2/83.

***   Live veraBra 2034 CD
As above, except omit Rajagopal, add Ramesh Shotham (*chatam, morsing, tavil*). 2/89.

Only fans of a certain age remember Joe Harriott's and John Mayer's *Indo-Jazz Fusions* experiments, released by Columbia in 1966 and 1967, hailed as the Next Big Thing, and then consigned to collector status. With a tonal approach not unlike Harriott's and a similar awareness of the boundaries of tonality and abstraction, Mariano's albums with the Karnataka College of Percussion make a perfectly valid comparison. The saxophone is paired with R. A. Ramamani's expressive voice, and it's unfortunately easy to ignore the intricate rhythmic canvas being stretched behind them by the other players; the live session is a little more even-handed in this regard, but on *Jyothi* (with the close-miked and lapidary sound typical of ECM), most of the emphasis is on Mariano's fervid upper-register playing.

**(*)   It's Standard Time Fresh Sound FSR 97 CD
Mariano; Tete Montoliu (*p*); Horacio Fumero (*b*); Peer Wyboris (*d*). 4/89.

Mariano has not been closely associated with standards jazz in recent years. Like Miles Davis (and only those who haven't heard the saxophonist play would consider the analogy absurd), he believes in confronting the 'music of today' rather than endlessly re-working changes. However, on the basis of a performance at the Kenton Festival in Oldham, Lancashire, where Mariano had played 'Stella By Starlight', producer Jordi Pujol persuaded him to cut a standards album in Barcelona with Catalan pianist Tete Montoliu and two other local players.

Mariano is in perfect voice. 'Stella' is wonderful, given a harmonically 'flatter' but more resonant reading than Lee Konitz tends to. He misfires briefly on 'Billie's Bounce' and makes a bit of a nonsense of 'Poor Butterfly', but it's a highly appealing album nevertheless, ideal for anyone who hasn't previously made contact with the saxophonist's work or who has a constitutional aversion to the *konakkol* or the *kanjira*.

***(*)   Innuendo Lipstick LIP 890082 CD
Mariano; Jasper van't Hof (*p, ky*); Marilyn Mazur (*d, perc*). 7 & 9/91.

More rhythmic and propulsive than *Sleep, My Love* as a result of Mazur's uncomplicated drumming, *Innuendo* hits a more orthodox jazz groove with 'Silk'. Playing down the atmospherics of the previous album makes it a slightly less distinctive set, and Mariano is very much less interesting, concentrating on high wails and big portamento effects that do little more than colour in the foreground. As an album, it scores well; as a *Mariano* album, it's something of a disappointment.

BRANFORD MARSALIS (born 1960)
TENOR AND SOPRANO SAXOPHONES

*** **Scenes In The City** Columbia 38951 CD/MC
Marsalis; John Longo (*t*); Robin Eubanks (*tb*); Mulgrew Miller (*p*); Ray Drummond, Ron Carter, Charnett Moffett, Phil Bowler (*b*); Marvin 'Smitty' Smith, Jeff Watts (*d*). 4–11/83.

** **Royal Garden Blues** Columbia 40363 CD/MC
Marsalis; Ellis Marsalis, Kenny Kirkland, Herbie Hancock, Larry Willis (*p*); Ron Carter, Charnett Moffett, Ira Coleman (*b*); Ralph Peterson, Marvin 'Smitty' Smith, Al Foster, Jeff Watts (*d*). 3–7/86.

*** **Renaissance** Columbia 40711 CD/MC
Marsalis; Kenny Kirkland (*p*); Charnett Moffett (*b*); Jeff Watts (*d*).

(*) **Random Abstract Columbia 44055 CD/MC
Marsalis; Kenny Kirkland (*p*); Delbert Felix (*b*); Lewis Nash (*d*). 8/87.

Articulate, hip, funny, the eldest of the Marsalis brothers has often seemed like the most likely to succeed. He started with Art Blakey's Jazz Messengers on alto; but his tenor playing is stonily powerful in the Rollins tradition, and he has stuck by the bigger horn on most of his solo records, with soprano – granted a sometimes reedy but usually impressive full tone – as second instrument. *Scenes In The City* was an entertaining debut, with a wry version of the Mingus title-tune (complete with dialogue), and the storming manifesto of 'No Backstage Pass' to show what he could do: but it's a bit of a jumble. *Royal Garden Blues* is a step down, the playing messy and subdivided among a bewildering variety of rhythm sections. *Renaissance* and *Random Abstract* emerge as accomplished but undecided sessions. On *Random Abstract* he seems to explore the mannerisms of a number of preceding tenor influences – Coltrane, Shorter, Coleman, even Ben Webster, whose celebration in a bathetic reading of 'I Thought About You' seems more of a parody than a tribute. The chief problem with all these sessions, though, is that Marsalis promises more than he delivers, both conceptually and in the heft and weight of his playing. While still sounding imaginative and technically top-line, he can't seem to focus an eloquent battery of remarks into a proper speech. Delfeayo Marsalis's production is idiosyncratic: his interest in 'more bass wood' tends to make the lower frequencies sound woolly and unclear.

*** **Trio Jeepy** CBS 465134 2CD/LP/MC
Marsalis; Milt Hinton, Delbert Felix (*b*); Jeff Watts (*d*). 1/88.

A rambling jam session (with, for once, extra music on the double-LP, not on the CD) illuminated by some brilliant moments. 'The Nearness Of You' is a mature ballad reading, 'Doxy' a convincing nod to Rollins, and 'Random Abstract' features the Marsalis/-Felix/Watts trio in full, exhilarating flight (the amazingly durable Hinton plays on most of the other tracks). While hailed (mystifyingly) as a breakthrough masterpiece in some quarters, it's actually a lightweight, fun record.

*** **Crazy People Music** CBS 466870 CD/MC
Marsalis; Kenny Kirkland (*p*); Robert Hurst (*b*); Jeff Watts (*d*). 1–3/90.

*** **The Beautyful Ones Are Not Yet Born** CBS 468896 CD/LP/MC
Marsalis; Wynton Marsalis (*t*); Robert Hurst (*b*); Jeff Watts (*d*). 5/91.

Hurst and Watts are musicians of resolute power and high craft, and they provide Marsalis with the bedrock he needs to contextualize his playing. *Crazy People Music* is a solidly realized tenor-and-rhythm date, full of elegant playing, but the music on *The Beautyful Ones Are Not*

Yet Born is better yet: the recording sounds warmer and more specifically focused, and the long, stretched-out improvisations insist that Marsalis has his perfect, singular setting in the trio with Hurst and Watts (brother Wynton makes a brief cameo appearance on one track, while Courtney Pine's alleged presence isn't clear). 'Citizen Tain', which has some of the wit of Sonny Rollins working against Philly Joe Jones on *Newk's Time*, 'Gilligan's Isle' and the steeply driven title-tune are aristocratic improvisations in which the leader finds a path away from merely discursive blowing. His soprano sounds pretty good, too. Recommended.

ELLIS MARSALIS (born 1934)
PIANO

*** **Piano In E** Rounder 2100 CD
Marsalis (*p* solo). 84.

*** **Ellis Marsalis Trio** Blue Note CDP 7961072 CD
Marsalis; Bob Hurst (*b*); Jeff Watts (*d*). 3/90.

*** **Heart Of Gold** Columbia 47509 CD/MC
Marsalis; Ray Brown (*b*); Billy Higgins (*d*). 91.

The founder of the Marsalis dynasty is no mean player himself. One can hear where Wynton got his even-handed delineation of melody from and where Branford's aristocratic elegance of line is rooted. Marsalis *père* isn't beyond tossing in the occasional surprise, such as a sudden right-hand rip in 'Just Squeeze Me' on the trio album, but both records offer mostly careful interpretations of standards, sparsely harmonized and delicately spelt out, with a few simple but cleverly hooked originals to lend a little extra personality. The trio records are stronger since Marsalis can leave rhythmic duties to bass and drums and concentrate on the path of the song, and on the Columbia album there are two lions in magisterial form. But all three discs are unassumingly well done and quietly enjoyable on their own terms.

WYNTON MARSALIS (born 1961)
TRUMPET

**** **Wynton Marsalis** Columbia 49021 CD/MC
Marsalis; Branford Marsalis (*ts, ss*); Herbie Hancock, Kenny Kirkland (*p*); Ron Carter, Charles Fambrough, Clarence Seay (*b*); Jeff Watts, Tony Williams (*d*). 81.

*** **Think Of One** CBS 25354 CD/LP
Marsalis; Branford Marsalis (*ts, ss*); Kenny Kirkland (*p*); Phil Bowler (*b*); Jeff Tain Watts (*d*). 83.

***(*) **Hothouse Flowers** Columbia CK 39530 CD/MC
Marsalis; Branford Marsalis (*ts, ss*); Kent Jordan (*af*); Kenny Kirkland (*p*); Ron Carter (*b*); Jeff Watts (*d*). 5/84.

**** **Black Codes (From The Underground)** Columbia CK 40009 CD/MC
Marsalis; Kenny Kirkland (*p*); Ron Carter, Charnett Moffett (*b*); Jeff Watts (*d*). 1/85.

**** **J Mood** CBS 57068 CD/LP
Marsalis; Marcus Roberts (*p*); Robert Leslie Hurst III (*b*); Jeff Watts (*d*). 12/85.

'Wynton is good for jazz. End of conversation.' Branford Marsalis is not, perhaps, an entirely impartial source of comment on his brother's worth, but the statement, quoted in *The Wire* magazine, has just the right mixture of self-assured arrogance and respect. It hasn't always worked reciprocally. Wynton responded to his saxophonist elder brother's signing up for a tour with Sting much as Michael Jackson did to the news that LaToya was taking 'em off for *Playboy*. Shock, family honour, darkened doorsteps. In the event, Marsalis *trompette* has delved a lot deeper into the 'white' tradition than Branford's untaxing and undoubtedly lucrative contributions to *Nothing Like The Sun* (for all its bardic allusions) or *Dream Of The Blue Turtles*, tackling Haydn, Hummel and 'the Brandenburgs' and culling as many awards for his classical recordings as for those done under the influence of the 'J Mood'.

Wynton Marsalis's purity of conception has made for good editorial copy, particularly when it brought him *mano a mano* with every youthful trumpeter's nemesis, the late Miles Davis, who ruthlessly snubbed Marsalis onstage in Vancouver in 1986. Marsalis thereafter complained of cultural sell-out, and Miles calmly rustled his campaign medals and bank statements. The sore never got a chance to heal, but did the Marsalis of 1986 really have enough artistic credits in the bank to dream of climbing up alongside Miles?

The earliest recordings, made at Bubba's in Fort Lauderdale in 1980, came a year after his recruitment to the Jazz Messengers, and they suggest that he did, in embryo at least. Though released on only relatively small labels, they bespeak a remarkable talent. Marsalis comes from a virtual dynasty of musicians (his father, Ellis, is a fine pianist, see below, and brother Delfeayo has produced albums for him) and it's tempting to see them as a jazz equivalent of the Kennedy clan: glitteringly gifted, with a combination of radicalism and deep cultural conservatism, given to assertion over argument, humane but often chillingly detached, and inevitably a target for every critical loner with a grudge who resents their remarkable success.

In 1981 he took leave of absence from the Messengers to tour and record with a top-drawer quartet consisting of Tony Williams, Ron Carter and Herbie Hancock, all of whom appear with him on the first of the CBSs. The opening 'Father Time', recorded by the trumpeter's 'own' band, which included Branford and Kenny Kirkland, is an astonishing major-label debut, a beautifully structured piece with inventive contrapuntal exchanges between the two horns and a marvellous sequencing of very different rhythmic profiles. Listen to the way Marsalis subtly adjusts his delivery for the shift into common time. Inevitably, though, most critical attention was directed towards the tracks with Williams, Carter and Hancock. The bassist's 'RJ' and Williams's slightly melancholic 'Sister Cheryl' bracket a furious stop-action Marsalis composition called 'Hesitation', which is actually a neo-bop variation on 'I Got Rhythm'; together these are the nub of a record which is programmed with unusual care and intelligence, closing on the lovely 'Twilight'. The trumpeter's solos lack the declamatory mannerisms that crept into some of his later records.

Hothouse Flowers was a slightly unfortunate title. By this stage in Marsalis's career, there was already considerable pressure on him to produce works of magisterial finish and almost classical perfection. His sound on the 1984 album is less forced and overheated than it is simply detached. Marsalis sounds increasingly as if he is playing under a bell jar. The tone-colours are almost astonishingly bright on 'Stardust', and 'When You Wish Upon A Star' is brilliantly confected out of nothing. Branford is much less effective here and, though he gets ample solo space, he seems to be used increasingly for backgrounds, much as Jordan is. Watts, however, is integral to the sound, crisp, subtle and able to vary furiously impacted rhythms with soft, almost melodic passages in Afro-waltz time. On *Black Codes (From The Underground)*, he is absolutely essential to the tight, tense sound of the trumpeter's best work to date. *Black Codes* is a highly committed record, not just in its references to the slave laws of the nineteenth century, but also in the sheer commitment of Marsalis's playing on the title-piece, 'Phryzzinian Man' and 'Chambers Of Tain' (a Kirkland composition dedicated to drummer Watts). On 'Black Codes' he sounds sorrowful but intense, anticipating the preaching style of *Majesty Of The Blues*; on 'Phryzzinian Man' he attempts variations which almost sound 'classical', diametrically opposed to the snarling fury of the drummer's feature, a track that recalls Miles's classic recordings. A thoroughly marvellous album and, along with the CBS debut, the best place to start with Marsalis's work.

Marsalis popped up out of a generation supposedly conditioned by funk and anti-musicianship very nearly fully formed. His tone, forged in the hot press of the Messengers, is bright and scalpel-sharp, and not above dipping down into dissonances that recall anyone you like between Bubber Miley and Leo Smith. On 'Later' (*Think Of One*), he is as 'contemporary' as anyone might ask; on 'Much Later' (*J Mood*; can these be references to Mr Davis's celebrated exit-line?) he is much more consciously in the tradition. He also sounds much better without a second horn, laying out the theme with the same thoughtful intensity that he brought to the still-underrated *Standard Time*, which featured the same band as *J Mood*.

The underlying proposition would seem to be that jazz is not an entity but a particular way of approaching musical performance, embellishing past musics with that same mixture of arrogant 'originality' and respect. To that extent, *J Mood* is philosophically very much in line with all three standards projects. 'Skain's Domain' and 'Presence That Lament Brings' touch the opposite boundaries of Marsalis's emotional range and illustrate that his greatest and most lasting virtue is not virtuosic flash and fire but his handling of the band as a whole. Though this is relatively conventional theme-and-solos jazz, it's the overall direction of each piece (and of the over-familiar staples on *Standard Time*) that evokes the most positive response, stimulating comparisons with the similarly aged Ellington, who achieved the same productive balance of individual and collective creative responsibility.

*** **Fathers And Sons** Columbia CK 37574 CD/MC
Marsalis; Branford Marsalis (*ts*); Ellis Marsalis (*p*); Charles Fambrough (*b*); James Black (*d*). 82.

A nice concept, bringing together the Marsalises with (on the second side) Chicagoan saxophonists Von and Chico Freeman, whose contributions are reviewed separately. For once, Wynton is almost entirely upstaged by his elder brother, who plays one solo on 'A Joy Forever' that makes one wonder why the saxophonist doesn't do it more often. Ellis is calmly authoritative throughout, playing with delicate sophistication on 'Lush Life'. Wynton's own finest moment comes on 'Nostalgic Impressions', which anticipates the quiet interchanges of *Standard Time: Volume 3*, below. Not an essential item in the Marsalis canon, but worth having for both family gatherings.

***(*) **Marsalis Standard Time: Volume 1** Columbia CK 40461 CD/MC
Marsalis; Marcus Roberts (*p*); Robert Leslie Hurst III (*b*); Jeff Watts (*d*). 5 & 9/86.

***(*) **Standard Time: Volume 2 – Intimacy Calling** Columbia CK 47346 CD/MC
Marsalis; Wes Anderson (*as*); Todd Williams (*ts*); Marcus Roberts (*p*); Robert Hurst, Reginald Veal (*b*); Herlin Riley, Jeff Watts (*d*). 9/87–8/90.

*** **Standard Time: Volume 3 – The Resolution Of Romance** Columbia CK 46143 CD/MC
Marsalis; Ellis Marsalis (*p*); Reginald Veal (*b*); Herlin Riley (*d*).

These were long anticipated by fans and sceptics alike, by the latter in order to see whether Marsalis really could cut it with a standards repertoire or whether the much-discussed vices of fussy formality and unswinging delivery would trip him up. The first of the series found himself establishing his own time-zone out of the pell-mell revisionist rush of the modernists, but by no means moving over into the fogeyish plains of the neo-traditionalists. *Marsalis Standard Time* still hasn't lost its burnish and, though there is a suspicion that the trumpeter is thinking through his strategies too far ahead of time to let them come across with spontaneity and freshness, the ideas are bright and individual. Two versions of 'Cherokee' particularly catch the ear; Marsalis's muted solo on the first is one of the finest things he has done on record and the piece is left in mid-flight, as if in anticipation of the more formal version which brings the album to a close.

Marsalis, bass and drums sit out 'Memories Of You', a fitting recognition that Roberts's sterling qualities are not just limited to accompaniment. The trumpeter also isn't heard on 'East Of The Sun (West Of The Moon)' on *Intimacy Calling*. The two later *Standard Time*s are less immediately impressive than the original, but the second volume is a deceptively simple record that constantly reveals new facets. Ellis Marsalis is a warm, unhurried player and the settings he lays out for his son are comfortable rather than challenging. Perhaps sensing that, Wynton relies on a larger-than-usual battery of muted effects, most notably the frail Harmon effects of 'Bona And Paul' and the wobbly wah-wah of 'The Seductress' (both actually originals). Ultimately, *The Resolution Of Romance* is rather forgettable, pretty but uninvolving, and certainly a lot less interesting than the Marsalis segment of *Fathers And Sons*.

***(*) **Live At Blues Alley** Columbia G2K 40675 2CD/2MC
Marsalis; Marcus Roberts (*p*); Robert Leslie Hurst III (*b*); Jeff Watts (*d*). 12/86.

Next question up was whether, after all the big-label attention and all the classical gigs in black-tie halls, Marsalis could still hack it in your standard-issue smoky club. Recorded shortly after the first volume of *Standard Time*, these Washington, D.C, performances are among Marsalis's best and clearly establish him as the heir of Fats Navarro, Clifford Brown, Freddie Hubbard and maybe even the uptight little cat who'd just frosted him off a stage in Vancouver. His tone ranges from bright clarions that seem to come from Roy Eldridge or Harry Edison, right through to tightly pinched notes that don't settle comfortably into the harmony, a sure sign that he has recognized some continuity between the occasional and untroubled use of atonality in classic jazz and the doctrinaire abandonment of harmony by the 1960s avant-garde, which he rejected so vehemently.

Virtually all the material is familiar from earlier CBS sessions. 'Knozz-Moe-King', from *Think Of One*, gets the set off to a ripping start and is reiterated as a band theme throughout. A reading of 'Au Privave' recalls the Messengers, but the real highlights are scalding performances of 'Skain's Domain', 'Delfeayo's Dilemma' and 'Chambers Of Tain' on which Marsalis's intensity is matched by a fine formal balance. His elaborations on 'Do You Know What It Means To Miss New Orleans' are also greatly inventive and conspicuously lack the slight self-consciousness that has occasionally crept into his embellishments of standard and traditional material.

The band is now thoroughly familiar to Marsalis-watchers, enough to register slight disappointment with the way Jeff Watts plays or has been recorded, making him sound blustery. Roberts is his usual tasteful self, but Hurst excels himself, cutting through a rather sibilant background with lovely rounded phrases and big, tantalizing harmonic ideas.

*** **The Majesty Of The Blues** Columbia CK 45091 CD/MC
Marsalis; Teddy Riley (*t*); Freddie Lonzo (*tb*); Dr Michael White (*cl*); Wes Anderson (*as*); Todd Williams (*ts, ss*); Marcus Roberts (*p*); Reginald Veal (*b*); Herlin Riley (*d*); Rev. Jeremiah Wright Jr (*v*). 10/88.

Wynton's tribute to the music of his native New Orleans combines inventive arrangements with a rather two-dimensional construction of his own role, which is largely limited to mimicking the growls, smears and vocalized tones of his artistic forebears. It's wrong to call *Majesty* a revivalist album; despite the presence of the clarinettist and scholar, Dr Michael White, on the 'New Orleans Function' suite, the music feels quite contemporary, certainly more so than on the later *Standard Time* sessions. Roberts's use of bop harmonies is on the title-track (also known as 'The Puheeman Strut'), and 'Hickory Dickory Dock' helps draw attention to Marsalis's restorative concern for the continuity of jazz music, which he believes was betrayed in the 1960s by a combination of scorched-earth experimentalism and commercial pop.

The long suite is essentially a funeral procession for 'The Death Of Jazz' and is dominated by a 17-minute sermon, 'Premature Autopsies', written by Stanley Crouch (who writes all of Marsalis's liner-notes, or the same liner-note umpteen times, depending on how persuasive you find him) and delivered by the Rev. Jeremiah Wright over an instrumental backing that deserves to be listened to carefully. Crouch's tribute to the nobility of jazz, and in particular the example of Duke Ellington, is surprisingly moving and shouldn't be dismissed as an uncomfortable distraction from the music. Interpreted discursively, it isn't up to much, written in the slightly breathless vein of liner-notes; as performed, though, it has a convincing majesty, even if it sounds closer to William Bradford Huie than to Martin Luther King Jr.

As 'concept' albums go, this is better than most, but it will disappoint anyone who wants to hear Marsalis in good blowing form; he is almost relegated to the status of guest artist, playing second trumpet to Teddy Riley on 'The New Orleans Function'.

*** **Crescent City Christmas Card** Columbia CK 45287 CD/MC
Marsalis; Wycliffe Gordon (*tb*); Wes Anderson (*as*); Todd Williams (*ts, ss, cl*); Alvin Batiste (*cl*); Joe Temperley (*bcl, bs*); Marcus Roberts (*p*); Reginald Veal (*b*); Herlin Riley (*d*); Kathleen Battle, Jon Hendricks (*v*). 89.

A pleasing enough confection and one that ties in very closely to the thinking of *Majesty Of The Blues*. If anything, the use of New Orleans devices and tonalities is *more* successful here than on the more serious *Majesty*, and there are moments of genuine beauty. Marsalis's attempt to combine the awe and sheer fun of Christmas works surprisingly well and the arrangements are very inventive. 'Hark! The Herald Angels Sing' is conceived as a dialogue between European harmony and a jazz groove, but it's 'The Little Drummer Boy' that really takes the breath away. Vocal features for Jon Hendricks (wonderful on 'Sleigh Ride') and soprano Kathleen Battle (upstaged by Wynton's own muted solo on 'Silent Night') and guest appearances by Todd Williams, Alvin Batiste and the evergreen Joe Temperley. Marcus Roberts devotes the usual solo piano slot to 'O Come All Ye Faithful'.

*** **Thick In The South** Columbia CK 47977 CD/MC
Marsalis; Joe Henderson (*ts*); Marcus Roberts (*p*); Bob Hurst (*b*); Elvin Jones, Jeff Tain Watts (*d*).

*** **Uptown Ruler** Columbia CK 47976 CD/MC
    Marsalis; Todd Williams (*ts*); Marcus Roberts (*p*); Reginald Veal (*b*); Herlin Riley
    (*d*).

***(*) **Levee Low Moan** Columbia CK 47975 CD/MC
    Marsalis; Wessel Anderson (*as*); Todd Williams (*ts*); Marcus Roberts (*p*); Reginald
    Veal (*b*); Herlin Riley (*d*).

Three simultaneous 1991 releases from Columbia's capacious vault, issued under the more or
less meaningless rubric 'Soul Gestures in Southern Blue'. *Thick In The South* is the closest to
the earlier quartet sessions, with Watts more than making up for Roberts's apparent lack of
interest in the rhythmic progress of pieces and Joe Henderson checking in with some magisterial
pronouncements from down the generations (by contrast, Elvin Jones's two guest slots are
pretty pointless). *Uptown Ruler* is a tighter but less incisive album, with a thin overall sound,
and far more of the emphasis falls on the leader's wonderfully contained and unruffled blues
playing; 'Down Home With Homey' is particularly good (and you have to be aware of the
ambiguity of 'home' and 'homey' in black parlance).
    The final session, though, is the best. Marsalis is able to let his sound trickle out through the
rich, Delta mud voicings of the saxophones (and the ever-present Roberts), and the leader's
contribution on 'Jig's Jig' has a startling flavour like a freshet of river water welling up through
the salt.

*** **Tune In Tomorrow . . .** CBS 467785 CD/LP/MC
    Marsalis; Wycliffe Gordon (*tb*); Alvin Batiste, Dr Michael White (*cl*); Wes Anderson,
    Harvey Estrin (*as*); Herb Harris (*ts*); Todd Williams (*ts, ss, cl*); Joe Temperley (*bs*);
    Marcus Roberts (*p*); Warren Bernhardt, Lucky Peterson (*org*); Reginald Veal (*b*);
    Herlin Riley (*d*); Johnny Adams, Shirley Horn (*v*). 90.

The film bombed but, as with Miles Davis's score for the forgotten *Siesta*, the music took on an
independent existence. Set in New Orleans, Jon Amiel's movie was an adaptation of Mario
Vargas Llosa's *Aunt Julia And The Scriptwriter*. Setting and plot afforded Marsalis an
opportunity to develop the ensemble language he sketched out on *Crescent City Christmas Card*
and to give coherence to a complex interplay of leitmotifs corresponding to the characters. The
result confirms Marsalis's growing stature as a composer/arranger, using the entire range of
instruments available to him. Even oddities like the mock Balkan folk of 'Albanians' somehow
fits snugly with the rest of the music and the music hangs together a great deal more succinctly
than the film. Joe Temperley and Alvin Batiste express two sides of the hero, Pedro, while the
two organists set up the Crescent City ambience on sucessive tracks. Shirley Horn (who's had
Marsalis guesting on recent albums) sings 'I Can't Get Started' with typical feeling, and the
whole suite turns back on itself with the elegiac 'Double Rondo On The River', dropping
Pedro's brighter, clarinet theme down into range of the baritone and trombone, underlining the
ambiguity of the character.
    Thoughtful, appealing music, but still inevitably rather limited in focus. As Miles Davis
showed with his score for *L'ascenseur pour l'échafaud*, the creative dividends of second-order
commissions of this sort can be considerable.

WARNE MARSH (1927–87)
TENOR SAXOPHONE

***(*) **Live In Hollywood** Xanadu 151 LP
    Marsh; Hampton Hawes (*p*); Joe Mondragon (*b*); Shelly Manne (*d*). 12/52.

**** **Ne Plus Ultra** Hat Art 6063 CD
    Marsh; Gary Foster (*as*); Dave Parlato (*b*); John Tirabasso (*d*). 69.

***(*) **Jazz Exchange** Storyville SLP 4001 LP
    Marsh; Lee Konitz (*as*); Ole Kock Hansen (*p*); Niels-Henning Ørsted-Pedersen (*b*);
    Svend Erik Norregaard, Alex Riel (*d*).

***(*) **Warne Marsh – Lee Konitz** Storyville SLP 4096 LP
    As above, except omit Riel. 12/75.

***(*) **Live At The Montmartre Club** Storyville SLP 4026 LP
Marsh; Lee Konitz (*as*); Dave Cliff (*g*); Peter Ind (*b*); Al Levitt (*d*). 12/75.

***(*) **Star Highs** Criss Cross Criss 1002 CD/LP
Marsh; Hank Jones (*p*); George Mraz (*b*); Mel Lewis (*d*). 8/82.

*** **A Ballad Album** Criss Cross Criss 1007 CD/LP
Marsh; Lou Levy (*p*); Jesper Lundgaard (*b*); James Martin (*d*). 4/83.

*** **Posthumous** Interplay IP 8604 CD/LP
Marsh; Susan Chen (*p*); George Mraz (*b*); Akira Tana (*d*). 85.

*** **Back Home** Criss Cross Criss 1023 CD/LP
Marsh; Jimmy Halperin (*ts*); Barry Harris (*p*); David Williams (*b*); Albert Heath (*d*).
3/86.

*** **Two Days In The Life Of . . .** Interplay/Storyville IP8602 LP / STCD 4165 CD
Marsh; Ron Eschete (*g*); Jim Hughart (*b*); Sherman Ferguson (*d*). 87.

By far the most loyal and literal of the Tristano disciples, Warne Marsh sedulously avoided the 'jazz life', cleaving to a improvisatory philosophy that was almost chilling in its purity. Anthony Braxton called him the 'greatest vertical improviser' in the music, and a typical Marsh solo was discursive and rhythmically subtle, full of coded tonalities and oblique resolutions. He cultivated a glacial tone (somewhat derived from Lester Young) that splintered awkwardly in the higher register and which can be off-putting for listeners conditioned by Bird and Coltrane.

Marsh's reputation still falls far short of that of his exact contemporary, Lee Konitz. Where Konitz changed down the years, Marsh remained a dogged strict-constructionist, perhaps the last major exponent of Tristano's 'Cool School'. If the *Live In Hollywood* sessions belie Marsh's reputation as a cool, even cold, player, that is largely Hawes's doing. He consistently pushes the pace, kicking off 'Fine And Dandy' at a lively pace, clattering through 'Buzzy' with a hot blues feeling and stoking up impressive, blindfold-testable solos from the saxophonist on 'I'll Remember April' and 'I Got Rhythm', which he surely has.

Marsh is disappointingly served on record, and his best work is so far mostly unavailable on CD. The reissued *Ne Plus Ultra* is certainly the most important thing currently available. With a less assertive group, the Tristano influence bounces back with a vengeance. Marsh plays with considerable energy, stretching out his line on 'Lennie's Pennies' and ducking away from the obvious resolutions the band would seem to prefer. The Criss Crosses are also good, with *Star Highs* definitely the one to plump for (listen to the straightened-out 'Moose The Mooche'), though Barry Harris and Albert Heath are highly responsive on *Back Home*, with the pianist playing in a boppish, blues idiom similar to that of Hawes, 30 years before, and Halperin contributing a second tenor on 'Two, Not One'.

The Storyvilles were all recorded within a week on the 'reunion tour' of Scandinavia with Konitz at the end of 1975. Marsh found the famously exact Danish rhythm sections more than conducive and played with great authority. The Parker and Parker-associated tunes on *Warne Marsh – Lee Konitz* provide an excellent point of entry for newcomers, but there are more typical performances elsewhere: 'You Stepped Out Of A Dream' on *Jazz Exchange* and 'Foolin' Myself' and 'Darn That Dream' on *Montmartre* stand out. On the latter album there are also 'formal' pieces for 'Two Voices', marked *Allegro* and *Allegro tranquillo*. That was Marsh's range of pace and mood. By no means a barnstorming or histrionic player, he needs to be listened to patiently and carefully. The booming sound and awkward balances of the Storyvilles don't help, but Marsh's is a voice vulnerable to well-intentioned 'sweetening' by transfer technicians. The two Interplay sessions (with a Storyville CD option on the latter) suffer the same problems. The group performances are less than inspiring, but Marsh (who was once featured on an album of solo edits, like the Benedetti Parkers) is magnificent on 'Unheard Of', 'Parisian Thoroughfare', a CD bonus 'My Romance' (all *Posthumous*), 'Initially K.C.' and, rather improbably, 'All God's Chillun Got Rhythm' (*Two Days*), overcoming a very brittle and clattery sound in both cases. Fans may conclude that it's better to persist with vinyl's shortcomings than to risk distorting one of the genuinely unique voices in jazz. Just before Christmas 1987, Marsh collapsed and died at Donte's; he was playing 'Out Of Nowhere'.

EDDIE MARSHALL (born 1938)
DRUMS

(*) **Dance Of The Sun Timeless SJP CD 109 CD
Marshall; Manny Boyd (*ss*, *ts*); Bobby Hutcherson (*vib*); George Cables (*p*); James Leary III (*b*). 5/77.

Eddie Marshall's single album as a leader shines brightest when the group locks into a groove: it happens best during Hutcherson's ebullient solos, where the shimmer and sparkle of the vibes are reflected in the pulse of the rhythm section. The best tune here is Hutcherson's sole original, 'The Stroll', although all concerned have fun on a breakneck 'Salt Peanuts'. Boyd is an unfortunately perfunctory lead voice, and the other tunes – all by Marshall – lack much original spirit, but the disc is worth hearing for Hutcherson's sheer energy. CD remastering adds little to the LP sound.

PAT MARTINO (born 1944)
GUITAR

(*) **El Hombre Original Jazz Classics OJC 195 CD/LP/MC
Martino; Danny Turner (*f*); Trudy Pitts (*org*); Mitch Fine (*d*); Abdu Johnson, Vance Anderson (*perc*). 5/67.

*** **Strings!** Original Jazz Classics OJC 223 CD/LP/MC
Martino; Joe Farrell (*ts*, *f*); Cedar Walton (*p*); Ben Tucker (*b*); Walter Perkins (*d*); Ray Appleton, Dave Levine (*perc*). 10/67.

*** **East!** Original Jazz Classics OJC 248 CD/LP/MC
Martino; Eddie Green (*p*); Tyrone Brown, Ben Tucker (*b*); Lenny McBrowne (*d*). 1/68.

** **Baiyina (The Clear Evidence)** Original Jazz Classics OJC 355 CD/LP/MC
Martino; Gregory Herbert (*as*, *f*); Bobby Rose (*g*); Richard Davis (*b*); Charlie Persip (*d*); Reggie Ferguson (*perc*); Balakrishna (*tamboura*). 6/68.

*** **Desperado** Original Jazz Classics OJC 397 CD/LP/MC
Martino; Eric Kloss (*ss*); Eddie Green (*p*); Tyrone Brown (*b*); Sherman Ferguson (*d*). 3/70.

After graduating from soul-jazz organ combos and the John Handy group, Martino led his own bands on a series of records for Prestige, all of which have now been reissued in the OJC series. Both *El Hombre* and *Strings!* depend on blues-based formulas and are typical of the genre; but Martino's maturing style – heavily indebted to Grant Green and Wes Montgomery, but built for bigger speed than either of those masters – is good enough to transcend the settings. *Strings!* is noteworthy for a long, burning treatment of Gigi Gryce's 'Minority', where Farrell's thunderous tenor solo is matched by equally flying statements by Martino and Walton. Aside from the prophetically 'mystical' title-track, *East* offers some of Martino's clearest and most articulate soloing against a straightforward rhythm section. *Baiyina* nodded towards incense and peppermints with its noodling rhythm parts, but Martino's own playing remained tough underneath, and the rambling themes sometimes dissolved in the face of his improvising. *Desperado* is a little-known stab at fusion: Martino plays electric 12-string against rumbling electric piano and bass, and the results are akin to a tighter, less violent *Lifetime*. 'Express' and 'Desperado' hit a particularly compelling movement, although Green isn't a very stimulating partner (Kloss plays on only one track, 'Blackjack'). All the OJC remastering is good, although *Desperado*'s original production betrays how engineers didn't really know how to deal with that sort of music at the time.

*** **Live!** Muse M 5026 CD/LP
Martino; Ron Thomas (*p*); Tyrone Brown (*b*); Sherman Ferguson (*d*). 9/72.

(*) **Consciousness Muse M 5039 CD/LP
As above, except Eddie Green (*p*) replaces Thomas. 10/74.

***   **Exit** Muse MR 5075 CD/LP
Martino; Gil Goldstein (*p*); Richard Davis (*b*); Billy Hart (*d*). 2/76.

***   **We'll Be Together Again** Muse MR 5090 LP
Martino; Gil Goldstein (*p*). 2/76.

Martino spent the early 1970s with Muse, producing another strong and undervalued series of records. *Live!* consists of three long, rocking workouts which show how the guitarist can rework simple material into sustained improvisations of elegant and accessible fire: even when he plays licks, they sound plausibly exciting. Both *Consciousness* and *Exit* are a little more ballad-orientated, although the new quartet on the latter backs the leader with some intensity. A few days after he made that, Martino returned to the studios with Goldstein to conduct a sequence of duets which are as thoughtfully paced out as the best of Bill Evans and Jim Hall.

***   **The Return** Muse M 5328 CD
Martino; Steve LaSpina (*b*); Joey Baron (*d*). 2/87.

After signing for Warners in 1976, the results of which are now out of print, in 1980 Martino became ill and had to work his way back following a bout of amnesia. This live set shows all his old fluency intact on four long tunes, closely matched by LaSpina and Baron. If it seems a little less exciting than before, that may be because Martino's technique can seem more commonplace – or even more classical – in an age when guitars are more likely to be used as deadly weapons.

GREG MARVIN
TENOR SAXOPHONE

***   **I'll Get By** Timeless SJP 347 CD
Marvin; Hank Jones, Susan Chen (*p*); George Mraz (*b*); Billy Higgins, Akira Tana (*d*). 12/86–3/87.

***   **Workout!** Criss Cross Jazz Criss 1037 LP
Marvin; Tom Harrell (*t*); Kenny Barron (*p*); George Mraz (*b*); Kenny Washington (*d*). 1/88.

(*)   **Taking Off! Timeless SJP 348 CD
Marvin; Tom Harrell (*flhn*); Joe Locke (*vib*); George Cables (*p*); Eric Von Essen (*b*); Sherman Ferguson (*d*). 11/89.

The callow, impassive sound which Marvin finds in the tenor's upper register is a clue to his inspiration, Warne Marsh; and his improvisations have much of the lean, endlessly unspooling quality which Marsh bequeathed to modern saxophone. Marvin also likes to keep things on a steady simmer, which suits the situation on all three records listed here. *I'll Get By* is a reissue of a couple of small-label LPs; with Jones, Mraz and Higgins at their professional best, it's a date full of felicities: Marvin sustains the very long ballad form of 'Our Angel' with real insight and, while some of his quicker solos seem like mere exercises, he obviously loves to play. Three tracks feature him with fellow Marshite Susan Chen on piano. The two subsequent dates carry on where the previous one left off and, with Barron and Harrell sounding fine, Original Jazz Classics *Workout!* is attractive stuff. But the relatively plain *Taking Off!* suggests that Marvin could already use a change of pace, at least in the studios: it's agreeable but blander than the earlier sets.

KESHAVAN MASLAK aka KENNY MILLIONS
ALTO SAXOPHONE, BASS CLARINET, SYNTHESIZERS, OTHER INSTRUMENTS

**   **Loved By Millions** ITM 0011 LP
Maslak; Pamela Lyons (*v*); Steve Peskoff (*g*); Alex Ponomarenko (*b*); Codaryl Moffett (*d*).

***   **Mother Russia** Leo CD LR 177 CD
Maslak (solo) and with Misha Alperin (*p*); Anatoly Vapirov (*ts*); Vladimir Tarasov (*d*). 89.

A talented but slightly enigmatic figure, Maslak cultivates a broadly satirical tone, as in the rock-influenced fantasies of *Loved By Millions* and in 'Kenny Meets Misha Meets Hieronymus Bosch' on *Mother Russia*. The Leo set was recorded during a tour of Lithuania and Maslak's ancestral Ukraine (he was born in New York). His technique is boppish, but with elements of abstraction; the satire in no way deflects or compromises his virtuosity. An extraordinarily overblown passage in the duet with pianist Alperin is sustained over nearly a minute by circular breathing, punctuating a folksy romp, some funeral music and a couple of cheesy dance tunes.

The duets with Vapirov, 'One/Two/Three/Four Million Little Russians', are more intense but sound very dated. The real core of the album, and best confirmation of Maslak's quality, is the long duet with percussionist Tarasov, recorded on a remarkable tour of the then Soviet Union. Considerably more accessible than most native Russian improvisation, Maslak's work is worth a look and *Mother Russia* is the ideal place.

MASQUALERO
GROUP

***(*)   **Bande A Part** ECM 1319 CD/LP
      Nils Petter Molvaer (*t*); Tore Brunborg (*ts, ss*); Jon Balke (*p, ky*); Arild Andersen (*b*); Jon Christensen (*d*). 8 & 12/85.

***   **Areo** ECM 1367 CD
      as above, but Frode Alnaes (*g*) in for Balke.

***(*)   **Re-Enter** ECM 1437 CD
      As for *Bande A Part*, but omit Balke.

Rooted on one of the finest rhythm sections in Europe, Masqualero occasionally sound like a self-conscious pastiche of the ECM sound: bleak, atonal passages grafted on to rippling polyrhythms, interspersed with sound-for-sound's-sake patterns from the horns, and quiet, folksy melodies. What is interesting about the group's development over three albums is the abandonment (tactical or enforced) of harmony instruments in favour of a very stripped down melodic approach that casts the bassist and drummer into appropriately high profile. It's routine to say that the two young front men are not up the quality of the 'rhythm section', but Molvaer and Brunborg spound fresh and unaffected on the first album and have matured considerably in the five years since then. Their contributions to 'Li'l Lisa', 'Re-Enter' and 'Gaia' on the most recent album are quite adventurous and certainly far in advance of anything attempted on the atmospheric *Bande A Part*.

It's still probably the best of the three. *Areo* is not so good, for indefinable reasons that don't have anything obvious to do with the change in personnel. *Re-Enter* sounds a little tentative again, but it does sketch out some promising ways forward. Needless to say, recording quality on all three is absolutely top-notch.

CAL MASSEY (1928–72)
TRUMPET

***   **Blues To Coltrane** Candid 9029 CD
      Massey; Julius Watkins (*frhn*); Hugh Brodie (*ts*); Patti Brown (*p*); Jimmy Garrison (*b*); G. T. Hogan (*d*). 1/61.

Massey arranged 'The Damned Don't Cry' for Coltrane's May 1961 session [*The Mastery Of John Coltrane: Trane's Mood*, Impulse MCA 254650] and then promptly disappeared again. Though he was widely respected as a writer, and co-wrote Archie Shepp's *Lady Day* for the Brooklyn Academy of Music, he recorded only once under his own name, and that was thanks to Nat Hentoff's generosity. For years the only part of the January 1961 session to be made available was an excerpt [*Jazz Life*, Candid 9019 LP] of the long 'Father And Son', with which *Blues To Coltrane* closes.

Its overdue release does nothing to reshape the jazz or even the trumpet pantheon, but it does confirm Massey as an impressive composer whose performing range is no narrower than many a player who went on to rack up a dozen albums. The opening 'Blues To Coltrane' is a slightly raggy tribute, with Massey sounding somewhat like Wilbur Harden and Brodie reading out the Trane times in a rather flat, announcer's diction. 'Bakai' was originally written for the great saxophonist and recorded in 1957, with trumpeter Johnny Splawn and baritonist Sahib Shihab on the eponymous *Coltrane* (OJC 020 CD/LP). Massey's own version is far less smooth, but possibly closer to its keening clamour, implied by the Arabic title.

'These Are Soulful Days' was written for Lee Morgan's *Leeway* [Blue Note 84034 LP]. Again, the composer's own version has more unplaned edges. The rhythm section, here and throughout, really isn't up to much, with Garrison curiously disappointing on his double-time solo. Only with 'Father And Son', which extends to 11 minutes, does the band start to gel, by which time it's all over. Not a classic, but a valuable solitary glimpse of a briefly influential and slightly tragic figure.

MARK MASTERS (born 1958)
ARRANGER

***   **Priestess** Capri 74031-2 CD
Louis Fasman, Carl Saunders, Les Lovitt, Clay Jenkins (*t*); Rick Culver, Dave Woodley, Fred Simmons, Jimmy Knepper (*tb*); Clint Sandusky, Allan Morrissey (*btb*); Danny House (*as, f*); Jerry Pinter (*ts, f*); Terry Federoff (*ts, f, af*); Bill Harper (*ts*); Mike Turre (*bs, bcl, f*); Tommy Gill (*p*); Dean Taba (*b*); Randy Drake (*d*).

Conservative but not humdrum, this is a finely honed and smartly played record that speaks of only a modest ambition for Masters. Knepper and Harper are cast as the two principal soloists and both play with gusto and charm, although Harper is matched by Jerry Pinter on 'Naima'. Only Gill is a less than strong soloist. The material, unusually, has no composing by Masters (Harper himself contributes four tunes, including the minor classic 'Priestess' itself): he is content to do the arranging, which is skilful but unwilling to draw attention to itself. Both 'Naima' and 'Giant Steps' throw a little fresh light on Coltrane by concentrating on the themes themselves, and although the title composition was handled more vividly by Gil Evans, it's a failsafe tune to have in the band's book.

RONNIE MATHEWS (born 1935)
PIANO

***(*)   **Selena's Dance** Timeless SJP 304 CD
Mathews; Stafford James (*b*); Tony Reedus (*d*). 1/88.

***(*)   **Dark Before The Dawn** DIW 604 CD
Mathews; Ray Drummond (*b*); Billy Higgins (*d*). 10/90.

A venerable sideman, Mathews has made only rare excursions as a leader. He's an exemplar of the skilful and self-effacing modal pianists who came in the wake of McCoy Tyner's eminence in the 1960s. While there's nothing to pull the listener out of their seat on either of these records, each says much about the dedication and craft of the five men involved. Mathews likes generously voiced chords and momentous rhythmic drive, and his partners on both discs complement his playing with great insight. Yet they are very different recitals. With James – an old friend and playing companion – and Reedus, Mathews tries a wide variety of settings: 'Stella By Starlight' becomes a bass feature after a lovely out-of-tempo intro by James, 'My Funny Valentine' is an unexpectedly hard-hitting swinger, 'Body And Soul' starts with an improvisation on the verse, and the title-track is built on locomotive rather than dance rhythms, sustained with terrific power by all three men. *Dark Before The Dawn* is less variegated but, if anything, even more accomplished, in part because Higgins – whose work on cymbals is particularly well caught by the sumptuous sound – is so masterful. This time Mathews builds 'Theme From MASH' on to a Tynerish vamp, starts a reading of 'You Don't Know What Love Is' with a solo section from 'Don't Explain' and freshens up two infrequently visited standards in 'The End Of A Love Affair' and 'You Leave Me Breathless', which open and close the record with decisive authority. Two very satisfying records.

TURK MAURO (born 1944)
TENOR SAXOPHONE, BARITONE SAXOPHONE

***   **The Underdog** Storyville SLP 4076 LP
Mauro; Al Cohn (*ts*); Hugh Lawson (*p*); Bob Cranshaw, Tom Ramey (*b*); Ben Riley
(*d*). 10/77.

The curiously under-recorded Mauro has always worn his stylistic heart on his sleeve. One of
the peaks of his career was a tribute performance at Zoot Sims's funeral. Al Cohn guests on *The
Underdog*, and the stand-out track – albeit *sans* Cohn and his smoothy tenor – is called 'Zoot
And Al'.

So there you have it. Not the most challenging of lineages in many respects, but one which
Mauro graces with a firm inventiveness and a rousing tone. The best of the album comes in the
tracks with Cohn – 'Underdog', 'Turquoise' and 'Until'.

GUIDO MAZZON
TRUMPET, FLUGELHORN, VOICE

***(*)   **Other Line** Splasc(h) H 317 CD
Mazzon; Umberto Petrin (*p*); Tiziano Tononi (*d*). 4–5/90.

Guido Mazzon has been seeking new forms for jazz trumpet for many years. He recorded an
all-solo record as far back as 1975 and another with the sole support of vocalist Marco Magrini
in 1979; but none of his albums have been much distributed outside Italy. All the more cause to
welcome this fine trio session for Splasc(h). While there is some studio doctoring – the
multiple-horns effect on 'Secret Music' and a stern reading of Ornette Coleman's 'Lonely
Woman' – it's mostly the highly detailed interplay between the three musicians which the album
relies on to make its mark. Mazzon never comes on as a great virtuoso and prefers a more
circumspect approach, picking over melodic fragments and using the false areas of the horn very
sparingly. Petrin responds with a similarly restrained style, allusively hinting at tonalities in
some pieces and taking a linear course in others; Tononi plays timekeeper and colourist with
marvellously adept touches. A couple of the slower pieces perhaps outstay their welcome, but
otherwise a fine encounter.

LES McCANN (born 1935)
PIANO, VOCAL

***   **In New York** Pacific Jazz CDP 7929292 CD
McCann; Blue Mitchell (*t*); Stanley Turrentine, Frank Haynes, Curtis Amy (*ts*); Bobby
Hutcherson (*vib*); Herbie Lewis (*b*); Ron Jefferson (*d*). 60–61.

Although he has recorded dozens of albums, very little of Les McCann's output is currently in
print – fortunately for his reputation, since most of his output has been disfigured by faddish
vocals and arrangements and feeble material. This early record is untypical, since it presents a
case for McCann as a might-have-been Horace Silver – funky settings, top-rate soloists,
infectious beats. The first six tracks (cut live) feature the smashing front-line of Mitchell,
Turrentine and the rarely heard Haynes, while Amy takes one feature elsewhere and
Hutcherson enlivens two tracks. McCann's own playing is righteously simple and, while this
hardly challenges either Blakey or Silver, it's a distinctive hard-bop brew. Sound is
unfortunately rather cloudy in parts.

**   **Swiss Movement** Atlantic 781 365-2 CD
McCann; Benny Bailey (*t*); Eddie Harris (*ts*); Leroy Vinnegar (*b*); Donald Dean (*d*).
6/69.

A hit album in its time, but its appeal has faded fairly drastically. Cut live at Montreux, it's a
ragged set of soul-jazz vamps, with a probably definitive version of McCann's 'Compared To
What'. The excitement is mitigated by what remains atrocious sound, even for a live session.
Bailey's solo on 'You Got It In Your Soulness' offers the best moment, but overall the revival
of interest in soul-jazz has uncovered many better records than this.

**   **Les Is More** Night VNCD 4 CD
McCann; Jeff Elliott (*t*); Nat Adderley (*c*); Cannonball Adderley, Gerald Albright
(*as*); Eddie Harris, Stanley Turrentine, Bobby Bryant Jr (*ts*); Roberta Flack (*p, v*); Joe
Sample, Norman Simmons (*p*); Leroy Vinnegar, Curtis Robertson Jr, Sam Jones, Ray
Brown, Jimmy Rowser (*b*); Frank Severino, Tony St James, Louis Powers, Louis
Hayes, Donald Dean (*d*); Buck Clarke (*perc*); Carmen McRae (*v*). 60s–70s.

A bizarre audio-documentary of McCann's interest in recording both his own gigs and other
people's. There are glimpses of Roberta Flack as a night-club singer and of Cannonball
Adderley's band, as well as desultory snatches of a wide range of the leader's own groups.
There's some interesting music, of the kind one expects to turn up on bootleg records, but it's a
collection for McCann devotees only, and even they will probably only want to dip into it.
Sound-quality varies wildly but is mostly quite listenable.

RON McCLURE (born 1941)
DOUBLE BASS

****   **Descendants** Bellaphon 660 56 007 CD
McClure; Tom Harrell (*flhn*); John Scofield (*g*); Mark Gray (*p*); Jimmy Madison (*d*).
7/80.

***   **Yesterday's Tomorrow** EPC 884 CD
McClure; John Abercrombie (*g*); Aldo Romano (*d*). 7/89.

***(*)   **McJolt** Steeplechase SCCD 31262 CD
McClure; John Abercrombie (*g*); Richard Beirach (*p*); Adam Nussbaum (*d*). 12/89.

***   **Never Forget** Steeplechase SCCD 31279 CD
McClure; Eddie Henderson (*t*); Vincent Herring (*as*); Kevin Hayes (*p*); Bill Stewart
(*d*). 10/90.

McClure's fusion group, Fourth Way, extended the jazz-rock idiom he had helped create with
Blood, Sweat and Tears and the Charles Lloyd Quartet into more adventurous compositional
territory. A fine bassist, with an excellent arco technique (see 'Tainted Rose' on *Yesterday's
Tomorrow*), he is also an exceptional composer who draws on non-jazz tonalities with great
confidence.
     The material on *Descendants* was written in 1980 for the group that recorded it. It opens
brightly on 'Boat People', a deceptively funky theme that allows McClure to show how
inventive he can be at the lower end of the bass without sounding glum or sententious. His line
on 'Descendants' and 'Sunny Day' strongly recalls Scott LaFaro, who pioneered the rapid,
multi-note approach McClure has adapted to a more straightforward rhythmic context. Like
Eddie Henderson on the later and rather disappointing *Never Forget*, Tom Harrell has a rich,
dark-edged tone that always sounds as if it ought to be registering a fifth down from what is
actually being played. As such, it's the ideal complement to McClure.
     The bassist sounds less persuasive in a conventional horn-led quintet, though, and Herring
has an uneasy time of it on the 1990 session. McClure's preferred instrumentation is one that
trackily pairs guitar and piano, usually allowing the keyboard player long, developed lines,
while the guitarist plays 'free' over the top. The unstructured lines of 'Life Isn't Everything' on
Descendants are a tongue-in-cheek version of open-form experiments McClure had
participated in with Lloyd, and the guitar's role is made quite explicit here. He's also very
interested in the way Miles Davis extended the language of modern jazz but constraining it
harmonically, and uses both Abercrombie and Scofield (who played with Miles) in ambitious
combinations with the rhythm line. Madison's drumming is a feature of the 1980s album that
deserves to be highlighted. Madison has played with Carmen McRae, Jack Walrath and Roland
Kirk, as well as with Harrell in the inventive Michael Cochrane quintet; like his leader, he's also
a good pianist and adjusts his articulation very exactly to changes of key.
     McClure's preference for players with a similar sound is obvious from the trio session with
Romano and Abercrombie (whose guitar synthesizer takes the place of an electric piano). This
is more abstract, impressionistic music, and very different from the standards approach of
McJolt, where McClure develops the LaFaro sound very impressively on tracks like 'Nardis',
'Stella By Starlight' and 'Once I Had A Secret Love'. The trio set, released on the

Montpellier-based EPC, is slightly short on conventional jazz virtues but features some of McClure's best writing and some of his best arco work since 'Line' on *Descendants*. 'Midi Evil' presumably refers to the south of France rather than to MIDI technology. The set *is* rather dominated in places (on 'Panchito' to a great extent) by Abercrombie's effects, sometimes at the expense of McClure's and Romano's more delicate interchanges. The sound is also a bit overcooked.

ROB McCONNELL (born 1935)
TROMBONE, VALVE TROMBONE

***   **Live In Digital** Sea Breeze CDSB 105 CD
McConnell; Arnie Chycoski, Erich Traugott, Guido Basso, Sam Noto, Dave Woods (*t, flhn*); Ian McDougall, Bob Livingston, Dave McMurdo (*tb*); Ron Hughes (*btb*); George Simpson, Brad Warnaar (*frhn*); Moe Koffman (*ss, as, f*); Jerry Toth (*as, f cl*); Eugene Amaro (*ts, f*); Rick Wilkins (*ts, cl*); Bob Leonard (*bs, bcl*); James Dale (*p*); Ed Bickert (*g*); Don Thompson (*b*); Terry Clarke (*d*); Marty Morell (*perc*). 12/80.

(*)   **All In Good Time Sea Breeze CDSB 106 CD
As above, except John McLeod (*t, flhn*); Jim McDonald (*frhn*), Brian Leonard (*perc*) replace Warnaar, Bickert and Morell. 82.

Despite the accepted wisdom that a big band is a broke band, McConnell, a veteran of the Canadian dance-band scene of the 1950s and '60s, has kept his Boss Brass together on and off for 25 years. Initially they did without any kind of sax section, but by the time of these records the size of the band had grown. McConnell's charts suggest expansiveness as the band's signifying element: although the leader worked with Maynard Ferguson for a spell, the brassiness of the BB is exploited for sonority rather than clout, and there's a kind of reluctance to even their toughest arrangements. The music is skilfully handled, but the various editions of the orchestra never seem to marshal the kind of players to set light to the charts. Even where McConnell seeks to evade cliché, he can't altogether shrug off the MOR atmosphere which hangs round most of their records. The live disc is arguably their best, if only because the setting gives them a pinch of adrenalin which their studio records (there are several on Canadian labels) tend to miss. *All In Good Time* was a Grammy winner, but that tends to prove the even-tempered pitch of a band that ought to show a few more claws.

**   **Old Friends, New Music** Unisson 1001 LP
McConnell; Guido Basso (*t, flhn*); Rick Wilkins (*ts*); Ed Bickert (*g*); Steve Wallace (*b*); Terry Clarke (*d*). 5/84.

**   **The Rob McConnell Jive 5** Concord CCD 4437 CD/MC
McConnell; Rick Wilkins (*ts*); Ed Bickert (*g*); Neil Swainson (*b*); Jerry Fuller (*d*). 8/90.

Nothing to cause a scratch here, either. Away from the big band, McConnell reveals himself as a merely workaday soloist, and Wilkins is a carbon of Zoot Sims on a middling day. Pleasant, but both discs are sheep in sheep's clothing.

**   **The Brass Is Back** Concord CCD 4458 CD/MC
McConnell; Arnie Chycoski, Steve McDade, John Macleod, Guido Basso, Dave Woods (*t, flhn*); Ian McDougall, Bob Livingston, Jerry Johnson (*tb*); Ernie Pattison (*btb*); Gary Pattison, James MacDonald (*frhn*); Moe Koffman, John Johnson (*ss, as, f, cl*); Eugene Amaro (*ts, cl, f*); Rick Wilkins (*ts, cl*); Bob Leonard (*bs, bcl, cl, f*); Don Thompson (*p*); Ed Bickert (*g*); Steve Wallace (*b*); Terry Clarke (*d*); Brian Leonard (*perc*). 1/91.

This 'return' album by the Boss Brass is as accomplished as before, but there's too much lingering over detail and texture for a band where details tend to disperse its impact. Most of the scores unfold at far too languorous a pace, each track clocking in between seven and eleven minutes. Moe Koffman's vigorous (in Boss Brass terms, splenetic) alto feature on 'All The Things You Are' is the most interesting event.

SUSANNAH McCORKLE
VOCAL

***(*)   **No More Blues** Concord CCD 4370 CD/MC
McCorkle; Ken Peplowski (*cl, ts*); Dave Frishberg (*p*); Emily Remler (*g*); John Goldsby (*b*); Terry Clarke (*d*). 11/88.

***(*)   **Sabia** Concord CCD 4418 CD/MC
McCorkle; Scott Hamilton (*ts*); Lee Musiker (*p*); Emily Remler (*g*); Dennis Irwin (*b*); Duduca Fonseca (*d*); Cafe (*perc*). 2/90.

***   **I'll Take Romance** Concord CCD 4491 CD/MC
McCorkle; Frank Wess (*ts, f*); Allen Farnham (*p*); Howard Alden (*g*); Dennis Irwin (*b*); Keith Copeland (*d*). 9/91.

McCorkle's records in the 1970s – now all missing in action – established her as a major songbook interpreter, uncovering rarities and seldom-heard verses from some of the best American composers. But they did her few commercial favours. Her current tenure with Concord points her in a more successful direction, though the material is often less challenging. *No More Blues* benefits from a superbly integrated band, with Peplowski and Remler chiming in with pithy solos and Frishberg adding the most alert and gracious of accompaniments: McCorkle's big, courageous voice, which has been compared to Doris Day but will remind more listeners of Julie London, is huskily entreating on the ballads and assuredly swinging on the faster tunes. She's an interpreter rather than an improviser, which sees her through the Brazilian songs on *Sabia*: the task here is to drift through the coolly appealing melodies rather than swinging them to pieces, and McCorkle does it with perfect aplomb. A couple of the ballads sound too stretched, but her take on Astrud Gilberto on 'So Danço Samba' is wholly beguiling, and Hamilton (in the Stan Getz role) and Remler (in her final studio date) are marvellous.

I'll Take Romance is perhaps a shade disappointing as a follow-up. Nothing wrong with the arrangements and the players, with Wess defining his role as strong-but-tender tenorman. But the material – all of it very well known, and excessively so in the case of 'Lover Man' and 'That Old Feeling' – seems like a deliberate attempt to play down McCorkle's knack for discovering forgotten gems, and some of her interpretations sound like false trails towards 'new' transformations. 'My Foolish Heart' and 'I Concentrate On You' are studied enough to suggest caricature, although occasionally – as on a wonderfully sustained 'It Never Entered My Mind' – it works out, and the faster pieces are magical. All three discs are recorded with fine lustre.

JACK McDUFF (born 1926)
ORGAN

(*)   **Tough 'Duff Original Jazz Classics OJC 324 LP/MC
McDuff; Jimmy Forrest (*ts*); Lem Winchester (*vib*); Bill Elliott (*d*). 7/60.

***   **Honeydripper** Original Jazz Classics OJC 222 LP/MC
McDuff; Jimmy Forrest (*ts*); Grant Green (*g*); Ben Dixon (*d*). 2/61.

(*)   **Brother Jack Meets The Boss Original Jazz Classics OJC 326 LP/MC
McDuff; Gene Ammons, Harold Vick (*ts*); Eddie Diehl (*g*); Joe Dukes (*d*). 1/62.

Titles like 'The Honeydripper', 'Whap!' and 'I Want A Little Girl' don't offer much promise of a delicate and subtle sensibility. However 'Brother' Jack McDuff managed to shake loose from a basic Jimmy Smith influence to explore a subtler and less heavy-handed approach to organ jazz. Forrest was the ideal partner, certainly more sympathetic than Ammons, whose guest status is complicated by the quite unnecessary inclusion of Harold Vick, a less than inspiring player. *Honeydripper*, from the old Prestige catalogue, is certainly the best of the bunch, with the bonus of Grant Green's developing guitar. There are some interesting moments on *Tough 'Duff*, when the vibraharpist kicks back against McDuff's reeling lines; one wonders what Bobby Hutcherson might have been able to do, but 'Smooth Sailing' and 'Mean To Me' are impressively organized, and the album is worth digging out of the organ racks.

HOWARD McGHEE (1918–87)
TRUMPET

***   **The Bop Master** Affinity AFF 765 CD
McGhee; Bennie Green (*tb*); Roland Alexander (*f, as*); Pepper Adams (*bs*); Sahib Shihab (*bs, as*); Tommy Flanagan, Duke Jordan (*p*); Ron Carter, Percy Heath (*b*); Walter Bolden, Philly Joe Jones (*d*). 10/55, 6/60.

***   **Maggie's Back In Town** Original Jazz Classics OJC 693 CD
McGhee; Phineas Newborn (*p*); Leroy Vinnegar (*b*); Shelly Manne (*d*). 6/61.

***(*) **Sharp Edge** Black Lion BL 760110 CD
McGhee; George Coleman (*ts*); Junior Mance (*p*); George Tucker (*b*); Jimmy Cobb (*d*). 12/61.

(*) **Just Be There Steeplechase SCS 1204 CD/LP
McGhee; Per Goldschmidt (*t*); Horace Parlan (*p*); Mads Vinding (*b*); Kenny Clarke (*d*). 12/76.

***   **Jazz Brothers** Storyville SLP 4077 LP
McGhee; Charlie Rouse (*ts*); Barry Harris (*p*); Lisle Atkinson (*b*); Grady Tate (*d*); Juan Curtis (*perc*). 10/77.

***   **Home Run** Storyville SLP 4082 LP
McGhee; Benny Bailey (*t*); Sonny Red (*ts*); Barry Harris (*p*); Lisle Atkinson (*b*); Bobby Durham (*d*). 10/78.

***(*) **Young At Heart** Storyville SLP 4080 LP

***   **Wise In Time** Storyville SLP 4081 LP
McGhee; Teddy Edwards (*ts*); Art Hillery (*p*); Leroy Vinnegar (*b*); Billy Higgins (*d*). 10/79

The relentlessly self-destructive McGhee helped shape a convincing synthesis between swing and bop, much as Roy Eldridge was to do. Fats Navarro, a colleague in the Andy Kirk band, was his first and most important model, and the two can be heard together on *The Fabulous Fats Navarro* (Blue Note 781531/781532 CD). McGhee never achieved anything like Navarro's astonishing poise at speed (nor Gillespie's pure energy), settling instead for Eldridge's sharply toned medium tempo without the roof-lifting high notes. A firebrand when a younger man (he wrote the show-stopping 'McGhee Special' while with Andy Kirk), he developed into a thoughtful and rather inward player who could be banal or unorthodoxly brilliant in successive tracks.

McGhee isn't well represented on CD, but he can be heard in characteristic, if not ideal, voice on the Affinity compilation of material from the drug-haunted 1950s. Riding over Philly Joe's energetic drumming, he produces nicely balanced phrases on 'I'll Remember April' which fit together with deceptively subtle logic but which are quite unlike the long lines of more conventional bop trumpeters. 'Lover Man' and 'Lullaby Of The Leaves' expose a slightly soft centre, but the classic 'Dusty Blue', recorded in 1960, with Tommy Flanagan and Ron Carter holding together the middle, is back in the trumpeter's favoured medium pace, and is beautifully voiced.

On *Maggie's Back In Town!* McGhee sounds straightened out and clear-headed, tackling 'Softly As In A Morning Sunrise' and 'Summertime' at a hurting pace that sounds good in the ensembles but flags a little when McGhee is soloing. The opening 'Demon Chase', dedicated to Teddy Edwards's son, is similarly hectic, but is good-natured enough. 'Brownie Speaks', included in homage to Clifford Brown, stretches him a little more convincingly, but by then the set is over; it's interesting to compare the version on *Home Run*, with Benny Bailey cutting him for sheer tone and delivery. There is really only one ballad on *Back*, and 'Willow Weep For Me' takes a slightly hysterical edge (as do one or two of the other tracks) from Newborn's very tensed-up accompaniment. *Jazz Brothers* is roughly contemporary, and it's Harris's patient chording and coaxing right-hand cues that appear to lift the trumpeter half a notch.

McGhee's association with Edwards, with whom he had worked in the 1940s, was among the happiest of his career. Their reunion *Together Again!* (OJC 424 CD/LP) is a minor classic. Unhappily, the much later Scandinavian sessions on Storyville are not as appealing, though more so than the dismal *Just Be There*. While Edwards has matured considerably and is playing with some elegance and subtlety, McGhee sounds rather abrupt, unable to string individual ideas along a single harmonic or melodic thread as he had once done. The Parker tracks on *Young At Heart* are more successful than the slightly more ambitious material on *Wise In Time*, but McGhee's enunciation on 'Moose The Mooche' is almost bitter (perhaps its associations ran too close to home) and 'Relaxin' At Camarillo' and 'Yardbird Suite' are both very unfinished. 'I Remember Clifford', 'Crescent' and 'Ruby, My Dear' on the second album (which comes from the same dates) push Edwards into some uncomfortable banalities.

It's an uncomfortably thin legacy from (on his day) one of the finest trumpeters of the period. Enthusiasts might also want to check out McGhee's contributions to Sonny Criss's 1947 *California Boppin'* (Fresh Sound FSR 156 CD) and to Sonny Stitt's 1962 *Autumn In New York* (Black Lion 60130 CD/LP).

KEN McINTYRE (born 1931)
ALTO SAXOPHONE, FLUTE, OBOE, BASSOON

*** **Looking Ahead** Original Jazz Classics OJC 252 LP
McIntyre; Eric Dolphy (*as, bcl, f*); Walter Bishop Jr (*p*); Sam Jones (*b*); Art Taylor (*d*).

*** **Hindsight** Steeplechase SCS 1014 LP
McIntyre; Kenny Drew (*p*); Bo Stief (*b*); Alex Riel (*d*). 1/74.

***(*) **Home** Steeplechase SCS 1039 LP
McIntyre; Jaki Byard (*p, electric p*); Reggie Workman (*b*); André Strobert (*d*). 6/75.

***(*) **Open Horizon** Steeplechase SCS 1049 LP
McIntyre; Kenny Drew (*p*); Buster Williams (*b*); André Strobert (*d*). 11/75.

***(*) **Introducing The Vibrations** Steeplechase SCS 1065 LP
McIntyre; Terumaso Hino (*t*); Richard Harper (*p*); Alonzo Gardner (*b*); André Strobert (*d*); Andy Vega (*perc*). 10/76.

***(*) **Chasing The Sun** Steeplechase SCS 1114 LP
McIntyre; Hakim Jamil (*b*); Beaver Harris (*d*). 7/78.

It has been McIntyre's misfortune to be remembered chiefly for his brief association with Eric Dolphy. The 1960 Prestige sessions were by no means the best thing either man did. Originally inspired by Parker (but hear his offbeat 'Now's The Time' on the later *Introducing The Vibrations*), McIntyre developed a multi-instrumental style less dramatic than Dolphy's and less self-consciously exotic than Yusef Lateef's, but the perfect vehicle for his much-underrated writing. McIntyre favours curious time changes and (literally) eccentric themes, which give the music a toppling, unstable quality that feeds challenging rhythmic cues to his sidemen.

Taken up by Steeplechase, McIntrye recorded a number of exceptional albums in the 1970s, marred only by a rather unforgiving sound-mix which could be rectified on transfer to CD. *Hindsight* is rather dull, and McIntyre's treatment of standards – 'Naima', 'Sonnymoon For Two', 'Body And Soul', 'Lush Life' – is inclined to seem eccentric rather than genuinely progressive. *Home* ranges from bouncy, Caribbean impressions to funkier 'portraits' and dark-toned essays which bring him together with Byard and Workman in tight, adventurous arrangements. *Open Horizon* covers a similar range of material (no standards), but with a wider improvisational purview, and McIntyre appears to use his alternative horns structurally rather than for cosmetic effect. One of the few jazz players to make convincing use of bassoon (Illinois Jacquet was another), he generally keeps to the centre of its huge range, much as he does with bass clarinet, eschewing Dolphy's furious overblowing.

The two later sessions occupy extremes of scale but are of consistent quality. McIntyre has only rarely featured a trumpeter; Hino suits his angular approach, popping out bright clusters of notes and underpinning them with shadowy commentary. A word of praise, too, for the little-known Strobert, who is an impressive technician. The trio is much more open and the writing more adventurous. Working without piano presents well-known challenges, but Jamil and the marvellous Harris more than paper over the cracks.

McIntyre is more than a curiosity. Don't be put off by the absence of CDs.

KALAPARUSHA MAURICE McINTYRE (born 1936)
TENOR SAXOPHONE, BASS CLARINET, FLUTE, PERCUSSION

***   **Peace And Blessing** Black Saint BSR 0037 LP
        McIntyre; Longineu Parsons (*t, flhn, f, sno/s/a rec*); Leonard Jones (*b*); King I. Mack
        (*d*). 6/79.

African-accented modernism from an impressive instrumentalist and composer who sounds not
unlike label-mate Billy Harper. Kalaparusha lacks Harper's gospely swing, and is inclined to be
a little abstract, but 'African Procession' and the closing 'Hexagon' are very fine, and
multi-instrumentalist Parsons creates interesting textures. Recommended.

DAVE McKENNA (born 1930)
PIANO

***(*)   **Left Handed Complement** Concord CCD 4123 CD/MC
         McKenna (*p* solo). 12/79.

***   **My Friend The Piano** Concord CCD 4313 CD/MC
         As above. ?.

***(*)   **Dancing In The Dark** Concord CCD 4292 CD/MC
         As above. 8/85.

***(*)   **Live At Maybeck Recital Hall: Volume 2** Concord CCD 4410 CD/MC
         As above. 11/89.

***   **No More Ouzo For Puzo** Concord CCD 4365 CD/MC
         McKenna; Gray Sargent (*p*); Monty Budwig (*b*); Jimmie Smith (*d*). 6/88.

Dave McKenna hulks over the keyboard. He is one of the most dominant mainstream pianists
on the scene, with an immense reach and an extraordinary two-handed style which distributes
theme statements across the width of the piano. That's particularly evident on the good 1979
Left Handed Complement, a mixture of moody ballads and sharp, attacking modern themes
(there's also an original 'Splendid Splinter') which keeps turning up fresh ideas. He doesn't
threaten, he just plays. Long a 'players' player', he has grown in popularity and stature in
recent years, not least through his association with the young Scott Hamilton.

The *Maybeck Hall* recital is among the latest and best of McKenna's solo performances. He
medleys – a frequently tiresome practice – with considerable ingenuity and absolute logic,
switching hands, reversing the direction of the new theme and carefully disguising the welds.
The 'Knowledge Medley' sounds odd and contrived on paper – 'Apple For The Teacher', 'I
Didn't Know What Time It Was', 'I Wish I Knew', 'You'll Never Know', but you get the idea?
– and works superbly in performance. The final 'Limehouse Blues' is archetypal.

Jazz players owe Arthur Schwartz an enormous debt. There are well over 50 versions of
'Alone Together' in the current catalogue, a record that approaches old warhorses like 'Body
And Soul' and 'All The Things You Are'. McKenna treats the tunes with considerable respect,
preserving their shape rather than just winkling out the meat of the chords. 'A Gal In Calico'
and 'I See Your Face Before Me', both routinely sentimentalized, are played with exemplary
taste and 'Dancing In The Dark' has almost as much innate energy as a much later composition
of the same name by a Bruce Springbok or Springstream, something like that. *My Friend* is the
weakest of the bunch. The two medleys – 'Summer' and 'Always' – are slacker, and
McKenna's very physical relationship with his instrument is slightly off-balance. Normally he
sounds as if he might be able to pick it up and put it away in a case.

The quartet might just as well be a solo performance. Sargent (whose possibly misprinted
name sounds like the medieval Grey Sergeant who haunts the battlefield) isn't quite the death's
head the opening number suggests, but *rigor* has set in somewhere. Budwig is as loose and
flowing as ever, and Smith clatters along with more enthusiasm than finesse. There's a 'Talk'
medley this time, but you'll have to guess.

McKINNEY'S COTTON PICKERS
GROUP

**** The Band Don Redman Built (1928–1930) Bluebird ND 90517 CD/LP
John Nesbitt, Langston Curl, Joe Smith, Leonard Davis, Sidney De Paris, George
'Buddy' Lee (*t*); Rex Stewart (*c*); Claude Jones, Ed Cuffee (*tb*); Don Redman,
George Thomas (*reeds, v*); Milton Senior, Prince Robinson, Jimmy Dudley, Benny
Carter, Coleman Hawkins, Ted McCord (*reeds*); Todd Rhodes, LeRoy Tibbs, Fats
Waller (*p*); Dave Wilborn (*bj, g, v*); Ralph Escudero, Billy Taylor (*tba*); Cuba Austin,
Kaiser Marshall (*d*); Jean Napier (*v*). 6/28–11/30.

***(*) McKinney's Cotton Pickers 1928–29 Classics 609 CD
As above. 6/28–11/29.

***(*) McKinney's Cotton Pickers 1929–1930 Classics 623 CD
As above, except add James P Johnson (*p*). 11/29–11/30.

Despite the title of the Bluebird compilation, it was primarily John Nesbitt who built
McKinney's Cotton Pickers (although Jean Goldkette, who booked the band into his Graystone
Ballroom in 1927, gave them their name). Redman's arrival in 1928 brought his distinctive
touch as arranger to the band's book – there are 12 of his charts on the Bluebird disc – but
Nesbitt's driving and almost seamless charts were as impressive and remain so, over 60 years
later. Bluebird have compiled a 22-track set which works well as a sampler of the band.
McKinney's Cotton Pickers were among the most forward-looking of the large bands of their
era: while the section-work retains all the timbral qualities of the 1920s, and the rhythm section
still depends on brass bass and banjo, the drive and measure of the arrangements and the
gleaming momentum of their best records both suggest the direction that big bands would take
in the next decade.

On the later, New York sides, guest soloists include Coleman Hawkins, Rex Stewart and Fats
Waller, and Benny Carter has one of his sharpest early outings on 'I'd Love It'. But Nesbitt,
Robinson and Redman himself are significant players on the earlier sides, and the precision and
verve of the band *in toto* is the main point of most of these tracks. Some of the vocals are banal,
but most of the sides worst affected by that malaise of the period have been left off the
Bluebird set at least, which offers a 22-track compilation while the Classics pair of CDs cover
twice as much ground – though there are no alternative takes (several exist) and it also includes
all the weaker material. As a one-disc representation, the Bluebird set works well. The sound is
a mixed bag. Most of the tracks come across in a full-bodied way, but one or two have some
surface whistling and others blast at loud points. The Classics CDs are also variable – smooth
and clear on some tracks, less gratifying on others. It's good that the complete set of the band's
individual titles is avilable on CD, but one feels that there may be a better job to be done yet.

HAL McKUSICK (born 1924)
ALTO SAXOPHONE

*** Bird Feathers Original Jazz Classics OJC 1735 CD
McKusick; Billy Byers (*tb*); Eddie Costa (*p*); Paul Chambers (*b*); Charles Persip (*d*).
12/57.

A careful, swing-influenced stylist, McKusick took a thoughtful, melodic approach to soloing,
keeping the tune in view at all times, rarely straying off into vertical fantasies. He's perhaps best
known for his clarinet work with Charlie Parker and for the fine *Cross Section Saxes* [Decca
DL 9209 LP], where he mixes ballad standards, 'Now's The Time' and 'Stratusphunk' by
George Russell, a composer with whom he had a close relationship.

Bird Feathers isn't quite the Parker nestling compilation it is made to sound. Shared with
Jackie McLean and fellow-altoist John Jenkins (who play the title-piece) and with Phil Woods
and Gene Quill. It's nice to hear McKusick without the complication of a second alto. Byers is
an excellent player with a big dynamic range. The two horns are particularly good on 'Con
Alma', which is the archetypal McKusick performance.

JOHN McLAUGHLIN (born 1942)
GUITARS, GUITAR SYNTHESIZER

***** **Extrapolation** Polydor 841598 CD
McLaughlin; John Surman (*bs, ss*); Brian Odges (*b*); Tony Oxley (*d*). 1/69.

Extrapolation is one of the finest jazz records ever made in Europe. Ranging between gently meditative runs, as on 'Peace Piece', and furious 13/8 scrabbles, it combines all of McLaughlin's virtues (accuracy, power, vision) on a single disc. It has transferred to CD reasonably well, though Odges and some of McLaughlin's lower runs sound slightly artificial.

The band was state-of-the-art for 1969. Oxley's drumming has the firmness of a rock beat, even when the count is extremely irregular, and Surman's playing is cast midway between folksy melodizing and complete abstraction. Tie to a chair any British jazz fan who came of age between 1967 and 1972 and a substantial number will confess that 'Binky's Beam' is their favourite track of all time. Forget (for the moment) *The Inner Mounting Flame* and the *Mediterranean Concerto*. This is essential and timeless.

**** **Mahavishnu Orchestra/The Inner Mounting Flame** Columbia 31067 CD/MC
McLaughlin; Jan Hammer (*p, syn*); Jerry Goodman (*vn*); Rick Laird (*b*); Billy Cobham (*d*). 71–73.

***(*) **Mahavishnu Orchestra/Birds Of Fire** Columbia 468224 CD
As above.

*** **Mahavishnu Orchestra/Between Nothingness And Eternity** Columbia 468225 CD
As above.

*** **Mahvishnu Orchestra/Best Of** Columbia 468226 CD
As above.

One of the few jazz-rock bands of the early 1970s whose (early) work is guaranteed to survive, the Mahavishnu Orchestra combined sophisticated time signatures and chord structures with drum and guitar riffs of surpassing heaviness. Wielding a huge double-neck incorporating 6-and 12-string guitars, McLaughlin produced chains of blistering high notes, often with considerable sustain, that represent a coherent and significant assimilation of post-Hendrix guitar to what was still essentially a jazz context. Less obviously dominant than on *Extrapolation*, McLaughlin works his group collectively, like an orchestra, rather than a theme-and-solo outfit. Billy Cobham's whirlwind drumming was and remains the key to the group's success, underpinning and embellishing McLaughlin's and Hammer's often quite simple lines. His opening press-roll and subsequent accents on (the still incorrectly titled) 'One Word' (*Birds Of Fire*) clear the way for Rick Laird's finest moment on record. Even where he is poorly recorded on the live album, he is still dominant. Goodman came from the American 'progressive' band Flock, and is used largely for embellishment, but his rather scratchy sound contributed a great deal to the overall impact of *Inner Mounting Flame*, still the group's best album, and he has no apparent difficulty playing in 13/8.

The first Mahavishnu album was one of the essential fusion records, largely because it was more generously promoted and more obviously rock-derived than *Extrapolation*. Ironically, just as he was pushing the iconic guitar solo to new heights of amplification and creative abandon, McLaughlin was also working against the dominance of electricity, and setting a new standard for 'acoustic' performance. 'Thousand Island Park' and 'Open Country Joy' on *Birds of Fire* recalls the beautiful acoustic 'A Lotus on Irish Streams' from the first album. They ought to have done more in that vein, and McLaughlin's subsequent work with Shakti [CBS 467905 CD] suggested strongly that it was far from exhausted. Unfortunately, Columbia have not drawn the Great Veil of Kindly Oblivion over the expanded Orchestra's subsequent recordings, *Apocalypse* [Columbia 467903 CD] and *Visions of the Emerald Beyond* [Columbia CBS 467904 CD], which are available in some territories; apart from flashes of quality from replacement violinist Jean-Luc Ponty, these were as drearily directionless as the three quintet albums were forceful, developing the line McLaughlin had begun with *Extrapolation* and *Where Fortune Smiles*. The *Best Of* compilation is, therefore, very nearly that, though most people would have swapped the live tracks for more from *Inner Mounting Flame*.

*** **Shakti** Columbia 46868 CD/MC
McLaughlin; L. Shankar (*vn*); R. Raghavan (*mridangam*); T. S. Vinayakaram (*perc*);
Zakir Hussain (*tabla*). 75.

Sweetly complex acoustic music that was initially hard to absorb after the fantastic energy of the original Mahavishnu Orchestra, but which was infinitely more impressive than the OTT gestures and uneasy syntheses of Mk II. Shankar quickly went on to personal stardom, but the real drama of this set (which is much superior to the later *Handful Of Beauty*) is the interplay between McLaughlin and the tabla and clay pot percussion. Though it appeared to many fans that McLaughlin had simply gone native, it's easier in hindsight to see the continuity of all his work, in bop-influenced advanced rock, fusion, flamenco and Eastern forms, rather than its apparent breaks and changes of direction.

*** **Johnny McLaughlin: Electric Guitarist** CBS 467093 CD
McLaughlin; David Sanborn (*as*); Patrice Rushen (*p*); Chick Corea (*p, syn*); Stu Goldberg (*electric p, org, syn*); Tom Coster (*org*); Carlos Santana (*g*); Jerry Goodman (*vn*); Stanley Clarke, Jack Bruce, Neil Jason, Fernando Saunders (*b*); Alphonso Johnson (*b, b pedals*); Billy Cobham, Jack DeJohnette, Tony Smith, Narada Michael Walden, Tony Williams (*d*); Alyrio Lima, Armando Peraza (*perc*); collective personnel. 78.

To some extent, *Electric Guitarist* was an attempt to distance McLaughlin from the Mahavishnu image of a rather intense, mystically inclined artist in white cheesecloth and sandals, plugging direct into the Godhead. The original album cover featured a hand-tinted school photo with pinned to it a cod business card as if McLaughlin were a jobbing guitarist: weddings, functions, recording sessions – competitive rates. Here, it seemed to be saying, is an ordinary bloke playing with a selection of his mates, none of your metaphysical fannying about.

Unfortunately, the musical content was very much a case of steady as you go, and more than one reviewer mistook this star-studded session for a compilation of out-takes from previous bands. There is a neo-Mahavishnu track, 'New York on My Mind' with Goodman, Cobham and draftees Goldberg and Saunders; a 'Friendship' is co-fronted with 'Devadip' Carlos Santana, in recollection of the now unfairly sneered at *Love, Devotion & Surrender* album (*two* cheesecloth shirts, *four* sandals); while 'Every Tear From Every Eye' brings in David Sanborn for a single hot solo, much like the one on Gil Evans's *Priestess*.

Side two opens with a Coltrane tribute, 'Do You Hear The Voices That You Left Behind?' with Corea, Clarke and DeJohnette and reaches its peak with a superb duet with Cobham. In between, 'Are You The One? Are You The One?' reunites three-quarters of the second version of Lifetime only to prove how essential Larry Young was to the sound. Bruce's yawing bass might almost have been supplied by a machine at this point in his career, so unimaginative was his playing, and McLaughlin is reduced to big wah-wah shapes like a child's paper cutouts. The closing 'My Foolish Heart' is a rare chance to hear McLaughlin tackle a standard. Like the rest of the album, a split decision.

*** **Live At The Royal Festival Hall** JMT 834436 CD/LP/MC
McLaughlin; Kai Eckhardt (*b*); Trilok Gurtu (*perc*). 11/89.

Twenty years on, with Lifetime, the Mahavishnu Orchestra(s), Shakti, the One Truth Band, and a wobbly 1980s mostly behind him, McLaughlin again sounds on good form, punching out rows of notes which are almost as impressive for their accuracy as for their power. Eckhardt is a subtler and more involving player than his predecessor Jonas Hellborg and Gurtu, as with the revivified Oregon, gives excellent value. The themes are no longer as obviously visionary and Eastern-influenced and the guitarist seems content to re-run many of the stylistic devices he had adopted from the days with Miles Davis through the ringing harmonics of Shakti and back out into a more obviously jazz-grounded idiom. These days, though, they have a clear organic function in the music. Less indulgent than formerly, McLaughlin can afford to let his strengths show through.

**** **Qué Alegría** Verve 837280 2 CD
McLaughlin; Kai Eckhardt, Dominique De Piazza (*b*); Trilok Gurtu (*d*). 11 & 12/91.

Designer stubble on the liner photo and the most robust set from McLaughlin in a long time. Gurtu has always been a pulse-driven percussionist, rarely content merely to provide exotic colours round the edges of the music, and he and the bassists (Eckhardt appears on

'Reincarnation' and '1 Nite Stand', the two most forceful tracks) push McLaughlin's acoustic but subtly MIDI-ed lines almost to the limits. Very little sign of the rather soft-centred flamenco approach and Indo-fusions that have dominated his work for many years. Excellent.

JACKIE McLEAN (born 1932)
ALTO SAXOPHONE

***(*)   **Lights Out** Original Jazz Classics OJC 426 CD/LP/MC
McLean; Donald Byrd (t); Elmo Hope (p); Doug Watkins (b); Arthur Taylor (d).
1/56.

***   **4, 5 And 6** Original Jazz Classics OJC 056 CD/LP/MC
McLean; Donald Byrd (t); Hank Mobley (ts); Mal Waldron (p); Doug Watkins (b);
Art Taylor (d). 7/56.

***   **McLean's Scene** Original Jazz Classics OJC 098 CD/LP
McLean; Bill Hardman (t); Red Garland, Mal Waldron (p); Paul Chambers, Arthur
Phipps (b); Arthur Taylor (d). 12/56, 2/57.

***   **Jackie's Pal** Original Jazz Classics OJC 1714 CD
McLean; Bill Hardman (t); Paul Chambers (b); Philly Joe Jones (d).

***   **Alto Madness** Original Jazz Classics OJC 1733 CD/LP
McLean; John Jenkins (as); Wade Legge (p); Doug Watkins (b); Art Taylor (d).

***   **Makin' The Changes** Original Jazz Classics OJC 197 LP/MC
McLean; Webster Young (t); Curtis Fuller (tb); Gil Coggins, Mal Waldron (p); Paul
Chambers, Arthur Phipps (b); Louis Hayes, Art Taylor (d). 2/57.

***   **A Long Drink Of The Blues** Original Jazz Classics OJC 253 LP/MC
As above. 8/57.

(*)   **Jackie McLean & Co. Original Jazz Classics OJC 074 LP/MC
McLean; Bill Hardman (t); Ray Draper (tba); Mal Waldron (p); Doug Watkins (b);
Art Taylor (d). 2/57.

***   **Fat Jazz** Fresh Sound FSR CD 18 CD
McLean; Webster Young (t); Ray Draper (tba) Gil Coggins (p); George Tucker (b);
Larry Richie (d). 12/57.

Charlie Parker once invited Jackie McLean to kick him in the ass as pay-off for some typically selfish transgression. There were those who felt that McLean in turn could have used similarly robust encouragement in the 1950s, when his life and career teetered towards the edge.

These come from a turbulent but productive period in McLean's career. The OJCs mine almost to exhaustion the mid-1956 and early-1957 sessions with Waldron, filling in with other Prestige and New Jazz materials. McLean's pure, emotive blues tone, characteristically taking off with a wail at the break, has already become a manner, but there is a searching, troubled quality to his work on 'Abstraction' (4, 5 And 6), 'Flickers' and 'Help' (& Co), and the two takes of 'Long Drink of the Blues' (OJC 253, which also includes desirable versions of 'I Cover the Waterfront', 'Embraceable You' and 'These Foolish Things'). Given the range and familiarity of material, this might seem a good place to start, but Scene ('Mean to Me' and 'Old Folks') and Changes ('I Hear a Rhapsody' and 'Chasin' the Bird') are more challenging, pointing a way out of the still-dominant Parker influence.

Perhaps the best of the group is the earliest. Lights Out has a directness and simplicity of diction that is not so evident elsewhere and where McLean does attempt something more adventurous, as in the 'bagpipe' introduction and carefully harmonized final chorus of 'A Foggy Day', he does so with taste and precision. As on 4, 5 And 6, Byrd is a fine collaborator, soloing in a sweet, Dorham-influenced tone on the ballad 'Lorraine' and 'Kerplunk', both of which were written by the trumpeter. Hardman, a 'pal' from the Hard Bop-vintage Jazz Messengers, is almost equally good and Philly Joe cooks up an accompaniment very nearly as forceful as Blakey's.

The Fresh Sound is desirable not least because of the CD format but also for freshly minted charts, and the inventive brass interplay of Young and Draper (who led his own session with John Coltrane a year later – *A Tuba Jazz*, Fresh Sound CD 20). 'Tune Up' is one of McLean's leanest and most daring performances of the period.

***   **Jackie's Bag** Blue Note B21Y 46142 CD
McLean; Blue Mitchell (*t*); Tina Brooks (*ts*); Sonny Clark, Kenny Drew (*p*); Paul Chambers (*b*); Philly Joe Jones, Art Taylor (*d*). 1/59, 9/60.

The least satisfactory of the Blue Notes. Neither session fully catches light and though the tough, bluesy frontline of Mitchell and Brooks works ambitiously far away from home base, attempting the unobvious charts of 'Appointment In Ghana' and 'Isle Of Java', the usually reliable Byrd (a matter of months before his own fine *Byrd In Hand* Blue Note) sounds very uninspired, often relying on pure sound to carry him through poorly thought out progressions.

****   **New Soil** Blue Note CDP 784013 CD
McLean; Donald Byrd (*t*); Walter Davis (*p*); Paul Chambers (*b*); Pete LaRoca (*d*). 5/59.

Transitional and challenging, *New Soil* seems reasonably tame by present-day standards. McLean had passed through difficult times and was visibly reassessing his career and direction. The extended 'Hip Strut' is perhaps the most conventional thing on the album, but the saxophonist is straining a little at the boundaries of the blues, still pushing from the inside, but definitely looking from a new synthesis. 'Minor Apprehension' has elements of freedom which are slightly startling for the period and wholly untypical of McLean's previous work. Davis contributes a number of compositions, including the previously unreleased 'Formidable' (which isn't). Byrd is still a more than viable player. The transfer isn't as good as usual, with a lot of mess on the drummer's tracks, but the music is important enough to be labelled historic.

***(*)   **Bluesnik** Blue Note B21Y 84067 CD
McLean; Freddie Hubbard (*t*); Kenny Drew (*p*); Doug Watkins (*b*); Pete LaRoca (*d*). 1/61.

Tough, unreconstructed modern blues that reveal considerable depths on subsequent hearings. That's particularly noticeable on the outwardly conventional title-track, on which McLean's solo has a formidably unexpected logic. The other soloists tend to take up space that one might prefer to have seen left to the on-form leader, but Hubbard is dashing and Drew affectingly lyrical. A word, too, for the seldom-discussed Watkins, who gives his lines a lazy-sounding drag that nonetheless holds the beat solidly together. An excellent record, that should be an high priority for anyone interested in McLean's music.

***   **Tippin' The Scales** Blue Note B21Y 84427 CD
McLean; Sonny Clark (*p*); Butch Warren (*b*); Art Taylor (*d*). 9/62.

Given his dominance as a soloist and his intensely personal approach, McLean recorded with rhythm only surprisingly rarely. This has to be seen as a set of preliminary exercises for the magnificent *Let Freedom Ring* that followed in 1963, below. There are already signs of a relaxation in McLean's attachment of bebop orthodoxies though his rhythmic conception (if not his harmony) on 'Rainy Blues' and 'Nursery Blues' is very close to Parker's. As on *Jackie's Bag*, Clark provides a muscly, provocative accompaniment that sounds quite raw in places, single notes struck with a force that distorts the tone in intriguing ways. The sound isn't quite up to Blue Note's norm and one wonders if Warren had to be brought forward. In places he sounds almost overdubbed.

****   **Let Freedom Ring** Blue Note 7465272 CD
McLean; Walter Davis Jr (*p*); Herbie Lewis (*b*); Billy Higgins (*d*). 63.

A classic. Influenced by Ornette Coleman – with whom he was to record for Blue Note on *Old and New Gospel* – McLean shrugged off the last fetter of bop harmony, and pushed through to a more ruggedly individual post-bop that in important regards anticipated the avant-garde of the later 1960s. McLean's phenomenally beautiful tone rings out on 'Melody for Melonae', 'I'll Keep Loving You', 'Rene' and 'Omega'. Higgins's bright, cross-grained drumming is exemplary and the band is generously recorded, with plenty of bass.

***(*)   One Step Beyond Blue Note B21Y 46821 CD
McLean; Grachan Moncur III (*tb*); Bobby Hutcherson (*vib*); Larry Ridley (*b*); Tony Williams (*d*). 4/63.

'Saturday And Sunday' and 'Frankenstein' see McLean pushing harder still at the envelope of bop and coming up with something that, in its remarkable rhythmic independence, strongly anticipates Eric Dolphy's classic *Out To Lunch!* The addition of Moncur is significant, too, placing sustained portamento effects under McLean's unmetrical slithers across a blues progression. Challenging music that.

***(*)   Dr Jackle Steeplechase SCS 6005 CD/LP
McLean; Lamont Johnson (*p*); Scott Holt (*b*); Billy Higgins (*d*). 12/66.

**(*)   Tune Up Steeplechase SCS 6023 LP
As above.

The later 1960s were a somewhat dead time for McLean, and it looked as though the huge strides he had taken at the beginning of the decade led nowhere. He acted in Jack Gelber's *The Connection*, and played some of the script for real. His playing of the time has a slightly tired edge, and a hesitancy that comes not from lack of confidence but from a seeming lack of motivation to develop ideas. *Dr Jackle* includes a take of 'Melody for Melonae' which is quite discouraging in its diffidence and defensive show; McLean clearly isn't helped by the rhythm section, but Higgins alone should have been enough to spur him to better things.

***(*)   Demon's Dance Blue Note BCT 84345 CD
McLean; Woody Shaw (*t*); Lamont Johnson (*p*); Scott Holt (*b*); Jack DeJohnette (*d*). 12/67.

An undervalued item in the McLean canon. DeJohnette gives it the same rhythmic complexity the saxophonist had previously looked to Tony Williams and Billy Higgins to provide, but the most important single contribution comes from Woody Shaw. Shaw is bell-like and assertive one moment, achingly tender the next and his playing on the title tune and 'Sweet Love Of Mine' counts as some his finest in a tragically under-achieving career.

****   Live At Montmartre Steeplechase SCS 1001 LP

***   A Ghetto Lullaby Steeplechase SCS 1013 LP
McLean; Kenny Drew (*p*); Bo Stief (*b* on *Live* only); Niels-Henning Ørsted-Pedersen (*b* on *Lullaby* only); Alex Riel (*d*). 8/72, 7/73.

For sheer *joie de vivre*, albeit with a chastened edge, *Live At Montmartre* is hard to beat. Full-voiced and endlessly inventive, McLean romps through 'Smile', adding the a-haircut-*bay-rum*' cadence to the end of his first statement with an almost arrogant flourish. 'Parker's Mood' is perhaps the best of his later bebop essays, shifting out of synch with Drew's excellent chording for a couple of measures. *Lullaby* is less immediately appealing, though NHØP adds a significant element to the group's harmonic output, and he is a much solider player than Stief. 'Mode for Jay Mac' is interesting, and the title-track calls up some of McLean's most purely emotive playing.

**(*)   Ode To Super Steeplechase SCS 1009 CD/LP
McLean; Gary Bartz (*as*); Thomas Clausen (*p*); Bo Stief (*b*); Alex Riel (*d*). 7/73.

A disappointing confrontation that recalls the *Alto Madness* session with John Jenkins, above. Bartz already sounds as if he has set his sights on a rock/fusion future and McLean battles against Clausen's apparent insistence on closing up the harmonies. 'Monk's Dance' makes a promising but unfulfilled opening, and 'Great Rainstreet Blues' bogs down rather too quickly.

***   The Meeting Steeplechase SCS 1006 CD/LP
McLean; Dexter Gordon (*ts*); Kenny Drew (*p*); Niels-Henning Ørsted-Pedersen (*b*); Alex Riel (*d*). 7/73.

***   The Source Steeplechase SCS 1020 CD/LP
As above.

For once, Steeplechase's obsessive over-documentation makes sense. Recorded over two nights, this isn't a good album and a makeweight, but a 'double' of genuine quality. Gordon and McLean were poles apart stylistically, but temperament and geography suggested such a meeting was inevitable. The first volume is darker and more sensitive and the opening 'All Clean' hits close to home. McLean is usually quicker to the punch, but Gordon spins out his ideas (particularly on the standards) with confidence and some in reserve. 'Half Nelson' and 'I Can't Get Started' (*The Source*) depend to a large extent on Drew's teasing out of the chords. The sound isn't spectacularly good, with a tendency to fragment round the edges; no better on the CD unfortunately, but the playing makes up for it.

***   **New York Calling** Steeplechase SCS 1023 CD/LP
McLean; Billy Skinner (*t*); Rene McLean (*ts, ss*); Billy Gault (*p*); James Benjamin (*b*); Michael Carvin (*d*). 10/74.

***   **Antiquity** Steeplechase SCS 1028 LP
McLean; Michael Carvin (*d, perc, v*). 8/74.

New York Calling is a respectable performance from a band capable of better. The Cosmic Brotherhood featured McLean's talented and indoctrinated-from-the-cradle son, René. Far from sounding like a chip, he shows considerable individuality on both his horns, carving out intriguing counter-melodies and straightforward responses, neither over-respectful nor wilfully defiant. The charts are impressively varied, but *New York Calling* isn't a first choice for CD transfer. The sound is unaccountably flat. McLean *père* takes his best solo early, on the title-track, and finds little to add to it. Skinner sounds as if he could do with a bottle of valve oil and has intonation problems throughout (unless he intends some of his middle register notes to be flatted). Once again, it's the drummer who attracts positive attention.

The duo with Carvin is as far out as anything McLean has attempted. The core of the session is an impressionistic account of slave days. The saxophonist's passions seem a trifle muted, but there are moments when the two spiral up on a single motif and the music starts to fire up. Then there's no mistaking McLean's mastery.

****   **Dynasty** Triloka 181 2 CD
McLean; René McLean (*ts, as, ss, f*); Hotep Idris Galeta (*p*); Nat Reeves (*b*); Carl Allen (*d*). 11/88.

***(*)   **Rites Of Passage** Triloka 188 2 CD
As above, except add Lenny Castro (*perc*). 1/91.

Both sessions start with McLean originals, but responsibility for producing new material for the Dynasty band has largely fallen on René and South African-born pianist Galeta. Their work introduces a range of altered changes and curious tonalities that are drawn from African and Asian musics ('Zimbabwe', 'Muti-Woman', Stanley Wiley's 'Third World Express' on *Dynasty*, 'Naima's Love Poem' and 'Destiny's Romance' on *Rites*), and to which McLean responds very positively, confirming how much on the outside of conventional bop language he always was. The unmistakable tone is still very much intact and infuses even a rather bland vehicle like Bacharach's 'A House Is Not A Home' with considerable feeling.

His son simply can't match him for either speed or articulation or beauty of tone, having a rather vinegary sound on his two main horns and a bleary version of Richie Cole's reedy whine on the alto. He is, though, a fine flute player and it would be good to hear him more often on that horn. Both albums are a must for McLean fans and the first (recorded in front of a studio audience) can be confidently recommended to anyone interested in the finest modern jazz.

JIM McNEELY (born 1949)
PIANO, KEYBOARDS

***   **The Plot Thickens** Muse MCD 5378 CD/LP
McNeely; John Scofield (*g*); Mike Richmond (*b*); Adam Nussbaum (*d*). 79.

***   **From The Heart** Owl 045 CD/LP
McNeely; Marc Johnson (*b*); Adam Nussbaum (*d*). 10/84–2/85.

***   **Winds Of Change** Steeplechase SCS/SCCD 1256 CD/LP
McNeely; Mike Richmond (*b*); Kenny Washington (*d*). 7/89.

Having worked with Mel Lewis, Stan Getz and Joe Henderson, McNeely has acquired a substantial reputation which these albums confirm in their unfussy way. A clever writer and a mercurial though restrained soloist, McNeely likes a lot of space to develop ideas in: the unfolding of, say, 'Chelsea Litany / Feng Liu' on *The Plot Thickens* takes some 13 minutes, and the Steeplechase session includes five originals that fill most of the record without any sense of time-wasting. The Muse session includes some good early Scofield on the two longest tracks, his lines running in parallel with the pianist's, and the Owl record is closely argued; but the best of the three is certainly *Winds Of Change*. Each of the five originals has a specific turn of phrase, while 'Bye-Ya' is a particularly fluent reading of a Monk piece that not many tackle. Richmond, whose voluble yet lightly weighted lines are entirely apt, is certainly his ideal bass partner.

JOHN McNEIL
TRUMPET, FLUGELHORN

(*) **Embarkation Steeplechase SCS 1099 LP/MC
McNeil; Bob Berg (*ts*); Joanne Brackeen (*p*); Rufus Reid (*b*); Billy Hart (*d*). 3/78.

*** **Faun** Steeplechase SCS 1117 LP
McNeil; Dave Liebman (*ss, ts, f*); Richard Beirach (*p*); Buster Williams (*b*); Billy Hart, Mike Hyman (*d*). 4–5/79.

** **Look To The Sky** Steeplechase SCS 1128 LP
McNeil; Tom Harrell (*t, flhn*); Kenny Barron (*p*); Buster Williams (*b*); Billy Hart (*d*). 4/79.

** **The Glass Room** Steeplechase SCS 1133 LP
McNeil; Bill Bickford (*g*); Tom Warrington (*b*); Mike Hyman (*d*). 11/79.

(*) **Clean Sweep Steeplechase SCS 1154 LP
McNeil; Dave Liebman (*ss*); Joanne Brackeen (*p*); Rufus Reid (*b*); Billy Hart (*d*). 5/81.

*(*) **I've Got The World On A String** Steeplechase SCS 1183 LP
McNeil; Doug Raney (*g*); Jesper Lundgaard (*b*); Aage Tanggaard (*d*). 9/83.

** **Things We Did Last Summer** Steeplechase SCS 1231 CD/LP
McNeil; Dave Liebman (*ss, f*); Ron McClure (*b*); Ed Soph (*d*). 8/83.

McNeil's work as a leader has been consistent enough. He writes themes which don't sound much like anyone else's, even if they can't be called especially distinctive, and he plays trumpet in a cautious, rather flat-footed way, as if in fear for his technique but still wishing to fly from sequence to sequence. All his records have been made for Steeplechase, and they all seem to have been made in one five-year period (the last one listed above, a live date from 1983, wasn't released until 1988). It's tempting to go even further and say that they all sound the same, but that's not quite fair, or accurate. The earlier sessions reach a peak in *Faun*, where the excellent band work with interest through six originals, one of which ('Iron Horse') is a duet between McNeil and Hyman. *Embarkation* is well played but routine post-bop, while *Look To The Sky*, although interesting for its scarce front-line of two trumpets, is less than happy because Harrell outplays McNeil throughout. *The Glass Room* lacks a performer of strong character to take charge of the music, which ends up as a series of plain episodes.

Clean Sweep musters another excellent band – Reid's huge sound anchors the tunes, Liebman is in zestful form, and Brackeen and Hart are dependably themselves. But they sound unfamiliar with the material, which consequently doesn't take off, although the unstormy 'Zephyr' and 'Where's Rialto?' at least seem striking enough. The live album with Liebman covers similar ground, but the villain here is the engineer, who delivers a noisy, tangled sound-mix in which McClure often disappears. *I've Got The World On A String* sites McNeil in Chet Baker territory with a watchful bass–drums duo (Raney appears on only one track) and a set of standards, but this doesn't suit him at all, and the playing sounds clumsy and contrived.

MARIAN McPARTLAND (born 1920)
PIANO

***   **At The Hickory House** Jasmine JAS 312 CD
McPartland; Bill Crow (*b*); Joe Morello (*d*). 55.

Now that the double-LP of Marian McPartland's Savoy recordings is out of print, this reissue is all that remains in the catalogue of her earlier work. Her lyrical, insistently swinging style is ideally portrayed in these 12 brief tracks, from the opening reharmonization of 'I Hear Music' through a hard-hitting 'Tickle Toe' to a charming but clear-headed treatment of 'Skylark' and 'Mad About The Boy'. A harp and strings intrude here and there, but the pianist does her best to sidestep this producer's distraction. Crow and Morello work marvellously in support. The sound is clear enough, though scarcely an improvement over the original (Capitol) LP. While McPartland worked regularly at the Hickory House in New York during the time the record was made, this is a studio session.

***   **From This Moment On** Concord CCD 4086 CD/MC
McPartland; Brian Torff (*b*); Jake Hanna (*d*). 12/78.

****   **Portrait Of Marian McPartland** Concord CCD 4101 CD/MC
As above, plus Jerry Dodgion (*as, f*). 5/79.

***(*)   **Personal Choice** Concord CCD 4202 CD/MC
McPartland; Steve LaSpina (*b*); Jake Hanna (*d*). 6/82.

***   **Willow Creek And Other Ballads** Concord CCD 4272 CD/MC
McPartland (*p* solo). 1/85.

McPartland's playing and composing have remained amazingly fresh and interested. Besides performing, she has hosted a long-running American radio series which features her with a different jazz pianist on every edition; and, perhaps as a result, her own playing seems sensitive to all the possible directions in contemporary jazz piano. Even though this would be classed by most as ostensibly 'mainstream jazz', there are inflexions in it which would be unknown to most of McPartland's immediate contemporaries. *From This Moment On* offers a tight, generous reading of familiar standards, but *Portrait* goes a notch higher by adding Dodgion's bristling alto and beautifully articulated flute to the mix. An incisive version of Herbie Hancock's 'Tell Me A Bedtime Story', a tart Dodgion blues called 'No Trumps' and an ideal treatment of the pianist's gorgeous 'Time And Time Again' are the highlights. *Personal Choice* is another catholic programme, with tunes by Jobim, Brubeck and Pettiford, but a surprisingly tough 'I'm Old-Fashioned' and a reflective solo 'Melancholy Mood' turn out the best. If the solo set is a shade behind the others, it's only because McPartland uses the resources of a trio so intelligently that she seems relatively quiescent by herself.

While her treatments of the likes of 'Someday I'll Find You' are typically original, it would be agreeable to hear her tackle an entire set of her own compositions.

***   **Plays The Music Of Billy Strayhorn** Concord CCD 4326 CD/MC
McPartland; Jerry Dodgion (*as*); Steve LaSpina (*b*); Joey Baron (*d*). 3/87.

***(*)   **Plays The Benny Carter Songbook** Concord CCD 4412 CD/MC
McPartland; Benny Carter (*as*); John Clayton (*b*); Harold Jones (*d*). 1/90.

Two fine excursions into repertory by McPartland. Strayhorn's suave impressionism is hard to evoke, let alone sustain for an entire album, but this is at least as successful as any similar homage. Despite a couple of less successful entries – 'A Flower Is A Lovesome Thing', for instance, is a little too doleful – the quartet have the measure of this deceptive music. There is a witty, unpredictable revision of 'Take The "A" Train', a springy 'Intimacy Of The Blues' and a purposefully crafted 'Lush Life' by the trio without Dodgion. The meeting with Carter, who plays on six of the eleven tunes chosen from his book, is flawlessly paced. Though his technique is still astonishing for a man in his eighties, Carter's sound and delivery are rather old-world compared to McPartland's astute command. Trio versions of 'When Lights Are Low', the beautiful 'Key Largo' and 'Summer Serenade' are probably the most distinguished moments on the record. Both sessions are recorded excellently.

***(*)   **Live At Maybeck Recital Hall Vol. 9** Concord CCD 4460 CD/MC
   McPartland (*p* solo). 1/91.

Her latest solo recital finds the pianist in characteristically adventurous mood. The composers represented here include Alec Wilder, Ornette Coleman, Mercer Ellington and Dave Brubeck; there are her latest reflections on the tune she startled Ellington himself with, 'Clothed Woman', and one of the most affecting of her own themes, 'Twilight World'. Each interpretation contains nothing unnecessary in the way of embellishment, yet they all seem ideally paced, properly finished. She makes it sound very easy. Ripe, in-concert recording, typical of this series from Concord.

JOE McPHEE (born 1939)
TENOR SAXOPHONE, POCKET-CORNET, FLUGELHORN, ELECTRONICS

***(*)   **Old Eyes & Mysteries** hat Art 6047 CD
   McPhee; Urs Leimgruber (*ss, ts*); André Jaume (*bcl, ts*); Jean-Charles Capon (*clo*); Raymond Boni, Steve Gnitka (*g*); Pierre-Yves Sorin (*b*); Milo Fine (*p, d*); Fritz Hauser (*d, perc*). 5/79.

***   **Topology** hat Art 6027 CD
   McPhee; Radu Malfatti (*tbn, elec*); Irene Schweizer (*p*); André Jaume (*as, bcl*); Daniel Bourquin (*as, bs*); François Mechali (*b*); Michael Overhage (*clo*); Raymond Boni (*g*); Pierre Favre (*perc*); Tamia (*v*). 3/81.

****   **Linear B** hat Art 6057 CD
   McPhee; André Jaume, Urs Leimgruber (*ss, ts*); Raymond Boni, Christy Doran (*g*); Léon Francioli (*b*); Fritz Hauser (*perc*). 1/90.

Time has softened some of the anger in McPhee's playing. He is, nonetheless, one of the most consistently impressive and adventurous composer/instrumentalists in the music. He bridges 'straight', thematic improvisation and total freedom, acoustic and electronic sound-sources in a way that is reminiscent of fellow-radicals George Lewis and Anthony Braxton (who are also, of course, like-minded traditionalists when the spirit moves them).

Over the past decade, McPhee has been involved with the creation of a large-scale cycle of works: *Topology*, *Linear B* and the latter's companion piece *Old Eyes & Mysteries*, with which it shares a liner-note. McPhee's aesthetic is based on the notion of 'provocation' as a source of improvisational cues, but it's interesting that its most common metaphoric underpinning relates to codes, mysteries, secrets, hidden languages (Linear B is an ancient Minoan language, which proved as tough to crack as the Second World War Enigma code). Listening to the music on all three albums is a little like encountering a private language, initially off-putting, but increasingly logical and self-consistent as time passes until it forms an entire, self-sufficient system that lacks for nothing but some point of reference outside of itself.

Perhaps the most confusing aspect of McPhee's work has been his willingness to combine total improvisation with 'standards' and progressive jazz repertoire. *Topology* is a surprisingly 'cool' confrontation with some impressive European modern/free players. The take of Charles Mingus's 'Pithecanthropus Erectus' develops the more abstract features of Mingus's original conception in ways that anticipate McPhee's own 'Topology', a two-part performance that sees Malfatti switch from trombone to a computer, another sign of the way McPhee is always looking for new musical codes that go beyond 'instrumentalism'. 'Blues for New Chicago' is more straightforward, but is still a challenging variation on traditional values.

Linear B is less dense and much more theatrical in direction, a token of the way McPhee's work as a whole has been developing during the 1980s. The 13 tracks are taken from a total of nearly 60 recorded over a three-day session. The record centres on a long performance of Wayne Shorter's 'Footprints', played with considerable lyricism, as is 'Here's That Rainy Day', which is dedicated to the late Chet Baker. The music here and on *Eyes/Mysteries* is credited to Po Music, not as in 'po' white', but as in the popular psychologist Edward De Bono's hypothesis of a realm of thought 'beyond yes and no' and predicated on the *po*ssible, the *po*sitive, the *po*etic and the hy*po*thetical. McPhee's 'compositions' are thus no more than poetic hypotheses, blueprints of what the players might possibly play, but in no way restrictively so. The result is a kind of orderly freedom which is perhaps best heard in the series of 'Little Pieces', duos with percussionist Hauser, which follow 'Footprints' and serve as a kind of mid-point primer or résumé.

McPhee is a major figure and hat Art (who are also responsible for recording maverick traditionalists like Franz Koglmann) have performed a valuable service in documenting one of the most intriguing extended improvisations of recent times.

CHARLES McPHERSON (born 1939)
ALTO SAXOPHONE

***   **Be Bop Revisited** Original Jazz Classics OJC 710 CD
McPherson; Carmell Jones (*t*); Barry Harris (*p*); Nelson Boyd (*b*); Tootie Heath (*d*).

(*)   **Siku Ya Bibi Mainstream MDCD 713 CD
McPherson; Lonnie Hillyer (*t*); Nico Bunink, Barry Harris (*p*); Gene Bertoncini, Earl Dunbar, Carl Lynch (*g*); Ron Carter, Sam Jones (*b*); Leroy Williams (*d*); strings. 71, 72.

****   **Beautiful!** Xanadu 115 LP
McPherson; Duke Jordan (*p*); Sam Jones (*b*); Leroy Williams (*d*). 8/75.

McPherson credits the relatively unsung Barry Harris, present on the first two albums above, for his schooling in bebop, but it's clear that Parker has marked his saxophone playing so deeply that he will always be identified as a faithful disciple. The straightforward bop covers on *Revisited* have an energy and clarity of tone that is completely missing from the later, overproduced sessions now reissued on Mainstream. The strings overpower already rather tottery arrangements, but there's a certain logic to the sound in what is intended as a tribute to Billie Holiday and McPherson's elastic phrasing and singing tone are still appealing. Only one track from 1972, an indifferent 'My Funny Valentine' that overdoes the electric guitars. Jones and (fellow Mingus graduate) Hillyer, who is miscredited as 'Hilliard' on the sleeve both play well, but the real focus of the music in both cases is Harris's patient boppish comping.

McPherson opens the fine Xanadu session with a Latin arrangement of Irvin Berlin's 'They Say It's Wonderful', followed by two Van Heusen–Burke tunes that suggest there is also a Johnny Hodges influence at work. 'It Could Happen To You' is tastefully and imaginatively done, opening out of tempo and and sticking closely to the rather complex original melody. 'Lover' is played very much faster than usual, but with references to Bird sewn into the bridge section. 'Body And Soul' is a magisterial performance, pretty much handed over to McPherson. No CD, but that shouldn't put anyone off this fine album.

CARMEN McRAE (born 1922)
VOCAL

***(*)   **Here To Stay** MCA GRP 16102 CD/MC
McRae; Jimmy Maxwell, Richard Williams, Al Stewart, Lennie Johnson, Ernie Royal (*t*); Jimmy Cleveland, Bill Byers, Mickey Gravine (*tb*); Paul Faulise (*btb*); Phil Woods, Vinnie Dean, Porter Kilbert (*as*); Zoot Sims, Budd Johnson (*ts*); Sol Schlinger (*bs*); Herbie Mann (*f*); Dick Katz, Billy Strayhorn (*p*); Ma Mathews (*acc*); Mundell Lowe (*g*); Wendell Marshall, Tommy Williams (*b*); Kenny Clarke, Floyd Williams (*d*). 6/55–11/59.

***   **The Ultimate Carmen McRae** Mainstream MDCD 705 CD
McRae, with orchestra conducted by Peter Matz or Don Sebesky. 64–72.

***   **Woman Talk** Mainstream MDCD 706 CD
As above. 64–72.

An accomplished pianist, Carmen McRae was something of a late starter as a featured vocalist, not recording a vocal session under her own name until 1954. Her fame has always lagged behind that of her close contemporaries Sarah Vaughan and Billie Holiday, but in her senior years she has finally achieved something like the honour she deserves, and her commitment to jazz singing has been unflinching. Thus far, her early work has been unjustly ignored by CD reissues: until recently, virtually nothing was available from her Decca period of the 1950s, which means that great records like *Torchy* or *Carmen For Cool Ones* must languish as collectors' items. But *Here To Stay* at least brings back two albums, *Something To Swing About* and *By Special Request* to the catalogue. One is a small group session, the other is with a big band and charts by Ernie Wilkins, but both display McRae's muscular phrasing, aggressive timbre and impeccable timing to high effect. There's always a tigerish feel to her best vocals – no woman has ever sung in the jazz idiom with quite such beguiling surliness as McRae – and on, say, 'Just One Of Those Things' she gets closer to the tough spirit implied by the lyrics than anyone ever has. The remastering is very good.

The 1960s, too, are under-represented, but at least these two compilations collect the best of several sessions for Mainstream, including two dates from 1964–5, both of which reveal more about McRae. Her scrupulous musicianship makes her the least obviously demonstrative of jazz singers, yet she alters melody lines as often as Vaughan, toys with rhythm as assuredly as Torme and still manages to deceive an uncommitted listener into thinking they're hearing the song just as it was written. While equally comfortable with big orchestras or small groups, she handles different settings with different inflections: here, with 40-piece orchestras behind her, she takes it easy, yet opens out her voice on big lines and seems to soak up the lyrics. *The Ultimate* is marginally superior for a few memorable pieces – a slow, almost indolent 'Sweet Georgia Brown' and a perfectly controlled 'Who Can I Turn To?' among them. The arrangements are merely functional, but McRae has the measure of them. Capable CD remastering.

**(*) Velvet Soul LRC CDC 7970 CD
McRae; Zoot Sims (*ts*); Dick Shreve, Tom Garvin (*p*); Larry Bunker (*vib, perc*); Bucky Pizzarelli, Joe Pass (*g*); Ray Brown, Paul West (*b*); Jimmy Madison, Frank Severino (*d*). 72–73.

McRae is in good voice on this useful collection of 19 tracks, running at a generous 73 minutes, although the material is a mixed batch of strong standards and glossy pop fillers. The documentation is also suspect: an unannounced orchestra turns up on four tracks, and 'All The Things You Are' is mysteriously credited to Oscar Hammerstein and Gene Lees! Zoot Sims contributes some reliably enthusiastic playing to a few tracks from the 1973 session.

** Heat Wave Concord CCD 4189 CD/MC
McRae; Al Bent, Mike Heathman (*tb*); Mark Levine, Marshall Otwell (*p*); Cal Tjader (*vib*); Rob Fisher (*b*); Vince Lateanoi (*d*); Poncho Sanchez, Ramon Banda (*perc*). 1/82.

*** You're Lookin' At Me Concord CCD 4235 CD/MC
McRae; Marshall Otwell (*p*); John Collins (*g*); John Leftwich (*b*); Donald Bailey (*d*). 11/83.

**(*) Fine And Mellow Concord CCD 4342 CD/MC
McRae; Red Holloway (*ts*); Phil Upchurch (*g*); Jack McDuff (*org*); John Clayton Jr (*b*); Paul Humphrey (*d*). 12/87.

While none of her records for Concord is outstanding, these three albums have enough good McRae to make them all worth hearing. The session with Tjader is blemished by the vibesman's usual flavourless Latin-jazz stylings, which offer no backbone to the singer's efforts, and the Stevie Wonder tunes on the record scarcely suit a vocal personality which has a pronounced streak of cussedness when she warms up. Yet *Fine And Mellow* goes to the other extreme without much more conviction: McRae is too sophisticated a stylist to convince as an earthy R&B singer, which this programme and these accompanists are tailored for. The other record is a tribute to Nat Cole, and while she doesn't sound very taken with the likes of 'I'm An Errand Girl For Rhythm', the ballads and the more subtle lyrics garner her full attention, with a cool, attentive rhythm section in support.

***(*) Any Old Time Denon 33CY-1216 CD
McRae; Clifford Jordan (*ts*); Eric Gunnison (*p*); John Collins (*g*); Scott Colley (*b*); Mark Pulice (*d*). 6/86.

As her voice has grown heavier, Ms McRae has hung back on the beat more often, but in at least two instances here – 'Tulip Or Turnip', an Ellington rarity hardly ever done by a singer, and 'I Hear Music' – one can hear how fast tempos can be handled by a singer who wants to take her time: it's a masterful display. This is probably the best of her latter-day sessions, with a tuned-in rhythm section, two excellent soloists in Collins and Jordan (both sparingly used), impeccable programming and sympathetic production. 'Love Me Tender' and 'This Is Always' are slow and graceful yet expunged of mush, while 'Prelude To A Kiss' embodies the idea of a musician spontaneously recasting a song she's probably sung throughout her whole career.

***   **Carmen Sings Monk** RCA Novus 83086 CD/MC
McRae; Clifford Jordan (*ss, ts*); Charlie Rouse (*ts*); Eric Gunnison, Larry Willis (*p*); George Mraz (*b*); Al Foster (*d*). 1–4/88.

***(*)   **Sarah – Dedicated To You** RCA Novus 90546 CD/MC
McRae; Shirley Horn (*p*); Charles Ables (*b*); Steve Williams (*d*). 10/90.

The singer worked very hard on the Monk collection, perhaps too much so, for some of the life seems to have been smothered out of it. While the familiar 'Round Midnight' sits up straight, too many of the other tracks suffer from the awkwardness of the lyric fitting into Monk's music, and with her own voice less limber than it once was, McRae makes heavy weather of some of them. But the two different quartets involved play well (Rouse on what was almost his farewell appearance), and a sense of commitment shines through.

The tribute to Sarah Vaughan, though, is better. It's far more about McRae herself than it is about Vaughan. In what might be a valedictory record, she muses through 'I've Got The World On A String' and 'Poor Butterfly' with a strikingly improvised air, and her 'Send In The Clowns' is as personal as any reading without betraying any of the gushing sentiment which the song is wont to bring out in most interpreters. The voice is frayed but resolutely defiant: no *Lady In Satin* nonsense here. And Horn's accompaniments are perfectly sympathetic.

JAY McSHANN (born 1916)
PIANO, VOCAL, BANDLEADER

**   **Roll 'Em** Black & Blue 233022 CD
McShann; Candy Johnson (*ts*); Claude Williams (*g, v*); T-Bone Walker (*g*); Roland Lobligeois, Gene Ramey (*b*); Paul Gunther, Gus Johnson (*d*). 3/69–3/77.

(*)   **Kansas City Memories Black & Blue 590572 CD
McShann; Arnett Cobb (*ts*); Milt Buckner (*org*); Al Casey, Clarence Gatemouth Brown (*g*); Roland Lobligeois (*b*); Paul Gunther (*d*). 11/70–7/73.

McShann's orchestral recordings of the 1930s and '40s – where Charlie Parker made his debut in the studios – are currently difficult to find on dedicated compilations. He has worked and recorded prodigiously enough in recent years, however, to have finally overcome a mere notoriety as the man who gave Bird his start. These reissues are rather slight, jam sessionish stuff, and although a meeting of McShann, Cobb and Buckner could hardly fail to create a few sparks, the material offers only slim pickings from a scattering of sessions. Better is to come.

**   **Best Of Friends** JSP CD 224 CD
McShann; Al Casey (*g*); Kenny Baldock (*b*); Robin Jones (*d*). 4/82.

***   **Swingmatism** Sackville 2-3046 CD
McShann; Don Thompson (*b*); Archie Alleyne (*d*). 10/82.

(*)   **Airmail Special Sackville 2-3040 CD
McShann; Neil Swainson (*b*); Terry Clarke (*d*). 8/85.

***   **At Café Des Copains** Sackville 2-2024 CD
McShann (*p* solo). 8/83–9/89.

McShann has recorded many albums for Sackville and they are starting to reappear on CD. At his best, he blends a wide variety of mannerisms into a personal kind of swing-stride-blues piano; at anything less than that, he can sound like a less than profound and overly eclectic performer. Most of these records feature moments where he's caught between both positions. The meeting with Al Casey is jolly, unprepossessing stuff, both men jogging along to no great end except to have a bit of fun. *Swingmatism* is rather better: focused by a decent rhythm section, McShann sets his mind to a programme that depends heavily on Ellington for source material, and 'The Jeep is Jumpin'' and 'The Mooche' are good accounts of less frequently heard tunes. *Airmail Special* is alright, if a bit uneventful, but the best disc is probably the solo set. McShann thinks through a wide spectrum of material – going as far back as Fredie Grofe's 'On the Trail' and ending up with Michel LeGrand – and the good piano and live atmosphere elicit a sound series of interpretations, recorded over several visits over a period of six years.

MIKE MELILLO (born 1939)
PIANO

(*)   **Sepia Red VPA 170 LP
Melillo (*p* solo). 3/84.

(*)   **Live And Well Red VPA 188 LP
Melillo (*p* solo). 3/85.

***(*)   **Alternate Choices** Red NS 211 LP
Melillo; Massimo Moriconi (*b*); Giampaolo Ascolese (*d*). 87.

Melillo has lived and worked in Italy for a decade, but before that he played gigs in New Jersey and eventually ended up in the Phil Woods Quartet. These albums for Red display a crisp, bop-orientated attack which – despite a dedication to Charles Ives on *Sepia* and a few dreamier themes here and there on the two solo records – is pointed and mostly free of rhetoric. That said, the trio album is certainly the most interesting, dedicated (aside from Melillo's title-track) entirely to Bud Powell compositions. After all the salutes to Thelonious Monk, this one's a refreshing change: the outstanding piece is a remarkable revision of 'Bouncing With Bud', which includes an unexpected fantasy on the introduction and an equally surprising gentle pace for the theme itself. But Melillo honours Powell throughout with incisive and commanding variations on the material, while bass and drums keep excellent time. It's only a pity that the studio sound is a little hard and clattery.

GIL MELLE
BARITONE SAXOPHONE, KEYBOARDS

***(*)   **Primitive Modern** OJC 1712 LP
Melle; Joe Cinderella (*g*); Bill Phipps (*b*); Ed Thigpen (*d*). 4–6/56.

****   **Gil's Guests** OJC 1753 LP
Melle; Art Farmer, Kenny Dorham (*t*); Hal McKusick (*as, f*); Julius Watkins (*frhn*); Don Butterfield (*tba*); Joe Cinderella (*g*); Vinnie Burke (*b*); Ed Thigpen (*d*). 8/56.

Melle's original sleevenote for *Primitive Modern* suggests that 'modern jazz at its best is a wedding of the classics with the more modern developments native to jazz', and while that implies third-stream dogma, at least Melle put the notion to very striking use. Anyone who lists Bartók, Varèse and Herbie Nichols as major influences is going to do something more than hard bop, and the leader's attempts at shifting the parameters of standard jazz form remain surprising and invigorating. The fast-moving complexities of 'Ironworks', the mysterious dirge 'Dominica' and the Russell-like 'Adventure Swing' mark out a path very different from most other developments of the time. Cinderella reveals himself as a fine soloist and perceptive interpreter of Melle's needs, and the rhythm section are also fine; while Melle himself is content to play an often reserved role, although his improvisations are melodically as strong as those of Lars Gullin, the baritone player he admits to admiring most. There are a couple of drawbacks – the original studio sound is rather flat, with the leader a little remote in the mix, and some of the structures are delivered a little stiffly by the quartet – but otherwise this is a significant and far too little-known record.

If anything, *Gil's Guests* is even better, thanks to Rudy Van Gelder's superior engineering and the opportunities which a bigger ensemble permits for Melle to create heightened colours, more vivid texture and counterpoint, and a smoother transition between his classically inspired ideas and a jazz execution. Even a conventional feature such as 'Sixpence', written for Kenny Dorham, has an ingenious arrangement for tuba and guitar at the beginning. 'Ghengis' is a direct borrowing from Bartók, and the shifting voicings of 'Block Island' merge brilliantly into a theme that works just as well as a blowing vehicle. An outstanding record, well remastered, although we must hope that both the above sessions – as well as the currently unavailable *Quadrama* – will be made available on CD in due course.

MISHA MENGELBERG (born 1935)
PIANO, COMPOSER

***   **Einepartietschtennis** FMP SAJ 03 LP
       Mengelberg; Han Bennink (*d, perc, v*). 5/74.

***(*) **Change of Season** Soul Note SN 1104 CD/LP
       Mengelberg; George Lewis (*tb*); Steve Lacy (*ss*); Arjen Gorter (*b*); Han Bennink (*d*).
       7/84.

****   **Impromptus** FMP 7 CD
       Mengelberg (*p* solo). 6/88.

Robert Frost once characterized free verse as 'playing tennis with the net down'. Improvisers like Dutchmen Mengelberg and Bennink have been very largely concerned with putting the net back, sometimes up to badminton height, searching for ways of combining the freedoms of improvisation with traditional jazz and even more formal structures.

Mengelberg is also a 'legitimate' composer, albeit one in the Louis Andriessen mould, with a very strong jazz influence in his work. The collectivism that was so strong a component of the Dutch 1960s avant-garde is evident in the autonomy granted to the performers (all of them expert players) on *Change Of Season*. Lewis seems most comfortable in the mixed idiom, though Lacy (a purist's purist) sounds a little glacial. As on the earlier FMP set, Bennink whips up little rhythmic storms, but he plays with unwonted reserve and an often unrecognized sensitivity.

He's less restrained on the fine *Einepartietschtennis*, swatting ideas about, dropping back-handed references into Mengelberg's court. Throughout both sets Mengelberg plays with great assurance and a graceful disposition of apparently self-contained and discontinuous ideas that is more reminiscent of the Swiss Irene Schweizer than of his compatriots, Fred Van Hove and Leo Cuypers. Interesting, if for no other reason, that there are other directions for 'free' piano than the one taken and dominated by Cecil Taylor.

Impromptus makes a generic nod to a (minor) classical form. The 13 individual pieces aren't obviously linked by theme or as variations, but they follow a barely discernible logic that can be picked up via Mengelberg's untutored vocalise, which is of the Bud Powell/Keith Jarrett/Cecil Taylor persuasion.

HELEN MERRILL (born 1930)
VOCAL

***(*) **Jazz 'Round Midnight: Helen Merrill** Verve 846011-2 CD
       Merrill; Clifford Brown (*t*); Jimmy Cleveland, Joe Bennett (*tb*); John LaPorta, Jerome
       Richardson, Danny Bank (*reeds*); Dick Marx, Hank Jones, John Lewis, Marian
       McPartland, Jimmy Jones (*p*); Freddy Rundquist, Barry Galbraith, Bill Mure (*g*);
       John Frigo, Oscar Pettiford, Al Hall, Milt Hinton (*b*); Joe Morello, Sol Gubin, Osie
       Johnson, Bobby Donaldson, Johnny Cresci, Jery Slosberg (*d*). 12/54–5/76.

The kind of singer who makes strong men and intellectuals go weak at the knees – and any doubts about that should be dispelled by the sleeve-notes to either this compilation of her records for Mercury or Piero Umiliani's notes on the Liuto disc listed below. Merrill sings at a consistently slow pace, unfolding melodies as if imparting a particularly difficult confidence, and she understands the harmonies of the songs as completely as she trusts her way with time. That gives these lingering performances a sensuality which is less of a come-hither come-on than the similarly inclined work of a singer such as Julie London. Merrill thinks about the words, but she improvises on the music too. This is a fine cross-section of her work for Mercury, all of it – bar a 1976 pairing with John Lewis, for a particularly haunted 'Angel Eyes' – dating from the 1950s. But it's a pity that the individual albums are currently out of print.

***(*) **Helen Merrill In Italy** Liuto LRS 0063/5 CD
Merrill; Nino Culasso, Nino Rosso (*t*); Dino Piana (*tb*); Gianni Basso (*ts*); Gino
Marinacci (*f*); Piero Umiliani, Renato Sellani (*p*); Enzo Grillini (*g*); Berto Pisano,
Giorgio Azzolini (*b*); Sergio Conti, Ralph Ferraro, Franco Tonani (*d*); strings. 59–62.

This is flawed by the sometimes unlovely sound, but it's an otherwise compelling collection of
all the pieces Merrill recorded on various trips to Italy. Three songs by Umiliani for film scores
have lyrics by the singer, and those for 'My Only Man' and 'Dreaming Of The Past' are
original and hard to forget. Most of the others are standards, again treated to the most rarefied
of ballad settings – 'The More I See You' is almost impossibly slow – but the four closing
tracks, sung in Italian with an orchestra conducted by Ennio Morricone, have a *Lieder*-like
quality that's disarmingly direct.

***   **No Tears . . . No Goodbyes** Owl 038 CD/LP
Merrill; Gordon Beck (*ky*). 11/84.

***(*) **Music Makers** Owl 044 CD/LP
Merrill; Steve Lacy (*ss*); Gordon Beck (*ky*); Stéphane Grappelli (*vn*). 3/86.

Meditations on the song form have assumed centre-stage in Merrill's exceptional recent work.
These aren't entirely satisfying records since the approach is at times a little too studied: on *No
Tears* . . . the selection of, say, 'The Thrill Is Gone' is too calculated a shot at isolating the
singer in a lonely world, and the better pieces – 'When I Look In Your Eyes' or 'Bye Bye
Blackbird' – are those which purvey a more spirited demeanour. Beck's piano parts, deftly
embellished here and there by electronics, are fetchingly done, though at times there seems to
be little genuine movement between him and the vocalist. *Music Makers* features Lacy in the
first half and Grappelli in the second, and the odd mix of personalities doesn't always work: if
Merrill can seem inexplicable in her handling of a lyric, unstitching the line with strange
deliberation, Lacy especially seems to be communing with himself, although piecemeal
music-making is very much his *forte*. The second half, with Grappelli, is much more engaging,
with the violinist pouring on the Gallic charm in 'As Time Goes By' and playing a very
sprightly duet with Beck on 'A Gal In Calico'.

***   **Collaboration** EmArcy 834205-2 CD
Merrill; Shunzo Ono (*t, flhn*); Lew Soloff (*t*); Jimmy Knepper (*tb*); Dave Taylor (*btb*);
Chris Hunter (*ss, as, f, cl, ob, picc*); Jerry Dodgion (*ss, f*); Steve Lacy (*ss*); Danny Bank
(*bs, f, bcl*); Phil Bodner (*bcl, f, af*); Wally Kane (*bcl, bsn*); Roger Rosenberg (*bcl*); Gil
Goldstein (*ky*); Harry Lookofsky, Lamar Alsop (*vn*); Theodore Israel, Harold
Colletta (*vla*); Jesse Levy (*clo*); Joe Beck, Jay Berliner (*g*); Buster Williams (*b*); Mel
Lewis (*d*); Gil Evans (*cond*). 8/87.

One of the strangest singer-and-orchestra records ever made. Merrill's voice has grown
weightier over the years, and she casts it very slowly on the waters of Gil Evans's arrangements
here, the charts laying down thick, barely moving textures which suggest a mildewing
romanticism. Her favourite slow tempos recur throughout, and it's Evans's often magical way
with three different ensembles (one with strings, one with trombone and woodwinds, another
led by brass) which stop the music from trudging to a stop. Lacy appears for a tart commentary
on two tracks, but otherwise it's the long, carefully held tones of the vocalist which act on the
music. Sometimes, as in an arrangement of 'Summertime' which harks back directly to *Porgy
And Bess*, Evans seems to be reminiscing on his own past, too.

PAT METHENY (born 1954)
GUITAR

***   **Bright Size Life** ECM 1073 CD/LP
Metheny; Jaco Pastorius (*b*); Bob Moses (*d*). 12/75.

***   **Watercolours** ECM 1097 CD/LP
Metheny; Lyle Mays (*p*); Eberhard Weber (*b*); Danny Gottlieb (*d*). 2/77.

**   **Pat Metheny Group** ECM 1114 CD/LP
As above, except Mark Egan (*b*) replaces Weber. 1/78.

(*) **New Chautauqua ECM 1131 CD/LP
Metheny (*g* solo). 8/78.

(*) **American Garage ECM 1155 CD/LP
Metheny; Lyle Mays (*ky*); Mark Egan (*b*); Danny Gottlieb (*d*). 6/79.

Metheny emerged as a cool, limpid-toned guitarist at just the moment when the world seemed to want such a player. His first two ECM albums are a little untypical – each depends more on its respective star bassist to give it some clout – but, like the ones that follow, they are pleasant, hummable records with a degree of fine playing which the high-grade production values and sometimes over-sensitive musicianship can occasionally block out with sheer amiability. At this time Metheny favoured a clean open tone with just enough electronic damping to take the music out of 'classic' jazz-guitar feeling, but he clearly owed a great debt to such urban pastoralists as Jim Hall and Jimmy Raney, even if he seldom moved back to bebop licks.

The Metheny Group albums settled the guitarist's music into the niche which he still works from: light, easily digested settings that let him play long, noodling solos which can as often as not work up a surprising intensity. His companions, Mays especially, can seem like much-too-nice influences on a player whose inclinations (as in the album with Ornette Coleman) may be far more interesting than most of his records allow.

*** **80/81** ECM 1180/1 2CD/2LP/2MC
Metheny; Dewey Redman, Michael Brecker (*ts*); Charlie Haden (*b*); Jack DeJohnette (*d*). 5/80.

At the time this sounded like an almost shocking departure, but Brecker and Redman adapt themselves to Metheny's aesthetic without undue compromise and Haden and DeJohnete play with great purpose. There's too much music here and many dreary spots, but some excellent moments too.

(*) **As Falls Witchita, So Falls Witchita Falls ECM 1190 CD/LP
Metheny; Lyle Mays (*ky*); Nana Vasconcelos (*perc*). 9/80.

** **Offramp** ECM 1216 CD/LP
As above, except add Steve Rodby (*b*), Danny Gottlieb (*d*). 10/81.

*** **Travels** ECM 1252/3 2CD/2LP
As above. 7–11/82.

The Metheny band rolled on. The two studio albums suggested a drying up of ideas, and though the impish Vasconcelos added a little extra gumption to it all, Mays's relentlessly uninteresting parts continued to be a source of aggravation. *Travels*, though, summed up the band's tenure with ECM with a studious and densely packed live set that will do for those who want a single set from the period.

***(*) **Rejoicing** ECM 1271 CD/LP
Metheny; Charlie Haden (*b*); Billy Higgins (*d*). 11/83.

It might seem conservative to pull out such a traditional record as Metheny's best up to this point, but he finds a loneliness in Horace Silver's 'Lonely Woman' and a happiness in Ornette Coleman's 'Rejoicing' which more severe interpreters of those composers don't seem to have time or room for. By itself the playing isn't so remarkable, but pairing him with Haden and Higgins, on a programme of mostly Coleman and Metheny originals, sheds new lustre on both himself and on music that's often somewhat neglected.

** **First Circle** ECM 1278 CD/LP
Metheny; Lyle Mays (*ky*); Steve Rodby (*b*); Paul Wertico (*d*); Pedro Aznar (*perc, v*). 2/84.

*** **Works** ECM 823270-2 CD

The last ECM album is nothing much: a retread of paths already foot-hollowed enough; the collection is a decent introduction.

**** **Song X** Geffen 924096 CD/MC
Metheny; Ornette Coleman (*as, vn*); Charlie Haden (*b*); Jack DeJohnette, Denardo Coleman (*d*). 12/85.

About the only problems with this record are DeJohnette – a great drummer, but not the right one for Ornette Coleman – and the sense that some of the best and most extreme material was left off the record (which Metheny has subsequently confirmed). Otherwise it's the most astonishing move ever made by any musician perceived as a middle-of-the-road jazz artist. Not only does the guitarist power his way through Coleman's itinerary with utter conviction, he sets up opportunities for the saxophonist to resolve and creates a fusion which Coleman's often impenetrable Prime Time bands have failed to come to terms with. Melody still has a place here, which suggests that Metheny's interest in the original Coleman legacy may be carrying forward in his own work more intently than it is in the composer's. Either way, on many of the more raving episodes here, both men sound exultant with the possibilities. Highly recommended.

***   **Question And Answer** Geffen 24293 CD/MC
Metheny; Dave Holland (*b*); Roy Haynes (*d*). 12/89.

Metheny's subsequent albums for Geffen have taken on something of a light-rock feel which leaves them largely outside our jurisdiction, but this session – which seems to be the kind of periodic vacation which Metheny takes from his regular band, and may it continue – finds the guitarist, bassist and especially the drummer playing with great brio and suppleness. The tunes are another mix of standards, Coleman and Metheny tunes; and if some of the charm of the ECM trio date is missing, and a few tunes seem to end up nowhere, it's well worth hearing.

MEZZ MEZZROW (1899–1972)
CLARINET, SAXOPHONES

***   **The King Jazz Story: Volume 1 – Out Of The Gallion** Storyville SLP 6004 LP

***   **The King Jazz Story: Volume 2 – Really The Blues** Storyville SLP 6005 LP

****   **The King Jazz Story: Volume 3 – Gone Away Blues** Storyville SLP 6006 LP

***(*)   **The King Jazz Story: Volume 4 – Revolutionary Blues** Storyville SLP 6007 LP

***(*)   **The King Jazz Story: Volume 5 – I'm Speaking My Mind** Storyville SLP 4115 LP

***(*)   **The King Jazz Story: Volume 6** Storyville SLP 226 LP

***(*)   **The King Jazz Story: Volumes 7 & 8** Storyville SLP 820/1 2LP

***   **Masters Of Jazz: Sidney Bechet** Storyville SLP 4104 LP
Mezzrow; Sidney Bechet (*ss*); Hot Lips Page (*t, v*); Sammy Price, Fitz Weston, Sox Wilson (*p*); Danny Barker (*g*); Wellman Braud, Pops Foster (*b*); Sid Catlett, Baby Dodds, Kaiser Marshall (*d*); Douglas Daniels, Coot Grant, Pleasant Joe (*v*); other personnel unidentified. 7 & 8/45, 9/46, 12/47.

***(*)   **Mezz Mezzrow In Paris, 1955** Jazz Time 252 712 CD
Mezzrow; Peanuts Holland, Guy Longnon (*t*); Maxim Saury (*cl*); Milton Sealey (*p*); Eddie De Haas (*b*); Kansas Fields (*d*). 5 & 7/55.

Nobody came closer to living the life of Norman Mailer's 'White Negro' than Milton 'Mezz' Mezzrow. Eddie Condon nicknamed him 'Southmouth' in ironic recognition of his obsessive self-identification with Black musicians and self-consciously disenchanted and unironic pursuit of a 'negro' lifestyle. (He claims to have insisted being put in the black cells of a segregated police block, on the grounds that he was only 'passing for white').

His nickname also carries an echo of Louis Armstrong's soubriquet 'Satchelmouth'. Mezzrow idolized the trumpeter and once worked for him as factotum and grass distributor (this was a *long* time before 'Hello, Dolly' and 'Wonderful World'). His music was considerably more 'authentic' than his personal manners: sinuous lines, a dry, slightly sharp tone (compare George Lewis's) and a flow of ideas which, if not endless, were always imaginatively permed and varied. The pre-war *Panassié Sessions* [RCA] made with Bechet and Tommy Ladnier are sadly no longer available, but the immediate post-war material from the King Jazz label is very nearly as good.

The Storyville series brings together all the material made for the original label, including alternate takes for a good many items. In a leaflet about the recordings prepared by Storyville, Mezzrow is quoted as saying that much of the material was improvised spontaneously and there are many good solos worked out over backgrounds that are either hesitant or completely awry. There is, though, a considerable emphasis on collective improvisation, as on two 1945 versions of 'Revolutionary Blues' (confusingly on Volume 2; compare the later versions on Volume 3), on which the whole group plays throughout, with no conventional soloing. 'Blood On The Moon' from Volume 1, credited to Mezzrow and Hot Lips Page (who was identified as Papa Snow White for contractual reasons), is one of the most interesting things in the entire sequence, superbly structured and tightly executed. There are also intriguing oddities, like Pops Foster's arco solo on 'Bowin' The Blues'.

The September 1946 sessions for King Jazz, irritatingly misdated by a full year in Storyville's full discography, included one classic Mezzrow solo on 'Breathless Blues', the kind of playing that must have overcome any of Bechet's doubts about the white clarinettist (though Bechet's doubts had a great deal more to do with musical ability than with skin pigment). Musically the sessions were very mixed. The vocal tracks are slight and largely forgettable and there are fluffs and uneasy vamps all over the place, but when the group really fires, as on 'Breathless Blues', the performances are of the highest calibre.

The Bechet compilation consists largely of reorganized material from the series; the band was known as the Mezzrow–Bechet Xtet, depending on numbers, and though Mezzrow largely called the shots musically, it's Bechet who is now (properly) identified as the more significant musician. Classics like 'The Sheikh of Araby', 'Minor Swoon', 'Jelly Roll', 'Revolutionary Blues', 'Perdido Street Stomp' are all included (the middle pair with alternate takes). Musically, it's pure pleasure, but it's important to recognize Mezzrow's contribution and that's best heard on the complete sequence.

The legendary *A La Schola Cantorum* sessions were made in 1955 with a multiracial Franco-American band. Essentially, the May sessions consist of two long takes each of the first (slow) and second (fast) parts of 'Blues Aven Un Pont'. Mezzrow's improvisations on the bridge are as clearly enunciated as any he was to record and the later, July sessions are nowhere near as interesting, despite some exciting solos. If the music appeals, try to take in Mezzrow's ghosted and at least partly fictional 'autobiography' *Really the Blues*. It's an absolute gas.

PALLE MIKKELBORG (born 1941)
TRUMPET, FLUGELHORN, COMPOSER

***(*)   **Heart To Heart** Storyville SLP 4114 LP
    Mikkelborg; Kenneth Knudsen (*ky*); Niels-Henning Ørsted-Pedersen (*b*). 86.

A player of enormous technical capability and lyrical strength, Mikkelborg has always worn his influences on his sleeve. The 1984 composition *Aura* was a harmonically coded dedication to Miles Davis (on which Davis was to play a guest role). Much of Mikkelborg's most important work in the late 1970s and '80s has been for large-scale conventional forces, much like his sometime collaborator, the guitarist-composer Terje Rypdal, but he remains more deeply rooted in jazz than the Norwegian, having served an impressively documented apprenticeship with the exiled Dexter Gordon (Blue Note 746397 CD, Steeplechase SCS 1145 LP).

Mikkelborg is one of the few convincing exponents of electric trumpet which he uses, unlike Don Ellis, to produce great sheets of harmonic colour against which he dabs acoustic notes of surprising purity. *Aura* underlined the Miles influence to the apparent exclusion of any other; but he is perhaps closer in conception to Chet Baker and, even on an impressionistic set like *Heart To Heart*, he can sound astonishingly like both Clifford Brown and Howard McGhee.

The opening track is an unashamed Miles rip-off, though played with a clear, brassy resonance that is Mikkelborg's own. Fortunately, perhaps, it doesn't set a tone for the set, which is quite varied in temper, though mainly in a meditative mood. Knudsen's keyboard structures are always highly effective and NHØP is far better recorded than usual. Recommended.

JOAKIM MILDER
TENOR SAXOPHONE

****   **Life In Life** Dragon DRLP 166 LP
    Milder; Jan Allan (*t*); Steve Dobrogosz (*p*); Christian Spering, Palle Danielsson (*b*);
    Rune Carlsson (*d*). 3/88.

***(*)   **Still In Motion** Dragon DRCD 188 CD
As above, except omit Allan and Danielsson. 9/89.

***(*)   **Consensus** Opus 3 CD 9201 CD
Milder; Johan Hölén (*as*); Anders Persson (*p*); Christian Spering (*b*); Magnus Gran
(*d*). 2/92.

Milder sounds like one of the most adventurous and least conformist of players to emerge from
the Swedish scene in the 1980s. As an improviser, he eschews both easy licks and long, heavily
elaborate lines, preferring a scratchy tone to the open-voiced timbre of most tenor players and
fragmenting his lines with silences, rushes and retards, anything he can think of that varies the
attack. Yet there is Rollins-like logic to some of his melodic paths, and on a standard such as 'It
Could Happen To You' (on *Life In Life*) he keeps the sense of the song to hand even as he
takes it crabbily apart. The first Dragon session is split between quartet, quintet and trio pieces,
and his original themes are as surprising as his treatments of Shorter, Strayhorn and Richard
Rodgers. The all-original *Still In Motion* is a more unified but fractionally less compelling
session, since nothing quite aspires to the interplay with Danielsson and Carlsson on the earlier
set. *Consensus* returns to standards – there are 12 of them here – and again refuses to take any
obvious routes. 'My Funny Valentine', for instance, hints only obliquely at its melody, 'Some
Day My Prince Will Come' gets a notably sour treatment – the tune almost exploded by Gran's
crackling toms – and the use of a second saxophone to counterpoint some of the tenor parts is
always different to what might be expected. Milder's own playing sounds more sewn-up than
before, suggesting that he may be losing some of his interesting rough edges, but this is still a
fine continuation of a very impressive discography.

MULGREW MILLER (born 1955)
PIANO

***   **Keys To The City** Landmark LLP/LCD 1507 CD/LP/MC
Miller; Ira Coleman (*b*); Marvin 'Smitty' Smith (*d*). 6/85.

***   **Work!** Landmark LLP/LCD 1511 CD/LP/MC
Miller; Charnett Moffett (*b*); Terri Lyne Carrington (*d*). 4/86.

***   **Wingspan** Landmark LLP/LCD 1515 CD/LP/MC
Miller; Kenny Garrett (*as*); Steve Nelson (*vib*); Charnett Moffett (*b*); Tony Reedus
(*d*). 87.

***   **The Countdown** Landmark LLP/LCD 1519 LP/MC/CD
Miller; Joe Henderson (*ts*); Ron Carter (*b*); Tony Williams (*d*). 8/88.

***   **From Day To Day** Landmark LLP/LCD 1525 CD/LP/MC
Miller; Robert Leslie Hurst III (*b*); Kenny Washington (*d*). 3/90.

Miller's sonorous touch and pensive improvising lend him great dignity, if not great distinction:
like so many other modern pianists, he is a marvellous executant and an indifferent personality,
at least in the studio. He's a valuable sideman and accompanist, and turns up on countless other
dates, but those under his own leadership achieve a fleeting excellence: a few of his originals,
such as 'The Countdown' or 'Sublimity' (*Work!*), stand out, and the rest are functional settings
for a technique that has enough virtuosity to handle most situations.

His early experience, with Mercer Ellington, Betty Carter and Art Blakey, was comparatively
diverse, but hard bop is Miller's natural métier, and most of this music could as easily stand as
the trio sections of a Blakey record. Smith, Carrington and Washington all support him on
exactly those lines, although Williams, who makes at least as much noise as Blakey would have
done, is in other respects the least like him, and *The Countdown* is certainly the most individual
of these records, with Henderson following his own private path and the trio combusting behind
him. There is little to choose between the others; *Work!*, though, has a particularly pleasing
programme of themes. Orrin Keepnews' production is unobtrusive and faithful to the music.

KENNY MILLIONS – see KESHAVAN MASLAK

MILLS BLUE RHYTHM BAND
GROUP

***   **Blue Rhythm** Hep CD 1008 CD
Wardell Jones, Shelton Hemphill, Ed Anderson (*t*); Harry White, Henry Hicks (*tb*);
Crawford Wethington (*cl, as, bs*); Charlie Holmes (*cl, as*); Ted McCord, Castor
McCord (*cl, ts*); Edgar Hayes (*p*); Benny James (*bj, g*); Hayes Alvis (*bb, b*); Willie
Lynch (*d*); Dick Roberston, Chick Bullock, George Morton (*v*). 1–6/31.

***(*)   **Rhythm Spasm** Hep CD 1015 CD
As above, except add George Washington (*tb*), Gene Mikell (*cl, as*), Joe Garland (*cl,
ts, bs*), O'Neil Spencer (*d*), Billy Banks (*v*). 8/31–8/32.

Although it lacked any solo stars, the Mills Blue Rhythm Band – the name derived from
manager Irving Mills – was a very hot outfit when these records were made, even though it was
originally used by Mills as a substitute band for either Ellington or Calloway. The lack of a
regular front-man and a rag-tag sequence of arrangers prevented the band from ever
establishing a very clear identity of its own, but it still mustered a kind of fighting collectivism
which comes through clearly on its best records. These two chronological CDs tell the first part
of the band's story. Cover versions of Ellington ('Black And Tan Fantasy') and Calloway
('Minnie The Moocher') reveal what the band's purpose was to start with, and the most
interesting thing about the earlier tracks is usually the soloists' role, particularly the impassioned
and badly unvervalued trumpeter, Ed Anderson. But by the time the music on *Rhythm Spasm*
was made, the band was energizing itself in splendid charts such as 'The Growl' and the
overwhelmingly swinging 'White Lightning', which reveals the dynamism of Hayes Alvis and
O'Neil Spencer in the rhythm section. There are some cringingly awful vocals from such experts
as Billy Banks and Chick Bullock, but those used to music of the period will know what to
expect. John R. T. Davies remasters with his usual care and attentiveness to the music.

IRVING MILLS (1884–1985)
VOCAL

***   **Irving Mills And His Hotsy Totsy Gang Vol. 1** Retrieval FJ 122 LP
Mills; Jimmy McPartland, Al Harris, Bill Moore (*c*); Jack Teagarden, Tommy Dorsey,
Glenn Miller (*tb*); Jimmy Dorsey, Benny Goodman, Gil Rodin (*cl, as*); Fud
Livingston (*cl, ts*); Jack Pettis (*Cmel, ts*); Dudley Fosdick (*mel*); Larry Binyon (*ts*);
Vic Breidis (*p, cel*); Al Goering (*p*); Jack Cornell (*acc*); Ed Bergman, Al Beller (*vn*);
Bill Schumann (*clo*); Eddie Lang (*g*); Clay Bryson, Dick Morgan, Perry Botkin (*bj*);
Harry Goodman (*bb, b*); Merrill Kline (*bb*); Ben Pollack, Dillon Ober (*d*); Elisabeth
Welch (*v*). 7/28–5/29.

***   **Irving Mills And His Hotsy Totsy Gang Vol. 2** Retrieval FJ 123 LP
Manny Klein, Phil Napoleon, Bill Moore, Leo McConville (*t*); Miff Mole, Tommy
Dorsey (*tb*); Jimmy Dorsey, Arnold Brilhart (*cl, as*); Pee Wee Russell (*cl, ts*); Larry
Binyon, Babe Russin (*ts*); Hoagy Carmichael (*p, cel, v*); Frank Signorelli (*p*); Jack
Cornell (*acc*); Dick McDonough (*g, bj*); Joe Tarto (*bb*); Chauncey Morehouse, Gene
Krupa (*d*); Bill 'Bojangles' Robinson (*v*). 7/29–1/30.

***   **Irving Mills And His Hotsy Totsy Gang Vol. 3** Retrieval FJ 127 LP
Charlie Teagarden (*t, v*); Manny Klein, Bill Moore, Ruby Weinstein, Ray Lodwig (*t*);
Bix Beiderbecke (*c*); Jack Teagarden (*tb, v*); Tommy Dorsey (*tb*); Benny Goodman,
Gil Rodin, Matty Matlock (*cl, as*); Babe Russin, Larry Binyon (*ts*); Jack Pettis (*Cmel*);
Min Leibrook (*bsx*); Joe Mooney (*p, acc, v*); Hoagy Carmichael, Vic Breidis (*p*); Al
Beller, Ed Bergman, Joe Venuti, Matty Malneck (*vn*); Dick Morgan (*g*); Dick
McDonough (*bj*); Joe Tarto (*bb*); Harry Goodman (*b*); Gene Krupa, Ray Bauduc (*d*);
Dick Robertson, Dan Mooney (*v*). 2/30–5/31.

Irving Mills had little to do with performing on any of the records under his own name. He was best known as a manager and a publisher, heavily involved in the early days of Duke Ellington's career, and lyricist for some of Duke's early hits. He sang occasionally and he turns up as a vocalist on a few tracks on the first record above, but otherwise he was no more than a nominal leader on what were pick-up sessions. Nevertheless, these are unusually literate and well-turned hot dance records, with several players given more room than in many of their session chores. Manny Klein in particular emerges as a forceful and exciting soloist on several tracks on *Volume 2*, especially 'Nobody's Sweetheart' and 'High And Dry'. The outstanding pieces on the first record include an early cover of Ellington's 'Diga Diga Doo' and the fine 'Futuristic Rhythm', with Goodman and Teagarden, and the third record – though it peters out in a dreary 1931 session by a mostly anonymous band – includes both Teagardens on 'St James Infirmary' and 'Farewell Blues' and a session with Beiderbecke, even though he doesn't have much to do. But the second record is the most interesting, largely through Carmichael's role. His arrangements on 'March Of The Hoodlums', 'Stardust' and the splendid 'Manhattan Rag' and 'What Kind A Man Is You' are convincingly integrated and powerful, with the use of a string section as important as the brass and reed charts (unfortunately, Carmichael fell out with Mills after the January 1930 session). As a genre exercise, there's little to complain about with these LPs, and they've been assiduously remastered. Mills's other achievement – to have outlived even Eubie Blake and chalked up 101 years on the planet – was as remarkable as anything else he did.

CHARLES MINGUS (1922–79)
DOUBLE BASS, PIANO, COMPOSER

****   **The Complete Debut Recordings** Debut 12DCD 4402 12CD
    Mingus; Spaulding Givens, Hank Jones, John Mehegan, Phyllis Pinkerton (*p*); George Koutzen, Jackson Wiley (*clo*); Al Levitt, Max Roach (*d*); Bob Benton, George Gordon, George Gordon Jr, Honey Gordon, Richard Gordon, Jackie Paris (*v*);

(*)   **Jazzical Moods Fresh Sound CD 62 CD
    Mingus; Thad Jones (*t*); John LaPorta (*cl, as*); Teo Macero (*ts, bs*); Jackson Wiley (*clo*); Clem De Rosa (*d*). 12/54.

(*)   **Welcome To Jazz: Charles Mingus Koch 321 974 CD
    As above.

***   **Abstractions** Affinity AFF 750 CD
    As above.

Huge, paradoxical and immensely influential, Mingus's true significance has taken a long time to be recognized, though most of his innovations have long since been absorbed by the modern/avant-garde movement. In that regard, he is very different from the broadly comparable Monk, whose work is still not fully assimilated and understood but who has been almost casually canonized. In addition to pioneering modern bass-playing, Mingus is responsible for some of the greatest large-scale compositions in modern 'jazz', beside which overblown efforts like Ornette Coleman's *Skies Of America* look positively sophomoric; he also transformed the conception of collective improvisation, restoring the energies and occasionally the sound of early jazz to an identifiably modern idiom. He pioneered overdubbing and editing, thereby paving the way for Miles Davis and Teo Macero, who appears on these curiously lifeless, virtually identical compilations from two albums recorded for Period.

These can really only be mined for pointers to more impressive work later. 'Four Hands' experiments with overdubbed piano (not quite like Claude Williamson's two-piano essays on the same label), and there are out-of-tempo sections that anticipate later, more radical experiments. 'What Is This Thing Called Love' undergoes interesting transformations, in keeping with Mingus's palimpsest approach to standards and new composition, and the use of cello (one of Mingus's first instruments) is intriguing.

The problem lies in the playing. Macero – later to achieve his apotheosis as producer/arranger for Miles Davis – is unpalatably dry, and the drummer tackles his part with no discernible enthusiasm. The Affinity and Fresh Sound also contain Macero's Third Streamish 'Abstractions', but that's a fairly minor plus. For serious Mingus scholars only.

That's equally true of Debut's pricey 12-CD boxed set covering the years 1951–7. The musician-owned label was started by Mingus and Max Roach as a way of getting their own adventurous music recorded and was briefly influential. With nearly 170 individual tracks, including many alternative takes, it's an exhaustive and occasionally exhausting compilation, well out of the range and probable requirements of the average fan; it does, however, include Mingus's own tape-recording of the famous Massey Hall, Toronto, 'Quintet Of The Year' gig of 15 May 1953, and it's good to know that even some of the lesser material remains in circulation.

*** **Mingus At The Bohemia** Original Jazz Classics OJC 045 CD/LP/MC
Mingus; Eddie Bert (*tb*); George Barrow (*ts*); Mal Waldron (*p*); Willie Jones, Max Roach (*d*). 12/55.

The Jazz Workshop in fine, searching form. Jones, who was to figure on the classic *Pithecanthropus Erectus* but who nowadays is little regarded, came to Mingus at Thelonious Monk's behest. The opening theme is a Monk dedication (with Waldron recreating an authentic cadence) that underlines Mingus's increasing emphasis on the rhythm section as a pro-active element in improvisation.

'Septemberly' is a characteristic hybrid of 'Tenderly' and 'September In The Rain', and 'Percussion Discussion' a duet between Mingus, on bass and cello, and Max Roach, just one of a long line of challenging duos set up by or for the great drummer. The rest of the material from this session was issued on a Prestige album called simply *Charles Mingus* [HB 6042], not to be confused with the Denon set reviewed below.

**** **Pithecanthropus Erectus** Atlantic 81456 CD
Mingus; Jackie McLean (*as*); J. R. Monterose (*ts*); Mal Waldron (*p*); Willie Jones (*d*). 1/56.

One of the truly great modern jazz albums. Underrated at the time, *Pithecanthropus Erectus* is now recognized as an important step in the direction of a new, freer synthesis in jazz. To some extent, the basic thematic conception (the story of mankind's struggle out of chaos, up and down the Freytag's Triangle of hubris and destruction, back to chaos) was the watered-down Spenglerism which was still fashionable at the time. Technically, though, the all-in ensemble work on the violent C section, which is really B, a modified version of the harmonically static second section, was absolutely crucial to the development of free collective improvisation in the following decade.

The brief 'Profile Of Jackie' is altogether different. Fronted by McLean's menthol-sharp alto, with Monterose (a late appointee who wasn't altogether happy with the music) and Mingus working on a shadowy counter-melody, it's one of the most appealing tracks Mingus ever committed to record, and the most generous of his 'portraits'. McLean still carried a torch for orthodox bebop and soon came to (literal) blows with Mingus; the chemistry worked just long enough. 'Love Chant' is a more basic modal exploration, and 'A Foggy Day' – re-subtitled 'In San Francisco' – is an impressionistic reworking of the Gershwin standard, with Chandleresque sound-effects. Superficially jokey, it's no less significant an effort to expand the available range of jazz performance, and the fact that it's done via a standard rather than a long-form composition like *Pithecanthropus* gives a sense of Mingus's Janus-faced approach to the music.

*** **The Clown** Atlantic 790142 CD
Mingus; Jimmy Knepper (*tb*); Shafi Hadi (*as, ts*); Wade Legge (*p*); Dannie Richmond (*d*); Jean Shepherd (*v*). 2 & 3/57.

With the first appearance of 'Reincarnation Of A Lovebird' and the *mano a mano* simplicities of 'Haitian Fight Song' (which saw Mingus build a huge, swinging performance out of the simplest thematic material), this is not a negligible record. It has never, though, been a great favourite.

'Blue Cee' is a dedication to Mingus's wife and has an almost gloomy cast. Throughout the album, the bassist grunts and hollers encouragement to himself and his players; perhaps he was still thinking about Bud Powell, who was apt to vocalize over his solos, because he had planned a 'portrait' of Powell before these sessions. The title-track is a reminder of Mingus's obsession with words and texts; Jean Shepherd's narration is fine, but one quickly longs for the instrumental versions that Mingus included in club sets thereafter. This is one of the few quality albums of Mingus's which is routinely neglected. That seems a pity.

***(*) **New Tijuana Moods** RCA PL 85635 2CD

***(*)   **New York Sketchbook** Charly CD 19 CD
Mingus; Clarence Shaw (*t*); Jimmy Knepper (*tb*); Shafi Hadi (*as*); Bill Triglia (*p* on
Tijuana only); Bill Evans, Bob Hammer, Horace Parlan (*p* on *Sketchbook* only);
Dannie Richmond (*d*); Frankie Dunlop (*perc* on *Tijuana* only); Ysabel Morel
(*castanets* on *Tijuana* only); Lonnie Elder (*v* on *Tijuana* only). 7 & 8/57, 57.

New Tijuana Moods combines the original release with the complete (that is, unedited)
performances from which the label not always successfully spliced together LP-length tracks.
'Ysabel's Table Dance' / 'Tijuana Table Dance' is the classic track, with Mingus's structures
constantly erupting into group improvisations. Nothing else quite compares with that track,
though 'Dizzy Mood' is also very fine, and 'Los Mariachos' is an impressive piece of writing.

There is inevitably a bit more room on the longer versions for the soloists to stretch out; but,
apart from that, most seasoned listeners will probably still want to cue the original releases on
their CD players rather than the restored versions. What *Tijuana Moods* called for was better
editing, not no editing.

Sketchbook is a CD reissue of the atmospheric *East Coasting*, with three additional tracks
from the original session. 'Conversation' and 'West Coast Ghost' are brilliantly realized
collective performances and, while none of the pieces is quite as ambitious as the *Tijuana*
structures, they all pay tribute to Mingus's growing stature as a grand synthesizer of blues, bop
and swing, with the shadow of something entirely new hovering on the music's inner horizons.

***   **Charles Mingus Trios** Jazz Door 1213 2CD
Mingus; Hampton Hawes, Bud Powell (*p*); Roy Haynes, Dannie Richmond (*d*). 7/57,
unknown.

Not normally heard in this context (though he performs beautifully on the Ellington *Money
Jungle* (Blue Note 746398 CD) with Max Roach), Mingus explores a range of bebop staples with
Powell and a more romantic repertoire with the emotive, bluesy Hawes. Constantly searching
for new configurations of familiar material, he combines 'Laura' and 'Tea For Two' in a
harmonically and rhythmically exciting way, to which Hawes responds with understanding and
wit. Powell is a more dominant, but also a more responsive player, and the familiarity of the
material shouldn't be allowed to distract listeners from some sophisticated explorations.

****   **Mingus At Antibes** Atlantic 90532 2CD
Mingus; Ted Curson (*t*); Eric Dolphy (*as, bcl*); Booker Ervin (*ts*); Bud Powell (*p*);
Dannie Richmond (*d*). 7/60.

Charles Delaunay memorably likened Mingus's performance in the mellow warmth of Juan les
Pins to a 'cold shower'. Certainly in comparison with the rest of the Antibes line-up, the 1960s
band was intellectually recherché and somewhat forceful. Unreleased until after Mingus's death
– the tapes had lain, unexamined, in Atlantic's vault – the set contains a valuable preview of
some of the material to be recorded that autumn for Candid, below, and for a thumping 'I'll
Remember April' with the exiled Bud Powell guesting. Mingus himself gets behind the piano on
a number of occasions, perhaps trying to give the slightly chaotic ensembles more shape. The
essence of the performance lies in the solos. Ervin is fine on 'Better Git Hit In Your Soul', as is
Dolphy, still sounding like a renegade Parker disciple, on a first version of the gospelly 'Folk
Forms', which reappears on *Presents*, below. The bass/bass clarinet sparring on 'What Love'
isn't quite as over-the-top as the later studio version, but it shows how far Dolphy was prepared
to move in the direction of Ornette Coleman's new synthesis.

Not just another 'previously unreleased' money-spinner, the *Antibes* set contains genuinely
important material. The chance to hear a Mingus concert in its entirety offers valuable clues to
his methods at the time.

****   **Charles Mingus Presents Charles Mingus** Candid CS 9005 CD/LP

***(*)   **Mingus** Candid CS 9021 CD/LP

***   **Reincarnation Of A Love Bird** Candid CS 9026 CD/LP
Mingus; Ted Curson, Lonnie Hillyer (*t*); Roy Eldridge (*t* on *Reincarnation* only)
Jimmy Knepper (*tb;* not on *Presents*); Britt Woodman (*tb* on *Mingus* only); Eric
Dolphy (*as, bcl*); Charles McPherson (*as;* not on *Presents*); Booker Ervin (*ts;* not on
Presents); Paul Bley (*p;* not on *Presents*); Nico Bunink (*p* on *Mingus* only); Tommy

Flanagan (*p* on *Reincarnation* only); Jo Jones (*d* on *Reincarnation* only) Dannie Richmond (*d*). 10/60, 10/60, 11/60.

Mingus's association with Candid was brief (though no briefer than the label's first existence) and highly successful. His long club residency in 1960 (interrupted only by festival appearances) gave him an unwontedly stable and played-in band to take into the studio (he recorded a fake – and uncommonly polite – night-club intro for the set), and the larger-scale arrangement of 'MDM' negatively reflects the solidity of the core band. *Presents* is for pianoless quartet and centres on the extraordinary vocalized interplay between Dolphy and Mingus; on 'What Love' they carry on a long conversation in near-comprehensible dialect. 'Folk Forms' is wonderfully pared down and features a superb Mingus solo. 'All The Things You Could Be By Now If Sigmund Freud's Wife Was Your Mother' has a wry fury (Mingus once said that it had been written in the psych ward at Bellevue) which is more than incidentally suggestive of 'harmolodic' and 'punk' procedures of the 1980s. The 'Original Faubus Fables' was a further experiment in the use of texts, here a furious rant against what Mingus later called 'Nazi USA', and his later '60s brothers 'Amerika'. It's powerfully felt but less well integrated in its blend of polemic and music than Max Roach's *Freedom Now Suite* on the same label (Candid CS 9002 CD/LP).

If *Presents* is a classic, *Charles Mingus* falls slightly short. The augmented band on 'MDM' sounds uninspired, either unfamiliar or unhappy with the material (which isn't exceptionally demanding). 'Stormy Weather', also released on *Candid Dolphy*, below, features a monster introduction by the saxophonist. Like 'ATTYCBBNISFWWYM' above, 'Lock 'Em Up' makes some reference to Bellevue (or to Charlie Parker's 'holiday' in Camarillo), if only because it's taken at the same hare-brained pace, and Mingus bellows instruction to his troops in a voice that sounds on the brink.

At producer Nat Hentoff's suggestion, he had attempted to vary the existing band and recreate the energy of the 'Newport rebels' anti-festival by bringing in past associates. The most notable of these was Roy Eldridge, who is featured (with Knepper, Flanagan and Jo Jones also guesting, as the Jazz Artists guild) on the long 'R & R', a superb 'Body And Soul', and a previously unreleased 'Wrap Your Troubles In Dreams'.

'Reincarnation Of A Love Bird' and 'Bugs' are both Parker-inspired. The title-track features Hillyer, McPherson and Ervin over Dolphy's uncredited bass clarinet (Curson isn't listed either, and is only mentioned in Brian Priestley's characteristically detailed liner-note). By no means a classic Mingus album, it restores some fascinating performances and alternates from a critical period in his career. Needless to say, worth having (and enthusiasts should take note of another 'Reincarnation' along with the Dolphy-led 'Stormy Weather' on the label compilation, *Candid Dolphy* (CCD 9033)).

***   **Oh Yeah** Atlantic 7567 90667 CD
    Mingus; Jimmy Knepper (*tb*); Rahsaan Roland Kirk (*ts, manzello, stritch, f, siren*);
    Booker Ervin (*ts*); Doug Watkins (*b*); Dannie Richmond (*d*). 11/61.

The addition of Rahsaan Roland Kirk gave the Mingus band the kind of surreality evident on the spaced-out blues 'Ecclusiastics', which Mingus leads from the piano. Kirk is also the main attraction on 'Wham Bam, Thank You Ma'am', a typically de-romanticized standard. On the closing 'Passions Of A Man' Mingus overdubbed a bizarre, associative rap, which is rather more effective than the instrumental backing. Odd. Damned odd, even; but a significant instance of Mingus's often desperate conflation of music and words in the search for some higher synthesis.

(*)   **Live At Birdland, 1962 Jazz View 028 CD
    Mingus; Richard Williams (*t*); Ed Armour (*flh*); Don Butterfield (*tba*); Charles
    McPherson (*as*); Booker Ervin (*ts*); Pepper Adams (*bs*); Jaki Byard (*p*); Dannie
    Richmond (*d*). 3 & 10/62.

These airshots document two hectic residencies at the great New York club. The sound isn't particularly good, but the performances hang together remarkably well and the band sounds well rehearsed and played-in on both occasions. In his excellent Mingus discography, Mingus lists Toshiko Akiyoshi as the piano player on the March date, and there seems no reason to doubt him, for it certainly doesn't sound like Byard's spiky approach, which is more evident on the later tracks.

The March session consists of three tracks: a rousing 'Take The "A" Train', a version of 'Fables Of Faubus' and first of two takes of the theme 'Eat That Chicken'. From October, 'The Search' is a barely altered 'I Can't Get Started', 'King Fish' of 'Monk, Bunk [or Funk] and Vice Versa' and 'Moonboy' of 'Please Don't Come Back From The Moon'. These are the last known recordings of Mingus before the magnificent *Black Saint And The Sinner Lady* sessions, so they take on an additional resonance from that. What's immediately clear is Mingus's now superbly confident control of his musicians and their music; whatever shortcomings these recordings betray, they're of considerable musical and historical interest.

*****   **The Black Saint And The Sinner Lady** MCA MCAD 5649 CD
Mingus; Rolf Ericson, Richard Williams (*t*); Quentin Jackson, Don Butterfield (*tba*); Jerome Richardson (*as, bs, f*); Booker Ervin (*ts*); Dick Hafer (*ts, f*); Charlie Mariano (*as*); Jaki Byard (*p*); Dannie Richmond (*d*). 1/63.

***(*)   **Mingus Mingus Mingus Mingus Mingus** MCA MCAD 39119 CD
As above, except add Britt Woodman (*tb*); Jay Berliner (*g*). 1 & 9/63.

Black Saint is Mingus's masterpiece. Almost everything about it was distinctive: the long form, the use of dubbing, the liner-note by Mingus's psychiatrist. On its release, they altered its usual slogan, 'The new wave of jazz is on Impulse!', to read 'folk', in line with Mingus's decision to call the group the Charles Mingus New Folk Band. Ellingtonian in ambition and scope, and in the disposition of horns, the piece has a majestic, dancing presence, and Charlie Mariano's alto solos and overdubs on 'Mode D/E/F' are unbelievably intense. There is evidence that Mingus's desire to make a single continuous performance (and it should be remembered that even Ellington's large-scale compositions were relatively brief) failed to meet favour with label executives; but there is an underlying logic even to the separate tracks which makes it difficult to separate them other than for the convenience of track listing. Absolutely essential.

Mingus etc. comes from the same and one later session. It includes 'Celia' and 'I X Love', both older pieces, both distinguished by great Mariano performances, with 'Theme For Lester Young', which is a variant on 'Goodbye, Pork Pie Hat', and 'Better Git Hit In Your Soul'. Nothing comes close to *Black Saint*, but the pair give an even better account of Mingus's thinking at the time. Whatever the compromises forced upon him in the past by musicians (or now by his label), he is creating music of classic scope and lasting value.

****   **Town Hall Concert 1964** Original Jazz Classics OJC 042 CD/LP

****   **Portrait** Prestige P 24092 2LP

***   **Concertgebouw Amsterdam: Volume 1** Ulysse Aroc 50506/7 2LP

***   **Concertgebouw Amsterdam: Volume 2** Ulysse Aroc 50608 CD/LP

***(*)   **Live In Stockholm** Royal Jazz RJD 517 2 CD

(*)   **Live In Oslo, 1964 Jazz Up JU 307 CD

(*)   **Astral Weeks Moon MCD 016 CD

***   **Mingus In Europe: Volume 1** Enja 3049 LP/MC

***   **Mingus In Europe: Volume 2** Enja 3077 CD/LP

****   **Meditations On Integration** Bandstand BDCD 1524 CD

***   **Meditation** France's Concert FCD 102 CD

***   **Live In Paris, 1964: Volume 2** France's Concert FCD 110 CD
Mingus; Johnny Coles (*t*; on *Town Hall, Oslo, Stockholm* and *Meditations* only); Lonnie Hillyer (*t* on *Portrait* only); Eric Dolphy (*as, fl, bcl*); Charles McPherson (*as* on *Portrait* only); Clifford Jordan (*ts*); Jaki Byard (*p*); Dannie Richmond (*d*). all 4/64, except *Portrait*: 4/64, 65.

This is undoubtedly the most heavily documented period of Mingus's career. The Town Hall concert predated the European tour, and this set consists of two long tracks which strongly feature Dolphy (the dedicatee) on each of his three horns. The release shouldn't be confused with a 1962 recording of the same name [Blue Note BNS 40034], which contains entirely different material. The *Portrait* version also contains sides recorded in the summer of 1965 with a slightly later band; a further Eric Dolphy tribute is grouped with an appealing standards medley.

For the record, on the European itinerary the Amsterdam concerts were recorded on 10 April, the Swedish and Norwegian dates (which included the magnificent *Meditations On Integration*) around the 13th, *Astral Weeks* on the 14th, *Meditation* in Paris on 18–19 April, and the Enjas on the 26th in Wuppertal. Specialists will argue about the respective merits of individual performances, for the repertoire overlaps very considerably. From the point of view of value, the FCDs and the single-box Royal are the most desirable. All the sets contain 'Peggy's Blue Skylight', 'Orange Was The Color Of Her Dress, Then Blue Silk' and 'Fables Of Faubus' (except the Dutch, which misses the first, but includes 'A.T.F.W.U.S.A. (A.T.F.W.Y.O.U.)', and the Norwegian, which only has 'Orange' but throws in a wild bonus cover of 'Take The "A" Train') . The Royal and France's Concert include 'Meditation On Integration' (there's a version on the Amsterdam date) and the Royal also includes a hesitant false start on 'Meditation', together with a bizarre 'When Irish Eyes Are Smiling' and two versions of 'So Long Eric' which, targeted on 'Goodbye, Pork Pie Hat', is also on the second of the French sets and the Norwegian. This is sometimes described as a threnody or epitaph to the multi-instrumentalist, who died on 29 June of that year, but there he is playing it; the piece was actually supposed to be a reminder to Dolphy (who'd decided to try his luck in Europe for a while) not to stay 'over there' too long. Sadly, by the time the *Portrait* version was recorded in Minneapolis, it had become a memorial to the late saxophonist.

Mingus's solo on the French performance of 'Peggy', shortly before which trumpeter Johnny Coles collapsed with a serious stomach ailment, is exemplary, but rather murkily recorded. Dolphy's keening, forceful alto pairs well with Cliff Jordan's leathery sound. They make excellent use of the extra space left by Coles. Though not credited for it, Dolphy also plays flute, and there is a fascinating three-way discourse on 'Meditation' between it, a dark-toned Mingus and Byard.

A bonus on the Enjas is a flute–bass duo credited to Dolphy as 'Started', but actually based on 'I Can't Get Started'. 'Fables' is awkwardly split on the LP format (Volume 1), but there are two versions (one complete, one not) and not much else on the Moon CD. Completists self-evidently will pounce on them all and uncover all manner of circumstantial variations. The less committed and underfunded will have to plump for one of the CD sets; they may find the Royal better value, though the recently released Bandstand has perhaps the single finest performance in the concluding 'Meditations'. Dolphy, rather subdued up to that point, plays magnificently on both flute and bass clarinet, and Mingus's bowed figures are very moving. The horns are generally not very well recorded and there are a couple of awkward drop-outs, but Byard is well miked and uncovers his most ironic touches on 'Fables Of Faubus', taking off 'Yankee Doodle' completely out of tempo; he's more conventionally swinging on 'Orange Was The Color . . .'

*** **Right Now** Original Jazz Classics OJC 237 CD/LP/MC
Mingus; John Handy (*as*); Clifford Jordan (*ts*); Jane Getz (*p*); Dannie Richmond (*d*). 6/64.

Two long cuts – 'Meditation (On A Pair Of Wire Cutters)' and a revised 'Fables Of Faubus' – which were originally released on Fantasy, featuring Mingus's Californian band of that summer. Handy comes in only on 'New Fables' but sounds funky and a lot more abrasive than McPherson. Jane Getz is by no means well known, and is certainly less individual than the otherwise-engaged Byard, but she acquits her piano duties more than adequately.

*** **Charles Mingus In Paris, 1970** DIW 326/7 2CD/2LP
Mingus; Eddie Preston (*t*); Charles McPherson (*as*); Bobby Jones (*ts*); Jaki Byard (*p, arr*); Dannie Richmond (*d*). 10/70.

** **Charles Mingus** Denon DC 8565 CD
As above, except omit McPherson; add Toshiyuki Miyama (*ld*); Shigeo Suzuki, Hiroshi Takamu (*as*); Masahiko Sato (*p*); Yoshisaburo Toyozumi (*d*); other personnel unknown. 1/71.

A rather straightforward, almost bland, concert recording from the city and country where Mingus had some of his more torrid moments. The repertoire combines recent arrangements with the well-worn but constantly evolving Ellington medley, and yet another version of 'Orange Was the Color . . .'.

The eponymous Denon is a rather dreary recording, made in Tokyo with a typically well-coached but utterly uninspired Japanese band. They follow Byard's charts – 'The Man Who Never Sleeps', the Oscar Pettiford dedication 'OPOP' (which also appear on *In Paris* and *Portrait*) – to the letter, leaving Mingus and his small touring group to inject what energy they can. Dispensable.

***   **Live In Chateauvallon, 1972** France's Concert FCD 134 CD
Mingus; Charles McPherson (*as*); John Foster (*p*); Roy Brooks (*d*). 8/72.

According to the English version of the liner-note, 'The charm of this tuesday evening arose from a preposterous alt of approximate music.' Anyone who takes the trouble to puzzle this one out will miss Mingus's superb opening statement on 'Stormy Monday'. The 'charming tuesday' came in the middle of an almost ridiculously antagonistic tour, which reduced the band to a quartet (France's Concert seem to specialize in truncated line-ups!) but the music is first rate, with McPherson – soon to be an ex-employee himself – playing with grace and fire on the non-vocal 'Fables' and on 'Body And Soul', where Mingus again solos beautifully. 'Blues For Some Bones' is a long and intermittently successful improvisation which features (presumably) Foster singing the blues and Brooks playing a musical saw with, how you say?, preposterous alt. Could have done with a couple of extra players, though.

***   **Three Or Four Shades Of Blues** Atlantic SD 1700 CD
Mingus; Jack Walrath (*t*); George Coleman (*ss, ts*); Ricky Ford (*ts*); Bob Nellums, Jimmy Rowles (*p*); Philip Catherine, Larry Coryell, Jimmy Scofield (*g*); George Mraz (*b*); Dannie Richmond (*d*). 3/77.

Despite Mingus's deep and vocal reservations, this was one of his commercially most successful albums. The addition of guitarists clearly pitched it in the direction of the younger rock-buying audience that Atlantic had targeted, and the record also included staples like 'Goodbye, Pork Pie Hat' and 'Better Git Hit In Your Soul' (presumably with a view to initiating that younger audience). The title-track, though, is rather too broad in its catch-all approach and sounds almost self-parodic. Mingus's health was beginning to break down in 1977, and there are signs of querulousness throughout, not least on 'Nobody Knows The Trouble I've Seen'.

(*)   **Cumbia And Jazz Fusion Atlantic AMCY 1039 CD
Mingus; Jack Walrath (*t, perc*); Dino Piana (*tb*); Jimmy Knepper (*tb, btb*); Mauricio Smith (*f, picc, as, ss*); Quarto Maltoni (*as*); George Adams (*ts, f*); Ricky Ford (*ts, perc*); Paul Jeffrey (*ts, ob*); Gary Anderson, Roberto Laneri (*bcl*); Anastasio del Bono (*ob, eng hn*); Pasquale Sabatelli, Gene Scholtes (*bsn*); Bob Neloms (*p*); Danny Mixon (*p, org*); Dannie Richmond (*d*); Candido Camero, Daniel Gonzalez, Ray Mantilla, Alfredo Ramirez, Bradley Cunningham (*perc*). 3 & 4/76, 3/77.

'Cumbia And Jazz Fusion' is a slightly messy piece that levels some doubts at Mingus's remaining talents as arranger and instrumentator. The ensembles are all rather congested, which mars a fine and vibrant piece which ranks as one of his best late compositions. There is a regularity to the basic metre and a simplicity of conception that make the rather opaque surface all the more disappointing. The fault doesn't seem to lie with the recording, which is well transferred.

'Music for *Todo Modo*' was written (sight unseen) as soundtrack to the film by Elio Petri. The ten-piece Italo-American band works a typically volatile score, which includes a variant on 'Peggy's Blue Skylight' and some fine blues.

***   **Mingus Plays Piano** Mobile Fidelity MFCD 783 CD
Mingus (*p* solo). 7/63.

Mingus played something more than 'composer's piano' throughout his career. His touch and harmonic sense were so secure that, though hardly virtuosic, he more than passes muster on a very resonant and richly toned instrument with what sounds like a very brisk action. It's interesting to hear themes like 'Orange Was The Color Of Her Dress, Then Blue Silk' reduced to their essentials in this way, though the true highlights are 'When I Am Real' and a thoroughly unabashed 'Body And Soul'. Not in the front rank of Mingus albums, but certainly not just for collectors.

PHIL MINTON (born 1940)
VOICE, TRUMPET

***(*)   **The Berlin Station** FMP SAJ 57 LP
Minton; Peter Brötzmann (*ts, perc*); Michel Waisisz (*syn*); Ernst Reijseger (*clo*);
Sven-Ake Johansson (*perc, acc, v*); Hugh Davies, Tony Oxley (*elec*). 2/84, 10/85, 1/86.

***   **Ways** ITN 1420 CD/LP
Minton; Veryan Weston (*p*). 2/87.

Minton is perhaps the most impressive vocal performer working in Europe today, and singing
has virtually overtaken his trumpet playing. Associated with Mike Westbrook on a number of
text-based projects, he is also a stunning vocal improviser, with a tonal and timbral range that
seems quite uncanny. The duos and occasional trios on *Berlin Station* are for the most part
highly abstract. Brötzmann's saxophone playing is a virtual guarantee of emotional intensity,
and Minton responds with typical flexibility, exploring the interstices, shifting from harsh,
primal-scream catharses to caressingly gentle insinuations.

The duos with Weston seem much more formalized and lack the sheer power of the slightly
earlier work with Roger Turner on *AMMO* (Leo Records), but they are compelling all the
same. Anyone who has heard Minton's work with Westbrook will want to explore this
extraordinary artist further.

BOB MINTZER
TENOR SAXOPHONE, BASS CLARINET

(*)   **Incredible Journey dmp CD 451 CD
Mintzer; Marvin Stamm, Randy Brecker, Laurie Frink, Bob Millikan (*t*); Dave
Bargeron, Bob Smith, Keith O'Quinn, Dave Taylor (*tb*); Lawrence Feldman, Peter
Yellin, Michael Brecker, Bob Malach, Roger Rosenberg (*reeds*); Don Grolnick (*p*);
Lincoln Goines (*b*); Peter Erskine (*d*); Frankie Malabe (*perc*). 2–4/85.

***   **Camouflage** dmp CD 456 CD
As above, except Chris Seiter (*tb*) replaces Bargeron, Zev Katz (*b*) replaces Goines,
Michael Brecker omitted. 6/86.

(*)   **Spectrum dmp CD 461 CD
As above, except Dave Bargeron (*tb*) replaces Seiter, Lincoln Goines (*b*) replaces
Katz, add Phil Markowitz (*p*), John Riley (*d*). 1/88.

**   **Urban Contours** dmp CD 467 CD
As above, except add Joe Mosello (*t*), Jim Pugh (*tb*), Jeff Mironov, Chuck Loeb (*g*).
2–3/89.

**   **Art Of The Big Band** dmp CD-479 CD
As above, except Mike Davis and Matt Finders (*tb*) replace Smith and Pugh, Scott
Robinson (*reeds*) replaces Malach, add Michael Formanek (*b*), omit Grolnick and
Mironov. 9/90.

The main attraction for many in these records may be the full-flushing digital sound secured by
engineer Tom Jung. Using a carefully positioned single, central microphone to record the brass
and reeds, Jung creates a tremendous sonic impact. Once past that, though, the band begins to
sound rather less exciting. Mintzer is an accomplished soloist and arranger, but his actual
themes often lack a specific identity, and while he tries to get the most out of his orchestra, too
many of the scores seem to consist of the piling on of effects. He seldom seeks to create genuine
contrast or thematic interest, and some of his charts for the non-originals can sound irritatingly
cute.

The earlier records tend to work better, especially *Camouflage*, which has a few smart,
memorable tunes in the unpromisingly titled 'Techno Pop', 'Mr Fone Bone' and 'Hip Hop'.
Spectrum is nearly as good, with some gripping solos by some of the illustrious sidemen. But
Urban Contours includes a couple of feeble variations on pop tunes, which seems a pointless
move when Mintzer works best with his own material, and *Art Of The Big Band*, which
numbers a trite revision of 'Moonlight Serenade' and a couple of near-MOR charts among its

tracks, implies that Mintzer, who clearly loves the sound of the band, can't find much of interest for them to do. Or possibly that the virtues of an auspiciously drilled mainstream big band are starting to seem anachronistic in the 1990s. A pity, since the sonic range of the discs has improved further: the later records are warmer than the earlier ones.

*(*)   **One Music** dmp CD-488 CD
Mintzer; Russell Ferrante (*ky*); Jimmy Haslip (*b*); William Kennedy (*d*); Don Alias (*perc*). 91.

**   **I Remember Jaco** RCA Novus 90618 CD/MC
Mintzer; Joey Calderazzo (*ky*); Jeff Andrews, Michael Formanek (*b*); Peter Erskine (*d*). 3/91.

Mintzer's facility and snap don't lend themselves to these small-group sessions at all well. The dmp date is compositionally empty, with the leader's big, musclebound sound running up modal blind alleys. The tribute to Pastorius lacks any line to earth, the music drifting around in a haze on the slower tunes and stamping on the spot on the faster ones. Erskine and Formanek play with their customary finesse, but the improvisations are tedious and wearisome.

BILLY MITCHELL (born 1926)
TENOR SAX

***   **The Colossus Of Detroit** Xanadu 158 LP
Mitchell; Barry Harris (*p*); Sam Jones (*b*); Walter Bolden (*d*). 4/78.

***(*)   **De Lawd's Blues** Xanadu 182 LP
Mitchell; Benny Bailey (*t*); Tommy Flanagan (*p*); Rufus Reid (*b*); Jimmy Cobb (*d*). 6/80.

Although he was born in Kansas City, Billy Mitchell did most of his 'prentice work in Detroit – hence the title of his first Xanadu album. While he recorded with Thad Jones in the early 1950s and went on to take one of the chairs in Count Basie's sax section, Mitchell hasn't made very many records; a splendid 1963 session, also with Jones and once issued in the UK on Fontana, has yet to appear on CD, and only the two sets listed above are in current circulation. The quartet record features what was virtually the Xanadu house rhythm section in the 1970s, and they offer fearless support to the big-toned, heavyweight tenorman. Better still, though, is *De Lawd's Blues*. Flanagan, an old friend from the early Detroit days, is a model of unassuming insight, Bailey sounds incisive with the mute and bluesily swinging on the open horn, and the leader takes some tremendous solos. Three long blows on 'B&B', 'De Lawd's Blues' and 'Perpetual Stroll' are superbly sustained: Mitchell is as leathery and unquenchably exuberant as his old Basie colleague, Lockjaw Davis, and shapes his solos round a similar blend of blues colloquialisms and mean-tempered hollers. The recording is a little dry but very upfront, obscuring nothing.

BLUE MITCHELL (1930–79)
TRUMPET, CORNET

****   **Big Six** Original Jazz Classics OJC 615 CD/LP/MC
Mitchell; Curtis Fuller (*tb*); Johnny Griffin (*ts*); Wynton Kelly (*p*); Wilbur Ware (*b*); Philly Joe Jones (*d*). 7/58.

***(*)   **Out Of The Blue** Original Jazz Classics OJC 667 CD/MC
Mitchell; Benny Golson (*ts*); Cedar Walton, Wynton Kelly (*p*); Paul Chambers, Sam Jones (*b*); Art Blakey (*d*). 1/59.

***(*)   **Blues On My Mind** Original Jazz Classics OJC 6009 CD/LP
Mitchell; Curtis Fuller (*tb*); Benny Golson, Johnny Griffin, Jimmy Heath (*ts*); Wynton Kelly (*p*); Paul Chambers, Sam Jones, Wilbur Ware (*b*); Art Blakey, Philly Joe Jones (*d*). 7/58, 1/59, 9/59.

***   **Blue's Moods** Original Jazz Classics OJC 138 LP/MC
Mitchell; Wynton Kelly (*p*); Sam Jones (*b*); Roy Brooks (*d*). 8/60.

***   **The Thing To Do** Blue Note 784178 CD
Mitchell; Junior Cook (*ts*); Chick Corea (*p*); Gene Taylor (*b*); Al Foster (*d*). 7/64.

A stalwart of the Horace Silver band, Mitchell took it over in 1964, replacing the former leader with the young Chick Corea. The debut recording isn't particularly memorable; though Corea has a fine grasp of the required idiom, which is blues-and-gospel-drenched hard bop of the kind Silver pioneered, it never quite ignites. The heavy-duty line-up on the Riverside reissues on OJC is much more satisfactory and *Big Six* is unquestionably the trumpeter's finest achievement. Griffin and Golson sound to have paid *lots* more dues than Cook. Mitchell shows that he can be sensitive, too, with a lovely quartet 'Blue Soul', ranging with unusual freedom over Kelly's blues lines. They're essential to the success of *Blue's Moods*, where the leader punches out cornet lines, forceful on 'Scrapple From the Apple' and, down a dynamic notch, touching on 'When I Fall in Love'. The *Blues On My Mind* compilation is, for most casual purchasers, a good buy, bringing together 'Brother Ball' and 'There Will Never Be Another You' from OJC 615 and 'It Could Happen To You' and a rousing 'Saints' from *Out Of The Blue*.

***   **Blue's Blues** Mainstream MDCD 710 CD
Mitchell; Herman Riley, John Mayall (*hca*); Joe Sample (*p*); Freddie Robinson (*g*); Darrel Clayborn (*b*); John Guerin, Ray Pounds (*d*); collective personnel. 72, 74.

(*)   **Graffiti Blues Mainstream MDCD 709 CD
Mitchell; Jim Bossy, Jon Faddis, Markie Markowitz, Herman Riley, Frank Vicari (*ts*); Joe Farrell (*ts, f*); Seldon Powell (*ts, bs*); Walter Bishop Jr, Joe Sample (*p*); Joe Beck, Sam Brown, Freddie Robinson, John Tropea (*g*); Don Bailey (*hca*); Wilbur Bascomb, Darrell Clayborn, Michael Moore (*b*); John Guerin, James Madison, Ray Pounds (*d*); collective personnel. 73, 74.

The better part of a decade on, Mitchell had made a surprisingly comfortable and uncompromised accommodation to the newly fashionable blues-rock scene. His brief association with British bluesman John Mayall (who guests on *Blue's Blues* as a harmonica player) probably brought him to the attention of more younger listeners than had all the dedicated gigging and recording of the past decade. Both albums are firmly plugged into an early-1970s electro-blues style. The rhythm backings are mostly banal and forgettable, with an excess of wah-wah and fuzz effects on some tracks, but Mitchell's solos are still clear and funky.

RED MITCHELL (born 1927)
DOUBLE BASS, PIANO

***   **When I'm Singing** Enja 4058 LP
Mitchell solo. 10/82.

***   **Simple Isn't Easy** Sunnyside SSC 1016 CD
As above. 9/83.

Known for a fluent improvising style in which pulled-off (rather than plucked) notes in a typically low register (Mitchell uses a retuned bass) suggest a baritone saxophone rather than a stringed instrument; Scott LaFaro was later sanctified for a broadly similar technique. Mitchell is also an accomplished pianist, with a hint of the romantic approach of his former colleague, Hampton Hawes. The Sunnyside originals – with titles like 'I'm A Homeboy' and 'It's Time To Emulate The Japanese' – quash any notion that Mitchell is merely a standards hack, though he is more approachable in that territory. *Simple Isn't Easy* is entirely for piano and voice, and to that extent isn't typical. Set it beside *When I'm Singing*, though, and it's clear that the same shaping intelligence is at work: harmonically limber, melodically sophisticated and rhythmically just dynamic enough (certainly in contrast to someone like Richard Davis, who has a comparable sound) to be listenable. Mitchell's really interesting work lies mostly in the past.

***(*)   **Presenting Red Mitchell** Original Jazz Classics OJC 158 LP
Mitchell; James Clay (*ts, f*); Lorraine Geller (*p*); Billy Higgins (*d*). 3/57.

An excellent late-bop excursion that survives the tragic Lorraine Geller's rather awkward comping. By contrast a great survivor, Clay places notes with nice judgement and without overtaxing himself. 'Scrapple From The Apple' proves that Mitchell wasn't just a mellow stylist, though he clearly does prefer medium to slow tempi when he can deploy the full range of his not-yet-lowered instrument. More than many a player, Mitchell stands to benefit from careful CD transfer. Though there hasn't so far been a rush, this would be the obvious choice.

**(*)   Chocolate Cadillac Steeplechase SCS 1161 LP
Mitchell; Idries Sulieman (*t*); Nisse Sandstrom (*ts*); Horace Parlan (*p*); Rune Carlsson (*d*). 12/76.

The writing is good and Mitchell is playing well (top form on a couple of tracks). The band is simply not behind him. Parlan, normally a stylistic chameleon, seems to have his mind on something else, and the two horns lock only infrequently. Disappointing.

***   The Red Barron Duo Storyville 4137 LP
Mitchell; Kenny Barron (*p*). 8/86.

This is the closest Mitchell came to duetting with himself before the item below. Barron shares his harmonic and rhythmic preoccupations to a productive degree, and their exploration of quite basic themes, 'Oleo', 'The Sunny Side Of The Street', is compellingly inventive.

(****)   A Declaration Of Interdependence Four Leaf Clover FLC CD 105 CD
Mitchell. overdubbed solo. 88.

So seriously strange is this record that it's very difficult to give an objective assessment of it. Technically, it's a problem, with Mitchell overdubbing piano, bass and vocal lines in undisclosed order; the sound has a demo-ish quality and slight irregularity of pulse that may be off-putting. Mitchell tackles 'Come Rain Or Come Shine', 'But Beautiful', 'I'm Glad There Is You' and 'My Romance' in a Chet Baker growl that rises on an eldritch 'break' for the odd top note. More astonishing, though, are the original songs. They sound, to be frank, horrible, but they also reveal Mitchell as a song-writer of quite astonishing lyrical resource, sometimes reaching a par with the wilder shores of Sondheim's earlier work. 'You Can Take Your Funny Money And Run, Honey', allegedly about a squabble over funding, is a devastatingly ironic hooker's lament which includes the (you'll agree) mawkishly sentimental line, 'Fuck you, you whore'. 'A Declaration Of Interdependence' is a rather weird hymn to polymorphous perversity (black and white, straight and gay, young and old) which Donna Summer may consider covering as a companion to 'State Of Independence'; someone else may consider how Mitchell can claim to have 'written' what is clearly 'Lover, Come Back To Me' with a revised hook to the chorus. The theme is further developed in the concluding 'Poles Apart', a small-world conceit that's certainly the tightest compositional performance of the set.
  An enigma.

ROSCOE MITCHELL (born 1940)
REEDS, PERCUSSION

****   Sound Delmark DS 408 LP
Mitchell; Lester Bowie (*t, flhn, hmca*); Lester Lashley (*tb, clo*); Kalaparush Maurice McIntyre (*ts*); Malachi Favors (*b*); Alvin Fielder (*d*).

Though still relatively little-known, this is one of the crucial documents of the new jazz of the 1960s. It was the first recording by musicians from Chicago's Association for the Advancement of Creative Musicians (AACM), under Mitchell's nominal direction, and the three pieces here are as radical and dramatic as anything produced at the time: the rationalization of energy playing in the compressed 'Ornette'; the use of 'little instruments' (harmonica, recorder, bits and pieces of percussion) in the pointillistic 'The Little Suite'; and the utterly extraordinary 'Sound' itself, which explores relationships between sound and silence by placing one in the context of the other, fragments of music juxtaposed with nothingness, musical interplay elongated into slow-motion conversations. It's still a thrilling and surprising record after 25 years. Luckily – unlike some of the other Delmark albums of the period – the recording is clear, if dry, and good enough to let the listener hear many of the tonal subtleties which these ultra-sensitive players were using.

***   **Roscoe Mitchell** Chief CD 4 CD
Mitchell; Leo Smith (*t, pkt-t, flhn*); George Lewis (*tb, sous, tba*); Thurman Barker,
Anthony Braxton, Don Moye, Douglas Ewart, Joseph Jarman, Henry Threadgill,
Malachi Favors (*perc*). 7–8/78.

Several of Mitchell's crucial recordings have disappeared with the apparent demise of Chicago's
Nessa label, but the above reissue of one of them returns some of his most significant 1970s
work to the catalogue. Away from the Art Ensemble Of Chicago, this dedicated reed
theoretician and experimenter has sought out some very rarified terrain. There are three long
pieces here: a trio for woodwinds, high brass and low brass, with Smith and Lewis; a
phantasmagoria for eight percussionists, 'The Maze'; and almost 18 minutes of Mitchell blowing
as softly as he can through the soprano sax, 'S II Examples', drifting through a world of
shadowy microtones. A remarkable programme, but there are drawbacks: the 'L-R-G' trio is
full of fascinating juxtapositions and echoes of countless other composers, yet its deliberately
piecemeal nature seems laboured next to the spontaneous structures conceived as a matter of
course by European improvisers. 'The Maze' has a burnished, glistening quality, but the fact
that only two 'genuine' drummers are among the percussionists makes one wonder what
Mitchell could have achieved with the involvement of eight full-time drum exponents. As it
stands the piece is a matter of shifting textures, when it might have transcended that. 'S II
Examples' is, too, more of an intriguing idea than a valuable musical one – or, at least, one more
important to Mitchell than to the listener. All that said, it's a rather bewitching set altogether,
and a useful notebook on what Chicago's playing elite were looking into at the period. The
equally significant *Nonaah* from the same period has yet to appear on CD.

***   **Sketches From Bamboo** Moers Music 02024 LP
Mitchell; Leo Smith, Kenny Wheeler, Hugh Ragin, Michael Philip Mossman, Rob
Howard (*t*); George Lewis, Ray Anderson, Alfred Patterson (*tb*); Anthony Braxton,
Douglas Ewart, Wallace McMillan, Dwight Andrews, Mart Ehrlich (*reeds*); Marilyn
Crispell (*p*); Bobby Naughton (*vib*); Pinguin Moschner (*tba*); Wes Brown (*b*);
Pheeroan AkLaff (*d*). 6/79.

A rare opportunity to record some of his big-band work allowed Mitchell to make this album,
which consists of two versions of 'Sketches Of Bamboo' and a ponderously swinging account of
'Linefine Lyon Seven', which here emerges as a kind of concerto for his own alto. The first
'Sketches' is a compelling, slowly collecting composite of horn lines and the second seeks to
amplify that tendency into what is, at the end, a vast, swirling collage that is nevertheless very
precisely directed and sustained. If there's a problem, it's in a possible unsureness on the
composer's part of how to use the rhythm players in a context almost overpowered by horns,
and the recording isn't quite transparent enough to let one hear all the detail of the lines. Still,
for the vividness of the first two tracks, this is well worth having.

***   **3 = 4 Eye** Black Saint 0050 LP
Mitchell; Hugh Ragin (*t, picc-t, flhn*); Spencer Barefield (*g*); Jaribu Shahid (*b, perc*);
Tani Tabbal (*d*). 2/81.

***(*)   **More Cutouts** Cecma 003 LP
As above, except omit Barefield and Shahid. 2/81.

****   **Roscoe Mitchell And The Sound And Space Ensembles** Black Saint BSR 0070 LP
Mitchell; Mike Mossman (*t, flhn*); Gerald Oshita (*ts, bs, Conn-o sax, cbsrsn*); Spencer
Barefield (*g, v*); Jaribu Shahid (*b, v*); Tani Tabbal (*d, v*); Tom Buckner (*v*). 6/83.

The first two records above were cut only a day apart. On the first, Mitchell and a picked team
tiptoe through and around some varied themes, including his tribute to Jarman, 'Jo Jar', and the
ironic 'Variations On A Folk Song Written In The Sixties'. The second record, by the trio, is
lighter, more pointillist, yet more free-spirited: Ragin and Mitchell sometimes burst out of the
leader's iron restraints. Improvisation becomes a matter of formal variation rather than
blowing, yet the leader's idiosyncratic deployment of sound and space (terms which he adopted
to describe his groups) make it often extraordinary. Better yet is the collision secured on the
next Black Saint record, perhaps the best introduction to Mitchell's strange discography. The
trio of Mitchell, Oshita – on some of the oddest reed instruments ever made – and the classical
tenor Tom Buckner perform a ghostly mixture of Kurt Schwitters and Wilton Crawley, before
an hilarious pseudo-funk rave-up by the whole ensemble, which features probably the only

recorded solo on the contrabass sarrusphone. The two ensembles blend again on the second side in two long, beautiful tracks, the needle-fine 'Linefine Lyon Seven' and the scuttling, drifting 'Variations On Sketches From Bamboo'. Vividly, closely recorded and strongly recommended.

**   **The Flow Of Things** Black Saint BSR 0090 CD/LP
Mitchell; Jodie Christian (*p*); Malachi Favors (*b*); Steve McCall (*d*). 6–9/86.

(*)   **Live At The Muhle Hunziken Cecma 1008 LP
Mitchell. 9/86.

***   **Live In Detroit** Cecma 1010/1011 2LP
Mitchell; Hugh Ragin (*t, picc-t, flhn*); Spencer Barefield (*g*); Jaribu Shahid (*b*); Tani Tabbal (*d*). 10/88.

Mitchell's later work in the 1980s was finally disappointing. While a colleague such as Anthony Braxton worked out many directions through obsessive recording, Mitchell scarcely recorded at all. The only studio date, *The Flow Of Things*, is a static and tamely conventional reeds-and-rhythm date which yields little advance on his earlier experiments. The solo concert features him on soprano, alto and bass sax, but his use of different techniques as thematic material is cumbrous next to Braxton's similar approaches, and he has little of the vitality of Evan Parker or Peter Brötzmann. *Live In Detroit* finds the Sound Ensemble in splendid form: the first of two versions of 'Snurdy McGurdy And Her Dancing Shoes' features superbly sustained solos by the leader (on alto) and especially Ragin, who here sounds like a major voice: Barefield, Shahid and Tabbal create touch-sensitive interplay which is candidly revealed by the excellent sound, and there's a long, burning rendition of Lester Bowie's 'Me Bop'. But elsewhere Mitchell's own playing and direction again sound like an awkward reprise of his earlier work.

***   **After Fallen Leaves** Silkheart SHCD 126 CD
Mitchell; Arne Forsén (*p*); Ulf Aokerhielm (*b*); Gilbert Matthews (*d*). 10/89.

(*)   **Songs In The Wind Victo 011 CD
Mitchell; Vartan Manoogian (*vn*); Vincent Davis, Richard Davis (*d*); Steve Sylvester (*bullroarers, windwands*). 6–8/90.

The haphazardness of Mitchell's recording regimen has made it difficult to take a balanced view of a musician whose work, had it been documented as extensively as, say, Anthony Braxton's, may have had a far more profound impact on the new music of the 1980s and '90s. As it is, Mitchell's marginalization has made records like these latest two seem like hurried odds and ends from his workshop. *After Fallen Leaves* features him with the Swedish Brus Trio, and there are many good moments – the boiling alto solo on 'Mr Freddie' and the long patchwork improvisation 'Come Gather Some Things' – without the session really making a coherent impact, since the trio seem eager but too unfamiliar with Mitchell's methods. *Songs In The Wind* is even more fragmented, the thirteen pieces ranging through solo, duo and trio explorations of mood and form: Mitchell is at his most unflinchingly austere here, and the oddball contributions of Sylvester seem like nothing more than a textural distraction. Hopefully, if Mitchell's plans to create a large repertory ensemble come to fruition, there'll be more opportunities to hear him at length on record in future.

HANK MOBLEY (1930–86)
TENOR SAXOPHONE

***   **The Jazz Message Of Hank Mobley** Savoy SV-0133 CD
Mobley; Donald Byrd (*t*); John LaPorta (*as*); Ronnie Ball, Horace Silver (*p*); Doug Watkins, Wendell Marshall (*b*); Kenny Clarke (*d*). 1–2/56.

(*)   **The Jazz Message Of Hank Mobley Vol. 2 Savoy SV-0158 CD
Mobley; Lee Morgan, Donald Byrd (*t*); Hank Jones, Barry Harris (*p*); Doug Watkins (*b*); Art Taylor, Kenny Clarke (*d*). 7–11/56.

Mobley's early records are customarily ignored, but these two discs for Savoy are probably as strongly delivered as anything he did in the 1950s. The first four tracks on the first *Jazz Message* (he doesn't play on the final three, which feature LaPorta) are played with great feeling and sensitivity, with 'Madeline' being an especially worthwhile ballad; even Byrd plays slightly above his usual faceless competence. The second *Message* sounds less forthright, with the programme clearly thrown together and the players sometimes watching the clock, but there are still some sinuous declamations on the blues from the leader. The remastering is good.

*** **The Hank Mobley Quintet** Blue Note B21Y-46816 CD
Mobley; Art Farmer (*t*); Horace Silver (*p*); Doug Watkins (*b*); Art Blakey (*d*). 3/57.

*** **Peckin' Time** Blue Note B21Y-81574 CD/MC
Mobley; Lee Morgan (*t*); Wynton Kelly (*p*); Paul Chambers (*b*); Charlie Persip (*d*). 2/58.

Now available only as American issues, Mobley's earlier Blue Notes are somewhat formula-bound examples of the hard bop session, although it's an impressive formula. The quintet album is lifted by the superlative rhythm section, and the lead-off 'Funk In Deep Freeze' is a near-classic of hard bop writing. *Peckin' Time* finds Morgan as much in the driving seat as Mobley, and both men work through improvisations of typical authority.

**** **Soul Station** Blue Note CDP 7465282 CD
Mobley; Wynton Kelly (*p*); Paul Chambers (*b*); Art Blakey (*d*). 2/60.

**** **Roll Call** Blue Note B21Y-46823 CD
As above, except add Freddie Hubbard (*t*). 11/60.

***(*) **Workout** Blue Note CDP 7840802 CD
Mobley; Wynton Kelly (*p*); Grant Green (*g*); Paul Chambers (*b*); Philly Joe Jones (*d*). 3/61.

*** **Another Workout** Blue Note CDP 7844312 CD
As above, except omit Green. 3–12/61.

Mobley's classic statements. Some have written him off as a lightweight among the hard men of hard-bop tenor, but any who hear these records must wonder why: there's nothing sickly about his tone, even if, as Mobley himself claimed, he sought a 'round sound' rather than a direct punch. His rhythmic subtlety is his strongest suit, accenting unexpected beats and planting emphases in places that take his phrasing out of the realms of cliché, but his slightly foggy undertone is another distinctive trait, and all this is combined with an overall mastery of the horn which – though seldom remarked on – is certainly the equal of almost any of his contemporaries. *Soul Station* is the one Mobley album which should be in every collection: his interplay with Blakey is superbly realized throughout, but especially in 'This I Dig Of You', while his ballad playing on 'If I Should Lose You', played at a slightly hopped-up tempo which always suits the saxophonist, is entirely sugar-free. *Roll Call* is very nearly as good and benefits also from Hubbard's youthful bravado, while *Workout* only slips down a notch for the thinner blues material and Green's occasionally routine playing. *Another Workout*, cut later the same year, is a rerun at a lower voltage. Respectable rather than startlingly good remastering to CD.

***(*) **No Room For Squares** Blue Note CDP 7841492 CD
Mobley; Lee Morgan (*t*); Andrew Hill (*p*); John Ore (*b*); Philly Joe Jones (*d*). 10/63.

*** **The Turnaround** Blue Note B21Y-84186 CD/MC
Mobley; Freddie Hubbard, Donald Byrd (*t*); Barry Harris, Herbie Hancock (*p*); Paul Chambers, Butch Warren (*b*); Billy Higgins, Philly Joe Jones (*d*). 2/65.

*** **Dippin'** Blue Note CDP 7465112 CD
Mobley; Lee Morgan (*t*); Harold Mabern (*p*); Larry Ridley (*b*); Billy Higgins (*d*). 6/65.

*** **A Caddy For Daddy** Blue Note CDP 7842302 CD
Mobley; Lee Morgan (*t*); Curtis Fuller (*tb*); McCoy Tyner (*p*); Bob Cranshaw (*b*); Billy Higgins (*d*). 12/65.

(*)   **Straight No Filter Blue Note B21Y-84435 CD
Mobley; Lee Morgan, Freddie Hubbard, Donald Byrd (*t*); McCoy Tyner, Barry Harris,
Herbie Hancock (*p*); Paul Chambers, Butch Warren, Bob Cranshaw (*b*); Philly Joe
Jones, Billy Higgins (*d*). 3/63–6/66.

***   **Hi Voltage** Blue Note B21Y-84273 CD/MC
Mobley; Blue Mitchell (*t*); Jackie McLean (*as*); John Hicks (*p*); Bob Cranshaw (*b*);
Billy Higgins (*d*). 67.

(*)   **Far Away Lands Blue Note CDP B21Y-84425 CD
Mobley; Donald Byrd (*t*); Cedar Walton (*p*); Ron Carter (*b*); Billy Higgins (*d*). 5/67.

Mobley recorded regularly for Blue Note in the mid-1960s and his records have remained
popular with a younger jazz audience. Frankly, most of them are solid and dependable rather
than outstanding sessions, and the mix'n'match out-takes of *Straight No Filter* and desultory
blowing of *Far Away Lands* add little more than loose jottings to the Mobley story. *No Room
For Squares* has a terrific Mobley solo on 'Three Way Split' and includes Andrew Hill on four
tracks, while the quintet responsible for half of *The Turnaround* – Mobley, Hubbard, Harris,
Chambers and Higgins – is a dream hard-bop band that isn't sustained for the whole record.
Dippin' might have been sharper, and the intriguing personnel on *A Caddy For Daddy* doesn't
quite live up to expectations: with scores of Blue Note sessions behind him, Mobley might have
been feeling his age at the label a little. Certainly the soul-jazz title-track of *Hi Voltage* hardly
suits him at all, and Jackie McLean sounds much more interested. The slightly earlier Blue
Notes remain the best place to get acquainted with Mobley's beguiling playing.

MODERN JAZZ QUARTET
GROUP

John Lewis (*p*); Milt Jackson (*vib*); Percy Heath (*b*); Connie Kay (*d*); Kenny Clarke
(*d*; pre-1955).

***(*)   **The Artistry Of The Modern Jazz Quartet** Prestige 60 016 CD
With Kenny Clarke (*d*), Sonny Rollins (*ts*). 12/52, 6 & 10/53, 12/54, 1/55, 7/55.

***(*)   **Django** Original Jazz Classics OJC 057 CD/LP/MC
6/53, 12/54, 1/55.

***(*)   **MJQ** Original Jazz Classics OJC 125 CD/LP/MC
With Henry Boozier (*t*), Horace Silver (*p*). 6/54, 12/56.

***   **Concorde** Original Jazz Classics OJC 002 CD/LP/MC
7/55.

***   **Fontessa** Atlantic SD 1231 LP
1 & 2/56.

***   **Live 1956** Jazz Anthology 550062 CD
56.

(***)   **The Legendary Performances** Suisa JZCD 340 CD
10/57, 1/58.

***   **Compact Jazz: Modern Jazz Quartet Plus** Verve 833290 CD
10/57.

***(*)   **At Music Inn: Volume 2** Atlantic SD 1299 CD
With Sonny Rollins (*ts*). 8/58.

***   **Longing For The Continent** LRC CDC 7678 CD
With Jazz Group de Paris. 58.

***(*)   **Pyramid** Atlantic 781340 CD
8 & 12/59, 1/60.

**   **Blues On Bach** Atlantic 781393 CD
Date not known.

***(*) **Lonely Woman** Atlantic SD 1381 2 CD
62.

*** **Comedy** Atlantic 1390 2 CD
With Diahann Carroll (*v*). 10/60, 1/62.

*** **The Sheriff** Atlantic AMCY 1026 CD
5 & 12/63.

(*) **Live At The Lighthouse Original Master Recordings MPCD 827 CD
67.

*** **The Last Concert** Atlantic 81976 CD
11/74.

(*) **Reunion At Budokan Pablo 2308243 LP/MC
82.

(*) **Together Again Pablo Live 2308344 CD/LP/MC
7/82.

*** **Together Again – Echoes** Pablo 2312142 CD/LP/MC
3/84.

*** **Topsy – This One's For Basie** Pablo 2310917 CD/LP/MC
6/85.

*** **Three Windows** Atlantic 254833 CD/LP/MC
With New York Chamber Symphony. 87.

*** **For Ellington** East West 790926 CD/LP/MC
2/88.

(*) **The Best Of The Modern Jazz Quartet Pablo 2405 423 CD/LP/MC
80s.

The MJQ is something of an enigma. Frequently dismissed – as unexciting, pretentious, bland, Europeanized, pat – they have been hugely popular for much of the last thirty years, filling halls and consistently outselling most other jazz acts (who else's catalogue has made such a comprehensive transition to CD?). So, they're commercial, then, MOR entertainers in tuxes with no real jazz credentials?

The enigma lies in that 'Modern', for inasmuch as the MJQ shift more product than anyone else, they are also radicals (or maybe nowadays that American hybrid, radical-conservatives) who have done more than most barnstorming revolutionaries to change the nature and form of jazz performance, to free it from its changes-based theme-and-solos clichés. Leader/composer John Lewis has a firm grounding in European classical music, particularly the Baroque, and was a leading light in both Third Stream music and the *Birth of the Cool* sessions with Gerry Mulligan and Miles Davis. From the outset, he attempted to infuse jazz performance with a consciousness of form, using elements of through-composition, counterpoint, melodic variation and, above all, fugue to multiply the trajectories of improvisation. And just as people still, even now, like stories with a beginning, middle and end, people have liked the well-made quality of MJQ performances which, on their night, don't lack for old-fashioned excitement.

The Modern Jazz Quartet was born viviparously out of the post-war Dizzy Gillespie band. The fact that it had been Gillespie's rhythm section (with Ray Brown on bass originally and Kenny Clarke on drums, both soon replaced) led people to question the group's viability as an independent performing unit. The early recordings more than resolve that doubt.

Concorde combines a swing that would have been brighter if recording quality had been better with some superb fugal writing. Lewis has never been an exciting performer (in contrast to Jackson, who is one of the great soloists in jazz), but his brilliant grasp of structure is evident from the beginning. Of the classic MJQ pieces – 'One Bass Hit', 'The Golden Striker', 'Bags' Groove' – none characterizes the group more completely than Lewis's 'Django', first recorded in the session of December 1954. The Prestige is a useful CD history of the early days of the band, but it's probably better to hear the constituent sessions in their entirety. The budget-price *Legendary Performances* contains several of the classic pieces, recorded in concert at Donaueschingen and, early the following year, San Remo, but the sound is atrocious and does the group no service whatsoever. Some of the material on the original Prestige two-disc vinyl format has been removed to make way for a Sonny Rollins/MJQ set ('No Moe', 'The Stopper', 'In A Sentimental Mood', 'Almost Like Being In Love'), which is a pity, for this material was long available on OJC 011 and on another Prestige album.

Kay slipped into the band without a ripple. His cooler approach, less overwhelming than Clarke's could be, was ideal, and he sounds right from the word go. His debut was on the fine *Concorde* which sees Lewis trying to blend jazz improvisation with European counterpoint. Though the integration is by no means always complete, it's more apealling in its very roughness than the slick Bach-chat of the Atlantic, with Lewis tinkling on harpsichord.

Though home-grown compositions reappear throughout the band's history (there's a particularly good 'Django' on *Pyramid*), there are also constant references to standard repertoire: 'How High the Moon' on the same album, 'Mean to Me' on *The Sheriff* (sitting alongside a slice of Villa-Lobos), 'Nature Boy' on the late, post-reunion Basie tribute.

By the same inverted snobbery that demands standards rather than 'pretentious classical rubbish', it's long been a useful cop-out to profess admiration only for those MJQ albums featuring right-on guests. The earlier Silver collaboration isn't as well known as the justly famous Rollins encounter at Music Inn, where he joins them on 'Bags' Groove' and 'A Night in Tunisia'. This is one of the group's very best recordings and conjures some of Jackson's most dazzling solo work, as well as some crisp interventions from Heath (the unsung soloist of the group) and Kay.

Lewis's first exploration of characters from the *commedia dell'arte* came in *Fontessa*, an appropriately chill and stately record that can seem a little enigmatic, even off-putting. He develops these interests considerably in the simply titled *Comedy* which largely consists of dulcet character sketches with unexpected twists and quietly violent dissonances. The themes of *commedia* are remarkably appropriate to a group who have always presented themselves in sharply etched silhouette, playing a music that is deceptively smooth and untroubled, but which harbours considerable jazz feeling and, as on both *Fontessa* and *Comedy*, considerable disruption to conventional harmonic progression.

Given Lewis's interests and accomplishments as an orchestrator, there have been surprisingly few jazz group-with-orchestra experiments. More typical, perhaps, than the 1987 *Three Windows* (a project that significantly included music written for a Roger Vadim film 30 years earlier and including the classic 'Golden Striker' in a magnificent triple fugue, also 'Django') is what Lewis does on *Lonely Woman*. One of the very finest of the group's albums, this opens with a breathtaking arrangement of Ornette Coleman's haunting dirge and then proceeds with small group performances of three works – 'Animal Dance', 'Lamb, Leopard' and 'Fugato' – which were originally conceived for orchestral performance. Remarkably, Lewis's small group arrangements still manage to give an impression of symphonic voicings.

There is little question that the energy and inventiveness of the band was diluted by time. By the early 1970s, the MJQ had become stylists first and improvisers only then. They disbanded in 1974, after a final flourish, but got together again and were still producing vital music (once again largely composed) in the 1980s. Lewis' explorations into the wider ramifications of jazz composition have drawn him closer and closer to Ellington and the ducal tribute on East West combines the original title-track and 'Maestro E.K.E.' – standing for Edward Kennedy Ellington – with classics like 'Ko-Ko', 'Jack The Bear', 'Prelude To A Kiss' and 'Rockin' In Rhythm'. Invigorated by that contact, the MJQ sound as if they could go on for ever.

***(*) **MJQ 40** Atlantic 7 82330 2 4CD
  With Bernie Glow, Joe Newman, Ernie Royal, Clark Terry, Snooky Young (*t*); Jimmy Cleveland, Garnett Brown, Tony Studd, Kai Winding (*tb*); Jimmy Giuffre, Bill McColl (*cl*); Bob de Domenica (*f*); Manny Zeigler (*bsn*); Paul Desmond, Charlie Mariano, Phil Woods (*as*); Richie Kamuca, Seldon Powell (*ts*); Wally Kane (*bs*); Laurindo Almeida, Howard Collins (*g*); Joe Tekula (*clo*); Betty Glauman (*hp*); The Swingle Singers (*v*). 52–88.

A magnificently packaged ruby-anniversary celebration which draws on all stages and aspects of the group's career. Fifty-four tracks on four CDs taking in music from such records as *Plastic Dreams* (once mildly notorious for its un-MJQ-ish cover painting of a blow-up sex doll), *Live At The Lighthouse*, *Third Stream Music*, and from the fine 1966 concert in Japan. As an introduction to the group's music, the accompanying booklet (which includes a complete discography) could hardly be bettered.

LOUIS MOHOLO (born 1940)
DRUMS, PERCUSSION

***(*)   **Tern** FMP SAJ 43/44 2LP
Moholo; Larry Stabbins (*ts, ss*); Keith Tippett (*p*). 11/82.

In the 1960s, radical American improvisers (with separatist agenda firmly in mind) renewed their interest in African percussion. What was quickly evident was that traditional African musics frequently anticipated the methodologies of free jazz and that the sometimes anarchic energies of contemporary African jazz were already more abstract than the prevailing American models. In Europe, for a variety of reasons, this was perceived much more readily and there was a quicker and less ideological trade-off between African jazz and popular music on the one hand, and free music.

Louis Moholo, more than most of the South African exiles active on the jazz scene in Britain (but much like the late Johnny Dyani and the late Dudu Pukwana), was able to make the transition without undue strain. His own bands – Spirits Rejoice, Viva La Black, the African Drum Ensemble – have always contained free or abstract elements, and Moholo has always been in demand as a more experimental improviser, where his drive and intensity are comparable to that of Americans Milford Graves and Andrew Cyrille.

Tern features the drummer in a very powerful improvising trio. Tippett is similarly eclectic, ranging effortlessly from furiously pounded clusters (derived from Cecil Taylor) to delicate ripples and single-note quasi-melodies. Stabbins has been consistently underrated, and any re-assessment of his muscular lyricism might usefully begin here. He plays economically and in assimilable musical units (perhaps in contrast to the energetic flow of his partners) and seems remarkably free of undigested influences.

***   **Exile** Ogun OGCD 003 CD
Moholo; Sean Bergin, Steve Williamson (*reeds*); Paul Rogers (*b*). 90.

From Viva La Black, a hot, dangerous session, with Bergin's ferocious statements in constant opposition to Williamson's much cooler delivery, and with Rogers and Moholo working independently of the horns most of the time. 'Wathinta Amododa' is the main piece, but most of its initial power is thrown away in an overlong development-cum-denouement.

LARS MØLLER (born 1967)
TENOR SAXOPHONE

***(*)   **Copenhagen Groove** Stunt STUCD 18902 CD
Møller; Thomas Clausen (*p*); Niels-Henning Ørsted-Pedersen (*b*); Jimmy Cobb (*d*).
5/88.

'Ingen Mas' – no sweat – gives some sense of Møller's astonishing gifts, which seem to be conveyed almost effortlessly. In fact, as Dave Liebman points out in an admiring liner-note, the young Dane is a serious-minded and dedicated student of the music and takes a uniquely thoughtful line on performance that prevents from accepting ready solutions.

Perhaps inevitably, Coltrane is the dominant influence. Møller's version of 'The Night Has A Thousand Eyes' is immediately identifiable as a gloss on the original version on *Coltrane's Sound*, but the youngster has imposed his own rhythmic framework and ventures a couple of harmonic ideas towards the middle of a carefully wrought solo. The five originals on *Copenhagen Groove* are all patiently and rather modestly worked out, in which enterprise the experienced Clausen is an ideal partner, and NHØP and Cobb the kind of rhythm section young players dream of. The disc may not be easy to find, but it shouldn't be passed up under any circumstances.

GRACHAN MONCUR III (born 1937)
TROMBONE

****   **Evolution** Blue Note CDP 784153 CD
Moncur; Lee Morgan (*t*); Jackie McLean (*as*); Bobby Hutcherson (*vib*); Bob
Cranshaw (*b*); Tony Williams (*d*).

Evolution wasn't the first or the last attempt to convey the broader movements of mankind in a
jazz setting: there was Mingus's hugely inventive *Pithecanthropus Erectus* and, more recently,
George Russell's *The African Game* and Marilyn Crispell's *Gaia*. Moncur's composition is less
ambitious than any of these; the track is much shorter for a start, but it hovers between bop
orthodoxy (reflected in Moncur's strong J. J. Johnson influence) and later developments in free
jazz. Moncur was probably the only major American trombonist to attempt the synthesis
(though Roswell Rudd and, in Europe, the towering Albert Mangelsdorff had similar
ambitions).

On *Evolution* he deploys a stellar band with great skill. Whatever slackness there is in the
title-track is largely due to his desire for individual freedom within the group context.
Elsewhere, it's clearer that he conceives the rhythm section as an independent unit, much as
Eric Dolphy did, and it's significant that Hutcherson and Williams also played on Dolphy's
epochal *Out To Lunch*. The opening 'Air Raid' makes that connection even more obvious, and
'The Coaster' has a freely accented flow that subordinates metre to pulse, a device typical of
Thelonious Monk, who is celebrated in the fourth track, 'Monk In Wonderland'. It's the most
rigorous of the tracks, completing an invigorating and intellectually satisfying set by a musician
whose subsequent career has been rather muted.

THELONIOUS MONK (1917–82)
PIANO

*****   **Genius of Modern Music: Volume 1** Blue Note 781510 CD

****   **Genius of Modern Music: Volume 2** Blue Note 781511 CD
Monk; Kenny Dorham, Idrees Sulieman, George Taitt (*t*); Lou Donaldson, Sahib
Shihab, Danny Quebec West (*as*); Billy Smith, Lucky Thompson (*ts*); Milt Jackson
(*vib*); Nelson Boyd, Al McKibbon, Bob Paige, Gene Ramey, John Simmons (*b*); Art
Blakey, Max Roach, Shadow Wilson (*d*). 10 & 11/47, 7/48, 7/51, 5/52.

Monk is one of the giants of modern American music, whose output ranks, with that of Morton
and Ellington, as *composition* of the highest order. Though no one questions his skills as a
pianist (they were compounded of stride, blues and a more romantic strain derived from Teddy
Wilson and filtered through Monk's wonderfully lateral intelligence), it is as a composer that he
has made the greatest impact on subsequent jazz music. Even so, it is vital to recognize that the
music and the playing style are necessary to each other and precisely complementary. Though
he has attracted more dedicated interpreters since his death than almost any musician (Ornette
Coleman and John Coltrane perhaps approach his standing with other players, but from very
different perspectives), Monk tunes played by anyone else always seem to lack a certain
conclusive authenticity.

Frequently misunderstood by critics and fans (and also by the less discerning of his fellow
musicians), he received due public recognition only quite late in his career, by which time
younger pianists originally encouraged by him and his example (Bud Powell is the foremost)
had recorded and died and been canonized. It's now questioned whether Monk was ever, as he
once appeared, a founding father of bop. Though some of his work, like 'In Walked Bud' on
Genius Of M~ ~ ~usic, utilized a straightforward chord sequence, and though 'Eronel', one
~ ~ ~ ~ ~ks from the critical July 1951 session with Milt Jackson, is relatively
~ ~ ~ interest in tough, pianistic melody, displaced rhythm and often extreme
~ ~ in his treatment of 'Carolina Moon') rather sets him apart from the bop

~ssential Monk recordings, no less achieved and magisterial for being his
~orded only intermittently over the next ten years, which makes them
~warted first by an American Federation of Musicians recording ban
~tence and a blacklisting, Monk took time to regain the highs of these

remarkable sides. The earliest of the sessions, with Sulieman, Danny Quebec West and Billy Smith, is not particularly inspired, though the pianist's contribution is instantly identifiable; his solo on 'Thelonious', built up out of minimal thematic potential, is emotionally powerful and restlessly allusive. A month later he was working with a more enterprising group (the difference in Blakey's response between the two sessions is remarkable) and producing his first classic recordings – of 'In Walked Bud' and ' 'Round About Midnight'.

The addition of Milt Jackson exactly a year later for the session that yielded 'Epistrophy' and 'Misterioso' was a turning point in his music, enormously extending its rhythmic potential and harmonic complexity. Jackson who, because of his association with the Modern Jazz Quartet, is now rather apt to be dismissed as a player lacking in improvisational excitement, makes an incalculable contribution to the music, here and on the session of July 1951 which yielded the classic 'Straight, No Chaser'. The later recordings on the set are much more conventionally arranged and lack the excitement and sheer imaginative power of the earlier cuts, but they do help overturn the received image of Monk as a man who wrote one beautiful ballad and then so dedicated the rest of his career to intractable dissonance as to set him apart entirely from the main currents of modern jazz.

Between 1952 and 1955, when he contracted to Riverside Records, Monk's career was relatively in the doldrums. However, he had already recorded enough material to guarantee him a place in any significant canon. No jazz fan should be without either of these records.

****   **Thelonious Monk Trio / Blue Monk: Volume 2** Prestige CDJZD 009 CD
Monk; Ray Copeland (*t*); Frank Foster (*ts*); Percy Heath, Gary Mapp, Curley Russell (*b*); Art Blakey, Max Roach (*d*). 10 & 12/52, 5 & 9/54.

***(*)   **Thelonious Monk** Original Jazz Classics OJC 010 CD/LP
Monk; Percy Heath, Gary Mapp (*p*); Art Blakey, Max Roach (*d*). 10 & 12/52, 9/54.

***(*)   **Thelonious Monk / Sonny Rollins** Original Jazz Classics OJC 059 CD/LP/MC
Monk; Sonny Rollins (*ts*); Julius Watkins (*frhn*); Percy Heath, Tommy Potter (*b*); Art Blakey, Willie Jones, Art Taylor (*d*). 11/53, 9 & 10/54.

***(*)   **MONK** Original Jazz Classics OJC 016 CD/LP/MC
Monk; Ray Copeland (*t*); Julius Watkins (*frhn*); Sonny Rollins, Frank Foster (*ts*); Percy Heath, Curley Russell (*b*); Art Blakey, Willie Jones (*d*). 11/53, 5/54.

The end of Monk's Prestige period included some remarkably inventive and adventurous, which isn't always played as well as it deserves. The trios with Heath and Blakey remain among the best performances of his career, however, and should on no account be missed.

The first of this group is a valuable twofer reissue of Prestige P 7027 and 7848, with original liner-notes in each case; though it involves repetition with the OJCs, it's a useful way of getting the best of the material on a single CD. OJC 010 repeats all the material save for four quintet tracks from May 1954 featuring Copeland and Foster on 'We See', 'Smoke Gets In Your Eyes', 'Locomotive' and the too little played 'Hackensack', all of which are taken from *MONK*. The latter album also includes additional material from the November 1953 recordings with Sonny Rollins which yielded OJC 059. That date was marked by the astonishing 'Friday The 13th', a brilliant use of simultaneous thematic statements which doesn't quite come off in this performance but sufficiently survives the group's uncertainty to mark it out as daring.

The September 1954 session with Heath and Blakey was originally the basis of the Prestige *Monk's Moods* and it's good to have it filled out with the additional 'Work' and 'Nutty', which are also on *Monk/Rollins*. Even with a repeat of 'Blue Monk' (*the* definitive version) and the solo slot 'Just A Gigolo', the Prestige is unbeatable value, clocking in at nearly 78 minutes.

Monk's treatment of standards is remarkable. When Monk strips down a tune, he arranges the constituent parts by the numbers, like a rifleman at boot camp, with the overall shape and function always evident. On 'These Foolish Things' and 'Sweet And Lovely' he never for a moment loses sight of the melody and, as with the originals, builds a carefully crafted performance that is light years away from the conventional theme-solo-theme format into which even relatively adventurous jazz performance seemed to be locked. A vital episode in modern jazz; the precise format chosen will depend on level of interest and budget, for it's almost impossible to go wrong.

***   **Plays Duke Ellington** Original Jazz Classics OJC 024 CD/LP/MC
Monk; Oscar Pettiford (*b*); Kenny Clarke (*d*). 7/55.

***   **The Unique Thelonious Monk** Original Jazz Classics OJC 064 CD/LP/MC
       Monk; Oscar Pettiford (*b*); Art Blakey (*d*). 3–4/56.

A curious start. Orrin Keepnews remembers that Monk spent an age simply picking out the Ellington tunes at the piano and trying to get them straight. It's a respectful nod from one master to another, but not much more. *The Unique* is a standards album which doesn't quite go to the extremes of demolition which Monk chose when dropping a standard into one of his otherwise original dates, and Pettiford doesn't seem like the best choice for bassist.

****   **Brilliant Corners** Original Jazz Classics OJC 026 CD/LP/MC
       Monk; Clark Terry (*t*); Ernie Henry (*as*); Sonny Rollins (*ts*); Oscar Pettiford (*b*); Max Roach (*d*). 12/56.

A staggering record, imperfect and patched together after the sessions, but one of the most vivid insights into Monk's music. The title tune was so difficult that no single perfect take was finished (after 25 tries), and what we hear is a spliced-together piece of music. Full of tensions within the band, the record somehow delivers utterly compelling accounts of 'Pannonica', 'Bemsha Swing', 'Ba-Lue Bolivar Ba-lues Are' as well as the title piece, and Monk ties it up with a one-take reading of 'I Surrender Dear'.

****   **Thelonious Himself** Original Jazz Classics OJC 254 CD/LP/MC
       Monk; John Coltrane (*ts*); Wilbur Ware (*b*). 4/57.

****   **Thelonious Monk With John Coltrane** Original Jazz Classics OJC 039 CD/LP/MC
       Monk; Ray Copeland (*t*); Gigi Gryce (*as*); Coleman Hawkins, John Coltrane (*ts*); Wilbur Ware (*b*); Shadow Wilson, Art Blakey (*d*). 4–6/57.

****   **Monk's Music** Original Jazz Classics OJC 084 CD/LP/MC
       Monk; Ray Copeland (*t*); Gigi Gryce (*as*); Coleman Hawkins, John Coltrane (*ts*); Wilbur Ware (*b*); Art Blakey (*d*). 6/57.

Thelonious Himself is a first solo album, and one of his definitive statements up to this point. Alone at last, Monk's prevarications on his own pieces begin to sound definitive as each progresses: he unpicks them and lays them out again with an almost scientific precision, but the immediacy of each interpretation is anything but detached. 'Functional' was probably never given a better reading than here, and his accompanying interpretations of standards are scarcely less compelling, melody and rhythm placed under new lights in each one. Capping it is the trio version of 'Monk's Mood' with Coltrane and Ware, and again, even with all the many versions of this tune which are extant, this one is unlike any other.

The sessions which made up *Thelonius Monk With John Coltrane* and *Monk's Music* are arguably the most compelling records with horns that he ever made. The first is actually by the quartet with Coltrane, Ware and Wilson on three tracks (frustratingly, the only ones the quartet made, despite working together for no less than six months at a New York residency), which include a lovely reading of 'Ruby My Dear', and throughout Coltrane seems to play humbly, in almost complete deference to the leader. This contrasts pretty strikingly with Hawkins on the second session, of which two alternative takes are also on OJC 039. The sonorous qualities of the horns make this one of the most beautiful-sounding of Monk sessions, and his inspired idea to start the record with an acapella arrangement of 'Abide With Me' sets an extraordinary atmosphere at the very start. There are still problems: the group play stiffly on these rhythms, Hawkins comes in wrongly a couple of times, and as fiercely as everyone is trying it often sounds more like six men playing at Monk rather than with him. But the flavour of the session is fascinating, and Monk himself sounds wholly authoritative.

***(*)   **Thelonious In Action** Original Jazz Classics OJC 103 CD/LP/MC
       Monk; Johnny Griffin (*ts*); Ahmed Abdul-Malik (*b*); Roy Haynes (*d*). 8/58.

***(*)   **Misterioso** Original Jazz Classics OJC 206 CD/LP/MC
       Monk; Johnny Griffin (*ts*); Ahmed Abdul-Malik (*b*); Roy Haynes (*d*). 8/58.

It might, on the face of it, seem improbable that such a headstrong and unmysterious character as Johnny Griffin could be such a masterful interpreter of Monk. But their partnership was an inspiring one, the tenorman unperturbed by any idea that Monk's music was difficult, and the quartet is on blistering form on these dates, recorded live at New York's lamented Five Spot.

***(*) **At Town Hall** Original Jazz Classics OJC 135 CD/LP/MC
    Monk; Donald Byrd (*t*); Eddie Bert (*tb*); Bob Northern (*frhn*); Phil Woods (*as*);
    Charlie Rouse (*ts*); Pepper Adams (*bs*); Jay McAllister (*tba*); Sam Jones (*b*); Art
    Taylor (*d*). 2/59.

Although Monk regarded this Town Hall concert as a triumph, the results seem rather mixed now. The long and suitably grand attempt at 'Monk's Mood' sounds rather lugubrious, and in general the ensemble catches only elements of Monk's intentions: his peculiar truce between a sober gaiety, bleak humour and thunderous intensity is a difficult thing for a big band to realize, and while there is some fine playing – by Woods and Rouse in particular – the band could probably have used a lot more time to figure out the composer's vision. Still, it's a valuable document of Monk's one personal involvement on a large-scale reading of his music.

***   **5 By Monk By 5** Original Jazz Classics OJC 362 CD/LP/MC
    Monk; Thad Jones (*t*); Charlie Rouse (*ts*); Sam Jones (*b*); Arthur Taylor (*d*). 6/59.

A relatively little-known Monk session but a very good one. Jones is another not much thought of as a Monk interpreter, but he carries himself very capably and commits a brilliant improvisation to 'Jackie-Ing', even though (as Orrin Keepnews remembers) he had to struggle with what was then a new piece that Monk attempted to teach everybody by humming it. The CD includes the first two (rejected) takes of 'Played Twice', another new tune.

**** **Thelonious Alone In San Francisco** Original Jazz Classics OJC 231 CD/LP/MC
    Monk (*p* solo). 10/59.

Another ruminative solo masterwork. Besides six originals, here is Monk elevating (or destroying, depending on one's point of view) 'There's Danger In Your Eyes, Cherie' and 'You Took The Words Right Out Of My Heart'. As a primer for understanding his piano playing, there is probably no better introduction than this one.

***   **At The Blackhawk** Original Jazz Classics OJC 305 CD/LP/MC
    Monk; Joe Gordon (*t*); Charlie Rouse, Harold Land (*ts*); John Ore (*b*); Billy Higgins
    (*d*). 4/60.

Live in San Francisco. Land and Gordon were late additions to the band but both men play well. It's not a classic Monk date by any means – despite another tune making its debut, 'San Francisco Holiday' – but there seems to be a good spirit in the playing and the leader sounds at his most genial.

***   **The First European Concert** Magnetic MRCD 120 CD
    Monk; Charlie Rouse (*ts*); John Ore (*b*); Frankie Dunlop (*d*). 4/61.

***(*) **Monk In Bern** Magnetic MRCD 126 CD
    As above. 5/61.

***(*) **Live In Stockholm** Dragon DRLP 151/2 2LP
    As above. 5/61.

***(*) **Live In Stockholm** DIW 315/6 2CD
    As above. 5/61.

The 1961 European tour and the subsequent Columbia contract put the seal on Monk's critical reputation. It's arguable that the end of his great association with Riverside marked the watershed in his creativity and that nothing he did after 1962 had the inventiveness and authority of the Blue Note, Prestige and Riverside years. Certainly, these three concert recordings from the 1961 tour have a strange *fin de siècle* quality, with a more than usually repetitive carry-over of ideas and very little sign of the pianist's usual ability to reinvent songs night after night. It's ironic that he should have been so warmly received in Europe, for Monk's compositional sense and his playing style were largely overdetermined by American models, rarely (as was the case with Bud Powell) by direct or ironic reference to the European classical tradition. What may have appealed to European audiences, even Swedes weaned on marathon blowing sessions by American exiles, was precisely his emphasis on *compositions*, rather than schematic chord progressions, as the basis of improvisation.

As so often, Rouse is the bellwether, uneasy and aggressive by turns in the presence of a rather diffident Monk on the first of the records (see 'Off Minor') but finding his feet with a vengeance in Bern and Stockholm. The DIW sound is very clear and pristine, but lacks the warmth and sheer 'feel' of the two-disc Dragon and those who already have that needn't feel they have to update urgently. Of the group, the Bern concert is perhaps the most rounded, with a wonderful, spiky-romantic version of 'I'm Getting Sentimental Over You' and the staple 'Blue Monk'. The Swedish date offers welcome performances of 'Ba-Lue Bolivar Ba-Lues Are' from *Brilliant Corners*, and a fine 'Body And Soul'. 'Just a Gigolo' is a solo performance, played in a self-consciously distracted manner, as if saying It's a *hell* of a job, but someone has to do it.

***   **Monk's Dream** Columbia 40786 CD/MC
Monk; Charlie Rouse (*ts*); John Ore (*b*); Frankie Dunlop (*d*). 10 & 11/62.

This was Monk's first album for CBS and, as Peter Keepnews points out in the reissue notes, it established the pattern for those that followed. Each contained a mixture of originals – most of them now getting quite long in the tooth – and standards, and marked a slight softening of Monk's once rather alien attack. The standards performances – 'Body And Soul', 'Just A Gigolo', 'Sweet And Lovely' – are not always immediately identifiable with the brittle, lateral-thinking genius of the Blue Notes and Riversides and are increasingly dependent on rather formulaic solutions. 'Monk's Dream' and 'Bye-Ya' are slightly tame and the changes of title on 'Bolivar Blues' (weirdly phoneticized in its first version) and 'Five Spot Blues' (originally 'Blues Five Spot') suggest how much Monk was unconsciously and partially moving towards the mainstream.

No one seems to have told Charlie Rouse, who really takes over on some of these tracks. The saxophonist sounds jagged and angular where the rhythm has been somewhat rationalized, intensely bluesy where the harmony begins to sound legitimate. Worthy of three stars for Rouse alone.

***   **The Composer** CBS 463338 2 CD
Monk; Charlie Rouse (*ts*); Larry Gales, John Ore, Butch Warren (*b*); Frankie Dunlop, Ben Riley (*d*); unidentified band conducted by Oliver Nelson. 11/62, 2, 3 & 5/63, 10/64, 3/65, 11/68.

A reasonable sampling of mostly live material from relatively late in Monk's active life. There's a previously unreleased version of 'Blue Monk', arranged for big band and conducted by Oliver Nelson, and two other tracks ('Brilliant Corners' and 'Reflections') from the same session. As Lee Jeske points out in his liner-note, Monk was often criticized from performing the same material over and over again, and this does represent something of a problem for the collector, who may well lose track of how many solo performances of 'Round Midnight' or 'Ruby, My Dear' he actually owns. Though these performances all date from the mid-1960s, all the compositions are from the immediate post-war decade, a further sign of the way Monk's genius as a composer diminished after the mid-1950s. Obviously pitched at newcomers as a useful compilation of the most important themes, this is a slightly muted introduction to Monk. Almost everything is available in a better and more varied form elsewhere.

***   **Criss Cross** Sony/Columbia COL 469184 CD
Monk; Charlie Rouse (*ts*); John Ore (*b*); Frankie Dunlop (*d*). 63.

One of the drabbest of the Columbias, *Criss Cross* nonetheless contains two sterling tracks, a vibrant 'Don't Blame Me' and a subtly varied 'Eronel'. The rhythm section are slightly better recorded than on some of the sessions, as if to make up for Monk's occasional lack of enterprise.

***   **Solo Monk** Columbia 09149 CD
Monk (*p* solo).

A rather lacklustre collection of unaccompanied performances, this doesn't compare with earlier, more focused endeavours. Monk's solos always seems to work better in the wider context of group albums, but it may prove useful now and again to concentrate on the bare bones, and from that perspective, this is a useful introduction to Monk's still underrated piano style.

***   **Tokyo Concerts** Sony/Columbia COL 466552 CD
Monk; Charlie Rouse (*ts*); Butch Warren (*b*); Frankie Dunlop (*d*).

Monk's reputation in Japan was cemented much quicker even than in Europe and this documents his first successful visit. The stand-out performances are 'Pannonica' and a marvellous 'Hackensack'. By his own high standard, Rouse is rather anonymous and plays surprisingly little of consequence, but the set as a whole is well worth hearing.

***(*)   **It's Monk's Time** Sony/Columbia COL 468405 CD
Monk; Charlie Rouse (*ts*); Butch Warren (*b*); Ben Riley (*d*). 64.

One of the best sessions of the period, recorded at the height of Monk's critical standing. In 1964, he was subject of a cover story in *Time* magazine, one of only three jazz artists (all piano players, but no more clues) to have been accorded that accolade. There's certainly nothing compromised or middle-market about this tough, abrasive set. Monk's sound had softened considerably over the past decade, partly as a result of playing on better instruments, partly because of more sensitive recording set-ups. He still sounds angular and oblique, but does so without the percussive edge he was wont to bring to theme statements like 'Lulu's Back In Town', 'Stuffy Turkey' and 'Shuffle Boil' which stand out from the rest for the piquancy of the melodic invention.

***(*)   **Blue Monk** Bandstand BD 1505 CD/LP
Monk; Charlie Rouse (*ts*); Larry Gales (*b*); Ben Riley (*d*). 64.

***   **Evidence** France's Concert FCD 105 CD
Monk; as above, and with John Ore, Butch Warren (*b*); Frankie Dunlop (*d*). 3/63, 2/64, 3/66.

***   **Live In Paris, Alhambra 1964** France's Concert FCD 135 CD

(*)   **Live In Paris, 1964 France's Concert FCD 132 2CD
Monk; Charlie Rouse (*ts*); Butch Warren (*b*); Ben Riley (*d*). 2/64.

The lacklustre performances on FCD 132 certainly don't merit double-length presentation and rather contradict the liner-note's earnest assurance that these two discs are not merely the 'febrile searchings of an unpublished Monkian'. Even with judicious selection and editing, it would scarcely rank with the best of Monk's live albums, and there's a slightly rote feel to the programme with Rouse a great deal more muted than usual and Riley half asleep at his kit on the first take of 'Epistrophy' (which may explain why they give it a more than usually exuberant clatter at the end in its theme slot).

The Alhambra session was recorded the previous day and is in every respect brighter and more to the point. 'Blue Monk', 'Rhythm-A-Ning' and 'Epistrophy' are the only tracks in common, but the existence of a reasonable single CD should deter all but the most febrile searchers from the double set. Those whose Monkian temperature still remains low might prefer to sample the Gallic selections on the *Evidence* compilation (which mustn't be confused with Milestone M 9115) or, better still, the ranking performances of 'Light Blue', 'Evidence', 'Blue Monk' and 'Hackensack' on the nicely balanced (but acoustically unpredictable) Bandstand.

***   **Standard Monk** Bandstand BDCD 1529 CD
Monk; as for *Blue Monk*, above. 61–5.

Looking to Monk for an album of standards might seem a little like asking Pele to play at centre half. You know he could have done it, but it wasn't exactly what he was best at. These sessions, culled from live European sessions, range from miniatures like the unaccompanied 'Just A Gigolo' and 'Body And Soul', which clock in at just over a minute and three and a half minutes respectively, to massive 17-minute explorations of 'Sweet And Lovely' and 'Lulu's Back In Town'. Monk's affection for the surprisingly little-covered Warren and Dublin tune is amply borne out, as he and Rouse nudge away at its jaunty, rag-tinged melody, playing deliberately out of synch with one another on the theme statements. It's recorded in a echo-y acoustic, as if the band are playing in an empty gymnasium. The three unaccompanied Ellington tracks – 'Sophisticated Lady', 'Caravan' and 'Solitude' – are also marred by murky sound-quality and there are places where the original tape seems to have slowed fractionally. Worth having all the same for Monk's completely committed and individual response to the repertoire, and for the rugged intelligence of Rouse's replies.

***   **Live At The It Club** Sony/Columbia COL 4691862 CD
Monk; Charlie Rouse (*ts*); Larry Gales (*b*); Ben Riley (*d*). 10/64.

***   **Live At The Jazz Workshop** Sony/Columbia COL 4691832 CD
        As above. 11/64.

Established connoisseurs of live Monk material will value the later of these for a fizzing performance of the challenging 'Hackensack' and for a rhythmically adroit 'Bright Mississippi', on which Monk calls the shots to his rhythm section. The earlier session is more convincing all round, though, with particularly fine readings of 'Misterioso', 'Blue Monk' and 'Ba-Lu Bolivar Ba-Lues Are'. As with several of these reissues, the sound reveals significantly more of the bass and drums than on earlier sessions. Good, but it would be hard to argue Monk's greatness on the strength of these alone.

***(*)   **Olympia, 23 May 1965** Disc Trema 710377/8 2CD
        Monk; Charlie Rouse (*ts*); Larry Gales (*b*); Ben Riley (*d*). 5/65.

Darkly recorded but musically very fine concert material from Paris. It's a fairly exhaustive example of what the band were doing at this time and for that reason might be seen to replace one or more of the items above. 'Teo' and 'Bright Mississippi' receive sharp, well-directed readings, characteristic of the material as a whole.

***   **Straight, No Chaser** Sony/Columbia 468409 CD
        Monk; Charlie Rouse (*ts*); Larry Gales (*b*); Frankie Dunlop (*d*). 66.

Includes the intriguing 'Japanese Folk Song' and a spanking version of 'We See', but this is as late as Monk gets really interesting. There are already *longueurs* and too many of the eccentricities seem carefully studied. Much of the material is derived from a film made about Monk that further raised his critical standing without contributing substantially to awareness of what truly made him distinctive.

***(*)   **Live In Switzerland, 1966** Jazz Helvet JH 06 2CD
        Monk; Charlie Rouse (*ts*); Larry Gales (*b*); Ben Riley (*d*). 3/66.

(*)   **Live In Paris, 1967 France's Concert FCD 113 CD

***   **The Paris Concert** Charly CD 074 CD

***   **On Tour In Europe** Charly CD 122 CD
        Monk; Ray Copeland, Clark Terry (*t*); Jimmy Cleveland (*tb*); Phil Woods (*as*); Johnny Griffin, Charlie Rouse (*ts*); Larry Gales (*b*); Ben Riley (*d*). 67.

By this stage, things are getting seriously silly. There are probably two dozen (mostly live) performances of 'Blue Monk', with at least some overlapping (the versions on *Live In Paris, 1967* and *On Tour* are identical) and with less fundamental variation in the solo material. By the mid-1960s, Monk has a polished and relatively settled stage show and begins to sound like a man casting imitation pearls before real swine. There are Las Vegas-y spatters of applause at the start of numbers and even the most banal (consciously so?) of solos receives tumultuous acclaim.

  On balance, the Jazz Helvet set is a good buy, taking in all the obvious tunes. It may be hard to find, though, and the sound isn't wonderful. The two Charlys are the next best bet; *On Tour* takes in some of the same Nonet/Orchestra sessions as on the France's Concert, but the reproduction is crisper and truer. By this stage, though, all but the most feverish Monkians have turned back to their Riversides and early Blue Notes.

(*)   **Monk Underground Sony/Columbia 460066 CD
        Monk; Charlie Rouse (*ts*); Larry Gales (*b*); Ben Riley (*d*). 12/67, 2 & 12/68.

The contrived surrealism of the cover, with Monk seated at the piano in an overstuffed junk basement, a machine pistol slung over his shoulder, may have been intended to appeal to a younger, rock audience. The music within is equally ersatz, perfectly straightforward interpretations lent a modicum of credibility by angular, out-of-tempo theme statements, bizarre shifts of metre and key and a lazy, self-defeating approach to the solos that replaces Monk's usual careful craftsmanship with a loose, unsteady approach to chord changes.

***(*)   **The London Collection: Volume 1** Black Lion BL 760101 CD/LP

***   **The London Collection: Volume 2** Black Lion BL 760116 CD

***   **The London Collection: Volume 3** Black Lion TKCB 30083 CD
Monk; Al McKibbon (*b*); Art Blakey (*d*). 11/71.

The solo performances on Volume 1 offer a fair impression of how Monk's ability to invest improvisations on self-written or standard ('Lover Man', 'Darn That Dream') themes with the same logical development and sense of overall form that one might look for in a notated piece. It isn't clear that Blakey was an entirely sympathetic accompanist and some of the faster paced numbers sound a little overpowered. Certainly, McKibbon is difficult to hear over clustered accents on the bass drum. There is a wonderful improvisation, mockingly called 'Chordially' on Volume 3, which is presumably meant to refute the charge that Monk's apparent indifference to conventional changes playing was a token of limited technique rather than a conscious strategy. Useful and often enjoyable sessions, these are still rather late in the day for genuine fireworks.

***   **Monk In Italy** Original Jazz Classics OJC 488 CD/LP/MC
Monk; Charlie Rouse (*ts*); John Ore (*b*); Frankie Dunlop (*d*).

***   **Monk In France** Original Jazz Classics OJC 670 CD/MC
Monk; Charlie Rouse (*ts*); John Ore (*b*); Frankie Dunlop (*d*).

A couple of European tour dates which Riverside released as contract-closers with Monk. Both feature the quartet in quite sunny mood, but both also contain the seeds of routine which would trouble many of the 1960s recordings.

***(*)   **The Thelonious Monk Memorial Album** Milestone 47064 CD

***(*)   **Thelonious Monk And The Jazz Giants** Riverside 60-018 CD

*****   **The Complete Riverside Recordings** Riverside 022 15CD/22LP
As above OJC discs.

The two compilations are perfectly adequate snapshots of Monk's Riverside period, though casual listeners would be better off zeroing in on the four-star records listed above. *The Complete Riverside Recordings* is another monument for the shelves, but there is so little flab and so much music in this set that it defies criticism. Superbly annotated by producer Keepnews, and including many out-takes and extras absent from the original records (though many of those have now been restored to the CD reissues of the appropriate albums), this is enough for a lifetime's study. On that basis alone we award it a fifth star.

J. R. MONTEROSE (born 1927)
TENOR SAXOPHONE, SOPRANO SAXOPHONE

***   **A Little Pleasure** Reservoir RSR CD 109 CD
Monterose; Tommy Flanagan (*p*). 4/81.

Monterose's recording debut with soprano saxophone casts him in mostly reflective mood with the tirelessly lyrical Flanagan. There are two good originals by the saxophonist: the 3/4 'Pain And Suffering . . . And A Little Pleasure' and the less satisfying 'Vinnie's Pad'. Monterose stays with his flutey soprano for 'A Nightingale Sang In Berkeley Square' (with Flanagan playing the verse) and on 'Central Park West', whose solo underlines just how little dependent on Coltrane Monterose has been down the years. It's very intimately miked, and Monterose's breathing is very audible. Recommended.

WES MONTGOMERY (1925–68)
GUITAR, BASS GUITAR

***   **A Dynamic New Jazz Sound** Original Jazz Classics OJC 034 CD/LP

(*)   **Boss Guitar Original Jazz Classics OJC 261 CD/LP

***   **Portrait Of Wes** Original Jazz Classics OJC 144 CD/LP
Montgomery; Mel Rhyne (*org*); Paul Parker (*d* on *Dynamic*); Jimmy Cobb (*d* on Boss Guitar); George Brown (*d* on *Portrait*). 10/59, 4/63, 10/63.

Wes Montgomery gave off that sense of effortlessness that is always bad karma in jazz. A little *sweat* and preferably some pain are almost considered *de rigueur*. But Montgomery used to loose off solos as if he was sitting on his back porch talking to friends. He used a homely thumb-picking technique, rather than a plectrum or the faster finger-picking approach. Stylistically, he copied Charlie Christian's Ur-bop, and added elements of Django Reinhardt's harmonic conception. It's interesting and ironic that Montgomery's most prominent latter-day disciple George Benson should have made almost exactly the same career move, trading off a magnificent improvisational sense against commercial success.

In career terms, Montgomery really did seem to prefer his back porch. During the 1950s, which should have been his big decade, he hung around his native Indianapolis, playing part time. When his recording career got going again, he was still capable of great things. Guitar–organ trios take a little getting used to nowadays, but these contain some of the guitarist's most vibrant recordings. While some of the best of the material – ''Round Midnight', 'Fried Pies', and so on – has been sampled on the Milestone sets below, these are worth hearing and having in their entirety. For no readily discernible reason, *Boss Guitar* sounds flatter than the others.

***(*)   **Far Wes** Pacific Jazz 94475 CD/LP
Montgomery; Pony Poindexter (*as*); Harold Land (*ts*); Buddy Montgomery (*p*); Monk Montgomery (*b*); Tony Bazley, Louis Hayes (*d*); collective personnel. 4/58, 10/59.

A welcome reissue (of the better 1958 sessions particularly). Montgomery plays fluently if a trifle dispassionately, but emerges here as a composer of some substance. The title-track is in relatively conventional bop idiom but has an attractive melodic contour (which Land largely ignores) and a well-judged 'turn' towards the end of the main statement. The later sessions are a trifle disappointing, though the great Louis Hayes weighs in at the drum kit with characteristic confidence. It's worth buying for the first half dozen tracks alone.

****   **Incredible Jazz Guitar** Original Jazz Classics OJC 036 CD/LP
Montgomery; Tommy Flanagan (*p*); Percy Heath (*b*); Albert Heath (*d*). 1/60.

Probably the best Montgomery record currently available. His solo on 'West Coast Blues' is very nearly incredible, though there are hints of banality even there, in his trademark octave runs, which he borrowed from Django. Flanagan may have slipped the engineer a sawbuck, for he's caught beautifully, and nicely forward in the mix. His lines on Sonny Rollins's buoyant 'Airegin' are exactly complementary to the guitarist's. There's a 'D-natural Blues' and covers of 'In Your Own Sweet Way' and 'Polka Dots and Moonbeams', which further hint at Montgomery's eventual artistic inertia, but for the moment he sounds like a master, and this is the one to go for.

***(*)   **So Much Guitar** Original Jazz Classics OJC 233 CD/LP
Montgomery; Hank Jones (*p*); Ron Carter (*b*); Lex Humphries (*d*); Ray Barretto (*perc*). 8/61.

Originally released on Riverside, Montgomery's smooth and uncannily fluent lines and Jones's elegant two-handedness lift 'Cotton Tail' out of the ordinary. Never a blindingly fast player (he picked with his thumb rather than a plectrum, a technically risky decision which paid off in a warmer, slightly muted tone), Montgomery specialized in sweeping oppositions of register that lend an illusion of pace to relatively stately passages.

***   **Encores** Milestone M 9110 LP/MC
Montgomery; James Clay (*f, ts*); Victor Feldman (*p*); Wynton Kelly (*p*); Buddy Montgomery (*p*); Mel Rhyne (*org*); Milt Jackson (*vib*); Kenny Burrell (*g*); Paul Chambers, Sam Jones, Monk Montgomery (*b*); Jimmy Cobb, Osie Johnson, Louis Hayes, George Brown (d). 10/60, 1 & 12/61, 4 & 11/63.

***   **Wes And Friends** Milestone M 47013 2LP
Montgomery; Wynton Kelly, George Shearing (*p*); Buddy Montgomery (*vib*); Mel Rhyne (*org*); Milt Jackson (*vib*); Sam Jones, Monk Montgomery (*b*); Philly Joe Jones, Walter Perkins (*d*); Richard Chimelis, Armando Peraza (*perc*). 10 & 12/61.

***(*)   **Movin' Along** Original Jazz Classics OJC 089 CD/LP
Montgomery; James Clay (*ts, f*); Victor Feldman (*p*); Sam Jones (*b*); Louis Hayes (*d*). 10/60.

***(*)   **Full House** Original Jazz Classics OJC 106 CD/LP
Montgomery; Johnny Griffin (*ts*); Wynton Kelly (*p*); Paul Chambers (*b*); Jimmy Cobb (*d*). 6/62.

***   **The Alternative Wes Montgomery** Milestone M 47065 CD/LP
Montgomery; Johnny Griffin (*ts*); James Clay (*f*); Victor Feldman, Wynton Kelly, Buddy Montgomery (*p*); Mel Rhyne (*org*); Milt Jackson (*vib*); Paul Chambers, Sam Jones, Monk Montgomery (*b*); George Brown, Jimmy Cobb, Louis Hayes, Philly Joe Jones, Bobby Thomas (*d*); orchestra. 10/60, 1 & 12/61, 6/62, 4 & 11/63.

A mass of material, and no maps. Some of Montgomery's better later performances are buried in the Milestone sides, but the cumulative impression is of incipient commercial longueur. Only *Friends* has much discographical consistency, taken from sessions in the autumn and winter of 1961. Almost all the rest, understandably in the case of the alternatives, less so elsewhere, is cobbled together like a cold buffet, with tastes impinging on each other uncomfortably.

Montgomery himself claimed to have been at his best a full decade before, but he spent most of the 1950s out of the limelight. He still sounds much more authoritative in the small groups, and *Movin' Along* and *Alternative* are much better records, including two fine sessions from October 1960 and June 1962. (Listen for Montgomery's warmly resonant bass guitar passages.) The latter brings together a good deal of valuable unreleased material, including sessions with Johnny Griffin (also on *Movin'/Full House*) and Milt Jackson (the preferred cut of 'Stairway to the Stars' is on *Friends*), who's also featured on *Encores*. For 'Round Midnight' addicts (and the law of supply suggests there may be a few), Montgomery's trio version with organist Rhyne and drummer Parker, is also available on the one-track-minded *Round Midnight* compilation (Milestone M 9144 CD/LP), which gives a fair impression of Milestone's distinctive combination of market shrewdness and completist redundancy. Who'd want all these? Only the most dogged of fans, one supposes.

***(*)   **Round Midnight** Charly CD 13 CD

***   **Live In Paris** France's Concert FCD 108 CD

***   **Straight, No Chaser** Bandstand BD 1504 CD/LP
Montgomery; Clark Terry (*t* on *Straight* only); Johnny Griffin (*ts* on *Round Midnight* only); Harold Mabern (*p*); Arthur Harper (*b*); Jimmy Lovelace (*d*). 3/65.

The Charly and FCD make a useful pair from a single French session, with no overlap of material. Mabern is an underrated pianist, with a strong blues feel. A version of Coltrane's 'Impressions' acts as reminder that Montgomery once worked the frontier with the best of them (he had a 1960 encounter with the saxophonist whose latter-day extravagances made the once-adventurous guitarist seem positively old hat). The surprise addition of Griffin adds muscle to ''Round About Midnight' without damaging the tracery of Montgomery's finely spun lines. His interchanges with Terry and Mabern on Monk's 'Straight, No Chaser' on the Bandstand are remarkably acute. Though increasingly perceived as a middle of the road entertainer, he maintained his improvisational skills in a live context, and it's as well not to dismiss his later work out of hand.

(*)   **Tequila Verve 831671 CD
Montgomery; George Devens (*vib*); Ron Carter (*b*); Grady Tate (*d*); Ray Barretto (*perc*); strings. 3 & 5/66.

Montgomery rather wearily putting in his time with the Claus Ogerman Orchestra. 'Bumpin' On Sunset' is of course a long-standing favourite (subsequently revived by Brian Auger's Oblivion Express in the jazz equivalent of minimalist trance music). Montgomery is still harmonically inventive, but the arrangements are too pre-packaged for very much in the way of surprises.

(*)   **Compact Jazz: Wes Montgomery Verve 831372 CD

(*)   **Compact Jazz: Wes Montgomery Plays The Blues Verve 835318 CD
Montgomery; as for *Tequila*; Donald Byrd, Mel Davis, Bernie Glow, Joe Newman, Jimmy Nottingham, Ernie Royal, Clark Terry, Snooky Young (*t*); Wayne Andre, Jimmy Cleveland, Urbie Green, Quentin Jackson, Melba Liston, John Messner, Danny Moore, Tony Studd, Bill Watrous, Chauncey Welsch (*tb*); Don Butterfield (*tba*); Jimmy Buffington (*fr hn*); Bob Ashton, Danny Bank, Ray Beckenstein, Walter Knie,

Romeo Penque, Jerome Richardson (*reeds*); Jerry Dodgion, Phil Woods (*as*); Stanley Webb (*ts*); Herbie Hancock, Roger Kellaway, Wynton Kelly, Bobby Scott (*p*); Jimmy Smith (*org*); Bucky Pizzarelli (*g*); Ron Carter, Paul Chambers, Bob Cranshaw, Richard Davis, George Duvivier (*b*); Jimmy Cobb, Grady Tate (*d*); Ray Barretto (*perc*). 11/64, 12/65, 5 & 9/66.

By 1966, Montgomery had been overtaken on both flanks by rock and roll and by a much more radical persuasion in jazz. His attempts at an up-to-date repertoire with the Mamas and the Papas' 'California Dreaming' (on *Wes Montgomery*) sound rather lame, though there are good versions of 'Caravan' and 'How Insensitive' that just about reach escape velocity from the prevailing schmaltz (arrangements courtesy of Ogerman, Oliver Nelson and Don Sebesky). 'Bumpin' on Sunset', 'Tequila' and 'Movin' Wes' put in predictable appearances.

The *Blues* compilation is only superficially more authentic and the definition of 'blues' appears to have been stretched like an A string. A later version of 'West Coast Ditto' for mid-size band merely deepens the frustration at Montgomery's lapses, for he is still evidently capable of much more. There is a nice 'Willow, Weep For me' with the redoubtable Wynton Kelly and a thoroughly weird 'Round Midnight' with organist Jimmy Smith and the Oliver Nelson Orchestra.

As compilations of the later Montgomery, these are still questionable. As introductions to Montgomery *period*, they should be avoided.

TETE MONTOLIU (born 1933)
PIANO

*** **A Tot Jazz** Fresh Sound CD
Montoliu; Erik Peter (*b*); Billy Brooks (*d*). 65.

Montoliu is, along with Martial Solal, Giorgio Gaslini, Alex Schlippenbach and Howard Riley, one of the reasons why Europe has a jazz piano tradition of its own in post-bop jazz. Dazzlingly fast in execution, his improvisations are mostly based on a standard bebop repertoire, yet at his best he seems driven to making his music fresh and new from record to record. From moment to moment he might suggest Tatum, Powell or Garner, and his feeling for blues playing is particularly sharp. He began recording in 1958, but until recently most of his '60s sessions as a leader were hidden on obscure, out-of-print Spanish labels (for contemporaneous work as a sideman, see under Dexter Gordon's entry). Frustratingly, a live set for Impulse at the Village Vanguard in 1967, with Richard Davis and Elvin Jones, has never been released. This record proves how able Montoliu was, even after working in the comparatively barren jazz environment of Spain. The piano is less than ideal and Peter and Brooks are no more than willing accomplices, but the pianist displays a feast of invention on an elaborate 'Stella By Starlight', 'Fly Me To The Moon' and Parker's 'Au Privave' among the up-tempo pieces, while 'I Guess I'll Hang My Tears Out To Dry' is a sinewy, rather tense ballad treatment.

***(*) **Songs For Love** Enja 2040 LP
Montoliu. 9/71.

*** **That's All** Steeplechase SCS 1199 LP
Montoliu. 9/71.

*** **Lush Life** Steeplechase SCS 1216 LP
Montoliu (*p* solo). 9/71.

***(*) **Body And Soul** Enja 4042 LP
Montoliu; George Mraz (*b*); Joe Nay (*d*). 71.

Montoliu opened a prolific decade of recording with a single session in Munich, half of which was released at the time by Enja, the remainder turning up many years later on two Steeplechase albums. Little to choose between the three discs, but the first has a few originals by Tete and a thoughtful improvisation on 'Two Catalan Songs'. The question of Montoliu's employment of his Catalan roots in a jazz environment is an interesting one: his oft-quoted remark, 'Basically, all Catalans are blacks', isn't very helpful, but there's little doubt that he is exceptionally responsive to using his native music in a post-bop setting. *Body And Soul* is a concert set which opens on a gloriously swinging delivery of Blossom Dearie's waltz 'Sweet

Georgie Fame' and moves through a rocketing 'Blues' and a long, detailed 'Body And Soul'. It's also recorded with great presence.

*** **Catalonian Fire** Steeplechase SCS 1017 LP
Montoliu; Niels-Henning Ørsted-Pedersen (*b*); Albert 'Tootie' Heath (*d*). 5/74.

***(*) **Tete!** Steeplechase SCS 1029 CD/LP
Montoliu; Niels-Henning Ørsted-Pedersen (*b*); Albert 'Tootie' Heath (*d*). 5/74.

***(*) **Tete A Tete** Steeplechase SCS 1054 LP/MC
As above. 2/76.

***(*) **Tootie's Tempo** Steeplechase SCS 1108 CD/LP/MC
As above. 2/76.

*** **Words Of Love** Steeplechase SCS 1084 LP
Montoliu (*p* solo). 3/76.

*** **Yellow Dolphin Street / Catalonian Folk Songs** Timeless SJP 107/116 CD
Montoliu (*p* solo). 2–12/77.

Montoliu seemed to release a lot of records in the 1970s, but actually had only two or three concentrated bursts of recording. The four albums by the trio with Pedersen and Heath remain his most impressive offerings: played with both elegance and fire, his improvisations on favourite themes – Montoliu is seldom very adventurous in his choice of material, preferring the same clutch of harmonically interesting standards and bebop themes – have a poise and dash which makes one overlook the frequent appearance of many familiar runs and manipulations of the beat. Pedersen, who loves to play with a pianist of outsize technique, holds nothing back in his own playing, while Heath's rather gruff and unfussy drumming makes him a nearly ideal timekeeper for the situation. Of the four Steeplechases, *Tootie's Tempo* and *Tete!* are particularly good, but any one is highly entertaining. The two solo records are slightly less interesting, though the Timeless session – combining an LP of standards and one of Catalonian tunes – has some thoughtful moments.

*** **Live At Keystone Corner** Timeless SJP 138 CD
Montoliu; Herbie Lewis (*b*); Billy Higgins (*d*). 9/79.

*** **Boston Concert** Steeplechase SCS 1152/3 2LP/2MC
Montoliu (*p* solo). 3/80.

*** **Lunch In L.A.** Contemporary C 14004 LP
Montoliu; Chick Corea (*p*). 80.

(*) **I Want To Talk About You Steeplechase SCS 1137 LP
Montoliu; George Mraz (*b*); Al Foster (*d*). 3/80.

Playing in America, Montoliu simply carries on with different rhythm sections. Higgins is dependably on top of things on the Timeless album, more so than Foster and Mraz on their meeting with the pianist, and the long *Boston Concert*, though it has its dead patches, includes a few particularly detailed solos. *Lunch In L.A.* includes a duet with Chick Corea, though it's not clear who had to foot the bill. Either way, Tete sounds better by himself.

*** **Catalonian Nights Vol. 1** Steeplechase SCS 1148 CD/LP
Montoliu; John Heard (*b*); Albert 'Tootie' Heath (*d*). 5/80.

*** **Catalonian Nights Vol. 2** Steeplechase SCS 1241 CD/LP
As above. 5/80.

A very exciting meeting, this one, but it's let down by an indifferent balance – Montoliu is almost drowned out by Heath at times – and a suspiciously battered piano. The second disc is worth having for the almost ecstatically driving 'I'll Remember April', but the music maintains a high standard throughout.

*** **Face To Face** Steeplechase SCS 1185 LP
Montoliu; Niels-Henning Ørsted-Pedersen (*b*). 4/82.

*** **The Music I Like To Play Vol. 1** Soul Note SN 1180 LP
Montoliu (*p* solo). 12/86.

***   **The Music I Like To Play Vol. 2** Soul Note SN 1200 LP
           As above. 12/86.

A duo album with Pedersen was an opportunity for both men to indulge in a cutting contest, and some of the fancier footwork here suggests that climate, but musicality mostly prevails; textures, though, are sometimes muddy. The two solos for Soul Note number among the most finished of Montoliu's albums, with a superior studio sound and one or two unexpected choices: Bobby Hutcherson's 'Little B's Poem', for instance, on the first record. But some routine improvisations betray that the pianist can defer to familiar patterns on some tunes that he knows a little too well.

***   **Sweet 'N Lovely Vol. 1** Fresh Sound FSR-CD 161 CD
           Montoliu; Mundell Lowe (*g*). 9/89.

***   **Sweet 'N Lovely Vol. 2** Fresh Sound FSR-CD 162 CD
           As above. 9/89.

The clean and persuasive interplay here suggests a friendly empathy that makes this unlikely combination work out very well: Lowe keeps to his unassumingly skilful swing-based style, and the ease with which it slips alongside Montoliu's playing suggests that the pianist is more of a conservative than his more ferocious moments suggest. Both discs were recorded on the same day, and as pleasing as they are, one will be enough for most listeners.

***   **The Man From Barcelona** Timeless SJP 368 CD
           Montoliu; George Mraz (*b*); Lewis Nash (*d*). 10/90.

***   **A Spanish Treasure** Concord CCD 4493 CD/MC
           Montoliu; Rufus Reid (*b*); Akira Tana (*d*). 6/91.

Up-to-scratch trio dates: Reid and Tana sound a bit too boisterous for Montoliu's sprightly lines to cut through as they should, and the more reserved Mraz and Nash work out better. As capable as the playing here is, though, one wishes Montoliu would seek out a new format for his studio dates, which are sounding very much the same. The quintet session with Peter King and Gerard Presencer on *Morning '89* (Fresh Sound FRS-117, 2LP; now deleted) was a nice blast of fresh air.

JAMES MOODY (born 1925)
TENOR SAXOPHONE, ALTO SAXOPHONE, SOPRANO SAXOPHONE, FLUTE, VOCALS

***(*)   **Hi Fi Party** Original Jazz Classics OJC 1780 CD
           Moody; Dave Burns (*t*); Bill Shepherd (*tb*); Numa Moore (*bs*); Jimmy Boyd (*p*); John
           Latham (*b*); Clarence Johnson (*d*); Eddie Jefferson (*v*). 9/54.

***(*)   **Wail, Moody, Wail** Original Jazz Classics OJC 1791 CD
           As above, except omit Jefferson. 1, 8 & 12/55.

***   **James Moody's Moods** Original Jazz Classics OJC 188 LP
           Moody; Dave Burns, Leppe Sundewall (*t*); Bill Shepherd (*tb*); Arne Domnérus (*as*);
           Gosta Theselius (*ts*); Per Arne Croona, Numa Noore (*bs*); Jimmy Boyd, Sadik Hakim,
           Thore Swanerud (*p*); Yngve Akerberg, John Latham (*b*); Andrew Burton, Joe Harris,
           Clarence Johnston (*d*); Eddie Jefferson (*v*). 9/54, 1, 8 & 12/55.

Moody's affability and slightly zany vocals have led some to dismiss him as a lightweight. Even on the song with which he is now inextricably associated he demonstrates fine if unorthodox improvisational skills. His debut 'I'm In The Mood For Love', recorded with a Scandinavian group in 1949, was a big hit, establishing him as a bopper (he does 'Au Privave' on the sometimes interesting *Bird Lives* compilation – Milestone 9166 CD/LP – and 'Confirmation' on *Sweet and Lovely* below) with a quirky tonal sensibility and a distinctive sinuous approach which became even more obvious when he added soprano saxophone to his kit.
    He's also joined on *Hi Fi Party* and on the extra 'I Got The Blues' on *Moods* by Eddie Jefferson, who re-worked a vocal version of the hit, thereby (allegedly) giving King Pleasure the idea for adding his own lyrics to bebop tunes. Moody has a strongly vocalized tone, and frequently appears to shape a solo to the lyric of a tune rather than simply to the chords or the written melody, and that vocalized sound is perhaps more evident on his alto playing, though he

even adapts it later in his career to flute, using a 'legitimate' version of Roland Kirk's vocalization. The saxophonist was off the scene for much of the 1970s, certainly as far as significant recording was concerned, and his reputation went into something of a decline. Without star names, though, both *Hi Fi Party* and the rather less gimmicky and straight-ahead *Wail* establish a strong, individual sound that deserves to be more widely known and which certainly stands up very strongly alongside later works.

***   **Something Special** Novus/RCA PD 83008 CD/LP
Moody; Kirk Lightsey (*p*); Todd Coolman (*b*); Idris Muhammad (*d*). 7/86.

(*)   **Moving Forward Novus/RCA PL 83026 CD/LP
Moody; Kenny Barron (*p*); Onaje Allan Gumbs (*syn*); Todd Coolman (*b*); Akira Tana (*d*). 11/87.

***   **Honey** Novus/RCA PD 83111 CD/LP
As above, except omit Gumbs. 10/90.

(*)   **Sweet And Lovely Novus/RCA PL 83063 CD/LP/MC
Moody; Dizzy Gillespie (*t, v*); Marc Cohen (*p, syn*); Todd Coolman (*b*); Akira Tana (*d*). 3/89.

On the sleeve to *Sweet and Lovely*, Moody mock-complains that people are still shouting for 'Moody's Mood for Love': 'I love it!' On *Something Special* he delivers, backed by a superb band. The recent *Honey* which reunites the equal-rated 1987 group, features Moody's intricate but unfussy soprano, and some lovely ballad performances ('Someone to Watch Over Me', 'When You Wish Upon a Star'). *Sweet and Lovely* is just a shade too saccharin, and Cohen's organ-like synth accompaniments are horrible (Gumbs does it with a wry style on *Moving*); Dizzy's singing also takes some handling, though he plays with great wit.

     Unlike his old teacher, Moody sat it out as long as rock seemed to be the only thing anyone wanted. He's back in fine, if mellow, form.

BREW MOORE (1924–73)
TENOR SAXOPHONE

***   **The Brew Moore Quintet** Original Jazz Classics OJC 100 LP
Moore; Dickie Mills (*t*); Johnny Marabuto (*p*); Max Hartstein (*b*); Gus Gustafsson (*d*). 2/55–2/56.

***   **Brew Moore** Original Jazz Classics OJC 049 LP
Moore; Harold Wylie (*ts*); Cal Tjader (*vib*); Johnny Marabuto, Vince Guaraldi (*p*); John Mosher, Dean Reilly (*b*); John Markham, Bobby White (*d*). 11/57–58.

***(*)   **Svinget 14** Black Lion BLCD 760164 CD
Moore; Sahib Shihab (*as*); Lars Gullin (*bs*); Louis Hjulmand (*vib*); Bent Axen (*p*); Niels-Henning Ørsted-Pedersen (*b*); William Schioppfe (*d*). 9/62.

***   **If I Had You** Steeplechase SCC 6016 LP
Moore; Atli Bjorn (*p*); Benny Nielsen (*b*); William Schioppfe (*d*). 4/65.

***   **I Should Care** Steeplechase SCC 6019 CD/LP
As above. 4/65.

(*)   **No More Brew Storyville SLP 4019 LP
Moore; Lars Sjösten (*p*); Sture Nordin (*b*); Fredrik Norén (*d*). 2/71.

Moore was a terrific but star-crossed tenor player, at his best as good as Getz and Sims but never able to get a career together as they did. He left only a small number of records behind him and to have even five of them available is some kind of bounty. The two OJCs are actually rather slight and unemphatic dates: decently handled, but the accompoanying players are lightweights and Moore needs a firmer challenge. The Black Lion disc originally appeared on Debut and is full of fine blowing: 'Ergo' and the title piece are superb improvisations with Moore at full stretch, his lightly foggy tone rounding all the corners and easing through problems without a murmur, while two duets with Gullin and a fierce blow with Shihab on 'The Monster' are outstandingly fine. The only problem is with the sound, which seems to break up into distortion quite often. The Steeplechase albums are surviving mementoes from a stay in Copenhagen on a radio-studio session, the other cut at the Montmartre: solid, but not quite Brew at his best. *No More Brew* also emanates from a live session, and there is a good rhythm section this time; but some of the fire seems to have gone out of Moore's playing. A PS to a career that was always unfinished. Moore died when he fell down some stairs in Copenhagen in 1973.

RALPH MOORE
TENOR SAXOPHONE, SOPRANO SAXOPHONE

***   **Round Trip** Reservoir RSR CD 104 CD
Moore; Brian Lynch (*t, flhn*); Kevin Eubanks (*g*); Benny Green (*p*); Rufus Reid (*b*); Kenny Washington (*d*). 12/85.

***(*)   **623 C Street** Criss Cross Criss 1028 CD
Moore; David Kikoski (*p*); Buster Williams (*b*); Billy Hart (*d*). 2/87.

****   **Rejuvenate!** Criss Cross Criss 1035 CD
Moore; Steve Turre (*tb, conch*); Mulgrew Miller (*p*); Peter Washington (*b*); Marvin Smitty Smith (*d*). 2/88.

***(*)   **Furthermore** Landmark LCD 1526 CD/LP/MC
Moore; Roy Hargrove (*t*); Benny Green (*p*); Peter Washington (*b*); Victor Lewis, Kenny Washington (*d*). 3/90.

London-born Moore has a muscular and very distinctive tone, not yet accompanied by much profundity in the solos which follow orthodox hard-bop lines. There's still of plenty good music to squeeze out of the idiom, and Moore does nothing to ironize it or spice it up with contemporary references (other, perhaps, than Kevin Eubanks' soupy guitar on parts of *Round Trip*, for which he also wrote the final track).

Rudy Van Gelder has been engineering this kind of material for longer than even he cares to remember, and all four records are technically flawless. The performances are equally unexceptionable but may prove a little cool. Though his writing skills have sharpened considerably ('Hopscotch' on *Furthermore*, 'Josephine', 'C. R. M.' and 'Song For Soweto' on *Rejuvenate*), he draws much of his material from piano-centred late bop – Bud Powell's 'Un Poco Loco' on *623 C Street*, 'Monk's Dream' on *Furthermore* – though rarely anything as ambitious as Elmo Hope's inventively Monkish 'One Second, Please', which appears on Moore's currently deleted *Images* [Landmark LLP 1520].

His soprano playing, restricted to 'Cecilia' and 'Christina' on *623 C Street*, still needs thinking out, and he seems to have some intonation and breath-control problems, neither of which are remotely evident in his supremely confident tenor playing. One to watch, not so much because he promises to shake the foundations, but simply because he's so consistently good.

CLAUDIO MORENGHI
TENOR SAXOPHONE

(*)   **Sky Gates Splasc(h) H 347-2 CD
Morenghi; Pampa Pavesi (*p*); Raimondo Meli Lupi (*g*); Gianmarco Scaglia, Otello Savoia (*b*); Paolo Mozzoni (*d*). 5/90–3/91.

Jazz from Brescello, in southern Italy. Morenghi is a skilful player, but not one to stand out in a crowd of tenormen: he writes most of the tunes himself, and there are a couple of pretty themes in 'Children Turnaround' and 'One Year, A Theme For You'; but the playing is really no more than serviceable in a post-bop mould. The pick is a quite intense reading of Mal Waldron's 'Soul Eyes'.

FRANK MORGAN (born 1933)
ALTO SAXOPHONE

***(*) **Gene Norman Presents Frank Morgan** Fresh Sound FSR CD 71 CD
Morgan; Conte Candoli (*t*); Wardell Gray (*ts*); Carl Perkins (*p*); Wild Bill Davis (*org*); Howard Roberts (*g*); Bobby Rodriguez, Leroy Vinnegar (*b*); Jose Mangual, Lawrence Marable (*d*); Ralph Miranda, Uba Nieto (*perc*). 55.

Frank Morgan's story is not just about paid dues. He also had to serve a stretch in San Quentin, after years of barely controllable drug abuse. Debts paid to society, he reappeared in the mid-1980s, purveying a brand of chastened bop, his initially bright and Bird-feathered style only slightly dulled by a spell in the cage.

In the mid-1950s, he was one of a group of saxophonists who hung on Charlie Parker's coat-tails. The currently deleted Savoy sessions aren't the best place to pick up on what Morgan was doing at the time, partly because the material is relatively unfamiliar, and because the dominant figure on the session is Milt Jackson, who is already thinking in new directions. The Fresh Sound CD is a much better place to begin, though the septet tracks with Wild Bill Davis and three Latin percussionists are a touch crude; 'I'll Remember April' succumbs almost completely. Wardell Gray lends his easy swing to 'My Old Flame', 'The Nearness of You' and four other tracks and Carl Perkins's bouncy clatter at the piano keeps the textures attractively ruffled.

*** **Easy Living** Contemporary C 14013 LP/MC
Morgan; Cedar Walton (*p*); Tony Dumas (*b*); Billy Higgins (*d*). 6/85.

***(*) **Lament** Contemporary C 14021 CD/LP/MC
As above, except Buster Williams (*b*) replaces Dumas. 4/86.

***(*) **Double Image** Contemporary C 14035 CD/LP/MC
Morgan; George Cables (*p*). 5/86.

***(*) **Bebop Lives!** Contemporary C 14026 CD/LP/MC
Morgan; Johnny Coles (*flhn*); Cedar Walton (*p*); Buster Williams (*b*); Billy Higgins (*d*). 12/86.

***(*) **Major Changes** Contemporary C 14039 CD/LP/MC
Morgan; McCoy Tyner (*p*); Avery Sharpe (*b*); Louis Hayes (*d*). 4/87.

*** **Yardbird Suite** Contemporary C 14045 CD/LP/MC
Morgan; Mulgrew Miller (*p*); Ron Carter (*b*); Al Foster (*d*). 11/88.

**** **Reflections** Contemporary C 14052 CD/LP/MC
Morgan; Joe Henderson (*ts*); Bobby Hutcherson (*vib*); Mulgrew Miller (*p*); Ron Carter (*b*); Al Foster (*d*). 89.

*** **Quiet Fire** Contemporary C 14064 CD
Morgan; Bud Shank (*as*); George Cables (*p*); John Heard (*b*); Jimmy Cobb (*d*). 89.

*** **Mood Indigo** Antilles 791230 CD/MC
Morgan; Wynton Marsalis (*t*); George Cables, Ronnie Mathews (*p*); Buster Williams (*b*); Al Foster (*d*). 6/89.

*** **A Lovesome Thing** Antilles 848213 CD/MC
Morgan; Roy Hargrove (*t*); George Cables (*p*); David Williams (*b*); Lewis Nash (*d*); Abbey Lincoln (*v*). 9/90.

San Quentin must have been a rough woodshed. Outwardly, there's no immediate sign of change. Modern recording makes his sound more intimate, grainier, anyway, so there's no reason to suppose that occasional huskiness is especially significant. Nor has Morgan forgotten where he came from. Almost the first thing he did on his comeback in 1985 was a brightly intelligent 'Now's The Time' (it's also excerpted on *Bird Lives!* (Milestone M 9166)), and there's a trawl of Parker-associated material on *Yardbird Suite*, with Jackie McLean's 'Little Melonae' thrown in on *Bebop Lives!*.

What *is* noticeable, even with these closely focused recordings, is that he has grown quieter and more reflective. The Antilles sessions hover on the edge of being mood pieces and are often rescued by the quality of the other players: guest star Marsalis, trumpet prodigy Hargrove, the redoubtable Buster Williams (who earns an unaccompanied track on *A Lovesome Thing* and is the lynchpin of *Bebop Lives!*), and George Cables, with whom Morgan enjoys a sympathetic playing relationship.

He seems rather hung up on Cables's 'Lullaby', which gets played with the group on *Mood Indigo* and then twice as a duo on *A Lovesome Thing*. Some of that softness comes through on the duo *Double Image*, which is reminiscent of Marion Brown's collaborations with Mal Waldron; Cables lacks the broad harmonic grasp of a McCoy Tyner, who provides the focus of *Major Changes*.

By far the best of the comeback albums is the complex *Reflections*, with Henderson and Morgan doing a straight-shooting thing over a patiently cross-hatched rhythm backing, in which Hutcherson plays a typically intelligent part. 'Black Narcissus' and 'O.K.' are crisp late-bop and the CD bonus 'Caravan' is one of the best recent versions. Miller plays rather lushly, but makes for contrast with Hutcherson's rather acid sound.

The excellent Miller sounds rather too respectful on *Yardbird Suite*; at this point in time, isn't it legitimate to interrogate that material a bit more vigorously? That's broadly what Tyner and Walton do on their respective albums, and they're all the better for it.

Morgan in turn is treated very respectfully by all concerned on the Antilles dates, and the effect is emotionally fulsome (there is an icky spoken thanks at the end; 'kiss the kids', 'smile at your neighbours', 'let's work for world harmony', what, now?) to the point where the tunes lack all internal tension, merely providing vehicles for Morgan's floating lines. In the same way, Abbey Lincoln's take on the Chris Connor staple 'Ten Cents a Dance' sounds unlived-in and *ersatz*, which in the circumstances is rather ironic. As albums, the Antilles pair are lovely to listen to, but not that durable. The real action is elsewhere.

LEE MORGAN (1938–72)
TRUMPET

***   **Candy** Blue Note 746508 CD
Morgan; Sonny Clark (*p*); Doug Watkins (*b*); Art Taylor (*d*). 2/58.

***   **Indestructible Lee** Affinity AFF 762 CD
Morgan; Clifford Jordan (*ts*); Eddie Higgins, Wynton Kelly (*p*); Paul Chambers, Art Davies (*b*); Art Blakey (*d*). 2 & 10/60.

***(*)   **Take Twelve** Original Jazz Classics OJC 310 CD/LP
Morgan; Clifford Jordan (*ts*); Barry Harris (*p*); Bob Cranshaw (*b*); Louis Hayes (*d*). 1/62.

***(*)   **The Sidewinder** Blue Note 784157 CD
Morgan; Joe Henderson (*ts*); Barry Harris (*p*); Bob Cranshaw (*b*); Billy Higgins (*d*). 12/63.

***(*)   **Search For The New Land** Blue Note 784169 CD
Morgan; Wayne Shorter (*ts*); Grant Green (*g*); Herbie Hancock (*p*); Reggie Workman (*b*); Billy Higgins (*d*). 2/64.

***   **The Rumproller** Blue Note 746428 CD
Morgan; Joe Henderson (*ts*); Ronnie Mathews (*p*); Victor Sproles (*b*); Billy Higgins (*d*). 4/65.

***   **Cornbread** Blue Note 784222 CD
Morgan; Jackie McLean (*as*); Hank Mobley (*ts*); Herbie Hancock (*p*); Larry Ridley (*b*); Billy Higgins (*d*). 66.

***   **Tom Cat** Blue Note 784446 CD
Morgan; Curtis Fuller (*tb*); Jackie McLean (*as*); McCoy Tyner (*p*); Bob Cranshaw (*b*); Art Blakey (*d*). 8/64.

***   **Dizzy Atmosphere** Original Jazz Classics OJC 1762 CD/LP/MC
Morgan; Al Grey (*tb*); Billy Mitchell (*as, ts*); Billy Root (*bs, ts*); Paul West (*b*);
Charlie Persip (*d*).

***   **Live At The Lighthouse** Fresh Sound FSR CD 140/2 2CD
Morgan; Bennie Maupin (*ts*); Harold Mabern (*p*); Jymie Merritt (*b*); Mickey Roker
(*d*). 7/70.

Morgan was a member of a vintage Jazz Messengers, cutting two – *Moanin'* (Blue Note 746516 CD) and *A Night In Tunisia* (Blue Note 784049 CD) – of Art Blakey's vintage performances. He had a punchy, bluesy tone that sounded a generation old but which yet proved adaptable to contemporary requirements. To some extent he dined out for a long time on a hit with 'The Sidewinder', but he was stretching the bounds of what he had learnt from Clifford Brown before and after that.

Recorded around the time the youthful Morgan graduated from section player with Dizzy Gillespie to featured soloist with the Messengers, *Candy* has a frosting of arrogant self-confidence which is rather attractive. Sonny Clark is a current rediscovery from the hard bop era, as is Mabern, both of whom were eclipsed by Herbie Hancock and, to a lesser extent, Wynton Kelly, who gives a fine bluesy texture to *Indestructible*. On *Candy*, Clark works his call-and-response style into something really quite substantial, feeding new ideas back to Morgan and Henderson.

Take Twelve was the first post-Messengers album. Hayes is a less dominant drummer than the trumpeter's ex-boss, and he leaves a lot more room for Morgan to develop his blues phrasing asymmetrically and with added notes that hint (distantly) at polytonality. Compositions like Elmo Hope's title-track suggest that Morgan was looking for something more challenging than straightforward hard bop. Ironically, *The Sidewinder* nearly foreclosed on further experimentation by being a resounding hit. Funky and danceable, the title-track has become a staple, known to people who think a Blue Note is a kind of aerogram. Unfortunately, it has obscured some other good material on the album ('Totem Pole', 'Hocus Pocus', 'Gary's Notebook' and 'Boy, What A Night') and reinforced the notion that Morgan took a commercial route in 1963, never again to be a serious contender.

The Rumproller was more or less intended to repeat the formula. In some ways it's a tighter and better-organized album than its routinely overpraised predecessor, but it conspicuously lacks the searching, inquisitive edge that Morgan could put on his more committed solos and which transformed the unusually textured *Search For The New Land*, a rare instance of Morgan varying his favoured quintet line-up. Green adds coloration; Shorter adds a harmonic dimension not even Henderson had been able to supply. A bold, refreshing album, it's surprisingly little known. 'Melancholee' (such puns are endemic, as to Lee Konitz records) is quite conventional, but 'Mr Kenyatta' and 'The Joker' represent a step on from Brown's quite contained solo-building.

Unfortunately, that opening up of the chorus-structure did tempt Morgan towards a more sterile, grandstanding approach, heard on *Cornbread* and *Tom Cat*. These are entertaining enough, and McLean is hot, but they represent a step back towards a middle-of-the-road approach that Morgan was easily capable of transcending. His ability to arrange effectively for a more substantial horn front-line is evident on *Dizzy Atmsophere*, which includes valuable alternates of 'Whisper Not' and 'Over The Rainbow', both of which run a spectrum from sentimental to hard-edged.

Live At The Lighthouse is an incendiary confrontation with next-generation players, who seem bent on pushing the leader to the limit. The sound is all over the place on CD, but the excitement is palpable and it's a generous length. Two years after it was recorded, and on the opposite side of the country, Morgan was shot dead at Slugs club in New York City, after a fight with a ladyfriend.

***(*)   **The Best Of Lee Morgan** Blue Note 791138 CD
Morgan; Joe Henderson, Hank Mobley, Wayne Shorter (*ts*); Pepper Adams (*bs*);
Sonny Clark, Herbie Hancock, Barry Harris, Harold Mabern, Ronnie Mathews,
Bobby Timmons (*p*); Bob Cranshaw, Larry Ridley, Victor Sproles, Butch Warren,
Doug Watkins (*b*); Billy Higgins, Art Taylor (*d*). 9 & 11/57, 12/63, 4, 7 & 9/65.

'The Sidewinder', 'The Rumproller', 'Night In Tunisia' from 1957, 'Since I Fell For You', 'Ceora' and 'Speedball'. Who's arguing?

LAWRENCE BUTCH MORRIS
CORNET, COMPOSER

****   Current Trends In Racism In Modern America Sound Aspects sas 4010 CD
Morris; John Zorn (*as, game calls*); Frank Lowe (*ts*); Brandon Ross (*g*); Eli Fountain
(*vib*); Zeena Parkins (*hp*); Curtis Clark (*p*); Tom Cora (*clo*); Christian Marclay
(*turntables*); Thurman Barker (*d, mar, perc*); Yasunao Tone (*v*). 2/85.

***(*)   Homeing Sound Aspects sas 4015 CD/LP
Morris; J. A. Deane (*tb, elec*); Vincent Chancey (*frhn*); Daniel Werts (*ob*); Eli
Fountain (*vib*); Curtis Clark (*p*); Pierre Dørge (*g*); Jason Hwang (*vn*); Jean-Jacques
Avenel (*b*); Oliver Johnson (*d*); David Weinstein (*elec*); Shelly Hirsch (*v*). 11/87.

Most visible lately as the *eminence grise* behind some of saxophonist David Murray's most
challenging music, Morris is an exponent of what he calls 'conduction', a kind of
directed improvisation by which improvising players respond moment to moment to the
conductor's signals.
    Current Trends may sound like a Ph. D. topic but is in fact a turbulent and often disturbing
piece whose subtitle, 'A Work In Progress', is as much a polemical comment as a
formal disclaimer. It certainly isn't 'finished' music and the surface is kept in a state of
considerable flux, but there is a logic to it which is reflected inindividual performances.
Zorn's anarchic duck-calls and honks camouflage a sophisticated bop player with a fine
structural sense; Lowe's Coltrane-derived screams are combined wth an easy swing that comes
from Don Byas and Chu Berry.
    Morris's interest in non-standard instrumentations is more obvious on *Homeing, which*
dispenses with saxophones. Zeena Parkins overturns most of the usual associations of harp-
playing, as does Cora with his cello. *Homeing* has a more settled surface and a gentler
timbre, but it's still extremely forceful music.

WILBER MORRIS
BASS

***   Wilber Force DIW 809 CD
Morris; David Murray (*ts, bcl*); Dennis Charles (*d*). 2/83.

While flawed – there are too many bass solos for Morris to sustain with comfort and the
material is repetitive – this concert set has a fine intensity of spirit. The best piece is the opening
number, 'Randy', which features some superb interplay between the three musicians over a
series of shifting metres. Murray's characteristically rambling improvisations muster their usual
ornery temperament and his bass clarinet showcase on 'Afro-Amer. Ind' is marvellously
articulated. The sound is rather restricted but not too distracting.

JELLY ROLL MORTON(1890–1941)
PIANO, VOCAL

***   Blues And Stomps From Rare Piano Rolls Biograph BCD111 CD
Morton (*p roll*). 24–26.

Piano rolls tend to make all pianists sound the same, no matter what their stylistic differences,
and Morton's nine original rolls don't offer any exception to a rule that blunts rhythmic and
dynamic subtleties and neuters touch and voicings. But Morton's music survives better in this
context than does Fats Waller's: the refinement and complexity of his compositions can be
heard with crystal clarity in these performances, and if it tends to isolate some aspects of his art,
it doesn't destroy it. And there are interesting variations with his solo playing on record: the
gentler reading of 'Grandpa's Spells', for instance. One or two pieces are rarer matters, too,
such as 'Tom Cat Blues', which was only recorded as a duet with King Oliver (even if it is a
development of 'Mr Jelly Lord'). Purely on its own terms, this is a very enjoyable disc, and the
player-piano sound is fine.

*****   The 1923–24 Piano Solos Fountain FJ 104 LP
Morton (*p* solo). 7/23–6/24.

****   **Jelly Roll Morton 1923–1924** Classics 584 CD
Morton; Tommy Ladnier, Natty Dominique (*c*); Zue Roberston (*tb*); Wilson Townes,
Boyd Senter, Horace Eubanks (*cl*); Arville Harris (*as*); W. E. Burton (*d, kazoo*); Jasper
Taylor (*d*). 6/23–6/24.

The self-styled originator of jazz and stomps started on record here, and showed the door to all
other pretenders. The old, discredited idea was that the piano solos collected on the Fountain
LP were sketches for the band sessions he recorded for Victor, but Morton's all-embracing
mastery of the keyboard makes these 19 solos a sublimation of everything jazz had done up to
this point. He combines the formal precision of ragtime with a steady melodic flow and a
portfolio of rhythms that are tirelessly varied: if Louis Armstrong finally liberated jazz rhythms,
Morton had already set out the possibilities to do so. As a series of compositions, this was a
storehouse of ideas which has yet to be exhausted: here are the first versions of two of jazz's
most enduring masterworks, 'King Porter Stomp' and 'Wolverine Blues', as well as such
definitive Morton portraits as 'The Pearls' and the brilliantly delivered 'Shreveport Stomp'.
His timing is ambitious yet miraculously secure: listen to the poetic elegance of 'New Orleans
(Blues) Joys', or the famous 'Spanish Tinge' in 'Tia Juana'. Considering the roughness of the
original recordings, the fact that the record remains utterly compelling throughout its 19 tracks
is testament to Morton's greatness. The piano sound is still pretty awful to modern ears, and
some of the (often very rare) originals are clearly in less than perfect shape, but this is essential
music. The Classics CD scarcely improves on the Fountain LP, and although it adds what were
really some false starts in Morton's career – two very cloudy 1923 tracks for Paramount, with a
band that may or may not include Tommy Ladnier, a not-much-better session for Okeh with the
feeble Dominique, Robertson and Eubanks and a fairly disastrous 'Mr Jelly Lord' where he's
buried behind Boyd Senter and some kazoo playing – some may feel that it simply devalues the
consistency of the solos.

****   **The Complete Jelly Roll Morton 1926–1930** RCA Bluebird ND82361 5CD
Morton; Ward Pinkett, Edward Anderson, Edwin Swayze, David Richards, Boyd
'Red' Rosser, Henry 'Red' Allen, Bubber Miley, Sidney de Paris (*t*); George Mitchell
(*c*); Kid Ory, Gerald Reeves, Geechie Fields, William Cato, Charlie Irvis, J. C.
Higginbotham, Wilbur De Paris, Claude Jones (*tb*); Sidney Bechet, Paul Barnes (*ss*);
Omer Simeon, Ernie Bullock (*cl, bcl*); Barney Bigard, Darnell Howard, Johnny
Dodds, George Baquet, Albert Nicholas (*cl*); Russell Procope (*cl, as*); Walter Thomas
(*as, bs*); Stump Evans (*as*); Joe Thomas (*cl, ts*); Joe Garland, Happy Caldwell (*ts*);
Rod Rodriguez (*p*); J. Wright Smith, Clarence Black (*vn*); Howard Hill, Bernard
Addison, Bud Scott, Lawrence Lucie, Will Johnson (*g*); Johnny St Cyr, Lee Blair (*bj,
g*); Barney Alexander (*bj*); Bill Benford, Billy Taylor (*bb, b*); Pete Biggs, Harry
Prather, Bill Moore, Quinn Wilson (*tba*); Pops Foster, Wellman Braud, John Lindsay
(*b*); Andrew Hilaire, Tommy Benford, Baby Dodds, Manzie Johnson, William Laws,
Cozy Cole, Paul Barbarin, Bill Beason, Zutty Singleton (*d*). 9/26–9/39.

*****   **Jelly Roll Morton Volume One** JSP CD 321 CD
Morton; George Mitchell (*c*); Gerald Reeves, Kid Ory (*tb*); Omer Simeon, Darnell
Howard, Barney Bigard, Johnny Dodds (*cl*); Stump Evans (*as*); Clarence Black, J.
Wright Smith (*vn*); Johnny St Cyr (*bj, g*); Bud Scott (*g*); Quinn Wilson (*bb*); John
Lindsay (*b*); Andrew Hilaire, Baby Dodds (*d*). 9/26–6/27.

****   **Jelly Roll Morton Volume Two** JSP CD 322 CD
Morton; Ed Anderson, Ed Swayzee, Boyd Rosser, Walter Briscoe, Henry 'Red' Allen
(*t*); William Cato, Charlie Irvis, J. C. Higginbotham (*tb*); Albert Nicholas, Barney
Bigard (*cl*); Russell Procope, Walter Thomas, Paul Barnes, Joe Garland, Joe Thomas
(*reeds*); Rod Rodriguez (*p*); Barney Alexander, Lee Blair (*bj*); Will Johnson (*g*);
Henry Prather, Bill Moore (*bb*); Pops Foster (*b*); Manzie Johnson, Paul Barbarin,
William Laws, Zutty Singleton (*d*). 12/28–12/29.

****   **Jelly Roll Morton Volume Three** JSP CD 323 CD
Morton; Ward Pinkett, Bubber Miley (*t*); Geechie Fields, Wilbur de Paris (*tb*); Albert
Nicholas (*cl*); Happy Caldwell, Joe Thomas, Walter Thomas (*reeds*); Bernard
Addison, Howard Hill (*g*); Lee Blair (*bj*); Billy Taylor (*bb, b*); Bill Benford, Pete
Biggs (*bb*); Cozy Cole, Tommy Benford (*d*). 3–10/30.

****   **Jelly Roll Morton Volume Four** JSP CD 324 CD
As Volumes One and Two, above.

****   **Jelly Roll Morton Volume Five** JSP CD 325 CD
As Volumes Two and Three, above.

****   **Jelly Roll Morton Vol. 1 1926–27 'Doctor Jazz'** Black & Blue 59.227-2 CD
As JSP Volume One, above. 26–27.

****   **Jelly Roll Morton Vol. 2 1928–39 'Didn't He Ramble'** Black & Blue 59.228-2 CD
As appropriate discs above. 28–39.

***   **Jelly Roll Morton 1924–1926** Classics 599 CD
Morton; Lee Collins, King Oliver, George Mitchell (*c*); Roy Palmer, Kid Ory, Ray
Bowling (*tb*); Omer Simeon (*cl, bcl*); Barney Bigard (*cl, ts*); Balls Ball, Volly De Faut,
Darnell Howard (*cl*); Alex Poole (*as*); W. E. Burton (*kazoo*); Clarence Black, J.
Wright Smith (*vn*); Johnny St Cyr (*bj, g*); John Lindsay (*b*); Clay Jefferson, Andrew
Hilaire (*d*); Edmonia Henderson (*v*).9/24–12/26.

****   **Jelly Roll Morton 1926–1928** Classics 612 CD
Morton; Ward Pinkett (*t*); George Mitchell (*c*); Kid Ory, Gerald Reeves, Geechie
Fields (*tb*); Omer Simeon, Johnny Dodds (*cl*); Stump Evans (*as*); Bud Scott, Johnny
St Cyr (*g*); Lee Blair (*bj*); Bill Benford, Quinn Wilson (*tba*); John Lindsay (*b*);
Andrew Hilaire, Tommy Benford, Baby Dodds (*d*).12/26–6/28.

****   **Jelly Roll Morton 1928–1929** Classics 627 CD
Morton; Ed Anderson, Edwin Swayze, Boyd 'Red' Rosser, Walter Briscoe, Henry
'Red' Allen, Freddie Jenkins (*t*); William Cato, Charlie Irvis, J. C. Higginbotham
(*tb*); Russell Procope, Albert Nicholas, Wilton Crawley, George Baquet (*cl*); Paul
Barnes (*ss*); Joe Thomas, Johnny Hodges (*as*); Joe Garland, Walter Thomas (*ts*); Luis
Russell, Rod Rodriguez (*p*); Lee Blair, Will Johnson (*g*); Barney Alexander (*bj*); Bill
Moore, Harry Prather (*tba*); Pops Foster (*b*); Manzie Johnson, William Laws, Paul
Barbarin, Sonny Greer (*d*). 12/28–12/29.

We should first deal with the three Classics CDs, which include material that the Bluebird and
JSP discs have ignored. Classics 599 starts with a 1924 date with Morton's (so-called) Kings Of
Jazz, and horrible it sounds, too, poorly transferred from grim originals and featuring diabolical
clarinet from the suitably named 'Balls' Ball and even worse alto by Alex Poole. Trio versions
of 'My Gal' and 'Wolverine Blues' with Volly de Faut aren't much better, but a fine 1926 solo
date for Vocalion *is* included, and these tracks (unavailable elsewhere) must make the disc
attractive to Morton specialists. Two sides with (allegedly) King Oliver and Edmonia
Henderson are a further bonus. They then go into the Victor sequence, which continues through
Classics 612 and 627, although the latter adds an unremarkable session at the end under Wilton
Crawley's leadership, with (somewhat mystifyingly) a number of Ellingtonians present.

Morton's recordings for Victor are a magnificent body of work which has been done splendid
but frustratingly mixed justice by some of the various reissues now available. His Red Hot
Peppers band sides, particularly those cut at the three incredible sessions of 1926, are
masterpieces which have endured as well as anything by Armstrong, Parker or any comparable
figure at the top end of the jazz pantheon. Morton seemed to know exactly what he wanted:
having honed and orchestrated compositions like 'Grandpa's Spells' at the piano for many
years, his realization of the music for a band was flawless and brimful of jubilation at his getting
the music down on record. Mitchell, Simeon and the others all took crackling solos, but it was
the way they were contextualized by the leader which makes the music so close to perfection.
The 1926–27 dates were a summary of what jazz had achieved up to that time: as a development
out of the New Orleans tradition, it eschewed the soloistic grandeur which Armstrong was
establishing, and preferred an almost classical poise and shapeliness. If a few other voices
(Ellington, Redman) were already looking towards a more modern kind of group jazz, Morton
was distilling what he considered to be the heart of hot music, 'sweet, soft, plenty rhythm', as
he later put it.

While the earliest sessions are his greatest achievements, it's wrong to regard the later work
as a decline. There are the two trio tracks with the Dodds brothers, with Morton tearing into
'Wolverine Blues'. The 1928 sessions feature his ten-piece touring band on the fine 'Deep
Creek' and a small group handling the beautiful 'Mournful Serenade', while 1929 saw a

memorable solo session which produced 'Pep', 'Fat Frances' and 'Freakish', and an exuberant band date that uncorked swinging performances in 'Burnin' The Iceberg' and 'New Orleans Bump'. But the sessions from 1930 onwards suffer from personnel problems and a vague feeling that Morton was already becoming a man out of time, with New York and territory bands moving into a smoother, less consciously hot music. His own playing remains jauntily commanding, but sidemen become sloppy and a piece like the complex 'Low Gravy', from July 1930, never reaches its potential on record. His last session for Victor until 1939 produced a final shaft of Mortonian genius in 'Fickle Fay Creep', but a feeling was now deep-set that the pianist was a declining force, and he didn't record for Victor again until the end of the decade. The 1939 tracks show the old master in good spirits, singing 'I Thought I Heard Buddy Bolden Say' and 'Winin' Boy Blues' with his old panache, and directing an authentic New Orleans band with resilient aplomb. It is very old-time music for 1939, but it's still very different from the early Peppers sides and none the worse for either.

Morton's music is fine enough to demand a comprehensive representation in all collections, and the current choices on disc are somewhat confusing. The most convenient method is to acquire the Bluebird set, which is handsomely documented and pretty well remastered; but there are problems with some of the tracks, which are from imperfect sources, and a couple of mistakes let down the project to some extent. Some may prefer to have the alternative takes – which are, frankly, revealing only in that Morton had a firm idea of what he wanted by the time take one was recorded each time – set apart, as the JSP series does, rather than on top of each other, as here. Nevertheless, it makes an impressive package. For sheer quality of transfers, though, the JSP sequence is clearly superior. John R. T. Davies's painstaking work from top-quality originals outfaces that secured by the Bluebird engineers, which even use latter-day tape transfers in some cases. The first volume, which includes the early Peppers dates, is unequivocally a five-star record. There are a couple of chronology problems, though, with the JSP series, since the 11 June 1928 session doesn't appear until Volume 4, along with the various alternative takes on the 1926–30 sessions complete. JSP also omit the 1939 tracks. But the first three volumes, which otherwise include all the master takes of the 1926–30 material, are our strong first recommendation. The Classics CDs follow the company's customary chronological path, but also suffer from patchy sound, and while the music remains outstanding they can only be a secondary choice. The newly arrived CDs from Black & Blue cover all the important Red Hot Peppers dates but, on Volume 2, jump rather suddenly from 1929 to the last Victor sessions of 1939. So many important tracks are missing; but the remastering is mostly very good. To add to the glut of issues, there are also sets available from Memoria (*The Complete Jelly Roll Morton, 1926–1930*, 2CD) and EPM (*Creole Genius*, 3CD) which go over the same ground. The RCA Bluebird 'sampler' of their complete edition, *The Pearls* (Bluebird 86588 CD), is also still in circulation. We feel that there are now surely enough issues available to provide a lasting choice!

***(*)   **The Library Of Congress Recordings Vol. 1** Classic Jazz Masters CJM 1 LP
Morton (*p, v*). 5–6/38.

***(*)   **The Library Of Congress Recordings Vol. 2** Classic Jazz Masters CJM2 LP
Morton (*p, v*). 5–6/38.

***(*)   **The Library Of Congress Recordings Vol. 3** Classic Jazz Masters CJM3 LP
Morton (*p, v*). 5–6/38.

***(*)   **The Library Of Congress Recordings Vol. 4** Classic Jazz Masters CJM4 LP
Morton (*p, v*). 5–5/38.

***(*)   **The Library Of Congress Recordings Vol. 5** Classic Jazz Masters CJM5 LP
Morton (*p. v*). 5–6/38.

***(*)   **The Library Of Congress Recordings Vol. 6** Classic Jazz Masters CJM6 LP
Morton (*p. v*). 5–6/38.

****   **The Library Of Congress Recordings Vol. 7** Classic Jazz Masters CJM7 LP
Morton (*p, v*). 5–6/38.

****   **The Library Of Congress Recordings Vol. 8** Classic Jazz Masters CJM8 5–6/38.
Morton (*p, v*). 5–6/38.

***(*)   **The Library Of Congress Recordings** Affinity AFS 1010-3 3CD
          Morton (*p, v*). 5–6/38.

In the summer of 1938, broke and almost finished, Morton was recorded – almost by chance at
first – by Alan Lomax at the Library Of Congress, and when Lomax realized the opportunity he
had on his hands, he got Morton to deliver a virtual history of the birth pangs of jazz as it
happened in the New Orleans of the turn of the century. His memory was unimpaired, although
he chose to tell things as he preferred to remember them, perhaps; and his hands were still in
complete command of the keyboard. The results have the quality of a long, drifting dream, as if
Morton were talking to himself. He demonstrates every kind of music which he heard or played
in the city, recreates all of his greatest compositions in long versions unhindered by 78 playing
time, remembers other pianists who were never recorded, spins yarns, and generally sets down
the most distinctive document we have on the origins of the music. The sessions were made on
an acetate recorder, and while the sound may be uncomfortably one-dimensional to modern
ears, everything he says comes through clearly enough, and the best of the piano solos sound as
invigorating as they have to be. The Classic Jazz Masters set spreads the recordings over eight
separate LPs: the final two are arguably the most essential, since Volume 7 is made up entirely
of piano solos and Volume 8 includes five classic solos – his reading of 'Creepy Feeling' is an
astonishing *tour de force* – as well as his 'Discourse On Jazz', which is a useful primer even
now. Although these are still vinyl-only, and were remastered as long ago as 1970, we still
recommend these as the best way to hear what are indispensable records for anyone interested
in jazz history.

The Affinity set, although it has many of the virtues of the CJM edition, is finally a bit
disappointing. There is an hour's worth of material missing, in order to squeeze the rest on to
three CDs, and the use of the CEDAR process for remastering has blurred the piano tone and
put a light fog over the sound, even if it has taken some of the rasp out of the tone of the LPs.

PINGUIN MOSCHNER
TUBA

***   **Tuba Love Story** Sound Aspects sas 005 LP
          Moschner (*tba* solo). 4/84.

(*)   **Heavy Metal – Light Industry FMP 1200 LP
          Moschner; Larry Fishkind, Melvin Poore, Benita Veridaz (*tba*). 9/87.

Tuba Love Story is, so far, the only solo tuba record in this book, and a worthy example of *sui
generis* at that. Moschner plays both F and B flat instruments on his recital, eight pieces
recorded in real time, and, while he touches no extremes of brass playing already conquered by
such peers as Gunther Christmann and Paul Rutherford, he conducts a wry and warm-hearted
battle with the perceived tubbiness of a supposedly intractable instrument. Not a record to play
very often, but an engaging one nevertheless.

Moschner also organizes the European Tuba Quartet, which puffs through the FMP album.
Here the preponderance of low tones becomes a little wearisome at times, but smart
arrangement and the players' sheer mastery of their horns overcomes the numbing anticipation
of 40 minutes of four tubas.

BOB MOSES (born 1948)
DRUMS

***(*)   **Visit With The Great Spirit** Gramavision GR 8307 CD
          Moses; Tiger Okoshi (*t, flhn, electric t*); John D'Earth (*electric t*); Michael Gibbs (*tb*);
          David Sanborn (*as*); David Liebman (*ss*); David Gross (*as, f*); George Garzone (*ts,
          ss*); Bob Mintzer (*ts, b*); Tony Coe (*ts*); Howard Johnson (*bs, tba, b*); Steve Kuhn (*p*);
          Delmar Brown, Cliff Korman (*syn*); Bill Frisell (*g*); Eddie Gomez, Lincoln Goines,
          Jerome Harris (*b*); Ron DeFrancesco, Janet Levatin, Bill Martin, Manoel Montero,
          Claudio Silva (*perc*); Kyoki Baker, Hiroshi Hieda, Rayko Shiota (*v*). 83.

A somewhat aggressive populist, Moses is also a superb arranger with an instinct for tone-colours that matches Michael Gibbs's. The drummer's former boss is persuaded to blow his rarely seen trombone on 'Macchu Picchu', a dark piece heavily laden with bass guitars, and 'Carinho'. Moses's slightly mystical bent tinges only a couple of the tracks. His Latin effects have the brooding ambiguity and repressed violence which the Spanish call *duende*. There are big, structural references to Miles Davis and to Monk. *Visit* is forceful, imaginative and resonant.

DAVID MOSS
VOICE, PERCUSSION, ASSORTED INSTRUMENTS

****   **Full House** Moers 02010 LP
Moss; John Zorn (*as, game calls*); Tom Guralnick (*bsx, ts, ss*); Fred Frith (*g*); Arto Lindsay (*g, v*); Bill Laswell (*6-string b*); Jamaaladeen Tacuma (*b*); Fred Maher (*d*); Christian Marclay (*turntables*); David Van Tieghem (*perc*); Phil Minton (*v*). 10/83 & 1/84.

***   **Dense Band** Moers 02040 LP
Moss; John Zorn (*as, game calls*); Fred Frith (*g, b, 6-string b, v*); Tom Cora (*clo*); Wayne Horvitz (*DX7 syn*); Arto Lindsay (*g, v*); Christian Marclay (*turntables*); Jules Moss (*d*); Tenko (*v*). 2 & 3/85.

Moss originally turned to singing to add colour to his percussion work. Blessed with a huge mouth, which gives him a huge range and volume of sound, he has turned singing into the pivot of his work (the disc label on these Moers discs includes a drawing of Moss with the spindle-hole slap in the middle of his beard). He mixes pure sound – 'simple chances in the physical world' – with language to a quite disconcerting extent, often raising expectations of a 'lyric' that remain wilfully unsustained.

Full House, the better of the two sets, is a series of 19 duets with ten musicians. Only four of the pieces are multi-tracked, the rest are real-time improvisations of remarkable focus and depth. Though the pieces don't lack for external references of one sort or another, there's a steady resistance to rhythmic or semantic grooves. The degenerate funk fragments of 'The Man With Rain Colored Legs', with Tacuma and a Linn Drum programme, are all the more unsettling for *seeming* to accord to conventional structure. The only disappointment is the solitary duet with Maher (it also features turntable inserts from Marclay) which falls a bit flat. Everywhere else, Moss demonstrates the great improviser's gift of allowing his partners to sound like themselves even as they're bent to the leader's conception. This is even more emphatically Moss's album than the ostensibly more collective *Dense Band*, which turns the rigours of *Full House* into a much more mannered style and, despite the suite-like themes of side one, at least feels very much more fragmentary and hesitant.

MICHAEL MOSSMAN (born 1959)
TRUMPET, PICCOLO TRUMPET, FLUGELHORN

***   **Granulat** Red 123240-2 CD
Mossman; Daniel Schnyder (*ss, ts, f*); Wladislaw Sendecki (*p*); Hami Hammerli (*b*); Guido Parini (*d*). 4/90.

Mossman has done time in many worthwhile European bands, and this group – which he co-leads with Schnyder – gives him a little more space than usual. The compositions are nearly all by Schnyder (the sole exception is Mossman's own 'Cage Of Ice') and display his brainy method as capably as the records under his own name, with the quicksilver lines of the title-track and 'Bifurcat' posing difficult tasks for the players which all five solve with impressive assurance. The rhythm section set down usefully straightforward grooves while the horns follow the pirouetting lines of Schnyder's melodies: some of them, such as 'Blue Tinjokes', have a crackpot demeanour which can seem slightly too cute, but they're mastered so smartly that it usually works. Mossman's bright tone and crisply accurate attack thrive in a situation like this.

SAM MOST (born 1930)
FLUTE, CLARINET, ALTO SAXOPHONE

*** **Bebop Revisited Vol 3.** Xanadu 172 LP
  Most; Doug Mettome (*t*); Urbie Green (*tb*); Bob Dorough (*p*); Percy Heath (*b*);
  Louie Bellson (*d*). 12/53.

*** **Mostly Flute** Xanadu 133 LP
  Most; Duke Jordan (*p*); Tal Farlow (*g*); Sam Jones (*b*); Billy Higgins (*d*). 5/76.

** **Flute Flight** Xanadu 141 LP
  Most; Lou Levy (*p*); Monty Budwig (*b*); Donald Bailey (*d*). 12/76.

** **From The Attic Of My Mind** Xanadu 160 LP
  Most; Kenny Barron (*p*); George Mraz (*b*); Walter Bolden (*d*); Warren Smith (*perc*).
  4/78.

*** **Flute Talk** Xanadu 173 LP
  Most; Joe Farrell (*f*); Mike Wofford (*p*); Bob Magnusson (*b*); Roy McCurdy (*d*); Jerry
  Steinholz (*perc*). 1/79.

Though he appears to have switched almost exclusively to the flute, Sam Most's clarinet playing was at least as important on his early records. Two excellent albums from the mid-1950s, *Sam Most Sextette* and *Plays Bird, Bud, Monk And Miles*, have yet to appear on CD, so only the session on Xanadu 172 (split with Tony Fruscella and Kai Winding sessions) survives from the period.

The later records see Most making as good a case as anybody has for the flute as a prime jazz instrument – in other words, not a very good case. As pretty as the playing is, an impression of blandness can't help overtaking the music. Most plays with winning agility, but that very virtuosity tells against him in the long run – it leads to mere acrobatics, no matter how intense the leader sounds. Farlow and Jordan add some spark to the earliest session, but the next two are all too forgettable, despite a brief glimpse of clarinet in *Flute Flight*'s 'Am I Blue'. The meeting with Farrell is much more entertaining, with a terrific work-out on Charlie Parker's 'Kim' and Farrell's fizzier manner contrasting well with Most's ineffable poise.

BENNIE MOTEN (1894–1935)
PIANO, BANDLEADER

(*) **Bennie Moten 1923–1927 Classics CLAS 549 CD
  Moten; Lammar Wright, Harry Cooper, Ed Lewis, Paul Webster (*c*); Thamon Hayes
  (*tb, v*); Harlan Leonard (*cl, ss, as*); Woody Walder (*cl, ts*); Jack Washington (*cl, as,
  bs*); LaForest Dent (*as, bs, bj*); Sam Tall, Leroy Berry (*bj*); Vernon Page (*tba*); Willie
  Hall, Willie McWashington (*d*). 9/23–6/27.

Moten's band was the most important group to record in the American southwest in the period, and luckily it made a large number of sides for OKeh and Victor: but the quality of the music is very inconsistent, and much of the earlier material is of historical rather than musical interest. This first CD in the complete edition on Classics couples the band's 14 sides for OKeh from 1923–5 with the first recordings for Victor. The OKeh tracks are a curious mixture: the very first two, 'Elephant's Wobble' and 'Crawdad Blues', are little more than strings of solos, while the subsequent 'South' and 'Goofy Dust' are driving, rag-orientated tunes which emphasize the ensemble. Wright is the only really interesting soloist from the period, and Walder, the apparent star, indulges in some idiotic antics on the clarinet but, even so, the lumpy rhythms and clattery ensembles yield some strong, hard-hitting performances, sometimes redolent of Sam Morgan's New Orleans band of a few years later. The early Victors don't show a very great advance, despite electrical recording, and one must wait for the later sides for Moten's band to really shine. Decent remastering of what are very rare originals, although not superior to the old Parlophone LP which first collected the OKeh tracks.

(*) **Bennie Moten 1927–1929 Classics CLAS 558 CD
  As above, except omit Wright, Cooper, Tall and Hall, add Booker Washington (*c*);
  Buster Moten (*p, acc*); James Taylor, Bob Clemmons (*v*). 6/27–6/29.

***   **South (1926–1929)** Bluebird ND 83139 CD/LP
As above. 12/26–7/29.

***   **Bennie Moten 1929–30** Classics CLAS 578 CD
As above, except William 'Count' Basie (*p*) replaces Bennie Moten; add Hot Lips
Page (*t*); Eddie Durham (*tb, g*); Jimmy Rushing (*v*). 7/29–10/30.

Moten's band progressed rather slowly, handicapped by an absence of both truly outstanding soloists and an arranger of real talent. The surprisingly static personnel did the best they could with the material, but most of the tunes work from a heavy off-beat. Walder has barely improved, and the arrival of Bennie's brother, Buster, with his dreaded piano-accordion was enough to root the band in novelty status. The second Classics CD still has some good moments – in such as 'The New Tulsa Blues' or 'Kansas City Breakdown' – but sugary saxes and pedestrian charts spoil many promising moments. Matters take an immediate upward turn with the joint arrival of Basie and Durham in 1929. 'Jones Law Blues', 'Band Box Shuffle' and 'Small Black' all show the band with fresh ideas under Basie's inspirational leadership (and soloing – here with his Earl Hines influence still intact). 'Sweetheart Of Yesterday' even softens the two-beat rhythm. The Bluebird CD chooses a compilation from the 1926–9 period, stopping just prior to Basie's arrival, and, while they pick the best tracks, the music is still no better than the sum of its parts. Little to choose in sound between the two: the Bluebird is cleaner but somewhat thinner.

****   **Basie Beginnings (1929–1932)** Bluebird ND 90403 CD/LP
Moten; Ed Lewis, Booker Washington (*c*); Hot Lips Page, Joe Keyes, Dee Stewart (*t*);
Thamon Hayes, Dan Minor (*tb*); Eddie Durham (*tb, g*); Harlan Leonard, Jack
Washington, Woody Walder, Eddie Barefield, Ben Webster (*reeds*); Count Basie (*p*);
Buster Moten (*acc*); Leroy Berry (*bj, g*); Vernon Page (*tba*); Walter Page (*b*); Willie
McWashington (*d*); Jimmy Rushing (*v*). 10/29–12/32.

****   **Bennie Moten 1930–32** Classics CLAS CD
As above. 30–32.

Under Basie's effective leadership, the Moten orchestra finally took wing, and its final sessions were memorable. There were still problems, such as the presence of Buster Moten, the reliance on a tuba prior to the arrival of Page, and a general feeling of transition between old and new; but, by the magnificent session of December 1932, where the band created at least four masterpieces in 'Toby', 'Prince Of Wails', 'Milenberg Joys' and 'Moten Swing', it was a unit that could have taken on the best of American bands: Page, Rushing, Webster, Durham and especially Basie himself all have key solo and ensemble roles, and the sound of the band on 'Prince Of Wails' and 'Toby' is pile-driving. Ironically, this modernism cost Moten much of his local audience, which he was only recovering at the time of his death in 1935. The Bluebird record compiles the best of the period, with all but the two least-important of the final titles, but some may prefer the chronological completion of the Classics series. Bluebird's sound is again crisper but a shade synthetic in the remastering.

PAUL MOTIAN (born 1931)
DRUMS, PERCUSSION

***   **Le Voyage** ECM 1138 LP
Motian; Charles Brackeen (*ts, ss*); Jean-François Jenny-Clark (*b*). 3/79.

***   **Psalm** ECM 1222 LP
Motian; Joe Lovano (*ts*); Billy Drewes (*ts, as*); Bill Frisell (*g*); Ed Schuller (*b*). 12/81.

***   **The Story Of Maryam** Soul Note SN 1074 CD

***(*)   **Jack Of Clubs** Soul Note SN 1124 CD

****   **Misterioso** Soul Note SN 1174 CD/LP
Motian; Jim Pepper (*ts, ss*); Joe Lovano (*ts*); Bill Frisell (*g*); Ed Schuller (*b*). 7/83,
3/84, 7/86.

***(*)   **It Should've Happened A Long Time Ago** ECM 1283 CD/LP

***   **One Time Out** Soul Note SN 1224 CD/LP
        Motian; Joe Lovano (*ts*); Bill Frisell (*g, syn*). 7/84, 9/87.

***(*)   **Monk In Motian** JMT 834421 CD/LP
        Motian; Joe Lovano, Dewey Redman (*ts*); Geri Allen (*p*); Bill Frisell (*g*). 3/88.

***   **Paul Motian On Broadway: Volume 1** JMT 834430 CD/LP/MC

***   **Paul Motian On Broadway: Volume 2** JMT 834440 CD/LP/MC
        Motian; Joe Lovano (*ts*); Bill Frisell (*g*); Charlie Haden (*b*). 11/88, 9/89.

****   **Bill Evans** JMT 834445 CD/LP/MC
        Motian; Joe Lovano (*ts*); Bill Frisell (*g*); Marc Johnson (*b*). 5/90.

Not a conventionally swinging drummer, Motian spins a shimmering web of cymbal lines and soft, delicately placed accents. He belongs to the Max Roach school of musical, almost melodic drummers, but is wholly undemonstrative in his commitment to group performance, with a built-in resistance to the grandstanding solo.

Between 1959 and 1964, Motian played with the enormously influential Bill Evans trio, an association that subordinated time-keeping to a more subtle semi-harmonic role, and that steered Motian in his own music towards a fragile blend of orthodox harmony with atonality, jazz with folk or classical themes, freedom and restraint. Motian has generally preferred to work with familiar and sympathetic players than to mix and match bands. In the 1980s, his most frequent collaborators have been tenor saxophonist Joe Lovano and post-Hendrix guitarist Bill Frisell. In their common tendency to mix delicacy with unbridled power, they make a superficially unlikely combination for a tribute album of Bill Evans tunes, but the chemistry works and it's testimony both to Evans's durable writing and to Motian's taste and control that Frisell's guitar effects on the classic 'Re: Person I Knew' sound perfectly apposite (which is doubly remarkable in that they also have to stand in for a piano part).

The early *Le Voyage* introduces Motian's folksy angularity, supported again by a 'strong' saxophone player and a bassist of considerable tonal range. 'Drum Music' reappears on the later *Jack Of Clubs* and 'Folk Song For Rosie' on the wonderful *Misterioso* by the same mid-1980s band, by which time they have acquired a riper self-confidence, accentuated by the combination of Lovano with Jim Pepper, a North American Indian who plays with a distinctive yodelling vibrato and shares Motian's interest in non-Western resolutions. *Psalm*, on which the little-known Billy Drewes played second saxophone, now seems an interim album, a proving ground for Frisell and Lovano, who emerged most spectacularly on *It Should Have Happened A Long Time Ago* and *One Time Out*.

Typically nonlinear in focus, there's no more conventional time-keeping on *Bill Evans* than on the slightly earlier *Monk In Motian*. Perhaps if anything unites the two great pianists, it's the sense that their rather different conceptions of swing shared the common characteristic of being rooted in the melody, rather than being tacked on underneath; for comparison, consider 'Monk's Mood' on the earlier *One Time Out* or 'Pannonica' on the Monk-titled *Misterioso*. *Monk In Motian* also drafts in pianist Geri Allen (for 'Ruby My Dear' and 'Off Minor') and a thoroughly ineffectual Dewey Redman (for 'Straight No Chaser' and 'Epistrophy', where the two-tenor front line really doesn't work), but the best tracks are down to the familiar trio. Motian never dominates and here is content to disappear altogether for periods, as he does on 'Ugly Beauty'.

That's a fair generic description of the *Broadway* treatments. Of the quartet, only Frisell wasn't obviously raised on the standards. Lovano, for all his tearing at the pages, certainly was, and the bassist and drummer have been coming across this repertoire for years. With Haden at hand, there are signs that Motian might be content to slip into conventional patterns – noticeably on 'Someone To Watch Over Me' (*Volume 1*), more insidiously on 'But Not For Me' and the creaking gate 'Body And Soul' (both *Volume 2*). Nevertheless, these are very beautiful records and highly original in their approach to far-from-virginal territory. Best starting-place remains *Misterioso*, with a quick backtrack to *Should've Happened* and then forward to the Monk and Evans tributes. One of the most solidly impressive drummer-led outputs of recent times.

BOB MOVER (born 1952)
ALTO AND SOPRANO SAX

(*) **In The True Tradition Xanadu 187 LP
Mover; Rufus Reid (*b*); Bobby Ward (*d*). 6/81.

(*) **Things Unseen! Xanadu 194 LP
Mover; Steve Hall (*ts*); Albert Dailey (*p*); Ray Drummond, Rufus Reid (*b*); Bobby
Ward (*d*). 6/81–12/82.

Mover is an interesting, awkward player whose improvisations take an unpredictable route
without moving too far from bebop grammar. His very hard, astringent tone makes him sound
more plangent than he often is, and on ballads he's a romantic in a hard shell. The trio album
finds him perhaps a shade too exposed, although 'Something To Live For' and 'Evidence'
feature terse, memorable solos. *Things Unseen!* varies the settings: 'Yesterdays' is a gnarled
duet with Dailey; 'Twardzik', an original that's perhaps too contrived in its angularity, finds
him on soprano with Hall guesting on tenor, and 'Little Man You've Had A Busy Day' is done
as a somewhat pointless alto solo. Interesting rather than compelling records.

*** **You Go To My Head** Jazz City 660.53.013 CD
Mover; Steve Hall (*ts*); Benny Green (*p*); Rufus Reid (*b*); Victor Lewis (*d*). 11/88.

A welcome return for Mover, although the circumstances offer little more than a blowing date,
capably dispatched by all concerned. The rhythm section is a stellar one.

BHEKI MSELEKU
PIANO, TENOR SAXOPHONE, VOCAL

*** **Celebration** World Circuit WC 019 CD/MC
Mseleku; Steve Williamson, Courtney Pine (*ss*); Jean Toussaint (*ts*); Eddie Parker (*f*);
Michael Bowie (*b*); Marvin 'Smitty' Smith (*d*); Thebe Lipere (*perc*). 91.

The South African-born Mseleku has waited a long time for this debut record, and with 71
minutes of music it's a substantial manifesto. But while it's a positive and big-hearted set, full of
grand major themes and impassioned playing from a distinguished cast, Mseleku has, on this
evidence, little to add to the firm base established by SA expatriates such as Louis Moholo and
Dudu Pukwana. His piano playing owes its weight and impetus to McCoy Tyner – 'Blues For
Afrika' might have come off any of Tyner's Milestone albums of the 1970s – and his tunes are
full of the call-and-response ingredients of such writers as Abdullah Ibrahim and Randy
Weston. Not that the music lacks any inner conviction: Bowie and Smith lend transatlantic
muscle which raises the temperature several degrees on the faster pieces, and Jean Toussaint
comes off best among the sax stars with a measured improvisation on 'The Age Of Inner
Knowing'. Enjoyable, but perhaps best as a basis for future work.

MTUME – see JAMES MTUME HEATH

SERGEI MUCHIN
BASS

(*) **Sergei Muchin Quartet Dragon DRLP 135 LP
Muchin; Gunnar Lindgren (*ts*); Harald Svensson (*p*); Anders Kjellberg (*d*). 9/86.

Muchin doesn't take a high profile on his own record until the final two tracks, which are
original themes with some space for the leader as a soloist. The main impression here is of a
ramshackle but not unrewarding quartet session that depends on lots of lusty blowing and some
brooding sensitivity on the slower tunes. Lindgren is a tempestuous if shaky improviser, and one
listens more closely to Svensson, whose fierce lyrical edge is akin to Keith Jarrett's ('Memories
Of Tomorrow' is the closing theme from Jarrett's *Koln Concert* recital) – or, to bring matters
closer to home, Bobo Stenson's. Not bad.

GERRY MULLIGAN (born 1927)
BARITONE SAXOPHONE, PIANO, SOPRANO SAXOPHONE

***   **Mulligan Plays Mulligan** Original Jazz Classics OJC 003 CD/LP
Mulligan; Jerry Hurwitz, Nick Travis (*t*); Ollie Wilson (*tb*); Allen Eager (*ts*); Max
McElroy (*bs*); George Wallington (*p*); Phil Leshin (*b*); Walter Bolden (*d*); Gail
Madden (*perc*). 8/51.

The most important baritone saxophonist in contemporary jazz, Mulligan took the turbulent
Serge Chaloff as his model, but blended his fast, slightly pugnacious delivery with the elegance
of Johnny Hodges and Lester Young. This produced an agile, *legato* sound which became
instinct with the cool West Coast style, the flipside of bebop. Mulligan's – and Claude
Thornhill's – major role in what became to be known as Miles Davis's *Birth of the Cool* is now
increasingly acknowledged, as is his genius as a composer/arranger. On the model of the *Birth
Of The Cool* nonet, his big bands have the intimacy and spaciousness of much smaller groups,
preferring subtlety to blasting power. His small groups, conversely, work with a depth of
harmonic focus that suggests a much larger outfit.

In his short story 'Entropy', the novelist Thomas Pynchon takes Mulligan's early-1950s
pianoless quartets with Chet Baker as a crux of post-modernism, improvisation without the
safety net of predictable chords. The revisionist argument was that Mulligan attempted the
experiment simply because he had to work in a club with no piano. The true version is that there
was a piano, albeit an inadequate one, but that he was already experimenting with a much more
arranged sound for small groups (to which the baritone saxophone was peculiarly adaptable)
and that the absence of a decent keyboard was merely an additional spur.

These early sessions already demonstrate what a fine composer and arranger the saxophonist
was (he arranged 'Disc Jockey Jump' for Gene Krupa when he was only 20). In comparison to
later work, they're slightly featureless and Mulligan's playing is very callow. It's perhaps best to
come back to this stuff.

***(*)   **The Best Of The Gerry Mulligan Quartet With Chet Baker** Pacific Jazz CDP 7 95481 2
CD
Mulligan; Chet Baker (*t*); Henry Grimes, Carson Smith, Bobby Whitlock (*b*); Dave
Bailey, Larry Bunker, Chico Hamilton (*d*). 8 & 10/52, 2, 4 & 5/53, 12/57.

***(*)   **The Gerry Mulligan Quartet: Paris 1954, Los Angeles 1953** Vogue 655616 CD
Mulligan; Chet Baker (*t*); Bob Brookmeyer (*v tbn*); Red Mitchell, Carson Smith (*b*);
Larry Bunker, Frank Isola (*d*). 5/53, 6/54.

***(*)   **Reunion** Pacific Jazz CDP 7 46857 2 CD
Mulligan; Chet Baker (*t*); Henry Grimes (*b*); Dave Bailey (*d*). 12/57.

Let's face it. We are all, deep down, suckers for 'My Funny Valentine', just as Miles Davis fans
play 'Time After Time' a good deal more often than they do *Agharta*. Don't be misled by the
line-up details on *Quartet*. This *isn't* the Chet Baker version (a live version with Chet can be
found on *The Best Of*), but one led after the trumpeter's departure by Bob Brookmeyer, who
makes a much brisker, folksy job of it, a little like having your valentine written by the village
scribe. The two Baker tracks – 'Lady Bird' and 'Half Nelson' – are quickly recognizable.

The Pacific Jazz compilation, drawn from singles (including the classic 'Soft Shoe' /
'Walkin' Shoes' combination) and subsequent 10' LPs is an excellent sampling of Mulligan's
11-month association with Chet, with a single item, 'Festive Minor' from the same December
1957 sessions that yielded *Reunion*. It's fair (to Chet, at least) to record that it was Mulligan,
not the famously unreliable trumpeter, who brought the line-up to an end. In June 1953, shortly
after recording the live 'My Funny Valentine' and the slightly earlier studio covers of 'Darn
That Dream' and 'I'm Beginning To See the Light', Mulligan was gaoled for several months on
a drugs offence. It is perhaps as well that the group was folded at its peak. Generously recorded
in a warm close-up, the sessions convey all of Mulligan's skill as a writer and arranger, with the
saxophone and a very foregrounded bass filling in the space normally occupied by piano. Chet's
own 'Freeway', Carson Smith's 'Carson City Stage' and Mulligan's own 'Jeru' and
'Swinghouse' are largely upstaged by the standards, with 'My Old Flame' receiving its finest
reading since Parker recorded it for Dial.

Reunion is by no means a disappointment. Mulligan's arrangement of 'My Heart Belongs To Daddy' is virtuosic, with Chet playing a very straight 'countermelody' and variation to a rather unfamiliar statement of the theme. 'Ornithology' has a sharp, staccato bounce one doesn't associate with this group but Mulligan's solo is a faithful extension of Parker's original, while on 'I Got Rhythm' and 'All The Things You Are' he plunges straight into Bird's source material. Only one track is in stereo; only mono masters survive for the rest.

The live sessions on Vogue usefully bridge the two Mulligan bands and offer a decently recorded sampling of familiar and one-off material. On balance, the earlier sessions with Chet come off less well in comparison. Brookmeyer's soloing is assured and quietly lyrical.

****　　**California Concerts: Volume 1** Pacific Jazz CDP 746860 CD
　　　　　Mulligan; Jon Eardley (*t*); Red Mitchell (*b*); Chico Hamilton (*d*). 11/54.

***　　**California Concerts: Volume 2** Pacific Jazz CDP 746864 CD
　　　　　Mulligan; as above; Bob Brookmeyer (*vtb, p*); Zoot Sims (*ts*); Larry Bunker (*d*).
　　　　　12/54.

Post-Chet. Somehow California is where this music was made to be heard. Sunny, cooled-out, elaborated but determinedly un-profound, it smacks very strongly of a time and place. No less than the slightly epicene Baker, the crew-cut, square-jawed Mulligan became a kind of icon, in sharp counter-definition to the long-hair, goatee and beret image of jazz. If it's surprising to think of Mulligan tackling 'Yardbird Suite' as he does on Volume One, it's done with a broad, open-air swing that blows away the hectic, claustrophobic atmosphere that hangs around the original.

****　　**Compact Jazz: Gerry Mulligan** Mercury 830697 CD
　　　　　Mulligan; Jon Eardley, Art Farmer, Don Ferrara (*t*); Bob Brookmeyer (*vtb*); Zoot
　　　　　Sims (*ts*); Warren Bernhardt (*p*); Jim Hall (*g*); Bill Crow, Eddie Gomez (*b*); Peck
　　　　　Morrison (*b*); Dave Bailey (*d*). 9/55, 9/63, 6 & 7/66.

If it's the purpose of a compilation to cut through the discographical chaff and give an uninitiated listener a well-cross-sectioned impression of what an artist does, without leaving a more informed fan (who wants it for the car or a Walkman, perhaps) feeling that he's been fobbed off with tag ends, then this is as good as one could hope for, within the availability open to the label.

It doesn't purport to be a 'best of . . . ', nor does it cover big-band material. But it does give a clear sense to an attentive listener of how Mulligan shapes a tune, how he responds as a player to different instrumental combinations (with or without a piano), and how he puts together a solo. Typically, the small groups (particularly those involving Brookmeyer) behave like the skeleton of much larger formations and there's a three-dimensionality to all the tracks which CD (though probably not a car or personal system) shows off from the very first bars.

****　　**At Storyville** Pacific Jazz 7944722 CD
　　　　　Mulligan; Bob Brookmeyer (*vtb, p*); Bill Crow (*b*); Dave Bailey (*d*). 12/56.

Despite what may sometimes be implied, Mulligan didn't give up using a piano in 1952. In later bands, he and Brookmeyer divided keyboard responsibilities, depending on which horn a particular track was voiced for. In the *At Storyville* sessions, recorded in Boston, the part-writing is typically elegant and exact and the backgrounds endlessly subtle (usually calling for two or three hearings to deliver their full import). 'Bweediba Bobbida', also on *Plays Mulligan*, above, has the two front men sounding like Bill and Ben, with their low-toned abstractions making only occasional sense to the outside. It's wonderfully entertaining, of course, and endlessly suggestive. The valve trombone has a softer, mellower tone than the blarting slide instrument, which is one reason why Brookmeyer so easily filled Baker's shoes in the quartet. In those days, Mulligan was a much more upfront player, and it's Brookmeyer who sounds closer in mood to the Mulligan one might recognize from the 1970s and after. There are half a dozen new tracks on this CD reissue, which comes highly recommended.

***(*)　　**Live In Stockholm, 1957** Nueva JU 324 CD
　　　　　Mulligan; Bob Brookmeyer (*vtb*); Joe Benjamin (*b*); Dave Bailey (*d*). 5/57.

Something of a 'favourites' set and thus warmly recommendable to anyone who doesn't have a surfeit of 'My Funny Valentine', 'Lullaby Of The Leaves', 'Baubles, Bangles And Beads', 'Walkin' Shoes' and so on already. Brookmeyer sounds as though he's loosened his top button for a change, and he's well forward on the mix, to the detriment of the rhythm section and, very occasionally, to Mulligan himself. A strong representative selection, with a convincing concert feel to the run of the tracks.

(*)   **Mulligan LRC CDC 7682 CD
Mulligan; Ruby Braff, Art Farmer (*t*); Bud Freeman (*ts*); Tom Fay, Billy Taylor, Claude Williamson (*p*); Dave Samuels (*vib*); Mike Santiago (*g*); Buddy Clarke, Bill Crow, George Duvivier, Benny Moten (*b*); Dave Bailey, Osie Johnson, Mel Lewis, Bobby Rosengarden (*d*). 58, 60, 11/76.

An oddly balanced compilation, that brings together some good late-1950s performances (including 'Festive Minor' from the quartet that recorded *A Night in Rome*, below) with some uncertain mid-1970s tracks which offer a glimpse of Mulligan's querulous soprano saxophone. The sextet with Braff and Freeman, and Benny Moten on bass, is perhaps his most backward-looking band ever. This isn't for the generalist and may only appeal to the serious collector who doesn't mind the absence of discographical material (some issues give no dates) and Fay's role on the last three tracks is uncredited.

***   **Americans In Sweden** Tax CD 3711 CD
Mulligan; Art Farmer (*t*); Bill Crow (*b*); Dave Bailey (*d*). 5/59.

***(*)   **A Night In Rome: Volume 1** Fini Jazz FJ 8801 CD/LP
As above. 6/59.

***   **A Night In Rome: Volume 2** Fini Jazz FJ 8802 CD/LP
As above. 59.

***(*)   **Walkin' Shoes** Bandstand BDCD 1536 CD
As above.

Francesco Fini's small label was also responsible for the release of Jimmy Giuffre's *Princess*, a concert recording from the same month as these excellent Mulligan tracks. Farmer doesn't quite have the lyrical authority of Chet Baker in this setting, but he has a full, deep-chested tone (soon to be transferred wholesale and exclusively to flugelhorn) which combines well with Mulligan's baritone. 'Walkin' Shoes', a reasonable test case for any comparison with Baker, has a jaunty urgency underneath its regular gait but 'I Can't Get Started' becomes a little hung up on its own elaborations.

These are both from the slightly superior first volume. The second is less compressed and has none of the compact lyricism of 'Baubles, Bangles And Beads', again on the first. The sound is above average for a live recording of this vintage, and the CD is sensibly balanced.

The Swedish CD is not so well organized or remastered. There is a fair bit of material in common: 'Spring Is Sprung', 'I Can't Get Started', 'Blueport' and 'Just In Time', but the earlier set also contains 'Utter Chaos', a fine Mulligan conception medleyed with two separate tracks on *At Storyville*, above, but here played on its own.

There's a good deal of overlap on these sets, but the Bandstand selection is probably the best of the bunch. Farmer's opening and subsequent solo on 'Blueport' is dazzling, setting a very high standard for the rest of the set, which is brightly remastered and free from extraneous noise. There's also a useful reprint of Mulligan's admirably cogent explanation of the thinking and techniques behind the pianoless quartets.

***   **Gerry Mulligan Meets Ben Webster** Verve 841661 CD
Mulligan; Ben Webster (*ts*); Jimmy Rowles (*p*); Leroy Vinnegar (*b*); Mel Lewis (*d*). 11 & 12/59.

(*)   **The Silver Collection: Gerry Mulligan Meets The Saxophonists Verve 827436 CD
Mulligan; Conte Candoli, Don Ferrara, Nick Travis (*t*); Bob Brookmeyer (*vtb, p*); Wayne Andre, Alan Ralph (*tb*); Paul Desmond, Johnny Hodges, Dick Meldonian, Gene Quill (*as*); Stan Getz, Zoot Sims, Ben Webster (*ts*); Gene Allen (*bcl, bs*); Lou Levy, Jimmy Rowles, Claude Williamson (*p*); Joe Benjamin, Ray Brown, Buddy Clark, Leroy Vinnegar (*b*); Dave Bailey, Stan Levey, Mel Lewis (*d*); 8 & 10/57, 11 & 12/59, 60.

***(*)   **Compact Jazz: Gerry Mulligan Concert Jazz Band** Verve 838933 CD

***(*) **New York – December 1960** Jazz Anthology 550072 CD
Mulligan; Conte Candoli (*t* on *Concert Jazz Band* only); Don Ferrara, Clark Terry,
Nick Travis (*t*); Bob Brookmeyer (*vtb*); Willie Dennis, Alan Ralph (*tb*); Gene Quill
(*as, cl*); Bob Donovan (*as*); Jim Reider (*ts*); Zoot Sims (*ts* on *Concert Jazz Band* only);
Gene Allen (*bs, bcl*); Bill Crow (*b*); Mel Lewis (*d*). 11 & 12/60, 12/60.

In Mulligan's book, everyone (by which he presumably means soloists as well as punters) profits
from the 'good bath of overtones' you get standing in front of a big band. The great
saxophonists lined up on *The Silver Collection* sound mostly constrained rather than inspired by
the small-to-medium-scale arrangements, steered in the direction of Mulligan's recitalist's cool
rather than to any new improvisational heights. Webster is magisterial on the sessions of
November and December 1959 ('Chelsea Bridge' and 'Tell Me When' are excerpted on *The
Silver Collection*), and the two saxophones blend gloriously in the lower register; something
wrong with the balance on the rhythm section, though. Hodges probably sounds the happiest of
the lot on the compilation, but then he was used to quite reasonable arrangements; these tracks
were originally issued backed by the Paul Desmond sessions, which made perfect sense all
round.

The *Compact Jazz* and *December 1960* sets are usefully complementary. Recorded at the
Village Vanguard (but not sounding at all clubby in quality), there are no serious overlaps,
beyond 'Lady Chatterley's Mother/Sister', and they make an attractive pair. The Verve also
has material recorded in Europe. 'Go Home', co-written with Webster, coaxes out one of
Mulligan's more unrestrained and intense solos.

***(*) **Monk Meets Mulligan** Original Jazz Classics OJC 301 CD/LP
Mulligan; Thelonious Monk (*p*); Wilbur Ware (*b*); Shadow Wilson (*d*). 8/57.

Not an entirely probable encounter, but Mulligan more than keeps afloat on the Monk tunes,
sounding least at ease on 'Rhythm-a-Ning', but absolutely confident on 'Straight, No Chaser'
and, of course, 'Round About Midnight'.

The dark, heavy sound of Wilbur Ware's bass is sufficiently 'below' Mulligan's horn and his
intervals sufficiently broad to tempt the saxophonist to some unusual whole-note progressions.
Monk darts in and out like a tailor's needle, cross-stitching countermelodies and neatly abstract
figures.

*** **Little Big Horn** GRP 91003 CD/LP
Mulligan; Alan Rubin (*t*); Keith O'Quinn (*tb*); Lou Marini (*as*); Michael Brecker (*ts*);
Marvin Stamm (*t*); Dave Grusin (*electric p, syn*); Richard Tee (*p*); Jay Leonhart,
Anthony Jackson (*b*); Buddy Williams (*d*).

Mulligan's hostility to (over-)amplification hasn't prevented him using electric instruments
when the need arises. Few electric piano players have given the instrument the grace and
sophistication Dave Grusin brings to it on 'I Never Was A Young Man' and 'Under A Star'.
Doubled with Richard Tee on 'Bright Angel Falls' he sounds less spacious, but one sees what
Mulligan is doing, trying to invest a small group with the breadth and harmonic range of a big
band (as he had tried to do, ironically, with the pianoless quartets of the 1950s). The addition of
brass on the title-track makes this even clearer, but it also underlines how much better it would
have sounded with a full-size band.

**** **The Age Of Steam** A&M CDA 0804 CD
Mulligan; Harry Edison (t); Bob Brookmeyer (*vtb*); Jimmy Cleveland, Kenny Shroyer
(*tb*); Bud Shank (*as, f*); Tom Scott (*ts, ss*); Ernie Watts (*reeds*); Roger Kellaway (*p*);
Howard Roberts (*g*); Chuck Domanico (*b*); John Guerin (*d*); Joe Porcaro (*d, perc*).
2–7/71.

Almost unrecognizably long-haired and bearded, posed in denims in front of one of the
locomotives that are his other great passion, Mulligan might almost be a footplateman on some
lonely Mid West branch line. In 1971, he hadn't recorded on his own account for nearly seven
years and so *The Age Of Steam* was awaited with considerable anticipation by those who had
followed Mulligan's career, and with delight by many who were coming to him for the first
time. The instrumentation (and Stephan Goldman's fine production job) are both identifiably
modern, with Mulligan making extensive use of electric piano and guitar. Both 'Country
Beaver' and 'A Weed In Disneyland' include strong rock elements (notably Roberts's strong
solo on the latter) and there's a strong dash of country swing to the opening 'One To Ten In

Ohio', which reunites him with Brookmeyer. The two finest tracks, though, are the long 'Over The Hill And Out Of The Woods', which Mulligan opens on piano, comping for an extensive range of horns out of which Harry Edison emerges for a strong solo, and the hauntingly beautiful 'Grand Tour'. The latter must be counted among the saxophonist's most beautiful composition, its meditative theme and misty timbre explored by Mulligan and Bud Shank. 'Golden Notebooks' is a further statement of Mulligan's long-sustained feminism. It's a light, almost floating piece from the yin side of his imagination.

Even allowing for the rather static dynamics of both tracks, the most striking characteristic of *The Age Of Steam* is its strongly rhythmic cast. Even when playing solidly on the beat, Mulligan's is an unmistakable voice and this is an important return to form after awkward years in the creative wilderness.

**   **Gerry Mulligan/Astor Piazzolla 1974** Accord 556642 CD
Mulligan; Astor Piazzolla (*bandoneon*); Angel Pocho Gatti (*pipe org*); Alberto Baldan, Gianni Zilolli (*mar*); Filippo Dacci (*g*); Umberto Benedetti Michelangeli (*vn*); Renato Riccio (*vla*); Ennio Morelli (*clo*); Giuseppe Prestipino (*b*); Tullio Di Piscopo (*d*). 74.

A nice idea that doesn't quite happen. The problem is not with the instrumentation or the arrangements, nor that Mulligan is not in sympathy with Piazzolla's *nueva tango* approach. It's simply that the performances are so drably uninflected (certainly in comparison to what the two principals do on their own account) as to render the experiment non-consequential.

***   **Soft Lights And Sweet Music** Concord CJ 300 CD/MC
Mulligan; Scott Hamilton (*ts*); Mike Renzi (*p*); Jay Leonhart (*b*); Grady Tate (*d*). 1/86.

What a session this might have been with Dave McKenna at the piano. As it is, Mulligan is left to carry too much of the harmonic weight, and his solo excursions seem cautious in consequence, rarely straying far from the most logical progression. There is also a tendency for the next phrase to be exactly the one you thought he was going to play. Hamilton shows off, but with forgivable charm and adroitness.

***(*)   **Lonesome Boulevard** A & M 395326 CD/MC
Mulligan; Bill Charlap (*p*); Dean Johnson (*b*); Richie De Rosa (*d*). 3 & 9/89.

Tonally sparse, but immensely suggestive of Mulligan's magisterial achievement as a writer/arranger. 'Flying Scotsman' is a small-group version of a piece reflecting Mulligan's affection for steam locomotives and commissioned for the 1988 Glasgow Jazz Festival. Far from lacking the impact of the big-band version, this account exposes the workings of the piece far more clearly, like a cut-away illustration in *Popular Railways*, and the subtlety of Mulligan's conception shows up.

The playing is softer, but also more varied, than the rather discursive voice of the 1950s. Mulligan's soprano saxophone isn't in evidence, which is a pity on the title-track and 'Splendor In The Grass', but his higher-register work on both is quite compelling. He may be spending more time on his orchestral work these days, but he can still produce deeply compelling jazz when the opportunities arise.

***   **Re-Birth Of The Cool** GRPGRD 9679 CD
Mulligan; Wallace Roney (*t*); Dave Bargeron (*tb*); John Clark (*frhn*); Bill Barber (*tba*); Phil Woods (*as*); John Lewis (*p*); Dean Johnson (*b*); Ron Vincent (*d*); Mel Torme (*v*). 1/92.

There has been some rewriting of the history books over the past year or two on behalf of Mulligan and pianist/arranger John Lewis *vis-à-vis* the original *Birth Of The Cool*. Mulligan is on record as feeling that the project was subsequently hijacked in Miles Davis's name. Though Miles 'cracked the whip', it was Lewis, Gil Evans and Mulligan who gave the music its distinctive profile. In 1991, Mulligan approached Miles regarding a plan to re-record the famous numbers, which were originally released as 78s and only afterwards given their famous title. Unfortunately, Miles died before the plan could be taken any further and the eventual session featured regular stand-in Roney in the trumpet part.

With Phil Woods in for Lee Konitz, the latter-day sessions have a crispness and boppish force that the original cuts rather lacked. Dave Grusin's and Larry Rosen's production is ultra-sharp and is perhaps too respectful of individual horns on 'Deception' and 'Budo', where a degree less separation might have been more effective (unless this is an impression based entirely on folk-memories of the original LP). The mix works rather better on the boppish 'Move' and 'Boplicity', and on the vocal 'Darn That Dream'. An ineresting retake on a still misunderstood experiment, *Re-Birth* (not to be confused with a funk-rap album of the same name, issued some time previously) sounds perfectly valid on its own terms.

MARK MURPHY (born 1932)
VOCAL

***(*)   **Rah** Original Jazz Classics OJC 141 LP/MC
Murphy; Ernie Wilkins Orchestra. 9–10/61.

***   **That's How I Love The Blues** Original Jazz Classics OJC 367 CD/LP/MC
Murphy; Nick Travis, Snooky Young, Clark Terry (*t*); Bernie Leighton, Dick Hyman (*org*); Roger Kellaway (*p*); Jim Hall (*g*); Ben Tucker (*b*); Dave Bailey (*d*); Willie Rodriguez (*perc*). 62.

Mark Murphy's been hip all his professional life. His earliest records, of which these are two, found him looking to emulate Eddie Jefferson rather than Frank Sinatra (or Bobby Darin – Murphy looked a little like a bobbysoxer himself back then), and while his delivery is sometimes self-consciously cool in its use of dynamics and bent notes, he's always an impassioned singer – sometimes too much so, such as on an overwrought 'Blues In My Heart' on the *Blues* collection. That record may annoy some with its showmanlike approach to a set of downbeat material, but Murphy is no more overbearing than Billy Eckstine or Al Hibbler. *Rah*, pitched as a college man's text of hipsterism, is marginally more enjoyable, but both records benefit from the singer's strong, flexible tenor – he's enough of his own man never to shoot for black pronunciation – and canny arrangements by Ernie Wilkins and (on *Blues*) Al Cohn.

***   **Beauty And The Beast** Muse M 5355 CD/LP/MC
Murphy; Brian Lynch (*t, flhn*); Bill Mays (*ky*); Lou Lausche (*vn*); Michael Formanek, Steve LaSpina (*b*); Joey Baron (*d*). 85–86.

***   **Kerouac Then And Now** Muse M 5359 CD/LP/MC
Murphy; Bill Mays (*ky*); Steve LaSpina (*b*); Adam Nussbaum (*d*). 11/86.

***   **What A Way To Go** Muse MCD 5419 CD/MC
Murphy; Danny Wilensky (*ts*); Pat Rebillot (*p*); John Cobert, Larry Fallon (*ky*); David Spinozza (*g*); Francisco Centeno (*b*); Alan Schwartzberg, Chris Parker (*d*); John Kaye, Sammy Figueroa (*perc*). 11/90.

Many Murphy albums are still awaited on CD. These three offer a useful round-up of his interests and techniques. *Beauty And The Beast* is almost a sampler of his latterday work, with a poem read as an accompaniment to Wayne Shorter's title theme, a fine 'I Can't Get Started' and an example of his mastery of bebop singing on Sonny Rollins's 'Doxy'. A useful cast of players are on hand in support. His fascination with Kerouac coninues on *Then And Now*, where there are tunes chosen to suggest the writer's tastes, episodes from some of his works read to music, and even a re-creation of a Lord Buckley routine. If it doesn't always work – Murphy can't help but sound self-conscious, even if he has a passion for this kind of thing – it's an interesting attempt at updating or rekindling beat repertory for an audience that would otherwise find this stuff quaintly hipsterish. *What A Way To Go* is his most recent set, and returns to a mixture of standards and jazz tunes: Murphy has started to exaggerate some of his bent notes and rhythmic risks, to compensate for a voice that is starting to turn grey at the edges, and some may dislike what he does with 'I Fall In Love Too Easily', to pick one. But he still sets himself the most inventive of programmes – Lee Morgan's 'Ceora', Ray Brown's 'Clown In My Window' – and makes them happen.

TURK MURPHY (1915–87)
TROMBONE

***   **Turk Murphy's Jazz Band Favourites** Good Time Jazz 60-011 CD
Murphy; Don Kinch, Bob Scobey (*t*); Bill Napier, Skippy Anderson, Bob Helm (*cl*);
Burt Bales, Wally Rose (*p*); Bill Newman (*g, bj*); Pat Patton, Dick Lammi, Harry
Mordecai (*bj*); Squire Gersback, George Bruns (*b, tba*); Stan Ward, Johnny Brent (*d*).
49–51.

**   **Turk Murphy And His San Francisco Jazz Band Vol. 1** GHB 091 CD
Murphy; Leon Oakley (*c*); Jim Maichak (*tb*); Phil Howe (*cl*); Pete Clute (*p*); Carl
Lunsford (*bj*). 4/72.

**   **Turk Murphy And His San Francisco Jazz Band Vol. 2** GHB 092 CD
As above. 4/72.

Murphy's music would be a little more credible if he hadn't gone on making it for so long. At
the time of his earliest recordings, when he was a member of the Lu Watters circle, the
Californian traditional jazz movement had some nous as revivalists of music which had lain,
unjustly neglected, for many years. In that light, the Good Time Jazz compilation, hammy
though much of the playing is, and painfully as opposed to authentically untutored, is both an
interesting and an enjoyable one. But after more than 20 years of this kind of thing, Murphy's
one-track traditionalism sounds tiresome and soulless on the two GHB CDs, taken from a single
1972. It might be cheerful and boisterous enough, and Murphy's own playing has achieved a
ready constituency, but there are many better arguments for revivalism than this music.

DAVID MURRAY (born 1955)
TENOR SAXOPHONE, BASS CLARINET

***   **Solo Live: Volume 1** Cecma 1001 LP

***   **Solo Live: Volume 2** Cecma 1002 LP
Murray solo. 5 & 8/80.

***(*)   **Live At The Peace Church** Danola BA 001 LP
Murray; Fred Hopkins (*b*); Stanley Crouch (*d*). 76.

***   **Flowers For Albert** West Wind 2039 CD
Murray; Lawrence Butch Morris (*c*); Don Pullen (*p*); Fred Hopkins (*b*); Stanley
Crouch (*d*). 9/77.

***   **Live At The Lower Manhattan Ocean Club** India Navigation IN 1032 CD
Murray; Lester Bowie (*t*); Fred Hopkins (*b*); Phillip Wilson (*d*). 12/77.

Over the last decade David Murray would seem to have confirmed Ornette Coleman's famous
claim that the soul of black Americans is best expressed through the tenor saxophone. A pivotal
figure in contemporary jazz (and one of the most comprehensively documented), Murray has
patiently created a synthesis of the radical experimentation of John Coltrane and (particularly)
Albert Ayler with the classic jazz tradition. As such, his music is virtually uncategorizable,
exploring freedom one moment, locked in bright swing structures the next, moving without
strain from astonishing aggression to openly romantic expression (much of it dedicated to his
wife, Ming).

He has worked with the World Saxophone Quartet and the Music Revelation Ensemble but
since 1976 has released nearly 25 albums under his own name, some of which are already
accorded classic status. He has an expansive tone that is readily adaptable to fast, aggressive
cross-cutting and slower, more expressive ballad performance. The unaccompanied
improviasations on the 1980 pair are, in their way, as significant as Sonny Rollins's celebrated
Solo Album, with the same associative freedom but with a much stronger tinge of free jazz than
Rollins would ever have allowed.

'Flowers For Albert' has been much reworked during Murray's subsequent career but the
unaccompanied version has a raw simplicity and directness. On the second volume of *Solo Live*,
he takes apart 'Body And Soul', an experiment to be repeated in a group context later. It's
appropriate to find him on the revived India Navigation label which was so influential in the

1960s. *Ocean Club* introduces material – 'Bechet's Bounce' and 'Santa Barbara And Crenshaw's Follies' – that also reappears later; remastered from the LPs, it has Murray doubling rather unconvincingly on soprano saxophone, though Bowie is on top form. *Peace Church* is a lot freer and more episodic. Any initial suspicion at yet another 'rediscovered' live set should be laid to rest: it's a powerful album that, better than any other single concert performance, lays Murray's stylistic roots bare. Stanley Crouch, who has reappeared regularly since, as a writer of sleeve-notes for Murray, was one of the central personal influences on the saxophonist's career, as is the superb Fred Hopkins.

***   **Interboogieology** Black Saint BSR 0018 CD
       Murray; Lawrence Butch Morris (*c*); Johnny Dyani (*b*); Oliver Johnson (*d*); Marta
       Contreras (*v*). 2/78.

Two compositions each by Murray and his most significant collaborator, Butch Morris. The opening 'Namthini's Song' is a stately procession, marked by Morris's typically unpredictable voicings. Marta Contreras sings wordlessly, somewhere up near the cornet's register; it's certainly a more convincing use of her voice than the Abbey Lincoln mannerisms of the title-track. 'Home' is a huge duet from Murray and Dyani, with the bassist's solid chant underpinning a free-flowing improvisation. 'Blues For David' is uncharacteristically direct for Morris, a fine blowing number with the leader's most shaped solo contributions of the set.

    This album probably set the pattern for Murray's subsequent and now very substantial output. A tireless experimenter, he also has a strong and canny urge to communicate, and there is a thread of populism running through his music that belies the easy critical association with Ayler and makes a nonsense of many critics' professed surprise at his rejection of unmediated avant-gardism in favour of a 'back to the future' examination of the whole sequence of black musical tradition.

***   **3D Family** hat Art 6020 CD
       Murray; Johnny Dyani (*b*); Andrew Cyrille (*d*). 8/78.

Murray's solitary album on hat Art is a curious mixture of fantastic potential in some directions and overachieved mastery in other, less promising ones. As a collaborative trio, it's absolutely sussed, but the material doesn't always do any more than trip up what sound like excitingly spontaneous ideas. Cyrille is a whirlwind, and a duo performance would be worth arranging. '3D Family', which reappears on *Home*, is among the saxophonist's best charts, and Dyani gives it a vibrant surge that recalls their duet on the *Interboogieology* version of 'Home'. (By this time, the permutation of tunes and performances has become quite bewildering.)

***   **The People's Choice** Cecma 1009 LP
       Murray; Hugh Ragin (*t, flhn*); Abdul Wadud (*clo*); Fred Hopkins (*b*).

Perhaps the least well-known of Murray's albums, this drummerless project was billed as a 'Chamber Jazz Quartet'. The stylistic emphasis, though, is 1960s rather than 1950s. Ragin's skittering trumpet rises like an exotic bird over a thick vegetation of string sounds which come across very cleanly. Murray's African figures are experimental in the best and most limited sense, and the overall impression is of conscious thought rather than spontaneity, though there is a heartfelt tribute to Johnny Dyani. It's an impressive performance, but certainly in the second division of David Murray albums.

****   **Sweet Lovely** Black Saint BSR 0039 CD
       Murray; Fred Hopkins (*b*); Steve McCall (*d*). 12/79.

Stripped down to basics, this anticipates *The Hill*. The first version of 'Hope / Scope', which has a slightly odd subsequent history, is the clearest, pivoted on Hopkins's booming bass. 'Coney Island' and 'The Hill' are at opposite ends of Murray's repertoire, but the trio gives them an unexpected coherence.

****   **Ming** Black Saint BSR 0045 CD/LP
       Murray; Olu Dara (*t*); Lawrence Butch Morris (*c*); George Lewis (*tb*); Henry
       Threadgill (*as*); Anthony Davis (*p*); Wilber Morris (*b*); Steve McCall (*d, perc*). 7/80.

***(*)   **Home** Black Saint BSR 0055 CD/LP
       As above. 11/81.

For many fans, *the* jazz album of the 1980s was recorded before the decade was properly under way. *Ming* is an astonishing record, a virtual compression of three generations of improvised music into 40 minutes of entirely original jazz. The opening 'Fast Life' has a hectic quality reminiscent of another of Murray's household gods, Charles Mingus. 'Jasvan' is a swirling 'Boston' waltz that gives most of the band, led off by the marvellous Lewis, ample solo space. 'Ming' is a sweet ballad which follows on from the troubling, almost schizophrenic 'The Hill', a piece that occupies a central place in Murray's output, perhaps an image of the jazz *gradus ad Parnassum* that he is so studiously and passionately scaling.

Recorded by the same octet, *Home* is very nearly the better album. The slow opening title-piece is a delicately layered ballad with gorgeous horn voicings. 'Last Of The Hipmen' is one of his best pieces, and the Anthony Davis vamp that leads out of Steve McCall's intelligent and exuberant solo is a reminder of how close to Ellington's bandleading philosophy Murray has come by instinct rather than design.

***   **Murray's Steps** Black Saint BSR 0065 CD/LP
     Murray; Bobby Bradford (*t*); Lawrence Butch Morris (*c*); Craig Harris (*tb*); Henry
     Threadgill (*as, f*); Curtis Clark (*p*); Wilbur Morris (*b*); Steve McCall (*d, perc*). 7/82.

This hasn't quite the sharpness of Murray's other octets and has to be considered, absurd as this will sound to anyone who has heard the disc, an off-day. The retake of 'Flowers For Albert' is an important index of how unwilling Murray has always been to leave his own output alone; there are more convincing versions; but, if the dedicatee represents some sort of magnetic north for Murray, then the piece is a good navigational aid.

***(*)   **Morning Song** Black Saint BSR 0075 CD/LP
     Murray; John Hicks (*p*); Reggie Workman, Ray Drummond (*b*); Ed Blackwell (*d*).
     9/83.

Compare the version of 'Body And Soul' – the tenor saxophonist's shibboleth – here with the unaccompanied one on the first item above. It is more assured, less willed and less concerned with deconstructing a piece that has been rendered virtually abstract by countless hundreds of improvisations. Note how Murray restores the tune in segments during his later statements of a freely arrived-at counter-theme.

Hicks is a wonderfully supportive and sensitive partner, particularly on the standard (enthusiasts should check out their duo, *Sketches of Tokyo*, DIW 8006 CD/LP, which features a (then surprisingly rare, but now more frequent) take on Coltrane by the saxophonist), and Blackwell's drumming touches all the right bases. A pity they haven't done more together.

***   **Live At Sweet Basil: Volume 1** Black Saint BSR 0085 CD/LP

***   **Live At Sweet Basil: Volume 2** Black Saint BSR 0095 CD/LP
     Murray; Olu Dara (*c*); Baikida Caroll, Craig Harris (*t*); Bob Stewart (*tba*); Vincent
     Chancey (*frhn*); Steve Coleman (*ss, as*); John Purcell (*as, cl*); Rod Williams (*p*); Fred
     Hopkins (*b*); Billy Higgins (*d*); Lawrence Butch Morris (*cond*). 8/84.

Volume 2 kicks off with a version of the wonderfully cheesy 'Dewey's Circle' from *Ming*, one of those compositions of Murray's that many listeners swear they have heard somewhere before. It's not quite the best piece on the set, but it's the one where most of the constituent elements are coming together. 'Bechet's Bounce' and 'Silence' on the first volume redirect some of Murray's increasingly familiar obsessions in quite new ways. The final track is a brief dedication to Marvin Gaye; by this stage in his career Murray is name-checking at an impressive rate.

The live context, with a hefty band pushing from behind, makes for some inventive conjunctions, but Murray's tone is uncharacteristically acid. There's no obvious explanation for it; the production is well up to Black Saint's careful standard.

***   **Children** Black Saint BSR 0089 CD/LP
     Murray; Don Pullen (*p*); James Blood Ulmer (*g*); Lonnie Plaxico (*b*); Marvin Smitty
     Smith (*d*). 10 & 11/84.

Rededicated to his son, David Mingus Murray, this is one of the poorer 1980s albums. Smith and Plaxico dominate unnecessarily, and Ulmer and Pullen consistently get in each other's way. That's another two bankable modern names to tick off against Murray's list, with 'All The Things You Are' for anyone who's bird-watching the standards.

*** **Recording NYC 1986** DIW 8009 CD/LP
Murray; James Blood Ulmer (*g*); Fred Hopkins (*b*); Sunny Murray (*d*). 86.

***(*) **I Want To Talk About You** Black Saint BSR 0105 CD/LP
Murray; John Hicks (*p*); Ray Drummond (*b*); Ralph Peterson Jr (*d*). 3/86.

Those who were disturbed by Murray's apparent abandonment of avant-garde might have been reassured by his firm rejection of the backward-looking stance of Wynton Marsalis and others. It's clear from the live *I Want To Talk About You* that, while the saxophonist is looking increasingly to an earlier generation of saxophone players, Sonny Rollins pre-eminently, but also synthesizers like the fated Ellingtonian Paul Gonsalves, he is doing so with instincts very explicitly conditioned by Coltrane and Ayler. His reading of 'I Want To Talk About You' has to be heard in the context of Coltrane's own version; as a ballad player, Murray is vibrant and expansive and 'Heart To Heart' (written by Hicks) is one of his most nakedly emotional recorded performances.

'Morning Song' reappears, its robust R&B stretched out into something altogether stronger than the album version. 'Red Car', from *Recording NYC* has him switch to bass clarinet; if the technique ultimately derives from Dolphy, Murray has managed to extend his great predecessor's somewhat predictable upper-register devices, making use of more of the horn.

Ulmer is another to have apparently turned his back on the avant-garde in pursuit of a more marketable neo-populism. In practice, of course, the more conservative Ulmer is also the one who digs deepest into black tradition, and so it turns out to be with Murray.

*** **In Our Style** DIW 819 CD
Murray; Fred Hopkins (*b*); Jack DeJohnette (*d, p*). 9/86.

Murray played in DeJohnette's Special Edition band, notably on *Album Album* (ECM 1280 CD/LP), but their duo confrontation feels slightly uncomfortable, as if they're doing no more than sounding one another out. DeJohnette's piano backgrounds, though uncharacteristically basic, are more effective foils than the drummed tracks, where DeJohnette seems to restrict himself to a disappointingly narrow range of devices, some of them overpoweringly recorded. It all makes a bit more sense when Fred Hopkins comes in on the title-track and 'Your Dice'.

**** **The Hill** Black Saint BSR 0110 CD/LP
Murray; Richard Davis (*b*); Joe Chambers (*d*). 11/86.

One of the peaks of Murray's career. The title-piece, pared down from eight voices to three, doesn't fall apart but retains its rather mysterious and troubling presence. Murray has significantly toned down his delivery from the immediately previous sessions and sounds altogether more thoughtful. The material, by now, is quite self-consciously programmed, with 'Chelsea Bridge' and 'Take The Coltrane' mixed in with the originals. 'Herbie Miller' contains Murray's best-recorded bass clarinet solo; pitched against Richard Davis's rich arco, he develops an intense thematic discourse that takes enough time to vary its accents in keeping with the changing emotional climate of the piece. By contrast, 'Fling' is exactly as throwaway as it sounds.

This is an essential modern album.

*** **Hope Scope** Black Saint BSR 0139 CD/LP
Murray; Hugh Ragin, Rasul Siddik (*t*); Craig Harris (*tb*); James Spaulding (*as*); Dave Burrell (*p*); Wilber Morris (*b*); Ralph Peterson (*d*). 5/87.

Only released in 1991 (by which time Murray was recording for DIW), this is a bright, exuberant album, full of the band's palpable delight in what they're doing. This version of 'Hope / Scope' is much less convoluted than the one on *Special Quartet*, below, but it inspires some raggedly spirited ensemble improvisations. The tributes to Lester Young and Ben Webster are closer to pastiche than usual (see also DIW 851, below), reflecting a rather lightweight side to the album that is initially appealing but increasingly puzzling as the layers come off it.

*** **The Healers** Black Saint BSR 0118 CD/LP
Murray; Randy Weston (*p*). 9/87.

Though Weston's sense of structure is much like Murray's, which turns out to be inhibiting rather than particularly productive, he tends to conceive developments in discontinuous units rather than in Murray's uninterrupted flow. Several times, the pianist falls back on set licks, which make him sound a less sophisticated player than he is. 'Mbizo' is a further version of a dedication to Johnny Dyani, who died the previous year. A by-way on Murray's increasingly determined course, *The Healers* takes Murray down a road he has seemed disinclined to pursue. Which is a pity.

****   **Deep River** DIW 830 CD
      Murray; Dave Burrell (*p*); Fred Hopkins (*b*); Ralph Peterson Jr (*d*). 1/88.

****   **Ballads** DIW 840 CD
      As above.

***(*) **Spirituals** DIW 842 CD
      As above.

****   **Special Quartet** DIW 843 CD
      Murray; McCoy Tyner (*p*); Fred Hopkins (*b*); Elvin Jones (*d*). 90.

Murray's move away from the Italian-based Black Saint (who had generously supported his work in the absence of any major-label bites) to the Japan-based DIW did nothing to stem the flow of material. Releasing records in threes quickly became the norm. These albums, with their explicitly traditionalist agenda, all come from a single New York session and are not quite as varied as the 1991 batch. *Ballads* has become one of the most popular of the saxophonist's albums, with *Spirituals* also touching a popular nerve; but spare a moment for *Deep River*, with 'Dakar's Dance' and 'Mr P.C.'. The latter is topped only by a riveting version of another Coltrane track on the 1990 album. *Special Quartet*? It certainly is, and a fine piece of arrogance on Murray's part to put half the classic Coltrane band back together, but it's no better than the 1988 group, even if Tyner is in sparkling form.

***(*) **Tea For Two** Fresh Sound FSRCD 164 CD
      Murray; George Arvanitas (*p*). 5/90.

Headed 'George Arvanitas Presents: The ballad artistry of . . . David Murray', there's a rabbit-out-of-hat quality to the ellipsis. Though no one's surprised any more to find Murray playing 'in the tradition', it's still rare to find him doing it quite this uncomplicatedly. The menu of standards doesn't really stretch him technically and there's a hint of a more mannered approach in his takes of past giants, almost as if he's over-anxious to inscribe himself into the history of jazz saxophone before the fortieth birthday comes up. For the record (this is a relatively undiscovered Murray album), the track listing is 'Chelsea Bridge', 'Polka Dots And Moonbeams', 'Star Eyes', 'Body And Soul' again, 'Tea For Two', 'I'm In The Mood For Love', an original 'Blues For Two', and 'La Vie En Rose'.

***   **Remembrances** DIW 849 CD
      Murray; Hugh Ragin (*t*); Dave Burrell (*p*); Wilber Morris (*b*); Tani Tabbal (*d*). 7/90.

On the cover a tiny child kneels, a toy saxophone pressed to its lips, the bell raised in exact mimicry of, yes! Albert Ayler at his most impassioned (or of Murray himself on the cover of *Deep River*). *Remembrances* digs down into the same influences that conditioned Murray's great predecessor. Much of this material is in the spirit of the black church (and thus of *Spirituals* and *Deep River*), its abstractions emerging out of impassioned witness, its resolutions an expression of acceptance rather than of will.

The tonal integrity of Ragin and Burrell is extraordinarily beautiful, with the trumpeter pealing away with a much fuller sound than he often uses and Burrell laying fat, rolling chords over the rhythmic pattern. Very lovely, very accomplished, and absolutely of its time and place.

***(*) **Shakill's Warrior** DIW 850 CD
      Murray; Don Pullen (*org*); Stanley Franks (*g*); Andrew Cyrille (*d*). 3/91.

A much more personal dredge of the past. *Shakill's Warrior* plugs Don Pullen into a Hammond B3 and Murray into his R&B roots. He even looked up his old pal, Stanley Franks, from their teenage band, Notations of Soul. Franks does damn-all on the album, but the remaining trio is red-hot. Pullen, working to a broadly similar concept, goes back virtually all the way with Murray; Cyrille is a new factor and, if he doesn't at first seem ideally suited to this line-up, it's the drummer's 'High Priest' that dominates the album.

***	**David Murray Big Band** DIW 851 CD
Murray; Graham Haynes, Hugh Ragin, Rasul Siddik, James Zollar (*t*); Craig Harris,
Frank Lacy, Al Patterson (*tb*); Vincent Chancey (*frhn*); Bob Stewart (*tba*); Khalil
Henry (*f, picc*); John Purcell (*as*); James Spaulding (*as, f*); Patience Higgins (*ts, ss*);
Don Byron (*bs, cl*); Sonelius Smith (*p*); Fred Hopkins (*b*); Tani Tabbal (*d*); Joel A.
Brandon (*whistle*); Andy Bey (*v*); Lawrence Butch Morris (*cond*). 3/91.

There are further versions of 'Lester' and 'Ben' from *Hope Scope* and a dedication to Paul
Gonsalves, acknowledged as an influence on Murray. The former pair are given an altogether
more complex and detailed reading but, by and large, the performances on this album are
disappointingly trite, and certainly lacking in the multi-layered obliqueness one expects from
Morris (who, significantly or not, doesn't contribute as a composer, other than the shared credit
on 'Calling Steve McCall').
The band is impressively constructed, on a scale Murray hasn't attempted before, but it
seems a pity to have got them all together and fired up and then to give them so little of
consequence to play.

***	**Lucky Four** Tutu 888108 CD/LP
Murray; Dave Burrell (*p*); Wilber Morris (*b*); Victor Lewis (*d, perc*). 9/88.

Moonlighting under the alias of Lucky Four, Murray and two long-standing collaborators turn
in a slightly lacklustre session that, despite interesting variants on both 'Valley Talk' and 'As I
Woke', never seems to grab the attention firmly. 'Chazz', dedicated to Mingus, and 'Strollin'',
to Michel Basquiat, are both slightly woolly.

SUNNY MURRAY (born 1937)
DRUMS

***(*)	**Live At Moers Festival** Moers Music 01054 CD/LP
Murray; David Murray (*ts, bcl*); Malachi Favors (*b, perc*); Cheik Tidiana Fall (*perc*).
6/79.

Despite his involvement with such crucial recordings as Cecil Taylor's 1962 Café Montmartre
sessions and Albert Ayler's *Spiritual Unity*, Murray has made scandalously few appearances on
record, and the recent rehabilitation of many of the early free jazz masters has entirely passed
him by as far as studio work is concerned. The leader's playing on this concert set remains
utterly distinctive, using a simple kit to create waves of rhythm and colour, dispersing marked
time and controlling without dominating all the different areas of the music. David Murray is at
something near his early, blistering best and, while the music is more a jam session than a
charted course, the four themes provide enough material for the group to roister along. The
in-concert sound is no more than acceptable, but the excitement survives any fidelity problems.

MUSIC REVELATION ENSEMBLE
GROUP

***	**No Wave** Moers 01072 CD/LP

**(*)	**Music Revelation Ensemble** DIW 825 CD/LP

***	**Elec. Jazz** DIW 841 CD/LP
David Murray (*ts*); James Blood Ulmer (*g*); Amin Ali (*b*); Jamaaladeen Tacuma (*b* on
MRE only); Ronald Shannon Jackson (*d;* not on *Elec. Jazz*); Cornell Rochester (*d* on
Elec. Jazz only). 6/80, 2/88, 3/90.

Music Revelation Ensemble bears out Bill Shankly's famous dictum about football being played
on grass, not on paper. *Music Revelation Ensemble*, on paper the most impressive-looking of the
three, is actually a rather dismal supergroup session that takes an inordinately long time to catch
light. Murray enters very late – and with some diffidence – on the opening 'Bodytalk', and
throughout the album he sounds as if he's just sitting in on someone else's date. Only with the
third track, 'Nisa', do things get moving, by which time more than 20 tedious minutes of
abstract noodling have already gone by. 'Blues For David', like all the tracks, is an Ulmer

composition, and not the Butch Morris of the same name on Murray's *Interboogieology* (Black Saint 0018 CD/LP/MC); the saxophonist plays a melancholy intro and then takes the front over a surprisingly bland accompaniment. The closing 'Burn!' is a silly pile-up. Prime Time and Last Exit (and Murray) fans may be tempted, but would be advised to leave well alone.

With a change of personnel in the engine-room, *Elec. Jazz* is rather better and sounds more like the product of a working group. Organized almost like a suite, with two parts each to 'Exit' and 'Big Top', it has far more shape than the first album and affords a better balance of ensemble and solo work. The musicians too are arrayed more logically in the mix, with Murray and Ulmer front and centre, bass and drums nicely divided across the near background. (In contrast, *MRE* sounded as if all four players – stars to a man – were queueing or jostling for a single spotlight.) *No Wave* is the rawest and most directly to-the-point, which may well recommend it; the sound, though, is often very wayward.

MWENDO DAWA
GROUP

**   **Free Lines** Dragon DRLP 33 LP
Ove Johansson (*ts*); Susanna Lindborg (*ky*); Ulf Wakenius (*g*); Anders Jormin (*b*); David Sundby (*d*). 3/81.

**   **New York Lines** Dragon DRLP 41 LP
As above, except Lars Danielsson (*b*) replaces Wakenius and Jormin. 6/82.

(*)   **Four Voices Dragon DRLP 47 LP
As above. 2/83.

(*)   **Live At Northsea Jazz Festival Dragon DRLP 79 LP
As above. 7/83.

**   **Street Lines** Dragon DRLP 72 LP
As above. 12/83.

**   **City Beat** Dragon DRLP 92 LP
As above. 1/85.

**   **Dimensions** Dragon DRLP 123 LP
As above, except Stefan Pettersson (*b, ky*) replaces Danielsson. 8/86.

**   **Human Walk** Dragon DRLP 155 LP
As above. 5/87.

This popular Swedish fusion band made a lot of records for Dragon – there are two earlier, deleted LPs as well – but their music is rather too tight and unyielding to allow space for the players to really shine. Johansson is a good, often belligerent tenor player who sounds roped-up in the plain rhythm charts, and Lindeborg is often content to deliver the melodic vamps on which many of the themes are based. When she has more freedom – as in the piano solo, 'Cool Beauty', on *Human Walk*, or the ballad, 'Chords', on *Dimensions* – she's impressively fluent. But the aim of the band seems to be to create a type of jazz-fusion that uses electronics in the same way as when adopted by the earliest jazz-rock groups: simple sequences over strict rhythms with a little improvisational decoration on top.

The band's best period was marked by the presence of bassist Lars Danielsson, whose compositions – such as 'Cold Winter' on *City Beat* – have an extra measure of substance which eludes Lindeborg's and Johansson's tunes. The Northsea set has a little more heat than they normally muster, and *Four Voices* is perhaps their most consistent set of original material. But otherwise the records are all prepared and delivered on much the same lines.

AMINA CLAUDINE MYERS (born 1943)

PIANO, KEYBOARDS, VOCALS

***   **Song For Mother E** Leo LR 1000 LP
Myers; Pheeroan AkLaff (*d*).

***(*)   **Salutes Bessie Smith** Leo CDLR 103 CD
Myers; Cecil McBee (*b*); Jimmie Lovelace (*d*).

***(*)   **The Circle Of Time** Black Saint BSR 0078 CD
Myers; Don Pate (*b*); Thurman Barker (*d*). 2/83.

***   **Country Girl** Minor Music 1012 LP
Myers; Patience Higgins (*f, as, ss*); Carlos Ward (*f, as*); Ricky ▓▓▓▓▓, ▓erome Harris
(*b, v*); Reggie Nicholson (*d, perc, v*); Bola Idowu (*perc, v*); collective personnel. 4/86.

(*)   **Amina RCA PL 83030 CD/LP
Myers; Jerome Harris (*g*); Reggie Nicholson (*d, tambourine, bells*); Bola Idowu
(*perc*); Ray Mantilla (*perc*); David Peaston, Catherine Russell (*v*). 11/87.

**   **In Touch** RCA PL 83064 CD/LP/MC
Myers; Jerome Harris (*g, b, v*); Reggie Nicholson, Flare Funston (*d, perc*).

A figure of enormous significance whose career seems to have temporarily succumbed to major label pressures, Myers combines a passionate commitment to soul, gospel and blues, with a more radical grounding in the AACM, the legendary proving ground from 1960s improvising radicals. Much like Mary Lou Williams before her, she is capable of tremendous musical subtlety (as on much of the free-ish *Circle of Time* and the long-deleted Marion Brown interpretations on *Poems for Piano* [Sweet Earth]), while preserving a raw emotionalism that is nevertheless laden with ambiguity.

Significantly, her finest single work to date is the Leo tribute to Bessie Smith, a much more convincing and rooted performance than the initially impressive but increasingly short-circuited *Songs For Mother E*, which kicked off one of the most significant independent labels of recent times and one with a particularly strong commitment to female improvising artists. Without attempting to pastiche the great blues singer, Myers gets inside Bessie's music completely. It's doubly unfortunate that her recent work should have been so blandly commercial. There is undoubtedly a substantial market for the two RCAs, and Myers deserves success more than most musicians, but her dull soul-funk, laden with brittle synthesizer patterns, scarcely reflects her real gifts.

FATS NAVARRO (1923–50)

TRUMPET

*****   **The Fabulous Fats Navarro: Volume 1** Blue Note B21Y 81531 CD

****   **The Fabulous Fats Navarro: Volume 2** Blue Note B21Y 81532 CD
Navarro; Howard McGhee (*t*); Ernie Henry (*as*); Allen Eager, Wardell Gray, Sunny Rollins, Charlie Rouse (*ts*); Tadd Dameron, Bud Powell (*p*); Milt Jackson (*p, vib*); Nelson Boyd, Tommy Potter, Curley Russell (*b*); Kenny Clarke, Roy Haynes, Shadow Wilson (*d*); Chano Pozo (*perc*). 9/47, 9 & 10/48, 8/49.

***(*)   **Fats Navarro Featured With The Tadd Dameron Band** Milestone M 47041 CD
Navarro; Tadd Dameron (*p*); Rudy Williams (*as*); Allen Eager (*ts*); Milt Jackson (*vib*); Curly Russell (*b*); Kenny Clarke (*d*). 48.

Like Howard McGhee, Navarro came up through the Andy Kirk band, having already worked with Snookum Russell. Overweight, with a high, rather effeminate voice (and nicknamed either 'Fat Boy' or 'Fat Girl'), he had by 1945, when he replaced Dizzy Gillespie in the Billy Eckstine orchestra, developed a trumpet style which replaced Gillespie's burp-gun lines with a more elegantly shaped approach that emphasized a bright, burnished tone. The open texture of his solos was altogether better suited to the Tadd Dameron band, which became his most effective setting.

Fabulous is one of the peaks of the bebop movement and one of the essential records. Navarro's tone and solo approach were honed in big band settings and he remarkable ability to maintain a graceful poise even when playing loudly and at speed. contrast with McGhee (it seems extraordinary that some of their performances together been misattributed) is very striking. Their duelling choruses on 'Double Talk' from a marvellous October 1948 session is one of the highpoints of the record; there is, as with several other tracks, an alternate take, which shows how thoughtful and self-critical an improviser the young trumpeter was, constantly refining, occasionally wholly rethinking his approach to a chord progression, but more frequently taking over whole segments of his solo and re-ordering them into a more satisfying outline. Navarro is rhythmically quite conservative, but he plays with great containment and manages to create an illusion, most obvious on 'Boperation', from the same session, that he is floating just above the beat; by contrast, McGhee sounds hasty and anxious. One hears the same effect rather more subtly on both takes of 'Symphonette' and on an alternate take of 'The Squirrel'.

There is an excellent version of 'Symphonette', also from 1948 on the Milestone Navarro/Dameron compilation. Milt Jackson is again present, but these performances, which also include 'The Squirrel', 'Dameronia' and two fine versions of 'Anthropology' are not up the standard of the Blue Notes.

For the time being, and certainly until Denon develop their reissue of Savoys, this is all that is available of the trumpeter's work. It's worth looking out for the unfortunately named *Fat Girl* [Savoy/Vogue 650115 CD] and *Fat Again* [Savoy/Vogue 650150 CD]. There are problems with both (including a degree of uncertainty whether Navarro or Dorham is playing on some cuts and the known fact that some of Navarro's solos were spliced in), but the quality of his playing shines through time and again on these earlier cuts. That talent only dimmed slightly towards the end, and the August 1949 sessions with Sonny Rollins and Bud Powell are not his best. Eight tracks (including the alternate master of 'Bouncing With Bud' from the same session are available on *The Amazing Bud Powell* (Blue Note CDP 781503 CD).

Navarro died of tuberculosis exacerbated by drug abuse. As an artist he was already astonishingly mature and it's slightly ironic that many of the stylistic innovations and developments attributed to Clifford Brown were actually instigated by Navarro. Small as his legacy is, it is one of the finest in all of jazz.

OLIVER NAYLOR (born 1903)
PIANO, BANDLEADER

**   Oliver Naylor's Seven Aces Fountain FJ 103 LP
         Naylor; Edward 'Pinky' Gerbrecht (*c*); Charles Hartman, Pete Beilman (*tb*); Bill
         Cregar (*cl, as*); Jerry Richel, Cecil Bailey (*as*); Newton Richardson (*ts*); Carl Rettie
         (*p*); Jules Bauduc (*bj*); Carl Hansen, Sam Olver (*tba*); Louis Darrough (*d*); Jack
         Kaufman (*v*). 2/24–1/25.

Naylor was from Birmingham, Alabama; several of his star musicians were from New Orleans, including Gerbrecht and Cregar; but the band was recorded in New York, by Gennett, and their entire output for the label, 17 sides, is included here. The original 78s are very rare, but Retrieval's customary attention to detail provides excellent remastering, even though the LP was first released in 1971. The music can't count as much more than a footnote in jazz history, and several of the tracks are no more than dance tunes of the day, but Gerbrecht and Cregar were capable players, and 'Ringelberg Blues' and 'Ain't That Hateful' offer interesting moments. Naylor continued working as a bandleader through the 1930s, and a later session for Victor includes at least one track – 'Slowin' Down Blues' – worthy of reissue.

BUELL NEIDLINGER
DOUBLE BASS

***(*)   Locomotive Soul Note 1161 CD/LP
         Neidlinger; Marty Krystall (*ts*); Brenton Banks (*vn*); John Kurnick (*mand*); Buell
         Neidlinger (*b*); Billy Osborne (*d*). 6/87.

Neidlinger was an essential component of Cecil Taylor's vital 1960 band (and features prominently on a rash of Candid reissues from that time). In later years he has developed in individual and unexpected directions, delving back into jump and swing, and even leading a bluegrass outfit.

At first glance, *Locomotive* is closer to what he was doing which (with?) Buellgrass (as he called it) than to his work with Taylor; but a closer comparative look at 'Jumpin' Punkins' here and on the Candid Taylor compilation of that name suggests much about the wellsprings of the pianist's work at that time, and also about Neidlinger's contribution to it. A strong, uncomplicated player, he drives this unusually shaped band through a roster of Monk and Ellington tunes in a manner that emphasizes the two composers' similarities rather than their differences. Though the pace is as abrupt as on a John Zorn record, there are few obvious modernist concessions. Banks plays like a folk fiddler, not in the scratchy microtonal style of Leroy Jenkins or Billy Bang, and, if there are already very few mandolin players, none of them bears useful comparison with what Kurnick is doing. Wholly original and absolutely riveting.

OLIVER NELSON (1932–75)
ALTO SAXOPHONE, SOPRANO SAXOPHONE, TENOR SAXOPHONE, CLARINET, COMPOSER, ARRANGER

***   **Meet Oliver Nelson. Featuring Kenny Dorham** Original Jazz Classics OJC 227 LP
Nelson; Kenny Dorham (*t*); Ray Bryant (*p*); Wendell Marshall (*b*); Art Taylor (*d*). 10/59.

(*)   **Soul Battle Original Jazz Classics OJC 325 LP
Nelson; King Curtis, Jimmy Forrest (*ts*); Gene Casey (*p*); George Duvivier (*b*); Roy Haynes (*d*). 9/60.

***   **Screamin' The Blues** Original Jazz Classics OJC 080 CD/LP/MC
Nelson; Richard Williams (*t*); Eric Dolphy (*as, bcl, fl*); Richard Wyands (*p*); George Duvivier (*b*); Roy Haynes (*d*). 5/60.

***(*)   **Straight Ahead** Original Jazz Classics OJC 099 CD/LP
As above, except omit Williams. 3/61.

****   **Blues And The Abstract Truth** MCA
Nelson; Freddie Hubbard (*t*); Eric Dolphy (*as, f*); George Barrow (*bs*); Bill Evans (*p*); Paul Chambers (*b*); Roy Haynes (*d*). 2/61.

Nelson did apprenticeship with Louis Jordan and with the Erskine Hawkins and Quincy Jones big bands. In style he was probably closer to Jones than to anyone else (liking to combine sophisticated intervals with a raw, bluesy feel) and eventually drifted off in the same direction, wasting his last few years on cop-show themes (and 'The Six Million Dollar Man'). One might almost say Nelson played 'arranger's sax', a slightly backhanded term usually reserved for piano players. His alto solos were direct and to the point, and with the original theme very much in view. They contrasted sharply and well with Eric Dolphy's more adventurous approach, though it's immediately evident from both *Screamin'* and *Straight Ahead* that Dolphy also prefers to explore the inner space of a tune rather than take the path of least resistance and go 'out'.

Like *Soul Battle*, these are slightly misleading titles, accentuating Nelson's forcefulness over his undoubted subtlety as an arranger and composer. The leader's alto solo on 'Six and Four' (*Straight Ahead*) is usefully representative of what he does; the two horn players indulge in some instrumental banter on the long 'Ralph's New Blues' (reminiscent of the kind of thing Dolphy did with Mingus) with Nelson switching briefly to tenor.

Through his contributions to *Screamin'* Williams isn't altogether missed on the later album, perhaps underlining Nelson's greater enthusiasm for saxophone writing. Dorham, on the earlier OJC, is used largely as a guest soloist, floating over Nelson's tight blues arrangements. Though more than capable of shaping an exciting solo, Williams isn't up to the standard of the great bopper, or of his descendant Freddie Hubbard who'd worked with Nelson a month before *Straight Ahead* on what was to be his best record.

Blues and the Abstract Truth is a wonderful set and nothing else Nelson did came close to it. Again featuring Dolphy, with Bill Evans and Paul Chambers joining the redoubtable Haynes in the rhythm section, it has a broader harmonic spectrum than the OJC pair, though it remains based on the 12-bar blues and the changes of 'I Got Rhythm', which were so significant in the development of bebop. It also contains Nelson's two best compositions, 'Hoe Down' and 'Stolen Moments', the former a theme based on 44 bars and developed from the opening two notes, the second a minor blues with challenging internal divisions. 'Stolen Moments' features Dolphy on his flute and a fine tenor solo from Nelson. 'Teenie's Blues', dedicated to his sister, is an attempt to reduce the harmonic range to just three progressions, with transpositions in the two altos to give the piece the required tension and release. (The later *More Blues and the Abstract Truth* [Impulse AS 75 CD] is frankly a disappointment.)

The two tenors on *Soul Battle* aren't known for thoughtful abstraction, but Nelson seems able to steer them to a degree of imaginative sophistication, much as later in his *Swiss Suite* [Flying Dutchman] he managed to put such drastically different horn players as Eddie Cleanhead Vinson and Argentinian screamer Gato Barbieri on stage together.

*** **Taking Care Of Business** Original Jazz Classics OJC 1784 CD
Nelson; Lem Winchester (*vib*); Johnny Hammond Smith (*org*); George Tucker (*d*); Roy Haynes (*d*). 3/60.

*** **Nocturne** Orginal Jazz Classics OJC 1795 CD
Nelson; Lem Winchester (*vib*); Richard Wyands (*p*); George Duvivier (*b*); Roy Haynes (*d*). 8/60.

Nelson's writing and arranging are consistently impressive, but these are rather drab sessions. Winchester is prominently featured on both, but isn't an entirely convincing soloist, with a tendency to repeat ideas he likes. 'Trane Whistle' (*Taking Care*) is a little-known tribute to the great saxophonist in his *Blue Train* uniform, and Nelson continues to work new changes on the basic blues sequence. *Nocturne* is a nice album, but a little hyper-subtle to make it into the front rank.

*** **Sound Pieces** Impulse GRD 103 CD
Nelson; Gabe Baltazar, Bill Green, Plas Johnson, Jack Nimitz, Bill Perkins (*reeds*); John Audino, Bobby Bryant, Conte Candoli, Ollie Mitchell, Al Porcino (*t*); Mike Barone, Billy Byers, Richard Leith, Dick Noel, Ernie Tack (*tb*); Bill Hinshaw, Richard Perissi (*frhn*); Red Callender (*tba*); Steve Kuhn, Mike Melvoin (*p*); Ray Brown, Ron Carter (*b*); Grady Tate (*d*); collective personnel. 9/66.

Like Toshiko Akiyoshi, Nelson tended to 'think high' as an arranger, and to some extent his personal switch to soprano saxophone was quite predictable. Even with the stern example of John Coltrane on the same label, Nelson sounds relaxed and surprisingly original, with a tight, hard-edged sound and no sign of intonation problems, except perhaps among the top notes on 'The Shadow of Your Smile'. The five small group tracks – with Kuhn, Carter and Tate – are not hard to place as Nelson's work, even allowing for the unfamiliarity of the instrument, but they're not entirely successful. 'Straight No Chaser' and the interesting original 'Example 78' were first released on *Three Dimensions*.

The first of the large-scale pieces, 'Sound Piece for Jazz Orchestra', was written for a German radio big band and covered by Stan Kenton's Newophonic Orchestra. With the solo part transposed up from his more usual horn, it has a vibrant, dramatic property, that doesn't carry over into the brief and skittish 'Flute Slas' (which is distinguished by a good Candoli solo), or 'The Lady from Girl Talk', which lacks Nelson's usual coherence of arrangement. Altogether rather disappointing.

*** **Black, Brown And Beautiful** RCA NL 86993 CD/LP/MC
Nelson; Randy Brecker, Ernie Royal, Marvin Stamm, Snooky Young (t); Oscar Brashear, Bobby Bryant (*t, flh*); Garnett Brown, Al Grey, Quentin Jackson, Tom Mitchell (*tbn*); Bob Ashton, Jerome Richardson (*reeds*); Jerry Dodgion, Johnny Hodges (*as*); Bill Green, Billy Perkins (*ts*); Joe Farrell, Frank Wess (*ts, fl*); Danny Bank (*bs*); Earl Hines, Hank Jones, Mike Morand (*p*); Lonnie Liston Smith (*electric p, p*); Mike Wofford (*p, syn*); Dennis Budimir, Hugh Burns, David Spinozza (*g*); Chas Hodges (*g, v*); Joe Jammer, Lee Ritenour (*el g*); Ron Carter, Chuck Domanico (*b*); Pat Donaldson (*el b*); Pete Gavin, Jimmy Gordon, Grady Tate (*d*); Willie Bobo, Shelly Manne (*perc*); Leon Thomas (*v*); collective personnel. 3/70.

A good example of Nelson's skills as an arranger. The high point of this Duke tribute was Johnny Hodges in the last few weeks of his life performing 'Creole Love Call' and Nelson's fine 'Yearning'. A good mix of older and younger players, and the typical balancing of approaches that applies, but Nelson's *Black, Brown and Beautiful* stands as witness to a misdirected talent.

STEVE NELSON (born 1956)
VIBES

***   **Live Session One** Red RR 123231 CD
Nelson; Bobby Watson (*as*); Donald Brown (*p*); Curtis Lundy (*b*); Victor Lewis (*d*). 7/89.

***   **Live Session Two** Red RR 123235 CD
As above. 7/89.

**   **Full Nelson** Sunnyside SSC 1044D CD
Nelson; Kirk Lightsey (*p*); Ray Drummond (*b*). 8/89.

**   **Communications** Criss Cross Jazz Criss 1034 CD
Nelson; Mulgrew Miller (*p*); Ray Drummond (*b*); Tony Reedus (*d*). 10/89.

Nelson is a late starter as a leader but, since these four records were issued almost simultaneously, he may be making up for lost time. Unfortunately, the two studio dates don't show this strong and much-admired player in a very appealing light. *Communications* suffers from a dislikeable sound-mix, with the vibes poorly focused and Reedus obscuring too much detail; while the material, aside from the attractive 'Blues For Bob', is rather tepid and lacking in sparkle. *Full Nelson* is a ballad session that unreels at a snail's pace and, by the time of the concluding, 14-minute ramble through 'Chelsea Bridge', most of the interest has trickled away. Lightsey tends to chime too closely with Nelson's lines to create enough contrast, and the thoughtful ballad, 'There Are Many Angels In Florence', is lost in the otherwise somnolent programme.

The live material is a different matter. While there are jam session *longueurs* here and there – 'Afro Blue' on *One* runs for over 20 minutes, for instance – the rhythm section has energy in abundance and Nelson and Watson both take extravagant, mercurial solos on both records. Recording, while not ideal, isn't too distracting.

ROGER NEUMANN
TENOR SAX

***   **Introducing Roger Neumann's Rather Large Band** Sea Breeze SBD 102 LP
Neumann; Gary Grant, Rick Baptist, Jack Coan, Larry Lunetta, Jack Trott (*t, flhn*); Alan Kaplan, Bob Enevoldsen, Herbie Harper, Morris Repass (*tb*); Dave Edwards, Eric Marienthal, Herman Riley, Bob Hardaway, Lee Callett (*reeds*); Tom Ranier (*p*); John Heard (*b*); John Perrett (*d*); Terry Schonig (*perc*). 4–6/83.

A bright, entertaining session by a band that manages to let professional gloss vie with enthusiastic playing. Neumann doesn't seek innovative charts; he likes to let the band rip and varies the section writing with intelligent craft rather than quirky individuality. The band is a mix of old familiars and younger pros, with an assertive team of soloists: Trott shines on the fast, funny 'Flintstones Theme', Rainer has a couple of good moments in the long piece conceived for Blue Mitchell, 'Blue', and everybody dispatches a flag-waving 'Cherokee' with great aplomb. Side one is analogue, side two digital, but both are splendidly recorded.

PHINEAS NEWBORN (1931–90)
PIANO

***(*)   **A World Of Piano** Original Jazz Classics OJC 175 LP
Newborn; Paul Chambers, Sam Jones (*b*); Louis Hayes, Philly Joe Jones (*d*); collective personnel. 61.

****   **The Newborn Touch** Original Jazz Classics OJC 270 LP
Newborn; Leroy Vinnegar (*b*); Frank Butler (*d*). 4/64.

***   **The Great Jazz Piano Of Phineas Newborn Jr** Original Jazz Clasics OJC 388
CD/LP/MC
Newborn; Sam Jones, Milt Turner, Leroy Vinnegar (*b*); Louis Hayes (*d*).

***   **Please Send Me Someone To Love** Contemporary C 7622 LP
Newborn; Ray Brown (*b*); Elvin Jones (*d*). 2/69.

***(*)   **Harlem Blues** Contemporary C 7634 LP
As above.

***   **Solo** L + R CDLR 45020 CD
Newborn solo. 75.

***   **Back Home** Contemporary C 7648 LP/MC
Newborn; Ray Brown (*b*); Elvin Jones (*d*). 9/76.

***   **Look Out – Phineas Is Back** Pablo 2310801 CD/LP
Newborn; Ray Brown (*b*); Jimmie Smith (*d*). 12/76.

A player of tremendous technical ability, often likened to Oscar Peterson (who had come on to the East Coast scene with similar suddenness and plaudits), the younger Newborn was flashy, hyped-up, and explosive, eating up themes like Clifford Brown's 'Daahoud' and Rollins's 'Oleo' like buttered toast. Underneath the super-confident exterior of *A World of Piano* and *The Newborn Touch*, though, there was a troubled young man whose personal and artistic problems somewhat recall Bud Powell's.

Newborn suffered a serious nervous collapse, from which he only partially recovered and the remainder of his career was interspersed with periods of ill health. His later recording output is spasmodic to say the least, marked by a chastened blues sound that contrasts sharply – in style and quality – with the early work. The two Contemporarys from 1969 are still characterized by trademark high-speed runs and a bouncing lyricism, but there are dark clouds too and some ideas remain curiously elided. The L+R solo record is a technically accomplished but aesthetically rather numbing medley of standards with 'Confirmation' thrown in as a test piece. Despite top-drawer rhythm players, the two later trios are very anonymous. Newborn's best performances may be found on the Teddy Edwards–Howard McGhee classic *Together Again!* (Original Jazz Classics 0JC 424 CD/LP) and on McGhee's *Maggie's Back in Town* (Contemporary C 7596 CD/LP).

DAVID 'FATHEAD' NEWMAN (born 1933)
TENOR, ALTO AND SOPRANO SAXOPHONES, FLUTE

**   **Back To Basics** Milestone 9188 CD/MC
Newman; Wilbur Bascomb, Jimmy Owens, Milt Ward (*t*); Earl McIntyre (*tb*); Babe Clark (*ts*); Clarence Thomas (*bs*); Kenneth Harris (*f*); Pat Rebillot, George Cables, Hilton Ruiz (*ky*); George Davis, Lee Ritenour, Jay Graydon (*g*); Abraham Laboriel (*b*); Idris Muhammad (*d*); Bill Summers (*perc*); strings. 5–11/77.

***   **Resurgence!** Muse M 5234 LP
Newman; Marcus Belgrave (*t*); Cedar Walton (*p*); Ted Dunbar (*g*); Buster Williams (*b*); Louis Hayes (*d*). 9/80.

***   **Still Hard Times** Muse M 5283 CD/LP
Newman; Charlie Miller (*t*); Hank Crawford (*as*); Howard Johnson (*bs*); Steve Nelson (*vib*); Larry Willis (*p*); Walter Booker (*b*); Jimmy Cobb (*d*). 4/82.

Fathead by name, but not by nature: Newman is an ornery, driving saxophonist whose R&B background – including 12 years with Ray Charles – has left him with a consummate knowledge in the use of riffs and licks in a soul-to-jazz context. He always swings, and his unmistakable Texan sound is highly authoritative, but like so many musicians of a similar background he's had trouble finding a fruitful context. His early Atlantic albums are all out of print. The Milestone album is a waste of his time: puling backings, strings and horns sweeten up already saccharine material, and Newman's surviving solos are the only reason to listen. But the Muse albums, sympathetically produced by Michael Cuscuna, are much more like it. *Resurgence* is still awkwardly balanced between blues-orientated sax blowing and more modish, funk-related concepts, but *Still Hard Times* reunites Newman with his old Ray Charles colleague Crawford, and they simple lay back and dig into the blues. Newman's solo on the opening 'Shana', a steadily mounting chorus of wails, is typical of the musician at his best, and also why Newman's records seldom sustain interest: he hasn't enough to say as a leader to keep a record's momentum going.

** **Fire! Live At The Village Vanguard** Atlantic 81965-2 CD
Newman; Hank Crawford (*as*); Stanley Turrentine (*ts*); Steve Nelson (*vib*); Kirk Lightsey (*p*); David Williams (*b*); Marvin 'Smitty' Smith (*d*). 12/88.

** **Blue Greens And Beans** Timeless SJP 351 CD
Newman; Marchel Ivery (*ts*); Rein De Graaff (*p*); Koos Serierse (*b*); Eric Ineke (*d*). 5/90.

(*) **Blue Head Candid CCD 79041 CD
Newman; Clifford Jordan (*ss, ts*); Budy Montgomery (*p*); Ted Dunbar (*g*); Todd Coolman (*b*); Marvin 'Smitty' Smith (*d*). 9/89.

Solid records, but they all lack some vital spark to make them come alive. *Fire!* never lives up to its title: Turrentine and Crawford help out in the front line, but the rhythm section shambles along, Nelson is entirely wasted, and most of the tracks never build up a genuine head of steam. *Blue Greens And Beans* is a two-tenor quintet which lacks all of the punch one has come to expect in the aftermath of the the the Lockjaw–Griffin records. *Blue Head* is much better, thanks to Jordan's energetic solos, Montgomery's dextrous piano, and the tremendously shifting rhythms laid down by Coolman and Smith. But six very long jam tunes is probably at least one too many.

JOE NEWMAN (1922–92)
TRUMPET

**** **The Count's Men** Fresh Sound FSR CD 135 CD

***(*) **I Feel Like A New Man** Black Lion BLCD 760905 CD/LP
Newman; Benny Powell (*tb* on *Count's Men* only); Bill Byers (*tb* on *New Man* only); Gene Quill (*as* on *New Man* only); Frank Foster (*ts*); Frank Wess (*f, ts*); John Lewis (*p* on *New Man* only); Sir Charles Thompson (*p*); Freddie Green (*g* on *New Man* only); Milt Hinton (*b* on *New Man* only); Eddie Jones (*b*); Osie Johnson (*d* on *New Man* only); Shadow Wilson (*d*). 9/55, 9/55 & 4/56.

*** **Good'n'Groovy** Original Jazz Classics OJC 185 LP
Newman; Frank Foster (*ts*); Tommy Flanagan (*p*); Eddie Jones (*b*); Bill English (*d*). 3/61.

***(*) **Jive At Five** Original Jazz Classics OJC 419 CD/LP/MC
Newman; Frank Wess (*ts*); Tommy Flanagan (*p*); Eddie Jones (*b*); Oliver Jackson (*d*).

***(*) **Hangin' Out** Concord CJ 262 LP
Newman; Joe Wilder (*t, flhn*); Hank Jones (*p*); Rufus Reid (*b*); Marvin Smitty Smith (*d*). 5/84.

Though included on the Savoy compilation *The Bebop Boys* (Savoy WL 70547 2LP), Newman was never an orthodox modernist. His sharp attack and bright sound were derived almost entirely from Louis Armstrong and, though he was chief cadre of the 'Basie Moderns' in the 1950s, he maintained allegiance to the Count's music over any other. *Good'n'Groovy* was recorded at about the time of his departure from the Basie band (and *Jive At Five* has very much the same feel). Newman always sounds good round Frank Foster, and the album bounces with enough vigour to cut through a rather flat mix.

Better to start with the Black Lion and Fresh Sound CDs from a pair of mid-1950s sessions, recorded while Newman was still trumpet star with the Basie band. 'East Of The Sun' on *New Man* is touched by Parker, but 'Diffugality', with the larger Byers/Quill/Foster front line, seems to be hamstrung between two idioms, offering a slightly ironic slant to Leonard Feather's famous characterization of the trumpeter's style as 'neutralist-modern'.

As a useful compare-and-contrast exercise, try 'A. M. Romp' on *The Count's Men* with the same tune on *Good'n'Groovy*. The later version is slightly wilder, but it's the tighter version with Sir Charles Thompson that really impresses, and newcomers to Newman's entertaining sound would do well to begin with the mid-1950s stuff.

A canny and enterprising musician (who represents a 'positive' counter-image to many of the musicians of his generation), Newman headed the educational/promotional Jazz Interactions trust in the later 1960s, a thin time for the music, and expanded his interests to include large-scale composition (a direction that reflected more of his New Orleans background than it did the turbulent classicism of his exact contemporary, Charles Mingus). In the 1980s, Newman was still playing vibrant trumpet, and the set co-led with Joe Wilder and distinguished by Hank Jones's expert comping is evidence of his artistic longevity and stamina. Newman also appears on a *Friends Of Boogie Woogie* project with pianist Axel Zwingenberger (Vagabond VR 8.85005 CD/LP) which is worth digging out.

NEW ORCHESTRA WORKSHOP
GROUP

***(*) **The Future Is N.O.W.** Nine Winds NWCD 0131 CD
Daniel Lapp, Bill Clark (*t*); Graham Ord, Coat Cooke, Bruce Freedman, Roy Stiffe (*reeds*); Paul Plimley (*p*); Clyde Reed, Paul Blaney, Ken Lister (*b*); Claude Ranger, Gregg Simpson, Roger Baird, Stan Taylor (*d*). 90.

Vancouver's New Orchestra Workshop is a co-operative venture inspired by Chicago's AACM. This CD offers the chance to sample the work of five different bands which have grown out of NOW. The outstanding piece is the opening track by Plimley's Octet, a swirling, compelling montage of rhythmic and melodic figures that is gripping throughout its nine-minute length; but there isn't a bad track among the six here. The harmolodically-inspired quartet Lunar Adventures contribute two tracks; Chief Feature is a quartet that brews up a long, blustering workout reminiscent of early Archie Shepp; and Unity purvey a vivacious free improvisation, with excellent work by Lapp, Blaney, Ord and Baird. Only the muddled piece by Turnaround is in any way disappointing. A valuable introduction to the work of some otherwise little-known players.

NEW ORLEANS RHYTHM KINGS
GROUP

(****) **New Orleans Rhythm Kings Vol. 1** Village VILCD 010-2 CD
Paul Mares (*c*); George Brunies (*tb*); Leon Roppolo (*cl*); Jack Pettis (*Cmel, ts*); Elmer Schoebel, Mel Stitzel (*p*); Lou Black (*bj*); Arnold Loyacano (*b*); Frank Snyder, Ben Pollack (*d*). 8/22–3/23.

(****) **New Orleans Rhythm Kings Vol. 2** Village VILCD 013-2 CD
As above, except add Santo Pecora (*tb*); Don Murray (*cl, as*); Glenn Scoville (*as, ts*); Charlie Cordella (*cl, ts*); Jelly Roll Morton, Kyle Pierce, Glyn Lea 'Red' Long (*p*); Bob Gillette, Bill Eastwood (*bj*); Chink Martin (*bb*); Leo Adde (*d*); omit Schoebel, Brown and Black. 7/23–3/25.

One of the major groups of jazz records, from the first stirrings of the music in recording studios, the New Orleans Rhythm Kings sessions still sound astonishingly lively and vital 70 years later. The band recorded in Chicago but had come from New Orleans: Mares was already a disciple of King Oliver (who hadn't yet recorded at the time of the first session here), Roppolo played fluent, blue clarinet, and even Brunies made more of the trombone – at that time an irresponsibly comical instrument in jazz terms – than most players of the day. The rhythms tend towards the chunky, exacerbated by the acoustic recording, but the band's almost visionary drive is brought home to stunning effect on the likes of 'Bugle Call Blues' (from their very first session in August 1922), the relentlessly swinging 'Tiger Rag' and the knockabout 'That's A Plenty'. On two later sessions they took the opportunity to have Jelly Roll Morton sit in, and his partnership with Roppolo on 'Clarinet Marmalade' and 'Mr Jelly Lord' – something of a sketch for Morton's own later version – invigorates the whole band. 'London Blues' and 'Milenberg

Joys' find Morton more or less taking over the band in terms of conception. The two final sessions they made, in early 1925, are slightly less impressive because of Brunies's absence, and there are moments of weakness elsewhere in the original records: the use of saxes sometimes swamps the initiative, Mares isn't always sure of himself, and the beats are occasionally unhelpfully overdriven. But this is still extraordinarily far-sighted and powerful music for its time, with a band of young white players building on black precepts the way that, say, Nick LaRocca of the ODJB refused to acknowledge.

The two CDs include almost all of the alternative takes of the band's records. Unfortunately, the transfers here are less than ideal. Given the rarity of fine copies of the originals and the poor fidelity of the Gennett 78s to start with, it's fairly clear and bright overall; but there is an astonishingly high level of surface blemishes carried through to the remastering, which makes one query the 'de-noising' credit listed on the CD insert. We have yet to examine the second volume, which was not finally available in time for this edition, but must assume that a similar caution has to apply there.

FRANKIE NEWTON (1906–54)
TRUMPET

***(*)   **Frankie's Jump** Affinity CDAFS 1014 CD
Newton; Cecil Scott (*cl, ts*); Edmond Hall (*cl, bs*); Mezz Mezzrow (*cl*); Pete Brown, Russell Procope, Tab Smith, Stanley Payne, Gene Johnson (*as*); Kenneth Hollon (*ts*); Don Frye, James P. Johnson, Kenny Kersey (*p*); Frank Rice, Al Casey, Ulysses Livingstone (*g*); Richard Fulbright, John Kirby, Johnny Williams (*b*); Cozy Cole, O'Neil Spencer, Eddie Dougherty (*d*); Clarence Palmer, Slim Gaillard, Leon LaFell (*v*). 3/37–8/39.

***   **At The Onyx Club** Tax M-8017 LP
As above, except add Buster Bailey (*cl*); Babe Russin (*ts*); Claude Thornhill, Billy Kyle (*p*); James McLin (*g*); Maxine Sullivan, Midge Williams (*v*); omit Procope, Johnson, Casey, Gaillard. 3–10/37.

Newton was an intriguing, unguessable player whose small number of recordings represents the rare strain of swing-era small groups at their most interesting. In some ways he was an old-fashioned hot player, using a terminal vibrato borrowed directly from Armstrong and turning in oblique, poetic solos on otherwise slight material. He worked extensively at New York's Onyx Club in the late 1930s, when the tracks on these two records were made. The Affinity CD is inevitably more comprehensive, including all eight tracks on the first side of the Tax LP, as well as the results of several later sessions. 'Who's Sorry Now' features a Newton solo which summarizes his style: the quirky lyricism and sudden bursts of heat make him exhilaratingly hard to predict. There are other good solos from Brown and Hall scattered through these sides, and one or two more challenging tunes, including 'Vamp' and the odd 'Parallel Fifths' from the final (1939) session. The Tax LP includes the results of two sessions missing from the Affinity record, each featuring Newton backing either Maxine Sullivan or Midge Williams. It's slighter stuff; but both singers perform with some charm, and the band support with seemingly genuine enthusiasm. The Tax LP has more surface noise but a more tangible presence than the punchier but rather brittle-sounding CD transfers.

JAMES NEWTON (born 1953)
FLUTE

***   **Crystal Texts** Moers 01048 LP
Newton; Anthony Davis (*p*). 11/78.

****   **Axum** ECM 1214 CD/LP
Newton (*f* solo). 81.

***   **James Newton** Gramavision GR 8205 CD
Newton; Slide Hampton (*tb*); Jay Hoggard (*vib*); John Blake (*vn*); Anthony Davis (*p*); Cecil McBee (*b*); Billy Hart (*d*). 10/82.

***(*)   **Luella** Gramavision GR 8304 CD
Newton; Jay Hoggard (*vib*); Kenny Kirkland (*p*); John Blake, Gayle Dixon (*vn*);
Abdul Wadud (*clo*); Cecil McBee (*b*); Billy Hart (*d*). 83.

***(*)   **Water Mystery** Gramavision GR 8407 CD
Newton; John Carter (*cl*); Greg Martin (*ob*); John Nunez (*bsn*); Charles Owens (*Eng
hn, ss*); Red Callender (*tba*); Alan Iwohara (*koto*); April Aoki (*hp*); Roberto Miguel
Miranda (*b*); Anthony Brown (*perc*). 1/85.

****   **The African Flower** Blue Note 746292 CD
Newton; Olu Dara (*c*); Arthur Blythe (*as*); Jay Hoggard (*vib*); John Blake (*vn*);
Roland Hanna (*p*); Rick Rozie (*b*); Billy Hart (*d*); Pheeroan AkLaff (*d, perc*); Milt
Grayson (*v*). 6/85.

One of the relatively few contemporary players to own to a direct Eric Dolphy influence,
Newton started out as a Dolphyish multi-instrumentalist but gave up alto saxophone and bass
clarinet towards the end of the 1970s to concentrate on the least developed aspect of the
Dolphy legacy. As a virtuoso flautist, he too has worked in both formal and improvised contexts
and has developed a wholly original means of vocalizing while he plays. This is by no means
new (Roland Kirk was exceptionally proficient at it), but Newton has taken the technique far
beyond unisons and harmonies to a point where he can sing contrapuntally against his own flute
line. The results are frequently dazzling, as on the solo *Axum*, an African-influenced set which
represents the most important piece of flute improvisation since Dolphy's 'Gazzeloni' (Blue
Note 764524 CD). Newton's vocalizations allow his pieces to develop with unprecedented
depth, and his tone is quite remarkable.
   Newton's recording career is an odd one, divided almost exactly between smaller
independent or borderline 'classical' labels (India Navigation, BvHaast) and the top-ranking
jazz labels of the last couple of decades, who may have found his uncompromising artistic
nature a difficult trade-off for his undoubted virtuosity and imagination. In 1985 he made a
remarkable group recording with Blue Note. *African Flower* is a more obviously accessible
work than the solo venture (partly because the bulk of the material is by Ellington) but is no
less successful as a synthesis of Afro-American musics. Typically, and as on *Luella*, it features a
non-standard line-up, with John Blake's violin constantly undermining its own references to the
European classical tradition. Blythe and Dara are both excellent, and Newton, though
inevitably less prominent in a group setting, runs his flutes through some wildly unfamilar
harmonic intervals and 'false' notes. The slightly later *Romance And Revolution* [Blue Note
746431 CD], a tribute to 'Forever Charles' Mingus and featuring an impressive group of young
M-Base players, is currently out of the catalogue.
   Luella is still identifiably a jazz album, and 'Mr Dolphy' puts Newton's heart throbbingly on
his sleeve. However, the line-up also refers to a more formal tradition. Later Gramavision
sessions were more obviously 'sheet-driven' and it's significant that the jazz tribute on *Water
Mystery* should be to Billy Strayhorn. As a set of contemporary chamber pieces, it's hard to
fault and the orchestration of winds and (unconventional) strings is quite beautiful; like his
colleague, Anthony Davis, with whom he duets on the fine Moers set, Newton is pushing hard at
the boundaries that divide musical traditions. If, like Davis, he has been accused of desiccation,
he's still capable of living with a swinging player like Slide Hampton (on the 1982 *James
Newton*) and coming out just ahead.

ALBERT NICHOLAS (1900–73)
CLARINET, SAXOPHONE

***(*)   **This Is Jazz** Storyville SLP 4068 LP
Nicholas; Wild Bill Davison (*c*); Jimmy Archey, George Brunies (*tb*); Dan Burley,
James P. Johnson, Charles Queener, Joe Sullivan, Ralph Sutton (*p*); Danny Barker
(*g*); George Pops Foster (*b*); Warren Baby Dodds (*d*). 3–8/47.

[***   **A Tribute To Jelly Roll Morton** Storyville SLP 4050 LP]
Nicholas; Bobby Greene (*p*); Jens Solund (*b*); Knud Ryskov Madsen (*d*). 8/70.

The war years were rocky ones for the most mellifluous of the New Orleans clarinettists, and his career only began to run true again in the revivalist fervour that overtook jazz after hostilities ceased and the European appetite for 'hot' music began to make a significant impact on the American scene. Nephew of cornettist Wooden Joe Nicholas, pupil of Lorenzio Tio Jr and a childhood friend of Sidney Bechet, Nicholas had a smooth and supple tone that lent itself perfectly to his sophisticated conception of the blues.

The 1947 sessions have all the smoothed-out finesse one expects of the period, but that suits Nicholas remarkably well. His phrasing on 'Rose Room' and 'I've Got A Feeling I'm Falling' (with Davison and Brunies) is flawless. It's simply that the foil isn't as darkly contrasting as he might like; Nicholas seemed to prefer situations (such as he had experienced with Jelly Roll Morton) with a hint of ambiguity and tension against which to pitch his beautifully resolved lines.

In 1953 Nicholas went to live in Europe. He died in Basle 20 years later. In between, like Bechet, he'd parlayed a substantial solo career as a founding father of the music. The tribute to Morton recalled their 1939 encounters. By now, backing groups were not so much a dynamic component in Nicholas's improvisation as a relatively passive backdrop to it. Compare this 'Wolverine Blues' with the earlier version. There's not a lot to choose between the readings, but the later session lacks the dialogue that Nicholas constructed with his favourite partners. The Scandinavian rhythm players know their material inside out, but they err on the side of correctness and a rather self-conscious 'authenticity' which doesn't ring true.

HERBIE NICHOLS (1919–63)
PIANO

[***   **M & N** Savoy 650112 CD]
Nichols; Danny Barker (g); Chocolate Williams (b, v); Shadow Wilson (d); probable personnel. 3/52.

****   **The Bethelehem Sessions** Affinity CD AFF 759 CD
Nichols; George Duvivier (b); Dannie Richmond (d). 11/57.

Despite being (posthumously) included in A. B. Spellman's important book *Four Lives in the Bebop Business* and despite the more practical advocacy of younger piano players like Geri Allen, Herbie Nichols has remained a strangely marginal figure. Less obviously offbeat in technique than either Richard Twardzik or Carl Perkins, he is most immediately likened to Thelonious Monk (with whom he shares the Savoy album, above) but his distinctive approach might also usefully be compared to Eric Dolphy's, particularly with regard to the way both men used fixed keys and conventional thematic structures. Whereas Dolphy pushed out the harmonic envelope, however, Nichols preferred to concentrate on motivic and thematic variation, with considerable rhythmic innovation. His was a more engaging, less alienating sound than Monk's and much less stressed than the later Bud Powell's, though the sudden interpolation of a 6-or 10-bar measure in the middle of a song is as unsettling for the listener as it must have been for his fellow players.

Not primarily a standards player, he is nevertheless capable of doing astonishingly subtle things with a familiar tune. 'All The Way' is played with cocktail, but at a topplingly slow pace and with a tremendous inertia in the left hand; it only just avoids falling apart, and without a relatively conventional rhythm section Nichols might have pushed it further still. His writing, which frequently hovers close to deliberate banality, has to be lived with for a while before it gives up its most interesting elements: 'Portrait Of Ucha', '45 Degree Angle', the romantic-ironic 'Infatuation Eyes' and 'S'Crazy Pad' and 'Love, Gloom, Cash, Love' (which gave its name to the original Bethlehem release) are among the best of Nichols's small output of songs. Nichols died of leukaemia in 1963, having spent his last few years accompanying singers, most notably Sheila Jordan. *The Bethelehem Sessions*, which was his last recording, is an absolute gem, and it's sad that there are no alternative takes available as there are on a couple of tunes on *M & N*. The long-deleted Blue Note *This World* from the previous year should be fought for if it ever turns up in a second-hand rack.

RED NICHOLS (1905–66)
CORNET, TRUMPET

***   **Red Nichols 1925–28** Fountain DJF 110 2LP
Nichols; Wingy Manone, Brad Gowans (*c*); Miff Mole (*tb*); Jimmy Dorsey, Fred
Morrow (*cl, as*); Pee Wee Russell (*cl, ts*); Dick Johnson (*cl*); Lucien Smith (*ts*); Arthur
Schutt, Rube Bloom, Bill Haid (*p*); Eddie Lang, Dick McDonough (*g*); Nick Lucas
(*bj*); Joe Tarto (*bb*); Vic Burton (*d*); Arthur Hall, Arthur Fields, Frank Gould, Irving
Kaufman (*v*). 11/25–9/28.

It seems strange at this distance to recall that Nichols was once considered the *sine qua non* of
jazz trumpet – at least, among many British musicians and fans, who regarded the New York
school of the 1920s as the most sophisticated jazzmen of the time. That judgement still has much
truth in it – harmonically and conceptually, Nichols's Five Pennies recordings were rare feats of
musicianship – but most now point to the anodyne tone of the music and the cool delivery as
black (or, rather, white) marks against the musicians. As principal ringleader, Nichols had
furthest to fall. But his records hold more than period charm for listeners who enjoy
Beiderbecke (the rival whose reputation has endured far more healthily than Nichols's) as well
as Armstrong.

Fountain's double-LP collects 24 sides by The Red Heads, two by We Three and six by The
Six Hottentots, all groups with the same nucleus of Nichols and Mole, with Dorsey, Schutt, Lang
and Burtonas their most frequent collaborators. The material is often in the genre of hot dance
music, but there are some surprising transformations of stricter jazz material: it's interesting to
conjecture what Morton would have thought of The Red Heads's 'Black Bottom Stomp', which
is as carefully arranged as the Red Hot Peppers version, if less red hot. Most of these tracks
create an exacting balance between breaks, solos and punctiliously neat ensembles, with Mole's
sometimes quirky trombone parts a wry foil to Nichols's dancing, angular solos. On the
three-and four-man tracks, which are basically trumpet solos with rhythm accompaniment,
Nichols has few problems in sustaining a melodic linear improvisation; both 'Plenty Off Centre'
and 'Trumpet Sobs' are impressive efforts for a man of 20.

Thirty-two tracks of this sort are a little hard to take in one go; they're best heard an LP side
at a time. Connoisseurs of period vocals should hear Irving Kaufman, the most stentorian singer
of the 1920s, on three tracks. Unfortunately, most of the originals were made for Pathé
Actuelle, whose distant and noisy recording seldom transfers well, and while the (*1974*) LP
sounds good enough, it's surely time to have this material remastered.

(*)   **Red & Miff (1926–1931) Saville SVL 146 LP
Nichols; Tommy Gott, Leo McConville, Manny Klein, Bob Ashford, Ruby Weinstein
(*t*); Miff Mole, Bill Rank, Glenn Miller (*tb*); Arnold Brilhart (*cl, as, f, ob*); Alfie Evans
(*cl, as, bs*); Jimmy Dorsey (*cl, as*); Harold Sturr, Pee Wee Russell, Fud Livingston (*cl,
ts*); Benny Goodman (*cl*); Max Farley, Sid Stoneburn (*as*); Babe Russin (*ts*); Frankie
Trumbauer (*Cmel*); Adrian Rollini (*bsx*); Joe Raymond, Joe Venuti (*vn*); Abe
Borodkin (*clo*); Nat Shilkret (*cel*); Irving Brodsky, Arthur Schutt, Lennie Hayton,
Roy Bargy (*p*); Tony Colucci (*g, bj*); Carl Kress, Eddie Lang (*g*); Arthur Campbell,
Jack Hanson (*bb*); Art Miller (*b*); Chauncey Morehouse (*d, vib, v*); Vic Berton, Stan
King, Gene Krupa (*d*); Franklyn Baur, Dick Roberston, Jim Miller, Charlie Farrell,
Paul Small (*v*). 9/26–1/31.

(*)   **Rhythm Of The Day ASV AJA 5025 CD
Nichols; Manny Klein, Leo McConville, Donald Lindley, James Kozak, Charlie
Teagarden, Wingy Manone, Johnny Davis (*t*), Miff Mole, Glen Miller, Will Bradley
(*tb*), Dudley Fosdick (*mel*); Ross Gorman (*cl, as, bs*), Alfie Evans (*cl, as, vn*), Harold
Noble (*cl, as, ts*), Jimmy Dorsey, Benny Goodman (*cl, as*); Billy McGill, Fud
Livingston (*cl, ts*); Pee Wee Russell (*cl*); Babe Russin (*ts*); Adrian Rollini, Barney
Acquelina (*bsx*), Nick Koupoukis (*f, picc*), Murray Kellner, Joe Venuti, Jack Harris,
Saul Sharrow (*vn*), Milton Susskind, Arthur Schutt, Edgar Fairchild, Jack Russin,
Fulton McGrath (*p*), Eddie Lang, Tony Colicchio, Carl Kress (*g*), Tony Starr (*bj*),
Artie Bernstein, Art Miller (*b*), Victor Engle, Chauncey Morehouse, Vic Berton,
David Grupp (*d*). 10/25–2/32.

Saville's LP represents a cross-section of the kind of studio work that Nichols and Mole handled virtually every day in the 1920s. Eight tracks by Roger Wolfe Kahn's orchestra offer polished hot dance music of the day, with 'The Tap Tap' and 'Say Yes Today' emerging slightly ahead; 'Feeling No Pain' is one of four versions by Nichols, this one credited to Red And Miff's Stompers. The 1928 and 1930 tracks by a larger Nichols-led aggregation are far less interesting than his earlier sides. The transfers are rather dull and flat compared to what can be done with these records.

The ASV CD is something of a missed opportunity, since it purports to be a Five Pennies compilation yet includes two tracks by Mole's Molers and one by Ross Gorman's dance band, as well as including several of the later, lesser records. At least the 1925-7 selections – including 'Alabama Stomp', 'Buddy's Habits' and 'Cornfed' – are among the best of the Pennies. But until a superior selection is released on CD, one must turn to the CJM LPs listed below. ASV's remastering is quite bright.

***   **Red Nichols Vol. 2** Classic Jazz Masters CJM 25 LP
Nichols; Leo McConville, Manny Klein (*t*); Miff Mole (*tb*); Dudley Fosdick, Bill Trone (*mel*); Arnold Brilhart, Jimmy Dorsey, Walter Livingston (*cl, as*); Fud Livingston (*cl, ts*); Pee Wee Russell (*cl*); Adrian Rollini (*bsx, gfs*); Arthur Schutt, Lennie Hayton (*p*); Murray Kellner (*vn*); Eddie Lang, Dick McDonough, Carl Kress (*g*); Art Miller (*b*); Vic Berton (*d*); Scrappy Lambert (*v*). 6/27–3/28.

***   **Red Nichols Vol. 3** Classic Jazz Masters CJM 27 LP
As above, except add Joe Venuti (*vn*), Joe Tarto (*bb*), Chauncey Morehouse (*d*), omit Rollini, Hayton and McDonough. 3–5/28.

CJM's chronological survey of Nichols's Five Pennies recordings has been blemished by the deletion of the first – and most consistently interesting – volume. The Pennies could range from a five-to a fifteen-piece band. Miff Mole remembered that they never played in public and it was a unit conceived either for jamming or to make records: unusually pure jazz motives for the day. But the smaller and more informal groups were confined to the 1926-7 records, and later sides were by an orchestra playing the tunes of the day rather than 'Hurricane' or 'Boneyard Shuffle'. The first side of Volume Two still contains some of the best Pennies records: 'Mean Dog Blues', 'Riverboat Shuffle', 'Eccentric' and 'Feelin' No Pain'. But 'Nobody's Sweetheart', included in two takes, has splendid Mole and Russell, and only the closing tracks feature blander, sweeter arrangements.

***   **Red Nichols Vol. 4** Classic Jazz Masters CJM 28 LP
Nichols; Leo McConville, Manny Klein (*t*); Miff Mole, Glenn Miller (*tb*); Dudley Fosdick (*mel*); Benny Goodman, Jimmy Crossan (*cl, as*); Jimmy Dorsey (*as*); Fud Livingston (*cl, Cmel, ts*); Arnold Brilhart (*ts*); Arthur Schutt (*p*); Kurt Dieterle, Murray Kellner (*vn*); Carl Kress, Perry Botkin (*g*); Hank Stern (*bb*); Vic Berton, Chauncey Morehouse, Gene Krupa (*d*); Scrappy Lambert, Tom Edwards, Richard Roberts, Charles Small (*v*). 6/28–1/29.

***   **Red Nichols Vol. 5** Clasic Jazz Masters CJM 30 LP
As above, except add Pete Pumiglio, Alfie Evans (*cl, as*), Adrian Rollini (*bsx, hot fountain pen*); Lennie Hayton (*p*), Art Miller (*b*), Dave Tough (*d*). 2–4/29.

Nichols approached the end of the jazz age with all his best work almost behind him: yet he was still only 25 in 1930, the veteran of hundreds of recording sessions. Both these last two volumes in the CJM series are weakened by several tracks of fairly straight dance music, but the best music is as feisty as the hottest of the Five Pennies sides. 'Marhie'opens volume 4 in fine style, and the closing tracks feature Goodman and the surprisingly soulful trombone of Miller, who arranged the date. It continues on Volume 5 with an excellent Goodman solo on 'Chinatown', followed by a very fine session dominated by Adrian Rollini, whose bass sax never sounded bigger and more resonant than it does here. The very last two tracks, under the name 'Louisiana Rhythm Kings', actually return to the quintet format, and Nichols, Goodman, Miller, Schutt and Tough close the era in rousing form on 'Ballin' The Jack' and 'I'm Walking Through Clover'. Nichols's many later Dixieland sessions have yet to make their way to CD.

MAGGIE NICOLS (born 1948)
VOCALS, ASSORTED INSTRUMENTS

***(*)   **Nicols/Tippetts** FMP SAJ 38 LP
Nicols; Julie Tippetts (*v, assorted instruments*). 6/78.

***(*)   **Nicols 'N' Nu** Leo LR 127 LP
Nicols; Pete Nu (*p*).

***   **Don't Assume** Leo LR 145 LP
As above.

A remarkable vocal performer, Scottish-born Nicols (who has French and Berber forebears) works in a personal style that combines orthodox singing with a homely *Sprechstimme* (as on 'Ooh, Me Poor Feet' on the duo album with Julie Tippetts) which is dramatic, moving and very funny within a generously undoctrinaire feminist agenda. The duets with Nu explore some of the territory mapped out by her earlier vocal groups Okuren and Voice, frequently moving into abstract territory but constantly reasserting the lyrical potential of personal experience. She is most convincing in company with Tippetts and pieces like 'Rabbiting', 'Moon Fire', 'Wind Forest' and 'Whailing' confirm a still ludicrously underrated talent.

Nicols has also recorded with Loverly (ITM Records 0019 CD), Perfect Trouble (Moers 02070 CD) and with saxophonist and electronics expert Uli Lask (*Sucht Und Ordnung*, ECM 1268 LP). She combines the avant-garde techniques of Cathy Berberian with the simplicity and directness of a folk singer and deserves much wider recognition.

LENNIE NIEHAUS (born 1929)
ALTO SAXOPHONE

***(*)   **The Quintets** Original Jazz Classics OJC 319 LP
Niehaus; Jack Montrose (*ts*); Bob Gordon (*bs*); Monty Budwig (*b*); Shelly Manne (*d*). 7/54.

****   **The Octet 712: Volume 3** Original Jazz Classics OJC 1767 LP
Niehaus; Bill Holman (*t*); Stu Williamson (*t, vtb*); Bob Enevoldsen (*tb*); Jimmy Giuffre (*reeds*); Pete Jolly (*p*); Monty Budwig (*b*); Shelly Manne (*d*).

Over-ripe for reassessment, Niehaus is a fine altoist with a smooth West Coast veneer that tends to belie his imaginative compositions and standards arrangements. It's clear from the opening bars of 'You Stepped Out Of A Dream' (*Quintets*) that something unusual is in progress. *The Octet* is better still, full of inventive and sophisticated arrangements that make up for a hint of blandness and propriety in the performances. Sadly, these fine sessions coincided with the beginning of a second stint with the Stan Kenton band. Niehaus also appears on a wilderness of Kenton albums (though there's little point looking for him there), after which he turned his music into a day job, writing and arranging for television and the movies. A loss and a lack.

JUDY NIEMACK
VOCAL

(*)   **Blue Bop Freelance FRL CD 009 CD
Niemack; Curtis Fuller (*tb*); Cedar Walton (*p*); Ray Drummond (*b*); Joey Baron (*d*). 9/88

Judy Niemack is a strong presence, but she also performs like a member of the band, which justly elevates her accompanists – Fuller (who appears only on three tracks), Walton, Drummond and Baron all play with superb authority. It's a strong programme, with some jazz themes as well as a sound mix of standards: Niemack turns 'Dizzy Atmosphere' into an all-scat vehicle, reshapes King Pleasure's take on 'Parker's Mod' and swings through a duet with Drummond on 'Softly As In A Morning Sunrise'. But while she exudes confidence, some of her approaches don't always ring true: she has a sometimes breathy, overblown way with her phrasing, and a certain light-opera plumminess detracts from her intensity. 'Gentle Rain', for instance, is mishandled, some lines rushed, others sounding too ripe. She's best on the tunes where she's most integrated with the band, such as Walton's memorable 'Bolivia'. The recording is clear if a little resonant.

***   **Long As You're Living** Freelance FRL-CD 014 CD
Niemack; Joe Lovano (*ts*); Fred Hersch (*p*); Scott Colley (*b*); Billy Hart (*d*). 8/90.

***   **Heart's Desire** Stash ST-CD-548 CD
Niemack; Kenny Barron (*p*); Erik Friedlander (*clo*). 91.

Long As You're Living is a set of jazz standards and a challenging programme: 'Daahoud', 'Infant Eyes', 'Monk's Dream', even Ornette Coleman's 'To Welcome The Day'. Niemack handles them all with breezy assurance. Any who found her earlier record a little overbearing, though, will probably feel the same about this. 'Waltz For Debby' comes out as merely sticky, and Cedar Walton's embarrassing 'The Maestro', a dedication to Ellington, doesn't transcend its feeble lyric. But there is superb accompaniment from the band, with Lovano taking some choice solos and Billy Hart playing with brilliant touch: at times, as on the title-track, he seems to be duetting with the singer, finding all sorts of ingenious strokes. *Heart's Desire* is a reflective series of duets with Barron (Friedlander underscores on only three tracks). Mostly standards, with a couple of pop tunes from Joni Mitchell and Stevie Wonder, Niemack sings with a little more restraint and Barron is his customarily masterful self: nothing hits any special heights, but it's a pleasing record.

GERRY NIEWOOD
FLUTE, ALTO SAXOPHONE

(*)   **Share My Dream dmp CD 450 CD
Niewood; Joe Beck (*g*); Michel Camilo (*p, syn*); Jay Leonhart, Wayne Pedsiwiatr (*b*); Dave Weckl (*d*); Jim Saporito (*perc*). 2 & 3/84, 1/85.

Despite a successful association with Gil Evans (whose open-mindedness included a sympathetic attention to rock composers like Jimi Hendrix), Niewood is an unreconstructed fusion player whose jazz credentials are dependent on sporadic outbreaks of improvisational flair. As a composer/bandleader, he is firmly locked into the over-produced sound of another of his employers, flugelhornist Chuck Mangione. Despite intelligent contributions from Camilo, Leonhart and Weckl, *Share My Dream* suffers from unhappy generic associations.

STEVE NOBLE
PERCUSSION

***   **Live At Oscar's** Incus LP52 LP
Noble; Alex Maguire (*p*). 88.

****   **Ya Boo, Reel And Rumble** Incus CD06 CD
Noble; Alex Ward (*cl, as*). 3/89, 7/90.

***(*)   **Tumba La Casa!: Trios Volume 1** VOTP VOCA 907 MC
Noble; Billy Jenkins (*g*); Oren Marshall (*tba*). 11/90.

***(*)   **Tumble Shakedown: Trios Volume 2** VOTP VOCA 911 MC
As above, except omit Marshall, add Roberto Bellatalla (*b*). 3/91.

Steve Noble came to wider notice during the 'Company Week' of 1987, when he joined one of Derek Bailey's most adventurous collectives for a week of improvisation. The best of those performances, including a fine duo between Noble and bassist Barre Phillips are preserved on *Once* (Incus CD04). At the same time, Noble and his occasional partner, Alex Maguire, were winning a reputation in the London free music community for improvised performances that combined intense, sometimes ferocious interplay with a rare infusion of wit. Their recording debut was less than wholly inspired. *Live At Oscar's*, so named from the performance location at the Wilde Theatre, Bracknell, covers a familiar enough range of idiom and contains a respectable quota of humour, but on cold (and acoustically rather dead) vinyl the music doesn't come across with any great conviction.

Remarkably, reeds player Alex Ward was only in his mid-teens when the first of the performances of *Ya Boo, Reel And Rumble* were recorded. A virtuosic player with a strong background in modernist formal repertoire, he plays with considerable authority, matched move for move by Noble's quick-witted percussion. The opening '8th and How' may still be Noble's best performance on record, but it's matched by moments on two roughly produced tapes made in association with 'spazz' anarchist, Billy Jenkins (*q. v.*), and released on Jenkins's cottage label VOTP (Voice of the People). (The partnership began with Jenkins's name foremost on the guitarists's *Big Fights* series (VOTP VOCA 909 MC), reviewed elsewhere, but also worth catching.) Each of the trio tapes features a long, whole-side improvisation, with several other, more structured pieces that call on the guitarist's uncategorizable anti-technique. Noble plays a more conventional drummer's role on *Tuba La Casa!* (with Oren Marshall's tuba filling in the bass parts), cutting satirical swathes through everything from post-bop harmony to rock and roll to the clichés of 'free' music. *Tumble Breakdown* is freer and much more varied in texture. Bellatalla plays a more interventionist role than Marshall and is a more conventionally virtuosic player. Noble hauls out his back-up bugle and musical saw, revelling in the unique atmosphere Jenkins generates.

Both sets are highly recommended to all but the very po-faced and owners of excessively sensitive tape decks.

MIKE NOCK (born 1940)
PIANO

**   **Talisman** Enja 3071 LP
Nock (*p* solo). 4/78.

**   **Piano Solos** Timeless SJP 134 LP
Nock (*p* solo). 9/78.

(*)   **In Out And Around Timeless SJP 119 CD
Nock; Michael Brecker (*ts*); George Mraz (*b*); Al Foster (*d*). 7/78.

***   **Climbing** Tomato 2696502 CD
Nock; Tom Harrell (*flhn*); John Abercrombie (*g, mand*); David Friesen (*b*); Al Foster (*d*). 1/79.

**   **Ondas** ECM 1220 CD
Nock; Eddie Gomez (*b*); Jon Christensen (*d*). 11/81.

A New Zealander by birth, Nock came to the US in the 1960s and stayed until 1985: he is on some records by Yusef Lateef and John Handy from the '60s, and tried jazz-rock before reverting to acoustic music in the '70s. Something of a burst of recording around 1979–80 has left these records in the catalogue. His earlier hard bop style is eschewed on the solo and trio records for a much windier, overcooked method which seeks to feel every note and succeeds in communicating very little. There's a certain charm in the solo records, since Nock has a penchant for nostalgic-sounding ballads, but the trio set, which looks to be conceived as a great statement, sounds like second-hand Jarrett, particularly the interminable 'Forgoten Love'. Gomez sounds bemused and it's left to the reliable Christensen to find a line to earth for Nock's airy meanderings. The Tomato set and the quartet date for Timeless are far better, if less than essential, since the other players are first-rank. Brecker gets off some good solos on *In Out And Around* and *Climbing* features the intriguing combination of Abercrombie and Harrell, two essentially conservative spirits whose lyricism always endures through fast tempos and full-blooded playing. In a subsidiary role, Nock sounds fine: like many a journeyman pianist, he's only vulnerable when exposed to a solo spotlight.

(*)   **Dark & Curious VeraBra vBR 2074 CD
Nock; Tim Hopkins (*ts, rec*); Cameron Undy (*b*); Andrew Dickeson (*d*). 90.

A bulletin from Nock's Antipodean base. Hopkins sounds like an accomplished saxophonist, with a sanded, morose tone and a way of undulating long lines through the rhythm section, but there's something wearisome about the way the quartet plays: it's too ponderous, too full of portent, even when worthwhile ideas – as on a steady, well-turned piece like 'Resurrection' – are clearly there. Nock's own improvisations suggest that he remains a little too hung up on his delivery. The kind of record which ultimately gives the term 'interesting' a bad name. Clear and truthful studio sound.

JIMMIE NOONE (1895–1944)
CLARINET

***   **The Complete Recordings Vol. 1** Affinity AFS 1027-3 3CD
Noone; George Mitchell (*c*); Fayette Williams (*tb*); Joe Poston (*cl, as, v*); Earl Hines, Alex Hill, Zinky Cohn (*p*); Bud Scott (*bj, g*); Junie Cobb, Wilbur Gorham (*bj*); Lawson Buford, Bill Newton (*bb*); Johnny Wells (*d*); Lillie Delk Christian (*v*). 6/26–6/30.

Complete with all the alternative takes, this is an exhaustive survey of the key period of Jimmie Noone's work on record. Noone has long been reckoned as one of the premier jazz clarinettists, but his records have fallen out of wide renown and listeners will find this set hard work. Track after track is spoiled by weak material, unsuitable arrangements, poor sidemen or a sentimental streak which eventually comes to dominate the playing. These are all familiar characteristics of the period, but Noone seemed oblivious to the excessive sweetness which overpowered so many of the records with his Apex Club band, named after his resident gig in Chicago. He had a mellifluous, rather sad-sounding tone and preferred his solos to be insinuating rather than fierce: where Johnny Dodds, the other great New Orleans player of the day, was comparatively harsh, Noone sought to caress melodies. But the plunking rhythm sections, still dominated by banjos even in 1928–9, and the unsuitable front-line partners failed to give Noone the kind of sympathetic settings which would have made his romantic approach more feasible. Poston tarnishes many of the tracks, and his replacement, Pollack, is even worse; even Earl Hines, who plays on 18 tracks on the first disc, can provide only flashes of inspiration. Mitchell arrives for a single session, and even that is ruined by some awful vocals, a final burden which afflicts far too many of these tracks.

There are, nevertheless, examples of the great musician Noone could be. The ballad-playing on 'Sweet Lorraine' and 'Blues My Naughty Sweetie Gives To Me' is of a very high order and investigates a rare, cool vein in the Chicago jazz of the period. 'Oh, Sister! Ain't That Hot?', 'El Rado Scuffle', 'It's Tight Like That' and 'Chicago Rhythm' are further isolated successes, but otherwise one has to pick out Noone amidst an otherwise discouraging backdrop. The Classics series has also released two discs covering the period, *Jimmie Noone 1928–1929* (Classics 611 CD) and *Jimmie Noone 1929–1930* (Classics 632 CD); they don't include any of the alternative takes, but those who might prefer just a single disc of Noone at work may find the earlier of the two holds the best of the original sides. Remastering is fairly good, if rather muffled, in both sets.

FREDRIK NORÉN
DRUMS

***   **Joao Carlos** Dragon DRLP 138 LP
Norén; Gustavo Bergalli (*t*); Joakim Milder (*ts*); Esbjörn Svensson (*p*); Christian Spering (*b*). 5/87.

***   **To Mr J** Sonet SNTCD1037 CD
Norén; Johan Horlen (*as*); Joakim Milder (*ts*); Carl Fredrik Orrje (*p*); Hans Backenroth (*b*). 1/90.

Norén is a veteran Swedish hard bopper who not only blows up the kit with Blakeyish aplomb but also hires the pick of the local young turks – the eldest man on the Sonet set aside from the leader is Milder, 25 at the time of the recording. Bergalli is a rather more experienced hand and he and Milder make a substantial front line on *Joao Carlos*, which goes at a typically no-nonsense pace, its ten tracks wrapped together with tight solos and Norén's watchful timekeeping, although there are interestingly dark moments provided by two themes by Svensson, 'Vinterport' and 'Vändpunkten'. *To Mr J* goes at a similar clip: eight originals and two standards are crisply despatched in less than 50 minutes, and while a couple of the themes aren't characterized strongly enough, Milder's 'Rollo's Little Sister' and Orrje's 'Damerance' have plenty of harmonic intrigue, which the two-horn front-line thrives on. Milder confirms a growing reputation as a budding master, while Horlen isn't far behind. Upfront and full-bodied studio sound.

WALTER NORRIS
PIANO

****   **Drifting** Enja 2044 CD
Norris; George Mraz, Aladar Pege (*b*). 8/74, 5/78.

***(*)   **Winter Rose** Enja 3067 LP
Norris; Aladar Pege (*b*). 5/78; 6, 8 & 9/80.

A fine and sensitive pianist, who worked with Chet Baker near the end of the trumpeter's life, Norris has a moody, intense delivery best suited to introspection. His favoured recording format – without drummer – heightens a sense of almost static harmony, though Norris can swing when he chooses. Stylistically, he is probably closest to George Mraz's better-known piano partner, Tommy Flanagan.

A CD reissue brings together the original *Drifting* with a slightly later album *Synchronicity*, another duo session but featuring Aladar Pege in place of the wonderful George Mraz. It's Mraz who really lifts the earliest of these sessions, subtly adumbrating Norris's occasional uncertainties. The versions of 'Spacemaker' and 'A Child is Born', both Norris originals, are more clearly articulated than the performances from *Synchronicity* and *Winter Rose* respectively, and Mraz's inside-out familiarity with a standard like 'Spring Can Really Hang You Up the Most' gives it a singing confidence. Pege's virtuosity (impressive enough to win him the late Charles Mingus's role in the Mingus Dynasty) sometimes clutters essentially simple themes and is in marked contrasted to Mraz's clearness of line. *Winter Rose* is a digital record but is superseded for sheer aural impact by the CD reissue/compilation of the earlier sets.

RED NORVO (born 1908)
VIBRAPHONE

***(*)   **Time In His Hands** Xanadu 199 LP
Norvo; Johnny Bothwell, Otto Hardwick (*ts*); Charlie Ventura (*ts*); Harry Carney (*bs*); Johnny Guarnieri, Jimmy Jones (*p*); Bill DeArango, Chuck Wayne (*g*); John Levy, Slam Stewart (*b*); Morey Feld, Specs Powell (*d*). 5, 7 & 8/45.

***(*)   **Red Norvo's Fabulous Jam Session** Spotlite SPJ 127 LP
Norvo; Dizzy Gillespie (*t*); Charlie Parker (*as*); Flip Phillips (*ts*); Teddy Wilson (*p*); Slam Stewart (*b*); J. C. Heard, Specs Powell (*d*). 6/45.

***(*)   **Red Norvo Trio** Original Jazz Classics OJC 641 CD/LP/MC
Norvo; Jimmy Raney (*g*); Red Mitchell (*b*). 53, 54.

***   **The Red Norvo Trios** Prestige P 24108 LP
As above, except add Tal Farlow (*g*). 55.

***(*)   **Just A Mood** Bluebird ND 86278 CD
Norvo; Harry Edison, Shorty Rogers (*t*); Jimmy Giuffre (*cl*); Ben Webster (*ts*); Buddy Collette (*f*); Pete Jolly, Jimmy Rowles (*p*); Tal Farlow (*g*); Monty Budwig, Red Callender, Bob Carter (*b*); Larry Bunker, Bill Douglass, Chico Hamilton (*d*). 8 & 9/54, 1/57.

***   **Music To Listen To Red Norvo By** Original Jazz Classics OJC 155 LP
Norvo; Buddy Collette (*f*); Bill Smith (*cl*); Barney Kessel (*g*); Red Mitchell (*b*); Shelly Manne (*d*). 57.

***(*)   **Swing That Music** Affinity AFF 776 CD
Norvo; Barney Kessel (*g*); George Wein (*p*); Larry Ridley (*b*); Don Lamond (*d*). 10/69.

Norvo's early recorded work, before he made the switch from xylophone to vibraharp, is usefully sampled on a BBC swing sampler (BBC REB 666 CD/LP/MC). It illustrates the problem of placing so self-effacing an instrument in a conventional jazz line-up and it's sometimes difficult to separate technical limitations and compromises from conscious dynamic strategies in Norvo's recorded work. The last year of the war was a good one for Norvo. The sessions on *Time In His Hands* offer a good impression of what he could do with just paino and rhythm, anticipating on 'The Voice Of The Turtle' and 'On The Upside Looking Down' some of Milt Jackson's and John Lewis's innovations with the Modern Jazz Quartet in the 1950s. The slightly later session with horns is marked by the lovely 'Blue At Dawn', which counts among Norvo's most openly romantic performances, matched only by Ben Webster's laid-back phrasing and Giuffre's low, throbbing clarinet on the excellent Bluebird compilation. The supersession with the young Gillespie and Parker brings together originals and alternate masters in a way that underlines the problems encountered in recording his instrument. In those early, 'hands-off' days, he frequently encountered engineers who would unilaterally boost the sound on quieter numbers or adjust the balances to accord with conventional expectations.

Most of those were overturned in the 1950–1 trio in which Charles Mingus was the outwardly unlikely replacement for Red Kelly. Just as Norvo made a pioneering contribution to the use of vibraphone in jazz, so too did the early trios contribute enormously to the development of a style of 'cool' or 'chamber' jazz that became dominant much later in the decade. One of the more significant aspects of the early trio (it may also reflect the bassist's personality to some extent, particularly in the context of an otherwise white group) is the unprecedentedly prominent role assigned to Mingus. Unfortunately, this material currently awaits reissue, but can be picked up in vinyl on the 2LP *Savoy Sessions* [WL 70540].

The later trios with Raney or Kessel and Mitchell are much less obviously adventurous, though again it's the bassist's singing lines that carry much of the interest. Kessel saves his best solo with Norvo for the concluding track on *Swing That Music*, recorded 15 years later. The two albums are also linked by one of the tunes that best exemplifies Norvo's group approach. As Alun Morgan underlines in his useful liner note to the Affinity set, 'Lullaby of the Leaves' calls for a particularly strong bass line. Mitchell plays it with much more feeling and depth; the later band has a wider harmonic and dynamic range but it doesn't quite recapture the intensity of the mid-1950s version.

Sooner or later when dealing with so-called 'chamber jazz', the question of its supposed 'pretentiousness' is bound to come into play. Norvo's 1954 quintet with Buddy Collette on flute, Tal Farlow on guitar strongly recalls fellow-member Chico Hamilton's sophisticated chamber jazz, with its soft, 'classical' textures and non-blues material. Titles like 'Divertimento In Four Movements' on *Music To Listen To Red Norvo By* are apt to be seen as red rags by hard-nosed boppers. It's clear, though, from the album title if not immediately from the music itself, that there is a hefty dose of humour in Norvo's work. Structurally, the 'Divertimento' is unexceptionable, with a beautiful division of parts and as lightweight as the genre demands. Other tracks, like 'Red Sails' and the boppish thematic puns of 'Rubricity', suggest a 'different' side to Norvo which is actually present throughout his work, even in his sixties.

Swing that Music is shared with an Armstrong tribute by cornettist Ruby Braff, using the same quartet. Norvo kicks off with a bouncy 'Spider's Webb' (a long-standing favourite), then sticks mainly to standards material. 'The Girl From Ipanema' is a slightly surprising inclusion; but played without vibrato as if originally conceived for marimba or xylophone, it works very well indeed. Though by no means a one-dimensional figure, Norvo has held to a steady course from the early days of bebop to the beginnings of a swing revival in the 1960s and '70s. His technique is superb and prefigures much of Milt Jackson's best MJQ passage-work. The early trios are unquestionably the place to begin, but there's plenty of good music later, particularly the 1954 and 1957 sessions on Bluebird, and newcomers shouldn't be prejudiced by the instrumentation. Norvo plays modern jazz of a high order.

SAM NOTO (born 1930)
TRUMPET, FLUGELHORN

(*)   **Entrance! Xanadu 103 LP
    Noto; Barry Harris (*p*); Leroy Vinnegar (*b*); Lenny McBrowne (*d*). 3/75.

***   **Act One** Xanadu 127 LP
Noto; Joe Romano (*ts*); Barry Harris (*p*); Sam Jones (*b*); Billy Higgins (*d*). 12/75.

***   **Notes To You** Xanadu 144 LP
Noto; Joe Romano (*ts*); Ronnie Cuber (*bs*); Jimmy Rowles (*p*); Sam Jones (*b*);
Freddie Waits (*d*). 5/77.

(*) **Noto-Riety Xanadu 168 LP
Noto; Sam Most (*f*); Dolo Coker (*p*); Monty Budwig (*b*); Frank Butler (*d*). 10/78.

Noto is a pleasure to hear – a trumpeter bathed in the light of Gillespie, Navarro and Brown
who plays as if those masters were the only musicians he's ever heard. But he can't do much
more than personify their best licks, which may be why he had to wait until he was 45 before
cutting a record under his own name. *Entrance!* offers plenty of fun, with Noto fizzing through a
familiar-sounding bebop programme, but, once past the virtuoso display of the opening 'Fats
Flats', one feels that he's already used up his repertoire. The rhythm section are professional but
somewhat indifferent. *Act One* and *Notes To You* are superior, thanks partly to the arrival of
Romano whose flat-toned but supple improvisations offer the foil needed to bring out the best
in Noto. The writing on *Act One* isn't very interesting, but the players sound in good spirits, and
the rhythm section hits harder this time. *Notes To You* has Cuber as a useful extra ingredient,
and the originals are a little more interesting – 'Quasinoto' inspires one of the trumpeter's
sharpest solos, and 'Parley' provokes a tense round-robin of improvisations. Unfortunately
Waits is too splashy to suit the horns; the crisper Higgins would have been a better choice.
Noto-Riety is all right, but Most's flute is less interesting than Romano, and the session seems to
play out by rote.

**   **2–4–5** Unisson DDA 1007 CD/LP
Noto; Pat LaBarbera (*ts*); Gary Williamson (*p*); Steve Wallace, Neil Swanson (*b*);
Bob McLaren (*d*). 11/86.

Noto spent the intervening period between albums as a local star in his new home base of
Toronto, where he used indigenous players for this date, which is made up of duos with
Swanson, two trumpet-and-rhythm tracks and four for the quintet – hence the title. Some of
the fire seems to have gone out of his playing: the duets with Swanson offer only a routine
virtuosity, and the quartet and quintet tracks are personable but lack punch.

HOD O'BRIEN
PIANO

***   **Opalessence** Criss Cross Criss 1012 LP
O'Brien; Tom Harrell (*t, flhn*); Pepper Adams (*bs*); Ray Drummond (*b*); Kenny
Washington (*d*); Stephanie Nakasan (*v*). 9/84.

(*) **Ridin' High Reservoir RSR CD 116 CD
O'Brien; Ray Drummond (*b*); Kenny Washington (*d*). 8/90.

30 years ago, Hod O'Brien made an impressive contribution to Belgian guitarist René Thomas's
Guitar Groove (Original Jazz Classics OJC 1725), playing alongside mavericks like J. R.
Monterose and Albert Heath. Recent years have seen him associated with Chet Baker (on
Blues for a Reason, Criss Cross 1010 CD/LP) and with saxophonist Ted Brown (*In Good
Company*, Criss Cross 1020 LP, and *Free Spirit*, Criss Cross 1031 CD/LP), strong bop
credentials with a label not exactly short of respectable pianists.
     Unfortunately his work as leader hasn't matched up to his sterling reliability and propulsive
strength as a sideman. His solos seems studied to the point of predictability and he suffers from
an irritating odd-handedness that sees him switching almost on cue from 'rhythm' to 'lead' like
an electric guitarist. With players of Harrell's elegance and with Adams beefing up the
arrangements, *Opalessence* is the more interesting of the two albums but, like the semi-precious
sheen of the title, it seems all surface and no depth or durability. The trio album reintroduces
standards material. 'You And The Night And The Music' reflects O'Brien's innate
romanticism, but at opposite extremes 'Willow Weep For Me' and 'Yardbird Suite' simply
expose his limitations.

ANITA O'DAY (born 1919)
VOCALS

****   **Tea For Two** Moon M 023 CD/LP
O'Day; Jimmy Jones, Tete Montoliu (*p*); Whitey Mitchell, Eric Porter (*b*); Billy
Brooks, John Poole (*d*). 7/58, 7/66.

(*)   **Mello'day GNP Crescendo 2126 LP
O'Day; Ernie Watts (*f, as, ts*); Lou Levy (*p*); Laurindo Almeida (*g*); Harvey Newmark
(*b*); John Poole (*d*); Paulinho Da Costa (*perc*). 11/78.

Anita O'Day lived the jazz life. She tells about it in *High Times, Hard Times* (1983). As a young
woman she worked as a singing waitress and in punishing dance marathons. And she shot horse
until her heart began to give out in the 1960s and she was forced to battle her demons cold. As
is immediately obvious from her combative, sharply punctuated scatting and line in stage patter,
O'Day was a fighter. As a 'chirper' with the Gene Krupa band in 1941, she refused to turn out
in ballgown and gloves and appeared instead in band jacket and short skirt, an unheard-of
practice that underlined her instinctive feminism. With Stan Kenton, she gave a humane edge to
a sometimes pretentiously modernist repertoire. O'Day's demanding style had few successful
imitators, but she is the most immediate source for June Christy and Chris Connor, who
followed her into the Kenton band.

The most familiar image of O'Day is at the Newport Festival in 1958, a set preserved in the
movie *Jazz on a Summer's Day*. In a spectacular black dress and a hat that must have accounted
for half the egrets in Louisiana, she resembles one of those subtly ball-breaking heroines in a
Truman Capote story. The voice even then is unreliably pitched, but there's no mistaking the
inventiveness of 'Tea For Two' and 'Sweet Georgia Brown'. The woman who sang 'The *Boy*
from Ipanema' with a sarcastic elision of the 'aahhs' was every bit as capable as Betty Carter of
turning Tin Pan Alley tat into a feminist statement.

The 1958 performances are well above average and perfect examples of O'Day's wittily
daring rhythmic sense. From the mid-1950s, her closest musical associate was drummer, John
Poole; she sticks close by him, leaving the pitched instruments to do their own thing, and, but
for the words, she might almost be involved in a percussion duet. The 1970s sessions are rather
low-key, with a definite loss of exuberance and stamina. Elsewhere there are scattered
performances with Oscar Peterson, but the pianist tends to overpower her. It's to be hoped that
the excellent trio-backed *Once Upon A Summertime* [Jasmine CD 2531], featuring live
European and American studio sessions, will return from limbo.

***(*)   **Swings Cole Porter With Billy May** Verve 849 266 CD
O'Day; main tracks with Billy May Orchestra, unknown personnel; other tracks include
Conte Candoli, Roy Eldridge, Lee Katzman, Al Porcino, Jack Sheldon, Ray Triscari,
Stu Williamson (*t*); Milt Bernhart, Bob Edmondson, Lloyd Elliot, Bill Harris, Joe
Howard, Lou McCreary, Frank Rosolino, Si Zetner (*tb*); Kenny Shroyer (*btb*); Al
Pollan (*tba*); Charlie Kennedy, Joe Maini (*as*); Budd Johnson, Richie Kamuca, Bill
Perkins (*ts*); Jimmy Giuffre (*reeds, arr*); Jack Nimitz, Cecil Payne (*bs*); Ralph Burns,
Lou Levy, Jimmy Rowles, Paul Smith (*p*); Tal Farlow, Al Hendrickson, Barney Kessel
(*g*); Monte Budwig, Buddy Clark, Al McKibbon, Joe Mondragon, Leroy Vinnegar
(*b*); Larry Bunker, Don Lamond, Mel Lewis, Lawrence Marable, Jackie Mills, Alvin
Stoller (*d*); Buddy Bregman, Bill Holman (*arr*). 1/52, 4/54, 11 & 12/55, 4/59.

O'Day never sounds quite as effective with a full band, and May's beefy arrangements tend to
overpower her subtler rhythmic skills. Fortunately, this reissue includes six bonus tracks,
including band arrangements by Buddy Bregman and Bill Holman, together with a magnificent
small-group 'From This Moment On', a second, rather smoothed-out version of 'Love For
Sale' to compare with May's, and Jimmy Giuffre's superb, throbbing arrangement of 'My
Heart Belongs To Daddy'. The May tracks are virtually all at accelerated tempos (in contrast to
the Rodgers and Hart sequel), but varied with Latin ('I Get A Kick Out Of You') or 'Eastern'
('Night And Day') settings. Even so, one would much prefer to hear O'Day swing Porter to the
basic accompaniment of bass and drums. She sounds unusually husky at extremes of pitch, as if
from the effort of projecting over the band, but these are still more than worthwhile
performances, and a great deal wittier and more stimulating than most of the 'songbook'
sessions that were rife at the time.

***(*)   **At Vine St Live** Disques Swing 8435 CD
O'Day; Gordon Brisker (*ts, f*); Pete Jolly (*p*); Steve Homan (*g*); Bob Maize (*b*);
Danny D'Imperio (*d*). 8/91.

The pitching is more than a little uncertain in places, but O'Day was never a singer who depended on beauty of tone. She begins with a daringly off-balance 'You'd Be So Nice To Come Home To', leaning into the rhythm of the song, as far ahead of the beat as she can be. It's a remarkable performancek, unmistakable and individual. Her accompanists are slick, perhaps a little bland, but Brisker and Jolly seem to understand her requirements pretty well and the live sound is well balanced and resonant. It's an attractive programme, mixing old standards ('Old DEvil Moon', 'S'posin'', 'It Don't Mean A Thing') with less familiar material like the Earl Hines, Melvin Dunlap, Charles Carpenter croon 'You Can Depend On Me', Leon Russell's 'A Song For You' and Lennon/McCartney's 'Yesterday', cleverly segued into 'Yesterdays'. Professional vocal jazz that bursts with personality.

STAFFAN ODENHALL
COMPOSER, ARRANGER

*(*)   **Big Ears Big Band** Dragon DRLP 144 LP
Joan Kohlin (*t, flhn*); Fredrik Norén, Lars Lindgren, Ulf Adaker (*t*); Olle Holmqvist,
Mats Hermansson, Walter Brolund, Mats Lundberg (*tb*); Hakan Broström, Jonas
Knutsson (*ss, as*); Pauer Lauenstein (*ts, f*); Par Grebacken (*ts*); Hans Arktoft (*bs*);
Andreas Aarflot (*ky*); Max Ahman (*g*); Mats Lindberg (*b*); Anders Gustavsson (*d*);
Rafael Sida (*perc*). 5/87.

Odenhall is a young arranger and composer who wears his influences all too heavily, at least on the strength of this record. The most important one seems to be latter-day Miles Davis: 'Mahler Meets Miles' has very little Gustav Mahler in it and is fractured half-way through by a central episode that seems to be an orchestration of a funky Davis vamp. 'Fangs' is more of the same; but in neither case do Odenhall's charts sound convincing. His more straightforward big-band swing is handled more comfortably by what is a skilful orchestra, but the results are no different from what a score of American college bands can do.

ITARU OKI
TRUMPET, FLUGELHORN

***   **One Year – Afternoon And Evening** FMP 0720 LP
Oki; Michel Pilz (*bcl*); Ralf Hubner (*d*). 10/78.

Another in the series of improvised concerts caught on the wing by FMP in the 1970s, this features two basically conservative free players in friendly confrontation over Hubner's drums. Pilz, perhaps the only modern player to devote himself chiefly to the bass clarinet, is a piquant partner for Oki's lambent trumpet phrasing, and the organization of the five pieces seems intuitively tight.

OLD AND NEW DREAMS
GROUP

***(*)   **Old And New Dreams** ECM 1154 CD/LP
Don Cherry (*t, p*); Dewey Redman (*ts, musette*); Charlie Haden (*b*); Ed Blackwell (*d*).
8/79.

***   **Playing** ECM 1205 CD/LP
As above. 6/80.

***(*)   **One For Blackwell** Black Saint 120113 CD/LP/MC
As above. 11/87.

One wonders if this is how the classic Ornette Coleman Quartet might have sounded with modern recording techniques and a more democratic sound-balance. Now that Coleman is concentrating largely on his electric Prime Time band and on large-scale projects, Old and New Dreams are perhaps the foremost interpreters of his acoustic small-group music. The dirges – 'Lonely Woman' on the first album and 'Broken Shadows' on *Playing* – are by no means as dark as the composer made them, and Redman adheres much more closely to a tonal centre on all the pieces, a role he performed in the Coleman quintet of the late 1960s/early 1970s (see *Crisis*). Cherry also seems to be using orthodox concert trumpet on at least the majority of the tracks, and its fuller tone sits more comfortably alongside Redman than the squeaky pocket cornet. Redman's eldritch musette, a two-reed oboe with a sound not unlike a shawm, gives 'Song Of La-Ba' (OND) a mysterious timbre.

Ed Blackwell has always been prominently featured with the band; the tribute album, recorded live at a Blackwell festival in Atlanta, Georgia, is entirely appropriate, given his multifarious commitment to New Orleans music, modern free jazz and, of course, the work of Ornette Coleman, to which he often stood as *il miglior fabbro*. The live versions of Ornette's 'Happy House' (from *Playing*) and the Ghanaian theme, 'Togo' (from the first album), are slightly rawer and more extended but show no significant differences over the studio versions. Indeed, the main difference between the live album and the others is the extent to which the drummer solos. It's in his work that the 'old' and 'new' of the band title truly resonates. Drawn to the rough second-line drumming of the marching bands, he adds the sibilant accents familiar from bebop, and also a strong element of African talking drum. His rhythmic patterns are dense, coded and allusive but, taken whole, refreshingly entire and self-sufficient. Altogether, these three albums are a monument to a crucially important figure on the modern-jazz scene, who has kept out of the critical pantheon by a mixture of chance (circumstances dictated that he didn't play on the early Coleman records, whose music he had done so much to create) and persistent ill-health.

JOE 'KING' OLIVER (1885–1939)
CORNET, TRUMPET

***** **King Oliver Volume One 1923 To 1929** BBC RPCD/ZCRP 787 CD/MC
Oliver; Louis Armstrong (*c*); Tommy Dorsey, Bob Shoffner (*t*); Honoré Dutrey, Kid Ory, Ed Atkins (*tb*); Johnny Dodds (*cl*); Albert Nicholas (*cl, ss, as*); Billy Paige, Darnell Howard (*cl, as*); Barney Bigard (*cl, ts*); Stump Evans (*ss, as*); Charlie Jackson (*bsx*); Lil Hardin, Jelly Roll Morton, Luis Russell (*p*); Arthur Schutt (*harm*); Eddie Lang, Lonnie Johnson (*g*); Bud Scott, Bill Johnson (*bj, v*); Bert Cobb (*bb*); Jimmy Williams (*b*); Baby Dodds, Paul Barbarin, Stan King (*d*). 4/23–5/29.

The third King of New Orleans, after Buddy Bolden and Freddie Keppard, remains among the most stately and distinguished of jazz musicians, although newer listeners may wonder if Oliver's records are really so important in the light of what his protege Louis Armstrong would do in the years after the Oliver Jazz Band records of 1923. Joe Oliver was in at the inception of jazz, and it's our misfortune that his group wasn't recorded until 1923, when its greatest years may have been behind it: accounts of the band in live performance paint spectacular images of creativity which the constricted records barely sustain. Yet they remain magnificent examples of black music at an early peak: the interplay between Oliver and Armstrong, the beautifully balanced ensembles, the development of polyphony, the blues-drenched colours of Dodds, the formal but driving rhythms. If the music is caught somewhere between eras – summing up the aftermath of ragtime and the move towards improvisation and individual identity represented by Armstrong – its absolute assurance is riveting, and presents a Ledare who knew exactly what he wanted. Oliver's subsequent band, the Dixie Syncopators, was far less successful, troubled by a feeble reed section and cluttered arrangements, but its best sides – such as the furiously paced 'Wa Wa Wa' – are as good as anything from their period.

There are 37 surviving sides by the Oliver (Creole) Jazz Band, although only ten of them appear on the first volume of Robert Parker's BBC compilation. Yet Parker's work here is astonishingly good. If these primitive recordings have been transferred many times, none has appeared in such fine sound as here: Parker's search for only the finest originals pays off handsomely, and as he gathers the missing discs he will surely proceed until the Oliver story is complete. In the meantime, here are 'Dippermouth Blues' (the Gennett version), 'Riverside

Blues', 'Sweet Lovin' Man' and other records which pace out the first distinctive steps of black jazz on record. Parker adds one of the duets with Jelly Roll Morton, 'King Porter'; seven sides by the Dixie Syncopators; the pair of tracks by 'Blind Willie Dunn's Gin Bottle Four', a session with Eddie Land and Lonnie Johnson where Oliver's presence is in some doubt; and a track with Tommy Dorsey on trumpet which allows scholars to compare his work with that of the hornman on the previous session. This is a model reissue in almost every way.

***(*) **King Oliver Volume Two 1927 To 1930** BBC RPCD/ZCRF 788 CD/MC
Oliver; Tick Gray, Ed Allen (*c*); Dave Nelson, Henry 'Red' Allen (*t*); James Archey, Kid Ory, Ed Cuffee (*tb*); Omer Simeon, Arville Harris, Ernest Elliott, Barney Bigard, Benny Waters, Buster Bailey, Bobby Holmes, Glyn Paque, Hilton Jefferson, Charles Frazier, Walter Wheeler, Paul Barnes (*reeds*); Clarence Williams (*p, cel, v*); Luis Russell, Don Frye, Norman Lester, Henry Duncan, Eric Franker (*p*); Eddie Lang (*g, vn*); Bud Scott, Leroy Harris, Arthur Taylor (*bj*); Bert Cobb, Cyrus St Clair, Clinton Walker, Lionel Nipton (*bb*); Paul Barbarin, Edmund Jones, Fred Moore (*d*); Justin Ring (*perc*); Texas Alexander (*v*). 4/27–9/30.

*** **1926–1931 Complete Vocalion/Brunswick Recordings** Affinity AFS 1025-2 2CD
Oliver; Bob Shoffner, Ed Anderson (*c*); Ward Pinkett (*t, v*); Tick Gray, Dave Nelson, Bill Dillard, Louis Metcalf (*t*); Kid Ory, James Archey, Ed Cuffee, J. C. Higginbotham, Ferdinand Arbello (*tb*); Buster Bailey, Johnny Dodds (*cl*); Albert Nicholas, Barney Bigard, Billy Paige, Omer Simeon, Stump Evans, Ernest Elliott, Arville Harris, Henry L. Jones, Bingie Madison, Fred Skerritt, Teddy Hill, Charlie Holmes (*reeds*); Luis Russell, Leroy Tibbs, Gene Rogers (*p*); Bud Scott, Leroy Harris, Will Johnson (*bj*); Goldie Lucas (*g, v*); Cyrus St Clair, Lawson Buford, Richard Fulbright (*tba*); Paul Barbarin, Bill Beason (*d*); Andy Pendelton, Willie Jackson (*v*). 3/26-4/31.

*** **King Oliver 1926–1928** Classics 618 CD
As appropriate records above. 3/26–6/28.

*** **The New York Sessions 1929–1930** RCA Bluebird ND 90410 CD/LP/MC
Oliver; Dave Nelson, Henry 'Red' Allen (*t*); James Archey (*tb*); Bobby Holmes, Glyn Paque, Charles Frazier, Hilton Jefferson, Walter Wheeler (*reeds*); Don Frye, James P. Johnson, Henry Duncan, Eric Franker, Norman Lester (*p*); Roy Smeck (*stg, hmca*); Arthur Taylor (*bj, g*); Clinton Walker (*bb*); Fred Moore, Edmund Jones (*d*). 9/29–9/30.

*** **King Oliver 1928–1930** Classics 607 CD
As appropriate records above. 6/28–3/30.

*** **King Oliver And His Orchestra 1930–1931** Classics 594 CD
As above, except omit Frye, Johnson, Smeck and Jones, add Ward Pinkett (*t, v*), Bill Dillard (*t*); Ferdinand Arbello (*tb*) Buster Bailey (*cl*), Henry L Jones, Bingie Madison, Fred Skerritt (*reeds*), Gene Rodgers (*p*); Goldie Lucas (*g, v*); Richard Fulbright (*bb*), Bill Beason (*d*). 4/30–4/31.

Oliver's later recordings are a muddle in several ways. Illness and problems with his teeth steadily cut down his instrumental powers, and some celebrated career errors – such as turning down a New York engagement which subsequently went to Duke Ellington – ruined his eminence. The first 13 tracks on the second BBC compilation trace his decline in fortunes, with nine underrated tracks by the Dixie Syncopators to start, two obscure blues accompaniments with Sara Martin and Texas Alexander to follow, and a session with Clarence Williams and Eddie Lang to complete the picture. Oliver could still play very well: his phrasing is usually simple and unadorned, a very different tale to Armstrong's vaulting mastery, but the quality of his tone and the starkness of his ideas can be both affecting and exhilarating. Parker concludes the disc with seven tracks from the King's Victor sessions. The Bluebird disc includes 16 tracks from that period, including a previously unheard take of 'Olga'. The Classics series takes a chronological route from the first Dixie Syncopators sides to the final Vocalion session of 1931, while the Affinity double-CD includes all the Dixie Syncopators tracks, three obscure blues accompaniments which are unavailable elsewhere, and the three final Vocalion sessions from 1931. A complex situation!

The Victor sessions were often plodding and routine orchestral jazz that ran aground on some inept material ('Everybody Does It In Hawaii' features a bizarre appearance by steel guitarist Roy Smeck), and Oliver's own contributions are in much doubt: it's very hard to know where and when he plays, for he may even have asked some of his trumpeters to play in his own style. Nevertheless, there are still many records with interesting passages and a few genuinely progressive items, such as 'Freakish Light Blues' and 'Nelson Stomp'. On a piece such as 'New Orleans Shout', where the soloist does sound like Oliver, he shows he can still play with the kind of sombre authority which befits a King. We primarily recommend the second BBC compilation as an inroduction to this period of Oliver's work, while the Affinity double-set – which is quite well remastered, if occasionally cloudy – is useful in bringing together all of the Dixie Syncopators sides. Otherwise, for completists, the Classics series can be safely recommended, although reproduction is, as usual, varied.

PAULINE OLIVEROS (born 1932)
ACCORDION

***(*)   The Roots Of The Moment hat Art CD 6009 CD
Oliveros solo, in acoustic environment devised by Peter Ward. 11/87.

Pioneer of a discipline known as 'Deep Listening', Oliveros occupies an unusual position (perhaps compounded by her gender) on the borders of jazz/improvisation, 'straight' music, and performance art. *The Roots Of The Moment* is perhaps her most thoroughly improvisational work, paralleling some of trombonist George Lewis's interactive works with computer. Oliveros uses an accordion tuned in just intonation (that is, in non-standard perfect fifths) with contact and air microphones which feed into a complex digital delay system that constructs acoustic environments to which which she must respond but which are responsive in turn to shifts in her performance. Perhaps marginal to jazz-based improvisation (though what better definition of the discipline could there be than 'roots of the moment'?), Oliveros's music is consistently challenging, and this continuous, hour-long performance is both accessible and very beautiful.

PETER O'MARA
GUITAR

***   Avenue 'C' Enja 6046 CD/LP
O'Mara; Joe Lovano (*ts*); Roberto Di Gioia (*p*); Dave Holland (*b*); Adam Nussbaum (*d*). 10/89.

O'Mara has made a couple of rockier records, but this intelligently paced set seems more like a dry run for John Scofield's albums with Joe Lovano. The saxophonist is probably the most interesting soloist here, with his dry tone and broken-up phrasing characteristically in place, but the guitarist takes plenty of well-utilized space for himself, his improvisations comfortably sustained. Holland is as marvellous as always but Nussbaum doesn't sound like the right man for the drum seat: he makes too much noise, and the straight rock beat for 'Uptown' sets the wrong metre at the start. A worthwhile listen.

SHUNZO ONO
TRUMPET, FLUGELHORN

**   Manhattan Blue Electric Bird K28P 6454 LP
Ono; Mike Stern (*g*); Kenny Kirkland (*p, syn*); Gil Goldstein, Pete Levin (*syn*); Darryl Jones (*b*); Victor Lewis, Steve Thornton (*d*). 11/86.

Messy techno-jazz from a good big-band trumpeter who has seen service with both Machito and Gil Evans. His version of 'Blue Bossa' has some of the marks of the former, but 'Summertime' sounds like a gross misrepresentation of Evans's method. Stern howls and clatters away above featureless arrangements but produces much of the solo interest. Ono's contributions are ill-thought-out and occasionally quite banal. Victor Lewis is much cruder than usual; the fact that he's given as 'Louis' may suggest a genetic link to the Brown Bomber.

OPPOSITE CORNER
GROUP

(*)   **Low-High Caprice CAP 1267 LP
Gunnar Lindberg (*ts*); Aoke Johansson (*p*); Kjell Jansson (*b*); Mats Hellberg (*d*); Annika Skoglund (*v*). 12/81.

(*)   **Back From Where We Came Dragon DRLP 70 LP
As above, except Leroy Lowe (*d*) replaces Hellberg. 12/83.

This was a popular band in Sweden in the 1970s and '80s, with most of the writing done by Jansson, although what emerges from their records is a good tenor-and-rhythm group. Lindberg's manner suggests a thoughtful energy saxophonist, and he and Johansson – who plays with quite as much spirit as he does on his own albums for Dragon – work through a lot of dialogue across the two albums which are still in catalogue. The Caprice album has a reticent sound mix, and Hellberg sounds diffuse as a result. Skoglund, though, seems to be an untoward addition, her vocal parts stiffly tacked on to the rest of the music. Destined for obscurity, perhaps, but the kind of thing that comes off the shelf as a pleasant surprise every so often.

ORANGE THEN BLUE
GROUP

***   **Orange Then Blue** GM 3006 CD
Roy Okutani, Tommy Smith, Tim Hagans, Kerry MacKillop (*t, flhn*); Swami Harisharan, Gary Valente (*tb*); Peter Cirelli (*btb, euph*); Matt Dariau, Adam Kolker, Dave Mann (*reeds*); Bruce Barth (*ky*); Dave Clark (*b*); George Schuller (*d*); Pat Hollenbeck (*perc*). 12/85–3/86.

***   **Jumpin' In The Future** GM 3010 CD
Roy Okutani, Andy Gravish, Ken Cervenka, Greg Hopkins, Richard Given (*t, flhn*); Rick Stepton, Curtis Hasselbring, Kenny Wenzel, Peter Cirelli (*tb*); Krista Smith, Mark Taylor (*frhn*); Robert Carriker (*tba*); Howard Johnson (*tba, bcl*); Matt Dariau, Allan Chase, Dave Finucane, Adam Kolker, George Garzone, Bob Zung (*reeds*); Katharine Halvorsen (*ob*); Andrew Strasmich (*f*); Bevan Manson (*p*); Ben Sher (*g*); Dave Clark (*b*); George Schuller (*d*); Gunther Schuller (*cond*). 3–5/88.

(*)   **Where Were You? GM 3012 CD
As above, except Matt Simon (*t, flhn*) replaces Given, omit Wenzel, Smith, Taylor, Carriker, Chase, Zung, Halvorsen, Strasmich and Sher, add George Adams (*ts*), Bruce Barth (*p*) and Russ Gold (*perc*). 5/87–3/88.

The band is led by George Schuller, son of Gunther, and is based in the Boston area. Their three records should tempt anyone interested in the development of post-bop jazz, since they consist of 'historical' material as translated through a contemporary set of inflexions. *Orange Then Blue* includes Mingus's 'Nostalgia In Times Square' and Monk's 'Think Of One' along with originals such as 'Ornette's Music'; *Jumpin' In The Future* is a set of Gunther Schuller's charts dating from the mid-1940s to the mid-1960s, conducted by the arranger himself. Both records strike a sometimes uneasy but often revealing alliance between the essential period quality of the music with the freedoms of a more modern jazz vocabulary. Schuller's scores especially show a concern with form which tends to override individual contributions, but the slow and peculiarly bleak reading of 'When The Saints Go Marching In' and the misty voicings of 'Summertime' provide their own rewards.

The third record is in some ways less successful, drawn from three live concerts by the band: although the choice of material includes pieces culled from the books of Miles Davis and Paul Motian as well as Monk and Mingus, the band play a little stiffly, and the presence of George Adams on three tracks tends to show up the other soloists as merely workmanlike. But when the music takes off, as on Garzone's 'New York', it makes an impressive sound.

OREGON
GROUP

****	**Music Of Another Present Era** Vanguard VSD 79326 CD
****	**Distant Hills** Vanguard VSD 79341 CD
***(*)	**Winter Light** Vanguard VSD 79350 CD
***(*)	**The Essential Oregon** Vanguard VSD 109/110 2LP
***	**Oregon** ECM 1258 CD/LP
**(*)	**Crossing** ECM 1291 CD/LP

Ralph Towner (*g, 12-string g, p, syn, c, mellophone, frhn*); Paul McCandless (*ob, Eng hn, ss, bcl, tin f, musette*); Glen Moore (*b, cl, vla, p, f*); Collin Walcott (*tabla, perc, sitar, dulc, cl, v*); Zbigniew Seifert (*vn* on *Essential Oregon* only); David Earle Johnson (*perc* on *Essential* only); collectivized instrumentation also relates to items below. 73, 73, 73–74, 2/83, 10/84.

Hugely talented and *sui generis*, Oregon have always managed to stay just a step ahead of critical prejudice. The band was formed in 1970, an offshoot of the Paul Winter Consort, at a point of low commercial ebb for jazz. By the time jazz had come to seem viably marketable again, the group had evolved far enough beyond their filigreed chamber-music origins and towards much more forcefully pulsed instrumental combinations to avoid the (still occasionally registered) charge that they were 'merely' a Modern Jazz Quartet for the 1970s. In much the same way, their assimilation of ethnic sources from Asian and native American music was complete long before 'world music' became a marketing niche and a critical sneer.

The early records were largely, but not exclusively, devoted to Towner compositions and were characterized by delicate interplay between his 12-string guitar and Paul McCandless's equally 'classical' oboe. The music on *Music Of Another Present Era* and *Distant Hills* was widely perceived as ethereal and impressionistic, and there was a tendency (perhaps encouraged by intermittent sound-balance on the original vinyl releases) to underestimate the significance of Glen Moore's firm bass-lines (see 'Spring Is Really Coming' on *Present Era*) or the forcefulness of Collin Walcott's tablas. The music combined evocative thematic writing ('Aurora' on *Present Era*, recently re-recorded on the last item below; the classic 'Silence Of A Candle' and McCandless's 'The Swan' on *Distant Hills*) with abstract, collectively improvised pieces (like the 'Mi Chirita Suite' on *Distant Hills*; a neglected aspect of the band's career), and forcefully rhythmic tunes like 'Sail' (*Present Era*) which should have confounded a lingering belief that the band were too professorial to rock.

Winter Light was in some respects a transitional album. Simpler in outline and in its commitment to song forms, it is nevertheless curiously muted, lifted only by 'Deer Path' and by a version of Jim Pepper's 'Witchi-Tai-To', an item that has remained a staple of Oregon performances ever since. The album is also interesting for its (relative) avoidance of so-called ethnic elements in favour of native American elements; Pepper is a North American Indian. The *Essential Oregon* compilation tends to highlight this side of the band's work, certainly at the expense of more abstract treatments, but offers a much less balanced picture of the band's work than the original releases; the additional tracks featuring Johnson and Seifert are something of a distraction.

Oregon went through something of a slump in the later 1970s. Two studio albums for Elektra, *Out Of The Woods* [ELK K 52101 LP] and *Roots In The Sky* [ELK K 52169 LP], represent perhaps their weakest moments on record, though a live double-album [ELK K 62028 2LP] contained some excellent individual work and a further sample of the group's free mode. The way forward had, however, been plotted by an astonishing collaboration with drummer Elvin Jones, also in Vanguard's back-catalogue, an unlikely combination of forces that in retrospect seemed perfectly logical. Though received wisdom has it that Jones taught them how to swing, it's clear that his polyrhythmic method was *already* part of the group's language. During this same period, the most obvious changes of focus were a gradual subordination of Towner's guitar playing in favour of piano (and later synthesizer) and McCandless's decision to double on the much more forceful soprano saxophone.

Oregon represents a partial return to form in the new, upbeat manner. Clearly, too, the group sound benefited enormously from ECM's state-of-the-art production. However, the writing seems remarkably tame and formulaic, a tendency reinforced on its successor. *Crossing* has acquired a slightly sentimental aura, since it is the last Oregon record on which Walcott appeared; between recording and release, he and the group's road manager were killed in an auto accident while on tour in Europe. It is, though, a very unsatisfactory record with few compelling themes and some of the group's most banal playing.

(*)   **Ecotopia ECM 1354 CD/LP

***   **45th Parallel** VeraBra CDVBR 2048 CD

***   **Always, Never And Forever** VeraBra CDVBR 2073 CD/MC
As above, but Trilok Gurtu (*tabla, perc*) replaces the late Collin Walcott; Nancy King (*v* on *45th Parallel* only). 3/87, 8 & 9/88, 90.

It is, of course, idle to speculate what might have happened had Walcott survived. A hugely talented musician, with a recording career of his own (*q.v.*), he was in some senses the most wayward of the group's members. To some extent, the range of his skills was at a premium in the 'new' Oregon. However, he was a vital component of the group's sound, and his death was a shattering blow which almost sundered the band permanently. Trilok Gurtu was recruited only after much heart-searching and because he combined many of Walcott's strengths with an individuality of voice and technique. His group debut on *Ecotopia* is uncertain, though the album's flaws can hardly be laid to his account. The group were still in personal and artistic shock, and there is a nostalgic rootlessness inscribed in every aspect of the album, from the title onwards. *45th Parallel* is better and more firmly demarcated, with some swinging piano from Towner (and a partial return to form on guitar) and a better balance of material. It's marred by Nancy King's preposterous vocal on 'Chihuahua Dreams', but there's a clear sense that the band has re-established contact with its own past output (that is made clear in the brief 'Epilogue') and with its own sense of development. Whether that is equally succsssfully signalled in the new version of 'Aurora' on the second VeraBra album is a matter of conjecture; but the turn of the group's third decade does seem to represent a promising new dawn.

ORIGINAL DIXIELAND JAZZ BAND
GROUP

***   **Original Dixieland Jazz Band/Louisiana Five** Retrieval FJ 101 LP
Nick LaRocca (*c*); Eddie Edwards (*tb*); Larry Shields (*cl*); Henry Ragas (*p*); Tony Sbarbaro (*d*). 8/17.

***(*)   **Sensation!** ASV AJA 5023R CD
As above, except add Emil Christian (*tb*); Bennie Krueger (*as*), J. Russel Robinson, Billy Jones (*p*). 2/17-11/20.

***(*)   **In England** EMI France Jazztime 252716-2 CD
As above. 4/19–5/20.

****   **The 75th Anniversary** RCA Bluebird ND 90650 CD
As above. 2/17–12/21.

Whatever effects time has had on this music, its historical importance is undeniable: the first jazz band to make records *may* have been less exciting than, say, the group that King Oliver was leading in the same year, but since no such records by Oliver or any comparable bandleader were made until much later, the ODJB assume a primal role. Harsh, full of tension, rattling with excitement, the best records by the band have weathered the years surprisingly well. Although the novelty effects of 'Barnyard Blues' may seem excessively quaint today, the ensemble patterns which the group created – traceable to any number of ragtime or march strains – have remained amazingly stable in determining the identity of 'traditional' jazz groups ever since. The blazing runs executed by Shields, the crashing, urgent rhythms of Sbarbaro and LaRocca's thin but commanding lead cornet cut through the ancient recordings. Although the band were at the mercy of their material, which subsequently declined into sentimental pap as their early excitement subsided, a high proportion of their legacy is of more than historical interest.

Fifty-four of their recordings between 1917 and 1922 have survived, but there is no comprehensive edition currently available. The Retrieval album is shared between the ODJB and the contemporaneous though inferior Louisiana Five, and it includes their complete 1917 sessions for Aeolian Vocalion, in very convincing transfers. The ASV CD includes 18 tracks and offers a good cross-section of their work, although a couple of undistinguished later pieces might have been dropped in favour of the absent and excellent 'Mournin' Blues' or 'Skeleton Jangle'. The EMI France CD duplicates nine tracks with the other disc and has some weak closing items, but it also includes five rare tracks by other jazz-influenced bands from the London scene of the same period, including the black groups Ciro's Club Coon Orchestra (doing perhaps the first-ever version of 'St Louis Blues' on record) and Dan and Harvey's Jazz Band. Each disc varies in its remastering almost from track to track, with some items obviously dubbed from poorer copies than others, although we find that the EMI France disc is overall a shade livelier in its reproduction, as well as offering some 15 minutes' more music.

The best overall recomendation, though, must go to the new Bluebird compilation, which includes 23 tracks and covers the band's entire issued Victor output up to the end of 1921. The transfers use the NoNOISE system and, while one feels that the sound could be more persuasive still, it's at least as good as the other discs listed here.

ORNICAR BIG BAND
GROUP

***   **Le Retour D'Ornicar** IDA 009 LP
Claude Egea, François Biensan, Michel Delakian, Jacques Berecochea (t); William Treve, Philippe Gibrat, Jacques Erard, Herve Defrance (tb); Jean-Marc Fritz, Claude André-Broutigny, René Gervat, Jean-Michel Proust, Claude Tissendier, Gilles Miton (reeds); Alain Bernard (p); Laurent Petit (g); Pierre Maingourd (b); François Laudet (d); Vincent Cordelette, Pierre Guignon (perc). 8/86.

Carried through on section-work that's exexcuted with whipcrack precision, this ironic, funny, modern big band settles down into convention as often as it goes for extremes; Philippe Laudet, who writes the material, is sometimes happy just to let the brass and the reeds trade punches, as on the bountiful 'Pygmalion'. But the opening, slyly treated satire on big-band funk, 'Chronodrome', lets you know that there's a certain Gallic wit involved. Soloists are perhaps less impressive, but it's the swing of the ensemble which counts. Impressively full recording, too.

NIELS-HENNING ØRSTED-PEDERSEN (born 1946)
DOUBLE BASS

***(*)   **Jaywalkin'** Steeplechase 1041 CD/LP/MC
Ørsted-Pedersen; Philip Catherine (g); Ole Kock Hansen (p); Billy Higgins (d). 9 & 12/75.

***   **Pictures** Steeplechase 1068 LP/MC
Ørsted-Pedersen; Kenneth Knudsen (ky). 12/76.

****   **Double Bass** Steeplechase 1055 CD/LP/MC
Ørsted-Pedersen; Sam Jones (b); Philip Catherine (g); Albert Heath, Billy Higgins (d, perc). 2/76.

****   **Live At Montmartre: Volume 1** Steeplechase 1083 LP/MC

***(*)   **Live At Montmartre: Volume 2** Steeplechase 1093 LP/MC
Ørsted-Pedersen; Philip Catherine (g); Billy Hart (d). 10/77.

****   **Dancing On The Tables** Steeplechase 1125 CD/LP/MC
Ørsted-Pedersen; Dave Liebman (ts, ss, af); John Scofield (g); Billy Hart (d). 7 & 8/79.

****   **The Viking** Pablo 2310894 CD/LP
Ørsted-Pedersen; Philip Catherine (g). 5/83.

***   **The Eternal Traveller** Pablo 2310910 LP
        Ørsted-Pedersen; Ole Kock Hansen (*p*); Lennart Grustvedt (*d*); Anna Marie (*v*). 6 &
        11/84.

NHØP's credits as a sideman almost defy belief. Currently, he plays on something over 150
currently available LPs and CDs, backing the likes of Chet Baker, Kenny Drew, Lee Konitz,
Ben Webster and (crucially) Dexter Gordon and Oscar Peterson. He has recorded with
younger-generation players as far apart in style as Niels Lan Doky and Anthony Braxton. If his
playing on the two Steeplechases from the Club Montmartre in Copenhagen sounds particularly
confident, that is because he spent much of his later twenties as house bassist there. His
technique as a young man was staggering, combining forceful swing with great melodic and
harmonic sense and a sure-fingeredness that gave his big, sonorous tone an almost horn-like
quality. While still in his teens, he was invited to join the Basie band, but decided against it.

Equally consistent as a leader, NHØP probably hasn't received his due of praise for his own
records. They are all broadly of a piece, largely standards-based, with the group sessions placing
greater emphasis on swing, and the duos on a more musing, intimate quality, and the ratings
above give a reasonable sense of their respective merits. The bassist has enjoyed a particularly
fruitful relationship with guitarist Philip Catherine, who shares many of his virtues, and the two
in combination are responsible for some formidably beautiful music, notably on *The Viking*.
The duos with Kenneth Knudsen are slightly soft-centred in places, but the keyboard man has a
gift for softly textured themes; they are joined by Palle Mikkelborg on the lovely *Heart To Heart*
(Storyville SLP 4114, reviewed under the trumeter's name). The punning *Double Bass* is an
interesting experiment that almost falters when a second drummer joins the group, doubling not
just the bass lines but the whole rhythm section; Catherine is left with an unenviable continuity
job, but 'Au Privave' (Oscar Peterson's favourite Charlie Parker theme) and Coltrane's 'Giant
Steps' fare remarkably well. *Dancing On The Tables* explores less familiar materials and
tonalities. Liebman's saxophone playing is sufficiently light and spacious not to swamp the
foreground, and NHØP produces some intriguing rapid-fire counterpoints to the guitarist.

Perhaps only *The Eternal Traveller*, with its opening and closing 'Moto Perpetuo' and its
rather irresolute structure, can be seen as a major disappointment. Set against the standard of
the bassist's other work, it's a much less pressing item, but it shouldn't be dismissed. Few
modern players have developed mainstream bass to anything like this extent and
Ørsted-Pedersen is overdue a comprehensive assessment.

ANTHONY ORTEGA (born 1928)
ALTO SAXOPHONE

***(*)   **New Dance** Hat Art 6065 CD
        Ortega; Chuck Domanico, Bobby West (*b*); Bill Goodwin (*d*). 10/66–1/67.

Ortega's earlier records as a leader – he apprenticed with Lionel Hampton in the early 1950s –
are obscure, and the two sessions included here would be too if it hadn't been for a very
enterprising reissue by Werner Uehlinger's Hat Hut operation. The leader was an untypical
West Coast saxman in that he chose to move some way beyond the customary neat, quicksilver
playing of his peers and began instead to investigate what there was in the new music of
Ornette Coleman for him. Like Art Pepper, Ortega blended elements of that freedom into a
style that still depended on bebop shapes and symmetries. When he strays too far into open
space, as at the end of 'New Dance' itself, his tonal distortions begin to sound affected. Most of
this material is based on standards, though, and with a flicker of a sequence in the background,
Ortega sounds completely confident. Several tracks are open-ended duets with Domanico (two
bass solos from the original Revelation albums have been omitted here) which are like coiled
lines slowly drawn into straightness: 'The Shadow Of Your Smile' does it with the ballad form,
while the pell-mell pace of 'I Love You' does it at full tilt. The trio tracks with West and
Goodwin are less dramatic, yet Ortega's sinuous lines and startlingly pure tone sound utterly
distinctive in both settings. The original recordings were rather cloudy but the remastering does
the music no disservice. Ortega's one later record, for Discovery, is out of print, but he does
turn up on a Mike Wofford session.

KID ORY (1886–1973)
TROMBONE, VOCALS

****   **Kid Ory's Creole Jazz Band** Good Time Jazz 12022 LP
Ory; Mutt Carey (*t*); Darnell Howard, Omer Simeon (*cl*); Buster Wilson (*p*); Bud
Scott (*bjo, v*); Ed Garland (*b*); Minor Ram Hall, Alton Redd (*d*). 8/44, 8, 9 & 11/45.

[***   **New Orleans Legends** Vogue 655603 CD]
Ory; Teddy Buckner, Mutt Carey (*t*); Joe Darensbourg, Jimmie Noone (*cl*); Lloyd
Glenn, Buster Wilson (*p*); Bud Scott (*g*); Ed Garland (*b*); Minor Ram Hall, Zutty
Singleton (*d*). 4 & 10/44.

***(*)   **Kid Ory's Creole Jazz Band, 1954** Good Time Jazz 12016 CD/LP
Ory; Alvin Alcorn (*t*); George Probert (*cl*); Don Ewell (*p*); Bill Newman (*g, bj*); Ed
Garland (*b*); Minor Hall (*d*).

***   **Sounds Of New Orleans: Volume 9** Storyville SLP 6016 LP
Ory; Alvin Alcorn (*t*); Albert Burbank, Phil Gomez, George Probert (*cl*); Don Ewell
(*p*); Ed Garland (*b*); Minor Ram Hall (*d*). 5, 7 & 11/54, 1 & 2/55.

***(*)   **The Legendary Kid** Good Time Jazz 12016 CD/LP
Ory; Alvin Alcorn (*t*); Phil Gomez (*cl*); Lionel Reason (*p*); Julian Davidson (*g*);
Wellman Braud (*b*); Minor Ram Hall (*d*). 11/55.

***   **Favorites!** Good Time Jazz 60-009 CD
Ory; Alvin Alcorn (*t*); Phil Gomez (*cl*); Cedric Haywood (*p*); Julian Davidson (*g*);
Wellman Braud (*b*); Minor Hall (*d*).

Kid Ory's 1940s albums (on Good Time Jazz) had Creole cooking tips printed on the sleeves.
On his comeback, after nearly a decade out of music fattening up chickens, the trombonist's
rhythmic tailgating style was still as salty as blackened kingfish and as spicy as good gumbo.
Ironically, he spent much of his life away from Louisiana, going to California for his health just
after the First World War, where he recorded the first ever sides by an all-black group, 'Ory's
Creole Trombone' and 'Society Blues', in 1922.

    A man can learn a lot watching chickens forage. Ory's comeback coincided with the big
Dixieland revival, and he turned an instinct for self-marketing to lucrative effect. Notoriously
difficult to work for, he was particularly demanding of his trumpet players. When Mutt Carey
died in 1948, Ory used the equally brilliant Teddy Buckner and later Alvin Alcorn in what was
to be one of the best and most authentic of the revivalist bands. Kid Ory's Creole Jazz Band
lasted until the 1960s, by which time his exemplary stamina was failing and the big glissandi and
slurs were sounding slightly breathless. Ory was a fine technician who cultivated a sloppy,
'rough' effect that led some listeners to dub him a primitive. Like all the great Delta players,
though, he thought of the whole group as a single instrument into which his own voice slotted
perfectly.

    The best of the available records are the two Good Time Jazz sets. The later is available on
CD, but the sound is rather glassy and *Creole Jazz Band* is to be preferred, with its excellent
readings of 'Maple Leaf Rag', 'Ory's Creole Trombone', 'Careless Love Blues' and 'Oh,
Didn't He Ramble', but not, unfortunately, his own 'Muskrat Ramble', which was one of the
revival hits of the mid-1950s. It's to be found on the good Storyville, with Alvin Alcorn's
trumpet going sharp as a tack in and out of the melody. There are also a couple of good tracks
on the Vogue compilation. Sound-quality varies on the vinyl selections but isn't significantly
better or worse than norm for the period, and Ory himself always took care to come through at
the front, loud and firm, just in case anyone forgot his name.

MIKE OSBORNE (born 1941)
ALTO SAXOPHONE

****   **All Night Long** Ogun OG700 LP
Osborne; Harry Miller (*b*); Louis Moholo (*d*). 4/75.

***(*)   **Tandem** Ogun OG210 LP
Osborne; Stan Tracey (*p*). 76.

***   **Marcel's Muse** Ogun OG810 LP
Osborne; Mark Charig (*t*); Geoff Green (*g*); Harry Miller (*b*); Peter Nykyruj (*d*). 77.

For the past 10 years illness has silenced one of the most powerful and emotionally stirring voices in British jazz. A Mike Osborne gig, with whatever line-up, was a furious dance of disparate parts: simple hymnic tunes, wild staccato runs, sweet ballad formations and raw blues, all stitched together into a continuous fabric that left most listeners exhausted, and none unmoved.

Osborne's early album, *Outback* [Turtle], is rarely seen and highly collectable. Most of the rest of his recorded output consists of chunks culled from live concerts in the mid-1970s. The studio album, *Marcel's Muse*, is edgily formalized and the short-track format doesn't suit Osborne's freewheeling style. *All Night Long*, though, is resolutely buccaneering and headlong, with Miller and Moholo (the latter much missed on *Marcel's Muse*) in stupendous form, certainly more intently attuned to Osborne's needs than on *Border Crossing* [Ogun OG300 LP], an earlier live set recorded in London. *All Night Long*, recorded at Willisau in Switzerland, consists of two long concert edits, each weaving together a multiplicity of material. The second side begins, as did *Border Crossing*, with an original, 'Ken's Tune', but then proceeds to transform it into a spontaneous piece retrospectively entitled 'Country Bounce', before reprising the opening 'All Night Long' and setting up a crashing finale. The first side works in the same way but, in the middle, Osborne, acting on the barest harmonic clues, suddenly switches into a marvellous, double-time reading of 'Round Midnight'.

He does something similar on *Tandem*, which ends with a beautifully simple statement of the theme from 'Goodbye, Pork Pie Hat'. Osborne had recorded one previous live concert with Stan Tracey, but *Original* [Cadillac] is no longer available. *Tandem*, recorded at the Bracknell jazz festival in 1976, follows the same spontaneous format, evolving thematic material and evoking standards with no prearranged sequence. Impossible now to judge what Osborne might have gone on to do. All that's left is to hear his music and wish him well.

GREG OSBY
ALTO AND SOPRANO SAXOPHONES, FLUTE, KEYBOARDS

(*)   **Greg Osby And Sound Theatre JMT 834411 CD/LP
Osby; Michele Rosewoman (*p*); Fusako Yoshida (*koto*); Kevin McNeal (*g*); Lonnie Plaxico (*b*); Paul Samuels, Terri Lyne Carrington (*d*). 6/87.

***   **Mindgames** JMT 834422 CD/LP
Osby; Geri Allen, Edward Simon (*ky*); Kevin McNeal (*g*); Lonnie Plaxico (*b*); Paul Samuels (*d*). 5/88.

(*)   **Season Of Renewal JMT 834435 CD/LP/MC
Osby; Edward Simon, Renee Rosnes (*ky*); Kevin Eubanks, Kevin McNeal (*g, gsyn*); Lonnie Plaxico (*b*); Paul Samuels (*d*); Steve Thornton (*perc*); Cassandra Wilson, Amina Claudine Myers (*v*). 7/89.

**   **Man Talk For Moderns Vol. X** Blue Note CDP 795414-2 CD
Osby; Steve Coleman (*as*); Gary Thomas (*ts, f*); Edward Simon, Michael Cain (*ky*); David Gilmour (*g, gsyn*); Chan Johnson (*g*); James Genus, Lonnie Plaxico (*b*); Billy Kilson (*d*); Steve Moss (*perc*); Hochmad Ali Akkbar (*v*). 10–11/90.

Osby is a hip, creative mind in search of a context that can do something worthwhile with a talent that gets wasted on most of these records. He plays alto sax in the sharp, coolly incisive manner which has become a standard among many of the younger New York-based players, and his agility and rhythmic acuity on the horn is unanswerable: he can move in the most complex time and make it sound effective, and the impassive tartness of his tone serves to harden the edge of his improvising. But too much of the music here seems to stand as a mere creative exercise for skilful players, and at its most rarefied Osby's composing suggests a kind of intellectual fusion which comes dressed in unyielding funk rhythms. The debut album for JMT is still the best under his own name, since it forges a genuine creative partnership – with pianist Michele Rosewoman, whose improvisations make Osby's tunes sound stronger than they are – and works through a range of options, from romantic ballads to tight, flat-out blowing. *Mindgames* moves the keyboards to a more textural role, and Osby turns up the guitar: there's also less variation in pulse and delivery. *Season Of Renewal* runs aground on some heartless material – five of the tracks are sung as songs, and Osby is no great songwriter – but his own playing sounds exactingly up to the mark. A move to Blue Note doesn't seem to have done him any artistic favours, though. *Man Talk For Moderns Vol. X* is so modish that it ought to have a sell-by date on it, and the record's compromised by some tracks which sound like a direct bid at American jazz-radio crossover. Osby has done better work elsewhere, notably on the exciting Strata Institute project with Steve Coleman, and also on the two recent Blue Note sets by Andrew Hill, where his playing hits an impressive note of assurance in the very difficult confies of Hill's music.

OSLO 13
GROUP

***   **Anti-Therapy** Odin 07 LP/MC

****   **Off-Balance** Odin NJ 4022-2 CD
Nils Petter Molvaer (*t*); Torbjorn Sunde, Dag Einar Eilertsen (*tb*); Erik Balke (*as, bs*); Tore Brunborg (*ts*); Arne Frang (*ts, bsx*); Olave Dale (*bs*); Jon Balke (*ky*); Carl Morten Iversen (*b*); Audun Klieve (*d*). 8/87.

The sound of a Norwegian sax section is surely an unique one in contemporary music, with the mournful vibrato and wind-chilled timbre seemingly a national characteristic. Jon Balke, who arranges and composes most of the music for this band, first formed in 1980 as a forum for young Oslo-based jazzmen, makes the most of that sound. Much of their music is based on the textural possibilities of the reeds, either skirling in opposition to the brass and rhythm or drifting in still, barren space. The earlier record is interesting if less coherently organized, but *Off-Balance* is a superb effort: Balke's scores offer something different in every track, the soloists are uniformly excellent, the balance of the band – trombones in tart opposition to the reeds, Molvaer a strong lone voice on trumpet, and Klieve's drum parts never content with playing time – is radically out of synch with any other contemporary large ensemble. They are also served with brilliant recording by Jan Erik Kongshaug.

***   **Nonsentration** ECM 1445 CD/LP
Per Jørgensen, Nils Petter Molvaer (*t*); Torbjørn Sunde (*tb*); Morten Halle (*as*); Tore Brunborg, Arne Frang (*ts*); Jon Balke (*ky*); Audun Klieve, Jon Christensen (*d*); Finn Sletten, Miki N'Doye (*perc*). 9/90.

Both livelier and more inert than the previous records, this is a vaguely disappointing continuation. Balke's interest in texture and line continues to create some fascinating music, and the group again plays with real finesse and cumulative intensity, but the addition of funkier percussion on several tracks contrasts uneasily with the motionless mood pieces which still take up a lot of the record. It all sounds unfinished.

ROBERTO OTTAVIANO
SOPRANO AND ALTO SAXOPHONE, MANZANO

***   **The Leap** Red NS 213 LP
Ottaviano; Ray Anderson (*tb*); Fabio Mariani (*g*); Piero Leveratto (*b*); Tiziano Tononi (*d*). 4/87.

***(*)   **Mingus: Portrait In Six Colours** Splasc(h) H 169 LP
Ottaviano; Luca Bonvini (*tb*); Martin Mayes (*frhn*); Fiorenzo Gualandris (*tba*); Sandro Cerino (*cl, bcl, f*); Mario Arcari (*ob*); Tiziana Ghiglioni (*v*). 6–7/88.

***   **Sotto Il Sole Giaguro** Solstice SOLCD 1000 CD
Ottaviano; Stefano Battaglia (*p*); Piero Leveratto (*b*); Ettore Fioravanti (*d*). 5/89.

***(*)   **Items From The Old Earth** Splasc(h) H 332 CD
Ottaviano; Roberto Rossi (*tb*); Mario Arcari (*ss, ob, cor*); Martin Mayes (*frhn*); Sandro Cerino (*cl, bcl, f, bf*); Fiorenzo Gualandris (*tba*). 12/90.

He has done significant work as a sideman with Ran Blake, Franz Koglmann and Tiziana Ghiglioni among others, but Ottaviano's albums as a leader offer some of the best indication of his powers. *The Leap* is an entertaining ramble through various sorts of setting – comic post-bop, twisting free blowing, modal ballads – helped enormously by the inspired casting of Ray Anderson, whose solos tend to overshadow those of the leader and the less interesting Mariani. 'In A Milky Way' is a particularly engaging theme.

Ottaviano returns to the soprano for the well-sustained quartet record for Solstice. He has clearly worked very hard on his tone, for he gets an unusually pure and unaffected sound on the horn, rarely going for a squawk or anything remotely expressionist, and it lends his improvisations a clear if somewhat terse intensity. Six of the nine themes are by him – the other players have one writing credit each – and although some are less impressive, such as the fractured freebop of 'Our Kind Of Wabi', others work splendidly. 'Feu De Glui' concentrates the quartet into a single voice, 'Freaks' has an ingeniously jabbing theme which sets up some pithy improvising, while Leveratto's 'Memories Memories' has a soprano solo of lucid beauty over walking bass and brushes. Excellent digital sound.

Mingus and *Items from The Old Earth* are both by Ottaviano's all-horns group, Six Mobiles. The Mingus tribute is surely the most unsual devised to date, eight of his original themes – including such unexpected choices as 'Myself When I Am Real', 'Boogie Stop Shuffle' and 'Prayer For Passive Resistance' – ingeniously rearranged and quite densely scored for the sextet. While there is space for improvisation to make a mark, the ebb and flow of the horns is the point of the music, and it's performed with great wit and insight by the players. *Items From The Old Earth* is something of a repeat performance on original themes by the group. This time the sonorities are even harder to predict, brassy at some points, woody at others, and the compositions are crwoded (perhaps excessively so at times) with both ideas and techniques, some of which beg comparison with European composition rather than jazz. But Ottaviano's own solos add a sudden brightness at moments when the ensemble threatens to turn wholly academic. Both discs are strongly recommended.

***   **Above Us** Splasc(h) H 330-2 CD
        Ottaviano; Stefano Battaglia (*p*); Piero Leveratto (*b*); Ettore Fioravanti (*d*). 11/90.

**   **Otto** Splasc(h) H 340-2 CD
        Ottaviano (*ss* solo). 1/91.

Ottaviano returns to more conventional ground on the quartet record, which matches him with the gifted Battaglia: loose modal blowing seems to be the mainstay of the date, and it's done with aplomb, although some of the music lacks anchor and compass. *Otto* takes a stab at a solo album but seems a mite too cleverly conceived: reverb and overdubs distract from the point of Ottaviano's improvising, and some of the solos seem like mere technical points-winners. A pretty record, though, when the saxophonist locates an attractive line.

MAKOTO OZONE

PIANO, KEYBOARDS

**   **Starlight** JVC JD-3323 CD/MC
        Ozone; Malta (*as*); Fumiaki Ogawa (*ky*); Fujimaru Yoshino, Kazuhiko Michishita, Masaki Matsubara, Kazuhiko Iwami (*g*); Akira Okazawa, Tatsuhiko Hizawa, Kohki Itoh (*b*); Yuichi Togashiki, Scott Latham, Shuichi Murakami (*d*); strings. 90.

Ozone did some sound work as a Gary Burton sideman; here he's content to decorate a series of light-fusion backdrops with some fleet and admittedly not unpleasing piano parts. There's nothing here that hasn't been done by the likes of David Benoit and his ilk, but Ozone tackles the tasks with as much commitment as anyone in the field, and the mysterious Malta takes a couple of nods to David Sanborn in his solos.

HOT LIPS PAGE (1908–54)
TRUMPET

***   **The Chronological Hot Lips Page, 1938–1940** Classics 561 CD
Page; Bobby Moore, Eddie Mullens (*t*); George Stevenson, Harry White (*tb*); Ben
Smith, Buster Smith (*cl, as*); Jimmy Powell (*as*); Ulysses Scott, Don Stovall (*as*); Ben
Williams (*as, ts*); Don Byas, Sammy Davis, Ernie Powell, Sam Simmons, Benny Waters
(*ts*); Pete Johnson, Jimmy Reynolds (*p*); John Collins, Connie Wainwright (*g*); Abe
Bolar, Wellman Braud (*b*); A. G. Godley, Ed McConney, Alfred Taylor (*d*);
Romayne Jackson, Bea Morton, Delores Payne, Ben Powers, The Harlem Highlanders
(*v*). 3, 4, 6/38, 1, 11 & 12/40.

(*)   **Americans In Sweden: Hot Lips Page, 1951 Jazz Society AA 513 LP
Page; Ake Persson (*tb*); Carl-Eric Lindgren (*ts*); Ingemar Westberg (*p*); Simon Brehm
(*b*); Sven Bohlerm (*d*). 9/51.

An Armstrong imitator who never quite made it out of that constricting sack, Page has always
hovered just below the threshold of most fans' attention. Realistically, he is a much less
accomplished player who wasted much of his considerable talent on pointless jamming and
dismal but lucrative rhythm and blues. The material recorded for Bluebird in April 1938
features a band that might have gone places had Page not had to disband it. At the beginning of
1940 he was recording with the remarkable Buster Smith, a Texan out of Ellis County (Page was
from Dallas), who became a mainstay of the Kansas City sound during the war years and after.
These are fine sides, but they're surpassed by the four cuts made for Decca towards the end of
the year with Pete Johnson and Don Byas, which (leaving aside an indifferent vocal by Bea
Morton) are among the best of the period and unjustly neglected.

The 1951 Swedish material is a sample of the kind of thing Page wasted time and talent doing
all through his career. In this case, he's playing well if unadventurously (he died only three years
later), uninspired, but for a moment or two on 'Cavalcade' and 'Home Boy', by a very
pedestrian band. Page deserves better representation than this.

WILLIE PAJEAUD
TRUMPET, VOCAL

*(*)   **Willie Pajeaud's New Orleans Band 1955** 504 LP31 CD/LP
Pajeaud; Raymond Burke (*cl*); Danny Barker (*g, bj, v*); Len Ferguson (*d*); Blue Lu
Barker (*v*). 55.

Pajeaud is best known as a principal in the Eureka Brass Band, but this memento of a jam
session on Bourbon Street in 1955 finds him leading a small group of New Orleans stalwarts.
Frankly, it's more of historical interest than anything else: Danny and Blue Lu Barker take
three of the numbers virtually by themselves, and the remainder are enthusiastic but ragged
accounts of the kind of tunes these men must have played every night of their professional lives.
The recording is an amateur one. The rest of the LP is devoted to Kid Thomas Valentine and is
listed under his name.

PAPA BUE'S VIKING JAZZ BAND
GROUP

***(*)   **A Tribute To Wingy Manone** Storyville SLP 210 LP
Arne Bue Jensen (*tb*); Wingy Manone (*t, v*); Finn Otto Hansen (*t*); Jorgen Svare (*cl*);
Jorn Jensen (*p*); Bjarne Liller Petersen (*bjo*); Jens Sjolund (*b*); Asger Rosenberg (*v*).
12/67.

(*)   **Live In Dresden Storyville SLP 815/6 2LP
As above, except omit Manone, add Knud Ryskov Madsen (*d*). 1/71.

***   **On Stage** Timeless TTD 511 CD/LP
Arne Bue Jensen; Ole Stolle (*t, v*); Jorgen Svare (*cl*); Jorn Jensen (*p*); Jens Sollund
(*b*); Soren Houlind (*d, v*). 4 & 9/82.

The Viking empire once stretched as far south as the Mediterranean, and considerable ingenuity has been expended in attempting to prove that a Norseman beat Christopher Columbus across the Atlantic. Arne Bue Jensen represents circumstantial evidence that the Vikings made it not just to a slippery rock off Newfoundland, but all the way down to New Orleans.

Nonsense about 'authenticity' apart, Papa Bue's long-running band is one of the finest revival outfits ever to emerge north of the Mason–Dixon line. The emphasis, inevitably, is on ensemble playing rather than soloing, and these are as confidently relaxed as anyone might wish for, with none of the stiffness that creeps into more studied revivalism. The rhythm players have a particularly good feel, and Madsen is one of the finest Scandinavian percussionists, with elastic wrists and a nice sound.

The collaboration/tribute with Wingy Manone – Bing Crosby's one-time funny man – is perhaps the best, not least because it shows off the Vikings in the kind of company they'd long emulated. 'When You're Smiling', 'Dark Eyes' and 'Black And Blue' are perhaps the best of the set, but the tribute pieces, with the two-armed Finn, Otto Hansen, in for Manone, stand up well. *Live In Dresden* is slightly chaotic and there really isn't enough top-flight material to justify a double album; 'Tar Paper Stomp', also on the Manone record, really isn't up to scratch, and there are hesitancies elsewhere. *On Stage* is tighter again and much more coherent, with a rousing 'Tiger Rag' and genuinely affecting 'Just A Closer Walk With Thee'; the CD helps. Erik the Blue would have been very proud.

SAKIS PAPADIMITRIOU
PIANO

***   **Piano Plays** Leo LR 111 LP
Papadimitriou (*p* solo).

(*)   **First Move Leo LR 128 LP
As above.

Improvising pianists now regard direct contact with the strings as a basic performing resource. Papadimitriou has taken what for most is an incidental and additional range of sounds one step further, concentrating very largely and often exclusively on playing 'inside'. Strings are stroked, plucked, stopped with the fingers and softly harmonized, creating effects that mimic kotos, zithers, steel drums, even violins. The best of Padimitrious's Leo albums *Piano Oracles* [LR 163 LP] is currently out of stock, but the two remaining titles are well worth investigating.

CHARLIE PARKER (1920–55)
ALTO SAXOPHONE, TENOR SAXOPHONE

****   **The Complete Dean Benedetti Recordings** Mosaic MD7-129 7CD/10LP
Parker solos, with Miles Davis, Howard McGhee (*t*); Hampton Hawes, Duke Jordan, Thelonious Monk (*p*); Addison Farmer, Tommy Potter (*b*); Roy Porter, Max Roach (*d*); Earl Coleman, Kenny Hagood, Carmen McRae (*v*); other unknown personnel. 3/47–7/48.

Parker's innovation – improvising a new melody line off the top, rather than from the middle, of the informing chord – was a logical extension of everything that had been happening in jazz over the previous decade. However, even though the simultaneous inscription of bebop by different hands – Dizzy Gillespie, Charlie Christian and Thelonious Monk all have their propagandists – suggests that it was an evolutionary inevitability, any artistic innovation requires quite specific and usually conscious interventions. With its emphasis on extreme harmonic virtuosity, bop has become the dominant idiom of modern jazz and Parker's genetic fingerprint is the clearest.

The British saxophone virtuoso, John Harle, has spoken of the remarkable *clarity* of Parker's music, and in particular his solo development. Even at his most dazzlingly virtuosic, Parker always sounds logical, making light of asymmetrical phrases, idiosyncratically translated bar-lines, surefooted alternation of whole-note passages and flurries of semiquavers, tampering with almost every other parameter of the music – dynamic, attack, timbre – with a kind of joyous arrogance. Dying at thirty-five, he was spared the indignity of a middle age given over to formulaic repetition.

Because, in theory at least, he never repeated himself, there has been a degree of fetishization of Parker's solos, many of them, like 'The Famous Alto Break' from the Dial recordings, below, or some of the later Verve material, in which a solo is either preserved out of the fullest context on an incomplete take or executed with insouciant disregard of bland or faulty accompaniments. There is, though, an explanation that usefully combines mythology with sheer pragmatism. In his faulty biography of Parker, *Bird Lives!*, Ross Russell introduced a composite figure called Dean Benedetti (the Kerouac resonance was inescapable) who follows Bird throughout the United States capturing his solos (and the solos only) on a primitive wire-recorder. Though unreleased until 1990, the Dean Benedetti archive has enjoyed cult reputation with Parker fans, the Dead Sea Scrolls of bebop, fragmentary and patinized, inaccessible to all but adepts and insiders, but containing the Word in its purest and most unadulterated form.

The real Benedetti, routinely characterized by Russell as a saxophonist *manqué*, remained a practising player, and these remarkable recordings fall into place ever more clearly if one starts towards the end, with Benedetti's amateurishly dubbed attempts to play along with Parker records, and then accepts the absoluteness of his identification with his idol. Dean Benedetti died of myasthenia gravis (a progressive atrophying of the musculature) two years after Bird. Benedetti was already fatally ill when he heard of Charlie Parker's death. He wrote: '*Povero C. P. anche tu. Dove ci troveremmo?*' (Poor Bird. You too. Where will we meet again?) The answer is: here. Benedetti's archive was left in the care of his brother, Rick, who in turn died just too soon to witness the release of these astonishing records.

The Mosaic set, lovingly restored and annotated by Phil Schaap, consists of 278 tracks and a boggling 461 recordings of Charlie Parker, made between 1 March 1947 and 11 July 1948 in Los Angeles and New York (a much smaller span of time and geography than legend finds comfortable). The famous wire-recorder certainly existed but was not used for recording Bird. Benedetti worked with 78-r.p.m. acetate discs, and only later with paper-based recording tape. A good many of the recordings are vitiated or distorted by swarf from the cutting needle (which an assistant was supposed to brush away as a recording progressed) getting in the way; since the cutter moved from the outer edge of the disc towards the centre, there was also a problem with torque, and the inner grooves are often rather strained and indistinct. The sound-quality throughout is far from impressive. What is remarkable, though, is the utter dedication and concentration Benedetti brought to his task. Some of the tracks offer fully developed solos occupying several choruses; others, to take two examples only from a recording made in March 1947 at the Hi-De-Ho Club in Los Angeles, last as little as three ('Night And Day'!!) or seven (possibly 'I Surrender Dear') *seconds*.

As an insight into how Parker approached the same tune with the same group on successive nights (there are six separate solos from 'Big Noise'/'Wee' between 1 and 8 March 1947) or how he continued to tackle less familiar material associated with pre-bop figures like Coleman Hawkins (three helpings of 'Bean Soup' in the same period), it is an unparalleled resource. There is also valuable documentation of a rare meeting with Thelonious Monk, recorded on 52nd Street in July 1948. The density of background material (titles, durations, key signatures, in some cases transcriptions) is awesome, and though some of the material has been available for some time as *Bird On 52nd Street* (Original Jazz Classics OJC 114 LP) the vast bulk of it has not been in the public domain. As such, *The Dean Benedetti Recordings* represent the last step in the consolidation of Parker's once inchoate and shambolic discography. Though there is a vast muddle of live material and airshots, there is a surprisingly small corpus of authorized studio material. Parker's recording career really lasts only a decade, from 1944 to 1953, and is enshrined in three main blocks of material, for Savoy (1944–8), for Dial (1946 to December 1947) and for Norman Granz's Verve (1948–53); throw in the significant Royal Roost live sessions and, but for the Benedetti archive, the main pillars of Parker's reputation are in place.

The painter, Barnett Newman, once said that aesthetics was for artists like ornithology was for the birds, and the unintended reference can usefully be appropriated in this context. Though essentially for specialists (and rather well-heeled experts at that) who are untroubled by the abruptly decontextualized nature of these performances, the Benedetti material represents a quite remarkable auditory experience. The initially exasperating sequence of sound-bites gives way to an illusion of almost telepathic insight, a key to the inner mystery of who and what Parker was.

*****   **The Charlie Parker Story** Savoy SV-0105 CD
Parker; Miles Davis (*t*); Dizzy Gillespie (*p, t*); Bud Powell (*p*); Curley Russell (*b*);
Max Roach (*d*). 11/45.

****   **Charlie Parker Memorial: Volume 1** Savoy SV-0101 CD
Parker; Miles Davis (*t*); Duke Jordan, John Lewis, Bud Powell (*p*); Nelson Boyd,
Tommy Potter, Curly Russell (*b*); Max Roach (*d*). 12/47.

****   **Charlie Parker Memorial: Volume 2** Savoy SV-0103 CD
As above. 5/47, 9/48.

****   **The Genius Of Charlie Parker** Savoy SV-0104 CD
as above; also Jack McVea (*ts*); Tiny Brown (*bs*); Sadik Hakim, Dodo Marmarosa (*p*);
Slim Gaillard (*p, g, v*); Zutty Singleton (*d*). 12/45, 5 & 12/47, 9/48.

The sides Parker cut on 26 November 1945 were billed by Savoy on the later microgroove
release as 'The greatest recording session made in modern jazz'. There's some merit in that.
The kitchen-sink reproduction of fluffs, false starts and breakdowns gives a rather chaotic
impression. Miles Davis, who never entirely came to terms with Parker's harmonic or rhythmic
requirements, doesn't play particularly well (there is even a theory that some of the trumpet
choruses – notably one on a third take of 'Billie's Bounce' – were played by Dizzy Gillespie in
imitation of Miles's rather uncertain style), and some of Bud Powell's intros and solos are
positively bizarre; step forward, pianist Argonne Thornton, who remembers (though he's the
only one who does) being at the sessions. Despite all that, and Parker's continuing problems
with a recalcitrant reed, the session includes 'Billie's Bounce', 'Now's The Time' and 'Ko-Ko'.
The last of these is perhaps the high-water mark of Parker's improvisational genius and the
justification for a five-star rating.

Though this is undoubtedly the zenith of Parker's compositional skill as well (in later years
he seems to have created fewer and fewer original themes), it is noticeable that virtually all of
the material on these sessions draws either on a basic 12-bar blues or on the chord sequece of 'I
Got Rhythm', the Ur-text of bebop. 'Ko-Ko' is based on the chords of 'Cherokee', as is the
generic 'Warming Up A Riff', which was intended only as a run-through after Parker had
carried out running repairs on his squeaking horn. The remainder of Parker's material was
drawn, conventionally enough, from show tunes; 'Meandering', a one-off ballad performance
on the November 1945 session, unaccountably elided after superb solos from Parker and
Powell, bears some relationship to 'Embraceable You'. What is striking about Parker's playing,
here and subsequently, is the emphasis on rhythmic invention, often at the expense of harmonic
creativity (in that department, as he shows in miniature on 'Ko-Ko', Dizzy Gillespie was
certainly his superior).

Availability on programmable CD means that listeners who find the staccato progression of
incomplete takes disconcerting are able to ignore all but the final, released versions.
Unfortunately, though these are usually the best *band* performances, they do not always reflect
Bird's best solo playing. A good example comes on 'Now's The Time', a supposedly original
theme, but one which may retain the outline of an old Kansas City blowing blues (or may have
been composed – that is, played – by tenor saxophonist Rocky Boyd). There is no doubt that
Parker's solo on the third take is superior in its slashing self-confidence to that on the fourth,
which is slightly duller; Miles Davis plays without conviction on both.

None of the other three volumes contains a single recording session, nor do any of the
constituent sessions match up to the erratic brilliance of 26 November 1945. There are seven
other dates represented, notably intermittent in quality. The sessions with Slim Gaillard,
creator of 'Vout', an irritating hipster argot apparently still used by Ronald and Nancy Reagan
in affectionate moments (if such a situation can be visualized with equanimity), are pretty corny
and time-bound; a bare month after 'Ko-Ko', Parker seems to have come down to earth. An
early session with guitarist Tiny Grimes and an unusual August 1947 date (under Miles Davis's
control) on which Bird played tenor saxophone have been excluded from this CD reissue. Of
the remaining dates, that of 8 May 1947, a rather uneasy affair, nevertheless yielded 'Donna
Lee' and 'Chasing The Bird'; by contrast, on 21 December 1947, Parker seems utterly confident
and lays down the ferocious 'Bird Gets The Worm' and 'Klaunstance'; the sessions of 18 and
24 September 1948 yielded the classic 'Parker's Mood' (original take 3 is suffused with
incomparable blues feeling) and 'Marmaduke' respectively.

The other key figures on these recordings are Max Roach, barely out of his teens but already playing in the kind of advanced rhythmic count that Parker required, and Dizzy Gillespie. Miles Davis was demonstrably unhappy with some of the faster themes and lacked Parker's ability to think afresh take after take; by the time of the 'Parker's Mood' date, though, he had matured significantly (he was, after all, only nineteen when 'Ko-Ko' and 'Now's The Time' were recorded). A word, too, for Curly Russell and Tommy Potter, whose contribution to this music has not yet been fully appreciated and who were rather sorely used on past releases, often muffled to the point of inaudibility.

The Genius Of Charlie Parker brings together original masters only from the six sessions, with an introduction by Al 'Jazzbeau' Collins. It's an attractive package, ideal for those who find the archaeology of recording sessions less than inspiriting. But for sheer majesty of performance and the best available representation of Parker's ability to pack the inner space of his phraseology with musical information, listeners should try to ignore the naff cover-art (one side features an unrecognizable portrait that makes him look like a hip dentist from Barksdale) and go for *The Charlie Parker Story*.

***** **Charlie Parker On Dial: Volume 1** Spotlite SPJ 101 LP
Parker; Miles Davis, Dizzy Gillespie, Howard McGhee (*t*); Lucky Thompson (*ts*); Jimmy Bunn, George Handy, Dodo Marmarosa (*p*); Arvin Garrison (*g*); Ray Brown, Bob Kesterson, Vic McMillan (*b*); Stan Levey, Roy Porter (*d*). 2, 3 & 7/46.

**** **Charlie Parker On Dial: Volume 2** Spotlite SPJ 102 LP
Parker; Errol Garner (*p*); Red Callender (*b*); Harold Doc West (*d*); Earl Coleman (*v*). 2/47.

**** **Charlie Parker On Dial: Volume 3** Spotlite SPJ 103 LP
Parker; Howard McGhee (*t*); Wardell Gray (*ts*); Russ Freeman, Dodo Marmarosa (*p*); Barney Kessel (*g*); Red Callender, Arnold Fishkind (*b*); Don Lamond, Jimmy Pratt (*d*). 2/47.

***** **Charlie Parker On Dial: Volume 4** Spotlite SPJ 104 LP
Parker; Miles Davis (*t*); Duke Jordan (*p*); Tommy Potter (*b*); Max Roach (*d*). 10/47.

***** **Charlie Parker On Dial: Volume 5** Spotlite SPJ 105 LP
Parker; Miles Davis, Dizzy Gillespie (*t*); Flip Phillips, Lucky Thompson (*ts*); Duke Jordan, Dodo Marmarosa, Teddy Wilson (*p*); Red Norvo (*vib*); Vic McMillan, Tommy Potter, Slam Stewart (*b*); Roy Porter, Specs Powell, Max Roach (*d*); and as for *Volume 2*. 6/45, 3/46, 2 & 11/47.

**** **Charlie Parker On Dial: Volume 6** Spotlite SPJ 106 LP
Parker; Miles Davis (*t*); J. J. Johnson (*tb*); Duke Hordan (*p*); Tommy Potter (*b*); Max Roach (*d*). 12/47.

**** **Bird Blows The Blues** Dial 901 LP
Collective personnel and dates as above.

**** **Alternate Masters: Volume 1** Dial 904 LP
As above.

***(*) **Alternate Masters: Volume 2** Dial 905 LP
As above.

***** **The Legendary Dial Masters: Volume 1** Stash ST CD 23 CD
As above.

**** **The Legendary Dial Masters: Volume 2** Stash ST CD 25 CD
As above.

**** **The Charlie Parker Anthology** Accord 500122 2CD
As above.

On 26 February 1946, Parker signed what was intended to be an exclusive recording contract with Dial Records, an outgrowth of the Tempo Music Shop on Hollywood Boulevard in Los Angeles. The co-signatory was Tempo owner, Ross Russell, subsequently author of *Bird Lives!* and disseminator of some of the more lasting myths about Parker.

A contemporary headline declared rather enigmatically: 'West Coast Jazz Center Enters Shellac Derby With Be-Bop Biscuits'. Russell's original intention to specialize in classic jazz (largely ignoring swing, in other words) had been confounded by an unanticipated demand for bop 78s. With typical perspicacity, he lined up Parker, Gillespie and others, gave them unprecedented free rein in the studio and backed his commitment with the best engineers available. The investment predictably took some time to recoup. Parker's Dial period straddles a near-catastrophic personal crisis and a subsequent period of almost Buddhist calm, when his playing takes on a serene logic and untroubled simplicity which in later years was to give way to a blander sophistication and chastened professionalism.

On Volume 1 of the Spotlite Dial, a solitary February 1946 cut ('Diggin' Diz') under Gillespie's leadership predates the remarkable session seven weeks later which yielded 'Moose The Mooche', 'Yardbird Suite', 'Ornithology' and 'A Night In Tunisia', four of his classic performances. Parker's solo on the third take of 'Ornithology' is completely masterful, by turns climbing fiercely and soaring effortlessly, always on the point of stalling but never for a moment losing momentum; close study reveals the daring placement of accents and a compelling alternation of chromatic runs (first refuge of beginners or those suffering temporary harmonic amnesia, but never handled with such grace) and dazzling intervallic leaps. Multiple takes of virtually every item (the six Spotlite volumes take in 39 tunes but 88 separate performances) demonstrate the extent to which Parker was prepared to re-take at constantly shifting tempi, never wrong-footing himself but often having to pull some of the rhythm players along in his wake. The 'Famous Alto Break', 46 seconds of pure invention on the saxophone, is all that remains of a first take of 'A Night In Tunisia'; before the Benedetti materials were made available, 'The Famous Alto Break' was Parker's best-known cameo solo.

In contrast to Curley Russell and Max Roach, Vic McMillan and Roy Porter can sound a little stiff, but Dodo Marmarosa (an undervalued player whose present whereabouts are unknown – if, indeed, he is still living) has a bright, sharp-edged angularity which suits Parker perfectly and which is picked up generously by good digital remastering. On 29 July 1946, Parker was in the C. P. Macgregor Studios, Hollywood, with Howard McGhee, a fellow addict, in for Miles Davis or Dizzy Gillespie. Bird was practically comatose during the recording of 'Lover Man' (but nevertheless managed a brutal, convoluted solo that is a rare converse to his usual formal clarity) and collapsed shortly after the session, setting off a train of disasters that landed him in the State Hospital at Camarillo.

Heroin addiction permits surprisingly extended activity at a high level, but usually at a high rate of interest. There has been a tendency again to festishize work born out of appalling physical and psychological anguish at the expense of less troubled performances. In the summer of 1946 Parker was writing cheques that his body and normally indomitable spirit could no longer cash. 'Lover Man', like so many club and concert solos from the preceding years, was done on autopilot. Bird's headlong flight was briefly halted.

He emerged healthier than he had been for a decade. Rest (as in 'Relaxin' At Camarillo'), detoxification and the occasional salad had done him more good than any amount of largactil. A rehearsal session held at Chuck Kopely's house on 1 February 1947 is included on Volume 3, but the recording is very poor (Howard McGhee allegedly kept a hand-held mike pointing at Bird throughout); there are two more tracks from the same occasion on Stash ST CD 25, below. Parker's first post-release recording for Dial cast him in the unlikely company of Errol Garner and the singer, Earl Coleman. Garner's intriguing two-handedness, offering apparent independence in the bass and melody lines, was a valuable prop for Parker, and he sounds remarkably composed. Coleman's singing on 'This Is Always' and 'Dark Shadows' is uncomplicated and rather appealing (a further take of the latter pointlessly turns up on Volume 5 as well, along with a further 'Moose The Mooche' and a take of 'Hallelujah', recorded with Red Norvo in 1945). The meat of the sessions comes with 'Bird's Nest' and the marvellous 'Cool Blues', again attempted at very different tempi. The fourth – or 'D' – take of 'Cool Blues' is positively lugubrious; 'B' and 'D' are included on Dial 901, below. The soloing is limpid and logical, and not much circumstantial knowledge is required to hear the difference between these tracks and the tortured 'Lover Man' of six months before.

A week later, Parker returned to the studio with McGhee and Marmarosa. 'Relaxin' At Camarillo' was allegedly written in the back of a cab en route to the date. Cast in familiar blues form but with an intriguing tonality that suggested Bird was beginning to exercise greater inventiveness along the other, relatively neglected, axis of his work. Unfortunately, the 26 February performances are rather cluttered (Wardell Gray's tenor adds nothing very much; Barney Kessel sounds rather blocky) and the sound isn't up to previous standards.

Volume 3 marked Parker's last West Coast recording for Dial. The selections from 28 October and 4 November 1947 on Volumes 4 and 5 are some of the most lyrical in Parker's entire output. 'Bird Of Paradise' is based on the sequence of 'All The Things You Are', with an introduction (Bird and Miles) that was to become one of the thumbprints of bebop. Parker reinvents his solo from take to take, never exhausting his own resources, never losing contact with the basic material. 'Embraceable You' and the gentle 'Dewey Square' (October; Volume 4), 'Out Of Nowhere' and single takes of 'My Old Flame' and 'Don't Blame Me' (November; Volume 5) don't reach quite the same heights, but the third (unissued) take of 'Out Of Nowhere' is further demonstration of how much magnificent music had to be picked off the editing-room floor. The November session also included two of Parker's finest originals, 'Scrapple From the Apple' and the bizarrely entitled 'Klact-oveeseds-tene' (apparently a quasi-phonetic transcription of 'Klage, Auf Wiedersehen' – some give it as 'Klact', meaning 'bad noise' – which could be taken to mean something like 'Farewell To The Blues'), which is a raw and slightly neurotic theme played entirely out of kilter.

Roach's grasp of Bird's requirements was by now completely intuitive. Only he seems to have been entirely in tune with the saxophonist's often weirdly dislocated entries, and there is a story that Roach had to shout to Duke Jordan not to elide or add beats or half-bars, knowing that Parker would navigate a course back to the basic metre before the end of his solo choruses. This intuitive brilliance is particularly easy to trace on the slower ballad numbers, where the saxophone's entry is often breathtakingly unexpected and dramatic, underlined by Miles Davis's increasingly confident ability to work across the beat, especially at lower tempi.

Bird's final recording session for Dial and with the great quintet was held in New York City on 17 December 1947, with the addition of trombonist, J. J. Johnson. 'Crazeology' is fast and furious and Parker's solos on both the 'C' and (released) 'D' takes are impeccable; he was allegedly playing with a new horn and his tone is more than usually full and precise. Johnson was certainly the first trombone player to understand bop completely enough to make a meaningful contribution to it. His solos on 'Crazeology' and 'Bird Feathers' are excellent, rhythmically much more daring than anyone had previously dared to be on slide trombone.

The Parker Dials, though perhaps of less concentrated brilliance than the Savoys, are among the greatest small-group jazz of all time; masters were cut in October 1949 and the album released shortly thereafter. They are also of considerable significance in that Dial 901, *Bird Blows The Blues*, above, was the first long-playing record devoted to jazz performance. It was distinctive in two regards. In the first place, Russell favoured the 12-inch format, which maintained its hegemony (until the rise of tape cassette and the compact disc) over the more usual 10-inch format, which was the record dealers' preference. Dial later bowed to market pressure, but subsequent 10-inch releases were pressed on a poor-quality vinyl mix that created a great deal of background noise. In the second place, Russell began to include alternative takes of many tracks, setting in motion a discographical mania that has haunted Parker fans ever since. Solos are sipped like vintages and too often spat into a bucketful of matrix numbers rather than fully savoured and absorbed.

For those who have problems on both counts, the availability of master performances on good-quality CD and without the distraction of multiple takes may well be a godsend, and the first volume of the Stash compilation should perhaps be considered essential to anyone building up a non-vinyl jazz collection from scratch; the Accord is a good second option, with 33 tunes from the Dial sessions but no alternatives. However, the fully documented Spotlite Dials are all available separately on vinyl, as well as in a six-volume boxed set. Volume 2, though it takes in half the 4 November 1947 session and all of the subsequent sextet masters, also includes nine representative alternatives: 'Yardbird Suite', 'The Famous Alto Break', 'Cool Blues', 'Relaxin' At Camarillo', 'Bird Of Paradise', 'Scrapple From The Apple', 'Out Of Nowhere' and two tracks not previously mentioned, 'Drifting On A Reed' (another of Parker's themeless improvisations) and 'Bongo Beep' (a December 1947 track that shouldn't be confused with the slightly earlier 'Bongo Bop'). Volume 2 also takes in two themeless blues recorded at the same home rehearsal at Chuck Kopely's that yielded 'Home Cooking', two versions of which are included on Dial 905, three (as if anyone might really want them) on Volume 3 of the Spotlite. The Stash also includes some other material that has already appeared on *Lullaby In Rhythm* (Spotlite 107 LP, below); the trumpeters (McGhee, Rogers, Broiles) are scarcely audible and sit it out on the Spotlite title-track. Some copies of a 1988 double album of the Dial masters entitled *Bird Lives!* and sponsored by the *NME* (Spotlite JU-6-733333 2LP) may still be in circulation, desirable chiefly for a magnificent Herman Leonard cover. Parker's later work for Norman Granz has now been released in exhaustive CD form, below, and a complete CD of the

Dials must surely be in the offing. Until it appears, beginners and enthusiasts have a choice, depending on level of commitment and pocket, among the three versions above.

****   Bird: The Complete Charlie Parker On Verve Verve 837141 10CD
Parker; Mario Bauza, Buck Clayton, Paquito Davilla, Kenny Dorham, Harry Edison, Roy Eldridge, Dizzy Gillespie, Chris Griffin, Benny Harris, Al Killian, Howard McGhee, Jimmy Maxwell, Doug Mettome, Carl Poole, Al Porcino, Bernie Privin, Rod Rodney, Charlie Shavers, Al Stewart, Ray Wetzel. Bobby Woodlen (*t*); Will Bradley, Bill Harris, Lou McGarity, Tommy Turk, Bart Varsalona, Bart Varsalona (*tb*); Vinnie Jacobs (*frhn*); Hal McKusick, John LaPorta (*cl*); Benny Carter, Johnny Hodges, Gene Johnson, Toots Mondello, Sonny Salad, Freddie Skerritt, Willie Smith, Harry Terrill, Murray Williams (*as*); Coleman Hawkins, Jose Madera, Pete Mondello, Flip Phillips, Hank Ross, Sol Rabinowitz, Ben Webster, Lester Young (*ts*); Manny Albam, Danny Bank, Leslie Johnakins, Stan Webb (*bs*); Artie Drelinger (*reeds*); Walter Bishop Jr, Al Haig, Rene Hernandez, Hank Jones, Ken Kersey, John Lewis, Thelonious Monk, Oscar Peterson, Mel Powell, Arnold Ross (*p*); Irving Ashby, Billy Bauer, Jerome Darr, Freddie Green, Barney Kessel (*g*); Ray Brown, Billy Hadnott, Percy Heath, Teddy Kotick, Charles Mingus, Tommy Potter, Roberto Rodriguez, Curly Russell (*b*); Kenny Clarke, Roy Haynes, J. C. Heard, Don Lamond, Shelly Manne, Buddy Rich, Max Roach, Arthur Taylor, Lee Young (*d*); Machito, Jose Manguel, Luis Miranda, Umberto Nieto, Chano Pozo, Carlos Vidal (*perc*); Ella Fitzgerald, Dave Lambert Singers (*v*); woodwinds; strings. 1/46–12/54.

After the extraordinary Savoys and Dials, the sessions for Norman Granz's label mark an inevitable diminuendo. However, it must never be forgotten that Granz was a passionate and practical advocate of better treatment for black American musicians, and it was he who brought Parker to the attention of the wider audience he craved. For the saxophonist, to be allowed to record with strings was a final rubber-stamp of artistic legitimacy. Just as his association with Granz's Jazz at the Philharmonic jamborees are still thought to have turned him into a circus performer, the Parker With Strings sessions (fully documented here) have attracted a mixture of outright opprobrium and predictable insistence that Bird's solos be preserved and evaluated out of context; the point, though, would seem to be that Parker himself, out of naïvety, a wakening sense of self-advancement, or a genuine wish to break the mould of 'jazz' performance, was every bit as concerned with the context as he was with his own place in it. There is a fair amount of saccharin in the first strings performances, but Parker is superb on 'April In Paris' and 'I Didn't Know What Time It Was', and the release of the material in January 1950 propelled Parker on to a new national stage. From February he toured with strings opposite Stan Getz. These experiments weren't always a perceived success. A vocal set to Gil Evans arrangements foundered after 15 takes of just four numbers; there are major problems with balances (and Schaap has fulfilled Evans's wish by re-weighting the rhythm section), but the performances are by no means the disaster they're commononly thought to be.

Parker's signing with Verve almost coincided with a recording strike that was called by the AFM for 1 January 1948. Verve boss Norman Granz managed to fit in two hasty recordings before that time, both of which were for a compilation album called *The Jazz Scene*, but neither of them did Parker much justice. There is some controversy as to the exact circumstances of his recording 'Repetition' with Neil Hefti's orchestra. Some sources suggest that Bird is overdubbed; he sounds merely overpowered by a lush arrangement, but manages to throw in a quote from *The Rite Of Spring* (Stravinsky was currently high on his playlist). 'The Bird' was recorded by a scratch quartet (Hank Jones, Ray Brown, Shelly Manne) and apparently done at speed. Parker fluffs a couple of times and the rhythm section accelerate and stutter like courtiers trying to keep an even 10 paces behind the king.

The same group (with the unsuitable Buddy Rich in for the elegant Manne) sounded much better two and a half years later. On 'Star Eyes', 'I'm In The Mood For Love' and 'Blues (Fast)' Parker plays remarkably straight and with little of the jagged angularity of earlier recordings. The CD compilation adds no new material or alternatives, in sharp contrast to a session recorded two months later, in June 1950, for which Granz, ever on the look-out for eye-catching combinations, brought together Dizzy Gillespie, Thelonious Monk (their solitary studio encounter), Curley Russell (Bird's most sympathetic partner on bass) and, again, the wholly unsuitable Buddy Rich, who thrashes away to distraction. The new material consists of little more than tiny canapés of studio noise, false starts and run-downs, but there are previously undiscovered or unreleased takes of 'Leap Frog' and 'Relaxin' With Lee', tunes Parker is said to have composed spontaneously when it was discovered that he had forgotten to bring sheets with him. 'Ballade', apparently recorded for use in a film by Gjon Mili, partners Bird with Coleman Hawkins, their only known studio recordings together.

The most substantial single item uncovered by Phil Schaap in his painstaking trawl through the vaults is an acceptable master of Chico O'Farrill's 'Afro-Cuban Jazz Suite', recorded in December 1950 with Machito. Less adept at Latin rhythms than Dizzy Gillespie, Parker had nevertheless experimented with 'south of the border' sessions (there's a fine 1952 session with Benny Harris, co-composer of 'Ornithology') and solos with great flourish on the 17-minute 'Suite'.

There are more Latin numbers on disc 6, which encapsulates Parker's finest studio performances for Granz. It covers three sessions recorded in January, March and August 1951. The earliest, with Miles, Walter Bishop Jr, Teddy Kotick and Max Roach, featured the classic original 'Au Privave', 'She Rote', 'K. C. Blues', and 'Star Eyes'. The 'Au Privave' solos (two takes) are rapid-fire, joyous Bird, deliberately contrasting with Miles's soft touch; on the alternative, Parker really pushes the boat out and Miles cheekily responds with mimicry of the last couple of bars. The tune is now an influential bebop staple, but it was originally issued as the B-side to 'Star Eyes' which, like the later 'My Little Suede Shoes', recorded in March with a Latin beat, enjoyed enormous success as a single. The August sessions featured a racially integrated line-up fronted by Parker and the young white trumpeter, Red Rodney, whose fiery playing reflected his nickname and hair coloration much more than it did his race, which presented a problem to some 'authenticity'-obsessed critics. The most poignant moment is a re-run, played at first with great correctness but with a bubbling eagerness coming up from underneath, of 'Lover Man', which had been the on-mike flashpoint of Parker's disastrous collapse in 1946. It is said that Bird was upset that the Dial performance was ever released; five years later, he gets his own back with an airy, problem-free reading (he even anticipates his own entry) and a snook-cocking 'Country Gardens' coda, a device Parker used frequently but which he intended here to be deflationary.

Swedish Schnapps (which covers the original LP of that name, the wonderful January 'Au Privave' sessions, and three alternatives from the May 1949 sessions with Kenny Dorham) has been available as a separate CD (Verve 849 393 CD) and is an ideal second-hand purchase for anyone not yet ready or not well-enough funded for the kitchen-sink approach of the 10-CD set.

The small-group material thins after this point. There is a good December 1952/January 1953 quartet recording ('The Song Is You', 'Laird Baird', 'Cosmic Rays', 'Kim') with Jones, Kotick and Roach, and two late flourishes from an increasingly erratic Parker in July 1953 and March and December 1954. The latter sessions, which were to be the last studio recordings of his life, were devoted to Cole Porter themes. Parker plays much more within the beat than previously and, but for a near perfection of tone, some of these later performances could safely be relegated. Schaap has found a long alternative of 'Love For Sale', however, which suggests how thoroughly Parker could still rethink his own strategies. It also conveniently brings the whole extraordinary package full circle.

Bird will already have superseded the eight-volume vinyl *Definitive Charlie Parker* in most serious collections. The most important additional material, apart from a couple of genuinely valuable alternatives and the restored 'Afro-Cuban Jazz Suite', is a substantial amount of live performance recorded under the umbrella of Granz's JATP. The earliest item in the collection is a live jam from January 1946 at which Parker encountered (and, on 'Lady Be Good', totally wiped out) his great role-model, Lester Young, then already in his post-war doldrums. The two men met once again at Carnegie Hall in 1949, but it's the earlier encounter that conveys the drama of Bird's precarious grasp on the highest perch. Absent at the beginning of the performance, he comes onstage to thunderous applause and tosses something on to Bud Powell's piano strings, creating a weird jangle. It may be his reed guard, but Phil Schaap suggests (rather improbably, one would have thought) that it was a hypodermic and spoon. The beauty of the 1946 concert lies in its spontaneity. The later, June 1952, 'alto summit' with Johnny Hodges and the veteran Benny Carter is by contrast rather stilted, with an 'after you' succession of solo appearances. (Oscar Peterson, being groomed for stardom by Granz, is also present.)

Pricey and perhaps a little overcooked for non-specialists, *Bird* is nevertheless a model of discographical punctiliousness. The sound is excellent, the notes detailed and fascinating (often backed by anecdotal material from interviews Schaap has conducted with surviving participants) and the packaging very attractive. Less committed collectors would do well to look around for a copy of *Swedish Schnapps*.

****   **Bird At The Roost: Volume 1** Savoy/Vogue 650124 CD
Parker; Miles Davis (*t*); Tadd Dameron (*p*); Curley Russell (*b*); Max Roach (*d*). 9 & 12/48.

****   **Bird At The Roost: Volume 2** Savoy/Vogue 650125 CD
Parker; Conte Candoli, Kenny Dorham (*t*); Bennie Green (*tb*); Flip Phillips, Lucky Thompson, Charlie Ventura (*ts*); Al Haig (*p*); Shelly Manne, Tommy Potter (*b*); Max Roach, Ed Shaughnessy (*d*). 2 & 3/49.

****   **Bird At The Roost: Volume 3** Savoy/Vogue 650126 CD
Parker; Fats Navarro (*t*); Bud Powell (*p*); Tommy Potter (*b*); Roy Haynes (*d*). 5/50.

****   **Bird At The Roost: Volume 4** Savoy/Vogue 650127 CD
Parker; Kenny Dorham (*t*); Lucky Thompson (*ts*); Al Haig (*p*); Milt Jackson (*vib*); Tommy Potter (*b*); Max Roach (*d*); Dave Lambert, Buddy Stewart (*v*). 3/49.

Anyone in possession of the Savoys, Dials, Verves, the Dean Benedetti collection (if they can afford it) and the Royal Roost recordings can reasonably feel they have a purchase on the major outcrops of Parker's career. Of the very many live sessions and airshots in circulation, only these should be considered absolutely essential. These CD reissues mark one significant advance over earlier vinyl issues in reducing to a minimum the announcements of 'Symphony Sid' Torin, who always manages to sound like an alternative comedian mimicking an American radio presenter. This may have the negative effect of spoiling the 'live atmosphere' of the LPs; atmospherics, though, represent a serious problem on vinyl, and the CDs deliver the music in a much cleaner signal, if a little sharply in places.

There are moments when Parker is very nearly eclipsed by Fats Navarro, whose death was not far away when they recorded the astounding 'Street Beat' (one of a couple of less familiar numbers) in May 1950. Somebody calls out, 'Blow, Girl!' (Navarro's unkind nickname was 'Fat Girl') as he puts together possibly the finest and most completely balanced solo of his career. Elsewhere, he is superb on 'Cool Blues' and an even later 'Ornithology'. Dorham is much less convincing and sounds very jaded indeed in places on the early 1949 sessions (though a rocky sound-balance doesn't favour his middle-register work, which is subtler than first appears), tending to play formulaically and in rather staccato, predetermined bites. At this period Miles Davis plays very much more consistently in club situations than under the stop–start discipline of the recording studio.

Parker, of course, is sublime. He even manages to make something extraordinary out of 'White Christmas', a tongue-in-cheek concession to the calendar on the 25 December 1948 set. His career was powerfully in the ascendant at this point, whatever 'personal problems' skulked around the edges; the recording ban was lifted and the substantial backing he was getting from Norman Granz allowed to think ever more expansively. In a club context, too, he was able to freewheel in a way that wasn't possible in the studio and, though few of the individual performances are very long (the norm is still three to five minutes, perhaps a concession to commercial times), there is a palpable sense of relaxation about his playing that comes through even on these rather one-dimensional recordings.

****   **The Quintet/Jazz At Massey Hall** Original Jazz Classics OJC 044 CD/LP/MC

aka

[***(*)   **The Greatest Jazz Concert Ever** Prestige P 24024 MC]
Parker; Dizzy Gillespie (*t*); Bud Powell (*p*); Charles Mingus (*b*); Max Roach (*d*). 5/53.

Perhaps the most hyped jazz concert ever, to an extent that the actuality is almost inevitably something of a disappointment. Originally released on Debut (a musician-run label started by Mingus and Roach), the sound, taken from Mingus's own tape-recording, is rather poor and the bassist subsequently had to overdub his part. However, Parker (playing a plastic saxophone and billed on the Debut release as 'Charlie Chan' to avoid contractual problems with Mercury, Norman Granz's parent company) and Gillespie are both at the peak of their powers. They may even have fed off the conflict that had developed between them, for their interchanges on the opening 'Perdido' crackle with controlled aggression, like two middleweights checking each other out in the first round. There is a story that they didn't want to go on stage, preferring to sulk in front of a televised big game in the dressing room. Parker's solo on 'Hot House', three-quarters of the way through the set, is a masterpiece of containment and release, like his work on 'A Night In Tunisia' (introduced by the saxophonist in rather weird French, in deference to the Canadian – but the wrong city, surely? – audience). Perhaps because the game was showing, or perhaps just because Toronto wasn't hip to bebop, the house was by no means full, but it's clear that those who were there sensed something exceptional was happening.

Powell and Roach are the star turns on 'Wee'. The pianist builds a marvellous solo out of Dameron's chords and Roach holds the whole thing together with a performance that almost matches the melodic and rhythmic enterprise of the front men. The Massey Hall concert is a remarkable experience, not to be missed. (A cassette version of the full concert, with Bud Powell's trio set, is still advertised.)

***(*) **The Band That Never Was** Spotlite SPJ 141 LP
Parker; Miles Davis (*t*); Duke Jordan (*p*); Tommy Potter (*b*); Max Roach (*d*). 3/48.

***(*) **Bird On 52nd Street** Original Jazz Classics OJC 114 LP
As above. 7/48.

These New York City performances (from The Three Deuces and The Onyx respectively) are miniaturized on the Dean Benedetti set, but they gain immeasurably from being heard in full context, for Parker was always trying to reorganize the overall sound of the conventional jazz group, to lend it a coherence it was apt to lose when the solo was the chief focus. Roach's polyrhythmic drumming, perhaps 20 years ahead of its appointed time, is the key here, though the recording is of such quality that one has to strain a little for the bass accents. Potter isn't treated any more generously; but the overall sound isn't bad and there is still a reasonable level of detail in the faster ensembles.

***(*) **Bird At St Nick's** Original Jazz Classics OJC 041 LP
Parker; Red Rodney (*t*); Al Haig (*p*); Tommy Potter (*b*); Roy Haynes (*d*). 2/50.

An attractively varied package of material (including 'Visa', 'What's New', 'Smoke Gets In Your Eyes' and other, more familiar themes) from a tight and very professional band who sound as if they've been together for some time. Haynes is no Max Roach, even at this period, but his count is increasingly subtle and deceptive, and he cues some of Rodney's better releases brilliantly. Worth watching out for and much more compelling than the rag-bag of material on *Bird's Eyes: Volume 1*.

***(*) **Bird's Eyes: Last Unissued – Volume 1** Philology 214 W 5 LP
Parker; Miles Davis (*t*); Walter Bishop Jr, Duke Jordan (*p*); Tommy Potter (*b*); Roy Haynes, Max Roach (*d*); Candido Camero (*perc*). 37 or 40?, 48, 11/52.

The most startling items on this collection are two unaccompanied recordings of 'Body And Soul' and 'Honeysuckle Rose', apparently made in a booth. Both are also included on Stash STCD 535, below, where they are improbably dated 1937. Philology's suggestion of May 1940 seems much more realistic. Parker had recently heard Art Tatum playing in New York City and had experienced the much-discussed epiphany while playing 'Cherokee', which led him to improvise on the higher intervals of the chord. Though the voice on these crude recordings is still unmistakably Parker's, the music (a fairly basic set of harmonic variations) is still unsophisticated and rhythmically unenterprising; of course solo performance was not the norm, and it's unrealistic to expect more from what was probably a very casual self-documentation.

The 1948 live material with the great quintet is well up to scratch, with Miles producing some distinctively fragile solos and Roach, when he is clearly audible, steadily elaborating the rhythmic vocabulary he had limned on the Dial sessions. The later Parker With Strings tracks (two takes of 'Just Friends' and a theme) are pretty forgettable.

***(*) **Bird's Eyes: Last Unissued – Volume 2** Philology 214 W 12 LP
Parker; Red Rodney (*t*); Al Haig (*p*); Tommy Potter (*b*); Max Roach (*d*). 11/49.

***(*) **Bird's Eyes: Last Unissued – Volume 3** Philology 215 W 15 LP
As above.

Something of a rag-bag of long and short edits. Rodney had joined Parker only rather diffidently, uncertain of his own abilities. He was frequently ill during their earlier association but allowed himself to become addicted to narcotics (perhaps in a misguided gesture of identification). There's a degree of strain in these early sets that is much less evident on the Jazz Anthology and *At St Nick's* sessions, below and above.

***(*) **'Bird' Charlie Parker** Forlane UCD 19009 CD
Parker; Dizzy Gillespie, Fats Navarro, Red Rodney (*t*); Al Haig, Bud Powell (*p*); Tommy Potter (*b*); Roy Haynes, Max Roach (*d*). 12/49, 5/50, 3/51.

*** **Live At Carnegie Hall** Bandstand BD 1518 CD/LP
As above; also Walter Bishop Jr (*p*); Walter Yost (*b*); Candido Camero (*perc*); woodwinds; strings. 12/49, 11/52.

The sleeve omits personnel for the first five (1949) items, but these feature concert performances (presumably not continuous, given the variation in sound from 'Ornithology' to 'Cheryl') featuring Rodney, Haig, Potter and Haynes. Parker's skiddling solo on 'Ko-Ko' and his varied opening to 'Bird Of Paradise' are worth the price on their own, but there are plenty of good things from the later sessions with Navarro (from the Royal Roost period) and Gillespie. The discographical documentation is untrustworthy (Haynes and Blakey seem to be transposed) but the music is excellent and the stereo reprocessing acceptably unobtrusive and natural.

The 1949 materials are also available on the Bandstand with a Parker With Strings concert from 1952. Nothing to write home about on the latter count, and the Forlane seems a better bet in every respect.

*** **More Unissued: Volume 1** Royal RJD 505 CD
Parker; Charlie Walp (*t*); Bill Harris, Earl Swope, George Swope (*tb*); Buddy DeFranco (*cl*); Teddy Edwards, Zoot Sims (*ts*); Dick Cary, Bill Shanahan, Lennie Tristano, Teddy Wilson (*p*); Mert Oliver, Eddie Safranski (*b*); Roy Haynes, Don Lamond, Lawrence Marable (*d*); Kenny Clarke (*brushes*); other personnel unidentified. 8/51, 3 & 10/52.

***(*) **More Unissued: Volume 2** Royal RJD 506 CD
Parker; Tony Fruscella, Red Rodney (*t*); Kenny Drew (*p*); Curley Russell (*b*); Art Blakey (*d*); other personnel unidentified. 12/50, 53.

Useful but not essential back-up documentation. Volume 1 includes some rehearsal tracks with Tristano and Clarke (who brushes the rhythm on a telephone book), an intriguing 'Cool Blues' with Teddy Wilson, an All Stars session with the tromboning Swopes, and an odd session under Jerry Jerome's leadership and including Bill Harris and Buddy DeFranco on 'Ornithology'. Volume 2 is a little more valid, with some good Red Rodney tracks from New York which also feature a surprisingly familiar-sounding Kenny Drew. Sound-quality is very intermittent, and these are really only for quite serious students.

*** **Rare Bird** Recording Arts Reference Edition RARECD 04/05 2CD
Parker; Kenny Dorham, Dizzy Gillespie, Fats Navarro, Herbie Williams (*t*); Wardell Gray, Frank Socolow, Lucky Thompson (*ts*); Walter Bishop, Rollins Griffith, Al Haig, Dick Hyman, John Lewis, Bud Powell (*p*); Sandy Block, Teddy Kotick, Al McKibbon, Tommy Potter, Curly Russell, Jimmy Woode (*b*); Art Blakey, Kenny Clarke, Marquis Foster, Joe Harris, Roy Haynes, Max Roach, Charlie Smith (*d*); Chubby Newsome (*v*); strings; other personnel unidentified. 9/47–1/54.

Some of this material has been around before. Four airshots from a Carnegie Hall concert on 29 September 1947 were released on a Columbia (Europe) release called *Portrait* (issued on the Roost label in the USA). Technically, they're of intermittent quality and the bassist and drummer are painfully amateur, but Parker's solos on 'A Night In Tunisia', 'Confirmation' and a version of 'Ko-Ko' not included on *Portrait* provide an excellent study of the way Parker continued to rethink not only his own solos but also the overall configuration of a tune (on which he presumably exercised final say-so). His introductory break on 'A Night In Tunisia' is exceptional: fleet, distinct and, once again, utterly logical.

Not all the material reaches this standard. A traditional 'Mambo' and 'Lament For The Congo', recorded at Birdland or the Renaissance Ballroom with an unidentified Afro-Cuban band, is largely of curiosity value, though Parker typically manages to find something of substance to say. Among the later material is a version of Gerry Mulligan's 'Rocker' (recorded nine days after the Verve studio version of 17 September 1950) featuring oboe (Tommy Mace again?) and unidentified string players; there's also a broadcast 'Easy To Love' featuring the popular formula of Parker and strings. There are good versions of 'Scrapple From The Apple' from New York in April 1951 and of 'Hot House', lifted from the soundtrack of a Channel 5 (NY) television broadcast of March 1952 and the only known film of Parker in action. There are also two reasonable performances ('Star Eyes' and 'Moose The Mooche'/'Lullaby Of Birdland') in 1953; but bebop enthusiasts will probably value the set most for the early Carnegie Hall sessions and for the five tracks recorded (like the two immediately above) at Birdland, but rather earlier, at the end of June 1950. Undistinguished in sound-quality (which is ropey even by contemporary airshot standards), these stand out as records of Fats Navarro's last public appearance before his death on 7 July. Though there's nothing on 'Round Midnight', 'Out Of Nowhere', 'Little Willie Leaps', 'Ornithology' or 'Embraceable You' to match the trumpeter's astonishing performances a month earlier at the Royal Roost (q.v.), he sounds in excellent voice and coaxes some vibrant playing out of Parker as they exchange rapid-fire fours.

Probably only seasoned ornithologists will have the stamina to probe the fuzz of surface noise and radio atmospherics on these 25 cuts, valuable as they are.

***   **Lullaby In Rhythm** Spotlite SPJ 107 LP
Parker; Melvyn Broiles, Dizzy Gillespie, Howard McGhee, Shorty Rogers (*t*); John LaPorta (*cl*); Russ Freeman, Hampton Hawes, Lennie Tristano (*p*); Billy Bauer (*g*); Ray Brown, Addison Farmer, Arnold Fishkind (*b*); Jimmy Pratt, Roy Porter, Max Roach (*d*). 2, 3 & 9/47.

[****   **The Great Sessions, 1947/8** Jazz Anthology 550082 CD]
Parker; Fats Navarro, Red Rodney (*t*); John LaPorta (*cl*); Allen Eager (*ts*); Al Haig, Lennie Tristano (*p*); Billy Bauer (*g*); Tommy Potter (*b*); Roy Haynes, Buddy Rich (*d*). 11/47, 12/49.

In September 1947, Barry Ulanov organized a radio 'duel' between representatives of the Dixieland and bop tendencies in jazz. Boxing out of the red corner opposite a band made up of Wild Bill Davison, Edmond Hall, Jimmy Archey, Ralph Sutton, Danny Barker, Pops Foster and Baby Dodds (who are not represented on this Spotlite release), Parker's beboppers ran through highly convincing readings of 'Ko-Ko', 'Hot House' and 'Fine And Dandy' (with a truncated band also playing 'I Surrender Dear'). LaPorta's contributions are almost as involving as Bird's in places, and the interplay on 'Hot House' is particularly interesting, with a much fuller acompaniment than he often enjoyed. The second round, recorded at Mutual a week later, was better still. 'On The Sunny Side Of The Street', 'How Deep Is The Ocean' and 'Tiger Rag' draw fierce, hooking solos from both Bird and Dizzy; the last piece is of considerable historical importance in the argument over bebop's place in the continuum (or was bop a sudden fracture?) of jazz.

The Jazz Anthology compilation includes further sides ('Groovin' High', 'Donna Lee', 'Fats Flats') with Tristano and Bauer from a return bout that was broadcast on 8 November 1947; there are also four good (but apparently misdated) tracks with Red Rodney, including a fizzing 'Ornithology' and some additional Lennie Tristano material, with Sarah Vaughan as guesting vocalist.

Of the other items on the Spotlite, 'Lullaby In Rhythm' was part of the first session Parker played after his release from Camarillo State Hospital and is included (for what it's worth) on the Stash Dial compilation, above. The sound is extremely poor and only Bird is properly audible. If that balance of emphasis smacks of Dean Benedetti, the last two items ('Dee Dee's Dance', parts 1 and 2) were taken from a Benedetti recording (but, again, *not* a wire recording) at the Hi-De-Ho in Los Angeles in March 1947. These are unusual in that they do include solo work by Howard McGhee and Hampton Hawes as well.

There is a good deal of live Parker material on Spotlite, and collectors may like to track down SPJ 108 (with Navarro, Gray, Eager – 1948), SPJ 118 (in Paris with Bechet and Hot Lips Page – 1949, see below), SPJ 120 (early material with Jay McShann (*q. v.*)), SPJ 123 (with Miles and Joe Albany – 1946), and SPJ 138 (with Machito, McGhee, Milt Jackson – 1948). Swedish material from 1950 is considered below.

***(*)   **Bird In Sweden** Spotlite SPJ 124/125 2LP
Parker; Rolf Ericson, Rowland Greenberg (*t*); Lennart Nilsson, Gosta Theselius (*ts, p*); Thore Jederby (*b*); Jack Noren (*d*). 1/50.

Record of a hectic week during Parker's second visit to Europe. He had had great success at the Paris Jazz Festival the previous year and was revered in Scandinavia, where bebop took deep and lasting root. A measure of that is the quality of the local musicians, who more than hold their own (Rolf Ericson, of course, acquired a substantial American reputation later in his career). Though Parker also played in Stockholm and Gothenburg, the materials are taken from sets in the southern towns of Hälsingborg and Malmö, plus a remarkable restaurant jam session at an unknown location. This last yielded the most notable single track, a long version of 'Body And Soul', more usually a tenor saxophonist's shibboleth but given a reading of great composure. This item was previously known in an edited form (which dispensed with solos by Theselius, who plays piano on the other selections, and Greenberg); but the restored version is very much more impressive, again by virtue of relocating Parker's improvisation in the wider context of a group performance.

The remaining material is pretty much a 'greatest hits' package with two versions each of 'Anthropology' and 'Cool Blues'. Worthwhile, but not essential.

****   Charlie Parker At Storyville Blue Note BT 85103 CD/LP
Parker; Herb Pomeroy (t); Red Garland, Sir Charles Thompson (p); Bernie Griggs, Jimmy Woode (b); Kenny Clarke, Roy Haynes (d). 3/53, 9/53.

First released in 1985, these Boston club dates are the only Parker performances on Blue Note. The tapes, made on a Rube Goldberg home-made system by John Fitch (aka John McLellan, the compère), have been magically reprocessed by Jack Towers and are among the most faithful live recordings of Parker from the period. Of the performances, it is necessary only to say that Parker is magisterial. Pomeroy strives manfully but seems to be caught more than once in awkward whole-note progressions which start well but then lapse back into cliché. Local bassist Griggs (who appears again on Stash's compilation of rarities, below) chugs along manfully on the March sessions, but Roy Haynes is a heavy-handed disappointment. The September quintets are generally less enterprising, and there are even signs that Parker may be repeating himself. In an interview recorded in June of the same year, McLellan pointed to an increasingly noticeable tendency for Parker to play old and established compositions. By the turn of the 1950s, the flow of new variations on the basic blues or on standards had virtually dried up. Despite that, Parker's ability to find new things to say on tunes as well-worn as 'Moose The Mooche', 'Ornithology' and 'Out Of Nowhere' (March) or 'Now's The Time', 'Cool Blues' and 'Groovin' High' (September) is completely impressive. The addition of relatively unfamiliar pieces like 'I'll Walk Alone' and 'Dancing On The Ceiling' contributes to a highly attractive set.

The McLellan interview concludes with one of Parker's most quoted articles of faith: 'You can never tell what you'll be thinking tomorrow. But I can definitely say that music won't stop. It will continue to go forward.'

***(*)   The Complete Birth Of The Bebop; Bird On Tenor, 1943 Stash STCD 535 CD
Parker; Chet Baker, Miles Davis, Billy Eckstine, Dizzy Gillespie (t); Jimmy Rowles, Hazel Scott (p); Milt Jackson (vib); Red Callender, Oscar Pettiford, Carson Smith (b); Hurley Ramey, Efferge Ware (g); Roy Haynes, Shelly Manne, Harold Doc West (d); Bob Redcross (brushes); Benny Goodman Trio and Quartet on record; other personnel unidentified. 5/40, 9/42, 2/43, 12/45, ?50, 11/53.

(***(*))   The Bird You Never Heard Stash ST-280 CD/LP/MC
Parker; Herb Pomeroy, Bud Powell (p); Charlie Mingus (b); Art Taylor (d); Candido Camero (perc); other personnel unidentified. 8/50.

(***(*))   Rara Avis/Rare Bird Stash ST-CD-21 CD
Parker; Miles Davis, Max Kaminsky, Herb Pomeroy, Shorty Sherrock (t); Will Bradley, Kai Winding (tb); Joe Marsala, Sidney Bechet (ss); Joe Bushkin, Mike Caluccio, Dean Erle, Joe Sullivan (p); Bernie Griggs, Chubby Jackson (b); Specs Powell, Max Roach, George Wettling (d); Ann Hathaway (v); other personnel unidentified. 2/49, 3/52, 54.

Barrel-scrapings, perhaps, but with Parker there was valid music to record every time he put a reed between his lips. Among the earliest items on *Birth Of The Bebop* are two examples of Bird's rare use of tenor saxophone; his only 'official' tenor recording was on a Miles Davis Prestige date, where he appeared as 'Charlie Chan' for contractual reasons. The first is a jammed 'Sweet Georgia Brown' with Dizzy Gillespie and Oscar Pettiford, the second a fascinating hotel-room recording with Gillespie and Billy Eckstine on trumpets and the rhythm shuffled out on a suitcase lid. Of the remaining material, by far the most interesting are the solo 'Body And Soul' and 'Honeysuckle Rose' (which Stash date from May 1940), two sets of duos with guitarists Ware (Bird on alto) and Hurley Ramey (tenor), and remarkable recordings of Parker improvising over Benny Goodman 78s of 'Avalon' and 'China Boy'. The original LP included tracks from 1953 with the 24-year-old Chet Baker on 'Ornithology', 'Barbados' and 'Cool Blues', but this has not been carried over.

The remaining Stashes are marred by very poor airshot sound and, in the case of *Rara Avis*, an excess of stilted badinage. Parker's *Dumont Centre Stage* appearance (see 'Hot House' on the item above) is the only surviving television performance; however, Parker appeared frequently on New York local stations in the early 1950s, and several soundtracks have been preserved. Performances are much briefer than equivalent club or concert versions, presumably to accommodate commercial slots, and the material is something of a mish-mash. There is, though, an interesting 1949 'I Can't Get Started' and a blues jam which features Sidney Bechet. The two saxophonists shared a booking agency at the time and played a number of gigs together in the first months of 1949. Parker was on the WPIX show to receive a *Down Beat* poll winner's plaque from the critic and jazz promoter Charles Delaunay (this is implicit in the Frenchman's comments in the intro to 'Now's The Time' but oddly is not mentioned in the liner-notes). Brief and noisy as it is, the encounter is of considerable historical interest, more so than a rather contrived 'Bop Vs Dixieland' 'bout' organized by WCBS in March 1952, as part of its *Adventures in Jazz* programme. (This was similar to Barry Ulanov's September 1947 experiment, referred to apropos *Lullaby In Rhythm*, above.) Parker's two solos on another truncated 'Blues Jam' are head and shoulders above anyone else on the bill, and the result has to be considered a TKO for the boppers.

There's nothing quite so unusual on *The Bird You Never Heard*. Sound-quality is the poorest of the three overall, but the performances are all first class. Four tunes ('Ornithology', 'Out Of Nowhere', 'My Funny Valentine', 'Cool Blues') come from Parker's January 1954 residency at the Hi-Hat in Boston, presumably the same sessions which appear undated but fully attributed on *Rara Avis* (local trumpeter Pomeroy figures on the Blue Note *At Storyville*, see above, from the previous year, and obviously enjoyed Parker's confidence).

The anonymous author of the liner-notes offers an interesting sidelight on Parker's behaviour during such performances, pointing to his joshing and 'kvelling' with MCs and implying that the image of Bird as a lonely genius who refused to don motley and clown for his audience is not borne out by the recorded facts. A point to ponder.

ERROL PARKER (born 1930)
DRUMS, PIANO

** **Compelling Forces** Cadence CJR 1043 LP
Parker (*p* solo). 85.

*** **A Night In Tunisia** Sahara 1015 CD
Parker; Philip Harper, Michael Thomas (*t*); Tyrone Jefferson (*tb*); Doug Harris (*ss*); Donald Harrison (*as*); Bill Saxton (*ts*); Patience Higgins (*bs*); Cary De Nigris (*g*); Reggie Washington (*b*). 4/91.

Parker has had a rather extraordinary career, often as a drummer, which he became after many years as a pianist. But he's seldom had the opportunity to record. His own label Sahara Records has released some of his ensemble records, but until recently the only accessible disc was this solo piano set made for the American Cadence company. His style sets deliberately simple left-hand lines against wandering, bitonal fantasies conjured up by the right. It's curious and hard to classify and not very rewarding.

The recent CD on Sahara is much more involving. Parker's 'A Night In Tunisia' is dramatically different to almost any other version: he breaks down both the melody and the rhythm (his drumming uses a modified kit where the snare is replaced by a conga and there are more tom toms and fewer cymbals in use) to make it more like a bouncing, dishevelled fantasy on the original theme. Since Parker is Algerian-born, it scarcely be a more authentic recreation, though. Originals such as 'Daydream At Noon' and 'The Rai' move to rhythms and grooves unfamiliar to the contemporary mainstream, most of them drawn from Parker's African background, and it places a compelling new context on the otherwise familiar solos of Harrison, Harper and Jefferson. The unglamorous sound, with the drums mixed right at the front, will knock out its appeal for many, but in a way this rough-and-ready mix suits what is a deliberately non-conformist session from a leader who deserves respect and attention.

EVAN PARKER (born 1944)
SOPRANO SAXOPHONE, TENOR SAXOPHONE

***(*)   **Incision** FMP SAJ 35 LP
      Parker; Barry Guy (*b*). 3/81.

****   **Atlanta** Impulse IMP 18617 CD/LP
      Parker; Barry Guy (*b*); Paul Lytton (*d, perc*). 12/86.

***   **Hall Of Mirrors** MM&T 01 CD
      Parker; Walter Prati (*elec*). 2/90.

***   **Process And Reality** FMP CD 37 CD
      Parker (*ts, ss solo and with multitracking*). 91.

There's a certain irony in the fact that Evan Parker, now almost universally acknowledged as one of the finest and most virtuosic instrumentalists working in improvised music today, should at one crucial stage in his career have been associated with an improvisational attitude that rejected instrumentalism altogether. In the late 1960s, improvisers became concerned that 'the instrument' (with its apparently repertoire of pitches and timbres) had become too narrow and restrictive a conduit for the kind of free-flowing, spontaneous music they were concerned to create. The alternative was to create sound-sources (inevitably, most of them were percussive) for the nonce, never allowing them or their users the comfort of 'technique'. Enthusiasts for improvised music (and its detractors, who had always suspected something of the sort) became used to seeing the kitchen cupboard and toolshed raided for sound-producing objects – bicycle pumps, pot lids, squeaking hinges, off-station radios – which were untouched by the formal, canonical, hierarchical properties associated with concert instruments.

Since the early 1970s, Parker's work has been a sustained rejection of that approach. Taking what is admittedly still a *parvenu*, perhaps the only genuinely new musical instrument of the last 150 years, Parker has vastly increased its potential range. By means of circular breathing (a technique which allows a wind player to inhale while maintaining air pressure on the reed), he is able to improvise uninterrupted for astonishingly long periods. So rapid and constant is his articulation that sceptical listeners have been moved to suggest that some of his purportedly solo recordings 'must' be the result of overdubbing; it was more than a little ironic when, on *Process And Reality*, he did just that.

In addition to eliminating the need to improvise in breath-groups, Parker has confronted the treacherous pitching of the soprano saxophone as a positive resource to be exploited rather than a technical difficulty to be overcome. Parker has created a unique repertoire of multiphonic effects and split notes which allows him to make progressive microtonal adjustments to a melodic cell. The effect of his music is of organic change over considerable durations. Though his music is now almost wholly abstract, it is clear that among its fundamental inspirations are the immensely long para-harmonic improvisations created by John Coltrane during his final years (see, for instance, *Live In Japan*, Impulse! GRP 4102-2 4CD) and Parker's tenor saxophone playing is still often reminiscent of Coltrane's intent examination of 'wrong' or 'ugly' notes. Though not a single-minded soprano specialist like Steve Lacy (another profound influence and the man who inspired Coltrane to try the straight horn), the soprano has become Parker's more effective and distinctive horn.

Unfortunately, the Parker discography is currently rather attenuated. His remarkable solo works for Incus (the improvised music label he co-founded with Derek Bailey and Tony Oxley in 1970) are no longer available. A limited edition box which includes masterworks like *Monoceros* and *The Snake Decides* sold out rapidly (and no one in his right mind is going to trade it in second-hand). The FMP duo with Guy will disappear as vinyl stocks decline, but is worth catching up with now. The title is a fair representation of the music. Lesser musicians might have turned six 'Incisions' into the aural equivalent of a slash movie, but Parker and Guy play with an exploratory exactness that is as tensely compelling as surgery.

The partnership is revived on *Atlanta*, a much more open and accessible performance that heralds an unprecedented user-friendliness in Parker's work. Where previously he might have entered at an absurd altitude and pace and continued from there, perhaps alienating as many unprepared listeners as impressing converts, here he seems content to build up the level of energy and complexity of interplay more slowly, approaching the summit from foothills mapped and contoured by the free jazz movement of the late 1960s and early '70s rather than simply overflying. Lytton's contribution can't be underestimated; he is one of Europe's most inventive percussionists, and a master in this context.

Hall Of Mirrors and *Process And Reality* might almost have swapped titles. It's the solo multi-tracked album that suggests the *mise-en-abîme* effects of a mirror gallery, while Walter Prati's delicate acoustic environments perform a function closer to West Coast composer Morton Subotnick's electronic 'ghost scores', suggesting a numinous significance lying underneath Parker's surprisingly vocalized lines. The pieces on *Process And Reality* are much briefer (there are 16 of them) and melodically coherent than has been typical of his work. 'Diary Of A Mnemonist' (inspired by Luria?) is perhaps the most reachable and humane thing Parker has yet to commit to record. As such, it stands at an opposite pole to the remarkable duos with Lacy on *Chirps* (FMP SAJ 53 LP), which are the ten-minute egg of hard-boiled abstraction and a tough breakfast for the uninitiated.

KIM PARKER (born 1953)
VOCAL

**   **Havin' Myself A Time** Soul Note SN 1033 LP
       Parker; Kenny Drew (*p*); Mads Vinding (*b*); Ed Thigpen (*d*). 11/81.

(*)   **Good Girl Soul Note 1063 LP
       Parker; Tommy Flanagan (*p*); Jesper Lundgaard (*b*); Ed Thigpen (*d*). 4/82.

**   **Sometimes I'm Blue** Soul Note SN 1133 CD/LP
       Parker; Mal Waldron (*p*); Isla Eckinger (*b*); Ed Thigpen (*d*). 5/85.

Parker, who is Chan Parker's daughter, is a sensitive singer, but there is little in these records to impress listeners who seek something more than a light, jazz-flavoured recital of familiar standards, although she picks a few more interesting themes – 'Azure', 'Star-Crossed Lovers', 'Fiesta In Blue' – as well. Of the three central accompanists, the masterful Flanagan is easily the most engaging, and the material on *Good Girl* is perhaps the most interesting too, with the wistful 'Hooray' a standout. Since she doesn't have a big voice, the slightly mixed-down vocals add to an impression of reticence.

LEO PARKER (1925–62)
BARITONE SAXOPHONE

***(*)   **Let Me Tell You 'Bout It** Blue Note CDP 784087 CD
       Parker; John Burks (*t*); Bill Swindell (*ts*); Yusef Salim (*p*); Stan Conover (*b*); Purnell
       Rice (*d*). 60.

Like Zeppo Marx, Leo is the saxophone-playing Parker whom people tend to forget. Like Zeppo, too, he quit the scene early, dying of a heart attack aged only 37. His best-known recordings were with Fats Navarro and Illinois Jacquet, having switched under Billy Eckstine from alto to baritone; he plays both on an early Prestige compilation. Just as the Eckstine Orchestra was always known, *tout court*, as 'The Band', so Leo was 'The Kid' or 'Lad'. Though fate didn't give him much personal leeway, there's a sense in which he never entirely grew up musically either, but *Let Me Tell You 'Bout It* suggests that he had the makings of a good, uncomplicated theme-writer. Tunes – 'Blue Leo' and the title-track most obviously – are apt to open with a slow, mournful intro, followed by big, whole-note statements and steady, patient developments, underpinned by Yusef Salim's fine bluesy piano. As relative unknowns – John Burks, incidentally, isn't a *nom de session* for John Birks Gillespie, but a little-known bopper with a tight, controlled tone – the band work well, concentrating on basics. An overlong cut of 'Low Brown' was held over from the original album release with the unfulfilled intention of issuing it as a double-sided jukebox single (like Ike Quebec, co-writer of 'Blue Leo', Parker enjoyed brief success in Harlem dance-joints); it's a good performance, better than the issued version. 'The Lion's Roar' is an offcut from Parker's Blue Note follow-up, *Rollin' with Leo* [Blue Note BST 84095 LP], which was issued only posthumously in 1980 and has since disappeared again. Though by no means a giant, Parker's unpretentious jazz merits a small corner in the oversubscribed family plot.

HORACE PARLAN (born 1931)
PIANO

***(*)   **Musically Yours** Steeplechase SCS 1141 LP
            Parlan (*p* solo). 11/79.

****   **The Maestro** Steeplechase SCS 1167 LP
            As above.

Parlan's most moving single performance is arguably the unaccompanied 'Lament For Booker Ervin', posthumously tacked on to the Ervin album of that title (Enja 2054 LP). None of his other solo recordings evinces that much intensity or attention to detail. A middle-order bop pianist in a highly oversubscribed field, Parlan only catches the attention for his tough bass chords and highly restricted melody figures (an attack of infantile paralysis crabbed his right hand) which contributed substantially to *Mingus Ah Um* and accorded closely with the bassist/composer's preference for highly rhythmic and unorthodox pianists.

Parlan has developed a blues-influenced repertoire marked by a substantial inclusion of Thelonious Monk themes, heavily left-handed melodies like 'Lullaby Of The Leaves' (as on *Musically Yours*), and throbbing swingers like Randy Weston's 'Hi-Fly', which reappears throughout his recorded work. The gentler material on *Maestro* (from the same session) is less immediately impressive, revealing its depth of understanding only on subsequent hearings. The repetition of 'Ruby My Dear' is odd but useful.

***   **Arrival** Steeplechase SCS 1012 LP
            Parlan; Idrees Sulieman (*flhn*); Bent Jaedig (*ts*); Hugo Rasmussen (*b*); Ed Thigpen
            (*d*). 12/73.

***   **No Blues** Steeplechase SCS 1056 LP
            Parlan; Niels-Henning Ørsted-Pedersen (*b*); Tony Inzalaco (*d*). 12/75.

***   **Frankly Speaking** Steeplechase SCS 1076 LP
            Parlan; Frank Strozier (*as*); Frank Foster (*ts*); Lisle Atkinson (*b*); Al Harewood (*d*).
            2/77.

****   **Blue Parlan** Steeplechase SCS 1124 CD/LP
            Parlan; Wilbur Little (*b*); Dannie Richmond (*d*). 11/78.

***   **Pannonica** Enja 4076 LP
            Parlan; Reggie Johnson (*b*); Alvin Queen (*d*). 2/81.

***(*)   **Like Someone In Love** Steeplechase SCS 1178 LP
            Parlan; Jesper Lundgaard (*b*); Dannie Richmond (*d*). 3/83.

***(*)   **Glad I Found You** Steeplechase SCS 1194 CD/LP
            Parlan; Thad Jones (*flhn*); Eddie Harris (*ts*); Jesper Lundgaard (*b*); Aage Tanggaard
            (*d*). 7/84.

(*)   **Little Esther Steeplechase SCS 1145 CD/LP
            Parlan; Per Goldschmidt (*bs*); Klavs Hovman (*b*); Massimo De Majo (*d*). 3/87.

Perhaps the best of Parlan's group work was made for Blue Note in the 1960s. The best of those, *Happy Frame Of Mind*, which featured his friend Ervin, was briefly available on CD [CDP 784134 CD] but has subsequently disappeared again. The excellent 1960 sessions with the Turrentine brothers are no longer available. Like other American players of the time, facing a slackening demand for jazz recording, Parlan emigrated to Scandinavia where he has pursued a workmanlike and unspectacular career, documented by Steeplechase from *Arrival* onwards with almost redundant thoroughness. The only highspots that call for separate treatment are the fine 1978 trio with Wilbur Little and Dannie Richmond (also, of course, a Mingus man) and the much later *Glad I Found You*, where Parlan and the late Thad Jones shrug off a rather diffident setting to produce some sparkling performances. For the rest, cautious sampling is perhaps the best bet. One of the least cliché-bound of players, Parlan is still somewhat repetitive in the structuring of his solos, and he's rarely as challenging as like-minded figures such as Roland Hanna, Jaki Byard or even Duke Jordan (whose Steeplechase discography marches on to the crack of doom). Parlan's duos with Archie Shepp (*q. v.*) underline the saxophonist's considerable limitations as a standards player but are still worth checking out.

JOE PASS (born 1929)
GUITAR

****   **Virtuoso** Pablo 2310-708 CD/MC
Pass (*g* solo). 12/73.

***   **Portraits Of Duke Ellington** Pablo 2310-716 CD/LP/MC
Pass; Ray Brown (*b*); Bobby Durham (*d*). 6/74.

***(*)   **Live At Donte's** Pablo 2620-114 2LP
Pass; Jim Hughart (*b*); Frank Severino (*d*). 12/74.

***   **At The Montreux Jazz Festival 1975** Pablo 2310-752 LP/MC
Pass (*g* solo). 7/75.

***(*)   **Virtuoso No. 2** Pablo 2310-788 CD/LP/MC
Pass (*g* solo). 10/76.

***   **Virtuoso No. 3** Original Jazz Classics OJC 684 CD
Pass (*g* solo). 5–6/77.

***   **Montreux '77** Original Jazz Classics OJC 382. CD/LP/MC
Pass (*g* solo). 7/77.

(*)   **Tudo Bem! Original Jazz Classics OJC 685 CD
Pass; Don Grusin (*p*); Oscar Castro Neves (*g*); Octavio Bailly (*b*); Claudio Slon (*d*); Paulinho Da Costa (*perc*). 5/78.

***   **I Remember Charlie Parker** Original Jazz Classics OJC 602 CD/LP/MC
Pass (*g* solo). 2/79.

(*)   **Live At Long Bay Beach College Pablo 2308-239 LP/MC
Pass (*g* solo). 1/84.

**   **Whitestone** Pablo 2310-912 CD/LP/MC
Pass; Don Grusin, John Pisano (*g*); Abe Laboriel, Nathaniel West, Harvey Mason (*d*); Paulinho Da Costa (*perc*); Armando Compean (*v*). 2–3/85.

***   **University Of Akron Concert** Pablo 2308-249 CD/LP/MC
Pass (*g* solo). 85.

***   **Blues For Fred** Pablo 2310-931 CD/LP/MC
Pass (*g* solo). 2/88.

***   **One For My Baby** Pablo 2310-936 CD/LP/MC
Pass; Plas Johnson (*ts*); Gerald Wiggins (*p, org*); Andrew Simpkins (*b*); Albert 'Tootie' Heath (*d*). 4/88.

***   **Summer Night** Pablo 2310-939 CD/LP/MC
Pass; John Pisano (*g*); Jim Hughart (*b*); Colin Bailey (*d*). 12/89.

***   **Appassionato** Pablo 2310-946 CD/MC
Pass; Jim Hughart (*b*); Colin Bailey (*d*).

Taste, refinement and an unflappable rhythmic poise are the hallmarks of a style which has made Joe Pass the benchmark player for mainstream jazz guitar. Pass smoothes away the nervousness of bop yet counters the plain talk of swing with a complexity that remains completely accessible. An improvisation on a standard may range far and wide, but there's no sense of him going into territory which he doesn't already know well. There's nothing hidden in his music, everything is absolutely on display, and he cherishes good tunes without sanctifying them. His tone isn't distinctive but it is reliably mellifluous, and he can make every note in a melody shine. Compared with Tal Farlow or Jimmy Raney, Pass takes few risks and sets himself fewer genuine challenges, but any guitarist will recognize a performer who has a total command over the instrument. His career went through a muddled phase in the 1960s – he first recorded as a member of a Synanon Rehabilitation Centre house band – but the string of albums he made for Pacific Jazz during the decade are all currently out of general circulation. On signing for Pablo in the 1970s, Pass effectively became the house guitarist, and a steady flow of albums under his own name has been supplemented by many guest appearances with Oscar Peterson, Milt Jackson and the rest of the company stable.

One could complain that Pass has made too many records, but even taking a few deletions into account it only amounts to about one a year under his own name. The problem is more that his favourite context tends to be quiet, reflective and insufficiently various to make one want to own more than one or two of them. *Virtuoso*, his debut for Pablo, remains the obvious place to start: at a time when traditional jazz guitar playing was being sidelined by the gradual onset of fusion, this seemed to reaffirm the deathless virtues of the straight-ahead instrument, and Pass has never sounded sharper or warmer on a set of standards, played with all the expertise which the title suggests. The three subsequent volumes (number four is deleted) are replays with lightly diminishing returns. Concert situations don't seem to affect Pass's concentration: he plays with the same careful diligence as he does in the studio, so the live solo albums sound much alike. *Blues For Fred* is a particularly attractive set of tunes in tribute to Fred Astaire, and although the Parker album could have been a bit more exciting than it turned out – Pass's first allegiance is certainly to bebop – it may be because it set him to work on the sort of standards which Bird covered during his Verve era, rather than bop originals. Of the trio albums, the best is certainly *Live At Donte's*, a consistently exhilarating two-LP set which unfortunately has yet to make its way to CD. From the first tune, an improbably hard-swinging reading of Melanie Kafka's 'What Have They Done To My Song', the empathy between the trio is close and dynamic. 'Darn That Dream' and 'What Are You Doing The Rest Of Your Life' find Pass at his most ineffably charming. The Ellington album with Ray Brown and Bobby Durham is a shade disappointing. *Summer Nights* is something of a tribute to Django Reinhardt, and Pass sounds contented and thoughtful, while the recent *Appassionato*, which benefits from a wider and more modern sound on CD, chooses terser material than usual – 'Grooveyard', 'Relaxin' At Camarillo', 'Nica's Dream' – and finds a cutting edge which some of Pass's records pass by. The odd records out are *One For My Baby*, which sets the guitarist up in a sort of down-home kind of roadhouse band with mixed success, although Johnson contributes a few lively solos; and the two Latin-styled albums, both of which are gently scuppered by Dave Grusin's penchant for light-music triviality, as prettily as everyone plays.

***   **The Best Of Joe Pass** Pablo 2405-419 CD/LP/MC
As Pablo albums, above.

A respectable cross-section from the Pablo albums, though almost any one of the three- or four-star recommendations above will do at least as good a job for the casual listener.

JACO PASTORIUS (1951–87)
BASS GUITAR

***(*)   **Jaco** DIW 312 CD/LP
Pastorius; Paul Bley (*p*); Pat Metheny (*g*); Bruce Ditmas (*d*). 6/74.

***   **PDB** DIW 827 CD
Pastorius; Hiram Bullock (*g, ky*); Kenwood Dennard (*d*). 2/86.

***(*)   **Punk Jazz** Big World Music BW 1001 CD
Pastorius; Jerry Gonzalez (*t, perc*); Alex Foster, Butch Thomas (*sax*); Michael Gerber (*p*); Delmar Brown (*ky*); Hiram Bullock (*g*); Kenwood Dennard (*d*).

(*)   **Honestly Jazzpoint JP 1032 CD
Pastorius (*b* solo). 3/86.

***(*)   **Live In Italy** Jazzpoint JP 1037 CD
Pastorius; Bireli Lagrene (*g*); Thomas Borocz (*d*). 3/86.

***   **Jazz Street** Timeless SJP 258 CD/LP
Pastorius; Brian Melvin (*d, perc, d prog*); Rick Smith (*sax, d prog*); Jan Davis (*p, syn*);
Paul Mousavizadeh (*g*); Keith Jones (*b*); Bill Keaney (*perc, syn*). 10 & 11/86.

It takes something extraordinary to get the public to part with hard-won cash for somewhat over an hour of solo bass guitar playing. There is absolutely no doubt that Pastorius was a remarkable player, but (to use Max Roach's valid distinction) how good a *musician* was he? The untitled improvisations on *Honestly* frequently seem no more than a Sears catalogue of exotic harmonics and effects, put together with diminishing logic and questionable taste. Needless to say, the Italian crowd shout cheer it to the echo, though they don't respond at all to an early quote from 'My Favorite Things'; but they don't rise to 'America the Beautiful' or the riff from 'Purple Haze' either, so what does that suggest about their musical expectations?

Put Pastorius in a group context, however, and he is transformed. Before his sanctification as the Hendrix of the bass guitar (followed by near-canonization when he was killed in 1987), he lent his considerable lyricism and power to Weather Report and to the ever more self-consciously jazzy Joni Mitchell; he is also increasingly recognized and covered as a composer. The quartet with Metheny and Paul Bley is pretty much how you'd expect it to sound at that vintage. Metheny's playing is articulate but not profound and a great pianist (even on an electric instrument) is lost in a sound mix that resonates in all the wrong places.

With a larger group, *Punk Jazz* is more impressive. Pastorius's wish to be considered a jazz man (albeit a punk jazz man) prompts an athletic, snappy 'Donna Lee', dedicated by Charlie Parker to the only substantial woman bassist of the bebop era (and by all accounts a very courageous one). The remainder of the set is good, hot-sauce electric jazz, surprisingly conventional when set alongside the 'punk' aesthetic of Zorn, Lindsay, Marclay and company.

PDB is considerably more subtle and tasteful than the ingredients might lead you to expect. Pastorius's lines sing and throb without any serious aspiration to lead guitar status, preferring to explore the curious hammered-on steel drum effects that have always peppered his solos. Bullock in turn plays with great restraint and considerable jazz finesse. Only Kenwood Dennard tends to mix it, blatting out coarse rock figures at inopportune moments. They do 'Dolphin Dance', but they also do 'Ode to Billy Joe', and who's to say it's any less viable? The sound is good, though Dennard might have been eased back in the mix a smidgeon. Make that a *big* smidgeon.

Live in Italy is almost the guitarist's album. In contrast to Metheny's Wes Montgomery fixation, Lagrene is in thrall to his countryman Django Reinhardt. His opening improvisaton more or less focuses the mind on what he's doing thereafter, to the virtual exclusion of a slightly subdued and acoustically recessed Pastorius. They do a creditable version of 'Satin Doll', Joe Zawinul's Weather Report theme 'Black Market' and a creditable version of Bob Marley's pop-reggae 'I Shot The Sheriff', which underlines Pastorius's childhood closesness to Caribbean music of all sorts.

Honestly is very much for specialized tastes, but the group albums should be sampled before writing Pastorius off as just another histrionic showman. A sincere and troubled artist, he was prey to alcoholism and bouts of clinical depression towards the end of his life. His death has been rewritten many times to imply a form of martyrdom; drunk and disordered, he was beaten by a club manager who had several times banned Pastorius from his premises, and died of his injuries several days later.

PAT BROTHERS

GROUP

***(*)   **The Pat Brothers** Moers Music 02052 CD/LP
Wolfgang Puschnig (*as, f, ky*); Wolfgang Mitterer (*elec*); Wolfgang Reisinger (*d*);
Linda Sharrock (*v*). 3/86.

A great, unclassifiable one-shot record. Puschnig scatters thin-toned, squealing alto and flute lines over Resinger's mixture of backbeats and looser time, but the key man in the group is Mitterer, who uses electronics and samples in an ingenious, non-stop cut-up of ideas that pinball around the sound-mix until everything seems to be spinning; yet it's a very melodic, songful, almost tender record at times. Linda Sharrock's cool, sung-spoken words only occasionally veer off into the gymnastics she once essayed with former partner Sonny, and the larger impression is of a band that combine songs, funky immediacy and improvisational flair with a far higher success rate than anything the M-Base collective have so far come up with.

JOHN PATITUCCI
BASS

* **John Patitucci** GRP 9560-2 CD
Patitucci; Michael Brecker (*ts*); John Beasley, Dave Witham, Chick Corea (*ky*); Dave Weckl, Peter Erskine, Vinnie Colaiuta (*d*); Rick Riso (*v*). 12/87.

* **On The Corner** GRP 9583-2 CD
As above, except omit Erskine, add Judd Miller (*EVI*), Eric Marienthal (*ss*), Kirk Whalum (*ts*), Paul Jackson (*g*), Al Foster, Alex Acuna (*d*). 89.

** **Sketchbook** GRP 9617-2 CD
Patitucci; Jonathan Crosse (*ss*); Michael Brecker (*ts*); Judd Miller (*EVI*); John Beasley, David Witham (*ky*); John Scofield, Ricardo Silveira (*g*); Peter Erskine, Vinnie Colaiuta, Terri Lyne Carrington (*d*); Dori Caymmi (*v*). 90.

All these records are full of clever playing and flawless technique, but they bespeak an icy indifference to conceptual substance or melodic warmth. Patitucci is a sought-after electric bassist and he isn't shy about featuring himself on his own albums. Guest spots by Brecker and Corea on the first two records don't disguise the tuneless nature of the material, and tracks such as 'A Better Mousetrap' from *On The Corner* will impress only bass players who are looking to be impressed by superfast fingering. *Sketchbook* is a little hotter, with Scofield and Brecker playing more meaningful roles and the leader pausing to think up a couple more worthwhile tunes. But it's hardly essential music. All are recorded with stinging digital clarity, in the house style.

CECIL PAYNE (born 1922)
BARITONE SAXOPHONE

*** **Patterns Of Jazz** Savoy SV 0135 CD
Payne; Kenny Dorham (*t*); Duke Jordan (*p*); Tommy Potter (*b*); Arthur Taylor (*d*). 5/56.

Payne cut his teeth as a soloist with Dizzy Gillespie's late 1940s Cuban-bop big band. Along with the lighter-sounding Leo Parker (*q. v.*), he did much to adapt the hefty baritone to the rapid transitions and tonal extremities of bebop. Charlie Parker was his main influence, but in 1956, with Parker gone, he was beginning a fruitful association with pianist Randy Weston, who contributes two of the most interesting compositions on *Patterns of Jazz*. Payne has not recorded prolifically under his own name, and this is a welcome and overdue reissue.

Weston's 'Chessman's Delight' is a dark, minor theme geared to Payne's lower register. As on the preceding ballad, 'How Deep Is The Ocean?', the solo is stately and fluid, with no sign of Leo Parker's rather slack embouchure. Dorham lifts the second Weston composition considerably; 'Saucer Eyes' has an engaging two-part melody-line, alternating a soft, four-note glide with a rhythmic bounce; and once again Payne is meditative rather than forceful in his solo. At this point at least his own writing isn't up to Weston's scratch. 'Arnetta', dedicated to his mother, is an attractive, rhythmic theme, but both 'Bringing Up Father' and the collaborative 'Man Of Moods', co-written with the excellent Jordan, are rather derivative. Just to acknowledge the source of the derivation, the set ends on a rousing 'Groovin' High', from Dizzy Gillespie's book.

Compared to Serge Chaloff, Gerry Mulligan and the affectionately remembered Leo Parker, Payne is still known to the record-buying public only as a useful sideman. *Patterns of Jazz* suggests a more substantial, albeit transitional, figure in the development of bebop.

GARY PEACOCK (born 1935)
DOUBLE BASS

[****   **Partners** Owl 058 CD]
Peacock (*b* solo). 12/89.

****   **Tales Of Another** ECM 1101 CD/LP
Peacock; Keith Jarrett (*p*); Jack DeJohnette (*d*). 2/77.

(*)   **Shift In The Wind ECM 1165 CD/LP
Peacock; Art Lande (*p*); Eliot Zigmund (*d*). 2/80.

***   **Voice From The Past/Paradigm** ECM 1210 LP
Peacock; Tomasz Stanko (*t*); Jan Garbarek (*ts, ss*); Jack DeJohnette (*d*). 8/81.

(*)   **Guamba ECM 1352 CD/LP
Peacock; Palle Mikkelborg (*t, flhn*); Jan Garbarek (*ts, ss*); Peter Erskine (*d, d syn*).
3/87.

Set Gary Peacock's solo numbers on *Partners* (the album is shared with Paul Bley) alongside Glen Moore's *Trios/Solos* with Ralph Towner (ECM 1256 CD/LP) and it's immediately obvious how much more rooted Peacock is in the jazz tradition. Pouncing on a minor programmatic coincidence, it may be instructive to compare Peacock's 'Pleiades Skirt' with Moore's 'Belt Of Asteroids' and trace his careful negotiation of a balance between formal progression and abstraction.

Peacock's career has rarely hewn to the centre. After a brief apprenticeship in Europe, he moved to the West Coast and worked with the likes of Bud Shank and Shorty Rogers, before absorbing himself in the challenging formal structures of Don Ellis, Bill Evans, Jimmy Giuffre and George Russell, maintaining the while a powerful involvement in avant-garde transformations of early jazz, notably with Albert Ayler, Roland Kirk and Steve Lacy. His playing style combines elements of Jimmy Blanton's and Wilbur Ware's sonority with something of Oscar Pettiford's rapid disposition of wide intervals.

Peacock's own records have been rather mixed and can't be taken as representative of his abilities. The earliest, *Tales Of Another*, is performed by the band that was to become known as Keith Jarrett's 'Standards Trio' six years later. In the late 1960s, Peacock had turned his back on the music scene and gone to Japan to study macrobiotics. However uncertain he may have been about a return to bass playing (and he may have been persuaded by ECM chief, Manfred Eicher), there is a wonderful coherence to his solo work on 'Vignette' (with piano rippling underneath) and on 'Trilogy I/II/III' that quashes any suggestion that this is another Jarrett album, politely or generously reattributed; it is, in fact, his last but one appearance as a sideman. Even so, the pianist is clearly at home with Peacock's music and there is a level of intuition at work which became the basis of their later standards performances, but it is unmistakably Peacock's record.

Sadly, he never sounds quite so poised or concentrated again. *Shift In The Wind* is merely enigmatic, and there seems to be little positive understanding (beyond, that is, an agreement not to tread on one another's toes) among the trio. The later quartets further obscure Peacock's playing, and though *Voice From The Past* is particularly good, it is chiefly memorable for the atmospheric interplay of Garbarek and Stanko. Mikkelborg's hyperactive style dissipates much of the concentration of Peacock's writing on *Guamba*, and Erskine seems a poor substitute for DeJohnette's brilliant out-of-tempo colorations.

WAYNE PEET
PIANO

***   **Down-in Ness** Nine Winds NWO111 LP
Peet (*p* solo). 9/81.

An absorbing solo recital. Peet's avant-garde manner is a rare one in that he seems mostly untouched by the obvious influence of Cecil Taylor: while he doesn't go quite to the other extreme, these seven improvisations are marked by a shrewd husbandry of resources. In 'Ballad: To The Edge (Grace City)', the movement from a kind of prelude to a hyperactive series of arpeggios seems entirely natural, and as disparate as his ideas are, there's nothing strained about the transition from one point to another. He's amusing, too: 'Plow And Angel' is a cunning variation on a hot piano stomp, and the ebb and flow of 'Neon Leon' suggests a bebop vocabulary which has found its way out of the vertical prison of chords. The piano sound is quite truthful and pleasing. Recommended, although Nine Winds LPs are now a little difficult to find.

HARRY PEPL
GUITAR, GUITAR SYNTHESIZER, PIANO

***(*)   **Cracked Mirrors** ECM 1356 CD/LP
          Pepl; Herbert Joos (*flhn*); Jon Christensen (*d*). 2/87.

***   **Schoenberg Improvisations** Amadeo 843086 CD/LP
          Pepl; Dave Liebman (*ss*); Johannes Enders (*ts*); Wolfgang Reisinger (*d, perc*). 11/89.

Pepl's characteristically melancholy style is tempered by a firmness and concision that make him an ideal group-player. His is one of the more impressive contributions on Adelhard Roidinger's *Schattseite* (ECM 1221 LP) and he has also worked with bandoneon player, Dino Saluzzi, another ECM artist. His own recordings of the late 1980s tend to overplay a rather limited imagination and Pepl resorts over and over again to a restricted code of octave runs, out-of-tempo scales with electronically divided pitches, and clusters of grace notes that obscure interesting melodic ideas. The later album, with its challenging exploration of late-romantic atonality, could perhaps have been scored more effectively without a drummer and with either trombone or bass clarinet in place of the tenor saxophone. But for the presence of the subtly swinging Christensen, the very fine *Cracked Mirrors* might almost be one of Austrian flugelhorn player Franz Koglmann's meditative essays on the jazz literature. The interplay between Pepl and Joos recalls some of Koglmann's work with guitarist Burkhard Stangl. Even without conscious reference to standards, Pepl's work is closer to orthodox jazz but draws on a wide stylistic spectrum as if to suggest that post-Schoenbergian music really is a cracked mirror, giving back a creatively splintered image of harmony.

KEN PEPLOWSKI
CLARINET, ALTO SAXOPHONE, TENOR SAXOPHONE

(*)   **Double Exposure Concord CCD 4344 CD/MC
          Peplowski; Ed Bickert (*g*); John Bunch (*p*); John Goldsby (*b*); Terry Clarke (*d*).
          12/87.

***   **Sunny Side** Concord CCD 4376 CD/MC
          Peplowski; Howard Alden (*g*); David Frishberg (*p*); John Goldsby (*b*); Terry Clarke
          (*d*). 1/89.

***   **Mr Gentle And Mr Cool** Concord CCD 4419 CD/MC
          Peplowski; Scott Hamilton (*ts*); Bucky Pizzarelli (*g*); Hank Jones (*p*); Frank Tate (*b*);
          Alan Dawson (*d*). 2/90.

***   **Illuminations** Concord CCD 4449 CD/MC
          Peplowski; Howard Alden (*g*); Junior Mance (*p*); Dennis Irwin (*b*); Alan Dawson (*d*).
          90.

There was once a *Punch* cartoon of a balding pipe-and-slippers man drowsing in front of the fire and telly while his wife and a friend look on: 'Oh, yes, Ken *does* have another side, but it's exactly the same as this one.' Pure coincidence, of course, but there is something slightly one-dimensional about Peplowski's sweetly elegant saxophone and clarinet playing. Certainly in comparison with Scott Hamilton, doyen of the young fogey swing revivalist boom, he is a very limited technician, who relies on rather meretricious cosmetic effects.

Mr Gentle and Mr Cool emphasizes just how much he could do with a little of Dr Jekyll's elixir. The two sextet tracks with Hamilton lift the album two notches. There's nothing comparable to lift *Illuminations* from later the same year, though Junior Mance's piano playing impresses, as does the impeccable Hank Jones. A clarinettist first, with a method half-way between Benny Goodman and the great swing saxophonists, he seems locked on to a single dynamic wavelength.

The two earlier albums show slight leanings towards the harmonic upsets of bop, but Peplowski's solos are the musical equivalent of what used, disgustingly, to be called heavy petting, ending just when he seems to be getting somewhere. There's a ready market for material like this, but it's by no means up to Concord's usual high scratch.

ART PEPPER (1925–82)
ALTO AND TENOR SAXOPHONES, CLARINET

*** **Surf Ride** Savoy SV-0115 CD
Pepper; Jack Montrose (*ts*); Russ Freeman, Hampton Hawes, Claude Williamson (*p*); Bob Whitlock, Joe Mondragon, Monty Budwig (*b*); Bobby White, Larry Bunker (*d*). 2/52–12/53.

*** **The Late Show/A Night At the Surf Club Vol. 1** Xanadu 117 CD/LP
Pepper; Hampton Hawes (*p*); Joe Mondragon (*b*); Larry Bunker (*d, vib*). 2/52.

*** **The Early Show/A Night At The Surf Club Vol. 2** Xanadu 108 CD/LP
As above. 2/52.

*** **With Sonny Clark 1953 Vol. 1** Time Is CD
Pepper; Sonny Clark (*p*).

Pepper's remains one of the most immediately identifiable alto sax styles in post-war jazz. If he was a Parker disciple, like every other modern saxophonist in the 1940s and '50s, he tempered Bird's slashing attack with a pointed elegance that recalled something of Benny Carter and Willie Smith. He was a passionate musician, having little of the studious intensity of a Lee Konitz, and his tone – which could come out as pinched and jittery as well as softly melodious – suggested something of the duplicit, cursed romanticism which seems to lie at the heart of his music. After a brief period with Californian big bands, he began recording as a leader and sideman on the Hollywood studio scene of the early 1950s. *Surf Ride* includes his earliest tracks as a leader: these clipped, rather brittle records find him a little wound up, and the six tracks with Jack Montrose in the front line – who sounds untypically hesitant on a couple of his solos – are standard West Coast fare. A better glimpse of the early Pepper is offered by the club recordings on the two Xanadu discs. Hawes and Pepper hit it off with superb elan, and their various attempts at standards and the blues suggest a rare balance between professional expertise and quizzical, exploratory music-making. The problem lies with the recording, which was made by a fan and does the pianist in particular a disservice, his tone sounding frankly awful in places. It's a comment on the quality of the music that it nevertheless remains very listenable. The Time Is disc with Sonny Clark offers scarcely less absorbing music: Clark is no match for Hawes, but his erudite comping offers Pepper a springboard which the altoist takes full advantage of. Sound is again less than ideal, but the energy in the music endures.

*** **The Artistry Of Pepper** Pacific Jazz CDP 7971942 CD
Pepper; Don Fagerquist (*t*); Stu Williamson (*vtb*); Bill Perkins, Bill Holman (*ts*); Bud Shank (*bs*); Jimmy Rowles, Russ Freeman (*p*); Red Callender (*tba*); Monty Budwig, Ben Tucker (*b*); Mel Lewis, Shelly Manne (*d*). 12/56–8/57.

*** **The Return Of Art Pepper** Blue Note CDP 7468632 CD
Pepper; Jack Sheldon (*t*); Red Norvo (*vib*); Gerald Wiggins, Russ Freeman (*p*); Leroy Vinnegar, Ben Tucker (*b*); Shelly Manne, Joe Morello (*d*). 8/56–1/57.

**** **Modern Art** Blue Note CDP 7468482 CD
Pepper; Russ Freeman, Carl Perkins (*p*); Ben Tucker (*b*); Chuck Flores (*d*). 12/56–4/57.

**** **The Art Of Pepper** Blue Note CDP 7468532 CD
As above, except omit Freeman. 4/57.

Pepper's sessions for Aladdin, collected on the three Blue Note albums, have been overshadowed by his records for Contemporary (see below). *The Return Of Art Pepper* (the altoist had been in prison for narcotics offences, a problem that would plague his career) puts together a fair if patchy quintet session with Jack Sheldon – the two ballad features without Sheldon, 'You Go To My Head' and 'Patricia' are easily the best things – with a set originally led by Joe Morello, with Red Norvo in the front line. *Artistry* couples a pleasing quintet date with Bill Perkins with a nonet playing Shorty Rogers arrangements and featuring Pepper as principal soloist: rather stylized in the West Coast manner, but the altoist plays impeccably. The really valuable records, though, are the two quartet discs. *Modern Art* is a deceptively quiet and tempered session: the opening 'Blues In' is a seemingly hesitant improvised blues which typifies the staunchless flow of Pepper's ideas, and the following 'Bewitched' and a quite exceptional reworking of 'Stompin' At The Savoy' are so full of ideas that Pepper seems transformed. Freeman responds with superbly insightful support. Yet the succeeding *Art Of Pepper* is even better, with bigger and more upfront sound and Carl Perkins spinning along in accompaniment. 'Begin The Beguine' is both beguiling and forceful, the dizzying lines of 'Webb City' are an entirely convincing tribute to Bud Powell, and the melodies unravelled from 'Too Close For Comfort' and 'Long Ago And Far Away' – which Pepper returns to on the Contemporary sessions – show a lyrical invention which few players of the day could have matched.

***(*) **The Way It Was!** Original Jazz Classics OJC 389 CD/LP/MC
Pepper; Warne Marsh (*ts*); Ronnie Ball, Red Garland, Dolo Coker, Wynton Kelly (*p*); Ben Tucker, Paul Chambers, Jimmy Bond (*b*); Philly Joe Jones, Gary Frommer, Frank Butler, Jimmy Cobb (*d*). 11/56–11/60.

**** **Meets The Rhythm Section** Original Jazz Classics OJC 338 CD/LP/MC
Pepper; Red Garland (*p*); Paul Chambers (*b*); Philly Joe Jones (*d*). 1/57.

**** **Modern Jazz Classics** Original Jazz Classics OJC 341 CD/LP/MC
Pepper; Pete Candoli, Jack Sheldon, Al Porcino (*t*); Dick Nash (*tb*); Bob Enevoldsen (*vtb, ts*); Vince DeRosa (*frhn*); Herb Geller, Bud Shank (*as*); Charlie Kennedy (*ts, as*); Bill Perkins, Richie Kamuca (*ts*); Med Flory (*bs*); Russ Freeman (*p*); Joe Mondragon (*b*); Mel Lewis (*d*). 3–5/59.

***(*) **Gettin' Together** Original Jazz Classics OJC 169 CD/LP/MC
Pepper; Conte Candoli (*t*); Wynton Kelly (*p*); Paul Chambers (*b*); Jimmy Cobb (*d*). 2/60.

**** **Smack Up** Original Jazz Classics OJC 176 CD/LP/MC
Pepper; Jack Sheldon (*t*); Pete Jolly (*p*); Jimmy Bond (*b*); Frank Butler (*d*). 10/60.

**** **Intensity** Original Jazz Classics OJC 387 CD/LP/MC
Pepper; Dolo Coker (*p*); Jimmy Bond (*b*); Frank Butler (*d*). 11/60.

Pepper's records for Contemporary, all of which have been reissued in the OJC series, make up a superlative sequence. *The Way It Was!* remained unissued until the 1970s, but the first half of it – a session with Warne Marsh, which secures a brilliant interplay on 'Tickle Toe' and exposes all Pepper's lyricism on 'What's New' – is as good as anything in the series (the other tracks are outtakes from the succeeding sessions). The playing of the quartet on *Meets The Rhythm Section* beggars belief when the circumstances are considered: Pepper wasn't even aware of the session till the morning of the date, hadn't played in two weeks, was going through difficult times with his narcotics problem and didn't know any of the material they played. Yet it emerges as a poetic, burning date, with all four men playing above themselves. *Modern Jazz Classics* is in some ways more prosaic, with Marty Paich's arrangements of Monk, Gillespie, Giuffre, Mulligan and more working from the by now over-familiar West Coast glibness, yet the sound of the ensemble is beautifully rich, Paich conjures new things out of 'Bernie's Tune' and 'Anthropology', and Pepper – who also brings out his clarinet and tenor – alternately glides through the charts and dances his way out of them. There isn't a great deal to choose between the three remaining sessions: *Smack Up* finds Pepper playing Ornette on 'Tears Inside' as well as a memorable version of Duane Tatro's haunting 'Maybe Next Year', and the appropriately titled *Intensity* is a wistful series of ballads and standards where Pepper, a peculiarly astringent romantic, seems to brood on the words of the songs as well as their melodies and changes: 'Long Ago And Far Away', for instance, seems a perfect transliteration of the song's message. Throughout these records, the saxophonist's phrasing, with its carefully delivered hesitations and sudden flurries, and his tone, which sometimes resembles a long, crying ache, communicate matters of enormous emotional impact. They demand to be heard. Remastering of all of them is well up to the fine OJC standards.

(*)   **Art Pepper Quartet '64 In San Francisco Fresh Sound FSCD-1005 CD
Pepper; Frank Strazzeri (*p*); Hersh Hamel (*p*); Bill Goodwin (*d*). 5–6/64.

Devastated by his personal problems, Pepper didn't make another studio record (aside from a Buddy Rich session in 1978) until 1973. These tracks come from a 1964 TV appearance and another at a San Francisco club. Not long released from prison, his style had changed dramatically: hung up on Coltrane and a fear that his older style would be out of touch, he sounds in a bizarre transition from the former, lyrically confident Pepper to a new, darker, often incoherent style based around tonal investigations and timbral distortions as much as anything. It's a trait he would rationalize with his 'normal' self in the 1970s, but here he's finding his way. He's still musician enough to make it an intriguing document, too, with the first version of 'The Trip' and a long 'Sonnymoon For Two'. The sound is rough, not much better than an average bootleg, but Pepperphiles will want to hear it. There is also an interview track with presenter Ralph Gleason.

**   **I'll Remember April** Storyville STCD 4130 CD
Pepper; Tommy Gumina (*polychord*); Fred Atwood (*b*); Jimmie Smith (*d*). 2/75.

***(*)   **Living Legend** Original Jazz Classics OJC 408 CD/LP/MC
Pepper; Hampton Hawes (*p*); Charlie Haden (*b*); Shelly Manne (*d*). 8/75.

***   **The Trip** Original Jazz Classics OJC 410 CD/LP/MC
Pepper; George Cables (*p*); David Williams (*b*); Elvin Jones (*d*). 9/76.

(*)   **A Night In Tunisia Storyville STCD 4146 CD
Pepper; Smith Dobson (*p*); Jim Nichols (*b*); Brad Bilhorn (*d*). 1/77.

(*)   **No Limit Original Jazz Classics OJC 411 CD/LP/MC
Pepper; George Cables (*p*); Tony Dumas (*b*); Carl Burnett (*d*). 3/77.

Pepper's re-emergence blossomed into the most remarkable comeback of its kind. He became a symbol of jazz triumph-over-adversity, and though in the end it didn't last very long, there was a stubborn, furious eloquence about his later playing that makes all his records worth hearing, even when he struggles to articulate a ballad or has to fight to get his uptempo lines in shape. The earlier sessions, following the *Living Legend* set, continue his struggle to digest Coltrane and reconcile that influence with his honourable past achievements: on both *the Trip* and *No Limit* he gets there some of the time, and the former at least includes his haunting blues line 'Red Car'. But *Living Legend* itself is the one to hear first. 'Lost Life' is one of his gentle-harrowing ballads, a self-portrait rigorously chewed out, and the whole session seems inbued with a mixture of nerves, relief and pent-up inspiration which the other players – an inspiring team – channel as best they can. The two Storyville discs chronicle a couple of live dates with local players in the rhythm sections. *I'll Remember April* is marred by a gymnasium sound and Gumina's odd-sounding polychord, but Pepper blows very hard throughout. *A Night In Tunisia* is better – Dobson is a useful player, and there is another strong version of 'Lost Life' – but the studio albums merit prior attention.

***(*)   **Thursday Night At The Village Vanguard** Original Jazz Classics OJC 694 CD/LP/MC
Pepper; George Cables (*p*); George Mraz (*b*); Elvin Jones (*d*). 7/77.

***   **Friday Night At The Village Vanguard** Original Jazz Classics OJC 695 CD/LP/MC
As above. 7/77.

***   **Saturday Night At The Village Vanguard** Original Jazz Classics OJC 696 CD/LP/MC
As above. 7/77.

***   **More For Les: At The Village Vanguard Vol. 4** Original Jazz Classics OJC 697 CD/LP/MC
As above. 7/77.

Four exhaustive nights from one engagement. The ballads, again, are the compelling things here, with 'Goodbye' (*Thursday*) and 'But Beautiful' (*Friday*) particularly acrid and wrenching. But by now Pepper is beginning to enjoy himself and there's some of his old light returning to the quicker tunes. Cables, Mraz and Jones keep up a decent flame underneath him, and the location recording is excellent.

*** **Live In Japan Vol. 1** Storyville STCD 4128 CD
Pepper; Milcho Leviev (*p*); Bob Magnusson (*b*); Carl Burnett (*d*). 3/78.

*** **Live In Japan** Storyville STCD 4129 CD
As above. 3/78.

*** **Art Pepper Today** Original Jazz Classics OJC 474 CD/LP/MC
Pepper; Stanley Cowell, Cecil McBee (*b*); Roy Haynes (*d*); Kenneth Nash (*perc*). 12/78.

***(*) **New York Album** Galaxy 5154 MC
Pepper; Hank Jones (*p*); Ron Carter (*b*); Al Foster (*d*). 2/79.

*** **Artworks** Galaxy 5148 MC
Pepper; George Cables (*p*); Charlie Haden (*b*); Billy Higgins (*d*). 3/79.

*** **Landscape** Original Jazz Classics OJC 676 CD
Pepper; George Cables (*p*); Tony Dumas (*b*); Billy Higgins (*d*). 7/79.

***(*) **Straight Life** Original Jazz Classics OJC 475 CD/LP/MC
Pepper; Tommy Flanagan (*p*); Red Mitchell (*b*); Billy Higgins (*d*); Kenneth Nash (*perc*). 9/79.

**** **Winter Moon** Original Jazz Classics OJC 677 CD
Pepper; Stanley Cowell (*p*); Howard Roberts (*g*); Cecil McBee (*b*); Carl Burnett (*d*); strings. 9/80.

*** **One September Afternoon** Original Jazz Classics OJC 678 CD
As above, except omit strings. 9/80.

*** **APQ: The Maiden Voyage Sessions Vol. 3** Galaxy 5151 MC
Pepper; George Cables (*p*); David Williams (*b*); Carl Burnett (*d*). 8/81.

*** **Art Lives** Galaxy 5145 MC
As above. 8/81.

*** **Roadgame** Galaxy 5142 MC
As above. 8/81.

*** **Goin' Home** Original Jazz Classics OJC 679 CD
Pepper; George Cables (*p*). 5/82.

The later records for Galaxy are in some ways all of a piece, and it's rather appropriate that the Fantasy group have chosen to issue a colossal boxed-set of the whole output (see below). Pepper remained in fragile health, as robustly as he played and carried himself, and the sense of time running out for him imparted an urgency to almost everyting he played: ballads become wracked with intensity, uptempo tunes spill over with notes and cries. Studio and live dates are the same in that respect. Of these many lkate albums, four ask to be returned to: *New York Album*, unfortunately not yet on CD, with a terrific rhythm section; *Straight Life*, with another fine quartet; *Landscape*, a sharp set by the band Pepper worked most frequently with in his last years; and above all the profoundly beautiful *Winter Moon*, a strings album which far surpasses the norm for this kind of record, Pepper uncorking one of his greatest solos against the rhapsodic sweep of Bill Holman's arrangement on 'Our Song'. The two Japanese live albums are also well worth seeking out.

**** **The Complete Galaxy Recordings** Galaxy 1016 16CD
As above OJC/Galaxy albums. 77–82.

A vast and surprisingly payable archive – most such monuments seldom come off the shelf, but Pepper's resilience, febrile invention and consistency of commitment makes this music endure far beyond expectations. There are dead spots, inevitably, and it's a costly undertaking, but there is also a lot of music unavailable elsewhere, including many alternate takes, outtakes and Japanese-only issues – 53 unissued tracks in all. Sumptuous packaging and a fine essay by Gary Giddins are included.

***   **Art & Zoot** West Wind 2071 CD
       Pepper; Zoot Sims (*ts*); Victor Feldman (*p*); Ray Brown, Charlie Haden (*b*); Billy
       Higgins (*d*). 9/81.

A surprise meeting between Pepper and Zoot Sims, recorded at a Los Angeles concert in 1981. Pepper does a slowburning 'Over The rainbow', Sims breezes through a carefree 'In The Middle Of A Kiss' and the two play together on 'Wee' and an impromptu blues. Given that Sims sounded comfortable with almost anybody, and Pepper is at his most accommodating, the music has no problems, and the improvisations unfurl with a good deal of inventiveness. The sound is less than ideal, a good amateur recording, and devotees of Pepper's Galaxy recordings might find this an interesting but middleweight supplement.

JIM PEPPER
TENOR SAXOPHONE

***   **Dakota Sound** Enja 5043 CD
       Pepper; Kirk Lightsey (*p*); Santi Wilson Debriano (*b*); John Betsch (*d*). 1/87.

***(*)   **The Path** Enja 5087 CD
       As above, with Stanton Davis (*t*); Arto Tuncboyaci (*perc*); Caren Knight (*v*). 3/88.

***   **West End Avenue** Nabel 4633 CD/LP
       Pepper; Christoph Spendel (*p*); Ron McClure (*b*); Reuben Hoch (*d*). 2/89.

***   **Camargue** Pan PMC 1106 CD
       Pepper; Claudine François (*p*); Ed Schulller (*b*); John Betsch (*d*); Kendra Shank (*v*).
       5/89.

Pepper is best known as the composer of 'Witchi-Tai-To', a jauntily haunting theme reflecting his American Indian roots and turned into an album and concert hit by Oregon. A melodic player with a strong roots feel and a resistance to abstraction, Pepper performs best against a highly lyrical background with a firm pulse. Lightsey seems an ideal accompanist and *The Path* (which includes 'Witchi-Tai-To' as well as the pianist's 'Habiba') is his most accomplished album. The later pair, on smaller labels, lack the emotional urgency that Pepper frequently brings to his work, and it's worth sampling his performances alongside fellow saxophonist Joe Lovano on Paul Motian's excellent mid-1980s albums, *The Story of Maryam*, *Jack of Clubs* and *Misterioso* (Soul Note 1074, 1124, 1174 CD).

BILL PERKINS (born 1924)
TENOR AND BARITONE SAXOPHONE, FLUTE, BASS CLARINET

***   **Tenors Head-On** Pacific Jazz CDP 7971952 CD
       Perkins; Richie Kamuca (*ts*); Hampton Hawes, Pete Jolly (*p*); Red Mitchell (*b*); Stan
       Levey, Mel Lewis (*d*). 7–10/56.

Perkins and Kamuca are in steaming form on the uptempo tunes, cavalier on the ballads, and the effortless cut of the music is typical of Pacific's barometric approach to the Californian music of the day: it was always fair weather. Bill Perkins was and remains a very supple and thoughtful soloist, though, and in the just-slightly-wounded romanticism of Kamuca he foud a very amenable partner for these gentlemanly tear-ups. 'Cotton tail' is taken at a whirlwind tempo, but since it sounds as if nobody is perspiring, it suggests a band gliding in rather than hustling their way through the tune. Perkins picks up the flute and the bass clarinet for a bit of local colour here and there, but mostly this is about two tenors, head on. Bright remastering.

***   **Quietly There** Original Jazz Classics OJC 1776 CD/LP
       Perkins; Victor Feldman (*p, org, vib*); John Pisano (*g*); Red Mitchell (*b*); Larry
       Bunker (*d*). 11/66.

This was one of only two sessions that Perkins made under his own name in the 1960s. Gentle, pretty, but closely thought-out, this is easy-listening jazz as it could be at its best. The nine tracks are all Johnny Mandel compositions, and Perkins devises a different setting for each one, some decidedly odd: baritone sax and organ for 'Groover Wailin'', for instance, which mainly proves that Feldman was no good as an organist. But Perkins's grey, marshy tone makes a charming matter of 'The Shining Sea', the flute and vibes treatment of 'A Time For Love' is ideal, and tempos and textures are subtly varied throughout. A welcome reissue of a little-known record.

** **Many Ways To Go** Sea Breeze SB-2006 LP
Perkins; Gordon Goodwin (*ss, as, ts, ky*); Clare Fischer (*org*); Bob Magnusson (*b*); Vince Lateano (*d*). 3/80.

(*) **Journey To The East Contemporary C-14011 LP
Perkins; Frank Strazzeri (*p*); Joel Di Bartolo (*b*); Peter Donald (*d*). 11/84.

Perkins has spent most of his career in studio work but these sessions recall something of the most halcyon West Coast days of 30 years before, where he was a more significant figure. *Many Ways To Go* includes a couple of attractive arrangements on Ellington themes, but with synthesizers and Goodwin as modish counterweights little of Perkins's personality breaks through to the surface. *Journey To The East* is more rewarding. The ten tracks are all concisely delivered, and here and there one might detect a tribute to other saxophonists as a subtext: 'Moose The Mooche' has a Parker-like fluency, and 'I'm An Old Cowhand' does sound like a nod to Rollins. Perkins does a version of 'Blood Count' which is far more gentle and wistful than Stan Getz's treatment, but it isn't much less affecting. Overall, though, the session has a fleeting and rather tossed-off quality.

CHARLI PERSIP (born 1929)
DRUMS, PERCUSSION

*** **In Case You Missed It** Soul Note 1079 CD/LP
Persip; Eddie E. J. Allen, Frank Gordon, Ambrose Jackson, Ron Tooley, Jack Walrath (*t*); Clarence Banks, Jason Forsythe, David Graf (*tb*); Carl Kleinstuber (*tba*); Bobby Watson (*as*); Monty Waters (*as*); Orpheus Gaitanopoulos, Alan Givens, Bill Saxton (*ts*); Fred Houn (*bs*); Richard Clements (*p*); Anthony Cox (*b*); Eli Fountain (*perc*). 9/84.

***(*) **No Dummies Allowed** Soul Note 1178 CD/LP
Persip; Torry Barrero, Ambrose Jackson, Genghis Nor, Jack Walrath (*t*); Nathan Duncan, Jason Forsythe, Matt Haviland, Herb Huvel (*tb*); Sue Terry, Sayyd Abdul Al-Khabyyr (*as, f*); Orpheus Gaitanopoulos, Craig Rivers (*ts, f*); Pablo Calajero (*bs*); Darrel Grant (*p*); Melissa Slocum (*b*); Eli Fountain (*perc*). 11/87.

Drummer Persip and his Superband have attempted to maintain a collectivist, internationalist and (intermittently) non-sexist approach without any of the pomposity and attitudinizing that has marred some otherwise excellent work by the Afro-Asian Ensemble, a broadly similar outfit co-led by baritonist Fred Houn. Houn also appears on the brawling *In Case You Missed It*.

Persip's track record is quite extraordinary and his technique is now honed to perfection. He's something of a hybrid of Blakey and Big Sid Catlett, but he has also paid attention to Cozy Cole and Shadow Wison. They're all performance players, big sounds but with sufficient sense of space (compare Rich or Krupa) to let things happen around them. Persip's inspirational qualities (mustn't say leadership) are evident in *No Dummies Allowed*, a dumb title for such a spanking set of big-band arrangements. Alto saxophonist Sue Terry's work on the Billie Holiday medley 'Strange Crazy Heartache' suggests that she has a formidable musical intelligence; her solo statement catches something of Lady's voice, and Jack Walrath does some terrific back-of-the-stand stuff.

'Vital Seconds' and 'Desert Ship' are both composed by saxophonist Orpheus Gaitanopoulos, a robust player who occasionally disrupts the band's surprising finesse. Both albums are worth finding, but the later set is the better by some distance.

HOUSTON PERSON
TENOR SAXOPHONE

**(*)   Goodness! Original Jazz Classics OJC 332 LP
Person; Sonny Phillips (*org*); Billy Butler (*b*); Frankie Jones (*d*); Buddy Caldwell (*perc*). 8/69.

***   Something In Common Muse 600633 CD
Person; Ron Carter (*b*). 2/89.

Recorded 20 years apart, these could hardly be more different, even allowing for the fact that Person's muscular approach has changed not one jot in that time. In 1969, jazz musicians struggling against industry-backed competition from rock either gave in gracelessly or else defended the high aesthetic ground. Both Person and Carter tried to make some accommodation. Person basically added a funky rhythm backing to what he would have been doing anyway, which was a soul–blues derivative of bop, and plodded on regardless. Butler's bass guitar sounds thick-fingered and inopportune, and the organ is all over the place.

Carter also briefly turned to amplified and 'piccolo' bass guitars, as was the fashion. The difference was that he tried to get inside a different instrument, rather than treating it as if it was merely a souped-up bull fiddle. On *Something In Common*, it's clear that a lot of the rhythmic and textural brushwood of that period has been lopped out. It's a clean-limbed and often quite affecting album, with some beautiful contributions from both men on a mixture of pieces from before and after bop. 'Anthropology' doesn't quite come off (and that's Carter's fault) but it's generally a very acceptable set.

***   The Party Muse MCD 5451 CD/MC
Person; Randy Johnston (*g*); Joey DeFrancesco (*org*); Bertell Knox (*d*); Sammy Figueroa (*perc*). 11/89.

Squarely in the soul–jazz mould. Person sounds like a latter-day Ike Quebec, wailing with unabashed self-indulgence over a thick Hammond stew from boy wonder DeFrancesco, who could be Jimmy McGriff reborn. The opening two tracks, 'Love Me Tender' and 'Blue Velvet', serve much the same function as the old Blue Note juke numbers. The rest is rather more interesting: a fine version of Lee Morgan's 'Ceora', which successfully negotiated the soul–jazz/mainstream–modern divide; a really excellent reading of Betty Comden, Adolph Green and Jules Styne's 'The Party's Over'; and a knocked-together curtain-piece called 'True Blues', which is no more than a blowing session but which tempts both Person and DeFrancesco into some of their most unhackneyed playing. For a party, cranked up loud and with lots of bottom, it could hardly be better.

***(*)   Why Not! Muse MCD 5433 CD
Person; Philip Harper (*t*); Joey DeFrancesco (*org*); Randy Johnston (*g*); Winard Harper (*d*); Sammy Figueroa (*perc*). 10/90.

Ably abetted by the Harper brothers, Person turns in a more reflective and inventive set than the above, bringing his unique timbre to the hokey 'As Times Goes By' and an unexpected bustle to Gene DePaul's 'Namely You'. DeFrancesco's organ and Figueroa's rippling percussion effects may be a little obtrusive for some tastes, but the basic ingredients are as wholesome as cornbread.

EDWARD PETERSON
TENOR SAXOPHONE

***   Upward Spiral Delmark 445 CD
Peterson; Brad Williams (*p*); Fareed Haque (*g*); Rob Amster (*b*); Jeff Stitely (*d*). 6/89.

This is a part-studio, part-live account of a band that has worked regularly on the contemporary Chicago scene. Peterson is the dominant voice, walking the line bwteen bop form and a freer conception with an unfussy confidence, and his solos contrast with the cloudier effects of Haque. Williams, Amster and Stitely provide competent support, but the extra grit and swing of the first four tracks – which were cut live in Chicago – suggest that the band has yet to find its feet in the studio. Since comparatively little is heard of Chicago's newer jazz, a welcome document.

HANNIBAL MARVIN PETERSON (born 1948)
TRUMPET

*** **Hannibal In Antibes** Enja 3011 LP
Peterson; George Adams (*ts, f*); Diedre Murray (*clo*); Steve Neil (*b*); Makaya
Ntoshko (*d*). 7/77.

***(*) **The Angels Of Atlanta** Enja 3085 LP
Peterson; George Adams (*ts*); Kenny Barron (*p*); Diedre Murray; Cecil McBee (*b*);
Dannie Richmond (*d*); Pat Peterson (*v*); Harlem Boys' Choir conducted by Walter
Turnbull. 2/81.

Though he lacks an instantly recognizable sound, Peterson has dug so deep into the tradition
that he seems to encapsulate the whole black music tradition from field songs through gospel
and soul to bop and free and onward to the kind of ambitious formal composition one
associates with Charles Mingus. There is a basic continuity between these apparently
inconsistent elements. The long live version of 'Swing Low, Sweet Chariot' on *Hannibal In
Antibes* gives the traditional theme the grandeur and structural solidity of a 'classical' piece,
but embeds popular and avant-garde elements within it. In the same way, the suite-like
succession of tracks that follow 'The Angels Of Atlanta' (a piece that addresses the same
atrocious child-murders that sparked James Baldwin's essay, 'The evidence of things not seen')
utilize a broad spectrum of formal and timbral devices, not least Diedre Murray's unexpectedly
vivid cello, to create a movement of stylistic and thematic associations towards the concluding
'Sometimes I Feel Like A Motherless Child'.
    In neither case is the sound-quality commensurate with the music, and the ratings above take
account of a considerable reservation on that point. It's to be hoped that both works will be
made available on CD and that Peterson's considerable talents will be given fuller and freer
rein.

***(*) **Kiss On The Bridge** Ear Rational 882 454909 CD
Peterson; Johannes Barthelemes (*ts, ss*); Michael Henning (*p*); Fred Stern (*b*);
Michael Landmesser (*d*). 90.

Another fine, polished set from the trumpeter that confirms his profound historical
understanding. Though rather harshly recorded, he ranges effortlessly from high, bell-like tones,
often dipping slightly at the end, to noisy, Bubber Miley-like smears and groans. The band are
accomplished if slightly anonymous, and only Landmesser really captures the attention. Full
marks to the leader, though.

OSCAR PETERSON (born 1925)
PIANO, ORGAN, ELECTRIC PIANO, CLAVICHORD

***(*) **Compact Jazz: Oscar Peterson & Friends** Pablo 835315 CD
Peterson; Roy Eldridge (*t*); Sonny Stitt (*as*); Stan Getz, Flip Phillips, Ben Webster,
Lester Young (*ts*); Lionel Hampton (*vib*); Milt Jackson (*vib*); Herb Ellis, Barney
Kessel (*g*); Ray Brown (*b*); J. C. Heard, John Poole, Buddy Rich, Alvin Stoller, Ed
Thigpen (*d*); Fred Astaire, Ella Fitzgerald, Anita O'Day (*v*). 1952–61.

*** **The George Gershwin Songbook** Verve 823249 LP
Peterson; Barney Kessel (*g*); Ray Brown (*b*). 11 & 12/52.

[*** **Jazz At The Philharmonic, Hartford 1953** Pablo Live 2308240 CD/LP]
Peterson; Roy Eldridge, Charlie Shavers (*t*); Bill Harris (*tb*); Benny Carter, Willie
Smith (*as*); Flip Phillips, Ben Webster, Lester Young (*ts*); Herb Ellis (*g*); Ray Brown
(*b*); J. C. Heard, Gene Krupa (*d*). 5/53.

***(*) **Compact Jazz: Oscar Peterson Plays Jazz Standards** Verve 833283 CD
Peterson; Herb Ellis (*g*); Ray Brown (*b*); Ed Thigpen (*d*). 53–62.

[*** **Jam Session 1955** Moon 029 CD/LP]
Peterson; Roy Eldridge, Dizzy Gillespie (*t*); Bill Harris (*tb*); Buddy DeFranco (*cl*);
Herb Ellis (*g*); Ray Brown (*b*); Louie Bellson (*d*). 2/55.

***(*)   At Zardis' Pablo Live 2620118 CD
Peterson; Herb Ellis (*g*); Ray Brown (*b*). 55.

No single moment ever gave a clearer impression of Oscar Peterson's fabled technique th̶ tiny incident on one of those all-star Jazz at the Philharmonic events released in rafts by th̶ Pablo label. Count Basie has just stated the opening notes of a theme in his inimitable elided style when there is a pause and then, presto! showers of sparkling notes. Any suspicions about what the Count might have ingested in his few bars of silence are allayed by the liner-note. What had happened, quite simply, was that Basie had spotted Oscar Peterson standing in the wings and had dragged him on for an unscheduled 'spot'.

Peterson has been almost as prolific as he is effusive at the piano. He appears on literally dozens in solo and trio setting, but also with horn-led groups and orchestras. He is one of the finest accompanists in swing-orientated jazz, despite which he served no real apprenticeship as a sideman, being introduced to an American audience (he was born and raised in Canada) by impresario and record producer Norman Granz in 1949. He has ridden on the extraordinary momentum of that debut ever since, recording almost exclusively for Granz's labels, Verve and, later, Pablo. He quickly became a favourite at JATP events and the *Hartford 1953* and *Friends* sessions anticipate the walk-on/walk-off sensation he was to become in the 1970s.

Peterson is perhaps best as a trio performer. During the 1950s these tended to be drummerless, and with a guitarist. Barney Kessel sounds rather colourless on the Gershwin album and Herb Ellis is much more responsive to Peterson's technique, as was his much later replacement, Joe Pass. After 1960, the stalwart Ray Brown was joined by a drummer, first by Ed Thigpen then by Louis Hayes. This coincided with Peterson's consolidation as a major concert and recording star and his early work, influenced primarily by Nat Cole, is now rather less well known. Of the mid-1950s sets, *At Zardi's* and the excellent *Standards* compilation (which covers the early years of the later trio as well) are certainly the best.

There has long been a critical knee-jerk about Peterson's Tatum influence. This was very much a later development. Tatum died in 1956 and only then does Peterson seem to have taken a close interest in his work. Even then it overlay the smoothed-out, ambidextrous quality he had found in Cole. With the turn of the 1960s and international stardom, Peterson's style changes only in accordance with the context of specific performances, particularly between the big, grandstanding 'all star' events and more intimate occasions with his own trio, where he demonstrates an occasional resemblance to Hampton Hawes and, more contentiously, to Bill Evans. Peterson's powerfully swinging style does tend on occasion to overpower his melodic sense and he is apt to become repetitious and, less often, banal. After four decades in the business, though, he understands its workings better than anyone. Above all, Peterson *delivers*.

***   The Silver Collection Verve 823447 IMS CD
Peterson; Ray Brown (*b*); Ed Thigpen (*d*); Nelson Riddle Orchestra. 8/59 & 63.

***   The Trio – Live From Chicago Verve 823008 IMS CD
As above, except omit orchestra. 9 & 10/61.

***(*)   Very Tall Verve 827821 CD
As above, except add Milt Jackson (*vib*). 9/61.

****   Night Train Verve 821724 CD/LP/MC
As above. 12/62.

***   We Get Requests Verve 810047 CD/LP
As above. 10 & 11/64.

After 30 years, *Night Train* is well established as a hardy perennial and is certainly Peterson's best-known record. Dedicated to his father, who was a sleeping-car attendant on Canadian Pacific Railways, it isn't the dark and moody suite of nocturnal blues many listeners expect but a lively and varied programme of material covering 'C-Jam Blues', 'Georgia On My Mind', 'Bag's Groove', 'Honey Dripper', 'Things Ain't What They Used To Be', 'Band Call', 'Hymn To Freedom', and a couple of others. Though by no means a 'concept album', it's one of the best-constructed long-players of the period and its durability is testimony to that as much as to the quality of Peterson's playing, which is tight and uncharacteristically emotional.

We Get Requests and *Live* reverse the polarity totally. Cool but technically effusive, Peterson gets all over two sets of (mostly) romantic ballads, played with a portrait of Nat Cole perched on the soundboard in front of him. *The Silver Collection* has four excellent trio tracks fighting

e syrupy orchestrations that might have worked for another pianist but ot in Peterson's line of sight.

n from John Lewis's unemphatic keyboard approach that there's not *Very Tall* might be mistaken for an MJQ record. One of the great zz, Jackson is the undoubted star of the session, finessing 'On Green tle counterpoint and adding a tripping bounce to 'A Wonderful Guy'.

car Peterson Mercury 830698 CD

Terry (*t*); Herb Ellis (*g*); Ray Brown (*b*); Louis Hayes, Ed Thigpen (*d*). 8/64, 5, 10 & 12/65, 5/66.

Absolutely excellent value and by far the best introduction to the bassist's music. The combination of Brown and Thigpen ('Django', 'Autumn Leaves', 'Wheatland', 'Misty' and with Clark Terry on 'Roundland', 'If I Were A Bell' and 'Mack The Knife') is arguably the best Peterson ever recruited, though Louis Hayes is equally impressive on the dangerously schmaltzy 'Shadow Of Your Smile', 'If I Were A Bell' again, and 'Stella By Starlight'. A single track with Ellis, 'Easy Listening Blues', is gently ironic.

Peterson's huge arpeggiations and dense harmonic argument at this period in his career are still always subject to the overall logic of a piece, never suggesting virtuosity for its own sake. If there's a single Oscar Peterson album to own, this is probably it.

***(*) My Favorite Instrument MPS 821843 CD
Peterson (*p* solo). 4/68.

'Body And Soul' and the closing 'Take The "A" Train' are the best two performances on this unexceptional set of solo pieces. Peterson is in uncharacteristically sardonic form on a couple of tracks (and it suits him). He has himself a fine piano, with a solid, bell-like resonance, and it's more than agreeable to bathe in its rich overtones.

*** The Trio Pablo 2310701 CD/LP

*** The Good Life Pablo Live 2308241 CD
Peterson; Joe Pass (*g*); Niels-Henning Ørsted-Pedersen (*b*). 73.

For some fans, this is Peterson's best vintage and most effective partnerships. *The Trio* concentrates largely on blues material, with a withers-wringing 'Secret Love' as a curtain piece. On the other album, 'Wheatland' needs the rhythmic drive that Ed Thigpen brought to the tune on *Compact Jazz*, above; but by and large the drummerless trio is a setting that suits Peterson's Tatumesque delivery. Only five tracks, and little sense of significant development on any of them as Peterson's technique becomes increasingly pleased with itself.

*** Oscar Peterson & Dizzy Gillespie Pablo 2310740 CD/LP
Peterson; Dizzy Gillespie (*t*). 11/74.

This instrumentation goes all the way back to 1928, when Louis Armstrong and Earl Hines recorded 'Weather Bird'. There are, inevitably, hints of a later Bird in Gillespie's blues style, but there is also a slackness of conception similar to what overtook Armstrong in later years, and Peterson's overblown accompaniments don't help. The ballads are better, but only because they're prettier.

***(*) Jousts Pablo 2310817 LP/MC
Peterson; duos with Harry Edison, Roy Eldridge, Jon Faddis, Dizzy Gillespie, Clark Terry (*t*). 11 & 12/74, 5 & 6/75.

If boxing provides one of the informing metaphors for avant-garde duo improvisation, jousting perfectly captures the highly formalized and bloodless character of most of these. End-to-end stuff with periodic clashes in the middle. The Eldridge ('Crazy Rhythm' and 'Summertime') and Gillespie ('There Is No Greater Love' and 'Stella By Starlight') material comes from the same sessions as the items above, but without overlap of tracks. Only Eldridge and Gillespie seem to grasp fully the rationale of such sessions. By contrast, Faddis, Edison and even the splendid Clark Terry sound a little overpowered.

***(*)   **At The Montreux Jazz Festival 1975** Pablo 2310747 MC
Peterson; Milt Jackson (*vib*); Toots Thielemans (*hca*); Joe Pass (*g*); Niels-Henning Ørsted-Pedersen (*b*); Louie Bellson (*d*). 7/75.

Notable for the inclusion of Parker's 'Au Privave', a bebop classic that has been a favourite of the pianist's but which still sits rather awkwardly alongside Peterson's usual diet of blues and swing. In the event, it's an effective enough performance, though the logic of his solo is rather lost in the showers of notes he plays. Thielmans underlines how good an improviser he can be, but Pass is very muted.

***   **Porgy And Bess** Pablo 2310779 MC
Peterson; Joe Pass (*g*). 1/76.

Peterson's choice of clavichord for the *Porgy And Bess* session looked initially promising but ultimately suggests nothing more than a way of freshening up rather stale performances. It's perhaps the least known of the keyboard family, covering between three and five octaves (Peterson seems to be using the larger model) and distinguished from the piano and harpsichord by the fact that the strings are struck (rather than plucked, as with the harpsichord) by metal tangents which can be left in contact with the string rather than rebounding, altering its distinctive vibrato. Peterson certainly hasn't mastered that aspect of the instrument and plays it with a pianist's 'clean' touch that loses him the delicious bluesy wavers and bends it could have brought to these rather stolid, Gershwin interpretations.

***   **Montreux '77** Original Jazz Classics OJC 383 CD/LP
Peterson; Ray Brown, Niels-Henning Ørsted-Pedersen (*b*). 7/77.

***   **Montreux '77** Original Jazz Classics OJC 378 CD/LP
Peterson; Dizzy Gillespie, Clark Terry (*t*); Eddie Lockjaw Davis (*ts*); Niels-Henning Ørsted-Pedersen (*b*); Bobby Durham (*d*) 7/77.

The first of these is an intriguing two-bass experiment from the much-documented 1977 festival, where Peterson had become a recognized draw. Brown tends to take on some of the responsibilities of a guitarist, alternating his familiar 'walk' with clipped strums reminiscent of Herb Ellis's guitar and leaving the darker sonorities to the great Dane. The material, with the exception of 'There Is No Greater Love', is perhaps not ideally suited to the two string-players and they're often left with a rather subsidiary role. Peterson was just about blown out of sight by Tommy Flanagan's excellent performance earlier in the weekend, but he's generally in good if undemanding form. He can also be heard on other sets from the same event: with Roy Eldridge (OJC 373), Eddie Lockjaw Davis (OJC 384) and on an All-Star Jam (OJC 380, all CD/LP); there are festival highlights on OJC 385.

***   **The Paris Concert** Pablo Live 2620112 2LP
Peterson; Niels-Henning Ørsted-Pedersen (*b*); Joe Pass (*g*). 10/78.

Again, much of the interest focuses on two Parker tracks, 'Donna Lee' and 'Ornithology', both of which receive the kind of scalping treatment meted out by the army barber at boot camp. There's a 'who's next?' feel to the succession of tracks that makes you wish someone had shouted out, 'Excursion On A Wobbly Rail' or 'Three Blind Mice' . . . *anything* to wrong-foot the man. Playing without drums, as he did a lot around this time, Peterson seems rhythmically yet more commanding, but he also opens up his phrasing quite noticeably, highlighting the stresses and accents. Good value and surely a stronger candidate for CD transfer than the Northsea set below?

***(*)   **Skol** Original Jazz Classics OJC 496 CD/LP
Peterson; Stéphane Grappelli (*vn*); Joe Pass (*g*); Niels-Henning Ørsted-Pedersen (*b*); Mickey Roker (*d*). 7/79.

Peterson as group player. He defers more than usual to his colleagues – 'Nuages' and 'Making Whoopee' have Grappelli's thumbprint on them, after all – and contributes to a surprisingly rounded performance. The music is still on the soft side, but Peterson is as unfailingly sensitive as an accompanist as he is as a leader, and his solo spots are all the more striking for being tightly marshalled. A good choice for anyone who prefers the pianist in smaller doses, or who enjoys Grappelli. The fiddler suffers broadly similar critical problems. A player of consummate skill and considerable improvisational gifts, he has been somewhat hijacked by television and has come (quite wrongly) to seem a middle-of-the-road entertainer rather than a 'legitimate' jazz man. There is still probably more thought and enterprise in just one Grappelli solo than on a whole raft of albums by Young Turk tenor saxophone players.

(*)   **Digital At Montreux Pablo Live 2308224 CD
         Peterson; Niels-Henning Ørsted-Pedersen (*b*). 7/79.

Very much a middle-market package for the hi-fi enthusiast who wants to watch the dials glow and twitch. This is a rather dead spell in Peterson's career, and listening to him negotiate 'Caravan' or 'Satin Doll' for the umpteenth time is a little like watching a snooker professional clear the table according to the book. One longs for a few near-misses. Collectors and dial-twitchers only.

(*)   **The Personal Touch Pablo Today 2312135 CD
         Peterson; Clark Terry (*t, flhn*); Ed Bickert, Peter Leitch (*g*); Dave Young (*b*); Jerry
         Fuller (*d*); orchestra conducted by Rick Wilkins. 1 & 2/80.

Rick Wilkins's orchestrations aren't as drowningly fulsome as one might have feared, and both Peterson and Clark Terry are forceful enough players to rise above them. All the same, it's hard to see how a fairly unenterprising set would have been much different for quintet alone. Peterson's brief switch to electric piano (see 'The World Is Waiting For The Sunrise' for a quick sample) underlines the instrument's limitations rather than the player's.

*(*)   **A Royal Wedding Suite** Pablo Today 2312129 LP
         Peterson; orchestra conducted by Rick Wilkins. 4/81.

Composed in honour of the Wales nuptials. Movements include 'The Announcement', 'Lady Di's Waltz' and 'The Empty Cathedral'. Ghastly.

(*)   **Live At The Northsea Jazz Festival Pablo Live 2620115 LP
         Peterson; Toots Thielemans (*hca*); Joe Pass (*g*); Niels-Henning Ørsted-Pedersen (*b*).
         7/80.

If it's July, it must be . . . The Hague! Though Peterson is never less than fluently inventive, experienced listeners may detect more than a hint of weariness about this one. It's a quieter, less dynamic set than many of the festival albums from the period (which suits Thielmans particularly well) but isn't particularly reflective. The Nat Cole references are well to the forefront if you care to look for them, but this shouldn't be considered an urgent purchase.

***(*)   **Nigerian Marketplace** Pablo Live 2308231 CD/LP/MC
         Peterson; Niels-Henning Ørsted-Pedersen (*b*); Terry Clark (*d*). 7/81.

The title-track has a vivid 'live from Lagos' bustle about it that carries on into 'Au Privave', by now established as Peterson's favourite Charlie Parker item. The middle of the programme is on much more familiar turf with 'Nancy', 'Misty' and, perhaps more surprisingly, Bill Evans's lovely 'Waltz For Debby'. Peterson hasn't shown a great deal of interest in Evans's book (and it's difficult to judge whether his occasional Hawes and Evans touches show a direct influence), but he handles this theme with characteristic amplitude and not too much depth. Newcomer Clark performs well if rather busily.

***   **If You Could See Me Now** Pablo 2310918 CD/LP/MC
         Peterson; Joe Pass (*g*); Niels-Henning Ørsted-Pedersen (*b*); Martin Drew (*d*). 11/83.

If You Could See Me Now includes 'Limehouse Blues' and the bassist's feature, 'On Danish Shore'. These are about the best things on offer, but it's a thin set altogether.

(*)   **Oscar Peterson Live! Pablo 2310940 CD/LP
         Peterson; Joe Pass (*g*); David Young (*b*); Martin Drew (*d*). 11/86.

***(*)   **Time After Time** Pablo 2310947 CD/MC
         As above.

Consists largely of the deutero-classical 'Bach Suite', a more gainly and authentic pastiche than anything of Jacques Loussier's, but with an awful predictability about it as well. 'City Lights', 'Perdido' and 'Caravan' are tacked on at the end to keep the strict-constructionists happy. Better on harpsichord?

Time After Time restores the balance considerably. An original *Love Ballade* revives Peterson's reputation as a melodist, and the closing 'On The Trail' allays any doubts about failing stamina.

***(*) **Live At The Blue Note** Telarc CD 83304 CD
    Peterson; Herb Ellis (*g*); Ray Brown (*b*); Bobby Durham (*d*). 3/90.

Whatever stiffness has crept into Peterson's fingers over the last few years has served only to increase the feeling he injects into his playing. It's hard to relate 'Peace For South Africa' to the torrents of sound Peterson conjured up in his big-hall Pablo days. This is quieter, more intimate and more thoughtful, and the ballad medley at its centre shows genuine melodic inventiveness. A must for Peterson fans, and 'Honeysuckle Rose' offers a good – albeit second-gear – impression of the Tatum-derived technique which overlaid his earlier commitment to Nat Cole.

RALPH PETERSON
DRUMS, CORNET

*** **Triangular** Blue Note CDP 7927502 CD
    Peterson; Geri Allen (*p*); Essiet Okon Essiet (*b*). 88.

*** **V** Blue Note CDP 7917302 CD
    Peterson; Terence Blanchard (*t*); Steve Wilson (*ss, as*); Geri Allen (*p*); Phil Bowler
    (*b*). 4/88.

*** **Volition** Blue Note CDP 7938942 CD
    As above. 2/89.

Peterson's music exemplifies the virtuosity which has trademarked much of the new jazz of the 1980s and '90s: fast, skilful, heavy with inner complexities, it nevertheless pretends to no genuine radicalism but looks towards a way of reconciling the blowing excitement of hard bop with more sophisticated ideas of form. His own drumming is breathtakingly energetic: on first impression, it sounds as if he's constantly overplaying, never content to let a simple 4/4 stand and blurring the lines between each part of his kit. It sounds as if he studied on Elvin Jones but got caught up in what Coltrane was playing just as much. Yet his accents are razor-sharp, his cymbals choked with pinpoint precision, and he's always listening. As a composer, the verdict is less clear. The originals on *Triangular* aren't very interesting, and although this trio date will appeal to fans of Allen, the most interesting moments emerge when the trio acts as one and delivers a new slant on an established theme: Denzil Best's 'Move', for instance, has surely never been played this way before. The two quintet albums are superior since it takes the hard bop band instrumentation and makes it sound like something else altogether: Blanchard has never played as daringly as he does on, say, 'Enemy Within' on *V*, and though Wilson sounds as yet lacking a clear persona, he never stumbles in what is often difficult music to play. The multiple themes of 'Monief', for instance, are played so assuredly that the complexity of the piece sounds benign. Bowler, a very quick-witted bassist, is a great help here. But both *V* and *Volition* lack a final degree of sparkle or intensity which would raise the records in the top bracket: more studio time might have helped.

***(*) **Presents The Fo'Tet** Blue Note CDP 7954752 CD
    Peterson; Frank Lacy (*tb, flhn*); David Murray (*ts, bcl*); Don Byron (*cl, bcl*); Bryan
    Carrott (*vib*); Melissa Slocum (*b*). 12/89.

*** **Ornettology** Blue Note CDP 7982902 CD
    As above, except omit Lacy and Murray. 8/90.

An impressive step forward for Peterson. The Fo'Tet's instrumentation recalls some of the West Coast experimentalism of the 1950s, and while that's intended as a compliment, Peterson also ensures that charges of soulless cleverness won't stand up, with a drum commentary which passes through the session like a single, ever-evolving solo. Murray and Lacy make rousing guest appearances, but the other four players are the heart of the music, with Byron's playing suggesting new trails for the clarinet in a contemporary context and Carrott fusing the roles of rhythm, colour and lead voice. *Ornettology* doesn't quite match up to the earlier record, even though the quartet play with as much animation as before. There are surprising reflections on Monk, Shorter and Coleman in 'Iris', 'I Mean You' and 'Congeniality' respectively, which suggest that the drummer is offering enthusiastic assistance with the newly emerging sense of jazz repertory; but some of the originals sound aimless, and even though the group's make-up is hardly a take-off of the Benny Goodman Quartet, Goodman's band were rather better at stepping lightly through their more audacious ideas than this one is – as yet.

ERNST-LUDWIG PETROWSKY
ALTO SAXOPHONE, TENOR SAXOPHONE, SOPRANO SAXOPHONE, CLARINET

***   **Just For Fun** FMP 0140 LP
Petrowsky; Conrad Bauer (*tb*); Klaus Koch (*b*); Wolfgang Winkler (*d*). 4/73.

***   **Synopsis/DDR** FMP 0240 LP
Petrowsky; Conrad Bauer (*tb*); Ulrich Gumpert (*p*); Günter Baby Sommer (*d*). 3/74.

***   **SelbViert** FMP 0760 LP
Petrowsky; Heinz Becker (*t, flhn*); Klaus Koch (*b*); Günter Baby Sommer (*d*). 11/79.

***(*)   **SelbDritt** FMP 0890 LP
As above. 12/80.

A participant in both the Berlin Contemporary Jazz Orchestra and Peter Brötzmann's Clarinet Project, Petrowsky is an able multi-reeds player who combines a wryly romantic tone with an individual repertoire of timbral effects. Essentially a miniaturist, he sounds best in the company of quite propulsive players like Bauer and Sommer. It's extremely difficult to separate the available recordings qualitatively, but *SelbDritt* is the most confidently argued. It may be significant that on this occasion Petrowsky reduces his usual armoury of horns to just alto and baritone saxophones.

MICHEL PETRUCCIANI (born 1962)
PIANO

***   **Michel Petrucciani Trio** Owl 025 CD
Petrucciani; Jean-François Jenny-Clark (*b*); Aldo Romano (*d*). 4/81.

***   **Oracle's Destiny** Owl 032 CD/LP
Petrucciani (*p* solo). 10/82.

****   **100 Hearts** Concord GW 3001/CCD 43001 CD/LP
Petrucciani (*p* solo). 83.

***(*)   **Note'n Notes** Owl 037 CD/LP
Petrucciani (*p* solo). 10/84.

****   **Live At The Village Vanguard** Concord GW 3006/CCD 43006 2CD/LP
Petrucciani; Palle Danielsson (*b*); Eliot Zigmund (*d*). 3/84.

***   **Cold Blues** Owl 042 CD/LP
Petrucciani; Ron McClure (*b*). 1/85.

There's a freshness and quicksilver virtuosity about Michel Petrucciani's early records which is entirely captivating. While he is an adoring admirer of Bill Evans – 'Call me Bill,' he once suggested to Jim Hall, who demurred – his extrovert attack places Evans's harmonic profundity in a setting that will energize listeners who find Evans too slow and quiet to respond to. Petrucciani was already a formidable talent when he began recording for Owl, and while some of these discs have been criticized for being the work of a pasticheur, that seems a curmudgeonly verdict on someone who enjoys the keyboard so much. *Trio*, *Oracle's Destiny* and *Note'n Notes* feature mostly original programmes and he's a witty composer, his uptempo pieces feasts of bright articulation and ideas that seem to run around each other until the pianist ties them up as neatly as, say, Oscar Peterson might, although his streak of intellectual charm more often recalls Martial Solal or Tete Montoliu, two other European masters. *100 Hearts* is arguably the best of these sessions, if only for the marvellous title-tune which skips and leaps around its tone centre: in themes like this, Petrucciani stakes a claim as one of the great romantic virtuosos in contemporary jazz. *Live At The Village Vanguard* captures a typically rumbustious concert set by Petrucciani's trio of the day: 'Nardis' and 'Oleo' offer fresh annotations on well-worn classics, and there are sparkling revisions of his own originals, 'To Erlinda' and 'Three Forgotten Magic Words'. *Cold Blues* is a shade more prosaic in the interplay with McClure, but there's still some glittering work from the pianist.

***   **Pianism** Blue Note CDP 746295-2 CD
Petrucciani; Palle Danielsson (*b*); Eliot Zigmund (*d*). 12/85.

***(*)   **Power Of Three** Blue Note CDP 746427-2 CD
Petrucciani; Wayne Shorter (*ss, ts*); Jim Hall (*g*). 7/86.

***   **Michel Plays Petrucciani** Blue Note CDP 748679-2 CD
Petrucciani; John Abercrombie (*g*); Gary Peacock, Eddie Gomez (*b*); Roy Haynes, Al Foster (*d*); Steve Thornton (*perc*). 9–12/87.

Petrucciani's move to Blue Note gave him a bigger sound, courtesy of Blue Note's engineering; and the first three albums provided a variety of challenges. *Pianism* is another excellent batch of six work-outs by the trio who made the earlier live album, and if Zigmund and Danielsson sometimes sound a little perfunctory, that's partly due to the leader's brimming improvisations. *Power Of Three* is a slightly fragmented but absorbing concert meeting of three masters, skittish on 'Bimini' and solemnly appealing on 'In A Sentimental Mood'.

Plays Petrucciani is an all-original set which lines the pianist up against two magisterial rhythm sections, with Abercrombie adding some spruce counterpoint to two pieces. The smart hooks of 'She Did It Again' suggest that the pianist has a good living as a pop writer if he decides to quit the piano, but the more considered pieces show no drop in imagination, even if some of the themes seem to be curtailed before the improvisations really start moving.

(*)   **Music Blue Note CDP 792563-2 CD
Petrucciani; Joe Lovano (*ss*); Gil Goldstein (*acc*); Adam Holzman (*ky*); Romero Lubambo (*g*); Anthony Jackson, Chris Walker, Andy McKee, Eddie Gomez (*b*); Lenny White, Victor Jones (*d*); Frank Colon (*perc*); Tania Maria (*v*). 89.

***   **Playground** Blue Note CDP 795480-2 CD
Petrucciani; Adam Holzman (*ky*); Anthony Jackson (*b*); Omar Hakim, Aldo Romano (*d*); Steve Thornton (*perc*). 90.

If it seems churlish to criticize these records for 'going electric', it's only because they occasionally fall prey to modish airplay considerations: for much of both of them, Petrucciani is on top form. *Music* has a couple of trivial tunes, and the light backwash of electric keyboards which decorates most of the tracks is superfluous, if not exactly intrusive. But 'Bite' shows how much point and zest the pianist can bring to a simple ballad, and 'Happy Birthday Mr K' is a tremendous display of fireworks. *Playground* sites Petrucciani even more firmly in the centre of things, and a bravado effort like 'Brazilian Suite No. 3' finds him warming to even a fusion rhythm section; but the brief duration of most of the tracks finds them running out before he has.

OSCAR PETTIFORD (1922–60)

BASS, CELLO

***(*)   **Discoveries** Savoy 650142 CD
Pettiford; Gene Roland (*t*); Paul Quinichette (*ts*); Herbie Mann (*f*); Chasey Dean (*bcl*); Eddie Costa, Hank Jones, Nat Pierce, Billy Taylor (*p*); Joe Roland (*vib*); Doyle Salathiel (*g*); Matt Mathews (*acc*); Charles Mingus (*b*); Osie Johnson, Charlie Smith, Ed Thigpen (*d*). 2/52, 8/56, 10/57.

****   **The New Oscar Pettiford Sextet** Original Jazz Classics OJC 112 LP
Pettiford; Julius Watkins (*frhn*); Phil Urso (*ts*); Walter Bishop Jr (*p*); Charles Mingus (*b*); Percy Brice (*d*). 12/53.

***   **Jazz Legacy Baden Baden: Unreleased Radio Tapes** Jazzline JL 20827 CD/2LP
Pettiford; Dusko Goykovich (*t*); Rolf Kuhn (*cl*); Don Byas, Hans Koller (*ts*); Lucky Thompson (*ss*); Helmut Brand, Johnny Feigl, Rudi Flierl (*bs*); Hans Hammerschmid

(p); Attila Zoller (g); Hartwig Bartz, Kenny Clarke, Jimmy Pratt (d); Monica Zetterlund (v). 7 & 12/58, 6 & 7/59, 3/60.

***   **Vienna Blues: The Complete Session** Black Lion BLCD 760104 CD/LP
Pettiford; Hans Koller (ts); Attila Zoller (g, b); Jimmy Pratt (d). 1/59.

Like Charlie Haden's, Pettiford's playing career began in a family orchestra, under the tutelage of his father, Harry 'Doc' Pettiford. Like another great bassist, Charles Mingus, he never quite outgrew the turbulences of his early upbringing, and there was an undercurrent of anger and frustration just below the surface of Pettiford's wonderfully propulsive bass-playing. In terms of jazz history, he marks a middle point between Jimmy Blanton and his exact contemporary, Mingus; had he lived longer and closer to the centre, he might well now be acknowledged the more influential player.

As it is, he didn't live to see forty and spent his last years as a European exile. As a musical environment, it suited him rather well, encouraging his underlying classicism and allowing him to experiment with more flexible contexts. The best of the surviving albums is unfortunately on LP only, but *The New Oscar Pettiford Sextet* underlines his interest in non-standard jazz tonalities and instrumentations. Only Ron Carter among bassists has shown a commensurate interest in the cello, and Carter very much followed Pettiford's example. Here, he concentrates on the higher-pitched instrument – nearly always played pizzicato – for every track except 'Tamalpais', where he reverts to bass. As a front-line voice, the cello sounds good, but the basis of its success is the close interplay with the two other horns, notably on Quincy Jones's 'Stockholm Sweetnin'' and the vigorous 'Fieldstalker'. (Some issues include bonus tracks, 'Fru Brüel' and 'I Succumb To Temptation', featuring a vibraharpist and additional pianist.)

Both *Discoveries* and the Baden Baden tapes demonstrate the extent to which Pettiford was experimenting with the basic jazz ensemble at the end of the 1950s. A 1956 track on the former has him playing bass alongside flute, bass clarinet, vibraphone, accordion and drums, elsewhere using accordion in place of piano or guitar. On the airshot Jazzline, 'Low Idea' has him playing both his fiddles with a section of four baritone saxophones (one wonders if Peter Brötzmann and Bill Laswell, who recorded a bass–bass saxophone album called *Low Life*, took notice). There is less cello material on the Baden compilation, and some of the best tracks are those with Austrian saxophonist Koller, who also features prominently on *Vienna Blues*. The version of 'Blues In The Closet' on Jazzline is better by the thickness of Kenny Clarke's drumming, but the Black Lion includes one outstanding ballad, 'The Gentle Art Of Love'.

Pettiford's work with Monk and Ellington (who recognized both the break and the continuity with Blanton) survives on disc, and it's worth concentrating on the bassist's performances. It should also be noted that, though credited to Bud Powell, Black Lion's *The Complete Essen Jazz Festival Concert* (BLCD 760105 CD, *q. v.*) documents a performance by the Oscar Pettiford Trio and (with Coleman Hawkins) Quartet from April 1960. Six months later Pettiford died in his adoptive city of Copenhagen of what was then still called 'infantile paralysis'.

JACK PETTIS (born 1902)
C-MELODY AND ALTO SAXOPHONES, CLARINET

****   **Jack Pettis Volume 3** Retrieval FJ-129 LP
Pettis; Bill Moore, Don Bryan, Mannie Klein, Phil Hart, Mike Mosiello (t); Tommy Dorsey, Paul Weigan, Glenn Miller, Jack Teagarden (tb); Benny Goodman, Don Murray, Len Kavash, Tony Parenti (cl, as); Al Goering, Lennie Hayton (p, cel); Jack Cornell (p); Matty Malneck, Nat Brusiloff, Nicky Gerfach (vn); Dick McDonough (g, bj); Eddie Lang, Carl Kress (g); Clay Bryon (bj); Merrill Klein (bb, b); Harry Goodman (b); Dillon Ober (d); Eugene Ramey, Erwin McGee, Irving Mills (v). 6/28–5/29.

A valuable and superbly remastered collection of some little-known records. Pettis was, along with Frankie Trumbauer, the only man to specialize on the C-melody saxophone, although he plays as much alto here; and this set brings together a number of sessions for Victor and Okeh from 1928–9, where he leads several all-star bands. The earliest date, by a nine-piece outfit, sounds much like one of the Trumbauer groups, while the later sides boast a top-notch big band working through unusually hot material: there are very few intrusive vocals, and plenty of interest in the arrangements, but it's the quality of the soloists which is remarkable. Goodman and Teagarden are both generously featured and both are in their best early form; Tony Parenti plays some searing clarinet on three titles; and Pettis himself, while not quite at his colleagues' highest level, is a thoughtful and agile improviser too. The two versions of 'Freshman Hop' and 'Bag O'Blues', 'Wild And Woolly Willie' and 'Companionate Blues' are about as good as New York jazz of the day gets: little is yielded to the more famous studio bands of the time. In a model reissue, four of the tracks come from previously unissued test-pressings. Highly recommended, although it should be noted that the first two volumes have actually yet to appear!

DAS PFERD
GROUP

**   **Das Pferd** ITM 0016/1416 CD/LP
      Reiner Winterschladen (*t*); Wolfgang Schmidtke (*reeds, ky, v*); Klaus Bernatzki
      (*reeds*); Suppi Huhn (*ky*); Markus Wienstroer (*g*); Tom Cora (*clo*); Jan Kazda (*b, ky,
      v*); Diethard Stein (*d*); Poncho Valdez (*perc*); Sabine Sabine (*v*). 87.

(*)   **Kisses ITM 0030/1430 CD/LP
      Randy Brecker (*t*); Wolfgang Scmidtke (*reeds, ky*); Peter Brötzmann (*ts*); Tobias
      Becker (*ky*); Billy Bang (*vn*); Markus Wienstroer (*g*); Jan Kazda (*b, ky*); John
      Lindberg (*b*); Marilyn Mazur (*d*); Oscar Sanders, Rosay Wortham (*v*). 88.

**   **Ao Vivo** VeraBra 29 CD
      As above, except Kurt Billker (*d*) replaces Mazur, omit Brötzmann, Bang, Lindberg,
      Sanders and Wortham. 5/89.

Exotic, sometimes humourless fusion, set down by an accomplished if oddball group, apparently led by Schmidtke and Kazda. The brief, clipped episodes on the first record suggest a Teutonic variation on some of New York's electric jazz of the period, although the deliberately stumbling rhythms are an excessively arch way of putting the music across. *Kisses* is enlivened, marginally, by some guest spots from unlikely participants such as Brötzmann and Bang but finally isn't much different. The surprise is the presence of Brecker, who plays throughout the live (third) record, which is the most expansive of the three without offering many more rewards. Tinny studio sound on the first records, while the live set is sonically more atmospheric.

BARRE PHILLIPS
DOUBLE BASS, ELECTRONICS

****   **Mountainscapes** ECM 1076 LP
      Phillips; John Surman (*bs, ss, bcl, syn*); John Abercrombie (*g*); Dieter Feichtener
      (*syn*); Stu Martin (*d*). 3/76.

***   **Die Jungen; Random Generators** FMP 0680 LP
      Phillips; Peter Kowald (*b*). 3/79.

***   **Journal Violone II** ECM 1149 LP
      Phillips; John Surman (*ss, bs, bcl, syn*); Aina Kemanis (*v*). 6/79.

***(*)   **Camouflage** Victo 08 CD
      Phillips solo. 5/89.

It's galling to record that two of bassist Phillips's very finest records (and there are few enough of them to begin with) are currently out of catalogue. The solo *Call Me When You Get There* [ECM 1257 LP] from 1983, with its lyrical journeyings and unfussy philosophical musings, covers similar musical territory to the much earlier but equally fine *Moutainscapes*, a suite of subliminally interrelated pieces that demonstrate the astonishing transformations visited on basic musical perspectives by very slight changes in the angle of vision. Almost all of Phillips's output operates in that way. Whatever is being hidden on the recent solo *Camouflage*, it can scarcely be the artist himself. Recorded in almost disturbing close-up (an effect necessarily heightened by CD reproduction), one can almost hear the bassist thinking as he investigates the sometimes fugitive tonalities of his instrument. Something of the same relationship between *Call Me* and *Mountainscapes* applies (recognizing the lapse in time) between *Camouflage* and *Journal Violone II*. The 1979 trio again makes use of Surman's melancholy soliloquizing, but in a rather more colouristic way that is reminiscent of *Three Day Moon* [ECM 1123 LP, with Terje Rypdal, Feichtner and Trilok Gurtu], another deletion casualty but Phillips's most accessible work.

Looking at the bassist's career only in the context of his recent solo work or of his improvisational activities with Derek Bailey's Company collective tends to cast it as something rarefied and dauntingly inward of gaze (the duo *Figuring* with Bailey (*q.v.*), Incus CD05, might attract that charge) but it's as well to remember that Phillips was Archie Shepp's bass player at the 1965 Newport Festival and that, with Surman and the late Stu Martin, also on *Mountainscapes*, he was a member of The Trio, one of the most dynamic free jazz units of the late 1960s. There is a dancer's grace and concentration in Phillips's playing, an internal balance and rhythm that, as on *Camouflage*'s 'You And Me', makes it virtually impossible to separate man and instrument.

***   **Aquarian Rain** ECM 1451 CD/LP
Phillips; Alain Joule (*perc*). 5/91.

Phillips made the first-ever album of solo bass improvisations as long ago as 1968. At the time, as Steve Lake relates in the liner-note to *Aquarian Rain*, he believed he was providing material for an electronic score, but composer Max Schubel thought the bass parts stood more than adequately on their own, and *Unaccompanied Barre* was eventually released. Nearly twenty-five years later, Phillips produces an album which does make significant use of electronic processing of instrumental performance. The effect suggests that Schubel's instincts were sound, for *Aquarian Rain* is the most diffuse and least focused album the bassist has released. Phillips's own description of the process of 'collective composition', by which tapes were sent back and forth between his French home in Puget-Ville and the Studio Grame in Lyon where Jean-François Estager and James Giroudon worked the filters and gates, may have yielded exemplary music for live performance (a suite called 'Brick On Brick' was created, incorporating pieces like 'Inbetween I And E' and 'Promenade De Mémoire') but it sounds rather stilted and contrived when digitalized and fixed. Enthusiasts for the bassist's work will find much of value but, compared to the duos with Guy, these interchanges with percussionist Joule lack even that tiny spark of electricity that rescues processed improvisation of this sort from becoming acoustic set-dressing.

FLIP PHILLIPS (born 1915)
TENOR SAX

(*)   **A Sound Investment Concord CCD 4334 CD/MC
Phillips; Scott Hamilton (*ts*); John Bunch (*p*); Chris Flory (*g*); Phil Flanigan (*b*); Chuck Riggs (*d*). 3/87.

***   **A Real Swinger** Concord CCD 4358 CD/MC
Phillips; Dick Hyman (*p*); Howard Alden, Wayne Wright (*g*); Jack Lesberg (*b*); Butch Morris (*d*). 5–6/88.

These are perhaps surprisingly able-bodied and big-hearted records from a tenorman who is still most notoriously remembered for long, tedious solos at Jazz At The Philharmonic appearances, some 40 years earlier. In his elder-statesman years, Phillips sounds warmly charismatic, pacing his solos with some flair and digging in just when he has to: the session where he is the sole horn sounds fine, with 'September Song' and 'Poor Butterfly' to remind one of his authoritative ballad playing. The set with Hamilton is sometimes too much of a good thing, with both tenors thickening the romantic broth a little too generously at times, but one can't deny the heartiness of it all.

MAURIZIO PICCHIO
DRUMS

***   **Biri San** Splasc(h) H 172 LP
Picchio; Klaus Lessman (*ss, as, cl*); Riccardo Galardini (*g*); Ramberto Ciammarughi
(*ky*); Franco Fabbrini (*b*). 1–2/88.

Pensive, steadily inventive fusion from a fine and unassuming quartet. Picchio is content to lead
from the rear – he takes only a couple of discreet solos and contributes only one theme – while
Galardini and Lessmann, the latter playing mainly soprano and clarinet, take the major solo
honours, Ciammarughi appearing on only two tracks. Galardini has trouble with the
guitar-synthesizer he occasionally uses – it tends to hoot – but otherwise the spare, loose
textures here are coolly amiable and insinuating.

ENRICO PIERANUNZI
PIANO

***   **New Lands** Timeless SJP 211 CD/LP
Pieranunzi; Marc Johnson (*b*); Joey Baron (*d*). 2/84.

***   **Autumn Song** Enja 4094 LP
Pieranunzi; Massimo Urbani (*as*); Enzo Pietropaoli (*b*); Fabrizio Sferra (*d*). 11/84.

***   **Deep Down** Soul Note SN 1121 CD/LP
Pieranunzi; Marc Johnson (*b*); Joey Baron (*d*). 2/86.

***   **What's What** yvp 3006 CD/LP
Pieranunzi (*p* solo). 6/85.

(*)   **Moon Pie yvp 3011 CD/LP
Pieranunzi; Enzo Pietropaoli (*b*); Roberto Gatto (*d*). 5–6/87.

***   **No Man's Land** Soul Note SN 1221 CD/LP
Pieranunzi; Marc Johnson (*b*); Steve Houghton (*d*). 5/89.

Pieranunzi's music is a persuasive and accomplished indexing of some of the options thrown
open to pianists in the aftermath of Tyner, Hancock, Taylor and – to cite one source away from
Afro-America – Martial Solal. Pieranunzi is not a virtuoso in the manner of any of those players
– though his rather self-effacing manner recalls something of Hancock – but he uses their
ground-breaking discoveries in modality, rhythm and the broadening of pianistic devices to his
own ends. As with the Space Jazz trio, which he apparently leads with bassist Pietropaoli, this is
convincingly post-modern jazz, where the pianist sounds perfectly self-aware yet concerned to
introduce elements of abstraction and emotional flow alike. Perhaps the two discs to seek out
are the ruminative but pointedly argued solo set, *What's What*, and the excllent trio session, *No
Man's Land*, though the earlier *New Lands* and *Deep Down* are both very good too. Urbani's
winsome bop manner adds some variation to the Enja album, though not enough to make it a
compelling difference; and *Moon Pie* sounds a little under-baked.

BILLY PIERCE
TENOR AND SOPRANO SAXOPHONES

(*)   **The Complete William The Conqueror Sessions Sunnyside SSC 9013D CD
Pierce; James Williams, James 'Sid' Simmons (*p*); John Lockwood (*b*); Keith
Copeland (*d*). 5/85.

**   **Give And Take** Sunnyside SSC 1026 D CD
Pierce; Terence Blanchard (*t*); Mulgrew Miller (*p*); Ira Coleman (*b*); Tony Reedus
(*d*). 6-10/87.

***   **Equilateral** Sunnyside SSC 1037 D CD
Pierce; Hank Jones (*p*); Roy Haynes (*d*). 1/88.

Another Jazz Messengers tenorman steps out on his own, with characteristically mixed results. Pierce is as easily tempted by bland competence as the next saxophonist, and nothing memorable happens on either of the two earlier discs: it's especially disappointing with regard to *Give And Take*, which from moment to moment suggests a genuinely heavyweight encounter but over the long stretch delivers nothing much at all. *Equilateral* starts out with two advantages: the presence of Jones and Haynes, still among the best props a young musician could hope to find alongside him, and the unusual bassless instrumentation, which isn't intrusive but at least proposes a different balance to the usual. The programme is nearly all standards, and on some of them – particularly 'You Don't Know What Love Is' and 'Come Rain Or Come Shine' – Pierce summons the gravitas of greater players without surrendering too much of himself. Worth watching, if future releases continue to set up a context of some purpose.

DAVE PIKE (born 1938)
VIBES, MARIMBA

(*)   **Pike's Groove Criss Cross Jazz Criss 1021 LP
          Pike; Cedar Walton (*p*); David Williams (*b*); Billy Higgins (*d*). 2/86.

***   **Bluebird** Timeless SJP 302 CD/LP
          Pike; Charles McPherson (*as*); Rein De Graaff (*p*); Koo Serierse (*b*); Eric Ineke (*d*). 10–11/88.

Pike is another musician whose several recordings have suffered at the hands of the deletions axe; *Pike's Peak*, a 1961 date with Bill Evans, was reissued in 1990 on Portrait but seems to have disappeared again already. Although he once worked with Paul Bley in the late 1950s, Pike's main interests are more conservative than that association might suggest: both the above records are light but undeniably skilful bebop sessions. *Pike's Groove* matches him with the most propulsive of rhythm sections and, thanks to Walton's craft and sensitivity to tone-colours, vibes and piano don't cancel each other out as they often do in such situations. Seven familiar pieces, but everyone is crisply on top of them.

The Timeless set features eight Charlie Parker themes, three by Pike and the rhythm section, four by the quintet, and one by the rhythm section alone. While the music is entirely regressive – the Dutch players are content to be model executants and Pike's own playing isn't charcterful enough to transcend bop routine – the themes are at least covered with great finesse, and McPherson, one of the premier exponents of bop repertory, is marvellously agile. Sharp, full sound.

MICHEL PILZ
BASS CLARINET

***   **Carpathes** FMP 0250 LP
          Pilz; Peter Kowald (*b*); Paul Lovens (*d*). 8–9/78.

Pilz may be the only improviser to concentrate solely on the bass clarinet. While he doesn't exactly evade the influence of Eric Dolphy, he sounds less like him than most practitioners: he loves the low register of the horn, growling on notes that seem to emanate from his midriff, and, rather than trying to make the ungainly beast of the clarinet family seem agile, he insists on its freakishness, his vocalizations guttural and unlovely. Yet he likes melody too, which gives these trio improvisations the quality of baleful songs: his two solos, 'Carpathes' and 'Krebsauel', are strange, clumping recitations. Kowald and Lovens creak and stamp around him, and there are some lovely moments on side two, particularly when the percussionist gets out his singing saw on 'Pikolo für den Glockner von Notre Dame'. The result is one of the most vivid FMP albums of its time, recorded aggressively close, which heightens the intimacy.

COURTNEY PINE (born 1964)

TENOR, ALTO AND SOPRANO SAXOPHONES, BASS CLARINET, FLUTE, ALTO FLUTE

(*)   **Journey To The Urge Within Island CID 9846 CD/MC
Pine; Kevin Robinson (*t*); Ray Carless (*bs*); Julian Joseph (*p*); Roy Carter (*ky*);
Orphy Robinson (*vib*); Martin Taylor (*g*); Gary Crosby (*b*); Mark Mondesir (*d*); Ian
Mussington (*perc*); Susaye Greene, Cleveland Watkiss (*v*). 7–8/86.

***   **Destiny's Song And The Image Of Pursuance** Island CID CD/MC
Pine; Julian Joseph, Joe Bashorun (*p*); Paul Hunt, Gary Crosby (*b*); Mark Mondesir
(*d*).

***   **The Vision's Tale** Antilles ANCD 8746 CD/MC
Pine; Ellis Marsalis (*p*); Delbert Felix (*b*); Jeff Watts (*d*). 1/89.

**   **Closer To Home** Mango 846528 CD/MC
Pine; Ian Fraser (*bs*); Robbie Lynn (*ky*); Cameron Pierre (*g*); Danny Browne, Delroy
Donaldson (*b*); Cleavie (*d*); Pam Hall, Carroll Thompson (*v*).

***   **Within The Realms Of Our Dreams** Antilles ANCD 8756 CD/MC
Pine; Kenny Kirkland (*p*); Charnett Moffett (*b*); Jeff Watts (*d*). 1/90.

British readers will have had a difficult time of it separating Pine the musician from Pine the marketing phenomenon, since, starting around the time of the first record above, he was fruitfully presented as the face of young British jazz in the 1980s. It was a move that brought unprecedented attention to the music in the UK, but the fallout has been a certain suspicion among many who are wary of media hype, as well as a problem in evaluating the records purely on their musical worth. Fortunately, Pine himself is a saxophonist of clear and outstanding capabilities: whatever flaws these records may have, his own contributions are of a consistently high standard. *Journey To The Urge Within*, his hit debut, emerges as a sampler for young British talent, with Joseph, Mondesir, Crosby, Robinson and Watkiss all making interesting debut appearances and Pine leading the pack. There are good moments, and the sense of a group of players seiing their time is palpable, but inexperience and fragmentation take their toll on the record's impact and it tends to work out as a series of half-fulfilled gestures. *Destiny's Song* was a strong follow-up: tunes such as 'Sacrifice' show that Pine has a knack for turning catchy riffs into feasible melodies, and an emerging dialogue with Mondesir (Pine's Dannie Richmond, if not quite his Elvin Jones) gave the session real clout. But both this and the subsequent *The Vision's Tale* hint at a talent that is taking a long time to work out what it wants to do: to many of the double-time solos and pyrotechnics smack of pointless virtuosity, and several improvisations sound like sketches for real achievements that have to be left unfinished. *The Vision's Tale* (a penchant for obfuscatory titles shouldn't put listeners off) put Pine in the hands of an American rhythm section, with Marsalis at his wiliest in accompaniment, and if a reading of 'I'm An Old Cowhand' seems to be asking for trouble – Pine has often been accused of balling together a host of unassimilated influences, though Coltrane rather than Rollins is the leading name involved – it's dealt with in enough good humour to lend a self-deprecatory note.

 Close To Home (or *Get Busy*, as it is also known) returns Pine to roots which no American jazz musician can really claim: like so many young black British musicians, he started in reggae and funk bands, and this lightly shuffling reggae set is a very pleasant if finally inconsequential disc. It has the merit, though, of reminding that Pine's records never sound like American jazz albums, for all his leaning towards familiar role models: rhythmically, tonally, harmonically, all his music – and that of many of his British sidemen – is informed by sources (Jamaican reggae being a prime example) which seldom filter through to the post-bop mainstream of American jazz. *Within The Realms Of Our Dreams* puts him back with a formidable American rhythm section, and there's no hint of difficulty for the leader. Originals such as 'Zaire', which features a double-time passage on soprano which is quite breathtaking in its technical aplomb, and 'The Sepia Love Song' show a maturing sense of detail as a composer, and 'Una Muy Bonita' and 'Donna Lee' sweep through Coleman and Parker with ferocious accomplishment. There are still too many notes, and too few ideas channelled down a single route to resolution, but this multifariousness of idea and delivery is clearly Pine's way.

ARMAND PIRON (1888–1943)
VIOLIN, VOCAL

**   **Piron's New Orleans Orchestra 1923–1925** Retrieval FJ-128 LP
Piron; Peter Bocage (*t*); John Lindsay (*tb*); Lorenzo Tio Jr (*cl, ts*); Louis Warnevcke
(*as*); Steve Lewis (*p*); Charles Bocage (*bj, v*); Jose Ysaguirres (*bb*); Louis Cottrell Sr
(*d*). 12/23–3/25.

Historically, the 18 tracks collected here are of some importance, since they comprise the
complete recorded output of one of the new black New Orleans bands to be recorded in the
1920s (although most of the sides were actually made in New York). The results, though, will
disappoint all but the most committed of scholars. Where they play material also recorded by
other bands – such as 'Do-Doodle-Oom' and 'West Indies Blues', both covered by Fletcher
Henderson – Piron's orchestra sounds tame and barely musters even a sense of hot dance music.
The playing is sprightly enough and, as each track goes on, they tend to loosen up as the last
chorus approaches, but pickings are slim. This is despite the presence of Tio, a New Orleans
legend, who seldom gets much of a look-in, and Peter Bocage, a decent trumpeter. The original
records suffer from rough acoustic recording, but the remastering is up to the house standards.
It must be accounted a great loss that Piron never made any records with his Olympia Band,
which he led in New Orleans around 1912. In the front line were King Oliver and Sidney
Bechet.

BUCKY PIZZARELLI (born 1926)
GUITAR

****   **The Complete Guitar Duos (The Stash Sessions)** Stash ST CD 536 CD
Pizzarelli; John Pizzarelli (*g*). 80, 84.

Pizzarelli's finest recording of recent years remains the unfortunately deleted solo *Love Songs*
[Stash ST 213 CD], a set of gentle swing improvisations on his favoured seven-string guitar
(which nevertheless sounds quite conventionally tuned). Pizzarelli maintained a highly
successful swing duo with George Barnes until the latter died in 1977, since when he has worked
with his son, John Pizzarelli Jr, an excellent family act reminiscent of the Raneys but untouched
by their bop leanings. John Pizzarelli was still developing an individual style over the period
covered by the two sessions; on the earlier tracks he sounds like an able accompanist but rarely
stamps any real personality on a piece. The later sessions sound much more like an equally
balanced duo, and the material is marginally more challenging in response, with a wonderfully
shuffling 'Four Brothers' and a near-perfect 'Lush Life'. Highly recommended.

JOHN PIZZARELLI
GUITAR, VOCAL

***   **My Blue Heaven** Chesky JD38 CD
Pizzarelli; Clark Terry (*t, v*); Dave McKenna (*p*); Bucky Pizzarelli (*g*); Milt Hinton
(*b*); Connie Kay (*d*). 2/90.

***   **All Of Me** RCA Novus PD 90619 CD/MC
Pizzarelli; Randy Sandke, John Frosk, Anthony Kadleck, Athony Ponella (*t*); Jim
Pugh, Rock Ciccarone, Michael Davis (*tb*); Paul Faulise (*btb*); Walt Levinsky, Phil
Bodner (*as*); Scott Robinson (*ss, ts, f*); Frank Griffith (*ts*); Sol Schlinger (*bs*); William
Kerr, Lawrence Feldman (*f*); Ken Levinsky (*p*); Bucky Pizzarelli (*g*); Martin Pizzarelli
(*b*); Joe Cocuzzo (*d*); Gordon Gottlieb (*perc, vib*); strings. 91.

One of the two sons of Bucky Pizzarelli – the other is bassist Martin, who plays on the Novus
album – John Pizzarelli follows in father's footsteps by using a guitar style that owes an obvious
debt to paternal influence: quick, clean picking, a Django-like tone and a penchant for the
humorous aside in the middle of otherwise terse improvisations. While this makes for solid,
gratifying mainstream, Pizzarelli isn't really a young fogey: there's a coolness about his manner
which detaches him a little from the material and, while some of his song choices are as
neo-classic as one can get, he sounds a little dreamier than the Concord crew of mainstreamers.

Besides, he sings – and this is what looks destined to make his fortune. Whether by design or not, the Novus album in particular is customized to home in on the market created by Harry Connick. Pizzarelli was doing this sort of thing long before Connick, and his singing (which actually owes more to Chet Baker than to Nat Cole) and playing is accomplished in its own right; but the tenor of the later records is unmistakably tuned to Connick's huge audience.

My Blue Heaven is beautifully recorded and shrewdly programmed, with Clark Terry tossing in some characteristic obbligatos and the instrumental pieces – including a very sharp-witted 'Don't Get Around Much Any More' – finding a real, spontaneous zest. *All Of Me* is Pizzarelli's stab at the big time: cleverly pitched between the big band charts and the nucleus of the singer and the rhythm section, it's artfully realized but a legitimate musical success by dint of Pizzarelli's trust of the material. His three original songs are, though, no special achievement. The recording and mix are superbly full and wide-bodied.

LONNIE PLAXICO
ELECTRIC BASS, BASS KEYBOARD

**   **Iridescence** Muse MCD 5427 CD
Plaxico; Greg Osby (*as, ss*); David Jones (*as*); Lance Bryant (*ts*); Mike Cain, Darryl G. Ivey (*ky*); David Gilmore (*g*); Bryan Carrot (*vib*); Kenny Davis (*b*); Gene Jackson (*d*); Terri Davis Plaxico (*v*); Brenda Brunson Bey (*wardrobe*). 12/90.

Another fine bassist falls victim to the Lead Guitar Syndrome. But where players like Ron Carter, Stanley Clarke and Jaco Pastorius had enough basic musical nous to avoid the charge of mere posturing, *Iridescence* trades in convincing musicianship for a thin patina of style. Like his solos, the leader's own compositions are cliché-ridden and lame, with the solitary exception of 'Intersection', the most straightforward and jazz-orientated piece (with a fine Sanborn-ish alto solo from Jones) on an overproduced album dotted with Janet Jackson, Anita Baker and Joe Sample covers. This surely isn't what M-Base's street revolution was all about?

KING PLEASURE (born 1922)
VOCALS

[***   **King Pleasure Sings** Original Jazz Classics OJC 217 CD/LP/MC]
Pleasure; Ed Lewis (*t*); J. J. Johnson, Kai Winding (*tb*); Charles Ferguson, Lucky Thompson (*ts*); Danny Banks (*bs*); Jimmy Jones, John Lewis, Ed Swanston (*p*); Paul Chambers, Percy Heath, Peck Morrison (*b*); Kenny Clarke, Joe Harris, Herbie Lovelle (*d*); Betty Carter, Jon Hendricks, Eddie Jefferson, The Dave Lambert Singers, The Three Riffs (*v*). 12/52, 9/53, 12/54.

***   **Golden Days** Original Jazz Classics OJC 1772 CD/LP
Pleasure; Matthew Gee (*tb*); Teddy Edwards, Harold Land (*ts*); Gerald Wiggins (*p*); Wilfred Middlebrooks (*b*); Earl Palmer (*d*).

Born plain Clarence Beeks, in plain old Oakdale, Tennessee, Pleasure won an amateur night at the Apollo in 1951 and went on to scoop enormous success with 'Moody's Mood For Love', a vocalese version of James Moody's saxophone solo on 'I'm In The Mood For Love', and later with 'Red Top'. Eddie Jefferson claimed to have invented the practice of fitting lyrics to bop solos, but it was Pleasure who garnered the praise and what cash was going. (Just to confirm Jefferson's luck, he was blown away outside a Detroit club in 1979, just as his career was reviving; Jefferson, Jon Hendricks and The Three Riffs all feature on two 1954 tracks from *Sings*.)

The earlier of the two OJCs is shared with Annie Ross, who sings the classic vocalization of Wardell Gray's 'Twisted', along with 'Moody's Mood For Love' and Pleasure's 'Parker's Mood' (on *Golden Days* and *Sings*) the best-known vocalese performance. Pleasure has something of Ross's honeyed smoothness of tone but combines it with a more biting articulation that can sound remarkably like Charlie Parker's alto saxophone (or more frequently the smooth tenor sound of Teddy Edwards and Lucky Thompson). Using less sophisticated arrangements and generally less witty lyrics than Jon Hendricks's for Lambert, Hendricks and Ross, Pleasure more often relies on the quality of the voice alone. The accompaniments are generally good, but the Quincy Jones backings to 'Don't Get Scared' and 'I'm Gone' are exceptional. Something of an acquired taste, though this by-way of jazz has assumed greater retrospective significance in recent years.

PAUL PLIMLEY
PIANO, MARIMBA

***   **Both Sides Of The Same Mirror** Nine Winds 0135 CD
Plimley; Lisle Ellis (*b*)/ 11/89.

Although the tune titles ('Moving The Twin Entrances Of Light', 'Reflections Of A Persistent Mirage') suggest a trip into New Age wonderland, Plimley's music – he is a veteran of Canada's free-jazz movement – is a good deal thornier than that. He and Ellis have worked together for many years, and a thread of experience runs through all the playing here. Plimley's employment of clusters suggests Cecil Taylor or Don Pullen without really bowing to either man, and when he picks up the marimba mallets for 'Mirage', he expands on the percussiveness of his approach with a fine understanding of his own strengths. Ellis counterpoints with arco of guitar-like lines, and on a version of Jimi Hendrix's 'Third Stone From The Sun' he sounds as impressive a soloist as Plimley. The CD seems a little long at almost an hour – a concentrated 40 minutes might have made a better impression – but it's a solid introduction to these players.

HERB POMEROY (born 1930)
TRUMPET

***   **Life Is A Many Splendored Gig** Fresh Sound FSR-CD 84 CD
Pomeroy; Lennie Johnson, Augie Ferretti, Everett Longstreth, Joe Gordon (*t*); Joe Ciavardone, Bill Legan, Gene DiStachio (*tb*); Dave Chapman, Boots Mussulli (*as*); Varty Haritounian, Jaki Byard, Zoot Sims (*ts*); Deane Haskins (*bs*); Ray Santisi (*p*); John Neves (*b*); Jimmy Zitano (*d*). 6/57.

Although this session was recorded in New York, Pomeroy worked mostly in Boston, and led some fine orchestras at The Stables in the late 1950s. He made disappointingly few records as a leader, and of those, *Jazz In A Stable* and *Band In Boston* are still awaited on CD. There's a touch of sessionman gloss on this set, originally made for Roulette, which Zoot Sims tends to dominate as guest soloist, and the charts are more concerned with straight-ahead swing than challenging ideas, but the band play with meaty insistence and the rhythm section – close colleagues of Pomeroy's – establish a commanding base for such as Tadd Dameron's 'Our Delight' and a version of 'It's Sand Man' that's as good as a prime Basie workout. Scholars may note that 'Aluminium Baby' is something of an answer to Ellington's 'Satin Doll' (from Byard, who provides a rare sighting on tenor). Good sound, although a forthcoming Roulette reissue may hopefully provide extra material from these sessions. Pomeroy also leads a strange ensemble with Ornette Coleman and Ian Underwood for three tracks on *Lenox School Of Jazz Concert* (Royal RJD 513), discussed in the Various Artists section.

VALERY PONOMAREV (born 1943)
TRUMPET

***   **Trip To Moscow** Reservoir RSR CD 107 CD
Ponomarev; Ralph Moore (*ts*); Hideki Tadao (*p*); Dennis Irwin (*b*); Kenny Washington (*d*). 4/85.

Valery Ponomarev left Russia in 1973, when pre-*glasnost* winds were still blowing chill. From 1977 to 1980 he held the trumpet chair in the Jazz Messengers and has adopted the idiom with unabashed aplomb.

The stint taught him how to juggle changes. Blakey used to let him loose nightly on 'I Remember Clifford' (acknowledging the obvious stylistic influence) and there's a marvellous version on Ponomarev's own deleted *Means Of Identification* [Reservoir RSR 101 LP]. The same combination of sinew and tenderness on 'For You Only' here underlines the fact that he isn't just a fast-valve showman but has absorbed the subtler cadence of Brown's approach. British-born Ralph Moore is in fine form, as is the drafted-in pianist, who had to read a projected guitar part and pulls it off with great credit.

JEAN-LUC PONTY (born 1942)
VIOLIN

***   **Compact Jazz** MPS 835320-2 CD
Ponty; Stéphane Grappelli, Sven Asmussen (*vn*); George Shearing, Kenny Drew, Wolfgang Dauner, Marc Hemmeler (*p*); Larry Coryell, Diz Disley, Philip Catherine, Ike Isaacs (*g*); Niels-Henning Ørsted-Pedersen, Eberhard Weber, Isla Eckinger, Andrew Simpkins (*b*); Alex Riel, Rusty Jones, Kenny Clare, Daniel Humair (*d*). 9/66–1/79.

In the 1960s, Ponty seemed like the natural successor to Stéphane Grappelli as Europe's great jazz-violin romantic. But his interest in Coltrane led him into altogether thornier areas, even though his recordings with the three-fiddle Violin Summit, some of which are collected on this compilation, showed him to be perfectly compatible with such old-timers as Grappelli and Sven Asmussen. His albums as a leader from this period are out of print, but three tracks from the 1967 *Sunday Walk* album turn up here, revealing the bristling modern improviser in romantic clothing. The remaining six tracks feature Grappelli in various settings.

***   **Aurora** Atlantic 19158-2 CD
Ponty; Patrice Rushen (*ky*); Daryl Stuermer (*g*); Tom Fowler (*b*); Norman Fearington (*d*). 12/75.

***   **Imaginary Voyage** Atlantic 19136-2 CD
Ponty; Allan Zavod (*ky*); Daryl Stuermer (*g*); Tom Fowler (*b*); Mark Craney (*d*). 7–8/76.

**   **Enigmatic Ocean** Atlantic 19110-2 CD
Ponty; Allan Zavod (*ky*); Allan Holdsworth, Daryl Stuermer (*g*); Ralph Armstrong (*b*); Steve Smith (*d*). 6–7/77.

***   **Cosmic Messenger** Atlantic CD
Ponty; Allan Zavod (*ky*); Peter Maunu, Joaquin Lievano (*g*); Ralph Armstrong (*b*); Casey Scheuerell (*d*). 78.

(*)   **Mystical Adventures Atlantic 19333-2 CD
Ponty; Chris Ryne (*p*); Jamie Glaser (*g*); Randy Jackson (*b*); Rayford Griffin (*d*); Paulinho Da Costa (*perc*). 8–9/81.

**   **Individual Choice** Atlantic 780098-2 CD
Ponty; George Duke (*ky*); Allan Holdsworth (*g*); Randy Jackson (*b*); Rayford Griffin (*d*). 3–5/83.

**   **Open Mind** Atlantic 780185-2 CD
Ponty; Chick Corea (*ky*); George Benson (*g*); Casey Scheuerell, Rayford Griffin (*d*). 6/84.

**   **Fables** Atlantic 781276-2 CD
Ponty; Scott Henderson (*g*); Baron Browne (*b*); Rayford Griffin (*d*). 7–8/85.

***   **Storytelling** Columbia 45252 CD
Ponty; Grover Washington (*ss*); Jamie Glover (*g*); Patrice Rushen, Wally Minko (*ky*); Clara Ponty (*p*); Baron Browne (*b*); Kurt Wortman (*perc*). 89.

Ponty had always amplified his violin, but by the 1970s he was making it a major part of his aesthetic, trying out echo and other effects to colour an approach which had fundamentally changed little since his earliest recordings. He had recorded a session with Frank Zappa, *King Kong*, in 1969, and Zappa's punishingly difficult kind of instrumental rock was a significant influence on the sort of fusion which Ponty recorded once he signed with Atlantic in 1975. Tunes were built out of complicated riffs or trance-like harmonic patterns, with modal solos played at blistering speed to create the excitement. Unusually, though, the music is more interesting than the average fusion band of the period allows, since the lyrical tang of the leader's violin sustains the mood of most of the records.

The earlier records, especially *Aurora* and *Imaginary Voyage*, are the best, if only because the sound of the group is at its freshest. Players like Stuermer and Zavod are capable technicians, but it's always Ponty whose fire ignites the music. Some of the Atlantics from this period are currently out of print, and after *Mystical Adventures* the music grew a little stale: *Individual Choice* and *Open Mind* are almost solo albums by the leader, with Duke, Holdsworth and Benson turning up only in guest spots, and the music lacks much sense of interplay. *Fables* returns to a quartet format, but Ponty seems uninterested in the overall sound. *Storytelling*, though, is a return to form. Aside from a Chopin prelude, improvised against Clara Ponty's solitary piano, the music is a bright set of surprisingly insidious melodies, with the violinist in fetching form.

ODEAN POPE
TENOR SAXOPHONE

***   **Almost Like Me** Moers Music 01092 CD/LP
        Pope; Gerald Veasley (*b*); Cornell Rochester (*d*). 10/90.

***   **Out For A Walk** Moers Music 02072 CD
        As above.

***(*)   **The Saxophone Choir** Soul Note 1129 CD/LP
        Pope; Robert Landham, Julian Pressley, Sam Reed (*as*); Bootsie Barnes, Arthur Daniel, Bob Howell (*ts*); Joe Sudler (*bs*); Eddie Green (*p*); Gerald Veasley (*b*); Dave Gibson (*d*). 10/85.

****   **The Ponderer** Soul Note 1229 CD/LP
        Pope; Byard Lancaster, Julian Pressley, Sam Reed (*as*); Glenn Guidone, Bob Howell, Middy Middleton, John Simon (*ts*); Joe Sudler (*bs*); Eddie Green (*p*); Tyrone Brown, Gerald Veasley (*b*); Cornell Rochester (*d*). 3/90.

Pope gave notice of interesting things to come in his work with Catalyst, a toughly modern, under-recorded outfit who received far less than their fair share of critical attention. A sophisticated composer and arranger, Pope has turned the Saxophone Choir into an exciting studio group which responds gamely to rather intricate charts. The whole ensemble plays 'I Wish I Knew' on *The Ponderer* (the album's only standard) with a snap and finesse that recalls the Ellington horn section. Many of Pope's voicings seem to derive from Duke's late suites, with their 'oriental' scales and off-centre rhythms. As with Ellington albums, though, much of the drama derives from the alternation of solo and ensemble sections. Pope has a powerful tone, somewhat reminiscent in phrasing of Charlie Rouse, but drawing elements from John Coltrane, Sam Rivers and from funk and soul.

The earlier of the Choir albums is still a little ragged, but the opening 'Saxophone Shop' is done with a light, almost ironic touch that makes up for some technical shortcomings, and 'Elixir' is one of the best things in Pope's book to date. The two parts of 'Out For A Walk' on *The Ponderer* have a strong Latin feel, and direct attention to Pope's characteristic latticing of rhythm lines, doubling two electric bassists (one upright, one on guitar) with the powerful drumming of trio colleague Cornell Rochester, who is also a much more robust large group player than Gibson. The Ellington influence is strongly evident on 'Phrygian Love Theme', which has a minor feel and a strong 'Spanish tinge'. As elsewhere, it's the bass lines that carry the code, and Pope characteristically plays in a lower register, closer to the saxophone's 'cello' tones, rather than an octave-plus above the accompaniment.

Out For A Walk takes the rattling swing of the Messengers (where Pope paid some dues) to a place well beyond bop. 'Out for a Brisk Run' might have been more appropriate; the saxophonist and his two cohorts take the material at a furious pace, drawing in devices and references from the boundaries of jazz and avant-rock. Veasley's electric bass is far more propulsive than an upright and it is he who seems to tow the music along, like a powerboat with two water skiers in his wake. Inevitably, there are sometimes terminal splashes and duckings, as pieces seem to fall apart, but it's basically good, hi-NRG stuff that might well appeal to anyone who finds the sound of 1960s free jazz a bit too austere and who's been weaned on anything from Prince to Prime Time.

MICHEL PORTAL (born 1935)
TENOR SAXOPHONE, BASS CLARINET

***   **Arrividerci Le Chouartse** hat Art CD 6022 CD
Portal; Léon Francioli (*b*); Pierre Favre (*d*). 10/80.

***(*)   **Men's Land** Label Bleu LBL 6513 LP
Portal; David Liebman (*ss*); Harry Pepl (*g*); Jean-François Jenny-Clark (*b*); Jack
DeJohnette (*d*); Mino Cinelu (*perc*). 5/87.

Portal is a highly accomplished instrumentalist who has taken in modern and free jazz, as well as
avant-garde 'straight' music. In 1970 he was working with John Surman and a decade later was
still exploring that idiom. The hat Art is more structured and large-scale than any of Surman's
work with The Trio, but the improvisational configuration is broadly the same, with a forceful,
all-in feel. The rather better *Men's Land* takes a step back from the music and examines it more
coolly. The saxophones offer a high-register commentary on Jenny-Clark's studied bass and
DeJohnette's rippling drums on 'Ahmad', while on the title-track there is a murky dialogue
between Portal's bass clarinet and Cinelu's intelligently balanced percussion (he also wrote the
piece). Portal stays in Dolphyish mood with the low-toned horn for 'Easy 'Nuff', a huge piece
occupying the whole second side which bounces Bud Powell echoes off the kind of shifting
rhythmic background that the great pianist (long a resident of France) used to value.

BUD POWELL (1924–66)
PIANO

****   **The Genius Of Bud Powell** Verve 827901 CD
Powell (*p* solo) and with Ray Brown (*b*); Buddy Rich (*d*). 7/50, 2/51.

Bud Powell was probably the most important jazz pianist between Art Tatum and Cecil Taylor.
He appropriated the former's improvising style to a large extent and anticipated the latter's
pianistic ferocity (the frequent suggestion that Powell played like a saxophonist is patently
absurd). His life was almost archetypically tragic, and the parallel path of his downfall and death
with Charlie Parker's has perhaps clouded the pianist's independence of resource and
development.

Powell was committed in 1951, suffering from variously diagnosed mental disorders. The
Verve documents his solo playing just before that catastrophic breakdown, together with three
takes of 'Tea For Two' for trio, recorded the previous summer. Powell's virtuosity shines
through the bustling 'Parisian Thoroughfare' (a piece which, like 'Un Poco Loco', always
precisely reflects his mood at the moment of playing) and on 'A Nightingale Sang In Berkeley
Square', which draws heavily on a Tatum influence. Solo recordings of Powell are extremely
precious, and this is one of the best, only recently transferred to CD.

****   **The Amazing Bud Powell: Volume 1** Blue Note 781503 CD
Powell; Fats Navarro (*t*); Sonny Rollins (*ts*); Tommy Potter (*b*); Roy Haynes (*d*). 8/49,
5/51.

****   **The Amazing Bud Powell: Volume 2** Blue Note 781504 CD
Powell (*p* solo) and with George Duvivier, Curly Russell (*b*); Max Roach, Art Taylor
(*d*). 5/51 & 8/53.

***   **Autumn Sessions** Magic Music 30007 CD
As above. 9/53.

***   **In March With Mingus** Magic Music 30005 CD
Powell; Charles Mingus (*b*); Roy Haynes (*d*). 3/53.

***   **Charles Mingus Trios** Jazz Door 1213 CD
As above.

***(*)   **Jazz At Massey Hall** Original Jazz Classics OJC 111 LP
Powell; Charles Mingus (*b*); Max Roach (*d*). 5/53.

***   **Summer Sessions** Magic Music 30006 CD
        Powell; Charlie Parker (*as*); George Duvivier, Charles Mingus (*b*); Art Taylor (*d*);
        Candido Camero (*perc*). 5, 6 & 7/53.

****   **The Amazing Bud Powell: Volume 3 – Bud** Blue Note 784173 CD
        Powell; Curtis Fuller (*tb*); Paul Chambers (*b*); Art Taylor (*d*). 56.

***(*)   **From Birdland, New York City, 1956** Jazz Anthology 550202 CD
        As above, except omit Fuller. 3/57.

****   **The Amazing Bud Powell: Volume 4 – Time Waits** Blue Note 746820 CD
        Powell; Sam Jones (*b*); Philly Joe Jones (*d*). 5/58.

Despite the linking name and numbered format, the four Blue Note CD transfers can quite comfortably be bought separately; indeed Volume 1 – with its multiple takes of 'Bouncing With Bud' (one of which was previously on *The Fabulous Fats Navarro: Volume 1* [Blue Note 781531 CD]), the bebop classic 'Ornithology' and Powell's own barometric 'Un Poco Loco' – was out of print for some time, and the fourth volume was issued only in 1987, after which the whole series was made available again at a very acceptable mid-price. The multiple takes of 'Un Poco Loco' are perhaps the best place for more detailed study of Powell's restless pursuit of an increasingly fugitive musical epiphany. 'Parisian Thoroughfare' contrasts sharply with the unaccompanied version, above, and is much tighter; Powell had a more than adequate left hand; however, since he conceived of his music in a complex, multi-linear way, bass and drums were usually required, not for support, but to help proliferate lines of attack. The quintet tracks are harshly tempered, but with hints of both joy and melancholy from all three front men; Navarro's almost hysterical edge is at its most effective, and Powell plays as if possessed.

    Volume 2 contains one of the most famous Powell performances, the bizarre, self-penned 'Glass Enclosure', a brief but almost schizophrenically changeable piece. There are also alternative takes of 'A Night In Tunisia', 'It Could Happen To You', 'Reets And I' and 'Collard Greens And Black Eyed Peas' (better known as 'Blues In The Closet', see below). The cheap *Autumn Sessions* contains club material by the same personnel as the August 1953 studio sessions. The sound-quality is poor, with the drummer almost completely inaudible and Powell's timing well off, but these are worthwhile back-up documents. *In March With Mingus* catches him earlier in the same year; no drums audible again, but brighter performances of mostly standard material. *Jazz At Massey Hall* is the rhythm section's spot from the classic Parker and Gillespie concert in Toronto (Prestige/Debut 98.471 CD), which has become a trig point for bop fans. If for no other reason, these tracks redirect attention to the enormous influence all three players had on bebop. Powell's schizophrenic opposition of delicate high-register lines and thudding chords is most obvious on 'Cherokee'. He displaces 'Embraceable You' entirely, losing his two colleagues in the middle choruses as he works out his own romantic agony.

    Volumes 3 and 4 of the Blue Note sequence are the least compelling of the series. Powell's personal problems were increasing steadily and he never again sounds as good, though there is no mistaking the intensity and sometimes anguish of the later work. On *Bud*, though, he was in good spirits and most of the pieces were done in single takes, reflecting the understanding apparent on the earlier Birdland recording by the same trio; it included 'Tea For Two', 'Ornithology' (played in full rather than merely quoted), and 'Lover Come Back To Me'. On *Bud*, trombonist Curtis Fuller guests for the final three tracks, a variant on Powell's preferred trio, which doesn't quite come off. *Time Waits*, by contrast, contains some of his brightest and least anguished later work. 'Sub City' and the ballad title-track are among his best compositions, though 'John's Abbey' (in two takes) is something of a throwback. (It's worth mentioning, particularly in the context of *Salt Peanuts* and *Essen*, below, that 'John's Abbey' is also known as 'Bean And The Boys' and may have been written by Coleman Hawkins.)

***   **New York All Star Sessions** Bandstand BD 1507 CD/LP
        Powell; George Duvivier, Curly Russell (*b*); Max Roach (*d*). 49 & 57.

Compilation of NYC airshots and other material, also featuring Powell with Charlie Parker, Miles Davis and Benny Harris groups. The Powell-led tracks are 'Lullaby Of Birdland', 'I've Got You Under My Skin' and 'Hallelujah' from 1957, and 'All God's Chillun' with Russell and Roach from the less well-documented late 1940s. The sound is about as good as expected, though the CD seems unnecessarily sharp and ringing.

*** **The Legacy** Jazz Door 1204 3CD
Powell; Dizzy Gillespie (*t*); Zoot Sims (*ts*); Michel Gaudry, Jean-Marie Ingrand, Pierre
Michelot, Charles Mingus, Oscar Pettiford (*b*); Kenny Clarke, Roy Haynes, Art
Taylor (*d*). 3/53, 57, 4/60, 60–1, 64.

A mixed-bag but rather attractive three-CD set which concentrates largely on the later,
European years, but taking in the same Mingus sessions on *Magic Music* above, and a version of
'How High The Moon' featuring Dizzy Gillespie from 1957. Though Michelot and the exiled
Clarke were reliable and inventive sidemen, Powell had to rely in his late years on some less
than special partners, and Gaudry on the 1964 date is less than adequate. There's a certain
irony in the title, because Powell's legacy was a vast body of uneven material, out of which
enthusiastic listeners have to pan tiny nuggets of genius. Sometimes, though, it's hard to ignore
settings and sound.

** **More Unissued** Royal Jazz RJD 507 CD
Powell; Clark Terry (*t*); Barney Wilen (*ts*); Pierre Michelot, Charles Mingus, Oscar
Pettiford (*b*); Roy Haynes (*d*); Joe Timer Orchestra. 4/53, 12/55, 57, 12/59.

Heigh ho. *More* unissued. Doesn't that sound exciting? This is another bits-and-pieces
compilation, more or less chucked into circulation on the assumption that almost anything by
Powell is going to appeal·to a certain kind of collector and to the odd curious passer-by looking
for a respectable sample. The first will doubtless want it, for the stuff with Wilen and Terry, if
for nothing else; the hypothetical second should avoid it.

*** **My Devotion** Jazz Society (Vogue) 670512 CD
Powell; George Duvivier, John Ore, Curly Russell (*b*); Kenny Clarke, J. C. Moses,
Max Roach, Art Taylor (*d*). 1/47, 9/53, 10/60, 9/64.

Like the above, this isn't put together with flawless artistic logic. Nevertheless it's a cheap and
cheerful collection of mostly standard material, and will appeal to anyone who wants a taste of
Powell's work.

*** **The Complete Essen Jazz Festival Concert** Black Lion BLCD 760105 CD
Powell; Coleman Hawkins (*ts*); Oscar Pettiford (*p*); Kenny Clarke (*d*). 4/60.

Announced by MC Joachim Berendt as the Oscar Pettiford Trio, it's not until the third track
and Pettiford's superb introduction to 'Willow Weep For Me' that the nominal leader begins to
assert himself. Powell has already got in two brisk solos, with only a couple of misfingerings on
the hectic 'Shaw Nuff'. A few minutes later, the bassist is referring to Powell, putative composer
of 'John's Abbey' as 'your favourite'.

Hawkins (the other claimant for that credit) comes in for the last three tracks. He'd played
'Stuffy' many times before, but it's rare to hear him on 'All The Things You Are', which gets
an unusually jaunty reading and some nice stretching of tempo on later choruses, closing with
the familiar bop arrangement. The sound is well balanced and clean, and Powell seems to have
lucked out on a decent instrument for a change.

(*) **At The Golden Circle: Volume 1 Steeplechase SCS 6001 CD/LP
Powell; Törbjorn Hultcrantz (*b*); Sune Spangberg (*d*). 4/62.

(*) **At The Golden Circle: Volume 2 Steeplechase SCS 6002 CD/LP
As above.

(*) **At The Golden Circle: Volume 3 Steeplechase SCS 6009 LP
As above.

** **At The Golden Circle: Volume 4** Steeplechase SCS 6014 LP
As above. ·

** **At The Golden Circle: Volume 5** Steeplechase SCS 6017 LP
As above.

We're now firmly in the era of an important discographical sub-genre: the Bud
Powell-live-in-Europe album. There are a great many of these. Some are good, others awful, but
the majority don't really stand up on their own terms. Steeplechase have long been guilty of
excessive documentation. One sharply edited disc from the 19 April 1962 gig would have been
more than adequate. The Copenhagen session finds Powell wavering between the hesitant and

the near-brilliant. The rhythm section play about as much part in the music as Rosencrantz and Guildenstern do in *Hamlet*, though, like most Scandinavian players, they seem well enough versed in the idiom.

Volume 3 has a second version of 'I Remember Clifford' from later in the residency; the last three all come from 23 April and are of more than passing interest, but by this stage the whole exercise seems rather redundant, we're back to vinyl only, and any pleasure in the music is seriously diluted. Five volumes of Powell at his *best* would still call for stamina.

***   **Bouncing With Bud** Storyville SLP 4113 CD/LP
        Powell; Niels-Henning Ørsted-Pedersen (*b*); William Schiopffe (*d*). 4/62.

Recorded three days after the later Golden Circle session, this has the pianist nosing again at 'I Remember Clifford', apparently dissatisfied with something in the theme. Otherwise, it's quite predictable fare, played with discipline but not much passion.

***(*)   **Salt Peanuts** Black Lion BLCD 760121 CD/LP/MC
        Powell; Johnny Griffin (*ts*); Guy Hayat (*b*); Jacques Gervais (*d*). 8/64.

You can almost smell the garlic and the sweat. Wonderfully authentic club jazz from the latter end of Powell's career, with Johnny Griffin doing his familiar unexpected sit-in on 'Wee', 'Hot House' and 'Straight, No Chaser'. Powell has an awful piano to play and the rhythm section isn't up to much, but (odd though the analogy may sound) much like Keith Jarrett in years to come, Powell always played best at moments of greatest adversity, and here he sounds supercharged. The title-track, 'Move' and '52nd Street Theme', for trio, bring France to Harlem. If 'Bean And The Boys' is familiar, the reason is explained above, apropos *Time Waits*. Wonderful, but don't expect audiophile sound.

(*)   **Blues For Bouffemont Black Lion BLCD 760135 CD/LP
        Powell; Michel Gaudray, Guy Hayat (*b*); Jacques Gervais, Art Taylor (*d*). 7/64, 8/64.

Johnny Griffin doesn't sweep in like the 7th Cavalry to rescue this one and Powell is left to plod his lonely course on the July session. Bouffemont was the convalescent equivalent of Charlie Parker's Camarillo, but there's nothing very relaxed about these tracks. Further material from the *Salt Peanuts* line-up is enough to convince anyone that Black Lion got it right first time. Second rank, even by the rather relative standards of late Powell recordings.

***(*)   **Earl Bud Powell** Mythic Sound MS 6001-6010 10CD/10LP
        consists of:

***(*)   **Early Years Of A Genius, 44–48** Mythic Sound MS 6001 CD/LP
        Powell; Benny Harris, Ermet Perry, Tommy Stevenson, George Treadwell, Cootie
        Williams, Lammar Wright (*t*); Ed Burke, Ed Glover, Bob Horton, J. J. Johnson (*tb*);
        Buddy DeFranco (*cl*); Eddie Cleanhead Vinson (*as, v*); Frank Powell (*as*); Eddie
        Lockjaw Davis, Budd Johnson, Lee Pop, Sam Taylor (*ts*); Eddie Deverteuil, Cecil
        Payne (*bs*); Leroy Kirkland, Chuck Wayne (*g*); Nelson Boyd, Norman Keenan, Carl
        Pruitt (*b*); Vess Payne, Max Roach (*d*); Ella Fitzgerald (*v*). 1 & 7/44, 12/48.

****   **Burning In USA, 53–55** Mythic Sound MS 6002 CD/LP
        Powell; Dizzy Gillespie (*t*); Charles Mingus, Oscar Pettiford, Franklin Skeetes (*b*); Art
        Blakey, Roy Haynes, Sonny Payne, Max Roach (*d*). 2, 3 & 5/53, 55.

***(*)   **Cookin' At Saint Germain, 57–59** Mythic Sound MS 6003 CD/LP
        Powell; Clark Terry (*t*); Barney Wilen (*ts*); Pierre Michelot (*b*); Kenny Clarke (*d*). 57,
        11/59.

***   **Relaxin' At Home, 61–64** Mythic Sound MS 6004 CD/LP
        Powell; Michel Gaudry (*b*); Francis Paudras (*brushes*). 61–64.

***(*)   **Groovin' At The Blue Note, 59–61** Mythic Sound MS 6005 CD/LP
        Powell; Dizzy Gillespie (*t*); Zoot Sims, Barney Wilen (*ts*); Jean-Marie Ingrand, Pierre
        Michelot (*b*); Kenny Clarke (*d*). 57?, 5 & 6/60, 1/61.

***   **Writin' For Duke, 63** Mythic Sound MS 6006 CD/LP
        Powell; Gilbert Rovère (*b*); Kansas Fields (*d*). 2/63.

(*)   **Tribute To Thelonious, 64 Mythic Sound MS 6007 CD/LP
        Powell; John Ore (*b*); J. C. Moses (*d*); Francis Paudras (*brushes*). 2/64.

****   **Holidays In Edenville, 64** Mythic Sound MS 6008 CD/LP
        Powell; Johnny Griffin (*ts*); Guy Hayat (*b*); Jacques Gervais (*d*). 8/64.

****   **Return To Birdland, 64** Mythic Sound MS 6009 CD/LP
        Powell; John Ore (*b*); J. C. Moses (*d*). 9/64.

***(*) **Award At Birdland, 64** Mythic Sound MS 6010 CD/LP
        As above. 10/64.

Here, then, is the basic story-board for *Round Midnight*, the almost obsessional but unmistakably sincere attachment of a young French fan and musician *manqué* to an ageing and disturbed American jazzman whose talent and emotions alike are as brilliant and as fragile as light bulbs. Francis Paudras lovingly recorded Bud Powell in performance at clubs like the Paris Blue Note, at home, and on recuperative holiday at Edenville. The story of his association with Powell is told in Paudras's book, *Dance of the Infidels*, on which Bernard Tavernier's movie was based.

In 1979, Paudras willed his archive of private recordings of Bud Powell to the pianist's daughter, Cecilia Barnes Powell, who subsequently permitted their release. The material is patchy in the extreme and shouldn't be seen as a comprehensive compilation of Powell material between 1944 and 1964. Given the circumstances of recording, the quality is not always up to scratch, and some of Powell's later performances are unbearably weary. The earliest material suggests an able accompanist with some skill as an arranger. Powell's version of Mary Lou Williams's 'Roll 'Em', underlines his skill in juxtaposing areas of dissonance (something he did constantly on the keyboard) while preserving the continuity of harmonic development. The early-1950s tracks include material from the legendary Massey Hall concert, and also excellent versions of 'Star Eyes', 'Like Someone In Love' and Pettiford's 'Blues In The Closet' from Birdland in September of that same year. The French sessions on *Cookin' at Saint Germain* are almost equally fine, though the rhythm sections lack the robust challenge posed by Pettiford and Roach. The later Blue Note (club, not label) recordings are alternately more abrupt and rather elided. Aesthetically, the effect is a little like taking the sound-board off the piano to expose the strings, for the workings of Powell's increasingly troubled mind are sometimes painfully evident.

Thanks to the generosity of Frank Sinatra, Powell was able to record a rare studio session in Paris in 1963, to be made under the supervision of Duke Ellington. Resources clearly didn't stretch to a reasonable rhythm section – both Rovère and Kansas Fields are pretty dire – but this supplement to the released *Bud In Paris* is of more than historical value, and Bud's performance of 'Satin Doll', whistled to him by its composer as he sat at the keyboard, is one of his most remarkable.

Much of the rest of the material is rather more ephemeral. The home recordings of Powell working through half a dozen Monk compositions are neatly balanced by five similarly focused tracks from autumn 1964, during his emotional return to Birdland. After his release from the sanatorium in the summer, Paudras had taken a convalescent Powell on holiday to Edenville on the Normandy coast, where he played now legendary sessions with a ropey local rhythm section and a piano that was one stage beyond clapped out. Johnny Griffin sat in, and the music has a strangely evocative quality, more redolent of a time long gone and of a man no longer living than many a professional recording.

A month or two later, a fitter, chubbier Powell received an ecstatic reception at Birdland, playing the last great sessions of his life (and receiving the Schaeffer award; Paudras notes his disappointment that Schaeffer was a brand of beer rather than a musical foundation) with the workmanlike support of Ore and Moses. The playing is full of familiarly unexpected dissonances – intentional here – but also a kind of quiet joy, exactly the quality that comes through on *Relaxin' At Home*, where Paudras scuffs out a brush rhythm over Powell's unselfconscious improvisations.

The 10 albums are available separately and should perhaps be sampled one at a time. Paudras's extensive liner-notes are fulsome and occasionally mawkish – and the music often tells a different story – but the pictures are wonderful (reason perhaps for choosing the LP option while it's around) and Powellites will treasure the set.

PRESTIGE BLUES SWINGERS
GROUP

(*)   **Outskirts Of Town** Original Jazz Classics OJC 1717 LP
    Art Farmer, Idrees Sulieman (*t*); Buster Cooper (*tb*); Jerome Richardson (*as, f*);
    Jimmy Forrest (*ts*); Pepper Adams (*bs*); Ray Bryant (*p*); Tiny Grimes (*g*); Wendell
    Marshall (*b*); Osie Johnson (*d*). 8/58.

Jerry Valentine's arrangements are functional rather than inspiring, but this conglomeration of
conservative modernists *circa* 1958 sound happy enough to play at being All Stars on one
August day. The material consists mainly of Count Basie staples, and at least one of them –
'Sent For You Yesterday And Here You Come Today' – gets a happier treatment than Basie
himself would have mustered at the time. A potboiler, but an entertaining one.

ANDRÉ PREVIN (born 1929)
PIANO

***   **Double Play** Original Jazz Classics OJC 157 LP
    Previn; Russ Freeman (*p*); Shelly Manne (*d*). 4 & 5/57.

***   **Gigi** Original Jazz Classics OJC 407 CD/LP/MC
    Previn; Red Mitchell (*b*); Shelly Manne (*d*). 4/58.

***   **West Side Story** Original Jazz Classics OJC 422 CD/LP/MC
    As above. 8/59.

(*)   **Like Previn!** Original Jazz Classics OJC 170 LP
    Previn; Red Mitchell (*b*); Frank Capp (*d*). 2 & 3/60.

***   **After Hours** Telarc Digital 83002 CD
    Previn; Joe Pass (*g*); Ray Brown (*b*). 3/89.

(*)   **Uptown** Telarc Digital 83303 CD
    As above, except Mundell Lowe (*g*) replaces Pass. 3/90.

(*)   **Old Friends** Telarc Digital 83309 CD
    As above, except omit Lowe. 8/91.

André Previn likes to tell the story of how, while working as a cinema accompanist, he so lost
himself in a piece of improvisation that he looked up some time later to see that he had vamped
'Tiger Rag' right through the Crucifixion scene in D. W. Griffiths's *Intolerance*. It's often
forgotten that Previn, now a highly popular orchestral conductor and media personality, began
his professional life as a jazz pianist, once considered hip enough (by Hollywood standards,
anyway) to appear as the stage band in a film adaptation of Jack Kerouac's *The Subterraneans*.
    Previn first recorded as a teenager, and the earliest sessions now available find him confident
and accomplished, though in a rather cluttered two-piano setting which doesn't flatter either
player and isn't quite redeemed by Manne's accurate and sensitive drumming. The show-tune
sessions with Mitchell and Manne are much more successful. Previn's minimal opening
statements on 'Something's Coming' on *West Side Story* give way to a brash and tightly belted
solo which exactly suits the emotional temper. Typically, though, it degenerates into rather
technical figuring, octave jumps and altered chords which are impressive without being very
involving. The CD pairs the Bernstein sessions with Shelly Manne's *My Fair Lady* which also
features Previn, with Leroy Vinnegar instead of the sonorous Mitchell. *Gigi* has a more dated
charm and *Like Previn!* is downright dull.
    Like Dudley Moore (but with ideas remaining), Previn has recently returned to his first love.
At sixty, he lacks the range and emotional complexity of his earlier work, but he is still a
formidable technician who will appeal to fans of laid-back piano trio jazz.

BOBBY PREVITE
DRUMS, PERCUSSION

***   **Bump The Renaissance** Sound Aspects sas 08 CD
Previte; Tom Varner (*frhn*); Lenny Pickett (*ts, bcl*); Richard Shulman (*p*); David
Hofstra (*d*). 6/85.

****   **Empty Suits** Gramavision GV 79447 CD
Previte; Robin Eubanks (*tb*); Marty Ehrlich (*as*); Steve Gaboury (*ky*); Allan Jafee,
Elliott Sharp (*g*); Skip Krevens (*pedal steel g*); Jerome Harris (*b, g, lap steel g, v*);
Carol Emmanuel (*hp*); Roberta Baum (*v*); David Shea (*turntables*). 5/90.

Empty Suits is a joyous, all-in set that touches all the bases. Previte's compositions and
arrangements are absolutely spot on (as they are on the smaller acoustic canvas of *Bump The
Renaissance*) and the guitars are used to maximum effect. 'Great Wall' is a dedication to the
minimalist composer John Adams, who may well have had an impact on Previte's repetitive but
shifting structures.

As a drummer, he combines the swing era with latter-day power *à la* Ronald Shannon
Jackson, but never overpowers an intelligently balanced mix. Strongly recommended.

EDDIE PRÉVOST (born 1942)
DRUMS, PERCUSSION

****   **Live: Volume 1** Matchless MR 01 LP

****   **Live: Volume 2** Matchless MR 02 LP
Prévost; Gerry Gold (*t*); Geoff Hawkins (*ts*); Marcio Mattos (*b*). 79.

***(*)   **Continuum** Matchless MR 07 LP
Prévost; Larry Stabbins (*ts, ss*); Veryan Weston (*p*); Marcio Mattos (*b*). 83.

***   **Resound** Matchless MR 08 LP
Prévost; Pete McPhail (*as, sno, f*); Tony Moore (*d*). 85.

Like his exact contemporary Han Bennink, Prévost is a free player who understands how to
swing. Influenced primarily by Max Roach, but also by Ed Blackwell, he can also play with the
stark simplicity of the early jazz drummers or with the ritualized freedoms of a Korean court
musician. Like Bennink again, he is very much a kit drummer, and though the early days of
AMM (the influential improvising ensemble of which Prévost is a founding member)
demanded a very radical diversification of sound-producing technics, he has shown remarkably
little interest in exotic or 'ethnic' percussion.

Prévost's own groups have tended to remain within the British free-jazz tradition, governed
to some degree by structures, but never constrained by them. The 1979 albums are a joy, veering
dramatically between moments of austere fury and jovial rave-ups fuelled by Prévost's tireless
invention. (That an album called *Live* should have a skull on the cover is a token of Prévost's
refusal to treat even quite abstract music-making with deathly seriousness.) Trumpeter Gerry
Gold (who has also played with the radical improvising group Coherents) is one of the buried
treasures of British jazz. He has a bright, generous tone, which he can turn on the instant into a
thin, acidulous stream of off-pitch comments. Mattos has an enormous sound, not so well
recorded here as on *Continuum*, but put to more dramatic use. The later record is more
abstract (the result, almost certainly, of Weston's rather fussy play) but Stabbins is always a joy,
following Prévost along of the most dramatically freewheeling courses either has attempted on
record.

Live kicked off Prévost's own cottage-industry label (and it's to be hoped that a CD reissue
can be set up). Since 1980, Matchless has built up a remarkable body of material within the
free-jazz to free spectrum. Like Supersession below, Resoundings can't be considered to
Prévost's own group, but it works according to a more hierarchical principle than the freer and
more abstract units. McPhail inscribes neat, enigmatic shapes on the backgrounds – sometimes
generous, sometimes plain awkward – laid out for him by the bass and drums. Moore (who also
plays with Prévost in the Free Jazz Quartet, q.v.) is a less resonant player than Mattos, a
pragmatist rather than a romantic.

***(*) **Supersession** Matchless MR 17 CD
Prévost; Evan Parker (*ss, ts*); Keith Rowe (*g, elec*); Barry Guy (*b, elec*). 9/84.

This is more problematic. The whole ethos of Supersession is opposed to the idea of leadership (or of avant-gardism in the old-fashioned sense) and can only be laid to Prévost's credit because he is the organizer and provides in the liner note an admirably brief and cogent discussion of the differences that prevail between the bland, self-exhausting alienation strategies of the avant-garde and an improvisational approach which 'supersedes' such ideologies and approaches music-making with confidence, mutual regard and without undue triumphalism.

It is, of course, a 'supersession' in another sense, bringing together the backbone of AMM and two of the most distinguished improvisers and composers on the British scene. The music – a single continuous performance – is rather better value for money than its meagre duration might suggest. It's typically difficult, and pointless, to separate individual performer, but it's Parker's chirping soprano harmonics and Prévost's exuberant battering outbreaks that one remembers.

SAM PRICE (born 1908)
PIANO, VOCAL

** **Midnight Boogie** Black & Blue 59.025-2 CD
Price (*p* solo). 11/69.

** **Fire** Black & Blue 59.079-2 CD
Price; Doc Cheatham (*t*); Gene Connors (**tb*); Ted Buckner (*as*); Carl Pruitt (*b*); J. C. Heard (*d*). 5/75.

** **Boogie And Jazz Classics** Black & Blue 59.111-2 CD
As above. 5/75.

Sam Price's recordings for King Jazz are scattered through the Storyville LPs discussed under Mezz Mezzrow and Sidney Bechet. Although he has remained active as a player ever since, his records have been few in number and were often made for minor labels in inauspicious situations. The Black & Blue CDs are, along with the fine duo session with Doc Cheatham on Sackville, the most representative of his later records. But they're finally rather dull. *Midnight Boogie* is an entirely straightforward selection of boogie and blues, played with a slow momentum which sounds weary rather than intense. Price's pieces are full of routine configurations, and tend to prop up the theory that boogie piano is tediously one-dimensional in its impoact. All 15 tracks are virtually interchangeable, and while any one of them makes a plausible performance, it's hard to see why anyone would want to work through an entire CD's worth of this sort of playing. The full band plays on eight of the 15 tracks on *Fire* and on only two on *Boogie And Jazz Classics*, and bring a little more spirit to the proceedings, even if all three horn players sound ragged at times. The trio tracks, though, are distinctly plain. Price plays his boogie with a steadily rocking pulse, but it tends to pall rather than become hypnotic, as the best boogie piano should. Pruitt and Heard play the most functional of rhythm roles and the tunes are mostly one-paced originals.

*** **Barrelhouse And Blues** Black Lion BLCD 760159 CD
Price; Keith Smith (*t*); Roy Williams (*tb*); Sandy Brown (*cl*); Ruan O'Lochlainn (*g*); Harvey Weston (*b*); Lennie Hastings (*d*). 12/69.

Price is rather better served by this enjoyable occasion, where he was recorded in London with a British band. The music is split between solo and ensemble tracks, and although the pianist is rather less glib than usual on the reflective 'Honey Grove Blues', the numbers with the full band turn out rather better: O'Lochlainn's oddball solos are a neat touch of local colour, and the lamented Brown contributes deep-set solos to each of two takes of Leroy Carr's 'In the Evening'. The CD runs to nearly 73 minutes and the remastering is fine.

JULIAN PRIESTER (born 1935)
TROMBONE, ELECTRONICS

***   **Polarization** ECM 1098 LP
Priester; Ron Stallings (*ts, ss*); Ray Obiedo (*g*); Curtis Clark (*p*); Heshima Mark
Williams (*b*); Augusta Lee Collins (*d*). 1/77.

Priester's Marine Intrusion band play in a spacious modern idiom, with carefully deployed
electronics overlaid on essentially conventional structures. Individual pieces are atmospheric
but without sacrifice of linear energies. 'Wind Dolphin' and 'Anatomy Of Longing' flirt with
banality but come out on top. Impressive stuff from an instrumentalist and composer who
played in a classic Max Roach outfit in the 1960s and has since been rather overlooked, despite
being one of the finest trombonists to emerge since J. J. Johnson and Curtis Fuller.

JIM PUGH
TROMBONE

(*)   **The Pugh–Taylor Project dmp CD-448 CD
Pugh; Dave Taylor (*btb*); George Young (*ss, f, kazoo*); Gerry Niewood (*ss, ts, f, picc*);
Lew Del Gatto (*cl, bcl, f, picc, bs*); Shelly Woodworth (*ob, ky*); Kirk Nurock, Bill
Dobbins, Ethyl Will (*p*); Keith Foley (*ky*); Jesse Levine, Olivia Kopell (*vla*); Jesse
Levy, Nathan Stutch (*clo*); John Beal (*b*); David Ratajczak (*d*); Gordon Gottlieb,
David Friedman (*perc*). 8–11/84.

An intriguing third-stream project, although one with rather mixed results, this offers six
composer-arrangers the chance to score something for the trombone duo of Pugh and Taylor
with various augmentations. The range is dramatically wide, with the entirely scored piece for
two trombones and drum machine, John Clark's '747', sitting at the far remove from Bob
Brookmeyer's elliptical, serio-comic 'Red Balloons'. Mike Abene contributes an arrangement
of the Ellington–Strayhorn double-bill 'Passion Flower/Single Petal Of A Rose', and Keith
Foley sets the horns to improvise against a pre-set sequence for eight synthesizers on 'Futures'.
Some of the themes seem more like exhibitions designed to show off everybody's virtuosity
rather than meaningful pieces of music, and 'Futures', for one, is impressive mainly as an
exercise in recording techniques: the results scarcely compete with George Lewis's improvising
against a computer. But the skill and enthusiasm of both principals offer many felicitous
moments, and it's an engaging collection, for all its weaknesses.

DUDU PUKWANA (1938–90)
ALTO SAXOPHONE, SOPRANO SAXOPHONE, VOCALS

***(*)   **In The Townships** Earthworks/Virgin CDEWV 5 CD
Pukwana; Mongezi Feza (*t, perc, v*); Biso Mngqikana (*ts, perc, v*); Harry Miller (*b*);
Louis Moholo (*d*). 73.

(*)   **Cosmics Chapter 90 Ah Um 05 CD
Pukwana; Lucky Ranku (*g*); Roland Perrin (*ky*); Eric Richards (*b*); Steve Arguelles
(*d*); Fats Ramobo Mogoboya (*perc*); Pinise Saul (*v*). 11/89.

Whatever Yeats feared, the best can also be full of passionate intensity. Larger than life, Dudu
Pukwana was a much-loved presence on the British music scene. A South African exile, he had
been a member of Chris McGregor's multi-racial Blue Notes (which also included Mongezi
Feza and Louis Moholo, and which was barred from performing in the Republic of South
Africa) and later the pianist's Brotherhood of Breath. An able composer with a heated alto
(and, later, soprano) saxophone style, Pukwana was able to work in African, mainstream and
free/abstract settings with equal ease; as with Moholo, he tended to bring the virtues and
techniques of each to the others, playing *kwela* music with considerable harmonic and thematic
latitude, free music with the kind of fire normally heard only in the shebeens.

    Recorded in 1973, *In The Townships* is a minor classic. Originally credited to Pukwana and
his band Spear, it uses *kwela* rhythms in a way that reflects a deep understanding of bop. Vocals
and additional percussion suggest a much larger band. It's sad to note that, of the 1973 line-up,

Feza, Miller and Pukwana are all now dead (as is the catalytic Chris McGregor) and Moholo has suffered major heart problems.

If exile and rootlessness were corrosive, it rarely showed in Pukwana's stage manner, which was unboundedly joyous. Towards the end of his life, though, his music took on a more inward character and was increasingly abstract in manner. This development was reflected in his turn to soprano saxophone, which is strongly featured on the rather disappointing *Cosmics Chapter 90*. Though Pukwana is still able to generate considerable excitement, there is a tiredness in his playing, and much of the emphasis of his band – now known as Zila – rests with vocalist Pinise Saul and guitarist Lucky Ranku.

***(*)   **Mbizo Radebe** Affinity AFF 775 CD
       Pukwana; John Stevens (*d, bugle*). 1/87.

Passionate free jazz, pairing Pukwana (in top form) with the godfather of free drumming in Britain. Recommended.

DON PULLEN (born 1944)
PIANO, ORGAN, COMPOSER

***(*)   **Solo Piano Album** Sackville 3008 LP
       Pullen (solo). 2/75.

***   **Healing Force** Black Saint BSR 0010 LP
       As above. 76.

****   **Evidence Of Things Unseen** Black Saint BSR 0080 CD/LP
       As above. 9/83.

(*)   **Plays Monk Paddle Wheel K28P 6368 CD/LP
       As above. 11/84.

***   **Capricorn Rising** Black Saint BSR 0004 CD/LP
       Pullen; Sam Rivers (*ts, ss, f*); Alex Blake (*b*); Bobby Battle (*d*). 10/75.

***(*)   **Warriors** Black Saint BSR 0019 CD
       Pullen; Chico Freeman (*ts*); Fred Hopkins (*b*); Bobby Battle (*d*). 4/78.

***(*)   **The Sixth Sense** Black Saint BSR 0088 CD/LP
       Pullen; Olu Dara (*t*); Donald Harrison (*as*); Fred Hopkins (*b*); Bobby Battle (*d*). 6/85.

****   **New Beginnings** Blue Note 791785 CD
       Pullen; Gary Peacock (*b*); Tony Williams (*d*). 12/88.

****   **Random Thoughts** Blue Note 794347 CD
       Pullen; James Genus (*b*); Lewis Nash (*d*). 3/90.

Don Pullen's solo records demand comparison with Cecil Taylor's. Pullen's traditionalism is more obvious, but the apparent structural conservatism is more appearance than fact, a function of his interest in boogie rather than Bartók, and he routinely subverts expected patterns. The *Solo Piano Album* betrays a 'classical' interest in large masses of sound, sometimes to the detriment of forward progress. The pieces are all long ('Suite (Sweet) Malcolm' checks in at 15½ minutes) and relatively static but laden with harmonic detail in a way that Taylor's more dancing line is not. *Evidence Of Things Unseen* is by far the best of the three originals. It bespeaks roughly the same dark-and-light opposition as Andrew Hill or Ran Blake, though Pullen is more of a free player than either, and certainly less of an ironist than Blake.

He favours exotic dissonances within relatively conventional chordal progressions and, to that extent, is a descendant of Monk. His tribute album is very uneven, with completely wrong-headed effects on "Round Midnight' and some of the aimlessness that creeps into his duos with George Adams (*q. v.*). *Healing Force* (an echo of one of Albert Ayler's most misunderstood experiments) is less cathartic than *Evidence*, largely because its climaxes seem, if not faked, then certainly forced.

Of the groups with horns, the best are those fronted by Freeman and Dara, where Pullen develops spiky, almost spasmodic graph-lines of improvisational material in the midst of inventive and often rather Ivesian structures; the technique is reminiscent of Mingus, with whom Pullen played in the mid-1970s. Rivers is too floaty and ethereal to be entirely effective in this context, though he noticeably tailors his approach to Pullen's cues.

The best work of all is in the two late-1980s trios. The first, with its big-name rhythm section, explodes in the fury of 'Reap The Whirlwind', where Williams's scything cymbal lines and almost military patterns give a very fair taste of apocalypse. Though less revelatory than *Evidence*, Pullen's piano-playing seems trance-like, rooted in voodoo, pentecostalism and the Old Religion. By contrast, *Random Thoughts*, with its less experienced bass player and drummer, is calmer and less intense (though Pullen's right hand swirls on 'Andre's Ups And Downs' and 'Endangered Species: African American Youth', which makes its thematic point by systematically eliding beats, are absolutely characteristic). The closing 'Ode To Life' is unaccompanied and almost child-like, with echoes of 'Falling In Love Again' and 'Lili Marlene' in the first and second halves of the brief phrase out of which it's constructed.

IKE QUEBEC (1918–63)
TENOR SAXOPHONE

(*)   **The Tenor Sax Album: The Savoy Sessions Savoy WL 70812 2LP
Quebec; Johnny Guarnieri (*p*); Bill De Arango (*g*); Billy Taylor (*b*); Cozy Cole (*d*). 8/45.

***   **Blue And Sentimental** Blue Note 784098 CD
Quebec; Sonny Clark (*p*); Grant Green (*g*); Paul Chambers (*b*); Philly Joe Jones (*d*). 12/61.

***   **The Complete Blue Note 45 Sessions** Mosaic MR 3121 3LP
Quebec; Edwin Swanston, Sir Charles Thompson, Earl Vandyke (*org*); Skeeter Best, Willie Jones (*g*); Milt Hinton (*b*); J. C. Heard, Wilbert Hogan (*d*). 59, 60, 62.

Blue Note's last recording date in Hackensack and first in its new headquarters at Englewood Cliffs were both by Ike Quebec. Little known to younger fans, the saxophonist was nevertheless a figure of considerable influence at the label, acting as musical director, A&R man and talent scout (Dexter Gordon and Leo Parker were two of his 'finds'). He was also an important Blue Note recording artist, producing some marvellous sessions for the label just after the war and steering the label in the direction of a more contemporary repertoire. Mosaic had already issued a compilation of mid-1940s work by Quebec and John Hardee (who also features on the Savoy compilation). *The Complete Blue Note 45 Sessions* brings together 27 popular sides Quebec made for the thriving juke-box market. By no means wholly organ-dominated, as such 45s tended to be, the sessions strongly feature Quebec's still-underrated tenor style. There is considerable subtlety even in such tunes as 'Buzzard Lope' and 'Zonky', with Quebec sounding like a cross between Wardell Gray and Dexter Gordon. His style had consolidated rather than developed from the immediate post-war tracks with Johnny Guarnieri and Cozy Cole, and he is still immediately identifiable in the more challenging context provided by Jones, Chambers, Clark (one track only) and Green.

The latter was another one-time Blue Note stalwart who fell on hard critical times. Quebec has several times teetered on the brink of major rediscovery, but each time interest has flagged. He is, admittedly, a rather limited performer when set beside Gordon or any of the other younger tenor players emerging at the time, but he has a beautiful, sinuous tone and an innate melodic sense that negotiates standards with a simplicity and lack of arrogance that is refreshing and even therapeutic. *Blue And Sentimental*, with fine performances on 'Minor Impulse', 'Don't Take Your Love From Me' and 'Count Every Star', is an excellent place to start.

PAUL QUINICHETTE (1916–83)
TENOR SAXOPHONE

(*)   **On The Sunny Side Original Jazz Classics OJC 076 LP
Quinichette; Curtis Fuller (*tb*); John Jenkins, Sonny Red (*as*); Mal Waldron (*p*); Doug Watkins (*b*); Ed Thigpen (*d*). 5/57.

***   **Six Classic Tenors** EPM Musique 5170 CD
Quinichette; Kenny Drew (*p*); Freddie Green (*g*); Gene Ramey (*b*); Gus Johnson (*d*).
12/52.

Was he or wasn't he merely Lester Young-and-water? On the basis of these two albums (one of them a compilation which casts Quinichette in very exalted company indeed), we'd have to invoke Scots law and say, Not Proven. The OJC is too overcooked with three saxophones and a trombone, and Jenkins culls more than his share of the honours, so final judgement isn't possible.

It's good to find Quinichette on CD at all, and the four tracks on *Six Classic Tenors* are much closer to the meat of his true worth as a soloist. Ironically, he sounds closer to Don Byas (also featured on the compilation, along with Ben Webster, Coleman Hawkins, Eddie Lockjaw Davis and the second-division John Hardee) than to Pres, with a warmer, less oblique tone and a fine phrase-making talent. The compilation won't be of much use to those who already have good Hawkins and Webster collections, but it's worth looking out.

BOYD RAEBURN (died 1966)
BASS SAXOPHONE, TENOR SAXOPHONE, BARITONE SAXOPHONE, BANDLEADER

***(*)   **The Man With The Horns** Savoy WL 70534 LP
Raeburn; Tom Allison, Frank Beach, Conte Candoli, Buddy Colaneri, Norman Faye, Bob Fowler, Bernie Glow, Carl Groen, Alan Jeffries, Ray Linn, John Napton, Dale Pierce, Nelson Shalladay (*t*); Milt Bernhart, Jackie Carman, Leon Cox, Burt Johnson, Tommy Pedersen, Hal Smith, Bart Varsalona, Ollie Wilson, Britt Woodman, Si Zentner, Fred Zito (*tb*); Ethmer Roden (*f, as*); Lloyd Otto, Albert Richman, Evan Vail (*frhn*); Jules Jacobs (*ob, eng hn, ts*); Bill Starkey (*eng hn, bsx*); Buddy DeFranco (*cl*); Jimmy Giuffre (*cl, as*); Leonard Green, Hal McKusick (*as*); Wilbur Schwartz (*as, cl*); Harry Klee, Jerry Sanfino (*as, f*); Stuart Anderson, Frank Socolow, Sam Spumberg, Lucky Thompson (*ts*); Gus McReynolds (*ts, bs*); Ralph Lee (*ts, bsn*); Hy Mandel, Shirley Thompson (*bs*); Dodo Marmarosa, Ray Rossi, Hal Schaefer (*p*); George Handy (*p, v*); Gail Laughton, Loretta Thompson (*hp*); Dave Barbour, Hayden Causey, Steve Jordan, Tony Rizzi (*g*); Harry Babasin, Joe Berise, Ed Mihelich (*b*); Irv Kluger, Jackie Mills (*d*); Ginnie Powell (*v*). 10/45, 5, 6, 9 & 11/46, 8/47.

In 1944 an unexplained fire at the Palisades Pleasure Park in New Jersey destroyed the instruments and music of one of the most challenging big bands of the period. Typically of Boyd Raeburn, his reformed band and new book were even more adventurous than what had gone before. Raeburn's was a musicians' band, held in the highest esteem by his peers, regarded with some suspicion by those who believed that bands were for dancing.

Raeburn had an intelligent awareness of classical and twentieth-century forms – 'Boyd Meets Stravinsky', from the above, gives a sense of his range – and was as comfortable with Bartók and Debussy as he was with Ellington and Basie. 'Tonsilectomy', 'Rip Van Winkle' and 'Yerxa', from the earliest of these sessions, are among the most remarkable of modern band pieces. Hal McKusick was a featured soloist, and the Raeburn bands of the time (like Kirk's or McShann's) are well worth scouring for the early work of prominent modernists. From these sessions, in addition to McKusick, one might list Jimmy Giuffre, Dodo Marmarosa, Conte Candoli, Buddy De Franco and Charles Mingus's buddy and inspiration, Britt Woodman.

It may be that simple market forces pushed Raeburn back in the direction of the swing mainstream. The latest of the Savoy selections, from the summer of 1947, are 'The Lady Is A Tramp', 'How High The Moon' and 'St Louis Blues', still intelligently and uncompromisingly arranged (by Johnny Richards), but less immediately powerful than earlier sessions.

FREDDY RANDALL (born 1921)
TRUMPET

***   **His Great Sixteen** Dormouse DM5 LP
Randall; Geoff Sowden, Norman Cave, Roy Crimmins (*tb*); Bruce Turner (*ss, cl*); Bernie Stanton, Archie Semple, Al Gay (*cl*); Betty Smith (*ts*); Stan Butcher, Art Staddon, Dave Fraser, Lennie Felix, Harry Smith, Eddie Thompson (*p*); Lew Green

(*g, bj*); Don Cooper, Bobby Coram (*g*); Ron Stone, Ted Palmer, Ken Eaglefield, Jack Peberdy (*b*); Lennie Hastings, Stan Bourke (*d*); Billy Banks (*v*). 1/51–2/56.

The three stars are for Randall himself: the bands he led, even though such musicians as Felix and Turner are involved here and there, played forgettable British trad, but the trumpeter makes an altogether more vivid impression. The material is staple stuff for this kind of setting, yet Randall's solos arrive with the force of small explosions, simple phrases strung together with a vehemence which drives the music relentlessly while he is stage-centre. The other main point of interest is the presence of Billy Banks on two tracks; this is the same Billy Banks who recorded the memorable Rhythmakers tracks of 1932 with Henry Allen and others; it's amusing to note that his singing hasn't improved to any noticeable degree since then. Randall, though, plays as if determined to make his footnote status in jazz history mean something. The music has been faithfully transferred.

ENZO RANDISI
VIBES

***   **Ten Years After** Splasc(h) H 346-2 CD
Randisi; Salvatore Bonafede (*p*); Giuseppe Costa (*b*); Mimmo Cafiero (*d*). 12/90.

Enzo Randisi is a veteran Italian vibes player who hasn't recorded much: the title refers to the date of his last record prior to this one. He has nothing out of the ordinary to say and ambles through most of this session at a slow to medium tempo, working through a series of familiar ballads. Yet it all works out very well. Bonafede sees through the problems of making piano work with vibes, Costa and Cafiero play patiently and unemphatically, and Randisi is left to concentrate on his lines, which sidestep the kind of overplaying that vibes players tend to be tempted into and seek out clear, ringing melodies instead. He can pick up gears when he wants to – the gathering power of his solo on 'Poor Butterfly' is particularly well handled – but most of the time he doesn't have to, and sounds the better for it.

DOUG RANEY (born 1957)
GUITAR

***   **Introducing Doug Raney** Steeplechase SCS 1082 CD/LP/MC
Raney; Duke Jordan (*p*); Hugo Rasmussen (*b*); Billy Hart (*d*). 9/77.

***   **Cuttin' Loose** Steeplechase SCS 1105 CD/LP/MC
Raney; Bernt Rosengren (*ts*); Horace Parlan (*p*); Niels-Henning Ørsted-Pedersen (*b*); Billy Hart (*d*). 8/78.

***(*)   **Listen** Steeplechase SCS 1144 LP/MC
Raney; Bernt Rosengren (*ts*); Jesper Lundgaard (*b*); Billy Hart (*d*). 12/80.

***   **I'll Close My Eyes** Steeplechase SCS 1166 LP
Raney; Bernt Rosengren (*ts, af*); Horace Parlan (*p*); Jesper Lundgaard (*b*); Ole Jacob Hansen (*d*). 7/82.

***   **Meeting The Tenors** Criss Cross Criss 1006 LP
Raney; Bernt Rosengren (*ts, f*); Ferdinand Povel (*ts*); Horace Parlan (*p*); Jesper Lundgaard (*b*); Ole Jacob Hansen (*d*). 4/83.

(*)   **Blue And White Steeplechase SCS 1191 LP

***   **Lazy Bird** Steeplechase SCS 1200 CD/LP

***(*)   **Something's Up** Steeplechase SCS 1235 CD/LP
Raney; Bernt Rosengren (*ts* on *Lazy Bird* only); Ben Besiakov (*p*); Jesper Lundgaard (*b*); Aage Tanggaard (*d* on *Blue And White* only); Ole Jacob Hansen (*d* on *Lazy Bird* only); Billy Hart (*d* on *Something's Up* only). 4/84, 2/88.

***   **Guitar Guitar Guitar** Steeplechase SCS 1212 CD/LP
Raney; Mads Vinding (*b*); Billy Hart (*d*). 7/85.

****   **The Doug Raney Quintet** Steeplechase SCS 1249 CD/LP
Raney; Tomas Franck (*as*); Bernt Rosengren (*ts*); Jesper Lundgaard (*b*); Jukkis Uotila (*d*). 8/88.

Raised to the family craft, Doug Raney quickly established his own identity and a more contemporary idiom that also seemed to draw on swing guitar (missing out, that is, much of the bebop influence his father has sustained). The 20-year-old sounds assured on *Introducing* and, while Steeplechase house pianist Jordan doesn't seem the ideal choice or partner on themes like Coltrane's 'Mr P.C.', they romp through 'Bluebird' and a Coltrane-tinged 'Like Someone In Love' as if they'd been doing the stuff for years.

Less robust rhythmically than his father, Raney slots more conventionally into a horn-and-rhythm set-up. His trio, *Guitar Guitar Guitar*, is highly accomplished but it has a one-dimensional quality, noticeable on more familiar material like 'Solar' and 'My Old Flame'. CD doesn't flatter his technique, which sounds slightly scratchy and lacks Jimmy Raney's smooth, Jim Hall-like legato.

The closing 'Moment's Notice' (also by Coltrane) on *Listen* is one of Raney's best performances on record. There is a steady modal shift on his theme statements, and the soloing is robust without losing the tune's innate romanticism. Rosengren's Coltraneisms are reasonably well assimilated, and he modulates well, as on *Cuttin' Loose*, *Lazy Bird*, and *I'll Close My Eyes*, between a smooth swing and a more aggressive modernism. He seems a very different, much less confident player on *Meeting Of The Tenors*, which, with *Blue And White*, is Raney's most disappointing album. Things pick up sharply again with the 1988 album. Besiakov is nowhere near as commanding a player as Parlan, but he has sharpened considerably over the four years since *Blue And White* and lends a genuine presence to 'Good Morning Heartache' and 'Upper Manhattan Medical Group'.

The '88 quintet album is excellent in every department. There is another fine version of 'Speedy Recovery' (also on *Something's Up*). The extra horn and absence of piano restores certain harmonic responsibilities to the guitar, but it also generates a very different texture through which he has to play with just a little more force than usual. It's difficult to know where else to start with Raney. The late 1980s albums are completely accomplished, but one misses the freshness of the earlier material. Follow the stars.

JIMMY RANEY (born 1927)
GUITAR

****   **A** Original Jazz Classics OJC 1706 LP
Raney; John Wilson (*t*); Hal Overton (*p*); Teddy Kotick (*b*); Art Mardigan, Nick Stabulas (*d*). 5/54, 2 & 3/55.

Perhaps of the bop-inspired guitarists, Raney combines lyricism with great underlying strength. Essentially a group player, he sounds good at almost any tempo but is most immediately appealing on ballads. *A*, which contains some of his loveliest performances, is overdue for CD transfer. Overton anticipates some of the harmonic devices employed by Hank Jones (below) and bebop bassist Kotick plays with a firm authority that synchronizes nicely with Raney's rather spacious and elided lower string work. Wilson adds a dimension to the lovely 'For The Mode' and to four more romantic numbers, including 'A Foggy Day' and 'Someone To Watch Over Me'.

***(*)   **Two Jims And Zoot** Original Master Recordings MFCD 833 CD
Raney; Zoot Sims (*ts*); Jim Hall (*g*); Steve Swallow (*b*); Osie Johnson (*d*).

A valuable mid-period recording, beautifully transferred to CD. While one doesn't think of Raney responding particularly well to saxophonists, Sims's lush developments and bell-like tones are an exception. Hall, oddly, is a little too close in conception, and there is a tendency for the guitarists to repeat each other's figures (not always on the same track!). Otherwise, excellent value.

****   **Here's That Raney Day** Black & Blue 59.756 CD
Raney; Hank Jones (*p*); Pierre Michelot (*b*); Jimmy Cobb (*d*). 7/80.

****   **The Master** Criss Cross Criss 1009 CD
Raney; Kirk Lightsey (*p*); Jesper Lundgaard (*b*); Eddie Gladden (*d*). 2/83.

****   **Wisteria** Criss Cross Criss 1019 CD/LP
         Raney; Tommy Flanagan (*p*); George Mraz (*b*). 12/85.

The early 1980s saw some vintage Raney on record. The quartet with Hank Jones is valuable largely for the inclusion of alternative takes that give a clearer idea of how subtly the guitarist can shift the dynamic of a piece by holding or eliding notes, shuffling the rhythm and increasing the metrical stress. *Raney Day* is distinguished by a couple of bebop staples, 'Au Privave' and 'Scrapple From The Apple', which are taken medium-fast but with great control. Jones is bettered as an accompanist only by Flanagan and, at moments, Lightsey, both of whom are more elaborate and romantic players.

The Master offers second takes of 'The Song Is You' and 'Tangerine' (but not, unfortunately, the vibrant 'Billie's Bounce'), revealing how thoughtful an accompanist Lightsey is. The rhythm players are slightly too stiff for him, but he compensates by breaking up their less elastic figures with single-note stabs and scurrying runs at the next bar-line.

Flanagan's right hand is lost in a rather woolly mix, but the material on this marvellous album more than makes up for any purely technical shortcomings. From the opening 'Hassan's Dream', with its big, dramatic gestures, to 'I Could Write A Book', the drummerless group plays at the highest level and 'Out Of The Past' is very special indeed.

****   **Duets** Steeplechase SCS 1134 CD/LP/MC

***   **Stolen Moments** Steeplechase SCS 1118 CD/LP/MC

***   **Raney '81!** Criss Cross Criss 1001 LP

***(*)   **Nardis** Steeplechase SCS 1184 LP
         Raney; Doug Raney (*g*); Jesper Lundgaard (*b* on *Raney '81* only); Michael Moore (*b*
         on *Stolen Moments* only); Eric Ineke (*d* on *Raney '81!* only); Billy Hart (*d* on *Stolen*
         Moments only). 4/79, 4/79, 2/81, 3/83.

If you can't hire 'em, breed 'em. Raney's partnership with his son Doug has been one of the most productive and sympathetic of his career. Their duos are masterpieces of guitar interplay, free of the dismal call-and-response clichés that afflict such pairings, and often unexpectedly sophisticated in direction. Generally, the repertoire is restricted to standards, but Raney is also an impressive composer and frequently surprises with an unfamiliar melody.

Duets is probably still the best available performance and is available on all formats. The closing 'My Funny Valentine' would melt a heart of stone and Doug Raney, with the lighter, less strongly accented style that was so responsive to Chet Baker's needs, is particularly good on 'My One And Only Love' and 'Have You Met Miss Jones'. The addition of rhythm doesn't alter the basic conformation of the music, but it does increase the tempo and spices up the slightly unlikely samba. The curtain number is that old duo warhorse, 'Alone Together'.

Nardis is slightly unusual in that it seems to move forward and back in time. Beneath the calm surface of the title-track there is an unexpected urgency which suggests a more contemporary idiom, and yet 'All God's Chillun' is absolutely in the tradition. Raney's bop genes don't seem to have got through to his son, who favours a more measured phraseology, with a definite swing influence. *Raney '81* isn't officially credited to Raney & Son Ltd, but Doug's part in it is considerable. The wonderfully titled 'Chewish Chive And English Brick' is a Raney favourite and gets a rousing performance, to be compared with the two takes on *Here's That Raney Day*, above.

ENRICO RAVA (born 1943)
TRUMPET, FLUGELHORN

***   **The Pilgrim And The Stars** ECM 1063 LP
         Rava; John Abercrombie (*g*); Palle Danielsson (*b*); Jon Christensen (*d*). 1/75.

****   **Enrico Rava Quartet** ECM 1122 LP
         Rava; Roswell Rudd (*tb*); Jean-François Jenny-Clark (*b*); Aldo Romano (*d*). 3/78.

***   **Rava String Band** Soul Note SN 1114 LP
         Rava; Augusto Mancinelli (*g*); Giovanni Tommaso (*b*); Tony Oxley (*d*); Nana
         Vasconcelos (*perc*); string quartet. 4/84.

***(*)   **Secrets** Soul Note SN 1164 CD
Rava; Augusto Mancinelli (*g, g syn*); John Taylor (*p*); Furio Di Castri (*b*); Bruce
Ditmas (*d*). 7/86.

***   **Animals** Inak 8801 CD
As above, except omit Taylor; Mauro Beggio (*d*) replaces Ditmas. 6/87.

***   **Enrico Rava Quintet** Nabel 4632 CD/LP
Rava; Ullmann Gebhard (*ts, ss, bf*); Andreas Willers (*g*); Martin Willichy (*b*);
Nikolaus Schauble (*d*). 3/89.

Born in the 'international city' of Trieste, Rava evolved a richly esperantist style (originally but
not slavishly influenced by Miles Davis) which allows him access to a broad range of musics
from the highly formal to the near-free. The earlier of the ECMs has an almost eerie beauty,
with Rava's sustained, curving notes and sudden tangents effectively accented by
Abercrombie's guitar, and a firm compositional logic that breaks through even the most
outward of the improvisational passages. Rava worked with trombonist Rudd in the early
1970s, and their slightly later collaboration remains perhaps his best single album. The absence
of saxophones undoubtedly suits both men. The solitary standard, ''Round About Midnight', is
slightly estranged without a piano, and Rava reshapes the melody twice. The original
compositions are good.

It's a pity that the 1981 *Opening Night* [ECM 1224 LP] is currently out of print. Featuring
Franco D'Andrea, Di Castri and Romano, it's one of the trumpeter's best group performances.
In the early 1980s, he worked with (mainly) Italian bands, relying heavily on Mancinelli's
Abercrombie-derived guitar. Tony Oxley's recorded contribution is restricted to the less than
wholly successful *String Band* project, which reflects Rava's growing interest in formal
composition for orchestral groups. *Secrets* gains immeasurably from the presence of another
Englishman, John Taylor, whose cultured accompaniments and understated soloing are
probably more widely recognized outside the British Isles. The recent Nabel underlines how
much a player of Rava's warmth and sensitivity owes to CD. The band is less interesting than
any he has previously mustered (and Gebhard is a rather bland colourist), but the leader's tone
and invention on two takes of 'Fourteen Days' are impressive indeed.

Much of his best work is recorded elsewhere, and a good deal of his own is now available on
vinyl only. Nevertheless, Rava is an individual stylist who completely transcends his stylistic
roots and has created a consistently interesting and appealing body of work.

JASON REBELLO (born 1970)
PIANO, KEYBOARDS

(*)   **A Clearer View Novus PD 74805 CD/MC
Rebello; David O'Higgins (*ss, ts*); Julian Crampton, Lawrence Cottle (*b*); Jeremy
Stacey (*d*); Karl van den Bosch (*perc*). 90.

A debut of considerable impact, although Rebello's first disc as leader – he can also be heard on
Alan Skidmore's *Tribute To 'Trane* (Miles Music) – suffers a little from its modish settings and
sometimes anodyne material. The interesting thing is how much his own man Rebello already
sounds here: influences such as Herbie Hancock and McCoy Tyner have been firmly
assimilated, and there's no rush or excess in his solos – all the notes sound thoughtfully
fingered, even where the improvisations miss a distinctive final shape. The use of electric
keyboards gets in the way as often as it provides a logical backdrop but otherwise Rebello
concentrates the music around the individual contributions. O'Higgins, a talented saxophonist,
has one of his best solos on the chattering 'Tone Row' and elsewhere sounds commanding if
not especially individual. A follow-up record from a musician who quickly became one of the
young 'names' of British jazz has been a trifle slow in forthcoming, but he was reported to be
recording again in the summer of 1992.

FREDDIE REDD (born 1927)
PIANO

(*)   **Piano: East/West Original Jazz Classics OJC 1705 LP
Redd; John Ore (*b*); Ron Jefferson (*d*). 2/55.

***   **San Francisco Suite** Original Jazz Classics OJC 1748 CD/LP
Redd; George Tucker (*b*); Al Dreares (*d*). 10/57.

***   **Live At The Studio Grill** Triloka 182 2 CD
Redd; Al McKibbon (*b*); Billy Higgins (*d*). 5/88.

***   **Everybody Loves A Winner** Milestone MCD 9187 CD
Redd; Curtis Peagler (*as*); Teddy Edwards (*ts*); Phil Ranelin (*tb*); Bill Langlois (*b*);
Larry Hancock (*d*). 90.

Redd's amiable West Coast bop soundtracks an unscripted (but you've seen it) Bay Area movie: bustling streetcars, pretty girls flashing their legs, sudden fogs and alarms, an apology for a narrative. The *San Francisco Suite* is cliché from start to finish, but like the very much later *Winner* (Redd has been only a sporadic recorder in recent years), the hackneyed moods are unpretentiously and engagingly done.

The younger Redd gave no frights to Hampton Hawes, with whom he shares *Piano: East/West*; 'Things We Did Last Summer' has a warm bounce, but no real substance. The *Suite* works better on CD, where it can be left on in the background; 'View of the Golden Gate Bridge from Sausalito' is a fair sample of the impressionism, while 'Blue Hour' rearranges some Chandler chestnuts.

Redd's two good Blue Notes (*Shades of Redd* and *The Connection*) were reissued as a limited edition double CD on Mosaic (MD 124, see introduction), but despite that apparent apotheosis, his career has been largely static since the late 1950s. The Studio Grill sessions document a career-reviving residency in the Santa Monica Boulevard restaurant. 'I'll Remember April' has a vivid bounce that contrasts well with the blunt block chords Redd favours in his own compositions. It and the closing 'All The Things You Are' are the two longest cuts of the set, suggesting perhaps a degree of Redd's frustration at the lack of sympathetic recording opportunities over the years. 'Waltzin' In' is the best of the originals, a bright, hummable melody that like 'Don't Lose The Blues', sounds as if ought to be a long-serving standard. 'Round Midnight' (credited to Monk, Bernice Hanighan and Cootie Williams) is beautifully executed, with just a hint of Redd's impressionism creeping back in.

Everybody Loves A Winner again highlights his talent as a composer (and some of his limitations as a performer). The addition of horns gives him some room for experiment, certainly more than with a conventional piano trio, but only Curtis Peagler's youthful alto in any way attempts to break the mould. An interesting figure, but by no means a 'neglected genius'. His critical standing is just about right.

DEWEY REDMAN (born 1931)
TENOR SAXOPHONE, CLARINET, MUSETTE, ALTO SAXOPHONE

***   **Redman And Blackwell In Willisau** Black Saint BSR 0093 CD/LP
Redman; Ed Blackwell (*d*). 8/80.

(*)   **The Struggle Continues ECM 1225 LP
Redman; Charles Eubanks (*p*); Mark Helias (*b*); Ed Blackwell (*d*). 1/82.

***(*)   **Living On The Edge** Black Saint BSR 123 CD
Redman; Geri Allen (*p*); Cameron Brown (*b*); Eddie Moore (*d*). 9/89.

Redman's career has been notably erratic and, though he recorded classic solo albums as far back as 1966 (*Look For The Black Star*, Arista Freedom) and 1973 (*Ear Of The Beharer*, Impulse), he has attained proper recognition as a performer in his own right only in the 1980s, from which decade all his surviving material derives. Alternately volatile and magisterial, Redman is a difficult player to characterize. For much of his career, his critical visibility was limited by his role in Charlie Haden's Liberation Music Orchestra, and by his ultimately self-destructive behaviour in Keith Jarrett's American band; *The Survivor's Suite* (ECM 1085) was a masterpiece, *Eyes Of The Heart* (ECM 1150) an unmitigated disaster. He acted as an almost normative presence in Ornette Coleman's inflammable 1970s quintet, and, as Ornette's 'double' in the band Old and New Dreams (*q. v.*), has since become perhaps the most significant explorer on saxophone of the elder Texan's compositional output.

There are few direct traces of Ornette's approach in Redman's recent work, yet they demonstrably come from a single source. To the hard-toned 'Texas tenor' style, Redman has brought a strong Middle Eastern influence, most noticeable on the fine duos with Blackwell, where he also uses the twin-reed musette, exploring almost microtonal territory a long way removed from the blues. Blackwell's chiming, resonant sound is one of the redeeming aspects of *The Struggle Continues*, an awkward, aesthetically shapeless album that renewed doubts about Redman's contradictory personality.

By the end of the 1980s he appeared to have achieved some sort of psychological and artistic breakthrough. *Living On The Edge* preserves much of the menace Redman can generate, but with a new simplicity of emotion and with a tone notably less forced than on previous outings. Allen is an ideal partner, in that she is willing to examine intervals that fall outside the usual geometry of blues and bebop, but she also has an unfailing rhythmic awareness that keeps Redman within bounds. Strongly recommended (and *Dark Star* and *Behearer* should be looked out for as well).

DON REDMAN (1900–64)
ALTO SAXOPHONE, SOPRANO SAXOPHONE, OTHER INSTRUMENTS, BANDLEADER

***   **McKinney's Cotton Pickers 1928–30** Zeta ZET 743 CD
Redman; unknown personnel.

***   **The Chronological Don Redman, 1931–1933** Classics 543 CD

***   **The Chronological Don Redman, 1933–1936** Classics 553 CD
Redman; Henry Allen, Shirley Clay, Bill Coleman, Langston Curl, Reunald Jones, Sidney De Paris (*t*); Claude Jones, Benny Morton, Fred Robinson, Gene Simon (*tb*); Jerry Blake (*cl, as, bs*); Robert Cole, Edward Inge (*cl, as*); Harvey Boone (*as, bs*); Robert Carroll (*ts*); Horace Henderson, Don Kirkpatrick (*p*); Talcott Reeves (*bj, g*); Bob Ysaguirre (*bb, b*); Manzie Johnson (*d, vib*); Chick Bullock, Cab Calloway, Harlan Lattimore, The Mills Brothers (*v*); Bill Robinson (tap dancing). 9 & 10/31, 2, 6, 9, 10 & 12/32, 2, 4, 8, 10 & 11/33, 1/34, 3 & 5/36.

***   **Shakin' The African** Hep 1001 LP

(*)   **Doin' The New Low Down Hep 1004 LP
Redman; Henry Red Allen, Bill Coleman, Shirley Clay, Langston Curl, Sidney De Paris, Leonard Davis (*t*); Claude Jones, Benny Morton, Fred Robinson (*tb*); Quentin Jackson (*tb* on *Low Down* only); Rupert Cole, Edward Inge (*as*); Robert Carrol (*ts*); Horace Henderson (*p*); Talcott Reeves (*g, bjo*); Bob Ysaguirre (*b, tba*); Manzie Johnson (*d*); Cab Calloway, Don Mills, The Mills Brothers (*v* on *Low Down* only); Lois Deppe (*v* on *Shakin'* only); Harlan Lattimore (*v*); Bill Bojangles Robinson (tap dancing on *Low Down* only). 9 & 10/31, 2, 6, 9, 10 & 12/32, 2 & 4/33.

***   **For Europeans Only** Steeplechase SCC 6020/1 2LP
Redman; Peanuts Holland (*t, v*); Alan Jeffries, Bob Williams (*t*); Jackie Carman, Quentin Jackson (*tb*); Tyree Glenn (*tb, vib*); Chauncey Haughton (*as, bs*); Pete Clark (*as, bs, cl*); Don Byas (*ts*); Ray Abrams (*ts*); Billy Taylor (*p*); Ted Sturgis (*b*); Buford Oliver (*d*); Inez Cavanaugh (*v*). 9/46.

He was small, compact, well-loved. He played a mean alto and sang in a soft, almost ethereal whisper. He arranged and composed. And he conducted with his left hand.

Redman's reputation has been in progressive eclipse since the war, but he remains one of the essential figures of the Big Band era. He started out as lead saxophonist and staff arranger with Fletcher Henderson's band, infusing the charts with a breathtaking simplicity and confidence, eventually leaving in 1928 to front the highly successful McKinney's Cotton Pickers. The Zeta is a welcome CD transfer. Technically, it's quite sound, though the bass (possibly Ralph Escudero) is poorly registered and there are some lapses of balance. The material was kept pretty basic, with a hokey blues content and Redman's characteristically unfussy arrangements.

Redman quickly moved on to form a 'name' band. The material on *Chronological* almost exactly reduplicates the two vinyl-only Heps, which halt with a session of April 1933 that included a better-than-average 'Sophisticated lady'. *Shakin' the African* and the earlier *Chronological* feature the band's remarkable theme-tune, 'Chant Of The Weed', Redman's brilliant and justly celebrated arrangement of 'I Got Rhythm' and two cuts of the title-track. The band at this time also featured Harlan Lattimore, one of the few genuinely challenging singers of the era, who was once described by George T. Simon as sounding like a rather hip Bing Crosby; one man or the other is spinning in his coffin even now. The later material, which fractionally overlaps a February 1933 session on both options, is by no means as good. The arrangements are well up to scratch, and there is more impressive work from Lattimore. Bojangles Robinson tip-taps on one version of the title-piece, but the better cut features the Mills Brothers and Cab Calloway.

Redman's bandleading career effectively ended with America's entry into the Second World War. He became a professional arranger and writer, working freelance for Harry James and others. He did, though, have one significant fling in 1946, when he led the first American band to visit Europe since peace broke out. *For Europeans Only* is patchy, but there are excellent, brassy readings of 'Chant Of The Weed', 'I Got Rhythm', 'The World Is Waiting For The Sunrise', 'All The Things You Are' and 'How High The Moon'.

ERIC REED (born 1970)
PIANO

**(*) Soldier's Hymn Candid CCD 79511 CD
Reed; Dwayne Burno (*b*); Gregory Hutchinson (*d*). 11/90.

Although intended as a showcase debut for Reed, who is currently pianist in the Wynton Marsalis band, this is much more of a trio record. Originals like the title piece (present in two different versions) and 'Coup De Cone' are conscious evaluations of the manner of a Jazz Messengers rhythm section (Art Blakey is the album's dedicatee) and elsewhere Reed's chord-based solos and call-and-response interplay suggest the influence of Ahmad Jamal or even Ramsey Lewis. This works out well on the less ambitious pieces – 'Soft Winds' is an impressive update of the old Benny Goodman tune – but on the more portentous tracks, such as 'Things Hoped For' or the half-baked medley which Reed does as a solo turn, the music sounds more like a demo session than a finished record. The first version of the title-track shows the trio in ideal balance, and it's a pity that they decided to record it a second time. The studio sound, though, is impeccable, and reveals all the detail in the music.

TONY REEDUS (born 1959)
DRUMS

***(*) The Far Side Jazz City 660.53.016 CD
Reedus; Bill Evans (*ss, ts*); Mulgrew Miller (*p*); Charnett Moffett (*b*). 11/88.

***(*) Incognito Enja 6058 CD
Reedus; Gary Thomas (*ts, f*); Steve Nelson (*vib*); Dave Holland (*b*). 12/89.

That these two outstanding records are very different from each other says something about the itch to diversify which attends virtually all young jazz musicians nowadays. Reedus is typical of the masterful generation of young virtuosos who are directing the music in America today: his drumming is big, loud and intense, but he plays for his bands, and he's no more egocentric than, say, Max Roach when it comes to directing the music. The Jazz City CD is the more concentrated set: despite a couple of distractions, such as a straight reading of Michael Jackson's 'I Just Can't Stop Loving You', the playing has elegant rigour and a passionate harshness in equal measure, with the undervalued Evans taking a few inspired solos – his Coltraneisms on the title-piece are especially exciting – and Miller anchoring matters when they threaten to slip into abstraction. *Incognito* is more considered, less of a blow-out, and the choice of players is ingenious: Nelson's delicate pointers, Holland's wiry lyricism and Thomas's stone-faced urgency (on tenor – his flute is surprisingly sweet and cultured) concoct a heady brew among them.

Sometimes Thomas's grim playing makes the music a little too dark, but it's absorbing. The drums are very forward on both records, though it shouldn't trouble anyone unduly.

REUBEN REEVES (1905–55)
TRUMPET

***   **Reuben 'River' Reeves And His River Boys** Retrieval FJ-126 LP
Reeves; Gerald Reeves (*tb*); Omer Simeon, Darnell Howard (*cl, as*); Cecil Irwin (*ts*); Jimmy Prince (*p*); Cecil White (*bj, g*); Jasper Taylor (*d*); Blanche Calloway (*v*). 5–9/29.

Reeves was an engaging if derivative trumpeter who made only a few records; all but a single 1933 session with a larger band are collected on this LP. The first track, 'River Blues', sounds curiously like a Red Nichols Five Pennies record, but Reeves, who is the principal soloist throughout, creates raw, excitable improvisations that give the music a gritty feel. He sometimes plays in a growl manner reminiscent of Bubber Miley, but is more usually found hitting harsh top notes with a wide vibrato that suggests the inevitable Armstrong influence. The first four tracks, by a quintet, are the most interesting; the later sides add extra players and are stodgier in feeling, although Reeves does his best to liven things up when he cuts through. Calloway does a fine job on a remarkably intense reading of Waller's 'Black And Blue', but some other tracks are marred by a terrible (and thankfully unidentified) male vocalist. John R. T. Davies does his usual marvellous job in remastering from rare originals.

HANS REICHEL
GUITAR, PREPARED GUITAR, DAXOPHONE/DACHSOPHON, OTHER INSTRUMENTS

(*)   **Wichlinghauser Blues FMP 0150 LP
Reichel (solo). 4–6/73.

***   **Bonobo** FMP 0280 LP
As above. 7 & 10/75.

***(*) **The Death Of The Rare Bird Ymir** FMP 0640 LP
As above. 2/79.

***   **Bonobo Beach** FMP 0830 LP
As above. 4/81.

***(*) **The Dawn Of Dachsman** FMP 1140 LP
As above. 5/87.

***   **Coco Bolo Nights** FMP CD 10 CD
As above. 12/88.

(*)   **Erdmannchen FMP 0400 LP
Reichel; Achim Knipsel (*g*). 6/77.

***   **Buben** FMP 0530 LP
Reichel; Rudiger Carl (*concertina*). 5/78.

***   **Angel Carver** FMP CD 15 CD
Reichel; Tom Cora (*clo, cellodax*). 10/88.

Riveting free-form guitar with a strong narrative flavour and a complete absence of the 'I've suffered for my art, now it's your turn' aggression of much solo improvised music. Reichel clearly desires to communicate and to convey a story, however notionally and abstractly. His playing is unfussy and uncluttered and he's generally best heard solo, though Cora and Carl offer stimulating support. The 'prepared' effects of *Bonobo* are less effective than his admirably disciplined straight performances, though he coaxes intriguing sounds from a group of personalized instruments which have some connection to the life and life-philosophy of Herr Dachsman.

This, and the marvellous *Death Of The Rare Bird Ymir* are by far the best of the albums and should be heard before the more abstract duos and before such tentative early efforts as *Wichlinghauser Blues*. An original and an offbeat entertainer, Reichel more than repays a little initial effort.

RUFUS REID (born 1944)
DOUBLE BASS

(*)   **Perpetual Stroll Theresa TR 111 LP
Reid; Kirk Lightsey (*p*); Eddie Gladden (*d*). 1/80.

A solitary outing as leader by the man who has underpinned Andrew Hill's recent work and launched the prodigious Geoff Keezer in such a way that the youngster's suspect left hand wasn't noticed unduly. With Lightsey, he's on easier and more productive ground. Themes like 'Habiba' and 'Tricotism' were made by and for the pianist, and he pulls the themes together with almost disdainful ease. 'One Finger Snap' was made for the bassist, and he thuds and thrums through it with a typically dark sonority, cracking out top notes with an almost New Orleans accent. 'Waltz For Doris' and 'Perpetual Stroll' are both beautifully done, but the sound calls for a bit of fiddling on the amplifier to get the balances right. Worth a look.

DJANGO REINHARDT (1910–53)
GUITAR

****   **Swing From Paris** ASV CD AJA 5070 CD
Reinhardt; Stéphane Grappelli (*vn*); Roger Chaput, Pierre Ferret, Joseph Reinhardt, Eugene Vees (*g*); Robert Grassnet, Tony Rovira, Emmanuel Soudieux, Louis Vola (*b*). 9 & 10/35, 1, 6 & 8/38, 3 & 8/39.

****   **Swing In Paris 1936–40** Affinity AFS 1003 5CD
Reinhardt; Rex Stewart (*c*); Pierre Allier, Philippe Brun, Bill Coleman, André Cornille, Lester Shad Collins, Gus Deloof, Bill Dillard, Al Piguillem (*t*); Alex Renard (*t, b t*); Benny Carter (*t, as*); Josse Breyere, Pierre Deck, Gaston Moat, Guy Paquinet, Dicky Wells (*tb*); Maurice Cizeron (*f*); Barney Bigard (*cl, d*); Christian Wagner (*cl, as*); Frank Big Boy Goudie, Bertie King, Hubert Rostaing (*cl, ts*); Fletcher Allen, Max Blanc, André Ekyan, Charles Lisée (*as*); Coleman Hawkins, Jacques Helian (*ts*); Alix Combelle (*ts, cl*); Larry Adler (*hca*); Stéphane Grappelli (*vn, p*); P. Bartel-Swetschin, Charlie Lewis, Eddie South, Michel Warlop (*vn*); Emil Stern, Yorke De Souza (*p*); Marcel Bianchi, Roger Chaput, Pierre Ferret, Louis Gaste, Joseph Reinhardt, Eugene Vees (*g*); Paul Cornonnier, Richard Fulbright, Eugene d'Hellemmes, Francis Luca, Wilson Myers, Tony Rovira, Lucien Simoens, Emmanuel Soudieux, Billy Taylor, Louis Vola (*b*); Bill Beacon, Tommy Benford, Maurice Chaillou, Jerry Mengo (*d*); Freddy Taylor (*v*). 36–40.

***(*)   **Django Reinhardt** Forlane UCD 19001 CD

****   **Bruxelles / Paris** Musidisc 403222 CD
Reinhardt; Roger Guerin, Bernard Hullin (*t*); Hubert Rostaing (*cl*); Hubert Fol (*as*); Stéphane Grappelli (*vn*); Martial Solal, Maurice Vander (*p*); Raymond Fol (*p* on *Bruxelles / Paris* only); Roger Chaput, Pierre Ferret, Alan Hodgkiss, Jack Llewelyn, Joseph Reinhardt, Eugene Vees (*g*); Fats Sadi (*vib*); Coleridge Goode, Pierre Michelot, Emmanuel Soudieux, Barney Speler, Louis Vola (*b*); Pierre Fouad, Pierre Lamarchand (*d*). 1938–53, 47–53.

***(*)   **Swing De Paris** Arco 3 ARC 110 CD
Reinhardt; Gerard Leveque, Maurice Meunier, Hubert Rostaing (*cl*); Joseph Reinhardt, Eugene Vees (*g*); Eddie Bernard (*p*); Ladislav Czabancyk, Emmanuel Soudieux (*b*); Andre Jourdan, Jacques Martinon (*d*); collective personnel. 7, 8 & 11/47.

One of the Christian-name-only mythical figures of jazz, Django embodies much of the nonsense that surrounds the physically and emotionally damaged who nevertheless manage to parlay their disabilities and irresponsibilities into great music. Django's technical compass, apparently unhampered by loss of movement in two fingers of his left hand (result of a burn which had ended his apprenticeship as a violinist), was colossal, ranging from dazzling high-speed runs to ballad-playing of aching intensity.

There are a number of good value CDs available. The Affinity set is essential, offering all the recordings made between 1936 and the fall of Paris. There are important sessions with visiting Americans – such as Benny Carter and Coleman Hawkins – who took back home the news that at last there was a European jazz man who seemed to be doing something new. In bulk, though, the music begins to sound slightly tired and dated and Django's astonishing technique almost *too* pefect.

The ASV is beautifully remastered by Colin Brown, an example of how historical recordings can be restored without intrusive sweetening or inauthentic balances. At 66 minutes, it's also excellent value. It's good to be reminded how extraordinarily forceful the drummerless Hot Club could sound. Even with the chugging background, 'Appel Direct' is remarkably modern and it's easy to see why Django continues to exert such an influence on guitarists of later, technically more sophisticated generations. The titles are confusingly similar, but this is the best single-volume option.

Of the latter pair, the Forlane reaches back further in time, and is thus more representative (with a snippet – 'I Got Rhythm', also on the ASV – from the original Hot Club de France), but the Musidisc offers a more extensive sample of the important sessions of 21 May 1947 (with Hubert Rostaing and the reconstituted Hot Club; the albums share 'Just One Of Those Things') and of 8 April 1953, the month before his death (with Martial Solal; they share a marvellous 'I Cover The Waterfront'), as well as good-quality material from 1951: 'Nuits De St Germain-Des-Prés', 'Crazy Rhythm', 'Fine And Dandy'. Anyone insistent on 'Nuages' will need the Forlane, which has an immediately post-war reading.

Bruxelles / Paris has a marginally tougher version. In 1947, Django was battling with amplification (not always successfully), coping with the repercussions of a not entirely ecstatic reception with Ellington in the USA (ditto), and slipping backwards into the moral vagrancy that undoubtedly shortened his life. On the better tracks, on 'Blues For Barclay', 'Manoir De Mes Rêves', 'Mélodie Du Crépuscule', and 'Nuages', his instincts seem to be intact. He picks off clusters of notes with tremendous compression, holds and bends top notes like a singer and keeps a deep, insistent throb on the bottom string that, when it makes it up through the lo-fi hiss and drop-out, is hugely effective.

*** **Swing Guitar** Jass J-CD-628 CD
Reinhardt; Herb Bass, Robin Gould, Jerry Stephan, Lonnie Wilfong (*t*); Bill Decker, Don Gardner, Shelton Heath, John Kirkpatrick (*tb*); Jim Hayes (*cl, as*); Joe Moser (*as*); Bernie Calaliere, Bill Zickenfoose (*ts*); Ken Lowther (*bs*); Larry Mann (*p*); Bob Decker (*b*); Red Lacky (*d*). 10 & 12/45, ?3/46.

Django and the European Division Band of the Air Transport Command recorded from the American Forces Network *Bandstand* and *Beaucoup De Music* (*sic.*) broadcasts, in rehearsal and live at the Salle Pleyel in the months immediately following the end of the war in Europe. Eric Bogart likens the ATC band to one of the 'scrapping, blues-heavy' territory bands of the interwar years, of which only Basie's made it to the big time. They certainly have a tougher feel than one normally associates with such outfits, and the opening 'Djangology' gets more than a run for its money, with an altered bridge by arranger Lonnie Wilfong. There is a fine interpretation of 'Belleville', with the first really classy guitar solo. Django excels himself on the unaccompanied 'Improvisation No. 6', taken from a slightly later small-group session, after which the group returns for rather more routine runs through 'Honeysuckle Rose' and 'Sweet Sue', the latter featuring a surprisingly effective penny whistle solo by Lieber. There's a second 'Djangology' and, rounding out the session, six cuts without the guitarist, but including spirited readings of 'Swing Guitars' and 'Manoir De Mes Rêves' and other tunes not immediately associated with Django, of which 'Perdido' and Strayhorn's 'Midriff' are the most impressive. As Django sessions go, this is about beta-plus, but the ATC outfit are consistently impressive and are well worth checking out. Jack Towers's 'audio restoration' has been done with common sense and good taste.

***(*) **Djangology 1949** Bluebird/BMG ND90448 CD/LP
Reinhardt; Stéphane Grappelli (*vn*); Gianni Safred (*p*); Carlo Recori (*b*); Aurelio de Carolis (*d*). 1 & 2/49.

A final opportunity to hear Reinhardt and Grappelli playing together, albeit with a dud rhythm section. In an intelligent sleeve-note (which includes useful track-by-track comments on all 20 CD items), guitarist Frank Vignola warns against making comparisons between these rather edgy and competitive sessions and the great days of the pre-war Quintette du Hot Club. The most evident token of changing musical times, and a legacy of Django's relatively unsuccessful American trip, is a boppish cast to several of the tracks, most significantly the Ur-text of bebop, 'I Got Rhythm'.

Fortunately for the session, both Django and Grappelli got rhythm to spare, for the local musicians are a positive hindrance. On 'All The Things You Are' Safred chords morosely in the background while Recori and de Carolis go off for a *grappa*. Django's frustration comes through in places, but it's clear that at least some of the aggression is directed at his one-time junior partner who now claims his full share of the foreground. For all its shortcomings, this is a worthwhile addition to the discography.

EMILY REMLER (1957–91)
GUITAR

(*)   **Firefly Concord CJ 162 MC
Remler; Hank Jones (*p*); Bob Maize (*b*); Jake Hanna (*d*). 4/81.

***   **Catwalk** Concord CJ 265 MC
Remler; John D'Earth (*t*); Eddie Gomez (*b*); Bob Moses (*d*). 8/84.

****   **East To Wes** Concord CCD 4356 CD/MC
Remler; Hank Jones (*p*); Buster Williams (*b*); Marvin 'Smitty' Smith (*d*). 5/88.

Remler's senseless early death (from heart failure while on tour in Australia) deprived us of a talent that seemed on the point of breakthrough. While her early role-models were conservative ones in terms of her instrument – Christian and Montgomery, specifically – her tough-minded improvising and affinity with hard-hitting rhythm sections let her push a mainstream style to its logical limits. Of a number of Concord albums, the above are still in print. *Firefly* was her debut for the label and is fluent if a little anonymous, although she handles the diversity of 'Strollin'' and 'In A Sentimental Mood' without any hesitation. *Catwalk* is one of two albums made with the somewhat unusual partnership with D'Earth whose crisp, pinchy solos make an interesting foil to the leader's more expansive lines. The best available set, though, is the impeccable Montgomery tribute, *East To Wes*. Smith proves to be an ideal drummer for the guitarist, his busy cymbals and polyrhythmic variations on the bebop pulse perfectly cast to push Remler into her best form: 'Daahoud' and 'Hot House' are unbeatable updates of each tune. Jones, imperturbable as ever, takes a cool middle course. While conceived as a Montgomery homage, Remler's playing actually shows how unlike Wes she really was: harder of tone, her solos more fragmented yet equally lucid.

****   **Retrospective, Vol. One: Standards** Concord CCD 4453 CD

***   **Retrospective, Vol. Two: Compositions** Concord CCD 4463 CD
As above records, except add Larry Coryell (*g*), James Williams (*p*), Don Thompson (*b*), Terry Clarke (*d*). 81–88.

Two excellent compilations of Remler's Concord years. The first volume is superior, with an intelligent choice of standards, two beautiful duets with Larry Coryell and an unaccompanied solo on 'Afro Blue'. Her original themes are rather less memorable, but the playing on the second volume remains enticing throughout.

DON RENDELL (born 1926)
SOPRANO AND TENOR SAX, CLARINET, FLUTE

**   **Live At The Avgarde Gallery Manchester** Spotlite SPJ 501 LP
Rendell; Pete Martin (*t, flhn*); Joe Palin (*p*); Ian Taylor (*b*); Gordon Beckett (*d*). 10/73.

***   **Just Music** Spotlite SPJ 502 LP
Rendell; Barbara Thompson (*ss, ts, f*); Peter Lemer (*ky*); Steve Cook (*b*); Laurie
Allen (*d*). 1–6/74.

**   **Earth Music** Spotlite SPJ 502 LP
Rendell; Dick Pearce, Paul Nieman (*tb*); Pete Hurt (*as*); Alan Wakeman (*ss, ts*); John
Williams (*bs*); Pete Saberton (*p*); Paul Bridge (*b*); Trevor Tomkins (*d*). 6/79.

***   **Set 2** Spotlite SPJ 516 LP
Rendell; Alan Wakeman (*ss, ts*); Pete Saberton (*p*); Paul Bridge (*b*); Trevor Tomkins
(*d*). 6/79.

None of Don Rendell's records from the 1950s – for Decca, Nixa and Tempo – have ever been
reissued, and the very fine series of quintet sessions with Ian Carr which he cut in the 1960s
have been similarly neglected. All of which has conspired against this excellent saxophonist
from acquiring a wider following among younger listeners – unlike, say, the much-talked-of
Tubby Hayes and Joe Harriott. Rendell broadened a swing-to-bop vocabulary with what he
learned from Coltrane and Rollins, and by the 1970s he was a masterful all-round stylist. These
Spotlite records, though, are rather patchy, catching him at various live dates rather than
affording the opportunity for decently prepared studio sessions, although *Just Music* is a little
more detailed. The Manchester set features a competent but not especially inspiring band which
Rendell tends to outclass. He has always liked another saxophonist in the front line, and
Thompson's punchy tenor and soprano are a good foil on *Just Music*, which is split between a
six-part 'Wensleydale Suite' and five other originals. *Earth Music* is another suite for a nonet,
although the writing is rather indifferent and the main point lies in the improvising; but *Set 2*,
recorded on the same day with Wakeman and the rhythm section, features arguably his best
work among the four records: Wakeman's slightly freer methods make a piquant contrast, and
the improvising on 'Becclesology' and the trenchant 'It Could've Happened To You' is
impressive. Only Saberton's solos lack focus.

REPERCUSSION UNIT
GROUP

***   **In Need Again** CMP 31 CD/LP/MC
John Bergamo; Jim Hildebrandt, Gregg Johnson, Ed Mann, Lucky Mosko (*perc*);
Larry Stein (*perc, ky, v*). 6/87.

The Repercussion Unit is more obviously satirical in conception than John Bergamo's solo
project, but concentrating on tonal and textural interplay of a high order, out of which it's
difficult or redundant to pick individuals other than Bergamo. 'The Grand Ambulation Of The
B72 Zombies' is one of the great tune titles, but there's nothing on the album that matches the
power and beauty of Bergamo's own work.

MELVIN RHYNE (born 1936)
ORGAN

***   **The Legend** Criss Cross Jazz Criss 1059 CD
Rhyne; Brian Lynch (*t*); Don Braden (*ts*); Peter Bernstein (*g*); Kenny Washington
(*d*). 12/91.

Best known for his part in the Wes Montgomery trios on Riverside, this is Rhyne's first
recording as a leader, done impromptu after the organist had finished a Criss Cross session for
trumpeter Brian Lynch.

Rhyne immediately sounds different from the prevailing Jimmy Smith school of organ
players. Instead of swirling, bluesy chords, he favours sharp, almost staccato figures and lyrical
single-note runs that often don't go quite where expected. The format for the session is the
same as that for the classic Montgomery recordings, and Kenny Washington makes a
particularly strong impact.

The set opens with Eddie Lockjaw Davis's 'Licks A-Plenty', kicks along with 'Stompin' At The Savoy', Wes Montgomery's 'The Trick Bag' and Dizzy Gillespie's 'Groovin' High'; there are two evocative ballads, 'Serenata' and 'Old Folks' and the session closes with a long 'Blues For Wes', with Lynch and saxophonist Braden sitting in. It's remarkable that a talent as individual as Rhyne's hasn't been more widely exposed.

MARC RIBOT
GUITARS, OTHER INSTRUMENTS

*** **Rootless Cosmopolitans** Antilles 842577 CD
Ribot; Curtis Fowlkes (*tb*); Don Byron (*cl, bcl*); Roy Nathanson (*sax*); Anthony Coleman (*ky, sampler*); Arto Lindsay, David Sardi (*g*); Melvin Gibbs, Brad Jones (*b*); Ralph Carney (*sona*); Michael Blair (*d, v*); Richie Schwarz (*d, sampler*).

Accused of superficiality and pointless eclecticism, former Lounge Lizard Ribot might respond that both of these are precisely the point, that surfaces and choices are all contemporary music can be made of. 'Rootless cosmopolitanism' entered the language from Stalin via Allen Ginsberg and means more or less what the Red Queen says it means. Ribot takes it as licence for a wildly divergent sample of sources as far afield as Ellington ('Mood Indigo'), Jimi Hendrix (a shaky vocal from Ribot on 'The Wind Cries Mary') and George Harrison (an unaccompanied 'While My Guitar Gently Weeps'). The two solo overdubs suggest possibilities that aren't even skirted, and much of the record is given over to pseudo-rock productions that wouldn't pass as demos in Chartsville. So why three stars? Because it's great listening from soup to nuts, is why.

BUDDY RICH (1917–87)
DRUMS, VOCAL

** **One Night Stand** Bandstand BDCD 1528 CD
Rich; Pinky Savitt, Louis Oles, Bitsy Mullens, Karl Warwick (*t*); Earl Swope, Morty Bullman, Al Lorraine, Sam Hyster (*tb*); Les Clarke, Mario Daone (*as*); George Berg, Mick Rich (*ts*); Sid Brown (*bs*); Tony Nichols (*p*); Joe Shulman (*b*); Stan Kay (*d*); Dorothy Reid (*v*). 3/46.

This was one of Rich's first bands as a leader after leaving Tommy Dorsey the year before. Eighteen tracks are drawn from a couple of live broadcasts from Hollywood, in acceptable sound for the period. While the band has few distinctive players, it's already typical of the kind of groups Rich liked: functional, unpretentious, ruthlessly swinging. The charts and original material, though, are decidedly routine. At the very end is the most surprising score of the lot, Tadd Dameron's 'Cool Breeze'.

**** **Compact Jazz: Buddy Rich** Verve 833 295-2 CD
Rich; Conrad Gozzo, Harry Edison, Pete Candoli, Emmett Bery, Joe Ferrante, Stan Fishelson, Jimmy Nottingham, Tommy Turrentine, Marky Markowitz, Rolf Ericson (*t*); Frank Rosolino, Eddie Bert, Bill Byers, Jimmy Cleveland, Willie Dennis, Julian Priester (*tb*); Bob Enevoldsen (*vtb, ts*); Earle Warren, Phil Woods, Sonny Criss (*as*); Ben Webster, Bob Cooper, Al Cohn, Benny Golson, Stanley Turrentine, Seldon Powell (*ts*); Buddy Collette (*bs, f*); Steve Perlow (*bs*); Sam Most (*f*); Jimmy Rowles, John Bunch, Paul Smith, Dave McKenna, Johnny Morris (*p*); Bill Pitman, Sam Herman, Howard Roberts (*g*); Mike Mainieri (*vib*); Joe Mondragon, Phil Leshin, Earl May, Wyatt Ruther (*b*); Max Roach, Alvin Stoller (*d*). 11/55–8/61.

Although he spent much of the 1950s and early '60s with the Harry James orchestra, Rich continued to lead his own bands on record, orchestras and small groups alike. Most of them – including *The Wailing Buddy Rich*, *Rich Verses Roach* and *Burnin' Beat* – have yet to appear on CD. But this intelligent compilation creams off several characteristic tracks, which in total showcase the drummer's virtuosity at every level. 'Jumpin' At The Woodside' and 'Jump For Me' come from an excellent Basie tribute album. 'Toot, Toot, Tootsie' pairs him off against Max Roach in a right royal encounter. 'A Night In Tunisia' is almost as over-the-top as Art Blakey's celebrated Blue Note reading; while a long, luxuriant 'Broadway' with Criss and

Edison displays his brushwork. In very bright and punchy sound, which belies the age of the original tracks, this is perhaps the best single introduction to Rich on record. There is also a single example of his vocal style, which nearly tempted him away from drummming for a while. It's not unpleasant, in a lowbrow-Sinatra kind of way.

***   **The Cinch** Spotlite SPJ 149 LP
Rich; Ole Jacob Hansen (*tb*); Sonny Criss (*as*); Kenny Drew (*p*); Phil Leshin (*b*); Dave Lambert Singers (*v*). 11/58.

Two broadcasts from Birdland in New York catch Rich leading a fiery quintet. Criss is in typically explosive mood and matches the leader for sheer firepower, but Hansen isn't far behind and stands his ground with great aplomb. Drew's 'The Cinch' and a blistering march through 'Four' stand out from a strong programme, which airshot sound serves respectably enough.

***(*)   **Illusion** Sequel NXT CD 181 3CD
Rich; Buck Clayton, Roy Eldridge, Dizzy Gillespie, Charlie Shavers, Joe Newman, Harry Edison, Pete Candoli, Conrad Gozzo, Joe Wilder, Nick Travis, Don Goldie, Al Stewart, Bobby Shew, John Sottile, Yoshito Murikami, Walter Battagello, Chuck Findley, Russell Iverson, Oliver Mitchell, Greg Bowen, Derek Watkins, Stan Reynolds, Ronnie Hughes, Johnny McLeavy (*t*); Tommy Turk, Bill Harris, Frank Rosolino, Bob Enevoldsen, Frank Rehak, Jimmy Cleveland, James Trimble, Johnny Boice, Ron Myers, Bill Wimberley, Jack Spurlock, Samuel Burtis, Robert Brawn, Cliff Hardie, Keith Christie, John Marshall, Jack Thirlwall, Bobby Lamb, Ray Premru (*tb*); Dennis Allan Good (*btb*); Buddy DeFranco (*cl*); Charlie Parker, Willie Smith, Benny Carter, Sonny Criss, Ronnie Chamberlain, Alan Branscombe (*as*); Flip Phillips, Lester Young, Paul Quinichette, Illinois Jacquet, Bob Cooper, Duncan Lamont, Jimmy Philip (*ts*); Buddy Collette (*bs, f*); Ken Dryden (*bs*); Nick Busch, Colin Horton, John Pigneguy, Tony Lucas, Nick Hill (*frhn*); Sam Marowitz, Eddie Wasserman, Jerry Sanfino, Danny Bank, Daniel Quill, Peter Yellin, Jay Corre, Martin Flax, Stephen Perlow, Quinn Davis, Ernie Watts, Robert Keller, James Moscher, Meyer Hisch (*saxes*); Nat Cole, Kenny Kersey, Hank Jones, Bud Powell, Stan Freeman, Bernie Leighton, Oscar Peterson, Count Basie, Teddy Wilson, Jimmy Rowles, Ronnie Ball, John Bunch, Ray Starling, Russel Turner Jr, Steve Gray (*p*); Irving Ashby, Billy Bauer, Barney Kessel, Freddie Green, Herb Ellis, Bill Pittman, George Barnes, Howard Collins, Barry Zweig, Richard Resnicoff (*g*); Billy Hadnott, Ray Brown, Eddie Safranski, Gene Ramey, John Simmons, Peter Ind, Carson Smith, Joe Mondragon, Herman Alpert, James Gannon, Arthur Watts (*b*); Gene Krupa (*d*); Tristan Fry (*perc*). 3/46–12/71.

If anyone ever doubted the comprehensiveness of Rich's career, they need only browse through this excellent three-CD compilation. The pianists alone make an impressive list. It starts with small-group sides from the late 1940s, with Parker, Young and others; moves through a number of Jazz At The Philharmonic sessions, which Rich was born to participate in; takes in a number of near-novelty dates, such as the drummer sitting in with Woody Herman's band and one of his drum battles with Gene Krupa; and concludes with a variety of big-band sessions, leading up to another guest appearance with a British orchestra dating from 1971. If the JATP and some other tracks highlight the full propensity of Rich's boorishness, many more display his concern for detail and need to make a band swing in order to create something useful. His steady impetus on a Lionel Hampton Quartet session from 1954, for instance, is beautifully controlled, as are three flag-waving numbers from a Hollywood club date of 1967, particularly the almost preternaturally crisp 'Big Swing Face'. All of this music is exceptionally vivid, even where the drummer is a disadavantage (as on the tracks with Parker) rather than an asset, and the remastering has been admirably done. Highly recommended.

***   **Time Being** RCA Bluebird ND 86459 CD/LP
Rich; Lin Bivano, Jeff Stout, Wayne Naus, John Deflon, Greg Hopkins (*t*); Bruce Paulson, Tony Dimaggio, Eric Culver, Alan Kaplan (*tb*); John Leys, Bill Reichenbach (*btb*); Brian Grivna, Jimmy Mosher, Pat LaBarbera, Don Englert, Joe Calo, Richard Centalonza (*reeds*); Bob Peterson, Bob Dogan, George McFetridge (*p*); David Spinozza, Walt Namuth (*g*); Paul Kondziela, Bob Daugherty, Joel Di Bartolo (*b*); Phil Kraus, Candido Camero (*perc*). 8/71–8/72.

Compiled from three RCA albums, *Time Being* catches Rich's 'comeback' band, originally formed in 1966, at its peak. Few bands of the period could match the collective clout which the leader forced out of his men – although this was a time when there were scarcely any big bands on tour in any case. There is one significant soloist aside from Rich, tenorist Pat Labarbera, who gets off a couple of leathery statements; but the point of the music is the sound of brass and reeds fusing in the glare of Rich's snare-to-tom fusillades and perpetually hissing cymbals. Monk's 'Straight No Chaser' is stripped of its mystery and the only genuinely inventive scores are Bill Holman's title-tune and John Labarbera's 'Best Coast', with an eccentric trombone outburst from Eric Culver; still, the whole thing never stops swinging. Four tracks were recorded live at the Ronnie Scott Club in London. The sound is a little bass-heavy and lacking in real focus.

**   **Ease On Down The Road** LRC CDC 8511 CD
         Rich; Greg Hopkins, Charlie Davis, John Hoffman, Larry Hall, Lloyd Michaels,
         Richard Hurwitz, Ross Konikoff, Danny Hayes, Charles Camilleri (*t*); Alan Kaplan,
         Keith O'Quinn, Barry Maur, Gerald Chamberlain (*tb*); Anthony Salvatori, John Leys
         (*btb*); Joe Romano, Bob Martin, Pat LaBarbera, Peter Yellin, Bill Blaut, Steve Marcus,
         Bob Mintzer, Bob Crea, Roger Rosenberg, John Laws (*reeds*); Buddy Budson, Gerg
         Kogan (*p*); Joe Beck, Wayne Wright, Cornell Dupree, Cliff Morris (*g*); Tony Levin,
         Ben Brown (*b*); Sam Woodyard, Ray Armando (*perc*). 10/73–6/74.

***   **Tuff Dude** LRC CDC 7972 CD
         Rich; Sonny Fortune (*ss, as*); Sal Nistico (*ts*); Kenny Barron, Mike Abene (*p*); Jack
         Wilkins (*g*); Anthony Jackson (*b*); Jimmy Maeulen (*perc*). 5/84.

Although the two main sessions on *Ease On Down The Road* were recorded less than a year apart, they feature two big bands with entirely different personnel from each other, aside from Rich – and he manages to make them sound virtually identical. Not bad, but only dedicated Rich admirers will warm to the session as a whole. Three choruses into 'Donna Lee', on *Tuff Dude*, Rich is already impatient with soloist Fortune and is driving himself into the spotlight. This set was recorded at the New York club, Buddy's Place, and is a rare example of latter-day Rich with a small group. Fortune and Nistico are two beefy soloists who know how to play to a hilt, and there are some wild solos from Wilkins too, as well as a suitably tough slow blues called '2nd Avenue Blue'. Respectable location recording and a little over an hour of music.

***   **Class Of '78** BBC Century CJCD 832 CD
         Rich; Chuck Schmidt, Dean Pratt, John Marshall, Danny Hayes (*t*); Matt Johnson,
         Dale Kirkland (*tb*); Edward Eby (*btb*); Chuck Wilson, Alan Gauvin, Steve Marcus,
         Gary Bribek, Greg Smith (*reeds*); Barry Keiner (*ky*); Tom Warrington (*b*). 10/77.

Worth having for the astonishing reading of Joe Zawinul's 'Birdland', which became a concert favourite in Rich's final years, this session – formerly made for a direct-to-disc operation – has a meagre playing-time of less than 30 minutes but blazes forth exactly as the leader would have wished. Steve Marcus is the principal soloist, although the leader's undiminished power remains the *raison d'être* of the music.

(*)   **Lionel Hampton Presents Buddy Rich Kingdom GATE 7011 CD
         Rich; Steve Marcus (*ss, ts*); Gary Pribek, Paul Moen (*ts*); Barry Kiener (*p*); Lionel
         Hampton (*vib*); Tom Warrington (*b*); Candido Camero (*perc*). 77.

An engaging reunion for Hampton and Rich, with Marcus and Pribek coming from Rich's big band and Moen arriving from Hamp's. Two Coltrane themes give the tenors a chance to smoke, and the vibes and rhythm section trade plenty of fours. Nothing surprising happens, but all concerned seemed to enjoy the date.

DANNIE RICHMOND (1935–88)

DRUMS

***   **Ode To Mingus** Soul Note SN 1005 LP
         Richmond; Bill Saxton (*ts*); Danny Mixon (*b*); Mike Rixon (*d*). 11/79.

***   **Plays Charles Mingus** Timeless SJP 148 LP
Richmond; Jack Walrath (*t*); Ricky Ford (*ts*); Bob Nellums (*p*); Cameron Brown (*b*). 8/80.

There probably wasn't a closer relationship in jazz than that between Charles Mingus and Dannie Richmond. Richmond's ability to anticipate Mingus's sudden shifts of tempo made them seem like two aspects of a single turbulent personality and, when Mingus died in 1979, it looked very much as though Richmond's legacy was merely to answer questions from journalists and to trim the flame.

Unfortunately, the only currently surviving Richmond albums tend to reinforce that view. It's usually forgotten that the drummer had a lively and productive career as an independent leader and co-leader. The fine 1980 *Dannie Richmond Quintet* [Gatemouth] is no longer available, and *Dionysius* [Red VPA 161 LP], a more stimulating performance by the *Plays Charles Mingus* quintet, has disappeared.

The two that survive are well worth having. Mingus's ghost actually hangs more heavily over the first, where *hommage* teeters in the direction of pastiche. 'Olduvai Gorge' is a nod in the direction of *Pithecanthropus Erectus* and sounds a little strained (certainly Saxton sounds strained); the best two tracks are 'Love Bird' and the too-brief 'Drum Some Some Drum'.

Plays is by no means a straightforward 'Greatest Hits'. 'Goodbye, Pork Pie Hat' was perhaps inevitable, but 'Wee' (which you can *almost* hear Mingus playing on recordings of the infamous Massey Hall concert) was an inspired choice, opening up the band for some genuinely inventive improvisation. The spirited Walrath doesn't combine particularly well with Ford's rather callow sound, but, much as Mingus might, Richmond makes a virtue of any shortcomings.

One rather sad irony attaches to both these records. Where Mingus (presumably it was Mingus) always ensured that his *doppelgänger*-drummer got a fair shake in the mix, Richmond sounds as if he's been lagged in asbestos on his own sessions. Why?

KIM RICHMOND
ALTO SAX

***   **Looking In Looking Out** Nine Winds NW 0125 LP
Richmond; Mike Fahn (*vtb*); John Gross (*ts, f*); Tad Weed, Wayne Peet (*p*); Ken Filiano (*b*); Billy Mintz (*d*).

Richmond has performed in many jazz and rock settings, and his debut as a leader reflects catholic and well-informed preferences. There are six good originals here, with flavoursome tone-colours and a harried rhythmic undertow that won't let the music settle into mere mainstream blowing. Try the clever use of valve-trombone against flute in 'Specifico Americano' or the straggling, vaguely inebriated treatment of 'Nardis'. Richmond takes some acerbic solos but is smart enough to give Fahn, Gross and Weed – all interesting soloists – the same measure of space. The leader's sleeve-note speaks of 'simultaneous improvisation' and, while this is of a comparatively ordered nature – at least compared with some of the other discs in the Nine Winds catalogue – it brings off a fine record.

MIKE RICHMOND (born 1948)
BASS

***   **On The Edge** Steeplechase SCS 1237 LP
Richmond; Larry Schneider (*ss, ts, f*); Adam Nussbaum (*d*). 88.

***(*)   **Dance For Andy** Steeplechase SCCD 31267 CD
Richmond; Larry Schneider (*ss, ts*); Jim McNeely (*p*); Keith Copeland (*d*). 89.

The title-track which opens *On The Edge* is a superb trio improvisation that has Schneider and Richmond almost locking horns before Nussbaum's resolving solo. The rest of the record doesn't quite match up, but the leader – whose wide experience with leaders such as DeJohnette, Getz and Silver has granted him a steadfast mainstream-modern reputation – pilots the trio with great enthusiasm. *Dance For Andy* is one of those rare CDs which sustain interest through a 70-minute-plus duration. Richmond's four originals are nothing special – aside, perhaps, from the witty, sanctified licks of 'Gospel' – but there is a serene trio reading of 'I

Remember Clifford', a fast and swingng 'You And The Night And The Music' and a reading of Jim Pepper's 'Witchi-Tai-To' which manages to supplant Jan Garbarek's glorious version in the memory. Schneider deploys his Brecker influence to gripping effect on both records.

KNUT RIISNAES (born 1945)
TENOR AND SOPRANO SAX

***   **Flukt** Odin LP05 LP
    Riisnaes; Dag Arnesen (*p*); Bjorn Kjellemyr (*b*); Jon Christensen (*d*). 5/82.

***(*)   **Confessin' The Blues** Gemini GMCD 63 CD
    Riisnaes; Red Holloway (*as, ts*); Kjell Ohman (*p, org*); Terje Venaas (*b*); Egil Johansen (*d*). 8/89.

Gifted with a huskily rich and weighty tone, Riisnaes is an Oslo-born jazzman who, like so many musicians from Northern Europe, deserves a far wider reputation than he has (his brother, Odd, is also a fine tenorman). *Flukt* won a Norwegian Grammy award and its carefully pointed dialogue between Riisnaes and the rhythm section is sustained through eight absorbing tracks. If anything, though, *Confessin' The Blues* is even better. The session was organized to document Red Holloway's visit to the Oslo Jazz Festival in 1989, and the sympathetic interplay between all five men belies the hasty circumstances of the occasion. While there are some straightforward blowing tracks, such as an ebullient 'Billie's Bounce', the highlight is probably the almost indecently languorous stroll through 'All Blues' at the beginning, which is paced out by both tenormen to sumptuous effect. If Holloway is the more perkily bluesy of the two saxophonists, Riisnaes emerges as at least his equal, taking a solo 'My Romance' which methodically opens out the melody to superb effect. The rhythm section, with Ohman playing mostly organ, is absolutely on top of things, and the digital sound is excellent.

LEE RITENOUR (born 1952)
GUITAR

*(*)   **Rio** GRP GRD 9524 CD
    Ritenour; Jerry Hey, Gary Grant (*t*); Larry Williams (*ts*); Dave Grusin (*ky*); Jeff Miranov (*g*); Marcus Miller (*b*); Buddy Williams (*d*). 10/79.

*(*)   **On The Line** GRP GRD-9525 CD
    Ritenour; Ernie Watts (*as*); Dave Grusin, Don Grusin (*ky*); Anthony Jackson (*b*); Harvey Mason (*d*). 3/83.

*   **Harlequin** GRP GRD-9255 CD
    Ritenour; Dave Grusin (*ky*); Jimmy Johnson (*b*); Carlos Vega (*d*); Paulinho Da Costa (*perc*). 11/84.

*   **Earth Run** GRP GRD-9538 CD
    Ritenour; Greg Mathieson (*ky*); Carlos Vega (*d*); Paulinho Da Costa (*perc*). 4/86.

*   **Portrait** GRP GRD-9553 CD
    Ritenour; Jerry Hey (*t*); Larry Williams (*ts, ky*); Barnaby Finch (*ky*); Djavan (*g, v*); Tim Landers (*b*); Vinnie Colaiuta (*d*); Paulinho Da Costa (*perc*). 1/87.

*   **Festival** GRP GRD-9570 CD
    Ritenour; Dave Grusin (*ky*); Joao Bosco (*g, v*); Anthony Jackson (*b*); Omar Hakim (*d*); Paulinho Da Costa (*perc*); Gracinha Leporace (*v*). 5/88.

*   **Color Rit** GRP GRD-9594 CD
    Ritenour; Larry Williams, Dave Witham (*ky*); Jimmy Johnson (*b*); Carlos Vega (*d*); Paulinho Da Costa (*perc*); Phil Perry (*v*). 3/89.

*(*)   **Stolen Moments** GRP GRD-9615 CD
    Ritenour; Ernie Watts (*ts*); Alan Broadbent (*p*); Mitch Holder (*g*); John Patitucci (*b*); Harvey Mason (*d*). 12/89.

**   **Collection** GRP GRD-9645 CD
        Personnel as on above eight records. 79–89.

For all his technical acumen, Ritenour is a disappointingly unstimulating player. Not for nothing was he nicknamed 'Captain Fingers'. His GRP albums, in glistening digital sound, include any number of fast, spankingly clean and accurate solos, but Ritenour's own reluctance to categorize himself with a jazz clientele is borne out by the excessive number of rock licks and fretboard exercises which go to make up most of his improvisations. There is very little to differentiate the first seven records listed above: busy but not unruly rhythm sections predominate in the music, which Ritenour decorates with tireless proficiency.

On the face of it, *Stolen Moments* is a little more interesting, with Ritenour for once playing a Montgomery-styled electric set against an all-acoustic band, but it seems like a successful man's indulgence rather than a meaningful musical decision. The *Collection* set, compiled from all eight of the previous studio albums, should satisfy the curious.

SAM RIVERS (born 1930)
TENOR SAXOPHONE, SOPRANO SAXOPHONE, FLUTE, PIANO, VOCALS

***(*)   **Waves** Tomato 2696492 CD
        Rivers; Joe Daley (*tba, bar hn*); Dave Holland (*b, clo*); Thurman Barker (*d, perc*).
        8/78.

***   **Jazzbuhne Berlin '82** Repertoire REPCD 4910 CC CD
        Rivers; Oliver Beener, Jack Walrath (*t*); Robin Eubanks, Dick Griffin, Douglas
        Purviance (*tb*); Vincent Chancey (*frhn*); Patience Higgins (*f, bs*); Anthony Cox (*b*);
        Eli Fountain (*d*). 6/82.

***(*)   **Colors** Black Saint BSR 0064 CD
        Rivers; Marvin Blackman (*f, ts, ss*); Talib Kibwe (*f, cl, ss, ts*); Chris Roberts (*f, ss*);
        Steve Coleman (*f, as*); Bobby Watson (*f, as*); Nat Dixon (*f, cl, ts*); Bill Cody (*ob, ts*);
        Eddie Alex (*picc, ts*); Jimmy Cozier, Patience Higgins (*f, bs*). 9/82.

***   **Lazuli** Timeless CD SJP 291 CD
        Rivers; Darryll Thompson (*g*); Real Wesley Grant (*b*); Steve McCraven (*d*). 10/89.

Rivers's significance to Black American music is scarcely reflected by his current catalogue; two important Blue Notes – *Fuchsia Swing Song* [BNJ 71044 LP] and *Dimensions And Extensions* [BST 84261 CD/LP] – and an excellent ECM – *Contrasts* [1162 LP] – are currently out of print. Though none matches these three, what is left is of consistently challenging quality. Rivers's association with Dave Holland, as on the bassist's marvellous *Conference Of The Birds* (ECM 1027 CD/LP) and the item below, helped foster his growing interest in piano playing and afforded him the kind of regular and sensitive partnership he had lacked since the end of the 1960s.

Waves is a fine and highly intelligent album. Holland and Barker combine as productively as they do on *Contrasts*, backing the leader with a rich, harmonic tissue rather than keeping time. As he shows on all these albums except the more conventionally structured *Lazuli*, Rivers pays little attention to a fixed rhythmic pattern, preferring to build his Coltrane-influenced lines in a kind of gravity-defying isolation that, spider-like, seems to bridge space with a web of ideas that reveals its structure only at the final juncture.

The excellent rhythmless Winds of Manhattan project, *Colors*, with its flute-dominated orchestra, takes this technique beyond small-group confines and on to a much larger scale. It's broadly successful but slightly dry, a flaw also of the East Berlin Rivbea Orchestra set on Repertoire, which never catches fire.

Until Rivers's classic sets are reissued on well-balanced CD, he is likely to remain an unworthily marginalized figure on the current scene, universally admired by players and by his students, but increasingly unknown to younger fans.

***(*)   **Dave Holland / Sam Rivers** Improvising Artists Inc 123843 CD
        Rivers (*ts, ss*); Dave Holland (*b*). 2/76.

Awarded to Rivers purely on grounds of seniority (and because he takes the composition credits), this is a finely balanced duo performance which reunites the more interesting axis of Holland's *Conference Of The Birds* quartet. Composition students are always warned to be wary of verse-settings which will tempt them into predictable descending scales on words like 'Waterfall'. Rivers and Holland tackle the idea – following up with 'Cascade', the only other track – with no obvious desire to create a literal tone-poem. The music is too sharply focused to be impressionistic, and the broader intervals of the first piece, on which Rivers plays soprano, are deployed in a manner which is both highly abstract and movingly lyrical, a characteristic of Holland's work. The tenor lines on 'Casacade' become muddied when Holland is working in a parallel register, and it's unfortunate that the most interesting parts of the longer track come when the two players separate, either working solo or with minimal accompaniment. A pity, too, that Holland doesn't use his cello on the session. Paul Bley's production is predictably intimate. An intriguing album, strongly recommended for anyone who found the ECM quartet compelling.

RMS
GROUP

*(*)   **Centennial Park** MMC CDP 7900102 CD
Henry Lowther (*flhn*); Derek Watkins (*flhn*); Malcolm Griffiths (*tb*); Ronnie Asprey (*as, ss, af*); Ray Russell (*g, g syn*); Mo Foster (*b, syn*); Simon Phillips (*d*); Peter Van Hooke (*perc*); Kim Goody (*v*).

Dismal fusion from a battery of good British players who sound good individually (Lowther and Griffiths especially) but obstinately refuse to add up to anything more than the sum of their parts. Probably not worth worrying about.

MAX ROACH (born 1924)
DRUMS, PERCUSSION

***   **Max Roach** Original Jazz Classics OJC 202 CD/LP
Roach; Idries Sulieman (*t*); Leon Comegys (*tb*); Gigi Gryce (*as*); Hank Mobley (*ts*); Walter Davis Jr (*p*); Frank Skeete (*b*). 4 & 10/53.

****   **In Concert** Vogue 655602 CD
Roach; Clifford Brown (*t*); Harold Land, Teddy Edwards (*ts*); Richie Powell, Carl Perkins (*p*); George Morrow, George Bledsoe (*b*). 4 & 8/54.

****   **Daahoud** Original Master Recordings MFCD 826 CD
As above, except omit Edwards, Perkins, Bledsoe. 6 & 8/54.

A great educator and activist as well as a consummate musician, Roach was the most complete of the bebop drummers. Stylistically, he stands mid-way between swing drummers like Dave Tough, Jo Jones, Gene Krupa and Big Sid Catlett and the avant-garde of the 1960s. His most immediate influence was the transitional Kenny Clarke, whose ideas he developed and carried forward. He was Charlie Parker's best drummer, bar none, and Sonny Rollins owes more to Roach than to any other player. In the 1970s, he became a tutelary genius of the new wave, almost reversing one-time collaborator Cecil Taylor's definition of the piano as 88 tuned drums.

Roach frequently made the drum kit (and he has tended to play a relatively conventional set-up) sound as tuneful and harmonically rich as a keyboard instrument. His on-and off-beat alternations and dense contrapuntal narratives have taken him close to his own ambition to transmit Bach's achievement in jazz terms. Some of Roach's most interesting solo performances have to be dug out of samplers; there are characteristic solo drum 'Conversations' on the intriguing and valuable *Autobiography In Jazz* (OJC 115 LP), on *At Last!* (OJC 480 CD/LP) and on *The Big Beat* (Milestone M 47016 CD/2LP). Most drum samplers of any pretension have something by him.

Roach began leading bands 40 years ago. The early sessions, like those on *Max Roach*, convey much promise but little real sense of the grandeurs to follow. The 1953 dates are unpretentious and bop-dominated, but with flashes of originality and the beginnings of Roach's characteristic emphasis on darkling themes and timbral density from the horns. In later years, rather than view a band as immutable, he liked to break it up into smaller units; there's some evidence of that happening here (though the rider 'collective personnel' doesn't indicate anything other than that six of the tracks were for quartet – Mobley and rhythm only – and without the brass and second saxophone that made 'Sfax' and 'Orientation' so vibrant).

Roach's career as leader really took flight only when he formed a tragically short-lived quintet with trumpeter Clifford Brown. While the other personnel changed, Brown and Roach established a rapport only briefly matched by that with the fated Booker Little, a few years later. Roach missed the road accident which killed Brown and Richie Powell, but his career faltered and nearly succumbed; listening to these concert recordings from 1954, when the band was only just coming together and two years before the accident, it's tempting to suggest that never again would Roach forge such a promising partnership. The music crackles through a dodgy recording (*In Concert* is also reviewed in the section on Clifford Brown.)

Brown's trumpet on 'Tenderly' is state of the art. Full and brassy, with a controlled but generous vibrato, it works the theme imaginatively, concentrating on the melody rather than more abstract 'changes'. Guesting, Teddy Edwards is almost as good as Land (they don't appear together) and Carl Perkins's unmistakably tinkling piano is a provocative foil for the drummer's own cymbal figures, in some ways more stimulating than Powell's orthodox bop. Marvellous. ('Jordu', 'Tenderly' and 'Clifford's Axe' – actually 'The Man I Love' – can also be found on a useful CD compilation of Brown material under his own and Gigi Gryce's leadership, entitled *Blue and Brown*, Jazz Society 670505.)

Brown's inventiveness – and his sometimes overlooked ability as a composer – is in further evidence on the marvellous Original Master dust-down. Valuable alternative takes of 'I Get A Kick Out Of You' and 'JoySpring' offer insights into Roach's endlessly adaptable and inspirational play. Brown's 'Daahoud' is marvellous, as are the standards, 'I Don't Stand A Ghost Of A Chance With You' and an unusually accented 'These Foolish Things'. All of this material is included on the essential ten-CD *Brownie* (Emarcy 838 306–16), and is reviewed in the section on Clifford Brown.

**** Deeds Not Words Original Jazz Classics OJC 304 CD/LP
Roach; Booker Little (*t*); Ray Draper (*tba*); George Coleman (*ts*); Art Davis (*b*). 9/58.

It's tempting to draw a moral from the title of this superb album and simply say: go out and buy it. Coleman was by far the most bruising of Roach's tenor players, but he was harmonically exacting in a way that Hank Mobley was not, and the drummer didn't find a saxophonist with the same balance of sheer power and finesse till the advent of Odean Pope in the late 1970s. Set against Draper's chesty valvings and Davis's accurate bass, drummer and young trumpeter weave intricate lines that were among the most ambitious in contemporary 'hard bop'. Whatever that unsatisfactory label really serves, this is it.

**(*) The Hardbop Academy Affinity AFF 773 CD
Roach; Kenny Dorham (*t*); Hank Mobley (*ts*); Ramsey Lewis (*p*); George Morrow (*b*). 58.

Marketed, with reasonable justification, as a taste of the two pre-eminent bop drummers at the height of their respective powers. Art Blakey's share of the album is probably of marginally superior quality to Roach's. This wasn't his best band, though Dorham and Mobley are both in excellent form, and Ramsey Lewis presents a fair simulacrum of the late Richie Powell. Neither for the beginner (who'll be misled) nor for the completist (who'd expect a more detailed documentation), but respectable value for money.

***(*) Max Roach And Friends: Volume 1 Jazz View 018 CD
Roach; Clifford Jordan (*ts*); Coleridge Perkinson (*p*); Eddie Khan (*b*). 60.

Above-average offering from the limited-edition Italian label. The long opening 'Night Mountain' is constructed over Roach's distinctive cymbal-ism and all four players take effective solos (Perkinson and Khan magically emerge from a fuzzy background to do so) with Jordan scoring alpha minus for his and the pianist getting extra credit for sounding more like Sonny Clark than the unrepeatable Powell, whose disciples were ubiquitous in 1960. Roach's own contribution, anchored by occasional pedal notes from bass and piano is typically tuneful. Also included are Roach's 'Ceciliana', with Khan bowing sonorously under Perkinson's formal, hymnic intro, and good versions of 'Jordu' and 'Sophisticated Lady' and a Kenny Clarke composition, 'Mop Mop'. Jazz View have a second volume projected and a collaboration with

Tommy and Stanley Turrentine. Roach will also feature in a trio set with Sonny Clark and George Duvivier.

*** **Drum Conversation** Enja 4074 LP
Roach; Tommy Turrentine (*t*); Julian Priester (*tb*); Stanley Turrentine (*ts*); Bobby Boswell (*b*). 60.

(*) **European Tour LRC CDC 7683 CD
As above.

Unfortunately not available on CD, *Drum Conversation* is a tough, rousing performance and, incidentally, the closest Roach was to come to the roistering sound of the Jazz Messengers, led by his poll rival and stylistic opposite number, Art Blakey. So tuneful is Roach's playing that the characteristic absence of piano isn't noticed. The Turrentine brothers were regulars in the drummer's 1959–60 band and are in excellent shape here, fulfilling Roach's preference for unfussy, even reticent instrumentalists. The sound-quality isn't absolutely reliable, and some of Roach's crucial cymbal lines sound distorted, but the music is of a high standard and the album worth collecting.

European Tour is shared between Roach's band and the Thelonious Monk Quintet, recorded some years earlier. Most of the virtues of *Drum Conversation* are in place and there's no material overlap with the Enja, but the CD format presents no conspicuous advantage. Collectors will want to have it, though.

**** **We Insist!: Freedom Now Suite** Candid CS 9002 CD/LP
Roach; Booker Little (*t*); Julian Priester (*tb*); Walter Benton, Coleman Hawkins (*ts*); James Schenck (*b*); Ray Mantilla, Olatunji, Thomas Du Vall (*perc*); Abbey Lincoln (*v*). 8 & 9/60.

***(*) **Speak, Brother, Speak** Original Jazz Classics OJC 646 CD/LP/MC
Roach; Clifford Jordan (*ts*); Mal Waldron (*p*); Eddie Khan (*b*). 62.

Another extensive improvisatory composition with Roach in spectacular form. Some slight misgivings about Mal Waldron's rather nay-saying and reticent approach, though rhythmically it fits the drummer's conception suprisingly well. The sound is better than on the original Fantasy album.

***(*) **Live In Europe – Freedom Now Suite** Magnetic MRCD 110 CD
Roach; Clifford Jordan (*ts*); Coleridge Perkinson (*p*); Eddie Khan (*b*); Abbey Lincoln (*v*). 1/64.

Overtaken by the furies of the Black Power movement (and the associated New Thing in jazz), *We Insist!* has a slightly corny feel today which utterly belies its significance as an American cultural document. The album made a major composer of Roach (though one mustn't forget the lyrical contributions of Oscar Brown Jr), and it transformed the drummer's then wife, Abbey Lincoln, from a night-club 'shan-tooze' of limited credibility into one of the most convincing vehicles of Black American experience since Billie Holiday.

The opening 'Driva' Man' is wry and almost sarcastic, enunciated over Roach's work-rhythms and Coleman Hawkins's blearily proud solo. It's followed by 'Freedom Day' which, with 'All Africa', was to be part of a large choral work targeted on the centenary of the Emancipation Proclamation. 'Freedom Day' follows Roach's typically swinging address, but is distinguished by a Booker Little solo of bursting, youthful emotion, and a contribution from the little-regarded Walter Benton that matches Hawkins' for sheer simplicity of diction.

The central 'Triptych' – originally conceived as a dance piece – is a duo for Roach and Lincoln. 'Prayer', 'Protest' and 'Peace' was not a trajectory acceptable to later militants, but there is more than enough power in Lincoln's inchoate roars of rage in the central part, and more than enough ambiguity in the ensuing 'Peace', to allay fears that her or Roach's politics were blandly liberal. The closing 'Tears For Johannesburg' has more classic Little, and also good things from Priester and Benton. It follows 'All Africa', which begins in a vein remarkably close to Billie Holiday, briefly degenerates into a litany of tribal names and slogans, but hinges on a 'middle passage' of drum music embodying the three main Black drum traditions of the West: African, Afro-Cuban and Afro-American. Its influence on subsequent jazz percussion is incalculable, and it remains listenable even across three decades of outwardly far more radical experimentation.

The *Freedom Now Suite* is one of the classic modern albums; its slightly dated feel (there are moments when it sounds closer in spirit to the Harlem Renaissance than to the era of Sharpeville and Watts) is no more than incidental. It's a little more critical on Magnetic's valuable live documentation. The less resistant European air gives the music a slightly triumphal blandness that it wouldn't have had in, say, San Antonio or even Chicago. Roach's allusive approach on the studio version, drawing in references to everything from Civil War marches to voodoo, is much more conservatively 'jazz'-centred in the live version. No disgrace in the fact that the concert band is less impressive. It lacks the vital bite of brass and is further normalized by a piano; Jordan sounds well settled in but lacks Hawkins's casual gravitas or Benton's sublime naïvety. Lincoln isn't in the best of voice, either, and the sound-mix doesn't flatter anybody. Even so, this is a worthwhile acquisition (there is one extra track, 'Who Will Buy?') that both confirms the importance and underlines the venial flaws of the original.

***(*) **Drums Unlimited** Atlantic AMCY 1043 CD
Roach (*d* solo) and with Freddie Hubbard (*t*); Roland Alexander (*ss*); James Spaulding (*as*); Ronnie Mathews (*p*); Jymie Merritt (*b*). 10/65, 4/66.

Three mildly disappointing group tracks (though 'St Louis Blues' with Hubbard and the two saxophones is excellent) are more than made up for by Roach's three solo features. The title-track is a meticulously structured and executed essay in rhythmic polyvalence that puts Sunny Murray's and Andrew Cyrille's more ambitious works in context; the second is an exploration of Roach's characteristic waltz-time figurings; the last a heart-felt tribute to Big Sid Catlett.

Roach's Catlett-like reflexes and responses are evidenced on countless recordings. On 'In The Red' here, he uses his own composition as the basis for a remarkably free but beautifully cadenced embellishment of the slow central theme. The band don't seem to be up to the task, though Hubbard – familiar with an autonomous rhythm section from work with Eric Dolphy and others – sounds assured. Marvellous – and particularly good on CD, which recovers some of Roach's more fugitive effects.

**** **Birth And Rebirth** Black Saint BSR 0024 CD
Roach; Anthony Braxton (*as, ss, sno, f, cl, cbcl*). 9/78.

*** **One In Two – Two In One** hat Art 6030 CD
As above. 8/79.

In their anxiety, critics couldn't decide who was climbing into who's pigeon-hole on these. Did *Birth And Rebirth* illustrate '*avant-gardist*' Braxton's accommodation to the mainstream, or did it prove what a radical old Roach actually was? The answer, of course, made nonsense of the question. Few supposed radicals have been so firmly rooted 'in the tradition' than the instrumentalist Braxton, and few hard-boppers have been so cerebrally adventurous as the veteran drummer.

Together, they made music of a very high and challenging order, comparable to Roach's historic duos with Cecil Taylor at Columbia University in 1979 (Soul Note SN 1100 2LP). Braxton's references to bop have tended to be both respectful and subversive; with Roach, he pushes their harmonic ambiguity to the limits, constantly 'breaking down' into dissonances that are as sharply percussive in attack as Roach's melorhythms are legato-smooth.

The later album gives off a far greater impression of contrivance than the inspired spontaneity the two players achieve on the Black Saint. A suite of four notionally connected arguments, used as the basis for extended improvisation, the prevailing tone is argumentative and divisive rather than the unity-in-diversity suggested by the title. Braxton's wider range of instruments – he adds flute, his least successful horn, and the still unassimilated contrabass clarinet – helps out in places, but only cosmetically. It was a great idea, but it didn't last.

*** **Pictures In A Frame** Soul Note SN 1003 CD
Roach; Cecil Bridgewater (*t, flhn*); Odean Pope (*ts, f, ob*); Calvin Hill (*b*). 1 & 9/79.

*** **In The Light** Soul Note SN 1053 CD
As above. 7/82.

But for the bassist, this is Roach's 1980s working band just before the point when the drummer began to turn slightly away from his own compositional output and towards a re-engagement with jazz history. The writing is strong, if a little sombre, and the drums are 'featured' even when someone else is purportedly soloing. Pope's doubling on oboe and flute varies the textures. Good-quality performances all around, but with an underlying sense of change in the air; much of the music is for fractions of the basic band, and not always simply duets with the leader. The next decade found Roach facing in a quite different direction, and anyone who caught up with him only in the 1980s may find this a useful benchmark.

In The Light already sounds more stripped-down and less tentative. Pope concentrates on tenor, Bridgewater clarifies his lines, and the fulcrum of the session is a pair of Monk readings – 'Ruby, My Dear' and 'Straight, No Chaser' – with Roach repositioning the rhythmic commas like the master he is. 'Good Bait' is worth comparing with the even more laid-back version on *Jazzbuhne Berlin '84*, below.

(*)   **Collage** Soul Note SN 1059 LP
Roach; Kenyatte Abdur-Rahman (*xyl, cabasa, perc*); Eddie Allen (*woodblocks, perc, cym*); Roy Brooks (*steel d, slapstick, musical saw, perc*); Joe Chambers (*xyl, mar, vib, b mar*); Eli Fountain (*cowbell, xyl, crotales, orchestral bells*); Fred King (*tym, concert bells, vib*); Ray Mantilla (*bells, chimes, perc*); Warren Smith (*b mar, perc*); Freddie Waits (*concert tom-toms, gongs, bass d, shaker*). 10/84.

Credited to the percussion collective M'Boom, which Roach formed in the 1970s, this is a slightly chaotic and rackety affair, more interesting episodically than in its entirety. Roach plays a relatively limited, honoured-patron's role, playing bass and snare drums and marimba, and the music lacks his sterling discipline and formal control.

***   **Live At Vielharmonie Munich** Soul Note SN 1073 CD/LP
Roach; Cecil Bridgewater (*t, flhn*); Dwayne Armstrong (*ts*); Phil Bower (*b*); string quartet. 11/83.

***(*)   **Easy Winners** Soul Note SN 1109 CD/LP
Roach; Cecil Bridgewater (*t, flhn*); Odean Pope (*ts*); Tyrone Brown (*b*); Ray Mantilla (*perc*); string quartet. 1/85.

Two of several experiments in 'doubling' the basic jazz quartet with strings. Typical of much of his 1980s work, the 1983 German concert is a retrospective homage to two of the drummer's most stimulating artistic partnerships. 'Booker Little' recalls the brilliant young trumpeter who died in 1961 after recording several classic sides with Roach; 'Bird Says' is an altogether more complex and angular work, exploring the Parker legacy.

The sound isn't always absolutely up to scratch, and there are problems in the balance of the strings. Armstrong has a rather wearying tone, and Bower's electric bass sits rather awkwardly in front of the 'acoustic' fiddles, robbing them of some of their punch; why not an upright bass? or none at all, leaving the lower-register figures to the cello and to Roach's right foot? Intriguing, and as challenging as ever, but by no means a great record.

The drummer's daughter, Maxine Roach, a talented violist, plays with the Uptown String Quartet on *Easy Winners*. The album contains a further snippet of Roach's memorialization of Booker Little and a further, tougher reading of 'Bird Says'. The reappearance of percussionist Mantilla (who'd appeared on *We Insist*) for the latter adds nothing of any great substance, but the sound is better, the string players have considerably more rosin on their bows and grease in their elbows, and the album as a whole is to be preferred to the earlier one, which sounds almost academic in comparison.

***   **Scott Free** Soul Note SN 1103 CD/LP
Roach; Cecil Bridgewater (*t, flhn*); Odean Pope (*ts*); Tyrone Brown (*b*). 5/84.

***(*)   **Jazzbuhne Berlin '84** Repertoire RR 4902 CC CD
As above. 6/84.

The Soul Note is a hefty two-part suite dedicated to the brilliant young bassist, Scott La Faro, who died in a motor accident in 1961, within four months of Booker Little (see above). Roach's ability to sustain interest over the length of the piece is traceable not just to the seamless cymbal-beat which gave the classic bebop sessions their fantastic excitement but also to a mathematically complex interference with common time. Roach's variations on a basic 4/4 metre give the characteristically sombre themes a vividness and motion they might otherwise lack. This is the same band as featured on *Easy Winners*, but they sound more clean-lined without the strings; as before, the band breaks down into challenging duos. As a unit they work

917

within more basic codes, but Bridgewater and Pope have good contrapuntal instincts and play with considerable dash and eloquence (the former with more than a whiff of Roach's beloved Clifford Brown, whose death left the biggest hole in his artistic life). Not a classic, but further evidence of Roach's extraordinary inventiveness.

The East Berlin set is an unashamed crowd-pleaser with only two originals out of eight long tracks. 'Six Bits' is over-long and the two final cuts brief enough to suggest perfunctory pre-curfew encores, but the meat of the set – 'Good Bait', 'I Remember Clifford' (played, unaccompanied, by Pope), 'Jordu', 'Giant Steps' (which features a superbly judged drum solo) and 'Perdido' – affords a valuable glimpse of Roach's approach to a standards repertoire. On the opening Dameron composition Brown turns in a solo of a quality that suggests there's a lot more to him than was previously obvious.

The generally well-recorded Repertoire series, of which this is the second, is an eclectic sample of concerts promoted by GDR Radio (others included are Betty Carter, Barbara Dennerlein, Yosuke Yamashita, Ornette Coleman, and Egberto Gismonti and Nana Vasconcelos). The East Berlin crowd either don't know the tunes or are too polite to clap them in; they applaud each performance to the echo, though.

***(*) **Survivors** Soul Note SN 1093 CD/LP
Roach; string quartet. 10/84.

A further extension of the strings experiment, this dispenses with the conventional jazz group altogether and launches into the kind of territory the Kronos Quartet were claiming as their sole preserve only a couple of years later. 'The Drum Also Waltzes' reappears from way back when, but the best of the material is the vibrant 'Billy The Kid' and the African-influenced 'Smoke That Thunders'.

Roach alternates dotted rhythms and more conventional string sweeps to build up music of remarkable depth and texture. The effect may still be a little academic for some but, even aimed at the head rather than the gut or feet, it's unquestionably exciting.

**** **To The Max!** Enja 7021 22 2CD
Roach; Cecil Bridgewater (*t*); Odean Pope (*ts*); George Cables, Tyrone Brown (*b*); Uptown String Quartet: Diane Monroe, Lesa Terry (*vn*); Maxine Roach (*vla*); Eileen Folson (*clo*); M'Boom: Roy Brooks, Joe Chambers, Omar Clay, Eli Fountain, Fred King, Ray Mantilla, Francisco Mora, Warren Smith (*perc*); The John Motley Singers: Priscilla Baskerville, Florence Jackson, Karen Jackson, Lucille J. Jacobsen, Sarah Ann Rodgers, Robbin L. Balfour, Brenda Lee Taub, Christopher Pickens, Abraham Shelton, Thomas Young, Games Gainer, Greg Jones, T. Ray Lawrence, John Motley, Ronnel Bey (*v*). 11/90, 4 & 6/91.

A massive celebration of Roach's recent career. Disc 1 is dominated by the three-part 'Ghost Dance', scored for orchestra and chorus, with an extraordinary central section by M'Boom, and recommendable to anyone who found Philip Glass's Amerindian-inspired *Koyaanisqatsi* excessively bland and pretentious. The piece has an almost formal elegance, but it is still deeply rooted in the blues and the closing section, marked by a speaker-threatening recording of an atomic blast, balances choral passages and steamingly intense passages from both Pope and Cables.

The very beautiful 'A Quiet Place' (played by M'Boom) almost comes in too quickly. Characterized by soft chimes and a swaying marimba pulse, it conjures up images of a drowned church, its bells pealing in the tides and currents. 'The Profit' is the first of four quartet tracks. Roach's jazz drumming is as inventive and propulsive as ever, pushing along Bridgewater's Clifford Brown-derived solo. The later 'Tricotism' is an Oscar Pettiford tune and appropriately a feature for Tyrone Brown, who continues to grow in stature. 'Tears' is an instrumental version of an Abbey Lincoln performance from *Freedom Now Suite*, while the long 'A Little Booker' brings on Maxine Roach and the Uptown strings for a superb double quartet.

Roach takes two solo slots, 'Self Portrait' and 'Drums Unlimited'. The latter was first recorded in 1966 and is every bit as fresh. Roach's technique has remained pristine, and even these live recordings reflect more of its subtlety than the badly miked studio originals.

For anyone who hasn't yet approached Roach's solo and leader work, this is an essential purchase, full of extraordinary riches.

HANK ROBERTS
CELLO, FIDDLE, I2-STRING GUITAR, VOICE

*** **Black Pastels** JMT 834417 CD/LP
Roberts; Ray Anderson, Robin Eubanks (*tb*); Dave Taylor (*btb*); Tim Berne (*as*); Bill
Frisell (*g, bjo*); Mark Dresser (*b*); Joey Baron (*d, perc*). 11 & 12/87.

** **Birds Of Pray** JMT 834437 CD/LP/MC
Roberts; Mark Lampariello (*g, v*); Jerome Harris (*b, v*); Vinnie Johnson (*d, v*); D. K.
Dyson (*v*). 1 & 2/90.

Though somewhat removed from the scratch-and-scrabble of more *avant* improvising cellists,
Roberts has a style that identifiably owes something to post-Hendrix guitarists like Bill Frisell
(with whom he played on *Lookout for Hope* (ECM 1350 CD/LP) and who returns the
compliment on the excellent *Black Pastels*) and several generations of play-or-die country and
bluegrass fiddlers. As middle man on the Arcado totem pole, he gave the music much of its
harmonic oomph, and that's evident too on the albums as leader.

Black Pastels treads the same splintery boards as Frisell's cracked C&W, but the brasses give
the music an almost medieval darkness that is quite unsettling. 'Granpappy's Barn Dance
Death Dance' and 'Scarecrow Shakedown' are both superb, while 'Lucky's Lament' (which
may contain a reference to Coltrane's folksy 'Lonnie's Lament') draws an emotional resonance
from the one-track-only addition of Arcado bass-man Dresser.

Birds of Pray is inferior in almost every conceivable direction; a disappointing and slightly
over-anxious follow-up that never takes flight.

MARCUS ROBERTS
PIANO

(*) **The Truth Is Spoken Here Novus 3051 CD/LP/MC
Roberts; Wynton Marsalis (*t*); Charlie Rouse, Todd Williams (*ts*); Reginald Veal (*b*);
Elvin Jones (*d*). 7/88.

*** **Deep In The Shed** Novus PD 83078 CD/LP/MC
Roberts; E. Dankworth, Scotty Barnhard (*t*); Wycliffe Gordon (*tb*); Wessel Anderson
(*as*); Todd Williams, Herb Harris (*ts*); Reginald Veal, Chris Thomas (*b*); Herlin Riley,
Maurice Carnes (*d*). 8–12/89.

Despite an almost obsessive sobriety and respectfulness to his own idea of 'the tradition',
Roberts's records are impressive statements. As a composer he packs the themes with technical
detail which his different groups negotiate without hesitation, and his own playing is marked by
a pensive assurance. He has listened to and learned from Monk, Ellington and many others. But
one can't help longing for a more direct melody or a less weighty construction even as the music
makes its absorbing points. Marsalis, who was Roberts's boss in the four years leading up to the
1988 album, plays imperiously (it's rumoured that he may also be the mysterious 'E.
Dankworth') and the solos by Rouse are a moving farewell to a musician who died not long
after the record was made. *Deep In The Shed* investigates blues tonality with five-, six-
and seven-strong groups, and its masterclass air is more frequently undercut by smart use of
ensemble colour than was the debut. But the music will either captivate or induce boredom,
depending on one's taste.

(*) **Alone With Three Giants Novus PD 83109 CD/LP/MC
Roberts (*p* solo). 6–9/90.

** **Prayer For Peace** Novus PD CD/LP/MC
Roberts (*p* solo).

Alone With Three Giants is an audacious recital, uniting six tunes each by Monk and Ellington
and three by Jelly Roll Morton. Roberts is good with Monk, his primary influence, and his
Ellington choices are interesting: 'Shout 'Em Aunt Tillie' and 'Black And Tan Fantasy' aren't
in anybody else's solo piano repertoire. But he seems less sure with Morton: 'The Crave'
entirely misses the loose-limbed courtliness of the composer's own. Engaging, but a certain
didacticism hovers over it. The Christmas collection, *Prayer For Peace*, is as well done as any

such records, but Roberts isn't exactly a great humorist, and we prefer Ramsey Lewis's 'Rudolph The Red Nosed Reindeer' to the one here.

HERB ROBERTSON
TRUMPET, POCKET TRUMPET, CORNET, FLUGELHORN, OTHER INSTRUMENTS

(*)   **Transparency JMT 834402 LP
Robertson; Tim Berne (*as*); Bill Frisell (*g*); Lindsay Horner (*b*); Joey Baron (*d*). 4/85.

***(*)   **The Little Trumpet** JMT 834407 LP
Robertson; Robin Eubanks (*tb*); Bob Stewart (*tba*); Tim Berne (*as*); Bill Frisell (*g*); Warren Smith (*vib, mar*); Anthony Cox (*b*); Reggie Nicholson (*d*). 7/86.

***   **X-cerpts: Live At Willisau** JMT 834413 CD/LP
Robertson; Tim Berne (*as*); Gust William Tsilis (*vib*); Lindsay Horner (*b*); Joey Baron (*d*). 1/87.

***(*)   **Shades Of Bud Powell** JMT 834420 CD/LP
Robertson; Brian Lynch (*t*); Robin Eubanks (*tb*); Vincent Chancey (*frhn*); Bob Stewart (*tba*); Joey Baron (*d, perc*). 1 & 2/88.

Herb Robertson doesn't play a single solo on Tim Berne's *The Ancestors* (Soul Note 121 061 CD/LP/MC), but he stamps his personality all over the music, shadowing the saxophonist in much the same way that Don Cherry became part of Ornette Coleman's own voice on the great early Atlantics. It's indicative of Robertson's individuality that he has managed to take 'the little trumpet' in a direction that very seldom invites meaningful comparison with Cherry's. Like many – perhaps the majority of – younger players, his most obvious stylistic influence is Miles Davis, an emotional, slightly pinched tone and a preference for across-the-beat phrasing.

The Miles influence is most obvious on *Transparency* and the live album, but it surfaces elsewhere as well. These are the least ambitious of Robertson's records and are, in many respects, indistinguishable from a whole rack of Young Turk recordings by Berne and his cohorts. Far more interesting musically are the *Little Trumpet* suite, which draws on Monk and Miles references, and the inventive brass ensembles of *Shades Of Bud Powell*, which directs 'Un Poco Loco' and 'Glass Enclosure' in unexpected and throughly stimulating directions.

Robertson's role on *The Ancestors* is almost prototypical, for he isn't the most stimulating soloist. The interest in his work lies in his manipulation of textures and in his arrangements, which are always valid and stretching.

JIM ROBINSON (1892–1976)
TROMBONE

***   **Birthday Memorial Session** GHB BCD-276 CD
Robinson; Yoshio Toyama (*t*); Paul 'Polo' Barnes (*cl*); James Miller (*p, v*); Keiko Toyama (*bj*); Chester Zardis (*b*); Cie Frazier (*d*). 73.

The doyen of New Orleans trombonists – along with Big Eye Louis Nelson – Robinson had turned eighty when he made this session, but his simple, perfectly appropriate playing wasn't too bothered by the pasing of time, and he performs here much as he did on all of the sessions he appeared on over a space of some 35 years. The material is as predictable as all such sessions, with only 'The Waltz You Saved For Me' and 'Hurry Down Sunshine' standing as anything out of the ordinary, but the band play with undimmed enjoyment of the occasion. The presence of the Toyamas, the Japanese couple who lived and worked on Bourbon Street for a spell in the late 1960s, invigorates the other old-timers involved on the date, with Yoshio's admiration for Bunk Johnson letting him fit into the occasion without any sense of strain. The remastering for CD has freshened the music up a little.

PERRY ROBINSON (born 1938)
CLARINET

**(*)   Nightmare Island – Live At The Leverkusener Jazztage West Wind 0026 CD/LP
Robinson;

Long – and apparently apron-stringed – association with Gunther Hampel and the Galaxie Dream Band tended to blur Robinson's critical reputation. A formidable technician on a unfashionable instrument (he is a collateral descendant of Tony Scott and Jimmy Giuffre, but with a pronounced rock influence), Robinson inherited a fine structural sense from his composer father and builds solos out of daring architectural swoops and apparently unsupported harmony, much like Sonny Rollins.

SPIKE ROBINSON
TENOR SAXOPHONE

***   The Music Of Harry Warren Discovery DSCD-937 CD
Robinson; Charles Owens (*t*); Victor Feldman, George Cables (*p*); Ray Brown, Red Callender (*b*); John Guerin, Roy McCurdy (*d*). 81–82.

***(*)   At Chesters Vol. 1 Hep CD 2028 CD
Robinson; Eddie Thompson (*p*); Len Skeat (*b*); James Hall (*d*). 7/84.

***   At Chesters Vol. 2 Hep CD 2031 CD
As above. 7/84.

Robinson is an American who has made a secure reputation for himself in Britain, having first arrived here on a Navy posting. Although he plays tenor now, he was an altoman entirely under Parker's spell when he made these tracks in London in 1951. Robinson's switch to tenor may have deprived us of a fine Bird-man, but his command of the bigger horn is scarcely less impressive on what were comeback recordings. His models now are Getz, Sims and – at the insistence of some – Brew Moore, but Robinson is deft enough to make the comparisons sound fuly absorbed. The Discovery album is perhaps a shade prosaic, but the two live records, made in Southend on a 1984 British visit, are wonderfully light and swinging, as if the tenor were an alto in his hands. Volume 1 has the edge for a couple of ethereal ballads and the swing which is piled into 'Please Don't Talk About Me When I'm Gone'. Vivid location recording.

***   In Town Hep CD 2035 CD
Robinson; Brian Lemon (*p*); Len Skeat (*b*); Alan Ganley (*d*); Elaine Delmar (*v*). 10/86.

***   The Odd Couple Capri 74008 CD
Robinson; Rob Mullins (*ky*); Fred Hamilton (*b*); Jill Fredericsen (*d*). 8/88.

***   Jusa Bit O'Blues Capri 74012 CD
Robinson; Harry Edison (*t*); Ross Tompkins (*p*); Monty Budwig (*b*); Paul Humphrey (*d*). 9/88.

***   Jusa Bit O'Blues Vol. 2 Capri 74013 CD
As above. 9/88.

The Capri records provide Robinson with some of his most encouraging settings. All three find Robinson drifting through a clutch of standards with carefree ease, and any preference between them might depend on the choice of songs on each. Edison is reliably lyrical and both rhythm sections play their part without complaint; the only qualm might be the essential sameness which accompanies such seasoned and professional music-making. In other words, they're more satisfying than exciting.

***   Three For The Road Hep CD 2045 CD
Robinson; Janusz Carmello (*t*); David Newton (*p*); Louis Stewart (*g*); Paul Morgan (*b*); Mark Taylor (*d*). 7/89.

**(*)   Stairway To The Stars Hep CD 2049 CD
Robinson; Brian Kellock (*p*); Ronnie Rae (*b*); John Rae (*d*). 10/90.

Robinson continues on his steady way. *Three For The Road* makes for an amiable blowing match between a seasoned cast: nothing fancy, and nothing untoward. *Stairway To The Stars*, though, is a trifle dull – Robinson never plays with less than a professional commitment, but on this occasion he sounds as though he might have been a bit tired. What he may be in need of now is context and a producer: there are enough off-the-cuff live dates in his discography already.

BETTY ROCHE (born 1920)
VOCAL

*** **Singin' And Swingin'** Original Jazz Classics OJC 1718 LP
Roche; Jimmy Forrest (*ts*); Jack McDuff (*org*); Bill Jennings (*g*); Wendell Marshall (*b*); Roy Haynes (*d*). 1/61.

Roche had two separate spells with Duke Ellington, in the 1940s and again in the early '50s, but she made only a handful of sides with the orchestra: her set-piece was a version of 'Take The "A" Train' which incorporated a long scat episode. Duke liked her style: 'she had a soul inflexion in a bop state of intrigue'. Her Bethlehem records of the 1950s have been available but are now out of print; this 1961 session, with a terrific band behind her, is a modest but enjoyable memento of her art. Bop appears with 'Billie's Bounce', but her huskier ballad delivery takes some of the slush out of 'When I Fall In Love', and her Anita O'Day influence shows through in a certain wry sidelong-delivery of some of the lyrics. A second Prestige album, *Lightly And Politely*, would make a welcome follow-up to this reissue.

BOB ROCKWELL (born 1945)
TENOR SAXOPHONE

(*) **No Rush Steeplechase SCS 1219 CD/LP
Rockwell; Butch Lacy (*p*); Jesper Lundgaard (*b*); Jukkis Uotila (*d*). 11/85–2/86.

*** **On The Natch** Steeplechase SCS 1229 CD/LP
As above. 87.

*** **The Bob Rockwell Trio** Steeplechase SCS 1242 CD/LP
Rockwell; Rufus Reid (*b*); Victor Lewis (*d*). 1/89.

*** **Reconstruction** Steeplechase SCCD 31270 CD
Rockwell; Joe Locke (*vib*); Rufus Reid (*b*); Victor Lewis (*d*). 3/90.

An American who's relocated to Copenhagen, Rockwell is an assured player who can create exciting music without suggesting a singular vision. He touches on freedom and tonal exploration in the manner of Sonny Rollins – and he seldom goes further than touching – but there's no special adherence to the Rollins sound, or to any slavish worship of Coltrane, though Rockwell's facility (particularly on soprano) again recalls that towering influence. His solos are often about momentum rather than melody, and he can get knotted up in the twists and turns of a theme, but it makes it more interesting to see how he'll extricate himself. Which he usually does. *No Rush* is a composite of various sessions at the Cafle Montmartre, and the similarly constructed *On The Natch* goes off at the same pitch, although the later session seems slightly more energetic. Aside from a ballad on each disc, the material is all originals by Rockwell and Lacy, and they run into the familiar problem of faceless modal themes, useful enough as lift-off points but not very absorbing for a listener. At its best – on 'Nightrider' from *On The Natch* – the quartet push and challenge each other into a dense and plausible group music, but in isolation the improvising sounds a trifle introverted and uptight.

The two later records give Rockwell a better chance to shine. The trio set has some tenor blowing of unmistakable power, the leader pacing himself over the long haul with fine assurance and winding up with the feeling that he has more to say yet; Reid and Lewis, two outstanding talents in themselves, add to the lustre. *Reconstruction* brings in the vibes of Joe Locke on a rarely encountered instrumentation, faintly reminiscent of the Milt Jackson–Lucky Thompson sessions of the 1950s, and while the playing here is much more studied in its intensity, all four men avoid meaningless blowing for most of the date.

CLAUDIO RODITI (born 1946)
TRUMPET, FLUGELHORN

**(*)   Gemini Man Milestone M 9158 CD/LP
Roditi; Daniel Freiberg (*ky*); Roger Kellaway (*p*); Nilson Matta (*b*); Ignacio Berroa,
Akira Tana (*d*); Rafael Cruz (*perc*). 3/88.

**(*)   Slow Fire Milestone M 9175 CD/LP
Roditi; Jay Ashby (*tb*); Ralph Moore (*ts*); Danilo Perez (*p*); David Finck (*b*); Akira
Tana, Ignacio Berroa (*d*); Rafael Cruz (*perc*). 89.

Roditi's bright tone and fizzing delivery have served him well in several bands, and these dates
of his own are intermittently exciting. His Brazilian roots turn up in the varous samba-derived
rhythmic bases which account for several of the tunes, but like so many of the current wave of
Latin American jazz musicians he owes a great stylistic debt to Dizzy Gillespie. Neither date has
perhaps quite the final ounce of weight that would make it outstanding, but the first has
Kellaway's astute comping and the second adds Ashby and Moore to beef up the sound of the
band, which otherwise tends to resolve itself in the percussion section.

**   Two Of Swords Candid CCD 79504 CD
Roditi; Jay Ashby (*tb*); Edward Simon, Danilo Perez (*p*); Nilson Matta, David Finck
(*b*); Duduka Fonseca, Akira Tana (*d*). 9/90.

Not bad, but this is a bit of a potboiler. Roditi splits the session between a 'jazz' and a
'Brazilian' group, and both perform in much the same direction, although the Brazilian band
has Ashby in the front line to add some tonal colour. Roditi's fat-toned flugelhorn gets a little
more exposure than usual but the music lacks much character. Another CD which doesn't really
justify its 72-minute length.

**(*)   Milestones Candid CCD 79515 CD
Roditi; Paquito D'Rivera (*cl, as*); Kenny Barron (*p*); Ray Drummond (*b*); Ben Riley
(*d*). 11/90.

An absolutely top-class band with everybody feeling fine and playing hard – yet the results are,
as with the records above, vaguely disappointing. One can't fault the virtuosity of either of the
horn players, and D'Rivera, especially, gets off some breathtaking flights on both alto and
clarinet, but the final impression is of too many notes and too much said. The jam-session
material doesn't assist matters much – the bailad 'Brussels In The Rain' is the only departure
from familiarity – and with playing time at almost 70 minutes it does start to sound like too
much of a good thing. The live recording is clear if a little dry.

RED RODNEY (born 1927)
TRUMPET

****   Modern Music From Chicago Original Jazz Classics OJC 048 LP
Rodney; Ira Sullivan (*t, as, ts*); Norman Simmons (*p*); Victor Sproles (*b*); Roy Haynes
(*d*). 6/55.

This one is long overdue for CD transfer. Rodney was perhaps the first white trumpeter to take
up the challenge of bebop, which he played with a crackling, slightly nervy quality. It sat well
with Parker's, and Rodney was an integral part of Bird's quintet in 1950 and 1951, having first
worked with him slightly earlier than that.
  Parker cast a long shadow, and the recordings Rodney made under his own name, before his
long sabbatical in non-improvising session work, have been rather eclipsed. *Modern Music* is a
splendid album, full of fire and zest. The track-listing throws up no obvious Bird references,
and the playing has the rough, bluesy quality associated with Chicago – the multi-instrumental
Sullivan's adoptive city; Rodney is a Philadelphian – rather than the KC-NY axis that
dominated bop.
  On 'Clap Hands, Here Comes Charlie', Rodney recalls Shavers's up-market vulgarity
(though that isn't why the song was chosen). Elsewhere, his descending runs sound like the
zipper going down on a dress, staticky with promise, but also rather dry.

Sullivan is a remarkable player. From the 1960s he has largely restricted his field of operations to South Florida, where he enjoys legendary status. He and Rodney got together again at the end of the 1970s, but they've never again sounded this good.

***(*) **Bird Lives!** Muse 5371 CD/LP/MC
Rodney; Charles McPherson (*as*); Barry Harris (*p*); Sam Jones (*b*); Roy Brooks (*d*). 7/73.

. . . and, for a moment or two, it's possible to believe that he actually does. McPherson carries the Bird part with the alternate confidence and anxiety of a typecast actor. Here, he sounds perfectly convincing, though his solo structure is often telegraphed several measures ahead (as on 'I'll Remember April' and 'Donna Lee') and there are occasional eccentricities of intonation.

This is an unashamedly nostalgic record, one of the first Rodney made after a long, drug-haunted lay-off in commercial session work. It came at a time when it was ideologically OK to discuss bebop again, and the trumpeter seems content to butterfly-net the original raptures of the music rather than dig any deeper into it. So far as it goes, that's fine, but it became a manner, and a respectably marketable one, which Rodney wasn't able to set aside. Listening to this and later albums, one always suspects him capable of something more than he wants to deliver. But beautiful.

***(*) **Red Giant** Steeplechase SCS 1233 CD/LP
Rodney; Butch Lacy (*p*); Hugo Rasmussen (*b*); Aage Tanggaard (*d*). 4/88.

(*) **No Turn On Red Denon CY 73 149 CD
Rodney; Dick Oatts (*as*); Garry Dial (*p*); Jay Anderson (*b*); Joey Baron (*d*). 8/86,

*** **One For Bird** Steeplechase SCS 1238 CD/LP
As above, except John Riley (*d*) replaces Baron. 7/88.

(*) **Red Snapper Steeplechase SCS 1252 CD/LP
As above.

Nowhere was bebop accorded higher sentimental status than in Scandinavia. House bands and rhythm sections have excellent chops (the same is true of Japanese players) but with a strongly authentic 'feel' as well. Of these 1988 sessions *Red Giant* is undoubtedly the best, with Rasmussen, Tanggard and the rough-diamond Lacy all contributing substantially. Compare the versions of 'Greensleeves' and a curiously but effectively tempoed 'Giant Steps' with those on *Red Snapper* which seem merely curious. Steeplechase has long been notorious for indiscriminate and prodigal release of marginally differentiated material. The sessions of 11 and 12 July 1988 have been used for one Bird and one non-Bird release, which may not make absolute artistic sense but may clarify matters for potential purchasers (who should nevertheless be warned that this is no pastiche band but a revisionist and quite challenging outfit with ideas of its own about the bop heritage). The original material on *Red Snapper* and *No Turn On Red* is perhaps more interesting, but there's very little doubt where Rodney's heart lies. At sixty-plus, he sounds chastened but undeterred, and his playing reveals a depth of reference that wasn't there previously.

SHORTY ROGERS (born 1924)
TRUMPET, FLUGELHORN

**** **Short Stops** RCA/Bluebird ND 90209 CD
Rogers; Pete Candoli, Maynard Ferguson, Conrad Gozzo, John Howell, Ray Linn (*t*); Harry Betts, Milt Bernhart, Bob Enevoldsen, John Haliburton, Jimmy Knepper (*tb*); John Graas (*frhn*); Gene Englund, Paul Sarmento (*tba*); Herb Geller (*as*); Art Pepper (*as, ts*); Bud Shank (*as, bs*); Bill Holman, Bill Perkins (*ts*); Bob Cooper, Jimmy Giuffre (*ts, bs*); Russ Freeman, Hampton Hawes, Marty Paich (*p*); Curtis Counce, Joe Mondragon (*b*); Shelly Manne (*d*). 1, 3, 4 & 7/53.

*** **Swings** RCA/Bluebird ND 83012 CD
Rogers; Buddy Childers, Conte Candoli, Pete Candoli, Al Porcino, Don Fagerquist, Bob Enevoldsen, Carroll Lewis, Ray Linn, Oliver Mitchell, Ray Triscari (*t*); Harry Betts, Marshall Cram, Richard Nash, Frank Rosolino, Ken Schroyer, David Wells (*tb*); Jimmy Giuffre (*cl*): Paul Horn, Bud Shank (*as*); Bob Cooper, Herb Geller, Bill

Holman, Richie Kamuca (*ts*); Charles Gentry (*bs*); Pete Jolly (*p*); Larry Bunker,
Eugene Estes, Red Norvo (*vib*); Barney Kessel, Howard Roberts (*g*); Joe Mondragon
(*b*); Mel Lewis (*d*). 12/58, 2 & 12/59.

***(*) **America The Beautiful** Candid CCD 79510 CD
Rogers; Bud Shank (*as*); Conte Candoli (*t*); Bill Perkins (*bs, ts, ss*); Bob Cooper (*ts*);
Pete Jolly (*p*): Monty Budwig (*b*); Lawrence Marable (*d*). 8/91.

Much influenced by the Davis–Mulligan–Lewis *Birth Of The Cool*, Shorty Rogers turned its
basic instrumentation and lapidary arranging into a vehicle for relaxedly swinging jazz of a high
order. The excellent *Short Stops* gathers material from three important 1953 issues, the
10-inchers *Shorty Rogers And His Giants* and the legendary *Cool And Crazy* from the spring,
and *The Wild One* (originally an extended-play 45 of material written for the Brando biker
flick) from July.

The July pieces were written by Leith Stevens, 'The Pesky Serpent' by Jimmy Giuffre;
everything else is by Rogers, which may be one reason why this is so much better than the
bland charts the players have to contend with on *Swings*. The tracks are arranged in matrix
order (which makes some sense but yields no particular insights) and are cleanly if a little
asymmetrically transferred by Ed Michel and Ray Mann, who might have made a better fist of
the thudding *Swings*.

'Bunny' is basically a vehicle for Art Pepper's torrid alto, and 'Diablo's Dance' for the
equally emotional Hawes, who gives the music its energizing infusion of blues. There are
excellent solos from Giuffre ('Pesky Serpent'), Shelly Manne (typically inventive on 'Tale Of
An African Lobster') and Bill Perkins, who sounds gorgeously bruised on 'Blues For Brando',
the perfect aural equivalent of watching the actor sulk into a room.

Rogers himself was never a memorable soloist. His arrangements, though, are among the
best of the time. If they lack the gelid precision that Lewis and Mulligan brought to *Birth Of
The Cool*, Rogers charts combine the same intricate texture with an altogether looser jazz feel;
'Boar-Jibu' exactly bridges the distance between Giuffre's 'Four Brothers' for Woody Herman
and *Birth*. It works fine when the basic material is strong, but most of *Swings* was written by Al
Stillman and Robert Allen and has a carousel blandness. The 1959 stuff is better because the
basic melodies – 'Get Happy', 'Blues In The Night', 'Let's Fall In Love' and 'That Old Black
Magic' – fill in their old familiar *Gestalt*s, strongly outlined where the Stillman and Allen stuff is
like mist. Giuffre's sound on 'Blues' is a delight, but there's too little of it. *Short Stops* should be
considered an essential purchase, but *Swings* might just as well be left with the roundabouts.

There is then something of a hiatus. For much of the intervening period, Rogers
concentrated on film music. His 1980s comeback found him in strong voice and, alongside Bud
Shank, in musically conducive company. Shank takes 'Lotus Bud' on alto saxophone, rather
than alto flute this time. The solo intro is huskily beautiful (with grace notes and colours that
make you wonder who has been listening to whom: Bud Shank or Bobby Watson?), and
surpassed only by Bill Perkins's eerily cadenced soprano solo on another Bud's 'Un Poco
Loco'.

'Here's That Old Martian Again' continues a series of similar conceits, done in reassuringly
un-alien blue rather than green, but with a hint of 'Blue In Green' in the shift across the line.
The Lighthouse All Stars play beyond themselves, with big credits to drummer Marable.
Recommended.

(*) **Big Band: Volume 1 Time Is TI9804 CD
Rogers; Maynard Ferguson, Conrad Gozzo, Ruben McFall, Don Dennis (*t*); Bob
Edmondson, Bob Enevoldsen, Herbie Harper (*tb*); Herb Geller, Bill Holman, Bill
Perkins, Jack Montrose (*saxes*); Lorraine Geller (*p*); John Simmons (*b*); Chuck Flores
(*d*). 53.

There are problems with this one. Not only are the track listings unreliable and the personnel
details incomplete, the music is stodgy in the extreme, with a tediously uninspired nine-minute
version of 'Short Stop' and a dismal hash of both 'C Jam Blues' and 'Perdido'. The
sound-balance is very wayward (it is a live set) and some of the subtler ensembles are swamped
by the rhythm section. For collectors only.

ADELHARD ROIDINGER (born 1941)
DOUBLE BASS

*(*) **Schattseite** ECM 1221 LP
Roidinger; Heinz Sauer (*ts*); Harry Pepl (*g*); Werner Pirchner (*vib, mar*); Bob Degen
(*p*); Michael DiPasqua (*d*); Aina Kemanis (*v*). 11/81.

Though Roidinger has played to great effect and with genuine beauty on other people's records
– most notably Braxton's wonderful *Seven Compositions (Trio) 1989* (hat Art 6025 CD) with
Tony Oxley – this is a bleak and rather cheerless record. That's not so much because of any tacit
programme (though 'When Earth Becomes Desert' doesn't sound exactly sanguine) but
because the playing is so stilted. By no means a strong candidate for urgent CD transfer.

ADRIAN ROLLINI (1904–56)
BASS SAXOPHONE, GOOFUS, VIBES

***(*) **Swing Low** Affinity AFS 1030 CD
Rollini; Wingy Manone (*t, v*); Manny Klein, Dave Klein, Irving Goodman, Jonah
Jones, Bunny Berigan, Johnny McGhee (*t*); Bobby Hackett (*c*); Jack Teagarden (*tb*);
Benny Goodman, Paul Ricci (*cl*); Sid Stoneburn, Joe Marsala (*cl, as*); Art Drelinger,
Arthur Rollini, Larry Binyon (*ts*); Putney Dandridge (*p, v*); Howard Smith, Fulton
McGrath, Jack Russin (*p*); George Van Eps, Nappy Lamare, Dick McDonough, Frank
Victor, Gwynn Nestor (*g*); Artie Bernstein, George Hnida, Sid Weiss, Harry Clark
(*b*); Stan King, Sam Weiss, Al Sidell, Phil Sillman, Buddy Rich (*d*); Jeanne Burns,
Ella Logan, Pat Hoka (*v*). 10/34–1/38.

(*) **Adrian Rollini His Quintet, His Trio Tax M-8036 LP
Rollini; Bobby Hackett (*c*); Frank Victor (*g*); Harry Clark (*b*); Buddy Rich (*d*); Sonny
Schuyler, The Tune Twisters (*v*). 1/38–5/40.

There are few instruments which can claim a single performer as their undisputed master, but
it's true of the bass asxophone and Adrian Rollini. Until recently it was ironic that the only LP
under his own name should feature not a single note of bass sax. The Affinity CD, though, has
restored to circulation seven sessions, most of which feature the great rumbling sound of
Rollini's bass sax: he played bass and melody lines with equal facility, could move through an
ensemble with disarming ease, and never gave the impression that the instrument was anything
but light and easy in his hands. Still, it remained a sound rooted in the 1920s, and as intriguing as
these sessions are – one with a Wingy Manone outfit, another with Goodman and Teagarden, a
fine 'Bugle Call Rag' with Jonah Jones, four titles with Irving Goodman on trumpet, and a
single track with Bunny Berigan – they're out of the mainstream of the jazz of the day.
Remastering is occasionally rather surfacey, but is usually clear. By the late 1930s, with the
instrument out of favour, Rollini had switched almost exclusively to vibes, which he plays on the
Tax LP, with a lightly swinging approach that is actually far from unpleasing: try his playing on
'I Wish I Had You', for instance. But the cocktail-trio sides which occupy the second side are
very slight. The eight tracks on the first side are all lumbered with tedious vocals, but each has
sublime, guileful playing by Bobby Hackett, whose solos and obbligatos are unfailingly fresh
and handsome: he's the reason the record is worthwhile. The transfers are mostly good, but
some, such as 'Small Fry', seem to have been dubbed from inferior 78s. The best Rollini is still
the music he made in the 1920s with Beiderbecke, Trumbauer and Nichols, and readers are
directed to their entries to find more of him; but it's good to have at least two records in the
catalogue which celebrate the king of an instrument which, many years after his death, is
actually recognized again in the avant garde and in some revivalist outfits.

SONNY ROLLINS (born 1930)
TENOR AND SOPRANO SAXOPHONE

(*)   **Sonny Rollins With The Modern Jazz Quartet Original Jazz Classics OJC 011
CD/LP/MC
Rollins; Miles Davis, Kenny Drew, John Lewis (*p*); Percy Heath (*b*); Art Blakey,
Kenny Clarke, Roy Haynes (*d*).1/51–10/53.

***   **Moving Out** Original Jazz Classics OJC 058 CD/LP/MC
Rollins; Kenny Dorham (*t*); Thelonious Monk, Elmo Hope (*p*); Percy Heath, Tommy
Potter (*b*); Art Blakey, Art Taylor (*d*). 8–10/54.

Rollins's most important early session is with Miles Davis on *Bags Groove* (OJC 245). The nine
1951 tracks on OJC 011 are cursory bop singles, and the MJQ – despite the headline billing –
appear on only three tracks, in a meeting that took place a second time on an Atlantic album
some years later. One track, 'I Know', has the novelty of Miles Davis on piano. *Moving Out* is
more substantial, though it still stands as a stereotypical blowing date, even with a single track –
'More Than You Know' – from a session with Monk. The most interesting contributor here is
probably Hope, whose off-centre lyricism still turns heads.

***(*)   **Work Time** Original Jazz Classics OJC 007 CD/LP/MC
Rollins; Ray Bryant (*p*); George Morrow (*b*); Max Roach (*d*). 12/55.

***(*)   **Sonny Rollins Plus 4** Original Jazz Classics OJC 243 CD/LP/MC
Rollins; Clifford Brown (*t*); Richie Powell (*p*); George Morrow (*b*); Max Roach (*d*).
3/56.

****   **Tenor Madness** Original Jazz Classics OJC 124 CD/LP/MC
Rollins; John Coltrane (*ts*); Red Garland (*p*); Paul Chambers (*b*); Philly Joe Jones
(*d*). 5/56.

*****   **Saxophone Colossus** Original Jazz Classics OJC 291 CD/LP/MC
Rollins; Tommy Flanagan (*p*); Doug Watkins (*b*); Max Roach (*d*).

***(*)   **Sonny Rollins Plays For Bird** Original Jazz Classics OJC 214 CD/LP/MC
Rollins; Kenny Dorham (*t*); Wade Legge (*p*); George Morrow (*b*); Max Roach (*d*).
10/56.

****   **Tour De Force** Original Jazz Classics OJC 095 CD/LP/MC
Rollins; Kenny Drew (*p*); George Morrow (*b*); Max Roach (*d*); Earl Coleman (*v*).
12/56.

***   **Sonny Rollins Volume 1** Blue Note CDP 7815422 CD
Rollins; Donald Byrd (*t*); Wynton Kelly (*p*); Gene Ramey (*b*); Max Roach (*d*). 12/56.

An astounding year's work on record. Rollins was still a new and relatively unheralded star
when he was working through this series of sessions, and – in the aftermath of Parker's death –
jazz itself had an open throne. There was a vast distance between Rollins and the tenorman
who was winning most of the polls of the period, Stan Getz, but though Sonny evaded the
open-faced romanticism and woozy melancholy associated with the Lester Young school, he
wasn't much of a Parkerite, either. Rollins used the headlong virtuosity of bop to more
detached, ironical ends. The opening track on *Work Time* is a blast through 'There's No
Business Like Show Business', which prefigures many of his future choices of material. Parker
would have smiled, but he'd never have played it this way. Still, Rollins's mastery of the tenor
was already complete by this time, with a wide range of tones and half-tones, a confident
variation of dynamics, and an ability to phrase with equal strength of line in any part of a solo.
If he is often tense, as if in witness to the power of his own creative flow, then the force of the
music is multiplied by this tension. The most notable thing about the records is how dependent
they are on Rollins himself: Roach aside, whose magnificent drum parts offer a pre-echo of
what Elvin Jones would start to develop with John Coltrane, the sidemen are often almost
dispensable. It is Rollins who has to be heard.

If *Worktime* is just a little sketchy in parts, that is only in comparison with what follows. *Plus
Four* is one of Rollins's happiest sessions. With both horn players in mercurial form, and Roach
sensing the greatness of the band he is basically in charge of, the music unfolds at a terrific clip

but has a sense of relaxation which the tenorman would seldom approach later in the decade. His own piece 'Pent-Up House' has an improvisation which sets the stage for some of his next advances: unhurried, thoughtful, he nevertheless plays it with biting immediacy. *Tenor Madness* features Coltrane on, alas, only one track, the title tune, and it isn't quite the grand encounter one might have wished for: but the rest of the record, with Miles Davis's rhythm section, includes surging Rollins on 'Paul's Pal' and 'The Most Beautiful Girl In The World'. The undisputed masterpiece from this period is *Saxophone Colossus*, and although Rollins plays with brilliant invention throughout these albums, he's at his most consistent on this disc. 'St Thomas', his irresistible calypso melody, appears here for the first time, and there is a ballad of unusual bleakness in 'You Don't Know What Love Is', as well as a rather sardonic walk through 'Moritat' (alias 'Mack The Knife'). But 'Blue Seven', as analysed in a contemporary piece by Gunther Schuller, became celebrated as a thematic masterpiece, where all the joints and moving parts of a spontaneous improvisation attain the pristine logic of a composition. If the actual performance is much less forbidding than it sounds, thanks in part to the simplicity of the theme, it surely justifies Schuller's acclaim. *Plays For Bird*, though it includes a medley of tunes associated with Parker, is no more Bird-like than the other records, and a reading of 'I've Grown Accustomed To Her Face' establishes Rollins's oddly reluctant penchant for a tender ballad. *Sonny Rollins* ended the year in somewhat more desultory fashion – the session seems to return to more conventional horns-and-rhythm bebop – but *Tour De Force*, recorded two weeks earlier, is almost as good as *Colossus*, with the ferocious abstractions of 'B Swift' and 'B Quick' contrasting with the methodical, almost surgical destruction of 'Sonny Boy'. The OJC reissues are all remastered in splendid sound, even if it's not especially superior to the original vinyl.

***(*) **Way Out West** Original Jazz Classics OJC 337 CD/LP/MC
Rollins; Ray Brown (*b*); Shelly Manne (*d*). 3/57.

***(*) **Sonny Rollins Vol. 2** Blue Note CDP 7815582 CD
Rollins; J. J. Johnson (*tb*); Horace Silver, Thelonious Monk (*p*); Percy Heath (*b*); Art Blakey (*d*). 4/57.

***(*) **The Sound Of Sonny** Original Jazz Classics OJC 029 CD/LP/MC
Rollins; Sonny Clark (*p*); Percy Heath (*b*); Roy Haynes (*d*). 6/57.

**** **Newk's Time** Blue Note CDP 7840012 CD
Rollins; Wynton Kelly (*p*); Doug Watkins (*b*); Philly Joe Jones (*d*). 9/57.

**** **A Night At The Village Vanguard Vol. 1** Blue Note CDP 7465172 CD
Rollins; Donald Bailey, Wilbur Ware (*b*); Pete LaRoca, Elvin Jones (*d*). 11/57.

**** **A Night At The Village Vanguard Vol. 2** Blue Note CDP 7465182 CD
As above. 11/57.

Rollins continued his astonishing run of records with scarcely a pause for breath. A visit to Los Angeles paired him with Brown and Manne on a session which, if it occasionally dips into a kind of arch cleverness, features some superb interplay betwen the three men, with Rollins turning 'I'm An Old Cowhand' into a jovial invention. The CD edition includes three alternative takes, which are also available on the *Alternate Takes* album listed below. One of the compelling things about this sequence is the difference in drummer from session to session: Blakey's inimitable pattern of rolls and giant cymbal strokes sounds, for once, a little inappropriate, with Philly Joe Jones using the same kind of drama to far more effect on *Newk's Time*. Jones, still in his formative phase, matches all of Rollins's most imperial gestures, and 'Striver's Row' and 'Sonnymoon For Two' become tenor-drums dialogues which must have directed the drummer towards his later confrontations with Coltrane. The undervalued player here, though, is Haynes, whose playing on *The Sound Of Sonny* is ingeniously poised and crisp. The Blue Note *Vol. 2* finds Rollins a little cramped by his surroundings, but Johnson's sober playing is a far more apposite accompaniment than Byrd's was, its deadpan line a wry rejoinder to the tenor parts. *The Sound Of Sonny* is unexpectedly cursory in its treatment of some of the themes: after the longer disquisitions which Rollins had accustomed himself to making, these three-and four-minute tracks sound bitten off. But the grandeur of Rollins's improvisations on 'Just In Time' and 'Toot-Toot-Tootsie' is compressed rather than reduced, and a solo 'It Could Happen To You', though a little snatched at, celebrates the breadth of his sound. We are somewhat divided on the merits of *Newk's Time* and the *Village Vanguard* sessions. If Rollins is arguably self-absorbed on some of the studio session, the extraordinary motivic development of 'Surrey With The Fringe On Top' is one of his most powerful creations and 'Blues For Philly Joe' takes the work done on 'Blue Seven' a step further. The live material, originally cherry-picked for a single peerless LP, has been stretched across two CDs with a certain diminution of impact, yet the leader is again in rampant form, and working with only bass and drums throughout leads him into areas of freedom which bop never allowed. If Rollins's free-spiritedness is checked by his ruthless self-examination, its rigour makes his music uniquely powerful in jazz. On the two versions of 'Softly As In A Morning Sunrise' or in the muscular exuberance of 'Old Devil Moon', traditional bop-orientated improvising reaches a peak of expressive power and imagination. Overall, these are records which demand a place in any collection. The remastering is mostly fine, although some of the Blue Notes seem a trifle recessed compared with original vinyl.

*** **The Best Of Sonny Rollins** Blue Note CDP 7932032 CD
As Blue Note records above. 56–57.

*** **Alternate Takes** Contemporary 7651 LP/MC
Rollins; Hampton Hawes (*p*); Victor Feldman (*vib*); Barney Kessel (*g*); Ray Brown, Leroy Vinnegar (*b*); Shelly Manne (*d*). 3/57–10/58.

*** **The Essential Sonny Rollins On Riverside** Riverside FCD-60-020 CD
Rollins; Kenny Dorham (*t*); Ernie Henry (*as*); Sonny Clark, Thelonious Monk, Hank Jones, Wynton Kelly (*p*); Percy Heath, Paul Chambers, Oscar Pettiford (*b*); Max Roach, Roy Haynes (*d*); Abbey Lincoln (*v*). 56–58.

The two best-of's score lower marks only because the original albums are indispensable. The Riverside set does, though, include tracks which are otherwise under the leadership of Dorham or Monk. *Alternate Takes* is a useful round-up of material rejected from *Way Out West* and *Sonny Rollins And The Contemporary Leaders*, but its appearance is anticlimactic when the original albums are as good as they are.

***(*) **The Freedom Suite** Original Jazz Classics OJC 067 CD/LP/MC
Rollins; Oscar Pettiford (*b*); Max Roach (*d*). 2/58.

***(*) **The Sound Of Sonny/Freedom Suite** Riverside CDJZD 008 CD
Rollins; Sonny Clark (*p*); Percy Heath, Paul Chambers, Oscar Pettiford (*b*); Roy Haynes, Max Roach (*d*). 6/57–2/58.

*** **Sonny Rollins And The Contemporary Leaders** Original Jazz Classics OJC 340 CD/LP/MC
Rollins; Hampton Hawes (*p*); Victor Feldman (*vib*); Barney Kessel (*g*); Leroy Vinnegar (*b*); Shelly Manne (*d*). 10/58.

** **European Concerts** Bandstand BD 1503 CD/LP
Rollins; Milt Jackson (*vib*); Kenny Drew (*p*); Percy Heath, Henry Grimes (*b*); Art Blakey, Billy Higgins (*d*). 57–58.

***(*) **In Sweden 1959** Dragon DRLP 73 LP
Rollins; Henry Grimes (*b*); Pete LaRoca (*d*). 3/59.

*** **Aix-En-Provence 1959** Royal Jazz RJD 502 CD
Rollins; Henry Grimes (*b*); Kenny Clarke (*d*). 3/59.

Rollins hasn't shown much interest in composition – the early 'Airegin' and 'Oleo' remain in jazz repertory, and that's about all – but his piece 'The Freedom Suite' takes a stab at an extended work, although its simple structure makes it more of a sketch for an improvisation than anything else. The enigineers caught his sound with particular immediacy on this date, and it's more a celebration of his tone and dynamic variation than a coherent, programmatic statement (Orrin Keepnews's sleeve-notes seem to deliberately fudge the directness of whatever Rollins was trying to say about black freedom).The (British) Riverside CD usefully couples both *The Freedom Suite* and *The Sound Of Sonny*. Despite a self-conscious clustering of stars for the Contemporary 'Leaders' date, Rollins takes a determined path through one of his most bizarre programmes; 'Rock-A-Bye Your baby', 'In The Chapel In The Moonlight', 'I've Told Ev'ry Little Star'. Following this, he departed for Europe, where some live recordings have survived. The Dragon set is the best, although the studio programme which makes up most of the record isn't quite up to the storming concert recording of 'St Thomas' which opens it. The Royal Jazz date is another good one, though fidelity problems keep it out of the front rank, while the provenance of the Bandstand record – which apparently includes Milt Jackson on two of the three tracks – is doubtful, and the sound (especially on the long and otherwise strong trio reading of 'Lover') is poor. Throughout these records, though, is a feeling that Rollins is coming to the end of a great period, having balanced his own achievements within a straight bop milieu and realized that, as a singular figure, he is remote from the ideas of interplay within a group (and particularly between horns) which almost everyone else in jazz was pursuing.

***(*) **The Quartets** RCA Bluebird ND85643 CD/MC
Rollins; Jim Hall (g); Bob Cranshaw (b); Mickey Roker, Ben Riley, Harry T. Saunders (d). 1–5/62.

*** **On The Outside** RCA Bluebird ND 82496 CD/MC
Rollins; Don Cherry (t); Bob Cranshaw, Henry Grimes (b); Billy Higgins (d). 7/62–2/63.

*** **Live In Paris 1963** Magnetic MRCD 101 CD
As above, except omit Grimes. 63.

*** **All The Things You Are** RCA Bluebird ND82179 CD/MC
Rollins; Coleman Hawkins (ts); Paul Bley, Herbie Hancock (p); Jim Hall (g); Bob Cranshaw, Teddy Smith, Ron Carter, David Izenson, Henry Grimes (b); Roy McCurdy, Stu Martin, Mickey Roker (d). 7/63–7/64.

***(*) **Alternative Takes** RCA Bluebird ND CD/MC
Rollins; Jim Hall (g); Herbie Hancock (p); Ron Carter, David Izenzon, Teddy Smith (b); Roy McCurdy, Stu Martin (d). 1/64–7/64.

The saxophonist disappeared for two years before returning to the studio for the sessions reissued on *The Quartets*, originally issued on albums called *The Bridge* and *What's New?* On the face of it, little had changed: though Ornette Coleman's revolution had taken place in the interim, the music sounded much like the old Rollins. But this is his most troubled and troubling period on record. The first track on *The Quartets* is a reading of 'God Bless The Child' which is starkly desolate in feeling, and although there are lighter moments in such as a shuffle-beat version of 'If Ever I Would Leave You', Rollins plays with a puzzling melancholy throughout. Hall, though, is an unexpectedly fine partner, moving between rhythm and front-line duties with great aplomb and actually finding ways to communicate with the most lofty of soloists. It's an often compelling record as a result. The meetings with Cherry and Hawkins are much less successful. *On The Outside* was hailed as Rolins's head-on collision with the new thing, as exemplified by Cherry, but hardly anything the two men play bears any relation to the other's music: recorded live, they may as well be on separate stages. On an exhaustively long 'Oleo', the tenorman's pent-up outburst might almost be an expression of rage at the situation. Cherry, peculiarly, sounds like a pre-echo of the older Rollins in his crabby, buzzing solo on 'Doxy'. Three brief studio tracks at the end are a feeble postscript. But the subsequent Paris concert recording suggests a more peaceful co-existence: 'On Green Dolphin Street' and 'Sonnymoon For Two' are rambling, sometimes tortuous workouts that find Cherry in his most lyrical form, while Rollins pushes towards all the barriers he can reach short of complete abstraction. The concert sound is surprisingly good. The encounter with Hawkins, which takes up half of *All the Things You Are*, is much more respectful, even if Rollins seems to be satirizing the older man at some points, notably in his weirdly trilling solo on 'Yesterdays'. Again, though, there's relatively little real interplay, aside from a beautifully modulated 'Summertime'. The rest of the record consists of quartet sessions with Herbie Hancock: aimless, encumbered by his own genius, Rollins sounds bored with whatever tune he's playing but can't help throwing in the occasional brilliant stroke. It's a fascinating if frustrating experience to hear, and there's much more of it on *Alternative Takes*, which pools a series of fragments and offcuts from the workbench: Rollins plugs through impromptu cadenzas, wrecks some tunes, elevates others, while Hancock and the others gamely try to read what he's doing. For aficionados only, perhaps, but a strangely absorbing record.

***(*) **On Impulse!** Impulse! CD
Rollins; Ray Bryant (p); Walter Booker (b); Mickey Roker (d). 7/65.

(***)   **Live In Europe '65** Magnetic MRCD 118 CD
Rollins; Niels-Henning Ørsted-Pedersen (*b*); Alan Dawson (*d*). 11/65.

(*)   **East Broadway Rundown Impulse! CD
Rollins; Freddie Hubbard (*t*); Jimmy Garrison (*b*); Elvin Jones (*d*). 5/66.

Another problem period. 'Three Little Words', from *On Impulse!*, showed that when he had a mind to, Rollins could still outplay any other saxophonist, with a superbly driving and witty development out of the melody. But the inconclusive treatment of the other themes continued to suggest a dissatisfaction, and the European concert recording (in only fair, bootleg-quality sound) finds him lost in space: he could play this kind of staggering, over-extended improvisation for ever, but even he seemed to be missing structure and point. *East Broadway Rundown* is spoilt by the incompatible rhythm section, and the long title-track spends a lot of time going nowhere: only a gnarled 'We Kiss In A Shadow' approaches the real Rollins. After this session, he disappeared for another five years.

***   **Next Album** Original Jazz Classics OJC 312 CD/LP/MC
Rollins; George Cables (*p*); Bob Cranshaw (*b*); David Lee (*d*); Arthur Jenkins (*perc*). 7/72.

**   **Horn Culture** Original Jazz Classics OJC 314 LP/MC
Rollins; Walter Davis Jr (*p*); Yoshiaki Masuo (*g*); Bob Cranshaw (*b*); David Lee (*d*); James Mtume (*perc*). 6–7/73.

(*)   **The Cutting Edge Original Jazz Classics OJC 468 CD/LP/MC
Rollins; Rufus Harley (*bagpipes*); Stanley Cowell (*p*); Yoshiaki Masuo (*g*); Bob Cranshaw (*b*); David Lee (*d*); James Mtume (*perc*). 7/74.

**   **Nucleus** Original Jazz Classics OJC 620 CD/LP/MC
Rollins; Raoul de Souza (*tb*); Bennie Maupin (*ts, bcl, lyr*); George Duke (*p*); Bob Cranshaw, Chuck Rainey (*b*); Roy McCurdy, Eddie Moore (*d*); James Mtume (*perc*). 9/75.

*(*)   **The Way I Feel** Original Jazz Classics OJC 666 CD/MC
Rollins; Oscar Brashear, Chuck Findlay, Gene Coe (*t*); George Bohannon, Lew McCreary (*tb*); Marilyn Robinson, Alan Robinson (*frhn*); Bill Green (*ss, f, picc*); Patrice Rushen (*ky*); Lee Ritenour (*g*); Don Waldrop (*tba*); Alex Blake, Charles Meeks (*b*); Billy Cobham (*d*); Bill Summers (*perc*). 8–10/76.

(*)   **Don't Stop The Carnival Milestone 55005 CD
Rollins; Donald Byrd (*t, flhn*); Mark Soskin (*p*); Aurell Ray (*g*); Jerry Harris (*b*); Tony Williams (*d*). 4/78.

(*)   **Milestone Jazzstars In Concert Milestone 55006 CD/2LP/MC
Rollins; McCoy Tyner (*p*); Ron Carter (*b*); Al Foster (*d*). 9–10/78.

Rollins returned to action with *Next Album*, a very happy album which sounded much more contented than anything he'd recorded in over a decade. 'Playin' In The Yard' and 'The Everywhere Calypso' were taken at a joyous swagger, 'Poinciana' showcased his debut on soprano, and 'Skylark' was the tenor tour de force of the record, the saxophonist locking into a persuasively argued cadenza which shook the melody hard. But at root the album lacks the sheer nerve of his early music. This reining-in of his darker side affects all of his 1970s records to some degree. *Horn Culture* makes a more oppressive use of the electric rhythm section, none of whom play to Rollins's level, and while the two ballads are pleasing, elsewhere the music gets either pointlessly ugly ('Sais') or messy with overdubs and overblowing ('Pictures In The Reflection Of A Golden Horn'). *The Cutting Edge*, recorded at Montreux, is a muddle, with only a lovely reading of 'To A Wild Rose' to save it. *Nucleus* and *The Way I Feel* both court outright disaster. The former has at least some interesting material, and Rollins's very slow path through 'My Reverie' is perversely compelling, but the band have his feet chained, and none of the tracks takes off. The latter, with its dubbed-in horn section, is plain feeble.

    Don't Stop The Carnival has two great set-pieces, a ravishing 'Autumn Nocturne' and a fine display of virtuosity on 'Silver City', but the mismatched band – Williams tends towards extravagance, and Byrd prefigures his astonishingly total decline of the 1980s – let him down. The *Jazzstars* live session is another disappointment, with the all-star group playing well but to no special purpose and with nothing to show at the end of the record. The almost sublime frustration of this period was provided by reports of (unrecorded) concerts where Rollins was reputedly playing better than ever.

*** **Sunny Days, Starry Nights** Milestone 9122 CD/LP/MC
Rollins; Clifton Anderson (*tb*); Mark Soskin (*p*); Russel Blake (*b*); Tommy Campbell (*d*). 1/84.

Some of Rollins's records from this period are out of print. This one features the nucleus of the band he's kept until now, built around Soskin and Anderson. Nobody else is remotely on Rollins's level, and he seems to prefer it that way: certainly his best performances have arisen out of a certain creative isolation. This is another good-humoured date, with the melody of 'I'll See You Again' coming in waves of overdubbed tenor and jolly themes such as 'Kilauea' and 'Mava Mava' tempting the leader out of himself, and it's as enjoyable as any of his later records.

(*) **The Solo Album Milestone 9137 LP/MC
Rollins. 7/85.

Alone at last. But the solo Rollins isn't necessarily the same thing as a Rollins solo. While his cadenzas on standard tunes have usually been concert highlights, this anchorless solo concert too often relies on scales and practice patterns, as if he were woodshedding for the real thing. It's an opportunity to hear and study his grainy, utterly distinctive tone at length, but note for note this scarcely stands with solo sax albums which the avant-garde masters have produced.

***(*) **G Man** Milestone 9150 CD/LP/MC
Rollins; Clifton Anderson (*tb*); Mark Soskin (*p*); Bob Cranshaw (*b*); Marvin 'Smitty' Smith (*d*). 8/86–4/87.

*** **Dancing In The Dark** Milestone 9155 CD/LP/MC
As above, except Jerome Harris (*b, g*) replaces Cranshaw. 9/87.

*** **Falling In Love With Jazz** Milestone 9179 CD/LP/MC
As above, except add Branford Marsalis (*ts*), Tommy Flanagan (*p*); Bob Cranshaw (*b*), Jeff Watts, Jack DeJohnette (*d*), omit Smith. 6–9/89.

*** **Here's To The People** Milestone 9194 CD/MC
As above, except add Roy Hargrove (*t*), Al Foster (*d*), Steve Jordan (*perc*), omit Marsalis and Flanagan. 91.

The live show which produced the title-track of *G Man* caught Rollins on his most communicative form: it might not be his most profound playing, but the sheer exuberance and tumbling impetus of his improvising sweeps the listener along. *Dancing In The Dark* seems tame in comparison, though the leader plays with plenty of bite: tracks such as 'Just Once', though, seem to have been designed more for radio-play than anything else, and the band's snappy delivery of 'Duke Of Iron' is a well-crafted routine, not a spontaneous flourish. His two most recent studio sessions follow a similar pattern, with the guest horn player on each date doing no more than blowing a few gratuitous notes. *Falling In Love With Jazz* has a quite irresistible version of 'Tennessee Waltz', and there are two Rollins flights through 'Why Was I Born?' and 'I Wish I Knew' on *Here's To The People*, where his tone seems grouchier and less tractable than ever before. Both discs, though, sound excessively studio-bound, suggesting that Rollins could use a change of scene here. In his sixties, though, he is probably content to work at his own whim, which – on the basis of the extraordinary catalogue listed above – he has surely earned.

ALDO ROMANO (born 1941)
DRUMS

*** **Ritual** Owl 050 CD/LP

*** **To Be Ornette To Be** Owl 057 CD
Romano; Paolo Fresu (*t, flhn, syn*); Franco D'Andrea (*p*); Furio Di Castri (*b*). 2/88, 11/89.

If, at first glance, the Ornette Coleman 'tribute' seemed an improbable date for Romano, a few bars of 'The Blessing' are sufficient reminder of the Sicilian-born drummer's deep roots in progressive rock and in the 'harmolodic' autonomy of the rhythm line. The band dig a lot deeper here than on *Ritual*, which is much more obviously generic. The earlier album, though, has an emotional presence (or, as in the homage to the recently dead Chet Baker, 'Absence') which the Ornette covers don't communicate. Neither hesitant nor over-intellectualized (as the Hamlet tag might have warned), they're done with a rather casual assertiveness that is true to the spirit of the music (and its creator's personality) but which jars slightly with the band. Fresu has an open tone and an agreeably sensitive touch; on 'Absence', his phrasing sounds disconcertingly like Tom Harrell's. D'Andrea is an excellent performer, too, if a little fulsome for this repertoire, and only Di Castri seems rather anonymous. The leader, too sophisticated ever to be likened to Denardo Coleman, nevertheless has some of that bashing power, more like Charles Moffett's, perhaps. On 'W. R. U.' and the slithering 'Skies Of America' theme he resembles a cross between drummers at opposite ends of Ornette's career, Billy Higgins and Jack DeJohnette. And that's a mark of his quality, still underpraised.

DOM UM ROMAO (born 1925)
PERCUSSION

***(*)   **Samba De Rua** Muse 6012 CD
Romao; William Campbell (*t*); Jimmy Bossey (*tb*); Lloyd McNeil (*f*); Jerry Dodgion (*as, f*); Mauricio Smith (*ts, ss, f*); Joe Beck (*g*); Amaury Tristao (*g*); Dom Salvador (*p, electric p*); Richard Kimball (*syn*); Sivuca (*org, p, g*); Frank Tusa, Stanley Clarke (*b*); Eric Gravatt, Portinho (*perc*). 6 & 11/73, 75.

Dom Um Romao succeeded his pupil, Airto Moreira, as percussionist with Weather Report. He is still probably better known for his contributions to *I Sing The Body Electric* and *Sweetnighter* than for the two excellent albums above. *Samba De Rua* – the title means 'samba of the streets' – also features the unpredictable Eric Gravatt, Weather Report's greatest-ever drummer, in a percussion-dominated session that beats into craven submission all those lame *bossa nova* records that sold in tens of thousands. Romao boxes the entire Afro-Brazilian compass, switching from one drum to another and between the carefully systematized *ritmos*. The guitar-dominated arrangements are mostly convincing and only pall when they are self-consciously accommodated to jazz structures. His later work is in every way less impressive; the Muse was his first American recording and it remains the best. The energy level is consistently impressive and the instrumental pool intelligently deployed. Most of those who profess an allergy to 'Latin-American' treatments are actually suffering secondary reactions to unsuccessful crossovers. *Samba De Rua* is the real thing, a wholly successful fusion.

WALLACE RONEY (born 1960)
TRUMPET

***(*)   **Verses** Muse 5335 CD/LP
Roney; Gary Thomas (*ts*); Mulgrew Miller (*p*); Charnett Moffett (*b*); Tony Williams (*d*). 2/87.

***(*)   **Intuition** Muse 5346 CD/LP/MC
Roney; Kenny Garrett (*as*); Gary Thomas (*ts*); Mulgrew Miller (*p*); Ron Carter (*b*); Cindy Blackman (*d*); collective personnel. 1/88.

***   **The Standard Bearer** Muse 5371 CD/LP/MC
Roney; Gary Thomas (*ts*); Mulgrew Miller (*p*); Charnet Moffett (*b*); Cindy Blackman (*d*); Steve Berrios (*perc*). 3/89.

****   **Obsession** Muse 5423 CD
Roney; Gary Thomas (*ts, f*); Donald Brown (*p*); Christian McBride (*b*); Cindy Blackman (*d*). 90.

Wallace Roney brought a brief touch of edgy subtlety to the Jazz Messengers (see Arco 3 ARC 107 CD), a willingness to drift obliquely across and behind the beat which elicited knee-jerk and quite misleading comparisons with Miles Davis. While the open, modal charts and strong, independent rhythm of *Intuition* recalls the Davis bands of the early 1960s (Ron Carter confirms the lineage), Roney has a far more dynamic approach to phrasing than His Unpleasantness, recalling Fats Navarro and, at rather slower tempi, Howard McGhee, rather than Miles. Only on 'Willow Weep For Me', arranged for quartet with no reeds, does the comparison really hold. 'Blue In Green' on *Verses* is a clearly stated tribute that almost makes explicit the younger man's point of departure from Miles's influence.

Elsewhere on *Intuition*, Roney lays his deceptively discontinuous statements at an angle to the powerful rhythm section (Cindy Blackman is an impressive simulacra of Tony Williams, who contributes enormously to the success of *Verses*). The trumpeter sounds particularly good on the generously constructed 'For Duke', where the full sextet sounds like twice the band, an effect co-producers Williams and Michael Cuscuna achieve on the earlier album. 'Intuition' and 'Opus One Point Five' (minus Thomas) sound a little more pinched, with Garrett in acidulous form, keeping his blues tones deliberately flat and elided.

Verses is an album that gets better as it goes along and gains immeasurably from repeated hearings. Roney's variations on 'Blue In Green' at the close of the first half are very subtle and the second side of the original LP is brilliantly constructed, lifting the pace again with Cindy Blackman's 'Topaz', followed by Williams's harmonically subtle 'Lawra', closing with a long blowing blues called 'Slaves', on which Roney produces some of his finest touches.

The (George) Coleman sound-alike Thomas can't match Kenny Garrett's dry, funky delivery, but he is a more impressive performer on other people's albums than he is on his own increasingly funk-derived releases. 'The Way You Look Tonight' and 'Con Alma' on *Standard Bearer* suggest a greater interest in exploring standard material which Roney develops impressively on the recent *Obsession*. On the earlier album, 'Giant Steps' pushes the quintet into a more demanding format than orthodox hard bop. Thomas sits it out on 'Don't Blame Me' and 'When Your Lover Has Gone' and on the intriguing trumpet plus two percussion of 'Loose'. A fine album, but not up to the thoughtful presence of *Intuition*.

Obsession is the best of the bunch to date, and in some respects the most conventional. Roney seems to have settled for a more direct and expressive approach, reaching back to Navarro's balance of virtuosity and lyricism. The set includes a breakneck version of the bop staple 'Donna Lee' and a far from creaking version of the overworked 'Alone Together', on which Thomas respectfully emulates Eric Dolphy's flute playing. An impressively mature record from Thomas, who has only just turned 30.

BERNT ROSENGREN (born 1937)
TENOR SAX

** **Surprise Party** Steeplechase SCS 1177 LP
Rosengren; Horace Parlan (*p*); Doug Raney (*g*); Jesper Lundgaard (*b*); Aage Tanggaard (*d*). 3/83.

** **Live!** Dragon DRLP 55 LP
Rosengren; Maffay Falay (*t, flhn*); Hakan Nyquist (*frhn*); Tommy Koverhult (*ss, ts*); Krister Andersson (*ts, cl*); Gunnar Bergsten (*bs*); Goran Lindberg (*p*); Doug Raney (*g*); Torbjörn Hultcrantz (*b*); Ole Jacob Hansen (*d*). 9/83.

(*) **Summit Meeting Phontastic PHONT 7560 LP
Rosengren; Nisse Sandstrom (*ts*); Goran Lindberg (*p*); Olle Steinholtz (*b*); Leroy Lowe (*d*). 1/84.

Rosengren has a considerable reputation and as a result these unassuming records are a bit disappointing. *Surprise Party* emerges as just another Steeplechase hard-bop session, well done and without any surprises. *Live!* features ten standards in sanguine arrangements that perk up only with the solos: 'Blue In Green' is sparely done, but the same technique makes 'Darn That Dream' merely lugubrious. The two-tenor session with Lindstrom gives the best indication of what Rosengren can do: his Zoot Sims-like tone and bursts of double-time phrasing are a bright if not exactly potent match for Sandstrom's similar improvising.

MICHELE ROSEWOMAN
PIANO

****   **Quintessence** Enja 5039 CD/LP
Rosewoman; Steve Coleman (*as*); Greg Osby (*as, ss*); Anthony Cox (*b*); Terri Lyne
Carrington (*d*). 1/87.

***   **Contrast High** Enja 5091 CD/LP
Rosewoman; Greg Osby (*as, ss*); Gary Thomas (*ts, f*); Lonnie Plaxico (*b*); Cecil
Brooks III (*d*). 7/88.

Like Geri Allen's, Michele Rosewoman's music is deeply marked by an intensive study not just
of the jazz tradition in its widest construction but of a huge range of other musics. Though she
now rarely plays in a straightforward 'Latin' context, the propulsive rhythms of Caribbean –
and particularly Cuban – music are always evident, almost casually intermingled with an angular
approach synthesized from Monk and Cecil Taylor. Less fêted than either Allen or Marilyn
Crispell, she is a player and composer of consummate skill.

Quintessence is the better of the two albums, and the most representative of the range of her
skills. The opening 'For Now And Forever' has a stop-start theme which is momentarily
reminiscent of the early-1970s Ornette Coleman. 'Lyons', a twin-alto tribute to the late Jimmy
Lyons, is cast in a robust late-bop mode that paves the way for the more adventurous
Taylorisms of 'Springular And Springle'; after that, the ironic ballad 'The Thrill-of-Real-Love'
comes as rather less of a shock. Osby sounds better with Coleman than with the occasionally
wayward Gary Thomas on *Contrast High*, and the *Quintessence* rhythm section is much better
attuned to Rosewoman's unpredictable metre.

The later album swings with all of Rosewoman's characteristic exuberance but sounds more
of an artefact, a great deal less adventurous and dangerous. *Quintessence* communicates the
kind of imaginative range and adaptability she shares with Geri Allen and which has allowed
her to work successfully in almost every setting, from conventional piano trio up to the New
Yoruba big band, which she leads. One of the best jazz albums of the late 1980s.

RENÉE ROSNES (born 1962)
PIANO, KEYBOARDS

(*)   **Renée Rosnes Blue Note CDP 7935612 CD
Rosnes; Branford Marsalis (*ss, ts*); Wayne Shorter (*ss*); Ralph Bowen (*ts*); Herbie
Hancock (*p*); Ron Carter (*b*); Lewis Nash (*d*). 4/88–2/89.

***(*)   **For The Moment** Blue Note CDP 7948592 CD
Rosnes; Steve Wilson (*ss, as*); Joe Henderson (*ts*); Ira Coleman (*b*); Billy Drummond
(*d*). 2/90.

Rosnes is a Canadian who came to early attention in an all-female rhythm section which backed
Joe Henderson for a time (she has continued to work with Henderson in his touring band).
These two sessions are pleasing records that don't quite catch fire but have plenty of solid
playing in them. She has a sensitive touch and her classical background persuades her into
offering hints of some study-composers in her voicings, and she can swing very hard, too.
Marsalis and Shorter take rather glib guest-star roles on the first record, but the second benefits
from Henderson's magisterial presence and there is a very good 'Four In One' and a dazzlingly
executed version of the standard, 'Summer Night', which goes through seemingly endless
rhythmical variations. Coleman and Drummond might not be her ideal rhythm section but they
play very gamely.

FRANK ROSOLINO (1926–78)
TROMBONE

****   **Free For All** Original Jazz Classics OJC 1763 CD/LP/MC
Rosolino; Harold Land (*ts*); Victor Feldman (*p*); Leroy Vinnegar (*b*); Stan Levey (*d*).

Coming of age in Gene Krupa's post-war band, Rosolino developed a style that seemed to combine elements of bop harmony with the more durable virtues of swing. A wonderfully agile player, with a tone that could be broad and humane, almost vocalized, one moment, thinly abstract the next, Rosolino brings a twist of humour to almost everything he plays. The OJC rounds out a fine session done for the Speciality label with some valuable alternative takes ('There Is No Greater Love', 'Chrisdee' and 'Don't Take Your Love From Me') and some great performances from the band that belie the undisciplined mood suggested by the title. Rosolino's end could hardly have been grimmer. In the autumn of 1978, suffering from depression, his murdered his children and then took his own life.

ANNIE ROSS (born 1930)
VOCALS

[*** **Annie Ross Sings** Original Jazz Classics OJC 217 CD/LP/MC]
Ross: George Wallington, Teacho Wiltshire (*p*); Ram Ramirez (*org*); Percy Heath (*b*); Art Blakey (*d*). 10/52.

***(*) **Sings A Song With Mulligan** Pacific Jazz CDP 7488522 CD
Ross; Chet Baker, Art Farmer (*t*); Gerry Mulligan (*bs*); Bill Crow, Henry Grimes (*b*); Dave Bailey (*d*). 12/57.

*** **A Gasser!** Pacific Jazz CDP 7468542 CD
Ross; Bill Perkins, Zoot Sims (*ts*); Russ Freeman (*p*); Billy Bean, Jim Hall (*g*); Monty Budwig (*b*); Frank Capp, Mel Lewis (*d*). 3/59.

Though best known as one-third of Lambert, Hendricks and Ross, the leading exponents of vocalized bop and swing, Annie Ross has had a substantial solo career. This album, shared with King Pleasure (q.v.), is all that survives under her own name. Fortunately, it preserves the remarkable 'Twisted', a tongue-knotting vocal version of Wardell Gray's tenor saxophone solo, recently revived by the young soul singer Crystal Waters. Ross's dark humour (improbably, she is the half-sister of Scots 'comedian' Jimmy Logan) is a characteristic quality of her work, most notable on 'Twisted', but also evident on 'Farmer's Market' and the wry 'Annie's Lament'.
    Technically, she is an extraordinary performer; her soft but inch-perfect scatting led to an inevitable comparison with Ella Fitzgerald, but there's a lorn weariness in her delivery (see particularly 'You're Nearer' on *A Gasser!*) which Ella wouldn't have risked. The 1959 sessions are much less successful than the slightly earlier Pacifics. Ross's voice is a shade uncertain and she seems to have difficulty holding even middle register notes, as if she is suffering breathing difficulties.
    Without any doubt, her timing is not as exact as it is on 'I Guess I'll Have To Change My Plan' on *With Mulligan* and the baritonist is a much more sensitive accompanist than Sims, who seems to take each song off in a different direction, leaving Ross to bring it back when the instrumental solos are over. The earlier album includes a couple of interesting alternate takes and has a slightly more even sound. Ross probably did her best work with Dave Lambert and John Hendricks; as a 'straight' singer, she's inclined to be predictable. But for the fact that the OJC is only a share of an album, it would be the album of choice.

THOM ROTELLA (born 1954)
GUITAR

* **Thom Rotella Band** dmp CD 461 CD
Rotella; Mark Minchello (*ky*); Wayne Pedzwater (*b*); Clint DeGanon (*d*); David Charles (*perc*). 8/87.

*(*) **Home Again** dmp CD 469 CD
Rotella; Jim Studer, Mike Lang (*ky*); Abe Laboriel (*b*); Carlos Vega (*d*); Lenny Castro, Michito Sanchez (*perc*). 4/89.

*(*) **Without Words** dmp CD 476 CD
Rotella; Phil Ayling (*rec*); Jim Studer, Mike Lang (*ky*); Jolyon Pegis (*clo*); Abraham Laboriel (*b*); Carlos Vega (*d*); Alex Acuna (*perc*). 5/90.

Rotella's first record for dmp claims a 'band' status for his accompanists, but it's difficult to see their role as other than limp background players for a guitarist whose pretty solos are consistently vapid and lacking in substance. By the second and third records, familiar sessionmen had taken over the backing. The results are marginally more appealing, but no more interesting. The recording maintains the company's impeccable digital standards.

CHARLIE ROUSE (1924–88)
TENOR SAXOPHONE

***(*) **Takin' Care Of Business** Original Jazz Classics OJC 491 CD/LP/MC
Rouse; Blue Mitchell (t); Walter Bishop (p); Earl May (b); Arthur Taylor (d). 5/60.

***(*) **Unsung Hero** Columbia 46181 CD/MC
Rouse; Billy Gardner, Gildo Mahones (p); Peck Morrison, Reggie Workman (b);
Dave Bailey, Arthur Taylor (d). 12/60, 7/61.

*** **Moment's Notice** Storyville JC 4 LP
Rouse; Hugh Lawson (p); Bob Cranshaw (b); Ben Riley (d). 10/77.

**** **Epistrophy** Landmark 1521 CD/LP/MC
Rouse; Don Cherry (t); George Cables (p); Buddy Montgomery (vib); Jeff Chambers
(b); Ralph Penland (d); Jessica Williams (v). 10/88.

Rouse always played saxophone as if he had a cold in the head. There were those who questioned whether his slightly adenoidal, wuffling tone was ever appropriate to Thelonious Monk's music. However, Rouse became one of Monk's most loyal and stalwart supporters, and an essential part of some of Monk's finest quartet recordings. Rouse also carried the banner posthumously in his band Sphere, and in such tribute recordings as the not entirely successful *Epistrophy*, recorded just a month before his death.

Much as Monk was actually more influenced by classic jazz and swing than by bebop, so Rouse drew unashamedly on Ben Webster, particularly in his ballad playing. 'When Sunny Gets Blue' and 'There Is No Greater Love' on the aptly titled *Unsung Hero* are excellent examples. On more upbeat numbers, he reverts to the slightly staccato address familiar from the Monk group and reconstructed on the Landmark set.

Even without undue hindsight, *Epistrophy* sounds like a final throw. He runs through the songbook – 'Nutty', 'Ruby, My Dear', 'Blue Monk', 'Round Midnight', 'Epistrophy', and a CD bonus 'In Walked Bud' – with magisterial calm; much of the interest comes from the still undiscovered Jessica Williams, a fine piano player and singer, and from Buddy Montgomery's spikey vibes. Rouse invests each of the numbers with the kind of rhythmic slant that is inalienably bound up with Monk's legacy. Among the earlier sessions, 'Well You Needn't' on *Moment's Notice* is a classic performance. 'Pretty Strange', 'Wierdo' and 'Upptankt' on *Takin' Care of Business* show how well Rouse anticipated Monk's approach and appreciated the level of resistance to it. A communicator rather than a pioneer, he must have found it strange and galling to be pushed out of view with the rest of the 'avant-garde'. On the strength of each of these, Rouse was 'in the tradition', centrally and majestically.

ROVA
GROUP

** **This, This, This, This** Moers Music 01080 LP
Larry Ochs, Bruce Ackley, Andrew Voight, Jon Raskin (reeds). 8/79.

ROVA made their first five albums within a space of twelve months, but this is the only one still available. Along with the World Saxophone Quartet, they helped to popularize the all-sax ensemble and suggest the multiplicity of directions which such a unit could explore. ROVA's principal energies were directed at different goals to the WSQ: whereas the other group were more interested in refashioning the swing and harmonic richness of big-band sax sections, ROVA sought to extend the areas explored by the Chicago avant-garde of the 1960s and '70s. Their collectivism is based on more abstract kinds of interaction, as suggested by the ongoing sequence of 'Trobar Clkus' compositions, and their ideas have as much to do with sound and space as with conventional kinds of counterpoint and harmony. There are very few instances of solos-with-accompaniment in what they do. An absence of any rhythmic imperatives does, though, make their music rather hard going. This early release offers a glimpse of the group in some creative flux: sour and sometimes laborious sequences make it hard going, but there are rewarding moments in 'Exiles' in particular.

***   **Saxophone Diplomacy** Hat Art CD 6068 CD
    As above. 6/83.

ROVA's 1983 tour of the Soviet Union resulted in this concert set, easily the most vivid evidence of their work up to that point. It includes two of their Steve Lacy arrangements, an extended revision of 'Flamingo Horizons' from the Moers album, and one long piece – 'Paint Another Take Of The Shootpop' – which personifies their virtues, starting with a methodically intense tenor solo by Ochs and marching into a complex development from there. The section on the original vinyl release which also featured two Russian musicians has been omitted from the CD issue. The concert recordings are of mixed quality, but there are no distracting shortcomings.

***   **Favourite Street** Black Saint BSR 0076 CD
    As above. 11/83.

***(*)   **Beat Kennel** Black Saint BSR 0126 CD/LP
    As above. 4/87.

Steve Lacy has been belatedly recognized as a major patrician influence on a wide spectrum of modern players, and ROVA's homage to him on *Favourite Street* pays overdue tribute. The bony rigour of Lacy's themes focuses ROVA's meandering, no matter how adventurous their earlier trips had been: Lacy's music is a good way to clear the head of distractions, either as listener or performer, and in their thoughtful elaborations on seven favourite themes they clear away some of the more baroque elements of their work. The subsequent *Beat Kennel* appears to build on this: in 'The Aggregate' and 'Sportspeak', their assured rhythms and tone colours pull them closer to a jazz tradition, and in their vibrant reading of a Braxton composition (superior to anything on their disappointing collaboration with the saxophonist himself, listed under Braxton's name) they create distinctive jazz repertory. It's the best record they've made.

JIMMY ROWLES (born 1918)
PIANO, VOCAL

****   **We Could Make Such Beautiful Music Together** Xanadu 157/EPM 5152 CD/LP
    Rowles; George Mraz (*b*); Leroy Williams (*d*). 4/78.

***   **Isfahan** Sonet SNTCD/ZCSN 790 CD/MC
    Rowles; George Mraz (*b*). 5/78.

His vast experience with both big bands and vocalists gave Rowles a matchless repertoire of songs, and since the early 1970s he has appeared as a significant figure in his own right. A number of albums have disappeared from print, including his early sessions as a leader from the 1950s, but those still available provide a fine portrait of this humorous, profound musician. The Xanadu is an almost perfect introduction to his work: eight standards range from warhorses such as 'I Can't Get Started' to the nearly forgotten 'How Do You Do Miss Josephine', and in each case the treatment is inimitable. He begins with a bossa nova version of 'Stars And Stripes Forever', the melody altered with sublime cunning, salutes his friend Errol Garner with 'Shake It But Don't Break It' and insinuates 'The Girl From Ipanema' into 'In The Still Of The Night'. His ideal rhythm section is a bassist who plays a rich, songful counterpoint and a drummer who keeps well out of the way, and Mraz and Williams do exactly what's required. The EPM CD issue includes ten minutes of extra material. *Isfahan* is a shade less involving although superior sound reveals more of Rowles's sonorities.

(*)   **The Jimmy Rowles/Red Mitchell Trio Contemporary C-14016 LP
    Rowles; Stacy Rowles (*t, flhn*); Red Mitchell (*b*); Colin Bailey (*d*). 3/85.

**   **Looking Back** Delos DE 4009 CD
    Rowles; Stacy Rowles (*t, flhn, v*); Eric Von Essen (*b*); Donald Bailey (*d*). 6/88.

*** **Sometimes I'm Happy, Sometimes I'm Blue** Orange Blue 003 CD
Rowles; Harry Edison (*t*); Stacy Rowles (*t, flhn*); Ray Brown (*b*); Donald Bailey (*d*); Clementine (*v*). 6/88.

*** **Trio** Capri 74009 CD
Rowles; Red Mitchell (*b*); Donald Bailey (*d*). 8/89.

Rowles recorded through the 1980s, and while none of these records is less than good, it must be said that the energy level on some of them is occasionally negligible. The pianist's talent for reordering tunes and imparting felicities hasn't diminished, but he has taken things much easier of late. His trumpet-playing daughter Stacy plays a useful guest role on some sessions, playing agreeable solos which recall a more boppish Harry Edison, whose own appearance on the Orange Blue CD underlines the comparison, although the two never play together. The Contemporary session is more mixed, and the Delos record is sluggish, the players becoming so ruminative that the music slows to a tepid pace. But *Trio* restores some of the impishness which is an essential in Rowles's best music, as he investigates such hoary themes as 'Dreamer's Lullaby' and 'You People Need Music'. Red Mitchell, who plays on three of the above sessions, is a favourite companion, and his voluminous sound is a wry partner for Rowles's particular tale-spinning; Bailey, though, is less in tune, and occasionally sounds indifferent to the conversation.

RICK ROZIE
DOUBLE BASS

*(*) **Afro Algonquin** Moers 01078 LP
Rozie; Lee Rozie (*ts, ss, f, perc*); Rashied Ali (*d*). 5/80.

Almost as stylistically confused as the title suggests, this seems to trade in individual skills for a remarkably bland group sound that struggles to hold the attention. Nominally a Rozie Trio record, it's the bassist and drummer who capture the bulk of attention, leaving the saxophone player to run through what sounds like a check-list of modernist devices and quasi-politicized aesthetic gestures. No.

GONZALO RUBALCABA (born 1963)
PIANO

(*) **Discovery: Live At Montreux Blue Note CDP 7954782 CD
Rubalcaba; Charlie Haden (*b*); Paul Motian (*d*). 7/90.

**** **The Blessing** Blue Note CDP 7971972 CD
As above, except Jack DeJohnette (*d*) replaces Motian. 5/91.

Rubalcaba is the most recent and perhaps the most singular of those Cuban musicians who have made an impact on the American jazz scene of late. While he plays with as much grandstanding power as his countrymen, there is also a compensating lightness of touch which one sometimes misses in the perpetually ebullient tone of most Cuban jazz. *Discovery*, a record of his sensational debut appearance at the Montreux Festival of 1990, suffers from an excess of tumult which finally makes the record wearisome, impressively played though it all is. From the first, terrifically overheated workout on Monk's 'Well You Needn't', it sounds as if Rubalcaba is out to impress at any cost, and Motian and Haden can only anchor him as best they can. Much exhilaration, but not a record to play often.

The subsequent studio record, *The Blessing*, is a huge step forward. The pianist rations his outbursts to a handful and instead negotiates a thoughtful but no less compelling way through a delightful programme: Haden's 'Sandino' emerges with just the right note of troubled dignity, 'Giant Steps' is reharmonized and made new through brilliant use of repetition, DeJohnette's charming 'Silver Hollow' rivals the composer's own version, and 'The Blessing' and 'Blue In Green' remodel Coleman and Evans. Best of all, perhaps, is a beautifully chiselled treatment of 'Besame Mucho' which eliminates all sense of kitsch that the tune may possess, suggesting instead a flinty sort of romanticism. Rubalcaba's touch and finesse are marvellous throughout, and DeJohnette is clearly the ideal drummer for the situation, his unassuming virtuosity meeting all the challenges head on. Highly recommnded.

ROSWELL RUDD (born 1935)
TROMBONE

***(*) **Regeneration** Soul Note SN 1054 CD/LP
Rudd; Steve Lacy (*ss*); Misha Mengelberg (*p*); Kent Carter (*b*); Han Bennink (*d*).
6/82.

It's been a matter of intense frustration that Rudd has made so few records, since his work with the New York Art Quartet and Archie Shepp in the 1960s announced a marvellously vivid and unpredictable spirit in the new jazz of the period. Rudd, like Ayler, suggested a return to primordial jazz roots while remaining entirely modern. His trombone style recalled the more expressionist methods of an earlier age – slurs and growls, blustering swing, a big, sultry tone – while remaining aware of the technical sophistry of the few boppers who'd taken to the horn. Yet he has led fewer than ten albums over a long, interrupted career.

This one, at least, is very satisfying although, for a demonstration of Rudd's latter-day style, Enrico Rava's *Quartet* album for ECM is a more comprehensive example. *Regeneration* is a tribute to the pianist-composer Herbie Nichols, whom Rudd worked with in the early 1960s. The trombonist has campaigned against Nichols's neglect ever since; and with the similarly inclined Lacy – who also once worked with Rudd, in a band which only played Thelonious Monk tunes – he devised a tribute programme which includes three pieces by each composer. The Nichols tunes are the most absorbing, if only because they're much less familiar than 'Monk's Mood', 'Friday The 13th' and 'Epistrophy'.

HILTON RUIZ (born 1952)
PIANO

**** **Piano Man** Steeplechase SCS 1036 CD/LP
Ruiz; Buster Williams (*b*); Billy Higgins (*d*). 7/75.

Ruiz's desire to give jazz a Latin accent runs a little deeper than the usual South-of-the-Border trimmings. Born in Puerto Rico, he has a profound understanding of an impressive range of popular forms – samba, *soca*, *clave* – and makes them an integral element in his writing and reworking of standards and classics. This is perhaps Ruiz's best album; it's certainly his most impressive group, with Williams's singing bass and Higgins's tuneful drums complementing his own two-handed style. 'Straight Street' and 'Giant Steps' are the most ambitious (and successful) tracks. Strongly recommended.

*** **Excition** Steeplechase SCS 1078 LP
Ruiz; Richard Williams (*t*); Frank Foster (*ts, ss*); Buster Williams (*b*); Roy Brooks (*d*).

(*) **Steppin' Into Beauty Steeplechase SCS 1158 LP
As above, except add Hakim Jamil (*b*), Steve Solder (*d*). 2/77.

(*) **New York Hilton Steeplechase SCS 1094 LP
Ruiz; Hakim Jamil (*b*); Steve Solder (*d*). 2/77.

Though much less compelling than the earlier trio, the combination of Jamil and Solder is highly responsive to Ruiz's concept. *New York Hilton* leads off with a dedication to Mary Lou Williams, which calls for a much larger arrangement. Otherwise, the trio seems to be Ruiz's natural turf, accommodating his easy swing and allowing him room for some of his more ambitious, long-lined solos. The addition of horns works well on the up-beat *Excition*, and Richard Williams is always worth hearing. *Steppin'* merely rounds out the busy early February sessions from 1977 and is much less coherent as a package.

*** **Strut** Novus/RCA PL 83053 CD/LP/MC
Ruiz; Lew Soloff (*t*); Dick Griffin (*tb*); Sam Rivers (*ts, ss*); Rodney Jones (*g*);
Francisco Centeno (*b*); Robert Ameen (*d, perc*); Steve Berrios, Mongo Santamaria
(*perc*). 11 & 12/88.

Ruiz's attempt to Latinize the standards repertoire continues. 'Lush Life' has long been susceptible to Latin readings, but this is more convincing and integral than most. The *soca*-flavoured 'Serenade' is slightly wishy-washy, but 'The Sidewinder' has some of the bite one associates with Ruiz's better work. Top-ranking talent in the brass, reeds and percussion, and a convincing fusion exercise all told.

*** **Doin' It Right** Novus/RCA PD 83085 CD/MC
Ruiz; Don Cherry (*t*); Jimmy Ronson, Ruben Rodriguez (*b*); Steve Berrios (*d, perc*); Daniel Ponce (*perc*). 11/89.

More self-consciously eclectic (as Cherry's brief presence may indicate) than either its predecessors or successors, *Doin' It Right* is a more demanding package than most of Ruiz's 1980s recordings. Beautifully recorded and balanced, its immediate accessibility peels away to reveal a well-structured exploration of post-Bud piano styles. Shedding his occasional dips into modal blandness, Ruiz plays with considerable fire at the far right of the keyboard. 'Stella By Starlight' conjures up one of his most evocative and technically impressive solos, and the other material – 'The Blessing', 'Scottish Blues', 'I Didn't Know What Time It Was' foremost – is expertly sequenced with something close to Ahmad Jamal's genius for putting together a coherent and emotionally satisfying set. Somehow it's the *feel* of the group as a whole that lets this one down.

**** **A Moment's Notice** Novus/RCA PD 83123 CD/MC
Ruiz; George Coleman (*ts*); Kenny Garrett (*as*); Dave Valentin (*f*); Andy Gonzales, Joe Santiago (*b*); Steve Berrios (*d, perc*); Endel Dweno, Daniel Ponce (*perc*). 2 & 3/91.

A superb set that takes in Coltrane, Kenny Dorham's 'Una Mas' and Jimmy Van Heusen's 'Like Someone In Love'. The concluding 'Naima' sounds slightly odd over the neurotic voodoo percussion, but the romantic urgency of Kenny Garrett's fine solo is focused rather than blunted by it; turning the spotlight on the alto helps recentre the piece. 'Moment's Notice' is more readily recast in Ruiz's now familiar mode, but the two horns find less to say. 'Jose' is a generous but questionable solo feature for bassist Joe Santiago. Forgivable at less than a minute and a half, and perfectly OK in a club or concert context, it seems rather out of place here, interrupting a finely judged and flowing set that shows Ruiz at the height of his considerable powers.

JIMMY RUSHING (1903–72)
VOCAL

***(*) **The Essential Jimmy Rushing** Vanguard VCD 65/66 CD
Rushing; Pat Jenkins, Emmett Berry (*t*); Henderson Chambers, Lawrence Brown, Vic Dickenson (*tb*); Ben Richardson, Rudy Powell (*as*); Buddy Tate (*ts*); Sam Price, Pete Johnson, Clarence Johnson (*p*); Marlowe Morris (*org*); Freddie Greene, Roy Gaines (*g*); Walter Page, Aaron Bell (*b*); Jo Jones (*d*). 12/54–3/57.

Jimmy Rushing began recording in 1929, with Bennie Moten, and continued for 40 years. Many of his finest performances are with Count Basie and are listed under the bandleader's name, but Rushing also cut plenty of good records under his own name. This CD creams off the pick of three sessions done for Vanguard in the mid-1950s. The first includes a near-definitive 'How Long Blues' with some effulgent piano from Sam Price and the most boisterous 'Sent For You Yesterday' which he ever recorded; the second is backed by an all-star band (Tate, Brown, Berry, Johnson) on five variations of the blues; the third is more of the same, with Dickenson's trombone as a bonus. Rushing is in good voice throughout.

***(*) **The You And Me That Used To Be** Bluebird NL/ND/NK 86460 CD/LP/MC
Rushing; Ray Nance (*c, vn*); Budd Johnson (*ss*); Zoot Sims, Al Cohn (*ts*); Dave Frishberg (*p*); Milt Hinton (*b*); Mel Lewis (*d*). 4/71.

Jimmy's last record. His own voice sounds bruised after four decades of blues shouting, but his spirit is undimmed, and the two groups involved – one with Sims and Nance, the other with Cohn and Johnson – work magnificently. Frishberg (who also did the arrangements) plays quirky piano against Hinton and Lewis at their most swinging, and Nance is simply extraordinary – his violin introduction to 'When I Grow Too Old To Dream' is enough to make the record essential, and his cornet solos are as good as anything he did with Ellington. Rushing and Frishberg go on to perform a duet version of 'I Surrender Dear' which is a moving farewell to a great jazz singer.

GEORGE RUSSELL (born 1923)
COMPOSER, BANDLEADER, PIANO, ORGAN

***(*)   **Jazz Workshop** Bluebird/BMG ND 86467 CD
Russell; Art Farmer (*t*); Hal McKusick (*as, f*); Bill Evans (*p*); Barry Galbraith (*g*); Milt Hinton, Teddy Kotick (*b*); Joe Harris, Osie Johnson, Paul Motian (*d*). 3, 10 & 12/56.

***   **Stratusphunk** Original Jazz Classics OJC 232 LP
Russell; Alan Kiger (*t*); Dave Baker (*tb*); Dave Young (*as*); Chuck Israels (*b*); Joe Hunt (*d*). 10/60

****   **Ezz-thetics** Original Jazz Classics OJC 070 CD
Russell; Don Ellis (*t*); Dave Baker (*tb*); Eric Dolphy (*as, bcl*); Steve Swallow (*b*); Joe Hunt (*d*). 5/61.

***(*)   **Outer Thoughts** Milestone 47027 2LP
Russell; Don Ellis, Alan Kiger (*t*); Dave Baker, Garnett Brown (*tb*); Eric Dolphy (*as, bcl*); John Pierce (*as*); Paul Plummer, Dave Young (*ts*); Chuck Israels, Steve Swallow (*b*); Joe Hunt, Pete La Roca (*d*); Sheila Jordan (*v*). 10/60, 5/61, 1/62, 8/62.

***(*)   **The Stratus Seekers** Original Jazz Classics OJC 365 CD/LP/MC
Russell; Dave Baker, Don Ellis (*t*); John Pierce (*as*); Paul Plummer (*ts*); Steve Swallow (*b*); Joe Hunt (*d*).

(*)   **The Outer View Original Jazz Classics OJC 616 CD/LP/MC
Russell; Garnett Brown (*tb*); Paul Plummer (*ts*); Steve Swallow (*b*); Pete La Roca (*d*); Sheila Jordan (*v*).

It would be difficult to overstate George Russell's significance within jazz or the degree to which he has been marginalized by the critical and commercial establishment. Russell is responsible for what remains the most significant single theoretical treatise written about the music. *The Lydian Chromatic Concept Of Tonal Organization*, completed in the early 1950s, was the direct source of the modal or scalar experiments of John Coltrane and Miles Davis. Sometimes falsely identified with the original Greek Lydian mode, it is not in fact the same at all. In diatonic terms, it represents the progression F to F on the piano's white keys; it also confronts the diabolic tritone, the *diabolus in musica*, which had haunted Western composers from Bach to Beethoven.

Russell's conception assimilated modal writing to the extreme chromaticism of modern music. By converting chords into scales, and overlaying one scale on another, it allowed improvisers to work in the hard-to-define area between non-tonality and polytonality. Like all great theoreticians, Russell worked analytically rather than synthetically, basing his ideas on how jazz *actually was*, not on how it could be made to conform with traditional principles of Western harmony. Working from within jazz's often tacit organizational principles, Russell's fundamental concern was the relationship between formal scoring and improvisation, giving the first the freedom of the second, freeing the second from being literally esoteric, 'outside' some supposed norm.

Russell's theories also influenced his own composition. 'A Bird In Igor's Yard' was a (rather too) self-conscious attempt to ally bebop and Stravinsky – it was also a young and slightly immature work – but it pointed the way forward. Russell's music always sounds both familiar and unsettlingly alien. His versions of staples like Charlie Parker's 'Au Privave', Thelonious Monk's equally precocious 'Round Midnight', and Miles Davis's almost oriental 'Nardis' on *Ezz-thetics* (and on the compilation *Outer Thoughts*, which also brings together material from *The Stratus Seekers* and *The Outer View*; the latter includes a remarkable performance of 'You Are My Sunshine') create new areas for the soloists to explore; in Don Ellis and Eric Dolphy he has players particularly responsive to expansions of the harmonic language (Dolphy in particular preferred to work the inner space of a piece, rather than to go 'out'). Other important originals on *Outer Thoughts* include the much-covered 'Stratusphunk' and 'The Stratus Seekers', further instances of Russell's doubly punning style; both titles and tunes suggest two directions of meaning. 'Ezz-thetic' first appeared on the classic 1956 *Jazz Workshop* sessions, reissued in a very welcome CD format as Bluebird ND 86467; it also contains the wonderful 'Night Sound' (with its Chopin and Bartók resonances) and 'Round Johnny Rondo' which, like 'Concerto For Billy The Kid', suggests a Copland influence. These and the excellent *Outer Thoughts* make a very good start to a Russell collection, but there's a case to be made for the two individual LPs, and *Ezz-thetics* in particular, with its fine Dolphy contributions. Coincidentally or not, the year of the saxophonist's death also marked the beginning of Russell's long exile in Europe and a mutual alienation from the American scene.

**   **Othello Ballet Suite/Electronic Organ Sonata No. 1** Soul Note 1014 CD/LP
         Russell; Rolf Ericson (*t*); Arne Domnérus (*as*); Bernt Rosengren (*ts*); Jan Garbarek
         (*ts*); Jon Christensen (*d*); others unknown. 1/67.

Conducting the exuberant big bands of the 1980s, Russell bore a striking physical resemblance to the choreographer, Merce Cunningham. There was a dancemaster's precision to his gestures that was communicated through his music as well. Russell's conception of harmonic space is somewhat like a modern choreographer's. The *Othello Ballet Suite* is only the most obvious example of how his imagination turns on movement – in this case, the curiously inward movements of Shakespeare's play – and on the formation of black identity in the West.

The music is more stately than passionate, with an almost ritualistic quality to its development. Russell's orchestration is curiously reminiscent of Ravel, and cloys in consequence; the saxophones sound slightly out of pitch. The *Electronic Organ Sonata* is rather superficial, too obvious an essay in Russell's harmonic and structural ideas to be entirely involving. The sound on both pieces, though, is good, and both are highly significant in his development of a non-canonical but systematic musical language.

***   **Electronic Sonata For Souls Loved By Nature** Soul Note SN 1034 LP
         Russell; Manfred Schoof (*t*); Jan Garbarek (*ts*); Terje Rypdal (*g*); Red Mitchell (*b*);
         Jon Christensen (*d*). 4/69.

(*)   **Electronic Sonata For Souls Loved By Nature 1980 Soul Note SN 1009 LP
         Russell; Lew Soloff (*t*); Robert Moore (*ts, ss*); Victor Gomer (*g*); Jean-François
         Jenny-Clark (*b*); Keith Copeland (*d, perc*). 6/80.

**   **Trip To Prillargui** Soul Note SN 1029 LP
         Russell; Stanton Davis (*t*); Jan Garbarek (*ts*); Terje Rypdal (*g*); Arild Andersen (*b*);
         Jon Christensen (*d*). 3/70.

For all the quality of the performances, these are conceptually woolly and rather abstract works that add no more than grace-notes to Russell's remarkable compositional output. In the triumvirate of great arrangers, Russell is closer to the open texture of Gil Evans than to Quincy Jones's lacquered surface. There is a sense, though, with these performances that surface is all that matters. The original *Electronic Sonata* has a depth of perspective and firmness of execution that the still-puzzling 1980 revision totally lacks. Conceived for tapes and ensemble, the piece is again chiefly concerned with the relationship between scored and improvised materials. *Trip To Prillargui* is beautifully played but sounds curiously emptied of significance and yields no more on repeated hearings.

(*)   **Listen To The Silence Soul Note SN 1024 LP
         Russell; Stanton Davis (*t*); Jan Garbarek (*ts*); Bobo Stenson (*electric p*); Webster
         Lewis (*org*); Terje Rypdal (*g*); Arild Andersen (*b*); Jon Christensen (*d*); solo voices;
         chorus. 6/71.

Billed as 'A Mass For Our Time', *Listen To The Silence* betrays all the aesthetic and philosophical confusions of Michael Tippett's blues-influenced post-war oratorio, *A Child Of Our Time*. To argue that it is not strictly a 'jazz' work is to miss a critical point about Russell's musical language, which exists in rather special, simultaneously respectful and ironic, relation to the 'jazz' tradition. Russell habitually divides his works into 'events' rather than movements, suggesting irreducibility rather than progression. The upshot is that there is only incidental emotional and structural connection between the segments and the whole founders. Russell's handling of voices is uneasy, and the vocal and instrumental lines don't sit comfortably with one another. There is a fine live version of Parts One and Two on Soul Note SN 1039, which shows how the music might be unfrozen; as it stands, it is like an old-fashioned tridentine Mass, impressive but more than forbidding.

**(*)   Vertical Form VI Soul Note SN 1019 LP
Russell; Americo Bellotto, Bertil Lovgren (*t, flhn*); Hakan Hyquist (*t, flhn, frhn*); Jan Allan (*t, frhn*); Ivar Olsen (*frhn*); Bengt Edvarsson, Jorgen Johansson, Lars Olofsson (*tb*); Sven Larsson (*btb, tba*); Arne Domnérus (*cl, as, ss*); Jan Uling (*f, as, ts*); Lennart Aberg, Bernt Rosengren (*f, as, ts, ss*); Erik Nilsson (*f, bcl, bs*); Rune Gustafsson (*g*); Bjorn Lind (*electric p*); Vlodek Gulgowski (*electric p, syn*); Monica Dominique (*electric p, cel, org, clavinet*); Stefan Brolund, Bronislaw Suchanek, Lars-Urban Helje (*b*); Lars Beijbon, Leroy Lowe (*d*); Sabu Martinez (*perc*). 3/77.

If we're looking for appropriate visual analogies, *Vertical Form VI* is less like an upright menhir than another kind of standing stone. The dolmen has a huge, slabby top perched on unfeasibly skinny supports. By that analogy Russell's piece has considerable mass and gravitational force, but seems to rest on nothing more than the bare uprights of theory, with little or no emotional engagement. The band is well drilled and produces a big, generous sound that might well benefit from CD transfer. Once encountered, though, the music seems just to sit there, much involved with its own enigma and a few intelligent guesses about its origins. Towards the end of the 1970s and during the following decade, Russell began to receive some of the attention he had long deserved.

***(*)   New York Big Band Soul Note SN 1039 CD
Russell; as above, plus: Stanton Davis, Terumasa Hino, Lew Soloff (*t*); Gary Valente (*tb*); Dave Taylor (*btb*); John Clark (*frhn*); Marty Ehrlich (*as*); Ricky Ford (*ts*); Roger Rosenberg (*ts*); Carl Atkins (*bs, bcl*); Mark Slifstein (*g*); Stanley Cowell, Gotz Tangerding (*p*); Ricky Martinez (*electric p, org*); Cameron Brown (*b*); Warren Smith (*d*); Babafumi Akunyon (*perc*); Lee Genesis (*v*). 77–78.

***(*)   Live In An American Time Spiral Soul Note SN 1049 CD/LP
Russell; Stanton Davis, Tom Harrell, Brian Leach, Ron Tooley (*t*); Ray Anderson, Earl McIntyre (*tb*); Marty Ehrlich (*as, f*); Doug Miller (*ts, f*); Bob Hanlon (*bs*); Jerome Harris (*g*); Jack Reilly, Mark Soskin (*ky*); Ron McClure (*b*); Victor Lewis (*d*). 7/82.

New York Big Band includes a vital (in every sense) performance of the epochal 'Cubana Be, Cubana Bop', written in collaboration with Dizzy Gillespie and first performed in 1947. With its structural and not just decorative use of African and Caribbean metres, the piece opened out a whole new direction for jazz writing, paving the way for *The African Game* 25 years later. *Big Band* also includes two sections from *Listen To The Silence* and a wonderful and unexpected 'God Bless The Child' that derives something from Dolphy's long engagement with the piece.

The main piece on *Live* is a concert performance of 'Time Spiral' from *So What*. Concerned again with the larger, almost meta-historical movements of human life, the charts have a slightly dense philosophical feel on the studio album, but open up considerably in a live setting. The album also includes a fine reading of 'Ezz-thetic' and the faintly ironic 'D. C. Divertimento', given force by a (mostly) young and enthusiastic band.

HAL RUSSELL (born 1926)
SAXOPHONES, TRUMPET, VIBRAPHONE, DRUMS, BANDLEADER

***   Generation Chief 5 CD
Russell; Chuck Burdelik (*cl, as, ts*); Charles Tyler (*as, cl, bs*); Brian Sandstrom (*g, b, t*); Curt Bley (*b*); Steve Hunt (*d, vib*). 9/82.

***(*)   The Finnish/Swiss Tour ECM 1455 CD/LP
Russell; Mars Williams (*ts, ss, didgeridoo*); Brian Sandstrom (*b, t, g*); Kent Kessler (*b, didgeridoo*); Steve Hunt (*d, vib, didgeridoo*). 11/90.

There is nothing else in contemporary jazz quite like Hal Russell's NRG Ensemble. Playing just one instrument is considered rather wimpish, especially when the old man drifts back and forth between vibes, cornet and high-register Ayler-influenced saxophone. Russell actually set out as a drummer; he was recruited by Miles Davis in 1950 and by the radical Chicagoan Joe Daley, now little known outside free-jazz circles in the United States, a decade later. Towards the end of the 1970s he took up trumpet again for the first time since student days and learned to play the saxophone.

In its blend of forceful, rock-inflected ostinati, extreme dynamics and broadly satirical approach, the NRG Ensemble bears some kinship to Frank Zappa's Mothers of Invention; in his liner-note, Steve Lake also notes Russell's physical resemblance to Charles Ives, which isn't so far away, either. On *The Finnish/Swiss Tour*, a record of the Ensemble's first and rather surreal European itinerary, the leader quotes from Keith Jarrett and for 'Linda's Rock Vamp' dons Prince of Darkness shades over his prescription specs, as the liner booklet shows, in dubious homage to his former employer. The band have the huge, dark sound of the mid-1970s Miles Davis units, the days when Miles was Abstract Expressionist rather than neo-Figurative. 'Compositions' are treated as reference points and performances frequently develop into all-out jams that nevertheless give off a strong aura of control. The sheer *size* of the sound suggests a much larger outfit. Sandstrom's stripped guitar playing, Steve Hunt's ferocious time-keeping and the occasional use of twinned basses generate astonishing volume, with Mars Williams (formerly of the rock band, Psychedelic Furs) overblowing furiously beside the leader on the powerful 'Temporarily'. 'For MC' is for didgeridoos, electric guitar and cornet; the Zappa-sounding 'Hal The Weenie' is also an Aylerish invocation of ghosts and spirits.

Generation is slightly disappointing, sounding forced where *Tour* appears spontaneous, disorderly where the later album conforms to some logic. Nevertheless it's powerful stuff, the sound is better, and there isn't that much of Russell available. Watch out for 'Generation' itself, and the scissorhands 'Poodle Cut'.

JOHN RUSSELL
GUITAR

****   Conceits Acta 1 LP
Russell; John Butcher (*ss, ts*); Phil Durrant (*vn, tb*). 4/87.

British guitarist Russell has made only a few appearances on record, mostly with Gunter Christmann's Vario projects. This trio has worked together for some years, but this is their only record to date; and it's a superb one. Russell's style may remind one of Derek Bailey, but his dogged, relentless scratchings and choked chords become more than a vivid personalization of some of Bailey's methods. In collaboration with Butcher, whose minimal soprano and tenor lines are eerily apposite, and Durrant, principally a violinist but here an occasional trombonist as well, Russell fashions a tersely beautiful series of improvisations. The 11 pieces here range from just under two minutes to a little over six in length: 'Fine Sharp And Leighton Buzzard' starts with a shocking wail from Butcher, rolls on Russell's clenched strumming and has Durrant pecking out a separate commentary before tying itself up in 3:10. Each piece has a character of its own and, as unlovely and drawn-in as the music is, it seems to build its own aesthetic: by the end, one feels one has joined in with the improvisation. The recording is aggressively dry and close, which is just right for the music. An exemplary account of British improvisers at their most challenging.

LUIS RUSSELL (1902–63)
PIANO, BANDLEADER

****   Savoy Shout JSP CD 308 CD
Russell; Louis Metcalf, Henry Allen, Bill Coleman, Otis Johnson (*t*); J. C. Higginbotham, Vic Dickenson (*tb*); Albert Nicholas (*cl, ss, as*); Charlie Holmes (*ss, as*); Teddy Hill, Greely Walton (*ts*); Will Johnson (*g, bj*); Bass Moore (*tba*); Pops Foster (*b*); Paul Barbarin (*d, vib*); Walter Pichon (*v*). 1/29–12/30.

Russell was an indifferent pianist, but he led one of the great orchestras of its period, having originally put it together in New Orleans in 1927, with such young local stars as Allen, Nicholas and Barbarin in attendance. *Savoy Shout* collects their 18 essential sides from seven remarkable sessions in New York, where the band had secured a prime Harlem residency at the Saratoga Club (they also backed Louis Armstrong on some of his contemporary dates). This was a sophisticated band: first, in its soloists, with Higginbotham dominating the earlier sides and Allen, Nicholas and Holmes adding their own variations to the later ones; and, secondly, in its increasing stature as an ensemble. 'Louisiana Swing', 'High Tension', 'Panama' and 'Case On Dawn' all show the orchestra swinging through the more advanced new ideas of counterpoint and unison variation while still offering chances for Allen and the others to shine as soloists. It's a pity that their six 1934 tracks aren't included here, since the band all together never sounded better, though with a rather different personnel.

These tracks have been compiled before on Parlophone and VJM LPs, but the excellent JSP remastering by John R. T. Davies supersedes the earlier editions, and it must stand as one of the most entertaining as well as historically valuable overviews of the period.

PEE WEE RUSSELL (1906–69)
CLARINET

***   **Jack Teagarden/Pee Wee Russell** Original Jazz Classics OJC 1708 CD/LP/MC
Russell; Max Kaminsky (*t*); Dickie Wells (*tb*); Al Gold (*ts*); James P. Johnson (*p*); Freddie Green (*g*); Wellman Braud (*b*); Zutty Singleton (*d, v*). 8/38.

He might have been a Dickensian grotesque, with his mile-long face and shopworn demeanour, and his clarinet playing had a raddled, asthmatic tone that tended to conceal most of the creativity which had gone into it. Yet Russell's music is a connoisseur's jazz, transcending schools and securing a personal voice that can stand with any of the most idiosyncratic spirits in the music. He began with the New York players of the 1920s – Nichols, Mole, Beiderbecke – but was more readily linked with Condon's Chicagoans in the 1930s and '40s. The 1938 session here (the rest of the LP features a Teagarden-led group) features a surprising line-up on five standards and a blues, two tracks featuring Russell and the rhythm section alone. Kaminsky and Wells are the most confident-sounding voices but it's Russell's queer sense of line and wobbly pitch that take the ear. His partnership with Johnson is just one of a series of unlikely alliances he formed with pianists on record, which would later include George Wein and Thelonious Monk.

***(*)   **We're In The Money** Black Lion BLCD 760909 CD
Russell; Doc Cheatham, Wild Bill Davison (*t*); Vic Dickenson (*tb*); George Wein (*p*); John Field, Stan Wheeler (*b*); Buzzy Drootin (*d*); Al Bandini (*v*). 53–54.

***(*)   **Portrait Of Pee Wee** Fresh Sound FSR-CD 126 CD
Russell; Ruby Braff (*t*); Vic Dickenson (*tb*); Bud Freeman (*ts*); Nat Pierce (*p*); Steve Jordan (*g*); Walter Page, Charles Potter (*b*); George Wettling, Karl Kniffe (*d*). 2–9/58.

***(*)   **Over The Rainbow** Xanadu 192 CD
Russell; Bobby Hackett (*c*); Nat Pierce, Dave Frishberg (*p*); Steve Jordan (*g*); Walter Page, George Tucker , Tommy Potter (*b*); Oliver Jackson, Karl Kiffe, George Wettling (*d*). 3/58–9/65.

***(*)   **Jazz Reunion** Candid CS 9020 CD
Russell; Emmett Berry (*t*); Bob Brookmeyer (*vtb*); Coleman Hawkins (*ts*); Nat Pierce (*p*); Milt Hinton (*b*); Jo Jones (*d*). 2/61.

There probably isn't a single definitive Pee Wee Russell record: he turned up in unlikely settings and played improbable material until the end of his life. But these three dates give a splendid account of what he could do. *We're In The Money* includes two dates by basically the same band, although the substitution of Davison for Cheatham lends a different feel: the former's irascible, barking playing is a startling contrast to Cheatham's politely hot phrasing. Russell listens to each man and pitches his remarks for due contrast himself. Dickenson, a kindred spirit, kibitzes from the sidelines and the recording is fine. The Fresh Sound disc collects the results of two LPs, and the session with Braff, Dickenson and Freeman is a smooth Chicago-style outing which Russell subverts just enough to give the music a little more needle. The other eight tracks have Pee Wee as sole horn, and though the voltage seems rather reduced it does isolate some of the aspects of his approach to a melody: wheezing through one part of a line then turning clear and tender for another, shaking a note till it comes out right or pulling up short if he's had enough. The same session takes up a little over half of the Xanadu LP, which is filled out with three lovely quartet tracks, including a quintessential 'Pee Wee's Blues', and a single (and rather low-fi) performance from a 1965 concert with Hackett and Frishberg, though the cornetist barely registers. As a single-disc representation of Pee Wee, this might be the best. The *Reunion* was with Hawkins – one of the tracks, *If I Could Be With You One Hour Tonight*, they'd recorded together as far back as 1929 – and it caught both men in excellent form, Hawkins's solos delivered in his most leathery autumnal manner which makes Russell's nagging at notes sound minimalist. Jones, in particular, reads everybody's moves superbly, although Berry and Brookmeyer especially seem rather irrelevant. All four of the above are warmly recommended, though there is plenty more good Pee Wee which has yet to find its way to CD.

NIELS RYDE
BASS

**   **Traffic Jam** Olufsen DOC 5113 CD/LP
Ryde; Mikael Sloth (*ss, ts*); John Tchicai (*ts*); Morten Elbek (*as*); Johannes Grønager (*bs, sitar*); Kaev Glimann (*ky*); Uffe Steen (*g*); Jesper Bo Knudsen (*d*); Claus Rahuage (*perc*). 11/90.

A modish and fragmented record which suggests interesting ideas without realizing them. Ryde crams a lot of twists and turns into compositions that never take a coherent form, and guest-star turns by Tchicai and Steen embellish but don't transform the modal settings and thin jazz-funk gestures. The leader noodles on bass in the Pastorius fashion: 'Blues For Jaco' pays the obvious dues.

TERJE RYPDAL (born 1947)
ELECTRIC GUITAR, GUITAR, SOPRANO SAXOPHONE, FLUTE, OTHER INSTRUMENTS AND EFFECTS

(*)   **What Comes After ECM 1031 CD

(*)   **When Ever I Seem To Be Far Away ECM 1045 LP

***   **Waves** ECM 1110 CD/LP
Rypdal; Palle Mikkelborg (*t, flhn, syn, ring modulator;* on *Waves* only); Olle Ullberg (*frhn* on *Far Away* only); Erik Niord Larsen (*ob* on *What Comes After* only); Pete Knutsen (*mellotron, electric p* on *Far Away* only); Barre Phillips (*b* on *What Comes After* only); Sveinung Hovensjo (*b*); Jon Christensen (*d*); Helmut Giger (*vn* on *Far Away* only); Christian Hedrich (*vla* on *Far Away* only); unidentified oboe and clarinet on *Far Away*; strings on *Far Away* only. 8/73, 74, 9/77.

***   **Odyssey** ECM 1067/8 CD
Rypdal; Torbjorn Sunde (*tb*); Brynjulf Blix (*b*); Svein Christiansen (*d*). 8/75.

In the later 1980s, Terje Rypdal was increasingly seen at the head of an impressive train of opus numbers. 'Straight' composition was, in fact, his third string. His professional career had begun as a rock performer, in the pit band at a Scandinavian production of *Hair!* (chilblains were doubtless a problem) and as accompanist to his sister, Inger Lise Rypdal (who added soft vocal colours to the otherwise solo and now deleted *After The Rain* [ECM 1083 LP]). In the 1970s, under the influence of George Russell (directly) and of Jimi Hendrix (less so), Rypdal made a series of highly atmospheric guitar-led albums which combined elements of classical form with a distinctive high-register sound and an improvisational approach that drew more from rock music than from orthodox jazz technique. (It's worth noting that *After The Rain* refers to a Rypdal composition, not Coltrane's.)

If there is an 'ECM sound', in either a positive or a more sceptical sense, it may be found in the echo-y passages of these albums. Rypdal's music is highly textural and harmonically static, its imagery kaleidoscopic rather than cinematic. At worst, Rypdal's solo excursions sound merely vacuous. The title and mood of 'Silver Bird Is Heading For The Sun' on ECM 1045 are reminiscent of Pink Floyd's woollier moments; the long title-track (which Rypdal calls an 'image', a useful generic description of his work) is, on the other hand, highly effective in its balance of winds, guitar and strings. ('Live' strings are more effective than the cumbersome and now outmoded mellotrons and 'string ensembles' that the guitarist uses elsewhere.)

Waves and *Odyssey* are the most interesting of this group. Rypdal favours brass with an almost medieval quality and, despite Mikkelborg's baroque embellishments, the trumpeter fits that prescription surprisingly well. Hovensjo and Christensen don't play as an orthodox rhythm section but as a shifting backdrop of tones and pulses; the bassist doubles on a 6-string instrument which is effectively a rhythm guitar.

Popular in their day, all these albums now sound a shade dated. Nevertheless they are still well worth hearing.

***(*) **Descendere** ECM 1144 CD/LP
Rypdal; Palle Mikkelborg (*t, flhn, ky*); Jon Christensen (*d, perc*). 3/79.

***(*) **Terje Rypdal / Miroslav Vitous / Jack DeJohnette** ECM 1125 CD/LP
Rypdal; Miroslav Vitous (*b, p*); Jack DeJohnette (*d*). 6/78.

*** **To Be Continued** ECM 1192 LP
As above. 1/81.

There have always been charges that Rypdal is not 'really' an improviser, just a high-powered effects man. At the root of the misconception is a prevailing belief that improvisation takes place only on a vertical axis, up and down through chord progressions and changes. Rypdal's genius is for juxtapositions of textures, overlays of sound that act as polarizing lenses to what his companions are doing. A broad, open chord laid close over a drum pattern takes the 'percussive' stringency out of DeJohnette's line, making him sound as if he were playing piano (as in other and later company he might well be) or adding harmonics to Vitous's huge bass notes. There is also, of course, a great deal of straightforward interplay which in itself helps refute the charge that Rypdal is a mere techno-freak.

The other trio is less conventional in format, though Mikkelborg's palette-knife keyboard effects mean that there's very little sense of 'missing' piano or bass. The trumpeter, who has an approach broadly similar to Rypdal's, tends to lay it on a little thick, and there is a suspicion of either muddle or overkill on a couple of tracks. That apart, *Descendere* still sounds fresh and vital and stands out as a high point in Rypdal's output.

***(*) **Works** ECM 825428 CD/LP
Rypdal; Palle Mikkelborg (*t, ky*); Olle Ulleberg (*frhn*); Jan Garbarek (*f*); Eckehart Fintl (*ob*); Brynjulf Blix (*org*); Pete Knutsen (*mellotron*); Arild Andersen, Sveinung Hovensjo, Miroslav Vitous (*b*); Jon Christensen, Jack DeJohnette (*d*). 1974–81.

Whether or not this represents a 'best of' Rypdal's pre-1980s work, it does provide a useful sample for newcomers. The tracks with Mikkelborg, and with Vitous and DeJohnette inevitably stand ahead of the rest and, though there's little sense of how Rypdal operates on long-form pieces, these offer convincing testimony of his sometimes queried improvising credentials. Recommended.

*** **Eos** ECM 1263 CD/LP
Rypdal; David Darling (*clo, 8-string electric clo*). 5/83.

The scorching power chords of the opening 'Laser' tend to mislead, for this a remarkably subtle and sophisticated record, making the fullest use of the players' astonishing range of tone-colours and effects. Darling conjures anything from Vitous-like bass strums to high, wailing lines that are remarkably close in timbre to Rypdal's souped-up guitar. He is still mostly reliant on rock-influenced figures played with maximum sustain and distortion, but his rhythm counts are consistently challenging, and the pairing of instruments sets up an often ambiguous bitonality. The title-track wavers a bit at over 14 minutes, but the two closing numbers, 'Mirage' and 'Adagietto', are particularly beautiful.

(*) **Chaser** ECM 1303 CD/LP
Rypdal; Bjorn Kjellmyr (*b*); Audun Klieve (*d*). 5/85.

** **Blue** ECM 1346 CD/LP
As above. 11/86.

(*) **The Singles Collection ECM 1383 CD/LP
As above, with Allan Dangerfield (*ky*). 8/88.

It may say something about Rypdal's psychic economy that, at a time when his scored, formal music was achieving new heights of sophistication and beauty, he should have gone on road and record with a power trio of minimum finesse. *Chaser* is a harsh clunking slice of nonsense that does Rypdal very little credit. *Blue* at least shows signs of thought, notably on 'The Curse' and 'Om Bare'.

How many people have been thrown by the ironically titled *Singles Collection*? It's not utterly improbable that Rypdal might have been sneaking out the odd seven-incher over the years, but this is a wholly new album of wry, generic samples. Basically, it's a tissue of rock guitar styles, with the changing of stylistic season marked by Dangerfield's progress from apoplectic Hammond to a rather under-programmed synth. Rypdal has expressed interest in Prince's music (and 'U.'N.I.' is presumably a reference to the Small One's trademark elision of titles) but it isn't clear whether he is drawn more to Paisley Park production techniques or to Prince's Carlos Santana-derived (rather than Hendrix-derived) guitar playing. Rypdal emerges as a surprisingly good *pasticheur*, and there is plenty to think about in this slightly odd, deliberately regressive set. It's certainly his best work since forming the Chasers.

HELMUT JOE SACHSE
GUITAR, FLUTE

***   **Solo** FMP 1070 LP
       Sachse solo. 12/84.

***(*)   **Berlin Tango** ITM 1448 CD
       Sachse; George Lewis (*tb*); David Moss (*d, perc, elec, v*). 12/86, 10/87.

***(*)   **European House** FMP CD41 CD
       Sachse solo. 90.

On *European House*, as on the ironically titled 'Der Wohltemperierte Schraubenzieher oder Joe's Mechanikerverständnis' on *Solo* (it also kicks off the live *Berlin Tango*), Sachse thinks nothing of cutting across a chaotically abstract passage with a sudden rock riff or Wes Montgomery-style octave run. An eclectic of a fairly radical sort, he has synthesized whole tracts of modern and contemporary guitar playing. The earlier solo record is rather thinly recorded and misses much of Sachse's quieter gestures.

Typically, *Solo* also contains a modestly reconstructed standard, 'Round About Midnight'; *European House* is rather less respectful of 'Epistrophy' and Coltrane's 'Impressions'. It's this element one misses on the anarchic *Berlin Tango*; 'Lover Man' may mislead, for it's actually a bizarre parody of all-stops-out soul, with Moss's surreal falsetto scats alternated with sexy murmurs and Sachse's lead guitarist posturing. Lewis plays a rather diffident role throughout and was presumably present on only one or other of the dates. The best of the group is undoubtedly the later FMP solo set; without Moss's clatteringly intrusive effects, Sachse improvises percussion on the guitar body and carrying case.

AKIRA SAKATA (born 1945)
ALTO SAX, BASS CLARINET

(*)   **Dance Enja 4002 LP
       Sakata; Hiroshi Yoshino (*b*); Nobu Fuji (*d*). 6/81.

Not, perhaps, the best place to hear this funny, spine-chilling saxophonist: he's made some exuberant cameo appearances elsewhere, with Last Exit and Manfred Schoof, and Yosuke Yamashita's *Ghosts* maps out his allegiances to Albert Ayler's music. The four pieces here are a little more mediated, and Yoshino and Fuji are too much the generic free-jazz rhythm section; but there's still some exhilarating blowing: the title of the first piece, 'Right Frankenstein In Seigne-Legier', gives you the idea of what's going on.

ANTONELLO SALIS
PIANO, KEYBOARDS

*(*)   **Salis!** Splasc(h) H136 LP
         Salis. 9/87.

Salis recorded an earlier solo session for Hat Hut; this one includes a six-part suite as well as 'Fool On The Hill' among its 10 tracks. On the evidence of this record at least, he's a rather too eclectic stylist, switching rapidly between prepared-piano bashing and sweet-natured ballad interludes. Some interesting moments, but not enough to sustain a whole record.

DINO SALUZZI
BANDONEON, FLUTE, PERCUSSION, VOICE

***   **Kultrum** ECM 1251 CD/LP
        Saluzzi solo. 11/82.

***(*) **Andina** ECM 1375 CD/LP
        As above. 5/88.

***   **Argentina** West Wind WW 2201 CD
        As above. 90.

***(*) **Once Upon A Time ... Far Away In The South** ECM 1309 CD/LP
        Saluzzi; Palle Mikkelborg (*t, flhn*); Charlie Haden (*b*); Pierre Favre (*d*). 7/85.

***   **Volver** ECM 1343 CD/LP
        Saluzzi; Enrico Rava (*t*); Harry Pepl (*g*); Furio Di Castri (*b*); Bruce Ditmas (*d*). 10/86.

Though it was the Argentinian *nueva tango* master, Astor Piazzolla, who sparked the recent revival of interest in bandoneon and accordion, it has been Dino Saluzzi who has performed some of the most significant new music on an instrument that always held a peculiar fascination for the avant-garde; this partly because of its slightly kitsch image, but also because it permits an astonishing range of harmonic and extra-harmonic devices (wheezes, clicks, terminal rattles) that lend themselves very readily to improvisational contexts.

Saluzzi's compositions and performances (and he is usually best heard solo) cover a wide spectrum of styles, from sombre, almost sacred pieces (like 'Choral' on *Andina*, his best record), to a semi-abstract tone-poem like 'Winter' on the same album, which takes him much closer to the exploratory work of radical accordionist, Pauline Oliveros. While both *Kultrum* and the later *Argentina* are well worth hearing, *Andina* is the one to plump for; richly and intimately recorded, although doubtless less authentic in idiom, it has infinitely greater presence than the later album.

Saluzzi tends to recede a little in a group setting, perhaps because European ears have not been conditioned to listen to button accordion as anything other than a bland portable organ useful for dancing and local colour. Both Rava and (especially) Mikkelborg are rather dominant players and occupy more than their fair share of the foreground. *Once Upon A Time* is better because Haden and Favre are so responsive; *Volver* takes a bit of getting used to.

***   **Mojotoro** ECM 1447 CD/LP
        Saluzzi; Celso Saluzzi (*bandoneon, perc, v*); Felix Cuchara Saluzzi (*ts, ss, cl*); Armando Alonso (*g, v*); Guillermo Vadalá (*b, v*); José Maria Saluzzi (*d, perc, v*); Arto Tuncboyaci (*perc, v*). 5/91.

At first hearing remarkably similar to one of Edward Vesala's accordion-led pieces, 'Mojotoro' is dedicated to the universalization of musical culture. It draws on tango, Bolivian *Andina* music, Uruguayan *Candombe* and other folk forms, travelling between deceptively spacious but highly intricate bandoneon figures and passionate saxophone outcries, which suggest a hybrid of Gato Barbieri with another ECM alumnus, Jan Garbarek. The multi-part 'Mundos' is less effective than the title-piece and the strongest performances are on the more conventionally structured pieces, 'Tango A Mi Padre' and Pintin Castellanos's wonderful *milonga*, 'La Punalada'. Instrumental colours are expertly handled, but the main drama comes from the interaction between Saluzzi and his kinsman 'Cuchara', who is a marvellously evocative clarinettist.

JOE SAMPLE (born 1939)
KEYBOARDS

(*)   **Fancy Dance Sonet SNTCD 788 CD
Sample; Red Mitchell (*b*); J. C. Moses (*d*). 4/69.

A straight-ahead piano trio date for the erstwhile keyboard player with The Crusaders. It's a potentially intriguing mix of personalities, but the material is rarher plain stuff and Mitchell and Moses play within themselves rather than pushing Sample into tougher areas. Still, 'Fancy Dance' and 'Another Blues' are spruce variations on the blues which Sample – a gospely, expansive stylist – is well equipped to make good on.

***   **Rainbow Seeker** MCA MCAD 31067 CD/MC
Sample; Robert O'Bryant, Jay Daversa, Steven Madaio (*t*); Garnett Brown (*tb*); Ernie Watts (*ss, ts, f*); Fred Jackson (*ts*); William Green (*ts, f*); Ray Parker (*g*); Robert Popwell (*b*); Stix Hooper (*d*); Paulinho DaCosta (*perc*). 78.

***   **Carmel** MCA MCAD 37210 CD/MC
Sample; Hubert Laws (*f*); Dean Parks, Paul Jackson Jr (*g*); Abe Laboriel, Byron Miller (*b*); Stix Hooper, Robert Wilson (*d*); Paulinho Da Costa (*perc*). 79–81.

***   **Voices In The Rain** MCA MCAD-27077 CD/MC
Sample; Dean Parks (*g*); Abraham Laboriel (*b*); Stix Hooper (*d*); Josie James (*v*); strings. 80.

(*)   **The Hunter MCA MCAD-1471 CD/MC
Sample; Dean Parks (*g*); Abraham Laboriel (*b*); Paulinho Da Costa (*perc*); Stix Hooper (*d*). strings. 82.

**   **Roles** MCA MCAD-5978 CD/MC
Sample; Dean Parks (*g*); Abraham Laboriel (*b*); Sonny Emory (*d*); Lenny Castro (*perc*); strings. 83.

***   **Collection** GRP GRD-9658 CD/MC
As above MCA discs.

Joe Sample continued on a solo career while still with The Crusaders, and the MCA records offer a thoughtful variation on his work with the 'parent' band. After working with Robert Popwell and Stix Hooper for so long, Sample wasn't going to give up on a strong beat – and Hooper appears on these records anyway. The arrangements are a little sweeter and Sample puts himself in the solo forefront, but the music is more about textures than solos – careful arrangements make the most of the pianist's knack for a tune and economic parts, more embellishment than improvisation. If it's scarcely challenging music, it's easy-listening jazz with a far firmer centre than most such players allow. *Carmel* is also available with *Voices In The Rain*, on which Sample played all-acoustic parts, as a double-play cassette (MCA MCAC2-6945). The *Collection* set is a neat cross-section of his solo career through the late 1970s and '80s, with the music growing more mellow but no less intelligent as it proceeds.

***   **Ashes To Ashes** Warner Bros 26318 CD/LP/MC
Sample; Jerry Hey (*t, flhn*); Larry Williams (*saxes, f*); Ricky Peterson (*ky*); Michael Landau, St Paul (*g*); Marcus Miller (*b*); Omar Hakim (*d*); Lenny Castro (*perc*). 90.

Sample's set for Warner Bros continues his earlier work with no startling changes, but the subtleties abide: 'The Road Less Traveled', for instance, floats an almost concealed riff inside a carefully cushioning arrangement, with Sample's closing solo emerging as a glittering coda to the tune, and there's much more like that. Tommy Lipuma's production is luxurious without smothering the spirit.

DAVE SAMUELS (born 1948)
VIBES, MARIMBA

**   **Double Image** Enja 2096 LP
Samuels; David Friedman (*vib, marim, perc*); Harvie Swartz (*b*); Michael DiPasqua (*d*). 6/77.

*(*)   **Ten Degrees North** MCA MCACD 6328 CD
Samuels; Eddie Daniels (*cl*); Clifford Carter (*ky*); Julio Fernandez (*g*); John Patitucci (*b*); Alex Acuna (*d, v*). 89.

**   **Natural Selection** GRP 9656-2 CD
Samuels; Jeff Beal (*t, flhn, ky*); Jay Beckenstein (*reeds*); Russell Ferrante (*ky*); Bruce Hornsby (*p*); Julio Fernandez (*g*); Jimmy Haslip (*b*); William Kennedy (*d*); Marc Quinones (*perc*). 90.

Joining the hugely successful pop-jazz group Spyro Gyra was either the making or the undoing of Samuels. Like David Friedman, his partner in the group Double Image, whose sole Enja album is an interesting if unfulfilled idea of a double-vibes band, Samuels is as much interested in the vibes as a source of rhythm and percussive power as in their melodic capabilities. But it must have been his ability to play pretty which won his spurs with Spyro Gyra, and pretty is the best thing one can say about the two subsequent solo albums. The least one can ask from such records is a set of good, hummable tunes, but Samuels isn't that kind of writer and his originals are staccato, jumpy affairs at up-tempo, hard and unripe at slow. *Ten Degrees North* is flat and prosaic; *Natural Selection* has a couple of stronger tunes, but the best was written by guest trumpeter Jee Beal, who contributes to only one track. Admirers of Spyro Gyra may enjoy, but there's nothing here that Samuels doesn't do on their records.

DAVID SANBORN (born 1945)
ALTO AND SOPRANO SAXOPHONE

(*)   **Taking Off Warner Bros 927295-2 CD
Sanborn; Randy Brecker (*t*); Tom Malone (*tb*); Peter Gordon, John Clark (*frhn*); Michael Brecker (*ts*); Howard Johnson (*bs, tba*); Don Grolnick (*ky*); Steve Khan, Buzzy Feiten, Joe Beck (*g*); Will Lee (*b*); Chris Parker, Rick Marotta (*d*); Ralph MacDonald (*perc*); strings. 75.

**   **Heart To Heart** Warner Bros 3189-2 CD
Sanborn; Jon Faddis, Lew Soloff, Randy Brecker (*t*); Michael Brecker (*ts*); Mike Mainieri (*vib*). 1/78.

***   **Voyeur** Warner Bros 256900 CD/MC
Sanborn; Tom Scott (*ts, f*); Michael Colina (*ky*); Hiram Bullock, Buzzy Feiten (*g*); Marcus Miller (*b, g, ky, d*); Buddy Williams, Steve Gadd (*d*); Lenny Castro, Ralph MacDonald (*perc*). 81.

**   **As We Speak** Warner Bros 923650-2 CD/MC
Sanborn; Bill Evans (*ss*); Bob Mintzer (*bcl*); Robert Martin (*frhn*); Don Freeman, Lance Ong, George Duke (*ky*); James Skelton (*org*); Michael Sembello (*g, v*); Buzzy Feiten (*g*); Marcus Miller (*b*); Omar Hakim (*d*); Paulinho Da Costa (*perc*). 82.

Whatever palatable, easy-listening trimmings are applied to David Sanborn's records, his own contributions always cut deeper than that. For someone who originally took up sax playing as a therapeutic exercise (he was affected by polio as a child), Sanborn has made the most of his medicine. He already had a signature sound by the time of *Taking Off*, his solo debut, having worked in rock and blues bands for ten years already, and while he is shy of jazz as a basis for his own music, his high, skirling tone and succinct phrasing have inspired countless other players. The problem with *Taking Off* and *Heart To Heart* (as well as the deleted *Sanborn* and *Promise Me The Moon*) is context: other than delivering vague funky instrumentals, there's little for Sanborn to bite on here, and the original tunes aren't much more than 1970s funk clichés. *Voyeur* is the album that raises the game a notch: the sound assumes a hard gleam and a tightness which would be constricting for most players replaces any sense of a loose gait. The altoman thrives in the context, cutting sharp circular patterns like a skater on ice, with the prettiness of 'It's You' and 'All I Need Is You' balancing the bright, airless funk of 'Wake Me When It's Over'. *As We Speak*, though, was a disappointing repeat run, with sentimental fluff courtesy of guitarist-singer Sembello taking up too much room.

***   **Backstreet** Warner Bros 923906-2 CD/MC
Sanborn; Marcus Miller (ky, g, b, perc); Michael Colina (*ky*); Hiram Bullock (*ky, g*); Buzzy Feiten (*g*); Steve Gadd (*d*); Ralph MacDonald (*perc*). 83.

***   **Straight To The Heart** Warner Bros 925150-2 CD/MC
Sanborn; Randy Brecker, Jon Faddis (*t*); Michael Brecker (*ts*); Don Grolnick (*ky*); Hiram Bullock (*g*); Marcus Miller (*b, ky*); Buddy Williams (*d*); Errol Bennett (*perc*). 84.

**   **A Change Of Heart** Warner Bros 925479-2 CD/MC
Sanborn; Michael Brecker (*EWI*); Marcus Miller (*ky, g, b*); Don Grolnick, Rob Mounsey, Michael Colina, John Mahoney, Michael Sembello, Bernard Wright, Philippe Saisse, Ronnie Foster, Randy Waldman (*ky*); Mac Rebennack (*p*); Hiram Bullock, Hugh McCracken, Nicky Moroch, Carlos Rios (*g*); Anthony Jackson (*b*); Mickey Curry, John Robinson (*d*); Paulinho Da Costa, Mino Cinelu (*perc*). 87.

***(*)   **Close Up** Reprise 925715-2 CD/MC
Sanborn; Marcus Miller (*ky, g, b*); Richard Tee, Ricky Peterson (*p*); Hiram Bullock, Nile Rodgers, Steve Jordan, Jeff Mironov, G. E. Smith, Paul Jackson (*g*); Andy Newmark, Vinnie Colaiuta, William House (*d*); Paulinho Da Costa, Don Alias (*perc*); Michael Ruff (*v*). 88.

Marcus Miller had been playing and composing for Sanborn's records before, but with *Backstreet* he began producing as well, intensifying further the almost abstract neo-funk which the saxophonist had behind him. *Backstreet* featured some agreeable tunes as well as the beat, though, and in the title piece, 'A Tear For Crystal' and 'Blue Beach' Sanborn wrung the most out of each situation. His sound was sometimes almost frozen in the still space of the studio, but his tone remained uniquely capable of emoting in this context. Cut before a studio audience, *A Change Of Heart* simulated one of Sanborn's live shows, and while it has some tedious features it's a rare chance to hear the leader in more extended solos than usual, which are strong enough to belie his insistence that a jazz context is inapporpriate for him.

A Change Of Heart was a false step. Four different producers handle the eight tracks and the result is a mishmash of styles where each man tries to affix Sanborn's trademark wail in his own setting. Only Miller's work is truly effective, although Michael Sembello gave Sanborn one of his most insistently catchy melodies in 'The Dream'; the rest is over-produced pop-jazz at its least amiable. *Close-Up*, however, was a brilliant return to form. This time Miller handled the whole project and turned in tunes and arrangements which took Sanborn to the very limit of this direction. Having experimented with different keyboard and drum-programme sounds on the earlier records, Miller built backing tracks of enormous complexity which barely gave the saxophonist room to breathe, yet the madly exciting riff-tune 'Slam', sweet melodies of 'So Far Away' and 'Lesley Ann' and staccato snap of 'Tough' squeezed Sanborn into delivering some of his smartest ideas. It's a little like a modernization of West Coast jazz, where soloists were required to put a personal stamp on 16 bars in the middle of a skintight arrangement. The sound is artificially brilliant but entirely suitable for the music.

***   **Another Hand** Elektra Musician 7559-61088-2 CD/MC
Sanborn; Art Baron (*tb, btb*); Lenny Pickett (*cl, ts*); Terry Adams, Marcus Miller (*p*); Leon Pendarvis (*org*); Bill Frisell, Marc Ribot, Al Anderson, Dave Tronzo (*g*); Greg Cohen, Charlie Haden, Marcus Miller (*b*); Joey Baron, Steve Jordan, Jack DeJohnette (*d*); Don Alias (*perc*); Syd Straw (*v*). 90.

A striking if sometimes uneasy change of direction. After working with a wide range of players on his American TV series *Night Music*, Sanborn (and producer Hal Willner) sought out less familiar territory and came up with this curious fusion of jazz, R&B and the kind of instrumental impressionism which participants Frisell and Ribot have been associated with. Sanborn sounds interested but not entirely sure of himself at some points, and happiest on the less rhythmically taxing pieces such as the infectious lope of 'Hobbies' and two tracks with the

Millers and DeJohnette. The film music medley arranged by Greg Cohen emerges as a queer pastiche. Possibly more important to its maker than his audience, but well worth hearing.

***(*) **Upfront** Elektra 7559-61272 CD/MC
Sanborn; Earl Gardner, Laurie Frink, Randy Brecker, Paul Litteral, Herb Roberston (*t*); Dave Bargeron, Art Baron (*tb*); Stan Harrison (*as*); Lenny Pickett, Arno Hecht (*ts*); Crispin Cioe (*bs*); Richard Tee (*org*); John Purcell (*ts, saxello*); William Patterson, Eric Clapton (*g*); Marcus Miller (*b, ky, g, bcl*); Steve Jordan (*d*); Don Alias, Nana Vasconcelos (*perc*). 91.

Looser, funkier, free-flowing where the last one was bound up in itself, this is Sanborn sounding better than he has for a long time. His own playing doesn't change so much from record to record but he sounds a lot more comfortable back here in Marcus Miller's grooves than he did on Hal Willner's on the previous disc – and a lot happier than Miles Davis ever did, too. The hip, updated treatment of Ornette's 'Ramblin'' works out a treat, with Herb Robertson adding squittery trumpet, but the whole record has a lot of fine playing – in a live-in-the-studio atmosphere – that stands up to plenty of listening.

PHAROAH SANDERS (born 1940)
TENOR SAXOPHONE

(*) **Journey To The One Theresa TR 108/9 CD/2LP
Sanders; Eddie Henderson (*flhn*); Joe Bonner, John Hicks (*p*); Paul Arslanian, Bedria Sanders (*harmonium*); Mark Isham (*syn*); Chris Hayes, Carl Lockett (*g*); James Pomerantz (*sitar*); Yoko Ito Gates (*koto*); Ray Drummond, Joy Julks (*b*); Randy Merrit, Idris Muhammad (*d*); Phil Ford (*tabla*); Babatunde (*perc*); Claudette Allen, Donna Dickerson, Bobby McFerrin, Vicki Randle, Ngoh Spencer (*v*).

*** **Rejoice** Theresa TR 112/3 CD/2LP
Sanders; Danny Moore (*t*); Steve Turre (*tb*); Bobby Hutcherson (*vib*); John Hicks (*p*); Joe Bonner (*p, v*); Peter Fujii (*g, v*); Lois Colin (*hp*); Art Davis (*b*); Jorge Pomar (*b, v*); Billy Higgins, Elvin Jones (*d*); Babatunde, Big Black (*perc*); Flame Braithwaite, William S. Fischer, B. Kazuko Ishida, Bobby London, Sakinah Muhammad, Carol Wilson Scott, Yvette S. Vanterpool (*v*).

*** **Heart Is A Melody** Theresa TR 118 LP
Sanders; William Henderson (*p*); John Heard (*b*); Idris Muhammad (*d*); Paul Arslanian (*bells, whistle*); Andy Bey, Flame Braithwaite, Cort Cheek, Janie Cook, William S. Fischer, Mira Hadar, Debra McGriffe, Jes Muir, Kris Wyn (*v*). 1/82.

*** **Live** Theresa TR 116 LP
Sanders; John Hicks (*p*); Walter Booker (*b*); Idris Muhammad (*d*). 4/82.

*** **Shukuru** Theresa TR 121 CD/LP
Sanders; William Henderson (*syn*); Ray Drummond (*b*); Idris Muhammad (*d*); Leon Thomas (*v*).

***(*) **Africa** Timeless SJP 253 CD/LP
Sanders; John Hicks (*p*); Curtis Lundy (*b*); Idris Muhammad (*d*). 3/87.

*** **Moon Child** Timeless SJP 326 CD/LP
Sanders; William Henderson (*p*); Stafford James (*b*); Eddie Moore (*d*); Cheikh Tidiane Fale (*perc*). 10/89.

Hearing that Pharoah Sanders has made an album of standards is a little like learning that Marvin Hagler gives flower-arranging classes. In the 1960s, Sanders was easily the most fearsome tenor saxophonist. Born in Little Rock, Arkansas, in 1940, and thus at the very intersection of every contradictory impulse facing young black males in America, he developed a tone of oxyacetylene heat, much influenced by Albert Ayler, but far harsher. He played on most of the late Coltrane albums and, rootless after Coltrane's death, made two shockers of his own, *Tauhid* [Impulse AS 9138] and *Thembi* [AS 9206], both safely deleted.

The saxophonist remained largely silent for the rest of the 1970s. His return wasn't anything like the grotesque flabby-middleweight comeback that everyone feared. Sanders had, perhaps inevitably, toned down the desperate inarticulacy which stood in place of conventional harmonic or melodic development (and was quite appropriate in the context of Coltrane's *Ascension*); what emerged in its place was a dry, philosophical voice that sought to persuade by logic and rhetoric rather than sheer power.

During the 1980s, Sanders regularly returned to Coltrane material: 'After The Rain' on both *Journey To The One* and the apparently deleted *A Prayer Before Dawn* [Theresa TR 127], the weakest of the recent sets, 'Moment's Notice' and 'Central Park West' on *Rejoice*, 'Ole' on *Heart Is A Melody*, 'Naima' on *Africa*, and a decidedly Coltraneish 'Night Has A Thousand Eyes' on *Moon Child*. Sanders has also been increasingly interested in standard material – with the tenor saxophonist's shibboleth 'Body And Soul' on *Shakuru* – which may represent a belated recognition that composing is not his trump.

Only a hardened cynic would suggest that dotting Coltrane themes throughout a rather densely packed programme of releases was a shrewd commercial tactic. It's clear that Sanders feels the music deeply, from the inside, and he is arguably the most authentic and thoughtful interpreter of this material on the scene today.

At the back of the mind of course is the nudging recognition that this *is* Pharoah Sanders (a little like the dilemma confronting fans of the Visigothic Peter Brötzmann when he release *Fourteen Love Poems* (FMP 1060 LP)). There are now too many Sanders albums from too short a period. *Journey To The One* was a shaky start, and the Max Roach-and-Ayler-influenced singing there and on *Heart Is A Melody* is wholly unsuccessful. There are still too many meandering, Afro-mystical themes and Nilotic fantasies, and too many ill-thought-out instrumental combinations. In Bonner, Henderson and Hicks though, luck, label politics or good judgement has delivered up to the saxophonist three players who understand his chastened romanticism.

ARTURO SANDOVAL (born 1949)
TRUMPET, FLUGELHORN, KEYBOARDS, PERCUSSION, VOCAL

(*)   **No Problem Jazz House JHR001 CD/LP
Sandoval; Hilario Duran Torres (*p*); Jorge Chicoy (*g*); Jorge Reyes Hernandes (*b*); Bernardo Garcia Carreras (*d*); Reinaldo Valera Del Monte (*perc*). 8/86.

**   **Flight To Freedom** GRP GRD-9634 CD/MC
Sandoval; Ed Calle (*ts, f*); Chick Corea, Mike Orta, Danilo Perez, Richard Eddy (*ky*); Rene Luis Toledo (*g*); Anthony Jackson, Nicky Orta (*b*); Dave Weckl, Orlando Hernandez (*d*); Long John, Portinho (*perc*). 91.

In person, Sandoval is one of the most ebullient trumpet ambassadors since Dizzy Gillespie, his great mentor. On record, this Cuban exile and scintillating virtuoso is a less convincing figure, though that may be due to overheated expectations. The live record is a fair sample of the kind of music he serves up at the venue on his regular visits, and while the playing bubbles with Latin fire and brilliance, battle fatigue tends to overtake the listener. Sandoval may be a great technician, but it's often hard to detect any reason for the galloping runs other than a love of showmanship. The band provide zesty accompaniment. The GRP set was his first 'American' statement after defecting to the USA, and the irony is that it often falls into international muzak: GRP house-bands provide faceless backing tracks which the trumpeter dances over with a sometimes light but more often crashingly heavy footfall. If Sandoval is going to make significant records, he'll need to think carefully about material, musicians and producers alike.

***   **I Remember Clifford** GRP GRP-96682 CD/MC
Sandoval; Ernie Watts, David Sanchez, Ed Calle (*ts*); Felix Gomez (*ky*); Kenny Kirkland (*p*); Charnett Moffett (*b*); Kenny Washington (*d*). 91.

Tribute albums are becoming a bore, but this is easily the best record under Sandoval's name to date. The material is all in dedication to Clifford Brown, and most of it emanates from Brownie's own repertoire, including 'Joy Spring', 'Daahoud' and the like. The up-tempo pieces are as thrilling as Sandoval can make them: 'Cherokee' is taken at a preposterously fast tempo, and the trumpeter still pulls off a solo which outpaces everybody else. Watts and Sanchez also fire off some exciting solos of their own, and the rhythm section is absolutely on top of it, with Kirkland at his most dazzling. Yet there remains a gloss of routine on the music, which can sound utterly unyielding, and the production decision to create some trumpet parts by feeding them through a harmonizer only adds to the sense of a spirit tamed by the demands of making successful records.

MONGO SANTAMARIA (born 1922)
PERCUSSION

***   **Yambu** Original Jazz Classics OJC 276 LP/MC
Santamaria; Al McKibbon (*b*); Francisco Aguabella, Willie Bobo, Modesto Duran, Pablo Mozo, Carlos Vidal (*p*); Mercedes Hernandez, Israel Del Pino (*v*). 12/58.

***   **Sabroso** Original Jazz Classics OJC 281 LP/MC
Santamaria; Marcus Cabuto, Louis Valizan (*t*); Rolando Lozano (*f*); Jose Silva (*ts, vl*); Felix Legarreta (*vl*); Rene Hernandez (*p*); Victor Venegas (*b*); Willie Bobo (*perc*); Pete Escovedo, Byardo Velarde (*v, perc*); Rudi Calzado (*v*). 60.

***(*)   **Skins** Milestone 47038 CD
Santamaria; Paul Serrano, Marty Sheller (*t*); Nat Adderley (*c*); Hubert Laws (*f, picc, ts*); Al Abreu, Pat Patrick (*f, sax*); Bob Capers (*as, bs*); Chick Corea, Rodgers Grant (*p*); Jose De Paulo (*g, perc*); Victor Venegas (*b*); Ray Lucas (*d*); Julio Collazo, Carmelo Garcia, Wito Kortwright, Osvaldo Chihuahua Martinez, To-Tiko (*perc*); Carmen Costa, Marcellina Guerra, Elliott Romero (*v*); chorus. 64, 7/72.

***(*)   **Mongo At The Village Gate** Original Jazz Classics OJC 490 CD/LP/MC
Santamaria; Marty Sheller (*t*); Pat Patrick (*f, sax*); Bob Capers (*as, bs*); Rodgers Grant (*p*); Victor Venegas (*b*); Frank Hernanadez, Osvaldo Chihuahua Martinez, Julian Cabrera (*perc*).

***(*)   **Summertime** Original Jazz Classics OJC 626 CD/LP/MC
Santamaria; Dizzy Gillespie (*t*); Doug Harris (*f, ts*); Allen Hoist (*f, bs, clo*); Toots Thielemans (*hca*); Milton Hamilton (*p*); Lee Smith (*b*); Steve Berrios (*perc*). 7/80.

(*)   **Soy Yo Concord 327 CD/MC
Santamaria; Eddie E. J. Allen (*t*); Sam Furnace (*as, bs, f*); Tony Hinson (*ts, f*); Bob Quaranta (*p, ky*); Ray Martinez (*b*); John Andrews (*d, perc*); Pablo Rosario, Steve Thornton, Valentino (*perc*); Ada Chabrier, Denice Nortez Wiener (*v*). 4/87.

(*)   **Soca Me Nice Concord 362 CD/MC
Santamaria; Ray Vega (*t, flhn*); Bobby Porcelli (*as, bs, f*); Mitch Frohman (*ts, f*); Bob Quaranta (*p*); Ray Martinez (*b*); Johnny Almendra Andreu, Humberto Nengue Hernandez (*perc*); Angelo-Mark Pagen (*v*). 5/88.

***   **Ole Ola** Concord 387 Cd/MC
Santamaria; Ray Vega (*t, flhn*); Bobby Porcelli (*as, bs, f*); Mitch Frohman (*ts, f*); Bob Quaranta (*p*); Bernie Minoso (*b*); Johnny Almendra Andreu, Humberto Nengue Hernandez (*perc*); Jil Armsbury, Bobbi Cespedes, Claudia Gomez (*v*). 5/89.

Born in Cuba, Santamaria moved to the United States in 1950. Originally an orthodox *charanga* player, leading a group fronted by violin and flute, he introduced trumpets and saxophones and experimented with jazz voicings. Despite a resurgence of activity in the later '80s, and two fine sessions for Concord, his reputation is now much less than it was in the 1960s and early '70s, when he was seen as largely responsible for the introduction of Latin-jazz and soul elements into the mainstream, developments which had a profound impact on players like Chick Corea and Hubert Laws, both of whom play on *Skins*, a compilation of sessions nearly a decade apart, and certainly the best place to begin. The once popular *Watermelon Man* appears only to be available in cassette form, but the best of the material is now available on *At The Village Gate*. This and the *Summertime* OJC are lively club and concert recordings and give a good sense (though neither is particularly well registered) of the high level of excitement Santamaria can generate. The latter is properly co-credited to Dizzy Gillespie, whose Afro-Cuban experiments owe a good deal to the percussionist's influence.

SAHEB SARBIB
BASS, PIANO, ORGAN, SHENAI

**   **UFO Live On Tour** Cadence CJR 1008 LP
Sarbib; Mark Whitecage, Daunik Lazro (*as*); Martin Bues (*d*). 3/79.

**   **Live At The Public Theater** Cadence CJR 1001 LP
Sarbib; Roy Campbell, Ryuichi Homma, Jack Walrath (*t*); Vincent Holmes Jr, Art
Baron, Tim Sessions (*tb*); Paul Shapiro, Talib Qadr, Lee Rozie (*ss*); James Ford,
Jemeel Moondoc, Mark Whitecage (*as*); Booker T, David Pate, Pete Chavez (*ts*);
David Sewelson (*bs*); William Brown, Steve Groves (*g*); David Hofstra (*b*); Richard
Baratta (*d*); Guilherme Franco (*perc*). 10/80.

**   **Aisha** Cadence CJR 1010 LP
As above, except Steven Bernstein (*t*), Rick Davies (*tb*), Mel Ellison (*ss*), Lee
Goodall (*as*), Frank Wright (*ts, v*) replace Homma, Walrath, Holmes, Baron, Qadr and
Ford. 7–8/81.

(*)   **Seasons Soul Note SN 1048 LP
Sarbib; Mel Ellison (*ss, as, ts*); Mark Whitecage (*as*); Paul Motian (*d*). 11/81.

(*)   **It Couldn't Happen Without You Soul Note SN 1098 LP
Sarbib; Joe Ford (*ss, as*); Pete Chavez, Joe Lovano (*ts*); Kirk Lightsey (*p*); Rashied
Ali (*d*). 1–2/84.

Primarily a bassist, Sarbib has attracted some interesting players to his sessions, but the results
tend to be unconvincingly diffuse. The Cadence albums are a disappointing lot: the UFO small
group gets lost in meandering duels between Whitecage and Lazro, who've both done better
work elsewhere, and the two big band records are noisy and discouragingly directionless
sessions, indifferently recorded, despite a few more rousing moments. Both *Seasons* and *It
Couldn't Happen Without You* are more pointed: the former has some pleasing melodies among
its eight tracks, and the impressive cast on *It Couldn't Happen Without You* works through a
series of dedications (to Parker, Monk and Dennis Charles) with thoughtful commitment.
Lovano is fine, and it's interesting to hear Ali on 'Crescent'. But a feeling persists that Sarbib
lacks the authority to bind these sessions together.

SAX APPEAL
GROUP

***   **Flat Out** Hep CD 2050 CD
Derek Nash, Nigel Hitchcock (*ss, as*); Dave O'Higgins, Scott Garland, Mornington
Lockett (*ts*); Gary Plumley (*as, ts*); Bob McKay (*bs, f*); Simon Hale (*ky*); Phil Mulford
(*b*); Mike Bradley (*d*). 91.

While this studio record doesn't quite capture the clout and panache which this group exude in a
club, it's a sharp and entertaining set of themes. Leader Derek Nash does most of the writing,
and while he's no great original, he knows how to make the most of a five-sax front line,
developing riffs into grand harmonic set-pieces and winging them over a rhythm section that's
comfortable in either bebop or jazz-rock time. Crisp, clear recording and plenty of space for the
principal soloists – mostly O'Higgins and Hitchcock – to go through their paces.

ANTONIO SCARANO
GUITAR

(*)   **Hot Blend Splasc(h) H 183 LP
Scarano; Felice Reggio (*t, flhn*); Luca Bonvini (*tb*); Sandro Cerino (*ss, as, cl, bcl, bf*);
Giulio Visibelli (*ss, ts, f*); Riccardo Viggore (*b*); Stefano Bagnoli (*d*); Roberta
Gambarini (*v*). 5–6/89.

**   **Apreslude** Splasc(h) H 356-2 CD
Scarano; Sandro Cerino (*bcl, cbcl*); Amerigo Daveri (*clo*); Loredana Gintoli (*hp*);
Roberta Gambarini (*v*). 5–6/91.

Two very different records, although Scarano and Gambarini are common to both. *Hot Blend* comes in the light modal-jazz flavours which are characteristic of the new wave of Italian musicians, and there are good tunes and pleasing solos which drift by without making too much impression. Gambarini takes a subdued role there; but *Apreslude* is basically a voice-and-guitar duo record, with the other players chipping in on only two tracks. It's a challenge to the two principals and one which Gambarini is frankly not up to yet: her scat readings of Ornette Coleman's 'Ramblin'' and Miles Davis's 'Nefertiti' are pretty but featherweight, and her voice is best used as a colour rather than a lead instrument. Scarano fills in behind her with honest toil, but the record doesn't amount to much.

ALEXANDER VON SCHLIPPENBACH (born 1938)
PIANO

***   **The Living Music** FMP 0100 LP
Schlippenbach; Manfred Schoof (*c, t*); Paul Rutherford (*tb*); Peter Brötzmann (*ts, bs*); Michel Pilz (*bcl, bs*); Buschi Niebergall (*b, btb*); Han Bennink (*d, perc*). 4/69.

***(*) **Payan** Enja 2012 LP

****   **Piano Solo** FMP 0430 LP
Schlippenbach (*p* solo). 2/72, 2/77.

*****   **Pakistani Pomade** FMP 0110 LP

***   **Three Nails Left** FMP 0210 LP

***(*) **The Hidden Peak** FMP 0410 LP

****   **Detto Fra Di Noi** Po Torch PTR/JWD 10/11 2LP

****   **Elf Bagatellen** FMP CD 27 CD
Schlippenbach; Evan Parker (*ss, ts*); Peter Kowald (*b* on *Three Nails Left* and *The Hidden Peak* only); Paul Lovens (*d*). 11/72; 6/74 & 2/75; 1/77; 6/81; 5/90.

***   **Live At The Quartier Latin** FMP 0310 LP

***   **Kung Bore** FMO 0520 LP
Schlippenbach; Sven-Ake Johansson (*d, acc*). 4/76, 11/77.

Schlippenbach's clean, atonal lines are far more reminiscent of Thelonious Monk than of Cecil Taylor, the figure who is usually adduced as ancestor for this kind of free music. By 1970 Schlippenbach had to some extent turned away from total abstraction and was showing an interest not only in formal compositional principles (serialism, orthodox sonata form, aspects of *ricercare*) but in renewing his own initial contact with early and modern jazz, blues and boogie-woogie. These interests were still obvious even underneath the radical freedoms of his influential collective, Globe Unity Orchestra (*q. v.*), but they became much clearer in his work with the later Berlin Contemporary Jazz Orchestra (*q.v.*) (ECM 1409 CD), where he uses the conventionally swinging drummer, Ed Thigpen, and trumpeter, Benny Bailey, in among the free men. Schlippenbach's conception of freedom has nearly always resulted in densely layered explorations of tonality, with a pronounced rhythmic slant. It's this which renders him surprisingly accessible as a performer.

His association with the Swedish drummer/accordionist has been among the most fruitful of his career. Their occasional examination of standards – 'Round About Midnight' on *Quartier Latin*, 'Over The Rainbow' on *Kung Bore* – simplifies understanding of Schlippenbach's angular lyricism. Something of the same quality is evident in the extreme chromaticism of 'Prelude To A Magic Afternoon Of Miss Yellow Sunshine' on the excellent *Payan*. If it's tempting to recommend this as the best point of entry into Schlippenbach's work, it's only fair to underline the significance of Free Music Production (FMP) in making available Schlippenbach's music, and that of many of his contemporaries. *Piano Solo* is a virtuosically extended performance, marked by tonal divisions of alarming suddenness and deft rhythmic displacements that frequently recall Monk. *The Living Music*, an excellent representation of his free-group performances of the time, comes at a vintage juncture in the FMP catalogue, wedged in between sax Goth Peter Brötzmann's extraordinary *Machine Gun* and his own trio, *Pakistani Pomade*, which, along with the later *Detto Fra Di Noi* (recorded on Paul Lovens's small label), represents the apex of Schlippenbach's free improvisatory approach. The later album, consisting of three long pieces ('Fra Di Noi' unfortunately is split between sides two and three, clear case for a future CD transfer), has a unity and unanimity of voice that replaces the briefer and rather more antagonistic (in the word's neutral sense) confrontations of *Pakistani Pomade*. The addition of Kowald on *Three Nails Left* seems to break down lines of communication between Parker and the pianist, and there is a slight air of uncertainty on parts of 'Range', recorded at Moers, which is absent from the later, Berlin-recorded performances. *The Hidden Peak* is a crashing return to form, an ascent in five mysterious climbs, marred only by the dullness of the sound and some loss of resolution on Lovens's characteristically unpredictable percussion.

Elf Bagatellen almost merits *Pakistani Pomade*'s fifth star, not just for its markedly improved sound-quality, but also for the sheer untrifling intensity of the trio's performances, which are unsurpassed in latter, quieter days. Like the earlier record, this is a studio performance rather than a live set, and it acts as a very conscious summation of the trio's near-two-decade career. It is, inevitably, rather more predetermined than a more spontaneous performance, and there are shards of melody scattered throughout. 'Sun-Luck: Revisited' refers to 'Sun-Luck Night-Rain', one of the finest pieces on the 1972 album, while 'Yarak: Reforged' provides a similar gloss on a piece from *Payan*. Parker and Lovens have rarely played better together and if Schlippenbach seems a trifle mild-mannered in places, the richness of the sound more than compensates for a slight drop in pulse-rate. Tremendous stuff.

****   **Smoke** FMP CD 23 CD
       Schlippenbach; Sunny Murray (*d*). 10/89.

Despite being tossed with insulting casualness into that overstuffed category, Schlippenbach is a very different kind of player from Cecil Taylor. By the same token, Sunny Murray is a very different kind of player *now* from what he was when he played with Taylor back in 1960. *Smoke* is an intriguing collaboration, in which both men hang up their 'free music' armour and get down to what sounds like a set of phantom standards. There are a dozen or more teasing echoes, more elusive than allusive, but only one outwardly identifiable theme, Monk's 'Trinkle Tinkle'. Beautifully recorded, and superbly played, it warms slowly from a rather misterioso opening. Only on 'Down The Mission' does the Taylor parallel make complete sense. Elsewhere, Monk and even Herbie Nichols seem more valid points of reference. Murray's 'Angel Voice' uses material that he has developed over two decades; cymbal overtones create an illusion of choral effects, studded by tight accents and the familiar poly-directional lines. Beautifully recorded.

****   **Das Höhe Lied** PoTorch PTR/JWD 16/17 2LP
       Schlippenbach; Evan Parker (*ss, ts*); Alan Silva (*b*); Paul Lovens (*d*). 11/81.

Inspired by the 'Song of Songs' and graced with extravagantly beautiful titles – 'Blow On My Garden and Press Out The Spices', 'Let The Heart Shower Kisses On You' – the music is less effusive than one might expect. Schlippenbach's brand of freedom increasingly seems to resolve into 'compositional' forms, but these advance and disappear with not the slightest suggestion that they are intended to structure an improvisation, merely reflecting an internal and very involved perception of it. Parker and Lovens play as brilliantly as one has come to expect, but a word for bassist Silva, on his day one of the most dramatic bassists in free music, and an ambitious composer/leader in his own right. There are moments here that strongly recall his Celestial Communication Orchestra projects of the early 1970s (some of which are recorded on BYG). Overall, this is precise, intelligent music, governed by sheer intelligence, and in most regards the antithesis of the radical freedoms claimed by an earlier avant-garde.

ROB SCHNEIDERMAN (born 1957)
PIANO

**   **New Outlook** Reservoir RSR 106 CD
       Schneiderman; Slide Hampton (*tb*); Rufus Reid (*b*); Akira Tana (*d*). 1/88.

Solid, contemporary hard bop. Slide Hampton is an unusual choice as the sole horn and his mild-mannered fluency suits Schneiderman's approach perhaps a little too well: the music tends to settle down into blandishments of the kind that have been committed to record many times before. Despite a couple of interesting ideas – such as the prickly waltz tempo chosen for Alec Wilder's 'While We're Young' – the music never quite lifts off the ground.

DANIEL SCHNYDER
TENOR AND SOPRANO SAXOPHONE

***   **Secret Cosmos** Enja 5055 CD/LP
Schnyder; Max Helfenstein (*t*); Hugo Helfenstein (*tb*); Hans Peter Hass (*btb*); Han Bergstrom (*frhn*); Matthias Ziegler (*f*); Urs Hammerli (*b*).

***   **The City** Enja 6002 CD/LP
Schnyder; Lew Soloff, Michael Philip Mossman (*t*); Ray Anderson (*tb*); Vladislaw Sendecki (*p*); Michael Formanek (*b*); Ronnie Burrage (*d*). 9/88.

***   **Decoding The Message** Enja 6036 CD
As above, except add Matthias Ziegler (*f*), Daniel Pezzotti (*clo*), Robert Mark (*perc*). 5/89.

A fluent player, Schnyder's real interest is in composing and aranging, and he's attracted some imposing names for his three Enja albums. Post-bop orthodoxy is ignored in favour of a wide-ranging approach which is often as close to contemporary European composition as it is to jazz: Schnyder tinkers with textures and lines, tries tone rows and motivic variations as bases for themes, and generally asks a lot of his musicians. There's something good on all the records, and perhaps the third, with a couple of impeccably scored pieces in 'The Sound Of The Desert' and 'A Call From Outer Space', is the best. But nothing ever quite manifests itself as a genuinely heavyweight piece, and the substance of some of the themes is dissipated by what might be a low boredom threshold: the shortness of several of the pieces isn't so much a refreshing brevity as a hint that Schnyder could be a bit of a gadfly.

MANFRED SCHOOF (born 1936)
TRUMPET

***   **Voices** L + R 41005 LP
Schoof; Gerd Dudek (*ts*); Alexander Von Schlippenbach (*p*); Buschi Niebergall (*b*); Jackie Liebezeit (*d*). 5/66.

***   **The Early Quintet** FMP 0540 LP
As above. 12/66.

****   **European Echoes** FMP 0010 LP
As above, except add Enrico Rava, Hugh Steinmetz (*t*); Peter Brötzmann (*ts*); Evan Parker (*ss*); Paul Rutherford (*tb*); Derek Bailey (*g*); Fred Van Hove, Irene Schweizer (*p*); Arjen Gorter, Peter Kowald (*b*); Han Bennink, Pierre Favre (*d*); omit Liebezeit. 6/69.

***   **Distant Thunder** Enja 2066 LP
Schoof (*t* solo) and with Yosuke Yamashita (*p*); Akira Sakata (*as*); Takeo Moriyama (*d*). 6/75.

(*)   **Light Lines Japo 60019 LP
Schoof; Michel Pilz (*bcl*); Jasper Van't Hof (*p, electric p, org*); Gunter Lenz (*b*); Ralf Hubner (*d*). 12/77.

***   **Shadows And Smiles** Wergo WER 80007 CD
Schoof; Rainer Bruninghaus (*p, ky*). 10/87 & 5/88.

The surprise of finding a jazz musician recording on Wergo, a label largely dedicated to adventurous modern composition, is partially explained by the fact that Schoof is also a composer of some significance, who has outdone even Wynton Marsalis by *writing* and performing his own trumpet concerto. Schoof's handling of large groups is best exemplified in the superb *European Echoes*, which is like a family gathering of the top-ranking European improvisers of the time. The doubling and sometimes trebling of instruments – as with the

Globe Unity Orchestra – leads to occasional congestion of the sound. Its continuous two-part structure would also benefit from CD transfer. There are hints of classical music, Bruckner even, in the brass voicings.

The earlier quintet consciously eschewed external reference of any sort, striving for an initial conceptual 'emptiness'. Empirically, the music is far from a blank canvas; it's abstract expressionist in the same sense that the later *Light Lines* is neo-realist and *Shadows And Smiles* neo-formalist.

Schoof's trumpet playing has a slightly stark quality, sharpened by his earlier use of cornet, warmed by his more recent occasional preference for flugelhorn. Like most trumpeters of his generation (and particularly the Europeans), he is conscious of Miles Davis, but looks back to the more pungent and abstract sound of Booker Little.

DIANE SCHUUR
VOCAL, KEYBOARDS

**   **Talkin' 'Bout You** GRP 9567 CD
Schuur; Tom Scott (*as, ts*); Lenny Pickett (*ts*); Ronnie Cuber (*bs*); Richard Tee, Mitch Forman (*ky*); Steve Khan (*g*); Will Lee (*b*); Steve Gadd (*d*); strings; Edwin Hawkins Singers (*v*).

**   **Pure Schuur** GRP 9628 CD
Schuur; Frank Szabo, Nolan Smith, Steve Huffsteter, Oscar Brashear, Gary Grant, Chuck Findley (*t*); Charles Loper, Garnett Brown, Dick Hyde, Maurice Spears (*tb*); David Duke, Marni Robinson, Art Mawby, Richard Perissi (*frhn*); Larry Williams, Fred Jackson, Ernie Fields, Joel C. Peskin (*as*); Dan Higgins (*ts*); Kim Hutchcroft, Jack Nimitz (*bs*); David Benoit, Tom Garvin (*p*); Mitchel Ruff, Mark Hugenberger Larry Steelman (*ky*); Dean Parks, Grant Geissman (*g*); Neil Stubenhaus, Jim Hughart (*b*); Carlos Vega, André Fischer, Harold Jones (*d*); Joe Williams, Denise DeCaro, Lynn Davis, Maxine Anderson, Bobby Womack (*v*); strings.

**   **Deedles** GRP 9510 CD
Schuur; Stan Getz (*ts*); Dave Grusin, Don Grusin (*ky*); Howard Roberts, Steve Khan (*g*); Don Dean (*b*); Moyes Lucas (*d*); strings.

**   **Schuur Thing** GRP 9531 CD
Schuur; Larry Williams, Stan Getz (*ts*); Dave Grusin (*ky*); Lee Ritenour (*g*); Abe Laboriel, Chuck Domanico (*b*); Carlos Vega (*d*); Paulinho Da Costa (*perc*); Jose Feliciano (*v*); strings.

**   **Timeless** GRP 9540 CD
Schuur; Chuck Findley, Jerry Hay, Gary Grant, Warren Luening (*t*); Charles Loper, Bill Reichenbach, Bill Watrous (*tb*); Tommy Johnson (*tb, tba*); Stan Getz, Bill Perkins, Tom Scott, Pete Christlieb, Gary Herbig, Jack Nimitz (*reeds*); Randy Kerber, Mike Lang, Dave Grusin (*ky*); Lee Ritenour (*g*); Chuck Domanico, Buell Neidlinger (*b*); Steve Schaeffer (*d*); Michael Fisher, Larry Bunker (*perc*); strings.

**   **Diane Schuur And The Count Basie Orchestra** GRP 9550 CD
Schuur; Bob Ojeda, Byron Stripling, Sonny Cohn, Melton Mustafa (*t*); Clarence Banks, Bill Hughes, Mel Wanzo, Dennis Wilson (*tb*); Danny House, Danny Turner (*as*); Frank Foster, Kenny Hing, Eric Dixon (*ts*); John Williams (*bs*); Donald T. Carson (*p*); Freddie Green (*g*); Lynn Seaton (*b*); Dennis Mackrel (*d*).

Schuur is a singer who tries too hard. She has become one of the most successful jazz-associated singers of her time, but the association does little honour to the music. Most of the above sessions are essentially polished bourgeois pop with the occasional sax solo thrown in to suggest a jazz sensibility: soothingly produced in the GRP house style, there are undeniable plesantries on all the records. But Schuur's mannerisms are no more appealing than, say, Linda Ronstadt's when she does her ersatz classic-vocal records, and in some cases – such as her knack for breaking into a scream when she feels overwhelmed by an inner drama – they are rather less so. The material is an unappetizing blend of standards and mildly risible contemporary songs. Although Getz turns up on a couple of sessions, they are scarcely important moments in his discography. The meeting with the latter-day Basie orchestra has a couple of respectable swingers, but compared with Basie's own team-ups with Tony Bennett, Sammy Davis or Sarah Vaughan, this one hardly raises the temperature. There is a compilation available, *Collection* (*GRP 9591*), which may be the best choice for the curious.

**(*)   In Tribute GRP 20062 CD/MC
Schuur; big band and strings. 91.

While it's not exactly a great step forward, this set is marginally more appealing than Schuur's other records. Conceived as a tribute to a dozen other jazz vocalists, the record's strength is that Schuur doesn't try to ape the mannerisms of the designated singers, and in the process of being herself she seems to actually convey more of herself in the music. While some of the songs – including the opening volley through 'Them There Eyes' – suggest, gratingly, that she has to be careful about choosing material, there are some quite effective ballad interpretations scattered through the programme. The blowsy orchestrations are too much, as usual, but Schuur is the kind of singer who asks for a lot anyway.

IRENE SCHWEIZER (born 1941)
PIANO

***   Wilde Senoritas FMP 0330 LP
Schweizer (*p* solo). 11/76.

***(*)   Hexensabbat FMP 0500 LP
As above. 10/77.

****   Piano Solo: Volume 1 Intakt 020 CD
As above. 5/90.

****   Piano Solo; Volume 2 Intakt 021 CD
As above.

***   Early Tapes FMP 0590 LP
Schweizer; Uli Trepte (*b*); Mani Neumeier (*d*). 1/67.

**(*)   Goose Panne 1e FMP 0190 LP
Schweizer; Rudiger Carl (*ts*); Arjen Gorter (*b*); Heinrich Hock (*d*). 9/74.

***   Messer FMP 0290 LP

**(*)   Tuned Boots FMP 0550 LP
Schweizer; Rudiger Carl (*ts, as, cl*); Louis Moholo (*d*). 5/75; 11/77, 3/78.

***   Die V-Mann Suite FMP 0860 LP
Schweizer; Rudiger Carl (*concertina, bcl, ts*). 10/80.

***(*)   Free Mandela! Intakt 003 LP
Schweizer; Louis Moholo (*d*). 87.

***   Schweizersommer Intakt 007 LP
Schweizer; Günter Sommer (*d*). 88.

****   The Storming Of The Winter Palace Intakt 003 LP
Schweizer; George Lewis (*tb*); Joëlle Léandre (*b*); Günter Sommer (*d*); Maggie Nicols (*b*).

Almost inevitably saddled with a 'female Cecil Taylor' tag, Schweizer is nevertheless a highly distinctive player whose premises diverge quite sharply from Taylor's essentially percussive approach. Like Marilyn Crispell (with whom she has recently duetted on record) and Geri Allen, though earlier than the rather younger Americans, she has proved her worth in almost aggressively masculine company and emerged with an aesthetic which is unmistakably and uncompromisingly female, fulfilling Mary Lou Williams's assertion that 'working with men . . . you automatically become strong, though this doesn't mean you're not feminine'.
   Like Crispell (but again much earlier), Schweizer has turned that initial and superficial Cecil Taylor influence into a combatively romantic approach to free playing. Even *Wilde Senoritas*, the most Taylorish of her records, is marked by a melodic warmth which the American wholly lacks. She is probably best heard solo, though the early trio is a fascinating glimpse into a style

that is not so much 'developing' as prematurely developed and cornered by its own idiomatic assurance. The two solo records, made in 1990 in her native Switzerland, are without doubt the place to begin. The sonority of CD recording suits her touch very well, and the ambience – or ambiences, since one of the records is made in front of an invited audience – is warmer than on most of the FMPs. Brief and apparently inconsequential structures are delivered without elaboration. There is none of the swirling intensity she conjures up in the presence of Rudiger Carl, Louis Moholo or Baby Sommer, and there is a meditative stillness about 'The Ballad Of The Sad Café' (a title derived from Carson McCullers's soft-tough story) that is unlike anything on the earlier work, even the fine *Messer*, but which is clearly derived wholly from it.

'Sisterhood Of Spit' (the name relates to an all-female collective of the 1970s) is dedicated to the late Dudu Pukwana, also name-checked in happier days on *Wilde Senoritas*, and to the late Chris McGregor, whose Brotherhood of Breath was a lasting example of the possibility of reconciling lyrical expressiveness and improvisational freedom. As the title suggests, Schweizer has taken her own route to that end. Her part in the powerful improvised *Canaille* (Intakt 002/88 LP) from the International Women's Festival of Music is somehow rather lost. She's much more impressive on another Intakt release, *The Storming Of The Winter Palace*, which was recorded live in Switzerland, featuring a superb group of improvisers who combine mature freedom with a capacity for tremendous lyricism; the record won a German Record Critics Award in 1988.

Despite her avowed feminism, Schweizer doesn't belong in the neutral enclave of 'women's music', but in the mainstream of European improvisation, a fact duly recognized by Barry Guy's *Theoria*, a fiftieth-birthday composition for her (yet to be released on record) in which two generations of mostly male European improvisers pay overdue court to her.

LOUIS SCLAVIS
BASS CLARINET, TENOR SAXOPHONE, SOPRANO SAXOPHONE

****   **Clarinettes** IDA 004 CD/LP
Sclavis solo, and with Christian Rollet, Christian Ville (*perc*). 9/84, 1/85.

***(*)   **Chine** IDA 012 CD/LP
Sclavis; François Raulin (*p, syn, perc*); Dominique Pifarely (*vn*); Bruno Chevillon (*b*); Christian Ville (*d, perc*). 7 & 9/87.

***(*)   **Chamber Music** IDA 022 CD
Sclavis; Ives Robert (*tb*); Michel Godard (*tba*); Dominique Pifarely (*vn*); Philippe Deschepper (*g*); François Raulin (*p, syn*); Bruno Chevillon (*b*). 7 & 9/89.

Potentially the most important French jazz musician since Django Reinhardt, Louis Sclavis has attempted to create an 'imaginary folklore' that combines familiar jazz procedures with North African and Mediterranean music, French folk themes and music from the *bal musette*. He is not yet an absolutely convincing recording artist and is best heard in concert. Nevertheless, early exposure on the mostly solo *Clarinettes* confirmed word-of-mouth reports from France that he was a performer to be reckoned with.

Unlike Sidney Bechet, who may have been a dim ancestral influence, his clarinet work is a great deal more forceful than his soprano saxophone playing, and Sclavis is one of the foremost of a growing number of younger jazz musicians who have rescued the clarinet from desuetude as an improvising instrument. His bass clarinet work is particularly original, drawing little or nothing from the obvious model and condensing most of Sclavis's virtues: melodic invention, timbral variation, rhythmic sophistication. Perhaps the most striking track on *Clarinettes* is 'Le Chien Aboie Et La Clarinette Basse' a husky duo with percussionist Ville which puns on a French gypsy saying: the dog barks '*et le caravane passe*'.

For all his interest in European folk and popular themes, Sclavis considers himself unequivocally a jazz musician. A duo version of 'Black And Tan Fantasy' on the same album suggests he has much to contribute to standards playing. Most of his work, however, has been original and this, coupled with his obvious straining at the conventions of the orthodox jazz ensemble (particularly as regards the drummer, whom Sclavis considers to be excessively dominant) has temporarily held back his development as a soloist. *Chine* is a fine and original set of pieces, but its unfamiliar tonal components only partially mitigate an overall lack of development. *Chamber Music*, as the title implies, throws still more weight on compositional values, but there are signs that Sclavis is working through his dilemmas. In Chevillon he has an understanding and highly effective foil. There seems little doubt that he is poised to make a substantial contribution to the music.

***(*) **Rouge** ECM 1458 CD/LP/MC
Sclavis; Dominique Pifarely (*vn*); François Raulin (*p, syn*); Bruno Chevillon (*b*); Christian Ville (*d*). 9/91.

Sclavis's ECM debut is a challenging and surprisingly abstract set that rarely allows itself to settle into a jazz groove. The first four tracks are moodily atmospheric, with a strong suggestion of North African music; 'Nacht' is particularly effective, with dissonant flashes of multi-tracked clarinet echoed by the softly bouncing thunder of Ville's bass drum, before giving way to an evocative solo by Chevillon. Pifarely comes into his own on 'Reeves', teasing out a long unison statement with Sclavis and then soloing on his own 'Moment Donné'. Several tracks sound as if they are through-composed, and apart from the later stages of 'Les Bouteilles' and a delicious waltz tag on the title piece, the emphasis is all on textures and rather brooding melodic outlines rather than on linear development. The longest track 'Face Nord' echoes 'Reflet' in the way it suspends Sclavis's high, swooping clarinet lines over a dense chordal background (that on 'Face Nord' suddenly erupts into a convincing simulacrum of a flat-out electric guitar solo, all done on Raulin's imaginatively programmed synth).

Rouge establishes Sclavis as an enterprising and thought-provoking composer. If it does so at the expense of rhythmic energy (a strategy consistent with his ambivalence about jazz percussion), it doesn't short-change in other departments.

JOHN SCOFIELD (born 1951)

GUITAR

**   **East Meets West** Black-Hawk BKH 533 CD/LP
Scofield; Terumasa Hino (*t*); Clint Houston (*b*); Motohiko Hino (*d*). 8/77.

(*)   **Live Enja 3013 CD/LP
Scofield; Richard Beirach (*p*); George Mraz (*b*); Joe LaBarbera (*d*). 11/77.

***   **Rough House** Enja 3033 LP
Scofield; Hal Galper (*p*); Stafford James (*b*); Adam Nussbaum (*d*). 11/78.

***   **Who's Who?** Novus PD 83071 CD/LP/MC
Scofield; Dave Liebman (*ss, ts*); Kenny Kirkland (*p*); Steve Swallow, Anthony Jackson, Eddie Gomez (*b*); Steve Jordan, Billy Hart, Adam Nussbaum (*d*); Sammy Figueroa (*perc*). 79–80.

John Scofield was perhaps the last of Miles Davis's sidemen to break through to a major career, but the records listed above, all made prior to his joining Davis in 1982, bespeak a substantial talent already making waves. He had played with a diverse group of leaders – Charles Mingus, Lee Konitz, Gary Burton, Billy Cobham – before forming the band that made the 1977 live album (the meeting with Hino is a rather desultory studio jam). Beirach is a little too cool to suit Scofield's needs and Gomez is all tight virtuosity rather than loosely funky, but the music is still impressive, since the leader's own playing is an intriguing mix of a classic, open-toned bop style and a blues-rock affiliation. He gets the same sound on the studio date with Galper, but this is a tougher record, with the pianist flying directly alongside the guitarist on tunes which unreel at a uniformly fast tempo: Nussbaum gives them both plenty of push. *Who's Who?* offers a varierty of groups – quintet with Kirkland, quartet with Liebman, trio with Nussbaum and Swallow. The first group suggests the funk style which Sco would adopt on his Gramavision sets, the quartet holds to the post-bop manner, and the four trio cuts propose a course between the two points: it's an excellent sampler of the guitarist's methods in this period, and at least one of the tunes – 'The Beatles' – is a potential standard.

***(*) **Shinola** Enja 4004 CD/LP
Scofield; Steve Swallow (*b*); Adam Nussbaum (*d*). 12/81.

***(*) **Out Like A Light** Enja 4038 CD/LP/MC
Scofield; Steve Swallow (*b*); Adam Nussbaum (*d*). 12/81.

Scofield's final Enja albums were recorded at a live date in Munich. Good though the earlier records are, these loose, exploratory tracks are his most interesting so far: the trio functions as a single probing unit, Swallow's fat sound counterpointing the guitar, and the space and drift of such as 'Yawn' from *Shinola* opens Scofield's horizon. With pianists, he was putting in as many notes as Coltrane on occasion, but here – with Nussbaum restlessly decorating the pulse – the guitarist sounds as if he doesn't see the need to cover every harmonic area. Good digital sound.

**   **Electric Outlet** Gramavision GR 8045 CD
Scofield; Ray Anderson (*tb*); David Sanborn (*as*); Pete Levin (*ky*); Steve Jordan (*d*). 4–5/84.

****   **Still Warm** Gramavision GR 8508 CD
Scofield; Don Grolnick (*ky*); Darryl Jones (*b*); Omar Hakim (*d*). 6/85.

***   **Blue Matter** Gramavision 18-8702 CD
Scofield; Mitch Forman (*ky*); Hiram Bullock (*g*); Gary Grainger (*b*); Dennis Chambers (*d*); Don Alias (*perc*). 9/86.

***   **Loud Jazz** Gramavision 18-8801 CD
As above, except Robert Aries, George Duke (*ky*) replace Forman, Bullock omitted. 12/87.

***   **Pick Hits Live** Gramavision 18-8805 CD
As above, except omit Duke and Alias. 10/87.

***(*)   **Flat Out** Gramavision 18-8903 CD
Scofield; Don Grolnick (*org*); Anthony Cox (*b*); Johnny Vidacovich, Terri Lyne Carrington (*d*). 12/88.

Scofield's six Gramavision albums are a coherent and highly enjoyable body of work. *Electric Outlet* was a false start: the band seems gimcracked around a dubious idea of highbrow pop-jazz, Sanborn and Anderson are there only for colour, and the attempted grooves and stiff and unyielding. But *Still Warm* solved matters at a stroke. Steve Swallow's production calorified the sound without overpowering the fluidity of Scofield's arrangements, Grolnick added thoughtful keyboard textures, and Jones and Hakim (colleagues from the Miles Davis band) were tight and funky without being relentlessly so. Scofield's own playing here assumes a new authority: tones are richer, the hint of fuzz and sustain is perfectly integrated, and his solos are unflaggingly inventive: for a single sample, listen to the sharp, hotly articulated solo on 'Picks And Pans'.

The band which the guitarist then formed with Grainger and Chambers bolstered the funk-fusion side of his playing: the drummer, especially, is a thunderous virtuoso in the manner of Billy Cobham, and the next three albums are all fired up with his rhythms. Scofield's writing revolves around ear-catching melodic hooks and a favourite device of a riff repeated over a shifting harmonic base, and the two studio albums are full of naggingly memorable themes. But the music was formulaic in the end: the live record is a feast of hard-nut jazz-funk showmanship, but it starts to sound clenched by the end. *Flat Out* comes as a welcome change of pace: Vidacovich and Carrington, who split chores between them through the record, are swinging but no less busy drummers: hear the consummately controlled rave-up on 'The Boss's Car' (a cheeky rip-off of Bruce Springsteen's 'Pink Cadillac'). Two standards, a Meters tune and a rollicking turn through 'Rockin' Pneumonia' also lighten the programme.

****   **Time On My Hands** Blue Note CDP 792894-2 CD/MC
Scofield; Joe Lovano (*ts*); Charlie Haden (*b*); Jack DeJohnette (*d*). 11/89.

***(*)   **Meant To Be** Blue Note CDP 795479-2 CD/MC
Scofield; Joe Lovano (*ts, cl*); Marc Johnson (*b*); Bill Stewart (*d*). 12/90.

Scofield's move to Blue Note has moved his career and his music substantially forward. Lovano is an inspired choice of front-line partner, renegotiating the jazz roots of Sco's approach without surrendering the feisty attack which he amplified through his Gramavision records. *Time On My Hands* provides some of his best writing, including the lovely ballad of 'Let's Say We Did' and the twining melodies of 'Since You Asked'. 'Fat Lip' is acoustic jazz-rock which Haden and DeJohnette jump on with brilliant ferocity. Superb studio sound throughout. If *Meant To Be* seems a shade less invigorating, it's only because it seems like a second run through the same territory. Both are very highly recommended.

***(*) **Grace Under Pressure** Blue Note CDP 7981672 CD/MC
    Scofield; Randy Brecker (*flhn*); Jim Pugh (*tb*); John Clark (*frhn*); Bill Frisell (*g*);
    Charlie Haden (*b*); Joey Baron (*d*). 12/91.

Though given a mixed reception on its release, this is a strong and thoughtfully realized continuation of Scofield's work for Blue Note. If he's starting to seem over-exposed as a player, turning up in countless guest roles as well as on his own records, the ten themes here display a consistent strength as a writer: variations on the blues, slow modal ballads, riffs worked into melodies, Scofield makes them all come up fresh, and he creates situations where the rhythm players can line the music with intensities and colours of their own. There are hard, swinging solos on the title-track and 'Twang', and if the interplay with Frisell can sometimes seem more like cheese and chalk, there are piquant contrasts which sometimes blend with surprising effectiveness: 'Honest I Do' is the kind of haunting, downbeat melody which Scofield has made his own. The brass are used very sparingly to underscore a few tracks.

RONNIE SCOTT (born 1927)
TENOR SAXOPHONE

***(*) **Never Pat A Burning Dog** Ronnie Scott's Jazz House JC 012 CD/LP/MC
    Scott; Dick Pearce (*t*); Mornington Lockett (*ts*); John Critchinson (*p*); Ron
    Mathewson (*b*); Martin Drew (*d*). 10 & 11/90.

Club owner, philosopher and wit (he asked us to say), Ronnie Scott has long been recognized as one of the most authentic and blues-rinsed of the European saxophonists. An active performer, Scott has recorded only sparingly and *Never Pat A Burning Dog* (seems obvious, but you never know) will appeal to those who have worn out their copy of *Serious Gold*, his late-1970s Pye album, though they may also be surprised at how far his harmonic thinking has developed since then. A muted, almost elegiac set (recorded live at Ronnie Scott's Club in Soho) begins with a stunning version of McCoy Tyner's 'Contemplation', full of glassy harmonies and tender, dissonant flourishes. Scott's choice of material is typically adventurous and tasteful: Jimmy Dorsey's 'I'm Glad There Is You', David Sanborn's 'White Caps', Cedar Walton's 'When Love Is New', a slightly unsatisfactory reading of Freddie Hubbard's 'Little Sunflower' with the less than inspiring Lockett in for Pearce, and two standards, 'All The Things You Are' and the still-under-recorded 'This Love Of Mine'.
    Scott's tone is deep and subtly modulated and his phrasing has the kind of relaxed precision and inner heat one associates with Paul Gonsalves or Zoot Sims. Despite the variety of material, it's a remarkably consistent set, perhaps even a little unvaried in treatment.

SHIRLEY SCOTT (born 1934)
ORGAN

*** **Blue Flames** Original Jazz Classics OJC 328 LP/MC
    Scott; Stanley Turrentine (*ts*); Bob Cranshaw (*b*); Otis Finch (*d*). 8/65.

Scott was no slouch when it came to mixing in heavy company: in 1955, in her native Philadelphia, she was working in a trio with John Coltrane. But it was her association with Eddie Lockjaw Davis which made her name and led to dozens of albums for Prestige, Impulse, Atlantic and Cadet through the 1970s. All of them have disappeared from print except the above Prestige session, now reissued as an Original Jazz Classic. Scott wasn't a knockabout swinger like Jimmy Smith and didn't have the bebop attack of Don Patterson, but there's an authority and an unusual sense of power in reserve which keeps her music simmering somewhere near the boil. She is a strong blues player and a fine accompanist. She was also married to Stanley Turrentine, and they made a number of records together, including the above – nothing more or less than some cooking tenor and organ on some blues and a ballad. Decent remastering, but it has to be played very loud to approximate the impact which the group must have had live.

*** **Oasis** Muse M 5388 CD/LP/MC
    Scott; Virgil Jones (*t*); Charles Davis, Houston Person (*ts*); Arthur Harper (*b*); Mickey
    Roker (*d*). 8/89.

After a long absence from the studios, Scott returned with a record as good as any she's made. Producer Houston Person, who plays on only one track, gets a smooth sound which suits the band, since the music is less about solos and more to do with ensemble timbre and the gently rocking grooves which Scott, Harper and Roker seem to relish. The title-track and 'Basie In Mind' are delectable slow swingers, but Scott's set-piece treatment of J. J. Johnson's 'Oasis' is the standout.

TOM SCOTT (born 1948)
ALTO AND TENOR SAX, LYRICON

** **Streamlines** GRP 9555 CD
Scott; Michael Landau, Eric Gale (g); Richard Tee, Joseph Conlan, Randy Kerber (ky); Neil Stubenhaus (b); Vinnie Colaiuta (d); Michael Fisher (perc). 7/87.

** **Flashpoint** GRP 9571 CD
As above, except Alan Pasqua (ky) replaces Tee, add Lynne Scott (v). 88.

** **Them Changes** GRP 9613 CD
Scott; David Koz (saxes); Eric Gale, Pat Kelley (g); Barnaby Finch, Jerry Peters (ky); Tim Landers (b); Art Rodriguez (d). 90.

* **Keep This Love Alive** GRP 9646 CD
Scott; David Paich (ky); Eric Gale, Dean Parks (g); Abe Laboriel, Will Lee (b); Brenda Russell, Diane Schuur, Bill Champlin (v). 91.

He might have started out with Oliver Nelson and Don Ellis, but Scott's jazz roots are negligible, and as such he's surely better placed than such recanting saxophonists as Eric Marienthal to make the most of a career as a king of MOR sax noodling. The first three GRP albums will do fine if you're after the kind of featherlight instrumentals which can double as TV theme tunes or in-car painkillers (they can hardly count as distractions). *Keep This Love Alive*, though, spoils it by bringing in vocalists. Scott sounded better behind Joni Mitchell.

TONY SCOTT (born 1921)
CLARINET, BARITONE SAXOPHONE, PIANO, ELECTRONICS

**** **A Day In New York** Fresh Sound FSR CD 160/2 2CD
Scott; Bill Evans (p); Clark Terry (t); Jimmy Knepper (tb); Sahib Shihab (bs); Henry Grimes, Milt Hinton (b); Paul Motian (d). 11/57.

***(*) **Dedications** Core COCD 9.00803 CD
Scott; Bill Evans, Horst Jankowski (p); Juan Suastre (g); Shinichi Yuize (koto); Scott LaFaro, Peter Witte (b); Paul Motian, Herman Mutschler (d). 57–59.

In 1959, Tony Scott turned his back on America, wounded by the death of several friends (Hot Lips Page, Billie Holiday, Charlie Parker, Lester Young) and by what he considered the 'death' of the clarinet in jazz terms. Since then he has been a wanderer, exploring the culture and music of the East, trading in the sometimes aggressive assertions of bebop for a meditative approach to harmony that at its best is deeply moving, at its least disciplined a weak ambient decoration.

These beautiful *Dedications* (some of which were available under the title *Sung Heroes* [Sunnyside SSC 1015 CD] and may still be found in that format) record Scott's reactions to a group of figures who have figured iconically in his life: Billie Holiday (the dedicatee of a delicate quartet, 'Misery'); Anne Frank (an overdubbed duet with himself on clarinet and baritone saxophone that might seem inept were it not so moving); Art Tatum; Hot Lips Page; an unnamed African friend; the Schoenbergian composer, Stefan Wolpe (who receives the homage of an atonal blues); his father; Israel; the bullfighter, Manolete; and Charlie Parker. There are also Japanese-influenced pieces, based on traditional verse and images.

The high clarinet protestations of 'Blues For An African Friend' and the succeeding 'Atonal Ad Lib Blues' suggest what a remarkable talent Scott's was, giving the instrument the power and immediacy of soprano saxophone without sacrificing its distinctive timbre. Influenced primarily by Ben Webster, he seems to condense and process an enormous acreage of jazz history in his enticingly miniaturist structures.

Scott enjoyed a close and fruitful relationship with Bill Evans, and perhaps his best recorded work is the session of 16 November 1957 with the Evans trio and guests, tackling a copious roster of originals and well-worn standards (including a lovely 'Lullaby Of The Leaves' with Knepper). The clarinettist's opening statements on Evans's 'Five' are almost neurotically brilliant and a perfect illustration of how loud Scott could play. 'Portrait Of Ravi' and 'The Explorer' are Scott originals, directed towards the concerns that were increasingly to occupy him. Evans's light touch and immense harmonic sophistication suited his approach ideally. Scott was at the top of his professional tree and enjoyed great critical acclaim. More recent years have found him a relatively forgotten figure. But he is unmistakably an original.

** **Music For Zen Meditation** Verve 817209 CD
Scott; Hozan Yamamoto (*shakuhachi*); Shinichi Yuizi (*koto*). 2/64.

Scott's absorption in Buddhist thinking ultimately resulted in some intriguing cross-cultural experiments like this one. His interest in Indian *raga* (as in his ahead-of-the-pack dedication to Ravi Shankar on the Fresh Sound, above) and in African musics, below, bespeaks certain philosophical premises which are rather difficult to judge on purely artistic grounds. How efficacious *Music For Zen Meditation* may be for its professed purpose is beyond the scope of this book to determine, but it's slightly disappointing to note how quickly Scott seemed prepared to abandon the taut harmonic arguments of his work with Evans, LaFaro and Motian in favour of the bland affirmations here.

***(*) **African Bird** Soul Note SN 1083 CD
Scott; Glenn Ferris (*tb*); Giancarlo Barigozzi (*f, bf*); Chris Hunter (*as, f*); Duncan Kinnel (*mar*); Rex Reason (*kalimba*); Robin Jones, Karl Potter (*perc*); Jacqui Benar (*v*). 81, 5/84.

Conceived and performed before 'World Music' had become a sneer, *African Bird* is a largely convincing synthesis of Scott's African and Afro-American concerns into a suite of songs with an impressive level of coherence and developmental logic. To all intents and purposes it is a solo record, with largely incidental colorations from all but Barigozzi and Kinnel, who both play beautifully. For a flavour of where Scott has been since 1960, this is ideal.

*** **Lush Life: Volume 1** Core COCD 9.00666 CD

*** **Lush Life: Volume 2** Core COCD 9.00667 CD
Scott; Bill Frisell (*g*); Ed Schuller (*b*); Tony D'Arco (*d*); Billy Strayhorn (*p, v*); Monica Sciacca (*v*). 81–4.

First blows in a promised seven-part dissection of Billy Strayhorn's great song, which has haunted his career. One can hear it almost subliminally quoted in umpteen Scott solos, most notably in 'Misery (to Lady Day)' on *Dedications*, above. This is far from a classical theme-with-variations. Scott provides a rap version; a recitation delivered over some heavily treated Frisell guitar; a quartet piece that stands in the same relation to the tune as a hangover to a great night out; solo piano, baritone saxophone, and clarinet performances; he has his young daughter (Sciacca is the family name) sing it; and he even includes an imperfect Strayhorn performance. Though there have been 'Round Midnight' albums by divers hands, rarely has a tune been subjected to such microscopic attention and loving deconstruction by a single individual. The effect is bizarre, kaleidoscopic and unsettlingly hypnotic.

(***) **Astral Meditation; Voyage Into A Black Hole 1** Core COCD 9.00590 CD

(**) **Astral Meditation: Voyage Into A Black Hole 2** Core COCD 9.00591 CD

(**) **Astral Meditation: Voyage Into A Black Hole 3** Core COCD 9.00592 CD
Scott solo instrumental and electronic treatments. 88.

It is, let's face it, none too difficult to dismiss projects of this New Age kind sight unseen. There is a certain conventional wisdom about their musical (if not their spiritual and therapeutic) worth that has critics reaching for their typewriters before the cellophane is off the record. In keeping with everything else he has ever done, Scott's exploration of electronics is maverick, highly personal, alternately riveting and galling. For him, synthesizers have opened up whole new harmonic territories that help draw together his interest in trance and process musics in the context of more conventional post-bop harmony. On the debit side, he shows no firm command of electronic processes and only a dull perception of the possibilities of *musique concrète*. The fundamental problem with *Astral Meditation* is that the music is largely insufficient to support the cosmic architecture Scott has erected around it; Parts 2 and 3, 'Astrala' and 'Astrobo', pall rapidly. In the context of this book, it's rather difficult to make a settled judgement; Scott's work is *sui generis*, but if the New Age is going to sound like this it may not be as boring as we'd feared.

JOEY SELLARS
TROMBONE

*** **Something For Nothing** Nine Winds NWCD 136 CD
Sellars; Greg Varlotta, Clay Jenkins (*t, flhn*); Alex Isles, Bruce Fowler (*tb*); Danny Hemwall (*btb*); Kim Richmond (*ss, as, cl, f*); John Schroeder (*ss, ts, cl, f*); Rob Verdi (*bs, bcl, f*); Kei Akagi (*p*); Ken Filiano (*b*); Billy Mintz (*d*). 2/89.

Although some of the big-band music on Nine Winds has been of a free-spirited nature, Sellars here leads a band of pros who could sit comfortably with any studio chores on the Los Angeles session-scene. The one cursory nod to any kind of dissembled structure on 'American Standard' is the least convincing moment on the record: the rest is sharply drilled and punchily phrased modern big band music, with Sellars throwing opportunities to soloists who can eat up changes and modal settings alike. His own trombone improvisations are as strong as anybody's, but a special mention to the splendid baritone of Verdi on the title tune. Some measure of the success of the arrangements comes in the point that although only five themes stretch across some 70 minutes of music, no track runs right out of steam.

BUD SHANK (born 1926)
ALTO SAXOPHONE, FLUTE; ALSO PENNY WHISTLE

*** **Misty Eyes** West Wind WW 0031 CD/LP
Shank; Claude Williamson (*p*); Don Prell (*b*); Jimmy Pratt (*d*). 4/58.

*** **California Concert** Contemporary C 14012 LP/MC
Shank; Shorty Rogers (*flhn*); George Cables (*p*); Monty Budwig (*b*); Sherman Ferguson (*d*). 5/85.

**** **That Old Feeling** Contemporary C 14019 LP/MC
Shank; George Cables (*p*); John Heard (*b*); Albert Heath (*d*). 2/86.

*** **At Jazz Alley** JVC/Fantasy VDJ 1120 CD
Shank; Dave Peck (*p*); Chuck Deardorff (*b*); Jeff Hamilton (*d*). 10/86.

*** **Serious Swingers** Contemporary C 14031 CD/LP/MC
Shank; Bill Perkins (*ts*); Alan Broadbent (*p*); John Heard (*b*); Sherman Ferguson (*d*). 12/86.

*** **Tomorrow's Rainbow** Contemporary C 14048 CD/LP/MC
Shank; Marcos Silva (*ky*); Ricardo Peixoto (*g*); Gary Brown (*b*); Michael Spiro (*d*).

Somewhat like Lee Konitz, Shank cast off a slightly wimpish initial reputation as a bland cocktail of Charlie Parker, Benny Carter and Johnny Hodges to re-emerge with a tougher and more abrasive approach that is reflected in his 1980s performances. *At Jazz Alley* is slightly rough and ready, certainly in comparison to *Serious Swingers*, co-led with Perkins a couple of months later; with the exception of Hamilton, the Jazz Alley group rarely finds a comfortable groove behind the leader. *That Old Feeling* is significantly better. Cables's subtle voicings provide the saxophonist with the kind of harmonic left-off that he seems to need, and his soloing is assured and mostly subtle, though occasionally marred by pointless *macho* mannerisms presumably intended to suggest strong emotion or a public recantation of the smooth pop he peddled in the later 1960s.

Like Shorty Rogers, with whom he appears on the so-so *California Concert*, Shank spent much of his middle years as a session musician. Perhaps ironically, the experience made him a more complete jazz musician. His work with the highly successful L.A.4 and to a lesser extent with the Lighthouse All Stars is inclined to be over-processed and self-consciously crowd-pleasing, but, as with the Modern Jazz Quartet, a superficial blandness masks formidable musicianship. Paired with Rogers's flugelhorn, he sounds much sweeter than when playing as sole wind, but the detailed attention he gives to themes as unalike as 'Makin' Whoopee' and the bop staple 'Ah-Leu-Cha' is highly instructive. One only misses the sound of his second horn; Shank is one of the few mainstream boppers to play convincing jazz flute.

Tomorrow's Rainbow teams him with Marco Silva's fusion group Intersection, for a lively, Latin set that keeps the temperature well up. There are valuable glimpses of Shank's early work on a Jazzline airshot compilation called *Hello Baden-Baden* [JL 280828 CD], where he plays with European luminaries Albert Mangelsdorff and Joe Zawinul. There is, though, little else of his pre-MOR, soft-bop phase, and (despite some good flute and a *tour de force* 'Tribute to the African Penny Whistle') *Misty Eyes* is a disappointingly thin offering, by no means as good a sample as the deleted *Live at the Haig* [Concept VL2 LP] recorded in 1956 with Williamson, Prell and drummer Chuck Flores. There are also a number of later Concords in the back catalogue, but these are of patchy quality.

LAKSHMINARAYANA SHANKAR (born 1950)
VIOLIN, DOUBLE VIOLIN

***   **Who's To Know** ECM 1195 CD/LP
Shankar; Umayalpuram K. Sivaraman (*mridangam*); Zakir Hussain (*tabla*); V. Lakshminarayana (*tala keeping*). 11/80.

***   **Vision** ECM 1261 CD/LP
Shankar; Jan Garbarek (*ts, ss, bsx, perc*); Palle Mikkelborg (*t, flhn*). 4/83.

(*)   **The Epidemics ECM 1308 CD/LP
Shankar; Caroline (*syn, tamboura, v*); Steve Vai (*g*); Gilbert Kaufman (*syn*); Percy Jones (*b*). 85.

***   **Pancha Nadal Pallavi** ECM 1407 CD/LP
Shankar; Zakir Hussain (*tabla*); Vikku Vinayakram (*ghatam*); Caroline (*talam, sruthi*). 7/89.

Subheaded 'Indian classical music' (a designation that has caused some controversy in quarters unamused by Shankar's syncretism of subcontinental idioms), *Who's To Know* poses a sly challenge to the Western listener. Is this 'authentic' Indian music? How would we know even if it wasn't? ECM's initial resistance to liner-notes and tendency to throw uncontextualized music at purchasers has changed in recent years (not least with the advent of the classically orientated New Series), but if Shankar's extraordinary music is be saved from a reductive categorization with 'ethnic', 'World Music' or 'New Age' materials, then more needs to be known about its rhythmic and harmonic premisses than is usually forthcoming.

Shankar's performing style is clearly not authentic in the sense that it is not constrained by traditional formulae and proscriptions. Shankar has played with saxophonist, Jan Garbarek, and with Eastward-stepping guitarist, John McLaughlin, in Shakti, the group that introduced him to a wider European audience. The association with Garbarek and Mikkelborg was a particularly fruitful one, demonstrating how readily Shankar's idiosyncratic 10-string double violin (whose twin necks can be played separately or simultaneously) and largely microtonal language translate to a Western improvisational idiom. There is nothing floatingly 'ethnic' about the music on *Vision*, which contains unprecedented bass saxophone work from Garbarek; it is a thoroughly contemporary and extremely intense performance from all three participants. The enigmatically titled *M.R.C.S.* is a re-recording of a solo project, with tabla master, Zakir Hussain, more than taking the place of the original rhythm box, and the other musicians helping to create a taut rhythmic web that trades up Shankar's almost pedestrian melodic notions into music of extravagant dimensions.

Pancha Nadal Pallavi is very much closer to Indian classical idiom and is consequently less penetrable from a Western point of view. Like the excellent *Nobody Told Me* [Music/ECM 08123162], these are American sessions centred on the interplay between Shankar's remarkable double-necked instrument (dimly reminiscent of John McLaughlin's trademark double-neck guitar in Mahavishnu days) and Zakir Hussain's virtuosic tabla. The singing is intricate and insistently rhythmic. The Music album also features the acoustic violin of Shankar's father, V. Lakshminarayana, and the drones (a technical device, no slur intended) of his wife Caroline (who seems to have shed a surname). She also appears on *The Epidemics*, a title used for Shankar's touring band, albeit with different personnel. This is the weakest of the albums, too far removed from the tradition that nourishes the best of them.

ELLIOTT SHARP
ELECTRIC GUITAR, STEEL GUITAR, BASS GUITAR, SOPRANO SAXOPHONE, BASS CLARINET, OTHER INSTRUMENTS AND TREATMENTS

***   **Datacide** Enemy EM 116 CD/LP
Sharp; Zeena Parkins (*electric hp, ky*); Samm Bennett (*perc, d, samples*); David Linton (*d*).

***   **In New York** Enemy EM 114 CD/LP
Sharp; Bachir Attar (*rhaita, guimbri, f, v*); Jane Tomkiewicz (*bendir*).

The latter title almost seems redundant. Where else might music as aggressively eclectic as this come from? In insisting, as its admirers do, that the New York downtown scene shows more variety than homogeneity, it's also important to register some slight suspicion that an absence of aesthetic fixity has become an end in itself, that all instrumental or stylistic combinations have become equally viable. Sharp's long-standing band, Carbon (to which *Datacide* is credited), produce a scaled-up version of his surprisingly accessible packaging of hardcore styles. It isn't either possible or worthwhile to assess Sharp as an instrumentalist because his whole playing ethos is devoted to instrumentalism in the philosophical sense, using his tools neutrally to achieve specific and predetermined ends. To that extent, this music doesn't sound improvised in the expected sense. Its surprise value is largely a function of timbre and dynamic rather than of content. Where *Datacide* falls neatly into the slot left by the slow retreat of art-punk, *In New York* is capital-of-the-twentieth-century stuff with greater emphasis on cultural *dis*continuities than on 'world music', and to that extent it may be salutary. (Sharp can also be heard in similar contexts on Korean zither player Jin Hi Kim's *Sargeng* (Ear-Rational 1014 CD) and, for some tracks only, on Kalle Laar and Takashi Kazamaki's *Return To Street Level* (Ear-Rational 1022 CD), though to little advantage on the former.)

JACK SHARPE
BARITONE SAXOPHONE

(*)   **Roarin' Jazz House JHCD 016 CD
Sharpe; Derek Watkins, Jimmy Deuchar, Mark Chandler, Stuart Brooks, Simon Gardner (*t*); Geoff Wright, Chris Pyne, Pete Beachill, Dave Stewart (*tb*); Andy Mackintosh (*as*); Jamie Talbot, Dave Bishop (*ts*); Dave Hartley (*p*); Chris Laurence (*b*); Harold Fisher (*d*). 5/89.

Although the sleevenote-writer avers that this 'may be the best big band ever put together outside America', it is actually an impressive outfit, creaming off some of the most proficient of British players to execute a sequence of tough and forceful scores. Mackintosh and Bishop are the two major soloists and they have virtuoso features on 'Old Folks' and Tubby Hayes's '100% Proof' respectively; while Mackintosh, in particular, may aspire to the kind of thing Chris Hunter or David Sanborn would do with the Gil Evans orchestra, it sounds more like routine pyrotechnics here. The only soloist who makes any real impression is Jimmy Deuchar, who sounds halting and imprecise on 'I'm Beginning To See The Light' beside the others, yet still seems to be more his own man than any of them. The band sound as if they need to relax more: only the closing 'J And B', a Deuchar theme, achieves a less forced take-off. Recorded live at Ronnie Scott's Club, the sound is constricted but clear enough.

SONNY SHARROCK (born 1940)
GUITAR

****   **Guitar** Enemy 102 CD/LP
Sharrock. 86.

Sharrock might have remained a lost legend if Bill Laswell hadn't provided him with a new context in Last Exit and egged him into this solo album, which shatters a former reputation for avant-garde 'weirdness'. His subsequent rise has completed the circle for a man who began by singing in a doo-wop group in the 1950s and spent seven years with Herbie Mann. *Guitar* is a textbook of what the electric instrument can be made to do in the hand of a master: Sharrock eschews fast picking in favour of blizzards of chords, walls of noise on the edge of feedback, drones that create a sort of violent timelessness and the first serious use of slide guitar in a 'jazz' context. 'Blind Willie', a dark nod to blues'n'gospel masters Johnson and McTell, is as severe as 'Like Voices Of Sleeping Birds' is beautiful.

(*)   **Seize The Rainbow Enemy EMY 104 CD/LP
Sharrock; Melvin Gibbs, Bill Laswell (*b*); Abe Speller, Pheeroan AkLaff (*d*). 5/87.

***   **Live In New York** Enemy EMY 108 CD/LP
Sharrock; Dave Snyder (*ky*); Melvin Gibbs (*b*); Pheeroan AkLaff (*d*); Ron 'The Burglar' Cartel (*v*). 7/89.

***   **Highlife** Enemy EMY 119 CD/LP
Sharrock; Dave Snyder (*ky*); Charles Baldwin (*b*); Abe Speller, Lance Carter (*d*). 10/90.

After the opening-round knockout of *Guitar*, these band albums are a mite disappointing. *Seize The Rainbow* rationalizes rather than extends Sharrock's ideas within a brawny blues-rock format with hints of exotica. The live album unleashes a little more ferocity, without surrendering Sharrock's oft-obscured romantic streak, which peeks through on 'My Song'. Gibbs and AkLaff play relatively straight but concentrated rhythms behind him. *Highlife* returns to polish rather than spit for its nine tracks – the guitarist is never one for rambling, unending solos – but gruff, clenched workouts like 'Chumpy' suggest that Sharrock's kind of fusion is good for many more records yet. Bass-heavy recordings on all these records, but crystalline clarity isn't what one should be looking for with music like this.

***   **Faith Moves** CMP CD 52 CD
Sharrock; Nicky Skopelitis (*g, b, sitar etc*). 90.

****   **Ask The Ages** Axiom 422-848-957 CD/MC
Sharrock; Pharoah Sanders (*ss, ts*); Charnett Moffett (*b*); Elvin Jones (*d*). 91.

There is some charming, sparkly music on *Faith Moves*, which depends on the folk-like interaction of Sharrock and the uncategorizable guitarist Skopelitis (who also uses 'world' instruments such as the Iranian tar and the Turkish saz on the session). Much shimmering and interweaving of lines, and though it's scarcely a riveting record compared with what Sharrock's already done, it's an agreeable alternative.

Ask The Ages, though, is of a different order. Here Sharrock uncorks some of his most ecstatic playing, and there are no more suitable players to accompany such a flight than Sanders and Jones, who quickly move in on the guitarist's space and both exalt and liberate his electric waving and crying. Moffett is a bit of a helpless bystander but the interplay of the other three men is magnificently evocative of some kind of bliss.

CHARLIE SHAVERS (1917–71)
TRUMPET, VOCALS

***   **Live** Black & Blue 59.302 CD
Shavers; Budd Johnson (*ts, ss*); André Persiany (*p*); Roland Lobligeois (*b*); Oliver Jackson (*d*). 2/70.

One of the great trumpeters of the swing era, and in many regards a more complete stylist than Roy Eldridge, his friend and closest rival, Shavers is represented disappointingly in the catalogue. By 1970 he was suffering the early stages of thoracic cancer and he sounds curiously disconsolate in the company of a rather plodding French rhythm section, leaving much of the work to saxophonist Johnson. There are still flashes of the old Shavers on 'Lester Leaps In', 'Prelude To A Kiss' and a couple of untitled blues, but this is a thin and indifferently recorded legacy from the man whose mouthpiece was placed in Louis Armstrong's casket.

ARTIE SHAW (born 1910)
CLARINET

**(*) Artie Shaw And His New Music Affinity AFS 1028 CD
Shaw; John Best, Malcolm Crain, Tom di Carlo (*t*); Hary Rogers, George Arus (*tb*); Les Robinson, Harry Freeman (*as*); Tony Pastor, Jules Rubin (*ts*); Les Burness (*p*); Al Avola (*g*); Ben Ginsberg (*b*); Cliff Leeman (*d*); Leo Watson, Beatrice Wain, Dolores O'Neil, Nita Bradley (*v*). 8–12/37.

*** Artie Shaw And His Rhythm Makers 1938 Tax CD 3709-2 CD
As above, except omit Watson, Wain and O'Neil. 2/38.

(**) Thou Swell ASV AJA 5056 CD
As above, except add Willis Kelly, Lee Castaldo, Dave Wade, Zeke Zarchey (*t*); Mark Bennett, Mike Michaels, Buddy Morrow (*tb*); Tony Pastor (*ts*); Joe Lippman, Fulton McGrath (*p*); Julie Schechter, Lou Klayman, Jerry Gray, Frank Siegfeld (*vn*); Sam Persoff (*vla*); Jimmy Oderich, Bill Schumann (*clo*); Wes Vaughan, Gene Stultz (*g*); Hank wayland, Ben Ginsberg (*b*); Sam Weiss, George Wettling (*d*); Peg La Centra, Leo Watson (*v*). 6/36–12/37.

Anyone familiar with the facts of his extraordinary life – with its sensational marriages and vast range of interests, overseen by a shrewd, restless mind – may find Artie Shaw's records a little lacking in fire. Yet he remains one of the most outstanding of instrumentalists, playing clarinet with a piercing mastery that outdoes any player of his day, and a musician whose search for superior settings has left an intriguing body of work behind him. He was the first swing bandleader to make much use of strings, and the 1936 sides collected on the ASV reissue chart his early interest in the projection of strings against the other sections (although Glenn Miller had already tried this sort of thing). The problem with all of Shaw's 1936–7 sessions, though, is a peculiarly old-fashioned feel to the rhythm section. Though his own solos were already close to impeccable, the bands lacked singular voices and the beat stuck close to a pulse that other rhythm sections were already streamlining into the smoother manner of the swing era. The ASV disc we must discount because of the very poor transfers, which are muddy and reverberant at the same time. The 1937 sides collected on Affinity's compilation, in much better sound, even though some scruffy originals were used for dubbing, are rather better than the earlier sessions, with Shaw – on arrangements such as 'Free Wheeling' – outclassing everybody else in the band with little apparent effort. The Tax disc covers a single day's recording of radio transcriptions and is perhaps the best representation of what Shaw's band could do – not a great deal. In character with its backward feel, one of the strongest tracks is a version of the oddball tune of some years earlier, 'The Call Of The Freaks'.

There are a few other real successes – 'Blue Fantasy' and a spirited 'Indian Love Call' among them – and trumpeter John Best takes some decent solos alongside Shaw's own. But otherwise the band sounds very so-so, and distinctly reluctant to catch fire. The transfers to CD have been excellently done.

***(*) Begin The Beguine RCA Bluebird ND 82432 CD/LP/MC
Shaw; Chuck Peterson, John Best, Claude Bowen, Bernie Privin, Charlie Margulis, Manny Klein, George Thow, Billy Butterfield, George Wendt, J. Cathcart, Harry Geller (*t*); Jace Cave (*flhn*); George Arus, Les Jenkins, Harry Rogers, Randall Miller, Bill Rank, Babe Bowman, Ray Conniff, Jack Jenney, Vernon Brown (*tb*); George Koneig, Hank Freeman, Les Robinson, Blake Reynolds, Bud Carlton, Jack Stacey, Bus Bassey, Neely Plumb (*as*); Tony Pastor, Ronnie Perry, Georgie Auld, Dick Clark, Les Robinson, Jerry Jerome (*ts*); Joe Krechter (*bcl*); Morton Ruderman (*f*); Phil Nemoli (*ob*); Johnny Guarnieri (*p, hpschd*); Les Burness, Bob Kitsis, Stan Wrightman

(*p*); Bobby Sherwood, Al Avola, Al Hendrickson, Dave Barbour (*g*); Sid Weiss, Jud DeNaut (*b*); Cliff Leeman, Buddy Rich, Carl Maus, Nick Fatool (*d*); Helen Forrest, Billie Holiday (*v*); strings. 7/38–1/41.

Although 'Begin The Beguine' made him a success – Shaw switched the original beguine beat to a modified 4/4, and its lilting pulse was irresistible – the huge hit he scored with it was greeted with loathing when it dawned on him what it meant in terms of fawning fans and general notoriety. He never seemed satisfied with his bands, and the four different orchestras on this compilation played through a series of breakdowns and disbandments by the leader. The second band, with arrangements by Jerry Gray and with Buddy Rich powering the rhythm section, was a far harder-hitting outfit than the old Shaw 'New Music'. But their best sides are still scattered. *Begin The Beguine* includes such hits as the title piece, 'Nightmare' (Shaw's first theme), 'Any Old Time' (the one title Billie Holiday recorded with Shaw), 'Traffic Jam' and 'Frenesi', as well as sides with Helen Forrest handling vocals and two tracks by the Gramercy Five, which has another CD to itself. The 1940 band includes Billy Butterfield and Johnny Guarnieri, and 'Star Dust' and 'Moonglow' hint at Shaw's romantic-symphonic aspirations, which troubled him at a time when listeners might have preferred to jitterbug. The remastering has been smartly done, though the NoNOISE system is, as usual, not to all tastes.

***   **The Complete Gramercy Five Sessions** RCA Bluebird ND 87637 CD/LP/MC
Shaw; Billy Butterfield (*t*); Johnny Guarnieri (*hpschd*); Dodo Marmarosa (*p*); Al Hendrickson, Barney Kessel (*g*); Jud DeNaut, Morris Rayman (*b*); Nick Fatool, Lou Fromm (*d*). 9/40–8/45.

Shaw's small group let him work off some more of his chamber-jazz hankerings, and though there are kitsch elements which outdo even Benny Goodman's 'Bach Goes To Town' – such as the very sound of Guarnieri's harpsichord and bouncing-ball tunes like 'Special Delivery Stomp' – the best of the Gramercy Five sounds surprisingly fresh, thanks mainly to the leader's unflinching dexterity and the heat generated by Butterfield (who sounds much like Cootie Williams in Goodman's small groups) and Eldridge. Youngsters like Marmarosa and Kessel also squeeze in solo parts. But the sense of a band working on artifice alone tends to drain off what excitement the group produces. The transfers sound rather thin.

***(*)   **Blues In The Night** RCSA Bluebird ND 82432 CD/LP/MC
Shaw; Hot Lips Page, Max Kaminsky, Lee Castle, Steve Lipkins, Roy Eldridge, Ray Linn, Jimmy Pupa, George Schwartz, Bernie Glow, Paul Cohen, Stan Fishelson (*t*); Jack Jenney, Ray Conniff, Morey Samuel, Charlie Coolidge, Pat McNaughton, Harry Rodgers, Ollie Wilson, Bob Swift, Gus Ischia (*tb*); Les Robinson, Charlie DiMaggio, Tom Mace, Les Clarke, Rudolph Tanza, Lou Prisby (*as*); George Auld, Mickey Folus, Hervie Steward, Jon Wealton, Ralph Rosenlund (*ts*); Chuck Gentry, Art Baker (*bs*); Johnny Guarnieri, Dodo Marmarosa (*p*); Mike Bryan, Barney Kessel (*g*); Eddie McKimmey, Morris Rayman (*b*); Dave Tough, Lou Fromm (*d*). 9/41–7/45.

Two more Shaw bands are featured here. The 1941 edition features Hot Lips Page as one of the main soloists along with Shaw, and there are three outstanding arrangements by Paul Jordan, one of which, 'Suite No. 8', is one of the few instances where the strings which Shaw loved were usefully integrated into the sound of his band. The second band features Roy Eldridge and includes Eddie Sauter's splendid reworking of 'Summertime', as well as a couple of good Ray Conniff charts. Shaw's own playing is by now showing a peerless command of the clarinet, and the compilation puts his playing in context rather than dwelling on indulgences such as the earlier 'Concerto For Clarinet'. A comprehensive survey of Shaw's music is, though, still awaited on CD.

***(*)   **The Last Recordings** Musicmasters/Limelight 65071-2 2CD
Shaw; Hank Jones (*p*); Tal Farlow (*g*); Joe Roland (*vib*); Tommy Potter (*b*); Irv Kluger (*d*). 54.

This was Shaw's last document and it's valuable to have it back in circulation, with ten new tracks. The music is poised somewhere between the swing principles which Shaw remained faithful to and the faintest wisp of bop-styled modernism, which such fellow crossovers as Farlow and Jones also make the most of. Lithe, piercing, but fundamentally relaxed and even-tempered, this is high-calibre chamber jazz which leaves the Shaw story tantalizingly unfinished, even if the man himself is still sporadically active as a conductor.

CHARLES BOBO SHAW
DRUMS, PERCUSSION

***   **Streets Of St Louis** Moers 02020 LP
Shaw; Lester Bowie (*t*); Joseph Bowie (*tb*); KJulius Hemphill (*as*); Hamiet Bluiett
(*bs*); Dominique Gaumont (*g*); Abdul Wadud (*clo*). 9/74.

Shaw's influence on other players through his Human Arts Ensemble and the St Louis Creative
Ensemble has been much greater than has ever filtered through to the record-buying public.
Shaw is not an extravagantly virtuosic player, preferring (as the insistence on 'ensemble'
suggests) to concentrate on collective aspects of music making. His impact on the
avant-traditionalism of such as David Murray and David Newton is incalculable, and it is
slightly disappointing that the current catalogue offers nothing more than a single, indifferently
recorded set, nearly twenty years old.

Streets Of St Louis features some fine growling trumpet from Bowie and passages of great
sophistication where Wadud and Bluiett interact on relative pitches. However, there is
something slightly dated about the approach, and those sufficiently interested to follow up on
Shaw would be well advised to search out *The Human Arts Ensemble Live* [Circle RK
9-23578/9 LP] a taut trio that explores some of the same territory as a British free group of the
1970s, Amalgam, led by drummer John Stevens and saxophonist Trevor Watts.

WOODY SHAW (1944–89)
TRUMPET

***   **Song Of Songs** Original Jazz Classics OJC 180 LP
Shaw; Emanuel Boyd (*fl, ts*); Bennie Maupin, Ramon Morris (*ts*); George Cables (*p, el
p*); Henry Franklin (*b*); Woodrow Theus (*d, perc*). 9/72.

***(*)   **The Moontrane** Muse MR 5058 LP
Shaw; Steve Turre (*tb*); Azar Lawrence (*ts, ss*); Onaje Allan Gumbs (*p, el p*); Cecil
McBee, Buster Williams (*b*); Victor Lewis (*d*); Guilherme Franco, Tony Waters
(*perc*). 12/74.

***   **Love Dance** Muse MR 5074 LP
Shaw; Steve Turre (*tb, btb*); René McLean (*as, ss*); Billy Harper (*ts*); Joe Bonner (*p*);
Victor Lewis (*d*); Guilherme Franco (*perc*). 76.

***   **Lotus Flower** Enja 4018 LP
Shaw; Steve Turre (*tbn*); Mulgrew Miller (*p*); Stafford James (*b*); Tony Reedus (*d*).
1/82.

***   **Woody Shaw With The Tone Jansa Quartet** Timeless SJP 221 CD/LP
Shaw; Tone Jansa (*ts, ss, fl*); Renato Chicco (*p*); Peter Herbert (*b*); Dragan Gajic (*d*).
4/85.

***(*)   **Solid** Muse MCD 5329 CD
Shaw; Kenny Garrett (*as*); Peter Leitch (*g*); Kenny Barron (*p*); Neil Swainson (*b*);
Victor Jones (*d*). 3/86.

***(*)   **Imagination** Muse MCD 5338 CD
Shaw; Steve Turre (*tbn*); Kirk Lightsey (*p*); Ray Drummond (*b*); Carl Allen (*d*). 6/87.

****   **In My Own Sweet Way** In + Out 7003 CD
Shaw; Fred Henke (*p*); Neil Swainson (*b*); Alex Deutsch (*d*). 2/87.

Woody Shaw's career judgement was almost as clouded as his actual vision. A classic
under-achiever, his relatively lowly critical standing is a function partly of his musical purism
(which was thoroughgoing and admirable) but also more largely of his refusal or inability to get
his long-term act together. A sufferer from *retinitis pigmentosa* (which severely restricted his
sight-reading), he fell under a subway train in the spring of 1989 and died of his injuries.

It was Eric Dolphy who taught Shaw to play 'inside and outside at the same time', but it was
listening to the classics that wakened a player with perfect pitch to the subtler nuances of
harmony. Like all imaginative Americans, Shaw was violently stretched between opposites and

inexorably drawn to the things and the places that would destroy him. Europe drew him for all the usual extramusical reasons, but there is a sense, too, that Shaw's foreshortened career represented a sustained fugue from the racially constrained job-description of the 'jazz musician'.

However hardly won, Shaw's technique sounded effortless, which disguised the awful disquiet at the root of his music. His influences were not settling ones: at the one extreme Debussy, the most inside-and-outside of the pre-Schoenberg composers; at the other his Newark friend, the organist Larry Young, with whom he recorded the superb *Unity*, and who taught him, across the grain of the earlier Hubbardly aggression and linearity, the value of chaos and meditative acceptance. 'The Organ Grinder' on *In My Own Sweet Way* is dedicated to Young, a typical asymmetrical Shaw theme. The first recorded version of Shaw's best-known composition, 'The Moontrane', was on *Unity*. As title piece on the 1974 Muse, it's arranged very differently, sounding lighter and much less funky, which is in keeping with a remarkably delicate album. The longest track, 'Sanyas', is a Latin rocker with beautifully cadenced work by all three horns. There's also a dedication to West Coast pianist-composer Horace Tapscott, written by the Azar Lawrence. on which Shaw and the saxophonist add dark undertones to the sunlit theme. It's difficult to tell which of the harmonic influences that entered Shaw's work in the late 1960s (see parts of *Song Of Songs*) came from contemporary free jazz and what from classical models. The early sessions, which contain a heartfelt tribute to Dolphy, contain non-standard harmonies and considerable rhythmic alteration, but always implicitly contained with bop models. His solos, delivered in a rich but melancholy tone, were always masterpieces of development and could on occasion almost sound written out, were they not so vibrantly immediate.

The 1976 concert at the Berlin Jazz Festival is poorly recorded, largely to the detriment of Louis Hayes's inspirational drumming, but it's good to hear Shaw stretched out and Joe Chambers's gentle theme 'Hellow To The Wind' is an ideal opener for a fine group. Shaw makes effective use of René McLean's flute and, whether by design or accident, Stafford James's bass comes through very strongly indeed. The group was credited as Shaw's Concert Ensemble and there is a curious formality to the arrangements which nevertheless doesn't prevent some searing solos.

Almost all the 1980s albums are worth having. Shaw's bands of the period were either the product of good luck, sympathetic label handling, or else they belie the received image of a guy perpetually nodding out on the practicalities, lost in a world of immaterial musical purity. (The only place he ever *sounded* that otherworldly was in his heavily Echoplexed work on *Zawinul*, the Weather Report keyboard man's Atlantic solo.) *Solid* is a good indication of how successfully he'd translated the freedoms of the early years and the pure-sound effects he offered Zawinul into straight, but carefully arranged jazz on the changes. 'There Will Never Be Another You' and 'You Stepped Out Of A Dream' are both fresh as paint. The long 'It Might As Well Be Spring' adds a substantial footnote to Miles Davis's treatment while at the opposite end of the scale 'The Woody Woodpecker Song' is taken at a manic, chucklehead pace.

Steve Turre was an ideal partner (and *Imagination* the better of their encounters), with the ability to counterpoise Shaw's inward examinations with bounce and fire. Their exchanges on 'Dat Dere' and Turre's down-home replies on 'Stormy Weather' are absolutely marvellous'. *In My Own Sweet Way* features a good working band (by contrast, the Jansa sessions aren't nearly as coherent) working an imaginatively varied book of tunes. Even the Brubeck plodder of the title gains an exceptional lyricism and depth of focus.

Shaw should be investigated by anyone who thinks they already have the recent history of jazz trumpet playing neatly sussed.

GEORGE SHEARING (born 1919)
PIANO

**   **Compact Jazz: George Shearing** MPS 833284-2 CD
       Shearing; Stephane Grappelli (*vn*); Louis Stewart, Sigi Schwab (*g*); Andrew Simpkins, Niels-Henning Ørsted-Pedersen (*b*); Rusty Jones, Stix Hooper (*d*); Chino Valdes, Carmelo Garcia (*perc*). 7/74–9/79.

(*)   **Blues Alley Jazz Concord CCD 4110 CD/MC
       Shearing; Biran Torff (*b*). 10/79.

***   **Two For The Road** Concord CCD 4128 CD/MC
Shearing; Carmen McRae (*v*). 80.

(*)   **On A Clear Day Concord CJ 132 MC
Shearing; Brian Torff (*b*). 8/80.

***   **Alone Together** Concord CCD 4171 CD/MC
Shearing; Marian McPartland (*p*). 3/81.

***   **First Edition** Concord CJ 177 MC
Shearing; Jim Hall (*g*). 9/81.

**   **Live At the Café Carlyle** Concord CCD 4246 CD/MC
Shearing; Don Thompson (*b*). 1/84.

**   **Grand Piano** Concord CCD 4281 CD/MC
Shearing (*p* solo). 5/85.

**   **Plays The Music Of Cole Porter** Concord CCD 42010 CD/MC
Shearing; Barry Tuckwell (*frhn*); strings. 1/86.

(*)   **More Grand Piano Concord CCD4318 CD/MC
Shearing (*p* solo). 10/86.

***   **Breakin' Out** Concord CCD 4335 CD/MC
Shearing; Ray Brown (*b*); Marvin 'Smitty' Smith (*d*). 5/87.

(*)   **Dexterity Concord CCD 4346 CD/MC
Shearing; Neil Swainson (*b*); Ernestine Anderson (*v*). 11/87.

(*)   **The Spirit Of 176 Concord CCD 4371 CD/MC
Shearing; Hank Jones (*p*). 3/88.

(*)   **George Shearing In Dixieland Concord CCD 4388 CD/MC
Shearing; Warren Vaché (*c*); Gorge Masso (*tb*); Kenny Davern (*cl*); Ken Peplowski
(*ts*); Neil Swainson (*b*); Jerry Fuller (*d*). 2/89.

George Shearing has always been on the periphery of jazz rather than anywhere inside it, even when he's been making records with genuine jazz musicians. His early tinkerings with a kind of cocktail bop have yet to make it to CD – earlier records for Capitol have been reissued, but they are entirely made up of middle-of-the-road albums with strings – and the MPS compilation is a record of an undistinguished period. But his many records for Concord have put some focus on his work, and have drummed up a few more worthwhile situations. Some of his best work willbe found on records under Mel Torme's name, but a few others listed here are also worth hearing. When Shearing sets aside his incessant borrowings from other players and eschews middlebrow ideas of what's tasteful to play in the jazz idiom, he can come up with some nice ideas: the partnerships with McPartland and Jones find him adapting to the far greater range of both of those players with some success, and he even holds his own with the trio with Brown and Smith. Carmen McRae's recital finds her in good, typically grouchy form, and Shearing accompanies with deference and good humour. One of the best discs, with Jim Hall, who can make any situation interesting, has unfortunately yet to make it to CD.The albums which lose their way are those where he has to provide most of the musical interest hmself: the solo sets and duos with bassist usually have one or two clever or gracious reworkings of standards, but they don't really sustain or repay close attention. The 'Dixieland' album is routine but pleasing enough, while the Cole Porter set is MOR prettiness.

JACK SHELDON (born 1931)
TRUMPET, VOCAL

(*)   **Hollywood Heroes Concord CJ/CCD 339/4339 CD/LP/MC
Sheldon; Ray Sherman (*p*); Doug McDonald (*g*); Dave Stone (*b*); Gene Estes (*d*).
9/87.

Sheldon has been something of a polymath: an ingenious comedian, a very hot cool-school trumpeter, a slight but charming vocalist – and for two of those attributes he owes something to Chet Baker. But he works best with a straight man, or at least a foil – in the Curtis Counce group of the 1950s, or on an early Jimmy Giuffre LP, he fires up on the challenge of the other horns. Here, with a useful rhythm section behind him, the results are pleasant rather than exciting, although Sheldon is probably taking it a bit easier these days anyway. *Hollywood Heroes* is lively, yet Sheldon has no real context, and the result sounds too much like a nice trumpet–voice–rhythm section date to make any deep impression.

ARCHIE SHEPP (born 1937)
TENOR SAXOPHONE, SOPRANO SAXOPHONE, ALTO SAXOPHONE, PIANO, VOICE

****   Archie Shepp & The New York Contemporary Five Storyville SLP 1010 LP
Shepp; Don Cherry (*c*); John Tchicai (*as*); Don Moore (*b*); J. C. Moses (*d*). 11/63.

Archie Shepp once declared himself something 'worse than a romantic, I'm a sentimentalist'. Shepp has tended to be a theoretician of his own work, often expressing his intentions and motivations in off-puttingly glib and aphoristic language. He has, though, consistently seen himself as an educator and communicator rather than an entertainer (or even an Artist) and is one of the few Afro-American artists who has effected any sort of convincing synthesis between black music (with its tendency to be depoliticized and repackaged for a white audience) and the less comfortable verbal experiments of poets like LeRoi Jones (Imamu Amiri Baraka). The dialectic between sentiment and protest in Shepp's work is matched by an interplay between music and words which, though more obvious, is also harder to assess. A playwright who also wrote a good deal of influential stage music, Shepp devised a musical style that might be called dramatic or, at worst and later in his career, histrionic.

Though strongly associated in most people's minds with John Coltrane (he worked on the augmented *Love Supreme* sessions and on *Ascension*), Shepp's most potent influence among the modernists was the radical populism of Ornette Coleman. Unlike Coltrane, the Texan saw no need to dismantle or subvert the tradition in order to use it, and Shepp was much affected by Ornette's rediscovery of the freedoms inherent in earlier forms. The New York Contemporary Five (which grew out of a Coleman-influenced quartet co-led with trumpeter Bill Dixon) was perhaps the ideal context for a player and tyro composer of Shepp's sensibilities. 'O.C.' and 'When Will The Blues Leave?' are both Coleman compositions; if Tchicai and Cherry are perhaps the most prominent soloists here and elsewhere, that is partly because of the familiarity of the alto–cornet combination in this repertoire, but also because Shepp has always been a strangely diffident soloist whose sentimentalism is best conveyed by his paradoxical alternation of silence and sudden chaotic torrents, as on 'Cisum'.

The NYCF helped shape his conception of a pianoless group with several horns in the front line. It also marks his debut as a composer. 'The Funeral' was originally dedicated to the murdered civil rights activist, Medger Evers (and later pressed into service as a threnody for Malcolm X), and focuses largely on the chilly melancholy of Cherry's Last Post, never explicitly stated but underlying his solo. Shepp attempted more ambitious things in years to come, but few of his later recordings have the straightforwardness and unselfconsciousness of this early set.

***   The House I Live In Steeplechase SCC 6013 LP
Shepp; Lars Gullin (*bs*); Tete Montoliu (*p*); Niels-Henning Ørsted-Pedersen (*b*); Alex Riel (*d*). 11/63.

Primarily of historical interest, this awaits the great Gullin rediscovery or a comprehensive reassessment of Shepp's career, whichever should come earlier, before making the much-needed transition to CD. The opening 'You Stepped Out Of A Dream' is perhaps the best of the set, the closing 'Sweet Georgia Brown' giving off the air of a hastily agreed encore. Shepp and NHØP met again on record in 1980, below.

***(*)   Fire Music MCA MCAD 39121 CD
Shepp; Ted Curson (*t*); Joseph Orange (*tb*); Marion Brown (*as*); David Izenzon, Reggie Johnson (*b*); Joe Chambers, J. C. Moses (*d*). 2 & 3/65.

One of the best of Shepp's albums (though sounding rather brittle on CD), *Fire Music* is the saxophonist's most balanced synthesis of *agitprop* and lyricism, avant-gardism and traditionalist deference. 'Hambone', the long opening track, is a blues-rooted but unconventional theme, cast in irregular time-signatures, tough and citified. At the opposite extreme, there is a slightly kitsch 'Girl From Ipanema' with a reworked bridge; Shepp's colonization of pop tunes is less subversive than Coltrane's (for the most obvious comparison, see 'My Favorite Things' on *New Thing*, below) because he always remains half sold on the sentiments therein, but he makes a persuasive job of the Jobim tune. 'Los Olvidados' is dedicated to the youthful underclass of the city, the 'forgotten ones', those who will not be beguiled by Sandy Becker's 'Hambone' television character. The main focus of the piece is on Marion Brown's desolate middle passage, conjuring up thwarted promise in a hectic but unheeding environment; Shepp's own solo, as became his norm, is a rather pat summing-up, musical Method-acting, that slightly detracts from the sophistication of the composition. 'Malcolm, Malcolm – Semper Malcolm', scored for just Shepp, Izenzon and Moses and dominated by Shepp's sonorous recitation, is a brief foretaste of the later but no more convincing 'Poem For Malcolm', below. Clipped and re-dedicated from a longer and more ambitious work ('The Funeral' on SLP 1010, above), it runs a slight risk of being ironized by 'Prelude To A Kiss' and the Jobim tune that follow; Shepp's ironies, though, are maintained not just between but also within compositions.

It's interesting to note that the trajectory of the album is (roughly) from populist experimentalism to a kind of experimental populism. The absence of piano is significant because it prevents the music (and particularly the two familiar themes) from sinking into comfortable tone-centres, thus maintaining its ambiguous, questing nature.

[*** **New Thing At Newport** Impulse GRP 11052 CD]
    Shepp; Bobby Hutcherson (*vib*); Barre Phillips (*b*); Joe Chambers (*d*). 7/65.

With the classic Coltrane Quartet on the other side of the original album, this gave an explicit and, in the circumstances, slightly ironic blessing to Shepp's emergence as one of the leading lights of the New Thing. Again, the balance of apparently contradictory motivations is just about right, with a less than wholly subversive 'My Favorite Things' set against the inner furies of 'Call Me By My Rightful Name' and 'Skag', and the surreal 'Rufus (Swung His Face To The Wind . . .)' from *Four For Trane*. On the whole, though, the music is far from radical in impact, and Shepp's spoken interpolations serve, as throughout his career, to mitigate any slight shift towards abstraction at this stage. Perhaps because of the circumstances and the eventual packaging of the music, Shepp's Newport performance has been somewhat overrated.

Again pianoless, the quartet takes a sharp, percussive edge from Hutcherson's tightly pedalled vibes. Phillips fares deservedly better on the CD and can be heard for the remarkable influence he was on the group. Shepp sounds quite self-consciously like a latter-day descendant of Webster and Hawkins, aggravating swing rhythms and phraseology with devices borrowed from R&B and early rock (and, more immediately, from the unabashed populist radicalism of Ornette Coleman). On the other side, Coltrane already sounds tired, but with the understandable weariness of a man whose path would be hard to follow.

(**) **Freedom JMY 1007 CD
    Shepp; Grachan Moncur III, Roswell Rudd (*tb*); Jimmy Garrison (*b*); Beaver Harris (*d*); Ted Joans (*v*). 12/67.

A heavily qualified rating, for the music is as stupendous as the sound-quality is awful, taken from a French concert performance. Shepp's clogged stuttering and sudden, passionate outbursts must have been stunning heard up close, and the long version of 'Portrait Of Robert Thompson (As A Young Man)' is one of the best extended improvisations we have from him. The band is just about as good as it gets for the period; post-Trane, Garrison did some quite special things, and Harris has never received the plaudits reserved for Elvin Jones, Sunny Murray or Milford Graves. Highly recommended.

***(*) **Yasmina/Poem For Malcolm** Affinity AFF 771 CD
    Shepp; Clifford Thornton (*c*); Lester Bowie (*t*); Grachan Moncur III (*tb*); Arthur Jones (*as*); Hank Mobley (*ts*); Roscoe Mitchell (*bsx*); Vince Benedetti, Dave Burrell, Burton Greene (*p*); Malachi Favors, Earl Freeman, Alan Silva (*b*); Claude Delcloo, Philly Joe Jones, Sunny Murray (*d*); Art Taylor (*rhythm logs*); Laurence Devereux (*balafon*). 8/69.

***(*)   **Blasé** Charly CD 77 CD
Shepp; Lester Bowie (*t, flhn*); Chicago Beau, Julio Finn (*hca*); Dave Burrell (*p*); Malachi Favors (*b*); Philly Joe Jones (*d*); Jeanne Lee (*v*). 8/69.

Yasmina/Poem For Malcolm catches Shepp at one of the increasingly rare points of confluence where his claims on 'the tradition' and his political progressivism seem to meld into something greater than a sum of influences and intentions. 'Mama Rose' was to become one of his most clichéd pieces, but the two title-pieces have a simple grandeur which transcends their historical moment. The twin-tenor 'Sonny's Back' with Hank Mobley demonstrates the degree to which Shepp's approach was conditioned by 'hard bop' norms rather than 'New Thing' vanguardism, while 'Body And Soul', with Burrell, Favors and Jones, anticipates David Murray's dredgings by a decade and more. *Blasé* is a welcome CD issue of a fine, if rather chaotic, session, recorded with overlapping personnel a couple of days later and originally released in Claude Delcloo's BYG 'Actuel' series, which helped sustain more than one American radical during dark days back home. Significantly or not, *Blasé* inverts the outline of *Fire Music*, ending on 'Touareg' with a combustible trio that dispenses with voice, piano and harmonicas. Finn and Beau are far less impressive here than on Philly Joe Jones's remarkable self-named (and now deleted) Impulse release, and there's some evidence that they simply happened by. Lester Bowie, on the other hand, slips perfectly into the spaces behind Jeanne Lee's voice on his only track, 'There Is A Balm In Gilead'. Lee sounds at her best here, merely wry on 'Sophisticated Lady'. The two long opening tracks are almost schematically opposite in tone, with 'My Angel' a fierce scatting prowl over the two mouth harps (and occasional interjections from Shepp), 'Blasé' a slow, soulful purr with a gynaecologically forthright vocal.

***   **There's A Trumpet In My Soul** Freedom F 41016 CD/LP
Shepp; Roy Burrowes, Alden Griggs (*t, flhn*); Charles Greenlee (*tb*); Ray Draper (*tba*); Dave Burrell (*p*); Walter Davis Jr (*electric p*); Brandon Ross (*g*); Jimmy Garrison, Vishnu Wood (*b*); Beaver Harris (*d*); Zahir Batin, Nene Defense (*perc*); Semenya McCord, Bill Willingham (*v*); Bill Hasson (*narr*). 4/75.

***   **Montreux One** Freedom F 41027 CD/LP
Shepp; Charles Greenlee (*tb*); Dave Burrell (*p*); Cameron Brown (*b*); Beaver Harris (*d, perc, v*). 7/75.

***   **A Sea Of Faces** Black Saint BSR 0002 CD/LP
As above, except add Charles Greenlea (*ts, tamb, v*); Bunny Foy (*v, perc*); Rafi Taha (*v*). 8/75.

It's unfair to put too much emphasis on chance juxtapositions in the catalogue, but there's an obvious comparison to be made between *A Sea Of Faces*, item number two in the Black Saint list, and Billy Harper's label-eponymous debut. *Black Saint* synthesizes virtually the same materials – R&B, Ellington, Ben Webster, free form, gospel – but does so with an integral self-confidence that Shepp, by this stage working as an academic at Amherst (of all places), seems to have traded in for a rather plodding stylistic crib that becomes more intrusive the more ambitiously he writes. *Trumpet* is desperately overcooked, full of *faux-naïf* gestures and bland thematic transitions that are signalled several measures ahead by a kind of whispering nervousness in the band. The solos and all-in collective passages are, predictably, the best of it, but Shepp himself is increasingly disposed to act as summarizer and moral-pointer. *A Sea Of Faces*, with its shorter, discontinuous tracks, is much more convincing. Shepp plays soprano on the title-track and (but for a brief snatch of piano under a Bunny Foy vocal) sticks to tenor elsewhere, pairing effectively with Charles Greenlea on 'Hipnosis' and 'Song For Mozambique'. The strengths and weaknesses of Shepp's working group of the time are underlined on the Montreux Festival album. 'Lush Life' (see also below) is as brutal as it is sentimental, like a drunk alternately maudlin and violent. The originals ('Crucificado' in particular) are better, but the sound-balance pushes Shepp so far forward that Greenlee and the rest of the band are periodically lost.

***(*)   **Steam** Enja 2076 CD/LP
Shepp; Cameron Brown (*b*); Philly Joe Jones (*d*). 76.

Perhaps the last point in his career at which Shepp can truly be considered a contender. The heavyweight 'Message For Trane' almost sounds like a gesture of farewell, a turning back once again from the trailing edge of the avant-garde to explore the roots, but also a slightly sorrowful recognition that the astral channels have grown too congested for many more such messages to get through. 'Steam' is brash and open, infinitely better here than the awful vocal version on the deleted *Attica Blues*, one of Shepp's worst and most ill-judged albums. 'Solitude' has the romantic quietly closing the door on the sentimentalist. Shepp doubles on piano but, given the space to develop his ideas (there are only those three tracks), the album is notable for the unwonted coherence of his saxophone solos.

(*)   Ballads For Trane Denon DC 8570 CD
Shepp; Albert Dailey (*p*); Reggie Workman (*b*); Charles Persip (*d*). 5/77.

First and most inevitable of a series of tributes to the great players. Shepp's desire to write himself into the tradition rapidly became overweening and rather tiresome. With Coltrane, though, he could claim a degree of discipleship. Whether one chooses to hear or to dismiss the phantom 'second tenor' at the end of Coltrane's masterpiece, *A Love Supreme*, depends somewhat on a desire to see Shepp pick up the fallen torch and carry it onward. On *Four For Trane* he showed some sign of doing just that. On this, coinciding neatly with the tenth anniversary of Coltrane's death and with Shepp's own *crise de quarante*, he sounds like a man going through all sorts of elaborate motions in order to conjure up an emotion commensurate with the occasion. It doesn't work. 'Soul Eyes', written by Mal Waldron and immortalized by Coltrane, is a mess, with Dailey making a hash of the piano part and only Workman and Persip working at anything like a thoughtful level.

(*)   Bird Fire West Wind WW 0006 CD/LP
Shepp; Everett Hollins (*t*); Siegfried Kessler (*p*); Bob Cunningham (*b*); Clifford Jarvis (*d*). 79.

***(*)   Looking At Bird** Steeplechase 1150 CD/LP/MC
Shepp; Niels-Henning Ørsted-Pedersen (*b*). 2/80.

Never short of a handy phrase and ever mindful of a need to resist the condescending nomenclature of 'jazz', Shepp prefers to consider bebop as the Baroque period of Afro-American classical music. Given the brutal accretions of his approach, it's an accurate but still slightly misleading designation. His Parker readings are irregular pearls with a raw, slightly meretricious beauty but with only questionable currency as serious re-examinations of the tradition. There is a rather better version of 'Now's The Time' (one of Parker's most traditionally rooted tunes and the one to which Shepp seems to be drawn) on the later *I Didn't Know About You*. With the exception of Jarvis, the *Bird Fire* band is nothing to write home about; only the drummer seems to be thinking about what he is playing.

The great NHØP cut his teeth on this repertoire and sounds completely at home with it, bouncing and singing through a more or less predictable roster of bebop anthems. It's probably easier for bass players who don't have to negotiate a dense and anxiety-inducing archaeology of previous readings to make their own statements, but the Dane does seem to encourage Shepp to some of his most relaxed and probing performances in the bebop canon. (It's worth listening to this in the context of two saxophone–bass duo takes of 'Davis' with Buell Neidlinger on Cecil Taylor's *Cell Walk for Celeste*, Candid 9034.)

(*)   Passport To Paradise West Wind WW 0002 LP
Shepp; Charles McGhee (*t*); Charles Eubanks (*p*); Santi Wilson Debriano (*b*); Michelle Wiley (*v*).

John Coltrane worked his way 'back to Bechet' with patience and understanding. Shepp brings no more than the now familiar angry-discursive approach and a raw and ill-mannered soprano tone. 'Petite Fleur' is a soft target and Shepp very nearly gets aways with it because the tune is so familiar, but the set as a whole is dull and, what's worse, unworthy of its dedicatee.

(*)   I Know About The Life Sackville SK 3062 CD
Shepp; Ken Werner (*p*); Santi Debriano (*b*); John Betsch (*d*). 2/81.

***   Soul Song** Enja 4050 CD/LP/MC
Shepp; Ken Werner (*p*); Santi Wilson Debriano (*b*); Marvin Smitty Smith (*d*). 12/82.

(*)   Down Home New York Soul Note SN 1102 CD/LP
Shepp; Charles McGhee (*t, v*); Ken Werner (*p, v*); Saheb Sarbib (*b*); Marvin Smitty Smith (*d, v*); Bartholomew Gray (*v*). 2/84.

(*)   **Live On Broadway Soul Note SN 1122 CD/LP
Shepp; George Cables (*p*); Herbie Lewis (*b*); Eddie Marshall (*d*); Royal Blue (*v*).
5/85.

After about 1975, Shepp's reputation held up more robustly in Europe than in the USA, in part because it may have been easier to sustain the mien of cool, magisterial fury when removed from the company of younger black Americans who either did it better or rejected the premisses and methodology. Smith takes a more pragmatic line on American racism, and he plays on *Down Home New York* (as on the earlier Soul Note) with a brisk self-confidence that rather shames the leader's dull rhythmic sense and increasingly formulaic phrasing. On both albums, it's the group rather than the leader that impresses.

Perhaps because the rhythm section is less ebullient, Shepp plays better on *Live On Broadway*, but 'My Romance', 'A Night In Tunisia', 'Giant Steps' and a vocal 'St James Infirmary' still leave the residual impression of an illustrated lecture. *I Know About The Life*, the earliest of the group, is simply drab.

**   **Mama Rose** Steeplechase SCS 1169 CD/LP/MC
Shepp; Jasper van't Hof (*ky*). 2/82.

(*)   **The Fifth Of May L + R Records LR 45004 CD/LP
As above. 5/87.

***   **Archie Shepp & Jeanne Lee** West Wind 2036 CD
Shepp; Jeanne Lee (*v*). 10/84.

Successive recordings of 'Mama Rose' (and there seem to be droves of them) are probably the most useful gauge of Shepp's progress or decline. Jeanne Lee puts back some of the dew. By contrast, the version with van't Hof is vulgarly overblown and recorded in horrible close-up. *The Fifth Of May* is rather better; the pianist limits himself to synthesizer and a slightly hollow-sounding grand, and there's a respectable though hardly inspired 'Naima'. Nothing, though, on a par with Shepp's longer-standing partnership with Horace Parlan. Lee was one of the high points of *Blasé*; in the intervening years she has become a more subtle but also a more adventurous singer – paradoxically, by daring to sing with absolute simplicity. They dust down 'Sophisticated Lady' from the 1969 album and for a moment cut through the dreary paid-by-the-hour accompaniments. Though still far short of the best work of either, this one's worth catching.

(*)   **Splashes L + R Records LR 45005 CD/LP
Shepp; Horace Parlan (*p*); Harry Emmery (*b*); Clifford Jarvis (*d*). 5/87.

A tribute to bassist Wilbur Little, comprising the now familiar blend of bebop staples ('Relaxin' At Camarillo', 'Groovin' High') and recycled originals ('Steam', 'Arrival') which bespeak little more than Shepp's loss of impetus as a composer. He plays his tenor throughout, but without the passionate conviction he used to bring to his first horn. Parlan has been one of his most stalwart and sympathetic supporters, and their early duo performance, below, contains some exquisite moments.

***(*)   **Goin' Home** Steeplechase 1079 CD/LP/MC
Shepp; Horace Parlan (*p*). 4/77.

***(*)   **Trouble In Mind** Steeplechase 1139 CD/LP/MC
As above. 2/80.

***   **Reunion** L + R Records LR 45003 CD/LP
As above. 5/87.

***   **First Set** 52e Rue Est RECD 015 CD
As above. 10/87.

***   **Second Set** 52e Rue Est RECD 016 CD
As above.

Parlan's slightly raw, bluesy style suits Shepp almost perfectly. The earliest of these, a moving compilation of gospel tunes, is by far the best and most concentrated. *Trouble In Mind*, which takes the same line on 11 blues staples, is perhaps a little too earnest in its pursuit of authenticity but achieves a chastened dignity. The later sets dig into Shepp's own back catalogue and obsessions – and it's unlikely that any but the staunchest fan will get excited about yet another 'Mama Rose' or 'Steam' (*First Set*) or even 'Sophisticated Lady' (*Second Ditto*). The best of the material once again is the blues, but no one who has the (better recorded) Steeplechases need bother hunting out the French CDs.

** **Lover Man** Timeless SJP 287 CD/LP
      Shepp; Dave Burell (*p*); Herman Wright (*b*); Steve McCraven (*d*); Annette Lowman
      (*v*). 1/88.

On *Bird Fire* Shepp managed to give no hint of the tragic associations that still hover round 'Lover Man' as a result of Parker's catastrophic breakdown while attempting to record the song. Here, he simply manages to sound inept. 'Lover Man' and 'Lush Life' are robbed of all pathos (and, what's worse, dignity), while 'My Funny Valentine' is full-choked sentimentality of a no longer appealing sort. Avoid.

*** **En Concert à Banlieues Bleues** 52e Rue Est RECD 017 CD
       Shepp; Chris McGregor (*p*); Harry Beckett, Dave Defries, Claude Deppa (*t, flhn*);
       Annie Whitehead, Faez Virji (*tb*); Julian Arguelles (*f, ss*); Frank Williams (*as, ss*);
       Talib Kibwe (*acl, as*); Jeff Gordon (*f, cl, ts*); Robert Juritz (*as, bsn*); Ernest Mothle
       (*b*); Gilbert Matthews (*d*); Tony Maronie (*perc*); Sonti Mndébélé (*v*). 3/89.

Valuable largely for a late glimpse of Chris McGregor's new-generation Brotherhood of Breath, recorded not long before his untimely death. 'Steam' and 'Bessie Smith's Blues' (previously sung by Annette Lowman) sit reasonably well with McGregor's well-drilled but by no means robotic band, but the pianist's big, African-tinged charts are much more interesting and tempt Shepp into some of his most unrestrained melodic playing.

***(*) **I Didn't Know About You** Timeless CD SJP 370 CD
         Shepp; Horace Parlan (*p*); Wayne Dockery (*b*); George Brown (*d*). 11/90.

There have long been signs that Shepp regards himself as one of the last surviving heirs of the bop tradition. He switches to alto here for 'Hot House' and the title-track, sounding rather closer to Hodges than to Charlie Parker but not, at first hearing of these tracks, instantly recongizable as himself. He opens, after a brief historical excursus, with 'Go Down Moses (Let My People Go)', vocalizing through his horn before singing the verse with quiet passion. Shepp has always had problems coming to terms with Monk's output, but Parlan (here as on their duo encounters) coaches him along; this time it's 'Ask Me Now', one of their very best recordings. The sound is bright and closely recorded, favouring saxophone and piano, and the album represents an encouraging return to form.

ANDY SHEPPARD (born 1957)
TENOR SAXOPHONE, SOPRANO SAXOPHONE, FLUTE

***(*) **Andy Sheppard** Antilles ANCD 8720 CD/LP
         Sheppard; Dave Buxton (*ky*); Pete Maxfield (*b*); Simon Gore (*d*); Mamadi Kamara
         (*perc*). 87.

*** **Introductions In The Dark** Antilles ANCD 8742 CD/LP
       As above, but add Oprhy Robinson (*vib*); Steve Lodder (*ky*); Chris Watson (*g*); Dave
       Adams (*perc*). 88.

By no means the precocious youngster the music press liked to think he was, Sheppard had actually been around for some time when he made his first album for Antilles. It's an assured and vividly executed debut, dominated by Coltranisms (as everything else was that year), but seen from a more individual perspective that anticipated the formal restlessness which was to be typical of Sheppard's subsequent career, which has taken in large-scale composition for his regular ensemble and for big-band, Miles-tinged rock–jazz, and (with his West Country friend, Keith Tippett, *q. v.*) an album of free improvisations disconcertingly entitled *66 Shades Of Lipstick*.

First indications that Sheppard would not be satisfied with transferring straightforward blowing gigs to record came with *Introductions In The Dark*. The album is dominated by the optimistically Ellingtonian 'Romantic Conversations (Between A Dancer And A Drum)', a huge two-part composition built out of attractively modest materials and then just slightly overcooked. Sheppard plays some engaging flute on Part One, but the later tenor work bogs down in an endless 'ethnic' vamp that is really rather dull and makeweight, redeemed only by vibraharpist Orphy Robinson's surprisingly pungent swing. There are signs that *Introductions*, produced with mixed success by Steve Swallow, was intended as an all-bases-touched presentation of Sheppard as a 'complete' musician. 'Optics' is a rather obvious Garbarek take-off, done in a bargain version of ECM's glacial acoustic. 'Where The Spirit Takes You' (CD only) loops along danceably, and only 'Rebecca's Glass Slippers' approaches anything like the fierce blowing of the first record.

***(*) **Soft On The Inside** Antilles ANCD 8751 CD/LP/MC
As for *Andy Sheppard*, but add Claude Deppa (*t*); Kevin Robinson (*t, flhn*); Gary Valente (*tb*); Chris Biscoe (*as, ts, ss*); Pete Hurt (*ts, bcl*); Steve Lodder (*ky*); Orphy Robinson (*vib, mar*); Mano Ventura (*g*); Ernst Reijseger (*clo*); Han Bennink (*d*). 11/89.

Sheppard's best album is boldly arranged, with many of the instruments 'paired' with a self-conscious opposite, bringing the univocal immediacy and rhythmic suppleness of his basic sextet to his first venture in big-band scoring. Sheppard had worked with both George Russell and Carla Bley European bands and draws elements of his scoring and a new melodic obliqueness from the experience. 'Carla Carla Carla Carla' makes one debt clear, calling on Lodder for a wry, accordion-like synth solo. 'Rebecca's Silk Stockings' turns a Morse message from the brass into another freewheeling rave (shudder to think how 'Rebecca's Suspender Belt' – she sounds the kind of woman who'd wear one – is going to sound) that is topped only by the percussive batter of 'Adventures In The Rave Trade', another whole-side two-parter that is much more finely conceived and scored than 'Conversation' on the earlier record. Outstanding among the soloists are Robinson ('Carla' and 'Rave Trade'), Reijseger (the opening 'Soft On The Inside'), Deppa ('Silk Stockings') and Valente, another Bley man, on the opening episode of 'Rave Trade'. The sound is big but rather compressed towards the middle. Enthusiasts might like to note that a video is also available, on Island Visual Arts IVA 047.

*** **In Co-Motion** Antilles ANCD 8766 CD/LP/MC
Sheppard; Claude Deppa (*t, flhn*); Steve Lodder (*ky*); Sylvan Richardson (*g, b*); Dave Adams (*d, perc, tb*). 2/91.

The clipped tracks' titles ('A.S.A.P.', 'Movies', 'Upstage', 'Circles', and nary a glimpse of Rebecca's underwear) immediately suggest a change of direction. The opening 'A.S.A.P.', with Deppa muzzled and dangerous, comes on like Miles's *Live-Evil* (Ydna Drappesh?), but there's too much again of *Introductions*' run-through feel of moods and styles. 'Eargliding' bears a disconcerting resemblance to 'The Girl From Ipanema', and there are satirical elements to both 'Let's Lounge', a sexy blur that provokes Sheppard's best solo, and 'Pinky', a co-credit with Lodder, who often sounds as if he's marbling Sheppard's scores with oil paint. The introduction of Richardson's six-string bass does nothing but smooth out the lower registers.

BOBBY SHEW (born 1941)
TRUMPET, FLUGELHORN, SHEW-HORN

*** **Trumpets No End** Delos DE 4003 CD
Shew; Chuck Findley (*t, flhn, tb*); Art Resnick (*p*); John Patitucci (*b*); Sherman Ferguson (*d*); Jerry Joyce (*v*). 10/83.

Shew has been a loyal foot-soldier in many big bands, and he turns up to fine effect on records by Toshiko Akiyoshi and Louis Bellson in particular. But more recently he's turned his attention to small groups and has visited the UK on many occasions in the last 10 years. This is a lighthearted date, where his glowing tone and pliable phrasing sound to fine advantage on swing material, with a couple of Clifford Brown tunes to remind one of a favourite influence. Findley makes a good partner and the rhythm section sound fine.

SAHIB SHIHAB (born 1925)
SOPRANO, ALTO AND BARITONE SAX, FLUTE

***   **Jazz Sahib** Savoy SV-0141 CD
Shihab; Phil Woods (*as*); Benny Golson (*ts*); Hank Jones, Bill Evans (*p*); Paul
Chambers, Oscar Pettiford (*b*); Art Taylor (*d*). 9–11/57.

The former Edmund Gregory is probably still best remembered for his work on some of
Thelonious Monk's Blue Note sessions. Since relocating to Europe in the 1960s, though, he has
turned up on many a continental big-band date. Shihab played alto with Monk but had
switched to baritone as his first instrument by the time he made this session for Savoy: bop
certainly needed no more altomen, and Woods could probably have smoked the leader if he'd
got his alto out on this date anyway. As it is, the programme provides a good-natured blow on
the blues via some fairly undemanding Shihab originals: all three hornmen take gratifying solos,
and the two rhythm sections make sure the rhythms are well sprung. Bright and full-bodied
digital remastering.

(*)   **Sentiments Storyville SLP 1008 LP
Shihab; Kenny Drew (*p*); Niels-Henning Ørsted-Pedersen (*b*); Jimmy Hopps (*d*). 3/71.

Shihab plays soprano and alto flute on this agreeable but fleeting session from 1971, which
includes perhaps his one composition to nudge standard status, 'Companionship'. A couple of
sessions for Vogue made in the mid-1960s deserve reissue; or perhaps we will have some new
recordings, since Shihab has now returned to the US.

CHARLIE SHOEMAKE (born 1937)
VIBES

(*)   **I Think We're Almost There Discovery DSCD-924 CD
Shoemake; Tom Harrell (*t, flhn*); Phil Woods (*as*); Ted Nash (*ts*); Mike Wofford,
Terry Trotter (*p*); Peter Sprague (*g*); Ray Drummond, Andy Simpkins (*b*); Billy Hart,
Dick Berk (*d*). 7/80–5/83.

(*)   **Sometime Yesterday Discovery DSCD-971 CD
As above, except add Hank Jones (*p*); Ed Schuller (*b*), Paul Motian (*d*), Sandi
Shoemake (*v*). 7/80–3/84.

**   **Satin Nights** Discovery DSCD-972 CD
Shoemake; Carl Saunders, Don Rader (*t, flhn*); Conte Candoli (*t*); Pete Beltran (*tb,
btb*); Andy Martin (*tb*); Ron Loofbourrow (*frhn*); Ted Nash (*as, ts, ss, f*); Phil Woods
(*as, cl*); Bob Cooper (*ts, f*); Alan Broadbent, Terry Trotter (*p*); Monty Budwig (*b*);
Jeff Hamilton, Harvey Mason (*d*). 1/85–9/86.

Shoemake is an accomplished if sometimes diffident vibes player, not especially connecetd to a
school or style but comfortably at home in the kind of easy-going jazz that came out of the
Discovery studios in the 1980s. The first two CDs are compilations from a number of LPs:
Woods, Nash and Harrell provide the most interest with their solos, and Bill Holman's
arrangements on the larger-group record drift attractively if a little aimlessly around
Shoemake's lazy shimmerings. Woods again rises to the occasion – his solos on 'In Acapulco
Bay' and 'Who Is Kidding Who?' are good enough to raise the temperature anywhere – but the
later disc is marred by the sequence of decidedly unmemorable songs written by Shoemake and
the plain and unappealing singing by his wife, Sandi, which takes up a lot of the playing time.

WAYNE SHORTER (born 1933)
TENOR SAXOPHONE, SOPRANO SAXOPHONE

***   **The Vee Jay Years** Affinity CD CHARLY 121 CD
Shorter; Lee Morgan (*t*); Wynton Kelly, Cedar Walton (*p*); Paul Chambers, Bob
Cranshaw (*b*); Art Blakey, Jimmy Cobb (*d*). 11/59, 10/60.

***(*) **Night Dreamer** Blue Note BCT 84173 CD
Shorter; Lee Morgan (*t*); McCoy Tyner (*p*); Reggie Workman (*b*); Elvin Jones (*d*).
4/64.

***(*) **Juju** Blue Note 746514 CD
As above, except omit Morgan.

**** **Speak No Evil** Blue Note 746509 CD
Shorter; Freddie Hubbard (*t*); Herbie Hancock (*p*); Ron Carter (*b*); Elvin Jones (*d*).
12/64.

**** **Adams Apple** Blue Note 746403 CD
Shorter; Herbie Hancock (*p*); Reggie Workman (*b*); Joe Chambers (*d*). 2/66.

*** **Super Nova** Blue Note B21Y 84332 CD/LP/MC
Shorter; Walter Booker, John McLaughlin, Sonny Sharrock (*g*); Miroslav Vitous (*b*);
Chick Corea (*vib, d*); Jack DeJohnette (*d, perc*); Airto Moreira (*perc*); Maria Booker
(*v*). 9/69.

*** **Odyssey Of Iska** Blue Note BCT 84363 CD
Shorter; Dave Friedman (*vib, mar*); Gene Bertoncini (*g*); Ron Carter, Cecil McBee
(*b*); Billy Hart, Alphonse Mouzon (*d*); Frank Cuome (*d, perc*). 8/70.

*** **The Best Of Wayne Shorter** Blue Note 791141 CD
Shorter; Freddie Hubbard (*t*); Curtis Fuller (*tb*); James Spaulding (*as*); Herbie
Hancock (*p*); Ron Carter, Reggie Workman (*b*); Joe Chambers, Elvin Jones, Tony
Williams (*d*); collective personnel. 12/64, 3/65, 2/66, 3/67.

Anyone who has encountered Shorter only as co-leader of Weather Report will know him primarily as a colourist, contributing short and often enigmatic brushstrokes to the group's carefully textured canvases. They may not recognize him as the formidable heir of Rollins and Coltrane (scale up and repitch those brief soprano saxophone statements and the lineage becomes clear). They will emphatically not know him as a composer. As Weather Report's musical identity consolidated, Joe Zawinul largely took over as writer. However, much as Shorter's elided 'solos' (in a group that didn't really believe in solos) still retained the imprint of a more developed idiom, so his compositions for the early records – 'Tears' and 'Eurydice' in particular – convey in essence the virtues that make him one of the most significant composers in modern jazz, whose merits have been recognized by fellow-players as far apart as Art Blakey, Miles Davis ('ESP', 'Dolores', 'Pee Wee', 'Nefertiti') and Kirk Lightsey (a challenging tribute album).

Known as 'Mr Weird' in high school, Shorter cultivated an oblique and typically asymmetrical approach to the bop idiom. His five years with the Jazz Messengers are marked by an aggressive synthesis of his two main models, but with an increasingly noticeable tendency to break down his phrasing and solo construction into unfamiliar mathematical subdivisions. The early material on *The Veejay Years* (culled from the debut album *Blues A La Carte* and its successor *Second Genesis*) finds him still in the powerful hold of John Coltrane, but the writing is impressive and there are signs of something new bubbling underneath. As a measure of how independently Shorter was thinking, *Blues A La Carte* was recorded on the same day as the Jazz Messengers' *Africaine*, on which he sounds a rather more conventional hard bopper. Working with Miles Davis between 1964 and 1970 (a period that coincides with his most productive phase as a solo recording artist), he moved toward a more meditative and melancholy style – with an increasingly dependence on the soprano saxophone – which is consolidated on the fine *Super Nova*, where he also makes unusually inventive use of Jekyll–Hyde guitar partnership of Mclaughlin and Sharrock. Shorter's recordings at this time relate directly to his work on Miles's *In a Silent Way* and to his work with Weather Report over the following decade.

Shorter's most individual work, however, remains the group of albums made for Blue Note in the mid-1960s, ending in 1970 with the low-key *Odyssey Of Iska*. The *Best Of* selection reproduces the enigmatic valuation Blue Note have placed on Shorter's output, completely ignoring the early *Juju*, which, like the undervalued and compositionally daring *Night Dreamer*, pits him with one version of the classic Coltrane quartet and has him playing at his most Coltrane-like. Fortunately, it is currently available on CD, along with *Adam's Apple* (also for quartet) and the excellent *Speak No Evil*, which is Shorter's most completely satisfying work (albeit one that has exerted a baleful influence on a generation of imitators).

There has always been some controversy about Freddie Hubbard's role on the session, with detractors claiming that, unlike Shorter, the trumpeter was still working the hand dealt him in the Messengers and was too hot and urgent to suit Shorter's growing structural sophistication. In fact, the two blend astonishingly well, combining his own instinctive exuberance on 'Fee-Fi-Fo-Fum' with something of the leader's own darker conception; interestingly, Shorter responds in kind, adding curious timbral effects to one of his most straight-ahead solos on the record.

As with *Adam's Apple* (which includes the classic 'Footprints'), much of the interest lies in the writing. Shorter has suggested that 'Dance Cadaverous' was suggested by Sibelius's 'Valse Triste'; 'Infant Eyes' is compounded of disconcerting nine-measure phrases that suggest a fractured nursery rhyme; the title piece pushes the soloists into degrees of harmonic and rhythmic freedom that would not normally have been tolerated in a hard bop context. Set *Speak No Evil* alongside Eric Dolphy's more obviously 'revolutionary' *Out To Lunch*, recorded by Blue Note earlier the same year, and it's clear that Shorter claims the same freedoms, giving his rhythm section licence to work counter to the line of the melody, and freeing the melodic Hancock from merely chordal duties. It's harder to reconstruct how alien some of Shorter's procedures were because by and large he does remain within the bounds of post-bop harmony, but it's still clear that *Speak No Evil* is one of the most important jazz records of the period.

** **Native Dancer** Columbia 467095 CD
Shorter; Milton Nascimento (*g, v*); Herbie Hancock (*p*); Airto Moreira (*perc*); with Dave McDaniel, Roberto Silva, Wagner Tiso, Jay Graydon, Dave Amaro (instrumentation not listed). 12/74.

A decade to the month after *Speak No Evil* finds Shorter in a bland samba setting which does more to highlight Nascimento's vague and uncommitted vocal delivery than the leader's saxophone playing. There is a hint of the old Shorter in the oblique introduction to 'Lilia' and some fine tenor work on 'Miracle of the Fishes' but much of the rest could have been put together by a competent session *pasticheur*. Reviewers tended to go one way or another on *Native Dancer*, but the consensus was that it was a 'surprise' and a 'new departure'. In fact, Shorter had long shown an interest in Latin American rhythms and progressions; 'El Gaucho' on *Adam's Apple*, above, is one of his finest compositions and *Native Dancer* is almost exactly contemporary with Weather Report's Pan-American *Tale Spinnin'*. The 'surprise' lay in the lush, choking arrangements and unnecessary verbiage. Shorter encountered similar resistance when his 1980s band flirted with discofied funk-jazz, stripped-down settings that pushed his distinctive tenor sound to the forefront again.

BEN SIDRAN
PIANO, VOCAL

(*) **Have You Met ... Barcelona? Orange Blue OB 002 CD/LP
Sidran; Johnny Griffin (*ts*); Jimmy Woode (*b*); Ben Riley (*d*); Clementine (*v*). 10/87.

A waggish songwriter and respectable pianist, Sidran's main appeal probably lies in his singing: he sounds like a slightly cooler, hipper Mose Allison, though he lacks any of the more idiosyncratic traits which make the style interesting. This set, with the surprising presence of Griffin, concentrates on standards as well as originals and includes a version of 'New York State Of Mind' which probably sums up Sidran's approach to music-making. It's certainly the ideal song for him to sing. Griffin, Woode and Riley are for certain the best band he's ever fronted. Clementine, who has an album of her own that was recorded in part at the same sessions, appears only on 'Girl Talk', suitably enough.

** **Past Masters** Go Jazz vBr 2096-2 CD
Sidran; Ricky Peterson (*ky*); Howard Arthur (*g*); Billy Peterson (*b*); Steve Miller, Patty Peterson, Dr John (*v*). 85.

** **A Good Travel Agent** Go Jazz vBr 2095-2 CD
As above, except add Phil Woods, Gordy Knudtson (*d*), omit Patty Peterson, Dr John. 3/86.

(*)   **Enrivre D'Amour Go Jazz vBr 2097-2 CD
As above, except add Bob Malach (*ts*), John Dela Silva (*g*), Lucia Newell (*v*), omit Miller, Woods. 87.

(*)   **Cool Paradise Go Jazz vBr 2041-2 CD
Sidran; Bob Malach (*ts*); Billy Peterson (*b*); Gordy Knudtson (*d*). 91.

Sidran's new contract has allowed the reissue of some of his old records. *Past Masters* stayed unreleased at the time, and wisely so: it's bombastic with synths and drum machines and mostly charmless. *A Good Travel Agent* is a live set with Woods taking some cameo solos, but Sidran's persona can become insufferably cool on occasion and will drive many out of the room, espcially on the long rap on the title-track. *Enrivre D'Amour* still suffers from fashionable production values, but it's quite appealing in its soft-core, driving-music way: Sidran's song, 'Critics', leaves one in no doubt that he has little time for such critiques, anyway. *Cool Paradise* is more of the same. For someone who always seems to have an axe to grind about 'jazz', it's a trifle odd that Sidran seems to want his records to sound like hip adult rock.

HORACE SILVER (born 1928)
PIANO

***   **Horace Silver Trio** Blue Note B21Y-81520 CD
Silver; Percy Heath (*b*); Art Blakey (*d*). 10/53.

***(*)   **Horace Silver And The Jazz Messengers** Blue Note CDP 746140-2 CD
Silver; Kenny Dorham (*t*); Hank Mobley (*ts*); Doug Watkins (*b*); Art Blakey (*d*). 11/54.

***   **Silver's Blue** Portrait 45138 CD
Silver; Joe Gordon, Donald Byrd (*t*); Hank Mobley (*ts*); Doug Watkins (*b*); Kenny Clarke, Art Taylor (*d*). 7/56.

Horace Silver's records present the quintessence of hard bop. He not only defined the first steps in the style, he also wrote several of its most durable staples, ran bands that both embodied and transcended the idiom and perfected a piano manner which summed up hard bop's wit and trenchancy and popular appeal. Yet he has recorded comparatively little in the last 20 years, and his back catalogue is in general disrepair as far as current availability is concerned.

The Blue Note *Jazz Messengers* album might be the one that started it all: two sessions, originally issued as a brace of ten-inch LPs, with a definitive hard bop cast. While the finest music by this edition of the original Jazz Messengers was probably recorded at the Cafe Bohemia the following year (listed in Art Blakey's entry), this one is still fresh, smart but properly versed in the new language (or, rather, the new setting for the old language). The trio album sets out Silver's own expertise: a crisp, chipper but slightly wayward style, idiosyncratic enough to take him out of the increasingly stratified realms of bebop piano. Blues and gospel-tinged devices and percussive attacks give his methods a more colourful feel, and a generous good humour gives all his records an upbeat feel.

***   **Six Pieces Of Silver** Blue Note B21Y-81539 CD
Silver; Donald Byrd (*t*); Hank Mobley (*ts*); Doug Watkins (*b*); Louis Hayes (*d*). 11/56.

***   **Finger Poppin'** Blue Note B21Y-84008 CD
Silver; Blue Mitchell (*t*); Junior Cook (*ts*); Gene Taylor (*b*); Louis Hayes (*d*). 2/59.

***   **Blowin' The Blues Away** Blue Note B21Y-46526 CD
As above. 8/59.

***   **Horace-Scope** Blue Note CDP 784042-2 CD
Silver; Blue Mitchell (*t*); Junior Cook (*ts*); Gene Taylor (*b*); Roy Brooks (*d*). 7/60.

****   **Song For My Father** Blue Note CDP 784185-2 CD
As above, except add Carmel Jones (*t*); Joe Henderson (*ts*); Teddy Smith (*b*); Roger Humphries (*d*). 10/64.

***(*)   **Cape Verdean Blues** Blue Note CDP 784220-2 CD
Silver; Woody Shaw (*t*); J. J. Johnson (*tb*); Joe Henderson (*ts*); Bob Cranshaw (*b*); Roger Humphries (*d*). 10/65.

****   **The Jody Grind** Blue Note CDP 7842502 CD
Silver; Woody Shaw (*t*); James Spaulding (*as, f*); Tyrone Washington (*ts*); Larry Ridley (*b*); Roger Humphries (*d*). 11/66.

Although Silver went on to record some 25 further albums for Blue Note, only the above are currently available as CD reissues. It's hard to pick the best of the seven albums since Silver's consistency is unarguable: each album yeilds one or two themes which haunt the mind, each usually has a particularly pretty ballad, and they all lay back on a deep pile of solid riffs and intensely worked solos. Silver's own are strong enough, but he was good at choosing sidemen who weren't so characterful that the band would overbalance: Cook, Mitchell, Mobley, Shaw, Jones and Spaulding are all typical Silver horns, and only Johnson (who was guesting anyway) and Henderson on the above records threaten to be something rather more special. The two choicest records, though, are surely *Song For My Father*, with its memorable title tune, the superb interplay of Jones and Henderson, and the exceptionally fine trio ballad 'Lonely Woman'; and *The Jody Grind*, which hits some sort of apex of fingersnapping intensity on the title tune and 'Mexican Hip Dance'. *Doin' The Thing*, cut live at New York's Village Gate, is another good one, *Blowin' The Blues Away* includes the soul-jazz classic 'Sister Sadie', and *The Cape Verdean Blues* includes Henderson, Shaw and Johnson on three tracks for one of Silver's most full-bodied front lines.

***   **The Best Of Horace Silver Vol. 1** Blue Note CDP 791143-2 CD

***   **The Best Of Horace Silver Vol. 2** Blue Note CDP 793206-2 CD

Both utterly solid. Volume 2 has the edge, perhaps, for 'Song For My Father', 'The Jody Grind' and 'Que Pasa', but both are very good one-disc samplers.

SONNY SIMMONS (born 1933)
ALTO SAXOPHONE

***   **Backwoods Suite** West Wind 2074 CD
Simmons; Joe Hardin (*t*); Al Thomas (*tb*); Michael Marcus (*bs*); Joe Bonner (*p*); Herbie Lewis (*b*); Billy Higgins (*d*). 1/82.

Isolated from the main currents of the music, Sonny Simmons has never built on the interest he created with a handful of records in the 1960s and '70s, which revealed a liaison between Ornette Coleman's freedoms and a terse, bop-orientated lyricism. The best of those – for ESP, Arhoolie and Contemporary – are long out of print, and this slightly mysterious session has recently appeared as if from nowhere. It's a little raw and imperfect, with the other horns splashing around and the excellent rhythm section sometimes adrift in the mix, but when Simmons locks in and wails, as he does on the title-track with Hardin and Thomas cleared away, the music ignites and burns very hard. The title seems particularly appropriate: Simmons suggests an affinity with the roots-music forms of John Carter, and his rural-sounding fierceness suggests a new link with the Coleman of 'Ramblin''.

ALAN SIMON
PIANO

(*)   **Rainsplash Cadence CJR 1027 LP
Simon; Ralph Lalama (*ts*); John Goldsby (*b*); Neil Tufano, Tim Pleasant (*d*). 5/83–8/84.

With the exception of one trio piece, this is a solid (and sometimes solidified) bop recital, distinguished mainly by Lalama (whose recent session for Criss Cross Jazz shows him in a slightly more characterful light). Simon is capable but undistinguished on this evidence.

TIZIANA SIMONA
VOCALS

** **Gigolo** ITM 1414 CD/LP
Simona; Kenny Wheeler (*t, flhn*); Giuseppina Runza (*clo*); Jean-Jacques Avenel (*b*); Nene Limafilho (*d, perc*). 2/86.

(*) **Flakes ITM 1437 CD/LP
Simona; Mal Waldron (*p*); Steve Lacy (*ss*); Enrico Rava (*t, flhn*); Giulio Visibelli (*f, af*). 8 & 9/88.

Unconvincing vocal surrealism for the most part from a singer with considerable talent but a slightly suspect diction and a rather too pleased-with-itself range of cultural reference. The title-track of *Flakes*, music by Steve Lacy, is a dedication to painter Mark Rothko; a later piece obliquely namechecks Marcel Duchamp. There are compositions by Lawrence Butch Morris, Rava, Visibeli and there's a version of David Murray's 'Flowers For Albert', which is a piece of up-to-date repertoire that calls for a singer of Sheila Jordan's stature. Waldron, who seems to act as sponsor and patron, plays typically fulsomely, and there are more oblique instrumental contributions from saxophonist and trumpeter; Visibeli's breathy alto flute occupies the final track, but it's not clear why. The set with Wheeler is in many regards more conventional, which means that it lacks much of the surprise of *Flakes*. Better to come, surely.

NANA SIMOPOULOS
GUITAR, BOUZOUKI, GUITAR SYNTHESIZER, VOICE

*** **Wings And Air** Enja 5031 CD/LP
Simopoulos; Don Cherry (*t, doussn'gouni*); Jim Pepper (*ts, f*); Matthias Sudholter (*didjeridu*); Ara Dinkjian (*oud*); Charlie Haden (*b*); Nana Vasconcelos (*berimbau, perc*); Jerry Granelli (*d*); Arto Tuncboyaci (*perc, v*). 6/86.

***(*) **Still Waters** Enja 6010 CD/LP
Simopoluos; Marty Fogel (*sax, f*); Mark Josefsberg (*vib syn, mar*); Chip Jackson (*b*); Christos Gotsinos (*d*); Hamid Drake (*d, tablas, bandir*); Christine Bard (*doumbek, perc*); John Harvey, Lue Simopoulos, Laura Toy (*v*). 4/88.

Nana Simopoulos brings considerable rhythmic inventiveness to her music, drawing heavily on Greek traditional and other ethnic musics. 'Don to Earth', which opens the fine *Still Waters*, is a demanding 9/4 by combining the Greek *zemebekiko* with an Afro shuffle. Elsewhere on the album she attempts similar combinations with equal success, even tacking on a choral reggae coda to the traditional *syrto* of the closing track, *Elements*.
Simopoulos plays it pretty straight, sticking to gut-strung and classical guitar for all but two tracks, switching to bouzouki for a change of colour. Her partners are mostly unobtrusive, and there is little of the earlier album's tendency to break down into duets. Despite the stellar line-up on *Wings And Air*, it is the later album which impresses. There is little of the 'world music' air of its predecessor and the tunes are much stronger and thought out. An impressive stylist, Simopoulos will be worth watching in the 1990s.

ZOOT SIMS (1925–85)
TENOR AND SOPRANO SAXOPHONES, VOCAL

*** **Quartets** Original Jazz Classics OJC 242 LP
Sims; John Lewis, Harry Biss (*p*); Curley Russell, Clyde Lombardi (*b*); Don Lamond, Art Blakey (*d*). 9/50–8/51.

***(*) **Zoot!** Original Jazz Classics OJC 228 CD/LP/MC
Sims; Nick Travis (*t*); George Handy (*p*); Wilbur Ware (*b*); Osie Johnson (*d*). 12/56.

Like Jack Teagarden, Zoot Sims started out mature and hardly ever wavered from a plateau of excellence throughout a long and prolific career (oddly enough, Sims's singing voice sounded much like Teagarden's). As one of Woody Herman's 'Four Brothers' sax section, he didn't quite secure the early acclaim of Stan Getz, but by the time of these sessions he was completely himself: a rich tone emboldened by a sense of swing which didn't falter at any tempo. He sounded as if he enjoyed every solo, and if he really was much influenced by Lester Young – as was the norm for the 'light' tenors of the day – it was at a far remove in emotional terms. *Quartets* sets up the kind of session Sims would record for the next 35 years: standards, a couple of ballads, and the blues, all comprehensively negotiated with a rhythm section that strolls alongside the leader: neither side ever masters the other. 'Zoot Swings The Blues' has Sims peeling off one chorus after another in top gear, while a seemingly endless 'East Of The Sun' shares the solos around without losing impetus. The original Prestige recording is grainy. *Zoot!* goes up a notch for the inspirational pairing of Sims and Travis, a minor figure who probably never played as well on record as he does here: 'Taking A Chance On Love' is a near-masterpiece, and Ware and Johnson play superb bass and drums.

***   **Tonite's Music Today** Black Lion BLCD 760907 CD
Sims; Bob Brookmeyer (*vtb*); Hank Jones (*p*); Wyatt Reuther (*b*); Gus Johnson (*d*). 1/56.

***(*)   **Morning Fun** Black Lion BLCD 760914 CD
As above, except Bill Crow (*b*) and Jo Jones (*d*) replace Reuther and Johnson. 8/56.

***(*)   **Zoot Sims In Paris** EMI/Pathé Jazztime 794125 CD
Sims; Jon Eardley (*t*); Henri Renaud (*p*); Eddie de Haas, Benoit Quersin (*b*); Charles Saudrais (*d*). 3/56.

***   **Down Home** Charly CD 59 CD
Sims; Dave McKenna (*p*); George Tucker (*b*); Dannie Richmond (*d*). 7/60.

***   **Live At Ronnie Scott's '61** Fresh Sound FSR-CD 134 CD
Sims; Stan Tracey (*p*); Kenny Napper (*b*); Jackie Dougan (*d*). 11/61.

The albums with Brookmeyer and Eardley were recorded while they were in Gerry Mulligan's Sextet: 'Lullaby Of The Leaves', included on *Morning Fun*, was one of the staples in Mulligan's repertoire, and the mood here (and throughout the sessions with Brookmeyer) owes much to him. But the atmosphere on both dates is of an utterly relaxed, good-pals jam session, refereed by the eternally sweet-natured Jones. *Morning Fun* just has the edge, perhaps, for the knockout tempo of 'The King' and a couple of lovely ballads (Zoot also sings 'I Can't Get Started'). The session in Paris is even more informal, but Sims here sounds magisterial, partly because the microphones catch his sound very close-up: Eardley, in comparison, is a bit recessed, and the drums are clattery on the first half of the date. A splendidly virile blowing date, nevertheless. *Down Home* is a good session, but Zoot doesn't have quite enough space: McKenna gets equal time in the front line, and while his mercurial solos are diverting, he had yet to develop the full-blooded orchestral style which makes his more recent work attractive. Richmond and Tucker aren't alawys in perfect time, either; but Sims sweeps through the likes of 'There'll Be Some Changes Made' with impervious enthusiasm. The live set, with what was a Scott house rhythm section, has no problems over space, and 'Blues In E Flat' is a rigorous demonstration of a basic skill, blowing on the blues, which Sims can apparently sustain indefinitely. A fondly remembered session, orginally issued on Fontana in the UK.

***   **Somebody Loves Me** LRC CDC 8514 CD
Sims; Teddy Wilson (*p*); Lionel Hampton (*vib, v*); Bucky Pizzarelli (*g*); George Duvivier, Milt Hinton (*b*); Buddy Rich (*d, v*); Stanley Kay (*d*).

It's not clear when this dates from, but it finds Sims and Pizzarelli – in a partnership pre-empting the duo set with Pass for Pablo – in a mood of some empathy. Some of the tracks are a trifle too short, and the final three, where Lionel Hampton and Teddy Wilson arrive, are unexceptional jams, but three impeccably drawn ballads for tenor and guitar alone are the outstanding things here, with Sims turning the melody of 'Memories Of You' into a sumptuous meditation.

***(*)   **Zoot Case** Sonet SNTCD 1044 CD
Sims; Al Cohn (*ts*); Claes Croona (*p*); Palle Danielsson (*b*); Peter Ostlund (*d*). 6/82.

Sims's long-standing partnership with Al Cohn actually left comparatively few recordings, which makes this impromptu session with a house rhythm section all the more valuable. If both men were usually content to take a relaxed path through their music, the energy quotient here is startling, with 'Zoot Case' and 'After You've Gone' taken at a snorting pace and the two tenors coming as close as they ever did to a cutting contest. The rhythm section struggles to keep the platform steady at times, though Danielsson is a rock, and the recording is only a little below studio standard.

****   **Zoot Sims And The Gershwin Brothers** Original Jazz Classics OJC 444 CD/LP/MC
Sims; Oscar Peterson (*p*); Joe Pass (*g*); George Mraz (*b*); Grady Tate (*d*). 6/75.

***   **Soprano Sax** Pablo 2310-770 LP
Sims; Ray Bryant (*p*); George Mraz (*b*); Grady Tate (*d*). 1/76.

**   **Hawthorne Nights** Pablo 2310-783 LP
Sims; Snooky Young (*t, flhn*); Oscar Brashear (*t*); Frank Rosolino (*tb*); Jerome Richardson (*ss, as, ts, cl, f*); Richie Kamuca (*ts, cl*); Bill Hood (*bs, bcl, f*); Ross Tompkins (*p*); Monty Budwig (*b*); Nick Ceroli (*d*); Bill Holman (*arr*). 9/76.

****   **If I'm Lucky** Original Jazz Classics OJC 683 CD
Sims; Jimmy Rowles (*p*); George Mraz (*b*); Mousie Alexander (*d*). 10/77.

***(*)   **Warm Tenor** Pablo 2310-831 CD/MC
As above. 9/78.

***(*)   **For Lady Day** Pablo 2310-942 CD/LP/MC
As above, except Jackie Williams (*d*) replaces Alexander. 4/78.

***(*)   **Just Friends** Original Jazz Classics OJC 499 CD/.LP/MC
Sims; Harry Edison (*t*); Roger Kellaway (*p*); John Heard (*b*); Jimmie Smith (*d*). 12/78.

***   **Blues For Two** Original Jazz Classics OJC 635 CD/LP/MC
Sims; Joe Pass (*g*). 3–6/82.

***   **Quietly There** Pablo 2310-903 MC
Sims; Mike Wofford (*p*); Chuck Berghofer (*b*); Nick Ceroli (*d*); Victor Feldman (*perc*). 3/84.

**   **The Best Of Zoot Sims** Pablo 2405-406 CD/LP/MC
As above Pablo albums.

When Sims signed to Norman Granz's Pablo operation, he wasn't so much at a crossroads as contentedly strolling down an uneventful path. For a man who could fit effortlessly into any situation he chose – admittedly, he never chose a situation that might cause trouble – Sims could have spent his final years as a nebulous figure. But his Pablo albums set the seal on his stature, sympathetically produced, thoughtfully programmed and with enough challenge to prod Zoot into his best form. *Gershwin Brothers* is a glorious sparring match with Peterson, rising to an almost overpowering charge through 'I Got Rhythm' via a simmering 'Embraceable You' and a variation on Coltrane's approach to 'Summertime'. *Soprano Sax* is a reasonable proposition, given Sims's interest in the soprano as a second horn, but it feels like a pointless exercise asking the man responsible for one of the most distinguished of tenor saxophone timbres to do a whole set on soprano, where he's recognizably Zoot but not a great deal more. It's the ravishing tone which makes the session with Pass so attractive: with drums and bass cleared away, the tenor sound is swooningly beautiful. A pity, though, that Pass sounds so perfunctory throughout. *Hawthorne Nights* puts Zoot in front of a disappointing set of Bill Holman charts, for a band that seems neither small nor large enough for the occasion; and the session with Harry Edison, though it has its moments, is blemished by studio arrangements that sound stiff and by a horrible-sounding eletric piano on a couple of tracks. The sessions with Jimmy Rowles at the piano, though, are indispensable examples of Zoot at his best. *If I'm Lucky* is, narrowly, the pick, for its ingenious choice of material – '(I Wonder Where) Our Love Has Gone' counts as one of Sims's most affecting performances – and the uncanny communication between saxophonist and pianist throughout. *Warm Tenor* is only a shade behind, and the recently discovered set of tunes associated with Billie Holiday, *For Lady Day*, is another plum choice, with an amble through 'You Go To My Head' that dispels the happy-sad clouds of Holiday's oeuvre with a smouldering lyricism. Two other sessions with Rowles, *The Swinger* and *I Wish I Were Twins*, are still awaited on CD. Although only a year away from his death when he made *Quietly There*, a set of Johnny Mandel themes, Sims was still in absolute command. Feldman's percussion adds a little extra fillip to the likes of 'Cinnamon And Clove', although Sims himself sounds undistracted by anything: his winding, tactile improvisation on the melody of 'A Time For Love', to pick a single instance, speaks of a lifetime's preparation. The *Best Of* is a mysteriously ill-chosen retrospective: better to pick any one of the albums with Rowles if a single disc is all that's required.

LARS SJØSTEN (born 1941)
PIANO

***   **Select Notes** Caprice CAP 1216 LP
Sjøsten; Jan Allan (*t*); Lars Olofsson (*tb*); Willy Lundin, Ulf Andersson (*as*); Hector Bingert (*ts*); Erik Nilsson (*bs, bcl*); Sture Nordin (*b*); Egil Johansen (*d*); Rudi Smith (*steel pans*). 4/80.

***   **Bells, Blues And Brotherhood** Dragon DRLP 46 LP
Sjøsten; Bertil Lovgren, Jan Kohlin (*t, flhn*); Lars Olofsson, Christer Torge, Torgny Nilsson (*tb*); Hakan Nyquist, Petter Carlsson (*frhn*); Jan Kling (*as*); Hector Bingert (*ts*); Erik Nilsson (*bs*); Sven Larsson (*tba, b*); Sture Nordin (*b*); Egil Johansen (*d*). 5–12/81.

Although characterized as a bop pianist, Sjøsten's albums under his own name – he began recording as a leader in 1971 – reveal a broader range of sympathies. The Caprice album is an apposite introduction to what he can do, since it features nine original themes in solo, trio, quartet, quintet and octet contexts. While the material suggests a conservative stylist content with a rhythmic shift or an unusual tonality to typify a composition, he's a deft and economical pianist, and his players bring plenty of life to the music: Olofsson is a memorably tart soloist, Smith adds steel pans to the interesting 'Third Call', and the closing 'capricious, irregular and complaining octet', as Sjøsten has it, is delivered with a flourish. His first album for Dragon makes more good use of an octet and a nonet.

***   **In Confidence** Dragon DRCD 197 CD
Sjøsten; Jan Kohlin (*t*); Bertil Strandberg (*tb*); Dave Castle (*as*); Krister Andersson (*ts*); Gunnar Bergsten (*bs*); Petter Carlsson (*frhn*); Oystein Baadsvik (*tba*); Patrik Boman (*b*); Nils Danell (*d*). 11–12/90.

Sjøsten's latest record suggests a steady late-maturity rather than any special growth. These are pleasing, good-natured compositions, deftly arranged, without hidden depths but not short on imagination. The 10 pieces are arranged for trio, quartet (with Bergsten), sextet and a ten-piece band and, while the theme statements by the horns could be tighter, the casual complexion suits the music rather well. Bergsten, Strandberg and Castle are the most inventive soloists, and Sjøsten rounds matters off with a thoughtful trio version of 'You'd Be So Nice To Come Home To'.

ALAN SKIDMORE (born 1942)
TENOR SAXOPHONE

***(*)   **Tribute To 'Trane** Miles Music CDMM075 CD
Skidmore; Jason Rebello (*p*); Dave Green (*b*); Stephen Keogh (*d*). 2/88.

Like his saxophonist father, Jimmy, who was a stalwart of the British mainstream scene in the 1950s and early '60s, Alan Skidmore is much less well known than he ought to be. In a wilderness of clones, he stands out – admittedly older and therefore wiser – as one of the few who have submitted the Coltrane legacy to thoughtful consideration, rather than taking it as licence for frenzied harmonic activity and emotional streaking. Skidmore is rather poorly represented in the current catalogue, though he can also be heard on the eponymous *S.O.S.* with fellow-saxophonists Mike Osborne and John Surman; two records by the challenging SOH (Skidmore, drummer Tony Oxley and bassist Ali Haurand) are also well worth looking out for.

The first of these – released on the small, German-based view label – featured a majestic interpretation of Coltrane's 'Lonnie's Lament', a theme he returns to on *Tribute To 'Trane*. With typical self-effacement, Skidmore asks that the album, one of a flood marking the twentieth anniversary of the great saxophonist's death, be regarded as a 'thank you' rather than as another god-bothering ritual by a disciple. The choice of material is interesting. 'Naima' and

'Mr P.C.' represent a more predictable closing sequence, but 'Resolution', 'Bessie's Blues', 'Crescent' and 'Dear Lord', together with the outstanding 'Lonnie's Lament' (on which Rebello and Keogh are both superb, incidentally) suggest the depth of Skidmore's understanding of the music. The performances are not in themselves self-consciously *de profundis*, and there are no overpowering histrionics. Well recorded in medium close-up, this takes its place behind McCoy Tyner *et al.*'s *Blues For 'Trane* as the best of the twentieth-anniversary votes of thanks.

BILLY SKINNER
TRUMPET, FLUGELHORN

***   **Kosen Rufu** Accurate 3333 CD
    Skinner; Henry Cook (*as, f*); Salim Washington (*ts, f*); Ichi Takato (*b*); Bobby Ward (*d*). 7/88.

Alternately breezy and wistful, this is a very attractive record with elements of free bop and more traditional playing mixed confidently together. Skinner writes simple but hauntingly effective melodies and seasons the programme with some favourite covers, including 'Mood Indigo' and a cleverly melded bebop sequence. His own playing has something of the free elegance of Bobby Bradford, though occasionally he seems a little too caught up in the music to make a decisive point, and Cook and Washington are good if relatively undemonstrative players.

JABBO SMITH (1908–90)
TRUMPET, VOCAL

****   **Jabbo Smith Vol. 1** Retrieval FJ 131 LP
    Smith; Garvin Bushell (*cl, as, bsn*); Omer Simeon, Darnell Howard (*cl*); Millard Robins (*bsx*); Fats Waller (*org*); Cassino Simpson, James P. Johnson, William Barbee (*p*); Ikey Robinson (*g, bj*); Hayes Alvis (*tba*). 3/28–2/29.

****   **Jabbo Smith Vol. 2** Retrieval FJ 132 LP
    Smith; Omer Simeon, Willard Brown (*cl, as*); Leslie Johnakins, Ben Smith (*as*); Sam Simmons (*ts*); Cassino Simpson, Kenneth Anderson, Alex Hill, James Reynolds (*p*); Ikey Robinson (*bj*); Connie Wainwright (*g*); Hayes Alvis, Lawson Buford (*tba*); Elmer James (*b*); Alfred Taylor (*d*). 3/29–2/38.

Until his rediscovery in the 1960s, Smith was legendary as Armstrong's most significant rival in the 1920s, a reputation built mostly on the records reissued on these two indispensable LPs. He had already made a name for himself with Charlie Johnson's orchestra, but it was the 20 sides he cut with his Rhythm Aces which have endured as Smith's contribution to jazz. The first record opens with a 1928 session by the Louisiana Sugar Babes, which included both Johnson and Waller, and three alternative takes are also present; but more exciting is a peppery 1929 session by Ikey Robinson's group, including the astonishingly hyperactive 'Ready Hokum'. The LP closes with the first seven Rhythm Aces titles, including 'Jazz Battle', the storming 'Little Willie Blues' and the nicely melancholy 'Sleepy Time Blues'. The other 13 Aces titles are on *Volume Two*, together with four tracks from a single 1938 session by Smith's then eight-strong group. Smith's style is like a thinner, wilder variation on Armstrong's. He takes even more risks in his solos – or, at least, makes it seem that way, since he's less assured at pulling them off than Louis was.

    Some passages he seems to play entirely in his highest register; others are composed of handfuls of notes, phrased in such a scattershot way that he seems to have snatched them out of the air. If it makes the music something of a mess, it's a consistently exciting one. Organized round Smith's own stop-time solos and dialogue with the rhythm, with the occasional vocal – a quizzical mix of Armstrong and Don Redman – thrown in too, the records seem like a conscious attempt at duplicating the Hot Five sessions, although in the event they sold poorly. Simeon is curiously reticent, much as Dodds was on the Hot Fives, and alto players Brown and James do no more than behave themselves. The livewire foil is, instead, the extraordinary Robinson, whose tireless strumming and rare, knockout solo (as on 'Michigander Blues') keep

everything simmering. Shrill and half focused, these are s[...]
poorly documented talent (who reappeared in his seventie[...]
The transfers have been splendidly done by the indefatigable [...]

JIMMY SMITH (born 1925)

ORGAN

***(*) **House Party** Blue Note CDP 746546-2 CD
Smith; Lee Morgan (*t*); Curtis Fuller (*tb*); George Colema[...]
Brooks (*ts*); Eddie McFadden, Kenny Burrell (*g*); Donald [...]
8/57–2/58.

*** **The Sermon** Blue Note CDP 746097-2 CD
As above. 8/57–2/58.

**** **Cool Blues** Blue Note CDP 784441-2 CD
Smith; Lou Donaldson (*as*); Tina Brooks (*ts*); Eddie McFadden (*g*); Donald Bailey,
Art Blakey (*d*). 4/58.

** **Crazy Baby** Blue Note B21Y-84030 CD
Smith; Quentin Warren (*g*); Donald Bailey (*d*). 3/60.

(*) **Midnight Special Blue Note B21Y/841E-84078 CD/MC
Smith; Stanley Turrentine (*ts*); Kenny Burrell (*g*); Donald Bailey (*d*). 4/60.

(*) **Back At The Chicken Shack Blue Note CDP 746402-2 CD
As above. 4/60.

As Coleman Hawkins is to the tenor saxophone, so James Oscar Smith is to the Hammond
organ. Amazingly, he didn't even touch the instrument until he was 28, but he quickly
established and personified a jazz vocabulary for the instrument: tireless walking bass in the
pedals, thick chords with the left hand, quickfire melodic lines with the right. It was a formula
almost from the start, and Smith has never strayed from it, but he so completely mastered the
approach that he is inimitable. At his best, he creates a peerless excitement which is seldom
sustained across an entire album but which makes every record he's on something to be
reckoned with.

Cool Blues is the ideal starting point for anyone wanting to hear what Smith can do.
Recorded on a single evening at Small's Paradise in New York, it earns its four stars on the basis
of the leader's astounding solo on 'Groovin' At Small's', a brilliant instance of how Smith deals
with a blues. There's also the opportunity to hear the seldom-recorded Brooks, whose brand of
cool hard bop is consistently compelling, and, although there are plenty of scrappy moments,
the music is never less than vibrant – even with nearly 75 minutes' playing time.

House Party and *The Sermon* are studio sessions at an only slightly lower flame, with fine
contributions from all the horns, while *Back At The Chicken Shack* has Turrentine confronting
Smith to somewhat lesser effect, although the title blues blows very warmly.

Midnight Special and *Crazy Baby* are still available as US releases. The former was recorded
at the same session as *Chicken Shack* and is more of the same, while the latter is a more prosaic
studio set devoted to standards that don't really get Smith started.

***(*) **Compact Jazz** Verve 831374-2 CD
Smith; Joe Newman, Doc Severinsen, Joe Wilder, Ernie Royal, Jimmy Maxwell, Bernie
Glow, Clark Terry, Marky Markowitz, Thad Jones (*t*); Tommy Mitchell, Urbie Green,
Jimmy Cleveland, Britt Woodman, Bill Byers (*tb*); Babe Clark, Jerome Richardson,
Jerry Dodgion, Robert Ashton, Phil Woods, George Barrow, Danny Bank, Romeo
Penque (*reeds*); Jim Buffington, Ray Alonge, Bill Correa, Earl Chapin (*frhn*); Barry
Galbraith, Kenny Burrell (*g*); Don Butterfield (*tba*); George Duvivier, Vince
Gambella (*b*); Ed Shaughnessy, Grady Tate, Mel Lewis (*d*); Phil Kraus (*perc*).
3/62–9/66.

Smith has recorded more than 60 albums, yet most await any kind of reissue, and this attractive
compilation gives only a glimpse of what he recorded for Verve in the 1960s and '70s. There are
five settings for him within a big band arranged by Oliver Nelson, and the irresistible swagger
of Elmer Bernstein's 'Walk On The Wild Side' suits Smith perfectly; besides these, Lalo

In The Night' and 'The Cat', and the organist and his long-time
...rrell, trade punches on 'Blue Bash' and 'Satin Doll'. The remastered sound

For Whatcha Know Blue Note (US) B21Y-46297/4BT-85125 CD/MC
Smith; Stanley Turrentine (*ts*); Monty Alexander (*p*); Kenny Burrell (*g*); Buster
Williams (*b*); Grady Tate, Kenny Washington (*d*); Errol Bennett (*perc*). 1/86.

The old man's return to Blue Note resulted in a disappointingly workmanlike date, even though
Smith has hardly lost his touch. Turrentine plays with prepackaged vigour, and one or two
modish touches – including a grim reading of Michael Jackson's tearful 'She's Out Of My Life'
– sound clangingly wrong. They should have just put Smith in the studio with Burrell and Tate
and let them all blow.

***   **Prime Time** Milestone M 9176 CD
Smith; Curtis Peagler (*as*); Herman Riley, Ricky Woodard (*ts*); Phil Upchurch (*g*). 89.

Much more like it – Smith romping through familiar ground with some old and new associates
with no concessions to pop material.

(*)   **The Best Of Jimmy Smith Blue Note CD

A serviceable compilation which includes 'Back At The Chicken Shack' and 'The Sermon' as
well as a couple of lesser items: concessions to being 'representative' have perhaps told against
the final choice here.

LEO SMITH (born 1941)
TRUMPET, FLUGELHORN, PERCUSSION, VOICE

****   **The Mass On The World** Moers 01060 LP
Smith; Dwight Andrews (*as, ts, bcl, af, picc, gongs*); Bobby Naughton (*vib, bells*). 5/78.

***   **Budding Of A Rose** Moers 02026 LP
Smith; Rob Howard, Michael Philip Mossman, Hugh Ragin, Kenny Wheeler (*t*); Ray
Anderson, George Lewis, Alfred Patterson (*tb*); Pinguin Moschner (*tba*); Dwight
Andrews, Anthony Braxton, Marty Ehrlich, Douglas Ewart, Wallace McMillan (*reeds*);
Marilyn Crispell (*p*); Bobby Naughton (*vib*); Wes Brown (*b*); Pheeroan AkLaff (*d,
perc*). 6/79.

***(*)   **Touch The Earth** FMP 0730 LP
Smith; Peter Kowald (*b*); Günter 'Baby' Sommer (*d*). 11/79.

***(*)   **Go In Numbers** Black Saint BSR 0053 LP
Smith; Dwight Andrews (*ts, ss, f*); Bobby Naughton (*vib*); Wes Brown (*b, odurogyaba
f*). 1/80.

****   **Procession Of The Great Ancestry** Chief CD6 CD
Smith; Joe Powell (*ts*); Bobby Naughton (*vib*); Louis Myers (*g*); Mchaka Uba, Joe
Fonda (*b*); Kahil El Zabar (*d, perc*). 2/83.

Smith is one of the few jazz musicians to have embraced Rastafarianism. That he has done so
from a fastness in Iceland seems even more extraordinary. It isn't really possible to divide his
career into earlier and later phases, since his concerns are remarkably consistent. He plays
trumpet and flugelhorn with a strong Miles Davis influence (particularly when muted), but he
has also absorbed other swing and bop players. The magnificent *Procession Of The Great
Ancestry*, accompanied by 'seven mystical poems of jahzz in 17 links', is a series of tributes to
models like Miles, Booker Little, Roy Eldridge, Dizzy Gillespie, Roy Eldridge and the Rev.
Martin Luther King Jr. Less pastiche than sincere invocation, the individual pieces follow the
ritual character of the title-track. The dominant combination, as so often in Smith's career, is of
trumpet and Bobby Naughton's post-Hutcherson vibes.
  This is the key to the earlier – but equally ritualistic – *Mass To The World*, a genuinely
uplifting piece marred by indifferent sound. Andrews's multi-instrumentalism is also an
important dimension, for Smith avoids settled formations in favour of *ad hoc* pairings. Nothing
else is quite so starkly minimal as the trio with Kowald and Sommer, which offers a glimpse of

996

the trumpeter's free-form playing. (The trio have also recorded under Kowald's name, the intriguingly titled *If You Want The Kernels, You Have To Break The Shells* (FMP 0920 LP), but it's a less impressive record than this.)

The huge *Budding Of A Rose* marshals an impressive roster of European and American avant-gardists for a composition that combines the ritual formality of Mary Lou Williams's large-scale pieces (and there is an allusion to Williams in the title) with the freedoms of collective improvisation. Though again the sound is barely adequate, with some distortion on the vital trumpet parts, Smith's imaginative grasp is firm and the album has a satisfying coherence.

Credited to the New Dalta Ahkri, *Go In Numbers* is in Smith's rapt, prophetic manner. Without a drummer, Naughton's vibes become the focal point. Time, perhaps, for some duo performances.

LOUIS SMITH (born 1931)
TRUMPET, FLUGELHORN

(*)   **Just Friends Steeplechase SCS 1096 LP/MC
Smith; George Coleman (*ts*); Harold Mabern (*p*); Jamil Nasser (*b*); Ray Mosca Jr (*d*). 3/78.

**   **Prancin'** Steeplechase SCS 1121 LP/MC
Smith; Junior Cook (*ts*); Roland Hanna (*p*); Sam Jones (*b*); Billy Hart (*d*). 6/79.

**   **Ballad For Lulu** Steeplechase SCCD 31268 CD
Smith; Jim McNeely (*p*); Bob Cranshaw (*b*); Keith Copeland (*d*). 3/90.

Fondly remembered for two impressive Blue Note albums made in 1958, Smith's more recent work is much less exciting. His first records for 20 years were hesitant and lacking in conviction so far as his own playing was concerned: both teams of musicians outplay him on *Just Friends* and *Prancin'*, with the redoubtable Coleman surging through on the earlier disc. The third record is a collection of ballads which Smith plays with exaggerated care: his tone is clear and strong, but the phrasing seems indolent, and McNeely's accompaniment and sweeping solos are the principal attraction in a set which is rather too generous at 70 minutes in length. Better to wait for the reissue of the Blue Note albums if you want to hear Smith at his best.

MARVIN SMITTY SMITH
DRUMS

***   **Keeper Of The Drums** Concord CCD 4325 CD
Smith; Wallace Roney (*t*); Robin Eubanks (*tb*); Steve Coleman (*as*); Ralph Moore (*ts*); Mulgrew Miller (*p*); Lonnie Plaxico (*b*). 3/87.

***   **The Road Less Travelled** Concord CCD 4379 CD
As above, except James Williams (*p*) and Robert Hurst (*b*) replace Miller and Plaxico; add Kenyatte Abdur-Rahman (*perc*). 2/89.

One wonders if this is how Max Roach or Philly Joe Jones might have sounded on their own albums if recording techniques in the 1950s had been up to present-day standards. Drummer albums, even by some of the masters, used to be vulnerable to the Tedious Solo Syndrome, overlong and overmiked excursions that rattled the fillings. In a sense, Smitty Smith never stops soloing. His is the most insistent voice throughout almost every track, a maelstrom of furiously paced percussion that seems out of all proportion to the relatively modest bop-to-M-BASE foregrounds.

The debut *Keeper Of The Drums* is marginally the better of the two because the themes seem fresher. 'Miss Ann', not the Dolphy classic of that name, works a variation on the classic Spanish interval. 'Just Have Fun' and 'Song Of Joy' are directly reminiscent of 1950s models, and most people, offered a sample of 'The Creeper', will claim they've got it on a Blue Note somewhere.

The writing is less varied and more predictable on *The Road Less Travelled*. There's no significant difference between the line-ups, except that Miller and Plaxico are marginally more sensitive, but the later set is brittle where the earlier album bends and moulds to the context. Smith's off-beats and compressed rolls are technically impressive but ultimately rather wearing. In his backwash one tends to lose sight of some excellent work from Moore and Roney in particular.

Smith may yet be acknowledged as the Max Roach of his day. Or maybe just the Art Blakey. His sideman credits are impressive. But it will take something a little more distinctive than these to put him on a par with his role models.

MIKE SMITH
ALTO SAXOPHONE

(*)   **Unit 7 A Tribute To Cannonball Adderley** Delmark DE 444 CD/LP
Smith; Ron Friedman (*t, flhn*); Jodie Christian (*p*); John Whitfield (*b*); Robert Shy (*d*). 90.

***   **On A Cool Night** Delmark DE 448 CD
As above, except Jimmy Ryan (*p*) and Bob Rummage (*d*) replace Christian and Shy. 91.

Hard bop from contemporary Chicago. Smith is frankly under the spell of Cannonball Adderley: he doesn't have the rasping, bluesy timbre down as well as Vincent Herring does, but the line of descent is clear from a few bars of any solo, and *Unit 7* is a proper genuflection in the direction of Cannon's work. But this young altoman looks a little further out, too: he organizes his bands with pithy discretion and seeks contrast in his choice and arrangement of material. 'Don't Scare Me None', for instance, the opening track on *On A Cool Night*, is a nicely measured bebop variation with a cunning tempo change to keep everyone awake. The first record begs direct comparison with the source of inspiration, and takes only a goodish second place as a result, but *On A Cool Night* is more personal and hints at an emerging voice. Friedman is the more unusual player, though, if only for his curiously ingested tone – as if he were an avant-gardist trying to play it relatively straight. A useful reminder that New York doesn't have it all its own way as regards new American talent.

STUFF SMITH (1909–67)
VIOLIN, VOCALS

[***   **Complete After Midnight Sessions** Capitol CDP 7483282 CD]
Smith; Nat King Cole (*p, v*); John Collins (*g*); Charles Harris (*b*); Lee Young (*d*). 9/56.

***   **Violins No End** Pablo 2310907 LP
Smith; Stéphane Grappelli (*vn*); Oscar Peterson (*p*); Herb Ellis (*g*); Ray Brown (*b*); Jo Jones (*d*). 5/57.

***(*)   **Live In Paris** France's Concert FCD 120 CD
Smith; George Arvanitas, Eddie Bernard, Joe Turner (*p*); Paul Rovere, Jacky Samson, Jimmy Woode (*b*); Marcel Blanche, Kenny Clarke, Charles Saudrais (*d*); Jean-Claude Pelletier Orchestra – personnel unknown. 1 & 5/65.

***(*)   **Swingin' Stuff** Storyville SLP 4087 LP

***(*)   **Live At The Montmartre** Storyville SLP 4142 LP
Smith; Kenny Drew (*p*); Niels-Henning Ørsted-Pedersen (*b*); Alex Riel (*d*). 3/65.

It's hard to imagine how Billy Bang's or Leroy Jenkins's mordant new-wave fiddling would have come about had it not been for the example of Stuff Smith. Initially influenced by Joe Venuti, Smith devised a style based on heavy bow-weight, with sharply percussive semiquaver runs up towards the top end of his range. Like many 1920s players, Smith found himself overtaken by the swing era and only re-emerged as a recording and concert artist (though he had a thriving club career in the meantime) after the war, when his upfront style and comic stage persona attracted renewed attention.

The mid-1950s sessions with sound-alikes Nat King Cole and Oscar Peterson are slightly watered-down versions of Smith's greatest work and can only be considered second-string performances. The sessions involving the other great violinst of the period are highly entertaining and a useful exercise in comparative stylistics, with Grappelli's smooth *legato* washing around Smith's blunt outcrops of melody on 'Don't Get Around Much Any More' and 'The Lady Is A Tramp'.

The later European sessions, recorded within a couple of years of Smith's death in Munich, are very much better. Sound-quality is less than ideal on the France's Concert compilation of performances, of which those with Arvanitas's trio ('Perdido', 'Take The "A" Train') are absolutely excellent. The long blues jam with Pelletier's stiff-sounding band is much less appealing. Though two tracks with Joe Truner's trio from the same date sound perfectly all right, the band mix is rather treacherous, alternately swamping and stranding the violinist in mid-chorus.

The two Storyvilles represent the best of Smith currently available, though a single edited CD of the two sets would be more than welcome. 'Old Stinkin' Blues', 'Mack The Knife', 'Bugle Blues' and 'Take The "A" Train' appear on both sessions (recorded five days apart, during a residency), which seems an unnecessary reduplication. The rhythm section give him more to chew on than Peterson and Cole, and the old boy responds accordingly.

TAB SMITH (1909–71)
ALTO AND TENOR SAXOPHONES

***   Jump Time Delmark DD-447 CD
Smith; Sonny Cohn (*t*); Leon Washington (*ts*); Lavern Dillon, Teddy Brannon (*p*); Wilfred Middlebrooks (*b*); Walter Johnson (*d*); Louis Blackwell (*v*). 8/51–2/52.

Smith jobbed around the Harlem big bands of the 1930s and eventually found a niche with Count Basie. But he won his wider fame as an R&B soloist in the 1950s, and for a while jockeyed with Earl Bostic on the nation's jukeboxes. This CD collects 20 such performances. Backed by an unobtrusive small group, Smith works through ballads, the blues and more roisterous outings. His sound is more graceful than Bostic's: he always seems to have something in reserve, and the hollow sound he sometimes gets in the alto's upper register reminds that he often made use of the soprano, too, although not here. Given the sameness of the format and the repetitive formulas Smith had to apply, this is a surprisingly engaging CD, although 20 tracks will be more than enough for all but the most devout followers. Very clean remastering, although since this kind of music is meant to be greasy and unkempt, it doesn't always sound right.

TOMMY SMITH (born 1967)
TENOR SAXOPHONE

**(*)   Forward Motion: The Berklee Tapes Hep 2026 LP
Smith; Terje Gewelt (*b*); Laszlo Gardonyi (*p*); Ian Froman (*d*). 11/84.

***   Step By Step Blue Note 791930 CD
Smith; John Scofield (*g*); Mitch Forman (*p, ky*); Eddie Gomez (*b*); Jack DeJohnette (*d*). 9/88.

***(*)   Standards Blue Note BLT 1003 CD/LP
Smith; Niels Lan Doky (*p*); Mick Hutton (*b*); Ian Froman (*d*). 1/91.

Sadly with quite unreasonable expectations as a fifteen-year-old whiz, Tommy Smith has made slow progress into major-label recording. His Blue Note debut, *Step By Step*, had a stellar rhythm section and a nervous, hasty quality that suggested Smith was trying to show off all his (by now considerable) talents in one brief session. In contrast to rather home-made sessions like *Taking Off* and *Giant Strides*, recorded at home in Scotland, it was a remarkably callow performance, and Smith's insistence on using his own material didn't help his cause. At Berklee, Smith had been taken up by vibraharpist and composer Gary Burton and played in Burton's

Whiz Kids band (ECM 1329 CD/LP). The experience simplified and straightened out his playing, stripping it of some of the Coltrane clichés and X-raying in on the harmonic skeleton of a piece. Though the opening 'Ally The Wallygator' and 'Ghosts' are admirably well argued, Smith sounds overpowered by the company he's keeping, and the production is decidedly foggy; though the sound hardly accords with ECM standards, Smith seems increasingly inclined to withdraw (as on 'Ghosts') into a tentative and watered-down version of Jan Garbarek's demanding and deceptively imitable style.

For his second American album, the currently deleted *Peeping Tom* [Blue Note BLT 1002], Smith settled for a more modest and sympathetic line-up than the one which had given him such an uncertain send-off. Ian Froman and Terje Gewelt are also present on the unsatisfactory *Berklee Tapes*, properly credited to the band, Forward Motion (and occasionally to the Terje Gewelt Quartet), but universally received as a Smith album. On *Peeping Tom*, the young saxophonist sounded more focused, more in touch with his surroundings, and much more himself.

Throughout Smith's brief but precocious career, grizzled veterans had comforted themselves that he hadn't yet been proved in a standards setting. With Froman again, and the Danish-Vietnamese pianist, Niels Lan Doky, in for Gewelt, he makes a more than interesting job of an unpredictable roster of standard material. There is still some sign of over-reaching. A gratuitously tacked-on coda to the Latin-boppish 'Star Eyes' is quite horrendous, and Smith's tone, which has sharpened, wavers rather badly. 'Night And Day' has all the irresoluteness of a November afternoon in Edinburgh; it's hard to separate dark from light, irony from a hint of ineptitude, and Smith parts company with the band. 'My Secret Love', on the other hand, is a big production number. Evasive but emotional, it goes all round the houses before it declares itself. If there's a new input to explain Smith's changes of diction and tone, it may well be Johnny Griffin, whose 'Mil-Dew' falls exactly mid-set.

Backhanded though it sounds, with *Standards* Smith seems to have recaptured the way he played as a teenager. After some wavering, he looks ready for a substantial step forward.

PAUL SMOKER
TRUMPET

***   **Mississippi River Rat** Sound Aspects sas 006 LP
Smoker; Ron Rohovit (*b*); Phil Haynes (*d*). 6/84.

****   **Alone** Sound Aspects sas 018 CD/LP
As above. 8/86.

***(*)   **Come Rain Or Come Shine** Sound Aspects sas 024 CD
As above. 8/86.

***   **Joint Venture** Enja 5049 CD/LP
Smoker; Ellery Eskelin (*ts*); Drew Gress (*b*); Phil Haynes (*d*). 3/87.

***   **Joint Venture/Ways** Enja 6052 CD
As above. 1/89.

Paul Smoker is a Mid-West academic who plays free-form jazz of surpassing thoughtfulness. Though by no means averse to tackling standards, he creates a lot of his own material, cleaving to quasi-classical forms which, coupled with a tight, rather correct diction, sometimes recall Don Ellis. *Alone* was among the most interesting recordings of the mid-1980s and an object-lesson in group improvisation. The dynamics (as throughout Smoker's work) are almost too self-consciously varied, with tracks seguing into one another, giving the whole a suite-like feel. Working without a harmony instrument and with only occasional stabs at pedal notes from Smoker, the rhythm section is called on to perform an unusually active function, which (as 'Mingus Amongus' seems to suggest) is reminiscent of what the great bassist did with his bands. Rohovit bows long, hold-steady notes over whispering percussion on 'Prelude' (Haynes often works at the boundaries of audibility) until Smoker enters, sounding as if his last gig was Hummel or Haydn. The standards – Armstrong's 'Cornet Chop Suey' and Ellington's 'Caravan' – are imaginatively stitched in, and the performance gives off an aura of quiet power which is wholly missing on the more eclectic and ironic charts of *Mississippi River Rat* and *Come Rain Or Come Shine*.

It's interesting to compare the trio version of 'Chorale And Descendance' on the latter with the one recorded by Smoker's Joint Venture band on its first recorded outing. The saxophone adds nothing much to the turbulent formality of the piece, but 'Lush Life' takes on a wonderfully awkward grace, like a drunk getting the walk right just long enough to get to the other side of the bar where the girl is sitting. Beautiful, but not a patch on the sober stillness of *Alone*. Strongly recommended.

GARY SMULYAN
BARITONE SAXOPHONE

***	**The Lure Of Beauty** Criss Cross Jazz Criss 1049 CD
Smulyan; Jimmy Knepper (*tb*); Mulgrew Miller (*b*); Ray Drummond (*b*); Kenny Washington (*d*). 12/90.

A staunch section-player, Smulyan worked with Woody Herman and Mel Lewis and has as good a grasp of baritone technique as any of the younger players of what's still a rare instrument. It was a smart idea to bring Jimmy Knepper to this session, a frequent associate of Pepper Adams and a player whose manner is individual enough to lift the music out of the hard bop rut which several Criss Cross sessions have fallen into. The group work up a great head of steam on 'Canto Fiesta', the rhythm section grooving hard enough to sustain the feel over more than ten minutes, and there are a couple of pretty if functional balad performances; but at 74 minutes, the record could have lost a couple of items and been none the worse for it.

JIM SNIDERO
ALTO SAXOPHONE

**(*)	**Mixed Bag** Criss Cross Criss 1032 CD
Snidero; Brian Lynch (*t*); Benny Green (*p*); Peter Washington (*b*); Jeff Tain Watts (*d*). 12/87.

Disclaimers and denials aside, the title just about says it all. Much as Lynch and Green have done elsewhere, Snidero's latter-day hard bop tries to touch too many bases too quickly and without the authority that comes with what used to be called dues-paying. The overall effect is a rather superficial self-confidence and blandness of conception. The solos, most noticeably on 'Pannonica', come by rote, and few of them are properly thought out. Snidero's introductory cadenza on 'Blood Count' is his only really distinctive moment. That being said, this is a perfectly inoffensive set, free from false grandeur or pretentiousness, and, as far as it goes, quite enjoyable.

***	**Storm Rising** Ken 660 56 006 CD
Snidero; Mulgrew Miller (*p*); Peter Washington (*b*); Jeff Hirshfield (*d*). 4/90.

A more enterprising set of originals from the saxophonist, interspersed by Wayne Shorter's 'Virgo' and Sam Rivers's 'Beatrice'. Snidero trots out some of his Coltranisms on the first track and thereafter leaves them well alone, concentrating on shaping well-crafted solos out of quite modest and unassuming materials. Snidero is unlikely to set the world on fire, but this album is a definite step in the right direction.

***(*)	**Live** Red RR 123228 LP
Snidero; Marc Cohen (*p*); Peter Washington (*b*); Victor Lewis (*d*). 7/89.

There are moments when this might easily be mistaken for a Bobby Watson record. The label is right; the unmistakable drumming of Watson associate Victor Lewis is right; there's just something in the saxophonist's tone and approach, drier, sharper, more abrupt in phrasing that gives the game away. Outside the studio and with what sounds like a working band, Snidero is transformed. This is certainly the record that shows off his skills to best advantage. The originals 'Blue Walk' and 'Toro' are finely conceived and crafted, but there's also a fine version of Duke Jordan's rarely covered 'You Know I Care', which has only been recorded recently by Allan Farnham's quartet on their Concord set. Washington and Lewis maintain a high level of energy and inventiveness and if Cohen slightly lacks for pace, he more than makes up for any purely dynamic shortcomings in his carefully crafted and admirably thoughtful solos.

MARTIAL SOLAL (born 1927)
PIANO

***   **Martial Solal With The Kentonians** Vogue 655007 CD
Solal; Vinnie Tanno (*t*); Carl Fontana (*tb*); Don Rendell (*ts*); Curtis Counce (*b*); Mel Lewis (*d*). 5/56.

***(*) **Solal Series: Zo-Ko-So** MPS 843107 IMS CD
Solal; Hans Koller (*ts*); Attila Zoller (*g*). 1/65.

****   **Plays Hodeir** OMDCD 5008 CD
Solal; Roger Guerin, Eric Le Lann, Bernard Marchais, Tony Russo (*t*); Jacques Bolognesi, Christian Guizien (*tb*); Jacques Di Donato (*cl*); François Jeanneau (*cl, ts, ss*); Jean-Pierre Debarbat (*ts, ss*); Jean-Louis Chautemps (*bcl, as, ss*); Pierre Gossez (*bs, cl*); Philippe Mace (*vib*); Frederic Sylvestre (*g*); Césarius Alvim (*b*); Andre Ceccarelli (*d*). 3 & 4/84.

Solal's reputation, such as it currently stands, rests largely on his solo and trio work (with Daniel Humair, Jean-François Jenny-Clark and others) and on his film music; he wrote an unforgettable score for Godard's *À Bout de Souffle*. Fashion, a hint of prejudice and the economics that militate against such ventures have conspired against wider appreciation of his genius as an arranger and big-band leader. Two sets from the 1980s stand out: the Gaumont *Big Band* session of 1981 (long deleted) and the truly superb Hodeir set, recorded at Radio France three years later.

Trumpeter Roger Guerin of course is there and is, as always, striking, notably on the closing Monk tribute 'Cimin' on the Hudson'. 'Transplantation I' is a companion-piece to 'Flautando', not included here, and features Debarbat's ringing tenor. 'D Or No' is for sextet and, like the full-band 'Le Desert Recommence', highlights Solal at his most ironically Gallic.

There is little enough of that on record. The deleted *RCA Sessions* [NL 70791 LP/MC] were still the best bet for an impression of the Algerian-born Frenchman's oversauced solo performances until the release of Soul Note's *Bluesine* in the mid-1980s, when Solal's reputation took a brief and deserved lift. A useful live compilation from two and half decades [Accord 239963 CD], released at the time of that short-lived revival, is no longer available. 'Arranger's piano' tends to suggest a minimal, chords-only style; but Solal, like Tatum, is able to make the piano sound like a whole orchestra on a mainly standards set. The three unaccompanied jazz staples on *Zo-Ko-So* are almost as good, full of richly flavoured ideas and startling harmonic transitions. The remaining trios, duos and solos (some not involving the pianist) are excellent. The originals underline his musical wit, and a duo 'Stella By Starlight' with Zoller is one of the highpoints of the album.

'Kentonian' has only rarely – and in limited quarters – been a term of approbation. Like Kenton, Solal is frequently accused of pretentiousness and desiccation. It's not clear how the term may be thought to apply to the Vogue sessions. Featuring solid big-band musicians, they have the weight of much larger ensembles, and 'The Way You Look Tonight' for sextet could almost be a study piece for orchestrators.

LEW SOLOFF (born 1944)
TRUMPET, FLUGELHORN

(*) **Hanalei Bay Electric Bird K28P 6365 CD/LP
Soloff; Gil Evans (*electric p*); Hiram Bullock (*g*); Pete Levin (*syn*); Mark Egan (*b*); Kenwood Dennard or Adam Nussbaum (*d*); Manolo Badrena (*perc*). 3/85.

***   **Yesterdays** Paddle Wheel K28P 6448 CD/LP
Soloff; Mike Stern (*g*); Charnett Moffett (*b*); Elvin Jones (*d*). 9/86.

***   **But Beautiful** Paddle Wheel K28P 6468 CD/LP
Soloff; Kenny Kirkland (*p*); Richard Davis (*b*); Elvin Jones (*d*). 6/87.

New Yorker Soloff's career has been almost absurdly various. Classically trained and a featured soloist on several significant concerti, he spent his early twenties working a mainly Latin circuit before his recruitment in 1968 to the influential Blood, Sweat and Tears. Subsequently he was employed by one of the few bandleaders unembarrassed by an association with rock. Gil Evans used Soloff on mid-1970s tours to the Far East and elsewhere, on the excellent *Little Wing* (West Wind 2042 CD) and, in the 1980s, in his Monday Night Orchestra (Electric Bird K19P 6421/2 & 6455/6 CD/LPs).

Evans gave his blessing – and his slightly uncertain, 'arranger's' touch on electric piano – to *Hanalei Bay*, a less than wholly successful set that gives Soloff's virtuoso technique very little to chew on and digest. The later, smaller groups show less of Evans's influence and are more straightforwardly jazz-based. If standards remain a touchstone, the trumpeter's handling of 'All Blues' and 'Yesterdays', and of 'Speak Low' and 'Stella By Starlight' on *But Beautiful* suggest that he's more confident as a melodic improviser than on more complex modalities. Stern offers him fewer harmonic leads than Kirkland and makes little attempt to push him along, preferring to vary and embellish. Moffett's bass-lines are sometimes too heavy-handed, but the two rhythm sections are quite differently conceived, and each seems valid on its own terms. The fact that Jones, hyperactive as ever, sits comfortably in both is testimony to his remarkable powers of assimilation and adaptation.

The best of Soloff's work still has to be sought in isolated solos on other people's records, but these do at least offer a concentrated distillation of what he is capable of, and there is more than enough good material to satisfy casual curiosity.

GÜNTER SOMMER
DRUMS, PERCUSSION, ETC.

**   **Hörmusik** FMP 0790 LP
     Sommer (solo). 8/79.

Once East Germany's answer to Han Bennink, Sommer's partnership with Ulrich Gumpert and an appearance on Cecil Taylor's Berlin project constitute his chief apearances on record. This solo session from a Berlin Festival appearance features a lot of interesting noise which loses a fair amount, perhaps, in the translation, not helped by FMP's less than gratifying documentary sound. A subsequent solo album for Nato, as well as a pleasing group record, have yet to make it to CD.

S.O.S.
GROUP

***   **S.O.S.** Ogun OG400 LP
     John Surman (*bs, ss, bcl, syn*); Mike Osborne (*as*); Alan Skidmore (*ts, d*). 74.

Enormously impressive in a live context, S.O.S. sounded rather muted on record and the experiment was never repeated. The very idea of a saxophone trio without rhythm section was virtually unheard-of in the early 1970s, and the group made the fatal mistake of diluting their extraordinary, contrapuntal force with bland synthesizer *ostinati* (Surman's use of electronics has advanced by bounds since then) and Alan Skidmore's barely functional drumming. All three men have performed better elsewhere, but this was an interesting and, for its time, unusual project.

SPACE JAZZ TRIO
GROUP

***   **Space Jazz Trio: Volume 1** yvp 3007 CD/LP

***(*)   **Space Jazz Trio: Volume 2** yvp 3015 CD/LP
     Enrico Pieranunzi (*p*); Enzo Pietropaoli (*b*); Fabrizio Sferra (*d; Volume 1*); Alfred
     Kramer (*d; Volume 2*). 6/86, 11/88.

The title conjures up the possibility of an offshoot from Sun Ra's Intergalactic Arkestra. The reality is more earthbound, but by no means mundane. Able accompanists, having worked with Chet Baker (posthumously namechecked on *Volume 2*) and Lee Konitz, their own material is highly intelligent, open-minded and, yes, spacious. Pieranunzi (*q. v.*) is a solo recording artist of some standing, and it isn't entirely clear where his eponymous trio ends and the SJT begins (they have Pietropaoli in common). However, the bonus version of 'Autobahn' on *Volume 2* is much more demandingly coherent than that on the pianist's 1987 *Moon Pie* (yvp 3011 CD/LP), confirming other indications that the recruitment of Kramer has helped gel the group identity. The 'Open Events' (one to four, distributed across both sets) are impressively improvised. The Sun Ra analogy may well be viable after all, for this is thoroughly post-modern music, deeply eclectic and simultaneous in its choice of traditions, abstract and emotional by turns. Recommended with only minor qualifications about the recordings, which are unflattering.

MUGGSY SPANIER (1906–67)
CORNET

***(*) **Muggsy Spanier 1924–1928** Retrieval FJ 108 LP
Spanier; Dick Fiege, Charlie Altier (*c*); Guy Carey, Jack Reid (*tb*); Frank Teschmacher, Maurie Bercov (*cl, as*); Mezz Mezzrow (*cl, ts*); Volly De Faut (*cl*); Charles Pierce (*as*); Ralph Rudder (*ts*); Mel Stitzel, Dan Lipscomb, Joe Sullivan (*p*); Marvin Saxbe (*bj, g*); Stuart Branch, Eddie Condon (*bj*); Johnny Mueller (*b, bb*); Joe Gish, Jim Lannigan (*bb*); Ben Pollack, Paul Kettler, Gene Krupa (*d*); Red McKenzie (*v*). 2/24–4/28.

Spanier was only seventeen when he made the earliest sides here – by The Bucktown Five, in Richmond, Indiana – but he was already a confident lead player, if less impressive as a soloist (his chorus on 'Hot Mittens' is a well-meaning near-disaster). These seven tracks are nevertheless thoroughgoing jazz performances by a young group which had absorbed many of the latest developments in the music. The LP also includes two 1925 tracks by The Stomp Six, seven rare 1928 Paramount sides by Charles Pierce's Orchestra and two by the Jungle Kings, a prototype Chicagoan group with Teschmacher, Mezzrow, Sullivan, Condon and Krupa. Spanier is a full-fledged master by now and Teschmacher's snappy clarinet makes a hot foil to the cornetist's pungent improvising. Most of the originals suffered from famously low-fi sound, but the remastering has made them as listenable as modern ears will ever find them. Recommended.

***** **Muggsy Spanier 1931 And 1939** BBC REB/ZCF/CD 687 CD/LP/MC
Spanier; Dave Klein (*t*); George Brunies (*tb, v*); Sam Blank (*tb*); Ted Lewis (*cl, v*); Benny Goodman (*cl, as*); Rod Kless (*cl*); Louis Martin (*as, bs*); Hymie Wolfson, Ray McKinstrey, Bernie Billings, Nick Caizza (*ts*); Fats Waller (*p, v*); George Zack, Joe Bushkin (*p*); Sam Shapiro, Sol Klein (*vn*); Tony Gerhardi, Bob Casey (*g, b*); Pat Pattison, Harry Barth (*b*); John Lucas, Marty Greenberg, Don Carter, Al Sidell (*d*). 3/31–12/39.

**** **At The Jazz Band Ball** Bluebird NK/ND/NL 86752 CD/LP/MC
Spanier; Leonard Davis, Max Kaminsky (*t*); Jack Teagarden, George Brunies (*tb, v*); Brad Gowans (*tb*); Rod Kless, Pee Wee Russell (*cl*); Mezz Mezzrow (*Cmel*); Happy Caldwell, Ray McKinstrey, Bernie Billings, Nick Caizza, Bud Freeman (*ts*); Joe Sullivan, George Zack, Joe Bushkin (*p*); Bob Casey (*g, b*); Eddie Condon (*g*); Clyde Newcomb, Pat Pattison (*b*); George Stafford, Marty Greenberg, Don Carter, Al Sidell, Danny Alvin (*d*). 2/29–12/39.

Spanier's 1939 Ragtime Band recordings are among the classic statements in the traditional jazz idiom. Bob Crosby's Bob Cats had helped to initiate a modest vogue for small Dixieland bands in what was already a kind of revivalism at the height of the big-band era, and Spanier's group had audiences flocking to Chicago clubs, although by December, with a move to New York, they were forced to break up for lack of work. Their recordings have been dubbed 'The Great Sixteen' ever since. While there are many fine solos scattered through the sides – mostly by Spanier and the little-remembered Rod Kless – it's as an ensemble that the band impresses: allied to a boisterous rhythm section, the informal counterpoint between the four horns (the tenor sax perfectly integrated, just as Eddie Miller was in The Bob Cats) swings through every performance. The repertoire re-established the norm for Dixieland bands and, even though the material goes back to Oliver and the ODJB, there's no hint of fustiness, even in the rollicking effects of 'Barnyard Blues'. 'Someday Sweetheart', with its sequence of elegant solos, is a masterpiece of cumulative tension, and Spanier himself secures two finest hours in the storming finish to 'Big Butter And Egg Man' and the wah-wah blues-playing on 'Relaxin' At The

Touro', a poetic tribute to convalescence (he had been ill the previous year) the way Parker's 'Relaxin' At Camarillo' would subsequently be.

While Robert Parker's stereo remastering may not be to all tastes, he honours the music with beautifully clear transcriptions, and as a bonus the BBC album includes four tracks by the 1931 Ted Lewis band, with Spanier and Goodman and Fats Waller as star guests. An essential record.

The Bluebird disc, though very clean, in comparison sounds flatter. Although they also offer all 16 sides, an inferior alternative take of 'Someday Sweetheart' has been substituted for the original. But they also include four tracks from an excellent Bud Freeman session of 1939, including 'China Boy' and 'The Eel', and the two 1929 tracks by Eddie Condon's Hot Shots, which features some superb Jack Teagarden. Collectors may find the choice between the two discs a personal matter!

***   **Muggsy Spanier** Everybody's 1020 LP
Spanier; Lou McGarity (*tb*); Pee Wee Russell (*cl, v*); Peanuts Hucko (*cl*); Boomie Richmond, Bud Freeman (*ts*); Dave Bowman, Jess Stacy (*p*); Hy White (*g*); Bob Haggart, Trigger Alpert (*b*); George Wettling (*d*). 10/44–10/45.

(*)   **Rare Custom 45's** IAJRC 42 LP
Spanier; George Brunies (*tb*); Peanuts Hucko, Charlie Spero (*cl*); Floyd Bean (*p*); Remo Biondi (*g*); Cy Nelson (*b*); Doc Cenardo, Frank Rullo (*d*). 4/56.

Spanier has disgracefully few of his later recordings in print. but the Everybody's LP includes some enjoyable Dixieland by a couple of fine bands, made for V-Disc. While the record is almost worth having for Pee Wee Russell's bizarre vocal on 'Pee Wee Speaks', there are also plenty of good spots for Spanier, Russell and Freeman. Crackly but listenable transfers. The IAJRC LP offers 18 sides made for jukebox 45s and, while Muggsy remains in righteous form, the material – all by now very routine Dixieland fare – is dispiriting, and the bands are only competent. Brunies, though, is in joshing high spirits, and one lovely ballad – 'I Cried For You' – makes one wish that Spanier had been able to record a wider variety of tunes more often. We should point out that IAJRC records are hard to find in the UK.

JAMES SPAULDING (born 1937)
FLUTE, ALTO SAXOPHONE, SOPRANO SAXOPHONE, PICCOLO, BASS FLUTE

***   **Plays The Legacy Of Duke Ellington** Storyville SLP 4034 LP
Spaulding; Steve Nelson (*vib*); Cedar Walton (*p*); Sam Jones (*b*); Billy Higgins (*d*); James M'tume (*perc*); Avery Brooks (*v*). 12/76.

****   **Brilliant Corners** Muse 600610 CD
Spaulding; Wallace Roney (*t*); Mulgrew Miller (*p*); Ron Carter (*b*); Kenny Washington (*d*). 11/88.

(*)   **Gotstabe A Better Way!** Muse M5413 CD/LP/MC
Spaulding; Monte Croft (*vib*); Mulgrew Miller (*p*); Ron Carter (*b*); Ralph Peterson (*d*); Ray Mantilla (*perc*). 5/88.

Spaulding is something of an enigma. A brilliant group-player under other leaders – Freddie Hubbard pre-eminently, but also Max Roach and David Murray – he seems curiously po-faced on his own records. The Ellington performances are obviously striving after something (though *what* isn't clear), and the closing 'It Don't Mean A Thing If It Ain't Got That Swing' might seem ironic in the circumstances. On *Gotstabe* he tries in a more oblique and personal way to write himself into the jazz tradition, but the album passes in a blur of drearily polished arrangements, redeemed only by Miller in Wynton Kelly mode, the interplay of two fine percussionists, and occasional exchanges between Spaulding and Croft. (The vibes/piano combination seems to cover a whole passle of arranging sins.)

Significantly, perhaps, the leader cuts his instrumental armoury down to just two on *Brilliant Corners*. He has all the chops required of a hard-bop saxophonist and sounds good on the Monk title-track, flagging only slightly when juxtaposed on four romping tunes with Roney's bright and confident trumpet. An uneasy output so far, and surely not representative of the reedman's skills.

CHRISTOPH SPENDEL
PIANO, KEYBOARDS

**   **Back To Basics** Blue Flame 40072 CD
Spendel; Thomas Heidepriem (*b*); Kurt Bilker (*d*). 3/87.

**   **So Near So Far** L+R LR 40024 CD/LP
Spendel; Michael Stagmeister (*g*).

(*)   **Ready For Take-Off L+R 45010 CD/LP
Spendel; Annie Whitehead (*tb*); Stefan Rademacher (*b*); Kurt Bilker (*d*); Michael
Küttner (*perc*). 9/88.

Spendel's playing puts him squarely in the middle ranks of European keyboard players. *Back To Basics* is a straightforward piano trio date with little to raise it out of the merely accomplished on modal staples such as 'Dolphin Dance', while the duo meeting with Stagmeister noddles around various electronic possibilities without coming to much of a result. The most spirited music comes on *Ready For Take-Off*, which is at least valuable for an opportunity to hear Whitehead, whose funky, agile trombone has had too few outings on record.

PETER SPRAGUE
GUITAR, ELECTRIC GUITAR

**   **Na Pali Coast** Concord CJ 277 LP
Sprague; Steve Kujala (*f*); Tripp Sprague (*ts*); Bob Magnusson (*b*); Peter Erskine (*d*).
2/85.

Lightweight, floaty New Age jazz (the Coltrane tribute was a mistake) which relies heavily on Erskine's intelligent percussion to give it a bit of bottom. Kujala has worked with Chick Corea (one of the 'Children's Songs' is included), and the whole album cries out for a piano player of Corea's eclectic sensibilities to give the harmonies a bit of direction. Tripp Sprague may not be giving up his day job just yet.

SPYRO GYRA
GROUP

***   **Point Of View** MCA MCAD 6309 CD
Jay Beckenstein (*as, ts, ss*); Tom Schuman (*ky*); Jay Azzolina (*g*); Julio Fernandez (*g*); Dave Samuels (*mar, vib, syn*); Oscar Cartaya (*b*); Richie Morales (*d*); Roger Squitero (*perc*). 89.

(*)   **Fast Forward GRP GRD 9608 CD
As above, except omit Squitero; add Jeff Beal (*t*); Barry Danelian (*t, flhn*); Randy Andos (*tb, btb*); Scott Kreitzer (*ts*); Marc Quiñones (*perc*); David Broza (*v*). 90.

For a quick working definition of 'crossover appeal', look no further than this astonishing fusion group, formed in Buffalo in 1975 and who in 1978 enjoyed the unprecedented accolade of simultaneous appearance in six *Billboard* charts. Quieter of late, they nevertheless remain a huge concert draw, purveying a bland but undeniably energetic synthesis of Latin jazz and stadium rock. *Fast Forward*, for the first time 'featuring' saxophonist and co-founder Jay Beckenstein (original partner Wall no longer plays with the group), is marred by intrusive production and a rather slabby mix; '4MD', written by co-founder Jeremy Wall, skirts Miles Davis–Marcus Miller territory with some conviction, but most of the rest is bland in the extreme. The more coherent and disciplined *Point Of View* suggests a parallel (and perhaps a direct reference on the melancholy 'Unknown Soldier') with Weather Report in one of its Latinized incarnations, but without Zawinul's firm compositional and structural control. Apart from Beckenstein, the most prominent voice is Dave Samuel's marimba and vibraphone (and his distinctive mallet-driven synthesizer). The band's two best albums, *Morning Dance* [MCA 250420 LP/MC] and the jazz-orientated *Freetime* [MCA 250417 LP/MC], are currently unavailable.

TOMASZ STAŃKO (born 1942)
TRUMPET

***   **The Montreux Performance** ITM 1423 CD/LP
Stańko; Janusz Skowron (*p, syn*); Witold E. Sczurek (*b*); Tadeusz Sudnik (*syn, elec*).
7/87.

Stańko's music looks at first as if it bears closer kinship to the abstract experimentalism of the Polish avant-garde than to orthodox or even free jazz. This is deceptive, for the trumpeter is deeply versed in all the defining elements of jazz, and even when the setting is ostensibly abstractionist, as in this relatively recent Freelectronic performance, there is still an underlying jazz 'feel', expressible both as a pulse (though there is no drummer) and as dimly familiar harmonies and structures (though nothing close to a blues is attempted). Not for every taste. The early-1970s performances that followed Stańko's nomination as European Jazz Musician of the Year may well be more immediately accessible.

***(*)   **Bluish** Power Bros 00113 CD
Stańko; Arild Andersen (*b*); Jon Christensen (*d*). 10/91.

A marvellous record from the Rybnik-based Polish label, which deserves the widest distribution. Paired with Northern Europe's premier rhythm section (with Andersen alone on the opening 'Dialogue') Stańko seems content to work a long way clear of the basic pulse, except perhaps on the title piece which begins on a more straightforward metre but compensates with a curiously unresolved harmonic profile and breaks down into a superb solo from Christensen, heralded by hesitations and silences. The second part of 'If You Look Enough' (it comes first for some reason) is an eerie, out-of-tempo meditation punctuated by smears and growls which is much closer to Stańko's Freelectronic work; the first part (placed last in the set) features the same chordal effects, which may be processed bass, and a nagging, insect-like chitter from Christensen. The drummer creates remarkable effects with damped cymbals on the long 'Bosanetta', a tune that resembles one of Edward Vesala's pastiches, as does the succeeding 'Third Heavy Ballad', on which Stańko plays with a quiet lyricism that will suggest Kenny Wheeler to many listeners. Strongly recommended (if you can find it).

JEREMY STEIG (born 1942)
FLUTE, PICCOLO, ALTO FLUTE, BASS FLUTE, ELECTRONICS

****   **Outlaws** Enja 2098 CD/LP
Steig; Eddie Gomez (*b*). 12/76,

***   **Lend Me Your Ears** CMP 3 LP
As above, except add Joe Chambers (*d, perc*). 6/78.

***(*)   **Music For Flute And Double Bass** CMP 6 LP
As above, except omit Chambers. 78.

***   **Rain Forest** CMP 12 LP
Steig; Eddie Gomez (*b*); Karl Ratzer (*g*); Mike Nock (*electric p, syn*); Nana
Vasconcelos (*perc, berimbau*); Jack DeJohnette, Steve Gadd (*d*); Ray Barretto (*perc*).
2/80.

***   **Something Else** LRC CDC 8512 CD
Steig; Jan Hammer (*electric p, gongs*); Eddie Gomez (*b*); Gene Perla (*b*); Don Alias
(*d, perc*).

A virtuoso performer on all the flutes, Steig has greatly expanded the instrument's performing range by incorporating a range of unorthodox devices into his playing and writing. These include finger and pad noises, audible breathing and, in a manner reminiscent of Roland Kirk, fierce overblowing. Some of these effects were becoming part of contemporary concert music for flute (like Brian Ferneyhough's unaccompanied piece, *Unity Capsule*) and Steig has shown an interest in that genre; his third album with regular associate, Eddie Gomez, is an example of latter-day Third Stream.

Steig's interest in electronics, though, comes not so much from the avant-garde as from jazz–rock. Joachim Berendt cites his now largely forgotten 1970s band, Jeremy and the Satyrs, as an influence on the fusion movement, and there are elements of a more populist cross-over on both *Rain Forest* (where Steig restricts himself to concert flute and bass flute) and *Something Else*. (The resemblance of title to Ornette Coleman's emphatically revolutionary *Something Else!* is quite incidental.) His most effective disposition of electronics is on the surprisingly forceful *Lend Me Your Ears*.

Steig's duets with Gomez are very effective, utilizing extremes of sonority and sophisticated structures. The earliest, *Outlaws*, is the most obviously jazz-centred and includes two beautifully redrafted standards, 'Autumn Leaves' and 'Nardis'. Much of the rest of their work together moves in apparrently irreconcilable directions, towards greater formal abstraction and towards a strict-tempo immediacy. Drummers Chambers, Alias and DeJohnette contribute very different musical personalities to different contexts (and DeJohnette has developed his own, more successful version of Steig's world-consciousness elsewhere).

An adventurous and technically remarkable player, Steig has yet to break through to a wider audience. That shouldn't put anyone off.

NORBERT STEIN
SOPRANO AND TENOR SAXOPHONES

(*) **Die 5 Tage Jazz Haus Musik JHM 31 LP
Stein; Thomas Heberer, Reiner Winterschladen, Joachim Gellert (*t*); Achim Fink (*tb*); Wollie Kaiser (*ss*); Gerhard Veeck (*ss, as*); Hennes Hehn (*ts*); Michael Heupel (*f*); Matthias Von Welck (*vib, marim*); George Ruby (*p*); Martin Kastenholz (*ky*); Ulla Oster (*b*); Reinhard Kobialka, Fritz Wettek (*d*). 6/87.

(*) **Pata Trio: Lucy Und Der Ball Jazz Haus Musik JHM 34 LP
Stein; Hennes Hehn (*s, ts, cl*); Reinhard Kobialka (*d*). 6/88.

*** **Die Wilden Pferde Der Armen Leute** Jazz Haus Musik JHM 39 CD/LP
Stein; Thomas Heberer (*t*); Joachim Gellert (*tb*); Achim Fink (*tb, tba, thn*); Andreas Gilgenberg (*as, cl, picc-f*); Hennes Hehn (*ts, cl*); Albrecht 'Ali' Maurer (*ky, v*); Reinhard Kobialka (*d*). 1/90.

***(*) **New Archaic Music** Jazz Haus Musik JHM 42 CD
Stein; Achim Fink (*tb, tba, euph*); Joachim Gellert (*tb, tba*); Andreas Gilgenberg (*ss, as, cl, bcl, f*). 8/90.

Stein works in Cologne at the centre of the city's effervescent new jazz scene, and he stands squarely in the modern German tradition of the Globe Unity Orchestra, orchestrating big-band weight and power with a freewheeling approach to structure and composition. The Pata Orchestra is respnsible for the first and third albums listed above, with *Lucy Und der Ball* credited to the Pata Trio and *New Archaic Music* to Pata Horns. *Die 5 Tage* is a bit stiff and lumbering in places, wearing its weight a little heavily, but Kastenholz's electronics add an unexpected flavour, and the shifts in texture and mass make for some absorbing music, which, at 39 minutes, doesn't overstay a welcome. Stein and Hehn duel their way through *Lucy Und Der Ball* with plenty of fire, Kobialka's drums pacing them and establishing the different climates for each piece: this time, though, some of the tracks could have stood a longer development. *Die Wilden Pferde Der Armen Leute* pares the Orchestra back to an octet, and the streamlined band moves a little more easily as a result: 'Wunder, Oh, Wunder' features Maurer on viola in a tune that hints at the folk-fusion ambitions which a lot of this music seems to point towards, away from any kind of modern bop. The Pata Horns take that a step further in their series of two reeds, two brass workouts. Stein's more sarcastic side comes out in the likes of 'So Long, Hippie', and there's a wriggle of impatience which keeps coming up in the playing here. Often, though, they're content to bask in the sonorities in their instruments, and rustic melodies mingle with urban uproar in the cut of the music. This isn't meant to be music with a rhythm section, but the brass players manage to suggest a bass line throughout in anycase. Recommended, and Stein's future work is clearly going to be worth seeking out.

LENI STERN
GUITAR

***(*) **Clairvoyant** Passport PJ 88015 CD/LP/MC
Stern; Bob Berg (*ts*); Bill Frisell (*g*); Larry Willis (*p*); Harvie Swartz (*b*); Paul Motian (*d*). 12/85.

***(*) **Secrets** Enja 5093 CD/LP
Stern; Bob Berg (*ts*); Wayne Krantz, Dave Tronzo (*g*); Lincoln Goines, Harvie Swartz (*g*); Dennis Chambers (*d*); Don Alias (*perc*). 9 & 10/88.

**** **Closer To The Light** Enja 6034 CD/LP
Stern; David Sanborn (*as*); Wayne Krantz (*g*); Lincoln Goines, Paul Socolow (*b*); Dennis Chambers, Zachary Danziger (*d*); Don Alias (*perc*). 11 & 12/89.

Stern quickly backed out of the fusion *cul-de-sac* to create albums of subtle presence that depend on interplay rather than very sophisticated themes. Perhaps oddly (or perhaps because she rejects conventional axe-man *machismo*), she has preferred to surround herself with other, often more dominant guitarists (Frisell on *Clairvoyant*) and her established duo partner, Wayne Krantz, on the excellent *Secrets*. Krantz's title-track on that album is one of the few false notes: a busy, hectic theme that overpowers the band. Stern herself works best with easy-paced melodies and settings that leave room for delicate, spontaneous touches. Though Frisell and Motian seem admirably suited to that intention, *Clairvoyant* is slightly uneasy in execution, and Berg's contributions seem much less appropriate than on the later record. Sanborn, perhaps surprisingly, fits in much better on his two tracks on the well-balanced *Closer* (which also seems to have been released as *Phoenix*). Stern's duos with Krantz and the two-guitar quartets (with Goines and Chambers or Socolow and Danziger backing them) are the best she's so far committed to record.

** **Ten Songs** Lipstick LIP 890092 CD
Stern; Bob Malach (*ts*); Billy Drewes (*ss*); Gil Goldstein (*ky*); Wayne Krantz (*g*); Alain Caron, Michael Formanek, Lincoln Goines (*b*); Dennis Chambers, Rodney Homes (*d*); Donal Alias (*perc*); Badal Roy (*tablas, perc*). 10/91.

Stern was a more interesting player on her earlier, bare-faced sessions, with their scrubbed-down sound. For the Lipstick set, she's given herself a rather blowsy funk sound, with every instrument puffed up and over-loud. The two best tunes are credited to Wayne Krantz; 'Our Man's Gone Now' sounds as if it might be a tribute to Miles, who is (or rather Marcus Miller is) the main influence on the arrangements; 'If Anything' features Stern on her Spanish and slide guitars, which are consitently her most effective instruments (only Sonny Sharrock has made a more developed use of slide guitar in a jazz context). A rather inconsequential set that somehow reflects the slightly throwaway title.

MIKE STERN (born 1954)
GUITAR

*** **Time In Place** Atlantic 781840 CD/MC
Stern; Bob Berg, Michael Brecker (*ts*); Don Grolnick (*org*); Jim Beard (*ky*); Jeff Andrews (*b*); Peter Erskine (*d*); Don Alias (*perc*). 12/87.

(*) **Jigsaw Atlantic 782027 CD/MC
Stern; Bob Berg (*ts*); Jim Beard (*ky*); Jeff Andrews (*b*); Peter Erskine, Dennis Chambers (*d*); Manolo Badrena (*perc*). 2/89.

First impressions of Stern were unfortunate, since he seemed set on treating the Miles Davis group of the early 1980s as a jazz-metal band while working out a sideman tenure. His albums for Atlantic are much more palatable, pushing through the kind of muscular, musicianly fusion which is the standard alternative to the wispy variety suggested by Windham Hill's roster. The problem, as usual, is the material, which is little more than a springboard for solos – which are tidy and intermittently powerful (especially Berg's) on both sets. Chambers and Erskine provide other interest with their interactive parts, but while the band has acquired a substantial reputation on the live circuit, it's too much a rational and unsurprising group in the studios. A live record might serve them better.

JOHN STEVENS (born 1940)
DRUMS, PERCUSSION, BUGLE

****   **The Longest Night: Voloume 1** Ogun OG 120 LP

***(*)   **The Longest Night: Volume 2** Ogun OG 420 LP
Stevens; Evan Parker (*ss*).

***   **Touching On** Konnex KCD 5023 CD
Stevens; John Calvin (*sax*); Dave Cole, Allan Holdsworth (*g*); Nigel Moyse (*g*); Jeff Young (*p*); Ron Mathewson, Nick Stephens (*b*).

Stevens is an agile and forceful drummer. Initially inspired by Phil Seamen, his most obvious influences are the proto-bop of Kenny Clarke and the polydirectional geometries of Elvin Jones. From the mid-1960s he has worked simultaneously in both orthodox-modern jazz and in free music. His Spontaneous Music Ensemble/Orchestra was one of the most influential improvising groups of the period, while Splinters maintained an interest in structures. This became even more overt in groups like the Dance Orchestra and the rock-defined Away. In more recent years Stevens has been much involved in music education and he plays less often.

The Longest Night is undoubtedly his finest recorded performance and one of the landmarks of British free improvisation, distilling the freedoms of the SME/O into a form that never lapses into bland conversational exchange but concentrates intently on its own processes. Stevens breaks down severe, almost militaristic, figures into passages of dissipated melody, matching Parker's patient examination of harmonics and overtones. A measure of weariness creeps in on the second volume and there are one or two signs of repetition but, in the absence of a single-CD edit (which would be welcome), this should be considered a priority item for anyone interested in the progress of contemporary improvised music.

The Konnex is a freeish, jazz–rock session that only intermittently reflects Stevens's talents. Perhaps the most interesting tracks are those that feature Allan Holdsworth (*q. v.*). (Stevens can also be heard in free mode on a moving duo with the late Dudu Pukwana (*q. v.*) on *Mbizo Radebe*, Affinity AFF 775.)

SLAM STEWART (born 1914)
DOUBLE BASS, VOICE

***   **The Complete Savoy Sessions: Volume 1** Savoy WL 70521 LP
Stewart; Errol Garner (*p*); Mike Bryan (*g*); Harold Doc West (*g*). 1/45.

***(*)   **Slam Stewart** Black & Blue 233027 CD
Stewart; Milt Buckner, Wild Bill Davis (*p*); Al Casey (*g*); Jo Jones, Joe Marshall (*d*). 4/71, 6/72.

***   **Fish Scales** Black & Blue 233109 CD
Stewart; Wild Bill Davis, Johnny Guarnieri, Gene Rodgers (*p*); Al Casey, Jimmy Shirley (*g*); Jo Jones, Joe Marshall, Jackie Williams (*d*). 3/75, 7/72.

[***   **Two Big Mice** Black & Blue 59.124 CD]
Stewart; Major Holley (*b*, *v*); Hank Jones (*p*); George Duvivier (*b*); Oliver Jackson (*d*). 7/77.

***   **Shut Yo' Mouth** Delos 1024 CD
Stewart; Major Holley (*b*, *v*); Oliver Jackson (*d*).

Stewart was already a star when he appeared in the movie, *Stormy Weather*, in 1943. During the 1930s he had been a stalwart of the New York scene, playing with Art Tatum and forming an evergreen partnership (love it, hate it; it sold records) with Slim Gaillard which exploited the less serious side of Stewart's virtuosic self-harmonizing on bass and vocals. However corny he now seems, few modern bass players have taken up the technical challenge Stewart posed (though Major Holley had a stab and joins up with his role model on *Two Big Mice*), and the purely musical aspects of his work are of abiding value.

The Savoy Sessions is split between January 1945 material under Stewart's name and featuring Errol Garner (who wrote much of the bassist's stuff at the time) and rather later, and in some respects better, tracks by Garner's own trio. The very oddity of Stewart's technique is initially off-putting, but on repeated listening its complexities begin to make an impact. It's perhaps easier to begin, or stick with, the two excellent Black & Blue CDs from very much later in his career. Much of the manic energy has gone, but 'The Flat Foot Floogie' (a massive hit with Gaillard; Ronald Reagan could remember the words even when he couldn't remember whether or not he'd ever met Oliver North) is as nutty as it always was, while the versions of 'On Green Dolphin Street' and 'All The Things You Are' (all three from *Slam Stewart*) are absolutely impeccable modern standards performances. Perhaps more of *Fish Scales* is given over to comedy material, but 'Willow Weep For Me' with Davis, Casey and Marshall is genuinely affecting.

It's perhaps a shame that Stewart wasn't able – or didn't choose – to record with more of the younger modern bassists. If Mingus and Pettiford are now thought to have set the instrument free, much of what they did was already implicit in Stewart's work of the 1930s. The *Two Big Mice* sessions, which include fine trio performances under Holley's name, suggest how productive such encounters could have been. (See also under Slim Gaillard.)

REX STEWART (1907–67)
CORNET, VOCALS

***(*) **Finesse** Affinity CD AFS 1029 CD
Stewart; Lawrence Brown, George Stevenson (*tb*); Jack Teagarden (*tb, v*); Barney Bigard (*cl, d*); Otto Hardwicke (*as*); Rudy Powell (*as, cl*); Bingie Madison, Ted Nash, Ben Webster (*ts*); Harry Carney (*bs*); Billy Kyle, Ram Ramirez (*p*); Brick Fleagle, Django Reinhardt (*g*); Wellman Braud, John Levy, Billy Taylor (*b*); Cozy Cole, Jack Maisel, Shelly Manne, Dave Tough (*d*). 12/34, 4/39, 7 & 12/40.

***(*) **Rex Stewart And The Ellingtonians** Original Jazz Classics OJC 1710 CD/LP
Stewart; Lawrence Brown (*tb*); Barney Bigard (*cl*); Billy Kyle (*p*); Brick Fleagle (*g*); Wellman Braud, John Levy (*b*); Cozy Cole, Dave Tough (*d*). 7/40, 46.

[**(*) **Americans In Sweden – Rex Stewart 1947** Jazz Society AA 514 LP
Stewart; Sandy Williams (*tb*); John Harris (*cl*); Vernon Story (*ts*); Don Gais (*p*); Simon Brehm (*b*); Ted Curry (*d*); Honey Johnson (*v*). 11/47.

The poet John Keats once wrote about the way very great artists erect a Great Wall across their respective genres, Shakespeare in the drama, Milton in the poetic epic. For trumpeters of the 1920s, Louis Armstrong fell into that category. His achievement was so primal and so pre-eminent that it was extraordinarily difficult to see a way round or over it. Rex Stewart, a self-confessed Armstrong slave (though he also loved Bix), experienced the problem more directly than most when he took over Armstrong's chair in the Fletcher Henderson orchestra.

In reaction to the inevitable but invidious comparisons, Stewart developed his distinctive 'half-valving' technique. By depressing the trumpet keys to mid-positions, he was able to generate an astonishing and sometimes surreal chromaticism which, though much imitated, has only really resurfaced with the avant-garde of the 1960s. As a maverick, Stewart was ideal for the Ellington orchestra of the mid-1930s, and the earlier of the above sessions brought him together with band colleagues for a free-blowing session that includes septet and (less satisfactory) quartet tracks and features Stewart's superheated cornet style. 'Bugle Call Rag' compresses most of what he had learned with Henderson, Luis Russell and with Ellington; it and three other tracks, 'Cherry', 'Solid Rock' and 'Diga Diga Doo', are also included on *Finesse*, which takes in material with Django Reinhardt on his first American visit, four tracks under Jack Teagarden's leadership, and two early cuts. Audio restoration is by the CEDAR system and not entirely satisfactory, but the musical material is excellent.

Stewart's vocalized style had few imitators, though Clark Terry gave it a more contemporary slant, bridging the gap with the modernists. The 1947 Swedish sessions – shared with some intermittent work by Hot Lips Page, another trumpeter who had to confront the Armstrong nemesis – are sub-standard but remain valuable in the absence of fuller documentation.

In later life, Stewart became one of the most persuasive writers on jazz and his *Jazz Masters of the '30s* is required reading for students of the period.

SONNY STITT (1924–82)
ALTO, TENOR AND BARITONE SAXOPHONES

*** **Sonny Stitt/Bud Powell/J. J. Johnson** Original Jazz Classics OJC 009 CD/LP/MC
Stitt; J. J. Johnson (*tb*); Bud Powell, John Lewis (*p*); Curly Russell, Nelson Boyd (*b*);
Max Roach (*d*). 10/49–1/50.

(*) **Prestige First Sessions Vol. 2 Prestige 24115 CD
Stitt; Al Outcalt, Matthew Gee (*tb*); Gene Ammons (*bs*); Kenny Drew, Duke Jordan,
Junior Mance, Clarence Anderson (*p*); Tommy Potter, Earl May, Gene Wright (*b*);
Art Blakey, Teddy Stewart, Wesley Landers, Jo Jones (*d*); Larry Townsend (*v*).
2/50–8/51.

*** **Kaleidoscope** Original Jazz Classics OJC 060 CD/LP/MC
Stitt; Bill Massey, Joe Newman (*t*); Kenny Drew, Charles Bateman, Junior Mance,
John Houston (*p*); Tommy Potter, Gene Wright, Ernie Shepard (*b*); Art Blakey,
Teddy Stewart, Shadow Wilson (*d*); Humberto Morales (*perc*). 2/50–2/52.

Considering the size of his discography – there are at least one hundred albums under Stitt's own name – the saxophonist has relatively little left in the catalogue, although the desultory nature of many of his records suggests that perhaps it is better this way. Stitt took every opportunity to record, often with undistinguished pick-up groups, and while he's impassive professionalism meant that he seldom sounded less than strong, his records need careful sifting to find him genuinely at his best. Originally, he was acclaimed as a rival to Charlie Parker, and the derivation of his style – which may have been arrived at quite independently of Bird – is a famously moot point. Whatever the case, by the time of the 1949 sessions on OJC 009, he was in complete command of the bop vocabulary and playing with quite as much skill as any man in the milieu. This disc finds him exclusively on tenor, which he plays with a rather stony tone but no lack of energy. Powell contributes some superb playing on such uptempo pieces as 'All God's Children Got Rhythm', and the 1950 group with Johnson and Lewis, though less obviously hot, finds Stitt at his best on the urgent improvisation on 'Afternoon In Paris'. Both the Prestige collection and *Kaleidoscope* bring together bits and pieces from the early days of the label, and though some of the tracks sound foreshortened, Stitt dominates throughout both discs. he occasionally played baritone, too, and there's a surprisingly full-blooded ballad treatment of 'P.S. I Love You' on *Kaleidoscope* which suggests that his use of the bigger horn was by no means offhand. The boxy sound of the originals carries over into all the CD issues.

(*) **In Boston 1954 Fresh Sound FSR-CD 1002 CD
Stitt; Dean Earle (*p*); Bernie Griggs (*b*); Marquis Foster (*d*). 2/54.

(*) **Jazz At The Hi-Hat Roulette CDP 7985822 CD
As above. 2/54.

Both CDs are drawn from the same club recording, with many tracks duplicated: the Fresh Sound disc has an extra 15 minutes of material, but Roulette have a second volume in the works. Stitt is in good form and switches between alto, tenor and baritone, playing all three on 'Tri-Horn Blues'. 'Every Tub', a familar Basie blues, shows how easily Stitt could move between swing and bop formations, but the prosaic choice of material and blandness of the rhythm section sets the tone for many of the sessions which Stitt would record for the rest of his life. The sound seems to be the same on both discs – flat and lacking in any shine, though the saxophonist always cuts through.

***(*) **Sonny Stitt Sits In With The Oscar Peterson Trio** Verve 849396 CD/MC
Stitt; Oscar Peterson (*p*); Herb Ellis (*g*); Ray Brown (*b*); Ed Thigpen, Stan Levey (*d*).
10/57–5/58.

A memorable meeting. Stitt plays alto and tenor here, and sounds unusually at ease with a pianist who might have brought out his most sparring side: instead, on the likes of 'Moten Swing' and 'Blues For Pres', they intermingle their respective many-noted approaches as plausibly as if this were a regular band (in fact, they never recorded together again). The CD includes three tracks from a session a year earlier, previously unreleased, with a storming 'I Know That You Know' emerging as the highlight. Excellent CD remastering.

(*)   **Sonny Stitt Meets Brother Jack Original Jazz Classics OJC 703 CD
Stitt; Jack McDuff (*org*); Eddie Diehl (*g*); Art Taylor (*d*); Ray Barretto (*perc*). 2/62.

*(*)   **Made For Each Other** Delmark DS 426 LP
Stitt; Don Patterson (*org*); Bill James (*d*). 7/68.

Whatever the state of jazz's declining fortunes in the 1960s, Stitt worked and recorded incessantly, if often carelessly. A lot of run-of-the-mill albums for Roulette and Cadet are currently unavailable; these two scarcely break the mould. With McDuff, Stitt strolls unblinkingly through a programme of rootless blues. With Patterson, he's saddled with then-fashionable electric attachments on his saxes. Wait for the later records.

****   **Tune-Up!** Muse M 5334 LP/MC
Stitt; Barry Harris (*p*); Sam Jones (*b*); Alan Dawson (*d*). 2/72.

****   **Constellation** Muse MCD 5323 CD/LP/MC
As above, except Roy Brooks (*d*) replaces Dawson. 6/72.

Despite the apparently unexceptional circumstances of these records – Stitt had by now settled into a regimen of sax-and-rhythm dates that offered no deeper challenges than some familiar standards and a touch of the blues – the results were vivid and masterful examples of a great bopper at his best. The tempos are a fraction sharper, the tunes a little more interesting, the settings zestier – Harris is a quietly compelling foil, his discreetly appropriate comps and solos the earth to Stitt's skywriting, but bassist Jones is equally important, roving all over the bass with inspired aplomb. There's almost nothing to choose between these two sessions. Stitt rifles Parker's 'Constellation' with scathing abandon, and follows that with a piercingly clear-headed take on 'I Don't Stand A Ghost Of A Chance With You', alto following tenor throughout both dates, with *Constellation* having perhaps just the edge.

***   **12!** Muse MR 5006 LP
As above, except Louis Hayes (*d*) replaces Brooks. 12/72.

***   **The Champ** Muse MCD 5429 CD/MC
Stitt; Joe Newman (*t*); Duke Jordan (*p*); Sam Jones (*b*); Roy Brooks (*d*). 4/73.

***   **Mellow** Muse M 5067 LP
Stitt; Jimmy Heath (*ss, ts, f*); Barry Harris (*p*); Richard Davis (*b*); Roy Haynes (*d*). 2/75.

***   **My Buddy: For Gene Ammons** Muse MR 5091 LP
Stitt; Barry Harris (*p*); Sam Jones (*b*); Leroy Williams (*d*). 7/75.

***   **Blues For Duke** Muse MR 5129 LP
As above, except Billy Higgins (*d*) replaces Williams. 12/75.

Stitt loved to play with Barry Harris behind him, and the pianist assists on most of his subsequent Muse dates. That makes for consistency, but not necessarily the same pitch of excitement: they never quite recapture the zip of the first two discs. Of the three quartet dates, the nods to Ammons and Ellington are more craftsmanlike than heartfelt, and the spirited *12!* is the most engaging, but there's little to choose. Jimmy Heath plays a walk-on part in the Stitt discography with *Mellow*, which isn't as laid back as the title implies, but doesn't have the more exciting gunplay which goes on between Stitt and Joe Newman on *The Champ*: the title-track is a smartly orchestrated feast of bop licks which sets up the session, and Stitt sounds at his creamiest on the succeeding 'Sweet And Lovely'; Jordan's scholarly touch is a nice bonus on the date. None of these records is particularly great, but Stitt always does enough on each of them to earn the three stars.

**   **In Brasil – With Zimbo Trio** Fresh Sound FSR-CD 118 CD
Stitt; Amilson Godoy (*p*); Luis Chaves (*b*); Rubens A. Barsotti (*d*). 79.

(*)   **Back To My Own Home Town Black & Blue 59574-2 CD
Stitt; Gerald Price (*p*); Don Mosley (*b*); Bobby Durham (*d*). 11/79.

***   **Sonny's Back** Muse MR 5204 LP
Stitt; Ricky Ford (*ts*); Barry Harris (*p*); George Duvivier (*b*); Leroy Williams (*d*).
4–7/80.

***   **In Style** Muse MR 5228 LP
Stitt; Barry Harris (*p*); George Duvivier (*b*); Jimmy Cobb (*d*). 3/81.

***   **The Last Stitt Sessions** Muse MCD 6003 CD
Stitt; Bill Hardman (*t*); Junior Mance, Walter Davis (*p*); George Duvivier (*b*); Jimmy
Cobb (*d*). 6/82.

Stitt died a few weeks after making *The Last Stitt Sessions*, but he betrayed only a few signs of
failing powers. The pick-up dates in Brazil and France (Black & Blue) are as rote as one might
imagine, the Fresh Sound disc, in a peculiarly glassy sound, barely passing muster. But *Sonny's
Back* and *In Style* are both injected with superior solos, the latter having a particularly fine
ballad reading of the ironically appropriate 'I'll Walk Alone', a swansong for a quintessential
singleton musician. The final sessions have no valedictory feel, and seem more like just another
capable Sonny Stitt date: Davis plays rather eccentrically on his share of duty, and the leader
sounds a shade tired here and there, but the dudgeon which sustained him through so many
sessions endures here, too.

MARKUS STOCKHAUSEN
TRUMPET, FLUGELHORN, SYNTHESIZER

(*)   **Cosi lontano . . . Quasi dentro ECM 1371 CD/LP
Stockhausen; Fabrizio Ottaviucci (*p*); Gary Peacock (*b*); Zoro Babel (*d*). 3/88.

***   **Aparis** ECM 1404 CD/LP
Stockhausen; Simon Stockhausen (*sax, syn*); Jo Thones (*d, electric d*). 8/89.

Markus Stockhausen came to prominence as Michael, the main soloist in his father's opera,
Donnerstag, the first part of the colossal *Licht* cycle, which bids fair to become the twenty-first
century's *Ring*. As an improvising performer he has the same purity of tone all through the
range but lacks entirely the dramatic force he draws from his father's global conception on
'Michaels Reise um die Erde'. Though the material is quite impressive, the conventional
quartet set-up on *Cosi lontano* . . . suits his approach not one bit. His solos are vague and
unanchored and, without Peacock's patient figuring, it would all fall apart. *Aparis*, written and
co-led with saxophonist brother, Simon Stockhausen, is more straightforwardly impressionistic
and altogether more successful. Neo-funk tracks like 'High Ride' sit rather uneasily, but
Thones's acoustic and electric drums and Simon's intelligent sequencing bring a propulsive
energy to even the quieter, watercoloured pieces. Still, it's hard to shake the feeling that this is
just relaxation from working in the old man's shop.

STOCKHOLM JAZZ ORCHESTRA
GROUP

***   **Dreams** Dragon DRCD 169 CD
Jan Kohlin, Fredrik Norén, Lars Lindgren, Stig Persson, Gustavo Bergalli (*t, flhn*);
Bob Brookmeyer (*vtb*); Mikael Raoberg, Bertil Strandberg, Mats Hermansson (*tb*);
Sven Larsson (*btb*); Dave Castle (*ss, as, cl*); Hakan Broström (*ss, as, f*); Ulf
Andersson, Johan Alenius (*ss, ts, cl*); Hans Arktoft (*bs, bcl*); Anders Widmark (*ky*);
Jan Adefeldt (*b*); Johan Dielemans (*d*). 8/88.

***   **Jigsaw** Dragon DRCD 213 CD
As above, except Peter Asplund (*t, flhn*), Anders Wiborg (*tb*), Johan Hörlén (*ss, as, cl,
f*), Jan Levander (*ts, cl, f*), Joakim Milder (*ts*), Jim McNeely (*p*), Martin Löfgren (*d*)
replace Lindgren, Brookmeyer, Larsson, Broström, Alenius, Widmark and Dielemans.
3/91.

Originally a rehearsal band, and now an occasional enterprise under a nominal leadership from Fredrik Norén, the SJO has recorded two CDs to celebrate working with guest arrangers: *Dreams* with Bob Brookmeyer, and *Jigsaw* with Jim McNeely. While the two sessions are unlike in tone and delivery, each is rewarding. Brookmeyer, who spends much time as a resident composer with West German Radio, knows European orchestras, and his themes make the most of the prowess of the band: difficult scoring in 'Missing Monk' and 'Cats' is despatched without much effort by the group, and while the soloists take a lesser role, they're perfectly in tune with Brookmeyer's quirkily structured pieces. Some of them seem like no more than eccentrically linked episodes, but there are many striking passages – the first three tracks are an informal suite, with 'Lies' a particularly intriguing patchwork – which deserve a close listen.

Jigsaw is a more conventional record. One gets the feeling that McNeely is a more meticulous and thoroughgoing composer than Brookmeyer but a less inspirational one. The modern orchestral bop of 'Off The Cuff', for instance, or the concerto for Milder in 'The Decision' are convincing and tersely wound set-pieces, but the freewheeling demeanour of the earlier record is missed. Still, it may suit some tastes better. Both discs are excellently recorded, doing justice to a very skilful band.

GORAN STRANDBERG (born 1949)
PIANO

***   **Silent Traces** Dragon DRLP 39 LP
         Strandberg; Red Mitchell, Olle Steinholtz (*b*); Rune Carlsson (*d*). 8/80–9/82.

***   **Ringvida** Dragon DRLP 105 LP
         Strandberg; Jan Adefelt (*b*); Rune Carlsson (*d*). 5/85.

Strandberg hasn't recorded much, but these two albums are stringently personal statements. He plays a kind of stripped-down hard bop, Monk-like in some ways but never really sounding like the master: his rather stolid and unconvincing treatment of 'Round Midnight' is probably the weakest thing on the first record. The abstruse but simply voiced harmonies and broken rhythms are more like those of a second generation figure such as Ran Blake. *Silent Traces* is divided between originals and covers of Carla Bley, Mike Gibbs, Monk and Charlie Haden, with a surprisingly straightforward reading of 'What Is This Thing Called Love' to go with them: Strandberg varies the pace with long and short tracks, solos and duos and trios. 'Fragment', a duet with Carlsson, is beautifully paced by the drummer's brushwork; two tracks with Mitchell on bass sound almost indecently rich in sonority; and the pianist's meditations on Haden's 'Silence' and his own 'Fragment' are sombrely refined. *Ringvida* is an all-original programme for the trio, with Adefelt matching all the moves of Strandberg's left hand and Carlsson working through a range of tattoos and shuffles, lending an air of dance to the mostly short pieces, themes that suggest a *haiku*-like concentration. Strandberg's pianism is resolutely unflashy, but he seems to have a great deal to say. He also has a superb solo on the Dragon *Anthology Of Swedish Jazz Piano*.

BILLY STRAYHORN (1915–67)
PIANO, COMPOSER, ARRANGER

***(*)   **Great Times!** Original Jazz Classics OJC 108 CD/LP
         Strayhorn; Duke Ellington (*p*); Wendell Marshall (*b*); Oscar Pettiford (*b, clo*); Lloyd Trottman (*b*); Jo Jones (*d*). 9, 10 & 11/50.

They were like two aspects of a single complex self. Where Duke Ellington was immodest, priapic and thumpingly egocentric, his longtime writing and arranging partner, Billy Strayhorn, was shy, gay and self-effacing. It's now very difficult, given the closeness of their relationship and their inevitable tendency to draw on aspects of the other's style and method, to separate which elements of an 'Ellington–Strayhorn' composition belong to each; but there is no doubt that Swee' Pea, as Ellington called him, made an immense impact on his boss's music. Even if he had done no more than write 'Lush Life' (see below) and 'Take The "A" Train', Strayhorn would still have been guaranteed a place in jazz history. Just after his painful death from cancer in 1957, Ellington recorded the tribute *And His Mother Called Him Bill* (RCA). After the session was over, but with mikes still on, the Duke sat on at the piano and played an impromptu epitaph that counts as one of the most moving farewells from one musician to another ever played.

Strayhorn was not a particularly inspiring pianist (he could sound like Duke on an off-day) and wasn't, of course, an instinctive performer. There is next to nothing on record, but in fairness the 1950 *Great Times!* might be credited to Strayhorn's account. In performance terms he's oversahdowed by his boss, playing much more 'correctly' and inside the key than the Duke found comfortable. It's easier to separate them on the inevitable '"A" Train' and 'Oscalypso', when Strayhorn switches to celeste. There probably is no better aural impression of their wildly diverging personalities.

(One further extraordinary tribute to Strayhorn exists on disc. In the early 1980s clarinettist Tony Scott (*q. v.*) recorded an astonishing two-volume exploration of 'Lush Life', Core COCD 9.00666/7 (see under Scott). It includes nine versions of the song, mostly solo performances on saxophones, clarinet and electric piano, but also including spin-off improvisations for duo and trio, an unaccompanied vocal version by Monica Sciacca, and, of course, Strayhorn himself on piano and vocals, establishing the Ur-text.)

FRANK STRAZZERI (born 1930)
PIANO

***   **I Remember You** Fresh Sound FSR-CD 123 CD
       Strazzeri; Horacio Fumero (*b*); Peer Wyboris (*d*). 11/89.

***   **Little Giant** Fresh Sound FSR-CD 184 CD
       As above. 11/89.

A journeyman pianist who's worked under many a famous leader, Strazzeri's kind of jazz glides off surfaces rather than cutting deep, and these sunny, cool, rounded sessions are as close to definitive as he'll ever find himself on record. Conservative in terms of harmony and rhythm, his distinctiveness comes out in his touch: he plays with a delicacy that makes all his solos flow evenly across each chorus, with nothing struck very hard and no phrase emerging out of kilter with the others. In other situations it might result in merely dull music, but Strazzeri picks tunes like a man who's easily bored. *Little Giant* was a session organized at a few hours' notice, and the temptation to go for easy old warhorses must have been hard to avoid: instead, there's scarcely anything which isn't out of the ordinary, including 'Don'cha Go 'Way Mad', Carl Perkins's 'Grooveyard', George Shearing's 'Conception' and Ellington's 'I'm Gonna Go Fishin''. Fumero and Wyboris keep spontaneously good time on both records.

STRING TRIO OF NEW YORK
GROUP

****   **First String** Black Saint BSR 0031 LP
       Billy Bang (*vn, yokobue, f*); James Emery (*g, soprano g, mand*): John Lindberg (*b*).
       6/79.

***(*)   **Area Code 212** Black Saint BSR 0048 LP
       As above. 11/80.

***   **Common Goal** Black Saint BSR 0058 LP
       As above. 11/81.

***(*)   **Rebirth Of A Feeling** Black Saint BSR 0068 LP
       As above. 11/83.

***(*)   **String Trio Of New York And Jay Clayton** West Wind WW 0008 CD/LP

[***   **As Tears Go By** ITM 0029 CD/LP]
       James Emery (*g*); Charles Burnham (*v*); John Lindberg (*b*); with Jay Clayton (*v*).
       12/87.

In the interests of neatness it would be convenient to shorthand these albums: 'with Billy Bang – good', 'without – not'. Despite a general critical consensus to that effect, it simply isn't as simple as that. Though Bang's ducks-and-drakes approach to tonality is a vital component of the first four albums, Burnham is a perfectly adequate replacement, and it's clear that much of the impetus of the band comes from the bassist (who is also an impressive writer). The addition of singer Jay Clayton (who bears some generic resemblance to Jeanne Lee) somewhat recentres the music but doesn't dilute it significantly, parcelling out Bang's inimitable voice between two musicians. The ITM album samples three tracks – 'Naturals Know', 'Shining Sea' and 'Waltz For Two' – from the preferable West Wind, but it also includes duo, String Trio and John Lindberg Trio (with Marty Ehrlich and Thurman Barker) material which is worth having.

Whatever the merits of the post-Bang STNY, there's no doubt that their best albums are those involving him. *First String* is divided into just three tracks, of which 'East Side Suite' (first of the band's wryly impassioned poems to New York) and 'Subway Ride With Giuseppi Logan' (dedicated to the now-neglected New Thing multi-instrumentalist) are by far the most impressive. Lindberg's shifting tone-centres and firm rhythmic cues launch Bang on some of his most extravagant car-chase excursions, with Emery filling in the middle ground. 'Catharsis In Real Time' is more mannered and fails to meet its own stated objective. The later albums (regrettably none available on CD) are less coherent, and *Common Goal* seems an almost ironic title for a record which accentuates individual contributions to the detriment of the whole. Some sign of recovery with *Rebirth Of A Feeling*, which includes the marvellous 'Karottenkopf' and 'Utility Grey'.

***(*) **Ascendant** Stash ST532 CD
6/90.

Ascendant may not be the best album yet. It's certainly the most entertaining, with a Kronos-style take on Jimi Hendrix's 'Manic Depression', some Satie and, to keep jazz credentials afloat, Monk, Charlie Parker and Jimmy Garrison. 'Ah-Leu-Cha' is tender, almost melancholic, but the title-track – credited to Coltrane's bassist – has an earthy grind. There are moments when it all sounds like one of John McLaughlin's gut-strung Mahavishnu Orchestra tracks, with Jerry Goodman's violin floating above. And none the worse for that.

FRANK STROZIER
ALTO SAXOPHONE, FLUTE

**** **Remember Me** Steeplechase SCS 1066 LP
Strozier; Danny Moore (*flhn*); Howard Johnson (*tba*); Harold Mabern (*p*); Lisle Atkinson (*b*); Michael Carvin (*d*). 11/76.

A heartfelt plea from an album unlikely to survive the Great Format Shift. Strozier has a somewhat featureless, Bird-influenced solo style, but he puts together tracks and albums with sophisticated layers of sound and takes an unconventional line on the rhythm section. Mabern and Carvin are far more inventive than appears on the surface, and Johnson and Atkinson fill out the lower registers. Moore plays flugelhorn like a 'first' horn rather than trumpet-made-easy. 'Kram Samba' is ruggedly unsentimental and full of unexpected rhythmic equations. The other originals are equally good. Not many of this one left in captivity, so it would be worth heeding.

JOHN STUBBLEFIELD
TENOR SAXOPHONE, SOPRANO SAXOPHONE

***(*) **Confessin'** Soul Note SN 1095 CD/LP
Stubblefield; Cecil Bridgewater (*t, flhn*); Mulgrew Miller (*p*); Rufus Reid (*b*); Eddie Gladden (*d*). 9/84.

*** **Prelude** Storyville SLP 1018 LP
Stubblefield; Cecil Bridgewater (*t, flhn*); Onaje Allan Gumbs (*ky*); Cecil McBee (*b*); Joe Chambers (*d*); James M'tume (*perc*).

***(*) **Bushman Song** Enja 5015 CD/LP
Stubblefield; Geri Allen (*p, syn*); Charnett Moffett (*b*); Victor Lewis (*d, perc*); Mino Cinelu (*perc, v*). 4/86.

**** **Countin' The Blues** Enja 5051 CD/LP
Stubblefield; Hamiet Bluiett (*bs*); Mulgrew Miller (*p*); Charnett Moffett (*b*); Victor Lewis (*d*). 5/87.

David Murray's (temporary) replacement in the World Saxophone Quartet has attracted much less attention as a solo recording artist than his predecessor. Stubblefield is a more narrowly focused player, without Murray's extraordinary fluency in almost every dialect of the jazz tradition, but he has a strongly individual voice, constructs solos with impeccable logic, and his own music has a rootsy immediacy and appeal.

Of these albums, the vinyl-only *Prelude* is the least compelling. Bridgewater's abrasively edged brass comes across far more strongly on *Confessin'*. 'Spiral Dance' and 'Waltz For Duke Pearson' (dedicated to the now underrated pianist) are well constructed, with something of the WSQ's emphasis on improvisation *within* the basic structure of the piece (compare some of the Art Ensemble of Chicago references on *Bushman Song*, which traces Stubblefield's engagement with a wider than usual spectrum of black music), and 'Confessin'' brings the set to a fine climax.

The more recent *Countin' The Blues* reunites Stubblefield with his WSQ colleague, Bluiett. Unlike Murray, who left the smaller horn aside in favour of tenor and bass clarinet, Stubblefield has worked steadily on soprano saxophone. Pitched 'parallel' to Bluiett's baritone, it heightens the tonal impact of both horns. Miller is excellent (as he is on *Confessin'*), but it's left to Moffett and the increasingly confident Lewis to give the arrangements the forward thrust they get on *Bushman Song* from a rock-tinged Geri Allen and from Moffett.

With David Murray albums going around in threes and catching all the plaudits, it would be easy to forget about Stubblefield. Spare him a moment.

IRA SULLIVAN (born 1931)
TRUMPET, FLUGELHORN, SOPRANO, ALTO AND TENOR SAXOPHONES

*** **. . . Does It All!** Muse MR 5242 LP
Sullivan; Red Rodney (*t, flhn*); Mike Rabinowitz (*bsn*); Garry Dial (*p*); Jay Anderson (*b*); Steve Bagby (*d*). 9/81.

Ira Sullivan is something of a minor enigma, seldom playing far away from his local (Florida) scene, and although he's been leading record sessions since 1956, very little remains available. He has been playing alongside Red Rodney for most of this period – he's on Rodney's fine *Modern Music from Chicago* session, reissued on OJC – and the Muse album is an early example of a session by a band they kept together through much of the 1980s. Sullivan started out in bop, but he sought a way out of the ground rules of the form: along with his surprising mastery of both brass and reeds, this led to an interest in what Coltrane had achieved, and there's a hint of the master in the soprano readings of 'Amazing Grace' and 'The More I See You' here (there's also a version of Trane's 'Central Park West'). Sullivan hasn't left bop behind – and Rodney certainly hasn't – but the record strikes an attractive balance between styles, with the brassy 'Sovereign Court' showing what Sullivan can do on flugelhorn. Rabinowitz is used as an ensemble player on two tracks.

MAXINE SULLIVAN (1911–87)
VOCAL

***(*) **It's Wonderful** Affinity AFS 1031 CD
Sullivan; Frankie Newton, Charlie Shavers (*t*); Bobby Hackett (*c*); Buster Bailey (*cl*); Jimmy Lytell, Paul Ricci, Slats Long, Chester Hazlett (*cl, as*); Bernie Kaufman, Pete Brown (*as*); Babe Russin, Bud Freeman (*ts*); Eddie Powell (*f*); Claude Thornhill, Milt Rettenberg (*p*); Ken Binford (*g*); John Kirby, Ed Barber (*b*); O'Neil Spencer, Buddy Rich, Ed Rubsam (*d*). 8/37–12/38.

'Loch Lomond', the first track here, was the novelty hit which launched Maxine Sullivan's career, part of a faintly ludicrous vogue for turning folk tunes and 'light music' into swing vehicles. The song (and 'Darling Nellie Gray', 'It Was A Lover And His Lass' and others here) still works, though, because of Sullivan's transparent, almost ghostly singing. She didn't really swing her material so much as give it a lilting quality, floating it on phrasing that was measured and controlled without sounding excessively polite. Her version of 'St Louis Blues' sounds mousey next to a voice like Bessie Smith's, but the demure melancholy she invests it with is surprisingly compelling. Claude Thornhill's arrangements work with unusual, pastel colours – one session uses cornet, four reeds, flute and rhythm section – and if the tone of these 24 tracks is sometimes monotonously low, Sullivan's thoughtful attention is always interesting. Though scarcely as well known, they make an intriguing pendant to Billie Holiday's work with Teddy Wilson. The remasering is unfortunately variable, with some tracks sounding muffled, but the best of them are fine.

*** **Maxine Sullivan Sings 1955–56** Fresh Sound FSR-CD 178 CD
Sullivan; Charlie Shavers (*t*); Buster Bailey (*cl*); Jerome Richardson (*as, ts, f*); Hilton Jefferson, Russell Procope (*as*); Dick Hyman (*p, hpschd, org*); Leonard Feather (*hpschd*); Billy Kyle (*p*); Oscar Pettiford, Milt Hinton, Wendell Marshall, Aaron Bell (*b*), Osie Johnson, Louie Bellson, Specs Wright (*d*). 6/55–8/56.

Two full-length albums are packed on to this CD. One was a tribute to Andy Razaf and covers 12 of his songs; the otheris mostly remakes of some of Sullivan's old hits from the 1930s. The Razaf session is rather peculiarly introduced as if it were a radio broadcast, and the material on the later date is starting to sound tired, but the singer deals with it all patiently, even though the backing group – Shavers behaves himself, but the music is very stiffly arranged and delivered – is too tame by half.

*** **Great Songs From The Cotton Club** Mobile Fidelity MFCD 836 CD
Sullivan; Keith Ingham (*p*). 11/84.

*** **Uptown** Concord CCD 4288/CJ 288 CD/LP/MC
Sullivan; Scott Hamilton (*ts*); John Bunch (*p*); Chris Flory (*g*); Phil Flanigan (*b*); Chuck Riggs (*d*). 1/85.

*** **Swingin' Street** Concord CCD 4351 CD
As above. 9/86.

** **Spring Isn't Everything** Audiophile 229 CD
Sullivan; Loonis McGlohon (*p*); Jim Stack (*vib*); Terry Peoples (*b*); Bill Stowe (*d*). 7/86.

Sullivan retired in the 1950s but later returned to regular singing (she also played flugelhorn and valve-trombone) and by the 1980s was as widely admired as she had ever been. Her manner didn't change much, but as recording improved, her intimate style and meticulous delivery sounded as classic as any of the great jazz singers. In her seventies, there was inevitably a decline in her voice's powers, but careful production ensured that her albums sounded very good. Some earlier LPs for Audiophile are still awaited on CD, but the later *Spring Isn't Everything*, one of her last sessions, features a 'songbook' recital (the tracks are all by Harry Warren) which finds her still in excellent shape. Unfortunately, the studio balance doesn't favour her at all. Better to turn to the two Concord dates with Hamilton's smooth neo-classic band, which do as fine a job for her as they do for Rosemary Clooney, and what was an award-winning album with Keith Ingham, dedicated to tunes associated with the Cotton Club. Her voice sometimes trembles more than it should, but she always knows how to pace herself.

STAN SULZMANN (born 1948)
TENOR SAXOPHONE, ALTO SAXOPHONE, SOPRANO SAXOPHONE, ALTO FLUTE

***(*) **Feudal Rabbits** Ah Um 011 CD
Sulzmann; Patrick Bettison, Mick Hutton (*b*); Steve Arguelles (*d*). 12/90.

A classic case of a Talent Deserving Wider Recognition who has consistently failed to break through to the audiences his talent and commitment would seem to merit. Chronically under-recorded, Sulzmann made what looked like a promising return to his late-1970s form

(*Krark* was a much-underrated record) with the curiously titled *Feudal Rabbits*. In the event, it's electric bassist Bettison who steals most of the honours, heavily featured on a number of tracks and name-checked on 'Feeling Bettison'. Sulzmann's delivery is introspective and melancholic and there's hardly an up-tempo track on the afternoon. Perhaps inevitably, but a little disturbingly, the best single piece is a version of Kenny Wheeler's '3/4 In The Afternoon' recorded on the trumpeter's ECM *Deer Wan*.

Pleasantly downbeat jazz that asks to be played late at night. One feels there ought to be a more challenging context for one of Britian's unsung instrumentalists.

SUN RA (born 1914)
ORGAN, PIANO, SYNTHESIZER

***(*)   **Sound Sun Pleasure!!** Evidence ECD 22014 2 CD
Sun Ra; Hobart Dotson, Ahktal Ebah, Art Hoyle (*t*); Bob Northern (*flhn*); Marshall Allen, Danny Davis (*as*); John Gilmore (*ts*); Charles Davis, Pat Patrick (*bs*); Danny Thompson (*reeds*); Stuff Smith (*vn*); Ronnie Boykins, Vic Sproles (*b*); Robert Barry, Nimrod Hunt, James Jackson, Clifford Jarvis (*d*); Hatty Randolph, Clyde Williams (*v*).?53–60.

***(*)   **Supersonic Jazz** Evidence ECD 22015 2 CD
Sun Ra; Art Hoyle (*t*); Julian Priester (*tb*); James Scales (*as*); Pat Patrick (*as, bs*); John Gilmore (*ts*); Charles Davis (*bs*); Wilburn Green, Victor Sproles (*b*); Robert Barry, William Cochran (*d*); Jim Herndon (*perc*). 56.

*****   **Jazz In Silhouette** Evidence ECD 22012 2 CD
Sun Ra; Hobart Dotson (*t*); Julian Priester (*tb*); Marshall Allen, James Spaulding (*as, f*); John Gilmore (*ts*); Charles Davis (*bs*); Pat Patrick (*bs, f*); Ronnie Boykins (*b*); William Cochran (*d*). 58.

***   **Monorails And Satellites** Evidence ECD 22013 2 CD
Sun Ra (*p* solo). 66.

***   **Holiday For Soul Dance** Evidence ECD 22011 2 CD
Sun Ra; Phil Corhan (*c*); Danny Davis, Akh Tal Ebah, Wayne Harris (*t*); Ali Hassan (*tb*); Marshall Allen, Danny Thompson (*as*); John Gilmore (*ts*); Pat Patrick (*bs, b*); Robert Cummings (*bcl*); Bob Barry (*d*); James Jackson, Carl Nimrod (*perc*); Ricky Murray (*v*). 68–69.

(*)   **Fondation Maeght Nights: Volume 1 Jazz View 006 CD

***   **Fondation Maeght Nights: Volume 2** Jazz View COD 007 CD
Sun Ra; Kwame Hadi (*t*); Akh Tal Ebah (*t, c*); Marshall Allen (*as, f, picc*); John Gilmore (*ts, d, v*); Pat Patrick (*bs, as, f*); Robert Cummings (*cl, d*); Absholom Ben Shlomo (*cl, f, as*); James Jackson (*cl, f, perc*); Danny Davis (*f, bs, perc*); Rashied Salim IV (*vib, d*); Alan Silva (*b, clo, vn*); Nimrod Hunt (*d*); John Goldsmith, Lex Humphries (*d, perc*); Verta Grosvenor, Gloristena Knight, June Tyson (*v, dancer*).

****   **The Solar Myth Approach** Affinity AFF 760 CD
Sun Ra; Kwame Hadi (*t*); Akh Tal Ebah (*t, space-dimension mellophone*); Ali Hassan, Charles Stevens (*tb*); Marshall Allen (*as, ob, f, picc*); Danny Davis (*as, acl, f*); John Gilmore (*ts, perc*); Pat Patrick, Danny Thompson (*bs, f*); James Jackson (*ob, f, Egyptian d*); Ronnie Boykins (*b*); Lex Humphries, Clifford Jarvis (*perc, d*); Nimrod Hunt (*hand d*); June Tyson (*voc*). 70–71.

***   **Reflections In Blue** Black Saint BSR 0101 CD/LP
Sun Ra; Randall Murray (*t*); Tyrone Hill (*tb*); Pat Patrick (*as, cl*); Marshall Allen (*as, f, ob, picc*); Danny Ray Thompson (*as, cl, bcl*); John Gilmore, Ronald Wilson (*ts*); James Jackson (*bsn, African d*); Carl LeBlanc (*g*); Tyler Mitchell (*b*); Thomas Hunter, Earl Buster Smith (*d*).

(*)   **Hours After Black Saint BSR 0111 CD/LP
As above. 12/86.

***   **Cosmo Omnibus Imaginable Illusion** DIW 824 CD/LP
Sun Ra; Michael Ray (*t, v*); Ahmed Abdullah (*t*); Tyrone Hill (*tb*); Marshall Allen (*as*); John Gilmore (*ts, perc*); Danny Thompson (*bs*); Leroy Taylor (*cl, bcl*); Bruce Edwards (*g*); Rollo Rodford (*b*); Eric Walter (*b*); Earl Buster Smith (*d*); June Tyson (*v, vn*); Judith Holton (*dancer*). 8/88.

***(*)   **Blue Delight** A & M SP 5260 CD
Sun Ra; Ahmed Abdullah, Fred Adams, Tommy Turrnetine (*t*); Tyrone Hill, Julian Priester (*tb*); Al Evans (*flhn, frhn*); Marshall Allen (*as, f, ob, picc, cl*); Noel Scott (*as, perc*); Danny Ray Thompson (*as, bs, f, perc*); John Gilmore (*ts, cl, perc*); Elmo Omoe (*bcl, as, contra acl, perc*); James Jackson (*bsn, f, perc*); Bruce Edwards, Carl Leblanc (*g*); John Ore (*b*); Billy Higgins, Earl Buster Smith (*d*); Elson Nascimento (*perc*). 12/88.

***(*)   **Purple Night** A & M SP 5324 CD
Sun Ra; Ahmed Abdullah, Jothan Collins, Fred Adams, Al Evans, Don Cherry (*t*); Tyrone Hill, Julian Priester (*tb*); James Spaulding (*as, f*); Marshall Allen (*as, f, perc*); John Gilmore (*ts, perc, v*); James Jackson (*f, d*); Reynold Scott (*bs, f*); John Ore, Rollo Radford (*b*); June Tyson (*v, vn*); Earl Buster Smith, Eric Walker, Thomas Henderson (*d*); Elson Nascimento, Jorge Silva (*perc*). 11/89.

A much-maligned and hugely influential figure, Sun Ra was either born in Chicago under the earth-name Herman Sonny Blount, as the birth-roll insists, or on Saturn, as the man himself has been heard to claim. This, and the paraphernalia of an Arkestra concert (dancers, space suits, lights), has tended to divert attention from Sun Ra's considerable three-decade output. He is one of the most significant big-band leaders of the post-war period, drawing on Ellington and the swing era (he did arrangements for Fletcher Henderson after the war), but also on the bop-derived avant-garde, and on collective improvisation; he is one of the few genuinely virtuosic synthesizer players, but also a pianist of great facility (the only solo piano record currently available unfortunately is the reissued *Monorails And Satellites*); and he has maintained a solitary independence from the music industry, releasing records on his own Saturn label, sustained by a group of remarkably loyal and dedicated musicians.

Foremost among these is the ever-present John Gilmore, who was considered in the 1950s to be the coming man on tenor saxophone (and a potent inspiration for John Coltrane) but who threw in his lot with Sun Ra and has remained – along with Marshall Allen and Pat Patrick – his most significant soloist. Gilmore's solo on the tenor saxophonist's proving ground, 'Body And Soul' (*Holiday For Soul Dance*) suggests something of what Coltrane found in his work. Much less well-known, Hobart Dotson also emerges strongly as an underrated player deserving of reassessment.

For the first time in many years, it's now possible to get hold of the important self-released Saturn material, which is being re-released *in toto* by Evidence (who work out of Conshohocken, Pennsylvania), a colossal project that will presumably take many years. Sound-quality is remarkably good, given the often shaky balance of the original masters and the fact that they've been subjected to uncertain storage conditions. *Holiday For Soul Dance* is entirely a standards set, but for the brief snippet of cornetist Corhan's 'Dorothy's Dance', which may have been conceived in homage to Oz. Sun Ra's opening solos on 'Holiday For Strings' and 'I Loves You Porgy' amply confirm his *bona fides* as a 'straight' swing soloist. He has a surprisingly light touch (which he later carried over to his synthesizer work) and gently alternates emphasis on left-and right-hand figures. There are few warp-speed runs on *Monorails And Satellites*; rather, a gently spacey version 'arranger's piano' that always seems to suggest cues for an absent band.

The bands themselves are terrific, of course. The baritone solo on the short 'Saturn' (*Jazz In Silhouette*), most probably Patrick, is an extension of Sun Ra's brilliantly individual voicings; he makes considerable use of the baritone and flutes, but also included a specialist flugelhorn player on *Sound Sun Pleasure!!*, and elsewhere makes distinctive use of electric bass, tympani and log drums.

The great surprise of these recordings (though presumably no surprise to those who have taken the Saturnian aesthetic fully on board) is their *timelessness*. Listening to 'Enlightenment', given an uncharacteristically straightforward reading on *Jazz In Silhouette*, it's very difficult to guess a date for the performance; by contrast, the chanted version which opens the set on the disappointing *Fondation Maeght Nights* seems very much of its time; Jazz View don't quite get round to saying what that time is, but it's presumably late 1960s. As Francis Davis suggests in a useful liner-note, the *Jazz In Silhouette* 'Enlightenment' is ideal 'blindfold test' material that might have been recorded at any point from the 1940s to the late 1980s. Only the long drum passage on 'Ancient Aiethopia' and the astonishing Dotson solo and chants that follow sound unequivocally 'modern'. Inevitably, the next track, 'Hours After', is orthodox swing.

The original *Sound Sun Pleasure!!* has been filled out for CD by material from the 1950s which was released in 1973 as *Deep Purple*. The earliest material appears to come from as early as 1953, a useful round-number indicator of Sun Ra's remarkable longevity, and features violinist Stuff Smith on the lo-fi, home-recorded title-track. *Supersonic Jazz* comes from the same period. Again, it is a set of originals combining conventional harmony and orchestrations with a thoroughly individual 'voice' (conveyed in occasional devices like Wilburn Green's use of electric bass on 'Super Blonde' and the closing 'Medicine For A Nightmare') and a striking gentleness that contrast sharply with the often brutal aspect of contemporaneous hard bop. So good is Julian Priester's own brief 'Soft Talk' (the only non-Sun Ra composition) that one immediately wishes for more. All the Evidence reissues have original cover art, crude by present standards but wildly unconventional in the late 1950s and '60s.

Newcomers and/or sceptics (including those who frisbee'd their copy of *The Heliocentric Worlds Of Sun Ra* across the room and who might be tempted to do the same with the dreary *Fondation Maeght Nights*, a limited-edition release which will appeal only to dedicated collectors) should certainly start with the marvellous *Jazz In Silhouette*, which will now surely be recognized as one of the most important jazz records since the war. The closing 'Blues At Midnight' is sheer excitement: start with the excellent Affinity. After years of noisy and low-fidelity LPs, the Arkestra comes through with great clarity and separation. The big electronic washes are both atmospheric and structurally subtle, suggesting a 'ghost' band of brasses in alien counterpoint to the remarkably tuneful main themes. One tends not to remember individual Sun Ra compositions, but 'Outer Spaceways Inc' has become a staple.

Of the latter-day Arkestra performances, the DIW, recorded live in Tokyo, combines a suite of mythic themes with a surprisingly straight 'Prelude To A Kiss'. Edit out the chants and some of the more self-conscious FX and it sounds like one of Sun Ra's most complete and convincing recordings of the last 15 years. *Reflections In Blue* and, from the same sessions, *Hours After* concentrate exclusively on mainstream composition (though the latter is punctuated by a chaotic 'Dance Of The Extra Terrestrians' and 'Love On A Far Away Planet', which are more typical of past snippets from the Arkestra's anarchic shows). This is broadly the pattern of *Blue Delight* and *Purple Night*, somewhat unexpectedly released on A & M ('I AM A SUN RA FAN' – HERB ALPERT CONFESSES). The appearance of guest stars on both albums underlines the unusually slick, showbizzy feel to both, and it's hard to avoid 'Jazz at the Philharmonic goes to Mars' jokes. Don Cherry seems a perfect choice for otherworldly settings, but it's slightly startling to find trumpeter Tommy Turrentine and the Louis Armstrong-influenced Ahmed Abdullah in such company. As the track title has it: 'Your Guest Is As Good As Mine'. *Blue Delight* mixes 'Out Of Nowhere' and 'Days Of Wine And Roses' with 'They Dwell On Other Planets'. The arrangements are tight and uncontroversial, confidently swinging, and may be a little difficult to square with the Spacemaster's joke-shop reputation. These are neither 'way out' nor uncomfortably 'radical', nor anything but highly accomplished. So listen.

***(*)   Sunrise In Different Dimensions hat Art 6099 CD
Sun Ra; Marshall Allen (*as, ob, f*); John Gilmore (*ts, cl, f*); Noel Scott (*as, bs, f*); Danny Thompson (*bs, f*); Kenneth Williams (*ts, bs, f*); Michael Ray (*t, flhn*); Chris Henderson, Eric Walker (*d*). 2/80.

Perhaps the most valuable of the recent live issues, this was recorded in Switzerland as long ago as 1980. Sun Ra is on piano only and the relatively small band deployed spaciously – so to speak – with more emphasis on unaccompanied soloing than earlier or later. The mix of material is by now familiar, with 'Limehouse Blues', 'King Porter Stomp', 'Cocktails For Two' and a delightfully jagged ''Round Midnight' and other swing era classics from Noble Sissle, Fletcher Henderson and Erskine Hawkins also in evidence. Entertaining and provocative.

****   Mayan Temples Black Saint 120121 CD/LP
Sun Ra; Ahmed Abdullah, Michael Ray (*t, v*); Tyrone Hill (*tb*); Noel Scott (*as*); Marshall Allen (*as, f*); John Gilmore (*ts, perc*); James Jackson (*bsn, perc*); Jothan

Callins (*b*); Clifford Barbaro, Earl Buster Smith (*d*); Ron McBee, Elson Nascimento, Jorge Silva (*perc*); June Tyson (*v*). 7/90.

As Francis Davis points out in his liner note, this studio session concentrates more than usually for an Arkestra session on Sun Ra's piano playing. His introductions and leads are absolutely in the line of Ellington, and the voicings are supple, open-ended and often quietly ambiguous, leaving considerable emphasis on the soloists. As always, Gilmore is a giant and Marshall Allen's searing solo on 'Prelude To Stargazers' is a model of controlled fury. He re-records 'El Is A Sound Of Joy' (see *Super-Sonic Jazz*, above), a late-1950s theme that sounds completely contemporary and brings a freshness and simplicity to 'Alone Together' that is quite breathtaking. 'Discipline No 1' is a lovely ballad, illustrating Sun Ra's ability to give simple material an unexpected rhythmic profile (Davis rightly points to the example of Mingus in this case) and the closing 'Sunset On The Night On The River Nile' is one of his very best space anthems. Few Sun Ra albums give a better sense of his extraordinary versatility; this is much preferable to the majority of recent live sets.

SUPERBLUE
GROUP

***   **Superblue** Blue Note 791731 CD
Don Sickler (*t, arr*); Roy Hargrove (*t, flhn*); Frank Lacy (*tb*); Bobby Watson (*as, arr*); Bill Pierce (*ts*); Mulgrew Miller (*p*); Bob Hurst (*b*); Kenny Washington (*d*). 4/88.

A cheerful, oddly uplifting album, with an undemanding, old-fashioned feel. Don Sickler's arrangements are tight and often quite sophisticated (particularly on Curtis Fuller's 'Time Off') but the main emphasis is on the solos. Everyone gets a bit of space to do their thing, though inevitably it's Bobby Watson (on 'Summertime', 'Time Off' and his own 'Conservation', the only non-Sickler arrangement) and trumpet whiz Hargrove ('Summertime', Marty Sheller's 'Marvellous Marvin', Hank Mobley's 'M & M' and, of course, 'I Remember Clifford') who attract most attention. Trombonist Lacy is worth a listen, too, and Miller is his elegant self; Washington trades some energetic eights with the horns on the closing Mobley number. There's a slightly programmed feel to Superblue that might have been less noticeable in a live context, but this is still a thoroughly enjoyable record. (*Superblue 2* [Blue Note 792997 CD] follows the same pattern of durable standards – 'Autumn Leaves' and 'Round Midnight' – with more adventurous bop compositions by Duke Jordan, Horace Silver, Elmo Hope and Sonny Clark. Unfortunately, now deleted.)

JOHN SURMAN (born 1944)
BARITONE SAXOPHONE, SOPRANO SAXOPHONE, BASS CLARINET, SYNTHESIZERS, PIANO, RECORDER

***   **Upon Reflection** ECM 1148 CD/LP

***   **Withholding Pattern** ECM 1295 CD/LP

(*)   **Private City ECM 1366 CD/LP

***(*)   **Road To St Ives** ECM 1418 CD/LP
Surman solo. 5/79, 12/84, 12/87, 4/90.

****   **The Amazing Adventures Of Simon Simon** ECM 1193 CD/LP
Surman; Jack DeJohnette (*d, electric p, perc*). 1/81.

***(*)   **Such Winters Of Memory** ECM 1254 CD/LP
Surman; Karin Krog (*v, ring modulator, tambura*); Pierre Favre (*d*). 12/82.

A rather solitary though much admired figure who has spent much of his professional career on the Continent, Surman turned an absence of satisfying commissions to (creative) advantage on a series of multi-tracked solo projects on which he improvised horn lines over his own synthesizer accompaniments. In the early 1960s, he had modernized baritone saxophone playing, giving an apparently cumbersome horn an agile grace that belied its daunting bulk and adding an upper register much beyond its notional range (somewhat as Eric Dolphy had done with Surman's second instrument, the bass clarinet, and Albert Mangelsdorff with the trombone). At the end of the 1960s, Surman co-founded The Trio, a remarkable free-jazz group; later augmented by Mangelsdorff and known as Mumps, it left behind a small but impressive recording legacy which is worth finding. Surman also performed on the classic John McLaughlin album, *Extrapolation*. In 1973 he moved closer to his most recent conception with a three-saxophone group known (after the initials of fellow members Mike Osborne and Alan Skidmore) as SOS. A band called Morning Glory included electric guitarist, Terje Rypdal, and Soft Machine drummer, John Marshall; at this point, Surman had abandoned baritone saxophone in favour of the tonal extremes of bass clarinet and soprano saxophone. The Brass Project revived his association with the Canadian arranger, John Warren (with whom he had made *Algonquin Suite*), and also his baritone playing, but Surman had already embarked on solo recording.

Upon Reflection quickly established the rather withdrawn, inward mood that became almost a vice on *Withholding Pattern* (it's hard not to read too much into the titles), but it also revived the folkish mode of Surman's solo *Westering Home*, which had mixed free passages with piano songs and even a sailor's dance on what sounds like harmonica. Surman's work of the 1980s under the aegis of ECM has updated that experiment and allied it to the stark and unadorned 'Northern' sound associated with Jan Garbarek and the better parts of Rypdal. This is at its coolest and most detached on *Secret City*, which was based on dance scores and sounds rather inconsequential outside that context.

Withholding Pattern is a curious combination of mock jauntiness ('All Cat's Whiskers And Bee's Knees') and similar untypical abstraction, with some of his best baritone playing for years, marred by bland waterdrop synthesizer patterns. 'Doxology' reflects an early interest in church music which re-emerges in the 'organ' opening to 'Tintagel' on *Road To Saint Ives*. The 1990 album isn't intended to be directly evocative of places, but it is one of Surman's warmest and most humane performances, in which the absence of 'live' accompaniment seems less constricting. Surman is a highly rhythmic player, but his multi-tracked backgrounds are often very unresponsive.

This wasn't a problem on Surman's live and studio collaborations with percussionist and keyboard player, Jack DeJohnette. *The Adventures Of Simon Simon* re-creates the quasi-narrative style of Surman's 1970s duo collaborations with the Trio drummer, Stu Martin, who died suddenly in 1980 (*Live At Woodstock Town Hall* is rare, but worth the hunt). DeJohnette's more explicit jazz background gives the music a more linear thrust, and less of the '(with)holding pattern' stasis that sometimes creeps into it, and creeps again into the otherwise excellent collaboration with singer Sheila Jordan and percussionist Pierre Favre.

Surman is a major figure whose earlier albums (those mentioned above and the big-band *How Many Clouds Can You See?*) are among the most significant European jazz performances of the last three decades. His isolation is as regrettable as its achievements have been impressive.

RALPH SUTTON (born 1922)
PIANO

***(*)   **Partners In Crime** Sackville SKCD 2-2023 CD
Sutton; Bob Barnard (*t*); Milt Hinton (*b*); Len Barnard (*d*). 8/83.

****   **At Café Des Copains** Sackville SKCD 2-2019 CD
Sutton (*p* solo). 6/83–1/87.

Sutton has been playing top-drawer stride and swing piano for fifty years, and shows few signs of slowing down. He has made only a few albums under his own name – a series for the Chaz Jazz company are unfortunately missing in action – but at least these two show him at his best. The quartet date with the Barnard brothers has a timeless feel, since the trumpeter seems wholly unselfconscious about an Armstrong influence, and their opening romp through 'Swing That Music' shows how beautifully swing repertory can turn out when delivered in the right hands. Sutton's accompaniments are as sharp as his solos: when he leans in and clears the decks, his huge two-handed manner gives the clearest impression of what stride masters such as Waller and Johnson would have sounded like if they'd been recorded on contemporary equipment. The solo record, drawn from a series of broadcasts over a five-year period, uses scarce material – 'Russian Lullaby', 'Laugh Clown Laugh' and a rollicking 'Somebody Stole My Gal', with its rhythms cunningly displaced – which Sutton relishes, acknowledging the melodies but steamrollering past them into areas of what might be called 'pure' stride piano. Excellent recording on both discs.

EWAN SVENSSON
GUITAR, GUITAR-SYNTHESIZER

*** **Present Directions** Dragon DRCD 218 CD
Svensson; Palle Danielsson (*b*); Magnus Gran (*d*). 9/90–6/91.

The range of settings explored by such American guitarists as John Abercrombie, John Scofield and Bill Frisell have mapped out plenty of fresh terrain for the electric instrument, and while Svensson may not be doing anything very new, he explores that ground with great skill. Across 12 compositions and over an hour of music, he alternates between fast, neatly picked solos and broader expressive washes via the guitar-synthesizer. What makes the difference is the exacting support offered by Danielsson, as strong a bassist as one could ask for in this setting, and Gran's busy and intelligent drumming. This won't disappoint anyone who's enjoyed what we might tacitly call post-modern guitar.

STEVE SWALLOW (born 1940)
BASS GUITAR

*** **Carla** XtraWatt/2 CD/LP
Swallow; Carla Bley (*org*); Larry Willis (*p*); Hiram Bullock (*g*); Victor Lewis (*d*); Don Alias (*perc*); Ida Kavafian (*vn*); Ikwhan Bae (*vla*); Fred Sherry (*clo*). 86–87.

A thin trawl for one of the most accomplished bassists of recent times and certainly the most significant living exponent of the bass guitar. The writing on *Carla* barely reflects the quality of classics like 'Arise Her Eyes' and 'Hotel Hello', which represent Swallow's other main contribution to modern jazz. But for the absence of the dedicatee's abrasive melodic mannerisms, this might just as well be a Carla Bley album (which will be sufficient recommendation for Bley fans). ECM have deleted the interesting *Home* [ECM 1160 LP], Swallow's settings of Robert Creeley poems for singer Sheila Jordan.

***(*) **Swallow** XtraWatt 6 CD
Swallow; Steve Kuhn (*p*); Carla Bley (*org*); Karen Mantler (*ky, hca*); Gary Burton (*vib*); Hiram Bullock, John Scofield (*g*); Robert Ameen (*d*); Don Alias (*perc*). 9–11/91.

There's a touch of sameness about the writing, but Swallow's arrangements are impeccable and he's seldom sounded better. The tunes are mostly mid-tempo Latino grooves with plenty of solo scope. Guest players Burton and Scofield don't figure all that prominently and the most arresting voice is Karen Mantler's harmonica; her brief solo on 'Slender Thread' sets the bassist up for one of his delicate, single note constructions, built up over Bley's organ chords and a soft, shuffle beat. It could do with just one ripping tune, but that isn't Swallow's forte. On its own perfectly respectable terms, this is a beauty.

THORE SWANERUD (1919–90)
PIANO

**** **More Than You Know** Dragon DRLP 85 LP
Swanerud; Bosse Broberg (*t*); James Moody (*as, f, v*); Putte Wickman (*cl*); Bernt Rosengren (*ts*); Red Mitchell, Sture Akerberg, Claes Lindroth (*b*); Pelle Hulten, Rune Carlsson (*d*). 10–12/84.

**** **Stardust** Dragon DRLP 100 LP
As above. 10–12/84.

These delightful records are a summary of a lifetime's work in jazz. Swanerud began his career in the 1930s and clearly kept his ears open: he sounds as easeful with younger pros Rosengren (in three splendid duets) and Broberg as he does with contemporaries Moody – with whom he made the original 'Moody's Mood For Love', heard here in a joshing remake – and Wickman, who plays the pristine reading of 'Stardust' on the second album. The records were made together at four different sessions and range from solos through to quartet tunes – mostly standards, although Swanerud contributes a charming original in 'Sodermalm' to *More Than You Know*. His aristocratic touch is perhaps best heard in the solo pieces, including a slow 'Misty' that would be somnolent if it weren't articulated so deftly, yet each theme is so graciously done that they feel like fresh but definitive interpretations. Excellent digital recording throughout, and there is nothing to choose between the two records in terms of the music.

HARVIE SWARTZ
DOUBLE BASS

*** **Urban Earth** Gramavision GR 8503 CD
      Swartz; Bob Mintzer (*ss*); David Sanborn (*as*); Mike Stern (*g*); Ben Aronov (*p*); Victor Lewis (*d*); Manolo Badrena (*perc*). 2/85.

***(*) **Smart Moves** Gramavision GR 8607 CD
      Swartz; Charlie Mariano (*as*); John Stubblefield (*ts*); Mike Stern (*g*); Ben Aronov (*p*); Victor Lewis (*d*); Mino Cinelu (*perc*). 2/86.

Vigorously impressive sessions from a bass player whose recording credits include work with singer Sheila Jordan (a duo as well as a more conventional quartet), and with fusion guitarist, Al DiMeola, where he was paired on some tracks with an electric bass player. The fusion elements are inevitably slightly more evident on *Urban Earth* and the material (which ends with a ropey 'Round Midnight') is less impressive than on the later album. Swartz himself has a good line and a firm, lyrical tone that lends itself especially to the slower tracks, though without compromising on pace for the upbeat numbers.

Coltrane's 'Equinox' and the standard 'My Romance' give the horns something to do. The partnership isn't quite right, but Mariano is in excellent form and produces some lovely slithers round the theme. The sound on both albums is very sharp, though Swartz tends to get wiped out by Berg's lower register in the ensembles. Recommended.

DUNCAN SWIFT
PIANO

(*) **The Broadwood Concert Big Bear BEARCD 34 CD/MC
      Swift (*p* solo). 90.

In the somewhat rare category of British stride, Duncan Swift works as idiomatically as anyone this side of Keith Ingham. This is an entertaining live show, with the pianist hammering through a lengthy programme of mostly fast showcase pieces, but its impact is diminished by the lack of light and shade: the great stride players knew when to cool off, and Swift is less convincing in the more placid moments.

LEW TABACKIN (born 1940)
TENOR SAXOPHONE, FLUTE

***(*) **Desert Lady** Concord CCD 4411 CD/MC
      Tabackin; Hank Jones (*p*); Dave Holland (*b*); Victor Lewis (*d*). 12/89.

It's a trifle unfortunate that nothing by the Akiyoshi–Tabackin big band is in the current catalogue, for that has been the area in which the saxophonist (who married Toshiko Akiyoshi in 1970) has made the greatest impact. On the other hand, Tabackin is a stylish and greatly underrated saxophone soloist who inclines towards Sonny Rollins's melodic improvisation. His solos sound both expertly structured and wholly spontaneous, and he is an able and effective flautist, with an attractively orientalized tone, picked up osmotically (so he claims) from his wife.

Both sides of his playing style are evident on *Desert Lady*, on which he is supported by an absolutely first-rate rhythm section. 'Chelsea Bridge' and Strayhorn's 'Johnny Come Lately' are constructed in such a way that the melody is implicit in each phrase and the harmonic progressions, though quite daring, are impeccably logical and thought out. Tabackin's tone isn't particularly distinctive and his flute playing is often more immediately arresting. 'Desert Lady' and 'Yesterdays' are worth investigating on an album that doesn't pall on repeated hearings.

JAMAALADEEN TACUMA
BASS

***   **Show Stopper** Gramavision GR 8301 CD
Tacuma; Olu Dara (*c*); James R. Watkins (*as, cl*); Julius Hemphill (*as*); Anthony Davis (*p*); James Blood Ulmer, Ricj Iannacone (*g*); Ann Sullivan (*hp*); Chuck Hammer (*g-syn*); Cornell Rochester, Anthony McLary, Daryl Burgee (*d*); Ron Howerton, Dennis Alston (*perc*); Wilhelmina Wiggins Hernandez, Barbara Walker (*v*); Ebony String Quartet. 82–83.

***   **Renaissance Man** Gramavision GR 8308 CD
Tacuma; Olu Dara (*c*); James R. Watkins (*as, cl*); Ornette Coleman (*ts*); David Murray (*ts*); Vernon Reid (*g*); Charles Ellerbee (*b*); Bill Bruford, Cornell Rochester (*d*); Darryl Burgee, Ron Howerton (*perc*); Ebony String Quartet. 83–84.

Tacuma is a bassist whose interests are almost absurdly wide-ranging, if the records under his own leadership are any guide. He has played with Ornette Coleman and David Murray, both of whom turn up as sidemen here, and he seems willing to learn from or live it up with any genre he turns his ear to. On both these records he explores funk, harmolodic jazz, a willowy sort of New Age music, a small-group third-stream fusion, and more. Both are enjoyable, and both have predictable dead spots. The best thing on the first record is the title-track, with a blistering alto part by Hemphill and a relatively straightforward structure. The second has two great pieces, 'Sparkle' with the unlikely grouping of Murray, Reid and Bruford, and a revision of 'Dancing In Your Head' with Coleman and a couple of drum machines. There's too much insubstantial or unfocused material padding both records out, but Tacuma's own playing – melodic, tuneful but bitingly fast – adds an inspirational edge to almost everything that gets played. A couple of later albums in a similar mould are currently out of print.

HORACE TAPSCOTT (born 1934)
PIANO

[****   **West Coast Hot** Novus/BMG ND 83 107 CD]
Tapscott; Arthur Blythe (*as*); David Bryant, Walter Savage Jr (*b*); Everett Brown Jr (*d*). 4/69.

***(*)   **Flight 17** Nimbus NS 135 LP
Tapscott; Archie Johnson, Lester Robertson (*tb*); Bob Watt (*frhn*); Red Callender (*tba, b*); Aubrey Hart, Kafi Roberts (*f*); Adele Sebastian (*f, v*); Herbert Callies (*acl*); Michael Session (*as*); Jesse Sharps (*ss, ts, bamboo f*); Billy Harris, Sabia Mateen (*ts*); James Andrews (*ts, bcl*); John B. Williams (*bs*); Linda Hill (*p*); Louis Spears (*clo*); David Bryant, Alan Hines, Roberto Miguel Miranda, Kamonta Lawrence Polk (*b*); Everett Brown Jr, Billy Hinton (*d*); William Madison (*d, perc*); Mike Daniels, Daa'oud Woods (*perc*).

***(*)   **The Call** Nimbus NS 246 LP
As above.

***   **Live At The I.U.C.C.** Nimbus NS 357 LP
As above.

***   **At The Crossroads** Nimbus NS 579 LP
Tapscott; Everett Brown Jr (*d*).

***(*)   **Dial 'B' For Barbara** Nimbus NS 1147 LP
Tapscott; Reggie Bullen (*t*); Gary Bias (*as, ss*); Sabia Mateen (*ts*); Roberto Miguel Miranda (*b*); Everett Brown Jr (*d, perc*).

****   **Live At Lobero** Nimbus NS 1369 LP
Tapscott; Roberto Miguel Miranda (*b*); Sonship Phaeus (*d, perc*).

***   **Live At Lobero: Volume 2** Nimbus NS 1258 LP
Tapscott; Roberto Miguel Miranda (*b*). 11/81.

****   **The Tapscott Sessions: Volume 1** Nimbus NS 1581 LP
Tapscott (*p* solo). 6/82.

****   **The Tapscott Sessions: Volume 2** Nimbus NS 1692 LP
As above. 11/82.

****   **The Tapscott Sessions: Volume 3** Nimbus NS 1703 LP
As above. 4/83.

***(*)   **The Tapscott Sessions: Volume 4** Nimbus NS 1814 LP
As above. 9/82.

****   **The Tapscott Sessions: Volume 5** Nimbus NS 1925 LP
As above. 1/84.

***(*)   **The Tapscott Sessions: Volume 6** Nimbus NS 2036 LP
As above. 10/83.

***(*)   **The Tapscott Sessions: Volume 7** Nimbus NS 2147 LP
As above. 2/83.

****   **The Dark Tree: 1** hat Art 6053 CD

***(*)   **The Dark Tree: 2** hat Art 6083 CD
Tapscott; John Carter (*cl*); Cecil McBee (*b*); Andrew Cyrille (*d*). 12/89.

There was, inevitably, a darker side to the cool 'West Coast sound' and to the conventionally sunny image of California. One hardly thinks of Eric Dolphy or Charles Mingus as 'West Coast' players, yet that is what they were, and they conveyed a fundamental truth about the region's culture that is reflected in Horace Tapscott's grievously unrecognized work.

Tapscott was and is a community musician. His decision to remain in Los Angeles as a performer–activist has undoubtedly thwarted wider recognition, but so too did the fact that he conformed to no readily marketable pigeonhole; 'West Coast Hot' was considered something of a pleonasm in the business, and there was a measure of suspicion regarding Tapscott's political agenda. In 1961 he helped establish the Union of God's Musicians and Artists Ascension, out of which grew the Pan-Afrikan People's Arkestra, both attempts to find uncompromised work for talented, young, black musicians. Their work is fiercely disciplined, somewhat reminiscent of Fred Houn's Afro-Asian Ensemble; pieces such as 'Horacio' (*Flight 17*), 'Nakatini Suite' and 'Peyote Song No. 3' (*The Call*), and 'Desert Fairy Princess' (*Live*) are built up out of deceptively simple elements, but with subtle polychordal shadings that reflect Tapscott's solo work and his intriguing duos and trios with members of the PAPA.

Tapscott's own first inspiration was the radical West Coast bandleader and arranger, Gerald Wilson (Dolphy's gratefully acknowledged 'G. W.'), and Tapscott's recording career took off as an arranger, turning out uncharacteristically formal and gentle charts for Sonny Criss. At the same time, though, his own long-deleted *The Giant Is Awakened* (revived on the valuable *West Coast Hot*, which also includes John Carter/Bobby Bradford material) took its central impetus from the angry separatism of black cultural nationalism. Perhaps as a result, Tapscott has recorded disappointingly rarely and has restricted himself in recent years largely to solo recitals on the sometimes hard-to-find Nimbus label.

Tapscott characteristically builds pieces over sustained *ostinati* in the bass clef (he uses two bass players on the 1969 date, and features McBee very strongly in his late-1980s band), building solos out of simple but often enigmatic themes. The most obvious influence is Monk, there are clear parallels with Randy Weston and Dollar Brand (Abdullah Ibrahim), but there is also a 'correctness' of touch and development that recalls classical technique in its purest form, not a Third Stream dilution. Over this, Tapscott likes to place a freer-sounding horn, the young pretender, Arthur Blythe, in 1969 (he's never played like this again) and the more abstract Carter two decades later. There are now four versions of 'The Dark Tree' available. That on *West Coast Hot* is terse and pungent, those on the hat Arts (one per volume) much cooler and more developed, but also exposing more of the piece's deceptive structure. The one on *Live At Lobero*, which also features 'Sketches Of Drunken Mary', one of the best of the hat Art tracks, is looser but has much to recommend it.

Not a frequent standards players (though there are respectable *Sessions* versions of 'Alone Together' on *Volume 1* and of 'Round Midnight' on the otherwise rather disappointing *Volume 7*, Tapscott favours curiously angled melodies, often juxtaposing quite alien time-signatures, as he does on 'Lino's Pad' (*The Dark Tree, Live At Lobero: Volume 2*). March cadences, reminiscent of Ayler, recur, and Tapscott also shows a fondness for easy 'Boston' waltzes, with the bass in fours counterpointing the main development. The second volume of *The Dark Tree* is marginally less compelling than the first (which stands quite acceptably on its own); however, first exposure to Tapscott creates an immediate appetite for more of his gloriously dissonant music. At least one of these should be in every serious collection.

BUDDY TATE (born 1915)
TENOR SAX, CLARINET

***   **Tate-A-Tate** Original Jazz Classics OJC 184 LP/MC
Tate; Clark Terry (*t, flhn*); Tommy Flanagan (*p*); Larry Gales (*b*); Art Taylor (*d*). 10/60.

Buddy Tate is one of the greatest and most durable of swing tenormen, a major performer for over half a century and a much-loved and amiable man; but the records under his own name are perhaps a little disappointing in the light of his grand reputation, and his reticent standing as a leader may account for why he's never quite secured the wider fame of some of his peers. His great records were made with Basie – whom he joined following Herschel Evans's death in 1939 – and his old friend from the band, Buck Clayton; but the session above is interesting because he succeeds in slowing everything down to his favourite, steady-rolling pace. Flanagan, Gales and Taylor are obliged to take things very steadily, and Clark Terry, at something like his sly best, treats the sequence of sneaky-sounding blues as a series of exchanged nudges and winks with the leader. Only the breezy reading of 'Take The "A" Train' steps out. 'Just lead-ins and lead-outs, and we just played,' opined Tate.

***   **Broadway** Black & Blue 590542 CD
Tate; François Biensan (*t*); Wild Bill Davis (*org*); Floyd Smith (*g*); Chris Colombo (*d*). 5/72.

**   **Midnight Slows Vol. 4** Black & Blue 194682 CD
Tate; Milt Buckner (*org*); Jo Jones (*d*). 1/74.

(*)   **The Texas Twister New World 352 CD
Tate; Paul Quinichette (*ts*); Cliff Smalls (*p*); Major Holley (*b*); Jackie Williams (*d*). 75.

(*)   **Tate A Tete At La Fontaine Storyville SLP 4030 LP
Tate; Tete Montoliu (*p*); Bo Stief (*b*); Svend Erik Norregaard (*d*); Finn Ziegler (*v*). 9/75.

***   **Kansas City Joys** Sonet SNTCD 716 CD
Tate; Paul Quinichette (*ts*); Jay McShann (*p, v*); Claude Williams (*vn*); Ted Sturgis (*b*); Herbie Lovelle (*d*). 3/76.

Tate's records in the 1970s have a desultory, pick-up feel to them, but there's still plenty of ingratiating music here. *Broadway* grants him the lavish support of Wild Bill Davis, whose splayed hands and continuous pumping of the mixture stop on the organ paints in all the spaces in the music. On a blues set-piece like 'Blues In My Heart' Tate's sound becomes massive, unstoppable, an Easter Island figure come to life. Over CD length it grows wearisome, though, and the bonus of four previously unreleased tracks is dubious. The disc in Black & Blue's 'Midnight Slows' series is even more stately in pace, and even more mixed in virtues: it's too sluggish to suit such a heavyweight at length, and Buckner and Jones merely plod alongside.

The sound on both is a little too bright, with organ and cymbals aggressively forward on the *Broadway* set. The meeting with Montoliu, already a veteran accompanist of Dexter Gordon and Ben Webster, is a knowing meeting of minds, even if the music is set back by a vocalist on a couple of tracks and by moments of waywardness. Tate does some singing of his own on *The Texas Twister*, and at least he sounds better than Zoot Sims or Phil Woods in this role. It otherwise interrupts an attractive two-tenor workout for the leads which offers a scarce glimpse of Quinichette in his later days: as does the Sonet CD, which adds McShann and his then frequent partner, Williams, for an authentic class of Kansas City swing. Shrewdly paced if not quite rising to the best of occasions, none of them do themselves any dishonour. 'Tickle Toe' rekindles much of the light spark of the Basie sax section.

(*)　**Just Jazz Reservoir RSR CD 110 CD
　　Tate; Al Grey (*tb*); Richard Wyands (*p*); Major Holley (*b, v*); Al Harewood (*d*). 4/84.

(*)　**Long Tall Tenor Calligraph CLG 008 LP
　　Tate; Humphrey Lyttelton (*t*); Pete Strange (*tb*); Bruce Turner (*cl, as*); John Barnes
　　(*cl, bs*); Stan Greig (*p*); Paul Bridge (*b*); Adrian Macintosh (*d*). 12/85.

The Reservoir disc is a reissue of an earlier LP with a couple of alternative takes to beef up playing time. Nothing very exciting here, but dependable playing from the principals and Grey in particular taking a witty role. Tate's appearance as an *éminence grise* with the Lyttelton band is sometimes discouraging, for it seems that Tate can't finally muster his old assurance with any consistency. His ballad reading of 'I Cover The Waterfront' is decidedly shaky, and his solos sound too much like an old man talking for them to sit comfortably within the typically buoyant charts devised by Humph, who is himself on very good form.

ART TATUM (1910–56)
PIANO, CELESTE

***(*)　**Art Tatum 1932–1934** Classics 507 CD
　　Tatum (*p* solo). 3/33–10/34.

***(*)　**Art Tatum 1934–1940** Classics 560 CD
　　Tatum; Lloyd Reese (*t*); Marshall Royal (*cl*); Bill Perkins (*g*); Joe Bailey (*b*); Oscar
　　Bradley (*d*). 10/34–7/40.

****　**Classic Early Solos 1934–1939** MCA GRD 607 CD
　　Tatum (*p* solo). 8/34–11/37.

The enormity of Tatum's achievements makes approaching him a daunting proposition even now. His very first session, cut in New York in 1933, must have astonished every piano player who heard any of the four tracks (only available on Classics 507). 'Tiger Rag', for instance, becomes transformed from a rather old-fashioned hot novelty tune into a furious series of variations, thrown off with abandon but as closely argued and formally precise as any rag or stomp at one-quarter of the tempo. If Tatum had only recorded what is on these first CDs, he would be assured of immortality; yet, like Morton's early solos, they are both achievements in their own right and sketchbooks for the great works of his later years.

There are just a few distractions in the music leading up to 1940: Adelaide Hall sings a couple of vocals on one session, and Tatum's Swingsters record one 1937 session (which also includes Tatum on celeste). The MCA disc only goes as far as the superb final session of 1937, but the Classics CDs cover everything up to 1940. The MCA disc, though, is in considerably superior sound.

****　**The Standard Transcriptions** Music & Arts CD-673 2CD
　　Tatum (*p* solo). 35–43.

(***)　**Standards** Black Lion BLCD 760143 CD
　　Tatumn (*p* solo). 35–43.

Tatum's transcription discs for radio were made at several sessions over a period of several years and have survived as rather indifferently stored acetates. The Music & Arts double-CD does an heroic job in getting the best out of them. They are as valuable in their way as the later sessions for Norman Granz: briefer, many solos almost casually tossed off, and some blemished by the poor recording (Tatum never finally received the kind of studio sound which his work demanded), but it's a magnificent archive, spread here over two lengthy CDs. Some of them, such as 'I Wish I Were Twins', have the melody abstracted into a monstrously fast chunk of stride piano; others, like 'The Man I Love', become tender but firm ballads, while others begin at a medium tempo before hurtling forward in double-time. Trifles such as Dvorak's 'Humoresque' are treated with Tatum's peculiar knowing gaucheness, while his treatment of such as 'I'm Gonna Sit Right Down And Write Myself A Letter' are like destructive tributes to such colleagues as Waller and Johnson: immensely superior in terms of technique, Tatum nevertheless pays them a kind of offhand homage by adopting elements of their manner to his own vast vocabulary. 'All God's Chillun Got Rhythm', meanwhile, prefigures Powell and bebop intensity. Highly recommended, and the package comes with a superb essay by Don Asher. It completely supercedes the Black Lion disc, which includes 20 solos (as compared with 61 in the Music & Arts set) in inferior mastering and with what seem to be some pitching problems created by uncertain speeds.

***   **The V Discs** Black Lion BLCD 760114 CD
Tatum; Tiny Grimes (*g*); Oscar Pettiford, Slam Stewart (*b*); Sid Catlett (*d*). 44–46.

***   **The Complete Capitol Recordings Vol. 1** Capitol CDP 7928662 CD
Tatum; Everett Barksdale (*g*); Slam Stewart (*b*). 7–12/52.

***   **The Complete Capitol Recordings Vol. 2** Capitol CDP 7928672 CD
As above. 9–12/52.

The V Discs is an interesting supplement rather than an essential part of the Tatum discography. Mostly solos, with the other musicians sitting in on only three tracks, these sessions for American forces overseas include some typically acomplished Tatum, but the variable sound quality – some tracks are quite clean, others are badly marked by surface noise – makes listening through the disc a sometimes jolting experience. 'Lover', 'I'm Beginning To See The Light' and a Gershwin medley are, though, top-class Tatum. The Capitol sessions date from the period when Tatum was working with a trio, but Barksdale and Stewart actually appear on only four tracks on each disc. These are mostly fine rather than great Tatum performances: from most other pianists they would be astonishing work, but ranked next to his other recordings these are on a comparatively lower flame. There are hints of the routine which he would often settle into on particular tunes, and one or two tracks where he sounds relatively indifferent to the occasion. On others – 'Someone To Watch Over Me' or 'Somebody Loves Me', both on the first disc – he is the great Tatum. The sound has been well enough handled in the remastering.

***(*)   **Masters Of Jazz Vol. 8: Art Tatum** Storyville STCD 4108 CD/LP
Tatum (*p* solo). 8/32–1/46.

***   **Piano Solos 1944–48** Zeta/Jazz Archive ZET 708 CD
Tatum (*p* solo). 12/44–48.

The Storyville disc is a hotchpotch of solos covering the 1930s and '40s. The music is unimpeachable but it makes little sense as a chronological compilation. The source of the Zeta material isn't entirely clear but it covers a good cross-section of Tatum solos from the mid-1940s, though nothing that one can't find in better shape on the Capitol discs.

***(*)   **In Private** Fresh Sound FSR-CD 127 CD
Tatum (*p* solo). c.48.

(*)   **At The Crescendo** Vogue 655615 CD
Tatum (*p* solo). 54.

A few private recordings of Tatum have survived away from the studios, and the Fresh Sound disc, though in low fidelity, finds him in brimming form on 11 standards. The Vogue disc also has some excellent Tatum but has been ruined by the overdubbing of not only applause but also a continuous background chatter. A preposterous abuse of Tatum's art.

****   **The Art Tatum Solo Masterpieces Vol. 1** Pablo 2405-432 CD
Tatum (*p* solo). 12/53.

****   **The Art Tatum Solo Masterpieces Vol. 2** Pablo 2405-433 CD
Tatum (*p* solo). 12/53.

****   **The Art Tatum Solo Masterpieces Vol. 3** Pablo 2405-434 CD
Tatum (*p* solo). 12/53.

****   **The Art Tatum Solo Masterpieces Vol. 4** Pablo 2405-435 CD
Tatum (*p* solo). 4/54.

****   **The Art Tatum Solo Masterpieces** Pablo 2405-436 CD
Tatum (*p* solo). 4/54.

****   **The Art Tatum Solo Masterpieces** Pablo 2405-437 CD
Tatum (*p* solo). 1/55.

****   **The Art Tatum Solo Masterpieces** Pablo 2405-438 CD
Tatum (*p* solo). 1/55–56.

*****   **The Complete Pablo Solo Masterpieces** Pablo 4404 7CD
As above seven discs. 12/53–1/55.

Tatum's extraordinary achievement was set down in no more than four separate sessions over the course of a little over a year. Twenty years after his first solo records, this abundance of music does in some ways show comparatively little in the way of 'progression': he had established a pattern for playing many of the tunes in his repertoire, and changes of inflection, nuance and touch may be the only telling differences between these and earlier variations on the theme. But there are countless small revisions of this kind, enough to make each solo a fresh experience, and mostly he is more expansive (freed from playing-time restrictions, he is still comparatively brief, but there can be a major difference between a two-and-a-half-minute and a four-minute solo), and more able to provide dynamic contrast and rhythmic variation. He still chooses Broadway tunes over any kind of jazz material and seems to care little for formal emotional commitments: a ballad is just as likely to be dismantled as it is made to evoke tenderness, while a feeble tune such as 'Taboo' (Vol. 7) may be transformed into something that communicates with great power and urgency. Tatum's genius (these records were originally known as 'The Genius Of Art Tatum') was a peculiar combination of carelessness – even at his most daring and virtuosic, he can sometimes suggest a throwaway manner – and searching commitment to his art, and those contradictory qualities (which in some ways exemplify something of the jazz artist's lot) heighten the power of these superb solos. While it is invidious to single out particular discs, we suggest that the uncommitted start with discs four and six. The boxed-set edition includes all the music, and demands a fifth star. It is tantalizing to conjecture what Tatum might have done in contemporary studios, for his whole discography is marred by inadequate recording – even these later solos are comparatively unrefined by the studio – but the CD versions are probably the best to date.

****   **The Tatum Group Masterpieces Vol. 1** Pablo 2405-424 CD
Tatum; Benny Carter (*as*); Louie Bellson (*d*). 6/54.

***(*)   **The Tatum Group Masterpieces Vol. 2** Pablo 2405-425 CD
Tatum; Roy Eldridge (*t*); Larry Simmons (*b*); Alvin Stoller (*d*). 3/55.

***(*)   **The Tatum Group Masterpieces Vol. 3** Pablo 2405-426 CD
Tatum; Lionel Hampton (*vib*); Buddy Rich (*d*). 8/55.

***(*)   **The Tatum Group Masterpieces Vol. 4** Pablo 2405-427 CD
As above. 8/55.

***(*)   **The Tatum Group Masterpieces Vol. 5** Pablo 2405-428 CD
Tatum; Harry Edison (*t*); Lionel Hampton (*vib*); Barney Kessel (*g*); Red Callender (*b*); Buddy Rich (*d*). 9/55.

****   **The Tatum Group Masterpieces Vol. 6** Pablo 2405-429 CD
Tatum; Red Callender (*b*); Jo Jones (*d*). 1/56.

****   **The Tatum Group Masterpieces Vol. 7** Pablo 2405-430 CD
Tatum; Buddy DeFranco (*cl*); Red Callender (*b*); Bill Douglass (*d*). 2/56.

****   **The Tatum Group Masterpieces Vol. 8** Pablo 2405-432 CD
Tatum; Ben Webster (*ts*); Red Callender (*b*); Bill Douglass (*d*). 9/56.

**** **The Complete Pablo Group Masterpieces** Pablo 401 6CD
As above eight discs. 6/54–8/56.

Even after the solo sessions, Tatum wasn't finished. Norman Granz recorded him in eight different group settings as well. The overall quality isn't so consistently intense, since Tatum's partners are sometimes either relatively incompatible or simply looking another way: the cheery Hampton and Rich, for instance, work well enough in their trio record, but it seems to lighten the music to an inappropriate degree. Yet some of this music is actually undervalued, particularly the trio session with Callender and Douglass, the group working in beautiful accord. The sextet date with Edison, Hampton and Kessel is comparatively slight, and the meeting with Eldridge, while it has moments of excitement, again sounds like two virtuosos of somewhat contrary methods in the same room. The meetings with Carter, DeFranco and Webster, though, are unqualified masterpieces: the Carter session is worth having just for the astonishing 'Blues In C', and elsewhere – as with the DeFranco session – Carter's aristocratic elegance chimes perfectly with Tatum's grand manner. The meeting with Webster might on the face of it have been unlikely, but this time the contrasts in their styles create a moving alliance, the heavy, emotional tenor floating poignantly over the surging piano below. All the music sounds good in this remastering.

ART TAYLOR (born 1929)
DRUMS

*** **Taylor's Wailers** Original Jazz Classics OJC 094 LP
Taylor; Donald Byrd (*t*); Jackie McLean (*as*); John Coltrane, Charlie Rouse (*ts*); Ray Bryant, Red Garland (*p*); Wendell Marshall, Paul Chambers (*b*). 2–3/57.

Art Taylor was a prolific visitor to the studios in the 1950s, drumming for Red Garland, John Coltrane, Miles Davis and many others on countless sessions, most of them for Prestige. The company gave him this shot at a leadership date and, while it's a well-cooked hard-bop session, it doesn't go much further than that. The album is actually compiled from two sessions, one with Coltrane, who works up a patented head of steam on 'C.T.A.', and another with Rouse, whose more circumspect passions are rather well caught in his solo on 'Batland'. 'Off Minor' and 'Well You Needn't' feature in Thelonious Monk's own arrangements but the band sound no more committed here than elsewhere, with Byrd his usual, blandly confident self. The leader's own playing is authoritative, although his more fidgety mannerisms leave him a grade below such hard-bop giants as Blakey. Another fine session, *Taylor's Tenors*, has yet to be reissued, and his Blue Note set, *AT's Delight*, is currently out of print again.

BILLY TAYLOR (born 1921)
PIANO

(*) **Cross-Section Original Jazz Classics OJC 1730 LP
Taylor; Earl May (*b*); Percy Brice (*d*); Charlie Smith, Jose Mangual, Ubaldo Nieto, Machito (*perc*). 5/53–7/54.

*** **The Billy Taylor Trio With Candido** Original Jazz Classics OJC 015 LP
Taylor; Earl May (*b*); Percy Brice (*d*); Candido Camero (*perc*). 9/54.

While he has become best known as one of the most experienced and respected forces in jazz education in America, Billy Taylor's talents as a piano player should be recognized more than they are. He played with everyone from Stuff Smith to Charlie Parker on 52nd Street in the 1940s, and having worked with Machito stood him in good enough stead to make these Latin-flavoured outings sound plausible. Taylor's affinities are essentially with bop, but his sensibility is akin to Teddy Wilson's: cultivated, gentlemanly, his improvisations take a leisurely route through his surroundings, alighting only on points which are germane to the setting but managing to suggest a complete grasp of the material and task at hand. *Cross-Section* features eight tracks by his trio with May and Brice and four with Machito's rhythm section: dainty but substantial, the music is very engaging and, although the second session is transparently fixed to feature Candido – whose conga and bongo solos tend to bore when heard at length – the slow and almost luxuriant reading of 'Love For Sale' and the swinging 'Mambo Inn' suggest Taylor's careful preparation for the date. There is no dramatic sense of Latin-jazz fusion on either record, just a calm and logical pairing of one genre with another.

*** **You Tempt Me** Taylor-Made 1003 CD/LP/MC
Taylor; Victor Gaskin (*b*); Curtis Boyd (*d*). 6/85.

*** **White Nights And Jazz In Leningrad** Taylor-Made 1001 LP/CD/MC
Taylor; Victor Gaskin (*b*); Bobby Thomas (*d*). 88.

*** **Solo** Taylor-Made 1002 LP/CD/MC
Taylor. 8/88.

*** **Billy Taylor And The Jazzmobile All Stars** Taylor-Made 1004 CD/LP/MC
Taylor; Jimmy Owens (*t, flhn*); Frank Wess (*ss, ts, f*); Ted Dunbar (*g*); Victor Gaskin
(*b*); Bobby Thomas (*d*). 4/89.

Taylor's move into education has left his back-catalogue in some disrepair, and we must await the reappearance of such as the fine *Billy Taylor At The London House* from 1956. Establishing his own label in the 1980s has, though, made Taylor more available now than for many years. Of the four discs so far released, *White Nights* is an attempt to re-create the experience of a visit to Leningrad, and the earlier *You Tempt Me* is largely made up of a sequence of themes from the pianist's suite, 'Let Us Make A Joyful Noise', intended to evoke something of the spirit of Ellington's Sacred Concerts: although the most interesting piece is his unexpected reworking of 'Take The "A" Train' which reharmonizes Strayhorn's melody at a steady, compelling gait. Both sessions are good, but the *Solo* date is a better or at least more comprehensive display of Taylor's powers. There are perhaps two tunes too many in a long (72 minutes) CD, but Taylor's exact, finely wrought treatments make durable new statements out of the likes of 'Old Folks' and 'More Than You Know', as well as some of his own originals.

The sextet session is distinguished by Taylor's uncompromising choice of material: there's nothing familiar, aside perhaps from Lee Morgan's 'Ceora', and the carefully positioned features for Owens and Wess are thoughtfully handled by the hornmen.

CECIL TAYLOR (born 1930)
PIANO, VOICE

**** **Jazz Advance** Blue Note CDP 7844622 CD
Taylor; Steve Lacy (*ss*); Buell Neidlinger (*b*); Dennis Charles (*d*). 9/56.

One of the most extraordinary debuts in jazz, and for 1956 it's an incredible effort. Taylor's 1950s music is even more radical than Ornette Coleman's, though it has seldom been recognized as such, and while Coleman has acquired the plaudits, it is Taylor's achievement which now seems the most impressive and uncompromised. While there are still many nods to conventional post-bop form in this set, it already points to the freedoms which the pianist would later immerse himself in. The interpretation of 'Bemsha Swing' reveals an approach to time which makes Monk seem utterly straightforward; 'Charge 'Em' is a blues with an entirely fresh slant on the form; Ellington's 'Azure' is a searching tribute from one keyboard master to another. 'Sweet And Lovely' and 'You'd Be So Nice To Come Home To' are standards taken to the cleaners by the pianist, yet his elaborations on the melodies will fascinate any who respond to Monk's comparable treatment of the likes of 'There's Danger In Your Eyes, Cherie'. Lacy appears on two tracks and sounds amazingly comfortable for a musician who was playing Dixieland a few years earlier. And Neidlinger and Charles ensure that, contrary to what some may claim, Taylor's music swings. The CD reissue sounds very well.

***(*) **Looking Ahead!** Original Jazz Classics OJC-452 CD/LP/MC
As above, except Earl Griffith (*vib*) replaces Lacy. 6/58.

The most pensive of Taylor's early records may be the best place to start in appreciating his music. The A minor blues of 'Luyah! The Glorious Step', Griffith's charming 'African Violet' and the remarkable fantasy on 'Take The A Train', 'Excursion On A Wobbly Rail', mark the pianist's transitional explorations of jazz form, while 'Toll' embarks on a new journey towards his own territory. 'Wallering', named in tribute to Fats Waller, is a wonderfully constructed improvisation on 'two improvised figures that are simultaneous', as Taylor says in the sleevenote. Griffith combines edginess with inborn lyricism which works surprisingly well in context, but it's Neidlinger and Charles who are again central to Taylor's search for rhythmical freedom.

****   **The World Of Cecil Taylor** Candid CCD 79006 CD
As above, except Archie Shepp (*ts*) replaces Griffith. 10/60.

***(*)   **Air** Candid CCD 79046 CD
As above. 1/61.

****   **Jumpin' Punkins** Candid CCD 79013 CD
As above, except add Clark Terry (*t*), Roswell Rudd (*tb*), Steve Lacy (*ss*), Charles Davis (*bs*), Billy Higgins (*d*). 1/61.

***(*)   **New York City R&B** Candid CCD 79017 CD
As above. 1/61.

***(*)   **Cell Walk For Celeste** Candid CCD 79034 CD
As above. 1/61.

The 1961 recordings for Candid – some of them under the nominal leadership of Neidlinger – secure a final balance between Taylor's insistent unshackling of familiar organization and his interest in standard material. *The World Of Cecil Taylor* introduced Shepp into the pianist's difficult universe, and it is a memorable encounter: Shepp's scrawling tenor battles through 'Air' with courageous determination, but it's clear that he has little real idea what's going on, and Taylor's own superbly eloquent improvisation makes the saxophonist seem like a beginner. It's even more apparent on the alternative takes of the piece (there were 18 attempts at it in the studio), many of which are on the Mosaic boxed-set of this music (see Introduction), and three of which are on *Air* (a collection of alternates which includes two different takes of 'Number One' and one of 'Port Of Call'). But the same sessions also included the lovely and (for Taylor) surprisingly impressionistic 'Lazy Afternoon' and the blues fantasy of 'O.P.'. The larger band tackles only two tunes, both by Ellington, 'Things Ain't What They Used To Be' and 'Jumpin' Punkins', though they sound more like the Monk ensembles of *Monk's Music* than any Ellington band. Finally, there are the trio pieces: 'E.B.', which approximates a sonata and includes a superb piano improvisation, and the wholly improvised yet seemingly finished 'Cindy's Main Mood' are outstanding. The original records are *The World* and *New York City R&B*, but the various collections of outtakes are equally revealing.

***   **Unit Structures** Blue Note BCT-84237 CD
Taylor; Gale Stevens Jr (*t*); Jimmy Lyons (*as*); Ken McIntyre (*as, bcl, ob*); Henry Grimes, Alan Silva (*b*); Andrew Cyrille (*d*). 5/66.

***   **Conquistador** Blue Note B21Y-84260 CD
Taylor; Bill Dixon (*t*); Jimmy Lyons (*as*); Henry Grimes, Alan Silva (*b*); Andrew Cyrille (*d*). 10/66.

With the very important Cafe Montmartre recordings of 1962 currently out of print, there's something of a gap before these two albums for Blue Note. But these are also important and very singular entries in Taylor's progress. *Unit Structures* is both as mathematically complex as its title suggests and as rich in colour and sound as the ensemble proposes, with the orchestrally varied sounds of the two bassist – Grimes is a strong, elemental driving force, Silva is tonally fugitive and mysterious – while Stevens and McIntyre add other hues and Lyons, who was steadily becoming Taylor's most faithful interpreter, improvises with and against them. The title piece is a highly refined but naturally flowing aggregation of various cells which create or propose directions for improvisation, combinations of players and tonal and rhythmical variations. *Conquistador* consists of two long pieces, one of which is a free, open piece, the other a development out of a particularly haunting slow theme, with a rare documentation of Dixon's playing in this period – he was recorded even less often than Taylor, yet was aassertive enough to make him sound like the most free-spirited member of the group aside from Taylor himself. Blue Note's recording wasn't ideal for this music but it's good enough.

***   **Student Studies** Charly AFF 770 CD
Taylor; Jimmy Lyons (*as*); Alan Silva (*b*); Andrew Cyrille (*d*). 11/66.

***   **Fondation Maeght Nights Vol. 1** Jazzview COD 001 CD
Taylor; Jimmy Lyons (*as*); Sam Rivers (*ts, ss*); Andrew Cyrille (*d*). 7/69.

***   **Fondation Maeght Nights Vol. 2** Jazzview COD 002 CD
As above. 7/69.

***   **Fondation Maeght Nights Vol. 3** Jazzview COD 003 CD
As above. 7/69.

One of Taylor's most difficult periods. *Student Studies* features Alan Silva on bass in addition to the trio, and while 'Amplitude' is a mysterious, whispering piece and the title-track is a compelling four-way argument, the blistering 'Niggle Feuigle', unrelieved energy music, pointstowards the music on the *Fondation Maeght* records (once available as *The Great Concert Of Cecil Taylor*). This single two-hour concert (somewhat clumsily spread over three CDs) is manic, maddening stuff, filled with ultra-violent playing and making almost intractable demands on the listener. Rivers and Lyons sound as if they're constantly on the point of bursting through to some higher dialogue that never quite arrives, but the comparatively inefficient recording may be obscuring detail in what is very hard work for even Taylor devotees.

****   **Indent** Arista Freedom FCD-41038 CD
Taylor (*p* solo). 3/73.

****   **Silent Tongues** Arista Freedom FCD-41005 CD
Taylor (*p* solo). 7/74.

Taylor's first solo records remain marvellous achievements. *Indent* is fashioned in three layers, with a thoughtful opening section leading to a second part of contrasting effects and conflicts, before moving to the astonishing, grandstanding arpeggios which sound like the keyboard being levered apart: Taylor may eschew showmanship in some ways, but it's telling that this brings cheers from the audience, and it certainly creates a memorable catharsis. *Silent Tongues* is built in shorter passages. The five parts each have a distinct character of their own, built out of rhythmic or harmonic notions as specifically (if more elaborately and mysteriously) as in his great early work; and the two encores he offers show how satisfied he was with the occasion. *Indent* is very well recorded, but the piano isn't quite so clearly focused on the second disc.

***   **Cecil Taylor Unit** New World NW 201 CD
Taylor; Raphe Malik (*t*); Jimmy Lyons (*as*); Ramsey Ameen (*vn*); Sirone (*b*); Ronald Shannon Jackson (*d*). 4/78.

***   **3 Phasis** New World NW 203 CD
As above. 4/78.

****   **One Too Many Salty Swift And Not Goodbye** hat Art 2-6090 2CD
As above. 6/78.

This was a superb group, full of contrast but bursting with the spirit of Taylor's music and exultant in its ability to make it work. The two New World albums are studio recordings, but they're performed with the intensity of a live set; the hat Art set is an overwhelming concert where conflicts with the promoters (Taylor was disallowed the use of a superior piano) seem to inspire a torrential exhibition of playing. These are colourful records: Ameen is a key member of the group, his fiddling vaguely reminiscent of Michael Sampson with Albert Ayler (a group which Jackson also played in), and there are moments (particularly the closing section of *One Too Many*) where he aspires to a very close kinship with the pianist. But textures are only one part of this music. Malik and Lyons play bright or wounded or bitingly intense lines, and they play their part in a group chemistry which sometimes has the players contrasting with each other, sometimes combining to push the music forward, sometimes providing a textured background to Taylor's own sustained flights of invention. After the ferocity of his playing and organization in the late 1960s, there is more obvious light and shade here, the freedoms more generously stated, the underlying lyricism more apparent. If there's a slight problem, it's with Jackson, who – ingenious and masterful though he is – hasn't quite the same grasp of Taylor's designs as Sunny Murray or Andrew Cyrille. The studio sessions are very well recorded, the concert rather less so, but the music transcends any problems.

***(*)   **It Is In The Brewing Luminous** hat Art CD 6012 CD
Taylor; Jimmy Lyons (*as*); Ramsey Ameen (*vn*); Alan Silva (*b, clo*); Jerome Cooper, Sunny Murray (*d*). 2/80.

This must have been a crushing experience in the tiny confines of New York's Fat Tuesday club. There is a long piano solo, though, which personifies the new currents of feeling in Taylor's work: small motifs, pensive longer lines and the familiar thunder realigned within an accessible but uncompromised method. The balance of the recording is again slightly problematical.

***   **The Eighth** Hat Art CD 6036 CD
Taylor; Jimmy Lyons (*as*); William Parker (*b*); Rashid Bakr (*d*). 11/81.

****   **Garden Part One** hat Art CD 6050 CD
Taylor (*p* solo). 11/81.

****   **Garden Part Two** hat Art CD 6051 CD
As above. 11/81.

The Eighth is a relatively disappointing session, with Parker and Bakr seemingly remote from the intense communication between Taylor and Lyons and a certain sourness afflicting the music. But *Garden* is a triumphant solo recording. Taylor uses an excellent Bosendorfer piano, is well recorded – two conditions which have infrequently attended his recording career – and he takes advantage of both in three long improvisations and a sequence of brief, supplementary solos which follow his latter-day habit of epigrammatic encores.

****   **Winged Serpent (Sliding Quadrants)** Soul Note SN 1089 CD/LP
Taylor; Enrico Rava, Tomasz Stanko (*t*); Jimmy Lyons (*as*); Frank Wright (*ts*); John Tchicai (*ts, bcl*); Gunter hampel (*bs, bcl*); Karen Borca (*bsn*); William Parker (*b*); Rashid Bakr (*d*); Andre Martinez (*d*). 10/84.

An important and insufficiently recognized record. Taylor's four compositions here begin from melodic cells: an eight-note motif starts 'Taht', a sort of riff (which at one point seems ready to turn into a locomotive piece, very much in an Ellingtonian tradition!) emerges in 'Womb Waters', but mainly these are exploding, brilliantly coloured ensemble improvisations where the horns (all very well caught by the recording) make superbly euphoric collective statements. As densely characterized as Taylor's music is, these musicians make their way into it with the highest courage, and the results are extradrinarily compelling.

****   **For Olim** Soul Note SN 1150 CD/LP
Taylor (*p* solo). 4/86.

By now, Taylor had built an impressive discography of solo recordings, and there is nothing rote in this further addition to it. 'Olim' is the only long piece, at some 18 minutes in duration; the others are sometimes only a couple of minutes long, isolating an idea, delivering it up, and then closing it down. What emerges most clearly from such a session is the refinement of his touch, sometimes obscured by the messier live mixes he's had to contend with, the absolute integration of favourite devices – clusters, call-and-response – into a a peerless mastery of the techniques available to the pianist, and his communicative abilities: nothing here does anything but speak directly to an attentive listener.

****   **Live In Bologna** Leo LR 100 CD
Taylor; Carlos Ward (*as, f*); Leroy Jenkins (*vn*); William Parker (*b*); Thurman Barker (*d, marim*). 11/87.

****   **Live In Vienna** Leo LR 174 CD
As above. 11/87.

(***)   **Chinampas** Leo LR 153 CD
Taylor (speech). 11/87.

Carlos Ward is hardly the man one thinks of when citing Taylor's saxophonists, and he is hardly a match for Jimmy Lyons; but his more directly responsive and familiar lines make an agreeable change in their way, and Jenkins is a formidable presence on both records, adding rustic colours and primeval textures to the mix, which also includes marimba and bell sounds from Barker. These are records of two more great concerts, recorded within days of each other, and though they are comparatively indifferently recorded they are still enormously exhilarating experiences. Some editing has been done from the original vinyl to fit onto single-CD release.

Chinampas may appeal only to hardcore Taylor devotees, since there is no piano, only the man reading some of his poetry. It's a fascinating adjunct to a monumental body of work; but inevitably, it's of limited appeal.

***(*) **In Florescence** A&M 395286-2 CD
Taylor; William Parker (*b*); Gregg Bendian (*perc*). 6/89.

Taylor's debut major-label album is a rather charming affair. There are three major pieces and scattered smaller ones in a programme which seems like a playful reflection on a master's achievements by the protagonist himself. Parker and Bendian proffer discreet rather than interactive accompaniment.

**** **Erzulie Maketh Scent** FMP CD 18 CD
Taylor (*p* solo). 7/88.

**** **Pleistozaen Mit Wasser** FMP CD 16 CD
Taylor; Derek Bailey (*g*). 7/88.

**** **Leaf Palm Hand** FMP CD 6 CD
Taylor; Tony Oxley (*d*). 7/88.

**** **Spots, Circles And Fantasy** FMP CD 5 CD
Taylor; Han Bennink (*perc, etc*). 7/88.

**** **Regalia** FMP CD 3 CD
Taylor; Paul Lovens (*perc*). 7/88.

**** **Remembrance** FMP CD 4 CD
Taylor; Louis Moholo (*d*). 7/88.

**** **The Hearth** FMP CD 11 CD
Taylor; Evan Parker (*ss, ts*); Tristan Honsinger (*clo*). 7/88.

**** **Riobec** FMP CD 2 CD
Taylor; Günter Sommer (*d*). 7/88.

*** **Legba Crossing** FMP CD 0 CD
Taylor; Heinz-Erich Godecke (*tb*); Ove Volquartz (*ss, ts, bcl*); Joachim Gies (*as*); Brigitte Vinkeloe (*as. ss, f*); Daniel Werts (*ob*); Sabine Kopf (*f*); Harald Kimmig (*vn*); Alexander Frangenheim, Uwe Martin, George Wolf (*b*); Paul Plimley (*p*); Lukas Lindenmaier, Peeter Uuskyla, Trudy Morse (*v*). 7/88.

**** **Alms / Tiergarten (Spree)** FMP CD 8/9.
Taylor; Enrico Rava (*t, flhn*); Tomasz Stanko (*t*); Peter Van Bergen (*ts*); Peter Brötzmann (*as, ts*); Hans Koch (*ss, ts, bcl*); Evan Parker (*ss, ts*); Louis Sclavis (*ss, cl, bcl*); Hannes Bauer, Wolter Wierbos, Christian Radovan (*tb*); Martin Mayes (*frhn*); Gunter Hampel (*vib*); Tristan Honsinger (*clo*); Peter Kowald, William Parker (*b*); Han Bennink (*d*). 7/88.

This unprecedented set of records is a towering achievement, even in Taylor's work. A document of his visit to a celebratory festival of his music in Berlin, it matches him with several of the finest European improvisers in meetings which secure an empathy that is almost beyond belief, given the comparative lack of formal preparation. An unparalleled inspiration to all these players, he makes almost all of them play above themselves, and the climactic concert with the full orchestra is a monumental event, the colossal sonic impact tempered by Taylor's own unflinching control and a grasp of dynamics and dramatic possibility which is breathtaking. Originally issed as a single boxed-set, and now available as individual records, no collection should be without at least some of these, as examples of the expressive power and liberating which this central figure has introduced into jazz and twentieth-century music in general. We would single out the encounters with Bailey, Parker, Honsinger, Oxley and Bennink as particularly brilliant examples of Taylor's adaptive capabilities and his partners' own contributons, but every one of these records is both thought-provoking and individually inspiring to any listener prepared to give themselves over to Taylor's music. Only the Woreksop record, *Legba Crossing*, which Taylor merely directs, is in anyway less than essential. As a collective achievement this stands as one of the major jazz recording projects, and were the original boxed-set still available we would have no hesitation in awarding it a fifth star.

**** **In East Berlin** FMP CD 13/14 2CD
Taylor; Günter Sommer (*perc*). 6/88.

**** **Looking (Berlin version)** FMP CD 28 CD
Taylor (*p* solo). 11/89.

***(*) **Looking (Berlin Version)** Corona FMP CD 31 CD
Taylor; Harald Kimmig (*vn*); Muneer Abdul Fataah (*clo*); William Parker (*b*); Tony
Oxley (*d*). 11/89.

**** **Looking (The Feel Trio)** FMP CD 35 CD
Taylor; William Parker (*b*); Tony Oxley (*d*). 11/89.

And yet more Cecil Taylor. The duets with Sommer were recorded a month prior to the Berlin
sessions: thunder and lightning, light and shade, and brimful of music, even across two long
CDs. The three editions of *Looking* take a *Rashomon*-style look at the same piece of music,
one solo (dense, heavily contoured, lots of pedal-sustain), one trio (magnificent interplay with
Parker and Oxley, who has become a frequent Taylor confere), and one with the somewhat
more awkward string stylings of Kimmig and Fataah, the latter meshing unconvincingly with
Parker. The incredible richness of event continues, with barely a pause, and one can only look
forward to what Taylor – now in his sixties, though it's hard to believe – will do next.

MARTIN TAYLOR (born 1956)
GUITAR

*** **Don't Fret** Linn AKD 014 CD
Taylor; David Newton (*p*); Dave Green (*b*); Alan Ganley (*d*). 9/90.

*** **Change Of Heart** Linn AKD 016 CD
Taylor; David Newton (*p*); Brian Shiels (*b*); John Rae (*d*). 6/91.

Taylor's unassuming virtuosity is probably a match for any guitarist of today in terms of
technique and bebop feel: his lines are so cleanly articulated that there seems to be no distance
between thought and execution. That said, these aren't very exciting records, partly because the
Linn studio sound is so blemish-free and partly through the expert but uninvolving work of the
rhythm sections. *Change Of Heart* includes a blues, 'You Don't Know Me', that Taylor takes to
the cleaners, but the anodyne brilliance of his tone takes some of the pith out of the playing and
certainly undermines the conviction of the rock-orientated 'Angel's Camp'. The earlier record
is more solidly in the jazz camp, thanks mostly to Ganley's civil adaptation of Art Blakey's beat,
but the more four-square Rae does no harm to the second session. Both finally suggest, for all
their undoubted pleasures, that Taylor is best positioned with a saltier horn player to work
against.

JOHN TCHICAI (born 1936)
ALTO SAXOPHONE, SOPRANO SAXOPHONE, TENOR SAXOPHONE, FLUTES

*** **John Tchicai Solo Plus Albert Mangelsdorff** FMP SAJ 12 LP
Tchicai solo and with Albert Mangelsdorff (*tb*). 2/77.

**** **Real Tchicai** Steeplechase SACS 1075 LP
Tchicai; Pierre Dørge (*g*); Niels-Henning Ørsted-Pedersen (*b*). 3/77.

**** **Darktown Highlights** Storyville SLP 1015 LP
Tchicai; Simon Spang-Hansen (*ts*); Peter Danstrup (*b*); Ole Romer (*d*). 3/77.

***(*) **John Tchicai And Strange Brothers** FMP SAJ 15 LP
As above. 10/77.

***(*) **Ball At Louisiana** Steeplechase SCS 1174 LP
Tchicai; Pierre Dørge (*g, v, perc*). 11/81.

*** **Timo's Message** Black Saint BSR 0094 CD/LP
Tchicai; Thomas Dürst, Christian Kuntner (*b*); Timo Fleig (*d, perc*). 2/84.

(*) Put Up The Fight Storyville SLP 4141 LP
Tchicai; Bent Clausen (*vib, g, syn*); Peter Danstrup (*b, syn*); Ole Romer (*d, perc, g*).
11/87.

Tchicai is not, as is commonly supposed, an American exile in Scandinavia, one of the generation who sought personal and artistic sanctuary in the 1950s and '60s, but a Copenhagen-born Dano-Congolese. He moved to the United States in the early 1960s and joined Archie Shepp and Bill Dixon in the New York Contemporary Five; but he went on to lead a more significant, if less well-known, group with percussionist Milford Graves and trombonist Roswell Rudd, known as the New York Art Quartet. In the following year he played alongside fellow altoist Marion Brown (whom he somewhat resembles in approach) on John Coltrane's epic *Acension*, before returning to Europe to work on a number of individual projects.

Though slightly quieter of late, Tchicai has been a very significant presence in the European avant-garde for a quarter of a century. A stripped-down version of his Cadentia Nova Danica big band can be heard on a fine self-titled CD (still a rare item in the Tchicai discography), originally recorded in 1968 [Freedom 32 JDF 179] and released in Japan. It perfectly illustrates Tchicai's attachment to large, very rhythmic *ostinati* as a basis for his high, keening saxophone sound. Though most obviously influenced by Ornette Coleman and, to a lesser extent, Eric Dolphy, Tchicai's very individual tonality has more often been likened to that of Lee Konitz, and his performing style has followed a similar trajectory, turning away from a rather cool and dry approach towards a rootsier and more forceful delivery. It's interesting to compare Tchicai's encounter with Albert Mangelsdorff with that of Konitz (*The Art Of The Duo*, Enja 5059 LP); in addition to the duo, 'One Soft, One Hard', it features a fine solo version of 'På Tirsdag' from *Cadentia Nova Danica* and a feverish 'Snakebite'. A later duo performance with Pierre Dørge (in whose New Jungle Orchestra the saxophonist was to play in the mid-1980s) is more developed and considered.

One doesn't normally consider Tchicai a standards player. However, on *Ball At Louisiana* he turns in superb performances of 'Go Down Moses' and 'I Can't Get Started' that suggest a growing interest in beauty of tone; a previous encounter with Dørge (with NHØP also on board) made him sound rather vinegary, though that tone perfectly suited a reading of 'Monk's Mood'. From the above it looks very much as though Tchicai's best work was concentrated in the mid-to late 1970s. His best surviving material is certainly the earlier of the two Strange Brothers albums. *Darktown Highlights* contains some of his most effective writing, notably 'Gromyko Lik Lak' and the multi-part suite that begins with 'Bright Shadows'. On 'Mao', he uses bamboo flute in a manner reminiscent of Don Cherry.

The FMP lacks some of the spark of the earlier set and is unevenly recorded, with Tchicai sounding rather remote.

The two 1980s sets are marked by Tchicai's shift away from alto saxophone. His tenor and soprano work is forceful but rather anonymous. There is a fine 'Stella By Starlight' on *Timo's Message*, which is the better of the pair, but again the weight of interest falls largely on Tchicai's now quite varied compositional style, which included calypso and rock elements.

JACK TEAGARDEN (1905–64)
TROMBONE, VOCAL

***(*) That's A Serious Thing** RCA Bluebird ND 90440 CD
Teagarden; Bobby Hackett (*c*); Louis Armstrong (*t, v*); Leonard Davis, Tommy Gott, Manny Klein, Jimmy McPartland, Ruby Weinstein, Henry Red Allen, Pee Wee Irwin, Jerry Neary, Nate Kazebier, Nat Natoli, Charlie Teagarden, Harry Goldfield, Eddie Wade, Harry James, Charlie Spivak, Bunny Berigan, Sonny Dunham, Max Kaminsky, Billy Butterfield (*t*); Tommy Dorsey, Joe Harris, Jack Fulton, Bill Rank, Hal Matthews, J. C. Higginbotham (*tb*); Benny Goodman, Peanuts Hucko (*cl*); Mezz Mezzrow, Happy Caldwell, Arnold Brilhart, Alfie Evans, Gil Rodin, Larry Binyon, Albert Nicholas, Otto Hardwicke, Charlie Holmes, Hymie Schertzer, Toots Mondello, Dick Clark, Arthur Rollini, Benny Bonaccio, Jack Cordaro, Charles Strickfadden, Frankie Trumbauer, Bud Freeman, Eddie Miller, Ernie Caceres (*reeds*); Red McKenzie (*kz, v*); Joe Sullivan, Vic Briedis, Arthur Schutt, Fats Waller, Frank Froeba, Roy Bargy, Bob Zurke, Dick Cary, Gene Schroeder, Johnny Guarnieri (*p*); Vincent

Pirro (*acc*); Joe Venuti, Joe Raymond, Eddie Bergman, Alex Beller (*vn*); Eddie Lang, Allan Reuss, Mike Pingatore, Carl Kress, Carmen Mastren, Jack Bland, Dick Morgan (*g*); Al Casey (*g*); Eddie Condon, Will Johnson (*bj*); Arthur Campbell, Norman McPherson (*tba*); Al Morgan, Harry Goodman, Art Miller, Bob Haggart, Jack Lesberg, Al Hall, Leonard Gaskin (*b*); George Stafford, Larry Gomar, Vic Berton, Kaiser Marshall, George Wettling, Ray Bauduc, Josh Billings, Gene Krupa, Herb Quigley, Bob White, Dave Tough, Cozy Cole (*d*); Helen Ward, Ben Pollack, Johnny Mercer (*v*). 3/28–7/57.

The trombone had a difficult time of it in the 1920s and was one of the last instruments to receive rhythmic emancipation through jazz. But once Teagarden and, to some extent, Jimmy Harrison had begun recording, matters changed. Miff Mole had all the flexibility and technique which Teagarden had, but for all his greatness Mole's deadpan approach had less of the mellifluous flow which for Teagarden seemed as natural as his singing voice, a sleepy Texas drawl. Besides, Teagarden was an infinite master of blues playing, and his meetings with Armstrong gave Louis the front-line partner who should have been at his shoulder for longer than he was. Teagarden made a lot of records, starting as a dance-band player and working through the big-band and revivalist periods, but there are comparatively few top-drawer albums under his own name: he was a victim of his own consistency, since there are scarcely any moments when he sounds less than wonderful. This Bluebird compilation is a useful starting-point. His very first record, 'She's A Great Great Girl' with Roger Wolfe Kahn, is here and, although the earlier material is a bit of a hotchpotch – tracks with Paul Whiteman, an early Goodman date, two pieces with Fats Waller's Buddies, a Red McKenzie session and a 1939 All Star Band where Bunny Berigan is a match for Tea – the trombonist illuminates every appearance with either the horn or the voice. Most will have the two tracks from the 1947 Town Hall concert with Armstrong on other issues, but the final, 1957 tracks, with a band led by Bud Freeman, are as stately and authoritative as anything here, with a dolorous 'I Cover The Waterfront' defining several aspects of Tea's art. The transfers are mostly from metal masters and count as one of the best remasterings in this Bluebird series.

*** **I Gotta Right To Sing The Blues** ASV AJA 5059 CD
Teagarden; Leonard Davis, Red Nichols, Ray Lodwig, Manny Klein, Charlie Teagarden, Ruby Weinstein, Sterling Bose, Dave Klein, Harry Goldfield, Nat Natoli, Frank Guarente, Leo McConville, Charlie Spivak (*t*); Jack Fulton, Glenn Miller, Ralph Copsey, Bill Rank (*tb*); Benny Goodman (*cl*); Mezz Mezzrow, Arthur Rollini, Charles Strickfadden, Benny Bonaco, John Cordaro, Chester Hazlett, Jimmy Dorsey, Art Karle, Eddie Miller, Matty Matlock, Joe Catalyne, Pee Wee Russell, Max Farley, Happy Caldwell, Arnold Brilhart, Bernie Day, Sid Stoneburn, Babe Russin, Larry Binyon, Gil Rodin, Irving Friedman, Adrian Rollini, Min Leibrook (*reeds*); Red McKenzie (*kz, v*); Fats Waller (*p, v*); Joe Sullivan, Jack Russin, Lennie Hayton, Arthur Schutt, Gil Bowers, Joe Moresco, Roy Bargy, Vincent Pirro, Howard Smith (*p*); Joe Venuti, Matty Malneck, Mischa Russell, Harry Struble, Walter Edelstein, Alex Beller, Ray Cohen (*vn*); Carl Kress, Jack Bland, Nappy Lamare, Eddie Lang, Dick McDonough, Perry Botkin, Mike Pingitore, George Van Eps (*g*); Treg Brown (*bj, v*); Eddie Condon (*bj*); Artie Bernstein, Art Miller, Jerry Johnson, Harry Goodman, Al Morgan (*b*); Norman McPherson (*tba*); Ray Bauduc, George Stafford, Herb Quigley, Stan King, Gene Krupa, Josh Billings, Larry Gomar (*d*). 2/29–10/34.

Another compilation, with 12 different bands and 18 tracks, which points up how easily Teagarden could make himself at home in bands of the period. One celebrated example is the treatment meted out to a waltz called 'Dancing With Tears In My Eyes', under Joe Venuti's leadership: Teagarden contravenes everything to do with the material and charges through his solo. Two early sessions under his own name have him trading retorts with Fats Waller on 'You Rascal You' and delivering his original reading of what became a greatest hit, 'A Hundred Years From Today'. Stricter jazz material such as two tracks by The Charleston Chasers is fine, but no less enjoyable are such as Ben Pollack's 'Two Tickets To Georgia', where Teagarden's swinging outburst suggests that he treated every setting as a chance to blow. One or two of the transfers are noisy, but most of the remastering is agreeably done.

***   **A Hundred Years From Today** Conifer 153 CD

Teagarden; Charlie Teagarden, Claude Whiteman, Sterling Bose, Frank Guarente (*t*); Pee Wee Russell, Benny Goodman (*cl*); Chester Hazlett, Jimmy Dorsey, Rod Cless (*cl, as*); Joe Catalyne, Max Farley, Dale Skinner, Mutt Hayes (*cl, ts*); Frankie Trumbauer (*Cmel*); Bud Freeman (*ts*); Adrian Rollini (*bsx*); Casper Reardon (*hp*); Fats Waller (*p, v*); Joe Meresco, Terry Shand, Charlie LaVere (*p*); Walter Edelstein, Joe Venuti, Lou Kosloff (*vn*); Nappy Lamare (*g, v*); Dick McPartland, Perry Botkin, Frank Worrell (*g*); Artie Bernstein, Eddie Gilbert, Art Miller (*b*); Stan King, Bob Conselman, Larry Gomar, Herb Quigley (*d*). 10/31–9/34.

Seventeen tracks all issued under Teagarden's leadership and, although two of them also appear on the ASV disc, this is a neat round-up of five sessions, including the rare title 'I Got The Ritz From The One I Love' from the 1931 session with Fats Waller. 'Junk Man', which features harpist Casper Reardon, is another famous piece, but as usual Teagarden dominates proceedings, even with Goodman and Jimmy Dorsey on hand. Some of the tunes are more vocal than instrumental and reveal the leader's peculiar ability to swing even at indolent tempos. Adequate sound.

**   **It's Time For Tea** Jass J-CD-624 CD

Teagarden; John Fallstich, Pokey Carriere, Sid Feller, Truman Quigley (*t*); Jose Gutierrez, Joe Ferrall, Seymour Goldfinger (*tb*); Danny Polo, Tony Antonelli, Joe Ferdindo, Art Moore, Art Beck (*reeds*); Ernie Hughes (*p*); Arnold Fishkind (*b*); Paul Collins (*d*); David Alle, Lynn Clark, Marianne Dunn (*v*). 1–6/41.

Teagarden had started leading a big band in 1939, but it wasn't until 1941 – as revealed in the excellent notes here – that it achieved much commercial success. On the evidence of the 24 sides collected here, it was done at the expense of much jazz content. Most of the tracks work politely through forgettable pop material of the day, along with leaning on a fashionable penchant for jazzing the classics: there are charts for 'Anitra's Dance' and Ravel's 'Afternoon Of A Faun' here, as well as 'Casey Jones'. It isn't until 'Harlem Jump' (number 21) that we get a thoroughgoing swing performance. There are glimmers of Teagarden – who, after all, was the band's only feasible soloist apart from Polo – but not nearly enough. For collectors only, though the remastering is painstakingly done.

(*)   **Accent On Trombone Fresh Sound FSR-CD 138 CD

Teagarden; Ruby Braff (*t*); Sol Yaged (*cl*); Lucky Thompson (*ts*); Kenny Kersey (*p*); Sidney Gross (*g*); Milt Hinton (*b*); Denzil Best (*d*). 54.

This might have been a riveting session, and it's certainly an intriguing mix of personalities, but the weary choice of material and the fairly terrible sound – half the players seem to be in one hall and the rest in another, and Best sounds like a merciless mistreater of cymbals – destroy many of its good intentions. Teagarden sounds in low spirits for the vocals, but his trombone solos are as distinctive as usual, and Braff is in sometimes meteoric form: a carousing 'After You've Gone' shows off what might have been. But the rest is often a mess. CD remastering has done nothing for the sound.

**   **Jack Teagarden And His All Stars** Jazzology 199 CD

Teagarden; Dick Oakley (*c*); Jerry Fuller (*cl*); Don Ewell (*p*); Stan Puls (*b*); Ronnie Greb (*d*). 58.

**   **Texas Trombone** Star Line 403 CD

As above. 7/58.

Teagarden drifted through his final years in a way that looks as careless and slipshod as some of Armstrong's later efforts: the numerous renditions of 'St James Infirmary' and 'Rockin' Chair' (both included here) eventually sound as fatigued as his perennially tired voice. The Jazzology release is a well-recorded club date, made in Cleveland in 1958, but it features a dusty band and a leader content to amble along. The set-list was much the same in Seattle, Washington, where the Star Line set was made, and there's no cause to revise opinions for this one.

TOMMY TEDESCO
GUITAR

(*)   **My Desiree Discovery DSCD 959 CD
Tedesco; Gene Cipriano (*cor, f, ob*); Jon Kurnick (*g*); Paul Capritto (*b*); Frank
Severino (*d*). 6/78–10/81.

**   **Carnival Time** Trend TRCD 534 CD
Tedesco; Jon Kurnick, Jim Bruno (*g*). 9/83.

(*)   **A Hollywood Gypsy Discovery DSCD 928 CD
Tedesco; Jim Bruno (*g*); John Leitham (*b*).

Tedesco plays acoustic and electric guitar with a soft, precise fluency: he likes to double-time
slow and medium tempos and occasionally gives the impression that he's going faster than he
actually is. The results are coolly pleasant if not very profound music, broadly in a Django/Bireli
Lagrene manner, although Tedesco's self-styling as a 'Hollywood gypsy' is more fanciful than
accurate. His own compositions tend towards a pastel shade of boring but, when focused by a
good standard – such as 'I'll Remember April' on *My Desiree* or 'Stella By Starlight' on
Hollywood Gypsy – he gives a better account of himself. The three-guitar *Carnival Time* is less
appealing unless one loves this kind of multiple pile-up. *My Desiree* compiles most of two earlier
LPs for Revelation.

RICHARD TEITELBAUM (born 1939)
PIANO, SYNTHESIZERS, ELECTRONICS

***(*)   **Concerto Grosso (1985)** hat Art CD 6004 CD
Teitelbaum; George Lewis (*tb, elec*); Anthony Braxton (*reeds*). 5/85.

***   **The Sea Between** Victo 02 LP
Teitelbaum; Carlos Zingaro (*vn*).

A key member of the extremely important Musica Elettronica Viva, Teitelbaum is a pioneering
exponent of electro-acoustic combinations in improvised music. The performance with Zingaro
is typically challenging, but ultimately rather dry, and is perhaps returned to after hearing
Teitelbaum's engrossing collaboration with two other significant performers of radical
'cross-over' music. With *Concerto Grosso*, he takes an intriguing step back from the aggressive
futurism of the avant-garde to examine the implications for improvisation of another, older
tradition.

The bracketed date is partially intended as a *caveat emptor* directed at anyone who might
think they're buying a 'grand ensemble' form the Baroque period; the original form differed
from a solo concerto in setting a small group, known as the *concertino*, in antiphonal relation to
a large ensemble of 'replenishing' *ripieni*, who play the *tutti*. Teitelbaum's full and correct title
is *Concerto Grosso (1985) for Human Concertini and Robotic Ripieno*. The idea is to place
instrumental improvisers in relation to a machine-generated background of
deutero-instrumental effects which is nevertheless responsive to what the improvisers
themselves choose to play.

Logic and the laws of thermodynamics suggest that the only possible outcome is utter chaos
and entropy. However, the responses of the human *concertini* (all of whom have shown an equal
commitment to 'freedom' and 'structures' elsewhere in their careers) are so intelligently
disciplined that it becomes possible to discern the fleeting ghost of an orthodox thematic
development, carried on at such a level of abstraction that it is never explicitly stated. Divided
into 'Invenzione', 'Fantasia' and 'Capriccio', the piece has a nicely ironic current which saves it
from pomposity or from any suggestion of pastiche. Not by any means for every taste, but
Braxton and Lewis are worth hearing whatever the context and Teitelbaum's contribution
merits wider recognition.

JOE TEMPERLEY (born 1929)
BARITONE AND SOPRANO SAXOPHONES

***   **Nightingale** Hep CD 2052 CD
         Temperley; Brian Lemon (*p*); Dave Green (*b*); Martin Drew (*d*). 4/91.

A delightful record. Temperley has seldom figured in record sessions in the UK since his move to America, and there has been very little under his own leadership, but this opportune session establishes his mastery of the baritone beyond doubt. A seamless, singing manner belies the difficulties of the instrument and, though his sometimes bubbly timbre at fast tempos may not be to all tastes, the quality of his improvisations is unanswerable. There's a glowing 'Body And Soul' to stand against the finest versions and a beautiful Ellington rarity in 'Sunset And A Mocking Bird', in which Temperley's sound never makes one think of Harry Carney. He ends on an *a capella* 'My Love Is Like A Red, Red Rose' that sums up the sound he can get from the horn. The weakness lies in the rhythm section: nothing very wrong, but the sheer ordinariness of the playing – Lemon sounding like Hank Jones on a budget, and Drew barely exerting himself – offers little encouragement to the saxophonist.

THE TENNESSEE TOOTERS
GROUP

***   **The Tennessee Tooters And The Hottentots** Retrieval DFJ-117 2LP
         Red Nichols, Harry Gluck, Phil Napoleon, Earl Oliver (*c*); Vincent Grande, Miff
         Mole, Charles Panelli, Sammy Lewis (*tb*); Arnold Brilhart, Dick Johnson (*cl, as*); Fred
         Morrow (*cl, ts*); Chuck Muller, Alfie Evans (*as*); Lucien Smith, Larry Abbott (*ts*);
         Rube Bloom, Frank Signorelli (*p*); John Cali (*bj*); Joe Tarto (*bb*); Vic Berton, Harry
         Lottman (*d*). 12/24–9/26.

This set may appeal to some listeners rather more than Fountain/Retrieval's Red Nichols album of the same period: it collects another 29 tracks by New York small groups of the period, with Nichols and Miff Mole helming most of the front lines and the musicians wrestling their way awkwardly out of the rhythmically square dance-tunes of the day. The difference is that these discs were originally made for Vocalion, whose recording was superior to Pathé's Nichols sides, and the quality of transfers of both the acoustic and the electric originals is marvellous. The Tooters account for three of the LP sides: much of the material is consistently hot, and there are superb moments for Mole in particular – his solo on 'How Come You Do Me Like You Do' is little short of astounding for a trombonist in 1925. Nichols has his felicitous passages, but there's an equal opportunity to glimpse such seldom-heard men as Phil Napoleon and Harry Gluck, whose vibrato is as shaky as Natty Dominique's but who still manages a game solo in 'Jimtown Blues'. The Hottentots' seven tracks are leaner and more swaggering, and even unpromising titles such as 'Pensacoila' and 'Nobody's Rose' turn out well. For those who've acquired the taste for the jazz of this period only, perhaps, but fine on its own terms.

CLARK TERRY (born 1920)
TRUMPET, FLUGELHORN

***   **Serenade To A Bus Seat** Original Jazz Classics OJC 066 LP
         Terry; Johnny Griffin (*ts*); Wynton Kelly (*p*); Paul Chambers (*b*); Philly Joe Jones (*d*).
         4/57.

Though not reducible to his 'influences', Terry hybridizes Dizzy Gillespie's hot, fluent lines and witty abandon with Rex Stewart's distinctive half-valving and Charlie Shavers's high-register lyricism; he is also a master of the mute, an aspect of his work that had a discernible impact on Miles Davis. Miles, though, remained unconvinced by Terry's pioneering development of the flugelhorn as a solo instrument; later in his career he traded four-bar phrases with himself, holding a horn in each hand. An irrepressible showman, with a sly sense of humour, Terry often fared better when performing under other leaders. His encounter with the Oscar Peterson Trio in 1964 [EmArCy 818840 CD] is often judged his best work (there are samples on Mercury 830698 CD) and it's hard to see where and when he played better. The 'early' – he was thirty-seven – *Serenade To A Bus Seat* combines a tribute to civil rights activist, Rosa Parks, with pungent versions of 'Stardust' and Parker's 'Donna Lee'. Terry isn't an altogether convincing bopper, but he's working with a fine, funky band, and they carry him through some slightly unresolved moments.

***   **Duke With A Difference** Original Jazz Classics OJC 229 CD/LP
Terry; Quentin Jackson, Britt Woodman (*tb*); Tyree Glenn (*tb, vib*); Johnny Hodges (*as*); Paul Gonsalves (*ts*); Jimmy Jones, Billy Strayhorn (*p*); Luther Henderson (*cel*); Jimmy Woode (*b*); Sam Woodyard (*d*); Marion Bruce (*v*). 7 & 9/57.

In 1957 Terry was most of the way through his eight-year stint with Ellington (he'd already worked with Charlie Barnet and Count Basie and was bound for a staff job with NBC, the first black man to get his feet under that rather clubby table) and a successful partnership with trombonist Bob Brookmeyer. It's the slide brass men he cleaves to on this mildly impertinent tribute to his boss. He undercuts both Jackson and Hodges on a beautifully arranged 'In A Sentimental Mood' (which features Strayhorn on piano and Luther Henderson on celeste) and cheerfully wrecking 'Take The "A" Train' in spite of Gonsalves's best efforts to keep it hurtling along the rails. Marion Bruce's vocals are nothing to write home about, but the band is as good as the form book says it ought to be.

****   **In Orbit** Original Jazz Classics OJC 302 CD/LP
Terry; Thelonious Monk (*p*); Sam Jones (*b*); Philly Joe Jones (*d*). 5/58.

Terry's solitary excursion on Monk's *Brilliant Corners*, a vivid 'Bemsha Swing', underlined the degree to which Monk himself still drew sustenance from swing. *In Orbit* is firmly Terry's album. If the material is less stretching, the arrangements are surprisingly demanding, and the interplay between flugelhorn (used throughout) and piano on 'One Foot In The Gutter' and the contrasting 'Moonlight Fiesta' is highly inventive.

****   **Color Changes** Candid 9009 CD/LP
Terry; Jimmy Knepper (*tb*); Yusef Lateef (*ts, f, eng hn, ob*); Seldon Powell (*ts*); Tommy Flanagan, Budd Johnson (*p*); Joe Benjamin (*b*); Ed Shaughnessy (*d*). 11/60.

Terry's best record, and ample evidence that swing was still viable on the cusp of the decade that was to see its demise as anything but an exercise in nostalgia. What is immediately striking is the extraordinary, almost kaleidoscopic variation of tone-colour through the seven tracks. Given Lateef's inventive multi-instrumentalism, Powell's doubling on flute and Terry's use of flugelhorn and his mutes, the permutations on horn voicings seem almost infinite. 'Brother Terry' opens with a deep growl from Terry, a weaving oboe theme by composer Lateef and some beautiful harmony work from Watkins (who a matter of days later was to make such a contribution to Benny Bailey's superb Candid session, *Big Brass* [9011 CD]), and who interacts imaginatively with Knepper on Terry's 'Flutin' And Fluglin''. Again arranged by Lateef, this is a straightforward exploration of the relation between their two horns; Terry has written several 'odes' to his second instrument, and this is perhaps the most inventive.

'Nahstye Blues', written by and featuring Johnson, in for the unsuitably limpid Flanagan, comes close to Horace Silver's funk. Terry is slightly disappointing, but Lateef turns in a majestic solo that turns his own cor anglais introduction completely on its head. The closing 'Chat Qui Pêche' is an all-in, solo-apiece affair that would have sounded wonderful in the Parisian *boîte* it celebrates and brings a marvellous, expertly recorded record to a powerful finish. Needless to say, it comes highly recommended.

***(*)   **The Power Of Positive Swinging** Mainstream MDCD 723 CD
Terry; Bob Brookmeyer (*vtb*); Roger Kellaway (*p*); Bill Crow (*b*); Dave Bailey (*d*). 65.

***   **Gingerbread** Mainstream MDCD 711 CD
Terry; Bob Brookmeyer (*vtb*); Hank Jones (*p*); Bob Cranshaw (*b*); Dave Bailey (*d*). 72.

Though running counter to the advanced language of the time, the Terry–Brookmeyer alliance – known to the trade as Mumbles'n'Grumbles – managed to combine an uncomplicated and joyous mainstream approach with inventive and unhackneyed structural devices, unusual rhythmic variations and a useful range of tonal and timbral touches. Mutes are not just wedged into place at the beginning of a tune to vary it from the last, but inserted and removed for local effect. Terry is a particular master at this.

Their approach to 'Battle Hymn Of The Republic' on *Positive Swinging* sums up the approach pretty well. Played more or less straight for several choruses, Terry lights the touchpaper with a cluster of high, sharp notes and then brings it all to a close with an irreverent trademark growl. The use of riffs (including one borrowed from Eddie Harris's 'Freedom Jazz Dance' on *Positive Swinging*'s opener, 'Dancing On The Grave') is strikingly effective and lends what might otherwise be tame swing an earthy 'bottom' over which even the sardonic Brookmeyer sounds cheerfully unbuttoned. He comes to the fore on *Gingerbread*, which is otherwise less effusive, and more forced, perhaps illustrating the contrast between the two bands. The 1965 unit, which reunited Brookmeyer with the rhythm section from Gerry Mulligan's 1956 quartet, had worked together for some time; though Jones and Cranshaw are more than adequate replacements, the sound, which depends so much on exact timing and instinctive variation of tone, is far less coherent, leaving Terry and Brookmeyer with more to do on their own. Their Mutt and Jeff vocals on an earthy 'My Gal' (whose rear resembles 'two pigs in a gunny-sack') contrast nicely with a seen-it-all 'Mood Indigo'. Terry slyly quotes 'The Girl From Ipanema' on the closing 'Bye Bye Blackbird'.

**(*)   Mother! Mother!! – A Jazz Symphony Pablo Today 2312115 LP
Terry; Zoot Sims (*ts, ss*); Jimmy Maxwell (*t*); Susan Palma (*f*); Anand Devendra (*cl*); Jeanne Ingraham (*vn*); Christopher Finckel (*clo*); Donald Palma (*b*); Gilbert Kalish (*ky*); Anthony Cinardo, Raymond Des Roches (*perc*); Joan Heller (*v*); Arthur Weisberg (*cond*). 2/79.

A bold but ultimately rather inconsequential attempt at large-scale composition for chamber ensemble and soloists. Almost inevitably, the individual contributions of Terry and co-leader Zoot Sims are far more interesting than the rather slackly conceived ensembles. Recording quality is rather remote in places, making what was presumably a continuous performance sound like a series of overdubs.

****   Memories Of Duke Original Jazz Classics OJC 604 CD/LP
Terry; Joe Pass (*g*); Jack Wilson (*p*); Ray Brown (*b*); Frank Severino (*d*). 3/80.

Obvious, really, but exquisitely done. The interplay between Pass and Brown touches unsuspected areas of 'Cotton Tail' and 'Sophisticated Lady' (compare the version with Red Mitchell, below) and, though Severino might have been dispensed with for at least a couple of the softer tracks, the overall sound is excellent.

**(*)   Squeeze Me Chiaroscuro CRD 309 CD
Terry; Virgil Jones (*t*); Al Grey, Britt Woodman (*tb*); Heywood Henry, Red Holloway, Phil Woods (*reeds*); John Campbell (*p*); Marcus McLaurine (*b*); Butch Ballard (*d*).

Good arrangements but a rather knotted sound that strips some fine horn players of any real individuality. The rhythm section sounds under-rehearsed and the tempo is always either lagging behind or rushing to catch up. Disappointing.

***   Clark Terry–Red Mitchell Enja 5011 CD/LP/MC

***(*)   Jive At Five Enja 6042 CD/LP
Terry; Red Mitchell (*b, p, v*). 2/86, 7/88.

Jive At Five is the more musicianly of these rather knockabout sets by one frustrated crooner and one master of verbal salad, whose 'Hey Mr Mumbles' gets its 5,000th airing on the earlier album. As a purely musical dialogue, these have no right to work half as well as they do, but Terry is in excellent lip on the later version of 'Big'n And The Bear' and the Ellington material. Mitchell's comping skills come into their own on 'Cotton Tail' (two nicely varied takes), 'Sophisticated lady' and 'Prelude To A Kiss'.

***(*)   Portraits Chesky JD 2 CD
Terry; Don Friedman (*p*); Victor Gaskin (*b*); Lewis Nash (*d*). 12/88.

***   Having Fun Delos DE 4021 CD
Terry; Bunky Green (*as*); Red Holloway (*as, ts*); John Campbell (*p*); Major Holley (*b, tba*); Lewis Nash (*d*). 4/90.

By the 1980s, Terry was more than satisfied with his billing as an elder statesman and trotted out all his tricks with almost indulgent ease. The big production numbers like 'Ciribiribin' sound good on *Portraits*, but the album overall almost sounds like an audiophile test disc, so exact and limpid is the reproduction. *Having Fun* means what it says, with jokey-straight versions of the Flintstones theme (one of the most irritating melodies ever committed) and 'It's Not Easy Being Green'. Holley is a marvellous partner; a duo record, with the two men vocalizing at full throttle, would be something to hear.

***(*) **Live At The Village Gate** Chesky JD 49 CD
Terry; Jimmy Heath (*ts, ss*); Paquito D'Rivera (*as*); Don Friedman (*p*); Marcus McLauren (*b*); Kenny Washington (d). 11/90.

Recorded three weeks short of Terry's 70th birthday, this is a good-natured set of uncomplicated jazz. Terry alternates his trumpet ('my driver') and flugelhorn ('putter'), favouring a soft, blurred-edge tone that in no way compromises the clarity of his bop-influenced lines. Jimmy Heath is dry without being sterile and takes a lovely solo on 'Pint Of Bitter', a dedication to the late Tubby Hayes. D'Rivera only shows up for a single track, the appealing 'Silly Samba'.

The recording is impeccably handled, with a light sound that still captures the live ambience; on 'Keep, Keep, Keep On Keepin' On', Terry has the entire audience singing along, and so he can't resist throwing them 'Hey Mr Mumbles' at the end. 'If Sylvester Stallone can make *Rocky 3, 4, 5*, I don't see why I can't make Mumbles 8, 9 and 10.'

LILIAN TERRY
VOCAL

(*) **A Dream Comes True Soul Note SN 1047 CD/LP
Terry; Tommy Flanagan (*p*); Jesper Lundgaard (*b*); Ed Thigpen (*d*). 4–5/82.

** **Oo-Shoo-Be-Doo-Be ... Oo, Oo ... Oo, Oo** Soul Note SN 1147 CD/LP
Terry; Dizzy Gillespie (*t, perc, v*); Kenny Drew (*p*); Isla Eckinger (*b*); Ed Thigpen (*d*). 5/85.

Terry has exemplary support from the most experienced of accompanists, Tommy Flanagan, on the first record, and she tackles a standard set of jazz material: 'Lover Man', ''Round Midnight' and so forth, although 'Star Crossed Lovers' is at least a little more unusual. There's nothing here to challenge other versions of these songs, and on the second record she defers entirely to Gillespie, who is meant to be a guest star. Even so, he scarcely adds to his own reputation on this modest record.

HENRI TEXIER
DOUBLE BASS

*** **La Companera** Label Bleu LBLC 6525 CD
Texier; Michel Marre (*t, flhn*); Louis Sclavis (*cl, ts*); Philippe Deschepper (*g*); Jacques Mahieux (*d*). 2/83.

**** **Izlaz** Label Bleu LBLC 6515 CD/LP

*** **Colonel Skopje** Label Bleu LBLC 6523 CD
Texier; Joe Lovano (*ts, ss, cl, f, perc*); John Scofield (*g on Colonel Skopje* only); Steve Swallow (*b*); Aldo Romano (*d*). 5/88, 7/88.

Texier's double bass style is a freer and lighter version of Wilbur Ware's (he eulogizes the great Chicagoan on *Barret/Romano/Texier*, Carlyne VG 651 695013 CD). Texier likes to work the lower end of the register, with a throbbing, wobbling sound in ensembles that gives way to a full-voiced lyricism as a soloist. The earliest of these sets is distinguished by some fine work from Sclavis (at that time still relatively unknown outside France), but the band takes off when only Marre is added for two excellent quintet tracks.

Izlaz is credited to Texier's Transatlantik Quartet. So disinclined is he to dominate it that he brings in a second bass player, albeit a bass guitarist. Swallow's upbeat, rock-tinged swing and confident navigation of the melody allow Texier a measure of freedom that he exploits much more fully here than on the disappointing mixed-bag, *Colonel Skopje*. 'Ups And Downs' bears very little relation to Bud Powell's composition of that name but it has a nice, slightly aggrieved bounce, and the title-track is impressively crafted, with Lovan well to the fore. The mix is rather heavy-handed, presumably to bring Texier forward; in the event, Romano, who's always good to listen to, is simply too loud. On the later set, Texier seems determined to allow everyone his head, and the abiding impression is of disconnected solo 'features'. Scofield and Lovano play with characteristic fire and urgency, though, and the 'rhythm section' do their stuff like they're enjoying it.

***   **Paris–Batignolles** Label Bleu LBLC 6506 CD
         Texier; Louis Sclavis (*ss, bcl*); Joe Lovano (*ts*); Philippe Deschepper (*g*); Jacques
         Mahieux (*d*). 5/86.

Swirling dance pieces and misterioso folk themes from a fine band, caught live at the Amiens Jazz Festival in 1986. Sclavis and Lovano inevitably, but guitarist Deschepper makes some effective interventions. The closing 'Noises', which sounds like an encore piece, is a delightful crowd-pleaser.

EJE THELIN (1938–90)
TROMBONE

**   **Eje Thelin Group** Caprice CAP 1091 LP
         Thelin; Harald Svensson (*p*); Bruno Raberg (*b*); Leroy Lowe (*d*). 12/74.

***   **Live At Nefertiti** Dragon DRLP 115 LP
         Thelin; David Wilczewski (*ss, ts*); Stefan Blomqvist (*ky*); Bobo Stenson (*p*); Anders
         Jormin (*b*); Andre Ferrari (*d*); Marilyn Mazur (*perc*). 7/86.

Thelin was an important Swedish musician who worked his way from Dixieland to free playing with an entirely plausible logic, having developed a formidable agility on the trombone early on. Records made prior to 1970 have long since disappeared from circulation, and the quartet set for Caprice is period stuff: wobbly electric piano, a drummer who bashes around rock and jazz time, and a general lack of disciplined form which almost shouts out the date of the session. Yet Thelin salvages some remarkable moments, with his fuming opening solo on 'There Is Something Rotten In Denmark' and the closing, multiphonic showcase of 'Capricorn'.

The music recorded at Stockholm's Nefertiti has further evidence of Thelin's continued mastery of the horn: 'Dimensions' squares his free thinking with more conventional modal playing. But the group, collectively known as E. T. Project, is unconvincing: Blomqvist's electronic touches seem tacked on, and there's no real shape to the playing. A disappointing finale.

MARTIN THEURER
PIANO

***(*)   **Moon Mood** FMP 0700 LP
         Theurer (*p* solo). 7/79.

***   **Der Traum Der Roten Palme** FMP 0950 LP
         Theurer; Paul Lovens (*d, zither*). 11/81.

Theurer is an aggressive improviser who should have made more records than he has. *Moon Mood* groups together a dozen striking episodes, most no more than two or three minutes long, but all of them realized with gripping thoroughness. In 'Kommen Und Gehen' he seems to tear the keyboard apart, yet winds up the piece with tiptoe delicacy. 'Improvisation 3' creates a great whirl of ideas that seem to move in opposing directions at once – melody bound into clusters, fracturing and falling apart – while 'Balance' and 'Shang On' offer the most extreme kind of prepared piano, the strings and hammers treated until the sound becomes eerily unnatural. He has a clipped, percussive style in the tradition of all post-Cecil Taylor piano, but he doesn't sound much like any other free pianist; and he's recorded with a direct, upfront clarity by Jost Gebers. The album with Lovens is a shade less involving, perhaps because some of the drummer's responses are akin to things that Theurer can handle himself at the piano, but it's another rewarding series of improvisations.

TOOTS THIELEMANS (born 1922)
HARMONICA, GUITAR, WHISTLING

***(*) **Man Bites Harmonica** Original Jazz Classics OJC 1738 CD/LP
Thielemans; Pepper Adams (*bs*); Kenny Drew (*p*); Wilbur Ware (*b*); Arthur Taylor (*d*).

**** **Live** Polydor 831694 CD
Thielemans; Wim Overgaauw, Joop Scholten (*g*); Rob Franken (*electric p*); Victor Kaihatu, Rob Langereis (*b*); Bruno Castellucci (*d*); Cees Schrama (*perc*). 4/75.

*** **The Silver Collection: Toots Thielemans** Polydor 825086 CD
Thielemans; Ferdinand Povel (*ts*); Rob Franken (*ky*); Wim Overgaauw, Joop Scholten (*g*); Victor Kaihatu, Niels-Henning Ørsted-Pedersen (*b*); Bruno Castellucci, Evert Overweg (*d*); Ruud Boos Orchestra; collective personnel, other details unknown. 4/74, 4/75.

*** **Apple Dimple** Denon DC 8563 CD
Thielemans; Masahiko Sato (*ky*); Tsunehide Matsuki (*g*); Akira Okazawa (*b*); Yuchi Togashiki (*d*); Tadomi Anai (*perc*); unknown horns and strings. 11/79.

*** **Just Friends** Jazzline JL 20812 CD/LP/MC
Thielemans; Ack Van Rooyen (*flhn*); Johnny Teupen (*hp*); Paul Kuhn (*p*); Jean Warland (*b*); Bruno Castellucci (*d*). 5/86.

**** **Do Not Leave Me** Stash ST CD 12 CD
Thielemans; Fred Hersch (*p*); Marc Johnson (*b*); Joey Baron (*d*). 6/86.

**** **Only Trust Your Heart** Concord CCD 4355 CD/MC
Thielemans; Fred Hersch (*p*); Marc Johnson, Harvie Swartz (*b*); Joey Baron (*d*). 4 & 5/88.

***(*) **Footprints** Emarcy 846650 CD/MC
Thielemans; Mulgrew Miller (*p*); Rufus Reid (*b*); Lewis Nash (*d*).

Thielemans frequently finds himself in the awkward and unsatisfactory position of coming first in a category of one or consigned to 'miscellandous instruments'. Though ubiquitous in the blues, the harmonica has made remarkably little impact in jazz, and there are no recognized critical standards for his extraordinary facility as a whistler. Thielemans's pop and movie work has tended further to downgrade his very considerable jazz credentials. Surprisingly, to those who know him primarily as a performer of moodily atmospheric soundtrack pieces (*Midnight Cowboy* pre-eminently) or as composer of the undemanding 'Bluesette' (included in *The Silver Collection*), his roots are in bebop and in the kind of harmonically liberated improvisation associated with John Coltrane. That's perhaps most obvious in the dark, Chicago-influenced sound of *Man Bites Harmonica* (which includes a wonderful 'Don't Blame Me') and on the very recent *Only Trust Your Heart* and *Footprints*, which mark a considerable revival of Thieleman's jazz playing.

Born in Belgium, he was originally an accordionist and harmonica player but was sufficiently moved by hearing Django Reinhardt play that he added guitar to his repertoire, and he continues to play it. There are good solo performances of 'Muskrat Ramble', 'The Mooche' and a slightly off-beam 'You're My Blues Machine' on *The Silver Collection*, a useful sample which establishes his bop *bona fides* with 'My Little Suede Shoes' and is marred only by a set of rather dreary band arrangements by Bos. There's no real overlap with *Live* which appears to confirm a long-standing belief that Thielemans is not a successful studio performer but needs the resistance and charge of a live audience. There's certainly something rather overprogrammed about the Japanese sessions on *Apple Dimple*. Haunting versions of 'Harlem Nocturne' and the movie themes 'Looking For Mr Goodbar' and 'Midnight Cowboy' are marred by deep-pile arrangements and a high-tech gloss that don't suit Thielemans's honest and straightforward approach. *Just Friends* is better, but the choice of material (including yet another 'Days Of Wine And Roses') is dull; no one should be put off by the unusual instrumentation, though.

A studio jazz recording by Thielemans is now a rarity, but *Only Trust Your Heart* is his masterpiece. His playing, restricted on this occasion to harmonica, is superb. The choice of material (and Fred Hersch's arranging) is impeccable and challenging and the production first rate, with Thielemans front and centre and the band spread out very evenly behind him. The set kicks off with a marvellous reading of Wayne Shorter's 'Speak No Evil', includes 'Sophisticated Lady', Monk's 'Little Rootie Tootie' and Thad Jones's 'Three And One', transposed unfamiliarly high to bring it within the range of Thielemann's instrument, which takes on the slightly yodelling timbre of soprano saxophone.

It's by no means an MOR or easy-listening set. Thielemans's solo development merits the closest attention, particularly on the original 'Sarabande', the better of two duets with Hersch. The pianist's other composition, 'Rain Waltz', merits wider distribution. Allegedly nearly all first takes, each of the dozen tracks represents Thielemans's undervalued art at its finest.

Do Not Leave Me was recorded in Brussels a year or two earlier and has all the qualities of a sentimental homecoming. The opening 'Ne Me Quitte Pas', by Jacques Brel, another native of the city, is drenched with emotion. 'Stardust' is dedicated to Benny Goodman, who had died a few days previously. It follows a long medleyed version of Miles Davis's 'All Blues' and 'Blue 'N' Green', the latter co-written with Bill Evans. Thielemans had played with the pianist in 1978, at which session he met Marc Johnson. 'Autumn Leaves' is a bass and drums feature, with an astonishing solo from Baron that brings up the temperature for a the samba rhythms of 'Velas', which Thielemans takes on guitar. A fine set closes with 'Bluesette', which he calls his 'calling card or, better yet, social security number'. Everyone whistles along.

ED THIGPEN (born 1930)
DRUMS

***   **Easy Flight** Reckless RR 9902 CD
        Thigpen; Tony Purrone (*g*); Johnny O'Neal (*p*): Marlene Rosenberg (*b*). 11/89.

Ed Thigpen (whose father Ben was a stalwart of Andy Kirk's much-travelled Clouds of Joy) has always been an easy-swinging drummer of great competence and minimum pretension. He's heard to great effect on a surprisingly effective compilation called *Explosive Drums* (Black & Blue 59.080 CD) in a trio with Gerald Wiggins and Major Holley, but is probably best sampled in more depth on Teddy Edwards's and Howard McGhee's marvellous *Together Again!* (Original Jazz Classics OJC 424 CD/LP) as well as on a host of Ella Fitzgerald and Oscar Peterson records.

Easy Flight gives only a muted and rather unappealing impression of his normally buoyant style. The band, however professional, clearly aren't entirely at ease with the material, and the sound is ludicrously top-heavy. 'Chelsea Bridge' and the 1960s shibboleth, 'Freedom Jazz Dance', are worth hearing, though, for the leader's tight and almost melodic figures.

***   **Mr Taste** Justin Time JUST 43-2 CD
        Thigpen; Tony Purrone (*g*); Mads Vinding (*b*). 4 & 7/91.

An astonishingly varied and adventurous session by a master percussionist. Drummer-led trios are often less than tuneful, but Thigpen plays very musically and lets a group sound develop naturally over a dozen mostly blues-based numbers that also touch on samba rhythms, Max Roach style 3/4 ballads and, remarkably, near-abstraction. 'Round Midnight' is one of the oddest versions ever, taken at a furious clip, rhythmically much denser than usual and marked by the sound of a pedal-tunable tom-toms. On 'Some Time Ago', one of the waltzes, and Thomas Clausen's 'You Name It', he uses brushes to great effect. Purrone isn't the most exciting soloist but like Vinding is a fine group player, who works well in tightly structured ensembles. His work on Charlie Parker's little covered 'Dewey Square' is exemplary.

JESPER THILO
TENOR SAXOPHONE

(*)   **Swingin' Friends Storyville SLP 4065 LP
Thilo; Kenny Drew (*p*); Mads Vinding (*b*); Billy Hart (*d*). 12/80.

***   **Jesper Thilo Quintet Featuring Harry Edison** Storyville SLP 4120 CD/LP
Thilo; Harry Edison (*t*); Ole Kock Hansen (*p*); Ole Ousen (*g*); Jesper Lundgaard (*b*);
Svend Erik Norregaard (*d*). 2/86.

(*)   **Shufflin' Music Mecca CD 1015 2 CD
Thilo; Ole Kock Hansen, Søren Kristiansen (*p*); Henrik Bay (*g*); Jesper Lundgaard,
Hugo Rasmussen (*b*); Svend-Erik Nørregaard (*d*); Ann Farholt (*v*). 9/90.

Thilo plays the kind of straight-ahead swing that the Scandinavians have now virtually patented.
There's a tranquillizing predictability about his solo development, an untroubled *déjà vu* that
has him play exactly the sequence of notes you were expecting. The set with Edison would be by
far the more impressive were it not for the dullness of the accompaniments; however, the
trumpeter does kick-start 'There Will Never Be Another You' and there are some graceful
moments on a romantic medley recorded on a later – and better – night. Nice, but not much
more than nice. *Sufflin'* is very much in the same vein, a professional club set that doesn't really
bear frequent repetition at home. The bebop flourishes on 'How High The Moon', with Ann
Farholt's rather strained voice acting as second horn, are quite dramatic, and there are enough
imaginative flourishes on a long roster of standards to sustain interest; but, again, nothing to
write home about.

GARY THOMAS
TENOR SAXOPHONE, FLUTE

***   **Seventh Quadrant** Enja 5047 CD/LP
Thomas; Paul Bollenback (*g, syn*); Renee Rosnes (*p*); Anthony Cox (*b*); Jeff Tain
Watts (*d*). 4/87.

(*)   **Code Violations Enja 5085 CD/LP
Thomas; Paul Bollenback (*g, syn*); Tim Murphy (*p, ky*); Anthony Cox, Geoff Harper
(*b*); Dennis Chambers, Steve Williams (*d*). 7/88.

***   **By Any Means Necessary** JMT 834432 CD/LP/MC
Thomas; Geri Allen, Tim Murphy (*p, syn*); Anthony Cox (*b*); Dennis Chambers (*d*);
Nana Vasconcelos (perc). 5/89.

***   **While The Gate Is Open** JMT 834439 CD
Thomas; Kevin Eubanks (g); Renee Rosnes (*p, syn*); Anthony Cox, Dave Holland (*b*);
Dennis Chambers (*d*). 5/90.

(*)   **The Kold Kage JMT 849151 CD
Thomas; Kevin Eubanks (*g*); Paul Bollenback (*g, syn*); Mulgrew Miller (*p*); Michael
Caine, Tim Murphy (*p, syn*); Anthony Perkins (*syn*); Anthony Cox (*b*); Dennis
Chambers (*d*); Steve Moss (*perc*); Joe Wesson (*v*). 3, 5 & 6/91.

Thomas comes on very much like a latter-day Wayne Shorter. He has the same acidulous tone
and preference for enigmatic and occasionally gnomic phraseology, but with little of the overall
structural awareness that saves funk grooves from sounding stuck. Growing up in a musical
environment required to prove itself not primarily on standards, he makes an impressive fist of
half a dozen well-worn themes on the untypical *While The Gate Is Open*. His work with Seventh
Quadrant is more directly funk-based than Steve Coleman's with Five Elements and is inclined
to lapse into dim, Miles-influenced abstractions that have none of his former boss's taste and
grasp of theatricals. Purchasers of the disappointing *Kold Kage* are warned to be careful if
listening to the opening 'Threshhold' while driving; one suspects that this is precisely where
Thomas's later recordings will have their biggest market impact, as urban-freeway soundtracks.
　The original *Seventh Quadrant* suggested an imagination aligned to Shorter's quasi-mystical
side (in the manner of his *Ju-Ju* and *Odyssey of Iska*), but this gave way on the poor,
over-produced *Code Violations* to a programme of black urban sc-fi (titles such as 'Maxthink',

'Traf', 'Zylog', 'Sybase', 'Adax') that falls victim to its own insufficiently worked-out premisses. This is the manner, too, of *Kold Kage*, in which Thomas adds raps to a flagging funk manner that is only streety in a dilettante, 33rd floor way.

Though it's not clear whether *By Any Means Necessary* is intended to access political sensibilities not directly evident on the other records (the title was a slogan of Malcolm X), there is a directness to both conception and production that allows two keyboard players to work together effectively and without taking each other's turf. It restores the virtues of 'Foresight, Preparation And Subterfuge', 'No' and 'The Eternal Present' on the first album. Thomas's palpable hurry to touch all the bases has probably diluted his first few records. He is, though, an extremely talented younger generation player whose main impact is yet to come.

LUTHER THOMAS
ALTO SAXOPHONE, VOICE

(*)   **Yo'Momma Moers Music 01088 LP
Thomas; Frank Cruz, John K. Mulkerin (*t*); Marvin Neal (*tb*); Billy Paterson (*g, v*); Ronald Muldrow (*g*); Stanley Banks (*b*); Warren Dengel Benbow (*d*); Steve Kron (*perc*); Flame Braithwaite, Rickie Arlita Byars (*v*); Clement Cann, Carol Edwards, Axel Markens, L. C. Petty (*handclaps*). 5/81.

Not quite as banal as it may sound. Thomas's Dizzazz band turn out vibrant, rootsy jazz-funk with a sound that falls between that of the St Louis Creative Ensemble (of which he is a member) and a second-generation Art Ensemble of Chicago. Disappointingly, the sound really isn't up to the music, with terrible loss of resolution on the rather good brasses. Extra percussion is provided by The Claps. They're perfectly audible.

RENÉ THOMAS (1927–75)
GUITAR

****   **Guitar Groove** Original Jazz Classics OJC 1725 LP
Thomas; J. R. Monterose (*ts*); Hod O'Brien (*p*); Teddy Kotick (*b*); Albert Heath (*d*). 9/60.

***(*)   **Blue Note, Paris, 1964** Royal RJD 512 CD
Thomas; Pony Poindexter (*as, ss, v*); George Arvanitas (*p*); Michel Gaudry, George Lucas (*b*); Michel Delaporte, Jean-Louis Viale (*d*). 10/64.

A fatal heart attack cut short a career that was already rather overshadowed by a more colourful and charismatic guitarist, Thomas's Belgian compatriot, Django Reinhardt. Though Django must have been the unavoidable comparison when Thomas moved to North America – he spent some time in Canada in addition to New York – there really wasn't very much in common between them and Thomas's modernist credentials allowed him to fit into the American scene more comfortably than his illustrious predecessor.

Guitar Groove is a fine product of his American sojourn and is one of the high points of a poorly documented career. The original 'Spontaneous Effort' combines firm boppish melody with an easy swing. Monterose is too raw-throated for 'Milestones' but slots into 'Ruby My Dear' with impressive ease. He sits out for 'Like Someone In Love' and O'Brien joins him on the bench for the duration of 'How Long Has This Been Going On'. The sound is better balanced on these tracks than when the horn is present, but overall it sounds very good indeed.

The French sessions are by no means as impressive, though Thomas's personal contributions are impeccable. Pony Poindexter's vocal contributions are an irritation, but he plays convincing bop on 'Au Privave' and 'Marmaduke', switching to soprano for some tracks. Thomas alternates sharp thematic statements with octave runs that somehow manage to avoid the predictability that had crept into Wes Montgomery's playing of the time. An underrated talent, he's not easy to collect on record, but the earlier of these is at least representative of his gifts.

BARBARA THOMPSON (born 1944)
SAXOPHONES, FLUTES, SOPRANINO RECORDER, KEYBOARDS

*** **Mother Earth** VeraBra CDVBR 2005 CD/LP
Thompson; Anthony Oldridge (*vn, electric vn*); Colin Dudman (*ky*); Dill Katz (*b*); Jon Hiseman (*d, perc*). 82.

(*) **Shadow Show VeraBra No 10 CD
Thompson; Rod Argent (*ky, v*); David Sancious (*syn*); Clem Clempson (*g*); John Mole (*b*); Jon Hiseman (*d, perc*); Gary Kettel (*perc*). 83.

(*) **Pure Fantasy VeraBra No 8 CD
Thompson; Rod Dorothy (*electric vn*); Bill Worrall (*ky*); Dave Ball (*b*); Jon Hiseman (*d, perc*). 1/84.

***(*) **Heavenly Bodies** VeraBra CDVBR 2015 CD/LP
Thompson; Guy Barker, Stuart Brooks, John Thirkell (*t*); Bill Geldard (*btb*); David Cullen, Pete Lemer, Steve Melling (*ky*); Paul Dunne (*g*); Dave Ball, Andy Paak (*b*); Rod Dorothy, Patrick Halling, Robin Williams (*vn*); Tony Harris (*vla*); Quentin Williams (*clo*); Jon Hiseman (*d, perc*). 8/86.

*** **A Cry From The Heart** VeraBra CDVBR 2021 CD/2LP
Thompson; Paul Dunne (*g*); Pete Lemer (*ky*); Phil Mulford (*b*); Jon Hiseman (*d, perc*). 11/87.

***(*) **Breathless** VeraBra CDVBR 2057 CD
Thompson; Pete Lemer (*ky*); Malcolm Macfarlane (*g*); Jon Hiseman (*d*). 90.

(*) **Songs From The Center Of The Earth Black Sun 15014 CD
Thompson solo. 8/90.

An astonishingly talented multi-instrumentalist, Thompson encompasses straight-ahead jazz, rock and fusion but incorporates an interest in ethnic, formal and (on her atmospheric *Songs From The Center Of The Earth*) elements of ambient and 'New Age' music. She is difficult to categorize and has therefore rarely received the critical attention she merits (though in 1979 an hour-long television documentary was devoted to her and her drummer husband, whom she met in 1965 while both were playing with the New Jazz Orchestra). Thompson is a forceful soloist who regularly introduces unusual harmonic juxtapositions by playing two instruments simultaneously, a device associated with Roland Kirk but perhaps borrowed from fellow-Briton, Dick Heckstall-Smith.

Thompson's band, Paraphernalia, has never perhaps been as effective in the studio as in a live setting. Earlier recordings such as *Mother Earth* and *Pure Fantasy* (originally released in Britain on her own Temple Music label) demonstrate her facility for synthesis of quite eclectic materials. The earlier combines quite orthodox jazz structures (albeit influenced by rock) with an underlying formal 'programme' that conforms thematically to her concern with quasi-theosophical connections between human beings and the planet they inhabit. This is done most effectively on *Heavenly Bodies*, her best currently available record, in which the musical surface and the improvisational logic are both much more highly developed. *Pure Fantasy* is largely drawn from one of Thompson's ambitious large-scale compositions, *In Search Of Serendip*, and derives much of its material from Singhalese folk music; it also features her facility on sopranino recorder, of which she is one of the very few serious exponents in jazz.

Shadow Show is the most rock-based of her current records. Like the more successful (but now deleted) *Ghosts*, it features her work with keyboardist Rod Argent, whose larger-scale compositions for his progressive rock band, Argent, are strongly reminiscent of Thompson's own. At the opposte extreme in performance, though drawing on the same folk and traditional materials, is the unaccompanied *Songs From The Center Of The Earth*. Recorded in the extraordinary acoustic of the Abbey de Thoronet in Provence, these 14 pieces have a meditative and almost ritual character that occasionally belies their this-worldly character. Impressive as it is, one still misses the excellent solo performances on the long-deleted *Lady Saxophone*.

Breathless, though, more than makes up for the gap. A fine balance of bop and funk energies, it contains some of her best solo work for years, notably on 'Jaunty' and 'Cheeky'. 'Sax Rap' starts well and fades, but 'Gracey' (her middle name) is a brilliantly conceived and surprisingly abstract composition. Thompson gives the band plenty of room to develop their own ideas, but her democratic instincts may have led her to drop her own increasingly distinctive voice back too far in the mix. She has a lot to be upfront about.

SIR CHARLES THOMPSON (born 1918)
PIANO, ORGAN

[**(*)   **Midnight Shows: Volume 8** Black & Blue 193582 CD]
Thompson; George Duvivier (*b*); Sam Woodyard (*d*). 11/77.

The Basie-influenced composer of 'Robbin's Nest' shows up rather poorly in the current catalogue. If he's known at all to younger fans, it's for his appearance on *Charlie Parker At Storyville* (Blue Note 785108 CD), which is by no means typical of his work. The Black & Blue is paired with a club session from Illinois Jacquet. Only three tracks: 'Georgia', 'Rockin' Chair' and a pleasant 'Stella By Starlight'. Thompson doubles on organ. The sound is agreeably rich for a live recording, but it's probably better to hope for the speedy return of *Portrait Of A Piano* [Sackville 3037 LP].

DANNY THOMPSON (born 1939)
DOUBLE BASS

****   **Whatever** Hannibal HNCD 1326 CD
Thompson; Paul Dunmall (*ts, ss, bs, cl;* on *Next*); Tony Roberts (*ts, ss, af, bf, Northumbrian pipes*); Bernie Holland (*g*). 88.

***   **Whatever Next** Antilles ANCD 8743 CD/LP
As above. 89.

***   **Elemental** Antilles ANCD 8753 CD/LP
Thompson; as above, except that John Etheridge replaces Holland, and add: Henry Lowther, Derek Watkins (*t*); Chris Pyne (*tb*); Alan Skidmore (*ss*); Stan Tracey (*p*); Kevin Dempsey (*g*); Maire Na Chathasaigh (*Irish hp*); Paul Brooke, Tony Levin (*d*); Gary Kettel (*perc*). 90.

Thompson came to wider attention as a member of Pentangle, a highly successful folk–rock group that set higher-than-average store by musicianship and which included (presumably at Thompson's behest) a version of fellow-bassist Charles Mingus's 'Goodbye Pork Pie Hat' in its act. On its demise, Thompson disappeared into session work and, until the formation of the highly original jazz-ethnic fusion group, Whatever, was most closely associated with the singer and guitarist, John Martyn, to whom 'Wildfinger' on *Whatever Next* is dedicated. Thompson was, though, also associated with the free jazz movement and is an improviser of greater range than is evident from his rock work. His bass playing is reminiscent of Charlie Haden's; Thompson prefers to explore the lower end of his range and, though he can play with explosive, percussive intensity, he prefers to hold long notes (played either pizzicato or arco) and and delve into their overtones.

Whatever perform a music compounded of elements of jazz, rock, traditional English and Middle Eastern idioms. The native British elements are perhaps foremost on *Whatever Next*, the band's second and least successful record. Three of the tracks are based on traditional themes and rhythms, often exploiting drones (but conveyed without a drummer), from which the two saxophonists derive most of their solo material. Dunmall, also a member of Spirit Level and of the as-yet-unrecorded Mujician, is perhaps the more impressive, but Roberts's multi-instrumentalism gives the music considerable range. Its predecessor, one of the most intriguing group debuts in British music of the 1980s, puts together its sources in a way that is quite irreducible. Though virtually none of the material is strictly jazz-derived, it has a free-flowing, improvisational surface and a strong emotional impact.

On *Elemental*, Thompson marshals a much wider instrumental spectrum and, in many regards, a more conventional sound, augmenting the basic quartet (in which Etheridge replaces Holland) with a large ensemble and, on 'Fair Isle Friends', uncredited strings. However, his distribution of voices is highly varied and consistently imaginative. 'Fair Isle Friends' and 'Searchin'' have some rather bland, movie soundtrack elements, but 'Women In War' and the whirling 'Beirut' are forceful performances and the long 'Musing Mingus', featuring veteran

British pianist Stan Tracey and the Coltrane-influenced approach of Alan Skidmore, is Thompson's most significant composition to date. The choral underpinnings to 'Freedom' are atmospheric but do little more than paper over the cracks in its three-part structure. New member Etheridge performs superbly, adding a distinctive bottleneck guitar part to 'Women In War'.

Uncategorizable, and well worth investigating.

LUCKY THOMPSON (born 1924)
TENOR SAXOPHONE, SOPRANO SAXOPHONE

****   **Accent On Tenor Sax** Fresh Sound FSCD 2001 CD
       Thompson; Ernie Royal (*t*); Jimmy Hamilton (*cl*); Earl Knight, Billy Taylor (*p*);
       Sidney Gross (*g*); Oscar Pettiford (*b*); Osie Johnson (*d*). 54.

****   **Lucky Strikes** Original Jazz Classics OJC 194 CD/LP
       Thompson; Hank Jones (*p*); Richard Davis (*b*); Connie Kay (*d*). 9/64.

[***   **Live In Switzerland 1968/9** Jazz Helvet JH 03 CD]
       Thompson; Buddy Tate (*ts*); Geo Voumard (*p*); Milt Buckner (*org*); Bob Jacquillard
       (*b*); Walter Bishop, Stuff Combe (*d*). 9/68, 9/69.

***(*)   **Lucky Thompson** LRC CDC 9029 CD
       Thompson; Cedar Walton (*p, electric p*); Sam Jones, Larry Ridley (*b*); Billy Higgins
       (*d*).

Thompson's disappearance from the jazz scene in the 1970s was only the latest (but apparently the last) of a highly intermittent career. He recorded with Charlie Parker just after the war (a rare example of that chimera, the bebop tenor player), but then returned to his native Detroit, where he became involved in R&B and publishing. Like Don Byas, whom he most resembles in tone and in his development of solos, he has a slightly oblique and uneasy stance on bop, cleaving to a kind of accelerated swing idiom with a distinctive 'snap' to his softly enunciated phrases and an advanced harmonic language that occasionally moves into areas of surprising freedom.

There is some good 1947 material included on *Esquire's All-American Hot Jazz Sessions* (RCA NL 86757 CD/LP/MC), but his best performances as leader are on the *Accent On Tenor Sax* and *Lucky Strikes*, where his partners are first rate. Thompson's rich, driving style coaxes some astonishing playing out of Jimmy Hamilton, who contributes 'Mr E-Z' to the session. Thompson's tenor has a smooth, clarinet quality on 'Where Or When', gliding over the changes with total ease. Though very far back in the mix, Pettiford and Johnson play superbly and the bassist checks in with one fine composition, 'Kamman's A'Comin''. For the last four tracks, including a superb 'Mood Indigo', Ernie Royal comes in on trumpet and Earl Knight replaces the guesting Billy Taylor.

Lucky Strikes is tighter and more precise. In the meantime, Thompson had made significant bounds in his understanding of harmonic theory, and he attempts transitions that would have been quite alien to him a decade earlier. All his characteristic virtues of tone and smooth development are in place, though. He subtly blurs the melodic surface of 'In A Sentimental Mood' (a curious opener) and adjusts his tone significantly for the intriguing 'Reminiscent', 'Midnite Oil' and 'Prey Loot'. The Swiss concert material is far more conventional, perhaps in deference to the ticket office, but more probably because the group is so stiffly unswinging. The undated and annoyingly unannotated LRC CD, which comes from a catalogue of classic material produced by Sonny Lester, develops Thompson's soprano work considerably, confirming its significance within his output. Apart from the brief opening 'Home Come'n', the overall impression is of soft, soul-tinged late-night jazz, but there is considerable sophistication even on the superficially undemanding 'Tea Time' and 'Sun Out', both soprano tracks. The former gives a first taste of Cedar Walton's subtly modulated electric piano voicings (he even manages a tinkling celeste-like opening to 'Then Soul Walked In' before switching back to an acoustic instrument).

Thompson has something of a cult following, but is still known to the average modern jazz fan only for a walk-on in the Parker discography. He's well worth investigating more closely.

HENRY THREADGILL (born 1944)
ALTO SAXOPHONE, TENOR SAXOPHONE, CLARINET, BASS FLUTE

***   **You Know The Number** RCA PL 83013 LP
Threadgill; Rasul Siddik (*t*); Frank Lacy (*tb*); Diedre Murray (*clo*); Fred Hopkins (*b*); Pheeroan AkLaff, Reggie Nicholson (*d, perc*). 10/86.

***   **Easily Slip Into Another World** RCA PD 83025 CD/LP
Threadgill; Rasul Siddik (*t*); Frank Lacy (*tb, flhn, frhn*); Diedre Murray (*clo*); Fred Hopkins (*b*); Pheeroan AkLaff, Reggie Nicholson (*d*); Asha Putli (*v*). 9/87.

***(*)   **Rag, Bush And All** RCA PD 83052 CD/LP/MC
Threadgill; Ted Daniels (*t, flhn*); Bill Lowe (*btb*); Diedre Murray (*clo*); Fred Hopkins (*b*); Newman Baker, Reggie Nicholson (*d, perc*). 12/88.

***(*)   **Spirit Of Nuff . . . Nuff** Black Saint 120134 CD/LP
Threadgill; Curtis Fowlkes (*tb*); Edwin Rodriguez, Marcus Rojas (*tba*); Masuhjaa, Brandon Ross (*g*); Gene Lake (*d*). 11/90.

The free-for-all theatricality of the Art Ensemble of Chicago was out of favour in the more hidebound 1980s, subordinated to a revival of interest in form. Classically trained and an inventive composer, Threadgill did sterling service with Air, another of the Chicago groups to emerge out of the legendary AACM proving ground, and one distinguished by a strong interest in early jazz and its procedures.

In line with that, Threadgill is not an effusive soloist, putting much greater emphasis on often very unusual ensemble arrangements that have gradually eroded the conventional triumvirate of lead, harmony and rhythm instruments. Threadgill habitually uses low brasses (sometimes instead of string bass, as in the earliest jazz groups), twinned drummers (and, more recently, electric guitarists, in the manner of Ornette Coleman's Prime Time), and he has regularly used Diedre Murray's highly effective cello.

The earliest two of the currently available albums still betray their AACM derivation. The sound is 'democratic', matted and slightly chaotic, though some of the fault for that lies in the production, since Threadgill's arrangements are admirably open-textured. It is, though, hard to imagine him working precisely in the manner of 'Bermuda Blues' or 'Black Hands Bejewelled' again. *Rag, Bush And All* still stands out as one of the finest albums of the later 1980s. Uncategorizable, but marked throughout by Threadgill's distinctive tonal, timbral and rhythmic devices, it shifts the emphasis away from smaller-scale blowing tunes to generously proportioned themes which gradually reveal, as on the opening 'Off The Rag' and the long concluding 'Sweet Holy Rag', a firm structural logic. Daniels is also a more interesting player than Siddik.

Threadgill's Very Very Circus appears to be the culmination of a cycle in his work. *Spirit of Nuff . . . Nuff* (his titles are nothing if not enigmatic) deploys the band in a way that recalls 1960s experiments with structures and free improvisation, but with far more discipline. Threadgill's writing has been quite muted in emotional timbre and 'Unrealistic Love', in which Threadgill's solo is announced by a long guitar passage, is typical. The arrangements on 'First Church Of This' (on which he plays flute) and 'Driving You Slow And Crazy' (which opens with a fractured chorale from the brasses) are consistently inventive, but it's increasingly clear that Threadgill, like Anthony Braxton, has now almost reached the limits of what he can do with a more or less conventional jazz instrumentation. It will be interesting to see whether he is able to develop a new instrumental idiom or whether he will choose – or be forced – to remain within the conventions.

THE THREE SOUNDS
GROUP

***   **Babe's Blues** Blue Note 784434 CD
Gene Harris (*p*); Andrew Simpkins (*b*); Bill Dowdy (*d*). 8/61, 3/62.

Sole survivor of the Sounds' Blue Note output, and in many respects one of the most appealing. Harris's firm swing and two-handed approach propels the trio through an uncomplicate set of standards and repertoire pieces. Outstanding among them are 'Shiny Stockings' (listen for

Dowdy's softly placed accents) and a marvellous 'Stairway To The Stars'. Still worth looking out for are *Introducing* [Blue Note CDP 746531 CD] and *Here We Come* [Blue Note BST 84008 LP], both of which embody the group's uncluttered professionalism and easy melodic invention.

STEVE TIBBETTS
GUITAR, MANDOLIN, SITAR, KEYBOARDS, KALIMBA

***   **Northern Song** ECM 1218 CD/LP
      Tibbetts; Marc Anderson (*perc*). 10/81.

***   **Bye Bye Safe Journey** ECM 1355 CD/LP
      Tibbetts; Bob Hughes (*b*); Marc Anderson, Steve Cochrane, Tim Wienhold (*perc*). 83.

***   **Yr** ECM 1355 CD/LP
      As above. 80.

***   **Big Map Idea** ECM 1380 CD/LP
      Tibbetts; Michelle Kinney (*clo*); Marc Anderson, Marcus Wise (*perc*). 87–88.

Steve Tibbetts and Marc Anderson are Minnesota-based musicians whose methodical, dreamy patchworks of guitars and percussion are surprisingly invigorating, taken a record at a time. Tibbetts's favourite device is to lay long, skirling electric solos over a bed of congas and acoustic guitars; at its best, the music attains a genuinely mesmeric quality. While their pieces are mostly short in duration, an interview included in the notes to *Big Map Idea* reveals that many are excerpts from much longer jamming situations, and Tibbetts's self-deprecating stance – 'When I tape four hours of sound, only ten minutes have any potential, and only 30 seconds ends up being used' – is refreshing. Anderson is clearly as important an influence in the music, and his pattering, insinuating rhythms are an appealing change from the usual indiscriminate throb of world-music situations. *Bye Bye Safe Journey* is perhaps the best of these albums: Tibbetts plays at his most forceful, and there's very little slack in the music. 'Running', which features the ingenious use of a tape of a child running, shows how inventively Tibbetts can use found sound. *Yr* is a reissue of his first album, previously available on an independent label, and *Northern Song* is a bit too quiet and rarefied. *Big Map Idea* opens with a charming treatment of Led Zeppelin's 'Black Dog' and, although some of the tracks suggest that Tibbetts has been listening to Bill Frisell – dreaminess overtaking the rhythmic impetus at times – it suggests that he has more to explore yet. *Exploded View*, recorded in 1985–6 and another strong effort, seems to be out of the catalogue at present.

TIMELESS ALL STARS
GROUP

***   **It's Timeless** Timeless SJP 178 CD/LP
      Curtis Fuller (*tb*); Harold Land (*ts*); Bobby Hutcherson (*vib*); Cedar Walton (*p*);
      Buster Williams (*b*); Billy Higgins (*d*). 4/82.

(*)   **Timeless Heart Timeless SJP 182 CD/LP
      As above. 4/83.

This short-lived band were All Stars indeed, and their London visit at the time of the earlier session resulted in some lovely music. The records, though, are comparatively lightweight. The standards on the first record are performed with assurance rather than intensity: Hutcherson's 'My Foolish Heart' ballad feature is, for instance, better on his own *Solo/Quartet* record, and Land and Walton play with professional elegance. The originals on the second set aren't terribly uplifting: nobody was saving their best writing for this band. In many ways the star of both records is Billy Higgins, whose commitment to swinging is as consistent as always, and his sound is captured well by the recording.

BOBBY TIMMONS (1935–74)
PIANO

***(*)   **This Here Is Bobby Timmons** Original Jazz Classics OJC 104 CD/LP
Timmons; Sam Jones (*b*); Jimmy Cobb (*d*). 1/60.

****   **In Person** Original Jazz Classics OJC 364 CD/LP/MC
Timmons; Ron Carter (*b*); Albert Heath (*d*).

This Here is a pun on 'Dat Dere', Timmons's second-best-known tune, to which Oscar Brown Jr subsequently added a lyric. Timmons will for ever be remembered, though, as the composer of 'Moanin'', recorded by the Jazz Messengers in 1958 on a marvellous album of that name and a staple of live performances thereafter. *This Here* was recorded two years later, just before his second stint with Art Blakey. It features both the hit tracks; as a disc, it is probably less good value than a now deleted Milestone compilation, also called *Moanin'* [M 47031 2LP], which includes material from the January 1960 session, together with excellent tracks recorded over the next three years.

Timmons's characteristic style was a rolling, gospelly funk, perhaps longer on sheer energy than on harmonic sophistication. The live *In Person* is surprisingly restrained, though Timmons takes 'Autumn Leaves' and 'Softly, As In A Morning Sunrise' at an unfamiliar tempo. The LP features a second, briefly thematic take of 'Dat Dere', included full length on the CD as an alternative alongside a valuable 'They Didn't Believe Me'. The drummer is probably better suited to Timmons's style than Cobb, but there's nothing between Carter and Jones. Timmons's handling of more delicate material here is rather better than expected and certainly better than on *This Here*; there, 'My Funny Valentine' (also on the Milestone *Moanin'*) and 'Prelude To A Kiss' leave a lot to be desired, and the unaccompanied 'Lush Life' (a song whose subject-matter was rather close to home) is uncomfortably slewed. Traces of Bud Powell in his approach at this time slowly disappeared over the next few years. 'Sometimes I Feel Like A Motherless Child', from an August 1963 session on the Milestone *Moanin'*, is perhaps the most typical if not the best trio performance on record. The OJCs will more than suffice, though.

KEITH TIPPETT (born 1947)
PIANO, OTHER INSTRUMENTS

***(*)   **Mujician** FMP SAJ 37 LP
Tippett solo. 12/81.

***(*)   **Mujician II** FMP SAJ 55 LP
As above. 6/86.

****   **Mujician III (August Air)** FMP CD 12 CD
As above. 6/87.

Though routinely likened to Cecil Taylor (he actually *sounds* much more like Jaki Byard), Tippett is unique among contemporary piano improvisers. He shows little interest in linear or thematic development, but creates huge, athematic improvisations which juxtapose darks and lights, open-textured single-note passages and huge, triple-*f* ostinati in the lowest register. On *Mujician III*, his most accomplished work, these sustained rumbles persist so long that the mind is drawn inexorably towards tiny chinks in the darkness, like points of light in a night sky.

Tippett has always insisted that listeners should not concern themselves with *how* particular sounds are made in his performances, but absorb themselves in what he clearly sees as a highly emotional and spontaneous process in which 'technique' is not separable from the more instinctual aspects of the music. In addition to now relatively conventional practices like playing 'inside', he makes use of distinctive sound-altering devices, such as laying wood blocks and metal bars on the strings, producing zither and koto effects. Though there are similarities, this is very different from John Cage's use of 'prepared piano'. Cage's effects, once installed, are immutable; Tippett's are spontaneous and flexible.

Though he is still remembered for such quixotic projects as the 50-strong Centipede band, for whom he wrote *Septober Energy*, Tippett is still best heard as a solo and duo performer. It may turn out that the three *Mujician* albums (the word was his daughter's childish version of her father's vocation) will be regarded as among the most self-consistent and beautiful solo improvisations of the 1980s and a significant reprogramming of the language of piano. Though there are unmistakable gestures to the presence of Cecil Taylor (especially on the first album), the differences of basic conception could hardly be greater.

The long 'August Air' is one of the essential performances of the decade. Nothing else quite touches it; but the three albums do seem to draw themselves into a cycle, whose development can only be experienced and intuited, not rationalized. FMP may yet transfer the original, rather sour, vinyl recordings of *Mujician* and *Mujician II* to CD; the final volume reaches tonalities and holds decays and overtones which are completely lost on its predecessors.

*** **No Gossip** FMP SAJ 28 LP
Tippett; Louis Moholo (*d*). 3/80.

This never quite reaches the level of the duo's later partnership with saxophonist Larry Stabbins (on *Tern*, FMP SAJ 43/44), where improvisational discoveries, however urgent, are allowed time to develop and assimilate. *No Gossip* is almost hasty by comparison. To what extent that is a function of the music's liberationist programme isn't clear, but there's a discursive quality to Tippett's playing that is completely absent from his later work. Moholo is typically driving, marking his way with crisp snare accents, but lacks his usual lyrical balance.

(*) **A loose kite in a gentle wind / floating with only my / will for an anchor Ogun OGD 007/8
Tippett; Marc Charig (*c*); Nic Evans (*tb*); Elton Dean (*as, saxello*); Paul Rogers (*b*); Tony Levin (*d*). 86.

A disappointingly verbose and undisciplined performance from almost all concerned. Concentrate on the piano trio at its heart, though, and something rather stronger emerges. It may be telling that the title isn't one of Tippett's trademark *haikus* but a quote from Maya Angelou's *And The Caged Bird Sings*. Something slightly second-hand about the music, too.

*** **Couple In Spirit** Editions EG EGED 52 LP
Tippett; Julie Tippetts (*rec, zither, shaker, v*). 89.

A continutation of the free-improvisational line Tippett and his wife, the former Julie Driscoll (who has retained the final 's' her husband has dropped from his surname), began with their highly regarded group, Ovary Lodge. *Couple In Spirit* is friendlier in manner than the rather austere imagism of the earlier group, and it draws much more comfortably, as with 'Brimstone Spring Lullaby', on recognizable thematic material. However spontaneous the improvisations, it is clear that they do not begin from a blank page and that gestures are consciously layered and directed towards specific ends. 'Marching (We Shall Remember Them)' has a warlike, destructive tread that is untypical of Tippett's music, but 'Grey Mist With Yellow Waterfall Entwines Evening Turquoise' exactly reflects the quasi-pictorial style of Ovary Lodge.

*** **66 Shades Of Lipstick** Editions EG EGED 64 CD/LP/MC
Tippett; Andy Sheppard (*ts, ss*). 7/90.

A much-vaunted album that failed to deliver on the promise of Sheppard's and Tippett's long association as a duo. Perhaps inevitably, given his market cachet, the record was widely perceived as the saxophonist's, but it is clearly Tippett who gives each of the 16 tracks – 14 on LP – its coherence and direction. Sheppard often sounds as if he is embellishing and, though his soprano lines in particular are highly atmospheric, they rarely sound as if they are in gainful communication with Tippett's brusque rolls and sweeping arpeggiations. Hints of identifiable tunes keep surfacing, but it's best to hear the album as a continuous suite whose breaks are only incidental.

**** **The Dartington Concert** Editions EG 2106-2 CD
Tippett (*p* solo). 8/90.

Just when it looked as though Tippett's marvellous cycle of solo recordings was over for the time being, the best of the lot popped up. Recorded in the Great Hall at Dartington on an old brown-wood Steinway that used to belong to Paderewski, this is probably the most emotionally entire performance that Tippett has released. The recording dynamics are not all they might be, but the music is exceptional.

It begins over a very basic alternation in the right hand, which continues for some time, continually feeding harmonic information into one of Tippett's most fully realized melodic developments. The first of two furiously extended high-register trills gives way to a long dark passage that quotes Satie's 'Gymnopédies', before returning to a long trill that fibrillates like a damaged heart. It ends in darkness but with the startling sound of Tippett calling the name Dudu into the piano strings, which resonate softly in response. The performance was dedicated to the South African saxophonist Dudu Pukwana, who had died a matter of weeks before, and the haunting sound of his name seems half invocation, half blessing.

CLAUDE TISSENDIER
ALTO SAXOPHONE

(*)   **Tribute To John Kirby IDA 006 LP/MC
Tissendier; Michel Delakian (*t*); Jean Étève (*cl*); Bernard Rabaud (*p*); Pierre Yves Sorin (*b*); François Laudet (*d*). 85.

***   **Saxomania** IDA 017 CD/LP
Tissendier; François Biensan (*t*); Jean Étève (*as, cl*); Benny Carter (*as*); Nicholas Montier, Claude Braud (*ts*); Stan Laferriere (*p*); Pascal Chebel (*b*); François Laudet (*d*). 1/88.

Any contemporary performer who opens his recording contract with a tribute to John Kirby, of all musicians, is clearly worthy of a listen. Tissendier emerges on these records as a young fogey with a single-minded interest in swing-era forms and their re-creation. He makes no attempts at neo-classic revision: this is a straightforward exercise in playing old tunes as if bebop had been a mere distracting interlude. Except, of course, he's clearly aware that there *has* been other jazz, and that swing material will sound valid only if it's done with a sense of urgency. There was never anything urgent about the John Kirby Sextet, and tunes such as 'Beethoven Riffs On' and 'Bounce Of The Sugar Plum Fairy' don't sound significantly less artificial than they did the first time around, even with conspicuously committed performances. But committed the playing certainly is: Étève takes the Barney Bigard parts with fetching style, and Delakian is rather more than a revivalist. If, in the end, Tissendier doesn't make a wholly convincing case for reviving Kirby's efforts, it's still a project worth noting.

The set with his later band, Saxomania, includes Carter as a guest, and one can hardly ask for a more authoritative sound to have on hand on another programme of swing staples. Besides Carter's own 'Doozy', the material includes some unexpected choices: Ernie Wilkins's 'Stereophonic' and 'Sixteen Men Swinging', Ellington's 'B.P. Blues'. The five-sax front line assumes a rather studied richness, perhaps inescapably since they're playing repertory at all levels. But the improvisations are model statements of appropriateness and the gentle swing has the steady inevitability of a pendulum.

CAL TJADER (1925–82)
VIBES, PERCUSSION, VOCAL

(*)   **Mambo With Tjader Original Jazz Classics OJC 271 LP/MC
Tjader; Manuel Duran (*p*); Carlos Duran (*b*); Edward Rosalies, Edward Verlardi, Bernardo Verlardi (*perc*). 9/54.

***   **Tjader Plays Mambo** Original Jazz Classics OJC 274 LP/MC
As above, except add Dick Collins, John Howell, Al Porcino, Charlie Walp (*t*). 8–9/54.

(*)   **Latin Kick Original Jazz Classics OJC 642 CD/LP/MC
Tjader; Brew Moore (*ts*); Manuel Duran (*p*); Carlos Duran (*b*); Luis Miranda, Bayardo Velarde (*perc*). 56.

(*)   **Jazz At the Blackhawk Original Jazz Classics OJC 436 CD/LP/MC
Tjader: Vince Guaraldi (*p*); Gene Wright (*b*); Al Torres (*d*). 1/57.

(*)   **San Francisco Moods Original Jazz Classics OJC 277 LP/MC
Tjader; Manuel Duran (*p*); Eddie Duran (*g*); John Mosher (*b*); John Markham (*d*). 58.

**   **Latin Concert** Original Jazz Classics OJC 643 CD/LP/MC
Tjader; Vince Guaraldi (*p*); Al McKibbon (*b*); Willie Bobo, Mongo Santamaria
(*perc*); strings. 9/58.

***   **A Night At The Blackhawk** Original Jazz Classics OJC 278 LP/MC
Tjader; Joe Silva (*ts*); Vince Guaraldi (*p*); Al McKibbon (*b*); Willie Bobo, Mongo
Santamaria (*perc*). 59.

(*)   **Monterey Concerts Prestige P24026 CD/2LP
As above, except Paul Horn (*f*) and Lonnie Hewitt (*p*) replace Silva and Guaraldi.
4/59.

**   **Concert On The Campus** Original Jazz Classics OJC 279 LP/MC
Tjader; Lonnie Hewitt (*p*); Eddie Coleman (*b*); Willie Bobo, Mongo Santamaria
(*perc*). 60.

**   **Cal Tjader Plays, Mary Stallings Sings** Original Jazz Classics OJC 284 LP/MC
Tjader; Paul Horn (*f*); Lonnie Hewitt, Clare Fischer (*p*); Freddie Schreiber, Victor
Venegas (*b*); Johnny Rae (*d*); Mary Stallings (*v*).

**   **Plays Harold Arlen** Original Jazz Classics OJC 285 LP
Tjader; Buddy Motsinger, Red Mitchell, Al McKibbon (*b*); Willie Bobo, Johnny Ray
(*d*); strings. 61.

Cal Tjader was a great popularizer whose musical mind ran a lot deeper than some have allowed. As a vibes player, he was an able and not quite outstanding soloist, but his interst in Latin rhythms and their potential for blending with West Coast jazz was a genuine one, and his best records have a jaunty and informed atmosphere which denigrates neither side of the fusion. He made a lot of records, and many of them have been awarded reissue, which makes it dificult to choose particular winners. Tjader helped to break Willie Bobo and Mongo Santamaria to wider audiences, and the steps towards an almost pure salsa sound are documented on most of the records listed above. *Tjader Plays Mambo* is a fine introduction: the brief tracks seem foreshortened, and there's no chance to establish any sort of extended groove, but the simple brass charts for 'Fascinatin' Rhythm' and 'It Ain't Necessarily So' still create shivers of excitement. *Latin Kick*, which has Brew Moore guesting on tenor, is another good one, and *A Night At The Blackhawk* is a superior live session. *Jazz At The Blackhawk* is the most straight-ahead of these records, and while it's scarcely up to the level of a top-drawer Milt Jackson session, Tjader sounds at ease on standard material. *Latin Concert*, though, starts to run the formula down, and the intrusion of strings marks the inevitable move towards wallpaper which Tjader seemed shameless enough about. The later concert albums are similarly doomed to niceness and, while most have moments when the band transcends the clip-clop pace, they're sparsely rewarding at best. The album with Mary Stallings is strictly a sessionman chore for Tjader, and the big-voiced singer blows right past him. It's worth having for Richard Hadlock's astonishingly discouraging sleeve-notes, though.

(*)   **La Onda Va Bien Concord CCD 4113 CD/MC
Tjader; Roger Glenn (*f, perc*); Mark Levine (*p*); Rob Fisher (*b*); Vince Lateano (*d*);
Poncho Sanchez (*perc*). 7/79.

**   **Gozame! Pero Ya ...** Concord CCD 4133 CD/MC
As above, except add Mundell Lowe (*g*). 6/80.

***   **The Shining Sea** Concord CCD 4159 CD/MC
Tjader; Scott Hamilton (*ts*); Hank Jones (*p*); Dean Reilly (*b*); Vince Lateano (*d*).
3/81.

(*)   **A Fuego Viva Concord CCD 4176 CD/MC
Tjader; Gary Foster (*ss, as, f*); Mark Levine (*p*); Rob Fisher (*b*); Vince Lateano (*d*);
Poncho Sanchez, Ramon Banda (*perc*). 8/81.

**   **Good Vibes** Concord CCD 4247 CD/MC
As above, except omit Banda. 83.

Tjader had something of a comeback when he joined Concord, though the music wasn't very different from what he'd been doing 20 years earlier. Cleaner, crisper recording and highly schooled musicianship put a patina of class on these records, but it still emerges as high-octane muzak from track to track. *Good Vibes*, in particular, is an unseemly farewell. The best things happen on *The Shining Sea* and *A Fuego Viva*: the former introduces Hamilton, and Jones and can't really fail from that point, while Gary Foster's experience with Clare Fischer stands him in useful stead for the latter record. Too softcore for real Latin aficionados, too lightweight for a sterner jazz audience, Tjader fell between stools to the end, but, if one can take the trouble to sift through his records, there are rewards to be found.

CHARLES TOLLIVER
TRUMPET, FLUGELHORN

***(*)   **Grand Max** Black Lion BLCD 760145 CD
      Tolliver; John Hicks (*p*); Reggie Workman (*b*); Alvin Queen (*d*). 8/72.

****   **Impact** Strata East 660 51 004 CD
      Tolliver; Jon Faddis, Larry Greenwich, Virgil Jones, Richard Williams (*t*); Garnett
      Brown, John Gordon, Jack Jeffers, Kiane Zawadi (*tb*); Charles McPherson (*as*); James
      Spaulding (*as, ss, picc, f*); Harold Vick (*ts, ss, f*); Charles Davis (*bs*); Stanley Cowell
      (*p*); Clint Houston, Cecil McBee (*b*); Clifford Barbaro (*d*); Big Black, Billy Parker,
      Warren Smith (*perc*); strings. 1/75.

The particular challenge of Tolliver's music is its dramatic simplicity. In place of the complex chord sequences favoured by most composers of his generation, he favours very basic motifs, often consisting of only four or five notes, repeated in *ostinato*. It's very much harder to play inventively over such a background than where the chords offer endless permutations of 'changes', but Tolliver develops solo material apparently without limit in a highly lyrical mainstream style that recalls Clifford Brown. Nowhere is the bricks-without-straw impression more forceful than on 'Peace With Myself', one of six remarkable originals on Tolliver's 1968 solo debut, *Paper Man* [Arista Freedom AL 1002 LP] and, together with the title-track (which featured Gary Bartz), one of his finest performances.

After coming to prominence with Jackie McLean, Tolliver played with Bartz in one of Max Roach's best small groups (they recorded the still-underrated *Members Don't Git Weary* (Atlantic)), and the powerful, rhythmic 'Grand Max' is dedicated to the drummer. The big-band version on *Impact* is probably preferable for sheer excitement, but the brisk, live feel of the Black Lion gives a better representation of Tolliver's method. The trumpeter formed his Music Inc. group with Stanley Cowell in 1969. There is an earlier (but now deleted) *Impact* [Enja 2016 LP] with a superb version of the exciting title-track, but Tolliver's solo on the Strata-East is one of his most fluid, with a pronounced Spanish tinge and a typically sophisticated internal rhythm that contrasts well with the endlessly repeated basic motif.

Spaulding, Cowell and Coleman are the main soloists on the album after Tolliver. The final 'Mournin' Variations' is a beautiful, string-led feature in double time for the tenorist. *Grand Max* seems to lack some of the bite of earlier and later albums, and it might have benefited from a saxophone player of Coleman's or Bartz's skills; but it's Tolliver who occupies the foreground, a superb technician with an utterly distinctive voice. He deserves wider recognition.

TOLVAN BIG BAND
GROUP

***(*)   **Split Vision** Dragon DRLP 44 LP
      Roy Wall, Sten Ingelf, Martin Cronstrom, Lars G. Flink, Rolf Ekstrom (*t, flhn*);
      Carl-Olof Lindberg, Sven Berggren, Anders Arner, Stefan Wikstrom, Bjorn Hangsel
      (*tb*); Per Backer, Lars Strom, Helge Albin, Cennet Jonsson, Bernt Sjunnesson (*saxes,*
      f); Torbjorn Brorsson (*p*); Anders Lindvall (*g*); Per Nilsson (*b*); Lennart Gruvstedt
      (*d*). 3/82.

*** **Montreux And More** Dragon DRLP 61 LP
As above, except Anders Gustavsson, Fredrik Davidsson, Anders Bergcrantz (*t, flhn*); Mats Larsson (*tb*); Bo Stief (*b*) replace Cronstrom, Flink, Ekstrom and Nilsson. 12/83.

Under the direction of tenorman Helge Albin, this Swedish big band has made some superb records. Albin's arrangements are highly personal and colouristic: he gets a strikingly individual sound out of the reed section in particular, with extensive use of flutes in the tonal palette and a gripping demonstration of contrast with the brass. The soloists are unpredictably adventurous: on *Split Vision*, Roy Wall's flugelhorn on 'I Got It Bad And That Ain't Good' is notably restrained; Bergcrantz is as fine as ever on his two features on the live Montreux recording, and only Albin's own tenor misses the best results: he can sound a little adrift in rhythmic terms. But the arrangements are consistently fine, with countless new points made on such familiar modern pieces as Shorter's "Speak No Evil' and 'Pinocchio', Miles Davis's 'Circle', Coleman's 'Broadway Blues' and two John Scofield themes. The recording is wonderful on both sessions, with a depth of clarity that illuminates everything in the scores.

*** **Colours** Phono Suecia PSCD 47 CD
Roy Wall, Anders Gustavsson, Sten Ingelf, Fredrik Davidsson, Anders Bergcrantz (*t, flhn*); Vincent Nilsson, Olle Tull, Ola Akerman, Stefan Wikstrom (*tb*); Bjorn Hangsel (*btb*); Helge Albin (*as, f*); Per Backer (*as, syn*); Cennet Jonsson (*ss, ts, syn*); Inge Petterson (*ts*); Bernt Sjunnesson (*bs, f*); Lars Jansson (*ky*); Anders Lindvall (*g*); Lars Danielsson (*b*); Lennart Gruvstedt (*d*); Bjarne Hansen (*perc*). 12/89.

In a way, this is a disappointing set after the two Dragon albums (a third Dragon set with guest soloist Dave Liebman is currently unavailable). All 10 themes are by Albin and, while he's an interesting composer, it's his variations on other standards which are compelling on the earlier records. Some of these pieces fail to muster a genuine melodic weight. But there are still marvellous moments – the five-way saxophone rumpus on 'Gold Ochre', Danielsson's thoughtful bass pattern on 'Zinnober', the cut-and-thrust of 'Kobolt' – and Jansson and Petersson are worthy new members of the band. The recording is perhaps a shade too bright on CD.

BRUNO TOMMASO
BASS

** **Su Un Tema Di Jerome Kern** Splasc(h) HP 18 LP
Tommaso; Otello Garofoli (*flhn*); Vittorio Gennari (*as*); Bruno Palombini (*ts, cl*); Stefano Catani (*ts, f*); Valerio Galavotti (*bs, f*); Paolo Renosto (*p*); Michele Iannocone (*vib*); Augusto Mancinelli (*g*); Massimo Manzi (*d*). 4/81.

*** **Barga Jazz** Splasc(h) HP 06 LP
Tommaso; Paolo Fresu (*t, flhn*); Sergio Gistri, Marco Bartalini, Andrea Vangi, Mauro Peccioli (*t*); Mauro Malatesta, Stefano Scalzi, Toni Constantini, Luca Begonia (*tb*); Paolo Mannelli (*as, cl*); Diego Carraresi (*ss, as*); Mario Codacci (*ts*); Roberto Luccarini (*ts, f*); Enrico Ghelardi (*bs, bcl, bf*); Luca Flores (*p*); Alessandro Di Puccio (*vib*); Tommaso Lama (*g*); Lello Pareti (*b*); Alessandro Fabbri (*d*). 8/87.

While he takes an important solo role in the 1981 recording, Tommaso's main involvement here is as a composer–arranger. The earlier record is a curious set of what seem to be variations suggested by Jerome Kern's 'Yesterdays', which appears as the first track: the bassist's solo parts, which move to an extreme of arco scraping, are set against doleful minor-key musings by the ensemble. Mysterious, but not terribly interesting. The big-band set is much more engaging, with Fresu and Flores numbering among the more familiar names in what is a typically characterful modern Italian ensemble. While most of the programme is devoted to originals by Tommaso, three standards – 'Lady Be Good', 'Slap That Bass' and 'Somebody Loves me' – appear as encores.

RADKA TONEFF (1952–82)
VOCALS

***(*)   **Fairy Tales** Odin CD 03 CD
Toneff; Steve Dobrogosz (*p*). 11/79.

Radka Toneff's tragically untimely death robbed jazz of one its most stylish and emotionally involving younger singers. Apparently of gypsy extraction, Toneff had a light, sensual tone that wavered slightly in the lower register (she has some trouble with the first few phrases of 'My Funny Valentine') and often sounded better when the tempo was slightly faster than average. *Fairy Tales* is an imaginatively mixed set, with some emphasis on Fran Landesman lyrics (music by Toneff, Dobrogosz and Dudley Moore), but including 'Nature Boy', the beautiful Weill/Anderson 'Lost In The Stars', Blossom Dearie's 'Long Daddy Green', Elton John and Bernie Tapin's 'Come Down In Time'; there is even a setting (by Dobrogosz) of Emily Dickinson's poem, 'I read my sentence'. The opening 'The Moon Is A Harsh Mistress' is outstanding even by the standards of a fine set. Sad that there was to be no substantial follow-up. Toneff is much missed.

MARCELLO TONOLO
PIANO

**   **D.O.C.** Splasc(h) H 119 LP
Tonolo; Davide Boato (*t*); Pietro Tonolo (*ts*); Piero Leveratto (*b*); Alfred Cramer (*d*). 7/86.

Tonolo is a pianist of unambitious temperament. On what is basically a trio album – Boato and Pietro Tonolo appear on one track only – he develops a Bill Evans influence into something not quite personal enough to stand out. It's good, sensitive playing, but the music is gone as soon as it's over. He gives the rubbery lines of Leveratto plenty of space, but it's not until the horn players sit in that the music takes on a wider interest.

TIZIANO TONONI
DRUMS

***   **Going For The Magic** Splasc(h) HP 13 LP
Tononi; Gianluigi Trovesi (*cl, bcl*); Daniele Cavallanti (*ss, ts*); Andrew Cyrille (*d*); Maggie Nicols (*v*). 9/87.

A pretty strange meeting. Tononi's other records have found him in a more familiar timekeeping role in sundry post-bop settings, but this one seems like a passage to an altogether darker heart, though the drummer (who appears in full face-paint on the sleeve) is hardly first choice as a partner for Cyrille – even if the notes reveal that Tononi studied with the American master. The music is basically a series of rising and falling rhythm-shuffles, with Nicols, Cavallanti (side one) and Trovesi (side two) decorating in their own way. 'Life Flowing', with a sharp improvisation by Cavallanti and an overdubbed chorale by Nicols, is the most interesting piece here, and it's good to find the singer given a context to work in; but the other pieces tend to drift off to sleep. Cyrille turns in some typically grand strokes, but there's otherwise little to study on. Excellent recording, though.

SUMI TONOOKA (born 1956)
PIANO

***   **Taking Time** Candid CCD 79502 CD
Tonooka; Craig Handy (*ss, ts*); Rufus Reid (*b*); Akira Tana (*d*). 11/90.

***   **Here Comes Kai** Candid CCD 79516 CD
Tonooka; Rufus Reid (*b*); Lewis Nash (*d*). 3/91.

Sumi Tonooka made a couple of small-label albums in the 1980s to little response, but these Candid records are strong and intelligent statements. *Taking Time* has its impact dispersed a little by the presence of Handy, who plays well enough but who tends to distract from the trio, Tonooka's most productive setting. She has an assertive touch which lacks nothing in technique, but her interest in breaking up her phrasing into horn-like lines clears away a lot of the excess which many modern pianists can't resist. She writes good tunes, too: 'It Must Be Real' and 'In The Void', both from the second record, have their melodies integrated into arrangements which involve Reid and Nash closely enough to make this a real group at work. Reid, especially, responds with some of his most alert playing. Excellent sound, on the second session in particular.

MEL TORME (born 1925)
VOCAL, DRUMS

***   **A Foggy Day** Musicraft MVSCD 54 CD
          Torme; The Mel-Tones (*v*); studio orchestras. 45–47.

***   **There's No One But You** Musicraft MVSCD 60 CD
          As above. 45–47.

The young Torme's voice was honey-smooth, light, limber, ineffably romantic and boyish; and it's amazing how many of those qualities he has kept, even into old age. His tracks for Musicraft date from his bobbysoxer days, some way below Sinatra but surprisingly considered and always insistently musical: the measured look at 'It Happened In Monterey' or 'A Cottage For Sale' says much about how personally Torme regarded his art. he was already an intersting writer, too, and it's a pity that his early recording of his own 'County Fair' has been omitted from both of these CDs. The sound is sometimes almost as foggy as that day in London town, but the voice glides through.

****   **Lulu's Back In Town** Charly CD 5 CD
          Torme; Pete Candoli, Don Fagerquist (*t*); Bob Enevoldsen (*vtb*); Vince DeRosa, John Cave (*frhn*); Bud Shank (*as*); Bob Cooper, Jack Montrose (*ts*); Jack Dulong (*bs*); Marty Paich (*p*); Albert Pollan (*tba*); Red Mitchell (*vb*); Mel Lewis (*d*). 1/56.

***(*)   **Mel Torme Sings Fred Astaire** Charly CD 96 CD
          As above, except Herb Geller (*as*), Max Bennett (*b*) and Alvin Stoller (*d*) replace Shank, Cave, Mitchell and Lewis. 11/56.

***   **Live At The Crescendo** Charly CD 60 CD
          Torme; Howard McGhee, Don Fagerquist (*t*); Larry Bunker (*vib, perc*); Marty Paich (*p, acc*); Ralph Sharon (*p*); Max Bennett (*b*); Mel Lewis, Stan Levey (*d*). 56–57.

****   **Mel Torme Swings Shubert Alley** Verve 821581 CD/MC
          Torme; Al Porcino, Stu Williamson (*tb*); Frank Rosolino (*tb*); Vince DeRosa (*frhn*); Art Pepper (*as*); Bill Perkins (*ts*); Bill Hood (*bs*); Marty Paich (*p*); Red Callender (*tba*); Joe Mondragon (*b*); Mel Lewis (*d*). 1–2/60.

****   **The Ellington & Basie Songbooks** Verve 823248-2 CD
          Torme; Jack Sheldon (*t*); Frank Rosolino, Stu Williamson (*tb*); Joe Maini (*as*); Teddy Edwards (*ts*); Bill Perkins (*bs*); Jimmy Rowles (*p*); Al Hendrickson (*g*); Joe Mondragon (*b*); Shelly Manne (*d*). 12/60–2/61.

****   **Compact Jazz: Mel Torme** Verve 833282-2 CD
          Torme; Stu Williamson (*t, vtb*); Al Porcino, Jack Sheldon (*t*); Frank Rosolino (*tb*); Vince DeRosa (*frhn*); Art Pepper, Joe Maini (*as*); Teddy Edwards, Bill Perkins (*ts*); Bill Hood (*bs*); Marty Paich, Jimmy Rowles (*p*); Red Callender (*tba*); Joe Mondragon (*b*); Mel Lewis, Shelly Manne (*d*); The Mel-Tones (*v*); Wally Stott Orchestra, Tony Osborne Orchestra, Russ Garcia Orchestra. 58–61.

This is arguably Torme's greatest period on record, and these four all capture the singer in full flight. Torme's range has grown a shade tougher since his 1940s records, but his voice is also more flexible, his phrasing infinitely assured, and the essential lightness of timbre is used to suggest a unique kind of tenderness. Marty Paich's arrangements for the three studio albums are beautifully polished and rich-toned, the french horns lending a distinctive colour to ensembles which sound brassy without being metallic. There may be only a few spots for soloists – notably Fagerquist, Montrose, Cooper and Shank or Geller – but they're all made to count, in the West Coast manner of the day. The showstopper is *Swings Shubert Alley*, which is loaded with note-perfect scores from Paich and a coupe of pinnacles of sheer swing in 'Too Darn Hot' (a treatment Torme has kept in his set to this day) and 'Just In Time', as well as a definitive 'A Sleepin' Bee'. *Lulu's Back In Town* has another marvellous choice of material – familiar pieces along with choice rarities such as 'I Like To Recognize The Tune', 'I Love To Watch The Moonlight' and the wonderfully feelingful 'Keepin' Myself For You'. The Astaire collection is enlivened by Paich's search for the unexpected: 'The Way You Look Tonight' becomes a swinger rather than a ballad, and the corn of 'Let's Call The Whole Thing Off' is dispersed by the slippery rhythms which both singer and band make their way through. The Ellington/Basie set is another winner: Torme loves this material, and his own words for 'Reminiscing In Tempo' are movingly delivered, as well as the uptempo set-pieces of the order of 'I'm Gonna Go Fishin''. All the albums were superbly recorded at the time, and the transfers are fine, if no particular improvement on the vinyl. The live session picks up more of the vaudevillian traits which Torme cheerfully acknowledges as a part of his concert routines, and is that much less satisfying, but there is still some superb singing, as well as cameo parts for McGhee and Fagerquist.

The *Compact Jazz* compilation is a marvellous cross-section of Torme's work for verve, and includes at least four tracks from *Swings Shubert Alley*, as well as four numbers from sessions cut in London (including his own durable 'Christmas Song') and splendid takes on 'Sent For You Yesterday' and 'Don't Get Around Much Any More'.

***   **Round Midnight** Stash ST-CD-4 CD
Torme; Pete Candoli, Don Fagerquist, Don Rader, Joe Newman, Sonny Cohn, Flip Ricard, Al Aarons (*t*); Shorty Rogers (*flhn*); Bob Enevoldsen (*vtb*); Ken Shroyer (*bt*); Henry Coker, Benny Powell, Grover Mitchell, Urbie Green, Jerry Collins, Carl Fontana, Henry Southall (*tb*); Paul Horn (*cl, as, f*); Marshall Royal, Woody Herman (*cl, as*); Bud Shank (*as, f*); Eric Dixon, Frank Wess, Frank Foster (*as, ts*); Bob Cooper, Bob Pierson, Louis Orenstein, Sal Nistico (*ts*); Arthur Herfurt, Buddy Collette (*reeds*); Bill Hood (*bcl, bsx, tba*); Tom Anastos, Charlie Fowlkes, Jack DuLong (*bs*); Count Basie, Don Trenner, Marty Paich, Lou Levy, Nat Pierce (*p*); Allen Reuss, Freddie Greene (*g*); Verlye Mills (*hp*); Albert Pollan (*tba*); Red Mitchell, Perry Lind, Monty Budwig, Buddy Catlett, Tony Leonardi (*b*); Ronnie Zito, Sonny Payne, Mel Lewis, Larry Bunker, Benny Barth (*d*); Chester Ricord, Ralph Hansell (*perc*); Mort Lindsay Orchestra. 56–68.

Pieced together from various off-the-air recordings, this is an intriguing stroll through a dozen years of Torme's career. He plays drums with Woody Herman on 'Four Brothers', joshes through 'Lil' Darlin'' with Basie's band, and acompanies himself elsewhere on both piano and baritone ukulele. There are 27 songs here, many of them unavailable on any other Torme record, and on such as 'Don't Let That Moon Get Away' and 'Lonely Girl' the singer sounds at his most thoughtful and determined, wasting nothing in the lyrics. the sound quality is often indifferent, and there are some merely throwaway pieces, so this might be for hardened Torme collectors rather than a casual listener, but it's hard not to enjoy such a surprising set. Admirable sleevenotes by Will Friedwald.

***   **Sunday In New York** Atlantic 780078-2 CD
Torme; studio orchestras directed by Shorty Rogers, Dick Hazard and Johnny Williams. 12/63.

Not a classic Torme session but it's nice that Atlantic have kept something from his tenure with them in circulation. The tunes are all to do with New York and it's not a bad concept with 'Autumn In New York', 'Harlem Nocturne' and a charming rarity, 'There's A Broken Heart For Every Light In Broadway', in the setlist.

***   **An Evening With George Shearing And Mel Torme** Concord CCD 4190 CD/MC
Torme; George Shearing (*p*); Brian Torff (*b*). 4/82.

***   **Top Drawer** Concord CCD 4219 CD/MC
Torme; George Shearing (*p*); Don Thompson (*b*). 3/83.

***   **An Evening At Charlie's** Concord CCD 4248 CD/MC
As above, except add Donny Osborne (*d*). 10/83.

(*)   **Mel Torme–Rob McConnell And The Boss Brass Concord CCD 4306 CD/MC
Torme; Arnie Chycoski, Erich Traugott, Guido Basso, Dave Woods, John McLeod (*t, flhn*); Rob McConnell, Ian McDougall, Bob Livingston, Dave McMurdo (*tb*); Ron Hughes (*btb*); George Stimpson, James MacDonald (*frhn*); Moe Koffman (*ss, as, cl, f*); Jerry Toth (*as, cl, f*); Euegene Amaro (*ts, f*); Rick Wilkins (*ts, cl*); Robert Leonard (*bs, bcl, f*); Jimmy Dale (*p*); Ed Bickert (*g*); Steve Wallace (*b*); Jerry Fuller (*d*); Brian Leonard (*perc*). 5/86.

***   **A Vintage Year** Concord CCD 4341 CD/MC
Torme; George Shearing (*p*); John Leitham (*b*); Donny Osborne (*d*). 8/87.

***   **Reunion** Concord CCD 4382 CD/MC
Torme; Warren Luening, Jack Sheldon (*t*); Bob Enevoldsen (*vtb*); Lou McCreary (*tb*); Gary Foster (*as*); Ken Peplowski (*ts*); Bob Efford (*bs*); Pete Jolly (*p*); Jim Self (*tba*); Chuck Berghofer (*b*); Jeff Hamilton (*d*); Joe Porcaro, Efrain Toro (*perc*). 8/88.

(*)   **In Concert Tokyo Concord CCD 4382 CD/MC
As above, except add Dan Barrett (*tb*), Allen Farnham (*p*), John Von Ohlen (*d*), omit Jolly, Hamilton, Porcaro and Toro. 12/88.

***   **Night At The Concord Pavilion** Concord CCD 4433 CD/MC
Torme; John Campbell (*p*); Bob Maize (*b*); Donny Osborne (*d*); Frank Wess Orchestra. 8/90.

***   **Fujitsu–Concord Jazz Festival 1990** Concord CCD 4481 CD/MC
As above. 11/90.

**   **Mel And George Do World War Two** Concord CCD 4471 CD/MC
Torme; George Shearing (*p*); John Leitham (*b*). 90.

Torme's contract with Concord has given him the chance to record a long run of albums that should provide his final legacy as a singer. Even though most singers would be thinking about easing up at this stage, Torme's workload and enthusiasm both seem limitless. The voice has throttled back a little, and there is a greyness at the edges, but he still makes his way to high notes very sweetly and will sometimes cap a song with an extraordinary, long held note that defies the rules on senior singers.

If there's a problem with these records, it's the formulaic settings which Concord tend to encourage for some of their regulars. The duo setting with Shearing is actually a good one, since both men seem to admire each other's work to the point where some of thre sessions threaten to slip into mutual congratulations; and context is given to both Shearing's sometimes dinky playing and to Torme's romantic sweeps. Of their records together, both *Top Drawer* and *An Evening With* are splendid, and *An Evening At Charlie's* isn't far behind; but there are too many live albums here, where Torme can slip into an ingratiating showmanship and an intrusive audience distracts from what is really a close and intimate kind of jazz singing. The World War Two disc founders on the terrible material, as charmingly as the principals deal with it.

Of the other discs, the meeting with Rob McConnell's band is marred by a certain glibness on both sides; the two albums with Paich don't quite recapture their great collaborative feel of the 1950s, but *Reunion* sparkles, with a lovely 'Bossa Nova Potpourri' and a hip reading of Donald Fagen's 'The Goodbye Look'; and the two 1990 concert sessions find Torme in ebullient form, delivering a gorgeous 'Early Autumn' on *Concord Pavilion* and two equally distinctive ballads in 'Wave' and 'Star Dust' on *Fujitsu-Concord*. As long as he goes on, he still sounds terrific.

DAVID TORN
GUITARS, DRUMS, VOICE, KEYBOARDS, ELECTRONICS

***   **Best Laid Plans** ECM 1284 CD/LP
Torn; Geoffrey Gordon (*perc*). 7/84.

(*)   **Cloud About Mercury ECM 1322 CD/LP
       Torn; Mark Isham (*t, picc-t, flhn, syn*); Tony Levin (*b, syn*); Bill Bruford (*d, electric d, perc*). 3/86.

*(*)   **Door X** Windham Hill WD 1096 CD
       Torn; Chris Botti (*t*); Antony Widoff (*ky, cl*); Doug Lunn (*b*); Mick Karn (*b, bcl*); Bill Bruford, Gary Burke (*d*); Geoffrey Gordon, Kurt Wortman (*perc*); Vida Vierra (*v*). 90.

Torn has recently taken to referring to himself in lower-case, which accords rather better than he might have hoped with his Joe Ordinary populism. His early ECM work with the rather good Everyman Band (ECM 1234 LP, and the later *Without Warning*, ECM 1290 CD/LP) was acute and often beautiful, in approximately the same idiom as the first Bass Desires album or Bill Frisell's less hectic solo ventures. *Best Laid Plans*, recorded shortly before *Without Warning*, is an intelligent duo with the little-known Gordon. 'The Hum Of Its Parts', 'In The Fifth Direction' and 'Angle Of Incidents' are pleasantly abstract, with a hint of Frisell's crazed Nashville in the guitar parts.

    Cloud About Mercury is rather more arch (one wonders what New York No-Waver Arto Lindsay might have made of the same material) and slightly overpowered by its own technology. Bruford is one of the few men around to make Simmons drums sound as resonantly natural as conventional skins, and he and Levin create a densely interlocked background for some inconsequentially impressionistic figures from the two front men. Isham is never less than pretty and has a fine instinct for atmospheric effects, but one always feels a need for images to accompany the sounds.

    The Windham Hill label has largely been associated with so-called New Age music, and *Door X* represents a further dilution of Torn's abilities. Bruford and former Japan man Karn enliven a handful of tracks, including an otherwise ponderous version of 'Voodoo Chile' but for the most part it's a stew of treatments, aptly named 'hypnodrones' and over-processed guitar. A door best left shut.

JEAN TOUSSAINT
TENOR AND SOPRANO SAXOPHONES

***   **What Goes Around** World Circuit WCD 029 CD/MC
       Toussaint; Tony Remy (*g*); Julian Joseph, Jason Rebello, Bheki Mseleku (*p*); Wayne Batchelor, Alec Dankworth (*b*); Mark Mondesir, Clifford Jarvis (*d*); Cleveland Watkiss (*v*). 9/91.

An ex-Jazz Messengers tenorman who now lives and works in London, Jean Toussaint's leadership debut is finally let down a little by its eclecticism. The various combinations of rhythm section – a clutch of contemporary British stars – are all worthwhile in themselves, but the three tracks with Joseph, Dankworth and Mondesir are concentrated and direct in a way that makes one wish Toussaint had stuck to this quartet for the entire record. He's generous in allotting solo space to others and, as a result, the impact of his own playing is diminished, but his firm tone and picked phrasing suggest a player not much interested in bluster. Two Monk tunes put his own original material in a poorer light, but the title-piece is a curt, nicely weighted theme that hangs in the mind, and only Watkiss's feature, 'Lower Bridge Level', sounds misplaced.

RALPH TOWNER (born 1940)
GUITAR, CLASSICAL GUITAR, 12-STRING GUITAR, PIANO, FRENCH HORN, SYNTHESIZER, CORNET

***(*)   **Trios / Solos** ECM 1025 CD
       Towner solo and with Paul McCandless (*ob*); Glen Moore (*b*); Collin Walcott (*tabla*). 11/72.

****   **Diary** ECM 1032 CD
       Towner solo. 4/73.

***(*)   **Solo Concert** ECM 1173 CD
       As above. 10/79.

**(*)   Blue Sun ECM 1250 CD/LP
          As above. 12/82.

Towner once told the critic Joachim Berendt that he preferred to treat the guitar 'like a piano trio'. Towner's classical interest pre-dates his involvement in jazz and his work retains many of the qualities of European chamber music, but he's by no means as unswinging as that may sound; in the same interview with Berendt he talked about his 'one-man-band approach' to solo performance.

The best measure of that philosophy is his fine *Solo Concert*, where he alternates delicate contrapuntal runs over plummy harmonics and 'Eastern' drone effects with sharp, percussive passages involving flamenco-style slaps on the sound-box. In the studio, though, as with his highly influential band, Oregon, Towner has been notably willing to use overdubs. It doesn't work on the rather perverse *Blue Sun*, Towner's least impressive record, but it succeeds admirably elsewhere. What appears to be a solitary duo on the beautiful *Trios/Solos* album actually features Moore on bass and Towner on both guitar and piano. Not usually known for playing standards or jazz repertoire, he gives a persuasive reading of Bill Evans's 'Re: Person I Knew', a tune tailor-made for his delicate approach; Miles Davis's 'Nardis', on *Solo Concert*, is also associated with Evans. On *Diary*, 'Icarus' is a highly effective overdub, but 'The Silence Of A Candle', one of the most beautiful melodies of recent times, seems to be calling out for the crisp guitar harmonics Towner brought to the piece on the Oregon album, *Music Of Another Present Era*. As a solo piano player, he is slightly thick-fingered, with too much arm-weight and not enough space around the notes, the antithesis of his qualities as a guitarist.

In solo performance, Towner has rarely attempted the level of abstraction which played a significant role on the two earliest Oregon albums and which has remained an aspect of their concert performances. 'Erg' on *Diary* is a rather brittle and glaring piece, in sharp contrast to 'Silence Of A Candle', which follows, but the most abstract and ambitious piece on *Trios/Solos* is Glen Moore's remarkable unaccompanied 'A Belt Of Asteroids'. Towner's '1×12' and 'Suite: 3×12' on the same album resemble little academic blues exercises with elements of Viennese dodecaphony thrown in. Effective, but rather slight. 'Raven's Wood' brings in McCandless for a single track, echoing the nascent Oregon sound; its nocturnal, elegiac quality looks forward to the days when the group would, once again, have to work without Collin Walcott, who guests on the opening 'Brujo'.

****   Solstice ECM 1060 CD/LP

***(*)   Sound And Shadows ECM 1095 CD/LP
          Towner; Jan Garbarek (*ts, ss, f*); Eberhard Weber (*b, clo*); Jon Christensen (*d, perc*).
          12/74, 2/77.

If Oregon was never an orthodox jazz group, this (and a guest appearance on Weather Report's *I Sing The Body Electric*) placed Towner in rhythmic contexts which suggested, if not a theme-and-solos approach, then at least a more straightforwardly jazz-orientated setting. The *Solstice* band, though, was particularly attuned to Towner's conception. The rhythm section has a high degree of autonomy and, though 'Distant Hills' on the later *Sound And Shadows* is treated very differently from the Oregon version of the same composition, it's clear that Weber and Christensen don't play merely supportive roles. 'Drifting Petals' on *Solstice* illustrates a rather sentimental streak in Towner's work (and, again, his rather stiff piano style) but Weber's 'Piscean Dance' is taut and vigorous and the bassist/cellist's highly melodic playing helps give both sets a complex contrapuntal rhythm over which Garbarek floats, sometimes plaintive, sometimes hostile.

Christensen's sensitive drumming is almost matched by Jack DeJohnette on the gentle trio, *Batik* [ECM 1121 LP], which has temporarily fallen out of favour.

***(*)   Old Friends, New Friends ECM 1153 CD/LP
          Towner; Kenny Wheeler (*t, flhn*); David Darling (*clo*); Eddie Gomez (*b*); Michael
          DiPasqua (*d, perc*). 7/79.

A curiously tentative set that, but for Kenny Wheeler's tensely lyrical passages, sounds remarkably like a watered-down version of Oregon. One can see how Jan Garbarek might have fitted into Darling's slot.

***   Slide Show ECM 1306 CD/LP
          Towner; Gary Burton (*vib, mar*). 5/85.

Matchbook, a previous record by this pairing, was credited to Gary Burton. *Slide Show* is in every respect a comedown, lacking entirely the coherence of the earlier record. The material is certainly more sophisticated but seems to get badly snagged in the awkward textures set up by vibes and 12-string guitar. Burton sounds more convincing on marimba in this context.

** **Works** ECM 823268 CD/LP
Towner; Kenny Wheeler (*t, flhn*); Jan Garbarek (*ts, f*); Eddie Gomez (*b*); Eberhard Weber (*b, clo*); David Darling (*clo*); Jon Christensen, Michael DiPasqua (*d, perc*). 74–82.

It's hard to see the rationale for this weird sample of Towner's ECM material. Nothing whatever from *Diary* or *Trios / Solos*; instead, two tracks from the weak and unrepresentative *Blue Sun*, a shapeless duo with cellist Darling from *Old Friends, New Friends*, plus another group track from that album and, making up the numbers, two of the more obvious cuts from the *Solstice* band. Neither musically compelling nor great value for money.

** **Open Letter** ECM 1462 CD/LP
Towner; Peter Erskine (*d*). 7/91.

'Volcanic' isn't a word normally applied to Ralph Towner or his playing. If the cover and title are intended as a distant echo of *Diary*, they're clearly also intended to suggest that this is a very different album. In place of the quiet seascape of the earlier album, there's a huge pall of smoky ash, dark and threatening. The addition of drums and of Towner's increasingly confident Prophet backgrounds certainly gives the music more immediate clout than the rather delicate structures of *Diary*, but repeated hearings don't tend to confirm that Towner's 'open letter' is any less inward and personal than his more private musings, and there's some evidence that Erskine's contributions were added as an afterthought; they certainly don't sound like an integral element. The turn to heaviness also begins to sound a touch contrived, with Erskine largely restricted to sombre, tymp effects (presumably using soft mallets on his tom-toms) and skitteringly unmetrical cymbal touches. Fans may regret what looks like a pointless trading-off of Towner's most distinctive qualities.

TINO TRACANNA
SOPRANO, ALTO AND TENOR SAXOPHONES

(*) **Mr Frankenstein Blues Splasc(h) H 158 LP
Tracanna; Riccardo Bianchi (*g*); Marco Micheli (*b*); Christian Meyer, Ettore Fioravanti (*d*); Naco (*perc*); Mariapia De Vito (*v*). 4/88.

*** 292 Splasc(h) H 322 CD
Tracanna; Paolo Fresu (*t, flhn*); Massimo Colombo (*ky*); Marco Micheli (*b*); Francesco Sotgiu (*d*); Naco (*perc*); Mariapia De Vito, Marti Robertson (*v*). 6/90.

Tracanna is another member of Italy's young jazz vanguard, and these two entertaining albums offer some brisk impressions of his manner. He plays tenor on the first half of *Mr Frankenstein Blues*, soprano on the second, and although he plays his solos a little carefully, his querulous tone and zigzag phrasing catch the attention. Bianchi's brittle, resonant electric guitar parts become a little tiresome over the course of the whole record, and the rest of the group scatter the initiative, but Tracanna's subversion of form – on a blues, a waltz and an oddball calypso – is unselfconsciously done.

The second record is more considered and more confidently finished. Tracanna plays soprano as his first horn here, although there's a startling, helter-skelter alto solo on 'P.F.C. Concept', and his meditations on 'Argomenti Persuasivi' and the pretty ballad 'Notti Eluse Ed Attese Deluse' (which also appears as a song delivered by De Vito) are very well done. Fresu and Colombo are also more suitable and challenging partners than Bianchi. The recording on the first disc is rather metallically bright, but the second has a warmer and more agreeable timbre.

TRINITY
GROUP

***   **Trinity** L + R 40002 LP
Hans Koller (*sax*); Roland Hanna (*p*); Attila Zoller (*g*).

No relation between this neat swing-to-modern outfit and the Ferres' string trio and album of the same name, below. Koller was one of the heroes of the European resistance to Nazism, continuing to play during the *Anschluss*. The material on *Trinity* is good and largely conditioned by Koller's enthusiasm for the Tristano school. Hanna, whose *Piano Soliloquy* sits consecutively in the L + R catalogue (40003 LP), is slightly out of place but produces intriguingly cross-grained figures on a number of tracks. Zoller is as tight and disciplined as always.

TRINITY
GROUP

***(*)   **Trinity** Steeplechase SCS 1171 LP
Boulou Ferre, Ellios Ferre (*g*); Niels-Henning Ørsted-Pedersen (*b*). 11/82.

A surprisingly modern set from this fine one-off trio, *Trinity* mixes Gillespie's 'Groovin' High', a delicate 'Out Of Nowhere', two Lee Konitz pieces, and an original 'De Moscou A Odessa'. It adds up to a set of delcate melodic interchange, with NHØP frequently taking the lead line over unison chords from the Ferres, and elsewhere showing his abilities as a soloist. Worth checking out.

THE TRIO
GROUP

***   **By Contact** Ogun OG529 LP
John Surman (*bs, ss, bcl, c*); Barre Phillips (*b*); Stu Martin (*d*). 4/71.

The Trio's first album, released on Dawn in 1969, is now a collectable rarity. There is an even rarer German festival session and an intriguing duo performance by Surman and Stu Martin, *Live At Woodstock Town Hall*, which turns up occasionally in the pricier second-hand racks. And that was pretty much it for one of the best jazz and improvisation groups working on the British and European scene, until in 1987 these unreleased tracks were belatedly put out on LP.

    By Contact lacks the taut, almost song-like progressions of *The Trio*, but gives an unequalled insight into Surman's brilliantly linear, improvisational approach at the time and his sympathetic interplay with two of the finest rhythm players of the time; Martin died suddenly in 1980, his fellow-American, Phillips, is now an established player on the European free scene. Only the opening (and weakest) track is by Surman, most of the compositional emphasis falling on the more experienced Phillips and Martin. The second side is dominated by a sequence of three pieces performed in continuous sequence. Surman plays soprano on the final, collectively improvised 'In The Round' and his bass clarinet on the beautiful 'Cant', a canticle-like theme that most strongly recalls the earlier album. On 'Noninka', though, he makes a very rare (unrepeated?) foray on cornet, sounding rather like a cross between Ornette Coleman and the British cornettist, Mark Charig. Sheer industry inertia and incomprehension meant that large amounts of fine music from this period never saw the light of day. Musically, *By Contact* probably doesn't match up to its own historical significance.

TRIO CON TROMBA
GROUP

***   **Who's Sorry Now?** Dragon DRLP LP
Jan Allan (*t*); Bengt Hallberg (*p*); Georg Riedel (*b*). 12/84.

Although it might seem rather late in their careers for these musicians to be producing some of their best work, this is jazz of a high order. Credit goes primarily to Hallberg, whose restless intelligence seems never to settle for the obvious continuation. He sets most of the tempos here – more so than Riedel, who sits out on a few tracks – and devises a number of surprising ideas: the tick-tock backdrop for 'Star Dust', a snatch of stride for 'Some Of These Days', or the ingenious improvisation in 'Time On My Hands', built with exacting logic. If the music recalls something of Ruby Braff's more chamberish dates, with Allan's cloudy tone reminiscent of the American cornetist's manner, it's not quite as salty as that: Allan sometimes fritters away a phrase when it should be delivered on the nose, and Riedel is a little stolid. But there's nothing routine or calculated here.

LENNIE TRISTANO (1919–78)
PIANO

***(*)   **First Sessions: 1949/50** Prestige P 24081 2LP
Tristano; Lee Konitz (*as*); Billy Bauer (*g*); Arnold Fishkin (*b*); Shelly Manne (*d*).

[***(*)   **Subconscious-Lee** Original Jazz Classics OJC 186 LP]
As above. 1/49.

****   **Requiem** Atlantic AMCY 1048 CD
Tristano; Lee Konitz (*as*); Peter Ind, Gene Ramey (*b*); Jeff Morton, Art Taylor (*d*).
6/55.

If Charlie Parker can be made to seem the Schoenberg of modern jazz, then Tristano is certainly its Webern; he represents its 'difficult' phase. Whereas most horn-led post-bop delved into uncomfortable psychic regions and cultivated a scouring intensity, Tristano ruthlessly purged his music of emotion, in sharp contrast to the highly expressive playing of his disciple, Bill Evans. Perhaps because his basic instruction to his horn players – the best known of whom were, of course, Lee Konitz and Warne Marsh – was that they should use a deliberately uninflected and neutral inflexion, concentrating instead on the structure of a solo, Tristano has remained a minority taste, and a rather intellectual one.

This is a pity, because Tristano's music is always vital and usually exciting. Though he abandoned the rhythmic eccentricities of bop in favour of an even background count, his playing is far from conventional, deploying long sequences of even semiquavers in subtly shifting time-signatures, adding sophisticated dissonances to quite basic chordal progressions. If his emphasis on structural rigour and technical (rather than emotional) virtuosity still alienates some listeners, there is a problem for the beginner in the nature of the Tristano discography, much of which involves indifferent live recordings and posthumously released private tapes. However, far from being the cerebral purist of legend, the blind Tristano was fascinated by every possibility of music-making and was a pioneer in studio overdubbing and in speeding up half-speed recordings to give them a cool, almost synthesized timbre.

That track was 'Requiem', perhaps the most striking single item on the 1955 Atlantic sessions. Dedicated to Charlie Parker, it further confounds an unspoken suspicion that Tristano had no feel for the blues. The pianist's experiments with multi-tracking and overdubbing were to have a profound effect on Bill Evans (notably *Conversations With Myself*) and others; here, they seem perfectly logical and quite in keeping with the tenor of the music which is not as glacial as is sometimes supposed; hear 'Turkish Mambo'.

Because Tristano regarded conventional jazz gigging with some disdain, there are few recorded 'club dates'. The second half of *Requiem* (which was originally released as *Lines*) comes from a New York City restaurant, significantly, perhaps, the Confucius, where Tristano played with a quartet fronted by his pupil, Lee Konitz. The saxophonist sounds dry and slightly prosaic on 'If I Had You' and much more like his normal self on a beautiful 'I Don't Stand A Ghost Of A Chance'. Tristano's own solos are derived, as almost always, from the refined and twice-distilled melodic code of standard material.

The *First Sessions* tracks and the near-identical *Subconscious-Lee* are not the earliest Tristano material on record – there is a 1947 track on *The Great Sessions* (Jazz Anthology 55082 CD) and 'Coolin' Off With Ulanov' from the same year is on a Verve sampler *Jazz Club: Piano* (840032 CD) – but they represent perhaps the best available sample of his remarkable powers as an improviser. 'Judy' (on both) is one of his most engaging performances, encapsulating his skill as a vertical improviser. Though an isolated figure, he blends superbly with his sidemen and, if the interplay with Bauer is less complete than on his October 1946 sessions for Keynote (see another Verve sampler, *Jazz Club: Guitar*, 840035 CD, for a fine take of 'Interlude'), it is nevertheless highly impressive.

JOHN TROPEA

GUITAR

(*) **NYC Cats Direct dmp CD 453 CD
Tropea; Lou Marini (*ss, ts, f*); Lewis Del Gatto, George Young (*ts, f*); Warren Bernhardt, Don Grolnick, Tom McFaul, Richard Tee (*ky*); David Spinozza, Jack Cavari (*g*); Anthony Jackson, Neil Jason (*b*); Steve Gadd, Alan Schwarzberg, Jimmy Maelen (*d*). 10–11/85.

There's something appealingly knowing about this session, headed by one of the super-sessionmen of the New York studio scene of the 1970s and '80s. Nothing happens that hasn't happened elsewhere, and it was probably these men who made it happen elsewhere as well; but tracks such as the opening 'Free Lunch' and 'NYC Direct' have a slick, smart edge to them that just about overcomes the kind of ennui which usually afflicts such occasions. Tropea's clean, crisp style is heard to no better advantage here than on his appearances with George Young or Warren Bernhardt, but at least he got it out of his system.

GIANLUIGI TROVESI

ALTO AND SOPRANO SAXOPHONES, BASS CLARINET, PICCOLO

** **Dances** Red VPA 181 LP
Trovesi; Paolo Damiani (*b, clo*); Ettore Fioravanti (*d*). 1/85.

** **Les Boites A Musique** Splasc(h) H 152 CD/LP
Trovesi; Luciano Mirto (*elec*); Tiziano Tononi (*perc*). 3/88.

The *Dances* record has six tracks – the first five are dances, and the last is entitled 'Sorry I Can't Dance', which implies that Trovesi has some sense of humour, although the music suggests not very much. He's a wracked, lugubrious stylist and, although Damiani and Fioravanti lighten things up with a wide variation of rhythms, the bassist switching between acoustic, electric and cello, the music is rather hard going. So is *Les Boites A Musique*. Luciano Mirto is credited as 'computer operator' and he establishes harsh, jangling washes of sound which Trovesi decorates with a mirthless intensity while Tononi patters away in the background. Interesting of its type, but the genre has been handled with better results elsewhere.

FRANKIE TRUMBAUER (1901–56)

C-MELODY SAXOPHONE, ALTO SAXOPHONE

(**) **The Studio Groups, 1927 EMI 2605271 LP
Trumbauer; Bix Beiderbecke (*c*); Bill Rank (*tb*); Jimmy Dorsey (*cl, as*); Don Murray (*cl, as, bs*); Bobby Davis, Stanley Ryker (*as*); Adrian Rolini (*bsx*); Paul Mertz, Itzy Riskin, Frank Signorelli (*p*); Eddie Lang (*bj*); Joe Venuti (*vn*); Chauncey Morehouse (*d*); Seger Ellis (*v*). 2, 5 & 9/27.

A major influence on the young Benny Carter and on Lester Young, Trumbauer was one of the few instrumentalists to play convincing jazz on the C-melody saxophone, a horn rarely seen today (though Anthony Braxton uses one) but pitched awkwardly between alto and tenor. Trumbauer had a light, rather cool tone that became a perfect foil for Bix Beiderbecke's romanticism and for Paul Whiteman's lush orchestrations. 'Trumbology' and the marvellous original pairing of 'Clarinet Marmalade' and 'Singin' The Blues' are the cream of Trumbauer's 1927 recordings as leader with Beiderbecke as featured soloist, but only a careful CD transfer will restore the fine trios made with Bix and guitarist Eddie Lang to acceptable standards; sound-quality has to be a major reservation. (A good job has been done on the BBC *Jazz Classics In Digital Stereo* sequence, and Trumbauer can be heard briefly on the Beiderbecke volume, REB 601, all formats, and on material dedicated to Joe Venuti and Eddie Lang, REB 644 and 680, tracks recorded in 1928 and 1929.)

A *Down Beat* headline in 1940 announced: 'Frank Trumbauer Quits Jazz'. It was clear that his delicate, understated style was out of keeping with the vogue for swing and the nascent bebop style. After a spell working with the Civil Aeronautics Authority (he used to fly himself to engagements) during the war, Trumbauer more or less disappeared from the scene, dying relatively young. With Bix, though, he recorded some of the very finest white jazz of the classical period.

GUST WILLIAM TSILIS
VIBRAPHONE, MARIMBA

***   **Pale Fire** Enja 5061 CD/LP
Tsilis; Arthur Blythe (*as*); Allen Farnham (*ky*); Anthony Cox (*b*); Horace Arnold (*d*); Art Tuncbayaci (*perc, v*).

***(*)   **Sequestered Days** Enja 6094 CD
Tsilis; Joe Lovano (*ts, f*); Peter Madsen (*p*); Anthony Cox (*b*); Billy Hart (*d*). 3/91.

Tsilis's Enja debut was a curious mixture of earthy modern jazz and slightly awkward, post-Weather Report atmospheric pieces that never quite took shape. His use of marimba veered towards an ironic imitation of electronic blips and waterdrops, a device that recurs on 'Not Ever Quite', one of the less dynamic tracks on the altogether better *Sequestered Days*. Even in his current fine form, Blythe is a rather one-dimensional player when compared to Lovano, who can conjure up anything from smooth swing insinuations, as on the opening 'Mahalia', to a more brittle sound over freer passages. On 'Lisa Robin', he opens on flute over Tsilis's marimba in what sounds like one of Joe Zawinul's folksier themes; the piece develops into an evocative solo from Cox, who underpins the long 'Crazy Horse'. Tsilis's vibraharp work on 'Evening In Paris' is less than wholly convincing, but elsewhere he lets the rhythm prod him towards a livelier delivery, as on 'Medger Evers', which is perhaps the best tune of the set. Its real find is the fluent Madsen, who takes over from the leader and punches out a fine, two-handed solo over Hart's clattering, swishing percussion, before handing over to Lovano in his Coltrane hat to take it out. The title-track is a strong modal theme one would like to see tackled by a much bigger band, for, as on *Pale Fire*, it's clear that Tsilis knows what he wants from his musicians; the arrangements are full of promise.

MICKEY TUCKER (born 1941)
PIANO, ORGAN

(*)   **Triplicity Xanadu 128 LP
Tucker; Jimmy Ponder (*g*); Gene Perla (*b*); Eddie Gladden (*d*). 12/75.

**   **Sojourn** Xanadu 143 LP
Tucker; Bill Hardman (*t*); Junior Cook (*ts*); Ronnie Cuber (*bs*); Cecil McBee (*b*); Eddie Gladden (*d*). 3/77.

(*)   **The Crawl Muse MR 5223 LP
Tucker; Slide Hampton (*tb*); Junior Cook (*ts*); Billy Hart (*d*).

Tucker worked in rock and soul in the 1960s before joining first James Moody and then the Thad Jones–Mel Lewis Orchestra. His albums as a leader in the 1970s are competent but discouragingly un-together, which may not always be Tucker's fault. *Sojourn*, for instance, is an ambitious sextet session of all-original material, but the band sound badly under-rehearsed on difficult charts such as 'Tunisian Festival' and 'Fast Train To Zurich' and the harmonies of 'Norwegian Nights – Norwegian Days' are very sour. *Triplicity* is better, although the sound isn't very ingratiating, and Tucker's organ work tends to reduce the setting to that of a routine guitar–organ combo. *The Crawl* is solid '70s hard bop, with Hampton and Cook on reliable though unsurprising form; at least Hart is a more authoritative and focused drummer than Gladden.

***   **Blues In Five Dimensions** Steeplechase SCCD 31258 CD
Tucker; Ted Dunbar (*g*); Rufus Reid (*b*); David Jones (*d*). 6/89.

Tucker's return to leading his own sessions is justly celebrated on this pleasing effort. Essentially, this is a collaboration between Tucker and Dunbar: Reid and Jones provide pulse and flow, but the most creative thinking comes from piano and guitar, the lines intersecting and parrying each other with consummate empathy. Tucker contributes only the title-track, while Dunbar's 'A Nice Clean Machine For Pedro' makes light work of a testing piece. The fine recording serves Tucker better than any of his previous records, his subtle touch and expressive facility clear at last.

BRUCE TURNER (born 1922)
ALTO SAXOPHONE, CLARINET

***   **The Dirty Bopper** Calligraph ZCLG 003 LP/MC
Turner; Dave Cliff (*g*); Dave Green (*b*); Eddie Taylor (*d*). 2/85.

Forever associated with Humphrey Lyttelton's band – and hence with a mistaken identity as a traditionalist – Turner's playing is more like that of an Anglophile Lee Konitz: dry, poised, and usually without much discernible strain, though he is less limber than he once was. His solos have an airy elegance which can disguise both good and bad days: Turner plays with the kind of even dynamic which allows him to coast or burn and still get the same response. This enjoyable date sounds at times like a xerox of a Lee Konitz–Billy Bauer session, with Cliff's insidious guitar shadowing the leader and a version of Tristano's 'April' sounding like, well, the real thing. 'Toddington Toddle' and a low clarinet feature on 'Laura' make a more individual mark, but even as repertory the record works out very well. Turner can be heard to advantage on many of Lyttelton's records, too.

STEVE TURRE
TROMBONE, CONCHES

***(*)   **Right There** Antilles ANCD 8768 CD/MC
Turre; Wynton Marsalis (*t*); Benny Golson (*ts*); Dave Valentin (*f*); John Blake (*vn*); Benny Green, Willie Rodriguez (*p*); Akua Dixon Turre (*clo, v*); Buster Williams (*b*); Billy Higgins (*d*); George Delgado, Herman Olivera, Manny Oquendo (*perc*). 3/91.

A player of formidable technique, who has previously recorded with Woody Shaw, Ralph Moore and Dizzy Gillespie, Turre had yet to prove himself as a leader when this album was recorded. It's clear, though, that he is now established as a major figure on the least fashionable and most problematic of the major horns. The writing is fairly basic and most of Turre's inventive energy has gone into arranging and playing. Though he's the dominant voice, with a sound that recalls aspects of Curtis Fuller's best work, he allows sufficient room for the band to assert itself. Violinist Blake makes some interesting contributions but is under-used and, but for a few solo excursions, under-recorded. Guest spots by Wynton Marsalis ('Woody And Bu', and the vocal 'Unfinished Rooms') and Benny Golson ('Woody And Bu') lend a touch of variety to the front line. No problems whatever about the rhythm section. Higgins and Williams are *huge*, and Benny Green plays out of his skin, confirming at least some of the promise as yet unfulfilled on his own projects. The two songs are interesting, so long as you concentrate on Akua Dixon Turre's voice on 'Duke's Mountain' and not on her husband's lyric. The couple perform an odd and not altogether successful duet on Ellington's 'Echoes Of Harlem'. If the idea of a jazz man playing seashells bothers you, be reassured that it's restricted to the shambolic final track and sounds perfectly in place there.

STANLEY TURRENTINE (born 1934)

TENOR SAXOPHONE

***   **Look Out** Blue Note B21Y 46543 CD
Turrentine; Horace Parlan (*p*); George Tucker (*b*); Al Harewood (*d*). 6/60.

***   **Blue Hour** Blue Note B21Y 84057 CD/LP/MC
Turrentine; The Three Sounds: Gene Harris (*p*); Andrew Simpkins (*b*); Bill Dowdy
(*d*). 12/60.

***   **Z.T.'s Blues** Blue Note B21Y 84424 CD/LP/MC
Turrentine; Grant Green (*g*); Tommy Flanagan (*p*); Paul Chambers (*b*); Art Taylor
(*d*). 9/61.

***(*)   **That's Where It's At** Blue Note B21Y 84096 CD/LP/MC
Turrentine; Les McCann (*p*); Herbie Lewis (*b*); Otis Finch (*d*). 1/62.

***   **Jubilee Shout** Blue Note B21Y 84122 CD
Turrentine; Tommy Turrentine (*t*); Kenny Burrell (*g*); Sonny Clark (*p*); Butch Warren
(*b*); Al Harewood (*d*). 10/62.

***   **The Man** Time BCD 1038 CD
Turrentine; Sonny Clark, Tommy Flanagan (*p*); George Duvivier (*b*); Max Roach (*d*).
63.

(*)   **Joyride Blue Note B21Y 46100 CD
Turrentine; Ernie Royal, Eugene Snooky Young (*t*); Jimmy Cleveland, Henry Coker,
J. J. Johnson (*tb*); Phil Woods (*as, cl*); Jerry Dodgion (*as, f, af, cl, picc*); Albert
Johnson (*ts, ss, cl, bcl*); Bob Ashton (*ts, cl*); Danny Bank (*bs, cl, bcl, f, af*); Herbie
Hancock (*p*); Kenny Burrell (*g*); Bob Cranshaw (*b*); Grady Tate (*d*). 4/65.

***   **Let It Go** Impulse GRP 1104 CD
Turrentine; Shirley Scott (*org*); Ron Carter, Bob Cranshaw (*b*); Otis Finch (*d*). 66.

***   **Straight Ahead** Blue Note B21Y 46110 CD/MC
Turrentine; George Benson (*g*); Jimmy Smith (*org*); Ron Carter (*b*); Jimmy Madison
(*d*). 12/84.

***(*)   **The Best Of Stanley Turrentine: The Blue Note Years** Blue Note B21Y 93201
CD/LP/MC
Turrentine; Blue Mitchell (*t*); Curtis Fuller, Julian Priester (*tb*); James Spaulding (*as*);
Pepper Adams (*bs*); Herbie Hancock, Gene Harris, Les McCann, Horace Parlan,
McCoy Tyner (*p*); Shirley Scott, Jimmy Smith (*org*); George Benson, Kenny Burrell,
Grant Green (*g*); Ron Carter, Bob Cranshaw, Major Holley, Herbie Lewis, Andy
Simpkins, George Tucker (*b*); Bill Dowdy, Otis Finch, Al Harewood, Clarence
Johnston, Jimmy Madison, Mickey Roker, Grady Tate (*d*). 60–84.

(*)   **Wonderland Blue Note B21Y 46762 CD/LP/MC
Turrentine; Mike Miller (*g*); Ronnie Foster (*p*); Eddie Del Barrio, Don Grusin (*ky*);
Stevie Wonder (*hca*); Abe Laboriel (*b*); Harvey Mason (*d*); Paulinho Da Costa
(*perc*). 86.

(*)   **La Place Blue Note 790261 CD
Turrentine; Freddie Hubbard, Michael Stewart (*t*); Bobby Lyle (*ky*); Paul Jackson Jr,
Phil Upchurch, David T. Walker (*g*); Gerald Albright, Kevin Brandon, Abe Laboriel
(*b*); Michael Baker, Tony Lewis (*d*); Paulinho Da Costa (*perc*); strings. 89.

Turrentine's bluesy soul-jazz enjoyed considerable commercial success in the 1960s and after;
Let It Go, which features the saxophonist's then wife Shirley Scott, is probably the best available
example of that vein, though *Jubilee Shout* and the sessions with Les McCann are almost equally
good. *Blue Hour* with The Three Sounds is marred only by a very soft-centred mix and range of
material, though the closing 'Willow Weep For Me' is affectingly played. Turrentine has a big,
slightly raw tone that sometimes, as on 'Soft Pedal Bues' and brother Tommy's composition
'Light Blue' (*That's Where It's At*), is subtler than first appears. The Blue Note *Best Of* is
thoroughly recommended, picking nine longish tracks (the shortest are a lovely, brief 'God

Bless The Child' from the deleted *Never Let Me Go* and the previously unreleased 'Lonesome Lover', a Max Roach composition).

Despite a partial return to jazz structures in subsequent decades, Turrentine appears to have moved over permanently to pop, like his collaborator on the thumping *Straight Ahead*, George Benson; McCann, another cross-over artist, also has a couple of tracks with his own group on the 1984 album. *Joyride* features a big, overproduced reading of 'A Taste Of Honey' which now compares rather badly with Turrentine's often quite imaginative interpretations of pop tunes; an album of Stevie Wonder covers, *Wonderland* features some of his best playing (and an unmistakable guest appearance by Wonder, playing mouth harp on 'Boogie On, Reggae Woman'). *La Place* is mostly dull and too many tracks are guitar-or synth-ridden; 'Terrible T' is good, though, and 'La Place Street', significantly the only track arranged by Turrentine himself, has a fine jazz feel.

With his roots in R&B, Turrentine has only rather infrequently shown off his skills as an orthodox harmonic improviser and jazz enthusiasts will have to settle for odd, tantalizing flashes rather than sustained invention. *The Man* is typical of Time's notably laid-back sessions, though the saxophonist's steaming solo on 'Mild Is The Mood' completely belies the title. By contrast, his improvisation on 'Time After Time' is almost introspective and full of musical material. The band is exceptionally good, with piano duties shared between the elegant Flanagan (superb on 'Let's Groove') and Sonny Clark, who stacks up the rhythmic fuel on 'Mild Is The Mood', leaving Roach to embellish the melody.

TOMMY TURRENTINE (born 1928)
TRUMPET

***   **Tommy Turrentine** Time BCD 1047 CD
Turrentine; Julian Priester (*tb*); Stanley Turrentine (*ts*); Horace Parlan (*p*); Bob Boswell (*b*); Max Roach (*d*).

The elder Turrentine is much less well-known than his saxophonist brother and is very poorly represented on record in the current catalogue. The debut Time session strongly suggests that he's a player whose compositional work should also be re-evaluated. There are no fewer than five originals, one of which is co-credited to fellow Pittsburgher, John Spencer, and another – 'Long As You're Living' – to Julian Priester. The trombonist's solo on the latter is a measure of how much he has managed to build on the pioneering example of J. J. Johnson (whom he resembles much more on the Bud Powell tune, 'Webb City') and Roach's distinctive polyrhythms sustain a rather staccato delivery which is initially difficult to place stylistically. The trombonist also dominates 'Too Clean', another original; but Tommy has very little to add to the basic outline of this, leaving the way clear for a big-hearted solo from Stanley. 'Two, Three, One, Oh!' is the trumpeter's one outstanding track, but again he's virtually eclipsed by Priester's delicate improvisation and Stanley's bustling impatience with the niceties. A fine record, but Turrentine himself is consistently outplayed by his own team.

FRANK TUSA
BASS

**   **Father Time** Enja 2056 LP
Tusa; Dave Liebman (*ss, ts, f, perc*); Richard Beirach (*p*); Frank Williams (*d*); Badal Roy (*perc*). 7/75.

Characteristic of its mid-1970s time-frame, this is very much a period piece: Tusa works up half a dozen different pieces and six different combinations and leaves with a meandering, half-realized set of musings. The best piece is 'String Beans', a trio with Liebman and Williams, while the aimless jam of 'Doin' It', which involves everybody, is the most typical one. Students may look back on such a disc in some years' time and marvel at what was indulged in at recording sessions of the day.

TWENTY-NINTH STREET SAXOPHONE QUARTET
GROUP

(*)   **Watch Your Step New Note NN 1002 LP
Ed Jackson, Bobby Watson (*as*); Rich Rothenberg (*ts*); Jim Hartog (*bs*). 85.

***(*)   **The Real Deal** New Note NN 1006 LP/CD
As above. 1/87.

***(*)   **Live** Red RR 123223 LP/CD
As above. 7/88.

At once the most fun and the most coherent and self-challenging of the saxophone quartets, 29th Street was first put together at the behest of Jackson and Hartog, who both met Rich Rothenberg independently of each other and then persuaded Bobby Watson to enlist. If Watson is in many ways the key member of the group – his are the most distinctive improvisations, and his romantic streak softens the edges of some of their repertoire to beneficial effect – there's an exceptional uniformity of ideas and abilities in this band. Since they never double on other instruments, there's a special concentration on individual and collective timbre, which has been raised to a very high level, and their interaction is now so advanced that they're close to that fabled point where improvisation and structure merge into one. Yet it's a high-spirited, funky and contagiously exciting group to listen to. They like to enjoy themselves.

The first New Note album is strong enough in its way, but it seems like sketchwork compared to the later efforts: Hartog's 'T.P.T.' and the very long 'Hotel De Funk' are comparatively stilted, and much of the music sounds like procedural try-outs rather than anything spontaneous. *The Real Deal* is an enormous advance. Watson's 'Free Yourself' and the wistfully beautiful ballad, 'The Long Way Home', explore a songful side not much exploited by all-sax groups, and three bebop revisions – 'I Mean You', 'Un Poco Loco' and 'Confirmation' – are bristling with imaginative strokes. Recorded in single takes on one day in the studio, it's as close to live as they can be – aside, that is, from *Live* itself, arguably their most vivid record. While there are occasional flaws – at least by their own prodigiously high standards – the sheer exuberance of the playing is phenomenal. Hartog's 'New Moon' must be the prettiest of all their ballads, and the way Jackson's yelping alto leads into the collective barnstorming of Kevin Eubanks's 'Sundance' is enough to elicit cheers from any listener. Very close and clear recording.

***(*)   **Underground** Antilles 422-848415 CD/MC
As above, except add Hugh Masekela (*flhn*); Benny Green (*p*); Curtis Lundy (*b*);
Victor Lewis (*d*); Pamela Watson (*v*). 91.

The Quartet's debut for a major company is just short of the knockout punch which they might have delivered. It's not so much that the programme is compromised by two tracks with a vocal and a rhythm section, though the additional forces do little except dilute the original impact of the group, but that they seem to have directed all their energies at virtuoso showmanship and have lost a little of their looseness in the process. 'In Case You Missed It', 'What Happened?' and the glittering raid on 'Manteca / Freedom Jazz Dance' are served up with an almost ruthless precision, and it might have been more impressive if these had been tempered by a few sweeter interludes. That said, it's a set of great firepower which most will surely find compelling.

CHARLES TYLER
ALTO SAXOPHONE, BARITONE SAXOPHONE

***(*)   **Definite** Storyville SLP 4099 LP
Tyler; Earl Cross (*t, mel*); Kevin Ross (*b*); Steve Reid (*d*). 10/81.

***   **Autumn In Paris** Silkheart SH 118 CD/LP
Tyler; Arne Forsen (*p*); Ulk Akerheim (*b*); Gilbert Matthews (*d*). 6/88.

Tyler has never sounded as distinctive under his own name as he
Rainbow Gladiator (Soul Note SN 1016 CD/LP). *Definite* was mad
seething Bang session, and Tyler comes across as uncertain in tone a
stance on the tradition. *Autumn In Paris* is more settled in tone, b
Tyler's free tonal approach significantly narrowed down; 'Legend
specific point of comparison, its rooted, black sound considerably (
group. The later album also includes none of his fierce, Hamiet Blu
High point of the two records is an alto–drums duet on *Definite*, 'Hip Da

McCOY TYNER
PIANO, KOTO, FLUTE, PERCUSSION

***(*)   **Inception/Nights Of Ballads And Blues** MCA/Impulse! 42000 CD
Tyner; Art Davis, Steve Davis (*b*); Elvin Jones, Lex Humphries (*d*). 1/62–3/63.

***   **Today And Tomorrow** GRP/Impulse! GRD-106 CD
Tyner; Thad Jones (*t*); Frank Strozier (*as*); John Gilmore (*ts*); Jimmy Garrison, Butch
Warren (*b*); Elvin Jones, Tootie Heath (*d*). 6/63–2/64.

(*)   **Plays Ellington MCA/Impulse! 33124 CD
Tyner; Jimmy Garison (*b*); Elvin Jones (*d*); Willie Rodriguez, Johny Pacheco (*perc*).
12/64.

Tyner was still with John Coltrane's group when he started making records under his own name,
and while these early sessions add little to what he was doing with the saxophonist, they do
reveal what the pianist was doing more clearly than the engine-room of the Coltrane band
could allow. *Inception/Nights Of Ballads And Blues* couples two trio sessions on to one CD, and
they are among Tyner's sunniest and most lyrical efforts. He had yet to build his playing into
the massive, orchestral concept which came later, and his variations on 'There Is No Greater
Love' and his own 'Inception' and 'Blues For Gwen' from the first date are beautifully bright
and lively. The second session is, as suggested, all ballads and blues, and Tyner responds as
though it were a welcome breather from Coltrane's thunder. *Today And Tomorrow* is split
between three sextet pieces and six with Garrison and Heath, three of the latter drawn from
material that was originally issued on sampler albums. The sextet pieces are sometimes lamely
delivered: Jones sounds mystified, Gilmore is his private self, and Strozier plays vigorous but
inappropriate bebop. Better are the trio pieces, with a glittering 'Autumn Leaves' emerging as
especially fine. The Ellington album is disappointing: Tyner's romanticism emerges, but his
interpretative bent seems untested by the likes of 'Satin Doll', and the addition of the
percussionists on four tracks seems like nothing but a gimmick.

****   **The Real McCoy** Blue Note CDP 7465122 CD
Tyner; Joe Henderson (*ts*); Ron Carter (*b*); Elvin Jones (*d*). 4/67.

A key album in Tyner's discography. On the face of it, the music might be a direct extension of
the Coltrane group, with Henderson substituting for Trane. But with Tyner calling the tunes, it
sounds quite different: dynamics are much more varied, form is more finely articulated, and
while the band pushes at limits of tonality and metre alike, it never quite breaches them. The
opening 'Passion Dance' is a definitive Tyner composition: structured around a single key but
pounding through a metre which the leader noted as 'evoking ritual and trance-like states', it
gathers power through the piano and saxophone statements until it sounds ready to explode, yet
the concluding regrouping and subsequent variations are resolved immaculately.
'Contemplation', 'Four By Five' and 'Search For Peace' explore this brinkmanship further,
through 3/4, 4/4 and 5/4 rhythms and fragments of melody which are enough to fuel all of the
band's manoeuvres. Henderson is superbly resolute in avoiding cliché, Carter and Jones work
with dramatic compatability, and Tyner's own playing exults in some of his discoveries learned
over the previous three years: his grand pedal chords and fluttering right-hand lines establish
the classic patterns of call-and-reponse which have dominated his manner ever since, and the
sound he gets is peculiarly translucent, enabling one to hear through the clusters and follow all
of his complex lines. Very highly recommended.

er Moments Blue Note BCT-84275 CD

yner; Lee Morgan (*t*); Julian Priester (*tb*); Bob Northern (*frhn*); James Spaulding (*as, f*); Bennie Maupin (*ts*); Howard Johnson (*tba*); Herbie Lewis (*b*); Joe Chambers (*d*). 12/67.

***   **Time For Tyner** Blue Note BCT-84307 CD/MC

Tyner; Bobby Hutcherson (*vib*); Herbie Lewis (*b*); Freddie Waits (*d*). 5/68.

***(*)   **Expansions** Blue Note B21Y-84338 CD/MC

Tyner; Woody Shaw (*t*); Gary Bartz (*as, f*); Wayne Shorter (*ts, cl*); Ron Carter (*clo*); Herbie Lewis (*b*); Freddie Waits (*d*). 8/68.

Tyner's late-1960s Blue Notes offer some of his freshest music, a point mid-way between his hard bop fundamentals and the panoramic acoustic fusions of his 1970s bands. *Tender Moments* includes the intriguing melody of 'The High Priest' and the Coltrane tribute 'Mode To John', while *Time For Tyner*, recorded at a university concert, features the quartet on 'I Didn't Know What Time It Was', the trio on 'Surrey With The Fringe On Top' and a meditative solo reading of 'I've Grown Accustomed To Her Face'. The pick of the three is *Expansions*, which has a rare sighting of Wayne Shorter on clarinet on 'Song Of Happiness' (his churning solo on 'Vision' is much more typical). Tyner's own playing is less heated and rushing than it was on *The Real McCoy*, but he rounds off his ideas with the same finesse, now becoming imperious with time. 'Smitty's Place', with its sequence of duets between the musicians, is as audacious an arrangement as any which Tyner has created. These three albums are now only available as US imports.

***   **Sahara** Original Jazz Classics OJC 311 CD/LP/MC

Tyner; Sonny Fortune (*ss, as, f*); Calvin Hill (*b, perc*); Alphonse Mouzon (*d, t, f*). 1/72.

Another important record for Tyner. After leaving Blue Note, his career floundered until he was signed by Milestone: his first release, *Sahara*, was a poll-winning record which established his course for the 1970s. Mouzon couldn't have played the way he does but for Elvin Jones, yet his choked cymbals and relentless emphasis of the beat are very different to Jones's polyrhythmic swells. Fortune plays with uproarious power and velocity, and his solo on 'Rebirth' is electrifying, but his is essentially a decorative role, while the pianist drives and dominates the music. The group acts as the opposing face to Cecil Taylor's brand of energy music: controlled by harmonic and metrical ground-rules, nobody flies for freedom, but there is a compensating jubilation in the leader's mighty utterance. 'Sahara' and 'Ebony Queen' best express that here, although the piano solo 'A Prayer For My Family' is a useful oasis of calm. Later Tyner records would be better engineered and realized, but this one remains excitingly fresh.

***   **Song For My Lady** Original Jazz Classics OJC 313 CD/LP/MC

As above, except add Charles Tolliver (*flhn*), Michael White (*vn*), Mtume (*perc*). 9–11/72.

***(*)   **Echoes Of A Friend** Original Jazz Classics OJC 650 CD/LP/MC

Tyner. 11/72.

(*)   **Song Of The New World Original Jazz Classics OJC 618 CD/LP/MC

Tyner; Virgil Jones, Cecil Bridgewater, Jon Faddis (*t*); Garnett Brown, Dick Griffin (*tb*); Julius Watkins, Willie Ruff, William Warnick III (*frhn*); Hubert Laws (*picc, f*); Sonny Fortune (*ss, as, f*); Harry Smyles (*ob*); Kiane Zawadi (*euph*); Bob Stewart (*tba*); Junie Booth (*b*); Alphonse Mouzon (*d*); Sonny Morgan (*perc*); strings. 4/73.

***(*)   **Enlightenment** Milestone MCD-55001-2 CD

Tyner; Azar Lawrence (*ss, ts*); Junie Booth (*b*); Alphonse Mouzon (*d*). 7/73.

***(*)   **Atlantis** Milestone MCD-55002-2 CD

Tyner; Azar Lawrence (*ss, ts*); Junie Booth (*b*); Willy Fletcher (*d*); Guilherme Franco (*perc*). 8–9/74.

***   **Paris Bossa** Moon MCD 034-2 CD

As above. *c.* 84.

**   **Fly With The Wind** Milestone M/MCD-9067 CD/LP
     Tyner; Hubert Laws (*f, af*); Paul Renzi (*picc, f*); Raymond Duste (*ob*); Linda Wood
     (*hp*); Ron Carter (*b*); Billy Cobham (*d*); strings. 1/76.

Following the success of *Sahara*, Tyner embarked on a regular schedule of recording and found himself a popular concert draw at last. The music certainly sounded at home among 'progressive' trends in rock and beyond, although the pianist's beefy romanticism had a lot more profundity in it than most such music-making. *Song For My Lady* varied the cast of the previous disc by adding Michael White and Charles Tolliver to two open-ended pieces, but it was the lyricism of the title-track and Tyner's solo outing 'A Silent Tear' which were most impressive. *Echoes Of A Friend* is a solo tribute to John Coltrane which resounds with all the grand exhortation which the pianist can wring from the keyboard. *Atlantis* and *Enlightenment* are two huge, sprawling concert recordings which will drain most listeners: Tyner's piano outpourings seem unstoppable, and Lawrence comes on as an even fierier spirit than Fortune, even if both are in thrall to Coltrane. The *Enlightenment* set, cut at Montreux, is marginally superior, if only for the pile-driving 'Walk Spirit, Talk Spirit'; but *Atlantis* is still very strong, with a majestic turn through 'My One And Only Love' and another torrential group performance on the title piece. *Paris Bossa*, although dated '1970' on the CD sleeve, is surely from the same period, and features two 20-minute workouts on 'Atlantis' and 'Sahara Love Bossa': Lawrence is a towering voice and Tyner is as primevally powerful as always, although the disc is best seen as a supplement to the two Milestone sessions. Unusually excellent sound from a company which issues many indifferent recordings.

It was this kind of incantatory performance which began to make Tyner's output sound overcrowded with effort: without the ability to soar away from structure, the music could seem bloated, as if packed with steroids. His other Milestone records of the period compensate with varied settings: *Song Of The New World* adds brass and string sections, *Fly With The Wind* sets up an orchestra behind him. But the latter seems to have its energy papered over with the strings, and *Song Of The New World* uses the extra musicians to no very bountiful purpose. Some fine albums from the period are currently deleted – including *Sama Layuca*, *The Greeting* and *Passion Dance* – and though they all contain music of lesser power than *Enlightenment*, Tyner's search for strength and tenderness in equal measure remains compelling.

***(*)   **Supertrios** Milestone MCD 55003-2 CD
     Tyner; Ron Carter, Eddie Gomez (*b*); Tony Williams, Jack DeJohnette (*d*). 4/77.

Shrewdly balanced between showtunes, jazz standards and Tyner originals, this double-trio event, with Tyner meeting Gomez and DeJohnette on one date and Carter and Williams on the other, is a memorable one. Almost fifteen years after his first trio records, Tyner's methods have taken on an invincible assurance, and with musicians like these he is working at his highest level. The session with Carter and Williams is slightly the more invigorating, with pianist and drummer working trenchantly through 'I Mean You' and a 'Moment's Notice' which stands out among many versions the pianist has played.

(*)   **It's About Time Blue Note B21Y-46291/4BT-85102 CD/MC
     Tyner; Jon Faddis (*t*); Jackie McLean (*as*); Ron Carter, Marcus Miller (*b*); Al Foster
     (*d*); Steve Thornton (*perc*). 4/85.

After a desultory period with Columbia, Tyner returned to Blue Note with this frankly inauspicious meeting with McLean, who was himself working his way back into regular playing. While there are useful moments, and the Tyner–Carter–Foster section can hardly fail to ignite, it's nothing special at all.

(*)   **Double Trios Denon 33CY-1128 CD
     Tyner; Avery Sharpe, Marcus Miller (*b*); Louis Hayes, Jeff Watts (*d*); Steve Thornton
     (*perc*). 6/86.

***   **Bon Voyage** Timeless SJP 260 CD/LP
     Tyner; Avery Sharpe (*b*); Louis Hayes (*d*). 6/87.

(*)   **Live At The Musicians Exchange Kingdom GATE 7021 CD
     As above. 7/87.

(*)   **What's New? West Wind 2041 CD
     As above. 7/87.

(*)   **Live At Sweet Basil Paddle Wheel 292E 6033 CD
As above, except Aaron Scott (*d*) replaces Hayes. 5/89.

(*)   **Live At Sweet Basil Vol. 2 Paddle Wheel 292E CD
As above. 5/89.

Moving from a larger unit back to a trio as his regular working line-up stymied Tyner's progress to some degree. These records are listenable enough but there's little here which he hasn't done better on previous records, and the preponderance of concert recordings does less than complete justice to a format which, because of the leader's fondness for lots of pedal and high-density playing, is hard to record truthfully. *Double Trios* has a bewitching original in 'Dreamer' and a good 'Lover Man', but the session with the second rhythm section (Marcus Miller and Jeff Watts) is misconceived and features the leader on a tinny electric piano at one point. *Bon Voyage* features mostly standards, while it appears that the Kingdom and West Wind records may actually have the same music, a functional set of unprepossessing originals. The Sweet Basil discs are good enough, the first volume opening with a titanic rush through Coltrane's 'Crescent', but the feeling that there's a lot of muscle for muscle's sake predominates, and the sound fails to accomodate whatever inner voicings Tyner intends to field. Sharpe, Hayes and (subsequently) Scott do what they can to shadow the great boxing presence of the leader, even if at times that seems to mean merely crashing alongside.

***(*)   **Uptown/Downtown** Milestone M 9167 CD/LP/MC
Tyner; Virgil Jones, Earl Gardner, Kamau Adilefu (*t*); Robin Eubanks (*tb*); Steve Turre (*tb, dij*); John Clark (*frhn*); Joe Ford, Doug Harris (*ss, as*); Ricky Ford, Junior Cook (*ts*); Howard Johnson (*tba*); Avery Sharpe (*b*); Louis Hayes (*d*); Steve Thornton (*perc*). 11/88.

A memorable departure for Tyner. The six charts here build on the sweep of his groups of the 1970s, and the miracle is that it comes across as expansive and uncongested. Although he hardly seems like a big-band pianist, his own solos seem able to raise the already grand sound of the orchestra to an even higher level, and the choice of horn soloists – Ford, Turre, Cook, Ford – makes for a thrillingly coloured and barnstorming effect. Five of the pieces are Tyner originals, the sixth is by Steve Turre, and nothing misfires; even the live sound is good enough to expose the few touches of under-rehearsal which slip through.

***(*)   **Revelations** Blue Note CDP 7916512 CD
Tyner. 10/88.

***(*)   **Things Ain't What They Used To Be** Blue Note CDP 7935982 CD
Tyner; George Adams (*ts*); John Scofield (*g*). 89.

Tyner has returned to Blue Note as a solo artist, and these albums are prized examples of a great player in his late prime. Turning fifty, the pianist recorded *Revelations* as a solo 'studio' recital at New York's Merkin Hall, and after a number of years of live recordings, the excellent sound here reminds one of his mastery of touch and the refinement he can summon when not required to create climax after climax. While some of the standards are a little too familiar – one wishes he would play an all-jazz programme, or a full set of his own originals – he approaches them all with a diligence that lends weight to the usual romantic flourishes. *Things Ain't What They Used To Be* is more of the same, although some of the tracks are duets with either Scofield or Adams. Again, Tyner sees no reason to check his customary flow, and the three tracks with Scofield sound too full as a result, but the duet with Adams on 'My One And Only Love' is gloriously realized, and some of the solos – particularly his latest thoughts on 'Naima' – are Tyner at his finest.

***   **Blue Bossa** LRC CDC 9033 CD
Tyner; Claudio Roditi (*t, flhn*); Avery Sharpe (*b*); Aaron Scott (*d*); Rafael Cruz (*perc*). 2/91.

***   **New York Reunion** Chesky JD 51 CD
Tyner; Joe Henderson (*ts*); Ron Carter (*b*); Al Foster (*d*). 4/91.

***(*)   **44th Street Suite** Red Baron AK 48630 CD/MC
Tyner; Arthur Blythe (*as*); David Murray (*ts*); Ron Carter (*b*); Aaron Scott (*d*). 5/91.

Tyner often seems to find himself heading up all-star sessions, and these three are predictably enjoyable if not quite indispensable dates. *Blue Bossa* starts with a hyperactive reading of Kenny Dorham's title tune, and once into the similarly hectic 'Recife's Blues' it seems as if the whole disc will be nothing but energy music – Roditi's typically buzzing trumpet suitably going at top velocity. But 'I'll Take Romance' cools matters off, and from there it settles into a nice, unemphatic blowing date. The *New York Reunion* never quite catches fire: Henderson doesn't know how to be boring, but his occasional diffidence on such as 'What is This Thing Called Love?' suggests he isn't fully involved, and even the duet with Tyner on 'Ask Me Now', which starts with four minutes of unaccompanied tenor, is finally more interesting as an exercise than a piece of music one wants to return to. Blythe and Murray are as ebullient as always on the Red Baron session: there is a voluptuously rich 'Bessie's Blues'; an improvised two-part title-track, which Murray sits out and Blythe opens by quoting 'Softly As In A Morning Sunrise', digging in harder than he almost ever has; and casual themes such as 'Blue Piano' and 'Not For Beginners' which are show-off pieces that the musicians transcend through sheer force of playing. Great fun, although Bob Thiele's studio sound may strike some as artifically heavy and fat-sounding.

***(*)   **Soliloquy** Blue Note CDP 7964292 CD/MC
          Tyner (*p* solo). 2/91.

Tyner's third solo outing for Blue Note completes a tryptych that sums up his art: rushing, open-hearted, grand of gesture, ineffably romantic, muscular, florid. He still takes every chance to overplay his hand, but that is his way: 'Willow Weep For Me', for instance, is about as aggressive a version of this tune as has ever been recorded. Yet his best melodies – either written or improvised out of tunes by Powell, Coltrane and, surprisingly, Dexter Gordon – are as communicative as they are powerful. He has written for long enough to make his own choices of tune a reflection on his own dynasty: 'Effendi' dates back to his earliest Impulse sessions, 'Espanola' – a haunting use of the Spanish tinge – is brand new, and both are performed with fine evocative skill. The piano sound (the album was, like its predecessors, recored at Merkin Hall in New York) is superb.

JAMES BLOOD ULMER (born 1942)
GUITAR, VOCALS

***(*)   **Revealing** In + Out 7007 CD
          Ulmer; George Adams (*ts, bcl*); Cecil McBee (*b*); Doug Hammond (*d, perc*). 77.

***   **Got Something Good For You** Moers 02046 CD/LP
          Ulmer; George Adams (*ts, v*); Amin Ali (*b*); Grant Calvin Weston (*d*). 9/85.

***(*)   **Original Phalanx** DIW 8013 CD/LP

***(*)   **In Touch** DIW 8026 CD/LP
          Ulmer; George Adams (*ts, ss, f*); Sirone (*b*); Rashied Ali (*d*). 2/87, 2/88.

(*)   **Blues Allnight In + Out 7005 CD
          Ulmer; Ronnie Drayton (*g, v*); Amin Ali (*b, v*); Grant Calvin Weston (*d, v*); Winnie Leyh (*v*). 5/89.

**   **Black And Blues** DIW 845 E CD
          Ulmer; Ronnie Drayton (*g*); Amin Ali (*b*); Grant Calvin Weston (*d*). 91.

Often described as a student of Ornette Coleman's still-unassimilated 'harmolodics' – a theory which dispenses with the normal hierarchy of 'lead' and 'rhythm' instruments, allowing free harmonic interchange at all levels of a group – Ulmer had actually started to devise similar ideas independently. In the late 1960s he played with organists Hank Marr and Big John Patton (as he did later on the great Larry Young's *Lawrence of Newark* [Perception]), promoting a harsh modern derivative of soul–jazz. His work with drummer Rashied Ali (who rejoined one of the more abstract of Ulmer's late-1980s bands, Original Phalanx/Phalanx) brought him to the attention of Ornette Coleman.

During the 1970s, the guitarist toured regularly with Coleman and played superbly on Arthur Blythe's excellent *Lenox Avenue Breakdown* [CBS]. Ulmer's breakthrough album was the remarkable *Tales Of Captain Black* [Artist's House] which featured Coleman, his mallet-fisted son, Denardo Coleman, and bassist Jamaaladeen Tacuma, and included a detailed discussion of Ulmer's harmolodic approach. Whatever critics and fans thought, A&R men were none the wiser and Ulmer found himself and his music increasingly marginalized. Partly in reaction, he turned towards the less outwardly complex, funk-based approach which is evident on most of the current releases. As with Coleman's music, this emphasized the extent to which the guitarist's 'radicalism' was based on traditional procedures. Most of Ulmer's characteristic distortions of pitch and loud riffing are part of a long-established electric blues idiom; what distinguishes Ulmer is the extremity to which he pushes such devices (to the point of tonal abstraction) and the bitter, inchoate quality of his playing.

None of the current releases matches up to the quality of *Tales* or the later *Are You Glad To Be In America?* [Rough Trade]. *Revealing* is by far the best of the albums with Adams (a live German session from 1985 is available under Adams's name on Repertoire REPCD 4912 CC CD), with 'Raw Groove' and 'Overtime' outstanding. The Moers is fine, but poorly recorded. *Blues Allnight* is dull funk-rock, uncharacteristically overproduced and soft-centred; *Black And Blues* is just dull.

UNITED JAZZ + ROCK ENSEMBLE
GROUP

***   **About Time, Too!** VeraBra CDVBR 2014 CD
Ian Carr, Ack Van Rooyen, Kenny Wheeler (*t, flhn*); Albert Mangelsdorff (*tb*); Charlie Mariano (*as*); Barbara Thompson (*as, f*); Wolfgang Dauner (*p, syn*); Steve Melling (*ky*); Volker Kriegel (*g*); Rod Dorothy (*v*); Eberhard Weber (*b*); Jon Hiseman (*d, perc*).

Founded in 1975 by keyboard player, Wolfgang Dauner, the UJ+RE began life as house band on a quietly politicized Sunday evening German television programme directed by Werner Schretzmeier. In addition to giving airtime to young unknowns, Schretzmeier promoted his 'Band of Bandleaders' so successfully that in 1977 the group began to give live concerts. In the same year, the German contingent in the band formed Mood Records with the express intention of promoting its music. A decade later, a boxed set containing six of the group's records was released, to considerable public acclaim.

Unfortunately, *About Time, Too!*, which grafts Dorothy and Melling, members of Barbara Thompson's Paraphernalia, on to the basic UJ+RE line-up, is rather disappointing. The large-scale structures achieve a nice balance between jazz freedoms and more accessible rock reference points, but there is an uncharacteristic lack of focus and substance in the solos, and the whole set seems grossly overproduced. It may be preferable to dig out second-hand copies of *Opus Sechs* or the earlier *Break-Even Point* and *Live In Berlin*.

UNIVERSITY OF NORTHERN COLORADO JAZZ LAB BAND
GROUP

***   **Alive VIII** Night Life CDNLR-3005 CD
Paul Quist, Darryl Abrahamson, Mike Krueger, Suzanne Higinbotham, Stan Baran (*t*); David Glenn, Brad Schmidt, David Wiske, Ray Heberer, Tim Carless (*tb*); Dav Hoof, Brian Bayman, Michael Cox, Tobin Rockley, Todd Wilkinson (*saxes*); Dan Geisler (*ky*); Eric Thorin (*b*); Dave Rohlf (*d*). 88.

***   **Alive, 1989** Sea Breeze SB 2040 CD
Paul Quist, Darryl Abrahamson, Todd Kelly, Suzanne Higinbotham, Dave Scott (*t*); Brad Schmidt, Mike Buckley, Dave Wiske, Dan Gauper, Tom Matta (*tb*); Dav Hoof, Rick Nelson, Michael Cox, Jill Geist, Fritz Whitney (*saxes*); Skip Wilkins (*p*); Eric Thorin (*b*); Terry Vermillion (*d*); Tom Van Schoick, Mike Packer (*perc*). 89.

There's no better indicator of the fierce standards in American college bands than the UNC Jazz Lab Band. Under director Gene Aitken, they've secured a level of expertise which seems to be consistent from year to year, even with an orchestra which must inevitably be in a state of constant flux. After seven albums of limited distribution, the band signed to the Sea Breeze/Night Life operation and have so far released two further sets of crisp, hard-hitting big-band music. The arrangements tend towards showmanship of a no-nonsense sort: some charts seem designed to give either reeds or brass a tough exercise programme, while others are based around stop-on-a-dime dynamics. As a result, the band can't help but be a little impersonal: the aesthetic has little to do with characterful timbre and, although the principal soloists – Michael Cox, Dav Hoof and Dave Scott – have space enough to let fly, their improvisations are studied rather than individual. But it would be churlish to deny the excitement the band creates at its best – as on the chase between Hoof and Cox on Wayne Shorter's 'Yes And No', from *Alive, 1989!*, the brimful arrangement of Bob Mintzer's 'Flying', on *Alive VIII*, or the convincing elaboration of Mike Stern's 'Upside, Downside' on *Alive, 1989!*. The sound on both discs is suitably bright and full.

UPPER MANHATTAN JAZZ SOCIETY
GROUP

***(*) **The Upper Manhattan Jazz Society** Enja 4090 LP/MC
Benny Bailey (*t*); Charlie Rouse (*ts*); Albert Dailey (*p*); Buster Williams (*b*); Keith Copeland (*d*). 11/81.

Nom de session for a bunch of seasoned campaigners who still know how to cut it. The yin and yang of the group lies in the deep, romantic sound of Dailey and Williams on the one side, the tougher, angular approach of Bailey and Rouse on the other. So rhythmic are all four that Copeland's relative anonymity, badly recessed on the up-tempo numbers, scarcely seems to matter. Stand-out tracks are 'Spelunke' and a marvellous reading of 'Naima's Love Song' – not the Coltrane ballad, but a thematically similar composition by pianist John Hicks.

MASSIMO URBANI
ALTO SAXOPHONE

** **Easy To Love** Red NS 208 LP
Urbani; Luca Flores (*p*); Furio Di Castri (*b*); Roberto Gatto (*d*). 1/87.

** **Duet Improvisations For Bird** Philology 214 W 4 LP
Urbani; Mike Melillo (*p*). 3/87.

A post-bop saxophonist whose hard tone and demanding solos aren't very attractive, Urbani is a musician whose work one tends to respect rather than warm to. He grafts timbral extremes into his playing in ways which aren't wholly convincing, and he can run out of steam when improvising at length. The quartet session finds him in assertive company, with Gatto an attacking drummer, and it's plain but wholesome fare. We prefer the duo improvisations with Melillo, who isn't distinctive enough to outplay Urbani but is sufficiently shrewd to counter his more blustering lines with lyricism. The material is made up of standards rather than bebop themes, but the Bird associations just about fit, even if the leader is scarcely on the same level.

MICHAEL URBANIAK
ELECTRIC VIOLIN

*** **My One And Only Love** Steeplechase SCS 1159 LP
Urbaniak; Gene Bertoncini (*g*); Michael Moore (*b*). 7/81.

*** **Take Good Care Of My Heart** Steeplechase SCS 1195 LP
Urbaniak; Horace Parlan (*p*); Jesper Lundgaard (*b*); Aage Tanggaard (*d*). 8/84.

**** **Songbird** Steeplechase SCCD 31278 CD
Urbaniak; Kenny Barron (*p*); Peter Washington (*b*); Kenny Washington (*d*). 10/90.

Like his tragic fellow-countryman and -instrumentalist, Zbigniew Seifert, Urbaniak began his career as a Coltrane-influenced saxophonist, concentrating increasingly on violin as he found an individual voice. In contrast to Seifert, who died in his early thirties in 1979, Urbaniak has shown less interest in free music than in accommodating conventional jazz structures and those folk elements which seem most adaptable to his instrument. In the 1970s he also showed a strong interest in electronics, experimented with the wind-generated lyricon, and made a number of successful albums with his singer wife, Ursula Dudziak; the fusion side of Urbaniak's work is sampled on *Jazz Club: Violin* (Verve 840039 CD) along with a beautiful Seifert track, 'Stillness'.

Of the available material, the recent *Songbird* is quite the most impressive, a mature set of originals that see the violinist finally come into his own as a wholly convincing harmonic and melodic improviser. His tone on the amplified instrument is cleaner and less raw-edged than previously, but he clearly knows how to vary bow-weight and left-hand stopping in order to create a range of articulations which do not so much mimic the saxophone as raise the violin to the same expressive level in this context. The early sets are pretty much of a piece, but less coherent, and never quite attain the authority of the *Songbird* band. 'Mazurka' on *My One And Only Love* is a reminder of Urbaniak's native roots, with its syncopated first beat and curious off-beats, elements he has introduced almost subliminally into his solo on the title-track. All three records underline the growing consistency and independence of his vision.

WARREN VACHÉ (born 1951)
CORNET

***   **Easy Going** Concord CCD 4323 CD/LP/MC
       Vaché; Dan Barrett (*tb*); Howard Alden (*g*); John Harkins (*p*); Jack Lesberg (*b*); Chuck Riggs (*d*). 12/86.

**   **Warm Evenings** Concord CCD 4392 CD/MC
       Vaché; Ben Aronov (*p*); Lincoln Milliman (*b*); Giampaolo Biagi (*d*); Beaux Arts String Quartet. 6/89.

A triumph of style over substance, Warren Vaché's mellifluous cornet is instantly attractive, but gallingly lacking in content. Though jazz players value 'sound' above all else, one is always conscious of a missing element in Vaché's playing. A traditionalist in the same young fogey vein as tenor saxophonist Scott Hamilton, with whom he has performed, Vaché harks back to the days of classic swing, but with a rather detached, 'chamber jazz' feel. The most obvious measure of his virtuosity, his ability to play extremes of pitch very quietly, is something of a mixed blessing, and can be seen to rob his music of much of its dramatic tension.

Easy Going is well named. Mannerly enough to be completely ignorable, it cries out for some modulation of mood and attack. The tunes are almost all brief and relatively undeveloped and, while there is no intrinsic objection to Vaché's concentration on melody ('playing the changes' can be as arid as integral serialism), he seems rather unwilling to stamp his own personality on the music. Porter's 'You'd Be So Nice To Come Home To' and the closing 'Moon Song' (significantly the longest track) suggest some willingness to put himself on the line, but not enough to save the set. Dan Barrett is an unexpected revelation.

It's as well not to dismiss *Warm Evenings* out of hand. Charlie Parker made the 'with strings' format perfectly respectable, if a trifle restrictive. Vaché chooses to be constrained by Jack Gale's arrangements, and he makes them sound more banal than they actually are; in point of fact, Gale seems to appreciate tunes like 'A Flower Is A Lovesome Thing' more thoroughly than the cornettist. The four (jazz) quartet tracks don't redeem a very dull and slightly craven album that grossly undersells Vaché's considerable talent.

KID THOMAS VALENTINE (1896–1987)
TRUMPET

***(*)   **Echoes From New Orleans** Storyville SLP 212 LP
       Valentine; Harrison Barnes (*tb*); Emil Barnes (*cl*); George Guesnon (*bj, v*); Babe Philip (*b*); George Henderson (*d*). 9/51.

'Kid' Thomas Valentine arrived in New Orleans rather late – in 1922. By the time he made his first records, almost 30 years later, he had led bands all over Louisiana but remained based in the city, where he continued to play for a further 35 years. He approached this awesome career with an almost Zen simplicity, reducing the New Orleans sound to its essentials and creating a lifetime's work from them. A fascinating lead-trumpeter, his methods – including a severe observance of the melody, a blunt, jabbing attack and a vibrato that sounds like an angry trill – manage to create high drama and lyrical depth alike, and though he seldom took solos he dominates every performance. His band, the Algier Stompers, are responsible for seven of the tracks on this set – the others are by Wooden Joe Nicholas and Louis Delisle – and they rattle through staples such as 'Panama', 'Sister Kate' and 'Bucket's Got A Hole In It' with typical gusto.

*** **Kid Thomas' Dixieland Band** 1957 504 LP 30 LP
Valentine; Louis Nelson (*tb*); Ed Washington (*as*); Joe James (*p*); Burke Stevenson (*b*); Sammy Penn (*d, v*); Joe Jeremiah (*v*). 57.

Crudely recorded, full of mistakes, this is a marvellous record. It was made up from a tape of an informal session at the Associated Art Gallery in New Orleans, one of the regular events which eventually led to the formation of Preservation Hall in the city, and the programme is a mix of jazz standards – 'Tiger Rag', 'Dippermouth Blues' – and standards of the order of 'Smile Darn Ya Smile'. Ed Washington's alto evokes the kind of lugubrious gaiety which one can hear on, say, Sam Morgan's records of the 1920s, but it's the team of Nelson and Valentine which is compelling. Their version of 'Dippermouth' makes the 1923 King Oliver record sound ultra-modern, yet it's impossible not to be exhilarated by this music. Docked one star only for the poor sound and the sometimes overbearing vocals on a few tracks.

** **A Portrait Of Kid Thomas Valentine** Storyville SLP 233 LP
Valentine; Louis Nelson (*tb*); Soren Sorenson (*ts*); Eric Hansen (*p*); Niels Richard Hansen (*bj*); Derek Cook (*b*); Keith Minter (*d*). 12/72.

** **Kid Thomas & Louis Nelson In Denmark Vol. 2** Storyville SLP 246 LP
As above, except Jon Marks (*p*) replaces Eric Hansen. 1/73.

There is much great Kid Thomas waiting to be reissued. In the meantime, these later recordings will have to do: made on a visit to Denmark, the two old hornmen – then only in their late seventies – do their best in the incongruous situation of playing with dedicated Danish New Orleanians. Curious material – 'On A Coconut Island', 'After The Ball' – but it was always Valentine's aim never to turn down a request.

JOE VAN ENKHUIZEN
TENOR SAXOPHONE

*** **Back On The Scene** Criss Cross Jazz Criss 1013 LP
Van Enkhuizen; Cees Slinger (*p*); John Clayton (*b*); Alvin Queen (*d*). 9/84.

*** **Joe Meets The Rhythm Section** Timeless SJP 249 CD/LP
Van Enkhuizen; Horace Parlan (*p*); Rufus Reid (*b*); Al Harewood (*d*). 7/86.

*** **Blues Ahead** Timeless SJP 356 CD/LP
Van Enkhuizen; Carlo Dewys (*org*); Han Bennink (*d*). 12/88–4/89.

This tenorman sounds as if he could have worked in southern R&B bands: he has the ripe, swaggering quality which makes the *Blues Ahead* organ-combo session sound entirely authentic. But he's from Holland. *Back On The Scene* and *Joe Meets The Rhythm Section* are hard-bop repertory sessions enlivened by a couple of mix'n'match rhythm sections and some out-of-the-way choices of material: Jimmy Heath's 'Picture Of Heath', for instance, on the Criss Cross Jazz disc. Little to choose between them. *Blues Ahead* offers a rare glimpse of Bennink on a straight-ahead kind of session and, with Dewys enthusiastically copying Jack McDuff and Shirley Scott, the leader's fuming solos emerge with gutsy vividness. Highly enjoyable.

FRED VAN HOVE
PIANO, ACCORDION, ORGAN

*** **Verloren Maandag** FMP SAJ 11 LP

***(*) **Church Organ** FMP SAJ 25 LP

**** **Solo** FMP SAJ 39 LP

***(*)   **Letzte** FMP SAJ 58 LP
> Van Hove solo; Ivo Vanderbroght (*bells* on *Verloren Maandag* only). 1/77, 8/79, 11/81, 6/86.

***(*)   **ML DD 4 / Was Macht Ihr Denn?** FMP SAJ 42 LP
> Van Hove; Mark Charig (*t, ahn*); Phil Wachsmann (*v, elec*); Günter Baby Sommer (*perc*). 3/82.

***(*)   **ML BB 1: Berliner Begegnung** FMP SAJ 47 LP
> Van Hove; Wolfgang Fuchs (*sno, cl, bcl*); Peter Hollinger (*d, perc*). 6/83.

****   **Berliner Begegnung: Wo Der Kopf Sitzt** FMP SAJ 56 LP
> Van Hove; Wolfgang Fuchs (*sno, bcl*); Paul Lytton (*perc, elec*). 6/86.

Van Hove is a Belgian improviser of highly distinctive aspect. Unlike many of his brethren, he has tended to prefer shorter, more compact performances (sometimes with an air of the classical impromptu or *étude*) to very long, freewheeling explorations. An exception, 'Begegnung 1a', which occupies side two of *Berliner Begegnung*, is rather diffuse when compared to the shorter tracks. In the same way, the unaccompanied performances on the 1981 *Solo* are far more coherent than those on *Letzte*, which pursue certain structural notions almost to exhaustion; the 1986 album is valuable, though, for a second performance of 'Lest', which conveys a good deal about Van Hove's principles of organization.

His approach is based very largely on clusters, sometimes performed quite abstractly, sometimes giving an impression of arpeggiated chords, opened out in such a way that any sense of harmonic or even rhythmic progression from one cluster to the next is little more than subliminal and thoroughly untrustworthy. The most dramatic instance of this approach is the superb *Church Organ* record, one of only a handful of successful experiments in this field (though, in the classical field, organ is one of the few instruments for which there is a substantial improvisational literature). Van Hove's non-linear approach avoids the technical difficulty of the church organ's huge delay; his is not music that is intended to swing. He uses the keyboard and stops to extend greatly the range of clusters and varying decays available to him; this also relates to his work on accordion, which can be heard on the fine group record, *Was Macht Ihr Denn?*. Not the least of the virtues of the organ record is its sheer audibility. Though some of the more extreme resonances overpower a rather lo-fi reproduction, one has less sense that Van Hove's characteristically quiet figures are being lost, as is the case on *Verloren Maandag* (a record that briefly exploits bells) and on the group records. Eventual CD transfer may help re-evaluate the pianist's work.

All of his bands have been headed with the initials MLA and ML. The suffix BB relates to 'Berliner Begegnung' – Berlin Encounters – a series of performances organized while Van Hove was a DAAD artist-in-residence in the city in 1983. The superiority of *Wo Der Kopf Sitzt* can without question be laid to Paul Lytton's account; his astonishingly subtle percussion and use of electronic effects confirms his standing as one of the most significant European improvisers, still widely unrecognized. The four 'Kritische Studien' which occupy the first side are sophisticated improvised essays, each with an evolving logic. Fuchs's bat-squeak sopranino and softly nudging figures reinforce a sense on both records that we are listening to a distant cousin of blues-based jazz filtered through any number of stylistic and historical gates, processed to a point of maximum abstraction. Only Hollinger seems uncertain in the idiom.

Van Hove is a major figure. Few improvisers are so seriously undersold by the limitations of vinyl reproduction; few stand to gain as much by sharper and more faithful transcription.

JASPER VAN'T HOF (born 1947)
PIANO, KEYBOARDS

***(*)   **Solo Piano** Timeless SJP 286 CD/LP
> Van't Hof solo. 10/87.

****   **Eyeball** CMP 11 LP

***   **Jazzbuhne Berlin '80** Repertoire REPCD 4908 CC CD
> Van't Hof; Bob Malach (*ts*); Didier Lockwood (*vn*); Bo Stief (*b*); Aldo Romano (*d*). 1/80, 5/80.

***   **Dinner For Two** M.A. Music International A 803 CD/LP/MC
        Van't Hof; Bob Malach (*ts*).

Solo Piano shows off a side of van't Hof which for much of his career has remained buried under a rather showy, Chick Corea-derived keyboard style. The Timeless sessions include a slightly blowsy 'Prelude To A Kiss'. There's also a well-etched reading of 'Dinner For Two' which compares more than favourably with one on the duo with Malach, a performance that recalls van't Hof's work with Archie Shepp. Identified for much of his career as a fusion player given to sweeping synthesizer gestures and melancholy romanticism, the Dutchman's touch on a concert grand is suprisingly like McCoy Tyner's, with the same confident absorption of idiom.

In the mid-1970s, van't Hof led the excellent group, Pork Pie. His long association with saxophonist Charlie Mariano and guitarist Philip Catherine (the three are heard together on the romantic *Sleep, My Love*, CMP 5 CD/LP) began then, and drummer Aldo Romano, also in the group, turns up again on *Eyeball*. The 1980 band is less compelling than either Pork Pie or the Afro-modernist Pili Pili, but it features the Coltrane-influenced violin of Frenchman Didier Lockwood in addition to Romano's superb drumming. 'Zbiggy' on the CMP studio album is dedicated to the Polish violinist, the late Zbigniew Seifert; the three tracks in common with the live Berlin recording – 'Ready Go', 'Some People', 'Time Is Up' – are all superior in the studio versions and, as always, Walter Quintus's production at CMP is immaculate.

TOM VARNER
FRENCH HORN

(*)   **Tom Varner Quartet Soul Note SN 1017 LP
        Varner; Ed Jackson (*as*); Fred Hopkins (*b*); Billy Hart (*d*). 8/80.

***   **Motion/Stillness** Soul Note SN 1067 LP
        As above, except Ed Schuller (*b*) replaces Hopkins. 3/82.

Varner's eloquence on an instrument which jazz has seldom bothered with as a solo voice is undeniable: a blindfold test on unwary listeners may induce the feeling that they're listening to a trombone, and these Soul Note albums find the leader mostly set on proving that the horn can work as a vehicle for solo agility. Some of the tunes are more like exercises than compositions – and titles such as 'Study No. 1' on *Motion/Stillness* ask for trouble – but the passionate dexterity of the playing, matched by Jackson and underscored by Hart on both records, is pleasing, sometimes uplifting.

***   **Jazz French Horn** New Note NN 1004 LP
        Varner; Jim Snidero (*ss, as*); Kenny Barron (*p*); Mike Richmond (*b*); Victor Lewis
        (*d*). 10/85.

(*)   **Covert Action New Note NN 1009 LP
        Varner; Mike Richmond (*b*); Bobby Previte (*d*). 1/87.

Jazz French Horn is, from the title inwards, reminiscent of those introducing-a-surprise-horn albums which used to showcase unlikely instruments in the 1950s. Varner and Snidero play with fearsome speed and nerve on the likes of 'What Is This Thing Called First Strike Capability?', and the ballads are handled with a tenderness that is touchingly effective, especially on the finely honed original 'April Remembrance'. The rhythm section sometimes play with a detached style, but Snidero is excellent. *Covert Action* finds Varner biting the bullet of being the sole horn, and he doesn't quite convince that the french horn can really handle it: the interplay with Richmond and Previte is genuinely inspiring as well as analytical, but tonally the record lacks a final sense of contrast.

***   **Long Night Big Day** New World NW 80410-2 CD
        Varner; Frank London (*t*); Steve Swell (*tb*); Ed Jackson, Thomas Chapin (*as*); Rich
        Rothenberg (*ts*); Lindsey Horner (*b*); Phil Haynes (*d*). 3/90.

Varner's most ambitious record is finally let down by a failure or two, despite the excellence of several pieces. The basic unit is three horns, bass and drums (London, Swell and Chapin appear only on 'Wind Trio +') and, if the earlier records were designed to display Varner's powers as an improviser, it's his sense of structure which gets tested here. 'Big Day', 'Search For Sanity' and especially 'Prince Of Jamaica (Queens)' manage to transcend their compositional complexities, while 'Wind Trio +' is a fascinatingly realized set-piece for two wind trios and percussion. But 'Arts And Leisure' is a terribly unconvincing mixture of tone rows and twelve-bar blues, and the title-piece merely rambles in search of coherence. Still a record well worth investigating, with fine studio sound.

NANA VASCONCELOS (born 1944)
BERIMBAU, PERCUSSION, VOICE

**(*)   Saudades ECM 1147 CD/LP
       Vasconcelos solo and with Egberto Gismonti (8-string g); strings. 3/79.

***   Lester Soul Note SN 1157 CD/LP
       Vasconcelos; Antonello Salis (g, acc, v). 12/85.

Unike his slightly older compatriot, Airto Moreira, who was propelled into independent stardom by a stint with Miles Davis and on the strength of his wife Flora Purim's astonishing voice, Vasconcelos has largely suffered from the old and patronizing Hollywood syndrome of 'specialist extra' recruitment: 'Six Chinees for a street scene in Kowloon!' . . . 'One Lascar and a Hottentot!' Vasconcelos has played bit-parts on countless Latin-modern sessions, bringing a distinctive range of sounds largely based on the Afro-Latin berimbau, a bow with a wire string plucked with a coin or stroked with a stick, its sound modified by a gourd or shell resonator pressed against the player's abdomen. Whereas Moreira was inclined to put together a rhythmic background like a pizza chef, throwing in aural ingredients with more sense of drama than of taste, Vasconcelos is a much more concentrated musician, capable of sustained performance on his own and as a full member of improvising groups; some of his best work is with guitarist Egberto Gismonti, who guests on Saudades, but also with Codona (q.v.).

The problem has been how to make Vasconcelos's intensely rhythmic but rather specialized music accessible to a Western audience. Saudades is, alas, not the solution. In addition to overdubbing his vocal parts (which seems completely redundant), the album places him in highly chromatic string settings which are utterly European in conception. Vasconcelos's Tarzan cry on the opening 'O Berimbau' appears to startle the orchestral players for a moment; it certainly throws the whole set into perspective.

Lester is very much truer to the Brazilian's enormous talents, though Salis is a surprisingly passive partner, following rather than confronting. There is an interesting Antilles set, Bush Dance [ANCD 8701 CD], but this is not currently available, and Vasconcelos still, regrettably, has to be sought on other leaders' albums. The three Codona sets probably remain the best bet.

SARAH VAUGHAN (1924–90)
VOCAL, PIANO

***   It's You Or No One Musicraft MVSCD 55 CD
       Vaughan; studio orchestras conducted by Tadd Dameron, George Treadwell or
       Richard Maltby. 5/46–4/48.

**(*)   Tenderly Musicraft MVSCD 57 CD
       As above. 46–48.

**(*)   Time And Again Musicraft MVSCD 61 CD
       As above. 46–48.

***(*)   The Divine Sarah Vaughan: The Columbia Years 1949–1953 Columbia 465597
       2CD/2MC
       Vaughan; Miles Davis, Billy Butterfield, Taft Jordan, Andrew Ferretti, Bernie Privin,
       Yank Lawson, Carl Poole, Ziggy Elman (t); Will Bradley, Jack Satterfield, William
       Rausch, Benny Green, John D'Agostino, William Pritchard (tb); Tony Scott (cl);
       Hymie Schertzer, Art Drelinger, George Kelly, Toots Mondello, Al Klink, Bill
       Versaci, Richard Banzer, Bill Hitz, Budd Johnson (saxes); Jimmy Jones (p); Freddie
       Green, Al Caiola, Mundell Lowe (g); Frank Carroll, Eddie Safranski, Jack Lesberg,
       Billy Taylor, Bob Haggart (b); J. C. Heard, Terry Snyder, Norris Shawker, Bill Coles

(*d*); strings; studio orchstras led by Percy Faith, Paul Weston and Norman Leyden. 1/49–1/53.

Her vocal on the 1946 Dizzy Gillespie Sextet record of 'Lover Man' was Sarah Vaughan's banner arrival, but these sessions for Musicraft and Columbia were her first significant body of records, following her stint with the Billy Eckstine Orchestra. The Musicraft tracks – reissued in a somewhat haphazard order on three CDs – are middleweight 1940s pop, not very clearly recorded, and the presence of Tadd Dameron as arranger on one session and a few jazzmen scattered through the ranks of the studio bands doesn't add much jazz status to the discs. The bulk of theColumbia sessions are also scarcely jazz-orientated sessions, with full orchestras and hefty ballads, but two sessions from May 1950 put Vaughan in front of a small band including Miles Davis, Tony Scott and Budd Johnson for eight fine tracks. Vaughan's musical insight – she was a more than capable pianist – and involvement with bop's early days gave her a hip awareness that went with a voice of vast range and power, and her early Billy Eckstine influence – both singers use vibrato to the same enormously ripe effect – makes her sound like a close relation of Eckstine's on all these tracks. Far from disguising the operatic qualities of her voice, Vaughan insists on them, sometimes dispersing the sense of a lyric while luxuriating in depth of her own voice. Luckily, the material on the Columbia sessions is good enough to withstand such indulgence, and it's a very enjoyable double-set, acceptably if not outstandingly remastered.

****   **Sarah Vaughan With Clifford Brown** EmArcy 814641 CD/MC
       Vaughan; Clifford Brown (*t*); Paul Quinichette (*ts*); Herbie Mann (*f*); Jimmy Jones (*p*); Joe Benjamin (*b*); Roy Haynes (*d*). 12/54.

A glorious occasion, and one that was repeated far too infrequently during the rest of Sarah's career. A blue-chip band (even Mann doesn't disgrace himself) on a slow-burning set of standards that Vaughan lingers over and details with all the finesse of her early-mature voice: 'Lullaby Of Birdland' (with an extra take on the CD edition) is taken at a pace that suspends or lets time drift, and the very slow pace for 'Embraceable You' and 'Bill' doesn't falter into a trudge. Perhaps there could have been one or two more speedier numbers – 'It's Crazy' is about the only one – and Brown and Quinichette are perhaps not quite as commanding as they might have been. But it's still a superb set, with Jones in particular following every turn of the singer's delivery. Excellent remastering.

***(*)   **Compact/Walkman Jazz: Sarah Vaughan** Mercury 830699 CD/MC
       Vaughan; Thad Jones, Joe Newman, Snooky Young, Clark Terry, Charlie Shavers, Freddie Hubbard, Clifford Brown, Ernie Royal, Bernie Glow (*t*); J. J. Johnson, Kai Winding, Henry Coker, Al Grey, Benny Powell (*tb*); Marshall Royal (*as, cl*); Phil Woods, Cannonball Adderley, Sam Marowitz (*as*); Frank Wess (*ts, as, f*); Jerome Richardson (*ts, f*); Zoot Sims, Paul Quinichette, Frank Foster, Billy Mitchell, Benny Golson (*ts*); Charlie Fowlkes (*bs*); Jo Hrasko, William Boucaya, Marcel Hrasko (*saxes*); Herbie Mann (*f*); Jimmy Jones, John Malachi, Ronnell Bright, Bob James (*p*); Michel Hausser (*vib*); Pierre Cullaz, Freddie Green, Turk Van Lake (*g*); Joe Benjamin, Richard Davis (*b*); Roy Haynes, Sonny Payne, Kenny Clarke (*d*); strings. 2/54–67.

***(*)   **Compact/Walkman Jazz: Sarah Vaughan Live!** Mercury 832572 CD/MC
       Vaughan; Thad Jones, Wendell Culley (*t*); Henry Coker (*tb*); Frank Wess (*ts*); Ronnell Bright, Kirk Stuart (*p*); Buster Williams, Richard Davis (*b*); George Hughes, Roy Haynes (*d*). 8/57–7/63.

These two compilations are a choice introduction to Vaughan's records for Mercury. The studio set concentrates on her mid-1950s work, aside from two stray tracks from 1967, and includes the brilliant scat miniature 'Shulie A Bop', a swinging 'How High The Moon' with Cannonball Adderley, a finely rhapsodic 'Misty' and a very heavyweight 'Lover Man'. The live set finds her in mostly ebullient form, with three tracks from the otherwise-unavailable *After Hours At The London House* and most of the *Sassy Swings The Tivoli* set listed below.

***   **The Rodgers And Hart Songbook** Emarcy 842864-2 CD
       Vaughan; Hal Mooney Orchestra. 9–10/56.

***   **In The Land Of Hi-Fi** EmArcy 826454-2 CD
       Vaughan; Hal Mooney Orchestra. 56.

***   **The George Gershwin Songbook Vol. 1** Emarcy 846895-2 CD
       Vaughan; Hal Mooney Orchestra. 57.

***   **The George Gershwin Songbook Vol. 2** Emarcy 846896-2 CD
       Vaughan; Hal Mooney Orchestra. 57.

***(*)   **The Irving Berlin Songbook** Emarcy 822526-2 CD
       Vaughan; Hal Mooney Orchestra; Billy Eckstine (*v*). 57.

***   **Golden Hits** Mercury 824891-2 CD
       Vaughan; Hal Mooney Orchestra. 58.

***   **Misty** Emarcy 846488-2 CD
       Vaughan; Zoot Sims, Jo Hrasko, William Boucaya, Marcel Hrasko (*saxes*); Ronnell
       Bright, Maurice Vander (*p*); Michel Hausser (*vib*); Pierre Cullaz (*g*); Richard Davis,
       Pierre Michelot (*b*); Kenny Clarke, Kansas Fields (*d*); strings. 7/58.

Vaughan's later Mercury sessions are sometimes a shade self-conscious – not in any sense an embarrassment to Vaughan, but in the way that she can get hung up on the sound of her own voice, the criticism most often levelled at her. Musicality and the comparative brevity of each piece usually win through, though, and while her 'songbook' collections miss some of the simple swing and infectiousness of the contemporaneous Ella Fitzgerald records in the same style, Vaughan's grandness and the lavish Mercury recording make these rich sonic experiences. Eckstine joins in on the Irving Berlin session to make matters even more resplendent. *Misty* includes Zoot Sims on a session recorded in Paris, and *In The Land Of Hi-Fi* and *Golden Hits* offer some of the best cross-sections of material, although the occasional stuffiness of the studio orchestras discourages any hint that Vaughan might use the occasions as springboards for more idiomatic jazz singing. Her coloratura tones and sweeping phrasing work instead to a different aesthetic, and one that is as individually creative. The remastering will find few quarrels with most listeners.

***(*)   **Sassy Swings The Tivoli** Mercury 832788-2 2CD
       Vaughan; Kirk Stuart (*p*); Charles Williams (*b*); Georges Hughes (*d*). 7/63.

***   **Sassy Swings Again** Emarcy 814587-2 CD
       Vaughan; Clark Terry, Charlie Shavers, Joe Newman, Freddie Hubbard (*t*); J. J.
       Johnson, Kai Winding (*tb*); Phil Woods (*as*); Benny Golson (*ts*); Bob James (*p*);
       others. 1/67.

These are very good rather than great live sets by Vaughan. *Tivoli* is a good balance between the unbridled grandeur of her range and the more loose-limbed jazz-musician stance – despite the grandiloquence of her voice, most of her best records have been done with small groups rather than orchestras – and *Swings Again* sets her up with a star-studded group that she does, nevertheless, seem less happy with, and the band have a bought-in feeling too. As a single live disc from the period, the *Compact Jazz* collections (which includes much of *Tivoli* anyway) is a better bet.

***   **I'll Be Seeing You** Vintage Jazz Classics VJC 1015-2 CD
       Vaughan; Clark Terry, Willie Cook, Francis Williams, Ray Nance, Dick Vance, Sonny
       Cohn, Thad Jones, Joe Newman, Snooky Young (*t*); Henry Coker, Benny Powell, Al
       Grey, Juan Tizol, Britt Woodman, Quentin Jackson (*tb*); Woody Herman (*cl*); Jimmy
       Hamilton, Paul Gonsalves, Johnny Hodges, Harry Carney, Russell Procope, Willie
       Smith, Marshall Royal, Frank Foster, Frank Wess, Billy Mitchell, Charlie Fowlkes
       (*reeds*); Jimmy Jones, Ronnell Bright, Count Basie (*p*); Freddie Green (*g*); Eddie
       Jones, Richard Davis, Joe Benjamin (*b*); Sonny Payne, Roy Haynes, Percy Bryce (*d*);
       Nat Cole (*v*). 49–60.

A collection of concert rarities, a few with Ellington (in very dusty sound) and Basie (a sweet duet with Joe Williams on 'Teach Me Tonight'), but mostly trio material from 1960–61 sessions. She is in very good voice for the latter, and there's fine readings of 'All Of Me', 'Misty' and others; but this is really a supplement for Vaughan fanatics. The sound is (aside from the Ellington pieces) vivid enough, though inevitably short of the studio records.

****   **After Hours** Roulette CDP 7932712 CD
       Vaughan; Mundell Lowe (*g*); George Duvivier (*b*). 61.

(*)   **The Singles Sessions Roulette CDP 7953312 CD
Vaughan; studio orchestras. 5/60–2/62.

(*)   **Sarah Slightly Classical Roulette CDP 7959772 CD
Vaughan; studio orchestras. 5–7/63.

***   **Sarah Sings Soulfully** Roulette CDP 7984452 CD
Vaughan; Carmell Jones (*t*); Teddy Edwards (*ts*); Ernie Freeman (*org*); unknown g, b;
Milt Turner (*d*). 6/63.

***(*)   **The Roulette Years Vols 1 & 2** Roulette CDP 7949832 CD
As above, plus Count Basie Orchestra, Barney Kessel (*g*), Joe Comfort (*b*). 60–64.

Vaughan's Roulette records veer between an hypnotic beauty and a wearisome, cod-operatic fulsomeness. The latter trait is caught particularly on *Sarah Slightly Classical*, which isn't a classical record by any means: it merely transposes Vaughan's most full-flushing manner into a setting that takes material such as 'Intermezzo' and hoses it down with a heaving orchestra. That said, her musical instincts endure and there are some breathtaking moments for those who admire the sheer scope of her voice. *The Singles Sessions* is a compilation of various one-off tracks, some of them pleasing – a fine 'Green Leaves Of Summer' and 'Don't Go To Strangers' – and others, such as 'Wallflower Waltz', let down by the scrappy material. *The Roulette Years* compilation is a good-value set with 24 tracks from 11 original Roulette albums, including her collaboration with the Basie band, two from *After Hours* and its lesser-known repeat of the formula, *Sarah Plus Two*, and various arrangements by Benny Carter (a very fine 'The Man I Love'), Quincy Jones and Don Costa. The single best disc, though, is the almost peerless *After Hours*. Though short measure (32 minutes – it's over so quickly one is left hungry for more), the intimate setting lets Vaughan throttle her voice back without losing any of her control of detail and nuance. Comparing her version of 'Ev'ry Time We Say Goodbye' with the famous one by Ella Fitzgerald underlines some of the differences between them: where Fitzgerald shows an easy-going naturalism, Vaughan prefers to let us know that we're in the presence of a great singer, yet her skills are put at the service of the song, and she makes us hear music, not technique. Lowe and Duvivier have to do little more than pad along in support, but they do it very well. *Sarah Sings Soulfully* puts the singer in front of a combo dominated by Freeman's organ, but it's not a bad session: 'Sermonette' swings brightly, and there's an impressively smouldering ''Round Midnight'. The only drawback is Milt Turner's noisy drumming. Other Roulette tracks are also available on *The Man I Love* (Jazz Society 670504 CD), which duplicates some of the above discs.

**   **1963 Live Guard Sessions** Jazz Band CD
Vaughan; Bill Chase, Paul Fontaine, Dave Gale, Ziggy Harrell, Gerry Lamy (*t*); Phil
Watson, Eddie Morgan, Jack Gale (*tb*); Woody Herman (*cl, v*); Sal Nistico, Larry
Cavelli, Gordon Brisker (*ts*); Frank Hitner (*bs*); Nat Pierce (*p*); Chuck Andrus (*b*);
Jake Hanna (*d*). 63.

A disappointing account of what could have been a fascinating match. Unfortunately, Vaughan met Woody Herman's band solely for a Forces radio advertising programme, and the music has to make way at times for insufferable scripted dialogue between Martin Block, Herman and an audibly contemptuous Vaughan. A few good moments survive, and the sound is clear if a little reverberant.

*(*)   **A Time In My Life** Mainstream MDCD 704 CD
Vaughan; studio orchestras. 71–72.

***(*)   **Live In Japan Vol. 1** Mainstream MDCD 701 CD
Vaughan; Carl Schroeder (*p*); John Gianelli (*b*); Jimmy Cobb (*d*). 9/73.

***(*)   **Live In Japan Vol. 2** Mainstream MDCD 702 CD
As above. 9/73.

***   **Round Midnight** Zeta 701 CD
As above, except Bob Magnusson (*b*) replaces Gianelli. 75.

**   **Sarah Vaughan With Michel Legrand** Mainstream MDCD703 CD
Vaughan; Michel Legrand Orchestra. 72–74.

Until she took up a contract with Pablo, much of Vaughan's 1960s and '70s work was only patchily available, but the recent reissue of some Mainstream albums on CD has filled in a few gaps. Both *A Time In My Life* and the collaboration with Michel Legrand are disappointing: the former is scuppered by some terribly weak material which even Vaughan can't do much with – saddling her with Carly Simon's 'That's The Way I've Always Heard It Should Be' was about as low as one of her producers ever went – and the Legrand record is simply at too low a voltage, though conceivably she could have made a great record of Legrand songs. *Live In Japan* returns her to her best setting: in front of a warm audience and with a responsive but not too pushy rhythm section behind her. The trombone-like low notes on 'Poor Butterfly' and 'Wave' suggest that her voice was getting even deeper and fuller, but throwaways like 'A Foggy day' or 'On A Clear Day' show how lightly she could step with uptempo material. There is some showbiz nonsense here and there on the two discs, and occasionally – as on a very ripe 'My Funny Valentine' – she simply overdoes things. But it's an exhilarating occasion for the most part. The Zeta album catches another and broadly similar set from the same period.

***(*)   **How Long Has This Been Going On?** Pablo 2310-821 CD/MC
Vaughan; Oscar Peterson (*p*); Joe Pass (*g*); Ray Brown (*b*); Louie Bellson (*d*). 4/78.

***(*)   **Duke Ellington Song Book One** Pablo 2312-111 CD/LP/MC
Vaughan; Waymon Reed (*t, flhn*); J. J. Johnson (*tb*); Eddie Vinson (*as, v*); Frank Wess (*ts, f*); Frank Foster, Zoot Sims (*ts*); Jimmy Rowles, Mike Wofford (*p*); Joe Pass, Bucky Pizarelli, Pee Wee Crayton (*g*); Andy Simpkins, Bill Walker (*b*); Grady Tate, Charles Randell (*d*); big band. 8–9/79.

***(*)   **Duke Ellington Song Book Two** Pablo 2312-116 CD/LP/MC
As above. 8–9/79.

****   **Copacabana** Pablo 2312-125 CD/MC
Vaughan; Helio Delmiro (*g*). 10/79.

***   **Send In The Clowns** Pablo 2312-230 CD/LP/MC
Vaughan; Sonny Cohn, Frank Szabo, Willie Cook, Bob Summers, Dale carley (*t*); Booty Wood, Bill Hughes, Denis Wilkson, Grover Mitchell (*tb*); Kenny Hing, Eric Dixon, Bobby Plater, Danny Turner, Johnny Williams (*saxes*); George Gaffney (*p*); Freddie Green (*g*); Andy Simpkins (*b*); Harold Jones (*d*). 2–5/81.

****   **Crazy And Mixed Up** Pablo 2312-137 CD/LP/MC
Vaughan; Roland Hanna (*p*); Joe Pass (*g*); Andy Simpkins (*b*); Harold Jones (*d*). 3/82.

Vaughan's Pablo albums will endure as some of her most finely-crafted music. *How Long Has This Been Going On?* introduced a new note of seriousness into her recording career, after several years of indifferent efforts and a seemingly careless approach to the studios. The voice has never been better or more closely recorded, and the picked session players and uniformly strong material makes these six albums the most consistent of her career. *How Long* has the odd flaw, but there are beautiful readings of 'I've Got The World On A String' and the title tune, and when Vaughan takes it in turns to do a duo with each member of the band it's a marvellous display of her ability. The Ellington albums gave her – at last – the opportunity to stamp her identity on the greatest of jazz songbooks, and while again there are a few disappointments – a second-class 'Solitude' that should have been a classic, the sometimes overbearing heft of Bill Byers's arrangements and the slightly problematical balance – there are some exceptionally bountiful treatments, of 'In A Sentimental Mood', 'I'm Just A Lucky So-And-So' and 'Chelsea Bridge' to cite three. Both discs stand as a worthy counterpoint to Fiztgerald's celebrated Ellington collaboration.

Send In The Clowns features the Basie orchestra minus Basie, and it's good – the gliding 'All the Things You Are' and a lovely 'Indian Summer' especially – the hard power of the band and Vaughan's own superhuman technique sometimes secure a coldness rather than any warmth of interpretation. *Copacabana* is the neglected album of the bunch, with the sparest of accompaniments to support the great, glowing voice, and the boss/samba material proving unexpectedly strong material for Vaughan. Best of all, perhaps, is *Crazy And Mixed Up*, a disappointingly short (about 32 minutes) but ideally paced and delivered set of standards with the most sympathetic of accompaniments.

GLEN VELEZ
PERCUSSION

***   **Internal Combustion** CMP 23 CD
        Velez; Layne Redmond (*frame d, v*). 5/85.

***(*)   **Seven Heaven** CMP 30 CD
        Velez; Steven Gorn (*bamboo f*); Layne Redmond (*perc*). 5/87.

****   **Assyrian Rose** CMP 42 CD
        Velez; John Clark (*frhn*); Steven Gorn (*bamboo f, South American f*); Howard Levy
        (*hca, p*); Layne Redmond (*perc, v*). 6/89.

A regular with oud player Rabih Abou-Khalil's groups (*q.v.*), Velez favours instruments with natural resonance, accentuating their constituent materials. He will make quite different use of the small Spanish *pandero* than of a larger frame drum, the Moroccan *bendir*, and exploits metal percussion like the Caribbean steel drum (notably on 'Assyrian Rose') and a Chinese opera gong for very specific tonal and timbral effects. In performances as seamlessly produced as those on the 1989 album, the precise configuration of instruments is of only specialist interest. On *Internal Combustion*, though, and the more varied *Seven Heaven*, there is a far greater concentration on the individual characteristics of fewer instruments whose language and properties are explored at length and enshrined in self-descriptive titles like 'Bodhran' and 'Bendir' (a device also used on Don Cherry's similarly disposed *Multi Kulti* album).

All but two tracks on *Seven Heaven* are for a trio of bamboo flute, *mbira* (kalimba) and percussion that glosses the traditional jazz format of horn, piano and drums. Velez explores subtly polyrhythmic structures which often reveal surprisingly simple components, and it's the essence of his music that it resists self-serving complexity, preferring to build up colour and detail in delicate brush-strokes. *Assyrian Rose* is a masterpiece, evidence of Velez's growing confidence and originality as a writer-arranger. Clark and Levy are used with great sophistication, and co-writer Gorn's bamboo and (what sound like) ceramic flutes provide an unembellished top line of great clarity. There are moments, as at the opening of 'Assyrian Rose', when the music is more awkwardly impressionistic, like the leitmotifs of a spaghetti-Western score, but such occasions are rare, as are more rarefied and extended percussion exercises later on the album; despite Gorn's evocative flute, 'Amazonas' palls well before its nine and a half minutes are up. Though there is no doubt which of these is going to have longest shelf-life in the average collection, it's useful to hear Velez's recordings in chronological order; there is a fine performance of 'Ramana' from *Seven Heaven* on an Enemy compilation, *Live At Knitting Factory: Volume 2* (EMCD 112 CD/LP), where it sits alongside Joey Baron's solo electro-percussion 'Pause Of The Clock', from another tradition entirely.

CHARLIE VENTURA (1916–92)
TENOR SAXOPHONE

***   **Gene Norman Presents A Charlie Ventura Concert** MCA 42330 CD/LP
        Ventura; Conte Candoli (*t*); Bennie Green (*tb*); Boots Mussulli (*as*); Roy Kral (*p, v*);
        Kenny O'Brien (*b*); Ed Shaughnessy (*d*); Roy Cain (*v*). 49.

Trading under the slogan 'Bop For The People', Ventura purveyed a brand of modernism much adulterated by R&B and still awkwardly dependent on an initial swing influence. Ventura played with Charlie Parker at the Royal Roost some time before the above material was recorded, and 'How High The Moon' underlines how awkward his Hawkins-derived phrasing could sound in such company. The Bop For The People septet featured the underrated vocal talents of Jackie Cain, often in duet with her husband-to-be, Roy Kral. Given unreliable recording-levels for the horns, it's the two vocalists who offer the best fix in this music, which is genial, competent and relatively undemanding. Ventura did much to secure a wider understanding for bebop, but he can't be accounted a major figure.

JOE VENUTI (1903–78)
VIOLIN, PIANO

****   **Joe Venuti And Eddie Lang Vol. 1** JSP 309 CD
Venuti; Jimmy Dorsey (*cl, as, bs*); Don Murray (*cl, bs*); Adrian Rollini (*bsx, goofus, hot fountain pen*); Arthur Schutt, Rube Bloom, Frank Signorelli (*p*); Eddie Lang (*g*); Justin Ring (*d*). 9/26–9/28.

****   **Joe Venuti And Eddie Lang Vol. 2** JSP 310 CD
Venuti; Jimmy Dorsey (*t, cl, as, bs*); Frankie Trumbauer (*Cmel, bsn*); Pete Pumiglio (*cl, bs*); Adrian Rollini (*bsx, goofus, hot fountain pen*); Lennie Hayton (*p, cel*); Rube Bloom, Frank Signorelli, Itzy Riksin (*p*); Eddie Lang (*g*); Joe Tarto (*b*); Justin Ring, Paul Graselli (*d*); Harold Arlen (*v*). 6/28–9/31.

***   **Joe Venuti And Eddie Lang** BBC CD/REB/ZDF 644 CD/LP/MC
As above two discs, except add Tommy Dorsey (*t, tb*); Charlie Margulis, Leo McConville, Charlie Teagarden, Red Nichols (*t*); Bix Beiderbecke, Andy Secrest (*c*); Jack Teagarden (*tb, v*); Miff Mole, Bill Rank (*tb*); Benny Goodman (*cl*); Charles Strickfadden, Bobby Davis (*as*); Izzy Friedman (*cl, ts*); Min Leibrook (*bsx*); Red McKenzie (*kzo, v*); Phil Ward, Fulton McGrath (*p*); Dick McDonough (*g*); Eddie Condon (*bj*); Ward Lay (*b*); Stan King, Neil Marshall, Vic Berton, Chauncey Morehouse (*d*). 11/26–5/33.

***(*)   **Violin Jazz 1927–1934** Yazoo 1062 CD
Similar to above. 27–34.

While there was a danger that Joe Venuti would be best remembered for his practical jokes rather than his violin playing, these marvellous reissues should allay any such fears. Venuti wasn't the only violinist to play jazz in the 1920s but he established the style for the instrument as surely as Coleman Hawkins did for the saxophone. He was a key figure on the New York session scene of the era, and appears on many dance band records alongside Beiderbecke, Trumbauer and the Dorseys, but his most important association was with Eddie Lang, and although their partnership was curtailed by Lang's death in 1933 it was a pairing which has endured like few other jazz double-acts. The tracks they made together as a duo and as part of Venuti's Blue Four are collected on the two JSP CDs. Some of them – 'Wild Cat', 'Doin' Things' – are like spontaneous bursts of virtuosity, Venuti's reeling melody lines counterpointed by Lang's driving accompaniment and subtle variations of dynamic; others, especially the Blue Four tracks, feature oddball instruments – Trumbauer on bassoon on 'Running Ragged', Jimmy Dorsey on trumpet on 'My Honey's Lovin' Arms', Rollini on everything he plays on – to create a kind of jazz chamber music of improbable zip and bravado. There are touches of kitsch in the style, too, and the occasional indiferent vocal (even if the singer on one session was none other than Harold Arlen!), but Venuti's irascible swing makes sure that every record is an event. Flawlessly remastered, the two JSP discs honour the music, and present it in chronological order, leaving out only those sessions where Venuti headed up a bigger band called Venuti's New Yorkers (which are much more like conventional dance-band records). Robert Parker's BBC compilation gets lower marks since it presents only a cross-section of various tracks featuring Venuti and Lang and the remastering isn't one of Parker's better efforts. The Yazoo disc is a splendid compilation and there are a few rare alternative takes – of 'Raggin' The Scale', 'Hey! Young Fella' and 'Jig-Saw Puzzle Blues' – included among the 14 tracks. Remastering leaves a lot of the surface hiss alone, but the music itself comes through very brightly. The important 1931 session by the Venuti–Lang All Star Orchestra can be found on *BG And Big Tea In New York* (*MCA*), listed under Benny Goodman's name.

***(*)   **Joe Venuti And Zoot Sims** Chiaroscuro CRD 142 CD
Venuti; Spiegel Wilcox (*tb*); Zoot Sims (*ts*); Dick Hyman, John Bunch (*p*); Bucky Pizzarelli (*g*); Milt Hinton (*b*); Cliff Leeman, Bobby Rosengarden (*d*). 5/74–5/75.

***(*)   **Sliding By** Sonet SNTCD 734 CD
Venuti; Dick Hyman (*p*); Bucky Pizzarelli (*vn*); Major Holley (*b*); Cliff Leeman (*d*). 4/77.

****   **Alone At The Palace** Chiaroscuro CRD 160 CD
Venuti; Dave McKenna (*p*). 4/77.

Venuti's Indian summer in the studios is currently represented by only these three records. He remained in such good form to the end of his playing life that all his final records are precious. The partnership with Zoot Sims has perhaps been a shade overrated, since Sims's bluff swing is no different to anything he plays on his own records and sounds occasionally a little glib, whereas Venuti's own playing – coloured by unexpected bursts of pizzicato, oddball kinds of bowing and resinous streams of melody that seem to go on forever – is of a different order. *Sliding By* continued a profitable association with Dick Hyman, but it's *Alone At The Palace* which is Venuti's valedictory masterpiece. McKenna's granitic swing and authority are just the kind of bedrock the violinist loved, and whether they play 'At the Jazz Band Ball' or 'Runnin' Ragged' (almost exactly 50 years after Venuti's original version) or a slush-free 'Send In The Clowns', it's all superbly achieved. Four months later, Joe was gone. The CD reissue of the original LP includes four new tracks and three alternative takes, all equally welcome, and the sound is admirably clear.

HARRY VERBEKE
TENOR SAXOPHONE

(*)   **Short Speech Timeless SJP 136 LP
Verbeke; Irvin Rochlin (*p*); Harry Emmery (*b*); Max Bolleman (*d*). 7/79.

***(*)   **Gibraltar** Timeless SJP 144 LP
Verbeke; Rob Agerbeek (*p*); Herbie Lewis (*b*); Billy Higgins (*d*). 11/79.

***   **Seven Steps** Timeless SJP 173 LP
Verbeke; Rob Agerbeek (*p*); Harry Emmery (*b*); James Martin (*d*). 12/82.

***   **Plays Romantic Ballads** Timeless SJP 230 CD/LP

(*)   **Mo De Bo Timeless SJP 246 LP
Verbeke; Carlo De Wijs (*org*); Hein Van De Geyn (*b*); Arnoud Gerritse (*d*). 6/85, 6 & 8/85.

A solitary CD suggests that Verbeke's subtly inflected swing phrasing hasn't always been well served on record. In company with Agerbeek he's capable of fine things, and *Gibraltar*, with its up-market rhythm section, should be checked out for highly romantic readings of 'Laura' and 'Stardust'. A version of Mingus's 'Peggy's Blue Skylight' on *Short Speech* promises a great deal more than it delivers, and Verbeke rarely attempts anything so ambitious again. The solo on 'Polka Dots And Moonbeams' on the *Romantic Ballads* CD is far more subtle than that on *Short Speech*, but De Wijs's breathy organ is a distraction and might have been replaced by a more incisive guitarist. *Mo De Bo* cobbles together more (and definitely inferior) material from the same sessions with slightly later tracks to which either growing familiarity or more sympathetic material have added a degree more snap.

EDWARD VESALA (born 1945)
DRUMS, PERCUSSION, OTHER INSTRUMENTS

***(*)   **Nan Madol** ECM 1077 CD/LP
Vesala; Kaj Backlund (*t*); Mirce Stan (*tb*); Charlie Mariano (*as, f, nagaswaram*); Juhani Aaltonen (*ts, ss, f*); Pentti Lahti (*ss, bcl*); Seppo Paakkunainen (*ss, f*); Sakari Kukko (*f*); Elisabeth Leistola (*hp*); Juhani Poutanen (*vn, alto vn*); Teppo Hauta-aho (*b*). 4/74.

*****   **Lumi** ECM 1339 CD/LP
Vesala; Esko Heikkinen (*t, picc-t*); Tom Bildo (*tb, tba*); Pentti Lahti (*as, bs, f*); Jorma Tapio (*as, cl, bcl, f*); Tapani Rinne (*ts, ss, cl, bcl*); Kari Heinilä (*ts, ss, f*); Raoul Björkenheim (*g*); Taito Vainio (*acc*); Iro Haarla (*hp*); Häkä (*b*). 6/86.

****   **Ode To The Death Of Jazz** ECM 1413 CD/LP
Vesala; Matti Rikonen (*t*); Jorma Tapio (*as, bcl, f*); Jouni Kannisto (*ts, f*); Pepa Päivinen (*ts, ss, bs, f, cl, bcl*); Tim Ferchen (*mar, bells*); Taito Vainio (*acc*); Iro Haarla (*p, hp, ky*); Jimi Sumen (*g*); Uffe Krokfors (*b*). 4 & 5/89.

Edward Vesala bears an uncanny physical resemblance to Richard Brautigan and weaves narratives and textures which, like the late American novelist's, are magically suffused, wry and tender by turns. Vesala is one of very few percussionists capable of sustaining interest as a solo performer (an early-1980s recording of extracts from the Finnish epic, *Kalevala*, rivets the attention despite the minimalist accompaniment and the fact that no English translation is provided); despite this, Vesala has been sparing of solo tracks on his records (the brief 'Call From The Sea' on *Nan Madol* is an exception), preferring to elevate his light, pulse-driven but often non-metrical drumming until it occupies the forefront of a piece. Recording with ECM has greatly enhanced his capacity in this regard. Vesala's groups have a unique sound, compounded of folk and popular references, but with a grasp of orchestration that, for all his commitment to themes and solos, is more typical of through-composed concert music. He favours extremes of timbre, alternating very dark themes exploiting sombre modes and tonalities with light, airy arrangements of flutes, soprano saxophones and harp; typically, though, he reverses the expressive polarity, investing light-toned pieces like 'The Wind' (on *Nan Madol*, re-recorded later) with a sinister quality, often reserving darker instrumentation for tongue-in-cheek compositions based on popular forms.

Vesala has produced one masterpiece. *Lumi* is one of the finest jazz albums of the 1980s. Even its cover, of a shrouded, Golem-like figure on an empty road under a threatening sky, suggests something of Vesala's distinctive combination of almost Gothic intensity and sheer playfulness. A re-recording of 'The Wind' shows how much he has advanced since 1974. It is spare, subtly voiced, less dependent on literal reference than its predecessor, but not a whit less evocative. 'Frozen Melody' is a superb exercise in static harmony; Vesala works variations on a descending repetition of four notes of the same pitch, gradually unpicking the rhythmic implications. 'Fingo', like 'A Glimmer Of Sepal' on *Ode To The Death Of Jazz*, is based on tango rhythms and illustrates Vesala's interest in extreme stylistic repetitions. This is evident on the later album, too, in 'Winds Of Sahara', which begins in spooky 'ethnic' mode, wobbles a bit, and then breaks into a camel-racing flag-waver of Maynard Ferguson proportions; 'Calypso Bulbosa' evokes similar incongruities.

Vesala works slowly and has not been a prolific recorder. Each of his records has been a superb balance of careful organization and arrangment and all-out freedom. Though not too much should be invested in chance resemblances and coincidences, it's interesting to note a parallel between Vesala's method on 'The Way Of . . .' (*Nan Madol*) and that of British drummer Tony Oxley on his classic, 1969 CBS album *The Baptised Traveller*, notably the extraordinary 'Stone Garden', composed by Charlie Mariano, who appears on two tracks on Vesala's album. The descending sequences are, though, entirely characteristic of Vesala and owe no apparent debt to anyone else.

Lumi remains his most convincing marshalling of quite disparate elements, and the addition of Raoul Björkenheim's dog-howls and (on 'Camel Walk') percussive choke rhythms is probably enough to lift it a peg above the others. Vesala is not a regular tourer in the English-speaking countries and has concentrated most of his energies on the burgeoning music scene in Helsinki. He is, though, a major musical presence, and deserves the widest recognition.

****   **Invisible Storm** ECM 1461 CD/LP
Vesala; Matti Riikonen (*t*); Jorma Tapio (*as, bcl, f, bf, perc*); Jouni Kannisto (*ts, f*); Pepa Päivinen (*ts, ss, bs, f, af*); Jimi Sumen (*g*); Pekka Sarmanto (*b*); Marko Ylönen (*clo*); Mark Nauseef (*perc*).

The opening four tracks of *Invisible Storm* represent the most powerfully dramatic work Vesala has yet to commit to record. It opens with an extraordinary recitation, 'Sheets And Shrouds', a cracked voice in an unfamiliar tongue (and Finnish has a quality that is both ancient and curiously Asian) before giving way to 'Murmuring Morning', a slow chorale highlit by Ylönen's cello, and then exploding in the thudding fury of 'Gordion's Flashes'. The fourth piece – and each is successively longer – also features a spoken vocal; 'Shadows On The Frontier' is in English but preserves the tranced quality of the opening. Though there is no explicit reason to connect them, they do seem to cohere in a way that later tracks do not. Of these, 'Somnanblues' is another of Vesala's brilliant generic parodies, and the closing 'Caccaroo Boohoo' is dryly witty. The longest single item, 'The Wedding Of All Essential Parts', and the title-track are less impressive – but only relative to Vesala's now absurdly high standard. His melodic inventiveness grows apace, concentrating on sinuously extended figures that evade conventional rhythmic resolution but underneath which there beats a powerful, even dramatic, pulse. *Lumi* remains the record of choice, but it's hard to put this lower than essential in terms of contemporary recording. Needless to say, the studio work and mastering are impeccable.

VIENNA ART ORCHESTRA & CHOIR
GROUP(S)

***(*) **Concerto Piccolo** hat Art 6038 CD
Matthias Rüegg (*comp, arr*); Karl Fian (*t*); Herbert Joos (*t, flhn, double t, bhn, alphorn*); Christian Radovan (*tb*); Billy Fuchs (*tba*); Harry Sokal (*f, ts, ss*); Wolfgang Puschnig (*picc, f, as*); Roman Schwaller (*ts*); Stefan Bauer (*vib*); Uli Scherer (*p, ky*); Jürgen Wuchner (*b*); Joris Dudli (*d*); Wolfgang Reisinger (*perc*); Lauren Newton (*v*). 10/80.

*** **Suite For The Green Eighties** hat Art 6054 CD
As for *Concerto Piccolo*, but Woody Schabata (*vib*) replaces Stefan Bauer, Ingo Morgana (*ts*) replaces Roman Schwaller, and add Janusz Stefanski (*d, perc*). 6 & 10/81.

*** **Serapionsmusic** Moers 02050 LP
Matthias Rüegg (*leader*); Karl Fian (*t*); Christian Radovan (*tb*); Wolfgang Puschnig, Harry Sokal (*reeds*); Woody Schabata (*vib*); Uli Scherer (*ky, melodica*); Wolfgang Reisinger (*d*); Lauren Newton (*v*); Vienna Art Choir. 3/84.

***** **The Minimalism Of Erik Satie** hat Art 6024 CD
Matthias Rüegg (*p, arr*); Karl Fian, Hannes Kottek (*t, flhn*); Herbert Joos (*t, flhn, bhn, alphorn*); Christian Radovan (*tb*); John Sass (*tba*); Co Strieff (*as, f*); Harry Sokal (*ts, ss, f*); Roman Schwaller (*ts*); Woody Schabata (*vib*); Uli Scherer (*ky, perc*); Heiri Kaenzig (*b*); Wolfgang Reisinger (*d*); Ima (*tamboura*); Lauren Newton (*v*); 9/83 & 3/84.

**** **Nightride Of A Lonely Saxophoneplayer** Moers 02054/5 2CD/2LP
As for *Minimalism*, but omit Co Strieff, add Erich Dorfinger (*sound effects*); Andy Manndorff (*g*); Tom Nicholas (*perc*). 10/85.

*** **Two Little Animals** Moers 02066 CD/LP

***(*) **Inside Out** Moers 02062/3 CD/2LP
As for *Minimalism*, but omit Co Strieff, add Andy Manndorff (*g*). 10 & 11/87.

***(*) **Blues For Brahms** Amadeo 839105 2CD/2LP
As for *Minimalism*, but without Puschnig, Strieff, Schabata, Ima. 11/88.

***(*) **Innocence Of Clichés** Amadeo 841646 2CD/2LP
As for *Blues For Brahms*, but add Erich Dorfinger (*sound effects*). 9/89.

Erik Satie thought that the beauty of jazz lay in how the world ignored its scream of sorrow. One of his abiding concerns was the degree of attention that was or could be directed towards music; it is not, after all, seriously possible to listen to all of his *Vexations*, 840 'very slow' repetitions of a single theme, occupying 28 hours of playing time. Whereas patrons of concert music (Satie's parodic targets) are expected to concentrate all their attention on it, jazz has had to grow up in an environment of profound inattention. With the Vienna Art Orchestra the Swiss composer and pianist, Matthias Rüegg, has attempted to square the formal demands of concert music with the freedoms of the century's most significant *musique pauvre*.

Like Willem Breuker, H K Gruber and the British composer, Mike Westbrook, Rüegg takes a broadly theatrical approach, drawing parallels between jazz soloing and Satie's 'face-pulling' exercises in incidental music (this is made explicit on the marvellous *Minimalism* record, still perhaps the best *entrée* into the VAO's methodology). Rüegg consistently makes reference to classic jazz, using tuba to mimic the brass bass of the New Orleans bands, rejecting strings in favour of unruly brasses and reeds. Though he also 'covers' standards in a relatively conventional way ('Cry Me A River' on *Inside Out*, 'In A Sentimental Mood' on *Innocence Of Clichés*, 'Body And Soul' on *Blues For Brahms*), Rüegg generally prefers to create large-scale pastiches of jazz and pre-jazz styles (like 'Ragtime' on *Nightride Of A Lonely Saxophoneplayer*) or curious thematic hippogriffs ('You Are The Ghost Of A Romance In

June' on *Two Little Animals*, 'What Is This Thing Called Free Jazz' on *Blues For Brahms*) whose titles clearly reflect his interest in Mingus's compositional strategies. ('Jelly Roll But Mingus Rolls Better' on *Concerto Piccolo* is an explicit homage.)

Rüegg is, like Satie, deeply motivated by a sympathy for the dispossessed, and it is important not to miss the emotional underpinning of music that, unheard, might seem forbidding and excessively formal. His titles are full of references to imprisonment and oppression, characteristically expressed in puns like 'Bars & Stripes' (*Blues For Brahms*), and his attraction to Satie's 'Gnossiennes' is not so much for their formal mystery as for the fact that they express the oppression of a people (a Greek scale is used throughout) whose culture has been frozen in stone and appropriated as required, just as Western classical music has ossified, calling on jazz only where and as it suits a formal or social purpose.

The Minimalism Of Erik Satie is one of the most important recordings of recent years and, though there are excellent things on all the VAO's recordings to date, this is the one that commands attention. Most of the tracks briefly articulate Satie's original theme before proceeding to work variations on it. The orchestral voicings are bright and spare, with most of the space devoted to solo material. 'Gnossienne No. 1' has a superb sopranino solo by Puschnig that immediately recalls Lindsay Cooper's work with Mike Westbrook (*q. v.*) on his Rossini project, a vivid, snake-charming improvisation that sways up out of Satie's theme. Most remarkable of all are the three essays on *Vexations*. These originally occupied sides 3 and 4 of the original LP set and are unusual in being for permutations of only three musicians: singer Lauren Newton in a Berberian-derived vocalise, Roman Schwaller on tenor saxophone, Wolfgang Puschnig on bass clarinet, each duetting with vibraharpist, Woody Schwabata, who maintains a steady chordal pulse underneath. The final 'Vexations 2105' with Puschnig is a masterful redefinition of jazz as a sorrow song. Quite wonderful.

****   From No Art To Mo(z)-Art Moers 02002 LP/CD
Matthias Rúegg (*leader*); Kurt Azesberger, Maria Bayer, Renate Bochdansky, Patricia Caya, Peter Jelosits, Lis Malina, Sharon Natalie, Lauren Newton, Christof Prinz, Karen Reisner (*v*); accompanied by George Lewis, Christian Radovan (*tb*); Wolfgang Puschnig (*reeds*). 5/83.

****   Five Old Songs Moers 02036 CD/LP
As above, but accompanied by Herbert Joos (*flhn, alphorn*); George Lewis, Christian Radovan (*tb*); Wolfgang Puschnig (*reeds*); Woody Schabata (*xy, dulcimer*). 5/84.

***(*)   Swiss Swing Moers 02060 CD/LP
Karl Fian (*t*); Woody Schabata (*vib*); Hans Hassler (*acc*); Uli Scherer (*ky*); Heiri Kaenzig (*b*); Wolfgang Reisinger (*d*); Elfi Aichinger, Sarah Barrett, Marie Bayer, Renate Bochdansky, Lauren Newton (*v*). 3/86.

The Vienna Art Choir was formed in 1983, broadly in accordance with the same principles as the VAO. The original *From No Art To Mo(z)Art* is a huge syllabic fantasy which calls on a wide range of vocal technique, from the free-form vocalise Newton brought to 'Vexations' to more conventional, modern choral devices. *Five Old Songs*, like the 'Ländler für funf Stimme' on *Swiss Swing* (which is more strictly a VAO record, but may be usefully compared with the Choir's work) are more formal in conception. Accompaniments are basic but highly imaginative, and the overall impact is very powerful. Also strongly recommended.

LEROY VINNEGAR (born 1928)
DOUBLE BASS

***(*)   Leroy Walks! Original Jazz Classics OJC 160 CD/LP
Vinnegar; Gerald Wilson (*t*); Teddy Edwards (*ts*); Victor Feldman (*vib*); Carl Perkins (*p*); Tony Bazley (*d*). 6 & 9/57.

**(*)   Leroy Walks Again! Original Jazz Classics OJC 454 CD/LP/MC
Vinnegar; Fred Hill (*t*); Teddy Edwards (*ts*); Mike Melvoin (*p*); Victor Feldman (*p, vib*); Roy Ayers (*vib*); Ron Jefferson, Milton Turner (*d*). 8/62.

A versatile, much-recruited sideman, Vinnegar's outwardly conventional 'walking' style contains considerable internal variation (he rarely actually solos) and additional left-hand accents which keep the beat absolutely solid and 'live'. It may be that Vinnegar's dense, slightly undifferentiated tone and those open accents have had an influence on the development of rock bass guitar; he once did sessions for the bass-less Doors.

The earlier of the two records is much superior. The material on *Walks Again!* is far less suited to Edwards's smooth, bluesy approach; in addition, Hill is a rather flat player with nothing particularly distinctive to say. One also misses the interplay of Perkins and Feldman, two individualists who understood each other's idiom and performing techniques intimately. Perkins's crab-wise technique is still not fully appreciated, and this is one of his best recorded performances. The 'walking' theme is flogged to death (except 'On The Sunny Side Of The Street', every track makes reference to ambulation), but there's nothing pedestrian about the music, which swings generously. Vinnegar's career has been rather curtailed of late due to ill-health, but the elastic phrasing hasn't changed since these records (one excellent, the other still worthwhile) were cut. Like many rhythm players, he still awaits proper critical assessment and the CD transfers bring him usefully forward in the mix.

EDDIE 'CLEANHEAD' VINSON (born 1917)
ALTO SAXOPHONE, VOCALS

****   **Cleanhead & Cannonball** Landmark 1309 CD/LP/MC
Vinson; Cannonball Adderley (*as*); Nat Adderley (*c*); Joe Zawinul (*p*); Sam Jones (*b*); Louis Hayes (*d*). 9/61, 2/62.

***   **Kidney Stew** Black & Blue 233021 CD
Vinson; Al Grey (*tb*); Eddie Lockjaw Davis, Hal Singer (*ts*); T-Bone Walker (*g*); Jay McShann (*p*); Wild Bill Davis, Bill Doggett (*org*); Floyd Smith (*g*); Milt Hinton, Roland Lobligeois (*b*); Paul Gunther, J. C. Heard (*d*). 3/69, 7/72.

***   **I Want A Little Girl** Pablo 2310866 CD/LP
Vinson; Martin Banks (*t*); Rashied Jamal Ali (*ts*); Cal Green (*g*); Art Hillery (*p, org*); John Heard (*b*); Roy McCurdy (*d*). 2/81.

A hugely entertaining singer/saxophonist, Vinson became a festival favourite in the 1970s, guesting with anyone who thought they could take his pace, playing Parker-tinged R&B with disconcerting self-possession. Some claim to find a Louis Jordan influence in Vinson's work, but this may have more to do with his performing personality than with any stylistic borrowing. 'Kidney Stew' was a major hit and, later, something of a millstone; it appears on both the Black & Blue, which brings together some interesting but unexceptional material, and the very fine Landmark, on which there's a nice balance of instrumental numbers to offset the vocals; the CD has a bonus performance of 'Vinsonology', one of the more obvious of his takes on Parker's blues style.

The Pablo features Vinson the festival personality with a slightly heavy-fisted band and a bag of blues numbers that contains a surprising 'Straight, No Chaser' and an excellent version of Pettiford's 'Blues In The Closet'.

VISBY BIG BAND
GROUP

**   **Fine Together** Dragon DRCD 210 CD
Magnus Appelholm, Hans Dyvik, Christer Linde, Bo Strandberg (*t*); Matts Siggstedt, Ingvar Sandström, Mimmi Hammar, Rickard Sandström (*tb*); Putte Wickman (*cl*); Lennart Löfrgen (*btb*); Bernt Eklund, Thomas Andersson (*as*); Bengt Öslöf, Göran Cderlöf (*ts*); Lars Olov Ahnell (*bs*); Lars-Åke Larsson (*p*); Andreas Petterson (*g*); Jörgen Smeby (*b*); Marton Löfgren (*d*). 3/91.

A disappointing encounter. The Visby Big Band's earlier records have featured a more commanding personnel, and under Öslöf's leadership they sound effortful and wanting in sparkle. Wickman is the guest soloist for the session, and he plays with his usual civilized excellence, but the scores are no more than functional settings for him. Fine, lucid recording, though.

MIROSLAV VITOUS (born 1947)
DOUBLE BASS

(*) **Miroslav Freedom 41040 CD/LP
Vitous; Don Alias, Armen Halburian (*perc*). 12/76, 7/77.

**** **Journey's End** ECM 1242 LP
Vitous; John Surman (*ss, bs, bcl*); John Taylor (*p*); Jon Christensen (*d*). 7/82.

***(*) **Emergence** ECM 1312 CD/LP
Vitous solo. 9/85.

It's not clear why a performer of Vitous's quality has seemed to be marginalized by ECM, a label to whose basic aesthetic he conforms majestically. There is no sign yet of *Journey's End*, probably his most accomplished work to date, being transferred to CD; there is no sign at all of the very fine, earlier *Miroslav Vitous Group* [ECM 1185], which had the equally lyrical Kenny Kirkland in place of John Taylor.

After leaving Weather Report in 1973, having recorded three classic albums (he appears only briefly on *Mysterious Traveller*, the group's fourth release), Vitous experimented with various 'lead' and 'piccolo' basses, but doesn't seem to have acquired the confidence in their use that made Stanley Clarke and a later Weather Report member, Jaco Pastorius, such charismatic figures (compare Vitous's and Pastorius's work with guitarist Bireli Lagrene, and that becomes clear). It took Vitous some time to re-establish the musical identity stamped all over his marvellous pre-Weather Report solo debut, *Infinite Search* (later re-released on Atlantic as *Mountain In The Clouds*), and there's an awkwardness to the piano and synthesizer shelters he digs for himself on *Miroslav*. The ECM is far more accomplished and begins to reintegrate the classical and folk-impressionistic elements on the earlier record (tracks such as 'Concerto In E Minor' and the Zawinul-influenced 'Pictures Of Moravia') into a much more coherent performance.

No problems with the recording-quality on *Journey's End* – the sound is rich and warm – but the absence of CD closes this fine period of Vitous's career to non-vinyl users. *Emergence* is both a step forward and a summation. 'Morning Lake Forever' relates back to a composition on *Weather Report*, and there's a new solo version of 'When Face Gets Pale' from *Miroslav Vitous Group*. It begins with an 'Epilogue', which suggests a degree of self-reassessment, and though the 'Atlantis Suite' is rather too floating in conception there is a new solidity of purpose to his playing. Originally influenced by Scott LaFaro's remarkable performances with the Bill Evans Trio, Vitous has returned to something close to those singing lines. Though *Emergence* is a triumph, Vitous's best work still has to be sought out on the albums of other leaders, notably Chick Corea and Jack DeJohnette. There are interesting duo performances with guitarist Larry Coryell on *Dedicated To Bill Evans And Scott LaFaro* (Jazzpoint JP 1021 CD/LP/MC).

URS VOERKEL
PIANO

*** **S'Gcschank** FMP 0300 LP
Voerkel (*p* solo). 5/76.

*** **Voerkel–Frey–Lovens** FMP 0340 LP
Voerkel; Peter K. Frey (*b*); Paul Lovens (*d*). 5/76.

Despite the dedication to Tristano and a version of 'I Remember Clifford', Voerkel is a charter member of the FMP roster of pianists: fragmented lines, atonal clusters, scattershot rhythmic bravado. But a certain conservatism links him to a less frantic kind of free jazz, and both the solo album and the more intense trio record point up some of the links between form and content in the improvising of the period.

(***) **Goldberg** Po Torch ptr/jwd 15 LP
Voerkel; Paul Lovens (*d*). 2/89.

A compelling meeting between two now-veteran players in German free music. The four pieces here feature cut and thrust of tirelessly varied power and intensity, with the first piece – moving from a quietly scurrying opening to series of gradually intensifying climaxes – a particularly fine one. But the amateur recording has been restored only partially by the subsequent studio work, and some will find it too muddled to offer a real hearing of the music, hence our reservations.

PETRAS VYSNIAUSKAS
SOPRANO SAXOPHONE, ALTO SAXOPHONE, BASS CLARINET, FLUTE

***   **Viennese Concert** Leo CDLR 172 CD
        Vysniauskias; Vyacheslav Ganelin, Kestutis Lusas (*p, syn*); Mika Markovich (*d*);
        Gediminas Laurinavicius (*perc*). 6/89.

(*)   **Lithuania ITM 1449 CD
        Vysniauskias; Arkadij Gotesman (*d, perc*). 6/90.

Vysniauskias is a gifted young Lithuanian who demonstrates extraordinary command of all the saxophones, clarinets and flute. Like the Ganelin Trio, he favours what has been called a 'mixed composition technique', combining free improvisation with predetermined structures. In performance, he has a disconcerting habit of concentrating on the upper registers of the low-pitched instruments, and the lower register of his soprano saxophone and flute. This creates a very distinctive timbre that bears an unmistakable echo of folk music and Vysniauskias has made a significant use of Lithuanian forms in his compositions and performances.

Both of his available recordings suffer from considerable *longueurs* where the music doesn't seem to be going anywhere. The opening item of the *Viennese Concert* is a rather wistful soprano saxophone solo called 'Plunge' that has an inconsequential, practice-tape quality. The long – and presumably partly scored – 'Salto Mortale Op. 8' is a collage of free tonal, abstract and quasi-bop passages, all played with considerable restraint. Kestutis Lusas, who can also be heard in extended improvsation with the saxophonist on Leo's enormous 8CD *Document* (see 'Various Artists'), is a much more effective collaborator than Ganelin, who has become increasingly mannered and self-conscious in settings other than those which he completely dominates. Lusas's solemn, hymnic synthesizer accompaniment to the saxophonist's distracted wailing on 'Salto Mortale' gives the piece some shape and restores interest in an album that really could have done with an early change of pace and intensity.

The duos with Gotesman are more obviously folkish. The opening 'Sonet' is dedicated to Lithuania and includes apparent references to pre-war anthems and popular songs. Like Markovich, Gotesman is quite prepared to make use of silence and of acoustically minimal gestures, tiny fragments of sound that barely register on the hearer. Vysniauskias plays bass clarinet and flute in addition to his saxophone, following his normal practice of concentrating on extremes of pitch. Ironically, this is something he avoids on the *Viennese Concert*, where his soprano playing is strikingly reminiscent of the rather dry tonality one associates with Steve Lacy.

Interesting music, but perhaps a little too rarefied for most tastes.

COLLIN WALCOTT (1945–84)
TABLAS, SITAR, PERCUSSION INSTRUMENTS, VOICE

****   **Cloud Dance** ECM 1062 CD/LP
        Walcott; John Abercrombie (*g*); Dave Holland (*b*); Jack DeJohnette (*d*). 3/75.

***(*) **Grazing Dreams** ECM 1096 CD/LP
        Walcott; Don Cherry (*t, f, doussn'gouni*); John Abercrombie (*g, electric mand*); Palle
        Danielsson (*b*); Dom Um Romao (*perc*). 2/77.

***   **Dawn Dance** ECM 1198 CD/LP
        Walcott; Steve Eliovson (*g*). 1/81.

***(*) **Works** ECM 837276 CD
        Walcott; Don Cherry (*t, f, doussn'gouni*); John Abercrombie (*g*); Palle Danielsson,
        Dave Holland, Glen Moore (*b*); Dom Um Romao (*perc*); Nana Vasconcelos
        (*berimbau, perc*). 75–84.

Walcott's sudden death in a road accident in East Germany robbed contemporary music of a remarkable player who, more than any other individual of his generation (except, perhaps, his friend and colleague, Don Cherry, with whom he formed the group Codona (*q.v.*)), was possessed of a genuinely global understanding. It's significant that the classically trained Walcott, who also studied tabla under Alla Rakha and sitar under Ravi Shankar, should have spent some professsional time with clarinettist Tony Scott, one of the first American musicians to understand and explore the trade-off between Eastern and Western musics. What is often forgotten about Walcott is that, for all his occasionally ethereal effects, he is capable of a thumpingly compelling beat on tablas and robust bass-lines on the normally 'atmospheric' sitar. Like most musicians of his generation, Walcott was much influenced by the John Coltrane quartet. However, few have so thoroughly explored the implications of Coltrane's masterful rhythm section. Walcott was instrumental in inviting drummer Elvin Jones to collaborate on a (long-deleted) recording by Oregon, a venture which emphasized and reinforced the group's solid rhythmic foundation.

ECM's 'Works' series is only occasionally recommendable. Though it's obviously preferable to encounter Walcott's albums in their carefully modulated entirety, the posthumous sampler is a fair and honest representation of his solo work, the three Codona albums, and a late track with Oregon, recorded only a month before his death. Though *Grazing Dreams* has much to recommend it, *Cloud Dance* has a freshness and originality that sustain its appeal. 'Prancing', for just tablas and double bass, is one of the most exciting performances in the ECM catalogue and convincing evidence of Walcott's desire to extend the idiom of the Garrison/Jones rhythm section. Of the other duos, 'Padma', for sitar and guitar, works less well; but the album as a whole can quite reasonably be heard as a suite of related pieces that dance towards their thematic source in the closing title-piece. The quartet format on *Grazing Dreams* inevitably anticipates Walcott's and Cherry's work with Codona, and the long 'Song Of The Morrow' is a perfect encapsulation of the group's idiom. (All the tracks cited, with the exception of 'Cloud Dance', are included on *Works*.)

Walcott's duo record with guitarist Eliovson is undeservedly little known (the only sample on *Works* is a Walcott solo) and is well worth investigating.

MAL WALDRON (born 1926)
PIANO

***   **Mingus Lives** Enja 3075 LP

***(*)   **Update** Soul Note SN 1130 CD
Waldron (*p* solo). 9/79, 3/86.

An immensely gifted and prolific player whose professional roots are in the raw soul-jazz of Big Nick Nicholas and Ike Quebec, Waldron typically builds up solos from relatively simple ideas (his classic, much-covered 'Soul Eyes' could hardly be less elaborate), paying great attention to colour and shading, and to space. He favours block chords rather than rapid single-note runs, a style which has lent itself equally to large ensembles and smaller blowing groups (he worked with Mingus and Coltrane in the mid-1950s and early 1960s), sensitive accompaniment (he spent more than two years with Billie Holiday), and free playing.

Though it's clear that Waldron's main influences are Bud Powell and Thelonious Monk, he has developed independently and sounds quite unlike either. He has not been a prolific solo performer, and these two records, made some time apart, are by no means his best music. But they do allow closer inspection of his compositional and improvising style and they do establish the brand identity of two labels which have consistently supported Waldron's work, Enja giving him a darker and more lugubrious sound, Soul Note a sunnier, clearer focus. *Mingus Lives*, recorded one week after the great bassist's death, is not an album of covers (Waldron rarely plays standards or other composers' work) but a set of originals. Even 'Snake Out', which has become his most durable theme, scarcely seems solid enough to support the interpretative weight Waldron has placed on it. The solo version moves, typically, in steady, cumulative segments, with no false climaxes or dramatic resolutions.

Update is unusual in including a standard (in addition to 'Night In Tunisia', there is a very individual gloss on a Frank Loesser tune); it also further adjusts Waldron's polite reserve *vis-à-vis* free playing, which he explored with the 1969 *Free At Last* trio, below. Taken together, 'Free For C. T.' and 'Variations On A Theme By Cecil Taylor' firmly underscore Waldron's rugged individualism and refusal to be colonized by what has become the most invasive of contemporary piano styles. The variations are subtly rhythmic and beautifully proportioned. This is an important album in Waldron's career, coming at a time when his group performances were also at a peak. It merits the closest attention.

***   **Mal – 1** Original Jazz Classics OJC 611 CD/LP
Waldron; Idrees Sulieman (*t*); Gigi Gryce (*as*); Julian Euell (*b*); Arthur Edgehill (*d*). 11/56.

***   **Mal – 2** Original Jazz Classics OJC 671 CD/MC
Waldron; Bill Hardman (*t*); Jackie McLean, Sahib Shihab (*as*); John Coltrane (*ts*); Julian Euell (*b*); Arthur Taylor, Ed Thigpen (*d*). 4 & 5/57.

***(*)   **One And Two** Prestige P 24068 2LP
As above. 11/56, 4 & 5/57.

***(*)   **Wheelin'** Prestige P 24069 2LP
As for *One And Two* only, with Paul Quinichette (*ts*); Frank Wess (*f, ts*); Doug Watkins (*b*). 4 & 9/57.

Despite Sulieman's and Gryce's bursting expressiveness, the OJC is a low-key selection from Waldron's Prestige period, which saw Waldron concentrating on sophisticated harmonic patterns and cross-rhythms. The sound – as they used to say about serving girls – is no better than it ought to be but, given the anonymity of the rhythm section, not much is lost. A fine 'Yesterdays' picks things up a bit at the end. All the material is available on the Prestige *One And Two*, and if anything sounds rather sharper. The later tracks with Coltrane and McLean are inevitably of greater interest, though there's a bit of padding on *Wheelin'* where the alternative takes don't really amount to more than make-weights.

In 1957, Coltrane had finally decided to rid himself of a deeply rooted drug and alcohol dependency. It isn't reading too much into basically conventional performances to suggest that his solos have a new maturity, coupled with an emotional vulnerability, which McLean seems to comprehend better than the rather single-minded Shihab, but round which Waldron steals with unfailing tact and supportive ease. No classic tracks, though 'Don't Explain' (with McLean) and 'The Way You Look Tonight' (with Shihab) are a cut above the rest.

***   **Impressions** Original Jazz Classics OJC 132 LP
Waldron; Addison Farmer (*b*); Albert Heath (*d*). 3/59.

Waldron made substantial strides as a composer towards the end of the 1950s. That isn't reflected here, in a rather bland selection of standard material with remarkably little personal input. Heath seems to anticipate all the pianist's needs, and it's a pity they have not recorded together more (as they might have done, given their mutual gravitation to Europe). There is some fine romantic material, but this should be considered a low-priority item.

***(*)   **The Quest** Original Jazz Classics OJC 082 LP
Waldron; Eric Dolphy (*as, cl*); Booker Ervin (*ts*); Ron Carter (*clo*); Joe Benjamin (*b*); Charles Persip (*d*). 6/61.

Often adduced as a Dolphy record, this fine session was firmly under Mal Waldron's hand. Despite that, he comes out rather badly in a soft, very homogenized mix. The album is most valuable for the insight it offers into Waldron's writing at the time, which ranges between the firmly anchored 'Status Seeking' and a drifting romanticism on 'Duquility' and 'Warm Canto'. The latter is a rare outing for Dolphy's concert clarinet; he otherwise sticks to alto saxophone and blows an outclassed Ervin all round the studio. Given the inadequacies of the original LP, it's unfortunate that *The Quest* hasn't (yet) been selected for CD transfer; it is, though, also available on a second-string Dolphy compilation *Fire Waltz* (Prestige P 24085 2LP), where it is paired with *Looking Ahead*, an album made under Ken McIntyre's leadership.

***(*)   **Free At Last** ECM 1001 CD
Waldron; Isla Eckinger (*b*); Clarence Beckton (*d*). 11/69.

To describe Waldron as 'unmelodic' is a description, not a criticism. He has rarely written memorable tunes, concentrating instead on subtly coded tonal cells out of which, as his career has continued, longer and longer improvisations can be developed. *Free At Last* was a conscious attempt to come to terms with free jazz; in Waldron's own words, it represented his desire to play 'rhythmically instead of soloing on chord changes'. At the same time, Waldron utterly rejects any notion of free jazz as 'complete anarchy or disorganized sound'. At first glance, these half-dozen tracks are disappointingly constrained and modest in scope. The long 'Rat Now' (a typical Waldron pun) and 'Rock My Soul' point a way forward for extended improvisation that does not depend on chord sequences; but, interestingly, both have the same 'feel' as more conventionally harmonic music because Waldron's clusters always seem to gravitate towards specific resolutions.

A useful trivia question, especially for anyone who wields the 'ECM sound' *canard* too freely, is to ask what the label's very first release was. If one quality characterizes ECM's output, it has been a search for new principles of organization in jazz, its only constraint a rejection of anarchic disorganization. *Free At Last* was a fine send-off.

***   **Black Glory** Enja 2004 LP

(*)   **Plays The Blues Enja 5021 LP

***(*)   **A Touch Of The Blues** Enja 2062 LP
         Waldron; Jimmy Woode (*b*); Pierre Favre (*d* on *Black Glory* and *Plays The Blues*);
         Allen Blairman (*d* on *A Touch Of The Blues*). 6/71, 5/72.

Waldron also kicks off the current Enja catalogue (further testimony to his dependence on European labels) with this rather mixed trio session. Favre and Woode don't entirely gel as a rhythm section and a version of 'Rock My Soul' borders on the chaotic. The curiously titled 'Sieg Haille' (arranged for sextet on *Moods*, below) is an instance of Waldron's Mingus-influenced black pride, not untouched by irony. *Plays The Blues*, with the same personnel, is one of Waldron's disappointing records; for completists only.

A Touch Of The Blues opens with a wryly romantic Beatles tune, 'Here, There And Everywhere' (see also *Mingus Lives*, above). 'The Search' and the title-piece make up the remainder, a three-part format which Waldron favours, both on record and for live sets. Performances are sharp and often moving.

****   **Up Popped The Devil** Enja 2034 LP
         Waldron; Carla Poole (*f*); Reggie Workman (*b*); Billy Higgins (*d*). 12/73.

One of the Waldron's finest records and greatly overdue for CD transfer. It includes a sterling performance of one of his most durable themes; 'Snake Out', written around an eminently pianistic F minor chord, has become a staple item in Waldron's group performances; there is a solo version on *Mingus Lives*, above. The title-track has the dark, gospelly roll one associates with his work at this time. 'Space Walk' is less compelling.

****   **Hard Talk** Enja 2050 LP
         Waldron; Manfred Schoof (*t*); Steve Lacy (*ss*); Isla Eckinger (*b*); Allen Blairman (*d*).
         5/74.

***(*)   **One-Upmanship** Enja 2092 LP
         Waldron; Steve Lacy (*ss*); Jimmy Woode (*b*); Makaya Ntoshko (*d*). 2/77.

***(*)   **Moods** Enja 3021 CD/2LP
         Waldron solo, and with Terumasa Hino (*t*); Hermann Breuer (*tb*); Steve Lacy (*ss*);
         Cameron Brown (*b*); Cameron Ntoshko (*d*). 5/78.

The mid to late 1970s was a vintage spell in Waldron's career. His improvisations were stretching out and growing more adventurous as he absorbed the lessons of free playing. In this regard, the association with Lacy was of paramount importance. Though they seem fundamentally opposed in basic aesthetics, it's clear that Lacy's dry abstraction is only a continual refinement of his Dixieland roots. He swings with absolute conviction on all these sides.

Hard Talk remains the most compelling. Consisting of just three tracks, it allows Waldron and his colleagues to stretch out, constructing elaborate patterns out of very basic material. 'Snake Out' charms, as always, with Lacy playing as magnificent a lead as he has done in duo performances with Waldron. Schoof sounds less confident on 'Russian Melody' but finds a bright, hard-edged sound for the title-track. 'Hooray For Herbie' on *One-Upmanship* is a Monkish vamp that Lacy and Waldron have performed at length elsewhere. It sounds a little overcooked with the full quartet; Woode in particular seems uneasy with it and falls back on a relentless repetition of the basic figure. *Moods* is much more varied, with an extra horn in the ensembles and a valuable sample of Waldron's rather mournful solo style; 'Soul Eyes' and 'I Thought About You' are beautiful and serve as reminders of the pianist's contact with Coltrane; but 'Anxiety', 'Lonely', 'Thoughtful' and 'Happiness' sound like 'face-pulling' exercises, and the soft, Monkish figurations of 'Duquility' are rather too elliptical. Waldron hits the keys with uncommon firmness, perhaps unused to or unsatisfied with the piano, perhaps merely trying new levels of attack.

***(*)   **What It Is** Enja 4010 LP
Waldron; Clifford Jordan (*ts*); Cecil McBee (*b*); Dannie Richmond (*d*). 11/81.

A rather dark and enigmatic set, overshadowed by Charles Mingus's turbulent spirit. Jordan is one of only a handful of saxophonists who have sounded effective in Waldron's company. His very individual tone contributes significantly to 'Hymn From The Inferno' and to the remarkable 'Charlie Parker's Last Supper', which is one of Waldron's most dramatic conceptions. Richmond and McBee are a solid presence, but the overall sound is rather shadowy and the upper levels aren't well balanced in relation to the prevailing sombreness.

***(*)   **You And The Night And The Music** Paddle Wheel K28P 6272 LP
Waldron; Reggie Workman (*b*); Ed Blackwell (*d*). 12/83.

A rather self-conscious exception to Waldron's long-standing resistance to standard repertoire. Indvidual performances all carry his unmistakable stylistic stamp, but there are no real revelations or surprises (nor is the sound anything to write home about) and the album merits its extra half-star only on the strength of its thorough enjoyability. Workman and Blackwell are superb, of course. For the record: 'The Way You Look Tonight', 'Bags' Groove', 'Round About Midnight', 'Georgia On My Mind', 'Billie's Bounce' and the title-piece. There's also an affecting 'Waltz For My Mother'.

***   **Dedication** Soul Note SN 1178 CD/LP
Waldron; David Friesen (*b*). 11/85.

Something of an oddity, but an enjoyable one. Friesen's floating, soft-edged bass-lines (played on an amplified, bodyless instrument, credited as 'Oregon bass') actually work rather well over Waldron's dark mutterings, and the set as a whole has a coherence and unity that begin to sound slightly repetitive only on subsequent hearings.

****   **Songs Of Love And Regret** Freelance FRL CD006 CD

***(*)   **Much More!** Freelance FRL CD010 CD
Waldron; Marion Brown (*as*). 11/85, 11/88.

****   **Sempre Amore** Soul Note SN 1170 CD/LP
Waldron; Steve Lacy (*ss*). 2/86.

For straightforward beauty these are unsurpassed in Waldron's output. Clearly there is a sharp difference between Brown's waveringly pitched emotionalism and Lacy's dry phrasing; but in all cases the two saxophonists get inside the song, concentrating in a manner one doesn't normally associate with Waldron on developing the melody. *Sempre Amore* is dedicated to Ellington–Strayhorn material, which must have made an intriguing change from Lacy's specialized diet of Monk. The two Freelances are more eclectic, taking in 'All God's Chillun Got Rhythm' and 'Now's The Time' (*Much More!*), McCoy Tyner's 'Contemplation' and (for comparison with the Lacy set) 'A Flower Is A Lovesome Thing' (*Love And Regret*). The earlier set opens with a slightly hesitant 'Blue Monk' (the CD reissue includes a rejected take that comes in at double the length and is far superior) which is then glossed in Waldron's own 'A Cause De Monk' and Brown's own 'To The Golden Lady In Her Graham Cracker Window', a typically delicate tune.

All three are strongly recommended, but they aren't for cynics.

***(*)   **Space** Vent Du Sud VSCD 107 CD
Waldron; Michel Marre (*t, flhn*); Doudou Gouirand (*as, ss*). 2/86.

Hard to find, perhaps, but well worth the effort. Both the material and the instrumentation are intriguingly varied, and even stalwarts like 'Soul Eyes' take on a fresh sheen that it's tempting to attribute to Marre's and Gouirand's Gallic inflexions, but for the fact that Waldron himself seems to be playing with unwonted bounce and motion.

****   **Left Alone '86** Paddle Wheel K28P 6453 CD/LP
       Waldron; Jackie McLean (*as*); Herbie Lewis (*b*); Eddie Moore (*d*). 9/86.

Recorded at the beginning of a vintage month for Waldron groups (see items below) in what was already a vintage year for the pianist, *Left Alone* has a searing melancholy. Basically a tribute to Billie Holiday, it consists of four tracks associated with her – 'Lover Man', 'Good Morning Heartache', 'All Of Me' and 'God Bless The Child' – interspersed with Waldron originals that are calculated to accentuate the mood of solitude and bluesy ennui Lady Day gave off in her final couple of years (when Waldron was her accompanist). McLean's alto playing has regained all its old fire; this is one his best performances of recent years.

***(*)   **The Git Go** Soul Note SN 1118 CD/LP

****   **The Seagulls Of Kristiansund** Soul Note SN 1148 CD/LP
       Waldron; Woody Shaw (*t, flhn*); Charlie Rouse (*ts, f*); Reggie Workman (*b*); Ed
       Blackwell (*d*). 9/86.

Two top-flight sets from a single night of a fine week's engagement at the Village Vanguard in New York City. All six compositions are Waldron's and his playing is supremely economical, sketching in tonal centres with a minimum of elaboration, soloing on the faster tracks with a positive touch, shading beautifully on the slow 'Seagulls Of Kristiansund'. This shows a side of Waldron's work which some critics have likened to American minimalism: a slow accretion of almost subliminal harmonic and rhythmic shifts steadily pile up until the music seems ready to overbalance.

Perhaps oddly – for subsequent releases from live or studio sessions rarely match up to the original albums – the second album is more appealing. *The Git Go* consists of no more than the title-piece and an overlong 'Status Seeking', which seems to have lost much of the terse discipline Waldron brought to it on *The Quest*.

On the second album, Waldron kicks off 'Snake Out' with a menacing bass pulse that builds up almost unbearable tension before loosing Woody Shaw on one of his most unfettered solos. Rouse's solo is more compact and provides a taut bridge between Shaw and Waldron, who plays lyrically over a bleak vamp. Blackwell and Workman both solo effectively, though the drummer's finest moment comes at the end of 'Judy', the middle track of the set and a tribute to Waldron's great supporter, Judy Sneed. Shaw's solo is astonishing. Blackwell shines again on 'Seagulls', producing non-metrical effects on his splash cymbal; Workman's foghorn and seabird effects are straight out of Mingus's bag.

The Git Go has some *longueurs*, but its successor is thoroughly and straightforwardly enjoyable, and should be tried for size.

****   **Our Colline's A Tresure** Soul Note SN 1198 CD
       Waldron; Leonard Jones (*b*); Sangoma Everett (*d*). 4/87.

Still on a high. Waldron's handling of 'The Git Go' is markedly different from that on the Village Vanguard sessions, tighter in conception, if not in length, and with most of the solo space inevitably restored to the composer. The opening 'Spaces' is a superb example of direct motivic improvisation and lets in Jones for the first of several fine contributions. Everett, a neighbour of Waldron's in Munich, is less well known but sounds more than competent. The title-piece (and the mis-spelt word is probably deliberate) is dedicated to a young French friend of Waldron's, who may grow up to tresure the beautiful waltz-tune better than she will the picture on the cover.

***(*)   **Live At Sweet Basil** Paddle Wheel K28P 6471 CD/LP
       Waldron; Steve Lacy (*ss*); Reggie Workman (*b*); Eddie Moore (*d*). 8/87.

Billed as the Super Quartet, this one is far less stellar than the Village Vanguard group. The music has a drier, less varied texture and features another saxophonist whose adoration for Monk ('Evidence') came from further off but went every bit as deep as Rouse's. Lacy's tightly pinched phrases are like accents on Waldron's bold, sans-serif lettering; Moore and Workman underscore firmly, sometimes overpowering the foreground.

***   **Mal Dance And Soul** Tutu 888102 CD/LP

***(*)   **Quadrologue At Utopia** Tutu 888118 CD
       Waldron; Jim Pepper (*ts*); Ed Schuller (*b*); John Betsch (*d*). 11/87, 10/89.

Good, mostly new material from Waldron's late-1980s band. As with Clifford Jordan, above, it is Pepper's peculiar tonality that fits him for this context. The saxophonist, who is of American Indian descent, appears only on 'Soulmates' in the 1987 session, but he is a full-blooded presence on the aptly named *Quadrologue* and is especially good on the atmospheric 'Mistral Breeze'. Though less versatile than Joe Lovano (with whom he used to work in the Paul Motian group), Pepper has an enormous emotional range and the kind of innate rhythmic sophistication that Waldron requires. The leader sounds faintly muted on 'Ticket To Utopia' but warms towards an excellent finish on 'Funny Glasses & A Moustache'.

***   **No More Tears (For Lady Day)** Timeless SJP 328 CD
       Waldron; Joey Cardoso (*b*); John Betsch (*d*). 11/88.

Unlike *You And The Night And The Music*, this one doesn't really get off the ground. Waldron has clearly reached a point in his career where he is prepared to re-examine a more traditional jazz repertoire, and it would be cynical to suggest that the choice of material was conditioned by his sidemen's limitations. Betsch is one of the finest European-based drummers, but Cardoso is a plodding fellow whose solo on the opening 'Yesterdays' begins to pall before he has got himself properly warmed up. This comes from a Timeless series dedicated to the preservation of the traditional piano trio (almost as if they were steam engines or an endangered species). Fortunately, Waldron does a fine conservation job on his own, injecting new life into warhorses like 'Smoke Gets In Your Eyes' and 'Alone Together', which used to be as plentiful in the catalogue as buffalo on the plains of Wisconsin but which seem to have been exploited to death and appear much more rarely on standards sets of late.

BENNIE WALLACE (born 1946)
TENOR SAXOPHONE

***   **The Fourteen Bar Blues** Enja 3029 LP
       Wallace; Eddie Gomez (*b*); Eddie Moore (*d*). 1/78.

***   **Live At The Public Theater** Enja 3045 LP
       Wallace; Eddie Gomez (*b*); Dannie Richmond (*d*). 5/78.

***   **The Free Will** Enja 3063 LP
       As above, except add Tommy Flanagan (*p*). 1–2/80.

***(*)   **Bennie Wallace Plays Monk** Enja 3091 LP
       As above, except Jimmy Knepper (*tb*) replaces Flanagan. 3/81.

***   **The Bennie Wallace Trio And Chick Corea** Enja 4028 CD/LP
       As above, except Chick Corea (*p*) replaces Knepper. 5/82.

***(*)   **Big Jim's Tango** Enja 4046 LP
       Wallace; Dave Holland (*b*); Elvin Jones (*d*). 1–2/82.

***   **Sweeping Through The City** Enja 4078 CD/LP
       Wallace; Ray Anderson (*tb*); Pat Conley (*p*); John Scofield (*g*); Mike Richmond, Dennis Irwin (*b*); Tom Whaley (*d*); The Wings Of Song (*v*). 3/84.

A traditionalist of the best kind, Bennie Wallace has made a lot of highly entertaining records without quite finding the bigger audience his populist music might reach. The trio albums give him the space he enjoys, and set up his Sonny Rollins influence to its most effective ends: the grand, swaggering rhythms and tonal exaggerations buttress an improvising style which owes much to R&B and roadhouse music, a greasiness which can distract from the intense strcutures which Wallace can work together. He isn't a licks player, doesn't dawdle in clichés, and the essential heartiness of his music is deceptive, for he provides greater rewards for listeners who are prepared to work with him. The first two trio albums suffer just a little from a slightly awkward mix of personalities: Gomez's rubbery virtuosity doesn't always suit Wallace's moves, even if they clearly enjoy playing together, and the following *The Free Will* is also too gentlemanly, through Flanagan's characteristically professorial touch. The Monk collection, though, is bountiful stuff: the players tear into the tunes instead of tiptoeing round them or going for anything 'quirky', the usual options in Monk tributes, and Knepper's inspirational playing adds line and length to Wallace's helter-skelter solos. 'Ask Me Now' is about as uproarious a wake for Monk as one could wish for. Chick Corea's guest appearance doesn't do anything much for the trio – only Corea could contribute a tune called 'Mystic Bridge' to follow a Wallace original titled 'The Bob Crosby Blues' – and while Gomez follows the pianist, Richmond tends to stick with the tenorman. The Wallace–Holland–Jones trio is, though, a rattling little ensemble. 'Monroe County Moon' posits Wallace's background (he comes from Tennessee) as a harbinger of a new roots jazz, 'Big Jim Does the Tango For You' is probably the only example of Elvin Jones playing a tango beat on record, and the mighty blow-outs of 'Green And Yellow' and another version of 'The Free Will' are enjoyable rounds of three heavyweights flexing their muscles. *Sweeping Through The City* invents some gospel roots for Bennie via the roistering contribution of The Wings Of Song on two tracks; the rest is neo-bop and blues with Anderson and Scofield adding their own characteristic thoughts to the mixture.

***(*)   **Brilliant Corners** Denon 32CY-2430 CD
         Wallace; Yosuke Yamashita (*p*); Jay Anderson (*b*); Jeff Hirshfield (*d*). 9/86.

****   **The Art Of The Saxophone** Denon 33CY-1648 CD
         Wallace; Oliver Lake (*as*); Jerry Bergonzi, Harold Ashby, Lew Tabackin (*ts*); John
         Scofield (*g*); Eddie Gomez (*b*); Dannie Richmond (*d*). 2/87.

Two outstanding and insufficiently known records. The quartet date with Yamashita leans heavily on Monk's repertoire and with the pianist playing in a kind of overdriven-Monk manner it's almost akin to a modernization of the quartet with Rouse (whose tonalities Wallace can occasionally evoke). Lucid, scathingly sharp, this is a bristling instance of post-bop repertory. *The Art Of The Saxophone* goes a notch better by inviting four other masters in for various duets: Tabackin and Wallace do an acapella 'All Too Soon', Ashby feathers his way through 'Prelude To A Kiss', Lake tears through 'Prince Charles' and Bergonzi makes three attacking appearances. Wallace and Scofield bind the appearances together and make everybody at home.

***(*)   **Twilight Time** Blue Note B21Y-46293 CD
         Wallace; Ray Anderson (*tb*); Rabbit Edmonds (*ts*); Dr John (*p, org*); John Scofield
         (*g*); Eddie Gomez, Bob Crandshaw (*b*); Jack DeJohnette, Bernard Purdie, Chris
         Parker (*d*). 85.

***(*)   **Bordertown** Blue Note CDP 7480142 CD
         Wallace; Ray Anderson (*tb*); Dr John (*org, p, v*); John Scofield, Mitch Watkins (*g*);
         Eddie Gomez, Jay Anderson, Will Lee (*b*); Chris Parker, Herlin Riley, Jeff Hirshfield
         (*d*). 6/87.

It's possible to accuse Wallace of being too calculatedly eclectic, and here he sets himself up in a New Orleans-goes-to-New York groove with Dr John as guest player and producer. But the results are so winningly infectious and the leader's own playing so quickly in key with the louche rhythms, that it's hard to dislike the results. Anderson and Scofield do pretty much what they did before, but Dr John's own rollicking keyboards and singing suit everything to a T. Both of these discs are ripely entertaining, with the first glorying in one of Wallace's most extravagant solos on 'Is It True What They Say About Dixie?' and a fulsome reading of the title-track, giving it just the edge over *Bordertown*; but either one is a strong portrait of the musician and his cast of cronies.

THOMAS 'FATS' WALLER (1904–43)
PIANO, ORGAN, VOCAL

(*)   **Classic Jazz From Rare Piano Rolls Biograph BCD 104 CD
         Waller, James P. Johnson, Lawrence J. Cook (*piano rolls*). 3/23–1/29.

***   **Low Down Papa** Biograph BCD 114 CD
         Waller; James P. Johnson (*piano rolls*). 5/23–6/31.

Thomas Waller was already deputizing for James P. Johnson and playing film and stage-show accompaniments when he started making piano rolls for the QRS company in 1923. These two discs transfer some of his many rolls to CD. Most of the tunes are typical light blues novelties of the day, and they're played with a crisp, courtly demeanour, although individuality is to some extent suppressed by the machinery of the roll system: certainly Waller's first piano records show much more idiosyncrasy than any of these tracks. There are a couple of items with Johnson, Waller's great mentor, and one on the earlier disc which was credited to Waller but is actually by Lawrence Cook. Ebullience and good humour are persistent to the point of becoming exasperting here, and perhaps these pieces are best sampled a few at a time: there are only a few genuinely Walleresque touches such as the abrupt doubling of tempo in 'Your Time Now', on *Low Down Papa*. The rolls have been brightly recorded, although *Low Down Papa* is less glassy and generally has the better selection of themes.

*(*) Fats At The Organ ASV AJA 5007R CD
Waller (*org*). 23–27.

A unique record, if a bizarre one. Waller made several pipe organ solos early in his career, but this set consists of organ transcriptions of piano roll solos: Waller is heard twice-removed. If the piano roll discs listed above sound artificial, it's hard to hear much of Waller in here except in the merry rhythmic gait of the original rolls: all the choices of registration are made by Ronald Curtis, admittedly after studying Waller's original organ records, and any authenticity which remains comes off a second-best to whatever a 78 can produce.

** The Complete Early Band Works 1927–29 Halcyon HDL 115 CD/MC
Waller; Tom Morris (*c*); Charlie Gaines, Henry Allen, Leonard Davis (*t*); Jack Teagarden (*tb*); Jimmy Archey, J. C. Higginbotham (*tb*); Arville Harris (*cl, as, ts*); Albert Nicholas, Charlie Holmes (*cl, as*); Larry Binyon (*ts*); Bobbie Leecan (*g*); Will Johnson, Eddie Condon (*bj*); Pops Foster, Al Morgan (*b*); Eddie King, Gene Krupa, Kaiser Marshall (*d*); The Four Wanderers (*v*). 5/27–12/29.

*** Fats And His Buddies RCA Bluebird 90649 CD/MC
As above, except add Jabbo Smith (*c*), Garvin Bushell (*cl, as, bsn*), James P Johnson (*p*). 5/27–12/29.

Waller doesn't sing anywhere on these records (which basically duplicate each other), and given the nightmarish vocals by The Four Wanderers on two tracks, perhaps he was numbed into silence. The seven tracks by Fats with Tom Morris's Hot Babies are a garish mismatch of pipe organ and cornet-led hot band, and since the resonances and overtones of the organ tamp down everything the other players do, it's hard to imagine how anyone could have thought that the group would work. The eight tracks by Fats Waller & His Buddies (the best of which are also included on some of the Bluebird records which follow) are merely loose-knit New York jazz of the period (1929). Where Bluebird score is in including six tracks by the Louisiana Sugar Babes, which are otherwise available under Jabbo Smith's name. The original sides have been nicely handled in the remastering on both discs.

*** Jazz Classics: Fats Waller 1927–1934 BBC REB/CD.ZEF 598 CD/LP/MC
As above, except add Rex Stewart, Muggsy Spanier (*c*); Dave Klein, Herman Autrey (*t*), George Brunies, Sam Blank, Floyd O'Brien (*tb*), Benny Goodman, Jimmy Lord, Mezz Mezzrow (*cl*), Don Redman, Benny Carter (*cl, as*), Louis Martin (*as, bs*), Coleman Hawkins, Hymie Wolfson, Pee Wee Russell (*ts*); Sam Shapiro, Sol Klein (*vn*), Tony Gerhardi, Jack Bland, Al Casey (*g*), Cyrus St Clair (*bb*); Harry Barth, Pops Foster, Billy Taylor (*b*), George Stafford, Zutty Singleton, John Lucas, Harry Dial (*d*), Billy Banks (*v*).

A superior handling of what was a complicated period of Waller's life, as far as studio work was concerned. He turns up here as a guest with Ted Lewis, Billy Banks's Rhythmakers and the Little Chocolate Dandies, and there are various tracks from the Hot Babies and Buddies sessions, as well as some piano solos and an organ version of 'Sugar'. Cleverly programmed, this is a disc that works as both an overview and a playable compilation, ending with an early Rhythm track and the piano solo, 'Alligator Crawl'. This was one of Robert Parker's earliest stereo remastering efforts, and the sometimes over-resonant acoustic may bother some ears, even if the originals are obviously in fine condition.

(****)   **Turn On The Heat** RCA Bluebird ND 82482 2LP/2CD/2MC
Waller. 2/27–5/41.

***(*)   **Piano Masterworks Vol. 1** EPM 5106 CD
Waller. 10/22–9/29.

Musically, the Bluebird set is the one Waller record which should be in every collection: it collates the results of all the solo sessions he recorded for Victor. Deplorably, for a pianist of his stature, he was allowed to cut only two sessions as a soloist after 1934, so most of these tracks date from 1929–34, with a solitary title, 'Blue Black Bottom', coming from 1927. Waller's inventiveness within the idiom of stride piano is astonishingly fecund, particularly in the two sessions made in August 1929: 'Valentine Stomp', 'Sweet Savannah Sue' and 'Baby Oh Where Can You Be' are among his finest statements on record, organized with sober attention to formality but graced with an inimitable energy and a delicate humour that's quite unlike the Waller of the 1930s. Almost as good are 'Smashing Thirds' and the rather cheeky miniatures of 'Clothes Line Ballet' and 'African Ripples', while the 1941 solos, culminating in a masterful treatment of James P Johnson's 'Carolina Shout' find him reflecting on a career that was consistently directed away from such 'serious' studies. The double-CD and album includes several alternative takes, some of which – particularly those for 'I've Got A Feeling I'm Falling' and 'Love Me Or Leave Me' – show some surprising variations in manner (the LP issue omits some of these). But the project is marred by the very variable quality of the remasterings. Some tracks are excessively noisy (which tends to make a mockery of a transfer system called NoNOISE) and the variety of sources – the sleeve credits metal masters, 78s and even tape copies – has clearly resulted in a patchwork product. Waller's pianism still emerges clearly enough but it's a pity that the restoration lacks consistent credibility. The EPM disc collects all the solos up to 1929, including two little-known sides for OKeh from 1922, and although the sound is also somewhat erratic here, it's rather more acceptable.

(*)   **You Rascal You ASV AJA 5040 CD
Waller; Henry Red Allen, Leonard Davis, Bill Coileman, Herman Autrey, Charlie Gains, Charlie Teagarden, Sterling Bose (*t*); Jack Teagarden (*tb, v*); Charlie Irvis, Tommy Dorsey, J. C. Higginbotham, Charlie Green (*tb*); Arville Harris, Ben Whittet, Artie Shaw, Albert Nicholas, Larry Binyon (*cl, as*); Gene Sedric, Larry Binyon (*cl, ts*); Bud Freeman (*ts*); Al Casey, Dick McDonough (*g*); Eddie Condon (*bj*); Billy Taylor, Pops Foster, Artie Bernstein (*b*); Stan King, Kaiser Marshall, Harry Dial (*d*). 3/29–11/34.

Waller's early band sides, picked out in this cross-section of 1929–34 sessions, suggested a mercurial talent pondering on its ultimate direction. The two sides by Fats Waller's Buddies are frantic small-band New York jazz of the day (1929), with little of the slyness of the Rhythm sides represented by seven 1934 tracks, and the guest-star role he takes on a Jack Teagarden version of 'You Rascal You' offers little more than inspired mugging, entertaining as it is. A few solos, including the enchanting 'My Fate Is In Your Hands', suggest the other side of Waller's art, and the complexity of his personality. Mixed reproduction again, alas: some sides sound very dull, others are clear and strong.

***(*)   **Fats Waller & His Rhythm** BBC REB/CD/ZEF 684 CD/LP/MC
Waller; Herman Autrey, Bill Coleman (*t*); Rudy Powell (*cl, as*); Gene Sedric (*cl, ts*); James Smith, Al Casey (*g*); Charles Turner, Billy Taylor (*b*); Harry Dial, Arnold Bolden, Slick Jones (*d*). 8/34–11/36.

(***)   **The Joint Is Jumpin'** RCA Bluebird ND 86288 CD
Waller; Charlie Gaines, Herman Autrey, John 'Bugs' Hamilton, Bunny Berigan, Nathaniel Williams, Benny Carter (*t*); Charlie Irvis, Tommy Dorsey, George Robinson, John Haughton, Slim Moore (*tb*); Arville Harris, Rudy Powell, Gene Sedric, William Allsop, James Powell, Fred Skerritt, Lonnie Simmons, Gene Porter (*reeds*); Al Casey, John Smith, Dick McDonough, Irving Ashby (*g*); Charlie Turner, Cedric Wallace, Slam Stewart (*b*); Harry Dual, Slick Jones, George Wettling, Zutty Singleton (*d*). 3/29–1/43.

A competent choice of some of Waller's best on the Bluebird disc: hits such as 'Your Feet's Too Big', two versions of 'Honeysuckle Rose' (including one from the 1937 'Jam Session At Victor' date) and a shrewd selection of ten of his best solos, in a generous 23 tracks. But the CD is again badly let down by the remastering, which sounds bright and clear on only a very few of the tracks – very sloppy work. The BBC disc concentrates on the earlier sessions by the Rhythm, and while any personal choice is going to be idiosyncratic, these 18 tracks include at least two of the best of the earlier sides in 'Whose Honey Are You?' and 'If It Isn't Love'. Robert Parker's remastering is authoritatively done, if the use of reverb is to one's taste, and until there's a definitive collection of the earlier Rhythm sides, this will be a firm first choice.

***   **The Definitive Fats Waller, His Rhythm, His Piano** Stash ST-CD-528 CD
Waller; Herman Autrey (*t*); Rudy Powell (*cl, as*); Gene Sedric (*cl, ts*); Al Casey (*g*);
Cedric Wallace, Charles Turner (*b*); Slick Jones, Harry Dial (*d*). 35–39.

A generous (76 minutes) helping of Waller and the Rhythm from broadcasts in 1935 and 1939. The material is staple Waller fare and the exuberance is as expected, in surprisingly good sound for the period and the sources. While the 'new' versions aren't strikingly revelatory of any different side to Waller, they confirm his ability to create happy music out of the thinnest of tunes.

***   **London Sessions 1938–1939** EMI Pathe/Jazztime 251271-2 CD
Waller; Dave Wilkins (*t*); George Chisholm (*tb*); Alfie Kahn (*cl, ts*); Ian Sheppard (*ts, vn*); Alan Ferguson (*g*); Len Harrison (*b*); Hymie Schneider, Max Levin, Edmundo Ros (*d*); Adelaide Hall (*v*). 8/38–6/39.

Waller visited Europe twice in the late 1930s, and recorded in London on both trips. Two sessions in 1938 found him handling organ and piano with a British band, cutting six organ solos (including a surprisingly bleak and unsettling 'Deep River') and backing Adelaide Hall for two further songs. Next year, he worked alone or with drum-only support. There are six wistful miniatures, the 'London Suite', and a rather mournful 'Smoke Dreams Of You', which go to suggest the reflective side of Waller's art which rarely made it to record yet which is always touted by supporters as his shamefully overlooked inner self. Whatever the case, these are slight but charming pieces. Unfortunately the original pressings were in poor shape and remastering has done little for the later tracks, although the earlier session rings out clearly.

***(*)   **The Last Years 1940–1943** RCA Bluebird ND 90411 4LP/3CD/3MC
Waller; Herman Autrey, John 'Bugs' Hamilton, Bob Williams, Joe Thomas, Nathaniel Williams, Benny Carter (*t*); George Wilson, Ray Hogan, Herb Flemming, Alton Moore (*tb*); Jimmy Powell, Dave Macrae, George James, Lawrence Fields, Gene Porter (*as*); Gene Sedric (*cl, ts*); Bob Carroll (*ts*); John Smith, Al Casey, Irving Ashby (*g*); Cedric Wallace, Slam Stewart (*b*); Slick Jones, Arthur Trappier, Zutty Singleton (*d*); Kathryn Perry, The Deep River Boys (*v*). 4/40–1/43.

If Waller was ultimately trapped by his non-stop funny-man image, the routine of his 'Fats Waller And His Rhythm' records at least helped to focus a talent that was sometimes in danger of merely running ragged. The dozens of throwaway tunes he lampooned may have had little intrinsic merit, and he often falls back on favourite lines and devices, but – like Armstrong in the same period – Waller remains an inimitable talent, and the space limitations of the records often results in performances full of compressed excitement. A little-known track such as 'You're Gonna Be Sorry' (1941) works up an explosive swing which Waller, Hamilton and Sedric turn to exciting advantage. Nor is it true to say that the Rhythm recordings declined in quality: the 1941–42 sessions include some of the finest sides the band made, and Hamilton, Sedric and Autrey, all minor figures who nevertheless played handsomely at the right moment, lend a more urgently swinging touch to the music than anything provided by, say, the Louis Jordan band (compare Waller's 'Your Socks Don't Match' or 'Don't Give Me That Jive', two very Jordanesque tunes, with any of the altoman's records – next to Jordan's calculating burlesques, Waller's wit sounds wholly spontaneous). With the disappearance of the US Bluebird complete Waller set on LP, this is the only comprehensive look at the later sessions, and given the large number of less familiar tunes, it's a surprisingly playable set, with fine sessions like the 1941 big-band date which pulled off a terrific 'Chant Of The Groove', the non-vocal Rhythm sides including 'Pantin' In The Panther Room' and the final studio date that included Benny Carter on trumpet and delivered a valedictory 'Ain't Misbehavin''. The remastering is rather better than the other Bluebird discs, and we must recommend the set to even cautious Waller listeners.

JAN WALLGREN
PIANO

***   **Love Chant** Dragon DRLP 10 LP
Wallgren; Bengt Ernryd (*t, flhn*); Tomasz Szukalski (*ts*); Pawel Jarzebski (*b*); Eric Dahlberg (*d*). 4/76.

(*)   **Ballad An Den Ruhr Dragon DRLP 24 LP
Wallgren; Bengt Ernryd (*t, flhn*); Buschi Niebergall (*b*); Conny Sjokvist (*d*). 11/79.

(*)   **Lavoro In Corso Dragon DRLP 89 LP
Wallgren; Bengt Ernryd (*t, flhn*); Gustavo Bergalli (*t*); Håkan Nykvist (*t, frhn*); Lasse Olofsson (*tb*); Sven Larsson (*btb*); Lennart Aberg (*ss, as, f*); Krister Andersson (*ts, cl*); Erik Nilsson (*bs, bcl*); Palle Danielsson (*b*); Peter Ostlund (*d*); Örjan Fahlström, Bengt Berger (*perc*). 3/84.

***   **Blueprints** Dragon DRLP 147 LP
Wallgren. 4/87.

Although now associated rather peripherally with jazz, Wallgren is a humane and wonderfully lyrical pianist whose affection for bebop piano often breaks through music which is otherwise dependent on multifarious strands of the European tradition. The Swedish group on the first two albums (Buschi Niebergall sits in on the second set) offer somewhat polite reflections on their own growing post-bop tradition, but Wallgren's wasteless composing – his charming 'Khalida's Lullaby', which appears in a solo version on *Blueprints*, will probably go down as his greatest hit – makes the most of the situation, and Ernryd is an attractive trumpeter. The Swedish Radio Group appear on *Lavoro In Corso*, which tests some of Wallgren's investigations into wider areas of music: 'Alexander Scriabin's Raga-Time Band' suggests something of its scholarly air and, while the players don't always breathe freely, there are too many excellent musicians here for the project to fall down. *Blueprints*, a solo set, is – as so often with pianists going it alone – the clearest path to Wallgren's heart. His twelve-part 'Hints & Suggestions' is a captivating set of miniatures, with a homage to Hampton Hawes as well as the expected impressionist ponderings and, while the other two sequences – 'Six Blueprints', based only on six notes, one for each episode, and six short pieces 'For Arnold, Alban and Anton' written by fellow-pianist Lasse Werner – are a shade more procedural, Wallgren's craftsmanship is so impeccable that the music remains absorbing. Securing this much lyricism with such economy of effort offers a lesson to many more renowned and saleable piano-players.

PER HENRIK WALLIN
PIANO

**   **The New Figaro** Dragon DRLP 4 LP
Wallin; Lars-Goran Ulander (*ss, as*); Peter Olsen (*d*). 4/75.

(*)   **River High Running Dragon DRLP 22 LP
Wallin; Torbjörn Hultcrantz b); Erik Dahlback (*d*). 4/79.

(*)   **Trio Caprice CAP 1185 LP
As above. 5–6/79.

**   **Raw Material** Dragon DRLP 48 LP
Wallin; Kevin Ross (*b*); Steve Reid (*d*). 10/81.

***   **Blues Work** Dragon DRLP 35 LP
Wallin; Torbjörn Hultcrantz (*b*); Erik Dahlback (*d*). 3/82.

Wallin is a strange admixture of styles: he can't seem to stay still for long, and a low boredom threshold combines with a maniacal energy to distil an edgy, whirling kind of piano jazz. If he resembles anyone, it might be McCoy Tyner, for his grandstand climaxes and hammering at the keyboard certainly evoke one of Tyner's displays of pianistic bravado. But in with this is mischievious humour, a plastic sense of form and an obsessive need to create moment-by-moment contrasts. Wallin never builds towards anything: big moments arrive like something crashing through a ceiling. These trio albums all benefit to greater or lesser degrees from his playing methods. *The New Figaro* is a confusion of free jazz and more conventional language, and Ulander and Olsen sound well meaning but lost. *River High Running* finds more sympathetic partners, but this one is troubled by second-rate mono recording and poor editing – the opening 'Norma' simply outstays its welcome over 20 minutes. *Trio* and *Blues Work* are better paced, and on the latter especially – where 21 themes are crammed into 45 minutes of music! – Wallin connects properly with the hitherto careless drumming of Dahlback. *Raw Material* seems like more of a jam on two long pieces (again recorded live at the ubiquitous Fasching Club in Stockholm) and wanders through highs and lows. Get *Blues Work* to start with, although any of the above may also appeal to liberal tastes.

***   **Knalledonia** Dragon DRLP 77 LP
Wallin; Gustavo Bergalli, Ann-Sofi Soderqvist (*t*); Stanislaw Cieslak (*tb*); Thomas Jaderlund (*as*); Thomas Gustafsson, Stefan Isaksson (*ts*); Hans Arktoft (*bs, cl, bcl*); Torbjörn Hultcrantz (*b*); Erik Dahlback (*d*). 9/84.

A vast, cantankerous suite for a ten-piece band, which exemplifies something of Wallin's manner – wild, apparently slapdash episodes are juxtaposed with intensely organized written ensembles. His own improvisations are at the heart of the music, with the second part a torrential feature for the trio, but the horns have their say too, especially Cieslak's mocking trombone and Gustafsson's bilious tenor commentary on part four. Recorded live, but the balance presents few problems.

***(*)   **One Knife Is Enough** Caprice CAP 1273 LP
Wallin. 1/82.

***   **Moon Over Calcutta** Dragon DRLP 143 LP
Wallin. 6/87.

These solo albums find Wallin at his best, for however much he may be stimulated by the presence of other players, they tend to get in his way more often than not. His own, apparently improvised themes on the Caprice record have a brilliant momentum, an all-embracing view of the keyboard which is a match for any contemporary virtuoso: the overwhelming yet deftly delivered lines of 'East River Carousel' and the blend of daintiness and flat-out attack in 'Vattern' are typical. Six of the ten pieces on *Moon Over Calcutta* are jazz and show-tune standards, and while Wallin makes each into a densely voiced structure, they're comparatively humdrum variations on the tune. A fulsomely detailed reading of Monk's 'Evidence' is, though, something special. The recording on the later record comes with a slightly more resonant acoustic.

***(*)   **Dolphins, Dolphins, Dolphins** Dragon DRCD 215 CD
Wallin; Mats Gustaffson (*ss, ts, bs*); Kjell Nordeson (*d*). 8/91.

Hospitalized after a crippling accident in 1988, Wallin has come back with none of his power depleted. The shade most closely evoked here is Thelonious Monk, since 'Nu Nu Och Dao Nu Gaor Dao Och Nu' sounds like a perversion of 'Round Midnihght' and other Monkish melodies drift through the remaining tunes. But the level of interplay here – confrontational and conspiratorial in equal proportion – gives the lie to the suggestion above that Wallin's best by himself, although his long solo 'J.W.' is a wonderfully expressive tribute to a painter friend. Gustafsson is gothically powerful and jagged, Nordeson works with military intensity, and it's all splendidly recorded.

GEORGE WALLINGTON (born 1924)
PIANO

***(*)   **The George Wallington Trio** Savoy SV-0136 CD
Wallington; Jerry Floyd (*t*); Kai Winding (*tb*); Brew Moore (*ts*); Gerry Mulligan (*bs*); Curley Russel (*b*); Charlie Perry, Max Roach (*d*); Buddy Stewart (*v*). 5/49–11/51.

***(*)   **The George Wallington Trios** Original Jazz Classics OJC 1754 CD/LP
Wallington; Chuck Wayne (*mandola*); Charles Mingus, Oscar Pettiford, Curley Russel (*b*); Max Roach (*d*). 9/52–5/53.

More so even than Joe Albany or Dodo Marmarosa, George Wallington is the underrated master of bebop piano: his name is still best known for his composing 'Lemon Drop' and 'Godchild'. His speed is breathtaking, his melodies unspooling in long, unbroken lines, and he writes tunes which are rather more than the customary convoluted riffs on familiar chord-changes. His touch on these early sessions – the first eight trio tracks were cut in 1951, the two bigger-band pieces and the final trio tracks dating from two years earlier – is percussive without suggesting aggression, and there's an aristocratic flavour to the writing of 'Hyacinth' and the latterly ubiquitous 'Polka Dot'. The two band pieces are lithe shots of cool bebop, with Brew Moore superb on 'Knockout', but the trio music is the stuff to hear. A few tracks have reverberations on the piano, but the remastering is mostly good. The OJC *Trios* disc is all piano, bass and drums, and there are marvellous, flashing virtuoso pieces like the ultrafast 'Cuckoo Around The Clock', although the elegance of 'I Married An Angel' is a harbinger of Wallington's later work.

(*)   **Jazz For The Carriage Trade Original Jazz Classics OJC 1704 CD
Wallington; Donald Byrd (*t*); Phil Woods (*as*); Teddy Kotick (*b*); Art Taylor (*d*). 1/56.

***   **Jazz At Hotchkiss** Savoy SV-0119 CD
Wallington; Donald Byrd (*t*); Phil Woods (*as*); Knobby Totah (*b*); Nick Stabulas (*d*). 11/57.

While these are serviceable hard-bop entries, it's prosaic stuff after the fine fierceness of the earlier records. Wallington's playing seemed to turn inward, and his improvisations are at an altogether cooler temperature: the best piece on either record, his own theme 'Before Dawn', is a starless ballad of surprisingly desolate feeling. Byrd muddles through the first date and is approaching his faceless self on the second, while Woods hits every note he needs to with his usual accuracy. The Savoy album is preferable and comes in splendid remastering. Wallington has been recording again in recent years after a very long absence, but the discs have been of Japanese provenance.

JACK WALRATH
TRUMPET

***   **In Europe** Steeplechase SCS 1172 LP
Walrath; Glen Ferris (*tb*); Michael Cochrane (*p*); Anthony Cox (*b*); Jimmy Madison (*d*). 7/82.

***(*)   **Wholly Trinity** Muse 600612 CD
Walrath; Chip Jackson (*b*); Jimmy Madison (*d*). 3 & 4/86.

***   **Killer Bunnies** Spotlite SJP LP 25 LP
Walrath; Spirit Level: Paul Dunmall (*ts*); Tim Richards (*p*); Paul Ansley (*b*); Tony Orrell (*d*). 5/86.

****   **Master Of Suspense** Blue Note B21Y 46905 CD/LP

****   **Neohippus** Blue Note B21Y 91101 CD/LP/MC
Walrath; Steve Turre (*tb*); Kenny Garrett (*as*); Carter Jefferson (*ts*); James Williams (*p*); Anthony Cox (*b*); Ronnie Burrage (*d*). 9/86, 88.

In a period dominated largely by the saxophone and by the muted, melted edges of Miles Davis's trumpet style, it's good to find a player who restores some of brass's authentic ring and bite. Walrath is a hugely talented player with a tough, almost percussive sound. A high-note man in several contemporary big bands (Charles Mingus's *Cumbia And Jazz Fusion* and *Three Or Four Shades Of Blues* spring immediately to mind, but he has also done sterling service with Charlie Persip Superbands), Walrath has so far not made his deserved impact as a leader. Two good Blue Notes (look particularly for *Neohippus*) are currently out of the catalogue in Europe, and there is a two-volume live set on Red which is worth searching for. Of those that are left, *Wholly Trinity* is the most successful. Working without a harmony instrument or second horn is a bold stroke for a trumpeter, but Walrath sounds completely assured. A first take of 'Killer Bunnies' (Walrath is a horror-movie freak and dedicated his Blue Note debut to the *Masters Of Suspense*) is better than the muscular Spotlite version, though one wouldn't want to miss Dunmall's muscular soloing on that album. Compositions like 'Spherious' and 'Spontooneous', also on the Muse, point not just to Walrath's rather zany sense of humour but also to his oblique, Monk-like compositional sense, which often makes use of folk and popular elements in a highly original way.

Unlike the Spotlite, the Steeplechase betrays all the disadvantages of vinyl, with a rather murky sound and uneven balance. A pity, because this notably brazen band was one of Walrath's best, and 'Duesin' In Dusseldorf' and 'Reverend Red' are among his best performances on record, with the two-horn front line chasing all over the place.

CEDAR WALTON (born 1934)
PIANO

***   **Blues For Myself** Red NS 205 LP
Walton (*p* solo). 2/86.

Walton has not yet been widely recognized as a significant jazz composer. Tunes like 'Bolivia', 'Ojos De Rojo', 'Maestro' and 'Ugetsu' rival McCoy Tyner's work for sophisticated inventiveness. Unfortunately, *Blues For Myself* contains none of them. Despite Walton's extended bop lines and accompanist's sense of space and shading, it's a rather monochrome set and the piano sounds rather leaden.

***(*)   **Cedar!** Original Jazz Classics OJC 462 CD/LP/MC
Walton; Kenny Dorham (*t*); Junior Cook (*ts*); Leroy Vinnegar (*b*); Billy Higgins (*d*). 7/67.

****   **Cedar Walton Plays Cedar Walton** Original Jazz Classics OJC 6002 CD/LP
As above, plus Blue Mitchell (*t*); Clifford Jordan (*ts*); Bob Cranshaw, Richard Davis (*b*); Jack DeJohnette, Mickey Roker (*d*). 7/67, 5/68, 1/69.

During the 1970s Walton was anchoring Clifford Jordan's Magic Triangle band. They seem to have struck up an immediate rapport on these earlier sessions, made for Prestige. *Plays* contains a useful sample of the earlier quartet and quintet stuff with Dorham and Cook, but the compilation misses a fine trio, 'My Ship'. Paired with the characteristically blunt Mitchell, Jordan takes the direct route to goal, with no sign of his irritating tendency to mark time in mid-solo. 'Higgins Holler' and 'Jakes Milkshakes' also feature sterling work by DeJohnette, who still sounds rather eager to please. There's an excellent trio performance of Walton's 'fantasy in D', 'Ugetsu', with Roker and Cranshaw. Though there's good stuff on OJC 462, the compilation has to be a better bet.

****   **Eastern Rebellion** Timeless SJP 101 CD/LP
Walton; George Coleman (*ts*); Sam Jones (*b*); Billy Higgins (*d*). 12/75.

***(*)   **Eastern Rebellion 2** Timeless CD SJP 106 CD
As above, except Bob Berg (*ts*) replaces Coleman.

***(*)   **First Set** Steeplechase 1085 CD/LP/MC
As above. 1 & 10/77.

***(*)   **Second Set** Steeplechase 1113 CD/LP
As above.

***   **Third Set** Steeplechase 1179 LP
As above.

This was a vintage period for Walton. His European gigs were models of tough contemporary bop and, though the incidence of covers is higher than one might like, the standard of performance is consistently high, and for once Steeplechase's exhaustive documentation seems justified. The original *Eastern Rebellion* is one of the pianist's finest albums; his version of 'Naima', with Coleman sounding magisterial as he cuts through the harmonies, compares more than favourably with that on the excellent *Bluesville Time*. Berg turns in an excellent performance on another Coltrane tune on *Second Set*. There are several good Monk performances, but the opening 'Off Minor' on *First Set* is the most dynamic. The original 'Ojos De Rojo' appears on both *First Set* and the later of the Timeless sets. Better sound on the Timeless CDs. The vinyl-only *Third Set* sounds a little ragged.

***(*)   **Cedar Walton–Ron Carter–Jack DeJohnette** Limetree MLP 0021 CD/LP
     Walton; Ron Carter (*b*); Jack DeJohnette (*d*). 12/83.

The young DeJohnette had proved his value to Walton on the 1968 Prestige sessions; 15 years made a substantial difference to the drummer's chops. In 1983 he's confident enough to play less and quieter, and all three players are intuitively musical in approach, which encourages a tight, unembellished style. Walton's own 'Rubber Man' is the outstanding track, but there are also worthwhile performances of 'Alone Together' and 'All The Things You Are', tunes which can sound thoroughly shop-soiled when accorded only routine treatment.

***(*)   **Eastern Rebellion 4** Timeless SJP 184 LP
     Walton; Alfredo Chocolate Armenteros (*t*); Curtis Fuller (*tb*); Bob Berg (*ts*); David
     Williams (*b*); Billy Higgins (*d*). 5/83.

***(*)   **Bluesville Time** Criss Cross Criss 1017 CD/LP

****   **Cedar** Timeless SJP 223 CD/LP
     Walton; Dale Barlow (*ts* on *Bluesville Time* only); David Williams (*b*); Billy Higgins
     (*d*). 4/85, 4/85.

Williams and Higgins were the ground floor of Walton's fine 1980s groups. The drummer's ability to sustain and develop a pattern became increasingly important to the pianist as he simplified and reduced his delivery. *Eastern Rebellion 4* is scarcely a patch on its earlier namesakes; Armenteros comes into his own on 'Manteca', but otherwise seems a player of limited ingenuity and with a rather ingenuous approach to solo development. Fuller plays well but doesn't seem to get squarely on-mike. Barlow, on the later *Bluesville Time*, compares very favourably with the inventive Berg. The material is excellent – 'Naima' and 'I Remember Clifford' alongside distinctive originals like 'Rubber Man' and 'Ojos De Rojo' – but the playing, Higgins apart, isn't quite crisp enough. The drummer sounds great on *Cedar*, but the material doesn't give anyone enough to bite down on and there's too much filling for too little substance.

***(*)   **The Trio: Volume 1** Red 123192 CD

***(*)   **The Trio: Volume 2** Red 123193 CD

***   **The Trio; Volume 3** Red 123194 CD
     Walton; David Williams (*b*); Billy Higgins (*d*). 3/85.

Recorded live in Bologna, these represent a compelling mixture of originals ('Ojos De Rojo', 'Jacob's Ladder', 'Holy Land'), standards ('Lover Man', 'Every Time We Say Goodbye'), and challenging repertoire pieces (Ellington's 'Satin Doll', Fred Lacey's 'Theme For Ernie', S. R. Kyner's 'Bluesville'). Walton's brilliant phrasing and inbuilt harmonic awareness keeps thematic material in view at all times and his solos and accompaniments are always entirely logical and consistently developed. About Higgins there is very little more to add, but that he has inherited and fully deserved the mantle of Elvin Jones. Williams offers firm, unobtrusive support, but isn't a very exciting soloist.

***   **My Funny Valentine** Sweet Basil 660-55-010 CD
     Walton; Ron Carter (*b*); Billy Higgins (*d*). 2/91.

Noisy backgrounds contribute to the prized 'live feel', but these are rather bland sessions, stringing together all the clichés in the book – rhythmic downshifts, long chromatic transitions, endless quotation – into an attractive confection that never quite rises above a drab choice of standards material. Carter and Higgins are well up to scratch, but the bassist has developed irritating harmonic mannerisms which grate after a while.

CARLOS WARD
ALTO SAXOPHONE, FLUTE

***(*)   **Lito** Leo LR 166 CD
     Ward; Woody Shaw (*t*); Walter Schmocker (*b*); Alex Deutsch (*d*). 7/88.

Recorded live at the North Sea Festival and sounding a little as if the sound were being sent down a pipeline, this is nevertheless a valuable documentation both of Ward and of Woody Shaw, who sounds magnificent. An atmospheric player rather than a highly virtuosic one, Ward has a piercing, keening tone that works best on short, discontinuous phrases. Long association with Dollar Brand/Abdullah Ibrahim has given his work a distinctive, almost folksy quality; but what is interesting about *Lito* is how effective a writer the saxophonist is, spinning out ideas through the long title-suite, and in three shorter tracks on the second side, best of which is a tribute to Thelonious Monk entitled 'First Love'. Ward's flute chimes sympathetically with Shaw in the middle sections of 'Lito', and the trumpeter's middle-register responses rank with his best work on record.

DAVID S. WARE
TENOR SAXOPHONE, SAXELLO, STRITCH

***(*)   **Passage To Music** Silkheart SH 117 CD/LP
Ware; William Parker (*b*); Marc Edwards (*b*). 4/88.

A quasi-mystic journey from 'The Ancient Formula', through 'African Secrets' and down 'The Elders Path' to the final 'Mystery' of jazz. Ware's use of the stritch and saxello (horns related to the alto saxophone; the former is closely associated with Rahsaan Roland Kirk, and it would be interesting to know whether Ware was introduced to the other as a result of Silkheart man, Dennis Gonzalez's, work with a British group that included saxello player Elton Dean) is more than a respectful nod to Kirk's ghost. Ware allows the unfamiliar tonality of the stritch in particular to suggest the ambiguities and perils of a journey through jazz history. He touches on mysterious harmonies with an almost ritual intensity and detachment. Parker is a forceful trio bassist (watch out for his sessions with Jimmy Lyons soundalike Marco Einedi on the limited release *Vermont – Spring 1986* [Botticelli 1001 LP]) with a strong sense of harmony. It would have been interesting to hear him paired again with Silkheart regular Dennis Charles, as on Rob Brown's *Breath Rhyme* (Silkheart SH 122 CD/LP), one of the strongest rhythm-section performances of recent years.

***   **Great Bliss: Volume 1** Silkheart SHCD 127 CD/LP
Ware; Matthew Shipp (*p*); William Parker (*b*); Marc Edwards (*d, perc*). 1/90.

***(*)   **Flight of i** DIW 856 CD
As above. 12/91.

Ware's 1960s revivalism has never been more clearly stated than on the turbulent Silkheart, first of a two-volume set. His adoption of stritch and saxello, non-standard horns with off-centre pitching, has given him a distinctive sound which is obviously related to Roland Kirk's more wayward experimentations, but which, like Kirk's, is intimately bound up with an interest in primitive blues, field hollers, gospel shouts and rags. Pianist Matthew Shipp is a valuable acquisition, a patient, sober-sounding player who lacks conventional swing but creates big, throbbing pulses, often round a single key. Drummer Edwards makes dramatic use of tymps and bells and it's unfortunate that he is conventionally disposed on the DIW

The CD of *Great Bliss* has four tracks (twenty two and a half minutes of music) that are not on the LP configuration. The unaccompanied 'Saxelloscape One' would not be greatly missed, but not to have 'Angular' (saxello again) or 'Bliss Theme' (a throbbing tenor vehicle) would seriously lessen the impact of the album. Ware plays his stritch on the long, rather shapeless 'Cadenza' and his flute on the opening 'Forward Motion' and (CD only) 'Mind Time'. An exploratory album, its overall tone and approach strongly recall the 1960s avant-garde, and it may be that Ware hasn't yet worked that influence out of his system.

He sticks with his tenor on *Flight of i*, cleaving to a line between Rollins and Ayler, constantly reverting to the melody (as on 'There Will Never Be Another You') despite Shipp's exciting habit of bashing the original theme into submission; it would be interesting to hear the pianist let loose on a trio session. 'Flight of i' and the long 'Infi-Rhythms #1' suggest that the saxophonist has been paying attention to David Murray's long-standing rehabilitation of Ayler, building huge upper-register prayers out of very basic thematic material. The title-track is one of the most remarkably sustained saxophone performances of recent years and the album should be heard.

WILBUR WARE (1923–79)
DOUBLE BASS

***(*) **The Chicago Sound** Original Jazz Classics OJC 1737 CD/LP
Ware; John Jenkins (*as*); Johnny Griffin (*ts*); Junior Mance (*p*); Wilbur Campbell,
Frank Dunlop (*d*). 10 & 11/57.

Though much of what Ware did stemmed directly from Jimmy Blanton's 'Jack The Bear', he developed into a highly individual performer whose unmistakable sound lives on in the low-register work of contemporary bassists like Charlie Haden. Ware's technique has been questioned but seems to have been a conscious development, a way of hearing the chord rather than a way of skirting his own supposed shortcomings. He could solo at speed, shifting the time-signature from bar to bar while retaining an absolutely reliable pulse. Significantly, one of his most important employers was Thelonious Monk, who valued displacements of that sort within an essentially four-square rhythm and traditional (but not European-traditional) tonality; the bassist also contributed substantially to one of Sonny Rollins's finest recordings. He grew up in the sanctified church and there is a gospely quality to 'Mamma-Daddy', a relatively rare original, on *The Chicago Sound*. The only other Ware composition on the record, '31st And State', might have come from Johnny Griffin's head; the saxophonist roars in over the beat and entirely swamps Jenkins, whose main contribution to the session is a composition credit on two good tracks.

Though the Ware discography is huge (with numerous credits for Riverside in the 1950s), his solo technique is at its most developed on his own record. 'Lullaby Of The Leaves' is almost entirely for bass, and there are magnificent solos on 'Body And Soul' (where he sounds *huge*) and 'The Man I Love'. One wonders if a couple of alternative takes mightn't have been included on the CD. Ware's impact was enormous and one record (albeit a fine one) seems a poor trawl.

PETER WARREN
BASS, CELLO

(*) **Solidarity Japo 60034 LP
Warren; Ray Anderson (*tb*); John Purcell (*ss, as, ts*); John Scofield (*g*); Jack
DeJohnette (*d, p*). 5/81.

A sideman with Jack DeJohnette, who produced this record, Warren assembles a characterful cast which enlivens an otherwise ordinary programme: 'Riff-Raff' is a jam on a riff, 'Solidarity' a cumbersome dirge, 'Mlle Jolie' a lightweight ballad. Anderson, especially, plays the hell out of the first two pieces, perhaps excessively so, while the cooler Scofield and Purcell add more tempered thoughts of their own. DeJohnette plays piano and drums on one tune but otherwise does his usual effortless work at the kit.

DINAH WASHINGTON (1924–63)
VOCAL

*** **Mellow Mama** Delmark DD 451 CD
Washington; Karl George (*t*); Jewel Grant (*as*); Lucky Thompson (*ts*); Milt Jackson
(*vib*); Wilbert Baranco (*p*); Charles Mingus (*b*); Lee Young (*d*). 12/45.

Whether or not she counts as a 'jazz singer', Washington frequently appeared in the company of the finest jazz musicians, and while she was no improviser and stood slightly apart from such contemporaries as Fitzgerald or Vaughan, she could drill through blues and ballads with a huge, sometimes slightly terrifying delivery. Her start came with the Lionel Hampton band, and after leaving him she made these dozen tracks for Apollo Records in the company of a band organized by Lucky Thompson. While Washington herself sounds comparatively raw and unformed, the jump-blues material doesn't demand a great range, and she swings through the likes of 'My Voot Is Really Vout' as well as the more traditional 'Beggin' Mama Blues'. Thompson's team sound as if they're having fun, and the remastering is quite clear.

***(*)   **Dinah Jams** EmArcy 814639-2 CD
Washington; Clifford Brown, Clark Terry, Maynard Ferguson (*t*); Herb Geller (*as*);
Harold Land (*ts*); Junior Mance, Richie Powell (*p*); Keter Betts, George Morrow (*b*);
Max Roach (*d*). 8/54.

Washington's sole 'jazz' record is fine, but not as fine as the closely contemporary Sarah
Vaughan record with a similar backing group, and therein lies a tale about Washington's
abilities. She claimed she could sing anything, wich was probably true, but her big, bluesy voice
is no more comfortable in this strata of Tin Pan Alley than was Joe Turner's. Still, the long and
luxuriant jams on 'You Go To My Head' and 'Lover Come Back To Me' are rather wonderful
in their way, and there is always Clifford Brown to listen to.

***   **In The Land Of Hi-Fi** EmArcy 826453 CD
Washington; Hal Mooney Orchestra. 4/56.

***   **The Fats Waller Songbook** EmArcy 818930 CD
Washington; Ernie Royal, Johnny Coles, Joe Newman, Clark Terry (*t*); Melba Liston,
Julian Priester, Rod Levitt (*tb*); Eddie Chamblee, Jerome Richardson, Benny Golson,
Frank Wess, Sahib Shihab (*reeds*); Jack Wilson (*p*); Freddie Green (*g*); Richard Evans
(*b*); Charli Persip (*d*). 10/57.

***   **The Bessie Smith Songbook** EmArcy 826663 CD
Washington; Blue Mitchell (*t*); Melba Liston (*tb*); Harold Ousley (*ts*); Sahib Shihab
(*bs*); Wynton Kelly (*p*); Paul West (*b*); Max Roach (*d*). 7/58.

***   **What A Difference A Day Makes** EmArcy 818815-2 CD
Washington; studio orchestra. 59.

***   **Compact Jazz: Dinah Washington** Mercury 830700 CD
As above EmArcy discs, plus Quincy Jones Orchestra. 55–61.

***(*)   **Compact Jazz: Dinah Washington Sings The Blues** Mercury 832573-2 CD
As above. 54–61.

***   **'Round Midnight: Dinah Washington** Verve 510087 CD
As above, except add Nook Shrier Orchestra, Eddie Chamblee Orchestra, Tab Smith
Orchestra, Jimmy Cobb Orchestra. 10/46–12/61.

Washington's studio albums for EmArcy are a good if fairly interchangeable lot: the quality of
the backing doesn't much affect the calibre of her singing, and a frowsy studio orchestra is as
likely to generate a great vocal as a smoking jazz ensemble. Which is why the compilations,
especially *Sings The Blues*, are probably the best bet, although either of the two *Compact Jazz*
sets willl do fine for anyone wanting a one-disc representation of Dinah's albums from this
period.

***   **Drinking Again** Roulette CDP 7932702 CD
Washington; studio orchestra. 62.

(*)   **In Love Roulette CDP 7972732 CD
Washington; studio orchestra. 62.

***   **The Best Of Dinah Washington** Roulette CDP 7991142 CD
Washington; studio orchestras. 62–63.

(*)   **Dinah '63 Roulette 7945762 CD
Washington; studio orchestra. 63.

The title song of *Drinking Again* is one of the great saloon set-pieces, and Washington does it
great justice. The other Roulette albums merely continue what was a disappointing decline on
record, even though it's hard to define exactly where the problem lies. Washington sings
mightily and with no lack of attention throughout all these records, and an improvisational
gleam resides at the heart of many of these songs, especially 'Do Nothin' Til You Hear From
Me' (*In Love*) and 'Just Friends' (*Drinking Again*). But the relentlessly tasteful orchestrations
by Don Costa and Fred Norman turn down the heat all the way through, and Washington can
sound curiously alone and friendless on a lot of the tracks. The remastering has been
respectably done.

SADAO WATANABE (born 1933)
ALTO SAXOPHONE, SOPRANINO SAXOPHONE, SOPRANO SAXOPHONE, FLUTE

*** **Bossa Nova Concert** Denon DC 8556 CD

*** **Plays Ballads** Denon CD 8555 CD
Watanabe; Masabumi Kikuchi (*p*); Sadanori Nakamure (*g* on *Bossa Nova Concert* only); Masanaga Harada (*b*); Masahiko Togashi (*d*); Hideo Miyata (*perc* on *Bossa Nova Concert* only); strings. 7/67, 3/69.

***(*) **Dedicated To Charlie Parker** Denon DC 8558 CD
Watanabe; Terumasa Hino (*t*); Kazuo Yashior (*p*); Masanaga Harada (*b*); Fumio Watanabe (*d*). 3/69.

***(*) **Round Trip** Vanguard VMD 79344 CD
Watanabe; Chick Corea (*p*); Miroslav Vitous (*b*); Jack DeJohnette (*d*). 74.

*** **How's Everything** CBS C2X 36776 LP
Watanabe; Jon Faddis (*t*); Dave Grusin, Richard Tee (*p, ky*); Eric Gale, Jeff Mironov (*g*); Anthony Jackson (*b*); Steve Gadd (*d*); Ralph MacDonald (*perc*); orchestra. 7/80.

*** **Fill Up The Night** Elektra 60297 LP
Watanabe; Jorge Dalto (*p*); Richard Tee (*ky*); Paul Griffin (*syn*); Eric Gale (*g*); Marcus Miller (*b*); Steve Gadd (*d*); Ralph MacDonald (*perc*); Grady Tate (*v*). 2 & 3/83.

*** **Rendezvous** Elektra 60430 LP
Watanabe; Richard Tee (*ky*); Barry Eastmond (*syn*); Eric Gale (*g*); Marcus Miller (*b*); Steve Gadd (*d*); Anthony MacDonald, Ralph MacDonald (*perc*); Roberta Flack (*v*); strings. 2 & 3/84.

*** **Maisha** Elektra 60431 LP
Watanabe; Herbie Hancock (*p*); Russell Ferrante, Don Grusin (*ky*); Carlos Rios, David Williams (*g*); Nathan East, Jimmy Johnson (*b*); Harvey Mason, John Robinson (*d*); Paulinho Da Costa (*perc*); Brenda Russell (*v*). 12 & 2/85.

***(*) **Parker's Mood** Elektra 60475 CD/LP

***(*) **Tokyo Dating** Elektra WPCP 4327 CD/LP
Watanabe; James Williams (*p*); Charnet Moffett (*b*); Jeff Watts (*d*). 7/85.

(*) **Good Time For Love Elektra 60945 CD/LP
Watanabe; Kenji Nishiyama (*tb*); Ansel Collins, Onaje Allan Gumbs, Rob Monsey, Sohichi Noriki (*ky*); Keiichi Gotoh (*syn*); Bobby Broom, Radcliffe Bryan, Takayuki Hijikata, Tsunehide Matsuki, Jeff Mironov, Earl Smith, Tohru Tatsuki (*g*); Victor Bailey, Bertram McLean, Kenji Takamizu, Ken Watanabe (*b*); Will Lee (*b, v*); Poogie Bell, Carton Davis, Shuichi Murakami, Chris Parker, Hideo Yamaki (*d*); Mino Cinelu, Sue Evans, Sydoney Wolfe (*perc*); Eve (*v*); collective personnel. 2 & 3/86.

*** **Birds Of Passage** Elektra 60748 CD/LP
Watanabe; Freddie Hubbard (*flhn*); Hubert Laws (*f*); George Duke, Russell Errante (*ky*); Dan Huff, Paul Jackson (*g*); Abraham Laboriel (*b*); Vinnie Colaiuta, John Robinson, Carlos Vega (*d*); Alex Acuna, Paulinho Da Costa (*perc*); collective personnel. 87.

*** **Elis** Elektra 60816 CD/LP
Watanabe; Cesar Camargo Mariano (*ky*); Heitor Teixeira Pereira (*g*); Nico Assumpcao (*b*); Pulinho Braga (*d*); Papeti (*perc*); Toquinho (*v, g*). 2/88.

*** **Made In Coracao** Elektra WPCP 4331 CD
Watanabe; Toquinho (*v, g*); Amilson Godoy (*ky*); Edson Jose Alves (*g*); Ivani Sabino (*b*); William Caram (*d*); Osvaldo Batto, Papeti (*perc*). 3 & 4/88.

***(*) **Selected** Elektra WPCP 4332 CD
As for *Fill Up The Night*, *Rendezvous*, *Maisha*, *Good Time For Love*, *Birds Of Passage*, *Elis*, plus Robbie Buchanan (*ky*); Steve Erquiaga, Paul Jackson Jr (*g*); Keith Jones

(*b*); Andy Narell (*steel d*); William Kennedy, Chester Thompson (*d*); Kenneth Nash (*perc*). 83–88.

Like most Japanese of his generation (the composer Toru Takemitsu tells a very similar story), Sadao Watanabe heard nothing but Japanese traditional and German martial music during his teens, and was only exposed to Western popular music through American forces radio; he also cites Norman Granz's Jazz At The Philharmonic broadcasts as a big influence. Watanabe had already largely rejected Japanese music (his father was a teacher of *biwa*, a lute-like instrument). By the time he was twenty, he was sufficiently adept on the alto saxophone to join Toshiko Akiyoshi and perform in America.

He subsequently recorded with both Chico Hamilton (who was always on the look-out for unusual tonalities) and Gary McFarland, who turned Watanabe on to the fashionable sound of *bossa nova*. Perhaps because he encountered jazz at a relatively advanced stage in its development, Watanabe seemed able to take virtually any of its stylistic variants (swing, bop, Latin, Afro, and later fusion) on their own terms. Though his recent recordings have tended to be heavily produced, middle-market fusion, Watanabe has recorded with an impressive array of American heavyweights including (to mention only the piano players) Chick Corea, Herbie Hancock, Cedar Walton and Richard Tee. In 1967, he collaborated with Toshiko Akiyoshi's ex-husband Charlie Mariano, producing three fine albums of standards and oriental themes.

These, like most of Watanabe's output, were only released in Japan. Between 1961 and 1980, he made a total of 36 albums, some of which turn up second-hand. The best of them – *Round Trip* with Corea, *At Pit Inn* with Walton, and, one of several Parker tributes, *Bird Of Paradise* with Jones – are the more swinging, 'American' sets. Watanabe's Japanese bands have tended to be correct, but rather stiff, a criticism that might be levelled at his own playing but for the surpassing beauty of his tone. *Dedicated* and *Ballads* were both apparently recorded at the same concert; the latter is smothered in strings, the former has the benefit of Hino's bright Dorham-ish trumpet, varying a rather stolid group sound.

In recent years, following illness, Watanabe has given up flute, which he plays beautifully on the *Bossa Nova Concert* and *Round Trip*; he does, though, continue to double on sopranino, a treacherously pitched horn with an attractive, 'Eastern' quality. *Round Trip*, with its long title-track and gorgeously toned 'Pastoral', is a rare example of Watanabe's soprano playing, but he sounds much less original on the lower pitched horn than on the exotic sopranino. Watanabe is one of only a handful who have specialized on it and his theme statement on 'My Dear Life', included on *Selected*, is his signature piece.

Of the albums with an American release, the most interesting from a straight jazz point of view are the live Parker set and subsequent studio album with Williams, Moffett and Watts. The recent Brazilian sets will appeal to Latin fans, and these probably have a sharper rhythmic edge than the drifting studio fusion of most of the others. For all but determined collectors, *Selected* should be sufficient. There is a vocal and an unreleased instrumental version of the haunting 'My Dear Life', a fine live version of 'California Shower' (the original album of that name came out in 1978) and three good examples of Watanabe sopranino work – 'Pastoral' (*Birds Of Passage*), 'Desert Ride' (*Maisha*), 'Say When' (*Fill Up The Night*). You'd never guess he'd even heard of Charlie Parker, though.

BENNY WATERS (born 1902)
ALTO AND TENOR SAXOPHONES, CLARINET, VOCAL

(*)   Hearing Is Convincing Muse M 5340 CD/LP/MC
    Waters; Don Coates (*p*); Earl May (*b*); Ronnie Cole (*d*). 6/87.

The title is designed as a challenge to any who might think that an 85-year-old saxophonist, embarking on a stiff one-horn-and-rhythm date, might have trouble in keeping himself intact for the whole session. Waters, though, is an indomitable personality, surely the oldest practising swing hornman, and he gets through these nine pieces with apparently no bother at all. Restlessly switching between alto, tenor and clarinet, often within the space of a single tune, his improvisations have a crusty logic and resolution to them: the second tenor chorus on 'Everything Happens To Me' is a model of polished lyricism. That said, his tone and articulation are obviously impaired by advancing years, with vibrato more a matter of a continuous tremble than anything. As with Benny Carter, there's an unmistakable antiquarian feel to his manner: he's not so much a relic as someone who still phrases the saxophone in a way that players don't any more. His singing, though, is very lively indeed on 'Romance Without Finance'.

DEREK WATKINS
TRUMPET, FLUGELHORN

* **Increased Demand** MA Music A 705 CD/LP/MC
  Watkins; Stan Sulzmann (*ss, ts, f*); Tony Hymas (*ky*); Peter Tiehuis, Poul Halberg (*g*); Paul Westwood (*b*); Harold Fiher (*d*); Frank Ricotti, Ethan Weisgard (*perc*). 88.

Renowned as a lead trumpet player, blessed with the ability to hit top Cs with unerring capability, Derek Watkins was given some sort of chance to make a solo record here – and ended up with a set that sounds just like most of the commercial and film-theme music he earns his regular crusts on. Blunt, brutalizing settings loaded with electronic beats give neither Watkins nor Sulzmann any space to do much except blow hard enough to make themselves heard. Definitely not one for posterity.

BILL WATROUS (born 1939)
TROMBONE

*** **Bill Watrous In London** Mole CD 7 CD
  Watrous; Brian Dee (*p*); Len Skeat (*b*); Martin Drew (*d*). 3/82.

There can't be a more technically skilled trombonist than Bill Watrous. His singing tone, punctiliousness and meteoric speed are matters to marvel at, and he has accrued wide big-band and stduio experience, as well as fronting rhythm sections like this one on a London visit in 1982. The five-chorus solo on 'Dearly Beloved', for instance, features what must surely be the fastest trombone playing on record, and his unaccompanied intro to 'Straight, No Chaser', which includes a plethora of chord-sounds, is the sort of thing to have other trombonists shaking their heads. Whether this will appeal to listeners who might prefer a few less practised hairpin-turns in the music is debatable, but Watrous is alive to the dangers of mere proficiency, and his songful tone to some extent lightens the flawless delivery. The local rhythm section offer uncomplaining support and there's almost 80 minutes of music, mostly well recorded, although Watrous seems under-miked in places.

The trombonist has also made a couple of light-music albums for the Soundwings company: *Someplace Else* (SW 2100 CD) and *Reflections* (SW 2104 CD).

ERIC WATSON
PIANO

*** **Your Tonight Is My Tomorrow** Owl 047 CD/LP
  Watson; Steve Lacy (*ss*); Jean-Paul Celea (*b*); Aaron Scott (*d*). 5/87.

*** **The Amiens Concert** Label Bleu 6512 CD/LP
  Watson; Steve Lacy (*ss*); John Lindberg (*b*). 11/87.

Watson is an interesting player, but he's hard to characterize: influences such as Monk, John Lewis and Mal Waldron seem to drift in and out of his music, and his composing favours dark, sluggish structures that mysteriously relax into moments of pure lyricism. Intriguing – but sometimes hard to take over the course of a record, and the hints of humour suggested by his titles ('New Canaan Con Man', 'Substance Abuse') never really surface. Steve Lacy seems to have been attracted by Watson's grainy intensity, and he makes a fist of the settings on both of the above records without quite invading Watson's world. Some of the best moments on *Your Tonight Is My Tomorrow* do, indeed, happen when Lacy sits out and the trio work at the music. *The Amiens Concert* is a bleak, unsmiling recital, with four Watson themes and one apiece by the others: again, when Lacy absconds on 'Substance Abuse', Watson and Lindberg reach a scowling truce. Some of Watson's best work is on his solo *Bull's Blood*, once available as an Owl LP but currently deleted.

LU WATTERS (born 1911)
TRUMPET

***   **Dawn Club Favourites** Good Time Jazz 12001 LP
Watters; Turk Murphy (*tb*); Bob Helm (*cl*); Wally Rose (*p*); Harry Mordecai (*bj*);
Dick Lammi (*b*); Bill Dart (*d*). 46.

***   **San Francisco Style Vol. 2** Good Time Jazz 12002 LP
As above. 46.

***   **San Francisco Style Vol. 3** Good Time Jazz 12003 LP
As above. 46.

Watters has little real credibility in jazz history, yet it was his band which did more than any other to get the revival of interest in New Orleans and traditional jazz under way in the 1940s. Watters began leading his Yerba Buena Jazz Band every week at San Francisco's Dawn Club: with hardly anybody else playing in the strictly traditional idiom – bands like Eddie Condon's outfits were too full of idiosyncratic spirits to pay much mind to the letter of trad law – Watters schooled his groups with records and the result was a somewhat stiff but uncompromised repertory band. Rags and blues were mixed with items from the Hot Five, Moten, Henderson and Oliver bandbooks; solos were pared down to a minimum; and the climactic ride-out, the great feature of Watters's records, was worth waiting for, since the leader played a simple but convincing lead that would have stood him in good stead 15 years before. Scobey and Murphy, who quit to form their own bands in due course, match Watters's dedication, and the buoyant dispatching of tunes that nobody else was daring to play much still sounds well. Very little to choose among the three records which did so much to spark off a revival, and it'll depend on the choice of titles on each.

ERNIE WATTS
TENOR SAXOPHONE, ALTO SAXOPHONE, SOPRANO SAXOPHONE

***(*)   **Ernie Watts Quartet** JVC JLP 3309 CD/LP
Watts; Pat Coil (*p*); Joel Di Bartolo (*b*); Bob Leatherbarrow (*d*). 12/87.

One of the real delights of Charlie Haden's largely unsung Quartet West (*In Angel City*, Verve 837031 CD/LP) was Watts's tender-muscular sax and synth patterns, looming and shimmering out of Haden's Angelean fogs. This overdue solo venture also features his rawer-sounding alto and positively desolate soprano (which might have sounded good in Quartet West) in a broadly romantic set of themes. The rhythm section are nothing to write home about and Watts is left with most of the work on 'Body And Soul', but as a package it's an attractive set.

JEFF 'TAIN' WATTS
DRUMS

***   **Megawatts** Sunnyside SSC 1055D CD
Watts; Kenny Kirkland (*p*); Charles Fambrough (*b*). 7/91.

Watts emerged as one of the leading drummers of his time when he worked in the first Wynton Marsalis Quintet, and this debut set under his own name reunites the original rhythm section from that band. His two original tunes have no special interest: Watts makes noise as a player, not a composer, and his favourite devices – thumping interpolations on the toms, crash-cymbal strokes that seem to linger in their own time, and an iron-faced swing – are well in evidence here. Kirkland is gregariously on top of the material. It's a good record, if rather charmless: there is some light and shade, but the trio are really interested only when they have the burners up full. The engineering is good enough, but one feels that Watts is surprisingly short of prominence in the mix, considering it's his album.

WEATHER REPORT
GROUP

***   **Weather Report** Columbia 468212 CD
Joe Zawinul (*ky*); Wayne Shorter (*ts, ss*); Miroslav Vitous (*b*); Alphonse Mouzon (*d*);
Airto Moreira (*perc*). 71.

****   **I Sing The Body Electric** Columbia 468207 CD
Joe Zawinul (*ky*); Wayne Shorter (*ts, ss*); Miroslav Vitous (*b*); Eric Gravatt (*d*); Dom
Um Romao (*perc*); with Ralph Towner (*g*); Wilmer Wise (*t, picc t*); Hubert Laws (*f*);
Andrew White (*eng hn*); Joshie Armstrong, Yolande Bavan, Chapman Roberts (*v*).
72.

Columbia have now withdrawn the whole Weather Report catalogue on vinyl and embarked on
a programme of CD reissues. There appears to be some uncertainty still as to what will be made
available and when, but all of the above have been announced and, when reissue is complete,
one of the most significant bodies of work by any contemporary group – jazz, rock, fusion,
whatever – will again be generally available.

Two bitches straight off: no mention as yet of *Sweetnighter* and *Mysterious Traveller*, which
represent (or the year between them does) the group's point of take-off, the moment when
Weather Report, in the rhetoric of the first breathless liner-note, grew wings because it could
fly; less seriously, but irritatingly in line with other Columbia reissues, newcomers have to look
long and hard to sort out personnels. Reprinting old liner-notes and running self-serving and
misleading puffs in place of clear and straightforward information is something of a dereliction
(though absolutely in line with CBS's famously cavalier attitude to musicians and fans alike).

From its inception until its demise in 1986, Weather Report was a flexible ensemble. After
the first album, it was unmistakably Joe Zawinul's flexible ensemble. From that point, Zawinul
claimed the majority of composition credits (though Shorter, Pastorius and others chipped in)
and steered the band's increasingly rhythm-orientated conception. Zawinul compositions are
typically riff-centred bass-clef ideas built up in layers by the rest of the band. Those who had
followed Shorter's developing career were alternately baffled and horrified by the exiguous
squeaks and tonal smears that suddenly were passing for solos (solos, it had been pointed out,
were not the Weather Report way; 'we always solo and we never solo'). The first album was a
set of fey acrylic sketches, clearly derived from the pastel side of the 1969–70 Miles Davis band
(in which both Zawinul and Shorter saw service) but much rawer in tone. The opening 'Milky
Way' is a pleased-with-itself set of FX on electric piano and soprano saxophone; 'it has to do
with overtones and the way one uses the piano pedals?' Yeah? that's great, man. Most of the
rest is in similar vein. Many years later, Vitous rejigged his folksy 'Morning Lake' and made
something of it. The recording is thin and erratic, which is a shame, for Shorter's closing
'Eurydice' introduces some promise.

Everything about *I Sing The Body Electric* was very 1972: the title lifted from Whitman via
Ray Bradbury, the brilliant sci-fi artwork (an overdue hand, please, for Ed Lee, Jack
Trompetter and Fred Swanson), the psychobabble liner-note ('There is flow. There is
selflessness'). There was also a band on the brink of premature extinction. Side one is more or
less an extension of the debut album. The (presumably) anti-war 'Unknown Soldier' is almost
prettified. The only thing that redeems it from banality is a tense cymbal pulse that on the live
second side erupts into some of the most torrential and threatening percussion of the period.
Zawinul is on record as thinking that Gravátt was the finest drummer the group ever had. On
'Vertical Invader' he plays with a clubbing hostility that somehow intensifies the impression
that the group was heading off in four or five (Dom Um Romao was only a part-timer)
directions at once. These days, Gravátt works as a prison guard. *Plus ça change*.

Sweetnighter, *Mysterious Traveller* and *Tale Spinnin'* having been passed over for the
moment, next up is *Black Market*, which seems to combine their virtues (atmospheric
tone-poetry, thudding, joyous rhythms) in the first unambiguously satisfying Weather Report
album. With Pastorius arriving in time to cut the funky 'Barbary Coast', Zawinul has the
engine-room tuned to his obvious satisfaction. 'Black Market' is a wonderful, thunderous tune
that completely blows out Shorter's rather wimpy 'Three Clowns' and utterly wimpy lyricon
figures; galling, because on 'Cannon Ball', dedicated to Julian Cannonball Adderley, for whom
Zawinul played and wrote 'Country Preacher' and 'Mercy, Mercy, Mercy', Shorter signs in
again with some chunky tenor.

Heavy Weather was the breakthrough album in market terms. It allegedly shifted in excess of 400,000, largely on the strength of 'Birdland', a whistleable, riffy tune dedicated to the New York jazz club. No one had ever danced to 'Orange Lady' or 'Surucucú'; suddenly, Weather Report were big, a fact that comfortably disguised the detail that, 'Birdland' and 'A Remark You Made' apart, *Heavy Weather* was nothing much. Onstage, the band went decidedly *nouvelle riche*, tossing around techno-nonsense, indulging in pointless virtuosity.

All except Shorter. He is widely taken to be *Mr Gone* (at high school, they'd called him 'Mr Weird'), but he shows his taste, maintaining virtual silence on the band's worst record, lower than which it took them some time to dive. *Night Passage* was better, but it was already obvious that a decade was more than enough, the band had done its best work; the rest was for the fans, and CBS, not for the players, and that makes an important and unhappy difference.

CHICK WEBB (1909–39)
DRUMS

****   **Chick Webb 1929–1934** Classics 502 CD
Webb; Ward Pinkett, Louis Bacon, Taft Jordan (*t, v*); Edwin Swayzee, Mario Bauza, Reunald Jones, Bobby Stark, Shelton Hemphill, Louis Hunt (*t*); Robert Horton, Jimmy Harrison, Sandy Williams, Ferdinand Arbello, Claude Jones (*tb*); Hilton Jefferson, Louis Jordan, Benny Carter (*cl, as*); Pete Clark, Edgar Sampson (*as*); Elmer Williams (*cl, ts*); Wayman Carver (*ts, f*); Don Kirkpatrick, Joe Steele (*p*); John Trueheart (*bj, g*); Elmer James (*bb, b*); John Kirby (*b*); Chuck Richards, Charles Linton (*v*). 6/29–11/34.

***(*)   **Chick Webb 1935–1938** Classics 517 CD
As above, except add Nat Story, George Matthews (*tb*); Chauncey Houghton (*cl, as*); Ted McRae (*ts*); Tommy Fulford (*p*); Bill Thomas, Beverley Peer (*b*); omit Bacon, Swayzee, Jones, Hemphill, Hunt, Horton, Harrison, Arbello, Carter, Kirkpatrick, Richards, Linton. 6/35–8/38.

These two CDs include all of Webb's studio recordings aside from those with vocals by Ella Fitzgerald, which Classics have released under her name. The first two tracks on the earlier disc, by The Jungle Band of 1929, sound almost primitive in comparison with the ensuing sessions, driven as much by Trueheart's machine-like banjo strumming as by Webb, but its use of the reeds and Webb's already exciting playing point a way out of the 1920s and, by the time of the 1931 session – which includes a memorable arrangement by Benny Carter of his own 'Blues In My Heart' and a valedictory appearance by Jimmy Harrison, who died not long afterwards – Webb was running a great band, which eventually (in 1933) won him a long-running residency at Harlem's Savoy Ballroom. Edgar Sampson handled some of the best of the earlier arrangements, and the leader could boast fine soloists in Taft Jordan (later to join Ellington), Sandy Williams, Bobby Stark and Elmer Williams, as well as a rhythm section that was almost unrivalled for attack and swing. Webb's own mastery of an enormous drum-kit allowed him to pack a whole range of percussive effects into breaks and solos which never disjointed the momentum of the band. His distance from the showmanship of Gene Krupa, who would far surpass him in acclaim, was complete. Some of the best examples of what he could do are on the second disc, including the terrific drive of 'Go Harlem' and the breaks in 'Clap Hands! Here Comes Charley'. Once Fitzgerald had begun singing with the band and began to secure a wider fame, though, some of the zip went out of their playing and, although the worst material is confined to the Fitzgerald CDs, the closing tracks on Classics 517 show them cooling off. For the most part, though, both records chronicle the steady development of one of the most swinging bands of its day. The remastering, while not up to the highest standards for this kind of material, is mostly clean and effective.

***(*)   **Chick Webb And His Savoy Ballroom Orchestra 1939** Tax 3706-2 CD
Webb; Dick Vance, Bobby Stark, Taft Jordan (*t*); Sandy Williams, Nat Story, George Matthews (*tb*); Garvin Bushell, Hilton Jefferson (*cl, as*); Wayman Carver (*ts, f*); Ted McRae (*ts*); Tommy Fulford (*p*); Bobby Johnson (*g*); Beverly Peer (*b*); Ella Fitzgerald (*v*). 1–5/39.

The swing which Webb and the orchestra generate on these broadcasts, made not long before Webb's death later in 1939, belie any hint on the studio records that the band was getting fatigued. Twenty-two tracks from two sessions, the first with Fitzgerald absent, find all concerned in top form. Stark, Jordan and Williams are again the outstanding soloists, but Webb's own playing is certainly the most powerful thing on the second date, where he combines with the excellent Peer to turn unlikely tunes such as 'My Wild Irish Rose' into battlegrounds. The slightly superior sound gives it an advantage over the first session, but both are very listenable, and the treatment of Count Basie's showcase 'One O'Clock Jump' on the earlier set reminds that Webb managed to defeat Basie's orchestra in a 'battle of the bands' at the Savoy almost exactly a year before.

EBERHARD WEBER (born 1940)
BASS, CELLO, OCARINA, KEYBOARDS

***(*)   The Colours Of Chloe ECM 1042 CD
Weber; Ack van Rooyen (*flhn*); Rainer Bruninghaus (*ky*); Peter Giger, Ralf Hubner (*d*); strings. 12/73.

Having played straight-ahead jazz bass through the 1960s, Weber delivered this uncannily beautiful album to Manfred Eicher's ECM operation and won himself an award or two. If some passages now suggest a cooler version of *Tubular Bells*, with the overlapping themes of 'No Motion Picture' hinting at the tranquillizing pomposity of progressive rock, the singular beauty of the textures and Weber's discovery of a new world based around massed cellos and subtle electronic treatments remains insidiously affecting. While the improvisational content is carefully rationed against the measure of the themes, Bruninghaus and Weber himself emerge as thoughtful and surprisingly vigorous virtuosos. While the CD offers few improvements over the excellent original vinyl edition, the recording itself still sounds splendid.

****   Yellow Fields ECM 1066 CD/LP
Weber; Charlie Mariano (*ss, shenai*); Rainer Bruninghaus (*ky*); Jon Christensen (*d*). 9/75.

Weber's masterpiece is essentially a period piece which will surely outface time. The sound of it seems almost absurdly opulent: bass passages and swimming keyboard textures that reverberate from the speakers, chords that seem to hum with huge overtones. The keyboard textures in particular are of a kind that will probably never be heard on record again. But there's little prolixity or meandering in this music. Weber builds very keenly around riffs and rhythmical figures, and solos – Mariano sounding piercingly exotic on the shenai, heartbreakingly intense on soprano – are perfectly ensconced within the sound-field. The key element, though, is the inspirational series of cross-rhythms and accents which Christensen delivers, rising to an extraordinary crescendo towards the close of 'Sand-Glass', a sprawling performance built from simple materials. And the leader's own bass never sounded better.

*(*)   The Following Morning ECM 1084 CD/LP
Weber; Rainer Bruninghaus (*ky*); Oslo Philharmonic Orchestra. 8/76.

**(*)   Silent Feet ECM 1107 CD/LP
Weber; Charlie Mariano (*ss, shenai*); Rainer Bruninghaus (*ky*); John Marshall (*d*). 11/77.

**(*)   Fluid/Rustle ECM 1137 CD/LP
Weber; Gary Burton (*vib, marim*); Bill Frisell (*g, bal*); Bonnie Herman, Norma Winstone (*v*). 1/79.

The anchorless drifting of *The Following Morning* was a disappointing continuation, rhythmically dead and texturally thin, with Weber and Bruninghaus circling dolefully through their material and badly missing a drummer. *Silent Feet* introduced John Marshall, formerly of Soft Machine, into the Colours band which Weber was touring with and, while his stiffer virtuosity wasn't the same thing as Christensen's sober flair, he restored some of the punch to Weber's music. The record hasn't the memorable tunes and perfect empathy of the earlier discs, though. Nor is *Fluid/Rustle* much more than enervating, with Burton's blandly effortful playing and Frisell's as-yet-unfocused contributions adding little to Weber's pretty but uninvolving pieces.

***   **Little Movements** ECM 1186 LP
     Weber; Charlie Mariano (*ss, f*); Rainer Bruninghaus (*ky*); John Marshall (*d*). 7/80.

(*)   **Later That Evening ECM 1231 CD/LP
     Weber; Paul McCandless (*ss, cor, ob, bcl*); Lyle Mays (*p*); Bill Frisell (*g*); Michael
     DiPasqua (*d*).3/82.

Both these bands provided Weber with better results. *Little Movements* is his best since *Yellow Fields*, the intricacies of 'A Dark Spell' and Bruninghaus's 'Bali' fielded with no problems, and Marshall growing into a resilient timekeeper for the band. *Later That Evening* isn't quite as good, with Mays a poor substitute for Bruninghaus and McCandless missing Mariano's acute sense of context, but it has its moments.

**   **Chorus** ECM 1288 CD/LP
     Weber; Jan Garbarek (*ss, ts*); Manfred Hoffbauer (*cl, f*); Martin Kunstner (*ob, cor*);
     Ralf Hubner (*d*). 9/84.

(*)   **Orchestra ECM 1374 CD/LP
     Weber; Herbert Joos, Anton Jillich, Wolfgang Czelusta, Andreas Richter (*tb*);
     Winfried Rapp (*btb*); Rudolf Diebetsberger, Thomas Hauschild (*frhn*); Franz Stagl
     (*tba*). 5–8/88.

Weber has lacked a valuable context in recent years: having patented one of the most gorgeous of bass sounds, he doesn't seem to have much else to say with it. *Chorus* is heavy on the brooding-spirit element, with Garbarek delivering some of his most stentorian commentaries on what are less than riveting themes, as Weber and Hubner toil away in the background. As a sequence of mood-music cameos, it may appeal strongly to some, but it's a depressing listen over the course of an entire record. *Orchestra* will disappoint any who've attended Weber's highly entertaining solo concerts. He splits the album between bass soliloquies and counterpoint with a chilly brass section, yet the prettiest piece on the disc is the synthesizer tune, 'On A Summer's Evening'.

BEN WEBSTER (1909–73)
TENOR SAXOPHONE

****   **Soulville** Verve 833551-2 CD
     Webster; Oscar Peterson (*p*); Barney Kessel, Herb Ellis (*g*); Ray Brown (*b*); J. C.
     Heard, Stan Levey (*d*). 5/53–10/57.

The best-loved of all saxophonists, perhaps of all jazz musicians, Ben Webster created a style which is the most personal and immediately identifiable sound in all of the music. As he got older and less partial to any tempo above a very slow lope, he pared his manner back to essentials which still, no matter how often one hears them, remain uniquely affecting. The best of his early work is with Duke Ellington – he remained, along with Paul Gonsalves, one of only two tenormen to make a genuine impression on Ducal history – but his records as a solo player, from the early 1950s onwards, are a formidable legacy. There are some beautifully bleary sessions with strings from this period which have yet to make their way to domestic CD release, but this set finds Ben in terrific form. Peterson may seem an unlikely partner but, just as Webster played superbly next to Art Tatum, so he mastered the potentially open floodgates of Peterson's playing. There are lustrous ballads in 'Where Are You' and an eerily desolate 'Ill Wind', while 'Bounce Blues' brings out the raucous side of the tenorman. Three previously unissued tracks from the sessions are also included on the CD. The later *Ben Webster Meets Oscar Peterson* has been reissued on CD but seems to have disappeared again.

***   **At The Renaissance** Original Jazz Classics OJC 390 CD/LP/MC
     Webster; Jimmy Rowles (*p*); Jim Hall (*g*); Red Mitchell (*b*); Frank Butler (*d*). 10/60.

***(*)   **Ben And 'Sweets'** CBS 460613 CD
     Webster; Harry Edison (*t*); Hank Jones (*p*); George Duvivier (*b*); Clarence Johnston
     (*d*). 6/62.

Among friends and feeling fine. Nobody ever played 'My Romance' like Ben, and the version on *Ben And 'Sweets'* is very close to definitive, a chorus of melody and another of improvisation which unfold with unerring logic. His treatment of melody remains a compulsory point of study for aspiring improvisers: he respects every part of each measure, yet makes it his own by eliminating a note, adding another, or taking breaths at moments when no one else would think of pausing, lest the momentum fall down. Webster's inner clock never fails him. Edison, the wryest of sidekicks, noodles alongside in his happiest lazybones manner, and Jones takes a handful of princely solos. The remastering will sound a bit lifeless to those who've heard the original vinyl. *At The Renaissance* finds Webster in unusual company and, while Rowles reads him like a good book, the others sometimes sound a little too smartly present and correct. 'Gone With The Wind', though, is a beauty.

(*)   **Live At Pio's Enja 2038 LP
       Webster; Junior Mance (*p*); Bob Cranshaw (*b*); Mickey Roker (*d*). 63.

***   **Soulmates** Original Jazz Classics OJC 390 CD/LP/MC
       Webster; Thad Jones (*c*); Joe Zawinul (*p*); Richard Davis (*b*); Philly Joe Jones (*d*).
       9–10/63.

Ben was already settling into a favourite repertory of tunes when he made the live album: 'Sunday', 'How Long Has This Been Going On?' and 'Gone With The Wind' were three of them. Docked a notch for imperfect live sound and Mance's tiresome clichés at the piano, but Webster sounds well enough. *Soulmates* offered a strange pairing with the young Joe Zawinul, with Jones sitting in on four tracks, although Webster was happy with any pianist who stood his ground. Highlights include a poignant reflection on Billie Holiday's 'Trav'lin' Light' and the title blues.

***(*)   **Stormy Weather** Black Lion BLCD 760108 CD
       Webster; Kenny Drew (*p*); Niels-Henning Ørsted-Pedersen (*b*); Alex Riel (*d*). 1/65.

***(*)   **Gone With The Wind** Black Lion BLCD 760125 CD/MC
       As above. 1/65.

Recorded on a single long, long night at Copenhagen's Café Montmartre, these glorious records commemorate the start of Webster's lengthy European sojourn. Drew's scholarly blend of blues and bop phrasing lends gentlemanly support, while the two local youngsters on bass and drums behave respectfully without losing their enthusiasm. All, though, rests with Webster's now inimitable tone and delivery. Close to the microphone, he's often content barely to enunciate the melody in an exhalation which feathers down to a pitchless vibration as often as it hits an actual note. Up-tempo pieces tend to be throwaway bundles of phrases, but anything slower becomes a carefully orchestrated set-piece. Sometimes the pace becomes almost too stolid, and perhaps the records are best heard a few tracks at a time, but it's enormously characterful jazz.

***   **There Is No Greater Love** Black Lion BLCD 760151 CD
       As above. 9/65.

***   **The Jeep Is Jumping** Black Lion BLCD 760147 CD
       Webster; Arnvid Mayer (*t*); John Darville (*tb*); Niels Jorgen Steen (*p*); Henrik
       Hartmann, Hugo Rasmussen (*b*); Hans Nymand (*d*). 9/65.

Webster back at the Montmartre in September, with an only marginally less engaging set, including his latest thoughts on 'I Got It Bad And That Ain't Good'. The session with Arnvid Mayer's band hems the saxophonist in a little more, with the group plodding at points, although Webster himself is again serenely in charge.

(*)   **Ben Webster Meets Bill Coleman Black Lion BLCD 760141 CD
       Webster; Bill Coleman (*t, flhn, v*); Fred Hunt (*p*); Jim Douglas (*g*); Ronnie Rae (*b*);
       Lennie Hastings (*d*). 4/67.

A bit disappointing. Webster and Coleman were both in London (as was Buck Clayton, scheduled for the date but in the event indisposed) and they cut this session with Alex Welsh's rhythm section in support. It's pleasing enough, but something tired seems to have crept into the music: the tempos plod a little too much, holding back both hornmen – and, considering the quality of Webster's playing on 'For Max' (dedicated to Max Jones) and 'For All We Know', it's a shame.

***   **Masters Of Jazz Vol. 5: Ben Webster** Storyville 4105 CD/LP
Webster; Palle Mikkelborg, Perry Knudsen, Palle Bolvig, Allan Botschinsky (*t*); Per
Espersen, Torolf Moolgaard, Axel Windfeld, Ole Kurt Jensen (*tb*); Uffe Karskov,
Jesper Thilo, Dexter Gordon, Sahib Shihab, Bent Nielsen (*reeds*); Ole Kock Hansen,
Kenny Drew (*p*); Ole Molin (*g*); Niels-Henning Ørsted-Pedersen, Hugo Rasmussen
(*b*); Ole Steenberg, Albert 'Tootie' Heath, Bjarne Rostvold (*d*); strings. 68–70.

***(*)   **Live In Amsterdam** Charly 168 CD
Webster; Cees Slinger (*p*); Rob Langereis (*b*); Peter Ypma (*d*). 1/69.

***(*)   **For The Guv'nor** Charly CD 15 CD
Webster; Cees Slinger, Kenny Drew, Frans Wieringa (*p*); Niels-Henning
Ørsted-Pedersen, Jacques Schols (*b*); John Engels, Donald McKyre (*d*). 5–10/69.

***   **No Fool, No Fun** Spotlite SPJ142 LP
Webster; Niels-Henning Ørsted-Pedersen (*b*); Marty Peters, Freddy Albeck (*v*); rest
unknown. 10/70.

***   **Plays Ballads** Storyville 4118 CD/LP
As above, except add Erling Christensen, Flemming Madsen (*reeds*); William
Schiöppfe (*d*); John Steffensen (*perc*). 7/67–11/71.

***   **Makin' Whoopee** Spotlite SPJ9 LP
Webster; George Arvanitas (*p*); Jacky Sampson (*b*); Charles Saudrais (*d*). 6/72.

(*)   **My Man Steeplechase SCS 1008 LP
Webster; Ole Kock Hansen (*p*); Bo Stief (*b*); Alex Riel (*d*). 4/73.

Webster's final years found him based in Copenhagen, and his manner was by now so *sui generis*
that it's tempting to view the later work as a single, lachrymose meditation on the same handful
of favourite ballads and Ellington tunes. But Ben's own subtle variations on himself create
absorbing differences between each stately rendition of 'Prelude To A Kiss' or 'Old Folks'. He
was lucky in his accompanists: while several of the rhythm sections sound anonymous in
themselves, Webster's knack of helping them raise their game elicits some exceptionally
sympathetic playing from almost everybody. The two Storyville albums collect scatterings from
several sessions over a five-year period, including dates with strings, some heavenly ballads, and
a couple of dates with Teddy Wilson at the piano: both mixed bags, but plenty of vintage
Webster. *No Fool, No Fun* gives the lie to the idea that Webster was a careless inebriate in his
autumnal years: rehearsing a band through a broadcast, he knows exactly what he wants from
them and how best to get it. *Makin' Whoopee* and *My Man* are both middling sessions, the
latter (recorded on a typical late night at the Café Montmartre) a bit too relaxed, the former
finding Arvanitas a little too bright. It's the two 1969 records on Charly which are outstanding.
The only reservations about both relate to the sound: the live set favours the bass above
everybody else, with the piano often disappearing, but Webster is in absolutely prime form, with
a ravishing 'Come Sunday' and a perfectly cooked 'Johnny Come Lately' as only two
highlights. *For The Guv'nor*, dedicated primarily to Ellington, is distinguished by wonderful
playing from Slinger – his intros to 'Prelude To A Kiss' and 'In A Sentimental Mood' are close
to definitive – and Webster in respectful, solemnly effective mood; but the saxophonist is
sometimes swamped by the over-miked brushwork of Engels. Anyone who enjoys the sound of
Ben Webster will find something to enjoy in all these records.

DAVE WECKL

DRUMS

*(*)   **Master Plan** GRP GRD-9619 CD
Weckl; Scott Alspath, Jerry Hey (*t*); Bill Reichenbach (*tb*); Eric Marienthal (*ss, as*);
Michael Brecker (*ts*); Chick Corea, Jay Oliver (*ky*); Ray Kennedy (*p*); Peter Mayer (*g,
v*); Anthony Jackson, Tom Kennedy (*b*); Steve Gadd (*d*). 90.

Weckl's technique will appease the most demanding of listeners who want to hear difficult
drumming. For listeners who'd prefer to hear music, there is rather less on offer here. No
gainsaying his accomplishments, of course: Weckl's only peer in this kind of death-or-glory
fusion music is Steve Gadd, who appears here in 'Master Plan', which is akin to a

modernization of the old drum battles that performers such as Rich and Krupa would indulge in in times past. The rest of the music – much of it co-written with producer Jay Oliver, who isn't exactly weighted down with a cargo of melodies – offers a festival of bombast, some of it barely tolerable: the one all-acoustic treatment, a trio reading of 'Softly, As In A Morning Sunrise', seems like a cynical interlude to the principal action.

MICHAEL WEISS (born 1958)
PIANO

** **Presenting Michael Weiss** Criss Cross Jazz Criss 1022 CD
Weiss; Tom Kirkpatrick (*t*); Ralph Lalama (*ts*); Ray Drummond (*b*); Kenny Washington (*d*). 4/86.

This debut set is very much in the house style: no-frills contemporary bebop on a handful of jazz standards and a couple of originals. Nothing amiss, but nothing to create much excitement unless you're playing in the band. Kirkpatrick, a vaguely irascible trumpeter, is the most striking player here, given that Drummond and Washington seem to be watching the clock, and Weiss is a perfectly accomplished and uninteresting leader.

BOBBY WELLINS (born 1936)
TENOR SAXOPHONE

*** **Birds Of Brazil** Sungai BW11 CD
Wellins; Kenny Wheeler (*t, flhn*); Peter Jacobsen (*p*); Kenny Baldock (*b*); Spike Wells (*d*); Chris Karan (*perc*); The Delme Quartet (*strings*). 89.

This Scottish tenorman remains among the most distinctive stylists British jazz has produced, and it's a pity that he wasn't recorded more frequently in his prime: some of his best work, with Stan Tracey's group of the 1960s, has been out of print for many years, and a long period of musical inactivity left a gap in what should have been an important legacy. This recent recording, featuring a suite in dedication to the World Wide Fund for Nature, is all that's currently available on CD. The three-movement title-opus, orchestrated by Tony Coe, isn't the most profound piece of writing, but Wellins's sinewy lyricism and staunchless appetite for sending ideas in unexpected directions keeps blandness at bay, even though he was perhaps too generous in offering solo space to the others (Wheeler, though, appears only briefly). Three standards, included as makeweights, include a rapt, lovely 'Angel Eyes' and an authoritative 'In Walked Bud'.

DICK WELLSTOOD (1927–90)
PIANO

*** **I Wish I Were Twins** Swingtime 8204 LP
Wellstood (*p* solo) and with Dick Hyman (*p*). 3/83.

***(*) **Diane** Swingtime 8207 LP
Wellstood (*p* solo). 2/85.

A jobbing musician who is content to play supper-club dates, parties and tribute recordings to great predecessors like Waller, James P. Johnson and Art Tatum, Dick Wellstood is easily underestimated. Always up for a gig though he may be, he is also a practising lawyer, and his easy, engaging stride approach masks a steel-trap understanding of every wrinkle of piano jazz, an eclecticism that allows him to play in virtually every idiom from early ragtime to quasi-modal compositions from the shores opposite bop. Regrettably, much of his work has bloomed and faded in highly unappreciative settings and company, and he is not well represented in the current catalogue.

At the keyboard, he sounds most like a younger version of James P. Johnson, setting up big and forceful alternations in the left hand against a characteristic tremolo in the melody line. He favours huge, raw bass figures and counters their jagged outlines with wonderfully subtle fills and footnotes. The two Swingtimes are only a fair approximation of his best work. In his late fifties he has tempered his approach slightly, enough to admit an occasional ballad. 'Body And Soul' on the very good *Diane* is a perfect example of his delicate approach to a melody, leaving the original tune intact even as he explores more of the feasible variations than seems possible in the brief compass of the number. The duos with Hyman are much less interesting, with a jangly, piano-roll quality. There is, though, a wonderful solo Ellington medley on the compilation, *Piano Giants: Volume 2* (Swingtime 8202 LP) and it's worth looking out for any Chiaruscuro and Jazzology sets that make their way into the second-hand racks.

ALEX WELSH (1929–82)
CORNET, VOCALS

*** **Live At The Royal Festival Hall, 1954/5** Lake LA5008 LP
Welsh; Roy Crimmins (*tb*, *v*); Ian Christie (*cl*); Fred Hunt (*p*); Neville Skrimshire (*g*); Frank Thompson (*b*); Pete Appleby (*d*); George Melly (*v*). 10/54, 1/55.

*** **Dixieland To Duke/The Melrose Folio** Dormouse DM7 LP
Welsh; Roy Crimmins (*tb*); Archie Semple (*cl*); Fred Hunt (*p*); Nigel Sinclair (*g*); Chris Staunton (*b*); Billy Lock, Johnny Richardson (*d*). 2 & 3/57, 2 & 3/58.

**** **At Home With ...** Dormouse DM16 LP
Welsh; Roy Williams (*tb*); Johnny Barnes (*as*, *bs*); Al Gay (*ts*); Fred Hunt (*p*); Jim Douglas (*g*); Ronnie Rae (*b*); Lennie Hastings (*d*). 11/67.

***(*) **Classic Concert** Black Lion BLCD 760503 CD/MC
Welsh; Roy Williams (*tb*, *v*); John Barnes (*cl*, *as*, *bs*, *f*, *v*); Fred Hunt (*p*); Jim Douglas (*bj*, *g*); Harvey Weston (*b*); Lennie Hastings (*d*). 10/71.

Despite the surname, Welsh was a Scot. A taut wee man with a gammy leg, he didn't entirely look the part but was nevertheless a fine cornetist, influenced by Wild Bill Davison (though he emphatically denied this). When he died in 1982, Humphrey Lyttelton described the Welsh band's impact as a combination of 'romanticism and rage', a near-perfect characterization of its leader's buttoned-up ferocity. *Dixieland To Duke / The Melrose Folio* (the latter so named after the Chicago publisher of classic jazz) are both disconcertingly crude in places, but the Morton, Oliver and Spikes material on the second half is authentically and confidently delivered. Welsh was an ardent revivalist long before the trad boom really got under way; the mid-1950s Festival Hall material has to be heard in the context of often bitter partisanship within jazz; at the second of the two concerts, the band were pelted with coins and shouted suggestions that they 'play some jazz'!

The band changed markedly in approach during the 1960s, a period during which the once teetotal Welsh acquired a famous thirst for vodka, moving away from the ragged, Chicagoan 'Condon style' evident on the Dormice towards the more orthodox swing approach audible on *Classic Concert*; 'classic' should perhaps be understood in its exact sense, in other words, as the opposite of 'romantic'. The band's enormous success at Antibes in 1967 and at later American festivals seemed to do no more than reinforce internal divisions, but *At Home* (recorded in Edinburgh) is buoyed along by the thrill of that remarkable summer. Welsh's own playing has an unforced intensity even on pabulum like 'The Shadow Of Your Smile'; 'Wood Green', with Roy Williams's 'Sir John Barbirolli Patter', is a blues dedicated to the 'other' London trad club of the time. None of the other soloists has anything quite like Welsh's rough-edged command. Though less limber than the 1960 front line of Roy Crimmins and the wounded Archie Semple (it can be heard on the Verve *Compact Jazz: Best of Dixieland* (831375 CD) or on *The Best Of British Traditional Jazz* (Philips 818651 CD)), the 1971 line-up of Williams and the multi-talented Barnes was still capable of performing powerfully. Side by side, 'Sleepy Time Down South' and 'Maple Leaf Rag' confirm something of Lyttelton's description; set alongside the 'Clark And Randolph Blues', a previously unissued version of the Art Hodes tune on the Lake compilation, they're slightly wan. Welsh himself sounds tired but plays with great straightforwardness and a lovely tone. Watch out for the marvellous 1967 *Strike One*, a vintage Welsh recording which deserves reissue.

KENNY WERNER
PIANO, KEYBOARDS, VOCAL

**   **Beyond The Forest Of Mirkwood** Enja 3061 LP
Werner. 2/80.

(*)   **Introducing The Trio Sunnyside SSC 1038D CD
Werner; Ratzo Harris (*b*); Tom Rainey (*d*). 3/89.

***   **Uncovered Heart** Sunnyside SSC 1048D CD
Werner; Randy Brecker (*t, flhn*); Joe Lovano (*ss, ts*); Eddie Gomez (*b*); John Riley
(*d*). 90.

***(*)   **Press Enter** Sunnyside SSC 1056D CD
Werner; Ratzo Harris (*b*); Tom Rainey (*d*). 8/91.

Werner is a beguiling player, perfectly at home in either a solo, trio or a rhythm-and-horns date, and if he often seems a little too becalmed in his playing it does gradually draw an attentive listener in. The solo record is plagued by a bothersome new age concept that seeps into the music as well as the Tolkeinian titles, but the Sunnyside discs are far more satisfying. *Uncovered Heart* includes some good originals, and if the horns perform with mundane expertise, Werner himself stands up as a leader worthy of respect. The first trio album seems a little undercooked, with nods to Bill Evans that sometimes turn into slavish imitation, but the second, *Press Enter*, is beautifully handled and suggests a much stronger empathy among the three players. Werner's long out-of-tempo introduction to a very thoughtful 'Blue In Green' sets one of the keynotes for the record, an exploration of shifting rhythms, and Rainey's almost pointillistic stickwork is ideally directed. Certainly the best place to start listeneing to Werner.

FRANK WESS (born 1922)
TENOR SAXOPHONE, FLUTE

***   **North, East, South . . . Wess** Savoy SV 0139 CD
Wess; Frank Foster (*ts*); Henry Coker, Bennie Powell (*tb*); Kenny Burrell (*g*); Eddie
Jones (*g*); Kenny Clarke (*d*). 3/56.

***(*)   **Entre Nous** Concord CCD 4456 CD
Wess; Ron Tooley, Snooky Young (*t*); Joe Newman (*t, v*); Pete Minger (*t, flhn*); Art
Baron, Grover Mitchell, Doug Purviance, Dennis Wilson (*tb*); Curtis Peagler, Bill
Ramsay (*as*); Billy Mitchell (*ts*); Arthur Clarke (*bs*); Tee Carson (*p*); Ted Dunbar (*g*);
Eddie Jones (*b*); Dennis Mackrel (*d*). 11/90.

Inseparable in most people's minds from Frank Foster, with whom he replaced Herschel Evans and Lester Young in the Basie band, Wess's main claim to fame is his pioneering use of flute as a solo instrument in jazz. A forthright swing soloist, virtually unmarked by bop, Wess is probably less distinctive than Foster on the saxophone (the original *NESW* liner-note helpfully identified individual contributions); their highly successful quintet was probably most listenable when they exploited 'alternate' horns. *Opus De Jazz* was a bold and well-intentioned effort that didn't quite come off and sounds rather stiff and remote in places, chamber jazz that never gets up enough body heat to compel interest.

Wess's flute solo on the custom-built 'Entre Nous', title-piece of the fine 1990 concert album, recorded in Japan, shows off his burnished and now supremely confident tone to the utmost. Ironically, the live recording displays it better than the earlier Savoys, which are close-miked and rather brittle in sound. The twinned horns of *North, East, South . . . Wess* are only occasionally effective. There really isn't enough between Coker and Powell to give their contributions much in the way of dramatic differentiation. It's Foster who shines, with a superb solo on 'Dancing On The Ceiling'.

KATE WESTBROOK
VOCALS

***(*) **Goodbye, Peter Lorre** Femme/Line FECD 9.01060 CD
Westbrook; John Alley, Mike Westbrook (*p*); Fine Trash: Jacqueline Barron, Michael Doré, Simon Grant, Denise Shane, Carey Wilson (*v*). 7/91.

It's rather remarkable and disturbing that this should be Kate Westbrook's first record under her own name. It's nearly twenty years since she joined husband Mike Westbrook (see below) in the celebrated Brass Band, to which she contributed tenor horn and piccolo as well as an almost schizophrenic vocal range. Her singing takes in torchy languour, tortured shrieks, and a threatening growl that puts a death's head on the weary come-on of 'Love For Sale' (a torch song for the AIDS generation?). There's another version on the earlier Westbrook Trio album named after the tune, but this one is particularly powerful, drawn up into the atmosphere of toxic sexual promise, pathos and violence one associates with Peter Lorre and that forms the basis of Kate Westbrook's tribute to him.

Lorre's voice and bizarre hyperthyroid looks stick uncomfortably in the memory and Kate Westbrook's imaginative recreation of his ambience is tremendously effective. Using songs by Brecht (who admired the actor greatly) and Westbrook originals, she creates a moody cabaret out of her familiar array of accents and languages. The dressing-room sound effects on 'The Show Goes On' are a little too obvious, but the alternation of mood, language and vocal style is almost perfect and it's hard to imagine a better version of 'Surabaya Jonny', spoken/sung with hurt innocence just on the point of turning dangerous. The closing 'Toute Seule' is a generous and sympathetic gesture toward Lorre's memory.

The arrangements are excellent and the singing of Fine Trash on two tracks is wonderfully precise. If this is your first encounter with Kate Westbrook, you should quickly move to the items listed below . . .

MIKE WESTBROOK (born 1936)
COMPOSER, PIANO, TUBA

***(*) **Citadel/Room 315** Novus ND 74987 CD
Westbrook; Nigel Carter, Derek Healey, Henry Lowther, Kenny Wheeler (*t, flhn*); Malcolm Griffiths (*tb*); Paul Rutherford (*tb, euph*); Geoff Perkins, Alf Rece (*btb*); Mike Page (*as, f, bcl*); Alan Wakeman (*ts, ss, cl*); John Holbrooke (*ts, f*); John Surman (*bs, ss, bcl*); John Warren (*bs, f*); Dave MacRae (*p*); Brian Godding (*g*); Chris Laurence (*b*); Alan Jackson (*d*); John Mitchell (*perc*); collective personnel. 3/75.

*** **For The Record** Transatlantic/Line TACD 9.00785 CD
Westbrook; Phil Minton (*t, v*); Kate Westbrook (*thn, picc, v*); Dave Chambers (*reeds, v*); Paul Rutherford (*tb, euph, v*). 10/75.

***(*) **Love/Dream And Variations** Transatlantic/Line TACD 9.00788 CD
Westbrook; George Chisholm, Paul Cosh, Alan Downey, Henry Lowther (*t*); Malcolm Griffiths, Geoff Perkins , Paul Rutherford (*tb*); Dave Chambers, John Holbrooke, Mike Page, John Warren (*reeds*); Dave MacRae (*p*); Brian Godding (*g*); John Mitchell (*vib, perc*); Chris Laurence (*b*); Alan Jackson (*d, perc*). 2/76.

***(*) **The Westbrook Blake: Bright As Fire** Impetus IMP 18013 CD/LP/MC
Westbrook; Mike Davies, Dave Hancock, Henry Lowther (*t*); Phil Minton (*t, v*); Malcolm Griffiths (*tb*); Alan Sinclair (*tba*); Kate Westbrook (*thn, picc, v*); Chris Biscoe, Alan Wakeman (*reeds*); Georgie Born (*clo*); Chris Laurence (*b*); Dave Barry (*d*). 80.

**** **On Duke's Birthday** hat Art 6021 CD
Westbrook; Kate Westbrook (*thn [tenor horn], picc, bamboo f, v*); Phil Minton (*t, v*); Stuart Brooks (*t, flhn*); Danilo Terenzi (*tb*); Chris Biscoe (*as, ss, bs, picc, acl*); Brian Godding (*g*); Dominique Pifarely (*vn*); Georgie Born (*clo*); Steve Cook (*b*); Tony Marsh (*d*). 5/84.

***(*)   **Love For Sale** hat Art 6061 CD
Westbrook; Kate Westbrook (*t hn [tenor horn], picc, bamboo f, v*); Chris Biscoe (*as, ss, bs, acl*). 12/85.

***(*)   **Pierides** Core/Line COCD 9.00377 CD
Westbrook; Kate Westbrook (*thn [tenor horn], picc, v*); Peter Whyman (*as, cl*); Brian Godding (*g, g syn*). 3/86.

****   **Westbrook–Rossini** hat Art 6002 CD
Westbrook; Kate Westbrook (*thn [tenor horn], picc, v*); Paul Nieman (*tb*); Andy Grappy (*tba*); Lindsay Cooper (*sno*); Paul Whyman (*as*); Peter Fairclough (*d*). 86.

****   **London Bridge Is Broken Down** Venture VED 13 CD/LP
Westbrook; Kate Westbrook (*v, thn [tenor horn]*); Graham Russell (*t, flhn, picc t*); Paul Nieman (*tb, elec*); Chris Biscoe (*as, ss, bs, acl*); Peter Whyman (*as, ss, cl*); Brian Godding (*g*); Steve Cook (*b*); Tony Marsh (*d*); Le Sinfonietta De Picardie. 12/87.

***(*)   **Off Abbey Road** TipToe 888805 CD
Westbrook; Kate Westbrook (*thn [tenor horn], v*); Phil Minton (*t, v*); Alan Wakeman (*ss, ts*); Peter Whyman (*as*); Andy Grappy (*tba*); Brian Godding (*g*); Peter Fairclough (*d*). 8/89.

It's tempting to suggest that were Mike Westbrook American or German rather than English his career might already have been garlanded with the praise it so conspicuously deserves. Britain's neglect of one of its most distinguished contemporary composers amounts to a national disgrace. Westbrook's regular groups – the early Concert Band, which included John Surman, the mixed-media Cosmic Circus, which paved the way for much of his later theatrical work, the jazz-rock Solid Gold Cadillac, and most recently the Brass Band (which is responsible for the slightly disappointing *For The Record*) – have drawn from a startling range of musical and performance backgrounds. In a very real sense, Westbrook is not a jazz musician at all but a musical magpie; Rossini's 'La Gazza Ladra' and '*Lone Ranger*' theme may have touched a chord of self-awareness (great artists thieve, after all, and Westbrook is certainly a masked loner).

If he is also an improviser, and there is no doubt that he is, it is not as an instrumentalist. Instead, he improvises with genre and with the boundaries of genre. Purely musical influences like Ellington (who lies behind all the early and mid-period big-band compositions, such as *Metropolis* and the reissued *Citadel/Room 315* and whose 'Creole Love Call' is covered on the excellent *Love/Dream And Variations*) and Thelonious Monk are tempered by an interest in the boundaries of music and verse, theatre, the plastic arts and agit-prop, which has led Westbrook to reconsider the work of Brecht and Weill and The Beatles.

The only one of Westbrook's earlier large-scale compositions for band still surviving is *Citadel/Room 315*, so named for the room in Leeds Polytechnic where much of the music was written. It's reissued courtesy of Novus's very welcome Series '70, which has been putting out valuable material from a little considered but highly inventive decade in jazz. The piece is a typical mixture of bright, brassy themes, stretched over a hard rock beat, but with considerable rhythmic and harmonic variation. Surman is the featured soloist, on all three of his horns. Westbrook himself performs very little, leaving piano duties to the New Zealander Dave MacRae. There are hints of later developments in Westbrook's useof a children's skipping chant on 'View From The Drawbridge'. At the heart of the piece are two tender love songs, one called just that, a blowing piece called 'Pastorale' and, as on *Metropolis*, two collective improvisations: 'Bebop De Rigueur' and the magnificent 'Sleeper Awaking In Sunlight', mainly for clarinets and baritone saxophone, which justifies the cost of the CD on its own.

Together with the former Kate Barnard, Westbrook has since devised a remarkable series of performances/entertainments which blend elements of jazz, popular song, verse and theatre. The finest of these are *The Cortege* (which at press time had not yet been reissued by Enja) and its dark thematic twin, *London Bridge Is Broken Down* (which represents the same drama of life-in-death-in-life). Perhaps the purest and most straightforward, though, is the trio *Love For Sale*, which weaves a remarkable range of sources (including an old Westbrook touchstone, William Blake, and a range of standard and traditional tunes) into a coherent performance that balances social anger, sentiment and purely formal control. The unifying factor, as in many of Westbrook's pieces, is Kate Westbrook's remarkable voice. 'England Have My Bones' features it at its most Grand Guignol, but she is equally capable of a whisky-and-nicotine romanticism, as with 'Lush Life', and of a husky purity which is reminiscent of the classical contralto Kathleen Ferrier. Westbrook contributes simple, thought-out piano and tuba accompaniments, and most of the embellishment derives from Biscoe's generous array of horns. The vocal and instrumental recipe works nearly as well on *Pierides*, where Godding's guitar adds a further dimension to music that was originally conceived as a dance/theatre piece known as *Pier Rides*, a wry Anglicization of the collective name of the Greek Muses; it's also (to give a sense of the serendipitous way Westbrook's imagination seems to work) the name given to the nine Thessalian maidens who, having challenged the Muses to a singing contest and lost, are turned into magpies.

Westbrook's later orchestral works have been tighter and less detailed than the beautiful abstract impressionism of *Metropolis*, or the free-Ellingtonian style of *Citadel/Room 315*, which, along with the classic early *Marching Song*, is his best non-vocal work. Two of the later pieces afford an interesting comparative exercise. Unlike *Westbrook–Rossini*, which treats the 'Thieving Magpie' theme (one lent a curiously threatening resonance by its use in Stanley Kubrick's *A Clockwork Orange*) and other tunes almost as if they were show-tune standards on which solo improvisations, *On Duke's Birthday* is a set of original scores which reflect the spirit of Ellington's compositions and arrangements, but which refer to them only subliminally. Neither approach is that of a *pasticheur*. Westbrook's arrangements are clean-limbed and his big bands have a simplicity and directness of detail very little different from the vocal trios and quartets. The studio CD of *Westbrook–Rossini* replaces an earlier double album live set of the same material; some of the solos, from Lindsay Cooper's snake-charmer sopranino in particular, lack the spontaneity of the live set, but the sound is very much better.

The long *London Bridge* set derives something from Eliot's aural soundscapes in 'The Waste Land', drawing together musical elements from Berlin, Prague and Vienna. The final 'Picardie' section is one of his most successful settings, a pastoral contrast to the urban modernism celebrated in earlier parts. His use of the Sinfonietta de Picardie is spare, imaginative and unobtrusive.

Westbrook belongs to a long-standing English musical tradition one associates (though Westbrook is from semi-rural High Wycombe) with the Lancashire Catholic background out of which John Lennon emerged (and to which novelist/composer Anthony Burgess has paid tribute). Underneath its wry whimsicality there is a dark thread of social romanticism (particularly important on the Blake settings) and protest that breaks the surface weave more or less often, depending on how serious or angry the piece in question happens to be. The Beatles arrangements are mostly light in touch but highly ambiguous in import; 'Maxwell's Silver Hammer', 'She Came In Through The Bathroom Window' and 'Come Together' all make an impact out of reasonable proportion to their actual content, and even 'Mean Mr Mustard' and 'Polythene Pam' demand further hearings.

RANDY WESTON (born 1926)
PIANO

***(*)   **Nuit Africaine** Enja 2086 LP
Weston solo. n.d.

****   **Blues To Africa** Freedom 41014 CD/LP
As above. 8/74.

***   **Self Portraits** Verve 841314 CD/MC
Weston; Idris Muhammad (*d*); Eric Asante (*perc*).

***(*)   **Jazz A La Bohemia** Original Jazz Classics OJC 1747 CD/LP
Weston; Cecil Payne (*bs*); Ahmed Abdul-Malik (*b*); Al Dreares (*d*); collective personnel. 10/56.

****   **Carnival** Freedom 41004 CD/LP
Weston; Billy Harper (*ts, f*); William Allen (*b*); Famoudou Don Moye (*d, perc*); Steve Berrios (*perc*). 7/74.

Six-foot something-ridiculous in his stocking soles, Weston cuts such an impressive figure that his rather marginal critical standing remains an enigma. Though dozens of players every year turn to the joyous 'Hi-Fly' theme, few of them seem to have probed any deeper into Weston's output, which is considerable and impressive. Like many players of his generation, his main initial influence was Thelonious Monk. In later years, though, Weston was to explore African and Caribbean musics, somewhat in the manner of Dollar Brand/Abdullah Ibrahim and Andrew Hill, and to attempt larger-scale structures of a sort pioneered by James P. Johnson and Duke Ellington. Though a ruggedly beautiful performer, it is as a composer that he is most seriously underrated; the two sides come together in the group 'Tribute To Ellington' on *Carnival*.

Weston spent the late 1960s and early '70s living in North Africa, making a flurry of superb recording on his return to the United States. *Blues To Africa* is the best of the solo sets (though 'Little Niles' on *Nuit Africaine* may be his best single composition and performance) effecting a much more coherent synthesis of African and American elements. This is made explicit on 'African Village Bedford Stuyvesant', a piece that points to the tribalism (meant positively in this context) of the New York black music scene. 'Tangier Bay', 'Uhuru Kwanza' and the title-track are much more obviously derived from his five-year exile/homecoming in Morocco.

For the clearest sense of what Weston gained – harmonically, rhythmically, spiritually – from that period, it's only necessary to compare the excellent *Carnival* with the much earlier *Jazz A La Bohemia*. It isn't the case that Weston pasively 'discovered' African rhythms and tonalities on one of his early-1960s study trips. Art is seldom the product of accidents. As one can clearly hear from the Africanized inflections of the 1950s Riverside sessions, Weston went in search of confirmation for what he was already doing. 'You Go To My Head' has a quality quite unlike the average standards performance of the time, and Payne's rather solemn-sounding baritone on the other tracks can almost suggest the buzz and thump of Central African drones. Among younger generation players, probably only Billy Harper had the right combination of traditionalism and modernist, post-bop technique, though later Weston was to record successfully with the new avant-traditionalist of tenor saxophone, David Murray (*The Healers*, Black Saint BSR 0118 CD/LP).

KENNY WHEELER (born 1930)
TRUMPET, FLUGELHORN

***(*) **Gnu High** ECM 1069 CD/LP
Wheeler; Keith Jarrett (*p*); Dave Holland (*b*); Jack DeJohnette (*d*). 6/75.

**** **Deer Wan** ECM 1102 CD/LP
Wheeler; Jan Garbarek (*ts, ss*); John Abercrombie (*g, electric mand*); Ralph Towner (*12-string g*); Dave Holland (*b*); Jack DeJohnette (*d*). 7/77.

***(*) **Double, Double You** ECM 1262 CD/LP
Wheeler; Michael Brecker (*ts*); John Taylor (*p*); Dave Holland (*b*); Jack DeJohnette (*d*). 5/83.

***(*) **Visions** Justin Time JTR 8413 CD
Wheeler; Orchestre Chambre De Montréal; Tim Brady (*g*). 11/85, 6/88.

***(*) **Welcome** Soul Note SN 1171 CD/LP
Wheeler; Claudio Fasoli (*t, flhn*); Jean-François Jenny-Clark (*b*); Daniel Humair (*d*). 3/86.

*** **Flutter By, Butterfly** Soul Note SN 1146 CD/LP
Wheeler; Stan Sulzman (*ss, ts, f*); John Taylor (*p*); Billy Elgart (*d*). 5/87.

**** **Music For Large And Small Ensembles** ECM 1415/6 2CD/2LP
Wheeler; Alan Downey, Ian Hamer, Henry Lowther, Derek Watkins (*t*); Hugh Fraser, Dave Horler, Chris Pyne, Paul Rutherford (*tb*); Julian Arguëlles, Duncan Lamont, Evan Parker, Ray Warleigh (*sax*); Stan Sulzman (*ts, f*); John Taylor (*p*); John Abercrombie (*g*); Dave Holland (*b*); Peter Erskine (*d*); Norma Winstone (*v*). 1/90.

**** **The Widow In The Window** ECM 1417 CD/LP
Wheeler; John Abercrombie (*g*); John Taylor (*p*); Dave Holland (*b*); Peter Erskine (*d*). 2/90.

Where the hell did the time go? Kenny Wheeler's sixtieth birthday in 1990 was treated in many quarters with a kind of suspicious amazement, as if he'd been lying about his age down the years or someone had been fiddling with the clocks. The fact is that Wheeler has been a fixture on the British jazz scene since 1952, when he emigrated from his native Canada and did section work with some of the best bandleaders of the time, joining John Dankworth in 1959 and staying until the mid-1960s. Initially influenced by the bop trumpet of Fats Navarro and his equally short-lived descendant, Booker Little, Wheeler also took on board the clipped abstractions and parched romanticism of trumpeter and flugelhorn player, Art Farmer, a hugely underrated musician whose perfectionism resembles Wheeler's own. Under this combination of interests, Wheeler turned towards free playing, joining John Stevens's influential Spontaneous Music Ensemble, Alexander von Schlippenbach's Globe Unity Orchestra and Anthony Braxton's superb early-1970s quartet. More recently, Wheeler has played with Norma Winstone and her husband, John Taylor, in the impressionistic Azimuth, and became the last permanent member of the United Jazz + Rock Ensemble in 1979.

It was possible in 1990 to wonder at Wheeler's threescore years because he became a leader only rather late in his career. Famously self-critical, the trumpeter seemed to lack the basic ego-count required to front a working band. Association with Manfred Eicher's musician-friendly ECM made an enormous difference to Wheeler's self-perception, and since 1975 he has regularly recorded for the label whose painstaking technical virtues match his own and whose limpid studio ideally suits his bleak lyricism. With ECM, Wheeler has also made enormous strides as a composer; standards are now very rare in his recorded work and the Dietz/Schwartz 'By Myself' on ECM 1416 seems a significant exception. 'Ana', on *The Widow In The Window*, had already been given a notable reading by the Berlin Contemporary Jazz Orchestra (ECM 1409 CD/LP). *Music For Large And Small Ensembles* contains some of Wheeler's most distinctive scores (though *Visions*, for soloist and orchestra, and recorded in his native Canada, remains his most emphatic statement as a 'straight' composer) and is, perhaps, the best place to gain an understanding of how Wheeler's particular grasp of tonality and instrumental colour works in a mixture of scored and improvised settings. As in *Azimuth*, he uses Norma Winstone's voice to increase the chromaticism of his arrangements and further humanize unwontedly personal and self-revealing pieces, full of folk echoes and deeply embedded North American themes (the 'Opening' to 'Sweet Time Suite' sounds like a variant on a cowboy tune, and there's a wide-open quality to the voicings that can be heard in fellow-Canadian, Leonard Cohen's, eclectic jazz–buckskin–*musette*–rock syntheses).

The trios that conclude disc two (there are also three duets which do not involve Wheeler as a player) are closer to Wheeler's free-abstract work than to the thematic improvisations on his best-known ECM records. Significantly, the most abstract of the albums he has made for the label, *Around 6*, is currently deleted. The best of those that remain is undoubtedly *Deer Wan*. It includes Wheeler's most atmospheric brass effects and some of his most unfettered playing. The opening 'Peace For Five' is a straightforward blowing theme, with fine solos by each of the players. The three remaining tracks are more elliptical, but no less impressive, and only the relatively brief '3/4 In The Afternoon', featuring one of Ralph Towner's off-the-peg 12-string spots, is a mild disappointment.

Deer Wan's predecessor on ECM is distinguished by being Keith Jarrett's last session as a sideman. There is some evidence that the pianist was less than happy with the music, but he produces three startling performances that are matched by Wheeler's distinctive phraseology and impeccable tone. An important album for the trumpeter, it's still marked by a degree of diffidence, which persists through the later work. The two Soul Notes suffer from a flatter acoustic, which seems to rob Wheeler's higher-register passages of their ringing strength. Musically, they're well up to scratch; 'Everybody's Song But My Own' (*Flutter By*) and 'Invisible Sound' and 'Emptiness' (*Silence*) utilize the softly falling figures one has heard in Wheeler's work from the outset (and which are also, interestingly, typical of his fellow-Canadian, John Warren) but which increasingly play a structural role in the composition. The recent *Widow In The Window* recaptures – but for Garbarek – the sound of *Deer Wan*, while adding a new solidity of conception. Taken in conjunction with the contemporaneous *Music For Large And Small Ensembles*, it signals Wheeler's emergence as a major jazz composer. Late in the day by some standards, but none the less welcome.

(**)   Kayak Ah Um 012 CD
Wheeler; Dave Horler, Chris Pyne (*tb*); Dave Stewart (*btb, tba*); John Rook (*frhn*); Stan Sulzmann (*ss, ts, f*); Julian Arguëlles (*ss, ts*); John Horler, John Taylor (*p*); Chris Laurence (*b*); Peter Erskine (*d*). 5/92.

Marred by oddly balanced sound, but musically fascinating. The latter part of the set is taken up with a suite loosely centred on C: 'See Horse', the impressionistic 'Sea Lady' (with a fine flute solo from Sulzmann), 'C Man' (dedicated to bassist Laurence, who introduces the solos), and 'C. C. Signor!' (a rollicking tribute to Chick Corea that brings the album to a very effective close).

Wheeler distributes the solo space very even-handedly, concentrating exclusively on flugelhorn for his carefully crafted explorations. The writing is consistently excellent, mixing older material like '5 4 6' and 'Gentle Piece – Old Ballad', the latter strongly recalling the Wheeler of *Deer Wan*. Despite reservations about the production, strongly recommended.

JIGGS WHIGHAM
TROMBONE

(*)   The Jiggs Up Capri 74024-2 CD
Whigham; Bud Shank (*as*); George Cables (*p*); John Clayton (*b*); Jeff Hamilton (*d*). 7/89.

Whigham has lived and worked in Cologne since going there in the mid-1960s to join Kurt Edelhagen's big band, although this set was recorded on one of his return visits to the US. He has a smooth, chocolatey sound on the trombone, entirely unblemished by tonal exaggerations, and, while this can lead to blandness, he has an agility on the horn which is nearly the match of Bill Watrous, a player of similar style. This live session is an enjoyable blow for all involved: Shank sounds in happy mood, although some of his solos take on an aggressively opposing stance to his former, more controlled manner, and it doesn't always suit him. Cables, Clayton and Hamilton play with professional class. The best moments come with the ballads, especially Whigham's charming 'For Someone Never Known'. Unfortunately the recording is less impressive: Shank in particular frequently drifts off-mike, and the rhythm section sound distant.

MICHAEL WHITE (born 1954)
CLARINET

(*)   Shake It And Break It 504 LPS 6 LP
White; Reginald Koeller (*t*); Freddie Lonzo (*tb*); Frank Moliere (*p, v*); Les Muscutt (*bj*); Walter Payton Jr (*b*); Frank Parker (*d*).

(*)   T'Ain't Nobody's Business 504 LPS 11 LP
White; Vernon Gilbert (*t*); Clement Tervalon (*tb, v*); Sadie Goodson Cola (*p, v*); Chester Zardis (*b*); Stanley A. Stephens (*d*); Barbara Ann Shorts (*v*). 8/84.

Maintaining the traditions of New Orleans jazz has been difficult for a number of reasons, principal among them being the dixiefication of the city's music for tourist purposes and the migration of younger musicians away from the locale. The Marsalis family and Harry Connick have brought jazz fame back to New Orleans, but not by playing New Orleans jazz. Michael White, though, is one of the few of the younger players who've attempted to bridge the gap between the original styles and a more contemporary approach, without resorting to the marching-band style of Rebirth or Dirty Dozen. *Shake It And Break It*, his debut on record, finds him in mostly much older company: trombonist Lonzo is the only other musician under 40 on the date. It's much in the tradition of ramshackle but intuitively right ensemble playing, with suspect pitches and ragged textures made into a part of the aesthetic, and Lonzo and White are actually the most extreme players on the date, with the trombonist taking some hair-curling solos and White exploiting his George Lewis influence as far as he can. But Moliere's shambolic piano and a few other infelicities let the side down. *T'Ain't Nobody's Business* is another pairing of generations: Chester Zardis, who's the nominal leader of some of the tracks, and Sadie Goodson Cola were both in their eighties at the time of the session, and both actually played in the legendary Buddy Petit band of 60 years before. It's simple, boisterous music.

Sadie belies her age on her feature 'Sadie's Blues', and Shorts provides some spirited vocals elsewhere, but a feeling persists that the music is more bedraggled than it need be, and that White is sometimes playing down for the occasion.

***   **Crescent City Serenade** Antilles 848545 CD
White; Wendell Brunious, Wynton Marsalis, Teddy Riley (*t*); Greg Stafford (*c*); Freddie Lonzo (*tb*); Steve Pistorius (*p*); Don Vappie (*bj*); Reginald Veal, Walter Payton (*b*); Herlin Riley (*d*). 12/90.

A mostly convincing if sometimes laboured attempt to put White's New Orleans jazz into a contemporary-looking production. The music is compromised somewhat by the presence of Marsalis and two members of his rhythm section: they play a little too slickly, and Wynton's own trumpet contributions seem grotesquely caricatured. Where White gets to play his own way, with fellow spirits like Brunious and Lonzo, it makes a believable synthesis of old and new New Orleans, though it sounds no more authentic – or, indeed, playable – thn the 504 discs listed above.

DICK WHITTINGTON
PIANO

***   **In New York** Concord CCD 4498 CD/MC
Whittington; Steve Gilmore (*b*); Bill Goodwin (*d*). 10/86.

Since this set was recorded (it wasn't released until 1992), Whittington has perhaps become more renowned as the voice introducing each of Concord's Maybeck Recital Hall series; he's the owner of the venue. But he's no slouch as a piano player himself, owing something to Hampton Hawes and Red Garland in style. With even-handed support from Gilmore and Goodwin, erstwhile members of Phil Woods's rhythm section, he goes through ten pieces with great bounce and vigour: 'Manteca' is taken at a very fast clip, and Ahmad Jamal's 'New Rhumba' surrenders nothing to the composer's versions of the tune. While there are many such mainstream-into-post-bop dates, this one's as solidly entertaining as any.

PUTTE WICKMAN (born 1924)
CLARINET

***   **Desire / Mr Clarinet** Four Leaf FLC-CD 101 CD
Wickman; Lars Samuelson (*t*); Bjorn J-Son Lindh (*ky, f*); Janne Schaffer (*g*); Teddy Walter (*b*); Magnus Person, Per Lindvall (*d*). 4/84–6/85.

****   **Miss Oidipus** Dragon DRLP 132 LP
Wickman; Hal Galper (*p*); Steve Gilmore (*b*); Bill Goodwin (*d*). 11/86.

***(*)   **Wickman In Wonderland** Capitol CDP 7903372 CD
Wickman; Butch Lacy (*p*); Jesper Lundgaard (*b*); Bjarne Rostvold (*d*). 12/87.

***(*)   **The Very Thought Of You** Dragon DRCD 161 CD
Wickman; Red Mitchell (*b*). 12/87–1/88.

****   **Some O' This And Some O' That** Dragon DRCD 187 CD
Wickman; Roger Kellaway (*p*); Red Mitchell (*b*). 6/89.

Putte Wickman is still, after five decades, one of the best arguments for taking Swedish jazz seriously. An impeccable swing player who followed cool developments in the 1950s, Wickman has spent time away from jazz but seems fully aware of every kind of development in the music. None of his earlier recordings are, alas, in general circulation at present, but these examples of the modern Wickman are peculiarly satisfying. The Four Leaf CD couples two earlier albums, where the clarinettist works in a soft-fusion setting: it's slight stuff, the playing vitiated a little by the context, but Wickman finds things to say, and the music remains disarmingly pretty. The two quartet albums, though, are absolutely marvellous. The Capitol set (a German release) is sometimes a little stiff, but there are no problems at all with *The Very Thought Of You*, where Wickman meets Phil Woods's rhythm section and the music burns at a slow simmer throughout. The leader's quietly insistent tone never once approaches a squeak, yet he can phrase his way into untouchable registers and lights on a high note with pinpoint finesse. Galper, Gilmore and Goodwin sound impressed, and work at their own top level.

The other two Dragons also find Wickman in splendid fettle. The duo set with Mitchell is momentarily troubled by the bassist's capricious streak: his fascination with the lowest register sometimes strays into indulgence, and the huffing momentum won't be to all tastes. But Wickman goes on spinning out memorable improvisations, and they devise some unexpected variations on the (standard) material: Basie's 'Topsy' becomes rather intense and brooding, and the Ellington themes have no sniff of routine in them. When Kellaway joins in, the music spreads itself out (eight pieces take 72 minutes here, whereas there are 13 in 68 minutes on the duo record), and Kellaway's extravagant imagination is perfectly checked by Wickman's insidious, wily lines. They all play very hard. The recording is sometimes a little flat, since both discs were made in Red Mitchell's apartment rather than a studio, but it suits the intimacy of the music.

WIDESPREAD DEPRESSION ORCHESTRA
GROUP

***   **Downtown Uproar/Boogie In The Barnyard** Stash ST-CD-540 CD
Jordan Sandke (*t*); Tim Atherton (*tb*); Michael Hashim (*as*); Dean Nicyper (*ts*); David Lillie (*bs*); Mike LeDonne (*p*); Jonny Holtzman (*vib, v*); Phil Flanigan (*b*); John Ellis (*d*). 79–80.

Though they subsequently called themselves 'Widespread Jazz Orchestra', presumably to avoid using misery as a label, the two albums coupled on one CD here were by the WDO, which sets out to revivify midstream swing material in the classic manner: as if the Lu Watters Band had been reincarnated as a crew of New England youngsters, which is what most of the musicians were when they started out in 1972. For all the spirit and interpretative elegance of the players, this is a genre exercise, and the fact that they include plenty of collectors'-item tunes (Coleman Hawkins's 'Hollywood Stampede', for instance, or Brick Fleagle's 'Zaza' or Ellington's 'Downtown Uproar') only adds to the inky-fingered aura which surrounds the music. But it's plenty of fun taken a few tracks at a time (the 76 minutes here are perhaps rather too much), and no doubting the calibre of the soloists, especially Michael Hashim's Hodges-inspired alto. A later record for Columbia, *Paris Blues*, is also good but seems to have disappeared from print.

GERALD WIGGINS (born 1922)
PIANO

**   **Music From Around The World In Eighty Days In Modern Jazz** Original Jazz Classics OJC 1761 CD/LP/MC
Wiggins; Eugene Wright (*b*); Bill Douglass (*d*).

(*)   **Relax And Enjoy It! Original Jazz Classics OJC 1761 LP
Wiggins; Joe Comfort (*b*); Jackie Mills (*d*). 61.

Gerry Wiggins began with swing big bands, but he has pursued much of his career as an accompanist, originally with Lena Horne. On his own, with an appropriate rhythm section, he plays light, undemanding but beguiling swing-to-cool piano, rarely challenging the listener and preferring to make a few well-chosen remarks rather than refashioning a tune. The *Eighty Days* material is typical of many records that were worked up from popular contemporary film and show material and, while it's not bad, it sounds as perfunctory as most such genre entries. *Relax And Enjoy It!* is more like it, and more like the title: Wiggins's even touch suits the programme, with a thoughtful 'One For My Baby' as a standout.

***   **Wig Is Here** Black & Blue 590692 CD
Wiggins; Major Holley (*b*); Ed Thigpen, Oliver Jackson (*d*). 5/74–2/77.

Wiggins caught in two trio settings in Paris, with Holley present on both occasions. Little has changed since the OJC albums and, although he was now playing Stevie Wonder as well as 'The Lady Is A Tramp', the same reliable, tension-free swing is at hand.

***(*)   **Live At Maybeck Recital Hall Volume Eight** Concord CCD 4450 CD/MC
Wiggins. 8/90.

Wig's entry in this splendid ongoing series is arguably his best-ever record. On a good piano, with impeccable sound, the quality which Jimmy Rowles – very much a kindred stylistic spirit – refers to in his sleeve-note as 'natural relaxation' emerges in full bloom. It's not so much a matter of taking his time, since none of the pieces here runs to much more than five minutes in length, more a point of shaping a performance to precisely the right tempo and dynamic in order to set down the thoughts the pianist has in mind. Here, for instance, he treats 'I Should Care' as a kind of slow stride interpretation, and Ahmad Jamal's 'Night Mist Blues' has a rocking steadiness which even the composer has never quite realized. He doesn't dawdle over ballads, but nothing's played at any kind of a fast tempo either. Some of the tunes are perhaps over-familiar, even to Wig himself, who has little of significance to add to 'Take The "A" Train' or 'Body And Soul', but that is the privilege of senior status. The recording is as truthful as usual in this fine sequence of records.

JOHNNY WIGGS (1899–1977)
CORNET

***   **Sounds Of New Orleans Vol. 2: Johnny Wiggs** Storyville SLP 6009 CD/LP
Wiggs; Tom Brown, Jack Delaney (*tb*); Harry Shields, Raymond Burke (*cl*); Stanley Mendelson, Armand Hug (*p*); Edmond 'Doc' Souchon (*g, v*); Joe Capraro (*g*); Sherwood Mangiapane, Arnold 'Deacon' Loyacano, Phil Darois (*b*); Roger Johnston, Ray Bauduc (*d*). 50–55.

Johnny Wiggs played in the classic New Orleans style, but the distinctiveness of his sound goes to prove the breadth and variety of New Orleans jazz, even within the over-familiar repertoire here. Wiggs heard King Oliver in 1916, according to Chris Albertson's notes, and his use of a firmly placed terminal vibrato suggests a close kinship with the King; but 'I'm Coming Virginia', played as a duet with Armand Hug, shows how closely he listened to Bix Beiderbecke, too. These recordings date from the period of Wiggs's first 'comeback' – he had been a teacher for some 20 years before returning in the height of the N.O. revival – and feature two unusually assertive bands, with splendid clarinet from both Shields and Burke and a very rare glimpse of the somewhat legendary trombonist Tom Brown. Some of the tracks are more like informal jams, Wiggs blowing with just a rhythm section on five tracks, and even where the material is dusty, there's genuine spirit in all the playing: 'Congo Square' and 'King Zulu Parade March', both from the earliest session, suggest that Wiggs was a useful composer, too. Lifted from private tapes, the sound is inevitably less than perfect but it won't trouble anyone interested in this fascinating area of the music.

JOE WILDER (born 1922)
TRUMPET

***   **Wilder 'N' Wilder** Savoy SV-0131 CD
Wilder; Hank Jones (*p*); Wendell Marshall (*b*); Kenny Clarke (*d*). 1/56.

A rare outing as a leader for this much-travelled sideman and studio player. Although he emerged at the time of bop – he was with Dizzy Gillespie in the Les Hite band – Joe was a sweeter, more temperate player. The title is a misnomer: there's nothing very wild about the playing here, although 'Six Bit Blues', a 3/4 walking blues, features some growl trumpet which the leader evidently enjoys. 'Cherokee' is taken at a light medium tempo and strolls on for 10 minutes, while most of the others stand as ballads. Wilder's broad tone and lightly shimmering vibrato are set against Jones's customarily civilized playing to maximum effect. The remastering is clear and well focused.

BARNEY WILEN (born 1937)
SOPRANO, ALTO AND TENOR SAXOPHONE

**   **Barney Wilen Quintet** Fresh Sound FSR-CD 48 CD
Wilen; Hubert Fol (*as*); Nico Bunink (*p*); Lloyd Thompson (*b*); Al Levitt (*d*). 57.

***   **Newport '59** Fresh Sound FSR-CD 165 CD
Wilen; Clark Terry (*t*); Toshiko Akiyoshi, Bud Powell, Ewald Heidepriem (*p*);
Tommy Bryant, Eric Peter, Karl Theodor Geier (*b*); Roy Haynes, Kenny Clarke,
Eberhardt Stengl (*d*). 59.

Basically a tenor player, Wilen made his name when Miles Davis chose him to play in a group he was fronting in Europe in 1957. The *Quintet* disc dates from then, and it's not a very auspicious start – middling European bop, splashily recorded, with Wilen sounding only intermittently effective. His subsequent visit to play at Newport in 1959 is commemorated by the Fresh Sound CD, although there's only 20 minutes of music from that occasion: Akiyoshi plays exuberant bebop piano in support, and Wilen's even, supple tenor works patiently and impressively through 'Passport' and 'Barney's Tune', with what was then a rare appearance of the soprano on 'Round Midnight', where his tonal control is impressive. Two other tracks of unclear date find him with Powell (very subdued), Terry and Clarke, and Wilen's solo on 'No Problem' is typically artful – since the recording is subject to some vagaries of balance, he seems to emerge from the shadows here. There is also another ''Round Midnight' with a German rhythm section. The sound is very mixed throughout but it's listenable enough.

(*)   **La Note Bleue IDA 010 CD/LP
Wilen; Alain Jean-Marie (*p, org*); Philippe Petit (*g*); Riccardo Del Fra (*b*); Sangoma
Everett (*d*). 12/86.

***   **French Ballads** IDA 014 CD/LP/MC
Wilen; Michel Graillier (*p*); Riccardo Del Fra (*b*); Sangoma Everett (*d*). 87.

****   **Wild Dogs Of The Ruwenzori** IDA 020 2CD/LP/MC
Wilen; Alain Jean-Marie (*ky*); Riccardo Del Fra (*b*); Sangoma Everett (*d*); Henri
Guedon (*perc*). 11/88.

****   **Sanctuary** IDA 029 CD
Wilen; Philip Catherine (*g*); Palle Danielsson (*b*). 1/91.

Wilen's contract for IDA has created a comeback for a fine musician. In the 1980s he tinkered with jazz-rock and African rhythms (he went to live in Africa in the late 1960s) and his return to a bop-inflected style has something of the full-circle maturity which Stan Getz came to in his later work; Wilen's tenor sound does, indeed, have something of the magisterial sweep which Getz delivered, but the main character of his playing continues to lie in its even trajectory. His solos have a serene assurance which eschews dynamic shifts in favour of a single flowing line. With his tone still exceptionally bright and refined, it grants his playing a rare, persuasive power.

La Note Bleue was a disappointing start, though, because the record is so bitty: what seem to be little fragments and codas from longer pieces are made into whole tracks, the material is dryly over-familiar, and the pieces are cut short before the group can get going. With Wilen perfectly adept at long solos, this foreshortening sounds wrong. *French Ballads* is better, although some of the playing again seems proscribed, and Wilen despatches a few of the themes with a too casual finesse. *Wild Dogs Of The Rowenzori* finally establishes his second wind: it's beautifully programmed, with straight-ahead swingers, hints of calypso rhythm and a few deftly understated fusion pulses setting a delightful variation in tempos. The title tune and 'Pauline Extended' bond Wilen's solos into a tight electronic framework, but his latest reflections on Rollins in 'Little Lu' and the two versions of 'Oh Johnny' are flawlessly paced and delivered. The rhythm section does well on all three records.

Sanctuary continues Wilen's good run. Catherine switches between acoustic and electric instruments and Wilen chooses classical rapture or firm, propulsive lines depending on the tmpor. Danielsson's third voice is immensely rich and apposite. One might pick out the absolutely lovely reading of 'How Deep Is The Ocean', but there's scarcely a weak moment on the record.

ERNIE WILKINS (born 1922)
TENOR SAXOPHONE

***   **Ernie Wilkins And The Almost Big Band** Storyville SLP 4051 LP
Wilkins; Palle Bolvig, Vagn Elsberg, Tim Hagans (*t*); Richard Boone, Erling Kroner
(*tb*); Sahib Shihab (*f, ss, as*); Jesper Thilo (*f, ss, ts*); Bent Jaedig (*f, ts*); Per
Goldschmidt (*bs*); Kenny Drew (*p*); Mads Vinding (*b*); Ed Thigpen (*d*); 11/80.

***(*)   **Montreux** Steeplechase SCS 1190 LP
Wilkins; Willie Cook (*t*); Allan Botschinsky, Vagn Elsberg (*t, flhn*); Erling Kroner
(*tb*); Richard Boone (*tb, v*); Sahib Shihab (*as, ss, f*); Jesper Thilo (*f, ss, ts*); Bent Jaedig
(*ts, f*); Per Goldschmidt (*bs*); Kenny Drew (*p*); Mads Vinding (*b*); Aage Tanggaard
(*d*). 7/83.

A gifted writer and arranger, Wilkins was largely responsible for modernizing the post-war
Basie band and tightening up its flagging charts. The 1960s were a bleak time for the
saxophonist, with stories of drug problems and much less non-commercial work around for an
arranger of his skill and imagination. Europe speeded his personal and professional recovery,
and in 1980 he launched the Almost Big Band.

Where the two available releases are concerned, you pays your money . . . There really isn't
very much between them, and probably only committed Wilkins enthusiasts will want both. The
Montreux set is marginally more swinging and the arrangements may be more challenging. Both
albums feature excellent arrangements of Randy Weston's 'Hi-Fly' and a selection of fine
originals – 'Bird In A World Of People', 'A Song For Ben Webster' (*Montreux*), 'No More
Rat Race', 'Ballad For Paul' (*Almost Big Band*) – which accurately represent his distinctive
combination of tight logic with lots of surface detail. As a saxophonist, Wilkins is nothing to
write home about, but he's often more adventurous than the Wesses and Fosters who played
with Basie after him. A musicians' musician in the best sense.

BUSTER WILLIAMS
DOUBLE BASS

****   **Something More** In and Out 7004 CD
Williams; Wayne Shorter (*ts, ss*); Herbie Hancock (*p*); Al Foster (*d*). 3/89.

You're a bassist. You don't get to record under your own name too often. So when you *do* get
the chance, out comes the wish-list and you call in a couple of favours. The two most
encouraging things about *Something More* are the quality of Williams's writing and the quality
of Wayne Shorter's playing. The first is still largely unrecognized, even by fellow players; the
second had been in serious eclipse in the 1980s but is absolutely sterling here, step for step with
Williams's involved themes. Apart from a dispensable piccolo bass solo on 'Sophisticated
Lady', most of the leader's energies are directed to group playing; he favours a dark sonority
(which is why the Ellington piece is irritatingly unrepresentative) which falls somewhere
between Wilbur Ware and Jimmy Garrison, varying quite simple lines with passing notes and
soft, left-hand strums. What a band, though!

CLARENCE WILLIAMS (1893–1965)
PIANO, JUG, VOCAL

***   **Complete Sessions Vol. 1 1923** EPM/Hot 'N Sweet FDC 5107 CD
Williams; Thomas Morris (*c*); Charlie Irvis, John Mayfield (*tb*); Sidney Bechet (*cl, ss*);
Buddy Christian (*bj*); Sara Martin, Eva Taylor, Lawrence Lomax, Rosetta Crawford,
Mamie Smith, Margaret Johnson (*v*). 7–11/23.

***(*)   **Complete Sessions Vol. 2 1923–1925** EPM/Hot 'N Sweet FDC 5109 CD
As above, except add Louis Armstrong, Bubber Miley (*c*), Aaron Thompson (*tb*),
Buster Bailey, Lorenzo Tio (*cl, ss*), Don Redman (*as*), Virginia Liston, Maureen
Englin, Sippie Wallace (*v*), omit Martin, Lomax, Crawford and Smith. 11/23–3/25.

***   **Complete Sessions Vol. 3 1925–26** EPM/Hot 'N Sweet 15122 CD
As above, except add Johnny Dunn, Big Charlie Thomas, Edward Allen (*c*), Joe
'Tricky Sam' Nanton, Jimmy Harrison, Jake Frazier (*tb*), Bob Fuller (*cl*), Coleman
Hawkins (*cl, ts, bs*), Leroy Harris (*bj*), Cyrus St Clair (*tba*), Clarence Todd (*v*), omit
Thompson, Tio, Liston, Englin, Wallace. 7/25–4/26.

Williams ran a publishing business and was A&R man on countless record dates during the
1920s and early '30s. He wasn't a great pianist, handled vocals with clumsy enthusiasm and often
resorted to blowing a jug on his Jug Band records; but he was a brilliant hustler and a master at
making record dates come together. At his very first session, on the first CD listed above, he
secured the services of Sidney Bechet (also making his debut), and in fact Bechet appears on
every track on this disc. Later sessions brought in Armstrong alongside Bechet, Bubber Miley,
Lorenzo Tio and others. The material was mostly novelty tunes ('Who'll Chop Your Suey
When I'm Gone?') or vaudeville blues, with the occasional tougher piece – such as Sippie
Wallace's two tracks on Volume 2 – and some instrumentals as by Clarence Williams's Blue
Five.

This will be a remarkable achievement if the project is seen through, but so far only three
CDs have been released. The later sides are hotter, though Bechet makes a striking impact
throughout the first disc, and his partnership with Armstrong on 'Cake Walking Babies From
Home', 'Mandy Make Up Your Mind' and a few others is exhilarating enough to cut through
the acoustic recording. Volume 2 is perhaps the best disc to sample, but the third volume
introduces cornetist Ed Allen, Williams's most faithful sideman, who seldom recorded
elsewhere, and includes some rollicking band sides. Remastering is consistently good
considering the age of the records.

***(*)   **Clarence Williams 1927 To 1934** BBC CD/REB/ZDF 721 CD/LP/MC
Williams; Edward Allen, Louis Metcalf, Ed Anderson, Henry 'Red' Allen (*t*);
Geechie Fields (*tb*); Ben Whittet, Bennie Moten, Cecil Scott, Buster Bailey (*cl*);
Arville Harris, Russell Procope (*cl, as*); Prince Robinson (*cl, ts*); Willie 'The Lion'
Smith, James P Johnson, Herman Chittison (*p*); Leroy Harris, Ikey Robinson (*bj*);
Cyrus St Clair (*bb*); Floyd Casey, Willie Williams (*wbd*); Eva Taylor, Clarence Todd
(*v*). 1/27–7/34.

Some impressive names here, though Williams also used King Oliver on occasion, and the music
in this compilation covers Williams's Jazz Kings, Blue Seven, Novelty Band, Washboard Five
and Jug Band. This is still primarily knockabout music, and some of the tunes – such as the
opening strut for two clarinets, 'Candy Lips' – are still based on vaudeville routine rather than
jazz practice, but some of the musicians – Ed Allen especially – achieve a greater depth, and as
a record of a particular side of early black music it's highly playable and very entertaining.
Roberet Parker's transfers are admirably clean and clear.

CLAUDE WILLIAMS
VIOLIN, GUITAR

(*)   **Call For The Fiddler Steeplechase SCS 1051 LP
Williams; Horace Parlan (*p*); Lars Blach (*g*); Hugo Rasmussen (*b*); Hans Nymand (*d*).
2/76.

Williams seemed destined to be a very modest footnote in jazz history until, in his sixties, he
began working with Jay McShann. The violinist had played with Andy Kirk and Count Basie
(as guitarist, prior to Freddie Green's arrival) in the 1930s, but it was touring and recording with
McShann in the 1970s which finally brought him a measure of fame. The discs with McShann
probably hold his best playing, although this single effort as a leader is amiably done. Williams
swings through a set of somewhat weary swing staples and, although his original roots reach
back to the string bands of Oklahoma, where he grew up, the presence of a Scandinavian
rhythm section (Parlan apart) makes one think of Sven Asmussen's playing. McShann's *The
Man From Muskogee* (Sackville 3005), which has yet to appear on CD, is perhaps Williams's
happiest record.

COOTIE WILLIAMS (1910–85)
TRUMPET

(*)   **The Big Challenge Jazztone/Fresh Sound FSRCD 77 CD
Williams; Rex Stewart (*c*); Bud Freeman, Coleman Hawkins (*ts*); Lawrence Brown,
J. C. Higginbotham (*tb*); Hank Jones (*p*); Milt Hinton (*b*); Gus Johnson (*d*). 4 & 5/57.

Ellington wrote 'Do Nothing Till You Hear From Me' as a 'Concerto For Cootie', a feature for
the young growler he recruited at nineteen as a replacement for Bubber Miley. By the late
1950s, when *The Big Challenge* was set up (and set up is the operative term), Williams was
working with a rock-and-roll group, a drab routine that had significantly blunted the edge of his
tough, brassy sound. Much of his most effective playing on the set seems to derive from the
man in the opposite corner. He reduplicates Rex Stewart's half-valved style and gruff swoops
authentically but also rather redundantly, because the cornetist is in excellent, pungent form.
Williams plays most convincingly on 'Walkin' My Baby Back Home', where he throws in a
muted solo even the Duke would have liked. The two tenors compare more straightforwardly,
trading choruses on 'Alphonse And Gaston' with the polite brutality of a Larry Holmes fight.
The closing 'I Knew You When' is a carefully matched head arrangement that allows Williams
and Stewart to slug it out to a finish. Not altogether inspiring stuff and a sorry reminder of the
way in which Williams's independent career, thwarted by the draft and the recording ban, was
short-circuited into blandly commercial sessions that offered little scope for his towering talent.

JAMES WILLIAMS (born 1951)
PIANO

***   **Progress Report** Sunnyside SSC 1012D CD
Williams; Bill Easley (*as*); Bill Pierce (*ts*); Kevin Eubanks (*g*); Rufus Reid (*b*); Tony
Reedus (*d*); Jerry Gonzalez (*perc*). 85.

Williams, who comes from Memphis, made his first major mark with The Jazz Messengers, and
this session – there are earlier discs for Concord which are out of print – certainly keeps
Blakey's faith, with a typically muscular but lyrical approach. The horns, though, do little but
go through well-practised motions: it's a workmanlike, intermittently sparking record.

***   **I Remember Clifford** DIW 601 LP/CD
Williams; Richard Davis (*b*); Ronnie Burrage (*d*).

***   **Meet The Magical Trio** Emarcy 838 653 CD
Williams; Charnett Moffett (*b*); Jeff Watts (*d*). 9/88.

***   **Magical Trio Vol. 1** Emarcy 832 859 CD
Williams; Ray Brown (*b*); Art Blakey (*d*).

***   **Magical Trio Vol. 2** Emarcy 834 368 CD
Williams; Ray Brown (*b*); Elvin Jones (*d*).

Williams is finally just a touch too diffident to characterize these otherwise pleasing records as
best as he might. There is authoritative leadership but not quite the last ounce of personal brio
which might have taken these discs into the front rank. That said, the interplay on *I Remember
Clifford* is admirable, with Davis in shining form and the studio sound glistening with class, and
the two dates with Blakey, Brown and Jones are predictably grandmasterly. Moffett and Watts
are a little more uppity and needle Williams a little here and there, but his inner calm is finally
unaffected.

MARY LOU WILLIAMS (1910–81)
PIANO

***(*)   **The Chronological Mary Lou Williams, 1927–40** Classics 630 CD
Williams; Harold Baker, Henry McCord, Earl Thompson (*t*); Bradley Bullett, Ted
Donnelly (*tb*); Edward Inge (*cl*); Earl Buddy Miller (*cl, as*); Dick Wilson (*ts*); John

Williams (*as, bsx*); Ted Robinson, Floyd Smith (*g*); Joe Williams (*bj*); Booker Collins (*b*); Robert Price, Ben Thigpen (*d*). 1 & 2/27, 4/30, 3 & 4/36, 9/38, 10/39, 1 & 11/40.

****   **Greatest Lady Piano Player In Jazz** Suisa JZCD 357 CD
Williams; Harold Baker, Paul King, Harry Lawson, Frank Newton, Earl Thompson, Clarence Trice (*t*); Vic Dickenson, Ted Donnelly, Henry Wells (*tb*); Claude Greene, Edward Inge (*cl*); Earl Miller (*as*); John Harrington (*as, cl*); John Williams (*as, bs*); Don Byas, Dick Wilson (*ts*); Andy Kirk (*bs*); Claude Williams (*vn*); Ted Brinson, Floyd Smith (*g*); Booker Collins, Al Lucas (*b*); Jack Parker, Ben Thigpen (*d*). 3/36, 2, 9, 10 & 12/38, 1 & 11/40, 3/ & 6/44.

***(*)   **The Zodiac Suite** Vintage Jazz Classics VJC 1305 CD
Williams; unidentified big band, featuring Ben Webster (*ts*); New York Philharmonic Orchestra. 12/45.

****   **Free Spirits** Steeplechase SCS 1043 CD/LP
Williams; Buster Williams (*b*); Mickey Roker (*d*). 7/75.

***(*)   **Live At The Cookery** Chiaruscuro CRD 146 CD
Williams; Brian Torff (*b*). 11/75.

***(*)   **My Mama Pinned A Rose On Me** Pablo 2310819 LP
Williams; Butch Williams (*b*); Cynthia Tyson (*v*). 12/77.

Duke Ellington described her as 'perpetually contemporary'. Mary Lou Williams's career encompassed weary days of travel with Andy Kirk's Clouds of Joy band (she began as a part-time arranger and only grudgingly won recognition as a piano player), staff arranging for Ellington, and band-leading. Having divorced John Williams, who had taken her on the road with Kirk, she married trumpeter Harold Baker and co-led a group with him.

The Classics *Chronological* compilation covers some intriguing early stuff, including sides made with Jeanette's Synco Jazzers as Mary Leo Burley (her step-father's name) when she was only sixteen, and two good solo sides recorded for the Brunswick label in Chicago in 1930. There are also two useful solos from rather later; 'Mary's Special' from April 1936 has her doubling on celeste, and there's a fine 'Little Joe From Chicago', recorded for Columbia in October 1939. Most of the rest, though, is available on the cheap-and-cheerful *Greatest Lady Piano Player In Jazz*, by far the fullest account of her early years, even though a slightly qualified superlative passes over her already evident skill as a composer and arranger. The earliest item on the Suisa compilation is a 1936 Clouds of Joy 'Walkin' And Swingin'', with solos by Williams and Dick Wilson. There are good trios from the same month, with Booker Collins and Ben Thigpen (father of Ed Thigpen); the trio reappears on a 1938 recording which includes a superlative performance of Jelly Roll Morton's 'The Pearls', a good example of Williams's scholarly examination of classic jazz repertoire. There are two further Clouds of Joy tracks from the beginning and end of 1938; 'Little Joe From Chicago' and 'Mary's Idea' are classic Williams compositions, but it's a pity that the only version of 'Roll 'Em' is a Chosen Five performance from 1944 with Frank Newton and Vic Dickenson. The 1940 groups – Six Men and a Girl and the Kansas City Seven – featured Earl Thompson, Earl Miller and Dick Wilson, and Harold Baker, Ted Donnelly, Edward Inge and Dick Wilson respectively, but they find her more or less completely in charge; these are also represented on the *Chronological* compilation. Sound-quality on both options is more than acceptable, but it's a shame that there is no liner-note to give the music a bit of much-needed context and background.

In 1946, Williams gave a remarkable performance of her *Zodiac Suite* with the New York Philharmonic at Town Hall. It's a sequence of dedications to fellow-musicians (identified by their astrological characteristics), and combines straight orchestral writing of a slightly bland, film-soundtrack sort with jazz interpolations and occasional sections ('Taurus' and 'Gemini', significantly) where the two seem to coincide. Wiliams had been profoundly dissatisfied with a partial reading of the music recorded in 1957 for Norman Granz's Verve label [*Masters Of The Modern Piano*, Verve 2-2514 2LP] and rediscovery of the 'lost' tapes from the Town Hall concert is a significant addition to Williams's still thin discography. The sound isn't always very reliable, with occasional crackles and some loss of resolution in the string parts, but Williams is caught in close up. (Both the Suisa and the VJC include versions of a jam session first recorded for V-Disc in March 1944 and released in celebration of the great photographer Gjon Mili; the

Suisa has the brief original version, but the orchestral performance adds some interesting aspects.)

There followed a period away from the United States and then away from music altogether, during which she worked with drug addicts. Renewed activity from the late 1950s onwards included lecture-recitals on the history of jazz, large-scale sacred compositions – *Mary Lou's Mass* and *Black Christ Of The Andes* – reflecting her conversion, and stormy contact with the new avant-garde, as on her remarkable collaboration with Cecil Taylor. *Embraced* [Pablo Live 2620108 2LP] gives off little sense of the hostilities behind the scenes, but it underlines her ability to play from almost any stance within the black music tradition: gospel, blues, swing, bop, free. Typical of much of her extensive output, it's currently unavailable.

Williams was treated dismissively by male colleagues for much of her career (Kirk finds room for for only half a dozen references in his autobiography, and his acknowledgement of her 'tremendous influence' seems rather *pro forma*). In the 1970s she was releasing material on her own label, Mary Records, including the superb *Zoning* and the huge *Mary Lou's Mass*. A valuable *Solo Recital* [Pablo Live 2308218 LP] from Montreux in 1978 has also disappeared. 'What's Your Story, Morning Glory', one of her most durable compositions, also appears on *My Mama Pinned A Rose On Me*, a mostly blues duo performance with additional vocals from Tyson. Williams's formal and historical concerns turned almost every performance at this time into a lecture on the roots of black American music, and there's a rather programmatic feel to the sequence of tracks. But it's an important piece of work, all the more valuable for the present scarcity of alternatives. The rather earlier *Live At The Cookery* is a better bet. Jon Bates has done an excellent job of bringing the sound up to current standards, and there's a minimum of distortion and extraneous noise ('I'm recording. If you talk too loud, it'll be on the record'). It's not clear why she tolerated Brian Torff thudding away relentlessly in her left ear, but Williams had always tended to be a right-sided player and here more than ever concentrates on a middle and upper register. Her playing is superb throughout and there are vintage performances of 'Roll 'Em', 'The Surrey With The Fringe On Top' (an odd favourite of hers), 'The Man I Love' and Johnny Hodges's 'The Jeep Is Jumping'.

As a straightforward performance, *Free Spirits* is very much better. Williams's health was still robust (it began to break down towards the end of the 1970s) and her playing is much sharper and surer, also more relaxed and swinging. Typically, she mixes standards ('Temptation', 'Surrey With The Fringe On Top') with jazz staples (Miles's 'All Blues', Bobby Timmons's gospel-tinged 'Dat Dere') and her own work, 'Ode To Saint Cecilie', 'Gloria', 'Blues For Timme', unexpectedly adding two John Stubblefield compositions (two takes each of 'Baby Man' and 'Free Spirits') and a promising 'Pale Blue' by bassist Buster Williams, who provides a perfect complement to her light left hand.

Perhaps inevitably, she rejected the term 'jazz', not so much because it was a white construct, but because it was a fundamentally reductive one. However swinging and jazz-based her solo and small-group output, Williams transcended the conventional bounds of jazz composition and performance. With the rediscovery of *Zodiac Suite*, it may at last be possible to attempt a comprehensive reassessment of one of the most significant figures in black American music and one of its great teachers.

RICHARD WILLIAMS (born 1931)
TRUMPET

***(*)   **New Horn In Town** Candid CD 9003 CD
    Williams; Leo Wright (*as, f*); Richard Wyands (*p*); Reggie Workman (*b*); Bobby Thomas (*d*). 11/60.

Like Fats Navarro and Clifford Brown, Williams managed to combine great technical brilliance and a biting tone with a sweeping lyricism, probably best heard here on an unexpected 'Over The Rainbow'. The opening 'I Can Dream, Can't I?' draws quite explicitly from Brown's successful version of the standard, but the phrasing is Williams's own. 'I Remember Clifford' follows at once, with a fat, sentimental tone that sounds almost like flugelhorn, were it not so exact in articulation; Wright plays flute underneath. The three Williams originals don't bespeak a major compositional talent, but the closing 'Renita's Bounce' asks to be played again, and there are some good things about the jokey 'Blues In A Quandary', which never quite reaches a resolution; 'Raucous Notes', a version of his high-school nickname, shows how accurate he can be at speed. Richard Wyands's 'Ferris Wheel' is in keeping with his light, bouncing accompaniments.

Williams remained a well-kept secret from jazz fans throughout his career. His solitary Candid has given him a curious one-off reputation, but he deserves to be investigated more thoroughly through his work with Charlie Mingus, Duke Ellington, Gigi Gryce, Oliver Nelson, Rahsaan Roland Kirk and Red Garland, a CV so impressive that it is odd he didn't record more often.

ROY WILLIAMS (born 1937)
TROMBONE

***   **Royal Trombone** Phontastic 7556 LP
Williams; John Mclevy (*t*); Arne Domnérus (*as, cl*); Putte Wickman (*cl*); Nisse Sandstrom (*ts*); Bengt Hallberg (*p*); Rune Gustafsson (*g*); Len Skeat, Georg Riedel (*b*); Rune Carlsson (*d*). 12/83.

***   **Again! Roy Williams In Sweden** Phontastic 7579 LP
As above. 12/83.

Williams emerged as a second-eleven man in British trad, but his stay with the Alex Welsh band of the 1960s (and, subsequently, with Humphrey Lyttelton) revealed a much more accomplished and versatile performer than anything most of his colleagues could aspire to. He has a lovely, creamy sound on the trombone which, with its relatively quiet dynamic and effortless delivery, has drawn comparisons with Jack Teagarden that are surprisingly near the mark. He never plays with any plangency. What comes out is a singing, insistent, winding sound which works its way through a song until there's a completely personalized variation on the melody comfortably in position. These albums were both recorded at the same sessions, when Williams and John Mclevy were visiting Sweden and teamed up with an all-star group of locals. Standards make up most of the menu, although Hallberg pens a crafty twist on 'Exactly Like You' called 'Accurately Like You', and there's a lot of variation in voicings and instrumenmtations: 'I'm Old Fashioned' is a duet for trombone and piano, 'Gone With The Wind' blows out on trombone, clarinet and piano. Wickman aces out Williams from time to time and has a serene 'I Remember Clifford' to himself, but the guest leader plays admirably throughout.

TONY WILLIAMS (born 1945)
DRUMS

***(*)   **Life Time** Blue Note BCT 84180 CD
Williams; Sam Rivers (*ts*); Herbie Hancock (*p*); Bobby Hutcherson (*vib, mar*); Ron Carter (*b*); Richard Davis, Gary Peacock (*b*). 8/64.

***(*)   **Spring** Blue Note B21Y 46135 CD/MC
Williams; Sam Rivers, Wayne Shorter (*ts*); Herbie Hancock (*p*); Gary Peacock (*b*). 8/65.

***(*)   **Foreign Intrigue** Blue Note B21Y 46289 CD/LP/MC
Williams; Wallace Roney (*t*); Donald Harrison (*as*); Bobby Hutcherson (*vib*); Mulgrew Miller (*p*); Ron Carter (*b*). 8/85.

***(*)   **Civilization** Blue Note B21Y 46757 CD/LP/MC

***   **Angel Street** Blue Note CDP 7484942 CD/LP/MC
Williams; Wallace Roney (*t*); Billy Pierce (*ts, ss*); Mulgrew Miller (*p*); Charnett Moffett (*b*). 11/86, 4/88.

***   **Native Heart** Blue Note CDP 7931702 CD/LP/MC
Williams; Wallace Roney (*t*); Bill Pierce (*ts, ss*); Mulgrew Miller (*p*); Ira Coleman, Bob Hurst (*b*). 9/89.

Williams had his baptism of fire with Miles Davis at 17, anchoring one of the legendary rhythm section in one of the finest jazz groups of all time. After leaving Davis, for whom he created a matrix of rhythmic cues so encompassing as to allow the trumpeter to angle a phrase or an entire solo any way he chose, Williams formed the thunderous Lifetime, a group consisting of guitarist John McLaughlin, organist Larry Young, and, more briefly, bassist/singer Jack Bruce, which was a seminal influence on the development of jazz-rock. The Polydors are long deleted, but there's a brief snatch of Lifetime doing Coltrane's 'Big Nick' on a Verve drums sampler (840033 CD).

Williams's early Blue Notes are intense, sometimes rather inward-looking explorations of the rhythmic possibilities opened up by bebop. Working with Jackie McLean, whose advances on Parker's idiom are still not fully appreciated, gave him ample opportunity to break down the basic 4/4 into complex counter-patterns and asymmentrical rhythms. Much of that comes through on *Life Time* (not to be confused with the later jazz-rock outfit) on which Williams plays a staggering trio with Herbie Hancock and Bobby Hutcherson on 'Memory'. Rivers's angular approach probably suited the drummer's sound better than any other horn player around at the time (though the apotheosis of Williams's early career was, of course, his work with Hutcherson and Davis on Eric Dolphy's *Out To Lunch!*) and he is quite superb on the two-bass, two-part 'Piece Of One' and the more stripped-down 'Tomorrow Afternoon'. The addition of Shorter on *Spring* gives the music an enigmatic, brooding quality, but this, too, was an inspired piece of casting. *Foreign Intrigue* has a touch of passion that lifts it above the rather mechanical forcefulness of the later sessions. Roney's bright, diamond-cut lines are completely in keeping with Williams's splintery execution, and Hutcherson gives the rhythmic profile an intriguing, multi-dimensional character, but the later sets are foggy by comparison, with no obvious explanation as to why. From any other source, *Angel Street* could be considered finely, untroublingly professional. From Williams, it seems just bland, with overarranged ensembles and almost none of Lifetime's boiling intensity or even the pastiche-Miles of VSOP, a later jazz venture. This rather disappointing album by no means reflects the quality of Williams's subsequent live performances, some of which had misty-eyed older critics muttering about 1967 and *acoustic* Miles Davis bands. 'Red Mask' and 'Dreamland' dip into the deeper end of funk – the latter might have graced a Blue Note of much earlier vintage – but there's not much excitement in the run of tracks and it's not the kind of record that cries out to be heard.

Native Heart is even slicker. Miller's usual harmonic polish looks like veneer and there's an offputting up-market sheen to neo-funk numbers like 'Juicy Fruit'. Oddly, but perhaps significantly, the best number is the CD-only 'Liberty', which is a drums feature. Williams clearly still has the chops and one wonders what he might have done had he recruited different players for each of these sessions, rather than relying on a stable band.

CLAUDE WILLIAMSON (born 1926)
PIANO

(*)   **Claude Williamson Mulls The Mulligan** Fresh Sounds FSR-CD 54 CD
Williamson; Howard Roberts (*g*); Red Mitchell (*b*); Stan Levey (*d*). 58.

***   **The Fabulous Claude Williamson Trio** Fresh Sounds FSR-CD 51 CD
Williamson; Duke Morgan (*b*); Chuck Flores (*d*). 61.

Claude Williamson, the brother of trumpeter Stu, was a superior exponent of cool bop, and his mixture of influences – Teddy Wilson and Bud Powell in particular – led him to an unusually dapper, rhythmically fleet style that could still deliver a surprisingly pungent blues chorus when he wanted one. Neither of the above records is quite his best – an earlier session for Bethelehem is stronger, and the fine *Theatre Party* with Herb Ellis has yet to appear on CD – but they're not at all bad. *Mulls The Mulligan* is a set of variations on Gerry Mulligan themes, and the use of 'twin pianos' (one of them an overdub) clouds some of Williamson's ideas. *The Fabulous Claude Williamson Trio* features 11 standards which are dispatched a little too readily, although the pianist's speed masks some of the sharpness of his ideas: it's fluency rather than glibness which is on show here.

STEVE WILLIAMSON (born 1956)
TENOR SAXOPHONE, ALTO SAXOPHONE, SOPRANO SAXOPHONE

***(*) **A Waltz For Grace** Verve 843088 CD/LP/MC
Williamson; Julian Joseph (*p*); Dave Gilmore, Hawi Gondwe (*g*); Gary Crosby,
Lonnie Plaxico (*b*); Mark Mondesir (*d*); Abbey Lincoln (*v*). 90.

*** **Rhyme Time (That Fuss Was Us)** Polydor 511235 CD/LP/MC
Williamson; Dennis Rollins (*tb*); Joe Bashorun (*p*); Dave Gilmore, Tony Remy (*g*);
Gary Crosby, Michael Mondesir (*b*); Steve Washington (*d*); Cassandra Wilson (*v*). 91.

Like his near-contemporary and fellow-saxophonist, Courtney Pine, Steve Williamson was
welcomed by British jazz critics as a brand snatched from the burning. For the first time in
perhaps 25 years, young black British musicians were making jazz – rather than calypso, ska,
soul or reggae – the music of choice. Perhaps inevitably, given the weight of peer and market
pressure, many (Pine most notably) have since returned at least partially to earlier interests.
Williamson, though, appears to be exploring a wider range of possibilities within jazz. His
apparent conversion to the urban funk of M-BASE was confirmed when the American
saxophonist Steve Coleman produced the disappointingly second-hand *Rhyme Time*.
Disappointing, because on his debut (which included UK and New York sessions, and a mixture
of home and American players) Williamson had seemed close to finding a viable contemporary
synthesis of the prevailing New York style with a much older, Caribbean strain in British jazz.

There was a clear, and increasingly self-conscious, link between Williamson's alto sound and
that of Joe Harriott, a Jamaican-born British player who died in 1973. Harriott began as a more
or less conventional bopper but in the 1960s began to explore Eastern and West Indian
rhythms, free abstraction, and some elements of formal composition. What is lastingly
impressive about *Waltz For Grace* is its tremendous rhythmic variety. 'Groove Thang' (a
UK-recorded soprano–percussion duet) leads direct into the fuller-sounding 'Synthesis' from
New York, both largely dependent on Williamson's ability to balance a line over a jolting,
staccato pulse. The equally unpromisingly titled 'Straight Ahead' pretends to be orthodox
mid-tempo hard bop, but travels an awkward path, full of hesitations and silences.

Williamson's welcome insistence that British players develop their own sound is well out the
window on *Rhyme Time*. Williamson's playing is as impressive as always, with a nervy,
unpredictable edge to his soloing on all three horns. Apart from a rather banal ballad called
'The Rock', which dispenses with much of the hardware, the rest is a homogenized blur. Apart
from the saxophonist, Dennis Rollins and Gary Crosby are both impressive, and Cassandra
Wilson's vocal is much more suited to Williamson's thoroughly contemporary intentions than
Abbey Lincoln's guest slot on 'A Waltz For Grace'.

STU WILLIAMSON (born 1933)
TRUMPET, VALVE TROMBONE

*** **Stu Williamson Plays** Fresh Sound FSR-CD 116 CD
Williamson; Charlie Mariano (*as*); Claude Williamson (*p*); Max Bennett (*b*); Stan
Levey (*d*). 1/55–1/56.

A characteristic if plain example of the kind of playing which Stu Williamson set down many
times on West Coast sessions of the period. His exceptionally bright tone gave him good
section-leader credentials and his solos are burnished with the same gleam; and there is solid
work from Mariano and brother Claude throughout these 11 swiftly dispatched tracks. But
there's finally little enough to remember the date by, apart from its sheer professionalism.

JACK WILLIS (born 1920)
TRUMPET

*** **Orleans Street Shuffle** 504 LPS 5 LP
Willis; Freddie Lonzo (*tb*); Ralph Johnson (*cl, ts*); Sam Mooney (*p*); Les Muscutt (*bj,
g*); Brian Turnock (*b*); Stanley Williams (*d*). 8/82.

Joshua 'Little Jack' Willis is a sweet-toned, rather gentle trumpeter, not much like the typical New Orleans brassman. He fronts this mixed band – with two Englishmen, and New Orleans musicians from a couple of generations – on what is a sprightly and good-natured addition to the 504 series aiming to document NO practice in the 1980s. Freddie Lonzo takes the most spirited solos on trombone, and Ralph Johnson's clarinet and tenor complete a warm front line, but Willis's quiet and even-handed solos also make their mark. The material is a little downbeat – 'Deep Purple', 'Lead Me Saviour', 'Tell Me Your Dreams' – but the opening 'Bugle Boy March' dispels any idea that the band aren't up to swinging. Excellent, lifelike studio sound.

CASSANDRA WILSON
VOICE

***   **Point Of View** JMT 834404 CD/LP
Wilson; Grachan Moncur III (*tb*); Steve Coleman (*as, perc*); Jean-Paul Bourelly (*g*); Lonnie Plaxico (*b*); Mark Johnson (*d*). 12/85.

(*)   **Days Aweigh JMT 834412 CD/LP
Wilson; Steve Coleman (*as*); Rod Williams (*ky*); Jean-Paul Bourelly (*g*); Kevin Bruce Harris, Kenny Davis (*b*); Mark Johnson (*d*). 5/87.

***(*)   **Blue Skies** JMT 834419 CD/LP
Wilson; Mulgrew Miller (*p*); Lonnie Plaxico (*b*); Terri Lyne Carrington (*d*). 2/88.

**   **Jumpworld** JMT 834434 CD/LP/MC
Wilson; Graham Haynes (*t*); Robin Eubanks (*tb*); Steve Coleman (*as*); Rod Williams (*ky*); David Gilmore (*g*); Kevin Bruce Harris, Lonnie Plaxico (*b*); Mark Johnson (*d*); James Moore (*v*). 7–8/89.

***   **She Who Weeps** JMT 834443 CD/LP/MC
Wilson; Rod Williams (*p*); Jean-Paul Bourelly (*g, g-syn*); Kevin Bruce Harris, Herman Fowlkes, Reggie Washington (*b*); Mark Johnson, Tani Tabbal (*d*). 11–12/90.

***   **Live** JMT 849149-2 CD
Wilson; James Weidman (*ky*); Kevin Bruce Harris (*b*); Mark Johnson (*d*). 90.

Wilson is among the most interesting singers to appear in recent years, and her association with such musicians as Coleman and Bourelly has given her an acknowledged place in the so-called M-Base movement of New York players. But her records are often rather awkward compromises between a more traditonal jazz singing role and the funk and rap influences which dominate today's black music. Her own compositions are flavourless vehicles for her style, marked by rambling melodies, vaguely prescriptive lyrics and rhythmical staggers; the early records (up to *Blue Skies*) are an occasionally exciting but often unfocused attempt at finding a balance. She shows a marked Betty Carter influence rhythmically, but the timbre of her voice is cloudier, and it can throw an interesting spin on otherwise familiar songs. *Blue Skies* is the least typical but easily the best of her records: though made up entirely of standards with a conventional rhythm section, the recital finds Wilson investing the likes of 'Shall We Dance?' with a wholly unfamiliar range of inflexions and melodic extensions which is captivating. Her third-person version of 'Sweet Lorraine' is peculiarly dark and compelling and, while some of the songs drift a little too far off base, it's a remarkable record, and it makes the ensuing *Jumpworld*, a return to self-consciously 'modern' music, sound all the more contrived. *She Who Weeps* takes a middle ground, with a mostly acoustic backing and a programme which includes an overlong 'Body And Soul' and a wordless and rather effective 'Chelsea Bridge'. The live session confirms that Wilson can sustain a concert set which is essentially a seamless, ongoing vocal improvisation, but the slipshod attention to quality-control, as far as the material is concerned, is a point which a strong producer must attend to if Wilson is ever going to deliver the masterpiece which she seems capable of.

GERALD WILSON (born 1918)
TRUMPET, BANDLEADER

***(*) **Moment Of The Truth** Pacific Jazz CDP 7929282 CD
Wilson; Johnny Audino, Jules Chaikin, Fred Hill, Carmell Jones (*t*); Lou Blackburn,
Bob Edmondson, Lester Robinson, Kenny Shroyer (*tb*); Joe Maini, Bud Shank (*as*);
Teddy Edwards, Harold Land (*ts*); Jack Nimitz, Donald Raffael (*bs*); Jack Wilson (*p*);
Joe Pass (*g*); Jimmy Bond (*b*); Mel Lewis (*d*); Modesto Duran (*perc*). 9/62.

**** **Portraits** Pacific Jazz CDP 7934142 CD
Wilson; Julius Chaikin, Freddie Hall, Carmell Jones, Nathaniel Meeks, Al Porcino,
Ray Triscari (*t*); Bob Edmondson, Bob Ewing, Lew McCreary, Lester Robinson, Don
Switzer (*tb*); Bud Shank (*f*); Joe Maini, Jimmy Woods (*as*); Teddy Edwards, Harold
Land (*ts*); Jack Nimitz (*bs*); Jack Wilson (*p*); Joe Pass (*g*); Dave Dyson, Leroy
Vinnegar (*b*); Chuck Carter (*d*); Modesto Duran (*perc*). 63.

*** **Feelin' Kinda Blues** Pacific Jazz CDP 792 CD
Wilson; Bobby Bryant, Fred Hill, Nat Meeks (*t*); Anthony Ortega (*f, picc, as*); Teddy
Edwards (*ts*); Curtis Amy (*ss, ts*); Victor Feldman (*vib*); Phil Moore (*p*); Dennis
Budimir (*g*); other personnel unknown. 65 or 66.

***(*) **Love You Madly** Discovery DSCD 947 CD
Wilson; Rick Baptist, Oscar Brashear, Bobby Bryant, Hal Espinosa, Eugene Snooky
Young (*t*); Garnett Brown, Jimmy Cleveland, Thurman Green, Maurice Spears (*tb*);
Buddy Collette, Roger Hogan, Harold Land, Jack Nimitz, Anthony Ortega, Jerome
Richardson, Hank de Vega, Ernie Watts (*reeds*); Gerald Wiggins, Mike Wofford (*p*);
Milcho Leviev (*ky*); Bob Conti, Harold Land Jr, John Shuggie Otis (*g*); John B.
Williams (*b*); Clayton Cameron, Paul Humphrey (*d*). 88.

After cutting his teeth with the Jimmie Lunceford Orchestra, where he replaced another
trumpeter, Sy Oliver, as staff arranger, Wilson formed his own band and has continued to lead
and write ever since, preferring the warmth of California to the more cut-throat East Coast
scene. Wilson favours heavy block chord figures that have the rhythmic immediacy and
insistence of small-group jazz, but he frequently writes in multi-part harmony, as with the
middle passages of the beautiful 'Ay-Ee-En' on *Love You Madly*, a combination of Ellington
tunes and originals that features Wilson's 'Orchestra of the '80s'.

Comparing it with work recorded two decades earlier reveals that Wilson's successful
formula has changed very little over the years, other than to incorporate elements of rock
rhythm and occasional (very effective) use of electric guitar and keyboards. Wilson's earliest
West Coast bands were, however, notably modern in their use of unusual harmonies, and Eric
Dolphy, for one, was deeply influenced by his ability to work highly inventive variations on very
basic tonalities and dedicated an early composition, 'G.W.', to the bandleader. Wilson's best
work is finely wrought and never sounds like a mere run-down or head arrangement. For that
reason, it's best assimilated quite slowly, paying some attention to the layers of sound that build
up over the course of an arrangement. Look, as a single instance, at what he does to Miles
Davis's battle-scarred 'So What' on *Portraits*, first of a series of sensitive *hommages*. Wilson's
reading has all the delicacy and precision of the *Birth Of The Cool* sessions, but with all the
contained power that comes from a full brass and reeds line-up. Perhaps only Mulligan creates
the same balance of delicacy and strength.

Though *Portraits* is the most interesting of the early sessions, Wilson's work is in some
respects all of a piece and, in equally important regards, so varied that only a track-by-track
analysis would reveal his particular genius. Of the much later albums, *Jenna* is the one to go for
(there's also a fine session on Trend *Calafia* [TRCD 537 CD] which is worth finding);
stand-out tracks are Eddie Durham's 'Lunceford Special', with vibrant high-note work from
Baptist, 'B-Bop And The Song', which offers a special insight into some of Wilson's harmonic
roots, and the gorgeous title-piece. The Ellington numbers on *Love You Madly* receive a
thoroughly contemporary big-band treatment (with some brilliant piano work from Wiggins),
but the highlights of the album are his own bluesy 'See You Later', featuring son-in-law,
Shuggie Otis, 'Blues For Zubin', based on his symphonic composition *5/21/72*, and 'Lomelin',
another of his dedications to bullfighters (don't write to complain to *us*) with Brashear and
Land Senior giving big licks to the old 'Spanish tinge'.

Wilson's work covers an immense range of modern jazz and blues. Heavily marked by the blues, it nevertheless also touches on bebop, rock and modern 'straight' techniques, using devices from each in a quite unselfconscious and integral fashion. One of the great orchestrators in jazz, Wilson's reputation, always solid among players and in California, has begun to extend more widely.

GLENN WILSON
BARITONE SAXOPHONE

***   **Impasse** Cadence 1023 LP
Wilson; Harold Danko (*p*); Dennis Irwin (*b*); Adam Nussbaum (*d*). 3–7/84.

(*)   **Elusive Sunnyside 1030 LP/CD
Wilson; Jim Powell (*t, flhn*); Bob Belden (*ts*); Harold Danko (*p*); Dennis Irwin (*b*); Adam Nussbaum (*d*). 12/87.

Although, like so many baritone specialists, Wilson seems doomed to recording mostly as a section sideman, he plays with fine gusto and thoughtful intelligence on the two records made under his own leadership. The Cadence album works up a great head of steam on material that is informed by Danko's lightly penetrating touch as much as by Wilson's own improvisations. *Elusive*, in contrast, is a little too civilized: the baritone blow-out on 'McCoy's Passion' is excitingly realized, 'Ouformation' is a surprising on-the-spot four-way improvisation, and 'Adams Park' a well-sustained threnody for Pepper Adams. But the tracks where Wilson is joined by Belden and Powell emerge as routine post-bop, and the soft-edged production lacks the impact the music needs to collar attention.

JACK WILSON (born 1936)
PIANO

***   **Ramblin'** Fresh Sounds FSR-CD 152 CD
Wilson; Roy Ayers (*vib*); Monk Montgomery (*b*); Ward Barlow (*d*). 66.

***   **Autumn Sunset** Discovery DSCD 941 CD
Wilson; Allen Jackson, John Heard (*b*); Clarence Johnston, Joey Baron (*d*); Joe Clayton (*perc*). 8/77–3/79.

A very interesting piano player. Wilson can play hard bop and soul–jazz licks with a smooth facility, but he often suggests a preference for freer waters and he likes to cover Ornette Coleman tunes: 'Ramblin', 'Tears Inside' on the Discovery record, and a fine version of 'The Sphinx' on his deleted Blue Note record *Something Personal* (which could certainly stand reissue). *Ramblin'* is by a very swinging group and, even if they have to play 'The Sandpiper', they also get to groove through 'Impressions', 'The Sidewinder' and 'Stolen Moments'; and Ayers proves how strongly he could play before he struck it rich with soul. Wilson has an elegant touch and a knack for building quite complex solos that still keep a watchful eye on the essence of the tune. The Discovery CD boils down the best of two LPs on to one disc: there are some pleasing originals and well-shaped readings of 'Body And Soul' and 'Invitation'.

PHILLIP WILSON
DRUMS, PERCUSSION

***   **Live At Moers Festival** Moers 01062 LP
Wilson; Olu Dara (*t*); Frank Lowe (*ts*); Fred Williams (*b*). 5/78.

A fine, free-ish drummer with an almost classic, swing-era repertoire of rolls and paradiddles, Wilson has seen extensive service with Lester Bowie, but has only this slightly ropey concert recording under his own name. 'Broadway Rhumba' and 'Cha Cha' don't come out quite the way they sound; 'F & L' suggests an Ornette Coleman influence somewhere. Dara's Bowie-influenced figures have a sharpness one normally associates with cornet, and Lowe trades off Chu Berry licks with Coltrane-derived wails and screams. The concert must have been thoroughly enjoyable; the record struggles a bit. Wilson was brutally murdered in the spring of 1992.

TEDDY WILSON (1912–86)
PIANO

***(*)   Teddy Wilson 1934–35 Classics CL 508 CD
Wilson; Roy Eldridge, Dick Clark (*t*); Benny Morton (*tb*); Tom Macey, Benny Goodman, Cecil Scott (*cl*); Hilton Jefferson, Johnny Hodges (*as*); Chu Berry, Ben Webster (*ts*); John Trueheart, Lawrence Lucie, Dave Barbour (*g*); John Kirby, Grachan Moncur (*b*); Cozy Cole (*d*); Billie Holiday (*v*). 5/34–12/35.

***(*)   Teddy Wilson Vol. 1: Too Hot For Words Hep 1012 CD
As above. 1–10/35.

Few jazz records have endured quite as well as Teddy Wilson's 1930s music. Wilson arrived in New York as, on the basis of the four solo titles which open the first Classics CD, an enthusiastic young stride pianist, already under the spell of Earl Hines and of Art Tatum with whom he worked as a two-man piano team. But even here there are the signs of an individual whose meticulous, dapper delivery and subtle reading of harmony would be hugely influential. Amazingly, everything is in place by the time of the first band session in July 1935: the initial line-up includes Eldridge, Goodman and Webster, and the singer is Billie Holiday, who would feature as vocalist on most of Wilson's pre-war records. Two classics were made immediately – 'What A Little Moonlight Can Do' and 'Miss Brown To You' – and the style was set: a band chorus, a vocal, and another chorus for the band, with solos and obbligatos in perfect accord with every other note and accent. All the others seem to take their cue from the leader's own poise, and even potentially unruly spirits such as Eldridge and Webster behave. The first of Classics' comprehensive seven-disc series includes 11 piano solos and 12 band sides, and it's a delight from start to finish, even though there was better to come.

The reissue of these records has been complicated by Holiday's presence, for all of her tracks with Wilson are now also available on discs under her own name. Collectors will have to follow their own tastes, but we would opine that, of all the various transfers of this material, the Hep discs – which follow the Classics discs fairly closely in sequencing, if finally not quite as generous in the number of tracks on each disc – have the most truthful sound. Even so, the Classics CD above is consistently clean and enjoyable in sonic terms.

***(*)   Teddy Wilson 1935–36 Classics CL 511 CD
Wilson; Dick Clark, Gordon Griffin, Frank Newton, Roy Eldridge, Jonah Jones (*t*); Benny Morton (*tb*); Benny Goodman, Buster Bailey, Rudy Powell, Tom Macey (*cl*); Jerry Blake (*cl, as*); Vido Musso (*cl, ts*); Harry Carney (*cl, bs*); Johnny Hodges (*as*); Ted McRae, Chu Berry (*ts*); Dave Barbour, John Trueheart, Allan Reuss, Bob Lessey, Lawrence Lucie (*g*); Lionel Hampton (*vib*); Israel Crosby, Harry Goodman, Leemie Stanfield, Grachan Moncur, John Kirby (*b*); Gene Krupa, Sid Catlett, Cozy Cole (*d*); Helen Ward, Ella Fitzgerald, Red Harper, Billie Holiday (*v*). 12/35–8/36.

****   Teddy Wilson Vol. 2: Warmin' Up Hep 1014 CD
As above. 12/35–6/36.

***   Teddy Wilson 1936–37 Classics 521 CD
Wilson; Gordon Griffin, Irving Randolph, Henry Allen, Jonah Jones, Buck Clayton, Cootie Williams (*t*); Cecil Scott (*cl, as, ts*); Vido Musso (*cl, ts*); Harry Carney (*cl, bs*); Benny Goodman (*cl*); Johnny Hodges (*as*); Ben Webster, Prince Robinson, Lester Young (*ts*); Allan Reuss, Freddie Green, James McLin (*g*); Harry Goodman, Milt Hinton, Walter Page, John Kirby (*b*); Cozy Cole, Jo Jones, Gene Krupa (*d*); Billie Holiday, Midge Williams, Red Harper (*v*). 8/36–3/37.

****   Teddy Wilson Vol. 3: Of Thee I Swing Hep 1020 CD
Largely as above. 8/36–2/37.

Wilson hit his stride as this long series of sessions proceeded. The next two Classics CDs are laden with fine music, and Billie Holiday's contributions assume greatness: the 16 tracks she sings on Classics 521 number among her finest records, and the mixed quality of the material seems to make no difference to her. Just as Lionel Hampton began pilfering men from local big bands for his Victor sessions, so Wilson organized similar contingents for his records, and some of these bands are drawn from either the Goodman or the Basie orchestra, although one offbeat session features Henry Allen, Cecil Scott and Prince Robinson. The spotlight is off Wilson to some extent, but one of the major reasons for the success of these dates is the light, singing fluency of the rhythm section, and the pianist's unemphatic but decisive lead is the prime reason for that. Ella Fitzgerald sings on one session on Classics 511 and Midge Williams, Helen Ward and Red Harper take their turns at the microphone, but it's Holiday one remembers. Lester Young's association with the singer also starts here, but his solos are really no more memorable than the offerings by Buck Clayton, Benny Goodman or Roy Eldridge. Those collecting the Classics CDs may be dismayed by the erratic sound-quality on Classics 521 in particular, and once again we prefer the Hep series.

****   **Teddy Wilson 1937** Classics 531 CD
Wilson; Cootie Williams, Harry James, Buck Clayton (*t*); Buster Bailey, Benny Goodman, Archie Rosati (*cl*); Harry Carney (*cl, bs*); Johnny Hodges (*as*); Vido Musso, Lester Young (*ts*); Red Norvo (*xy*); Allen Reuss, Freddie Green (*g*); John Kirby, John Simmons, Harry Goodman, Artie Bernstein, Walter Page (*b*); Cozy Cole, Jo Jones, Gene Krupa (*d*); Helen Ward, Billie Holiday, Frances Hunt, Boots Castle (*v*). 3–8/37.

****   **Teddy Wilson Vol. 4: Fine & Dandy** Hep 1029 CD
Largely as above. 3–7/37.

***(*)   **Teddy Wilson 1937–1938** Classics 548 CD
Wilson; Harry James, Buck Clayton (*t*); Bobby Hackett (*c*); Benny Morton (*tb*); Pee Wee Russell, Prince Robinson (*cl*); Johnny Hodges, Tab Smith (*as*); Gene Sedric, Lester Young, Chu Berry, Vido Musso (*ts*); Red Norvo (*xy*); Allen Reuss, Freddie Green (*g*); Walter Page, Al Hali, John Simmons (*b*); Johnny Blowers, Jo Jones, Cozy Cole (*d*); Billie Holiday, Nan Wynn (*v*). 9/37–4/38.

****   **Teddy Wilson Vol. 5: Blue Mood** Hep 1035 CD
As above. 8/37–1/38.

****   **Teddy Wilson 1938** Classics 556 CD
Wilson; Jonah Jones, Harry James (*t*); Bobby Hackett (*c*); Trummy Young, Benny Morton (*tb*); Pee Wee Russell (*cl*); Benny Carter, Johnny Hodges, Toots Mondello, Ted Buckner, Edgar Sampson (*as*); Lester Young, Herschel Evans, Bud Freeman, Chu Berry, Ben Webster (*ts*); Allan Reuss, Al Casey (*g*); Al Hall, John Kirby, Milt Hinton, Walter Page (*b*); Johnny Blowers, Cozy Cole, Jo Jones (*d*); Billie Holiday, Nan Wynn (*v*). 4–11/38.

This is jazz of such a consistently high level that it seems churlish to offer criticism. The Classics CDs are mostly in pretty good, clean sound, with the occasional track sounding a little starchier: the Hep transfers continue to be our first recommendation, though the Classics 'uniform' editions may appeal more to some collectors. The first 1937 CD is magnificent, the first five sessions as strong in material as they are in performances: 'Mean To Me', 'I'll Get By', 'How Am I To Know?' and more. These are also among Holiday's greatest records. The 1937–8 disc includes the September 1937 session which included the memorable two-part 'Just A Mood' quartet with Harry James and Red Norvo, as well as a previously rejected date. The 1938 set sees Bobby Hackett arriving to play lead, as well as six solos originally made for the 'Teddy Wilson School For Pianists'. Wilson's mixture of lyricism and vigour is almost unique in the jazz of the period and it suggests a path which jazz doctrine has seldom explored since.

***   **Teddy Wilson 1939** Classics 571 CD
Wilson; Roy Eldridge, Karl George, Harold Baker (*t*); Floyd Brady (*tb*); Pete Clark (*cl, as, bs*); Rudy Powell (*cl, as*); Benny Carter (*as, ts*); Ben Webster, George Irish (*ts*); Danny Barker, Al Casey (*g*); Al Hall, Milt Hinton (*b*); Cozy Cole, J. C. Heard (*d*); Billie Holiday, Thelma Carpenter, Jean Eldridge (*v*). 1–9/39.

Inevitably, Wilson went on to lead his own big band, and musicians were more than impressed by its secure power and purposeful clarity of tone, a direct extension of Wilson's own manner. But it failed commercially, and its records don't quite match its reputation, largely through charts that are only so-so but which may have come alive in person. The 1939 sides are collected here, along with four more Wilson solos, including a sparkling 'China Boy'.

*** **Isn't It Romantic** Musicraft 058 CD
Wilson; Buck Clayton (*t*); Scoville Brown (*as*); Don Byas (*ts*); George James (*bs*); Remo Palmieri (*g*); Billy Taylor (*b*); J. C. Heard (*d*). 44–46.

*** **Central Avenue Blues** VJC 1013 CD
Wilson; Charlie Shavers (*t*); Benny Morton (*tb*); Joe Thomas (*reeds*); Ed Hall (*cl*); Red Norvo (*vib*); Remo Palmieri (*g*); Sid Catlett (*d*); Paul Baron Orchestra. *c.* 48.

Wilson's records for Musicraft are typical late-swing small-band music, the leader as impeccable as always, though the other players can tend towards the motley. The Musicraft CD features various settings, from solo to octet. *Central Avenue Blues* is a collection of V-Disc masters in excellently refurbished sound: Shavers will sound as overbearing as usual to some ears, but the more considered methods of Hall and Norvo should counterbalance that, and Wilson is Wilson.

** **Air Mail Special** Black Lion BLCD 760115 CD
Wilson; Dave Shepherd (*cl*); Ronnie Gleaves (*vib*); Peter Chapman (*b*); Johnny Richardson (*d*). 6/67.

** **Swedish Jazz My Way** Sonet SNTCD 618 CD
Wilson; Ove Lind (*cl*); Lars Estrand (*vib*); Rolf Berg (*g*); Arne Wilhelmsson (*b*); Per Hultén (*d*). 4/70.

(*) **The Dutch Swing College Band Meet Teddy Wilson Timeless CDTTD 525 CD
Wilson; Ray Kaart (*t*); Bert de Kort (*c*); Dick Kaart (*tb*); Bob Kaper (*cl*); Peter Schilperoot (*cl, ts, bs, p*); Arie Ligthart (*g*); Henk Bosch van Drakestein, Bob van Oven, Fred Pronk (*b*); Huub Janssen, Louis de Lussanet (*d*). 2/64–10/73.

** **Teddy Wilson Meets Eiji Kitamura** Storyville 4152 CD
Wilson; Eiji Kitamura (*cl*); Ichiro Masuda (*vib*); Masanaga Harada (*b*); Buffalo Bill Robinson (*d*). 10/70.

*** **With Billie In Mind** Chiaroscuro CRD III CD
Wilson. 5/72.

(*) **Blues For Thomas Waller Black Lion BLCD 760131 CD
Wilson (*p* solo). 1/74.

*** **Three Little Words** Black & Blue 233 094 CD
Wilson; Milt Hinton (*b*); Oliver Jackson (*d*). 7/76.

*** **Teddy Wilson** LRC CDC 9003 CD
Wilson; Benny Goodman (*cl*); Milt Hinton (*b*); Oliver Jackson (*d*).

Wilson's later music is frequently disappointing in the light of his earlier achievements. Lacking any commitment from a major label, he seemed to wander from session to session with a sometimes cynical approach to the occasion, careless of the company and relying on an inner light which had long since burned down to a routine. Only when a sympathetic producer was on hand did Wilson raise his game, and the solo records listed above include some of the best music of his later albums. *With Billie In Mind* is devoted to material he had recorded with Holiday in the 1930s and its graceful, characterisic atmosphere makes for a special occasion. Six titles are added to the original LP issue. The Waller collection is less happy; the mature Wilson was a very different pianist from Waller, and his brand of sober gaiety isn't well attuned to the bumptious themes here, although 'Black And Blue' is more like the familiar Wilson. *Three Little Words* is a fine trio date, Wilson very much at home with players he trusts; although undated, the LRC album probably comes from the same period: Goodman's appearance on six tracks emanates from an unidentified live session, and the sound is slightly inferior to the studio tracks. It all works out elegantly enough, and the studio pieces carry on where the Black & Blue album leaves off.

The other records are eminently missable. *Air Mail Special* features dreary British mainstream and Wilson doesn't bother to disguise his boredom. Eiji Kitamura and his companions do marginally better, but the music is mostly second-hand swing. Ove Lind comes off as the best of the three clarinettists on *Swedish Jazz My Way*, and the music has a pleasing lilt to it, although again it's scarcely sustained for an album's duration. The Dutch Swing College Band play with their customary zeal and Wilson sounds in good spirits on 'Limehouse Blues' in particular; but there's little to remark on, other than pleasant mainstream noodling (the tracks from the 1960s don't feature Wilson).

*** **Revisited The Goodman Years** Storyville SLP 4046 LP
Wilson; Jesper Lundgaard (*b*); Ed Thigpen (*d*). 6/80.

*** **Masters Of Jazz Vol. 11: Teddy Wilson** Storyville 4111 CD/LP
As above, except add Niels-Henning Ørsted-Pedersen (*b*); Bjarne Rostvold (*d*). 12/68–6/80.

Wilson carried on working into the 1980s, and these are among his final recordings. He still sounds much as he did nearly 50 years before. The material on both records – most of it comes from the same session, with the trio date with NHØP and Rostvold adding six tracks to the second CD – is still heavily reliant on the 1930s standards which Wilson always stood by. As good as anything he recorded later in life.

LEM WINCHESTER
VIBES

** **Winchester Special** Original Jazz Classics OJC 1719 CD/LP
Winchester; Benny Golson (*ts*); Tommy Flanagan (*p*); Wendell Marshall (*b*); Art Taylor (*d*). 9/59.

** **Lem's Beat** Original Jazz Classics OJC 1785 CD
Winchester; Curtis Peagler (*as*); Oliver Nelson (*ts*); Billy Brown (*g*); Roy Johnson (*p*); Wendell Marshall (*b*); Art Taylor (*d*). 60.

Winchester's two surviving albums are characterized more by the guest tenors than by the nominal leader. His vibes playing is vigorous enough, if sometimes flat-footed; Golson's gruff, argumentative tenor on the first record and Nelson's loamy sound on the second create most of the interest. The rhythm section on the latter date hint at some of the forthcoming extroversions of soul-jazz without quite leaving hard-bop routine behind, and the most interesting point is the title, 'Lem & Aide', a pun that is outrageous even by the standards of the era. *Another Opus* and *With Feeling*, two other Winchester albums from the same period, may yet be reissued on CD.

NORMA WINSTONE (born 1941)
VOCALS

***(*) **Somewhere Called Home** ECM 1336 CD/LP
Winstone; Tony Coe (*cl, ts*); John Taylor (*p*). 7/86.

Winstone's first entry on Mike Westbrook's remarkable road-movie of an album, *Metropolis*, is one of the most breathtaking in contemporary jazz, a pure, reed-like tone that suddenly rises up out of the growling 'male' horns. Very powerful. One of the things that makes Winstone so exceptional as a singer is her equal confidence with pure abstraction (as in much of her work with Azimuth) and the most straightforward vocal line; she has talked of a 'Radio 2' side to her work but has often proved to be a sensitive lyricist as well as a standards singer.

In the absence of the now-rare *Edge Of Time* (released by Deram in 1971) *Somewhere Called Home* is a more-than-acceptable sample of Winstone's atmospheric approach. It takes a certain amount of brass neck to include 'Hi Lili Hi Lo' and 'Tea For Two' on a set like this. Coe and Taylor (Mr Winstone when off duty) are able and sensitive partners, but one wonders whether it wouldn't have come off better with just Taylor's thoughtful acompaniments.

DIEDERIK WISSELS

PIANO

(*)   **Juvia** Timeless SJP 218 LP
Wissels; Steve Houben (*as, f*); Hein van de Geyn (*b*); Jan De Haas (*d*). 5/84.

(*)   **Tender Is The Night** B Sharp CDS 075 CD
Wissels; Philippe Aerts (*b*); Jan De Haas (*d*). 90.

Accomplished post-bop piano. Houben is a hard-hitting saxophonist on *Juvia*, and Wissels characterizes his material with nimble expertise; but one has the impression that neither musician has quite enough fresh thought to make the music stand out in a personal way. 'I Loves You Porgy' and 'Autumn Leaves', both on the Timeless LP, certainly show up the other tunes as wanting.

MIKE WOFFORD

PIANO

***   **Sure Thing** Discovery DSCD 942 CD
Wofford; Anthony Ortega (*as, ts*); Monty Budwig, Andy Simpkins (*b*); John Guerin, Jim Plank (*d*). 1/67–7/80.

***(*)   **Plays Jerome Kern** Discovery DSCD 5000 2CD
Wofford; Anthony Ortega (*as, ts, cl, f*); Andy Simpkins, Tom Azaarello (*b*); Jim Plank (*d*). 2–7/80.

***   **Funkallero** Trend TRCD 552 CD
Wofford; Paul Sundfor (*ss, as*); Andy Simpkins (*b*); Sherman Ferguson (*d*). 9/87.

***   **Plays Gerald Wilson – Gerald's People** Discovery DSCD 951 CD
Wofford; Rufus Reid (*b*); Carl Burnett (*d*); Richie Gajate Garcia (*perc*). 9–10/88.

Wofford is an oblique modern pianist, taking a broadly linear tack to post-bop methods. He makes his way through standard material in unpredictable ways: the best of these records is the Kern collection, put together from the original three LPs, which is a very ruminative and varied approach to a single composer. The melodies for 'Why Was I Born' or 'Dearly Beloved' are referred to only fleetingly, while other songs – such as a nearly perfect 'Smoke Gets In Your Eyes' – are cast as one-take miniatures. Plank appears more as a percussionist than a trap drummer, and there's the bonus of hearing the rarely sighted Ortega, whose rather acrid playing injects a little more vinegar into the music. *Sure Thing* includes the balance of various sessions, including an early (1967) date with Monty Budwig on bass, while the later records each start from interesting premisses – one paring Gerald Wilson big-band scores down to a quartet setting, and the other working through an idiosyncratic selection of modern composers, including Monk ('Skippy'), Ellington ('Isfahan') and Shorter ('Funkallero'). Sundfor's thoughtful improvisations work as seamlessly with Wofford as, say, Konitz with Tristano, and the comparison holds good for the emotional timbres here too. Start with the Kern double-set, but any of the later records are well worth hearing.

THE WOLVERINE ORCHESTRA

GROUP

***   **The Wolverine Orchestra** Fountain FJ 114 LP
Bix Beiderbecke (*c, p*); Jimmy McPartland (*c*); George Brunies (*tb, kazoo*); Al Gande (*tb*); Jimmy Hartwell (*cl, as*); George Johnson (*ts*); Dick Voynow (*p*); Bob Gillette (*bj*); Min Leibrook (*bb*); Vic Moore (*d*); Dave Harmon (*v*). 2–12/24.

Richard Sudhalter's notes to the Fountain LP sum up The Wolverines in one sentence: 'Bix apart, they weren't really a very good band.' The group had played engagements in and around Cincinnati, Ohio, when they were recorded by Gennett in Richmond, Indiana, in 1924. The material mixes currently hot pop-tunes with pieces that date back to the ODJB, and it's Beiderbecke who time and again illuminates the otherwise clumsy and unswinging playing with solos of astonishing tenderness, poise and lyrical grace. The improvisations on 'Jazz Me Blues' and 'Riverboat Shuffle', with their singing tone, finely controlled articulation and euphonious sense of melody, are as enduring as anything recorded at the time. The band improves as one session succeeds another, but none of the other contributions – especially the terrible tenor playing of Johnson – is destined for anything other than footnote status, although Brunies does a reasonable job on his arrival, and the teenaged McPartland struggles through with courageous energy, subbing for Bix on the final date. The original recordings have been handled kindly in the remastering and the group's youthful enthusiasm survives.

RICKY WOODARD (born 1956)
TENOR AND ALTO SAXOPHONES

***   **California Cooking!** Candid CCD 79509 CD
      Woodard; Dwight Dickerson (*p*); Tony Dumas (*b*); Harold Mason (*d*). 2/91.

At last, a young(ish) tenorman who isn't in thrall to either Coltrane or Rollins. Woodard is actually from Nashville but works in Los Angeles, and there's a flavour of West Coast sunshine about the music, which has a burnished, easy-going lilt to it without sacrificing anything in energy. Zoot Sims, surprisingly, is the stylist whose manner Woodard most closely resembles, but his tone is as close to unique as a tenorman's can be in an age of a thousand tenor players: lean but hard, with a dusky timbre that he sustains through all the registers. His alto playing is more in hock to soul–bop sax playing, but there's the same fluency and bite. Dickerson and the others keep up and take occasional solos, but everything here is down to Woodard, and he completely dominates the 66 minutes which include fine readings of Hank Mobley's 'This I Dig Of You' and Duke Pearson's rare 'Jeannine'. The piano sounds a fraction recessed, but sound is otherwise excellent. Woodard can also be heard with Frank Capp.

PHIL WOODS (born 1931)
ALTO AND SOPRANO SAXOPHONE, CLARINET, VOCAL

(**)   **Bird's Eyes** Philology W 57-2 CD
      Woods; Hal Serra (*p*); Joe Raich (*vib*); Sal Salvador (*g*); Chuck Andrews (*b*); Joe Morello (*d, v*).

***   **Woodlore** Original Jazz Classics OJC 052 CD/LP/MC
      Woods; John Williams (*p*); Teddy Kotick (*b*); Nick Stabulas (*d*). 11/55.

***   **Pairing Off** Original Jazz Classics OJC 092 CD/LP/MC
      Woods; Donald Byrd, Kenny Dorham (*t*); Gene Quill (*as*); Tommy Flanagan (*p*); Doug Watkins (*b*); Philly Joe Jones (*d*). 6/56.

**   **The Young Bloods** Original Jazz Classics OJC 1732 CD/LP
      Woods; Donald Byrd (*t*); Al Haig (*p*); Teddy Kotick (*b*); Charlie Persip (*d*). 11/56.

(*)   **Four Altos Original Jazz Classics OJC 1734 CD/LP
      Woods; Gene Quill, Sahib Shihab, Hal Stein (*as*); Mal Waldron (*p*); Tommy Potter (*b*); Louis Hayes (*d*). 2/57.

***(*)   **Phil & Quill** Original Jazz Classics OJC 215 CD/LP
      Woods; Gene Quill (*as*); George Syran (*p*); Teddy Kotick (*b*); Nick Stabulas (*d*). 3/57.

Phil Woods sprang into jazz recording with a fully formed style: tone, speed of execution and ideas were all first-hand borrowings from bebop, and, inevitably, Parker, but he sounded like a mature player from the first. The 1947 recordings must be discounted, since they're from private acetates and the fidelity is almost as poor as some of the worst Charlie Parker airshots. Yet the bristling insistence of the sixteen-year-old Woods is already astonishingly in evidence, assuming the date is accurate (there is some 30 minutes of music by this band on the CD; the rest continues the series of live Parker recordings). *Woodlore* is a relatively quiet business, considering that Woods thrived on blowing session shoot-outs at the time, and it's the prettiness of his sound which impresses on 'Be My Love' and 'Falling In Love All Over Again'; but 'Get Happy' is a burner. The rhythm section, with Williams sometimes barely in touch, is less impressive. *Pairing Off* and *Four Altos* milk the jam-session format which was beloved by Prestige at the time, and both dates come off better than most. *Pairing Off* features a couple of crackerjack blues in the title-tune and 'Stanley The Steamer', and only Byrd's relative greenness lets the side down; Philly Joe is superbly inventive at the kit. *Four Altos* is an idea that ought to pall quickly, but the enthusiasm of Woods and Quill in particular elevates the makeshift charts into something worthwhile. They made a very fine team: *Phil & Quill* doesn't have an ounce of spare fat in the solos, and the spanking delivery on, say, 'A Night At St Nick's' is as compelling as anything Prestige were recording at the period. Quill's duskier tone and more extreme intensities are barely a beat behind Woods's in terms of quality of thought (they also have two tracks on the subsequent compilation, *Bird Feathers*, OJC 1735 CD/LP). *The Young Bloods*, although interesting for a rare 1950s appearance by Al Haig, is beset by the familiar problem of Byrd's lack of authority, and sparks never fly between the horns the way Woods would probably have wished. All five discs are remastered to the customary high standards of OJC.

***   **Young Woods** Fresh Sounds FSR-CD 182 CD
Woods; Burt Collins (*t*); Eddie Bert (*tb*); Nat Pierce, Ralph Martin, John Williams (*p*); Eddie Costa (*vib*); Barry Galbraith, Sal Salvador (*g*); John Drew, Danny Martucci, Sonny Dallas (*b*); Gus Johnson, Joe Morello, Jimmy Campbell (*d*). 12/56–8/57.

Three sessions featuring Woods as a sideman. A quintet date with Burt Collins and Nat Pierce has little interest, but a quintet and a septet, both with Sal Salvador, are much more exciting. Salvador goes so clean and fast that he actually outblows Woods, and Bert's pungent solos are fine, too. The sound is foggy for the Pierce/Collins date, but the rest sound very good.

(***)   **The Birth Of The ERM** Philology 214 W 16/17 2LP
Woods; George Gruntz (*p*); Henri Texier (*b*); Daniel Humair (*d*). 6–10/68.

***   **Freedom Jazz Dance** Moon M 019 CD/LP
As above. 69.

***   **Stolen Moments** JMY 1012-2 CD
As above. No date.

Woods made few jazz records in the 1960s, working mostly on commercial studio dates, but a move to France in 1968 led him to form the European Rhythm Machine with the above trio. None of their official albums are in print, but these in-concert recordings, some of dubious origin, present a good picture of the band at work. Woods eschews bop's concentration for longer solos, labyrinthine variation and improvisations which owe as much to the methods of Coltrane and Rollins as to Parker, even if Woods himself might scoff at hints of prolixity in his manner. Texier and Humair are consistently imaginative, and there are points where bass and drums seem ready to spin off into their own orbit. Gruntz, too, is a fireball of activity: hear the groove which the trio hits on the 'Freedom Jazz Dance' on *Stolen Moments*. The problem with all three records is the sound, which is merely OK at best and sometimes is frankly terrible. The Philology set comes from the label run by Woods fanatic, Paolo Piangiarelli, whose devotion to the altoman extends to releasing concerts which would be tolerated only by the most dedicated of disciples: the second disc, recorded at Bologna, has a Dean Benedetti-like low fidelity. Authentic, perhaps, but not very enjoyable. Both the Moon and the JMY discs are much better, if still less than ideal; but, given that each disc features much the same material – long versions of 'Freedom Jazz Dance', 'Stolen Moments' and 'And When We're Young' – the less committed might choose only the JMY disc as a single selection.

***(*)   **Song For Sisyphus** BBC CJCD 831 CD
Woods; Mike Melillo (*p*); Harry Leahy (*g*); Steve Gilmore (*b*); Bill Goodwin (*d*). 11/77.

Woods returned to the US in 1973 and formed a new acoustic band, following a brief flirtation with electricity. He's stuck by Gilmore and Goodwin to this day and in a live setting prefers to play without even the house amplification. One listen to the sound of this band may explain why: they play with consummate finesse, but Woods sounds as if he could slice through tungsten with a tone that bites and a rhythmic attack which is by now almost non-pareil in the realm of bebop alto. 'Last Night When We Were Young' is sumptuously romantic and 'Change

Partners' shows what he can do with a less familiar standard. Cut originally for direct-to-disc, which may account for a high level of tape-hiss amd certainly for the short playing time of 34 minutes.

***   **The Macerata Concert** Philology 214 W 1/2/3 3LP
        As above, except omit Leahy, add strings. 11/80.

Another great extravagance from Philology – a three-decker LP-set covering a complete 1980 show, with a curious bonus version of 'Don't Despair' featuring Woods with strings. The sound is again variable and, while Woods is on assertive form, the disc could happily have lost half its length and been the better for it.

****   **Integrity** Red VPA 177 2LP/2CD
        Woods; Tom Harrell (*t, flhn*); Hal Galper (*p*); Steve Gilmore (*b*); Bill Goodwin (*d*).
        4/84.

This became a firm line-up, and any who heard the group in concert will surely want this live record, for it's a fine souvenir of one of the great touring bands of the 1980s. Harrell had worked for some years as a freelance in search of a context, and with Woods he secured a precise focus: the material here is a connoisseur's choice of jazz themes – including Neal Hefti's 'Repetition', Ellington's 'Azure', Wayne Shorter's 'Infant Eyes' and Sam Rivers's '222' – mediated through a very clear-headed approach to modern bop playing. Harrell's lucid tone and nimble, carefully sifted lines are as piquant a contrast with Woods as one could wish, without creating any clashes of temperament. Galper's pensiveness is occasionally a fraction too laid-back, but he moves as one with bass and drums. Woods himself assumes a role both paternal and sporting, stating themes and directions with unswerving authority but still taking risky routes to resolving an idea: his solo on Charlie Mariano's 'Blue Walls', for instance, is rhythmically as daring as any of his early work. Good in-concert recording.

***(*)   **Heaven** Black Hawk BKH 50401 CD/LP/MC
        As above. 12/84.

***   **Gratitude** Denon 33CY-1316 CD
        As above. 6/86.

***(*)   **Bop Stew** Concord CJ/CCD 345/4345 CD/LP/MC
        As above. 11/87.

***(*)   **Bouquet** Concord CJ/CCD 377/4377 CD/LP/MC
        As above. 11/87.

****   **Flash** Concord CCD 4408 CD/MC
        As above, except add Hal Crook (*tb*). 4/89.

As consistent a series of records as any in this period. Woods's facility seems ageless and, if his parameters remain tied to orthodox bop langauge, he has developed it as inventively as a player can, making the most of dynamic contrast and colour and granting every member of the band their own space. *Bop Stew* and *Bouquet* are from a fine Japanese concert; *Heaven* is a crisp studio session. *Gratitude* is docked one star for the studio sound, which seems rather distant and unfocused, although the playing time runs for a more-than-generous 70 minutes. *Flash*, the final album with Harrell (who has since been replaced by Hal Crook as the front-line horn), has the edge of some outstanding composing by the trumpeter – 'Weaver' and 'Rado' are particularly sound vehicles – and Crook's extra tones on a few tracks.

***   **All Bird's Children** Concord CCD 4441 CD/MC
        As above, except omit Harrell. 6/90.

As good as Crook is, with a sparkling fluency as a soloist and a canny arranger's ear, it's hard to evade the feeling that Harrell will be missed by the band. In other respects, it's another assured session by the Woods band. Highlight: the lush 'Gotham Serenade' by Galper, who has also since departed the group.

***   **Evolution** Concord CJ/CCD 361/4361 CD/LP/MC
        As above, except add Nelson Hill (*ts*); Nick Brignola (*bs*). 5/88.

***(*)   **Real Life** Chesky JD 47 CD
As above, except Jim McNeely (*p*) replaces Galper. 9/90.

***   **Here's To My Lady** Chesky JD 3 CD
Woods; Tommy Flanagan (*p*); George Mraz (*b*); Kenny Washington (*d*). 12/88.

Woods's Little Big Band builds on the virtues of the quintet with smart logic. Arrangements by Galper, Woods, Harrell and Crook leave the group without a specific identity, allowing it to shape a vocabulary through the charisma of the leader and the pro's pro feel of the ensemble. *Real Life* is the bigger and more confident record, with a couple of lovely ballad features for Woods and a burning memorial to his old sparring partner, 'Quill', in which Brignola takes the second alto part; but the somewhat eccentric Chesky studio sound, an attempt to secure analogue warmth and presence on digital equipment, may not be to all tastes. Similar remarks apply to the quartet Chesky session, although the blue-chip rhythm section are so apposite to Woods's needs that it makes one wish that he would take a vacation from his usual band a little more often. The mood here is rather more languid than usual, with nothing breaking into a gallop, and it's a useful appendix to his more full-blooded work in the 1980s.

***   **Embraceable You** Philology 214 W 25 CD/LP
Woods; Marco Tamburini, Flavio Boltro, Paolo Fresu (*t, flhn*); Danilo Terenzi, Hal Crook, Roberto Rossi (*tb*); Giancarlo Maurino (*ss, as*); Mario Raja (*ss, ts*); Maurizio Giammarco (*ts*); Roberto Ottini (*bs*); Danilo Rea (*ky*); Enzo Pietropaoli (*b*); Roberto Gatto (*d*). 7/88.

A passionate mess. Nothing wrong with the calibre of the band – these are some of Italy's finest. Woods, too, is in strong form and occasionally reaches exalted heights: the reading of 'Embraceable You', characterized with the purplest of prose in the sleeve-notes, is almost as good as the producer makes out. But Mario Raja's arrangements are cumbersome, the band seem under-rehearsed, and the studio sound is hopelessly ill-focused: Paolo Piangiarelli may be a great fan, but he should entrust production duties to someone else.

***   **Phil On Etna** Philology W 38/39 2CD
Woods; Giovanni La Ferlita, Mario Cavallaro, Giuseppe Privitera, Enzo Gulizia (*t*); Camillo Pavone, Paul Zelig Rodberg, Benvenuto Ramaci (*tb*); Salvo Di Stefano (*btb*); Carlo Cattano, Umberto Di Pietro (*as*); Salvo Famiani, Ercole Tringale (*ts*); Antonio Russo (*bs*); Giuseppe Emmanuele (*p*); Nello Toscano (*b*); Pucci Nicosia (*d*); Antonella Consolo (*v*). 3/89.

Another extravagant set from Philology, compiling 100 minutes of music from a concert with the Catania City Brass Orkestra, a young big band following up a week's tuition under Woods's direction. They're eager to please, and Woods himself plays with astonishing commitment as featured soloist throughout: several of the improvisations here rank with anything he's recorded in recent years. But the band lack any notable finesse and, faced with a demanding chart such as 'Pink Sunrise', they're audibly struggling. The few other soloists play with the trepidation of keen but bashful students. Good live sound, though.

REGGIE WORKMAN
DOUBLE BASS

***(*)   **Synthesis** Leo LR 131 LP
Workman; Oliver Lake (*reeds*); Marilyn Crispell (*p*); Andrew Cyrille (*d*). 6/86.

***   **Images** Music & Arts CD 634 CD
Workman; Don Byron (*cl*); Michele Navazio (*g*); Marilyn Crispell (*p*); Gerry Hemingway (*d*); Jeanne Lee (*v*). 1 & 7/89.

As befits the name, Workman has clocked up an astonishing number and range of sideman credits: with Coltrane (*Olé*, the 1961 European tour, the *Africa/Brass* sessions) and with Wayne Shorter, Mal Waldron, Art Blakey, Archie Shepp and David Murray. Workman is also a forceful leader who has moved on to explore areas of musical freedom influenced by African idioms and frequently resembling the trance music of the *griots*. Of the two available albums, *Synthesis*, a live performance from The Painted Bride in Philadelphia, is the more convincing. Workman bows, triple-stops and produces unreliably pitched sounds (presumably from below the bridge), leaving it to Crispell, as on *Images*, to give the performance its undoubted sense of coherence. Of the six tracks on *Synthesis*, it is her 'Chant' which sounds most like a fully articulated composition. Workman's ideas are developed less completely and, while they often lead to more adventurous solo excursions from the individual performers, they rarely do much more than peter out. 'Jus' Ole Mae' on *Synthesis* is '(Revisited)' on the later album, a brighter and more evocative performance, but one that lacks the sheer daring and adventurous seat-of-the-pants logic of the Philadelphia version.

WORLD SAXOPHONE QUARTET
GROUP

***(*)   **Point Of No Return** Moers 01034 CD/LP
Hamiet Bluiett (*bs, f, af, acl*); Julius Hemphill (*f, ss, as*); Oliver Lake (*ss, ts, as, f*); David Murray (*ts, bcl*). 6/77.

***   **Steppin'** Black Saint BSR 0027 CD/LP
As above. 12/78.

****   **W.S.Q.** Black Saint BSR 0046 CD
As above. 3/80.

***(*)   **Revue** Black Saint BSR 0056 CD
As above. 10/80.

***   **Live In Zurich** Black Saint BSR 0077 CD/LP
As above. 11/81.

***(*)   **Plays Duke Ellington** Elektra Musician 979137 CD/LP
As above. 4/86.

****   **Dances And Ballads** Elektra Musician 979164 CD
As above. 4/87.

***(*)   **Rhythm And Blues** Elektra Musician 60864 CD
As above. 11/88.

Market-leaders in the now well-attested saxophone quartet format, the WSQ were founded in 1977. The debut album was not particularly well recorded but it helped establish the group's identity as adventurous composer-improvisers who could offer great swinging ensembles (not quite as hokey as those of the 29th Street Saxophone Quartet) and remarkable duo and trio divisions of the basic instrumentation. On *Point Of No Return* the armoury of reeds is pretty modest, but increasingly after 1978 all four members began to 'double' on more exotic specimens, with Bluiett's alto clarinet (rarely used in a jazz context) and Murray's bass clarinet both lending significant variations of tonality and texture. 'Scared Sheetless' from the first album gives a fair impression of its not altogether serious appropriation of free-jazz devices. 'R & B' on the second album plays with genre in a friendlier and more ironic way.

The best of the earlier records, *W.S.Q.*, is dominated by a long suite that blends jazz and popular elements with considerable ingenuity and real improvisational fire. 'The Key' and 'Ballad For Eddie Jefferson' (dedicated to the inventor of jazz vocalese) are perhaps the most interesting elements, but the closing 'Fast Life' is as fine a curtain-piece as the group has recorded. With *Revue* (a significant pun), the centre of gravity shifts slightly towards rising star Murray and towards what looks like a reassessment of the group's development. Murray's 'Ming' is well known from his own records but has never been played with such fierce beauty.

The Ellington album marks a gentle, middle-market turn that has done the group no harm at all. Opening and closing with 'Take The "A" Train', they check out 'Sophisticated Lady' and 'I Let A Song Go Out Of My Heart', do a wonderful 'Come Sunday', and add a raw lyricism to 'Lush Life' and 'Prelude To A Kiss'. The sound is better than usual, with no congestion round about the middle, as on some of the earlier sets. There's a broader big-band sound to *Dances And Ballads*, achieved without the addition of outsiders as on *Metamorphosis*, below, which seems to draw something from the Ellington set. Hemphill contributes only two tracks, but there's a fine version of David Murray's Prez tribute 'For Lester' (later to appear on his octet, *HopeScope*), and Oliver Lake's 'West African Snap', 'Belly Up' and 'Adjacent' are among the best of his recorded compositions. The soul staples covered on *Rhythm And Blues* – including

'Let's Get It On', '(Sittin' On) The Dock Of The Bay', and, unforgettably, 'Try A Little Tenderness', with Murray's tenor going places Otis Redding never heard of – are done with absolute conviction and seriousness. Only *Steppin'* and the rather rough *Live In Zurich* are disappointments, though the latter has a fine reading of 'Steppin'' itself.

All four members have developed highly individual careers apart, Murray most of all; along with Hemphill, he is the most distinctive and flexible composer. The durability of the group lay in the degree to which personal strengths were encouraged and exploited rather than subordinated. With so many instrumental permutations and the possibility of internal subdivisions, the WSQ's exploratory sound has never settled into a manner.

***   **Metamorphosis** Elektra Nonesuch 979258 CD
        Oliver Lake (*as, ss, f*); David Murray (*ts, bcl*); Hamiet Bluiett (*bs*); Arthur Blythe
        (*as*); Melvin Gibbs (*b*); Chief Bey, Mar Gueye, Mor Thiam (*perc*). 4/90.

The departure of Julius Hemphill and arrival of Arthur Blythe couldn't have looked altogether propitious, given (a) Hemphill's importance as a writer for the group, and (b) Blythe's stuttering fortunes in recent years. The title-track, though, is given over to the new boy and he fills the outgoing man's shoes with impressive confidence, checking in with a powerful contrapuntal weave that is lifted a notch by the (initially disturbing; the WSQ used always to go it alone) presence of the three African drummers. In the event, they add a great deal more than bassist Gibbs, who clocks on for three tracks only, and might as well not have bothered. Murray's 'Ballad For The Black Man' is very much an individual feature and easily the most coherent single track; Lake's 'Love Like Sisters' has tremendous potential but might well sound better tackled by a more conventional horn-plus-inventive-rhythm outfit. A new departure? Or a rearguard action? Time will tell.

RICHARD WYANDS (born 1928)
PIANO

***   **Then, Here And Now** Storyville SLP 4083 LP
        Wyands; Lisle Atkinson (*b*); David Lee (*d*). 10/78.

Oakland-born Wyands is a considerably underrated composer with a keyboard style that falls around the romantic end of Red Garland's far broader spectrum. These trio pieces are a little sullen in register, but 'Lament' and 'Blue Rose' have a fragile beauty that suggests Bill Evans. Atkinson is an excellent bassist and can be heard again with Wyands on his own *Bass Contra Bass* (Storyville SLP 4084 LP), which makes an interesting, and in some ways preferable, companion work.

YOSUKE YAMASHITA
PIANO

***(*)   **Clay** Enja 2052 LP

***(*)   **Ghosts By Albert Ayler** West Wind 2050 CD
        Yamashita; Akira Sakata (*cl, as*); Takeo Moriyama (*d* on *Clay*). 6/74, 5/77.

***   **Banslikana** Enja 2080 LP
        Yamashita (*p* solo). 7/76.

***   **Inner Space** Enja 3001 LP
        Yamashita; Adelhard Roidinger (*b*). 6/77.

(**)   **Yosuke Yamashita – Hozan Yamamoto Enja 5003/4 2LP
        Yamashita; Hozan Yamamoto (*shakuhachi*). 7/85.

An intriguing stylist with a highly individual take on the modern jazz tradition, Yamashita has explored bop staples like 'A Night In Tunisia' (on the solo *Banslikana*), classic ballads like ''Round Midnight' (with shakuhachi player, Yamamoto) and an excellent solo 'Autumn Leaves', but has also delved into the turbulent sound-world of Albert Ayler, anticipating Giorgio Gaslini's *Ayler's Wings*. With a sharp but curiously delicate touch, Yamashita prefers to play in short, apparently discontinuous blocks of sound that often do not connect in accordance with accepted harmonic or even rhythmic logic. The piano–shakuhachi duets are particularly unusual in their approach to rhythm, and it's often the flute that holds a basic pulse while Yamashita ranges more freely. The duets with Roidinger are atmospheric but rather empty and compare poorly with the superb trios featuring the urgent tone of Akira Sakata's saxophone and clarinet. The long 'Nina's Second Theme' and 'Clay', a dedication to Muhammad Ali and title-track of the better set, reveal a bold touch as a composer which often doesn't receive full rein on later tracks. Enthusiasts might also like to try the intriguing *Distant Thunder* (Enja 2066 LP) with the trumpeter Manfred Schoof, who attempts an unaccompanied ''Round Midnight' to match Yamashita's solo title-piece.

JIMMY YANCEY (1894–1951)
PIANO

***(*)   **The Yancey–Lofton Sessions: Volume 1** Storyville SLP 238 LP
Yancey (*p* solo) and with Mama Yancey (*v*). 43.

***   **The Yancey–Lofton Sessions: Volume 2** Storyville SLP 239 LP
As above.

Acclaimed as the originator of boogie-woogie, Yancey spent much of his life in obscurity (though he seems to have considered it *the* job) as groundsman for the Chicago White Sox, playing piano only at rent parties. A 1936 recording by Meade Lux Lewis of 'Yancey Special' brought him to wider notice, and in the early 1940s he was recorded by Victor and other labels. The 1943 sessions are not a patch on 'Cryin' In My Sleep' and 'Death Letter Blues', but they feature the wonderful 'At The Window', on which Yancey's characteristic ability to realign a usually unvarying left-hand bass figure is heard to good advantage. His particular genius lay in an ability to make impressive music out of quite extraordinarily limited harmonic and rhythmic materials. So simple is his approach that tiny variations, as on 'Eternal Blues' and 'Yancey Special' (both *Volume 2*) assume great dramatic significance. These sessions also included material made with his wife, Mama Yancey, together with tracks by Alonzo Yancey (a marvellous 'Exstatic Rag') and fellow pianist Cripple Clarence Lofton.

KHALID YASIN – see LARRY YOUNG

GEORGE YOUNG
TENOR AND SOPRANO SAXOPHONES

***   **Burgundy** Paddle Wheel K 28P 6449 CD
Young; Toots Thielemans (*hca*); Warren Bernhardt (*p*); Ron Carter (*b*); Al Foster (*d*). 10/86.

***   **Oleo** Paddle Wheel K 28P 6481 CD
Young; Warren Bernhardt (*p*); Dave Holland (*b*); Jack DeJohnette (*d*). 11/87.

**   **Yesterday And Today** Paddle Wheel 292 E 6028 CD
Young; Gil Goldstein (*p*); Chip Jackson (*b*); Dave Weckl (*d*). 3/89.

Lacking any special characteristic to make him stand out from the ranks of modern tenors, Young is nevertheless a musician who can muster convincingly exciting music at will. A listener's reaction, as with the many records Young has made with the Manhattan Jazz Quintet, may depend on whether he or she is prepared to listen through the session-man gloss which tends to varnish over this kind of jazz and appreciate the ideas within. At times, as with most of *Yesterday And Today*, the music burnishes inspiration down to a matter of professional pride, and it's difficult to feel involved in what's going on. But with *Oleo*, where the accompanying trio are too good to be boringly excellent, Young's thesis on the achievements of Rollins and Coltrane takes on some stature of its own. *Burgundy* is enlivened by the appearance of Toots Thielemans on one track.

LARRY YOUNG (died 1979)
ORGAN

***(*)   **Testifying** Original Jazz Classics OJC 1793 CD
Young; Thornel Schwartz (*g*); Jimmie Smith (*d*).

Larry Young – later known as Khalid Yasin – was the first Hammond player to shake off the pervasive influence of Jimmy Smith (not to be confused with the drummer on this record) and begin the assimilation of John Coltrane's harmonics to the disputed border territory between jazz and nascent rock. Young's best-known work was with Tony Williams's Lifetime band, for whom he created great billowing sheets of sound, doubling until Jack Bruce's arrival as a (pedal) bass player. He can also be heard on John McLaughlin's *Devotion* (Douglas), prominent on such fire-eating numbers as 'Don't Let The Dragon Eat Your Mother'. Significantly, he also played a part in Miles Davis's epochal *Bitches Brew* (CBS 66236 CD).

It's profoundly unfortunate, though, that so little of of his already small but highly significant output should remain available. *Testifying* is an early recording, still rather stuck in the soul-jazz, Jimmy McGriff mould, out of which Young was fledging by the session (Schwartz, it should be noted, also worked for McGriff) but already showing some signs of the tonal sophistication of later work. James Blood Ulmer fans would sense an ancestral influence on tracks like 'Exercise For Chihuahuas', 'Some Thorny Blues' and the title-number. The sound is a bit shimmery and harsh, but adequate.

*****   **Unity** Blue Note BCT 84221 CD/LP/MC
Young; Woody Shaw (*t*); Joe Henderson (*ts*); Elvin Jones (*d*). 11/65.

Unity is a masterpiece, whipped along by Jones's ferocious drumming and Henderson's meaty tenor, even on a normally soft-pedal tune like 'Softly As In A Morning Sunrise'. Young contributes nothing as a writer, which doesn't in any way diminish the impact of his performance. Woody Shaw's 'The Moontrane', 'Zoltan' and 'Beyond All Limits' are a measure of *his* underregarded significance as a composer; the first of the three is the perfect test of Young's absorption of Coltrane's ideas, as he develops a rather obvious (if precocious, Shaw wrote it when he was 18) sequence of harmonics into something that represents a genuine extension of Coltrane, not just a bland repetition.

Anyone really interested in Young's music should also get hold of another fine but deleted Blue Note, the moving *Heaven On Earth* [BNJ 71040 LP].

LESTER YOUNG (1909–59)
TENOR SAXOPHONE

***(*)   **Prez's Hat: Volume 1** Philology 214 W 6 LP
Young; Buck Clayton, Harry Edison, Al Killian, Ed Lewis, Joe Newman (*t*); Ted Donnelly, Eli Robinson, Lou Taylor, Dickie Wells (*tb*); Jimmy Powell, Earl Warren (*as*); Buddy Tate (*ts*); Rudy Rutherford (*bs, cl*); Count Basie, Hank Jones, Harold Kauffman, Oscar Peterson, René Urtreger (*p*); Jimmy Gourley, Freddie Green, Barney Kessel (*g*); Ray Brown, Jean-Marie Ingrand, Pierre Michelot, Walter Page, Rodney Richardson (*b*); Kenny Clarke, Christian Garros, J. C. Heard, Jo Jones, Max Roach (*d*); Thelma Carpenter, Jimmy Rushing (*v*); collective personnel. 9/39, 5/44, 4/52, 3/53, 56, 3/59.

***(*)   **Prez's Hat: Volume 2** Philology 214 W 7 LP
Young; Harry Edison, Al Killian, Ed Lewis, Joe Newman (*t*); Ted Donnelly, Eli Robinson, Earl Swope, Lou Taylor (*tb*); Jimmy Powell, Earl Warren (*as*); Buddy Tate (*ts*); Rudy Rutherford (*bs, cl*); Count Basie, Bill Potts (*p*); Freddie Greemn (*g*); Rodney Richardson, Norman Williams (*b*); Jo Jones, Jim Lutch (*d*); Jimmy Rushing (*v*); collective personnel. 5/44, 12/56.

***   **Prez's Hat: Volume 3** Philology 214 W 8 LP
Young; Jesse Drakes (*t*); Horace Silver (*p*); Frank Skeete (*b*); Connie Kay (*d*); and as above, but minus Swope, Potts, Williams and Lutch; some personnel unidentified; collective personnel. 5/44, 4/53, 8/56.

***   **Prez's Hat: Volume 4** Philology 214 W 9 LP
Young; Jesse Drakes (*t*); and as for *Volume 2*, but minus Swope, Williams and Lutch; some personnel unidentified; collective personnel. 5/44, 9/56.

***(*)   **Live At The Royal Roost 1948** Jazz Anthology 550092 CD
Young; Jesse Drakes (*t*); Ted Kelly (*tb*); Freddie Jefferson (*p*); Ted Briscoe (*b*); Roy Haynes (*d*). 11/48, 3/49.

***(*)   **Lester Young & The Piano Giants** Verve 835316 CD
Young; Harry Edison, Roy Eldridge (*t*); Vic Dickenson (*tb*); Nat Cole, Hank Jones, John Lewis, Oscar Peterson, Teddy Wilson (*p*); Herb Ellis, Freddie Green (*g*); Ray Brown, Gene Ramey, Joe Shulman (*b*); Bill Clark, Jo Jones, Buddy Rich (*d*); collective personnel. 3 & 4/46, 7/50, 1/51, 12/55, 1/56.

***   **Prez Conferences** Jass J-CD-18 CD
Young; Buck Clayton (*t*); Coleman Hawkins (*ts*); Mike Caluccio, Nat King Cole, Kenny Kersey, Nat Pierce, Bill Potts, Sinclair Raney (*p*); Irving Ashby, Oscar Moore, Mary Osborne (*g*); Billy Hadnott, Johnny Miller, Gene Ramey, Doug Watkins, Norman Williams (*b*); Jim Lucht, Buddy Rich, Willie Jones, Specs Powell, Shadow Wilson (*d*). 3 & 4/46, 12/56, 58.

***   **Masters Of Jazz: Lester Young** Storyville SLP 4107 LP
Young; Jesse Drakes, Idrees Sulieman (*t*); John Lewis, Bill Potts, Horace Silver (*p*); Aaron Bell, Gene Ramey, Franklin Skeete, Norman Williams (*b*); Jo Jones, Connie Kay, Abram Lee, Jim Lucht (*d*); collective personnel. 5/51, 1/53, 12/56.

***   **Lester Young In Washington, D.C. 1956: Volume 1** Pablo Live CD 2308219 CD

***(*)   **Lester Young In Washington, D.C. 1956: Volume 2** Pablo Live CD 2308225 CD
Young; Bill Potts (*p*); Norman Williams, Jim Lucht (*d*). 12/56.

For every ten jazz fans who can whistle 'Goodbye, Pork Pie Hat', there's probably only one who can claim any real knowledge of Lester Young's music. Universally acknowledged as a major influence on the bop and post-bop schools, Young's own output is neglected and frequently misunderstood. Serious appraisal of his work is complicated by a irreconcilable controversy about the quality of Young's post-war work, from which virtually all the above recordings are drawn.

Young grew up in the jazz heartland near New Orleans and served a nomadic apprenticeship with Art Bronson's Bostonians, Walter Page's Blue Devils (and later the Thirteen Original Blue Devils), moving to Minneapolis in 1931. A year or so later, he had an encounter with Charlie Christian that must count as one of the significant episodes in the pre-history of bebop. In 1933, he joined the Bennie Moten band before signing up with Count Basie the following year on the strength of an impassioned postcard he had written to the bandleader he later christened 'The Holy Main'.

Young made his name in the Basie band, but only after an unhappy sojourn in Fletcher Henderson's orchestra, where the saxophone section ganged up on his unconventional approach and unusual sound. After brief stints with Andy Kirk and a tough spell as a 'single' in Kansas City, he returned to the Basie band. Young quickly became a major soloist, using a delivery that was the precise opposite of the dominant Coleman Hawkins style; they can be heard together on three 1946 shots recorded in Hollywood on the rather drab Jass compilation. Where Hawkins was bluff, aggressive and sensual, Young developed a sound that was dry, precise and almost delicate. Some of its curiosities of tone are traceable to the example of Jimmy Dorsey, a greatly underrated saxophonist who had created a vocabulary of alternate fingerings and low, almost unpitched breath-sounds through the horn. The only other predecessor to influence Young was Bix's sidekick Frank Trumbauer, though less for his sound (Trumbauer favoured a C-melody saxophone) than for his distinctive habit of building solos up out of brief thematic and melodic units which he subjected to seamless variation and augmentation, building up solos of great formal control which, coupled with his unmistakable sound, represent the single most important advance in saxophone improvisation until the advent of Charlie Parker. Unlike Hawkins, Young was little concerned with playing on harmonic changes.

Versions of what followed vary – and the precise emphasis matters significantly – but in 1944 Young was drafted and began a year-long nightmare in the US Army. Some accounts suggest that he was conscripted after being spotted smoking marijuana by a plain-clothes military whipper-in scouring the clubs for able-bodied men. Other sources suggest that Young's drug and later alcohol problems began *in reaction to* the repressive horrors of army life. A convenient mythology suggests that the army destroyed Young as a man and an artist and that the post-war recordings are sad dregs from a once-fine musician. Another tendency suggests that Young's later recordings are actually much more experimental and exploratory as he attempts to come to terms with the rise of bebop (a music he is credited with having influenced).

Listeners who have heard Young's classic solos – the 1936 'Lady Be Good' with Jo Jones and Carson Smith, 'Jumpin' At The Woodside' and the later 'Lester Leaps In' with Basie – will have to judge how much of a falling-off is evident in the material on the currently deleted Savoy sessions and on the rather shambolically put together *Prez's Hat*, which is culled from airshot and other material from France and the USA. Though the sound quality is rather uncertain, it's often preferable to contemporary studio recordings, which are recorded in unforgiving close-up, rather than from a single collector mike. The first side of Volume 1 consists of 'Flashes Of Prez' (the saxophonist was christened 'The President' by Billie Holiday), awkward edits from radio broadcasts, but it also includes a pre-war 'Lester Leaps In', which serves as a valuable comparative introduction for newcomers. Volume 2 mixes good Basie material with three duff 1956 tracks. Volumes 3 and 4 are patchier and despite some fine things could easily be left to one side for now in hopes that much of this material, like the Savoys, will soon be reissued on CD.

The Royal Roost sessions offer invaluable insights into what was happening in Young's music after the war. Though rarely as explicitly as in 'Bebop Boogie', he was exploring some of the rhythmic and harmonic innovations of the boppers. Already, though, there is evidence of some of the less desirable traits that crept into his 1950s work (a formulaic repetition and a self-conscious and histrionic distortion of tone and phrasing akin to his friend Billie Holiday's around the same time), it's clear that he is trying to rethink harmonic progression. A new device, much noted, is his use of an arpeggiated tonic triad in first inversion (i.e. with the third rather than the root in lowest position) which, whatever its technical niceties, smoothed out chordal progression from ever shorter phrases.

It's patent nonsense to suggest that the 1950s Young was merely a broken hack, mawkishly and as often as not drunkenly rehashing old solos, hanging behind the beat as he tried to keep one step ahead of a failing technique. However chastened, the 1950s recordings preserved a good deal of the original genius, but placed it in a new and unfamiliar, and therefore challenging, context. The Verve (again, a CD is very welcome) includes some excellent material recorded in January 1956 with Roy Eldridge, another stylistic bridge-builder, and Teddy Wilson, together with a 1950 version of 'Up'N'Adam' with Hank Jones, which is worth comparing with the rougher textured Horace Silver accompaniment on *Prez's Hat: Volume 2*. The 1956 Pablos further confound the notion of a man who had given up on life and art; though drastically reconceived and hardly abetted by Potts's backward-looking accompaniments (it was often Prez's sidemen who wanted to play in the 'old style' about which he became so painfully ambivalent), 'Lester Leaps In' and 'These Foolish Things' (both on the better Volume 2) are major jazz performances. Right to the very end, Young was capable of quite extraordinary things. 'There Will Never Be Another You', with Kenny Clarke, Jimmy Gourley, Harold Kauffman and Jean-Marie Ingrand (with one exception, not the company he deserved) was recorded within a fortnight of his death and still sounds vital, moving and full of musical intelligence.

Young's later years have been unhelpfully coloured by too many sorry anecdotes (about his drinking, world-weariness, and increasingly restricted conversational code) and, more recently, by Bernard Tavernier's composite anti-hero Dale Turner in *Round Midnight*, a character who is truer in spirit to the declining Bud Powell. Powell felt safe in the past and retreated into recreations of his best work. Throughout his life, Young had been brutally cut off from his own past; by its end the only direction he knew was uneasily forward.

(*) **The President: Volume 1** Jazz View 029 CD
Young; Jerry Elliott, Ted Kelly (*tb*); Freddie Jefferson, John Lewis, Junior Mance (*p*); Ted Briscoe, Gene Ramey (*b*); Roy Haynes, Jo Jones (*d*). 12/48, 4/49, 1, 2 & 3/51.

(*) **The President: Volume 2** Jazz View 030 CD
Young; Jesse Drakes (*t*); Earl Knight, John Lewis (*p*); Aaron Bell, Gene Ramey (*b*); Joe Harris, Joe Jones (*d*). 1, 5 & 8/51.

More evidence for the broken reed interpretation of Young's post-war work from a limited edition Italian label with an ambitious advance catalogue and little obvious discrimination. Mostly airshots, but with two earlier tunes from the Royal Roost in 1948/9, these are tired and inconsequential performances and only Lewis (apparently playing inside a lagged water tank) does anything interesting. In five versions of 'Up And At 'Em', three of 'Lester Leaps In', Pres seems to be going through the motions only.

There are, apparently, four more volumes to come. An unexciting prospect even with the fillip of built-in scarcity value.

SNOOKY YOUNG (born 1919)
TRUMPET

***(*)   **Snooky & Marshal's Album** Concord CCD 4055 CD
Young; Marshall Royal (*as*); Ross Tompkins (*p*); Freddie Green (*g*); Ray Brown (*b*); Louie Bellson (*d*); Scatman Crothers (*v*).

Though much in demand as a high-note man (a duty he performed for Basie, Benny Carter, Gerald Wilson and countless others), Young has made disappointingly little under his own name. Allied with saxophonist Royal, he sounds a little more thoughtful and measured, negotiating 'I Let A Song Go Out Of My Heart' with a gruff tenderness, but really stretching for the distinctive upper-register crackle only on the blues themes. The rhythm section is superb (Freddie Green's understated artistry deserves close examination), and Scatman Crothers, who played an effective role in Stanley Kubrick's skin-creeper, *The Shining*, creates much the same effect with his vocals. Beautifully recorded and balanced (though Royal isn't favoured in the ensembles), this is well worth a shot.

YOUNG TUXEDO BRASS BAND
GROUP

***(*)   **Jazz Continues** 504 LPS 10 LP
John 'Kid' Simmons (*t*); Joshua 'Little Jack' Willis (*c, mel*); Gregory Stafford (*c*); Clement Tervalon, Lester Caliste Jr (*tb*); Michael White (*cl*); Herman Sherman (*as*); Joseph Torregano (*ts*); Walter Payton Jr (*sou*); Charles Barbarin, Lawrence Trotter (*d*). 8/83.

Although the band has been a New Orleans fixture for many years, this was only the second record the Young Tuxedos had ever made (the first, cut for Atlantic in 1958, was called *Jazz Begins*). While the question of New Orleans 'authenticity' is a quarrelsome one, this music is about as close to the feel of a New Orleans marching band as one can find on record, and it runs the expected gamut of slow funeral pieces to the homeward-bound swagger which turns up in most of the items on side two. 'Just A Closer Walk With Thee' can never have been played at such a slow tempo as it is here and, although the ensembles and solos are just a shade tidier than they were in the 1958 edition of the band, the impression still lingers that they sometimes seek out wrong notes and tunings. The ragged flair of 'Tiger Rag' and 'Down In Honky Tonk Town', though, is unanswerable. The misdemeanours which trad musicians have visited on this kind of music make it hard to treat a 'genuine' article without scepticism, and the younger musicians here – including Michael White, whose subsequent records certainly reveal a sophisticated mind at work – may simply be guarding tradition with artifice, but in the end it's a spirited and uplifting set. Plain but truthful recording.

YOUR NEIGHBOURHOOD SAXOPHONE QUARTET
GROUP

(*)   **Boogie Stop Shuffle Coppens CCD 3004 CD
Allan Chase (*as, ss*); Bob Zung (*as*); Tom Hall (*ts*); Steve Adams (*bs*). 5/89.

**   **Plutonian Nights: The Music Of Sun Ra** Coppens CCD 3006 CD
As above, except Joel Springer (*ts*) replaces Hall. 90.

One of the less resolved saxophone foursomes on the scene at present, the YNSQ haven't yet solved the problem of how to give individual voices definition without losing the rapid-fire, collective transitions that are the rationale of such units. *Boogie Stop Shuffle* has an appealing rawness, best sampled on ''Da Fuk' and the hectic 'S.O.S.' (look out for the band and album of that name for *sophisticated* saxophone interplay). The Sun Ra tribute deserves a couple of stars for sheer bravado, but it really doesn't come off, sounding bland where the Man from Saturn sounds genuinely displaced, like a high-school marching band to the Arkestra's serious swing.

ATTILO ZANCHI
BASS

**   **Early Spring** Splasc(h) H 129 LP
         Zanchi; Paolo Fresu (*t, flhn*); Tino Tracanna (*ss*); Michele Bozza (*ts*); Ferdinando Arno (*ky*); Stefano Battaglia, Roberto Cipelli, Franco D'Andrea (*p*); Pierluigi Ferrari, Augusto Mancinelli (*g*); Gianpiero Prina, Ettore Fioravanti, Tiziano Tononi (*d*); Luis Agudo (*perc*). 3/86–3/87.

(*)   **Cats Splasc(h) H 164 LP
         Zanchi; Riccardo Lupi (*ss, ts, f, af*); Massimo Colombo (*ky*); Christian Meyer (*d*). 6–7/86.

Despite the formidable talents involved, this young bassist's debut for Splasc(h) fails to cohere as a record. Its constantly changing cast of players and search for something that sticks add up to a record of good moments and thin results. On *Cats*, a sound post-bop recital, Zanchi shows a fine, clean attack but an anonymous tone which leaves his solos – much more generously featured than on *Early Spring* – as interruptions in what's otherwise a promising session. Luppi seems to be there for instrumental colour – he prefers not to lead from the front – and his flute is a nice touch on the boisterous 'She Looks'. The writing is useful rather than outstanding, but the rhythm section cooks on some of the quicker tempos and Colombo turns out to be the best improviser on the date.

JOE ZAWINUL (born 1932)
PIANO

(*)   **The Beginning Fresh Sound FSR CD 142 CD
         Zawinul; George Tucker (*b*); Frankie Dunlop (*d*); Ray Barretto (*perc*). 9/59.

Many fans – and particularly those who associate him exclusively with Weather Report – will be largely unaware of Zawinul's career before he joined Miles Davis and gave the trumpeter 'In A Silent Way'. Some may know his *Soulmates* collaboration with Ben Webster (Original Jazz Classics OJC 109 LP) and the sharper-eyed may even have spotted his thinning pate in one of the less nerve-wracking scenes of the Clint Eastwood movie, *Play Misty For Me*, backing Cannonball Adderley, for whom he wrote 'Mercy, Mercy, Mercy'.

Zawinul came to the United States in January 1959 and was quickly recruited by Maynard Ferguson. The trio recordings on *The Beginning* give away little about what distinguished the young Austrian. He isn't a wildly exciting standards player, there are no original pieces, and the recording is a bit wooden. He has a disconcerting but also a curiously effective habit of softening his articulation on downward progressions; it works wonderfully on 'Love For Sale', less so on the closing 'Sweet And Lovely'. An unaccompanied 'Greensleeves' underlines his long-standing affection for simple, diatonic folk-melodies.

Listeners (particularly those who also know the disappointing post-Weather Report projects) will conclude that the band focused Zawinul's undoubted talents much better than anything else in his career.

MONICA ZETTERLUND (born 1938)
VOCAL

***	**Spring Is Here** Dragon DRLP 171 LP
Zetterlund; Benny Bailey, Donald Byrd, Bengt-Arne Wallin, Gösta Nilsson, Bernth
Gustavsson, Weine Renliden, Sixten Eriksson, Arnold Johansson, Jan Allan (*t*); Åke
Persson, Andreas Skjold, Kurt Järnberg, Gunnar Medberg, Folke Rabe (*tb*); Åke
Börkman (*frhn*); Arne Domnérus (*as*); Yngve Sandström (*af*); Bjarne Nerem, Rolf
Blomqvist, Lennart Jansson, Johnny Ekh, Georg Björklund, Harry Bäcklund, Rolf
Bilberg (*ts*); Lars Gullin, Rune Falk (*bs*); Bengt Hallberg, Gunnar Svensson (*p*); Lars
Bagge (*p, bsn*); Tage Lundgren, Åke Johansson, Karl Nilheim, Axel Herjö (*vn*); Claes
Lindroth, Georg Riedel, Lars Pettersson, Gunnar Almstedt (*b*); William Schiöppfe,
Joe Harris, Sture Kallin, Egil Johansen, Jack Noren (*d*). 6/58–6/60.

If Astrud Gilberto strikes a responsive (if not entirely responsible) note, then Monica
Zetterlund should surely do the same. She was barely out of her teens when she made these
tracks, compiled from various Swedish releases into a definitive look at her career at that point;
but her voice already sounds mature and fearless, even though her accent colours almost every
line. That, as with Gilberto, is part of the charm, especially on a tune such as 'I Want To Be His
Girl', which comes out as 'hees girl'. Zetterlund doesn't swing much and she tends to read off
lyrics, and still the music evokes an artless, sensitive understanding of the material in broad
strokes rather than word-by-word delivery. Essentially, she's a cool stylist, though, coming from
Hagfors, it's hard to see how she could be anything else. A bonus throughout is the witty and
economical arranging, mostly by Gunnar Svensson but also including a couple of thoughtful
scores by Lars Gullin, and there is plenty of space for fills by Domnérus, Persson and Gullin,
although the surprise appearances by Donald Byrd and Benny Bailey are pretty fine too. Easy
jazz listening that betters many an American record of the same style and period. The
remastering for this 1988 reissue has been excellently done and we hope a CD will be made
available in due course.

ATTILA ZOLLER (born 1927)
GUITAR, BASS

***	**Conjunction** Enja 3051 LP
Zoller (*g* solo). 10/79.

Like many quiet and understated players, Zoller has rarely received his fair share of critical
attention. Among fellow players, though, his stock remains very high. Recognized as a fine,
romantic accompanist, he is also highly regarded as a solo player and small-group leader.
Recorded direct-to-disc, *Conjunction* gives a clear, if occasionally over-bright, account of his
soft, sweeping lines, gentle harmonic runs, and occasional unexpected riff-like figures. The
title-piece is reminiscent in structure of some of McCoy Tyner's compositions.

****	**Zo-Ko-So** MPS 843107 CD
Zoller; Hans Koller (*ts*); Martial Solal (*p*). 1/65.

Released as part of a re-examination of Solal's scattered output and including impressive solo
performances by all three men (Zoller does little more than comp along gently to Koller on 'All
The Things You Are'). Zoller's solo 'After Glow' is finely wrought but much less interesting
than the dazzling contrapuntal lines of 'Stella By Starlight', in duet with Solal. 'Mr Heine's
Blues' and 'H.J. Meets M.A.H.' are trio performances, fleet and brimming with musical
intelligence.

***	**Dream Bells** Enja 2078 LP
Zoller; Frank Luther (*g*); Sonny Brown (*d*). 5/76.

***(*)	**Common Cause** Enja 3043 LP
Zoller; Ron Carter (*b*); Joe Chambers (*d*). 5/79.

***(*)	**The K & K In New York** L + R 40009 LP
Zoller; Hans Koller (*ts, sno*); George Mraz (*b*). 6/79.

Zoller sounds slightly overpowered by a drummer and the two Enjas compare unfavourably with the elegant counterpoint of a 1979 reunion with Koller (who tries out a reflective sopranino saxophone in addition to his smooth tenor). Mraz's melodic lines are featured on a fine duet, 'The Clown Down And Upstairs', with Koller, who rather steals the album. Carter and Chambers are probably too dynamically up-front for this kind of music, but the bassist is excellent on 'Lady Love', and 'Meet' brings rather scattered elements together for an impressive curtain.

***   **Jim And I** L + R 40006 LP
     Zoller; Jimmy Raney (g). 6/79.

***(*) **Jim And I – Live In Frankfurt** L + R 40013 LP
     As above. 10/80.

Marvellous, original guitar duos by exact contemporaries who fit together seamlessly. Bold to tackle this kind of performance without a bag of standards tucked under the chair, but they press ahead with some strikingly inventive themes – 'The Gallery', 'Two Beats Circa 1980' and, on *Live In Frankfurt*, 'A Common Nightmare'. The live sound is rather better than on the original record.

****   **Memories Of Pannonia** Enja 5027 LP
     Zoller; Michael Formanek (b); Daniel Humair (d). 6/86.

***(*) **Overcome** Enja 5063 LP
     As above, except add Kirk Lightsey (p). & 11/86.

The trio album is one of Zoller's best, graced with a lovely reading of 'Sophisticated Lady', which catches his restrained lyricism perfectly. *Overcome* is a fine if unusually conventional quartet date, with Lightsey in excellent form. A duo record would be more than welcome.

JOHN ZORN (born 1954)
ALTO SAXOPHONE, DUCK CALLS

***(*) **Cobra** hat Art CD 2034 CD
     Zorn; Jim Staley (tb); Carol Emanuel, Zeena Parkins (hp); Bill Frisell (g); Elliott Sharp (g, b); Arto Lindsay (g, v); Anthony Coleman, Wayne Horvitz (p, ky); David Weinstein (ky); David Klucevsek (acc); Bob James (tapes); Christian Marclay (turntables); J. A. Deane (tb synthesizer, elec); Bobby Previte (perc). 10/85, 5/86.

Listening to John Zorn is like flicking through a stack of comic books or watching endless Hanna–Barbera and Fred Quimby re-runs on a TV set whose brightness and contrast have been jacked up to migraine level. Zorn is not the first but is certainly the most thorough and considered post-modernist thrown up by jazz, and there's a certain appropriateness to his alphabetical position. More than any other individual musician, he appears to mark the point of transition between a period of high-value technical virtuosity and a new synthesis of art that does not presume to raise itself above the throwaway, five-minute, all-tastes-are-equal, recyclable culture. He is, when he chooses to be, a fine boppish saxophonist, using duck calls as ironic punctuations, much in the way that Rahsaan Roland Kirk, another underrated player and expert surrealist, used to end solos with raucous siren blasts. It's not surprising to find Zorn turning, as he does in *Spy Vs Spy*, below, to the music of Ornette Coleman, whose reconstitution of melody in jazz is probably the most significant technical advance since the advent of bebop. However, Zorn's fundamental premisses are in many regards the opposite of Coleman's. Insofar as he belongs to any creative tendency, Zorn is a 'free' player whose hectic collage-ism is only a populist version of the invent-your-own-language gestures of the free movement. An aficionado of game systems (and of other, more traditional aspects of Japanese culture and art: two-dimensionality, false persective, simultaneity, violence-as-aeçthetics), Zorn has frequently drawn on games and sports. Earlier works such as *Archery* (Parachute), *The Classic Guide To Strategy* (Lumina) and the marvellous *Yankees* (a Celluloid release with Derek Bailey and George Lewis; the instrumentation has been revived in the Lulu project, below) drew heavily on game-theory as a matrix for 'free' (ah, but no longer abjectly free) improvisation. The remarkable *Cobra* is perhaps the most developed example of this strand in Zorn's work and, with Butch Morris's 'conduction' (Zorn played on Morris's *Current Trends In Racism In*

Modern America, sound aspects sas CD 4010 CD), is perhaps the most radical recent attempt to restructure improvisation without imposing structures on it.

Cobra was inspired by the war-game of that name, and the title carries a suggestion of unpredictabiliy which suits Zorn's purpose (it may also suggest the snake-charming illusion by which he conjures players up out of a pre-informational 'basket'). Zorn stands in relation to *Cobra* as a game-programmer, not as a composer. His only sleeve credit is as a 'prompter'. Though unfettered by a notated score, players respond to his hand-signals, as in Morris's work, interpreting them pretty much according to their own lights. The result is by no means inchoate. Zorn attaches Italian tempo markings – 'Allegro', 'Violento', 'Lento/Misterioso' – and quasi-generic names – 'Fantasia', 'Capriccio' – to each of the movements, giving them an ironic formality. The music is often serendipitously beautiful, but Zorn typically refuses to allow any dalliance on lyrical or promisingly rhythmic passages, constantly changing the on-screen image like a station-zapping teenager. The juxtaposition of two versions of the game-piece is perhaps a nudging comment on the fetishization of 'live' performance in both jazz and rock. The live sections (recorded first) tend to be longer, but no more structurally developed.

Though sharply alienating in impact, *Cobra* remains the best point of entry into Zorn's intriguing sound-world. The only element missing is the appealing squawk and bite of his saxophone.

***(*) **Locus Solus** Eva/Wave WWCX 2035 CD
Zorn; Wayne Horvitz (*ky*); Arto Lindsay (*g*); Anton Fier, Mark Miller, Ikue Mori (*d*); Christian Marclay (*turntables*); Whiz Kid (*scratching*); Peter Blegvad (*v*). 83.

Only very recently reissued on CD, this is one of the sacred texts of '80s New York improv, a fierce, scrabbly set of asociations that draw heavily on the power trio aesthetic of rock bands like Hüsker Dü. Zorn favours the short, sharp shock approach to improvisation, steering sessions that are remarkably reminiscent of Billy Jenkins 12 x 3 minute round 'Big Fights', but for the fact that one player is always refereeing and sometimes even normalizing the music. Noted out of chronological sequence here, *Locus Solus* is one of those records that, in one respect very much of its time, also seems to float freely without obvious stylistic or fashion anchors. It's impressively compact but sometimes rather too abrupt.

***** **The Big Gundown** Elektra Nonesuch/Ikon 979139 CD/LP
Zorn; Jim Staley (*tb, btb*); Tim Berne (*as*); Vicki Bodner (*ob, eng hn*); Bill Frisell, Fred Frith, Jody Harris, Robert Quine, Vernon Reid (*g*); Arto Lindsay, Anthony Coleman (*p, ky*); Wayne Horvitz (*p*); Big John Patton (*org*); Orvin Acquart (*hca*); Toots Thielemans (*hca, whistling*); Ned Rothenburg (*shakuhachi, etc.*); Michihiro Sato (*shamisen*); Guy Klucevsek (*acc*); Carol Emanuel (*hp*); Polly Bradfield (*vn*); Melvin Gibbs (*b*); Anton Fier (*d*); Mark Miller, Bobby Previte (*d, perc*); Ciro Batista, Reinaldo Fernandes, Duduca Fonseca, Claudio Silva, Jorge Silva (*perc*); David Weinstein (*elec*); Bob James (*tapes*); Christian Marclay (*turntables*); Laura Biscotto, Diamanda Galas, Shelley Hirsch (*v*). 9/84–9/85.

Utterly remarkable in every way and one of the essential records of the 1980s. Ennio Morricone's soundtrack scores – to movies by Pontecorvo, Lelouch, Bertolucci, Petri and, most memorably, Sergio Leone – are among the most significant artistic collaborations of recent times, a simultaneous confirmation and dismantling of the *auteur* myth. Zorn appears to have been influenced every bit as much by Leone's weird pans, sustained close-ups and frozen poses (where a fly or a melting harmonica note on the soundtrack might command more attention than the actor), followed by bouts of violence which are ritualized rather than choreographed (as they would be in a Peckinpah movie).

Zorn assembles musicians with his usual puppet-master care, bringing on harmonica player Toots Thielemans to whistle plangently on 'Poverty' from *Once Upon A Time In America*, organist Big John Patton to grind out the 'Erotico' line from *The Burglars*, Diamanda Galas and Vernon Reid to lash up a storm on 'Metamorfosi', a theme from Petri's *La Classe Operaia Va In Paradiso*. Zorn's political concerns are engaged to the extent of his determination to raise preterite music to the gates of heaven, thereby overcoming what he considers the 'racist' compartmentalization of high and low, black and white, formal and improvised styles on which the music industry depends.

The Big Gundown establishes the pattern for much of Zorn's subsequent music. It is very much a 'studio' record, an artefact, and Zorn himself has adduced the example of George Martin and the Beatles, or the earlier works of another enormous, alphabetically and stylistically late-coming influence, Frank Zappa. Like Zappa, Zorn appears to trash the very musics he seems to be setting up as icons. The result is ambivalent, unsettling and utterly contemporary.

****   **Spillane** Elektra Nonesuch 79172 CD/LP

      Zorn; Jim Staley (*tb*); Anthony Coleman, Wayne Horvitz (*p, ky*); Big John Patton (*org*); Dave Weinstein (*ky*); Carol Emanuel (*hp*); Albert Collins, Bill Frisell (*g*); Melvin Gibbs (*b*); David Hofstra (*b, tba*); Bob James (*tapes, CDs*); Ronald Shannon Jackson (*d*); Bobby Previte (*d, perc*); Christian Marclay (*turntables*); Kronos Quartet; David Harrington, John Sherba (*vn*); Hank Dutt (*vla*); Joan Jeanreanaud (*clo*); Ohta Hiromi (*v*). 8/86, 6 & 9/87.

Zorn's own liner-notes to *Spillane* offer immensely valuable insights into his work and philosophy: his interest in Carl Stalling, composer of Bugs Bunny and other cartoon soundtracks; his Japan obsession (reflected here in 'Forbidden Fruit' for voice and string quartet); his conceptual-collage, file-card approach to 'Spillane' itself; the need for longer durations to accommodate Albert Collins's blues lines on 'Two-Lane Highway'; his overall conviction that 'the era of the composer as autonomous musical mind has just about come to an end'.

For all their apparent serendipity, Zorn's groups are selected with very great care. He approaches instrumental coloration much as a graphic artist might use a 'paintbox' package on a computer graphics screen, trying possibilities consecutively or even simultaneously, but making his gestures in a very precise, hard-edged way. 'Spillane' is a sequence of tiny sound-bites, evocative not so much of Mickey Spillane's fictional world (in the sense of dim bars, lonely roads, chalked outlines on the pavement) as of his language, which is notably fragmentary, clipped and elided, poised between literalism and the purst self-reference. Zorn has pointed to the fact that Schoenberg's earliest atonal works were given unity only by use of texts, and it's clear that Zorn's imagery works in much the same way, with 'Mickey Spillane's voices soundtracking the music rather than vice versa.

'Two-Lane Highway' follows a more systematic and structured groove, a concerto for bluesman and improvising orchestra, with Collins's guitar, voice, mere *presence* taking the part of the solo instrument. The final part, 'Forbidden Fruit', is actually more conventional and is by far the dullest thing Zorn has done on record, reminiscent of Ennio Morricone's non-film, squeaky-door compositions.

****   **Spy Vs Spy** Elektra Musician 960844 CD

      Zorn; Tim Berne (*as*); Mark Dresser (*b*); Joey Baron, Michael Vatcher (*d*).

In some respects a more straightforward tribute than the Morricone set, Zorn's take on the music of Ornette Coleman is a headlong, hardcore thrash that approaches levels of sheer intensity never attempted by Coleman's own Prime Time band. Only one of the first dozen tracks is over three minutes in length. 'Chronology', from Coleman's classic Atlantic album, *The Shape Of Jazz To Come*, lasts exactly 68 seconds, and half a dozen others, drawn from Coleman's output between 1958 and the 1980s, occupy no more than 15 minutes between them. It is these, rather than the more measured performances, which seem most faithful to the originals. The twinned altos, sharply separated by channel, scribble all over the white-noise drumming, brutal sgraffito effects which almost miraculously preserve Coleman's melodic outlines.

***(*)   **News For Lulu** hat Art CD 6005 CD

****   **More News For Lulu** hat Art CD 6055 CD

      Zorn; George Lewis (*tb*); Bill Frisell (*g*). 8/87, 1/89.

Named after a composition by Sonny Clark, a reviving reputation among bop piano players, *News For Lulu* and its live sequel offer the best-recorded instances of Zorn as bop saxophonist. (Zorn has also fronted a 'Sonny Clark Memorial Quintet', recording the pianist's compositions on an excellent Black Saint album, *Voodoo* [BSR 1019 CD/LP], which is not currently in the catalogue.) Lewis is the ideal partner, poised midway between total freedom and a more structured melodic/harmonic approach. Frisell takes a relatively modest role, painting backgrounds rather than the foreground figures but keeping his more extravagant washes and treatments in reserve for Zorn's thrash-core Naked City project, below. There are versions of Kenny Dorham's 'K.D.'s Motion', 'Lotus Blossom' and 'Windmill', Hank Mobley's 'Funk In Deep Freeze' and the title-piece on both; two studio cuts of Clark's 'Blue Minor' are supplemented by two more, better still, from the Paris concert.

More also features material by Freddie Redd, also the focus of some revisionist attention, and an original piece by Misha Mengelberg. The live sound is a bit flat and unresponsive, but the performances are a shade more vivid; read what you will into that.

***   **Naked City** Elektra Musician 79238 LP

***(*)   **Torture Garden** Earache Mosh 28 LP
Zorn; Wayne Horvitz (*ky*); Bill Frisell (*g*); Fred Frith (*g, b*); Joey Baron (*d*); Yamatsuka Eye (*v*). 89, 89–90.

A million stories in the naked city, and you might feel you've heard two-thirds of them in the average Naked City performance. The sequence of tracks on *Torture Garden* is almost absurdly kaleidoscopic, some of them mere blips of frantic noise, samples of noise coming in through the window of a cruising car. Items like 'Fuck The Facts' and 'Igneous Ejaculation' are repeated; but, for the most part, these sets sound like a random shuffle of Zorn's tastes and obsessions, with snippets of Ornette Coleman ('Lonely Woman'), cop-show funk, snuff-movie aggression, and homier TV and cartoon references like 'Batman' and 'Snagglepuss' (all *Naked City*) thrown in alongside more measured polemical statements like 'Jazz Snob Eat Shit' and the Japanese S/M soundtracks on *Torture Garden*.

****   **Filmworks: 1986–1990** Elektra Nonesuch 979270 CD
Zorn; Jim Staley (*tb*); Tom Varner (*frhn*); Vicki Bodner (*ob*); Marty Ehrlich (*ts, cl*); Ned Rothenberg (*bcl*); Bill Frisell, Robert Quine (*g*); Arto Lindsay (*g, v*); Anthony Coleman, Wayne Horvitz, David Weinstein (*ky*); Carol Emanuel (*hp*); Mark Dresser, Fred Frith, Melvin Gibbs, David Hofstra (*b*); Anton Fier (*d*); Robert Previte (*d, mar, perc, v*); Cyro Baptista, Nana Vasconcelos (*perc*); David Shea (*turntables, v*); Shelley Hirsch (*v*). 6/86–5/90.

Much to his disappointment, Hollywood didn't a beat a path to Zorn's door after the Spillane and Morricone tributes. Independent movie-maker Rob Schwebber did, however, commission a soundtrack for his short *White And Lazy* and Zorn put together a name band of downtown eclectics capable of the jump-cut style-switching that Zorn demands. The same sort of thing goes on a score for Raul Ruiz's *The Golden Boat*. This is a more developed sequence of stylistic bites, with Zorn's saxophone on 'Jazz I' sounding uncannily like Ornette Coleman for a few bars, more rockabilly, a touch of 'Horror Organ' and some Bernard Hermann harmonies. *She Must Be Seeing Things*, by Sheila McLaughlin, is a story of lesbian love and jealousy and Zorn's music, scored for saxophones, horns and keyboards, has a threatening, polymorphous quality that fits the movie's emotional temper very well. The long 'Seduction' is an extraordinary mood-swing blues, by far the most coherent thing Zorn has done in this idiom. There's one additional track. 'The Good, The Bad and The Ugly' was a try-out for a Camel cigarettes campaign for South East Asia (!). Zorn's submission, a typical cut-up, was close, but no cigar. So to speak.

Lighter and less compelling than the earlier film materials, this is a thoroughly entertaining and often provocative insight into the working methods of perhaps the most distinctive 'composer' (if he'd accept the term) in jazz music today. It's also beautifully recorded, with a big rock mix that demands to be turned up higher and higher.

AXEL ZWINGENBERGER
PIANO

***   **Boogie Woogie Live** Vagabond VR 8.85007 CD/LP
Zwingenberger (*p* solo).

(*)   **Boogie Woogie Jubilee Vagabond VR 8.81010 CD/2LP
Zwingenberger; Big Joe Turner (*v*); other personnel unknown. 81.

***(*) **Axel Zwingenberger & The Friends Of Boogie Woogie: Volume 6** Vagabond VR
8.85005 CD/LP
Zwingenberger; Joe Newman (*t*); Lloyd Glenn (*p*); Torsten Zwingenberger (*d*); Big
Joe Turner (*v*). 5/81, 1/82.

***(*) **The Boogie Woogie Album** Vagabond VR 8.88008 CD/LP
Zwingenberger; Lionel Hampton (*vib*); Barry Reis, Johnny Walker (*t*); Tom Chapin,
Yoshi Malta (*as*); Arnett Cobb, Ricky Ford, Illinois Jacquet, George Kelly (*ts*); Ralph
Hamperian, Arvell Shaw (*b*); Panama Francis (*d*); other personnel unknown. 1/82.

*** **Boogie Woogie Bros** Vagabond VR 8.89015 CD/LP
Zwingenberger; Torsten Zwingenberger (*d*). 2/88.

*** **Axel Zwingenberger & The Friends Of Boogie Woogie: Volume 6** Vagabond VR
8.90016 CD/LP
Zwingenberger; Torsten Zwingenberger (*d*); Champion Jack Dupree (*v*). 2/88.

Good-natured nonsense from a dedicated revivalist with a solo technique that would sit
comfortably alongside all the great boogie-woogie players. Zwingenberger has something of
Pinetop Smith's ability to vary 'the sixteens' in the bass, and his right-hand figures, which seem
to combine Smith with Meade Lux Lewis, are impressively modulated. His concentration of
energy is genuinely impressive and the music a great deal more varied than might ever have
been expected. The sessions with Newman and the rejuvenated Hampton are predictably the
best, but the duos with brother Torsten are rousing (try the splendidly entitled 'Two Eels
Walking On An Icecake'); only the vocal sides (there's also another Champion Jack Dupree
album, *Champ's Housewarming*, VR 8.88014 CD/LP) tend to pall rather quickly. The
recordings are excellent. It helps having a label all to yourself.

VARIOUS ARTISTS

In our view, compilation albums merit only a small significance, except in those cases where the
artists in question can't muster an album's worth of material by themselves. Far too many
indifferent various-artists albums clutter up jazz record ranks, many of them designed around
some dubious concept rather than as an hour or so of thematically linked music. Nor do we
subscribe to the view that various-artists albums are good introductions for newcomers to jazz.
An excellent Duke Ellington or Miles Davis or Louis Armstrong record is a far more satisfying
way in to the music.

  With this in mind, we have eschewed any attempt at comprehensiveness and have chosen for
this section only a very small number of records which we consider are worth discussing.

1920s: HOT DANCE

***(*) **Hot Coffee** Saville CDSVL 217 CD
Featuring: Savoy Orpheans, Jay Whidden, Debroy Somers, Piccadilly Revels Band,
Jack Hylton's Rhythmagicians, Jack Payne, Billy Cotton, New Mayfair Dance
Orchestra, Arcadians Dance Orchestra, Marius B. Winter, Ambrose, Ray Noble,
Geraldo. 7/25–9/38.

One of the most important ways that jazz was disseminated in Britain prior to 1940 was through
its enormously popular dance-band community: many of the musicians were avid jazz followers
and, while few of the bandleaders were similarly enlightened, there are countless examples of
dance records enlivened by a 16-bar improvisation by one of its instrumentalists. Occasionally
the leaders would go out on a limb and give their men the chance to make *bona fide* jazz titles,
and some of those are collected here, along with more straightforward examples of
jazz-inflected dance tunes. Among the outstanding pieces are Hylton's 'Grieving For You',
where a contingent from his band performed an arrangement modelled on Red Nichols's Five
Pennies; two surprisingly tough and modern-sounding titles by the 1927 Piccadilly Revels Band;
Jack Payne's 'Hot And Heavy', and the Arcadians Dance Orchestra's ''Leven Thirty Saturday
Night'. But just as intriguing are the normally polite Debroy Somers' band running through
'Brainstorm' and Marius B. Winter taking a shot at Frankie Trumbauer's 'Choo Choo'. A
fascinating release, and the original records – many of them very rare, which may say something

about how popular hot dance was before the war – have been faithfully remastered, if the sound is occasionally less vibrant than it might be.

** **Midway Special** Fountain DFJ-115 2LP
Tommy Gott (*t*); Murphy Steinberg, Frankie Quartell, Carl Rinker, Edward Gerbrecht (*c*); Jesse Barnes, Miff Mole, Pete Beilman, Santo Pecora (*tb*); Phil Wing, Art Kassel, Charlie Bezimek (*cl, as, ts*); Goof Moyer, Roy Kramer (*cl, as*); Jerry Richel (*cl*); Elmer Schoebel, Art Kahn, Clark Whipple, Arthur Schutt, Bob Zurke, Al Siegel, Mel Stitzel, Louis Klatt (*p*); Lou Black, Earle Roberts, Jules Bauduc (*bj*); Steve Brown (*bb*); Frank Snyder, Vic Berton, David Grupp, Bobby de Lys, Dick Dickson (*d*); Billy Meyers, Arthur Hall (*v*). 4/23–6/25.

Conceived originally as a record devoted to tracks featuring cornetist Murphy Steinberg, this motley collection will probably appeal only to scholars of the early dance music of the 1920s: there is jazz interest on every track, but much of the playing fumbles towards any grasp of improvisation, the rhythm sections barely swing, and even the best arrangements are stock routines. Still, Steinberg himself emerges as an interesting if minor player, and the occasionally manic intensity which dance music of the day could work up does break through on some of the tracks. Miff Mole, on his three appearances, makes the rest of the musicians sound like shambling amateurs. Luckily there are only three vocals among the 31 tracks. Fine remastering from acoustic recordings.

**** **Hot British Dance Bands** Timeless/CBC 1-005 CD
Kit-Cat Band; Devonshire Restaurant Dance Band; Fred Elizalde and His Cambridge Undergraduates; Piccadilly Revels Band; The Rhythmic Eight; The Rhythm Maniacs; Jack Hylton and His Orchestra; Arcadians Dance Orchestra; Spike Hughes and His Orchestra; Jack Payne and His BBC Dance Orchestra; Billy Cotton and His Band; Jimmy Wornell's Hot Blue-Bottles; Roy Fox and His Band; Lew Stone and His Orchestra; Joe Loss and His Band; Ray Noble and His Orchestra; Madame Tussaud's Dance Orchestra; The Six Swingers; Brian Lawrence and the Quaglino Quartet; Bond Street Swingers; Harry Roy and His Band; Ambrose and His Orchestra. 25–37.

The first issue of *Melody Maker* in January 1926 included a brief caption-story on the Kit-Cat Band, and a review of the group's first record. 'Riverboat Shuffle' heads up this fine collection of early British jazz from the Dutch Timeless label; the arranger was saxophonist Al Starita, recently recruited from the famous Savoy Orpheans. What is revealing about *MM* editor Edgar Jackson's review is his reference to 'dirt', that is, 'hot' breaks and syncopations, being 'thrown in'. In 1925, hotel and restaurant dance groups would, depending on the tastes and tolerance of the bandleader, periodically include 'hot' numbers as a little spice to a diet of strict-tempo dance tunes. 'Jazz' was still regarded as an element that could be added to otherwise straight music rather than as an integral principle. A perfect example follows the Kit-Cats' excellent version of the Hoagy Carmichael hit (a reading aparently independent of Bix Beiderbecke's, made the previous year) in Bert Firman's Devonshire Restaurant Dance Band, whose leader was more than usually disposed to 'hot' numbers. The third item, 'Stomp Your Feet' by the Spanish-American Fred Elizalde with a group of Cambridge students, illustrates the ways in which British players were still somewhat dependent on transatlantic leads.

However, 'hot' music had taken hold in Britain remarkably quickly and the Musicians' Union had quickly moved to block the importation of American players for recording. Less than a decade after the Original Dixieland Jass Band's first transatlantic tour in 1919 there was a thriving jazz scene. Bandleaders like Billy Cotton, BBC Dance Orchestra director Jack Payne, and Jack Hylton all strongly favoured 'hot' music and accelerated its acceptance by combining professional arrangements, excellent sound, friendly vocals (like Cotton's on 'Bessie Couldn't Help It'). At the same time, assisted by the MU embargo, British players were becoming more prominent. Trumpeter Nat Gonella worked for both Cotton and Roy Fox, and Norman Payne (claimed by Brian Rust in a slightly breathless liner-note as 'the greatest jazz trumpeter this country ever produced') found a niche with Spike Hughes; the 1930 Hughes orchestra also included saxophonist Buddy Featherstonehaugh, another fine British player.

As a broad-based sample, the Timeless collection is hard to beat, though it might have been preferable to have two volumes, slightly fewer bands and two or three sides from each. The sound, though, is impeccable and very natural and Chris Barber's CBC series imprimatur is a guarantee of authenticity and good taste.

1920s: MISCELLANEOUS

***(*) New Orleans Chicago New York** BBC 3CD 821 3CD
Including: Jelly Roll Morton's Red Hot Peppers; King Oliver's Jazz Band; Johnny
Dodds Orchestra; Louis Armstrong Hot Seven; Freddie Keppard's Jazz Cardinals;
Celestin's Original Tuxedo Jazz Orchestra; New Orleans Owls; Louis Dumaine's
Jazzola Eight; New Orleans Rhythm Kings; Henry Allen's New York Orchestra; Jones
& Collins Astoria Hot Eight; Monk Hazel & His Bienville Roof Orchestra; New
Orleans Feetwarmers; Louis Armstrong & Earl Hines; Johnny Dodds Trio; Jelly Roll
Morton Trio; Original Dixieland Jazz Band; King Oliver's Dixie Syncopators; Carroll
Dickerson's Savoyagers; Richard M. Jones's Jazz Wizards; Frankie Trumbauer
Orchestra; McKenzie & Condon's Chicagoans; Carmichael's Collegians; Mound City
Blue Blowers; McKinney's Cotton Pickers; Reuben 'River' Reeves & His River Boys;
J. C. Cobb & His Grains Of Corn; Eddie South & His Orchestra; Benny Goodman;
Chicago Foot Warmers; State Street Ramblers; Ma Rainey; Omer Simeon Trio; Earl
Hines Orchestra; Pinetop Smith; Dixieland Jug Blowers; Fletcher Henderson
Orchestra; Bessie Smith; Paul Whiteman Orchestra; Miff Mole's Molers; Eddie
Condon's Footwarmers; Fats Waller & His Buddies; Duke Ellington Orchestra; Charlie
Johnson Orchestra; Luis Russell Orchestra; Fess Williams Royal Flush Orchestra;
Lloyd Scott's Orchestra; Casa Loma Orchestra; The Jungle Band; Cab Calloway
Orchestra; Jimmie Lunceford Orchestra; Clarence Williams's Washboard Five; Freddy
Jenkins & His Harlem Seven; Eddie Lang–Joe Venuti All Star Orchestra. 7/18–9/34.

No compilation of any feasible size could provide a comprehensive overview of jazz as it stood
between 1917 and the beginning of the swing era; but this three-CD set, the result of combining
three separate LPs which looked at each of the three cities of the title, comes remarkably close
to it, even if that wasn't compiler Robert Parker's intention. While the transfers aren't entirely
satisfactory – these were early days for Parker's digital realizations of original material and his
use of reverberation is sometimes a little overdone – the actual selections provide a fascinating
cross-section of the jazz of the period. The 'New Orleans' disc is a little misleading in that few
of the tracks were actually made in New Orleans, and those by Armstrong, Morton, Oliver,
Dodds and Allen reflect what was going on in Chicago and New York more truthfully. But the
Monk Hazel, Celestin, New Orleans Owls and Jones–Collins tracks are rare and welcome
reissues. The 'Chicago' material also includes Oliver, Morton and Armstrong (with Carroll
Dickerson), but there is also Richard M. Jones's 'African Hunch', Omer Simeon's 'Beau Koo
Jack', and the barrelhouse music of the State Street Ramblers and Junie Cobb, as well as
(somewhat incongruously) Ma Rainey and Pinetop Smith, representing the blues. 'New York'
stretches from Charlie Johnson's splendid 'Hot Bones And Rice' to Miff Mole's 'Imagination',
and looks forward as far as the 1934 'Stratosphere' by Jimmie Lunceford – a hotchpotch
collection, but also a necessary diversity. The strong point about this set, which runs to 60 tracks
in all, is its unassuming breadth: it suggests that we pay as much attention to an obscure piece
such as Lloyd Scott's 'Happy Hour' as to an acknowledged classic like Morton's 'Dr Jazz'.
Parker has also chosen comparatively unhackneyed pieces by some of the most renowned
leaders: Armstrong's Hot Seven are represented by 'Alligator Crawl', Luis Russell by 'Dr
Blues'. One could argue against some of the selections, but it's a very stimulating set overall,
and one which might be the best introduction to the music of the period.

*** **Kansas City 1926 To 1930** BBC REB/CD/ZCF 691 LP/CD/MC
Including: Bennie Moten's Kansas City Orchestra; Andy Kirk & His Twelve Clouds Of
Joy; Walter Page's Blue Devils; Hatttie North; George E. Lee Orchestra. 12/26–10/30.

Another American city, compiled and remastered by Robert Parker. Most of the records here
are by Moten or Kirk, and both are well represented: Moten's 'Band Box Shuffle' and 'New
Vine Street Blues' and Kirk's 'Corky Stomp' and 'Mary's Idea' must number among the
outstanding records by the bandleaders, and the Page, Lee and North tracks round off the
overview of a city only sketchily documented by the jazz of the period. One oddity is the
opening 'Rite Tite' by Moten – a steal from Frankie Trumbauer's 'Singing The Blues' right
down to Harlan Leonard imitating all of Trumbauer's glisses. Parker has done one of his best
remastering jobs: it's very full and clear sound.

***   **Harlem Jazz 1921–1931** Classic Jazz Masters CJM 1 LP
Including: Jimmie Johnson's Jazz Boys; Henderson's Dance Orchestra; Texas Blues
Destroyers; Metropolitan Dance Players; Katharine Henderson; Marvin Smolev's
Syncopators; Harlem Hot Chocolates; Harlem Hot Shots; Cab Calloway Orchestra.
21–31.

There's no special logic to this compilation, but it's a very entertaining overview of the different
styles of black jazz which were recorded in New York during the period. Fletcher Henderson
and Duke Ellington (Harlem Hot Chocolates) are represented by some obscure tracks, but of
more immediate interest are the 1921 track by James P. Johnson's Jazz Boys, running through
an early version of his 'Carolina Shout'; the little-known duets by Bubber Miley and organist
Arthur Ray, the 'Texas Blues Destroyers', stiff but already showing off Miley's growl style; and
the amazing, runaway set-piece, 'The Terror', by the otherwise forgotten Marvin Smolev group.
Excellent transfers from fine original 78s.

***   **Americans In Paris Vol. 1 1918–1935** EMI Pathé/Jazztime 251276-2 CD
Including: 158th US Infantry Band; Scrap Iron Jazzorinos Jazz Band; Mitchell's Jazz
Kings; Orchestra Syncopated Six; Orchestra Pollard's Six; Billy Arnold; The Southern
Serenaders; The Playboys; Lud Gluskin's Versatile Juniors; Lud Gluskin's Orchestra;
Jean Cocteau & L'Orchestre; Dan Parrish; Sam Wooding's Orchestra; Lud Gluskin Et
Son Jazz; Willie Lewis & His Entertainers. 12/18–4/35.

The jazz word was spread quickly through Europe by such American bands that visited the old
world in the 1910s and '20s, and this French compilation collects a surprising diversity of
material, from the puffing post-ragtime of the two military bands which open the disc to the
sophistications offered by Sam Wooding and Willie Lewis. The Playboys, with the fine, Red
Nichols-ish trumpet of Eddie Ritten, and the various Lud Gluskin groups offer smart hot-dance
music of the period, but the two tracks which have to be heard to be believed are those where
Jean Cocteau recites two poems to the clanking accompaniment of a band led by Dan Parrish.
Did Jack Kerouac ever hear them? Mostly excellent transfers from rare originals.

(*)   **Black Jazz In Europe 1926–1930 EMI Pathé/Jazztime 252714-2 CD
Including: The Plantation Orchestra; Sam Wooding & His Chocolate Kiddies; Noble
Sissle's Sizzling Syncopators; James Boucher Et Son Jazz. 12/26–12/30.

Although there are some heavyweight names here – including Tommy Ladnier, Arthur Briggs,
Pike Davis and Johnny Dunn in the trumpet sections – most of these bands play black
vaudeville rather than black jazz. Sissle's two orchestras are let down by corny material and the
leader's egregious vocals, although there are two barnstorming performances in 'Kansas City
Kitty' and 'Miranda' with the remarkable violinist, Juice Wilson. Boucher's solitary side has
little interest, The Plantation Orchestra leave little space for soloists, and the interest is
otherwise with Sam Wooding, who was a pioneer in bringing jazz to Europe. His 11 sides here
were made in Barcelona in 1929 – Wooding had already travelled as far as the Soviet Union –
and the best of them are his own tunes, 'Bull Foot Stomp' and 'Carrie', although several are
again let down by weak vocals and arrangements which strive too hard for effect. An issue
mainly of documentary interest, even though the transfers (from very rare originals) are
splendid.

***(*)   **The Jazz Age: New York In The Twenties** Bluebird ND 83136 CD
Red and Miff's Stompers: Red Nichols (*c*); Miff Mole (*tb*); Jack Hansen (*tba*); Jimmy
Dorsey (*cl, as*); Fud Livingston, Pee Wee Russell (*cl, ts*); Lennie Hayton, Arthur
Schutt (*p*); Carl Kress (*g*); Tony Colucci (*bj*); Vic Berton (*d*); collective personnel. 2
& 10/27.
Red Nichols and His Orchestra: Red Nichols, Leo McConville (*t*); Miff Mole (*tb*);
Dudley Fosdick (*mellophone*); Fud Livingston (*cl, ts*); Carl Kress (*g*); Chauncey
Morehouse (*d, vib, v*); 6/28.
Ben Pollack and His Orchestra: Al Harris, Jimmy McPartland, Frankie Quartell (*c*);
Glenn Miller (*tb*); Benny Goodman (*cl, as, c*); Larry Binyon, Gil Rodin (*reeds*); Vic
Breidis (*p*); Dick Morgan (*bj*); Harry Goodman (*bb*); Ben Pollack (*d, v*). 12/27.
Ben Pollack and His Californians: as above, but Bud Freeman (*ts*) replaces Binyon;
omit Quartell and add Al Beller, Ted Bergman (*vn*). 4/28.
Ben Pollack and His Park Central Orchestra: as above, but Ruby Weinstein (*t*)

replaces Harris; Jack Teagarden (*tb*) replaces Miller, Larry Binyon returns, and add
Bill Schuman (*clo*); Belle Mann (*v*). 10/28, 3/29.
Ben's Bad Boys: Jimmy McPartland (*c*); Glenn Miller (*tb*); Benny Goodman (*cl*); Vic
Breidis (*p*); Dick Morgan (*bj*); Harry Goodman (*b*); Ray Bauduc (*d*); Ben Pollack
(*v*).
1/29.
Napoleon's Emperors: Phil Napoleon (*t*); Tommy Dorsey 9tb); Jimmy Dorsey (*cl, as*);
Joe Venuti (*vn*); Frank Signorelli (*p*); Eddie Lang (*g*); Joe Tarto (*b, bb*); Stan King,
Ted Napoleon (*d*). 5/29.
Joe Venuti's Blue Four: Joe Venuti (*vn*); Eddie Lang (*g*); Frank Signorelli (*p*); Pete
Pumiglio (*cl, bs*). 10/30.

In the 1920s, jazz recordings were ruthlessly targeted on mass and 'race' markets, with styles of
playing sharply polarized between the 'hot' extravagance of the black bands and the tighter and
smoother musicianship required of their white counterparts. Certainly the seven cuts by various
Ben Pollack bands included on *The Jazz Age* do very little to confirm his reputation as a
powerful drummer and swinging leader. Despite its obvious historical significance on the cusp
of the swing era and with significant swing leaders such as Benny Goodman, Glenn Miller, Bud
Freeman, Jack Teagarden and Jimmy McPartland in the band at different stages, as well as less
luminous talents like Fud Livingston, its recorded output is extremely disappointing.

Comparison between Pollack's 1929 'My Kinda Love' compares poorly with Phil
Napoleon's. Napoleon (confounding his adapted, adoptive surname) was an unassuming and
kindly man not altogether cut out for the tough world of band-leading, and he functioned much
more successfully with his Dixieland-based small groups. Napoleon's very important Original
Memphis Five (not represented here) had included the young Miff Mole, and profoundly
influenced Red Nichols; unfortunately, the copy had little of the energy of the original (perhaps
due to the selfsame that constrained Pollack). Napoleon had once claimed to have shown Bix
Beiderbecke some of his best licks; Red and Miff open the set with a version of Bix's
'Davenport Blues' that is cool and precise, but scarcely compelling, a criticism which can also
be levelled at the neat chamber jazz of Venuti and Laing, who sound here like the palest
forerunner of the Quintet du Hot Club de France. At the end of the 1920s Venuti (about whom
there are salacious stories by the drawerful) settled into the Paul Whiteman Orchestra, which
seems like a fit conclusion to the era.

One values some of the solos, those by Teagarden and Goodman particularly, but also Fud
Livingston's on 'Feeling No Pain' and 'Harlem Twist'. And there is no escaping a sensation
that *The Jazz Age* captures a music in the process of (quiet, evolutionary) transition to a new
hegemony. The digital transfers are done on the NoNoise system and there are no complaints
on that score.

1930s: EARLY SWING

*** **The Territory Bands** Tax M-8009 LP
Including: Blanche Calloway & Her Band; Jeter-Pillars Club Plantation Orchestra; Bob
Pope & His Orchestra; Carolina Cotton Pickers Orchestra; Original Yellow Jackets;
Bobby Gordon & His Rhythm; J. H. Bragg & His Rhythm Five; Original St Louis
Crackerjacks. 2/35–8/37.

A delightful trawl through the unfamiliar currents of American jazz in the mid-1930s. The bands
represented here hail from Chicago, Birmingham, Los Angeles, San Antonio and even Hot
Springs, Arkansas, in the case of the splendidly virile Original Yellow Jackets. While most of
the musicians are obscure figures, there are a few better-known names present – Vic Dickenson
and Prince Robinson are in Blanche Calloway's band, and Cat Anderson makes his teenage
debut with the Carolina Cotton Pickers. What's perhaps surprising is how good most of these
tracks are: only Bob Pope's group and the Jeter-Pillars Orchestra offer rather straightforward
dance records. The two Calloway tracks go at a terrific pace, the anonymous Gordon and Bragg
bands create rough-and-ready good fun, and the St Louis Crackerjacks perform a couple of
intricate scores with feisty aplomb. Remastering for LP has been carefully and vividly brought
off.

1930S: SMALL GROUPS

***(*)   **Swing Is Here: Small Band Swing 1935–1939** Bluebird ND/NK/NL 82180 LP/CD/MC
Including: groups led by Mezz Mezzrow, Gene Krupa, Gene Gifford, Frankie Newton,
Wingy Manone. 5/35–9/39.

A valuable compilation of tracks made by various small ensembles, most of them featuring
musicians working on New York's 52nd Street in the mid-1930s. Four tracks under Gene
Krupa's leadership feature an amazing group including Roy Eldridge, Benny Goodman and
Chu Berry: 'Swing Is Here', an almost frantic charge, sets the keynote for the whole record.
Bunny Berigan shines on three tracks by a Gene Gifford group, and while the name of Mezz
Mezzrow normally does little to heighten expectations, the eight tracks he plays on are elevated
by a number of other soloists, including Frankie Newton, Willie 'The Lion' Smith and James P.
Johnson. Which leaves seven tracks by various Wingy Manone groups, with Berry, Buster
Bailey, Joe Marsala and others. While few of the 22 pieces here (only 16 on LP and cassette) are
on the highest level, the mix of professionalism and loose-knit jamming which goes to make up
the character of the music makes a refreshing alternative to the more formal big-band sessions
of the period. The remastering, using Bluebird's usual NoNOISE methods, is full-bodied if
rather dry.

****   **The Metronome All Star Bands** RCA Bluebird ND 87636 CD
Harry James, Bunny Berigan, Charlie Spivak, Sonny Dunham, Ziggy Elman, Cootie
Williams, Harry Edison, Pete Candoli, Neal Hefti, Sonny Berman, Rex Stewart, Dizzy
Gillespie, Miles Davis, Fats Navarro (*t*); Tommy Dorsey, Jack Teagarden, J. C.
Higginbotham, Will Bradley, Bill Harris, Kai Winding, J. J. Johnson (*tb*); Benny
Goodman, Buddy DeFranco (*cl*); Hymie Schertzer, Toots Mondello, Benny Carter,
Johnny Hodges, Herbie Fields, Charlie Parker (*as*); Eddie Miller, Arthur Rollini,
Coleman Hawkins, Tex Beneke, Flip Phillips, George Auld, Charlie Ventura (*ts*);
Harry Carney, Ernie Caceres (*bs*); Fats Waller, Bob Zurke, Count Basie, Teddy
Wilson, Lennie Tristano (*p*); Red Norvo (*vib*); Dick McDonough, Carmen Mastren,
Tiny Grimes, Billy Bauer (*g*); Bob Haggart, Artie Bernstein, Chubby Jackson, Eddie
Safranski (*b*); George Wettling, Ray Bauduc, Buddy Rich, Dave Tough, Shelly Manne
(*d*). 3/37–1/49.

Although the recordings here span a dozen years, and the last two sessions date from the 1940s,
most of the music is swing-based. There are only 10 78-r.p.m. sides, along with five alternative
takes, but it's a modest feast of playing from a personnel which is stellar in make-up, all the
players on the sessions chosen from reader polls in *Metronome* magazine. The earliest sessions
feature a quintet with Berigan, Dorsey and Waller and a big band playing 'Blue Lou' and 'The
Blues': the latter is priceless for the only meeting on record between Dorsey and Teagarden –
and wonderful they sound together, too. The 1941 session includes Elman, Williams and James
in the trumpet section, Goodman at his bristling best, and Basie leading the rhythm section; the
1946 date is swing's last gasp, with a band that sounds Ellingtonian (Duke and Strayhorn
conducted the second of the two tunes, 'Metronome All Out'); and the tremendous 1949
session has Parker and Tristano both in mercurial form and an extraordinary three-way chase
between Gillespie, Davis and Navarro. As *ad hoc* as these sessions were, there's nothing very
disorganized or uncommitted about the playing, and it's a very playable compilation. There's a
little harshness in the transfers here and there, but the sound is mostly good.

1930S: MISCELLANEOUS

****   **Americans In Paris Vol. 2 1931–1940** EMI Pathé/Jazztime 251277-2
Including: Josephine Baker; Coleman Hawkins; Michel Warlop's Orchestra; Willie
Lewis & His Entertainers; Bill Coleman; Benny Carter's Orchestra; Arthur Briggs &
His Swing Band. 6/31–2/40.

The jewels here are the sessions featuring Hawkins and Carter. Both men were on extended
sojourns to Europe and both were at the height of their powers. Carter's arrangements for
Willie Lewis are translucent in their texture and refinement, and his own playing – trumpet and
alto with Hawkins's All Star Jam Band, trumpet on a 1938 session of his own – creates small
masterpieces of poise and elegance. Hawk turns in ballad improvisations of rather offhand

calibre with Michel Warlop, but he burns everyone off in the Jam Band date, with a version of 'Crazy Rhythm' that for once lives up to its title. There are four tracks by Bill Coleman to make the purchase almost mandatory, and rounding off is a rare glimpse of trumpeter Arthur Briggs on a 1940 date with Django Reinhardt, who turns up on several other tracks too. Fine sound that isn't afraid of 78 crackle if it means clear transfers.

***(*) **Americans In Paris Vol. 4 1935–1939** EMI Pathé/Jazztime 252715-2 CD
Including: Garnet Clark & His Hot Club's Four; Joan Warner; Willie Lewis & His Entertainers; Fletcher Allen & His Orchestra; Rex Stewart's Feetwarmers; Frank 'Big Boy' Goudie's Orchestra. 11/35–5/39.

Compared to the other volumes in this superb series, this is more of a collector's record: aside from the magnificent Rex Stewart session, none of these are well-known tracks or groups. But Clark's band includes Bill Coleman and Django Reinhardt, and elsewhere Herman Chittison, Arthur Briggs and (pianist) Joe Turner crop up. Allen and Goudie were saxophonists who were heading up a couple of sessions of their own and, if the music isn't outstanding, it provides – in the case of Allen's group at least – evidence that local players could handle small-group swing without sounding like second-hand copyists. The Stewart session – with Barney Bigard, Reinhardt and Billy Taylor – is one of the great moments of its era, the five tunes apparently tossed off yet each sounding perfectly orchestrated and crackling with intent. These sides are now available on the Affinity *Finesse* Stewart collection; but, if anything, the sound here is superior.

1930S: BIG BANDS

*** **Swinging The Blues** ASV AJA 5088 CD
Including: Duke Ellington; Tommy Dorsey; Bennie Moten; Count Basie; Spike Hughes; Dorsey Bros Orchestra; Luis Russell; Woody Herman; Artie Shaw, Connie's Inn Orchestra; Benny Goodman; Fletcher Henderson; Bob Crosby; Don Redman; Fats Waller's Buddies; Bunny Berigan; Louis Armstrong; Jimmy Dorsey. 9/29–4/39.

The point of this compilation is to collect big bands playing the blues, although not all of them are 'true' blues, even where they have the word 'blues' in the title. The earliest tracks, by Russell and Waller, date from 1929, but most come from the mid-1930s, and it's a quite shrewdly made selection. Putting the tracks in chronological order would have made more sense – in the given order, Ellington's 'Bundle Of Blues' is followed by Dorsey's 'Tin Roof Blues' from 1938, before rushing back to Moten in 1930 – but listeners can programme their disc to their own taste. It's useful to find Shaw's 'The Blues', Redman's 'Hot And Anxious' and Berigan's 'Jelly Roll Blues' – to name three very fine but lesser-known pieces – on the same compilation, along with the acknowledged hits such as Basie's 'Swinging The Blues' and Herman's 'At The Woodchoppers' Ball'. The transfers are good, if not quite of the first order, and there is full documentation of the personnels, but the sleeve-notes are feeble.

1940S: JAM SESSIONS

**** **Jazz Live And Rare: The First And Second Esquire Concert** Jazzline 95810-14 5CD/LP
Esquire Metropolitan Opera House Jam Session: Louis Armstrong (*t, v*); Roy Eldridge (*t*); Jack Teagarden (*tb, v*); Barney Bigard (*cl*); Coleman Hawkins (*ts*); Art Tatum, Teddy Wilson (*p*); Red Norvo (*vib, xyl*); Lionel Hampton (*vib, d*); Al Casey (*g*); Oscar Pettiford (*b*); Big Sid Catlett (*d*); Mildred Bailey, Billie Holiday (*v*).
Louis Prima Gang: Prima (*t*); Julian Lane (*tb*); Irving Fazola (*cl*); Peter Landeman (*p*); Frank Frederico, Mary Osborne (*g*); Bunny Franks (*b*); Charlie Darke (*d*).
Louis Armstrong & the Foundation Six: Armstrong, Bunk Johnson (*t*); J. C. Higginbotham (*tb*); Sidney Bechet (*cl, ss*); James P. Johnson (*p*); Richard Alexis (*b*); Paul Barbarin (*d*).
James P. Johnson (*solo p*).
Benny Goodman Quintet: Goodman (*cl*); Red Norvo (*vib*); Teddy Wilson (*p*); Sid Weiss (*b*); Morey Fields (*d*); Mildred Bailey (*v*).
Duke Ellington & His Orchestra: Ellington (*p*); Rex Stewart (*co*); Ray Nance (*t, vn*);

Cat Anderson, Shelton Hemphill, Taft Jordan (*t*); Lawrence Brown (*tb*); Claude Jones, Joe Nanton (*tb*); Jimmy Hamilton (*cl, ts*); Otto Hardwicke, Johnny Hodges, Willie Smith (*as*); Al Sears (*ts*); Harry Carney (*bs, cl, b cl*); Fred Guy (*g*); Junior Raglin (*b*); Hillard Brown (*d*); Billie Holiday, Anita O'Day (*v*).
Art Tatum (solo *p*).
Duke Ellington Quartet: Ellington; Al Casey (*g*); Junior Raglin (*b*); Big Sid Catlett (*d*).
Esquire Three-Way Jam: as above, plus Louis Armstrong (*t*); Benny Goodman (*cl*); Billy Strayhorn (*p*); Art Tatum (*p*); Al Casey (*g*); Big Sid Catlett (*d*).
January 18 1944, January 17 1945.

During the 1930s, *Esquire* magazine established itself as a major supporter of jazz in the United States. Not without a measure of condescension, though; Louis Armstrong's biographer James Lincoln Collier refers to an appalling 1935 issue in which the trumpeter's life story is told in teeth-grating Uncle Remus style, sho'nuff. Between 1943 and 1947, Armstrong received six (the arithmetic isn't wrong) of *Esquire*'s poll awards; part of the prize was a slot at an annual command performance of poll winners at the Met in New York.

Jazzline's compilation of the two inaugural concerts is, let's say, of greater historical than musical significance. It is, though, of considerable historical significance, and there are some more than worthwhile performances. The CD sound booms a bit, and the vinyl is more than acceptable. James P. Johnson, one of the great piano players, is given centre stage for a strongly accented solo 'Arkansas Blues'; Tatum later plays 'The Man I Love' with a near-perfect mimicry of Billie Holiday's drawled delivery in the early measures. The Benny Goodman Quintet are less fazed by the setting than some others and turn in a fine selection, including a fine 'Air Mail Special'. The jams are chaotic, funny, awkward, bland, inspired, dull by turns; the 1944 all-in (which is all there is from that year) sounds a shade more authentic, but there is some fine individual playing in the Ellingtonian jam on 'Things Ain't What They Used To Be'.

Which brings us to Armstrong. Only two of his *Esquire* awards were for trumpet; the others were for singing and the two wartime concerts really mark his final transition from musician to entertainer, Artist to Personage. His trumpet playing is often little more than empty daredevilry, punching out top notes with little reference to the dynamics of the piece. In the opening jam, he's already threatened by Roy Eldridge's strong, sweet tone.

There's an interesting career footnote to the career of another trumpeter on the album. Louis Prima – mysteriously rebaptized 'Leon' in some sources – showed every sign of going Armstrong's way, starting out as a hot, pungent horn player, ending up (doubtless wealthier) singing 'I'm the King of the Swingers' on Disney's *Jungle Book*. The *Esquire* concerts played a significant role in establishing hot jazz, not just swing, as an entertainment music. Elsewhere, proto-boppers watched with narrowing eyes.

**(*)   Harlem Odyssey Xanadu 112 LP
Joe Guy, Charlie Teagarden (*t*); Jack Teagarden (*tb, v*); Tab Smith, Willie Smith, Floyd 'Horsecollar' Williams, Murray McEachern (*as*); Danny Polo (*cl*); Joe Thomas, Skippy Williams, Buddy Tate, Al Sears (*ts*); Thelonious Monk, Dave Bowman (*p*); Nick Fenton (*b*); Kenny Clarke (*d*); Billie Holiday (*v*) 40–41.

A strange miscellany, but the fascoinating things here are all on the second side, which finds Thelonious Monk feeling his way towards the authentic Monk's music on a bunch of jam-session tunes, all of them fronted by Joe Guy, who sounds rather better here than on the featured Xanadu listed under his own name. 'Rhythm Riff' (alias 'I Got Rhythm') and 'You're A Lucky Guy' are especially interesting, although the piano is often at sea in what is barely average sound (these are all transcriptions from acetates). The other tracks find Holiday in very good form on two songs, Tab Smith and Jack Teagarden doing familiar routines, and Tatum interrupted by Murray McEachern on 'All The Things You Are', all of them recorded after-hours in Harlem.

1940s: SWING AND BOP

****   **Esquire's All-American Hot Jazz Sessions** Bluebird ND/NK/NL 86757 CD/LP/MC
Louis Armstrong (*t*, *v*); Charlie Shavers, Neal Hefti, Max Kaminsky, Buck Clayton (*t*);
Jack Teagarden (*tb*, *v*); J. J. Johnson (*tb*); Jimmy Hamilton, Peanuts Hucko (*cl*);
Benny Carter, Pete Brown, Johnny Hodges (*as*); Coleman Hawkins, Lucky
Thompson, Clifton Stickland, Don Byas, Allen Eager (*ts*); Bob Lawson (*bs*); Duke
Ellington, Billy Strayhorn, Dodo Marmarosa, Jimmy Jones, Teddy Wilson, Gene
Schroeder (*p*); Red Norvo (*vib*); Remo Palmier, Barney Kessel, Mary Osborne, John
Collins (*g*); Chubby Jackson, Jack Lesberg, Al McKibbon, Red Callender (*b*); Sonny
Greer, Shadow Wilson, Dave Tough, Shelly Manne, Jackie Mills (*d*). 1/46–4/47.

A superb collection. Esquire's poll-winners were chosen by a panel of elected experts, and the
resulting bands created an intriguing cross-section of stylists. the first date includes Ellington
and Armstrong (on their first date together) with Byas, Hodges and Shavers; the second has
Wilson, Hawkins, J. J. Johnson and Clayton. Shrewdly organized by Leonard Feather, the
tracks rise above the simple jam-session, and there are moments when bop seems to be
beckoning. Elsewhere, there's a magnificent blues feature for Teagarden, 'Blues After Hours',
and two tracks ostensibly led by Hawkins but mainly featuring Pete Brown and the outstanding
Allan Eager. But the session starring Lucky Thompson, with a group including Carter,
Marmarosa and Kessel, tops everything: the tenorman's playing on 'Just One More Chance'
and the heroically delivered 'Boppin' The Blues' is gloriously abandoned. The transfers are
mostly very good.

1940S: SMALL GROUPS

***(*)   **Giants Of Small Band Swing: Volume 1** Original Jazz Classics OJC 1723 CD/LP
Billy Kyle's Big Eight: Kyle (*p*); Dick Vance (*t*); Trummy Young (*tb*); Buster Bailey
(*cl*); Lee Davis (*cl*); John Simmons (*b*); Buddy Rich (*d*).
Russell Procope's Big Six: Procope (*as*); Harold Baker (*t*); John Hardee (*ts*); Billy
Kyle (*p*); John Simmons (*b*); Denzil Best (*d*).
Sandy Williams's Big Eight: Williams (*tb*); Pee Wee Irwin (*t*); Tab Smith (*as*); Cecil
Scott (*ts*, *bs*); Jimmy Jones (*p*); Brick Fleagle (*g*); Sid Weiss (*b*); Denzil Best (*d*).
Dicky Wells's Big Seven: Wells (*tb*); George Treadwell (*t*); Bud Johnson (*ts*); Cecil
Scott (*bs*); Jimmy Jomnes (*p*); Al McKibbon (*b*); Jimmy Crawford (*d*).
Jimmy Jones's Big Four: Jones (*p*); Bud Johnson (*ts*); Al Hall (*g*); Denzil Best (*d*). 46

***(*)   **Giants Of Small Band Swing: Volume 2** Original Jazz Classics OJC 1724 CD/LP
Dicky Wells's Big Seven: as above.
Sandy Williams's Big Eight: as above; or Williams; Joe Thomas (*t*); Johnny Hodges
(*as*); Harry Carney (*bs*); Jimmy Jones (*p*); Brick Fleagle (*g*); Sid Weiss (*b*); Denzil
Best (*d*).
Joe Thomas's Big Six: Thomas (*t*); Lem Davis (*as*); Ted Nash (*ts*); Jimmy Jones (*p*);
Billy Taylor (*b*); Shelly Manne (*d*).
J. C. Higginbotham's Big Eight: Higginbotham ((*tb*); Sidney De Paris (*t*); Tab Smith
(*as*); Cecil Scott (*ts*); Jimmy Jones (*p*); Brick Fleagle (*g*); Billy Taylor (*b*); Dave
Tough (*d*).
Jimmy Jones's Big Four: as above. 45 & 46.

These are not the forces one normally associates with 'the Swing Era', when the big bands held
sway, and there has been a tendency to play down – even dismiss – the significance of
small-group swing. In part, this has been encouraged by the absence of regularly functioning
smaller units (the John Kirby Sextet and various internal fractions of the Benny Goodman
Orchestra were important exceptions) during the classic period of swing. The sessions above are
'late' works, recorded at a point when swing had virtually ceded the field to bebop and other
modernist tendencies. There was another important aspect to the dearth of smaller swing
groups. When they did come together, it was usually as a break from the routine and disciplines
of section playing and full-band rehearsal, and while some of the sessions feature powerful
blowing and robust accompaniments (there are marvellous passages by Harold Baker, Dicky
Wells and Joe Thomas, which on their own make the two volumes worthwhile), there is usually

little polish and finish to the arrangements, and the playing has a stiffness that, as Orrin Keepnews suggests in an intelligent and sceptical liner note, suggests section work.

Because the above sessions permutate a relatively restricted number of players (they were recorded for the HRS label and subsequently released on Riverside), it's impossible to judge how representative this work is of small-group swing as a whole. It's clear with hindsight that much of this music was a rearguard action against modernism. There is a tiredness about Kyle's 'Contemporary Blues' that leaves the title wide open to the obvious ironic rebuff. The Ellingtonians – Hodges, Carney, Procope, Baker – are generally more adventurous, but the emphasis is squarely on a light, swinging sound, with solo space doled out like slices of cake. Historically significant in an elegiac sort of way, and unquestionably enjoyable, these are worthwhile sides for anyone interested in the jazz of the period.

***(*) **Trumpet Time** Jazz Society AA 511 LP
Louis Armstrong (*t, v*); Yank Lawson, Billy Butterfield, Johnny Maxwell, Andy Ferretti, Bill Graham, Buck Clayton, Roy Eldridge, Charlie Shavers, Chris Griffin (*t*); Bobby Hackett (*c, t*); Jack Teagarden, Trummy Young (*tb, v*); Lou McGarity, Cutty Cutshall, Henry Wells, Vernon Brown, Bill Mustarde, Ward Silloway, Billy Rauch (*tb*); Peanuts Hucko, Ray Eckstrand, Hank D'Amico (*cl*); Bill Stegmeyer (*cl, as*); Ernie Caceres (*cl, bs*); Hymie Schertzer, Ed Brown (*as*); Nick Caiazza, Henry Ross, Al Sears, Don Byas, Boomie Richmond, Bud Freeman (*ts*); Johnny Guarnieri, Dave Bowman, Bill Rowland, Buddy Weed, Kenny Kersey, Arnold Ross (*p*); Herb Ellis, Carl Kress, Carmen Mastren, Allen Hanlon, Eddie Condon, Mike Bryan, Remo Palmieri (*g*); Al Hall, Bob Haggart, Trigger Alpert, Irv Manning, Felix Giobbe (*b*); Cozy Cole, Johnny Blowers, Ray McKinley, Morey Feld, Bunny Chalker, Buddy Rich, Specs Powell, Jimmy Crawford, George Wettling (*d*); Connie Boswell, The Paulette Sisters, Ella Fitzgerald (*v*). 12/44–10/45.

The starry line-ups among the 10 groups collected here were all recorded for V-Disc, for 'entertaining the troops' purposes, and, while some of this kind of material has been issued more comprehensively in the past, this LP includes many more obscure dates. It concentrates on trumpeters, though there are also plenty of fine moments for other players: Cutty Cutshall on 'Fidgety Feet', Bill Stegmeyer on 'Tea For Two'. But the main point is to hear some of the best horns of the era: Armstrong is in imperious command on two titles, Roy Eldridge is superb on two more, Bobby Hackett solos with poised vitality on 'Fidgety Feet'. Ella Fitzgerald turns up on two titles – though sound is less good on these – and Chris Griffin, a Goodman sideman, takes off Rex Stewart on 'Boy Meets Horn'. A very enjoyable jumble, mostly well mastered.

**** **Confirmation: The Tempo Jazzmen/The Hermanites** Spotlite SPJ 132 LP
Dizzy Gillespie, Sonny Berman (*t*); Bill Harris (*tb*); Lucky Thompson, Flip Phillips (*ts*); Serge Chaloff (*bs*); Ralph Burns, Al Haig (*p*); Chuck Wayne (*g*); Ray Brown, Artie Bernstein (*b*); Stan Levey, Don Lamond (*d*). 2–9/46.

An important collection of sessions recorded for Dial, at the cusp between swing and bebop. Swing is represented by a Woody Herman aggregation, including Berman, Harris, Phillips and Chaloff, all at something near their best; though the accent is on reflective rather than powerhouse music, it's deeply satisfying playing. Harris gets two versions of 'Somebody Loves Me' almost to himself, Chaloff – yet to reach his best form, admittedly – is impressive on two readings of 'Blue Serge' (alias 'Cherokee') and there's a surprisingly feelingful treatment of Burns's 'Nocturne'. The rest of the LP includes the complete session by the Tempo Jazzmen, the name used for the band Dizzy Gillespie took to the West Coast in 1945–6. Parker was missing, but Lucky Thompson fills in beautifully, and Gillespie is simply magnificent, rampant at fast tempos and finding something to say even on the throwaway novelty of 'When I Grow Too Old To Dream'. This isn't among the best-known documents of early bop, but for Gillespie alone it's essential. Indifferent sound – which shouldn't, however, deter listeners.

(***) **Charlie Parker And The Stars Of Modern Jazz At Carnegie Hall, Christmas 1949** Jass J-CD-16 CD
Miles Davis, Red Rodney (*t*); Benny Green, Kai Winding (*tb*); Charlie Parker, Sonny Stitt, Lee Konitz (*as*); Warne Marsh, Stan Getz (*ts*); Serge Chaloff (*bs*); Al Haig, Bud Powell, Lennie Tristano, Jimmy Jones (*p*); Curley Russell, Tommy Potter, Joe Shulman (*b*); Max Roach, Roy Haynes, Jeff Morton (*d*). 12/49.

If the sound-quality weren't so poor for so much of this disc, it would be a major document of jazz as it stood in 1949, captured at a Carnegie Hall concert on Christmas night, with groups led by Parker, Getz, Tristano and Powell, as well as two songs from Sarah Vaughan and a jam session with Davis, Stitt and Chaloff. Powell opens proceedings with a hell-for-leather 'All God's Children Got Rhythm', and the ensuing jam is an exciting meeting of styles. Getz sounds diffident and Vaughan is barely listenable, owing to the terrible sound, and the subtleties of the Tristano–Marsh–Konitz band are also swamped by the low-fi. But the five closing tracks by Parker's quintet are, luckily, in much better sound, and there's a tremendous 'Ko Ko' and a long 'Bird Of Paradise' and 'Now's The Time' with the leader in imperious mood, even if his tone sounds a little less forthright than usual. Leaving aside the low-quality items, it's still an important record.

1950S: CONCERTS / JAM SESSIONS

*** **International Jam Sessions** Xanadu 122 LP
Rolf Ericson, Clifford Brown, Jorgen Ryg (*t*); Charlie Parker, Phil Woods (*as*); Frank Socolow (*ts*); Cecil Payne (*bs*); Gosta Theselius, Jorgen Bengtson, Duke Jordan (*p*); Thore Jederby, Erik Moseholm, Wendell Marshall (*b*); Jack Noren, Art Taylor (*d*). 11/50–8/57.

An entertaining if not especially profound hotchpotch of material. The four tracks with Parker in Sweden are available on Spotlite as part of *Bird In Sweden*, so the main interest centres on a 10-minute jam in Copenhagen featuring Clifford Brown, who delivers two richly imaginative solos on 'Indiana'. Sound-quality is fairly terrible, but Brown's power endures. The second half is taken up with two long jams on 'Yardbird Suite' and 'Scrapple From The Apple' featuring Woods and Payne (who both play splendidly), Socolow and Jordan. The sound isn't perfect but it's far superior to the tracks in the first half.

***(*) **Lenox School Of Jazz Concert** Royal Jazz RJD 513 CD
Don Cherry–Ornette Coleman Quartet: Don Cherry (*t*); Ornette Coleman (*as*); Ken McGarity (*tb, btb*); Ron Brown or Steve Kuhn (*p*); Lary Ridley (*b*); Bary Greenspan (*d*).
Kenny Dorham (*t*); unknown quintet.
Herb Pomeroy Ensemble: Tony Greenwald, Herb Pomeroy (*t*); Herb Gardner (*tb*); Dave Baker (*btb*); Ornette Coleman, Lenny Popkin (*as*); Ian Underwood (*f, as*); Ted Carter (*ts*); unknown (*vib*); Dave McKay (*p*); John Keyser (*b*); Paul Cohen (*d*). Other group unidentified. 8/59.

Ornette Coleman was sponsored by Atlantic Records to attend the summer 1959 School of Jazz at Lenox, Massachusetts, home of the Berkshire Music Center which was later known simply as 'Tanglewood'. Coleman's ideas were in a ferment and after leaving Lenox he and Cherry launched the first 'free jazz' experiments in New York City, thereby setting in motion the main stylistic drama of the 1960s. The Lenox concert is primarily of historical importance and retains an odour of Third Stream pretensions that is not particularly appealing now. The Cherry–Coleman tracks (and that order seems justified and close to the true innovative hierarchy at the time) are powerfully constructed, particularly 'The Sphinx', and there are some fine things from the rather more formal Herb Pomeroy group. Dorham plays well on 'D.C. Special' but is very badly recorded. There are five additional tracks by an unidentified group who tackle Monk and George Russell material with slightly tentative aplomb. A fascinating set, but too shakily registered for some tastes.

NEW ORLEANS

** **726 St Peter, New Orleans LA 1955–1960** 504 LP35 LP
Willie Pajeaud, Punch Miller, Dee Dee Pierce (*t, v*); Kid Thomas Valentine (*t*); Louis Nelson, Eddie Morris (*tb*); Raymond Burke (*cl*); Ed Washington (*as*); Emanuel Paul (*ts*); Sam Chartres, Joe James, Billie Pierce, Isidore 'Tuts' Washington (*p*); Danny Barker, Charlie 'Little Red' Lajoie (*bj*); Burke Stevanson, Sylvester Handy, Joseph 'Kid Twat' Butler (*b*); Len Ferguson, Alec Bigard, Sammy Penn (*d*). 55–60.

For the most part, this will only appeal to the diehard New Orleans enthusiast. While the players here are distinguished names, recorded more or less informally at the Associated Artists Studio in the city, most of the tunes are loose and untogether treatments: Valentine's band sound relatively routine, Billie and Dee Dee Pierce make an indifferent impression on their tracks, and the two tunes by a rarely heard Willie pajeaud band are very poorly recorded (nothing here counts as hi-fi). But there are two pieces by the idiosyncratic trumpeter Punch Miller which are little short of marvellous: he is sometimes preposterously ambitious as a soloist, going for impossible trills and runs, and it makes the music exciting in a way the other tracks aren't.

1950S: SMALL GROUPS

*** **The Modern Art Of Jazz** Biograph BCD 120 CD
Art Farmer (*t*); Bob Brookmeyer (*vtb*); Julius Watkins (*frhn*); Gigi Gryce (*as*); Zoot Sims, Al Cohn, Herbie Mann (*ts*); Dick Katz, Hank Jones, John Williams (*p*); Mat Matthews (*acc*); Joe Puma (*g*); Oscar Pettiford, Milt Hinton (*b*); Charlie Smith, Gus Johnson, Kenny Clarke, Osie Johnson (*d*). 56.

14 tracks made at various sessions for the Dawn label, all dating from 1956, with the emphasis on a cool, late-swing approach. The best music comes on four delightful trio outings by Hank Jones, Oscar Pettiford and Charlie Smith, where Pettiford's buoyant playing is given high prominence, and four tracks by Al Cohn with Jones, Hinton and Osie Johnson, which include a lithe 'Softly As In A Morning Sunrise'. Elswehere there are Sims and Brookmeyer, on a couple of loose-limbed blowing vehicles, and the little group led by accordionist Mat Matthews, playing a dated sort of chamber-jazz which still delivers a pretty reading of 'I Only Have Eyes For You'. Acceptable remastering of what were initially less than outstanding recordings.

1960S: JAM SESSIONS

(*) **Newport Jazz Festival Tribute To Charlie Parker RCA Bluebird ND 86457 CD/LP
Howard McGhee (*t*); J. J. Johnson (*tb*); Jackie McLean (*as*); Sonny Stitt (*ts*); Harold Mabern, Lamont Johnson (*p*); Arthur Harper Jr , Scott Holt (*b*); Max Roach, Billy Higgins (*d*). 7/64–2/67.

There was some potential for an event of real substance here, with a group of original beboppers reflecting on Parker at the Newport Festival of 1964. But Stitt, McGhee and Johnson play the whole occasion with such deadpan energy that what results is a highly professional 30 minutes of bop revivalism. McGhee plays well, Stitt is his usual unshakeably determined self, and it's left to Johnson to raise the game with a solo on 'Wee' of ironclad precision. Father Norman O'Conner, one of the great jazz chaplains, makes a few remarks which are usefully edited out by the CD facility. The record is banked up with two ballads by Jackie Mclean, recorded three years later, but he sounds miserably uninterested.

NEW ORLEANS REVIVAL

*** **The 77 Sessions** GHB 250 CD/LP
Cuff Billett, Kid Thomas Valentine, Keith Smith, Percy Humphrey (*t*); Louis Nelson, James Archey, Mike Sherbourne, Pete Dyer (*tb*); George Lewis, Darnell Howard, John Defferary (*cl*); John Handy, Bill Greenow (*as*); Alton Purnell (*p, v*); Graham Paterson, Richard Simmons, Lars Edegran (*p*); Alfred Lewis (*bj, v*); Brian Turnock, Pops Foster, Terry Knight (*b*); Barry Martyn, Louis Barbarin, Josiah Frazier, Dave Evans (*d*). 6/63–10/72.

This is a cross-section of previously unreleased performances from Doug Dobell's 77 label, prior to the back catalogue being transferred to CD by George Buck's GHB company. Dobell recorded a lot of jazz from many different sources, but 77 was a particular repository for New Orleans revivalism, and the bands represented here – Barry Martyn, Keith Smith, and two all-star pick-up groups – were a strong source of material. the highlights here all come from

Martyn's groups: with the fine Cuff Billett on trumpet, and guests Valentine, Lewis and Nelson on different occasions, the music manages to be faithful to New Orleans spirit and personal to Martyn's understanding of it. The New Orleans All Stars are disappointing on 'Pops' Blues', and Alton Purnell's scattershot singing won't be to all tastes on three tracks with Smith's band, but the momentum of the record never flags, and the recording, if less than top of the line, has been very clearly remastered.

1970S: JAM SESSIONS

(*)   **Xanadu At Montreux Volume One Xanadu 162 LP
        Sam Noto (*t*); Sam Most (*f*); Ronnie Cuber (*bs*); Dolo Coker (*p*); Sam Jones (*b*); Frank Butler (*d*). 7/78.

***   **Xanadu At Montreux Volume Two** Xanadu 163 LP
        Al Cohn, Billy Mitchell (*ts*); Barry Harris (*p*); Sam Jones (*b*); Frank Butler (*d*).7/78.

**   **Xanadu At Montreux Volume Three** Xanadu 164 LP
        As above, plus Sam Noto (*f*); Ronnie Cuber (*bs*); Dolo Coker (*p*); Ted Dunbar (*g*). 7/78.

**   **Xanadu At Montreux Volume Four** Xanadu 165 LP
        As above. 7/78.

Recorded on a single evening at the 1978 Montreux Jazz Festival, this celebration of Xanadu's leading artists of the day has a lot of fine jazz but, as with all such occasions, there are dead spots and throwaway jams which weaken the albums. Boiled down to a single double-album or CD, it would prove more valuable. The first record features some excellent work by Cuber on a solo 'Vamping' and 'But Not For Me', but Noto's 'Get Happy' reminds one of Ziggy Elman, and the very long 'So What' is deflated by Frank Butler's drum solo, which is one of those you-had-to-be-there features. *Volume Two* is easily the pick of the four, centred on Cohn and Mitchell duelling over a fine rhythm section, with Harris clearing a couple of fences of his own on 'Willow Groove' and 'All God's Chillun Got Rhythm'. Most is the prinicipal on the third record, with an arbitrary jam winding up the proceedings, although Dunbar's treatment of 'Half Nelson' is a sinewy outing. *Volume Four* is mostly left-overs. the recording is rather variable: Sam Jones is often hard to hear and Harris seems to be playing on a poorer piano than Coker (even if it is the same one).

*(*)   **The International Pescara Jam Sessions 1970–1975** Philology W-96-2 CD
        Chet Baker, Roy Eldridge, Cat Anderson, Randy Brecker (*t*); Charles McPherson (*as*); Paul Gonsalves, Dexter Gordon, Ben Webster, Michael Brecker (*ts*); Rein de Graaf, Joe Lubin, J. Colombo, John Lewis, Kenny Drew, Hampton Hawes, George Arvanitas (*p*); Didier Levallet, Henry Franklin, Jacky Samson, Charles Mingus, Will Lee, D. Hoveroecke (*b*); Eric Ineke, Franco Manzecchi, Charles Saudrais, Michael Carvin, Roy Brooks, Alvin Queen (*d*). 7/70–7/75.

Not much honour conferred on anyone here, although there are some extraordinary line-ups thrown up by this after-hours jam session compilation from various Pescara festivals: a trio of Ben Webster, Kenny Drew and Charles Mingus; Gerry Mulligan with Hampton Hawes; Roy Eldridge with Mingus and John Lewis. The bootleg-quality sound militates against enjoying anything much, though and, aside from a few entertaining moments – the Webster piece especially, where Ben growls out, 'That's E flat, ain't it?' to an unidentified miscreant – it's another personal oddity from the Philology set-up.

1980s

****   **Document: The '80s** Leo 801/8 8CD
        Irina Bogdanova (*v*); Alexander Simagin (*v, d*); Roman Dubinnikov (*v, acc, perc*); Vladimir Arbuzov (*v, b, perc*); Viktor Maltsev (*v, ts, ss, f, tba*).
        Vyacheslav Guyvoronsky (*t*); Vladimir Volkov (*b*).
        Valentina Goncharova (*solo electric vn, clo, v, d, rec*).
        Valentina Ponomareva (*v*); Mark Pekarsky, Alexander Suvorov, Dmitry Lazarev,

Nikolai L'govsky, Alexander Vinets (*perc*).
Jazz Group Arkhangelsk: Vladimir Rezitsky (*as, f, vargan, hca, v*); Vladimir Turov (*p, org, syn, t*); Nikolai Klishin (*b*); Oleg Yudanov (*d, f*); Sergey Belichenko (*perc*).
Datevik Hovhannesian (*v*); Vladimir Chekasin Big Band; no individual personnel.
Orkestrion: Ravil Azizov (*cl, tb, b, p, xyl, g, v, perc*); Sergey Karsaev (*perc, etc*); Yelena Chashchina (*v*); Oleg Lubimov (*Argentinian f* on one track only).
Petras Vysniauskas (*as, ss*); Kestutus Lusas (*p*).
Anatoly Vapirov (*reeds*); Sergey Kuryokhin (*p, perc*).
Tri-O': Sergey Letov (*sax, f, b cl*); Arkady Kirichenko (*tba, sous, v*); Arkady Shikloper (*frhn*).
Vladimir Chekasin (*cl, as, v, perc, g*); Sergey Kuryokhin (*p, v, perc, f*); Boris Grebenshchikov (*g, v, perc*).
Homo Liber: Yuri Yukechev (*p, f*); Vladimir Tolkachev (*f, ss, as*).
Alexander Sakurov (*sax, elec*); Yuri Dronov (*v*).
Sergey Kuryokhin (*p, metalophone*); Igor Butman (*as*); Alexander Pumpyan (*g*).
Moscow Improvising Trio: Andrei Solovyev (*t, bamboo f, baritoniphonium*); Igor Grigoriev (*g, syn*); Sergey Busakhin (*d, perc*); Mikhail Zhukhov (*perc*); collective personnel.
Vladislav Makarov (*clo, p, cym*); Mikhail Yudenich (*d, cym*); Valeri Dudkin (*g, cym*).
Ganelin Trio and solos/duo: Vyacheslav Ganelin (*syn*); Vladimir Chekasin (*reeds*) with Oleg Molokoedov (*p*); Vladimir Tarasov (*perc*).

**** **Conspiracy: Soviet Jazz Festival – Zurich 1989** Leo 809/12 4CD
Leningrad Duo: Vyacheslav Guyvoronsky (*t*); Vladimir Volkov (*b, v*).
Yuri Kuznetsov (*p*).
Anatoly Vapirov (*reeds*); Vladimir Tarasov (*d*). Askhat Sayfoolin (*b*).
Slava Ganelin (*p, syn, perc*); Mika Markovich (*d, perc*).
Aziza Mustafa-Zade (*p, v*); Askhat Sayfoolin (*b*); Antony Barakhovsky (*vn*); Sergey Belichenko (*d*); collective personnel.
Valentina Ponomareva (*v*); Sergey Letov, Werner Ludi (*reeds*); collective personnel.
Stephen Wittwer (*g*); Hans Koch (*reeds*); Vladimir Tarasov (*d*); Valentina Ponomareva (*v*); Arkady Kirichenko (*v, euph*); Martin Schutz (*clo*); Vyacheslave Guyvoronsky (*t*); Vladimir Volkov (*b*); collective personnel.
Veladimir Chekasin (*reeds, syn, v*); Oleg Molokoedov (*p, syn, t*); Vitas Labutis (*syn, reeds*); Arvidas Joffe (*d*).
Jazz Group Arkhangelsk: Vladimir Rezitsky (*reeds*); Vladimir Turov (*p, syn, t*); Oleg Yudanov (*d*); Nikolai Yudanov (*tb, perc*); Konstantin Sedovin (*balalaika, f, v*).
Anatoly Vapirov Big Band: Anatoly Vapirov (*ts*); Vyacheslav Guyvoronsky (*t*); Nikolai Yudanov (*tb*); Konstantin Sedovin (*f, v*); Vitas Labutis, Vladimir Rezitsky (*as*); Sergey Letov (*b cl*); Nikolai Klishin (*tba*); Arkady Kirichenko (*euph*); Vladimir Uvarov, Vladimir Volkov (*vib*); Askhat Sayfoolin (*b*); Oleg Molokoedov (*p, syn, t*); Vladimir Turov (*syn, t*); Oleg Yudanov (*d*); Sergey Belichenko (*perc*).
6/89.

The history and travails of Leo Records has been told by its owner and *de facto* producer Leo Feigin in his edited collection of essays *Russian Jazz – New Identity* (London, 1985). It is difficult to underestimate the label's role in broadening the foci of contemporary improvisation. In addition to recording some of the senior members of the American avant-garde – Cecil Taylor, Anthony Braxton – and promoting significant younger talent like Marilyn Crispell (Feigin's first release was by another woman pianist, Amina Claudine Myers), he has almost singlehandedly established the parameters of our understanding of new Russian jazz and improvisation. Many of the recordings he has released were made clandestinely in less than ideal circumstances and brought out of the Soviet Union by sympathetic fans. Rarely has a record producer been so beset by extra-artistic dilemmas of the sort Feigin has had to face. In releasing some of the material, he has had to consider the implications for musicians denied even the permissive diffidence accorded Western improvisers, whose very physical freedom remained in question.

Clearly, the situation has 'improved' somewhat with the Gorbachev thaw, but at least the first of these recordings illustrates one of the perils of sudden rises in temperature. Listeners confronted with *Document: The '80s* may feel flooded with what, after more than a decade of

Leo Records, was still an essentially alien music. There were few Western reference points for the slightly anarchic, jestering histrionics of performers like saxophonist Vladimir Chekasin, who turned a now notorious London performance by the vanguard Ganelin Trio into a dialogue of the deaf that made an ironic footnote to the stand-offs of the Cold War.

It is equally clear that in the accelerated exposure of Russian improvisers to their Western kin, considerable effort has been expended in reinventing the wheel. Work like that of the Jazz Group Arkhangelsk, Orkestrion and the Ganelin Trio itself, could in many essentials have emerged from the European or American avant-garde of the early 1960s. Many of the unfamiliar elements were simple folkloristic appurtenances, as in the work of Valentina Ponomareva and in the songs on 'Dearly Departed', the opening performance on *Document*.

One of the abiding criticism of this enormous, 8-CD set is that it represents a triumph of packaging over substance. Michael Bennion's box and booklet are *tours de force*, as is his slightly more muted cover for the smaller, later set, but there are question marks over some of the performances. (Most of the more significant performers are covered under their own names, and this isn't the place for detailed stylistic comment, but Feigin cheerfully admits to a degree of compromise in the selection of material for both sets.) It is perhaps best to take the title completely literally, and regard *Document* as an archive of material selected *faute de mieux* to fit the logistical constraints even of CD release. As such, it is a remarkable piece of work, but it seems a trifle monolithic and, price apart, is unlikely to be an urgent priority for most jazz and new music enthusiasts. However, like many of Leo Feigin's releases, it is issued in a limited edition of only 1000 and by that token alone must be considered highly collectable.

By 1989, the political situation in the Soviet Union had mellowed sufficiently to permit travel and performance overseas for the more prominent Russian improvisers. The music played at the Zurich Russian jazz festival is more relaxed and confident, but it has also, perhaps inevitably, lost a great deal of its tension and edge. It is a 'conspiracy' only in the sense now of a 'breathing together', but one might venture to suggest that the Swiss air is still a little thin to fuel absolutely convincing music. In the period between the two records, the flagship Ganelin Trio had broken up, revealing what more than a few critics in the West had suspected: that Vyacheslav Ganelin's ostensible leadership was merely a flag of convenience (in the Soviet Union, the band was apparently always known by a phonetic rendering of the members' cognomens, 'GeTeChe', never as the Ganelin Trio). There is a sloppy banality about Ganelin's performace at Zurich; naturalized and familiarized (and now known by the diminutive 'Slava'), he and some of the other performers seem bent on giving a Western audience precisely what they had seemed to expect of Russian improv.

Nevertheless again, the Zurich album is of considerable historical importance. The *samizdat* period is now over (one hopes permanently) and the process of 'normalization' symbolized by Zurich nearly complete. The Apocrypha and Pseudopographia of Russian improvised music will quickly be superseded by better and less over-determined performances, but *Document* and *Conspiracy* will remain essential texts of modern frontier music and permanent testimony to Leo Feigin's dogged belief in the music of his homeland.

GUITAR

**(*)   Jazz Guitar Classics 1953–1974 Original Jazz Classics OJC 6012 CD/LP/MC
Including: Barney Kessel; Eddie Duran; Kenny Burrell; Jimmy Raney; Tiny Grimes; Wes Montgomery; Billy Bean; Pat Martino; Billy Butler; Tal Farlow; Jim Hall; Herb Ellis; Joe Pass. 12/53–2/74.

The Fantasy group have some strong guitar records to choose from in order to make up a compilation, and that makes this so-so effort all the more disappointing. Significant quality seems to have been sacrificed in favour of being as eclectic as possible, while still remaining within a framework of the 'classic' open-toned jazz guitar. Hence there are dispensable tracks by Billy Bean and Eddie Duran, while Wes Montgomery is represented by a track which he originally rejected, and Burrell and Raney appear in a makeweight duet piece. Kessel's 'Salute To Charlie Christian' is a reminder of his gifts as a cool bopper, and the three best tracks come at the end: Farlow's effortless cruise through 'My Romance', Jim Hall duetting with Ron Carter on a lovely 'Autumn Leaves', and Ellis and Pass romping through a fun version of 'Seven Come Eleven'. The remastering is up to the usual good standards of the OJC enterprise.

HAMMOND ORGAN

***(*) **So Blue, So Funky** Blue Note CDP 796563-2 CD
   Blue Mitchell (*t*); George Braith (*ss, ts, stritch*); Lou Donaldson (*as*); Fred Jackson,
   Jay Arnold, Harold Vick, Claude Bartee, Joe Henderson, Sam Rivers (*ts*); Earl van
   Dyke, Billy Gardner, Jack McDuff, Jimmy McGriff, John Patton, Lonnie Liston Smith,
   Emmanuel Riggins, Freddie Roach, Jimmy Smith, Baby Face Willette, Larry Young
   (*org*); Willie Jones, Grant Green, Charlie Freeman, Morris Dow, Melvin Sparks,
   Eugene Wright (*g*); Jimmy Lewis (*b*); Wilbert Hogan, Hugh Walker, Sammy Creason,
   Jackie Mills, Ben Dixon, Idris Muhammad, Donald Bailey, Clarence Johnston, Elvin
   Jones (*d*); Candido Camero, Richard Landrun (*perc*). 2/62–1/70.

An ideal music for anthologies: while most of the albums these tracks are taken from would be
entirely routine by themselves, taken a track at a time they sound fine, and rounding up the best
of some otherwise one-shot players at least rescues some worthwhile music from oblivion
(many of the original sources of these tracks number among the most rare of Blue Note
releases). The pick of the 12 tracks includes John Patton's relentless 'The Silver Metre', Larry
Young's 'Plaza De Toros' with support from Sam Rivers, Grant Green and Elvin Jones, and
Freddie Roach's jostling 'Brown Sugar' with assistance from Joe Henderson. Much of this
music is aimed more at the feet than at the head, and tolerance has to be stretched a bit for the
likes of Fred Jackson's 'Hootin' And Tootin'', but it's an altogether entertaining set, expertly
programmed and remastered.

PIANO

(*) **Classic Jazz Piano 1927–1957 Bluebird ND 86754 CD
   Jelly Roll Morton, Earl Hines, Jimmy Yancey, Meade Lux Lewis, James P. Johnson,
   Fats Waller, Willie 'The Lion' Smith, Art Tatum, Teddy Wilson, Jess Stacy, Earl
   Hines, Duke Ellington, Billy Strayhorn, Count Basie, Mary Lou Williams, Erroll
   Garner, Oscar Peterson, Lennie Tristano, Bud Powell, Bill Evans (*p*). 6/27–2/66.

Piano jazz compilations might be a useful vehicle for telescoping aspects of jazz history into a
single disc, since piano jazz is both a tradition of its own and a central part of the main
continuum. If it had stopped with, say, Erroll Garner, this one would have been a useful
overview of traditional and swing piano styles, with many of the major practitioners
represented. But Tristano, Powell and Evans represent three very different strands of
modernism, and they unbalance the story, if not quite upending it. The choice of tracks to
represent the others is often strange, too. Morton's 'Mr Jelly Lord' with the Dodds brothers is
hardly superior to his 1929 solo tracks; Stacy's 'Daybreak Serenade' is pretty but slight; and
Evans gets in only on one of the few dates he recorded for RCA, George Russell's *Jazz
Workshop* session. But there are still plenty of classics here: Waller's 'Smashing Thirds',
Yancey's 'State Street Special' and Mary Lou Williams's 'All God's Children Got Rhythm'
among them. Covering 40 years of music as it does, the sound is variable – as usual, the
NoNOISE process has tended to dry out many of the 78 originals.

***(*) **Jazz Piano 1935–1942 Vol. 1** EMI Pathé Jazztime 251282-2 CD
   Including: Garnet Clark, Herman Chittison, Garland Wilson, Joe Turner, Ray Stokes,
   Leo Chauliac, Eddie Barclay, Pierre Cazenave (*p*). 11/35–5/42.

An impressive compilation of piano-playing in Paris in the period, both by visiting Americans,
such as the obscure but intriguing Garnet Clark (who died at twenty-four after developing
schizophrenia), Joe Turner and Garland Wilson, and by local men, including Barclay and
Cazenave, neither of whose sessions were even released at the time. While there's nothing
without interest here – hear, for instance, the impeccable 'Slidin' Thru'' by Ray Stokes – the
major pieces are by Wilson and Chittison. Garland Wilson, though derided at the time as
something of a show-off with a fondness for a crossed-hands technique, is an exacting blues
player with a bewitching touch in 'The Blues I Love To Play'; he also takes a charming solo on
celeste in 'Blue Morning'. Chittison, though, is the real master here: his Tatumesque touch and
complete relaxation at even the torrid pace which he chooses for his solos make one regret that
he made so few recordings. All the remastering for CD has been excellently done.

SAXOPHONE

**   **Jazz Around Midnight – Saxophone** Verve 840951-2
Including: Johnny Hodges; Coleman Hawkins; Ben Webster; James Moody; Georgie
Auld; Stan Getz; Lester Young; Herb Geller; Sonny Rollins; Sonny Criss; Benny
Golson; Joe Henderson; Sonny Stitt. 2/44–1/80.

The choice of musicians here makes a logical introduction to jazz saxophone, but the arbitrary
nature of the selections and the awkward programming only emphasize how hard it is to create
a feasible look at the instrument in jazz across the space of a single disc, even when the
intention is to view it purely as a purveyor of late-night ballads. Webster and Hawkins and Getz
are all masters of that approach, and their tracks are duly functional, although both the Getz
and Hawkins choices are odd ones. Less probable are Auld's 'Taking A Chance On Love' from
an obscure 1963 session, a dreary Lester Young, a latter-day Joe Henderson (with Chick Corea
in 1980) and Stitt playing 'Down Home Blues'. Good marks for avoiding obvious material, but
one feels that this is due more to bewilderment than to intention. The sound is clean, if a little
dry.

TRUMPET

***   **Great Trumpets** Bluebird ND 86753 CD
Including: Louis Armstrong, King Oliver, Bunk Johnson, Tommy Ladnier, Lee Collins,
Henry 'Red' Allen, Sidney De Paris, Jabbo Smith, Bix Beiderbecke, Red Nichols,
Bunny Berigan, Muggsy Spanier, Wingy Manone, Max Kaminsky, Harry James, Ziggy
Elman, Cootie Williams, Rex Stewart, Roy Eldridge, Hot Lips Page, Frankie Newton,
Buck Clayton (*t, c*). 2/27–5/54.

The title is a misnomer, since Beiderbecke, Nichols, Stewart, Smith and Spanier are all playing
cornets rather than trumpets. But this is otherwise a sensible overview of some of the major
brass stylists of the 1920s and '30s, as they recorded for Victor. The programming is intelligently
done: it starts with Armstrong, goes into the great 'primitive' stylists such as Oliver, Johnson
and Ladnier, the odd-men-out (Collins, Allen, Smith), the white New York players (Bix,
Nichols, Berigan) and the sweeter stylists of the swing era; and it ends with Armstrong again.
While some of the tune choices seem a trifle eccentric, at least there's nothing hackneyed here:
it's arranged for scholars and newcomers alike. Especial delights include Newton's wryly hot
'The Blues My Baby Gave To Me' and Sidney De Paris starring on Sidney Bechet's fearsomely
intense 'Nobody Knows The Way I Feel Dis Morning'. Clean if fairly dry sound throughout.

WOMEN ARTISTS

****   **The Women: Classic Female Jazz Artists** Bluebird ND 86755 CD
Mary Lou Williams Girl Stars & Trio; Beryl Booker Trio; Vivien Garry Quintet; Una
Mae Carlisle; International Sweethearts of Rhythm; Hazel Scott & the Sextet of the
Rhythm Club of London; Edythe Wright with Tommy Dorsey with Tommy Dorsey
and the Clambake Seven; Alberta Hunter; Ethel Waters; Mildred Bailey; Helen Ward
with Gene Krupa and his Swing Band; Helen Forrest; Barbara Carroll Trio; Kay Davis
with Duke Ellington and his Orchestra. 1939–52.

Just after the war, Leonard Feather and RCA released a compilation called *Girls in Jazz* (the
contrast of title with the above is by no means incidental). It contained tracks by pianists Mary
Lou Williams and Beryl Booker, bassist/leader Vivien Garry and the stalwart International
Sweethearts of Rhythm who through the 1940s had gamely worked against the innate prejudice
of the black theatre circuit.

    Given at least some change in attitudes since 1945 and the appearance of a revisionist history
like Linda Dahl's *Stormy Weather*, *The Women* isn't perhaps as significant a document as its
predecessor. Williams is now almost universally recognized as one of the essential
composer/pianists in modern jazz, and figures like Alberta Hunter, Ethel Waters, Mildred
Bailey and Hazel Scott all seem to have staked their own claim to a corner of jazz history.
However, it remains to be seen why someone like Mary Osborne, who recorded with Coleman

Hawkins (and who can be sampled on Jazzline JL 95810 and RCA NL 86757), should have slipped out of view, or why the 'vigorous' Vi Stansbery of the International Sweethearts should be little more than a vague memory.

The Bluebird compilation, which has been sensibly selected and carefully packaged, is a significant and thoroughly enjoyable attempt to redress the balance slightly. Leonard Feather's liner note is full, detailed and affectionate. The emphasis isn't just on singers, and while it's clear on the evidence of 'A Woman's Place Is In The Groove' and 'Operation Mop', the Vivien Garry Quintet would have been cut by the average club band of the time (Charlie Parker took a Dr Johnsonish stance on women bassists, but then wrote 'Donna Lee'), there's no excuse for oblivion. Mary Lou Williams still quite properly remains the flagship performer, but the quality of performance is generally high. Strongly recommended for anyone interested in the period in general or with a more ideological axe to grind. A sense of fun helps, too.

Index